INTERNATIONAL LITERARY MARKET PLACE 1980

R. R. BOWKER COMPANY
New York & London, 1980

Published by R. R. Bowker Company (a Xerox Publishing Company)
1180 Avenue of the Americas
New York, N.Y. 10036

Copyright © 1980 by Xerox Corporation

All rights reserved.
Reproduction of this work, in whole or in part,
without written permission of the publisher is prohibited.

International Standard Book Number 0-8352-1294-7
International Standard Serial Number 0074-6827
Library of Congress Catalog Card Number 77-70295

Printed and bound in the United States of America

The publishers do not assume and hereby
disclaim any liability to any party for
any loss or damage caused by errors or
omissions in *International Literary
Market Place*, whether such errors or
omissions result from negligence,
accident or any other cause.

Computer typeset by Millford Reprographics International Ltd, Luton, England.

INTERNATIONAL LITERARY MARKET PLACE
1980

LIBRARIES

UNIVERSITY OF MAINE

AT ORONO

RAYMOND H. FOGLER LIBRARY

ORONO

Contents

The material for each country is grouped under a series of subheadings to the main country heading. These subheadings appear always in the same order, and the omission of any of them from a particular country implies that no information is available. The headings are as follows:

General Information (language, population, currency, etc.)
Book Trade Organizations
Book Trade Reference Books and Journals
Publishers
Remainder Dealers (UK only)
Literary Agents
Book Clubs
Major Booksellers
Major Libraries
Library Associations
Library Reference Books and Journals
Literary Associations and Societies
Literary Periodicals
Literary Prizes
Translation Agencies and Associations

Preface	vii
Abbreviations	viii
Afghanistan	1
Albania	1
Algeria	2
Angola	2
Argentina	2
Australia	9
Austria	23
Bahamas	31
Bahrain	32
Bangladesh	32
Barbados	33
Belgium	33
Belize	46
Benin	46
Bermuda	47
Bolivia	47
Botswana	48
Brazil	48
Brunei	57
Bulgaria	58
Burma	59
Burundi	60
United Republic of Cameroun	60
Central African Republic	61
Chad	61
Chile	62
People's Republic of China	63
China (Taiwan)	64
Colombia	65
Popular Republic of Congo	67
Costa Rica	67
Cuba	68
Cyprus	69
Czechoslovakia	69
Denmark	74
Dominican Republic	80
Ecuador	81
Egypt	82
El Salvador	83
Ethiopia	84
Fiji	84
Finland	85
France	88
French Guiana	116
French Polynesia	116
Gabon	116
The Gambia	116
German Democratic Republic	117
Federal Republic of Germany	121
Ghana	174
Gibraltar	175
Greece	176
Guatemala	178
Guinea	179
Guyana	179
Haiti	179
Honduras	180
Hong Kong	180
Hungary	182
Iceland	184
India	186
Indonesia	199
Iran	201
Iraq	202
Republic of Ireland	203
Israel	205
Italy	211
Ivory Coast	223
Jamaica	224
Japan	225
Jordan	234
Kampuchea	235
Kenya	235
Democratic People's Republic of Korea	237
Republic of Korea	237
Kuwait	240
Laos	240
Lebanon	240
Lesotho	241
Liberia	242
Libya	242
Liechtenstein	243
Luxembourg	243
Macao	244
Democratic Republic of Madagascar	244
Malawi	245
Malaysia	245
Mali	248
Malta	248
Martinique	249
Mauritania	249
Mauritius	249
Mexico	249
Monaco	255
Mongolian People's Republic	255
Montserrat	255
Morocco	255
Mozambique	256
Namibia	257
Nepal	257
Netherlands	257
Netherlands Antilles	271
New Caledonia	271
New Zealand	271
Nicaragua	276
Niger	276
Nigeria	277
Norway	281
Pakistan	284
Panama	287
Papua New Guinea	288
Paraguay	288
Peru	289
Philippines	290
Poland	293
Portugal	298
Puerto Rico	302
Qatar	303
Réunion	303
Romania	303
Rwanda	306
Saudi Arabia	306
Senegal	306
Seychelles	307
Sierra Leone	307
Republic of Singapore	308
Somalia	310
Republic of South Africa	311
Spain	317
Sri Lanka	329
Sudan	330
Suriname	331
Swaziland	331
Sweden	331
Switzerland	339
Syria	357
Tanzania	357
Thailand	358
Togo	360
Trinidad and Tobago	361
Tunisia	361
Turkey	362
Uganda	364
Union of Soviet Socialist Republics	365
United Arab Emirates	368
United Kingdom	368
Upper Volta	422
Uruguay	422
Vatican City State	423
Venezuela	423
Socialist Republic of Viet Nam	425
Western Samoa	426
People's Democratic Republic of the Yemen	426
Yemen Arab Republic	426
Yugoslavia	426
Zaire	432
Zambia	433
Zimbabwe	434
INTERNATIONAL SECTION	437
Copyright Conventions	437
International Organizations	437
International Bibliography	444
International Literary Prizes	446
The ISBN System	452
BOOK TRADE CALENDAR	456
INDEX	462

Preface

The 1980 edition of *International Literary Market Place* is the fifth to be compiled in the United Kingdom. It embodies corrections received in response to more than 11,000 questionnaires despatched to virtually every country in the world apart from the USA and Canada. Questionnaires were also sent to 850 potential new entrants, whilst various information was collected from many other sources.

Over 5,000 replies were received, not only from publishers but from organizations of every kind – libraries, booksellers, book clubs, literary agents – which supply or use their products.

As usual, the editor owes an enormous debt to Linda Redman, who coped with day-to-day returns, dealt with queries and ensured generally that the whole operation ran smoothly. The careful processing of replies by Pat Brown, Dennis Corbyn, Rosemary Harley and Martha Ross was of immense value, and Derek French is also to be thanked for technical advice.

I am happy to have any suggestions for the improvement of *International Literary Market Place*. Please write to the editorial office at Bowker Publishing Company, Erasmus House, High Street, Epping, Essex, England CM16 4BU.

PETER FOUND
Editor

Abbreviations

*	Entries not based on questionnaires
+	Indicates membership of national Publishers' Association
AB	Aktiebolag (= limited company)
AG	Aktiengesellschaft (= public limited company)
Apdo	Apartado (= postbox)
ApS	Anpartsselskab (= private limited company)
A/S	Aksjeselskap, Aktieselskab (= limited company)
ASBL	Association sans but lucratif (= non-profit-making society)
Ave	Avenida, Avenue
Bldg	Building
Blvd	Boulevard, Bulevard
BP	Boîte postale (= postbox)
BV	Besloten Vennootschap (= private limited company)
CA	Compañía anónima (= public limited company)
Cie	Compagnie (= company)
Co	Company, Kompanie
CP	Caixa Postal, Casetta postale (= postbox)
Dir	Director
Dr	Drive
eV	eingetragener Verein (= registered society)
GmbH	Gesellschaft mit beschränkter Haftung (= private limited company)
Ho	House
Jl	Jalan (= street)
KG	Kommanditgesellschaft (= partnership)
Ltd	Limited
Man Dir	Managing Director
Nachf	Nachfolger(s) (= successor(s))
nám	náměstí (= square)
NV	Naamloze Vennootschap (= public limited company)
of	oficina (= office)
OY	Osakeyhtiö (= limited company)
Pl	Plac, Place, Plaza
Pty	Proprietary
PVBA	Personenvennootschap met Beperkte Aansprakelijkheid (= private limited company)
Rd	Road
SA	Sociedad Anónima, Sociedade Anônima, Société Anonyme (= public limited company)
Sàrl	Société à responsabilité limitée (= private limited company)
SCA	Sociedad en comandita por acciónes (= limited partnership)
SpA	Società per Azioni (= public limited company)
SPRL	Société de personnes à responsabilité limitée (= private limited company)
Sq	Square
SRL	Sociedad de responsabilidad limitada, Società à responsabilità limitata (= private limited company)
St	Street
Str	Straat, Strada, Strǎda, Straede, Strasse
u	utca
ul	ulica, ulice, Uliţă, ulitsa
VEB	Volkseigener Betrieb (= people's enterprise)
VZW	Vereniging zonder winstoogmerk (= non-profit-making society)

A limited company is a corporation owned by shareholders (or stockholders) who may contribute capital to the company but are not otherwise generally liable for its debts.

A public company may invite anyone to become a shareholder, and its shares (or stocks) are usually traded on a stock exchange. A private, or proprietary, company has a restricted number of shareholders and its shares are not traded on a stock exchange.

The owners of a partnership are generally liable for its debts, but a limited partnership has some owners who only contribute capital and are not otherwise liable for debts.

Afghanistan

General Information

Language: Pushtu. Most also speak Dari, ideally used in commerce. (English, French or German spoken by most educated people)
Religion: Predominantly Muslim (Sunni sect)
Population: 17.4 million
Bank Hours: 0800-1200, 1300-1600 Saturday-Wednesday; 0800-1300 Thursday
Shop Hours: Winter: 0900-1300, 1400-1700 Saturday-Thursday; Summer: 0800-1300, 1500-1800 Saturday-Thursday
Currency: 100 puls = 1 afghani
Export/Import Information: Duty on books 10%; children's picture books, 15%; some advertising matter, 35%. Additional taxes of 1 + 2% duty and 4% ad valorem. No import licence but importer must be licensed. Books of propaganda against State policies or Islam or publications causing moral corruption prohibited. Exchange controls
Copyright: Florence (see International section)

Publishers

Afghan Kitab*, Kabul
Subject: Translations

Baihaqi Book Publishing Institute*, BP 748 Kabul Tel: 26853
Founded: 1971 (by Government Press, Ministry of Information and Culture)

Book Publishing Institute*, Herat
Subjects: Fiction, History, Religion
Founded: 1970 (by cooperation of Government Press and citizens of Herat)

Franklin Book Programs Inc*, PO Box 332, Kabul

Government Press*, Kabul
Subjects: Afghan history & literature, Textbooks, Newspapers, Magazines, Journals
Founded: 1870
Miscellaneous: Under supervision of Ministry of Information and Culture

Historical Society of Afghanistan*, Kabul
Dir: M Yakub Wahidi
Founded: 1931
Subjects: Afghan History and Culture
Publications: Afghanistan (in English, French and German); *Aryana* (in Dari and Pashtu), both quarterly

Kabul University, Institute of Geography*, Kabul
Subject: Maps

Ministry of Culture and Information, Book Publishing Department*, Kabul

Ministry of Education, Department of Educational Publications*, Kabul
Subjects: Primary & Secondary Textbooks in Pushtu and Dari

Pushtu Toulana, Afghan Academy*, Kabul
Subjects: Pushtu Language

Major Booksellers

Behzad Bookshop*, Welayat Ave, Kabul

Behzad Bookstore*, Shop No 122, Chahra-hi-Malikasghar, Kabul

Haji Abdullah Jan Barban & Co*, Kandahar

Royal Afghanistan Press Department*, Kabul

University of Kabul Bookstores*, Ali-Abad, Kabul

Zuri Book Shop*, Shir Shah Meena, Kabul *also* Charahi-Sadarat, Kabul

Major Libraries

Institute of Education Library, Kabul University*, Kabul

Ministry of Education Library*, Kabul

Library of the **National Bank***, Kabul

Library of the **Press Department***, Kabul

Public Library*, Kabul

Library of the **Royal Palace***, Kabul

University Library*, Kabul

Library Associations

Anjuman Kitab-Khana-I-Afghanistan (Afghan Library Association)*, PO Box 3142, Kabul
Publication: Afghan Library Association Bulletin

Library Journals

Afghan Library Association Bulletin, Anjuman-Kitab-Khani-I-Afghanistan PO Box 3142, Kabul

Albania

General Information

Language: Albanian
Religion: Muslim, but Albania proclaimed an atheist state in 1967
Population: 2.6 million
Currency: 100 quintars = 1 lek
Export/Import Information: Importation of books is through State Trading Organization, Nah Shperndarjes Të (or NST) Librit, Blvd e Pezës, Tirana. Correspondence should be in Italian or French. Copies of correspondence to Albanian Legation in Rome. Import licences and strict exchange controls

Book Trade Organizations

Drejtoria Quëndrore e Përhapjes dhe e Propagandimit të Librit (Central Administration for the Dissemination and Propagation of the Book)*, Tirana

Book Trade Journals

The Albanian Book, National Library, Tirana

Articles from Albanian Periodicals, National Library, Tirana

Bibliografia kombëtare e Republikës Popullore të Shqipërisë (Albanian National Bibliography), Botim i Bibliotekës Kombëtare, Tirana

Libri (The Book), Rruga Konferenca e Pezës, Tirana

Publishers

'8' Nentori Publishing House*, Tirana
Subjects: Books and journals on Albania; documents and publications of the Albanian Party of Work

Naim Frasheri*, Tirana
Subject: Books in foreign languages

Ndërmarrja e Botimeve Ushtarake*, Tirana
Subjects: Military, Technology

N I S H Shtypshkronjave 'Mihal Duri'*, Tirana
Subjects: Government Publications, Education, Politics, Law

Major Booksellers

Nah Shperndarjes Të Librit (NST)*, Blvd e Pezës, Tirana
State trading organization controlling importation of books

Ndërmarrja e Librit*, Konfercenca e Pezës, Tirana Tel: 3323 Cable Add: Ndlibri Tirana
Distributor of books, journals and newspapers published in Albania in Albanian and foreign languages

Major Libraries

Biblioteka Kombëtare (National Library)*, Tirana Tel: 5887
Dir: Marika Vegli

Biblioteka Shkencore e Universitetit Shtetëror të Tiranës (Scientific Library of the State University of Tiranës)*, Tirana

Shkodër Public Library*, Shkodër

Library Associations

Council of Libraries, Rruga 'Abdi Toptani', No 3, Tirana
President: M Domi

Literary Associations and Societies

Union of Writers and Artists of Albania*, 37 Z Baboci St, Tirana
Chairman: Dritero Agolli
Publications: Nëndori; Drita

Literary Periodicals

Drita (The Light), Union of Writers and Artists of Albania, 37 Z Baboci St, Tirana

Nëndori (November), Union of Writers and Artists of Albania, 37 Z Baboci St, Tirana

Shejzat (Pleiades) (Albanian language and literature), Piazza della Balduina 59, I-00136 Rome, Italy

Algeria

General Information

Language: Arabic and French, the language for commerce
Religion: Muslim
Population: 17.7 million
Literacy Rate (1971): 26.4%
Bank Hours: Winter: 0745-1100, 1415-1700 Monday-Friday; Summer: 0715-1100, 1500-1730 Monday-Friday
Shop Hours: 0900-1200, 1500-1900 Monday-Saturday
Currency: 100 centimes = 1 Algerian dinar
Export/Import Information: Books not textbooks dutied 11.11%; children's picture books, 37.50%. Advertising matter other than single copies, 25%. Global Sole Production Tax levied on duty paid. Books may be imported or exported only by or with permission of SNED State Monopoly, 3 blvd Zirout Yousef, BP 49, Alger Strasbourg. There are also quota restrictions. Permission to import usually entitles holder to obtain necessary foreign exchange; strict controls are in effect
Copyright: UCC (see International section)

Book Trade Organizations

Syndicat des Librairies d'Algérie*, 18 ave de la Marne, Algiers
Association of Algerian Booksellers

Book Trade Journals

Bibliographie de l'Algérie, National Library, ave du Docteur Fanon, Algiers (The national bibliography, published bi-annually)

Publishers

Editions Populaires de l'**Armée***, 2 rue de Normandie, Algiers Tel: 620613
Telex: 52039
Man Dir: T Senhadji
Subjects: General Fiction, General Nonfiction, Belles Lettres, Poetry, History, Africana, Religion, Social Science
Miscellaneous: Distributed by SNED

Government Printer*, 7-13a ave Abdelkador Benbarek, Algiers

Société nationale d'Edition et de Diffusion (SNED)*, 3 blvd Zirout Youcef, BP 49, Algiers Tel: 639670 Cable Add: Sneda Alger
Man Dir: M Ouar; *Export Manager:* Abdelmalek H El-Djaziri
Subjects: General Fiction, General Nonfiction, Belles Lettres, Poetry, Biography, History, Africana, Philosophy, Religion, Juveniles, Arabic language & literature, Paperbacks, General & Social Science, University & Secondary Textbooks
Bookshop: Address as above
Founded: 1966

Major Booksellers

Librairie **Ferraris***, 43 rue Michelet, Algiers

Librairie **Maison** des Livres*, 12 rue Ali Boumendjel, Algiers

Librairie **S N E D** (Societe nationale d'Edition et de Diffusion)*, 13 blvd Zirout Youcef, Algiers
Sole importer, exporter and distributor of books and periodicals

Librairie du **Tiers Monde***, Pl Emir Abdelkader, Algiers

Major Libraries

Archives nationales*, Palais du Gouvernement, Esplanade d'Afrique, Algiers

Bibliothèque municipale*, Hôtel de Ville, Constantine

Bibliothèque nationale (National Library)*, ave du Docteur Fanon, Algiers Tel: 630632
Dir: Mahmoud Agha Bouayed
Publication: Bibliographie de l'Algérie (in Arabic and French, twice a year)

Bibliothèque universitaire, Université d'Alger*, 2 rue Didouche Mourad, Algiers Tel: 640215
Librarian: Zoulikha Bekadour

Ecole nationale polytechnique, Bibliothèque*, ave Pasteur, El-Harrach, Algiers

Bibliothèque de l'**Université de Constantine***, Route de Ain el Bey, Constantine Tel: 931125
Librarian: Sari Mahmoud

Université d'Oran, Bibliothèque*, rue du Colonel Lofti, Oran

Library Associations

Institut de Bibliothéconomie et des Sciences Documentaires (Institute of Library Management and Documentary Science)*, University of Algiers

Library Reference Books and Journals

Books

Bibliographie de l'Algérie (in Arabic and French, twice a year), Bibliothèque nationale, ave du Docteur Fanon, Algiers

Literary Associations and Societies

Union des Ecrivains algériens (Union of Algerian Writers)*, 12 rue Ali Boumendjel, Algiers

Literary Prizes

Union des Ecrivains algériens*
Awards annual literary prize for fiction, 10,000 Algerian dinars. Enquiries to Union des Ecrivains algériens, 12 rue Ali Boumendjel, Algiers

Angola

General Information

Language: Portuguese, U-Mbundu and other African languages
Religion: Christian, Animist
Population: 6.8 million
Currency: 100 centavos = 1 kwanza
Export/Import Information: No tariff on books and advertising. Very restricted issuance of import licences but books of cif value not exceeding 2500 escudos generally permitted. Advertising matter is currently given considerably lower priority. Exchange controls

Publishers

Nova Editorial **Angolana** SARL*, CP 1225, Luanda
Man Dir: Pombo Fernandes
Subjects: General Books, Educational Books
Founded: 1935

Industrias ABC*, CP 1245, Luanda
Subjects: General Nonfiction, Directories
Bookshop: Address as above

Lello & Cia Lda*, CP 1245, Luanda
Bookshop: CP 1300, Luanda
Subjects: General Fictionn n & Nonfiction, Secondary & Primary Textbooks

Major Booksellers

Albino Jose de Magalhes Lda*, CP 70, Lobito

Argente, Sentos & Cia Lda*, CP 1314, Luanda

Industrias ABC*, CP 1245, Luanda

Lello & Cia Lda*, CP 1300, Luanda

Major Libraries

Biblioteca Nacional de Angola (National Library)*, CP 2915, Luanda Tel: 37317
Director: D van Dunem

Universidade de Luanda Biblioteca*, CP 815, Luanda Tel: 764
Librarian: A C Ferraz Correia

Library Journals

Novas (News), National Library, CP 1281, Luanda

Argentina

General Information

Language: Spanish
Religion: Roman Catholic
Population: 26.1 million
Literacy Rate (1970): 92.6%
Bank Hours: 1200-1600 Monday-Friday
Shop Hours: 0900-1900 Monday-Saturday
Currency: 100 centavos = 1 peso
Export/Import Information: No tariffs on

books except children's picture books 5%, no VAT on books. Most advertising matter (more than one copy) subject to 130% duty. Added taxes of 7% on all imports. Import licences required, goods require prior deposit of 40%. Limited foreign exchange led to cancellation of most importation in 1975.
Copyright: UCC, Berne, Buenos Aires (see International section)

Book Trade Organizations

Cámara Argentina de Editores de Libros*, Maipú 359, 2° piso, of 31, Buenos Aires Tel: 451322
President: Hector Oscar Tucci
Association of Argentine Book Publishers

Cámara Argentina de Editoriales Tecnicas*, Venezuela 668, Buenos Aires
Argentinian Association of Technical Publishers

Cámara Argentina de Publicaciones*, Montevideo 48, 4° piso, Buenos Aires
President: Fernando Vidal Buzzi
Argentine Publications Association

Cámara Argentina del Libro*, Ave Belgrano 1580, 6° piso, 1093 Buenos Aires Tel: 388383
Secretary: A Sisco
Argentine Book Association

Federación Argentina de Librerías, Papelerías y Actividades Afines*, España 848, Losario, Santa Fé
Federation of Bookstores, Stationers and Related Activities

Publishers

Editorial **Abaco** de Rodolfo Depalma SRL+*, Avda Callao 441, 7° D, 1022 Buenos Aires Tel: 459604
Man Dir Editorial: Rodolfo Depalma; *Sales:* Raúl Wilkis; *Production:* Marcos José Azubel
Branch Off: Centenera 461, Buenos Aires
Subjects: Law, Economics, Sociology, Philosophy, History, Psychology
Founded: 1975

Editorial **Abeledo** Perrot SAEeI+*, Lavalle 1280-1328, 1048 Buenos Aires Tel: 352848
Man Dirs: Juan Carlos Abeledo, Emilio José Perrot; *Sales Dir:* Carlos Alberto Pazos
Subject: Law
Founded: 1901
Bookshop: Lavalle 1280-1328, 1048 Buenos Aires

Editorial **Acme** SA+*, Santa Magdalena 633, 1008 Buenos Aires Tel: 461662
Man Dir: Emilio I González
Subjects: General Fiction, Belles Lettres, Poetry, Biography, History, How-to, Juveniles, Paperbacks, Technical, University & Primary Textbooks
Founded: 1949

Aguilar Argentina SA de Ediciones+*, Ave Córdoba 2100, 1120 Buenos Aires Tel: 466400/466559
Man Dir: Antonio Sempere; *Sales Dir:* Manuel Rodríguez
Parent Company: Aguilar SA de Ediciones, Spain (qv)
Br Off: Deán Funes 501, Córdoba
Subjects: Philosophy, Literature, Art, Psychology, Economics, Technical, Juveniles
1977: 24 titles *Founded:* 1946

Librería **Akadia** Editorial+, Luis María Drago 389, 1414 Buenos Aires Tel: 549037
Man Dir: José F Patlallan
Subject: Medicine
Bookshop: At above address
Founded: 1967

Editorial **Albatros** SRL+*, Lavalle 3975, 1190 Buenos Aires Tel: 861215
Man Dir: Roberto R Canevaro
Subjects: Agriculture, Animal Care & Breeding, Technical, How-to, Social Sciences, Medicine, University Textbooks
Founded: 1967

Editorial **Alfa** Argentina SA+*, Defensa 599, 3er piso, 1065 Buenos Aires Tel: 331199/341473
Man Dir: Leonardo Milla; *Manager:* Héctor Allegrini
Subjects: General Fiction, Literature, Philosophy, Psychology, University Textbooks
Founded: 1971

Editorial Rodolfo **Alonso** SRL, Sánchez de Bustamante 923, 1173 Buenos Aires Tel: 891346
Man Dir: Rodolfo Alonso; *Sales Manager:* Raquel Rebaudi Basavilbaso
Subjects: General Fiction & Nonfiction
1977: 2 titles *1978:* 8 titles *Founded:* 1968

América Norildis Editores SA, Belgrano 624, 11 piso, Buenos Aires Tel: 349903
Man Dir & Editorial: Fernando Videl Buzzi; *Sales & Publicity:* Federico Alberto Catalano; *Production:* Jorge Draoz Bodi; *Rights & Permissions:* Teresa Vernengo
Parent Company: Crea SA (qv)
Associate Company: Editorial Huemul, Buenos Aires (qv)
Subjects: Secondary and University Textbooks, Fiction, Literature
1977: 38 titles *Founded:* 1970

Editorial **Américalee** SRL+*, Tucumán 353, 1049 Buenos Aires Tel: 323750/320958
Man Dir: Héctor E Landolfi; *Sales Dir:* Josefa A S de Landolfi
Subjects: Technical Science, Sports, Cooking
1978: 20 titles *Founded:* 1939

Editorial **Americana**+*, Brasil 675, 1154 Buenos Aires Tel: 238862
Man Dir: Manuel Rey Tosar
Subjects: History, Politics, Social Sciences, Arts, Fiction

Amorrortu Editores SA+*, Icalma 2001, Esq José A Salmún Feijóo, 1274 Buenos Aires Tel: 282630/282818
Man Dir: Horacio de Amorrortu
Orders to: Icalma 2001, 1274 Buenos Aires
Founded: 1967
Subjects: Anthropology & Religion, Economy, Philosophy, Psychology, Sociology, Argentine current affairs

Ediciones **Andromeda**+*, Mexico 625, pisa 1°, 1097 Buenos Aires Tel: 308280
Man Dir, Rights & Permissions: Carlos Samonta; *Editorial:* Jorge A Sanchez
Subjects: General Fiction, Literature
1977: 15 titles *Founded:* 1975

Arbó SACeI+*, Ave Martín García 653, 1268 Buenos Aires Tel: 280643/280647
Man Dir: Orestes Arbó; *Technical Dir:* J M Barcala; *Production:* Ariel Arbó; *Publicity:* Clotilde E H de Arbó
Subjects: Science & Technology
1977: 10 titles *Founded:* 1912

Editorial **Astrea** de Alfredo y Ricardo Depalma SRL+*, Lavalle 1208, 1048 Buenos Aires Tel: 351880
Man Dir: Alfredo Depalma; *Sales Dir:* Ricardo Depalma
Subjects: Law, Sociology, Politics, History, Philosophy, Economics
Bookshop: Librería Astrea, Lavalle 1208, 1367 Buenos Aires
1977: 32 titles *Founded:* 1968
Miscellaneous: Associate company of Ediciones La Bastilla, Buenos Aires (qv)

Editorial El **Ateneo**+, Pedro García SA, Patagones 2463, 1282 Buenos Aires Tel: 942/9002/9152/9052/9102 Cable Add: Ateneo
Dirs: Pedro García, Eustasio A García, Jorge I Letemeudía
Subjects: Medicine, Agronomy, Veterinary Science, Economics, Technical, Education, Business, University Textbooks
Founded: 1912
Bookshop: Florida 336, 340 & 344, 1005 Buenos Aires Tel: (46) 6801/6805

Editorial **Atlántida** SA+, Florida 643, 1005 Buenos Aires Tel: 315416 Cable Add: Ediatlán *Telex:* 121163 AR
Man Dir: Alfredo J Vercelli; *Sales Dir:* Fernando A Parodi
Subject: Juveniles, Textbooks
1977: 70 titles *1978:* 95 titles *Founded:* 1918
Bookshop: Florida 643, 1005 Buenos Aires

Asociación Ediciones La **Aurora**+, Doblas 1753, 1424 Buenos Aires Tel: 9215817/9224937
Dir: Pablo A La Moglie; *Editorial, Rights & Permissions:* Marcelo Pérez Rivas; *Sales Dir:* Mario C Ale
Subjects: Literature, History, Philosophy, Religion, Theology, Sociology, Psychology, Linguistics, Children's books
Bookclubs: Club del Libro Nuevo, Doblas 1753, 1424, Buenos Aires (qv)
Bookshop: Libreria La Aurora, Corrientes 728, 1043 Buenos Aires
1977: 42 titles *1978:* 25 titles *Founded:* 1923

B A E S A (Buenos Aires Edita SA)+*, Cordoba 1249, Buenos Aires
1977: 8 titles

Editorial Com Ind **Barry**, SRL+*, Talcahuano 860, 1013 Buenos Aires Tel: 447075

Ediciones la **Bastilla***, Lavalle 1208, 1048 Buenos Aires Tel: 351880
Man Dir: Alfredo Depalma; *Sales Dir:* Ricardo Depalma
Subjects: Politics, History
1977: 8 titles *Founded:* 1972
Miscellaneous: Associate company of Editorial Astria de Alfredo y Ricardo Depalma SRL, Buenos Aires (qv)

Asociacion **Bautista** Argentina de Publicaciones+*, Rivadavia 3464, 1203 Buenos Aires Tel: 888938, 888924
Man Dir: Hans Iver Jorgensen; *Assistant Manager:* Emanuel Benavídez; *Editorial Dir:* Arnoldo Canclini
Br Offs: San Martín 1572, 2000 Rosario, Santa Fe; Tucumán 351, 5000 Córdoba; San Martín 2242, 5500 Mendoza
Subject: Religion
1977: 2 titles *Founded:* 1906

SA Editorial **Bell**+*, Otamendi 215-17, 1405 Buenos Aires Tel: 901076/77/78 Cable Add: Edibell
Man Dir: Hugo O Varela; *Sales Dir:* C E Lippold; *Publicity Dir:* S Frasso;

4 ARGENTINA

Advertising Dir: Susana Tubal; *Rights & Permissions:* Mario Martínez
Subjects: How-to, General Science, Technical, Sports
Founded: 1927

Editorial **Beta** SRL+*, Tacuarí 237, 1071 Buenos Aires Tel: 389586
Man Dir: Miguel Angel Bini
Subjects: Medicine, Psychology, University Textbooks
Founded: 1948

Bias Editora*, Lavalle 1294, 1048 Buenos Aires Cable Add: Biasedita
Man Dir: Ival Rocca; *Editorial:* Ignacio Javier Barrio; *Sales:* Rodolfo Esteban Amigorana; *Production:* Francisco Spatafora; *Publicity:* Jorge O'Connor
Subjects: Law, Economics
Bookshop: Bias Editora (Libros Jurídicos), Lavalle 1294, 1048 Buenos Aires Tel: 354161
1977: 5 titles *Founded:* 1966

Librería **Bonum** SACI+*, Maipú 859-1° subsuelo, 1006 Buenos Aires Tel: 3929763 Cable Add: Bonum
Man Dir: Antonio Gremelspacher; *Sales Dir:* René Juan Trossero
Subjects: Religion, Textbooks
Founded: 1960

Ediciones **Botella** al Mar+*, Viamonte 2754-1° "5", 1213 Buenos Aires Tel: 898073

Editorial **Bruguera** Argentina*, Hipólito Irigoyen 646-650, Buenos Aires Tel: 301932/309255
Man Dir: Jorge Merlini
Parent Company: Editorial Bruguera SA, Spain (qv)

Editorial **Calicanto**+, Suipacha 831-3° 'C', 1008 Buenos Aires Tel: 317028
Man Dir: Eduardo Irazabal
Subjects: Literature & Criticism
Founded: 1975

Editorial **Cangallo** SACH+*, Ave Belgrano 609, 1092 Buenos Aires Tel: 338848/330204/332453
Man Dir: Norberto del Hoyo
Imprint: Talleres Graficos Mundial SRL
Subjects: Law, Economics, Business, University Textbooks
Bookshop: Ave Belgrano 609, 1092 Buenos Aires
1977: 7 titles *Founded:* 1968

Editorial **Cartago**+*, Viamonte 2617, 5° piso, of D, 1056 Buenos Aires Tel: 472783
Subjects: Politics, Economics, History

Editorial **Caymi**+*, 15 de Noviembre 1149, 1130 Buenos Aires Tel: 232474
Subjects: Popular Science & Medicine, Yoga, Judo & Karate, Magic & Fortune-Telling, Occultism, Sexology, Science Fiction, Spanish & South American Classics

Celcius — J J Vallory+*, Ave Belgrano 2815 - 1, Buenos Aires Tel: 932469/939414
Subjects: Medicine, Politics, History
1978: 4 titles

Centro Editor de America Latina SA*, Cangallo 1228, 2° D, 1038 Buenos Aires Tel: 359449/350142 Cable Add: Centroedit
Man Dir: José Boris Spivacow; *Sales Dir:* Aldo Antonio Sangoi
Subjects: Literature, Biography, History, Art, Psychology, How-to, Juveniles, General Science, Social Science, Educational Materials
Founded: 1966

El **Cid** Editor — Eduardo Varela-Cid+, Alsina 500, 1087 Buenos Aires Tel: 330071

Editorial **Científica** Argentina*, Paraguay 1300, Buenos Aires Tel: 443562
Man Dir: Fernando Duelo Cavero
Subjects: Argentine history, Pedagogy, Various

Editorial **Ciordia** SRL+*, Ave Belgrano 2271, 1094 Buenos Aires Tel: 481681
Man Dir: Eduardo B Ciordia; *Sales Dirs:* Manuel Ciordia, Carlos Danzini
Subjects: Literature, Philosophy, Psychology, University & Secondary Textbooks
Founded: 1938

Editorial **Claretiana**, Lima 1360, (1138) Buenos Aires Tel: 279250 Cable Add: Editorial Claretiana
Man Dir, Editorial, Rights & Permissions: Domingo A Beltrani; *Sales:* Eduardo Righetti; *Publicity:* José Luis Pérez
Subject: Religion
1977: 56 titles *1978:* 26 titles *Founded:* 1956

Editorial **Claridad** SA+*, San José 1627, Buenos Aires Tel: 235573 Cable Add: Claridad Baires
Man Dir: Dr Elio M A Colle; *Sales Manager:* José Zamora
Subject: General Literature
Founded: 1922

Editora **Close Up** SA+*, Thames 2450, 1414 Buenos Aires Tel: 7742926/1278

Club de Lectores+, Ave de Mayo 624, 1084 Buenos Aires Tel: 343955
Man Dir: Juan Manuel Fontenla; *Sales:* Carlos A Alvano; *Publicity:* María Inés Fontenla
Subjects: History, Philosophy, Religion, Psychology, Social Science, University Textbooks
1978: 36 titles *Founded:* 1938

Libreria del **Colegio** SA*, Humberto 1° 545, 1103 Buenos Aires Tel: 337867
Subjects: Educational Books, Textbooks

Colmegna SA+, San Martín 2546, 3000 Santa Fe Tel: 23102
Man Dir, Editorial, Sales: Nestor Lammertyn
Subjects: Literature, History, Poetry
Bookshop: San Martín 2546, 3000 Santa Fe
1977: 34 titles *Founded:* 1889

Editorial **Columba** SA+*, Sarmiento 1889-5°, 1044 Buenos Aires Tel: 451145
Man Dir: Ramón Columba
Subjects: Classics in translation, Twentieth century themes
Founded: 1953

Compañia Impresora Argentina SA+*, Alsina 2049, 1090 Buenos Aires Tel: 472308

Editorial **Conjunta** SRL+*, Fr J S M de Oro 2587, 1425 Buenos Aires Tel: 7741734

Ediciones **Contabilidad** Moderna SACIC+*, Independencia 3277/81, 1225 Buenos Aires Tel: 934918/19
Man Dir: Juan Carlos García Stella; *Sales Manager:* Oscar B Himschoot
Subject: Business
Founded: 1943

Editorial **Contempora** SRL+*, Sarmiento 643, of 522, 1041 Buenos Aires Tel: 451793
Subject: Architecture

Ediciones **Corregidon** SAICI & E+*, Talcahuano 463, 1013 Buenos Aires Tel: 35-3203/4598
Dir: Manuel Pampín
Subject: General Literature
Founded: 1972

Cosmopolita SRL+, Chile 474, 1098 Buenos Aires Tel: 348925
Man Dir: Eva Ruth F de Rapp
Subjects: Technical, Agriculture
Founded: 1940

Crea SA, Belgrano 624, 11 Piso, 1092 Buenos Aires Tel: 307891/09
Editorial, Sales Dir: Osvaldo Pierdominici; *Sales, Publicity:* Luis Alvarez; *Rights & Permissions:* Teresa Vernengo
Subsidiary Companies: América Norildis Editores SA, Editorial Huemul (qqv)
1978: 47 titles

Editorial **Crespillo** SA+*, Defensa 485, 1065 Buenos Aires Tel: 347384
Subjects: History, Arts, Maps

Depalma SRL+, Talcahuano 494, 1013 Buenos Aires Tel: 407306
Man Dir: Roque Depalma; *Sales Dir:* Alberto E Barón
Subjects: Law, History, Social Science, Business, University Texts
1977: 52 titles *1978:* 64 titles *Founded:* 1944
Bookshop: Talcahuano 494, 1013 Buenos Aires

Editorial **Difusión** SA+, Sarandí 1065, Buenos Aires Tel: 9410118
Man Dir: Luis Luchia Puig; *Sales Dir:* Domingo Palombella
Subjects: Literature, Philosophy, Religion, Juveniles, Education, Textbooks
Founded: 1936

Distasa*, Córdoba 2064, Buenos Aires
Associated Companies: See under Alianza Editorial SA, Spain

Ediciones **Dronte** Argentina SRL+*, Juàn de Garay 1323, Buenos Aires Tel: 267207/268015
Man Dir: Nestor Ricardo Gutierrez
1976: 22 titles *Founded:* 1972

E C A (Ediciones Culturales Argentinas)*, Ave Alvear 1690, 1014 Buenos Aires Tel: 444124
Man Dir: Luis Ricardo Furlan
Subjects: Argentine Literature, Publications of the Ministry of Culture & Education
Founded: 1961

E U D E B A (Editorial Universitaria de Buenos Aires)*, Rivadavia 1571-73, 1033 Buenos Aires Tel: 371527
Man Dir: Capt de Navio Francisco Suarez Battan; *Sales Dir:* Eduardo Suarez Corrado; *Advertising Dir:* Miguel A Molaccino
Br Off: Córdoba, Arg, México
Subjects: Literature, Biography, History, Art, Philosophy, Reference, Religion, Medicine, Psychology, Science & Technology, Social Sciences, Juveniles, Manuals, University & Secondary Textbooks
Founded: 1959

Edicient SAIC, Pte Luis Saenz Peña 1021, 1110 Buenos Aires Tel: 235115
President: Rubén S Coda; *Technical Dir:* Roberto J Fillmann; *Sales Dir:* Julio A Casati; *Publicity:* Horacio A Andrada
Subjects: Technical, Electronics

Editorial Sudamericana SA+, Humberto 1°
545, 1103 Buenos Aires Tel:
304232/337867 Cable Add: Librecol
President: Antonio López Llausas; *Man
Dir:* Jaime Rodrigué; *Editorial:* Enrique
Pezzoni; *Sales Dir:* Francisco La Falce;
Publicity Dir: Maria Eugenia Ramos Mejía;
Rights & Permissions: Gloria L Llovet de
Rodrigué
Associated Companies: Edhasa, Spain (qv);
Editorial Hermes, Mexico (qv)
Subjects: General Fiction & Nonfiction,
Literature, Biography, History, Philosophy,
Psychology
1977: 160 titles *Founded:* 1939

Editorial Universidad SRL+*, Corrientes
1250 – 4° 'J', 1043 Buenos Aires Tel:
356490/6850
Subject: Textbooks

Editorial Universitaria de Buenos Aires+*,
Ave Rivadavia 1571/73, 1033 Buenos Aires
Tel: 385478
Subject: Textbooks

Emecé Editores SA+*, Carlos Pellegrini
1069 9°, 1009 Buenos Aires Tel:
314710/314906/317327 Cable Add:
Emece/Baires
President: Dr Bonifacio del Carril;
Administration: Marcos I Fantin; *Sales
Dirs:* Oscar Guerrieri, Eduado Fantin;
Publicity Dir: Jose A Mateo; *Rights &
Permissions:* Jorge O Naveiro, José A
Mateo; *Editorial:* Jorge O Naveiro, Carlos
V Frias, Bonifacio P del Carril; *Production:*
Francisco F Del Carril
Orders to: Emece Distribuidora SA, Alsina
2062, 1090 Buenos Aires
Subsidiary Companies: Emecé Distribuidora
SA, Alsina 2062, 1090 Buenos Aires
Associated Companies: Ultramar Editores
SA, Mallorca 49, Barcelona 29, Spain;
Riomar Editora y Distribuidora, Atenas 42,
Mexico 6 DF
Book Club: Club 'El Libro del Mes' (qv)
Subjects: Fiction, Biography, Essays,
Nonfiction, Science Fiction, Mystery
1977: 100 titles *1978:* 110 titles *Founded:*
1939

Angel **Estrada** y Cía EICIEI & ASA+,
Bolivar 462-66, 1066 Buenos Aires Tel:
336521/27
Man Dir: Angel M de Estrada
Subjects: How-to, Primary & Secondary
Textbooks, Books for Infants, Teaching
Guides, Atlas
1978: 20 titles *Founded:* 1869

Fabril Editora SA+*, Armenia 2097 – 3°,
1289 Buenos Aires Tel: 213601
Subjects: General Nonfiction, Textbooks,
Reference Books, Arts, Humanities

Ediciones Librerías **Fausto**+*, Ave
Corrientes 1316, 1043 Buenos Aires Tel:
453914/456266
Manager: Rafael Zorrilla
Bookshops: see under Booksellers (Librerías
Fausto & Martín Fierro)

Ediciones de la **Flor** SRL+*, Uruguay 252,
Piso 1° B, 1015 Buenos Aires Tel: 405795
Man Dir: Daniel Divinsky; *Sales Dir:* Elisa
Miler; *Publicity & Advertising Dir:* Norma
M Vich; *Rights & Permissions:* Ricardo
Perugorría
Subjects: Fiction, Literature, History,
Psychology, Juveniles, Humour
1977: 20 titles *Founded:* 1967

Ediciones **Formentor** SRL+*, Ave Belgrano
1462, 1093 Buenos Aires Tel:
371657/382769

Man Dir: Ruben Duran; *Sales Dir:* Enrique
Celis
Subjects: Literature, Philosophy, Religion,
Social Sciences, Psychology, Engineering,
University Textbooks
Founded: 1971

Editorial **Freeland***, Casilla de Correo 5093,
Buenos Aires Tel: 457845
Man Dir: Jorge Enrique Freeland
Subjects: Fiction, History
Founded: 1953

Editorial **Galerna** SA*, Charcas 3741, 1425
Buenos Aires Tel: 711739 Cable Add:
Galerna
Dirs: Julio Martín Alonso, Hugo B Levin
Subjects: Literature, History, Social
Sciences, Paperbacks
Founded: 1967
Bookshops: Librerías Galerna, Talcahuano
487; Tucumán 1425; both in Buenos Aires
Subsidiary: Librería Piloto (foreign sales &
bibliographic service)

Fernando **García Cambeiro***, Ave de Mayo
560, 1380 Buenos Aires Tel: 332713
Man Dir: Fernando García Cambeiro
Subjects: Essays on Latin American Writers
1976: 5 titles *1977:* 4 titles

Librería y Papelería Casa **García** SA,
C Pellegrini 41, Resistencia Chaco Tel: 5930
Man Dir: José García Pulido; *Sales Dir:*
Luis Aguirre
Subjects: Fiction, Poetry, General Literature
& Literary Criticism, History, Geography,
Politics
Bookshop: C Pellegrini 41, Resistencia
Chaco
Founded: 1939

Editorial **Geminis** SRL+*, Barcena 2105 –
8, 1431 Buenos Aires Tel: 513491
1977: 2 titles

Ediciones G **Gili** SA*, Cochambra 154-158,
Buenos Aires
Parent Company: Editorial Gustavo Gili
SA, Spain (qv)

Editorial **Glem** SACIF+, Avda Caseros
2056, 1264 Buenos Aires Tel: 266641
President: José Alfredo Tucci; *Vice-
President:* Héctor Oscar Tucci; *Dir:*
Eduardo Anibal Tucci
Subjects: Technical, Psychology
Founded: 1933

Editorial y Librería **Goncourt***, Av Callao
1519, 1024 Buenos Aires Tel:
449032/449743
Man Dir: Jaime Fariña
Subjects: Fiction & Nonfiction
Bookshop: Callao 1519, 1024 Buenos Aires
1977: 15 titles *Founddded:* 1952

Goyanarte Editor SA+*, Esmeralda 923 –
3° 'B', 1007 Buenos Aires Tel:
320023/8362 Telex: Bs As Booth NBR 9
Finazzi 32.0023
Man Dir: César Amadeo López; *Sales Dir:*
Hugo Hanuel Vázquez
Subject: Fiction
Founded: 1969 (as Juan Goyanarte Editore)

Gram Editora+, Cochabamba 1652, 1148
Buenos Aires Tel: 268397
Dir: Manuel Herrero Montes
Subjects: Educational Books, Religion
1978: 6 titles *1979:* 12 titles *Founded:* 1925

Editorial Juan Carlos **Granda**+*, Corrientes
1243, 1043 Buenos Aires Tel: 356114

Granica Editor SA+*, Lavalle 1634, 3°
piso, 1048 Buenos Aires Tel: 461456
Man Dir: Juan Granica
Subjects: Fiction, Art, Social Sciences,
Juveniles, University Textbooks
Founded: 1971

Librería & Editorial Alfa **Graziano** SACI*,
Sarmiento 1343, 1° piso, 1041 Buenos Aires
Tel: 495349
Man Dir: Mauricio Domingo Graziano
Bookshop: Sarmiento 1343, 1041 Buenos
Aires
Subjects: Medicine, Law, Social Sciences,
Economics, General Culture

Grijalbo SA+*, Belgrano 1256, 1093 Buenos
Aires
Parent Company: Editorial Grijalbo SA
(Mexico)
Subjects: Fiction & Nonfiction

Editorial **Guadalupe**+*, Mansilla 3865, 1425
Buenos Aires Tel: 846066
Man Dir: José Gallinger; *Sales Dir:*
Clemente Hoffmann; *Publicity Dir:* Roberto
Bossio; *Production, Rights & Permissions:*
Manuel de Gracia
Subjects: Pedagogy, Social Sciences,
Religion, Literature
Founded: 1942
Bookshops: Librería Guadalupe, Mansilla
3865, 1425 Buenos Aires; Librería Verbo
Divino, Deán Funes 165, Local 27, Córdoba

Librería **Hachette** SA, Rivadavia 739-43,
1002 Buenos Aires Tel: 348481 Cable Add:
Aglibrairi Baires Telex: 17479 HACBA AR
President: Juan A Musset; *Vice-President:*
Carmen P de Picó; *Commercial Manager:*
José Manuel Caneda
Bookshop: Librería Hachette, Rivadavia
739-743, 1002 Buenos Aires Tel: 348481
Subjects: History, Travel, Literature,
Philosophy
1977: 14 titles *1978:* 14 titles

Editorial **Hemisferio** Sur SA+, Pasteur 743,
1028 Buenos Aires Tel: 489825, 488454
Man Dirs: Juan Angel Peri, Adolfo Luis
Peña
Associated Companies: Editorial
Agropecuaria Hemisferio Sur SRL, Alzaibar
1328, Montevideo, Uruguay; Librería
Agropecuaria SA, Pasteur 743, 1028 Buenos
Aires, Argentina
Subjects: Agriculture, Veterinary Science,
Natural Science
1977: 25 titles *1978:* 30 titles *Founded:*
1966

Editorial **Hobby***, Constitución 2348,
Buenos Aires Tel: 9414255
Man Dir: Marcelo Oscar Castroman; *Sales
Manager:* Norberto Luis Carca
Subjects: Technical
Founded: 1936

Editorial **Huemul** SA+*, Reconquista 1011,
5° piso, 1003 Buenos Aires Tel: 324037
President: Fernando Vidal Buzzi; *Vice-
President:* Juan Carlos Pellegrini
Parent Company: Crea SA (qv)
Associate Company: América Norildis
Editores SA, Buenos Aires (qv)
Subjects: Secondary & Primary Textbooks
Founded: 1961

Librería **Huemul**+, Ave Santa Fe 2237,
1123 Buenos Aires Tel: 831666
Man Dir, Editorial: Antonio Rego; *Sales,
Publicity, Rights & Permissions:* Carlos L
Sánchez
Subjects: University, Secondary & Primary
Textbooks, Children's Books

1977: 12 titles *1978:* 12 titles *Founded:* 1954
Bookshop: Ave Santa Fe 2237, 1123 Buenos Aires

Editorial **Humanitas**, Carlos Calvo 644, 1102 Buenos Aires Tel: 7821449 (Orders to: Tres Américas, Alsina 722, Buenos Aires)
Man Dir: Aníbal Villaverde; *Sales Dir:* Leandro Ameghino; *Publicity Dir:* Mauricio Faistman
Subjects: Social Sciences, Psychology, Education, Psychological Textbooks
1977: 8 titles *1978:* 6 titles *Founded:* 1955

Instituto de Publicaciones Navales+*, Córdoba 547, 1054 Buenos Aires Tel: 311011

Editorial **Inter-Médica** SAICI+, Junín 917, piso 1°, Casilla de Correo 4625, Buenos Aires Tel: 833234/833148/855572
President: Jorge Modyeievsky; *Vice-President:* Sonia M B de Modyeievsky
Subjects: Medicine, Dentistry, General Science, University Textbooks
1978: 8 titles *Founded:* 1959

Intersea*, México 924, Buenos Aires

Biblioteca Popular **Judía***, Casilla de Correo 20, Suc 53, 1453 Buenos Aires (Located at: Larrea 744, 1030 Buenos Aires) Tel: 486213 Cable Add: Worldgress Baires
Editorial: Roberto Brzostowski
Subjects: Jewish History & Biography, Jewish Latinamerican Conference publications

Ediciones & Librería **Jurídica***, Calle 45, No 532, 1900 La Plata Tel: 41427
Subject: Law

Editorial **Juventud** Argentina+*, Defensa 355, 1065 Buenos Aires Tel: 337756
Parent Company: Editorial Juventud SA, Spain (qv)
Subjects: History, Juveniles, Fiction, Maps

Editorial **Kapelusz** SA+, Moreno 372, 1091 Buenos Aires Tel: 346451/59, 3928905 Cable Add: Kapelusz
Man Dir: Ricardo Pascual Robles; *Editorial, Rights & Permissions:* Diego S Guidotti; *Sales:* Hernando Ferreres; *Publicity & Public Relations:* Atilio A Veronelli
Subjects: Psychology, Pedagogy, Juveniles, Primary, Secondary & University Textbooks
Bookshop: Corrientes 999, Buenos Aires
1976: 126 titles *1977:* 146 titles *Founded:* 1905

Editorial **Kier** SACIFI+, Ave Santa Fe 1260, 1059 Buenos Aires Tel: 410507/418243
President: Alfonso Florencio Pibernus; *Vice President:* José Grigna; *Man Dir:* Héctor Pibernus; *Sales Dir:* Alberto Pibernus
Subjects: Eastern Religions, Astrology, Tarots, Occultism, Rosicrucianism, Medicine
1977: 98 titles *1978:* 132 titles *Founded:* 1907
Bookshop: Santa Fe 1260, 1059 Buenos Aires

Editorial **Labor** Argentina SA+*, Venezuela 617, 1095 Buenos Aires Tel: 334135
Man Dir: Pedro Clotas Cierco
Parent Company: Editorial Labor, Spain (qv)

Ediciones **Larousse** Argentina SA+, Valentin Gómez 3530, 1191 Buenos Aires Tel: 876671 Telex: 0121783 Cable Add: Editlarousse
President: Georges Lucas
Subjects: Dictionaries, Encyclopaedias

Luis **Lasserre** y Cía, SACIFI*, Alsina 1666, 1088 Buenos Aires Tel: 405803/451693
Subjects: Textbooks, Public Health, Maps

Latina SCA, Ave de Mayo 953 – 11°, 1084 Buenos Aires Tel: 389108/4631
Editorial: Juan Carlos Orgueira; *Sales:* Nelson Guillermo Cositorto
Subjects: Pre-school books, Juveniles
1978: 4 titles *Founded:* 1971

Editorial Victor **Lerú** SA+, Don Bosco 3834, 1206 Buenos Aires Tel: 8116098/6198/8978 (Located at: Casilla 2793, Correo central, 1000 Buenos Aires)
Man Dir: Victor Nep; *Sales Dir:* León Nep
Orders to: Editorial Victor Lerú SA, Casilla 2793, Correo central, 1000 Buenos Aires
Subjects: Art, Architecture, Technology, Primary, Secondary & University Textbooks, Music, Dictionaries, History
Founded: 1944
ISBN Publisher's Prefix: 84-8205

La **Ley** SA Editora e Impresora+, Tucumán 1471, 1050 Buenos Aires Tel: 403421
Man Dir: Carlos Maria Oliva Vélez; *Commercial Dir:* Jerónimo Luis Oliva Vélez; *Commercial Manager:* Norberto Carlos Polo; *Production Dir:* Enrique Algorta
Subjects: Law, Economics, Philosophy, History
1977: 10 titles *Founded:* 1935

Ediciones Carlos **Lohlé** SA+, Tacuarí 1139, Casilla de Correo 1000, 1139 Buenos Aires Tel: 279969 Cable Add: Lohlé Baires
President: Carlos F P Lohlé; *Man Dir:* Francisco M Lohlé
Subjects: Literature, Poetry, Philosophy, Religion, Psychology, Social Science
Founded: 1953

López Libreros Editores+*, Junín 901, 1113 Buenos Aires Tel: 837744
Man Dir: Dr Pablo A López; *Sales Manager:* R Enrique Lohrmann
Subject: Medicine
Founded: 1927

Editorial **Losada** SA+*, Alsina 1131, 1088 Buenos Aires Tel: 387267/389902 Cable Add: Edilosada
President: Gonzalo Losada; *Man Dir:* Gonzalo Pedro Losada; *Sales Dir:* Manuel Taboada
Br Offs: Moneda 1576, Santiago, Chile; Calle 18A, No 7-37, Bogotá, Colombia; Jirón Contumaza 1050, Lima, Peru; Maldonado 1092, Montevideo, Uruguay
Subjects: Fiction & Nonfiction, Classics, Poetry, Literary Studies, Philosophy, Psychology, Biography, History, Pedagogy, Secondary Textbooks
Founded: 1938

Ediciones **Macchi**+*, Córdoba 2015, 1120 Buenos Aires Tel: 838355
Man Dir: Raúl Luis Macchi; *Sales Dir:* Julio Ricardo Mora
Subjects: Economic Sciences
Founded: 1947
Bookshop: Córdoba 2015, 1120 Buenos Aires

Marymar Ediciones SA, Chile 1432, 1098 Buenos Aires Tel: 380391
President: Isay Klasse; *Man Dir:* Hildegard Kupfer; *Dir of Production:* Saúl Cherny
Subjects: Social, Political & General Science, Economics, Philosophy, Architecture, Technology, Music, Cinema, History, Teaching, Library Science, Ecology, Fiction & Classics, Psychology
1978: 35 titles *Founded:* 1960

Librería y Editorial La **Médica**+*, Córdoba 2901, 2000 Rosario Tel: 397858
Man Dir: Cataline C de Radeff; *Sales Dir:* Ruben T Radeff, Ricardo A Radeff, Roberto A Radeff
Subject: Medicine
Miscellaneous: Major Distributor of Schoolbooks and General literature

Editorial **Médica** Panamericana SA+, Junín 831, 1A, 1113 Buenos Aires Tel: 838819/466171
Man Dir, Editorial: Roberto Brik; *Sales:* Hector Brik; *Production:* Daniel Brik; *Publicity:* Hugo A Brik
Subsidiary Companies: Generalísimo 30, piso 14, Izquierda, Madrid 16, Spain; Herschel 153, Colonia Nueva Anzures, Mexico City 5, Mexico DF; Rua Salvador Correa 80 (Alimacao) Cep 04109, Sao Paulo, Brazil; Centro Andrés Bello, 6° piso, Oficina 64-E, Caracas, Venezuela
Subjects: Medicine, Dentistry, Rehabilitation, Nursing
1979: 450 titles *Founded:* 1953

Editorial Librería **Mitre** SRL+*, Bartólome Mitre 2063, 1039 Buenos Aires Tel: 495856
Man Dir: Rodolfo Amura
Subject: Technical (especially Mechanics)
1977: 6 titles *1978:* 5 titles *Founded:* 1949

Editorial **Mundi** SAIC y F+, Casilla Correo 47, Suc 53 Codigo, 1121 Buenos Aires Tel: 839339, 839663
Production, Publicity, Rights & Permissions: Elena Garcia Mila
Subjects: Dentistry, Medicine
1978: 15 titles *1979:* 8 titles *Founded:* 1939

Editorial **Mundo** Técnico SRL+, Montevideo 205, piso 6° K, 1019 Buenos Aires Tel: 350738 Cable Add: Muntex
Man Dir: Gustavo A Marini; *Sales Dir:* Juan C García Venturini
Literary Rep: International Editors' Co, Buenos Aires
Subjects: Technical, Engineering, Atlases, How-to, School Dictionaries & Textbooks
1977: 15 titles *1978:* 15 titles *Founded:* 1972

Librería y Editorial **Nigar** SRL+*, Humberto 1° 667, 1103 Buenos Aires Tel: 331794

Editorial **Norte** SAIC+*, José Mármol 2131, 1255 Buenos Aires Tel: 9239507

Editttorial **Nova** SACI+*, Perú 858, 1068 Buenos Aires Tel: 348698
Man Dir: Horacio D Rolando; *Publicity & Sales Dir:* María del Pilar Lopez Soto de Rolando
Subjects: Literature, Biography, History, Art, Philosophy, Religion, Medicine, Psychology, Education, University & Secondary Textbooks
Founded: 1945

Ediciones **Nueva Visión** SAIC+*, Tucumán 3748, 1189 Buenos Aires Tel: 895050
Man Dir: Jorge José Grisetti; *Sales Manager:* Anibal Victor Giacone
Subjects: Social Sciences, Psychology, Architecture, Art, Theatre
Founded: 1954
Bookshop: Viamonte 500, Buenos Aires

La **Obra**+*, Ave Independencia 3124-32, 1225 Buenos Aires Tel: 974291
Subject: Primary Textbooks

Ediciones **Orion**+*, Guatemala 4745, 1425 Buenos Aires Tel: 712800
Subjects: General Fiction & Nonfiction

Editorial **Paidós**+, Defensa 599, 1° piso, 1065 Buenos Aires Tel: 332275
Man Dir, Rights & Permissions: Enrique Butelman; *Sales Dir:* Renato Modai
Subjects: Social Sciences, Psychology, Medicine, Philosophy, Religion, History, Biography, Literature, University Textbooks
Founded: 1945
Bookstore: Librería Paidos, Las Heras and Canning

Ediciones **Pannedille**+*, Chacabuco 129, Buenos Aires Tel: 354957
Man Dir: Oscar Buonano
Subjects: History, Law, Technical
Founded: 1970

Casa **Pardo** SAC*, Defensa 1170, 1065 Buenos Aires Tel: 346676 Cable Add: Pardoroman
Dir: Roman José Pardo
Founded: 1892
Subjects: General Literature, Humanism
Miscellaneous: Company are exporters

Ediciones **Paulinas**+*, Nazca 4249, Buenos Aires Tel: 5723926/5724810 Cable Add: Paulinas
Man Dir: Lucía Monterumici; *Sales Dir:* Paulina Tibaldo
Br Offs: Buenos Aires 837, Rosario; San Jerónimo 2136, Sante Fé; 24 de Setiembre 512, Tucumán; San Martín 980, Mendoza; Antártida Argentina 178, Resistencia; Calle 49, No 744, La Plata (all in Argentina)
Subjects: Education, Religion
Founded: 1940

A **Peña** Lillo SA+*, H Yrigoyen 1394-1086, Buenos Aires Tel: 370994
Man Dir: Arturo Peña Lillo; *Sales Dir:* María Luisa Comellí; *Production & Publicity:* Laura Peña
Orders to: Rivadavia 739, Buenos Aires (Librería Hachette SA)
Associate Company: Librería Hachette SA
Subjects: History, Political Science, Economics, Sociology, Literature
1977: 8 titles *Founded:* 1956
ISBN Publisher's Prefix: 84-8203
Miscellaneous: Firm is an importer and exporter

Ediciones **Periféria** SRL*, Cangallo 1730, 6° piso, of 68, 1037 Buenos Aires Tel: 450574
Subjects: Social Sciences, University Textbooks
Founded: 1971

Editorial Argentina **Plaza & Janés** SA+*, Lambaré 893, Buenos Aires Tel: 866769/866785
Man Dir: Jorge Perez; *Sales Dir:* Ernesto Pena
Subjects: General Fiction & Nonfiction

Editorial **Pleamar**, Corrientes 1994, 1° piso, Buenos Aires
Man Dir: Andrés Alfonso Bravo
Subjects: Political & Social Science
Founded: 1965

Editorial **Plus Ultra** SAI & C+*, Viamonte 1755, 1055 Buenos Aires Tel: 446605/446694/446788 Cable Add: Plusultra
Man Dirs: Rafael Román, Lorenzo Marengo, Diego Mazzitelli; *Editorial:* Carlos Alberto Lopreté; *Sales:* Ricardo Errea; *Production:* Francisco Barbati; *Publicity:* Fernando Sorrentino
Subjects: Literature, History, Law, Textbooks, Economics, Philosophy, Politics, Sociology, Psychology, Pedagogy, Children's Books
Bookshops: Viamonte 1755, 1055 Buenos Aires; Riobamba 265, 1025 Buenos Aires
1977: 78 titles *Founded:* 1964

Pomaire SA+*, Lavalle 1634 – 3° 'G', 1048 Buenos Aires Tel: 490669
Man Dir: Oscar Molina
Parent Company: Editorial Pomaire, Spain (qv)
Subject: Fiction

Prolam SRL (Ediciones Economia y Empresa)*, México 625, Buenos Aires Tel: 308280
Man Dir: Beatriz E P de Lambruschini
Subjects: Economics, Business, Science & Technology
Founded: 1958

Editorial **Proyección** SRL+*, Yapeyú 321, Buenos Aires Tel: 8115086
Man Dirs: Ernesto Portela, Noe Bursuck; *Sales Dir:* Carlos Garcia Iribarren
Subject: Political Science
Founded: 1968

Ricordi Americana SAEC+*, Cangallo 1558, 1037 Buenos Aires Tel: 409841/3 Cable Add: Ricordamericana Telex: 122580
Man Dir: Renzo Valcarenghi; *Manager:* Egilberto Chiti; *Editorial, Sales:* Ernesto Larcade
Associate Companies: Ricordi Brasileira, Sao Paulo, Brazil; G & C Ricordi, Italy (qv); G & C Ricordi, Mexico
Subjects: Music, Musical Teaching Methods
1977: 47 titles *Founded:* 1924

Ruy Diaz SAEIC+, Juan B Alberdi 3067, 1406 Buenos Aires Tel: 6126508/6125339 Cable Add: Ediruy
Man Dir: Rafael Zuccotti
Br Off: Casilla de Correo 45, Su cursal 6, 1406 Buenos Aires
Subjects: Educational, Atlases, Dictionaries
1977: 4 titles *1978:* 4 titles *Founded:* 1966

Editorial **Santiago** Rueda SRL+, Sarmiento 680 – 1°, 1041 Buenos Aires Tel: 491874/497860
Man Dir: Enrique S Rueda
Subject: Literature
Founded: 1940

Schapire Editor SRL+*, Uruguay 1249, 1016 Buenos Aires Tel: 440765
Man Dir: Miguel Schapire
Subjects: Literature, Biography, History, Art, Psychology, Social Science, Juveniles
Founded: 1935

Selcon SAEC & I (Selección Contable)*, Sarandí 1067, 1222 Buenos Aires Tel: 9410118
Man Dir: Luis Luchia Puig; *Sales & Advertising Dir:* Domingo Palombella
Subjects: Business, Economics
Founded: 1942

Santiago **Sentis** Melendo+*, Rivadavia 4076, 1205 Buenos Aires

Ediciones **Siglo XX** SAC & I+*, Maza 177, 1206 Buenos Aires Tel: 882758 Cable Add: Sigloveinte
Man Dir: Isidoro Wainer; *Sales Dir:* Carlos Zorrilla
Bookshop: At above address
Subjects: General Fiction & Nonfiction
Founded: 1943

Editorial **Sigmar** SACI+*, Belgrano 1580, 7°, 1093 Buenos Aires Tel: 373045/384474 Cable Add: Sigmar
Man Dir: Sigfrido Chwat
Subject: Juveniles
1977: 28 titles *Founded:* 1941

Ediciones del **Sol** SA*, Ave Roque Saénz Peña 974, 8° piso B, Buenos Aires Tel: 350473
Man Dir: Adolfo Colombres; *Sales Dir:* Manuel Valiz
Literary Rep: International Editors' Co, Buenos Aires
Subjects: Fiction, General Literature, Social Sciences
Founded: 1973

Editorial Ramon **Sopena** av Rio de la Plata SAI y C+*, Bolívar 430, Casilla de Correo 1075, 1066 Buenos Aires Tel: 309748/340748/345930
Subjects: Dictionaries, Language & Linguistics, Literature & Criticism, Spanish & Hispano-American classics, Chess, Health & Beauty, Practical Guides, Contemporary Politics, History, Children's Anthologies, all mainly paperback

Editorial **Stella**+*, Viamonte 1984, Buenos Aires
Subjects: Non-fiction, Textbooks

Studia Croatica*, Carlos Pelegrini 743.P.3, Buenos Aires Tel: 3927254

Editorial **Sur** SA+*, Viamonte 494 – 8°, 1053 Buenos Aires Tel: 325148

T E A (Tipográfica Editora Argentina)+*, Lavalle 1430, 1048 Buenos Aires Tel: 405668
Man Dir: Pedro San Martín; *Sales Dir:* María Teresa San Martín
Subjects: History, Social Science, Law, Economics, Philosophy
Founded: 1946

Talleres Graficos Mundial SRL, imprint of Editorial Cangallo (qv)

Instituto Torcuato di **Tella**, 11 de Septiembre 2139, 1428 Buenos Aires Tel: 7848255/7848264/7815013/7815015
Dir: Javier Villanueva
Subjects: Social Sciences, Economics, History, Political Science, Epistemology and Methodology of the Social Sciences
1977: 6 titles *1978:* 5 titles *Founded:* 1958

Ediciones **Theoria** SRL, Rivadavia 1255, 4° piso, of 407, Casilla de Correo 5096, 1033 Buenos Aires Tel: 380131
Man Dir: Jorge O Orús; *Sales Dir:* José Luis Menéndez
Subjects: Literature, Biography, History, Religion
1978: 8 titles *Founded:* 1954

Editorial **Tiempo** Contemporaneo*, Viamonte 1453, 10° piso, of 66, 1055 Buenos Aires Tel: 459640
Man Dir: Alberto Mario Serebresky; *Sales Dir:* José Fuster
Subjects: General Fiction, History, Philosophy, Psychology, Technical, Medicine, Social Sciences, University Textbooks
Founded: 1969

Ediciones **Tiempo de Hoy***, Casilla de Correo 66, Sucursal 32, 1432 Buenos Aires
Dir: Juan Carlos Nigro
Miscellaneous: Firm runs a writers' workshop, *Taller Literario*, offering tuition in writing techniques, and also provides a review service, API (see under Literary Associations)

Distribuidora **Tres Americas** SAC+*, Alsina 722, 1087 Buenos Aires Tel: 339063/9066/9101

Ediciones **Tres Tiempos** SRL+*, Ave Belgrano 225, 1092 Buenos Aires Tel: 342913/347184/338785
Man Dirs: José C Orríes e Ibars, Canio Carmelo Cillo; *Assistant Manager:* Jose Luis Tato; *Editor:* Luis F Coco; *Administration:* Luis Pirozzi; *Sales Dir:* Raul Villar; *Advertising & Promotion:* Florinda Minsk; *Rights & Permissions:* Teresa Cillo; *Imports/Exports:* Alejandro Luis Calegari
Orders to: Belgrano 225, 3° 23
Branch Off: Moreno 3201, Buenos Aires Tel: 936498
Subjects: Anthropology, Architecture and Urbanism, Arts, Cinematography and Theatre, Demography, Ecology, Economics, Education, Philosophy, Psychology, Management, Technology, Sciences, Social & Political Sciences, Novels, Fiction & Poetry
1977: 65 titles *1978:* 103 titles *Founded:* 1975

Editorial **Troquel** SA+*, San José 157-159, 1076 Buenos Aires Tel: 380118/380349 Cable Add: Troquelsa
President: Armando Silvio Ressia; *Sales Manager:* Alberto Meriggi
Subjects: General Literature, Technology, Textbooks
Founded: 1954

Turismo Editorial*, Corrientes 369, Buenos Aires

Turner Ediciones SRL, Alsina 1535, 8° piso, of 803, Buenos Aires 1088 Tel: 466477
Man Dir: Mary C Turner
Subjects: Reference, Bibliography
1977: 3 titles *1978:* 2 titles

Universidad SRL*, Corriente 1250, P 12 D, 1043 Buenos Aires Tel: 356490/356850
Man Dir, Production: Alfonso La Rocca; *Sales, Rights & Permissions:* Alejandro José Lo Iacono; *Publicity:* Raul Caracciolo
Subjects: Law (civil and commercial)
1977: 2 titles *1978:* 6 titles *Founded:* 1970

Javier **Vergara** Editor SRL+*, Juncal 691 9° y 10°, 1062 Buenos Aires Tel: 315653
Dir: Javier Vergara; *Rights:* Gabriela Cruz de Vergara
Br Offs: Cardenal Reig 18, Barcelona 14, Spain Tel: 3347754; Fresas 158, México 12 D F, Mexico Tel: 5756071; Ave Bulnes 80, Santiago, Chile Tel: 65921
Subjects: General Fiction, Nonfiction, Science Fiction
1978: 50 titles *Founded:* 1975

Victor P de **Zavalía**, Editor+, Alberti 835, 1223 Buenos Aires Tel: 9421274/9423046
Man Dir: Ricardo L de Zavalía; *Sales Dir:* Araceli L de Zavalía
Bookshop: Law School of the University of Buenos Aires
Subjects: Law
1977: 8 titles *1978:* 8 titles *Founded:* 1950

Literary Agents

International Editors' Co*, Nicolás Costa, Cabildo 1156, Buenos Aires Tel: 734613
Cable Add: Lifeplay
Also office in Spain (qv)

Lawrence **Smith**, Ave de los Incas, 3110 Buenos Aires 1426 Tel: 7845012 Cable Add: Litagent Baires

Book Clubs

Círculo de Lectores Argentina SA*, Esmeralda 155, 1035 Buenos Aires

Club del Libro Nuevo, Doblas 1753, 1424 Buenos Aires
Owned by: Asociación Ediciones La Aurora, Buenos Aires (qv)

Club 'El Libro del Mes'*, Alsina 2041, 1090 Buenos Aires
Owned by: Emecé Editores SA, Buenos Aires (qv)

Major Booksellers

Librería **A B C***, Florida 725, 1005 Buenos Aires Tel: 316848
Branches at: Avda Córdoba 685, 1054 Buenos Aires; Avda Libertador 13777, 1646 Martinez, Buenos Aires

American Books*, Tucumán 994, 1° piso, Buenos Aires Tel: 353704

El **Ateneo***, Florida 336, 340 & 344, 1005 Buenos Aires Tel: 466801

Bias Editora (Libros Jurídicos)*, Lavalle 1294, 1048 Buenos Aires Tel: 354161

Distribuidora **Cuspide***, Suipacha 764, 1008 Buenos Aires Tel: 3921727/3928868/3927434

Librería **Española***, Florida 943, 1005 Buenos Aires Tel: 323214/325850

Librerías **Fausto***, Ave Corrientes 1311, 1043 Buenos Aires Tel: 401222; Ave Corrientes 885, Buenos Aires Tel: 3927988 1043 Buenos Aires; Ave Santa Fé 1715, 1060 Buenos Aires Tel: 412708

Librería 'Martín **Fierro'***, Corrientes 1264, 1043 Buenos Aires Tel: 350444

Ediciones **Garriga** Argentinas SA+*, Talcahuano 897, Buenos Aires Tel: 443562

Librería Alfa **Graziano***, Sarmiento 1343, 1041 Buenos Aires Tel: 495349

Librería **Hachette**, Rivadavia 739-743, 1002 Buenos Aires Tel: 348481

Carlos **Hirsch** SRL, Florida 165, Galería Güemes 4° piso, Buenos Aires Tel: 332391/331787/307122

Librería **Huemul***, Ave Santa Fe 2237, 1123 Buenos Aires Tel: 831666

Librería **Kier**, Ave Santa Fe 1260, 1059 Buenos Aires Tel: 410507/418243

Librerías **MacKern** SA*, Lavalle 1765, Buenos Aires Tel: 460737

H F **Martínez** de Murguía*, Ave Córdoba 2270, Buenos Aires Tel: 486173

Librería **Morena***, Rivera Indarte 62, Ave Gral Paz 1, Ave Gral Paz 162, Córdoba Tel: 43600

Librería La **Nena***, Callao 410, Buenos Aires Tel: 450271/463562

Librería **Norte**, Las Heras 2225, Buenos Aires Tel: 843944

Nueva Visión*, Viamonte 500, Buenos Aires Tel: 326434

Librería General de Tomas **Pardo***, Maipú 618, Buenos Aires Tel: 3920496

Pigmalión*, Corrientes 515, Buenos Aires Tel: 494621

Librerías **Premier***, Corrientes 1583, Talcahuano 459, Callao 1180, Buenos Aires

Librería **Rodríguez**, Sarmiento 835, Buenos Aires Tel: 358125

Librería **Ross***, Córdoba 1347, Rosario Tel: 65378

Librería **Santa Fe***, Santa Fe 2386, Buenos Aires Tel: 835746; Santa Fe 2928, Buenos Aires Tel: 8219442

Librería **Sarmiento***, Libertad 1214-20, Buenos Aires Tel: 414792

Tres Américas Libros*, Alsina 722, Buenos Aires Tel: 339066

Major Libraries

Biblioteca del **Banco** Central de la República Argentina*, Reconquista 266, Buenos Aires
Library of the Central Bank

Biblioteca Nacional (National Library)*, México 564, Buenos Aires Tel: 347370

Biblioteca Nacional de Maestros*, Pizzurno 935, Buenos Aires
National Teachers' Library

Biblioteca Publico Central*, Calle 47, No 510, La Plata

Biblioteca de la **Associación Argentina** de Cultura Inglesa*, Juncal 851, Buenos Aires
British Council Library

Biblioteca del **Congreso** de la Nación*, Rivadavia 1850, Buenos Aires
National Library of Congress

Biblioteca **Lincoln***, Florida 935, Buenos Aires (USIS)

Biblioteca Pública Gratuita de 'La **Prensa**', Rivadavia 552, Buenos Aires

Instituto Bibliotecológico, **Universidad de Buenos Aires***, Casilla de Correo 901, 1000 Buenos Aires (Located at: Azcuénaga 280, Buenos Aires)

Biblioteca de la **Universidad del Salvador***, Callao 542, Buenos Aires

Biblioteca Mayor de la **Universidad Nacional de Córdoba** (Principal Library of the National University of Córdoba)*, Calle Obispo Trejo y Sanabria 242, Córdoba
Dir: Professor Joaquín García
Publications: Informativo (irregular), Monographs

Biblioteca Pública de la **Universidad Nacional de La Plata***, Plaza Rocha 137, La Plata, Provincia de Buenos Aires Tel: 24109
Dir: Mrs Haydée Cervantes de Artola
Publications: Bulletin 'Informaciones'

Library Associations

A B G R A (Asociación de Bibliotecarios Graduados de la República Argentina)*, Casilla de Correo 68, Suc 1, 1401 Ciudad de Buenos Aires
Association of Graduate Librarians of Argentina
Executive Secretary: Elida S Iriondo
Publications: Documentos Ocasionales, Reuniones Nacionales de Bibliotecarios (Documentos de Base; Actas); Memoria annual

Asociación Argentina de Bibliotecas y Centros de Información Científicos y Tecnicos*, Santa Fe 1145, Buenos Aires

Tel: 411405
Executive Secretary: Olga E Veronelli

Asociación de Ex-Alumnos de la Escuela Nacional de Bibliotecarios*, c/o Biblioteca Nacional, México 564, Buenos Aires

Centro De Documentación Bibliotecológica*
Universidad Nacional del Sur, Ave Alem 1253, Bahía Blanca
Dir: Atilio Peralta
Publications: Bibliografía Bibliotecológica Argentina, Quien es Quien en la Bibliotecología Argentina, Guía de las Bibliotecas Universitarias Argentinas, Documentacion Bibliotecologica, Indices de Revistas de Bibliotecología

Colegio de Bibliotecarios de la Provincia de Buenos Aires*, Calle 48, No 633, piso 3, oficina 315, 1900 La Plata

Dirección de Bibliotecas Municipales*, Talcahuano 1261, Buenos Aires

Instituto de Bibliográfia del Ministerio de Educación de la Provincia de Buenos Aires*, Calle 47, No 510, 6 piso, 1900 La Plata
Dir: María del Carmen Crespi de Bustos
Publications: Bibliografía Argentina de Historia, Boletín de Información Bibliográfica

Library Reference Books and Journals

Books

Bibliografía Bibliotecológica Argentina (Argentine Library Science Bibliography), Centre for Library Science Documentation, Ave Alem 1253, Bahía Blanca

Guía de las Bibliotecas Universitarias Argentinas (Guide to Argentine University Libraries), Centre for Library Science Documentation, Ave Alem 1253, Bahía Blanca

Journals

Boletín Informativo (Information Bulletin), Association of Graduate Librarians of Argentina, Talcahuane 1261, Dirección de Bibliotecas Publicas de la Municipalidad de Buenos Aires, Ciudad de Buenos Aires

Literary Associations and Societies

Academia Argentina de Letras*, Sánchez de Bustamante 2663, Buenos Aires
Secretary: Juan Carlos Ghiano
Publications: Boletín de la Academia Argentina de Letras (quarterly)
Library Publications: Serie de Clásicos Argentinos, Serie de Estudios Académicos, Serie de Discursos Académicos, Serie de Acuerdos acerca del Idioma, Boletín, Serie Estudios Lingüísticos y Filológicos

The **Dickens** Fellowship*, Basavilbaso 12A, Buenos Aires
Honarary Secretary: Miguel Alfredo Olivera

Instituto de Literatura*, Calle 47, No 625, La Plata
Dir: Arturo Cambours
Publications: Investigaciones, Boletín

P E N Club de la Argentina, Calle de Basavilbaso 1396, 1006 Buenos Aires
President of the Advisory Council: D Miguel Alfredo Olivera
Publications: Boletín and books

S A D E (Sociedad Argentina de Escritores)*, Uruguay 1371, 1016 Buenos Aires Tel: 413520/420773
Director: Horacio E Tarri; *Editorial:* Jorge Caldas Villar
Publication: Boletín de la SADE (Bi-monthly)

Sociedad General de Autores de la Argentina ('Argentores')*, Pacheco de Melo 1818-20, Buenos Aires Tel: 444518
Publications: Boletín Social (quarterly), *Argentores* (monthly)

Literary Periodicals

Boletín, Argentine Academy of Letters, Sánchez de Bustamante 2663, Buenos Aires

Boletín, Association of Argentine Writers, Uruguay 1371, 1016 Buenos Aires

Comentario, Tucuman 2137 y San Martin 663, Buenos Aires

Criterio, Alsina 840, Buenos Aires

Davar, Sociedad Hebraica Argentina, Sarmiento 2233, Buenos Aires

Histonium, Paraná 464, Buenos Aires

Igitur Revista Literaria, Republica de Israel 115, Córdoba

Sur, Viamonte 494, 8° piso, Buenos Aires

Literary Prizes

Argentine National Prize for Literature*
For best works of prose and Poetry. Awarded every three years. Enquiries to Argentinian Ministry of Education and Culture, General Directorate of Culture, Ave Alvear 1630, Buenos Aires

Alfredo A Bianchi Essay Prize*
For the best scholarly essay on any subject. Awarded annually. Enquiries to Association of Argentine Writers, Uruguay 1371, 1016 Buenos Aires

Buenos Aires Literary Prizes*
For the best works written or published during the year in Buenos Aires. Awards are given for fiction; essay (including biography and literary criticism); poetry. Awarded annually. Enquiries to Buenos Aires Municipality, Secretariat of Culture and Social Activities, Ave de Mayo 525, Buenos Aires

Carlos **Casavalle** Prize*
Awarded in turn for the best book published in Argentina in the following categories: fiction; poetry and drama; essay, including scientific writing. Awarded annually. Enquiries to Argentine Book Association, Paraguay 610, 7° piso, Buenos Aires

Premio **Emecé** Annual Prize*
For the best novel or short story by an unpublished writer. Enquiries to Emecé Editores SA, Carlos Pellegrini 1069 9°, 1009 Buenos Aires

First Book Prize*
For the first literary work written by an author under 30. Awarded annually. Enquiries to Argentine Book Association, Paraguay 610, 7° piso, Buenos Aires

Kraft Prize*
For the best unpublished novel, particularly by young and unknown authors. Awarded biennially. Enquiries to Guillermo Kraft Publishing Ltd, Moreno 872, Buenos Aires

Fernando **Moreno** Poetry Prize*
For outstanding work in Poetry. Enquiries to Association of Argentine Writers, Uruguay 1371, 1016 Buenos Aires

Premio de '**La Nación**' Prize*
Given by the newspaper *La Nación* for different types of literature. Enquiries to La Nación, Florida 343/San Martín, Buenos Aires CF

Pablo **Rojas** Paz Prize*
For the best unpublished biography. Enquiries to Association of Argentine Writers, Uruguay 1371, 1016 Buenos Aires

Ricardo **Rojas** Prize*
For prose work (imaginative writing, criticism, essay). Awarded biennially. Enquiries to Buenos Aires Municipality, Secretariat of Culture and Social Activities, Ave de Mayo 525, Buenos Aires

Medalla de Oro de la **S A D E** (Sociedad Argentina de Escritores)*
Annual prize for the total output of an author. Enquiries to Association of Argentine Writers, Uruguay 1371, 1016 Buenos Aires

Sarmiento Prize*
For the best book of prose written during the year. Awarded annually. Enquiries to Association of Argentine Writers, Uruguay 1371, 1016 Buenos Aires

Australia

General Information

Language: English
Religion: Predominantly Protestant
Population: 14.1 million
Bank Hours: 1000-1500 Monday-Thursday; 1000-1700 Friday
Shop Hours: 0900-1700 Monday-Friday; usually 0900-1200 Saturday
Currency: 100 cents = 1 Australian dollar
Export/Import Information: No tariffs on books. Advertising catalogues other than single copies or less than 1 kg gross weight dutied 35%. Most books, especially of literary or educational nature, free of sales tax. No import licences for books; no seditious literature permitted
Copyright: Signatory of UCC, Berne (see International section)

Book Trade Organizations

Association of Australian University Presses, Australian National University Press, PO Box 4, Canberra, ACT 2600
President: B Clouston
Incorporating Australian National University Press, Melbourne University Press, Sydney University Press, University of Queensland Press, University of Western Australia Press, University of New South Wales Press (qqv under Publishers)

Association of British Book Publishers Representatives in Australia*, 18-20 Collins St, Melbourne, Victoria 3000

Australian Book Publishers Association, 163 Clarence St, Sydney, NSW 2000 Tel: (02) 292570
Dir: Sandra Forbes
Publication: Directory of Members

10 AUSTRALIA

Australian Booksellers Association, Box 3254, GPO Sydney, NSW 2001 Tel: (02) 2325311

Australian Copyright Council*, 24 Alfred St, Milsons Point, NSW 2061 Tel: 921151
Chairman: G C O'Donnell (at above address)

Australian Independent Publishers' Association*, PO Box 4059, Mail Exchange, Melbourne, Victoria 3001
Secretary: Sally Milner

Australian Society of Indexers, Unit 4, 2 Erne St, Mont Albert, Victoria 3129
Secretary: Miss J Hagger

Book Trade Group (New South Wales)*, c/o Evan Grigor, Granada Publishing Australia Pty Ltd, 717 York St, Sydney, NSW 2000

Book Trade Group (Queensland)*, Barker, Conlan and Ferret Pty Ltd, Brisbane, Queensland 4000

Book Trade Group Secretary (Victoria)*, PO Box 4065, Mail Exchange, Melbourne, Victoria 3001 Tel: (03) 3599535
Secretary: Deborah Dare

Children's Book Council of Australia*, GPO 2428V, Melbourne, Victoria 3001
Secretary: Philip Sydenham
Branches in Australian Capital Territory, New South Wales, South Australia, Tasmania, Victoria, Western Australia

Christian Bookselling Association of Australia*, 125 New Line Rd, West Pennant Hills, NSW 2120
Secretary: Brian Geesing

Copyright Agency Ltd*, 24 Alfred St, Milsons Point, NSW 2061 Tel: 921151

Committee for **Freelance Writing***, The Secretary, PO Box 139, Caulfield South, Vic 3162

Galley Club of Sydney*, PO Box 91, Cammeray, NSW 2062

Imprint Society*, 125 Bank St, South Melbourne, Victoria 3205 Tel: 6999474
Secretary: Ian Green

National Book Council*, 4th Floor, 71 Collins St, Melbourne, Victoria 3000 Tel: (03) 638043
Executive Director: Stuart Edwards

New South Wales Booksellers' Association, 66 King St, Sydney 2000
Secretary: Ms Jean Abbey

Queensland Booksellers' Association*, Treasury Book Store, 14 Queen St, Brisbane 4000
Secretary: G Bott

Society of Editors*, c/o PO Box 176, Carlton South, Victoria 3053
Secretary: Christine Nicol

South Australia Booksellers' Association*, Adelaide University Bookshop Pty Ltd, GPO Box 498, Adelaide 5001
President: R M Amundsen

Tasmanian Booksellers' Association*, GPO Box 1415P, Hobart 7001
Secretary: M Tilley

United States Book Association*, PO Box 363, Crow's Nest, NSW 2065
Secretary: W Douglas

Victoria Booksellers' Association*, Collins Book Depot Pty Ltd, 86 Bourke St, Melbourne 3000
President: M G Zifcak

Western Australian Booksellers' Association, c/o Child Education Services, 13A Havelock St, West Perth, Western Australia 6005
Secretary: M Walton

Wholesale Booksellers Association of Australia*, c/o Book Supplies Pty Ltd, 35 York St, Sydney, NSW 2000 Tel: (02) 292620
Secretary: David Joel

Book Trade Reference Books and Journals

Books

Australian and Pacific Book Prices Current, OP Books Pty Ltd, PO Box 591, Brookvale, NSW 2100

Australian Book Publishers' Association: Guide to Book Outlets in Australia, Meldrum, Johnston and Weston, 163 Clarence St, Sydney, NSW 2000

Australian Books in Print, D W Thorpe Pty Ltd, 384 Spencer St, Melbourne, Victoria 3003

Books Australia (annual catalogue), PO Box 41, Glebe, NSW 2037

Current Australian Serials; a select list, National Library of Australia, Parkes Pl, Canberra, ACT 2600

Directory of Australian Booksellers, Australian Book Trade Advisory Committee, 163 Clarence St, Sydney, NSW

Journals

Australian Author, Australian Society of Authors, 24 Alfred St, Milsons Point, NSW 2061

Australian Book Review, 46 Porter St, Prahran, Vic 3181

Australian Books, National Library of Australia, Parkes Pl, Canberra, ACT 2600

Australian Bookseller & Publisher, D W Thorpe Pty Ltd, 384 Spencer St, Melbourne, Victoria 3003

Australian Government Publications, National Library, Parkes Pl, Canberra, ACT 2600

Australian National Bibliography, National Library of Australia, Parkes Pl, Canberra, ACT 2600

The Indexer, c/o Norman Hillyer, 139 The Ryde, Hatfield, Herts AL9 5DP, UK (Journal of Australian, American and British Societies of Indexers)

Weekly Book Newsletter, D W Thorpe Pty Ltd, 384 Spencer St, Melbourne, Victoria 3003

Publishers

A D I S Press Australasia Pty Limited+, PO Box 132, Balgowlah, NSW 2093 (Located at: 404 Sydney Road, Balgowlah, NSW 2093) Tel: 9492022 Cable Add: Adinfo Sydney Telex: ADIS AA25868
Chief Editorial Office: 15 Rawene Rd, PO Box 34-030 Birkenhead, Auckland 10, New Zealand Tel: 486125 Telex: NZ 21334 ADIS
Man Dir: William W Hughes; *Editorial:* Graeme S Avery; *Sales, Publicity:* Gervan McCune; *General Manager, Rights & Permissions:* David R Bleakley
Orders to: ADIS Press Australasia Pty Ltd, 404 Sydney Road, Balgowlah, NSW 2093
Associate Companies: ADIS Press International Ltd, Unit 5b, Fifth Floor, Gardena Court, Kennedy Terrace, Kennedy Rd, Hong Kong; ADIS Press USA Inc, 515 Madison Avenue, New York, NY 10022, USA; ADIS Press, Hummelsbuetteler Kirchenweg 36, 2000 Hamburg 63, Federal Republic of Germany
Imprints: ADIS Press
1977: 4 titles *1978:* 6 titles *Founded:* 1960
Subjects: Medicine
ISBN Publisher's Prefix: 0-9599827; 0-909337

A P C O L, an imprint of Alternative Publishing Co-operative Ltd (qv)

Acme Books*, 188 Weston St, Brunswick 3057 Tel: (03) 3873525
Publisher: Jim Hart

Addison-Wesley Publishing Co+, 31 Albany St, Crows Nest, NSW 2065 Tel: (02) 4381451 Cable Add: Adiwes Sydney
General Manager, Rights & Permissions: W Douglas; *Editorial:* James F Robins; *Sales:* Geoffrey Hasler (college and general), Chris Howard (school and juveniles); *Production:* Kenneth Markillie
Parent Company: Addison-Wesley Publishing Company, Reading, Mass, USA
Miscellaneous: Firm is an associate of Addison-Wesley Publishers Ltd, UK (qv for other associates)
Subjects: Educational Books, Scientific and Technical Books, Juveniles
1978: 37 titles

Adelaide University Union Press, PO Box 498, Adelaide 5001 Tel: 2234366 Telex: AA 89141 UNIVAD
Chief Executive: Ray Amundsen
Subjects: Poetry, Politics, Literature, Critiques
1978: 6 titles *1979:* 4 titles *Founded:* 1976
ISBN Publisher's Prefix: 09598309

Algona Publications Pty Ltd, PO Box 52, Montrose, Victoria 3765 Tel: 7283348
Chief Executives: John R Brownlie, Gloria E Harman
Subjects: Australian flora, fauna, history and landscape for travellers
1978: 3 titles *1979:* 1 title *Founded:* 1970
ISBN Publisher's Prefix: 0-909594

Allara Publishing*, 47 Deakin St, East Bentleigh 3165

George **Allen & Unwin** Australia Pty Ltd+, PO Box 764, North Sydney, NSW 2065 Tel: 9226399 Cable Add: Deucalion Sydney Telex: 24331 gaua
Man Dir: P A Gallagher; *Sales:* Roger Ward
Warehouse and Distribution: Bookstocks Pty Ltd, Cnr Bridge Rd & Jersey St, Hornsby, NSW 2077
Parent Company: George Allen & Unwin Ltd, UK (qv)
Associated Company: Allen & Unwin Inc, 198 Ash St, Reading, Mass 01867, USA
Subjects: Academic, Social Science, General Nonfiction
1978: 15 titles *Founded:* 1976
ISBN Publisher's Prefix: 0-86861

Alpha Books*, 280 Pitt St, Sydney 2000
Tel: (02) 265154
Head of Company: A W Sheppard

Alternative Publishing Co-operative Ltd+,
10 Shepherd St, Chippendale, Sydney 2008
Tel: (02) 2113837/591937
Chairman: Greg Crough; *Editorial, Sales,
Production, Publicity, Rights &
Permissions:* D K Cleaver
Imprints: APCOL
Branch Off: 4 Longbourne, North Clayton
3168
Subjects: Reference, High-priced
Paperbacks, Psychology, University &
Secondary Textbooks, History, Political
Science, Sociology, Economics
1978: 4 titles *1979:* 9 titles *Founded:* 1975

Angus & Robertson Publishers+, Unit 4, 31
Waterloo Rd, North Ryde, NSW 2113 Tel:
(02) 8872233 Cable Add: Fragment,
Sydney Telex: 26452
Chairman: Gordon Barton; *Publisher:*
Richard Walsh; *Publicity:* Alan Davidson;
Rights & Permissions: Gwenda Jarred
Branch Off: 627 Rathdowne St, North
Carlton, Victoria 3054
Subjects: General Fiction, Belles Lettres,
Poetry, Biography, History, How-to, Art,
Reference, Juveniles, Low- & High-Priced
Paperbacks, Medicine, Psychology, General
& Social Science, University
Founded: 1884
Bookshops: Angus & Robertson, 209 Pitt
St, Sydney, and many other branches
Subsidiaries: Angus & Robertson (South-
East Asia) Ltd, Singapore (qv); Angus &
Robertson (South-East Asia) Ltd,
135-C Dolores St, Pasay City, Metro
Manila, Philippines; Angus & Robertson
(UK) Ltd, UK (qv)
Miscellaneous: Firm is a division of Ipec
Holdings Ltd
ISBN Publisher's Prefix: 0-207

Ansay Pty Ltd+*, PO Box 90, 2040
Leichardt, NSW (Located at: 19-25 Beeson
St, Leichhardt 1) Tel: 5602044 Cable Add:
Cowboy Sydney
Man Dir: Philip Lindsay; *Editorial,
Production:* H E Lindsay; *Sales, Rights &
Permissions:* P S Lindsay; *Publicity:* C Rijks
Parent Companies: A L Lindsay & Co Pty
Ltd, Lindsays Leichardt Pty Ltd
Imprint: Dollar Books
Subjects: Fiction, Educational
1977: 8 titles *1978:* 12 titles *Founded:* 1972
ISBN Publisher's Prefix: 0-909245

Antipodean Publishers Pty Ltd*, 7 Lanceley
Pl, PO Box 277, Artarmon, NSW 2064 Tel:
(02) 4392616
Subjects: Australiana, History,
Psychological books by Australian authors
ISBN Publisher's Prefix: 0-86944

Apple Paperbacks, an imprint of Widescope
International Publishers Pty Ltd (qv)

Edward **Arnold** (Australia) Pty Ltd+, 373
Bay St, PO Box 146, Port Melbourne,
Victoria 3207 Tel: (03) 641346 Cable Add:
Edarnold Telex: 35974 AA
Man Dir: R D Blackmore
Subjects: Medicine, Psychology,
Engineering, Social Science, University &
Secondary Textbooks (especially Australian
studies)
1977: 12 titles *1978:* 22 titles *Founded:*
1966, changed name 1975
Miscellaneous: Firm is a subsidiary of
Edward Arnold (Publishers) Ltd, UK (qv)
ISBN Publisher's Prefix: 0-7267

Ashton Scholastic+, PO Box 579, Gosford,
NSW 2250 Tel: (043) 621401 Cable Add:
Tonash Sydney Telex: 24881
Shipping Add: Railway Crescent, Lisarow,
via Gosford
Man Dir: Terry T Hughes; *General
Manager:* Ken A Jolly; *Publishing, Rights &
Permissions:* Ruth A Hamilton; *Marketing
Manager:* Geoffrey S Gribble; *National
Sales Co-ordinator:* Gavin S Shepherd
Publicity: Derek A Harling
Imprints: Core Libraries, Impact, Read It
Again, Visuals of the Australian
Environment, Community Language
Children's Books
Br Off: 9-11 Fairfax Ave, Penrose,
Auckland, New Zealand
Subjects: Juveniles, Paperbacks, Secondary
& Primary Textbooks, Educational
Materials
Book Clubs: Arrow; Lucky; Teacher's
Bookshelf; Teenage
1977: 8 titles *1978/79:* 9 titles *Founded:*
1968
ISBN Publisher's Prefix: O-86896

Associated Book Publishers (Aust) Ltd+,
301 Kent St, Sydney, NSW 2000 Tel: (02)
291791 Cable Add: Asbook Sydney
Man Dir: W Mackarell; *Legal Division Dir:*
D S Lees; *Trade Division Manager:* J E
Coxhill
Parent Company: Associated Book
Publishers Ltd, UK (qv)
Subsidiary Companies: Atlantic Forlib Pty
Ltd; The Law Book Co Ltd (qv); Methuen
of Australia Pty Ltd (qv); Associated Book
Publishers (New Zealand) Ltd, New Zealand
(qv)
Branch Offs: 610-612 Church St, Richmond,
Vic 3121; IOOF House, Cnr Allenby and
Leichhardt Sts, North Brisbane, Queensland
4000; 6 Sherwood Court, Perth, WA 6000
Subjects: See subsidiary companies

Australasian Book Society Ltd*, PO Box A
161, Sydney South, NSW 2000 Tel: (02)
613229
Man Dir: N Zusman; *Sales, Publicity,
Advertising, Rights & Permissions:* D
Cleaver
Subjects: General Fiction, High-priced
Paperbacks, Social Science
1976: 3 titles *Founded:* 1951
ISBN Publisher's Prefix: 0-909916

Australasian Publishing Co Pty Ltd+,
Corner Bridge Rd and Jersey St, Hornsby,
NSW 2077 Tel: 4762000 Cable Add:
Publishing Hornsby
Man Dir: A S M Harrap; *Sales Dir:* G A
Rutherford; *Publicity:* John Cody, Mrs R
Onslow; *Rights & Permissions &
Production:* A S M Harrap
Br Offs: 83 Glen Eira Rd, Ripponlea,
Victoria 3183; 303 Adelaide St, Brisbane,
Queensland 4000; 33 Pirie St, Adelaide,
South Australia 5000
Subjects: General Fiction, Belles Lettres,
Juveniles, Education, General Science
ISBN Publisher's Prefix: 0-900882

Australia & New Zealand Book Co Pty
Ltd+, PO Box 459, Brookvale, NSW 2100
(Located at: 23 Cross St, Brookvale, NSW
2100) Tel: (02) 9382244 Cable Add:
Anzbook Sydney
Executive Chairman: Geoffrey King; *Man
Dir, Rights & Permissions:* G Ross King;
Publishing Dir: Peter Benjamin; *Marketing
Dir:* Wendy Livingston
Parent Company: G M King Investments
Pty Ltd
Subsidiary Companies: Book Exports
(Australia) Pty Ltd, Australia & New
Zealand Books International Ltd
Imprint: ANZ
Branch Offs: Brisbane and Melbourne,
Australia; Auckland, New Zealand
Subjects: Science, Technical, Medical,
General Nonfiction, Arts and Crafts, Sports
1978: 10 titles *1979:* 12 titles *Founded:*
1964
ISBN Publisher's Prefix: 0-85552

Australian Academy of Science+*, PO Box
783, Canberra City, ACT 2601 Tel: 486011
Orders to: Canberra Ho, Marcus Clarke St,
Canberra City, ACT 2601
Subjects: Scientific and Educational Books
ISBN Publisher's Prefix: 0-85847

Australian Council for Educational
Research+, Frederick St, PO Box 210,
Hawthorn, Victoria 3122 Tel: 8181271
Cable Add: Aceres
Man Dir: Dr J P Keeves; *Sales Dir:* Eric
McIlroy; *Publicity:* P Jeffery; *Editorial,
Production, Rights & Permissions:* Don
Maguire
Subjects: Education, Textbooks,
Educational materials
1977: 18 titles *Founded:* 1930
Bookshop: Frederick St, Hawthorn, Victoria
3122
ISBN Publisher's Prefix: 0-85563

Australian Encyclopaedia Pty Ltd, see The
Grolier Society of Australia Pty Ltd

Australian Government Publishing
Service+, PO Box 84, Canberra, ACT 2600
(Located at: 109 Canberra Ave, Griffith,
ACT 2603) Tel: (062) 952111 Telex:
AA62013
Warehouse & Shipping Add: Wentworth
Ave, Kingston, ACT 2604
Controller: P A Nott; *Editorial:* J Pitson;
Sales: L J Gwyther; *Production:*
J Thompson; *Publicity:* C Bucello; *Rights &
Permissions:* B P Shurman
Parent Company: Department of
Administrative Services
Subjects: Australian Government
Publications. Also sales agent for
publications of Canadian Government; New
Zealand Government Printer; HMSO (UK);
FAO, UNESCO, WHO (United Nations)
Bookshops: 12 Pirie Street, Adelaide; 294
Adelaide Street, Bisbane; 113 London
Circuit, Canberra; 162 Macquarie Street,
Hobart; 347 Swanston Street, Melbourne;
200 St George's Terrace, Perth; 309 Pitt
Street, Sydney
1977: approx 2800 *1978:* approx 3400
Founded: 1970
ISBN Publisher's Prefix: 0-642

Australian Institute of Aboriginal Studies+,
PO Box 553, Canberra City 2601 Tel: (062)
461111 Cable Add: Abinst
Warehouse: Acton Ho, Acton ACT 2601
Principal: Dr P J Ucko; *Executive Officer,
Publications & Rights & Permissions:*
Graham Pike
Subjects: Anthropology, Archaeology,
Ethnomusicology, Linguistics, Human
Biology, Prehistory, Material culture,
Aboriginal art, Education
ISBN Publisher's Prefix: 085575

Australian Institute of Criminology+, PO
Box 28, Woden, ACT 2606 (Located at:
10-18 Colbee Court, Phillip, Act 2606) Tel:
822111 Cable Add: Austcrim
Dir: William Clifford; *Editorial:* Peter Kay
Subject: Criminology
1978: 3 titles *1979:* 4 titles *Founded:* 1976
ISBN Publisher's Prefix: 0-642

Australian National University Press+*, PO
Box 4, Canberra, ACT 2600 Tel: (062)
492812 Cable Add: Natuniv Press,
Canberra
Shipping Add: Old Administration Area,
Australian National University, Canberra,
ACT
Dir: B Clouston; *Editor:* P Croft; *Sales,*

Publicity & Advertising: B Clouston; *Rights & Permissions:* P Croft
Subjects: Belles Lettres, Poetry, Biography, Geography, History, Reference, Social Science, Earth Sciences, University Textbooks, High-priced Paperbacks
1977: 37 titles *Founded:* 1965
ISBN Publisher's Prefix: 0-7081

Australian Universities Press Pty Ltd+*, Offset Ho, 169-171 Philip St, Waterloo, NSW 2017 Tel: (02) 695633/4
Man Dir: R G Hackett
Subjects: Cookery Books, Australiana, Children's Books
ISBN Publisher's Prefix: 0-7249

Bacchus Books*, 4A Alfred St, Woolwich, NSW 2110 Tel: (02) 892764
Man Dir: Boo Johnson
Orders to: Rical Enterprises Pty Ltd, GPO Box 2510, Sydney, NSW 2001
Subjects: Australia, Nonfiction, Humour
1977: 3 titles
ISBN Publisher's Prefix: 0-908003

S John **Bacon** Pty Ltd+, 13 Windsor Ave, PO Box 345, Mt Waverley, Victoria 3149 Tel: (03) 2773944 Cable Add: Interbac, Melbourne
Dirs: Mary Bacon, Joan Diemar, Neville Cuthbert; *Editorial:* Rosalind Beale; *Sales & Marketing:* Michael T Baker
Subjects: Theology, Christian Education, Devotional Music, Primary and Secondary Educational Books and Aids, Children's Books
Founded: 1938
Subsidiary: Lantern House Pty Ltd
ISBN Publisher's Prefix: 0-85579

Book People of Australia P/L, PO Box 313, Prahran, Victoria (Located at 590 Little Bourke St, Melbourne) Tel: (03) 679249/(02) 293911
Chief Executive, Editorial, Rights & Permissions: Richard Jones; *Sales:* Ken Wright; *Production:* John Gribic; *Publicity:* Sandra Birch
Associate Companies: Kelly Books (qv); Pentacle (qv)
Branch Offs: Suites 6-9, 2nd floor, 123 Clarence St, Sydney Tel: 293911; 332 Brunswick St, Fortitude Valley, Queensland Tel: 521794
Subjects: All subjects, particularly books by Australian authors or on Australian subjects
1978: 5 titles *1979:* 17 titles *Founded:* 1975
Miscellaneous: Firm is the largest distributor of independently published Australian titles
ISBN Publisher's Prefix: 0-908

Books for Pleasure*, 176 South Creek Rd, Dee Why West, Sydney, NSW 2099 Tel: (02) 9822344 Cable Add: Pleasbooks Sydney Telex: AA 21546
Chief Executive: Max Henry; *Marketing:* Ross Alexander; *Publishing:* Warwick Jacobson; *Export Rights & Sales:* Warwick Page
Parent Company: Paul Hamlyn Pty Ltd (qv)
Subjects: General Nonfiction
ISBN Publisher's Prefix: 0-7296

Bookwise (Australia) Pty Ltd, 104 Sussex St, Sydney 2000 Tel: 296437 Cable Add: Bookwise Sydney Telex: Naku AA 25691
Man Dir: John Redrup; *Editorial, Sales, Production:* Arthur Vella; *Publicity, Rights & Permissions:* Max Herford
Branch Off: 10/247 Riversdale Rd, Hawthorn, Vic 3123
Subjects: Oriental Arts, Social Sciences, Languages, Cooking and Quality Non-fiction generally

1977: 5 titles *1978:* 4 titles *Founded:* 1957
ISBN Publisher's Prefix: 0-8120

Michael **Booth** Publications, PO Box 66, Carnegie, Victoria 3163 Tel: 509 2333
Chief Executive: Michael Booth
Imprint: Tallboy Publications
Subject: Overland travel through Asia
1978: 1 title *Founded:* 1978
ISBN Publisher's Prefix: 0959595902

Butterworths Pty Ltd+, 586 Pacific Highway, Chatswood, NSW 2067 Tel: (02) 4123444 Telex: 22033
Man Dir: D J Jackson; *Editorial:* K Siebel; *Sales:* A R Tostevin (Medicine, Science & Technology); *Production:* B Coats; *Publicity:* G C Thomas; *Rights & Permissions:* K Siebel
Parent Company: Butterworth & Co (Publishers) Ltd, UK (qv)
Branch Off: 233 Macquarie St, Sydney NSW 2000; 343 Little Collins St, Melbourne, Vic 3000; Commonwealth Bank Bldg, King George Sq, Brisbane Q 4000; 49-51 St George's Terr, Perth WA 6000; Lensworth Chambers, 82 Flinders St, Adelaide, SA 5000
Subjects: Law, Business, Medicine, Science & Technology, Textbooks
1977: 40 titles *1978:* 57 titles *Founded:* 1910
ISBN Publisher's Prefix: 0-409

C S I R O (Commonwealth Scientific and Industrial Research Organization)+, 314 Albert St, PO Box 89, East Melbourne, Victoria 3002 Tel: (03) 4191333 Cable Add: Coresearch Melbourne Telex: 30236
Shipping Add: 19 Rokeby St, Collingwood, Victoria 3066
Publisher: B J Walby; *Sales and Publicity:* Ros McLeod; *Production:* Paul Lynch
Subjects: Engineering, General Science
1977: 35 titles *Founded:* 1926
ISBN Publisher's Prefix: 0-643

Cambridge University Press (Australia) Pty Ltd+, 296 Beaconsfield Parade, Middle Park, Victoria 3206 Tel: 5340457 Cable Add: Cantabaust
Man Dir: B W Harris
Subjects: Education, University, Secondary & Primary Textbooks
Miscellaneous: Firm is a branch of Cambridge University Press, UK (qv)
ISBN Publisher's Prefix: 0-521

Carroll's Pty Ltd+*, 566 Hay St, GPO Box M-954, Perth, Western Australia 6001 Tel: (09) 256377 Cable Add: Carroll's Perth WA 6000 Telex: AA 92842
Man Dir, Rights & Permissions, Editorial: Mark R Saunders; *Production:* Maxwell J McNamara; *Publicity:* G M Cameron
Branch Offs: 143 Denison St, Bondi Junction, NSW 2022; 141 Leveson St, North Melbourne, Vic
Subjects: Secondary & Primary Textbooks, Children's books, General Books
1977: 68 titles *Founded:* 1904
Bookshops: Reader and Artist, Cloisters Sq, Hay St, Perth, Western Australia 6001; 566 Hay St, Perth Western Australia 6001
ISBN Publisher's Prefix: 0-909994

Cassell Australia Ltd+*, PO Box 52, Camperdown, NSW 2050 (Located at: 31 Bridge Rd, Stanmore, NSW 2048) Tel: 5162155 Cable Add: Pachamac Sydney Telex: AA 21206
Man Dir: D C Field; *Publicity:* Beverley Eley
Br Off: 30-36 Curzon St, North Melbourne, Victoria 3051
Subjects: General Fiction, Biography, Education, Travel, History, Agriculture, Textbooks

1978: 42 titles
Miscellaneous: Firm is an associate company of Cassell & Co Ltd, UK (qv for other associates)
ISBN Publisher's Prefix: 0-7269

Cat and Fiddle Press+*, PO Box 153B, Hobart, Tasmania 7001 (Located at: 81 Murray St, Hobart, Tasmania 7000) Tel: (02) 346175
Dirs: Cedric Pearce, Chris Pearce, I P Pearce
Subjects: General, Fiction

Centre Publications, PO Box 114, Saint Kilda, Melbourne 3182 (Located at: 25 Chapel St, Saint Kilda, Melbourne 3182) Tel: (03) 514608
Man Dir: Paul Sumner
Parent Company: Yoco Pty Ltd, PO Box 114, Saint Kilda, Melbourne 3182
Associate Companies: The Helen Vale Foundation (qv); The Yoga Education Centre (at above address)
Subjects: Education, Health
1978: 2 titles *1979:* 2 titles *Founded:* 1974

Chatto, Bodley Head & Jonathan Cape Australia Pty Ltd+*, Suite 816, 121 Walker St, North Sydney, NSW 2060 Tel: 9294660 Telex: 24059
Man Dir: John Cody
Orders to: Australasian Publishing Co, Corner Bridge Rd and Jersey St, Hornsby, NSW 2077
Parent Company: Chatto, Bodley Head & Jonathan Cape Ltd, UK (qv)
Subjects: Fiction, Nonfiction, Reference, History, Childrens, Australiana
Founded: 1977

Cheshire, an imprint of Longman Cheshire Pty Ltd (qv)

Chevalier Press, PO Box 312, Moorabbin, Victoria 3189
Br Off: PO Box 13, Kensington, NSW 2033
1978: 2 titles *1979:* 5 titles

Childerset Pty Ltd+, 67 Katrina St, Blackburn North, 3130 Melbourne Tel: (03) 8775121 Cable Add: Childerset Melbourne Telex: 33571
Man Dir: Haworth H Bartram; *Sales, Publicity, Rights & Permissions:* Denise Burt; *Production:* Veronica Capper
Subjects: Juveniles, Educational Materials, Children's Picture Books, Foreign Language Picture Books, Classroom Pictures
1977: 7 titles *1978:* 42 titles *Founded:* 1970
ISBN Publisher's Prefix: 0-909404

Churchill-Livingstone, imprint of Longman Cheshire Pty Ltd (qv)

Circus Books, 14 Little Oxford St, Collingwood, Victoria 3066 Tel: (03) 412110 Cable Add: Circus Melbourne Telex: AA 35136 Outbac
Chief Executive, Editorial: Morry Schwartz; *Production:* Neil Conning; *Publicity:* Margaret Gee
Subjects: Fiction, General Non-fiction, in mass market paperbacks
1977: 35 titles *1978:* 40 titles *Founded:* 1977

Clearway Textbooks, see Sapphire Books Pty Ltd

R J **Cleary** Pty Ltd+, PO Box 282, Kings Cross, NSW 2011 (Located at: 155 Brougham St, Sydney, NSW 2011) Tel: (02) 3586144 Cable Add: 'Clearpub' Sydney Telex: 27031
Man Dir: R J Cleary
Subjects: Biography, History, How-to, Reference, Juveniles, High-priced

Paperbacks, Australiana, Series Books, Part-Works, Primary and Secondary Textbooks, Educational Materials, Children's Activities, Special Projects
1979: 100 titles *Founded:* 1969
ISBN Publisher's Prefix: 0–85567

The **Clifford** Press*, PO Box 120, Hawthorn, Victoria 3122 Tel: 810231
Shipping Add: 597 Burwood Rd, Hawthorn, Victoria
General Secretary: C K Moss; *Rights & Permissions, Publicity, Business Manager:* Alma M Widdicombe
Subjects: Religion, Juveniles, Educational Materials
Founded: 1956
ISBN Publisher's Prefix: 0–85044

Cole Publications+*, 3 Creswick St, Hawthorn, Victoria 3122 Tel: 8185640
Man Dir: Cole Turnley
Parent Company: Alterns Pty Ltd, same address
Subjects: Juveniles, Technical, Humour
1977: 1 title *Founded:* 1868
ISBN Publisher's Prefix: 0–909900

Collier Macmillan Australia*, 31–34 Bridge St, Stanmore, NSW 2048
Miscellaneous: Firm is an associate company of Cassell & Co Ltd, UK (qv for other associates)

William **Collins** Pty Ltd+, 55 Clarence St, Sydney, NSW 2000 Tel: (02) 2902066 Cable Add: Folio Sydney Telex: 26292 Folio
Warehouse and Shipping Add: Yarrawa Rd, Moss Vale, NSW 2577
Chairman: K W Wilder; *Paperback Sales Dir:* A J Horgan; *Special Projects Dir, Rights & Permissions:* A S Rein; *Editorial:* Anne Ingram, Mrs M Olds; *Production Dir:* J Hooker; *Publicity & Advertising:* Mrs J Garvan; *Foreign Rights:* Mrs B Potts; *Marketing Dir:* G S Rumpf
Parent Company: William Collins Sons & Co Ltd, UK (qv)
Br Offs: 62 Merivale St, South Brisbane, Qld 4101; 25 Trent St, Burwood, Vic 3125; 7–9 Maple Ave, Forestville, SA 5034; Boag St, Morley, WA 6062
Subjects: General Fiction, Biography, History, How-to, Music, Art, Philosophy, Reference, Religion, Juveniles, Low- & High-priced Paperbacks, University, Secondary & Primary Textbooks
1977: 24 titles *1978:* 40 titles *Founded:* 1872

Community Language Children's Books, imprint of Ashton Scholastic (qv)

Compendium Pty Ltd+*, RSD Birregurra South, Victoria 3242 Tel: (052) 334574
Editorial Dir, Rights & Permissions: Gregory Ket; *Sales Dir:* Penny Lane
Subjects: General, Technical, Children's
1977: 3 titles *Founded:* 1974
ISBN Publisher's Prefix: 0–9598495

Contempa Publications*, PO Box 68, Clifton Hill 3060 Tel: (03) 3876859
Manager: Phillip Edmonds
Subject: Poetry

Core Libraries, an imprint of Ashton Scholastic (qv)

Croft Press, see Gryphon Books Pty Ltd

Currawong Press Pty Ltd+*, PO Box 233, Milson's Point, NSW 2061 Tel: 9223404
Rights & Permissions: Phillip Mathews
Subjects: Books of general appeal by Australian writers, mainly non-fiction
Founded: 1946
Miscellaneous: Publishers of *The Australian Language, Men and Affairs, The Affairs of Women*
ISBN Publisher's Prefix: 0–85041

Currency Press Pty Ltd+, 87 Jersey Rd, Woollahra, NSW 2025 Tel: (02) 324481 Cable Add: Dramabooks, Sydney
Editorial, Rights & Permissions: Mrs K Parsons
Orders to: Cambridge University Press, 296 Beaconsfield Parade, Middle Park, Victoria
Subject: Drama, Films
1977: 6 titles *1978:* 7 titles *Founded:* 1971
ISBN Publisher's Prefix: 0–86937 (Currency Methuen) and 0–86819

John **Currey** O'Neil Publishers Pty Ltd+, 2B Frederick St, Windsor, Victoria 3181 Tel: 514251/5294259 Telex: 36472 AA
Man Dir: John Currey; *General Manager:* Geoff Currey
Associate Companies: Lloyd O'Neil Pty Ltd (qv); George Philip and O'Neil Pty Ltd
Subjects: Australian History, Art and General Nonfiction, Natural History
1978/79: 12 titles
ISBN Publisher's Prefix: 0–85902

Curriculum Development Centre+, PO Box 52, Dickson, ACT 2603 Tel: 433042 Telex: Education Canberra
Man Dir: Dr Malcolm Skilbeck; *Editorial and Rights & Permissions:* Chris Makepeace
Subjects: Educational
ISBN Publisher's Prefix: 642

Cypress Books+*, PO Box 6, Box Hill, Vic 3128 (Located at: 5 Bentley St, Surry Hills, Vic 3127) Tel: (03) 894908
Dir & Editorial: Harley Forster
Subject: Australian History

D J **Davies***, 18 South Valley Rd, Highton 3216 Tel: (052) 436862
Man Dir: David J Davies

Dollar Books, an imprint of Ansay Pty Ltd (qv)

Doubleday Australia Pty Ltd+, PO Box 184, Lane Cove, NSW 2066 (Located at: 14 Mars Rd, Lane Cove, NSW 2066) Tel: 4270377 Telex: 20901 Dubday
Man Dir: Peter B Madgwick; *Editorial, Rights & Permissions:* David J Standish; *Distribution Manager:* John D Madgwick; *Book Club Manager:* John W Liddell
Divisions: Tudor Distributors, 2A Woodcock Place, Lane Cove, NSW 2066 (distributor and wholesaler of books in Australia); Book Club Associates (operates book clubs in Australia)
Parent Company: Doubleday & Co Inc, New York, USA
Subsidiary Company: Doubleday New Zealand Ltd, New Zealand (qv)
Branch Offs: Unit 1, 57 Parkhurst Drive, Knoxfield, Vic 3180; 8 Taylors Rd, Morningside, Auckland 3, New Zealand
Subjects: General and Biographical Australian Nonfiction
Book Clubs: Doubleday Australia Pty Ltd, Book Club Associates Division (see Book Club section for individual clubs)
1978: 8 titles *1979:* 10 titles
ISBN Publisher's Prefix: 0–86824

Dove Communications Pty Ltd+*, PO Box 51, Caulfield East, Victoria 3145 (Located at: 203 Darling Rd, East Malvern, Victoria) Tel: (03) 2119177 Cable Add: Dovcom
Man Dir: J Garry Eastman; *Sales & Editorial:* David C Lovell
Subjects: Catholic theology, Religion, Moral Philosophy, Education
1977: 20 titles *1978:* 16 titles *Founded:* 1972
ISBN Publisher's Prefix: 0–85924

Drummond Publishing, associate company of Primary Education (Publishing) Pty Ltd (qv)

E J **Dwyer** (Australia) Pty Ltd+*, PO Box 492, Darlinghurst, NSW 2010 (Located at: Kippax and Waterloo Streets, Surry Hills, Sydney, NSW 2010) Tel: (02) 2114533 Telex: 26883
Subjects: Educational, Religion, Nonfiction
ISBN Publisher's Prefix: 0–85574

Educational Material Aid, 10 South St, Strathfield, NSW 2135 Tel: 767962
Dir: Yvonne McBurney
Subjects: Australian History and Novels designed to improve reading skills
Bookshop: 10 South St, Strathfield, NSW 2135
1978: 2 titles *1979:* 2 titles *Founded:* 1976
ISBN Publisher's Prefix: 0908053

Edwards & Shaw Pty Ltd+*, 184 Sussex St, Sydney, NSW 2000 Tel: (02) 29 6489
Dirs: Eric Edwards, Roderick Malcolm Shaw; *Rights & Permissions:* Eric Edwards; *Publicity:* R M Shaw
Subjects: Poetry, Belles Lettres
1977: 2 titles *1978:* 1 title
ISBN Publisher's Prefix: 0–85551

Encyclopaedia Britannica (Australia) Inc+*, Britannica House, 44 Miller Street, North Sydney, NSW 2060 Tel: (02) 9224799 Telex: Enbrit AA 23044
President: H W Deweese; *Sales & Marketing:* B Plasier
Subjects: Educational Reference, Dictionaries, Geography, Biography, Art, Science, Suitable for levels from Kindergarten to Tertiary Education, Audio Visual material and teaching aids
Miscellaneous: The Company is a wholly owned subsidiary of Encyclopaedia Britannica Inc of Chicago. It is an associate Company of Encyclopaedia Britannica International Limited UK (qv for other associate companies)
ISBN Publisher's Prefix: 0–909263

John **Ferguson** Pty Ltd+*, 133 Macquarie St, Sydney, NSW 2000 Tel: 273414
Man Dir: John R Ferguson
Subjects: Australian General & Historical
1977: 8 titles *Founded:* 1975
ISBN Publisher's Prefix: 909134

Fine Arts Press Pty Ltd+, 34 Glenview St, Gordon, NSW 2072 Tel: 4984656/4987452 Cable Add: Imprint Sydney
Publisher: Sam Ure Smith
Subjects: Australiana and the Fine Arts, Producers of Books for Other Publishers, *ART and Australia* (quarterly)
1978: 2 titles
ISBN Publisher's Prefix: 0–86917

Gazelle Publications Pty Ltd+, PO Box 43, Sth Yarra, Victoria 3141 (Located at: 59 E Station St, Bennettswood, Melbourne, Victoria 3125) Tel: 2889363
Man Dir: John R Brook; *Editorial:* Brian L Blackwell
Subjects: Fiction and Nonfiction (mostly paperbacks)
1977: 1 title *1978:* 4 titles *Founded:* 1977

Georgian House Pty Ltd+, 296 Beaconsfield Parade, Middle Park, Victoria 3206 Tel: 534 0457
Man Dir: Brian W Harris
Subjects: General Australian Literature
Founded: 1943
ISBN Publisher's Prefix: 0–85585

Golden Press Pty Ltd, 2–12 Tennyson Rd, Gladesville, NSW 2111 Tel: (02) 890421 Cable Add: Goldpress Telex: AA20514
Man Dir: Hugh Richardson; *Editorial & Rights & Permissions:* Robert Coupe; *Marketing Manager:* Peter Arentz; *Export Manager:* Charles Stempf; *Production:* Dennis Creer
Subsidiary Company: Shakespeare Head Press, Australia (qv)
Br Off: 16 Copsey Place, Avondale, Auckland, New Zealand
Subjects: Biography, History, How-to, Juveniles, Secondary & Primary Textbooks, Australiana, Nonfiction
1978: 17 titles
Miscellaneous: Associated imprints include Whitman, Australia Pty Ltd
ISBN Publisher's Prefix: 0–85558

Granada Publishing Australia Pty Ltd+, PO Box Q164, Queen Victoria Bldgs, Sydney, NSW 2000 Tel: (02) 295239 Cable Add: Granada
Dirs: W M Blanshard, W Carr, A R H Birch, E G Grigor, G Wallis-Smith; *Sales:* E G Grigor; *Publicity:* Bev Weynton
Subjects: General Books, Science, Technical Books, Yachting, Education, Juveniles, Fiction, Paperbacks
Miscellaneous: Firm is a branch of Granada Publishing, UK (qv)

Greenhouse Publications+*, 'Winooka' Riverview, Calder Highway, Kyneton, 3444 Victoria Tel: (054) 222425
Man Dir: Sally R Milner
Subjects: Technical, Sociology, Educational, Children's
Founded: 1975

The **Grolier** Society of Australia Pty Ltd+, PO Box 410 Crows Nest, NSW 2065 (Located at: 1 Campbell St, Artarmon, NSW 2064) Tel: (02) 4392355 Cable Add: Grolier Sydney Telex: 26584
Man Dir, Rights & Permissions: D Ashley-Wilson; *Editorial, Production:* R Appleton; *Publicity:* K Brown
Parent Company: Grolier Inc, New York, USA
Associate Companies: Grolier Inc, Canada, Latin America, UK, Europe, Africa, Far East, New Zealand; Franklin Watts Inc, USA and UK (qv)
Subsidiary Company: The Australian Encyclopaedia, Sydney
Subjects: Reference, Educational
Founded: 1960

Gryphon Books Pty Ltd, 106 Napier St, South Melbourne, Vic 3205 Tel: 6994541
Man Dir, Editorial: Richard Griffin; *Sales, Publicity:* Ann Nolan; *Production:* William Pate; *Rights & Permissions:* Elizabeth Michaels
Subsidiary Company: Pegasus Books (at above address)
Associate Company: Croft Press, 59 Osborne St, South Yarra, Vic 3141
Subjects: Limited Editions of Illustrated Books
1978/79: 10 titles *Founded:* 1977

Guyra Publishing Co Pty Ltd+, 25 Lang St, South Yarra, 3141 Victoria
Subjects: Pictorial Diaries of Australia, Sepik Art of New Guinea

Paul **Hamlyn** Pty Ltd, 176 South Creek Rd, Dee Why West, Sydney, NSW 2099 Tel: (02) 9822344 Cable Add: Pleasbooks Sydney Telex: AA21546
Chief Executive Books Div: Laurie Muller; *Marketing:* Peter Melville; *Export Sales:* Warwick Page; *Publishing & Production:* Warwick Jacobson; *Advertising:* Arthur Severn
Associated Companies: Paul Hamlyn, New Zealand (qv), Mereweather Press Inc, New York, UUSUSA
Imprints: Summit Books, Ure Smith, Lansdowne Press, Lansdowne Editions, Universal Books. (See separate entries for Summit Books, Ure Smith, Lansdowne Editions, Lansdowne Press, Books for Pleasure)
Br Off: 14 Lansdowne St, East Melbourne, Victoria 3002
Subjects: General, Children's Books, Australiana, Art, Maps and Road Guides

Harcourt Brace Jovanovich Group (Australia) Pty Ltd+, PO Box 300, North Ryde, NSW 2113 (Located at: Unit E, Centrecourt, 25–27 Paul St, North Ryde, NSW 2113) Tel: 888 3655 Cable Add: Jovan
Man Dir: Barry Dingley; *Editorial:* Grant Walker; *Sales:* Don Duff; *Marketing:* Don Conson; *Publicity:* Janet Taylor
Parent Company: Harcourt Brace Jovanovich Inc, 757 Third Ave, New York NY 10017, USA
Associate Companies: Academic Press Inc (London) Ltd, UK (qv); Academic Press, 111 Fifth Ave, New York, NY 10003, USA; Benefic Press, 1900N Narragansett, Chicago, Illinois 60639, USA; Grune & Stratton Inc, 111 Fifth Ave, New York, NY 10003, USA; Harcourt Brace Jovanovich Ltd, UK (qv); Instructor Publications Inc, Instructor Park, Dansville, NY 14437; Johnson Reprint Corporation, 111 Fifth Ave, New York, NY 10003, USA
Branch Off: 7C/622 St Kilda Rd, Melbourne, Vic 3004
Subjects: Educational, Science, Technical, Medicine, Reprints, Trade, Audiovisual software

Hargreen Publishing Co, PO Box 4582, Melbourne, Vic 3001 (Located at: 43 Walsh St, West Melbourne, Vic 3003) Tel: 3299714
Chief Executive: Michael Haratsis, Senior; *Editorial, Production, Rights & Permissions:* Tim Morfesse; *Sales:* Michael Haratsis, Junior; *Publicity:* Mary-Ann Haratsis
Parent Company: M and M A H Nominees Pty Ltd
Branch Off: Suite 16, 350 Victoria St, North Melbourne, Vic 3051
Subjects: Educational and Reference
1978: 3 titles *1979:* 6 titles *Founded:* 1972
ISBN Publisher's Prefix: 0-9596696

Harper & Row (Australasia) Pty Ltd+*, Cnr Reserve Rd and Campbell St, PO Box 226, Artarmon, NSW 2064 Tel: 4392250/4392265/4392281 Cable Add: Bookserv
Man Dir: M L Watson; *Publishing & Marketing:* Brian Wilder; *Editorial:* Neville Drury; *Trade Sales:* Harry Howell; *College Sales:* Adrian McComb
Parent Company: Harper & Row Inc, New York, NY 10022, USA
Miscellaneous: Associate company of Editora Harper & Row do Brasil Ltda, Sao Paulo (qv), Harper & Row Ltd, UK (qv), Harper & Row Latinoamericana-Harla, Mexico (qv)

The **Hawthorn** Press Pty Ltd+, 601 Little Bourke St, Melbourne, Victoria 3000 Tel: (03) 672544/672414
Man Dir: John Gartner; *Sales Dir:* Zelma Gartner; *Editorial & Publicity:* Rebecca Lines; *Production:* James McFadden
Subjects: Belles Lettres, Poetry, Biography, History, Reference, Religion, Political, Philately, Numismatics, Ships
1977: 26 titles *1978:* 21 titles *Founded:* 1945

Subsidiary: The Hawthorn Publishing Co Pty Ltd, 601 Little Bourke St, Melbourne, Victoria 3000
ISBN Publisher's Prefix: 07256

William **Heinemann** Australia Pty Ltd+, 60 Inkerman St, St Kilda, Victoria 3182 Tel: 534 0383 Cable Add: Sunlocks
Parent Company: William Heinemann Ltd, UK (qv)
Man Dir: John Burchall; *Sales Manager:* R Hellier
Subjects: General Fiction, Belles Lettres, Poetry, Biography, Juveniles, High-priced Paperbacks, History
1977: 5 titles *1978:* 4 titles *Founded:* 1948
ISBN Publisher's Prefix: 0–85561

Heinemann Educational Australia Pty Ltd+, 85 Abinger St, PO Box 133, Richmond, Victoria 3121 Tel: (03) 4293622 Cable Add: Hebooks Melb Telex: Heaust 35347
Man Dir: Nicholas J Hudson; *Editorial:* Tim Bass; *Sales Dir:* Jim Warburton; *Production:* Roger Seddon; *Publicity, Rights & Permissions:* Julie Morgan
Parent Company: Heinemann Educational Books Ltd, UK (qv)
Br Offs: PO Box 102, Neutral Bay, NSW 2089; Andrew House, 1 Wickham Terrace, Brisbane, Q 4000
Subjects: Plays, Drama, High-priced Paperbacks, Engineering, General & Social Science, University & Secondary Textbooks, Law, Educational Materials
1977/78: 31 titles *Founded:* 1967
ISBN Publisher's Prefix: 0–85859

Hicks Smith & Sons Pty Ltd, now Methuen of Australia Pty Ltd (qv)

Hill of Content Publishing Co Ltd+, 86 Bourke St, Melbourne, Vic 3000 Tel: (03) 6622711 Cable Add: Colbook
Man Dir, Rights & Permissions: M G Zifcak; *Editorial:* L Gregory; *Sales:* P Shaw
Orders to: 33 Lonsdale St, Melbourne, Vic 3000
Associated Company: Collins Booksellers Pty Ltd (qv under Booksellers)
Subjects: Australiana, Archive series, Australian Literature, Educational, Politics
1979: 15 titles *Founded:* 1965
ISBN Publisher's Prefix: 85572

Hodder & Stoughton (Australia) Pty Ltd+*, 2 Apollo Pl, Lane Cove 2066 Tel: (428) 1022 Cable Add: Expositor Telex: AA 248858
Man Dir: Edward Coffey; *Editorial:* Margaret Hamilton, Jane Wilton-Smith; *Publicity, Rights & Permissions:* Gabrielle King; *Sales & Marketing:* Bob Whiteside; *Production:* Margaret Hamilton
Parent Company: Hodder & Stoughton Ltd, UK (qv)
Br Offs: 164 High St, Ashburton 3149; 6th Floor, AGC House, 177 Edward St, Brisbane 4000; PO Box 46, Doubleview 6018
Subjects: General, Fiction, Children's Books, History, Education, Dictionaries, Religion, General Science, Travel, How-to
1977: 16 titles
ISBN Publisher's Prefix: 340

Holt-Saunders Pty Ltd+, 9 Waltham St, PO Box 154, Artarmon, NSW 2064 Tel: (02) 4393633 Cable Add: Aytcholt, Sydney Telex: 21217
Chairman of Dirs: A R Taylor; *General Manager (Education):* L Giles; *General Manager (Professional):* T MacLennan; *Advertising Manager:* S Stanton; *Production:* D Huffell

Br Off: 10 Moa St, Otahuhu, Auckland, New Zealand
Subject: Education
1978: 20 titles *1979:* 29 titles *Founded:* 1967
Miscellaneous: Firm is an associate company of Holt-Saunders Ltd, UK (qv for other associates)
ISBN Publishers' Prefix: 003

Horwitz Group Books Pty Ltd, Horwitz Cammeray Centre, 506 Miller St, PO Box 306, Cammeray, NSW 2062 Tel: (02) 9296144 Cable Add: Horbooks Sydney Telex: 27833 HORWTZ AA
Shipping Add: c/o Frank Cridland Pty Ltd, 154 Sussex St, Sydney, NSW 2000 (exclusive of Grahame Book Company Orders)
Man Dir: L J Moore; *Rights & Permissions:* Miss B Benjamin
Br Off: c/o U Spalinger and Co Ltd, PO Box 765, General Post Office, Hong Kong
Subjects: General Fiction, Biography, History, How-to, Reference, Low- & High-priced Paperbacks, Secondary & Primary Textbooks, Educational Materials
1977: over 400 titles *1978:* over 400 titles *Founded:* 1921
Bookshops: Grahame Book Co, Bankstown Square, Bankstown 2200; Grahame Book Co, Corner Pitt & Hunter Streets, Sydney 2000; Grahame Bookshop, 17 Alfred St, Circular Quay, Sydney 2000; Grahame Book Co, MLC Building, Miller St, North Sydney 2060; Grahame Bookshop, Imperial Centre, Gosford 2250 (all in Australia)
Miscellaneous: The Horwitz Group includes Martin Educational, Horwitz Publications, Scripts Publications (all at 506 Miller St, Cammeray, NSW 2062); Grahame Book Co Pty Ltd, Grahame Library & Subscription Service (both at 35-51 Mitchell St, North Sydney, NSW 2060)
ISBN Publisher's Prefixes: 0-7252 (Scripts), 0-7253 (Martin Educational), 0-7255 (Horwitz)

Hutchinson Group (Australia) Ltd+*, PO Box 2031, Richmond South 3121 (Located at: 30-32 Cremorne St, Richmond, Victoria 3121) Tel: (03) 423511 Cable Add: Kahminyah
Man Dir: Otto Hofner; *Sales Dir:* Paul Jaboor; *Man Editor, Rights & Permissions:* Elizabeth Douglas
Br Offs: 330-370 Wattle St, Ultimo, NSW 2007 Tel: (02) 2113233 Cable Add: Kahminyah Sydney; PO Box 151 Broadway 2007; 236 Elizabeth St, Brisbane 4000, Queensland
Subjects: Biography, History, How-to, Reference, Juveniles
1978: 28 titles
Miscellaneous: Firm is an associate company of the Hutchinson Publishing Group Ltd, UK (qv)
ISBN Publisher's Prefix: 0-09

Impact, an imprint of Ashton Scholastic (qv)

Inkata Press Pty Ltd+, 4 Lobourgne Ave, North Clayton, Victoria 3168 Tel: 5600272 Cable Add: Inkata Melbourne
Man Dir: C H Jerram
Subsidiary Company: Meredith Marketing
Subjects: Science, Technology, Natural History
1977: 1 title *1978:* 3 titles *Founded:* 1968
ISBN Publisher's Prefix: 0-909605

Island Press, PO Box R217, Royal Exchange, Sydney, NSW 2000
Man Dir: Philip Hammial
Subject: Poetry
1978: 4 titles *1979:* 4 titles *Founded:* 1973
ISBN Publisher's Prefix: 0-909771

Jacaranda Wiley Ltd+, GPO Box 859, Brisbane 4001 (Located at: 65 Park Road, Milton, Queensland 4064) Tel: (07) 362755 Cable Add: Japress Telex: AA 41845
Shipping Add: 172 Robinson Road, Geebung, Queensland 4034
Man Dir: John Collins; *Publishing Manager:* Colin Cunnington; *Marketing Managers:* John Braithwaite (school, general), John Collins (college); *Publicity:* Julie Smith (school), Shirley Macpherson (college); *Rights & Permissions:* Sheree Cavaye; *Production:* Alan Robbie
Orders to: 65 Park Rd, Milton, Queensland 4064
Parent Company: John Wiley & Sons, Inc, Publishers, 605 Third Avenue, New York, NY 10016, USA
Associate Companies: Editorial Limusa SA, Mexico (qv); Livros Tecnicos e Cientificos Editora SA, Brazil (qv); Wiley Eastern Ltd, India (qv); John Wiley & Sons Ltd, UK (qv); John Wiley and Sons Canada Ltd
Subsidiary Companies: Jacaranda Wiley (Hong Kong) Ltd, 19D, 257 Gloucester Rd, Causeway Bay, Hong Kong; Niugini Press Pty Ltd, PO Box 3395, Port Moresby, Papua New Guinea
Imprints: The Jacaranda Press, Niugini Press, John Wiley and Sons
Br Offs: 151 Victoria Rd, Gladesville, NSW 2111; 303 Wright Street, Adelaide, SA 5000; 83 Palmerston Crescent, South Melbourne, Vic 3205; 142 Colin Street, West Perth, WA 6005 (all in Australia); 32 Nikau Street, Mount Eden, Auckland, New Zealand; PO Box 3395, Port Moresby, Papua New Guinea
Subjects: Preschool, Primary, Secondary and Tertiary Textbooks, Atlases, Educational Multimedia Materials, General
1977: 74 titles *Founded:* 1954
ISBN Publisher's Prefix: 0-7016 (The Jacaranda Press, Niugini Press), 0-471 (John Wiley and Sons)

Kelly Books, PO Box 313, Prahran, Victoria (Located at: 590 Little Bourke St, Melbourne) Tel: (03) 679249/(02) 293911
Associate Companies: Book People of Australia P/L (qv); Pentacle (qv)

Kookaburra Technical Publications Pty Ltd+, PO Box 648, Dandenong, Vic 3175 Tel: 5600841
Man Dir, Production: Geoff Pentland; *Editorial:* Miss J Martin; *Sales:* Mr F Parks
Branch Off: 214 Kenmark Rd, Newark, Delaware 19713, USA; 1204 Campbell St, Joliet, Illinois 60435, USA
Subject: Aviation history
1978: 3 titles *1979:* 3 titles *Founded:* 1964
ISBN Publisher's Prefix: 0-85880

L & S Publishing Co Pty Ltd+, 99 Argus Street, Cheltenham, Melbourne, Victorria 3192 Tel: (03) 5506311 Cable Add: Scholib Melbourne Telex: AA 33626
A Division of L & S Educational Group
Man Dir, Rights & Permissions: Ian Stevenson; *Manager & Sales:* Brian Barratt; *Publicity, Advertising and Production:* Malcolm MacArthur
Branch Offs: Brisbane, Sydney, Orange, Canberra
Company Divisions: L & S Educational Equipment Pty Ltd, L & S School Library Service Pty Ltd, L & S Textbook & Stationery Co Pty Ltd, L & S Design Development & Export Co, L & S Map & Globe Co Pty Ltd
Subjects: Secondary & Primary Textbooks, Educational Materials
1979: 28 titles *Founded:* 1963
ISBN Publisher's Prefix: 0-86898

Lansdowne Editions, 14 Lansdowne St, East Melbourne, Vic 3002 Tel: (03) 4197493 Cable Add: Lansbooks Melbourne
Chief Executive: Duncan Maclellan; *Publisher:* Terry Greenwood; *Publicity Manager:* Carol Holyoake
Parent Company: Paul Hamlyn Pty Ltd (qv)
Subjects: Limited Editions on Fine Art, Natural History and Australiana
1978: 10 titles *1979:* 14 titles
ISBN Publisher's Prefix: 0-7018

The **Law** Book Co Ltd, 31 Market St, Sydney, NSW 2000 Tel: (02) 291611 Cable Add: Asbook
Man Dir: D S Lees; *Sales:* G M Smith; *Marketing Manager:* J K Leonard; *Rights & Permissions:* D S Lees; *Production:* P Finneran
Parent Company: Associated Book Publishers (Australia) Ltd (qv for associate companies)
Br Offs: 389 Lonsdale St, Melbourne, Victoria 3000; 27-35 Turbot St, Brisbane, Queensland 4000; 6 Sherwood Court, Perth, WA 6000
Subjects: Law, Accountancy, Commerce
1978: 32 titles
ISBN Publisher's Prefix: 0-455

Libra Books+*, GPO Box 292C, Hobart 7001 Tel: (002) 251479
Proprietor: B M Wicks
Subject: Horse racing and breeding

Lonely Planet Publications+, PO Box 88, South Yarra, Victoria 3141 Tel: (03) 4295268
Man Dir: Tony Wheeler; *Editorial:* Maureen Wheeler; *Sales:* Andy Nielsen
Branch Off: 15 Heatherway, Crowthorne, Berks RG11 6HG, UK
Subject: Travel guides
1977: 5 titles *1978:* 7 titles *Founded:* 1973
ISBN Publisher's Prefixes: 0-9598080, 0-908086

Longman Cheshire Pty Ltd+, Longman Cheshire House, 346 St Kilda Rd, Melbourne, Victoria 3004 Tel: 699 1522 Cable Add: Miscellany Melbourne Telex: AA 33501
Parent Company: Longman Group Ltd, UK (qv)
Man Dir: W P Kerr; *Editorial:* N J Ryan; *Sales Manager:* F R Priatel; *Rights & Permissions:* Mrs E Moody, N J Ryan; *Production:* P H R Hylands; *Publicity:* Mrs D Mathewson
Orders to: Penguin Books Australia, 487 Maroondah Highway, Ringwood, Victoria 3134
Imprints: Cheshire, Churchill-Livingstone, Oliver and Boyd
Br Offs: 33 Cooper St, Surry Hills, NSW 2010; 139 Merivale St, South Brisbane, Queensland 4101; 105 Gouger St, Adelaide, SA 5000; CWA Ho, 1174 Hay St, West Perth, WA 6005
Subjects: Educational (Primary, Secondary, Tertiary Textbooks)
1977: 135 titles *1978:* 43 titles *Founded:* 1976 (formed by merger of Longman Australia Pty Ltd and Cheshire Publishing Pty Ltd)
ISBN Publisher's Prefixes: 0-582 0-7015

Lothian Publishing Company Pty Ltd+, 4-12 Tattersalls Lane, Melbourne, Victoria, 3000 Tel: (03) 6634976 Cable Add: Thorough
Man Dir: Louis A Lothian; *Sales Director:* Peter H Lothian; *Publicity:* Sue Armstrong
Br Offs: 146 Sussex Street, Sydney, NSW 2000; c/o All Book Agencies, 11 Bishop Street, Kelvin Grove, Q'ld 4059; 139 Gilles

16 AUSTRALIA

St, Adelaide, SA 5000; c/o Graden Enterprises, 56 Twelfth Ave, Armadale, WA 6112; New Zealand: 88 Nelson Street, Auckland 1, NZ
Subjects: How-to, Juveniles, Agriculture, Local history, Non-fiction
1977: 5 titles *1978:* 7 titles *Founded:* 1910
Associate: Thomas C Lothian Pty Ltd, 4–12 Tattersalls Lane, Melbourne, Victoria, 3000
ISBN Publisher's Prefix: 0-85091

Lowden Publishing Co+, Lowdens Rd, Kilmore, Victoria 3601 Tel: (057) 821118 Cable Add: Lowden, Kilmore
Man Dir: Jim Lowden
Subjects: Biography, History, Reference, Religion, Transport
1978: 7 titles *1979:* 6 titles *Founded:* 1969
ISBN Publisher's Prefix; 0-909706

M C A, an imprint of Macmillan Co of Australia Pty Ltd (qv)

McGraw-Hill Book Co Australia Pty Ltd+, 4 Barcoo St, Roseville East, NSW 2069 Tel: (02) 4064288 Telex: 20849
Man Dir: P J Bradley; *Rights & Permissions:* P Donoughue; *General Manager Tertiary:* D Pegrem; *General Manager Service:* J H Fowlstone; *Production:* M Bagnato
Subjects: Technology, Management, Educational, Professional & Reference, General Interest, Secondary Textbooks
1977: 51 titles *1978:* 39 titles
Miscellaneous: Firm is a subsidiary company of McGraw-Hill, Inc New York
ISBN Publisher's Prefix: 0-07

The **Macmillan** Co of Australia Pty Ltd+, 107 Moray St, PO Box 440 South Melbourne, Victoria 3205 Tel: (03) 6998922 Cable Add: Scriniaire Melbourne Telex: AA34454
Man Dir: Brian Stonier; *Dir* (General Books): Robert S McKay; *Editorial* (General Books): John Ross, (Educational): John Rolfe; *Sales* (General Books): Peter Phillips, (Educational): Trevor Paparella; *Production:* George Smith; *Publicity* (General Books): Elsa Petersen-Schepelern, (Educational): Colin Wood, (College): Clarissa Gornall; *Rights & Permissions* (General Books): Pamela Reid; (Educational): Ann Paterson, (Serialization): Elsa Petersen-Schepelern
Parent Company: Macmillan London Ltd, UK
Associated Companies: Refer to Macmillan London Ltd, UK (qv)
Subsidiary: Sun Books Pty Ltd, Australia (qv)
Imprints: MCA, SUN
Branch Off: Unit 4, 6 George Pl, Artarmon, NSW 2064; PO Box 587, South Brisbane, Queensland 4101; 9 Hackney Rd, Hackney, South Australia 5069; 1325 Hay St, Perth West, WA 6005
Subjects: General Fiction, Biography, History, Music, Art, Religion, Juveniles, Paperbacks, Engineering, General & Social Sciences, University, Secondary & Primary Textbooks
Bookshops: Mary Martin Bookshop Pty Ltd, 68 Grenfell St, Adelaide South Australia; Canberra Arcade, Alinga St, Canberra, ACT; Shop M19, City Arcade, Perth, Western Australia; 269 Swanston St, Melbourne, Victoria; York St, Sydney, New South Wales
1977: 114 titles *1978:* 140 titles *Founded:* 1965
ISBN Publisher's Prefix: 0-333

McPhee Gribble Publishers+, 203 Drummond St, Carlton, Victoria 3053 Tel: (03) 3477428 Telex: AA 33626
Principals: H J McPhee, D M Gribble
Subject: Nonfiction Paperbacks, Children's Fiction and Nonfiction, Australian Fiction
Founded: 1975
ISBN Publisher's Prefix: 0-86914

Martin Educational, see Horwitz Group Books Pty Ltd

Martindale Press, associate company of A H & A W Reed Pty Ltd (qv)

Melbourne University Press+, PO Box 278, Carlton South, Victoria 3053 Tel: (03) 3473455 Cable Add: MUPRESS
Shipping Add: 138 Cardigan St, Carlton, Victoria 3053
Dir: P A Ryan; *Rights & Permissions:* Miss S A Hardiman; *Production:* P Jones
Br Off: A W Sheppard, Room 43, 4th Floor, 104 Bathurst St, Sydney, NSW 2000
Subjects: Belles Lettres, Poetry, Biography, History, Music, Art, Philosophy, Reference, Paperbacks, Medicine, Psychology, Engineering, General & Social Sciences, University & Secondary Textbooks
1978: 31 titles *Founded:* 1922
Bookshop: University Bookroom, University of Melbourne, PO Box 278, Carlton South, Victoria 3053
ISBN Publisher's Prefix: 0-522

Methuen of Australia Pty Ltd, Saint Martins Tower, 31 Market St, Sydney, NSW 2000 Tel: (02) 291791 Cable Add: Sydney Asbook
(For personnel see Associated Book Publishers (Aust) Ltd)
Branch Offs: Cnr Allenby and Leichhardt St, Brisbane, Queensland 4000; 610-612 Church St, Richmond, Vic 3121
Parent Company: Associated Book Publishers (Australia) Ltd (qv for associate companies)
Subjects: Education, General, Juveniles
ISBN Publisher's Prefix: 0-454

Minerva's Express, PO Box 71, Beaconsfield 2014 Tel: 6988013
Man Dir: D Hunter; *Editorial, Production:* J Power; *Sales, Publicity, Rights & Permissions:* P Henderson
Subject: Photographic Dictionary/Travel Aid in 12 languages
1979: 4 titles *Founded:* 1979

Modern Teaching Aids Pty Ltd+, 26–28 Chard Rd, PO Box 608, Brookvale 2100 Tel: 9392355 Telex: TEAID 27109
Br Off: Evandale Rd, Malvern 3144
Subject: Educational Books

Mullaya Publications+*, 17 Griott St, PO Box 54, Canterbury, Victoria 3126 Tel: 839300
Man Dir: M C Sayers
Subjects: History, Biography
Founded: 1972
ISBN Publisher's Prefix: 0-85914

Nadjuri+*, Mannanarie Stud Farm, PO Box 24, Jamestown, SA 5491 Tel: (086) 657061
Manager: David Robinson; *Editor:* Nancy Robinson
Subjects: Social & Folk History, Children's Literature, Social Issues, Fiction

National Library of Australia+, Parkes Pl, Parkes, Canberra, ACT 2600 Tel: (062) 621111 Cable Add: Natlibaust Canberra Telex: 62100
Dir: A T Bolton; *Editor:* Mrs J Abbott; *Publications Officer:* D Brown
Orders to: Australia and New Zealand Book Co. Pty Ltd, 23 Cross St, Brookvale, NSW 2100
Subjects: National bibliographical publications, publications based on materials in the Library's collections
1977: 153 titles *Founded:* 1960
ISBN Publisher's Prefix: 0-642

Thomas **Nelson** (Australia) Pty Ltd+, 19–39 Jeffcott St, West Melbourne, Victoria 3003 Tel: 329 5199 Cable Add: Thonelson Melbourne Telex: 33088
Man Dir: B Rivers; *Trade Editorial:* R Sessions; *Educational Editorial:* R Andersen; *Trade Sales:* J Attenborough; *Mass Market Paperback Sales:* J Smith; *Educational Sales:* D Nancarrow; *Production:* K Yendell; *Trade Publicity:* D Goss; *Educational Publicity:* E Curtain; *Rights & Permissions:* E McDonald
Parent Company: Thomson Books Ltd, a part of International Thomson Organisation Ltd (Canada)
Associated Companies: Bowmar/Noble Inc, USA; Hamish Hamilton Ltd, UK (qv); Michael Joseph Ltd, UK (qv); Thomas Nelson & Sons (Canada) Ltd; Thomas Nelson & Sons (UK) Ltd (qv); Sphere Books Ltd, UK (qv); Pelham Books Ltd, UK (qv); The Rainbird Publishing Group Ltd, UK (qv); TBL Book Services Ltd, UK; Thomas Nelson (Nigeria) Ltd, Nigeria
Branch Off: 7th Floor, Dunstan Ho, 236 Elizabeth St, Brisbane 4000; 89–97 Jones St, Ultimo 2007; Rooms 305-306, Orlit Ho, 95 Currie St, Adelaide 5000
Subjects: Fiction, General Non-fiction, Juveniles, Mass Market Paperbacks, History, Gardening; Educational: Reading programmes, Primary and Secondary Texts
1977: 80 titles *1978:* 66 titles
ISBN Publisher's Prefix: 0-17

New Australian Library Pty Ltd*, 104 George St, Hornsby NSW 2077 Tel: 01061/4762282 Telex: 21332
Subjects: Books by the World's most widely read authors (including Paperback); Publishers and Distributors of Part Works

Van **Nostrand** Reinhold Australia Pty Ltd+, 17 Queen St, PO Box 53, Mitcham, Victoria 3132 Tel: (03) 8741469
Man Dir: Mark A Tucker
Parent Company: Litton Educational Publishing Inc, New York, USA
Associate Companies: American Book Co, New York, USA; D Van Nostrand Co, USA; Delmar Publishers, Albany, New York, USA; McCormick-Mathers Publishing Co, New York, USA; Van Nostrand Reinhold Co, London, New York, Toronto
Subjects: Educational, Art and Craft, General Interest
1977: 8 titles *1978:* 9 titles *Founded:* 1967
ISBN Publisher's Prefix: 0-442

Anne **O'Donovan** Pty Ltd, 203 Drummond St, Carlton, Vic 3053 Tel: (03) 3470313
Man Dir: Anne O'Donovan
Subject: Adult Non-fiction
1979: 2 titles *Founded:* 1978
ISBN Publisher's Prefix: 0-908476

Oliver & Boyd, an imprint of Longman Cheshire Pty Ltd (qv)

Lloyd **O'Neil** Pty Ltd+, 19 Hornby Street, Windsor, Victoria 3181 Tel: 511325 Cable Add: Windsorpub 19 Hornby Street, Windsor 3181 Telex: AA36472 HORNBY
Man Dir: Lloyd O'Neil; *Editorial Dir:* Sue Donovan
Associated Companies: John Currey O'Neil Publishers Pty Ltd (qv); George Philip and O'Neil Pty Ltd; Blond Pty Ltd
Subjects: Educational, Primary & Secondary Atlases, Australiana
ISBN Publisher's Prefix: 0-85550

Outback Press Pty Ltd+, 14 Little Oxford St, Collingwood, Victoria 3066 Tel: (03) 412110 Cable Add: Circus Melbourne Telex: AA 35136 OUTBAC
Man Dir, Editorial: Alfred Milgrom; *Sales & Rights, Permissions:* Naomi Besen; *Production:* Neil Conning; *Publicity:* Margaret Gee
Associate Company: Melbourne House (Publishers) Ltd, UK (qv)
Br Off: 850 Seventh Ave, New York, NY, USA
Subjects: Fiction, General Nonfiction, Politics
Book Club: Australian Jewish Book Club Pty Ltd
1978: 30 titles *1979:* 42 titles *Founded:* 1973
ISBN Publisher's Prefix: 0-86888

Oxford University Press+, GPO Box 2784Y, Melbourne, Victoria 3001 (Located at: 7 Bowen Crescent, Melbourne, Victoria) Tel: (03) 263748 Cable Add: Oxonian Melbourne Telex: 35330
General Manager: David Cunningham; *Sales:* James Walker; *Publicity:* Vida Holswade
Subjects: Nonfiction, Juveniles
Miscellaneous: Firm is a branch of Oxford University Press, UK (qv)
ISBN Publisher's Prefix: 0-19

Pacific Publications (Australia) Pty Ltd+, GPO Box 3408, Sydney, NSW 2001 (Located at: 76 Clarence Street, Sydney, 2000) Tel: (02) 296693 Cable Add: Pacpub Telex: 21242
Publisher & Chief Executive: Stuart Inder; *Marketing:* John Berry; *Production Editor:* John McDonald
Parent Company: The Herald and Weekly Times of Melbourne
Br Off: Pacific Publications, 2nd Floor, Herald & Weekly Times Bldg, 61 Flinders Lane, Melbourne, Victoria
Subjects: Pacific Island Subjects — General & Reference, Australian Agricultural/Technical Handbooks. Publishers *Pacific Islands Yearbook*, *Papua New Guinea Handbook*
Founded: 1930
ISBN Publisher's Prefix: 0-85807

Pegasus Books, see Gryphon Books Pty Ltd

Penguin Books Australia Ltd+*, 487 Maroondah Highway, PO Box 257, Ringwood, Victoria 3134 Tel: (03) 870 3444 Cable Add: Penguinook Melbourne Telex: AA32458
Man Dir: T D Glover; *Deputy Man Dir:* R A Davis
Associate Companies: Penguin Books Ltd, UK (qv); Viking-Penguin Inc, USA
Subjects: Low & high-priced Paperbacks, Juveniles
1977: 24 titles
ISBN Publisher's Prefix: 0-14

Pentacle, 590 Little Bourke St, Melbourne, Victoria 3001 Tel: (03) 679249
Man Dir: Richard Jones
Associate Companies: Book People of Australia P/L (qv); Kelly Books (qv)
Subjects: Visual Arts, Occult

Pergamon Press (Australia) Pty Ltd, 19A Boundary Rd, Rushcutters Bay, NSW 2011 Tel: (02) 318211 Telex: Pergap AA27458
Dirs: Jerry Mayer (Managing), I R Maxwell (Chairman), R McLeod; *Editorial:* Beverley Barnes; *Sales Manager:* Ken Woods; *Publicity:* Dana Kuzmanova; *Rights & Permissions:* Ngaire Laundy
Sales Offs: Melbourne, Sydney
Subjects: Reference, Medicine, Psychology, Engineering, General & Social Science, University, Secondary & Primary

Textbooks, Educational Materials, High-priced Paperbacks
1978: 26 titles *1979:* 23 titles *Founded:* 1968
ISBN Publisher's Prefix: 0-80

Pinchgut Press, 6 Oaks Ave, Cremorne, NSW 2090 Tel: 905548
Chief Executives: Marjorie Pizer, Anne Spencer Parry
Subjects: Poetry, Fiction
1978: 1 title *1979:* 2 titles *Founded:* 1947
ISBN Publisher's Prefix: 09598913

Pioneer Design Studio Pty Ltd+, North Rd, Lilydale, Victoria
Subjects: History, Nature, Gardening
1978: 4 titles

Pitman Publishing Pty Ltd+, 158 Bouverie St, Carlton, Victoria 3053 Tel: (03) 3473055 Cable Add: Fono Telex: 30107
Man Dir: Philip Harris; *Editorial & Rights & Permissions:* Tudor Day; *Marketing:* Sandy Grant; *Sales:* Ken Pryse; *Production:* John Cook; *Publicity & Advertising:* Jeanette Webb
Subjects: How-to, Music, Art, High-priced Paperbacks, Medicine, Engineering, Social Science, University, Secondary & Primary Textbooks, Educational Materials
1977: 18 titles *1978:* 33 titles *Founded:* 1913
Miscellaneous: Firm is an associate company of Pitman Publishing Ltd, UK (qv)
ISBN Publisher's Prefix: 0-85896

The **Polding** Press, 343 Elizabeth St, Melbourne, Victoria 3000 Tel: (03) 671740/675157
Man Dir: John A Phillips SJ; *Sales Dir:* Marie-Thérèse Hilton
Bookshop: Central Catholic Library Bookshop, 343 Elizabeth St, Melbourne, Victoria 3000
Subjects: Biography, History, Religion, High-priced Paperbacks, Secondary Textbooks
1978: 2 titles *1979:* 6 titles *Founded:* 1968
Miscellaneous: Promotional and Wholesale marketing consortium formed in 1976 with Chevalier Press, Sydney, and Spectrum Publications, Melbourne, handling 90 titles

Prentice-Hall of Australia Pty Limited+, 7 Grosvenor Place, Brookvale, NSW 2100, Tel: (02) 9391333 Cable Add: Prenhall Sydney
Man Dir: Patrick F Gleeson; *Editorial:* Charles Lucas; *Australian Sales Manager:* James McGrath; *Sales Manager:* Max Reidy; *Publicity:* Jillian LePatourel; *Rights & Permissions:* Ruth Shaw
Br Off: 209 Glenhuntly Rd, Elsternwick, Vic 3185
Subjects: Elementary, Secondary and University Textbooks, Trade, Professional Reference, Art, Technical, Management, Medicine, Business, Nursing
Miscellaneous: Firm is a subsidiary company of Prentice Hall International, UK (qv for other associates and ISBN's)
ISBN Publisher's Prefix: 7248

Primary Education (Publishing) Pty Ltd+, PO Box 150, East Melbourne, Victoria 3002 (Located at: 2 The Crofts, Richmond, Victoria 3121) Tel: 4294822 Telex: 35347
Publishers: Don Drummond, Sheila Drummond
Associated Companies & Imprints: Drummond Publishing; Primary Education Pty Ltd
Subjects: Educational, Sociology, Politics
1978: 15 titles *1979:* 20 titles *Founded:* 1975
ISBN Publisher's Prefix: 0-909081

Prism Books (Poetry Society of Australia)+, Box N110 Grosvenor Street PO, Sydney 2000, NSW Tel: (02) 423861
Business Man: Cheryl Adamson
Subjects: Art, Poetry (Commercial & Collector's Editions), Art, Music, Photography
1977: 2 titles *1978:* 2 titles *Founded:* 1952
ISBN Publisher's Prefix: 0-909081

Ragman Productions, PO Box 54, Clifton Hill, Vic 3068 (Located at: 24 Urquhart St, Northcote, Vic 3070) Tel: (03) 4893925
Owner, Editorial, Rights & Permissions: Robert Kenny; *Sales, Publicity:* Retta Hemensley; *Production:* D O'Layshon
Imprint: Rigmarole of the Hours
Subjects: Innovative Fiction, Literary Criticism, Poetry
1978: 4 titles *1979:* 3 titles *Founded:* 1974
ISBN Publisher's Prefix: 0-909229

Reader's Digest Services Pty Ltd+, GPO Box 4353, Sydney (Located at: 26-32 Waterloo St, Surry Hills, NSW 2010) Tel: (02) 6990111 Cable Add: Readigest Sydney
Man Dir: M Maton; *Editorial:* Barbara Ker Wilson (Condensed Books), Nelson Kenny (Other Books); *Product Managers:* Richard Watson (Condensed Books), Sandra Step (Other Books)
Subjects: Condensed books, Reference, Educational, General
ISBN Publisher's Prefix: 0-909486

Read It Again, an imprint of Ashton Scholastic (qv)

A H & A W Reed Pty Ltd+, PO Box 126, Terry Hills, NSW 2084 Tel: (02) 4502555 Cable Add: Reedkoala Terrey Hills Telex: AA 27212 Reedoz
Man Dir, Rights & Permissions: Mrs E J Reed; *Marketing Dir:* K White; *Publisher:* W A Reed; *Editorial:* M English; *Production:* B E Robson
Parent Company: A H & A W Reed Ltd, New Zealand (qv)
Associate Company: Martindale Press Pty Ltd
Subjects: Books on Australia, General Non-fiction
1978: 120 titles *1979:* 120 titles *Founded:* 1964
ISBN Publisher's Prefix: 0-589

Review Publications Pty Ltd, 1 Sterling St, Dubbo, NSW 2830 Tel: 068 823283
Man Dir: William Hornadge
Subjects: Philatelic catalogues and handbooks, Australian history
1978: 14 titles *1979:* 13 titles *Founded:* 1947
ISBN Publisher's Prefix: 0-909895

Richmond Hill Press, 195 Bridge Rd, Richmond, Vic 3121 Tel: (03) 4295575
Man Dir, Editorial: John Curtain; *Sales, Publicity:* Peter Steer; *Production:* Michelle Johnston
Subjects: Limited Editions, Natural History, Australiana, Art
1978: 2 titles *1979:* 5 titles *Founded:* 1978
ISBN Publisher's Prefix: 0-908157

Rigby Ltd+, PO Box 104, Norwood, South Australia 5067 Tel: (08) 2235566 Cable Add: Rigbylim Telex: 88090
Chief Executive: N E Searle; *Editorial:* M F Page, J D Gilder, Mrs D Adamek; *Marketing Manager:* R M Gilmour; *Rights & Permissions:* J Hart; *Export:* M F Page
Orders to: 30 North Terrace, Kent Town, South Australia 5067
Br Offs: 28 Willoughby St, Kirribilli, NSW 2061; 122 Chetwynd St, North Melbourne, Vic 3051; 375 Montague Rd, West End,

18 AUSTRALIA

Queensland 4101
Subjects: General Fiction, Australiana, History, How-to, Art, Reference, Juveniles, Low- and High-priced Paperbacks, Secondary & Primary Textbooks, Educational Materials
Bookshop: Rigby Ltd, 24 James Pl, Adelaide, South Australia 5000
1977: 300 titles *1978:* 280 titles *Founded:* 1859
ISBN Publisher's Prefix: 0–85179, 0–7270

Rigmarole of the Hours, an imprint of Ragman Productions (qv)

Robin Books, PO Box 355, Wynyard, Tasmania 7321 Tel: (004) 422025
Man Dir, Editorial, Sales, Rights & Permissions: Barney Roberts; *Production, Publicity:* Bruce McM Roberts
Subjects: Poetry, Short Stories
1978: 1 title *1979:* 1 title *Founded:* 1976
ISBN Publisher's Prefix: 0-908030

Roebuck Books+D, Dr J S Cumpston, 42 Araba St, Aranda, ACT 2614 Tel: 513284
Man Dir: J S Cumpston
Subject: Australian History
1977: 2 titles *1978:* 5 titles *Founded:* 1970
ISBN Publisher's Prefixes: 0–9500858, 0–909434

Sapphire Books Pty Ltd+, PO Box 222, Strathfield, NSW 2135 (Located at: 21 Redmyre Rd, Strathfield, NSW 2135) Tel: 7641115/7631577
Man Dir: J Franklin
Subjects: Educational
1978: 12 titles
Miscellaneous: Also trading as Clearway Textbooks
ISBN Publisher's Prefixes: 0-909286, 0-85861

School Projects Ltd, see Associated Book Publishers (Aust) Ltd

Science Research Associates Pty Ltd+, 82–84 Waterloo Rd, North Ryde, NSW 2113 Tel: (02) 8887833 Cable Add: Sciresant North Ryde
Man Dir, Rights & Permissions: R J Barton; *Editorial:* J Alice Hofler; *Sales:* R W Duncan; *Advertising:* R W Duncan; *Production:* W Kavanagh
Subjects: Primary, Secondary, Tertiary & Other Textbooks, Multimedia Learning Systems
Miscellaneous: Firm is an associate company of Science Research Associates Ltd, UK (qv for other associates)
ISBN Publisher's Prefix: 0–574

Scripts Publications, see Horwitz Group Books Pty Ltd

Second Back Row Press Pty Ltd, PO Box 197, North Sydney, NSW 2060 (Located at: 8 Cliff Street, Milsons Point, NSW 2061) Tel: (02) 9222770
Man Dirs: Tom Whitton, Wendy Whitton
Subjects: Alternative Lifestyles, Technology, Politics, Education, Juveniles
1978: 4 titles *1979:* 7 titles *Founded:* 1973
ISBN Publisher's Prefix: 0909-325

Shakespeare Head Press, 2–12 Tennyson Rd, Gladesville, NSW 2111 Tel: (89) 0421 Cable Add: Goldpress
Man Dir: Hugh Richardson; *Marketing Manager:* P Arentz; *Editorial and Rights & Permissions:* R Coupe
Parent Company: Golden Press Pty Ltd (qv)
Subjects: Secondary & Primary Textbooks
Miscellaneous: Firm is a subsidiary of Golden Press Pty Ltd (qv)
1977: 3 titles *1978:* 7 titles
ISBN Publisher's Prefix: 0-85558

Sorrett Publishing Pty Ltd+*, 1227 Malvern Rd, PO Box 94, Malvern 3144 Tel: (03) 205486
Man Dir: Ian Coghill
Subjects: General, Secondary Textbooks, Educational Materials
1977: 7 titles *Founded:* 1972
ISBN Publisher's Prefix: 0–909752

South Head Press, 350 Lyons Rd, Five Dock, Sydney, NSW 2046 Tel: (02) 7139754
Man Dir: Grace Perry; *Sales & Publicity:* John Millet
Subjects: Poetry & Criticism
Founded: 1964
ISBN Publisher's Prefix: 0–901760

Spectrum Publications Pty Ltd+, PO Box 75, Richmond, Victoria 3121 Tel: 4291404
Man Dir: H Rohr; *Editorial:* Irene Aili
Subjects: Religion, Australiana, Art
1978: 7 titles
ISBN Publisher's Prefix: 909837

Sugar and Snails Books, see Women's Movement Children's Literature Co-op Ltd

Summit Books*, 176 South Creek Rd, Dee Why West, Sydney, NSW 2099 Tel: (02) 9822344 Cable Add: Pleasbooks Sydney Telex: AA21546
Chief Executive: Max Henry; *Marketing Manager:* Ross Alexander; *Publishing Manager:* Warwick Jacobson; *Export Rights & Sales:* Warwick Page
Parent Company: Paul Hamlyn Pty Ltd (qv)
Subjects: General Nonfiction, Juveniles, Maps & Guides, 'Softies', Cookery, Handcrafts, Do It Yourself, Australiana
1977: 34 titles
ISBN Publisher's Prefix: 0–7271

Sun Books Pty Ltd, 107 Moray St, South Melbourne, Victoria 3205 Tel: (03) 6998922 Cable Add: Sunbooks Telex: AA 34454
Man Dir: Brian Stonier; *Sales Dir, Rights & Permissions:* Robert S McKay
Parent Company: The Macmillan Co of Australia Pty Ltd (qv)
Subjects: General Fiction, Poetry, Biography, History, Music, Art, Philosophy, Reference, Low- & High-priced Paperbacks, Social Science, University & Secondary Textbooks
1978: 50 titles
ISBN Publisher's Prefix: 0–7251

Sydney University Press+, Press Bldg, University of Sydney, Sydney, NSW 2006 Tel: (02) 6604997 Cable Add: Sydpress *Dir:* Malcolm Titt; *Deputy Director (Design & Production):* David New; *Editor:* Lesley Glaysher
Subjects: Scholarly Books, University Textbooks
1977: 14 titles *1978:* 19 titles *Founded:* 1964
ISBN Publisher's Prefix: 0–424

Tallboy Publications, an imprint of Michael Booth Publications (qv)

D W Thorpe Pty Ltd+, 384 Spencer St, Melbourne 3003 Tel: (03) 3283359 Cable Add: Bookstat
Man Dir, Production, Rights & Permissions, Editorial: Joyce Nicholson; *Sales, Advertising Dir:* Pat White
Subject: Reference
1978: 3 titles *1979:* 8 titles *Founded:* 1921
ISSN Publisher's Prefix: 0067–172 X, 0-909532-05

Transworld Publishers (Australia) Pty Ltd+, 3 Bowen Crescent, Melbourne, Victoria 3004 Tel: (03) 263679 Cable Add: Transcable Telex: 33808
Sales & Marketing Dir: A Boardman
Subjects: Paperbacks, General, Fiction, Educational, Juveniles
Miscellaneous: Firm is an associate company of Transworld Publishers Ltd, UK (qv for other associates)

Turton and Armstrong, 21 Lister St, Wahroonga, NSW 2076 Tel: 485524
Publisher: P T Armstrong
Subjects: Industrial Archaeology, Special Interest, Technical
1978: 3 titles *1979:* 4 titles *Founded:* 1977
ISBN Publisher's Prefix: 908031

Universal Books*, 176 South Creek Rd, Dee Why West, 2099 Tel: 9822344 Cable Add: Pleasbooks Telex: AA21546
Man Dir: Max Henry; *Manager:* Michael Verran
Miscellaneous: Firm is a division of Paul Hamlyn Pty Ltd (qv)

University of New South Wales Press Ltd+, PO Box 1, Kensington, NSW 2033 Tel: (02) 6630351 ext 3503 and 3587
General Manager: D S Howie
Subjects: Biography, History, How-to, Philosophy, Reference, Engineering, General & Social Science, University Textbooks
Bookshop: College Shop, George St, Sydney
1978: 13 titles *Founded:* 1961
ISBN Publisher's Prefix: 0-86840

University of Queensland Press+, PO Box 42, St Lucia, Queensland 4067 Tel: (072) 3772127
Manager: Frank W Thompson; *Editorial:* Merril E Yule, C C Munro; *Sales:* Malcolm Beazley; *Publicity & Advertising:* Marilyn Bitomsky; *Rights & Permissions:* Merril E Yule; *Production:* Cyrelle Birt
Subjects: Belles Lettres, Poetry, Biography, History, Music, Art, Philosophy, Reference, Religion, Low- & High-priced Paperbacks, Medicine, Psychology, Engineering, General & Social Science, University & Secondary Textbooks, Educational Materials
1978: 65 titles *1979:* 60 titles *Founded:* 1948
Bookshop: University Bookshop, University of Queensland, St Lucia, Queensland 4067
ISBN Publisher's Prefix: 0–7022

University of Western Australia Press+, Nedlands, Western Australia 6009 Tel: (092) 3803182 Cable Add: Uniwest Perth
Manager, Rights & Permissions, Production: V S Greaves; *Editorial:* F A Brodalka, Mrs N Zeffertt; *Sales, Promotion:* A Kane
Subjects: Literary Criticism, Biological Sciences, Biography, History, Music, Art, Philosophy, Reference, Religion, Social Sciences, University & Secondary Textbooks
1977: 6 titles *1978:* 21 titles *Founded:* 1954
ISBN Publisher's Prefix: 0-85564

Ure Smith*, 176 South Creek Rd, Dee Why West, Sydney, NSW 2099 Tel: (02) 9822344 Cable Add: Pleasbooks Sydney Telex: AA21546
Chief Executive: Max Henry; *Man Editor:* Sue Wagner; *Production Manager:* Gary Baulman; *Publishing Manager:* Warwick Jacobson; *Marketing Manager:* Ross Alexander
Parent Company: Paul Hamlyn Pty Ltd (qv)
Subjects: Adult Nonfiction, Australiana,

'Softies', Cookery, Handcrafts, Do It Yourself
1977: 33 titles
ISBN Publisher's Prefix: 0-7254

V C T A Publishing Pty Ltd+, 304 Nicholson St, Fitzroy, Victoria 3065 Tel: 4191066
Director: John Brooke; *Editorial:* Fae Taylor
Parent Company: Victorian Commercial Teachers' Association
Subjects: Educational textbooks and teacher guides in Accountancy, Economics, Commercial and Legal Studies, Consumer Education, Secretarial Studies
1977: approx 25 *1978:* approx 27 titles
Founded: 1953
ISBN Publisher's Prefix: 0-86859

The Helen **Vale** Foundation, PO Box 114, Saint Kilda, Melbourne 3182 (Located at: 12 Chapel St, East Saint Kilda, Melbourne 3182) Tel: (03) 519861
Executive Dir: Kenneth J Ingbritsen
Associate Company: Centre Publications (qv)
Subjects: Education, Health
1979: 2 titles *Founded:* 1970
ISBN Publisher's Prefix: 0-909698

Visa, imprint of Widescope International Publishers Pty Ltd (qv)

Visuals of the Australian Environment, an imprint of Ashton Scholastic (qv)

Was Is Press, PO Box 2, Moreland 3058 Tel: (03) 3863166
Proprietor: Yvonne Rousseau

Wentworth Books Pty Ltd+, 48 Cooper St, Surry Hills, NSW 2010 Tel: 697286
Dirs: Walter W Stone, Walter P Stone
Subjects: Australian History, Literature, Biography, Educational, Bibliography
Associated Companies: Stone Printing Co Pty Ltd, Wentworth Press Pty Ltd
ISBN Publisher's Prefix: 0-85587

Westbooks Pty Ltd+*, PO Box 83, Bayswater, Western Australia 6053 Tel: 2714578
Dirs: Rayma and David Turton
Subjects: Educational, Juveniles

Whitcombe & Tombs Pty Ltd, 159-163 Victoria Rd, Marrickville, NSW 2204 Tel: (02) 5609888 Cable Add: Whitcombes Sydney
Publishing Dir: J Smytheman; *Editorial, Rights & Permissions:* J Pagan
Parent Company: Whitcoulls Ltd, New Zealand (qv)
Subjects: General Fiction, Belles Lettres, Poetry, Biography, History, Music, Art, Juveniles, High-priced Paperbacks, Engineering, General & Social Science, University, Secondary & Primary Textbooks, Educational Materials
Bookshops: Whitcombe & Tombs, Sydney, NSW; Richmond, Melbourne, Victoria and West Perth, Western Australia
1977: 5 titles *Founded:* 1882
ISBN Publisher's Prefix: 0-7233

Widescope International Publishers Pty Ltd+, PO Box 339, Camberwell, Victoria 3124 (Located at: 7 Cato St, Hawthorn East, Victoria 3124) Tel: (03) 207909 Cable Add: Widescope Melbourne Telex: AA 36035
Man Dir: Geoffrey M Gold
Imprints: Apple Paperbacks, Visa Books
Subjects: Politics, Sociology, History, Biography, Media and Communications, Sport, Economics, Health and Sexuality, Culture, Fiction

1978: 25 titles *1979:* 25 titles *Founded:* 1974
ISBN Publisher's Prefix: 0-86932

Wild & Woolley Pty Ltd+, PO Box 41, Glebe, NSW 2037 (Located at: 260 Kent St, Sydney, NSW 2000) Tel: (02) 295650
Man Dir: Pat Woolley
Associate Companies: Books Australia, ALLBOOKS
Branch Off: PO Box 10711, Eugene, Oregon 97440, USA
Subjects: Fiction, Cartoons, Art, Politics
1977: 8 title *Founded:* 1974
ISBN Publisher's Prefix: 0-909331

John **Wiley** & Sons Australasia Pty Ltd, see Jacaranda Wiley

Wobbledagger+, 5/1 Parkview Rd, Manly, NSW 2095 Tel: 949 2036
Man Dirs: Ian Hoyle, Sally Hoyle
Subjects: Children's Books
Founded: 1977

Women's Movement Children's Literature Co-op Ltd, PO Box 119, Mooroolbark, 3138 Vic Tel: 7283291
Chief Executive: Robyn Wallace; *All other offices:* Noelle McCracken
Subsidiary Company: Sugar and Snails Books
Subjects: Counter-sexist children's books, Fiction and Non-Fiction
1978: 3 titles *1979:* 4 titles *Founded:* 1974
ISBN Publisher's Prefix: 0-908092

Wren Publishing Pty Ltd*, 77 Shoreham Rd, Red Hill South, 3937 Victoria Tel: (059) 892152
Man Dir, Editorial, Sales Production: Dennis Wren; *Publicity, Rights & Permissions:* Dee Wren
Orders to: Hibbins Taylor & Co Pty Ltd, 69 Stanley St, West Melbourne, 3003 Victoria
Subjects: History, Travel, Fiction, Juveniles
1977: 2 titles *Founded:* 1971
ISBN Publisher's Prefix: 0-85885

Literary Agents

Dorothy **Blewett** Associates*, 50 View Hill Crescent, Eltham, Victoria 3095

Book People of Australia P/L, PO Box 313, Prahran, Victoria (Located at: 590 Little Bourke St, Melbourne) Tel: (03) 679249/(02) 293911
Contact: Richard Jones

Charter Books Pty Ltd*, Foveaux House, 63 Foveaux St, Surry Hills, NSW 2101
Contact: Bruce Semler, Malcolm Newell or Donald McLean

Curtis Brown (Australia) Pty Ltd, 86 William St, Paddington, Sydney, NSW 2021 Tel: 318301/336161 Cable Add: Browncurt Sydney
Contact: Tim Curnow, Barbara Mobbs

Hampton Press Features Syndicate*, 5 Dick St, Henley, NSW 2111
Man Dir: Michael Hervey

Yaffa Syndicate Pty Ltd, 432-436 Elizabeth St, Surry Hills, NSW 2010 Tel: (02) 699 7861 Telex: AA 21887

Book Clubs

Arrow, owned by Ashton Scholastic (qv)

Australasian Book Society Ltd*, PO Box A161, Sydney South, NSW 2000

Australian Jewish Book Club Pty Ltd
Owned by: Outback Press Pty Ltd (qv)

Doubleday Australia Pty Ltd, Book Club Associates Division, 14 Mars Rd, Lane Cove, NSW 2066
Man Dir: Peter B Madgwick; *Manager:* John W Liddell
Includes: Doubleday Book Club, The Literary Guild, Doubleday History Book Club, Reader's Choice (Australiana Book Club), Twentieth Century Classics

Doubleday Book Club, see Doubleday Australia Pty Ltd, Book Club Associates Division

Doubleday History Book Club, see Doubleday Australia Pty Ltd, Book Club Associates Division

The **Literary Guild**, see Doubleday Australia Pty Ltd, Book Club Associates Division

Lucky, owned by Ashton Scholastic (qv)

Reader's Choice (Australiana Book Club), see Doubleday Australia Pty Ltd, Book Club Associates Division

Reader's Digest Condensed Book Services Pty Ltd*, Box 4353 GPO, Sydney, NSW 2001

Teacher's Bookshelf, owned by Ashton Scholastic (qv)

Teenage, owned by Ashton Scholastic (qv)

Twentieth Century Classics, see Doubleday Australia Pty Ltd, Book Club Associates Division

Major Booksellers

Abbey's Bookshop, 477 George St, Sydney, NSW 2000 Tel: (02) 291093
Manager: Peter Milne

Angus & Robertson Bookshops (Head Office), 209 Pitt St, Sydney, NSW 2000 Tel: (02) 2314066 (about 60 branches)

Australian Government Publications, Mt Newman House, 200 St George's Terrace, Perth, Western Australia 6000 Tel: (093) 224737

Collins Booksellers Pty Ltd (Head Office)*, 86 Bourke St, Melbourne, Victoria 3000 Tel: (03) 6622711 (18 branches)

Dymock's Book Arcade Ltd*, 424 George St, Sydney, NSW 2000 Tel: (02) 254211 (several branches)

Foreign Language Bookshop, 94 Elizabeth St, Melbourne, Victoria 3000 Tel: (03) 6542883

Grahame Book Co Pty Ltd*, Pitt and Hunter Streets, Sydney, NSW 2000 Tel: (02) 2321966 (several branches)

Language Book Centre, 127 York St, Sydney 2000 Tel: 296643

Queensland Book Depot (Head Office), 61-63 Adelaide St, Brisbane, Queensland 4000 Tel: (072) 312331 (9 branches)

Rigby Ltd, 24 James Pl, Adelaide, South Australia 5000

John **Scott** Educational Books Supply*, 65 Park St, Abbotsford, Victoria 3067 Tel: 417041

University Co-op Bookshop Ltd*, 76–84 Bay St, Broadway, NSW 2007 Tel: (02) 2122211 (several branches)

Whitcombe & Tombs Pty Ltd, 159-163 Victoria Rd, Marrickville, NSW 2204 Tel: 5609888; 81 York St, Sydney Tel: 294743; 142 Colin St, West Perth, Western Australia 6005 Tel: 217044; 120 Chestnut St, Richmond, Victoria Tel: 421226

Major Libraries

Australia Archives*, Kingston, ACT 2604
Publications: Inventories, Guides (irregular)

Australian National University Library, PO Box 4, Canberra, ACT 2600 Tel: (062) 495111 Cable Add: Natuni Telex: AA 62760

The **Barr Smith** Library, The University of Adelaide, Adelaide, South Australia, 5001 Tel: (08) 2234333
Librarian: I D Raymond

C S I R O (Commonwealth Scientific and Industrial Research Organization), Central Information, Library and Editorial Section, 314 Albert St, PO Box 89, East Melbourne, Victoria 3002 Tel: (03) 4191333 Telex: 30236
Officer-in-Charge: P J Judge; *Editor-in-Chief:* B J Walby; *Chief Librarian:* P H Dawe; *Manager, Information Service:* C Garrow
Publications: CSIRO Index, Australian Science Index, Australian Renewable Energy Resources Index, Australian Sheep and Wool Information Service, Scientific Serials in Australian Libraries (microfiche), *Scientific and Technical Research Centres in Australia, Australian Scientific Societies and Professional Associations, CSIRO-SDI User Manual, Technical Communications, CILES Biennial Report*

Commonwealth Patents, Trade Marks and Designs Offices Library*, Scarborough House, Phillip, PO Box 200, Woden, ACT 2606

High Court of Australia Library, Taylor Sq, Darlinghurst, Sydney, NSW 2010 Tel: 2381423
Librarian: Mark Powell

The **Library Board and the State Reference Library of Western Australia**, Henley Ho, 102 Beaufort St, Perth, WA 6000 Tel: (09) 3287466
State Librarian: Robert Sharman

National Library of Australia, Parkes Pl, Canberra, ACT 2600 Tel: (062) 621111 Cable Add: Natlibaust Canberra Telex: 62100
Director of Publications: A T Bolton
Publications: Acquisitions Newsletter (five or six times yearly), *Australian Books* (annual), *Australian National Bibliography* (four times monthly), *Current Australian Serials* (irregular)

The **State Library of New South Wales**, Macquarie St, Sydney, NSW 2000 Tel: (02) 2211388

State Library of Queensland, William St, Brisbane, Queensland 4000
Includes the Oxley Library
Publication: Queensland Heritage (twice yearly) *Annual Statistical Bulletin of Queensland Public Libraries Services* 1968–, *Queensland Government Publications*, 1977- (quarterly)

State Library of South Australia, North Terrace, Adelaide, South Australia 5000 Tel: 2238911 Telex: 82074
Formerly Public Library of South Australia
Publications: South Australiana (twice yearly), *Pinpointer* (two-monthly), *Index to Australian Book Reviews* (quarterly), *Annual Report*

State Library of Tasmania, 91 Murray St, Hobart, Tasmania 7000 Tel: (002) 308033 Telex: 58222
Taking in Tasmanian Public Library
Publication: Annual report

State Library of Victoria, 328 Swanston St, Melbourne, Victoria 3000 Tel: 6634811

University of Melbourne Library, Parkville, Victoria 3052

University of New South Wales Library, PO Box 1, Kensington, NSW 3033 Tel: 6630351

University of Queensland Library*, St Lucia, Queensland, Australia 4067 Tel: (07) 3772304
University Librarian: F D O Fielding
Publication: Annual Report

University of Sydney Library*, Sydney, NSW 2006 Tel: (02) 692 1122 Telex: 20056

University of Western Australia Library*, Nedlands, Western Australia 6009 Tel: 803838

Library Associations

Australian Advisory Council on Bibliographical Services (AACOBS)*, National Library, Canberra, ACT 2600
Chairman: The Hon Sir Malcolm Peter Crisp

Australian Law Librarians' Group*, c/o Margaret McAleese, Law Librarian, Australian National University, PO Box 4, Canberra, ACT 2600
Convener: Margaret McAleese

Australian Library Promotion Council, Executive Director, 328 Swanston St, Melbourne, Victoria 3000 Tel: (03) 635994
President: Mrs Dulcie Stretton
Publications: Australian Library News (10 issues per year), *Bookmark* (Annual Directory/Diary)

Australian Library Technicians' Association*, GPO Box 313B, Melbourne, Vic 3001
President: Joe Lynam; *Secretary:* Lorraine Conway (at above address)

Australian School Library Association, PO Box 266, Goulburn, NSW 2580 Tel: (048) 212325
Executive Secretary: Bill Sommerville
Publications: School Libraries in Australia (official journal; irregular)

Australian Society of Archivists*, PO Box 83, O'Connor, ACT 2601
President: Mr G L Fisher; *Secretary:* Ms D Wheeler (at above address)

Bibliographical Society of Australia and New Zealand*, 18 Oakes St, Cook, ACT 2614
Secretary: Mr V Crittenden (at above address)
Publications: Bulletin (irregular); occasional papers

Commonwealth Archives Offices*, Commonwealth Centre, Cnr Hunter and Phillip Sts, Sydney, NSW 2000

International Association of Music Libraries, Australia/New Zealand Branch (IAMLANZ)*, Victorian College for the Arts, 234 Saint Kilda Rd, Melbourne, Vic 3004
President: Kenneth A R Horn; *Secretary:* Ian G Miller (at above address)
Publication: Continuo

Library Association of Australia, 35 Clarence St, Sydney, NSW 2000
General Secretary: Jeanette Knox
Publications: Australian Library Journal, Handbook, Directory of Special Libraries in Australia, Australian Academic and Research Libraries, Australian Special Libraries News, Orana, Cataloguing Australia, List of Translators and Translation Services in Australia, Conference Proceedings, The Variety of Librarianship: Essays in Honour of John Wallace Metcalfe, Libraries, Information and Education

The **Library Automated Systems** Information Exchange (LASIE), 10 Wattle Rd (PO Box 581), Brookvale, NSW 2100 Tel: 9382722/55
President: Dorothy G Peake; *Executive Officer:* Leslie Symes
Publication: LASIE (Information Bulletin)

Medical Librarians' Group*, Central Library, Australian Department of Health, PO Box 100, Woden, ACT 2606
Convener: Mrs S Liki (at above address)

Public Lending Right Committee*, The Administrator, Australia Council, PO Box 302, North Sydney, NSW 2060 Tel: 9222122

State Librarians' Council*, c/o State Library of Victoria, 328 Swanston Rd, Melbourne 3000
Chairman: K A R Horn

Library Reference Books and Journals

Books

Directory of Public Reference and Lending Libraries in Australia, Library Association of Australia, 35 Clarence St, Sydney, NSW 2000

Directory of Special Libraries in Australia, Library Association of Australia, 35 Clarence St, Sydney, NSW 2000

Library Association of Australia: Handbook, Library Association of Australia, 35 Clarence St, Sydney, NSW 2000

Journals

Acquisitions Newsletter (five or six times yearly), Sales and Subscriptions Unit, National Library of Australia, Canberra, ACT 2600

Archives and Manuscripts, A Lemon (Editor), 704 Toorak Rd, Malvern, Victoria 3144

Australian Academic and Research Library, 35 Clarence St, Sydney, NSW 2000

Australian Library Journal, Library Association of Australia, 35 Clarence St, Sydney

Australian Library News, Australian Library Promotion Council, c/o State Library of Victoria, 328 Swanston St, Melbourne, Victoria 3000

Australian Library Technicians Association (ALTA) News (6 issues a year), 55 Radnor St, Camberwell, Vic 3124

Australian School Librarian (quarterly), PO Box 280, East Melbourne, Vic 3001

Australian Special Libraries News, Library Association of Australia, Special Libraries Section, 32 Belvoir St, Surry Hills, NSW 2010

Biblia (monthly), Library Board of Western Australia, 102 Beaufort St, Perth, WA

Cataloguing Australia (quarterly), c/o School of Librarianship, University of NSW, Kensington, NSW 2033

Orana (Childrens Libraries Newsletter), Library Association of Australia, 35 Clarence St, Sydney NSW 2000

School Libraries in Australia, Australian School Library Association, PO Box 118, Carlton 3053

School Library Bulletin (quarterly), Education Department, Library Branch, 449 Swanston St, Melbourne, Vic 3000

Teacher-Librarian (quarterly), PO Box 21, Waverley, NSW 2024

Literary Associations and Societies

Australian Literature Society*, PO Box 55, Barooga, NSW 2739
Secretary: Mrs A Egan

Australian Society of Authors*, 24 Alfred St, Milsons Point, NSW 2061
Executive Secretary: Deirdre Hill
Publication: The Australian Author (quarterly)

Australian Writers' Guild, Suite 505, Fifth Floor, 83 York St, Sydney, NSW 2000 Tel: 291402
General Secretary: Angela Wales

Bibliographical Society of Australia and New Zealand*, Department of English, Monash University, Clayton, Vic 3168
Publication: Bulletin (twice yearly)

Book Collectors' Society of Australia*, 64 Young St, Cremorne, NSW 2090 Tel: 902184
President: Walter Stone (at above address)
Publications: Biblionews, Australian Notes and Queries (periodical)

Bread and Cheese Club, PO Box 272, East Melbourne 3002
Secretary: S J Czynski

Combined Literary Societies (Australia), PO Box 272, East Melbourne, Vic 3002
Secretary: Miss F N Breen

The **Dickens** Fellowship
29 Henley Beach Rd, Henley Beach, Adelaide, SA 5022
Honorary Secretary: G J Rowe
Also at:
Brisbane: Unit No 3, 12 Sydney St, New Farm, Queensland 4005
Honorary Secretary: Mrs G M Taylor
Melbourne: Flat 143, 200 Dorcas St, South Melbourne 3205, Victoria
Honorary Secretary: Mrs Barbara Barrett

Fellowship of Australian Writers NSW, GPO Box 3448, Sydney, NSW 2001
Secretary: Kate Wright

Publication: Bulletin (bi-monthly)
Fifteen regional branches in suburbs of Sydney and country towns

Literature Board of the Australia Council, PO Box 302, 168 Walker St, North Sydney, NSW 2060 Tel: 9222122
Director: Dr Michael Costigan

International **P E N** (Melbourne Centre), 17-1 Domain Park, 193 Domain Rd, South Yarra, Victoria 3141
Secretary: Jean Gittins

International **P E N** (Sydney Centre), Secretary, 422/290 Jersey Rd, Woollahra, NSW 2025 Tel: 325668
Secretary: Susan Yorke
Publication: Newsletter (quarterly)

Poetry Society of Australia, Box N110 Grosvenor Street PO, Sydney 2000, NSW *Secretary:* Cheryl Adamson
Publication: New Poetry (quarterly). Publishes poems, articles, reviews, notes and comments, cartoons, interviews, photographs

Society of Australian Writers*, Australia House, Strand, London, UK

Society of Women Writers*, PO Box 1388, Sydney, NSW 2001

Literary Periodicals

A U M L A, a journal of literary criticism, philology and linguistics (text in English and French), Australasian Universities Language and Literature Association, James Cook University of North Queensland, Townsville, Queensland 4811

The Australian Author, Australian Society of Authors, c/o 24 Alfred St, Milsons Point, NSW 2061

Australian Literary Studies, Department of English, University of Queensland, Saint Lucia, Queensland 4067

Australian Writers and Their Work, Oxford University Press, 7 Bowen Crescent, Melbourne, Victoria 3000

Index to Australian Book Reviews (quarterly), State Library of South Australia, North Terrace, Adelaide, SA 5000

Meanjin Quarterly, a magazine of literature, art and discussion, University of Melbourne, Parkville, Victoria 3052

New Poetry, Box 110, George St North PO, Sydney, NSW 2001

Overland, GPO Box 98a, Melbourne, Victoria 3001

Poetry Australia, 350 Lyons Rd, Five Dock, NSW 2046

Quadrant, Box C344, Clarence St Post Office, Sydney, NSW 2000

Reading Time, Children's Book Council of Australia, New South Wales Branch, PO Box 159, Curtin, ACT 2605

Southerly, a review of Australian literature (English Association, Sydney Branch), Department of English, University of Sydney, Sydney, NSW 2006

Westerly, English Department, University of Western Australia, Nedlands, WA 6009

Literary Prizes

A N Z Local History Award
Awarded by the Australian and New Zealand Bank, $500, plus commended prizes, for a book of Australian local or regional history published during the year (ending 31 December). Administered by Victorian Fellowship of Australian Writers. Entries close 31 December. Enquiries to J Hamilton, 1/317 Barkers Rd, Kew, Victoria 3101

'Age' Book of the Year
Awarded by *The Age*, $3,000 for an Australian book of outstanding literary merit which best expresses Australia's identity or character. Can include fiction, poetry and scholarly writing. Enquiries to *The Age*, 250 Spencer St, Melbourne, Victoria 3000

Angus & Robertson Writers' Fellowship
For a manuscript or book project of outstanding originality, preferably by a new author. Contract with advance of $2,000. Enquiries to The Publisher, Angus & Robertson Publishers, PO Box 290, North Ryde, NSW 2113 Tel: 8872233

Australian Industry Awards for Young Writers
Awarded by BHP, Shell, Ford and *Herald* and *Weekly Times* for poetry, stories, essays, scripts and collections; for young writers 15-21 years, varying conditions. It includes BHP-FAW Young Poets Publishing Project. Enquiries to J Hamilton, 1/317 Barkers Rd, Kew, Victoria 3101

Australian Literature Society Gold Medal*
Originated by Colonel, the Honourable R A Crouch. Enquiries to Secretary, Australian Literature Society, Alvie Egan, c/o PO Box 55, Barooga, NSW 2739

Australian Natives' Association Literature Award
Founded in 1978 as an award for a book on an Australian theme. 1978 winners were Jessica Anderson for *Tirra Lirra By The River* (Macmillan) and Ronald Conway for *Land of the Long Weekend* (Sun Books) who each received $150. Enquiries to J Hamilton, 1/317 Barkers Rd, Kew, Victoria 3101

Awgie Awards
Awarded annually by the Australian Writers' Guild to members, adjudicated by fellow members, for film, stage, radio and television scripts. Further enquiries to Secretary, Australian Writers Guild, Suite 505, Fifth Floor, 83 York St, Sydney, NSW 2000

Book Design Awards
Awarded annually by the Australian Book Publishers' Association. Closing date is 30 November and books must have been published during the previous calendar year. There is an entry fee of $10 per book and any type of book can be submitted, as judging is in several categories. Books must be contracted and designed in Australia, but may be printed anywhere. Enquiries to Director, ABPA, 163 Clarence St, Sydney, NSW 2000

Bookman of the Year Award*
Awarded by the National Book Council to a person who has made a substantial contribution to the promotion of books, but who might not necessarily be expected to be eligible for many of the other awards listed in this section. Awarded in 1978 to Marcie and Harry Muir (booksellers). Enquiries to

22 AUSTRALIA

National Book Council, 4th Floor, 71 Collins St, Melbourne, Victoria 3000

Bronze Swagman Award
Awarded annually for Bush Verse. Bronze statuette of The Swagman, sculpted by Daphne Mayo, valued at $500, and a Winton opal, valued at $50. Closes May 31st. Enquiries to Winton Tourist Promotion Association, PO Box 44, Winton, Queensland 4735

'**Canberra Times**' Short Story Award*
$2,000 and $700 awards for a short story. Awarded in 1978 to James Morlock. Enquiries to the 'Canberra Times', PO Box 443, Canberra City, ACT 2601

Ronald **Carson-Gold** Memorial Short Story Competition*
Awarded annually. Closes 23 April. Short Story by Australian with Australian setting. 1st Prize $600, 2nd Prize $300, 3rd Prize $100. Administered by the Union Fidelity Trust. Enquiries to Carson-Gold Short Story Competition, PO Box 339, Toowong, Brisbane, Queensland 4066

Children's Book of the Year Awards
Awarded annually by the Children's Book Council of Australia. The awards now fall into three sections: Book of the Year — primarily for literary merit but quality of production considered; Picture Book of the Year — for younger children; Best Illustrated Book of the Year. For the first Section the Literature Board makes $2,500 available of which at least $1,500 must go to the winner, who also receives the medal. The Picture Book Award does not carry any monetary prize: the Council's medal is presented to the artist. The award for illustrators is $2,500 and is from the Visual Art Board. The award is to the artist for the best illustrated book entered in any section: a minor portion may be given to the runner up. Authors and illustrators entered for awards must be Australian citizens, or resident in Australia for five of the last ten years, or provide evidence of intention to reside permanently in Australia. Closing date is 31 December, for books published during that year. Entries must be sent by publishers to the State Children's Book Council which is providing the executive for that particular year. Enquiries to L Rees, 50 Booroondara St, Reid, ACT or Library Services, 35 Mitchell St, North Sydney, NSW 2060

Tom **Collins** Poetry Prize*
Administered by Western Australia FAW. For West Australian residents. Prizes $100 and two at $50. First awarded in 1977. Enquiries to Secretary, Western Australia FAW, Tom Collins House, 9 Servetus St, Swanbourne, WA 6010

James **Cook** Australian Literary Studies Award
Not less than $500 from the Townsville Foundation for Australian Literary Studies at the James Cook University of North Queensland. The award is made to the author of the best book dealing with any aspect of Australian life. The book must have been published in Australia, even though printed elsewhere. The publication may be in any field of writing — fiction, poetry, drama, letters, biographical or historical. Closing date is 28 February. Enquiries to the Vice-Chancellor of the University, Townsville, PO, James Cook University, Queensland 4811

Colonel **Crouch** Gold Medal*
Enquiries to Secretary, Australasian Literary Society, Alvie Egan, PO Box 55, Barooga, NSW 2739

C J **Dennis** Award
$1,000, originally for a book about Australian flora and/or fauna, but not necessarily for that category in future. Award provided by Victorian Government and administered by Victorian Fellowship of Australian Writers. The 1978 winner was Robert F Zacharin for *Emigrant Eucalypts: Gum Trees as Exotics* (Melbourne University Press). Enquiries to J Hamilton, 1/317 Barkers Rd, Kew, Victoria 3101

Anne **Elder** Poetry Fund Award
$500 for a first book of poetry. Administered by Victorian Fellowship of Australian Writers. The 1978 winner was Lee Cataldi for *Invitation to a Marxist Lesbian Party* (Wild and Woolley). Enquiries to J Hamilton, 1/317 Barkers Rd, Kew, Victoria 3101

F A W-Barbara **Ramsden** Award
Awarded by the Victorian Fellowship of Australian Writers to both the author and to the editor of an outstanding work of quality writing and presentation published each year. It is the Fellowship's major national award for quality writing and was founded by public subscription to honour Barbara Ramsden, MBE, a publisher's editor of distinction. The winning author and editor are each presented with a plaquette specially designed by sculptor Andor Meszaros, depicting the origin of art. More than one work may be submitted by any publisher, author or publisher's editor in Australia. The 'editor' is to be that person the publisher regards as responsible for editing the work. The 1978 winners were Carol Bram (Publisher's Editor) and C M H Clark (Author) for *A History of Australia, Volume IV: The Earth Abideth for Ever 1851-1888* (Melbourne University Press). Entries close 31 December. Enquiries to J Hamilton, 1/317 Barkers Rd, Kew, Victoria 3101

F A W-John Shaw **Neilson** Poetry Award
Awarded by the Victorian Fellowship of Australian Writers. Closing date 31 December. Any kind of poem is acceptable with a minimum of 14 lines. Merit will be the criterion. First prize at least $150. The 1978 winner was Anne Odgers for *Ruth*. Enquiries to J S Hamilton, 1/317 Barkers Rd, Kew, Victoria 3101

FAW Regional Branch Awards
Various FAW regional branches such as Parramatta, Ballarat, Eastwood, Geelong, Latrobe Valley and North Central hold occasional or regular awards, usually in the area of stories and poetry, for small cash prizes and sometimes publication. They are sometimes open within the State or the Nation

Miles **Franklin** Award
Awarded annually, $A2,250 for a published novel portraying Australian life in any of its phases. Entrants must submit one copy of the published work to each of the five judges, and also one copy to the Permanent Trustee Co Ltd, within two months of its publication. Closing date is 31 January. Enquiries to The Manager, Permanent Trustee Co Ltd, Box 4270, GPO Sydney, NSW 2001

Robert **Frost** Award
Medallion supplied from America by the Friends of Robert Frost. Awarded to a poet in Australia whose work, particularly if sustained, achieves distinction. Entries not required. Administered by the Victorian Fellowship of Australian Writers. The 1978 winner was Rosemary Dobson. Enquiries to J Hamilton, 1/317 Barkers Rd, Kew, Victoria 3101

Gemini Awards*
Awarded by the Toowoomba Arts Festival, a prize of $100 for a short story. Enquiries to the Secretary, Gemini, PO Box 634, Toowoomba, Queensland 4350

Mary **Gilmore** Award*
Awarded annually on themes of significance to the life and aspirations of the Australian people. Subject matter — novel, short story, children's book, etc — varies year by year. $2,000 and a Mary Gilmore medallion will be awarded. Closing date is August. Enquiries to The Secretary, Mary Gilmore Award, Room 75, Trades Hall, Goulburn St, Sydney, NSW 2000

Grenfell 'Henry Lawson' Festival Prizes
Awarded annually in June with engraved bronze statuettes created by Sydney sculptor Alan Ingham, and cash. Awards are made for prose, verse, art and the words and music of an Australian popular song. Prose (a short story up to 4,000 words); Verse (up to 60 lines). Enquiries to Honorary Secretary, PO Box 77, Grenfell, NSW 2810

The Grace **Leven** Prize for Poetry
Instituted under the Will of William Baylebridge, the Australian poet, who died in 1942. This Prize of $200 is offered annually for 'the best volume of poetry published during the twelve months immediately preceding the year in which the award is made'. Competitors must be either Australian born, and writing as Australians, or they must be naturalized in Australia and have lived in that country for at least ten years. The volume chosen may have been published in any country, but copies of it must be freely obtainable in Australia. Enquiries to Perpetual Trustee Co Ltd, 39 Hunter St, Sydney, NSW 2000

Jessie **Litchfield** Memorial Award
A cash prize of $500 and a bronze plaque awarded annually by the Bread and Cheese Club, Melbourne, to encourage writers who, in the opinion of the Committee, may make a contribution to Australian literature. Entry forms available on request accompanied by return postage. Enquiries to S J Czynski, Bread and Cheese Club, Box 272, East Melbourne 3002

Literature Board of the Australia Council
The Literature Board supports the writing of all forms of creative literature, including novels, short stories, poetry and plays. Aid is also given to some nonfiction (especially biography, autobiography, history and the humanities). All individual applicants must use the Literature Board's application form. Annual closing dates: Fellowships, 31 May; Special Purpose Grants, 31 March. Enquiries to the Secretary, Literature Board, Australia Council, PO Box 302, North Sydney 2060

Alan **Marshall** Award
For the best unpublished manuscript that tells a good story in any literary form. Prize currently $500. The 1978 winner was Maria Lewitt for *Years Without Spring*. Administered by Victorian Fellowship of Australian Writers. Enquiries to J Hamilton, 1/317 Barkers Rd, Kew 3101, Victoria

National Book Council Awards*
Awarded by the National Book Council, first prize $3,000 ($600 to publisher) for book of highest literary merit, 2nd prize $2,000 ($400 to publisher) for book of highest literary merit in a category other than that of the book winning first prize. Enquiries to Executive Secretary, 4th Floor, 71 Collins St, Melbourne, Victoria 3000

John Shaw **Neilson** Poetry Award, see FAW–John Shaw Neilson Poetry Award

New Zealand Anzac Fellowships*
The New Zealand Government offers several Fellowships each year to Australians. Awards are tenable for periods of between 3 and 12 months and candidates should preferably be under 45. Enquiries to Secretary, Department of Education, PO Box 826, Woden, ACT 2606

Banjo **Paterson** Awards*
Competition run in conjunction with the Biennial Orange Festival of Arts (March 1979, 1981). Various categories — essays, poems, plays, short stories. Enquiries to The Honorary Secretary, Festival of Arts Committee, Cultural Centre, Sale St, PO Box 763, Orange, NSW 2800

Barbara **Ramsden** Award, see FAW—Barbara Ramsden Award

Shell Book of the Year Award
The 1978 winner was Robin Smith for *Birth of Australia* (Rigby Ltd). Enquiries to J Hamilton, 1/317 Barkers Rd, Kew, Victoria 3101

South Australia Biennial Literature Prize*
Two awards for literature were given by the South Australian Government in 1978. Each award was of $3,000, the first for a South Australian regional history or biography, the second (for writers who have had no more than two books published) for a work of poetry, fiction or drama. Enquiries to Arts Development Division, Premier's Department, PO Box 2343, Adelaide, SA 5001

South Australian Government Literature Prize*
For a regional history or biography. $3,000, biennial. For a published work of poetry, fiction or drama. $3,000, biennial. Enquiries to Arts Development Division, Premier's Department, Box 2343, GPO, Adelaide 5001

State of Victoria Short Story Awards
Awarded annually; prizes of $700, $250 and $200 to an Australian writer for an original short story. The 1978 winner was James McQueen for *Acorns*. There will also be commendatory awards. There are also two special awards of $50 each for unpublished writers. Stories should be unpublished and not exceed 4,000 words. More than one entry may be submitted in all sections. Closing date 31 December. Administered by Victorian Fellowship of Australian Writers. A stamped addressed envelope should be enclosed. Enquiries to J Hamilton, 1/317 Barkers Rd, Kew, Victoria 3101.

'**Sun News-Pictorial**' Holiday Short Story Festival Awards
Awarded by the Melbourne *Sun News-Pictorial* for short stories published during December/January each year. $1,000 first prize, and a prize of $250 to the best story by a writer under 30. Each story published receives publication fee of $100. Opens 1 September and closes 1 November. Enquiries to Marketing Director, *Sun News-Pictorial*, 44-74 Flinders St, Melbourne, Victoria 3000

Townsville Foundation for Australian Literary Studies Award
For the best book dealing with any aspect of Australian life. Annual award of $750. Enquiries to the Vice-Chancellor of the University, Townsville, Post Office, James Cook University, Queensland 4811

Warana Writers' Awards*
Awarded annually by the Fellowship of Australian Writers (Queensland Branch) for poetry, feature article and short story. Closes 25 August. Enquiries to Mrs Jean Scott, PO Box 339, Toowong, Brisbane, Queensland 4066

Con **Weickhardt** Award
Awarded for a published work of biography, autobiography or a memoir. $500, administered by the Victorian Fellowship of Australian Writers. Closing date 31 December. The 1978 winners were Ray Ericksen for *Ernest Giles—Explorer and Traveller 1835-1897* (William Heinemann) and John Kerr for *Matters of Judgement* (Macmillan). Enquiries to the Secretariat, 1/317 Barkers Rd, Kew, Victoria 3101

Patricia **Weickhardt** Award
Cash prize to an aboriginal writer. Administered by Victorian Fellowship of Australian Writers. The 1978 winner was Kevin Gilbert, a poet. Enquiries to J Hamilton, 1/317 Barkers Rd, Kew, Victoria 3101

Patrick **White** Award
Patrick White has applied his Nobel Prize money to establish a trust to make grants to Australian writers, to help relieve financial need of older writers of distinction. Submissions are not required. Enquiries to J Allison, Woollahra Municipal Library, Woollahra, NSW

Sir Thomas **White** Memorial Prize*
Annual award of the Society of Australian Writers (UK). Categories vary from year to year. Award is approximately $500. Enquiries to Secretary, Society of Australian Writers, Australia House, Strand, London, UK

Wilke Literary Award
For a book printed in Australia in field of Australiana. $100. Administered by the Victorian Fellowship of Australian Writers. The 1978 winner was W F Mandle for *Going It Alone: Australia's National Identity in the Twentieth Century* (Allen Lane/Penguin Books Australia). Enquiries to J Hamilton, 1/317 Barkers Rd, Kew, Victoria 3101

Austria

General Information

Language: German (English widely spoken)
Religion: Predominantly Roman Catholic
Population: 7.5 million
Bank Hours: 0800-1530 Monday-Wednesday, Friday; 0800-1730 Thursday
Shop Hours: 0800-1800 Monday-Friday; 0800-1200 or 1300 Saturday
Currency: 100 groschen = 1 schilling
Export/Import Information: Austria has own system of preferential tariffs. Books generally free, except children's picture books which are dutied at 20% (general rate) or 19% (GATT), but this has been temporarily reduced. Advertising matter is duty-free. 18% VAT on books and advertising. No import licences for books or advertising. No exchange controls.
Copyright: UCC, Berne, Florence (see International section)

Book Trade Organizations

Bundesgremium des Handels mit Büchern, Kunstblättern und Musikalien, Zeitungen und Zeitschriften, A-1011 Vienna, Bauernmarkt 13 Tel: (0222) 635763
Federal Group for Traders in Books, Prints and Sheet Music, Newspapers and Periodicals

Hauptverband der graphischen Unternehmungen Österreichs*, A-1010 Vienna 1, Grünangergasse 4
Austrian Graphical Association

Hauptverband des österreichischen Buchhandels, A-1010 Vienna 1, Grünangergasse 4 Tel: (0222) 521535 Cable Add: Buchverein, Vienna
Austrian Publishers' and Booksellers' Association
Secretary: Dr Gerhard Prosser
Miscellaneous: A number of subsidiary organizations are administered from the same office, e.g. Verband der Antiquaire (qv), Österreichischer Verlegerverband (qv), etc
Publications: Anzeiger des österreichischen Buchhandels (bi-monthly); *Adressbuch des österreichischen Buchhandels (Directory); Das österreichische Buch* (catalogue) (annual); *Bücher für Alle* (catalogue) (annual)

Landesgremium Kärnten des Handels mit Büchern, Kunstblättern, Musikalien, Zeitungen und Zeitschriften, A-9020 Klagenfurt, Bahnhofstr 40-42 Tel: 04222/80411
Carinthian Regional Group of Traders in Books, Art Prints, Sheet Music, Periodicals and Newspapers

Landesgremium Niederösterreich des Handels mit Büchern, Kunstblättern, Musikalien, Zeitungen und Zeitschriften*, A-1014 Vienna, Herrengasse 10 Tel: 636691
Lower Austria Regional Group of Traders in Books, Art Prints and Sheet Music, Periodicals and Newspapers

Landesgremium Oberösterreich des Handels mit Büchern, Kunstblättern, Musikalien, Zeitungen und Zeitschriften, A-4010 Linz, Hessenpl 3 Tel: 78444/328
Upper Austria Regional Trade Association of Traders in Books, Art Prints, Sheet Music, Periodicals and Newspapers

Landesgremium Salzburg des Handels mit Büchern, Kunstblättern, Musikalien, Zeitungen und Zeitschriften, A-5027 Salzburg, Julius-Raab-Platz 1 Tel: 71571/251 Telex: 3633
Salzburg Regional Group of Traders in Books, Prints, Sheet Music, Periodicals and Newspapers

Landesgremium Steiermark des Handels mit Büchern, Kunstblättern, Musikalien, Zeitungen und Zeitschriften*, A-8010 Graz, Burggasse 11 Tel: 76411
Styrian Regional Group of Traders in Books, Prints, Sheet Music, Periodicals and Newspapers

Landesgremium Tirol des Handels mit Büchern, Kunstblättern, Musikalien, Zeitungen und Zeitschriften, A-6020 Innsbruck, Meinhardstr 14/IV Tel: 35651/290
Tyrol Regional Group of Traders in Books, Art Prints, Sheet Music, Periodicals and Newspapers

24 AUSTRIA

Landesgremium Vorarlberg des Handels mit Büchern und Musikalien*, A–6800 Feldkirch, Wichnergasse 9 Tel: (05522) 2251148
Vorarlberg Regional Group of Traders in Books and Sheet Music
Man Dir: Heribert Eggler; *Secretary:* Dr Manfred Fiel

Landesgremium Wien des Handels mit Büchern, Kunstblättern, Musikalien, Zeitungen und Zeitschriften, A–1040 Vienna, Schwarzenbergpl 14 Tel: 657671
Vienna Regional Group of Traders in Books, Prints, Sheet Music, Periodicals and Newspapers

Literar-Mechana, Wahrnehmungsgesellschaft für Urheberrechte mbH, A–1060 Vienna VI, Linke Wienzeile 18 Tel: (0222) 572161
Organization for Copyright Protection
Man Dir: Franz Leo Popp

Musikverleger Union Österreich, Baumannstr 8-10, A–1030 Vienna
Union of Austrian Music Publishers

Österreichischer Verlegerverband*, A–1010 Vienna, Grünangergasse 4
Association of Austrian Publishers
President: Dr Wilhelm Schwabl; *Secretary-General:* Dr Gerhard Prosser

Staatlich Genehmigte Gesellschaft der Autoren, Komponisten und Musikverleger (AKM) reg Gen mbH, A–1030 Vienna III, Baumannstr 8-10 Tel: (0222) 731555
National Licensing Society of Authors, Composers and Music Publishers
President: Prof Dr Marcel Rubin

Staatlich genehmigte Literarische Verwertungsgesellschaft (LVG) reg Gen mbH, A–1060 Vienna VI, Linke Wienzeile 18 Tel: (0222) 572161
National Licensing Society for Literary Exploitation
President: Milo Dor; *Man Dir:* Franz Leo Popp

Verband der Antiquare Österreichs*, A–1010 Vienna, Grünangergasse 4
Austrian Antiquarian Booksellers' Association

Verband der Bühnenverleger Österreichs*, A–1120 Vienna, Kiningergasse 6 Tel: 8367103
Association of Austrian Theatrical Publishers

Verband österreichischer Kommissionäre, Grossobuchhändler und Auslieferer*, A–1010 Vienna, Grünangergasse 4 Tel: 521535
Association of Austrian Agents, Book Wholesalers and Distributors

Book Trade Reference Books and Journals

Books

Adressbuch des österreichischen Buch-Kunst-Musikalien-und Zeitschriftenhandels (Directory of Austrian Book, Art, Music and Magazine Trade), Austrian Publishers' and Booksellers' Associations, A–1010 Vienna, Grünangergasse 4

(See also reference books listed under Federal Republic of Germany)

Journals

Anzeiger des österreichischen Buchhandels (Austrian Book Trade Gazette), Austrian Publishers' and Booksellers' Association, A–1010 Vienna, Grünangergasse 4

Anzeiger des Verbandes der Antiquare Österreichs (Austrian Antiquarian Booksellers' Association Gazette), Austrian Publishers' and Booksellers' Association, A–1010 Vienna, Grünangergasse 4

Buch und Bildung (Book and Education), Holzwarth & Berger, A–1010 Vienna, Borseplatz 6

Österreichische Bibliographie (Austrian Bibliography), Austrian Publishers' and Booksellers' Association, A–1010 Vienna, Grünangergasse 4

Wiener Bücherbriefe (Viennese Book Letters), Druck- und Verlagsanstalt Forum Verlag, A–1050 Vienna, Sonnenhofgasse 8

Zeit im Buch (Today in the Book), A–1010 Vienna, Stephans Platz 6

Publishers

Adyar-Verlag+, A–8011 Graz, Wartingergasse 31, Postfach 655 Tel: (0316) 657055
Man Dir: Norbert Lauppert
Subjects: Specialist Publishing House for Theosophical Literature: The Occult, Mysticism, Yoga, Eastern Religions
1977: 4 titles *Founded:* 1947
ISBN Publisher's Prefix: 3-85005

Akademische Druck- und Verlagsanstalt+, A–8011 Graz, Auerspergggasse 12, Ruf 31 1-65, Postfach 598 Tel: 31165 Cable Add: Adeva Graz
Owner: Elsy Struzl; *Man Dir:* Hans Kögeler; *Editorial:* Dr Hans Biedermann, Dr Karl Gratzl, Dr Manfred Kramer, Inge Schwarz
Subjects: Reference, Bibliographies, Scholarly Reprints, Facsimile Editions, University Textbooks
1977: 60 titles *Founded:* 1948
ISBN Publisher's Prefix: 3-201

Aktuell-Verlag+, Neidhardgasse 18, A–3400 Klosterneuburg Tel: 6939 Cable Add: Aktuellverlag klosterneaburg
Publisher: Hademar Bankhofer; *Editorial:* Hans Lichtblau; *Sales:* Erich Bruckberger
1978: 3 titles

Amalthea-Verlag+*, A–1030 Vienna 3, Am Heumarkt 19 Tel: (0222) 723560
Dir: Dr Herbert Fleissner
Subjects: Belles Lettres, Art, Music, Fiction
Founded: 1917
Miscellaneous: Firm is a member of Verlagsgruppe Langen-Müller/Herbig, Federal Republic of Germany (qv)

Jörn **Andreas** Verlag, Hans-Seebach-Str 10, A–5020 Salzburg Tel: 06222/21310
Subjects: Popular Scientific and other Factbooks

Andreas und Andreas Verlagsbuchhandel+, A–5020 Salzburg, Hans-Seebach Str 10 Tel: 21318 Cable Add: Andreasverlag Salzburg Telex: 063212
Publishers: Wolf-Dietrich Andreas, Ingrid Andreas; *Dir:* Franz Pemwieser
Br Offs: Oskar Andreas Nachfolger Herzog & Co, Reise- und Versandbuchhandel, A–1170 Vienna, Parhamerpl 9; Andreas & Andreas Verlagsbuchhandel Zweigniederlassing, D–8228 Freilassing, Ludwig Zellerstr 40, Federal Republic of Germany; Andreas & Andreas Verlagsanstalt, FL–9490 Vaduz, Liechtenstein
Subjects: General Fiction
Founded: 1956
ISBN Publisher's Prefix: 3-85012

Ferdinand **Berger** und Söhne+, A–3580 Horn, Wiener Str 21-23, Postfach 14 Tel: 02982/2318 Cable Add: Berger Horn Telex: 078/77123
Subjects: Folk History, Art History, Anthropology, Archaeology, Reference, the Natural Sciences generally; *Periodicals:* Universum (all branches of science and technology); Sydorvia (mycology); Phyton (botany), etc
Founded: 1868

Bergland Verlag, Arbeitergasse 1-7, A–1051 Vienna Tel: 555641
Man Dir: Friedrich Geyer

Verlag 'Das **Bergland-Buch**' (R Kiesel & Co)+, A–5021 Salzburg, Rainerstr 19 Postfach 175 Tel: (06222) 73587 Cable Add: Berglandbuch Salzburg Telex: 06/3588
Man Dir: Gerald Nowothy; *Publicity:* Anna Hofbauer
Orders to: Dr Franz Hain, A–1220 Vienna (for Austria)
Subjects: General Fiction, Junior Nonfiction, History, General Science, Sport
1978: 19 titles *Founded:* 1929
ISBN Publisher's Prefix: 3-7023

Verlag Alexander **Bernhardt**+, A–6134 Vomperberg Tel: (5242) 2131
Associate Company: Verlag der Stiftung Gralsbotschaft, Federal Republic of Germany (qv)
Subject: Philosophy
Founded: 1945

Annette **Betz** Verlag, Postfach 60, A–1095 Vienna (Located at: Alser Strasse 24, A–1095 Vienna) Tel: (0222) 425684
Man Dir: Dr Otto Mang
Parent Company: Verlag Carl Überreuter (qv)
Associate Company: Meyster Verlag, Federal Republic of Germany (qv)
Subjects: Juveniles
Founded: 1962
ISBN Publisher's Prefix: 3-7631

Bibliographisches Institut GmbH, Vienna, see Bibliographisches Institut AG, Federal Republic of Germany

Bilderbuchstudio Neugebauer*, A–4822 Bad Goisern, Haus 8 Tel: (06135) 7164 Cable Add: Neugebauer Press Bad Goisern
Parent Company: Hermann Schroedel Verlag AG, Switzerland (qv)
Associate Companies: Bilderbuchstudio Neugebauer (im Hermann Schroedel Verlag), Switzerland (qv); Neugebauer Press Verlag, address as above
Subjects: Art, Juveniles

Verlag Hermann **Böhlaus** Nachf GmbH+*, A–1061 Vienna, Schmalzhofgasse 4, Postfach 167 Tel: (0222) 574783/4
Man Dir: Dr Dietrich Rauch; *Editorial:* Dr Peter Rauch; *Sales Dir:* Otto Sprung; *Production:* Heinz Müller; *Publicity:* Renate Redl; *Rights & Permissions:* Robert Reula
Associate Company: Verlagsbuchhandlung Hermann Böhlaus Nachfolger GmbH, Graz, Kroisbach, Ob Pflaffenweg 39
Br Off: Böhlau Verlag, D–5 Cologne 60, Schwerinstr 40, Federal Republic of Germany (qv)
Subjects: Theatre, Biography, History, Music, Art and the Arts generally, Philosophy, Religion, Psychology, General & Social Science, University Textbooks, Economics, Education, Law, Linguistics
1977: 35 titles *Founded:* 1947
Bookshop: Antiquariat Böhlau, A–1061 Vienna, Schmalzhofgasse 4
ISBN Publisher's Prefix: 3-205

Bohmann Druck und Verlag AG+, A-1010 Vienna 1, Canovagasse 5 Tel: 658685
Telex: 12312
Dir: Dr Rudolf Bohmann
Subjects: Trade, Technical, Industrial
Founded: 1936
ISBN Publisher's Prefix: 3-7002

Verlag Dr Gerda **Borotha-Schoeler**+*,
A-1190 Vienna, Glatzgasse 4
Tel: 3494382/3490365
Orders to: Lechner & Sohn, A-1010 Vienna, Seilerstätte 5
Subject: General Knowledge

Wilhelm **Braumüller** Universitätsverlag GmbH+, A-1092 Vienna, Servitengasse 5
Tel: 349124 Cable Add: Braumüller
Man Dir: Albert F Reiterer
Subjects: History, Philosophy, Psychology, General Nonfiction, Juveniles, Agriculture, Literature, Education, Social Science, Economics, Periodicals
1978: 28 titles *Founded:* 1783
ISBN Publisher's Prefix: 3-7003

Galerie und Werkstatt **Breitenbrunn**, Eisenstädterstr 8, A-7091 Breitenbrunn/Neusiedlersee Tel: (0043) 2683/5268
Dirs: Fria Elfen, Will Frenken
Branch Off: Stechbahn 28, D-4190 Kleve, Federal Republic of Germany
Subjects: Hand-Printed Books, Special Books of Various Kinds, Bibliophile Texts and Documents

Verlagsbuchhandlung Julius **Breitschopf**+*, A-1170 Vienna, Bergsteiggasse 5
Tel: 437203/4 Cable Add: Breitschopfbuch Vienna Telex: 074539
Subjects: Picture Books, Juveniles
Bookshop: A-1090 Vienna 9, Nussdorferstr 62
Founded: 1937
Miscellaneous: Associate Company: Julius Breitschopf KG, Verlags buchhandlung, D-8000 Munich 45, Federal Republic of Germany (qv)
ISBN Publisher's Prefix: 3-7004

Verlag **Carinthia**+, A-9010 Klagenfurt, Völkermarkter Ring 25, Postfach 197
Tel: (04222) 83651 Telex: 042204
Subjects: Fiction, Art, Religion
1977: 31 titles *1978:* 29 titles

Codices Selecti, A-8010 Graz, Auersperggasse 12, Postfach 598 Tel: (0316) 31165/31
Subject: Facsimile Editions

Compass Verlagsgesellschaft Rudolf Hanel und Sohn+, A-1013 Vienna 1, Wipplingerstr 32, Postfach 49
Tel: 636616/17/18 Cable Add: Compass Vienna
Man Dir: Werner Futter
Subjects: Austrian Industrial, Financial & Commercial Directories, Economics, Reference, Business
1979-80: 5 titles *Founded:* 1867
ISBN Publisher's Prefix: 3-85041

Cura Verlag GmbH+, A-1030 Vienna, Beatrixgasse 32, Postfach 49 Tel: 736480
Man Dir: Dr Anton Plattner
Associate Companies: Bayerische Verlagsanstalt Bamberg, Sankt Otto Verlag GmbH, both in the Federal Republic of Germany (qqv)
Subjects: Belles Lettres, Educational, Household, Song Books, Juvenile, Religious, Reference
1978: 6 titles

Danubia—Verlag, see Braumüller

Denzel Verlag Auto-und Wander Führer+*, A-6020 Innsbrück, Maximilianstr 9
Tel: (05222) 26880
Subjects: Geography, Atlases, Travel
Founded: 1952

Verlag Franz **Deuticke**+*, A-1011 Viie   , Helferstorferstr 4, Postfach 761 Tel: (0222) 634345/636429
Man Dir: Werner Riehl
Subjects: Nonfiction, Technical, Psychology, General Science, University & Secondary Textbooks, Earth Sciences (Geography, Cartography, Geology, Environmental Protection), Law
Founded: 1878
Bookshops: Buchhandlung Franz Deuticke, Antiquariat Franz Deuticke, A-1010 Vienna 1, Helferstorferstr 4
ISBN Publisher's Prefix: 3-7005

Ludwig **Doblinger** (Bernard Herzmansky) Musikverlag+, A-1010 Vienna 1, Dorotheergasse 10, Postfach 882
Tel: 523504
Man Dir: Christian Wolff
Subject: Music
Founded: 1876
ISBN Publisher's Prefix: 3-90035

Edition **Dumreicher**, an imprint of Rhombus-Verlag (qv)

Econ-Verlag GmbH*, A-1030 Vienna, Ziehrerpl 9 Tel: 724485
Subjects: Reference books on Culture, Science, Engineering, Economics

Wilhelm **Ennsthaler**+, A-4400 Steyr, Stadtpl 26 Tel: (07252) 22053
Subjects: Belles Lettres, Poetry, History
Founded: 1880
Bookshop: A-4400 Steyr, Stadtpl 26
ISBN Publisher's Prefix: 3-85068

Europa Verlags-GmbH+, A-1232 Vienna, Altmannsdorferstr 154-156 Tel: (0222) 672622 Cable Add: Europaverlag
Telex: 131326
Dir: Erich Pogats; *Editorial:* Dr Franz Haderer, Peter Aschner; *Sales, Publicity:* Christian Lunzer; *Production:* Georg Prechtl; *Rights & Permissions:* Anna Marchfeld
Subjects: Philosophy, Natural, Social & Political Science, Current Events, Literature, Economics, Law, Psychology, Belles Lettres
1977: 82 titles *1978:* 65 titles *Founded:* 1946
ISBN Publisher's Prefix: 3-203

Evangelischer Pressverband in Österreich*, A-1030 Vienna, Ungargasse 9
Tel: 725475/725461 Telex: 01/12818
Founded: 1925

Fackelverlag G Bowitz KG*, Postfach 216, Salzburg
Miscellaneous: Firm is a Branch Office of Fackelverlag, Stuttgart, Federal Republic of Germany (qv)

Facultas Verlag+*, A-1090 Vienna, Berggasse 4 Tel: 346198 Telex: 07-6529 ICPFA A
Subject: Sciences
1977: 12 titles *1978:* 7 titles

Forum Verlag GmbH+*, A-1050 Vienna 5, Sonnenhofgasse 8 Tel: 526411
Man Dir: Dr Franz Hentschel
Subjects: General Fiction, General Science, Art, Juveniles
Founded: 1952
ISBN Publisher's Prefix: 3-7006

Freytag-Berndt und Artaria, Kartographische Anstalt+, A-1071 Vienna 7, Schottenfeldgasse 62

Chairman: Dr W R Petrowitz, Harald Hochenegg
Orders to: Kohlmarkt 9, A-1010 Vienna; Wilhelm-Greil Str 15, A-6020 Innsbruck
Subjects: Geography, Atlases

George **Fromme** und Co*, A-1051 Vienna 5, Spengergasse 39 Tel: 555641
Man Dir: Friedrich Geyer
Subjects: Textbooks, General Science, Technology
1977-78: 40 titles *Founded:* 1748
ISBN Publisher's Prefix: 3-85086

Dr Heinrich **Fuchs***, Thimiggasse 82, A-1180 Vienna
1977: 2 titles

Gerlach & Wiedling Buch und Kunstverlag+*, A-1060 Vienna, Gumpendörferstr 51 Tel: 576326/27
Parent Company: Fa Hermann Waldbaur

Gerold & Co, A-1011 Vienna, Graben 31
Tel: 522235/525739 Cable Add: Geroldbuch Vienna Telex: 847136157 gerol a
Man Dirs: Dr Heinrich Neider, Hans Neusser
Subjects: Philosophy, Linguistics
Bookshop: A-1011 Vienna, Graben 31
ISBN Publisher's Prefix: 3-900190

Verlag für **Geschichte und Politik**+, A-1030 Vienna, Neulinggasse 26/12 Tel: 726258/753106
Man Dir: Dr Karl Cornides; *Sales Dir:* Gerda Adler; *Publicity & Advertising:* Dr Erika Rüdegger
Subjects: History, Sociology, Economics, Political Science
Miscellaneous: Associate Company: Verlag Oldenbourg, Vienna (qv)
1977: 9 titles *1978:* 15 titles *Founded:* 1947
ISBN Publisher's Prefix: 3-7028

'**Globus**' Zeitungs-, Druck- und Verlagsanstalt GmbH+, A-1201 Vienna 20, Höchstädtpl 3 Tel: 334501 Cable Add: Globusbuch Wien
General Manager: H Zaslawski
Subjects: Politics, Popular Sciences, Belles Lettres, Sports, Fiction, Newspapers
1977: 7 titles *Founded:* 1945
Miscellaneous: Firm are also general representatives and distributors

Alois **Göschl** & Co+*, A-1190 Vienna 19, Trummelhofgasse 12 Tel: 321180
Proprietor: Hilde Göschl
Subjects: Health, Domestic Science, Juveniles
Founded: 1949

Dr Franz **Hain***, Dr Otto Neurath-Gasse 5, A-1220 Vienna Tel: (0222) 221624
Associate companies: Verlag der Arche, Switzerland (qv); E Pfister GmbH, Federal Republic of Germany (qv); Sanssouci Verlag, Switzerland (qv)

Heimatland Verlag+*, Obere Landstrasse 12, A-3500 Krems

Verlag **Herder** und Co+, Wollzeile 33, A-1011 Vienna 1, Postfach 248 Tel: (0222) 521413 Cable Add: Herderbuch Wien
Telex: 011601 (inland); 11046 (foreign)
Man Dir: Fritz Wieninger
Associate Companies: Verlag Herder KG, Freiburg im Breisgau, Federal Republic of Germany (qv); Herder AG, Basel, Switzerland (qv); A G Ploetz KG, Würzburg, Federal Republic of Germany
Bookshop: Herder und Co, Wollzeile 33, A-1011, Vienna
Founded: 1886
Subjects: Religion, Reference, Psychology, Philosophy, Juveniles, History
ISBN Publisher's Prefix: 3-210

Herold Druck- und Verlagsgesellschaft mbH+, A-1081 Vienna 8, Strozzigasse 8, Postfach 321 Tel: (0222) 431551
Man Dir: J K Niedermaier
Associate Company: Herold Verlagsgesellschaft mbH, D-8000 Munich 90, Claude Lorrainstr 11, Federal Republic of Germany
Subjects: Art, History, Religion (Catholic)
Founded: 1893
ISBN Publisher's Prefix: 3-7008

Bernhard **Herzmansky**, see Ludwig Doblinger

Johannes **Heyn**+*, A-9020 Klagenfurt, Kraßniggstr 42 Tel: (04222) 72759/82522 Cable Add: Heyn Klagenfurt Telex: 042401
Man Dir: Kurt Zechner; *Sales:* Gerd Zechner
Subjects: General Fiction, Belles Lettres, Poetry, Biography, History, How-to, Music, Art, Reference, Juveniles, Low- & High-priced Paperbacks, General Science, University, Secondary & Primary Textbooks
Founded: 1868
Bookshop: Buchhandlung Johannes Heyn, A-9010 Klagenfurt, Kramergasse 2-4
ISBN Publisher's Prefix: 3-85366

Edition E **Hilger***, A-1010 Vienna, Dorotheergasse 2 Tel: (0222) 525315
Man Dir & Production: Ernst Hilger; *Sales & Publicity:* Gabriele Krombholz
Subjects: Collectors' Books, Art, Limited editions of original graphics
1977: 2 titles *Founded:* 1973

Ferdinand **Hirt** mbH & Co KG+*, A-1094 Vienna, Postfach 39 (Located at: A-1094 Vienna Widerhofergasse 8) Tel: (0222) 343558 Telex: 75014
Managers: Götz Hirt-Reger, Herwig Seebauer Sabine Hirt-Reger
Parent Co: Ferdinand Hirt, Federal Republic of Germany (qv)
Orders to: A-1080 Vienna, Lerchenfelder Str 138
Subjects: Science, Education
Founded: 1965
Miscellaneous: Publish serials Wegweiser für die Lehrerfortbildung, Veröffentlichungen der schleswigholsteinischen Universitätsgesellschaft, Hamburger geographische Studien, Wiener geographische Schriften, Schriften des Instituts für Österreichkunde, Hirts Stichwortbücher, Reihe Geocolleg
ISBN Publisher's Prefix: 3-7019

Brüder **Hollinek** und Co GmbH+, A-1130 Vienna, Gallgasse 40A Tel: 8257062
Man Dir: Dr R Hollinek; *Sales Dir:* Mag Ing R Hollinek; *Advertising Dir, Rights & Permissions:* E Kindler-Hollinek
Subjects: Reference, Medicine, Law
Founded: 1872
Bookshop: A-1130 Vienna, Gallgasse 40A
Subsidiary: Druckerei Brüder Hollinek, A-2351 Wiener Neudorf

Inn-Verlag+, Roseggerstr 30, Postfach 516, A-6021 Innsbruck Tel: (05222) 43240 Cable Add: Innverlag Innsbruck Telex: 05-3617 innvlg a
Publisher: Käte Glotz-Hagleitner; *Sales:* Günther Glotz; *Production:* Klaus Hagleitner
Subjects: Technical Books, History, Sport, School Books
Bookshop: Kommissions-Reise & Versandbuchhandlung, Roseggerstr 30, A-6020 Innsbruck
1977: 22 titles *1978:* 19 titles *Founded:* 1947
ISBN Publisher's Prefix: 3-85123

Jasomirgott-Verlag+*, Leopoldstr 19, A-3400 Klosterneuburg Tel: (02243) 7570
Man Dir: J Herbert Neumaerker

Jugend und Volk Verlagsgesellschaft mbH+, A-1014 Vienna, Tiefer Graben 7-9 Tel: 630771-0
Man Dir: Kurt Biak; *Sales Dir:* Friedrich Herda; *Production:* Helmut Leiter; *Publicity Dir:* Hubert Hladej; *Rights and Permissions:* Friedrich Themel
Subjects: Belles Lettres, Music, Art, Picture Books, Juveniles, High-priced Paperbacks, Psychology, Social Science, Education, Viennese Memorabilia, Secondary & Primary Textbooks, Educational Materials, Austrian post-war literature
1977: approx 360 titles *Founded:* 1921
Bookshop: Bücher am Heidenschuss, A-1010 Vienna, Heidenschuss 2
Subsidiary: Jugend und Volk Verlag GmbH, D-8000 Munich 90, Claude-Lorrain-Str 11, Federal Republic of Germany (qv)
Miscellaneous: Publishes journals, periodicals, reprints
ISBN Publisher's Prefix: 3-7141

Verlag **Jungbrunnen**+, A-1011 Vienna 1, Rauhensteingasse 5, Postfach 583 Tel: (0222) 521299
Man Dir: Hans Matzenauer; *Editorial, Rights and Permissions:* Wolf Harranth
Subjects: Juveniles, Psychology, Education
1978-79: 10 titles *Founded:* 1923
ISBN Publisher's Prefix: 3-7026

Juridica-Verlag GmbH+*, A-1070 Vienna, Wimbergergasse 33 Tel: 933292
Managers: Ing Werner Sopper, Karl Weidlich

Verlag A F **Koska**+, A-1095 Vienna, Zimmermanngasse 1, Postfach 61 Tel: (0222) 424689, 432137
Manager: Prof Alfred F Koska

Verlag **Kremayr und Scheriau**+, A-1120 Vienna, Niederhofstr 37 Tel: 834501 Telex: 131405
Man Dir: Dr Wolfgang Klesl
Orders to (Trade Dept): Zentralgesellschaft Dr Berger, A-1010 Vienna, Singerstrasse 12
Subjects: General Fiction, History, How-to, Music, Art, Juveniles
1978: 15 titles *1979:* 11 titles *Founded:* 1950
Book Club: Buchgemeinschaft Donauland
Bookshop: Buchhandlung und Zeitschriftenvertrieb Kremayr & Scheriau, A-1121 Vienna, Niederhofstr 37
Miscellaneous: Firm is part of Verlagsgruppe Bertelsmann, Federal Republic of Germany (qv)
ISBN Publisher's Prefix: 3-218

Elisabeth **Lafite**+, A-1010 Vienna 1, Hegelgasse 13 Tel: 526869
Subjects: Music books and periodicals
Founded: 1962
ISBN Publisher's Prefix: 3-85151

Langenscheidt-Verlag GmbH*, A-1010 Vienna, Singerstr 12
Subject: Foreign Languages
Miscellaneous: Firm is a subsidiary of Langenscheidt KG, Federal Republic of Germany (qv)

Leykam AG+, A-8011 Graz, Stempfergasse 3, Postfach 424 Tel: 0316 71691 Cable Add: Leykam Graz Telex: 031703
Man Dir: Dr Karl Schober
Subjects: Art, GGGeneral Fiction, Textbooks
1977: 17 titles *1978:* 17 titles *Founded:* 1585
Bookshops: A-8605 Kapfenberg, Kol Wallischpl; A-8700 Leoben, Am Durchbruch 5; A-8940 Liezen, Hauptstr 29; A-8680 Mürzzuschlag, Toni Schruf-Str 12; A-8330 Feldbach, Grazerstr 9
ISBN Publisher's Prefix: 3-7011

Löcker Verlag+*, Annagasse 5, A-1010 Vienna Tel: 520282
Gen Man: Erhard Löcker; *Publicity, Rights & Permissions:* Dr Helga Kaschl
Orders to: Pichlers Witwe und Sohn, Altmannsdorferstr 154-156, A-1232 Vienna
1978: 4 titles
Founded: 1974

Paul **Mangold** Verlag, A-8020 Graz, Josef Poschstr 117 Tel: (0316) 52536 Cable Add: Mangoldverlag
Man Dir: Paul Mangold
Subject: Juveniles
1978: 3 titles *1979:* 3 titles *Founded:* 1977
ISBN Publisher's Prefix: 3-900301

Manutiuspresse Wulf Stratowa Verlag+*, A-1011 Vienna 1, Postfach 587
Subjects: Biography, Ethnology, Travel, Juveniles, Music, Theatre, Philosophy
ISBN Publisher's Prefix: 3-85171

Manz'sche Verlags- und Universitätsbuchhandlung+*, A-1014 Vienna, Kohlmarkt 16 Tel: 631785
Man Dirs: Dkfm Franz Stein, Dr Anton C Hilscher
Subjects: Law, Economics, University Textbooks, Educational Materials
1977: approx 90 titles *Founded:* 1849
Bookshop: Manz'sche Verlags-und Universitätsbuchhandlung, A-1014 Vienna, Kohlmarkt 16
ISBN Publisher's Prefix: 3-214

Verlag Wilhelm **Maudrich**+, A-1097 Vienna 9, Lazarettg. 1, Postfach 21 Tel: 425241 Cable Add: Mandrich Verlag Wien
Man Dir: Gerhard Grois; *Advertising Dir:* Elisabeth Bernard
Subjects: How-to, Medicine, Psychology, University Textbooks
Founded: 1909
Bookshop: Buchhandlung Wilhelm Maudrich, A-1097 Vienna, Spitalg. 21a
ISBN Publisher's Prefix: 3-85175

Meyster Verlag*, Alserstr 24, Postfach 60, A-1095 Vienna Tel: 425684 Cable Add: Ueberreuter Vienna Telex: 07-4802
Man Dir: Thomas F Salzer; *Editorial:* Dr Andreas Hopf; *Sales:* Hermann Meyer; *Production:* Ing Günter Plass; *Publicity:* Klaus von Sobbe
Parent Company: Carl Ueberreuter Druck und Verlag in Salzer AG (qv)
Subsidiary Company: Meyster Verlag GmbH München, Federal Republic of Germany (qv)
Associate Company: Annette Betz Verlag (qv)
Subjects: Reference, Picture Books
1978: 11 titles *Founded:* 1977
ISBN Publisher's Prefix: 3-7057

Progress-Verlag Dr **Micolini's** Wtw+, A-8010 Graz, Glacisstr 57 Tel: (03122) 79508 Cable Add: Micolini Graz
Founded: 1934

Modulverlag GmbH*, Seilergasse 16, A-1010 Vienna

Verlag Fritz **Molden**+*, A-1190 Vienna Grinzing, Sandgasse 33 Tel: (0222) 323151 Cable Add: Moldenverlag Vienna Telex: 074306
Publisher: Fritz P Molden; *Man Dirs:* Dr Hans-Peter Übleis, Johannes Eidlitz; *Sales:* Klaus P Frank (Federal Republic of Germany), Josef Lukes (Austria, Switzerland); *Publicity:* Marianne Menzel (Munich), Dr Ursula Schramel (Vienna); *Advertising:* Gerhart Langthaler; *Rights & Permissions:* Marguérite Segur-Cabanac
Subsidiary Company: Buch ins Haus GmbH, Munich, Federal Republic of Germany

Subjects: General Fiction, Biography, History, How-to, Music, Art, Travel, Paperbacks, General & Social Science, Juvenile Literature
1977: 200 titles *Founded:* 1965
Affiliates: Verlag Fritz Molden GmbH, 8 Munich 19, Stievestr 9, Federal Republic of Germany (qv); Molden Press AG, Glarus, Switzerland; Buch in's Haus GmbH, Vienna; Eroica Verlagsgesellschaft mbH; Molden Taschenbuch Verlag, Vienna; Molden Edition Graphische Kunst, Vienna; Verlag Fritz Molden, A-6020 Innsbruck, Maria Theresienstr 10
ISBN Publisher's Prefix: 3-217

Otto **Müller** Verlag KG+, A-5021 Salzburg, Ernest-Thun Str 11, Postfach 167
Tel: 72152 Cable Add: Müller Verlag
Man Dir: Dr Richard Moissl; *Sales & Publicity:* Alexander Weiger
Subjects: Belles Lettres, Poetry, History, Religion, Psychology
1977: 12 titles *1978:* 16 titles *Founded:* 1937
ISBN Publisher's Prefix: 3-7013

Mundus, Österreichische Verlagsgesellschaft GmbH, see Paul Zsolnay Verlag GmbH, Vienna

Paul **Neff** Verlag KG+*, A-1060 Vienna 6, Gumpendorferstr 5 Tel: (0222) 574767
Cable Add: Neffverlag
Man Dir: Karl Andreas Edlinger
Subjects: General Fiction, Biography, Music, Art
Founded: 1829
Miscellaneous: Associate company of Paul Neff Verlag KG, Federal Republic of Germany (qv)
ISBN Publisher's Prefix: 3-7014

Edition **Neue Mitte**+, A-1033 Vienna, Postfach 12 (Located at: A-1030 Vienna, Landstrasser Hauptstrasse 13/43)
Tel: (0222) 733703
Man Dir: Kurt Sattlberger
Subjects: Political/Social: especially, alternatives to Marxism, future political projections; periodical *Integral*, a tribune for ideological discussion in East and West
1977: 1 title *Founded:* 1976
ISBN Publisher's Prefix: 85401

Neufeld-Verlag und Galerie*, A-6890 Lustenau Tel: 0577 3158 Cable Add: Neufeld
Editorial, Rights & Permissions: Kurt Prantl
Parent Company: Lopfe KG
Associate Company: Neufeld-Verlag, Switzerland (qv)
1977: 2 titles *Founded:* 1962

Wolfgang **Neugebauer**, Wiss Verlagsbuchhandlung, Postfach 64, A-5033 Salzburg (Located at: Alpenstr 12, A-5033 Salzburg)
1978: 6 titles

Neugebauer Press Verlag für bibliophile Drucke+*, A-4822 Bad Goisern, Haus 8
Tel: (06135) 7164 Cable Add: Neugebauer Press Bad Goisern
Parent Company: Hermann Schroedel Verlag AG, Switzerland (qv)
Associate Companies: Bilderbuchstudio Neugebauer, at above address; Bilderbuchstudio Neugebauer im Hermann Schroedel Verlag AG, Switzerland (qv)
Subject: Art
ISBN Publisher's Prefix: 3-85195

Wolfgang **Neugebauer**, A-5033 Salzburg, Postfach 64 Tel: (06222) 23136
Man Dir: Wolfgang Neugebauer
Subjects: Natural Sciences, Theology, Philosophy, Psychology, History, German Literature

Bookshops: Wolfgang Neugebauer, A-5033 Salzburg, Alpenstr 12
1977: 8 titles *1978:* 9 titles *Founded:* 1975
ISBN Publisher's Prefix: 3-85376

Verlag **Niederösterreichisches Pressehaus** mbH+, A-3100 St Pölten, Gutenbergstr 12
Tel: 02742/51561 Telex: 015512
Man Dir, Sales & Editorial: Dr Ingeborg Ornazeder; *Publicity, Production:* Ernst Ablöscher
Subjects: History, Literature, Architecture, Art
Orders to: R Lechner und Sohn, Heizwerkstr 10, A-1232 Vienna
Bookshop: Hippolyt-Buchhandlung, A-3100 St Pölten, Linzerstr 4
1977: 40 titles *1978:* 44 titles *Founded:* 1889
ISBN Publisher's Prefix: 3-85326

Obelisk-Verlag+*, Falkstr 1, A-6020 Innsbruck Tel: (05222) 20733
Proprietor: Helga Buchroithner
Subjects: Geography, Ethnology, Travel, Guidebooks

Oberösterreichischer Landesverlag+, A-4010 Linz, Landstr 41 Tel: (0732) 78121
Man Dir: Hubert Lehner
Subjects: Biography, History, Art, Religion
1977: 20 titles *1978:* 21 titles *Founded:* 1872
Bookshops: Linz, Landstr 41, Postfach 50; A-4810 Gmunden, Rodhauspl 1; A-4710 Grieskirchen, Stadtpl 42, Postfach 26; A-4910 Ried i Innkreis, Bahnhofstr 5-7, Postfach 116; A-4150 Rohrbach, Marktpl 28, Postfach 3; A-4690 Schwanenstadt, Stadtpl 45; A-4600 Wels, Bahnhofstr 16, Postfach 146; A-4820 Bad-Ischl, Pfarrgasse 11; A-4840 Vöcklabruck, Mühlbachgasse 4 (all in Austria)
ISBN Publisher's Prefix: 3-85214

Octopus Verlag, Erich Skrleta, A-1236 Vienna, Postfach 53 Tel: (0222) 7260645
Man Dir: Erich Skrleta
Subjects: Buddhism & Oriental Philosophies, Yoga
Bookshop: A-1030 Vienna, Dannebergpl 10
1977: 6 titles *1978:* 3 titles *Founded:* 1973
ISBN Publisher's Prefix: 3-900290

Verlag **Oldenbourg**+, Neulinggasse 26-12, A-1030 Vienna Tel: 726258/753106
Man Dir: Dr Karl Cornides; *Sales Dir:* Gerda Adler; *Publicity & Advertising:* Dr Erika Rüdegger
Parent Company: R Oldenbourg Verlag GmbH, Federal Republic of Germany (qv)
Subjects: History, Philosophy, Engineering, General & Social Science, University & Secondary Textbooks
Miscellaneous: Associated Company: Verlag für Geschichte & Politik, Vienna (qv)
1977: 45 titles *1978:* 32 titles *Founded:* 1957
ISBN Publisher's Prefix: 3-7029

Wirtschaftsverlag Dr Anton **Orac**+, A-1014 Vienna, Graben 17, Postfach 56 Tel: 528552
Man Dir, Sales, Production, Rights & Permissions: Dkfm Helmut Hanusch; *Editorial, Publicity:* Leo Mazakarini
Subjects: Economics, Jurisprudence, Management, Sport, General Nonfiction
Bookshop: address as above
1979: 60 titles *Founded:* 1946

Österreichische Verlagsanstalt GmbH+, Arbeitergasse 1-7, A-1051 Vienna Tel: 555641
Man Dir: Friedrich Geyer

Verlag der **österreichischen Akademie der Wissenschaften**+, (Publishing House of the Austrian Academy of Sciences) A-1010 Vienna, Dr Ignaz Seipel-Pl 2 Tel: (0222) 521586 Telex: 0112628
Man Dir: Brigitta Nowotny
Subjects: Archaeology, Architecture, Art, Belles Lettres, Biography, Byzantine and Oriental Studies, English Lang and Lit, History, Jurisprudence, Maps, Music, Numismatics, Philology & Dialect Studies, Philosophy, Psychology, Reference, Social Science, Theatre, Urbanism, Paperbacks
1977: 80 titles *1978:* 75 titles *Founded:* 1973
ISBN Publisher's Prefix: 3-7001

Verlag des **österreichischen Gewerkschaftsbundes** GmbH+, A-1232 Vienna 23, Altmannsdorfer Str 154-156 Tel: 67622
Man Dir: Erich Pogats
Founded: 1947

Österreichischer Agrarverlag, Druck- und Verlags- GmbH+, A-1014 Vienna, Bankgasse 1-3, Postfach 136 Tel: 639676
Cable Add: Agrarverlag
Man Dir: Dr Josef Enigl
Subjects: History, Domestic Science, Agriculture, Law, Periodicals
1977: 14 titles *1978:* 17 titles *Founded:* 1945
ISBN Publisher's Prefix: 3-7040

Österreichischer Bundesverlag GmbH+, A-1010 Vienna 1, Schwarzenbergstr 5
Tel: 522561 Cable Add: Bundesverlag Vienna
Orders to: Österreichischer Bundesverlag, A-2351 Wiener Neudorf, Postfach
Subjects: Belles Lettres, History, Juveniles, Textbooks, Reference, Educational Materials, Art, Music, General Fiction, General Science
Bookshop: Quirin Haslinger, A-4010 Linz a d D, Klosterstr 6, Postfach 53
1979: 70 titles *Founded:* 1772
Miscellaneous: Foundation administered by the State; *Dir:* Ministerialrat Dr Peter Lalics

Österreichisches Katholisches Bibelwerk+, A-3400 Klosterneuburg, Stiftspl 8, Postfach 48 Tel: (02243) 2938
Man Dir, Editorial, Rights & Permissions: Dr Norbert Höslinger; *Sales:* Gabriele Marrooscher, Gerlinde Bieder; *Technical Assistant, Production:* Ing Peter Ernst; *Publicity:* Brigitta Witzmann
Subjects: Bibles, Pius Parsch Institute texts, Scriptural Studies
1978: 8 titles *1979:* 7 titles *Founded:* 1966
Miscellaneous: Company is a member of AMB (qv under German Federal Republic) and WCBFA (World Catholic Federation for the Biblical Apostolate)
ISBN Publisher's Prefix: 3-85396

Pinguin-Verlag, Pawlowski KG+*, A-6021 Innsbruck, Lindenbühelweg 2 Tel: (05222) 29306/20360 Telex: 053173 Cable Add: Pinguinverlag Innsbruck
Man Dir: Herbert Pawlowski
Subjects: Art, Juveniles, Reference Books, Calendars
Founded: 1945
ISBN Publisher's Prefix: 3-7016

Ernst **Ploetz**+*, A-9400 Wolfsberg
Subjects: Education, Child Welfare, Textbooks
ISBN Publisher's Prefix: 3-85232

Georg **Prachner**+, A-1010 Vienna, Kärntnerstr 30 Tel: 528549
Man Dir: O G Prachner

Subjects: Architecture, Art, Belles Lettres, History, Fiction
Bookshop: A-1010 Vienna, Kärtnerstr 30

Prugg Verlag+*, A-7000 Eisenstadt, Haydngasse 10 Tel: (02682) 2114
ISBN Publisher's Prefix: 3-85238

Universitätsverlag Anton **Pustet**+*, A-5021 Salzburg, Bergstrasse 12, Postfach 144 Tel: (06222) 73507/76392 Cable Add: Pustet Salzburg
Br Off: D-8828 Freilassing, Reichenhallerstr 17, Postfach 498, Federal Republic of Germany
Subjects: Philosophy, Religion, Psychology, Education, Political Science, Law, Poetry and Iconographs of the University of Salzburg
Founded: 1598
ISBN Publisher's Prefix: 3-7025

Verlag Dr Herta **Ranner**+*, A-1070 Vienna, Zeismannsbrunngasse 1

Felizian **Rauch** Verlagsbuchhandlung+*, A-6010 Innsbruck, Innrain 6-8, Postfach 199 Tel: (05222) 23325 Cable Add: Bücherrauch Innsbruck
Subjects: Art, History, Religion, Philosophy
Founded: 1747
ISBN Publisher's Prefix: 3-85245

Residenz Verlag+, A-5020 Salzburg, Gaisbergstr 6 Tel: (06222) 25771
Man Dir: Wolfgang Schaffler; *Editorial:* Dr Jochen Jung, Renate Buchmann; *Sales Manager:* Christl Sennewald; *Publicity and Rights and Permissions:* Renate Buchmann
Subjects: Belles Lettres, Poetry, Music, Art, Architecture
Founded: 1956
ISBN Publisher's Prefix: 3-7017

Rhombus-Verlag, Edition Dumreicher, A-1132 Vienna, Postfach Tel: (0222) 859027
Man Dir: Vintila Ivanceanu
Orders to: Mohr, A-1010 Vienna, Singerstr 12; Lang, D-1000 Berlin 15, Sächsischestr 7, Federal Republic of Germany
Imprint: Edition Dumreicher
Subject: Experimental modern literature
1978: 7 titles *1979:* 7 titles *Founded:* 1977
ISBN Publisher's Prefix: 3-85394

Karl und Ina **Rinder***, Peuntstr 16, A-8621 Ebensfeld

E **Rötzer** Verlag+*, A-7001 Eisenstadt, Postfach 25 (Burgenland) Tel: (02682) 2473
Proprietor: Elfriede Weber
Subjects: Periodicals, Reference, Guidebooks

S N-Verlag, Salzburger Nachrichten Verlags GmbH & Co KG+, A-5020 Salzburg, Bergstr 14, Postfach 154 Tel: (06222) 775910
Subjects: Regional (Salzburg), Architecture, History, Music, Theatre

Verlag der **Salzburger Druckerei**+, A-5020 Salzburg, Bergstr 12, Postfach 144 Tel: (06222) 73507, Telex:
Subjects: Arts, Poetry, History and Chronicles of Salzburg
1978-79: 10 titles
ISBN Publisher's Prefix: 3-85338

Verlag für **Sammler**+*, A-8011 Graz, Kreuzgasse 45, Postfach 54 Tel: 348923
Subjects: History of Art, Culture, Manners & Morals, Folklore, Early History

Verlag **Sankt Gabriel**+, A-2340 Mödling Tel: 02236/2117
Man Dir: P Alfons Jochum; *all other offices:* Direktor Leo Schuler

Parent Company: Missionshaus Sankt Gabriel, A-2340 Mödling
Subjects: Books for Children and Young People, Religious Knowledge, Practical Theology, Belles Lettres, Travel, Education
Bookshops: A-2340, Mödling; A-1010 Vienna
1977: 22 titles *Founded:* 1905
Miscellaneous: Associate company of Steyler Verlag, Federal Republic of Germany (qv)
ISBN Publisher's Prefix: 3-85264

Verlag **Sankt Peter**+*, A-5010 Salzburg, Postfach 113 Tel: (06222) 42166 Telex: 06/3094
Man Dir: R M Rinnerthaler
Subjects: Austrian Church Art, Austrian Guidebooks, Austrian History
1977: 10 titles *Founded:* 1948
ISBN Publisher's Prefix: 3-900173

Paul **Sappl**, Schulbuch- und Lehrmittelverlag+*, A-6332 Kufstein, Eichelwang 406 Tel: (05372) 2835 Telex: 5119115
Br Off: A-1050 Vienna, Stolberggasse 31-33
Subjects: School Books, Driving School Text Books
1977: 42 titles *Founded:* 1953

Dr A **Schendl** GmbH & Co KG+, A-1041 Vienna, Karlsgasse 15, Postfach 29 Tel: (0222) 655593-96
Dirs: Dr Anna Schendl, Franz Ogg
Subjects: History, Ethnography, Geography, Folklore, Art, Literature, Music, Economy, Periodicals
1978: 6 titles *1979:* 5 titles

Franz **Schneider** Verlag*, Wallnerstr 8, A-1010 Vienna
Subject: Juveniles

Schönbrunn-Verlag GmbH+*, A-1010 Vienna 1, Schulerstr 1-3 Tel: 526905
Subject: Art
Founded: 1946

Anton **Schroll** & Co+, Buch und Kunstverlag, A-1051 Vienna 5, Spengergasse 39 Tel: 555641 Cable Add: Schrollverlag Vienna
Man Dir: Friedrich Geyer, Dieter Reisser
Br Off: D-8000 Munich 95, Boostr 15, Federal Republic of Germany
Subjects: Belles Lettres, History, Art
1977: 20 titles *1978:* 20 titles *Founded:* 1889
ISBN Publisher's Prefix: 3-7031

Verlagsbüro Karl **Schwarzer**+*, Dorotheergasse 6-8, A-1010 Vienna Tel: (0222) 521687
Man Dir: Karl Schwarzer
Subjects: Almanacs, Special Editions

Severin Presse, A-2346 Südstadt Vienna, Dobrastr 112, Postfach 15 Tel: (02236) 811744
Publisher: Peter Croy
Subject: Art (Original Engravings)

Josef Otto **Slezak**, A-1040 Vienna, Wiedner Hauptstr 42 Tel: (0222) 570259
Sales Managerial: Ilse Slezak
Subjects: Transport, especially historical accounts of railways and tramways in Austria and Europe generally
1977: 6 titles *1978:* 12 titles

Springer-Verlag KG+, A-1011 Vienna, Mölkerbastei 5, Postfach 367 Tel: (0222) 639614 Cable Add: Springerbuch Wien Telex: 074506
Man Dir: Dr Wilhelm Schwabl; *Sales Manager:* Rudolf Siegle; *Promotion, Rights & Permissions:* Dr Erna Ungersbaeck;

Production Dir: Bruno Skuhra
Associate Company: Springer-Verlag Inc, 175 Fifth Ave, New York, NY 10010, USA
Subjects: Medicine, Natural Sciences, Engineering, General & Social Science, Economics, Law, Philosophy, University Textbooks, Reference
1977: 62 titles *1978:* 66 titles *Founded:* 1924
Bookshop: Minerva Wissenschaftliche Buchhandlung GmbH, A-1010 Vienna, Schottengasse 7
ISBN Publisher's Prefix: 3-211

Dr Karl **Steinhauser**+*, A-2544 Leobersdorf, Südbahnstr 5
Subject: Arts

Leopold **Stocker** Verlag+, Bürgergasse 11, A-8011 Graz, Postfach 438 Tel: (0316) 71636 Cable Add: Stockerverlag Graz
Publisher: Dr Ilse Dvorak-Stocker; *Editorial Sales, Publicity, Rights and Permissions:* Dr Peter Strallhofer
Br Off: Agent in Vienna is: Rudolf Lechner & Sohn, Heizwerkstr 10, A-1232 Vienna
Subjects: Belles Lettres, Contemporary Literature, Hunting, Nature and Mountain Books, Specialist Books, Agricultural Textbooks and School Books
Founded: 1917

Verlag **Styria**+, A-8010 Graz, Schönaugasse 64, Postfach 435 Tel: 77561 Cable Add: Styriaverlag Graz Telex: 031782 Kleine Zeitung
Man Dir, Editorial: Dr Gerhard Trenkler; *Sales:* Wolfgang Fath; *Production:* Hans Paar; *Publicity:* Peter Altenburg; *Rights & Permissions:* Margarethe Katholnig
Parent Company: Katholischer Pressverein
Imprints: Verlag Styria Graz Wien Köln
Br Offs: Verlag Styria — Meloun & Co, D-5000 Cologne 51, Schillerstr 6, Postfach 511029, Federal Republic of Germany; Verlag Styria, Repräsentanz Wien, A-1010 Vienna, Lobkowitzpl 1
Subjects: Religion, History, Philosophy, Biography, Juveniles, Education, Books, Belles Lettres, Reference Books, Current Affairs
Bookshops: Buchhandlung Styria, A-1010 Vienna, Opernring 15; Buchhandlung Styria, A-8010 Graz, Albrechtgasse 5; Buchhandlung Ulrich Moser, A-8010 Graz, Herrengasse 23; Bücherbox, Goethestr 42, A-8010 Graz; Buchhandlung Styria, A-8750 Judenburg, Hauptplatz 15; Buchhandlung Styria, A-8720 Knittelfeld, Kapuzinerplatz 3, Postfach 72
1977: c 60 titles *1978:* 80 titles *Founded:* 1869
ISBN Publisher's Prefix: 3222

Editio **Totius** Mundi E E Maenner*, A-1090 Vienna, Gussenbauergasse 5-9 Tel: 347346 Cable Add: Baennermundi
Subjects: Art, Maps, Textbooks

Rudolf **Trauner** Verlag+, A-4020 Linz, Baumbachstr 4a Tel: (0732) 78241-3
Man Dir: Rudolf Trauner
Br Off: A-4020 Linz, Köglstr 14
Subjects: Popular Medicine, How-to, Art, Juveniles, Cookbooks, Sports, Maps, Nonfiction
1978: 7 titles *Founded:* 1946
ISBN Publisher's Prefix: 3-85320

Edition **Tusch**+*, A-1160 Vienna, Seitenberggasse 39 Tel: (0222) 452165 Cable Add: Editusch Wien Telex: 76262 tusch a
Subject: Art

Verlagsanstalt **Tyrolia**+, A-6020 Innsbruck, Exlgasse 20, Postfach 220 Tel: 81541 Cable

Add: Tyrolia-Verlag Innsbruck Telex: 05/3620
Dirs: Dr Kunzenmann, Dr Schiemer
Subjects: Theology, School Books, Juveniles, Tour Guides, Illustrated Books, General Nonfiction
Bookshops: in Innsbruck, Ehrwald, Fulpmes, Imst, Landeck, Lienz, Mayrhofen, St Johann, Schwaz, Wattens, Vienna
1977: 38 titles *1978:* 49 titles *Founded:* 1888
ISBN Publisher's Prefix: 3-7022

Verlag Carl Überreuter+, A-1095 Vienna, Alserstr 24, Postfach 60 Tel: (0222) 4256584 Cable Add: Überreuter Vienna Telex: 074802
Publisher: Thomas F Salzer, Andreas Salzer
Man Dir: Otto Mang; *Editorial:* Dr Marion Pongracz, Ingrid Weixelbaumer; *Sales, Publicity:* Thomas C Sacken
Subsidiary Companies: Annette Betz Verlag, Meyster Verlag, Austria (qqv); Meyster Verlag, Federal Republic of Germany (qv)
Br Off: A-2100 Korneuburg, Industriestr 1; D-6900 Heidelberg/Schlierbach, In der Aue 32A, Federal Republic of Germany
Subjects: Juveniles, Low-priced Paperbacks, Secondary & Primary Textbooks, Educational Materials
Founded: 1548
ISBN Publisher's Prefix: 3-8000

Universal Edition AG+*, A-1015 Vienna, Bösendorfer Str 12, Postfach 3 Tel: 658695 Cable Add: Musikedition Wien Telex: 1397
Dirs: Dr J Juranek, S Harpner, A Schlee
Subjects: Music, Musicology
Founded: 1901

Urban und Schwarzenberg+, A-1096 Vienna 9, Frankgasse 4, PoSach 102 Tel: (0222) 422731/2
Man Dir: Helmut Rieger
Bookshops: A-1096 Vienna Frankgasse 4, Postfach 102;
Subjects: Psychology, Medicine, Physics
Founded: 1866
Miscellaneous: Firm is a branch of Verlag Urban & Schwarzenberg, Federal Republic of Germany (qv)
ISBN Publisher's Prefix: 3-85327

Verband der wissenschaftlichen Gesellschaften Österreichs+, A-1070 Vienna, Lindengasse 37 Tel: 0222/932166/934756 Telex: 134981 VIRGOE A
Man Dir: Dr Rainer Zitta
Orders to: Austria: Verband, Vienna; All other countries: Proost en Brandt
1977: 24 titles *1978:* 29 titles *Founded:* 1954
ISBN Publisher's Prefix: 3-85369

Veritas-Verlag+*, A-4010 Linz, Harrachstr 5, Postfach 403 Tel: 0732/71081
Man Dir: Karl Grüber
Br Off: Veritas Passau, Theresienstr 42, D839 Passau
Bookshop: Veritas, Singerstr 26, A-1010 Vienna
1978: 24 titles *Founded:* 1945
Subjects: Religion, Music, Art, Textbooks,
ISBN Publisher's Prefix: 3-85329

Vorarlberger Verlagsanstalt GmbH, A-6850 Dornbirn, Schwefel 81 Tel: (05572) 62864/64697
Subject: Literature

Universitätsverlag Wagner GmbH+, Andreas-Hoferstr 13/1, A-6010 Innsbruck, Postfach 219 Tel: (05222) 27721 Cable Add: Universitätsverlag Wagner, A-6010 Innsbruck
Man Dir: Gottfried Grasl

Imprints: Universitätsverlag Wagner Innsbruck
Subjects: Scientific Works, Maps, Illustrated Motoring Guides, Literature, Lyrical Verse, Colloquial Poetry
1977: 12 titles *1978:* 14 titles *Founded:* 1554
ISBN Publisher's Prefix: 03-7030

Weilburg-Verlag*, Am Fischertor 5, A-2500 Baden bei Wien Tel: 02252/2906 Cable Add: Weilburg Verlag 2500 Baden
Subjects: Art Books, Lyrical Poetry, Numbered and Autographed Bibliophile Editions

Verlag Galerie **Welz** Salzburg, A-5010 Salzburg, Sigmund-Haffner-Gasse 16, Postfach 123 Tel: 41771
Publisher: Friedrich Welz; *Sales:* Hannes Lüftenegger; *Production Manager:* Franz X Eder
Subject: Art, Art Books, Art Prints, Art Post Cards, Art Posters

Wiener Dom-Verlag+, A-1080 Vienna, Strozzigasse 8
Subjects: Art, Education, History, General Science, Religion, Nonfiction
Founded: 1946
ISBN Publisher's Prefix: 0-85351

Wiener Urtext Edition-Musikverlag GmbH & Co KG*, A-1010 Vienna, Bösendorferstr 12 Tel: (publication) 658695, (sales) 657651 Cable Add: Musikedition Telex: 1397
Man Dir: Stefan G Harpner; *Sales Dir:* Vladimir Prusa; *Publicity & Advertising:* Friederike Zimmermann
Parent Company: Verlag B Schotts Söhne, Federal Republic of Germany (qv) and Universal Edition AG, Vienna, Austria
Subject: Music, especially *original scores* of Bach, Beethoven, Brahms, Chopin, Haydn, Mozart, Schubert, Schumann. All accompanying texts are in German and English
1978: 55 titles *Founded:* 1972

J **Wimmer** Druckerei und Zeitungshaus GmbH & Co+*, A-4010 Linz, Promenade 23, Postfach 269
Subjects: Juveniles, Geography, History, Commerce, Art

Alfred **Winter** Verlag+*, Gstöttengutstr 47, A-5020 Salzburg Tel: (06222) 35314
Gen Man: Alfred Winter; *Reader:* Volker E Horn
Founded: 1974
Subjects: Belles Lettres, Folklore, Local History and Geography, Art Books
ISBN Publisher's Prefix: 3-85380

Kunstverlag **Wolfrum**, A-1010 Vienna 1, Augustinerstr 10 Tel: 525398/524178 Cable Add: Witwolf Vienna
Man Dir: Hubert Wolfrum
Bookshop: A-1010 Vienna, Augustinerstr 10
Subjects: Art, Art Reproductions, Calendars
Founded: 1919
ISBN Publisher's Prefix: 3-900178

Wort und Welt Verlag+, A-6020 Innsbruck, Heiliggeiststr 21 Tel: (05222) 25923 Cable Add: Wortwelt Innsbruck
Publisher: Professor Dr Walter Miess; *Editorial:* Günther Schick; *Publicity:* Ingrid Obermayr
Orders to: Thaurdruck, A-6065 Thaur bei Innsbruck
Br Off: D-8031 Puchheim, Munich, Postfach 1169, Federal Republic of Germany
Subjects: Humour, Textbooks, Art, Belles Lettres, Factbooks
1978: 11 titles *1979:* 9 titles *Founded:* 1972
ISBN Publisher's Prefix: 3-85373

Paul **Zsolnay** Verlag GmbH+, A-1041 Vienna, Prinz-Eugen-Str 30 Tel: (0222) 657661 Cable Add: Zsolnayverlag Wien Telex: 01-31515 (ruleso) Lechner
Dirs: Hans W Polak, August Langer; *Sales Manager:* Wolfgang Dechant
Editors: Margarethe Venjakob, Reinhard Deutsch, Alexandra Auer; *Production:* Peter Baumgartner; *Rights & Permissions:* Olga Kaindl
Parent Company: Heinemann & Zsolnay Ltd, see The Heinemann Group of Publishers, UK
Associate Companies: Mundus, Österreichische Verlagsgesellschaft mbH, A-1041 Vienna 4, Prinz-Eugen-Str 30, Austria; Paul Zsolnay Verlag, Federal Republic of Germany (qv)
Br Off: Büro München, Hildegart Eichholz, Über der Klause 7a, D-8000 Munich 90, Federal Republic of Germany
Subjects: General Fiction, Belles Lettres, Poetry, Biography, History, How-to, Music, Juveniles, Social & Political Science, Art, Medicine, Sports
1979: 36 titles *Founded:* 1923
ISBN Publisher's Prefix: 3-552

Literary Agents

Copro International Verlagsgesellschaft mbH*, A-1134 Vienna, Biraghigasse 30 Tel: 825412 Cable Add: Coproint Vienna

Book Clubs

A B C Buchklub GmbH & Co KG*, A-1010 Vienna 1, Schubertring 3

Ing Johann **Brunner***, A-4400 Steyr, Rooseveltstr 2b

Bücherbund Buch- und Schallplattenhandel Verlagsgesellschaft mbH*, A-1150 Vienna 14, Thaliastr 68

Buchhandlung b Theater a d Wien*, Stein & Co, A-1060 Vienna VI, Linke Wienzelle 6-8

Rudolf **Buchner***, A-8280 Fürstenfeld, Hauptstr 13

Deutsche Buch-Gemeinschaft C A Koch's Verlag Nachfolger*, Zweigniederlassung Wien, A-1010 Vienna I, Wipplingerstr 23

Buchgemeinschaft **Donauland**,
Owned by: Kremayr & Scheriau (qv)

Erster Linzer Lesezirkel Heinrich Auer & Co, A-4020 Linz a d D, Lüttenegerstr 12, Postfach 52 Tel: (0732) 79053

Erster Moderner Lesezirkel Kreith & Schram*, A-1070 Vienna, VII, Mariahilfer Str 54 Tel: 935550

Erster Wiener Lesezirkel Gebrüder Kreith*, A-1070 Vienna, VII, Mariahilfer Str 54 Tel: 935550

Festungsverlag*, A-5020 Salzburg, Mirabellpl 7

Frau und Mutter Verlag*, J Lachner & Co, A-1014 Vienna, Kohlmarkt 11, Postfach 99

Reinfried **Fuchsbichler***, A-8021 Graz, Annenstr 53 and Querg. 1-3, Postfach 1026

Gertraude **Just***, A-3100 St Pölten, Kremsergasse 41

Eduard **Kaiser***, Verlag Buchgemeinde Alpenland OGH, A-9020 Klagenfurt, Brunnengasse 3, Postfach 30

Jos A **Kienreich***, A-8011 Graz, Sackstr 6, Postfach 428

Friedrich **Meixner***, A-8600 Bruck/M, Herzog-Ernst-Str 18, Postfach 123

Morawa & Co*, A-1011 Vienna, I, Wollzeile 11/4

Osterreichischer Buchklub der Jugend*, A-1080 Vienna, Fuhrmannsgasse 18a Tel: (0222) 431605

Elisabeth **Reiter***, A-6600 Reutte, Attlmayrstr 10

A & G **Tengler***, A-6010 Innsbruck, Bürgerstr 28, Postfach 214

Volksbuchverlag GmbH*, A-1232 Vienna, Altmannsdorferstr 154

Anna **Weber***, A-3500 Krems, Schmidgasse 13, Postfach 87 Tel: 02732/2857

Welt im Heim Morawa & Co*, A-1011 Vienna, I, Wollzeile 11/4 Postfach 606
Owned by: Morawa & Co

Herta **Winter***, A-8490 Radkersburg, Langg 21

Major Booksellers

Emil **Albrecht***, A-1014 Vienna, Wallnerstr 8 Tel: (0222) 632272 (wholesaler)

Hans **Fürstelberger***, A-4010 Linz, Landstr 49 Tel: (07222) 73177

Gerold & Co, A-1011 Vienna, Graben 31 Tel: 522235/525739 Telex: 847136157 GEROL A (export and library supplier)
Man Dirs: Dr Heinrich Neider, Hans Neusser

Anna **Hadwiger***, A-1010 Vienna, Johannesgasse 4 Tel: (0222) 524772/3 (wholesaler)

Dr Franz **Hain***, A-1220 Vienna, Dr Otto Neurath-Gasse 5 Tel: (0222) 221624 (wholesaler)

A L **Hasbach***, A-1010 Vienna, Wollzeile 9 Tel: 528876/528932

Leopold **Heidrich***, A-1010 Vienna, Plankengasse 7 Tel: 523701 (wholesaler)

Gebhard **Heinzle's** Erben, A-6700 Bludenz, Josef-Wolf-Platz 2 Tel: (05552) 2066 (export and library supplier)

Herder und Co, A-1011 Vienna, Wollzeile 33 Tel: (0222) 521413

Johannes **Heyn***, A-9020 Klagenfurt, Krassnigstr 42 Tel: (04222) 82024 (export and library supplier)

Buchhandlung Karl **Hofbauer**, A-8430 Leibnitz, Hauptpl 31, Postfach 68 Tel: (03452) 27-93 and 21-77

Eduard **Hollriegl***, A-5020 Salzburg, Sigmund-Haffner-Gasse 10 Tel: (06222) 41146 (export and library supplier)

Jos A **Kienreich***, Sackstrasse 6, A-8011 Graz
(export and library supplier)

Walter **Krieg***, Kärntnerstr 4, A-1010 Vienna Tel: (0222) 521193 (export and library supplier)

Rudolf **Lechner** & Sohn*, A-1010 Vienna, Seilerstätte 5 Tel: (0222) 523604 (wholesaler)

Franz **Leo** & Comp KG*, Universitätsbuchhandlung, A-1010 Vienna, Lichtensteg 1 Tel: (0222) 631451 (export and library supplier)

Manz'sche Verlags und Universitätsbuchhandlung, A-1014 Vienna, Kohlmarkt 16 Tel: (0222) 631785 (export and library supplier)

Wilhelm **Maudrich**, Buchhandlung und Verlag für medizinische Wissenschaften, A-1097 Vienna, Spitalg 21a Tel: (0222) 424712 (export and library supplier)

Robert **Mohr***, A-1010 Vienna, Singerstr 12 Tel: (0222) 525711 (wholesaler)

Marie **Mora** OHG*, A-5010 Salzburg, Residenzplatz 2 Tel: (06222) 43620 (export and library supplier)

Werner **Neugebauer** OHG, A-4010 Linz, Landstr 1, Taubenmarkt Tel: (0732) 71766 (export and library supplier)

Max **Pock**, Universitätsbuchhandlung*, A-8010 Graz, Hauptplatz 1 Tel: (03122) 75254/79042 Telex: 03-1873 (export and library supplier)

Georg **Prachner** KG, A-1010 Vienna, Kärntnerstr 30 Tel: 528549
Manager: O G Prachner

Schottentor*, A-1014 Vienna, Schottengasse 9

Styria*, A-8010 Graz, Albrechtgasse 5 Tel: 0316/79355; A-1010 Vienna, Opernring 15 Tel: 0222/577196

Tyrolia*, A-6010 Innsbruck, Maria Theresienstr 15 Tel: (05222) 24944

Urban und Schwarzenberg*, A-1096 Vienna 9, Frankgasse 4, Postfach 102 Tel: (0222) 422731/2

Wagner'sche Universitätsbuchhandlung, Museumstr 4, A-6021 Innsbruck Tel: (05222) 22316 Telex: 053793 (export and library supplier)
Dir: Ernst Angerer

Rupertusbuchhandlung Augustin **Weis** und Söhne KG, A-5024 Salzburg, Dreifaltigkeitsg 12, Linzer Gasse 29 Tel: (06222) 71661 (export and library supplier)

Fachbuchhandlung für **Wirtschaft und Recht**, A-1181 Vienna, Währinger Str 122 Tel: (0222) 38391 (export and library supplier)
Proprietor: Eleonore Stropek

Kunstverlag **Wolfrum**, A-1010 Vienna, Augustinerstr 10 Tel: (0222) 524178 (export and library supplier of art books)

Zentralgesellschaft für buchgewerbliche und graphische Betriebe*, A-1010 Vienna, Singerstr 12 Tel: (0222) 526136 (wholesaler)
Proprietor: Dr Gottfried Berger

Major Libraries

Archiv der Universität Wien*, Vienna 1

Bibliothek des **Benediktinerklosters***, A-3390 Melk Tel: (02752) 2312/21
Library of the Benedictine Monastery

Administrative Bibliothek und österreichische Rechtsdokumentation im **Bundeskanzeramt***, A-1010 Vienna, Herrengasse 23
Administrative Library and Law Documentation of the Chancellery

Bibliothek des **Kriegsarchivs Wien***, A-1070 Vienna, Stiftgasse 2
Library of the War Archives Dept of the Austrian State Archives
Librarian: Dr Edith Wohlgemuth

Bibliothek der **Österreichischen Akademie der Wissenschaften***, A-1010 Vienna, Dr Ignaz Seipelpl 2
Library of the Austrian Academy of Science

Österreichische Nationalbibliothek, A-1014 Vienna, Josefspl 1 Tel: (0222) 521684/525255
Austrian National Library

Bucherei des **Österreichischen Patentamtes**, A-1014 Vienna, Kohlmarkt 8-10
Library of the Austrian Patents Office
Publications: Österreichisches Patentblatt, Österreichischer Markenanzeiger, Patentschriften

Österreichisches Staatsarchiv, A-1010 Vienna 1, Minoritenpl 1
Austrian State Archives
Publication: Mitteilungen des Österreichischen Staatsarchivs

Universitätsbibliothek Graz, Universitätspl 3, Graz Tel: (0316) 31581/2 Telex: 031662
Publications: Jahresbericht; Fachliche Benützungsanleitungen für die Bibliotheken der Universität Graz, Heft 1 (1973); Bibliographische Informationen, 1 (1974); Schriftenreihe EDV-Projekt, 1 (1978); Grazer Zeitschriften-Verzeichnis, 1 (1974)

Universitätsbibliothek Innsbruck, Innrain 50, A-6010 Innsbruck Tel: (05222) 33601 Telex: 53708

Universitätsbibliothek Wien, A-1010 Vienna, Dr-Karl-Lueger-Ring 1 Tel: (0222) 4300, 2376, 2371

Wiener Stadt- und Landesarchiv, A-1082 Vienna, Magistratsabteilung 8, 1 Rathaus
Vienna Municipal Archives

Wiener Stadt und Landesbibliothek, A-1082 Vienna, Rathaus Tel: (0222) 42800/42809
Vienna Municipal and Country Library
Dir: Dr Franz Patzer

Library Associations

Dokumentationsstelle für neuere österreichische Literatur, A-1060 Vienna VI, Gumpendorferstr 15/1/13 Tel: (0222) 561249
Documentation Point for Newer Austrian Literature
General Secretary: Dr Heinz Lunzer

Österreichische Gesellschaft für Dokumentation und Information, c/o Austrian Centre for Efficiency and Productivity, A-1014 Vienna, Hohenstaufengasse 3
Austrian Society for Documentation and Information
Executive Secretary: B Hofer
Publication: ÖGDI-Mitteilungen

Österreichisches Institut für Bibliotheksforschung, Dokumentations- und Informationswesen*, A-1014 Vienna, Josefsplatz 1
Austrian Institute for Library Research, Documentation and Information

Secretary-General: Prof Dr Josef Mayerhöfer
Publication: Biblos

Verband österreichischer Archivare, c/o A-1010 Vienna, Minoritenpl 1
Association of Austrian Archivists
Publication: Scrinium (twice yearly)

Verband österreichischer Volksbüchereien und Volksbibliothekare, A-1080 Vienna, Lange Gasse 37 Tel: (0222) 439722
Association of Austrian Public Libraries
Man Chairman: Dr R Müller

Vereinigung österreichischer Bibliothekare, A-1014 Vienna, Josefspl 1 (Österreichische National-Bibliothek) Tel: 521684
Association of Austrian Librarians
President: Franz Kroller; *Secretary:* Manfred Lube
Publication: Mitteilungen (quarterly)

Library Reference Books and Journals

Books

Dokumentation und Information in Österreich (Documentation and Information in Austria), Brüder Hollinek, A-1030 Vienna, Landstrasser Hauptstr 163

Handbuch österreichischer Bibliotheken (Handbook of Austrian Libraries), Austrian National Library, A-1014 Vienna, Josefspl 1

Journals

Biblos, Austrian journal for book and library personnel, documentation, bibliography and bibliophily (text in English and German), c/o Austrian National Library, A-1014 Vienna, Josefspl 1

Mitteilungen der Vereinigung österreichischer Bibliothekare (Bulletin of the Association of Austrian Librarians), c/o Austrian National Library, A-1014 Vienna, Josefspl 1

ÖGDI-Mitteilungen (ÖGDI Bulletin) (Österreichische Gesellschaft für Dokumentation und Information), c/o Austrian Productivity Centre, A-1014 Vienna, Renngasse 5

Scrinium, Association of Austrian Archivists, c/o A-1010 Vienna, Dr Karl Luegar Ring 1

Literary Associations and Societies

Österreichische Exlibris-Gesellschaft, A-1040 Vienna, Johann Strauss-Gasse 28-18
Austrian Book-plate-collectors' Society
Chairman: Professor Dr Gustav Dichler
Publications: Jahrbuch, Mitteilungen, books on the art of the bookplate and bookplate-collecting

Österreichische Gesellschaft für Literatur, A-1010 Vienna, Herrengasse 5
Austrian Literary Society
President: Dr W Kraus

Österreichischer Schriftstellerverband*, A-1050 Vienna V, Kettenbrücken 11 Tel: (0222) 564151
Austrian Writers' Association
General Secretary: Wilhelm Meissel

Österreichisches Institut für Bibliographie*, Vienna 1, Rathauspl 4
Dir: Dr Oskar Langer

Österreichischer P E N-Club, Concordia Haus, A-1010 Vienna 1, Bankgasse 8
Secretary: Franz Richter

Wiener Bibliophilen-Gesellschaft*, A-1090 Vienna IX, Leichtensteinstr 61
Vienna Booklovers' Society
Chairman: Sekt Chef Dr Walter Sturminger

Wiener Goethe-Verein, A-1010 Vienna, Reitschulgasse 2
Secretary: Cornelia Kritsch and Gisela Herbeck
Publication: Jahrbuch (yearbook)

Literary Periodicals

Blätter für Volksliteratur (Popular Literature Magazine), Verein der Freunde der Volksliteratur, Graz, Naglergasse 22

Eröffnungen (Communications), magazine for literature and pictorial art (text mainly in German, occasionally in English or Slovene), Hubert Fabian Kulterer, A-1120 Vienna, Unter-Meidlinger Str 16-18

Eselsohr (Dog's Ear), G Pilz, A-4320 Perg, Stifterstr 4a

Literatur und Kritik (Literature and Criticism), Otto Müller Verlag, A-5021 Salzburg, Ernst-Thunstr 11

Literaturspiegel (Mirror to Literature), Vienna 4, Schleifmühlgasse 23-29

Manuskripte (Manuscripts); journal for literature, art, criticism, A-8010 Graz, Forum Stadtpark 1 Tel: (03122) 77734

Modern Austrian Literature (text and summaries in English and German), Arthur Schnitzler International Research Association, c/o Donald G Daviau, Editor, Department of German, University of California, Riverside, California 92502

Moderne Literatur (Modern Literature), Zeitschriftenverlag, Vienna, Favoritenstr 235/26

Das Pult (The Desk); literature, art, criticism, Klaus Sandler, A-3100 St Pölten, Schiessfach 12

Schrifttumsspiegel (Mirror to Literature), Gesellschaft für Ganzhehsforschung, A-1191 Vienna, Franz Klein Gasse 1

Sprachkunst (Art of Language) (text in English, French, German and Russian); contributions to the study of literature, Verlag der österreichischen Akademie der Wissenschaften, A-1010 Vienna, Dr Ignaz Seipelpl 2

Literary Prizes

Austrian literary prizes are generally not associated with a single work, and are not often awarded in a lump sum, because of the high taxes authors have to pay. In addition to those cited below, each province has its own prize

'Encouragement Prize'*
40,000 Schillings, awarded by jury. Submissions accepted. Enquiries to Bundesministerium für Unterricht und Kunst, Strozzigasse 2, Sektion IV/3, A-1080 Vienna

'Encouragement Prizes' for Books for Children and Young People
There are five categories (small children, children reading levels 1-4 and levels 5-8, books for young people, translation) total sum 150,000 Schillings. All awarded by a jury. Submissions accepted. Enquiries to Bundesministerium für Unterricht und Kunst, A-1014 Vienna, Postfach 65, Sektion V/Abteilung 3A

Great Austrian State Prize*
150,000 Schillings, for life's work. Awarded by Österreichischer Kunstsenat. No applications. Enquiries to Bundesministerium für Unterricht und Kunst, Strozzigasse 2, Sektion IV/3, A-1080 Vienna

New Writers Stipendium for Literature*
Four given each year. 6,000 Schillings each month for twelve months, awarded by jury. Submissions accepted. Enquiries to Bundesministerium für Unterricht und Kunst, Strozzigasse 2, Sektion IV/3, A-1080 Vienna

'Recognition Prize'*
75,000 Schillings. Awarded by jury. No applications. Enquiries to Bundesministerium für Unterricht und Kunst, Strozzigasse 2, Sektion IV/3, A-1080 Vienna

State Stipendium for Literature*
Eight given each year. 6,000 Schillings each month for twelve months, awarded by jury. Submissions accepted. Enquiries to Bundesministerium für Unterricht und Kunst, Strozzigasse 2, Sektion IV/3, A-1080 Vienna

Vienna Art Foundation (Wiener Kunstfonds)*
Prizes totalling 20,000 Schillings. Enquiries to Zentralsparkasse der Gemeinde Wien, A-1030 Vienna, Vordere Zollamtstr 13

Vienna Prize for children's and young people's literature*
For a distinguished book for children and young people. Awarded annually. Enquiries to Office for Culture, Education and School Administration, Vienna

Anton **Wildgans** Prize of Austrian Industry
Awarded annually, at the beginning of the autumn, to an Austrian lyric poet, dramatist, novelist or essayist, young or middle aged. The author must be an Austrian citizen, writing in German, who lives either in Austria or abroad. Maximum prize 50,000 Schillings. Awarded by a committee. No applications. 1978 prize went to Dr Wolfgang Kraus. Enquiries to Vereinigung österreichischer Industrieller, A-1031 Vienna

Translation Agencies and Associations

Vienna Übersetzungsbüro und Sprachinstitut, A-1010 Vienna, Universitätsstr 11

Bahamas

General Information

Language: English
Religion: Largest of 12 denominations are Baptist, Roman Catholic and Anglican
Population: 220,000

Bank Hours: 0930-1500 Monday-Thursday; 0930-1700 Friday
Shop Hours: 0900-1700 Monday-Saturday; noon closing on Friday
Currency: 100 cents = 1 Bahamian dollar
Export/Import Information: No tariffs on books and advertising matter. 1% stamp tax. Import licences required. Exchange controls
Copyright: Berne, UCC (see International section)

Publishers

Bright Advertising and Publishing Ltd*, PO Box N4181, Nassau

Etienne **Dupuch** Jr Publications Ltd*, PO Box N7513, Nassau
Subjects: Journals, Maps, Educational Colouring Books

Major Booksellers

Bahamas Anglo American Book Store*, PO Box N9046, 9 Nassau Arcade, Hoffer Bldg, Bay St Tel: 50388

Bahamas Book & Bible House*, PO Box N356 Tel: 23032

Calypso Distributors Ltd*, PO Box ES 6220, Chesapeake Rd Tel: 28986 (wholesaler)

Christian Book Shop, PO Box N4924, Shirley & Hall Lane Tel: (809) 325 8744
Manager: David Duame

The **Island** Shop*, PO Box N3947, Bay St Tel: 24183/21588

Lee's Book Centre*, Bank Lane, PO Box N-8196, Nassau Tel: 22128
Manager: Maria Lee

Mackey's Variety Stores*, Market St Tel: 52011

Tryma Book Shop*, PO Box N1243, Independence Shopping Centre Tel: 57478

United Book Shop & Stationers, PO Box ES6220, Oakes Field Shopping Centre Tel: 50316; Madeira St Shopping Centre Tel: 28597/28986

Major Libraries

Archival Institution, Public Records Office, Ministry of Education and Culture, PO Box N3913, Nassau

College of the Bahamas Library*, PO Box N4912, Nassau Tel: 36456/7

John **Harvard** Lending Library*, PO Box F40, Freeport, Grand Bahama

Nassau Public Library*, PO Box N3210, Nassau

Bahrain

General Information

Language: Arabic (English used commercially)
Religion: Muslim, officially
Population: 267,000
Literacy Rate (1971): 40.2%
Bank Hours: 0730-1200 Saturday-Wednesday; 0730-1100 Thursday
Bazaar Hours: 0800-1200, 1530-1830 Saturday-Thursday (few shops open Friday morning)
Currency: 1000 fils = 1 Bahrain dinar
Export/Import Information: Generally books dutied at 10%, most schoolbooks free of duty; none on advertising matter. No import licence required but no obscene literature permitted and for books (not for advertising) a Chamber of Commerce certificate is mandatory. No exchange controls

Major Booksellers

Al-Aadab Bookshop*, PO Box 384, Manama

Bahrain Bookshop*, PO Box 443, Manama Tel: 54415

Family Bookshop (Bahrain) WLL, PO Box 1, Manama Tel: 254288 Telex: 8444 FAMBAH BN

Islamic Cultural Bookshop*, PO Box 873, Manama

National Bookshop and Branches*, PO Box 594, Manama

Literary Associations and Societies

Bahrain Writers and Literators Association, PO Box 1010, Manama
Secretary: Ibrahim Abdullah Ghuloom

Bangladesh

General Information

Language: Bengali (English widely used commercially)
Religion: Muslim
Population: 82.7 million
Bank Hours: 0930-1330 Monday-Thursday; 0900-1100 Friday and Saturday
Shop Hours: 0900-2100 Monday-Friday; 0900-1400 Saturday
Currency: 100 paise = 1 taka
Export/Import Information: No tariff on books and advertising matter. Import licences; books may be imported by importers with valid Import Registration Certificate or certain actual users such as recognized universities. Books may be imported on sight draft, usance bill or letter of credit
Copyright: UCC

Book Trade Organizations

Bangladesh Pustak Prokashak o Bikreta Samity (Bangladesh Publishers' & Booksellers' Association)*, c/o Rahman Brothers, 5/1 Gopinath Datta, Kabiraj St (Babu Bazar), Dacca Tel: 282633
Secretary: Azhirul Islam Khan

Book Trade Journals

Boi (Text in Bengali), National Book Centre of Bangladesh, 67a Purana Paltan, Dacca 2

Publishers

Adeylebros & Co*, 60 Patuatuly, Dacca 1

Anwari Publications*, 5/1 Simson Rd, Dacca 1

Banga Sahitya Bhavan*, 144 Government New Market, Dacca

Bangladesh Books International Ltd*, PO Box 377, Dacca (Located at: 1, RK Mission Rd/Hatkhola, Dacca 3) Tel: 245265/7 ext 19 Cable Add: Bhabooks Dacca
Man Dir: Manzurul Islam
Subjects: Educational, Academic, Reference, General
1977: 14 titles *Founded:* 1975

Biswakosh*, 316 Government New Market, Dacca

Boighar*, 149 Government New Market, Dacca

Chalantika*, 177 Government New Market, Dacca

Continental Publications*, 18 Dhanmandi Hawkers Market, Dacca 5
Subjects: Science, Technical

Crescent Publishers*, 77 Patuatuly, Dacca 1

Kitabistan*, 3 Liaquat Ave, Dacca

Lekha Prokashani*, 18 Pyarids Rd, Dacca 1

Mullick Bros*, 3/1 Bangla Bazar, Dacca
Subjects: Education, Secondary & Primary Textbooks

Pak Kitab Ghar*, 39 Patuatuly, Dacca

Paramount Book Corporation*, Ashraf Chamber, 66 Bangladesh Ave, Dacca
Administrator: D H Khondker
Subject: Literature

Rahman Brothers*, Educational Publishers, 5/1 Gopinath Datta, Kabiraj St (Babu Bazar), Dacca Tel: 282633

Major Booksellers

Adeyle Brothers*, 60 Patnatully, Dacca

Ali Publications*, 77 Patnatully, Dacca

Dacca Book Mart*, 38 Banglabazar, Dacca

Golden Book House*, 38 Banglabazar, Dacca

Green Book House Limited*, 85 Motighlel, Dacca

Hakkim's Bookshop*, 33 Banglabazar, Dacca

Hamidia Library*, 65 Chawk Circular Rd, Dacca

Islamia Library*, 41/42 Islampur Rd, Dacca

Mohammadi Library*, Chawk Circular Rd, Dacca

Mullick Brothers*, 3/1 Banglabazar Dacca

Oriental Book Service, c/o Bangladesh Books International Ltd, PO Box 377, Dacca

Provincial Book Depot*, Dacca Stadium, Dacca

Provincial Library* , 109-A Sarat Gupta Rd, Narinda, Dacca

Puthigar Limited*, 74 Farashgunj, Dacca

Major Libraries

Bangladesh Institute of Development Studies Library, Adamjee Ct, Motij Heel Commercial Area, Dacca 2 Tel: 257360

British Council Library*, 5 Fuller Rd, Ramna, Dacca 2 POB 161
Librarian: G F Rowbotham

Dacca University Library*, Dacca 2

Central **Public Library**, Dacca*, Shahbagh, Dacca 2

University of Rajshahi Library*, Rajshahi

Library Associations

Bangladesh Granthagar Samity*, c/o Library, Bangladesh University of Engineering and Technology, Dacca 2
Library Association of Bangladesh
Secretary: Abù Bakr Siddique
Publication: Eastern Librarian (three times a year)

Directorate of Archives and Libraries*, 103 Elephant Rd, Dacca 5
Director: Dr K M Karim
Publications: Bangladesh National Bibliography (annually), *Article index* published in the daily newspapers, *Bulletin of the Dissertations on Social Science*

Library Journals

Bangladesh National Bibliography, Directorate of Archives and Libraries, 103 Elephant Rd, Dacca 5

Eastern Librarian (text in English), Library Association of Bangladesh, c/o Library, Bangladesh University of Engineering and Technology, Dacca 2

Literary Associations and Societies

Dacca Centre for International **P E N** Madhura, House 3, Road 13, Dhanmondi RA, Dacca 9
Secretary: Sanaul Huq

Society of Arts, Literature and Welfare*, Society Park, K C Dey Rd, Chittagong
General Secretary: Musharraf Hussain

Literary Prizes

Bengali Academy Literary Awards*
For an overall contribution to Bengali literature in the following categories: novel, short story, children's literature, poetry, essay, drama, literary research. Awarded annually. Enquiries to Bengali Academy, Burdwan House, Dacca

Barbados

General Information

Language: English
Religion: Anglican
Population: 254,000
Literacy Rate (1946): 89.8%
Bank Hours: 0800-1300 Monday-Thursday; 0800-1300, 1500-1750 Friday
Shop Hours: 0800-1600 Monday-Friday; 0800-1200 Saturday
Currency: 100 cents = 1 Barbados dollar
Export/Import Information: No tariff on books; advertising matter, 45%. Import licence covering exchange required; no obscene literature permitted

Publishers

Caribbean Universities Press*, 8 Rock Dundo Heights, Lodge Hill, Eagle Hall 15
Subjects: Academic, Education (English, Spanish & French), Journal of Caribbean History

The **C E D A R** Press, Publishing House of the Caribbean Conference of Churches, PO Box 616, Bridgetown
Editor: Dr David Mitchell; *Acting Publisher:* Mrs Muriel Forde
Subjects: Religion, Sociology, Education, Music, Agriculture, Communication, Politics, Caribbean History, Identity and Culture
1978: 4 titles

P P C Ltd*, Eldino, Gills Rd, St Michael Tel: 75505

Yoruba* Publishing and Typesetting, Mottley Ho, Coleridge St, Bridgetown Tel: 63927

Major Booksellers

Christian Literature Crusade*, St Michael Plaza, St Michael's Row, Bridgetown Tel: 65675

Cloister Book Store Ltd, Hincks St, Bridgetown Tel: 62662

Roberts Stationery Ltd*, 9 High, Bridgetown Tel: 65500

Sandy Beach Book Store*, Worthing Plaza and Shopping Centre, Bridgetown Tel: 89432

Wayfarer Book Store Ltd, Trident Ho, Broad St, Bridgetown Tel: 73760 (4 other branches)

Major Libraries

Public Library*, Coleridge St, Bridgetown

University of the West Indies*, Main Library, Cave Hill Campus, PO Box 64, Bridgetown
Librarian: Michael Gill

Library Associations

Library Association of Barbados*, PO Box 827E, Bridgetown Tel: 02191
Secretary: Joan Brathwaite
Publication: Bulletin (annual)

Library Journals

Bulletin of the Library Association of Barbados, PO Box 27E, Bridgetown

Belgium

General Information

Language: Dutch in the north, French in the south. Brussels is officially bilingual. (English widely used)
Religion: Predominantly Roman Catholic
Population: 9.8 million
Literacy Rate (1947): 96.7%
Bank Hours: Variable locally. Brussels: 0900-1300 Monday-Friday; 1400-1630 Monday and Friday; 1430-1530 Tuesday-Thursday. Antwerp: 0930-1500 Monday-Friday; 1630-1800 Friday
Shop Hours: Variable. Department stores: 0915-1800 Monday-Saturday; open until 2100 Friday
Currency: 100 centimes = 1 Belgian franc
Export/Import Information: No tariff on books except children's picture books, 13% from non-EEC; advertising other than single copies generally 10.6% with sales tax of 14%. VAT on books and advertising 6%. No import licence required, just Model A form of notice of declaration of payment. No exchange controls
Copyright: UCC, Berne, Florence

Book Trade Organizations

Algemene Vlaamse Boekverkopersbond, Frankrijklei 93, B-2000 Antwerp
Flemish Booksellers' Association

Association belge des Editeurs de Langue française (ABELF), 111 ave du Parc, B-1060 Brussels
Belgian Association of Publishers of French Language Books
Dir: J de Raeymaeker

Bond Alleenverkopers van Nederlandstalige Boeken (BANB)*, Dr Desmethlaan 4, B-1980 Tervuren
Association of Wholesalers of Dutch Books in Belgium
Secretary: J van den Berg

Centrale de l'Industrie du Livre*, Galerie du Centre, Bloc 2, B-1000 Brussels
Central Office of the Book Industry

Cercle Belge de la Librairie, BP 1, B-1040 Brussels (Located at: 5 rue du Luxembourg, B-1040 Brussels) Tel: (02) 5112158
Belgian Booksellers' Association
President: P Heroufosse; *Secretary General:* R Lohest; *Administration:* R Mertens
Publications: Journal de la Librairie (10 a year) *Annuaire du CBL* (next edition 1980)

Fédération des Editeurs belges, 111 ave du Parc, B-1060 Brussels Tel: (02) 5382167
Belgian Publishers' Association
Dir: Julien de Raeymaeker

Syndicat belge de la Librairie ancienne et moderne*, 112 rue de Trèves, B-1040 Brussels
Belgian Association of Antiquarian and Modern Booksellers

Union des Industries graphiques et du Livre (UNIGRA)*, 76 rue Renkin, B-1030 Brussels
Book & Graphics Industries Union

Vereniging ter Bevordering van het Vlaamse Boekwezen, Frankrijklei 93, Bus 3, B-2000 Antwerp Tel: (031) 324684
Association for the Promotion of Flemish Books
Publication: Iijdingen

34 BELGIUM

Vereniging van Uitgevers van Nederlandstalige Boeken, Frankriklei 93, Bus 3, B-2000 Antwerp Tel: (031) 324684
Association of Publishers of Dutch Language Books
Secretary: A Wouters

Book Trade Reference Books and Journals

Books

Annuaire des Editeurs belges (Belgian Publishers' Annual), Belgian Publishers' Association, 111 ave du Parc, B-1060 Brussels

Cercle belge de la Librairie Annuaire (Annual), Belgian Booksellers' Association, 111 ave du Parc, B-1060 Brussels

L'Edition en Belgique (Publishing in Belgium), Belgian Publishers' Association, 111 ave du Parc, B-1060 Brussels

Lijstenbook (List of Booksellers), Association of Publishers of Dutch Language Books, Frankriklei 93, Bus 3, B-2000 Antwerp

Liste des Sociétés savantes et littéraires de Belgique (List of Belgian Learned and Literary Societies), Service belge des Echanges Internationaux, 80-84 rue des Tanneurs, B-1000 Brussels

Livres belges (Books from Belgium), Belgian Publishers' Association, 111 ave du Parc, B-1060 Brussels

Journals

Belgica Selecta, Belgian Institute of Information, 3 rue Montoyer, B-1040 Brussels (lists new Belgian books)

Bibliographie de Belgique (Bibliography of Belgium), Bibliothèque royale Albert 1er, 4 blvd de l'Empereur, B-1000 Brussels

Boekengids (Guide to Books), Katholiek Centrum voor Lectuurinformatie en Bibliotheekvoorziening, Raapstr 4, Antwerp

Bulletin, Belgian Commission of Bibliography, 80-84 rue des Tanneurs, B-1000 Brussels

Journal de la Librairie (Book Trade Journal), Belgian Booksellers' Association, 111 ave du Parc, B-1060 Brussels

Livre et l'Estampe (The Book and the Print) (text in French), Royal Society of Bibliophiles and Iconophiles of Belgium, 4 blvd de l'Empereur, B-1000 Brussels

Répertoire annuel des principaux Travaux bibliographiques récents (Annual Catalogue of the Principal Recent Bibliographical Works), Belgian Commission of Bibliography, 80-84 rue des Tanneurs, B-1000 Brussels

Tijdingen (News), Association of Publishers of Dutch Language Books, Frankriklei 93, Bus 3, B-2000 Antwerp

Travailleur du Livre (Worker with Books), Central Office of the Book Industry, Galerie du Centre, Bloc 2, B-1000 Brussels

Publishers

Editions **A B C** Jeunesse SARL, 160 ave Gabriel E Lebon, B-1150 Brussels Tel: (02) 7346601
Publisher: Emile D Probst
Subject: Juveniles

Acco SV+*, Tiensestr 134-136, B-3000 Louvain Tel: (016) 233520 Telex: 62574
Dir: H van Steenbrouck
Orders to: (for all foreign orders except from Netherlands) Oyez, Muntstraat 10, B-3000 Louvain
Subjects: Classic Languages and Culture, Linguistics, Economics, Law, Social Sciences, Education, Pedagogy, Mathematics, General Science, History, Physiotherapy, Psychology, Medicine, Religion, Philosophy, Criminology, Ethics
Founded: 1960

Acta Medica Belgica ASBL+*, 43 rue des Champs Elysées, B-1050 Brussels Tel: (02) 6480468
Subject: Medicine
Founded: 1945

Actualquarto+, 20 allée des Bouleaux, B-6280 Gerpinnes Tel: (071) 216153
Subject: Educational

Agence belge des grandes Editions SA, 146 boulevard Adolphe Max, B-1000 Brussels Tel: (02) 2191872 Cable Add: Belgeditions
Man Dir: Monique de Smet
Subjects: Medicine, Educational Materials, Encyclopaedias, Games, Sports
Founded: 1928

Bibliotheca **Alphonsiana** VZW*, Dekenstr 28, B-3000 Louvain Tel: (016) 23470
Subjects: Religion, Juveniles, Textbooks
Founded: 1927

Altiora NV+, Abdijstr 1, B-3281 Averbode Tel: (013) 771751/4 Telex: 39104
Dirs: F Nauwelaerts, J Volkaerts; *Production:* N Vrancky
Subjects: Education, Juveniles, Religion, Periodicals
1978: 80 titles

Angelet+*, Potterie Rei 69, B-8000 Bruges Tel: (050) 335186
Dir: P Angelet
Subjects: Juveniles, Music
Founded: 1969

Editions Jacques **Antoine** SPRL+, 55-57 rue des Éperonniers, B-1000 Brussels Tel: (02) 5124337
Dir: J Antoine; *Sales, Publicity, Rights & Permissions:* Milly Colmant
Subjects: Literature, Linguistics, Arts
1977: 13 titles *1978:* 8 titles *Founded:* 1968

Antwerpse Lloyd NV, see Editions du Lloyd Anversois

Editions **Arcade-Fonds Mercator**+*, Lange Nieuwstr 76, B-2000 Antwerp Tel: (02) 3435183 Cable Add: Arcadebel Telex: ARCADE B 24381
Man Dir: J Martens; *Sales Dir:* C Hoessels
Associate Company: Fonds Mercator (qv)
Br Off: 299 ave Van Volxem, Brussels
Subject: Art
Founded: 1952
ISBN Publisher's Prefix: 2-8005

Editions **Arscia** SA+*, rue de l'Etuve, B-1000 Brussels Tel: (02) 5114272
Dir: C Pirson
Subject: Belles Lettres
Founded: 1957

SC **Artis-Historia**+, 19 rue Général Gratry, B-1040 Brussels Tel: (02) 7362000
Dir Secretary General: J M Ugeux
Subjects: Geography, History, Ethnography, Nature, Art, Travel
Bookshops: 70 throughout Belgium
1977: 4 titles *Founded:* 1949, companies merged to form Artis-Historia in 1976

Editions **Arts et Voyages***, 88 ave de Tervueren, B-1040 Brussels Tel: (02) 7343560/7343582
Man Dir: Lucien de Meyer; *Rights & Permissions:* Dominique Schoofs
Associate Company: Editions d'Art Lucien de Meyer (qv)
Subjects: Art, Literature, History, Juveniles, Management, Sports
1977: 40 titles *Founded:* 1954
ISBN Publisher's Prefix: 2-8016

Assimil, Uitgaven Nelis PVBA+, Steenstr 5-7, B-1000 Brussels Tel: (02) 5114502
Man Dir: R Nelis; *Commercial Dir:* A Van Damme
Subjects: Bibliography, Languages
ISBN Publisher's Prefix: 90-70077

Editions de **Association des Consommateurs** ASBL, see Uitgaven van de Verbruikersunie VZW

Association des Sociétés scientifiques médicales belges (ASBL)+, 43 rue des Champs Elysées, B-1050 Brussels Tel: (02) 6480468
Subjects: Medicine, Journals
Founded: 1945

ASTRID, see H-K de Jaeger Publications

Atlantis NV*, Kruishoftstr 205, B-2610 Wilrijk Tel: (031) 280986 Telex: 33164
Dir: A Jonckx
Subjects: Education, Pedagogy, Sports, Games, Juveniles, Journals
Founded: 1970
Miscellaneous: Firm is subsidiary of Beckers Groep (qv)
ISBN Publisher's Prefix: 90-6181

Audivox+*, Rubenslei 23, B-2000 Antwerp Tel: (031) 328465
Dir: W Gonnissen
Founded: 1953
Subjects: School Text Books
Miscellaneous: also Booksellers and Importers of Educational Books (Wholesale)

Aurelia Books+*, Bonekruidlaan 30, B-1020 Brussels Tel: (02) 2678126 Telex: 63 009 aurgam B
Dir: J Bauwens; *Editorial:* Jo Stevens; *Sales:* M Drieskens; *Production:* Jan Van Lier; *Publicity:* Jan Bauwens
Subjects: Training of Nurses, School Books, Flemish Folklore, Popular Devotion
Book Club: ABC (Aurelia Book Club)
1977: 29 titles *Founded:* 1972

De **Backer** Publishers PVBA+, Penitentenstr 14, B-9000 Ghent Tel: (091) 231013
Dir: Chr de Backer
Subjects: Bibliography, Languages, History of Pharmacy, History, Travel, Medicine, Literature, Music
Founded: 1972

Maison d'Editions **Baha'ies** ASBL+*, rue du Trône 205, 1050 Brussels Tel: (02) 6470749
Subject: Bahai
1977: 9 titles *Founded:* 1970

Banana Press NV+*, Rozenlaan 10, B-2080 Kapellen (Bos) Tel: (031) 667171
Dir: W Beckers
Parent Company: Beckers Groep, Kalmthout (qv)
Subjects: Bibliography, Languages, Education, Pedagogy, Sport, Games, Literature
Founded: 1972
Miscellaneous: Firm is subsidiary of Beckers Groep (qv)
ISBN Publisher's Prefix: 90-6180

Barbiaux (Drukkerij G — Uitgeverij de Garve) PVBA+*, Groene Poortdreef 27, B-8200 St-Michiels, Bruges Tel: (050) 318283
Dir: W Barbiaux
Subjects: Law, Political, Administrative & Social Sciences, Mathematics, General Science, Music
Founded: 1909

Editions **Beatrice-Nauwelaerts***, see NV Uitgeverij Nauwelaerts Edition SA

Beckers Groep*, Brasschaatsteenweg 200, B-2180 Kalmthout Tel: 667171 Cable Add: Walbeck
Man Dir: R Peeters; *Literary Agent:* A van Hageland
Subjects: General Fiction, Belles Lettres, Poetry, Biography, History, Juveniles, High-priced Paperbacks
Book Clubs: Vente Directe; Atlanta NV
Subsidiaries: Banana Press; De Beurs NV; Gutenberg; PP Rubens

Beckers SA Editions, Brasschaatsteenweg 200, B-2180 Kalmthout Tel: (031) 667171
Owned by: Beckers Groep

Belgisch Instituut voor Voorlichting en Documentatie (INBEL), see Institut belge d'Information et de Documentation

Uitgeverij van **Belle** PVBA+*, Steenweg op Ninove 116, B-1080 Brussels Tel: (02) 5213417/5210221
Dir: R van Belle
Subjects: Geography, History, Ethnography, Travel, Juveniles
Founded: 1938

De **Beurs** NV, see Beckers Groep

Editions **Beyaert***, 3 pl Hans-Memlinc, B-8000 Bruges Tel: (050) 33745
Man Dir: Jean-Marie Beyaert
Subjects: Education, Religion, Philosophy, Textbooks
Founded: 1842

Editions Gérard **Blanchart** & Cie SA+, 15 ave Ernest Masoin, B-1090 Brussels Tel: (02) 4783706
Man Dir: Charles Blanchart
Subjects: Art, Religion, Educational Materials
Founded: 1930

Maison d'Edition A de **Boeck** SA+, ave Louise 203 Bte 1, B-1050 Brussels Tel: 6407272
General Dir: Chr de Boeck; *Administrative Dir:* J van Nes
Subjects: Textbooks for primary and secondary schools, Higher education (educational psychology, methodology, social sciences, humanities), Technical and Professional textbooks (general and applied mechanics, machine tools)
1978: 70 titles *Founded:* 1883

Bordas-Dunod Bruxelles SA+, 44 rue Otlet, B-1070 Brussels Tel: (02) 5238133
Subjects: Textbooks, Education, Pedagogy, Sports, Mathematics, General Science, Geography, History, Juveniles, Paperbacks
Founded: 1969

Bourdeaux-Capelle SA+*, 69 rue Sax, B-5500 Dinant Tel: (082) 222283/222277
Dir: E Bourdeaux
Subjects: Bibliography, Languages, Journals
Founded: 1913

De **Branding** NV+*, Korte Winkelstr 13-15, B-2000 Antwerp Tel: (031) 332739
Dir: L Ruys
Subjects: Nautical
Bookshop: Belgisch Maritiem Centrum
Founded: 1956

Brepols IGP+, Baron F du Fourstr, B-2300 Turnhout Tel: (014) 415466/7 Telex: 34182
Chairman: Baron de Cartier de Marchienne; *Man Dir:* M Rolin
Br Off: Éditions Brepols, 9 rue Huysmans, 75006 Paris, France
Subjects: Religion (Patristics, Bibles, Prayerbooks), History

Vanden **Broele** PVBA+, Magdalenastr 41-47, B-8200 Bruges Tel: (050) 315074
Dir: E de Jonghe
Subjects: Law, Political, Administrative & Social Sciences, Popular Medicine
1977: 10 titles *1978:* 11 titles
ISBN Publisher's Prefix: 90-6267

A W **Bruna** & Zoon NV+, Antwerpsesteenweg 29a, B-2630 Aartselaar Tel: (031) 874018/9
Dir: J Raedschelders
Subjects: Juveniles, Literature, Paperbacks
Founded: 1966

Etablissements Emile **Bruylant** SA+, 67 rue de la Régence, B-1000 Brussels Tel: (02) 5129845
Man Dirs: Angèle Van Sprengel, Jean Vandeveld
Subjects: Law, High-priced Paperbacks, General & Social Science, University Textbooks
1977: 25 titles *1978:* 35 titles *Founded:* 1838
Bookshop: Etablissements Emile Bruylant, 67 rue de la Régence, B-1000 Brussels

J E **Buschmann** PVBA+*, Italiëlei 26, B-2000 Antwerp Tel: (031) 323130/325235
Dir: J Buschmann
Subjects: Arts, Geography, History, Ethnography, Travel, Journals
Miscellaneous: firm is both publisher and printer

Business Information Establishment SA+*, 2 rue de la Résistance, B-4400 Herstal Tel: (041) 642174 Telex: 041118
Dir: P Lardinois
Subjects: Textbooks, Law, Political, Administrative & Social Sciences, Mathematics, General Science, Journals
Founded: 1968
ISBN Publisher's Prefix: 2-87000

C E D-Samsom NV+*, 7 rue Philippe de Champagne, B-1000 Brussels Tel: (02) 5138570
Dir: O Chrispeels
Parent Company: NV ICU België, Belgium (qv)
Bookshops: CED-Samsom, 7 rue Philippe de Champagne, Brussels
Subjects: General & Social Science, Documentation, Textbooks, Literature, Law, Psychology
Founded: 1964

Editions **C E F A** (Centre d'Éducation à la Famille et à l'Amour)+, 58 rue de la Prévoyance, B-1000 Brussels Tel: (02) 5131749
Man Dir: Pierre de Locht; *Sales:* Mrs André
Orders to: above address or Librairie Novissima, 33 rue de la Concorde, B-1050 Brussels
Subjects: The Family, Sexual Education, Religion
Bookshops: Librairie Novissima, 33 rue de la Concorde, B-1050 Brussels
1977: 8 titles *1978:* 7 titles *Founded:* 1961

Editions **Calozet** SPRL+, 40 rue des Chartreux, B-1000 Brussels Tel: (02) 5116026
Dir: J de Groef
Subjects: Mathematics, Cuisenaire Materials (educational)
Founded: 1874

Carmelitana VZW ('De Karmelieten')+*, Burgstr 46, B-9000 Ghent Tel: (091) 255787
Dir: A Dupon
Subject: Religious books
ISBN Publisher's Prefix: 90-70092

Carto PVBA+, Gaucheretstr 139, B-1000 Brussels Tel: (02) 2161545 Cable Add: Cartopress
Man Dir: Wijnand Plaizier
Subjects: Geography, History, Secondary & Primary Textbooks, Educational Materials (Transparencies), Maps, Travel
Founded: 1950
Subsidiaries: Carpress, International Press Agency; European Cartographic Institute; Cremers Cartographic Institute (school maps)

Casterman+, rue des Soeurs noires 28, B-7500 Tournai Tel: (069) 224141 Cable Add: Casteredim Tournai Telex: 57328
Man Dir: Louis-Robert Casterman; *Sales Dir:* Jean-Jacques Dursin; *Rights & Permissions:* Pierre Servais, Ivan Noerdinger
Br Offs: 44 ave de Roodebeek, B-1040 Brussels; 66 rue Bonaparte, F-75006 Paris, France; De Morinel 25-29, NL-8251 HT Dronten, Netherlands
Subjects: General Fiction, Belles Lettres, Poetry, Biography, History, Music, Art, Philosophy, Reference, Religion, Juveniles, High-priced Paperbacks, Psychology, General & Social Science, University & Secondary Textbooks, Languages, Law, Geography, Sports, Travel, Medicine
1977: 210 titles *1978:* 220 titles *Founded:* 1780
ISBN Publisher's Prefix: 2-203 (French), 90-303 (Dutch)

Centre d'Education à la Famille et à l'Amour. see CEFA

Centre d'Etude et d'Edition Conjugale et Familiale ASBL+*, 27 rue du Congrès, B-1000 Brussels Tel: (02) 2182482
Dir: J Hinnekens
Associate Companies: Les 'Feuilles Familiales' ASBL, Belgium (qv); NFF (Nouvelles Feuilles Familiales), Belgium (qv)
Subject: Marriage and the Family
Founded: 1947

Centre international d'Etudes de la Formation religieuse Lumen Vitae ASBL, see Lumen Vitae (International Centre for Religious Education) ASBL

Centre national d'Etudes et de Recherches socio-économiques (CERSE) ASBL+*, 9 rue Vilain XIIII 9, B-1050 Brussels Tel: (02) 6495817
President: R Gubbels
Subjects: Law, Political, Administrative & Social Sciences
Founded: 1963

Centre national de Recherches 'Primitifs Flamands' ASBL+, 1 parc du Cinquantenaire, B-1040 Brussels Tel: (02) 7354160
Dir: R Sneyers; *Science Editor:* M Comblen; *Sales:* M Gierts; *Rights & Permissions:* R Sneyers
Subjects: Arts
Founded: 1950
ISBN Publisher's Prefix: 2-87033-000-6

Ceres+, Nukerkeplein 9, B-9681 Maarkedal Tel: (055) 211404
Dir: P de Riemaecker
Subjects: Geography, History, Ethnography, Travel
1978: 5 titles *Founded:* 1947

Chanlis+, 17 B rue de Lennery, B-6430
Walcourt Tel: (071) 326394/611770
Man Dir: Pierre Magain; *Sales:* M Nowak
Subsidiary Company: Chanlis, Route de
Mons 25A, B-6000 Charleroi
Subjects: Numismatics, Archaeology, Arts
Bookshop: Route de Mons 25A, B-6000
Charleroi
1978: 8 titles *Founded:* 1968
ISBN Publisher's Prefix: 2-87039

Editions **Chantecler**+, Cleydaellaan 8,
B-2630 Aartselaar, Antwerp Tel: (031)
878300 Telex: 31739 ZUIDB
Man Dir: Joris Schaltin; *Editorial:*
Emmanuel de Vocht; *Sales:* Jan Goetz;
Production: Eric Feyten; *Rights &
Permissions:* Wilfried Wuyts
Parent Company: Zuidnederlandse
Uitgeverij (qv)
Subjects: Children's Teaching Books,
Reading Books
1977: 265 titles *Founded:* 1947

La **Charte** NV+*, Oude Gentweg 108,
B-8000 Bruges Tel: (050) 331235
Dir: H Bogaerts
Subjects: Bibliography, Languages,
Textbooks, Law, Political, Administrative &
Social Sciences, Literature
Founded: 1948

De **Clauwaert**+*, Koning Albertlaan 17,
B-3040 Korbeek-Lo, Louvain Tel: (016)
462229
Man Dir: W Vanden Eynde; *Sales Dir:* J
Raymaekers
Subjects: General Fiction, Belles Lettres,
Secondary Textbooks
Founded: 1948
Miscellaneous: Firm is also a book club

Cogedi SA+, galerie des Princes 2-4,
B-1000 Brussels Tel: (02) 5132038
Dir: Pierre Mardaga
Subjects: Education, Pedagogy, Psychology,
Architecture
Founded: 1938

Colibrant-Uitgaven+*, Rode Beukendreef
17, B-9831 Deurle-Leie Tel: (091) 824697
Dir: J L de Belder
Subjects: Arts, Literature
Founded: 1950

Compagnie belge d'Editions, see Albert de
Visscher Editeur

Editions **Complexe** (Diffusion–
Promotion-Formation)+, 8b rue de
Châtelain, BP 10, B-1050 Brussels Tel: (02)
6496121/6496122 Telex: ASAEL B 33822
Man Dir, Sales, Publicity: Danielle Vincken;
Man Dir, Editorial, Rights & Permissions:
André Versaille; *Production:* Pierre Borgers
Parent Company: Alfred Eibel, Editeur,
France (qv)
Associate Company: Nouvelle Diffusion (at
above address)
Subjects: Psychological, Socio-Political,
Dialectics, Scientific, Ethnological series of
books
Bookshop: Le Nouveau Monde (at above
address)
1978: 20 titles *1979:* 27 titles *Founded:*
1973-74
Miscellaneous: Formerly Nouvelle Diffusion
Complexe (founded 1971)
ISBN Publisher's Prefix: 2-87027

Contact NV+*, Elsbos 33, B-2520 Edegem
Tel: (031) 572024/573486
Dir: A J H Binneweg
Subjects: Arts, Textbooks, Education,
Pedagogy, Sports, Games, Literature,
Paperbacks
1977: 17 titles *Founded:* 1946
ISBN Publisher's Prefix: 90-254

Creadif+, 14 blvd de l'Empereur bte 3,
B-1000 Brussels Tel: (02) 5114943
Dir: M Servais
Subjects: Geography, History, Ethnography,
Travel, Economy, Commerce
Founded: 1974

Crédit Communal de Belgique—Centre
Culturel+, 44 blvd Pacheco, B-1000
Brussels Tel: (02) 2193200 Cable Add:
Crédit Communal Brussels Cregem B 26354
Secretary General: C Swinnen
Subjects: History, Politics, Law, Sociology
Founded: 1977

Cremers (Schoollandkaarten) PVBA+,
Gaucheretstr 139, B-1000 Brussels Tel: (02)
2161545 Cable Add: Cartopress
Dir: Wijnand Plaizier
Parent Company: Carto PVBA (qv)
Subjects: Textbooks, Geography, History,
Ethnography, Travel, Journals
Founded: 1950

Crisp+*, 35 rue du Congrès, B-1000
Brussels Tel: (02) 2183226
Man Dir: J Gerard-Libois; *Editorial:* Xavier
Mabille; *Publicity:* M Julin
Subjects: Political Science, Industry,
Finance
Founded: 1958

Van **Cromphout** Frères & Soeurs
Imprimerie+*, 3 rue des Moulins, B-7860
Lessines Tel: (068) 332047/332182 Cable
Add: Cromphout Lessines Telex: 32047
Man Dir: Robert Cromphout
Subjects: Education, Textbooks, Sports,
Games, Pedagogy, Journals
Founded: 1853

Fondation **Cultura**-Stichting Cultura+,
avenue de Broqueville 17, bte 11, B-1200
Brussels Tel: (02) 5136103 ext 431
Man Dir: Fernand Duffaut
Parent Company: Fonds Mercator SA (qv)
Subject: Art
Founded: 1958

Editions **Culture et Civilisation**+, 115 ave
Gabriel Lebon, B-1160 Brussels Tel: (02)
7345005 Cable Add: JADAM
Man Dir: Jos Adam
Subjects: Biography, History, Geography,
Ethnography, Travel, Music, Art,
Philosophy, Reference, Religion, Medicine,
Psychology, University Textbooks,
Bibliography, Languages, Law, Social &
General Sciences, Literature
Founded: 1960
Subsidiary: Imprimerie Jos Adam, 115 ave
Gabriel Lebon, B-1160 Brussels

De **Dageraad** PVBA+*, Perenstr 13-15,
B-2000 Antwerp Tel: (031) 356866
Dir: R van Hevel
Founded: 1971

Uitgeverij **Dap-Reinart** SV*+, Industriepark
B4, B-9140 Zele Tel: (052) 445171
Dir: A van Acker
Parent Company: Standaard Uitgeverij en
Distributie BV, Netherlands (qv)
Subjects: Juveniles, Literature, Education,
Law, Religion
Founded: 1946
Miscellaneous: Firm is also a book club

Editions **Daphne**+, Mageleinstr 50, B-9000
Ghent Tel: (091) 253645
Man Dir: Albert Dubrulle
Subjects: Belles Lettres, Poetry, Music, Art,
Education, Juveniles
Founded: 1945
ISBN Publisher's Prefix: 90-70090

Daphne Diffusion SPRL+*, Poortakkerstr
19, B-9820 Gent Tel: (091) 214591
Telex: 11659
Dir: F Dubrulle

Davidsfonds VZW+, Blijde Inkomststr 79,
B-3000 Louvain Tel: (016) 221801
Dir: F Valvekens
Subjects: Arts, Law, Political,
Administrative & Social Sciences,
Education, Pedagogy, Sports, Games,
Juveniles, Religion, Philosophy, Literature,
Journals
Founded: 1875
ISBN Publisher's Prefix: 90-6152

Maison d'Editions Cl **Dejaie**+, 436 chaussée
de Dinant, B-5150 Wepion Namur
Tel: (081) 221516
Dir: M Cl M Dejaie
Subjects: Bibliography, Languages, Law,
Political, Administrative & Social Sciences,
Religion, Philosophy, Literature
1977: 8 titles *1978:* 8 titles *Founded:* 1972
ISBN Publisher's Prefix: 2-1491

Editions **Delta**, 92-94 sq Plasky, B-1040
Brussels Tel: (02) 5379412
Man Dir: Georges-Francis Seingry
Subjects: Reference books regarding EEC
and other European Organizations
1978: 6 titles *1979:* 12 titles *Founded:* 1976
ISBN Publisher's Prefix: 2-8029

Denis & Co PVBA+*, Sterckshoffel 28-30,
B-2100 Deurne Tel: (031) 213299/220804
Subjects: Art, Law, Education, History,
Juveniles, Philosophy

Desclée, Editeurs+*, 13 rue Barthélemy
Frison, B-7500 Tournai Tel: (069) 226101
Cable Add: Desclée-Tournai Telex: Gedit
57251
Dir: J Desclée
Parent Company: Gedit SA (qv)
Associate Companies: Editions Desclée et
Cie, France (qv); Editions Gamma (qv);
Nouvelles Editions Mame, France (qv)
Subjects: Religion, Philosophy, Missals,
Theology, Literature
Bookshop: At above address
Founded: 1872

Desclée de Brouwer SA+*, 217b rue de la
Loi, B-1040 Brussels Tel: (02)
352734/341169
Man Dir: Geoffroy de Halleux
Associate Companies: Desclée de Brouwer
& Cie SA, France (qv); Desclée de Brouwer,
Netherlands; Emmaus (qv)
Subsidiary Company: Orion (qv)
Br Offs: Bilbao, Montreal, Utrecht
Subjects: Religion, Juveniles, Philosophy,
Arts, Textbooks, Education, Sports, Games,
Languages, Paperbacks
Founded: 1873

Desmet-Huysmans PVBA+*, Dam 67,
B-8500 Kortrijk Tel: (056) 217242
Man Dir: G Desmet

Editions **Desoer** SA+, 17 rue Ste
Véronique, B-4000 Liège Tel: (041) 521175
Dir: J Quidonne
Subjects: Science, Medicine, Educational
Materials, Arts, Textbooks, Mathematics
1977: 1 title *Founded:* 1750

F **Dessain** SPRL+*, 7 rue Trappé, B-4000
Liège Tel: (041) 237882/3
Man Dir: Maximilien Dessain
Subjects: Religion, Mathematics, Textbooks,
Education, Pedagogy, Sports, Games,
General Science, Geography, History,
Ethnography, Travel
Founded: 1719

H **Dessain** NV*, Regenboog 5-9, B–2800 Mechelen Tel: (015) 416986
Man Dir: Patrick Dessain
Subjects: Juveniles, Medicine, Music, Religion, Reference, Geography, History, Ethnography, Travel
Founded: 1904

A **Dewallens***, 212 chaussée de Bruxelles, B–3020 Herent Tel: (016) 225857
Dir: A Dewallens
Subjects: Bibliography, Philology, Languages, Education, Pedagogy, Sports, Games, Journals
Founded: 1946

Editions Marcel **Didier** SA+, 1 pl de la Maison Rouge, B–1020 Brussels Tel: (02) 4256602/4256753
Man Dir: Paul Didier
Associate Companies: Librairie Marcel Didier, France (qv); Didier Canada, Montreal
Subsidiary Company: Didier Nederland BV, Postbus 5530, Amsterdam, Netherlands
Subjects: Reference, University, Secondary & Primary Textbooks, Educational Materials
Bookshop: Librairie Marcel Didier, 1 pl de la Maison rouge, B–1020 Brussels Tel: (02) 4256753
1977: 12 titles *1978:* 17 titles *Founded:* 1932

Diligentia-Uitgeverij+*, S B–9040 Oostakker Tel: (091) 511281
Dir: S de Weerdt
Subject: Textbooks
Founded: 1908
ISBN Publisher's Prefix: 90-70021

Distri BD SPRL+*, 47 rue de Namur, B–1000, Brussels Tel: (02) 5129675
Dirs: Mrs Micheline Vandesande, Miss Jacqueline Martin, André Leborgne
Orders to: 435 ave Van Volxem, B–1060 Belgium
Subject: Art
1977: 6 titles *Founded:* 1973

La **Documentation** Cistercienne+, Abbaye ND de St-Remy, B–5430 Rochefort Tel: (084) 213181 Cable Add: Trappistes-Rochefort
Dir: P Eug Manning
Subjects: Bibliography, Geography, Literature, History (especially Medieval), Heraldry
1977: 12 titles *1978:* 13 titles *Founded:* 1969

Editions Irène **Dossche** SPRL*, 1256 chaussée de Mons, B–1070 Brussels Tel: (02) 5239564
Dir: Mme I Dossche
Subject: Arts
Founded: 1969

Dossiers politiques*, 48 ave F D Roosevelt, B–1050 Brussels Tel: (02) 6475435/6499780
Dir: M P Vandenbossche
Founded: 1974

Editions J **Duculot** SA+*, rue de la Posterie, Parc industriel, B–5800 Gembloux Tel: 081/610061 Telex: 59309 Duculo B
Man Dir: Pierre De Bie; *Sales, Advertising & Publicity:* Georges David (Commercial Director); *Rights & Permissions:* Emmanuel Brutsaert and Christiane Lapp
Orders to: Presses de Belgique, rue du Sceptre 25, B–1040 Brussels
Subsidiary Company: Editions J Duculot, 16 rue Séguier, F–75006, Paris, France
Subjects: Belles Lettres, Art, Religion, Juveniles, Linguistics, General Science, University, Secondary & Primary Textbooks
1977: 57 titles *Founded:* 1918
ISBN Publisher's Prefix: 2-8011

Editions Jean **Dupuis** SA+*, 39 rue Destrée, B–6001 Marcinelle-Charleroi Tel: (071) 364080 Telex: 51370
Dirs: Charles and Marcel Dupuis
Br Off: Livornostr 97, B–1050 Brussels
Subjects: Art, How-to, Cinema, Paperbacks, Juveniles, Comics
Bookshop: Editions Jean Dupuis, 39 rue Destree, B–6001 Marcinelle-Charleroi
1977: 88 titles *Founded:* 1898
ISBN Publisher's Prefix: 2–8001

E P O+, Lange Pastoorstraat 25, B–2600 Berchem Tel: (031) 396874
Man Dir: Paul-Marie Doumen; *Editorial:* Hugo Durieux; *Sales:* Patrick van Buyten
Subjects: Literature, Politics
1978: 10 titles *1979:* 8 titles *Founded:* 1974
ISBN Publisher's Prefix: 90-6445

Edi-Art+*, 18 ave de Berchem Ste Agathe, B–1080 Brussels Tel: (02) 4269270
Man Dir: J Freydiger
Founded: 1975

Editeurs de Litterature Biblique+, Ch de Tubize 479, B–1420 Braine-L'Alleud Tel: (02) 3545402
Man Dir: M Cl Kroeker
Subjects: Education, Juveniles, Philosophy, Religion, Music, Pocketbooks
1978: 5 titles *Founded:* 1959

Editions interuniversitaires+, 14 boulevard de l'Empereur, Bte 3, B–1000 Brussels Tel: (02) 5114943
Dir: M Servais
Subjects: Geography, History, Ethnography, Travel
Founded: 1974

Editions techniques et scientifiques SPRL+*, 35-43 rue Borrens, B–1050 Brussels Tel: (02) 6401040
Man Dir: G Louis
Subjects: General Technology, Law, Mathematics, Science, Geography, History, Ethnography, Travel, General
Founded: 1919

Editions universitaires SA+*, 25 rue du Sceptre, B–1040 Brussels Tel: (02) 6488026 *Dir:* L Honhon
Subjects: Textbooks, Law Political, Administrative & Social Sciences, Education, Pedagogy, Sports, Games, Mathematics, General Science, Geography, History, Ethnography, Travel, Religion, Philosophy, Literature, Languages, Journals
Founded: 1944

Elsevier Séquoia+*, Leuvensesteenweg 325, B–1940 Woluwe Tel: (02) 7209090
Man Dir: Jean-Jacques Schellens; *Sales, Publicity & Advertising:* J Lamiroy; *Editorial:* Claude van Godtsenhoven; Roger Gheysens
Parent Company: NV Uitgeversmaatschappij Elsevier, Netherlands (qv)
Associate Company: Elsevier Sequoia, France (qv)
Subjects: Biography, History, Reference, Juveniles, Art, Practical Guides, Nature, Documentaries, Children's Books, Travel
1977: 60 titles *Founded:* 1960
Bookshop: Librairie universelle, 142 ave Louise, B–1050 Brussels
ISBN Publisher's Prefix: 2–8003

Emmaus-Desclée de Brouwer NV+*, Lieven Bauwensstr 19, B–8200 Bruges Tel: (050) 318157 Telex: 81068
Dir: A Goyvaerts
Associate Company: Desclée de Brouwer SA (qv)
Subjects: Textbooks, Religion, Philosophy, Journals, Paperbacks
Founded: 1960
ISBN Publisher's Prefix: 90264

Encyclopaedia Universalis+*, 8 pl Meiser, B–1030 Brussels Tel: (02) 7362787

Editions **Erasme** (NV Scriptoria)+, Belgiëlei 147a, B–2000 Antwerp Tel: (031) 395900 Telex: B Edista 31421
Man Dir: A Sap
Associate Company: Standaard Uitgeverij, Belgium (qv)
Subjects: Medicine, Science, Reference, Encyclopaedias, Arts, Textbooks, Juveniles
Founded: 1946
ISBN Publisher's Prefix: 90–020

Erel+, St-Sebastiaanstr 16, B–8400 Ostend Tel: (059) 701308
Dir: R Lanoye; *Publicity:* Monique Lanoye
Subjects: Arts, Bibliography, Languages, Education, Pedagogy, Sports, Games, Geography, History, Ethnography, Travel, Literature, Journals
Bookshop: At above address
1977: 6 titles *1978:* 8 titles *Founded:* 1946

Editions **Est-Ouest**+*, 66 rue St Bernard, B–1060 Brussels Tel: (02) 5386177
Dir: C André
Subjects: Art, Travel, Belles Lettres, Bibliography, Languages
Founded: 1939

Etablissements Généraux d'Imprimerie SA, 14 blvd de l'Empereur, B–1000 Brussels Tel: (02) 5118026
Man Dir: F Jacobs
Subject: Reference
Founded: 1831

Europa+*, Botermarkt 10, B–3290 Diest Tel: (013) 331187
Dir: R Peeters
Subjects: Arts, Geography, History, Numismatics, Folklore
ISBN Publisher's Prefix: 90–6188

European Press Scientific Publisher+, Kortrijksesteenweg 154, B–9000 Ghent Tel: (091) 213000/10/08 Telex: Eupress 11008
Man Dir: R Desmet; *Editorial, International Books Department:* M Guy
Branch Off: Citadellaan 36, B–9000 Ghent; Borluutstraat, B–9000 Ghent; Postbus Amsterdam, NL-3802 Amsterdam, Netherlands
Subjects: Science (especially Medicine and Pharmacology), Medical Periodicals, Scientific Translations
1978: 6 titles

Europress NV*, Lousbergskaai 86A, B–9000 Ghent Tel: (091) 255701 Cable Add: Europress Gent Telex: 11228 volkge b
Man Dir, Publicity, Rights & Permissions: S Vervloet; *Editorial, Sales, Production:* J Van Haverbeke
Orders to: J Van Haverbeke, Forelstraat 22, B–9000 Ghent
Subjects: Children's Books, Strip Cartoon Books
1977: 12 titles

Familia et Patria PVBA*, Kortemarkstr 26, B–8120 Handzame Tel: (051) 567336
Dir: M Mispelon
Subjects: Bibliography, Languages, Law, Political, Administrative & Social Sciences, Geography, History, Ethnography, Travel, Literature
Founded: 1966

Les '**Feuilles** familiales' ASBL+*, 27 rue du Congrès, B–1000 Brussels Tel: (02) 2183482
Associate Companies: NFF (Nouvelles Feuilles Famiales) (qv); Centre d'Etude et d'Edition Conjugale et Familiale (qv)
Subjects: Marriage & Family Relations, Psychology, Educational, Religion
Founded: 1937

Fonds Mercator SA+, Lange Nieuwstr 76, B–2000 Antwerp Tel: (031) 319859
Publisher: Dr Jan Martens; *Dirs:* Christian Hoessels, Jos Jansen
Associate Company: Editions Arcade-Fonds Mercator (qv)
Subsidiary Company: Fondation Cultura (qv)
Subjects: Arts, Geography, History, Ethnography, Travel, Literature, Music
1977: 5 titles *1978:* 7 titles *Founded:* 1965

Het **Fonteintje***, Grote Markt 1, B–3500 Hasselt Tel: (011) 224505
Man Dir: J Melis
Subject: Juveniles
Founded: 1949

Fonteyn Medical Books NV+, Fochplein 13, B–3000 Louvain Tel: (016) 222267 Telex: 26334
Man Dir: B Osaer
Subject: Medicine
Founded: 1836

Editions **Foyer** Notre-Dame, now incorporated in Editions Lumen Vitae

Editions de la **Francité** (Imprimeries Havaux)*, 37c rue A Levêque, B–1400 Nivelles Tel: (067) 226131
Dir: LL Havaux
Br Off: 20 rue du Pouvre, 75001 Paris, France
Subjects: Arts, Bibliography, Languages, Textbooks, Education, Pedagogy, Sports, Games, Geography, History, Ethnography, Travel, Medicine, Literature, Religion, Philosophy, Journals, Paperbacks

G I A SA+, 321 ave des Volontaires, B–1150 Brussels Tel: (02) 7620662
Art Director: J Carion; *Export:* M J Hellin
Subjects: Art, Medicine
Miscellaneous: Exporter of Belgian books

Editions **Gamma**+*, 11 rue Barthélemy Frison, B–7500 Tournai Tel: (069) 226105
Cable Add: Editions Gamma-Tournai
Telex: Gedit 57251
Dir: J Desclée
Parent Company: Gedit SA (qv)
Associate Companies: Desclée, Editeurs (qv); Desclée et Cie, France (qv); Editions Gamma, France (qv); Nouvelles Editions Mame, France (qv)
Subjects: Education, How-to, Science & Technology, Textbooks, Sports, Games, Mathematics, Juveniles
Founded: 1962

De **Garve** PVBA+*, Groene Poortdreef 27, B–8200 St-Michiels, Bruges Tel: (050) 318283/320707
Dir: W Barbiaux
Subjects: Bibliography, Languages, Textbooks, Law, Politics, Social Science, Mathematics, Physics, Technical, Music
Founded: 1909

Gedit SA+*, 13 rue Barthélemy Frison, B–7500 Tournai Tel: (069) 226105 Cable Add: Gedit Tournai Telex: Gedit 57251
Dir: J Desclée
Subjects: General (also printers)
Founded: 1872
Subsidiary Companies: Desclée, Editeurs (qv); Editions Desclée et Cie, France (qv); Editions Gamma (qv); Editions Gamma, France (qv); Nouvelles Editions Mame, France (qv)

Editions **Gérard** & Co SPRL, see Marabout SA

Girault **Gilbert** SPRL+*, 50 rue de l'Association, B–1000 Brussels Tel: (02) 2171430

Subjects: Cartography
Founded: 1928, Reconstituted: 1956

Uitgeverij het **Gouden** Spoor+*, Grotenhof 38, B–2510 Mortsel Tel: (03) 498415
Dir: M Saldien
Subjects: Juveniles, How-to, Medicine
Founded: 1951

De **Goudvink** NV*, Steenwinkelstr 644, B–2621 Schelle Tel: (031) 875318/9 Telex: 33866
Dirs: W L Detieger, W van den Hoek
Subjects: Arts, Education, Sport & Games, Geography, History, Ethnography, Travel, Juveniles
Founded: 1959
ISBN Publisher's Prefix: 90–270

Gutenberg, subsidiary of Beckers Groep, Kalmthout (qv)

Hachette (Département International)+*, Karthuizersstraat 5, B–1000 Brussels Tel: (02) 5111476 Teelex: Hachette Bru B 25028
Man Dir: D Pichon
Subject: General

Imprimeries **Havaux**, a division of Editions de la Francité (qv)

Imprimerie **Hayez** SPRL+, 4 rue Fin, B–1080 Brussels Tel: (02) 4287112
Man Dir: Serge Hayez; *Sales Dir:* Frédéric Hayez
Subjects: Belles Lettres, Poetry, Philosophy, Religion, Medicine, General Science
Founded: 1780

Heibrand*, Hoevebosstr 1, B–2460 Kasterlee Tel: (014) 557328
Dir: R Lievens

Heideland PVBA+*, Grote Markt 1, B–3500 Hasselt Tel: (011) 224505
Dir: L Nagels
Bookshop: Boekhandel Heideland, Hasselt (qv)
Founded: 1945
Subjects: Arts, Bibliography, Languages, Juveniles, Religion, Philosophy, Literature & Linguistics, Periodicals, Paperbacks, General

Heideland NV+, Grote Markt 1, B–3500 Hasselt Tel: (011) 224505
Dir: L Nagels
Subjects: Arts, Bibliography, Languages, Textbooks, Education, Sport & Games, Juveniles, Philosophy, Literature, Linguistics, General, Religion
Founded: 1945
ISBN Publisher's Prefix: 90–6440

Heideland-Orbis NV, Postbus 12/13, B–3500 Hasselt (Located at: Torenplein 6, B–3500 Hasselt) Tel: (011) 212112
Dirs: L Vandeschoor, F Smeets
Subjects: Encyclopaedias, Dictionaries, Language, Literature, Linguistics, Series, General
1978: 14 titles *Founded:* 1969
ISBN Publisher's Prefix: 90–291

Editions **Hemma**+*, 53 rue du Centre, BP 25 B–4081 Stoumont-Chevron Tel: (086) 433022 Cable Add: Hemma Telex: 41507
Dirs: Albert, Michel, Yvonne Hemmerlin
Subsidiary Company: Diffusion Hemma, 34–38 rue des Francs-Bourgeois, F–75003 Paris,France
Br Off: Diffusion Hemma, 34 rue des Francs-Bourgeois, F–75003 Paris, France
Subjects: Juveniles, Educational Materials
1977: about 60 titles *Founded:* 1952
ISBN Publisher's Prefix: 2–8006

Hernieuwen-Uitgaven PVBA+, Noordstr 100, B–8800 Roeselare Tel: (051) 201541
Subjects: Juveniles, Religion, Philosophy

Drukkerij-Uitgeverij **Hertoghs**+*, Turnhoutsebaan 319, B–2110 Wijnegem Tel: (031) 536040
Dir: J Hertoghs
Subject: Textbooks
Founded: 1945

M van **Hove** DPN*, Dorpstr 11, B–2080 Kapellen, Antwerp Tel: (031) 642407
Dir: M van Hove
Subjects: Religion, Philosophy, General
Founded: 1966

Van **Hyfte**-De Coninck*, Lindenlaan 28A–30, B–9068 Ertvelde Tel: (091) 447200
Dir: M van Hyfte

NV **I C U**-België*, Louizalaan 485, B–1050 Brussels Tel: (02) 6499026 Telex: 62067 Icubel
Parent Company: NV ICU, Netherlands (qv)
Subsidiary Companies: CED-Sansom nv, Belgium (qv); CNES-Sansom, Belgium; J B Wolters NV, Belgium (qv)
Subjects: Publishing, text processing, planning and administration systems, training, consulting, films and AV packages, literature distribution, social and fiscal information

I V A C SA, 691 chaussée de Mons, B–1070 Brussels Tel: (02) 5230190 Telex: 23958 IVAC B
Man Dir: Willy Simons
Subjects: Art, Education, History, General Science, Geography, Languages, Textbooks
Founded: 1949

Uitgeverij J van **In**+, Grote Markt 39, B–2500 Lier Tel: (031) 805511
Man Dir: Dr Laurent Woestenburg; *Editorial, Rights & Permissions:* Dr Laurent Woestenburg; *Sales:* Jacques van Hellemont; *Production:* Ives Crokaerts; *Publicity:* Ludo Verscuren
Parent Company: V N U NV, Netherlands (qv)
Subjects: Juveniles, University, Secondary & Primary Textbooks, Educational Materials, Law
Bookshop: At above address
1977: 233 titles *1978:* 115 titles *Founded:* 1833
ISBN Publisher's Prefix: 90–306

Infoboek+*, Roosterputstr 34, B–3990 Meerhout Tel: (014) 300477
Dir: W Verhaert
Subjects: Textbooks, Education, Sport & Games, Juveniles, Religion, Philosophy, Literature, Linguistics, Music
Founded: 1971

Institut national de Sténodactylographie+*, rue de l'Union 23, B–1030 Brussels Tel: (02) 2176859
Dir: H Pringels
Subject: Textbooks relating to study of typing and shorthand-typing
Founded: 1897

Institut royal des Relations internationales (Koninklijk Instituut voor Internationale Betrekkingen)+*, 88 ave de la Couronne, B–1050 Brussels Tel: (02) 6482000
Man Dir: Dr E Coppieters
Subjects: Political Science, Law, Economics
1977: 5 titles *Founded:* 1947
Miscellaneous: Publishes periodical *Studia Diplomatica*

Uitgaven van **Interbankendienst** NV+, Keizerslaan 14, B–3000 Brussels Tel: (02) 5132553

BELGIUM 39

Dir: L Dewincklear
Subjects: Law, Political & Social Science, Periodicals
Founded: 1968

Interéditions, see Reflets du Monde

International Publishers' Aid (IPA)+*, Potterie Rei 69, BP 89, B–8000 Bruges Tel: (050) 335186
Man Dir: Pierre Angelet
Subject: Juveniles
Founded: 1969
Miscellaneous: Specialists in work to be jointly edited, jointly produced, in a number of languages

De **Internationale Pers**+*, Karel Govaertsstr 56–58, B–2100 Deurne Tel: (031) 213873
Dir, Editorial, Publicity, Rights & Permissions: J A Walvisch; *Sales:* C J van Wolferen, E Jurres; *Production:* A Schödl
Subjects: Medicine, Juveniles, Periodicals
Founded: 1947

H-K de **Jaeger** Publications (ASTRID), K Astridlaan 89, B–9000 Ghent
Editor: H-K de Jaeger
Subject: ASTRID General Reference and Practical Information Science Series
1978: 1 title
ISBN Publisher's Prefix: 90-70078

J **Janssens**+*, Kruikstr 14, B–2000 Antwerp Tel: (031) 391220
Dir: J Janssens
Subjects: Arts, Education, Plays
Founded: 1876

Jecta*, A Gomandstr 24, B–1090 Brussels Tel: (02) 4268419
Dir: J Detremmerie
Subjects: Religion, Philosophy
Founded: 1961

Keesing — Internationale Drukkerij en Uitgeverij NV+, Keesinglaan 2-20, B–2100 Deurne Tel: (031) 243890 Cable Add: Systeka Telex: 32507
Dir: Mr Gillieron
Subjects: Education, Sport & Games, Medicine, Juveniles, Periodicals
Founded: 1911

Die **Keure** NV+*, Oude Gentweg 108, B–8000 Bruges Tel: (050) 331236
Dir: H Bogaerts
Subjects: Textbooks, Law, Political, Administrative & Social Sciences, Juveniles
Founded: 1948

NV Uitgeverij **Kluwer**+*, Santvoortbeeklaan 21–23, B–2100 Deurne Tel: (031) 247890/1/2
Dirs: R Roziers, J Wijnen
Founded: 1954
Subjects: Technical books and periodicals
Miscellaneous: Firm is part of Kluwer Group, Netherlands (qv)

Maarten **Kluwer's** Internationale Uitgeversonderneming NV+, Somersstraat 13-15, B–2000 Antwerp Tel: (031) 312900
Dirs: M Kluwer, E Boerwinkel
Subjects: Textbooks, Law, Political & Social Science, Education, Technical, Periodicals
1978: 25 titles *Founded:* 1972
Miscellaneous: Wholesaler (Dutch books)

Koninklijk Instituut voor Internationale Betrekkingen, see Institut royale des Relations internationales

Kritak uitgeverij+, Vesaliusstraat 1, B–3000 Leuven Tel: (016) 231264
Man Dirs: Rik Coolsaet, André Van Halewijck
Subjects: Politics, Social affairs, Literature

Bookshop: Vesaliusstraat 57, B–3000 Leuven
1978: 14 titles *1979:* 23 titles *Founded:* 1976
ISBN Publisher's Prefix: 90-6303

Editions **Labor**+, 342 rue Royale, B–1030 Brussels Tel: (02) 2168150
Man Dir: Alexandre André; *all other offices:* J Fauconnier
Orders to: 156–158 chaussée de Haecht, B–1030 Brussels
Subjects: Belles Lettres, Poetry, Biography, History, Philosophy, Reference, Psychology, General & Social Science, University & Primary Textbooks, Pedagogy
1977: 45 titles *1978:* 40 titles *Founded:* 1927
ISBN Publisher's Prefix: 2-82590039

Imprimerie **Laconti** SA+, 51 rue Bonaventure, B–1090 Brussels Tel: (02) 4784835 Cable Add: Impriilaconti
Dir: C Volters
Subject: Art
Founded: 1935
ISBN Publisher's Prefix: 2-87008

Editions **Lampe** d'Or ASBL+*, 23 ave Giele, B–1090 Brussels Tel: (02) 4279277
Man Dir: F M Van Dÿk
Subjects: Religion, Juveniles
Founded: 1955
ISBN Publisher's Prefix: 2-87001

Lannoo+, Kasteelstr 97, B–8880 Tielt Tel: (051) 402551 Cable Add: Lanoprint Telex: 81555
Man Dirs: Godfried Lannoo, Drs Johan Ducheyne
Subjects: Art, Philosophy, Religion, Juveniles, High-priced Paperbacks, Psychology, Education, Sports, Games, Travel
1977: 65 titles *1978:* 83 titles *Founded:* 1909
ISBN Publisher's Prefix: 90–209

Maison Ferdinand **Larcier** SA+*, 39 rue des Minimes, B–1000 Brussels Tel: (02) 5129679/5124712
Man Dir: Jean-Marie Ryckmans
Subjects: Social Science, Law (Belgian and International/European), Science & Technology, Periodicals: *Journal des Tribunaux* (weekly); *Journal des Tribuneaux du Travail* (fortnightly)
1977: 18 titles *Founded:* 1839

Latomus ASBL+, 60 rue Colonel Chaltin, B–1180 Brussels
Editorial: L Herrmann, M Renard; *Sales, Production, Publicity, Rights & Permissions:* G Cambier
Subjects: Bibliography, Philology, Roman Literature and History, Archaeology
1977: 4 titles *1978:* 5 titles *Founded:* 1937
ISBN Publisher's Prefix: 2-87031-000-5

Editions Paul **Legrain**+*, 72 rue Defacqz, B–1050 Brussels Tel: (02) 5387405
Dir: P Legrain
Subjects: Arts, Geography, History, Ethnography, Travel
Founded: 1946

Editions **Legrand***, rue Champs de Tignee, B–4511 Barchon Tel: (041) 628152 Telex: 41193 apal b
Deputy Administrator: Ch Legrand, 42 Rue des Chateaux, B–4510 Saive
Subjects: Children's activities

Editions **Lesigne**+*, 171 ave du Prince Héritier, B–1200 Brussels Tel: (02) 7332097
Dir: P Moorkens
Subject: Textbooks

Uitgavenfonds Leon **Lesoil** V Z W+, Washuisstr 12-14, B–1000 Brussels Tel: (02) 5128778
Man Dir: Monique Laenen
Subject: Politics
1978: 8 titles *1979:* 2 titles *Founded:* 1973

Leuven University Press, Krakenstr 3, B–3000 Leuven
Dir: Guido Declercq
1978: 16 titles *Founded:* 1971
Subjects: Theology, Psychology, Pedagogy, Economics, Sociology, Political Studies, Music, Mathematics, Medicine, Philosophy, etc
ISBN Publisher's Prefix: 90-6186

Editions de la **Librairie encyclopédique***, 40 rue du Luxembourg, B–1040 Brussels Tel: (02) 5132467
Man Dir: A C Leyenberger
Subjects: History, Reference, Law, Economics, Political & Social Science
nded: 1939
Bookshop: Librairie encyclopédique Exportation-Antiquariat, 40 rue du Luxembourg, B–1040 Brussels Tel: (02) 5113551

Librairie générale SA*, 51 rue de Namur, B–1000 Brussels Tel: (02) 5123073 Telex: 61486 pauli b
Subjects: General Fiction, History, Music, Art, General Science
Founded: 1919
Miscellaneous: Associate Company: Librarie Pauli SA (qv)

Editeurs de **Littérature** biblique (Biblical Publications)+, 479 chaussée de Tubize, B–1420 Braine-l'Alleud Tel: (02) 3845402
Dir: M Cl Kroeker
Subjects: Education, Pedagogy, Sport, Games, Juveniles, Religion, Philosophy, Music, Journals, Paperbacks
Founded: 1959

Editions du **Lloyd** Anversois SA (Antwerpse Lloyd NV)+*, Eiermarkt 23, B–2000 Antwerp Tel: (031) 340550 Telex: 31446
Man Dir: M R Jaumotte
Subjects: General & Social Science, Law, Bibliography, Philology, Languages, Textbooks, Mathematics, Literature
Founded: 1904

Lombard SA+*, ave Paul-Henri Spaak 1-11, B–1070 Brussels Tel: (02) 5225600 Cable Add: Lombarbel-Brussels Telex: 23097
Dir: G Leblanc; *Rights & Permissions:* Viviane Rousie
Subjects: Juveniles, Sports, Games, Education, Geography, History, Ethnography, Travel
Founded: 1946

Uitgeverij **Lotus**/Editions Lotus+, Leopoldstraat 43, B–2000 Antwerp Tel: (031) 327010/327001
Man Dir: Andreas Ausloos; *Editorial (Dutch language books for children):* Gerda de Visser; *Editorial, Sales, Rights & Permissions, Production, Publicity:* Andreas Ausloos, Jean-Pierre Zinjé
Orders to: (French language books) Garnier Frères, BP 168, 19 rue des plantes, F-75665 Paris; (Dutch language books, Belgium) Denis, Sterckshoflei 28-30, B–2100 Deurne; (Dutch language books, Netherlands) Centraal Boekhuis, Postbus 125, Erasmusweg 10, Culemborg
Subjects: Novels, Documentary Works, Juveniles
1978: 45 titles *1979:* 50 titles *Founded:* 1977
ISBN Publisher's Prefix: 90-6290 (Dutch language books); 2-87053 (French language books)

Editions **Lumen** Vitae (International centre for Religious Education) ASBL+, 184 rue Washington, B-1050 Brussels Tel: (02) 3441882
Man Dir: Jean Bouvy; *Sales Dir:* Albert Dreze
Subjects: Religion, High-priced Paperbacks, Psychology, Secondary & Primary Textbooks, Educational Materials
1977: 15 titles *1978:* 8 titles *Founded:* 1936

M I M, see Moderne Industrie Methoden

Uitgeversmaatschappij A **Manteau** NV+, 107 ave René Comhaire, B-1080 Brussels Tel: (02) 4650617 Telex: 33866
Man Dir: J Weverbergh; *Sales Dir:* W L Detiger
Subjects: General Fiction, Belles Lettres, Poetry, Biography, Art, Low & High-priced Paperbacks, Secondary Textbooks
1977: 103 titles *1978:* 116 titles *Founded:* 1932
Subsidiary: A Manteau NV
ISBN Publisher's Prefix: 90-223

Les Nouvelles Editions **Marabout** SA+, 65 rue de Limbourg, B-4800 Verviers Tel: (087) 339135
Man Dir: Jean-Etienne Cohen-Seat; *Sales Dir:* Jacques Closset
Br Off: 81 ave de Tervueren, B-1040 Brussels Tel: (02) 7359125; 34 avenue Marceau, F-75008 Paris Tel: 7237250
Subject: Paperbacks
Founded: 1977
Miscellaneous: Formerly Gérard et Cie SPRL

Pierre **Mardaga** SA+*, 2-4 galerie des Princes, B-1000 Brussels Tel: (02) 5132038
Man Dir: Pierre Mardaga
Subjects: Psychology, Social Science, Architecture
1977: 23 titles *Founded:* 1938
ISBN Publisher's Prefix: 2-87009

Maredsous ASBL+, 11 rue de Maredsous, B-5642 Denee Tel: (082) 699155
Dir: Père Léon-Nicolas Dayez
Subjects: Geography, History, Religion, Philosophy, General, Ethnography, Travel
Bookshop: Librairie de Maredsous, B-5642 Denee
Founded: 1924

Editions **Marie-Médiatrice** ASBL*, 172 ave Gevaert, B-1320 Genval Tel: (02) 6537613
Subjects: Juveniles, Religion, Paperbacks
Founded: 1941

Editions **Markus**+*, Schilsweg 23, B-4700 Eupen Tel: (087) 552108
Dir: M Schroder
Subjects: Bibliography, Languages, Textbooks, Geography, History, Ethnography, Travel, Religion, Philosophy, General

Frans **Masereel** Fonds VZW+*, Raveschootstr 4, B-9000 Ghent Tel: (091) 253853
Dir: L Brabans
Subjects: History, Current Affairs
Founded: 1971

Les Ateliers d'Art graphique **Meddens** SA+*, 141-143 ave de Scheut, B-1070 Brussels Tel: (02) 5227925
Dir: F Van Den Bremt
Subjects: Fine Arts, Geography, History, Music, Theology

Mercatorfonds SA, see Fonds Mercator SA

Mercatorfonds-Arcade, see Arcade

Editeur Paul F **Merckx**+*, 145a ave des Statuaires, B-1180 Brussels Tel: (02) 3744156/3744158
Subjects: Art, Geography, History, Educational Materials
Founded: 1958

Mercurius PVBA+*, Rodestr 44, B-2000 Antwerp Tel: (031) 333708/333762
Dir: K Schenck
Subjects: Geography, History, Ethnography, Travel
Founded: 1894

Editions d'Art Lucien de **Meyer** ASBL*, 88 ave de Tervueren, B-1040 Brussels Tel: (02) 7343560/7343582
Executives: As for Editions Arts et Voyages (qv)
Subject: Art
1977: 1 title *Founded:* 1977

D **Meyers-Trefois**+*, Pontstr 50, B-9230 Melle, Ghent Tel: (091) 521081
Dir: D Meyers

Meysmans+*, 23 rue de l'Union, B-1030 Brussels Tel: (02) 2176859
Dir: H Pringels
Subject: Textbooks
Founded: 1897

Michelin (Département Cartes & Guides) SA+*, 33 quai de Willebroek, B-1020 Brussels Tel: (02) 2186100 ext 238 Cable Add: Pneumiclin
Dir: R Cammaerts
Subjects: Travel Guides, Maps
Founded: 1913

Van **Mierlo-Proost** & Co NV*, Steenweg op Mol 60, B-2300 Turnhout Tel: (014) 414131 Cable Add: Vamipro Telex: 32906
Dir: J van Mierlo-Proost
Subjects: Law, Political & Social Sciences, General
Founded: 1918

Moderne Instructie Methoden (MIM) PVBA+*, Jules Moretuslei 760, B-2610 Wilrijk Tel: (031) 496271
Dir: M Callebaut
Subjects: Textbooks, Education, Sport & Games
Founded: 1971

Louis **Musin** Editeur+, 99 ave de la Brabançonne, B-1040 Brussels Tel: (02) 7363727/7341276
Dir: L Musin
Subjects: Textbooks, Juveniles, Literature, Linguistics, History
1978: 15 titles *Founded:* 1960

N F F (Nouvelles Feuilles Familiales)*, 27 rue du Congrès, B-1000 Brussels Tel: (02) 2183482
Dir: Jean Hinnekens
Associate Companies: Centre d'Etude et d'Edition Conjugale et Familiale ASBL, Belgium (qv); Les 'Feuilles familiales' ASBL, Belgium (qv)
Subjects: Marriage and Family Relations, Psychology, Educational, Religion, Pedagogy
Founded: 1937

NV Uitgeverij **Nauwelaerts** Edition SA+*, Muntstr 10, B-3000 Louvain Tel: (016) 220421 Telex: 25564
Man Dir: W Vandermeulen
Subjects: History, Philosophy, Theology, Medicine, Psychology, Social Science, Economics, University Textbooks, Educational Materials, Literature
Founded: 1938
Subsidiary: Editions Beatrice-Nauwelaerts, 4 rue de Fleurus, Paris 6, France

De **Nederlandsche Boekhandel** NV+, Kapelsestr 222, B-2080 Kapellen Tel: (031) 645320
Man Dir: J R L Pelckmans
Parent Company: Standaard Uitgeverij en Distributie BV, Netherlands (qv)
Subjects: History, Philosophy, Religion, Juveniles, Social Science, University, Secondary & Primary Textbooks
1977: 249 titles *1978:* 176 titles *Founded:* 1892
Bookshop: Sint-Jacobsmarkt 7, B-2000 Antwerp
ISBN Publisher's Prefix: 90-289

Nici*, Lousbergkaai 32, B-900 Ghent Tel: (031) 252897
Dir: G Vander Rol

Nomath*, 65 rue de Maizeret, B-5134 Loyers Tel: (081) 588592
Dir: M van Cutsem
Subjects: Textbooks, Mathematics, Physics, Technical
Founded: 1967
ISBN Publisher's Prefix: 2-87002

Het **Noordnederlands Boekbedrijf** NV+*, Paleisstr 23-25, B-2000 Antwerp Tel: (031) 374605/385506
Dir: F Doumh
Subjects: Bibliography, Philology, Languages, Textbooks, Law, Political & Social Sciences, Education, Sport & Games, Mathematics, Physics, Technical, Medicine, Juveniles, Religion, Philosophy, Literature, Linguistics, Music, Periodicals, General, Geography, History, Ethnography, Travel
Founded: 1951
ISBN Publisher's Prefix: 90-6154

Norma PVBA+*, St Baafsplein 30, B-9000 Ghent Tel: (091) 252815
Subject: Textbooks
Founded: 1938

Nouvelle Diffusion — Complexe+, see Editions Complexe

Les **Nouvelles Editions Marabout** SA, see Marabout

Nouvelles Editions Vokaer SA, see Vokaer

Nouvelles feuilles familiales, see NFF

Omega NV*, Lamorinièrestr 23, B-2000 Antwerp Tel: (031) 390614
Dir: A Lenaerts
Subject: General

Uitgeverij S V **Ontwikkeling**+*, Leeuwerikstr 41, B-2000 Antwerp Tel: (031) 338659
Dir: R Binnemans
Subjects: Novels, Poetry, History, Textbooks
Founded: 1923
Bookshops: Boekhandel Ontwikkeling, Ommeganckstr 35-37, Antwerp; Boekhandel Ontwikkeling, Dés Boucherystr 18-20, Mechelen; Boekhandel Ontwikkeling, J Brochhovenstr 28, Deurne, Antwerp (all in Belgium)

L **Opdebeek** Uitgeversfirma NV+, Kapelsestr 222, B-2080 Antwerp Tel: (031) 645320
Dirs: J Pelckmans, R Pelckmans
Subject: Juveniles
1978: 17 titles *Founded:* 1953
ISBN Publisher's Prefix: 90-6162

Orbis Boekhandel NV+*, Vekestr 16-18, B-2000 Antwerp Tel: (031) 318610
Dir: A Goyvaerts
Subjects: Geography, History, Ethnography, Travel
Founded: 1968

Ordina Editions+, 5 rue Forgeur, B-4000 Liège Tel: (041) 323472
Man Dir: Georges Derouaux
Subject: Problems of population
1978: 3 titles *1979:* 2 titles *Founded:* 1974
ISBN Publisher's Prefix: 87040

Uitgeverij **Orientaliste** PVBA*, Klein Dalenstr 42, B-3009 Winksele-Louvain Tel: (016) 488102
Man Dir: E Peeters
Subjects: History, Philosophy, Religion, Psychology, University Textbooks
Miscellaneous: Publish Oriental and foreign language books

Uitgeverij **Orion**+*, Lieven Bauwensstraat 19, B-8200 Bruges 2 Tel: 050 318157 Telex: 81068
Man Dir: A Goyvaerts; *Editorial, Rights & Permissions:* F Bonneure; *Sales, Publicity:* J de Stecker; *Production:* Ph Van Daele
Parent Company: Desclée de Brouwer (qv)
Br Off: B Gottmer, Nijmegen, Netherlands
Subjects: General Fiction, Literature, Essays, Poetry, Art, History, Hobbies
1977: 163 titles *Founded:* 1942
ISBN Publisher's Prefix: 90-264

De **Oude** Linden NV+*, Abdijstr 26, B-3180 Tongerlo-Westerlo Tel: (014) 544206
Dir: P de Mey*Subjects:* Juveniles, Religion, Philosophy
Founded: 1962

Oyez SA+*, 21 rue Defacqz, B-1050 Brussels Tel: (02) 5386973 Telex: 25564
Dirs: Michaël Bacon, W Vandermeulen; *Sales Manager:* Yvon Marechal
Orders to: Muntstraat 10, B-3000, Louvain
Associate Company: The Solicitors Law Stationery Society Ltd, UK, Oyez Publishing Ltd (qv), London, is a sister company of Oyez SA
Subjects: Law, Science, Practical books

Uitgeverij **Patmos**+, Kapelsestr 222, B-2080 Kapellen Tel: (031) 645320
Dirs: J and R Pelckmans
Subjects: Education, Juveniles, Religion
1978: 68 titles
ISBN Publisher's Prefix: 90-292

Pauli SA*, rue de Namur 51, B-1000 Brussels Tel: (02) 5123073 Telex: 61486 pauli b
Founded: 1930
Subjects: Geography, History, Ethnography, Travel
Miscellaneous: Associate Company: Librarie Générale SA (qv)

Peeters SPRL+*, BP 41, B-3000 Louvain Tel: (016) 488102
Dir: Mme Peeters
Subjects: Periodicals, General
Founded: 1970

Pink Editions & Productions+*, Venusstr 18A, B-2000 Antwerp Tel: (031) 332273
Dir: R Lowet de Wotrenge
Founded: 1973
Subjects: Art, Bibliography

Uitgeverij **Plantyn** SA NV+*, Santvoortbeeklaan 21-23, B-2100 Deurne, Antwerp Tel: (031) 247897
Dir: J Vrindts
Subjects: Education, all levels
Miscellaneous: Firm is a member of the Kluwer Group, Deventer, Netherlands (qv)
Founded: 1950

La **Presse** Internationale, see De Internationale Pers

Presses agronomiques de Gembloux ASBL+, 22 Ave de la Faculté d'Agronomie, B-5800 Gembloux Tel: (081) 611955
Dir: Mme C Dagnelie
Subjects: Agriculture, Botany, Chemistry, Mathematics, Physics, Technical, Periodicals
Founded: 1965
ISBN Publisher's Prefix: 2-87016

Presses universitaires de Bruxelles ASBL*, 42 ave Paul Heger, B-1050 Brussels Tel: (02) 6499780
President: Ed Burg; *Man Dir:* Marc Oostens; *Sales:* Françoise van den Dorpel
Subjects: University Textbooks, especially Philosophy, Medicine, Engineering, Economics, General Science, Architecture
Founded: 1958
Bookshops: Librairie des Presses Universitaires de Bruxelles, 42 ave Paul Heger, B-1050 Brussels; 162 rue aux Laines, B-1000 Brussels
1977: c. 40 titles *1978:* c. 60 titles *Founded:* 1958
ISBN Publisher's Prefix: 2-500

Presses universitaires de Liège ASBL+, Domaine du Sart Tilman, B-4000 Liège 1 Tel: (041) 562218
Dir: P Froidcoeur
Subjects: Law, Political & Social Sciences, Medicine, General
Founded: 1920

Presses universitaires de Namur+, Rempart de la Vierge 8, B-5000 Namur Tel: (081) 229061 Telex: 59222 facna b
Dir: P Pellemans
Subjects: Art, Biography, History, Literature, Philosophy, Religion, Medicine, General Scientific, Social Sciences, University Textbooks, Quality Paperbacks
1977: 4 titles *1978:* 5 titles
ISBN Publisher's Prefix: 2-87037

Het **Prisma** NV+*, Corverstr 13, B-3700 Tongeren Tel: (012) 231325
Dir: G Michiels
Subject: Textbooks

Pro Civitate, see Crédit Communal de Belgique—Centre Culturel

La **Procure**+*, 161 rue des Tanneurs, B-1000 Brussels Tel: (021) 5122672
Man Dir: J O Neukermans
Subjects: Travel, General & Political Science, Educational Materials
Founded: 1881

Prodim SPRL+, Boulevard Général Jacques 184, B-1050 Brussels Tel: (02) 6405970
Dir: P Nile
Subjects: Textbooks, Medicine, Science
Founded: 1968

Production et Diffusion medico-techniques SPRL, see Prodim SPRL

Henri **Proost** & Co, Everdongenlaan 23, B-2300 Turnhout Tel: (014) 416911 Telex: 33185
Man Dir: Jef Proost; *Sales Dir:* Frans Peeters
Subsidiary Company: Salamander Books Ltd, UK (qv)
Subjects: Religion, Juveniles, Cookery, Gardening, Travel, History

André de **Rache***, Editeur, 127 rue du Château d'Eau, B-1180 Brussels Tel: (02) 3743950
Man Dir: A de Rache
Subjects: Belles Lettres, Poetry, Biography, Art
Founded: 1954

Reader's Digest SA+*, 12a Grande Place, B-1000 Brussels Tel: (02) 4287100 Telex: 21876
Man Dir: P Kittel
Subjects: Education, Sport & Games, Geography, History, Travel
Founded: 1967

Reinaert Uitgaven, see DAP Reinaert Uitgaven

La **Renaissance** du Livre SA+*, 12 pl du Petit-Sablon, B-1000 Brussels Tel: (02) 5119914/5134751
Man Dir: Ch R Bousson
Subjects: Belles Lettres, History, Art, Juveniles, Law, Business, Reference, Educational Materials
Founded: 1923

Fondation André **Renard**+*, 9-11 pl St Paul, B-4000 Liège Tel: (041) 237940
Dirs: R Gillon, G Vandersmissen, M Hockers

La **Revue** nouvelle ASBL+, 3-5 rue des Moucherons, B-1000 Brussels Tel: (02) 3436798
Dir: M Delepeleire
Subjects: Bibliography, Languages, Law, Political & Social Sciences, Education, Religion, Philosophy, Literature, Linguistics, Periodicals
Founded: 1945

De **Riemaecker** Uitgeverij*, Kerkewijk 2, B-9681 Nukerke Tel: (055) 211404
Dir: P de Riemaecker
Founded: 1947

Roeland Kamer Fonds VZW*, Groenendaalsesteenweg 135, B-1990 Hoeilaart Tel: (02) 6572602
Man Dir: Rienk H Kamer

De **Roerdomp**+*, Vandereydtlaan 46, B-2160 Brecht Tel: (031) 138401
Dir: J Lombaerts
Subjects: Law, Political & Social Sciences, Literature, Linguistics
Founded: 1967

Rossel Edition SA+, 134 rue Royale, B-1000 Brussels Tel: (02) 2194190 Telex: 24298
Manager: J Gerlache; *Rights and Permissions:* André-Paul Duchâteau
Associate Company: Rossel Edition, France (qv)
Subjects: Education, Sports and Games, Documentary Reports, Period History, Juveniles; Periodicals
Founded: 1972

Roularta NV+*, Meiboomlaan 33, B-8800 Roeselare Tel: (051) 203191
Man Dir: W De Nolf
Subjects: Law, Political & Social Sciences

Roya Boudewijn*, Ravestraat 35, B-8000 Bruges Tel: (050) 331235

Rubens, see Beckers Groep

Saeftinge*, De Merodedreef 55, B-2180 Westerlo
Dir: J J A Verstappen
Subjects: Juveniles, Literature, Linguistics

Publications de **Saint-André**+, allée de Clerlande 1, B-1340 Ottignies Tel: (010) 417463
Subjects: Pastoral, Liturgical, Anthropology, Contemporary Architecture (all periodicals)

Publications des Facultés universitaires **Saint Louis**+*, 43 blvd du Jardin Botanique, B-1000 Brussels Tel: (02) 2177653

42 BELGIUM

Man Dir: M van de Kerchove; *Sales, Publicity:* M G Braive
Subject: Humanities
1977: 3 titles *1978:* 3 titles *Founded:* 1974
ISBN Publisher's Prefix: 2-8028

Samsom (CED), see CED-Samsom NV

Sanderus PVBA+, Rempardenstr 36, B–9700 Oudenaarde Tel: (055) 311130
Dir: M van den Abeele
Subject: Textbooks
Founded: 1959

Schaubroeck PVBA+*, Drapstr 23, B–9730 Nazareth Tel: (091) 854227
Dir: J Schaubroeck
Subjects: Law, Political & Social Sciences
Founded: 1911

Schott Frères SPRL (Éditeurs de Musique), 30 rue St-Jean, B–1000 Brussels Tel: (02) 5123980
Man Dir: Jean-Jacques Junne
Subject: Music
Founded: 1823

De **Schutter** SA*, Venusstraat 23, B–2000 Antwerp Tel: (031) 311750 Telex: 32339 DS Ant
Subjects: Fine Art Reprints and Facsimiles
1977: 1 title

Editions **Sciences et Lettres** SA+*, 13 rue de la Commune, B–4020 Liège Tel: (041) 426154
Man Dir: L Maraval
Subjects: History, Medicine, Psychology, University, Secondary & Primary Textbooks
Founded: 1946

De **Seizoenen** PVBA+*, Prins Leopoldlei 60, B–2510 Mortsel Tel: (031) 496034
Dir: P Vanhout
Subject: Juveniles
Founded: 1958

Service SC+, 232 blvd Em Bockstael, B–1020 Brussels Tel: (02) 4282627/4280520
Dirs: G Vanden Avyle, M Geets
Subjects: Law, Technical, Periodicals
Founded: 1949

Services interbancaires SA+, 14 boulevard de l'Empereur, B–2000 Brussels Tel: (02) 5132553
Dir: L Dewincklear
Subjects: Law, Political & Social Sciences, Periodicals
Founded: 1968

Uitgeverij De **Sikkel** NV+*, Kapelsestr 222, B–2080 Kapellen Tel: (031) 645320
Man Dir: Karel de Bock
Founded: 1919
Subjects: General Fiction, Belles Lettres, Art, History, General Science, Educational Materials
ISBN Publisher's Prefix: 90-260

Editions Le **Sillon** d'Or+*, Grotenhof 38, B–2510 Mortsel Tel: (031) 498415
Dir: M Saldien
Subject: General
Founded: 1951

Simon Stevin NV+*, Zennestr 37, B–1000 Brussels Tel: (02) 5121085/5138295 Telex: 23602 Boetis
Dirs: J Van Hoorick, M Strens-Van Horrick
Parent Company: N V Drukkerij De Bouwkroniek
Subjects: Law, Political & Social Sciences, Mathematics, Physics, Technical, Surveying, Architecture, Engineering Science, Periodicals
1977: 2 titles *Founded:* 1930

Sinite Parvulos+, B–3581 Achel Tel: (011) 641078
Dir: L van Gassel
Subjects: Devotional Literature and Miscellaneous

Sintal+*, Dekenstr 28, B–3000 Louvain Tel: (016) 223470
Dir: J Devos
Subjects: Geography, History, Ethnography, Travel
Founded: 1928

Snoeck-Ducaju & Zoon NV+, Begijnhoflaan 440, B–9000 Ghent Tel: (091) 234897
Dir: S Snoeck
Subjects: Snoeck's Literary Yearbook, Snoeck's almanakken
Founded: 1782

Société Biblique belge asbl+*, 160 rue du Trône, B–1050 Brussels Tel: (02) 6401112/6401575
Board Secretary: Rev R Catinus
Subjects: Editions of the Bible in many languages

Société d'Etudes morales, sociales & juridiques*, 39 rue Ernotte, B–5000 Namur
Subjects: Philosophy, Social Science, Law

Walter **Soethoudt**+*, Perenstr 15, B–2000 Antwerp Tel: (031) 367055
Dir: W Soethoudt
Subjects: Literature, Poetry, Paperbacks, General
Founded: 1964

Soledi (Imprimeur-Editeur) SA+, 37 rue de la Province, B–4020 Liège
Dir: P Mardaga
Subjects: Arts, Languages, Education, Philosophy, Architecture, Linguistics, General
Founded: 1919

Sonneville Press (Uitgeversmij) PVBA+*, Orchideeënlaan 3, B–8200 St-Andries, Bruges Tel: (050) 321112
Dir: J Sonneville
Subjects: Arts, Law, Political & Social Sciences, Education, Sport & Games, Geography, History, Ethnography, Travel, Religion, Philosophy, Literature, Linguistics, Music, Periodicals, Paperbacks
Founded: 1966

Het **Spectrum** NV+*, Bijkhoevelaan 12, B–2110 Wijnegem Tel: (031) 539800
Dirs: M Cornu, H C de Wit
Subjects: Arts, Bibliography, Philology, Languages, Law, Political & Social Sciences, Education, Sport & Games, Mathematics, Physics, Technical, Geography, History, Ethnography, Travel, Medicine, Religion, Philosophy, Literature, Linguistics, Music, Periodicals, General
Founded: 1946

Le **Sphinx** SA+*, 5 rue de Danemark, B–1060 Brussels Tel: (02) 5370437/5381044
Publisher: Marcel Leempoel
Subjects: General Fiction, Belles Lettres, General
Founded: 1951

Anciens Etablissements **Splichal** SA+*, Apostoliekenstr 105, B–2300 Turnhout Tel: (014) 413861
Man Dir: L Verwaest
Subject: Religion
Founded: 1856

Standaard Uitgeverij (NV Scriptoria)+, Belgiëlei 147a, Postbus 212, B–2000 Antwerp Tel: (031) 395900 Telex: Edista 31421
Man Dir: A Sap
Parent Company: Standaard Uitgeverij en Distributie BV, Netherlands (qv)
Associate Company: Editions Erasme (qv)
Subjects: General Fiction, How-to, Politics, Economics, Law, Reference, General Science, Textbooks, Encyclopaedias, Juveniles
Founded: 1946
Bookshops: Owns chain of Standaard-Boekhandel shops in Belgium and Netherlands
ISBN Publisher's Prefix: 90-021

NV Uitgeverij **Stappaerts**+, Letterkundestraat 138 A-B, B–2610 Wilrijk (Antwerp) Tel: (031) 288531 Telex: 71288
Man Dir: Jozee Stappaerts
Subject: Juveniles
1978: 78 titles *1979:* approx 45 titles
Founded: 1976

Steppe+*, Aalstersesteenweg 99–101, B–9400 Ninove Tel: (054) 332591 Cable Add: Steppe-Ninove
Subjects: Textbooks, Mathematics, Physics, Technical

De **Ster** PVBA+*, Lange Brilstr 9, B–2000 Antwerp Tel: (031) 322036
Dir: R De Smedt

E **Story**-Scientia PVBA+, van Duysplein 8, B–9000 Ghent Tel: (091) 255757
Dirs: E Story, L Van Opdenbosch, J Story
Subjects: Science, Humanities, History, Business, Agriculture, Medicine, Law, Education, Economics, Psychology
Bookshop: At above address
Founded: 1960

De **Techniek**+*, J De Bomstr 61, B–2000 Antwerp Tel: (031) 378567
Dir: J Roggen
Subjects: Textbooks, Mathematics, Physics, Technical
Founded: 1926

Uitgeverij De **Tempel**+, Tempelhof 37, B–8000 Bruges Tel: (050) 315505
Man Dir: Mrs M H Monseu
Subjects: Philosophy, Social Science (especially European unification), Archaeology
1977: 1 title *1978:* 2 titles *Founded:* 1905

Imprimerie-Editions Georges **Thone** Sciences et Lettres+*, 11–19 rue de la Commune, B–4020 Liège Tel: (041) 426154
Man Dir: L Maraval; *Sales, Publicity:* Mrs I Severyns; *Production, Rights & Permissions:* L Maraval
Parent Company: Imprimerio Georges Thone
Subjects: Scholastic Texts, Mathematics, Language, Chemistry, Law, Social History, Pedagogy, Education, Mechanics, Psysiology, Biology, Botany, Zoology, Science and Technology
1977: 8–10 titles *Founded:* 1908 ('Sciences et Lettres', 1946)

Toulon+*, Sportstr 35, B–8400 Ostend Tel: (059) 800927
Dir: P A Toulon
Subjects: Educational, Technical, Juveniles

Trois Arches+, 87 ave W Churchill, POB 18, B–1180 Brussels Tel: (02) 3447333/3587181
Also known as 3 Arches
Man Dir, Rights & Permissions: Hugues Boucher
Subjects: Literature, Fine Art, Architecture, Photography, Children's Books, Bibliography
1977: 2 titles *1978:* 3 titles *Founded:* 1976

Editions **U G A** (Uitgeverij voor Gemeente-Administratie)+*, Stijn Streuvelslaan 73, B–8710 Kortrijk-Heule Tel: (056) 355881
Dir: L Deschildre
Br Offs: 5 ave de Stassart, B–5000 Namur; 19 rue Guimard, Bte 2, B–1040 Brussels
Subjects: Administration, History, Social Science, Law, Language, Bibliography, Literature, Journals
Founded: 1948

U O P C, see Union et Orientation de Presse et de Culture

Union et Orientation de Presse et de Culture (UOPC) SA+*, 216 chaussée de Wavre, B–1040 Brussels Tel: (02) 6489689
Dir: Mme Lefebvre
Subjects: Religion, Philosophy
Founded: 1923

Universa PVBA+*, Hoenderstr 24, B–9200 Wetteren Tel: (091) 691563
Man Dir: A De Meester
Subjects: Textbooks, Geography, History, Ethnography, Travel, Music
Founded: 1958

Universitaire Boekhandel NV*, St-Amandstr 20, B–9000 Ghent Tel: (091) 231675/232311
Subject: Textbooks
Founded: 1964

Editions de l'**Université** de Bruxelles+, Parc Léopold, 137A rue Belliard, B–1040 Brussels Tel: (02) 2307705
Man Dir: Mrs S Unger
Subjects: Humanities, Social Sciences, Science, Medicine; Periodicals
1977: 36 titles *1978:* 35 titles *Founded:* 1950
ISBN Publisher's Prefix: 2-8004

Vademecum de Pharmacie+, 3 pl Rotenberg, B–4700 Eupen Tel: (087) 553271
Man Dir: Paul Schiltz
Subjects: Reference, Medicine
Founded: 1963

Imprimerie H **Vaillant** Carmanne SA+, rue Ste Véronique 17, B–4000 Liège Tel: (041) 529616
Man Dir: G Dengis
Subjects: Science, Education, Political Science, Belles Lettres, Religion, Medicine, Law, History, Science, Technical
1978: 5 titles *Founded:* 1838

Vander Publishing+, 148 Mechelsestraat, B–3000 Louvain
Man Dir: Willy Vandermeulen
Br Offs: Brussels Tel: (322) 7620662
Subjects: Psychology, Engineering, General & Social Science, University Textbooks, Law, Economics, Politics, Medicine, Reference, Languages, Architecture, Periodicals
Founded: 1880
ISBN Publisher's Prefix: 2-8008

Librairie **Vanderlinden** SA+*, 17 rue des Grands-Carmes, B–1000 Brussels Tel: (02) 5116140
Man Dir: J Vanderlinden
Bookshop: 17 rue des Grands-Carmes, B–1000 Brussels
Subjects: Art, General Fiction, Juveniles, Textbooks, Paperbacks, Science, Mathematics
Founded: 1897

L **Vanmelle** (Drukkerij) NV+*, Lt Willemotlaan 80, B–9910 Mariakerke (Ghent) Tel: (091) 233586 Telex: 11850
Dir: L Vanmelle
Subjects: Textbooks, Juveniles

Uitgaven **Verbeke-Loys***, rue Fossé aux Loups, B–8000 Bruges Tel: (050) 33254
Subjects: General Science, Juveniles, Textbooks, Educational Materials
Founded: 1872

Uitgaven van de **Verbruikersunie** VZW (Editions de Association des Consommateurs ASBL)+*, Hollandstr 13, B–1060 Brussels Tel: (02) 5378938 Telex: Test 26771 B
Dir: G Castelain
Subjects: Periodicals, Tests and Studies connected with consumers
1977: 4 titles *Founded:* 1957

Vereniging van de belgische medische Wetenschappelijke Genootschappen VZW, see Association des Sociétés scientifiques médicales belges ASBL

Editions **Verrycken**+, Wiegstraat 30, B–2000 Antwerp Tel: (031) 323378
Man Dir, Editorial, Rights & Permissions: Christian Vandekerkhove; *Sales:* R Canale; *Production:* E Droesbeke; *Publicity:* E Vandekerkhove
Orders to: Vedas Booksellers, Hoogstraat 68, B–2000 Antwerp
Subjects: Philosophy, Medicine, Parapsychology, Occult
Bookshops: Librairie Verrycken, Wiegstraat 30, B–2000 Antwerp; Occult Bookshop, Hoogstraat 68, B–2000 Antwerp
1978: 1 title *1979:* 4 titles *Founded:* 1976
ISBN Publisher's Prefix: 90-70181

De **Verzekeringswereld** PVBA*, Karel de Preterlei 146, B–2200 Borgehout Tel: (031) 365349
Dir: A Seghers
Subjects: Law, Political & Social Sciences
Founded: 1961

Les Editions **Vie** ouvrière ASBL+*, 305 ave van Volxem, B–1190 Brussels Tel: (02) 3456166
Subjects: Religion, Juveniles, Psychology, Social Science, University & Secondary Textbooks
1977: 7 titles *Founded:* 1958
ISBN Publisher's Prefix: 2-87003

Albert de **Visscher** Editeur+, Ave du Golf 31, B–1640 Rhode-St-Genèse Tel: (02) 3587423
Man Dir: Albert de Visscher
Subjects: Music, Art, Medicine, Engineering, General Science, Juveniles
Founded: 1944

Vlaamse Bijbelstichting*, St Michielsstr 2, B–3000 Louvain Tel: 337468
Subjects: Religious Literature connected with Catholic Bible production in Belgium, the Netherlands, Austria, Switzerland and Federal Germany
Miscellaneous: Company is a member of AMB (qv under German Federal Republic)

Vlaamse Toeristenbond VZW+*, Sint-Jacobsmarkt 45, B–2000 Antwerp Tel: (031) 317680/313615
Dir: R Rombaut

De **Vlijt** NV+*, Nationalestr 46, B–2000 Antwerp Tel: (031) 312880
Dir: J Huybrechts
Subjects: Arts, Educational, History, Geography

Nouvelles Editions **Vokaer** SA, 131 rue de Birmingham, B–1070 Brussels Tel: (02) 5240070
Subjects: Arts, Geography, History, Ethnography, Travel, General
Founded: 1969
ISBN Publisher's Prefix: 2-87012

Het **Volk** NV+, Forelstr 22, B–9000 Ghent Tel: (091) 255701
Dir: J van Haverbeke
Subject: Juveniles

C De **Vries** Brouwers PVBA, Haantjeslei 80, B–2000 Antwerp Tel: (031) 374180
Dir: I de Vries
Subjects: Education, Juveniles, History, Law
Founded: 1946

De **Vroente**+*, Bosakkerstr 10, B–2460 Kasterlee Tel: (014) 556160
Dir: S Debroey
Subjects: Arts, Textbooks, Education, Religion, Philosophy

PVBA Imprimerie-Editions **Vyncke**+, Savaanstr 92, B–9000 Ghent Tel: (091) 253960
Dir: H Vyncke; all other offices: Frans Pauwels
Subjects: Textbooks (for technical schools), Periodicals (on textiles, industrial equipment, water sports)
1978: 3 titles *Founded:* 1922

Eugène **Wahle**+, 14 A rue du Mèry, B–4000 Liège Tel: (041) 322113
Subjects: History, Art, Archaeology
1977: 5 titles *1978:* 3 titles
ISBN Publisher's Prefix: 2-87011

Wastiau-Jeukens+*, 9 rue de l'Industrie, B–1010 Brussels Tel: (02) 2303425
Dirs: R Wastiau, R Jeukens
Subjects: Arts, Literature, Linguistics
Founded: 1951
ISBN Publisher's Prefix: 2-87005

Wereldbibliotheek NV*, Leeuwerikstr 23, B–2000 Antwerp Tel: (031) 323642
Dir: L Reinalda
Subjects: Education, Sport & Games, Juveniles, General
Founded: 1947
ISBN Publisher's Prefix: 90-284

Maison d'Editions Ad **Wesmael**-Charlier SA+, 69 rue de Fer, B–5000 Namur Tel: (081) 220148
Subjects: Secondary & Primary Textbooks
Bookshops: At above address and 62 rue de la Loi, Brussels
1977: approx 100 titles *Founded:* 1790

Winkelhaak PVBA*, Perenstr 15, B–2000 Antwerp Tel: (031) 367055
Dir: R van Hevel
Founded: 1973

J B **Wolters** Leuven NV*, Blijde Inkomststr 50, B–3000·Louvain Tel: (016) 233488 Telex: 24525
Man Dir: W Vanden Eynde
Parent Company: NV ICU-België, Belgium (qv)
Subjects: Instruction and Education, Secondary & Primary Textbooks, Educational Materials
1977: 67 titles *Founded:* 1959
ISBN Publisher's Prefix: 90-309

Zuidnederlandse Uitgeverij NV+, Cleydaellaan 8, B–2630 Aartselaar, Antwerp Tel: (031) 878300 Telex: 31739 ZUIDB
Publishers: Emmanuel de Vocht, Joris Schaltin; *Sales:* Jan van de Velden; *Production:* Eric Feyten; *Rights & Permissions:* Wilfried Wuyts
Associated Companies: Centrale Uitgeverij, Netherlands; Editions Chantecler, France
Imprint: Deltas
Subjects: General Fiction and Nonfiction, Children's Books
1977: 288 titles *Founded:* 1946
ISBN Publisher's Prefix: 90-243

Literary Agents

Agence belge des grandes Editions SA*, 110–116 ave Louise, B-1050 Brussels Tel: (02) 6474902

Firma **Denis** & Co PVBA*, Sterckshoflei 28–30, B-2100 Deurne

A van **Hageland**, Blutsdelle 10, B-1641 Alsemberg (Beersel) Tel: 02-358 27 52.
General Manager: Albert van Hageland.
Represents authors, publishers and agencies in and for the Dutch and French territories.
Specialization: Fantasy and Science Fiction; Anthologies. Only printed works (no manuscripts)

International Literair Agentschap*, Blankenbergestr 23, B-9000 Ghent
Contact: Dr Hugo Tomme

Book Clubs

A B C (Aurelia Book Club)*, Bonekruidlaan 30, B-1020 Brussels
Owned by: Aurelia Books

L'**Académie** du Livre SA, 3 rue du Palais St Jacques, B-7500 Tournai Tel: (069) 226130

Atlanta NV, Brasschaatsteenweg 200, B-2180 Kalmthout Tel: (031) 667171
Owned by: Beckers Groep

Beckers NV Uitgeverij*, Brasschaatsteenweg 200, B-2180 Kalmthout Tel: (031) 667171
Owned by: Beckers Groep

Boekengilde de **Clauwaert***, Koning Albertlaan 17, B-3040 Korbeek-Lo, Louvain

D A P Reinaert Uitgaven*, Industriepark B4, B-9140 Zele

Interbooks, Holleweg 70, B-2550 Kontich Tel: (031) 570816/571395 Telex: 35521 INBOOK B

Editions **Rencontre***, 4 rue du Lombard, B-1080 Brussels

Major Booksellers

Audivox*, Rubenslei 23, B-2000 Antwerp Tel: (031) 328465
(Wholesalers of Imported Educational Books)

Boekhandel **Belis-Vinck***, Lange Leemstr 41, B-2000 Antwerp Tel: (031) 327448

Librairie **Bellens***, 13 rue de la Wache, B-4000 Liège Tel: (041) 237860

Librairie **Castaigne***, 34 rue du Fosse-aux-Loups, B-1000 Brussels Tel: (02) 2170424

Librairie **Halbart***, 11 rue des Carmes, B-4000 Liège Tel: (041) 232125

Boekhandel **Heideland***, Grote Markt 1, B-3500 Hasselt Tel: (011) 224505

Office international de Librairie*, 30 ave Marnix, B-1050 Brussels Tel: (021) 5136675

Standaard Hoofdstadboekhandel*, Adolf Maxlaan 146, B-1000 Brussels

E **Story**-Scientia PVBA, B-9000 Ghent, 8 P Van Duyseplein Tel: (091) 255757
Managers: E and J Story, L van Opdenbosch
(Also Importers)

Libris **Toison** d'Or SA, 29 ave de la Toison d'Or, B-1060 Brussels Tel: (02) 5116400 Telex: 24084

U O P C*, 216 chaussée de Wavre, B-1040 Brussels Tel: (02) 6489689

Librairie **Vanderlinden***, 17 rue des Grands-Carmes, B-1000 Brussels Tel: (02) 5116140

Boekhandel het **Volk**, Forelstr 22, B-9000 Ghent

Major Libraries

Archives générales du Royaume*, 2–6 rue de Ruysbroeck, B-1000 Brussels
National Archives

Bibliothèque royale Albert Ier (Koninklijke Bibliotheek Albert I)*, 4 blvd de l'Empereur, B-1000 Brussels Tel: (02) 5136180

Deutsche Bibliothek — Goethe Institut Brüssel*, rue Belliard 58, B-1040 Brussels

Bibliothèque **Fonds** Quetelet, 6 rue de l'Industrie, Brussels Tel: (02) 5127950
Library of the Ministry of Economic Affairs
Librarian: J de Buck
Publications: Accroissements de la Bibliotheque Centrale (Fonds Quetelet), monthly

Institut royal des Sciences naturelles de Belgique, Service de Documentation*, 31 rue Vautier, B-1040 Brussels

Katholieke Universiteit Leuven, Universiteitsbibliotheek, Bibliotheekcentrale, Mgr Ladeuzeplein 21, B-3000 Leuven Tel: (016) 238678 Telex: Kulbib 25715
Librarian: W Dehennin

Bibliothèque centrale du **Ministère de l'Education** nationale*, 27 rue de Louvain, B-1000 Brussels

Bibliothèque Universitaire **Moretus Plantin**, 19 rue Grangagnage, B-5000 Namur
Librarian: R P Matagne

Bibliothèque du **Musée royal de Mariemont**, 100 chaussée de Mariemont, B-6510 Morlanwelz-Mariemont Tel: (064) 221243/226563
Librarian: M-B Delattre

Museum Plantin-Moretus, Vrijdagmarkt 22, B-2000 Antwerp Tel: (031) 322455/330688

Bibliothèque du **Parlement***, 2 Palais de la Nation, pl de la Nation, Brussels

Bibliotheek van de **Rijksuniversiteit te Gent***, Rozier 9, B-9000 Ghent Tel: (091) 233821/257571/257611

Bibliotheek der Universitaire Faculteiten **Sint-Ignatius**, Prinsstr 13, B-2000 Antwerp

Stadsbibliotheek*, Hendrik Conscienceplein 4, Antwerp
Municipal Library

Bibliothèque centrale de l'**Université Catholique de Leuven**, see Katholieke Universiteit Leuven

Bibliothèque générale de l'**Université de Liège**, Place Cockerill 1, B-4000 Liège Tel: (041) 420080

Bibliothèques de l'**Université libre de Bruxelles**, 50 ave Franklin D Roosevelt, B-1050 Brussels Tel: 6490030

Library Associations

Association belge de Documentation, BP 110, B-1040 Brussels 26
Belgian Association for Documentation
Secretary: J C Smeets
Publication: Cahiers de la Documentation

Association des Archivistes et Bibliothécaires de Belgique*, Bibliothèque royale, Albert Ier, 4 blvd de l'Empereur, B-1000 Brussels
Belgian Association of Archivists and Librarians
General Secretary: Raphaël de Smedt
Publication: Archives et Bibliothèques de Belgique

Association des Bibliothécaires-Documentalistes de l'Institut d'Etudes sociales de l'Etat*, 24 rue de l'Abbaye, B-1050 Brussels Tel: 6493443
Association of Librarians and Documentalists of the State Institute of Social Studies
Secretary: Claire Gerard
Publication: Flash

Association des Bibliothécaires et du Personnel des Bibliothèques des Ministères de Belgique*, 22 rue des petits Carmes, B-1000 Brussels
Association of Librarians and Library Personnel in Belgian Government Departments
President: G Braive

Association nationale des Bibliothécaires d'Expression française*, 56 rue de la Station, B-5370 Havelange
National Association of French-speaking Librarians
Executive Secretary: J Peraux
Publications: Le Bibliothécaire: Revue d'Information culturelle et bibliographique

Centre national de Documentation scientifique et technique, 4 blvd de l'Empereur, B-1000 Brussels
Publications: Catalogue collectif belge et luxembourgeois des Périodiques étrangers en cours de publication; Inventaire permanent des Institutions belges de Recherche disposant d'une Bibliothèque ou d'un Centre de Documentation

Conseil national des Bibliothèques d'Hôpitaux, Croix-Rouge de Belgique, 98 chaussée de Vleurgat, B-1050 Brussels
National Council of Hospital Libraries
Librarian/Secretary: Françoise Delsemme
Publications: Issues annual report, Proceedings of workshops, seminars; book selections for hospital patients

Fédération nationale des Bibliothèques Catholiques*, 21 rue du Marais, B-1000 Brussels
National Federation of Catholic Libraries

Institut belge d'Information et de Documentation (INBEL), 3 rue Montoyer, B-1040 Brussels Tel: (02) 5126688 Telex: Inbel Bru 21716
Dir: F Coppieters

Vereniging van Religieus-Wetenschappelijke Bibliothecarissen, Minderbroederstr 5, B-3800 St Truiden
Association of Theological Librarians
Secretary: K Van de Casteele, Elsbos 16, B-2520 Edegem
Publication: VRB-Informatie (quarterly)

Vlaamse Vereniging van Bibliotheek-, Archief en Documentatie-Personeel*, Frans van Heymbecklaan 4–6, B-2100 Deurne Tel: (031) 252470
Flemish Association of Librarians, Archivists and Documentalists
General Secretary: J Bogaert
Publications: Bibliotheekgids (three monthly)

Library Reference Books and Journals

Books

Inventaire permanent des Institutions belges de Recherche disposant d'une Bibliothèque ou d'un Centre de Documentation Directory of Belgian Research Libraries and Documentation Services), National Centre for Scientific and Technical Documentation, 4 blvd de l'Empereur, B-1000 Brussels

Journals

Archives et Bibliothèques de Belgique (Archief- en Bibliotheekwezen in België) (Archives and Libraries of Belgium), (text in Dutch, English, French German, Italian, Latin and Spanish), Belgian Association of Archivists and Librarians, 4 blvd de l'Empereur, B-1000 Brussels

Le Bibliothécaire (The Librarian), National Association of French-speaking Librarians, 56 rue de la Station, B-5370 Havelange

Bibliotheekgids (Library Guide), Flemish Association of Librarians, Archivists and Documentalists, Blindestr 19, B-2000 Antwerp

Bulletin de Documentation (Verkeersdocumentatie Bulletin) (Bulletin of Documentation), (text in Dutch, English, French and German), Ministère des Communications et des PTT, 62 rue de la Roi, B-1040 Brussels

Cahiers de la Documentation (Bladen voor de Documentatie) (Journal of Documentation), (text in Dutch, English, French), Belgian Association for Documentation, 90 ave des Armures, B-1190 Brussels

Literary Associations and Societies

Académie royale de Langue et de Littérature françaises*, Palais des Académies, 1 rue Ducale, Brussels
Permanent Secretary: Georges Sion
Publications: Bulletin, Annuaire, Mémoires

Académie royale des Sciences, des Lettres et des Beaux-Arts de Belgique*, Palais des Académies, 1 rue Ducale, Brussels
Permanent Secretary: Maurice Leroy
Publications: Monthly Bulletin, Memoirs, Year Book

Association des Ecrivains belges de langue française*, Maison des Ecrivains, 150 chaussée de Wavre, B-1050 Brussels Association of Belgian Writers in the French Language
Secretary-General: Philippe Delaby
Publications: Nos Lettres Informations (ten a year)

Commission belge de Bibliographie, 80-84 rue des Tanneurs, B-1000 Brussels
Secretary: E Cosyns-Verhaegen
Publications: Bulletin (quarterly), *Bibliographia Belgica, Coll*

Icon, Lobergenbos 27, B-3200 Louvain
Secretary: Jozef Peeters
Association on marginal literature and art
Publication: Cahier Jean Ray (annual) in Dutch, English & French

The **Dickens** Fellowship*, Blvd Albert-Elisabeth 101, B-7000, Mons
Honorary Secretary: Georges C Haincourt

Koninklijke Academie voor Nederlandse Taal- en Letterkunde, Koningstr 18, B-9000 Ghent
Royal Academy of Dutch Language and Literature
Permanent Secretary: M Hoebeke

Koninklijke Academie voor Wetenschappen, Letteren en Schone Kunsten van België, Paleis der Academiën Hertogsstraat 1, B-1000 Brussels
Royal Academy of Science, Letters and Fine Arts
Permanent Secretary: G Verbeke
Publications: Proceedings, Memoirs, Year Book, Reports and Proposals, Special Editions

International **P E N Club, Flemish Centre**, Albert Heyrbautlaan 48, B-1710 Dilbeek
General Secretary: Willem M Roggeman
Publication: PEN-Club Tijolingen

International **P E N Club, Belgian French Centre**, 76 avenue du 11 novembre 76, BP 7, B-1040 Brussels
President: Baron de Radzitzky
General Secretary: Raymond Quinot

Société belge des Auteurs, Compositeurs et Editeurs (SABAM), 75-77 rue d'Arlon, B-1040 Brussels Tel: (02) 232660
Belgian Society of Authors, Composers and Publishers
Man Dirs: Joseph Dethier, Ernest van der Eyken
Publication: Bulletin (quarterly)

Société de Langue et de Littérature wallones ASBL, Université de Liège, 7 pl du XX août, B-4000 Liège
Secretary: Jean Rathmès
Publications: Bulletin de la Société de Langue et de Littérature wallonnes, Dialectes de Wallonie (both periodically), Literary & Philological collections

Société royale des Bibliophiles et Iconophiles de Belgique, blvd de l'Empereur 4, B-1000 Brussels
Director: Eugéne Rouir

Vereeniging der Antwerpsche Bibliophielen, Museum Plantin-Moretus, Vrijdagmarkt 22, B-2000 Antwerp Tel: (031) 322455
Editorial Secretary: Dr L Voet
Publications: De Gulden Passer (annual)

Literary Periodicals

Dietsche Warande en Belfort, journal for literature, art and spiritual life, Standaard Boekhandel NV, Belgiëlei 147a, B-2000 Antwerp

Flambeau (Torch), Belgian review of political and literary questions, 75 ave Emile de Beco, Brussels 5

Livres et Disques (Books and Records), Centre d'Action culturelle de la Communauté d'Expression française, 12 rue Saintraint, B-5000 Namur

Mandragora, journal for literature and art, (text in Dutch), Acacalaan 58, B-9620 Zottegem

Marginales (Marginalia), review of ideas and letters, Albert Ayguesparse, 118 rue Marconi, B-1180 Brussels

Nieuw Vlaams Tijdschrift (New Flemish Journal), Leeuwerikstr 41, Antwerp

Revue générale belge (General Belgian Review), 21 rue de la Limité, B-1030 Brussels

Revue nouvelle (New Review), 305 ave van Volxem, B-1190 Brussels

Ruimten (text in Dutch and German), Antwerpsesteenweg 488, Hoboken, Antwerp

Scarabée, Centre européen de Diffusion de la Culture, 137 rue de Livourne, Brussels

Streven, Sanderusstr 5, B-2000 Antwerp

Trefpunt (Meeting-point), Blankenbergs Literair Archief Trefpunt, Kerkstr 41, Te Blankenberge

Literary Prizes

Goblet d'**Alviella** Prize
For the best work of a strictly scientific and objective character relating to the history of religions, published by a Belgian author. 40,000 francs. Awarded every five years. Winner for tenth period (1971–1975), Michel Malaise. Enquiries to Académie Royale de Belgique, Palais des Académies, Brussels

Lode **Baekelmans** Prize
For the best literary work in Dutch — novel, poetry, play, radio play, essay, etc — dealing with the sea, sailors, navigation, the harbour, inland navigation or related topics. A prize of 40,000 BFr is awarded every 3 years: the recipients must be Belgian nationals. Enquiries to the Royal Academy of Dutch Language and Literature, Koningstr 18, B-9000 Ghent.

Beernhaert Prize*
For the most outstanding work of a Belgian author written in French language. Awarded annually. Enquiries to Royal Academy of French Language and Literature, Palais des Académies, 1 rue Ducale, Brussels

Belgian Government Prizes for Literature (Ministry of Flemish Culture)
Triennial State Prizes for prose, poetry, drama, essay and youth and children's literature. A triennial Great State Prize for a Literary Career. Each year two of these prizes may be awarded. The ordinary prizes amount to 200,000 Francs and the Great State Prize to 400,000 Francs. Enquiries to Ministerie van de Nederlandse Gemeenschap, Kolonliënstr 29-31, B-1000 Brussels

Belgian Government Prizes for Literature (Ministry of French Culture)*
An annual State Prize for Literature, in turn awarded for prose, drama and poetry. A quinquennial State Prize for Critique and Essay and a quinquennial State Prize for a Literary Career are also awarded. The annual State Prize amounts to 125,000 Francs, the Prize for Critique and Essay to 150,000 Francs, and the State Prize for a Literary Career to 200,000 Francs. An increase of these amounts is under consideration. Enquiries to Ministerie van Nationale Opvoeding en Nederlandse Cultuur, Kolonlënstr 29-31, B-1000 Brussels

Ernest **Bouvier-Parviliez** Prize*
For the entire work of a Belgian author written in French. Awarded every four years. Enquiries to Royal Academy of French Language and Literature, Palais des Académies, 1 rue Ducale, Brussels

Adelson **Castiau** Prize
For the Belgian author of the best work on means of improving the moral, intellectual and physical conditions of the poor (works relating to the lower middle classes are also admissible). 40,000 francs. Awarded every three years. No prize awarded for twenty-

fifth period (1975-1977). Last winner (1969-1971), Mme Nicole Lahaye. Enquiries to Académie Royale de Belgique, Palais des Académies, Brussels

Felix **Denayer** Prize*
For a single work or the entire literary work of a Belgian written in French. Awarded annually. Enquiries to Royal Academy of French Language and Literature, Palais des Académies, 1 rue Ducale, Brussels

Jules **Duculot** Prize
For a work in print or manuscript form, written in French, dealing with the history of philosophy. Awarded only to Belgians, or to foreigners holding an academic grade granted by a Belgian university. Printed work must have been published in the five years prior to the end of the relevant period. The prize is awarded for what appears the most deserving work, irrespective of whether it has been submitted for entry or not. 70,000 francs. Awarded every five years. Winner for the second period (1971-1975), Claude Troisfontaines. Enquiries to Académie Royale de Belgique, Palais des Académies, Brussels

Charles **Duvivier** Prize
For the Belgian author of the best work on the history of Belgian or foreign law, or on the history of Belgian political, judicial or administrative institutions. 40,000 francs. Awarded every three years. Winner for twenty-fourth period (1976-1978), M Magits. Enquiries to Académie Royale de Belgique, Palais des Académies, Brussels

Joseph **Gantrelle** Prize*
For a work in classical philology. 40,000 francs. Awarded biennially. Enquiries to Royal Academy of Science, Letters and Fine Arts, Division of Letters and Moral and Political Sciences, Palais des Académies, 1 rue Ducale, Brussels

Grand Franco-Belgian Literary Prize, see French literary prizes

Tobie **Jonckheere** Prize
For a work, in published or manuscript form, devoted to the educational sciences. 35,000 francs. Awarded every three years. Winners for seventh period (1974-1976), Mesdames Cl Botson and M Deliège. Enquiries to Académie Royale de Belgique, Palais des Académies, Brussels

Eugène **Lameere** Prize
For the best work in history teaching intended for use in primary or intermediate schools or teachers' training colleges in Belgium, in which pictures play an important rôle in the comprehension of the text. 45,000 francs. Awarded every five years. Winners for fourteenth period (1970-1975), Jean George and Jean Lefèvre. Enquiries to Académie Royale de Belgique, Palais des Académies, Brussels

Malpertuis Prize*
For an outstanding contribution to Belgian literature in the field of drama, poetry, short story or essay written in French. Awarded biennially. Enquiries to the Royal Academy of French Language and Literature, Palais des Académies, 1 rue Ducale, Brussels

Joseph-Edmond **Marchal** Prize
For the Belgian author of the best work, in print or in manuscript form, on national antiques or archaeology. 50,000 francs. Awarded every five years. Winners for twelfth period (1973-1977), Georges Rapsaet, Marie-Thérèse Rapsaet-Charlier, Monique Lesenne. Enquiries to Académie Royale de Belgique, Palais des Académies, Brussels

Albert **Mockel** Grand Prize for Poetry*
For the best Belgian poet writing in French. Awarded every five years. Enquiries to Royal Academy of French Language and Literature, Palais des Académies, 1 rue Ducale, Brussels

Emil **Polak** Prize*
For a distinguished literary work written in French, preferably by a poet. Awarded biennially. Enquiries to Royal Academy of French Language and Literature, Palais des Académies, 1 rue Ducale, Brussels

Victor **Rossel** Prize*
For the best novel of the year written in French by a Belgian author. 125,000 francs. Awarded annually. Enquiries to 'Le Soir' 112 rue Royale, Brussels

Saint-Genois Prize
For the author of the best historical or literary work written in Dutch. 50,000 francs. Awarded every five years. Winner for seventeenth period (1970-1975), John Everaert. Enquiries to Académie Royale de Belgique, Palais des Académies, Brussels

Suzanne **Tassier** Prize
For a Belgian woman who, following study at a Belgian university, has obtained at least a doctorate. The prize is awarded for a major scientific work, dealing with a subject from history, law, philology or the social sciences: failing a meritorious work from one of these branches, then for a subject from the natural sciences, medicine or mathematics. Preference will be given to a work of an historical nature, in its widest sense. 50,000 francs. Awarded every two years. Winner for the tenth period (1975-1976), Mme L Hadermann-Misguich. Enquiries to Académie Royale de Belgique, Palais des Académies, Brussels

Auguste **Teirlinck** Prize*
For a contribution to Flemish literature. 35,000 francs. Awarded every five years. Enquiries to Royal Academy of Science, Letters and Fine Arts, Division of Letters and Moral and Political Sciences, Palais des Académies, 1 rue Ducale, Brussels

Carton de **Wiart** Prize*
For a book in the field of literary history or on subjects which relate to Belgian life. Alternately awarded for a work in French and in Flemish. 10,000 francs. Awarded every five years. Enquiries to Belgian Ministry of National Education, 155 rue de la Loi, B-1040 Brussels

Translation Agencies and Associations

Centre belge de Traduction, 4 blvd de l'Empereur, B-1000 Brussels Tel: (02) 5136180 Ext 561 Telex: 21157
Dir: Mme I Clemens

Belize

General Information

Language: English (and Spanish)
Religion: Catholic and various Protestant denominations
Population: 149 million
Bank Hours: 0900-1500 Monday, Tuesday, Thursday, Friday; 0900-1130 Wednesday and Saturday
Shop Hours: 0730-1130, 1300-1600 Monday-Saturday (some open 1900-2100 evenings); generally early closing Wednesday
Currency: 100 cents = 1 Belize dollar
Export/Import Information: No tariff on books, but advertising 45% duty. General licence. Nominal exchange controls
Copyright: Berne, UCC (see International section)

Major Booksellers

Belize Book Shop*, 14 Albert St Tel: 2054

Beuhler's Shoppe*, Fort George Hotel Lobby Tel: 3491

Cathedral Bookshop*, 144 North Front St Tel: 2757

Christian Literature, Christian Literature Centre, PO Box 76 (Located at: 14 New Rd) Tel: 2593

The **Emporium***, 2 Bishop St Tel: 2566

Major Libraries

National Library Service, The Central Library, PO Box 287, Bliss Institute, Belize City Tel: 3367
Chief Librarian: L G Vernon

Library Association

Belize Library Association*, Central Library, PO Box 287, Bliss Institute, Belize City

Benin

General Information

Language: French
Religion: equally divided among Muslim, Christian, and traditional religions
Population: 3.29 million
Bank Hours: 0800-1130, 1430-1530 Monday-Friday
Shop Hours: 0800-1200, 1430-1730 Monday-Saturday. Larger ones close Monday, some open for a few hours Sunday morning
Currency: franc CFA
Export/Import Information: 2% tariff on books of non-EEC origin; 7% on atlases. Advertising matter (unless single copy) 25%, or 37% from non-EEC countries. 5% C.I.F. price Amortization Tax; Stamp tax (4% of duty paid) and small additional taxes. Import licence required. Exchange controls for non-franc zone.
Copyright: Berne (see International section)

Publishers

Government Printer*, BP 59, Porto Novo

Major Booksellers

Centre de Littérature Chrétienne*, BP 34, Cotonou

Librairie A B M*, Cotonou

Librairie-Papetiere **A B M***, Porto Novo

Librairie **Drouot** (Ets Robert Drouot)*, BP 33, Cotonou Tel: 3451

La **Maison** du Livre*, BP 341, Cotonou

Librairie **Nationale** (Ministère Education National)*, Porto Novo

Librairie SA Gaston **Nègre***, BP 52, Cotonou

Librairie **Notre Dame***, Ave Clozel, BP 714, Cotonou

Librairie **Protestante***, Ave Proche, BP 34, Cotonou

Major Libraries

Archives nationales de la République Populaire du Benin*, BP 3, Porto Novo
Director: A S Tidjari

Bibliothèque nationale (National Library)*, BP 401, Porto Novo Tel: 212585
Publication: Bibliographie nationale (in preparation)

Bibliothèque de l'**Université** du Benin*, BP 526, Cotonou

Bermuda

General Information

Language: English
Religion: Anglican
Population: 57,000
Literacy Rate (1960): 97.6%
Bank Hours: 0930-1500 Monday-Thursday; 0930-1500, 1630-1800 Friday
Shop Hours: 0900-1700 Monday-Saturday
Currency: 100 cents = 1 Bermuda dollar
Export/Import Information: No tariff on books and advertising matter. No import licence. Exchange controls on imports valued over $100
Copyright: Berne, UCC (see International section)

Publishers

Bermuda Press Ltd*, Reid St, Hamilton
Subject: Literature

Bermudian Publishing Co*, PO Box 283, Hamilton 5
Subjects: Law, Economics

Royal Gazette Ltd*, Reid St, Hamilton
Subject: Literature

Major Booksellers

Baxters*, Burnaby St, Hamilton Tel: 23292

Bermuda Book Store Ltd*, Queen St, Hamilton Tel: 53698

The **Book Mart***, Above annex on Reid St Tel: 51647

Major Libraries

Bermuda Archives, Par-la-Ville, Hamilton

Bermuda Library, Par-la-Ville, Hamilton 5-31 Tel: 52905
Librarian: Mary Skiffington

Bolivia

General Information

Language: Spanish
Religion: Roman Catholic
Population: 5.95 million
Literacy Rate (1950): 29.7%
Bank Hours: 0900-1200, 1400-1630 Monday-Friday
Shop Hours: 0900-1200, 1400-1800 Monday-Friday; 0900-1200 Saturday
Currency: 100 centavos = 1 peso Boliviano
Export/Import Information: No tariffs on books, except for 10% on luxury bindings. 10% ad valorem on children's picture books, 5% on atlases. Advertising matter dutied 10 pesos per kg gross weight and 5% ad valorem. 2% Services Rendered Tax on all. No import licences, except for textbooks, but no pornography allowed. No advertising that includes imitation money, stamps, etc allowed. No exchange controls
Copyright: Buenos Aires (see International section)

Book Trade Organization

Cámara Boliviana del Libro, Librería Selecciones*, Casilla 682, La Paz
Secretary: P Lewy S
Bolivian Booksellers' Association

Book Trade Reference Books and Journals

Books

Informativo Amigol literario ('Literary Friend'), Los Amigos del Libro, Casilla 450, Cochabamba

Journals

Bibliografía Boliviana, Los Amigos del Libro, Casilla 450, Cochabamba

Boletin Bibliografico Boliviano (text in Spanish, summaries in English and Spanish), Ediciones ISLA, Casilla N4311, La Paz

Publishers

Ediciones los **Amigos** del Libro*, Calle Mercado 1315, Casilla 4415, La Paz Tel: 22794 Cable Add: Amigol
Parent Company: Editorial los Amigos del Libro (qv)
Bookshop: Librería los Amigos del Libro: address as above
1977: 6 titles *Founded:* 1977

Editorial Los **Amigos** del Libro, Casilla 450, Cochabamba Tel: 2920 Cable Add: Amigol
Man Dir: Werner Guttentag; *Sales Dir:* Peter Lewy; *Foreign Sales Manager:* Eva Guttentag; *Production:* J Flores
Associate Companies: Grijalbo Boliviana Ltda (qv); Librería Interamericana, La Paz
Subsidiary Company: Ediciones los Amigos del Libro (qv)
Bookshops: Libreria Universal Bookstore, Casilla 4415, La Paz; Librería Los Amigos del Libro, Mercado 1315, La Paz (and other branches)
Subjects: Bolivia, South America
1977: 40 titles *1978:* 48 titles *Founded:* 1945

Editorial **Difusión**, Casilla 1510, La Paz (Located at: Ave 16 Julio 1601, La Paz) Tel: 328126
Man Dir: Jorge F Catalano; *Publicity & Advertising:* Carmelo Andrade
Bookshop: Librería Difusion, same address
Subjects: Bolivian literature & history, Politics, Social Studies
1978: 75 titles *Founded:* 1960

Editorial y Librería **Don Bosco***, Ave 16 de Julio 1899, Casilla 4458, La Paz
Bookshop: Address as above
Subject: Religion

Universidad Boliviana Tomás **Frías**, Div de Extensión Universitaria*, Casilla 36, Potosí
Subjects: Literature, History

Gisbert y Cia SA, Comercio 1270-80*, Casilla 195, La Paz Tel: 28484 Cable Add: Gisbercia
Dir: José Javier Gisbert
Subjects: Belles Lettres, History, Law, Textbooks

Grijalbo Bolivia Ltda*, Apdo 4415, La Paz
Publicity: Peter Lewy
Parent Company: Editorial Grijalbo SA, Mexico (qv)

Librería y Editorial **Juventud***, Plaza Murillo 519, Casilla 1489, La Paz
Tel: 41694 Cable Add: Juventud
Man Dir: Rafael Urquizo; *Assistant Dir, Publicity:* Gustavo Urquizo; *Sales:* Jefe de Ventas, Nancy de Aramayo; *Production:* Rafael Urquizo Mendoza
Orders to: Casilla 1459, La Paz
Subsidiary Company: Empresa Editora Urquizo SA
Br Off: Calle Mercado, Ayacucho
Subjects: Literature, Biography, History, Social Science, University, Secondary & Primary Textbooks; General Cultural Subjects
Bookshop: At above address
1977: 30 titles *Founded:* 1946

Universidad Mayor de San Andres*, Editorial Universitaria, Casilla 6548, La Paz

Major Booksellers

Librería Los **Amigos** del Libro*, Calle Mercado 1315, Casilla 4415, La Paz Tel: 22794 (7 other branches)

Librería **Difusión***, Ave 16 de Julio 1601, Apdo 1510, La Paz Tel: 28126

Librería **Don Bosco***, Ave 16 de Julio 1899, Casilla 204, La Paz Tel: 22191

Gisbert y Cía SA*, Calle Comercio 1270-80, Casilla 195, La Paz Tel: 28484

Librería **Icthus***, Ave 16 de Julio 1800, Casilla 8353, La Paz Tel: 54007

Librería **Juventud**, Plaza Murillo 519, Casilla 1489, La Paz Tel: 341694

Librería **La Paz**, Ingavi esq Yanacocha, Casilla 539, La Paz Tel: 53323

Librería **Selecciones***, Casilla 972, La Paz Tel: 24159

Alfonso **Tejerina** Ltda*, Comercio 1073, Casilla 834, La Paz

Librería **Universal Bookstore**, Casilla 4415, La Paz

Major Libraries

Biblioteca Universitaria Departamento de Bibliotecas Universidad Boliviana Tomás Frías*, CP 54, Potosí

Dir: Adolfo Vera del Carpio
Publications: Boletin de la Biblioteca Universitaria and occasional papers

Biblioteca ye Archivo Nacional de Bolivia (National Library and Archives)*, Calle Bolívar, Sucre

Biblioteca del **Congreso** Nacional*, Palacio Legislativo, La Paz

Biblioteca de la **Dirección de Cultura** (Library of Cultural Affairs Administration)*, Alcaldía Municipal, Casilla 1856, La Paz

Biblioteca Central de la **Universidad Mayor de San Andrés**, Ave Villazón 1995, Casilla 6548, La Paz

Biblioteca Central de la **Universidad Mayor de San Francisco Xavier***, Plaza 25 de Mayo, Apdo 212, Sucre

Biblioteca Central de la **Universidad Mayor de San Simón***, Ave Oquendo-Sucre, Cochabamba

Library Associations

Asociación Boliviana de Bibliotecarios (A B B), Casilla 658, Cochabamba
President: Dr Efraín Virreira Sánchez
Bolivian Library Association

Centro Nacional de Documentación Científica y Tecnológica, Casilla correo 3283, La Paz
Dir: Hugo Loaiza-Terán
National Scientific and Technological Documentation Centre

Centro Nacional de Documentación e Información Educativa*, c/o Ministerio de Educación y Cultura, La Paz
Dir: Rosa Melgar de Ipiña
National Centre of Documentation and Education Information

Literary Periodicals

Cultura Boliviana, Universidad Tecnica de Oruro, Departamento de Extension Cultural, Oruro

Presencia Literaria, Casilla 1913, La Paz

Literary Associations and Societies

P E N Club de Bolivia (Centro Internacional de Escritores) (International PEN Centre)*, Calle Goitia 17, Casilla 149, La Paz
Secretary: Yolanda Bedregal de Cónitzer

Literary Prizes

Bolivian Grand Prize for Literature*
For an outstanding achievement in the field of literature. Enquiries to the Bolivian Government, La Paz

Premio Nacional de **Cultura***
Enquiries to Ministerio de Educación, La Paz

Franjas Prizes*
For the best printing work done in Bolivia. Awarded annually. Enquiries to La Paz Municipal Mayor's Office, La Paz

Premio de Novela 'Erich **Guttentag**'
'Erich Guttentag' prize for novel of the year. First prize 25,000 Bolivian pesos, second prize 10,000 Bolivian pesos. Enquiries to Los Amigos del Libro, Casilla 450, Cochabamba

Franz **Tamayo** Prize*
For outstanding literary work. 25,000 Bolivian pesos, 15,000 pesos and 5,000 pesos. Awarded annually. Enquiries to La Paz Municipal Mayor's Office, La Paz

Botswana

General Information

Language: Setswana and English
Religion: Protestant
Population: 710,000
Bank Hours: 0830-1300 Monday-Friday; 0830-1100 Saturday
Shop Hours: 0800-1300, 1400-1700 or 1800 Monday-Saturday
Currency: South African currency
Export/Import Information: No tariffs on books or advertising matter. No import licence required; no obscene literature. Exchange controls

Book Trade Journals

The National Bibliography of Botswana, Botswana National Library Service, Private Bag 36, Gaborone

Publishers

Government Printer*, PO Box 87, Gaborone

Major Booksellers

Botswana Book Centre, PO Box 91, Gaborone Tel: 52931/2

Via Afrika Botswana Ltd, PO Box 332, Gaborone

Major Libraries

Botswana National Archives*, PO Box 239, Gaborone Tel: 5227

Botswana National Library Service, Private Bag 0036, Gaborone Tel: 52397/52288
Director of Library Services: G Seame

University of Botswana and Swaziland Library, Private Bag 0022, Gaborone Tel: 55115
Publications: Library Handbook, Library Report of the First Five Years 1971-76

Brazil

General Information

Language: Portuguese (some English spoken)
Religion: Roman Catholic
Population: 112 million
Literacy Rate (1970): 66.2%
Bank Hours: Generally 1000-1600 Monday-Friday
Shop Hours: 0900-1700 Monday-Friday (many open much later); 0900-1230 or 1300 Saturday
Currency: 100 centavos = 1 cruzeiro
Export/Import Information: No tariffs on books and advertising, but 85% ad valorem on luxury bindings, 100% on children's picture books. Import licences and exchange controls
Copyright: UCC, Berne, Buenos Aires, Florence (see International section)

Book Trade Organizations

Associação Brasileira de Livreiros Antiquarios (Brazilian Association of Antiquarian Booksellers)*, Rua Cosme Velho 800, Rio de Janeiro

Associação Brasileira do Livro*, Ave 13 de Mayo 23, 16° andar, Rio de Janeiro Tel: 2327173
Director: Alberjano Torres
Brazilian Booksellers' Association

Câmara Brasileira do Livro*, Ave Ipiranga 1267, 10° andar, CEP 01039, São Paulo 2 SP Tel: 333359/362364
Superintendent: José Gorayeb
Brazilian Book Association

Instituto Nacional do Livro*, Edifício Venâncio V, Setor de Diversões Sul, CEP 70000, Brasília Tel: 235628
Dir: María Alice Barroso
National Book Institute

Sindicato Nacional dos Editores de Livros, Ave Rio Branco 37, 15° andar, Salas 1503-6 e 1510-12, CEP 20097, Rio de Janeiro RJ Tel: 2336481/2335484 Cable Add: Sindelivros
Man Dir: Maria H Geordane
Brazilian Publishers' Association
Publications: Boletim Informativo Mensal (monthly bulletin)

Book Trade Reference Books and Journals

Books

O Mundo do Edição Luso-Brasileira (The World of Publishing, Portugal and Brazil), Publicações Europa-Americana, Apdo 8, Mem Martins, Portugal

Journals

Bibliografia Brasileira (Brazilian Bibliography), National Book Institute. Edifício Venâncio V, Setor de Diversões Sul, CEP 70000, Brasília

Bibliografia Classificada (Classified Bibliography), Centre of Investigation and Documentation, CP 23, Petropolis, Rio de Janeiro

Boletim Bibliográfico, National Library, Ave Rio Branco 219-31, ZC-21, Rio de Janeiro, GB

Boletim Bibliográfico Brasileiro (Brazilian Bibliographical Bulletin), Estante Publicações, Ave Rio Branco 138, 11° andar, Rio de Janeiro

O Editor do Livros, Revistas e Jornais (The Publisher of Books, Reviews and Journals), Editôra Métodos Ltda, Rua da Lapa 180, sala 607, CP 15085, Rio de Janeiro, GB

El Libro (The Book), Equilar Editores, Castillan 5, São Paulo 17

Livros Novos (New Books) (text in English and Portuguese), Atlantis Livros Ltda, CP 3752, 01000 São Paulo

Pregão de Livros ('Pawnbroker of Books'), J C Amaral Guimarães, Rua Conde de Sarzedas 246, 01512 São Paulo

Resumo Bibliográfico (Bibliographical Résumé), Brazilian Publishers' Association, Centro de Bibliotécnia, Ave Rio Branco 37, 15° andar, Salas 1503-6 & 1510-12, Rio de Janeiro, RJ

Revisto do Livro (Review of Books), (text in Portuguese and Spanish), Ministerio da Educação e Cultura, of 3068, Brasilia, DF

Publishers

A G I R (Artes Graficas Industrias Reunidas SA), Rua dos Invalidos 198, CP 3291, ZC-00, Rio de Janeiro Tel: 2528261 Cable Add: Agirsa
Man Dir: Alfonso D Faveret; *Editorial:* Ernst Fromm
Br Off: São Paulo, Belo Horizónte
Subjects: Literature, Juveniles, Social Science, Religion
1977: 12 titles *1978:* 7 titles *Founded:* 1944
Bookshop: Livraria Agir Editora, Rua México 98-B, Rio de Janeiro

Abril SA Cultural e Industrial*, Rua do Cortume 585, São Paulo Tel: (011) 2626222 Cable Add: Culturabril Telex: 23227
Man Dir: Roberto Civita; *Planning & Marketing Dir:* Jayme Almeida
Br Offs: Rua do Passeio 56, 11° andar, Lapa 20021, Rio de Janeiro
Subjects: General Literature, Science
Book Club: Círculo do Livro SA (owned jointly with Bertelsmann Aktiengesellschaft, Federal Republic of Germany (qv))
Founded: 1950

Agents Editores Ltda, Rua Almirante Baltazar 349, São Cristovão 20941, Rio de Janeiro RJ Tel: (021) 2845988/2640687/2649988 Cable Add: Agentsrio
Superintendent-Director: Francisco da Gama Lima Netto; *Editorial:* João Sergio Rao
Subjects: Security in Technical and Scientific fields (including Security, Counter-surveillance, Criminal investigation, Intelligence)
1978: 6 titles *1979:* 6 titles *Founded:* 1977

Editora Nova **Aguilar** S/A*, Rua Barão de Itambi 28, Botafogo, Rio de Janeiro RJ Tel: 2667474 Cable Add: Aguilar
Vice-President: Silvia Farré
Br Off: Av Jurema 767, São Paulo CEP 04079
Founded: 1958
Subjects: General Literature

Livraria Francisco **Alves** Editôra SA*, Rua Sete de Setembro 177, Centro, 20050 Rio de Janeiro RJ Tel: 2322009/2324064/2327188 Cable Add: Alvesia Telex: 2121637 LFAE BR
Man Dir: Paulo Roberto Rocco; *Editorial:* Carlos Leal; *Sales:* Harry Costa; *Publicity & Public Relations:* Mauro da Silveira Lobo
Parent Company: Companhia de Navegação Marítima Netumar, Av Presidente Vargas 482-3° 18, 23 e 27 andar, 20071, Rio de Janeiro, RJ, Brasil; Netumar International Inc, 67 Broad St, 28th floor, New York, NY, USA
Associate Company: Editora Vozes Ltda (qv)
Subsidiary Company: Hoje — Os Melhores Livros (The Book Digest Magazine), Rua Barão de Lucena 43, Botafogo, 22260 Rio de Janeiro, RJ
Imprints: São Paulo Editora; Museográfica; Prescolor; AGGS Indústrias Gráficas
Br Offs: Rua Pires de Mota 399, 01529 São Paulo, SP; Rua da Bahia 1060, 30000 Belo Horizonte, MG
Subjects University, High School and Primary Textbooks; Nonfiction, General Fiction, Crime etc.
Bookshops: Rua Farme de Amoedo 57, Ipanema; Rua do Ouvidor 166, Centro; Rua Sete de Setembro 177, Centro; Av Amaral Peixoto 427, loja 121, Nova Iguaçu (all in Rio); Rua da Bahia 1060, Belo Horizonte
1977: 97 titles *1978:* 97 titles *Founded:* 1854

Organização **Andrei** Editora SA*, Rua Conselheiro Nebias 1071, São Paulo SP Tel: 2207246 Cable Add: Carolandre
Dir: Edmondo L Andrei; *Sales Dir:* Alberto Mayer
Subjects: Medicine, Pharmacy, Veterinary Medicine
Founded: 1956

Antenna Edições Técnicas Ltda, Ave Mal Floriano 143, 20080 Rio de Janeiro RJ Tel: (021) 2231799
Man Dir: Gilberto A Penna; *Publicity:* J F Kempner
Associate Company: Seleções Eletronicas Editora Ltd (qv)
Br Off: Rua Vitoria 195, São Paulo
Subjects: Electronics, Telecommunications
Bookshops: Lojas do Livro Eletrônico, Ave Mal Floriano 148, Rio de Janeiro; Rua Vitória 379-383, São Paulo
1977: 5 titles *1978:* 11 titles *Founded:* 1926
Miscellaneous: the Company has its own printing works

Ao Livro Técnico SA Industria e Comércio, Rua Sá Freire 36-40, São Christovãó, Rio de Janeiro 20000 CP 3655 Tel: 2642474/2482566 Cable Add: Litecnico
Man Dir: Reynaldo Max Paul Bluhm; *Editorial:* J M Netto; *Sales:* Reynaldo Bluhm; *Production:* Sebastiao Feital; *Publicity:* Carlos B Figueiredo; *Rights & Permissions:* Paulo E Bluhm
Orders to: Rua sa Freire 36-40, São Christovãó, Rio de Janeiro 20000
Subsidiary Companies: AGIR-Litecnico Ltda; DISAL (Distribuidores Associados de Livros Ltda); LTC (Livros Tecnicos e cientificos Editora SA); A Nossa Livraría; A Nossa Livraría de Belo Horizonte Ltda
Subjects: Technical, Scientific, Children's books, Art, Language Textbooks, English Language Teaching, Schoolbooks
Bookshops: Ao Livro Técnico, Rua Miguel Couto 35, Loja C, ZC- 21, Rio de Janeiro (for other branches see under Booksellers); Diálogo Livraria e Editora Ltda, Rua da Conceição 204/6, Niterói, Rio de Janeiro
1977: 35 titles *Founded:* 1946

Apec Editôra SA, Rua Sorocaba 316, Botafogo, CP 15006, Rio de Janeiro 20000 Tel: 2663597/2663547/2664449/2664249 Cable Add: Editorapec
Br Off: Ave Ipiranga 890, 1° andar, 3 p, São Paulo
Subjects: Economics, Education, Law, History, Sociology, Reference Books

Aquarius Editora e Distribuidora de Livros Ltda, Rua Olavo Egidio 242, Santana, 02037 São Paulo SP Tel: 2902911/2994639
Man Dir: Alfredo Prata Ginja; *Sales:* Manuel Fonesca
1978: 15 titles *1979:* 38 titles *Founded:* 1976

Editôra **Artenova** SA*, Rua Belisário Távora 660, Laranjeiras, 20000 Rio de Janeiro RJ Tel: 2453063/2455649 Cable Add: Artnova
Man Dir: Alvaro Pacheco; *Editorial, Rights & Permissions:* Luzia Regina Alves; *Sales:* João Pacheco; *Publicity:* Nilo Dante de Giovanni
Associate Companies: Artenova Filmes Ltda; Artel Cinematografica Ltda; Studio Artenova de Publicidade Ltda
Br Off: Rua Cartão Abdala Chama 254, Benfica; Rua Prof Vahia de Abreu, 100 Saõ Paulo
Subjects: Literature, Sociology, Psychology, Occultism, Health, Cinema, History
Founded: 1971

Livraría Editôra **Artes** Medicas Ltda, Rua Dr Cesario Motta Jr 63, Vila Buorque, 01221 São Paulo SP Tel: PABX 2219033 Cable Add: LEAM
Man Dir: Henrique Hecht;;; *Editorial, Rights & Permissions:* M Hecht; *Sales:* C dos Santos; *Production:* W Steinhoff; *Publicity:* J Hecht
Subsidiary Companies: Editôra Artes Medicas Sul Ltda, Rua General Vitorino 277, 90000 Porto Alegre; Livraría Artes Medicas Norte Ltda, Recifé
Imprints: AGGS (Artes Graphicas Gomes de Souza SA); São Paulo Industria Grafica e Editora SA
Subjects: Medicine, Dentistry
1977: 15 titles *1978:* 18 titles *Founded:* 1964

Livraria **Atheneu** Ltda, Rua Bambina 74 Lojas A/B, Botafogo, 22251 Rio de Janeiro Tel: 2661295/2264793 Cable Add: Zigadag
Man Dir: Simão Rzezinski; *Editorial Dir, Rights & Permissions:* Paulo da Costa Rzezinski; *Sales Dir:* Marly Amorim Mattos; *Production Dir:* Moacyr Coelho
Br Offs: Rua Senador Dantas 56B, Rio de Janeiro RJ; Rua Jesuino Pascoal 30, Santa Cecilia, São Paulo
Subjects: Medicine, Nursing, Psychology
Bookshops: 25 outlets
1978: 28 titles *1979:* 28 titles *Founded:* 1928

Editora **Atica** SA*, Rua Barão de Iguape 110, Liberdade, CEP 01507, CP 8656 São Paulo Tel: 2789322 Cable Add: Bomlivro
President: Anderson Fernandes Dias*Br Offs:* Rua Barão de Ubá 173, Estácio, 20260, Rio de Janeiro
Subjects: University, Secondary & Primary Textbooks, Pre-school Books, Children's Books, Literature

Editôra **Atlas** SA*, Rua Helvétia 574–578, CP 7186, São Paulo Tel: 2219144 Cable Add: Atlasedita
Man Dir: Luiz Herrmann; *Editorial, Rights & Permissions:* J P Rossetti; *Sales, Publicity:* A B Brandão; *Production:* P Gerencer
Br Off: Rio de Janeiro, Brazilia, Amazonas, Ceará, Goiás, Paraná, Minas Gerais, Rio Grande do Sul, S Catarina
Subjects: Administration, Economics, Financial, Social Sciences
1977: 350 titles *1978:* 400 titles *Founded:* 1944

Atual Editora Ltda, Rua José Antonio Coelho 785, V Mariana, 04011 São Paulo Tel: 717795/5491720
Man Dirs: Gelson Iezzi, Osvaldo Dolce; *Editorial:* Gelson Iezzi; *Sales:* Osvaldo Dolce; *Production:* Iorge Fuzii; *Publicity, Rights & Permissions:* José Roberto Brauner
Associated Companies: Fimac—Distribuidora Livros Ltda, Rua da Bahia

478, Belo Horizonte MG; Editora e Distribuidora Pre-Universitária Ltda, Rua do Príncipe 470, Recife PE
Subject: Didactics
Bookshop: Livraria Alberjano Torres Ltda, Rua Barão de Mesquita 28A, Rio de Janeiro RJ
1978: 15 titles *1979:* 15 titles *Founded:* 1973

Gráfica Editôra **Aurora** Ltda*, CP 7041, ZC–58 Rio de Janeiro (Located at: Rua Frei Caneca 19, Centro, 20211 Rio de Janeiro) Tel: 2220654
Man Dir: Francesco Molinaro; *Sales Dir:* Natale A Molinaro; *Publicity Dir:* Solange de Paula; *Advertising Dir:* Socrates de Paula
Subjects: Secondary & Primary Textbooks, Literature, Pedagogy, How-to, Law, Business, Masonic themes
1978: 160 titles *Founded:* 1945
ISBN Publisher's Prefix: 85-30

Bloch Editores SA*, Rua Frei Caneca 511, Centro, 20211 Rio de Janeiro RJ Tel: 2321338/2831717
Publicity: Paulo Maia Poucinha
Subject: Textbooks

Editôra Edgard **Blücher** Ltda, Rua Pedrosa Alvarenga, 1245–2° andar conj 22, 01000 São Paulo Tel: 648114/815613 Cable Add: Blucherlivro
Man Dir: Edgard Blücher
Subjects: Engineering, Science, Business, University Textbooks
Founded: 1966

Editôra do **Brasil** SA*, Rua Conselheiro Nébias 887–889, Campos Elíseos, CP 4986, 01203 São Paulo SP Tel: 2211663/2220211/2220818 Cable Add: Editabras
Branch Off: Rua do Resende 89, Centro, 20231 Rio de Janeiro RJ
Subjects: Education, Reference, Juveniles, History, Psychology, Sociology

Editora **Brasília**/Rio Ltda*, Rua Muniz Barreto 16, Botafogo, 20000, Rio de Janeiro RJ Tel: 2663428/2869394
Man Dir: Dr José Jobim; *Editorial:* Lygia M Jobim Silveira; *Rights & Permissions:* Gilda Oswaldo Cruz
Subjects: Brazilian Literature, Social Science, Law, Psychology, Pre-school & Juveniles, Fiction, Cinema, Cookery, Law, History
1977: 13 titles *Founded:* 1974

Brasilia Editôra Ltda*, Rua Cinco 15, Jardim da Penha, 29000 Vitória ES Tel: 2271962 Cable Add: Brasilivros
Subjects: Textbooks, Home Economics, Mathematics

Editôra **Brasiliense** SA*, Rua Barão de Itapetininga 93, 12° andar, CP 30644, 01042 São Paulo Tel: 345693/346268 Cable Add: Edibrasa
Man Dir, Editorial, Rights & Permissions: C G Prado; *Sales:* C C Guerrato; *Production:* A Orzari
Subjects: Social Sciences, Humanities, Literature, Education, Juveniles
Bookshop: address as above
1977: 160 titles *Founded:* 1943

Livraría e Editôra Juridica José **Bushatsky** Ltda*, Riachuelo 195, CP 2826, 01007 São Paulo SP Tel: 344148/344149 Cable Add: Bushatsky
Man Dirs: José Bushatsky, Anna Bushatsky; *Sales, Publicity:* José Bushatsky; *Production:* Anna Bushatsky
Subject: Law
Bookshop: Ria Riachuelo 195, São Paulo
1977: 22 titles *Founded:* 1967

C E P A, see Centro Editor de Psicologia Aplicada Ltda

Cadernos Didáticos, Livros Cadernos Ltda*, Rua General Rocca 194, Tijuca, 20521 Rio de Janeiro Tel: 2481211

Editora **Campus** Ltda, Rua Japeri 35, Rio Comprido, 20261 Rio de Janeiro RJ Tel: 2848443/2842638
Man Dir, Editorial: Claudio M Rothmuller; *Sales, Publicity Dir:* Juarez Nery; *Production Dir:* Carlos Hamilton Rocha; *Rights & Permissions:* Emilia Fernandez
Subjects: Textbooks — all fields except Law and Medicine
1978: 14 titles *1979:* 26 titles *Founded:* 1976

Livraría Editôra **Cátedra** Ltda*, Rua Senador Dantas 20, Sala 806–807, Centro 20031 Rio de Janeiro Tel: 2227593
Subjects: Cookery, History, Children's Books, Reference Books, Sociology

Cedibra Editora Brasileira Ltda, Rua Filomena Nunes 162, Olaria, 20000 Rio de Janeiro Tel: 2807272 Cable Add: Edibras
Editorial: Rubens F Lucchetti; *Sales:* Marcos Arruda; *Production:* Albino M Marques; *Rights & Permissions:* Luiz T Rosemberg
Subjects: Juveniles, Fiction, Paperbacks
1978: 1500 titles *1979:* 1500 titles *Founded:* 1952

Centro Editor de Psicologia Aplicada Ltda (CEPA), CP 15131, ZC 06, 20031 Rio de Janeiro RJ (Located at: Rua Senador Dantas 118 s/901–907, Centro, 20031 Rio de Janeiro) Tel: 2427838/2324983 Cable Add: Edicepa
Man Dir: Antonio Rodrigues
Subject: Psychology Textbooks and Tests
1978: 10 titles *1979:* 5 titles *Founded:* 1952

Editôra **Civilização** Brasileira SA, Rua Muniz Barreto 91–93, 22251 Rio de Janeiro RJ Tel: 2869096 Cable Add: Civilização-Rio
Man Dir: Enio Silveira; *Administrative Dir:* Joaquim Ignacio Baptista Cardoso; *Editorial Dir:* Enio Silveira
Br Off: Rua das Palmeiras 260–262, São Paulo; Quadra 309, lojas 3 e 4, 70000 Brasilia DF
Subjects: General Fiction, Belles Lettres, Poetry, Social Science
1977: 167 titles *Founded:* 1932

Concordia SA—Artes Gráficas e Embalagens, CP 6150, 90000 Porto Alegre RS (Located at: Ave São Pedro 633 e 639, 90000 Porto Alegre) Tel: 422859 Cable Add: Concordia
Man Dir: Johanes Gedradt; *Sales, Publicity:* Luiz Ricardo Böttcher
Parent Company: Igreja Evangèlica Luterana do Brasil
Subject: Religion
1978: 10 titles *1979:* 20 titles *Founded:* 1923

Confraria dos Amigos do Livro Ltda*, Rua Maria Angélica 168, Lagoa, 22461 Rio de Janeiro RJ Tel: 2664928 Cable Add: Neofront Telex: 2122319 ENOF BR
Man Dir, Sales & Publicity: Elson Mancen; *Editorial:* Sebastião Lacerda
Parent Company: Editora Nova Fronteira SA (qv)
Subjects: Art books in special editions
1977: 2 titles *Founded:* 1976

Cortez e Moraes Ltda, Rua Ministro Godoy 1002, 05015 São Paulo SP Tel: (011) 8647849
Man Dirs: José Xavier Cortez, Orozimbo José de Moraes
Subjects: Education, Philosophy, Social Service, Literature, Communications
Bookshop: Rua Curt Nimuendajú 19, 05015 São Paulo
1978: 40 titles *1979:* 25 titles *Founded:* 1974

Editôra **Cultrix***, Rua Conselheiro Furtado 648–6° andar, sala 62, 01511 São Paulo SP Tel: 2784811
Man Dir: Diaulas Riedel
Subjects: General Literature, Social & General Science, Economics. Education, Philosophy, History, Children's Books, Psychology, Sociology
Founded: 1956

Editora **Cultura Médica** Ltda, CP 24052, 20550 Rio de Janeiro (Located at: Rua São Francisco Xavier 111, 20550 Rio de Janeiro) Tel: 2349798/2484888
Man Dir, Editorial, Rights & Permissions: Ezequiel Feldman; *Sales, Publicity Dir:* Ivo Feldman; *Production:* João Emanuel Paes de Andrade
Orders to: Av Heitor Beltão 61, Apto 801, Rio de Janeiro
Subject: Medicine
1978: 8 titles *1979:* 15 titles *Founded:* 1966

Difusão Editorial SA (DIFEL), Ave Vieira de Carvalho 40, 5° andar, 01210 São Paulo SP Tel: 2236923/2234619
Man Dir: Fernando Baptista da Silva; *Sales Dir:* Fernando G Barros; *Rights & Permissions:* Karin M Winkler
Subjects: Sociology, History, Geography, General Fiction, Physical Fitness, Arts, Economics, Philosophy, Psychology, Religion
1978: 66 titles *Founded:* 1951

Editora **Documentário** Ltda, Rua Muniz Barreto 12, 22251 Rio de Janeiro Tel: (021) 2666648
Man Dir: Marcos Margulies; *Editorial Dir:* Mario Bendetson; *Production Dir:* Elias Salgado; *Rights & Permissions:* Esther Mellinger
Subjects: Psychology, Sociology, History & Art History, Languages, Publicity & Marketing, Dictionaries, Brazil, Judaism
1978: 38 titles *1979:* 15 titles *Founded:* 1973

Livraría **Duas Cidades** Ltda*, Rua Bento Freitas 158, Vila Buarque, CP 433, CEP 01220 São Paulo SP Tel: 375257
Man Dir: José Petronillo de Santa Cruz; *Sales Dir:* Mitsuro Nagata; *Publicity Dir:* Mara Valles
Branch Off: Ave Rio Branco 9, Sala 116, Centro 20090 Rio de Janeiro RJ
Subjects: Literature, Philosophy, Religion, Psychology, Social Science, University Textbooks
Founded: 1956

E P U, see Editôra Pedagogica e Universitaria Ltda

Ebraesp Editorial Ltda, Rua Pamplona 254, Bela Vista, 01405 São Paulo Tel: 2884904/2848164 Cable Add: Ebraesp
Man Dir, Editorial: Fernando Santos Burguete; *Sales:* Henney Pertusi; *Production:* Antonio Baeza; *Publicity:* Heliodoro Teixeira Bastos; *Rights & Permissions:* Ibrahim Miguel Saad, Yolanda Lhullier Santos
Br Off: Rua Marechal Floriano Peixoto 16, s/Lj 208 e 210, Santos, 11100 São Paulo
Subjects: Philosophy, Anthropology, Communications
1978: 7 titles *1979:* 12 titles *Founded:* 1971

Edart (São Paulo Livraría Editôra Ltda)*, Rua Jaguaribe 47, Vila Buarque, CP 4108, CEP 01224, São Paulo SP Tel:

2214399/2203962, 2219933
Man Dir: Washington Luis José Helou; *Sales Dir:* Henrique Ademar Marques; *Publicity Dir:* Inácio Bueno; *Dir of Editions:* Antonio Orzari
Subjects: Medicine, Science, Technology, Psychology, History, Mathematics, How-to, Textbooks
Founded: 1966

Cía Editôra Americana*, Rua Visconde de Maranguape 15, Lapa, 20000 Rio de Janeiro
Subject: Literature in general

Editôra Interamericana do Brasil Ltda, Rua Coronel Cabrita 8, São Cristovão, CEP 20920 Rio de Janeiro RJ Tel: 2281693/2845645/2487969/2648617 Cable Add: Interbras Telex: 2123036
Man Dir: N B Cordeiro; *Editorial:* G M de Sousa; *Sales, Publicity:* L A de Carvallio; *Production:* J Belmonte
Br Offs: São Paulo, Porto Alegre, Salvador, Belo Horizonte, Recife, Curitiba
Subjects: Medicine and Related Sciences, Psychology, Business, Chemistry, Physical Education, Biology
1978: 16 titles *1979:* 33 titles *Founded:* 1972
Miscellaneous: Firm is an associate company of CIP-CBS International Publishing, USA

Editôra Moderna Ltda*, Rua Dr Elísio de Castro 369, Ipiranga, 04277 São Paulo SP Tel: 2731636
Br Off: Rua dos Araújos 50, Tijuca, 20521, Rio de Janeiro RJ
Subjects: Educational Books, Astronomy, Brazilian Literature

Cía Editôra Nacional*, Rua dos Gusmões 639, Santa Ifigênia, CP 7032, 01212 São Paulo SP Tel: (220) 1308/9881 Cable Add: Editora
Man Dir, Rights & Permissions: Ezio Távora dos Santos; *Editorial:* Carlos Rizzi; *Sales:* J R Breves; *Production:* R de B Lima; *Publicity:* L A Belia
Br Offs: Benjamin Constant 30–32, Glória, 20241 Rio de Janeiro, RJ; Rua dos Andradas 725, Porto Alegre; Dr José Mariano 94, Recife; Rua Sen Manuel Barata 122–130, Belem
Subjects: Pedagogy, History, Philosophy, Psychology, Technical, General & Social Science, Textbooks, Business, Fiction
1977: 199 titles *Founded:* 1925

Editôra Pedagogica e Universitaria Ltda (EPU)*, Praça Dom José Gaspar 106, 3° andar, S/loja 15, São Paulo
Subjects: Scientific, Technical
Founded: 1952

Seleções Eletrônicas Editôra Ltda, Ladeira do Faria 23, CP 771, 20221 Rio de Janeiro RJ Tel: (021) 2232644
Man Dir: Maria B A Penna; *Editorial:* José F Kempner
Associate Company: Antenna Edições Técnicas Ltda (qv)
Subjects: Electronics, Radio and TV Technology, Electricity
1977: 6 titles *Founded:* 1960

Editôra Espiritualista*, CP 7041, ZC-58 Rio de Janeiro (Located at: Rua Frei Caneca 19, Centro, 20211 Rio de Janeiro) Tel: 2220654
Man Dir: Francesco Molinaro; *Sales Dir:* Natale A Molinaro; *Publicity & Advertising Dir:* Socrates de Paula
Subjects: Philosophy, Religion
1978: 150 titles *Founded:* 1945
ISBN Publisher's Prefix: 85-94

Exped-Expansaõ Editorial Ltda, Rua Luís Câmara 319, 21030 Olaria Rio de Janeiro RJ Tel: 2804642 Telex: (021) 23186

Dir: Ferdinando Bastos de Souza; *Sales:* José Nicácio Itagyba de Oliveira; *Editor:* Maria Alice Barroso
Subjects: General Literature, Scientific & Technical
Founded: 1967

F E N A M E—Fundação Nacional de Material Escolar, Rua Miguel Ângelo 96, Maria da Graça, Rio de Janeiro RJ Tel: 2617750/2614140
Man Dir: Milton Durço Pereira; *Editorial Dir:* Tania Jatobá de Matos Menezes; *Sales Dir:* Murilo Alves Nunes; *Production Dir:* Antonio José de Britto; *Publicity Dir:* Ivan Estelita Campos; *Rights & Permissions:* José Ribeiro de Castro Neto
Subject: Textbooks
Bookshops: About 250 outlets throughout Brazil
1978: 22 titles *1979:* 20 titles *Founded:* 1967

Editôra F T D SA*, Rua do Lavapés 1023, Cambuci, CP 30402, 01519 São Paulo SP Tel: 2788264
President: João Tissi; *Man Dir:* Paulo Alves Ferraz
Br Offs: Rua Agenor Meira 4/67, Bauru, São Paulo; Rua Lavras 235, Carmo Sion, Belo Horizonte, MG; Rua Mal Deodoro 887, Curitiba, PR; Ave Goiás 1146, Goiânia, GO; Ave Rio Branco 185, Londrina, PR; Ave Tiradentes 963, Maringa; Ave Joana Angélica 3t963, Salvador, BA; Rua Prof Baltazar 12, Vitória, ES; Rua André Cavalcanti 78, Rio de Janeiro, GB; Rua Martins Junior 39, Recife, PE; Ave do Imperador 1203, Fortaleza, CE (all in Brazil)
Subject: Textbooks
Founded: 1897

Editôra Forense—Universitaria Ltda, CP 2284/ZC-00, 20020 Rio de Janeiro RJ (Located at: Ave Erasmo Braga 227-0° Grupo 309, Rio de Janeiro) Tel: 2526244/2831152/2831147

Editôra e Encadernadora Formar Ltda*, Rua dos Trilhos 1126, Mooca, CP 13250, 03168 São Paulo SP Tel: 935133 Cable Add: Formar
Subjects: Education, Scientific & Technical, Cookery, History, Geography, Children's Books, Reference Books

Livraría Freitas Bastos SA*, Rua 7 de Setembro 127–129, Centro, 20050 Rio de Janeiro RJ Tel: 2220250/2228858/2228973 Cable Add: Etiel
Br Off: Rua 15 de Novembro 62–66, São Paulo, SP
Bookshop: Rua 7 de Setembro 111, Rio de Janeiro
Subject: Law

Fundação Instituto Brasileiro de Geografia e Estatística, Ave Brasil 15671, ZC 91 Rio de Janeiro Tel: 2304747/3917788
Man Dir: Joaquim Fernandes Ramos Netto
Subjects: Statistics, Geography, Maps
Founded: 1936

Fundação Nacional de Material Escolar, see FENAME

Editôra Gustavo Gili do Brasil SA*, Rua Araripe Júnior 45, Andaraí, 20540 Rio de Janeiro RJ Tel: 2880881 Cable Add: Gustobras
Parent Company: Editorial Gustavo Gili SA, Spain (qv)
Subjects: Architecture, Engineering

Global Editora e Distribuidora Ltda, CP 45329, São Paulo SP (Located at: Rua José Antonio Coelho 814, 45329 São Paulo) Tel: 5493137/5442917

Man Dir, Sales: Luis Alves Jr; *Editorial, Production, Publicity, Rights & Permissions:* José Carlos Rolo Venancio
Imprint: Editora Parma Ltda
Subjects: Linguistics, Romance, Humour, UFOs, Politics
1978: 40 titles *1979:* 60 titles *Founded:* 1973

Editôra Globo SA, Av Getúlio Vargas 1271, CP 1520, 90000 Porto Alegre RS Tel: 331300 Cable Add: Dicionario
Editorial Dir, Rights & Permissions: José O Bertaso; *Sales Dirs:* Fernando José O Bertaso, Antonio C Leite
Parent Company: Livraria do Globo SA, Rua dos Andradas 1416, Pôrto Alegre
Subsidiary Company: Instituto Áudio-Visual e de Idiomas SA
Br Off: Rua Gen Belford 190-s/loja/201-202, Rocha, Rio de Janeiro RJ
Subjects: Education, Engineering, Dictionaries, Literature
1978: 88 titles (incl. re-editions) *1979:* 75 titles (incl. re-editions) *Founded:* 1954

Edições Graal Ltda, Rua Hermenegildo de Barros 31A, Glória, 20241 Rio de Janeiro RJ Tel: 2528582
Man & Editorial Dirs, and Rights & Permissions: André da Costa Santos, Paul Joseph Christoph Jr; *Sales Dir:* Francisco de Brito Magalhães Jr; *Production Dir:* Heyder Méndez de Matos; *Publicity Dir:* Maria Tereza Machado
Subjects: Social Sciences, Philosophy, Psychology, Medicine, Economics, History, Sociology
1978: 20 titles *1979:* 14 titles *Founded:* 1977

Ordem do Graal na Terra*, CP 128, 06800 Embu, São Paulo (Located at: Ave 7 de Setembro 29200, 06800 Embu, São Paulo)
Man Dir: Harry von Sass
Subjects: Religion, Philosophy, History
Founded: 1947

Editorial Grijalbo Ltda*, Rua 7 de Abril 264, loja B-2, 01044, São Paulo SP Tel: 369544
Man Dir: José Monfort
Subjects: Law, Technical
Founded: 1958
Miscellaneous: Firm is a subsidiary of Editorial Grijalbo SA, Mexico (qv)

Editôra Guanabara Koogan SA, Travessa do Ouvidor 11, 20000 Rio de Janeiro RJ Tel: 2328020 Cable Add: Edigua
Man Dir: Joao Pedro Lorch; *Editorial:* E M Carneiro; *Sales:* R Berardinelli Filho; *Production:* M P Costa; *Rights and Permissions:* P M da Silveira Jr
Subjects: Medicine, Dentistry, Life Sciences

Livraria Pioneira Editora Enio Matheus Guazzelli e Cia Ltda, Praça Dirceu de Lima 313, Casa Verde, 02515 São Paulo SP Tel: 2660926/2666507
Dir: Enio M Guazzelli; *Rights & Permissions:* Ricardo Guazzelli
Orders to: Praça Dirceu de Lima, 313, 02515 São Paulo
Subjects: Social Sciences, Business and Management, Linguistics, Brazilian Studies, Architecture and Urbanism; General Subjects, Children's Books
Bookshop: Praça Dirceu de Lima 313
1977: 31 titles *1978:* 36 titles *Founded:* 1960

H U C I T E C Ltda—Editora de Humanismo, Ciência e Tecnologia, Alameda Jau 404, Jardim Paulista, São Paulo SP Tel: (011) 2871825
Man Dirs: Adalgisa Pereira da Silva, Flávio

52 BRAZIL

George Aderaldo; *Editorial, Production, Rights & Permissions:* Flávio George Aderaldo; *Sales, Publicity:* Luiza Helena Alegro
Subjects: Textbooks, Education
1978: 50 titles *1979:* 50 titles *Founded:* 1971

Livraría **Hachette** do Brasil SA*, Rua Décio Vilares 278, Bairro, Peixoto, Copacabana, Rio de Janeiro

Harbra, an imprint of Harper & Row do Brasil Ltd (qv)

Harla, an imprint of Harper & Row do Brasil (qv)

Editora **Harper & Row** do Brasil Ltda, CP 45–312, 01000 Vila Mariana, São Paulo Tel: 703572 and 704891 Cable Add: Habra Sao Telex: (11) 25631 EHRB
Man Dir, Editorial, Rights & Permissions: Francisco Gutiérrez; *Sales:* Luiz Carlos de Matos; *Production:* Ma Lucia S Leife; *Publicity:* Tania Castro
Parent Company: Harper & Row Inc, New York, NY 10022, USA
Associate Companies: Basic Books Inc, New York, USA; T Y Crowell, New York, USA; J B Lippincott, Philadelphia, USA
Imprints: Harbra, Harla
Subjects: University and High School Text Books in Science, Mathematics, Engineering, Social Science, Business, Medicine, General Interest Books
1978: 30 titles *1979:* 20 titles *Founded:* 1976
Miscellaneous: Associate company of Harper & Row (Australasia) (qv), Harper & Row Ltd, UK (qv), Harper & Row Latinoamericana-Harla, Mexico (qv)

Hemus-Livraria Editora Ltda, Rua da Glória 312, CP 9686, 01510 São Paulo SP Tel: 2799911 Telex: 32005 HLEL BR
President: Eli Behar; *Man Dir:* Maxim Behar; *Financial Dir:* Uri Behar
Subjects: Technical & Engineering, Textbooks, Juveniles, Philosophy, Science Fiction, General Literature
1977: 67 titles *1978:* 82 titles *Founded:* 1965

Editora de **Humanismo**, Ciência e Tecnologia, see HUCITEC Ltda

I B A M, see Instituto Brasileiro de Administraçao Municipal

I B R A S A (Instituição Brasileira de Difusão Cultural SA), Rua 21 de Abril 97, Brás, CP 30927, 03047 São Paulo SP Tel: 939524
Man Dir: Jorge Leite
Orders to: IBREX Ltda, Rua 21 de Abril 101, CP 30927, São Paulo
Subjects: IBRASA Encyclopaedia, General Medical, Health & Sexuality, Parapsychology, Social Sciences, Psychology & Education, Philosophy, Politics, Economics, History, Classics of Democracy in translation, Exploration & Discovery, Modern Literature & Science
Founded: 1958

I P E A (Instituto de Planejamento Econômico e Social) Serviço Editorial, Caixa Postal 2672, Rio de Janeiro RJ (Located at: Rua Melvin Jones, 5–280 andar (ZC–21), Centro, Rio de Janeiro) Tel: 2428098 Cable Add: Planipea Telex: 963
Man Dir, Editorial, Production: A F Vilar de Queiro; *Sales, Publicity:* Gilberto V de Carvalho
Subject: Economics
1979: 110 titles *Founded:* 1971

Livro **Ibero-Americano** Ltda, Rua Hermenegildo de Barros 40, Caixa Postal 816, 20241 Rio de Janeiro RJ Tel: 2325248/2528814/2329048 Cable Add: Nebrija
Man Dir: Ramón Martín González
Br Offs: Rua Conselheiro Crispiniano 29, 1° pav, São Paulo SP Tel: 355827; Rua do Rosário 99, 3° e 4° andares, Rio de Janeiro RJ Tel: 2212026
Subjects: History, Philosophy, Reference, Religion, Medicine, Psychology, Textbooks (all levels)
Founded: 1946

Impacto, Editôrial e Serviços Ltda*, Ave Pres Vargas 534/1901, CEP 20000 Rio de Janeiro RJ Cable Add: Jovinorio
Man Dir: Jovino de Oliveira; *Sales Dir:* João Silva
Subjects: General Literature, Tourism
Founded: 1974

Instituição Brasileira de Difusão Cultural SA, see IBRASA

Instituto Brasileiro de Administraçao Municipal (IBAM), Largo IBAM 1, 22282 Rio de Janeiro RJ Tel: 2666622 Cable Add: Ibambras
Superintendent-General: Diogo Lordello de Mello; *Editor:* Alvaro Costa e Silva
Subjects: Law, Municipal Administration, Planning, O & M, Systems Analysis, Public Finance, Periodicals
Bookshop: at above address
1978: 12 titles *1979:* 6 titles *Founded:* 1952

Instituto Brasileiro de Edições Pedagógicas (IBEP)*, Rua Joli 294, Brás, CP 5312, 03016 São Paulo SP Tel: 2912355
Branch Off: Ave Lôbo Júnior 1011, Penha, 21020 Rio de Janeiro RJ
Subjects: Textbooks, Reference Books

Fundação **Instituto Brasileiro de Geografia** e Estatística, see under Fundação

Instituto Brasileiro de Informação em Ciência e Tecnologia (IBICT) (Brazilian Institute for Information in Science and Technology), Ave General Justo 171 4°, 20021 Rio de Janeiro Tel: (021) 2423453/2422915
Director: Carlos Augusto de Albuquerque
Subjects: Social, Natural and General Sciences, Technology, Bibliographies, Periodical *Ciencia da Informação*

Instituto Campineiro de Ensino Agrícola e Comércio Ltda, Rua Coronel Quirino 545, CP 1148, Campinas, SP Tel: 29333/88448 Cable Add: Icampi
Man Dir: Gervásio Souza Cavalcanti; *Sales Dir:* Vicente Botacini
Subject: Agriculture
Founded: 1955

Instituto de Planejamento Econômico e Social (IPEA), Rua Melvin Jones 5, 2000 Rio de Janeiro RJ Tel: 2225567/2240115
Subjects: Human & Social Science, Economics, Agriculture

Livraría **Interciencia** Ltda*, Ave Pres Vargas 435, 5° andar, Sala 504, Centro, CP 1825, 20071 Rio de Janeiro RJ Tel: 2216850/2210993
Man Dir: Edson do Nascimento Pereira; *Rights & Permissions:* Joel José Gomes
Subject: Science in general
Founded: 1969 (1975 as publisher)
Bookshop: Livraría Interciencia Ltda, Ave Pres Vargas 435, Rio de Janeiro

Junta de Educação Religiosa e Publicações da Convenção Batista Brasileira, CP 320, 20000 Rio de Janeiro RJ Tel: 2690772 Cable Add: Batistas
Superintendent-General: Prof H Victor Davis; *Editorial, Rights & Permissions:* Prof Darci Dusilek; *Sales, Publicity:* Prof Silvino Carlos Figueira Netto; *Production:* Dr Daniel dos Santos Nascimento
Subject: Religion
Bookshops: Rua do Rosário 141 s/Lj 201, Centro, 20041 Rio de Janeiro RJ (and others in Bandeira, Rio, Duque de Caxias, Niterói, Nova Iguaçu); Ave Visconde de São Lourenço 6, 40000 Salvador BA; Ave São João 816–820, 01000 São Paulo SP; SDS Bl G Lj 17, Conjunto Baracat, 70000 Brasilia DF; Rua Barão de Intapemirin 208, 29000 Vitória ES
1978: 38 titles *1979:* 72 titles *Founded:* 1907

Norberto R **Keppe**, Ave Rebouças 3115, Pinheiros, 05401 São Paulo Tel: 8536755/8535551
Man Dir, Editorial: André R Keppe; *Sales Dir:* José Calderoni; *Production Dir:* Regina Bertazoni; *Publicity Dir:* Omnypolis Fozolino
Subjects: Psychoanalysis, Psychology, Medicine, General Science
1978: 3 titles *1979:* 3 titles *Founded:* 1977

Livraría **Kosmos** Editôra*, Rua de Rosario 137, Centro, CP 3481, 20041 Rio de Janeiro RJ Tel: 2529534/2529552
Man Dirs: Walter and Stefan Geyerhahn
Subjects: Engineering, History, Linguistics, Music, Reference Books, Tourism
Founded: 1935

L I S A (Livros Irradiantes SA)*, Rua Castro Alves 139, CP 7873, Aclimação, 01532 São Paulo, SP Tel: 2788900/2797011/2797169 Cable Add: Lisalivros
Man Dir: Leonídio Balbino da Silva; *Sales Dir:* Francisco de Paula Oliveira Filho
Branch Off: Ave Presidente Vargas 446, Sala 1802, Centro, 20071 Rio de Janeiro RJ
Subjects: Textbooks, Reference, Education
Founded: 1965

L T r Editora Ltda, Rua Jaguaribe 571–585, Vila Buarque, 01224 São Paulo SP Tel: 660458
Man Dir: Armando C Costa; *Editorial, Publicity:* Marinho; *Sales:* Armando C Costa Jr; *Production:* Arnaldo C Costa
Branch Off: Rua Anfilófio de Carvalho 29, Salas 607/8, Castelo, 20030 Rio de Janeiro RJ
Subject: Law
1977: 130 titles *Founded:* 1937

Editorial **Labor** do Brasil SA, Rua Buenos Aires 104, CP 1519ZC00, Rio de Janeiro Tel: 2526554 Cable Add: Edilabor
Dir: Antonio Francisco Souza Filho
Parent Company: Editorial Labor, Spain (qv)
Br Off: Mal Floriano 13 7 andar, Gonj 71/73 Porto Alegre; Rua Aurora 858 2 Conj 23, São Paulo
Subjects: Art, Medicine, Science, Engineering, Technology

Editôra **Laudes** SA*, Ave Almirante Barroso 90, 3° andar, Castelo, 20031 Rio de Janeiro RJ Tel: 2682796/2689981
Subjects: Textbooks, Brazilian Literature

Lex Editora SA, CP 12888, 04106 São Paulo (Located at: Rua Machado de Assis 57, 04106 São Paulo) Tel: 5490122
Man Dir: Affonso Vitale Sobrinho; *Editorial:* Dra Dulce Eugênia de Oliveira; *Sales:* Oswaldo Messina Jr; *Production:* Paulo Celso Vitale
Branch Off: Rua Debret 23 conj 801, Rio de Janeiro

Subject: Law
1978: 10 titles *1979:* 10 titles *Founded:* 1937

Editôra **Lidador** Ltda+, Rua Paulino Fernándes 58, Botafogo, 20000 Rio de Janeiro RJ Tel: 2667179/2664105/2867593
Publicity Manager: Ruy Carvalho
Subjects: Economics, Music, Occultism, Sociology, Dramatic Art

Waldyr **Lima** Editora, Rua Dr Bulhões 947, 20730 Rio de Janeiro RJ Tel: (021) 2691332/2893995
Director-General, Rights & Permissions: Waldyr Lima; *Editorial (Research & Planning Dir):* Lilian Moreira Neves; *Sales, Production, Publicity Dir:* Richard Noel Taylor
Subjects: Didactics, English as a foreign language
1978: 57 titles *1979:* 63 titles *Founded:* 1967

Editora Max **Limonad** Ltda, Rua Quintino Bocaiuva 191 4° s/41, 01004 São Paulo SP Tel: 357393
Man Dir, Editorial: Sara Limonad
Subject: Law
1978: 5 titles *Founded:* 1944

Livraria Editora Tecnica Ltda (LITEC)*, Rua dos Timbirãs 257, CP 30869, São Paulo SP Tel: 2208983
Man Dir: Adalbert Walter Miehe; *Sales Dir:* José Lopes
Subjects: Electronics, Technical
Founded: 1971

Editora **Logosófica**, Rua Coronel Oscar Porto 818, 04003 São Paulo SP Tel: 701476/706574
Man Dir, Editorial: José Antonio Antonini; *Sales:* Expedito Jorge Leite; *Production:* Antonio Francisco Ocãna
Orders to: Rua Luiz Machado Pedrosa 96, 01431 São Paulo SP
Bookshops: Ave W-3 SQS 715 Bloco E Casa 78, 70000 Brasília DF; Rua Piauí 742, 30000 Belo Horizonte MG; Rua Barão de Rio Branco 63, s/1902, 80000 Curitiba PR; Rua Nunes Machado 14 s/35, 88000 Florianópolis SC; Rua 17A, 959 Setor Aeroporto, 74000 Goiânia GO; Rua Domingos de Sá 373, 24000 Niterói RJ; Rua General Polidoro 36, 20000 Rio de Janeiro; Rua Angélica 30, 38100 Uberaba MG; and others in Argentina, Mexico, Paraguay and Uruguay
Subject: Logosofia
1978: 4 titles *1979:* 2 titles *Founded:* 1964

Edições **Loyola** SA*, Rua 1822 No 347, Ipiranga, CP 42335, 04216 São Paulo SP Tel: 639695/2746028
2*Subjects:* Law, Education, Literature, Cinema, Economics, Philosophy, Psychology, Religion, Textbooks

Edicoes '**Lumen Christi**', CP 2666, 20000 Rio de Janeiro RJ (Located at: Rua Dom Gerardo 40, 20000 Rio de Janeiro) Tel: 2537122 Cable Add: Mosteiro Sanbento
Man Dir, Production, Publicity: D Hildebrando P Martins OSB; *Sales:* Nicolau Mueller OSB
Subjects: Liturgy, Theology, Spiritualism, Art
Bookshop: Edições men Christi' (at above address)
1978: 6 titles *1979:* 6 titles *Founded:* 1935

Editôra **McGraw-Hill** do Brasil Ltda*, Alameda Juruá 434, Alphaville, KM 23 da Rodovia Castelo Branco, 06400 Barueri SP
Man Dir: Jan Rais
Br Off: Editora McGraw-Hill Ltda, Rua Rosa, Damasceno 11, AB, Lisbon 2, Portugal

Subjects: Science & Technology
Founded: 1970
Miscellaneous: Firm is an associate company of McGraw-Hill Book Co (UK) Ltd (qv for other associates)

Editora **Manole** Ltda, CP 1489, 01327 São Paulo (Located at: Rua 13 de Maio 1026, 01327 São Paulo) Tel: 2870746
Man Dir, Editorial, Production, Rights & Permissions: Dinu Octau Manole; *Sales:* Gloria Vassuda; *Publicity:* Ilma Manole
Subjects: Physiotherapy and like Sciences
1978: 65 titles *1979:* 47 titles *Founded:* 1969

Mapa Fiscal Editora Ltda, PO Box 30027, Cambucí, 01540 São Paulo (Located at: Rua Miguel Telles Jr 394, Cambucí, São Paulo) Tel: 2784011 Cable Add: Mapa Fiscal Telex: 1130323 MFEL BR
Man Dir: Jayro Gonçalves; *Editorial, Sales, Production, Publicity Dir:* Roberto Mateus Ordine
Branch Off: Rua do Russel 680 terreo, Praia do Russel, Rio de Janeiro
Subject: Tax laws
Bookshop: Rua Barão de Paranapiacaba 93 6° of 63, Rio de Janeiro
1978: 64 titles *1979:* 26 titles *Founded:* 1952

Livraría **Martins** Editôra SA*, Rua Rocha 274, Bela Vista, 01330 São Paulo SP Tel: 2880667
Br Off: Rua Evaristo da Veiga 47, Rio de Janeiro, GB
Subjects: Literature, Juveniles, Art, Social Sciences, Law, Economics, Geography, History

Masson do Brasil, Ruo da Quitanda 20 s/301, 20011 Rio de Janeiro
Associate Companies: Masson Editeur, France (qv); Masson Editores, Dakota 383, Colonia Napoles, Mexico 18 DF, Mexico; Toray Masson, Spain (qv); Masson Publishing USA Inc, 111 West 57th St, New York NY, USA

Editora **Meca** Ltda, Rua Araújo 81, Vila Buarque, São Paulo Tel: 2599049/2599034
Man Dir, Editorial, Production: Cosmo Juvela; *Sales:* Anna Maria Santos Brasil; *Publicity:* Jorge de Jesus; *Rights & Permissions:* Guarany Gallo
Subjects: General
1978: 4 titles *1979:* 2 titles *Founded:* 1970

Companhia **Melhoramentos** de São Paulo, CP 8120, 01000 São Paulo (Located at: Rua Tito 479, 05051 São Paulo)
Tel: 2626866 Cable Add: Melhoraluz
Telex: 1123151 MELP BR
Man Dir: Hasso Weiszflog; *Dir:* Alfredo Weiszflog
Branch Off: Rua Pinto Guedes 24, Tijuca, 20511 Rio de Janeiro RJ
Bookshop: Livroluz, Largo do Arouche 167, São Paulo
Subjects: Children's Books, Dictionaries, Reference, General Literature
1977: 195 titles *1978:* 170 titles *Founded:* 1915

Mestre Jou SA, Rua Guaipa 518, Vila Leopoldina, São Paulo, CP 24090 Tel: 2602498/2611920 Cable Add: Mestrejou
Man Dir: Felipe Mestre Jou; *Sales, Publicity, Advertising & Rights Dir:* Antonio Bidin
Subjects: Literature, History, Philosophy, Psychology, Medicine, Technical & Engineering, Social Sciences
Bookshops: Rua Senador Dantas 19, S/206, Rio de Janeiro; Rua Augusta 2843, Rua Martins Fontes 99, Rua 7 de Abril 172 and Rua Alvaro de Carvalho 111 (all in São Paulo)

1977: 34 titles *Founded:* 1946
Miscellaneous: Firm is also an importer and distributor for all Brazil

Editôra **Monterrey** Ltda*, Rua Visconde de Pirajá 550, 14° andar, Sala 1401, Ipanema, 22410 Rio de Janeiro Tel: 2272795/2272602
Man Dir, Editorial: J Gueiros; *Sales:* J Fernandez; *Production:* W Teixeira; *Publicity:* C Marquez
Subjects: Fiction
1977: 241 titles *Founded:* 1963

Livraría **Nobel** SA Editôra*, Rua María Antonia 108, Vila Buarque CP 2373 São Paulo SP Tel: 2572144
Publicity: Ary Kuflik Benclowicz
Subjects: Textbooks, Agronomy, Mathematics, Statistics, Science, Engineering, Management & Economics, Public Relations, Dictionaries, Veterinary, Husbandry, Gardening
Bookshops: Rua Maria Antonio 108; Rua de Consolacão 49, São Paulo
1977: 119 titles *Founded:* 1943

Noblet Editora e Distribuidora Ltda, CP 15181, 01530 São Paulo (Located at: Rua Almeida Torres 119/163, 01530 São Paulo) Tel: 2786152 Cable Add: Altesse
Man Dir: Joseph Bekhor Abourbih; *Editorial:* Yasukazu Hamazaki; *Production:* Fausto Taoka; *Publicity:* Josette A H Savatovsky
Subjects: Fiction, Periodicals
1978: 8 titles *1979:* 8 titles *Founded:* 1968

Editorial **Nórdica** Ltda, Ave NS Copacabana 1189, 22070 Rio de Janeiro RJ Tel: (021) 2872169 Cable Add: Nórdica
Subjects: General Books, Juveniles, Humour, Politics, Cinema, Cookery, Economics, Sports, Occultism, Fiction

Editora **Nova Aguilar** SA, Rua Maria Angélica 168, 22461 Rio de Janeiro Tel: 2667474 Cable Add: Aguilar
President, Editorial, Production: Silvia Farré; *Sales:* A O Frazeres
Parent Company: Ed Nova Fronteira SA (qv)
Br Off: Av Jurema 767, 04079 São Paulo
Subjects: Luxury editions of complete works of important Brazilian, Portuguese and International writers and poets
1977: 21 titles *1978:* 1 title *Founded:* 1958

Nova Epoca Editorial Ltda*, Ave Angélica 55, Santa Cecilia, 01228 São Paulo SP Tel: 679505
Man Dir: Maria Dorell; *Sales Dir:* Dr Mark A Dorell; *Publicity Dir:* Poala Bassano; *Advertising Dir:* Roberto Zaccola; *Rights & Permissions:* Allan Delan
Subjects: General Fiction, Biography, History, Philosophy, Reference Books, Occultism
Founded: 1971

Editora **Nova Fronteira**, Rua Maria Angélica 168, 22461 Rio de Janeiro Tel: 2667474 Cable Add: Neofront
Man Dir: Sérgio Lacerda; *Editorial:* P P de Sena Madureira; *Sales:* A O Prazeres; *Rights & Permissions:* M A Bandeira
Subsidiary Companies: Nova Aguilar (qv); Confraria dos Amigos do Livro (qv)
Br Off: Av Jurema 767, 04079 São Paulo
Subjects: Fiction, Literature, Biography, Psychology, History, Brazilian Problems, Dictionaries
1977: 61 titles *1978:* 44 titles *Founded:* 1965

Livraria José **Olympio** Editora SA*, Rua Marquês de Olinda 12, Botafogo, CP 9018, 22251 Rio de Janeiro RJ Tel: 2660662/2665032 Cable Add: Jolympio
Dir: Hênio Rodrigues de Souza; *Sales Dirs:*

BRAZIL

Lidelmo Lima Terra, Harry de Almeida Costa
Foreign Rights: Gilda O Cruz Lehner
Br Offs: Rua dos Gusmões 100-104, Santa Ifigênia, 01212 São Paulo, SP; Rua Januária 258, Belo Horizonte, MG; Comércio local da S Q Sul 108, Bloco D, Loja 5, Brasília, DF; Rua dos Andradas 717, Porto Alegre, RS; (all in Brazil)
Subjects: Juveniles, General Science, General Fiction, Textbooks, Sports, Philosophy, History, Humour, Music, Reference Books, Psychology, Religion, Sociology
Founded: 1931

Pallas SA*, Editôra e Distribuidora, Rua Frederico de Albuquerque 44, Higienopolis, CP 7001, 21050 Rio de Janeiro Tel: 2700186
Man Dir: Martha Bozôti; *Editorial, Rights & Permissions:* D Marques; *Sales:* A C Fernandes
Subjects: Fiction, Social Sciences, National Literature, Economics, Law, Psychology, Occultism
1977: 16 titles *Founded:* 1975

Editora **Parma** Ltda, an imprint of Global Editora e Distribuidora Ltda (qv)

Edições **Paulinas**, Rua Dr Pinto Ferraz 183, CP 12899, 04117 São Paulo Tel: 716302/702688 Cable Add: Paulinas
Man Dir: Carlos D Vido; *Editorial:* Carlos Vido, M G Bordeghini; *Sales:* W P Bosio, Daniela Rodrigues; *Production:* Vitt Sarraceno; *Publicity:* W P Bosio, D Rodrigues; *Rights & Permissions:* C Vido, M Glória Bordeghini
Subjects: Religion, Philosophy, Biography, Juveniles, Secondary & Primary Textbooks, Theological, Biblical, Liturgical
Bookshops: Rua Dr Pinto Ferraz 183, and three more in São Paulo; Rua México 111-B and two more in Rio de Janeiro; one each in Belo Horizonte, Brasilia, Caxias do Sul, Curitiba, Fortaleza, Goiânia, Maringá, Niterói, Cuiabá, Porto Alegre, Recife and Salvador
1977: 192 titles *1978:* 203 titles *Founded:* 1930

Editôra **Paz e Terra**, Rua André Cavalcanti, 86 ZC-06, Fátima, 20231 Rio de Janeiro RJ Tel: 263-4399 Telex: 2122643
General Manager & Sales: Fernando Gasparian; *Editorial, Production, Publicity, Rights & Permissions Dir:* Decio Drummond
Subjects: Brazilian Studies, Latin-American Studies, Social Sciences, Philosophy, Cinema, Theatre, Political Science, Literature & Literary Theory
1977: 68 titles *Founded:* 1966

Editôra **Pensamento** SA*, Rua Conselheiro Furtado 648, 01511 São Paulo Tel: 2784811
Man Dir: Diaulas Riedel
Subjects: Philosophy, Religion
Founded: 1908

Editôra **Perspectiva***, Ave Brigadeiro Luíz Antônio 3025, Jardim Paulista, 01401 São Paulo SP Tel: 2888388/2886878
Man Dir: Mr Plinio
Subjects: Social Science, Humanities, Cinema, Economics, Education, History, Philosophy, Music, Psychology, Religion

Pink and Blue Editora Ltda, Rua Jandaia 180, Bela Vista, 01320 São Paulo Tel: 325886/350036
Man Dir: Maria Cecília de sá Quartim Barbosa; *Editorial Dir:* Francisco Quartim Barbosa; *Sales Dir:* Lucia Barbosa Lemos; *Production Dirs:* Genny M Ramalho, Maria Eugenia C Obniski; *Publicity Dir:* Lucilia Ribas Chaves; *Rights & Permissions:* Ana Maria Quartim Barbosa

Subject: English as a foreign language, primary & secondary stage
1978: 2 titles *1979:* 2 titles *Founded:* 1972

Editôra **Primor** Ltda, Ave Almirante Barroso 63 S/2716, 20031 Rio de Janeiro RJ Tel: (021) 2224122/2225977 Cable Add: Primor Telex: (021) 22150
Subsidiary Company: Gráfica Editora Primor SA (qv)
Subjects: Children's Books, Humour, Tourism, Illustrated Fiction and Nonfiction; International Co-Productions

Gráfica Editora **Primor** SA, Ave Almirante Barroso 63 S/2716, 20031 Rio de Janeiro RJ Tel: (5521) 3716622 Telex: (021) 22150
Man Dirs: Sergio Jacques Waissman, Simão Waissman; *Editorial:* Jaime Rodrigues; *Sales, Publicity:* Allen Josias; *Production:* Miguel Lerner; *Rights & Permissions:* Sergio Jacques Waissman
Parent Company: Editora Primor Ltda (qv)
Br Offs: Rua Cons Carrão 191/7, 01328 São Paulo SP
Subjects: Didactics, Pre-school & Juvenile Literature, Reference, Art, General Interest, Notebooks, Illustrated books
1977: 6 titles *1978:* 9 titles *Founded:* 1969

Editôra de **Publicações Científicas** Ltda, Rua do Russel 404, Grupos 901/2 Parte, Glória, 22210 Rio de Janeiro RJ Tel: 2654047/2654245/2258708/2451336
Man Dir: José Maria de Sousa e Melo; *Editorial:* Dr Ismar Chavés da Silveira; *Sales, Publicity:* Luiz Carlos Ávila de Souza; *Production:* Luiz Augusto Rodrigues
Associated Company: Editora de Publicações Médicas Ltda (EPUME) (at above address)
Br Off: Rua Borges Lagoa 126, São Paulo
Subject: General Medicine
Book Club: Estante do Livro Científico
1978: 3 titles *1979:* 5 titles *Founded:* 1959

Editôra **Raio** X Ltda*, Senador Dantas 117, S/640, 20000 Rio de Janeiro
Subject: Literature in general

Distribuidora **Record** de Serviços de Imprensa SA*, Ave Erasmo Braga 255, 8° andar, CP 884, Castelo, 20020 Rio de Janeiro Tel: 2524128 Cable Add: Recordist
President & General Manager: Alfredo C Machado; *Vice-President:* Sergio C Machado
Br Offs: R Pedro Alves 150 (ZC-14), Rio de Janeiro; Rua José Antônio Coelho 801, São Paulo SP; Av Augusto de Lima 233, Belo Horizonte MG
Subjects: General Fiction & Nonfiction, Biography, History, Philosophy, Juveniles, Primary Textbooks
Bookshop: Livraría Record, Ave Copacabana 249, Rio de Janeiro
1977: 317 titles *Founded:* 1942

Editôra **Resenha** Tributaria Ltda*, Rua Cel Xavier de Toledo 210, Cj 74, 7° andar, Centro, 01048 São Paulo Tel: 354445
Subjects: Law, Education

Editora **Reverté** Ltda*, Ave do Exército 49, CP 23001, Apt São Cristovão, 20910 Rio de Janeiro Tel: 284-5244
Man Dir: E Rosel Albero
Associate Companies: See under Editorial Reverté SA, Spain (qv)

Editôra **Revista** dos Tribunais Ltda*, Rua Conde do Pinhai 78, Centro, CP 8153, 01501 São Paulo SP Tel: 378689/379772
Man Dir: Nelson Palma Travassos; *Sales Dir:* Alvaro Malheiros
Subjects: Law, Economics, Philosophy, History, Reference Books, Sociology
Founded: 1955

Rio Grafica e Editora SA*, Rua Itapiru 1209-5° andar, Rio Comprido, 20000 Rio de Janeiro RJ Tel: (021) 2342000 Telex: 021464
Subjects: Comic Books, Sports and Games; Activity Books

Editôra Ana **Rosa***, Rua Aurora 858, 6° andar, São Paulo Tel: 2212211
Subjects: Fashion & Design

Saraiva SA, Livreiros Editores* Av do Emissario 1897, Barra Funda, CP 2362, 01139 São Paulo SP Tel: 8268422 Cable Add: Academica Telex: (11) 25642 (EDSA)BR
Man Dirs: Ruy Gonçalves, J E Saraiva; *Dir:* P Saraiva; *Editorial:* A Faccioli, S Corrêa, O Juarez; *Sales, Publicity:* N Lepera; *Production:* A Cardoso; *Rights & Permissions:* S Corrêa
Br Off: Ave Marchal Rondon 2231, Rio de Janeiro; Rua Celia de Souza 571, Belo Horizonte
Subjects: Law, Education, Business Administration, Economics, Primary, Secondary School Texts
Bookshops: 21 branches throughout Brazil
1977: 240 titles *1978:* 329 titles *Founded:* 1917

Sarvier — Editôra de Livros Medicos Ltda*, Rua Dr Amancio de Carvalho 459, Vila Mariana, CP 12927, 04012 São Paulo SP Tel: 713439
Man Dir: Cid A Balieiro
Subjects: Medicine, Dentistry
Founded: 1965

Scipione Autores Editores Ltda, Rua Princesa Leopoldina 431/445, Alto da Lapa, 05081 São Paulo SP Tel: 2605878/2612902
Man Dir, Editorial: Prof Dr Scipione di Pierro Netto; *Sales, Publicity:* Adonis Franco Martins; *Production:* José Augusto del Bianco; *Rights & Permissions:* Prof Dr Scipione di Pierro Netto, Luis Fernando di Pierro
Subsidiary: Módulus Orientação Pedagógica, Edição e Comercialização de Obras Didáticas Ltda (at above address)
Subject: Didactics
1978: 28 titles *1979:* 30 titles *Founded:* 1974

Seleções Editora Ltda, see Eletrônicas

Edições **Símbolo**, Rua General Flores 518, 01129 São Paulo SP Tel: 2200267/2215833 Cable Add: Simbolgraf
Man Dir: Moysés Baumstein; *Editorial Dir:* Alberto Baumstein; *Sales Dir:* Hélio Loyola
Parent Company: Simbolo SA: Industrias Gráficas
Subjects: Literature, Social Literature, University Textbooks, Sociology, History, Politics, Jungian Psychology, Education, Communications
1978: 18 titles *1979:* 10 titles *Founded:* 1976

Livraría **Sulina** Editôra, CP 357, 90000 Pôrto Alegre RS (Located at: Ave Borges de Medeiros 1030-36, Pôrto Alegre) Tel: 254765 Cable Add: Zipasul
President: Leopoldo Bernardo Boeck Jr; *Vice-President:* Vilson Nailor Noer
Parent Company: Organização Sulina de Representações S/A, Rua Cel Genuino 290, Porto Alegre (Distributor)
Subjects: Science, Technical, Law, Textbooks, Psychology
Bookshops: Above address and Rua Julio de Castilhos, 1657-Caxias do Sul; Av 7 de setembro 1169, L 12 Bagé; Rua Marechal Floriano 1000, c 63 Sta Maria, and 5 other bookshops in Porto Alegre
1977: 36 titles *1978:* 42 titles *Founded:* 1946

Edições **Tabajara***, Rua dos Andradas 1774, CP 1918, 90000 Pôrto Alegre RS Tel: 241073/247724
Assistant Manager: Maria Azambuja
Br Off: Rua Santa Ifigênia 72, São Paulo
Subjects: Linguistics, Social & General Science, Mathematics, Sociology, Dramatic Art, Education, Textbooks

Livros **Tecnicos e Cientificos** Editora SA, Ave Venezuela 131, Salas 301/8, Cais do Porto, 20220 Rio de Janeiro RJ Tel: 2435869/2437078 Cable Add: Litece
Man Dir: P Machado Alves; *Editorial, Production:* J R de Carvalho; *Sales, Publicity:* Novais de Paula; *Rights & Permissions:* J C Neder Cunha
Orders to: A Mesma
Associate Companies: John Wiley & Sons, UK (qv for other associates)
Br Off: Rua Dr V de Carvalho Pinto 301-7, São Paulo
Subjects: Scientific and Technical
1977: 50 titles *Founded:* 1968

Tecnoprint SA*, Rua Nova Jerusalém, 345, Bonsucesso, CP 1880, 21040 Rio de Janeiro RJ Tel: 2606122/2804090 Cable Add: Ediouro
Subjects: Cookery, Textbooks, Sports, Children's Books, Reference Books, Paperbacks
Founded: 1939

Edições **U R G S** (Universidade Federal do Rio Grande do Sul), Rua Jacinto Gomes 540, 5° andar, 90000 Porto Alegre RS Tel: 234221
Dir: Blasio H Hickman
Subjects: General & Academic
1979: 89 titles

Editora **Universidade de Brasília**, CP 040289, 70910 Brasília DF (Located at: Campus Universitário, Asa Norte Apt 15, 70910 Brasília) Tel: 2720000
President of Editorial Council: Prof Carlos Henrique Cardim; *Editorial, Sales:* Sérgio Sampaio Alexandre; *Production, Publicity:* Antonio Luiz Coelho
Br Offs: São Paulo, Rio de Janeiro
Subjects: Politics, General Non-fiction, Periodicals
Book Club: Clube do Livro Político

Editôra da **Universidade de São Paulo***, CP 11465, 05508 São Paulo SP (Located at: Edifício da Reitoria, 6° andar, Cidade Universitária 'Armando Salles Oliveira', Butantã, São Paulo) Tel: 2110011/1011 Cable Add: Ruspaulo
President: Mario Guimarães Ferri
Subjects: Scholarly, General Nonfiction
Founded: 1964

Livraria e Editora **Universitária de Direito** Ltda, Rua Benjamin Constant 171 1° S/1 a 5, 01005 São Paulo Tel: 356374/340314
Man Dir, Production: Armando Luiz Almeida Martins; *Editorial Dir:* Pedro Gellindo Sommavilla; *Sales Dir:* Armando des Santos Mesquita Martins
Subject: Legal works
1978: 16 titles *1979:* 8 titles *Founded:* 1968

Fundação Getúlio **Vargas**, Praia de Botafogo 188, CP 9052, 22253 Rio de Janeiro RJ Tel: 2863344 Cable Add: Fugevar
Man Dir: Mauro Gama; *Sales Dir:* Jorge Rangel da Matta
Subjects: Administration, Economics, Business, Sociology, Psychology, Education, Marketing, Accounting

Editôra **Vecchi** SA*, Rua do Resende 144, Centro, 20231 Rio de Janeiro RJ Tel: 2444522 Cable Add: Vekieditora
Dir & Vice-president: Lotario Campello Vecchi
Subjects: Biography, Cookery, Philosophy, Reference Books, Occultism, Religion, Juveniles
Founded: 1913

Editôra **Verbo** Ltda*, Rua Bueno de Andrade 480-484, Liberdade, CP8811, 01526 São Paulo SP Tel: 2792776 Cable Add: Verbo
Subjects: Art, Social Science, Reference, Juveniles, Cinema, Education, Geography, History, Psychology, Religion

Vertente Editora Ltda, Rua Dr Homem de Melo 446, 05007 São Paulo SP Tel: 8641758/8640077
Man Dir: Wladyr Nader; *Production Dir:* Maria Teresa Teixeira Ribeiro
Subjects: Literature, The Humanities, Periodicals *Escrita* and *Escrita/Ensaio*
Bookshop: Escrita (at above address)
1978: 9 titles *1979:* 7 titles *Founded:* 1968

Editôra **Vigília** Ltda, Rua Felipe dos Santos 508, Bairro de Lourdes, CP 2468, 30000 Belo Horizonte MG Tel: 3372744/3372363/3372834/3358720
Branch Off: Rua Pareto 23, Tijuca, 20550 Rio de Janeiro RJ
Subjects: Textbooks, Linguistics, Brazilian Literature, Religion

Editora **Visão** Ltda, Rua Alfonso Celso 243, 04119 Vila Mariana, São Paulo SP Tel: 5494344 Cable Add: Revistavisão Telex: (011) 23552 SEVL BR
Man Dir: Henry Maksoud; *Editorial Dir:* Isaac Jardanovski; *Sales Dir:* Carlos Alberto Borgneth; *Production Dir:* Antonio Lopes Colhado; *Publicity Dir:* Célio Corradini; *Promotions Dir:* Carlos Duailibi; *Rights & Permissions:* Ayrton Pedro de Oliveira
Associate Company: Visão SA Editorial (at above address)
Br Off: Conjunto Pacarat Sala 301, Brasilia DF
Subjects: Humanities, Economics, Finance, Agriculture, Cattle Breeding, Diet, Commerce, Hobbies, Tourism, Politics, Science, Technology
1978: 1 title *1979:* 1 title *Founded:* 1952

Vozes Editôra Ltda*, Rua Frei Luís 100, CP 23, 25600 Petrópolis RJ Tel: 435112 Cable Add: Vozes
Man Dir: Miguel Mourão de Castro
Associate Company: Livraria Francisco Alves Editôra SA (qv)
Br Offs: Rua Senador Dantas 118-1, Rio de Janeiro; Rua Senador Feijó 168, São Paulo; Rua Tupis 85, Loja 10, Belo Horizonte; Rua Riachuelo 1280, Pôrto Alegre; CRL/Norte, Q704 Bloco A 15, Brasília, DF; Rua Conselheiro Portela 354, Recife PE; Rua Alferes Poli 52, Curitiba, PR
Subjects: Belles Lettres, Linguistics, Communications, Philosophy, Religion, Administration, Psychology, Sociology
Founded: 1901

Zahar Editores+, Rua México 31, CP 207-ZC-00, Rio de Janeiro GB Tel: 2215079
General Manager: Jorge Zahar; *Sales Dir:* Jorge Zahar, Jr
Br Off: Alameda Nothaman 1067, São Paulo
Subjects: Social Science, Psychology
Founded: 1957

Zip Editora Ltda, CP 35034, 20000 Rio de Janeiro (Located at: Rua Filomena Nunes 162, Olaria, 20000 Rio de Janeiro) Tel: 2306470
Man Dir: Nildo Vicente; *Editorial:* Gilson B Soares; *Sales:* Mario P Vieira; *Production:* Walmir B Monteiro; *Rights & Permissions:* Luiz T Rosemberg
Subjects: Juveniles, Fiction, Paperbacks
1979: 100 titles *Founded:* 1978

Literary Agents

Carmen **Balcells** Agencia Literaria, Rua Joao Lira 97 202, Leblon, 20000 Rio de Janeiro RJ Tel: 2943248 Cable Add: Copyright
Manager: Carmen Balcells
Branch Off: also in Barcelona, Spain (qv)

Dr J E **Bloch** and Mrs Karin Schindler, Rua Oscar Freire 416, Apt 83, 01426 São Paulo Tel: 2823053 Cable Add: Copyright Sãopaulo

International Editors' Co*, Alameda IEU 402, São Paulo

Rômulo **Paes Barreto**, CP 16083, ZC-01 20000 Rio de Janeiro Tel: 2659478

Book Clubs

Círculo do Livro SA, CP 7413, São Paulo SP (Located at: Ave Paulista 326, São Paulo) Tel: 2852133 Cable Add: Cirlivro Telex: 1132900/1131747
Man Dir: Raymond Cohen
Owned by: Bertelsmann Aktiengesellschaft, Federal Republic of Germany (qv); Abril SA Cultural e Industrial (qv)

Estante do **Livro Científico**, Rua do Russel 404 9° andar, ZC-01, 22210 Rio de Janeiro
Owned by: Editora de Publicações Científicas Ltda (Rio de Janeiro) (qv)

Clube do **Livro Político**, CP 040289, 70910 Brasília DF (Located at: Campus Universitário, Asa Norte Apt 15, 70910 Brasilia)
Owned by: Editora Universidade de Brasília (qv)

Major Booksellers

Livraría **Agir**, Rua México 98-B, Rio de Janeiro Tel: 2428327

Ao Livro Técnico, Rua Miguel Couto 35, Loja C, ZC-21, CP 3655, 20000 Rio de Janeiro Tel: 2639377
Branches in Brasilia, Belo Horizonte, Minas Gerais, Rio de Janeiro, Niteroi, São Paulo
Also widespread wholesaler and distributors

Editôra **Brasiliense** SA*, Rua Barão de Itapetininga 93, São Paulo Tel: 367824

Livraria **Canuto** Ltda, Rua da Consolação 348, 2°, São Paulo Tel: 2564564

Livraría **Científica Técnica**, Rua Riachuelo 453, Loja 4, Recife PE 50000 Tel: 24933

Livraría **Civilização** Brasileira*, Rua Bettencourt da Silva 12-F, Rio de Janeiro Tel: 2216980

Cultura 70 Livraria e Editora S/A*, Rua Barão de Itapetininga, 93 to 99, 01042 São Paulo

Livraría **Duas Cidades***, Rua Bento Freitas 158, CP 433, São Paulo Tel: 2204702

A Casa do Livro **Eldorado** Ltda, Ave Copacabana 1189, 22070 Rio de Janeiro Tel: 2872147

Livraría **Freitas** Bastos*, Rua 7 de Setembro 111, Rio de Janeiro Tel: 332999

Livraría do **Globo***, Rua dos Andradas 1416, Pôrto Alegre Tel: 24811

Librairie **Hachette** SA do Brasil*, Rua Décio Villares 278, Bairro Peixoto, Copacabana, Rio de Janeiro

I B R E X- Distribuidora de Livros e Material de Escritório Ltda*, Rua 21 de Abril 101, São Paulo — SP Tel: 939524

Livro **Ibero-Americano**, Rua do Rosario 99, 3° & 4° andares, ZC-00, Rio de Janeiro Tel: 2212026 (see under Publishers)

Livraría **Kosmos***, Rua do Rosario 137, CP 3481, ZC-00, Rio de Janeiro Tel: 2529552

Livraría **L E R***, Rua México 31 Sobreloja, CP 4576, Rio de Janeiro Tel: 2215073/74/75/76 Cable Add: Livreril Also at Praça Olavo Bilac 28, Rio de Janeiro; Praça da República 71, São Paulo Importer, Exporter & Distributor

L I T E C-Livraria Editora Técnica Ltda, Rua dos Timbiras 257, CP 30869, São Paulo Tel: 2208983

Livraría D **Landy**, Rua 7 de Abril 252, 3°, São Paulo Tel: 355242

Livraría **Leonardo da Vinci***, Ave Rio Branco 185, L/2°, Rio de Janeiro Tel: 2577192/2241329

Mestre Jou SA, Rua Guaipá 518, Vila Lepoldina, 05089 São Paulo Tel: 2602498/2611920 Firm is also an importer and distributor for all Brazil

Livraría **Nobel***, Rua de Consolação 49, CP 2373, São Paulo Tel: 2593237

Livraría **Parthenón***, Rua Barão de Itapetininga 140-1°, S/14, 01042 São Paulo Tel: 372623

Livraría Científica Ernesto **Reichman**, Rua Dom José de Barros 168, 6° andar, Conj 61-62, 01000 São Paulo Tel: 342340

Livraría **Sulina**, Ave Borges de Medeiros 1030-36, CP 357, Pôrto Alegre Tel: 250287

Livraría **Triangulo** Ltda*, CP 30317, Rua Barão de Itapetininga 255, Loja 23-24, 01042 São Paulo Tel: 348243, 355830, 2390316

Major Libraries

Arquivo Nacionaal, Praça da República 26, Rio de Janeiro

Biblioteca Estadual*, Ave Presidente Vargas 1261, Rio de Janeiro
State Library

Biblioteca Municipal Mário de Andrade, Rua da Consolação 94, Caixa Postal 8170, São Paulo — SP Tel: 2394384/2565777
Dir: Maria Helena Guimarães da Costa e Silva

Biblioteca Nacional, Ave Rio Branco 219-239, 20042, Rio de Janeiro RJ Tel: 2320520 Telex: 02122941 BN RJ BR
Dir: Plinio Doyle

Biblioteca Publica do Estado do Rio de Janeiro*, Praça da República, Niterói, Rio de Janeiro

Centro de Documentação e Informaçao da Camara dos Deputados, Coordenaçaõ de Publiçacoẽs, Praça dos Tres Poderes, Brasilia DF
House of Representatives Centre of Documentation & Information

Biblioteca do **Ministerio das Relações Exteriores***, Esplanada dos Ministérios, Rio de Janeiro Tel: 2264305
Dir: P Penner Cunha (Minister)

Biblioteca da **Sociedade Brasileira** de Cultura Inglesa*, Ave Graça Aranha 327, 3° andar, CP 821, Rio de Janeiro

Universidade de Brasilia, Biblioteca Central, Ag Postal 15, 70910 Brasilia DF Tel: (061) 1083 Telex: 2720000, Ramal 2400

Divisão de Biblioteca e Documentação da **Universidade de São Paulo***, Cidade Universitaria, Butantan, CEP 05508, CP 8191, São Paulo
Library and Documentation Division of São Paulo University

Biblioteca da Faculdade Nacional de Medicina da **Universidade Federal do Rio de Janeiro**, Centro de Ciencias Medicas*, Cidade Univ, Ilha do Fundão, ZC-32, 20000 Rio de Janeiro
Medical School Library of the University of Rio de Janeiro

Universidade Federal do Rio Grande do Sul, Biblioteca Central, Edificio da Reitoría-térreo, Ave Paulo Gama, 90000 Porto Alegre RS Tel: (0512) 242431 Telex: 0511055
Librarian: H B Schreiner

Library Associations

Associação Brasileira de Bibliotecarios*, IBBD, Ave General Justo 171, 4° andar, Rio de Janeiro
Brazilian Library Association

Associação dos Arquivistas Brasileiros*, Praia de Botafoga 186 — sala B-217, 22253 Rio de Janeiro
President: Marilena Leite Paes
Association of Brazilian Archivists
Publication: Arquivo e Administração (4-monthly)

Associação Paulista de Bibliotecarios*, CP 343, 01327 São Paulo SP (Located at: Rua 13 de Maio 1100, 3° andar, G32 São Paulo)
Executive Secretary: Mirian L Honorato
Library Association of São Paulo

Associação Riobrandense de Bibliotecarios*, CP 2344, Pôrto Alegre, Rio Grande do Sul
Library Association of the State of Rio Grande do Sul

Centro de Investigação e Documentação*, CP 23, Petropolis, Rio de Janeiro

Comissao Brasileira de Documentaçao Agricola (CBDA)*, c/o Museu Paraense "Emilio Goeldi", CP 399, Belem, Para
Secretary: Cely Farias Raphael
Headquarters of Brazilian Commission for Agricultural Documentation
Publication: Agricolas

Conselho Federal de Biblioteconomia (CFB) (Federal Council of Librarianship)*, Edificio Márcia, Sala 211, SC Sul, Brasília, DF
Executive Secretary: Etelvina Lima

Federação Brasileira de Associações de Bibliotecários (FEBAB) (Brazilian Federation of Library Associations), Rua Avanhandava 40, conj 110, 01306 São Paulo SP Tel: 2579979
President: Antonio Gabriel
Editor: Neusa Dias de Macedo
Publication: Revista Brasileira de Biblioteconomia e Documentação Jornal da FEBAB

Federação Brasileira de Associações de Bibliotecários — Comissão Brasileira de Documentação Jurídica (FEBAB/CBDJ), Rua Prof Antônio Maria Teixera 120 ap 802, Leblon, 22430 Rio de Janeiro RJ Tel: 2592763
Brazilian Federation of Library Associations — Brazilian Committee of Legal Documentation
President: Nylma Thereza de Salles Velloso Amarante; *Executive Secretary:* Alba Regina C Facioli
Publications: Many publications dealng with legal and related matters

Instituto Brasileiro de Informação em Ciência e Tecnologia (IBICT) (Brazilian Institute for Information in Science and Technology)*, Ave General Justo 171, 4° andar CEP 20021, Rio de Janeiro Tel: (021) 2423453/2425051
Director: Carlos Augusto de Albuquerque
Publications: Notícias (bi-monthly bulletin), *Ciência da Informação* (2 a year)

Library Reference Books and Journals

Books

Guia de Bibliografía Especializada (Guide to Specialist Libraries), Brazilian Library Association, Ave General Justo 171, 4° andar, Rio de Janeiro (covers all Latin America)

Journals

Boletim Informativo (Information Bulletin), Library Association of São Paulo, Rua 13 de Maio 1100, 3° andar, G32, São Paulo

Jornal, Library Association of São Paulo, Rua 13 de Maio 1100, 3° andar, G32, São Paulo

Noticias (News), Brazilian Federation of Library Associations, Brazilian Committee of Legal Documentation, Rua Avanhandava 40, conj 110, São Paulo

Revista Brasileira de Bibliteconomia e Documentação (Brazilian Review of Librarianship and Documentation), Brazilian Federation of Library Associations, Rua Avanhandava 40, conj 110, São Paulo, ZP 3

Literary Associations and Societies

Academia Amazonense de Letras*, Rua Ramos Ferreira 1009, Manaus, 69000 Amazonas
President: Dr Mario Y Monteiro; *Secretary:* Tânia Regina Mesquita
Publication: Revista

Academia Cachoeirense de Letras*, Praça Jerônimo Monteiro 105, 2° andar, Cachoeiro de Itapemerim, Espírito Santo

Academia Catarinense de Letras*, Rua Tenente Silveira 6, Florianópolis, Santa Catarina
Secretary-General: Altino Flôres
Publication: Revista

Academia Cearense de Letras, Palácio Senador Alencar, Rua São Paulo s/n, 60000 Fortaleza CE
Secretary-General: Raimundo Girâo
Publication: Revista

Academia de Letras*, João Pessôa, Paraíba

Academia de Letras da Bahia*, Ave 7 de Setembro 283, CP 662, Salvador, Bahia
Secretary: Edith Mendes de Gama e Abreu
Publication: Revista (every 6 months)

Academia de Letras de Piauí*, Teresina, Piauí
Publication: Revista

Academia Feminina Espírito Santense de Letras*, Rua Bernardo Horta 30, Apdo 1, Jucutuara, Vitoria, Espírito Santo
Women's Academy of Letters

Academia Matogrossense de Letras*, Rua 13 de Junho 173, Cuiabá Mato Grosso
President: José de Merquita
Publication: Revista

Academia Mineira de Letras*, Rua Carijos 150, 6°, Belo Horizonte, Minas Gerais

Academia Paranaense de Letras, CP 8610, Curitiba, Paraná
President: Vasco José Taborda
Publication: Revista

Academia Paulista de Letras, Largo do Arouche 312, São Paulo
President: Francisco Marins
Publications: Revista da Academia Paulista de Letras, Biblioteca Academia Paulista de Letras

Academia Pernambucana de Letras, Av Rui Barbosa 1596, CP 50000, Graças, Recife, Pernambuco
President: Dr Mauro Mota; *Secretary:* Dr Andrade Lima Filho
Publication: Revista

Academia Riograndense de Letras*, Rua Candido Silveira 43, Pôrto Alegre, Rio Grande do Sul
Publication: Revista

Academia de Letras 'Humberto de **Campos'***, Rua 23 de Maio, Vila Velha, Espírito Santo

P E N Clube do Brasil (Associação Universal de Escritores) (International PEN Centre)*, Praia do Flamengo 172, 10°, Rio de Janeiro
President: Professor Marcos Almir Madeira
Publications: Boletim, novels, poetry

Literary Periodicals

Escrita (Writing), Vertente Editora Ltda, Rua Dr Homen de Melo 446, 05007 São Paulo SP

Jornal de Letras (Journal of Letters), Rua Barata Ribeiro 774 s/1-101, Copacabana-Rio, Estado da Guanabara

Opinião (Opinion), Ramos 78, Jardim Botanico, Rio de Janeiro

Verbum (The Word), Universidade Catolica, Rua Marques de São Vicente 209, Rio de Janeiro

Veritas (The Truth), Pontificia Universidade Catolica do Rio Grande do Sul, Ave Iparanga 6681, Pôrto Alegre

Literary Prizes

Graca **Aranha** Prize*
For the best Brazilian novel. Enquiries to PEN Clube do Brasil, Praia do Flamengo 172, 10°, Rio de Janeiro

Afonso **Arinos** Prize*
For the best work of fiction published or written during the two years preceding the year of award. Awarded annually. Enquiries to the Brazilian Academy, Ave Presidente Wilson 203, Rio de Janeiro

Arthur **Azevedo** Prize*
For the best works of drama, history of the theatre and theatrical criticism. Awarded anually. Enquiries to the Brazilian Academy, Ave Presidente Wilson 203, Rio de Janeiro

Olavo **Bilac** Prize*
For the best book of poetry. Awarded annually. Enquiries to the Brazilian Academy, Ave Presidente Wilson 203, Rio de Janeiro

Viriato **Correa** Prize*
To the author of the best unpublished book for children. Enquiries to National Book Institute, OF 3068, Brasilia, DF

Folklore Prize*
For outstanding research work on Brazilian folklore. 4,000 Cruzeiros. Awarded annually. Enquiries to Campaign for the Defence of Brazilian Folklore, Brazil

Fundepar Prize*
For best short stories in the Portuguese language. $17,000 distributed among the six winners. Awarded annually. Enquiries to Parana State Educational Foundation, CP 2854, 8000 Curitiba

Monteiro **Lobato** Prize*
For children's literature. Awarded annually. Enquiries to Brazilian Academy, Ave Presidente Wilson 203, Rio de Janeiro

Julia **Lopes** de Ameida Prize*
For the best unpublished or published literary work written by a woman, preferably for a novel or collection of short stories. Awarded annually. Enquiries to Brazilian Academy, Ave Presidente Wilson 203, Rio de Janeiro

Machado de Assis Prize*
For an outstanding Brazilian writer for the sum of his work. Awarded annually. One of Brazil's highest literary honours. Enquiries to Brazilian Academy, Ave Presidente Wilson 203, Rio de Janeiro

Odorico **Mendes** Prize*
For the best translation from foreign literature into the Portuguese language. Awarded annually. Enquiries to Brazilian Academy, Ave Presidente Wilson 203, Rio de Janeiro

National Book Institute Prizes*
For outstanding unpublished literary works of fiction, poetry, history and essays. In addition, one prize is awarded for the best unpublished work of children's literature and another for illustrations of books for children. Awarded annually. Enquiries to National Book Institute, Of 3068, Brasilia DF

National Cultural Awards*
For outstanding intellectual and artistic accomplishments in the fields of literature, theatre, sciences, social studies, music, cinematography and arts. Enquiries to Brazilian Government, Brasilia

Silvio Romero Prize*
For best works in literary criticism and history of literature. Awarded annually. Enquiries to the Brazilian Academy, Ave Presidente Wilson 203, Rio de Janeiro

Luisa Claudio de **Sousa** Prize*
For the best book published in the previous year. Novels, plays, literary history and criticism works are considered. Awarded annually. Enquiries to PEN Clube do Brasil, Praia do Flamengo 172, 10°, Rio de Janeiro

José **Verissimo** Prize*
For the best essay and a work of scholarship. Awarded annually. Enquiries to Brazilian Academy, Ave Presidente Wilson 203, Rio de Janeiro

Brunei

General Information

Language: Malay and other languages (English in business)
Religion: Predominantly Muslim
Population: 190,000
Literacy Rate (1971): 63.9%
Bank Hours: 0900-1200, 1400-1500 Monday-Friday; 0900-1100 Saturday
Shop Hours: 0730-1930 or 2000 Monday-Saturday in Bandar Seri Begawan, Tuesday-Sunday in*Shop Hours:* 0730-1930 or 2000 Monday-Saturday in Bandar Seri Begawan, Tuesday- Sunday in Seria, Wednesday-Monday in Kuala Belait
Currency: 100 cents = 1 Brunei dollar
Export/Import Information: No tariff on books. Advertising matter dutied at 25 cents per lb. No obscene literature allowed. Import licences not required. No exchange controls

Publishers

Leong Brothers*, 52 Jalan Bunga Kuning, PO Box 164, Seria Tel: Seria 22381 Cable Add: Leong

The **Star** Press*, Bandar Seri Begawan
Manager: F W Zimmermann
Founded: 1963

Major Booksellers

The **Brunei** Press, Jalan Sungai, Kuala Belait
Stockists and dealers for books handled by the Strait Times Press, Singapore

Sharikat Toko Buku **Kwang Hwa**, PO Box 1211, Brunei (Located at: 308A Kiaw Lian Bldg, B S Begawan, Brunei) Tel: 24075

Rainbow Photo & Book Store, 59 Jalan Pretty, Kuala Belait Tel: 2295

Rex Bookstore*, PO Box 500, Brunei Hotel, Jalan Chevalier Tel: 2060

Swan Book Store*, Shop No 2, Jalan Bunga Rambai, Kuala Belait Tel: 2639

Major Libraries

Language and Literature Bureau Library*, Jalan Elizabeth II, Bandar Seri Begawan

Bulgaria

General Information

Language: Bulgarian (English becoming common foreign language. Russian widely used)
Religion: Eastern Orthodox, Muslim
Population: 8.8 million
Literacy Rate (1965): 90.2% (94.8% Urban, 86.2% Rural)
Bank Hours: 0830-1145 Monday-Friday; 0800-1100 Saturday
Shop Hours: 0800-1300, 1600-1900 Monday-Saturday
Currency: 100 stotinki = 1 lev
Export/Import Information: Foreign trade is a state monopoly and tariffs are paid by enterprise involved. Books imported by the foreign trade organization 'Hemus', Russki blvd 6, Sofia. Exchange controls
Copyright: UCC, Berne (see International section)

Book Trade Organizations

Darzhavno Obedinenie 'Bulgarska Kniga', pl Slavejkov 11, Sofia Tel: 879111 Telex: 22927 lpms
State Association 'Bulgarian Book'

Suyuz Knigoizdatelite i Knizharite*, vu Solum 4, Sofia
Union of Publishers and Booksellers

Book Trade Reference Books and Journals

Books

Bulgarian Academic Books, Catalogue of the Books and Periodicals of the Bulgarian Academy of Sciences and the Academy of Agricultural Sciences in Bulgaria, Bulgarian Academy of Sciences, 7 Noemvri 1, Sofia

Bŭlgarski Knigi (Bulgarian Books), Jusautor, pl Slavejkov 11, Sofia

Journals

Bŭlgarski Knigopis (National Bibliography), Cyril and Methodius National Library, blvd Tolbuhin 11, Sofia

Publishers

Knigoizdatelstvo 'Georgi **Bakalov**'*, blvd Hristo Botev 3, Varna Tel: 25077
Subjects: Maritime, Economics

Izdatelstvo na **Bulgarskata Akademia** na Naukite*, ul Academician G Bonchev 1113, Sofia Tel: 724643
Publishing House of the Bulgarian Academy of Sciences
Subject: Science

Izdatelstvo na **Bulgarskata Komunisticheska Partiya***, blvd Lenin 47, Sofia Tel: 4631
Publishing House of the Bulgarian Communist Party
Subjects: Geodesy, Philosophy, Politics, Popular Sciences, Sociology, Political Economy

Bulgarski Houdozhnik, ul Moskovska 37, Sofia Tel: 884480/884275
Dir: Prof Petr Tchuchovski
Subjects: Art, Archaeology, Juveniles
1978: 84 titles *Founded:* 1952

Bulgarski Pissatel*, ul 6 Septemvri 35, Sofia Tel: 884734
Dir: Simeon Sultanov
Publishing House of the Union of Bulgarian Writers
Subjects: General Fiction, Belles Lettres

Izdatelstvo na **Bulgarskiya Zemedelski Naroden Suyuz***, ul Yanko Zabounov 1, Sofia Tel: 881951
Subjects: Social & Popular Politics, Agriculture, Fiction

Darzhavno Izdatelstov 'Christo G **Danov**'*, ul Petko Karavelov 17, 4000 Plovdiv Tel: 25232
Dir: Peter Anastassov: *Editorial:* Ivan Nikolov
Parent Company: Glavna Direkzia 'Knigoizdavane', pl Slaveikov 11, Sofia 1000
Subjects: Science, Agriculture, University Textbooks, Poetry, Fiction translations
1977: 100 titles *Founded:* 1855

Meditsina i Fizkultura, pl Slaveikov 11, Sofia 1000 Tel: 879111
Subjects: Biology, Geography, Hygiene, Medicine, Sports

Darzhavno Izdatelstvo '**Muzica**'*, blvd Georgi Traykov, 2a, Sofia Tel: 662031
Subjects: Music, Theory of Music

Narodna Kultura*, ul Gravril Genov 4, Sofia Tel: 862722
Subject: Belles Lettres

Narodna Mladezh*, ul Kaloyan 10, Sofia Tel: 8681
Manager: Marko Nedyalkov
People's Youth Publishing House
Subjects: Juveniles, Philosophy, Mathematics, General, Political & Social Science, Original and Translated Fiction

Darzhavno Izdatelstvo '**Narodna Prosveta**'*, ul Vasil Drumev 37, Sofia Tel: 442211
Dir: Paunka Gocheva
Subject: Educational

Izdatelstvo na **Natsionalniya Savet** na Otetchestveniya Front*, blvd Dandukov 32, Sofia Tel: 878481/882991
Publishing House of the National Council of the Fatherland Front
Subjects: History, Politics, Popular Sciences, Belles Lettres

Darzhavno Izdatelstvo **Nauka** i Izkustvo*, blvd Rousky 6, Sofia Tel: 875701
Dir: Philip Genev
State Publishing House 'Science & Art'
Subjects: History, Art, Music, Law, Philosophy, General & Social Science, Technology, Business, Languages
Founded: 1949

Izdatelstvo **Profizdat***, blvd Dondukov 82, Sofia Tel: 872501
Manager: Ivan Daskalov
Publishing House of the Central Council of Bulgarian Trade Unions
Subjects: General Fiction, Belles Lettres, Political Science, Philosophy, General & Social Science

Sinodalno Izdatelstvo*, ul Sveta Sofia 2, Sofia Tel: 883313
Synodal Publishing House
Subject: Liturgical Books

Sofia Press Agency*, ul Levski 1, Sofia Tel: 885831/885832 Cable Add: Sofia Press Telex: 22622
General Dir: Kristo Santov
Subjects: General Fiction, Belles Lettres, Poetry, Biography, History, Political Science, Music, Art, Philosophy, Reference, Guides
Founded: 1967
Bookshop: Levski St 1, Sofia

Technica*, blvd Ruski 6, Sofia Tel: 875701
Subjects: Encyclopaedias and Dictionaries, Textbooks

Voenno Izdatelstvo*, ul Ivan Vazov 12, Sofia Tel: 878116
Subjects: History, Social Sciences, Military

Darzhavno Izdatelstvo **Zemizdat***, blvd Lenin 47, 1000 Sofia, PB 422 Tel: 4631
Dir: Yosif Grigorov
State Agricultural Publishing House
Subjects: General Science, Agriculture, Textbooks, Hobbies, Nonfiction
Founded: 1949

Literary Agents

Jusautor*, pl Slavejkov 11, Sofia Tel: 884817 Cable Add: Jusautor, Sofia
Copyright Protection Agency
The agency is the exclusive representative of Bulgarian authors, and also acts as an intermediary between foreign authors, publishers and agencies and Bulgarian users of their works

Major Booksellers

'**Hemus**' Foreign Trade Company*, 11 Pl Slaveikov, Sofia Tel: 870365 Telex: 22267 HEMKIK

Major Libraries

Central Historical **Archives***, Sofia, ul Zhdanov 5, Sofia

Central **Archives** of the People's Republic of Bulgaria*, ul Slavanjska 4, Sofia

Central Library, **Bulgarian Academy of Sciences***, 7 Noemvri 1, Sofia Tel: 877731
Librarian: Elena Savova
Publications: Collected Papers (irregular)

Centre for Pedagogical Information and Documentation*, Lenin 125, Sofia

Cyril and Methodius National Library*, blvd Tolbuhin 11, 1504 Sofia Tel: 882811
Director: Ms K Kalajdzieva

Central Agricultural Library of the 'G **Dimitrov' Academy** of Agricultural Sciences*, Dr Cankov 6, Sofia

Central **Institute** for Scientific and Technical Information (of the State Committee for Science, Technical Progress and Higher Education)*, Chapaev 56, Sofia

Central Medical Library*, bul G Sofiiski 1, Sofia 1431
Director: Mrs N Kudreva

Municipal Library*, ul Gurko 1, Sofia

National Library 'Ivan Vazov*, 4000 Plovdiv, Nikola Vaptzarov 17 Tel: 22915
Dir: Johan Lautliev

Sofia City and District State Archives*, ul Vitosha 2, Sofia
There are 26 District State Archives

Sofiiski Universitet 'Kliment Ohridsky' Biblioteka (University of Sofia Library)*, blvd Ruski 15, Sofia

Central Library of the Higher **Technical Instituts***, Dr Cankov 2, Sofia

Central **Technical Library***, Gurko 16, Sofia

Library Associations

Bulgarian Union of Public Libraries*, ul Alabin 31, Sofia

Sekciya na Bibliotechnite Rabotnitsi pri Centralniya Komitet na Profesionalniya Sŭyuz na Rabotnitsite ot **Poligraficheskata Promishlenost i Kulturnite Instituti***, c/o Cyril and Methodius National Library, blvd Tolbuhin 11, Sofia Tel: 882811
President: Stefan Kánčev
Section of the Librarians at the Professional Organization of the Workers in Polygraphics and Culture
Publications: Issues annual reports, and occasional publications jointly with the National Library, eg on IBY

Library Reference Books and Journals

Books

Biblioteki Bolgarii (Bulgarian Libraries), Cyril and Methodius National Library, blvd Tolbuhin 11, Sofia
Bibliotekoznanie, Bibliografiya, Knigoznanie Nauchna Informatsiya (Library Science, Bibliography, Scientific Information), Cyril and Methodius National Library, blvd Tolbuhin 11, Sofia

Journals

Bibliotekar (The Librarian), periodical for library work, (Contents page in Bulgarian, English and Russian), Committee for Culture and Art and the Cyril and Methodius National Library, blvd Tolbuhin 11, Sofia

Statisticheski Danni za Bibliotekite v Bŭlgariya (Statistical Data on Libraries in Bulgaria), Cyril and Methodius National Library, blvd Tolbuhin 11, Sofia

Literary Associations and Societies

Bulgarian Academy of Sciences, Institute of Literature*, blvd Vitosha 39, Sofia C

Komitet za Izkoustvo i Koultoura, (Committee for Arts and Culture)*, blvd Stambolissky 18, Sofia

Society of Aesthetes, Art and Literary Critics*, pl Evtimij 48, Sofia
Secretary: Dr K Goranov

Union of Bulgarian Writers*, angel Kanchev 5, Sofia
President: Academician Pantelev Zarev
Publications: Literaturen front, Septemvri, Plamuk, Savremennik, Slaveyche

Literary Periodicals

Literatourna Missul (Literary Thought), (text in Bulgarian, contents page in English and French), Bulgarian Academy of Sciences, Institute of Literature, blvd Vitosha 39, Sofia C

Obzor (Survey), Bulgarian quarterly review of literature and the arts (text in English, Spanish and French), Union of Bulgarian Writers, Committee for Friendship and Cultural Relations with Foreign Countries, blvd Dondukov 39, Sofia

Plamŭk (The Flame), literature, art, publicity, Union of Bulgarian Writers, angel Kanchev 5, Sofia

Literary Prizes

A competition for the best Bulgarian book published abroad is held at the annual Sofia International Book Fair

Bulgarian Publishing Award*
For the best artistic and technical achievements in the art of book publishing. Awarded annually. Enquiries to the Bulgarian People's Republic Council of Ministers, Committee for the Press and the Union of Bulgarian Artists, Sofia

Burma

General Information

Language: Burmese (English used for foreign correspondence)
Religion: Buddhism
Population: 31.5 million
Literacy Rate (1953): 69.1%
Bank Hours: 1000-1400 Monday-Friday; 1000-1200 Saturday
Shop Hours: Generally 0800-1700 Monday-Saturday
Currency: 100 pyas = 1 kyat
Export/Import Information: Burma has own complex tariff system, but duties are paid by State Trading Corporation No 9, 550-552 Merchant St, Rangoon, and Printing and Publishing Corporation, 228 Theinbyu St, Rangoon, principally. No tariffs on advertising. Books exempt from sales tax. Import licence required. Exchange controls; priorities apply
Copyright: No copyright conventions signed

Book Trade Organizations

Burmese Publishers' Union*, 146 Bogyoke Market, Rangoon

Publishers

Hanthawaddy Book House*, 157 Bo Aung Gyaw St, Rangoon
Subjects: Textbooks, Multilingual Dictionaries

Knowledge Printing & Publishing House*, 130 Bogyoke St, Yegyaw, Rangoon
Subjects: Art, Education, Politics, Religion, Sociology

Kyi-Pwar-Ye Book House*, 84th St, Letsegan Mandalay
Subjects: Travel, Arts, Religion, Juveniles

Sarpay Beikman Board*, 529 Merchant St, Rangoon Tel: 16611 Cable Add: Sarbeikman
Chairman: U Mya Maung; *Secretary:* U Aung Tun; *Sales, Publicity & Advertising:* U Tin Myint; *Editorial:* U Kyaw Khin
Subjects: Encyclopaedia, General Information, Culture, History, Applied Science, Agriculture, Law, Literature, Biography
Founded: 1947
Book Club: Sarpay Beikman Book Club, 529 Merchant St, Rangoon
Bookshop: 529 Merchant St, Rangoon

Shumawa Book House*, 146 Bogyoke Aung San Market, Rangoon
Bookshop: 1 Sandwith Rd, Rangoon
Subjects: Mechanical Engineering, Technical

Shwepyidan Printing & Publishing House*, 12(A) Hninban St, Yegwaw Quarter, Rangoon
Subjects: Politics, Law, Religion

Smart & Mookerdum*, 221 Sule Pagoda Rd, Rangoon
Subjects: Arts, Juveniles, Cookery, Popular Sciences

Than Myit Baho Publishing House*, 230 Anawyatha Rd, Rangoon
Subjects: Scientific, Technical

Thudhammawaddy Press*, 55-56 Moung Khine St, Rangoon
Subject: Religion

Universities Administration Office*, Prome Rd, University Post Office, Rangoon
Chief Editor, Translations and Publications Department: U Wun

Book Clubs

Sarpay Beikman Book Club*, 529 Merchant St, Rangoon

Major Booksellers

Ava Bookshop (Government Bookshop)*, 2 Sule Pagoda Rd, Rangoon

Chindwin Book Distributors*, 180 47th St, Rangooooon

Gondu*, 209 33rd St, Rangoon

Hanthawaddy Bookshop*, 357 Bo Aung Gyaw St, Rangoon

Hna Lon Hla*, 5 100th St, PO Box 87, Kandawlay PO, Rangoon

Knowledge Book House, 130 Bo Gyoke Aung San St, Rangoon

Pagan Publishing House, 123 Myamagonyi St, Kandawlay, Rangoon

Sabe U*, 148-150 33rd St, Rangoon

Sarpay Beikman Bookshop, 529 Merchant St, Rangoon

Sarpay Lawka, 173 33rd St, Rangoon

Shumawa Publishing House, 1 Sandwith Rd, Rangoon

Thwe Thauk, 341 Bo Aung Gyaw St, Rangoon

Major Libraries

Arts & Science University Library, University Estate, Mandalay

Institute of Economics Library, University Estate, Rangoon

Institute of Education Library, University Estate, Rangoon

Institute of Technology Library, Insein PO, Rangoon

International Institute of Advanced Buddhistic Studies Library, Kaba-aye Pagoda Compound, Rangoon

Magwe College Library, Magwe

National Library, Town Hall, Rangoon

State Library, Moulmein

Universities' Central Library, University Estate, Rangoon

Library Associations

Burma Library Association, c/o International Institute of Advanced Buddhistic Studies, Kaba Aya, Rangoon

Jubilee Library Association, c/o Steel Road, Toungoo

Literary Associations and Societies

Department of Ancient Literature and Culture, Ministry of Culture*, 1 Church Rd, Rangoon

Literary Prizes

National Literary Awards

When the Burma Translation Society (now renamed Sarpay Beikman Board) was founded in 1947 it established the Best-Published-Novel-of-the-Year Prize. Min Aung won the prize for 1948 with his book *Mo Auk Mye Byin* (Land under the Sky). The prize money was K1000 (one thousand kyats).

The awards were gradually increased and in 1962 Sarpay Beikman was offering nine awards. They were for the best published novel of the year, the best collection of short stories, the best belles lettres, the best book of knowledge, the best book of poems, the best translation of a world classic, and the best published play of the year. In the absence of any official literary awards, the Sarpay Beikman literary awards were virtually honoured as national literary awards.

When Sarpay Beikman was taken over by the Revolutionary Government in August 1963 the Sarpay Beikman Literary Awards were transformed into National Literary Awards. More literary awards were gradually added and there are now 12 awards. The awards are for the best published novel of the year, the best collection of short stories, the best belles lettres, the best book of knowledge (arts), the best book of knowledge (science), the best book of poems, the best translation of a world classic, the best published play, the best book for children, the best book for youth, the best book on Burmese culture and the best book on political affairs. A panel of literary specialists is formed every two years by the State to adjudicate the published works.

Each national literary award now draws prize money of K5000. The awards are presented at a ceremony on Sarsodaw Day (Literary Day), which usually falls in December. Enquiries to the Secretary, Sarpay Beikman Board, 529 Merchant St, Rangoon

Sarpay Beikman Best Manuscripts Awards

In order to discover new writers and to enable promising manuscripts to be published, Sarpay Beikman Board has established a competition for the Best-Manuscripts-of-the-Year-Awards since 1963. There are 11 prizes for the best manuscripts of the year: for novels, short stories, belles lettres, general knowledge (arts), general knowledge (science), plays, children's literature, literature for youth, Burmese cultural affairs, political affairs and translations of a prescribed literary material. There are first, second and third prizes for each award and prize moneys are K500, K300 and K200 respectively.

All prize-winning manuscripts (except translations) are published by Sarpay Beikman. Only the manuscript which wins the first prize in translation is published by Sarpay Beikman. Payments for the manuscripts are made on royalty basis and are for the first publication rights only. Enquiries to the Secretary, Sarpay Beikman Board, 529 Merchant St, Rangoon

Burundi

General Information

Language: Kirundi, but French is main language commercially
Religion: Predominantly Catholic but many animists
Population: 3.97 million
Bank Hours: normally closed for cash transactions in afternoon but open for all other business morning and afternoon
Shop Hours: 0800-1200, 1400-1630 Monday-Friday; 0800-1200 Saturday
Currency: Burundi franc
Export/Import Information: advertising matter subject to 35% revenue duty. 3% ad valorem statistical tax on all imports. Import licence required over value of 20,000 Burundi francs

Publishers

Government Printer*, BP 1400, Bujumbura

Les Presses Lavigerie*, 5 ave de l'Uprona, BP 1640, Bujumbura

Major Booksellers

Librairie A Gennotte & Fils*, BP 420, Bujumbura

Imparudi*, BP 509, Bujumbura

Librairie Larousse Centrafrique*, BP 525, Bujumbura

Librairie Saint Paul*, BP 1360, Bujumbura

Major Libraries

Bibliothèque Publique*, BP 960, Bujumbura

Ecole normale supérieure, Bibliothèque*, BP 1065, Bujumbura Tel: 3544
Librarian: Deogratias Ndayizeye
Publication: Pédagogie

Institut Murundi d'Information et de Documentation (IMIDOC)*, 7 ave Malfeyt, BP 902, Bujumbura

Bibliothèque de l'Université du Burundi*, BP 1320, Bujumbura Tel: 5196/5446
Librarian: H Mununi

Literary Associations and Societies

Centre culturel du Burundi*, BP 1582, Bujumbura

United Republic of Cameroun

General Information

Language: French and English (officially bilingual)
Religion: Predominantly Roman Catholic in west and south, Muslim in centre and north
Population: 7.91 million
Bank Hours: East: 0800-1130, 1430-1530 Monday-Friday; West: 0800-1330 Monday-Friday
Shop Hours: 0800-1200, 1430-1730 (earlier closing in West) Monday-Friday; 0800-1200 Saturday
Currency: CFA franc
Export/Import Information: No tariff on books, 7.5% fiscal, 30% customs, 10% VAT, 5% turnover tax on advertising matter. Import licence, entitling holder to provision for necessary foreign exchange, required. Exchange controls on non-Franc zone (and Congo, Mauritania and Malagasy)
Copyright: UCC, Berne, Florence (see International section)

Publishers

Editions C L E (Centre de Littérature Evangélique), BP 1501, Yaoundé
Tel: 223554 Cable/Telex: CLE Yaoundé
General Manager: Jean Dihang; *Sales Manager:* Nicolas Amengou
Subjects: General Fiction & Nonfiction, Belles Lettres, Poetry, Biography, History/Africana, How-to, Study Guides, Philosophy, Religion, Juveniles, Paperbacks, Medicine, General & Social Science, University & Secondary Textbooks
Founded: 1963
ISBN Publisher's Prefix: 2-7235

Centre d'Edition et de Production de Manuels et d'Auxiliaires de l'Enseignement*, Elig-Essono, BP 808, Yaoundé Tel: 221323
Cable Add: Cepmae-Yaoundé Telex: 8338
Dir General: Martin Medjo; *Technical Adviser;* Henry Meier; *Sales Manager:* François Mele
Subjects: General Nonfiction, History/Africana, Paperbacks, Science &

Technology, General & Social Science, University & Secondary Textbooks
Founded: 1967

Government Printer*, BP 1091, Yaoundé

Librairie/Imprimerie **Saint Paul***, Ave Monseigneur Vogt, BP 763, Yaoundé
Subjects: Religion, Christian tracts, Paperbacks, Secondary & Primary Textbooks
Bookshop: Libairie St Paul, BP 763, Yaoundé

Editions **Semences** Africaines, BP 2180, Yaoundé-Messa
Man Dir, Production: Philippe-Louis Ombede; *Editorial, Rights & Permissions:* Martin King Mbida; *Sales:* Ateba Joseph Kono
Subjects: General Fiction, History, Africana, Religion, Paperbacks, Secondary & Primary Textbooks (in French and English only), Poetry, Theatre
Bookshop: address as above
1977: 4 titles *1979:* 6 titles *Founded:* 1976

Société Kenkoson d'Etudes Africaines*, BP 4064, Yaoundé
Chief Executive: Marie Salomé
Subjects: Academic, Law
Founded: 1975

Major Booksellers

Librairie '**Aux Frères Réunis**'*, BP 5346, Douala

Cameroun Book Centre, 2C Nambeke St, PO Box 123, Victoria Tel: 332255

L'Imprimerie **Coulouma***, BP 134, Yaoundé

La Librairie L'**Equatoriale***, BP 324, Yaoundé

Librairie-Papeterie Moderne*, BP 495, Yaoundé

Librairie-Papeterie Protestante CEBEC*, BP 225, Douala

Presbyterian Book Depot and Printing Press Ltd (PRESBOOK), PO Box 13, Victoria, Cameroun Tel: Victoria 337214/335246 Telex: 5613 KW
Branches: Presbook Mankon, PO Box 39, Bamenda; Presbook Kumbo, PO Box 4; Presbook Bura, PO Box 19; Presbook Kumba 87; Presbook Douala (Akwa)

Librairie **Saint Paul***, BP 763, Yaoundé

Major Libraries

Archives nationales du Cameroun*, BP 1053, Yaoundé

Bibliothèque nationale du Cameroun*, BP 1053, Yaoundé Tel: 220078

British Council Library*, BP 818, Yaoundé Tel: 221696

Centre culturel américain, Bibliothèque*, American Embassy, BP 817, Yaoundé Tel: 221633 ext 229
Librarian: Emile Mongo-Bebey

Centre culturel français, Bibliothèque*, BP 513, Yaoundé Tel: 220533

Collège camerounais des Arts, des Sciences et de la Technologie, Bibliothèque*, Bamili, BP Bamenda

De **Sautoy** College Library*, Pan African Institute for Development, PO Box 133, Buea, South-West Province Tel: 328216
Librarian: Eugene O Nwanosike

Université de Yaoundé, Bibliothèque*, BP 1312, Yaoundé Tel: 220744
Librarian: Peter Nkangafaok Chateh
Publications: Discours de la Rentrée Solennelle de l'Université (annual), *Newsletter de l'ABADCAM* (bi-monthly)

Library Associations

Association des Bibliothécaires, Archivistes, Documentalistes et Muséographes du Cameroun (ABADCAM)*, c/o P N Chateh, President, ABADCAM, Bibliothèque Universitaire, BP 1312, Yaoundé Tel: 220744
Secretary General: Th. Eno Belinga
Association of Librarians, Archivists, Documentalists and Museum Curators of Cameroun
Publications: Newsletter

Library Journal

Newsletter, Association of Librarians, Archivists, Documentalists and Museum Curators of Cameroun, c/o P N Chateh, President, Bibliothèque Universitaire, BP 312, Yaoundé

Literary Associations and Societies

Association nationale des Poètes et Ecrivains camerounais (APEC), BP 2180, Yaoundé-Messa
National Association of Cameroun Poets and Writers
Secretary-General: R Philombe
Publication: Cameroun littéraire

Centre d'Edition et de Production de Manuels scolaires de l'UNESCO*, Yaoundé

Forum littéraire camerounais*, BP 73, Yaoundé
Cameroun Literary Workshop

Literary Periodicals

Abbia, Editions CLE, BP 1501 Yaoundé
An influential literary and cultural magazine edited by Bernard Fonlon; publication has been rather irregular during the past few years

Cameroun littéraire (Literary Cameroun) (text in English and French), National Association of Cameroun Poets and Writers, BP 2180, Yaoundé-Messa

Ozila, Cameroun Literary Workshop, BP 73, Yaoundé

A 'little magazine' edited by Jean-Pierre Togolo and published by the Cameroun Literary Workshop

Central African Republic

General Information

Language: French
Religion: Christian and animist
Population: 2 million
Bank Hours: 0700-1200 Monday-Saturday
Shop Hours: 0700 or 0800-1200 or 1230, 1430 or 1500–1830 or 1900 Tuesday-Saturday, mostly
Currency: CFA franc
Export/Import Information: No tariff on books; advertising has 7.5% Fiscal Duty, 30% Customs Duty and 10% Turnover Tax. Import licence required but grant automatically to original six EEC members. Imports subject to quotas. Exchange controls outside franc zone
Copyright: Berne (see International Section)

Publishers

Government Printer (Imprimerie Centrale d'Afrique)*, BP 329, Bangui

Major Booksellers

Au Messager*, BP 823, Bangui

Librairie **Hachette***, BP 823, Bangui

Librairie évangélique*, BP 240, Bangui

Papeterie Centrale*, BP 1442, Bangui

'**Papyrus**'*, BP 920, Bangui

Major Libraries

Centre culturel français*, Bibliothèque, BP 971, Bangui Tel: 2927

Bibliothèque de l'**Université Jean-Bédel Bokassa** (National Library)*, BP 1450, Bangui Tel: 2424

Chad

General Information

Language: French
Religion: Muslim in north, Christian or animist in south
Population: 4.21 million
Bank Hours: 0700-1200 Monday-Saturday
Shop Hours: 0700 or 0800-1200 or 1230, 1430 or 1500-1900 Tuesday-Saturday
Currency: CFA franc
Export/Import Information: No tariff on books; total duty and taxes on advertising matter is 40%. Consumption tax on children's picture books and advertising 10%. Import licences required. Import Turnover Tax of 10% on advertising. Exchange controls on non-franc zone
Copyright: Berne (see International section)

Publishers

Government Printer*, BP 69, N'Djamena

Major Booksellers

Georges **Abtour** SA, Librairie-Papeterie*, BP 103, N'Djamena

Bielmas Librairie-Papeterie*, BP 71, N'Djamena

Librairie **Billeret***, BP 463, N'Djamena

Librairie **évangélique***, BP 127, N'Djamena

Librairie **Notre Dame***, BP 7, N'Djamena Tel: 3330

Major Libraries

Bibliothèque paroissiale (Parochial Library)*, Cathédrale Notre-Dame, BP 456, N'Djamena Tel: 3350

Centre culturel américain, Bibliothèque*, BP 3, N'Djamena Tel: 2846

Centre culturel français, Bibliothèque*, BP 901, N'Djamena Tel: 2920

Centre de Documentation Pédagogique, Bibliothèque*, BP 731, N'Djamena Tel: 2327

Bibliothèque de l'**Université du Tchad***, BP 1117, N'Djamena Tel: 2176

Chile

General Information

Language: Spanish
Religion: Roman Catholic
Population: 10.7 million
Literacy Rate (1970): 88.1% (92.4% Urban, 72.8% Rural)
Bank Hours: 0900–1400 Monday-Friday; 0900–1200 Saturday
Shop Hours (Santiago): 1500–1900 Monday; 1000–1900 Tuesday-Friday; 0900–1300 Saturday
Currency: 100 centavos = 1 peso
Export/Import Information: Ad valorem for books generally 20% (children's picture books 40%, atlases 30%); advertising matter 40%. Advertising material dutiable if not sent in envelopes, no more than 2 lb. 6% Sales Tax on advertising. Import licences and exchange controls
Copyright: UCC, Berne, Buenos Aires (see International section)

Book Trade Organizations

Cámara Chilena del Libro*, Av Bulnes 188, Casilla 2787, Santiago Tel: 81519
Secretary: A Newman N
Chilean Publishers' Association

Book Trade Reference Journal

Anuario de la prensa chilena (Yearbook of Chilean Publications), National Library, Ave Bernardo O'Higgins 651, Santiago

Publishers

Aguilar Chilena de Ediciones, subsidiary of Aguilar SA de Ediciones, Spain (qv)

Editorial **Andrés Bello**/Juridíca de Chile*, Ave Ricardo Lyon 946, Casilla 4256, Santiago Tel: 40041 Cable Add: Edibel
General Manager: Carlos Ducci Claro;
Editorial: Lucía Wormald Delpiano;
Commercial: Francisco Hoyl Sotomayor;
Publicity: María Teresa Herreros
Subjects: Medicine, History, Social Science, Literature Law
Bookshop: Librería Andrés Bello, Huérfanos 1158, Santiago Tel: 722116
1976: 52 titles *Founded:* 1947

Centro Latinoamericano de Demografía (CELADE)*, Edificio Naciones Unidas, Ave Dag Hammarskjöld, Casilla 91, Santiago
Subjects: Demography, Statistics, Sociology

Editorial Universitaria, Maria Luisa Santander 0447, Casilla 10220, Santiago Tel: 383405/234555 Cable Add: Edunsa
Man Dir: Eduardo Castro LeFort
Subjects: General Literature, General & Social Science, Technical, Textbooks
Founded: 1947

Editorial **Gustavo Gili** Ltda*, Santa Beatriz 120, Santiago
Parent Company: Editorial Gustavo Gili SA, Spain (qv)

Grijalbo y Cía Ltda*, Casilla 180–d, Santiago
Parent Company: Editorial Grijalbo SA, Mexico (qv)

Editora Nacional Gabriela **Mistral** Ltda*, Ave Santa María 076, Santiago Tel: 779522
Man Dir: José Harrison de la Barra; *Sales & Publicity Dir:* Jorge Sims Sn Roman
Subjects: Literature, Biography, History, Philosophy, Reference, Religion, How-to, Art, Juveniles, Secondary & Primary Textbooks
Miscellaneous: Government-owned

Editorial **Mundo Nuevo***, Pasaje Matte 342 of 16, Santiago Tel: 381646
Manager: Servando Salgado R
Miscellaneous: Associate company of Editorial El Sembrador, Santiago (qv)

Editorial **Nascimento** SA*, Chiloe 1433, Casilla 2298, Santiago Tel: 569405 Cable Add: Nascimento
Man Dir: Carlos George-Nascimento Marquez
Subjects: General Fiction & Nonfiction, Scholarly Books
Bookshop: Librería Nascimento, San Antonio 390 Tel: 32062
Founded: 1898

Editorial y Distribuidora **Orbe***, Miraflores 354, Santiago Tel: 36220/33698/303346
Subjects: General Fiction & Nonfiction
Founded: 1939

Editorial del **Pacifico** SA*, Alonso Ovalle 766, Casilla 3547, Santiago Tel: 397805/395317
General Manager: Arturo Valdes Phillips;
Editorial: Lidio Ramirez Rivera; *Sales:* Jose de Gregorio Aroca; *Production:* Emilio Pot Von; *Publicity:* Mrs Magali Zamorano Castro; *Rights & Permission:* Raul Zamora Messina
Associate Company: Ediciones Mar del Sur, Casilla 13844, Santiago
Subsidiary Company: Distribuidora Alonso Ovalle Ltda
Subjects: History, Politics, Economics, Literature, Educations, Primary, Secondary and University Textbooks
1977: 19 titles *1978:* 21 titles *Founded:* 1946

Ediciones **Paulinas***, Vicuña MacKenna 6299, Casilla 3429, Santiago Tel: 212832
Orders to: Centro Catequistico Paulino, Cienfuegos 60, Casilla 3429, Santiago Tel: 64650
Subjects: Catholic texts
Bookshop: Librería San Pablo, Ave Bernardo O'Higgins 1626, Santiago, Centro Catequistico Paulino, Cienfuegos 60, Santiago; Branches in Antofagasta, Concepción & Valparaiso

Pineda Libros*, Bandera 101, Casilla 13556, Santiago Tel: 721807
Man Dir: A Gonzalo Pineda
Subjects: Literature, History, Juveniles, Paperbacks
Bookshops: Pergola del Libro: Merced 838; Bandera 101 (both in Santiago)
Founded: 1944

Editorial **Pomaire** SA, Román Diaz 587, Santiago
Parent Company: Editorial Pomaire, Spain (qv)

Editorial El **Sembrador***, Pasaje Matte 342-344, Santiago Tel: 35295
Dir, Editorial: Servando Salgado R
Associate Company: Editorial Mundo Nuevo, Santiago (qv)
Bookshop: Librería El Sembrador, Pasaje Matte 342-344, Casilla 2037, Santiago

Ediciones **Universitarias de Valparaiso***, Universidad Católica de Valparaiso, Yungay 2872, Of 2, Casilla 1415, Valparaiso Tel: 59105/52900 Cable Add: Casilla 1415, Valparaiso Telex: Ucval 30389
Man Dir, Editorial: Renato C Flores;
Production: L A Briones Solis
Br Off: Moneda 673, 8° piso, Santiago Tel: 383137
Subjects: General Literature, Social Sciences, Engineering, Education, Music & Arts, Textbooks, Children's Books
1977: 27 titles *Founded:* 1970

Empressa Editora **Zig-Zag** SA*, Providencia 199, 4° piso, Casilla 84–D, Santiago Tel: 234675

Book Club

Studio Book Club, PO Box 1227, Santiago (Located at: Andres de Fuenzalida 36, Santiago) Tel: 259432/465799 Cable Add: Studio Telex: 40084 STUDI CL
Members: 200
Owned by: Elise Friedler Librería Studio
See also under Booksellers

Major Booksellers

Librería **Andrés Bello***, Huérfanos 1158, Santiago Tel: 722116

C E D I L (Centro Distribuidor de Libros)*, Arturo Prat 1477, Casilla 5454, Correo 3, Santiago Tel: 568029
Manager: Servando Salgado R

Cooperativa del Libro*, José Miguel Infante 22, Santiago Tel: 461747

Librería y Editorial Cultura*, Huérfanos 1179, Santiago Tel: 88830

Feria Chilena del Libro*, Huérfanos 1112, Santiago Tel: 721420

Librería Tecno-Ciencia*, Huérfanos 972, Of 409, Casilla 367, Santiago Tel: 64975

Librería Universitaria*, Ave Bernardo O'Higgins 1050, Casilla 10220, Santiago Tel: 84135

Librería Orellana*, Esmeralda 1148, Valparaiso Tel: 51821

Librería Parera*, Condell 1202–1206, Valparaiso Tel: 57162

Librería Pax-Chile*, Calle Huérfanos 770, Santiago Tel: 393822

Librería San Pablo*, Ave Bernardo O'Higgins 1626, Casilla 3746, Santiago Tel: 89145

Librería El Sembrador*, Pasaje Matte 342–344, Casilla 2037, Santiago Tel: 396675/35295 (two other branches in Santiago, and one in Arica)

Librería Studio, Andrés de Fuenzalida 36, Santiago Tel: 259432/465799 Cable Add: Studio Telex: 40084 STUDI CL Branches in Concepcion and Valparaiso

Major Libraries

Biblioteca Nacional*, Ave Bernardo O'Higgins 651, Santiago Tel: 381151

Biblioteca Nacional de Chile de la Dirección de Bibliotecas, Archivos y Museos*, Santiago
Dir: Enrique Campos Menendez
Administration of Libraries, Archives & Museums

Biblioteca del Congreso Nacional, Huérfanos 1117, 2° piso, Clasificador 1199, Santiago
Dir: Jorge Ivan Hübner Gallo; *Librarian:* Jose Miguel Vicuña Lagarrigue
Library of Congress
Publications include: Boletin bibliográfico; Efímeros

Biblioteca del Instituto Chileno-Británico de Cultura*, Casilla 3900, Santiago

Biblioteca Central de la Universidad Católica de Chile*, Ave Bernardo O'Higgins 340, Santiago Tel: 224236
Dir: María Teresa Sanz
Publications: Bibliografía Eclesiástica Chilena; Presentación del trabajo escrito

Biblioteca de la Universidad Católica de Valparaisod*, Casilla 4059, Valparaiso

Biblioteca Central de la Universidad de Chile*, Calle Arturo Prat 23, Santiago

Biblioteca Central de la Universidad de Concepción*, Casilla 1807, Concepción

Library Associations

Centro Nacional de Información y Documentación (CENID), Casilla 297–V, Santiago (Located at: Canada 308, Santiago)

Colegio de Bibliotecarios de Chile, Diagonal Paraguay 383, Torre II, Departamento 122, Casilla 3741, Santiago
President: Maria Teresa Sanz
Chilean Library Association
Publications: Boletin del Colegio de Bibliotecarios de Chile, Noticias del Colegio, Indices de Publicaciones Periodicas en Bibliotecología

Library Reference Books and Journals

Books

Guía de Bibliotecas y Centros de Documentación de Chile (Guide to Chilean Libraries and Centres of Documentation), National Centre of Information and Documentation, Bernarda Morín 560, Casilla 297–V, Correo 21, Santiago

Journals

Indices de Publicaciones Periodicas en Bibliotecología (Catalogue of Periodical Publications on Librarianship), Chilean Library Association, Diagonal Paraguay 383, Torre II, Departamento 122, Casilla 3741, Santiago

Literary Associations and Societies

Sociedad de Bibliófilos Chilenos*, Casilla 895, Santiago
Secretary: Ramón Eyzaguirre
Publication: El Bibliófilo Chileno (annual)

Literary Periodicals

El Bibliófilo Chileno (The Chilean Bibliophile), Society of Chilean Bibliophiles, Casilla 895, Santiago

Mapocho, Editorial Universitaria, Maria Luisa Santander 0447, Casilla 10220, Santiago

Revista Chilena de Literatura (Chilean Review of Literature), Editorial Universitaria, Maria Luisa Santander 0447, Casilla 10220, Santiago

Taller de Letras (Workshop of Letters), Editorial Universidad Católica, Diagonal Oriente 3300, Santiago

People's Republic of China

General Information

Language: Chinese
Religion: Atheistic state
Population: 866 million
Shop Hours: Generally 0900-1900 daily
Currency: 10 chiao (or 10 fen) = 1 yuan
Export/Import Information: Foreign trade is a state monopoly. The foreign distributor for Chinese publications is Guozi Shudian, PO Box 399, Peking. The importing organization is Waiwen Shudian, PO Box 88, Peking.

Book Trade Reference Journal

Quan guo xin shu mu bian ji bu (Chinese National Bibliography), Bei Zong Bu Hu Tong 33 Hao, Peking

Publishers

China Youth Publishing House*, Peking
Subjects: Literature, Journals
Founded: 1953

Chung Hua Book Co*, Peking
Subject: Chinese Classics

Commercial Press, 36 Wang Fu Jing St, Peking
Subject: Foreign translations

Foreign Languages Press*, Peking 37
Subjects: Languages, Translations

Hsinhua New China Book Agency*, Peking
Subjects: All

National Minorities Publishing House*, Peking
Subject: Books in languages spoken by minorities in China

People's Literature Publishing House*, Peking and Shanghai

People's Physical Culture Publishing House*, Peking
Subjects: Sport books & pictorial magazines

Publishing Department*, Peking
Special agency of the State Council; undertakes the major part of book publishing in China

Renmin-Jiyou-Chuban-She (People's Education Publishing Co)*, Peking
Subject: Education

'Sanlian Shudian' Publishing House, Peking
A state publishing house; general, political and literary

Workers' Press*, Peking
Publishing house of All China Federation of Trade Unions

Writers' Publishing House*, Peking
A state enterprise publishing reprints of Chinese literature

Youth Publishing House*, Peking

Major Booksellers

Guozi Shudian, China Publications Centre*, PO Box 399, Peking
Distributor abroad for Chinese publications

Waiwen Shudian*, PO Box 88, 38 Suchou Hutung, Peking
Importer for foreign publications

Major Libraries

The Library of Academia Sinica*, 9 Wang Fu Ta Chei, Peking

Beijing Tushuguan, see Pei-ching t'u shu kuan

Chekiang Library*, Hangchow

Ch'in-hua ta hsueh t'u shu kuan (Tsinghua University Library), Peking

Chung-kuo k'o hsueh yuan t'u shu kuan (Central Library of the China Academy of Sciences)*, 3 Wen-chin-chieh, Peking
Director: Tung Tseng-kung

Chungking Library*, Chungking

Chungshan Library of Kwangtung Province, Canton

Liaoning Library*, Shenyang (Mukden)

Nan-ching t'u shu kuan (Nanking Library)*, Nanking, Kiangsu

Pei-ching t'u shu kuan (National Library of Peking), Peking 7
Director: Liu Ji-ping

Pei-ching ta hsueh t'u shu kuan (Peking University Library)*, Peking
Director: Guo Song-nian
Includes the Library School

Shang-hai t'u shu kuan (Shanghai Library)*, Shanghai
Director: Pan Hao-ping

Yunnan Provincial Library*, Kunming
Director: Mo Tien-Chuang

Literary Periodicals

Chinese Literature (English and French editions), Foreign Languages Press, Peking 37. Subscriptions to Guozi Shudian, PO Box 399, Peking

China (Taiwan)

General Information

Language: Chinese (Amoy dialect)
Religion: Confucianism, Buddhism, Taoism, Christianity
Population: 7.6 million
Literacy Rate (1956): 45.5%
Bank Hours: 0900-1200 Monday-Friday; 0900-1530 Saturday
Shop Hours: 0800-1700 Monday-Saturday
Currency: 100 cents = 1 new Taiwan dollar
Export/Import Information: No tariffs on books and advertising. Import licences required; exchange available when licence presented at authorized bank
Copyright: No copyright conventions signed

Book Trade Reference Journals

Chinese National Bibliography (text in Chinese and English), National Central Library, 43 Nan Hai Rd, Taipei 107

Shu mo chi kan (Bibliography quarterly), (text in Chinese), Student Book Co Ltd, 298 Roosevelt Rd, 3rd Section, Taipei

Publishers

Business Publications Ltd, PO Box 58432, Taipei (Located at: Hui Feng Bldg 3rd/4th Fl, No 20 Lane 14 Chi Lin Rd, Taipei) Tel: 5216457/5218784 Cable Add: Andypandy Telex: 21032 ANDY
Man Dir: Michelle Yang; *Editorial:* Nigel White; *Sales, Publicity:* Hellen Tsai; *Production:* Dawn Chen; *Rights & Permissions:* Mark Van Roo
Associate Companies: Andy Pandy Pty Ltd (Hui Feng Bldg 3rd Fl); Business English Center (4th Fl)
Subjects: International Business, Business English Textbooks, Business Dictionary (English/Chinese), Periodical Magazine: *Current Business Affairs in Taiwan and International Trade*
Bookshop: (at above address)
1978: 5 titles *1979:* 10 titles *Founded:* 1978

Cheng Chung Book Co*, 20 Hengyang Rd, Taipei
Subjects: Academic

Chung Hwa Book Co Ltd*, 94 Chungking S Rd, Section 1, Taipei 100 Tel: 3117365/3117344/3113541 Cable Add: 2821 Taipei
Man Dir: D S Hsiung; *Sales Dir:* C C Ku; *Publicity Dir:* Mrs S M Sun
Subjects: General Fiction, Belles Lettres, Poetry, Biography, History, How-to, Music, Art, Philosophy, Reference, Religion, Juveniles, Low- & High-priced Paperbacks, Medicine, Psychology, Engineering, General & Social Science, University, Secondary & Primary Textbooks, Educational Materials
1977: 220 titles *Founded:* 1911

Eastern Publishing Co Ltd*, 121 Chungking S Rd, Section 1, PO Box 75, Taipei
Subjects: Geography, Atlases, Agriculture, General Technology

Far East Book Co*, 66 (10th Floor) Chungking S Rd, Section 1, Taipei
Manager: Peter Y K Pu
Subjects: Art, Education, History, Physics, Dictionaries, Shakespeare in translation

Fu-Hsing Book Co*, 44 Huai Ning St, Taipei
Subject: Textbooks

Great China Book Corporation*, 66 Chungking S Rd, Section 1, Taipei
Subject: Textbooks

Hua Kuo Publishing Co*, 6 Lane 180, Section 1, Ho-ping East Rd, Taipei
Publisher: T F Wang
Founded: 1950

San Min Book Co*, 77 Chung Ching S Rd, Section 1, Taipei
Subjects: History, Philosophy, Sociology

Tah Chung Book Co*, 37-1 Chung Shan N Rd, 2nd Section, Taipei
Subjects: Health, Music, Physics, Technical, Economics

World Book Co*, 99 Chungking S Rd, Section 1, Taipei

Yee Wen Publishing Co Ltd*, PO Box 969, Taipei
(Surburban Office Address: 14 Shiao-Chien St, Panchiao, Taipei, Taiwan 220) Tel: (02) 9616321

Major Booksellers

J Cynthia Co Ltd*, PO Box 24-92, Taipei, Taiwan 106

Great Publications Co Ltd*, PO Box 58213, Taipei

H C Ling Book Store & Co Ltd*, PO Box 322, Taipei, Taiwan 100

Mei Ya Publications Inc (Sueling, Inc)*, PO Box 22555, Taipei Tel: 5414915

The **National Book** Co*, 84-5 Sec 3, Sing Sung South Rd, Taipei

Southeast Book Co*, 105 Po Ali Rd, Taipei

Taipei Publications Trading Co, PO Box 59326, Taipei
Manager: Y C Huang

Unifacmanu Trading Co Ltd*, 3 Lane 292, Jia Shing St, Taipei Tel: 341-9646

Major Libraries

Fu Ssu-Nien Library Institute of History and Philology*, Academia Sinica, Taipei

Kuomintang Central Committee Library*, Taipei

National Central Library*, 43 Nan Hai Rd, Taipei Tel: 3113981 (Office of the Director); 3114501 (Reference and Readers' Service Department)

National War College Library*, Yangmingshan, Taipei

Taipei Municipal Library*, Hsin I Rd, Section 4, Taipei

Taiwan Branch Library, National Central Library*, 1 Hsinshen South Rd, Section 1, Taipei, Taiwan 106
Librarian: Henry H S Jeng

Library Associations

Library Association of China, c/o National Central Library, 43 Nan Hai Rd, Taipei
Executive Dir: Karl M Ku
Publication: Library Association of China Newsletter (quarterly in Chinese)

Library Science Society*, c/o Department of Library Science, National Taiwan University, Roosevelt Rd, 4th Section, Taipei
President: Professor Tsin-Fu Chow
Publication: Biblioteca (Bulletin of the Library Science Society, National Taiwan University); Chinese, partly in English

Library Reference Journals

Chung-kuo t'u-shu-kuan hsueh-hui hui-pao (Bulletin of the Library Association of China), National Central Library, 43 Nan Hai Rd, Taipei

Journal of Library and Information Science, National Taiwan Normal University, Department of Social Education, Taipei

Literary Associations and Societies

China National Association of Literature and the Arts*, No 4, Lane 22, Ningpo St West, Taipei

National Council of Ethnographic Arts and Literature of China*, 11 Terrace 5, Lane 5, Section 3, Jan-Ai Rd, Taipei

Literary Periodicals

Counter Attack, National Institute for Compilation and Translation, 247 Keelung Rd, Taipei

Tamkang Review, a journal mainly devoted to comparative studies between Chinese and foreign literatures (text in English), Tamkang College, Graduate Institute of Western Languages a Literature, King-Hua St, Taipei

Yeh ko (Evensongs) (text in Chinese or English), Tamkang College, English Department Evening School, Evensongs Association, No 5, Lane 199, King-hua St, Taipei

Translation Agencies and Associations

National Institute for Compilation and Translation*, 247 Keelung Rd, Taipei
Dir: Tien-Ming Wang
Publication: Counter Attack

Colombia

General Information

Language: Spanish (English widely used in business)
Religion: Roman Catholic
Population: 25 million
Literacy Rate (1964): 72.9%
Bank Hours: 0900-1500 Monday-Friday
Shop Hours: 0900-1230, 1430-1830 Monday-Saturday
Currency: 100 centavos = 1 peso
Export/Import Information: 7.5% added taxes on all imports; no sales tax on books. Ad valorem: none generally on books except 50% on books bound in leather or similar materials, 50% on photonovels of thrillers, detective stories etc, and horoscopes, 10% on children's picture books, 10% on atlases. Advertising catalogues 45%. No import licence for books. Exchange licence from Banco de la Republica required
Copyright: UCC, Buenos Aires (see International section)

Book Trade Organizations

Cámara Colombiana de la Industria Editorial, Carrera 7a, No 17-51 Oficinas 409 y 410, Apdo 8998, Bogotá Tel: 821117/428403
Executive Secretary: Hipólito Hincapié
Colombian Publishers' Association
Publication: Libros Colombianos

Cámara Colombiana del Libro*, Carrera 50, 52-126 of 411, Medellin Tel: 425714; Carrera 54, 52-15P3 Tel: 457778
Colombian Book Association

Book Trade Reference Books and Journals

Books

Guia de Editoriales, Distribuidores y Librerias de Bogotá, CERLAL, Calle 70 No. 9-52, Apdo 17438, Bogotá

Journals

Anuario Bibliográfico Colombiano 'Rubén Pérez Ortiz' (Colombian Bibliographical Annual), Instituto Caro y Cuervo, Apdo Aéreo 51502, Bogotá

Bibliografia Oficial Colombiana (Official Colombian Bibliography), Escuela Interamericana de Bibliotecología, Universidad de Antioquia, Apdo Aéreo 1226, Medellín

Libros Colombianos (Colombian Books), Colombian Publishers' Association, Apdo 8998, Bogotá

Publishers

Aguilar Colombiana de Ediciones+*, Calle 13 7-40, Bogotá Tel: 432046
Man Dir: Gustavo de Florza
Parent Company: Aguilar SA de Ediciones, Spain (qv)

Editorial **Bedout** SA+, Apdo Aéreo 760, Medellín (Located at: Calle 61 No 51-04, Medellín) Tel: 316900 Cable Add: Bedout
President: Manuel de Bedout del Valle;
Editorial: Hernando Londoño Arango; *Sales Dir:* Miguel Angel Rojas; *Production:* Libardo Maya Upegui; *Publicity:* Fabio Arango Saraz
Branch Offs: Ave Jiménez 9-47, Bogatá DE, Plaza de Caicedo, Edificio Lloreda Of No 301, Cali; Calle 45 No 36-50, Barranquilla; Carrera 51 No 61-27, Medellín
Subjects: Literature, Social Science, Textbooks, Juveniles
1977: 80 titles *1978:* 90 titles *Founded:* 1889

Editorial **Bruguera** Colombiana Ltda+*, Calle 18, 8-64, Bogotá Tel: 429610
Man Dir: Antonio Mourin
Parent Company: Editorial Bruguera SA, Spain (qv)

Instituto **Caro** y Cuervo, Apdo Aéreo 51502, Bogotá Tel: 557753
Man Dir: José Manuel Rivas Sacconi
Bookshops: Librería Yerbabuena, Carrera 11, 64-37, Bogotá; Librería Cuervo, Calle, 10, 4-77, Bogotá
Subjects: Belles Lettres, Linguistics, Philology, Reference
Founded: 1942

Carvajal SA, Apdo Aéreo 46, Cali Tel: 681111 Cable Add: Carvajales Cali Telex: 055555
Subsidiary Company: Editorial Norma (qv)
Subjects: Children's Pop-ups, Juveniles, Textbooks

Fundación **Centro** de Investigación ed Educación Popular (CINEP)*, Carrera 5 No 33 A 08, Apdo Aéreo 25916, Bogota Tel: 324440/698160
Man Dir, Rights & Permissions: Alejandro Angulo Novoa; *Sales Manager:* Gilberto Gómez Arango; *Production, Publicity:* María Cecilía de Roux de Salazar
Subjects: Colombian Politics & Economics, Sociology
1977: 17 titles *Founded:* 1959

Cultural Colombiana Ltda+, Calle 72 no 16-15/21, Apdo Aéreo 6307, Nacional 2169, Bogotá Tel: 355494/483311/483236 Cable Add: Culbiana
Man Dir: José Porto; *Editorial:* Jose Porto Vazquez; *Sales Dirs:* Hernando Salazar; *Production:* Maximilian Gomez
Associate Company: Cultural Colombiana de Occidente Ltda
Subjects: Primary & Secondary Textbooks
Bookshop: Carrera 9a, 16-72
1977: 32 titles *1978:* 83 titles *Founded:* 1951
ISBN Publishers Prefix: 84-8273

Edinorma Ltda y Cía SCA+, Calle 37 No 13-08, Apdo Aéreo 53550, Bogotá Tel: 2851600/853297 Cable Add: Edinorma
President: Alberto José Carvajal: *General Manager:* Humberto Serna Gómez *Editorial Dir:* Daniel Ordóñez
Subjects: Textbooks, Children's Books, Juveniles, General Interest, Magazines

Editorial **Interamericana** SA+*, Apdo Aéreo 6131, Bogotá (Located at: Carrera 17 No 33-71) Tel: 454786
General Manager: Angel Alonso Valdizán
Miscellaneous: Firm is an associate company of Holt-Saunders Ltd, UK (qv for other associates)

Fondo Educativo Interamericano SA+, Apdo Aéreo 29696, Bogotá Tel: 258839/2492088 Cable Add: Adiwes-Bogota Telex: 45581
Man Dir: Luis Felipe Martínez
Miscellaneous: This is the editorial department of Fondo Educativo Interamericano, of Panamá
Associate Company: Addison-Wesley Publishers Ltd, UK (qv for other associates)
Subjects: University Textbooks, School Texts, Trade Books
1978: 20 titles *1979:* 120 titles *Founded:* 1970

Editorial Gustavo **Gili** Ltda+*, Diagonal 45 No 16B-11 Bogotá Tel: 456760
Man Dir: Antonio Huidobro
Parent Company: Editorial Gustavo Gili SA, Spain (qv)

Editorial **Gran América***, Carrera 52, 67-35, Medellín

Editorial **Juventud** Ltda+*, Calle 63-A, 10-30, Bogotá 2 Tel: 481634
Man Dir: Santiago Preckler
Parent Company: Editorial Juventud SA, Spain (qv)

Editorial **Labor** Colombiana Ltda+*, Carrera 9a-A, 18-08 (Pasaje Comercial Calle 19), Bogotá Tel: 698301
Man Dir: Enrique Fajardo
Parent Company: Editorial Labor, Spain (qv)

Legislación Económica Ltda, Ave Las Americas 58-51, Apdo Aéreo 8646, Bogotá Tel: 2605200 Cable Add: Legislación
Man Dir: Tito Livio Caldas
Subsidiary Company: Legislación Económica Srl, URB Industrial la Urbina, Calle 8, Edifico Lec, Caracas, Venezuela
Subjects: Economics, Law, Commerce
Founded: 1952

Ediciones **Lerner** Ltda+, Ave Jiménez de Quesada 4-35 y Calle 8-A-No 68-A-41, Bogotá Tel: 430567/623-505/720/986 Cable Add: Edilerner Telex: 43195

COLOMBIA

Man Dir: Salomon Lerner Mutzmajer;
Editorial: Jack A Grimberg; *Sales:*
A Londono
Subjects: Literature, History, Medicine
Bookshop: address as above
Founded: 1959

Editorial **McGraw-Hill** Latinoamericana
SA+*, Calle 60, 15-99, Apdo Aéreo 11255,
Bogotá Tel: 2351952/2357741
Man Dir: Daniel Waingart; *Editorial:*
Michael Bates
Subjects: Engineering, Technology, Biology,
Physics, Chemistry, Mathematics,
Psychology, Sociology, Textbooks
1977: 21 titles

Editorial **Norma** y Cia SCA*, Calle 37 No
13-08, Apdo Aereo 53550, Bogotá Tel:
453152/2851600 Cable Add: Edinorma
Telex: 44855
Man Dir: Humberto Serna G; *Editorial:*
D Ordonez, J Camacho; *Sales:* G Mateus C;
Production: A Martinez (Infants and
Juveniles), J Bonfante (School Textbooks)
Parent Company: Carvajal SA (qv)
Subsidiary Company: Publicar Ltda
Branch Offs: at Bogota, Cali, Medellin,
Barranquilla, Cartagena, Manizales, Ibaqué,
Neiva, Bucaramanga, Cúcuta
Subjects: General, Juveniles, Primary &
Secondary Textbooks, Education
1977: 43 titles *Founded:* 1964

Editorial **Pluma** Ltda, Carrera 22 No 35-45,
Apdo Aéreo 345, Bogotá Tel: 2453458
Cable Add: Edipluma Telex: 044420
Subjects: Politics, Psychology, Social
Science, Philosophy, Essays, Co-publishers
of complete works of Trotsky in Spanish

Editorial **Pomaire** SA+*, Carrera 20, 53-47,
Bogotá
Parent Company: Editorial Pomaire, Spain
(qv)

Editora **Reverté** Colombiana SA+*, Calle
22 No 6-16, of 202, Bogotá Tel: 419330
Associate Companies: See under Editorial
Reverté, Spain

Siglo XXI Editores de Colombia Ltda+*,
Ave 3a 17-73 Primer Piso, Bogotá 8
Man Dir: Alberto E Diaz
Parent Company: Siglo XXI de España,
Editores SA, Spain (qv)
Associate Company: Siglo XXI Editores
SA, Mexico (qv)
Subjects: Anthropology, Sociology,
Psychology, History, Fiction, Linguistics,
Art, Architecture, Politics, Philosophy
1977: 150 titles *Founded:* 1966

Sopena Colombiana SA+*, Carrera 24, No
11-42, Bogotá Tel: 471597/379431
Man Dirs: David Fuente Fuente, Manuel
Bóix
Parent Company: Ramón Sopena SA,
Spain (qv)

Editorial **Temis** Ltda, Calle 13 No 6-45,
Apdos 5941 y 12008, Bogotá 1 Tel:
2694721/2699235/2445297
Cable Add: Editemis
Man Dir: Jorge Guerrero; *Sales Dir:* Erwin
Guerrero Pinzon
Subject: Law
Bookshop: Librería Temis Ltda, Calle 13,
No 6-45, Bogotá
1977: 48 titles *1978:* 52 titles *Founded:*
1951
ISBN Publisher's Prefix: 84-8272

Ediciones **Tercer** Mundo Ltda+*, Carrera
30 No 42-32, Apdo Aéreo 4817, Bogotá
Tel: 695129/695149 Cable Add: Tercer
Mundo

Man Dir: Luis Carlos Ibáñez
Subjects: General Literature, Social Science
Founded: 1961

Voluntad Editores Ltda y Cía SCA+*,
Carrera 13 No 38-99, Apartado 4692,
Bogotá Tel: 325520 Cable: Voluntad
President: Samuel de Bedout; *Vice-president:* Gastón de Bedout; *Vice-president
of Sales:* Luis Obregon; *Vice-president
Finance:* Guillermo Fernandez
Branches: Barranquilla, Bucaramanga,
Cartagena, Cali, Cúcuta, Manizales,
Medellín, Montería, Ibaque, Valledupar,
Tunja, Neiva, Pasto, Pereira, Villavicencio;
Voluntad Publishers Inc, 7800 Shoal Creek
Blvd, Austin, Texas, USA
Subjects: Kindergarten, Primary and
Secondary Textbooks
Bookshops: Voluntad Editores Carrera 13,
38-99 Bogotá
1977: 72 titles *1978:* 290 titles *Founded:*
1930
ISBN Publisher's Prefix: 84-8270

Book Clubs

Circulo de Lectores*, Calle 57, 6-35, 4°,
Bogotá Tel: 555676/555976

Major Booksellers

Librería **Aguirre**, Calle 53 No 49-123,
Medellín Tel: 424268 Cable Add: Laguirre

Librería **América**, Calle 51 No 49-58, apdo
11-92, Medellín Tel: 412878

Librería **Buchholz***, Ave Jiménez 8-40,
Bogá Tel: 341309/415896/426350

Librería **Casa del Libro***, Calle 18 No 6-43,
Bogotá Tel: 432668

Librería La **Gran Colombia***, Calle 18 No
6-30, Bogotá Tel: 421359/411755

Librería del **Ingeniero**, Ave Jiménez 7-45,
Apartado aéreo 14825, Bogotá
Tel: 412507/823610/343260

Librería **Lerner***, Ave Jiménez 4-35,
Bogotá Tel: 347826/430567

Librería **Central***, Calle 16 No 6-34,
Bogotá Tel: 426767

Librería **Continental***, Carrera 50 No 52-06,
Medellín Tel: 414948

Librería **Cultural** Colombiana, Calle 72 No
16-15, Bogotá Tel: 483236/483306
Also at Carrera 9a No 16-72, Bogotá

Librería **Nacional***, Carrera 5a No 11-50,
Cali Tel: 73250

Librería **San Pablo***, Carrera 9 No 15-01,
Bogotá Tel: 2433653/2345036Also at Calle
57 No 13-71 Tel: 494167

Librería del **Seminario**, Calle 57 No 49-44,
Medellín, Antioquia Tel: 428374
Distributors

Librería **Temis** Ltda, Calle 13 No 6-45,
Bogotá Tel: 423035/413325

Librería **Tercer** Mundo*, Carrera 30 No 42-
32, Bogotá Tel: 695129/695149

Major Libraries

Biblioteca Luis-Angel **Arango***, Banco de la
República, Calle 11 No 4-14, Bogotá
Tel: 439100

Archivo Nacional de Colombia, Biblioteca
Nacional*, Calle 24 No 5-60, 4° piso,
Bogotá

Biblioteca Nacional de Colombia*, Calle 24
No 5-60, Apdo Aéreo 27600, Bogotá
Tel: 414029

Biblioteca y Centro Nacional de
Documentación Pedagógica, Sección de
Servicios Bibliotecarios*, Apdo Nacional
8475, Bogotá
National Centre of Educational
Documentation

British Council Library*, Apdo Aéreo 4682,
Bogotá (Located at: Calle 11 No 5-16,
Bogotá 1) Tel: 2438181/2438184/2814922

Universidad de los Andes, Calle 18-A
Carrera 1-E, Bogotá

Universidad Nacional de Colombia,
Biblioteca Central, c/o Hugo Parra Acq
Libr, Apdo Aéreo 14490, Bogotá DE

Library Associations

Asociación Colombiana de Bibliotecarios*,
Calle 10 No 3-16, Apdo Aéreo 30883,
Bogotá Tel: 825798
Executive Secretary: Beatriz de Tabares
Colombian Library Association
Publication: Boletín

Bibliotecarios Agricolas Colombianos*, c/o
Biblioteca de Tibaitata, Apdo Aéreo 7984,
Bogotá DE
Secretary: Hector Galeano
Agricultural Librarians of Colombia

Colegio de Bibliotecarios Colombianos*,
Apdo Aéreo 3212, Bogotá
President: Martha Valencia H
Association of Colombian Librarians
Publication: Boletín Informativo

Departamento de Bibliotecas*, Universidad
de Antioquia, Apdo Aéreo 1226, Medellín

Library Reference Books and Journals

Books

*Bibliografía Bibliotecológica, Bibliográfica y
de Obras de Referencia Colombianas*
(Bibliography of Library Science,
Bibliography and Colombian Works of
Reference), Unversidad de Antioquia, Apdo
Aéreo 1226, Medellín

Journals

Boletín (Bulletin), Colombian Library
Association, Calle 10, 3-16, Apdo Aéreo
30883, Bogotá

Boletin Cultural y Bibliografico (Cultural
and Bibliographical Bulletin), Biblioteca
Luis-Angel Arango, Banco de la República,
Calle 11, 4-14, Bogotá

Boletin Informativo (Information Bulletin),
Association of Colombian Librarians, Apdo
Aéreo 3272, Bogotá

Boletin Informativo y Bibliografico
(Informative and Bibliographical Bulletin),
Universidad de Narino, Biblioteca Central,
Apdo Aéreo 505, Nacional 75, Narino

Literary Associations and Societies

Asociación de Escritores de Colombia*, Carrera 5a No 8–47, Bogotá
Association of Colombian Writers

Asociación Nacional de Autores de Obras Didacticas (AUCOLDI)*, Calle 14 No 12–15, Of 508, Bogotá Tel: 349845
National Association of Authors of Textbooks and Teaching Materials

Centro Filosófico-Literario*, Apdo Nacional 298, Manizales

P E N Internacional de Escritores de Colombia, Apdo Aéreo 51557, Bogotá
President: José María Acosta Acosta;
Secretary: Hernando Torres Neira
PEN International of Colombian Writers

Literary Periodicals

Letras Nacionales (National Letters), Calle 17, 7–71, Of 401, Bogotá

Razón y Fábula (Reason and Fiction), Universidad de los Andes, Apdo Aéreo 4976, Bogotá

Literary Prizes

Revista Vivencias and the Instituto Colombiano de Cultura have annual prizes

Colombian Novel Contest Awards*
For stimulating Colombian writers. 100,000 Colombian pesos. Awarded annually. Enquiries to the Liquor Industry of Valle, Cali, Valle

Cordoba Stories Prizes*
For stimulating and developing literary tastes. Diploma plus three prizes of 5,000, 3,000 and 2,000 Colombian pesos. Awarded annually. Enquiries to Cordoba Department, Secretary of Education, Montaria

National Story Prize*
For promoting literary development in Colombia. Diploma plus three prizes of 6,000 Colombian pesos, 3,000 pesos and 1,000 pesos. Awarded annually. Enquiries to University Day School of Colombia, Student Cultural Group 'El Candil', Carrera 16 No 24–25, Bogotá

Pamplona and its Culture Prize*
For stimulating a liking for reading in children. Awarded annually. Enquiries to Pedro de Orsua Public Library, Pamplona

José Ma **Vergara** y Vergara Prize*
For Colombian authors, to promote literary development. Diploma plus 10,000 Colombian pesos. Awarded annually. Enquiries to Colombian Ministry of National Education, Bogotá

Popular Republic of Congo

General Information

Language: French
Religion: Predominantly Roman Catholic
Population: 1.44 million
Bank Hours: 0700–1130 Monday-Saturday
Shop Hours: 0700 or 0800–1200 or 1300, 1500–1700 or 1730 Tuesday-Friday; 0700 or 0800–1200 or 1300 Saturday
Currency: CFA franc
Export/Import Information: 10% VAT on all goods, but goods for schools, the army, the police and health authorities are exempt. Import licences required for all goods. Favourable terms for imports from EEC countries
Copyright: Berne (see International section)

Publishers

Government Printer*, BP 58, Brazzaville

Société congolaise **Hachette***, BP 919, Brazzaville
Subjects: General Fiction, Belles Lettres, Education, Juveniles, Textbooks

Major Booksellers

Librairie **Hachette***, BP 2150, Brazzaville Tel: 2302

Librairie **Populaire***, BP 2212, Brazzaville

Maison de la Presse, Société congolaise Hachette*, BP 2150, Brazzaville

Office national des Librairies*, BP 577, Brazzaville

Major Libraries

Bibliothèque nationale populaire*, BP 114, Brazzaville Tel: 811287
Librarian: Francis Abaraka

Bibliothèque universitaire, Université Marieu N Gouabi*, BP 2025, Brazzaville Tel: 811430
Dir: François Wellot-Samba
Publications: Dimi; Annales; Repertoire d'auteurs congolais; Revue d'histoire anthropologie. Also other lists and catalogues

Centre culturel français, Bibliothèque*, BP 2141, Brazzaville Tel: 3852

Ecole normale supérieure de l'Afrique centrale, Bibliothèque*, BP 237, Brazzaville Tel: 4454

Library Associations

Direction générale des **Services** de Bibliothèques, Archives et Documentation*, BP 114, Brazzaville
General Management of Library, Archives and Documentation Services

Costa Rica

General Information

Language: Spanish
Religion: Roman Catholic
Population: 2.07 million
Literacy Rate (1963): 82.4%
Bank Hours: 0800–1100, 1330–1500 Monday-Friday; 0800–1100 Saturday
Shop Hours: 0800–1200, 1400–1800 Monday-Saturday (some close Saturday afternoon)
Currency: 100 centimos = 1 colon
Export/Import Information: Catalogues $0.03 per gross kg; other advertising material dutied at $1.50 per gross kg + 25% ad valorem. 10% Consumption Tax + 20% Exchange Surcharge on advertising. No import licences, but statistical recording prior to importation necessary. Imports over $300 must be registered with Banco Central to be eligible for foreign exchange allocation
Copyright: Berne, UCC, Buenos Aires (see International section)

Book Trade Reference Journal

Anuario bibliográfico costarricense (Costa Rican Annual Bibliography), Costa Rican Association of Librarians, Apdo 3308, San José

Publishers

Editorial **Costa Rica**, Apdo 10010, San José Tel: 234875/239303
Subject: Literature of Costa Rica
Founded: 1959

Editorial Universitaria Centroamericana (EDUCA)+, Apdo 64, Ciudad Universitaria 'Rodrigo Facio', San José (Located at San Pedro de Montes de Oca, San José) Tel: 258740/243727 Cable Add: Cosuca Educa
Editorial Dir, Publicity: Lic Julio Escoto;
Sales: Rodrigo Ortiz Astúa (International), Rodrigo Ortiz Astúa (National & International); *Production:* Alvaro Gómez Astúa
Subjects: Science, Art, Philosophy
1977: 34 titles *1978:* 35 titles *Founded:* 1969
ISBN Publisher's Prefix: 84–8360

Grijalbo Centroamerica y Panamá SA*, Apdo 362, San Pedro de Montes de Oca
Parent Company: Editorial Grijalbo SA, Mexico (qv)

Instituto Centro Americano de Administración Pública (ICAP)*, Dpto de Publicaciones, Apdo 10025, San José
Dir: Carlos Cordero d'Aubuisson
Subject: Technical
1977: 5 titles *Founded:* 1954

Instituto Interamericano de Ciencias Agricolas (IICA)*, Dpto de Publicaciones, Turrialba

Librería Imprenta y Litografía **Lehmann** SA*, Ave Central, Apdo 10011 San José Tel: 231212 Telex: 2540 LILL EH
Man Dir: Antonio Lehmann Struve;
Publicity: Orlando Mora
Bookshop: Librería Imprenta y Litografía Lehmann SA, Ave Central, Apdo 10011, San José Tel: 231212
Subjects: General Fiction & Nonfiction
Founded: 1894

COSTA RICA — CUBA

Ministerio de Cultura, Juventud y Deportes, Dpto de Publicaciones, Apdo 10227, San José
Subject: Literature in general
1978: 10 titles

Universal Librería, Imprenta y Fotolitografia (Carlos Federspiel & Co) SA*, Ave Fernández Guell 42-E, Apdo 1532, San José Tel: 222222
Subject: Textbooks

Universidad de Costa Rica*, Dpto de Publicaciones, Ciudad Universitaria Rodrigo Facio, San José Tel: 225555

Major Booksellers

Librería Universal Carlos **Federspiel***, Ave Fernández Guell 42-E, Apdo 1532, San José Tel: 222222

Librería Imprenta y Litografía **Lehmann** SA*, Ave Central, Apdo 10011, San José Tel: 231212

Librería **Trejos***, Calle 11-13, Ave Fernández Guell, Apdo 1313, San José Tel: 2285

Major Libraries

Biblioteca Nacional*, Calle 5, Ave 1-3, San José

Biblioteca del **Centro** Cultural Costarricense-Norteamericano*, Apdo 1489, San José
International Communication Agency Library

Biblioteca de la **Universidad de Costa Rica***, Apdo 3862, Ciudad Universitaria Rodrigo Facio, San José Tel: 257372
Publications: Lista de tesis de grado de la Universidad de Costa Rica no 1- 1958-; *San Pedro de Montes de Oca* (Serie de bibliotecología, no 12-14, 19-20, 22-25)

Library Associations

Asociación Costarricense de Bibliotecarios*, Apdo 3308, San José
Secretary-General: Nelly Kopper
Costa Rican Association of Librarians
Publication: Boletín

Colegio de Bibliotecarios de Costa Rica*, C/o Lupita Rodriguez Mendez, Encargada de Biblioteca, Instituto de Fomento Asesoria Municipal, San José
Library Association of Costa Rica

Library Journals

Boletín (Bulletin), Costa Rican Association of Librarians, Apdo 3308, San José

Literary Prize

Aquileo T **Echeverria** Prize*
For Costa Rican citizens who have excelled in the fields of literature (novel, short story, poetry, essay, scientific literature); history; theatre; music; fine arts. 40,000 colones divided between the selected works. Total sum of awards cannot exceed 8,000,000 colones. Awarded annually. Enquiries to Costa Rican Ministry of Culture, Youth and Sport, General Directorate of Arts and Letters, San José

Cuba

General Information

Language: Spanish
Religion: Roman Catholic predominantly; no established church
Population: 9.46 million
Literacy Rate (1953): 75.8%
Bank Hours: 0800-1200, 1415-1615 Monday-Friday; 0800-1200 Saturday
Currency: 100 centavos = 1 peso
Export/Import Information: Control of all import and export by Ministry of Foreign Trade; books imported by Cuban Book Institute, Belascoain 864, PO Box 210, Havana. No commercial advertising permitted in Cuba; brochures etc must be sent to the appropriate foreign trade organization. Exchange controlled by National Bank of Cuba
Copyright: UCC, Florence (see International section)

Book Trade Reference Journals

Revolutionary Cuba; a bibliographical guide, University of Miami Press, Coral Gables, Florida, USA (annual)

Publishers

Casa de las **Américas***, G y Tercera, Vedado 3, Havana
Dir: Roberto Fernández Retamar
Subject: Latin American Literature, *Música* (monthly)
Founded: 1960

Editorial **Arte** y Literatura, Calle G No 505e 21 y 23, Vedado, Havana
Director: Rosario Paz Llovera
Subjects: Art, Literature
1978: 86 titles

Ediciones **C O R***, Revolutionary Orientation Commission of the Communist Party, Havana
Subject: Politics

Editorial **Ciencias Sociales**, Calle 14 No 4104e Mendoza y 43, Playa, Havana
Director: Marcos Luit Lescailles
Subject: Social Sciences
1978: 152 titles

Editorial **Científico** Técnica, Calle 2 No 58e 3 y 5, Vedado, Havana
Director: Jorge Luis Victorero Gonta
Subjects: Science, Engineering
1978: 34 titles

Consejo Nacional de Cultura*, O'Reilly 126, Havana
President: Eduardo Muzio
Subjects: Art, Fiction, Periodicals

Cuadernos de Historia de la Salud Publica, Ministerio de Salubridad y Asistencia Social*, Historiador, Havana
Subject: History

Editorial **Gente Nueva**, Calle 8 No 469e 19 y 21, Vedado, Havana
Director: Elenia Rodríguez Oliva
Subject: Social Sciences
1978: 100 titles

Instituto Cubano del Libro*, Belascoaín 864, Apdo 6540, Havana
Dir: Rolando Rodríguez
Subject: Government Publications
Founded: 1967

Editorial **Letras Cubanas**, Calle G No 505e 21 y 23, Vedado, Havana
Director: Pablo Pacheco López
Subject: Literature
1978: 86 titles

Editorial **Orbe**, Calle 17 No 1057e 12 y 14, Vedado, Havana
Director: Humberto González Borduy
1978: 92 titles

Editorial **Oriente**, José Antonio Saco 356, Santiago
Director: Reinaldo Cuesta Reina
1978: 34 titles

Editorial **Pueblo** y Educación, Calle 15, 604e B y C, Vedado, Havana
Director: Ana María Santana Romero
Subject: Education
1978: 370 titles

Ediciones **Revolución***, Plaza Cívica, Havana
Subjects: Art, Culture

Universidad Central de la Villas, Carretera de Camajuani*, Km 10, Santa Clara
Subjects: Academic

Universidad de la Habana*, Apdo 3060, Havana 3 Tel: 325238/328815
Subjects: Academic
1977: 206 titles *Founded:* 1934

Major Booksellers

Cuban Book Institute*, Belascoain 864, PO Box 210, Havana
The organization for book importation

Major Libraries

Academia de Ciencias de la República de Cuba*, Biblioteca Central, Capitolio Nacional, Havana

Archivo Histórico Municipal de la Habana (Municipal Archives of Havana)*, Plaza de Catedral, Havana

Biblioteca Histórica Cubana y Americana (Cuban and American Historical Library)*, Municipio de la Habana, Oficina del Historiador de la Ciudad, Havana

Biblioteca Nacional José Martí (National Library)*, Plaza de la Revolución, Apdo Oficial 3, Havana Tel: 73613
Publications: Revista de la Biblioteca Nacional José Martí; Boletín Bibliotecas; Bibliografía Cubana; Indice General de Publicaciones; Trabajos de Investigación

Biblioteca del **Colegio de Abogados** (Library of the College of Advocates)*, Lamparilla 114 esq Cuba, Havana

Biblioteca del **Colegio de Belén** (Library of the Belén Jesuit College)*, Apdo 221, Marianao, Havana

Biblioteca 'José Antonio **Echeverría'***, Casa de las Americas, Tercera y G, Vedado, Havana

Biblioteca del **Instituto de Literatura** y Linguistica*, Salvador Allende 710, Havana

Biblioteca del **Instituto Pre-universitario** de la Habana (Library of the Pre-University Institute of Education)*, Zulueta y San José, Havana

Biblioteca del **Museo de Zoologia** (Library of the Zoological Museum), 42 No 3307, Marianao 13, Havana

Biblioteca 'Manuel **Sanguily***, Ministerio de Relaciones Exteriores, Calzada y G, Vedado, Havana

Biblioteca General de la **Universidad Central** de las Villas*, Santa Clara, Las Villas

Biblioteca Central 'Rubén Martínez Villena' de la **Universidad de la Habana**, Havana

Biblioteca Central de la **Universidad de Oriente***, Carretera de Cuabitos, Santiago

Library Associations

Colegio Nacional de Bibliotecarios Universitarios*, c/o National Library, Plaza de la Revolucion, Havana
National Association of University Librarians

Library Reference Books and Journals

Books

Guía de Bibliotecas y Centros de Documentación de la República de Cuba (Guide to Libraries and Centres of Documentation of Cuba), National Library, Plaza de la Revolución, Apdo Oficial 3, Havana

Journals

Bibliotecas (Libraries), National Library, Plaza de la Revolución, Apdo Oficial 3, Havana

Cuba Bibliotecológica (Cuban Library Science), Colegio Nacional de Bibliotecarios Universitarios, c/o National Library, Plaza de la Revolución, Apdo Oficial 3, Havana

Revista de la Biblioteca Nacional José Marti (Review of the National Library), National Library, Plaza de la Revolución, Apdo Oficial 3, Havana

Literary Associations and Societies

Unión de Escritores y Artistas de Cuba (Union of Writers and Artists of Cuba)*, Calle 17, 351, Vedado, Havana
Administrative Secretary: Benvenido Suarez

Literary Periodicals

Taller Literario (Literary Workshop), Universidad de Oriente, Escuela de Letras, Santiago de Cuba

Union, Union of Writers and Artists of Cuba, Calle 17, 351, Vedado, Havana

Cyprus

General Information

Language: Greek and Turkish (English widely spoken)
Religion: Greek Orthodox and Muslim (among Turks)
Population: 640,000
Literacy Rate (1960): 74.5%
Bank Hours: 0830–1200 Monday-Saturday
Shop Hours: Winter: 0830–1300, 1430–1730 Monday-Friday; 0800-1300, Saturday Summer 0800-1300, 1600-1830 Monday-Friday; 0800-1300 Saturday
Currency: 1000 mils = 1 Cyprus pound
Export/Import Information: No tariffs on books or advertising matter. No import licence specially required. Exchange control administered by Central Bank of Cyprus
Copyright: Berne, Florence (see International section)

Book Trade Organisations

Cyprus Booksellers Association*, Hatzisavva Bldg, Evagora Ave, Box 1455, Nicosia Tel: 49500/62312
Secretary: Panikos Michaelides

Book Trade Reference Journals

O Kosmos Tou Kypriakou Vivliou (The World of Cypriot Books), (text in Greek), PO Box 1722, Nicosia

Publishers

M A M, PO Box 1722, Nicosia Tel: (21) 72744
Subjects: Various, specialising in publications about Cyprus and works by Cypriot authors
Bookshop: PO Box 1722, Nicosia
Miscellaneous: authorized distributors of Cyprus Government publications and works about Cyprus, and of publications by United Nations agencies and major international organizations

Major Booksellers

Arcane Bookshop, 15 Saripolou St, PO Box 373, Limassol Tel: (051) 63541

Hellenic Distribution Agency (Cyprus) Ltd*, 1-9 Kostis Palamas St, Nicosia Tel: (021) 73662

A **Joannides** & Co, 30-32 Athens St, PO Box 141, Limassol Tel: (051) 62204
Bookshops: 30-32 Athens St, Limassol; Archbishop Makarios III Ave 147, Limassol

K P **Kyriakou** Books & Stationery, 3 Grivas Digenis Ave, Panagides Bldg, Limassol Tel: 68508

M A M, PO Box 1722, Nicosia Tel: (21) 72744
Specializes in publications about Cyprus and works by Cypriot authors. Authorized distributors of Cyprus Government publications and of publications of international organizations

K **Rustem** & Bro*, 24 Kyreniá St, Nicosia Tel: (021) 2681 Cable Add: Rustem Br 4

Iakovou **Yiannakis**, 22 Greg Xenopoulous St, Nicosia Tel: (021) 52197 Cable Add: Vivliopolis

Major Libraries

Library of the **Archbishopric***, PO Box 1130, Nicosia

British Council Library*, PO Box 1995, Nicosia (Located at: 3 Museum St, Nicosia) Tel: 42152/3

Library of the **Cyprus Museum**, PO Box 2024, Nicosia

Ministry of Education Library*, Didaskalikon Megaron, Archbishop Makarios III Ave, Nicosia

Municipal Library*, PO Box 41, Famagusta

Municipal Library*, Limassol

Library of the **Paedagogiki Academia** (Institute of Education Library)*, Nicosia

Library of **Phaneromeni***, PO Box 1637, Nicosia

Sultan's Library*, Evcaf, Nicosia

Turkish Public Library*, 49 Mecediye St, Nicosia

Library Association

Cyprus Library Association, PO Box 1039, Nicosia Tel: 402310
Secretary: Paris G Rossos

Library Journals

Deltion Vivliothikarion (Library Bulletin), Greek Library Association of Cyprus, PO Box 1039, Nicosia

Czechoslovakia

General Information

Language: Czech in Bohemia and Moravia, Slovak and Hungarian in Slovakia (German widely spoken)
Religion: Roman Catholic and Protestant
Population: 15 million
Bank Hours: 0800-1400 Monday-Friday
Shop Hours: 0900-1200, 1400-1800 Monday-Friday; most open half day Saturdays
Currency: 100 haler = 1 koruna
Export/Import Information: Import policy administered by Federal Ministry of Foreign Trade. Appropriate corporations for book importation are Artia, Prague 1, Ve Smĕckách 30, or Slovart, Bratislava, Gorkého 17. Exchange control administered by State Bank
Copyright: UCC, Berne (see International section)

Book Trade Organizations

Ministerstvo kultury CSR, Odbor knižní kultury*, Prague 1, Staré Mĕsto, Na Perštýnĕ 1
Czechoslovak Ministry of Culture, Department for Publishing and Book Trade

CZECHOSLOVAKIA

Slovenské ústredie knižnej kultúry*, Bratislava, nám SNP 12
Slovak Centre for Publishing and Book Trade

Společnost pro krásné písmo a typografii*, Prague 1, Malá Strana, Říční 5
Association of Design and Typography

Book Trade Reference Books and Journals

Book

Books in Czechoslovakia, a survey of Czech and Slovak publishers, book-museums and important libraries, Czechoslovak Ministry of Culture, Prague 1, Staré Město, Na Perštýně 1

Journals

Bibliografický katalog CSSR (Czech National Bibliography), consisting of: *České knihy* (Czech Books), State Library of the CSSR, 11000 Prague 1, Klementinum 190 (weekly); *Slovenská národná bibliografia* (Slovak National Bibliography), Slovak National Library, 13601 Martin, Mudróňova 13 (monthly); *České hudebniny* (Czech Music), State Library of the CSSR, 11000 Prague 1, Klementinum 190 (quarterly); *Slovenské hudebniny* (Slovak Music), State Library of the CSSR, 11000 Prague 1, Klementinum 190 (annual)

Czech Books in Print, Artia, 11127 Prague 1, Ve Smečkách 30, PO Box 790

Nové knihy (New Books), Prague 1, Vězeňská 5

Slovak Books in Print, Slovart Ltd, Foreign Trade Company, Bratislava, Gorkého 17

Věda a knihy (Science and Books), Academia, 11220 Prague 1, Vodičková 40

Publishers

Academia, Publishing House of the Czechoslovak Academy of Sciences, 11229 Prague 1, Vodičkova 40 Tel: 246241/8 Cable Add: Academybooks Prague
Man Dir: Radoslav Švec; *Export Manager:* Mrs Z Svobodová; *Publicity & Advertising:* J Vinkler; *Rights & Permissions:* L Zapletal
Subjects: History, Philosophy, Psychology, Economy, Archaeology, Linguistics, Mathematics, Physics, Chemistry, Engineering, Geology; Monographs and University Textbooks
Bookstore: Prague 1, Vodickova 40
Founded: 1953

Albatros, Prague 1, Ná Perštyně 1 Tel: 245151/6, 247741/6, 248851/6 Telex: 121605 alba c
Man Dir: Václav Mikeš; *Sales, Publicity & Advertising:* Jiří Lapáček
Subject: Books for Children and Young People
Book Club: KMC — Young Readers' Club
Founded: 1949

Alfa — Vydavateľstvo technickej a ekonomickej literatúry*, 89331 Bratislava, Hurbanovo nám 3 Tel: 331441/5 Cable Add: Alfa Bratislava
Dir: Rudolf Schaller; *Sales Dir:* Josef Bednárik
Publishers of technical and economic literature
Subjects: Engineering, General & Social Science, Special Dictionaries, University & Secondary Textbooks
Bookshop: Bratislava, Palackého ul 1
1977: 253 titles *Founded:* 1952
Miscellaneous: Sole importers of scientific and technical books from Western countries in Slovakia

Artia*, 11127 Prague 1, Ve Smečkách 30, PO Box 790 Tel: 246041 Cable Add: Artiapublish Telex: 121065/122775
Man Dir: Dr V Silar; *Sales Dir:* J Ružička
Foreign language publishers
1977: 38 titles *Founded:* 1953
Subjects: Art Books, Books on Nature, Children's Books

Avicenum, zdravotnické nakladatelství, 11802 Prague 1, Malostranské nám 28 Tel: 530640
Czechoslovak Medical Press
Subject: Medicine
1977: 84 titles *Founded:* 1953

Nakladatelství **Blok**, 60000 Brno, Rooseveltova 4
Dir: Ivo Odehnal
Subjects: Belles Lettres, Fiction, Regional Literature

Československý spisovatel, 11147 Prague 1, Národní 9 Tel: 239051 Cable Add: Spisovatel Prague
Dir: Ivan Skála
Czechoslovak Writers' Union Publishers
Subjects: General Fiction, Belles Lettres, Poetry, Biography, Philosophy, Juveniles
Book Club: Klub Přátel Poezie (Club of the Friends of Poetry)
Bookshops: Prague 1, Narodní 9; Brno, Česká 7 (both in Czechoslovakia)
Founded: 1949

Nakladatelství **Dopravy** a spoju*, 11578 Prague 1, Hybernská ul 5, Nové Město
Publishing House of the Ministry of Transport and Communications
Dir: Bohumil Klail
Subjects: Science & Technology, Transport

Kartografie NP*, 17029 Prague 7, Kostelní 42 Cable Add: Kartografie Prague
Man Dir: Adolf Chmelař; *Editorial Dir:* Dr I Caslavka
Orders to: Artia, Foreign Trade Corporation 11127 Prague 1, Ve Sméckách 30
Subject: Cartography
Founded: 1971

Kruh*, 50021 Hradec Králové, Klicperova 197 Tel: 22076/225458
Dir: Dr Josef Kubíček
Eastern Bohemian Regional Publishing House
Subjects: General Fiction, Biography, History, Music, Art, Low- & High-priced Paperbacks, Regional Literature
Founded: 1966

Landwirtschaftlicher Staatsverlag (Agricultural State Publishers), see Státní zemědělské nakladtelství

Lidové nakladatelství*, 11565 Prague 1, Václavské nám 36 Tel: 226383/5 Cable Add: Lidové Nakladatelství Prague
Dir: F J Kolár
Publishing House of the Union of Czechoslovak-Soviet Friendship
Subjects: General Fiction, Belles Lettres, Poetry, Biography, History, Philosophy, Juveniles, Low-priced Paperbacks, Social Science
Founded: 1968 (formerly Svět Sovětu)

Madáh*, Bratislava, Martarovicova 10
Publishing House for Books and Journals in the Hungarian Language
Subject: Books in Hungarian

Matica slovenská*, 63552 Martin, Mudroňova 35,
Subjects: Bibliographies, Museum Science, Information Processing

Melantrich, 11212 Prague 1, Václavské nám 36 Tel: 260341 Cable Add: Melantrich Telex: 121432
Man Dir: O Balabán; *Sales Dir:* K Voleský; *Editorial:* Ph Dr K Houba; *Production:* A Krákora
Publishing House of the Czechoslovak Socialist Party
Subjects: Belles Lettres, Poetry, Biography, Philosophy, High-priced Paperbacks, Textbooks
Bookshop: Na príkope 3, Prague 1
1979: 30 titles *1980:* 36 titles *Founded:* 1898

Mladá fronta*, 11222 Prague 1, Panská 8 Tel: 224141 Telex: 00245
Dir: Dr Kornel Vavrinčik
Publishing House of the Czechoslovak Union of Youth
Subjects: General Fiction, Belles Lettres, Poetry, Biography, History, How-to, Music, Art, Philosophy, Juveniles, Low-priced Paperbacks
Founded: 1945

Mladé letá, 89426 Bratislava, nám SNP 12 Tel: 50475 Telex: 93421 Cable Add: Mladéletá Bratislava
Man Dir: Rudo Móric; *Editorial:* Dr Juraj Klaučo; *Sales Dir:* Vlasta Strnadová; *Production:* Jan Columby; *Publicity:* Silvia Kršková; *Rights & Permissions:* Eva Hornišová
Young Years: Slovak Publishing House of Children's Literature
Subjects: Juveniles, Reference
Book Club: club of Young Readers
1978: 228 titles *Founded:* 1950
Bookshop: Detská Kniha (The Child's Book), Bratislava, Hurbanovo nám 7

Nakladatelství a distribuce knih **Naše Vojsko***, 12812 Prague 2, Na Děkance 3 Tel: 547241/8
Dir: Dr Lubomír Baroš
Publishing and Distribution House of Czechoslovak Army
Subjects: General Fiction, Medicine, Technical, Paperbacks, Juveniles, Military Science, Psychology, History, Aviation, Book Industry
Founded: 1945

Nakladatelství **Obelisk***, Prague 1, Mikulandská 10
Man Dir: Jiří Dvořák
Publishing House of Czechoslovak Artists
Subject: Art

Obzor, vydavateľstvo knih a casopisov národní podnik*, 89336 Bratislava, ul Ceskoslovenskej armády 29a Tel: 53062/57251 Cable Add: Vydavatelstvo Obzor Bratislava
Dir: Ján Mojžiš (acting)
Horizon: Slovak Book & Periodical Publishing House for People's Education
Subjects: General Fiction, Non-fiction, Encyclopaedias, Law, General Science, Textbooks, Paperbacks, Educational, Maps
Founded: 1953

Odeon, nakladatelství krásné literatury a umění, 11587 Prague 1, Národní 36 Tel: 247141 Cable Add: Odeon Praha
Dir: Josef Kuličék; *Assistant Dir:* Dr

Edvard Vonka; *Editorial:* Karel Boušek; *Sales:* Dr M Burkon; *Production:* Ing J Přib; *Publicity:* J Janovský; *Rights & Permissions:* Dr V Vocetková
Publishing House of Literature and Art
Subjects: General Fiction, Belles Lettres, Poetry, Biography, Art, Reproductions
Bookshop: Knihkupectví Odeon Na Florenci 3, 11586 Prague 1
Book Club: Odeon Book Club
1977: 170 titles *1978:* 140 titles *Founded:* 1953

Nakladatelství CSTV Olympia, 11588 Prague 1, Klimentská 1 Tel: 61639 Cable Add: Olympia Prague
Man Dir: Ludvík Uhlíř; *Sales Dir:* M Karas *Publicity & Advertising:* D Suchánková
Publishing House of Sports and Tourism
Subjects: Sports, Travel, Juveniles, Albums
Bookshop: Prague 1, Hybernská 34
1977: 74 titles *1978:* 59 titles *Founded:* 1954
Miscellaneous: Formerly Sportovní a turistické nakladatelství

Opus Records and Publishing House, 89923 Bratislava, Dunajská 18 Tel: 53241/50783/52665 Telex: 92219
Man Dir: Dr Ian Stanislav; *Editorial:* Marian Jurík; *Publicity:* Pavol Fellegi; *Rights & Permissions:* Dr Oldrich Horák
Subject: Music
1978: 41 titles (including sheet music)

Nakladatelství Orbis, dissolved in 1977, part of activity taken over by Nakladatelství a vydavatelství Panorama (qv); name Orbis now attached to Press Agency

Osveta, 03654 Martin, Skultétyho 1
Dir: Ján Krajč
Subjects: Education, Popular Sciences, Tourism, Medicine
1978: 92 titles

Vydavatel'stvo SFVU Pallas*, 88209 Bratislava, Štúrova 1/b
Publishing House of the Slovak Fund of Fine Arts
Subjects: Art, Literature, Biography

Nakladatelství a vydavatelství Panorama, PO Box 75, 12072 Prague 2, Hálkova 1 Tel: 245449 Cable Add: Panorama Prague II Telex: 122657
Man Dir: Dr František Hanzlík
Subjects: Popular Science, Local History, Picture Books, Law, Concise Encyclopedias, Travels, Juveniles, Periodicals, Postcards, Applied Arts, Publicity Materials
Founded: 1978
Formerly Orbis, nakladatelství a vydavatelství, Vinohradská tř 46, Prague 2

Panton, 11839 Prague 1, Říční 12 Tel: 538151/5 Cable Add: Panton
Publishers of the Czech Music Fund — Prague
Man Dir: Vladimir Ševčík
Subjects: Music (Instruction, Works, Biography, General), Juveniles, Educational Materials
Bookshops: Prague 1, Jungmanova 30; Brno, Ceská 14; Bratislava, Sedlářská 3
Founded: 1958

Peace and Socialism International Publishers, 16616 Prague 6, Thakurova 3 Tel: 325731/325132 Cable Add: CSSR Prag Srozt
Subjects: International Communist and Working-Class Movement (in English, French, German, Russian, Spanish), Periodicals, including *World Marxist Review* (in 34 languages), *Information Bulletin* (in English, French, German, Spanish)

Vydavatelstvo ROH 'Práca', 89717 Bratislava, Obrancov mieru 19 Tel: 330838/333779/332347/93283 Telex: 93329
Dir: Ján Duži
Publishing House of the Revolutionary Trade Union Movement
Subjects: Trade Unions (history and contemporary studies), Labour Problems, Social Security, Ergonomics, Labour Law, Work Safety, Needlework Handbooks, Economics
Bookshop: Knizna predajna PRACA, 89717 Bratislava, nám SNP 20
1977: 54 titles *1978:* 60 titles *Founded:* 1946

Práce*, 11258 Prague 1, Václavské nám 17, Nové Město
Dir: Vilém Kún
Publishing House of the Czech Trade Union Movement
Subjects: Belles Lettres, How-to, General, Social & Political Science, Juveniles, Law, Engineering, Fiction, Non-fiction
Book Club: ERB
Founded: 1945

Pragopress*, Prague Tel: 224651 Cable Add: Pragobublish Praha
Subjects: Reprints, Facsimilies

Nakladatelstvo Pravda, CS-88205 Bratislava, Gundulicova ul 12 Tel: 335574
Dir: Viliam Kačer
Subjects: Fiction, Biography, History, Political Science, Philosophy, Social Science, Law, Economics
Book Club: ČKP (Členská knižnica pravdy)
Miscellaneous: Firm is the publishing house of the Central Committee of the Communist Party of Slovakia

Príroda, vydavatel' stvo kníh a časopisov*, 89417 Bratislava, Krížkova 9 Tel: 47241
Dir: Vincent Šugár; *Editorial:* Ján Braun
Subjects: Agriculture, Veterinary Science, Biology, Husbandry, Forestry, Nature Protection, Phytopathology, Beekeeping, Mechanisation of Agriculture
1977: 196 titles *Founded:* 1949

Nakladatelství Profil*, 70100 Ostrava 1, Cihlářská 51 Tel: 53559, 55129
Dir: František Cečetka
Northern Moravian Publishing House
Subjects: General Fiction, Belles Lettres, Poetry, Biography, History, Music, Art, Reference, Juveniles, Social Science, Psychology
Founded: 1957

Nakladatelství ruže*, 37196 Ceské Budějovice, Zižkovo nám 5
Tel: 2250/5620/7693
Dir: František Podlaha
Southern Bohemian Publishing House
Subjects: General Fiction, Belles Lettres, History, Juveniles, Low-priced Paperbacks, Regional Literature
Founded: 1960

S N T L Nakladatelství technické literatury, 11302 Prague 1, Spálená 51 Tel: 295880
Man Dir: Ing Jindřich Sucharda; *Editorial:* Dr V Šesták
Subjects: Engineering and Applied Technology, Science, Economics, Dictionaries, Reference, Periodicals
Book Club: Klub čtenářu technické literatury (Club for Readers of Technical Literature), Prague 1, Spálená 51
Bookshop: Středisko technické literatury (Centre of Technical Literature), Prague 1, Spálená 51
1977: 497 titles *1978:* 443 titles *Founded:* 1895

Severoceské nakladatelství*, 40021 Ústí nad Labem, Velká Hradební 33
Dir: Jan Stuchl
North Bohemian Publishing House
Subjects: General Fiction, Belles Lettres, Poetry, Biography, History, Music, Art, Philosophy, Juveniles, General Science, Low-priced Paperbacks, Regional Literature
Founded: 1961

Slovenská kartografia NP, 82717 Bratislava-Krasňany, Pekná cesta 17
Slovak Cartographic Publishing House

Slovenské pedagogické nakladatelstvo*, Bratislava, Sasinkova 5 Tel: 64551/3 Cable Add: SPN Bratislava
Man Dir: František Mráz
Slovak Publishing House for Educational Literature
Subjects: History, Music, Art, Psychology, General Science, University, Secondary & Primary Textbooks, Education, Reference
1977: 17 titles *Founded:* 1920

Slovenské vydavatel'stvo podohospodarskej literatúry*, 80000 Bratislava, Krizková 7
Slovak Publishing House of Literature on Agriculture
Subjects: Agriculture, Biology, Industry, Veterinary Science

Vydavatel'stvo Slovenskej Akademie Vied, see Veda
Publishing House of the Slovak Academy of Sciences

Slovenský spisovatel', 89728 Bratislava, Leningradská 2 Tel: 333922
Man Dir: Vojtech Mihálik; *Editorial:* Vladimír Dudáš; *Sales, Production:* Rudolf Pernica; *Publicity:* Anna Sigmundová; *Rights & Permissions:* Olga Petková
Orders to: 89728 Bratislava, Leningradská 2
Publishing House of the Slovak Literary Fund
Subjects: General Fiction, Belles Lettres, Poetry, Literary Theory and Criticism
Book Clubs: SPKK — Spoločnosť priatel'ov' krásnych kníh; KMP — Kruh milovníkov poézie; NST — Nová sovietska tvorba; Vavrín
Bookshop: Dom knihy, 89728 Leningradská 2, Bratislava
1977: 119 titles *Founded:* 1950

Smena, 89714 Bratislava, Pražská 11 Tel: 48539/48541 Cable Add: Bratislava, Smena, 09341
Dir: Rudolf Belan
Publishing House of Slovak Central Committee of Socialist Youth Union
Subjects: General Fiction, Belles Lettres, Poetry, Biography, History, Philosophy, Low- & High-priced Paperbacks, Psychology, Social Science, Juveniles, Hobbies
Book Club: Máj, Bratislava, Prazská 11
Founded: 1949

Sport, 89344 Bratislava, Vajnorská 100
Dir: Ing František Mikloš
Subject: Sport
Miscellaneous: Firm is the publishing house of the Central Committee of the Slovak Physical Culture Organization

Statisticke a evidencni vydavatelství tiskopisu*, 11000 Prague 1, Malá strana, Trziste 9
Publishing House of Statistics and Data
Subject: Reference

Státní pedagogické nakladatelstvi*, 11301 Prague 1, Ostrovní 30, 1 Nově Město Tel: 293241/9 Cable Add: Stapena Prague
Man Dir: Bedřich Satrapa

State Publishing House for Educational Literature
Subjects: History, Juveniles, Medicine, Psychology, Engineering, Social Science, Secondary & Primary Textbooks, Pedagogical Journals, Reference
1977: 1295 titles *Founded:* 1775

Statní zemědělské nakladatelství, 11311 Prague 1, Nové Město, Václavské náměstí 47 Tel: 226641
Man Dir: Karel Koukal
Agricultural Publishing House
Subjects: Agriculture, Forestry, Veterinary Science, Agronomy, Hobbies

Středočeské nakladatelství knihkupectví*, 11000 Prague 1, U Prašné brány 3
Dir: František Pěkný
Central Bohemian Publishing House & Bookshop
Subjects: Regional Literature, Fiction, General, Belles Lettres

Supraphon, Prague 1, Palackého ul 1 Tel: 268141 Cable Add: Supraphon Praha Telex: 121218 SUNP
Man Dir: Viktor Kašák; *Foreign Connections, Rights & Permissions:* Pavel Smola; *Editorial:* Dr Olga Šotolová; *Commercial Director:* Vladimir Vobornik
Publishing House of Music, Recordings, Sheet Music and Musicological Literature
Subject: Music
Bookshops: 150 branches
1977: 12 titles, 214 music sheets *1978:* 13 titles, 212 music sheets *Founded:* 1946

Svepomoc*, 11000 Prague 1, Gorkého nám 10, Nové Město
Publishing House of the Central Cooperative Council

Svoboda*, 11303 Prague 1, Revoluční 15 Tel: 66851
Dir: Evžen Palonczy
Subjects: History, Philosophy, Politics, Belles-Lettres
Book Clubs: Friends of Antiquity, Svobodq
Miscellaneous: Firm is the publishing house of the Central Committee of the Communist Party of Czechoslovakia

Tatran*, 89134 Bratislava, Michalská 9 Tel: 30141/3 Cable Add: Tatran Michalská 9, 89134 Bratislava
Man Dir: Dr Anton Markuš; *Sales, Publicity & Advertising:* Margita Lehocká; *Rights & Permissions:* LITA, Slovak Literary Agency, Bratislava, ul Ceskoslovenskej armády 31/III
Slovak Publishing House of Belles Lettres
Subjects: Belles Lettres, Poetry, Art, Low-priced Paperbacks
Book Club: Hviezdoslavova knižnica
Bookshop: Tatran, Bratislava, Michalská 9
Founded: 1947

V E D A, vydavateľstvo Slovenskej akadémie vied, 89530 Bratislava, Klemensova 19 Tel: 50355 Cable Add: VEDA Bratislava
Man Dir: Ing Miroslav Murín; *Editorial:* Dr Ján Jankovič; *Publicity Manager:* Terézia Zelenáková
Publishing House of the Slovak Academy of Sciences
Subjects: Technical Sciences, Natural Sciences, Linguistics, History, Archaeology, Philosophy, Psychology, Encyclopedias, Dictionaries
Bookshop: Kníhkupectvo SAV, 89530 Bratislava, Dunajská 5
Founded: 1953

Východoslovenské vydavateľstvo np*, 040 01 Košice 1, Alejová 3
Man Dir: Mikuláš Jáger
Slovak Publishing House
Subjects: Belles Lettres, History, Political Science, Juveniles, Regional Literature

Vyšehrad*, Prague 1, ul 28, října 3
Publishing House of the Czech People's Party
Subjects: The Works of Christian Writers and Poets, Czech History, Philosophy, Social Sciences

Západočeské nakladatelství*, 30100 Plzeň, Moskevská 36
Dir: Václav Brašna
Western Bohemian Regional Publishing House
Subjects: General Fiction, Belles Lettres, History, Regional Literature, Juveniles

Literary Agents

D I L I A, Vyšehradská 28, Post Box 34, 12824 Prague 2 Tel: 296651/5 Cable Add: Dilia Prag Telex: 121367 DILI C
Theatrical and Literary Agency
Contact: Robert Jurák

L I T A, 89420 Bratislava, ul Cs Armády 37 Tel: 55007 Cable Add: LITA Bratislava
Slovak Literary Agency
Copyright organization representing Slovak authors in foreign transactions
Contact: Judr Matej Andráš

Book Clubs

C K P (Clenská knižnica Pravdy)*, CS-88205 Bratislava, Gunduličová ul 12
Owned by: Nakladateľstvo Pravda, Bratislava

Club of Young Readers, 89426 Bratislava, nám SNP 12
Owned by: Mladé letá, Bratislava

E R B*, 11258 Prague 1, Václavské nám 17, Nové Město
Owned by: Práce (Prague)

Friends of Antiquity*, 11303 Prague 1, Revoluční 15
Owned by: Svoboda

Hviezdoslavova knižnica*, 89134 Bratislava, Michalská 9
Owned by: Tatran (Slovak Publishing House of Belles Lettres), Bratislava

K M C — Young Readers' Club*, Prague 1, ná Perštýně 1
Owned by: Albatros, Prague
Subject: Juveniles

K M P (Kruh milovníkov poézie), 89728 Bratislava, Leningradská 2
Club for Poetry Lovers
Owned by: Slovenský spisovateľ, Bratislava

Klub čtenářu technické literatury, 11302 Prague 1, Spálená 51
Club for Readers of Technical Literature
Supervised by: SNTL-Nakladatelství technické literatury (qv)
Subjects: Engineering and Applied Technology, Science, Dictionaries, Applied Economics

Klub přátel poézie*, 11147 Prague 1, Národní 9
Club of the Friends of Poetry
Owned by: Československý spisovatel, Prague

Máj, 89714 Bratislava, Pražská 11
Owned by: Smena, Bratislava

N S T (Nová sovietska tvorba), 89728 Bratislava, Leningradská 2
Owned by: Slovenský spisovateľ, Bratislava

Odeon Book Club, 11697 Prague 1, Celetna 11
Members: 200,000
Owned by: Odeon, Prague
Subject: Fiction

S P K K (Spoločnosť priateľov krásnych kníh), 89728 Bratislava, Leningradská 2
Society of Friends of Beautiful Books
Owned by: Slovenský spisovateľ, Bratislava

Svoboda Book Club*, 11303 Prague 1, Revoluční 15 Tel: 66851
Owned by: Svaboda (Prague)
Subjects: History, Philosophy, Politics, Belles Lettres

Vavrín, 89728 Bratislava, Leningradská 2
Owned by: Slovenský spisovateľ, Bratislava

Major Booksellers

Artia*, 11127 Prague 1, Ve Smečkách 30, PO Box 790 Tel: 246041
Import/export organization

Slovart Ltd*, 80532 Bratislava, Gottwaldovo nam 48
Import/export organization

Kniha (The Book)*, Prague 2, Nové Město, 6 Zitna
The central purchasing place for single bookselling businesses in Czechoslovakia

Major Libraries

Státni knihovna **České socialistické republiky**, 11001 Prague 1, Klementinum 190 Tel: Main switchboard 266541; Dir 225192
State Library of the Czech Socialist Republic

Základní knihovna — ústředí vědeckých informací **Československé akademie věd***, 88618 Bratislava, Klemensova 19 Tel: 56321/51733 Telex: 93464
Main Library — Scientific Information Centre of Czechoslovak Academy of Sciences

Knihovna Národního muzea, 11579 Prague 1, Václavské nám 68 Tel: 269451/9
Dir: Dr Jaroslav Vrchotka CSc
National Museum Library
Publication: Sborník Národního muzea v Praze, řada C-literární historie (quarterly)

Matica Slovenská*, Martin 03652, Mudroňova 13 Tel: 31346-9/32184 Telex: 121207
Slovak National Library

Městská knihovna v Praze*, 11572 Prague 1, nám primátora dr V Vacka 1
Prague City Library

Památník národního pisemnictví, Strahovská knihovna*, 11838 Prague 1, Strahovské nádvoří 132 Tel: 538841
Museum of National Literature, Strahov Library

Slovenská technická knižnica*, Bratislava, Gottwaldovo nám 2
Slovak Technical Library

CZECHOSLOVAKIA 73

Štátní technická knihovna*, Prague 1, nám primátora Dr V Vacka 5
State Technical Library

Štátní technická knihovna v Brně*, Brno, Veveří 95
State Technical Library in Brno

Státní vědecka knihovna, Olomouc, Bezručova 2
State Scientific Library

Státní vědecká knihovna, 60187 Brno, Leninová 5-7 Tel: 58321 Telex: 62299
State Research Library

Universitná knižnica*, Bratislava, Michalská 1
University Library

Knihovny fakult a ústavu **University Karlovy***, Prague
Libraries of Faculties and Institutes of Charles University

Library Associations

Slovenská knižničná*, Ministerstvo kultúry SSR, Bratislava, Suvorovová 2
Chairman: Dr S Pasiar
Slovak Library Council

Ústřední knihovnická rada ČSSR*, Prague 1, Valdštejnká 30
Secretary: Jaroslav Lipovsky
Central Library Council of the Czechoslovak Socialist Republic
Publication: Knihovnik

Zväz slovenských knihovníkov a informatikov, Michalská 1, 88517 Bratislava Tel: 331151 Telex: 093255
Executive Secretary: Ing Štefan Kimlička
Association of Slovak Librarians and Information Scientists
Publication: Zväzový bulletin

Library Reference Books & Journals

Book

Knihy a pražné, addresses of libraries, printing houses and bookshops, Nakladatelství Orbis, 12041 Prague 2, Vinohrady, Vinohradská třída 46

Journals

Československá akademie věd. Ustřední archiv. Archivní zprávy (Czechoslovak Academy of Sciences. Central Archives. Archival Reports), Academia, 11229 Prague 1, Vodičková 40

Čitatel (The Reader) (text in Slovak, summaries in German and Russian), Slovak NatiOoonal Library, 13601 Martin, Mudroňova 13

Čtenář (The Reader) (text in Czech, contents page in German and Russian), Nakladatelství Orbis, 12041 Prague 2, Vinohrady, Vinohradská třída 46

Informačný bulletin (Information Bulletin), Association of Slovak Librarians, Bibliographers and Documentalists, Bratislava 8000, Michalská 1

Knihovnictví a bibliografie (Librarianship and Bibliography) (issued as supplement to Čtenář), Nakladatelství Orbis, 12041 Prague 2, Vinohrady, Vinohradská třída 46

Literary Associations and Societies

Výtvarná služba **Českého fondu** výtvarných umělcu, sekce krásné knihy a grafiky*, Prague 1, Nové Město, třída Politických vězňu 7
Creative service of the Czech Fund for Creative Artists, Section for the Well-designed Book and Prints

Kruh priatelov detskej knihy, 89426 Bratislava, nám SNP12
Association of Friends of Children's Books in Slovakia

Matice Moravská*, Brno, Gorkého 14
Secretary: Dr Bedřich Čerešňák
Moravian Society of History and Literature
Publication: Časopis matice Moravské (quarterly)

Společnost přátel knihy pro mládež*, 11000 Prague 1, Na Perštýně 1
Association of Friends of Children's Books
Publication: Bulletin (irregular)

Index-**Společnost pro Československou literaturu** v zahraničí, Postfach 410511, D–5000 Cologne 41, German Federal Republic
Society for the Promotion of Czechoslovak Literature Abroad

Spolek Českých bibliofilu*, Prague, Nové Město, Václavské nám 39
Association of Czech Bibliophiles

Svaz českých spisovatelu*, 11147 Prague 1, Národní třída 11
Chairman: Dr Jan Kozak
Union of Czech Writers
Publication: Literáarní měsíčník (literary monthly)

Zväz slovenských spisovateľov, 89008 Bratislava, ul Obrancov mieru 14
Chairman: Andrej Plávka
Union of Slovak Writers

Literary Periodicals

Červený Květ (The Red Flower), literature and art, Ostrava 1, Tyrsová 9

Česká literatura (Czech Literature) (text in Czech, summaries in English, French, German and Russian), Academia, Publishing House of the Czechoslovak Academy of Sciences, 11229 Prague 1, Vodičková 40

Literarní měsíčnik (Literary Monthly), Union of Czech Writers, 11147 Prague 1, Národní třída 11

Novinky literatury (Literary News), State Library, 11001, Prague 1, Klementinum 190

Sborník narodního muzea v Praže rada C: literarni historie (Magazine of the National Museum, Prague. Series 3: Literary History), (title also in Latin, summaries in English, French, German and Russian), National Museum, 11579 Prague 1, Václavské nám 68

Slovenská literatúra (Slovak Literature) (contents page and summaries in German and Russian), Slovak Academy of Sciences, Institute of Slovak Literature, Bratislava, Klemensová 27

Slovenské pohlady na literatúru a uměnie (Slovak View on Literature and Art), Slovenský spisovateľ, 80000 Bratislava, Gajová 9

Slowakei (Slovakia), literary, scientific and political review, Matus-Cernak-Institut, Kulturelles Zentrum der Slowaken in Deutschland, D-5000 Cologne 1, Postfach 100924, German Federal Republic

Svědectví (Czech literary journal published abroad), 6 rue du Pont de Lodi, Paris 6e, and Vienna V, Margaretenpl 7

Svetova literatura, review of foreign literature, Odeon, 11587 Prague 1, Národní 36

Literary Prizes

Bratislava Literary Prize*
For the best literary work relating to the town of Bratislava written during the preceding five years. Awarded annually. Enquiries to Bratislava City Council, Bratislava

Brno Literary Prize*
For the best book written and published in Brno. Awarded annually. Enquiries to Brno City Council, Brno

Frano **Kral** Prize*
For existing works or for outstanding achievements in the field of juvenile literature. The executive body of Frano Kral Prize is the Slovak Literary Fund, the Circle of Friends of Juvenile Literature and publishing house Mladé léta. The prize is awarded annually. Enquiries to Ministry of Culture of the Slovak Socialist Republic, Suvorova 16, Bratislava

Marie **Majerove** Prize*
The highest award for a life's work in the fields of Czech literature and art for children and young people. Awarded every other year. Enquiries to Association of Friends of Children's Books, 11000 Prague 1, Na Perštýně 1

Maladá Fronta Award*
For literary works of prose, poetry, journalism, popular science also translations, published by Mladá Fronta during the preceding year. Awarded annually. Enquiries to Mladá Fronta (Young Front) Publishing House, Panská 8, 11222 Prague 1

Mladé léta Prize
For the best book of juvenile literature. Awarded annually. Enquiries to Mladé léta (Young Years) Publishing House, 89426 Bratislava, nám SNP 12

Naše vojsko Prizes*
For a political book, a book on military theory and a book of fiction Monetary prize is divided between the winners in each category. Enquiries to Nakladatelství a distribuce knih nase vojsko (Publishing and Distribution House of Czechoslovak Army), Na Děkance 3, 12812 Prague 2

Prague Literary Prize*
For the best creative work which has enriched human knowledge, contributed to the construction of socialism and furthered the development of culture in the City of Prague. Awarded annually. Enquiries to Prague City Council, Prague

Denmark

General Information

Language: Danish (English and German widely spoken)
Religion: Lutheran
Population: 5.1 million
Bank Hours: 0900 or 1000-1500 or 1600 Monday-Thursday; open until 1800 Friday
Shop Hours: 0800 or 0900-1700 or 1730 Monday-Thursday; open until 1900 or 2000 Friday; open until 1400 Saturday
Currency: 100 øre = 1 krone
Export/Import Information: No tariff on books except children's picture books 10.4% from non-EEC. Advertising matter 7.2% from non-EEC. (Original six common customs tariff effective 1 July 1977). VAT 15%. No import licences required. Importers must use longest of alternative credit terms in contract, otherwise no exchange controls
Copyright: UCC, Berne, Florence (see International section)

Book Trade Organizations

Bog- og Papirbranchens Kreditor-Udvalg*, Kompagnistr 11, D-1208 Copenhagen K
Committee of Inspection for the Book and Paper Trade

Dansk Boghandlermedhjaelperforening*, Siljangade 6, DK-2300 Copenhagen S
Danish Book Trade Employees' Association
Publication: Bogormen

Dansk Bogtjeneste*, Rostrup Bogmarked, Østergade 20, DK-7400 Herning
Chairman: Frits Rostrup
Danish Collective Book Advertising Organization

Danske Antikvarboghandlerforening, Silkegade 11, DK-1113 Copenhagen K
Danish Antiquarian Booksellers' Association

Danske Boghandleres Bogimport A/S, Herlev Hovedgade 199, DK-2730 Herlev Tel: (02) 918311
Director: Hans Pedersen
Danish Booksellers Book Import

Danske Boghandleres Importørforening (DANBIF)*, Møntergade 19, DK-1116 Copenhagen K Tel: (01) 141195
Chairman: Niels Stubbe Ostergaard
Danish Booksellers' Import Association

Danske Boghandleres Kommissionsanstalt (DBK), Siljangade 6, DK-2300 Copenhagen
Man Dir: Jorgen G Hensen
Danish Booksellers Clearing House

Den Danske Boghandlerforening, Boghandlernes Hus, Siljangade 6, DK-2300 Copenhagen S
Secretary: Elisabeth Brodersen
Danish Booksellers' Association
Publication: De Danske Bogmarked (with Danske Forlaeggerforening)

Danske Forlaeggerforening, Købmagergade 11, DK-1150 Copenhagen K Tel: (01) 156688
Dir: Erik V Krustrup
Danish Publishers' Association
Publication: Det Danske Bogmarked (with Danske Boghandlerforening)

Fællesekspeditionen, Njalsgade 19, DK-2300 Copenhagen S
Joint Trade Counter

Forening for Boghaandvaerk, Nørre Farimagsgade 74, DK-1364 Copenhagen K
Danish Book-craft Association
Publication: Bogvennen

Forening for Forlagsfolk, Kurt Hartogsohn, Jul Gjellerup Forlagsaktieselskab, 11 Roemersgade, DK-1362 Copenhagen K
Association of Young Publishers

Book Trade Reference Books and Journals

Book

Fortegnelse over Samhandels-Berettigede Boghandlere MV (Register of Licensed Booksellers etc), Danish Publishers' Association, Købmagergade 11, DK-1150 Copenhagen K

Journals

Bogormen (The Bookworm), journal for book trade employees, Danish Book Trade Employees' Association, Boghandlernes Hus, Siljangade 6, DK-2300 Copenhagen S

Bogvennen (The Book Lover), Brolaeggerstr 4, DK-1211 Copenhagen K, Danish Book-craft Association, Nørre Farimagsgade 74, DK-1364 Copenhagen K

Dansk Bogfortegnelse (Danish National Bibliography), Bibliotekscentralen, Telegrafvej 5, DK-2750 Ballerup

Den Danske Bogmarked (The Danish Book Market), Danish Booksellers' Association, Boghandlernes Hus, Siljangade 6, DK-2300 Copenhagen S

Publishers

Akademisk Forlag, Store Kannikestr 6-8, DK-1169 Copenhagen K Tel: (01) 119826/112346
Man Dir: Jørgen Bruus
Subjects: History, Philosophy, High-priced Paperbacks, Psychology, Engineering, General Science, University Textbooks, Educational Materials
1977: 180 titles *Founded:* 1962
ISBN Publisher's Prefix: 87-500

Arnkrone Forlaget A/S+*, Fuglebækvej 4, DK-2770 Kastrup Tel: (01) 507000
Man Dir: J Juul Rasmussen
Subjects: Art, Cultural History, Popular Medicine
Founded: 1941
ISBN Publisher's Prefix: 87-87007

Aschehoug Dansk Forlag A/S+, Landemaerket 11, DK-1119 Copenhagen K Tel: (01) 135130 Cable Add: Asdanfo
Man Dir: Erik Ipsen; *Rights & Permissions:* Kaj Påskesen
Subsidiary Companies: J Fr Clausens Forlag, Denmark (qv); H Hagerups Forlag, Denmark (qv); H Hirschsprungs Forlag, Denmark (qv)
Subjects: School Books, Textbooks
Founded: 1914
ISBN Publisher's Prefix: 87-11

H M Bergs Forlag ApS+, Peder Skrams Gade 5, DK-1054 Copenhagen K Tel: (01) 135480
Man Dir: H M Berg
Subjects: General Non-fiction, Juveniles, Art
1977: 3 titles *1978:* 6 titles *Founded:* 1965
ISBN Publisher's Prefix: 87-7228

Berlingske Forlag A/S+, Antonigade 7, DK-1187 Copenhagen K Tel: (01) 157575 Cable Add: Berlingske Telex: 27094
Publisher: Henrik Fonss
Subjects: Crime Stories, Berlingske Encyclopaedic Series, Dictionaries, Reference Books
1977: 58 titles *1978:* 58 titles *Founded:* 1733
ISBN Publisher's Prefix: 87-19

Bibliotekscentralens Forlag+, Telegrafvej 5, DK-2750 Ballerup Tel: (02) 975555 Cable Add: Danliber Telex: 35370
Man Dir: Leo Alste; *Editor:* Jørgen Richøj
Subjects: Literature about Librarians, Bibliographical Manuals
1978: 12 titles *Founded:* 1939
ISBN Publisher's Prefix: 87-552

Bierman og Bierman A/S, Vestergade 120, DK-7200, Grinsttted Tel: (05) 320288/320481 Cable Add: Bierbook Grindsted
Man Dir: H A Bierman
Subsidiary Company: Helle Samuels & Co Ltd, 32 Bodmin Road, Luton, Beds, UK
Subjects: Children's Books, Culture
1978: 3 titles *1979:* 2 titles *Founded:* 1968

Bogans Forlag+*, Kastaniebakken 8, DK-3540 Lynge Tel: (03) 188055
Owner: Evan Bogan
Subjects: Quality Paperbacks (factual, general), Popular Science, Occult

Borgens Forlag A/S+, Mynstersvej 19, DK-1827 Copenhagen K Tel: (01) 312041
Man Dir: Jarl Borgen; *Dir and Editor-in-Chief:* Ole Thestrup; *Sales Dir:* Else-Marie Hyldekrog; *Rights and Permissions:* Mette Nymark
Orders to: Fællesekspeditionen Njalsgade 19, DK-2300 Copenhagen S Tel: (01) 541333
Subjects: General Fiction, Belles Lettres, Poetry, Biography, Music, Art, Philosophy, Religion, Reference, Juveniles, Low- & High-priced Paperbacks, Medicine, Psychology, General & Social Science, Textbooks
1977: 207 titles *1978:* 255 titles *Founded:* 1948
ISBN Publisher's Prefix: 87-418

Børsen Forlaget A/S, Moentergade 19, Box 2103, 1014 Copenhagen K Tel: 157250
Publishing Manager: Ib Topholm; *Editorial:* Jan Erik Olsen; *Sales Manager:* Peter Rodbro *Production:* Ole Clement
Subject: Management
ISBN Publisher's Prefix: 87-755

Branner og Korch's Forlag A/S+, Fuglebækvej 4, DK-2770 Kastrup Tel: (01) 505588 Cable Add: Bookbranner
Man Dir: Jørgen Martens
Subjects: General Fiction & Non-fiction, Technical, Juveniles, Reference, Textbooks, Politics
1977: 90 titles *1978:* 118 titles *Founded:* 1949
ISBN Publisher's Prefix: 87-411

Nyt Nordisk Forlag Arnold **Busck** A/S+, Købmagergade 49, DK-1150 Copenhagen K Tel: (01) 111103 Cable Add: Bookbusck
Man Dirs: Helge Arnold Busck, Ole Arnold Busck
Subsidiary Company: Det Schønbergske Forlag, Denmark (qv)
Subjects: General Fiction, Biography, History, How-to, Music, Art, Philosophy, Reference, Religion, High-priced Paperbacks, Medicine, Psychology, General

& Social Science, University, Secondary & Primary Textbooks
Bookshops: Arnold Busck International Booksellers, Købmagergade 49, DK-1150 Copenhagen K; Nordisk Boghandel, Ostergade 16, DK-1100 Copenhagen K; Arnold Busck Antiquarians, Fiolstr 24, DK-1171 Copenhagen K
1977: 285 titles *1978:* 290 titles *Founded:* 1896
ISBN Publisher's Prefix: 87-17

Carit Andersens Forlag I/S*, Amagertorv 31, DK-1160 Copenhagen K Tel: (01) 123327
Owners: Poul Carit Andersen, Ulrik Boesen
Subjects: Travel, Limited Editions, Handbooks, Psychology, Juveniles, Cookery

Carlsen if+*, Köbmagergade 9, DK-1001 Copenhagen K Tel: (01) 143596 Cable Add: Carlsenif Telex: 22426
Man Dir: Per Hjald Carlsen
Subject: Children's Picture Books

J Fr Clausens Forlag+, Landemaerket 11, DK-1119 Copenhagen K Tel: (01) 135130
Editorial, Rights & Permissions: Kaj Påskesen
Subject: Practical Handbooks
Miscellaneous: Firm is a subsidiary of Aschehoug Dansk Forlag, Denmark (qv)
ISBN Publisher's Prefix: 87-11

Forlaget **Danmark** A/S*, Frederiksholms Kanal 18, DK-1220 Copenhagen K Tel: (01) 129192
Man Dir: Erik Bastfeldt
Subjects: Handbooks, Encyclopaedias

Dansk Historisk Haandbogsforlag+, Klintevej 25, DK-2800 Lyngby Tel: (02) 888500 Telex: 37406
Owner, Man Dir: Henning Jensen
Subjects: Genealogy, Heraldry, Culture, Local History
1978: 50 titles

Dansk Videnskabs Forlag ApS (Danish Science Press Ltd)*, 32F Lyngbyvej, DK-2100 Copenhagen Ö Tel: (01) 297144/22
Chief Executive: H C Bjerg
Subjects: Scientific Works; Periodicals

Det **Danske Forlag**+, Roskildevej 65, DK-2620 Albertslund Tel: (02) 648765
Man Dir: N J Laursen
Orders to: Njalsgade 19, DK-2300 Copenhagen S
Subjects: Biography, History, Philosophy, Reference, Juveniles, Low- & High-priced Paperbacks, Psychology, General & Social Science
1977: 21 titles *1978:* 19 titles *Founded:* 1941
ISBN Publisher's Prefix: 87-422

Christian Ejlers' Forlag A/S+, Brolaeggerstr 4, DK-1211 Copenhagen K Tel: (01) 122114
Man Dir: Christian Ejlers
Subjects: Educational & Academic, Art, Bibliography
1978: 17 titles *Founded:* 1967
ISBN Publisher's Prefix: 87-7241

Chr Erichsens Forlag A/S+*, Kronprinsensgade 1, DK-1114 Copenhagen K Tel: (01) 159595 Cable Add: Bogerich
Man Dir: Mr Kay Holkenfeldt
Subjects: Fiction, Mysteries, How-to, Juveiles, Handbooks
Founded: 1902
ISBN Publisher's Prefix: 87-555

F A D L Forlag (Foreningen af danske Laegestuderendes Forlag), Blegdamsvej 84, DK-2100 Copenhagen 0 Tel: (01) 262826 Telex: 16698
Man Dirs: Hans Jespersen, Steen Brynitz
Subjects: Medicine, Biology
1976: 60 titles *1977:* 58 titles *Founded:* 1964
ISBN Publisher's Prefix: 87-7437

Forlaget for **Faglitteratur** A/S+*, Vandkunsten 6, DK-1467 Copenhagen K Tel: (01) 137900
Subjects: Medicine, Technology
ISBN Publisher's Prefix: 87-573

Flensteds Forlag*, Korup Aabakke 10, DK-5461 Korup Tel: (09) 64392
Owner & Man Dir: Margit Bundegaard Flensted
Subject: International Editions of Hans Christian Andersen
Founded: 1936
ISBN Publisher's Prefix: 87-7010

Palle **Fogtdal** A/S+*, Nørre Farimagsgade 49, DK-1364 Copenhagen K Tel: (01) 126612
Chief Man Dir: Erik Skipper Larsen
Subjects: Home Decoration, DIY, Cooking, Gardening, Motoring, Boating, Fashion, Needlework
1977: 18 titles *1978:* 20 titles *Founded:* 1959

Forum Publishers Ltd+, Åbenrå 31, DK-1124 Copenhagen K Tel: (01) 147714 Cable Add: Forumbooks
Man Dir: Jokum Smith
Subjects: General, Scientific, Educational, Juveniles, Mysteries, High-priced Paperbacks
1978: 80 titles *Founded:* 1940
ISBN Publisher's Prefix: 87-553

Fremad+*, Nørrebrogade 54, DK-2200 Copenhagen N Tel: (01) 394040 Cable Add: Bogfremad
Man Dir: Mogens Bang; *Editorial:* Erik Langkjaer
Subjects: General Fiction, Juveniles, Textbooks, Cheap Editions of Travel Books and International Novels, Periodicals
Bookshop: Boghandelen Fremad, Nørrebrogade 54, DK-2200 Copenhagen N
1977: 100 titles *Founded:* 1912
ISBN Publisher's Prefix: 87-557

J Frimodts Forlag+, Korskaervej 25, DK-7000 Fredericia Tel: (05) 926100
Man Dir: A Brendholdt
Associate Company: Lohses Forlag (qv)
Subjects: Religion, Fiction
1977: 1 title *1978:* 3 titles
ISBN Publisher's Prefix: 87-7446

Forlaget **G M T***, Mejlgaard, DK-8584 Tranehaus Tel: (06) 317511
Publishers: Hans Jørn Christensen, Erik Bjørn Olsen
Subjects: History, Aesthetics, Politics, Philosophy, Psychology, Sociology, General Fiction, Textbooks, Educational Materials
1977: 20 titles *Founded:* 1971
ISBN Publisher's Prefix: 87-7330

G E C Gads Forlag+, Vimmelskaftet 32, DK-1161 Copenhagen K Tel: (01) 150558 Cable Add: Boggad
Man Dirs: Ole Restrups, Kaj Lynnerup
Subjects: Religion, Psychology, General Science, Education, Textbooks, Art, Reference, Law, Management
Bookshop: G E C Gads Dansk og Udenlandsk Boghandel A/S, Vimmelskaftet 32, DK-1161 Copenhagen K
Founded: 1855
ISBN Publisher's Prefix: 87-12

Jul **Gjellerup** Forlagsaktieselskab+, Rømersgade 11, DK-1362 Copenhagen K Tel: (451) 137801 Cable Add: Gjellerupbooks
Man Dir: Svend E Pedersen; *Marketing Manager:* Ulf Thomsen
Subjects: Reference, University, Secondary & Primary Textbooks, Educational Materials
Bookshop: Jul Gjellerups Boghandel ApS, Sølvgade 87-89, DK-1307 Copenhagen K Tel: (01) 137233
1978: approx 300 titles *Founded:* 1884
ISBN Publisher's Prefix: 87-13

Grafisk Forlag A/S+, Klosterrisvej 7, DK-2100 Copenhagen O Tel: (01) 294000 Cable Add: Boggrafisk Telex: 16987
Man Dir: Birger Schmith; *Deputy Manager, Editor-in-Chief:* Otto Hans Steidl
Subjects: General Fiction, Juveniles, Secondary & Primary Textbooks, Educational Materials, Foreign Language Easy Readers
1977: 500 titles *1978:* 478 titles *Founded:* 1940
ISBN Publisher's Prefix: 87-429

Grevas Forlag+*, Skovfaldet 2 K, DK-8200 Århus N Tel: (06) 168387 Cable Add: Grevas Arhus
Man Dir: Eva Hemmer Hansen; *Sales Dir:* Luise Pihl
Subjects: General Fiction, Belles Lettres, Poetry, Biography, Art, Juveniles
Founded: 1966
ISBN Publisher's Prefix: 87-7235

Det **Grønlandske Forlag**, PO Box 1009, DK-3900 Godthåb, Greenland (Located at: Hans Egedesvej 21, DK-3900 Godthåb) Tel: 22122 Cable Add: Groefobo Telex: 90638
Man Dir: Poul Bay
The Greenland Publishing House
Subjects: Children's Books, Fiction
Bookshop: Atuagkat Bookstore, PO Box 1009, DK-3900 Godthåb, Greenland
1978: 47 titles *1979:* 60 titles *Founded:* 1956
ISBN Publisher's Prefix: 87-558

Gutenberghus Publishing Service, Vognmagergade 11, DK-1148 Copenhagen K Tel: (01) 151925 Cable Add: Gutenbergblade Telex: 16705
Dirs: Adolf Kabatek, Peter Jerichow, Peter Hammertoft; *Editorial:* Carsten Jacobsen, Per Då, Jørgen Sonnergaard
Parent Company: Gutenberghus Group, Copenhagen
Associate Companies: Oy Kirjalito, Finland; Ehapa-Verlag GmbH, Federal Republic of Germany (qv); Hjemmet A/S, Norway (qv); Hemmets Journal AB (qv) and Forlaget Kärnan AB, Sweden; Egmont Publishing Ltd, UK
Subjects: Juveniles, Albums
Book Club: Walt Disney Wonderful World of Reading

Gyldendalske Boghandel — Nordisk Forlag A/S+, Klareboderne 3, DK-1001 Copenhagen K Tel: (01) 110775 Cable Add: Gyldendalske Copenhagen Telex: 15887 Gyldaldk
Dirs: Kurt Fromberg, Mogens Knudsen, Ole Werner Thomsen, Eigil Winther, Ole Wivel; *Editorial:* Helge Dokkedal, Vagn Grosen, Peter Holst, Erik Vagn Jensen, Egon Schmidt; *Sales Manager:* Søren Melgaard; *Rights & Permissions:* Kirsten

76 DENMARK

Franke, Per Finn Jacobsen; *Co-Productions Manager:* Eyvind Thorsen
Subjects: General Fiction, Belles Lettres, Poetry, Biography, History, How-to, Music, Art, Philosophy, Reference, Juveniles, Low- & High-priced Paperbacks, Medicine, Psychology, General & Social Science, University, Secondary & Primary Textbooks, Educational Materials
Founded: 1770
Book Clubs: Gyldendals Bogklub, Gyldendals Børnebogklub, Samlerens Bogklub
ISBN Publisher's Prefix: 87-01

P **Haase** & Søns Forlag A/S+, Løvsttr r 8, DK-1152 Copenhagen K Tel: (01) 115999
Cable Add: Boghaase
Man Dir: Niels Jørgen Haase; *Secretary:* Nina Jensen; *Treasurer:* Mogens Koreska; *Product Manager:* Preben Bentzen; *Editorial Manager:* Knud Andersen; *Sales & Marketing:* Steen Folkersen
Subsidiary Company: N J Haases Bookimport ApS; Rasmus Navers Forlag, Denmark (qv)
Subjects: Juveniles, University, Secondary & Primary Textbooks, Educational Materials
Bookshop: P Haase & Sons Boghandel A/S, Løvstr 8, DK-1152 Copenhagen K
1977: 79 titles *1978:* 132 titles *Founded:* 1877
Miscellaneous: Part owner of AV Media A/S, Nørre Søgade 35A, DK-1370 Copenhagen K
ISBN Publisher's Prefix: 87-559

H **Hagerups** Forlag+, Landemaerket 11, DK-1119 Copenhagen K Tel: (01) 135130
Cable Add: Asdanfo
Man Dir: Erik Ipsen
Subjects: Juveniles, Secondary & Primary Textbooks
Miscellaneous: Firm is a subsidiary of Aschehoug Dansk Forlag A/S, Denmark (qv)
ISBN Publisher's Prefix: 87-11

Edition Wilhelm **Hansen**+, Gothersgade 9-11, DK-1123 Copenhagen K Tel: (01) 117888 Cable Add: Musikhansen Telex: 19912 musik dk
Owners: Hanne and Lone Wilhelm Hansen
Subjects: Music, Musicology, Art, Educational Materials
Miscellaneous: Also Literary Agent (see Section)
Founded: 1857
ISBN Publisher's Prefix: 87-7455

Edvard **Henriksens** Forlag*, Palaegade 4, DK-1261 Copenhagen K Tel: (01) 145151
Owner: Edvard Henriksen
Subjects: Handbooks, Art, Cultural History

Hernovs Forlag+, Bredgade 14-16, DK-1260 Copenhagen K Tel: (01) 156284/156209/113930
Man Dir: Johs G Hernov; *Publicity Dir:* P Leslie Holst
Subsidiary Company: Johs G Hernov, Vinimport ApS
Subjects: General Fiction, Juveniles
Book Club: Hernovs Book Club (qv)
Founded: 1941
ISBN Publisher's Prefix: 87-7215

H **Hirschsprungs** Forlag+, Landemaerket 11, DK-1119 Copenhagen K Tel: (01) 135130 Cable Add: Asdanfo
Man Dir: Erik Ipsen
Subjects: School Books, Textbooks
Miscellaneous: Firm is a subsidiary of Aschehoug Dansk Forlag, Denmark (qv)
ISBN Publisher's Prefix: 87-11

Hjorts Forlag ApS*, Hovedvagtsgade 8, DK-1103 Copenhagen K Tel: (01) 152292
Man Dir: Per Hjort
Subjects: Yachting, Needlework, How-to; Monthly magazines on Yachting and Needlework
ISBN Publisher's Prefix: 87-7300

Forlaget **Hönsetryk***, Godthåbsvej 15a, DK-3060 Espergaerde Tel: (03) 231074
Owner: Kirsten Hofstätter

Høst og Søns Forlag+, Bredgade 35, DK-1260 Copenhagen K Tel: (01) 155051/153031 Cable Add: Bookhøst
Man Dir: Mogens C Lind; *Editorial:* Kirsten Skaarup
Subjects: Hobbies & Crafts, Languages, Books on Denmark, Juvenile Paperbacks, Reference
1978: approx 80 titles
Founded: 1836
ISBN Publisher's Prefix: 87-14

Birgitte **Hövrings** Biblioteksforlag+, Teglgårdsvej 531, DK-3050 Humlebaek Tel: (03) 190926
Owner: Thorsteinn Stefánsson
1978: 1 title

Informations Forlag ApS, St Kongensgade 40, DK-1264 Copenhagen K Tel: (01) 141426 Telex: 22658
Man Dirs: Johs Feil, Asger Jepsen
Parent Company: Information Daily Newspaper
Subjects: Non-Fiction informative books on current issues, Educational
1977: 9 titles *1978:* 16 titles *Founded:* 1975
ISBN Publisher's Prefix: 87-87498

A/S **Interpresse**, PO Box 11, DK-2880 Bagsvaerd (Located at: 32 Krogshoejvej, DK-2880 Bagsvaerd Tel: 02985227 Cable Add: Stonepress Telex: 37416 STENBY DK
Man Dir: Arne Stenby
Subjects: Juveniles, Comics
1978: 65 titles *1979:* 80 titles *Founded:* 1954
ISBN Publisher's Prefix: 87-7529

Jespersen og Pios Forlag+*, Valkendorfsgade 22, DK-1151 Copenhagen K Tel: (01) 129642 Cable Add: Jespio
Man Dir: Iver Jespersen; *Rights & Permissions:* Elly Sandal
Subjects: General Fiction & Nonfiction, Juveniles, Paperbacks
1977: 50 titles *Founded:* 1865
ISBN Publisher's Prefix: 87-419

Lademann Ltd, Publishers+, Linnesgade 25, DK-1361 Copenhagen K Tel: (01) 131650 Cable Add: Boglademann Telex: 19149
Man Dir: J Lademann; *Dirs:* Svend Aage Jørgensen, Bent W Dahlström; *Production Dir:* Ove Mølbeck; *Advertising Dir:* Heinz Mueller; *Rights & Permissions:* Kirsten Jacobsen
Subsidiary Companies: Hamlet Ltd; Kolon Ltd; Komma Ltd; Sesam Ltd
Subjects: General
Book Clubs: Union Book Club, Union Crime Club, Union Novel Library, Union Harlekin Library, Union Classics Library
1977: 280 titles *1978:* 280 titles *Founded:* 1954
ISBN Publisher's Prefix: 87-15

Lentz og Jenssens Forlag ApS, Torpetvej 9, DK-4100 Ringsted Tel: (03) 613161
Man Dir: Børge Lentz
Subjects: How-to, Reference, High-priced Paperbacks, Engineering, Secondary Textbooks, Sports
1977-78: 17 titles *Founded:* 1971
ISBN Publisher's Prefix: 87-7554

Lindhardt og Ringhof+, Studiestr 14, DK-1455 Copenhagen Tel: (01) 111955
Cable Add: Eleteredit
Owners: Otto B Lindhardt, Gert Ringhof
Subjects: General Fiction, Biography, History, How-to, Philosophy, Paperbacks, Pre-school Materials
1977: 38 titles *1978:* 38 titles *Founded:* 1971
ISBN Publisher's Prefix: 87-7560

Lohses Forlag+, Korskaervej 25, DK-7000 Fredericia Tel: (05) 926100
Man Dir: A Brendholdt
Associate Company: J Frimodts Forlag (qv)
Subjects: Religion, Juveniles
1977: 23 titles *1978:* 18 titles *Founded:* 1868
ISBN Publisher's Prefix: 87-564

Martins Forlag+, Kompagnistrade 34.4.sal, DK-1208 Copenhagen K Tel: (01) 146665
Owner: Erik Halkier
Subjects: General Fiction, Nonfiction, Juveniles
ISBN Publisher's Prefix: 87-566

Medicinsk Forlag ApS+, Tranevej 2, DK-3650 Ölstykke Tel: (03) 176592
Man Dir: Anni Lindelöv
Subjects: Medical, Scientific

Forlaget **Modtryk** AMBA, Mejlgade 21-23, DK-8000 Aarhus C Tel: (0045) 6127991 Telex: 4556785 MOD
Man Dir: Frands Mortensen; *Editorial:* Jan Knus; *Sales:* Niels Jørgen Jensen; *Production:* Kjeld Vindum; *Publicity:* Carsten Vengsgård; *Rights & Permissions:* Preben Bach
Parent Companies: Politisk Revy Skt, Pederstræde 28B, DK-1453 Copenhagen K; Værtshuset Aesken, Anholtsgade 8, DK-8000 Aarhus C
Subjects: Political Writings and Essays (especially in the field of the 'New Left' movement), Children's Books, Fiction
Book Club: Socialistisk Bogklub ApS
1978: 25 titles *1979:* 30 titles *Founded:* 1972
ISBN Publisher's Prefix: 87-458, 87-620, 87-817

Munksgaard, International Booksellers & Publishers Ltd+, Nørre Søgade 35, DK-1370 Copenhagen K Tel: (01) 127030
Cable Add: Bogotto
Chairman of the Board: Per Saugman; *Man Dir:* Oluf V Møller; *Editorial:* Jørgen Bergmann, Peter Hartmann, Karen Margrethe Henriksen, Sven Erik Olsen; *Treasurer:* Jørgen Sandal
Subjects: Medicine, Nursing, Dentistry, Social Sciences, Psychology, Schoolbooks, Children's Books, Scientific Journals
Bookshop: Munksgaard Bookshop, Nørregade 6, DK-1165 Copenhagen K (subscription agency and export only)
1977: 498 titles *Founded:* 1917

Rasmus **Navers** Forlag+, Løvstr 8, DK-1152 Copenhagen K Tel: (01) 115999
Man Dir: Niels Jørgen Haase
Subjects: Humour, Art, Fiction
Miscellaneous: Firm is a subsidiary of P Haase & Søns Forlag A/S, Denmark (qv)

Nordisk Kolportage Forlag A/S*, Frederiksholms Kanal 18, DK-1220 Copenhagen K Tel: (01) 129192
Man Dir: Erik Bastfeldt
Subjects: Encyclopaedias, Handbooks

DENMARK 77

Nordisk Romanforlag A/S*,
Frederiksholms Kanal 18, DK-1220
Copenhagen K Tel: (01) 111876
ISBN Publisher's Prefix: 87-7489

M Normanns Forlag A/S+*, Kastanievej 3,
DK-5230 Odense M Tel: (09) 120697
Man Dir: Mogens Normann
Subjects: How-to, Secondary & Primary
Textbooks
Founded: 1942
ISBN Publisher's Prefix: 87-7032

Jörgen Paludans Forlag A/S+*, Fiolstr 32,
DK-1171 Copenhagen K Tel: (01) 116042
Man Dir: Jörgen Paludan
Subjects: Non-fiction, Psychology,
Sociology, History, Political Science,
Economics, High-priced Paperbacks
ISBN Publisher's Prefix: 87-7230

Politikens Forlag A/S+, Vestergade 26,
DK-1456 Copenhagen K Tel: (01) 112122
Cable Add: Polbooks
Man Dir: Johannes Ravn; *Sales Dir:* Sören
Seedorff
Subjects: General Nonfiction: Nature Study,
History and Documentary, Sports, Games,
Hobbies, Children's Folklore, Art,
Literature, Music, Maps and Atlases,
Travel, How-To
1978: 100 approx *Founded:* 1946
ISBN Publisher's Prefix: 87-567

C A Reitzels Forlag+, Nørre Søgade 35,
DK-1370 Copenhagen K Tel: (01) 117031
Man Dir: Jørgen Sandal
Subjects: General Science, Engineering ,
Textbooks
1977: 50 titles *1978:* 46 titles *Founded:*
1819
ISBN Publisher's Prefix: 87-421

Hans Reitzels Forlag A/S+, Snaregade 4,
DK-1205 Copenhagen K Tel: (01) 140451
Cable Add: Reitzelbooks
Man Dir: Hans Reitzel; *Editorial, Rights &
Permissions:* Line Schmidt-Madsen
Subjects: Psychology, General & Social
Science, University Textbooks, Philosophy,
Reference, High-priced Paperbacks
1977: 51 titles *1978:* 56 titles *Founded:*
1949
ISBN Publisher's Prefix: 87-412

Rhodos, International Science and Art
Publishers+*, Niels Brocks Gård,
Strandgade 36, DK-1401 Copenhagen K
Tel: (01) 543020 Cable Add: Sciencebooks
Man Dir: Niels Blaedel
Subjects: Art, High-priced Paperbacks,
General & Social Science, Handbooks,
Encyclopedias
Founded: 1959
ISBN Publisher's Prefix: 87-7496

Rosenkilde og Bagger+, Kron-Prinsens-
Gade 3, PO Box 2184, DK-1017
Copenhagen K Tel: (01) 157044 Cable
Add: Bogkunst
Man Dir: Finn Jacobsen
Subjects: Reprints, Facsimile Editions,
High-priced Paperbacks, General Science
Bookshop: Rosenkilde & Bagger, Kron-
Prinsens-Gade 3, PO Box 2184, DK-1017
Copenhagen K
1978: 49 titles *Founded:* 1941
ISBN Publisher's Prefix: 87-423

Samlerens Forlag A/S+, Christian den
Niendesgade 2, DK-1111 Copenhagen K
Tel: (03) 131023
Man Dir: Børge Priskorn
Subjects: General Fiction & Nonfiction,
History, Guides, Art, Social Science,
Paperbacks, Domestic Crafts, Games, Sport
1977: 60 titles *1978:* 60 titles
ISBN Publisher's Prefix: 87-568

Det **Schoenbergske** Forlag A/S (Nyt
Nordisk Forlag Arnold Busck A/S)+,
Landemaerket 5, DK-1119 Copenhagen K
Tel: (01) 113066 CablAdd: Schoenbook
Man Dir: Elsa Pedersen; *Dir:* Paul Monrad;
Sales Manager: Max-Erik Reinhold
Subjects: General Fiction, Belles Lettres,
Poetry, Biography, History, Music, Art,
Philosophy, Reference, Travel, Low- &
High-priced Paperbacks, Psychology, Trade
Books, University, Commercial School,
Secondary & Primary Textbooks
1977: 70 titles *1978:* 44 titles *Founded:*
1857
ISBN Publisher's Prefix: 87-570

A/S J H **Schultz** Forlag+, Møntergården,
Møntergade 21, DK-1116, Copenhagen K
Tel: (01) 121195 Cable Add: Bogschultz
Manager: H Borberg
Subjects: Nonfiction, Law, EEC
publications, Medical books
1978: 76 titles *Founded:* 1661
ISBN Publisher's Prefix: 87-569

Scientology Publications Organization
(AOSH DK Publ Dept ApS), Jernbanegade
6, DK-1608 Copenhagen V Tel: (01)
145128 Telex: 15387 rly PDK
Man Dir: Judy Graham; *Sales Manager:*
Neil Lumbsden; *Manufacturing Dir:* Marc
Dumas; *Rights & Permissions:* Annette dèl
Francia
Branch Off: Pubs UK, Saint Hill Manor,
East Grinstead, West Sussex RH19 4JY,
UK
Subjects: Philosophy, Religion,
Management, Education
1978: 13 titles *Founded:* 1967
ISBN Publisher's Prefix: 87-87347

Skarv-Nature Publications ApS,
Kongevejen 45, DK-2840 Holte Tel: (02)
424745
Man Dir: Soren Koustrup
Subjects: Nature & Wildlife Books, Modern
Biology, Geography, Animal Behaviour,
Ecology, Ornithology, Social Anthropology
1978: 22 titles *1979:* 25 titles *Founded:*
1976
ISBN Publisher's Prefix: 87-87581

A/S **Skattekartoteket**+, Palaegade 4,
DK-1261 Copenhagen K Tel: (01) 117874
Man Dir: V Spang-Thomsen
Subject: Taxation (national and
international)
1978: 2 titles

Sommer & Sörensen Forlag ApS+,
Siljangade 3, DK-2300 Copenhagen S
Tel: (01) 950945
Dirs: Erik Sommer, Aage Börglum Sörensen

A/S **Sparevirke**+*, Köbmagergade 62-64,
DK-1150 Copenhagen K Tel: (01) 151811
Man Dir: T G Söndergaard
Subjects: Handbooks, School Books
ISBN Publisher's Prefix: 87-7538

Strandbergs Forlag+*, Topstykket 17,
DK-3460 Birkeröd Tel: (02) 816397
Owner: Hans Jörgen Strandberg
Subject: Cultural History

Strubes Forlag og Boghandel A/S+*,
1 Söndergade, DK-4130 Gl Viby/Sjaelland
Tel: (03) 394250 Cable Add: Strubebooks
Man Dirs: Jonna and Povl Strube
Subjects: Psychic & Occult, Philosophy,
Art, Bibliophilic, Naval
Bookshop: at above address

Finn **Suenson** Forlag, Rosernörns Alle 18,
DK-1970 Copenhagen V Tel: (01) 359888
Man Dir: Finn Suenson
Subjects: Handbooks, Reference, Politics,
History
1978: 12 titles *1979:* 12 titles *Founded:*
1971
ISBN Publisher's Prefix: 87-201

Teknisk Forlag A/S+, Skelbaekgade 4,
DK-1717 Copenhagen V Tel: (01) 216801
Cable Add: Technipress Telex: 16368
TEFKO DK
Man Dir: Peter Müller
Subjects: Engineering, Manuals, Directories,
Guides
1977: 7 titles *1978:* 21 titles *Founded:* 1948
ISBN Publisher's Prefix: 87-571

Teknologisk Instituts Forlag+,
Gregersensvej, DK-2630 Tåstrup Tel: (02)
996611
Subjects: Technical, Special Literature and
Handbooks for Crafts and Industries
1977: 20 titles *1978:* 20 titles

Thaning og Appels Forlag+, Fuglaebækvej
4, DK-2770 Kastrup Tel: (01)
508100/508969
Man Dir: Thomas Blom
Subjects: General Fiction, Belles Lettres,
Art, History, Philosophy, Juveniles, Science
& Technical Education, Psychology,
How-to; Paperbacks
1977: 45 titles *1978:* 43 titles *Founded:*
1866
ISBN Publisher's Prefix: 87-413

Ungdommens Forlag & Aamodts Forlag
A/S*, Grundtvigsvej 37, DK-1864
Copenhagen K Tel: (01) 241500
Subjects: Special Literature, Juveniles
ISBN Publisher's Prefix: 87-7516

De **Unges** Forlag, Unitas Forlag+,
Amaliegade 24, DK-1256 Copenhagen K
Tel: (01) 159363
Subjects: Religion, Fiction
ISBN Publisher's Prefix: 87-7517

Vinten's Forlag +, Amagertorv 31,
DK-1160 Copenhagen K Tel: (01) 122121
Owner, Man Dir: Jeppe Vinten
Subjects: General Fiction, Belles Lettres,
Art, Philosophy, Juveniles, Low- & High-
priced Paperbacks, Psychology
1978: 31 titles *Founded:* 1950
ISBN Publisher's Prefix: 87-414

Wangels Forlag A/S+, Gammeltorv 8, PO
Box 1061, DK-1008 Copenhagen K
Tel: (01) 156111
Man Dir: Søren Bruhn
Subjects: General Fiction
Founded: 1946
Book Club: Danske Bogsamleres Klub
ISBN Publisher's Prefix: 87-7220

Wilkenschildts Forlag*, Gedevasevej 3,
DK-3520 Farum Tel: (02) 951828
Owner: Ebbe Wilkenschildt
Subjects: Handbooks, Nonfiction

Winthers Forlag ApS, Naverland 1A,
DK-2600 Glostrup Tel: (02) 960666 Cable
Add: Winnpub
Man Dir: Per Andreassen; *Rights &
Permissions:* Anni Groth
Subsidiary Companies: Wennerberg,
Finland; Wennerbergs Förlags AB, Sweden
Subjects: General Fiction, Juveniles, Low-
priced Paperbacks
Founded: 1945
ISBN Publisher's Prefix: 87-18

Wöldikes Forlag+*, Troels-Lundsvej 14, DK-2000 Copenhagen F Tel: (01) 748775
Owner & Man Dir: Arne Wöldike Schmith
Subjects: All types of books for the general trade market, Fiction & Nonfiction

Literary Agents

R P **Adam***, Brede Bovej 31, DK-2800 Lyngby, Copenhagen

A/S **Bookman**, Fiolstr 12, DK-1171 Copenhagen K Tel: (01) 145720 Cable Add: Bookman, Copenhagen

Bjorn **Hansen***, Hojskolevej 8, Rangsted Rust

International Children's Book Service, Kildeskovsvej 21, DK-2820 Gentofte Tel: (01) 653032 Cable Add: Bookchild

Georg **Juelner**, Smøgen 1, DK-3480 Fredensborg

Edith **Kiilerich***, Fiolstr 12, DK-1171 Copenhagen K
Miscellaneous: This company also acts as a Literary Agent for Finnish, Norwegian and Swedish writers

Preben **Klein**, PO Box 50, DK-3200 Helsinge
Also publishers representative

Albrecht **Leonhardt** ApS, Literary Agent, Studiestraede 35, DK-1455 Copenhagen K Tel: (01) 132523 Cable Add: Leolitag

Michaels og Licht, Osterbrogade 84, DK-2100 Copenhagen Tel: (01) 424608 Cable Add: Literagent

Svend **Mondrup** International Literary Agency, Holbergsgade 20, DK-1057 Copenhagen K Tel: (01) 149942/(01) 129666
Chief Executive: Svend Mondrup

Nordiska Teaterforlaget Edition Wilhelm Hansen, Gothersgade 9-11, DK-1123 Copenhagen Tel: (01) 117888
Branch Off: Norrlandsgatan 16, S-111 43 Stockholm (qv)

Carl **Strakosch** & Olaf Nordgreen*, Nyhavn 5, DK-1051 Copenhagen K

Book Clubs

Danske Bogsamleres Klub, Gammeltorv 8, PO Box 1061, DK-1008 Copenhagen K
Owned by: Wangels Forlag A/S (Copenhagen)

The **English Book** Club*, Raadhospladsen 55, DK-1500 Copenhagen
Owned by: Borge Boesen (qv under Booksellers)

Gyldendals Bogklub, 51 Pilestraede, DK-1001 Copenhagen K
Owned by: Gyldendalske Boghandel-Nordisk Forlag A/S (Copenhagen)
Subjects: Fiction and General Nonfiction
Associated Book Clubs: Gyldendals Børnebogklub, Samlerens Bogklub; both qv

Gyldendals Børnebogklub*, Pilestraede 51, DK-1001 Copenhagen K
Owned by: Gyldendalske Boghandel — Nordisk Forlag A/S (qv)

Hernovs Book Club, Bredgade 14-16, DK-1260 Copenhagen K
Owned by: Hernovs Forlag

Det Bedste fra **Reader's Digest** A/S*, PO Box 1160, Oestergade 61, DK-1010 Copenhagen K

Samlerens Bogklub*, Klareboderne 5, DK-1001 Copenhagen K
Owned by: Gyldendalske Boghandel-Nordisk Forlag A/S (Copenhagen)
Subjects: Fiction, Nonfiction, Political
Associated Book Clubs: Gyldendals Bogklub, Gyldendals Børnebogklub; both qv

Socialistisk Bogklub ApS, Mejlgade 21-23, DK-8000 Aarhus C
Owned by: Forlaget Modtryk AMBA (Aarhus)

Union Book Club*, Linnesgade 25, DK-1361 Copenhagen K
Subjects: Fiction, Illustrated Nonfiction
Owned By: Lademann Ltd, Publishers (Copenhagen)

Union Classics Library+, Linnesgade 25, DK-1361 Copenhagen K
Owned by: Lademann Ltd (Copenhagen)

Union Crime Club, Linnesgade 25, DK-1361 Copenhagen K
Owned by: Lademann Ltd, Publishers (Copenhagen)

Union Harlekin Library+, Linnesgade 25, DK-1361 Copenhagen K
Owned by: Lademann Ltd (Copenhagen)

Union Novel Library+, Linnesgade 25, DK-1361 Copenhagen K
Owned by: Lademann Ltd (Copenhagen)

Walt Disney Wonderful World of Reading, Vognmagergade 11, DK-1148, Copenhagen K
Owned by: Gutenberghus (Copenhagen)

Major Booksellers

Akademisk Boghandel, Universitetsparken, DK-8000 Århus C Tel: (06) 128844
Manager: Bent Kjeldsen

Biblioteksboghandelen ApS*, Kultorvet 2, DK-1175 Copenhagen K

Bierman & Bierman, Book Import and Sale, Vestergade 120, DK-7200 Grindsted Tel: 05/320288/320481

Borge **Boesen** (The English Bookshop)*, Raadhospladsen 55, DK-1550 Copenhagen V Tel: (01) 132550
Man Dir: Borge Boesen

Clemens **Bøger** og Papir I/S*, Skt Clemens Torv 17, DK-8000 Århus C

Boghallen*, Rådhuspladsen 37, DK-1585 Copenhagen V Tel: (01) 118511

Arnold **Busck** International Boghandel A/S, Købmagergade 49, DK-1150 Copenhagen K Tel: (01) 122453; Export Division (formerly Andr Fred Høst & Søn), Købmagergade 49, DK-1150 Copenhagen K Tel: (01) 122453
Associate Company: Nordisk Boghandel, Arnold Busck International Boghandel A/S, Østergade 16, DK-1100 Copenhagen K Tel: (01) 147007

Dansk Central-Boghandel*, Nørregade 49, DK-1165 Copenhagen K

The **English Bookshop**, see Borge Boesen

G E C **Gads** Dansk og Udenlandsk Boghandel A/S, Vimmelskaftet 32, DK-1161 Copenhagen K Tel: (01) 150558

Jul **Gjellerups** Boghandel ApS, Sølvgade 87-89, DK-1307 Copenhagen K Tel: (01) 137233 Telex: 19110 GJ BOOK DK

Magasin du Nord A/S, Book Department, The English Bookshop, Kongens Nytorv 13, DK-1095 Copenhagen K Tel: (451) 114433 Cable Add: Magdunord Telex 15975

Munksgaard, International Boghandel*, Nørregade 6, DK-1165 Copenhagen K Tel: (01) 126970

Nordisk Boghandel*, Östergade 16, DK-1100 Copenhagen K

Erik **Paludans** Boghandel*, Fiolstr 10, DK-1171 Copenhagen K Tel: (01) 150675

Polyteknisk Boghandel og Forlag, Anker Engelundsvej 1, DK-2800 Lyngby Tel: (02) 881488
Manager: Ove Dela

Universitetsbogladen (Panumbogladen/Naturfagsbogladen/Latinerbogladen), Blegdamsvej 3, DK-2200 Copenhagen Tel: (01) 351643 Telex: 16698 unbog dk
Branches: Blegdamsvej 3, DK-2200 Copenhagen N; Universitetsparken 13, DK-2100 Copenhagen O; Njalsgade 80, DK-2300 Copenhagen S
Manager: Hans Jespersen

Major Libraries

Århus Kommunes Biblioteker, Mølleparken, DK-8000 Århus C Tel: (06) 136622 Telex: 64850
Århus Public Library

Danmarks Tekniske Bibliotek, Anker Engelunds Vej 1, DK-2800 Lyngby Tel: (02) 883088 Telex: 37148
National Technological Library of Denmark

Erhvervsarkivet-Statens Erhvervshistoriske Arkiv, Vester Allé 12, DK-8000 Århus C
Danish National Business History Archives

Gentofte Kommunebibliotek, Öregaards Allé 7, DK-2900 Hellerup, Copenhagen Tel: 45162/7500
Chief Librarian: Helge Stenkilde
Gentofte Municipal Library

Københavns Kommunes Biblioteker, Kultorvet 2, DK-1175 Copenhagen K Tel: (01) 136070 Telex: 16648 kkbhb dk
Copenhagen Municipal Libraries

Københavns Stadsarkiv, Rådhuset, DK-1599 Copenhagen V
Copenhagen City Archives
Publication: Historiske Meddelelser om København (Historical Year-book)

Det **Kongelige Bibliotek***, Christians Brygge 8, DK-1219 Copenhagen Tel: (01) 150111 Telex: 15009
Royal Library

Det **Nordjyske Landsbibliotek**, Ved Vor Frue Kirke, DK-9000 Ålborg
Central Library for the County of North Jutland

Odense Centralbibliotek*, DK-5000 Odense
Odense County Library

Odense Universitetsbibliotek, Campusvej 55, DK-5230 Odense M
Odense University Library

Rigsarkivet, Rigsdagsgården 9, DK-1218 Copenhagen K
Chief Archivist: S Rambusch
National Record Office

Statsbiblioteket, Universitetsparken, DK-8000 Århus C Tel: (06) 122022 Telex: 64515
State and University Library

Universitetsbiblioteket, 1 afd: Humanities, Fiolstraede 1, DK-1171 Copenhagen K
Librarian: Torben Nielsen Tel: (01) 130875

Universitetsbiblioteket, 2 afd: Science and Medicine, Nørre allé 49, DK-2200 Copenhagen N
Librarian: Kell Prehn

Library Associations

Arkivforeningen*, Rigsarkivet, Rigsdagsgarden 9, DK-1218 Copenhagen K Tel: (01) 123878
Archives Society

Bibliotekarforbundet, Hyskenstr 2, DK-1207 Copenhagen K Tel: (01) 152811
Secretary: B Sørensen
Union of Librarians
Publication: Bibliotek 70

Bibliotekarforbundet for Forsknings- og Fagbiblioteker
Secretariat: Klaus Munck, Statsbiblioteket, Universitetsparken, DK-8000 Århus C
Union of Librarians for Research and Reference Libraries

Bibliotekscentralen, Telegrafvej 5, DK-2750 Ballerup Tel: (02) 975555 Cable Add: Danliber Telex: 35370
Man Dir: Leo Alster; *Editor:* Jørgen Rishøj
Danish Library Bureau
Subjects: Literature about Libraries, Bibliographical Manuals and Material
Publications: Dansk Bogfortegnelse (The Danish National Bibliography, Books), *Dansk Periodicafortegnelse* (The Danish National Bibliography, Serials)

Danmarks Biblioteksforening*, Trekronergade 15, DK-2500 Copenhagen Valby Tel: (01) 308682
Secretary: F Ettrup
Danish Library Association
Publications: Bogens Verden (Danish Library Journal); *Biblioteksvejviser* (Danish Library Guide); *Biblioteksårborg* (Danish Library Yearbook)

Danmarks Forskningsbiblioteksforening, The Royal Library, Christians Brygge 8, DK-1219, Copenhagen K Tel: (01) 150111
Danish Research Library Association:
Section 1 Research Libraries; Section 2 Staff members in Danish research libraries
President: P Birkelund
Publication: DF-Revy (in conjunction with Sammenslutningen af Danmarks Forskningsbiblioteker)

Danmarks Skolebibliotekarforening*, Rønnevej 7, DK-6880 Tarm
Association of Danish School Librarians
Publication: The School Librarian

Danmarks Skolebiblioteksforening, Vejlemosevej 21, DK-2840 Holte Tel: (02) 424930
Chief Executive: Jørgen Christiansen; *Manager:* Niels Jacobsen
Association of Danish School Libraries
Publication: Børn & Bøger; also books dealing with School Libraries and Youth Culture etc

Dansk Musikbiblioteksforening*, The Secretary, The Royal Library, Music Department, Christians Brygge 8, 1219 Copenhagen K
Association of Danish Music Libraries

Dansk Teknisk Litteraturselskab, Anker Engelunds Vej 1, DK-2800 Lyngby
Danish Society for scientific and technological information and documentation

Sammenslutningen af Danmarks Forskningsbiblioteker, a section of Danmarks Forskningsbiblioteksforening (qv)

Library Reference Books and Journals

Books

Biblioteksårbog (Library Yearbook), Danish Library Association, Trekronergade 15, DK-2500 Copenhagen Valby

Biblioteksvejviser (Library Guide), Danish Library Association, Trekronergade 15, DK-2500 Copenhagen Valby

Public Libraries in Denmark, Det Danske Selskab, Kulturvet 2, DK-1175 Copenhagen K

Udenlandsk Bibliotekslitteratur i Danske Biblioteker (Foreign Library Literature in Danish Libraries), Bibliotekscentralen, Telegrafvej 5, DK-2750 Ballerup

Journals

Bibliotek 70 (Library 70), Association of Librarians, Hyskenstr 2, 4, DK-1207 Copenhagen K

Biblioteken (The Library), Biblioteksskole, Birketinget 6, DK-2300 Copenhagen S

Bogens Verden (Library Journal), magazine for Danish library employees, Danish Library Association, Trekronergade 15, DK-2500 Copenhagen Valby

DF-Revy, Danmarks Forskningsbiblioteksforening, Statsbiblioteket, Universitetsparken, 8000 Århus C

Information for Forskningsbiblioteker (Information for Research Librarians), The Royal Library, Christians Brygge 8, DK-1219 Copenhagen K

Meddelelser frä Rigsbibliotekaren (Communications from the State Librarians), The Royal Library, Christians Brygge 8, DK-1219 Copenhagen K

Restaurator, International journal for the preservation of library and archival material (text in English, French, German and Russian), Restaurator Press, PO Box 96, DK-1004 Copenhagen K

The School Librarian, Association of Danish School Librarians, Rønnevej 7, DK-6880 Tarm

Literary Associations and Societies

Bogvennerne*, Madvigs Allé 2, DK-1829 Copenhagen
Friends of the Book

Dansk Bibliofil-Klub*, Hj Brantingspl 1iv, DK-2100 Copenhagen Ø
President: Dr Niels Gangsted
Danish Bibliophile Club

Dansk Exlibris Selskab*, PO Box 1519, DK-2700 Copenhagen Brh
Danish Bookplate Society
Publication: Exlibris-Nyt

Dansk Forfatterforening*, Forfatternes Hus, Nyhavn 21, Copenhagen K
Chairman: Hans Jørgen Lembourn
Danish Authors' Society
Publication: Forfatteren (8 a year)

Nyt **Dansk Litteraturselskab**, Bibliotekscentralen, Telegrafvej 5, DK-2750 Ballerup
Manager: Leo Alster
New Danish Society for Literature
Aims: Publication/Republication of books in short supply in libraries
Special activity: Magnaprint (large print books for partially-sighted)
Members: public libraries only

Danske Sprog-og Litteraturselskab, Frederiksholms Kanal 18A, DK-1220 Copenhagen
Administrator: Dr Erik Dal
Danish Language and Literature Society

Kongelige Danske Videnskabernes Selskab*, H C Andersens Boulevard 35, DK-1553 Copenhagen V Tel: (01) 113240
President: P J Riis; *Secretary:* Christian Møller
Royal Danish Academy of Sciences and Letters
Publications: Oversigt (annual) etc

Samfund til Udgivelse af Gammel Nordisk Litteratur, Kjaerstrupvej 33, DK-2500 Copenhagen Valby
Secretary: Agnete Loth
Society for the Publication of Old Norse Literature

Literary Periodicals

Bog-anmelderen (The Book Review), Bog-Anmelderens Tidsskrifter, Gammel Torv 16, DK-1457 Copenhagen

Børn og Bøger (Children and Books), Association of Danish School Libraries, Stationsvej 3, DK-4070 Kirke-Hyllinge

Exlibris-Nyt (Bookplate News), Danish Bookplate Society, PO Box 1519, DK-2700 Copenhagen Brh

Hvedekorn (Wheat Grain), Borgens Forlag, Mynstersvej 19, DK-1827 Copenhagen V

Language and Literature (text in English), Copenhagen University, English Institute, Lille Kirkestr 1, DK-1072 Copenhagen K

Orbis Litterarum, international review of literary studies (text mainly in English, occasionally in French and German), Munksgaard, Nørre Søgade 35, DK-1370 Copenhagen K

Literary Prizes

Emil **Aarestrup** Prize*
For a poet. 2,500 Danish crowns and a medal. Awarded annually. Enquiries to Danish Ministry of Cultural Affairs, Nybrogade 2, Copenhagen K

Hans Christian **Andersen** Prize
For the best Danish book for children.
Established in 1955 to commemorate the
150th anniversary of the birth of Andersen.
Awarded annually. Enquiries to Nyt
Nordisk Forlag Arnold Busck A/S,
Købmagergade 49, DK-1150 Copenhagen K

Danish Academy Prize for Literature
For an outstanding work of literature.
50,000 Danish crowns. Awarded annually.
Enquiries to The Danish Academy,
Rungstedlund, 109 Rungsted Strandvej,
DK-2960 Rungsted Kyst

Danish Authors' Colleagues Prize*
To a colleague who has published an
interesting work. 5,000 Danish crowns.
Awarded annually. Enquiries to Danish
Authors' Society, Forfatternes Hus, Nyhavn
21, Copenhagen K

Danish Authors' Lyric Prize*
For poetry. 5,000 Danish crowns. Awarded
annually. Enquiries to Danish Authors'
Society, Forfatternes Hus, Nyhavn 21,
Copenhagen K

Danish Critics Literary Prize*
For literary and art criticism. 5,000 Danish
crowns. Awarded annually, Enquiries to
Danish Publishers' Association,
Vesterbrogade 41B, DK-1620 Copenhagen
V

Danish Prize for Children's Literature*
For the best Danish books for children and
teenagers. Awarded annually. Enquiries to
Danish Ministry of Cultural Affairs,
Nybrogade 2, Copenhagen K

Johannes **Ewald** Prize*
For prose, poetry and dramatic works. 2,000
Danish crowns. Awarded annually.
Enquiries to Danish Authors' Society,
Forfatternes Hus, Nyhavn 21, Copenhagen
K

Adam **Gottlob** Oehlenschläger Prize*
For outstanding Danish writers. 2,000
Danish crowns. Awarded annually.
Enquiries to Danish Ministry of Cultural
Affairs, Nybrogade 2, Copenhagen K

Søren **Gyldendal** Prize
For authors from any field whose work is of
great literary value. 20,000 Danish crowns.
Awarded annually. Enquiries to
Gyldendalske Boghandel, Nordisk Forlag,
Klareboderne 3, DK-1001 Copenhagen K

Holberg Medal*
For outstanding contributions to Danish
literature. 5,000 Danish crowns and a
medal. Awarded annually. Enquiries to
Danish Authors' Society, Forfatternes Hus,
Nyhavn 21, Copenhagen K

Translation Agencies and Associations

Association of Translators*, Ribegade 8,
Copenhagen

Danish Translations Centre (DTC)*, Risø
Library, Risø National Laboratory,
DK-4000 Roskilde

Translatørforeningen, Bornholmsgade 1,
DK-1266 Copenhagen K
Association of Danish Sworn Translators

Dominican Republic

General Information

Language: Spanish
Religion: Roman Catholic
Population: 4.98 million
Literacy Rate (1970): 68.5%
Bank Hours: 0830-1230 Monday-Friday;
some open 0830-1130 Saturday
Shop Hours: 0800-1200, 1400 or 1500-1800
Monday-Friday; some open Saturday
Currency: 100 centavos = 1 peso oro
Export/Import Information: Children's
picture books dutiable at 25%, atlases 10%.
Advertising catalogues 10% ad valorem.
35% VAT FOB Internal Tax, 20%
Consumption Tax, and 4% surtax on all
imports. No import licences required for
books. Exchange licence and approval from
Central Bank required
Copyright: Buenos Aires (see International
section)

Publishers

Publicaciones **Ahora** C por A*, Ave San
Martin 236, Apdo 1402, Santo Domingo
Tel: 5655581 Cable Add: Ahora DR Telex:
326438
Editorial: R Molina Morillo; *Sales:* Luis R
Cordero; *Production:* José R Grau;
Publicity: Manuel Fco Santana

Juan Max **Alemany***, E Henriquez 12,
Santo Domingo

Editora **Alfa y Omega***, M Cabral 11, Santo
Domingo

Blas de la Rosa*, Yolanda Guzmán 105,
Santo Domingo

Editora El **Caribe***, Autop Duarte
Km 7 1/2, Santo Domingo

Editora **Colonial***, Moca 27-B, Santo
Domingo

Rafael **Corporan** de los Santos*,
S. Valverde 44, Santo Domingo

Editora **Cosmos***, Calle N No. 13, Feria,
Santo Domingo

Ediciones **Pedagógicas** Domincanas, C por
A*, Padre Billini 103, Apdo 1320, Santo
Domingo Tel: 6889711
Man Dir: Miguel González Cano
Imprint: Escobo
Subjects: School Books and Educational
Materials
Subsidiary Company: Editora Cultural
Dominicana SA
Founded: 1962

Editora **Cultural Dominicana***, San
Martín 236, Santo Domingo

Editora **Educativa Dominicana***,
Mercedes 45, Santo Domingo

Editora **Internacional***, Moca 31, Santo
Domingo

Editora y **Distribuidora** Nacional de
Libros*, Arzobispo Nouel, 80 esqina
Espaillat, Santo Domingo Tel: 98222
Cable Add: Edinalibros

President: Luis Franco
Subjects: History, Social Science, Law,
Philosophy
Founded: 1964

Editorama, SA*, Ave Tiradentes 56, Santo
Domingo

Editorial Librería Dominicana*, Mercedes
45-49, Santo Domingo Tel: 96293/23893
Cable Add: Sirviendo
Dir: Julio Postigo
Subjects: General Literature, Religion, Law,
Textbooks
Founded: 1937

Editora **Enriquillo***, I la Catolica 41, Santo
Domingo

Escobo, an imprint of Ediciones
Pedagógicas Dominicanas (qv)

P A **Gómez***, E Tejera 15, Santo Domingo

Editora **Horizontes** de América*,
A Fleming 2, Santo Domingo

La **Información***, M Gómez 16, Santiago

Editora **Listín** Diario*, Paseo de los
Periodistas 12, Santo Domingo

Editorial **Padilla***, San Fco Macorís 14,
Santo Domingo
Bookshops: see under Booksellers

Editora Colegial **Quisqueyana** SA*, Ave
Tiradentes, Centro Comercial Naco, Santo
Domingo Tel: 5661808/5654277/5671818
Subjects: Pre-school, Primary & Secondary
Textbooks and Educational Materials
Bookshop: address as above

Editora La **Razon**, J Verne 14, Santo
Domingo

Editorial **Stella***, Guayacanes 7, Santo
Domingo

Ultima Hora*, Paseo de los Periodistas 12,
Santo Domingo

Universidad Autónoma de Santo Domingo,
Ciudad Universitaria*, Apdo 1355, Santo
Domingo
Subjects: Academic

Departamento de Publicaciones de la
Universidad Católica Madre y Maestra*,
Autopista Duarte, Santiago de los
Caballeros Tel: 5825105 Cable Add:
Universidad Católica Madre y Maestra
Man Dir, Editorial: Héctor I Cabral; *Sales:*
Lourdes Tavares
Subjects: General
1977: 11 titles *Founded:* 1967

Major Booksellers

Caribe Grolier Inc*, L de Castro 203
Tel: 6897373; Hostos 208 Tel: 6888544

Ediciones **Coquito***, E Tejera 19
Tel: 6883021

Casa **Cuello***, El Conde 33 Tel:
6896226/6874242

Disesa*, Hostos 202 Tel: 6897644/6823533;
S Larga Tel: 6882163

Distribuidora Escolar SA*, Hostos 202 Tel:
6897644/6823533; S Larga 6882163

Encyclopaedia Britannica de
Venezuela SA*, El Conde 35 Tel: 6829260

Papeleria **Fersobe** Hnos*, Ave Duarte 177
Tel: 6894744; Ave Mella 156 Tel: 6881848

Casa **Herrera***, Mercedes 125, Santo Domingo Tel: 97568

Febio **Herrera***, Bolivar 40 Tel: 6878677
Importer

Librería y Papelería **Lope** de Vega*, L de Vega 55 Tel: 5658066

Mella*, Ave Duarte 27 Tel: 6886539

Niove*, 16 de Agosto 47 Tel: 6894088

Editorial **Padilla***, El Conde 511 Tel: 6820111/6880303; San Fco Macoris 14 Tel: 6823101; El Conde 109 Tel: 6880303

Editora Colegial **Quisqueyana** SA*, Tiradentes Tel: 5654277/5661808

Major Libraries

Archivo General de la Nación*, Calle M E Diaz, Santo Domingo
National Archives

Biblioteca Dominicana*, Santo Domingo

Biblioteca Nacional*, César Nicolás Penson 91, Plaza de la Cultura, Santo Domingo
National Library

Biblioteca de la **Cámara** Oficial de Comercio, Agricultura e Industria del Distrito Nacional*, Arzobispo Nouel 52, Altos, Santo Domingo
Library of the Chamber of Commerce, Agriculture and Industry

Biblioteca Municipal de **Santo Domingo***, Padre Billini 18, Santo Domingo

Biblioteca de la **Secretaría de Estado de Relaciones Exteriores***, Estancia Ramfis, Santo Domingo
Library of the Secretariat of Foreign Affairs

Biblioteca de la **Universidad Autónoma de Santo Domingo***, Ciudad Universitaria, Apdo 1355, Santo Domingo

Library Associations

Asociación Dominicana de Bibliotecarios (ASODOBI), Biblioteca Nacional, Santo Domingo Tel: 6884086
President: Prospero J Mella-Chavier;
Secretary-General: Verónica Regús de Tosca
Dominican Association of Librarians

Grupo Bibliografico Nacional de la Republica Dominicana*, c/o Emilio Rodriguez de Morizi, Director, Archivo General de la Nacion, Calle Chiclana de la Frontera, Santo Domingo

Servicio de Documentación y Biblioteca*, Palacio de Educación, Santo Domingo
Library and Documentation Service

Ecuador

General Information

Language: Spanish
Religion: Predominantly Roman Catholic
Population: 7.56 million
Literacy Rate (1962): 67.5% (88.1% Urban, 55.5% Rural)

Bank Hours: 0900-1200, 1500-1630 Monday-Friday
Shop Hours: 0830-1230, 1430-1830 Monday-Saturday. In Guayaquil, shops open in the afternoon Friday at 1530 and many are closed Saturday
Currency: 100 centavos = 1 sucre
Export/Import Information: Books and most advertising catalogues not dutiable. No import licences or exchange controls for books
Copyright: UCC, Buenos Aires (see International section)

Book Trade Organizations

Sociedad de Libreros del Ecuador*, Calle Bolivar 268 y Venezuela, Of 501, Quito
Secretary: Eduardo Ruiz
Booksellers' Society of Ecuador

Publishers

Ariel Ltda*, Coronel 2207, PPB 4285, Guayaquil Tel: 346400 Cable Add: Cromograf Telex: 3387 Ariel ED
Publisher: Dr Tomas Rivas
Subjects: Pocket Books, Juveniles

Fondo Editorial de **C I E S P A L** (Centro Internacional de Estudios Superiores de Comunicación para América Latina), Ave Diego de Almagro y Andrade Marín s/n, CP 584, Quito Tel: 544624/545831 Cable Add: Ciespal Telex: 2474 CIESPL ED
Dirs: Marco Ordóñez Andrade; Galo Viteri Pinto (Orders)
Subjects: Social Communication, Development Planning, Research and Documentation; Periodicals
Founded: 1960

Cromograf SA*, Coronel 2207, PPB 4285, Guayaquil Tel: 346400 Cable Add: Cromograf Telex: 3387 Ariel ED
Subjects: Juvenile/Children's Books; Paperbacks; Art Productions

Casa de la **Cultura** Ecuatoriana*, Ave 6 de Diciembre 332, Apdo 67, Quito
Tel: 230260 Cable Add: Casacultura
Br Offs: Núcleo del Azuay, Apdo 4907, Cuenca; Núcleo del Guayas, Guayaquil
Subjects: General Fiction & Nonfiction, General Science (Ecuadorian authors only)
Founded: 1944

Editorial Interamericana del Ecuador CA*, Ave America 542, Quito
Manager: Manuel de Castillo
Miscellaneous: Firm is an associate company of Holt-Saunders Ltd, UK (qv for other associates)

Editorial **Labor** del Ecuador SA*, Portoviejo 105 y 10 de Agosto, Edificio Carrera, CP–710A, Quito
Parent Company: Editorial Labor, Spain (qv)

Pontificia **Universidad Católica** de Ecuador*, 12 de Octobre 1076 y Carrion, Apdo 2184, Quito Tel: 529240
Subjects: Literatura, Art, Natural Sciences, Law, Anthropology, Sociology, Politics, Economics, Theology, Philosophy, History, Archaeology

Universidad Central del Ecuador*, Dpto de Publicaciones, Servicio de Almacén Universitario, Ciudad Universitaria, Quito

Universidad de Guayaquil*, Dpto de Publicaciones, Biblioteca Gral, Apdo 3834, Guayaquil Tel: 392430

Man Dir: Constantino Vinueza M
Subjects: General Literature, History, Philosophy, Fiction
Founded: 1930
Bookshop: Librería Universitaria*, Ciudad Universitaria, PO Box 3834, Guayaquil

Major Booksellers

Librería **Cervantes***, Vélez 416, Guayaquil Tel: 15573

Librería **Cima***, Ave 10 de Agosto 285, Quito Tel: 233066

Librería **Científica***, Apdo 2905, Quito Tel: 12556; Luque 223, Casilla 362, Guayaquil Tel: 14555

Librería **Española***, Venezuela 961 y Mejía, Casilla 356, Quito Tel: 212060; Librería Española Cía Ltda, Ave 10 de Agosto 1233, Casilla 356, Quito Tel: 543460

Librería **Universitaria**, García Moreno 739, Apdo 2982, Quito Tel: 212521
Dir: Ing Carlos E Wong Flores
Importer/Exporter

Una **Pequeña** Librería*, Ave 10 de Agosto 563, Quito Tel: 234296

Librería **Selecciones***, 9 de Octubre 735, Guayaquil; Calle Benalcázar 543, Quito

Su Librería*, Apdo 2556, Quito Tel: 210225

Major Libraries

Archivo Nacional de Historia*, Ave 6 de Diciembre 332, Apdo 67, Quito
National Historical Archives

Biblioteca Ecuatoriana 'Aurelio Espinosa Pólit'*, Apdo 160, Quito Tel: 530420

Biblioteca Nacional del Ecuador*, García Moreno y Sucre, Quito
National Library

Biblioteca de la **Casa de la Cultura Ecuatoriana***, Ave 6 de Diciembre 332, Apdo 67, Quito Tel: 230260
Library of Ecuadorian Culture

Museo y Biblioteca Municipal*, Ave 10 de Agosto y Calle Pedro Carbo, Guayaquil

Biblioteca de la **Universidad Central de Ecuador***, Ciudad Universitaria, Quito

Biblioteca General, **Universidad de Guayaquil***, Apdo 3834, Guayaquil

Library Association

Asociación Ecuatoriana de Bibliotecarios (AEB)*, Casa de la Cultura Ecuatoriana, Casilla 87, Quito Tel: 528840 Headquarters: 263474
Executive Secretary: Elizabeth Carrionee
Ecuadorian Library Association
Publications: Unidad Bibliotecaria

Library Journal

Unidad Bibliotecaria, Ecuadorian Library Association, Casa de la Cultura Ecuatoriana, Casilla 87, Quito

Egypt

General Information

Language: Arabic (English and French widely used)
Religion: Muslim
Population: 38.7 million
Bank Hours: Generally 0830-1230 Monday-Thursday; 1000-1200 Saturday
Shop Hours: 0830-1330, 1630-1900 Monday-Saturday
Currency: 100 piastres (1000 milliemes) = 1 Egyptian pound
Export/Import Information: No tariff on books, 25% on advertising in quantity. 10% Consolidation Duty, 1% statistical tax and small additional taxes apply. No import licences. Exchange control by Supreme Committee set up by Ministry of Finance, Economy and Foreign Trade. Banks authorized to execute foreign-exchange transactions. No longer government monopoly but some book importing done by Foreign Trade Company, Misr Import & Export Co, 6 Adly St, Cairo
Copyright: Berne, Florence (see International section)

Book Trade Organizations

General Egyptian Book Organization*, Corniche el Nil, Boulac, Cairo Tel: 972649
Cable Add: Gebo Telex: 92252 MENA
Chairman: D M el Sheniti
See also entry under Publishers

The **Public Organization** for Books and Scientific Appliances*, Cairo University, Orman, Ghiza, Cairo
Chairman: Kamil Seddik

Publishers

Al-**Ahram** Establishment*, Galaa St, Cairo Tel: 46460 Cable Add: Ahram Telex: 2001
Subjects: Original Works and Reprints, Microfiche and Microfilm, Periodicals
Miscellaneous: Firm also owns a Book Club

American University in Cairo Press, 113 Sharia Qasr el Aini, PO Box 2551, Cairo Tel: 29781 Cable Add: Victorious Telex: 92224 Auccai Un
Dir: John Rodenbeck
Subjects: Literature, Art, History, Africana, Anthropology, Arabic Language, Architecture, Coptology, Social Science, Textbooks, Guidebooks, Egypt and the Arab World, Religion, Natural Sciences, Reference Works, Periodicals
1978: 5 titles *1979:* 8 titles *Founded:* 1960

Al **Arab Publishing** House*, 23 Faggalah St, Cairo Tel: 908025 Cable Add: Arabukshop Cairo
Man Dir: Prof Dr Saladin Boustany; *Sales Manager:* George G Eddé
Subjects: General Fiction, Belles Lettres, Poetry, Biography, History, Africana, Philosophy, Reference, Religion, Arabic Language & Literature, Arabic Manuscripts, Paperbacks, Social Science, University & Secondary Textbooks
Bookshop: 28 Faggalah St, Cairo
Founded: 1900

Cairo University Press*, Guiza-Orman, Giza, Cairo Tel: 846144
Subject: University Textbooks

E S D U C K, see The Egyptian Society for the Dissemination of Universal Culture and Knowledge

Les **Editions universitaires** d'Egypte*, 41 Sharia Sherif Pasha, Cairo
Subject: University Textbooks

The **Egyptian Society** for the Dissemination of Universal Culture and Knowledge (ESDUCK), PO Box 21, Cairo (Located at: 1081 Corniche el Nil St, Garden City, Cairo) Tel: 20295/25079 Cable Add: Esduck
Man Dir: Ibrahim Abdel Rahman; *Editorial:* Inas Effat; *Production:* Amira Farid; *Rights & Permissions:* Shewikar Zaki, Nazli el Hitamy
Subjects: Trade Books, Textbooks, Children's Books, Reference
Founded: 1953 (as Franklin Book Programs Inc)
Miscellaneous: Acts as literary and translation agency for major publishers and as co-publisher with local and American firms. Representation covers all Arab countries. Has co-published over 1,000 titles since 1953

Franklin Book Programs Inc, now The Egyptian Society for the Dissemination of Universal Culture and Knowledge (ESDUCK) (qv)

General Egyptian Book Organization*, Corniche el Nil, Boulac, Cairo Tel: 972649, Cable Add: Gebo Telex: 92252
Chairman: D M el Sheniti
Foreign Distribution Centre: Samady & Salha Bldg, Syria St, Beyrouth, Lebanon
Subjects: Arab classic and modern books in all fields
Bookshops: International Book Centre, Cairo, 13 branches throughout Egypt
1977: 200 titles *Founded:* 1961
ISBN Publisher's Prefix: 977-201

The **General Organization** for Government Press Affairs*, 22 Al Nil St, Imbaba, Guiza, Cairo
This is the Government Printer

Government Printer, see The General Organization for Government Press Affairs

Dar Al-**Hilal** Publishing House, 16 Sharia Muhammad Ezz-El-Arab, Cairo Tel: 20610
Subjects: General Nonfiction, Magazines
Founded: 1892

Dar Al **Maaref***, 1119 Corniche el Nil St, Cairo Tel: 59263/8 Cable Add: Damaref Telex: UN 92199
President: Anis Mansour; *Man Dir:* Dr M Fouad Ibrahim; *General Manager:* Dr Salib Botros; *Sales:* Camile Fahim Mossad
Subsidiary company: Dar el-Maaref, Lebanon
Subjects: Academic, Scientific, General Islamic, Schoolbooks, Children's (in Arabic), University Textbooks (in English)
Bookshops: in Cairo, Alexandria, Assiut, Qena, Tanta, Shebin, El-Kom, Asswan
1977: 120 titles *Founded:* 1890
ISBN Publisher's Prefix: 977-247

Middle East Book Centre*, 45 Sharia Kasr el-Nil, Cairo Tel: 910980
Man Dir: Dr A M Mosharrafa; *Sales Manager:* A Ismail
Subjects: General Fiction, Belles Lettres, Poetry, Biography, History, Africana, Philosophy, Religion, Arabic Language & Literature, Paperbacks, General & Social Science, University & Secondary Textbooks
Founded: 1954

Maktabet **Misr** (Misr Bookshop)*, 3 Kamel Sidki St, PO Box 16, Cairo Tel: 908920
Man Dir: Amir Said Gouda El Sahhar
Subjects: General Fiction, Belles Lettres, Poetry, Biography, History, Books in Arabic language, University & School Textbooks
Bookshop: Maktabet Misr, 3 Kamel Sidki St, Cairo
Founded: 1932

Dar al-**Nahda** al Arabia*, 32 Sharia Abdel-Khalek Sharwat St, Cairo
Subjects: Arabic Language & Literature
Bookshop: At above address

Editions le **Progrès***, 6 Sharia Sherif Pasha, Cairo
Man Dir: Wedi Choukri

The **Public Organization** for Books and Scientific Appliances, Cairo University*, Orman, Ghiza, Cairo
Chairman: Kamil Seddik
Subject: University Textbooks
Founded: 1965

Senouhy Publishers*, 54 Sharia Abdel-Khalek, Sarwat, Cairo
Man Dir: Leila A Fadel
Subjects: General Nonfiction, Belles Lettres, Poetry, History, Africana, Religion
Founded: 1956

The **Sphinx***, Bookshop and Publishing House, 3 Shawarby St (Kasr El Nil), 3rd Floor, Apartment 305, Cairo Tel: 40616
Cable Add: Bulhall Cairo
Man Dir: Abd-el-Salam Hassan Sharara
Subjects: Educational and Academic Books
Founded: 1958

Literary Agent

The **Egyptian Society** for the Dissemination of Universal Culture and Knowledge (ESDUCK), PO Box 21, Cairo (Located at: 1081 Corniche el Nil St, Cairo) Tel: 20295/25079 Cable Add: Esduck

Book Club

Al-**Ahram** Establishment*, Galaa St, Cairo

Major Booksellers

Al **Ahd** Al Gadeed Bookstore*, Farouk Zaky & Co, 4-5 Kamel Sidky St, Cairo Tel: 900290/905296

Al-**Anglo** American Bookshop*, 55 Algomhouria St, Cairo Tel: 905262

Al-**Anglo** Egyptian Bookshop, 165 Mohamed Farid St, Cairo Tel: 914337
Proprietor: Sobhy Grais

Al **Arab** Bookshop, 28 Faggalah St (del PL 480), Cairo Tel: 908025 Agent of the Library of Congress PL 480

Librairie **Hachette***, 45 bis rue Champolion, Cairo

Al **Ittihad** Bookstore*, Mohamed Abdel Mouty Ismail, 3 Kamel Sidky St, Al Ezbekia, Cairo Tel: 916403

Dar Al **Kutub** Al Hadeetha*, Tewfik Afeefi Amer & Co, 14 Al Goumhouria St, Abdeen, Cairo Tel: 916107

Lehnert & Landrock*, 44 Sherif St, PO Box 1013, Cairo

Livres de France*, Immeuble Immobilia, rue Kasr el Nil, Cairo

Misr Bookshop, 3 Kamel Sidki St, Faggalah, Cairo Tel: 908920 Cable Add: Dameltibaa, Cairo
Manager: Amir Saïd El-Sahhar

Misr Import & Export Co*, 6 Adly St, Cairo
Importer/Exporter

Modern Cairo Bookshop*, 169 Tahreer St, Cairo

Saladdine Publications & Distributors*, 28 Talaat Harb St, Cairo Tel: 52542

Ahmed Shaker Al Ansary*, Midan Birkit Al Ratly, Sikit Al Ratly No 3, Bab Al Sharea, Cairo Tel: 932895

Major Libraries

Alexandria Municipal Library*, 18 Sharia Menasce Moharrem Bey, Alexandria

American University in Cairo Library, 113 Sharia Kasr El-Aini, Cairo Tel: 22969

Al-Azhar University Library*, Cairo Tel: 904051

Dar-ul-Kutub*, Midan Ahmed Maher, Bab El-Khalq, Cairo
Egyptian National Library

Institut français d'Archéologie orientale*, Bibliothèque, 37 rue Mourira, Cairo

Institut d'Egypte Library*, 13 Sharia Sheikh Rhane, Cairo

Institute of Arab Research & Studies Library*, 1 Tolombat St, Cairo

Ministry of Justice Library*, Midan Lazoghli, Abassia, Cairo Tel: 831546

National Archives*, Quasr 'Abindin, Maydan al-Jumhriyah, Cairo

National Assembly Library* Palace of the National Assembly, Cairo

National Information and Documentation Centre*, Sh Al-Tahrir, Dokki, Cairo

University of Alexandria Library*, 22 Al-Gueish Ave, Shatby, Alexandria Tel: 71675/8

University of Cairo Library*, Orman, Ghiza, Cairo Tel: 845186

Library Associations

Algamiia Almasriia Lilmaktabat Almadrasiia*, 35 Algalaa St, Cairo
Egyptian School Library Association
Publication: Sahifat al-Maktabát (Egyptian Library Journal)

Egyptian Association for Archives and Librarianship*, c/o Library of Fine Arts, 24 El Matbâa Al-Ahlia, Boulac, Cairo
Executive Secretary: Ahmed M Mansour
Publication: Alam al-Maktabát

National Information and Documentation Centre*, Al-Tahrir St, Dokki, Cairo

Library Reference Book and Journals

Book

Directory of Scientific and Technical Libraries, National Information and Documentation Centre, Al-Tahrir St, Dokki, Cairo

Journals

Alam al-Maktabát (Library World), Egyptian Association for Archives and Librarianship, c/o Library of Fine Arts, 24 El Matbâa Al-Ahlia, Boulaq, Cairo

Sahifat al-Maktabát (Egyptian Library Journal), Egyptian School Library Association, 35 Algalaa St, Cairo

Literary Associations and Societies

Permanent Bureau of Afro-Asian Writers*, 104 Kasr el-Aini St, Cairo

Atelier*, 1 Sharia St, Saba, Alexandria
Secretary-General: L Hergenstein
Society of Artists and Writers

High Council of Arts & Literature*, 9 Sharia Hassan Sabri, Zamalek, Cairo
Secretary: Youssef Al Sibai

Literary Periodical

Lotus; Afro-Asian Writings, 104 Kasr el-Aini St, Cairo
Important quarterly review published for the Permanent Bureau of Afro-Asian Writers

Translation Agencies and Associations

The Egyptian Society for the Dissemination of Universal Culture and Knowledge (ESDUCK), PO Box 21, Cairo (Located at: 1081 Corniche el Nil St, Cairo) Tel: 20295/25079

El Salvador

General Information

Language: Spanish
Religion: Roman Catholic
Population: 4.26 million
Literacy Rate: 1971, total population 56.9%; 1961, 49% total, 71.2% Urban, 33.7% Rural
Bank Hours: 0830-1130, 1430-1600 Monday-Friday; 0900-1130 Saturday
Shop Hours: 0800-1200, 1400-1800 Monday-Friday; 0800-1200 Saturday
Currency: 100 centavos = 1 colon
Export/Import Information: Catalogues dutied at $0.03 per gross kg. No import licences but exchange licence from Exchange Control Department of Central Reserve Bank required, if goods coming from outside Central America. Commercial banks authorize certain import payments
Copyright: UCC, Buenos Aires, Florence (see International section)

Publishers

Editorial Universitaria de la Universidad de El Salvador, Apdo Postal 1703, San Salvador (Located at: Ciudad Universitaria, San Salvador) Tel: 256604
Dir: Armando Herrara
Subject: Scholarly Books, Textbooks, General Literature
Founded: 1923

Ministerio de Educación, Dirección de Publicaciones, Pasaje Contreras 145, San Salvador Tel: 254605/259092
Man Dir, Rights & Permissions: Salvador Gálvez Rosales; *Editorial:* María Celia de Ormes; *Sales:* Salvador Cabezas; *Production:* Mauricio Gómez; *Publicity:* Mauricio Dueñas
Orders to: Gerencia de Distribución, 9a Calle Oriente 104 y Ave España, San Salvador
Subjects: Literature, Art, Sociology, History, General Textbooks
Bookshop: 9a Calle Oriente 104 y Ave España, San Salvador
1977: 63 titles *Founded:* 1953

U C A Editores, Apdo Postal (06) 668, San Salvador (Located at: Universidad Centroamericana José Simeón Cañas, Autopista Sur, Jardines de Guadalupe, San Salvador) Tel: 234491
Dir: Italo López Vallecillos
Subjects: Social Science, Religion, Economy and Scholarly Books
Founded: 1968

Major Booksellers

Librería Claudio Bernard, Calle Los Cedros 53, 100 metros al sur del IVU, San Salvador Tel: 256719

Clasicos Roxsil, 6a Ave Sur 1-6, Santa Tecla, San Salvador Tel: 281212

Librería Cultural Salvadoreña SA de CV, Calle Arce 423, San Salvador Tel: 27206/221307

Librería e Importadora Neruda, 29 Calle Poniente 222, Local No 6, San Salvador Tel: 251566

Librería Renacimiento SA de CV, Apdo Postal 852, San Salvador (Located at: Final Pasaje 5 No 126 y 2a diagonal, Urbanización La Esperanza, San Salvador) Tel: 254541/263198

Distribuidora Salvadoreña, Ave España 344, San Salvador Tel: 213438
Office: 9a Ave Norte 422, San Salvador Tel: 226983

Librería Universitaria de la Universidad de El Salvador, Apdo Postal 2028, San Salvador (Located at: Ciudad Universitaria, San Salvador) Tel: 258607/258022 ext. 132

Librería Universitaria UCA, Apdo Postal (06) 668, San Salvador (Located at: Universidad Centroamericana José Simeón Cañas, San Salvador) Tel: 240011 ext 193, 234491

Major Libraries

Biblioteca Nacional, 8a Ave Norte y Calle Delgado, San Salvador Tel: 213249
National Library

Biblioteca de la **Universidad Centroamericana José Simeón Cañas**, Apdo Postal (06) 668, San Salvador (Located at: Autopista Sur, Jardines de Guadalupe, San Salvador) Tel: 240011
Dir: Mélida Arteaga de Andino

Biblioteca Central de la **Universidad de El Salvador**, Apdo Postal 143, San Salvador (Located at: Ciudad Universitaria, San Salvador) Tel: 258022 ext. 115
Dir: Ana Aurora de Kapsalis
Publications: Boletín (monthly); *Lista de Adquisiciones Recientes* (monthly)

Library Associations

Asociación de Bibliotecarios de El Salvador*, Urbanización Gerardo Barrios Polígono, 'B' No 5, San Salvador Tel: 220409/253471
Secretary-General: Edgar Antonio Pérez Borja
El Salvador Library Association
Publication: Informa (Newsletter) (monthly)

Asociación General de Archivistas de El Salvador*, Apdo Postal No 664, Edificio Sede 8, Calle Oriente 314, San Salvador
Association of Archivists of El Salvador

Library Journal

Informa (Newsletter), El Salvador Library Association, Urbanización Gerardo Barrios Polígono, 'B' No 5, San Salvador

Literary Periodical

Guíon Literario (Literary Summary), Ministerio de Educacion del Gobierno de El Salvador, Dirección General de Publicaciones, Pasaje Contreras 145, San Salvador

Ethiopia

General Information

Language: Amharic (English, French and Italian spoken)
Religion: Ethiopian Orthodox (allied to Coptic Church)
Population: 29 million
Bank Hours: 0900-1200, 1500-1700 Monday-Friday; 0900-1200 Saturday
Shop Hours: Addis Ababa: 0900-1300, 1500-2000 Monday-Saturday. Asmara: 0800-1300, 1600-2000 Monday-Friday
Currency: 100 cents = 1 birr
Export/Import Information: No tariff on books, but additional taxes of 15% CIF +1% and 1% cif +1% Advertising subject to 10% customs and same taxes. No import licence required but Exchange Payment Licence necessary. Importer must be registered with Ministry of Commerce, Industry and Tourism
Copyright: No copyright conventions signed

Book Trade Reference Books and Journals

Book
List of Ethiopian Authors, Addis Ababa University Library, PO Box 1176, Addis Ababa

Journal
Ethiopian Publications (Ethiopian National Bibliography), Institute of Ethiopian Studies, Addis Ababa University, PO Box 1176, Addis Ababa

Publishers

Addis Ababa University Press, PO Box 1176, Addis Ababa Tel: 119148 Cable Add/Telex: University Addis
Editor: Innes Marshall
Subjects: Public Health, Hydrology, Climatology, Botany, Ornithology, Conservation, Geology, Philosophy; University Textbooks, Reference; works in English language
1977: 2 titles *1978:* 3 titles *Founded:* 1968

The **Bible** Churchmen's Missionary Society*, PO Box 864, Asmara, Eritrea Tel: 114267
Dir: John Coracher
Subjects: General Fiction, Belles Lettres, Poetry, Biography, History, Africana, Religion, Juveniles, Amharic Language & Literature
Bookshop: PO Box 864, Asmara, Eritrea

Government Printer, Government Printing Press, PO Box 980, Addis Ababa

Major Booksellers

Berhan Bookshop and Stationery*, PO Box 302, Addis Ababa

Bible Churchman's Society*, PO Box 1089, Addis Ababa

Bible Churchmen's Missionary Society*, PO Box 864 Asmara, Eritrea

The **City** Bookshop*, 9 Haile Selassie I Ave, PO Box 864, Asmara

Cosmos Bookshop*, PO Box 3393, Addis Ababa Tel: 111954

E C A Bookshop Co-op Society*, PO Box 60100, Addis Ababa

International Press Agency*, G P Giannopoulos, PO Box 120, Addis Ababa

Menno Bookstore*, PO Box 1236, Addis Ababa

S I M Bookshop*, PO Box 1151, Addis Ababa

Major Libraries

Addis Ababa University Library*, PO Box 1176, Addis Ababa Tel: 115673

American Library*, PO Box 1014, Addis Ababa Tel: 113377

Asmara Public Library*, 20 Haile Selassie I Ave, Asmara

British Council Library*, PO Box 1043, Addis Ababa (Located at: Artistic Bldg, Adua Ave, Addis Ababa)

Ethiopian Manuscript Microfilm Library*, PO Box 30274, Addis Ababa
Publication: Bulletin (quarterly)

National Library and Archives of Ethiopia*, PO Box 717, Addis Ababa Tel: 442241

Organization for African Unity Library*, PO Box 3243, Addis Ababa Tel: 157700 Cable Add: OAU Telex: 21046

Polytechnic Institute Library*, PO Box 26, Bahar-Dar

U N Economic Commission for Africa Library*, PO Box 3001, Addis Ababa Tel: 447200

University of Asmara Library*, PO Box 1220, Asmara Tel: 113600

Library Associations

Ethiopian Library Association*, PO Box 30530, Addis Ababa Tel: 110844 ext 353
Publications: Ethiopian Library Association Bulletin; Directory of Ethiopian Libraries

Library Reference Books and Journals

Books

Directory of Ethiopian Libraries, Ethiopian Library Association, PO Box 30530, Addis Ababa

Journals

Bulletin, Ethiopian Library Association, PO Box 30530, Addis Ababa

Bulletin, Ethiopian Manuscript Microfilm Library, PO Box 30274, Addis Ababa

Literary Prizes

Amharic Literature Award*
For the Ethiopian author or translator who has made the best recent contribution to the Amharic language. Gold medal, diploma and monetary prize of 10,000 Ethiopian dollars. Awarded annually. Enquiries to Haile Selassie I Prize Trust, PO Box 2320, Addis Ababa

Fiji

General Information

Language: English, Fijian, Hindi and Cantonese
Religion: Predominantly Protestant, with large minority of Hindus
Population: 596,000
Bank Hours: 1000-1500 Monday-Friday; 0930-1100 Saturday
Shop Hours: 0800-1630 or later Monday-Friday; early closing Wednesday or Saturday
Currency: 100 cents = 1 Fiji dollar
Export/Import Information: No tariffs on books and advertising. No import licences. Exchange control by central monetary authority; no specific exchange licence required and authorized banks perform

transaction upon application
Copyright: Berne, UCC (see International section)

Book Trade Journals

Publications Bulletin, Government Printing and Stationery Department, Suva

Publishers

Home Products Ltd*, Garrick Bldg, Suva Tel: 25196

Indian Printing and Publishing Co*, PO Box 151, Suva
Man Dir: S M Bidesi Jr
Subjects: Law, Administration, Business Management

Lotu Pasifika Productions, PO Box 208, Suva Tel: 24314 Cable Add: Lotupak
Manager: Aisake M Raratabu
Subjects: Education, Religion, Poetry, Cookery
1977: 8 titles *1978:* 8 titles

Oceania Printers*, PO Box 597, Suva Tel: 311044/311224
Subject: Literature

Sangam Saradā Printing Press*, PO Box 9, Nadi
Subjects: Literature, History, Geography

Tara Press*, Kings Rd, PO Box 923, Nasinu, Suva
Subjects: Literature, Music

Trans-Pacific Publishers*, PO Box 3083, Lami, Suva (Located at: Queens Rd, Lami, Suva) Tel: 361727

Major Booksellers

Desai Bookshops*, Head Office: Rajobhai Patel Rd, Suva Tel: 311188 (and 12 branches)

Suva Book Shop*, 97 Marks St, Suva Tel: 311355

Major Libraries

Library Service of Fiji, Western Regional Library, PO Box 150, Lautoka

National Archives of Fiji*, PO Box 2125, Government Buildings, Suva

Suva City Library, Victoria Arcade, Suva
Librarian: Edward David

Library Association

Fiji Library Association (FLA)*, c/o Hon Secretary, PO Box 2292, Government Bldgs, Suva
Publication: Fiji Library Association Newsletter; Fiji Library Journal

Library Journal

Newsletter, Fiji Library Association, c/o The Secretary, University of the South Pacific, Box 1168, Suva

Finland

General Information

Language: Finnish and Swedish (officially bilingual); English and German spoken widely
Religion: Lutheran
Population: 4.7 million
Bank Hours: 0915-1615 Monday-Friday
Shop Hours: 0830-1700 or later Monday-Friday; 0830-1500 or 1600 Saturday
Currency: 100 pennia = 1 markka
Export/Import Information: No tariff on books or advertising. 12.4% Turnover Tax, 3.1% Import Equalization Tax, 2-3% Port Charges. No import licences required
Copyright: UCC, Berne, Florence (see International section)

Book Trade Organizations

Kirja-ja Paperikauppiasliitto, Pieni Roobertinkatu 13-B26, SF-00130 Helsinki 13 Tel: (90) 603479
Finnish Booksellers' Association
Chief Executive: Pentti Kuopio

Kirjapalvelu (Book Service)*, Kalevankatu 16, SF-00100 Helsinki 10
Advertising and Public Relations Organization

Suomen Antikvariaattiyhdistys-Finska Antikvariatföreningen, P Makasiininkatu 6N, Magasinsgatan 6, SF-00130 Helsinki 13 Tel: 626352
Finnish Antiquarian Booksellers' Association

Suomen Kustannusyhdistys, Annankatu 31-33 C55, SF-00100 Helsinki 10 Tel: 641644
Publishers' Association of Finland
Secretary-General: U Lappi

Suomen Nortenkirjaneuvosto*, Helsinki 53
Finnish Council for Children's Books

Book Trade Reference Book and Journals

Book

Suomessa Ilmestyneen Kirjallisuuden Luettelo (Katalog över i Finland Utkommen Litteratur) (List of Books Published in Finland), Kirjavälitys Osakeyhtiö, Kalevank 16 SF-00100 Helsinki 10

Journals

Kirja Ja Paperi (Book and Paper), Finnish Publishers' Association, Kalevankatu 16, SF-00100 Helsinki 10

Kirjakauppalehti (Book Trade Journal), Finnish Publishers' Association, Kalevankatu 16, SF-00100 Helsinki

Libristi (Journal for Booksellers' Assistants), PO Box 10242, Helsinki 10

Suomen Kirjallisuus (Finlands Litteratur) (The Finnish National Bibliography), Helsinki University Library, Unioninkatu 36, PO Box 312 SF-00171 Helsinki 17

Publishers

Akateeminen Kustannusliike Oy, Mikonk 20 B 12, SF-00100 Helsinki 10 Tel: (90) 174002
Manager: M O Mattila; *Sales:* Riitta Mattila
Subjects: Secondary Textbooks, Religion, Fiction
Founded: 1927
ISBN Publisher's Prefix: 951-9023

Arvi A Karisto Oy+, Raatihuoneenkatu 1, PO Box 102, SF-13101 Hämeenlinna 10 Tel: (917) 23551 Cable Add: Arvikaristo
Man Dir: Onni-Sakari Karisto; *Editorial:* Ilmari Lehmusvaara (Finnish Literature), Ritva Makelä (Foreign Literature); *Sales:* Leo Räiha; *Production:* Onni Helin; *Advertising:* Olli Tuomi; *Foreign Rights:* Ritva Mäkelä
Br Off: Arvi A Karisto, Keskusk 3, Helsinki 10
Subjects: General Fiction and Nonfiction, Juvenile Fiction
Book Club: Uusi Kirjakerho Oy, PL 29, SF-00381 Helsinki 38 (owned jointly with Kirjayhtymä Oy (Helsinki), Weilin & Göös (Helsinki), K J Gummerus Osakeyhtiö (Jyväskylä)
1977: 147 titles *1978:* 160 titles *Founded:* 1900
ISBN Publisher's Prefix: 951-23

Ekenäs Tryckeri AB, PO Box 36, SF-10600 Ekenäs (Located at: Stationsvägen 1, Ekenäs) Tel: (911) 12800 Telex: 13150 vne sf
Man Dir: Sven Sundström
Subjects: History, Politics
Bookshop: Ekenäs Bokhandel — Boktjänst AB (at above address)
1978: 3 titles *1979:* 12 titles *Founded:* 1881
ISBN Publisher's Prefix: 951-9000

Etelä-Suomen Kustannus Oy*, Huoltomiehentie 1, SF-21420 Lieto Tel: (921) 777502
Subjects: War, Reference, Science Fiction Paperbacks, Comics
ISBN Publisher's Prefix: 951-9064

Edition **Fazer**, PO Box 260, 00101 Helsinki 10 (Located at: Höyläämotie 16, 00380 Helsinki 38) Tel: (90) 558991 Cable Add: Musicfazer Telex: 121738 MUFA SF
Man Dir (of Parent Company): John-Eric Westö; *Editorial, Production:* Einari Marvia, Kai Kavanto; *Sales, Publicity:* Liisa Aroheimo; *Rights & Permissions:* Mirjam Saksa
Parent Company: Oy Musiikki Fazer Musik AB, PO Box 260, 00101 Helsinki 10
Subjects: Music, Music Education
Bookshop: Aleksanterink 11, 00100 Helsinki 10
1978: 70 titles *1979:* 80 titles *Founded:* 1897
ISBN Publisher's Prefix: 951-757

Forsamlingsforbundets Forlags AB, PO Box 285, 00121 Helsinki 12 (Located at: Bangatan 29 A 1, 00120 Helsinki 12) Tel: 170221
Man Dir: Bjarne Boije; *Sales:* Aili Hellström; *Production:* Pia Hartman
Associate Company: Ab Fram (printing house), Vasaesplanaden 24, 65100 Vasa 10
Subject: Religion
Bookshop: Ab Gamlakarleby Bokhandel, Strandgatan 13, 67100 Karleby 10
1978: 19 titles *1979:* 15 titles *Founded:* 1920
ISBN Publisher's Prefix: 951-550

Government Printer*, Government Printing Centre, Valtion Painatuskeskus, Annankatu 44, Helsinki 10

K J **Gummerus** Osakeyhtiö+, Alasinkatu 1–3, PO Box 130, SF–40101 Jyväskylä 10 Tel: (941) 272522 Cable Add: Gummerus Telex: 28289
Man Dir: Pekka Salojärvi; *Editorial:* Jussi Sorjonen; *Publishing Dir:* Olli Arrakoski; *Rights & Permissions:* Anna Thorwall
Subjects: Fiction, General Nonfiction, Philosophy, Psychology, Education, Juveniles, Paperbacks, Textbooks
Book Club: Uusi Kirjakerho Oy (partly owned)
Bookshops: Jyväskylä, Jämsä, Mänttä, Seinäjoki (all in Helsinki)
1977: 210 titles *1978:* 240 titles *Founded:* 1872
ISBN Publisher's Prefix: 951-20

Karas-Sana Oy, PO Box 11, Vivamo, 08101 Lohja 10 Tel: (912) 87755
Man Dir, Rights & Permissions: Matti Valtonen; *Editorial:* Eva Mesiäinen; *Sales:* Kimmo Tepora
Parent Company: Kansan Raamattuseuran Säätiö (at above address)
Subject: Christian Religion
1978: 13 titles *1979:* 17 titles *Founded:* 1974
ISBN Publisher's Prefix: 951-655

Kustannusliike **Kirjaneliö**, Töölönkatu 55, SF–00250 Helsinki 25 Tel: (90) 440 561
Orders to: Raamattutalo, PO Box 8, SF–76101 Pieksämäki 10
Subjects: Religion, Fiction, Juveniles
1979: 37 titles *Founded:* 1905
ISBN Publisher's Prefix: 951-600

Kirjayhtymä Oy+, Eerikinkatu 28, SF–00180 Helsinki 18 Tel: 602566 Cable Add: Kirjayhtymä
Man Dir: Pentti Nurmio; *Publishing Dir:* Keijo Immonen; *Marketing Dir:* Viljo Salin; *Publicity Manager:* Heikki Rönnqvist; *Rights & Permissions:* Mrs Salonen
Subjects: Fiction, Nonfiction, Textbooks
Founded: 1958
Book Club: Uusi Kirjakerho Oy (partly owned)
ISBN Publisher's Prefix: 951-26

Lasten Keskus Oy, Uudenmaankatu 4 A 5, SF–00120 Helsinki 12 Tel: (90) 658800 Cable Add: Lasten Keskus
Man Dir: Pertti Rosenholm; *Publishing Manager, Production, Rights & Permissions:* Juhani Järvelä; *Head Salesman, Publicity:* Olli Nuosmaa
Associate Company: Yhteiskirjat, Uudenmaakatu 4 6, SF–00120 Helsinki 12
Subjects: Juveniles, Books for Parents and Teachers, Religion (Lutheran)
Bookshop: Lasten Kirjakauppa (Children's Bookshop), Fredrikinkatu 61, SF–00100 Helsinki 10
1978: 22 titles *1979:* 39 titles *Founded:* 1974
ISBN Publisher's Prefix: 951-626

Otava Kustannusosakeyhtiö+, Uudenmaankatu 8–12, PO Box 134, SF–00120 Helsinki 12 Tel: (90) 170471 Cable Add: Otava Helsinki Telex: 124560
Chairman: Heikki A Reenpää; *Man Dir:* Olli Reenpää; *Literary Dirs:* Dr Paavo Haavikko (Fiction), Pentti Huovinen (Nonfiction & Encyclopaedias); *Dir of International Relations; Rights & Permissions:* Erkki Reenpää; *Export Manager:* Matti Käki
Subjects: General Fiction, Belles Lettres, Biography, History, How-to, Music, Art, Philosophy, Reference, Religion, Juveniles, Low- & High-priced Paperbacks, Textbooks, Educational Materials
Book Club: Suuri Suomalainen Kirjakerho Oy (partly owned)
Bookshops: 8 branches throughout Finland
1977: 738 titles *1978:* 789 titles *Founded:* 1890
ISBN Publisher's Prefix: 951-1

Ristin Voitto ry*, PO Box 75, SF–01301 Tikkurila Tel: 826377
President: Eino Vanhala; *Publishing Dir:* Valtter Luoto
Book Club: Ristin Voitto ry PO Box 75, SF–01300 Tikkurila
Subjects: Christian Literature & Music
1977: 56 titles *Founded:* 1926
ISBN Publisher's Prefix: 951-605

Holger **Schildts** Förlagsaktiebolag, Annegatan 16, SF–00120 Helsinki 12 Tel: (00) 604892 Cable Add: Bokschildt
Man Dir: J af Hällström
Subjects: General Fiction, Belles Lettres, Poetry, Biography, History, Music, Art, Philosophy, University Textbooks, Reference, Juveniles, High-priced Paperbacks
1977: 135 titles *1978:* 132 titles *Founded:* 1913
ISBN Publisher's Prefix: 951-50

Söderström ja Co Förlagsaktiebolag+, Murbacksgatan 6, SF–00210 Helsingfors 21 Tel: 6923681 Cable Add: Söderströms
Man Dir: Göran Appelberg
Subjects: General Fiction, Belles Lettres, Poetry, Biography, History, How-to, Music, Art, Philosophy, Reference, Religion, Juveniles, Medicine, Psychology, General Science, University, Secondary & Primary Textbooks
1977: 309 titles *1978:* 302 titles *Founded:* 1891
ISBN Publisher's Prefix: 951-52

Suomalaisen Kirjallisuuden Seura (Finnish Literature Society), PO Box 259, SF–00171 Helsinki 17 (Located at: Hallituskatu 1, SF–00171 Helsinki 17) Tel: (90) 171229
Secretary-General/Director: Urpo Vento
Subjects: Folklore, Ethnology, Literary History, Linguistics
1978: 33 titles *1979:* 30 titles *Founded:* 1831
ISBN Publisher's Prefix: 951-717

Tammi Kustannusosakeyhtiö+, Hämeentie 15, SF–00500 Helsinki 50 Tel: 716522 Cable Add: Tammi Helsinki
Man Dir: Jarl Hellemann; *Editorial:* Sirkka Kurki-Suonio; *Marketing Dir:* Sakari Lahtinen; *Rights & Permissions:* Ritva Urnberg
Subjects: General Fiction, Belles Lettres, Poetry, Biography, History, How-to, Music, Art, Philosophy, Reference, Juveniles, High-priced Paperbacks, Psychology, Engineering, Social Science, University Textbooks, Easy Readers
Book Club: Suuri Suomalainen Kirjakerho Oy (jointly owned)
1978: approx 350 titles *Founded:* 1943
ISBN Publisher's Prefix: 951-30

Tietoteos Publishing Co, PO Box 40, SF–02211 Espoo 21 (Located at: Yläportti 1 A, SF–02211 Espoo 21) Tel: 881133
Man Dir: Jyrki K Talvitie
Associate Company: Transpico Ltd (at above address)
Subjects: Technical Dictionaries, Travel Guides, Finnish Air Force History series, Stock Market Manual, General Technical
1978: 5 titles *1979:* 5 titles *Founded:* 1948
ISBN Publisher's Prefix: 951-9035

Kustannus Oy **Uusi Tie**, PO Box 54, SF–00601 Helsinki 60 (Located at: Oulunkyläntie 5, SF–00600 Helsinki 60) Tel: (90) 799244
Man Dir: Eino J Honkanen; *Sales:* Olavi Maijala
Subjects: Christian Religion, Theology
1978: 9 titles *1979:* 9 titles *Founded:* 1964
ISBN Publisher's Prefix: 951-619

Amer-yhtymä Oy **Weilin + Göös**, Ahertajantie 5, SF–02100 Espoo 10 Tel: 461322 Cable Add: Weilingöös Telex: 122597 weigs sf
Man Dir: Seppo Saario; *Publishing Dir:* Ville Repo; *Editorial:* Maarit Tyrkkö, Jaakko Manninen, Eero Syrjänen; *Rights & Permissions:* Tuula Kuusi
Subjects: General Fiction & Nonfiction, Belles Lettres, Poetry, Biography, History, Business, Reference, Juveniles, Economics, Textbooks, Educational Materials
Book Club: Uusi Kirjakerho Oy, PL29, SF–00381 Helsinki 38 (owned jointly with Kirjayhtymä Oy (Helsinki), K J Gummerus Osakeyhtiö (Jyväskylä), Arvi A Karisto Osakeyhtiö (Hämeenlinna))
1977: 240 titles *1978:* 290 titles *Founded:* 1872
Bookshop: Kirjakievari, Mannerheimintie 40, Helsinki 10
ISBN Publisher's Prefix: 951-35

Werner **Söderström** Osakeyhtiö (WSOY)+, Bulevardi 12, PO Box 222, SF–00121 Helsinki 12 Tel: (90) 643521 Cable Add: WSOY Helsinki Telex: 122644 wsoy sf
Man Dir: Hannu Tarmio; *Publishing Dir:* Keijo Ahti (Nonfiction, Encyclopaedias, Educational); *Assistant Literary Dir:* Matti Snell (Foreign Relations, Fiction and Nonfiction); *Assistant Dirs:* Petri Arpo (Educational), Asko Rysa (Juveniles); *Rights & Permissions:* Satu Suomala
Subjects: General Fiction, Nonfiction, Juveniles, Textbooks, Encyclopaedias, Audio-Visual Materials, Educational Materials
1977: 822 titles *1978:* 865 titles, about 900 audio-visual titles *Founded:* 1878
Book Club: Suuri Suomalainen Kirjakerho Oy (Great Finnish Book Club) (jointly owned)
ISBN Publisher's Prefix: 951-0

Yritystieto Oy — Foretagsdata AB, PO Box 148, 00181 Helsinki 18 (Located at: Kalevankatu 45 A 1, 00181 Helsinki 18) Tel: (90) 648292/648293 Cable Add: Hibernia Telex: 121394 TLTX SF for Hibernia
Publisher: Börje Thilman
Subjects: Business, Directories, Reference
1978: 3 titles *1979:* 4 titles *Founded:* 1972
ISBN Publisher's Prefix: 951-9102

Literary Agents

Edith **Kiilerich**, Fiolstr 12, DK–1171 Copenhagen K, Denmark
This company also acts as a literary agent for Danish, Norwegian and Swedish writers

Werner **Söderström** Osakeyhtiö (WSOY), PL 222 Bulevardi 12, SF–00121 Helsinki 12

Book Clubs

Ristin Voitto ry*, PO Box 75, SF–01300 Tikkurila

FINLAND 87

Suuri Suomalainen Kirjakerho Oy,
Hietalahdenranta 15A, SF-00180 Helsinki
18 Tel: 601466 Telex: 121394 TLTX SF
KIRJAKERHO
Man Dir: Pertti Araviita
The Great Finnish Book Club Ltd
Owned by: Werner Söderström Osakeyhtiö
(Helsinki), Otava Kustannusosakeyhtiö
(Helsinki), Tammi Kustannusosakeyhtiö
(Helsinki)

Bokklubben Tre Böcker*, 02510 Oitbacka
Subjects: Classics, Current Affairs,
Dictionaries, Encyclopaedias, Detective
fiction, Periodicals

Uusi Kirjakerho Oy, PL 29, SF-00381
Helsinki 38
Subjects: Bestselling Novels, General
Nonfiction, Encyclopaedias
Owned by: Kirjayhtymä Oy (Helsinki), K J
Gummerus Osakeyhtiö (Jyväskylä), Oy
Weilin & Göös Ab (Helsinki), Arvi A
Karisto Osakeyhtiö (Hämeenlinna)

Major Booksellers

Akateeminen Kirjakauppa, Keskuskatu 1,
SF-00100 Helsinki 10 Tel: (90) 651122
Cable Add: Akateeminen Telex: 124773
Chief Executive: Heimo Salovaara
Br Off: Rautatienkatu 11, SF-15100 Lahti;
Kirkkobatu 29, SF-90100 Oulu 10

Gummeruksen Kirjakauppa, Kauppakatu
16, SF-40100 Jyväskylä 10 Tel: (941)
10760 Telex: 28289 KJGOY SF
Manager: Paavo Harju

Lahden Akateeminen Kirjakauppa*,
Rautatienkatu 11, SF-15100 Lahti 10 Tel:
(918) 44311

Lappeenrannan Kirjakauppa Oy*, Valtakatu
36, SF-53100 Lappeenranta 10 Tel: (953)
15117

Pohjalainen Kirjakauppa Oy*, Kirkkokatu
17, SF-90100 Oulu 10 Tel: (981) 24133

Savolan Kirjakauppa Oy*, Tulliportinkatu
33, SF-70100 Kuopio 10 Tel: (971) 16611

Suomalainen Kirjakauppa*,
Aleksanterinkatu 23, SF-00100 Helsinki 10
(5 other branches in Helsinki, and branches
in Kouvola, Oulu, Vaasa, Vantaa)

Tampereen Kirjakauppa Oy*, Hämeenkatu
27, SF-33200 Tampere 20 Tel: (931) 28380
Telex: 22521 Tamki SF

Turun Kansallinen*, PO Box 135, SF-20101
Turku 10 Tel: (921) 29451

Yliopistokirjakauppa Oy, Fredrikinkatu
30A, SF-00120 Helsinki 12 Tel: (90) 640109

Major Libraries

Eduskunnan Kirjasto*, SF-00102
Eduskunta
Library of Parliament

Helsingin Kaupunginkirjasto*,
Rikhardinkatu 3, Helsinki
Helsinki City Library

Helsingin Teknillisen Korkeakoulun
Kirjasto, Otaniementie 9, SF-02150 Espoo
15
Helsinki University of Technology Library

Helsingin Yliopiston Kirjasto, Unioninkatu
36, PO Box 312, SF-00171 Helsinki 17 Tel:
(1911) 1912742 Telex: 12-1538 HYK SF
Helsinki University Library

Jyväskylän Yliopiston Kirjasto*,
Seminaarinkatu 15, SF-40100 Jyväskylä 10
Tel: (941) 291211 Telex: 28219
Jyväskylä University Library

Lääketieteellinen Keskuskirjasto,
Haartmanink 4, SF-00290 Helsinki 29
Telex: 121498 Lkk sf
Central Medical Library

Oulun Yliopiston Kirjasto, PO Box 186,
SF-90101 Oulu 10 (Located at: Kasarmintie
7, SF-90100 Oulu 10) Tel: (981) 223455
Telex: 32256 oyk sf
Chief Librarian: Rae Murhu
Oulu University Library

Sibelius-Akatemian Kirjasto*, Pohj
Rautatiek 9, Helsinki
Sibelius Academy Library

Statistics Library, Annankatu 44 2nd Floor,
Box 504, SF-00101 Helsinki 10 Telex:
122656
Chief Librarian: Hellevi Yrjölä
Library of the Central Statistical Office of
Finland

Suomalaisen Kirjallisuuden Seura*,
Hallituskatu 1, PO Box 259, SF-00171
Helsinki 17
Finnish Literature Society

Tampereen Yliopiston Kirjasto*, Kalevantie
4, SF-33100 Tampere 10 (PL 617) Tel:
(931) 156111 Telex: 22263 tayk sf
Library of the University of Tampere

Tieteellisten Seurain Kirjasto*, PB248,
SF-00170 Helsinki 17
Library of Scientific Societies

Turun Yliopiston Kirjasto, SF-20500 Turku
50
Librarian: H Eskelinen
Turku University Library

Valtionarkisto (National Archives), PO Box
274, SF-00171 Helsinki 17

Library Associations

Arkistoyhdistys ry, Rauhankatu 17,
SF-00170 Helsinki 17 Tel: (90) 176911
Secretary-Treasurer: Ritva Pesonen
Archival Association

Kirjastonhoitajien Keskusliitto-
Bibliothekariers Centralforbund ry*,
Museokatu 18 A, SF-00100 Helsinki 10
Executive Secretary: Seija Ryömä
Central Federation of Librarians
Publication: Kirjastolehti (Library Journal)
(jointly with Finnish Library Association)

Kirjastopoliittinen Yhdistys-
Bibliotekspolitiska Föreningen*, c/o
Rautalamminkatu 5 C 3, SF-00550 Helsinki
55
Association for Library Politics

Kirjastovirkailijat-Biblioteksanstallda ry*,
c/o Helsinki University Library,
Unioninkatu 36, PO Box 312, SF-0017
Helsinki 17 Tel: (90) 1912737
Headquarters: Vipusentie 8, Helsinki
Tel: (90) 794276
Executive Secretary: Kirsti Tuominen
Association for Non-Professional Staff of
Public and Research Libraries
Publications: Volyymi

Suomen Kirjallisuuspalvelun Seura*, c/o
Helsinki University of Technology Library,
Otaniementie 9, SF-02150 Espoo 15
Finnish Association for Documentation

Suomen Kirjastonhoitajat — Finlands
Bibliotekarier ry*, Cygnaeuksenkatu 4 B 11,
SF-00100 Helsinki 10
Executive Secretary: Kari Turunen
Finnish Librarians

Suomen Kirjastoseura, Museokatu 18 A 4,
SF-00100 Helsinki 10 Tel: 492632
Secretary General: Hilkka M Kauppi
Finnish Library Association
Publication: Kirjastolehti (Library Journal)

Suomen Tieteellinen Kirjastoseura*, Central
Medical c/o Library Haartmaninkatu 4,
SF-00290 Helsinki 29 Tel: 418544 Telex:
121498 lkk sf
Secretary: Ms Pirjo Havia
Finnish Research Library Association

Tieteellisen Informoinnin Neuvosto*, PO
Box 312, SF-00171 Helsinki 17
Secretary: Liisa Rajamäki
Finnish Council for Scientific Information
and Research Libraries

Tieteellisten Kirjastojen Virkailijat —
Vetenskapliga Bibliotekens
Tjänstemannaförening ry, c/o Library of the
Soviet Institute, Armfeltintie 10, SF-00150
Helsinki 15
Executive Secretary: Raija Majamaa
Association of Research and University
Librarians
Publications: Issues newsletter to members

Library Reference Books and Journals

Book

Suomen Eríkoiskirjastojen Luettelo
(Directory of Special Libraries in Finland),
Finnish Association for Documentation, c/o
State Institute for Technical Research,
Lönnrotinkatu 37, SF-00180 Helsinki 18

Journals

Kirjastokalenteri (Library Calendar),
Finnish Library Association, Museokatu 18
A 4, SF-00100 Helsinki 10

Kirjastolehti (Library Journal), Finnish
Library Association, Museokatu 18 A 4,
SF-00100 Helsinki 10 (jointly with Central
Federation of Librarians)

Signum (text in Finnish and Swedish;
summaries in English), Finnish Research
Library Association, c/o Helsinki University
Library, Unioninkatu 36, SF-00170 Helsinki
17

Volyymi (The Volume), Association for
Non-Professional Staff of Public and
Research Libraries, c/o Helsinki University
Library, Unioninkatu 36, PO Box 312,
SF-00171 Helsinki 17

Literary Associations and Societies

Bibliofiilien Seura, Lauttasaarentie 5 C 29,
00200 Helsinki 20
President: Onni M Turtiainen
Society of Bibliophiles

Finlands Svenska Författareförening,
Runebergsgatan 32 C 27, 00100 Helsinki 10
Tel: (90) 446266
Secretary: Kerstin Nyqvist
Association of Swedish Authors in Finland

Kirjallisuudentutkijain Seura, Kotimaisen kirjallisuuden laitos, Fabianinkatu 33, 00170 Helsinki 17
Secretary: Pertti Lassila
Society of Literary Research Workers
Publication: Kirjallisuudentutkijain Seuran Vuosikirja (Annual of Literary Historians)

Suomalainen Tiedeakatemia*, Snellmaninkatu 9-11, SF-00170 Helsinki 17 Tel: (90) 636800
Secretary-General: Lauri A Vuorela
Finnish Academy of Science and Letters
Publications: Annales Academiae Scientiarum Fennicae; F F Communications; Documenta Historica; Sitzungsberichte (Proceedings); *Vuosikirja* (Yearbook)

Suomalaisen Kirjallisuuden Seura, PO Box 259, SF-00171 Helsinki 17 (Located at: Hallituskatu 1, SF-00171 Helsinki 17) Tel: (90) 171229
Secretary-General/Director: Urpo Vento
Finnish Literature Society
Publications: Studia Fennica; Suomi; Tietolipas; Toimituksia; (irregular)

Suomen Arvostelijain Liitto*, Lönnrotinkatu 15 A 7, SF-00120 Helsinki 12
Critics' Association of Finland

Suomen Kirjailijaliitto*, Runeberginkatu 32 C, Helsinki
Executive Secretary: Jarl Louhija
Association of Finnish Authors
Publications: Suomen Runotar, Suomalaisetkertojat

Suomen Nuortenkirjaneuvosto ry, Uudenkaupungintie 7 A 9, SF-00350 Helsinki 35
Finnish Section of the International Board on Books for Young People (IBBY)
President: Kaija Salonen, Haapaniemenkatu 16 C, SF-00530 Helsinki 53
Secretary: Lilian Hakkarainen (address as above)

Svenska Litteratursällskapet i Finland, Snellmaninkatu 9-11, SF-00170 Helsinki 17 Tel: (90) 636738
Swedish Literary Society in Finland
Publication: Skrifter

Svenska Österbottens Litteraturförening*, Hrvrattsesplanaden 5, Vasa SF-10
Swedish Österbottens Literary Association

Literary Periodicals

Katsaus (Review) (text mainly in Finnish, occasionally in Swedish), Kulttuurikeskus Kriittisen Korkeakoulun Kannatusyhdistys ry, Lehtikuusentie 6, SF-00270 Helsinki 27

Parnasso, Hietalahdenranta 13, SF-00180 Helsinki 18

Skrifter (Writings), Swedish Literary Society, Snellmaninkatu 9-11, SF-00170 Helsinki 17

Virittäjä (The Kindler) (Summaries in English, French, or German), Society for the Study of the Mother Tongue, Fabianink 33, SF-00170 Helsinki 17

Literary Prizes

Helsinki Prize*
For the best book written by an author connected with Helsinki. Awarded annually. Enquiries to Rudolf Koivu Foundation, c/o Ministry of Education, Rauhankatu 4, SF-00170 Helsinki

Tauno **Karilas** Prize
For the writer of the year's best Finnish book for children. Awarded annually. Enquiries to Suomen Nuorisokirjailijat ry, Uudenkaupungintie 7 A 9, SF-00350 Helsinki 35

Arvid **Lydecken** Prize
For the writer of the year's best Finnish book for children. Awarded annually. Enquiries to Suomen Nuorisokirjailijat ry, Uudenkaupungintie 7 A 9, SF-00350 Helsinki 35

State Prizes for Literature*
Twenty-one prizes for the best literary works. Awarded annually. Enquiries to the Rudolf Koivo Foundation, c/o Ministry of Education, Rauhankatu 4, SF-00170 Helsinki

Anni **Swanin** Prize
For the best children's book of the previous three years. Awarded every three years. Enquiries to Finnish Section of the International Board on Books for Young People, Haapaniemenkatu 16 C, SF-00530 Helsinki 53

Tampere Prize*
For the best authors connected with the city of Tampere. Awarded annually. Enquiries to Tampere City Government, Tampere

Topelius Prize*
For the writer of the year's best Finnish book for young adults. Awarded annually. Enquiries to Suomen Nuorisokirjailijat, Pajalahdentie 7A, 00200 Helsinki 20

Translation Agencies and Associations

Suomen Kääntäjäin Yhdists (Finnish Translators' Association)*, Oversättarförening ry, Fredrikinkatu 62 A 6, Helsinki 10

France

General Information

Language: French
Religion: Roman Catholic predominantly
Population: 53.1 million
Bank Hours: 0900-1600 Monday-Friday
Shop Hours: 0900-1200, 1400-1800 Tuesday-Saturday
Department Stores: 0930-1830 Tuesday-Saturday; open Monday in Paris
Currency: 100 centimes = 1 franc
Export/Import Information: No tariff on books, except children's picture books from non-EEC 13%. 1.8% on advertising. VAT on books 7%, 20% on most advertising matter. 2% Customs Stamp Tax (based on duty). Import licences not required. Nominal exchange controls over 1500-franc value. For imports over 50,000 francs, documents must be 'domiciliated' before any other transaction occurs. There is control of the book trade based on a number of legal and regulating provisions applying to the import of pirated publications, articles and writings that offend against morality, publications harmful to youth, writings forbidden by the Minister for the Interior, books, writings, printed matter, etc intended to provoke the crime of abortion; the customs official must submit articles subject to control for examination by the General Information Service of the Ministry of the Interior
Copyright: UCC, Berne, Buenos Aires, Florence (see International section)

Book Trade Organizations

Centre de la Productivité du Livre (Book Research Centre)*, 117 blvd St-Germain, F-75279 Paris. Official service of the Documentation française, 31 quai Voltaire, F-75008 Paris
Publication: Le Livre en France

Cercle de la Librairie (Syndicat des Industries et Commerces du Livre), 117 blvd St-Germain, F-75279 Paris cedex 06 Tel: 3292101
Booksellers' Circle of the Association of Book Trades and Industries
Man Dir: Michel Dupouey; *Director:* Patrick Lehideux
Publications: Bibliographie de la France; Notices établies par le Dépôt Légal (Copyright Depositions); *Les Livres de l'année—Biblio* ('Biblio' Books of the Year); *Les Livres Disponibles* (French Books in Print); *Le Répertoire International des Éditeurs et Diffuseurs de Langue Française* (International List of French Language Publishers and Distributors); *Répertoire des Livres au Format de Poche* (List of Paperback (or Pocket Edition) Books; *Livres et Matériel d'Enseignement* (Teaching Aids and Books); *Catalogue des Livres d'Étrennes* (Catalogue of New Year Gift Books); *Études et Statistiques sur le Livre français* (Statistics and Research on French Books); *Catalogue général des ouvrages parus en Langue française* (General Catalogue of Works which have appeared in the French Language)

Chambre syndicale des Editeurs d'Annuaires et de Publications similaires (Association of Publishers of Directories and Similar Publications), Permanent Secretariat, Cercle de la Librairie, 117 blvd St-Germain, F-75006 Paris Tel: (01) 3232101
President: Gérard Delaubier

Fédération française des Syndicats de Libraires (French Booksellers' Association)*, 117 blvd St-Germain, F-75279 Paris cedex 06
Publication: Lettre du Libraire

Office de Promotion de L'Edition Française, 117 blvd Saint-Germain, F-75279 Paris cedex 06 Tel: 3266166
Man Dir: Gustave Girardot
Miscellaneous: Function of the office is to organise the national stands of all French publishing companies at international book fairs as well as specific exhibitions throughout the world. It represents all French publishing houses

Syndicat National de la Librairie ancienne et moderne, 117 blvd St-Germain, F-75279 Paris cedex 06
(This is the National Association of Antiquarian and Modern Booksellers)

Syndicat des Représentants littéraires français (Association of French Literary Agents)*, 117 blvd St-Germain, F-75279 Paris cedex 06

Syndicat national de l'Edition (French Publishers' Association)*, 117 blvd St-Germain, F-75279 Paris cedex 06 Tel: (01) 3292101
Secretary: Michel Dupouey
Publications: Le Répertoire des Livres et Matériel d'Enseignement; Le Répertoire international des Editeurs et Diffuseurs de Langue française; Le Catalogue des Produits et Matériels audio visuels; La Classification décimale de Dewey; Le Catalogue des Livres au Format de Poche; Le Catalogue des Livres d'Etrennes; Les Livres disponibles (French Books in Print)

Syndicat national des Annuaires et Supports divers de Publicité, 40 blvd Malesherbes, F-75008 Paris Tel: 7421248
National Federation of Yearbooks and Sundry Publicity Aids

Syndicat national des Importateurs et Exportateurs de Livres, 117 blvd St-Germain, F-75279 Paris cedex 06
National Federation of Book Importers and Exporters

U D E F, 117 blvd Saint-Germain, F-75279 Paris cedex 06 Tel: 0338714
Dir: P Monnet
This is the Union of French Publishers, with the aim of international promotion of books in the French language. It has four associated Groups: Groupe des Editeurs d'Art, Groupe des Editeurs de Poésie, Groupe des Editeurs d'Erudition, Groupe des Editeurs de Réligion (Groups associated with Art, Poetry, Learning and Religion respectively)
Founded 1901

Union d'Editeurs Français, see U D E F

Unipress*, 14 rue de Bretagne, F-75140 Paris cedex 03
Non-profit-making organization, whose purpose is to extend knowledge of the French Press abroad

Book Trade Reference Books and Journals

Books

Catalogue de l'Edition française (Catalogue of French-language Publishing), 22 rue de Condé, F-75006 Paris

Guide du Livre Ancien et du Livre d'occasion (Antique and second-hand book guide), Hotel du Cercle de la Librairie, 117 Blvd St-Germain, F-75279 Paris cedex 06

Répertoire des Livres au Format de Poche (Catalogue of Paperback Books), 117 blvd St-Germain, F-75279 Paris cedex 06

Répertoire international des Editeurs et Diffuseurs de Langue française (International List of French Language Publishers and Distributors), Cercle de la Librairie, 117 blvd St-Germain, F-75279 Paris cedex 06

Répertoire international des Librairies de Langue française (International List of French Language Bookshops), Cercle de la Librairie, 117 blvd Saint-Germain, F-75279 Paris cedex 06

Journals

Art et Métiers du Livre (Art and Crafts of the Book), Cercle de la Librairie, 117 blvd St-Germain, F-75279 Paris cedex 06

La Bibliographie de la France — Biblio (French National Bibliography), Cercle de la Librairie, 117 blvd St-Germain, F-75279 Paris cedex 06

Book Promotion News (French edition), Unesco, 7 pl de Fontenoy, F-75700 Paris

Bulletin, Association of Antiquarian and Modern Booksellers, 117 blvd St-Germain, F-75279 Paris cedex 06

Bulletin critique du Livre français (Critical Bulletin on French Books) (text in English and Spanish), Association pour la Diffusion de la Pensée française, 21 bis rue la Perouse, F-75116 Paris

Bulletin du Livre (Book Bulletin), 18 rue Dauphine, F-75006 Paris

Connaissance et Formation (Knowledge and Training), France Expansion, 336-340 rue St-Honoré, F-75001 Paris (trade journal for the educational market)

La Documentation française; 'Bibliographie sélective' des Publications officielles françaises (French Documentation; 'Selective Bibliography' of French Official Publications), Secrétariat général du Gouvernement, Paris

Documentation — technique, scientifique et commerciale (Documentation — Technical, Scientific and Commercial) (text and summaries in English, French and German), Librairie Lavoisier, 11 rue Lavoisier, F-75008 Paris

Francophonie-Edition; revue bibliographique de l'Edition de Langue française dans le Monde, France Expansion, 336-340 rue St-Honoré, F-75001 Paris

Liens, Editions du Cap, Palais de la Scala, Monte Carlo

Livres (Books), Institut national de Recherches et de la Documentation pédagogique, 29 rue d'Ulm, F-75230 Paris

Livres-Actualité (Books of the Day), Information Promotion et Culture Sàrl, 17 rue de la Félicité, Paris 17e

Livres de France, 18 rue Dauphine, F-75006 Paris

Les Livres de l'Année — Biblio; annual cumulation of *Bibliographie de la France — Biblio* (qv)

Les Livres disponibles (French Books in Print), Cercle de la Librairie, 117 blvd St-Germain, F-75279 Paris cedex 06

New French Books (English extracts from *Bulletin Critique du Livre français*), Association pour la Diffusion de la Pensée française, 21 bis rue la Perouse, F-75116 Paris

Officiel de la Librairie (Booksellers' Official Journal), French Booksellers' Association, 117 blvd St-Germain, F-75279 Paris cedex 06

Publishers

A R E D I P (Agence Recherches Droits Internationaux et Promotion), 23 rue Cambon, F-75001 Paris Tel: 2603633 Telex: 240620
President/Man Dir: André Limansky
Subject: Juveniles

Edition de l'**Abbaye** d'Encalcat+*, F-81110 Dourgne Tel: 502837
Subject: Religion

Academy Editions, 70 rue des Saints-Pères, F-75007 Paris Tel: 2227897
Man Dir: Dr Andreas Papadakis; *Editorial:* Giada Ricci
Parent Company: Academy Editions, UK (qv)
Subjects: Art, Architecture
1979: 12 titles *Founded:* 1978

Advisor Editions*, 44 Rue Lamarck, F-75018 Paris Tel: (255) 2559
Subject: Children's Books and Games

Agence Parisienne de Distribution Sarl, see Editions Techniques et Scientifiques Françaises (ETSF)

Editions **Albin** Michel+, 22 rue Huyghens, F-75014 Paris Tel: (01) 3261350
President: Robert Esménard; *Man Dir:* Francis Esménard; *Sales Dir:* Georges Madamour; *Dir Foreign Department:* Ivan Nabokov; *Publicity:* Raymonde Leroux; *Advertising:* Richard Ducousset; *Rights & Permissions:* Béatrix Blavier
Subjects: General Fiction, Science Fiction, Fine Arts, History, Philosophy, Reference, Religion, How-to, General & Social Science, Popular Music, The Occult
1978: 160 titles *Founded:* 1902
ISBN Publisher's Prefix: 2-226

Almonde*, 2 Impasse Lebouis, F-75014 Paris Tel: (306) 4720
Subjects: Psychology, Ecology, Sexuality, Education, Science; Periodicals

Alpha Editions+*, 10 rue Chauchat, F-75009 Paris Tel: (01) 7709189
General Manager/President: Mme de Salm Salm
Subsidiary Company: Co-owner with Editions Atlas (qv) of Grange Batelière (qv)

Editions **Alpina**, 60 rue Mazarine, F-75006 Paris Tel: (01) 3298740
Man Dir: Alain Gründ
Subjects: Guide Books
Founded: 1928
Miscellaneous: Associate company of Librairie Gründ, Paris (qv)
ISBN Publisher's Prefix: 2-7000

Alsatia SA+*, 10 rue Bartholdi, F-68001 Colmar Tel: 411450 Telex: Alco 88200 F 508
Man Dirr: André Clemessy; *Sales, Publicity, Advertising, Rights & Permissions:* Auguste Rimelé
Subjects: Belles Lettres, Poetry, Biography, History, How-to, Religion, Low-priced Paperbacks, Medicine, Primary Textbooks, Educational Materials
Founded: 1896
Bookshops: Librairie Alsatia, 31 pl de la Cathédrale, F-67000 Strasbourg; Librairie Union, 4 pl de la Réunion, F-68000 Mulhouse; Librairie Union, 28 rue des Têtes, 68 Colmar; Librairie Union, 26 rue Charles de Gaulle, F-68130 Altkirch; Libraire Union, 3 rue St-Antoine, F-68500 Guebwiller
ISBN Publisher's Prefix: 2-7001

Editions **Alta**, 17 rue Jacob, F-75006, Paris Tel: 3290620
Man Dir: Sylvie Messinger
Parent Company: Editions Jean-Claude Lattès (qv)
Subjects: Novels, Sport, How-to, Nonfiction
1977: 20 titles *Founded:* 1977

Les **Amis** de Milosz, see Editions André Silvaire

Editions de l'**Amitié**+, G T Rageot, 15 rue de Verneuil, F–75007 Paris Tel: (01) 2612022
Man Dir: Jean Vilnet; *All other offices:* Mrs C Scob
Orders to: Librairie Hatier SA, 8 rue d'Assas, F–75006 Paris
Subject: Juvenile; mainly young peoples' fiction in the contemporary world
1978: 22 titles *Founded:* 1941
Miscellaneous: Editions de l'Amitié is an imprint of Librairie Hatier (qv)
ISBN Publisher's Prefix: 2–7002

Editions **Amphora** SA+, 14 rue de l'Odéon, F–75006 Paris Tel: (01) 3261087
Administration and Accounts: 51 blvd Saint-Michel, F–75005 Paris Tel: (01) 3253461
Man Dir: Roger Vaultier; *Editorial, Publicity:* Roland Antoine; *Sales, Production:* Michel Vaultier
Subjects: Sports and Leisure Activities
1978: 11 titles *Founded:* 1954
ISBN Publisher's Prefix: 2–85180

Anael*, 2 rue de Marly, F–78150 Parly Tel: (954) 9060

Annuaires Ravet **Anceau**, 42 rue Roger Salengro, F–59260 Hellemes-lez-Lille Tel: 567141
Man Dir: Daniel Melchior
Subjects: Professional Yearbooks/Directories
Founded: 1853

Antarès Editions d'Art*, 218 Bd Raspail, F–75014 Paris Tel: (01) 3223194
Subject: Publishers of original engravings

Editions **Anthropos** SA, 12 ave du Maine, F–75015 Paris Tel: (01) 5484258/2227682
Man Dir: Serge Jonas
Subjects: History, Philosophy, Social Sciences, Anthropology, Economy etc
1977: over 50 titles *1978:* 60 titles
Founded: 1965
ISBN Publisher's Prefix: 2–7157

L'**Arbalète**+*, Marc Barbezat, F–69150 Décines-Charpieu Tel: 495101
Subjects: Literature, Art

Publications **Aredit**, 357 blvd de Gambetta, F–59200 Tourcoing Tel: 267981/295963 Telex: 130372F
Subjects: Picture-Strip Books in instalments on War, Adventure, Westerns, Romance, Schoolgirl interests

Art et Valeur*, 20 rue Molitor, F–75016 Paris Tel: (01) 5206290
President & Man Dir: Yves Gauguet; *Assistant Man Dir:* R Poli; *Commercial Dir:* Mrs A Boisnier; *Marketing:* Mrs D Zwierz
Br Offs: 3 quai du Maréchal-Joffre, F–69002 Lyon; 18 rue du Congrès, F–06000 Nice
Subject: Art (specialized and limited editions)
Founded: 1971
Miscellaneous: Sales are more usually to individuals and certain galleries

Arted (Editions d'Art), 6 ave du Coq, 75009 Paris Tel: (01) 8747184
Subjects: Fine Arts; Sculpture, Painting
ISBN Publisher's Prefix: 85067

Editions **Arthaud** SA+*, 6 rue de Mézières, F–75006 Paris Tel: (01) 5443847 Cable Add: Artore Paris
President: Henri Flammarion; *Dir:* P-F Racine; *Rights & Permissions:* as for Flammarion (qv)
Subjects: Literature, Arts, History, Travel Books, Sailing, Mountaineering, Sports
Founded: 1890
ISBN Publisher's Prefix: 2–7003

Artisan du Livre (Guérin et Cie), 22 rue Guynemer and 2 rue de Fleurus, F–75006, Paris Tel: (01) 5483058
Subjects: Literary, Academic, Commentary on Classics, Music, Art etc

Editions d'**Artrey**+*, 17 rue de la Rochefoucauld, F–75009 Paris Tel: (01) 8744260
Subject: Education

Arts et Métiers Graphiques+*, 19 rue Racine, F–75006 Paris 6 Tel: (01) 3269220
Man Dir: Yves Rivière
Subject: Art
1977: 8 titles *Founded:* 1927
ISBN Publisher's Prefix: 2–7004

Compagnie Française des **Arts Graphiques** SA+, 3 rue Duguay-Trouin, F–75006 Paris Tel: (01) 5487285
President: V P Victor-Michel
Subject: Art
Founded: 1939
ISBN Publisher's Prefix: 2–85001

L'**Asiathèque**, 6 rue Christine, F–75006 Paris Tel: (01) 3253437
Editorial, Production: Alain Thiollier; *Sales, Publicity:* Oscar Ferreyros
Subjects: Far East (language, literature, etc)
Bookshop: At above address
1977: 17 titles *Founded:* 1973

Editions **Assimil** SA+, 13 rue Gay Lussac, PO Box 25, F–94430 Chennevières sur Marne Tel: 5768737 Cable Add: Publicode 777 Assimil Telex: 210311F
Dirs: J L Cherel, J le Gal; *Editorial:* J L Cherel; *Sales, Production, Publicity:* J le Gal
Subjects: The Teaching of Languages; Handbooks, Textbooks, Reference
Bookshop: 11 rue des Pyramides, F–75001 Paris
1978: 4 titles *Founded:* 1930
Miscellaneous: Assimil has a Language School at 29 Champs-Elysées, F–75008 Paris Tel: 2253664
ISBN Publisher's Prefix: 2–7005

L'**Astrolabe**, La Librairie du Voyageur, 46 rue de Provence, F–75009 Paris Tel: 2854295/2811603
Man Dir: Jacques P Nobecourt; *Editorial:* Raymond M Chabaud; *Sales:* Odile Nobecourt
Subsidiary Company: Librairie Blondel La Rougery (qv)
Subjects: Travel, Geography, Cartography
1978: 2 titles *1979:* 3 titles *Founded:* 1974
ISBN Publisher's Prefix: 2–86230

Editions **Atlas***, 10 rue Chauchat, F–75009 Paris Tel: (01) 7709189
Man Dir: M Bocs
Subsidiary Company: Co-owner with Alpha Editions (qv) of Grange Batelière (qv)

Aubanel SA+, 7 pl Saint-Pierre, F–84028 Avignon 90 Tel: (090) 824626
Man Dir: Laurent Theodore-Aubanel
Subjects: General Fiction, Psychology, Secondary Textbooks, Latin, Regional History, Tourist Guides, Provencal interest
1977: 17 titles *Founded:* 1744
ISBN Publisher's Prefix: 2–7006

Editions **Aubier-Montaigne** SA+, 13 quai Conti, F–75006 Paris Tel: (01) 3265559/6335917
Man Dir: Mrs M Aubier-Gabail; *Sales Manager, Rights & Permissions:* Patrice Mentha
Subjects: Belles Lettres, Poetry, History, Philosophy, Reference, Religion, Psychology, University Textbooks, Pedagogy, Sociology, Languages
1977: 31 titles *1978:* 40 titles *Founded:* 1924

Editions d'**Aujourd'hui**, F–83120 Plan de La Tour Tel: (94) 437079
Man Dir: Odette Charrière
Subjects: Literature, Music, Drama, Cinema, Poetry, Fiction, Human Sciences, Folklore, Esoteric
1978: 50 titles *1979:* 50 titles *Founded:* 1974
ISBN Publisher's Prefix: 2–7307

Editions Philippe **Auzou**, see Ed Michel de Lile

L'**Avant-Scène** Théâtre, Cinéma et Opéra, 27 rue St-André des-Arts, F–75006 Paris Tel: (01) 3255229
Man Dir: C Dupeyron
Subjects: Theatre, Cinema, Opera
1978: 46 titles *Founded:* 1949

Editions **B P I** (Bureau de Presse et d'Informations)+*, 79 ave des Champs-Elysées, F–75008 Paris 8 Tel: 7236870
Man Dir: J Milinaire
Subjects: Science & Technical, Hotels and Restaurants, Surface Treatments

Editions **B R G M**, see Bureau de Recherches Géologiques et Minières

Editions J-B **Baillière**+, 19 rue Hautefeuille, F–75279 Paris cedex 06 Tel: (01) 3269602
Man Dir: M Roux Dessarps
Subjects: Technical texts for professional and instructional use in: all branches of Medical, Dental, Surgical care; Agriculture and Horticulture; various branches of Technology and Industry
Founded: 1819
ISBN Publisher's Prefix: 2–7008

André **Balland**, 33 rue St-André-des-Arts, F–75006 Paris Tel: (01) 3257440
Publisher: André Balland; *Sales:* François Coupry; *Rights & Permissions:* Sabine Forest
Subjects: Fiction, Documentaries, Humour, Sexology
1977: 55 titles *1978:* 57 titles *Founded:* 1966
ISBN Publisher's Prefix: 2–7158

Les Editions de l'Illustration **Baschet** et Cie, 13 rue St-Georges, F–75009 Paris 9 Tel: (01) 2806118
Man Dir: Roger Allegret
Imprints: Les Editions Chantereine (qv); Editions de l'Illustration (qv)
Subjects: History, Art, How-to, Encyclopaedias, Travel, Science, Geography; The *Encyclopédie de La Maison* (6–vol work on interior decoration and appointments) etc
1978: 3 titles *Founded:* 1843
ISBN Publisher's Prefix: 2–7059

Bayard-Presse SA+*, 17 rue de Babylone, F–75007 Paris Tel: (01) 2229315/5484417
President: Jean Gelamur
Associate Company: Le Centurion (qv)
Subjects: Juveniles, Religion, Literature
Founded: 1873
ISBN Publisher's Prefix: 2–7009

Editions **Beauchesne**+, 72 rue des Saints-Pères, F-75007 Paris
Tel: (01) 5488028
Dir: Miss M Cadic
Subjects: Religion & Theology, Social and Political Science, Humanities, Reference, Current Affairs, Spirituality, The Church Today, Holy Scripture, Biography, History, Literature, Essays
1977: 42 titles *1978:* 45 titles *Founded:* 1851
ISBN Publisher's Prefix: 2-7010

Editions Pierre **Belfond**+*, 3 bis passage de la Petite-Boucherie, F-75006 Paris Tel: (01) 3252760 Telex: 260717F
Chairmen: Pierre Belfond, Franca Belfond; *Rights & Permissions:* Ghislaine de Montalembert
Subsidiary Companies: Nouvel Office d'Edition et de Diffusion (qv), Productions de Paris (both at 3 bis passage de la Petite-Boucherie, F-75006 Paris); Presses de la Renaissance (qv)
Subjects: General Fiction, Belles Lettres, Bibliophily, Poetry, Biography, History, Music, Art, Paperbacks
Founded: 1962

Editions le **Belier-Prisma** SA, see Editions Universitaires

Librairie Classique Eugène **Belin**+*, 8 rue Férou, F-75278 Paris cedex 06 Tel: (01) 3292142 Telex: Libelin 202978F
Man Dir & Chairman: Max Brossollet; *Editorial:* Marie-Claude Brossollet; *Documentation:* Soraya Eghbal-Dupouey; *Sales:* Maurice Farcy; *Publicity:* Pierre Chassagnol; *Production, Rights & Permissions:* Max Brossollet
Subjects: Secondary & Primary Textbooks, Educational Material, Literary & Scientific Magazines
Founded: 1777
ISBN Publisher's Prefix: 2-7011

Editions Les **Belles Images***, 53 rue St André-des-Arts, F-75006 Paris Tel: (01) 0338207 Telex: 202844F
Man Dir: Peter Watkins; *Sales:* Jacques-Edouard Tavernier
*Imprints*d1 Belles Images, Butterfly Books
Subjects: Children's Books, Posters and Puzzles, Educational Material
1977: 12 titles *1978:* 10 titles *Founded:* 1975

Société d'Edition 'Les **Belles Lettres**'+, 95 blvd Raspail, F-75006 Paris Tel: (01) 5487055
Man Dir: Pierre de Mijolla; *Editor:* Jean Malye; *Publicity & Advertising:* Christine Bonneton
Subjects: Poetry, History, Philosophy, Literature, Religion, Scholarly, University Textbooks, Ancient History
1978: 60 titles *Founded:* 1919
Bookshop: Librairie Guillaume Budé, 95 blvd Raspail, F-75006 Paris
Miscellaneous: This Société now incorporates the formerly independent firm Cathasia
ISBN Publisher's Prefix: 2-251

Berg International Editeurs*, 19 blvd Saint-Michel, F-75005 Paris Tel: (01) 3258443
Cable Add: Bergedit Paris
Man Dir: Monique Gougaud
Subjects: Art, History, General & Social Science, Heraldry, Music, Reference, Religion
ISBN Publisher's Prefix: 900269

Berger-Levrault+, 1 ave de l'Observatoire, F-75006 Paris Tel: (01) 3294450 Telex: 27797
Man Dir: Marc Friedel; *Editorial:* Didier Bonnet, Jean-Jacques Brisebarre, Hubert Cuny, Yves Robert; *Sales:* André Bourgeois; *Production:* Anne-Marie Veujoz; *Publicity:* Catherine Riand
Branch Off: 23 place Broglie, F-6700 Strasbourg
Subjects: Books on various regions of France and the World, Geographical, Historical, Leisure, Art, Literature, History, Architecture
Bookshop: Librairie Berger-Levrault, pl Broglie, F-67000 Strasbourg
1977: 50 titles *1978:* 70 titles *Founded:* 1676
ISBN Publisher's Prefix: 7013

Société Internationale des Ecoles **Berlitz** SA*, 31 blvd des Italiens, F-75002 Paris Tel: (01) 7420509 Cable Add: Berliscool Paris
Subjects: Education, Textbooks
Founded: 1907
ISBN Publisher's Prefix: 2-7014

Atelier **Beyer***, 7 rue de Genève, F-68300 St-Louis Tel: (89) 677876
Sales Manager: Marie-France Durisch
Publisher: Jochen Beyer
Subject: Art

Bias (Société Nouvelle des Editions) SA+, 26 rue Vauquelin, F-75005 Paris Tel: (01) 3376560
Man Dir: Georges Lauvaux; *Editorial, Production:* G Lauvaux; *Sales Dir:* Mrs A Gontier; *Publicity & Advertising:* Jean Lauvaux; *Rights & Permissions:* Jean Lauvaux
Subjects: Stories, How-to and Information Books for all age juveniles; Travel, Hobbies, Popular Science & Technology
1977: 300 titles *1978:* 320 titles *Founded:* 1941
ISBN Publisher's Prefix: 2-7015

Société **Biblique** Française+*, 58 rue de Clichy, F-75009 Paris Tel: (01) 8742850
Subject: Bibles
ISBN Publisher's Prefix: 2-85300

Blondel La Rougery SA+, 7 rue St-Lazare, F-75009 Paris Tel: (01) 8789554
Chairman: J Barbotte
Associate Company: L'Astrolabe (qv)
Subjects: Science & Technical, Maps & Charts
Founded: 1902
ISBN Publisher's Prefix: 2-7016

Bloud et Gay (Librairie) SA+, see Editions Desclée et Cie

Editions E de **Boccard**+, 11 rue de Médicis, F-75006 Paris Tel: (01) 3260037
Subjects: Archaeology, History
ISBN Publisher's Prefix: 2-7018

Editions André **Bonne**+*, 15-17 rue Las-Cases, F-75007 Paris Tel: (01) 5510609/5515953
Man Dir: André Bonne; *Editorial Dir:* Robert de Chateaubriant
Subjects: General Fiction, Belles Lettres, Reference, Religion
Founded: 1861
ISBN Publisher's Prefix: 2-7019

Boosey & Hawkes*, Société des Grandes Editions Musicales, 4 rue Drouot, F-75009 Paris Tel: 1770-7344 Telex: Sonorous, Paris
Parent Company: Boosey & Hawkes, UK (qv)

Editions **Bordas**, 37 rue Boulard, F-75686 Paris cedex 14 Tel: (01) 5392208; 17 rue Rémy Dumoncel, F-75686 Paris cedex 14 Tel: (01) 3201550 Telex: 270004
President: Jean-Manuel Bourgois; *Man Dir:* Jean-François Grollemund; *Editorial:* Michel Legrain, Jean Lissarrague; *Sales:* Dominique Desmottes, Fernand Joffre, (export) Luc Tiberghien; *Production:* Jacques Patry; *Publicity:* Philippe Fournier-Bourdier, Jean Ganem; *Rights & Permissions:* Mireille Debenne, Maryvonne Guérin
Orders to: 37 rue Boulard, F-75686 Paris cedex 14
Subsidiary Companies: Société Générale de Diffusion (SGED), BP 429, F-93104 Montreuil cedex; Société Gauthier-Villars, 70 rue de Saint-Mandé, F-93100 Montreuil; Société Bordas-Dunod-Bruxelles, Brussels, Belgium (qv); Bordas-Dunod-Montréal Inc, 350 Blvd Lebeau, Saint-Laurent, Montreal, Quebec, H4N IW6 Canada; also Librairie de Montaigne, 24-26 rue de l'Hôpital, F-75005, Paris; Librairie Dunod (see Bookshops)
Imprints: Bordas, Dunod, Gauthier-Villars
Subjects: Educational (from Elementary to Higher Levels), General Fiction and Nonfiction, Scientific, Technical, Reference (espec Dictionaries and Encyclopedias)
Book Club: Librairie de Montaigne
Bookshops: Librairie Dunod, 30 rue Saint-Sulpice, F-75006 Paris; Librairie Beranger, Liège, Belgium
1978: 200 titles *Founded:* 1946
ISBN Publisher's Prefix: 775-663347

Editions **Bornemann**+*, 15 rue de Tournon, F-75006 Paris Tel: (01) 3260588
Manager: Maurice Bornemann
Subjects: Art, How-to, Sports, Nature, Easy Readers
Founded: 1829
ISBN Publisher's Prefix: 2-85182

Boscher-Chapron+, 10 rue du Docteur-Robin, 22600 Loudéac Tel: (96) 280127
Publisher/Author: Mrs J Chapron
Subjects: Educational, Juvenile; the 'Boscher' Method of Infant Teaching

Editions N **Boubée** et Cie+*, 11 pl Saint-Michel, F-75006 Paris Tel: (01) 6330030
Subject: Biology
Founded: 1941
ISBN Publisher's Prefix: 2-85004

Christian **Bourgois**+, Editeur, 8 rue Garancière, F-75006 Paris Tel: (01) 3291280 Telex: Precite 204807F
Subject: Literature
Miscellaneous: Member of the Presses de la Cité group (qv)
ISBN Publisher's Prefix: 2-267

Editions Colin **Bourrelier**, 103 blvd Saint-Michel, F-75240 Paris cedex 05
Subjects: Juvenile: formerly awarded French Youth Prize

Bréa Éditions, 24 ave Ledru-Rollin, F-75012 Paris Tel: 3452090 Telex: Brea 250303 Public Paris
Man Dir: Eric Brébant; *Commercial Manager:* Jean Arcache
Orders to: Editions du Buot, 30 rue du Rendezvous, F-75012 Paris Tel: 3435903
Subjects: Economics, Tourist Guides, Practical Information books
1978: 1 title *1979:* 2 titles *Founded:* 1978

Editions **Brepols** SA+*, 6 rue du Vieux-Colombier, F-75006 Paris Tel: (01) 2224210
Subject: Religion
ISBN Publisher's Prefix: 2-85006

92 FRANCE

Michèle **Broutta** Oeuvres Graphiques Contemporaines*, 31 rue des Bergers, F-75015 Paris Tel: (01) 5779371/5779379
Man Dir: Michèle Broutta
Subject: Art
1977: 3 titles *Founded:* 1970
ISBN Publisher's Prefix: 900332

Editions **Buchet/Chastel**+*, 18 rue de Condé, F-75006 Paris Tel: (01) 0334599/0335047; (sales) (01) 3269200 Cable Add: Buchet/Chastel Paris
Man Dir: Guy Buchet; *Editorial Dir:* Edmond Buchet; *Sales Dir:* René Charbonnier; *Publicity & Advertising:* Guy Buchet; *Rights & Permissions:* Anne Buchet
Subjects: General Fiction, Belles Lettres, Biography, History, Philosophy, Music, Religion, Social Science, Medicine
Founded: 1930
ISBN Publisher's Prefix: 2-7020

Bureau de Presse et d'Information, see B P I

Bureau de Recherches Géologiques et Minières, BP 6009, F-45018 Orléans cedex (Located at: 6-8 rue Chasseloup Laubat, F-75737 Paris cedex 15) Tel: (01) 7839400 Telex: brgm 270844 f
Subjects: Texts connected with mineralogical and geological research (principally in France and Francophone areas of world); Maps and Charts
1977: 35 titles *1978:* 105 titles
Miscellaneous: Publisher for the French National Department of Geology; its catalogue includes geology-related works published by other government offices
ISBN Publisher's Prefix: 2-7159

C A L/Retz* (Culture Art Loisirs/Retz), 114 ave des Champs Elysées, F-75391 Paris cedex 08 Tel: 3598650 Telex: 290049
Man Dir: François Richaudeau; *Sales:* Jacques Cabuj; *Rights & Permissions:* Simone Bulteau-Jumin
Subsidiary Companies: CAL, Pully, Switzerland; L'Académie du Livre SA, Belgium (Book Club only) (qv)
Subjects: History, Psychology, Social Science, Arts, Encyclopaedias
Book Club: CAL, 114 Champs Elysées, F-75008 Paris
Founded: 1957
ISBN Publisher's Prefix: 2-7140

C D R, see Centre de Documentation Universitaire

C E D S, see Centre d'Etudes et de Documentation Scientifiques

C E F A G, see Centre d'Etudes et Fabrication Arts Graphiques

C E L S E (Compagnie d'Editions Libres, Sociales et Economiques SA)+, 68 rue Cardinet, F-75017 Paris Tel: (01) 2674123
Subjects: Road Transport (Vocational Training, Economics, Administration, Management, Social Science, Vocabulary of International Transport); Tourist interest
ISBN Publisher's Prefix: 2-85009

C E P A D, see Cepadues Editions SA

C E P L (Centre d'Etude et de Promotion de la Lecture)*, 114 ave des Champs-Elysées, F-75008 Paris Tel: (01) 2251483
Subjects: Education, Popular Reference Works

C L D, BP 2, 42 ave des Platanes, F-37170 Chambray-Les-Tours Tel: (47) 282068
Man Dir: Jean-Pierre Normand; *Editorial:* Hélène Richard; *Sales and Rights & Permissions:* Jack Normand; *Production:* Pierre Proust; *Publicity:* Bernadette Dusseau
Subjects: Regional Interest, Folklore, History, Architecture, Religion, Tourism, Hunting
1978: 22 titles *1979:* 25 titles *Founded:* 1960

C L E International, 11 rue Méchain, F-75014 Paris (Located at: 59-61 rue de la Santé, F-75013 Paris) Tel: 3376112
Man Dir: Gilbert Mitry; *Editorial, Production:* Anne Rebérioux; *Sales, Rights & Permissions:* Jean-Claude Richard; *Publicity:* Martine Borgomano
Orders to (outside France): as company address; (in France): Ed Fernand Nathan, 9 rue Méchain, F-75680 Paris
Subjects: Books for the Foreign Market, especially connected with teaching French as a foreign language; also teaching French as a second language
1978: 29 titles *1979:* 28 titles *Founded:* 1973

Editions du **C N R S** (Centre National de la Recherche Scientifique)+, 15 quai Anatole France, F-75700 Paris Tel: (01) 5559225 Telex: 260034
Man Dir: Henri Peronnin; *Sales:* Pierre Cohendy; *Publicity & Advertising:* Denis Cotard
Parent Company: Centre national de la recherche scientifique
Associate Company: CNRS Laboratoire Intergeo (qv)
Bookshop: Librairie du CNRS, 15 quai Anatole France, F-75700 Paris
Subjects: History, Geography, Literature, Linguistics, Music, Art, Philosophy, Reference, Religion, Medicine, Psychology, Engineering, Social Sciences, Education, Science & Technology, Law, Economics, Mathematics, Information Sciences, Electronics, Mechanics, Energy, Chemistry and Physics, Geology, Biology, Astronomy
1978: 151 titles *Founded:* 1939
ISBN Publisher's Prefix: 2-222

C N R S, Laboratoire Intergeo, see Intergeo

Editions **Cahiers d'Art***, 14 rue du Dragon, F-75006 Paris Tel: (01) 5487673
Man Dir: Marc de Fontbrune
Subject: Art
Founded: 1926
ISBN Publisher's Prefix: 2-85117

C R E R, see Coopérative Régionale de l'Enseignement Religieux

Les **Cahiers Fiscaux** Européens Sàrl+, 51 ave Reine Victoria, F-06000 Nice Tel: (93) 810326
Parent Company: Société d'Etudes Juridiques Internationales et Fiscales (JURIF)
Subjects: European Taxation Systems, Fiscal Law, Economics, Social Science (embraced in 3 separate series and 1 periodical)
1977: 8 titles *Founded:* 1968

Editions **Calmann-Lévy** Sàrl+*, 3 rue Auber, F-75009 Paris Tel: (01) 0730802/0735389/7423833 Cable Add: Caledit
Man Dirs: Robert Calmann-Lévy, Alain Oulman; *Sales Dir:* Philippe Cahen; *Publicity & Advertising:* Michèle Truchan; *Rights & Permissions:* Thérèse Scaroni, Suzanne Lescoat
Subjects: General Fiction, Science Fiction, History, Biography, Philosophy, Psychology, Social Sciences, Economics, Practical, Memoirs, Humour, Sport
1977: 51 titles *Founded:* 1836
ISBN Publisher's Prefix: 2-7021

Camugli+, 6 rue de la Charité, Lyon Cedex 1 Tel: (78) 426550 Telex: Camugli 370897F

Editions **Capendu**, 3 rue des Haudriettes, F-75003 Paris Tel: (01) 2721319
Man Dir: J F Capendu
Subject: Juveniles
ISBN Publisher's Prefix: 2-85124

editions andré **casteilla**, see Nouveautés de l'Enseignement

Editions **Casterman**+, 66 rue Bonaparte, F-75006 Paris Tel: (01) 3252005 Telex: 200001 F Edicast
President: Louis-Robert Casterman; *Dir:* Gabriel Chamozzi; *Sales Dir:* Christophe Veyrin-Forrer, Claude Lelan; *Publicity & Advertising:* Christophe Veyrin-Forrer; *Rights & Permissions:* Pierre Servais
Parent Company: Editions Casterman, Belgium (qv)
Branch Offs: 28 rue des Soeurs noires, 7500 Tournai, Belgium; De Morinel 25-29, Dronten, Netherlands
Subjects: Children's Books and Albums, Picture Strips, Religion, Economics, Politics, Practical Living, Urban questions, Architecture, Painting, Photography, Cinema, Music, Poetry, Fiction, Records, Diaries
1977: 130 titles *1978:* 130 titles *Founded:* at Tournai, 1780; in Paris, 1857
ISBN Publisher's Prefix: 2-203

Editions **Catalanes** de Paris*, 18 rue Jobbé-Duval, F-75015 Paris Tel: (01) 2501643
Man Dir: Paul Kipfer; *Sales Dir:* Angeli Castanyer; *Publicity & Advertising, Rights & Permissions:* Romà Planas
Subjects: History, Low-priced Paperbacks, Social Science (in the Catalan language)
Founded: 1969

Catalogue de l'Edition Française*, 9 rue Séguier, F-75006 Paris Tel: (01) 3256170
Man Dir: Serge Ciregna
Subject: Bibliography

Cathasia, see Société d'Edition 'Les Belles Lettres'

Editions **Cedic**+*, 93 ave d'Italie, F-75013 Paris Tel: (01) 5896185/5802562
Man & Sales Dir: François Robineau; *Publicity, Advertising, Rights & Permissions:* François Robineau
Subjects: Low-priced Paperbacks, Education, Mathematics, Secondary Textbooks, Languages
1977: 30 titles *Founded:* 1971
ISBN Publisher's Prefix: 2-7124

Editions **Cèdre***, 40 rue Grégoire-de-Tours, F-75006 Paris Tel: (01) 6339328
Man Dir: Bernard Dermineur
Subjects: History, Nonfiction, Encyclopaedias, Juveniles
Founded: 1976

Centre d'Etude et de Promotion de la Lecture, see C E P L

Editions du **Centre d'Etudes et de Documentation** Scientifiques (CEDS Editions)+*, 95 bis Ave Foch, F-76290 Montivilliers Tel: (35) 300527 Telex: 190406F
Dir: Mme A Huard; *Literary Dir:* Dr G Mathieu
Subjects: Science & Technology, Nature & Health, Humour, Practical guides
ISBN Publisher's Prefix: 2-85256

Centre d'Etudes et Fabrication Arts Graphiques (CEFAG)+*, 153 rue de Grenelle, F-75007 Paris Tel: (01) 7055105
Subjects: Religion, Audio Visual
Founded: 1958

Centre de Documentation Universitaire et Société d'Edition d'Enseignement Supérieur Réunis (CDU & SEDES)+*, 5 pl de la Sorbonne, F-75005 Paris Tel: (01) 3252323
Subjects: History, Philosophy, Social Science, Science & Technology, Economics, Education, School Books, Fiction, Literature, Psychology, Maps
Founded: 1933
ISBN Publisher's Prefix: 2-202

Centre national d'Art et de Culture Georges Pompidou+*, F-75191 Paris cedex 04 Tel: 2771233/2336178
President: Jean Millier; *Production:* Jean Seyrig; *Sales:* Marcel Lefranc
Orders to: Editions Flammarion, 27 rue Racine 75006, Paris (qv)
Subjects: Art (Modern Art, Contemporary Painting, Sculpture, Drawings, Photography); Industrial Design (Architecture, Environment, Urbanism); Musical and Acoustic Research (Modern Music, Music Composition); Various
1976: 14 titles *1977:* 40 titles
ISBN Publisher's Prefix: 2-85850

Centre national de la Recherche Scientifique, see CNRS

Editions du Centurion+, 17 rue de Babylone, F-75007 Paris Tel: (01) 2229315/5484417
Man Dir: Hervé Lauriot Prevost; *Editorial and Production:* Charles Ehlinger; *Sales:* Annie Valaise; *Publicity and Advertising:* Clotilde Manoury; *Rights and Permissions:* Magdeleine Leblanc
Orders to: Sofedis, 29 rue Saint Sulpice, F-75006 Paris
Parent Company: Bayard-Presse (qv)
Subjects: Religion, Juveniles, Social Sciences, General & Social Science, Paperbacks, How-to, Education
1978: 88 titles *1979:* 95 titles *Founded:* 1870
ISBN Publisher's Prefix: 2-227

Cepadues Editions (C E P A D) SA, 111 rue Nicolas Vauquelin, F-31300 Toulouse Tel: (61) 405736 Telex: message 520987F
Man Dir: Guy Collin
Subjects: Scientific, Technical, Data Processing
1978: 15 titles *1979:* 12 titles *Founded:* 1969
ISBN Publisher's Prefix: 2-85428

Editions Cercle d'Art SA+, 90 rue du Bac, F-75007 Paris Tel: (01) 5442890
Man Dir: Paul Labergère
Subjects: Art, History
1978: 8 titles *Founded:* 1950
ISBN Publisher's Prefix: 2-7022

Editions du Cerf+, 29 blvd La Tour Maubourg, F-75007 Paris cedex 07 Tel: (01) 5503407 Cable Add: Edicerf
General Dir: M Houssin; *Man Dir:* J Kopf; *Editorial Dir:* F Refoulé; *Sales Dir:* J Mignon; *Publicity & Advertising:* Mrs L Rossi; *Rights & Permissions:* Mrs F de Chasse
Subjects: Religion, History, Philosophy, Juveniles, Social Science, Paperbacks, Reference, Textbooks, Crafts, Psychology, Economics
Founded: 1929
ISBN Publisher's Prefix: 2-204

Editions R **Chaix**, 1 rue de Fleurus, F-75006 Paris Tel: 5444111/5485124
Man Dir, Rights & Permissions: J-Y Vincent; *Editorial:* R Chaix; *Sales:* J Farge
Subjects: Leisure pursuits, Practical
Founded: 1977

Editions du Chalet+, 8 rue Madame, F-75006 Paris Tel: (078) 252343
Subjects: Roman Catholic Devotional, Liturgical, Catechisms; Pictures and Posters
Orders to: (France) Begedis, 77 rue de Vaugirard, F-75006 Paris Tel: 5487860; (Foreign) Arc-en-Ciel International, 11 rue Barthélemy Frison, B-7500 Tournai, Belgium
1978: 24 titles *Founded:* 1946
ISBN Publisher's Prefix: 2-7023

Editions **Champ Libre**, 13 rue de béarn, F-75003 Paris Tel: (01) 2722700/2723480
Subjects: Classics, History, Social Science, Literature, Modern Theory
1978: 12 titles *Founded:* 1970
ISBN Publisher's Prefix: 2-85184

Librairie des **Champs-Elysées** SA+, 10 rue Marignan, F-75008 Paris Tel: (01) 3596616
Man Dir: Christian Poninski
Imprints: Le Masque, Club des Masques
Subjects: Several fiction series dealing exclusively with one theme; viz: Westerns; Science Fiction; Crime and Police Novels (Editions Le Masque, Club des Masques)
1977: 167 titles *Founded:* 1927
ISBN Publisher's Prefix: 2-7024

Chancerel Editions SA, 4 rue Aumont Thiéville, F-75017 Paris Tel: (01) 7660302 Telex: 640093 CHANCED F
Chairman: Philippe Chancerel; *Publisher, Manager:* Jean-Marie Ide; *Sales:* Patrick Erhard; *Production:* Claude Blanc
Associate Company: Chancerel Publishers Ltd, UK (qv)
Subjects: Educational strip cartoons; Sport; Hobbies; Homecraft; (in French and other European languages)
1977: 15 titles *1978:* 15 titles *Founded:* 1960
ISBN Publishers' Prefix: 2-85429

Les Editions **Chantereine**, 13 rue Saint-Georges, F-75009 Paris Tel: 2806118
Subjects: Do-it-Yourself Encyclopaedia
Miscellaneous: Imprint of Les Editions de l'Illustration Baschet et Cie (qv)

Editions du **Chêne**+, 40 rue du Cherche-Midi, F-75006 Paris Tel: (01) 2222852 Telex: 250302 Paris
Man Dir, Editorial, Rights & Permissions: Georges Herscher; *Sales, Publicity:* Anne de Margerie
Orders to: Groupe International Hachette, 254 blvd Saint-Germain, F-75006 Paris
Parent Company: Librairie Hachette (qv)
Subjects: Ancient, Graphic and Contemporary Art, Architecture, Photography, Cinema, Documentaries
1978: 49 titles *1979:* 37 titles *Founded:* 1939
ISBN Publisher's Prefix: 2-85108

Le **Cherche-Midi**, Éditeur+, 110 rue du Cherche-Midi, F-75006 Paris Tel: (01) 2227120
Dirs: Louis Aldebert, Jean Breton, Michel Breton, Jean Orizet; *Publicity:* Philippe Heracles
Subjects: Belles Lettres, Poetry, Paperbacks
1978: 5 titles *Founded:* 1978
Miscellaneous: Managing company responsible for Editions Saint-Germain-des-Près SA (qv)

Editions du **Chiendent** Sarl*, Marcevol Vinça F-66320 (Eastern Pyrenees) Tel: (68) 051263
Man Dir: Xavier d'Arthuys; *Sales:* Blandine Renauld; *Production:* Sophie d'Arthuys
Orders to: Blandine Renaud, 14 rue de Nanteuil, F-75015 Paris
Subjects: 4 series deal generally with (1) people in conflict with events; (2) man's conflict with his apparent destiny; (3) Eastern Pyrenees regional; (4) writings by children
1977: 2 titles *Founded:* 1977
ISBN Publisher's Prefix: 2-85999001

Editions de **Chiré**, an imprint of Diffusion de la Pensée Française (qv)

itions **Chiron**+*, 40 rue de Seine, F-75006 Paris Tel: (01) 6331893
Chairman: DeFerrando-Dufort; *Promotion & Marketing:* Henri Sinniger
Subjects: Education, Juveniles, Sports, Science & Technical
Founded: 1907
ISBN Publisher's Prefix: 2-7027

Chotard et Associés, Editeurs, 1 rue Garancière, F-75006 Paris Tel: (01) 2338065
Man Dir: Yvon Chotard; *Sales Dir:* Jacques Chapellon; *Rights & Permissions:* Anne Chotard
Orders to: 33 rue Beauregard, F-75002 Paris
Subjects: Psychology, Engineering, Social Science, University Textbooks, Educational Material
1977: 10 titles *1978:* 3 titles *Founded:* 1969
Miscellaneous: Firm is a subsidiary of Editions France Empire, 68 rue Jean-Jacques Rousseau, F-75001 Paris
ISBN Publisher's Prefix: 2-7127

Editions de la **Chronique** des Lettres Françaises+*, 33 rue de Verneuil, F-75007 Paris Tel: (01) 6477641
Editorial: Georges G Place; *Sales:* Mrs P Place
Orders to: 12 rue Pierre et Marie Curie, F-75005 Paris
Parent Company: Chronique des Lettres Françaises
Associate Company: Editions Jean-Michel Place (qv)
Subjects: Academic (Ancient and Modern), Bibliographies
1977: 2 titles *Founded:* 1922
ISBN Publisher's Prefix: 2-85185

Librairie Armand **Colin**+*, 103 blvd St-Michel, F-75005 Paris Tel: (01) 3291219 Cable Add: Arcolin Paris 91
Man Dir: Jean-Max Leclerc; *Sales Dir:* Rémy Bourrelier; *Publicity & Advertising:* Yvette Dardenne; *Rights & Permissions:* Michel Couché
Subjects: History, Philosophy, Reference, Psychology, Engineering, General & Social Science, University, Secondary & Primary Textbooks, Educational Materials
1977: 80 titles *Founded:* 1870
ISBN Publisher's Prefix: 2-200

Editions **Comindus**+*, 1 rue Descombes, F-75017 Paris Tel: (01) 3807916
Subject: Trade Annuals
Miscellaneous: Associate company of SEAP (Société d'Edition d'Annuaires Professionnels), Paris (qv)

Compagnie d'Editions Libres, Sociales et Economiques, see C E L S E

Compagnie Française d'Editions SA+*, 40 rue du Colisée, F-75008 Paris Tel: (01) 2961285
Subjects: Science & Technical

94 FRANCE

Le **Concours** Médical+, 37 rue de Bellefond, F–75009 Paris Tel: (01) 2850536
Subject: Medicine

Coopérative Régionale de l'Enseignement Religieux (CRER)+*, 7 rue du Parvis St–Maurice, BP 230, F–49003 Angers cedex Tel: 884695
Subject: Religion

Copernic, 13 rue Charles Lecocq, F–75737 Paris cedex 15 Tel: (01) 8888887
Man Dir: Jean-Claude Valla; *Sales:* Guy Devautoir; *Production, Rights & Permissions:* Gérard Landry; *Publicity:* Chantal de Chanterac
Associate Companies: Nouvelle École, Publeditec
Subjects: History, Documentary, Modern Thought, Philosophy/Religion, Myth and Fantasy
1978: 13 titles *1979:* 20 titles *Founded:* 1976
ISBN Publisher's Prefix: 2–85984

Courrier du Livre Sàrl+, 21 rue de Seine, F–75006 Paris Tel: (01) 3541891
Subjects: Philosophy, Religion, Ecology, Health and Nutrition, Organic Gardening, Yoga
ISBN Publisher's Prefix: 2–7029

Editions de la **Courtille***, 26 rue de Gramont, F–75002 Paris Tel: (01) 0738725/6 Telex: 27618
Man Dir: Denise Drouin; *Editorial:* André Rossel; *Sales, Rights & Permissions:* Denise Drouin; *Production:* André Casteilla; *Publicity:* Katia Favard
Associate Company: Editions Hier et Demain (qv)
Subjects: Biography, History, High-priced Paperbacks, Educational Materials, Collectors' Editions, Practical Guides, Encyclopedias
1977: 23 titles *Founded:* 1971
ISBN Publisher's Prefix: 2–1207

Editeurs **Crépin-Leblond** et Cie SA+, 12 rue Duguay-Trouin, F–75006 Paris Tel: (01) 5489350
Man Dir: Mrs A R Henry; *Sales:* Denise Bechu; *Publicity:* E–G Souquet
Subjects: Hunting, Shooting, Arms, Dogs, Horse-Riding, Nature
1977: 14 titles *1979:* 4 titles *Founded:* 1952
ISBN Publisher's Prefix: 2–7030

Editions **Cujas**+, 4, 6 & 8 rue de la Maison Blanche, F–75013 Paris Tel: (01) 5889657/5888436
Man Dir: Pierre Joly; *Publicity Dir:* Jacqueline Joly
Subjects: Politics, Economics, Education, mainly in France and Francophone countries, Social Sciences
Bookshops: Librairie J Joly, 19 rue Cujas, F–75005 Paris; Cujas Librairie, 2 rue de Rouen, F–92000 Nanterre
1977: 58 titles *1978:* 25 titles *Founded:* 1946
ISBN Publisher's Prefix: 2–254

Culture Art Loisirs/Retz, see CAL/Retz

Editions d'Art — Christophe **Czwiklitzer***, 54 rue Bonaparte, F–75006 Paris Tel: 00331/5049665
Subjects: Bibliophile Editions; Monographs; Bibliographies; Original Graphics; Aesthetics

D A F S A+, 125 rue Montmartre, F–75002 Paris Tel: (01) 2332123
Man Dir: Michel Vieillard
Subjects: Economics, Finance

Les Editions Roger **Dacosta**, 19 blvd Raspail, F–75007 Paris Tel: (01) 5441491
Man Dir: Jean Dacosta; *Sales Dir:* Mrs Stern
Subjects: Medicine, Medical History, Dentistry, Horse-riding, Hunting
1978: 2 titles
ISBN Publisher's Prefix: 2–85128

Jurisprudence Générale **Dalloz**+, 11 rue Soufflot, F–75240 Paris Cedex 05 Tel: (01) 3295080
President, General Manager: Patrice Verge; *Man Dir, Rights & Permissions:* Georges Alapetite; *Financial Dir:* Raymond Sibille; *Editorial, Production:* M Dunes; *Sales:* M Hapiot; *Publicity Dir:* A Stein
Bookshop: Dalloz, 14 rue Soufflot, F–75240 Paris cedex 05
Subjects: Law, Political Science, Reference, Business, Economics, Philosophy
1977: 120 titles *Founded:* 1845
ISBN Publisher's Prefix: 2–247

Editions **Dangles** SA+, 18 rue Lavoisier, BP 36, F–45800 St Jean-de-Braye Tel: (01) 38864180
Man Dir, Editorial, Production, Publicity, Rights & Permissions: J-Y Anstet Dangles; *Sales:* Alain Queant
Subjects: Naturopathy, Esotericism and Spirit Life, Psychology, Physical Culture
1977: 14 titles *1978:* 12 titles *Founded:* 1926
ISBN Publisher's Prefix: 2–7033

Editions **Dardalet** SA+*, 22 rue René-Thomas, F–38000 Grenoble Tel: 961631
Subject: Juveniles

Dargaud Editeur+*, 12 Blaise Pascal, BP 155, F–92201 Neuilly sur Seine Tel: 7471133 Cable Add: Editfranc Neuilly Telex: 62631
Editorial: Michel Greg
Publisher: Georges Dargaud; *Dir:* Louis Olivier; *Rights & Permissions:* Anthéa Shakleton
Subjects: Juveniles, Art, Strip Cartoons, Magazines
ISBN Publisher's Prefix: 2–205

SEF Philippe **Daudy***, rue de la Banque, F–75002 Paris Tel: (01) 2366221 Cable Add: Encybiblio
Subjects: Reference Books
Founded: 1966

Editions du **Dauphin**, 43–45 rue de la Tombe-Issoire, F–75014 Paris Tel: (01) 3277900/3275768
Manager: Anne Tromelin
Subjects: General Fiction, Poetry, Social Science, How-to, Dictionaries, Documentaries, Regional Studies
Founded: 1936
ISBN Publisher's Prefix: 2–7163

Éditions **De Vecchi** SA*, 20 rue de la Trémoille, F–75008 Paris Tel: 2255516
Man Dir: Robert Pinto; *Editorial:* Evelyne Level
Associate Companies: Giovanni De Vecchi Editore SpA, Italy (qv); Editorial De Vecchi SA, Spain (qv)
Subjects: Practical Guides on Legal Questions, Animals, Games, Leisure, Gardening, Health, Mystery, Cookery, History
Founded: 1971
ISBN Publisher's Prefix: 2–85177

Editions **Debard**+*, 17 rue du Vieux-Colombier, F–75006 Paris Tel: (01) 2225415
Subjects: Science & Technical, Encyclopaedias

Nouvelles Editions **Debresse**, 17 rue Duguay-Trouin, F–75006 Paris Tel: (01) 5481047
Man Dir: Pierre Moulin; *Editorial:* Paul Poncelet; *Sales:* Vincent Moulin; *Production, Publicity:* Josiane Muller
Subjects: General Fiction, Poetry, History, Social Science
Founded: 1933

Librairie Générale de l'Enseignement Mme **Decomble**, 4 rue Dante, Paris 5 Tel: (033) 0698
Title denotes: General Educational Publisher
Man Dir and Other Offices: Mrs Decomble
Subject: Botany
1978: 13 titles *1979:* 13 titles *Founded:* 1903

Défense de l'Occident, see Les Sept Couleurs

Editions **Delachaux** et Niestlé SA+*, 32 rue de Grenelle, F–75007 Paris Tel: (01) 2220586
Parent Company: Editions Delachaux et Niestlé, Switzerland (qv)
Subjects: Religion, Medicine, Psychology, Education, Social & Natural Science, Juveniles, Technical, Mathematics, Architecture, Sports
Founded: 1860
ISBN Publisher's Prefix: 2–7178

Librairie **Delagrave** Sàrl+, 15 rue Soufflot, F–75240 Paris cedex 05 Tel: (01) 3258866
Cable Add: Delagrave Paris Telex: 210311F Code 690
Manager: Fabrice Delagrave; *Sales Dir:* J Roustan; *Publicity:* F Simmonet; *Rights & Permissions:* Y Blaise
Subjects: Juveniles, General Science, University, Technical, Secondary & Primary Textbooks, Educational Materials, Languages
1977: 35 titles *1978:* 33 titles *Founded:* 1865
ISBN Publisher's Prefix: 2–206

Jean-Pierre **Delarge** SA+, 10 rue Mayet, F–75006, Paris Tel: 3069636, 7837070
Man Dir: Jean-Pierre Delarge; *Editorial:* Michel Gault; *Sales:* François Chagneau; *Rights & Permissions:* Chantal Galtier Roussel
Subjects: General Nonfiction; especially Popular Reference Works, Juveniles, Cookery, Reportage, Literature, History, Biography, Philosophy, Education, Religion, Games, Sports, Sociology; Paperbacks
1977: 60 titles *Founded:* 1942
ISBN Publisher's Prefix: 27113

Imprimeries **Delmas***, ave du Mirail, Artigues-près-Bordeaux, BP 14, F–33370 Tresses Tel: 863941
Subject: Literature
ISBN Publisher's Prefix: 2–7034

Editions J **Delmas** et Cie+, 13 rue de l'Odéon, F–75006 Paris Tel: (01) 3250832
Man Dir: Jacques Delmas; *Sales, Rights & Permissions:* Charles Hubert de Brantes; *Publicity:* Chantal Boutemy
Subjects: Accountancy, Law, Finance, Management, Insurance, Data Processing, Social and Factory Legislation, Dictionaries
1978: 4 titles *Founded:* 1947
ISBN Publisher's Prefix: 7034

Editions Robert **Delpire** SA*, 9 rue Georges-Pitard, F–75015 Paris Tel: (01) 8426800
Subject: Art
ISBN Publisher's Prefix: 2–85107

Editions **Denoël** Sàrl+, 19 rue de l'Université, F–75007 Paris Tel: (01) 2615085
Cable Add: EDEPEGE
Man Dir: Albert Blanchard; *Rights & Permissions:* Thérèse MaireSE
Parent Company: Editions Gallimard (qv)

Associate Company: Mercure de France (qv)
Subsidiary Company: Société Nouvelle des Editions Gonthier Sarl (qv)
Subjects: General and Science Fiction, Art, Reference, Sports, Documents, Political Science, Economics, De Luxe Editions
1977: 121 titles *1978:* 133 titles
ISBN Publisher's Prefix: 2-207

Editions **Desclée** et Cie+, 77 rue de Vaugirard, F-75006 Paris Tel: (01) 5487860 Telex: 202036 Blougay
Man Dir: Marcel Vervaet
Parent Company: Gedit SA, Tournai, Belgium (qv)
Associate Companies: Desclée Editeurs SA, Tournai, Belgium (qv); Editions Gamma, Paris (qv); Nouvelles Editions Mame, Paris (qv)
Subjects: History, Philosophy, Religion, Social Science
1977: 45 titles *1978:* 50 titles *Founded:* 1872
ISBN Publisher's Prefix: 2-7189

Desclée, De Brouwer SA+*, 76 bis, rue des Saints-Pères, F-75007 Paris Tel: (01) 5440763 Cable Add: Dedebrouw
Man Dir: François-Xavier de Guibert; *Editorial:* Jacques Deschanel; *Sales:* Michel Mugler; *Production:* Gerard Hoeltzel; *Publicity:* Odette Schwartz; *Rights & Permissions:* Yvonne Tomazi
Subjects: Belles Lettres, Poetry, Music, Art, Philosophy, Religion, Low-priced Paperbacks, Medicine, Psychology, Social Science
1977: 60 titles *Founded:* 1875
ISBN Publisher's Prefix: 2-220

Librairie **Desforges***, 27-9 quai des Grands-Augustins, F-75006 Paris Tel: (01) 0336054
Subjects: Technology, Commerce, Management, Education

Dessain et Tolra+, Lethielleux-Seneve Editorial Bouret, 10 rue Cassette, F-75006 Paris Tel: (01) 2229020
Man Dir: P Zech; *Rights & Permissions:* Mrs F Desgrandchamps, Mrs F Houssin
Subjects: Children's and Young Adults' books, Handcrafts and Do-it-yourself, Pastoral works and Catechisms
ISBN Publisher's Prefix: 2-249

Librairie André **Desvigne**+*, 53-54 Quai Pierre Scize, F-69321 Lyon cedex 1 Tel: (078) 286374
President: André Desvigne
Orders to: Ed André Desvigne, 6 bis rue de l'Abbaye, Paris 6
Subject: School Books, Higher Grade education
ISBN Publisher's Prefix: 2-7037

Les Editions des **Deux Coqs d'Or***, 28 rue de la Boétie, F-75008 Paris Tel: (01) 2561052 Cable Add: Deucodo Paris Telex: 650780
Man Dir: Philip A Jarvis; *Publicity & Advertising:* Claude Gille; *Rights & Permissions:* Regine Crowett
Subjects: Art, How-to, Juveniles, Reference, Paperbacks
Founded: 1949
Book Clubs: Education & Culture; Presses d'Or
ISBN Publisher's Prefix: 2-7192

La Maison du **Dictionnaire**, see Maison

John **Didier** Editions*, 1 rue des Chailles, F-92500 Roeil Malmaison Tel: 7514545 Telex: 25303 Service Didier 7227010 Cable Add: Johndid Neuillyseine
Man Dir & Editor: John Didier; *Assistant Editor:* Barbara Lyon; *Sales Dir:* C Perrin; *Advertising Dir:* R Mercier; *Publicity Dir:* L Meynier; *Rights & Permissions:* Miss R Camus
Subjects: Fiction, Nonfiction, General Trade, Belles Lettres, Biography, History, Theses, How-to, Art, Philosophy, Religion, Juveniles
Bookshop: The American Bookshop (at above address)
Founded: 1962

Librairie Marcel **Didier** SA+*, 15 rue Cujas, F-75005 Paris Tel: (01) 3292133
Associate Companies: Editions Marcel Didier SA, Belgium (qv); Didier Canada, Montreal
Subjects: Education, Audio Visual and Electronic Media
ISBN Publisher's Prefix: 2-208

Editions **Didier et Richard***, 9 Grande Rue, BP 137, F-38019 Grenoble cedex Tel: (076) 441286
Man Dir: Jacques Harel; *Sales:* F J Bach
Subjects: Cartography, Regional Literature
Bookshop: Librairie Didier & Richard, 9 Grande Rue, F-38000 Grenoble 51
Founded: 1924
ISBN Publisher's Prefix: 2-7038

Société **Didot-Bottin** SA+, 28 rue du Docteur Finlay, F-75738 Paris cedex 15 Tel: (01) 5786166 Telex: 204286F
Bookshop: at above address
Subjects: Encyclopaedias and Annuals concerning Business, Trades, International Commerce and Touring, French Administration, Transport, Motor Cycling etc.
Founded: 1796
ISBN Publisher's Prefix: 2-7039

Diffusion de la Pensée Française, Chiré-en-Montreuil, F-86190 Vouillé Tel: (049) 518304
Man Dir: Jean Auguy; *Publicity Dir:* Jean Sechet
Imprint: Editions de Chiré
Subjects: History, Social Science, Counter-revolution, Religion
1977: 5 titles *1978:* 7 titles *Founded:* 1966
Miscellaneous: Publish literary journal *Lecture et Tradition*, political journal *Lectures Françaises*

Editions **La Diffusion Scientifique**+*, 156 rue Lamarck, F-75018 Paris Tel: (01) 6270160
Subject: Literature
ISBN Publisher's Prefix: 2-85012

Société de **Documentation et d'Analyses** Financières, see D A F S A

La **Documentation Française** (Published by the Government General Secretary's Office), 29-31 quai Voltaire, F-75340 Paris cedex 07 Tel: (01) 2615010 Telex: 204826 DOCFRAN Paris
Man Dir: Jean-Louis Cremieux-Brilhac
Subjects: Reprints of documents and official reports bearing on French and Foreign Politics, Economics, Regional Administration, Environment, Social Problems, Science and Technology, Law, the Arts, Official Announcements; 40 Periodicals
Bookshops: 29-31 quai Voltaire, F-75007 Paris; 165 rue Garibaldi, F-69401 Lyons
Founded: 1945
Miscellaneous: Publishing House for the National Archives Administration, also comprises a library, a bookshop, a photographic library and an information service (all at the above address)
ISBN Publisher's Prefix: 2-86000

Doin Editeurs+, 8 pl de l'Odéon, F-75006 Paris Tel: (01) 3268650
Man Dir: M Abadie
Subjects: Medicine, Psychology, General & Social Science, University Textbooks
1978: 35 titles *Founded:* 1874
ISBN Publisher's Prefix: 2-7040

Domino*, 22 rue de l'Echiquier, 75010 Paris
Dirs: Jean Chapelle, Humbert Rusconi

Doubleday-France, 9 rue du Pré-Aux-Clercs, Paris 7 Tel: 2611898/2611899 Cable Add: Doubday Paris
Business Manager: Véronique Poderzay; *Editorial:* Beverly Gordey; *Rights & Permissions:* Ruth Grossman
Parent Company: Doubleday & Co, Inc, 245 Park Ave, New York, NY 10017, USA
Associate Company: Doubleday & Co, Inc, UK
Founded: 1959 (Doubleday-France)

Draeger Editeur+*, 46 rue de Bagneux, F-92120 Montrouge Tel: 6571154 Telex: 270294F
Man Dir: Claude Draeger
Subjects: Art, Architecture, Documents, Biography, De Luxe Editions
1977: 4 titles
ISBN Publisher's Prefix: 2-85119

Dragon's Dream Ltd, formerly of Paris, now in Netherlands (qv)

Droguet et Ardant+*, 41 rue Henri Giffard, BP 1010, F-87004 Limoges 57 cedex Tel: (055) 374306 Telex: 580934
Man Dir: Robert Ardant; *Publicity Dir:* Suzanne Pasteau
Subjects: R C Devotional; the Mass, Bibles, Prayer Books, Catechisms
1978: 10 titles
ISBN Publisher's Prefix: 2-7041

Librairie Générale de **Droit et de Jurisprudence**+, 20 rue Soufflot, F-75005 Paris Tel: (01) 0330719
Man Dirs: Françoise Marty, Jacqueline Hebert; *Sales Manager, Rights & Permissions:* Guy Hamonic
Subjects: Social Science, Law, University Textbooks, Jurisprudence
Bookshop: LGDJ, 24 rue Soufflot, Paris
Founded: 1836
ISBN Publisher's Prefix: 2-275

Dunod, see Bordas

Maison d'Editions J **Dupuis** Fils et Cie SA+, 8 rue Bellini, F-75008 Paris Tel: (01) 7277280
Subjects: Juveniles, Literature

G **Durassié** et Cie Sàrc*, 162 ave Pierre-Brossolette, F-92240 Malakoff Tel: 2535940
Dir: G Durassié
Subjects: Science & Technical
Founded: 1922
ISBN Publisher's Prefix: 2-85013

E P A, 83 rue de Rennes, F-75006 Paris Tel: (01) 6090005 Telex: 202891F
Man Dir, Editorial, Sales, Publicity, Rights & Permissions: Arnauld de Fouchier; *Production:* Gilles Blanchet
Orders to: E P A, 18 rue d'Issy, F-92100 Boulogne Billancourt
Parent Company: E T A I, 20-22 rue de la Saussière, F-92100 Boulogne Billancourt
Subjects: Aviation, Automobile, Railways, Military, Marine Interest, Photographic, Historical
Bookshops: 83 rue de Rennes, Paris 6; 92 rue Saint Lazare, Paris 9; 18 rue de

96 FRANCE

l'Ancienne Préfecture, Lyon
1978: 20 titles *1979:* 25 titles *Founded:* 1953
ISBN Publisher's Prefix: 2-85120

Editions **E S F** (Editions Sociales
Françaises)+, 17 rue Viète, F-75854 Paris
cedex 17 Tel: (01) 9246876/2275383/227901
President: Gérard Didier; *Man Dir:* Claude
Chichet; *Sales Dir:* Michel Henry
Subsidiary Company: Entreprise Moderne
d'Edition (qv)
Subjects: Education, Re-education,
Pedagogy, Problems of Handicapped
Children, Psychology, Social Problems and
Legislation, Health and Nutrition
Bookshop: sales from SABRI, 292 rue Saint-
Jacques, F-75005 Paris
1978: 20 titles *Founded:* 1928
ISBN Publisher's Prefix: 2-7101

E T P (Editions Techniques Professionnelles
et Régies Audiovisuelles)+*, 31 ave Pierre-
1er de Serbie, F-75784 Paris cedex 16
Tel: (01) 7236158/7236161
Subjects: Information Science in Business,
Management and Marketing, International
Relations

E T S F, see **Editions** Techniques et
Scientifiques Françaises

L'**Ecole**/L'Ecole des Loisirs+, 11 rue de
Sèvres, F-75006 Paris Tel: (01) 2229410
Cable Add: Librecole
Man Dir: Jean Fabre; *Export Sales
Manager:* H Doulmet; *Rights and
Permissions, Publicity and Advertising:* Jean
Delas
Subjects: Juveniles, High-priced Paperbacks,
University, Secondary & Primary Textbooks,
Educational Materials
1978: 90 titles
ISBN Publisher's Prefix: 2-211

Edhis, see Histoire Sociale

Les Editions **Edilec** SA*, 9 ave Robert
Schuman, F-75007 Paris Tel:
5556917/7055043 Telex: 22064F Ext 5506
Subjects: Encyclopaedias, Medicine,
Psychology, Education, Law, Economics

Ediscience, see McGraw-Hill Inc

Edisud*, La Calade, RN 7, F-13100 Aix-en-
Provence Tel: (42) 244135
Man Dir: Charles-Yves Chaudoreille; *Sales,
Production:* C-Y Chaudoreille; *Publicity:*
Anne-Marie Paolantonacci; *Rights &
Permissions:* C-Y Chaudoreille
Associate Company: Editions Marrimpouey
Jeune, 2 pl de la Libération F-64000 PAU
Subjects: Ecology, Agriculture, History,
Geography, Regional Interest (Provence);
General Topics
1977: 15 titles *Founded:* 1971
ISBN Publisher's Prefix: 2-85744

Société **Editart** Quatre Chemins*, 3 pl
St-Sulpice, F-75006 Paris Tel: (01)
0334073 Cable Add: Waledit
Dir: Mme A Gabrilovitch
Bookshop: Librairie des Quatre Chemins
Editart 3, Place St-Sulpice, Paris 6e
Subject: Art
Founded: 1924

Les **Editeurs Français** Réunis+, 21 rue de
Richelieu, F-75001 Paris Tel: (01) 2961410
General Dir: Madeleine Braun; *Man Dir:* Mr
Aragon; *Literary Dir:* Rouben Melik
Subjects: Belles Lettres, Theatre, Cinema,
Poetry, Novels, History, Paperbacks,
Fiction, Nonfiction, Art, Music
Founded: 1944
Miscellaneous: Publish literary review
Europe
ISBN Publisher's Prefix: 2-201

Les **Editeurs Réunis***, 11 rue de la
Montagne-Sainte-Geneviève, F-75005 Paris
Tel: (01) 6337446/0334381
Subjects: The company acts as sole agent for
YMCA Press (qv), Bradda Books and
Prideaux Press in publishing a very
comprehensive list of Russian books in the
original Russian

Les **Editions Internationales***, 47 rue
St-André-des-Arts, F-75006 Paris Tel: (01)
3267781
Subject: Political Science

Editions Maritimes et d'Outre-Mer SA+, 17
rue Jacob, F-75006 Paris Tel: (01) 3290620
Telex: 270461
Man Dir: Nicole Lattès
Subjects: General Fiction, Art, History,
How-to, Education, Juveniles, Science and
Technology, Geography, Ethnography,
Marine, Colonial Literature
Founded: 1839
Bookshops: Librairie EMOM, 17 rue Jacob,
F-75006 Paris
ISBN Publisher's Prefix: 2-7070

Editions Modernes Média*, 21 rue du
Cardinal-Lemoine, F-75005 Paris Tel: (01)
3268384
Subjects: Philosophy, Linguistics, Literature
ISBN Publisher's Prefix: 83398

Les **Editions Mondiales** SA+*, 2 rue des
Italiens, F-75009 Paris Tel: (01) 8244621
Cable Add: Editomondiales
Dir: Cino del Duca
Subjects: General Fiction, How-to, History,
Juveniles, Literature, Education, Philosophy,
Languages
Founded: 1932
ISBN Publisher's Prefix: 2-7074

Les **Editions Sociales**+, 146 rue du
Faubourg-Poissonnière, F-75010 Paris
Tel: (01) 2805225 Telex: 226 CDLP
Man Dir: Lucien Seve; *Editorial:* Richard
Lagache, Nicole Konopnicki; *Publicity,
Rights & Permissions:* Cecile Botlan
Orders to: Odeon Diffusion (at above
address)
Subjects: Philosophy, Social Science,
Politics, Literature, Education, Languages,
Economics
Book Club: Livre Club Diderot
Bookshop: Les Librairies de la Renaissance
1978: 50 titles *Founded:* 1920
ISBN Publisher's Prefix: 2-209

Editions Sociales Françaises, see E S F

Editions Techniques SA+, 123 rue d'Alésia,
F-75680 Paris cedex 14 Tel: (01) 5392291
Telex: Editec 270737F; 18 rue Séguier,
F-75006 Paris Tel: (01) 3292130
Man Dir: Philippe Durieux; *Assistant Dir:*
Robert Turberg; *Export Sales Dir:* J P
Chamoux
Subjects: Law, Medicine, Engineering,
University Textbooks, Encyclopaedias
Founded: 1907
ISBN Publisher's Prefix: 2-7110

Editions Techniques et Scientifiques França
+, 2-12 rue de Bellevue, F-75940 Paris
cedex 19 Tel: 2003305 Telex: PGV
230472F
Man Dir: Jean-Pierre Ventillard; *Editorial,
Sales, Production, Publicity:* Georges
Rochereau
Subjects: Technical books dealing with
radio, television, electronics and associated
themes: Periodicals on same subjects at
popular and professional level
1977: 30 titles *1978:* 35 titles

Editions Techniques Professionnelles, see
E T P

Les **Editions Universelles** Sàrl*, 140 blvd
St-Germain, F-75006 Paris Tel: (01)
3267382
Subjects: Literature, Medicine, Philosophy

Editions Universitaires-Éditions du Jour SA,
now Éditions Jean Pierre Delarge SA

Alfred **Eibel**, éditeur, Montparnasse-
Diffusion, 30 Blvd Sebastopol, F-75003
Paris Tel: (01) 2776661
President, Editorial, Rights & Permissions:
Alfred Eibel; *Sales:* Michel Ferloni;
Production, Publicity: Claude Schmitt
Orders to: Montparnasse-Diffusion, at same
address
Parent Company: Alfred Eibel, Editeur, 7
rue de Genève, CH-1002 Lausanne,
Switzerland
Associate Company: Claude Schmitt, 195
bis rue Raymond Losserand, F-75014 Paris
Subsidiary Companies: Editions L'Age
d'Homme, Switzerland (qv); Nouvelle
Diffusion, Belgium (qv); Agenzia Libraria
Salvatore Fozzi, 72-76 Via Toscana,
I-09100 Cagliari, Italy
Branch Offs: Claude Schmitt Tipografia
Editrice Giovanni Gallizzi, Via Venezia 5,
I-07100 Sassari, Sardinia, Italy
Subjects: China, South-East Asia, Travel,
Literature
Bookshops: Librairie Montparnasse-
Diffusion, 1 Quai de Conti, F-75006 Paris
1978: 10 titles *1979:* 4 titles *Founded:* 1974
ISBN Publisher's Prefix: 2-8274

Editions **Elsevier** Séquoia Sàrl*, 1 rue du 29
Juillet, F-75001 Paris Tel: (01) 2601556
Man Dir: Gabriel Bourdin
Parent Company: Elsevier, Netherlands (qv)
Associate Company: Elsevier Sequoia,
Belgium (qv)
Subjects: History, Reference, Juveniles,
Medicine and Health, Nature, Psychology,
Travel, Family, Sports and Hobbies,
Management, Education, Cookery
1977: 51 titles *Founded:* 1960
Miscellaneous: Firm is a subsidiary of NV
Uitgeversmaatschappij Elsevier,
Netherlands (qv)
ISBN Publisher's Prefix: 2-8003

Encyclopaedia Universalis France SA, 10
rue Vercingétorix, F-750014 Paris Tel:
5394539/5396114 Cable Add: Encyversal
Telex: 220064F Code 3121
President, Man Dir: Mr Baumberger;
Editorial: Mr Bersani; *Sales:* Mr Nepveu;
Production: Mr Schweizer; *Rights &
Permissions:* Mr Rabilloud
Subjects: Encyclopedias, Atlases
1978: 2 titles *1979:* 4 titles *Founded:* 1967
Miscellaneous: Club Français du Livre (qv)
and Encyclopaedia Britannica France are
partners in the distribution of the
Company's publications
ISBN Publisher's Prefix: 2-85229

Librairie Générale de l'**Enseignement** Sàrl*,
4 rue Dante, F-75005 Paris Tel: (01)
0330698
Man Dir: Mrs de Comble
Subjects: Botanical Studies, Bee-keeping;
Periodical: Revue Générale de Botanique
(monthly by subscription)
1977: 13 titles *Founded:* 1903
ISBN Publisher's Prefix: 2-85022

Editions **Entente**+, 12 rue Honoré-
Chevalier, F-75006 Paris Tel: (01) 2228070
Man Dir: Edouard Esmerian
Subjects: Ecology, Economics, Third World,
Essays, Monographs on Minorities,

Documentary Accounts, Novels etc
Bookshop: Librairie Entente, 12 rue Honoré Chevalier, F-75006 Paris
1979: 44 titles *Founded:* 1975
ISBN Publisher's Prefix: 2-7266

Entreprise Moderne d'Edition+, 17 rue Viète, F-75854 Paris cedex 17 Tel: 9246876
President: Gérard Didier; *Sales Manager:* Michel Henry
Parent Company: Editions E S F (qv)
Subjects: all aspects of Business Management; Personnel Training and Management; Data Processing; Technology; Periodicals
1979: 25 titles *Founded:* 1953
Miscellaneous: The merger between Entreprise Moderne and E S F dates from July 1979
ISBN Publisher's Prefix: 2-7043

Les Editions de l'**Epargne**+, 174 blvd St-Germain, F-75280 Paris cedex 06 Tel: (01) 5482452
Man Dir: René Laurent
Subjects: Investment, Savings Banks, Economy and Finance, Family Budgets, aspects of Law, Penal Codes
1977-78: 11 titles
ISBN Publisher's Prefix: 2-85015

Epi SA Editeurs+*, 68 rue de Babylone, F-75007 Paris Tel: (01) 5552554
Manager & Sales Dir: Yvon Paya; *Editorial, Sales, Production, Publicity:* Jean Boutry; *Rights & Permissions:* Anna-Marie Coquier
Subjects: History, Philosophy, Religion, Yoga, Juveniles, Psychoanalysis, Social Science
1977: 42 titles *Founded:* 1947
ISBN Publisher's Prefix: 2-7045

Publications **Estoup et Roy** Sàrl+*, 47 rue du Château-des-Rentiers, F-75013 Paris Tel: (01) 4028550
Subject: Education
ISBN Publisher's Prefix: 2-85016

Etudes Augustiniennes+*, 8 rue François-1er, F-75008 Paris Tel: (01) 2258337
Man Dir: Georges Folliet
Subjects: Theology and Church History, especially in relation to Saint Augustine; the Works of Saint Augustine
1977: 5 titles *1978:* 7 titles *Founded:* 1954
ISBN Publisher's Prefix: 2-85121

Eurédif (Société Européenne d'Edition et de Diffusion)+, 2 bis rue de la Baume, F-75008 Paris Tel: 2561480/2561559 Cable Add: Euredif
Man Dir: Guy Cécille; *Sales, Publicity, Rights & Permissions:* Marc Schweizer
Subjects: General Fiction, Low-priced Paperbacks
1978: 600 titles *Founded:* 1969
ISBN Publisher's Prefix: 2-7167

L'**Expansion** Scientifique Française+, 15 rue St-Benoît, F-75006 Paris Tel: (01) 2603950
Man Dir: Pierre Bergeaud
Subject: Medicine
Bookshop: Librairie des Facultés de Médécine et de Pharmacie, 174 blvd St-Germain, F-75006 Paris
1978: 40 titles *1979:* 40 titles *Founded:* 1925
ISBN Publisher's Prefix: 2-7046

Éditions **Eyrolles**+, 61 blvd St-Germain, F-75240 Paris cedex 05 Tel: (01) 3292199
Man Dir: Claude Schoedler; *Editorial:* Lucien Tournier
Subsidiary Company: Les Editions d'Organisation (qv)
Subjects: Comprehensive series covering Physical Sciences, Earth Sciences, Electricity, Mechanics, Transport, Building and Architecture, Agriculture, Management and Industry, the Arts, Sports and Hobbies
Bookshop: Librairie de l'Enseignement Technique, 61 blvd St-Germain, F-75240 Paris cedex 05
1977: 84 titles *1978:* 100 titles (incl reprints) *Founded:* 1918
ISBN Publisher's Prefix: 2-212

Editions La **Farandole**+, 11 bis rue de la Planche, F-75007 Paris Tel: (01) 5489529
Dir: Ghilaine Povinha
Subject: Juveniles
Founded: 1955
ISBN Publisher's Prefix: 2-7047

Librairie Arthème **Fayard**+*, 75 rue des Saints-Pères, F-75006 Paris Tel: (01) 5443845
Man Dir: Alex Grall; *Sales Dir:* Bernard Clesca; *Publicity Dir:* Marylène Bellenger; *Advertising Dir:* Claude Danis; *Rights & Permissions:* Josette Wittorski
Subjects: General Fiction, Belles Lettres, Poetry, Biography, History, Religion, Medicine, Social Science
Founded: 1854
ISBN Publisher's Prefix: 2-213

Des **Femmes***, 68 rue de Saint-Pères, F-75007 Paris Tel: (01) 2220208
Subjects: General Fiction, Essays, Documents, Belles Lettres, Poetry, Biography, Juveniles, Low-priced Paperbacks
Bookshops: Librairie 'Des Femmes', 2 pl des Célestins, Lyon 2; Librairie 'Des Femmes', 35 rue Pavillon, F-13006 Marseille; Librairie 'Des Femmes', 68 rue des Sts-Pères, F-75007 Paris
1978: 120 titles *Founded:* 1974
ISBN Publisher's Prefix: 2-7210

Groupe **Femmes d'aujourd'hui***, 14 Blvd de la Madeleine, F-75008 Paris Tel: (01) 2665171 Cable Add: Parisgraph Telex: 680200 Fer-Sen
Subjects: Domestic Crafts, Medicine, Bible
ISBN Publisher's Prefix: 2-87024

La **Fenêtre** Ouverte SA*, 3 rue de la Rochefoucauld, F-75008 Paris Tel: (01) 8745844
Subject: Literature

Editions du **Feu** Nouveau, 8 ave César-Caire, F-75380 Paris cedex 08 Tel: (01) 2257305
Subjects: Religion, Literature
Founded: 1946
ISBN Publisher's Prefix: 2-85017

Editions **Filipacchi**+, 63 Champs Elysées, F-75008 Paris Tel: (01) 3590179 Cable Add: JazMag Telex: UEM 29294
Sales, Publicity, Rights & Permissions: Anne-Marie Périer
Subjects: Art, General Fiction, How-to, Juveniles; Paperbacks
Founded: 1970
ISBN Publisher's Prefix: 2-85018

Firmin-Didot et Cie+*, 56 rue Jacob, F-75006 Paris Tel: (01) 5440026
Subjects: General Literature, History, Art, Language
ISBN Publisher's Prefix: 2-7196

Editions **Fiscado**+*, 7 rue Godot-de-Mauroy, F-75009 Paris Tel: (01) 0735004
Subject: Education

Librairie **Fischbacher**, International Art Book Distribution (import-export), 33 rue de Seine, F-75006 Paris Tel: (01) 3268487 Telex: Art & Edition 240896 (Garocie)
Man Dir, Production, Publicity, Rights and Permissions: H Earle-Fischbacher; *Editorial:* M C Galand; *Sales:* P Diani
Parent Company: Librairie Fischbacher SA
Subsidiary Companies: International Art Books Distribution and Office de Documentation Bibliographique et de Diffusion
Subjects: Art, Primitive Art, Architecture, Belles Lettres, Musicology, Philosophy, History, Education, Religion, Juveniles
Bookshop: 33 rue de Seine, F-75006 Paris
1977: 2 titles *1978:* 2 titles
Founded: 1850
ISBN Publisher's Prefix: 2-7179

Flammarion et Cie+, 26 rue Racine, F-75278 Paris Tel: (01) 3291220 Cable Add: Flammedit Telex: 204034F
Man Dirs: Henri Flammarion, Chas-Henri Flammarion; *Export Man:* Pierre-Alain Amiot; *Publicity:* Anne de Cazanova, Charles Rubinsztein, Micheline Amar; *Advertising:* Catherine Bachelez; *Rights & Permissions:* Catherine Cullaz
Subjects: General Fiction, Belles Lettres, Poetry, History, How-to, Art, Philosophy, Reference, Juveniles, Low- & High-priced Paperbacks, Economics, General & Social Science, University Textbooks, Education, Medicine
1977-78: 500 titles *Founded:* 1875
Bookshops: Libraries Flammarion: *France:* in Paris — 5 shops, in Lyons — 3, in Marseilles — 1, in Dijon — 1, in Bordeaux — 1; *Canada:* in Montreal — 7
ISBN Publisher's Prefix: 2-08

Editions **Fleurus** SA+*, 31 rue de Fleurus, F-75280 Paris cedex 06 Tel: (01) 5484995 Telex: 21023 Ogtel Ref 557
Man Dir: Jacques Anfray; *Editorial:* Ms M C Maine, Yves Jolly; *Sales Dir:* Jean Li Sen Lie; *Production:* Gérard Piassale; *Publicity:* Jean Ch Cornet; *Rights & Permissions:* R J Pintigny
Parent Company: Fleurus-Presse, 31 rue de Fleurus, Paris 6e
Subjects: Religion, Psycho-Sociological, Illustrated Children's Albums, Picture strip stories, Technical Manuals
Bookshop: Libraire du Soleil, 45 rue de Vaugirard, Paris 6
1977: 67 titles *Founded:* 1944
ISBN Publisher's Prefix: 2-215

Editions **Fleuve** Noir, 6 rue Garancière, F-75278 Paris cedex 06 Tel: 3292161 Telex: Flenoir 204870 F
Man Dir: Armand de Caro; *Editorial Dir:* Patrick Siry; *Sales Dir:* André de Caro; *Publicity Dir:* Eugène Moineau; *Rights & Permissions:* Jean-Marie Carpentier
Orders to: 35 rue Jean-Jacques Rousseau, F-94200 Ivry
Subjects: General Fiction (especially Crime and Science Fiction), Low-priced Paperbacks
Founded: 1946
Miscellaneous: Firm is a member of the Presses de La Cité group (qv)
ISBN Publisher's Prefix: 2-265

Fondeur d'Aujourd'hui*, 12 ave Raphael, F-75016 Paris Tel: 5047250
Man Dir: Pierre Brunschwig; *Editorial:* Mon Chupeau; *Sales, Production, Publicity, Rights & Permissions:* Mrs Zeilingher
Imprint: Editions Techniques des Industries de la Fonderie
Subject: Foundry technique
1977: 7 titles *Founded:* 1950
ISBN Publisher's Prefix: 7119

98 FRANCE

Les Editions **Foucher**+*, 128 rue de Rivoli, F–75001 Paris Tel: (01) 2363890
Founder-President: Ms Burgod-Foucher; *General Manager:* Bernard Foulon; *Sales Manager:* J C Richard
Subjects: Education, Medicine, Economics, General & Social Science
Founded: 1934
ISBN Publisher's Prefix: 2–216

Editions **France Empire**+*, 68 rue Jean-Jacques Rousseau, F–75001 Paris Tel: (01) 2365235/2332519 Telex: 680126
President, Man Dir: Yvon Chotard; *Editorial:* Herve le Boterf; *Sales Dir:* Jacques Chapellon; *Production:* Pierre Pousset; *Publicity:* Christine Collinet; *Rights & Permissins:* Anne Chotard
Subsidiary companies: Chotard et Associés, Editeurs (qv); Sofedis, 29 rue Saint Sulpice, Paris 6
Br Off: 13 rue des Lombards, F–27000 Evreux
Subjects: Biography, History, Documentary, Religion, Reference, Novels, Aviation, Marine Interest
Book Clubs: Club du Roman Féminin; Club du Livre de Guerre (both at 33 rue Beauregard, F–75002 Paris)
1977: 85 titles *Founded:* 1945

France Expansion+, 15 square de Vergennes, F–75015 Paris Tel: (01) 8281013 Cable Add: Francexpansion Paris Telex: Pubfran 20003 F
President: Jacques Dodeman; *Man Dir:* Pascal Paradis; *Foreign Rights:* Régine Le Meur
Subjects: Bibliography, Reference, Humanities, Linguistics, Management, Teaching French as Foreign Language
1978: 350 titles *Founded:* 1970
Miscellaneous: Publish *Les Livres disponibles* (French Books in Print), in association with the Cercle de la Librairie

France-Loisirs+*, 123 blvd de Crenelle, F–75015 Paris Tel: (01) 5373565
Subjects: Juveniles, Literature, Art

Les Editions **Franciscaines** SA+*, 9 rue Marie-Rose, F–75014 Paris 14e Tel: (01) 5407351/5407659
Imprint: Editions Franciscaines La Cordelle
Subjects: Saint Francis and the Franciscans
ISBN Publisher's Prefix: 2–85020

Le **François***, 91 blvd Saint-Germain, F–75006 Paris Tel: (01) 3265545
Subject: History, Medicine, Science
ISBN Publishers' Prefix: 2–85085

Editions **Fréal***, 4 rue des Beaux Arts, F–75006 Paris Tel: (01) 3265402
Subjects: Art, Architecture

J **Gabalda** et Cie (Librairie Lecoffre) SA+*, 90 rue Bonaparte, F–75006 Paris Tel: (01) 3265355
Proprietor: J Gabalda
Subject: Religion
Founded: 1845
ISBN Publisher's Prefix: 2–85021

Editions **Galilée***, 9 rue Linné, F–75005 Paris Tel: (01) 3312384
Man Dir: Michel Delorme
Subjects: History, Philosophy, Art, Social Science, Economics, Belles Lettres, Poetry, How-to, University Textbooks
Founded: 1971
ISBN Publisher's Prefix: 2–7186

Editions **Gallimard**+*, 5 rue Sébastien-Bottin, F–75007 Paris Tel: (01) 5443919 Cable Add: Enerefene Paris 044 Telex: 204121 Gallim
Man Dir: Claude Gallimard; *Editorial:* François Erval, Pierre Marchaad; *Rights and Permissions:* Ania Chevallier, Monique Poublan
Subjects: General Fiction, Belles Lettres, Poetry, Biography, History, Music, Art, Philosophy, Juveniles
Founded: 1911
Bookshop: Librairie Gallimard, 15 blvd Raspail, F–75007 Paris
Subsidiaries: Editions Denoël (qv); Mercure de France (qv)
ISBN Publisher's Prefix: 2–07

Editions **Gamma**+, 77 rue de Vaugirard, F–75006 Paris Tel: (01) 5487860 Telex: 202036 Blougay
Man Dir: Marcel Vervaet
Parent Company: Gedit SA Tournai, Belgium (qv)
Associated Companies: Desclée Editeurs, Tournai, Belgium (qv); Editions Desclée et Cie, Paris, France (qv); Editions Gamma, Belgium (qv); Nouvelles Editions Mame, Paris, France (qv)
Subjects: Science & Technology, Reference, Social Science, Juveniles, School Books
1977: 75 titles *1978:* 70 titles *Founded:* 1964
ISBN Publisher's Prefix: 2–7130

Imprimerie Librairie **Gardet**+, 16 rue du Pâquier, F–74000 Annecy Tel: (50) 454437
Man Dir: Clément Gardet
Subjects: Arts, Crafts, Hobbies, Educational
1978: 3 titles *Founded:* 1836
ISBN Publisher's Prefix: 2–7049

Éditions **Garnier** Frères+*, BP 168, F–75665 Paris cedex 14 (Located at: 19 rue des Plantes, F–75014 Paris) Tel: (01) 5409815 Telex: 270105 F TXFRA/Ref 665
Man Dir: Bernard Vereano; *Sales Dir:* Bertrand Cantegrit; *Rights & Permissions:* Hubert Deveaux
Subjects: Literary Classics, Juvenile, Strip Cartoons, Art, Travel Pictorial, History, Dictionaries
Founded: 1833

Société **Gauthier-Villars**, 70 rue de Saint-Mandé, F–93100 Montreuil
Parent Company: Editions Bordas, France (qv)
Associate Companies: Société Générale de Diffusion S G E D; Sté Bordas-Dunod, Brussels (Belgium) (qv); Bordas-Dunod-Montreal, Canada (see Editions Bordas)

Les Editions **Gautier-Languereau**+, 18 rue Jacob, F–75006 Paris 6 Tel: (01) 3250751 Cable Add: Editlangue
Man & Sales Dir: Bernard Moreau
Subjects: General Fiction, How-to, Juveniles
1978: 30 titles *Founded:* 1917
ISBN Publisher's Prefix: 2–217

Librairie **Gedalge***, A Wast & Cie, 54 rue des Sts–Pères, F–75006 Paris Tel: (01) 5485379
Subjects: General Fiction, Belles Lettres, Reference, Juveniles, Multi-Media
ISBN Publisher's Prefix: 2–85066

Editions M Th **Genin**, see Librairies Techniques

Librairie Orientaliste Paul **Geuthner** SA+*, 12 rue Vavin, F–75006 Paris Tel: (01) 3269027 Cable Add: Liborient Paris
Man Dir: Mrs Paul Geuthner
Subjects: Archaeology, Assyriology, Islam, Near & Far East, Linguistics, Numismatics, Religion
1977: 10 titles *Founded:* 1902

Miscellaneous: Specialists in Oriental & North African subjects
ISBN Publisher's Prefix: 2–7053, 0005 8

Gibert Jeune Sàrl+*, 27 quai St-Michel, F–75005 Paris Tel: (01) 0335732
Subject: Education
ISBN Publisher's Prefix: 2–900002

Editions De **Gigord**+*, 15 rue Cassette, F–75006 Paris Tel: (01) 5485521
Subjects: General Fiction, Belles Lettres, Education, Religion, University & Secondary Textbooks
Founded: 1830
ISBN Publisher's Prefix: 2–7054

Société Nouvelle des Editions **Gonthier** Sàrl, 19 rue de l'Université, F–75007 Paris Tel: (01) 2615085 Cable Add: EDEPEGE
Man Dir: Albert Blanchard; *Rights & Permissions:* Thérèse Mairesse
Subjects: Art, Philosophy, Education, Religion, Philology, Psychology, Sociology, Political Science & Economics, Women's Writing
1977: 17 titles *1978:* 25 titles *Founded:* 1964
Miscellaneous: Owned by Editions Denoël Sarl (qv)
ISBN Publisher's Prefix: 2–7197

Jacques **Grancher**, Editeur, 98 rue de Vaugirard, F–75006 Paris Tel: 2226480/5447028 Cable Add: Sce de Vente/Librairies 5480317, 14 rue Littre, F–75006 Paris
Man Dir: Jacques Grancher
Subjects: Military Series (Uniforms, Arms), Memoirs (Art World), Health, Diet, Cookery Series
Founded: 1952
ISBN Publisher's Prefix: 2–7146

Grange Batelière SA*, 10 rue Chauchat, F–75009 Paris Tel: (01) 7709189 Cable Add: Edibatel Maine
Man Dir: Herman Grégoire; *Dir:* Italo Milani; *Publicity & Advertising:* Ms Lemoine
Subjects: Encyclopaedias, General Fiction, Belles Lettres
Founded: 1967
Miscellaneous: The company has sold its business goodwill to Editions Atlas (qv) and Alpha Editions (qv)
ISBN Publisher's Prefix: 2–255

Société des Editions **Grasset et Fasquelle**+, 61 rue des Saints-Pères, F–75007 Paris Tel: (01) 5480771
Chairman: Bernard Privat; *Man Dir:* Jean-Claude Fasquelle; *Dir:* Claude Durand; *Editors-in-Chief:* Yves Berger, Françoise Verny; *Sales:* Gérard Porra; *Publicity and Advertising:* Monique Mayaud; *Production:* Jean Fournier; *Administrative Dir:* Philippe Méry; *Rights and Permissions:* Marie-Hélène d'Ovidio; *Public Relations:* Claude Dalla-Torre
Subjects: General Fiction and Nonfiction, Belles Lettres, Poetry, Philosophy, Juveniles
Founded: 1908
ISBN Publisher's Prefix: 2–246

Jean **Grassin** Editeur+, 50 rue Rodier, F–75009 Paris Tel: (01) 5269040
Man Dir: Jean Grassin
Orders to: Moulin de l'Ecluse, F–28210 Nogent-le-Roi Tel: 37 825154
Subjects: Literature, Poetry, History, Bibliophily
Book Club: Poètes Présents (Poets of Today) (qv)
1977: 32 titles *1978:* 34 titles *Founded:* 1957
ISBN Publisher's Prefix: 2–7055

FRANCE 99

Groupe Expansion*, 67 ave de Wagram, BP 570, F–75017 Paris cedex 17 Tel: (01) 7581295 Telex: 650242 manxpan
President and Man Dir: Jean-Louis Servan-Schreiber; *General Man:* Hubert Zieseniss; *Publicity Dir:* Philippe le Grix de la Salle
Associate Company: Publi-Union, Paris (qv)
Subjects: Economics, Politics, Social Sciences, Education, Literature, Law, Architecture, Scientific and Technical

Librairie **Gründ**+, 60 rue Mazarine, F–75006 Paris 6 Tel: (01) 3298740 Cable Add: Gründ Paris Telex: 27105 F TXFRA/ref 888
Man Dir: Michel Gründ; *Sales Dir:* Alain Gründ; *Rights & Permissions, Advertising:* P A Touttain
Subjects: Information and Reference books on Nature, Animals etc; Travel; Arts; How-to Books; Juvenile; 10-vol Benezit Biographical Dictionary of International Artists, Sculptors and Designers; Gift Books
1978: 23 titles *1979:* 47 titles *Founded:* 1880
Miscellaneous: Associate company of Éditions Alpina, Paris (qv)
ISBN Publisher's Prefix: 2–7000

Librairie **Guénégaud**+, 10 rue de l'Odéon, F–75006 Paris Tel: 3260791
Man Dir: Mr Pénau
Subjects: History, Topography (France)
1977: 12 titles *1978:* 12 titles *Founded:* 1947
ISBN Publisher's Prefix: 2–85023

Guérin et Cie, see Artisan du Livre

Editions d'Art Albert **Guillot**+*, 4 rue de Sèze, F–69006 Lyon Tel: (078) 523133
Subject: Art
ISBN Publisher's Prefix: 2–85096

Groupe International **Hachette***, 254 blvd St-Germain, F–75007 Paris Tel: (01) 2603822 Telex: Gihac 270357 F and Hachetr 260624
Dir: Jean-Marie Lepargneur; *Sales Managers:* Jean-Claude Diemer (North), Gérard Choquet (South); *Publicity Manager:* Jacques Leblanc
Subjects: General Fiction, Art Books, Classics, Juveniles, History, Educational Materials

Librairie **Hachette**+*, 79 blvd St-Germain, F–75006 Paris Tel: (01) 3291224 Cable Add: Hachechi Paris 25 Telex: Hacsieg Paris 24434
Man Dir: Gerard Worms; *Export Manager:* Jean-Marie Lepargneur; *Foreign Rights:* Jean-Loup Chiflet
Br Off: Hachette Inc, 2 Park Ave, New York, NY 10016
Subsidiary Companies: Hachette/Enseignment (qv); Hachette Guides Bleus (qv); Hachette-Jeunesse (qv); Hachette Littérature et Sciences Humaines (qv); Hachette Pratique (qv); Hachette Réalités (qv); Hachette-Sciences Humaines (qv); Editions Stock (qv)
Subjects: General Fiction, Nonfiction, History, How-to, Philosophy, Art, Travel, Reference, Education, Juveniles, Science, Paperbacks, Textbooks, Architecture, Bibliography, Engineering, Music, Politics, Social Science, Games, Sport, Languages, Economics
Bookshops: Bookshops throughout the world
Founded: 1826
ISBN Publisher's Prefix: 2–01

Hachette/Enseignement (Hachette Educational), 79 blvd Saint-Germain, BP 1506, F–75006 Paris Tel: 3252211 Cable Add: Hacheci-Paris 25 Telex: 26624 Hachepr Paris
Sales Manager: Jean-Claude Didelot
Parent Company: Librairie Hachette (qv)
Subjects: Pedagogic and para-pedagogic books on every subject and for every level from Nursery School to University

Hachette Guides Bleus*, 284 blvd St-Germain, F–75007 Paris Tel: (01) 5556061
Publisher: Gérald Gassiot-Talabot; *Rights & Permissions:* André Faure
Parent Company: Librairie Hachette (qv)
Subjects: Guides, Art

Hachette-Jeunesse, 79 blvd St-Germain, BP 1506, F–75006 Paris Tel: 3291224 Cable Add: Hacheci-Paris 25 Telex: Hacsieg-Paris 204434
Executives: Georges Berton, Roland Brénin, Philippe Schuwer; *Rights and Permissions:* Françoise Laurent, Raymonde Plomion-Lesellier, Paule Tschudin
Parent Company: Hachette (qv)
Subjects: Illustrated Childrens' Books, Reference, How-to, Collections, Novels for the Young

Hachette-Littérature, 6 ave Pierre Ier de Serbie, F–75116 Paris Tel: 7236163
Man Dir: Gérald Gassiot-Talabot; *Rights & Permissions:* Mrs Andrée Faure
Parent Company: Librairie Hachette (qv)
Subjects: Reference Works, Science, Historical, Essays, Biographical, Documentation
1977: 50 titles *1978:* 60 titles *Founded:* 1975

Hachette Pratique, 4 rue de Gallière, F–75116 Paris Tel: (01) 7236138
Publisher: Sylvie Diarte; *Rights and Permissions:* Andrée Faure
Subjects: Guides, Illustrated Albums, Handicraft Manuals

Hachette — Réalités*, 284 blvd St-Germain, F–75007 Paris Tel: (01) 5556001 Telex: 26624 Hachepr-Paris
Publisher: Claude Janicot; *Rights and Permissions:* Andrée Faure
Parent Company: Librairie Hachette (qv)
Subjects: Art, History, Reference
Founded: 1956

Editions Dominique **Halévy***, 26 pl Dauphine, F–75001 Paris Tel: (01) 3266127
Man Dir: Dominique Halévy
Subjects: Poetry, Juveniles
Founded: 1969
ISBN Publisher's Prefix: 2–85024

Le **Hameau**, Editeur, 15 rue Servandoni, F–75006 Paris Tel: 3290550
Man Dir, Rights & Permissions: Paule Truchaud; *Sales:* C Navelet; *Production:* C Noualhier; *Publicity:* A R L
Orders to: Le Hameau Diffusion, at above address
Subjects: Psychology, Psychoanalysis, Social Science, Medicine, Fiction, Essays, Poetry
Bookshop: address as above
1977: 20 titles *1978:* 20 titles *Founded:* 1973
ISBN Publisher's Prefix: 2–7203

Librairie **Hatier** SA+*, 8 rue d'Assas, F–75006 Paris Tel: (01) 5443838 Cable Add: Libhatier Paris Telex: 202 732
Man Dir: Michel Foulon; *Sales Dirs:* André Cazaux, Alain Jauson; *Rights & Permissions:* Marie-Blanche D'Ussel

Orders to: 8 rue d'Assas, F–75278 Paris cedex 06
Imprint: Editions de l'Amitié
Subjects: Children's Fiction, Travel, Tour Guides, Popular Natural History, Chess, Sport, How-to, DIY, Illustrated books
Bookshop: 59 blvd Raspail F–75006 Paris
Founded: 1880
ISBN Publisher's Prefix: 2–218

Pierre **Hautot** SA*, 36 rue du Bac, F–75007 Paris Tel: (01) 2611015
Subject: Art
Founded: 1952

Fernand **Hazan** Editeur SA+*, 35–37 rue de Seine, F–75006 Paris Tel: (01) 0336872
Chairman: B Panche; *Man Dir:* Henri van Raay
Subjects: Art, Reference, Juveniles, Paperbacks
Founded: 1945
Bookshop: Editions Fernand Hazan, 35–37 rue de Seine

Hermann (Editeurs des Sciences et des Arts) SA+, 293 rue Lecourbe, F–75015 Paris Tel: (01) 5574540 Cable Add: Piby Paris Telex: Hermann Paris 200595
Man Dir: Pierre Berès; *Rights & Permissions:* Mrs A Rulleau
Br Off: 6 rue de la Sorbonne, F–75005 Paris
Subjects: Science, Art, Medical and Technical, Textbooks, Reference, Paperbacks
Bookshop: 6 rue de la Sorbonne, F–75005, Paris
1977: 50 titles *1978:* 50 titles *Founded:* 1870
ISBN Publisher's Prefix: 2–7056

Editions de l'**Herne**, 41 rue de Verneuil, F–75007 Paris Tel: (01) 2612506
Man Dir, Rights & Permissions: Constantin Tacou; *Editorial, Press Attaché:* Miss Laurence Mauriac; *Sales:* Sodis; *Production, Publicity:* François Delaroière
Subjects: Belles Lettres, Poetry, Philosophy, Social Science, Politics, Art, Novels, Strategy
1977: 8 titles *1978:* 8 titles *Founded:* 1964
ISBN Publisher's Prefix: 5112

Editions d'Art Les **Heures Claires** SA+*, 19 rue Bonaparte, F–75006 Paris Tel: (01) 3265475
Owner: Jean Estrade
Subject: Art
Founded: 1945
ISBN Publisher's Prefix: 2–85026

Editions **Hier et Demain**+*, 26 rue de Gramont, F–75002 Paris Tel: (01) 0738725/6 Telex: 27618
Man Dir: Denise Drouin; *Editorial:* André Rossel; *Sales, Rights & Permissions:* Denise Drouin; *Production:* Nicole Sabot; *Publicity:* Katia Favard
Associate Company: Editions de la Courtille, France (qv)
Subjects: Biography, History, High-priced Paperbacks, Educational Materials, Collectors' Editions, Practical Guides, Encyclopaedias
1977: 8 titles *Founded:* 1971
ISBN Publisher's Prefix: 2–7199, 2–7206

Editions d'**Histoire et d'Art**, J & R Wittman*, 32 ave du Président Wilson, F–75016 Paris Tel: (01) 7270431
Subjects: History, Art
Founded: 1933

Editions d'**Histoire Sociale** EDHIS+, 23 rue de Valois, F–75001 Paris Tel: (01) 2614778
Man Dir: Léon Centner
Subjects: Social History, Revolutions in

France, Historical Documents
Bookshops: 23 rue de Valois, Paris; 144 Galerie de Valois, Paris 1e
1977: 19 titles *1978:* 37 titles *Founded:* 1967

Editions **Hommes et Techniques**+, 2 rue Benoît Malon, BP 128, F-92154 Suresnes Tel: 7723132 Telex: 62785
Man Dir: Paul Guyot
Subjects: Business Management, Organizational Development
1977: 13 titles *1978:* 15 titles *Founded:* 1945

Pierre **Horay** Editeur*, 22 bis passage Dauphine, F-75006 Paris Tel: (01) 3545390
Man Dir: Sophie Horay; *Editorial:* François Caradec; *Production:* Jean Paoli; *Rights & Permissions:* Colette Haro
Orders to: Editions Garnier, 19 rue des Plantes, F-75014 Paris
Subjects: General Fiction, Belles Lettres, Poetry, Biography, History, How-to, Music, Art, Juveniles, High-priced Paperbacks
1977: 15 titles *Founded:* 1946
ISBN Publisher's Prefix: 2-7058

Editions **Horizons** de France+*, 34 rue de Laborde, F-75008 Paris Tel: (01) 5227634
Man Dir: Pierre Lagrange
Subjects: History, How-to, Art, Music, General and Social Sciences, Natural History
ISBN Publisher's Prefix: 2-85027

Les **Humanoïdes** Associés, 15–17 passage des Petites Ecuries, F-75010 Paris Tel: 2464538
Man Dir, Rights & Permissions: Jean Pierre Dionnet, Isabelle Morin; *Editorial:* Philippe Manoeuvre; *Production:* Gennaro Russo; *Art Editor:* Janic Dionnet; *Publicity:* Catherine Philippot, Dominique Bosch
Subjects: Fantasy Fiction, Strip Cartoons, Reprints, Children's Books, Science Fiction, Erotica, Popular Art
1977: 40 titles *1978:* 60 titles *Founded:* 1975
ISBN Publisher's Prefix: 2-902-123

La **Hune***, 170 blvd St-Germain, F-75006 Paris Tel: (01) 5483585
Subject: Art
Bookshop: Librairie La Hune, at same address

Idea Books Distribution SA*, 24 rue du 4 Septembre, F-75002 Paris Tel: (01) 628785; 48 rue de Montreuil, F-75011 Paris Tel: (01) 3404003 Cable Add: Idea Books-Paris
Publisher: Giampaolo Grazzini
Subject: Communications, Artbooks, Architecture, Visual Arts

Éditions de l'**Illustration**, 13 rue Saint-Georges, F-75009 Paris Tel: (01) 8785319
Miscellaneous: Imprint of Les Editions de l'Illustration Baschet et Cie (qv)
Subjects: 8-vol pictorial Encyclopaedia of Everyday Life in France (Histoire de la Vie Française)

InterEditions Paris, 7 rue Sarrette, F-75014 Paris Tel: 3228362 Telex: 210311 Publi 147
Man Dir: Geoffrey M Staines; *Production:* Monika Neumann; *Rights & Permissions:* Claudine Antonin
Orders to: Bordas SA, 37 rue Boulard, F-75680 Paris cedex 14
Parent Company: Inter-European Editions, Amsterdam, Netherlands
Subjects: Scientific texts related to teaching and/or research, especially Biology, Chemistry, Physics, Mathematics; Commerce

1977: 7 titles *1978:* 8 titles *Founded:* 1976
ISBN Publisher's Prefix: 7296

CNRS Laboratoire **Intergéo** (Intergéo Laboratory of the French National Scientific Research Centre — CNRS), 191 rue Saint-Jacques, F-75005 Paris Tel: 6337431
Man Dir: R Brunet
Parent Company: Centre National de la Recherche Scientifique (CNRS)
Associate Company: Editions CNRS (qv)
Subjects: Geography, Documentation
1977: 3 titles *1978:* 3 titles *Founded:* 1947
ISBN Publisher's Prefix: 901560

Librairie **Istra** SàrI+*, 93 rue Jeanne-d'Arc, F-75013 Paris Tel: (01) 5851660 Telex: 25884
Subjects: Economics, Education (Primary & Secondary)
Founded: 1928
ISBN Publisher's Prefix: 2-219

Groupe **J A** (Editions J A), 3 rue Roquépine, BP 250, F-75017 Paris Tel: 7542920 Cable Add: Grupjia Paris Telex: 280674
Man Dir and Editorial: Mme Ben Yahmed; *Rights & Permissions:* Mme Ben Yahmed, Mme R Prétab
Subjects: Geography, Tourism, Cartography, Art, History
Bookshop: SAP, 17 ter, ave Habib Thámeur, Tunis
1977: 18 titles *Founded:* 1968
ISBN Publisher's Prefix: 2-85258

Editions **J'ai Lu**+*, 31 rue de Tournon, F-75006 Paris Tel: (01) 3267759 Telex: Jailu 202765
Subjects: General Fiction, Belles Lettres, Low-priced Paperbacks
Founded: 1958

Editions **Jeune Afrique**, 3 rue Roquépine, F-75008 Paris Tel: (01) 7665242/2656931 Cable Add: Grupjia Paris Telex: Grupjia 280674
President: Bechir Ben Yahmed; *General and Literary Manager:* Danielle Ben Yahmed; *Commercial Manager:* Rolande Prétat; *Foreign Rights:* D Ben Yahmed, R Prétat; *Press/Publicity:* Anne Simon, R Prétat
Subjects: History, Biography, Geography and Travel, Political, Reference Works, Natural Sciences, Fine Arts
1977: 10-12 titles *1978:* 15 titles *Founded:* 1966
Miscellaneous: Firm publishes periodicals Jeune Afrique, Annuaire de l'Afrique et du Moyen Orient, Marchés Nouveaux
ISBN Publisher's Prefix: 2-85258

Journal des Notaires et des Avocats SA+*, 6 rue de Mézières, F-75006 Paris Tel: (01) 5481210
Subject: Law
ISBN Publisher's Prefix: 2-85028

Edition **Judogi***, 107 blvd Beaumarchais, F-75003 Paris Tel: (01) 2729559
Subject: Sports

Editions René **Julliard**+*, 8 rue Garancière, F-75008 Paris Tel: (01) 3291280 Cable Add: Edijulliard Paris 110
Man Dir: Bernard de Fallois; *Publicity Manager:* Nadia Leser
Subjects: General Fiction, Poetry, Belles Lettres, History, Religion, Political Science
Founded: 1931
Miscellaneous: Firm is a member of the Presses de la Cité group (qv)
ISBN Publisher's Prefix: 2-260

Editions **Jupiter** SàrI+, 21-23 rue du Mont-Thabor, F-75001 Paris Tel: (01) 2607465/2607778
Dir: Pierre Legrand
Subjects: Law, Politics, Encyclopaedias
ISBN Publisher's Prefix: 2-7060

Jurif (Société d'Etudes Juridiques Internationales et Fiscales), see Cahiers Fiscaux Européens

Kent-Segep SA+, Editions-Publicité, 74 ave Kléber, F-75016 Paris Tel: (01) 5330080
Subject: Literature
1978: 1 title
ISBN Publisher's Prefix: 2-85029

Editions **Klincksieck**+, 11 rue de Lille, F-75007 Paris Tel: (01) 2603825
Man Dir: Andrée Laurent-Klincksieck; *Publicity, Rights & Permissions:* Marie-Françoise Vauquelin
Subjects: Social Sciences, Philology, Linguistics, Archaeology, History, Belles Lettres, Aesthetics, Reference, General & Social Science
Bookshop: Librairie C Klincksieck, 11 rue de Lille, F-75007 Paris
1977: 70 titles *Founded:* 1842
ISBN Publisher's Prefix: 2-252

Knowledge International Marketing*, 54 rue de Varenne, F-75007 Paris Tel: (01) 5442290, 2222961 Cable Add: Kim, 54, rue de Varenne Telex: 24488
Subject: Encyclopaedias

L J Productions*, 9 rue Méchain, F-75680 Paris cedex 14 Tel: (01) 5352816
Subjects: Juveniles, Games

Editions Robert **Laffont**+, 6 pl St-Sulpice, F-75006 Paris Tel: (01) 3291233 Cable Add: Edilaf Paris 110 Telex: 25877
Man Dir: Robert Laffont
Subjects: General Fiction, History, Documentary, Philosophy, Religion, Art, Biography, Juveniles, High-priced Paperbacks, Medicine, General & Social Science, Psychology, Textbooks, Hobbies, Translations
Founded: 1941
ISBN Publisher's Prefix: 2-221

Lafolye et Lamarzelle Editeurs SàrI+*, 2 pl des Lices, F-56000 Vannes Tel: (097) 661198
Subject: Religion

Librairie Léonce **Laget**+, 75 rue de Rennes, F-75006 Paris Tel: (01) 5489018 Cable Add: Liblaget Paris 110
Man Dir: Léonce Laget
Subjects: Art, History, Trades and Crafts
1978: 60 titles *1979:* 90 titles *Founded:* 1955
ISBN Publisher's Prefix: 2-85204

Editions **Lahumière**, 88 blvd de Courcelles, F-75017 Paris Tel: (01) 9240395/6224367
Publisher: Anne Margaréte Lahumière
Subject: Art

Editions **Lamarre-Poinat** SA+*, 47 rue Saint André-des-Arts, F-75006 Paris Tel: (01) 3265838
Subject: Medicine
ISBN Publisher's Prefix: 2-85030

Lamy SA+, 155 rue Legendre, F-75017 Paris cedex 17 Tel: (01) 6272890 Telex: 650790
Man Dir: Bernard Nitot; *Sales:* Mr Laquieze; *Publicity:* Mr Chareton; *Public Relations:* Pierre-Yves Odinot
Orders to: Sofrado, 38 rue Lantiez, F-75017 Paris
Subjects: Law (Social, Fiscal, Company,

Transport, Transport Methods)
1979: 39 titles *Founded:* 1949
ISBN Publisher's Prefix: 305-254 161000 14
APE 5 112

Librairie Fernand **Lanore** Sàrl, 1 rue
Palatine, F-75006 Paris Tel: (01) 3256661
Dir: François Sorlot
Subjects: Belles Lettres, History,
Philosophy, Secondary Textbooks,
Education, Religion, Languages, Touring,
Mountaineering
1977: 10 titles *1978:* 14 titles *Founded:* 1920

Editions J **Lanore** C L T+, Successeur de
Laurens, 4 rue de Tournon, F-75006 Paris
Associate Company: Librairie-Editions
J Lanore, 12 rue Oudinot, F-75007 Paris
Subjects: Pedagogy and Teaching Texts on
Cookery and Catering, Dressmaking, Home
Economy, Law, Technology, Careers
1978: 10 titles

Librairie **Larousse**+, 17 rue du
Montparnasse, F-75006 Paris Tel: (01)
5443817 Cable Add: Liblarous, 43 Paris
Telex: 250828
Man Dirs: Georges Lucas, Claude Moreau,
Jean-Louis Moreau; *Foreign Trade Dir:*
Francis Trébinjac; *Rights & Permissions:*
E Faguer, Agence SEU, 95 rue de Rennes,
F-75006 Paris
Subjects: Dictionaries, Encyclopaedias,
Reference, Textbooks, Juveniles,
Paperbacks, Technical, General & Social
Science, Linguistics
Subsidiaries & Affiliates: Ediciones Larousse
Argentina SA, Valentin Gomez 3530,
Buenos Aires R 13, Argentina; Larousse-
Belgique, 32 blvd du Jardin Botanique,
B-1000 Brussels, Belgium; Editora Larousse
do Brasil, Av Almte Barrosa, 63s/2609, Rio
de Janeiro, Brazil; Editions Françaises Inc,
192 rue Dorchester, Quebec 2, Canada;
Ediciones Larousse SA, Marsella 53, Esq
Nápoles, Mexico City 6, Mexico; Larousse
(Suisse) SA, 23 rue des Vollandes, CH-1211
Geneva 6, Switzerland; Larousse & Co Inc,
572 Fifth Ave, New York, NY, USA
1978: 148 titles *Founded:* 1852
ISBN Publisher's Prefix: 2-03

Editions Jean-Claude **Lattès**, 23 ave
Villemain, F-75014 Paris Tel: (01) 5392207
Man Dir: Jean-Claude Lattès; *Rights &
Permissions:* Ursula Veit
Subjects: General Fiction & Nonfiction,
Biography, Documents, Low-priced
Paperbacks, Music
1978: 100 titles *Founded:* 1968

Editions Henri **Laurens** Successeurs Sàrl,
see Editions J Lanore

Charles **Lavauzelle**, BP 8, F-87350 Panazol
Tel: (55) 341515
Man Dir: Jean Claude Mazaud; *Sales and
Publicity:* Geneviève Giry; *Production:*
Henri Chabrier
Subjects: Military History, Law, Horse-
Riding
1978: 15 titles *1979:* 18 titles *Founded:* 1880
ISBN Publisher's Prefix: 2-7025

Diffusion Bernard **Laville***, 3 rue
Garancière, F-75006 Paris Tel: (01)
6332930
Publisher: Bernard Laville; *Sales Manager:*
Eric Prevost
Subjects: Fiction, Social Science, Politics,
Juveniles, Religion, Art, Classics

Editions Guy **Le Prat**+, 5 rue des Grands-
Augustins, F-75006 Paris Tel: (01) 3265782
Man Dir: Guy Le Prat

Subjects: Reference, Leisure, Sports,
Oriental and Occult, Natural Medicine,
Environment, Ecology, Juvenile,
Management, Investment, Glues/Adhesives,
Fine Arts, Limited Editions; General
Literature, Reprints, Paperbacks
1978: 5 titles *Founded:* 1825
Miscellaneous: Formerly Editions Delarue
ISBN Publisher's Prefix: 2-85205

Editions **Lechevalier** Sàrl+, 19 rue
Augereau, F-75007 Paris Tel: (01)
5554369/5555510
Man Dir: Jacques Lechevalier
Subjects: Natural Sciences, Natural History,
Biology, Entomology, Mycology,
Ornithology, Silviculture, Botany, Zoology,
Periodicals
1977: 5 titles *1978:* 4 titles *Founded:* 1875

Francis **Lefebvre**+*, 44 rue de Villiers,
F-92300 Levallois-Perret Tel: 7581620
Dir: Francis Lefebvre
Subjects: Psychology, Educational Materials
Bookshop (affiliated): Librairie la
Salamandre, 41 rue des Trois Frères,
F-75018 Paris
ISBN Publisher's Prefix: 2-85115

Editions Robert **Léger** et Cie+, 27 rue de la
Harpe, F-75005 Paris Tel: (01) 3540450
Subject: Arts

Editions André **Lesot** Sàrl+*, 10 rue de
l'Eperon, F-75006 Paris Tel: (01) 3265673
Subject: Science & Technical
ISBN Publisher's Prefix: 2-7062

Editions Olivier **Lesourd**, 252 Faubourg
St-Honoré, F-75008 Paris Tel: (01)
9244070/2276930
Subject: Technical Reports (Energy)

Société Nouvelle des Editions **Letouzey** et
Ané Sàrl+, 87 blvd Raspail, F-75006 Paris
Tel: (01) 5488014
Dir: J Letouzey
Subjects: Dictionaries, Religion, History
Founded: 1885
ISBN Publisher's Prefix: 2-7063

Lettres Modernes Minard, see Minard

Librairie Commerciale et Technique (**Licet**)
Sàrl+, 110 rue de Rivoli, F-75001 Paris
Tel: (01) 2334729
Man Dir: Yves Defaucheux; *all other
offices:* J P Le Gall
Orders to: 110 rue de Rivoli, Paris 1er
Subjects: Accountancy, Typewriting,
Business Techniques, Economics, Law,
English, Statistics, Data Processing
1978: 13 titles *1979:* 10 titles *Founded:* 1963
ISBN Publisher's Prefix: 2-85232

**Librairie Générale de Droit et de
Jurisprudence**, see Droit et Jurisprudence

Librairie Générale Française SA+*, 14 rue
de l'Ancienne-Comédie, F-75006 Paris
Tel: (01) 3265393
Subject: Literature (Paperbacks)

Librairies Techniques SA+, 27 pl Dauphine,
F-75001 Paris Tel: (01) 3266090/3290771
Dir: Mme Argenson
Parent Company: Editions Techniques,
18 rue Séguier, F-75006 Paris
Branch Off: 26 rue Soufflot, F-75005 Paris
Subjects: Politics, Law, Commerce
1977: 51 titles *1978:* 36 titles
Miscellaneous: Firm incorporates Editions
M Th Genin
ISBN Publisher's Prefix: 2-7111

Licet, see Librairie Commerciale et
Technique

Editions de la **Licorne**+*, 95 rue La Boétie,
F-75008 Paris Tel: (01) 3436443
Subject: Education

Editions **Lidis** SA+, 23 rue des Grands-
Augustins, F-75006 Paris Tel: (01)
3292188 Cable Add: Elidis Paris Telex:
Elidis 270900 F
Man Dir, Rights & Permissions: Noël
Schumann; *Editorial, Production:* Claire de
la Pradelle; *Sales:* J Souci; *Publicity:* Sophie
Schumann
Subsidiary Companies: Editions Lidis SA —
Diffusion Benelux, 70 Chaussée de Charleroi,
B-1111060 Brussels, Belgium; La Diffusion,
23 rue des Grands Augustins, F-75006 Paris
Subjects: Encyclopaedias, Art
Book Club: Librairie Lidis, 208 rue de
Rivoli, F-75001 Paris
1977: 2 titles *1978:* 2 titles *Founded:* 1955
ISBN Publisher's Prefix: 2-85032

Editions **Ligel**+, 77 rue de Vaugirard,
F-75006 Paris Tel: (01) 5487860
Man Dir: Henri Creff; *Deputy Director:*
Jules Desmyetter
Subject: School Textbooks
Bookshop: 77 rue de Vaugirard, F-75006
Paris
1977: 18 titles *Founded:* 1909
ISBN Publisher's Prefix: 2-7064

Editions Michel de **Lile** et Philippe Azou, 1
rue du Dahomey, F-75014 Paris Tel: (01)
5421877
Man Dir: Michel de Lile
Subjects: Art Editions, Facsimile
Reproductions
1978: 1 title *1979:* 1 title *Founded:* 1978

Office Central de **Lisieux** SA, see under
Office Central

Editions **Lito**, 32 ave Oudinot, F-94340
Joinville le Pont Tel: 8832411 Cable Add:
Litofrance Paris Telex: Edlit 680284
Man Dir, Rights & Permissions: Lennart
Rosdahl; *Editorial, Publicity:* Janine
Ancelet; *Sales:* Yvette Mallay
Parent Company: Lito Interco, 15 ave Guy
Mocquet, 94340 Joinville le Pont
Subsidiary Companies: Litor Publishers Ltd,
UK (qv); Lito Editrice, Via Palazzetto 15,
I-10070 Mappano, Turin, Italy
Subjects: Children's Books, Puzzles,
Teaching Aids, Cutouts and Stick-Ons,
Transfers, Paperbacks
1978: 630 titles *Founded:* 1958
ISBN Publisher's Prefix: 2-244

Le **Livre de Paris***, 3-5 ave de Garlande,
F-92221 Bagneux Tel: (01) 6571140
Subjects: Art, How-to, Juveniles
ISBN Publisher's Prefix: 2-245

Le **Livre de Poche**, 12 rue Francois 1er,
F-75008 Paris Tel: (01) 3597959
Man Dir, Rights & Permissions: C Poninski
Subject: General Fiction
Founded: 1953

Lumiere Biblique, see Les Editions de la
Source SA

M C L*, 22 rue Bergère, 75009 Paris
Tel: (01) 7706183
Dirs: Jean Chapelle, Humbert Rusconi
Subjects: Occult, Medicine, Juveniles

Editions **M D I** (La Maison des
Instituteurs)+, Parc des 10 Arpents, Dept
113, PO Box 39, F-78630 Orgeval Tel:
9756381 Telex: MDI Edit 698094F
Man Dir: Alexandre Schajer
Subjects: Juveniles, History, Geography,
General Science, Secondary and Primary

Textbooks, Educational Materials
Founded: 1954
ISBN Publisher's Prefix: 2-223

McGraw-Hill Inc+, 28 rue Beaunier,
F-75014 Paris Tel: (01) 5409438/5406281
Telex: 250304
Man Dir, Rights & Permissions: Mrs
Jolanda von Hagen; *Editorial, Production:*
Danielle Duperrier
Parent Company: McGraw-Hill
International, 1221 Ave of the Americas,
New York, NY 10020, USA
Associate Companies: see McGraw-Hill, UK
Subjects: General Science, Technology,
Economics, Finance, Humanities, Current
Affairs
1978: 10 titles *1979:* 14 titles *Founded:*
1967
ISBN Publisher's Prefix: 2-7042

Maeght Editeur*, 13 rue de Téhéran,
F-75008 Paris Tel: (01) 3876149 Cable
Add: Galmaeght Paris 037 Telex: 28660
Dir: Jean Frémon; *Sales Manager:* François
Bruller
Subject: Art
ISBN Publisher's Prefix: 2-85087

Les Editions **Magnard** Sàrl+, 122 blvd
St-Germain, F-75279 Paris cedex 06
Tel: (01) 3294100
Dirs: Louis Magnard, Pierre Delas; *Sales
Dir:* Louis Magnard; *Literary Director,
Publicity:* Thérèse Roche-Magnard; *Export
Manager:* Jean-Claude Brouillet, Rés Les
Crêtes, Bat Géranium, Ave Marcel-
Camusso, F-1360 La Ciotat
Subjects: Juveniles, University, Secondary &
Primary Textbooks, Educational Materials
Bookshop: Librairie de France, 122 blvd
Saint-Germain, F-75006 Paris
1977: 233+ titles *Founded:* 1934
Miscellaneous: awarders of the Jeune
France Literary Prize (qv)
ISBN Publisher's Prefix: 2-210

La **Maison des Instituteurs**, see M D I

La **Maison du Dictionnaire**, 95 bis rue
Legendre, F-75017 Paris Tel: 2294836
Telex: 270105 ref 355 txfra b rungi
Man Dirs: Michel Feutry, Louis-Pierre
Leslie
Subjects: Technical, Specialized and General
Dictionaries in many languages
1978: 4 titles *1979:* 4 titles *Founded:* 1976
ISBN Publisher's Prefix: 2-85608

La **Maison** Rustique SA+, Librairie
Agricole et Horticole, 26 rue Jacob,
F-75006 Paris 6 Tel: (01) 3256700
Subjects: Natural Science, Horticulture,
Agriculture, Forestry
Founded: 1836
ISBN Publisher's Prefix: 2-7066

Adrien **Maisonneuve-Librairie d'Amérique
et d'Orient**+, 11 rue St-Sulpice, F-75006
Paris Tel: (01) 3268635
Man Dir: Jean Maisonneuve
Subjects: History, Philosophy, Religion,
Art, Social Science, Economics, Orientalia
1977: 40 titles *Founded:* 1926
ISBN Publisher's Prefix: 2-7200

Editions G P **Maisonneuve et Larose**+, 15
rue Victor-Cousin, F-75005 Paris Tel: (02)
3543270
Man Dir: J-P Pinardon
Subjects: Scholarly, Social Science,
Agriculture, Oriental & African Studies,
Folklore
1978: 29 titles *Founded:* 1961
Miscellaneous: Firms merged in 1961.
Founded 1853 & 1860, respectively
ISBN Publisher's Prefix: 2-7068

Librairie **Maloine**+, 27 rue de l'École-de-
Médecine, F-75006 Paris Tel: (01) 3256045
Telex: 203215F
Dir: Henry Grim; *Man Dir:* Antonin
Philippart; *Publicity & Advertising:* Jean
Philippart
Subjects: Medicine, Veterinary, Reference
1977: 121 titles *1978:* 116 titles *Founded:*
1881
ISBN Publisher's Prefix: 2-224

Nouvelles Editions **Mame*** (Division of SA
Gedit), 77 rue de Vaugirard, F-75006 Paris
Tel: 5487860 Telex: Blougay 202036
Man Dir: Marcel Vervaet; *Editorial, Sales,
Production:* Louis de Bouville; *Publicity,
Rights & Permissions:* Suzel Vervaet
Parent Company: Gedit SA, Tournai,
Belgium (qv)
Subjects: The Bible, Religious Literature,
Catechism, Liturgy
Miscellaneous: Associate Companies:
Desclée Editeurs SA, Tournai, Belgium (qv);
Editions Gamma, Paris, France (qv);
Editions Desclée et Cie, Paris, France (qv)
ISBN Publisher's Prefix: 2-7289

Éditions **Marrimpouey** Jeune et Cie, 2 pl de
la Libération, F-64000 Pau
Associate Company: Editions Edisud (qv)
Subjects: Travel and customs in the South
of France (especially Pyrenees and Basque
regions); including works in the Gascon
language

Editions **Martinsart***, 72 blvd de
Sébastopol, F-75003, Paris Tel: 8875128
Subjects: Luxury and Semi-Luxury
Editions, Collected Literary Works,
Encyclopaedias

François **Maspero** Editeur+, 1 pl Paul-
Painlevé, F-75005 Paris Tel: (01) 6334116
Man Dir: François Maspero
Subjects: Belles Lettres, Poetry, History,
Philosophy, Low- & High-priced
Paperbacks, Sociology, Political Economy
1978: 80 titles *Founded:* 1959
ISBN Publisher's Prefix: 2-7071

Editions Charles **Massin** et Cie+*, 2 rue de
l'Echelle, F-75001 Paris Tel: (01) 2603005
Subjects: Architecture, Interior Decoration,
Arts
Founded: 1910
ISBN Publisher's Prefix: 2-7072

Masson Editeur+, 120 blvd St-Germain,
F-75280 Paris cedex 06 Tel: (01) 3292160
Cable Add: Gemas Paris 025 Telex:
Massoned 260946
Dir: Dr Jérôme Talamon; *Man Dirs:*
P Lahaye, D de Costigliole; *Sales Dir:*
F Clouzet; *Rights & Permissions:* Françoise
Han
Associate Companies: Toray Masson,
Spain (qv); Masson Publishing USA Inc,
111 West 57th St, New York, NY USA;
Masson do Brasil, Rua da Quitanda 20,
Sala 301, 20011 Rio de Janeiro, Brazil;
Masson Editores, Dakota 383, Colonia
Napoles, Mexico 18 DF, Mexico
Subjects: Medicine, Scientific, Technical,
Social Science, Law, Economics
Founded: 1804
ISBN Publisher's Prefix: 2-225

Editions **Mazarine**, 34 ave Marceau,
F-75116 Paris Tel: (01) 7237250
Man Dir: J-E Cohen-Seat; *Sales:* Martine
Clairet; *Rights & Permissions:* Valérie-Anne
Montassier
Subjects: General Literature; Novels, Belles
Lettres, History, Current Events Reports
1979 (planned): 25 titles
ISBN Publisher's Prefix: 2-86374

Editions d'Art Lucien **Mazenod**+*, 33 rue
de Naples, F-75008 Paris Tel: (01) 5222366
Cable Add: Mazeditio Telex: 270105 F
TXFRA
Man Dir: Lucien Mazenod
Subjects: History, Art, Architecture
ISBN Publisher's Prefix: 2-85088

Editions **Mengès**, 22 rue Sébastien Mercier,
F-75015 Paris Tel: 5780408
Man Dirs: Bernard Blazin, Jean Paul
Mengès; *Editorial, Production:* J P Mengès;
Sales, Publicity: B Blazin; *Rights &
Permissions:* Cl Bay
Subjects: Humour, Documentaries,
Historical Novels, How-to, Illustrated
Books
1978: 35 titles *1979:* 40 titles *Founded:*
1975
ISBN Publisher's Prefix: 2-85620

Mercure de France SA+, 26 rue de Condé,
F-75006 Paris Tel: (01) 3292113
Man Dir: Simone Gallimard; *Editorial Dir:*
Michel Cournot; *Rights and Permissions:*
Nicole Boyer
Parent Company: Editions Gallimard (qv)
Associate Company: Editions Denoël Sarl
(qv)
Subjects: General Fiction, Belles Lettres,
Poetry, History, Philosophy, Juveniles,
Social Science, Psychology
1977: 65 titles *1978:* 72 titles *Founded:*
1891
ISBN Publisher's Prefix: 2-7152

Messageries Centrales du Livre*, 22 rue
Bergère, F-75009 Paris
Subjects: Cartoon strips, Juveniles
Miscellaneous: Firm is a member of the
Presses de la Cité group (qv)

Michelin et Cie (Services de Tourisme)+, 46
ave de Breteuil, F-75341 Paris cedex 07
Tel: (01) 5392500
Associate Company: Michelin Tyre
Company Ltd, 81 Fulham Rd, London
SW3 6RD, UK (qv)
Subjects: Travel Guides, Maps
1978: 4 titles

José **Millas-Martin***, 14 rue Le Bua,
F-75020 Paris
ISBN Publisher's Prefix: 2-241

Lettres Modernes **Minard**, 73 rue du
Cardinal Lemoine, F-75005 Paris Tel: (01)
3544609
Man Dir, Production: J Michel Minard;
Sales: Librairie Minard Diffusion; *Rights &
Permissions:* Danièle Morgat
Associate Company: Librairie Minard (qv)
Subjects: General Literature, University
Studies and Theses, Critical Studies
1977: c 50 titles *Founded:* 1954
ISBN Publisher's Prefix: 2-256

Librairie **Minard**, 73 rue du Cardinal
Lemoine, F-75005 Paris Tel: (01) 3544609
Man Dir: Michel Minard; *Sales:* Librairie
Minard Diffusion
Associate Company: Lettres Modernes
Minard (qv)
Subjects: University Studies and Theses
1978: 5 titles
ISBN Publisher's Prefix: 2-85210

Les Editions de **Minuit** SA+, 7 rue Bernard-
Palissy, F-75006 Paris Tel: (01) 2223794
Man Dir: Jérôme Lindon
Orders to: Sodis, 128 Ave du Maréchal-de-
Lattre de Tassigny, F-77400 Lagny
Subjects: General Fiction, Philosophy,
Social Science, History, Literary Works
Bookshops: Librairie Autrement Dit, 73
blvd Saint-Michel, F-75005 Paris; 9 rue
Bernard-Palissy, F-75006 Paris

1977: 27 titles *1978:* 25 titles *Founded:* 1942
ISBN Publisher's Prefix: 2-7073

Gérard Monfort, Saint-Pierre de Salerne, F-27800 Brionne Tel: (32) 448741
Man Dir: Gérard Monfort
Subjects: Literature, History, Art, Law, Archaeology, Ethnology
1978: 13 titles *1979:* 10 titles *Founded:* 1960

Editions du Moniteur, BP 47902, F-75065 Paris cedex 02 (Located at: 17 rue d'Uzes) Tel: 2334435 Telex: 680876F
President and Man Dir: Marc N Vigier; *Editorial:* Jean-Marc Pilpoul; *Sales:* Joseph Osman
Parent Company: C E P, 17 rue d'Uzes, F-75002 Paris
Subjects: Architecture, Building Construction, Public Works, Home Improvements, Laws and Regulations
Bookshops: Librarie du Moniteur, 15 rue d'Uzes, F-75002 Paris
1978: 28 titles *1979:* 52 titles
ISBN Publisher's Prefix: 2-86282

Editions Montchrestien SàrI+*, 158-160 rue St-Jacques, F-75005 Paris Tel: (01) 0331710
Subjects: Law, Political Science
ISBN Publisher's Prefix: 2-7076

Publications Photo-Cinema Paul Montel+, 189 rue St-Jacques, F-75005 Paris 5ème Tel: (01) 3294090
Man Dir: Pierre G Montel; *Editorial:* Yves Lorelle; *Sales:* Mr Sainsson; *Production:* Gérard Montel; *Publicity:* Xavier Bernard
Subjects: All aspects of photography and ciné-photography, filming; Periodicals
Founded: 1920
ISBN Publisher's Prefix: 2-7075

Montparnasse-Diffusion, see Alfred Eibel, Editeur

Editions de Montsouris SA+*, 9 rue d'Alexandrie, F-75002 Paris Tel: (01) 5080190
Br Off: 176 rue de Paris, F-91300 Massy
Subjects: Science and Technical
ISBN Publisher's Prefix: 2-85035

Editions Albert Morancé+, 1 rue Palatine, F-75006 Paris Tel: 6332455
Man Dir: Mrs G-A Morancé
Subjects: Fine Arts, Architecture
Founded: 1781
Book Club: Club du Livre d'Art
ISBN Publisher's Prefix: 2-85307

Editions Alain Moreau+, 5 rue Eginhard, F-75004 Paris Tel: (01) 2725151
Editorial, Rights & Permissions, Sales: Alain Moreau
Orders to: Groupe International Hachette, 58 rue Jean Beluzen, F-92170 Vanves
Subjects: Social, Economic & Political Sciences, History
1977: 13 titles *1978:* 14 titles *Founded:* 1972
ISBN Publisher's Prefix: 2-85209

Morel Editeurs*, 33 ave Victor Hugo, F-84400 Apt Tel: (90) 740217
Dirs: Robert Morel, François Morel
Associate Company: Editions 'R' (qv) at same address
Subjects: Belles Lettres, Poetry, Music, Art, Religion, Paperbacks, Architecture, Gastronomy, Folklore, Humour
Founded: 1961
Bookshops: La Fête, Montparnasse Diffusion, 1 quai de Conti, Paris 6; Di, Société Internationale de Diffusion, 33 ave Victor Hugo, F-84400 Apt; Galeria Pecanins, Hamburgo 103, México 6, DF, Mexico

Publications du Musée de l'Affiche et du Tract+*, 20 rue des Ecoles, F-75005 Paris Tel: (01) 0334132
Subject: Encyclopaedias

Editions de la Réunion des Musées Nationaux+, 10 rue de l'Abbaye, F-75006 Paris Tel: (01) 3292145
Subjects: Art, Guides, Science & Technology, Architecture
Founded: 1931
ISBN Publisher's Prefix: 2-7118

Editions du Muséum national d'Histoire naturelle, 38 rue Geoffroy Saint-Hilaire, F-75005 Paris Tel: (01) 3317124
Subjects: All aspects of Natural History; Natural History in the Middle East

Fernand Nathan Editeur+*, 9 rue Méchain, F-75014 Paris Tel: (01) 5898949 Cable Add: Nathaned Paris Telex: Nataned 24525 F
Dirs: Jean-Jacques Nathan, Pierre Nathan; *Publicity & Advertising:* André Broch
Subjects: History, How-to, Music, Art, Philosophy, Textbooks, Reference, Juveniles, Psychology, General & Social Science, Guides, Nature, Architecture, History, Education
Founded: 1881
ISBN Publisher's Prefix: 2-09

Librairie A-G Nizet+, 3 bis pl de la Sorbonne, F-75005 Paris Tel: (01) 3547976
Man Dir: A G Nizet
Publishers Represented: Renaissance du Livre, Belgium; Naaman Sherbrooke, Canada
Subjects: Belles Lettres, University Textbooks, Literary
1977: 29 titles *Founded:* 1922
ISBN Publisher's Prefix: 2-7078

F De Nobele, 35 rue Bonaparte, F-75006 Paris Tel: (01) 3260862 Cable Add: Denobelef Paris 110
Man Dir: F de Nobèle
Subjects: History of Art, Bibliography
1978: approx 70 titles *Founded:* 1880
ISBN Publisher's Prefix: 2-85189

Editions La Noria*, 13 ave Théophile Gautier, F-75016 Paris Tel: (01) 2881983/2604429
Man Dir: Nicolas Munoz de la Mata
Subjects: Belles Lettres, Juveniles, Educational Materials
Founded: 1975

Nouveautés de l'Enseignement-éditions andré casteilla, 25 rue Monge, F-75005 Paris Tel: (01) 0335650
Commercial Manager: Mrs Casteilla
Subjects: Textbooks for Technical, Commercial and Secondary Education; Economy, Legislation, Careers, Philately
1977: 30 titles
ISBN Publisher's Prefix: 2-7135

Nouvel Office d'Edition et de Diffusion (Les Productions de Paris — NOE)*, 3 bis passage de la Petite Boucherie, F-75006 Paris Tel: (01) 3262460
Parent Company: Editions Pierre Belfond (qv)
Subjects: Novels, History, How-to, Juveniles, Paperbacks, Social Science, Belles Lettres
Founded: 1969
ISBN Publisher's Prefix: 2-7144

Nouvelle Cité, 131 rue Castagnary, F-75015 Paris Tel: (01) 8281894
Man Dir, Rights & Permissions: Jean-Michel Merlin; *Editorial, Production, Publicity:* Jean-Pierre Rosa; *Sales:* Michel Visart
Associate Companies: Citta Nuova, Italy (qv); Neue Stadt, Federal Republic of Germany (qv); Ciudad Nueva, Spain (qv); Niewe Stad, St Stephanusstraat 11, Nijmegen, Netherlands; Cidade Nova, Rua Pio XII, 274 Paraiso São Paulo, Brazil; New City, 57 Twyford Avenue, London W3, UK
Subjects: Spiritual themes, Testimonies, Essays
1978: 4 titles *1979:* 8 titles *Founded:* 1963
ISBN Publisher's Prefix: 2-85313

Nouvelles Editions Françaises+, 13 rue St-Georges, F-75009 Paris Tel: (01) 8785319
Dir: Denis Baschet; *Man Dir:* Elaine Allegret; *Sales Dir:* Roger Allegret
Subject: Art
Founded: 1946
ISBN Publisher's Prefix: 2-7079

Nouvelles Editions Latines, 1 rue Palatine, F-75006 Paris Tel: (01) 0337742/3547742
Man Dir: Fernand Sorlot
Subjects: General Fiction, Belles Lettres, Poetry, History, Travel, Religion
1978: 80 titles *Founded:* 1928
ISBN Publisher's Prefix: 2-7233

Nouvelles Editions Rationalistes SA, 16 rue de l'Ecole-Polytechnique, F-75005 Paris Tel: (01) 6330350
Subjects: Philosophy, Religion, History of Ideas, Rationalist Themes
Book Club: L'Oeil Ouvert, 16 rue de l'Ecole-Polytechnique

O R S T O M, see Office de la Recherche Scientifique

Office Central de Librairie SàrI+*, 65 rue Claude-Bernard, F-75005 Paris Tel: (01) 7076210
Subject: Education

Office Central de Lisieux SA, 51 rue du Carmel, F-14100 Lisieux Tel: (31) 620188
Subject: Religion

Office de Documentation Bibliographique et de Diffusion, subsidiary of Librairie Fischbacher (qv)

Office de la Recherche Scientifique et Technique Outre Mer (ORSTOM), 24 rue Bayard, F-75008 Paris Tel: (01) 2253152 Cable Add: Orstom Paris
Man Dir: Professor G Camus
Publishing Dept and Orders to: Service des Publications, 70-74 route d'Alnay, F-93140, Bondy Tel: (847) 3195
Subjects: Scientific and Technical Texts, especially the Human Sciences connected with the Tropical and Mediterranean Areas of the World
1978: 44 titles *1979:* 40-50 titles *Founded:* 1943
ISBN Publisher's Prefix: 2-7099

Opera Mundi SA*, 100 ave Raymond Poincaré, F-75784 Paris cedex 16 Tel: (01) 5533421/7045320 Telex: Mundi Paris 611967
President: P Winkler; *Man Dir:* G Gauthier; *Dir:* C Ronsac
Subjects: Art, Social Science, History, General Fiction & Nonfiction, Juveniles

Editions Ophrys+*, 10 rue de Nesle, F-75006 Paris Tel: (01) 3268204

Man Dir: Albert-Yves Jean; *Publicity & Advertising:* Mrs B Monnier
Subjects: Linguistics, Belles Lettres, History, Philosophy, Education, Economics, Sociology
Founded: 1934
Bookshops: Librairie Ophrys, 61 rue Monsieur le Prince, F-70006 Paris; Editions Ophrys succursale de Paris, 10 rue de Nesle, F-75006 Paris
ISBN Publisher's Prefix: 2-7080

Editions de l'**Orante**+, 6 rue du Général-Bertrand, F-75007 Paris Tel: (01) 7835502
Man Dir: Simone Lafarge
Subjects: Belles Lettres, Poetry, History, Philosophy, Religion
Founded: 1940
ISBN Publisher's Prefix: 2-7031

Editions Oliver **Orban**, 7 rue Daunou, F-75002 Paris Tel: 2617601/2617804
Man Dir: Olivier Orban; *Editorial:* Françoise Roth, Anne Leclerc, Martine Laroche; *Rights & Permissions:* Marie-Ange Mosca
Subjects: General Fiction and Nonfiction
1977: 18 titles *1978:* 37 titles *Founded:* 1974
ISBN Publisher's Prefix: 2-85565

Les Editions d'**Organisation**+*, 5 rue Rousselet, F-75007 Paris Tel: (01) 5671840 Telex: 24133 f intedur
Dir: Dominique Bidart
Parent Company: Editions Eyrolles (qv)
Subjects: Business Management & Organization generally; especially Data Processing, Personnel Training, Sociology, Industrial Law
Bookshop: 5 rue Rousselet, F-75007 Paris
1977: 25 titles *Founded:* 1953
ISBN Publisher's Prefix: 2-7081

Michel de l'**Ormeraie**, 4 rue Labrouste, F-75015 Paris Tel: 8284070
Man Dir, Editorial: Michel de l'Ormeraie; *Sales:* Véronique Reiffers; *Publicity:* Frédéric Mercier; *Rights and Permissions:* Chantal Chazalet
Subjects: Exact Facsimiles (text and binding), of famous illustrated editions of French and other Literary Classics
Bookshop: Galerie Michel de l'Ormeraie, 17 rue Castagnary, F-75015 Paris
1977: 18 titles *Founded:* 1970
ISBN Publisher's Prefix: 2-85135

Editions Pierre Jean **Oswald***, 7 rue de l'Ecole Polytechnique, F-75005 Paris
Tel: (01) 0339007
Subjects: General Fiction, Poetry, Belles Lettres, Paperbacks, Music, Third World, Creative Literature
Founded: 1964
ISBN Publisher's Prefix: 2-7172

Ouest-Publicité (Annnuaire de Versailles)+*, 26 ave de St-Cloud, F-78000 Versailles
Tel: (01) 9508097
Subject: Annuals

Les Editions **Ouvrières** SA+*, 12 ave Soeur-Rosalie, F-75013 Paris Tel: (01) 3379385
Subjects: History, Religion, How-to, Education, Juveniles, Political & Social Science, Economics
Founded: 1939
ISBN Publisher's Prefix: 2-7082

Editions **P A C** (Presse-Auto-Conseil)+, 3 rue Saint Roch, F-75001 Paris
Tel: 2615017
Man Dir, Rights and Permissions: Thierry Schimpff; *Publicity:* Catherine Schimpff
Subjects: Sport, Cinema, Crime Novels, Commentaries and Documentaries,
Adventure Reports
1977: 18 titles *1978:* 32 titles *Founded:* 1975
ISBN Publisher's Prefix: 2-85336

P O F, see Publications Orientalistes de France

P U F, see Presses universitaires de France

P U L, see Université de Lille

P Y C Edition+, 254 rue de Vaugirard, F-75740 Paris cedex 15 Tel: (01) 5322719
Subjects: Mechanical Engineering, Heating, Air Conditioning, Solar Energy, Refrigeration, Metallurgy, Welding

Les Editions du **Pacifique**+*, 26 rue des Carmes, F-75005 Paris Tel: (01) 3251022 Telex: 203913 f edpac
Man Dir: Didier Millet; *Assistant Editor:* Robert Cooley; *Marketing Dir:* Rose Desbois
Orders to: Groupe International Hachette, 58 rue Jean Bleuzen, F-92170 Vanves
Associate Company: Les Editions du Pacifique, Papeete, Tahiti, French Polynesia (qv)
Subjects: General Nonfiction; Travel, Natural Sciences (for tropical environments), History, Gift Books
1977: 12 titles *1978:* 55 titles (Numbers refer to publications both in France and French Polynesia) *Founded:* 1971
ISBN Publisher's Prefix: 2-85700

Jean-Jacques **Pauvert** Editeur*, 8 rue de Nesle, F-75006 Paris Tel: (01) 6335640
Dir: Jean-Jacques Pauvert
Orders to: Distribution Hachette, 25 rue des Cevennes, F-75739 Paris cedex 15
International orders to: Distribution Hachette, 58 rue Jean Bleuzen, F-92170 Vanves
Subjects: Fiction, Belles Lettres, Art, History, Reference, Social Science, Paperbacks, Poetry, Philosophy, Juveniles, Photography, Languages
Founded: 1945
ISBN Publisher's Prefix: 2-85092

Le **Pavillon**, Roger Maria Editeur+*, 5 rue Rollin, F-75005 Paris Tel: (01) 3268429
Subjects: General Fiction, Belles Lettres, Philosophy, Religion, Social Science, History, Education
Founded: 1947
ISBN Publisher's Prefix: 2-85224

Editions **Payot**+, 106 blvd St-Germain, F-75006 Paris Tel: (01) 3297410
Man Dir: Jean-Luc Pidoux-Payot
Subjects: Biography, History, Philosophy, Reference, Religion, Low-priced Paperbacks, Education, Medicine, Law, Economics, General and Social Science, Psychology, Languages
1977: 70 titles *1978:* 80 titles *Founded:* 1912
ISBN Publisher's Prefix: 2-228

Pédagogie Moderne, 39 rue Chanzy, F-75011 Paris Tel: 3716878
Man Dir, Rights & Permissions: Louis-J Bonnet; *Editorial:* Françoise Poquin; *Publicity:* Yvonne Cartier
Orders to: Diffusion Bordas, 39 rue Boularrd, F-75680 Paris cedex 14
Parent Company: Groupe Bordas-Dunod, 17 rue Rémy Dumoncel, F-75680 Paris cedex 14
Subjects: Teaching Instruction (semi-scholastic)
1978: 21 titles *1979:* 27 titles *Founded:* 1931
ISBN Publisher's Prefix: 2-7294

Editions **Pédone**+, 13 rue Soufflot, F-75005 Paris Tel: (01) 3540597
Man Dir: Denis Pédone
Subjects: Law, Engineering, Agriculture, Mining, Management, Economics, Book Industry
1977: 39 titles *1978:* 36 titles *Founded:* 1837
ISBN Publisher's Prefix: 2-233

Pensée Moderne Jacques Grancher, see Jacques Grancher

Les **Périodiques** Parisiens+*, 150 ave des Champs-Elysées, F-75008 Paris Tel: (01) 2255837
Subject: Annuals

Librairie Académique **Perrin**, 8 rue Garancière, F-75006 Paris Tel: (01) 3291280
Chairman: Claude Nielsen; *Publicity Manager:* Nadia Leser; *Foreign Rights:* Josiane Bontron
Subjects: Belles Lettres, History, Reference, Scholarly, Bibliography, Fiction, Arts, Religion
Founded: 1827
Miscellaneous: Member of Presses de la Cité group (qv)
ISBN Publisher's Prefix: 2-262

Editions G M **Perrin** SA*, 61 ave Ledru-Rollin, F-75012 Paris Tel: (01) 3437512
Subjects: Audio Visual & Electronic Media, Education, Science & Technical
Miscellaneous: Firm is a member of the Presses de la Cité group (qv)
ISBN Publisher's Prefix: 2-85084

Olivier **Perrin** Editeur*, 198 blvd St-Germain, F-75007 Paris Tel: (01) 5485982/5489687
Man Dir: Olivier Perrin
Subjects: General Fiction, Reference, Art, Theatre, Scholarly, Medicine, Social Science, Sports, Education
Founded: 1948
ISBN Publisher's Prefix: 2-85053

Editions **Phébus**+, 17 rue Pierre Lescot, F-75001 Paris Tel: 2602394
Man Dir: Jean-Pierre Sicre
Orders to: Diffusion Littera, 4 rue de Tournon, F-75006 Paris
Subjects: General Literature, Oriental (Eastern) Literature, Literary Criticism, Fine Arts
1979: 31 titles

Editions A & J **Picard** Sàrl+*, 82 rue Bonaparte, F-75006 Paris 6 Tel: (01) 3269673
Man Dirs: Jacques Picard, Chantal Pasini
Subjects: General, Art, Legal, Religious, Literary and Local History; Archaeology, Architecture, Reference, Education, Bibliography, Folklore, Philology, Textbooks, Musicology, Antiquarian Books
1977: 10 titles *Founded:* 1869
ISBN Publisher's Prefix: 2-7084

Editions Marcel **Pierron**+*, Terrain Industriel, 4 rue Gutenberg, F-57206 Sarreguemines Tel: (087) 982003/951431 Telex: 860495 F
Subjects: Education, Audio Visual & Electronic Media

Editions Jean-Michel **Place***, 12 rue Pierre et Marie Curie, F-75005 Paris Tel: 6330511
Man Dir and other offices: Jean-Michel Place
Associate Company: Éditions de la Chronique des Lettres Françaises (qv)
Subjects: Literature and Literary Research; Bibliographies, Reference, Poetry, Fiction

Bookshop: 12 rue Pierre et Marie Curie, Paris
1977: 12 titles *Founded:* 1973
ISBN Publisher's Prefix: 2-85893

Editions **Plantyn** SA+*, 1 pl Gabriel-Fauré, BP 803, F-74016 Annecy-le-Vieux Tel: (50) 572838
Subjects: Education, Science & Technical
Miscellaneous: Firm is a member of the Kluwer Group, Deventer, Netherlands (qv)
ISBN Publisher's Prefix: 2-7136

Librairie **Plon** SA+, 8 rue Garancière, F-75006 Paris Tel: (01) 3291280 Cable Add: Ploédit Paris 110 Telex: 204807
Chairman: Claude Nielsen; *Foreign Rights:* Josiane Bontron
Subjects: General Fiction, History, Belles Lettres, Philosophy, How-to, Religion, Reference, Economics, Social Science, Scholarly, Arts, Maps, Travel, Anthropology, Trade Books
Founded: 1844
Miscellaneous: Member of Presses de la Cité group (qv)
ISBN Publisher's Prefix: 2-259

Presses **Pocket***, 8 rue Garancière, F-75006, Paris Tel: 3291280 Telex: Precite 204807 F
Subjects: Novels, Memoirs, War, Documentary, Science Fiction (all paperback)
Miscellaneous: Firm is a member of the Presses de la Cité group (qv)

Centre Georges **Pompidou** Edition, see Centre national d'art et de Culture Georges-Pompidou

Julien **Prélat** Sàrl+, 17 rue du Petit-Pont, F-75005 Paris Tel: (01) 3547763
Management, Rights & Permissions: H Dargent, S Kolf; *Publicity & Advertising:* Mr Lizeux
Subjects: Textbooks and specialist books connected with odontology, stomatology; also general dentistry and medicine
1977: 11 titles *1978:* 17 titles *Founded:* 1946
Bookshops: Librairie Odonto Stomatologie, 17 rue du Petit-Pont, Paris 5e; Librairie Psychologie, 2 rue du Cardinal Lemoine, Paris 5e
Miscellaneous: Publishes two quarterly journals
ISBN Publisher's Prefix: 2-85039

Société Nouvelle **Présence Africaine**+, 25 bis rue des Ecoles, F-75006 Paris Tel: (01) 0331374 Cable Add: Presafric Paris
Man Dir: Mme Alioune Diop; *Publicity & Advertising, Rights & Permissions:* H G Jones
Subjects: General Fiction, Belles Lettres, Poetry, Philosophy, History, Reference, Religion, Low-priced Paperbacks, Primary Textbooks, Politics (all subjects pertain to Africa)
1977: 15 titles *1978:* 23 titles *Founded:* 1947
Bookshop: 25 bis rue des Ecoles
ISBN Publisher's Prefix: 2-7087

Presse-Auto-Conseil, see P A C

Les **Presses d'Ile-de-France** Sàrl+*, 12 rue de la Chaise, F-75007 Paris Tel: (01) 2223730
Subject: Juveniles
ISBN Publisher's Prefix: 2-7088

Les **Presses de la Cité**+*, 8 rue Garancière, F-75006 Paris Tel: (01) 3291280 Cable Add: Svennil Paris
President and Distribution Dir: Claude Nielsen; *Publicity & Advertising:* Nadia Leser; *Rights & Permissions:* Josiane Bontron, Mrs Fréret
Subjects: General Fiction, History, How-to, Low- & High-priced Paperbacks
Founded: 1947
Presses de la Cité group: Librairie Plon (qv); G P Rouge et Or (qv); Solar (qv); Librairie Académique Perrin; Julliard (qv); Presses Pocket (qv); Fleuve Noir (qv); Messageries Centrales du Livre (qv); Editions Christian Bourgois (qv); Encyclopédie Internationale des Sciences & Techniques; 10/18; le Rocher; UGE
ISBN Publisher's Prefix: 2-258

Presses de la Fondation Nationale des Sciences Politiques+, 27 rue St-Guillaume, F-75341 Paris cedex 07 Tel: 2603960, 2220985
Man Dir: Louis Bodin; *Sales:* Marc Riglet
Subjects: Research Works and Periodicals connected with the Social Sciences, especially Political, Historical, Sociological, Economics
1977: 12 titles *1978:* 13 titles *Founded:* 1975
ISBN Publisher's Prefix: 2-7246

Presses de la Renaissance, 198 blvd Saint-Germain, F-75007 Paris Tel: 5485982/5489687 Telex: 260717 orem 158
Man Dir, Sales: Fabienne Delmote; *Editorial:* Tony Cartano; *Rights & Permissions:* Françoise Triffaux
Parent Company: Pierre Belfond, Paris (qv)
Associate Companies: Nouvel Office d'Edition et de Diffusion (qv), Productions de Paris
Subjects: General Fiction, Biography, Documentary, Folklore, Science Fiction, Psychology and the Para-Normal, Animals; French Classics, and Foreign Classics in Translation
1978: 30 titles *1979:* 30 titles *Founded:* 1971
ISBN Publisher's Prefix: 85616

Les **Presses Monastiques**, see Zodiaque

Presses universitaires de France (PUF)+, 108 blvd St-Germain, F-75279 Paris cedex 06 Tel: (01) 3291201 Telex: 600979 F
Registered Office: 17 rue Sfflot, F-75005 Paris; *General Management and Editorial:* 108 blvd Saint-Germain, F-75279 Paris; *Public Relations/Publicity:* 90 blvd Saint-Germain, F-75005 Paris
President: Pierre Angoulvent; *Dirs:* Robert Ruelle, Pierre Wittmann; *Sales Dir:* Jean-Pierre Giband; *Editorial:* Laurence Piel, Michel Prigent; *Publicity & Advertising:* Gabrielle Gelber; *Rights & Permissions:* Françoise Laye, Arlette Monsallier
Orders to: Bois de L'Epine, CE 1105, F-91002 Evry Cedex Tel: 0778205 Telex: PUF 600474 F
Subjects: Belles Lettres, Poetry, Biography, History, Music, Art, Philosophy, Reference, Religion, Engineering, Low- & High-priced Paperbacks, Psychology, Medicine, General, Social & Political Science, University Textbooks
1977: 450 titles *Founded:* 1921
Bookshops: Librairie générale des PUF, 49 blvd St-Michel, F-75005 Paris; Librairie Internationale, 17 rue Soufflot, F-75005 Paris

Presses universitaires de Grenoble, Domaine Universitaire, BP 47X, F-38400 St Martin d'Hères Tel: (76) 548178 Telex: Unisog 980910
Manager: Philippe Hardouin; *Commercial Manager:* Jean-Claude Naar, Lydie Valero
Orders to: Ophrys, 10 rue de Nesle, F-75006 Paris
Subjects: Architecture, Anthropology, Sociology, Law, Economics, Management, History, Statistics, Literature, Medicine, Data Processing, Physics, Politics
1977: 35 titles *1978:* 45 titles
ISBN Publisher's Prefix: 2-7061

Presses Universitaires de Lyon, 86 rue Pasteur, F-69365 Lyon cedex 2 Tel: (78) 692048
Man Dir: Joël Saugnieux
Subjects: History, Economics, University Textbooks, Linguistics, Lyons Regional Interest, Religious History, Law
1977: 10 titles *1978:* 25 titles *Founded:* 1976
ISBN Publisher's Prefix: 2-7297

Editions Edouard **Privat** SA+*, 14 rue des Arts, F-31000 Toulouse 61 Tel: (61) 230926
Man Dir: Pierre Privat; *Literary, Production:* Georges Hahn; *Sales Dir:* Jean Sacrispeyre; *Publicity & Press Relations:* André Rimailho; *Rights & Permissions:* Noëlle Lever
Subjects: French regional history and culture; Education, Psychology, Sociology, Philosophy, Pedagogy
1977: 50 titles *Founded:* 1834
ISBN Publisher's Prefix: 2-7089

Publi-Union+, 10 rue Lyautey, F-75016 Paris Tel: (01) 9243610
Man Dir: Michel Wenlersse
Associate Company: Groupe Expansion, Paris (qv)
Subjects: Law, Economics, Social Science, Education, Science & Technical
ISBN Publisher's Prefix: 2-85200

Publications Filmées d'Art et d'Histoire+, 9-15 rue Carvès, F-92120 Montrouge Tel: 6571413 (ext 78)
Man Dir: Marcel Hamelle; *Sales:* Georges Auger
Subjects: Books illustrated by slides on Art, History, and the Exploration of Space
1977: 3 titles
ISBN Publisher's Prefix: 2-85228

Publications Orientalistes de France (POF)+, 4 rue de Lille, F-75007 Paris Tel: (01) 2606705
Dir: Simone Maviel
Orders to: Ophrys, 10 rue de Nesles, F-75006 Paris
Subjects: Literature translated mainly from East European, Middle and Far East Languages; also Bibliographies, Vocabularies etc relating to these languages, Theatre, Economy; specialises in works covering all aspects of Eastern Europe and the Middle and Far East
1978: 23 titles
ISBN Publisher's Prefix: 2-7169

Editions **Pygmalion** — Gérard Watelet, 70 Ave de Breteuil, F-75007 Paris
Tel: 5674077
Man Dir, Editorial: Gérard Watelet; *Sales, Rights & Permissions:* Luce Watelet
Subjects: General Literature, History, Archaeology, Art
1978: 25 titles *1979:* 25 titles *Founded:* 1977
ISBN Publisher's Prefix: 2-85704

Librairie Aristide **Quillet** SA+, 278 blvd St-Germain, F-75006 Paris Tel: (01) 5514810 Cable Add: Ariquillet Paris 44
Man Dir: Guy Rocaut; *Rights & Permissions:* Philippe Leturc
Subjects: Science & Technology, Dictionaries, Encyclopaedias
Founded: 1898
ISBN Publisher's Prefix: 2-85041

106 FRANCE

Quoi de Nouveau*, 23 bis, blvd Brune,
75014 Paris Tel: (01) 5399189

Editions '**R**', Société Civile Typo, Graphique
et Littéraire, 33 ave Victor Hugo,
F-84400 Apt Tel: (90) 720598
Man Dir, Editorial, Rights & Permissions:
Robert Morel; *Production, Publicity:*
François Morel
Orders to: Morel, 5 rue du Mail, Paris 2
Tel: 2600738
Associate Companies: Morel Editeurs (qv),
at same address; "R" Editore, Via Larga 9,
Ortonovo (LS), Italy
Subjects: Rites, Myths and Symbols,
Sorcery, Encylopaedia of Tarot, Fiction,
Vocabulary Traditions and Images, Popular
Literature
1978: 35 titles *Founded:* 1977

R E C T A Foldex+*, 27 rue Trébois,
F-92300 Levallois-Perret Tel: 2701203
Man Dir: Mrs Costard
Subject: Maps, Charts etc
Miscellaneous: RECTA = Réalisations,
Études Cartographiques Touristiques et
Administratives (Cartographic design and
production in the touring and administrative
fields)

R E M I, see Réalisation pour
l'Enseignement Multilingue International

Editions **R S T**, see Editions Robert
Steindecker

Société des Editions **Radio**+*, 9 rue Jacob,
F-75006 Paris Tel: (01) 0331365
Subjects: Engineering (Books & Technical
Journals), Mass Media
Founded: 1934
ISBN Publisher's Prefix: 2-7091

Editions **Ramsay**, 27 rue de Fleurus,
F-75006 Paris Tel: 5665505
Man Dir: Jean-Pierre Ramsay; *Editorial:*
Erick Orsena, Gérard H Coury; *Sales:* Alain
Flatigny; *Production:* Nathalie Perpin;
Publicity: Catherine Royes; *Rights and
Permissions:* N E Nilleret
Orders to: Forum, 13 rue de la Glaciere,
F-75011 Paris
1978: 42 titles

Réalisations pour l'Enseignement
Multilingue International+ (REMI), 39 rue
de l'Abbé-Grégoire, F-75006 Paris Tel: (01)
2227090
Man Dir: Mrs D Holtzer
Subjects: Foreign language courses for
Primary schools (French, German, English);
Elementary French readers
Founded: 1966
ISBN Publisher's Prefix: 2-85134

Retz, see CAL/Retz

Revisematic+*, 61 rue Raymond Losserand,
F-75014 Paris Tel: (01) 3060915
Subjects: Education, Science & Technical

Editions Scientifiques **Riber** Sàrl+*, 54 rue
du Vert-Bois, F-75003 Paris Tel: (01)
2775772
Subjects: Science & Technical
ISBN Publisher's Prefix: 2-7091

Franco Maria **Ricci***, Galerie 12, 12 Rue
des Beaux-Arts, F-75006 Paris
Tel: 6339631
*Man Dir, Editorial, Production, Rights &
Permissions:* Franco Maria Ricci; *Sales:*
Yves Dantoing
Orders to: Sofedis, 88 rue de Lille, F-75007
Parent Company: Franco Maria Ricci,
Milan, Italy
Publishers Represented: Franco Maria
Ricci, Deco Press

Subjects: Art Books, Bodoni Editions,
Diderot Encyclopaedia, Bibliophile Editions,
Graphic Design (Deco Press)
Book Clubs: Les Amis de Franco Maria
Ricci, Société des Bibliophiles
Bookshop: 12 rue des Beaux Arts, F-75006
Paris
1977: 2 titles *Founded:* 1974

Editions **Richelieu** SA*, 12 rue Ernest-
Psichari, F-75007 Paris Tel: (01) 5519650
Subjects: Law, Economics, Social Science,
Academic, Art
ISBN Publisher's Prefix: 2-85043

Jacques **Riquier** Editions*, Champs Elysees,
F-75008 Paris Tel: 2562490
Subjects: Children's Books

Librairie Marcel **Rivière** et Cie+, 22 rue
Soufflot, F-75005 Paris Tel: (01) 0330718
Dir: R Abranson
Subjects: History, Philosophy, Social
Science, Economics, Scholarly Books,
Politics, Management
Founded: 1902
ISBN Publisher's Prefix: 2-85229

Editions E **Robert**+, L'École et la Famille,
BP 4384, F-69241 Lyons cedex 1 (Located
at: 28 rue du Bon-Pasteur, F-69001 Lyons)
Tel: (78) 284889
Man Dir: A Rouveyrol; *Sales, Publicity &
Advertising:* L Chauffour
Subjects: Primary Textbooks, Educational
Materials
1979: 4 titles *Founded:* 1873
ISBN Publisher's Prefix: 2-7093

Dictionnaire Le **Robert**, see Société du
Nouveau Littré (SNL)

Éditions **Rombaldi** SA*, 15-17 rue de
Rome, F-75008 Paris Tel: (01)
2618401/2618425 Telex: rombald 641854 F
President: Pierre Godfroid; *Man Dir:*
Michel Leroux; *Commercial Dirs:* Henri
Kaufman, Hervé le Henaff; *Production
Manager:* Henri Kaufman
Subjects: General Fiction, Belles Lettres,
Encyclopaedias, History
Founded: 1920
Book Clubs: Bibliothèque Du Temps
Présent and six others (sold by Ediclub
Rombaldi, qv under Book Clubs)
ISBN Publisher's Prefix: 2-231

E S F **Rosenwald**+*, 15 rue St-Benoît,
F-75006 Paris Tel: (01) 2225585
Subject: Annuals

Rossel Edition*, 73 rue d'Anjou, F-75008
Paris Tel: (01) 3874517
Associate Company: Rossel Edition,
Belgium (qv)
Subjects: Juveniles, Sport, Novels, Guides,
Gardening, Nature

Editions **Roudil**+*, 53 rue St-Jacques,
F-75005 Paris Tel: (01) 0334797
Man Dir: Henry Roudil; *Sales Dir:* Lucien
Drouot; *Publicity Dir:* Mr Roy; *Advertising
Dir:* Mr Brajon; *Rights & Permissions:*
Henry Roudil
Subjects: History, Philosophy, University &
Secondary Textbooks, Fiction
Founded: 1954
ISBN Publisher's Prefix: 2-85044

Editions **Rouff** SA+, 36 rue du Vieux-Pont-
de-Sèvres, F-92100 Boulogne-Billancourt
Tel: 6090140
Subjects: Humour, Shooting, Periodicals
ISBN Publisher's Prefix: 2-85045

G P **Rouge et Or***, 8 rue Garancière,
F-75006 Paris Tel: 3281280 Telex: Precite
204807 F

Subjects: Children's Literature
1978: 110 titles
Miscellaneous: Firm is a member of the
Presses de la Cité group (qv)

Publications **Roy**, now incorporated in
Publications Estoup et Roy (qv)

Ruedo Ibérico*, 6 rue de Latran, F-75005
Paris Tel: (01) 3255649
Man Dir: Mr Martínez
Bookshop: 6 rue de Latran, F-75005 Paris
Subjects: Studies of Recent and
Contemporary Spanish History, Spanish
Politics, Social Science etc, General Fiction
(many titles in Castilian)
Founded: 1962
ISBN Publisher's Prefix: 2-7153

S C E M I (Société Continentale d'Editions
Modernes Illustrées) Sàrl*, 25 quai des
Grands-Augustins, F-75006 Paris Tel: (01)
3260306
Subject: Encyclopaedias
ISBN Publisher's Prefix: 2-85046

S E A P (Société d'Edition d'Annuaires
Professionnels)*, BP 115, F-75825 Paris
cedex 17 (Located at: 1 rue Descombes,
F-75017 Paris) Tel: (01) 3807916
Subject: Annuaire Officiel de la Charcuterie
(Official Year Book of the Delicatessen
Trade)
Miscellaneous: Associate company of
Editions Comindus, Paris (qv)

S E C A (Société d'Exploitation et de
Diffusion des Codes Rousseau Sàrl)+, 7
quai du Brise-Lames, F-85100 bles-
d'Olonne Tel: 327731
Subjects: Education, Juveniles, Audio Visual
& Electronic Media
ISBN Publisher's Prefix: 2-7095

S E D E (Société d'Edition de Dictionnaires
et d'Encyclopédies)+*, 26 rue de Condé,
F-75006 Paris Tel: (01) 3264781
Subject: Reference
Founded: 1949
ISBN Publisher's Prefix: 2-85151

S E D E S, see Centre de Documentation
Universitaire

S E R T (Société d'Edition, de Publicité, de
Radio et Télévision) SA+*, 50 rue de la
Condamine, F-75017 Paris Tel: (01)
5085477
Subject: Literature

S I M E P SA, 38/46 rue de Bruxelles,
BP 1214, F-69611 Villeuisanne, cedex Tel:
(78) 899710
Name denotes Société d'Information
medicale et d'Enseignement post-
universitaire, Medical Information and Post-
University Teaching Company
Chairman: Bernard Duportet; *Man Dir:*
Micheline Duportet
Subject: Specialist texts on all aspects of
medicine; Periodicals
1977: 110 titles *1978:* 130 titles *Founded:*
1965
ISBN Publisher's Prefix: 2-85334

S N L, see Société du Nouveau Littré

Editions **S O S** (Editions du Secours
Catholique)+, 106 rue de Bac, F-75007
Paris Tel: (01) 5486066
Man Dir: Maurice Herr; *Publicity &
Advertising:* Georges Fanucchi
Subjects: History, Philosophy, Religion,
Social Science
Founded: 1949
ISBN Publisher's Prefix: 2-7185

S P E L D, 6 rue Victor-Cousin, F-75005 Paris
A group of French publishers specializing in Politics, Law and Economics

S R A (Société de Recherche appliquée à l'Education)+, 92 blvd de Latour-Maubourg, F-75007 Paris Tel: (01) 5517773
President: B de Luze
Parent Company: Science Research Associates Inc (USA)
Associate Companies: see Science Research Associates (UK)
Subject: Primary & Secondary Education materials
1978: 1 title
ISBN Publisher's Prefix: 2-274

S U D E L (Société Universitaire d'Editions et de Librairie)+*, 20 rue Corvisart, F-75640 Paris cedex 13 Tel: (01) 5354846
Subject: Education
ISBN Publisher's Prefix: 2-7162

Editions **Sageret**+, 5 et 7 rue Plumet, F-75015 Paris Tel: (01) 5674674/5674682
Subject: Publishes a General Directory of Building and Public Works

Les Editions du **Sagittaire** — Union des Techniques d'Editions, 61 rue des Sts-Pères, F-75006 Paris Tel: (01) 2229976
Dirs: Bernard Privat, Jean-Claude Farquelle
Subjects: Fiction, Biography, History, General Literature
Founded: 1929

Editions **Saint-Germain-des-Prés** SA, 110 rue du Cherche-Midi, F-75006 Paris Tel: (01) 2227120
Holding Company: Le Cherche-Midi (qv)
1978: 75 titles *Founded:* 1969

Editions **Saint-Paul** SA+, 6 rue Cassette, F-75006 Paris Tel: (01) 2221783 (Paris); 6422980 (Issy-les-Moulineaux)
Man Dir: M Dumas
Subsidiary Company: Editions Saint-Paul SA, Dept des Classiques Africains (qv)
Br Off: 184 ave de Verdun, F-92130 Issy-les-Moulineaux
Subjects: Religion, Religious History, Biography, Africana
Bookshop: Librairie Saint-Paul, 6 rue Cassette, F-75006 Paris
1978: 8 titles *Founded:* 1873
ISBN Publisher's Prefix: 2-85049

Editions **Saint-Paul, Departement Les Classiques Africains**, 184 ave de Verdun, F-92130 Issy-les-Moulineaux Tel: 6422980
Parent Company: Editions Saint Paul
Subjects: Black Africa Literature, Daily Life, Tropical Medicine, School Books
Bookshop: Librairie Saint-Paul, 6 rue Cassette, F-75005 Paris
1977: 15 titles *1978:* 15 titles

Editions **Salvator** SàrH+, BP 1175, F-68053 Mulhouse cedex (Located at: 9 Pont d'Altkirch) Tel: (89) 451430
Orders to: Editions du Cerf (qv), Paris or to Salvator at above address
Subject: Religion
1977: 8 titles *1978:* 10 titles *Founded:* 1924
ISBN Publisher's Prefix: 2-7067

K G **Saur** Editeur Sàrl, rue de Bassano 38, F-75008 Paris Tel: 7235518

Schott Frères Sàrl*, 35 rue Jean Moulin, F-94300 Vincennes Tel: 3743095

Scolavox, BP 429, F-86011 Poitiers Tel: 462766
Man Dir: Claude Moreau; *Sales Dir:* Albert Combe
Subjects: Poetry, Primary Textbooks, Educational Materials, including audio-visual slide programme
Founded: 1959
ISBN Publisher's Prefix: 2-85052

Editions du **Secours** Catholique, see S O S

La Société **Sécuritas** SA+*, 2 rue de Châteaudun, F-75009 Paris Tel: (01) 8787206
Subjects: Science & Technical, Law, Economics, Social Science, Audio Visual & Electronic Media
ISBN Publisher's Prefix: 2-7097

Seditas (Société d'Editions et de Diffusion Tambourinaire-Sofradel)+, 186 rue du Faubourg-St-Honoré, F-75008 Paris Tel: (01) 5619600
Orders to: 41 rue Washington, F-75008 Paris
Subjects: Management, Scientific, Technical, Electronics
ISBN Publisher's Prefix: 2-85179

Editions **Seghers** SA+, 31 rue Falguière, F-75725 Paris cedex 15 Tel: 3201421 Telex: Edilaf 250877
President and General Manager: Serge Godin; *Rights & Permissions:* Béatrix Vernet
Orders to: Inter Forum, 13 rue de la Glacière, F-75013 Paris Telex: 250055
Subjects: Belles Lettres, Poetry, History, Biography, Philosophy, Science & Technical, Music, Politics, Paperbacks
1977: 79 titles *Founded:* 1939
ISBN Publisher's Prefix: 2-232

Editions **Sélection** J Jacobs SA+*, 66 rue Falguière, F-75015 Paris Tel: (01) 3203188
Subjects: Technology, Fine Arts, How-to series
ISBN Publisher's Prefix: 2-7174

Les Editions du **Sénevé***, 10 rue Cassette, F-75006 Paris Tel: (01) 2229020
Subjects: Art, Juveniles, Religion, Religious Educational Materials
Founded: 1947

Les **Sept Couleurs***, 13 rue des Montiboeufs, BP 9775962, F-75020 Paris cedex 20 Tel: 3314015
Man Dir: Maurice Bardèche
Orders to: Diffusion Sofedis, 29 rue St Sulpice, F-75006 Paris
Subsidiary Company: Défense de l'Occident Sarl, at above adddress
Subjects: Belles Lettres, Poetry, History, Social Science, Philology, Politics
Bookshop: Librairie Française, 27 rue de l'Abbé Grégoire, F-75006 Paris
Founded: 1948
ISBN Publisher's Prefix: 2-85147

Editions **Serg** SRP*, 35 rue St-Lazare, F-75009 Paris Tel: 2851906
Subjects: Strip Cartoons, Applied Arts, French Regional Architecture, History of Architecture

Service Technique pour l'Education (Fonds Social Juif Unifié)+*, 19 blvd Poissonnière, F-75002 Paris Tel: (01) 5084756
Man Dir: Mrs Krief
Subjects: General Fiction, Belles Lettres, Poetry, Biography, History, Music, Art, Philosophy, Reference, Religion, Juveniles, Educational Materials, Judaica
Founded: 1962
Bookshop: 19 blvd Poissonnière, F-75002 Paris

Editions du **Seuil**+, 27 rue Jacob, F-75261 Paris cedex 06 Tel: (01) 3291215 Cable Add: Ediseuil Telex: 600605 F
Man Dir: Michel Chodkiewicz; *Editorial:* Anne Fréjer, Denis Roche, François Wahl, Bruno Flamand, Jean-Claude Guillebaud, Jean-Marie Borzeux; *Sales Dir:* Edouard de Andréis; *Production:* Anne Poulain; *Publicity:* Françoise Peyrot; *Rights & Permissions:* Jacqueline Lesschaeve
Subsidiary Company: Société d'Editions Scientifiques, Dimedia
Subjects: General Fiction, Literature, Poetry, Biography, History, How-to, Music, Art, Philosophy, Reference, Religion, Low- & High-priced Paperbacks, Psychology, General & Social Science, University Textbooks, Politics
1977: 206 titles *Founded:* 1935
ISBN Publisher's Prefix: 2-02

Editions **Siloé** SàrH+*, 8 pl St-Sulpice, F-75006 Paris Tel: (01) 3260057
Subject: Religion
ISBN Publisher's Prefix: 2-85054

Editions André **Silvaire**+, 20 rue Domat, F-75005 Paris Tel: (01) 5513613
Branch Off: 16 rue de Bellechasse, F-75007 Paris
Bookshop: Librairie des Lettres, 16 rue de Bellechasse, F-75007 Paris
Subjects: General Fiction, Belles Lettres, Poetry, Theatre, Philosophy, Social Sciences, Paperbacks, School Books
Founded: 1944
Miscellaneous: Associate company is Les Amis de Milosz, 6 rue José-Maria-de Heredia, F-75007 Paris
ISBN Publisher's Prefix: 2-85055

Sindbad+, 1-3 rue Feutrier, F-75018 Paris Tel: (01) 2553523
Man Dir: Pierre Bernard
Subjects: General Fiction, Belles Lettres, Poetry, History, Art, Philosophy, Reference, Religion, Social and Political Science. Specializes in the Arabic, Persian and Muslim worlds
1977: 12 titles *1978:* 14 titles *Founded:* 1972
ISBN Publisher's Prefix: 2-7274

Editions **Sirey**+, 22 rue Soufflot, F-75005 Paris Tel: (01) 3540718
Dir: Patrice Vergé; *Dir:* Georges Alapetite; *Sales:* Alain Hapiot
Subjects: History, Philosophy, Social Science, Law, Business, University & Secondary Textbooks, Economics
1977: 50 titles *Founded:* 1791
ISBN Publisher's Prefix: 2-248

Société Continentale d'Editions Modernes Illustrées, see S C E M I

Société d'Edition d'Annuaires Professionnels, see S E A P

Société d'Edition de Dictionnaires et d'Encyclopédies, see S E D E

Société d'Edition d'Enseignement Supérieur, see Centre de Documentation Universitaire

Société d'Edition, de Publicité, de Radio et Télévision, see S E R T

Société d'Editions Scientifiques, Dimedia, subsidiary company of Editions du Seuil (qv)

Société de Recherche appliquée à l'Education, see S R A

Société d'Exploitation et de Diffusion des Codes Rousseau, see S E C A

Société d'Information médicale et d'enseignement post-universitaire, see S I M E P

Société du Nouveau Littré (SNL) Dictionnaire 'Le Robert', 107 ave Parmentier, F-75011 Paris Tel: (01) 3577313
President, Man Dir: Charles-Albert de Waziers; *Commercial Manager:* Robert Crosa; *Technical Manager:* Jacques Pierre; *Publicity:* Miss de Ternay
Subject: Dictionaries
1978: 2 titles *Founded:* 1951
ISBN Publisher's Prefix: 2-85036

Société Encyclopédique Française (SEF), see SEF Philippe Daudy

Société Universitaire d'Editions et de Librairie, see S U D E L

Sodel (Editeur) SA+*, 336-340 rue St-Honoré, F-75001 Paris Tel: (01) 2603180
Subjects: Science & Technical
ISBN Publisher's Prefix: 2-7102

Sofiac (Société Française des Imprimeries Administratives Centrales), 8 rue de Furstenberg, F-75006 Paris Tel: (01) 3292129
Subjects: Economics, Social Science, Business Administration, Legal and Judicial, Accountancy
1977: 8 titles *1978:* 13 titles

Sofradel-Seditas, see Seditas

Sofradif Editions Philippe Auzou*, 1-1 bis rue du Dahomey, F-75011 Paris Tel: (01) 3714493
Publisher: Philippe Auzou; *Sales Manager:* Fred Frangeul
Subjects: Medicine, Law

Solar*, 8 rue Garancière, F-75006 Paris Tel: 329180 Telex: Precite 204807
Subjects: Practical Books, Cookery, Sport, Nature
Miscellaneous: Firm is a member of the Presses de la Cité group (qv)

Editions **Soleil Noir**+*, 2 rue Fléchier, F-75009 Paris Tel: (01) 2804702
Man Dir: François di Dio
Subjects: Poetry, Art, Social Science, Fiction
Founded: 1948
ISBN Publisher's Prefix: 2-85131

Editions d'Art Aimery **Somogy**+*, 91 rue de Seine, F-75006 Paris Tel: (01) 3268981 Telex: 204473
Man Dir: Aimery Somogy
Subject: Art
Founded: 1937
ISBN Publisher's Prefix: 2-85056

Editions **Sonzé***, 7 rue Alexandre-Cabanel, F-75015 Paris Tel: (01) 3064027
Subject: Education
ISBN Publisher's Prefix: 2-85057

Soprep (Editions de Bussac)+*, 2 cours Sablon, F-63000 Clermont-Ferrand Tel: (073) 923278

Soprode*, 3 rue Crébillon, F-75006 Paris Tel: (01) 3260158
Man Dir: Bernard Laville
Subjects: Philosophy, Social Sciences, Literature, History
ISBN Publisher's Prefix: 2-85240

Editions Louis **Soulanges** 'Le Livre Ouvert', 20 rue de l'Odéon, F-75006 Paris Tel: (01) 3262538/5240609
Man Dir, Sales Dir, Publicity: Louis Drouot Soulanges
Branch Off: 5-7 rue Abel Ferry, F-75016 Paris Tel: 5240609

Subjects: General Fiction, Philosophy, Reference, Religion, Juveniles
Founded: 1960

Les Editions de la **Source** SA+, 5 rue de la Source, F-75016 Paris Tel: (01) 5253007
Man Dir: Rev Father Dom André Gozier; *All Other Offices:* Rev Father Dom Norbert Balladur
Orders to: Office Général du Livre, 14 bis rue Jean-Ferrandi F-75006, Paris
Imprints: Lumière Biblique series
Subjects: Religion; Doctrine, Theology, Holy Scripture, Monasticism and Monastic History
Bookshop: Librairie Sainte Marie, 5 rue de la Source, F-75016 Paris
Founded: 1927
ISBN Publisher's Prefix: 2-900005

Les Editions Internationales Alain **Stanké**, 6 rue Saint Florentin, F-75001 Paris Tel: 2602332 Telex: 05561358
Man Dir, Editorial: Alain Stanké; *Sales:* Eric Ghedin; *Production:* Annie Creton; *Publicity:* Claire Dayan; *Rights & Permissions:* Lyn Franklin
Subjects: Current Affairs, Biography, Fiction, How-to, Cookery, Art, Pocket Editions
1978: 42 titles *1979:* 50 titles *Founded:* 1975
ISBN Publisher's Prefix: 2-7604

Editions Robert **Steindecker** (Editions RST)+*, 52 rue de Bassano, F-75008 Paris Tel: (01) 7201480
Man Dir: Robert Steindecker; *Sales Dir:* Guy Simbozel; *Publicity, Rights & Permissions:* Albert Monny
Subject: Juveniles
Founded: 1960
ISBN Publisher's Prefix: 2-7090

Editions **Stock**+, 14 rue de l'Ancienne Comédie, F-75006 Paris Tel: (01) 3292125
President, Man Dir: Christian de Bartillat; *Assistant Dir:* Claude Daillencourt; *Editorial Dir:* André Bay; *Sales Dir:* Alain Devanlay; *Production:* Jacques Menard; *Publicity & Advertising:* Marie-Pierre Lassus-Debat; *Rights & Permissions:* Janine Noël
Parent Company: Librairie Hachette (qv)
Subjects: French and Foreign Literature, Human Sciences, Medicine, Juveniles, Theatre, Music, Cinema, Paperbacks
1978: 130 titles *1979:* 150 titles *Founded:* 1780
ISBN Publisher's Prefix: 2-234

Editions **Studia** SA+*, 40 bis rue Maurice-Arnoux, F-92120 Montrouge Tel: 2533811
Subject: Education
ISBN Publisher's Prefix: 2-7104

Table Ronde (Les Editions de la)+*, 40 rue du Bac, F-75007 Paris Tel: (01) 2222891
Man Dir: Roland Laudenbach; *Publicity Dir:* Danielle Levêque; *Literary Dir:* Frédéric Musso; *Rights & Permissions:* Mahaut Pascalis
Subjects: General Fiction, Belles Lettres, Poetry, Biography, History, Religion, Medicine, Psychology, Social Science
Founded: 1944
ISBN Publisher's Prefix: 2-7103

Les Presses de **Taizé**+, F-71250 Taizé-Communauté (Saône et Loire) Tel: (85) 501414 Telex: Cotaize 800753F
Subject: Religious works
1977: 5 titles *1978:* 6 titles *Founded:* 1959

Librairie Jules **Tallandier**+, 17 rue Rémy-Dumoncel, F-75680 Paris cedex 14 Tel: (01) 3277770

Subjects: General Fiction (especially Romantic), Art, Belles Lettres, Reference, History, Geography, Paperbacks
Founded: 1865
ISBN Publisher's Prefix: 2-235

Editions **Tardy** SA+, 22 rue Joyeuse, BP 56, F-18002 Bourges Tel: 242986; 89 rue de Seine, F-75006 Paris Tel: (01) 3260058
Man Dir, Rights & Permissions: Pierre Tardy
Subjects: Religion, Catechisms, Parish Manuals, Religious Pedagogy
Founded: 1938
ISBN Publisher's Prefix: 2-7105

Editions **Taride** SàrI+*, 2 bis pl du Puits de l'Ermite, F-75005 Paris Tel: (01) 3364040
Cable Add: Cartaride Paris
Subjects: Geography, Travel
Founded: 1852
ISBN Publisher's Prefix: 2-7106

Claude **Tchou** Editeur, 8 rue du Pont Neuf, F-75001 Paris Tel: 2336118
Man Dir: Claude Tchou; *Rights & Permissions:* Agnes de Gorter
Subjects: General Fiction, Belles Lettres, Poetry, Biography, History, How-to, Music, Art, Juveniles, Reference, Paperbacks, Social Science, Geography, Psychology
Founded: 1963
ISBN Publisher's Prefix: 2-7107

Société des Éditions **Technip**+, 27 rue Ginoux, F-75737 Paris cedex 15 Tel: (01) 5771108
Dir: Jacques Ledésert; *Man Dir:* Anna Beraud
Subjects: Petroleum Science & Technology
1977: 20 titles *1978:* 40 titles *Founded:* 1956
ISBN Publisher's Prefix: 2-7108

Technique et Documentation (Librairie Lavoisier)+*, 11 rue Lavoisier, F-75008 Paris Tel: (01) 2657167
Subjects: Scientific and Technical covering: Engineering, Industrial Safety, Environment, Metallurgy, Hydraulics, Chemistry, Electro-Technology, Biology, Food Industry, Civil Engineering, Oceanography; Reference Works
1977: 25 titles
ISBN Publisher's Prefix: 2-85206

Technique et Vulgarisation SA+, 21 rue Claude Bernard, F-75005 Paris Tel: (01) 5811131
Dirs: Laurent Heilmann, Charles Miguet
Subjects: Industrial, General Technology, Educational Materials, Engineering, Secondary & Primary Textbooks
1978: 23 titles *Founded:* 1946
ISBN Publisher's Prefix: 2-7109

Techniques de l'Ingénieur Sàrl+, (Editorial), 21 rue Cassette, F-75006 Paris Tel: (01) 2223550; (Commercial Office) 123 rue d'Alésia, F-75014 Paris Tel: (01) 5392291
Man Dir: Jacques Debaene; *Editorial Manager:* Jean-Jacques Baron; *Publicity Manager:* Gérard Delepoulle (at Commercial Office address)
Subjects: Scientific, Technical
ISBN Publisher's Prefix: 2-85059

Editions **Techniques Professionels**, see ETP

La **Télédition***, Châtel-Gérard, F-89310 Noyers Tel: (01) 2605798; (Châtel) 29 Telex: Teledit 670541 F
Man Dir: Danielle Munoz de la Mata
Subjects: Belles Lettres, Poetry, Juveniles, Educational Materials
Founded: 1974

Tema — Editions*, 4 rue de la Michodière, F-75002 Paris Tel: (01) 7422302
Man Dir: Robert Jauze; *Sales Dir:* Jacqueline Feydel
Subjects: History, How-to, Psychology, Social Science
Founded: 1972
Subsidiary: Tema-Recherches, 4 rue de la Micholdière, F-72002 Paris
ISBN Publisher's Prefix: 2-7142

Librairie Pierre **Tequi** et Editions Tequi+, 82 rue Bonaparte, F-75006 Paris Tel: (01) 3260458
Subjects: Education, Literature, Religion, Juveniles
1977-78: 48 titles *1978-79:* 35 titles
ISBN Publisher's Prefix: 2-85244

Editions **Tests***, 41 rue de la Grange-aux-Belles, F-75483 Paris cedex 10 Tel: (01) 2022910
Subjects: Science & Technical, Audio Visual & Electronic Media

Editions **Touret** SA*, 11 rue La Boétie, Paris 8eme
Paris office: 32 rue Baudin, 92400 Courbevoie Tel: 7881699
President & Director General: Denise Louvet; *Administration:* Raphaël Peres; *Editorial:* Michel Bizet; *Publicity:* Caroline Levy
Br Off: Conty F80160 Tel: (22) 412324
Subjects: Children's and Young Peoples' books, Reading books, Colouring books, Cut-out books, Transfers
Founded: 1923
ISBN Publisher's Prefix: 2-7161

Editions de **Trévise**+, 34 rue de Trévise, F-75009 Paris Tel: (01) 8246713/7703604
Man Dir: Gérald Gauthier; *Literary Dir:* Alexis Ovtchinnikoff
Subjects: History, Encyclopaedias, Art, Reference, Languages, Novels & Short stories
Founded: 1956
ISBN Publisher's Prefix: 2-7112

Trianon Press, 125 ave du Maine, F-75014 Paris Tel: (01) 3220917
Man Dir: Arnold D Fawcus
Subjects: Art, Art History (specialize in the works of William Blake, Ben Shann, Abbé Breuil)
1977: 3 titles *Founded:* 1947
ISBN Publisher's Prefix: 2-85172

U G E*, 10/18, 8 rue Garancière, F-75006 Paris Tel: 3291280 Telex: Precite 204807 F
Subjects: University and Political series (various)
Miscellaneous: Member of the Presses de la Cité group (qv)
ISBN Publisher's Prefix: 2-264

Union Latine d'Editions SA*, 5 rue de Savoie, F-75006 Paris Tel: (01) 0330224
Subject: Collectors' editions
Book Clubs: Club Bibliophile de France SA, 5 rue de Savoie, F-75006 Paris
Founded: 1930
ISBN Publisher's Prefix: 2-85061

Presses **Universitaires** de Lille (PUL)+, BP 149, F-59653 Villeneuve d'Ascq cedex Tel: (20) 911300
Man Dir: University President; *Editorial:* Y M Hilaire; *Sales, Production/Publicity, Rights & Permissions:* D Rosselle
Orders to: PUL, BP 149, F-59650 Villeneuve d'Ascq cedex
Subjects: Social Sciences and Humanities, French and Foreign Literature, History, Philosophy, Law, Philology, Psychology etc

1978: 20 titles *1979:* 18 titles *Founded:* 1972
ISBN Publisher's Prefix: 2-85939

Editions de **Vaillant** — IGO+, 126 La Fayette, F-75010 Paris Tel: (01) 7709759 Telex: Edipif 64067
Subject: Juveniles

Vander-Oyez SA+, 4 rue de Fleurus, F-75006 Paris Tel: 5484092
Man Dir: Mr Kaatee
Parent Company: Oyez Publishing Ltd, UK (qv)
Associate Company: Oyez SA, Belgium (qv)
Subjects: How-to, Medicine, Social Science, Science & Technology, Economics, Architecture, Languages, Humanities, Arts, Agriculture, Mathematics, Education, Philosophy, Psychology, Law, Sports
Founded: 1971
Miscellaneous: This Company incorporates the former French firm Beatrice-Nauwelaerts, taken over by Oyez, UK, in 1975
ISBN Publisher's Prefix: 2-85247

Editions de **Vecchi**, see De Vecchi

Editions **Van de Velde**, La Peite Plaine, BP 22, Fondettes, F-37230 Luynes Tel: (47) 510623
Man Dir, Sales: Jean François Pitchal; *Editorial, Production:* Francis Van de Velde; *Publicity:* Sylvie Toussaint; *Rights & Permissions:* Boris Cattier
Subject: Musical Instruction
1978: 8 titles *1979:* 10 titles *Founded:* 1898
ISBN Publisher's Prefix: 2-85868

Editions Francis **Van de Velde**, 12 rue Jacob, F-75006 Paris Tel: (01) 3259343
Man Dir, Editorial: Francis Van de Velde; *Sales, Rights and Permissions:* Alain Gouiffes
Subject: Musicology

Editions de la Revue **Verve** Sàrl*, 4 rue Férou, F-75006 Paris Tel: (01) 3267705
Dir: E Teriade
Subjects: Art, Special Editions
Founded: 1937
ISBN Publisher's Prefix: 2-900015

Veyrier*, 12 rue de Nesle, F-75006 Paris Tel: 6332018/3258037
Man Dir: Henri Veyrier; *Editorial:* Chantal Noetzel-Aubry; *Sales:* Hélène Mai
Orders to: Anagramme, at above address
Parent Company: Anagramme, at same address
Subjects: Illustrated Books on Art, Cinema, Paris, Fiction
Bookshops: 17 ter ave de Clichy, F-75018 Paris; 20 rue J H Fabre, Saint Ouen
1977: 11 titles *Founded:* 1973

Editions André **Vial***, 67 rue Madame, F-75006 Paris Tel: (01) 2221315
Man Dir: André Vial
Subjects: Limited editions of illustrated books
Founded: 1947
ISBN Publisher's Prefix: 2-85062

Editions **Vialetay** Sàrl+*, 23 rue de l'Abbé-Grégoire, F-75006 Paris Tel: (01) 2221276
Subject: Art
ISBN Publisher's Prefix: 2-85063

Editions **Vigot** Frères+, 23 rue de l'Ecole-de-Médecine, F-75006 Paris Tel: (01) 3295450
Man Dir: Daniel Vigot
Subjects: Medicine, General Science, Sports, Veterinary

Bookshop: Librairie Vigot, at address above
1977: 29 titles *1978:* 30 titles
Founded: 1890
ISBN Publisher's Prefix: 2-7114

Editions **Vilo** SA+*, 5 rue de Savoie, F-75006 Paris Tel: (01) 5770805 Cable Add: Edivilo Paris Telex: 200305 F
Man Dir: M Larfillon
Subjects: Art, History, Religion, Architecture, Reference, Maps, Literature, Aviation, Medicine, Nonfiction, Sports, Languages, Tourism
ISBN Publisher's Prefix: 2-7191

Dominique **Vincent** et Cie+*, 4 rue des Beaux-Arts, F-75006 Paris Tel: (01) 3265402
Subjects: Science & Technical
ISBN Publisher's Prefix: 2-85064

Vingtième Siècle*, 13 rue de Nestle, F-75006 Paris Tel: (01) 3261823
Man Dir: I Potel

Emmanuel **Vitte** Editeur SA*, 117 ave Félix-Faure, F-69395 Lyon Tel: (78) 544707
Subjects: Religion, Education, Literature
ISBN Publisher's Prefix: 2-7115

Editions La **Voix** de l'Ain+*, 20 rue Lalande, BP 88, F-01003 Bourg-en-Bresse Tel: (74) 215384
Subject: Religion

Librairie Philosophique J **Vrin**+*, 6 pl de la Sorbonne, F-75005 Paris 5 Tel: (01) 0330347
Man Dir: Gérard Paulhac
Subjects: Philosophy, Reference, Religion, Psychology, University Textbooks, History
1977: 40 titles *Founded:* 1920
Bookshops (new and second hand books): Philosophy, Law, Religion at 6 Pl de la Sorbonne, Paris; Literature, Art, History at 71 re St Jacques, Paris
ISBN Publisher's Prefix: 2-7116

Librairie **Vuibert** SA+*, 63 blvd St-Germain, F-75005 Paris Tel: (01) 3256100 Cable Add: Vuibert Paris
President: Jean Adam; *Sales:* Serge Wils; *Production:* Pierre Bonnefond; *Publicity, Rights & Permissions:* Dominique Lallouette
Subjects: Mathematics, Physics, Chemistry, Biology, Earth Sciences, Schoolbooks, Children's Literature
1977: 60 titles *Founded:* 1877
ISBN Publisher's Prefix: 2-7117

Dominique **Wapler***, 63 rue Rennequin, F-75017 Paris Tel: 02 3807939
Subjects: General Fiction, Belles Lettres, Religion, Reference, Scholarly Books
Founded: 1945
ISBN Publisher's Prefix: 2-85161

Gerard **Watelet**, see Editions Pygmalion

Weber*, 90 rue de Rennes, F-75006 Paris Tel: (01) 5481251 Cable Add: Webart-Paris
Subjects: Art, Architecture, Social Science, Juveniles, Reference
Founded: 1967
ISBN Publisher's Prefix: 2-7190

Galerie Lucie **Weill**, Au Pont des Arts, 6 rue Bonaparte, F-75006 Paris Tel: 3547195
President: Lucie Weill
Subjects: Books with illustrations by famous artists
Book Club: Nouveau Cercle Parisien du Livre (qv)
Founded: 1930

110 FRANCE

Y M C A-Press+*, 11 rue de la Montagne Sainte-Geneviève, F-75005 Paris Tel: (01) 0337446
Subjects: Religion, Literature, Russian books (in Russian), in association with Bredda Books and Prideaux Press under imprint "Les Editeurs Réunis" (qv)
ISBN Publisher's Prefix: 2-85065

Editions Philateliques **Yvert et Tellier***, 35 bis rue de Provence, F-75009 Paris Tel: 7706298
Subjects: General, Encyclopaedias, Sports

Zodiaque, la Pierre-qui-Vire, F-89830 St-Léger-Vauban Tel: (86) 322123 Cable Add: Zodiaque-89830 St Léger
Man Dir: José Surchamp
Distribution in France: Weber Diffusion, 28 rue du Moulinet, F-75013 Paris
Distribution outside France: Marcel Weber, 13 rue du Monthoux, CH-1211 Geneva 2, Switzerland
Subjects: Ancient and Modern Art, Music
1977: 7 titles *1978:* 7 titles *Founded:* 1951

Literary Agents

Agence **Bataille***, 65 rue St André-des-Arts, F-75006 Paris
Contact: Marie-Claude Bataille

Jean-Pierre **Bosco***, 65 rue du Faubourg St-Honoré, F-75008 Paris

Mrs W A **Bradley**, 18 quai de Bethune, F-75004 Paris Tel: (01) 3547514

Mlle Sabine **Delattre***, 9 rue Christine, F-75006 Paris Tel: (01) 3262709

Mme Françoise **Germain***, 8 rue de la Paix, F-75002 Paris Tel: (01) 2616814

Agence **Hoffman**, 77 blvd St-Michel, F-75005 Paris Tel: (01) 0337115/0332327 Cable Add: Aghoff Paris Telex: 203605F
Contacts: Boris or Georges Hoffman or Mme Merrily de Douhet

Mme Michelle **Lapautre**, 6 rue Jean Carriès, F-75007 Paris Tel: (01) 7348241/7346450 Cable Add: Milalit Paris

Alice **Le Bayon***, 113 blvd St-Germain, Paris

Anne **Lenclud***, Agence Renault-Lenclud, 18 rue Blanche, F-75009 Paris Tel: (01) 5262679

McKee & Mouche, 16 rue du Regard, F-75006 Paris Tel: (01) 5484503/2224233

Matthias-Estienne*, 27 rue du Dragon, F-75006 Paris Tel: 2222912

La **Nouvelle Agence***, 7 rue Corneille, F-75006 Paris Tel: (01) 3258560
Contact: Mary Kling

Promotion Littéraire*, F-75116 Paris Tel: (01) 5004210 Cable Add: Promolit Paris
Contact: Mariella Giannetti

Mme Janine **Quet***, Bureau littéraire, 20 rue de la Michodière, F-75002 Paris Tel: (01) 0333850

Bureau littéraire international Marguerite **Scialtiel**, 14 rue Chanoinesse, F-75004 Paris Tel: (01) 3547116
Contact: Geneviève Ulmann

Mme Héléna **Strassova**, 4 rue Gît-Le-Coeur, F-75006 Paris Tel: (01) 6333457

W J **Taylor-Whitehead***, 60 rue Madame, F-75006 Paris

Le **Téléscope**, 10 rue Mayet, F-75006 Paris Tel: 3069636
Dir: Chantal Galtier Roussel

Mme Ellen **Wright**, 20 rue Jacob, F-75006 Paris

Book Clubs

Les **Amis** de Franco Maria Ricci*, Galerie 12, 12 rue des Beaux-Arts, F-75006 Paris
Owned by: Franco Maria Ricci (Paris)

L'**Amitié** par le Livre*, F-25310 Blamont
Dir General: Henri Frossard
Subjects: Prose fiction, Poetry, Philosophy & Religion
1976: 15 titles *1977:* 12 titles *Founded:* 1930
ISBN Publisher's Prefix: 2-7121

C A L (Culture Art Loisirs SA)*, 114 Champs Elysées, F-75008 Paris

Cercle du Bibliophile*, 22 rue de Cocherel, F-27 Evreux

Club Bibliophile de France SA*, 5 rue de Savoie, F-75002 Paris
Owned by: L'Union Latine d'Editions (Paris)
Subjects: Encyclopaedias, Collectors' editions

Club des Amis du Livre*, 8 rue de Berri, F-7500 Paris 8e

Club des Aventures de Guerre*, 33 rue Beauregard, F-75002 Paris
Owned by: Editions France Empire (Paris)

Club du Livre d'Art*, 1 rue Palatine, F-75006 Paris
Owned by: Editions Albert Morancé (Paris)

Club du Livre SA, 28 rue Fortuny, F-75017 Paris Tel: 9248055
Man Dir: Philippe Lebaud
Subjects: Art, De Luxe Editions

Club du Livre technique*, 28 rue du Faubourg-Poissonnière, F-75000 Paris 10e

Club du Roman féminin*, 33 rue Beauregard, F-75002 Paris
Owned by: Editions France Empire (Paris)

Club Français des Bibliophiles*, 5 & 7 rue Baudoin, F-75013 Paris 13ème Tel: 583 4330
Subjects: Encyclopaedic Collections: The Sciences of Man, Sociology, Biography and Memoirs, Leisure, Touring, Sport

Club Français du Livre, 7 & 9 rue Armand-Moisant, F-75015 Paris

Livre Club **Diderot**, 13 blvd Bourdon, F-75004 Paris Tel: (01) 8876519
Subjects: Political and Economic Science, History, Poetry, Literature
Owned by: Editions Sociales, Paris

Education et Culture*, 28 rue de la Boétie, F-75008 Paris
Owned by: Les Editions des Deux Coqs d'Or (Paris)

Femmes dans la Vie*, 61 rue des Sts-Pères, F-75006 Paris
Owned by: Editions du Centurion (Paris)

Libraire **Lidis***, 208 rue de Rivoli, F-75001 Paris
Owned by: Editions Lidis (qv)

Editions **Livre** Club de Libraire*, 11 rue de Sèvres, F-75006 Paris

Meilleure Bibliothèque*, 61 rue des Sts-Pères, F-75006 Paris

Nouveau Cercle parisien du Livre, 6 rue Bonaparte, F-75006 Paris
President: Daniel S Sickles
Subjects: Illustrated Books
Club is associated with publisher Galerie Lucie Weill (qv)

L'**Oeil** Ouvert, 16 rue de l'Ecole Polytechnique, Paris 5
Owned by: Nouvelles Editions Rationalistes (qv)
Subject: Historical texts expressing rationalist thought

Opta Editions*, 39 rue d'Amsterdam, F-75008 Paris Tel: 5266004

Poètes Présents, 50 rue Rodier, F-75009 Paris
Owned by: Jean Grassin Editeur (qv)
Subject: Poetry

Presses d'Or*, 28 rue de la Boétie, F-75008 Paris
Owned by: Les Editions des Deux Coqs d'Or (Paris)

Sélection du **Reader's Digest** Sàrl, 216 blvd St-Germain, F-75007 Paris
Subjects: General Fiction, History, How-to, Juveniles, Medicine, Science & Technology, Reference, Art, Architecture, Social Science, Economics

Ediclub **Rombaldi***, 222 blvd St-Germain, F-75007 Paris.
Selling organization for seven book clubs, including Bibliothèque du Temps Présent
Subjects: Mostly Fiction (mostly classics)

Société des Bibliophiles*, Galerie 12, 12 rue des Beaux-Arts, F-75006 Paris
Owned by: Franco Maria Ricci (Paris)

Société Editions Internationales Sàrl*, 150 Champs Elysées, F-75008 Paris

Major Booksellers

Brentano's*, 37 ave de l'Opéra, F-75002 Paris

F N A C*, 136 rue de Rennes, F-75006 Paris Tel: (01) 2771133

Flammarion*, 19 pl Bellecour, F-69002 Lyon Tel: (078) 380157; 54 La Canebière, F-13231 Marseille cedex 1 Tel: (091) 542520 (for other bookshops see under entry in Publishers)

Librairie '**Furet du Nord**'*, 11 pl du Gnl de Gaulle, F-59000 Lille Tel: (020) 541234

Librairie Joseph **Gibert**, 26 blvd St Michel, F-75006 Paris Tel: (01) 3292141

Librairie La **Hune***, 170 blvd St-Germain, F-75006 Paris Tel: (01) 5483585

Librairie **Laffitte***, 156 La Canebière, F-13000 Marseille

Librairie **Maupetit***, 142 La Canebière, F-13232 Marseille

Librairie **Mollat***, 15 rue Vital-Carles, F-33000 Bordeaux

Librairie **Montparnasse** Edition, 1 Quai de Conti, F-75006 Paris
Owned by: Alfred Eibel, éditeur (qv)

Presses universitaires de France, 49 blvd
St-Michel, F-75005 Paris Tel: (01) 3258340

Librairie de **Provence**, 31 cours Mirabeau,
F-13100 Aix en Provence

Sodexport-Grem, 117 blvd Saint-Germain,
F-75006 Paris
Exporters of scientific, technical and
medical books

Librairie **Sauramps**, Le Triangle, pl de la
Comédie, F-34000 Montpellier Tel: (67)
588515

Stechert-Macmillan Inc*, 54 rue Boissonade,
F-75014 Paris Tel: (01) 3257599 (library
suppliers for books and periodicals)

Librairie de l'**Université***, 17 rue de la
Liberté, F-21014 Dijon Tel: (80) 305117

Major Libraries

Archives nationales, 60 rue des Francs-
Bourgeois, F-75141 Paris cedex 03
1978: 8 titles
Publications: National Archive Documents,
which are published by La Documentation
Française, Publisher (qv)

Bibliothèque de l'**Arsenal**, 1 rue de Sully,
F-75004 Paris Tel: (01) 2774421
Chief Librarian: J Guignard

Bibliothèque mazarine, 23 quai de Conti,
F-75006 Paris Tel: (01) 3548948

Bibliothèque municipale, 1 rue de la
Bibliothèque, F-25000 Besançon Tel: (81)
812089

Bibliothèque municipale, blvd Maréchal
Lyautey, BP 1095, F-38021 Grenoble cedex
Tel: 440156/444250/444276

Bibliothèque municipale de la Ville de Lyon,
30 blvd Vivier-Merle, F-69431 Lyon
cedex 3 Tel: (078) 628520
Librarian: Jean-Louis Rocher

Bibliothèque nationale*, 58 rue de
Richelieu, F-75084 Paris cedex 02 Tel: (01)
2666262
National Library
*Publication: Bulletin de la Bibliothèque
Nationale; Bulletin des Bibliothèques de
France*

**Bibliothèque nationale et universitaire de
Strasbourg**, 5 rue du Maréchal Joffre, BP
1029/F, F-67070 Strasbourg cedex
Tel: (88) 360068 (main address and
Management and Legal Section); 6 place de
la République, BP 1029/F, F-67070
Strasbourg cedex Tel: (88) 360068
(Literature and Human Sciences Section); 3
bis rue du Maréchal Joffre, BP 1029/F,
F-67070 Strasbourg cedex Tel: (88) 360068
(Section dealing with Alsace region affairs);
6 rue Kirschleger, F-67085 Strasbourg
cedex Tel: (88) 362323 (Medical Section);
34 boulevard de la Victoire, BP 1037/F,
F-67070 Strasbourg cedex Tel: (88) 613323
(Scientific and Technical Section)

Bibliothèque littéraire Jacques **Doucet**, 10 pl
du Panthéon, F-75005 Paris
Tel: (01)3296100 (extensions 22, 56, 72)
Librarian: François Chapon
Publications: Exhibition Catalogues

Bibliothèque de l'**Institut de France***, 23
quai de Conti, F-75270 Paris cedex 06
Tel: (01) 3268540

Bibliothèque de l'**Institut national** des
Langues et Civilisations orientales, 2 rue de
Lille, F-75007 Paris Tel: (01) 2603458

Bibliothèque du **Musée de l'Homme**, Palais
de Chaillot, pl du Trocadéro, F-75116
Paris Tel: (01) 7045394
Librarian: Françoise Weil
*Publication: Liste des Périodiques reçus
regulièrement par la Bibliothèque du Musée
de l'homme*

Bibliothèque centrale du **Muséum national**
d'Histoire naturelle, 38 rue Geoffroy Saint-
Hilaire, F-75005 Paris 5 Tel: (01)
3317124/3319560

Bibliothèques des **Universités de Paris** (Paris
University Libraries):

Bibliothèque Interuniversitaire de Médecine,
12 rue de l'Ecole de Médecine, F-75270
Paris cedex 06

**Bibliothèque Interuniversitaire de
Pharmacie**, 4 ave de l'Observatoire, F-75270
Paris cedex 06 Tel: 3291208 ext 238, 311,
241 Telex: 200707 f
Librarian: Paul Roux-Fouillet

Centre de Géographie, Bibliothèque*, 191
rue St-Jacques, F-75005 Paris

Bibliothèque de **Documentation**
Internationale Contemporaine*, Centre
Universitaire, F-92001 Nanterre cedex

Bibliothèque d'Art et d'Archéologie
Fondation Jacques **Doucet**, 3 rue Michelet,
F-75006 Paris Tel: 3543527
Dir: Denise Gazier

Bibliothèque de la **Faculté de Droit***, 127
rue St-Jacques, F-75005 Paris

Muséum Calvet, Bibliothèque*, 65 rue
Joseph-Vernet, F-84000 Avignon Tel: (90)
863384
Chief Curator: Georges de Loÿe

Bibliothèque **Sainte-Geneviève***, 10 pl du
Panthéon, F-75005 Paris Tel: (01)
6330515/7

Bibliothèque de la **Sorbonne**, 47 rue des
Ecoles, F-75230 Paris cedex 05 Tel: (01)
3291213 (DAN 2194)
Chief Librarian: André Tuilier *Librarian:*
Jacquette Reboul

Service des Travaux Historiques de la **Ville
de Paris** et Bibliothèque historique de la
Ville de Paris, 24 rue Pavée, F-75004 Paris
Tel: (01) 2721018/2726836/2773975

Library Associations

The two following organizations administer
the libraries and archives:

Direction des **Archives** de France*, 60 rue
des Francs-Bourgeois, F-75141 Paris cedex
03 Tel: 2771130

Service des Bibliothèques, Ministère des
Universités, 61-65 rue Dutot, F-75732 Paris
cedex 15
Chief Librarian: Andrée Carpentier

Association de l'Ecole nationale supérieure
de Bibliothécaires, 17-21 blvd du 11
Novembre 1918, F-69100 Villeurbanne
Tel: (78) 524738
Association of the National School of
Librarianship
General Secretary: P J Lamblin
Founded: 1967

*Publication: Annuaire de l'Association de
l'Ecole nationale supérieure de
Bibliothécaires*

Association de l'Institut national des
Techniques de la Documentation
(Association of the National Institute for
Information Sciences), 32 rue des Bluets,
F-75011 La Garenne-Colombes
President: E Vallée

Association des Archivistes français, 60 rue
des Francs-Bourgeois, F-75141 Paris
cedex 03 Tel: 2771130
Association of French Archivists
President: Mr H Charnier
Publication: La Gazette des Archives
(quarterly)

Association des Bibliothécaires français*, 65
rue de Richelieu, F-75002 Paris
Tel: 7429879
Association of French Librarians
President: Marc Chauveinc; *Executive
Secretary:* Miss M Beaudiquez
Founded: 1906
Publication: Bulletin d'Information

Association des Bibliothèques ecclésiastiques
de France (ABEF), 6 rue du Regard,
F-75006 Paris
Executive Secretary: Paul-Marie Guillaume
Publication: Bulletin de Liaison de l'ABEF

Association des Diplômés de l'Ecole de
Bibliothécaires-Documentalistes (Association
of Graduates of the School of Librarians
and Documentalists), Bibliothèque du
Saulchoir, 43 bis rue la Glacière, F-75013
Paris Tel: 5870533
Executive Secretary: Miss A Piot
Publication: Bulletin d'Information

Association française des Documentalistes et
Bibliothécaires spécialisés (French
Association of Information Scientists and
Special Librarians), 5 ave Franco-Russe,
F-75007 Paris Tel: (01) 5555516
Publication: Documentaliste

Association nationale des Bibliothécaires
Municipaux (National Association of
Municipal Librarians)*, c/o M Baudin, Cité
Administrative, 17 blvd Morland, F-75004
Paris

Association pour la Mediathèque publique
(AMP), Bibliothèque municipale, 37 rue
Saint-Georges, F-59400 Cambrai

Centre d'Archives et de Documentation
politiques et sociales (Centre for Political
and Social Archives and Documentation)*,
86 blvd Haussmann, F-75008 Paris
*Publications: Informations politiques et
sociales; Est et Ouest*

Fédération des Amicales de Documentalistes
et Bibliothécaires de l'Education nationale
(Federation of Friends of Documentalists
and Librarians of National Education)*, 29
rue d'Ulm, F-75007 Paris

Library Reference Books and Journals

Books

Les Bibliothèques (The Libraries), Presses
Universitaires de France, 108 blvd
St-Germain, F-75279 Paris cedex 06

*Les Bibliothèques de France au Service de
Public* (Public Libraries in France),
Ministère de l'Education nationale,
Direction de Bibliothèque et de Lecture

publique, 1 rue du Périgord, F-31000 Toulouse

Les Bibliothèques publiques en France, ENSB-Presses, 17-21 blvd du 11 novembre 1918, F-69100 Villeurbanne

Répertoire des Bibliothèques et Organismes de Documentation (Catalogue of Libraries and Documentation Organisms), National Library, 58 rue de Richelieu, F-75084 Paris cedex 02

Libraries in France, Clive Bingley Ltd, 16 Pembridge Rd, London W11

Journals

Bulletin, Association of French Theological Libraries, 6 rue du Regard, F-75006 Paris

Bulletin d'Information (Information Bulletin), Association of French Librarians, 4 rue Louvois, F-75002 Paris

Bulletin de l'Unesco à l'intention des Bibliothèques (Unesco Bulletin for Libraries) (editions in English, French, Russian and Spanish), Unesco, pl de Fontenoy, F-75700 Paris

Bulletin de la Bibliothèque (Library Bulletin), Institut national de la Statistique et des Etudes économiques, 29 quai Branly, F-75000 Paris

Bulletin des Bibliothèques de France (Bulletin of French Libraries), Secretariat d'Etat aux Universités Service des Bibliothèques, 61-65 rue Dutot, F-75732 Paris, cedex 15

Documentaliste (Documentalist); review of documentary information and techniques, French Association of Information Scientists and Special Librarians, 61 rue du Cardinal-Lemoine, F-75005 Paris

La Gazette des Archives (Archives Gazette), Association of French Archivists, 60 rue des Francs-Bourgeois, F-75003 Paris

Informatique (Information Processing), Editions d'Informatique, 82 rue Lauriston, F-75116 Paris

Revue Bitrimestrielle (for specialist librarians), Inter-CDI, 7 Residence de Guinette, F-91150 Etampes

Literary Associations and Societies

Académie des Lettres et des Arts*, (Société du Vieux Montmartre), c/o Musée de Montmartre, 12 rue Cortot, F-75018 Paris Tel: 6066111
President: Romain Delahalle

Académie Goncourt, Société des Gens de Lettres*, 38 rue du Faubourg St Jacques, F-75014 Paris
Secretary-General: Armand Lanoux

Académie Montaigne*, Le Doyenné, Sillé-le-Guillaume (Sarthe)
Secretary: Constant Hubert

Association des Ecrivains combattants (Association of Combatant Writers)*, 8 rue Roquépine, F-75008 Paris
Secretary: Maurice Ch Renard
Publication: Bulletin

Centre national des Lettres, 6 rue Dufrénoy, F-75116 Paris
Secretary-General: M Auclaire

Jeunesses littéraires de France (French Literary Youth)*, 117 blvd St-Germain, F-75279 Paris cedex 06

La **Joie** par les Livres (Joy Through Books), 4 rue de Louvois, F-75002 Paris
An experimental library and a documentation centre on children's literature
Publications: La Revue des Livres pour Enfants and other special selections

Maison de Poésie (House of Poetry) (Fondation Emile Blémont)*, 11 bis rue Ballu, F-75009 Paris
President: Mme George-Day

P E N Club Français, 6 rue François Miron, F-75004 Paris Tel: 2773787
President: René Tavernier; *General Secretary:* Dimitri Stoly-pine
Publication: News Bulletins to members as occasion arises

Société d'Etudes dantesques, Centre universitaire méditerranéen, 65 promenade des Anglais, F-06100 Nice Tel: 868156
President: Louis Gautier-Vignal (of The Society for Dantesque Studies)

Société d'Histoire littéraire de la France, 14 rue de l'Industrie, F-75013 Paris
This is the French Literary History Association
Secretary: R Pomeau
Publications: Revue d'Histoire littéraire de la France (alternate months); *Bibliographie de la Littérature française* (annually)

Société des anciens Textes Français (Society of Ancient French Texts)*, 19 rue de la Sorbonne, F-75005 Paris
Sale of Publications from Ed A and J Picard (qv)
General Secretary: Professor J Monfrin

Société des Gens de Lettres (Society of Men and Women of Letters)*, Hôtel de Massa, 38 rue du Faubourg St Jacques, F-75014 Paris
General Secretary: Pierre Bearn

Société des Poètes français (Society of French Poets)*, 38 rue du Faubourg St Jacques, F-75014 Paris
Secretary-General: Roland le Cordier; *Assistant Secretary-General:* Brigitte Level
Publication: Bulletin Trimestriel

Société du Vieux Montmartre, see Académie des Lettres et des Arts

Syndicat des Critiques littéraires (Association of Literary Critics), 58 rue Claude Bernard, F-75005 Paris
Secretary: R André
Publication: Bulletin du Syndicat (quarterly)

Union des Ecrivains et Artistes latins (Union of Latin Writers and Artists)*, 11 rue de l'Estrapade, F-75005 Paris
Secretary: Mr Decremps
Publications: France latine and books in Langue d'Oc

Literary Periodicals

Bulletin des Lettres (Bulletin of Letters); review of criticism and of literary and bibliophilic information, Librairie Lardanchet, 10 rue du Président-Carnot, F-69002 Lyon

Critique (Criticism); general review of publications in France and abroad, Editions de Minuit, 7 rue Bernard Palissy, F-75006 Paris

Figaro littéraire (Literary Figaro), 14 Rond-Point des Champs-Elysées, Paris 8e

Information littéraire (Literary Information), Editions J-B Baillière, 19 rue Hautefeuille, F-75006 Paris cedex 06

Lecture et Tradition (Reading and Tradition), Diffusion de la Pensée Française, Chiré-en-Montreuil, F-86190 Vouillé

Lettres françaises (French Letters), 5 rue du Faubourg Poissonnière, Paris 9e

Lettres nouvelles (News Letters); literary review, 19 rue Aurelie, F-75007 Paris

Littérature (Literature), Larousse, 17 rue du Montparnasse, F-75280 Paris cedex 06

Magazine littéraire (Literary Magazine), Magazine-Expansion, 40 rue des Sts-Pères, Paris 7e

Nouvelles littéraires, Arts, Sciences, Spectacles (Literary News, Arts, Sciences, Entertainments), 146 rue Montmartre, Paris 2e

Parler (To Speak); literary review, Galerie 'Parti-Pris', 4 rue Alexandre 1er du Yougoslavie, Grenoble

Passerelle (Footbridge); literary review, Pierre Bearn, 60 rue Monsieur le Prince, F-75006 Paris

Quinzaine littéraire (Literary Fortnightly), 43 rue du Temple, F-75004 Paris 4

Revue de Littérature comparée (Review of Comparative Literature) (text in English, French, German, Italian and Spanish), Librairie Marcel Didier SA, 15 rue Cujas, F-75005 Paris

Strophes; literary review, Jean Fremon, 9 rue de Belfort, F-9200 Asnières

Literary Prizes

Academy of Thirteen Prize*
Known as 'Prix le Boisson' and given for a work of prose or poetry. Sixteen bottles of famous wine. Awarded annually. Enquiries to Academy of Thirteen, 166 rue de la Burgonce, Niort, Deux-Sèvres

Ambassadors' Prize*
To an author for his total work that best expresses the French spirit. Awarded annually. Enquiries to Secretariat, 75 rue Caumartin, F-75009 Paris

Guillaume **Apollinaire** Prize*
For modern poetry after the style of Apollinaire by a poet under 50 years of age. Awarded annually. Enquiries to Henri de Lescoët, 86 blvd de Cessole, F-06100 Nice

Francois-Joseph **Audiffred** Prize
For a published work best qualified to inspire love of virtue, and to discourage egoism and envy; or to instil patriotism. Enquiries to Academy of Moral and Political Sciences, Institut de France, 23 quai de Conti, F-75006 Paris

Aujourd'hui Prize*
For a historical or contemporary work on politics. Awarded annually. Enquiries to Secretariat, 12 rue du Quatre Septembre, F-75002 Paris

Joseph **Autran** Prize
Awarded to a poet for the whole of his work. Enquiries to Société des Poètes Français, 38 rue du Faubourg St Jacques, F-75014 Paris

René **Bardet** Prize*
For a poetic work. Awarded every two years. Enquiries to French Academy, Institut de France, 23 quai de Conti, F-75006 Paris

André **Barre** Prize*
For the work with the most original thinking and clearest style. Enquiries to French Academy, Institut de France, 23 quai de Conti, F-75006 Paris

Alice Louis **Barthou** Prize*
To a woman of letters. For one work or all of her work. Awarded annually. Enquiries to French Academy, Institut de France, 23 quai de Conti, F-75006 Paris

Louis **Barthou** Prize*
To a writer whose work or life has served the best interests of France. Awarded annually. Enquiries to French Academy, Institut de France, 23 quai de Conti, F-75006 Paris

Max **Barthou** Prize*
To a writer under 30 years of age whose talent has been proven or who has shown great promise. Awarded annually. Enquiries to French Academy, Institut de France, 23 quai de Conti, F-75006 Paris

Charles **Blanc** Prize*
For a written work, preferably treating issues in art. Awarded annually. Enquiries to French Academy, Institut de France, 23 quai de Conti, F-75006 Paris

Emile **Blémont** Prize*
For poetry inspired by France or one of its regions. Monetary prize of 100 francs. Awarded annually. Enquiries to Maison de Poésie, 11 bis rue Ballu, F-75009 Paris

Pascal **Bonetti** Grand Prize
Award of 1,000 francs for a poetic work of high quality, classical structure and lofty sentiments. Enquiries to Société des Poètes Français, 38 rue du Faubourg St Jacques, F-75014 Paris

Bordin Prize*
To encourage superior literature. Awarded annually. Enquiries to French Academy, Institut de France, 23 quai de Conti, F-75006 Paris

Broquette-Gonin Grand Prize*
To the author of a philosophical, political or literary work, inspiring the love of truth, beauty and virtue. Awarded annually. Enquiries to French Academy, Institut de France, 23 quai de Conti, F-75006 Paris

Louis **Castex** Prize*
For literary works such as reminiscences of important voyages or explorations. Works on discoveries in archaeology and ethnology are also considered. Awarded annually. Enquiries to French Academy, Institut de France, 23 quai de Conti, F-75006 Paris

Hercule **Catenacci** Prize*
To encourage the publication of de luxe illustrated books of poetry, literature, history, archaeology or music. Awarded annually. Enquiries to French Academy, Institut de France, 23 quai de Conti, F-75006 Paris

Chateauneuf-du-Pape Grand Prize
Instituted by the town of Chateauneuf-du-Pape and other cities in the same renowned area. Awarded every two years for a poetic work which, irrespective of subject, appears most deserving by virtue of its formal purity and lofty sentiments. 1,000 francs. Solely for a young poet. Enquiries to Société des Poètes Français, 38 rue du Faubourg St Jacques, F-75014 Paris

Honoré **Chavée** Prize
To encourage work in linguistics and in particular research on romance languages. Awarded biennially. Enquiries to Academie des Inscriptions et Belles-Lettres, Institut de France, 23 quai de Conti, F-75006 Paris

Combat Prize*
For a published or unpublished novel. Awarded annually. Enquiries to Combat Newspaper, 18 rue du Croissant, F-75002 Paris

François **Coppée** Prize*
For the work of a poet, preferably just beginning his career. Awarded every two years. Enquiries to French Academy, Institut de France, 23 quai de Conti, F-75006 Paris

Courteline Prize*
For best humorous novel of the year by an author over 50. Awarded annually. Enquiries to Société de Gens de Lettres, Hotel de Massa, 38 rue du Faubourg St-Jacques, F-75014

Constant **Dauguet** Endowment*
To the author of the best work on morals, particularly from the Catholic point of view. Awarded annually. Enquiries to French Academy, Institut de France, 23 quai de Conti, F-75006 Paris

Albert **Dauzat** Prize
Awarded for a poetic work extolling animals. Enquiries to Société des Poètes Français, 38 rue du Faubourg St Jacques, F-75014 Paris

Eve **Delacroix** Prize*
For a literary work, essay or novel expressing human dignity and responsibility of the writer to society. 5,000 francs. . Awarded annually. Enquiries to Secretariat, 56 ave Foch, F-75016 Paris

Deldebat de Gonzalva Prize
Given since 1941 (except 1948) to a small body of poems classical in form and noble in inspiration. Enquiries to Société des Poètes français, 38 rue du Faubourg St Jacques, F-75014 Paris

D'Erlanger Prize
Given since 1921 for poem, 150 lines maximum, written by someone who has served in front line of combat. Enquiries to Société des Poètes français, 38 rue du Faubourg St Jacques, F-75014 Paris

Marceline **Desbordes-Valmore** Prize
Founded 1937. To a member poetess in whom personality and talent are fully developed. Enquiries to Société des Poètes français, 38 rue du Faubourg St Jacques, F-75014 Paris

Deux Magots Prize*
For an avant-garde book by a young writer. Awarded annually. Enquiries to Café des Deux Magots, pl St-Germain-des-Prés, Paris

Dumas-Millier Prize*
To a writer over 45 whose work will be an honour to the French language and will contribute to the dissemination of French thought. Enquiries to French Academy, Institut de France, 23 quai de Conti, F-75006 Paris

Alfred **Dutens** Prize
For the most useful work on linguistics. Awarded every ten years. Enquiries to Académie des Inscriptions et Belles Lettres, Institut de France, 23 quai de Conti, F-75270 Paris

Fabien Prize*
To the author who has made the best suggestions for improving the moral and material position of the largest class. Awarded annually. Enquiries to French Academy, Institut de France, 23 quai de Conti, F-75006 Paris

Fantasia Prize, see Jeune France Prize

Jules **Favre** Prize*
For a literary work by a woman, poetry or prose, treating moral, educational, philogical or historical questions. Awarded every two years. Enquiries to French Academy, Institut de France, 23 quai de Conti, F-75006 Paris

Fémina Prize*
Founded in 1904 by review Femina to encourage writing and draw women of letters closer together. A jury of women of letters meets in Paris each December to select a literary work of imagination written in French, by man or woman, prose or poetry. 5,000 francs. Awarded annually. Enquiries to Secretary-General, 79 blvd St-Germain, F-75006 Paris

Fénéon Prize*
For outstanding published work of any kind by an author over 35. Awarded annually. Enquiries to Fénéon Foundation, 10 pl du Panthéon, F-75005 Paris

Jean **Finot** Prize
For a work with humanitarian social tendencies. Awarded every two years. Enquiries to Academy of Moral and Political Sciences, Institut de France, 23 quai de Conti, F-75006 Paris

Paul **Flat** Prize*
To the best critical work and the best novel published by a young writer (between 30 and 40 years of age). Awarded annually. Enquiries to French Academy, Institut de France, 23 quai de Conti, F-75006 Paris

Ernest **Fleury** Prize
Instituted by Marthe-Claire Fleury in memory of her father, the poet Ernest Fleury. It is awarded for a work of quality, and of a high order of spirituality. Enquiries to Société des Poètes Français, 38 rue du Faubourg St Jacques, F-75014 Paris

Marshal **Foch** Prize*
For a book on the nation's defence by an officer, engineer, scholar or philosopher. Awarded biennially. Enquiries to French Academy, Institut de France, 23 quai de Conti, F-75006 Paris

Pascal **Fortuny** Prize*
To the author of a poem of 200 lines or less, preferably written in the classical form. Awarded annually. Enquiries to French Academy, Institut de France, 23 quai de Conti, F-75006 Paris

114 FRANCE

Fouraignan Prize
Created in 1914 for volume of poems in 18th century style, inspired by current events. Enquiries to Société des Poètes Français, 38 rue du Faubourg St Jacques, F-75014 Paris

Fraternité Prize*
For a literary work or work of art (theatre, cinema or painting) that best contributes to fraternity between all people. Enquiries to Secretariat, 15 Faubourg Montmartre, Paris

French Catholic Grand Prize for Literature*
For a recent book or the sum of the work of a Catholic writer. Awarded annually. Enquiries to 11 rue Pachot-Laine, F-93190 Livry-Gargan

French Critics' Prize*
For the best literary work of prose or poetry published during the year. Awarded annually. Enquiries to Editions du Pavois, 1 bis rue Vaneau, F-75007 Paris

French Grand Prize for Humour*
For the best humorous writing published during the year, preferably a novel. Awarded annually by the Academy of Humour. Enquiries to Society of Dramatic Authors and Composers, 11 bis rue Ballu, F-75009 Paris

French Poets' Grand Prize*
For outstanding poetry. Awarded annually, Enquiries to French Poets' Society, 15 rue Plumet, F-75015 Paris

Gegner Prize
To a philosopher-writer whose works contribute to the science of philosophy. Awarded annually. Enquiries to Academy of Moral and Political Sciences, Institut de France, 23 quai de Conti, F-75006 Paris

Félix Georges Prize
Created in 1949 to honour a poem in classical form. Enquiries to Société des Poètes français, 38 rue du Faubourg St Jacques, F-75014 Paris

Giles Prize
For a work on China, Japan or the Far East. Awarded every two years to a French national only. Enquiries to Académie des Inscriptions et Belles Lettres, Institut de France, 23 quai de Conti, F-75270 Paris

Golden Feather of the *Figaro littéraire**
For a novel by someone 'forgotten' by the other prize commissions. Awarded annually. Enquiries to *Figaro littéraire*, 14 Rond Point des Champs Elysées, F-75008 Paris

Goncourt Prize
Founded by J and E de Goncourt, 21 December 1903, the annual prize honours a prose work by a younger writer with originality of spirit and form. The novel is the preferred medium. The award is the same as when the prize was originated, 50 francs. In 1979 the prize was awarded to Andrée Chedid for *Les Corps et le Temps* (Flammarion). Enquiries to Académie Goncourt, Armand Lanoux, 'Le Clapotis', ave Denis-Séméria, F-06290 Saint-Jean-Cap-Ferrat

**Grand Franco-Belgian Literary Prize*
Established 1956. For the sum of work of a Belgian author written in the French language, free from any political, religious or philosophical bias. Monetary prize of 2,000 French francs. Awarded annually. Enquiries to Association des Ecrivains d'Expression francaise de la Mer et de l'Outre-Mer (AEFMOM), 41 rue de la Bienfaisance, Paris 8, France

**Grand Prize for Literature*
To a prose-writer or poet for one or more works showing inspiration and style. 10,000 francs. Awarded annually. Enquiries to French Academy, Institut de France, 23 quai de Conti, F-75006 Paris

**Grand Prize for Mystery Stories*
To the writers of the two best mystery stories, one written in French and the other translated into French. Awarded annually. Enquiries to Secretariat, 19 rue Fontaine, F-75009 Paris

Grand Prize for Poetry Criticism
Awarded for a work or body of work of poetic criticism or exegesis. Enquiries to Société des Poètes Français, 38 rue du Faubourg St Jacques, F-75014 Paris

Grand Prize of French Poets
Given since 1936. Enquiries to Société des Poètes français, 38 rue du Faubourg St Jacques, F-75014 Paris

Edmond Haraucourt Prize
Replaces the J-M Renaitour Prize. Awarded annually for a complete poetic work, preferably in classical form. Enquiries to Société des Poètes Français, 38 rue du Faubourg St Jacques, F-75014 Paris

Marie Havez-Planque Prize*
One year for a collection of stories or news stories or for a psychological novel, the following year for a collection of classical poetry. Preferably to an author who has not yet been published. Awarded annually. Enquiries to French Academy, Institut de France, 23 quai de Conti, F-75006 Paris

Hermes Prize
To a young writer who is publishing his first novel. 2,000 francs. Awarded annually. Enquiries to Higher School of Commerce of Paris, 79 ave de la République, F-75011 Paris

Emile Hinzelin Prize*
For a volume of verse or a play in verse following the rules of French prosody, and showing the author's love for France. Awarded annually. Enquiries to French Academy, Institut de France, 23 quai de Conti, F-75006 Paris

Clovis Hugues Prize
Awarded to a poet whose work is inspired by the same sentiments of social brotherhood as moved Clovis Hugues. Enquiries to Société des Poètes Français, 38 rue du Faubourg St Jacques, F-75014 Paris

Interallié Prize
Awarded since 1930 for a high quality novel, preferably written by a journalist. Awarded annually. Enquiries to Roger Giron, 72 blvd de La Tour-Maubourg, F-75007 Paris

Max Jacob Prize*
For a poetical work published during the preceding year, preferably by a relatively unknown poet. Awarded annually. Enquiries to Librairie Le Pont Traversé, 16 rue St-Severin, F-75007 Paris

Jean-Christophe Prize
For poetry, preferably of classical form. Offered by Mme Alice Cluchier in memory of the young tragedian, her son. Awarded to young poet for manuscript of 10 poems, judged likely to inspire love of art and beauty and having fidelity of recollection. Enquiries to Société des Poètes français, 38 rue du Faubourg St Jacques F-75014 Paris

Jeune France Prize
For the best unpublished book for young people. The book can cover any field. Awarded every two years. Enquiries to Les Editions Magnard Sàrl, 122 blvd Saint-Germain, F-75279 Paris cedex 06

Juteau-Duvigneaux Prize*
For works on morality, especially from the Catholic point of view. Awarded annually. Enquiries to French Academy, Institut de France, 23 quai de Conti, F-75006 Paris

La Fontaine Prize*
For a moral literary work. Awarded biennially. Enquiries to French Academy, Institut de France, 23 quai de Conti, F-75006 Paris

Paul Labbé-Vauquelin Prize
Founded in 1924, and accorded to a collection of intimate poetry regionally inspired. Enquiries to Société des Poètes français, 38 rue du Faubourg St Jacques, F-75014 Paris

Georges Lafenestre Prize
Given since 1938, it was founded by the family of Georges Lafenestre on the occasion of the poet's centenary and goes to an unpublished poem of high inspiration and classical form, 150 lines maximum. Enquiries to Société des Poètes français, 38 rue du Faubourg St Jacques, F-75014 Paris

Lambert Prize*
To men of letters or their widows (if they deserve public recognition). Awarded annually. Enquiries to French Academy, Institut de France, 23 quai de Conti, F-75006 Paris

Langlois Prize*
For the best translation in verse or prose of a Greek, Latin or other foreign work into the French language. Awarded annually. Enquiries to French Academy, Institut de France, 23 quai de Conti, F-75006 Paris

Eugène Le Moël Prize
Founded in 1936 for a poem in any genre, but preferably inspired by Eugène Le Moël. Enquiries to Société des Poètes français, 38 rue de Faubourg St Jacques, F-75014 Paris

Sébastien-Charles Leconte Prize*
Given since 1935 to a poem of noble inspiration and strictly classical form, 150 line maximum. Enquiries to Société des Poètes français, 38 rue du Faubourg St Jacques, F-75014 Paris

Van Lerberghe Prize*
Founded in 1957 for French expression in poetry. 100 francs. Awarded annually. Enquiries to Maison de Poésie, 11 bis rue Ballu, F-75009 Paris

Literary Critics' Grand Prize*
For the best work of literary criticism or literary history. Awarded annually. Enquiries to Syndicate of Literary Critics, 1 rue Renault, F-94 St-Mande

Literary Prize of the Resistance*
For a work contributing to the history and spirit of the Resistance. 10,000 francs. Awarded annually by the Resistance Action Committee. The 1978 prize was awarded to General Guillandot for *Soldats bleus dans l'Ombre*. Enquiries to Secretariat, 10 rue de Charenton, F-75012 Paris

Paul Lofler Prize
Replaced the prize for the Sonnet in 1963. For the best regulated sonnet. Enquiries to Société des Poètes français, 38 rue du Faubourg St Jacques, F-75014 Paris

Jean Mace Prize*
For works of fiction or nonfiction either as published books or as manuscripts for readers aged fifteen to eighteen. Awarded annually. Enquiries to French Education League, 3 rue Recamier, F-75007 Paris

Maille-Latour-Landry Prize*
To a young writer who should be encouraged to follow a literary career. Awarded biennially. Enquiries to French Academy, Institut de France, 23 quai de Conti, F-75006 Paris

Maisondieu Prize
To the author or founder of a work contributing to the betterment of the working classes. Awarded every two years. Enquiries to Academy of Moral and Political Sciences, Institut de France, 23 quai de Conti, F-75006 Paris

Fernand Mazarde Prize*
For criticism of poetry or a critical edition of poets or chronicle of poetry in reviews or publications. Created in 1955. Enquiries to Maison de Poésie, 11 bis rue Ballu, F-75009 Paris

Médicis Prize*
Awarded to an avant-garde novel, story or collection whose publication has not been accompanied by the celebrity or fame the author's talent deserves. Founded in 1958. Enquiries to 20 rue Cortot, F-75108 Paris

Narcisse Michaut Prize*
For the best piece of French literature. Awarded biennially. Enquiries to French Academy, Institut de France, 23 quai de Conti, F-75006 Paris

Louis P Miller Prize*
For works furthering the love of virtue, in particular remembrance and gratitude. Awarded annually. Enquiries to French Academy, Institut de France, 23 quai de Conti, F-75006 Paris

Marcelle Millier Prize*
To a female writer over 45 whose work will be an honour to French literature. Enquiries to French Academy, Institut de France, 23 quai de Conti, F-75006 Paris

Charles Monselet Prize*
For a poetical work on the glory of French cuisine. Founded in 1954. Enquiries to Société des Poètes français, 38 rue du Faubourg St Jacques, F-75104 Paris

Montyon Prize*
For literary works of high moral character. Awarded annually, Enquiries to French Academy, Institut de France, 23 quai de Conti, F-75006 Paris

National Grand Prize of Letters
To the French writer who has contributed most to French literature. 20,000 francs. Awarded annually. Enquiries to French Ministry of Cultural Affairs, Direction du livre, Centre National des Lettres, 6 rue Dufrenoy, F-75116 Paris

Alfred Née Prize*
For a work showing originality of thought and style. Awarded annually. Enquiries to French Academy, Institut de France, 23 quai de Conti, F-75006 Paris

Novel Prize*
To a young prose-writer for an inspirational imaginative work. 20,000 francs. Awarded annually. Enquiries to French Academy, Institut de France, 23 quai de Conti, F-75006 Paris

Paris Grand Prize for Literature*
For different forms of literature such as novel, poetry, criticism, essay, history, philosophy. Awarded annually (each year for a different form). Enquiries to Paris City Council, Hôtel de Ville, F-75004 Paris

Paris Prize*
For a novel. Awarded annually. Enquiries to Academy of Letters and Arts, c/o Musée de Montmartre, 17 rue St-Vincent, F-75018 Paris

Petitdidier Prize*
To poets under 40, 300 francs. Awarded annually. Enquiries to Maison de Poésie, 11 bis rue Ballu, F-75009 Paris

De Pimodan Prize
Given since 1926 to regional poet celebrating his land. Enquiries to Société des Poètes français, 38 rue du Faubourg St Jacques, F-75014 Paris

Charles Pitou Prize
Founded 1928, reserved for poem in strictly classical form celebrating a French province, preferably Normandy. Enquiries to Société des Poètes français, 38 rue du Faubourg St Jacques, F-75014 Paris

Raymond Poincaré Prize*
For a literary work which creates a favourable climate for the army. Awarded to officers of the French army. 1,000 francs. Awarded annually. Enquiries to National Union of Reserve Officers, 17 ave de l'Opéra, F-75001 Paris

Racine Prize*
For a work on the life or works of Racine, containing previously unknown documents or new views. Awarded annually. Enquiries to Racine Society, BP 49 Neuilly Principal 92204, Neuilly, Seine

J-M Renaitour Prize, replaced by Edmond Haraucourt Prize (qv)

Théophraste Rénaudot Prize*
Founded by Gaston Picard in 1926. Same conditions as for Goncourt (qv). Awarded in 1978 to Conrad Detrez for *L'Herbe a Bruler*. Enquiries to 62 rue de Vaugirard, Paris

Léon Riotor Prize*
Founded 1953, and honours a critical essay or poetical story. 100 francs. Awarded annually. Enquiries to Maison de Poésie, 11 bis rue Ballu, F-75009 Paris

Roberge Prizes*
One year to a young poet who has published no more than two volumes of verse. The following year to a young author who has published no more than two novels. Enquiries to French Academy, Institut de France, 23 quai de Conti, F-75006 Paris

Roucoules Foundation Grand Prize for Poetry*
10,000 francs. Awarded annually. Enquiries to French Academy, Institut de France, 23 quai de Conti, F-75006 Paris

Saintour Prize*
For works (lexicons, grammars, editions of criticism, commentaries, etc) on the study of the French language, in particular from the 16th century to the present. Awarded annually. Enquiries to French Academy, Institut de France, 23 quai de Conti, F-75006 Paris

Dr Albert Schweitzer Prize*
For a literary work which arouses interest in the problem of infirmity and in society's responsibility for the disabled. 5,000 francs. Awarded annually. Enquiries to Confederation of the Blind, Deaf-Mutes and the Severely Disabled, 38 rue René-Boulanger, Paris

Sobrier-Arnould Prize*
To the authors of the two best works in moral literature which are instructive to youth. Awarded annually. Enquiries to French Academy, Institut de France, 23 quai de Conti, F-75006 Paris

Paul Teissonnière Prize*
For the best liberal work (printed or manuscript) on a moral, philosophical or religious subject. Enquiries to French Academy, Institut de France, 23 quai de Conti, F-75006 Paris

Lucien Tisserand Prize*
To a novelist between 40 and 50 years of age who has proved his talent. Awarded annually. Enquiries to French Academy, Institut de France, 23 quai de Conti, F-75006 Paris

Maurice Trubert Prize*
For a prose or verse work taking into account classical traditions and presenting morality from a Catholic point of view. Author must be under 30. Awarded biennially. Enquiries to French Academy, Institut de France, 23 quai de Conti, F-75006 Paris

Antony Valabrègue Prize*
To a young poet who has published one volume of verse. Awarded biennially. Enquiries to French Academy, Institut de France, 23 quai de Conti, F-75006 Paris

Valentine Abraham Verlain Prize*
To a woman of letters or for a needy female artist. Awarded annually. Enquiries to French Academy, Institut de France, 23 quai de Conti, F-75006 Paris

Paul Verlaine Prize*
Founded 1950 for all kinds of poetry. 100 francs. Awarded annually. Enquiries to Maison de Poésie, 11 bis rue Ballu, F-75009 Paris

Gabriel Vicaire Prize*
Founded 1948 for traditional poetry. 100 francs. Awarded annually. Enquiries to Maison de Poésie, 11 bis rue Ballu, F-75009 Paris

Claire Virenque Prize*
To young authors. One year for a collection of poems, the next for a novel or biography showing Christian inspiration. Enquiries to French Academy, Institut de France, 23 quai de Conti, F-75006 Paris

Volney Prize
For a work in comparative philology. Enquiries to Académie des Inscriptions et Belles-Lettres, Institut de France, 23 quai de Conti, F-75006 Paris

J J Weiss Prize*
For a prose work in the purest classic style on travel, literature, literary or dramatic criticism or politics. Awarded every two

years. Enquiries to French Academy, Institut de France, 23 quai de Conti, F-75006 Paris

Valentine de **Wolmar** Prize*
For the most beautiful novel or collection of poetry. Awarded annually. Enquiries to French Academy, Institut de France, 23 quai de Conti, F-75006 Paris

Translation Agencies and Associations

Société française des Traducteurs (French Union of Translators), 1 rue de Courcelles, F-75008 Paris

French Guiana

General Information

Language: French
Religion: Catholic
Population: 60,000
Literacy Rate (1967): 73.9%
Bank Hours: 0700-1130, 1400-1600 Monday-Friday
Shop Hours: 0800-1300, 1500-1800 Monday-Friday
Currency: 100 centimes = 1 franc
Export/Import Information: Tariff as for France. See France for domiciliation of documents. No import licences required. Same exchange restrictions as France

Major Booksellers

Mme **Beaufort***, 16 rue du Lieutenant-Brassé, BP 505, Cayenne Tel: 98

La **Boutique** Bleue*, ave Pasteur, BP 243, Cayenne

Emilio **Gratien***, 25 ave du Général de Gaulle, Cayenne Tel: 280

Librairie-Papeterie Universelle*, 26 rue Lallouette, Cayenne Tel: 240

Major Libraries

Bibliothèque Franconie*, 97300 Cayenne

Office de la Recherche Scientifique et Technique Outre-Mer (Office of Scientific and Technical Research Overseas)*, Centre ORSTOM de Cayenne, Bibliothèque, BP 165, Cayenne

Literary Associations and Societies

Association des Amis du Livre (Association of Book Lovers)*, 97300 Cayenne

French Polynesia

General Information

Language: French is the commercial language
Religion: Roman Catholic
Population: 136,000
Literacy Rate (1962): 94.5%
Bank Hours: 0900-1100, 1400-1600 Monday-Friday; 0900-1100, 1400-1500 Saturday
Shop Hours: 0730-1100, 1330-1700 Monday-Friday; 0730-1130 Saturday
Currency: 100 centimes = 1 franc CFP
Export/Import Information: No tariff on books except 8% customs duty on children's picture books; advertising matter subject to 8% customs duty, 5% import duty, although catalogues generally considered printed books. Advertising subject to 20 francs per unit Statistical Tax. Miscellaneous tax of 2% of customs value on books and advertising. No import licence required. Exchange controls

Publishers

Les Editions du **Pacifique**+, 10 ave Bruat, BP 1722, Papeete, Tahiti Tel: 26643 Telex: 293 fp tahiti
Man Dir: Didier Millet
Subjects: Travel Books, Natural Science (tropical environment), History, Nonfiction, Gift Books
1977: 12 titles *1978:* 12 titles (figures cover publications in both France and French Polynesia) *Founded:* 1971
ISBN Publisher's Prefix: 2-85700

Major Booksellers

Librairie **Au Ping-Pong***, 6 rue du Commandant-Destremeau, Papeete, Tahiti Tel: 133

Librairie **Klima**, La Boutique, BP 31, pl Notre-Dame, Papeete, Tahiti
Manager: Manuella Luciani

Librairie **Quartier-Latin***, BP 25, Papeete, Tahiti

Librairie du **Sagittaire***, 10 ave Bruat, BP 334, Papeete, Tahiti Tel: 610

Gabon

General Information

Language: French
Religion: About half Roman Catholic and half animist
Population: 534,000
Literacy Rate (1960-61): 14.8%
Currency: CFA franc
Export/Import Information: No tariff on books; 7.5% fiscal, 30% customs, 10% VAT, 5% tax turnover on advertising matter. Import licence required. Exchange controls on non-franc zone (and Congo, Mauritania and Madagascar)

Publishers

Government Printer (Imprimerie Centrale d'Afrique)*, BP 154, Libreville

Saint-Joseph*, BP 58, Libreville

Major Booksellers

Centre de Littérature Evangélique*, BP 206, Oyem

Librairie **Hachette***, BP 121, Libreville Tel: 733131 Telex: 5418 go

Librairie **Nouvelle***, BP 612, Libreville Tel: 3616

Librairie **Sogalivre***, BP 50, Port-Gentil Tel: 52319

Major Libraries

Archives et Bibliothèque nationale (National Library and Archives)*, BP 1188, Libreville Tel: 32543

Centre culturel américain*, Bibliothèque, BP 2237, Libreville Tel: 721558/722161

Centre culturel français St-Exupéry*, Bibliothèque, BP 2103, Libreville Tel: 721120

Centre **Bibliotheque** d'Information*, BP 3127, Libreville Tel: 21115

Collège Jésus Marie*, Bibliothèque, BP 120, Bitam Tel: 277

Ecole normale supérieure*, Bibliothèque, BP 16030, Libreville

Institut polytechnique de l'Afrique centrale*, Bibliothèque, BP 1158, Libreville

Bibliothèque de l'**Université** nationale du Gabon*, BP 11132, Libreville Tel: 32506

The Gambia

General Information

Language: English
Religion: Muslim
Population: 553,000
Bank Hours: 0800-1300 Monday-Friday; 0800-1100 Saturday
Shop Hours: 0800-1200, 1400-1700 Monday-Thursday; 0800-1200, 1500-1700 Friday; 0800-1200 Saturday
Currency: 100 butut = 1 dalasi
Export/Import Information: No tariff on books; 25% on some advertising matter. 1% Import Tax on all. No import licence required. National Trading Corporation has no monopoly. Exchange controls

Publishers

The **Government Press***, Banjul

Major Booksellers

Jeng's Bookshop*, PO Box 234, Banjul

The **Gambia** Methodist Bookshop Ltd*, PO Box 203, Banjul Tel: 8179

Major Libraries

Gambia National Library*, Independence Drive, PMB, Banjul Tel: 461
Senior Librarian: Sally P C N'Jie

Yundum College Library*, Yundum

German Democratic Republic

General Information

Language: German
Religion: Predominantly Protestant
Population: 17 million
Bank Hours: Generally 0800-1600 Monday-Friday; open Saturday morning
Shop Hours: Vary. Generally 0900 or 1000-1800 or 1900 Monday-Friday; open part day Saturday
Currency: 100 pfennige = 1 DDR mark or ostmark
Export/Import Information: Foreign trade is a state monopoly; books imported and exported by Buchexport, Leninstr 16, Postfach 160, DDR-701 Leipzig. Import licences required and Foreign Trade Bank handles all payments. No advertising materials to be sent to private individuals; for preparation of advertising, contact Interwerbung GmbH, Berlin
Copyright: UCC, Berne (see International section)

Book Trade Organizations

Börsenverein der Deutschen Buchhändler zu Leipzig (Association of German Democratic Republic Publishers and Booksellers in Leipzig)*, Gerichtsweg 26, DDR-701 Leipzig Tel: 293851 Cable Add: Buchbörse
Publications: Börsenblatt für den Deutschen Buchhandel

Buchexport — Volkseigener Aussenhandelsbetrieb der Deutschen Demokratischen Republik, (GDR Peoples' Export Undertaking), Leninstr 16, Postfach 160, DDR-701 Leipzig Tel: 7661 Telex: 051678
Publications: Nova, Wissen und Können, Buch der Zeit, Bücher aus deer DDR, DDR Gesamtkatalog, DDR Periodica. (See individual entries under Book Trade Reference Books and Journals).
The state organization for foreign trade. These catalogues contain particulars of the entire range of GDR publications.

Ministerrat der Deutschen Demokratischen Republik, Ministerium für Kultur, Hauptverwaltung Verlage und Buchhandel*, DDR-108 Berlin 8, Clara-Zetkin-Str 90 (Council of Ministers of the German Democratic Republic, Ministry of Culture, Main Department — Publishing and Bookselling)

Book Trade Reference Books and Journals

Books

Adressbuch des Volksbuchhandels der Deutschen Demokratischen Republik (Directory of the People's Booksellers of the DDR), Volksbuchhandel der DDR, Zentrale Zeitung, DDR-701 Leipzig, Friedrich-Ebert-Str 25

Die Deutsche Demokratische Republik, ein Land des Buches (The DDR, A Country of the Book), Association of German Publishers and Booksellers in Leipzig, Gerichtsweg 26, DDR-701 Leipzig

Deutsches Bücherverzeichnis (5-year German Book List), Deutsche Bücherei, Deutscher Platz, DDR-701 Leipzig

LKG Lagerkatalog (LKG Stock Catalogue), Leipziger Kommissions- und Grossbuchhandel, Leninstr 16, DDR-701 Leipzig

Schriftenreihen aus den Verlagen der Deutschen Demokratischen Republik (Series from the Publishers of the DDR), Buchexport, Leninstr 16, DDR-701 Leipzig

Titel-Information (Title-Information), Leipziger Komissions- und Grossbuchhandel, Leninstr 16, DDR-701 Leipzig

Verlage der Deutschen Demokratischen Republik (Publishers of the DDR), Association of German Publishers and Booksellers in Leipzig, Gerichtsweg 26, DDR-701 Leipzig

Journals

Beiträge zur Literaturkunde (Contributions to Literary Knowledge); bibliography of selected newspaper and periodical contributions, VEB, Bibliographisches Institut, Gerichtsweg 26, DDR-701 Leipzig

Bibliographie der Bibliographien (Bibliography of Bibliographies), Deutsche Bücherei, Deutscher Platz, DDR-701 Leipzig

Bibliographie der Übersetzungen deutschsprachiger Werke (Bibliography of Translations of German Language Works), Deutsche Bücherei, Deutscher Platz, DDR-701 Leipzig

Bibliographie fremdsprachiger Germanica (Bibliography of Germanics in Foreign Languages), Deutsche Bücherei, Deutscher Platz, DDR-701 Leipzig

Börsenblatt für den deutschen Buchhandel (German Book Trade Journal), Association of German Publishers and Booksellers in Leipzig, Gerichtsweg 26, DDR-701 Leipzig

Buch der Zeit (Books of the Day), (text in English and German), Buchexport, Leninstr 16, DDR-701 Leipzig

Bücher aus der DDR (Books from the German Democratic Republic) Lists of new books and reprint editions on German Language and Literature, German history and culture etc. pub by Buchexport, Leninstr 16, DDR-701 Leipzig. Published every 3 months

DDR Gesamtkatalog (German Democratic Republic Complete Catalogue), Buchexport (qv under Book Trade Organisations), Leninstr 16, DDR-701 Leipzig
A general catalogue in two vols, it covers all titles published in one year and appears annually, at the start of the following year

Deutsche National-Bibliographie (German National Bibliography), Deutsche Bücherei, Deutscher Platz, DDR-701 Leipzig

Informationsblatt (Information Sheet), Library Association of the German Democratic Republic, Hermann-Matern-Str 57, DDR-104 Berlin

Jahresverzeichnis der Verlagsschriften (Annual List of Publications), Deutsche Bücherei, Deutscher Platz, DDR-701 Leipzig

Nova; forthcoming books (table of contents and subtitles in English, German and Russian), Buchexport, Leninstr 16, DDR-701 Leipzig. Two issues per month

Selecta; titles immediately available from the publishers of the DDR, Buchexport, Leninstr 16, DDR-701 Leipzig

Wissen und Können (To Know and Be Able), Buchexport, Leninstr 16, DDR-701 Leipzig. A series of 26 Catalogues covering every branch of knowledge under the headings: I — Social Sciences; II — Art and Literature; III — Natural Sciences; IV — Technical Science/Engineering; V — Agriculture and Forestry, Veterinary Science; VI — Medicine. The Catalogues list all books under the particular subject selected which are available for sale, in print or in course of preparation.
Publication of each list is annual.

Publishers

Akademie-Verlag, Leipziger Str 3-4, Postfach 1233, DDR-108 Berlin Tel: 22360 Cable Add: Akademie-Verlag Berlin Telex: 114420 averl dd
Subjects: History, Philosophy, Literature, History of Art, Archaeology, Ethnography, Oriental, Biology, Geology, Mathematics, Physics, Chemistry, Medicine, Languages, Economics; Periodicals
1978: 350 titles *Founded:* 1946

Aufbau-Verlag Berlin und Weimar, Französische Str 32, Postfach 1217, DDR-108 Berlin Tel: 2202421 Cable Add: Aufbau Verlag Berlin
Subjects: General Fiction, Library of World Literature, Belles Lettres, Literary Criticism, Paperbacks
Founded: 1945
Miscellaneous: Associate Company: Verlag Rütten & Loening, German Democratic Republic

Johann Ambrosius **Barth** Verlagsbuchhandlung, Salomonstr 18b, Postfach 109, DDR-701 Leipzig Tel: 295245 Cable Add: Barth Leipzig
Man Dir: Klaus Wiecke
Orders to: LKG VA 221, Postfach 520, DDR-701 Leipzig
Subjects: Medicine, Dentistry, Stomatology, Psychology, Natural Science, Chemistry, Astronomy, Physics; Periodicals, Publications of the German Academy of Naturalists, *Leopoldina*
1977: 43 titles *1978:* 42 titles *Founded:* 1780
Miscellaneous: Publish 15 periodicals

GERMAN DEMOCRATIC REPUBLIC

VEB Verlag für **Bauwesen**, Französische Str 13-14, Postfach 1232, DDR-108 Berlin Tel: 20410 Cable Add: Bauwesenverlag Telex: 112229 Trave
Man Dir: Siegfried Seeliger; *Editorial:* Siegfried Schikora; *Sales:* Franz Rautenstrauch; *Production:* Günter Langer; *Publicity:* Marion Thiele
Subjects: Civil Engineering, Architecture and Building Construction, Materials and Mechanics; 10 Periodicals
1977: 80 titles *1978:* 60 titles (Figures include reprints) *Founded:* 1960

VEB **Bibliographisches Institut***, Gerichtsweg 26, Postfach 130, DDR-701 Leipzig Tel: 7801 Cable Add: Biblio Leipzig Telex: 051773
Man Dir: Helmut Bähring
Associate Companies: VEB Verlag für Buch und Bibliothekswesen (qv); VEB Max Niemeyer Verlag (qv); VEB Verlag Enzyklopädie (qv); all at above address
Subjects: General Dictionaries, Reference, Biography, Bibliographies, German Language, Library Science, Documentation, Literature, Languages, Periodicals
Founded: 1826
Miscellaneous: Publish periodicals

Hermann **Böhlaus** Nachfolger+, Meyerstr 50a, DDR-53 Weimar Tel: 2071 Cable Add: Böhlauverlag DDR-53 Weimar
Man Dir: Dr Leiva Petersen
Subjects: History of Law, Literature & Art, Critical Editions & Yearbooks, Medieval History
1977: 30 titles *1978:* 30 titles *Founded:* 1624

VEB **Breitkopf und Härtel** Musikverlag, Karlstr 10, Postfach 147, DDR-701 Leipzig Tel: 7351 Cable Add: Breitkopfs
Man Dir: Dr Günter Hempel; *Sales Dir:* Werner Hennig
Founded: 1719
Subjects: Music: Vocal and Instrumental Music, Biographies, Reference, Musicology, etc

VEB F A **Brockhaus** Verlag, Salomonstr 17, DDR-701 Leipzig
Subjects: Picture-books (relating to the German Democratic Republic and other countries), Reference, Travel, Popular Science
1979: 33 titles

VEB Verlag für **Buch- und Bibliothekswesen***, Gerichtsweg 26, Postfach 130, DDR-701 Leipzig Tel: 7801 Telex: 051773
Man Dir: Helmut Bähring
Subjects: Bibliography, Book Industry, Reference, Periodicals
Miscellaneous: Associate Companies: VEB Verlag Enzyklopädie (qv); VEB Bibliographisches Institut (qv); VEB Max Niemeyer Verlag (qv); all at above address

VEB **Deutscher Landwirtschaftsverlag**, Reinhardtstr 14, DDR-104 Berlin
Subject: Agriculture
1978: 80 titles

VEB **Deutscher Verlag der Wissenschaften**, Johannes-Dieckmann-Str 10, Postfach 1216, DDR-108 Berlin Tel: 22900 Cable Add: Devauwe Berlin Telex: 112063 dvw dd
Sales Dir: Mr Spiekenheuer; *Publicity Dir:* Mr Taufmann
Subjects: History, Philosophy, Psychology; General, Natural & Social Sciences; Physics, Chemistry, Mathematics
1978: 67 titles

VEB **Deutscher Verlag für Grundstoffindustrie**, Karl-Heine-Str 27, DDR-7031 Leipzig Tel: 44441 Cable Add: Grundstoffverlag Leipzig
The German Democratic Republic Publishing House for the Raw Material Industry
Subjects: Geological Sciences, Coal, Energy, Mining of Ores, Metallurgy, Potash, Chemistry and Chemical Process Technology; also Popular Scientific Literature, Periodicals
1977: 24 new, 79 reprint titles

VEB **Deutscher Verlag für Musik**, Karlstr 10, Postfach 147, DDR-701 Leipzig Tel: 7351 Cable Add: Demusica Leipzig
Man Dir: Dr Günter Hempel; *Sales Dir:* Werner Hennig
Subjects: Music: Vocal and Instrumental Music, Reference, Biographies, Children's and Young Peoples' Books on Music, Musicology, Facsimilies, Musical Belles Lettres
Founded: 1954

Dieterich'sche Verlagsbuchhandlung, Mottelerstr 8, Postfach 88, DDR-7022 Leipzig
Associate Companies: Insel-Verlag (qv); Gustav Kiepenhauer Verlag (qv); Paul List Verlag (qv)
Subjects: World literature in translation
1978: 3 titles

Dietz Verlag*, Wallstr 76-79, Postfach 273, DDR-102 Berlin Tel: 276361
Subjects: Social Science, Economics, Philosophy, Politics, History, Memoirs, Periodicals
Founded: 1946

VEB Verlag **Enzyklopädie***, Gerichtsweg 26, Postfach 130, DDR-701 Leipzig Tel: 7801 Telex: 051773
Man Dir: Helmut Bähring
Subjects: Languages, Dictionaries, Foreign Language Textbooks
Founded: 1956
Miscellaneous: Associate Companies: VEB Bibliographisches Institut (qv); VEB Verlag für Buch und Bibliothekswesen (qv); VEB Max Niemeyer Verlag (qv); all at above address

Eulenspiegel Verlag für Satir und Humor, Kronenstr 73-74, Postfach 1239, DDR-108 Berlin Tel: 2202126
Deputy Manager: Kurt Noack
Associate Company: Verlag Das Neue Berlin (qv)
Subjects: Humorous Publications generally: Satire, Caricature, Cartoons
1978: 73 titles

Evangelische Verlagsanstalt GmbH, Krautstr 52, Postfach 114, DDR-1017 Berlin Tel: 2700131
Dirs: Olkr von Brueck, Dr Forck
Subjects: Christian History, Devotional, Biblical Exegesis, Christian Fiction and Poetry, Biography, Art Books, Music; also Calendars, Periodicals
1978: 135 titles *Founded:* 1946

VEB **Fachbuchverlag**, Karl-Heine-Str 16, Postfach 67, DDR-7031 Leipzig Tel: 44021 Cable Add: Fachbuch Leipzig Telex: 51451 d d
Man Dir: Siegfried Hoffmann
Subjects: General Knowledge, Popular Science, Basic Technologies, Specific texts on variety of industries (e.g. food, leather, textiles etc)
1979: 127 titles *1980:* 100 titles *Founded:* 1949
Miscellaneous: Publish 20 periodicals

VEB Gustav **Fischer** Verlag, Villengang 2, Postfach 176, DDR-690 Jena Tel: Jena 27332 Cable Add: Fischerbuch Telex: 05886176
Parent Company: Volkseigene Verlage für Medizin und Biologie, Berlin, Jena, Leipzig
Associate Companies: VEB Georg Thieme (qv); VEB Verlag Volk und Gesundheit (qv)
Subjects: Medicine, Veterinary, Biology; Periodicals
1977: 82 titles *1978:* 72 titles *Founded:* 1878

VEB **Fotokinoverlag**, Karl-Heine-Str 16, Postfach 67, DDR-7031 Leipzig Tel: 44021
Man Dir: Siegfried Hoffmann
Subjects: Photography, Film
1979: 25 titles *1980:* 29 titles *Founded:* 1957
Miscellaneous: Publish three periodicals

Verlag für die **Frau**, Friedrich-Ebert-Str 76-78, Postfach 1005/1025, DDR-701 Leipzig
Subjects: Fashion, Family, Domestic Science, Periodicals

Akademische Verlagsgesellschaft **Geest und Portig** KG, Sternwarten Str 8, Postfach 106, DDR-701 Leipzig Tel: 293158/59/297535 Cable Add: Akabuch Leipzig
Man Dir: Ing Heinz Kratz
Associate Company: BSB B G Teubner Verlagsgesellschaft (qv)
Subjects: Chemistry, Physics, Mathematics, Engineering, History of Science, Geo-Sciences, Electro-Technology
Founded: 1906

Altberliner Verlag Lucie **Groszer**, Neue Schönhauser Str 8, Postfach 44, DDR-102 Berlin Tel: 2826749
Dir: Lucie Groszer; *Editorial:* Alfred Könner
Subject: Children's Books from infant age upwards
1978: 18 titles *1979:* 18 titles *Founded:* 1945

VEB Hermann **Haack**, Justus-Perthes-Str 3/9, Postfach 274, DDR-58 Gotha Tel: 3872-3874 Cable Add: Geokart Gotha Telex: 618583 telex hago dd
Imprint: Haack Gotha
Subjects: Maps, Atlases, Geographic and Cartographic Publications, Periodicals

Henschelverlag Kunst und Gesellschaft, Oranienburger Str 67-68, Postfach 220, DDR-104 Berlin Tel: 28790 Cable Add: Henschelverlag Berlin
Dir: K Mittelstädt
Subjects: General Fiction, Film, Theatre, Music, Art, Periodicals

VEB **Hinstorff** Verlag+, Kröpeliner Str 25, Postfach 11, DDR-25 Rostock Tel: 34441
Subjects: Contemporary Literature of the DDR, German Language Literature in Series, Scandinavian Literature in Translation, Homeland Literature and Studies, Maritime Literature

VEB Friedrich **Hofmeister** Musikverlag, Karlstr 10, Postschließfach 147, DDR-701 Leipzig Tel: 7351
Man Dir: Dr Günter Hempel; *Sales Dir:* Werner Hennig
Subjects: Vocal and Instrumental Music, Song Books, Musicians' Biographies
Founded: 1807

Insel-Verlag Anton Kippenberg, Mottelerstr 8, Postfach 88, DDR-7022 Leipzig Tel: 592356 and 52857
Associate Companies: Insel-Verlag issues a common catalogue with: Gustav

GERMAN DEMOCRATIC REPUBLIC

Kiepenhauer Verlag (qv); Dieterich'sche Verlagsbuchhandlung (qv); Paul List Verlag (qv)
Subjects: Literature, Art; Classics of World Literature in Translation
1978: 29 titles *Founded:* 1899

Verlag **Junge Welt**, Postfach 43, DDR–1056 Berlin (Located at: Mauerstr 39/40, DDR–108 Berlin) Tel: 22330
Man Dir: Manfred Rucht
Subjects: Juveniles, Education, Sports, Science, Technical, Periodicals
1979: 32 titles *Founded:* 1952

Gustav **Kiepenheuer** Verlag, Mottelerstr 8, Postfach 88, DDR–7022 Leipzig
Associate Companies: Dieterich'sche Verlagsbuchhandlung (qv); Insel-Verlag (qv); Paul List Verlag (qv)
Subjects: Literary Studies and Fiction, especially from the Far East; Literature in translation; Art
1978: 20 titles *Founded:* 1909

Der **Kinderbuchverlag** Berlin, Behrenstr 40–41, Postfach 1225, DDR–108 Berlin
Subject: Juveniles

Koehler und Amelang (VOB), Hainstr 2, DDR–701 Leipzig Tel: 282379
Associate Company: Union Verlag Berlin (VOB) (qv)
Branch Off: Talstr 3, DDR–701 Leipzig Tel: 209519
Subjects: Cultural History, Art History, Biographical
1978: 8 titles

VEB Verlag der **Kunst***, Spenerstr 21, DDR–8019 Dresden Tel: 34486
Subjects: Fine Arts, Reproductions

Edition **Leipzig***, Verlag für Kunst und Wissenschaft, Karl-Liebknecht-Str 77, DDR–703 Leipzig Tel: 32445 Cable Add: Edileip
Man Dir: Elmar Faber; *Sales Dir:* Fritz Becker
Subjects: Art, History of Civilization, Science, Scientific & Bibliophile Reprints
Founded: 1960

Paul **List** Verlag*, Paul-List-Str 22, Postfach 1062, DDR–701 Leipzig Tel: 35424
Associate Companies: Dieterich'sche Verlagsbuchhandlung (qv); Insel-Verlag (qv); Gustav Kiepenheuer Verlag (qv)
Subjects: Foreign Literature in translation
Founded: 1894

VEB **Militärverlag** der DDR, Storkower Str 158, Postfach 46551, DDR–1055 Berlin Tel: 4300618 Telex: 112673 mv
Subjects: Books, paperbacks and periodicals on military subjects; military theory, politics, history, specialised literature; Popular Science; Fiction, Periodicals
Founded: 1956

Mitteldeutscher Verlag, Thälmannplatz 2, Postfach 295, DDR–401 Halle/Saale Tel: 8730
Man Dir: Dr Eberhard Günther
Subjects: General Fiction & Nonfiction, Collected Works, Poetry, Belles Lettres, Biography, Novels
1977: 107 titles *1978:* 112 titles *Founded:* 1946

Buchverlag Der **Morgen**, Johannes-Dieckmann-Str 47, DDR–108 Berlin Tel: 2202181
Man Dir: Dr Wolfgang Tenzler
Subjects: General Fiction, Belles Lettres, Poetry, Biography, Political Monographs
1977: 45 titles *Founded:* 1958

Verlag der **Nation**, Friedrichstr 113, Postfach 74, DDR–104 Berlin Tel: 2825826
Dir: Günter Hofé
Subjects: Publications of the National Democratic Party of Germany, Current Politics, Biographical, Illustrated Texts, Historical Fiction, Belles Lettres, Cultural; Paperback Series
1978: 64 titles *Founded:* 1948

Verlag das **Neue Berlin**, Kronenstr 73/74, Postfach 1239, DDR–108 Berlin Tel: 2202126 Cable Add: Neuesberlinbuch Berlin
Associate Company: Eulenspiegel Verlag (qv)
Subjects: Crime Literature, Adventure, Science Fiction
1978: 50 titles

Verlag **Neues Leben**, Behrenstr 40–41, Postfach 1223, DDR–108 Berlin Tel: 2032765 Cable Add: Neuesleben Berlin
Man Dir: Rudolf Chowanetz
Subjects: General Fiction and Nonfiction; Juveniles, Science Fiction: Paperbacks
1977: 218 titles *1978:* 221 titles *Founded:* 1946

VEB Max **Niemeyer** Verlag*, Gerichtsweg 26, Postfach 130, DDR–701 Leipzig Tel: 7801 Telex: 51773
Man Dir: Helmut Baehring
Subjects: Philology, University Textbooks, Protestant Theology, Literature, Languages; Periodicals
Founded: 1869
Miscellaneous: Associate Companies: VEB Verlag Enzyklopädie (qv); VEB Bibliographisches Institut (qv); VEB Verlag für Buch und Bibliothekswesen (qv); all at above address

Prisma-Verlag Zenner und Gürchott, Leibnizstr 10, Postfach 1461, DDR–701 Leipzig Tel: 281411
Man Dir: Klaus Zenner; *Publicity Dir:* Fritz Gürchott
Subjects: Archaeology, Art and Cultural History, Fine Illustrated Editions, Historical Novels; many Non-fiction books have texts in German, English and Russian
1977: 10 titles *1978:* 6 titles *Founded:* 1957

Verlag Philipp **Reclam** jun, Nonnenstr 38, DDR–7031 Leipzig Tel: 44501 Cable Add: Reclam Leipzig
Man Dir: Hans Marquardt; *Sales Dir:* Gottfried Berthold; *Publicity & Advertising Dir:* Doris Lietz
Subjects: Reclam's Universal Library (a paperback series covering Belles Lettres, Philosophy, History, Aesthetics, Music, Biography), Literature
1977: 135 titles *1978:* 110 titles *Founded:* 1828

Verlag **Rütten und Loening** Berlin, see Aufbau Verlag

Sankt-Benno Verlag GmbH, Verlag für katholisches Schrifttum (Catholic Literature Publishing House), Thüringer Str 1–3, Postfach 98 and 112, DDR–7033 Leipzig Tel: 44161
Gen Managers: Prelate Hermann J Weisbender, Franz J Cordier
Subjects: Religion, Philosophy, Music, Catholic Literature in German and Latin Languages; Periodicals
1978: 78 titles

VEB E A **Seemann** Buch- und Kunstverlag, Jacobstr 6, Postfach 846, DDR–701 Leipzig Tel: 7736 Cable Add: Kunstsemann
Subjects: Art, Reference

Seven Seas Publishers, Glinkastr 13–15, DDR–108 Berlin Tel: 2202851 Cable Add: Sevenseasberlin
Man Dir: Kay Pankey
Parent Company: Verlag Volk und Welt (qv)
Subjects: General Fiction, Poetry, Biography, History, High quality Paperbacks (in English), Secondary Textbooks
1977: 9 titles *Founded:* 1957

Sportverlag, Neustädtische Kirchstr 15, Postfach 1218, DDR–108 Berlin Tel: 2202651 Cable Add: Sportverlag Berlin-DDR
Subjects: Sport, How-to
Founded: 1947

Staatsverlag der Deutschen Demokratischen Republik, Otto Grotewohl Str 17, DDR–108 Berlin Tel: 2272516 (Publicity); 2272497 (Export); 2272498 (Sales)
The official State Publishing Company of the German Democratic Republic
Subjects: History, Social & Political Theory, Economics, Law, International Relations, Government Publications; Periodicals

VEB Verlag **Technik**, Oranienburger Str 13–14, Postfach 293, DDR–102 Berlin Tel: 28700 Cable Add: Technikverlag Berlin Telex: Berlin 0112228 techn dd
Subjects: Science, Mechanical, Electrical and Electronics Engineering, Control Engineering and Automation, Cybernetics, Technical Dictionaries and Periodicals, Reference, University Textbooks
1978: 42 titles *Founded:* 1946

BSB B G **Teubner** Verlagsgesellschaft, Sternwartenstr 8, DDR–701 Leipzig Postfach 930 Tel: 293158/59 Cable Add: Teubnerianum Leipzig
Man Dir: Ing Heinz Kratz
Associate Company: Akademische Verlagsgesellschaft Geest und Portig KG (qv)
Subjects: Mathematics, Physics, History of Science, Geo-sciences, Building Technology, Philology, Greek and Latin Languages
Founded: 1811

VEB Georg **Thieme**, Verlag für Medizin und Naturwissenschaften, Hainstr 17–19, DDR–701 Leipzig Cable Add: Buchthieme Telex: 051533
Trade Dept: Villengang 2, DDR–69 Jena
Associate Companies: VEB Gustav Fischer Verlag (qv); VEB Verlag Volk und Gesundheit (qv)
Subjects: Medicine, Bio-Science, Periodicals
1977: 34 titles *1978:* 22 titles *Founded:* 1886

Transpress, VEB Verlag für Verkehrswesen, Französische Str 13–14, Postfach 1235, DDR–108 Berlin Tel: 20410 Cable Add: transpress Berlin Telex: 112229 travedd
Man Dir: Paul Kaiser
Subjects: Transport and Traffic (Railways, Shipping, Motor Traffic, Aviation), Post and Telecommunications, Philately, Numismatics, Popular Science; Periodicals
1977: 85 titles *1978:* 91 titles *Founded:* 1960

Union Verlag Berlin VOB, Charlottenstr 79, DDR–108 Berlin Tel: 2202711
Dir: Dr sc phil Hubert Faensen
Br Off: Talstr 3, DDR–701 Leipzig
Subjects: Political Science, Christian

Literature, Belles Lettres, Christian Art, History of Philosophy and Religion
1978: 40 titles
Miscellaneous: Associate Company: Koehler & Amelang (VOB), Leipzig (qv)

Urania-Verlag, Salomonstr 26–28, Postfach 969, DDR–701 Leipzig Tel: 7426
Subjects: Popular Science, Nonfiction, Cultural History, Hobbies; Periodicals
1978: 37 titles

VEB Verlag **Volk und Gesundheit***, Neue Grünstr 18, Postfach 53, DDR–102 Berlin Tel: 2000621 Cable Add: Volksgesundheit Telex: 0114488
Trade Dept: Villengang 2, DDR–69 Jena
Parent Company: Volkseigene Verlag für Medizin und Biologie, Berlin, Jena, Leipzig
Associate Companies: VEB Gustav Fischer Verlag (qv); VEB Georg Thieme (qv)
Subjects: Scholarship, Medicine
1977: 86 titles *1978:* 104 titles *Founded:* 1952

Verlag **Volk und Welt**, Glinkastr 13–15, DDR–108 Berlin Tel: 2202851 Cable Add: Volkwelt Berlin
Company is subtitled Verlag für internationale Literatur (Publishing House for international literature)
Man Dir: Jürgen Gruner
Subsidiary Company: Seven Seas Publishers (qv)
Subjects: General Fiction and Nonfiction of other countries, worldwide, in German translation: Poetry, Reportage; Periodicals
Book Club: buchklub 65
1977: 165 titles *1978:* 153 titles *Founded:* 1947

Volk und Wissen Volkseigener Verlag Berlin*, Krausenstr 50, Am Spittelmarkt, DDR–108 Berlin Tel: 20430 Cable Add: Volkwissen Berlin Telex: 112181 vowiv dd
Subjects: Schoolbooks, Pedagogy, Illustrated Instructional Material, Literary History, Sports Training
Founded: 1945

Verlag Die **Wirtschaft**, Am Friedrichshain 22, DDR–1055 Berlin
Subjects: Management, Economics, Statistics, Periodicals

Z A Reprints, see Zentralantiquariat der DDR

Verlag **Zeit** im Bild*, Julian-Grimau-Allee 10, DDR–801 Dresden
Manager: H Zumpe
Subjects: Politics, Foreign Languages, Economics, Periodicals

Zentralantiquariat der DDR – Reprintabteilung (ZA Reprints), Talstr 29, Postfach 1080, DDR–701 Leipzig 1 Tel: 293641–43, 295808
The Reprint Department of the Central Antiquarian and Second Hand Book Dealers' Office of the German Democratic Republic
Subjects: Special Editions, Reprints (generally of specialized texts), especially Near Eastern/Babylonic Cuneiform and History of Crime Series
1978: 89 titles

Literary Agents

Büro für Urheberrechte, Clara-Zetkin-Str 105, DDR–108 Berlin
Authors' manuscripts and publishing rights are submitted in the DDR without agents. Nevertheless agreements with individuals and firms outside the DDR must be sanctioned and handled by the above Büro

Book Clubs

buchclub 65, Glinkastr 13–15, DDR–108 Berlin
Owned by: Verlag Volk und Welt (Berlin)

Buchklub der Schüler*, Clara-Zetkin-Str 90, DDR–108 Berlin

Major Booksellers

Volksbuchhandlung **Haus des Buches***, Ernst-Thälmann-str 29, DDR–8010 Dresden

Volksbuchhandlung Edwin **Hoernle***, Ernst-Thälmann-Str 13, DDR–20 Neubrandenburg

Volksbuchhandlung Alexander von **Humboldt**, Am Platz der Einheit, DDR–15 Potsdam Tel: 22539/23574
Manager: Friedrich Richter

Humboldt-Buchhandlung*, Bahnhofstr 1, DDR–9001 Karl-Marx-Stadt

Ulrich v **Hutten** Volksbuchhandlung*, Karl-Marx Str 184, DDR–12 Frankfurt/Oder

Keysersche Buchhandlung*, Anger 11, DDR–50 Erfurt

Volksbuchhandlung Robert **Koch**, Universitätsring 7 and 10, DDR–40 Halle

L K G, see Leipziger Kommissions- und Grossbuchhandel

Leibnitz-Volksbuchhandlung*, Otto-Grotewohl-Str 3, DDR–27 Schwerin

Leipziger Kommissions- und Grossbuchhandel (LKG), Leninstr 16, DDR–701 Leipzig Tel: 70251
Dir: H Köhler
Leipzig Wholesale Booksellers and Distributors
Publications: LKG Lagerkatalog; Vorankündigungsdienst für den Buchhandel (Advance Information Service for the Book Trade)

Volksbuchhandlung Thomas **Mann**, Kollegiengasse, DDR–690 Jena

Buchhandlung für **Medizin***, Friedrichstr 128, DDR–1040 Berlin

Universitätsbuchhandlung*, Str der Freundschaft 77, DDR–22 Greifswald

Universitätsbuchhandlung*, Grimmaische Str 30, DDR–701 Leipzig

Universitätsbuchhandlung*, Kröpeliner Str 15, DDR–25 Rostock

Erich-**Weinert**-Buchhandlung, Wilhelm-Pieck-Allee 23–27, DDR–301 Magdeburg

Major Libraries

Ernst-Moritz-**Arndt** Universität Universitatsbibliothek, Rubenowstr 4, DDR–220 Greifswald

Berliner Stadtbibliothek*, Breitestr 37, Berlin C2

Deutsche Staatsbibliothek*, Unter den Linden 8, Postfach 1312, DDR–1086 Berlin Tel: 20780
German State Library

Humboldt Universität zu Berlin, Universitätsbibliothek, Clara-Zetkin-Str 27, DDR–108 Berlin Tel: 2078356
Librarian: Dr Waltraud Irmscher

Karl-Marx-Universität*, Universitätsbibliothek, Beethovenstr 6, DDR–701 Leipzig Tel: 34391

Landwirtschaftliche Zentralbibliothek (Agricultural Central Library)*, Krausenstr 38–39, Postfach 1295, DDR–1086 Berlin

Nationale Forschungs- und Gedenkstätten der klassischen deutschen Literatur – Zentralbibliothek der deutschen Klassik, Platz der Demokratie 1, DDR–530 Weimar
National Research and Memorial Foundation of Classical German Literature – Central Library of German Classicism

Wilhelm-Pieck-Universität **Rostock** Universitätsbibliothek*, Universitätsplatz 5, DDR–25 Rostock

Sächsische Landesbibliothek, Marienallee 12, DDR–806 Dresden Tel: 52677/57097
Dir: Prof Dr sc Bürghard Bürgemeister
Publications: Sächsische Bibliographie, Bibliographie Bildende Kunst, Bibliographie Illustrierter Bücher der DDR, Bibliographie Geschichte der Technik, Bibliographie Musik, Sozialistisches Musikschaffen in der Deutschen Demokratischen Republik — all Annual

Zentrales **Staatsarchiv**, Berliner Str 98–101, DDR–150 Potsdam
The National Archives of the German Democratic Republic

Stadt- und Bezirksbibliothek Leipzig*, Mozartstr 1, DDR–701 Leipzig Tel: 34216
Dir: Helga Laue

Universitäts- und Landesbibliothek Sachsen-Anhalt, August-Bebel-Str 13 & 50, DDR–401 Halle/Saale Tel: 38147

Universitätsbibliothek*, Goetheallee 6, DDR–69 Jena Tel: 8222239 Telex: 0588634
Dir: Prof Dr Lothar Bohmüller
Subjects: Various bibliographical works relating to Jena and the German Democratic Republic, and also to international themes; agricultural, historical, geographical, cultural

Universitätsbibliothek der Technischen Universität, Mommsenstr 13, DDR–8027 Dresden

Zentralbibliothek der deutschen Klassik, Pl der Demokratie 1, DDR–53 Weimar Tel: 3552 Telex: 618975 nfg dd

Library Associations

Bibliotheksverband der Deutschen Demokratischen Republik (Bibliotheksverband der DDR)*, Hermann-Matern-Str 57, DDR–104 Berlin Tel: 2362845
The Library Association of the German Democratic Republic
President: Gotthard Rückl; *Executive Secretary:* Wilfried Kern
Publications: Informationsblatt (Conference Reports, Publications relating to Librarianship)
1977: 11 titles *Founded:* 1964

Deutsche Bücherei (German Library), Deutscher Platz, DDR–701 Leipzig Tel: 88120
Dir: Prof Dr Helmut Rötzsch
Publications: Deutsche Nationalbibliographie und Bibliographie des im Ausland erschienenen deutschsprachigen Schrifttums, Reihe A, B, C (German National Bibliography and Bibliography of German Language Literature appearing abroad

Series A, B, C.); *Jahresverzeichnis der Verlagsschriften* (Annual List of Publications); *Deutsches Bücherverzeichnis* (5-Year German Book List); *Bibliographie der Übersetzungen deutschsprachiger Werke* (quarterly: Bibliography of Translations of German Language Works); *Bibliographie fremdsprachiger Germanica* (quarterly: Bibliography of Germanica in foreign languages); *Bibliographie der Bibliographien* (monthly: Bibliography of Bibliographies); *Jahresverzeichnis der Hochschulschriften der DDR, der BRD und Westberlins* (Annual List of Academy Texts; appearing in the GDR, the FRG, and in West Berlin); *Deutsche Musikbibliographie* (monthly: German Bibliography of Music); *Jahresverzeichnis der Musikalien und Musikschriften* (Annual List of Musical Scores and Texts); *Bibliographie der Kunstblätter* (Bibliography of Art Prints); *Jahrbuch der Deutschen Bücherei* (Annual of the German Library); *Die Deutsche Bücherei im Bild* (The German Library in Pictures); *Wissenwertes uber die Deutsche Bücherei* (Facts about the German Library); *Buch und Schrift von der Frühzeit bis zur Gegenwart* (Books and Print from the earliest times to the present day): also other regularly-appearing Bibliographies and Directories

Zentralinstitut für Bibliothekswesen, Hermann-Matern Str 57, DDR–104 Berlin
The Central Institute for Library Science
Publications: *Bibliothekar; Mitteilungen und Materialien; Die Entwicklung des Bibliothekswesen in der DDR* (Annual Report); *Informationsdienst Bibliothekswesen; Beiträge zu Theorie und Praxis der Bibliotheksarbeit*

Zentralinstitut für Information und Dokumentation, Köpenicker Str 80–82, DDR–102 Berlin Tel: 6576210 Telex: OWU 113070/113071 Cable Add: Zeniid Berlin
Central Institute for Information
Director: Mr Och

Library Reference Books and Journals

Books

Die Deutsche Bücherei im Bild (The German Library in Pictures), Deutsche Bücherei, Deutscher Platz, DDR–701 Leipzig

Die Entwicklung des Bibliothekswesens in der Deutschen Demokratischen Republik (The Development of Library Science in the DDR) (annual), Central Institute for Library Science, Hermann-Matern Str 57, DDR–104 Berlin

Jahrbuch der Bibliotheken, Archive und Informationsstellen der Deutschen Demokratischen Republik (Yearbook of the Libraries, Archives and Information Offices of the DDR), VEB Bibliographisches Institut, Gerichtsweg 26, Postfach 130, DDR–701 Leipzig

Sigel Liste der Bibliotheken der Deutschen Demokratischen Republik (Classification List of Libraries of the DDR), Deutsche Staatsbibliothek, Unter den Linden 8, DDR–108 Berlin

Wissenwertes über die Deutsche Bücherei (Facts About the German Library), Deutsche Bücherei, Deutscher Platz, DDR–701 Leipzig

Journals

Bibliothekar (Librarian) (text in German; contents page in English, French, German and Russian), Central Institute for Library Science, Hermann-Matern Str 57, DDR–104 Berlin

Informationsdienst Bibliothekswesen und Bibliographie der Literatur zum Bibliothekswesen (Information Service on Library Science and Bibliography of the Literature on Library Science), Central Institute for Library Science, Hermann-Matern Str 57, DDR–104 Berlin

Literatur zum Bibliothekswesen (Literature on Library Science), Central Institute for Library Science, Hermann-Matern Str 57, DDR–104 Berlin

Mitteilungen und Materialien (Communications and Materials), Central Institute for Library Science, Hermann-Matern Str 57, DDR–104 Berlin

Zentralblatt für Das Bibliothekswesen (Central Journal for Library Science) (text in German; contents page in English, French, German and Russian), VEB Bibliographisches Institut, Gerichtsweg 26, Postfach 130, DDR–701 Leipzig

Literary Associations and Societies

Institut für Literatur Johannes R **Becher** (Johannes R Becher Institute for Literature)*, Karl-Tauchnitzstr 8, Leipzig CI
Dir: Professor Max Walter Schulz

P E N Zentrum, Deutsche Demokratische Republik, Friedrichstr 194–199, DDR–108 Berlin
Secretary: Henryk Keisch

Literary Periodicals

Bücherkarren (Book-Cart), Verlag Volk und Welt, Glinkastr 13–15, DDR–108 Berlin

Deutsche Literaturzeitung (German Literature Newspaper), Akademie-Verlag, Leipziger Str 3–4, DDR–108 Berlin

Fontane-Blätter (Fontane Papers), Deutsche Staatsbibliothek, Theodor Fontane Archiv, Dortustr 30–34, Potsdam

Ich Schreibe (I Write), VEB Friedrich Hofmeister Musikverlag, Karlstr 10, Postschließfach 147, DDR–701 Leipzig

Kunst und Literatur (Art and Literature), Buchexport, Leninstr 16, Postfach 160, DDR–701 Leipzig

Literatur und Gesellschaft (Literature and Society), Buchexport, Leninstr 16, Postfach 160, DDR–701 Leipzig

Marginalien (Marginal Notes); journal for the art of the book and bibliophily, Aufbau-Verlag Berlin und Weimar, Französische Str 32, Postfach 1217, DDR–108 Berlin

Neue deutsche Literatur (New German Literature), Aufbau-Verlag Berlin und Weimar, Französische Str 32, Postfach 1217, DDR–108 Berlin

Sinn und Form (Sense and Form); contributions to literature, Deutsche Akademie der Künste, Rütten & Loening, Französische Str 32, Postfach 1217, DDR–108 Berlin

Weimarer Beträge (Weimar Contributions); journal for literature, aesthetics and culture, Aufbau-Verlag Berlin und Weimar, Französische Str 32, Postfach 1217, DDR–108 Berlin

Federal Republic of Germany

General Information

Language: German
Religion: Protestant and Catholic
Population: 62 million
Bank Hours: Vary. 0800 or 0830 or 0900-1400, or 0900-1200, 1400-1530 Monday-Friday; open until 1800 Thursday
Shop Hours: 0800 or 0830 or 0900-1800 Monday-Friday. Some have early closing one day a week. Open until 1330 or 1400 Saturday
Currency: 100 pfennige = 1 Deutsche mark
Export/Import Information: No tariff on books except children's picture books 13% from non-EEC. None on advertising to be distributed free, if exporter's country grants reciprocal treatment, otherwise 9%. 11% Import Turnover Tax on books and advertising. No import licence required. No exchange controls
Copyright: UCC, Berne, Florence (see International section)

Book Trade Organizations

Adressbuchausschuss der deutschen Wirtschaft (German Trade Directory Committee)*, Adenauerallee 148, D–5300 Bonn 1 Tel: (02221) 104306 Telex: 886805 diht d

Arbeitsgemeinschaft Buchgemeinschaften und verwandte Unternehmen im Börsenverein des Deutschen Buchhandels, Berliner Allee 6, D–6100 Darmstadt Tel: (06151) 8661
Alliance of Book Clubs/Societies and related concerns in the German Publishers' and Booksellers' Association

Arbeitsgemeinschaft der Vertriebsfachverbände*, c/o Verband Deutscher Buch-Zeitungs- und Zeitschriften-Grossisten eV, Theodor-Heuss-Ring 32, D–5000 Cologne 1 Tel: (0221) 123803
Organization of the Distributive Trades Associations

Arbeitsgemeinschaft Literarische und Sachbuchverlage (Alliance of Literary and Nonfiction Publishers)*, Charlottenstr 21c, D–7000 Stuttgart 1 Tel: (0711) 245272

Arbeitsgemeinschaft rechts- und staatswissenschaftlicher Verleger (Economics and Legal Publishers Alliance)*, Widenmayerstr 46/III, D–8000 Munich 22 Tel: (089) 479692

Arbeitsgemeinschaft von Jugendbuchverlegern in der Bundesrepublik Deutschland eV, Otto Maier Verlag, Marktstr 22–26, D-7980 Ravensburg Tel: 862231
The Alliance of Publishers of Children's Books in the Federal Republic of Germany:
Chairman: Christian Stottele

Aussenhandels-Ausschuss, Foreign Trade Committee of Börsenverein des deutschen Buchhandels eV (qv)

B A G Buchhändler-Abrechnungs-Gesellschaft mbH, Grosser Hirschgraben 17–21, Postfach 2422, D-6000 Frankfurt 1
Booksellers' Clearing-House Company

Berliner Verleger- und Buchhändlervereinigung eV, Lützowstr 105–107, D-1000 Berlin 30 Tel: (030) 2621040/2621049
Berlin Publishers' and Booksellers' Association

Börsenverein des deutschen Buchhandels eV, Grosser Hirschgraben 17–19, Postfach 2404, D-6000 Frankfurt am Main 1 Tel: (0611) 13061 Cable Add: Börsenblatt Telex: 413573 buchv d
German Publishers' and Booksellers' Association; also has a Foreign Trade Committee (Aussenhandels-Ausschuss)
Secretary: Dr Hans-Karl von Kupsch
Publications: Börsenblatt für den deutschen Buchhandel; Adressbuch für den deutschsprachigen Buchhandel; Deutsche Bibliographie; Neuescccheinungen-Sofortdienst (CIP); Archiv für die Geschichte des Buchwesens; Buch und Buchhandel in Zahlen; Die schönsten deutschen Bücher; Verzeichnis lieferbarer Bücher; Bibliothekswesen in Deutschland; LIT — Magazin für Kunden des Buchhandels; *How to obtain German books and periodicals;* and others

Bundesverband der deutschen Verlagsvertreter eV (National Association of German Publishers' Representatives)*, Zeil 65–69, D-6000 Frankfurt am Main
Tel: (06110 288891

Bundesverband der deutschen Versandbuchhändler eV (National Federation of German Mail-order Booksellers)*, Burchardstr 14, D-2000 Hamburg 1

Bundesverband des werbenden Buch- und Zeitschriftenhandels eV (National Federation of the Promotional Book and Periodical Trade)*, Brusseler Str 96, D-5000 Cologne 1 Tel: 514774
Publication: Der werbende Buch- und Zeitschriften Handel

Hessischer Verleger- und Buchhandler-Verband eV (Hessen Publishers' and Booksellers' Federation)*, Großer Hirschgraben 17–19, D-6000 Frankfurt am Main 1 Tel: (0611) 282643
Chairman: Dr Heribert Marré; *Manager:* Lisabeth Schubert, Frankfurt-am-Main

Informations-Zentrum Buch (Book Information Centre): an Association of prominent publishers who share information about their varied publishing programmes. Information can be obtained from any of the participating companies:
Artemis/Winkler, Bouvier, Carl, Deutscher Taschenbuch Verlag, Duncker & Humblot, Ehrenwirth, W Fink, Frommann/Holzboog, Hanser, Herder, Hiersemann, Kiepenheuer & Witsch, Kindler, Klett, Klinkhardt, Kösel, W Kohlhammer, Metzler, M Niemeyer, Nymphenburger, Piper, Quelle & Meyer, Reclam, E Schmidt (qqv)

Interessengemeinschaft Musikwissenschaftlicher Herausgeber und Verleger (IHMV), Heinrich-Schütz-Allee 33, D-3500 Kassel-Wilhelmshöhe Tel: 30011/16
Association of Musicology Editors and Publishers

Landesverband der Buchhändler und Verleger in Niedersachsen eV (Provincial Federation of Booksellers and Publishers in Lower Saxony), Hausmannstr 2, D-3000 Hanover 1 Tel: (0511) 14622

Landesverband der Verleger und Buchhändler Bremen-Unterweser eV (Bremen Provincial Federation of Publishers and Booksellers)*, Contrescarpe 17, D-2800 Bremen 1 Tel: 326949

Landesverband der Verleger und Buchhändler Rheinland-Pfalz eV (Rhineland-Palatinate Provincial Federation of Publishers and Booksellers), Schönbornstr 3, D-6500 Mainz 1 Tel: (06131) 27270

Landesverband der Verleger und Buchhändler Saar eV (LVBS) (Saar Provincial Federation of Publishers and Booksellers)*, Eisenbahnstr 68, D-6600 Saarbrücken Tel: (0681) 51471

Landesverband des werbenden Buch- und Zeitschriftenhandels von Südwestdeutschland eV (Provincial Federation of the Book and Periodical Trade of South-west Germany)*, Strohberg 38, D-7000 Stuttgart 1 Tel: (0711) 602088/604056

Münchner Arbeitsgemeinschaft der Verlagshersteller (Munich Association of Publishers' Production Managers)*, Scharnitzer Str 58, D-8032 Gräfelring Tel: 852238

Norddeutscher Verleger- und Buchhändler-Verband eV (North German Publishers' and Booksellers' Federation)*, Brahmsallee 24, D-2000 Hamburg 13 Tel: (040) 4103161

Verband bayerischer Buch- und Zeitschriftenhändler eV (Bavarian Booksellers' and Newsagents' Federation), Enzenspergerstr 9, D-8000 Munich 80 Tel: (089) 488533

Verband bayerischer Verlage und Buchhandlungen eV (Bavarian Publishers' and Booksellers' Federation)*, Enzenspergerstr 9, Postfach 800949, D-8000 Munich 80 Tel: (089) 484141

Verband der Schulbuchverlage eV (Association of Publishers of Schoolbooks), Zeppelinallee 33, Postfach 900540, D-6000 Frankfurt /AM 1 Tel: (0611) 703075 Telex: vsib 416213
Chief Executive: Dipl-Volkswirt H P Vonhoff

Verband der Verlage und Buchhandlungen in Baden-Württemberg eV (Federation of Publishers and Booksellers in Baden-Württemberg)*, Leonhardspl 28, D-7000 Stuttgart 1, Tel: (0711) 245959

Verband der Verlage und Buchhandlungen in Nordrhein-Westfalen eV, Marienstr 41, D-4000 Düsseldorf 1 Tel: (0211) 320951
Federation of Publishers in North Rhine-Westphalia

Verband des werbenden Buch- und Zeitschriftenhandels Gross-Berlin eV (Greater Berlin Federation of the Promotional Book and Periodical Trade)*, Leydenallee 70, D-1000 Berlin 41 Tel: (030) 720461

Verband deutscher Adressbuchverleger eV (Association of German Directory Publishers), Ritterstr 17–19, D-4000 Düsseldorf Tel: (0211) 320909

Verband deutscher Antiquare eV (German Antiquarian Booksellers' Association), Zum Talblick 2, D-6246 Glashütten im Taunus bei Frankfurt am Main
President: Godebert M Reiss

Verband deutscher Bahnhofsbuchhändler, Grosser Hirschgraben 19H, D-6000 Frankfurt am Main 1
Federation of German Station Booksellers

Verband deutscher Buch-Zeitungs- und Zeitschriften-Grossisten eV (Federation of German Wholesalers of Books, Newspapers and Periodicals)*, Theodor-Heuss-Ring 32, D-5000 Cologne 1 Tel: (0221) 123803 Telex: 08-885 203
Chairman: Dr Eberhard Nolte; *Manager:* Dr Hans Ziebolz

Verband deutscher Bühnenverleger eV (Federation of German Theatrical Publishers)*, Bundesallee 23, D-1000 Berlin 31 Tel: (030) 8618088

Verband deutscher Schulbuchhändler eV, Marienstrasse 41, D-4000 Düsseldorf Tel: (0211) 320951
Federation of German School Book Dealers

Verband katholischer Verleger und Buchhändler eV, Lehenstr 31, D-7000 Stuttgart 1 Tel: 642061
Federation of Catholic Publishers and Booksellers
Manager: Wolfgang Grossmann

Verband norddeutscher Buch- und Zeitschriftenhändler eV (Federation of North German Booksellers and Newsagents)*, An Der Rehbocksweide 22–24, D-3150 Hannoversch-Münden Tel: 4084/4089

Verband westdeutscher Buch- und Zeitschriftenhändler eV (West German Booksellers' and Newsagents' Federation)*, Dürener Str 251, D-5000 Cologne 41 Tel: (0221) 413704

Verein für Verkehrsordnung im Buchhandel, Frankfurt am Main 1, Postfach 2404, D-6000
Association for the Regulation of Trade in the Book Trade

Vereinigung evangelischer Buchhändler eV (Association of Protestant Booksellers)*, Silberburgstr 58/1, D-7000 Stuttgart 1 Tel: (0711) 622654

Vereinigung selbständiger Verlagsvertreter, Schatten 6 Gewand, D-7000 Stuttgart (Büsnau) 80 Tel: (0711) 681457
Association of Self-Employed Publishers' Representatives

Verlegervereinigung Rechtsinformatik eV (Association of Publishers of Legal Documentation)*, c/o Verlagsgesellschaft Recht und Wirtschaft GmbH, Häusserstrasse 14, D-6900 Heidelberg Tel: 256613 Telex: D461665
Director: Dr Jobst Gumpert

FEDERAL REPUBLIC OF GERMANY 123

Book Trade Reference Books and Journals

Books

Adressbuch für den deutschsprachigen Buchhandel (Directory of German-speaking Book Trade) (including Austria, Switzerland, and German-speaking publishers and booksellers in other countries), German Publishers' and Booksellers' Association, Großer Hirschgraben 17–21, D–6000 Frankfurt am Main 1

Anschriften deutscher Buchhandlungen (Addresses of German Booksellers), Verlag der Schillerbuchhandlung Hans Banger, Mainzer Str 24, D–714 Marbach 2

Anschriften deutscher Verlage und ausländischer Verlage mit deutschen Auslieferungen (Addresses of German Publishers and Foreign Publishers with German Distribution), Verlag der Schillerbuchhandlung Hans Banger, Mainzer Str 24, D–7142 Marbach

Die Begegnung (The Meeting); authors, publishers, booksellers, Elwert & Meurer, Hauptstr 101, D–1000 Berlin 62

Bibliographie des Buchhandels (Bibliography of the Book Trade), Saur KG, Pössenbacherstr 2, D–8000 Munich 71

Buch und Buchhandel in Zahlen (Books and the Book Trade in Figures), German Publishers' and Booksellers' Association, Großer Hirschgraben 17–21, D–6000 Frankfurt am Main 1

Buchhändler Kalender (Booksellers' Calendar), Bibliographisches Institut AG, Dudenstr 6, Postfach 311, D–68 Mannheim

Deutsches Verlagsregister (German Publishers' List), Stamm-Verlag GmbH, Goldammerweg 16, D–4300 Essen 1

Freude mit Büchern (Joy with Books); the German book catalogue, Verlag Bücherschiff Walter Reutin, Rheinstr 122, Postfach 210947, D–7500 Karlsruhe

Handbuch des Buchhandels (Handbook of the Book Trade), Verlag für Buchmarktforschung, Beim Strohhause 34, D–2000 Hamburg 2

How to Obtain German Books and Periodicals, Börsenverein des deutschen Buchhandels eV, Postfach 2404, D–6000 Frankfurt am Main 1

Was erscheint wo. Verlage, Titel, Redaktionen (What Appears Where. Publishers, Titles, Editors), Team Verlag, Helmut Müller GmbH & Co KG, Rossertstr 9, Postfach 2661, D–6000 Frankfurt am Main

Journals

AGB-Titeldienst (AGB-Title Service); recently published German-language books, Amerika-Gedenk-Bibliothek, Arbeitsstelle für das Bibliothekswesen, Fehrbelliner Platz 3, D–1000 Berlin 31

Antiquariat (Second-hand Bookshop), Dr Lothar Rossipaul, Verlagsgesellschaft mbH, Finkenweg 6, D–7261 Stammheim/Calw, (monthly)

Börsenblatt für den deutschen Buchhandel (German Book Trade Journal), German Publishers' and Booksellers' Association, Grosser Hirschgraben 17–21, D–6000 Frankfurt am Main 1

Buch Aktuell (Contemporary Books), Westfalendamm 57, Postfach 1305, D–4600 Dortmund

Buch und Leser (Book and Reader), German Publishers' and Booksellers' Association, Grosser Hirschgraben 17–21, Postfach 2404, D–6000 Frankfurt am Main 1

Buchhändler Heute (Bookseller Today), Verlag Buchhändler Heute, Jahnstr 36, Düsseldorf, (monthly)

Buchmarkt (Book Market), the largest independent journal for the book trade in German-speaking areas, Rochusstr 34, Postfach 320545, D–4000 Düsseldorf

Buchreport (Book Report), Westfalendamm 57, Postfach 1305, D–4600 Dortmund

Deutsche Bibliographie (German National Bibliography), German Publishers' and Booksellers' Association, Großer Hirschgraben 17–21, D–6000 Frankfurt am Main 1

Dokumentation deutschsprachiger Verlage (Documentation of German-speaking Publishers), Günter Olzog Verlag, Thierschstr 11, D–8000 Munich 22

Goldmann's Mitteilungen für den Buchhandel (Goldmann's Communications for the Book Trade), Wilhelm Goldmann Verlag GmbH, Neumarkterstr 22, Postfach 800709, D–8000 Munich 80

Mitteilungsblatt für Dolmetscher und Übersetzer (Interpreters' and Translators' News Sheet), Federal German Association of Interpreters and Translators, Blaulstr 1, D–6728 Germersheim (twice monthly)

Die Neuen Bücher (New Books), Dr Lothar Rossipaul, Verlagsgesellschaft mbH, Finkenweg 6, D–7261 StammheiAmm/Calw

Philobiblon; quarterly journal for books and graphic art, Dr Ernst Hauswedell & Co, Pöseldorfer Weg 1, D–2000 Hamburg 13

Taschenbücher, Halbjähriges Verzeichnis (Paperbacks, Half-yearly List), Verlag der Schillerbuchhandlung Hans Banger, Mainzer Str 24, D–7142 Marbach

Der Übersetzer (The Translator), Association of German-speaking Translators of Literary and Scientific Works, D–7400 Tübingen, Fürststr 17

Verzeichnis lieferbarer Bücher (German Books in Print), German Publishers' and Booksellers' Association, Großer Hirschgraben 17–21, D–6000 Frankfurt am Main 1

Welt der Bücher (World of Books), *Der werbende Buch- und Zeitschriftenhandel* (The Book and Periodical Trade), Bundesverband des werbenden Buch- und Zeitschriftenhandels eV, Brusseler Str 96, D–5000 Cologne 1

Publishers

Edition der **2**, see under der 2

A D A C Verlag, Baumgartnerstr 53, Postfach 700086, D–8000 Munich 70 Tel: (089) 156021 Cable Add: Adacverlag Telex: 52923135
Man Dir: Alfred Dietrich; *Editorial:* Bleinagel, Michael Dultz; *Sales Promotion:* Helmut Engerer; *Production:* Uto Rogner; *Rights & Permissions:* Alfred Dietrich
Subjects: Automobile Interest primarily: Touring, Holiday Guides, Car Buying, Repairs, Insurance, Driving Instruction etc Publishers of magazines *ADAC-Motorwelt* and *Deutsches Autorecht*
1977: 10 titles 1978: 13 titles *Founded:* 1958
ISBN Publisher's Prefix: 3–87003

A D L A F, see Arbeitsgemeinschaft Deutsche Lateinamerika-Forschung

A E G - Telefunken Zentralabteilung Firmenverlag, Hohenzollerndamm 150, D–1000 Berlin 33 Tel: 8282133 Cable Add: Elektron Berlin Telex: 183581
Man Dir: Heinz Ketterer; *Editorial:* R Lutgens; *Sales, Publicity, Rights and Permissions:* Detlef Lorenz; *Production:* Reinhard Eckardt
Subjects: Electrical Engineering, Electronics
1977: 10 titles 1978: 10 titles *Founded:* 1883
ISBN Publisher's Prefix: 3–87087

A M B (Arbeitsgemeinschaft mitteleuropäischer Bibelwerke), Association of Mid-European Biblical Presses, comprising Verlag Schweizerisches Katholisches Bibelwerk, Switzerland (qv), Vlaamse Bijbelstichting, Belgium (qv), Österreichisches Katholisches Bibelwerk, Austria (qv), and Verlag Katholisches Bibelwerk GmbH, German Federal Republic (qv)

Aar- Verlag+, Volkerstr 33, D–6200 Wiesbaden Tel: (06121) 88218
Proprietor: Iolanda Debus
Subject: General Literature
1978: 5 titles
ISBN Publisher's Prefix: 3–87945

Abakon Verlagsgesellschaft mbH*+, Söhtstr 3a, D–1000 Berlin 45 Tel: (030) 8333389 Telex: 182993
Man Dir: Dipl-Ing M Schneider; *Rights & Permissions:* Dr Achim Schneider
Orders to: Karl Halliant und Sohn, Albrechtstr 17–19, D–1000 Berlin 42
Imprints: Abakon; Edition Lichterfelde; Life Sciences Research Reports; Dahlem Konferenzen
Subjects: Science (in English language), Architecture, Art
1977: 10 titles 1978: 11 titles *Founded:* 1975
ISBN Publisher's Prefix: 3–8200

Abakus Schallplatten Barbara Fietz, Haversbach 1, D–6331 Ulmtal-Allendorf Tel: (06478) 2250
Man Dirs: B and S Fietz; *Editorial, Sales, Publicity:* B Fietz; *Production:* S Frietz
Associate Companies: Ulmtal Musikverlags GmbH Ulmtal; Melos Musikverlag, Munich
Subjects: Children's Song Books, Musical Scores; all with Christian religious emphasis
1978: 5 titles 1979: 5 titles *Founded:* 1974

Accidentia Druck- und Verlagsgesellschaft mbH, Graf-Adolf-Str 112, D–4000 Düsseldorf Tel: (0211) 350271 Telex: 08581986

Man Dir: H Sontowski
Subjects: Photography, Travel Calendar
Founded: 1959
ISBN Publisher's Prefix: 3-920005

Achberger Verlag GmbH*, Esseratsweiler Nr 23, D-8991 Achberg Tel: 08380/515544
Gen Mans: Wilfried Heidt, Peter Schata
Subjects: Publications connected with the "Third Way" political alternative; publications of the Institute of Social Research, Achberg
1977: 5 titles *Founded:* 1973
ISBN Publisher's Prefix: 3-88103

Verlag Andreas **Achenbach**+, Holzmühler Weg 63, Postfach 82, D-6304 Lollar Tel: (06406) 3639
Publisher: Andreas Achenbach; *Production:* Frederick Carl Schlotman; *Sales:* H F O Achenbach
Subjects: Social Science, Economics, Sport, Ethnology, Pedagogics
1977: 15 titles *Founded:* 1972
ISBN Publisher's Prefix: 3-87958

F A **Ackermanns** Kunstverlag, Wienerplatz 7-8, D-8000 Munich 80 Tel: (089) 488046 Cable Add: Kunstackermann Munich
Man Dir: Hubertus Weinert
Subjects: Art, Calendars, Photographic
1977: 70 titles *1978:* 70 titles *Founded:* 1874
ISBN Publisher's Prefix: 3-87002

Agis Verlag GmbH, Eberbachstr 7, Postfach 7, D-7570 Baden-Baden 19 Tel: (07221) 66810 Cable Add: Agis Baden-Baden
Subjects: Aesthetics, Cybernetics, Information Theory, Human and Natural Sciences, Philosophy
ISBN Publisher's Prefix: 3-87007

Agora-Verlag, Hanseatenweg 10, Postfach 210533, D-1000 Berlin 21 Tel: (030) 3913775 Cable Add: Agora
Man Dir, Production: Manfred Schlösser; *Sales & Publicity:* Monika Schlösser-Fischer
Subsidiary Company: Erato-Presse
Branch Off: Lucasweg 17, D-6100 Darmstadt
Subjects: Literary Criticism, Belles Lettres, Poetry, Juveniles, Music, Theatre, Literature by exiles
1977: 8 titles *Founded:* 1960
ISBN Publlisher's Prefix: 3-87008

L B **Ahnert**-Verlag, Niddaer Str 17, D-6363 Echzell-Bisses Tel: 06031/3131 Cable Add: Ahnert-Verlag Echzell Telex: 415961
Subjects: Sports, Horse Breeding, Nonfiction, Periodicals, Reproductions
ISBN Publisher's Prefix: 3-921142

Akademische Verlagsgesellschaft, Bahnhofstr 39, Postfach 1107, D-6200 Wiesbaden Tel: (06121) 39794 Cable Add: AKA Wiesbaden
Man Dir: Dr Claus Steiner; *Sales:* Gerland Stahl; *Publicity:* Margret Nerger
Subjects: Educational, Data Processing, Life Science, Chemistry, Physics, Maths, Electro-technology, Politics, Sociology; Periodicals
Founded: 1912
Subsidiary Company: Akademische Verlagsgesellschaft Athenaion (qv)
ISBN Publisher's Prefix: 3-400

Akademische Verlagsgesellschaft Athenaion, Bahnhofstr 39, Postfach 1107, D-6200 Wiesbaden Tel: (06121) 39794
Parent Company: Akademische Verlagsgesellschaft, Wiesbaden (qv)
Subjects: Literary Science, Linguistics with especial reference to English, German, Romance; History of Culture, History of Germany; Periodicals
ISBN Publisher's Prefix: 3-7997

Alba Buchverlag GmbH und Co KG, Römerstr 9, Postfach 320108, D-4000 Düsseldorf 30 Tel: (0211) 482069
Man Dir, Rights & Permissions: Alf Teloeken; *Sales:* D Wiesent; *Production:* K Hartung; *Publicity:* Dip Kfm K Harrer
Associate Company: Alba Publikation Alf Teloeken GmbH und Co KG (qv)
Subjects: Model Railways, Transport, Modelling
1979: 83 titles *Founded:* 1951
ISBN Publisher's Prefix: 3-87094

Alba Publikation Alf Teloeken GmbH und Co KG, Römerstr 9, Postfach 320109, D-4000 Düsseldorf Tel: (0211) 482069
Man Dir, Rights & Permissions: Alf Teloeken; *Sales:* D Wiesent; *Production:* K Hartung; *Publicity:* Dip Kfm K Harrer
Associate Company: Alba Buchverlag GmbH und Co KG (qv)
Subjects: Model Railways, Transport, Modelling; Periodicals covering modelling and bus and rail transport

Verlag Karl **Albér** GmbH*, Hermann Herder Str 4, D-7800 Freiburg im Breisgau Tel: (0761) 273495 Telex: 07721440 vh d
Man Dir: Dr Meinolf Wewel
Orders to: Auslieferungsgemeinschaft Herder, Postfach D-7800 Freiburg im Breisgau Tel: 0761/27171
Subjects: Logic, History & Theory of Science, Philosophy, Psychology, Pedagogy, History, Law, Sociology, Political Science
1978: 25 titles *Founded:* 1939
Miscellaneous: Firm is a subsidiary of Verlag Herder (qv)
ISBN Publisher's Prefix: 3-495

alpha 9 GmbH, Eschborn, Postfach 29, Königsbergerstr 9, D-6236 Eschborn II Tel: (06173) 62268/62368 Cable Add: alpha verlag eschborn
Subjects: Informative Books of Plates and Wall Calendars: speciality — book/calendar combinations

Alpha Literatur Verlag*, August-Siebert-Str 9, D-6000 Frankfurt am Main 1 Tel: (0611) 555325 Telex: 414890
Man Dir: Dr G Philipps
Subjects: Poetry, Belles Lettres, Theatre

Alternative Verlag GmbH, Postfach 150230, D-1000 Berlin 15 (Located at: Konstanzer Str 11, D-1000 Berlin 31) Tel: (030) 8811570/8815550
Man Dir: H Brenner; *Sales & Advertising Dir:* Peter B Schumann
Subjects: Literature, Social and Political Sciences, Philosophy, Literature, Theatre, Art
Founded: 1954

Amazonen Frauenverlag GmbH, Kantstr 125, D-1000 Berlin 12
Subjects: Women's Cultural and Historical; Poster-Calendars; Female Homosexual Themes; Lesbians in the Women's Movement

Anabas-Verlag Günter Kämpf KG, Am unteren Hardthof, D-6300 Lahn-Giessen 1 Tel: 0641/72455
Man Dir: Günter Kämpf
Orders to: Sova Verlagsauslieferung, 44 Franziusstraße, D-6000 Frankfurt am Main; (West Berlin) — Zirk und Ellenrieder, Lützowstr 105/106, D-1000 Berlin 30
Subjects: Belles Lettres, Poetry, History, Art, High-priced Paperbacks, Educational Materials
1977: 10 titles *1978:* 8 titles *Founded:* 1966
ISBN Publisher's Prefix: 3-87038

Andres Kalender und Buch Verlag GmbH, Lenaustr 2, D-2000 Hamburg 76 Tel: (040) 255047/48 Telex: 02-173065 akb-d
Publishing and Sales Manager: Heinrich Jessen
Associate Company: Umschau Verlag Breidenstein GmbH, Frankfurt am Main (qv for other Associates)
Subjects: Calendars, Books

Verlag Roland **Angst***, Achleitnerstrasse 1, D-8000 Munich 90 Tel: 640532
Publisher: Roland Angst
Subject: Modern Art
1977: 8 titles

Neithard **Anrich** Verlag, Neunkirchen 5, D-6101 Modautal 3 Tel: (06254) 7229
Man Dir: Gerold Anrich
Subjects: Juveniles, History
Founded: 1970
ISBN Publisher's Prefix: 3-920110

Arani-Verlag GmbH, Kurfürstendamm 126, D-1000 Berlin 31, Postfach 310829 Tel: (030) 8911008
Publisher: Horst Meyer
Orders to: Libri VA, Postfach 3584, D-6000 Frankfurt-am-Main 3
Subjects: Belles Lettres, Poetry, History, books on Berlin
1978: 55 titles *Founded:* 1947
ISBN Publisher's Prefix: 3-7605

Ararat Verlag GmbH, Reinsburgstr 199, D-7000 Stuttgart 1 Tel: 654350
Man Dir and Other Offices: Dr A I Dogan
Subjects: Turkish Literature in German translation; German-Turkish Twin-Language books
1978: 2 titles *1979:* 6 titles *Founded:* 1977
ISBN Publisher's Prefix: 3-921889

Verlag **Arbeiterbewegung und Gesellschaftswissenschaft**, Weidenhäuserstr 56, Postfach 564, D-3550 Marburg/Lahn Tel: (06421) 29983
Workers' Movement and Sociology Publishing Co
Man Dir: Karl-Heinz Flessenklemper; *Editors:* Wolfgang Abendroth, Frank Deppe, Georg Fülberth, Gerd Hardach, H-J Sandkühler
Subjects: Workers' Rights, Trade Unions, Social History
1977: 7 titles *1978:* 9 titles *Founded:* 1976
ISBN Publisher's Prefix: 921630

Arbeitsgemeinschaft Deutsche Lateinamerika-Forschung (ADLAF), Forschungsinstitut der Friedrich-Ebert-Stiftung, Godesberger Allee 149, D-5300 Bonn 2 Tel: (02221) 883267/883278 Telex: 885479 fest-d
German Association for Latin-American Studies
Subjects: Embracing the work of 20 academic Member Institutes and approximately 100 individual members in research areas of Archaeology, Ethnology, History, Literature, the Geo-Sciences, Economic and Social Sciences, Librarianship; also publish periodicals and Bibliographies

Arbeitsgemeinschaft mitteleuropäischer Bibelwerke, see AMB

Arbeitsgemeinschaft sozialistischer und demokratischer Verleger und Buchhändler (Co-operative of Socialist and Democratic Publishing Houses and Bookshops) comprises 18 Publishers, as follows:

Verlag Marxistische Blätter GmbH, Frankfurt am Main; Nachrichten-Verlags-GmbH, Frankfurt am Main; Pahl-Rugenstein-Verlag, Cologne; Röderberg-Verlag GmbH, Frankfurt am Main; Weltkreis-Verlags-GmbH, Dortmund; Damnitz-Verlag, Munich; Asso-Verlag, Oberhausen; Stimme-Verlag GmbH, Mainz; Verlag Atelier im Bauernhaus, Fischerhude; Institut für Marxistische Studien und Forschungen (IMSF), Frankfurt am Main; Monitor-Verlag, Düsseldorf; W Runge-Verlag, Hamburg; Neue Kommentare, Frankfurt am Main; Rochus-Verlag, Düsseldorf; Plambeck und Co Druck und Verlag GmbH, Neuss; Brücken-Verlag GmbH, Düsseldorf
Miscellaneous: the central marketing agency for this group is the Brücken-Verlag GmbH, Düsseldorf (qv)
see individual entries in respect of: Marxistische Blätter, Nachrichten, Pahl Rugenstein Röderberg, Weltkreis, Damnitz, Brücken-Verlag

Verlag Die **Arbeitswelt** GmbH, Grimmstr 27, D-1000 Berlin 61 Tel: (030) 6916536
Dirs: Ulrich Laube, Werner Jung
Subject: Politics (especially trade union studies)

Verlag für **Architektur***, Martiusstr 8, D-8000 Munich 44
Subjects: Collected Works of Leading World Architects, Studio Paperback Series, Works on Town Planning, Pre-Fabrication etc
Miscellaneous: Associate Companies: Artemis & Winkler Verlag, Munich (qv); Druckenmüller Verlag, Munich (qv); Artemis Verlag, Zürich, Switzerland (qv)

Arena-Verlag Georg Popp, Talavera 7-11, D-8700 Würzburg 1 Tel: (0931) 43061 Postfach 5169 Telex: 068833
General Manager, Publicity and Advertising Manager, Rights & Permissions: Georg Popp; *Sales Dir:* Günter Reich
Associate Company: Georg Popp, Würzburg (qv)
Subjects: General Nonfiction, Juveniles, Young Adult, Low-price Paperbacks
Bookshop: Arena-Buchhandlung, Domstr 26, D-8700 Würzburg 1
1978: 53 titles *1979:* 60 titles *Founded:* 1949
(1969 acquisition of Westermann Jugendbuchverlag)
ISBN Publisher's Prefix: 3–401

Arkana-Verlag, Fritz-Frey Str 21, D-6900 Heidelberg Tel: (06221) 46074-5 Cable Add: arkanaverlag
Man Dir: Dr E Fischer
Associate Companies: Karl F Haug Verlag GmbH & Co (qv); Verlag für Medizin Dr E Fischer GmbH (qv)
Subject: Popular Medicine
ISBN Publisher's Prefix: 3–920042

Verlag **Ars** Sacra Josef Müller*, Friedrichstr 9, D-8000 Munich 43 Tel: (089) 393045 Cable Add: Arssacra Munich
Man Dir: Dr E Dubler
Subjects: Religion, Juveniles
1978: 40 titles *Founded:* 1896
ISBN Publisher's Prefix: 3–7607

Art Address Verlag Müller GmbH und Co KG, Gr Eschenheimer Str 16, D-6000 Frankfurt am Main Tel: (0611) 284486 Telex: 041699 omf D
Man Dirs: J Müller, E Kohl
Subject: Art
Founded: 1949

Artemis und Winkler Verlag, Martiusstr 8, D-8000 Munich 40 Tel: (089) 348074 Cable Add: arte d Telex: 5215517
Man Dir: Dr Dieter Lutz; *Publicity Dir:* Anita Donat; *Advertising Dir:* Sunhild Pacheco; *Rights and Permissions:* Marianne Jahn
Orders to: Koch, Neff und Oetinger, Am Wallgraben 110, D-7000 Stuttgart 80
Associate Companies: Verlag für Architektur (qv); Alfred Druckenmüller Verlag (qv)
Subsidiary Company: Winkler-Verlag (qv)
Subjects: (Artemis Verlag) Belles Lettres, The Humanities, Children's, Illustrated Books, History of Antiquity, Collected Works, Classics, Oriental Studies; (Winkler Verlag) India Paper Editions and Special Editions of World Literature, Special series of Classics, Works of Zola, Germanistics
ISBN Publisher's Prefix: 3–7608

Aschendorffsche Verlagsbuchhandlung*, Soesterstr 13, D-4400 Münster/Westfalen Postfach 1124 Tel: (0251) 6901 Cable Add: Verlag Aschendorff Münster
Telex: 0892830
Man Dirs: Anton Wilhelm Hueffer, Maxfritz Hueffer
Subjects: History, Art History, Philosophy, Religion, Reference, Juveniles, Psychology, Law, Folklore, Social & Natural Science, Economics, Philology, Textbooks, Foreign Languages
Miscellaneous: Publish periodicals
Founded: 1720
ISBN Publisher's Prefix: 3–402

Aspekte Verlag GmbH*, Forsthausstr 9, D-6246 Glashütten 1 Tel: 06174/61116
Gen Man, Publicity, Rights & Permissions: Gerhard Hirschfeld; *Editorial & Advertising:* Stephan Bohnke; *Sales:* Annerose Bayer
Subsidiary Company: Verlag Frankfurter Kinderbücher (qv)
1976: 21 titles *Founded:* 1965
Subjects: Sociology, Political Science, Economic Sciences, Psychology
ISBN Publisher's Prefix: 3–921096

Assimil-Verlag KG+*, Grimmstr 4, Postfach 230147, D-4000 Düsseldorf 23 Tel: (0211) 683191
Publisher: Franz Wilhelm Kreft
Parent Company: Assimil, France (qv)
Subjects: Language courses, Linguistics; also Records and Cassettes
ISBN Publisher's Prefix: 2–7005

Asso Verlag Anneliese Althoff*, Josefplatz 3, D-4200 Oberhausen Tel: (0208) 802356
Orders to: VVA Reinhard Mohn OHG, Carl-Bertelsmann-Str 161, D-4830 Gütersloh 1; (West Berlin): Lützowstr 105-106, D-1000 Berlin 30
Subjects: Contemporary Political Literature in prose, poetry, songs, graphics; Miners' Solidarity
1978: 5 titles

Verlag **Association** GmbH & Co*, Postfach 501525, D-2000 Hamburg 50 Tel: (040) 393245
Subjects: Politics, Socialism, Social History, Political Ecology

Ästhetik und Kommunikation Verlags-GmbH, Fuggerstr 18, D-1000 Berlin 30 Tel: (030) 241084/241085
Man Dir, Editorial, Rights & Permissions: Eberhard Knödler-Bunte; *Sales:* Gudrun Fricke; *Production:* Richard Reitinger; *Publicity:* Jochen Rossbroich
Subjects: Contemporary Issues, Political Culture; Periodicals
1978: 3 titles *1979:* 8 titles *Founded:* 1969

FEDERAL REPUBLIC OF GERMANY 125

Atelier-Handpresse Verlag H Hoffmann*, Blücherstr 23, Postfach 475, D-1000 Berlin 61 Tel: 6933080
Subjects: Prose/Lyrical Poetry with original graphics in hand-printed editions, First Editions, Calendars, Reprints

Verlag **Atelier im Bauernhaus***, in der Bredenau 5, D-2802 Fischerhude
Tel: (04293) 671
Subjects: Regional Books; Prose and Poetry in Bibliophile Editions; Novels; Graphics

Atelier Verlag Andernach (AVA), Antel 74, D-547 Andernach Tel: 44432
Man Dir & Rights & Permissions: Rosa Werf; *Publicity Dir:* Fritz Werf
Subjects: Belles Lettres, Poetry, Art
1976: 1 title *1977:* 2 titles *Founded:* 1967
ISBN Publisher's Prefix: 3–921042

Athenaion, see Akademische Verlagsgesellschaft

Athenäum Verlag GmbH, Adelheidstr 2, Postfach 1220, D-6240 Königstein/TS Tel: (06174) 3026
Publisher: Dietrich Pinkerneil; *Editorial:* Dr Beate Pinkerneil; *Sales:* Rudolf Klein; *Publicity:* Karin Hirschfeld; *Rights & Permissions:* Hildegard Wilhöft
Subsidiary Companies: Anton Hain Verlag GmbH; Peter Hanstein Verlag GmbH; Scriptor Verlag GmbH (qqv)
Subjects: Philosophy, History, Textbooks, Paperbacks, Law, Linguistics, Paedagogic, Politics, Psychology, Social Science, Literary Criticism, Languages, Economics, General Nonfiction
1977: 40 titles *1978:* 77 titles *Founded:* 1949
ISBN Publisher's Prefix: 3–7610

Atlantis-Verlag GmbH & Co Kg*, Erwinstr 58-60, D-7800 Freiburg im Breisgau Tel: (0761) 71570
Man Dir: Georg Linke
Subjects: Poetry, Biography, History, Music, Art, Geography, Juveniles
Founded: 1930
Miscellaneous: Firm is a branch office of Atlantis Verlag AG, Zurich, Switzerland (qv)
ISBN Publisher's Prefix: 3–7611

Verlag Ludwig **Auer***, Heilig-Kreuz-Str 12, Postfach 239, D-8850 Donauwörth Tel: (0906) 3061 Cable Add: Auer Donauwörth Telex: 05-1845
Subjects: History, Religion, Education, Textbooks, Juveniles
Founded: 1875
ISBN Publisher's Prefix: 3–403

Aulis Verlag Deubner & Co KG, Antwerpener Str 6/12, D-5000 Cologne 1 Tel: (0221) 518051
Publisher: Karl-August Deubner; *Publicity Manager:* Wolfgang Deubner
Subjects: Nonfiction, Juveniles, Biology, Mathematics, Medicine, Physics, Psychology, Engineering, Maps, Geography, Education
ISBN Publisher's Prefix: 3–7614

Aurum Verlag GmbH & Co KG+, Erwinstr 60, Postfach 5204, D-7800 Freiburg im Breisgau Tel: (0761) 71034
Publisher: Günther Berkau; *Editorial:* Leon Düldig
Orders to: Walter-Verlag GmbH, Erwinstr 58-60, Postfach 1708, D-7800 Freiburg im Breisgau Tel: (0761) 71050 Telex: 0772676
Associate Company: Hermann Bauer Verlag KG (qv)
Subjects: Psychology, Mysticism, Religion,

Yoga, Meditation, Para-Medicine
1977: 25 titles *1978:* 38 titles
ISBN Publisher's Prefix: 3–591

Aussaat Verlag GmbH, Wittensteinstr 110–114, Postfach 200735, D–5600 Wuppertal 2 Tel: (0202) 80075/76
Dir: Hans Steinacker; *Assistant Dir:* Manfred Gieche; *Editorial:* Gerd Ulmer; *Production, Advertising:* Michael Lippkau
Orders to: Schriftenmissions-Verlag, Postfach 548, D–4390 Gladbeck
Subjects: Evangelical and Scriptural Texts, Religion, Education, Juveniles, Paperbacks
Bookshop: Rudolfstr 139, D–5600 Wuppertal 2
1977: 34 titles *1978:* 21 titles *Founded:* 1891
ISBN Publisher's Prefix: 3–7615

Verlag der **Autoren** GmbH & Co KG*, Staufenstr 46, D–6000 Frankfurt am Main Tel: (0611) 725222
Subjects: Texts for Theatre, Radio, Film and TV

Syndikat **Autoren-und Verlagsgesellschaft***, Savignystr 61–63, D–6000 Frankfurt am Main Tel: (0611) 751801/751781
Author/Publisher Syndicate Company
Orders to: VVA Reinhard Mohn OHG, Carl-Bertelsmann Str 161, D–4830 Gütersloh 1; (West Berlin): Lützowstr 1105–106, D–1000 Berlin 30
Subjects: mostly serious Nonfiction; Literary Criticism, Art Theory, Psychology, Psychoanalysis, Ethnology, Social Theory and Social History, Political Economy etc
1977: 24 titles

Auxilium Verlag*, Hasstr 7, D–8500 Nuremberg Tel: (0911) 313403
Subject: Educational Material
ISBN Publisher's Prefix: 3–920092

Axel-Juncker Verlag Jacobi KG, see Juncker

BLV Verlagsgesellschaft mbH, Lothstr 29, Postfach 400320, D–8000 Munich 40 Tel: (089) 38851 Cable Add: BLV Verlag Telex: 5215087
Man Dir: Dr A Egger; *Dir:* Dr Rudolf Schneider; *Editorial:* Wilhelm Eisenreich, Jürgen Kemmler; *Sales (International):* Curt Ablaßmayer; *Rights & Permissions:* Ursula Holkko, Monika Grill
Subjects: General Non-fiction: especially Nature, Sports, Field and Travel Guides, Horses, Hunting, Household and Garden, Geography, Bavaria; Technical books on Agriculture, Forestry, Environment, Biology, Nutrition; Education, School Textbooks
Founded: 1946
ISBN Publisher's Prefix: 3–405

B N V (Bohmann-Noltemeyer Verlag)*, Am Kronenburger Hof 9, Postfach 47, D–6901 Dossenheim Tel: (06221) 85755
Publisher: Werner Noltemeyer
Subjects: Engineering, Electronics, Technical

B S-Verlag Manfred Kerler, Marbacher Str 8, Postfach 450, D–7057 Winnenden-Stuttgart Tel: (07195) 8012
Subject: Transport

B V B, see Bayerische Verlagsanstalt Bamberg

J P **Bachem** Verlag GmbH*, Ursulaplatz 1, D–5000 Cologne 1 Tel: (0221) 135041 Cable Add: Bachemhaus Cologne
Dirs: Dr Peter Bachem, Gerd Horbach
Subjects: Religion, Social Science, Economics, Biography, Popular Psychology, Books on Cologne and the Rhenish lands
Founded: 1818
ISBN Publisher's Prefix: 3–7616

Karl **Baedeker**, Rosastr 7, D–7800 Freiburg im Breisgau Tel: (0761) 32915 Cable Add: Baedeker Freiburg
Man Dir, Editorial, Production: Karl Baedeker; *Sales, Publicity:* Dr Volkmar Mair
Subsidiary Company: Baedekers Autoführer-Verlag (qv)
Br Off: Mairs Geographischer Verlag, D–7302 Ostfildern
Subjects: Guide Books, Motoring Guides, Town and Regional Maps (in English and French), Facsimile early guidebooks
1977: 19 titles *Founded:* 1827
ISBN Publisher's Prefix: 3–87954

Baedekers Autoführer-Verlag GmbH*, Marco-Polo-Str 1, Postfach, D–7302 Ostfildern 4 (Kemnat) bei Stuttgart Tel: (0711) 4502262 Cable Add: Baedeker Stuttgart Telex: 721796 mair d
Man Dirs: Karl Baedeker, Dr Volkmar Mair; *Editorial:* Dr Peter Baumgarten
Associate Company: Karl Baedeker (qv)
Subject: Travel Guides, Motoring Guides
1977: 5 titles *Founded:* 1951 (Stuttgart; orig 1827 Leipzig)
ISBN Publisher's Prefix: 3–87036

Hans A **Baensch**, see Mergus Verlag

Baha'i Verlag GmbH+, Eppsteiner Str 89, D–6238 Hofheim-Langenhain Tel: (06192) 22921
Subject: The Baha'i Religion
1978: 5 titles
ISBN Publisher's Prefix: 3–87037

Friedrich **Bahn** Verlag GmbH, Zasiusstr 8, Postfach 1186, D–7550 Konstanz Tel: (07531) 23054/5
Man Dir: Dr Rudolf Weth; *Manager, Rights & Permissions:* Herbert Denecke
Parent Company: Christliche Verlagsanstalt GmbH (qv)
Subjects: Children's Books, Christian Instruction, Christianity
1978: 6 titles *1979:* 8 titles *Founded:* 1891
ISBN Publisher's Prefix: 3–7621

Bärenreiter Verlag, Karl Vötterle KG*, Heinrich Schütz Allee 29–37, D–35 Kassel-Wilhelmshöhe Tel: (0561) 300117 Cable Add: Bärenreiter, Kassel Telex: 992376
Management: Wolfgang Matthei, Dr Wolfgang Rehm, Barbara Scheuch-Vötterle
Br Offs: London, England; Tours, France; Basel, Switzerland
Subjects: Music, Calendars, Records, Reproductions of Ancient Topographical Maps
Founded: 1924
ISBN Publisher's Prefix: 3–7618

Verlag **Bartels und Wernitz** KG*, Reinickendorfer Str 113, Postfach 650380, D–1000 Berlin 65 Tel: (030) 4611011 Cable Add: Bartelswernitz Westberlin Telex: 181331 bawer d
Man Dir: Harry Bartels; *Editorial:* Hans-Jürgen Ehrlich; *Sales & Advertising Dir:* Monika Schuchardt-Bartels
Orders to: Georg Lingenbrink, Postfach 3584, D–6000 Frankfurt am Main
Subjects: Sport (including training and history)
1977: 12 titles *1978:* 16 titles *Founded:* 1926
ISBN Publisher's Prefix: 3–87039

Otto Wilhelm **Barth**-Verlag KG, Stievestr 9, D–8000 Munich 19 Tel: (089) 172237
Man Dir: Rudolf Streit-Scherz; *Editor:* Stephan Schuhmacher
Parent Company: Scherz Verlag AG, Berne, Switzerland
Subjects: Philosophy and Religions of the East, Mysticism
1977: 22 titles *1978:* 22 titles *Founded:* 1924
ISBN Publisher's Prefix: 3–87041

Barudio & Hess Verlag, Neuhaus Str 8, D–6000 Frankfurt am Main Tel: (0611) 5972455
Man Dirs: Dr Gunter Barudio, Stephan Hess; *Editorial:* Barudio, Hess, Maschke; *Sales, Production, Rights & Permissions:* S Hess; *Publicity:* Hess, Schmidt
Subjects: Literature, Politics, Art, History, Economics
1978: 1 title *1979:* 5 titles *Founded:* 1978
ISBN Publisher's Prefix: 3–922182

Basis-Verlag, Crellestr 22, D–1000 Berlin 62, Postfach 645, Berlin 15 Tel: (0311) 7848433
Subjects: Juveniles, Comics, Education, Media
ISBN Publisher's Prefix: 3–88025

Friedrich **Bassermann'sche** Verlagsbuchhandlung im Falken-Verlag Erich Sicker KG, Schöne Aussicht 21, Postfach 1120, D–6272 Niedernhäusern Tel: (06127) 3011 Telex: 4186585
Subjects: Sports, Wilhelm-Busch-Edition
ISBN Publisher's Prefix: 3–87043

Bastei-Verlag Gustav H Lübbe*, Scheidtbachstr 23–31, Postfach 1170, D–5070 Bergisch Gladbach 3 Tel: (02202) 1211 Cable Add: Scheidtbachstr 23–31 Telex: 887922
Man Dir: Gustav Lübbe; *Manager:* Günther Jakel; *Editorial:* Rolf Schmitz; *Sales:* H–J Karl; *Production:* D Deichmann (Fiction); J Dippmann (Juveniles and Paperbacks); *Publicity:* L Becker-Voss, I Sellmann
Associate Company: Gustav Lübbe Verlag (qv)
Subjects: Paperbacks
Founded: 1953
ISBN Publisher's Prefix: 3–404

Ernst **Battenberg** Verlag, Prinzregentstr 79, Postfach 800349, D–8000 Munich 80
Man Dir, Editorial, Sales, Rights & Permissions: Ernst Battenberg; *Production, Publicity:* Walter Lachenmann
Subjects: Art and Antiques, Numismatics, Heraldry, Orders and Decorations, Old Maps
1977: 20 titles *1978:* 21 titles *Founded:* 1956
ISBN Publisher's Prefix: 3–87045

Hermann **Bauer** Verlag KG, Staudingerstrasse 7, Postfach 167, D–7800 Freiburg Tel: 0761/43003 Telex: 0772821
Man Dir: Friedrich Kirner; *Editorial, Publicity, Rights & Permissions:* Gabriele Kirner; *Sales Manager:* Waltraud Kirner
Associate Company: Aurum Verlag GmbH & Co KG (qv)
Subjects: Astrology, Philosophy, Parapsychology, Yoga, Esoterica
1978: 12 titles
ISBN Publisher's Prefix: 3–7626

Bauverlag GmbH, Wittelsbacherstr 10, Postfach 1460, D–6200 Wiesbaden 1 Tel: (06121) 74951 Cable Add: Bauverlag Wiesbaden Telex: 4186792
Dir, Rights & Permissions: Reinhart Knapp; *Sales Dirs:* Eberhard Blottner, Karlheinz Gross; *Publicity & Advertising:* Eberhard Blottner
Subsidiary Companies: Verlag für Aufbereitung Schirmer & Zeh GmbH; Mauritius-Verlags-Messe- &

Werbegesellschaft GmbH (both in Wiesbaden, German Federal Republic)
Branch Off: Nikolsburger Str 11, D–1000 Berlin 31
Subjects: Civil Engineering, Architecture, Surveying, Town Planning, Building Materials, Dictionaries, Books and Periodicals in both German and English languages
1977: 85 titles *1978:* 82 titles *Founded:* 1929
ISBN Publisher's Prefix: 3-7625

Bayerische Verlagsanstalt Bamberg (B V B), Lange Str 22/24, D-8600 Bamberg Tel: (0951) 25252 Telex: 06 62860 otvl
Man Dir: Kurt Kiening; *Other Offices:* Norbert Goebel
Associate Company: Cura Verlag, Vienna, Austria (qv)
Subsidiary Company: Sankt Otto-Verlag GmbH, at address above
Subjects: Classics, World Literature Series, Poetry, Juveniles, Regional Literature
Bookshop: Goerres Buchhandlung at address above
1977: 10 titles *1978:* 15 titles *Founded:* 1949
ISBN Publisher's Prefix: 3-87052

Bayerischer Schulbuch-Verlag, Hubertusstr 4, Postfach 87, D-8000 Munich 19 Tel: (089) 174067/69 Telex: 526677
Dir: Heinz Klüter; *Sales Manager:* Hartmut Köppelmann
Orders to: BSV, Ohmstr 10, D-8047 Karlsfeld Tel: (08131) 95091 Telex: 526677 bsv d
Branch Off: Ohmstr 10, D-8047, Karlsfeld, Düsseldorf
Subjects: School textbooks on all subjects for teachers, and pupils of all ages; also Records, Audiovisual Materials, Periodicals
ISBN Publisher's Prefix: 3-7627

Bechtle*, Hubertusstr 4, D-8000 Munich 19 Tel: (089) 177041 Cable Add: Langenmüller Telex: 05215045
Dirs: Dr Herbert Fleissner, Otto Wolfgang Bechtle, Dr Friedrich Bechtle; *Man Dir:* Dr Georg Niebling
Orders to: VVA Reinhard Mohn, Carl-Bertelsmann-Str 161, D-4830 Gütersloh 1 Tel: (05241) 851 Telex: 0933827; (West Berlin) Halliant, Albrechtstr 17–19, D–1000 Berlin 42
Subjects: Poetry, Biography, History, Politics, High-priced Paperbacks, Series 'Bechtle Anekdoten'
1977: 11 titles *Founded:* 1868 (Book Department, 1949)
Miscellaneous: Firm is a member of Verlagsgruppe Langen Müller-Herbig (qv)
ISBN Publisher's Prefix: 3-7623

Verlag C H **Beck**, Wilhelmstr 9, Postfach 400340, D-8000 Munich 40 Tel: 381891 Telex: 05215085 beckd
Dirs: Dr Hans D Beck, Wolfgang Beck; *Editorial:* E Wieckenberg, Ursula Pietsch, Günther Schiwy, B Rüster; *Sales Dirs:* G Elze, E Hoppe; *Publicity Dir:* P Schunemann; *Rights & Permissions:* Eva von Freeden
Associate Companies: Franz Vahlen (qv); Biederstein Verlag (qv)
Branch Off: Palmengartenstr 14, D-6000 Frankfurt am Main
Subjects: Ancient and Modern History, Archaeology, Literary History, Linguistics, Social Sciences, Anthropology, Economics, Law, Popular Nonfiction, Art, Illustrated Books, Textbooks, Classics, Periodicals
1978: 520 titles *Founded:* 1763
ISBN Publisher's Prefixes: 3-406 (Beck), 3-8006 (Vahlen), 3-7642 (Biederstein)

Edition Monika **Beck***, Am Römer-Museum, D-665 Homburg-Schwarzenacker/Saar Tel: (06848) 554
Man Dir/Proprietor: Monika Beck; *Publicity Dir:* B O Beck
Branch Offs: Frankfurt, Kaiserslauten
Subjects: Bibliophile portfolios, First editions, Monograph portfolios
1977: 13 titles *Founded:* 1967
Bookclub: Kunstkreis für Bibliophile Mappen

Reinhard **Becker** Verlag, Friedrich-Ebert-Str 80, D-6520 Worms Tel: (06241) 51425
Man Dir, Editorial, Rights &Permissions: Reinhard Becker; *Sales:* Friedrich Becker; *Production:* Uschi Becker
Subjects: Current Events, Belles Lettres, Juveniles, Specialist Computer Operating Literature, Esoteric and Occult
Bookshop: Reinhard Becker Buchversand, at above address
1978: 5 titles *1979:* 10 titles *Founded:* 1977
ISBN Publisher's Prefix: 3-88325

M P **Belaieff**, see C F Peters Musikverlag Gmbh und Co KG

Chr **Belser** AG für Verlagsgeschäfte und Co KG, Falkerstr 73, Postfach 1002, D-7000 Stuttgart 1 Tel: (0711) 221359/221350 Cable Add: Belserverlag Telex: 0722334 belag d
Publishers: Hans Weitpert, Hilde Weitpert-Vogt; *General Manager:* Bernd Friedrich; *Managing Editor:* Michael Maegraith; *Sales Manager:* Herbert Lindauer; *Rights & Permissions:* Michael Maegraith, Elfriede Kurz
Subjects: Art, Architecture, Music, Biographies, Natural History, Non-fiction, Politics, Maps, Travel, Book/Record combinations, Periodical *Belser Kunst Quartal*
1977: 27 titles *Founded:* 1835
ISBN Publisher's Prefix: 3-7630

Beltz Verlag*, Am Hauptbahnhof 10a Werderstr, Postfach 1120, D-6940 Weinheim Tel: (06201) 61041 Telex: 465500
Man Dir: Dr Manfred Beltz-Rubelmann; *Sales:* Eberhard Hosemann, Anni Wetzel; *Publicity:* Gunter Holm; *Rights & Permissions:* Gisela Schroeder
Subjects: How–to, Juveniles, High-priced Paperbacks, Psychology, Social Science, Primary & University Textbooks
Founded: 1841
ISBN Publisher's Prefix: 3-407

Benziger Verlag*, Martinstr 16, D-5000 Cologne 1 Tel: (0221) 210925
Sales & Publicity: Klaus Opitz
Subjects: General Fiction, Juveniles, Education, Politics, Religion
Miscellaneous: Firm is a branch office of Benziger AG, Switzerland (qv)
ISBN Publisher's Prefix: 3-545

Johannes **Berchmans** Verlag GmbH, Münchhausenstr 4, D-8000 Munich 60 Tel: (089) 8114535
Gen Man: Dr Erich Lampey
Subjects: Philosophy, Contemporary History
1978: 3 titles
ISBN Publisher's Prefix: 3-87056

Edition Sven Erik **Bergh**, Goethestr 6, D-7400 Tübingen Tel: (07071) 22340 Telex: 7262891 mepo
Man Dir: Dr Sven-Erik Bergh; *Editor:* Liselotte Weiss
Parent Company: Berghs Förlag AB, Sweden (qv)

FEDERAL REPUBLIC OF GERMANY 127

Associate Company: Edition Sven Erik Bergh im Europabuch AG, Switzerland (qv)
Subjects: General Fiction & Nonfiction, Juveniles
Founded: 1971

Berghaus Verlag, D-8347 Ramerding Tel: (08571) 8102
Man Dir: Ursel Bader
Imprint: Berghaus International
Subjects: Art, High-priced Paperbacks
1977: 28 titles *1978:* 32 titles *Founded:* 1960
ISBN Publisher's Prefix: 3-7635

J F **Bergmann***, Agnes-Bernauer-Platz 8, D-8000 Munich 21 Tel: (089) 5803023 Cable Add: Bergmannverlag Munich Telex: 529029
General Managers: Dr Heinz Goetze, Dr Konrad F Springr, Claus Michaletz
Subjects: General Science, Medicine, Economics
Founded: 1878
ISBN Publisher's Prefix: 3-8070

Bergverlag Rudolf Rother GmbH, Landshuter Allee 49, Postfach 67, D-8000 Munich 19 Tel: (089) 160081
Publisher: Rudolf Rother; *Sales:* Christine Nat
Subjects: Mountaineering and Ski-ing
Bookshop: at above address
1977: 15 titles *1978:* 25 titles *Founded:* 1920
ISBN Publisher's Prefix: 3-7633

Berlin Verlag, Pacelliallee 5, D-1000 Berlin 33 Tel: (030) 8326232; Ehrenbergstr 29, D-1000 Ben 33 Tel: (030) 8313469/8326232
Proprietor, Publicity Manager: Arno Spitz
1977: 23 titles *1978:* 37 titles *Founded:* 1962
Subjects: International and Comparative Law, Economy, Politics, Bibliographic Guides to Social Science, Legal, Pedagogic Studies etc
ISBN Publisher's Prefix: 3-87061

Berliner Handpresse Wolfgang Joerg und Erich Schoenig, Kohlfurter Str 35, D-1000 Berlin 36 Tel: (030) 6148728/6142605/6141201
Publisher: Wolfgang Joerg
Subjects: General Fiction, Arts, First Editions, Children's Books
Founded: 1961

Berliner Union GmbH*, Verlag für Wissenschaft & Technologie, 80 Hessbruehlstr 69, D-7000 Stuttgart Tel: (0711) 78631 Cable Add: Berlinunion
Dir: Dr Jürgen Gutbrod; *Editor:* Alfred Beierl; *Sales Dir:* Gerd W Ludwig; *Rights & Permissions:* Dr Alexander Schweickert
Subjects: How-to, Reference, Engineering, Rubber Chemistry, Electronics, Electrical Engineering, Computer Programming, General Science
Founded: 1949
Miscellaneous: Firm is a subsidiary of Unternehmensgruppe Verlag W Kohlhammer GmbH, (qv)
ISBN Publisher's Prefix: 3-408

Bernard & Graefe Verlag, Hubertusstr 5, Postfach 380180, D-8000 Munich Tel: (089) 174021/174022
Subjects: Military, History, Politics, Textbooks
Founded: 1918
ISBN Publisher's Prefix: 3-7637

C **Bertelsmann** Verlag*, Steinhauserstr 1, Postfach 800360, D-8000 Munich 80 Tel: (089) 4136347 Cable Add: Bertelsmann

München Telex: 0523259
Dir: Reinhold G Stecher; *Publisher:* Olaf Paeschke; *Sales Manager:* Lothar Nalbach; *Press Chief:* Lionel von dem Knesebeck; *Sales and Publicity Manager:* Lothar Nalbach
Parent Company: Verlagsgruppe Bertelsmann GmbH (qv)
Subjects: General Fiction & Nonfiction, Juveniles, Arts, Biography
Founded: 1835
ISBN Publisher's Prefix: 3-570

Verlagsgruppe **Bertelsmann** GmbH*, Carl-Bertelsmann-Str 270, D-4830 Gütersloh Tel: (049) 80246 Cable Add: Bertelsmann Gutersloh Telex: 933646
President: Dr Ulrich Wechsler; *Vice-Presidents:* Franz Freiberg, Dr Horst Benzing
Subsidiary Companies: Verlagsgruppe Bertelsmann München, C Bertelsmann Verlag, Friedr Vieweg und Sohn GmbH (qqv)
Book Clubs: Bertelsmann Lesering; Europarings der Buch- und Schallplattenfreunde Federal Republic of Germany (qv); The Leisure Circle, UK (qv); Circulo de Leitores Lda, Portugal (qv); Circulo do Livro SA, Brazil (qv) (owned jointly with Abril SA Cultural e Industrial, Brazil (qv)
Founded: 1952
ISBN Publisher's Prefix: 3-570

Verlagsgruppe **Bertelsmann München***, Steinhauser Str 1, D-8000 Munich 80 Tel: (089) 41361 Cable Add: Bertelsmann Munich Telex: 523259
Man Dir: Olaf Paeschke; *Sales:* Lothar Nalbach; *Publicity:* Lionel v d Knesebeck; *Rights & Permissions:* Verlagsgruppe Bertelsmann International (*Dir:* Peter Gutmann)
Parent Company: Verlagsgruppe Bertelsmann GmbH (qv)
Branch Offs:
Düsseldorf: Pro Schule Verlag GmbH, Corneliusstr 9-11 *Dir:* Benno Hasselsweiler Gutersloh (parent company address): Bertelsmann Lexicon-Verlag *Editorial:* Werner Lenz; *Foreign Rights:* Wolfgang Zill. Prisma Verlag GmbH *Dir:* Aloys Hellmold
Hamburg: I L S — Institut für Lernsysteme GmbH, Doberaner Weg 10, D-2000 Hamburg 73 *Dir:* Bernhard v Minckwitz
Munich: C Bertelsmann Verlag GmbH (qv); Fachverlag Bertelsmann GmbH, Kreuzstr 14-16, D-8000 Munich 2 *Man Dir:* Dr Helmut Schachenmayer; Blanvalet Verlag GmbH (qv); Wilhelm Goldmann Verlag GmbH (qv); Mosaik Verlag GmbH (qv); R V Reise-und Verkehrsverlag GmbH (qv)
Wiesbaden: Betriebswirtschaftlicher Verlag Dr Th Gabler KG (qv); Friedr Vieweg und Sohn Verlagsgesellschaft mbH (qv); Westdeutscher Verlag GmbH (qv)
Parent Company: Verlagsgruppe Bertelsmann GmbH (qv)
Associate Company: Gütersloher Verlagshaus Gerd Mohn (qv)
Subjects: General Literature, Fiction & Nonfiction, Handbooks, Reference, Encyclopaedias, Dictionaries (see under individual branches)

Bertelsmann Lexikon-Verlag, a member of Verlagsgruppe Bertelsmann GmbH (qv)

Beton-Verlag (Concrete Publishing) GmbH, Postfach 110134, D-4000 Düsseldorf 11 Tel: (0211) 571068
General Manager: Emil Fuchs; *Advertising:* Walter Hauck; *Editorial:* Dieter Bausch; *Publicity and Marketing:* Peter Fischer

Orders to: Abteilung Fachbuch at above address
Subjects: Structural Engineering, Technology and Architecture
Founded: 1958
ISBN Publisher's Prefix: 3-7640

Annette **Betz** Verlag, formerly of Munich, removed to Austria (qv)

Elke **Betzel** Verlag, Bertha von Stuttner Ring 5a, D-6000 Frankfurt 70 Tel: (0611) 682600
Subjects: Art, Maps
Miscellaneous: Formerly Gruppe Hinterhaus

Beuroner Kunstverlag GmbH, D-7792 Beuron 1 Tel: (07466) 264 Cable Add: Beuroner Kunstverlag
Dir: Gabriel Gawletta; *Publicity Manager:* Siegfried Studer
Subjects: Calendars, Arts, Religion, Periodicals
Founded: 1898
ISBN Publisher's Prefix: 3-87071

Beuth Verlag GmbH+, Burggrafenstr 4-10, D-1000 Berlin 30 Tel: (030) 26011 Telex: 183622 bvb d
Man Dirs: Hans Hermann Plischke, Dr-Ing Helmut Reihlen; *Sales Dir:* Werner Schmitz; *Publicity & Advertising Dir:* Albrecht Geuther
Branch Off: Kamekestr 2-8, D-5000 Cologne 1 Tel: (0221) 57131
Telex: 8881332 bvk d
Associate Company: VDI-Verlag GmbH (qv) D-4000 Düsseldorf 1
Subjects: Science & Technical, DIN (German Standards) Handbooks and Textbooks
1978: 2,200 titles *Founded:* 1924
ISBN Publisher's Prefix: 3-410

Bibellesebund eV, Höfel Nr 6, Postfach 1129, D-5277 Marienheide 1 Tel: (02264) 7575
Scripture Union of Germany
Man Dir: Karl Schäfer; *Gen Man:* Helmut Klein
Parent Company: Scripture Union, UK (qv)
Subjects: Christian Literature for Juveniles and Adults
1977: 10 titles *1978:* 8 titles *Founded:* 1950
ISBN Publisher's Prefix: 3-87982

Bibliographisches Institut AG, Dudenstr 6, Postfach 311, D-68 Mannheim Tel: (0621) 39011 Cable Add: Biblio Telex: 04-62107 duden
Man Dirs: Karl Felder, Claus Greuner, Dr Michael Wegner; *Sales:* Rosita Throm; *Sales Dir, Rights & Permissions:* Claus Greuner
Subsidiaries: Bibliographisches Institut AG, Zurich (qv); Bibliographisches Institut GmbH, Vienna; Südbuch Vertriebgesellschaft mbH, Mannheim
Subjects: Technology, Arts and Sciences, German Language, General Knowledge, Juveniles, Low-priced Paperbacks, General Science, University Textbooks, Encyclopaedias, Geography
Founded: 1826
Miscellaneous: Publishers of the Duden series of Dictionaries and Lexicons
ISBN Publisher's Prefix: 3-411

Biederstein Verlag, Wilhelmstr 9, D-8000 Munich 40 Tel: (089) 381891 Telex: 05-215085
Man Dir: Wolfgang Beck; *Sales:* Günter Elze; *Rights & Permissions:* Eva von Freeden
Subjects: General Fiction, Poetry, Biography, History, Natural Science
Founded: 1945
Associate Companies: Verlag C H Beck

(qv); Franz Vahlen (qv)
ISBN Publisher's Prefix: 3-7642

Birkhäuser Verlag, Olgastr 53, D-7000 Stuttgart 1
Parent Company: Birkhäuser Verlag, Switzerland (qv)

Georg **Bitter** Verlag, Herner Str 62, Postfach 248, D-4350 Recklinghausen Tel: (02361) 25888/2140
Man & Sales Dir: Dr Georg Bitter; *Editorial:* Hans-Sigismund von Buch; *Publicity & Advertising, Rights & Permissions:* Hildegard Schäfer
Subjects: Juveniles, Picture Books
1978: 16 titles *1979:* 18 titles *Founded:* 1968
ISBN Publisher's Prefix: 3-7903

Blanvalet Verlag*, Steinhauser Str 1, Postfach 800360, D-8000 Munich 80 Tel: 41361 Cable Add: Blanvaletverlag Berlin Telex: 523259
Man Dir: Reinhold G Stecher
Subjects: Belles Lettres, Juveniles, Biographies
1977: 20 titles *Founded:* 1935
Miscellaneous: Firm is a member of Verlagsgruppe Bertelsmann (qv)
ISBN Publisher's Prefix: 3-7645

Blaukreuz-Verlag, Freiligrathstr 27, D-5600 Wuppertal 2 Tel: (0202) 621099 and 621090
Publisher: Hans-Jürgen Weidtke
Parent Company: Blaues Kreuz in Deutschland eV, Wuppertal
Subjects: Alcoholism, Christian Books and Texts
1978: 10 titles *1979:* 18 titles
Miscellaneous: Firm is a contributor to the Telos (qv) series of evangelical paperbacks
ISBN Publisher's Prefix: 3-920106

Bleicher Verlags-KG*, Holderäcker Str 14, Postfach 70, D-7016 Gerlingen Tel: (07156) 21033 Cable Add: Bleicherverlag
Publisher, Editorial, Rights & Permissions: Heinz M Bleicher; *Sales, Publicity:* Thomas Bleicher; *Production:* Rainer Abel
Subjects: Picture Books, Poster Books, Comic Verse, Periodicals
1977: 8 titles *Founded:* 1968
ISBN Publisher's Prefix: 3-921097

P Stephan **Blotzheim** Ostasiatischer Kunstverlag, see Ostasiatischer Kunstverlag

Böhlau-Verlag GmbH*, Niehler Str 272-274, Postfach 600180, D-5000 Cologne 60 Tel: (0221) 765368 Cable Add: Böhlau, Cologne 60
Man Dir: Dr Günter J Henz
Associate Company: Verlag Böhlau, Austria (qv)
Subjects: History, Music, Art, Philosophy, General & Social Science
Founded: 1951

Boje-Verlag, Holzstrasse 19, Postfach 1278, D-7000 Stuttgart 1 Tel: (0711) 247305/07 Cable Add: Bojeverlag
Proprietor: Hanns-Jörg Fischer; *Editorial:* Dr Doris Stephan; *Sales:* Michael Fischer; *Production:* Hildegard Schwarz; *Publicity:* Ursula Pfaffinger; *Rights & Permissions:* Erika Weiss
Subject: Juveniles
1977: 40 titles *1978:* 38 titles *Founded:* 1947
ISBN Publisher's Prefix: 3-414

Harald **Boldt** Verlag KG, Postfach 110, D-5407 Boppard am Rhein Tel: (06742) 2511
Man Dir, Publicity: Harald Boldt; *Sales Dir:* Heidrun Tschentke; *Production:* Peter

Boldt; *Rights & Permissions:* Edith Boldt
Associated Company: Boldt Druck Boppard GmbH
Subjects: Biography, History, Reference, General & Social Science
1977: 40 titles *1978:* 26 titles *Founded:* 1951
ISBN Publisher's Prefix: 3-7646

Bollmann-Bildkarten-Verlag GmbH & Co Kg, Lilienthalplatz 3, Postfach 1526, D-3300 Braunschweig Tel: (0531) 332069
Telex: 952546
Dir: Friedrich Bollmann
Subject: Maps

Verlag Aurel **Bongers** KG, Hubertusstr 13, Postfach 220, D-4350 Recklinghausen Tel: (02361) 26001/2 Cable Add: Bongers Recklinghausen
Proprietor, Publishing Dir, Rights & Permissions: Aurel Bongers Sr, Aurel Bongers Jr; *Sales Dir:* Renate Drygalla; *Publicity & Advertising Dir:* Aurel Bongers Jr
Subjects: Art (Modern and Classical Painting and Sculpture, Eastern Church Art), Archaeology, Calendars
1978: 8 titles *1979:* 9 titles *Founded:* 1931
ISBN Publisher's Prefix: 3-7647

Bonn Aktuell GmbH, Pforzheimer Str 377, Postfach 310807, D-7000 Stuttgart 31 Tel: (0711) 881149
Publisher: Horst Poller
Subjects: Politics, Current Affairs
ISBN Publisher's Prefix: 3-87959

Verlag Adolf **Bonz** GmbH*, Kaisersbacher Str 4, D-7012 Fellbach-Oeffingen Tel: (0711) 511070 Cable Add: Bonz-Verlag
Man Dir: Wolfgang Reinecker
Subjects: Pedagogics, Psychology, Psychoanalysis, Social Science
Founded: 1876
ISBN Publisher's Prefix: 3-87089

Gebrüder **Borntraeger** Verlagsbuchhandlung, Johannesstr 3A, D-7000 Stuttgart 1 Tel: (0711) 623541/3
Man Dirs: Dr Erhard Naegele (Production), Klaus Obermiller (Sales)
Subjects: Geology, Geomorphology, Geography, Geophysics, Meteorology, Metallography, Botany, Biology, Oceanography, General Science
Founded: 1790
Associate Company: E Schweizerbart'sche Verlagsbuchhandlung (qv)
ISBN Publisher's Prefix: 3-443

Gustav **Bosse** Verlag, Von-der-Tann-Str 38, D-8400 Regensburg Tel: (0941) 55455
Cable Add: Bosse Regensburg
Imprint: bmp (bosse musik paperback)
Subjects: Early Musical Training, New Religious Songs, Musicology, Musical Pedagogy, "Contributions to the Musical History of the 19th Century"; Periodicals, Music Paperbacks
1978: 28 titles

Oscar **Brandstetter** Verlag+, Stiftstr 30, Postfach 1708, D-6200 Wiesbaden Tel: (06121) 521002/3 Telex: 04186486 obra d
Man Dir: Martin Arndt; *Editorial:* Dr Antonin Kucera
Subjects: Language & Technical Dictionaries
1977-78: 4 titles *Founded:* 1862
ISBN Publisher's Prefix: 3-87097

Verlag G **Braun** GmbH, Karl-Friedrich-Str 14-18, Postfach 1709, D-7500 Karlsruhe Tel: (0721) 1651 Cable Add: Braunverlag Telex: 07826904

Man Dir: Dr Eberhard Knittel; *Dir:* Hans Fehrle
Subjects: General Science, Medicine, Secondary Textbooks, Music, Paperbacks
ISBN Publisher's Prefix: 3-7650

Literarischer Verlag Helmut **Braun** KG*, Dünnwalder Mauspfad 390, D-5000 Cologne 80 Tel: (0221) 601457
Publisher: Helmut Braun; *Editor:* Berndt Mosblech, Dr Burghard Busse; *Representatives:* Wolfgang Ohm, Cecilie Sprenger, Iris Bechmann, Sabine Hillebrand; *Press Chief:* Irene Peters
Orders to: VVA, Postfach 7779, D-4830 Gütersloh, (Berlin) Karl Halliant & Sohn, Albrechtstr 17-19, D-1000 Berlin 42
Subjects: General Fiction, Belles Lettres, Poetry, Juvenile
1977: 40 titles *Founded:* 1975
ISBN Publisher's Prefix: 3-88097

Verlag **Braun und Schneider***, Maximiliansplatz 9, D-8000 Munich 2 Tel: (089) 555580
Dirs: Dr Julius Schneider, Friedrich Schneider
Subjects: Juveniles, Paperbacks, Illustrated Books
Founded: 1843
ISBN Publisher's Prefix: 3-87099

Verlag die **Braunkohle**, see Droste Verlag

Werkstatt und Galerie **Breitenbrunn**, Stechbahn 28, D-4190 Kleve Tel: (0043) 2683/5268
A Branch Office of Galerie & Werkstatt Breitenbrunn, Austria (qv)
Dirs: Fria Elfen, Will Frenken
Subjects: Hand-Printed Books, Special Books of Various Kinds, Bibliophile Texts and Documents

Breitkopf und Härtel, Walkmühl-Str 52, Postfach 1707, D-6200 Wiesbaden 1 Tel: (06121) 402031 Cable Add: Breitkopfs Wiesbaden
Man Dirs: Lieselotte Sievers, Gottfried Möckel
Subjects: Music, Books, Education
1978: 30 book titles (plus sheet music)
Founded: 1719
ISBN Publisher's Prefix: 3-7651

Julius **Breitschopf** KG*, Verlagsbuchhandlung, Schleisseimerstr 37B, D-8000 Munich 45 Tel: (089) 3514747
Subjects: Juveniles, Television Tie-in Books
Miscellaneous: Associate Company: Verlagsbuchhandlung Julius Breitschopf, A-1170 Vienna, Austria (qv)
ISBN Publishers' Prefix: 3-87254

Breklumer Verlag, Bundesstr 5/Kirchenstr, Postfach Bredstedt 1220, D-2257 Breklum Tel: (04671) 2028 Cable Add: Breklumer Verlag Breklum
Publisher: Manfred Siegel
Subject: Religion
ISBN Publisher's Prefix: 3-7793

Brendow-Verlag, Gutenbergstr 1, Postfach 1280, D-4130 Moers 1 Tel: (02841) 41036
Telex: 8121162
Dir: Gerhard Köller
Subjects: Evangelical Religious Literature; firm is a member of the Telos (qv) group of evangelical paperback publishers

Brigg Verlag GmbH (formerly Verlag die Brigg), Hermanstr 33, Postfach 112323, D-8900 Augsburg 11 Tel: (0821) 30008
Man Dir: Franz-Josef Büchler
Subjects: Fiction, Illustrated and Bibliophile Books, Travel, Children's Regional Books, Belles Lettres, Poetry, Music, Art, Juveniles,

FEDERAL REPUBLIC OF GERMANY 129

University Textbooks, Sport and Physical Fitness
1977: 10 titles *1978:* 10 titles *Founded:* 1950
ISBN Publisher's Prefix: 3-87101

F A **Brockhaus**, Leberberg 25, Postfach 1709, D-6200 Wiesbaden 1 Tel: (06121) 521054 Cable Add: Brockhausverlag
Telex: 04186699
Dirs: Ulrich Porak; *Sales:* H-E Brandt, Gisela Reuter, Kurt Schreiner, Hansjorg Triebel; *Publicity:* Adelheid Schmitz-Valckenberg
Orders to: Publishing address; Hartwich for Berlin
Subjects: Encyclopaedias, Language and other Dictionaries; Biography, History, General Science, Travel, Music, Schopenhauer, Nature, Animals; Fiction
1978: 15 titles *Founded:* 1805
ISBN Publisher's Prefix: 3-7653

R **Brockhaus** Verlag*, Postfach 110197, D-5600 Wuppertall (Located at: Champagne 7, D-5657 Haan 2)
Tel: (02104) 6311/12/13
Publisher: Dr Ulrich Brockhaus, *Editorial:* Doris Hoppler, Wolfgang Steinseifer, Elisabeth Wetter; *Sales:* Karl-Heinz Eisner, Raimond Schmidt
Associate Company: Theologischer Verlag Rolf Brockhaus (qv)
Subjects: Popular Christian Literature, Biographies, Fiction, Juveniles, Song Books, Bible Study
1977: 43 titles *Founded:* 1853
Bookshop: Christliche Buchhandlung R Brockhaus, Kleine Klotzbahn 8, D-56 Wuppertal-Elberfeld
ISBN Publisher's Prefix: 3-417

Brönner Verlag Breidenstein KG+, Stuttgarter Str 18-24, D-6000 Frankfurt am Main 1 Tel: (0611) 26001 Cable Add: Brönnerdruck Frankfurtmain
Telex: 0411964
Dirs: Klaus-Jürgen Breidenstein, Klaus-Jürgen Schlotte; *Editorial:* Eberhard Urban; *Sales Manager:* Armin H Schwertfeger
Associate Company: Umschau Verlag Breidenstein GmbH (qv for other Associate Companies)
Subjects: Art, Calendars
1979: 50+ titles
ISBN Publisher's Prefix: 3-599

Broschek Druck GmbH & Co KG, Bargkoppelweg 61, D-2000 Hamburg 73
Publisher: Dr A Schneckenburger-Broschek
Subjects: Juveniles, Art History, Illustrated books
Miscellaneous: formerly Hamburger Fremdenblatt Broschek und Co B & T KG
Founded: 1913
ISBN Publisher's Prefix: 3-87102

Broschek Verlag*, Kleine Theaterstr 9/11, Postfach 301021, D-2000 Hamburg 36 Tel: (040) 341456 Cable Add: Christians Druck
Orders to: Hans Christians Druckerei & Verlag (qv)
Subjects: Hamburg regional literature

Brücken-Verlag GmbH Literaturvertrieb Import-Export*, Ackerstr 3, Postfach 1928, D-4000 Düsseldorf 1 Tel: (0211) 353883/353884/363277 Cable Add: Brücken-Verlag Telex: 8588674
Dir: Erich Mayer; *Sales Managers:* Alfons Clemens, Gerd Fiegweil
Subjects: Textbooks, Literary Criticism, Reprints, Periodicals
Miscellaneous: This firm is the central marketing agency for the

Arbeitsgemeinschaft sozialistischer und demokratischer Verleger und Buchhändler (qv)
ISBN Publisher's Prefix: 3–87106

Verlag F **Bruckmann** KG, Nymphenburger Str 86, D–8000 Munich 19 Tel: (089) 12571 Cable Add: Bruckmannkoge Munich Telex: 0523739
Editor: Erhardt D Stiebner; *Publishing Manager:* F Andreae; *Editorial Manager:* Dr K Beth; *Sales:* H Ludwig; *Publicity:* Fritz Scheuer; *Production:* K Liese
Associate Company: Studio Bruckmann Kunst im Druck (qv)
Subjects: Art, Illustrated Books, Handbooks, Reference, History, Mountaineering, Bavaria
1977: 28 titles *Founded:* 1858
Miscellaneous: Publish periodicals *Pantheon, Der Bergsteiger, Novum Gebrauchsgraphik*
ISBN Publisher's Prefix: 3–7654

Studio **Bruckmann Kunst** im Druck Fine Art GmbH, Nymphenburger Str 84, Postfach 27, D–8000 Munich 19 Tel: (089) 12571 Cable Add: Bruckmannkoge Telex: 0523739
Editor: E D Stiebner; *Publishing Man:* F Andreae; *Sales:* H Ludwig; *Publicity:* Fritz Scheuer; *Production:* K Liese
Associate Company: Verlag F Bruckmann KG (qv)
Subjects: Art; Special Editions
1977: 4 titles *Founded:* 1972
ISBN Publisher's Prefix: 3–7854

Brunnen-Verlag GmbH, Pestalozzistr 1, Postfach 5205, D–6300 Giessen Tel: (0641) 42029/42020
Man Dir: Wilfried Jerke; *Editorial:* Helmut Jablonski; *Rights and Permissions:* Rudolf Horn
Branch Off: CH–4001 Basel, Spalenberg 20, Switzerland (qv)
Subjects: Religion, Juveniles
1977: 50 titles *1978:* 40 titles *Founded:* 1919
ISBN Publisher's Prefix: 3–7655

Brunner Verlagsgellschaft*, Hauptstr 4, D–8500 Nuremberg Tel: (0911) 831614
Man Dir: Monika Popp
Subjects: Children's Books
Founded: 1976
ISBN Publisher's Prefix: 3–88194

Brunnquell-Verlag der Bibel-und Missions-Stiftung Metzingen, Karlstr 4, Postfach 99, D–7418 Metzingen Tel: (07123) 2280
Subject: Religion
ISBN Publisher's Prefix: 3–7656

C J **Bücher** GmbH, Hanauer Landstr 11, D–6000 Frankfurt am Main 1 Tel: (0611) 439503
Parent Company: Verlag C J Bücher AG, Switzerland (qv)

Buchholz Verlag, Brühlstrasse 19, Postfach 2320, D–3000 Hanover Tel: 15253 Telex: 923228 repro
Publicity Manager: Fritz Bütehorn; *Sales Manager:* Erich Grikscheit; *Production Manager:* Meinrad Schilling
Subjects: Juveniles, How-to, Educational

Selbstverlag Walter **Büchner***, Schwabacher Strasse 87, D–8510 Fürth/Bay
Publisher: Walter Büchner
Subjects: Anthologies, Poetry, Criticism

Bund-Verlag GmbH, Deutz-Kalker Str 46, Postfach 210140, D–5000 Cologne 21 Tel: (0221) 82821 Telex: 08873362
Man Dir: Tomas Kosta; *Sales:* Dr H Adam; *Production:* Heinz Biermann; *Publicity:* Waldemar Block; *Rights & Permissions:* Gunther Heyder, Inge Stalker
Subjects: Trade Union Policy, Industrial Law, Social Law, Legal Texts and Commentaries, WSI Studies (Industrial Series)
Bookshops: Bund-Verlag GmbH Buchhandlung at address above; Bund-Verlag Buchhandlung, Wilhelm-Leuschner Str 64, D–6000 Frankfurt; Bund-Verlag GmbH Buchhandlung, Schwanthalerstr 64, D–8000 Munich 2
1978: 50 titles *1979:* 50 titles *Founded:* 1947
ISBN Publisher's Prefix: 3–7663

Burckhardthaus-Laetare Verlag GmbH, Herzbachweg 2, D–6460 Gelnhausen Tel: (06051) 891 Cable Add: Burckhardthaus
Dir: Jürgen Schwarz
Orders to: PO Box 1140, D–6460 Gelnhausen
Branch Offs: Burckhardthaus-Buchhandlung, Stubenrauchstr 12, D–1000 Berlin 37
Subjects: Humanities, Arts, Textbooks, Multimedia, Music, Education, Philosophy, Psychology, Religion, Social Science, Games
Bookshops: Burckhardthaus-Buchhandlung, Langgasse 2, D–6460 Gelnhausen; Burckhardthaus-Buchhandlung, Teltower Damm 9, D–1000 Berlin 37; Wichern-Buchhandlung, PO Box 2025, D–6720 Speyer; Burckhardthaus-Buchhandlung Hackhauser Hof, D–5650 Solingen 11
1978: 64 titles
ISBN Publisher's Prefix: 3–7664

Verlag Aenne **Burda**, Am Kestendamm 2, Postfach 1160, D–7600 Offenburg Tel: (0781) 871 Telex: 752804
1978: 70 titles
Subjects: Hobbies, Cookery, Handicrafts; Periodicals
ISBN Publisher's Prefix: 3–920158

Burgert Handpresse, Lassenstr 22, D–1000 Berlin 33 Tel: (030) 8264348
Man Dir: Professor Hans-Joachim Burgert
Subjects: Early Lyrical Poetry, Limited Editions (hand-printed with original illustrations)
1978: 2 titles *1979:* 1 title *Founded:* 1962

Kartographischer Verlag **Busche** GmbH, Kaiserstr 129, Postfach 114, D–4600 Dortmund 1 Tel: (0231) 597088/89 Telex: 0822270
Man Dir: Günter Schiffmann; *Editorial:* Alfred Heinemann; *Publicity & Advertising Dir:* Herr Klaffka; *Rights & Permissions:* Herr Schiffmann
Subjects: Street Maps, Atlases
1979/80: 56 titles *Founded:* 1972
ISBN Publisher's Prefix: 3–921143

Busse Kunstdokumentation GmbH, (Busse Art Information) Parkstrasse 23, Postfach 1803, D–6200 Wiesbaden Tel: 06121/569111
Managing Partner: Joachim Busse
Subjects: Art Reference Books, especially *Internationales Handbuch aller Maler und Bildhauer des 19 Jahrhunderts, Busse Verzeichnis* (International Directory of all Painters and Sculptors of the 19th Century, Busse Index)
Founded: 1976

Bussesche Verlagshandlung GmbH, Brüderstr 30, Postfach 341, D–4900 Herford Tel: (05221) 72055 Cable Add: Westverlag Herford Telex: 934717
Publishing Dir: K–H Zirkmann; *Commercial Manager, Rights & Permissions:* Heinz Zimmermann
Associate Companies: Westdeutsche Verlagsanstalt GmbH, Postfach 335, D–4900 Herford; Buchdruckerei und Verlag Busse, Postfach 335, D–4900 Herford
Subjects: Leisure, Sport, Travel, Sailing, Games and Hobbies, Oriental Themes
1978: 15 titles *1979:* 15 titles *Founded:* 1947
ISBN Publisher's Prefix: 3–87120

Verlag **Butzon und Bercker** GmbH, Neustr 7–13, Postfach 215, D–4178 Kevelaer 1 Tel: (02832) 6081 Telex: 812207 bb kev Cable Add: Butzonbercker
Dirs: Edmund Bercker, Dr Edmund Bercker Jr; *Editorial:* Josef Heckens; *Sales:* Walter Roelofs; *Production:* Otto Paustian; *Publicity:* Werner Krebber; *Rights & Permissions:* Mrs I Eisenbach
Subjects: Catholic Religion and Theology, Prayer and Meditation, Liturgy, Religious Teaching Books for Children
1977: 40 titles *1978:* 40 titles *Founded:* 1870
ISBN Publisher's Prefix: 3–7666

Caann Verlag GmbH*, Postfach 710360, D–8000 Munich 71 Tel: (089) 796533
Man Dir: Klaus Wagn
Subjects: Idea-books, Belles Lettres, Philosophy, Psychology, Fiction, Nonfiction
Founded: 1969
ISBN Publisher's Prefix: 3–87121

Verlag Georg D W **Callwey**, Streitfeldstr 35, Postfach 800409, D–8000 Munich 80 Tel: (089) 405024 Cable Add: Callweyverlag
Man Dir: Helmuth Baur; *Editorial:* Günther Mehling, Dr Paulhans Peters; *Sales:* Traute Geier; *Production:* Christian Pfeiffer-Belli; *Publicity:* Ludger Marquardt
Subjects: Biography, History, Architecture, History of Art, Handicrafts, Landscape Architecture, Painting and Restoration, Stonemasonry; Periodicals
1977: 39 titles *1978:* 29 titles *Founded:* 1884
ISBN Publisher's Prefix: 3–7667

Calwer Verlag, Scharnhäuser Str 44, D–7000 Stuttgart 70 Tel: (0711) 452019
Dir: Christof Munz; *Sales, Publicity, Rights & Permissions:* Sibylle Fritz
Subjects: Reference, Encyclopaedias, Dictionaries, Education, Religion, Periodicals
1978: 30 titles *Founded:* 1836
ISBN Publisher's Prefix: 3–7668

Campus Verlag GmbH, Schumannstr 65, D–6000 Frankfurt am Main Tel: (0611) 751008
Man Dir: Frank Schwoerer; *Editor:* Adalbert Hepp; *Advertising Dir:* Jochen Woerner; *Editorial:* Solveig Ockenfuss; *Rights & Permissions:* Beate Koglin
Subjects: Social Sciences, Psychology, Pedagogics, Economics, Politics, History, University Textbooks
1977: 81 titles *1978:* 102 titles *Founded:* 1972 (as Herder & Herder) renamed Campus Verlag 1975
ISBN Publisher's Prefix: 3–593

Editio **Cantor**, Verlag für Medizin und Naturwissenschaften KG, Zollenreuterstr 11, Postfach 1310, D–7960 Aulendorf Tel: (07525) 431/432/433 Cable Add: Cantor Aulendorfwürtt Telex: 0732225 vebu d
Subjects: Medicine, Pharmacy, Periodicals, *Arzneimittel-Forschung* (Pharmaceutics Research); *Die Pharmazeutische Industrie*; *Drugs Made in Germany*; *Dermatosen in Beruf und Umwelt* (Skin Diseases in

Profession and Environment)
1978: 8 titles *Founded:* 1947
ISBN Publisher's Prefix: 3-87193

Verlag Hans **Carl** KG+, Breite Gasse 58-60, D-8500 Nuremberg 11 Tel: (0911) 203831
Cable Add: Carlverlag Telex: 623081
Man Dir, Editorial: Dr Tilman Schmitt; *Sales, Production:* Raimund Schmitt; *Advertising Dir:* Rudolf Weidinger; *Publicity Dir:* Günter Schmiedel
Subjects: General Fiction, Belles Lettres, Poetry, History, Art, Philosophy, General Science, Biochemistry, University Textbooks, Literature for Brewers
1977: 12 titles *1978:* 9 titles *Founded:* 1861
Bookstore: Fachbuchhandlung Hans Carl, Breite Gasse 58-60, Postfach 9110, D-8500 Nuremberg 11
ISBN Publisher's Prefix: 3-418

Carlsen Verlag GmbH, Dieselstr 6, D-2057 Reinbek bei Hamburg Tel: (040) 7224051
Telex: 217879 carl d
President: Per Hjald Carlsen; *Man Dir:* Herbert Voss; *Rights & Permissions:* Per Hjald Carlsen
Subject: Juveniles
1978: 180 titles
Founded: 1953
ISBN Publisher's Prefix: 3-551

Ceres-Verlag Rudolf-August Oetker KG, Brokstr 77, Postfach Bielefeld 85, D-4800 Bielefeld 1 Tel: (0521) 24024 Cable Add: Ceres Telex: 0932324
Man Dir: Ernst A Kobusch; *Editorial:* Werner Tiltz, Gisela Knutzen; *Sales:* Wolfgang Krauss; *Publicity:* Ralph Plüm, Werner Tiltz
Parent Company: August Oetker, Bielefeld
Subject: Cookery
1979: 8 titles *Founded:* 1951
ISBN Publisher's Prefix: 3-7670

Champion Verlag G Kowalski, Kurfürstendamm 229, D-1000 Berlin 15 Tel: (030) 8827290 Cable Add: Championpress Telex: 0184560
Man Dir: Gerhard Kowalski; *Rights & Permissions:* Silvia Behr
Orders To: MGS, Postfach 1344, D-8032 Gräfelfing, Munich
Subjects: Music, Folklore, Freelight Stage Directories
1977: 2 titles *Founded:* 1974
Miscellaneous: Company also runs a Literary Agency (qv under Kowalski)
ISBN Publisher's Prefix: 3-921793

Verlag **Chemie** GmbH+, Pappelallee 3, Postfach 1260/1280, D-6940 Weinheim/Bergstr Tel: (06201) 14031
Cable Add: Chemieverlag Weinheimbergstr
Telex: 465516
Man Dirs: Juergen Kreuzhage, Hans Schermer; *Editorial:* Dr Hans Friedrich Ebel, Dr Gerd Giesler, Dr Ulrich Herzfeld; *Production:* Maximilian Montkowski; *Sales, Publicity & Advertising:* Helmut Schmitzer; *Rights & Permissions:* Kornelia Herbig, Irmgard Doersam
Branch Off: Verlag Chemie International Inc, Plaza Centre, Suite G, 1020 NW 6th St, Deerfield Beach, Florida 33441, USA
Subsidiary Company: Physik Verlag GmbH (qv)
Subjects: Life Sciences, Physical Sciences with emphasis on Chemistry & Chemical Engineering; University Textbooks, Periodicals
1977: 70 titles *1978:* 60 titles *Founded:* 1921
Bookshop: Buchhandlung Chemie, D-6940 Weinheim/Bergstr, Boschstr 12, Postfach 1260/1280
ISBN Publisher's Prefix: 3-527

Christian-Verlag, Akademiestr 7, D-8000 Munich 40 Tel: (089) 398095
Man Dir: Christian Strasser
Subjects: Psychology, Educational Materials, Music, Art, Religion, High-priced Paperbacks, Social Science, General (illustrated) Nonfiction
Founded: 1949
ISBN Publisher's Prefix: 3-88472

Hans **Christians** Druckerei und Verlag*, Kleine Theaterstr 9-11, Postfach 301021, D-2000 Hamburg 36 Tel: (040) 341456
Cable Add: Christians Druck
General Manager: Jens Christians
1977: 86 titles *Founded:* 1740
Subjects: General Fiction, Book Industry, History, Arts, Maps, Nonfiction
ISBN Publisher's Prefix: 3-7672

Christliche Verlagsanstalt GmbH, Zasiusstr 8, Postfach 1186, D-7750 Konstanz Tel: (07531) 23054/5
Man Dir: Dr Theol R Weth; *Manager, Rights & Permissions:* Herbert Denecke
Subsidiary Company: Friedrich Bahn Verlag (qv)
Subjects: Novels, Biography, Philosophy, Religion, Juveniles, Low- & High-priced Paperbacks, Psychology, Educational Materials
Bookshop: Buchhandlung der Christlichen Verlagsanstalt, Zasiusstr 8, D-7750 Konstanz
1978: 14 titles *1979:* 11 titles *Founded:* 1892/1933
ISBN Publisher's Prefix: 3-7673

Christliche Verlagsgesellschaft mbH, Moltekestr 1, Postfach 168, D-6340 Dillenburg 1 Tel: (02771) 6312/6313 Cable Add: Christlicher Verlag Dillenburg
Man Dirs; Dieter Boddenberg, Günther Kausemann; *Editorial, Publicity:* Dieter Boddenberg; *Sales:* Siegfried Reh; *Production, Rights & Permissions:* Günther Kausemann
Subsidiary Company: Christliche Bücherstuben, at above address
Associate Company: Emmaus-Fernbibelschule Deutschland, at above address
Subjects: Working Texts for Scriptural Instruction, Evangelical Nonfiction
Bookshops: Marburger Tor 32, D-5900 Siegen 1; Alte Linner Str 124, D-4150 Krefeld 1; Moltkestr 1, D-6340 Dillenburg
1978: 6 titles *1979:* 8 titles *Founded:* 1957
ISBN Publisher's Prefix: 3-921292

Christliches Verlagshaus GmbH, Senefelderstr 109, D-7000 Stuttgart 1 Tel: (0711) 221301
Man Dir: Heinz Schäfer
Subjects: Religion (Juvenile & Young Adult); Paperbacks, Periodicals
1978: 40 titles *Founded:* 1872
ISBN Publisher's Prefix: 3-7675

Christophorus-Verlag Herder GmbH+, Hermann-Herder-Str 4, D-7800 Freiburg im Breisgau Tel: (0761) 27171 Telex: 07721440
Man Dir: Heribert Mohr
Subjects: Christian Religious for all ages, Leisure Crafts, Sheet Music
1977: 40 titles *1978:* 66 titles *Founded:* 1935
Miscellaneous: Firm is a subsidiary of Verlag Herder KG (qv)
ISBN Publisher's Prefix: 3-419

Verlag Ernst **Chur**, Dedersberg 3, Postfach 2114, D-5372 Schleiden Tel: (02445) 7112
Cable Add: Dedersberg 3 D 5372 Schleiden
Man Dirs: Ernst & Gisela Chur
Subjects: Juveniles, Art, Periodicals

1978: 3 titles *Founded:* 1969
ISBN Publisher's Prefix: 3-87995

Cicero verlagsgesellschaft mbH*, Stuttgarter Str 82, D-7000 Stuttgart 30 Tel: (0711) 850829 Telex: 7252147 ciro d
Man Dir, Editorial, Sales, Rights & Permissions: F K Rothenbacher; *Production, Publicity:* H V Platen
Parent Company: Art Edit AG, Drusbergstr 1, CH-8703 Erlenbach, Switzerland
Subjects: Art
1977: 26 titles *Founded:* 1970
ISBN Publisher's Prefix: 3-921165

Claassen-Verlag GmbH, Grupellostr 28, Postfach 9229, D-4000 Düsseldorf Tel: (0211) 360516 Cable Add: Claassen-Verlag Telex: 8587327
Publisher: Erwin Barth von Wehrenalp; *Sales Manager:* Herbert Borgartz; *Publicity Manager:* Michael Tochtermann
Subjects: General Fiction, Literary Criticism, Linguistics, Languages, Biography
Miscellaneous: Firm is part of Econ Verlagsgruppe (qv)
ISBN Publisher's Prefix: 3-546

Claudius Verlag GmbH, Birkerstr 22, D-8000 Munich 19 Tel: (089) 184031
Telex: 523718 epdm d
Dirs: Richard Kolb, Hans J Pfalzgraf; *Publicity:* Elfi Barth
Parent Company: Evangelischer Pressverband für Bayern eV
Subjects: Juveniles, Religion, Paperbacks, Records, University Textbooks, Educational Materials
Founded: 1954
ISBN Publisher's Prefix: 3-532

Colloquium Verlag Otto H Hess+, Unter den Eichen 93, D-1000 Berlin 45 Tel: (030) 8328085
Proprietors: Anja Hess, Otto H Hess; *Man Dir:* Otto H Hess; *Sales Dir:* Manfred Köppen; *Rights & Permissions:* Dr Gabriele Pangratz
Subsidiary Company: Zeitgeschichtlicher Buchversand GmbH, Unter den Eichen 93, D-1000 Berlin 45, (Mail-order Store)
Orders to: Koch, Neff, Oetinger & Co, Abt. Verlagsauslieferung, Am Wallgraben 110, D-7000 Stuttgart-Vaihingen
Subjects: Current Affairs, Latin-American Studies, History, Pedagogy, Biography, School TV, Research and General Knowledge, Politics
1977: 16 titles *1978:* 22 titles *Founded:* 1948
ISBN Publisher's Prefix: 3-7678

Verlag W A **Colomb***, D-7274 Haiterbach-Oberschwandorf
Editorial: Dr Hans Kittel
Parent Company: Verlag H Heenemann GmbH (qv)
Subjects: Specialist literature connected with enamels, coatings, corrosion protection

Columbus Verlag, Paul Oestergaard GmbH, Columbus Haus, Postfach 1180, D-7056 Weinstadt-Beutelsbach Tel: (07151) 68011
Cable Add: Columbus-verlag
Telex: 0724382
Publishers: Peter Oestergaard, Rudi Heubach; *Sales:* Gerhard Reuschle
Subjects: Cartography, Globes, Reference
Founded: 1909
ISBN Publisher's Prefix: 3-87129

Conradi-Reiseführer oHG*, Hans-Heinrich und Anneliese Feldhoff, Vordere Str 2, Postfach 1206, D-7012 Fellbach
Publicity Manager: Hans-Heinrich Feldhoff

Associate Company: Conradi-Verlagsgellschaft mbH (qv)
Subjects: Books concerning holidaymaking, especially travel guides to England, Scotland, Ireland and Wales

Conradi-Verlagsgellschaft mbH*, Vordere Str 2, Postfach 1206, D-7012 Fellbach
Publicity Manager: Hans-Heinrich Feldhoff
Associate Company: Conradi-Reiseführer OHG (qv)
Subject: Lore of the Theatre

Copress-Verlag, Schellingstr 39-43, Postfach 401280, D-8000 München 40 Tel: (089) 287202 Cable Add: Copress München Telex: 524368
Man Dir: Oskar Müller; *Editorial:* Karl-Heinz Huba; *Sales:* Helmut Simler
Subjects: Juveniles, Education, Nonfiction, Games, Sports
ISBN Publisher's Prefix: 3-7679

Cornelsen & Oxford University Press GmbH, Lützowstr 106, Postfach 3144, D-1000 Berlin 30 Tel: (030) 2621060/2621018 Telex: 184968 cvk b
Man Dirs: Peter Collier, Goetz Manth
Orders to: Cornelsen-Velhagen & Klasing VG (qv), Kammerratsheide 66, D-4800 Bielefeld 1
Parent Companies: Cornelsen-Velhagen & Klasing Verlag für Lehrmedien (Teaching Aids and Textbook Publisher) (qv); Oxford University Press, UK (qv)
Subjects: Secondary & Primary Textbooks in English Language Teaching
1978: 27 titles *Founded:* 1971
ISBN Publisher's Prefix: 3-8109

Cornelsen-Velhagen & Klasing Verlagsgesellschaft*, Kammerratsheide 66, Postfach 8729, D-4800 Bielefeld 1 Tel: (0521) 24071 Cable Add: Cevauka Bielefeld Telex: 932909 cvkbi d
Associate Company: Cornelsen & Oxford University Press
Subjects: Mainly Teaching Aids in National Sciences, Languages, History, Geography, Social Studies, Sexual Instruction

Cornelsen-Velhagen & Klasing GmbH & Co Verlag für Lehrmedien KG, Lützowstr 105, Postfach 3144, D-1000 Berlin 30 Tel: (030) 2621071 Cable Add: Cevaukamedien Telex: 184968
Man Dirs: Franz Cornelsen, Hans-H Kannegiesser, Manfred Lösing, Goetz Manth
Associate Companies: Cornelsen-Velhagen & Klasing VG (qv); Cornelsen & Oxford University Press GmbH (qv)
Subjects: Textbooks, Audio-Visual aids for all student levels and adults
Founded: 1968
ISBN Publisher's Prefix: 3-464

Corona Verlag KG, see Dipa-Verlag und Druck

Corvus Verlag*, Kurfürstendamm 157, Postfach 311120, D-1000 Berlin Tel: (030) 8854041 Telex: 0184212
Subjects: Popular Nonfiction, Lexicons, Handbook to divining-rod practice, Special commissions in Book Production

J **Cramer**, in den Springäckern 2, D-3300 Braunschweig Tel: (0531) 65951
Subject: Botany (Specialized Technical, Reprints, Texts in English, Latin, French etc)
1978: 156 titles *1979:* 200 titles *Founded:* 1811
ISBN Publisher's Prefix: 3-7682

Verlag **D und C***, Verlag für zeitgeschichtliche Dokumente und Curiosa, Luitpoldstr 58, D-8520 Erlangen Tel: (09131) 41505
Editorial: Hans Carl Hopferman; *Sales:* Martin Kirchner
Subject: History
ISBN Publisher's Prefix: 3-921295

D B V-Verlag*, Mühlenstr 9, Postfach 267, D-3508 Melsungen Tel: (05661) 6374
Founded: 1971
Subjects: Ornithology, Protection of Birds, Protection of the Environment/Nature
Periodical: Wir und die Vögel (The Birds and Ourselves)

D E B Verlag (Das Europäische Buch), Thielallee 34, D-1000 Berlin 33 Tel: (030) 8324051
Orders to: V V A, Postfach 7777, D-4840 Gütersloh
Dir: Tell Schwandt
Subjects: History, Philosophy, Politics, Economics, Marxism, Books on Bert Brecht
1977: 10 titles
ISBN Publisher's Prefix: 3-920303

D R W-Verlag Weinbrenner-KG, Fasanenweg 18, D-7022 Leinfelden-Echterdingen 1 Tel: (0711) 79891 Telex: 7255609 drw
Subsidiary Company: Verlagsanstalt Alexander Koch GmbH (qv)
Subjects: Forestry, Timber, Woodworking, Periodicals
ISBN Publisher's Prefix: 3-87181

D T V, see Deutscher Taschenbuch Verlag

D V A, see Deutsche Verlags-Anstalt GmbH

Damnitz Verlag GmbH+, Hohenzollernstr 144, D-8000 Munich 40 Tel: (089) 301015/301016
Man Dir: Otto Schmidl; *Sales Dir:* Erika Däbritz; *Publicity Dir:* Liesl Neumann; *Advertising Dir, Rights & Permissions:* Otto Schmidl
Subjects: General Fiction, Belles Lettres, Poetry, Biography, How-to, Music, Art, Low-priced Paperbacks, Social Science
Founded: 1965

Verlag **Darmstädter Blätter** Schwarz und Co*, Haubachweg 5, D-6100 Darmstadt Tel: (06151) 48196
Man Dir: Dr Günther Schwarz
Subjects: Semantics, Languages, Dictionaries, Philosophy, Reference, Psychology, Social Science, University, Secondary & Primary Textbooks
1977: 6 titles *1978:* 27 titles *Founded:* 1967
ISBN Publisher's Prefix: 3-87139

Werner **Dausien***, Frankfurter Landstr 32, D-6450 Hanau am Main Tel: (06181) 82353/22316
Man Dir: Werner Dausien; *Editorial:* Gerlinde Schneider
Orders to: Burgallee 67, 6450 Hanau/M Tel: (06181) 259052
Subjects: How-to, Music, Art, Reference, Juveniles, University Textbooks
Founded: 1949
Subsidiary: Verlag Müller & Kiepenheuer, German Federal Republic (qv)
Bookshop: Werner Dausien, Nürnberger-str 22, D-6450 Hanau am Main
ISBN Publisher's Prefix: 3-7684

R v **Decker's** Verlag G Schenck GmbH, im Weiher 10, Postfach 102640, D-6900 Heidelberg Tel: (06221) 489250 Telex: 0461727 huehd
Dir: Dr Hans Windsheimer
Associate Companies: Kriminalistik Verlag (qv); C F Müller Jüristischer Verlag GmbH (qv)
Subjects: Law, Economy, Admin, Post and Telecommunications, Defence, Defence Admin, Automation, Data Processing, Periodicals

Delius, Klasing und Co, Siekerwall 21, Postfach 4809, D-4800 Bielefeld 1, Tel: (0521) 67015 Cable Add: Buchklasing Telex: 0932934
Dirs: Konrad-Wilhelm Delius, Kurt Delius; *Production:* Leo Siebzehnrübl; *Publicity:* Wilhelm Meyerhenke; *Rights & Permissions:* Ilsemarie Steinbrinker
Subsidiary Company: Klasing und Co GmbH (qv)
Subjects: Yachting, Motor Boats, Seafaring and Navigation, Model Boat Building, Motor Cars
Founded: 1911
ISBN Publisher's Prefix: 3-7688

Delphin Verlag GmbH, Herzog-Wilhelm-Str 22, D-8000 Munich 2 Tel: (089) 557697/8 Cable Add: Delphinverlag Telex: 522522
Man Dir: Martin Grell; *Dir:* Klaus Müller-Crepon
Subsidiary Company: Delphin Verlag AG, Switzerland (qv)
Founded: 1963
ISBN Publisher's Prefix: 3-7735

Delp'sche Verlagsbuchhandlung, St Blasienstr 5, D-8000 Munich 40 Tel: (089) 358498 Telex: 61524
Man Dir: Heinrich Delp
Orders to: Delp, Kegetstr 11, D-8532 Bad Windesheim
Subjects: Politics, Poetry, Art, Asiatica
1978: 8 titles *Founded:* 1961
ISBN Publisher's Prefix: 3-7689

edition **der 2** Gerald Fritsch und Stefan Fritsch Buchverlag GmbH, Merseburger Str 7, D-1000 Berlin 62 Tel: (030) 7849346
Dir: Gerald Fritsch
Branch Off: Wissenschaftliche Abt, Kurfürstendamm 65, D-1000 Berlin 15
Subjects: Belles Lettres, Fiction, Poetry, Essays
1978: 3 titles *1979:* 6 titles *Founded:* 1974
ISBN Publisher's Prefix: 3-921347

Engelbert **Dessart** Verlag KG*, Wildstr 7, Postfach 1240, D-8202 Bad Aibling Tel: (08061) 4045
Man Dir: Johann Meisinger
See Siebert & Engelbert Dessart Verlag GmbH, German Federal Republic

Dr Peter **Deubner** Verlag GmbH*, Dürener Str 85, Postfach 410268, D-5000 Cologne 41 Tel: (0221) 405936
Publisher: Dr Peter Deubner; *Dir:* Jürgen Wagner
Subject: Jurisprudence (especially Fiscal Law)
1978: 50 titles *Founded:* 1974

Verlag Harri **Deutsch**, Gräfstr 47, D-6000 Frankfurt am Main 90 Tel: (0611) 777338/702467
Man Dir: Harri Deutsch; *All other offices:* Dr Anton Reiter
Subsidiary Company: Verlag Harri Deutsch, Riedstr 2, CH-3600 Thun, Switzerland
Bookshop: Naturwissenschaftliche Fachbuchhandlung Harri Deutsch, Gräfstr 47, D-6000 Frankfurt am Main 90
Subjects: Natural Sciences, Technical, Textbooks, Reference, Mathematics, Economics, Foreign Languages, Agriculture, Paperbacks
1977: 40 titles *1978:* 40 titles *Founded:* 1960
ISBN Publisher's Prefix: 3-87144

Deutsche Bibelstiftung (German Bible Foundation)*, Haupstätterstr 51, Postfach 755, D-7000 Stuttgart 1 Tel: (0711) 247341 Cable Add: Bibelhaus Stuttgart Telex: 721816 CSD
Man Dir: Dr Gernot Winter
Subject: Bibles
Founded: 1812
ISBN Publlisher's Prefix: 3-4380

Deutsche Buch-Gemeinschaft C A Koch's Verlag Nachfolger, Berliner Allee 6, Postfach 4131, D-6100 Darmstadt Tel: (06151) 8661 Cable Add: Lesestunde
Man Dir: Ernst Leonhard
Associate Company: Deutsche Buch-Gemeinschaft CA Koch's Verlag Nachfolger, Austria (qv)
Subjects: General Fiction, Belles Lettres, Poetry, Biography, History, How-to, Music, Art, Philosophy, Rerence, Juveniles
Book Club: Address as above
1977: 211 titles *1978:* 240 titles *Founded:* 1924

Deutsche Jugend-Presse-Agentur KG, see Dipa-Verlag und Druck

Deutsche Philips GmbH, see Philips GmbH

Deutsche Verlags-Anstalt GmbH (DVA), Neckarstr 121, Postfach 209, D-7000 Stuttgart 1, Tel:,(0711) 21511 Cable Add: deva Stuttgart Telex: 0722503
Man Dirs: Ulrich Frank-Planitz, Dr Hans Glücker
Foreign Rights: Mrs Märit Schütt
Subjects: Fiction, Poetry, Biography, History, Politics, Current Events, General Science, Architecture; Scientific and Specialist Magazines
Bookshop: Buchversand Herbert Krebs GmbH, Postfach 209, D-7000 Stuttgart 1
1978: 68 titles *Founded:* 1848
ISBN Publisher's Prefix: 3-421

Deutscher Apotheker Verlag Dr Roland Schmiedel GmbH und Co, Birkenwaldstr 44, Postfach 40, D-7000 Stuttgart 1 Tel: (0711) 292559 Telex: 23636 dazd
Man Dirs: Dr Hanskarl Hornüng, Hans Rotta
Associate Companies: Wissenschaftliche Verlagsgesellschaft mbH (qv); S Hirzel Verlag GmbH & Co (qv); Franz Steiner Verlag GmbH; all in Federal Republic of Germany
Subjects: Pharmacy, Periodicals
Founded: 1861
Bookshop: Deutscher Apotheker Verlag, Sortiments-Abteilung, at Company address above
ISBN Publisher's Prefix: 3-7692

Deutscher Betriebswirte-Verlag GmbH, Bleichstr 20-22, Postfach 230, D-7562 Gernsbach 1 Tel: (07224) 3091 Cable Add: dbv Gernsbach Telex: 78915 dbv-d
Man Dirs: Dr Casimir Katz, Christel Katz
Subjects: Business Administration, Management, Marketing, Company Organization, Accounting, Personnel
Bookshops: DBV-Bücherstube, Kelterplatzzentrum, Gernsbach
1978: 10 titles *1979:* 10 titles *Founded:* 1926
ISBN Publisher's Prefix: 3-921099

Deutscher Eichverlag, Burgplatz 1, Postfach 3367, D-3300 Braunschweig
Parent Company: Friedr Vieweg und Sohn GmbH (qv)

Deutscher Fachschriften-Verlag Braun GmbH & Co KG, Felsenstr 23, Postfach 2120, D-6200 Wiesbaden 1 Tel: (06121) 42785/86/87
Publisher: Dr Herbert Braun; *Publicity Manager, Rights & Permissions:* Friedrich Vohl
Subjects: Public Health, Law, Official Reports
ISBN Publisher's Prefix: 3-8078

Deutscher Fachverlag GmbH, renamed Lorch-Verlag GmbH (qv)

Deutscher Gemeindeverlag GmbH, Luxemburger Str 72, Postfach 100448, D-5000 Cologne 1 Tel: (0221) 426761 Telex: dgv köln 08882662
Br Offs: Hessbrühlstr 69, Postfach 800430, D-7000 Stuttgart 80; Alexanderstr 3, Postfach 1465, D-3000 Hanover Tel: (0511) 328721 Telex: dgv han 0922618
Jägersberg 17, Postfach 1865, D-2300 Kiel 1 Tel: (0431) 554857 Telex: dgv kiel 0292856
Philipp-Reis-Str 3, Postfach 421049, D-6500 Mainz 42 Tel: (06131) 59031/32 Telex: dgv mainz 04187768
Theresienstr, 124/1, Postfach 200625, D-8000 Munich 2 Tel: (089) 521359 Telex: dgv mu d 0523990
Postfach 2125, D-6200 Wiesbaden 1 Tel: (06131) 59031/32 Telex: dgv mainz 04187768
Parent Company: Verlag W Kohlhammer, Stuttgart (qv)
Subjects: The Company specialises in publishing texts connected with local government and laws, environmental protection, social services etc., each of the above Branch Offices being responsible for texts appropriate to the particular region, with associated computer tape and microfilm services, periodicals
ISBN Publisher's Prefix: 3-555

Deutscher Instituts-Verlag GmbH, Oberländer Ufer 84-88, Postfach 510670, D-5000 Cologne 51 Tel: (0221) 37041 Cable Add: Deutstitut Telex: 8882768
Man Dir, Rights and Permissions: Harald Schwer; *Editorial:* Wilhelm Weisser; *Sales:* Norbert Anselm; *Production:* Horst Schlechter; *Publicity:* Ludwig Matjasic
Parent Company: Institut der Deutschen Wirtschaft, Cologne (German Economics Institute)
Subsidiary Companies: Librex - Buchvertrieb der Deutschen Wirtschaft GmbH; Edition Agrippa GmbH
Subjects: Economic, Company and Educational Policy; Literature
1977: 62 titles *1978:* 65 titles *Founded:* 1951
ISBN Publisher's Prefix: 3-88054

Deutscher Kunstverlag GmbH, Vohburger Str 1, D-8000 Munich 21 Tel: (089) 564722
Subjects: Art, Pictorial Guidebooks, Regional Art Books, Guides to Artistic Monuments, Egypotology, Catalogues, Yearbooks, Periodicals
1977: 30 titles *1978:* 17 titles *Founded:* 1921
ISBN Publisher's Prefix: 3-422

Deutscher Taschenbuch Verlag GmbH & Co KG, Friedrichstr 1a, Postfach 400422, D-8000 Munich 40 Tel: (089) 397031 Telex: 05215396
Man Dir: Heinz Friedrich; *Editorial:* Maria Friedrich, Eberhard Gaupp, Dr Wolfram Goebel, Winfried Groth, Dr Walter Kumpmann; *Sales Dir:* Wolfgang Josephi; *Publicity & Advertising Dir:* Klaus Baeulke; *Rights & Permissions:* Konrad Jost
Subjects: General Fiction, Belles Lettres, Poetry, Biography, History, Music, Art, Philosophy, Reference, Religion, Juveniles, Medicine, Psychology, General and Social Science, Secondary & Primary Textbooks
1977: approx 250 titles
Founded: 1961
ISBN Publisher's Prefix: 3-423

Deutscher Verlag für Kunstwissenschaft GmbH, Lindenstr 76, D-1000 Berlin 61 Tel: (030) 2512028 Cable Add: Kunstbrief Berlin
Man Dirs: Professors Dr Heinz Peters, Dr Stephan Waetzoldt, Dr Henning Bock
Associate Company: Gebr Mann Verlag (qv)
Subject: Art in Germany, Periodicals
1978: 2 titles *Founded:* 1964
ISBN Publisher's Prefix: 3-87157

Deutscher Wirtschaftsdienst John von Freyend GmbH+, Fachverlag für Wirtschaft und Aussenhandel, Marienburger Str 22, D-5000 Cologne 51 Tel: (0221) 388011/388012 Cable Add: DWD
Sales, Rights & Permissions Dir: Peter John von Freyend; *Editorial, Production:* Edelgard Reiche; *Publicity:* Karl Ludwig Ostermann
Subjects: Loose-leaf systems covering current international economic questions; Chamber of Commerce publications; Finance, Commercial Law
1977: 3 titles *1978:* 5 titles
ISBN Publisher's Prefix: 3-87156

Eugen **Diederichs** Verlag, Brehmpl 1, Postfach 140163, D-4000 Düsseldorf 14; Bremer Str 5, Postfach 100526, D-5000 Cologne 1 Tel: (0211) 622035 (Düsseldorf); (0221) 137011 (Cologne)
Man Dirs: Dr Eugen Peter Diederichs, Ulf Diederichs; *Editorial:* Gabriele Pfau, Inge Diederichs, Christa Hinze; *Sales Dir:* Horst Biedermann; *Production:* Antje Ketteler; *Advertising & Publicity Dirs:* Ursula Albrecht, Eberhart May; *Rights & Permissions:* Christa Hinze
Orders to: Koch, Neff & Oetinger & Co, Am Wallgraben 110, D-7000 Stuttgart 80; (West Berlin) B A Claudius, Schillerstr 13, D-1000 Berlin 12
Subjects: Belles Lettres, Biography, History, Philosophy, Eastern Religion and Literature, Sociology; Illustrated collections of Folk and Fairy Tales from all countries
1977: 22 titles *1978:* 25 titles *Founded:* 1896
ISBN Publisher's Prefix: 3-424

Verlag Moritz **Diesterweg**/Otto Salle Verlag, Hochstr 31, D-6000 Frankfurt am Main 1 Tel: (0611) 13011 Telex: 413234 md d
Orders to: Koch, Neff & Oetinger & Co, Am Wallgraben 110, D-7000 Stuttgart 80
Man Dir: Dietrich Herbst; *Rights & Permissions:* Waltraud Soehnel
Subjects: Educational; Psychology, Social Science, University, Secondary & Primary Textbooks, Educational Materials
1978: 233 titles *Founded:* 1860
ISBN Publisher's Prefixes: 3-425 (Diesterweg), 3-7935 (Salle)

Verlag J H W **Dietz** Nachf GmbH, Godesberger Allee 143, Postfach 200189, D-5300 Bonn 2 Tel: (02221) 378021-378025
Orders to: Verlagsauslieferung Georg Lingenbrink, Postfach 3584, D-6000 Frankfurt am Main 1; (for Berlin) Zirk und Ellenrieder, Lützowstr 105 (bbz), D-1000 Berlin 30
Associate Company: Verlag Neue Gesellschaft GmbH (qv)
Subjects: History, Politics, Sociology, Economics, Legal, Reprints, Periodicals

134 FEDERAL REPUBLIC OF GERMANY

Dipa-Verlag und Druck GmbH & Co, Deutsche Jugend-Presse-Agentur KG, Weberstr 69-71, D-6000 Frankfurt am Main 1 Tel: (0611) 556188
Man Dir: K-W Hesse (*Administration:* Am Röckerkopf 26, D-6238 Hofheim-Lorsbach Tel: (06192) 8210
Subsidiary Company: Corona Verlag KG
Subjects: Biography, History, How-to, Music, Art, Reference, Psychology, Social Science, University Textbooks
1978: 76 titles *Founded:* 1948
ISBN Publisher's Prefix: 3-7638

Direkt Verlag*, Bremerstr 11, D-6236 Eschborn/Ts Tel: (06196) 46481
Owner, Rights & Permissions: Volker Abel
Founded: 1978
Subjects: Belles Lettres, Poetry, Social Subjects
1978: 2 titles *Founded:* 1972

Verlag **Dokumentation** Saur KG, now K G Saur Verlag KG (qv)

Don Bosco Verlag der Gesellschaft der Salesianer*, Sieboldstr 11, D-8000 Munich 80 Tel: (089) 4138349
Dir: Richard Feuerlein; *Man Dir:* Johann Ernstberger; *Editorial:* Reinhold Storkenmaier; *Sales:* Gerhard Sacher
Subjects: Education, How-to, Religion, Textbooks
Founded: 1948
Bookshop: Sieboldstr 11, D-8000 Munich 80
ISBN Publisher's Prefix: 3-7698

Dreisam-Verlag, Schwaighofstr 6, D-7800 Freiburg-im-Breisgau Tel: (0761) 77037
Subjects: Campaign literature to combat nuclear plants, military drafting; Civil Rights and student advice on dealing with authorities etc; Ecology, Socio-political, Literary Works (Prose and Poetry)
1978: 6 titles *1979:* 7 titles *Founded:* 1975
ISBN Publisher's Prefix: 3-921472

Galerie **Dreiseitel**, Richmodstr 25, D-5000 Cologne 1 Tel: (0221) 244165
Man Dir: H Dreiseitel
Subjects: Art, Illustrated Books (with original illustrations)
1977: 3 titles *1978/9:* 7 titles *Founded:* 1971

Cecilie **Dressler** Verlag*, Poppenbütteler Chaussee 55, Postfach 220, D-2000 Hamburg 65 Tel: (040) 6070484
Telex: 02174230
Man Dirs: Thomas Huggle, Uwe Weitendorf
Subjects: Fiction, Juveniles, Paperbacks
Founded: 1928

Droemersche Verlagsanstalt Th Knaur Nachf*, Rauchstr 9-11, Postfach 800480, D-8000 Munich 80 Tel: (089) 982501/3
Cable Add: Droemerverlag Telex: 522707
Man Dir: Willy Droemer; *Editorial:* Dr Dieter Harnack, Franz Nikolaus Mehling; *Sales Manager:* Ernst Linsmeier; *Publicity Manager:* Peter Breuer; *Rights & Permissions:* Alice Meyer
Subjects: General Fiction, Nonfiction, Dictionaries, Art, Juveniles, Reference, Paperbacks, Textbooks, Current Events, Architecture, Maps, Mathematics, Psychology
Founded: 1901
ISBN Publisher's Prefix: 3-426

Droste Verlag GmbH, Pressehaus am Martin-Luther-Platz, Postfach 1122, D-4000 Düsseldorf 1 Tel: 8851 Cable Add: Drosteverlag Düsseldorf
Man Dir: Dr Joseph Schaffrath; *Publishing Dir:* Dr Manfred Lotsch; *Editorial:* Heidemarie Alertz; *Sales:* Klaus Ehrke; *Production, Publicity:* Helmut Schwanen
Subsidiary Companies: Verlag Die Braunkohle, Postfach 1122, D-4000 Düsseldorf 1; Wilhelm Knapp Verlag (qv)
Subjects: History, Current Affairs, Politics, Economics, Social Sciences, Art, Belles Lettres, Humour and Satire, Picture Books, Düsseldorf local interest books
Bookshop: Buchhandlung Droste, Pressehaus am Martin-Luther-Platz, Postfach 1122, D-4000 Düsseldorf 1
1978: 72 titles *1979:* 62 titles *Founded:* 1711
ISBN Publisher's Prefix: 3-7700

Druckenmüller Verlag, Martiusstr 8, D-8000 Munich 40 Tel: (089) 348074
Telex: 5215517
Associate Companies: Artemis & Winkler Verlag, Munich (qv); Verlag für Architektur, Munich (qv); Artemis Verlag, Zürich, Switzerland (qv)
Subjects: Encyclopedia of Classical Antiquity, Classical Works, European Ancient History

Druffel-Verlag, Assenbucherstr 28, D-8131 Leoni am Starnbergersee Tel: (08151) 5326
Dir: Gert Sudholt; *Publisher:* Ursula Sündermann;
Subjects: Popular German History (especially relative to World War II), German Politics, Controversial Reportage
ISBN Publisher's Prefix: 3-8061

Monika **Dülk** Verlag*, Kaiserdamm 12, D-1000 Berlin 19 Tel: (030) 322585
Subjects: City maps, Travel Guides

Horst-Werner **Dumjahn** Verlag, Parcusstr 9, Postfach 1746, D-6500 Mainz 1 Tel: 06131/21010
Man Dir and Other Offices: Horst-Werner Dumjahn
Orders to: Vereinigte Verlagsauslieferung (VVA), Postfach 7777, D-4830 Gütersloh
Subjects: Railways and Railway History (Federal German and other countries)
Bookshop: Versandbuchhandlung und Antiquariat Horst-Werner Dumjahn at above address (Antiquarian Bookshop and Despatch Office)
1978: 2 titles *1979:* 3 titles *Founded:* 1974
ISBN Publisher's Prefix: 3-921426

Wolfgang **Dummer** und Co, see Verlag Moderne Industrie

Ferd **Dümmlers** Verlag, Kaiserstr 31-37, Postfach 1480, D-5300 Bonn 1 Tel: (02221) 223031 Cable Add: Dümmlerbuch
Man Dir: Helmut Lehmann
Subjects: Schoolbooks and Pedagogic books for Schools of all levels, Technical and Specialised School Textbooks in Natural Sciences, Arts, Linguistics; also Sports, Hobbies, History, Politics, Periodicals
1979: 40 titles *Founded:* 1808
ISBN Publisher's Prefix: 3-427

Duncker und Humblot, Dietrich-Schäfer-Weg 9, Postfach 410329, D-1000 Berlin 41 Tel: (030) 7912026
Subjects: History, Philosophy, General & Social Science, Law, University Textbooks
1977: 245 titles *1978:* 220 titles *Founded:* 1798
ISBN Publisher's Prefix: 3-428

Dustri-Verlag Dr Karl Feistle, Bahnhofstrasse 5, Postfach 49, D-8024 Deisenhofen-Munich Tel: (089) 6132352
Dirs: Dr Karl Feistle, Hans-Peter Eckardt
Subjects: Medicine, Reference, Paperbacks, Periodicals

E O S Verlag, Erzabtei Sankt Ottilien, D-8917 Sankt Ottilen Tel: 08193/71261
Man Dir: Dr P Bernhard Sirch
Subjects: Religion, Theology, Spiritual Life, Travel, Children's Books
Bookshop: Klosterladen, D-8917 Sankt Ottillen
1977: 15 titles *Founded:* 1904
ISBN Publisher's Prefix: 3-88096, 3-920289

E R Verlags GmbH, see Symposium-Verlag

Ebeling Verlag*, Langgasse 35, Postfach 2386, D-6200 Wiesbaden 1 Tel: (06121) 39081 Telex: 4186318
Parent Company: Hasso Ebeling Verlag, Luxembourg (qv)
Subject: Art

Echter-Seelsorge Verlag*, Juliuspromenade 64, Postfach 5560, D-8700 Würzburg
Subjects: Exegesis, Bible Research, Spirituality, Books of Plates, Art Books, Stories, Periodicals

Econ Verlagsgruppe, Grupellostr 28, Postfach 9229, D-4000 Düsseldorf 1 Tel: (0211) 360516 Cable Add: Econ-Verlag Telex: 8587327
Publisher: Erwin Barth von Wehrenalp; *Man Dir & Editor-in-Chief:* Joseph Nyssen; *Sales & Marketing:* Herbert Borgartz; *Advertising & Promotion:* Michael Tochtermann
Branch Off: Ziehrerplatz 9, A-1020 Vienna, Austria
Subjects: Biography, History, Politics, Music, Art, Travel, Reference, Religion, Archaeology, Medicine, Psychology, General & Social Science, Audio-visual Teaching Aids, General Fiction
Miscellaneous: Group comprises Claassen Verlag GmbH (qv), Econ Verlag GmbH, Marion von Schröder Verlag GmbH (qv)
ISBN Publisher's Prefix: 3-430

Egoist-Verlag*, Postfach 910207, D-3000 Hanover 91 Tel: (0511) 451354
Man & Sales Dirs: E Kreutzburg, A Seide; *Publicity & Advertising Dir:* Herr Barth; *Rights & Permissions:* Herr Kreutzburg
Subject: Modern Art, Design, Belles Lettres
1977: approx 12 titles

Ehapa Verlag GmbH*, Postfach 1215, D-7000 Stuttgart Tel: (0711) 790271 Cable Add: Ehata Stuttgart Telex: 7255581 ehpd
Dir: Walter Berning; *Manager:* Adolf Kabatek; *Editorial:* A Kabatek (comics), W Berning (special magazines); *Sales:* M Klieber; *Production:* S Eberspächer; *Publicity:* U Marbach, F Spes; *Rights & Permissions:* Christine Wagner, A Kabatek, W Berning
Parent Company: Gutenberghus Publishing Service, Denmark (qv)
Associate Companies: Gutenberghus Bladene, Denmark; Hjemmet A/S, Norway; Hemmets Journal AB, Forlaget Kärnan AB, Sweden (qqv)
Subjects: Hobbies, Nonfiction, Comics, Cartoons
Founded: 1951
Miscellaneous: Publish periodical *Das Magazin der Technik*

Ehrenwirth Verlag GmbH, Postfach 860348, D-8000 Munich 86 (Located at: Vilshofenerstr 8) Tel: (089) 989025 Telex: 0529667
Publisher: Martin Ehrenwirth; *Man Dir:* Frank Auerbach; *Sales, Publicity & Advertising Dir:* Gebhard von Doering; *Editorial:* Anneliese Starke, Reinhard Stachwitz; *Rights & Permissions:* Irmengard Staudinger

Distribution: Verlegerdienst München, Postfach 1280, D-8031 Gilching
Subjects: General Fiction, History, Poetry, Biography, How-to, Reference, High-priced Paperbacks, Psychology, Social Science, University, Secondary and Primary Textbooks, Educational Materials
1977: 150 titles *1978:* 90 titles *Founded:* 1945
ISBN Publisher's Prefix: 3-431

Verlag Rena **Ehresmann***, Nikolausstr 27, D-8911 Reichling/Obb Tel: (08194) 675
Man Dir: Rena Ehresmann; *Sales & Advertising Dir:* Heinz W Ehresmann
Subjects: General Fiction, Biography
1976: 3 titles *Founded:* 1973

Eldra Taschenbuchverlag, Postfach 950171, D-5000 Cologne 91 (Located at: Am Sommerberg 29, D-5064 Roesrath 3) Tel: (02205) 81849
Man Dir: A Osterhoff
Subjects: Epic, Lyrical and Dramatic Works in paperback form
1977: 3 titles

Elitera-Verlag GmbH, see AEG-Telefunken

Ellenberg Verlag, Am Urbacher Wall 35, D-5000, also Postfach 100705, D-5000 Cologne 1 Tel: (02203) 22675
Man Dir: Dr Eduard Ellenberg
Parent Company: Ellenberg GmbH
Subsidiary Company: Theaterverlag Ellenberg
Subjects: Belles Lettres, Anthologies, Documentaries, Politics, Theology, History, Philosophy, Economics, Art, Science, Poetry, Novels, Theatre, Literature, other areas of Scholarship; Periodicals
1977: 15 titles *1978:* 28 titles *Founded:* 1974
ISBN Publisher's Prefix: 3-921369

Verlag Heinrich **Ellermann** KG, Romanstr 16, D-8000 Munich 19 Tel: (089) 133737 Cable Add: Ellerbuch, Munich
Man Dirs: Berthold und Christa Spangenberg; *Editorial, Sales, Production, Publicity, Rights & Permissions:* Christa Spangenberg
Orders to: Koch, Neff & Oetinger, Am Wallgraben 110, D-7000 Stuttgart Tel: (0711) 78601
Imprints: Edition Spangenberg
Subjects: Belles Lettres, Juveniles
1978: 19 titles *1979:* 20 titles *Founded:* 1934
ISBN Publisher's Prefix: 3-7707

Otto **Elsner** Verlagsgesellschaft mbH & Co KG*, Schöfferstr 15, Postfach 4039, D-6100 Darmstadt Tel: (06151) 891630
Man Dir: Dr Franz-G Rudl
Subjects: Belles Lettres, Poetry, Reference, Engineering, Transportation, University Textbooks
1978: 5 titles *Founded:* 1871
ISBN Publisher's Prefix: 3-87199

Elwert und Meurer GmbH, Hauptstr 101, D-1000 Berlin 62 Tel: (030) 784001
Associate Company: Karl Ohm Verlag (qv)
Subjects: Cybernetics, Psychology, Philosophy, Law, Sociology, Politics
ISBN Publisher's Prefix: 3-7669

N G **Elwert** Verlag, Reitgasse 7-9, Postfach 1128, D-3550 Marburg an der Lahn Tel: (06421) 25024 Cable Add: Elwert Marburg
Man Dir: Dr W Braun-Elwert
Subjects: History, Religion, Law, German Language & Literary History, Social Science

1977: 42 titles *1978:* 36 titles *Founded:* 1726
ISBN Publisher's Prefix: 3-7708

Encyclopaedia Britannica, Berliner Allee 47, Postfach 200251, D-4000 Düsseldorf Tel: (0211) 324945
Manager: R J Ellmers
Miscellaneous: Firm is an associate company of Encyclopaedia Britannica International Ltd, USA (see UK entry for other associates)

Friedemann von **Engel** Verlag, Friedbergstr 5, D-1000 Berlin 19 Tel: (030) 3233145
Man Dir: F V Engel
Subsidiary Company: Globetrotter-Verlag, at same address
Subjects: "Tips für Trips" series of travel handbooks

Engelbert-Verlag, Gebr Zimmermann, Widukindplatz 2, Postfach 120, D-5893 Balve/Sauerland Tel: (02375) 631 Cable Add: Gezet Balve Telex: 827755 gezi d
Publisher: Heinz Zimmermann; *Reader:* Alfons Schumacher; *Production:* Heinz Droste; *Sales Manager:* Helmut Levermann
Subjects: Juveniles, Popular Science, Information Books; General Fiction and Nonfiction
Founded: 1930
ISBN Publisher's Prefix: 3-536

F **Englisch** Verlag GmbH, Webergasse 12, Postfach 2309, D-6200 Wiesbaden Tel: (06121) 39478/9 Telex: 4186741
Man Dir: F-I Englisch; *Editorial, Sales, Rights & Permissions:* R Fuhr; *Production, Publicity:* G Heigel
Orders to: Vereinigte Verlagsauslieferung (VVA), Reinhard Mohn OHG, Postfach 7777, D-4830 Gütersloh
Subjects: General Nonfiction, Folk and Myth, Facsimile editions
1978: 22 titles *1979:* 25 titles *Founded:* 1973
ISBN Publisher's Prefix: 3-88140

Ferdinand **Enke** Verlag, Herdweg 63, Postfach 1304, D-7000 Stuttgart 1 Tel: (0711) 20471 Cable Add: Enkebuch Telex: 721942
Man Dir: Dr med hc Günther Hauff, Dr Jur Albrecht Greuner, Frau Dr M Kuhlmann; *Sales Dir, Rights & Permissions:* Joachim Niendorf; *Publicity:* Jürgen Ritter
Subjects: MediCine, Psychology, Social Science, Veterinary, Geology, Chemistry, University Textbooks, Scientific Journals
1977: 65 titles *Founded:* 1837
ISBN Publisher's Prefix: 3-432

Ensslin und Laiblin Verlag GmbH & Co KG, Harretstr 6, Postfach 754, D-7412 Eningen Tel: (07121) 8471/2/3 Cable Add: Buchhaus Reutlingen Telex: 0729733
Man Dir: Joachim Ulrich Hebsaker; *Editorial:* Grit Hebsaker, Sylvia Novák; *Sales:* Gerda Uecker, Lisa Lutz; *Production:* Monika Conzelmann; *Publicity:* Ellen Abel; *Rights & Permissions:* J U Hebsaker, Grit Hebsaker
Branch Off: Harretstr 6, D-7412 Eningen
Subjects: Children's Books
1978: 26 titles *1979:* 19 titles *Founded:* 1818
ISBN Publisher's Prefix: 3-7709

Hans P **Eppinger***, Scheffelsteige 28, D-7170 Schwäbisch Hall Tel: (0791) 51652 Cable Add: Eppinger-Verlag Schwäbisch Hall
Man Dir: Hans Paul Eppinger
Subjects: Belles Lettres, Picture Books,

History, Anthropology, Juveniles
Founded: 1970
ISBN Publisher's Prefix: 3-87176

Horst **Erdmann** Verlag für Internationalen Kulturaustausch, Hartmayerstr 117, Postfach 1380, D-7400 Tübingen 1 Tel: (07071) 62061/2 Cable Add: Erdmannverlag Tübingen Telex: 7262741 erdm
Publicity & Sales Department: Milanweg 1, D-7400 Tübingen Tel: (07071) 64409
Man Dir: Horst J Erdmann; *Editorial and Production:* Dr Gernot Giertz; *Sales and Publicity:* Katja Tenholt; *Rights & Permissions:* Margarete Graf
Orders to: VA Koch, Neff & Oetinger, Postfach 800620, D-7000 Stuttgart 80
Branch Off: Horst Erdmann Verlag & Co, Bachofenstr 10, CH-4000 Basel, Switzerland
Subjects: General Fiction, Belles Lettres, Poetry, Biography, History, How-to, Reference, Educational Materials
1977: 23 titles *Founded:* 1956
ISBN Publisher's Prefix: 3-7711

Eremiten-Presse und Verlag (Huelsmanns und Reske GmbH), Fortunastr 11, Eremiten-Haus, Postfach 170143, D-4000 Düsseldorf 1 Tel: (0211) 660590
Man Dirs: Dieter Huelsmanns, Friedolin Reske
Subjects: General Fiction, Belles Lettres, Poetry, Music, Art, High- & Low-priced Paperbacks
1977: 20 titles *Founded:* 1949
ISBN Publisher's Prefix: 3-87365

Edition **Eres** Horst Schubert Musikverlag, Feldhäuser Str 94, Postfach 1220, D-2804 Lilienthal-Bremen Tel: (04298) 1676
Man Dir: Horst Schubert
Subjects: Music, Art, High-priced Paperbacks, University, Secondary & Primary Textbooks, Educational Materials
Founded: 1946
ISBN Publisher's Prefix: 3-87204

Wilhelm **Ernst** und Sohn Verlag für Architektur und Technische Wissenschaften, Hohenzollerndamm 170, D-1000 Berlin 31 Tel: (030) 860376/7/8 Telex: 0184143 Cable Add: Ernstsohn Berlin
Dir: Karlheinz Grassmann; *Editorial, Rights & Permissions:* Wolfgang Junge; *Sales:* Wilhelm Schreiber, H-J Winterstein; *Production:* W Schreiber; *Publicity:* Bärbel Schneider
Branch Off: Flüggenstr 13, D-8000 Munich 19; Am Haferkamp 37, D-4000 Düsseldorf 13
Subjects: Technical, Architecture
Bookshop: Gropius, Technische Fachbuchhandlung, Hohenzollerndamm 170, D-1000 Berlin 31
1977: 30 titles *1978:* 35 titles *Founded:* 1851
Miscellaneous: Member of ABV (Arbeitsgemeinschaft Baufachverlage)
ISBN Publisher's Prefix: 3-433

Erota-Press, see Odörfer-Verlags GmbH

Euphorion Verlag*, Egenolffstr 14, D-6000 Frankfurt am Main 1
Man Dir: H Imhoff; *Sales Manager:* Roderick Klein; *Publicity Dir:* Ulrich Raschke; *Rights and Permissions:* Peter Kochanski
Subjects: Belles Lettres, Poetry, Philosophy
Book Club: Freundeskreis des Euphorion Verlages, Neumannstr 13, D-6000 Frankfurt/M 50
Founded: 1963

Verlag **Europa-Lehrmittel**, Nourney, Vollmer & Co OHG, Postfach 201815, D-5600 Wuppertal 12 (Located at: Kleiner Werth 50) Tel: (0202) 556070
Managing Partner: Helmut Nourney; *General Manager:* Heinz Stühmer MA
Subjects: Textbooks for School and Professional use: in Metallurgy, Automobile, Electrical, Electronics, Physics, Building, Timber, Economics
1978: 87 titles *1979:* 92 titles *Founded:* 1947
ISBN Publisher's Prefix: 3-8085

Das **Europäische Buch**, see D E B Verlag

Europäische Gemeinschaften (European Communities)*, Zitelmannstr 22, D-5300 Bonn Tel: 238041 Telex: 886648
Subjects: Monographs, Documents, Periodicals on European integration, Official and Business Reports, Studies of Competition, Industry and Agriculture, European Instructional and Information Literature, Periodical — *EG Magazin*

Verlag **europäische Ideen**, Postfach 246, 1 Berlin 37 (Located at: Mühlenstrasse 17b) Tel: (030) 8111852
Subjects: Reprints of all the Works of Erich Mühsam, Anarchist, comprising some 33 titles, all of a socio-political nature

Europäische Verlagsanstalt GmbH*, Deutz-Kalker-Str 46, Postfach 210140, D-5000 Cologne 21 Tel: (0221) 82821 Telex: Bund d 8873362
Man Dir: Tomas Kosta; *Editorial:* Günther Heyder; *Sales Dir:* Karl-Ernst Sakobielski, Waldemar Block; *Rights & Permissions:* Lieselotte Vorwerk
Subjects: History, Philosophy, Psychology, Social Science, Judaica, Political Science, Economics, Trade Unions
1977: approx 40 titles *Founded:* 1946
Miscellaneous: Publication — *Kritische Justiz, Demokratie und Sozialismus*
ISBN Publisher's Prefix: 3-434

Europrisma-Verlag, Auf dem Gelling 7, D-5800 Hagen Tel: (02331) 46655
Dir: Stephan Ramrath

Verlag der **Evangelisch Lutherische Mission**, Schenkstr 69, D-8520 Erlangen Tel: (09131) 33064
Publisher: Christoph Jahn; *Sales Manager:* Eva Mueller
Subjects: Juveniles, Calendars, Religion, Social Science, Paperbacks
1978: 15 titles
ISBN Publisher's Prefix: 3-87214

Verlag und Schriftenmission der **Evangelischer Gesellschaft** für Deutschland GmbH, Kaiserstr 78, D-5600 Wuppertal 1 Tel: (0202) 301313
Publishing House and Scriptural Mission of the German Evangelical Society
Man Dir: Ulrich Affeld; *Sales, Production, Publicity:* Herbert Becker
Subjects: Religious Literature; Telos and Junior Telos texts (see Miscellaneous)
1977: 10 titles *1978:* 8 titles *Founded:* 1954
Miscellaneous: Firm is a member of the Telos group (qv) publishing evangelical paperbacks
ISBN Publisher's Prefix: 3-87857

Evangelischer Missionsverlag*, Postfach 1380, D-7015 Korntal-Münchingen 1 Tel: (0711) 831083
Man Dir: Erwin Scherer
Subjects: Religion, Juveniles, Educational Materials
Founded: 1920

Bookshop: Buchhandlung des Evangelischen Missionsverlag, D-7015 Korntal-Münchingen 1, Postfach 1380
1977: 1 title
ISBN Publisher's Prefix: 3-7714

Evangelischer Presseverband für Bayern eV, Birkerstr 22, D-8000 Munich 19 Tel: (089) 184031 Telex: 0523718
Bavarian Evangelical Press Union
Dirs: Richard Kolb, Hans-Joachim Pfalzgraf; *Publicity Manager:* Elfi Barth
Subsidiary Company: Claudius Verlag GmbH (qv)
Subjects: Evangelical Press Service, School Books, Song Books, Christian weekly periodical
Founded: 1932
ISBN Publisher's Prefix: 3-583

Evangelisches Verlagswerk GmbH, Stafflenbergstr 44, Postfach 927, D-7000 Stuttgart 1 Tel: (0711) 241495
Man Dir: Willy Collmer
Subject: Religion
1977: 5 titles *1978:* 6 titles *Founded:* 1947
ISBN Publisher's Prefix: 3-7715

Expanded Media Editions, Herwarthstr 27, D-5300 Bonn Tel: (02221) 655887
Editorial, Sales, Production, Publicity, Rights & Permissions: S Pociao; *Editorial, Production, Publicity:* Walter Hartmann
Associated Companies: see under Pro Media, Berlin (Major Booksellers)
Subjects: Belles Lettres, Poetry, Music, Art, High-priced Paperbacks
1978: 3 titles *Founded:* 1969
Bookshop: Pociao's Book Shop, Herwarthstr 27, D-5300 Bonn
ISBN Publisher's Prefix: 3-88030

Fackelträger-Verlag Schmidt-Küster GmbH, Ricklinger Stadtweg 118, D-3000 Hanover 91 Tel: (0511) 454088
Man Dir: Hans Rauschning; *Sales:* Siegfried Liebrecht
Subjects: General Fiction, Poetry, Biography, History, How-to, Art, Juveniles
1978: 12 titles *Founded:* 1949
ISBN Publisher's Prefix: 3-7716

Fackelverlag G Bowitz GmbH*, Herdweg 29-31, Postfach 442, D-7000 Stuttgart 1 Tel: (0711) 20171 Cable Add: Fackelverlag Stuttgart Telex: 0722875
Despatch Off: Schockenriedstr 46, D-7000 Stuttgart 80
Br Off: A-6971 Hard-Bei-Bregenz, Ankergasse 18a, Austria
Subjects: General Fiction, History, How-to, Reference, Dictionaries, Low-priced Paperbacks
Book Club: Fackel-Buchklub
Founded: 1919
ISBN Publisher's Prefix: 3-87220

Falk- Verlag für Landkarten & Stadtpläne Gerhard Falk GmbH, Burchardstr 8, Postfach 102122, D-2000 Hamburg 1 Tel: (040) 331981 Cable Add: falkverlag Telex: 02162175
Man Dir: Dr Helge Lintzhöft, Handelsregister AG Hamburg HRB 23204
Subjects: Maps, Guidebooks, Phrasebooks
1977: 14 titles *1978:* 12 titles *Founded:* 1945
ISBN Publisher's Prefix: 3-920317 and 3-88445

Falken-Verlag Erich Sicker KG, Schöne Aussicht 21, Postfach 1120, D-6272 Niedernhausen Tel: (06127) 3011/3015 Telex: 4186585
Publisher: Frank Sicker; *Sales:* Manfred Abrahamsberg; *Production:* Horst Gemmerich; *Rights & Permissions:* Jo Klein

Subjects: Health, Hobbies, Continuing Education, Family Life, Gardening, Cooking, Games, Sports
1977: 75 titles *Founded:* 1923
ISBN Publisher's Prefix: 3-8068

Dr Martin **Faltermaier**, see Juventa Verlag

Favorit-Verlag Huntemann & Co*, Stettiner Str 16, Postfach 1549, D-7550 Rastatt Tel: (07222) 22254/5 Cable Add: favoritverlag Telex: 0786630
Subjects: Juveniles, Calendars

Willy F P **Fehling** GmbH*, Spichernstr 22-26, Postfach 1960, D-3000 Hanover Tel: (0511) 315051 Cable Add: Fehlingwerk Hannover Telex: 0922758
Publisher: Werner von Holtzendorff-Fehling; *Man Dir, Editorial:* Günther Ostermeier; *Production:* Gerd Gerhold
Orders to: B L V, Lothstr 29, D-8000 Munich 40
Subject: Horticulture
1977: 6 titles *Founded:* 1912
ISBN Publisher's Prefix: 3-921144

Feuervogel-Verlag GmbH*, Gerh-Hauptmann Ring 107-109, Postfach 550122, D-6000 Frankfurt am Main Tel: (0611) 574257
Man Dir: Georg Treguboff
Subjects: Historical novels and documentation concerning post-1917 Russia
1977: 6 titles *Founded:* 1971
ISBN Publisher's Prefix: 3-921148

Wolfgang **Fietkau** Verlag*, Gabainstr 5, D-1000 Berlin 46 Tel: (030) 7743492
Publisher: Wolfgang Fietkau
Founded: 1959
Subject: Poetry, Belles Lettres
ISBN Publisher's Prefix: 3-87352

Emil **Fink** Verlag*, Heidehofstr 15, D-7000 Stuttgart 1 Tel: (0711) 465330
Publisher: Richard Scheibel
Subjects: Arts, Maps
ISBN Publisher's Prefix: 3-7717

J **Fink-Kümmerly & Frey** Verlag GmbH, Gebelsbergstr 41, D-7000 Stuttgart 1 Tel: (0711) 643091 Cable Add: Buch-Fink Telex: 723737 fkfd
Dir: Harry Neubauer; *Public Relations:* Gina Ahrend
Subjects: Touring and walking guides to regions of Germany and Europe and related Non-fiction
1978: 180 current titles
Miscellaneous: Firm has developed from an association between the German company J Fink (founded 1894) and the Swiss cartographic company Kümmerly und Frey (founded 1852). The latter firm also continues as an independent company in Switzerland (qv)
ISBN Publisher's Prefix: 3-7718

Wilhelm **Fink** Verlag KG, Nikolaistr 2, D-8000 Munich 40 Tel: (089) 340434/347246 Cable Add: Fink München
Subjects: History, Literature, Law Study, Art, Criticism, Philosophy, Linguistics, Languages, Music, Classical Archaeology, Sociology, Psychology
1978: 98 titles
ISBN Publisher's Prefix: 3-7705

Finken-Verlag, Zimmersmühlenweg 40, Postfach 1420, D-6370 Oberursel/Ts Tel: 53073 Cable Add: Finkenverlag Oberursel
Dir: Manfred Krick
Subjects: Juveniles, Textbooks, Education, Games
1978: 10 titles
ISBN Publisher's Prefix: 3-8084

Gustav **Fischer** Verlag+, Wollgrasweg 49, Postfach 720143, D-7000 Stuttgart 72 (Hohenheim) Tel: (0711) 455038 Cable Add: Fischerbuch
Man Dirs: Bernd von Breitenbuch, Dr W D von Lucius; *Sales, Advertising & Publicity Dir:* Gerhard Weber; *Rights & Permissions:* Dr W D von Lucius
Branch Off: Gustav Fischer, 175 Fifth Ave, New York, NY 10010, USA
Subjects: Medicine, Biology, Anthropology, Psychology, General & Social Science, Paperbacks, University Textbooks, Scientific Journals
1977: 120 titles *Founded:* 1878
ISBN Publisher's Prefix: 3-437

Rita G **Fischer** Verlag, Alt Fechenheim 75, D-6000 Frankfurt 61 Tel: (0611) 422069/412048
Man Dir: Rita G Fischer
Subjects: Medicine, Politics, Psychology, Engineering, General and Social Science, How-to, University Textbooks, High-priced Paperbacks
1978: 50 titles *1979:* 100 titles *Founded:* 1977
ISBN Publisher's Prefix: 3-88323

S **Fischer** Verlag GmbH, Geleitsstr 25, Postfach 700480, D-6000 Frankfurt am Main 70 Tel: (0611) 60621 Cable Add: Buchfischer Telex: 0412410
Man Dir: Monika Schoeller; *Editorial:* Ivo Frenzel; *Sales:* Ulrick Fritz; *Production:* Wilfried Meiner; *Publicity:* Ulrich Meier; *Rights and Permissions:* Cornelia Wohlfarth
Subsidiary Companies: Fischer Taschenbuch Verlag GmbH (qv); Wolfgang Krüger Verlag GmbH (qv)
Subjects: General Fiction and Nonfiction, Belles Lettres, Poetry, Biography, History, Philosophy, Low- & High-priced Paperbacks, Psychology, Social Science, University Textbooks, Music, Art, Reference Books for the layman
1977: 73 titles *Founded:* 1886
ISBN Publisher's Prefix: 3-10

W **Fischer** Verlag+*, Stresemannstr 30, Postfach 621, D-3400 Göttingen Tel: (0551) 62038/9 Telex: 96746
Dir: Wilhelm Fischer; *Sales Manager:* Hans-Walter Planke
Subject: Juvenile Fiction and Nonfiction
1977: 42 titles *Founded:* 1948
ISBN Publisher's Prefix: 3-439

Fischer Taschenbuch Verlag GmbH, Geleitstr 25, Postfach 700480, D-6000 Frankfurt am Main 70 Tel: (0611) 60621 Cable Add: Buchfischer Telex: 0412410
Man Dir: Monika Schoeller; *Editorial:* Iwo Frenzel; *Sales, Publicity:* Ulrich Meier; *Production:* Wilfried Meiner; *Rights & Permissions:* Cornelia Wohlfarth
Parent Company: S Fischer Verlag GmbH (qv)
Subjects: General Fiction & Nonfiction, Paperbacks
1977: 193 titles *Founded:* 1952
ISBN Publisher's Prefix: 3-596

Verlag Johannes **Fix***, Sonnenscheinstr 4, Postfach 1221, D-7060 Schorndorf Tel: (07181) 3236 Cable Add: Fix-Verlag Schorndorf
Man Dir: Johannes Fix
Subjects: Religion, Juveniles
ISBN Publisher's Prefix: 3-87228

Fleischhauer und Spohn Verlag, Maybachstr 18, Postfach 301160, D-7000 Stuttgart 30 Tel: (0711) 89241 Telex: 723113 umco d
Owned by: Dr Max Bez, Thomas Bez, Ursula Roth; *Man Dir:* Wolfgang Stammler

Associate Company: Barsortiment G Umbreit GmbH und Co, Maybachstr 18, D-7000 Stuttgart 30
Subjects: Belles Lettres, Travel Literature, Regional Literature
Founded: 1830
ISBN Publisher's Prefix: 3-87230

Focus-Verlag, Grünbergerstr 16, Postfach 110328, D-6300 Giessen Tel: (0641) 34760
Man Dirs: Herr Mende & Herr Schmidt; *Sales Dir, Rights & Permissions:* Herr Mende; *Publicity & Advertising Dir:* Herr Schmidt
Subjects: History, Reference, High-priced Paperbacks, Psychology, Social Science, University Textbooks
1977: 30 titles *Founded:* 1970
ISBN Publisher's Prefix: 3-920352

Alfred **Förg** GmbH & Co KG, see Rosenheimer Verlagshaus

Forkel-Verlag GmbH, Königsträssle 2, Postfach 104, D-7000 Stuttgart 70 Tel: (0711) 764032 Cable Add: Forkelverlag Stuttgart; also Felsenstr 23, Postfach 2120, D-6200 Wiesbaden-Dotzheim Tel: (06121) 42785
Man Dir: Dr Herbert Braun; *Sales & Advertising Dir, Publicity, Rights & Permissions:* Friedrich Vohl
Br Off: Felsenstr 23, Postfach 2120, D-6200 Wiesbaden 1
Subjects: Business Administration, Business Law, Promotion & Sales
Bookshop: Forkel-Kundendienst, Felsenstr 23, Postfach 2120, D-6200 Wiesbaden 1
1977: 17 titles *1978:* 16 titles
ISBN Publisher's Prefix: 3-7719

Rat für **Formgebung**, Eugen-Bracht-Weg 6, 6100 Darmstadt Tel: (06151) 44051
Editorial: Georg Buchner
Subjects: Industrial Design, Graphic Design, Architecture

Fortschritt für Alle-Verlag+, Schlossweg 2, D-8501 Feucht Tel: (09128) 3126 Cable Add: Fortschrit
Man Dir: Erika Herbst
Orders to: Auslieferung-Lebenskunde Vertrieb, Jägerstr 4, D-4000 Düsseldorf 1
Subjects: Popular Explanation of Scientific Advances
1978: 1 title *Founded:* 1974
ISBN Publisher's Prefix: 3-920304

Fox produktionen traude Aubeck, Postfach 1106, D-7550 Rastatt Tel: (07245) 5536
Subjects: Lyrical Poetry (individual vols and anthologies), Nonfiction by new authors

A **Francke** GmbH, Dachauer Str 42, Postfach 200909, D-8000 Munich Tel: (089) 594713 Cable Add: Franckeverlag Munich
Dir: C L Lang
Br Off: Francke Verlag, Hochfeldstr 113, Postfach, CH-Berne 26 Switzerland (qv)
Subjects: Philosophy, Literature, History, Reference, Paperbacks, Linguistics
Founded: 1959

Verlag der **Francke Buchhandlung** GmbH*, Am Schwanhof 19, Postfach 640, D-3550 Marburg/Lahn Tel: (06421) 25260
Man Dir, Editorial, Production, Publicity: Gerhard Kuhlmann; *Sales:* Liselotte Kerste
Subjects: Evangelical Theology, Biblical Studies, Christian Books for Children
Bookshops: in Marburg, Hebronberg, Gunzenhausen, Velbert, Lemförde, Oberursel
1976: 35 titles *1977:* 58 titles *Founded:* 1950

Miscellaneous: Firm is contributor to the Telos series of evangelical paperbacks (qv)
ISBN Publisher's Prefix: 3-88224

Franckh'sche Verlagshandlung W Keller & Co, Pfizerstr 5-7, Postfach 640, D-7000 Stuttgart 1 Tel: (0711) 21911 Cable Add: Kosmosverlag Stuttgart Telex: 0721669 kosm d
Dirs: R Keller, C Keller, E Nehmann; *Sales Dir:* A Düker; *Production:* H J Staelin; *Publicity Dir:* W Wollmann; *Rights & Permissions:* Mrs Ehrler
Subsidiary Companies: Franz Mittelbach-Verlag, Verlag Der Neue Schulmann (both at Pfizerstr 5-7, D-7000 Stuttgart 1); W Spemann Verlag (qv)
Subjects: Popular Science, Juveniles, General Reference, Technology, Railway Literature, Hobbies, Care of Pets/Animals, Nature Study, Aquarium; Periodicals and Records
Book Club: KOSMOS-Gesellschaft der Naturfreunde
Bookshop: Richard Bucholz, Alexanderstr 27, D-7000 Stuttgart 1
1977: 130 titles *1978:* 100 titles *Founded:* 1822
ISBN Publisher's Prefix: 3-440

Verlag **Frankfurter Bücher**, part of Societäts-Verlag (qv)

Frankfurter Fachverlag Michael Kohl GmbH & Co KG, Emil Sulzbach Str 12, Postfach 970115, D-6000 Frankfurt am Main 97 Tel: (0611) 778410 and 776513
Associate Company: Kohl's Technischer Verlag Erwin Kohl GmbH & Co KG (qv)
Subjects: Electrical Engineering, Electronics, Industries, Crafts, Textbooks
ISBN Publisher's Prefix: 3-87234

Verlag **Frankfurter Kinderbücher** GmbH*, Forsthausstrasse 9, D-6246 Glashuetten 1 Tel: (06174) 61116
Publisher: Gerhard Hirschfeld
Parent Company: aspekte verlag gmbH (qv)
Imprint: Verlag Frankfurter Kinderbücher, Glashuetten/Taunus
Subjects: Picture Books and Textbooks for Children
1977: 2 titles *Founded:* 1976
ISBN Publisher's Prefix: 3-88162

Fränkische Gesellschafts-Druckerei Würzburg/Echter Verlag*, Juliuspromenade 64, D-8700 Würzburg, Postfach 5560 Tel: (0931) 50258 Telex: 068862 Cable Add: Echterverlag
Dirs: Elmar Wegner, Franz L Schwarz
Subjects: Religion, Art, Fiction, Youth, Periodicals
Founded: 1900
Miscellaneous: Publish several magazines
ISBN Publisher's Prefix: 3-429

Frankonius Verlag GmbH, Wiesbadener Str 1, Postfach 140, D-6250 Limburg 1 Tel: (06431) 401211 Telex: 0484764 palan d
Man Dir: Engelbert Tauscher; *Publicity:* Klemens Holdener; *Editorial:* Ursula Mock
Subjects: Textbooks for modern teaching methods, covering: History, Languages, Social Sciences, Physical Sciences, Pedagogy and Training, Sports
1978: 20 titles *Founded:* 1976
ISBN Publisher's Prefix: 3-87962

Verlag Ernst **Franz** und Sternberg-Verlag, Max Planck Str 25, Postfach 1262, D-7430 Metzingen/Württemberg Tel: (07123) 6237 Telex: 07245334
Publisher: Gerhard Heinzelmann
Subjects: Christian comment and exegesis;

138 FEDERAL REPUBLIC OF GERMANY

Swabian devotions
1977: 4 titles *1978:* 6 titles
ISBN Publisher's Prefix: 3-7722

Franzis-Verlag, Karlstr 37, Postfach 370120, D-8000 Munich 2 Tel: (089) 5117/1 Telex: 522301
Dir: Peter Mayer; *Sales & Publicity Manager:* Georg Geschke; *Rights & Permissions:* Siegfried Pruskil
1978: 21 titles *Founded:* 1924
ISBN Publisher's Prefix: 3-7723

Frauen-Selbstverlag*, Gustav-Müller-Platz 4, D-1000 Berlin 62 Tel: (030) 7849129
Subjects: Literature by and about Women, Calendars, Stories, Pedagogy, Psychiatry, Medicine, Poetry, Economics
Miscellaneous: Distribution is by Frauenbuchvertrieb, Mehringdamm 32-34 D-1000 Berlin 61 Tel: (030) 2511666

Frauenbuchverlag, Kreittmayrstr 26, D-8000 Munich 2 Tel: (089) 192970
Parent Company: Weismann Verlag - Frauenbuchverlag GmbH (qv)
Subjects: Political Texts on Women's Emancipation, Reportage, Novels, Cartoons, Illustrated Books

Frauenkalender Selbstverlag*, Breitenbachplatz 17, D-1000 Berlin 33 Tel: (0611) 654151
Subjects: Literature by and about Women, Calendars

Verlag **Frauenoffensive**, Kellerstr 39, D-8000 Munich 80 Tel: (089) 485102
Dirs: U Bauer, R Guckert, S Kahn-Ackermann, S Kohlstadt, G Kowitzke, G Meixner; *Editorial:* S K-Ackermann, G Kowitzke; *Sales:* S Kohlstadt; *Production:* R Guckert; *Publicity:* G Meixner
Subjects: Feminist publications, Posters and Records on Feminist Themes
1977: 10 titles *1978:* 13 titles *Founded:* 1976
ISBN Publisher's Prefix: 3-12045

Verlag **Frauenpolitik**, see VFP GmbH

Verlag **Frech**, Vaihinger Landstr 4, D-7000 Stuttgart 1 Tel: (0711) 691011
Man & Sales Dir: E A Krauss; *Publicity Dir, Rights & Permissions:* Mrs I Euler; *Advertising Dir:* W Krauss
Subjects: "Topp" series of books on crafts, hobbies and popular electronics
1978: 240 titles *1979:* 320 titles *Founded:* 1954
ISBN Publisher's Prefix: 3-7724

Verlag **freies Geistesleben***, Haussmann Str 76, D-7000 Stuttgart Tel: (0711) 283255
Man Dir: Dr W Niehaus; *Sales:* Heinrich Didwiszus
Subjects: Belles Lettres, Poetry, Biography, History, How-to, Music, Art, Philosophy, Juveniles, High-priced Paperbacks, Medicine, Psychology, General & Social Science, Educational Materials
Founded: 1947
Bookshop: Buchhandlung freies Geistesleben, D-7000 Stuttgart, Alexanderstr 11

Verlag Dieter **Fricke** GmbH, Gr Bockenheimer Str 32, D-6000 Frankfurt 1 Tel: (0611) 285139
Man Dir: Dieter Fricke
Subjects: Photography, Art
1978: 7 titles *1979:* 12 titles *Founded:* 1976
ISBN Publisher's Prefix: 3-88184

Friedenauer Presse*, Jenaer Str 6, D-1000 Berlin 31 Tel: (030) 2115060
Subjects: Bibliophilia

Erhard **Friedrich** Verlag*, Im Brande 15, D-3001 Velber über Hannover 1 Tel: (0511) 480868 Cable Add: Friedrich Telex: 0922923
Subjects: Theatre, Opera, Film, Education, Hobbies, Arts
Founded: 1960
ISBN Publisher's Prefix: 3-7727

Frisia-Verlag GmbH, Mainzlarer Str 11, D-6301 Staufenberg 1 Tel: (06406) 3319
General Manager: Werner Struep; *Partner:* Gisela Struep
1977: 9 titles *1979:* 15 titles *Founded:* 1975
Subjects: North Sea Literature, Island Guides, Travel Guides
Miscellaneous: Agency for Posters and other publicity material
ISBN Publisher's Prefix: 3-88111

Edition der 2 Gerald **Fritsch** und Stephan Fritsch, see der 2

Verlag A **Fromm** GmbH & Co, Postfach 1948, D-4500 Osnabrück (Located at: Breiter Gang 11-14) Tel: (0541) 3101 Telex-; 94916 fromm d
Publisher: Leo V Fromm; *Man Dir:* Annette Harms-Hunold; *Sales Manager:* Annegret Busch; *Public Relations:* Ursula Malzahn
Associate Companies: Edition Interfrom AG, Zurich, Switzerland (qv); Fromm International Publishing Corp, 1212 Ave of the Americas, New York, NY 10036
Subjects: Authoritative texts by German-Speaking Authors on Politics, Economics, Society, Culture and Education, Nature, the Environment; also publish Periodicals and Newspapers
ISBN Publisher's Prefix: 3-7729

Frommann-Holzboog (Friedrich Frommann Verlag, Günther Holzboog GmbH & Co), König-Karl-Str 27, Postfach 500460, D-7000 Stuttgart 50 Tel: (0711) 569039
Man Dir & Editorial: Günther Holzboog, Eva-Maria Holzboog; *Sales Dir:* H Gündert; *Publicity & Advertising Dir:* U Vogel; *Rights and Permissions:* H Kruschwitz
Subjects: History, Philosophy, Political Science, Reference, Religion, Psychology, Social Science, Pedagogy, History of Science, University Textbooks, Philosophical Journal
Founded: 1727
ISBN Publisher's Prefix: 3-7728

Verlag Franz-Joachim **Gaber**, see megapress

Betriebswirtschaftlicher Verlag Dr Theodor **Gabler**, Taunusstr 54, Postfach 1546, D-6200 Wiesbaden 1 Tel: (06121) 5341 Cable Add: Gablerverlag Telex: 04186567
Parent Company: Verlagsgruppe Bertelsmann GmbH (qv)
Subjects: Business Administration; Personnel Management, Accounting, Material Procurement, Insurance, Banking, etc; Periodicalsss, Business Courses
1977: 92 titles

Verlag **Gaehme***, Henke, Kartäusergasse 24, D-5000 Cologne Tel: (0221) 321562
Publisher: Rolf Henke
Subjects: Politics, Literature of the Working Class

Verlag Werner **Gebühr***, Rosenwiesstr 7, D-7000 Stuttgart 80 Tel: (0711) 716630
Dir: Erika Gebühr
Subjects: General Fiction, Belles Lettres
Founded: 1972
ISBN Publisher's Prefix: 3-920014

Dr Max **Gehlen** Verlagsbuch-handlung*, Daimlerstr 12, Postfach 2247, D-6380 Bad Homburg vor der Höhe 1 Tel: (06172) 23056 Cable Add: Taunusbote Badhomburg
Man Dir: Dr Alexander Krebs-Gehlen
Subjects: Reference, Social Science, Commercial & Technical Textbooks, Periodicals
Founded: 1913

Geo Center Internationales Landkartenhaus GmbH, Honigwiesenstr 25, Postfach 800830, D-7000 Stuttgart 80 Tel: (0711) 735031 Cable Add: Geocentre Telex: 7255405 geo d
Dir: Bodo Neiss; *Sales Manager:* Wolfgang Völcker
Branch Offs: Liebherrstr 5, D-8000 Munich 22; Lützowstr 105-106, D-1000 Berlin 30
Subject: Maps, Travel Literature
Miscellaneous: The company also acts as supplier and distributor on behalf of some 30 other German and foreign publishing companies connected with Touring, Geography and Cartography
ISBN Publisher's Prefix: 3-920137

Geographische Verlagsgesellschaft Velhagen und Klasing und Hermann Schroedel GmbH und Co KG, Lützowstr 105, Postfach 3144, D-1000 Berlin 30 Tel: (030) 2616019
Man Dirs: Dr Ludwig Arentz, Goetz Manth
Parent Company: Velhagen & Klasing (qv), D-1000 Berlin 30
Subjects: Secondary & Primary Textbooks on Geography, Atlases
1978: 4 titles *Founded:* 1963
ISBN Publisher's Prefix: 3-7680

Verlag Dr Rudolf **Georgi***, Aureliusstr 42, Postfach 407, D-5100 Aachen Tel: (0241) 36866/30107 Telex: 832337
Man Dirs: Werner and Manfred Georgi
Subjects: History, How-to, Music, Art, Calendars, General Science
Founded: 1928
Bookshops: Fachbuchhandlung Dr Rudolf Georgi, Aureliusstr 42, Postfach 407, (and Wilhemstr 90), D-51 Aachen
ISBN Publisher's Prefix: 3-87248

Carl **Gerber** Verlag, see Schwaneberger Verlag GmbH

Gerhardt Verlag, Jenaer Str 7, D-1000 Berlin 31 Tel: (030) 8543009
Man Dir: Renate Gerhardt
Subjects: Belles Lettres, Poetry, Art, High-priced Paperbacks, Educational Materials
Founded: 1962
ISBN Publisher's Prefix: 3-920372

Gerstenberg Verlag, Postfach 390, D-3200 Hildesheim (Located at: Rathausstr 20) Tel: (05121) 37031 Telex: 0927108 gberg
Man Dir, Editorial: Martin Oesch; *Sales, Publicity:* W J Dietrich; *Production:* Reinhard Fabian; *Rights & Permissions:* Elisabeth Franke
Subjects: Bibliographies, History, Politics, Philosophy, Art, Music, Mathematics, Physics, Psychology, Religion, Linguistics, Literature, English, German, Roman Historical, Historical Reprints
1978: about 100 titles *1979:* about 100 titles *Founded:* 1969
ISBN Publisher's Prefix: 3-8067

Verlag Ernst und Werner **Gieseking***, Deckertstr 30, Postfach 130120, D-4800 Bielefeld 13 Tel: (0521) 14674 Telex: 932240
Publisher: Werner Gieseking
Subjects: Law, Music
ISBN Publisher's Prefix: 3-7694

Giesserei-Verlag GmbH (Foundry Press), Breitestr 27, Postfach 3503, D-4000 Düsseldorf 1 Tel: (0211) 88941
Telex: 8587086
Man Dir: Dietrich Schnell; *Sales Dir:* Günther Hecker
Associate Company: Verlag Stahleisen mbH (Iron and Steel Press), (qv)
Subjects: Scientific and Technical (relating to foundries)
1977: 3 titles *1978:* 4 titles *Founded:* 1927
ISBN Publisher's Prefix: 3-87260

Gillardon Verlag GmbH, Wilhelmstr 8, Postfach 1540, D-7518 Bretten 1
Tel: 07252/2319
Specialist publisher for various Financial and Interest Tables
Owners: E and H Gillardon; *Publicity:* Heinrich Gillardon; *Rights & Permissions:* Karin Gillardon
Subjects: Variety of Interest, Discount, Amortisation etc Tables
Founded: 1920
ISBN Publisher's Prefix: 3-921475, 3-88329

Gilles und Francke Verlag+, Blumenstr 67-69, Postfach 100764, D-4100 Duisberg 1
Publisher, Proprietor: Werner Francke; *Editorial:* Wolfgang Strähler, Dr K Körper; *Sales:* Barbara Francke; *Production:* Wolfgang Strähler; *Publicity:* Thomas Mühlenbrüch
Subsidiary Company: G & F Book and Periodical Sales
Subjects: Leisure Activities, Poetry, Anthologies, Music, Fiction, Essays, Periodicals
Bookshop: G & F Buch und Zeitschriftenhandlung
1977: 8 titles *1979:* 15 titles *Founded:* 1900
ISBN Publisher's Prefix: 3-12251

Verlag W **Girardet**, Girardetstr 2-38, Postfach 9, D-4300 Essen 1 Tel: (0201) 79961 Cable Add: Girardet Essen
Telex: 0857888
Publisher: Dr Paul Girardet; *Editorial:* Ulrich Melzer; *Publicity:* Marianne Faust
Subjects: Texts and Teachers' Texts for Technical Training Colleges and Institutions: Electro-Technology, Engineering, Basic Sciences, Business Administration, Languages etc
1978: 24 titles *Founded:* 1865
ISBN Publisher's Prefix: 3-7736

Globetrotter-Verlag see Friedemann von Engel Verlag

Glock und Lutz Verlag Heroldsberg*, Hans-Sachs-Str no 2, D-8501 Heroldsberg bei Nürnberg Tel: (0911) 560738
Subjects: Religion, Regional Guides, Biography, History, Art
1977: approx 25 titles *Founded:* 1923
Miscellaneous: Also publishes periodicals. Company is housed in the 1580 'Yellow Castle'
ISBN Prefix: 3-7738

PR Verlag Kurt **Glombig**, see Pinx-Verlag

Verlagsgesellschaft R **Glöss** und Co, Mörkenstr 7, Postfach 500344, D-2000 Hamburg 50 Tel: (040) 388573
Telex: 0215667
Publisher: Wolfgang Glöss
Subjects: Periodicals, Politics, Biography
ISBN Publisher's Prefix: 3-87261

Wilhelm **Goldmann** Verlag GmbH, Neumarkter Str 22, Postfach 800709, D-8000 Munich 80 Tel: (089) 492063
Cable Add: Goldmannverlag Munich
Man Dir: Gert Friederking; *Editorial:* Hans-Ulrich Göhler; *Sales:* Ulrich Scheele; *Publicity:* Josef Schaaf
Subjects: General Fiction, Crime, Science Fiction, Juvenile, Poetry, Biography, History, How-to, Art, Classics, Religion, Law, Medicine, Psychology & Education, General & Social Science, Cinema, Astrology
ISBN Publisher's Prefix: 3-442

Goldstadtverlag, see Karl A Schäfer Buch- und Offsetdruckerei Goldstadtverlag

Gondrom Verlag GmbH & Co Kg*, Bahnhofstr 15, Postfach 2606, D-8580 Bayreuth Tel: (0921) 21031 Telex: 642771
Publishing Dir: D H Klein
Subjects: Art, History, Juveniles, Literature
1977: 60 titles

V **Gorachek** KG, see Possev-Verlag

Lutz **Görner***, Eigenverlag, Herrnstr 11, D-8000 Munich 22 Tel: (089) 295322
Subjects: Illustrated editions of work by the Munich actor Lutz Görner

Grabert-Verlag, Am Apfelberg 18-20, Postfach 1629, D-7400 Tübingen
Tel: (07071) 61206 Cable Add: Grabert-Tübingen Telex: 7262863 grav d
Man Dir and Owner: Wigbert Grabert
Subjects: Belles Lettres, Biography, History (also pre-History and Contemporary History), High-priced Paperbacks, Annual Publication *Ihr Buchberater*
1978: 4 titles *1979:* 5 titles *Founded:* 1953
Book Club: Deutscher Buchkreis
ISBN Publisher's Prefix: 3-87847

Gräfe und Unzer GmbH, Isabellastr 32, Postfach 400709, D-8000 Munich 40
Tel: (089) 373791
Man Dir: Kurt Prelinger; *Editorial:* Hans Scherz; *Sales:* Fritz Petermuller; *Marketing:* Dieter Banzhaf; *Publicity:* Heinz Kraxenberger; *Rights & Permissions:* Ursula Feuerbacher
Orders to: Verlegerdienst München, Gutenbergstrasse, 8031 Gilching
Subjects: Cookery, Health, How-to, Nature, Animals, Reference
1978: 32 titles *1979:* 35 titles *Founded:* 1722
ISBN Publisher's Prefix: 3-7742

Verlag der Stiftung **Gralsbotschaft** GmbH, Lenzhalde 15, D-7000 Stuttgart 1
Tel: (0711) 294355
Grail Message Foundation Publishing Co
Associate Company: Verlag Alexander Bernhardt, Austria (qv)
Subjects: Philosophy, Religion

Greven Verlag Köln, Neue Weyerstr 1-3, D-5000 Cologne 1 Tel: (0221) 233333
Cable Add: Grevenverlag Köln
Telex: 8882249
Man Dir: Sigurd Greven
Subjects: Cologne and Region (Fine Art editions)
1977: 12 titles *1978:* 12 titles *Founded:* 1827
ISBN Publisher's Prefix: 3-7743

Ukvary **Griff** Verlag Kiado*, Titurelstr 2/II, D-8000 Munich 81 Tel: (089) 989423/989552
Publisher: Ursula von Ujváry; *Man Dir:* Dr Sandor A Ujváry
Associate Company: Irodalmi Uj Ság, Paris, France
Subsidiary Company: Griff Literary Agency
Subjects: Books in Hungarian
1977: 15 titles *Founded:* 1938

Julius **Groos** Verlag KG+, Hertzstr 6, Postfach 102423, D-6900 Heidelberg 1
Tel: (06221) 33621 Cable Add: Groos Heidelberg
Man Dir: Dieter Wolff; *Sales Dir:* Renate Wolff
Subjects: Linguistics, Textbooks on Modern Languages, Educational Materials
1977: 12 titles *1978:* 11 titles *Founded:* 1804
Miscellaneous: Publish journals *Iral, Hörgeschädigten Pädagogik, Journal of Literary Semantics,* Jahrbuch: *Deutsch als Fremdsprache*
ISBN Publisher's Prefix: 3-87276

Verlag und Landkartenhaus W **Grösschen** KG*, Suedwall 15, Postfach 170, D-4600 Dortmund 1 Tel: (0231) 528119 Telex: 822243 wigrod
Subjects: Maps, History, Schoolbooks

Grote'sche Verlagsbuch-handlung KG*, Luxemburger Str 72, D-5000 Cologne Tel: (0221) 426761 Cable Add: Groteverlag
Telex: dgv Köln 08882662
Dir: Friedrich Plagge
Branch Off: Luxemburger Str 72, Postfach 100448, D-5000 Cologne 1
Subjects: History, Law, Literature, Economics, Administration, Social & Political Science, Periodicals
Founded: 1661
Miscellaneous: Firm is a subsidiary of Unternehmensgruppe Verlag W Kohlhammer GmbH (qv)
ISBN Publisher's Prefix: 3-7745

Verlag **Grundlagen** und Praxis GmbH & Co, Wissenschaftlicher Autorenverlag KG, Bergmannstr 40, PostfA 507, D-2950 Leer
Tel: (0491) 61886
Man Dir: Mrs M Harms
Subjects: Homoeopathy, Graphology, Philology
1977: 2 titles *1978:* 2 titles *Founded:* 1972

Matthias-**Grünewald**-Verlag, Bischofsplatz 6, Postfach 3080, D-6500 Mainz Tel: (06131) 26341
Publisher: Dr Jakob Laubach; *Editorial:* Mr Bertram; *Sales Dir:* Ludwig Hahn; *Production:* Mr Wagner; *Publicity:* Käthe Hellbauer
Subjects: Religion, Biography, History, Juveniles
1978: 58 titles *1979:* 90 titles *Founded:* 1918
ISBN Publisher's Prefix: 3-7867

Walter de **Gruyter** & Co, Mouton Publishers, Genthiner Str 13, D-1000 Berlin 30 Tel: (030) 2611341 Cable Add: Wissenschaft Berlin 0184027
Man Dirs: Dr Kurt-Georg Cram, Dr Kurt Lubasch; *Sales:* Dietrich Rackow; *Publicity:* Joachim Oest
Associate Company: J Schweitzer Verlag (qv)
Subsidiary Companies: Aldine Publishing Company, New York, USA; Walter de Gruyter Inc, 3 Westchester Plaza, Elmsford, New York, NY 10523, USA; Mouton Publishers, The Hague (qv), New York, Paris
Subjects: Liberal Arts, especially Law, History, Linguistics, Philosophy, Theology, Anthropology, Natural Sciences, Literary Criticism; also Commerce, Technology, Social Sciences, Medicine; Works in German, English, French
1978: approx 300 titles
ISBN Publisher's Prefix: 3-11

Gryphius-Verlag*, Harretstr 6, Postfach 754, D-7410 Reutlingen Tel: (07121) 8471
Cable Add: Buchhaus Reutlingen
Telex: 0729733
Subjects: Special Editions and Reprints

Verlag Klaus **Guhl**, Königin-Elizabethstr 8, D-1000 Berlin 19 Tel: 3017482, 3011612
Man Dir: Klaus-Dieter Guhl; *Editorial:* H j von Hülst; *Sales:* Forian Guhl; *Production:* Robert Guhl; *Rights & Permissions:* Hans Paul Guhl
Branch Off: Oranienstr 188, D-1000 Berlin 36
Subjects: Politics, Literature, Textbooks on Jurisprudence, Literary Criticism
1978: 35 titles *1979:* 29 titles *Founded:* 1976
ISBN Publisher's Prefix: 3-88220

D **Gundert** Verlag*, Ostfeldstr 46, Postfach 710140, D-3000 Hannover-Kirchrode Tel: (0511) 522535
Publisher: Guy d'Hoedt
Subjects: Juveniles, Young Adult
Founded: 1878
ISBN Publisher's Prefix: 3-87279

Verlag August **Güse**, Hauptstr 103, D-6367 Karben 3 Tel: (06039) 2990/2991
Subjects: Calendars, Horticulture
1978: 3 titles *Founded:* 1954
ISBN Publisher's Prefix: 3-87278

Büchergilde **Gutenberg** Verlagsgesellschaft mbH*, Untermainkai 66, Postfach 16220, D-6000 Frankfurt am Main 16 Tel: (0611) 230131 Telex: 412063 buegi d
Subjects: Fiction, Reference, History, Politics, Biography, Art, Juveniles, 69 prizewinning 'Books of the Year' Records, Games

Gutenberg-Gesellschaft, Liebfrauenpl 5, D-6500 Mainz Tel: 06131/26420
Man Dir, President: J Fuchs; *Manager:* H Knauer; *Editorial:* Prof Koppitz
Subject: Printing
Founded: 1901

Gütersloher Verlagshaus Gerd Mohn, Königstr 23, Postfach 2368, D-4830 Gütersloh 1 Tel: (05241) 1831 Cable Add: Gütersloher Verlagshaus Telex: 0933868
Man Dir: Gerd Mohn; *Sales Dir, Publicity:* Otfrid Seippel; *Rights & Permissions:* Dr Heinz Kühne
Subjects: Religion, Philosophy, Politics, Juveniles, Paperbacks
Imprints: Gütersloher Taschenbücher Siebenstern (paperback series)
1977: 100 titles *1978:* 20 titles *Founded:* 1959
Miscellaneous: Affiliated with Verlagsgruppe Bertelsmann
ISBN Publisher's Prefix: 3-579

H A D U – Hagemann Lehrmittel und Verlagsgesellschaft mbH, Karlstr 20, Postfach 5129, D-4000 Düsseldorf Tel: (211) 353811 Cable Add: Hagemannverlag Telex: 8587623 hage d
Man Dir: Maria Schütte-Hagemann; *Editorial, Production:* Hans Peisker, Heinz W Schmidt; *Sales, Export, Finance:* W Kils-Hütten; *Publicity:* H W Schmidt; *Rights & Permissions:* W Kils-Hütten, Hans Peisker, H W Schmidt
Parent Company: Lehrmittelverlag Wilhelm Hagemann (qv)
Associate Company: Verlagsgesellschaft Schulfernsehen mbH, D-5000 Cologne
Subjects: Teaching Aids and Pedadogy
1977: 120 titles *1978:* 130 titles (also numerous teaching aids) *Founded:* 1929
ISBN Publisher's Prefix: 3-544

Haag und Herchen Verlag, Fichardstr 30, D-6000 Frankfurt am Main 1 Tel: (0611) 550911
Man Dir: Hans-Alfred Herchen
Subjects: How-to, High-priced Paperbacks, Medicine, Politics, Psychology, Engineering, General & Social Science, University Textbooks
1978: 80 titles *1979:* 140 titles *Founded:* 1975
ISBN Publisher's Prefix: 3-88129

Verlag Josef **Habbel**, Gutenbergstr 8, Postfach 339, D-8400 Regensburg 11 Tel: (0941) 96044 Cable Add: Pustet Telex: 65672
Man Dir: Dr Friedrich Pustet; *Sales and Advertising:* Dr Reinhold Röttger
Parent Company: Verlag Friedrich Pustet (qv)
Subjects: Christian Juvenile; Leisure reading for the Christian home
1977: 6 titles *Founded:* 1870
ISBN Publisher's Prefix: 3-7748

Rudolf **Habelt** Verlag GmbH, Am Buchenhang 1, Postfach 150104, D-5300 Bonn 1 Tel: (02221) 232015 Cable Add: Buchhabelt Bonn
Man Dirs: Dr Rudolf Habelt, Wolfgang Habelt; *Editorial, Production:* Renate Schreiber
Subjects: Pre-History, Archaeology, Ancient History, Regional, Folklore, etc

Walter **Hädecke** Verlag*, Postfach 1203, D-7252 Weil der Stadt Tel: (07033) 2264
Man Dir: Hilde Graff-Hädecke; *Sales & Advertising Dir, Rights & Permissions:* Joachim Graff
Subjects: Reference, High-priced Paperbacks, Cook Books, Public Health
Founded: 1919
ISBN Publisher's Prefix: 3-7750

Lehrmittelverlag Wilhelm **Hagemann**, Karlstr 20, Postfach 5129, D-4000 Düsseldorf Tel: (0211) 353811 Cable Add: Hagemannverlag Telex: 8587623 hage d
Sales: Walter Kils-Hütten; *Production, Rights & Permissions:* Hano Peisker, Heinz W Schmidt
Subsidiary Company: HADÜ – Hagemann Lehrmittel und Verlagsgesellschaft mbH (qv)
Subjects: Textbooks, especially on Biology, Chemistry, Electrical Engineering, Electronics, Public Health, Mathematics, Education, Physics, Politics; also Teaching Transparencies, Biological Wall Charts
ISBN Publisher's Prefix: 3-544

Buchvertrieb **Hager** GmbH, Mainzer Landstr 147, Postfach 119151, D-6000 Frankfurt Am Main 2 Tel: (0611) 730234 Telex: 04-13080 kuehl d
Managing & Sales Dir: Hermann Figge; *Publicity & Advertising Dir:* Bruno Fries
Subjects: Belles Lettres, Poetry, History, Music, Art, Philosophy, Juveniles, Low-priced Paperbacks, Social Science
Founded: 1974
ISBN Publisher's Prefix: 3-88145

Mary **Hahns** Kochbuchverlag*, Welserstr 10 & 12, Postfach 1443, D-1000 Berlin 30 Tel: (030) 245138
Subjects: Cookery, Home Economics
Miscellaneous: Firm is a member of Verlagsgruppe Langen-Müller/Herbig (qv)
ISBN Publisher's Prefix: 3-8004

Verlag Anton **Hain** KG*, Adelheidstr 2, Postfach 1220, D-6240 Königstein/Ts Tel: 06174/3026 Cable Add: Hain Telex: 042507
Man Dir: Dieter Hain; *Sales:* Rudolf Klein;

Editorial: Beate Pinkerneil; *Publicity:* Karin Hirschfeld
Associate Companies: Peter Hanstein Verlag GmbH; Athenaum Verlag GmbH; Scriptor Verlag GmbH & Co KG (qqv)
Subjects: Philosophy, Reference, Religion, Psychology, Social Science, University Textbooks
Founded: 1946
ISBN Publisher's Prefix: 3-445

Hallwag Verlag, Marco-Polo-Str 1, D-7302 Ostfildern 4 bei Stuttgart Tel: (0711) 4502266 Cable Add: Hallwagverlag Telex: 721796
Sales Manager: Ulrich Mailänder; *Publicity Manager:* Brigitte Buschmann
Subjects: Maps, Town Plans, Travel and Touring Guides and Books; Pocket Information series on General Knowledge; Reference, Music
Head Office: Hallwag Verlag AG, Berne, Switzerland (qv)
ISBN Publisher's Prefix: 3-444

Hamburger Fremdenblatt Broschek und Co, see Broschek Druck GmbH & Co KG

Hamburger Lesehefte Verlag Iselt und Co Nfl mbH, Nordbahnhofstr 2, Postfach 1480, D-2250 Husum Tel: (04841) 6081/3
Man Dir, Editorial, Rights & Permissions: Ingwert Paulsen Jr; *Sales:* Alfred Lorenzen; *Production:* Hajo Hartkopf; *Publicity:* Barbara Marquardt
Parent Company: Husum Druck- und Verlagsgesellschaft mbH u Co KG (qv)
Associated Companies: Matthiesen Verlag Ingwert Paulsen Jr (qv)
Subjects: Textbooks
Founded: 1953
ISBN Publisher's Prefix: 3-87291

Peter **Hammer** Verlag GmbH, Foehrenstr 33-35, Postfach 200415, D-5600 Wuppertal 2 Tel: (0202) 505066
Dir: Hermann Schulz; *Sales Manager:* Barbara Kehrein; *Rights & Permissions:* Helmut Lotz
Associate Company: Jugenddienst Verlag (qv)
Subjects: Latin America, The Third World, Literature, Current Affairs, Meditation, Christian Action
1977: 56 titles *1978:* 13 titles
ISBN Publisher's Prefix: 3-87294

Hansa Verlag Heinz W Hass*, Feldstrasse Hochhaus 1, D-2000 Hamburg 4 Tel: (040) 4300862
Subjects: Belles Lettres, Literary Criticism
ISBN Publisher's Prefix: 3-920421

Carl **Hanser** Verlag, Kolbergerstr 22, Postfach 860420, D-8000 Munich 86 Tel: (089) 985861 Telex: 05/22837
Man Dirs: Joachim Spencker, Christoph Schlotterer, Franz-Joachim Klock; *Editorial:* Fritz Arnold, Burkhart Kroeber, Michael Krüger, Hans Joachim Simm; *Sales Dirs:* Felicitas Feilhauer, Christoph Sickel; *Advertising Dir:* Wolfgang Nagel; *Publicity Manager:* Fritz Arnold
Subsidiary Companies: Part-owner of Deutscher Taschenbuch Verlag, Friedrichstr 1, D-8000 Munich 40 (qv) and of Verlegerdienst München, Gutenbergstr, Gilching
Subjects: General Fiction, Belles Lettres, Poetry, Biography, History, Philosophy, High-priced Paperbacks, Engineering, General Science, Macromolecular Chemistry, Plastics, Business & Management, Dentistry
1978: 180 titles *Founded:* 1928

FEDERAL REPUBLIC OF GERMANY 141

Miscellaneous: Publish 18 technical and other periodicals
ISBN Publisher's Prefix: 3-446

Hänssler-Verlag*, Friedrich Hänssler KG, Bismarckstr 4, Postfach 1220, D-7303 Neuhausen-Stuttgart Tel: (07158) 5001
Man Dir: Friedrich Hänssler; *Rights & Permissions:* Reinhold Lechler
Subjects: Music, Art, Religion, Low-priced Paperbacks
1977: 300 titles *Founded:* 1920
Bookshop: Laudate GmbH, Versandbuchhandlung Friedrich Hänssler, Bismarckstr 4, D-7303 Neuhausen-Stuttgart
Miscellanous: Firm is a member of the Telos (qv) series publishing group; it also publishes publications of the American Institute of Musicology
ISBN Publisher's Prefix: 3-7751

Peter **Hanstein** Verlag GmbH*, Adelheidstr 2, Postfach 1220, D-6240 Königstein/Ts Tel: 06174/3026
Publisher: Dietrich Pinkerneil; *Editorial:* Hans-Georg Beer; *Sales:* Rudolf Klein; *Publicity:* Karin Hirschfeld; *Rights & Permissions:* Hildegard Willhöft
Associate Companies: Athenaeum Verlag GmbH; Scriptor Verlag GmbH & Co KG; Hain Verlag GmbH (qqv)
Subjects: Law, Economic Sciences, Theology
1977: c 30 titles *Founded:* 1878
ISBN Publisher's Prefix: 3-7756

Harlekin-Presse, Mathystr 36, D-7530 Pforzheim Tel: (07231) 27084
Publicity Manager: Ulrike Strauss
Subject: Verse and other texts, with original illustrations

Harrach und Sabrow, Wöllsteiner Str 8, Postfach 745, D-6550 Bad Kreuznach Tel: (0671) 67073 Telex: 042815
Associate Company: Inter-Kunst und Buch GmbH (qv)
Subjects: Calendars etc connected with mineral collection; Children's Books; Poetry

Verlag Otto **Harrassowitz**, Taunusstr 6, Postfach 2929, D-6200 Wiesbaden 1 Tel: (06121) 521046 Cable Add: Otto Harrassowitz Wiesbaden Telex: 04186135
Man Dir: Dr Helmut Petzolt; *Sales & Publicity Manager:* Albrecht Weddigen
Subjects: History, Book Trade and Library Science, Orientalia, Linguistics, Slavic Studies, East European History, Religion, Education, Classical Philology, Ethnology, Middle East studies, Publication ZDB — Zeitschriften-Datenbank (Periodicals' Data Bank) in association with das Deutsche Bibliotheksinstitut and the Staatsbibliothek Preussischer Kulturbesitz (qv)
1977: 78 titles *1978:* 67 titles *Founded:* 1872
Bookshop: Otto Harrassowitz, D-6200 Wiesbaden, Taunusstr 5
ISBN Publisher's Prefix: 3-447

Verlag Karlheinz **Hartmann**, Rodheimer Str 17, D-6382 Friedrichsdorf im Taunus Tel: (06007) 622
Man Dir: Karlheinz Hartmann MA; *Editorial:* Roland Hunger
Subjects: Contemporary Literature, Reprints, Literary Criticism, Scenarios and Film Scripts, Modern Poetry, Horror
1977: 2 titles *Founded:* 1976
ISBN Publisher's Prefix: 3-87293

Verlag **Harwalik** KG*, Hohbuchstr 5, Postfach 714, D-7410 Reutlingen Tel: (07121) 22041 Cable Add: Harwalik
Subjects: Woodcut Prints, Graphics etc, Books illustrated by Woodcuts

Verlag Gerd **Hatje** GmbH+, Wildunger Str 83, Postfach 468, D-7000 Stuttgart 50 Tel: (0711) 561109 Cable Add: Hatjeverlag Stuttgart
Man Dir: Gerd Hatje
Subjects: Architecture, Interior Decoration, Art (especially Modern Art)
1977: 10 titles *Founded:* 1945
ISBN Publisher's Prefix: 3-7757

Haude und Spener Verlag, Postfach 147, D-1000 Berlin 62 (Located at: Grossgörschenstr 6) Tel: 030/7813514
General Manager: Volker Spiess
Subjects: Literary History, Bibliographies, Collected Works, History, Cultural History, Reminiscences of Berlin, Radio and TV
Associate Companies: Bruno Hessling Verlag (qv), Verlag V Spiess (qv), both at above address
1977: 16 titles *Founded:* 1614
ISBN Publisher's Prefix: 3-7759

Rudolf **Haufe** Verlag, Hindenburgstr 64, Postfach 740, D-7800 Freiburg im Breisgau Tel: (0761) 31560 Cable Add: Haufeverlag
Man Dirs: G Gaedeke, Dr G Friedrich, Dr M Jahrmarkt, G Osswald, F J Ruebsam; *Editorial:* Dr G Friedrich, Dr M Jahrmarkt; *Sales, Production:* F J Ruebsam
Subsidiary Company: WRS-Verlag, Wirtschaft, Recht, Steuern, Irmgardstr 1, D-8000 Munich 71 (qv)
Subjects: Business and Law; Financial, Management, Social Science, University Textbooks
1977: 35 titles *1978:* 35 titles *Founded:* 1934
ISBN Publisher's Prefix: 3-448

Karl F **Haug** Verlag GmbH und Co, Postfach 102840, D-6900 Heidelberg 1 (Located at: Fritz-Frey Str 21) Tel: (06221) 46074/5 Cable Add: haugverlag
Man Dir: Dr E Fischer
Br Off: Bergheimer Str 102, D-6900 Heidelberg
Subject: Medicine
Founded: 1903
Associate Companies: Arkana Verlag (qv); Verlag für Medizin Dr Ewald Fischer GmbH (qv)
ISBN Publisher's Prefix: 3-7760

Verlag H M **Hauschild** GmbH, Rigaer Str 3, D-2800 Bremen Tel: (0421) 385508
Dir: Ernst August Echtermann
Subjects: Art Books and Calendars, Art Catalogues, Information Books, Bremen Regional

Dr Ernst **Hauswedell** und Co, Magdalenen Str 8, D-2000 Hamburg 13 Tel: (040) 448798
Man Dir: Dr Ernst L Hauswedell; *all other offices:* Reinhold Busch
Subjects: Reference Works for Book and Print Collectors, Bibliographies, Illustrated Books
1978: 10 titles *1979:* 11 titles *Founded:* 1927
ISBN Publisher's Prefix: 3-7762

Heckners Verlag, Postfach 1260, D-3340 Wolfenbüttel Tel: (05331) 5166
Subjects: Vocational (Business), Economics
Founded: 1895

H **Heenemann** Verlagsgesellschaft mbH, Bessemerstr 83, Postfach 420320, D-1000 Berlin 42 Tel: (030) 7536031 Telex: 183 796 hekg d
Subsidiary Company: Verlag W A Colomb (qv)
Subjects: Fishery and Fishing, Sociology and Popular Science; Enamels and Coatings (Colomb)
ISBN Publisher's Prefix: 3-87903

Heering-Verlag GmbH, Ortlerstr 8, Postfach 700840, D-8000 Munich 70 Tel: (089) 7609023-27 Telex: 0522720
Man Dir: Gerfried Urban
Subjects: Photography, Cinematography, Mountaineering
Founded: 1932
ISBN Publisher's Prefix: 3-7763

Heidmük-Verlag Günther U Müller*, Cosimastr 2, D-8000 Munich 81 Tel: (089) 916414
Man Dir: Günther U Müller
Subjects: Juveniles, Games

Ernst **Heimeran** Verlag, Dietlindenstr 14, Postfach 400824, D-8000 Munich 40 Tel: (089) 399017/18
Man Dirs: Till Heimeran, Margrit Heimeran, Tillman Roeder; *Editorial:* Else Sommer; *Sales & Publicity, Rights & Permissions:* Thomas Kniffler
Subjects: Latin and Greek Classics (bilingual), Philology, Modern Text Editions, Music, Cultural Histories, Poetry, Humour, Bavarica
1977: 30 titles *1978:* 16 titles *Founded:* 1922
Associate Company: Kochbuchverlag Heimeran KG, German Federal Republic (qv)
ISBN Publisher's Prefix: 3-7765

Verlag Egon **Heinemann**, Chronik der Seefahrt, Kösliner Weg 16, D-2000 Norderstedt Tel: (040) 5232368/5239023/5239024
Publisher: Egon Heinemann
Subjects: Sailing, Sailing Ships, Nautical Literature
1977: 4 titles *1978:* 6 titles
ISBN Publisher's Prefix: 3-87321

Heinrichshofen's Verlag, Liebigstr 16, Postfach 620, D-2940 Wilhelmshaven Tel: (04421) 26555/202004 Cable Add: Heinrichshofen Wilhelmshaven
Man Dir: Otto Heinrich Noetzel; *Editorial:* Dr Viktor Kreiner, Florian Noetzel; *Production:* Johann Reiners
Associate Companies: Otto Heinrich Noetzel Verlag; Arthur Türk KG
Subjects: Music & Musicology, Ballet, Opera, Song Books, Paperbacks
1977: 25 titles *1978:* 30 titles *Founded:* 1797
ISBN Publisher's Prefix: 3-7959

Verlag Georg **Heintz**, Wasserturmstr 7, D-6520 Worms Cable Add: Heintz
Subjects: Bibliography, Exile Literature, Anti-Semitism

G **Henle** Verlag, Postfach 710466, D-8000 Munich 71 (Located at: Forstenrieder Allee 122) Tel: (089) 754096/7/8
Subject: Music, Original Editions, Reference Books (Music)
ISBN Publisher's Prefix: 3-87328

Henssel Verlag, Glienicker Str 12, D-1000 Berlin 39 Tel: (030) 8051493 Cable Add: Hensselverlag Berlin
Man Dir: Karl-Heinz Henssel; *Editorial:* Asta-Maria Henssel
Subjects: General Fiction, Humour, Travel, Literary Theory, Theatre, Poetry, Biography, Art, High-priced Paperbacks
1977: 4 titles *Founded:* 1938
ISBN Publisher's Prefix: 3-87329

F A **Herbig** Verlagsbuchhandlung*, Hubertusstr 4, D-8000 Munich 19 Tel: (089) 177041 Cable Add: Langenmüller Telex: 05215045
Man Dir: Dr Herbert Fleissner; *Editorial:* Dr Bernhard Strückmeyer; *Sales Manager:*

142 FEDERAL REPUBLIC OF GERMANY

Gisela Weichert; *Production Manager:* Dr Wolf Bachmann; *Publicity Manager:* Dr Brigitte Sinhuber-Erbacher; *Rights & Permissions:* Renate Werner
Orders to: Vereinigte Verlagsauslieferung Reinhard Mohn, Carl-Bertelsmann-Str 161, D-4830 Gütersloh
Subjects: Novels, Belles Lettres, Poetry, History, Art, Hobbies, Gift Books
Founded: 1821
Miscellaneous: Firm is a member of Verlagsgruppe Langen-Müller/Herbig (qv)*ISBN Publisher's Prefix:* 3-7766

Verlag **Herder** GmbH & Co, KG, Hermann-Herder-Str 4, Postfach, D-7800 Freiburg im Breisgau Tel: (0761) 27171 Cable Add: Herder Freiburgbreisgau Telex: 07721440 vhd
Man Dir: Fritz Knoch; *Sales Dir:* Franz Grossmann; *Publicity Manager:* Dr Ludwig Muth; *Rights & Permissions:* Alfred Zimmermann
Associate Companies: Verlag Herder & Co, Vienna, Austria (qv); Herder AG, Basel, Switzerland (qv); A G Ploetz KG, Wurzburg, Federal Republic of Germany (qv)
Subsidiaries: Christophorus-Verlag; Verlag F H Kerle (qv); Verlag Karl Alber; Verlag Ploetz KG; (qqv)
Book Club: Herder Buchgemeinde
Bookshops: Located in major cities throughout German Federal Republic
Subjects: General Fiction, Belles Lettres, Poetry, Biography, History, Art, Philosophy, Reference, Religion, Juveniles, Low- and High-priced Paperbacks, Psychology, Social Science, University, Secondary & Primary Textbooks, Educational Materials, Atlases, Encyclopaedias
1977: 600 titles *Founded:* 1801
ISBN Publisher's Prefix: 3-451

Herder und Herder GmbH, Verlag für Wirtschaft und Gesellschaft, Rathenauplatz 14, D-6000 Frankfurt 1
Associate Companies: Verlag Herder KG, Ploetz KG, Federal Republic of Germany (qqv); Herder AG, Switzerland (qv)
Subjects: Politics, Social Sciences, Economics
ISBN Publisher's Prefix: 3-585

Bert **Hering** Verlag*, Schellingstr 44, Postfach 40967, D-8000 Munich 40 Tel: (089) 288471
Subjects: Bibliographic Services; Title Search; Scientific and Technical Source Literature Information

Herold Neue Verlagsgesellschaft GmbH*, Waldgarten Str 66, D-8000 Munich 70, Postfach 700849 Tel: (089) 7147550 Cable Add: Heroldverlag Munich
Dir: Dr Joseph S Herold; *Sales Dir:* Inge Angelletti
Subjects: Culture Guides, Culture and Art History, Pharmacy, Business Management, University Textbooks
1977: 6 titles *Founded:* 1883 (Leipzig)
Affiliated Company: Vereinigte Herold Verlag GmbH (qv)
ISBN Publisher's Prefix: 3-920451

Herold Verlag Brück KG*, Alexanderstr 51, Postfach 507, D-7000 Stuttgart-S Tel: (0711) 240996
Dirs: Elisabeth Häring, Emmerich Müller; *Editorial:* Irma Sander and Christa Laufs
Subjects: Juveniles
Founded: 1871
ISBN Publisher's Prefix: 3-7767

Vereinigte **Herold** Verlage GmbH*, Waldgarten Str 66, Postfach 700849, D-8000 Munich 70 Tel: (089) 7148146 Cable Add: Heroldverlag Munich
General Manager & Editor: Dr Joseph S Herold; *Man Dir:* Fritz Walter
Subjects: Encyclopaedias (Herold Deutschland Bibliothek)
Founded: 1970
Book Club: Herold Buch-club
Affiliated Company: Herold Neue Verlagsgesellschaft GmbH, D-8000 Munich 70, Waldgarten Str 66

Bruno **Hessling** Verlag, Grossgörschenstr 6, Postfach 147, D-1000 Berlin 62 Tel: 030/7813514
General Manager: Volker Spiess
1977: 12 titles *Founded:* 1883
Subjects: Art and History of Berlin, Art, Medical History, Political Periodicals
Associate Companies: Haude & Spener Verlag (qv), Verlag V Spiess (qv), both at above address
ISBN Publisher's Prefix: 3-7769

Hestia-Verlag GmbH, Eduard-Bayerlein-Str 1, D-858 Bayreuth Tel: (0921) 22117 Telex: 642103
Dirs: Heinz G Konsalik, Dagmar Stecher
Subjects: General Fiction, History, Biography
Founded: 1954
ISBN Publisher's Prefix: 3-7770

B **Heymann** Verlag*, Edition Ethnos, Bertramstr 21, Postfach 3065, D-6200 Wiesbaden Tel: (06121) 302861
Publisher: Bernd Heymann; *Press Chief & Sales Manager:* Klaus Baumann; *Publicity, Rights & Permissions:* Peter Heiliginthal
Subjects: Anthropology, Ethnology, Social Science, Philosophy, Reprints

Carl **Heymanns** Verlag KG*, Gereonstr 18-32, D-5000 Cologne 1 Tel: (0221) 134022; Bonn (901) 234550; Berlin (030) 3913111/3913635/3917090; Munich (089) 224811 Cable Add: Köln Rechtsverlag; also Bonn/Munich/Berlin Rechtsverlag; Telex: Cologne 8881888; Munich 0524058; Berlin 0181811
Man Dir: Hans-Jörg Gallus; *Editorial:* K W Frohn, K Pompe, H E Wohlfarth; *Production:* C Free; *Publicity:* K. Brachvogel; *Sales:* N Langhahn
Subsidiary Companies: Gallus Druckerei KG, Berlin; Albert Nauck & Co, Cologne and Berlin; Gallus Verlag, Hans O Gallus KG, Munich; Euroliber Verlags- und Vertriebs-GmbH, Cologne; Gallus Verlag KG, Vienna, Austria; Scientia AG, Zug, Switzerland
Br Off: Adalbert-Stifter-Str 15, D-5300 Bonn; Steinsdorfstr 10, D-8000 Munich 22; Gutenbergstr 3-4, D-1000 Berlin 10
Subject: Law
Founded: 1815
ISBN Publisher's Prefix: 3-452

Wilhelm **Heyne** Verlag, Türkenstr 5-7, Postfach 201204, D-8000 Munich 2 Tel: (089) 288211/16 Cable Add: Heyneverlag München Telex: 0524218
Editorial: Roswitha Heyne, Wolfgang Jeschke, Manfred Kluge, Renate Matuschka, Reinhold G Stecher; *Sales Dir:* Friedhelm Koch; *Advertising Dir:* Horst Mikkat; *Rights & Permissions:* Traudel Eckardt
Subjects: Paperbacks only: General Fiction, Belles Lettres, Poetry, Biography, History, How-to, Music, Art, Juveniles, Psychology, Science Fiction and Westerns

1977: 450 titles *1978:* 500 titles *Founded:* 1934
ISBN Publisher's Prefix: 3-453

Anton **Hiersemann** Verlag, Rosenbergstr 113, Postfach 723, D-7000 Stuttgart 1 Tel: (0711) 638264/5
Man Dir: Karl G Hiersemann; *Editorial:* Dr R W Fuchs; *Rights & Permissions:* K G Hiersemann
Subjects: History, Art, Reference, Bibliography, Books about Books, Classical Studies, Germanic Literature, Theatre
1979: 35 titles *Founded:* 1884
Miscellaneous: publishes organ of the Literarischer Verein in Stuttgart (Stuttgart Literary Society) (qv)
ISBN Publisher's Prefix: 3-7772

Verlag **Hinder und Deelmann**, Postfach 1206, D-3554 Gladenbach (Hessen) Tel: (06462) 1301
Publishers: Johannes Deelmann, Rolf Hinder
Subjects: Philosophy, Religion, Social Science
1977: 5 titles *1978:* 4 titles
ISBN Publisher's Prefix: 3-87348

Gruppe **Hinterhaus**, now Elke Betzel Verlag (qv)

Hippokrates Verlag GmbH, Neckarstr 121, Postfach 593, D-7000 Stuttgart 1 Tel: (0711) 21511 Telex: 0722503 Cable Add: Hippokratesverlag
Dirs: Ehrenfried Klotz, P Eich; *Publicity:* H-G Zimnik; *Sales:* A Steiss
Associate Company: Paracelsus Verlag GmbH, Stuttgart
Subjects: Medicine, Psychology, University and Secondary Textbooks
1978: approx 45 titles *Founded:* 1925
ISBN Publisher's Prefix: 3-7773

Hirmer Verlag, Gesellschaft für Wissenschaftliches Lichtbild GmbH, Mareesstrasse 15, D-8000 Munich 19 Tel: (089) 1781011
Man Dirs: Dr Max Hirmer, Aenne Hirmer, Albert Hirmer; *Editorial:* Heinz Friedrich Blaesing
Subjects: Archaeology, History of Art
1979: 8 titles *Founded:* 1948
ISBN Publisher's Prefix: 3-7774

Ferdinand **Hirt**, Schauenburgerstr 36, Postfach 2580, D-2300 Kiel 1 Tel: (0431) 561066 Telex: 299873
Subsidiary Co: Ferdinand Hirt mbH & Co KG (qv), Widerhofergasse 8, A-1094 Vienna (Postal Add: A-1094 Vienna, Postfach 39) Austria
Subjects: Science, Education, Academic, Geographical, Teacher Training
Founded: 1832
Miscellaneous: Publish series *Wegweiser für die Lehrerfortbildung; Veröffentlichungen der schleswig-holsteinischen Universitätsgesellschaft; Hamburger Geographische Studien; Wiener Geographische Schriften; Schriften des Instituts für Österreichkunde; Hirts Stichwortbücher, Reihe Geocolleg*
ISBN Publisher's Prefix: 3-554, 3-7019

S **Hirzel** Verlag GmbH und Co, Birkenwaldstr 44, Postfach 347, D-7000 Stuttgart 1 Tel: (0711) 294482 Cable Add: Hirzelverlag, Stuttgart Telex: 0723636 daz d
Man Dirs: Hans Rotta, Dr Hanskarl Hornüng; *Sales Manager:* Karl Hübler; *Publicity Manager:* Barbara Schreck
Subjects: Philosophy, Medicine, Psychology, Engineering, General Science
Founded: 1853

Associate Companies: Wissenschaftliche Verlagsgesellschaft mbH (qv); Deutscher Apotheker Verlag Dr Roland Schmiedel (qv); Franz Steiner Verlag GmbH (qv); all in German Federal Republic
ISBN Publisher's Prefix: 3-7776

Hoch-Verlag, Kronprinzenstr 27, D-4000 Düsseldorf 1   Tel: (0211) 307001   Cable Add: Hochverlag
Man Dirs: Aenne Hafemann, Joachim Hoch, Hanns Kulmann, Eric Zinth de Kentzingen; *Sales & Publicity Dir:* Hans Kulmann; *Advertising Dir:* Joachim Hoch; *Rights & Permissions:* Eric Zinth de Kenzingen
Subject: Juveniles
1977: 15 titles   *Founded:* 1949
ISBN Publisher's Prefix: 3-7779

Hofacker Ing W GmbH Verlag*, Tegernseerstr 18, D-8150 Holzkirchen/Obb   Tel: 08024/7331
Man Dir, Rights & Permissions: Winfried Hofacker; *Editorial, Publicity:* J Maier; *Sales:* Evi Linkogel; *Production:* Th Kirschenhofer
Orders to: Ing W Hofacker GmbH, Tegernseer Str 18, D-8150 Holzkirchen
Subjects: Electronics, Micro-Computers, Micro-Processing
1977: 30 titles   *Founded:* 1968
ISBN Publisher's Prefix: 3-921682

Dieter **Hoffmann** Verlag*, Senefelderstr 25, D-6500 Mainz 41   Tel: (06136) 416   Telex: 4187213
Dir: Dieter Hoffman
Subjects: History of German Aviation (in German and English texts), Aircraft Modelling, Hunting and Shooting Handbooks
Founded: 1960
ISBN Publisher's Prefix: 3-87341

Julius **Hoffmann** Verlag, Pfizerstr 5-7, Postfach 788, D-7000 Stuttgart 1   Tel: (0711) 2191320
Man Dir: Kurt Hoffmann
Subject: Building and Architecture
1977: 4 titles   *1978:* 4 titles   *Founded:* 1827
Micellaneous: Texts of many books are in English and French
ISBN Publisher's Prefix: 3-87346

Hoffmann und Campe Verlag, Harvestehuder Weg 45, D-2000 Hamburg 13   Tel: (040) 441881   Cable Add: Hoca   Telex: 02214259
Man Dirs: Thomas Ganske, Eberhard Boeckel, Hans Helmut Roehring; *Editorial:* Hermann Josef Barth, Dr Ingeborg Hillmann, Dr Renate Jürgens, Ulrike Rickert, Dr Hans-Jürgen Schmitt, Dr Anneliese Schumacher-Heiss, Dr Helmut Wiemken; *Sales Dir:* Bruno Laudien; *Publicity Dir:* Baerbel Naporowski; *Advertising Dir:* Rudolf Sommer; *Rights & Permissions:* Helga Eberhard, Ulla Thomsen
Subjects: General Fiction, Belles Lettres, Poetry, Biography, History, How-to, Music, Art, Psychology, General & Social Science
1977: 65 titles   *1978:* 72 titles   *Founded:* 1781
ISBN Publisher's Prefix: 3-455

Verlag Karl **Hofmann***, Steinwasenstr 6-8, Postfach 1360, D-7060 Schorndorf   Tel: (07181) 7811   Cable Add: Hofmannverlag Schorndorf
Man Dir: Ottmar Hecht; *Sales, Publicity:* Mr Pastorek
Subjects: Sports, Technical Literature on glass utilization; Periodicals
1977: 25 titles
ISBN Publisher's Prefix: 3-7780

Hohenloher Druck- und Verlagshaus*, Verlag Hohenloher Tagblatt, Blaufelderstr 44, Postfach 80, D-7182 Gerabronn   Tel: (07952) 5126   Cable Add: HDV-Gerabronn   Telex: 74334
Publisher: Rolf Wankmüller
Subjects: Fiction, Poetry, Biography, Juveniles
ISBN Publisher's Prefix: 3-87354

Hohenstaufen Verlag Schumann KG, im Gries 17, Postfach 29, D-7762 Bodman/Bodensee   Tel: (07773) 5616   Cable Add: Hohenstaufen
Dir: Gerhard Schumann; *Sales:* Erika Schumann
Subjects: Belles Lettres, Memoirs, Contemporary History

Grafikverlag **Hohmann***, Kapellenstr 6, D-5307 Wachtberg-Werthoven   Tel: (02221) 344415
Subject: Children's Picture Books and Children's Posters

Verlag Wolfgang **Hölker**, Martinistr 2, Postfach 3820, D-4400 Munster   Tel: (0251) 42225   Cable Add: Martinistrasse 2   Telex: 892112 msfro d
Owner, Man Dir, Rights & Permissions, Sales: Wolfgang Hölker; *Editorial, Production, Publicity:* Axel Riepenhausen
Subject: Cookery Books of all types; books about Menus and Cooking
1978: 18 titles   *1979:* 17 titles   *Founded:* 1973
ISBN Publisher's Prefix: 3-88117

Holle Verlag GmbH*, Markgrafenstr 4, Postfach 320, D-7570 Baden-Baden   Tel: (07221) 23591   Telex: 0781108
Man Dir: G Du Ry van Beest Holle; *Sales & Advertising Dir:* F Litten
Subjects: History, Art, Encyclopaedias
Founded: 1933
Miscellaneous: Publish Holle Kunstbibliothek; Bild der Menschheit (10 vols); Holles Kunstgeschichte (3 vols complete); Enzyklopedie der Weltkunst (9 vols complete)
ISBN Publisher's Prefix: 3-87355

Holsten Verlag GmbH und Co KG*, Geschwister-Scholl-str 142, D-2000 Hamburg 20   Tel: (040) 470934
Man Dir: Wolf E Schenke
Subjects: History, Political Science
Founded: 1955

Verlag Gebr **Holzapfel**+, Kienhorststr 61-63, D-1000 Berlin 51   Tel: (030) 4133098
Publisher: Klaus-J Holzapfel
Subject: Politics
ISBN Publisher's Prefix: 3-921226

Gunther **Holzboog** GmbH & Co, see Frommann-Holzboog

Hans **Holzmann** Verlag GmbH und Co KG, Gewerbestr 2, Postfach 460 & 480, D-8939 Bad Wörishofen   Tel: (08247) 1031/8   Cable Add: Holzmann Verlag   Telex: 0539331
Man Dir: Peter Holzmann; *Sales Dir:* Alfred Stempfle
Subjects: Management, Handicraft
Founded: 1936
Bookshop: Versandbuchhandlung Hans Holzmann, D-8939 Bad Wörishofen, Postfach 460
ISBN Publisher's Prefix: 3-7783

Horatio-verlag und Agentur*, Dirnitzweg 5, D-8491 Zandt   Tel: (09944) 815
Dir: Genoveva Seydlitz; *Marketing Manager, Rights & Permissions:* Kurt Seydlitz; *Publicity:* Hans Köln
Subject: Humour; Jokes and Games

FEDERAL REPUBLIC OF GERMANY   143

Werner **Hörnemann** Verlag+, In der Wehrhecke 17, Postfach 130109, D-5300 Bonn 1   Tel: (02221) 251376
Subjects: Hobbies, Cookery, Art
1978: 15 titles
ISBN Publisher's Prefix: 3-87384

Horst-Werner Dumjahn Verlag, see Dumjahn

Edition Volker **Huber***, Berliner Str 218, Postfach 933, D-6050 Offenbach   Tel: (0611) 814523
Publisher: Volker Huber; *Sales Managers:* Rosemarie Grenz, Helga Schwinn
Subject: Art

Max **Hueber** Verlag, Krausstr 30, D-8045 Ismaning bei Munich   Tel: (089) 96021   Telex: 05-23613   Cable Add: Hubook
Dirs: Dr Ingomar Hauchler, Heinrich Schrand, Gernot Keuchen; *Sales Dirs:* Bert Rech, Ekkehard Ziegler, Ulrich Heinerz
Subsidiary Companies: Hueber-Holzmann, Pädagogischer Verlag (qv)
Subjects: Textbooks, Reference, Bilingual Dictionaries, German for Foreigners, Linguistics
Founded: 1921
Bookshop: Universitätsbuchhandlung Max Hueber, Amalienstr 77-79, D-8000 Munich 40
ISBN Publisher's Prefix: 3-19

Hueber-Holzmann, Pädagogischer Verlag, Krausstr 30, D-8045 Ismaning/Munich   Tel: (089) 96021   Cable Add: Hubook   Telex: 0523613
Dir: Gernot Keuchen
Subjects: Electrical Engineering, Electronics, Informatics, Data Processing, Textbooks, Mathematics, Music, Periodicals, Social Sciences, Arts
Miscellaneous: Firm is a subsidiary of Max Hueber Verlag, German Federal Republic (qv)
ISBN Publisher's Prefix: 3-8096

Hulsmanns Reske GmbH, see Verlag Eremiten-Presse

Humboldt-Taschenbuchverlag Jacobi KG, Neusser Str 3, Postfach 401120, D-8000 Munich 40   Tel: (089) 38301   Cable Add: Langenscheidt Munich   Telex: 5215379 Lkg md
Man Dir: Karl-Ernst Tieleber-Langenscheidt; *Editorial:* Lieselotte Wirth; *Sales Dir:* Peter Haering; *Advertising Dir:* Dieter Krause; *Sales, Promotion:* through Langenscheidt KG (qv); *Rights & Permissions:* Manfred Überall
Subjects: Nonfiction Paperbacks
1978: 24 titles   *1979:* 24 titles   *Founded:* 1970
Miscellaneous: Company is a member of the Langenscheidt Group (qv)
ISBN Publisher's Prefix: 3-581

edition **hundertmark**, Kolonie Kleeblatt, Blumenweg 12, D-1000 Berlin 42   Tel: (030) 7037732
Man Dir: Armin Hundertmark
Subjects: Contemporary Art Books, Literature; Periodicals
1977: 8 titles   *Founded:* 1970

Husum Druck- und Verlagsgesellschaft mbH und Co KG, Nordbahnhofstr 2, Postfach 1480, D-2250 Husum   Tel: (04841) 6081/3
Man Dir, Editorial, Rights & Permissions: Ingwert Paulsen Jr; *Sales:* Alfred Lorenzen; *Production:* Hajo Hartkopf; *Publicity:* Barbara Marquardt
Subsidiary Company: Hamburger Lesehefte Verlag Iselt & Co Nfl mbH (qv)
Associate Company: Matthiesen Verlag

Ingwert Paulsen Jr (qv)
Subjects: Belles Lettres, Regional Interest
Founded: 1973
ISBN Publisher's Prefix: 3-88042

Dr Alfred **Hüthig** Verlag GmbH, Postfach 102869, D-6900 Heidelberg (Located at: Im Weiher 10) Tel: (06221) 4891 Cable Add: Hüthigverlag Heidelberg Telex: 0461727
Production: Willi Mayer; *Publicity:* Ulrich Stiehl
Subjects: Chemistry, Chemical Engineering, Medicine, Dentistry, Cosmetics, Electronics
1978: 15 titles *Founded:* 1925
Miscellaneous: Publish 32 professional and scientific magazines
ISBN Publisher's Prefix: 3-7785

Hüthig und Pflaum Verlag GmbH & Co KG, Postfach 201920, D-8000 Munich 2 (Located at: Lazarettstr 4, D-8000 Munich 19) Tel: (089) 186051
Telex: 0529408
Publicity Manager: Hans-Georg Scheideler
Branch Off: Im Weiher 10, D-6900 Heidelberg 1
Subjects: Electrical Engineering, Electronics
Associate Company: Richard Pflaum Verlag KG, Munich (qv)
ISBN Publisher's Prefix: 3-8101

i-Punkt*, Zwernitzer Str 3, Postfach 662109, D-8000 Munich 60 Tel: 8714931, 870957
Subjects: Fred Dengers *Gott & Co;* Psalms and Aphorisms

I d W-Verlag GmbH*, Cecilienallee 36, Postfach 320580, D-4000 Düsseldorf 30 Tel: (0211) 434391 Cable Add: ideweverlag
Telex: 8584270
Subject: Business Administration, Tax Law, Finance, Auditing
1977: 12 titles
ISBN Publisher's Prefix: 3-8021

I L S (Institut für Lernsysteme) GmbH, member of Verlagsgruppe Bertelsmann GmbH (qv)

I S P-Verlag (Internationale Sozialistische Publikationen)*, Speicherstr 5, D-6000 Frankfurt am Main 2 Tel: (0611) 233012
Subject: Politics

I V A Verlag Bernd Polke GmbH, Am Lastnauer Tor 4, D-7400 Tübingen 1 Tel: (07071) 212314
Man Dir, Rights & Permissions: Bernd Polke; *Sales:* Herbert Grohmann; *Publicity:* Cornelia Voester
Orders to: VVA, D-4830 Gütersloh

Ibnassus Presse*, Postfach 930, D-3400 Göttingen Tel: (0551) 72659
Man & Sales Dirs: Bert Schlender, Detlev Pawlik
Subjects: Belles Lettres, Poetry, Art
Founded: 1972
Bookshop: Versandbuchhandlung Bert Schlender, Postfach 930, D-3400 Göttingen

Idion Verlag*, Nussbaumstrasse 10, D-8000, Munich Tel: 593504 Telex: 8579460 vam D
Dirs: Hans-Lothar Merten, Manfred Stölting; *Sales:* Manfred Mayer; *Production:* Johannes Rüger
Subjects: Popular Facsimilies

Index eV, Überlinger Str 13, Postfach 410511, D-5000 Cologne 41 Tel: (0221) 436939/372043
Publisher: Adolf Müller
Subjects: Belles Lettres, Poetry, Politics, Czech and Slovak Literature

Inform-Verlag, see Dreisam-Verlag

Insel Verlag, Lindenstr 29-35, Postfach 3325, D-6000 Frankfurt am Main
Tel: (0611) 740231 Cable Add: Inselverlag
Telex: 413972
Publisher: Dr Siegfried Unseld; *Man Dir:* Dr Heribert Marré; *Sales:* Dr Gottfried Honnefelder; *Publicity:* Claus Carlé; *Rights & Permissions:* Helene Ritzerfeld
Subjects: Belles Lettres, Poetry, Biography, History, Music, Art, Low-priced Paperbacks, Fiction, Philosophy, Psychology, Education, Juveniles
Founded: 1899
Miscellaneous: Associate Company: Suhrkamp Verlag (qv)
ISBN Publisher's Prefix: 3-458

Institut für Lernsysteme (ILS), member of Verlagsgruppe Bertelsmann GmbH (qv)

Institut für Marxistische Studien und Forschungen eV (IMSF) Frankfurt/AM (Institute for Marxist Studies and Research)*, Liebigstr 6, D-6000 Frankfurt/AM Tel: 724914
Man Dir: Prof Dr Schleifstein; *all other offices:* Dr Schmidt
Subjects: Publication of results of studies, research etc, commentary on current political questions; Periodical (quarterly) *Marxismus Digest*
1977: 8 titles *Founded:* 1968

Inter-Kunst und Buch GmbH*, Wöllsteinerstr 8, D-6550 Bad Kreuznach Tel: (0671) 67073 Telex: 042815
Associate Company: Harrach & Sabrow, Bad Kreuznach (qv)
Subjects: Art Books, Graphics, Bibliophile Editions

Verlag **Internationale Solidarität** Verlagsgesellschaft mbH*, Zugweg 10, D-5000 Cologne Tel: (0221) 327817 Cable Add: Zugweg 10
Sales, Production: Ole Callsen
Subject: Politics

Irisiana Druck und Verlag, Wengenerstr 8, D-8961 Haldenwang Tel: (08374) 1574
1978: 3 titles
Subjects: Eastern Religion, Feminine Interest

Verlag der **Islam***, Babenhäuserlandstr 25, D-6000 Frankfurt am Main 70 Tel: (0611) 653122 Cable Add: Islam
Man Dir: F I Anweri; *Publicity Dir:* Hadayatullah Hübsch
Subject: Religion

J R O-Kartografische Verlagsgesellschaft mbH, Leopoldstrasse 175, Postfach 400940, D-8000 München 40 Tel: (089) 381031
Cable Add: hochbild Telex: 5215802
Gen Managers: Dr Bernd Koberg, Karl E Keck; *Marketing and Publicity:* Frieder Neher; *Sales:* Ingo Kruck; *Production:* Max Hann
Parent Company: Süddeutscher Verlag GmbH, Sendlonger Str 80, Postfach 202220, D-8000 Munich 2
Subjects: Road Maps, Town Maps, Walking Maps and Guides, School Wall Maps, Organisational Charts, Atlases, Globes
Founded: 1922
ISBN Publisher's Prefix: 3-87378

Jacobi Verlag GmbH*, Mühlenweg 67, D-2822 Schwanewede 1 — Leuchtenberg Tel: (0421) 631413
Man Dir, Editorial: Friedrich Röver; *Sales:* Heyke Weinbecker
Subjects: World Literature of the late 19th/early 20th century
1977: 6 titles *Founded:* 1974
ISBN Publisher's Prefix: 13198

Jahreszeitenverlag*, Poßmoorweg 1, Postfach 601220, D-2000 Hamburg 60
Tel: (040) 27171 Cable Add: Jalag
Telex: 0213214
Subject: Belles Lettres

Verlag Eduard **Jakobsohn**, Glogauer str 22, D-1000 Berlin 36 Tel: 6181258
Orders to: PRO MEDIA Literaturvertrieb GmbH, Werner Voss Damm 54, D-1000 Berlin 42
Subjects: Alternative Living, Communes, Marxist Theory, Literature
1977: 4 titles *1979:* 10 titles

Jal-Verlag/Jal-Reprint Arnulf Liebing, Werner-von-Siemens-Str 5, Postfach 5840, D-8700 Würzburg 1 Tel: (0931) 21120/22821 Cable Add: Journalfranz
Publisher: Arnulf Liebing, Hildgund Holler
Imprints: Slavica, History of Pharmacy
Subjects: Slavistics, History of Pharmacy
1978: 11 titles
ISBN Publisher's Prefix: 3-7778

Stern-Verlag **Janssen** und Co, see Stern-Verlag

Reinhard **Jaspert**, see Safari-Verlag

Jourpart Redaktionsbüro und Verlagsgesellschaft mbH*, Gähkopf 3, D-7000 Stuttgart 1 Tel: (0711) 221121/3
Telex: 723615 jpar d
Publisher: Martin Rabe
Subjects: Art, Juveniles, Dictionaries, Encylopaedias, Politics

Jugend und Volk Verlag GmbH*, Claude-Lorrainstr, D-8000 Munich 40 Tel: (089) 374560
Parent Company: Jugend und Volk Verlagsgesellschaft mbH, Austria (qv)
Subject: Juveniles
ISBN Publisher's Prefix: 3-8113

Jugenddienst-Verlag, Foehrenstr 33-35, Postfach 200415, D-5600 Wuppertal 2
Tel: (0202) 551888
Dir: Hermann Schulz; *Sales Manager:* Barbara Kehrein; *Rights & Permissions:* Helmut Lotz
Associate Company: Peter Hammer Verlag (qv)
Subjects: Playgroups, Learning, Sexual Instruction, Meditation, Christian Action
1978: 12 titles
ISBN Publisher's Prefix: 3-7795

Axel-**Juncker**-Verlag Nachfolger Jacobi KG, Neusserstr 3, D-8000 Munich 40 Tel: (089) 38301
Man Dir: Karl Ernst Tielebier-Langenscheidt; *Sales Dir:* Peter Haering; *Publicity & Advertising:* Dieter Krause; *Sales, Promotion:* through Langenscheidt KG (qv); *Rights & Permissions:* Manfred Überall; *Export Dir:* Uwe Cordts
Subjects: Reference, Educational Materials
Titles in print: 42 *Founded:* 1902
Miscellaneous: Company is a member of the Langenscheidt Group (qv)
ISBN Publisher's Prefix: 3-558

Junior International, Postfach 285, D-7300 Esslingen (Located at: Liebigstr 1-11, D-7301 Deizisau) Tel: (07153) 22011 Cable Add: Verlag Schreiber Telex: 7266880 jfs d
Associate Company: Verlag J F Schreiber

Juventa Verlag, Dr Martin Faltermaier, Tizianstr 115, D-8000 Munich 19 Tel: (089) 155420
Man Dir: Dr Martin Faltermaier; *Publicity:* Elke Gerdes
Subjects: Mainly connected with young

people's training, education, etc
1977: 18 titles *1978:* 14 titles *Founded:* 1953
ISBN Publisher's Prefix: 3-7799

Verlag Gerhard **Kaffke***, Echzellerstr 1, Postfach 640125, D-6000 Frankfurt am Main 64 Tel: (06194) 21493
Man Dir: Gerhard Kaffke; *Manager:* Gisela Kaffke; *Sales:* Ursula Wieder
Subjects: Theology, Religion, Paperbacks
1977: 16 titles *Founded:* 1955
ISBN Publisher's Prefix: 3-87391

Chr **Kaiser** Verlag, Postfach 509, D-8000 Munich 43 (Located at: Isabellastr 20, D-8000 Munich 40) Tel: (089) 372097/378786
Dir: Manfred Weber; *Sales Dir:* Uwe Fleischle
Subjects: Christian apologetics and exegesis; Theology; Religion and Society
1977: 65 titles *1978:* 85 titles *Founded:* 1845
ISBN Publisher's Prefix: 3-459

Verlag Ferdinand **Kamp**, Widumestr 2-8, Postfach 101309, D-4630 Bochum
Tel: (0234) 15071
Subjects: Textbooks, Reference, Encyclopaedias, Dictionaries, Education, Nonfiction, Paperbacks, Periodicals
ISBN Publisher's Prefix: 3-592

S **Karger** GmbH, Verlag für Medizin & Naturwissenschaften, Angerhofstr 9, Postfach 2, D-8034 Germering, Munich
Tel: (089) 844021 Cable Add: Kargermedbooks Telex: 5248665
Man Dir: W Kunz
Subjects: Medicine, Psychology, Natural Science
Bookshop: Karger-Buchhandlung Ausstellung & Vertrieb internationaler medizinischer Fachliteratur, Angerhofstr 9, Postfach 2, D-8034 Germering, Munich
Miscellaneous: Firm is a branch of S Karger AG, Switzerland (qv)

Karo-Bücher, an imprint of A Weichert Verlag (qv)

Verlag **Katholisches Bibelwerk** GmbH*, Silberburgstr 121A, D-7000 Stuttgart
Tel: (0711) 629003
Editorial: Martha Buck
Dir: Horst Rauchecker; *Sales Manager:* Fritz Unger
Subject: Religious literature on practical aspects of Catholic Bible work in Belgium, Federal Germany, Netherlands, Austria and Switzerland
Miscellaneous: Company is a member of AMB (qv)
ISBN Publisher's Prefix: 3-460

Katzmann-Verlag KG+, Doblerstr 33, Postfach 1827, D-7400 Tübingen
Tel: (07071) 23115 Cable Add: Katzmann Verlag
Man Dir: Dr Volker Katzmann; *Sales Dir:* Sibylle Katzmann; *Production:* Margarete Knöpfle; *Publicity, Rights & Permissions:* Dr V Katzmann
Subjects: Sociology, Youth Work, Adult Education, Marriage and Family Counselling, Theology, Art, Religion, Periodical
1977: 10 titles *1978:* 11 titles *Founded:* 1945
ISBN Publisher's Prefix: 3-7805

Verlag Ernst **Kaufmann**, Alleestr 2, Postfach 1780, D-7630 Lahr/Schwarzwald
Tel: (07821) 26083 Cable Add: Ernstkauf Telex: 0754973
Man Dir: Heinz Kaufmann; *Chief Editor:* R Dessecker-Kaufmann
Subjects: Religious Education (books, materials); Children's Books
1977: 19 titles *1978:* 31 titles *Founded:* 1816
Miscellaneous: Member of Verlagsring Religionsunterricht (VRU = Religious Instruction Publishing Ring)
ISBN Publisher's Prefix: 3-7806

Verlag und Buchvertrieb E **Keimer***, Postfach 22, D-8014 Munich-Neubiberg
Tel: (089) 6014811
Dir: Wolfgang Reuter
Subject: Textbooks
ISBN Publisher's Prefix: 3-920536

Verlag **Keip** KG Antiquariat, Hainer Weg 46-48, D-6000 Frankfurt am Main 70 Tel: (0611) 614011 Cable Add: Antikeip Frankfurtmain Telex: D 689857 Keip
Publisher: Ulrich Keip; *Manager and Office Chief:* Johann Holler
Subjects: Law, Economics, History, Sociology, Socialism
1977: 500 titles *1978:* 100 titles *Founded:* 1967

Franckh'sche Verlagshandlung, W **Keller** & Co, see Franckh'sche

Verlag F H **Kerle**, Hermann-Herder Str 4, Postfach, D-7800 Freiburg Tel: (0761) 27171 Telex: 07721440
Man Dir: Franz Grossmann; *Sales:* Günther Zimmermann; *Publicity:* Hildegard Zoller
Parent Company: Verlag Herder GmbH & Co KG (qv)
Subjects: Belles Lettres (covering novels, memoirs, reportage)
ISBN Publisher's Prefix: 3-600

Keysersche Verlagsbuchhandlung GmbH, Widenmayerstr 41, Postfach 243, D-8000 Munich 22 Tel: (089) 225055
Publishers: Christian Neumann, Hans Joachim Neumann; *Production:* Joachim W Schmidt; *Public Relations, Advertising:* Silke Schreiber
Subjects: Art, Reference, Geography, Juveniles
1979: 10 titles *Founded:* 1777
ISBN Publisher's Prefix: 3-87405

Kibu-Verlag GmbH, Bräuckerweg 120, Postfach 329, D-5750 Menden 1 Tel: 02373 63131 Telex: 8202855
Dirs: Kunibert Birnkraut, Erhard Tamm
Subjects: Children's, Juveniles, Special Editions

Johannes **Kiefel** Verlag, Linderhauser Str 60, D-5600 Wuppertal 2 Tel: (0202) 642084/5 Cable Add: Kiefel, Wuppertal-2
Dir: Ingeborg Kiefel
Subjects: Religion, Juveniles, Textbooks
Founded: 1920
ISBN Publisher's Prefix: 3-7811

Friedrich **Kiehl** Verlag GmbH*, Pfaustr 13, Postfach 210747, D-6700 Ludwigshafen
Tel: (0621) 695041/2 Telex: 0464810
Dir: Ernst-Otto Kleyboldt; *Sales Manager:* Regina König
Subjects: Law, Economics, Commerce, Banking
Miscellaneous: Firm is a subsidiary of Verlag Neue Wirtschafts-Briefe GmbH (qv)
ISBN Publisher's Prefix: 3-470

Verlag **Kiepenheuer und Witsch***, Rondorfer Str 5, D-5000 Cologne-Marienburg
Tel: (0221) 387038 Cable Add: Kiepenbücher Cologne
Man Dir: Dr Reinhold Neven Du Mont; *Editorial:* Bärbel Flad, Erika Stegmann, Renate Matthaei; *Sales:* Heinz Biehn;

FEDERAL REPUBLIC OF GERMANY 145

Foreign Rights & Permissions: Alexandra von Miquel
Subjects: General Fiction, Belles Lettres, Poetry, Biography, History, Social Science, High-priced Paperbacks, University Textbooks
1977: 48 titles *Founded:* 1948
Miscellaneous: Associate company of Verlag für Politik und Wirtschaft (qv)
ISBN Publisher's Prefix: 3-462

Kilda Verlag*, Münsterstr 71, D-4402 Greven/Westfalen Tel: (0251) 36229 Cable Add: Kildagreven
Man Dir: Mr Pölking

Kindler Verlag GmbH*, Leopoldstr 54, Postfach 401043, D-8000 Munich 40
Tel: (089) 394041 Cable Add: Kindlerverlag Telex: 0521567
Editorial and Publicity: Traut Felgentreff; *Sales:* Elke Gerhart
Orders to: Vereinigte Verlagsauslieferung GmbH, Postfach 7777, D-4830 Gütersloh
Subjects: General Fiction, Belles Lettres, Biography, History, How-to, Art, Reference, Religion, Low- & High-priced Paperbacks, Medicine, Psychology, General & Social Science, University Textbooks, Educational Materials
Founded: 1951
Miscellaneous: Associate Company: Lichtenberg Verlag GmbH (qv)
ISBN Publisher's Prefix: 3-463

Klasing und Co GmbH, Siekerwall 21, Postfach 4809, D-4800 Bielefeld 1
Tel: (0521) 67015 Cable Add: Buchklasing Bielefeld Telex: 932934 Dekla
Publishers: Konrad-Wilhelm Delius, Kurt Delius; *Sales & Publicity Manager:* Wilhelm Meyerhenke; *Rights & Permissions:* Ilsemarie Steinbrinker
Parent Company: Delius, Klasing & Co (qv)
Subjects: Yachting, Motor Boats
ISBN Publisher's Prefix: 3-87412

Kunstverlag Woldemar **Klein**, Dr Rudolf Georgi, Aureliusstr 42, Postfach 407, 51 Aachen Telex: 832337 geac d
Tel: (0241) 26141
Subjects: Art Calendars, Art Books

Buchverlag **Klemmer und Muller***, Heisterweg 39, D-2900 Oldenburg
Tel: (0441) 31018/9 Telex: 25660 nopro d
Subjects: Poems and Non-Rhymes from Popular Humorist Heinz Erhardt

Klens Verlag GmbH, Prinz-Georg-Str 44, Postfach 320620, D-4000 Düsseldorf 32
Tel: (0211) 480023
Publisher: Viktor Nolden
Subjects: Popular Christian Aids, Juveniles, and Youth Training
1978: 5 titles
ISBN Publisher's Prefix: 3-87309

Ernst **Klett***, Rotebühlstr 77, Postfach 809, D-7000 Stuttgart Tel: (0711) 66721
Publisher: Michael Klett; *Publicity Manager:* Egon Schramm; *Foreign Relations:* Martin Veit; *Rights and Export Sales:* Joachim Lange
Subjects: Biology, Chemistry, History, Industries, Crafts, Arts, Textbooks, Reference, Encyclopaedias, Dictionaries, Literary Criticism, Mathematics, Multimedia, Education, Music, Physics, Games, Linguistics, Languages, Periodicals
Miscellaneous: Associate Companies: Klett-Cotta Verlag, Federal Republic of Germany (qv); Stuttgarter Verlagskontor, Federal Republic of Germany and Switzerland (qv); Klett & Balmer Verlag, Switzerland (qv)
ISBN Publisher's Prefix: 3-12

Klett Cotta Verlag*, Rotebühlstr 77, Postfach 809, D-7000 Stuttgart 1 Tel: (0711) 66721 Cable Add: Klettverlag Telex: 721715 klett d
Man Dir: Michael Klett; *Editorial:* Dr Arbogast, Dr Dieckmann, Friedrich Kür; *Foreign Relations:* Mr Veit; *Rights and Export Sales:* Joachim Lange
Imprints: Edition Alpha; Hobbit Presse
Subjects: Education, Psychology, Philosophy, History, Social Sciences, Dictionaries, Literature, Linguistics, Art, Easy Readers
Founded: 1844
Associate Companies: Klett-Balmer, Switzerland (qv); Ernst Klett; Stuttgarter Verlags Kontor, German Federal Republic (qv)
ISBN Publisher's Prefix: 3-12

Klinkhardt und Biermann Richard Carl Schmidt Co, Helmstedter Str 151, D-3300 Brunswick Tel: (0531) 73189
Owner: Ilse Gutsch
Subjects: Art, Antiques, Numismatics
Founded: 1907
ISBN Publisher's Prefix: 3-7814

Erika **Klopp** Verlag GmbH, Kurfürstendamm 126, Postfach 310829, D-1000 Berlin 31 Tel: (030) 8911008
Publisher: Horst Meyer
Subject: Juveniles
1978: 25 titles *Founded:* 1925
ISBN Publisher's Prefix: 3-7817

Vittorio **Klostermann**, Frauenlobstr 22, Postfach 900601, D-6000 Frankfurt am Main 90 Tel: (0611) 774011
Man Dirs: Michael Klostermann, Eckard Klostermann
Subjects: Philosophy, Bibliography, Romanistics, University Textbooks, General Science, History, Art, High-priced Paperbacks
1977: 50 titles *1978:* 50 titles *Founded:* 1930
ISBN Publisher's Prefix: 3-465

Ehrenfried **Klotz** Verlag, Theaterstr 13, Postfach 77, D-3400 Göttingen Tel: (0551) 54031/3
Man Dir: Dr Arndt Ruprecht; *Sales:* Robert-Bosch-Breite
Subject: Religion
Parent Company: Vandenhoeck & Ruprecht, Göttingen (qv)
1977: 1 title *1978:* 2 titles *Founded:* 1949
ISBN Publisher's Prefix: 3-525

Fritz **Knapp** Verlag GmbH, Neue Mainzer Str 60, D-6000 Frankfurt am Main 1 Tel: (0611) 280151 Cable Add: Schauinsland Telex: 411397
Man Dirs: Alfons Binz, Peter Muthesius; *Sales Dir:* Alexander Rausch von Traubenberg; *Publicity Manager:* Karlheinz Möller; *Production:* K M Tecklenburg; *Advertising Dir:* Dieter Belz; *Rights & Permissions:* Alfons Binz
Subjects: Money, Banking, Stock Exchange, Economics, Economic Science, Reference, High-priced Paperbacks, Specialist Dictionaries, German Law in English/French Translation
1977: 36 titles *1978:* 35 titles *Founded:* 1935
ISBN Publisher's Prefix: 3-7819

Wilhelm **Knapp** Verlag, Pressehaus am Martin-Luther-Platz, Postfach 1122, D-4000 Düsseldorf 1 Tel: (0211) 885608
Man Dirs: Dr Max Nitsche, Dr Joseph Schaffrath, Werner Gutzki; *Publishing Dir:* Dr Manfred Lotsch; *Production, Promotion:* Helmut Schwanen

Parent Company: Droste Verlag GmbH, Düsseldorf, (qv)
Subjects: Photography, Cinematography
1978: 15 titles *1979:* 12 titles *Founded:* 1838
ISBN Publisher's Prefix: 3-87420

Albrecht **Knaus** Verlag, Postfach 520447, D-2000 Hamburg 52 (Located at: Beselerstr 2) Tel: (040) 897401 Cable Add: knausbooks Hamburg
Man Dir: Dr Albrecht Knaus; *Sales:* Lothar Nalbach; *Production:* Johannes Eikel
Orders to: VVA, Postfach 7777, D-4830 Gütersloh 1
Subjects: Fiction and Nonfiction: Memoirs, History, Politics
1978: 10 titles *1979:* 20 titles *Founded:* 1978
ISBN Publisher's Prefix: 3-8135

Verlag Josef **Knecht**-Carolus Druckerei GmbH, Liebfrauenberg 37, D-6000 Frankfurt am Main 1 Tel: (0611) 281767
Dirs: Dr Josef Knecht, Dr H Herder-Dorneich, Fritz Knoch; *Editorial:* Dr Ursula Hegemann, Dr Marianne Regnier
Subjects: General Fiction, Paperbacks, Religion, Social Science, Philosophy, Nonfiction
1978: 15 titles *Founded:* 1946
ISBN Publisher's Prefix: 3-7820

Knorr und Hirth Verlag GmbH, D-3167 Ahrbeck vor Hanover Tel: (05136) 5501 Cable Add: Knorrhirth Ahrbeck
Man Dir: Berthold Fricke
Subjects: Art, Geography, Travel Guides, Almanacs; Editions also in English, French, Dutch, Italian, Spanish and Japanese; Several Bilingual Editions
1977-78: 40 titles *Founded:* 1894
ISBN Publisher's Prefix: 3-7821

Verlagsanstalt Alexander **Koch** GmbH, Postfach 3081, D-7000 Stuttgart 1 (Located at: Fasanenweg 18, D-7022 Leinfelden-Echterdingen 1) Tel: (0711) 79891 Telex: 7-255609 drw d
Man Dirs: Karl-Heinz Weinbrenner, L Drabarczyk; *Manager, Rights & Permissions:* Dr Erwin Schmid; *Editorial:* Max Fengler, Eberhard Höhn
Parent Company: DRW-Verlag Weinbrenner KG (qv)
Subjects: Architecture, Interior Decoration, Building Technology; Periodicals
1977: 5 titles *1978:* 3 titles *Founded:* 1890
ISBN Publisher's Prefix: 3-87422

Kochbuchverlag Heimeran KG, Dietlindenstr 14, Postfach 400824, D-8000 Munich 40 Tel: (089) 399017
Man Dir: Till Heimeran; *Editorial Production:* Tillmann Roeder; *Sales, Publicity, Rights & Permissions:* Thomas Kniffler
Associate Company: Ernst Heimeran Verlag (qv)
Subject: Cookery
1978: 12 titles *Founded:* 1969
ISBN Publisher's Prefix: 3-8063

C A **Koch's** Verlag Nachfolger, see Deutsche Buchgemeinschaft

K F **Koehler** Verlag*, Eberhardstr 10, Postfach 210, D-7000 Stuttgart 1 Tel: (0711) 782071 Telex: 0723308
Dir: Till Grupp
Subjects: Humanities, History, Politics, Law, Social Science, Geography
Founded: 1789
ISBN Publisher's Prefix: 3-87425

Koehlers Verlagsgesellschaft*, Steintorwall 17, Postfach 371, D-4900 Herford Tel: (05221) 3147/8 Cable Add: Koehlers Vlg Herford/Westf Telex: 934801
Publishers: Dr Kurt Schober, Gerhard Bollmann, Hans-Focko Koehler; *Sales:* Hans-Focko Koehler; *Publicity:* Gerhard Mindt
Associate Companies: Maximilian-Verlag, E S Mittler und Sohn GmbH, Verlag Offene Worte (all at above address)
Subjects: Fiction and Nonfiction, Shipping, Shipbuilding, Maritime and Offshore interest, Periodicals
ISBN Publisher's Prefix: 3-7822

Verlag Valentin **Koerner** GmbH+, Hermann-Sielcken-Str 36, Postfach 304, D-7570 Baden-Baden Tel: (07221) 22423
Publisher: Valentin Koerner
1978: 18 titles
ISBN Publisher's Prefix: 3-87320

Unternehmensgruppe Verlag W **Kohlhammer** GmbH+, Hessbrühlstr 69, Postfach 800430, D-7000 Stuttgart 80 Tel: (0711) 78631 Cable Add: Kohlhammer Stuttgart Telex: 07255820
Man Dirs: Dr Jürgen Gutbrod, Günter Haberland; *Sales Dir:* Gerd W Ludwig; *Rights & Permissions:* Dr Alexander Schweickert
Subsidiary Companies: Berliner Union GmbH (qv); Deutscher Gemeindeverlag (qv); G Grote'sche Verlagsbuchhandlung KG (qv); Kohlhammer und Wallishauser GmbH, Hechingen; (all in Federal Republic of Germany)
Branch Offs: Berlin, Cologne, Mainz
Subjects: History, Art, Orientalia, Philosophy, Humanities, Religion, Law, Public Administration, Linguistics, Literary History, Economics, Natural Sciences, Architecture, Travel
1977: 280 titles *1978:* 380 titles *Founded:* 1866
Miscellaneous: Subsidiary Deutsche Gemeindeverlag (qv) has Branch Offices in 8 major cities, each office producing literature appropriate to the particular region
ISBN Publisher's Prefix: 3-17

Kohl's Technischer Verlag Erwin Kohl GmbH & Co KG, Emil-Sulzbach-Str 12, Postfach 970115, D-6000 Frankfurt am Main 97 Tel: (0611) 778410 and 776513
Associate Company: Frankfurter Fachverlag Michael Kohl KG (qv)
Subjects: Civil & Mechanical Engineering
ISBN Publisher's Prefix: 3-87430

Kolibri-Verlag+, Else-Lasker-Schüler-Str 47-49, D-5600 Wuppertal 1 Tel: (0202) 443143
Dir: Maria Pfriem; *Sales:* Karin Bambek
Associate Company: Engelbert Pfrim Verlag (qv)
Subjects: Books for Children of all ages, on all subjects, Fiction and Nonfiction
1978: 26 titles *Founded:* 1950
ISBN Publisher's Prefix: 3-87434

Komar*, Oberaustr 1, Postfach 1132, D-8200 Rosenheim Tel: (08031) 1280/33477/33499 Telex: 0525793
Subjects: Juveniles, Psychology, Sports

Verlag **Kommentator** GmbH, Zeppelinallee 43, Postfach 970148, D-6000 Frankfurt am Main Tel: (0611) 774055
Man Dir: Dr Caspar van Kempen; *Editorial:* Gunter Herz, Ulrich Neuhaus; *Sales, Publicity:* Ernst F Grundl
Subject: Law, Taxation
Miscellaneous: Firm is a member of the Kluwer Group, Deventer, Netherlands (qv)

Associate Company: Alfred Metzner Verlag GmbH (qv)
ISBN Publisher's Prefix: 3-7824

Konkordia AG für Druck und Verlag*, Eisenbahnstr 31-33, Postfach 1240, D-7580 Bühl/Baden Tel: (07223) 22501/23631
Telex: 784533
Subject: Textbooks
ISBN Publisher's Prefix: 3-7826

Anton H **Konrad** Verlag*, Erlenweg 7, Postfach 3, D-7912 Weissenhorn Tel: (07309) 2657
Subjects: Arts, History
ISBN Publisher's Prefix: 3-87437

A **Korsch** Verlag, Bodenseestr 226-228, Postfach 662320, D-8000 Munich 66 Tel: (089) 870021 Telex: 05212901
Subjects: Travel, Scenic picture books

Kösel-Verlag GmbH & Co, Flüggenstr 2, D-8000 Munich 19 Tel: (089) 175077 Cable Add: Köselverlag Munich Telex: 5215492 kvmud
Man Dirs: Dieter Munz, Dr Christoph Wild; *Production:* Friedhelm Jochems; *Rights & Permissions:* Ingrid Fink; *Advertising:* Gudrun Loesel
Orders to: Flugplatzstr 1, D-8031 Gilching Tel: (08105) 9014 Telex: 524199 kvgid
Subjects: Pedagogy, Philosophy, Religion, Educational Materials, History, Textbooks, Social Science, Fiction
1977: 71 titles *1978:* 76 titles *Founded:* 1593
ISBN Publisher's Prefix: 3-466

G **Kowalski**, see Champion Verlag

Karin **Kramer** Verlag, Postfach 106, D-1000 Berlin 44 (Located at: Braunschweiger Str 22) Tel: (030) 6845055/6842598
Editorial and Publicity: Bernd Kramer
Subjects: Politics, Art, Literature, Education, Psychology, Anarchist Literature
1977: 12 titles *1978:* 12 titles *Founded:* 1970
ISBN Publisher's Prefix: 3-87956

Karl **Krämer** Verlag GmbH und Co, Schulze-Delitzsch-Str 15, Postfach 800650, D-7000 Stuttgart 80 Tel: (0711) 610700 Cable Add: Fachbuchkraemer Stuttgart
Man Dir, Rights & Permissions: Karl H Krämer; *Sales Dir:* Bernhard Prokop; *Production, Publicity:* Annemarie Bosch
Orders to: Rotebühlstr 40, Postfach 808, D-7000 Stuttgart 1
Associate Company: Verlag Karl Krämer & Co, Spiegelgasse 14, CH-8001 Zurich, Switzerland
Subjects: Town Planning, Architecture, Building Construction, Sociology
Bookshop: Fachbuchhandlung Karl Krämer, Rotebühlstr 40, Postfach 808, D-7000 Stuttgart 1
1977: 18 titles *Founded:* 1930
ISBN Publisher's Prefix: 3-7828

Dr Waldemar **Kramer** Verlagsbuchhandlung+, Bornheimer Landwehr 57a, Postfach 600445, D-6000 Frankfurt am Main Tel: (0611) 434325
Publishers: Waldemar Kramer, Henriette Kramer
Subjects: Science and Natural History, Biology, History, Art Education, Psychology, Geography, Nature Study, Environment; Publications of the Senckenberg Nature Study Association; Periodicals
1977: 15 titles *1978:* 18 titles
ISBN Publisher's Prefix: 3-7829

Krausskopf Verlag GmbH, Lessingstr 12, Postfach 2760, D-6500 Mainz Tel: (06131) 674041 Cable Add: Krausskopfverlag
Dirs: Hans Hauck, Jan Hendrik Stoel
Subjects: Technical Books & Periodicals
Founded: 1937
Miscellaneous: Firm is a subsidiary of NV Uitgeversmaatschappij Elsevier, Netherlands (qv)
ISBN Publisher's Prefix: 3-7830

Kreuz Verlag, Breitwiesenstr 30, Postfach 800669, D-7000 Stuttgart 80 Tel: (0711) 734281/733135
Man Dir: Dieter Breitsohl; *Editor:* Helmut Weigel, Hildegunde Wöller; *Publicity, Rights & Permissions:* Barbara Dressler; *Production:* Brigitte Gnieser
Subsidiary Company: Feuerseebuchhandlung, Breitwiesenstr 30, D-7000 Stuttgart 80 Tel: (0711) 732387
Branch Off: Lützelsteiner Weg 51, D-1000 Berlin
Subjects: Reference, Religion, Education, Juveniles, Psychology, Social Science, Periodicals
1978: 35 titles *Founded:* 1945
ISBN Publisher's Prefix: 3-7831

Kriminalistik Verlag GmbH, Postfach 102640, 6900 Heidelberg (Located at: im Weiher 10) Tel: 06621/498250 Telex: 04-61727 huedh
Associate Companies: R V Decker's Verlag G Schenck GmbH (qv); C F Müller Jüristischer Verlag GmbH (qv)
Subject: Criminology

Kronen-Verlag Erich Cramer, Donnerstr 5, Postfach 500903, D-2000 Hamburg 50 Tel: (040) 391207 Cable Add: Kronenverlag
Subjects: Natural Science Plates and Wall Charts in Biology, Calendars
ISBN Publisher's Prefix: 3-920567

Alfred **Kröner** Verlag, Reuchlinstr 4, Postfach 1109, D-7000 Stuttgart 1 Tel: (0711) 620221
Man Dirs: Arno Klemm, Walter Kohrs
Subjects: History, Music, Art, Philosophy, Reference, Psychology, Engineering, General and Social Science, Economics, Literature, Education
1977: 25 titles *Founded:* 1904
ISBN Publisher's Prefix: 3-520

Helmut **Krüger***, Oberkasseler Str 94, D-4000 Düsseldorf 11 Tel: 53524
Man Dir: Helmut Krüger
Subjects: Art, Photography
Founded: 1974

Wolfgang **Kruger** Verlag, Geleitsstrasse 25, Postfach 700480, D-6000 Frankfurt am Main 70 Tel: 0611/60621 Cable Add: buchfischer Telex: 0412410
Man Dir: Monika Schoeller; *Editorial:* Ivo Frenzel; *Sales, Publicity:* Ulrich Meier; *Production:* Wilfried Meiner; *Rights & Permissions:* Cornelia Wohlfarth
Parent Company: S Fischer Verlag GmbH (qv)
Subjects: General Fiction and Nonfiction
1977: 33 titles
ISBN Publisher's Prefix: 3-8105

Kübler Verlag GmbH, Postfach 242, D-6840 Lampertheim 1 (Located at: Gaußstr 21) Tel: (06206) 51055 Telex: 465738
Dir: Ulrich Schele
Subjects: Social Studies, Economics, Politics, Education, Picture Books
1977: 2 titles *1979:* 6 titles *Founded:* 1972
ISBN Publisher's Prefix: 3-921265

FEDERAL REPUBLIC OF GERMANY 147

Kubon & Sagner, see Verlag Otto Sagner

Kühl KG, Verlagsgesellschaft, Mainzer Landstr 147, Postfach 119151, D-6000 Frankfurt am Main 2 Tel: (0611) 730234 Cable Add: kuhl Telex: 0413080 kuehl d
Managed by: Communist Party of the Federal Republic of Germany (KBW)
Branch Offs: Hanover, Cologne and Munich
Subjects: Publications by the Central Committee of the Communist Party of the Federal Republic of Germany
1977: 10 titles *Founded:* 1973

Wilhelm **Kumm** Verlag, Tulpenhofstr 45, D-6050 Offenbach am Main Tel: 884349 Cable Add: Kummverlag
Proprietor & Man Dir: Wilhelm Kumm
Subjects: Belles Lettres, Poetry
Founded: 1967
ISBN Publisher's Prefix: 3-7836

Kunst und Wissen Erich Bieber OHG, Wilhelmstr 4, Postfach 46, D-7000 Stuttgart 1, Tel: (0711) 241152/4 Cable Add: Kunstwissen Telex: 0721929
Publishers: Erich, Jürgen and Wolfgang Bieber
Subjects: Technical Textbooks
ISBN Publisher's Prefix: 3-87953

Florian **Kupferberg** Verlag*, Postfach 2680, D-6500 Mainz Tel: (06131) 24977
Owner: Christian A Kupferberg
Subjects: Art, Architecture, Cultural & Literary History, Mass Media
Founded: 1797/1938
ISBN Publisher's Prefix: 3-7837

Verlag Helmut **Küpper** (formerly Georg Bondi)*, Boltensternstr 12, D-4000 Düsseldorf 1 Tel: (0211) 623801
Dir: Margarete Breuer
Subjects: General Fiction, Humanities, Education, Social Science, Economics, Philosophy
ISBN Publisher's Prefix: 3-7835

Kyrios-Verlag GmbH+, Luckengasse 8, Postfach 1740, D-8050 Freising Tel: (08161) 5527
Dir: Ursula Blum; *Sales Manager:* Eveline Kamm
Subjects: Religion, Social Work, Periodicals
1979: 12 titles *Founded:* 1916
ISBN Publisher's Prefix: 3-7838

L N-Verlag Lübeck, Lübecker Nachrichten GmbH*, Königstr 53-57, Postfach 2238, D-2400 Lübeck 1 Tel: (0451) 1441 Telex: 026801
Man Dirs: Charles Coleman, Jürgen Coleman, Bernd Ehrlich, Dr Günter Semmerow, Jürgen Wessel; *Editorial:* Jürgen W Scheutzow; *Sales Dir:* Elmar Bruns
Subjects: Series of pocket guidebooks to various countries world-wide, and areas of Germany
1977: 10 titles *1978:* 10 titles
ISBN Publisher's Prefix: 3-87498

Laetare, see Burckhardthaus-Laetare Verlag GmbH

Lahn-Verlag, Wiesbadener Str 1, Postfach 140, D-6250 Limburg Lahn 1 Tel: (06431) 401211 Telex: 0484764 palan d
Publisher: Engelbert Tauscher; *Editorial:* Ursula Mock; *Publicity Manager:* Raimund Zoellner
Subjects: Religion, Philosophy, Education
1978: 22 titles *Founded:* 1900
ISBN Publisher's Prefix: 3-7840

Lambertus Verlag GmbH+, Sternwaldstr 4, Postfach 1026, D-7800 Freiburg im Breisgau Tel: (0761) 70721/2
Man Dirs: Dr Lioba Knöbber, Gerhild Neugart
Subjects: Social Work (Community and Case Work etc, with youth, the old and disabled), Social Security
Bookshop: Freiburger Bücherdienst, Sternwaldstr 4, Postfach 1026, D-7800 Freiburg
1977: 16 titles *1978:* 18 titles *Founded:* 1898
ISBN Publisher's Prefix: 3-7841

Landbuch-Verlag GmbH, Kabelkamp 6, Postfach 160, D-3000 Hanover Tel: (0511) 632006 Cable Add: Landbuch Hanover Telex: 921169
Man Dir, Production, Rights & Permissions: Alice Gross; *Sales:* Willi Ludwig Kroeck; *Publicity:* Ulrich Knocke
Subjects: Arts, Agriculture, Animal Breeding, Forestry, Sports, Nature, Hunting, Wildlife; Periodicals
1977: 17 titles *1979:* 14 titles *Founded:* 1945
ISBN Publisher's Prefix: 3-7842

Landsberger Verlagsanstalt Martin Neumeyer*, Museumstr 14, Postfach 104, D-8910 Landsberg Tel: (08191) 4055
Subjects: History, Hobbies, Mass Media, the Art of Living, How-To, Regional Interest
ISBN Publisher's Prefix: 3-920216

Albert **Langen**-Georg Müller Verlag*, Hubertusstr 4, D-8000 Munich 19 Tel: (089) 177041 Telex: 05215045
Man Dir: Dr Herbert Fleissner; *Editorial:* Dr Katerina Horbatsch, Dr Herbert Greuèl, Dr Bernhard Struckmeyer; *Sales:* Gisela Weichert; *Publicity:* Dr Brigette Sinhuber; *Rights & Permissions:* Renate Werner
Subjects: General Fiction, Theatre, Reportage, Humour, Current Controversy
Founded: 1897
Miscellaneous: Firm is a member of the Verlagsgruppe Langen-Müller/Herbig (qv)
ISBN Publisher's Prefix: 3-7844

Verlagsgruppe **Langen-Müller**/Herbig*, Hubertusstr 4, D-8000 Munich 19 Tel: (089) 177041 Telex: 05215045
Man Dir: Dr Herbert Fleissner
Members of the Group: Bechtle Verlag (qv); Mary Hahn's Kochbuchverlag (qv); F A Herbig Verlagsbuchhandlung (qv); Albert Langen-George Müller Verlag (qv); Georg Lentz Verlag (qv); Limes Verlag (qv); Nymphenburger Verlagshandlung (qv); Safari-Verlag (qv); Universitas Verlag Dr Klaus Schweitzer KG (qv); Wirtschaftsverlag (qv) (all in German Federal Republic); Amalthea-Verlag, Austria (qv)

The **Langenscheidt Group**, Neusser Str 3, Postfach 401120, D-8000 Munich 40 Tel: (089) 38301
The Group consists of: Langenscheidt KG (qv); Langenscheidt-Longman GmbH (qv); Langenscheidt-Hachette GmbH (qv); Humboldt-Taschenbuchverlag Jacobi KG (qv); Polyglott-Verlag Dr Bolte KG (qv); Axel-Juncker-Verlag Nachfolger Jacobi KG (qv); Mentor-Verlag Dr Ramdohr KG (qv)

Langenscheidt KG, Neusser Str 3, Postfach 401120, D-8000 Munich 40 Tel: (089) 38301 Cable Add: Langenscheidt Munich Telex: Munich 5215379 Lkgm-d (also at An der Langenscheidtbrücke, D-1000 Berlin 62)
Man Dir: Karl-Ernst Tielebier-Langenscheidt; *Editorial:* Dr Walter Voigt, Dr Wolfgang Wieter, Dr Heinz F Wendt; *Production:* Helmut Wahl; *Sales Dir:* Peter Haering; *Advertising Dir:* Dieter Kräuse; *Export Dir:* Uwe Cordts; *Rights & Permissions:* Manfred Überall
Subsidiary Companies: Langenscheidt AG, Switzerland (qv); Langenscheidt-Verlag GmbH, Austria (qv)
Associate Companies: Axel-Juncker-Verlag Nachfolger Jacobi KG; Humboldt-Taschenbuchverlag Jacobi KG; Mentor-Verlag Dr Ramdohr KG, Polyglott — Verlag Dr Bolte KG (qqv)
Subjects: Foreign Languages, German for Foreigners; Dictionaries, Textbooks, Records, Tapes, Cassettes
1978: 20 titles *1979:* 45 titles *Founded:* 1856
ISBN Publisher's Prefix: 3-468

Langenscheidt-Hachette GmbH, Neusser Str 3, Postfach 401120, D-8000 Munich 40 Tel: (089) 38301 Cable Add: Langenscheidt Munich Telex: 5215379 lkgm d
Man Dirs: Karl-Ernst Tielebier-Langenscheidt, Gérard Lilamand; *Editorial:* Brigitte Peters; *Sales & Promotion:* Through Langenscheidt KG (qv)
Subjects: French (Language Teaching) for German-speaking people
1978: 61 titles *1979:* 50 titles *Founded:* 1977
Miscellaneous: Firm is an associate company of Langenscheidt KG, Munich and Hachette SA, Paris
ISBN Publisher's Prefix: 3-595

Langenscheidt-Longman GmbH, Neusser Str 3, Postfach 401120, D-8000 Munich 40 Tel: (089) 38301 Cable Add: Langenscheidt Munich Telex: 5215379 lkg md
Man Dirs: Karl-Ernst Tielebier-Langenscheidt, David Mortimer; *Publishing Executive:* Uwe Mäder; *Sales & Promotion:* through Langenscheidt KG
Subjects: English Language Teaching
1978: 105 titles *1979:* 50 titles *Founded:* 1972
Miscellaneous: Firm is an associate company of Langenscheidt KG, Munich, and Longman Group Ltd, UK (qv)
ISBN Publisher's Prefix: 3-526

Karl Robert **Langewiesche** Nachfolger Hans Koester KG+, Grüner Weg 6, Postfach 1327, D-6240 Königstein I Tel: (06174) 7333 Cable Add: Langewiesche Königsteintaunus
Man Dir, Production, Sales and Publicity, Rights & Permissions: Hans-Curt Koester; *Editorial:* Hans Koester, Hans-Curt Koester
Orders to: Koch, Neff & Oetinger & Co, Abt VA, Postfach 800620, D-7000 Stuttgart
Subjects: Art, Geography, Biography, History, How-to, Music, University Textbooks, Architecture, Landscape; Low- and High-priced Paperbacks
1979: 15 titles *Founded:* 1902
ISBN Publisher's Prefix: 03-7845

Langewiesche-Brandt KG, Abholfach (Poste Restante), D-8026 Ebenhausen bei München Tel: (08178) 4857
Man Dir: Kristof Wachinger
Subjects: Belles Lettres, Art Books, Autobiographical, Poetry; High-priced Paperbacks, Posters
1977: 6 titles *1978:* 5 titles *Founded:* 1906
ISBN Publisher's Prefix: 3-7846

Verlag **Laterna Magica** Joachim F Richter*, Stridbeckstr 48, D-8000 Munich 71 Tel: (089) 797091/4 Telex: 05-22425 color d
Publisher: Joachim F Richter; *Sales, Publicity:* Christian Klages; *Production:* E W Panckow
Orders to: Stridbeckstr 48, D-8000 Munich 71
Subjects: Photography, Periodicals
1977: 14 titles *Founded:* 1966
ISBN Publisher's Prefix: 3-87467

H **Laupp'sche** Buchhandlung, an imprint of J C B Mohr (Paul Siebeck) (qv)

August **Lax**, Postfach, Weinberg 56, D-3200 Hildesheim Tel: (05121) 81074/81075
Man Dir, Editorial, Rights & Permissions: Lorenz Lax; *Sales:* D Lax; *Production:* Th Ahrens
Associate Company: Filmsatz Gesellschaft at above address
Subjects: Archaeology, History, Pre-history, Folklore, Art History, Literature (Prose, Poetry, Dialect), Lower Saxony Historical
Bookshop: Buchhandlung August Lax, Bernwardstr 7, D-3200 Hildesheim
1978: 18 titles *1979:* 29 titles *Founded:* 1849
ISBN Publisher's Prefix: 3-7848

J F **Lehmanns** Verlag*, Agnes-Bernauer-Platz 8, Postfach 210140, D-8000 Munich 21 Tel: (089) 581031 Cable Add: Lehmennverlag
Dirs: Bernard Spatz, Otto Spatz, Volker Schwartz; *Sales Manager:* Günther Heck; *Publicity:* Rolf Wendeler
Parent Company: Springer-Verlag (qv)
Subjects: Medicine, Psychology, Arts, Aviation, Military
Founded: 1890
Bookshops: Buchhandlung Für Medizin Otto Spatz, Schillerstr 51; D-8000 Munich 15; D-8000 Munich 55, Sauerbruchstr 10; D-2000 Hamburg-Eppendorf, Breitenfelder Str 62 (all in German Federal Republic)
ISBN Publisher's Prefix: 3-469

Verlag Hermann **Leins**, see Rainer Wunderlich Verlag Hermann Leins

Leitfadenverlag Dieter Sudholt, D-8131 Berg 3 (Assenhausen) Tel: (08151) 5342
Publisher: Volker Sudholt
Subjects: Tax Directories, Business, Law, Economics
1978: 22 titles
ISBN Publisher's Prefix: 3-543

Verlag Otto **Lembeck**, Leerbachstr 42, D-6000 Frankfurt am Main 1 Tel: (0611) 721836 Cable Add: Lembeckdruck Frankfurtmain
Subject: Religion, Ecumenical Studies, Africa
1977: 14 titles *Founded:* 1945
ISBN Publisher's Prefix: 3-87476

Verlag Lambert **Lensing** GmbH, Kampstr 42, Postfach 875, D-4600 Dortmund 1 Tel: (0231) 148367 Cable Add: Lensingbuch Telex: 0822106
Man Dir: F C Lorson; *Editorial:* Dr Werner Jaeger; *Sales and Publicity:* S Binder; *Production:* G Marx
Subjects: Modern Languages, Modern Language Teaching, Educational Materials
1978: 38 titles *Founded:* 1870
Bookshop: Westenhellweg 86-88, Postfach 875, D-4600 Dortmund 1
ISBN Publisher's Prefix: 3-559

Georg **Lentz** Verlag, Romanstr 16, D-8000 Munich 19 Tel: (089) 162051
Subjects: Fiction and Nonfiction for Juveniles
Miscellaneous: Firm is a member of Verlagsgruppe Langen-Müller/Herbig Munich (qv)

Leske Verlag und Budrich GmbH,
Rennbaumstr 25, Postfach 300406, D-5090
Leverkusen 3 Tel: (02171) 45525
Man Dir: Edmund Budrich
Subjects: Social Science, Sexology, Middle
East, University, Secondary and Primary
Textbooks, Educational Materials
1977: 38 titles *Founded:* 1974
ISBN Publisher's Prefix: 3-8100

Leuchter-Verlag AG*, Industriestr 6-8,
Postfach 60, D-6106 Erzhausen
Tel: (06150) 7565
Man & Sales Dir: Karl-Heinz Neumann
Subjects: Religion, Low-priced Paperbacks
Founded: 1946

Leuchtturm-Verlag*, Kreuzlinger Str 54,
D-775 Konstanz 1 Tel: (07531) 26675
Man Dir: H-J Zebisch; *Sales Dir:* Frau von
Ulardt; *Publicity & Advertising Dir, Rights
& Permissions:* H-J Zebisch
Subjects: Engineering, General & Social
Science
1976: 20 titles *Founded:* 1974

Lexika-Verlag Hablitzel & Wippler KG*,
Maichinger Str 16, Postfach 2, D-7031
Grafenau 1 Tel: (07033) 7344 Cable Add:
fhwd Telex: 07265883 fhw
Publishers: Chris Hablitzel, Elmar Wippler
Subjects: Careers and Management
Training, Adult Education, Economic
Science, Reference Books, Periodicals
ISBN Publisher's Prefix: 3-920353

Liber Verlag GmbH, Hegelstr 45, Postfach
2946, D-6500 Mainz 1
Man Dir, Editorial: Tomo Matasić
Production, Publicity: Renate Ammersbach
Subjects: Literature, Literary Criticism,
Linguistics, Foreign Language Teaching,
Theses on Slavistics, History, Politics
1977: 2 titles *1978:* 3 titles *Founded:* 1977
ISBN Publisher's Prefix: 83111

Lichtenberg Verlag GmbH*, Leopoldstr 54,
Postfach 401043, D-8000 Munich 40
Tel: (089) 394041 Cable Add:
Lichtenbergverlag Telex: 05215678
Dirs: Peter Nikel, Klano Jost
Orders to: Vereinigte Verlagsauslieferung
GmbH, Postfach 7777, 483 Gütersloh
Founded: 1962
Subjects: General Fiction and Nonfiction,
Belles Lettres, Practical Guides, Humour
Miscellaneous: Associate Company: Kindler
Verlag GmbH (qv)
ISBN Publisher's Prefix: 3-7852

Lichtkreis Christi*, Feldwieser-Str 84,
Postfach 2, D-8212 Ubersee am Chiemsee
Tel: 08642/6744
Subject: Die Neue Bibel (The New Bible) in
12 vols, appearing in numerous languages

Verlag der **Liebenzeller Mission**, Liobastr 8,
Postfach 1223, D-7263 Bad Liebenzell 1
Tel: (07052) 2031
Publisher: Arthur Klenk
Subjects: Mission Reports, Theology,
Methodology, also Biographies and
Devotional
1978: 17 titles *1979:* 25 titles *Founded:*
1906
Miscellaneous: Member of the Telos (qv)
paperback series publishing group
ISBN Publisheer's Prefix: 3-88002

Arnulf **Liebing**, see Jal-Verlag/Jal-Reprint

Rudolf **Liebing**, see Physica-Verlag

Edition/Galerie **Lietzow**, Knesebeckstr 32,
D-1000 Berlin 12 Tel: (030) 8812895
Man Dir: Horst Hartmann; *Editorial:*
Godehard Lietzow; *Sales, Production,*
Publicity: Godehard Lietzow, Horst
Hartmann
Subjects: Biography, Art, Reference
1977: 4 titles *Founded:* 1970

Limes Verlag, Romanstr 16, D-8000
Munich 19 Tel: (089) 162051
Man Dir: Marguerite Schlüter; *Sales:*
Brigitte Nunner
Subjects: General Fiction, Belles Lettres,
Poetry, History, Music, Art
1977: 17 titles *1978:* 14 titles *Founded:*
1945
Miscellaneous: Firm is a member of
Verlagsgruppe Langen-Müller/Herbig (qv)
ISBN Publisher's Prefix: 3-8090

Limpert Verlag*, Ferdinandstr 18,
Postfach 1727, D-6380 Bad Homburg
vdH 1 Tel: (06172) 6038
Man Dir: H Farnung; *Sales:* Ruprecht
Sickel; *Rights & Permissions:* Hermann
Farnung
Subject: Sport and Recreation
1977: 17 titles *Founded:* 1921

Lingen Verlag*, Marienburger Strasse 17,
Postfach 510729, D-5000 Cologne
Tel: (0221) 380066 Telex: 8882138
Man Dir: Helmut Lingen
Subjects: Atlases, Language, Cookery,
Popular Nonfiction

Paul **List** Verlag KG, Goethestr 43, D-8000
Munich 2 Tel: (089) 530561 Telex: 0522405
Man Dir: Robert Schäfer; *Editorial:* Dr
Horst Ferle; *Sales:* Volker Neumann;
Publicity: Dr Rolf Cyriax; *Advertising:*
Michael Schindler; *Rights & Permissions:*
Gabriele Fentzke
Associate Companies: Südwest Verlag
GmbH & Co KG (qv); Süddeutscher Verlag
Buchverlag (qv)
Subjects: General Fiction, Belles Lettres,
Poetry, Biography, History, Music, Art,
Philosophy, Reference, Religion,
Psychology, General & Social Science,
Secondary & Primary Textbooks
1977: 27 titles *1978:* 28 titles *Founded:*
1919
ISBN Publisher's Prefix: 3-471

Literarisches Colloquium Berlin*, Am
Sandwerder 5, D-1000 Berlin 39 Tel: (030)
8035681
Man Dir: Walter Höllerer; *Sales Dir:*
Wilhelm Standke; *Publisher's Reader:*
Gerald Bisinger
Subjects: Belles Lettres, Poetry
Founded: 1963
ISBN Publisher's Prefix: 3-920392

Henry **Litolff's** Verlag, an imprint of
C F Peters Musikverlag GmbH und Co KG
(qv)

Loewes Verlag KG*, Bahnhofstr 15,
Postfach 2606, D-8580 Bayreuth
Tel: (0921) 21031 Cable Add: Loewesverlag
Bayreuth Telex: 642771
Man Dir: Volker Gondrom; *Publicity, Sales
Dir, Rights & Permissions:* Werner
Skambraks
Subject: Juveniles
Founded: 1863
ISBN Publisher's Prefix: 3-7855

Lorber-Verlag*, Hindenburgstr 3, Postfach
229, D-7120 Bietigheim Tel: (07142) 44446
Cable Add: Lorber, Bietigheim
Subject: Religion
Miscellaneous: Associate Company: Turm-
Verlag, 3 Hindenburgstr, D-7120
Bietigheim (qv)
ISBN Publisher's Prefix: 3-87495

Lorch-Verlag GmbH, Schumannstr 27,
Postfach 2625, D-6000 Frankfurt am Main
Tel: (0611) 7433448/9 Telex: 0411862
Man Dirs: Eva Lorch, Klaus Kottmeier
Associate Companies: Spohr-Verlag; Eder-
Verlag, Sponholz-Verlag
Subjects: Handbooks, Textile Trade Books,
Management
1977: 15 titles *Founded:* 1950
Miscellaneous: Formerly known as
Deutscher Fachverlag
ISBN Publisher's Prefix: 3-87496

Gustav **Lübbe** Verlag GmbH*,
Scheidtbachstr 29-31, Postfach 200127, D-
5060 Bergisch Gladbach 2 Tel: (02202)
1211 Telex: 887922
Man Dir: Gustav Lübbe; *Manager, Rights
& Permissions:* W Mertz; *Editorial:* A
Kleinlein; *Sales:* Hans-Jochen Mundt;
Publicity: Irmgard Sellmann
Associate Company: Bastei-Verlag Gustav
Lübbe (qv)
Subjects: General Fiction and Nonfiction,
Illustrated books on Archaeology and
History
1977: 16 titles *Founded:* 1964
ISBN Publisher's Prefix: 3-7857

Hermann **Luchterhand** Verlag GmbH & Co
KG*, Heddesdorfer Str 31, Postfach 1780,
D-5450 Neuwied 1 Tel: (02631) 8011
Telex: 0867853
Man Dir: Fritz Berger; *Dir:* Karl-Heinz
Westphal; *Marketing:* Dr Lothar Johannes
Associate Company: Druck- und- Verlag-
Gesellschaft mbH, Darmstadt
Br Off: Donnersbergring 18a, Postfach 4250,
D-6100 Darmstadt
Subjects: General Fiction and Nonfiction,
Belles Lettres, Juveniles, Social Sciences,
Law, Economics, Education
1977: c 90 titles *Founded:* 1924
ISBN Publisher's Prefix: 3-472

Verlag W **Ludwig**, Türltorstr 14, Postfach
86, D-8068 Pfaffenhofen/Ilm 1 Tel: (08441)
5051/5052 Telex: 55540
Man Dir: Wilhelm Ludwig; *Editorial,
Rights & Permissions:* Michael Ludwig;
Sales: Elfriede Maier; *Production:* Werner
Behrens; *Publicity:* Angelika Ludwig
Subsidiary Company: Afrika Verlag
Subjects: Popular Science, Current Affairs,
Belles Lettres, Poetry, History
1977: 26 titles *Founded:* 1950
ISBN Publisher's Prefix: 3-7787

Luther-Verlag GmbH+, Postfach 5660, D-
4800 Bielefeld 1 Tel: (0521) 44861 Telex:
0937325 epdbid
Dir: Dr Gerhard E Stoll
Subject: Religion
Bookshop: Luther Buchhandlung,
Cansteinstr 1, D-4800 Bielefeld 14
1977: 12 titles *1978:* 8 titles *Founded:* 1911
ISBN Publisher's Prefix: 3-7858

Lutherisches Verlagshaus, Mittelweg 111,
D-2000 Hamburg 13 Tel: (040) 452131
Subjects: Protestant Religious Texts on
Current Debates, Liturgy, Theology, Church
History

M F B (Phono- und Schriftenmission des
Missionstrupps Frohe Botschaft eV),
Nordstr 15, Postfach 1180, D-3432
Grossalmerode bei Kassel Tel: (05604) 361
and 5120
Man Dir, Rights & Permissions: W Heiner
Subjects: Christian Evangelical; covering
also Juvenile Interest, How-to, Paperbacks,
Texts in English, Periodicals *Das Frohe
Botschaft* ('Glad Tidings'), *AEE-news*
(Evangelization of Africa)
1977: 8 titles *1978:* 19 titles

150 FEDERAL REPUBLIC OF GERMANY

McGraw-Hill Book Co GmbH, Lademannbogen 136, D-2000 Hamburg 63 Tel: (040) 5382081-6 Telex: 2164048
Man Dir: Jolanda L von Hagen; *Sales:* Wolf Rudiger Ritter
Subjects: Medicine, Psychology, Engineering, General & Social Science, University & Secondary Textbooks, Educational Materials
1978-79: 30 titles under Schaum imprint *Founded:* 1969
Miscellaneous: Firm is an associate company of McGraw-Hill International Book Co New York (see UK entry for other Associate Companies). The Düsseldorf branch is the one from which all McGraw-Hill publications in English may be ordered from any point in Europe
ISBN Publisher's Prefix: 0-07

Magnus Verlag*, im Teelbruch 60-62, Postfach 185528, 4300 Essen 8 Tel: (02054) 7077/7078
Man Dir: Walter Stender
Subjects: Reference Books, Dictionaries

Otto **Maier** Verlag+, Marktstr 22-26 & Robert Bosch Str 1, Postfach 1860, D-7980 Ravensburg Tel: (0751) 861 Cable Add: Maierverlag Telex: 0732926/0732921
President: Otto J Maier, Dorothee Hess-Maier; *Man Dir:* Claus Runge; *Editorial:* Walter Diem, Peter Hille, Christian Stottele; *Rights & Permissions:* Frank Jacoby-Nelson
Subsidiary Companies: Ravensburger Spiele GmbH, Vienna, Austria; Editions Ravensburger SA, Attenschwiller, France; Fritz Löhmann GmbH, Ravensburger graph Betriebe Otto Maier GmbH, Ravensburger Verlag GmbH, (all in Ravensburg), Union Verlag mbH, Stuttgart, Federal Republic of Germany; Otto Maier Benelux BV, Amersfoort, Netherlands; Carlit & Ravensburger AG, Zurich, Switzerland
Subjects: Juvenile Fiction and Nonfiction, Adult Craft and Hobby, Art, Educational (Pedagogics, Art, Pre- and Elementary School Materials), Paperbacks
Founded: 1883
ISBN Publisher's Prefix: 3-473

Mairs Geographischer Verlag*, Marco-Polo-Str 1, D-7302 Ostfildern 4 (Kemnat) Tel: (0711) 454055 Cable Add: Mairverlag Telex: 721796
Man Dir: Dr Volkmar Mair; *Sales Dir:* Claus Benath
Subjects: Road Maps & Atlases
Founded: 1948
ISBN Publisher's Prefix: 3-87504

Mai's Reiseführer Verlag+, Unterlindau 80, D-6000 Frankfurt am Main 1 Tel: (0611) 723783
Man & Sales Dir: Ingo and Marie-Luise Schmidt di Simoni
Subjects: Pocket Guides and Travel Guides to non-European countries
1977: 15 titles *1978:* 13 titles *Founded:* 1951
ISBN Publisher's Prefix: 3-87936

Gebr **Mann** Verlag, Lindenstr 76, Postfach 110303, D-1000 Berlin 61 Tel: (030) 2512028/2591865 Cable Add: Kunstbrief Berlin Telex: 183723
Man Dir: Professor Dr Heinz Peters
Subjects: Archaeology, Art, Art Reproduction
1978: 29 titles *Founded:* 1917
Miscellaneous: Associate Company: Deutscher Verlag für Kunstwissenschaft (qv)
ISBN Publisher's Prefix: 3-7861

Manz Verlag, Anzinger Str 1, D-8000 Munich 80 Tel: (089) 403031 Cable Add: Manzverlag Telex: 522504
Publisher: Eduard Niedernhuber; *Sales:* Erna Schmidt; *Publicity:* Siegbert Seitz
Subjects: Educational Materials
Founded: 1830
Subsidiary: Erich Wewel Verlag (qv)
ISBN Publisher's Prefix: 3-7863

Tibor **Marczell**, Nederlinger Str 93, D-8000 Munich 19 Tel: (089) 155985
Man Dir: Tibor Marczell
Subjects: Medical, including History, Herbal and Fringe
Founded: 1964
ISBN Publisher's Prefix: 388015

Carl **Marhold** Verlagsbuchhandlung*, Hessenallee 12, Postfach 191409, D1000 Berlin 19 Tel: 3043732/3049032 Cable Add: Marholdverlag Berlin
Man Dir: Wolfgang Jaeh; *other offices:* Thomas Jaeh
Subjects: Special healing pedagogy; caring/nursing technologies; teaching of handicapped children
1977: 30 titles *Founded:* 1891
ISBN Publisher's Prefix: 37864

Maria-Verlag*, Rudolf-Diesel-Str 5, D6300 Giessen Tel: (0641) 4104143 Telex: 4821733 wsl d

Edition **Maritim**, Schwanenwik 27, D2000 Hamburg 76 Tel: (040) 2296656
Dirs: Frank Grube, Gerhard Richter
Subjects: Yachting, Nautical
ISBN Publisher's Prefix: 3922117

Maro Verlag*, Bismarckstr 7 1/2, D8900 Augsburg Tel: (0821) 577131
Dir: B Kaesmayr
Subjects: Modern Poetry and Fiction
1977: 4 titles *Founded:* 1969
2ISBN Publisher's Prefix: 3-87512

Verlag **Marxistische Blätter** GmbH, Heddernheimer Landstr 78a, D-6000 Frankfurt am Main 50 Tel: (0611) 571051
Publisher: Albert Maag; *Dir:* Max Schafer
Subject: Politics, Marxist Literature; *Periodical:* Marxistische Blätter
1978: 50 titles *1978:* 55 titles *Founded:* 1969
ISBN Publisher's Prefix: 3-88012

Hugo **Matthaes** Druckerei und Verlag GmbH & Co KG, Olgastr 87, Postfach 622, D-7000 Stuttgart 1 Tel: (0711) 21331 Cable Add: Matthaesverlag Telex: 721802
Subjects: Food Trade, Gastronomy

Matthes und Seitz Verlag GmbH, Postfach 401324, D-8000 Munich 40 (Located at: Dietlindenstr 14) Tel: (089) 333170
Editorial, Rights & Permissions: Axel Matthes; *Sales, Production, Publicity:* Claus Seitz
Subjects: Literature, Art and the Arts generally, Fiction, Memoirs
1978: 12 titles *1979:* 14 titles *Founded:* 1977
ISBN Publisher's Prefix: 3-88221

Matthias-Grünewald-Verlag, see Grünewald

Matthiesen Verlag Ingwert Paulsen Jr, Nordbahnhofstr 2, Postfach 1480, D-2250 Husum Tel: (04841) 6081/3
Man Dir, Editorial, Rights & Permissions: Ingwert Paulsen Jr; *Sales:* Alfred Lorenzen; *Production:* Hajo Hartkopf; *Publicity:* Barbara Marquardt
Associate Companies: Husum Druck- und Verlagsgesellschaft (qv); Hamburger Lesehefte Verlag Iselt & Co Nfl mbH (qv)
Subjects: Textbooks, Science, Reference
Founded: 1892
ISBN Publisher's Prefix: 3-7868

Maximilian-Verlag, Steintorwall 17, Postfach 371, D-4900 Herford Tel: (05221) 50001 Cable Add: Maximilian, Herford/Westf Telex: 934801
Publishers: Dr Kurt Schober, Gerhard Bollmann; *Sales:* Hans-Focko Koehler; *Publicity:* Gerhard Mindt
Subjects: Philosophy, Law, Administration, History, Social Sciences; Periodicals
Miscellaneous: Associate Companies: Koehlers Verlagsgesellschaft, E S Mittler & Sohn GmbH, Verlag Offene Worte: all at Maximilian-Verlag address
ISBN Publisher's Prefix: 3-7869

Karl-**May**-Verlag, Joachim Schmid & Co, Karl-May-Str 8, D-8600 Bamberg Tel: (0951) 22261
Main Publicity Dir: Joachim Schmid; *Sales Dir:* Lothar Schmid; *Production Dir:* Roland Schmid; *Rights & Permissions:* Joachim, Lothar and Roland Schmid
Subject: Children's Fiction
Founded: 1913
ISBN Publisher's Prefix: 3-7802

Edition Hansjörg **Mayer***, Engelhornweg 11, D-7000 Stuttgart 1 Tel: (0711) 282036
Man Dir: Hj Mayer
Br Offs: London, Reykjavik
Subjects: Belles Lettres, Poetry, Music, Art, High-priced Paperbacks
1977: 16 titles *Founded:* 1964

J A **Mayer'sche** Buchhandlung, Ursulinerstr 17-19, Postfach 467, D-5100 Aachen Tel: (0241) 48142 Cable Add: Mayer Aachen Telex: 832768
Man Dir, Publicity: Helmut Falter
Branch Off: Templergraben 44, D-5100 Aachen
Bookshops: at company and branch office addresses
1977: 22 titles *Founded:* 1817
ISBN Publisher's Prefix: 3-87519

Verlag für **Medizin**, Dr Ewald Fischer GmbH, Fritz-Frey Str 21, Postfach 105767, D-6900 Heidelberg 1 Tel: (06221) 46074-5 Cable Add: verlagfürMedizin
Man Dir: Dr E Fischer
Associate Companies: Arkana Verlag (qv); Karl F Haug Verlag GmbH & Co (qv)
Branch Off: Bergheimer Str 102, D-6900 Heidelberg
Subject: Medicine
Founded: 1967
ISBN Publisher's Prefix: 3-921003

Medizinisch-Literarische Verlagsgesellschaft mbH, Ringstr 9, Postfach 120/140, D-3110 Uelzen Tel: (0581) 19091 Cable Add: ML-Verlag 3110 Uelzen 1 Telex: 0916
Man Dir, Rights & Permissions: Jens Buettler; *Editorial:* Dr med Dipl ing H Schuldt; *Sales:* B Pianka; *Production:* S Horstmann, G Grätz; *Publicity:* U Rath, M Jess
Parent Company: C Beckers Buchdruckerei, 3110 Uelzen 1
Subjects: Medical, Acupuncture, Orthopaedics, Electro-Acupuncture texts in English; Periodicals
1977: 7 titles *1978:* 13 titles *Founded:* 1957
ISBN Publisher's Prefix: 3-88136

megapress-Verlag Franz-Joachim Gaber KG, Beethovenstr 64, PO Box 402, D-6078 Neu Isenburg-bei-Frankfurt am Main Tel: 06103/23817
Publisher: F J Gabert
Subjects: Politics, Socialist Magazine

Monthly Review (German Edition)
ISBN Publisher's Prefix: 3-87979

Felix **Meiner** Verlag+, Richardstr 47, D-2000 Hamburg 76 Tel: (040) 294870 Telex: 212120 hihe
Founded: 1911
Subjects: Philosophy, Periodicals
1977: 32 titles *1978:* 28 titles
ISBN Publisher's Prefix: 3-7873

Verlag Anton **Meisenheim** GmbH, Adelheidstr 2, Postfach 1220, D-6240 Königstein/TS Tel: (06174) 3026 Telex: 410664
Man Dir, Rights & Permissions: Dietrich Pinkerneil, Dieter Hain; *Editorial:* Beate Pinkerneil; *Sales:* Rudolf Klein; *Production:* Mr Langer; *Publicity:* Mrs Hirschfeld
Parent Company: Publishing Group Athenäum/Hain/Scriptor/Hanstein
Subjects: Academic, Science
1977: 90 titles *1978:* 41 titles *Founded:* 1946
ISBN Publisher's Prefix: 3-445

Otto **Meissner** Verlag, Schloss Str 10, Postfach 106, D-2122 Bleckede/Elbe Tel: (05852) 319
Dir: Reinhard Sonntag
Subjects: General Nonfiction, Hobbies, Humanities, Periodicals
Founded: 1848
ISBN Publisher's Prefix: 3-87527

Melanchton Verlag*, Moltkestr 1, D-1000 Berlin 45 Tel: 8334150
Subjects: Supply of Museum Catalogues etc

J CH **Mellinger** Verlag GmbH; Wolfgang Militz und Co KG, 55 Büssenstr, Postfach 131164, D-7000 Stuttgart 1 Tel: (0711) 463565/246401
Orders to: Koch, Neff, Oettinger & Co, Abt Verlagsauslieferung, Am Wallgraben 110, D-7000 Stuttgart 80
Proprietors & Man Dirs: Wolfgang Militz, Elisabeth Sambo
Subjects: Religions, Biography, Aesthetics, Literature, Juveniles, Games
Founded: 1926
ISBN Publisher's Prefix: 3-88069

Verlag Abi **Melzer** GmbH, Wildscheuerweg 1, Postfach 301117, D-6072 Dreieich-Buchschlag Tel: (06103) 63061/63062 Telex: 4185381 amp
Gen Man: Abraham Melzer
Orders to: VVA, Gütersloh
1977: 16 titles *1978:* 20 titles *Founded:* 1975
Subjects: Picture Strips, Graphics, Comics, Children's Books, General Literature
ISBN Publisher's Prefix: 3-8201

Melzer Verlag KG, Gutenbergstr, D-6101 Weiterstadt Tel: (06151) 86056 Telex: 419249
Man Dir: Horst Göhde; *Sales Dir:* Horst Beitlich
Subjects: Comics, Art, Juveniles
1977: 4 titles *Founded:* 1972
ISBN Publisher's Prefix: 3-7874

Verlag **Mensch und Arbeit***, Vogelweideplatz 10, D-8000 Munich 80 Tel: (089) 474051 Cable Add: Pronto Munich
Man Dir: Robert Pfützner; *Rights & Permissions:* Gerhart Kindl
Subjects: How-to, Art, Social Science, Professional, Technical
Founded: 1957

Mentor-Verlag Dr Ramdohr KG, Neusser Str 3, Postfach 401120, D-8000 Munich 40 Tel: 38301 Cable Add: Langenscheidt Munich Telex: 5215379 lkg md
Man Dir: Karl-Ernst Tielebier-Langenscheidt; *Editorial:* Katharina Baudach; *Sales Dir:* Peter Haering; *Advertising Dir:* Dieter Krause; *Sales, Promotion:* Through Langenscheidt KG (qv); *Rights & Permissions:* Manfred Überall
Subjects: Reference, Low-priced Paperbacks, Textbooks
Titles in print: 38 *1979:* 4 titles *Founded:* 1904
Miscellaneous: Company is a member of the Langenscheidt Group (qv)
ISBN Publisher's Prefix: 3-580

Mergus Verlag Hans A Baensch, Postfach 86, D-4520 Melle 1 (Located at: Bergstr 3) Tel: (05422) 3636 Cable Add: Mergus Melle Telex: 941550 megus d
Man Dir: Hans A Baensch
Subjects: Natural History, Care of Pets
1978: 2 titles *1979:* 4 titles *Founded:* 1977
ISBN Publisher's Prefix: 3-88244

Merlin Verlag Andreas Meyer Verlags GmbH und Co KG, Sierichstr 54, D-2000 Hamburg 60 Tel: (040) 2791140
Publisher: Andreas J Meyer; *Sales Manager:* Ilse Meyer
Subjects: History, Arts, Literature
ISBN Publisher's Prefix: 3-87536

Merve Verlag, Crelle Str 22, D-1000 Berlin 62 Tel: (030) 7848433
Man Dir: Hans-Peter Gente
1978: 9 titles

Methodik-Verlag Manfred Helfrecht, Markgrafenstr 27, D-8591 Alexandersbad Tel: (09232) 2655 Telex: 641180 thelf d
Dir: Josef Schmidt
Subject: Individual and Company planning methods
1978: 1 title *1979:* 1 title
ISBN Publisher's Prefix: 3-920986

J B **Metzlersche** Verlagsbuchhandlung, Kernerstr 43, Postfach 529, D-7000 Stuttgart 1 Tel: (0711) 225074/75/76 Cable Add: Metzlerverlag Stuttgart
Man Dir: Günther Schweizer; *Sales Dir:* Mr Cziszinsky; *Advertising Dir:* Ulrich Gensicke; *Rights & Permissions:* Dr Bernd Lutz
Orders to: (Book Trade): Goethestrasse 6, D-7400 Tübingen; (in Berlin) A Muschal & Sohn, Lützowstr 105-6, D-1000 Berlin 30
Subjects: Philology, Human Sciences, American Studies, Geodesy, Pedagogics, School Books
Founded: 1682
Miscellaneous: Associate Company: C E Poeschel Verlag (qv)
ISBN Publisher's Prefix: 3-476

Alfred **Metzner** Verlag GmbH, Zeppelinallee 43, Postfach 970148, D-6000 Frankfurt am Main Tel: (0611) 774055
Dir: Dr Caspar van Kempen; *Editorial:* Dr Günther Küpcke; *Publicity and Sales:* Ernst F Grundl
Subjects: Law, University Textbooks
Founded: 1909
Miscellaneous: Associate Company: Verlag Kommentator GmbH (qv). Alfred Metzner Verlag is a member of the Kluwer Group, Deventer, Netherlands (qv)
ISBN Publisher's Prefix: 3-7875

Meyster Verlag, Nymphenburger Str 139, D-8000 Munich 19 Tel: (089) 187069/187060 Telex: 522569 meyst d
Man Dir, Sales: Hermann Meyer; *Editorial:* at Georgenstr 24, D-8000 Munich 40; *Rights & Permissions:* Isolde Rieger
Parent Company: Verlag C Überreuter, Alser Str 24, A-1095 Vienna, Austria (qv)
Associate Company: Annette Betz Verlag, Austria (qv)
Subjects: Popular Science Works, Gift Books, the Family, Cookery, Illustrated Vols
1978: 11 titles *1979:* 18 titles *Founded:* 1978
ISBN Publisher's Prefix: 3-7057

Gertraud **Middelhauve** Verlag+, Wiener Platz 2, D-5000 Cologne 80 (Mülheim) Tel: (0221) 614982
Man Dir, Editorial, Rights & Permissions: Gertraud Middelhauve; *Publicity:* Annemarie Balkenhol
Orders to: Vereinigte Verlagsauslieferung, Carl-Bertelsmann Str 161, D-4830 Gütersloh 1
Subjects: General Fiction, Juveniles
1977: 10 titles *Founded:* 1947
ISBN Publisher's Prefix: 3-7678

Wolfgang **Militz** und Co KG, see J Ch Mellinger Verlag

Missionstruppe Frohe Botschaft, see M F B

E S **Mittler** und Sohn GmbH*, Steintorwall 17, Postfach 371, D-4900 Herford Tel: (05221) 3147/8 Cable Add: Mittler & Sohn, Herford/Westf Telex: 934801
Publishers: Dr Kurt Schober, Gerhard Bollmann; *Sales:* Hans-Focko Koehler; *Publicity:* Gerhard Mindt; *Production:* Heinz Kameier
Associate Companies: Koehlers Verlagsgesellschaft, Maximilian-Verlag, Verlag Offene Worte; all at above address
Subjects: Military, Political, NATO Affairs
Founded: 1789
ISBN Publisher's Prefix: 3-87547.3-8132

Verlag **Moderne Industrie** Wolfgang Dummer und Co, Ehrenbreitsteiner Str 36, D-8000 Munich 50 Tel: 14851 Telex: 05215566
Man Dir: Dr Reinhard Moestl; Christel Miczek; *Publicity:* Wolfgang Oster; *Rights & Permissions:* Rita Ploetz
Subjects: Management (Personnel Management, Sales Management, Accountancy, Advertising, Data Processing), Investment, Textbooks, Technical
1977: 150 titles *1978:* 150 titles *Founded:* 1952
ISBN Publisher's Prefix: 3-478

Moderne Verlags GmbH (MVG)*, Ehrenbreitsteiner Str 36, D-8000 Munich 50 Tel: (089) 1415051 Cable Add: Moderne Verlags GmbH Telex: 05215566
Subjects: Hobbies, Arts, Popular Sciences, Careers
ISBN Publisher's Prefix: 3-478

Gütersloher Verlag Gerd **Mohn**, see Gütersloher

J C B **Mohr** (Paul Siebeck), Wilhelmstr 18, Postfach 2040, D-7400 Tübingen Tel: (07071) 26064 Cable Add: Siebeck Tübingen Telex: 7262872 mohr d
Proprietor: Dr hc Hans Georg Siebeck; *Man Dir:* Georg Siebeck Jun; *Sales:* Johannes Krämer; *Production:* Rudolf Pflug; *Publicity:* Dr Arnulf Krais; *Rights & Permissions:* Maria Branse
Subsidiary Company: H Laupp'sche Buchhandlung (books on Tübingen and Suevia)
Subjects: History, Philosophy, Religion, General & Social Science, Economics, Law, University Textbooks
1977: 110 titles *1978:* 101 titles *Founded:* 1801
ISBN Publisher's Prefix: 3-16

152 FEDERAL REPUBLIC OF GERMANY

Verlag Fritz **Molden**, Stievestr 9, D-8000 Munich 19 Tel: (089) 176071 Telex: 5-29993
Publisher: Fritz P Molden; *Man Dir:* Klaus-Peter Frank; *Publicity:* Marianne Menzel
Parent Company: Verlag Fritz Molden, Vienna, Austria (qv)

Mönch-Verlag GmbH & Co, Heilsbachstr 26, D-5300 Bonn 1 Tel: (02221) 643066-68 Telex: 8869429 mvkb d
Man Dir: Manfred Sadlowski; *Sales Dir:* Joachim Latka; *Publicity Dir:* Heinz-Jürgen Witzke; *Advertising Dir:* Peter Konietschke; *Rights & Permissions:* Herr Latka
Branch Off: Mönch-Verlag, D-5401 Waldesch, Hübingerweg 33
Subjects: History, How-to, Engineering, General Science, High-priced Paperbacks

Edizioni del **Mondo***, Hollerborn 77, Postfach 2380, D-6200 Wiesbaden Tel: (06121) 420186
Publisher: Comm. Olaf Hein
Founded: 1971
Subjects: First world-edition of the complete works of Athanasius Kircher (Opera Omnia Athanasii Kircheri) in 66 vols, Arts, Reprints, Sciences, Books on Rome
ISBN Publisher's Prefix: 3-920228

Du **Mont** Buchverlag GmbH und Co KG, Apostelnkloster 21-25, Postfach 100468, D-5000 Cologne 1 Tel: (0221) 20531 Telex: 8882 975 dbe b d
Dir: Ernst Brücher
Subjects: Archaeology, Art History, Art, Art Calendars
Founded: 1805
ISBN Publisher's Prefix: 3-7701

Heinz **Moos** Verlag Munich, Rottenbucher Str 30, D-8032 Gräfelfing Tel: (089) 851311 Cable Add: Moosverlag
Man Dir: Heinz Moos
Subjects: Town Planning, History of Architecture, Preservation of Monuments, Fringe Areas of Science and Art, Book Production and Printing, Monographs, Current Affairs, German-American Dual Language (International Relations) Texts
Founded: 1959
ISBN Publisher's Prefix: 3-7879

Morsak Verlag, Kröllstr 5, Postfach 5, D-8352 Grafenau Tel: (08552) 1015/6 Telex: 57431
Man Dir, Production, Rights & Permissions: Erich Stecher; *Sales:* Rosa Zarham
Subjects: Bavaria, School books, Textbooks
1977: 12 titles *1978:* 10 titles *Founded:* 1884
ISBN Publisher's Prefix: 3-87553

Morus-Verlag*, Grunewaldstr 24, D-1000 Berlin 41 Tel: (030) 8210101/8213443
Sales Dir: Gertrud Sagner; *Publicity Manager:* Elisabeth Jagdt
Subject: Religion
Founded: 1945
ISBN Publisher's Prefix: 3-87554

Mosaik Verlag*, Steinhauserstr 1, Postfach 800360, D-8000 Munich Tel: (089) 4136/1 Cable Add: Bertelsmann München Telex: 0523487
Dir: Gerhard Zorn; *Advertising:* Lionel von dem Knesebeck; *Sales and Publicity:* Lothar Nalbach; *Rights & Permissions:* Udo Knispel
Subjects: How-to, Cookery, Health & Medicine, Gardening, Furnishing, Crafts, Hobbies, Reference, General Literature
Miscellaneous: Firm is a member of Verlagsgruppe Bertelsmann GmbH (qv)
ISBN Publisher's Prefix: 3-570

Motorbuch-Verlag, Böblinger Str 18, Postfach 1370, D-7000 Stuttgart 1 Tel: (0711) 642031 Cable Add: pico d Telex: 0722662
Man Dir: Wolfgang Schilling; *Sales:* Thomas Günther, Kurt Wölfle; *Rights & Permissions:* Brigitte Weller
Subjects: How-to, Reference, Engineering
1978: 112 titles *Founded:* 1962
Miscellaneous: Firm is a division of Buch- & Verlagshaus Paul Pietsch GmbH & Co KG
ISBN Publisher's Prefix: 3-87943

Verlag C F **Müller**, Rheinstr 122, Postfach 210940, D-7500 Karlsruhe 21 Tel: (0721) 555955 Telex: 7825909
Man Dir: Dr Christof Müller-Wirth; *Sales, Publicity:* Winfried Ammon; *Production, Rights & Permissions:* Jochen Schmitt
Subjects: Technical Specialist Books on Cold, Heat, Climate, Air, Environment, Energy and Solar Technology
1977: 12 titles *1978:* 8 titles *Founded:* 1797
ISBN Publisher's Prefix: 3-7880

C F **Müller Jüristischer** Verlag GmbH, Postfach 102640, D-6900 Heidelberg (Located at: im Weiher 10) Tel: (06221) 489250 Telex: 0461727 huehd
Associate Companies: Kriminalistik Verlag GmbH (qv); R v Decker's Verlag G Schenck GmbH (qv)
Subjects: Jurisprudence Textbooks; Commentaries and Law Practice; Academic Series

Verlag Josef **Müller**, Friedrichstr 9, Postfach 360, D-8000 Munich 43 Tel: (089) 393045 Cable Add: Arssacra München
Subjects: Hummel Pictures, Hummel Books, Advent Calendars, Picture Books, Bohatta Books and Puzzles
Founded: 1896
ISBN Publisher's Prefix: 3-7607

Verlagsgesellschaft Rudolf **Müller**, Stolberger Str 84, Postfach 410949, D-5000 Cologne 41 Tel: (0221) 542061 Telex: 08881256
Publisher: Walther Müller; *Dir:* Helmut Evers; *Sales Manager:* Peter von Klaudy; *Publicity Manager:* Peter Groth
Br Off: Johnsallee 53, D-2000 Hamburg 13
Subjects: Architecture, Electrical Engineering, Electronics, Textbooks, Education, Pets
ISBN Publisher's Prefix: 3-481

Verlag **Müller** und Kiepenheuer*, Frankfurter Landstr 32, Postfach 500, D-6450 Hanau am Main Tel: (06181) 22316/82353
Publisher: Werner Dausien
Subjects: General Fiction, Arts, Maps
Miscellaneous: Firm is a subsidiary of Werner Dausien, German Federal Republic (qv)
ISBN Publisher's Prefix: 3-7833

Verlag **Müller** und Schindler+, Sonnenbergstr 55, D-7000 Stuttgart Tel: (0711) 233204
Proprietor: Dr Rolf Müller
Subject: Facsimiles of manuscripts and historical prints relating to Art, Civilisation and the Natural Sciences
Founded: 1965

Rudolf **Müller** und Steinicke Verlag, Lindwurmstr 21, D-8000 Munich 2 Tel: (089) 265881
Publisher: Werner Gissler; *Sales:* Volker Keller
Subjects: Medicine and associated fields

Munin Verlag GmbH, Postfach 3023, D-4500 Osnabruck Tel: (0541) 572278
Subject: War History of the Waffen SS

1978: 3 titles *1979:* 3 titles *Founded:* 1955
ISBN Publisher's Prefix: 3-921242

Münster Verlag*, Hildastr 25, D-7800 Freiburg-im-Breisgau Tel: (0761) 35190
Subjects: Reference Works; Popular Fact-Books; Religious

Musterschmidt-Verlag*, Weender Str 80/82, Postfach 421, D-3400 Göttingen Tel: (0551) 55301 Cable Add: Musterschmidt Telex: 096860
Dirs: Hans Hansen-Schmidt, Eva Maria Gerhardy-Löcken
Br Offs: Rossmarkt 23, D-6000 Frankfurt am Main, German Federal Republic; Zürich, Waldmannstr 10a, Switzerland
Subjects: Biography, History, Anthropology, Medicine
Founded: 1905
ISBN Publisher's Prefix: 3-7881

N D V (Neue Darmstädter Verlagsanstalt), Hauptstr 72, D-5342 Rheinbreitbach Tel: (02224) 3232
Publisher: Klaus-J Holzapfel
Subject: Politics
ISBN Publisher's Prefix: 3-87576

Nachrichten-Verlags-GmbH, Glauburgstr 66, Postfach 180372, D-6000 Frankfurt am Main Tel: (0611) 599791
Man Dir: Dr Werner Petschick; *Sales Dir:* Elfriede Krüger; *Publicity & Advertising Dirs:* Renate Bastian, Gisela Mayer; *Rights & Permissions:* Ruth Malkomes
Subjects: How-to, Social Science
Founded: 1969

Gunter **Narr** Verlag, Postfach 2567, D-7400 Tubingen 1 (Located at: Stauffenbergstr 42) Tel: (07071) 24156
Manager and Sales Dir: Gunter Narr; *Publicity Dir:* Brigitte Narr; *Advertising Dir:* Horst Schmid; *Rights & Permissions:* Gunter Narr
Subjects: Linguistic studies (especially German, English and French); Literary Criticism; Romanesque Studies
1977: 38 titles *1978:* 46 titles *Founded:* 1969
ISBN Publisher's Prefix: 3-87808

Paul **Neff** Verlag KG, Herwarthstr 3, D-1000 Berlin 45 Tel: (030) 7725246
Man Dir: Fritz Pfenningstorff
Subjects: Novels, Belles Lettres, Poetry, Music, Art, Biography, History, Textbooks, Geography
1977: 7 titles *Founded:* 1829
Miscellaneous: Associate company of Paul Neff Verlag KG, Austria (qv)

Nerva-Verlag*, Romanstr 7-9, D-8000 Munich 19 Tel: (089) 132051 Cable Add: Nerva-Verlag Telex: 5215959
Man Dir: Johann Milleder; *Sales & Advertising Dir:* Ernst K Jost
Subject: Reference

Verlag Günther **Neske**, Kloster, Postfach 7240, D-7417 Pfullingen Tel: (07121) 71339 Cable Add: Neske-Verlag Pfullingen
Publisher: Günther Neske; *Editorial, Publicity:* Brigitte Neske
Subjects: General Fiction, Humanities, Literary Criticism, Philosophy, Politics, Poetry, Psychiatry, Theology, Swiridoff Picture Books
1977: 11 titles *1978:* 10 titles
ISBN Publisher's Prefix: 3-7885

Neue Darmstädter Verlagsanstalt, see N D V

Verlag **Neue Gesellschaft** GmbH, Godesberger Allee 143, D-5300 Bonn 2 Tel: (02221) 378021
Dir: Dr Heiner Lindner; *Editorial:* Dr Klaus

Kamberger, Charly Schüddekopf; *Sales:* Peter Marold
Orders to: Verlagsauslieferung Georg Lingenbrink, Postfach 3584, D–6000 Frankfurt am Main 1; or (Berlin): Zirk & Ellenrieder, Lützowstr 15 (bbz), D–1000 Berlin 30
Associate Company: Verlag J H W Dietz Nachf GmbH (qv)
Subjects: Politics, Legal, History, Sociology, Economics, Periodicals
ISBN Publisher's Prefix: 3–87831

Verlag **Neue Kritik** KG, Myliusstr 58, D–6000 Frankfurt am Main Tel: (0611) 727576
Orders to: Sozialistische Verlagsauslieferung, GmbH, Franziusstr 4, D–6000 Frankfurt am Main
Subjects: Mainly Socialist-orientated
1978: 8 titles *1979:* 8 titles *Founded:* 1965
ISBN Publisher's Prefix: 3–8015

Verlag Der **Neue Schulmann***, Pfizerstr 5–7, D–7000 Stuttgart 1, see Franckh'sche Verlagshandlung

Verlag **Neue Stadt** GmbH, Gleissner Str 87, D–8000 Munich 83 Tel: (089) 405081 Cable Add: Neue Stadt
Man Dir: Wolfgang Bader; *Sales Dirs:* Hans R Jurt, Enrico Giuliani; *Publicity and Advertising:* Hans R Jurt; *Rights:* Wolfgang Bader
Parent Company: Città Nuova Editrice Italy (qv)
Associate Companies: Cidade Nova, Rua Pio Xii, 274 Paraiso São Paulo, Brazil; Citta Nuova, Italy (qv); Ciudad Nueva, Spain (qv); New City, UK (qv); Niewe Stad, St Stephanusstraat 11, Nijmegen, Netherlands; Nouvelle Cité, France (qv)
Branch Offs: Trostr 116, A–1100 Vienna, Austria; Hammerstr 9, Postfach 218, CH–8032 Zurich, Switzerland
Subjects: Music, Art, Religion, Juveniles
1978: 15 titles *1979:* 15 titles *Founded:* 1965
ISBN Publisher's Prefix: 3–87996

Verlag **Neue Wirtschafts-Briefe** GmbH*, Eschstr 22, D–4690 Herne 1 Tel: (02323) 54071 Telex: 08229870 Cable Add: Steuerbriefe Herne
Man Dir: E–O Kleyboldt; *Sales Dir:* J Müller-Grote; *Advertising Dir:* H Werner
Subsidiary Company: Friedrich Kiehl Verlag GmbH (qv)
Subjects: Trade Journals and books on Tax and Company Law, Accountancy, Industrial Management, Political Economics, Vocational Training
Founded: 1947
ISBN Publisher's Prefix: 3–482

Neuer Jugendschriften-Verlag, Tiestestr 14, D–3000 Hanover 1 Tel: (0511) 813068 Cable Add: Buchweichert Telex: 0923872 awv d
Man Dir: Alfred Trippo
Associate Company: A Weichert-Verlag (qv)
Branch Off: Hans Feulner, Lindenallee 25, D–1000 Berlin 19
Subject: Juveniles
1978: 23 titles *1979:* 17 titles
ISBN Publisher's Prefix: 3–483

Verlag **Neuer Weg**, Heusteigstr 88a, D–7000 Stuttgart 1, Postfach 3080 Tel: (0711) 645894
Subjects: Marxist Politics, Communism, Novels, Song Books
Founded: 1971
ISBN Publisher's Prefix: 3–88021

Verlag Claus **Neugebauer***, Postfach 40, D–8521 Uttenreuth Tel: (09131) 24692
Publisher: Claus Neugebauer

Subjects: Fiction, Poetry
ISBN Publisher's Prefix: 3–921394

Neukirchener Verlag des Erziehungvereins GmbH, Andreas-Braem-Str 18–20, Postfach 216, D–4133 Neukirchen-Vluyn 2 Tel: (02845) 39222 Cable Add: Verlagshaus neukirchenvluyn
Man Dirs: Werner Braselmann, Hans-Martin Dahlmann; *Editors:* Dr K Adloff; *Sales Dir:* Thomas von Puskas; *Publicity & Advertising Dir:* Reinhard Lieber; *Rights & Permissions:* Werner Braselmann
Subsidiary Company: Kalendar-Verlag des Erziehungs-Vereins, D–4133 Neukirchen-Vluyn 2, Andreas-Braem Str 18–20 (Calendars)
Branch Off: Evangelische Schriften-Zentrale (esz), Barsortiment, Postfach 216, D–4133 Neukirchen-Vluyn
Subjects: Evangelical Christianity, Catholic and Reformed; Biblical Studies, Bible Archaeology, Belles Lettres
1977: 39 titles *1978:* 31 titles *Founded:* 1888
Bookshop: Neukirchener Buchhandlung, A–Braem-Str 20, D–4133 Neukirchen-Vluyn 2
ISBN Publisher's Prefix: 3–7887

Verlag J **Neumann-Neudamm** KG*, Muhlenstr 9, Postfach 267, D–3508 Melsungen Tel: (05661) 2374/6374
Subjects: Agriculture, Horticulture, Forestry, Hunting, Fishing, Natural Science, Aquarian Science
ISBN Publisher's Prefix: 3–7888

Neureuter Baumann mbH*, Pettenkoferstr 7, Postfach 482, D–8000 Munich 2 Tel: (089) 597186
Publishers: Thomas Neureuter, Kurt Baumann
Founded: 1972

Nicolaische Verlagsbuchhandlung GmbH und Co KG, Wilhelmsaue 11, D–1000 Berlin 31 Tel: 870497/98
General Manager: Dieter Beuermann
Subjects: All aspects of Berlin; Politics, European Art and Photography, Poetry
1978: 12 titles *1979:* 12 titles

Verlag C W **Niemeyer**+, Osterstr 19, Postfach 447, D–3250 Hameln 1 Tel: (05151) 200326 Cable Add: Dewezet Telex: 92859
Dir: Erich Schoeneberg; *Sales:* Gerda Pfab
Orders to: Hamburger Kommissionsbuchhandlung GmbH, Libri-Haus, 2 Hamburg 36
Subjects: Scenic Picture Books (Germany), Quality Illustrated Books, Humour
Founded: 1797
Miscellaneous: Associate Company of Adolf Sponholtz Verlag (qv)
ISBN Publisher's Prefix: 3–87585

Max **Niemeyer** Verlag, Pfrondorfer Str 4, Postfach 2140, D–7400 Tübingen Tel: (07071) 81104 Cable Add: Niemeyer Tübingen
Man Dir: Robert Harsch-Niemeyer; *Rights & Permissions:* Cornelia Linz; *Publicity and Marketing:* Manfred Korn
Subjects: General Literary Criticism; German, English & Romance Philology; Linguistics, Philosophy, History
1978: 71 titles *Founded:* 1870
ISBN Publisher's Prefix: 3–484

Verlag Friedrich **Nolte***, Postfach 475, D–1000 Berlin 61 Tel: (030) 6933080
Publisher: Friedrich Nolte; *Editorial:* Dr Franz Büchler, Dicter Straub
Subjects: Belles Lettres, Poetry, Modern Literature, Periodicals, Psychology
1977: 4 titles
ISBN Publisher's Prefix: 3–921177

FEDERAL REPUBLIC OF GERMANY 153

Nomos Verlagsgesellschaft mbH und Co KG, Waldseestr 3–5, Postfach 610, D–7570 Baden-Baden Tel: (07221) 3441 Telex: 0781201
Man Dir: Volker Schwarz; *Sales, Publicity:* Renatus Bräutigam
Associate Companies: Suhrkamp Verlag (qv); Insel Verlag (qv)
Subjects: Jurisprudence, Economics, European Economy, Admin Sciences, International Co-operation, Periodicals
1977: 66 titles *1978:* 104 titles *Founded:* 1936
ISBN Publisher's Prefix: 3–7890

Verlag Wissenschaft und Politik, Berend von **Nottbeck**, Salierring 14–16, D–5000 Cologne 1 Tel: (0221) 312878/315787 Cable Add: Politikbuch 5 Köln 1
Man Dir: Berend von Nottbeck; *Sales & Advertising Dir:* Siegmund Mindt; *Publicity Dir:* C P von Nottbeck
Branch Off: Redaktion 'Deutschland Archiv', D–5000 Cologne 51, Goltsteinstr 185
Subjects: Political Science, especially in context of East-West relations; International Law and Problems, Dialogue with the German Democratic Republic etc
1977: 19 titles *1978:* 24 titles *Founded:* 1960
ISBN Publisher's Prefix: 3–8046

NovaPart Verlag GmbH*, Schönfeldstrasse 13, D–8000 Munich 22 Tel: (089) 281038 Telex: 529891 nopa d
Editorial Off: Ismaningerstr 21, D–8000 Munich 80
Dir: Willi Hauck; *Editorial:* Rudolf Radler; *Sales, Publicity:* Werner Theidemann; *Production:* Anton Siesegger; *Rights & Permissions:* Barbara Hartl
Subsidiary Company: NovaBuch GmbH, Ismaningerstr 21, D–8000 Munich 80
Br Off: Novapart BV, Amsterdam, Netherlands
Subject: Part-works
Founded: 1976

Verlag Monika **Nüchtern***, Breisacherstr 14, D–8000 Munich 80 Tel: (089) 481230
Man Dir: Monika Nüchtern
Subject: Films
1977: 3 titles *Founded:* 1976

Numismatischer Verlag P N Schulten, Bornwiesenweg 34, D–6000 Frankfurt am Main 1 Tel: (0611) 550286 Telex: 4189154
Publisher: Peter N Schulten
Subjects: Coins, Medals, Reprints
Founded: 1974
ISBN Publisher's Prefix: 3–921302

Nusser Verlag, Kaufbeurerstr 3, Postfach 500411, D–8000 Munich 50 Tel: (089) 146788
Man Dir: Dr Horst Nusser; *Sales:* Katharina Mühlberger; *Rights & Permissions:* Horst Hodemacher, Axel Poldner GmbH Co KG, Munich (qv under Literary Agents)
Subjects: History, Geography, Popular Science, Art, Culture, Asiatic Topics
1978: 1 title *1979:* 3 titles *Founded:* 1972
ISBN Publisher's Prefix: 3–88091

Nymphenburger Verlagshandlung GmbH, Romanstr 16, D–8000 Munich 19 Tel: (089) 162051 Cable Add: Nymphenbuch Munich
Man Dir: Hans Adolf Neunzig; *Editorial:* Peter Brambӧck; *Sales:* Peter Karg, Brigitte Nunner; *Advertising and Rights and Permissions:* Gisela Günther
Subjects: General Fiction, Belles Lettres, Poetry, Biography, History, How-to, Music, Art, Philosophy, Sports, Hobbies, Mountaineering, General and Social Science, High-priced Paperbacks
1977: 35 titles *1978:* 34 titles *Founded:* 1946

FEDERAL REPUBLIC OF GERMANY

Miscellaneous: Firm is a member of Verlagsgruppe Langen-Müller/Herbig (qv)
ISBN Publisher's Prefix: 3-485

Oberbaumverlag*, Postfach 127, D-1000 Berlin 21 Tel: (030) 3953099
Man Dir: G Petermann; *Publicity & Advertising Dir:* Walter Knoblich
Subjects: Political (Left Wing, Revolutionary), Proletarian-Revolutionary Fiction, Materialism generally, pro-Mao, anti-Soviet Literature
Founded: 1966

Odörfer-Verlags GmbH, Mohrengasse 10, D-8500 Nuremberg Tel: (0911) 203611
Dir: Kurt Odörfer
Subjects: Sexual Literature, Pornography
1978: 24 titles

Oekumenischer Verlag Dr R-F Edel, D-355 Marburg an der Lahn, Cappelerstr 8, Postfach 1211 Tel: (02351) 83255
Publicity Manager: Dr Reiner-Friedemann Edel
Orders to: Annabergstr 46, D-5880 Lüdenscheid
Subject: Christian Evangelical and Devotional; Cultural, Philosophical, Art

Verlag Friedrich **Oetinger***, Poppenbütteler Chaussee 55, D-2000 Hamburg 65, Postfach 220 Tel: (040) 6070055 Cable Add: Oetingerbuch Telex: 02174230
Editorial: Else Marie Bonnet; *Sales:* Thomas Huggle; *Publicity:* Anke Ludtke; *Rights & Permissions:* Uwe Weitendorf
Subjects: Juveniles, Illustrated Books
Miscellaneous: Associate Company: Cecilie Dressler Verlag (qv)
ISBN Publisher's Prefix: 3-7891

August **Oetker**, see Ceres-Verlag

Verlag **Offene Worte***, Steintorwall 17, Postfach 371, D-4900 Herford Tel: (05221) 3147/8 Cable Add: Vlg Offene Worte, Herford/W Telex: 934801
Publishers: Dr Kurt Schober, Gerhard Bollmann; *Sales:* Hans-Focko Koehler; *Publicity:* Gerhard Mindt
Br Off: D-5300 Bonn, Bonngasse 3
Subjects: Military, Politics, Periodicals
Miscellaneous: Associate Companies: Koehlers Verlagsgesellschaft, Maximilian-Verlag, ES Mittler & Sohn GmbH (qqv)
ISBN Publisher's Prefix: 3-87599

Karl **Ohm** Verlag, Hauptstr 101, D-1000 Berlin 62 Tel: (030) 784001
Publisher: Kurt Meurer
Associate Company: Elwert und Meurer GmbH (qv)
Subject: Law
ISBN Publisher's Prefix: 3-87600

R **Oldenbourg** Verlag GmbH+, Rosenheimer Str 145, Postfach 801360, D-8000 Munich 80 Tel: (089) 41121 Cable Add: Rograph München Telex: 0523789
Man Dirs: Walter Oldenbourg, Dr Thomas von Cornides, Götz Ohmeyer
Orders to: Verlegerdienst München, Auslieferung R Oldenbourg Verlag, Gutenbergstr 1, Postfach 1280, D-8031 Gilching Tel: (08105) 9031/32/33
Branch Off: R Oldenbourg KG Wien, Neulinggasse 26/12, A-1030 Vienna, Austria (qv)
Subjects: Modern Science and Technology (Data Processing, Statistics etc); History and the Liberal Arts (Politics, Current Affairs, Philosophy, Art History, and especially Austrian and European History); Social Sciences, Psychology, Pedagogics and School Text Books, Periodicals

1977: 163 titles *1978:* 186 titles *Founded:* 1858
ISBN Publisher's Prefix: 3-486 (Munich), 3-7029 (Vienna)

Verlag **Olle und Wolter**, Paul Lincke Ufer 44a, Postfach 4310, D-1000 Berlin 30 Tel: (030) 6121973
Gen Man, Editorial, Rights & Permissions: Ulf Wolter; *Sales and Publicity:* Dieter Hartendoof; *Production:* Walle Bengs
Subjects: History of the Workers' Movement, Politics, Economics, Philosophy, Literature, Scientific; Periodical *Kritik* (Socialist Discussion)
1977: 21 titles *Founded:* 1972
ISBN Publisher's Prefix: 3-921241, 3-88395

Georg **Olms** Verlag, Hagentorwall 7, D-3200 Hildesheim Tel: (05121) 37007 Cable Add: Bookolms Hildesheim
Publisher: W Georg Olms, Dr E Mertens; *Sales:* Edith Olms; *Production:* J-P Pracht; *Publicity:* Johannes Koeltzsch; *Rights & Permissions:* Miss G Beutel
Subsidiary Company: Editions Olms AG, Haldenbachstr 17, CP 159, CH-8033 Zurich, Switzerland
Br Off: 52 Vanderbilt Ave, New York, NY 10017, USA
Bookshop: Georg Olms, Verlagsbuchhandlung, Hagentorwall 7, D-3200 Hildesheim
Subjects: Languages and Language History (especially Slavic, Germanic, Romance), Books in foreign languages (especially English, French), History (Classical, Renaissance etc), Geography and Travel, Literature and the Arts (Music, Theatre etc), Judaica, Science and Technology, Orientalia, Folklore, Theology, Law, Politics, Economics, Sociology, Psychology, Pedagogy, Philosophy, Paperbacks
1977: 428 titles *1978:* 452 titles *Founded:* 1945
Miscellaneous: The firm commenced production in 1976 of The *Bibliothek der Deutschen Sprache*, a complete library of significant writing in German from the earliest times till c.1900 in microfiche form (Olms Microform)
ISBN Publisher's Prefix: 3-487

Verlag **Ölschläger** GmbH, Amalienstr 81, D-8000 Munich 40
Man Dirs: Claus Ölschläger, Christina Ölschläger
Associate Company: Verlag für Wirtschaftsskripten (qv)
Subjects: Communications, Journalism, Economics, Business and Management, Sociology, Psycho-analysis
1978: 12 titles *Founded:* 1977
ISBN Publisher's Prefix: 3-88295

Verlag für Wirtschaftsskripten, Dipl Kfm C **Ölschläger** GmbH, see Wirtschaftsskripten

Günter **Olzog** Verlag GmbH, Thierschstr 11, D-8000 Munich 22 Tel: (089) 293272
Man Dir: Dr Günter Olzog; *Sales, Publicity & Advertising Dir:* Johann Hacker; *Rights & Permissions:* Dr Günter Olzog
Subjects: History, Social Science, Educational Materials, Politics, East European Economics
1977: 20 titles *1978:* 18 titles *Founded:* 1949
ISBN Publisher's Prefix: 3-7892

Oncken Verlag KG*, Postfach 110197, D-5600 Wuppertal 11 Tel: (02104) 6311/3
Subjects: Popular Religion: Biography, Devotional, Song Books etc
1977: 13 titles
ISBN Publisher's Prefix: 3-7893

Orangerie Galerie und Verlag, Gerhard F Reinz*, Helenenstr 2, D-5000 Cologne 1 Tel: (0221) 234684 Cable Add: Orangerie Telex: 8882939
Subject: Art

Orion-Heimreiter Verlag GmbH, Friedrich-Ebert-Str 5-7, Postfach 1324, D-6056 Heusenstamm Tel: (06104) 5013 Cable Add: Orionheimreiter
Publisher: Erich W Rüskamp; *Editorial:* Ernst Frank; *Sales, Production, Publicity:* Sigrun Wagner; *Rights & Permissions:* through Hodemacher-Poldner, 8 Munich 19
Subjects: Biography, Documentary, Local History, Art, History, Fiction
1977: 6 titles *1978:* 9 titles *Founded:* 1961
ISBN Publisher's Prefix: 3-87588

Verlag **Osterrieth**, part of Societäts-Verlag (qv)

PIAG, see Verlag Presse Information Agentur GmbH

P R Verlag Wiesbaden, H G Schwieger, Glückstr 12, D-6200 Wiesbaden Tel: (06121) 520030 Cable Add: PR Verlag, Wiesbaden
Man Dir: H G Schwieger
Subjects: Belles Lettres, Poetry, Educational Materials
Founded: 1974
ISBN Publisher's Prefix: 3-921261

Päd extra buchverlag in der pädex Verlags GmbH, Postfach 295, D-6140 Bensheim (Located at: Bahnhofstr 5) Tel: (06251) 6054/6055
Man Dir, Editorial, Sales: Jörg Jonas; *Production:* Christiane Bohm; *Publicity:* Hans Jürgen Blank
Parent Company: Pädex Verlags GmbH (at above address)
Subjects: Pedagogy, Social Sciences
1977: 12 titles *1978:* 14 titles *Founded:* 1976
ISBN Publisher's Prefix: 3-921450

Pädagogischer Verlag Schwann GmbH, Am Wehrhahn 100, Postfach 7640, D-4000 Düsseldorf 1 Tel: (0211) 360301 Cable Add: Schwannverlag Düsseldorf Telex: paed d 858 1345
Dirs: Dr Paul Böhringer, Wilhelm Biswanger; *Production:* Dr Hans Weymar; *Publicity Manager:* Hartwig Berthold
Subjects: University, Secondary and Primary Textbooks, Educational Materials, History, Arts, Linguistics, Children's Books, Records
1977: 75 titles *1978:* 74 titles *Founded:* 1821
ISBN Publisher's Prefix: 3-508

Pahl-Rugenstein Verlag*, Gottesweg 54, D-5000 Cologne 51 Tel: (0221) 364051
Dir: Paul Neuhöffer; *Editorial:* Jürgen Hartmann; *Sales Manager:* Hajo Leib
Subjects: History, Literature Criticism, Education, Philosophy, Politics, Psychology, Social Science, Paperbacks, Economics, Periodicals, Sports
ISBN Publisher's Prefix: 3-7609

Wilhelm **Pansegrau** Verlag, Bessemerstr 83, Postfach 420320, D-1000 Berlin Tel: 7536631
Subjects: Corrosion Protection, Plastics, Lacquer and Coatings

Parabel Verlag GmbH und Co KG, Bauerstr 20, Postfach 401024, D-8000 Munich Tel: (089) 374494 Telex: 055215697
Publisher: Nadine Lange-Siemens; *Sales:* Franz Eheberg; *Rights & Permissions:* Barbel Kistner
Subjects: Picture Books, Modern Literature
1978: 8 titles *1979:* 15 titles
ISBN Publisher's Prefix: 3-7898

Paracelsus Verlag GmbH, see Hippokrates Verlag GmbH

Verlag Paul **Parey**, Spitalerstr 12, Postfach 106304, D–2000 Hamburg 1; Lindenstr 44–47, D–1000 Berlin 61 Tel: (040) 321511 (Hamburg); (030) 2516011 (Berlin) Cable Add: Pareyverlag Hamburg or Berlin Telex: Hamburg 2161391; Berlin 184777
Man Dirs: Dr Friedrich Georgi, Dr Rudolf Georgi; *Sales, Publicity, Editorial Manager:* Gerhard Schwennesen; *Publicity:* Karlheinz Römer; *Rights & Permissions:* Gerhard Reichwald
Subjects: Biology, Veterinary Medicine, Foodstuff, Agriculture, Starch Research and Application, Brewery and Distillery, Forestry, Horticulture, Plant Medicine and Protection; Environment Protection, Hydro- and Cultural Technologies, Hunting, Sporting and Professional Fishing, Riding and Horses, Technical and Scientific Journals
1977: 79 titles *1978:* 92 titles *Founded:* 1848
ISBN Publisher's Prefixes: 3–490 (Hamburg), 3–489 (Berlin)

Parkland Verlag GmbH und Co Verlags- & Vertriebs-KG, Schwabstr 189, D–7000 Stuttgart 1 Tel: (0711) 292287
Man Dirs: Gerd Seibert, Dr Erhard Wendelberger; *Sales Dir:* Martina Deissner
Subjects: Nonfiction, especially Belles Lettres, Art etc
Founded: 1974

Verlag **Passavia**, Postfach 2147, D–8390 Passau 2 Tel: (0851) 51081/82/83 and 56947 Cable Add: Passavia Telex: 57837
Publishing Dir & Rights & Permissions: M Teschendorff; *Sales:* Katharina Moritz
Subjects: Bavarian Topics, Folklore, Humour, Homecare, Belles Lettres, Fiction
1978: 5 titles *1979:* 6 titles *Founded:* 1888
ISBN Publisher's Prefix: 3–87616

Galerie **Patio** Verlag, Laubestr 24H, D–6000 Frankfurt am Main 70
Man Dir: Walter Zimbrich; *Editorial:* Walter Richartz; *Sales:* Günter Scherer; *Production:* David Albrecht; *Publicity:* Manfred Linke
Subjects: Reprints of Rare Texts, Hand-Printed Texts, the *Parabü* series (Patio's Book Rarity Library)
1978: 8 titles *1979:* 7 titles *Founded:* 1964

Patmos Verlag GmbH, Am Wehrhahn 100, Postfach 6213, D–4000 Düsseldorf 1 Tel: (0211) 360301 Cable Add: Patmos Verlag Düsse: paed d 8581345
Dir: Dr P Böhringer; *Man Dir:* Gerhard Binder; *Sales:* Wilhelm Biswanger; *Publicity:* Hartwig Berthold
Subjects: Roman Catholic Theology, Religion, Education, Juveniles, Textbooks
1977: 55 titles *Founded:* 1910
ISBN Publisher's Prefix: 3–491

Paul **Pattloch** Verlag, Goldbacherstr 6, D–8750 Aschaffenburg Tel: (06021) 22187 Cable Add: Pattloch Aschaffenburg Telex: 4188517
Man & Sales Dir: Clemens Pattloch; *Editorial:* Dr B Pattloch
Subjects: Religion, Bibles
1978: 30 titles *1979:* 27 titles *Founded:* 1827
Bookshops: Buchhandlung Paul Pattloch, Herstallstr, D–8750 Aschaffenburg; City Galerie, Goldbacherstr 2, D–8750 Aschaffenburg
ISBN Publisher's Prefix: 3–557

Paulinus Verlag, Fleischstr 61, Postfach 3040, D–5500 Trier Tel: (0651) 46171 Telex: 04–72731
Dir: Werner Adrian
Parent Company: Paulinus Druckerei GmbH (at above address)
Associated Company: Spee Buchverlag GmbH (qv)
Subjects: Religion, Theology
ISBN Publisher's Prefix: 3–7902

Pawel Pan Presse*, Kennedystr 25, D–6072 Dreieich Tel: 06103/81347
Man Dir, Production: Sascha Juritz; *Editorial:* Hanne F Juritz
Subjects: Contemporary Literature, Educative Art, Poetry, First Publications in Bibliophile Editions
1977: 5 titles *1978:* 3 titles *Founded:* 1972
ISBN Publisher's Prefix: 3–921454

Manfred **Pawlak** Grossantiquariat und Verlagsgesellschaft mbH, Postfach 1149, D–8036 Herrsching (Located at: Gachenau Str 13) Tel: (08152) 1067–69 Telex: 0527724 mph d
Proprietor, Man Dir: Manfred Pawlak
Subjects: Biography, History, Music, Art
1979: about 600 titles *Founded:* 1949
Miscellaneous: The Company is a wholesale antiquarian and second-hand book dealer as well as a Publishing House

Pestalozzi-Verlag graphische Gesellschaft mbH, Am Pestalozziring 14, Postfach 2829, D–8520 Erlangen Tel: 09131/6116 Cable Add: Pestalozzi Erlangen Telex: 629766 Pevau
Man Dirs: Dr Reinhold Weigand, Norbert Franke; *Editorial:* Wolfgang Kaisere
Subjects: Children's Books
1977: 500 titles *1978:* 105 titles *Founded:* 1844
ISBN Publisher's Prefix: 3–876

Verlag J P **Peter**, Gebr Holstein, Herrngasse 1, Postfach 19, D–8803 Rothenburg Tel: (09861) 3001 Cable Add: Peterverlag
Man Dir: Bernhard Doerdelmann; *Sales Dir:* Rainer Holstein; *Publicity Dir:* Bernhard Doerdelmann
Subjects: Belles Lettres, Poetry, History, Religion, Travel, Educational Materials, Fiction; Periodicals
Founded: 1825
ISBN Publisher's Prefix: 3–87625

C F **Peters** Musikverlag GmbH und Co KG, Kennedyallee 101, Postfach 700906, D–6000 Frankfurt-am-Main 70 Tel: (0611) 633066 Cable Add: Petersedjt
Managing Partner: Dr Johannes Petschull
Associate Companies: Hinrichsen Edition Ltd, London, UK; C F Peters Corporation, New York, USA
Imprints: Edition Peters, Henry Litolff's Verlag, Edition Schwann, MP Belaieff
Subjects: Musical scores, Books on Music (all areas of Classical and Contemporary Music)
Founded: 1800
ISBN Publisher's Prefix: 3–87626

Dr Hans **Peters** Verlag*, Salisweg 56, Postfach 685, D–6450 Hanau Tel: (06181) 21632 *Man Dir:* Wolfgang A Nagel; *Editorial:* Rainer G Tripp; *Sales:* Christa Buschbeck; *Production:* Barbara Nagel
Subjects: Art Books, Pictorial Books, Picture Books for Children
1977: 11 titles *Founded:* 1952
ISBN Publisher's Prefix: 87627

Pfaffenweiler Presse*, Mittlere Str 23, D–7801 Pfaffenweiler Tel: (07664) 8999
Subjects: Small Literary Editions; hand-printed texts

Fachbuchverlag Dr **Pfanneberg** & Co, Postfach 110910, D–6300 Lahn-Giessen 11 (Located at: Schanzenstr 18) Tel: (0641) 74034
Man Dirs, Rights & Permissions: Dr Günther Pfanneberg, Gero Pfanneberg; *Editorial:* Gero Pfanneberg; *Sales:* Christa Horn; *Production:* Gerhard Duske
Subjects: Hotels and Catering Trade Textbooks, Technologies (automobile, electrical etc), Commerce, Botany, Textbooks for Trade Schools
Founded: 1949
ISBN Publisher's Prefix: 3–8057

Verlag J **Pfeiffer**, Herzogspitalstr 5, D–8000 Munich 2 Tel: (089) 2603036
Man Dir: Günter Müller; *Editorial:* A Arnold; *Sales, Publicity:* M Reile; *Production:* G Bitterauf; *Rights & Permissions:* I Grote-Haara
Subjects: How-to, Philosophy, Psychology, Religion, Juveniles, High-priced Paperbacks, Social Science, Educational Materials
1977: 21 titles *1978:* 22 titles *Founded:* 1882
Bookshop: Buchhandlung J Pfeiffer, Herzogspitalstr 5, D–8000 Munich 2
ISBN Publisher's Prefix: 3–7904

E **Pfister** GmbH*, Postfach 6485, Hussenstr 6, D–7750 Constance Tel: (07531) 23598
Associate Companies: Verlag der Arche, Switzerland (qv); Dr Franz Hain, Austria (qv); Sanssouci Verlag AG, Switzerland (qv)

Richard **Pflaum** Verlag KG, Postfach 201920, D–8000 Munich 2 (Located at: Lazarettstr 4, D–8000 Munich 19) Tel: (089) 186051 Cable Add: Pflaumverlag Telex: 529408
Sales & Publicity Manager: Hans-Georg Scheideler
Subjects: Electrical Engineering, Electronics, Hobbies, Medicine, Paperbacks, Periodicals
Associate Company: Hüthig & Pflaum Verlag (qv)
ISBN Publisher's Prefix: 3–7905

Engelbert **Pfriem** Verlag+, Else-Lasker-Schüler-Str 47–49, D–5600 Wuppertal 1 Tel: (0202) 447878
General Manager: Engelbert Pfriem
Associate Company: Kolibri Verlag (qv)
Subjects: Books and magazines for aquarium enthusiasts

Udo **Pfriemer** Verlag GmbH, Landwehrstr 68, Postfach 201940, D–8000 Munich 2 Tel: 531604 Telex: 0523398
Subjects: Energy, Alternative Energies, Maintenance Technology in Water, Gas, Helio systems; Sanitary, Health, Heating, Sewage Technology, History of Science and Technology

Philips GmbH, Fachbuch-Verlag, Mönckebergstr 7, Postfach 101420, D–2000 Hamburg 1 Tel: (040) 32971 Cable Add: Phihag Telex: 2161587 a dpu d
Man Dir: Wilfried von Hacht
Subjects: Electronics, Electrical Engineering, Radio & Television
1979: approx 100 titles
ISBN Publisher's Prefix: 3–87145

Physica-Verlag Rudolf Liebing GmbH und Co, Werner-von-Siemens-Str 5, Postfach 5840, D–8700 Würzburg 1 Tel: (0931) 22821
Man Dir: Arnulf Liebing
Branch Off: A–1010 Vienna, Seilerstätte 18, Austria
Subjects: University Textbooks (Management Science, Computing Science, Econometrics)
1977: 12 titles *1978:* 12 titles *Founded:* 1952
ISBN Publisher's Prefix: 3–7908

Physik Verlag GmbH+, Pappelallee 3, Postfach 1260-80, D-6940 Weinheim/Bergstr Tel: (06201) 14031 Telex: 465516
Man Dirs: Jürgen Kreuzhage, Hans Schermer; *Editorial:* Dr Hans-Friedrich Ebel, Dr Gerd Giesler; *Sales, Publicity and Advertising Dir:* Helmut Schmitzer; *Production:* Maximilian Montkowski; *Rights & Permissions:* Kornelia Herbig
Subjects: Science & Technology (especially Physics), University Textbooks
1977: 12 titles *1978:* 7 titles *Founded:* 1947
Miscellaneous: Firm is a subsidiary of Verlag Chemie GmbH (qv)
ISBN Publisher's Prefix: 3-87664

Buch- & Verlagshaus Paul **Pietsch** GmbH & Co KG, Postfach 1370, D-7000 Stuttgart 1 (Located at: Böblinger Str 18)
Subsidiary Division: Motorbuch-Verlag (qv)

Pinx-Verlag Kurt Glombig, Hartmann-Ibach-Str 68, D-6000 Frankfurt am Main 60 Tel: (0611) 461211, 454807
Publisher: Kurt Glombig
Subjects: Public Relations Texts in Popular editions; Pharmaceuticals; Travel Sketches; PR Paperbacks; Series of Primers; Animals

R **Piper** und Co Verlag+, Georgenstr 4, Postfach 430120, D-8000 Munich 40 Tel: (089) 397071 Cable Add: Piperverlag Munich Telex: 5215385
Shipping Add: Koch, Neff & Oetinger & Co, Am Wallgraben 110, D-7000 Stuttgart 80
Co-owner & President: Klaus Piper; *Man Dir:* Matthias Pflieger; *Editorial:* Walter Fritzsche, Dr Klaus Stadler; *Sales Dir:* Peter Wagner; *Rights & Permissions:* Dorothee Grisebach
Branch Off: R Piper & Co Verlag GmbH, Zurich, Zehntenweg 146, CH-4654 Lostorf
Subjects: Novels, Poetry, Biography, General and Social Science, Several series of Quality Paperbacks, Philosophy, Psychology, Arts, Education, Biology, Children's Books
1978: 88 titles *1979:* 83 titles *Founded:* 1904
ISBN Publisher's Prefix: 3-492

Plambeck & Co, Druck und Verlag GmbH, Xantener Str 7, Postfach 920, D-4040 Neuss Tel: 57081/88 Telex: 8517506 and 8517530
Subjects: Paperbacks, Pocket Books; Periodicals

Ploetz GmbH und Co KG, Hermann-Herderstr 4, D-7800 Freiburg-im-Breisgau Tel: (0761) 208387
Man Dir: Harald Glaeser
Orders to: Verlag Herder, address as above
1978: 21 titles *Founded:* 1880
Subjects: Illustrated Popular Reference Works on Historical, Biographical, Geographical Themes; School Books, Sociology, Linguistics
Miscellaneous: Company is an Associate of Verlag Herder KG, German Federal Republic (qv); of Herder AG, Switzerland (qv); of Verlag Herder & Co, Austria (qv); and of Herder & Herder GmbH, German Federal Republic (qv)
ISBN Publisher's Prefix: 3-87640

Podzun-Pallas Verlag GmbH, Markt 9, Postfach 14, D-6360 Friedberg 3-Dorheim Tel: (06031) 3131 Cable Add: Podzun, Friedberg Telex: 415961
Man Dir, Production, Rights & Permissions: Rainer Ahnert; *Editorial:* Mrs Neisel; *Sales:* Mrs Hergesell
Subjects: Modern History, Illustrated Books, Periodicals
1977: 7 titles *1978:* 12 titles
ISBN Publisher's Prefix: 3-7909

C E **Poeschel** Verlag, Kernerstr 43, Postfach 529, D-7000 Stuttgart 1 Tel: (0711) 225074-6
Man Dir: Mr Schweizer; *Sales Dir:* Mr Cziszinsky; *Advertising Dir:* Mr Kegler; *Rights & Permissions:* Mrs Kästing
Orders to: (German Federal Republic): Goethestrasse 6, D-7400 Tübingen; (in Berlin) A Muschal & Sohn, Lützowerstr 105-6, D-1000 Berlin 30
Associate Company: J B Metzlersche Verlagsbuchhandlung (qv)
Subjects: Economics, 'The Encyclopaedia of Industrial Management Theory'
1978: 25 titles *Founded:* 1902
ISBN Publisher's Prefix: 3-7910

Pohl Druckerei und Verlagsanstalt Otto Pohl, Herzog-Ernst-Ring 1, Postfach 103, D-3100 Celle Tel: (05141) 27081 Cable Add: Pohl, Celle
Dir: Manfred Senftleben
Subjects: Physical Education, Games, Sports, Gymnastics, Keep Fit
1978: 7 titles
ISBN Publisher's Prefix: 3-7911

Verlag für **Politik und Wirtschaft***, Rondorfer Str 5, D-5000 Cologne-Marienburg Tel: (0221) 387038 Cable Add: Kiepenbücher Köln Telex: 8881142
Subjects: Politics, Economics
Miscellaneous: Associate company of Verlag Kiepenheuer & Witsch (qv)

Verlag für **polizeiliches Fachschrifttum**, see Georg Schmidt-Römhild

Bernd **Polke** GmbH, see I V A Verlag

Polyglott-Verlag Dr Bolte KG, Neusser Str 3, Postfach 401120, D-8000 Munich 40 Tel: (089) 38301 Cable Add: Langenscheidt Munich Telex: 5215379 Lkg md
Man Dir: Karl-Ernst Tielebier-Langenscheidt; *Editor:* Dr Anton Schmuck; *Sales Dir:* Peter Haering; *Export Dir:* Uwe Cordts; *Advertising Dir:* Dieter Krause; *Rights & Permissions:* Manfred Überall
Subjects: Travel Guides & Phrasebooks, Maps
1978: 10 titles *1979:* 10 titles *Founded:* 1902
Miscellaneous: Company is a member of the Langenscheidt Group (qv)
ISBN Publisher's Prefix: 3-493

Polyglotte Buch- und Schallplatten-Verlag und Vertrieb*, Postfach 230147, D-4000 Düsseldorf Tel: 683191
Man Dir: F W Kreft
Subject: Educational Materials
ISBN Publisher's Prefix: 3-920754

Polygraph Verlag GmbH, Schaumainkai 85, Postfach 700940, D-6000 Frankfurt am Main Tel: 639066 Cable Add: Polygraphverlag Frankfurt am Main Telex: 0413562
Man Dir: H J Teichmann; *Sales Dir:* W Kissel; *Publicity Dir:* R Kreis; *Rights & Permissions:* Ulrike Schulz, H Sidoruk
Subjects: Textbooks and Reference Works for the Printing Industry and Allied Trades
1977: 130 titles *1978:* 24 titles *Founded:* 1947

Edition Georg **Popp**, Talavera 7-11, Postfach 5169, D-8700 Würzburg 1 Tel: (0931) 43061 Cable Add: Edition Popp Telex: 068833
Publisher, Editorial, Rights & Permissions: Georg Popp; *Sales:* Günter Reich
Associate Company: Arena-Verlag Georg Popp, Wurzburg (qv)
Subjects: Art Books, Books for the Bibliophile

Founded: 1975
ISBN Publisher's Prefix: 3-881

Possev-Verlag V Gorachek KG, Flurscheideweg 15, D-6230 Frankfurt am Main 80 Tel: (0611) 341265
Publisher, Editorial, Production, Rights & Permissions: Lev Rahr; *Sales, Publicity:* N Jdanoff
Subjects: Contemporary Russian authors in the original Russian and in German translation; Periodicals in Russian
1977: 12 titlees *1978:* 10 titles *Founded:* 1945

Praesentverlag Heinz Peter, Kleiststr 15, Postfach 2720, D-4830 Gütersloh Tel: (05241) 3188/9 Telex: 0933831
Publisher: Heinz Peter
Subjects: General Fiction, Hobbies, Reference Books, Travel, Cookery
ISBN Publisher's Prefix: 3-87644

Präsenz-Verlag der Jesus Bruderschaft*, Gnadenthal, D-6257 Hünfelden 2 Tel: (06438) 2001 Cable Add: Präsenz 6257 Gnadenthal
Dir: Bruder Viktor
Subject: Religion
ISBN Publisher's Prefix: 3-87630

Verlag **Presse** Informations Agentur GmbH (PIAG), Stefanienstr 4, D-7570 Baden-Baden Tel: (07221) 28994/25348 Cable Add: PIAG Baden-Baden Telex: 781217 piag-d
Man Dir: Dieter Brinzer; *Publicity & Advertising Dir:* Thea Gutzeit; *Sales Dir:* Klaus Pittner
Subject: Photography
1978: 24 titles *Founded:* 1963

Guido **Pressler** Verlag, Auf dem Strifft, D-5165 Hürtgenwald Tel: (0249) 1385
Subjects: Art, History, Literature, Bibliographies, History of Sciences
ISBN Publisher's Prefix: 3-87646

Prestel Verlag, Mandlstr 26, D-8000 Munich 40 Tel: (089) 333055 Cable Add: Prestelverlag Telex: 5216366
Man Dir, Sales Dir: Jürgen Tesch; *Advertising & Publicity Dir:* Ursula Wagner; *Rights & Permissions:* Miss Aasta Fischer
Subjects: General Nonfiction, Art, Reference, History
1977/78: 25 titles *Founded:* 1924
ISBN Publisher's Prefix: 3-7913

Helmut **Preussler** Verlag, Rothenburger Str 25, Postfach 2007, D-8500 Nuremberg Tel: (0911) 262323 Cable Add: Preussler-Verlag
Man Dir: Helmut Preussler; *Editorial:* Dr Walter Barbier; *Sales, Publicity:* Annemarie Seeberger; *Production:* Rolf Marienfeldt, Werner Eckstein
Bookshop: Ernst Gebhard, Rothenburger Str 23-25, D-8500 Nuremberg
1977: 25 titles *Founded:* 1973
ISBN Publisher's Prefix: 3-921332

Prisma Verlag GmbH, member of Verlagsgruppe Bertelsmann GmbH (qv)

Pro Schule Verlag GmbH, member of Verlagsgruppe Bertelsmann GmbH (qv)

Albert **Pröpster**+, Schillerstr 46, Postfach 2149, D-8960 Kempten Tel: 22797
Subjects: Cookery Books, Specialist Gastronomy Books, Picture Books, R Catholic Interest Books

FEDERAL REPUBLIC OF GERMANY 157

Propyläen Verlag, Lindenstr 76, D–1000 Berlin 61 Tel: (030) 25911 Cable Add: Ullsteinbuch Berlin Telex: vlgul d 183723
Dirs: W Joachim Freyburg, Hans F Erb, Viktor Niemann, Wolfgang Richter; *Publicity:* Margrit Osterwold; *Press:* Ingrid Schick
Parent Company: Verlag Ullstein GmbH (qv)
Subjects: Arts, History, Literature
ISBN Publisher's Prefix: 3–549

Verlag für **Psychologie**, Dr C J Hogrefe, Rohnsweg 25, Postfach 414, D–3400 Göttingen Tel: (0551) 54044
Proprietor: Dr C J Hogrefe; *Man Dir:* Dr H Lundberg; *Sales & Publicity Dir:* O Kohl; *Advertising, Production, Rights & Permissions Dir:* B Otto
Branch Offs: C J Hogrefe Inc, 525 Eglinton Ave East, Toronto, Ontario M4P 1N5; Verlag fur Psychologie, Dr C J Hogrefe, Zürich, Switzerland (qv)
Subjects: Psychology, Textbooks, Handbooks, Conference Reports, Yearbooks
1978: 200 titles *1979:* 230 titles *Founded:* 1949
ISBN Publisher's Prefix: 3–8017

Anton **Pustet** München* pA Tyrolia, Postfach 498, D–8228 Freilassing
Man Dir: Dr F. G Kuhn
Subjects: Philosophy, Religion, Psychology, Social Science, Music
Founded: 1958
Miscellaneous: Associate Companies: Universitätsverlag Anton Pustet, D–8228 Freilassing, German Federal Republic (Book Depot and Post Box)
ISBN Publisher's Prefix: 3–7025

Verlag Friedrich **Pustet**, Gutenbergstr 8, Postfach 339, D–8400 Regensburg 11 Tel: (0941) 96044 Cable Add: Pustet Telex: 65672
Man Dir: Dr Friedrich Pustet; *Editorial:* Monika Bock, Dr Gerd J Maurer; *Sales & Advertising Dir, Rights & Permissions:* Reinhold Röttger; *Production:* Karl Wittman
Subsidiary Company: Verlag Josef Habbel (qv)
Subjects: Christian Religion, Art, Monographs, Biography, Folklore, Bavaria
1977: 64 titles *1978:* 68 titles *Founded:* 1826
Bookshops: Buchhandlung Friedrich Pustet, Regensburg, Gesandtenstr 6; Kleiner Exerzierplatz 4, Passau; Grottenau 4, Augsburg
ISBN Publisher's Prefix: 3–7917

Quell-Verlag, Furtbachstr 12A, Postfach 897, D–7000 Stuttgart 1 Tel: (0711) 605746/8
Dir: Dr Helmut Riethmüller; *Sales & Publicity Dir:* Michael Jacob; *Editorial, Rights & Permissions:* Helmut Zechner
Subjects: General Fiction, Biography, History, Philosophy, Religion
1978: 13 titles *Founded:* 1830
Bookshop: Buchhandlung der Evangelischen Gesellschaft, Stuttgart
ISBN Publisher's Prefix: 3–7918

Quelle und Meyer Verlag†, Schloss-Wolfsbrunnen-Weg 29, Postfach 104480, D–6900 Heidelberg 1 Tel: (06221) 22443 Cable Add: Quellmeyer Heidelberg
Man Dir: Dr Walter Kissling; *Sales Dir:* Edith Teich; *Advertising & Publicity Dir:* Hermann Klippel; *Foreign Rights Dir:* Hildegard Müller
Orders to: KNOe, Stuttgart
Subjects: Philosophy, Religion, Psychology, Chemistry and Biology, General & Social Science, Education, Language and Literature, History and Geography, University, Secondary & Primary Textbooks
1978: 50 titles *Founded:* 1906
ISBN Publisher's Prefix: 3–494

R V, see Reise- und Verkehrsverlag

Radius-Verlag GmbH+, Kniebisstr 29, D–7000 Stuttgart 1 Tel: (0711) 283091/2
Man Dir: Wolfgang Erk; *Sales, Publicity & Advertising Dir:* Gerhard Schroeder
Subjects: General Fiction, Philosophy, Religion, High-priced Paperbacks, Psychology
1978: 9 titles *1979:* 17 titles *Founded:* 1963
Miscellaneous: Quarterly publication Radius
ISBN Publisher's Prefix: 3–87173

Rainer Verlag*, Körtestr 10, D–1000 Berlin 61 Tel: (030) 6916536
Man Dir: Rainer Pretzell; *Sales Dir:* Agnes Pretzell; *Publicity Manager:* Aldo Frei; *Advertising Dir:* Rainer Pretzell
Subjects: Belles Lettres, Poetry, Music, Art, High-priced Paperbacks
Founded: 1966

Raith Verlag*, Barstystr 6, D–8000 Munich 60 Cable Add: Raith Verlag München 2 H Heinrich 21
Subjects: Education, Social Sciences, Politics, Belles Lettres, Juveniles
ISBN Publisher's Prefix: 3–921121

Dokument und Analyse Verlag Bogislaw von **Randow**, Barerstr 43, D–8000 Munich 40 Tel: (089) 281414/2724200/283001
Publisher: Bogislaw von Randow
General Manager: Gerhard Fassmann; *Marketing Manager:* Renate Lotte; *Marketing Publicity:* Thomas Lingenthal; *Marketing Accounts:* Hannelore Igel
Orders to: above address
Subjects: Politics, Economics, Law, Sociology, Periodical Dokument & Analyse (monthly Current Affairs magazine)
Founded: 1972

Rathgeber Verlag*, Pettenkoferstr 10a, D–8000 Munich 2 Tel: (089) 597797
Publishers: Walter Rathgeber, Johanna Rathgeber-Knan
Subjects: Medicine, Social Science, Humanities
ISBN Publisher's Prefix: 3–921298

Rationalisierungs-Kuratorium der Deutschen Wirtschaft eV (RKW)*, Gutleutstr 163–7, Postfach 119193, D–6000 Frankfurt am Main Tel: (0611) 25651 Cable Add: erkawe Telex: 411154
Branch Offs: in all areas of the German Federal Republic
Subjects: Architecture, Electrical Engineering, Civil & Mechanical Engineering, Education, Economics, Industrial and Human Relations, Management Consultancy, Packaging, Innovation, Technology
1977: 93 titles *Founded:* 1921

Walter **Rau** Verlag, Benderstr 168a, Postfach 6508, D–4000 Düsseldorf Tel: (0211) 283095 Telex: 08586682
Dir: Gisela Rau
Subjects: Arts, Education, Nonfiction, Social Science, Literature, Translations, Chess
ISBN Publisher's Prefix: 3–7919

Karl **Rauch** Verlag KG, Am Wehrhahn 100, Postfach 6520, D–4000 Düsseldorf 1
Man Dir: Harald Ebner
Subjects: Documentation, History, Fiction, Book Industry, Translations
Founded: 1923
ISBN Publisher's Prefix: 3–7920

Agentur des **Rauhen Hauses** GmbH*, 2 Hamburg 76, Papenhuder Str 2 Tel: (040) 2201291
Dirs: Max Lenz, Dieter Gätjens
Subjects: Religion, Belles Lettres, Juveniles, Art
Founded: 1842
ISBN Publisher's Prefix: 3–7600

Druckerei und Verlag Gerhard **Rautenberg**, Blinke 8, Postfach 1909, D–2950 Leer/Ostfriesland Tel: (0491) 4288 Cable Add: Rautenberg Leer
Dir: Gerhard Rautenberg; *Editorial:* Gerhard Rautenberg Junior
Branch Off: Druckerei und Verlag Gerhard Rautenberg, Königstr 41, D–2208 Glückstadt
Subjects: Regional Guides within Germany, Humour, Popular Historical, General Fiction, Show Business, Pictorial Calendars
Bookshop: Rautenbergsche Buchhandlung, Postfach 1909, D–2950 Leer
1977: 10 titles *1978:* 12 titles *Founded:* 1825
ISBN Publisher's Prefix: 3–7921

Ravensburger Graphische Betriebe Otto Maier GmbH*, Robert-Bosch-Str 1, Postfach 1860, D–7980 Ravensburg Tel: (0751) 861 Telex: 732921
Subjects: Juveniles, Hobbies, Games

Ravensburger Verlag GmbH, Marktstr 22–6, Postfach 1860, D–7980 Ravensburg Tel: (0751) 861 Telex: 732921
Presidents: Otto J Maier, Dorothee Hess-Maier; *Man Dirs:* Dieter Breede, Erwin Glonegger (International); *Editorial:* Werner Schlegel, Alois Ströbl
Parent Company: Otto Maier Verlag (qv for Associate Companies)
Subjects: Games, Puzzles, Activity Materials for Children and Adults

Ravenstein Verlag GmbH, Wielandstr 31–35, D–6000 Frankfurt am Main Tel: (0611) 590722/23/24 Cable Add: Ravensteinverlag
Man Dirs: Helga Ravenstein, Rüdiger Bosse; *Sales Dir:* E Zeilfelder
Subjects: Country and Regional Touring and Walking Maps; Town Maps and Guides; Pictorial Guides
Founded: 1830
ISBN Publisher's Prefix: 3–87660

Verlagsgesellschaft **Recht und Wirtschaft** mbH, Häusserstr 14, Postfach 105960, D–6900 Heidelberg Tel: (06221) 25661 Cable Add: Rechtwirtschaft Heidelberg Telex: 461665
Subjects: Specialist Literature in fields of Law and Economics, Tax, Social and Industrial Questions; Tax Guide and other periodicals
Associate Company: I H Sauer Verlag, Heidelberg (qv)

Philipp **Reclam** Jun, Mönchstr 27–31, Postfach 466, D–7000 Stuttgart 1 Tel: (0711) 253016 Cable Add: Reclam Stuttgart
Publisher: Dr Heinrich Reclam; *Sales Dir:* Walter Maier; *Publicity Dir:* Christoph Wilhelmi; *Rights & Permissions:* Marianne Diehl
Subjects: General Fiction, Belles Lettres, Poetry, Music, Art, Philosophy, Reference, Religion, Low-priced Paperbacks, University, Secondary & Primary Textbooks
1977: approx 75 titles *Founded:* 1828
ISBN Publisher's Prefix: 3–15

Dr Ludwig **Reichert** Verlag, Reisstr 10, D–6200 Wiesbaden-Dotzheim Tel: (06121) 465686
Publisher: Ludwig Reichert

Subjects: Facsimile Reprints, Art, Books and Libraries, Orientalia, Linguistics
1977: 35 titles *1978:* 40 titles

Otto **Reichl** Verlag, 'Der Leuchter', Haus Herresberg, D–5480 Remagen Tel: 02642/22271
Man Dir: Herwart von Guilleaume
Subjects: Philosophy, Religion, Parapsychology, Mysticism, Supernatural
1977: 2 titles *1978:* 2 titles *Founded:* 1957
ISBN Publisher's Prefix: 3–87667

Verlag Knut **Reim***, Kleine Theaterstr 11, Postfach 302824, D–2000 Hamburg 36 Tel: (040) 342641
General Managers: Jens Christians, Knut Reim
Subjects: Juvenilia, Jurisprudence, Economics
1977: 6 titles *Founded:* 1958

Ernst **Reinhardt** GmbH & Co Verlag, Kemnatenstr 46, D–8000 Munich 19 Tel: (089) 170266
Man Dir, Production: Karl Münster
Orders to: Postfach 380280, D–8000 Munich 38
Br Off: Ernst Reinhardt Verlag AG, Basel, Sommergasse 46, Switzerland
Subjects: Psychology, Psychotherapy, Philosophy, Pedagogy
1978: 33 titles *Founded:* 1899
ISBN Publisher's Prefix: 3–497

Verlag Wilhelm G **Reinheimer**, see Edition Venceremos

Reise– und Verkehrsverlag (RV), Schockenriedstr 40a, Postfach 800863, D–7000 Stuttgart 80 Tel: (0711) 736379 Cable Add: Verkehrsverlag
Man Dirs: Peter Gutmann, Olaf Paeschke; *Editorial:* Helmut Schaub; *Sales Man, Publicity:* Wolfgang Kunth
Subjects: Maps, Atlases, Guides
Founded: 1927
Miscellaneous: Firm is a member of Verlagsgruppe Bertelsmann GmbH (qv)

Relief-Verlag-Eilers, Martin Greif Str 3, D–8000 Munich 2 Tel: (089) 537213
Man Dir: W Eilers
Subjects: General Fiction, Belles Lettres, Poetry, Biography, Juveniles, Periodical Publikation
Founded: 1961

Rembrandt Verlag GmbH, Schaperstr 35, D–1000 Berlin 15 Tel: (030) 2115503
Man Dir: Dr Klaus J Lemmer
Subjects: Biography, History, Music, Art, Social Science, Educational Materials
1977: 12 titles *1978:* 10 titles *Founded:* 1923
ISBN Publisher's Prefix: 3–7925

Verlag Klaus G **Renner***, Oesterreicher Str 15, D–8520 Erlangen Tel: (09131) 32177
Man Dir: Klaus Renner; *Editorial:* Thomas Milch; *Publicity:* Barbara Renner
Subjects: Belles Lettres, Poetry, Limited Editions
Founded: 1973
ISBN Publisher's Prefix: 3–921499

Reuter-Verlag*, Birkenstr 9, D–7903 Laichingen 4 Tel: (07333) 6166
Man Dir: Dieter Reuter; *Sales Dir:* Alfred Winkelmann; *Publicity & Advertising Dir:* Dieter Reuter; *Rights & Permissions:* Marlies Reuter
Subjects: General Fiction, Belles Lettres, Poetry
Founded: 1974

Rheingauer Verlagsgesellschaft mbH, Postfach 90, D–6228 Eltville am Rhein (Located at: Walluferstr 5a) Tel: (06123) 2312 Telex: 04182921 rvg d
Man Dir, Rights & Permissions: Bernd Ley; *Sales:* Mr Mätzel, Mr Hülzer, Mr Stärk; *Production:* Monika Ley; *Publicity:* Ingrid Bader
Orders to: Above address or Vereinigte Verlagsauslieferung Reinhard Mohn OHG, Postfach 7777, D–4830 Gütersloh
Subjects: Quality Illustrated Works, Low-priced Foreign Classics in Translation, Saga and Legend, Juvenile, General Non-fiction
1978: 25 titles *1979:* 14 titles *Founded:* 1975
ISBN Publisher's Prefix: 17319

Rheinland-Verlag GmbH, Landeshaus, Kennedy-Ufer 2, Postfach 210720, D–5000 Cologne 21 Tel: 82832687
Orders to: Rudolf Habelt Verlag GmbH, Bonn (qv)
Branch Off: Postfach 150104, D–5300 Bonn
Subjects: Rhineland excavations, Regional Knowledge, Folklore, Care of Art and Monuments
1978: 54 titles

Dr **Riederer** Verlag GmbH, Johannesstr 60, Postfach 447, D–7000 Stuttgart 1 Tel: (0711) 613000
Man Dir: M Groitzsch; *Sales Dir:* H Schneider
Subjects: Science, Engineering, Metallography
Founded: 1945
1978: 3 titles
ISBN Publisher's Prefix: 3–87675

Ritter Verlag GmbH*, Sonnenwinkel 1, Postfach 1221, D–8031 Wörthsee/Steinebach Tel: (08152) 1525
Man Dir: Reinhold Schröder
Subjects: Natural Healing, Practical Psychotherapy and Fringe Medicine

Ritzau KG Verlag Zeit und Eisenbahn+, Landsberger Str 24, D–8911 Pürgen Tel: (08196) 252
Subjects: History of German Railways; old Timetables and General History of Transport in Germany from late 19th Century
1978: 6 titles *1979:* 9 titles *Founded:* 1968
ISBN Publisher's Prefix: 3–921304

Röderberg-Verlag GmbH*, Schumannstr 56, Postfach 4129, D–6000 Frankfurt am Main 1 Tel: (0611) 751046 Telex: 414721
Editorial, Production: Peter Altmann; *Sales:* Hoerst Foerster
Subject: Politics
ISBN Publisher's Prefix: 3–87682

Rogner und Bernhard GmbH & Co Verlags KG, König-Marke-Str 5, D–8000 Munich 40 Tel: (089) 363024 Telex: 05215482 buch d
Dirs: Antje Ellermann, Thomas Landshoff, W H Schünemann
Subjects: General Fiction, Belles Lettres, Art, Photography
1977: 20 titles *1978:* 18 titles
ISBN Publisher's Prefix: 3–8077

Rudolf **Rolfs**, see Die Schmiere

Rombach und Co GmbH, Verlag & Buchdruckerei, Lörracher Str 3, Postfach 1349, D–7800 Freiburg im Breisgau Tel: (0761) 42323 Telex: 772820
Man Dir: Dr Hodeige
Subjects: History, Art, Philosophy, Religion, Psychology, Economics, Social & Political Science, University Textbooks
Founded: 1936

Bookshop: Rombach-Center, Bertoldstr 10, D–7800 Freiburg
ISBN Publisher's Prefix: 3–7930

Rose-Verlag und Edition Rose-Verlag*, Seestr 12, D–8221 Seebruck Chiemsee Tel: (08667) 420 Cable Add: Rose-Verlag 8221 Seebruck Telex: 0526144 M Piepenstock
Man Dir, Rights and Permissions: Marianne Piepenstock; *Editorial, Sales, Production:* Michael Piepenstock
Subjects: Education and Upbringing, Health, Food, Religion
1977: reprints only *Founded:* 1955
ISBN Publisher's Prefix: 3–920803

Rosenheimer Verlagshaus Alfred Förg GmbH & Co KG, Am Stocket 12, D–8200 Rosenheim 2 Tel: (08031) 86332 Cable Add: Rosenheimer Verlagshaus Rosenheim Telex: 525732 rosen d
Man Dir: Alfred Förg; *Sales:* Hansjörg Decker; *Rights & Permissions:* Thea Roscher
Subjects: General Fiction, Belles Lettres, Poetry, Biography, History, Music, Art Needlecraft, Bavarica
1978: 91 titles *1979:* 108 titles *Founded:* 1968
ISBN Publisher's Prefix: 3–475

Rösler und Zimmer Verlag, see Verlag Wolfgang Zimmer

Rotbuch Verlag GmbH, Potsdamer Str 98, D–1000 Berlin 30 Tel: (030) 2611196
Man Dirs: Eberhard Delius, Manfred Naber; *Editorial:* Marlies Janz; *Sales, Advertising:* Angela Tieger, Niels Kadritzke; *Publicity:* W D Pfäfferling; *Rights & Permissions:* Uta Ruge, Ingrid Karsunke
Subjects: Belles Lettres, Poetry, History, Social Science
1977: 29 titles
ISBN Publisher's Prefix: 3–88022

Verlag **Roter Morgen***, Wellinghoferstr 103, D–4600 Dortmund-Hörde (30) Tel: (0231) 433691/92
Orders to: GEWISO Buchvertrieb GmbH, Postfach 500568, D–2000 Hamburg
Subjects: Speeches and Writings of Stalin and Enver Hoxhas; Communism; Publications of the Communist Party of Germany (Marxist-Leninist); Periodical *Roter Morgen*
1977: 22 titles *Founded:* 1977
ISBN Publisher's Prefix: 3–88196

Verlag **Roter Stern***, Postfach 180147, D–6000 Frankfurt am Main Tel: (0611) 599999
Publishers: K D Wolff, Angelika Schwarz
Subjects: Textbooks, Periodicals
ISBN Publisher's Prefix: 3–87877

Erich **Röth**-Verlag, Kassel*, Korbacher Str 235, D–3500 Kassel-Nordshausen Tel: (0561) 401206 Cable Add: Röthverlag
Subjects: Belles Lettres, Poetry, Music, Art, Folklore
Founded: 1921
ISBN Publisher's Prefix: 3–87680

Bergverlag Rudolf **Rother**, see Bergverlag

Verlag Friedrich **Röver***, Mühlenweg 67, D–2822 Schwanewede 1 — Leuchtenberg
Man Dir, Editorial: Friedrich Röver; *Sales:* Heyke Weinbecker; *Publicity:* Ilse Windhoff
Subjects: Bremen Regional Interest, Ramblers' books, Photo Pictorial books, Scientific Publications
1977: 2 titles *Founded:* 1964
ISBN Publisher's Prefix: 15414

Rowohlt Taschenbuch Verlag GmbH, Hamburger Str 17, Postfach 1349, D-2057 Reinbek bei Hamburg Tel: (040) 72721 Cable Add: Rowohltverlag Reinbek Telex: 0217854
Man Dirs: Heinrich Maria Ledig-Rowohlt, Kurt Busch, Horst Varrelmann, Dr Matthias Wegner; *Editorial:* Freimut Duve, Richard K Flesch, Dr Uwe Wandrey, Dr Jürgen Manthey; *Rights & Permissions:* Eda Brigitta von Seebach
Subjects: Wide range of mainly low-priced, mainly Nonfiction Paperbacks; especially popular works on Life Sciences, History and Archaeology, Art, Politics, Psychology, Education, Philosophy, Religion, Social Sciences, Sports and Games
1977: 418 titles *Founded:* 1953
ISBN Publisher's Prefix: 3-499

Rowohlt Verlag GmbH, Hamburger Str 17, D-2057 Reinbek bei Hamburg Tel: (040) 72721 Cable Add: Rowohltverlag Reinbek Telex: 0217854
Man Dirs: Heinrich Maria Ledig-Rowohlt, Kurt Busch, Horst Varrelmann (Sales), Dr Matthias Wegner; *Production:* Erwin Steen
Subjects: General Fiction, Belles Lettres, Poetry, Biography, How-to, Philosophy, Reference, Psychology, General & Social Science, Education, History, Juveniles, Politics, Translations of International Literature
1977: 56 titles *Founded:* 1908
ISBN Publisher's Prefix: 3-498

Ruhland Verlag*, Goethestr 27, D-6000 Frankfurt am Main 1 Tel: (0611) 285604
Publisher: Erich Ruhland; *Publicity, Rights & Permissions:* Habdank Philipp
Subject: Instruction courses and texts on Secretarial Work, Commerce etc

Elsbeth **Rütten** Verlag*, Burggrafenstr 19, Postfach 428, D-4050 München-Gladbach 1 Tel: (02161) 37801 Cable Add: Rütten
Man Dir: Elsbeth Ebert; *Sales & Advertising Dir:* Kurt Ebert; *Publicity Dir:* Angelika Rütten
Subjects: General Fiction, Belles Lettres, Poetry, Biography, History, How-to, High-priced Paperbacks
Founded: 1975
ISBN Publisher's Prefix: 3-921447

VWK **Ryborsch** GmbH, see VWK

S A S S-Verlagsgesellschaft mbH und Co KG, Postfach 249, D-6440 Bebra (Located at: Nürnberger Str) Tel: 06622/2005 Telex: 493412

s t v, see Stolfuss Verlag

Safari Verlag (Reinhard Jaspert), Welserstr 10, Postfach 1443, D-1000 Berlin 30 Tel: 2131049
Man Dir: Hans-Heinrich Kuemmel
Subjects: Travel and Geography, Ancient History, Mythology, Popular Science and Nature Study, Religion, Art, Philosophy
Founded: 1921
Miscellaneous: firm is a member of Verlagsgruppe Langen-Müller/Herbig, Munich (qv)
ISBN Publisher's Prefix: 3-7934

Verlag Otto **Sagner***, Heßstr 39-41, Postfach 34, D-8000 Munich 34 Tel: (089) 522027 Cable Add: buchsagner München
Publisher: Otto Sagner; *Editorial:* Dr Peter Rehder
Orders to: Kubon und Sagner, Postfach 68, D-8000 Munich 34
Parent Company: Kubon und Sagner, Heßstr 39-41, D-8000 Munich 40
Subject: Slavistics (Language and History)
1976: 12 titles *1977:* 14 titles *Founded:* 1959
ISBN Publisher's Prefix: 3-87690

Otto **Salle** Verlag, see Verlag Moritz Diesterweg/Otto Salle Verlag

Salvator Verlag GmbH*, Hermann-Josef-Str 4, Postfach 220, D-5370 Kall Tel: (02441) 5047
Dir: Klaus Kupitz
Subject: Religion, Musicology

Eugen **Salzer** Verlag*, Titotstr 5, Postfach 3048, D-7100 Heilbronn 1 Tel: (07131) 68294 Cable Add: Salzerverlag
Man Dir: Hartmut Salzer; *Sales Dir:* J Glage
Subjects: Fiction, Belles Lettres, How-to, Reference, Juveniles
1977: 6 titles *1978:* 12 titles *Founded:* 1891
ISBN Publisher's Prefix: 3-7936

Dr Martin **Sändig** GmbH, Postfach 5120, D-6200 Wiesbaden 1 (Located at: Kaiser Friedrich Ring 70)
Dir: Ulfa von den Steinen
Orders to: Kraus-Thomson Organization Ltd, FL-9491 Nendeln, Liechtenstein (qv)
Parent Company: Kraus-Thomson Organization Ltd, Liechtenstein (qv)
Subjects: Natural Sciences, Linguistics, Fiction, Folklore, Music
ISBN Publisher's Prefix: 3-500

Verlag der **Sankt-Johannis-Druckerei** C Schweickhardt, Heiligenstr 24, Postfach 5, D-7630 Lahr 12 Tel: (07821) 43014 Cable Add: Veritas Lahrschwarzwäld
Man Dir: Walter Guthmann; *Editorial, Publicity, Rights & Permissions:* Karl-Heinz Kern; *Sales:* Johannes Walter; *Production:* Helmut Schlegel
Subjects: Christian Devotional: stories, commentaries, travel books for young people and adults
1977: 25 titles *1978:* 20 titles *Founded:* 1896
Miscellaneous: Member of the Telos (qv) group publishing evangelical paperbacks
ISBN Publisher's Prefix: 3-501

Sankt Otto Verlag GmbH, Lange Str 22-24, Abholfach, D-8600 Bamberg Tel: (0951) 25252 Telex: 0662860 etvl
Man Dir: Kurt Kiening; *Other Offices:* Norbert Göbel
Parent Company: Bayerische Verlagsanstalt Bamberg (qv)
Associate Company: Cura Verlag, Austria (qv)
Subjects: Roman Catholic Religious Literature; Guides for Pilgrims, Bamberg Diocesan interest, Hymn Books, Devotional
Bookshop: Goerres Buchhandlung at above address
1978: 5 titles
ISBN Publisher's Prefix: 3-87693

Sassafras Verlag, Bismarckplatz 43, D-4150 Krefeld Tel: (02151) 599555
Subject: Contemporary Writing

Satire Verlag GmbH, Auerstr 1, D-5000 Cologne 60 Tel: (0221) 735929
Man Dir: Saskia E Wollschon; *Editorial:* Reinhard Hippen, Gerd Wollschon
Subject: Satire
1978: 4 titles *1979:* 6 titles *Founded:* 1977
ISBN Publisher's Prefix: 3-88268

I H **Sauer** Verlag GmbH, Häusserstr 14, Postfach 105960, D-6900 Heidelberg Tel: (06221) 25661 Cable Add: Rechtwirtschaft Heidelberg Telex: 461665
Publicity: Oswald Preusse
Associate Company: Verlagsgesellschaft Recht und Wirtschaft (qv)
Subjects: Industrial Management, Economics, Organisation; Data Processing, Personnel Questions, Works Psychology, Leadership, Training, Rhetoric, Publicity; Series of Paperbacks for Industry

H R **Sauerländer** und Co, Finkenhofstr 21, D-6000 Frankfurt am Main 1 Tel: (0611) 555217
Partners: Helmut Baetz, Hans C Sauerländer
Parent Company: Sauerländer AG, Switzerland (qv)
Subjects: Juveniles, Fiction, Sciences
Founded: 1964
ISBN Publisher's Prefix: 3-7941

J D **Sauerländer's** Verlag, Finkenhofstr 21, D-6000 Frankfurt am Main 1 Tel: (0611) 555217
Publisher: Helmut A Baetz
Subjects: Forestry and Agricultural Sciences
1977: 10 titles *1978:* 11 titles *Founded:* 1816
ISBN Publisher's Prefix: 3-7939

K G **Saur** Verlag KG, Pössenbacherstr 2b, Postfach 711009, D-8000 Munich 70 Tel: (089) 798901/2/3 Cable Add: saur Telex: 5212067
Man Dir: Klaus G Saur; *Editorial:* Willi Gorzny, Dr Helga Lengenfelder; *Sales:* Ingo-Erich M Schmidt-Braul; *Production:* Horst Ahaus; *Rights & Permissions:* Dr Helga Lengenfelder
Subsidiary Companies: Minerva-Publikation Saur GmbH, Solnerstr 29, D-8000 Munich 71 (100%); Verlag Dokumentation Saur GmbH, Kagerbauerstr 13, D-8023 Pullach (100%); TR-Verlagsunion GmbH (qv); Uni-Taschenbücher GmbH (qv); K G Saur Publishing Inc, 175 5th Ave, New York NY 10010; K G Saur Editeur Sàrl, France (qv) (100%); Clive Bingley Ltd, UK (qv) (100%)
Branch Off: Hallgartenstr 49, D-6000 Frankfurt am Main 60
Subjects: Reference, Social Science, Library Management, Documentation and Information Science, Data Processing
1977: 148 titles *Founded:* 1948
Miscellaneous: Formerly known as Verlag Dokumentation Saur KG, Munich
ISBN Publisher's Prefix: 3-7940

Karl A **Schäfer** Buch-und Offsetdruckerei-Goldstadtverlag*, Finkensteinstr 6, D-7530 Pforzheim Tel: (07231) 42095 Cable Add: Goldstadtverlag
Publisher: Günter Schäfer
Orders to: Geo-Center, Honigwiesenstr 25, D-7000 Stuttgart 80
Subject: Travel Guides
1976: 84 titles *1977:* 96 titles *Founded:* 1956
ISBN Publisher's Prefix: 3-87269

Hermann **Schaffstein** Verlag, Postfach 1283, D-4600 Dortmund 1 Tel: (0231) 527496
Sales: Paul Lazar; *Rights & Permissions:* Hans-Georg Noack
Orders to: Schroedel-Verlagsauslieferung, Postfach 656, D-4600 Dortmund 1
Subjects: Juveniles, High-priced Paperbacks
Miscellaneous: Firm is a subsidiary of Hermann Schroedel Verlag KG (qv)
ISBN Publisher's Prefix: 3-7942

F K **Schattauer** Verlag GmbH*,
Lenzhalde 3, Postfach 2945, D-7000
Stuttgart 1 Tel: (0711) 221733-7
Telex: 721886
Publisher: Philipp Reeg; *Sales Manager:*
Jochen Hintermeier
Subject: All aspects of Medicine, including
hygiene, biochemistry, psychology etc. and
related sciences
1977: 40 titles
ISBN Publisher's Prefix: 3-7945

Moritz **Schauenburg** Verlag GmbH und Co
KG, Schillerstr 13, Postfach 2120, D-7630
Lahr 1 Tel: (07821) 23091 Cable Add:
Schauenburg Lahrschwarzwald
Telex: 0754943
Dir: Jörg Schauenburg
Subjects: General Fiction, Maps, Music,
Linguistics, Philosophy, Literature
1978: 10 titles *Founded:* 1794
ISBN Publisher's Prefix: 3-7946

Verlag Heinrich **Scheffler**, part of Societäts-
Verlag (qv)

Scherpe Verlag*, Glockenspitz 140, Postfach
2630, D-4150 Krefeld Tel: (02151) 59211
Telex: 0853892
Subjects: General Fiction, Juveniles, Arts,
Education, Illustrated Books, Belles Lettres,
Politics
ISBN Publisher's Prefix: 3-7948

Scherz Verlag GmbH, Stievestr 9, D-8000
Munich 19 Tel: (089) 172237/38
Telex: 5215282 sherz d
President: Rudolf Streit-Scherz; *Editorial
Dir:* Gert Woerner; *Sales Dir:* Wolfgang
Radaj; *Paperbacks:* Gabriele Schatz; *For
O W Barth Affairs:* Stephan Schuhmacher
Subsidiary Company: Otto Wilhelm Barth-
Verlag KG (qv)
Subjects: General Fiction, History, Politics,
Belles Lettres, Documentary Works
1977: 115 titles *1978:* 114 titles *Founded:*
1957
Miscellaneous: Company is a Branch Office
of Scherz Verlag, Switzerland (qv)
ISBN Publisher's Prefix: 3-502

Gertrud E **Scheuerer** Verlag, Miesbacher
Str 16a, D-8201 Raubling Tel: (08035) 2586
Man Dir: Gertrud Scheuerer; *Production:*
Otto Scheuerer
Subject: Art
1977: 8 titles *Founded:* 1975

Fachverlag **Schiele und Schön** GmbH*,
Markgrafenstr 11, D-1000 Berlin 61
Tel: (030) 2516029 Cable Add: schieleschön
Berlin
Man Dir: Peter Schön
Subjects: Medicine, Engineering,
Electronics, Industry, Reference,
Mathematics, Hobbies; Periodicals
1977: 22 titles *Founded:* 1946

Kurt **Schilling**, see Scientia Verlag

G **Schindele** Verlag GmbH, Rheinstr 5, D-
7512 Rheinstetten 3 Tel: (07242) 4786
Man Dir: Gerlinde Schindele
Subjects: Pedagogy, Psychology, Sociology,
Rehabilitation, Special Teaching, Social
Instruction
1978: 24 titles *1979:* 26 titles *Founded:*
1969

Schirmer/Mosel Verlag GmbH,
Nikolaistr 15, D-8000 Munich 40 Tel: (089)
393037/8
Man Dirs: L Schirmer, E Mosel; *Sales Dir:*
L Schirmer; *Publicity & Advertising Dir:*
Erik Mosel
Subjects: Photography, Art

Verlag Bert **Schlender***, Postfach 930, D-
3400 Göttingen Tel: (0551) 72659
Man Dirs: Bert Schlender, Detlev Pawlik
Associate Company: Edgar Wüpper (qv)
Subjects: General Fiction, Belles Lettres,
Poetry, Art, Low- & High-priced
Paperbacks
Founded: 1973
Bookshop: Versandbuchhandlung Bert
Schlender, Auf der Vessel 531, Postfach 930,
D-3400 Göttingen

Joachim **Schmid** und Co (Karl-May Verlag),
see Karl-May Verlag

Erich **Schmidt** Verlag, Genthiner Str 30G,
D-1000 Berlin 30 Tel: (030) 2611741
Branch Offs: Viktoriastr 44a, Postfach 7330,
D-4800 Bielefeld; Paosostr 7, D-8000
Munich 60
Subjects: History, How-to, Reference, High-
priced Paperbacks, Engineering, Economics,
Social Science, Law, University &
Secondary Textbooks, Educational
Materials
1977: 130 titles *1978:* 130 titles *Founded:*
1924
ISBN Publisher's Prefix: 3-503

Verlag Dr Otto **Schmidt** KG+, Ulmenallee
96-98, D-5000 Cologne 51 Tel: (0221)
373021
Man Dir: Dr H M Schmidt; *Editorial:*
Lopau Mechthild, Dr Katherine Knauth;
Sales Dir: Alois Wittig; *Publicity &
Advertising Dir:* Edmund Arand
Branch Off: Merlostr 4, D-5000 Cologne 1
Subjects: University Textbooks,
Jurisprudence, Tax Law
1977: 38 titles *1978:* 36 titles *Founded:*
1905
Bookshops: Buchhandlung Hermann Sack,
Bahnstr 61, D-4000 Düsseldorf 1;
Buchhandlung Hermann Sack,
Mercatorstr 27, D-6000 Frankfurt am Main
ISBN Publisher's Prefix: 3-504

Richard Carl **Schmidt** und Co, Helmstedter
Str 151, D-3300 Braunschweig Tel: (0531)
73189 Cable Add: Schmidtverlag
Man Dir: Ernst Raschka
Subjects: Engineering, Technical, Maps,
Aviation, Transport
Founded: 1897
ISBN Publisher's Prefix: 3-87708

Verlag für polizeiliches Fachschrifttum
Georg **Schmidt-Römhild**, Mengstr 16,
Postfach 2051, D-2400 Lübeck 1 Tel: 75001
Publisher: Norbert Beleke
Associate Company: Max Schmidt-Römhild
Verlag (qv)
Subjects: Psychology, Criminology,
Reference books for police officials, lawyers,
public authorities
1977: 30 titles *1978:* 25 titles *Founded:* 1892
ISBN Publisher's Prefix: 3-8016

Max **Schmidt-Römhild**, Verlag, Mengstr 16,
Postfach 2051, D-2400 Lübeck 1 Tel: 75001
Publisher: Norbert Beleke
Associate Company: Verlag für polizeiliches
Fachschrifttum Georg Schmidt-
Römhild (qv)
Subjects: History, Medicine, General &
Social Science; Reference books in
criminology, forensic medicine and for
lawyers, public authorities and medical and
chemical laboratories
1977: 30 titles *1978:* 30 titles *Founded:*
1579
ISBN Publisher's Prefix: 3-7950

Die **Schmiere** — Rudolf Rolfs*,
Karmeliterkloster, D-6000 Frankfurt am
Main Tel: (0611) 28066, 06074/90979
Subjects: Works of Rudolf Rolfs, Author
and Manager of unsubsidised satirical
Theatre *Die Schmiere*

Wilhelm **Schmitz** Verlag, Kattenbachstr 5,
D-6300 Lahn-Wissmar Tel: (06406) 2324
Dir: S Schmitz
Subjects: Art, Religion, Linguistics,
Languages, German Studies, Slav Studies,
East European Studies, Folklore
1979: 12 titles *Founded:* 1847

Galerie **Schmücking** Verlag, Lessingplatz 12,
D-3300 Braunschweig Tel: (0531) 44960
Branch Offs: D-2286 Archsum/Sylt,
Bobtäärp, Federal Republic of Germany;
Galerie Schmücking, Sattelgasse 2, CH-4000
Basel, Switzerland
Subject: Art

Franz **Schneekluth** Verlag, Postfach 466, D-
8000 Munich 22 (Located at: Widenmayer
Str 34) Tel: (089) 221391 Telex: 529070
Owned by: Ulrich Staudinger; *Editorial:*
Dr Michael Schmidt; *Sales and Publicity:*
Alf Jungermann; *Rights & Permissions:*
Ellen Reuter, Dr Michael Schmidt; *Public
Relations:* Sybille Maier
Subject: General Fiction
1978: 52 titles *Founded:* 1949
ISBN Publisher's Prefix: 3-7951

Franz **Schneider** Verlag GmbH und Co KG,
Frankfurter Ring 150, D-8000 Munich 46
Tel: (089) 381911 Telex: 05215804
Publisher: Franz Schneider; *Editor-in-Chief:*
Gisela Schneider; *Sales:* Christian Warweg;
Production: Josef Loher; *Publicity:* Dr
Schäfer
Subject: Juveniles
1977: 420 titles *1978:* 135 titles *Founded:*
1913
ISBN Publisher's Prefix: 3-505

Lambert **Schneider** Verlag GmbH,
Hausackerweg 16, Postfach 105802, D-6900
Heidelberg 1 Tel: (06221) 21354
Publisher: Lothar Stiehm
Associate Company: Lothar Stiehm
Verlag (qv)
Subjects: Belles Lettres, Poetry, Biography,
Literature, Humanities, History, Music, Art,
Judaica, Philosophy, Reference, Religion,
University & Secondary Textbooks
1977: 30 titles *1979:* 30 titles *Founded:*
1925
ISBN Publisher's Prefix: 3-7953

Verlag **Schnell und Steiner** GmbH und Co,
Paganinistr 92, D-8000 Munich 60 Tel:
(089) 8112015/8112016 Cable Add:
Schnellsteiner München
Man Dir, Rights and Permissions: Karl A
Stich; *Editorial:* Dr H Schnell, Dr P Mai;
Sales: N Dinkel; *Production:* J A Fink,
N Dinkel
Orders to: Schnell und Steiner,
Postfach 112, D-8000 Munich 65
Branch Off: Schnell & Steiner, CH-8260
Stein am Rhein, Switzerland
Subjects: Biography, History, History of
Art, Art Guides, Philosophy, Religion,
Juveniles, High-priced Paperbacks,
University and Secondary Textbooks, Travel
Literature
Bookshop: Pötzlstr 2, Postfach 1109, D-8595
Waldsassen
1977: 70 titles *1978:* 80 titles *Founded:*
1934
ISBN Publisher's Prefix: 3-7954

Verlag Die **Schönen Bücher** Dr Wolf Strache KG*, Friedhofstr 11, Postfach 1124, D-7000 Stuttgart Tel: (0711) 297116 Cable Add: Schönbücher
Subjects: Arts, Mass Media, Education
ISBN Publisher's Prefix: 3-7956

Ferdinand **Schöningh** Verlag, Jühenplatz am Rathaus, Postfach 2540, D-4790 Paderborn Tel: (05251) 21322 Cable Add: Schönbuch Paderborn
Subjects: Educational Publishers for Schools and Colleges, Earth Sciences, History, Literary Criticism, Mathematics, Education, Philosophy, Physics, Politics, Psychology, Law, Religion, Social Science, Linguistics, Languages, Paperbacks
1978: 167 titles
ISBN Publisher's Prefix: 3-506

B **Schott's** Söhne, Musikverlag+dl, Weihergarten, Postfach 3640, D-6500 Mainz 1 Tel: (06131) 10741 Cable Add: Scotson Mainz Telex: 4187821 scot d
Man Dirs: Ludolf Frhr von Canstein, Günther Schneider-Schott, Dr Peter Hanser-Strecker; *Sales & Export Dir:* Günther Schneider-Schott; *Editorial:* Friedrich Zehn, Friedrich Wanek; *Sales:* Hellmut Fischer; *Production, Publicity:* Dr Hanser-Strecker; *Rights & Permissions:* Heinz Wolf, Erhard Keller
Orders to: Carl-Zeiss Str 1, PO Box 3640, D-6500 Mainz-Hechtsheim Tel: (06131) 59035
Associate Companies: Wega Verlag GmbH, Mainz; Ars-Viva-Verlag GmbH, Mainz; Music Factory GmbH, Mainz; MGS Zimmerhansl, Munich; Schott & Co Ltd, 48 Great Marlborough St, London W1
Branch Offs: Schott Music Corp, New York, USA; Schott Japan Co Ltd, Tokyo, Japan
Subjects: Music and Music Reference, High-priced Paperbacks, Journals, University, Secondary & Primary Textbooks, Educational Materials
1978: 10 books, 160 sheet music *Founded:* 1770
ISBN Publisher's Prefix: 3-7957

Verlag J F **Schreiber**, Postfach 285, D-7300 Esslingen (Located at: Liebigstr 1-11, D-7301 Deizisau) Tel: (07153) 22011/3 Telex: 7266880 jfs d
Man Dirs: Gerhard Schreiber, Joachim Schreiber; *Sales:* H K Vahlbruch *Rights & Permissions:* Jutta Hinkelbein
Associate Company: Junior International, German Federal Republic (qv)
Branch Offs: Möhlstr 34, D-8000 Munich 80
Subjects: Juveniles, Educational Materials, Textbooks, Biology, Nonfiction
Founded: 1831
ISBN Publisher's Prefix: 3-480

Verlag und **Schriftenmission** der Ev Ges für Deutschland GmbH, see Evangelischer Gesellschaft

Schriftenmissions-Verlag*, Goethestr 79-81, Postfach 548, D-4390 Gladbeck Tel: (02143) 22654
Dir: Hans Steinacker; *Sales Manager:* Hermann Conrad; *Rights & Permissions:* Liesel Rennscheidt
Subjects: Periodicals, Religion
1977: 22 titles
ISBN Publisher's Prefix: 3-7958

Hermann **Schroedel** Verlag KG, Hildesheimerstr 202 and Zeisstr 10, Postfach 810620, D-3000 Hanover 81 Tel: (0511) 83881; (Despatch Dept) (05066) 2081 Telex: 923527 HSV HA
Manager: Hermann von Schroedel; *Man Dirs:* Joachim Günther, Dr Ilse Ebeler, H A Koeppel; *Sales, Publicity:* Hans Freiwald; *Production:* Peter Brück; *Advertising:* Rudolf Wegner; *Rights & Permissions:* Gudrun Ruiner
Associate Company: Hermann Schroedel Verlag AG, Switzerland (qv)
Subsidiary Companies: Hermann Schaffstein Verlag (qv)
Branch Offs: Lützowstr 105-106, D-1000 Berlin 30; Am Kavalleriesand 47, Postfach 1026, D-6100 Darmstadt; Marsstr 4, D-8000 Munich 2
Subjects: University, Secondary & Primary Textbooks; Art, Religion, Languages, Social Sciences, Pure Science, Philosophy, Psychology, Pedagogy, Technical Instruction, Sport
1977: 320 titles *Founded:* 1792
ISBN Publisher's Prefix: 3-507

Kurt **Schroeder** Verlag*, Am weissen Stein 48, D-5653 Leichlingen 1 Tel: (02175) 3355
Man Dir: Hannsgeorg Schroeder
Subject: Travel Guides to foreign countries world-wide; Plant Guides
1977: 3 titles *Founded:* 1919
ISBN Publisher's Prefix: 3-87722

Marion von **Schroeder** Verlag GmbH, Postfach 9229, D-4000 Düsseldorf (Located at: Grupellostr 28) Tel: (0211) 360516 Telex: 8587327
Publisher: Erwin Barth von Wehrenalp; *Sales Manager:* Herbert Borgartz; *Publicity Manager:* Michael Tochtermann
Subjects: Belles Lettres, Fiction, Foreign Literature, Biography, Fantastica
Founded: 1935
Miscellaneous: Firm is part of Econ Verlagsgruppe, German Federal Republic (qv)
ISBN Publisher's Prefix: 3-547

Anton **Schroll** und Co GmbH, Boosstr 15, D-8000 Munich 95 Tel: (089) 653590
Man Dirs: Friedrich Geyer, Dieter Reisser
Branch Off: Anton Schroll & Co, Austria (qv)
Subjects: Art, Travel
Founded: 1953

Verlag **Schule und Elternhaus**, Wilhelmshöher Allee 254-256, Postfach 410160, D-3500 Kassel Tel: (0561) 30076 Cable Add: Schule und Elternhaus Kassel-Wilhelmshöhe Telex: 0992450
Editorial: Claus Reineke
Associate Company: Druck- und Verlagshaus Thiele & Schwarz, Kassel (qv)
Subjects: Education, Vocabularies, Series by Young Writers
ISBN Publisher's Prefix: 3-88056

Schuler Verlagsgesellschaft mbH*, Gachenaustr 13, D-8036 Herrsching Tel: (08152) 1087 Telex: 526493
Man Dir, Rights & Permissions: Anton Bolza; *Editorial:* Dr Barbara Chabrowe; *Sales:* Klaus Sperlich; *Production:* Herstellungsbüro Rudolf Gorbach
Subjects: Art, Juveniles, Reference
Founded: 1946
ISBN Publisher's Prefix: 3-7796

Hermann **Schulte***, Sophienstr 23, Postfach 2580, D-6330 Wetzlar Tel: (06441) 8461 Telex: 483794
Publisher: Hermann Schulte; *Dir:* Klaus Gerth
Subjects: Music, Religion, Biography, Juveniles

Ludwig **Schultheis**, Verlag Haus und Heim*, Heilwigstr 64, D-2000 Hamburg 20 Tel: (040) 4602644
Subject: Art

Verlag R S **Schulz***, Berger Str 8-10, Seehang 4, D-8136 Percha-Kempfenhausen Tel: (08151) 13041 Telex: 0526427
Publisher: Rolf Simon Schulz
Subjects: Architecture, Fiction, Public Health, Law, Nonfiction, Social Science, Veterinary Science; Periodicals
ISBN Publisher's Prefix: 3-7962

Carl Ed **Schünemann** KG, Zweite Schlachtpforte 5-7, Postfach 106067, D-2800 Bremen 1 Tel: (0421) 36731/36351 Cable Add: Schünemanns Bremen
Man Dir: Klaus Kirchner; *Sales & Publicity Dir:* Herbert Kuhangel
Subjects: Belles Lettres, Art
Founded: 1810
ISBN Publisher's Prefix: 3-7961

Verlag K W **Schütz** KG, Am Osttor 12, Postfach 1180, D-4994 Preußisch Oldendorf Tel: (05742) 2073/4
Man Dir: Erwin Höke
Subjects: History, Juveniles
Founded: 1948
Bookshop: Versandbuchdienst Göttingen, Postfach 1180, D-4994 Preussisch Oldendorf
ISBN Publisher's Prefix: 3-87725

Schwabe und Co GmbH Verlag*, Postfach 758, D-7000 Stuttgart 1
Subjects: History, Medicine, Philosophy, Psychology
ISBN Publisher's Prefix: 3-7965

Schwabenverlag AG*, Senefelderstr 12, Postfach 4280, D-7302 Ostfildern 1 Tel: (0711) 412908 Telex: 0723556
Man Dir: Paul Löcher
Subsidiary Company: Süddeutsche Verlagsgesellschaft mbH (qv)
Subjects: Popular Christian Devotional; Juvenile Fiction and Nonfiction, Swabian Regional Interest
Bookshops: Schwabenverlag Buchhandlung, Bahnhofstr 21, D-7080 Aalen; Spitalstr 17, D-7030 Ellwangen
1978: 14 titles *Founded:* 1848
ISBN Publisher's Prefix: 3-7966

Verlag Haus **Schwalbach***, Bethelstr 35, D-6200 Wiesbaden Tel: (06121) 429288
Subjects: Textbooks, Education, Periodicals
ISBN Publisher's Prefix: 3-920427

Schwaneberger Verlag GmbH, Muthmannstr 4, D-8000 Munich 45 Tel: 381931 Cable Add: Schwanverlag München Telex: 5215342 gerb d
Man Dir: Hans Hohenester; *Editorial:* Gerhard Webersinke; *Sales:* Gerhard Recht; *Publicity:* Horst Rogg; *Rights & Permissions:* Hans Hohenester
Associate Company: Carl Gerber Verlag GmbH
Subject: Philately
1977: 16 titles *Founded:* 1910
ISBN Publisher's Prefix: 3-87858

Edition **Schwann**, an imprint of C F Peters Musikverlag GmbH und Co KG (qv)

Pädagogischer Verlag **Schwann** GmbH, se Pädagogischer

Verlag Otto **Schwartz** und Co, Annastr 7, D-3400 Göttingen Tel: (0551) 31051/2
Man Dir: Dr Herbert Weisser, Konrad Weisser
Subjects: Social Science, University Textbooks, Educational Materials

1978: 62 titles *Founded:* 1871
Bookshop: Fachbuchhandlung Otto Schwartz & Co, Annastr 7, D-3400 Göttingen
ISBN Publisher's Prefix: 3-509

Verlag Elke **Schwarz**, Ooser Luisenstr 23, D-7570 Baden-Baden 22 Tel: (07223) 52936
Publisher, Editorial: Dieter Schwarz; *Sales:* Elfriede Junker
Subjects: Belles Lettres, Poetry
1977: 5 titles *Founded:* 1974
ISBN Publisher's Prefix: 3-15859

Dr Wolfgang **Schwarze** Verlag*, Heckinghauser Str 65-67, Postfach 202015, D-5600 Wuppertal 2 Tel: (0202) 622005/6
Man Dir, Rights & Permissions: Dr Wolfgang Schwarze; *Sales, Office Chief:* Ursula Rumker-Schulze
Subsidiary Company: Kunst und Wohnen Verlag GmbH
Subjects: Art books on Antiquities, Illustrated books on the Home and Interior Architecture, Facsimile Engravings
1977: 25 titles *Founded:* 1968
ISBN Publisher's Prefix: 3-87741

Verlag der Sankt-Johannis-Druckerei G **Schweickhardt**, see Sankt-Johannis

J **Schweitzer** Verlag*, Genthiner Str 13, D-1000 Berlin 30 Tel: (030) 2611341 Cable Add: Wissenschaft Berlin Telex: 0184027
Br Off: Geibelstr 8/0, D-8000 Munich 80
Subjects: Jurisprudence, Legal Information

E **Schweizerbart**'sche Verlagsbuchhandlung, Johannesstr 3A, D-7000 Stuttgart 1 Tel: (0711) 623541/3
Man Dirs: Dr Erhard Naegele (Production), Klaus Obermiller (Sales)
Associate Company: Gebrüder Borntraeger Verlagsbuchhandlung (qv)
Subjects: Geology, Palaeontology, Mineralogy, Limnology, Botany, Fishery, Hydrobiology, Zoology, Anthropology; Periodicals (27 scientific journals)
Founded: 1826
ISBN Publisher's Prefix: 3-510

H G **Schwieger**, see P R Verlag

Verlag Junge Gemeinde E **Schwinghammer** KG+, Fangelsbachstr 11, Postfach 979, D-7000 Stuttgart 1 Tel: (0711) 643015/16 Cable Add: Jungegemeindeverlag
Dir: Siegfried Krumrey
Subjects: Religion, Juveniles, Educational Materials, Periodicals
1977: 3 titles *Founded:* 1928
ISBN Publisher's Prefix: 3-7797

Scientia Verlag und Antiquariat Kurt Schilling, Adlerstr 65, Postfach 1660, D-7080 Aalen 1 Tel: (07361) 41700 Cable Add: Scientia Aalenwuertt
Man Dir: Kurt Schilling; *Other Offices:* Günter Schilling
Subjects: Reprints in History, Education, Philosophy, Law, Social Science, Economics
1977: 80 titles *Founded:* 1953
ISBN Publisher's Prefix: 3-511

Scriptor Verlag, Adelheidstr 2, Postfach 1220, D-6240 Königstein/TS Tel: (06174) 3026
Publisher: Dietrich Pinkerneil; *Editorial:* Dr Beate Pinkerneil; *Sales:* Rudolf Klein; *Publicity:* Karin Hirschfeld; *Rights & Permissions:* Hildegard Willhöft
Associate Companies: Athenäum Verlag GmbH (qv); Verlag Anton Hain GmbH (qv); Peter Hanstein Verlag GmbH (qv)

Subjects: Linguistics, Communications, Literature, Sociology, Education, Reprints
1977: 40 titles *1978:* 64 titles *Founded:* 1973
ISBN Publisher's Prefix: 3-589

E A **Seemann** Verlag*, Nassestr 14, D-5000 Cologn 41 Tel: (0221) 411915
Man Dir: Elert A Seeeemann
Subjects: Artbooks and Colour Reproductions, 43-volume Thieme-Becker Artistlexicon
Founded: 1858

Seewald Verlag, Obere Weinsteige 44, Postfach 6, D-7000 Stuttgart 70 Tel: (0711) 765085 Telex: 7255361
Man Dirs: Dr Heinrich Seewald, Sixt A Seewald; *Sales Manager:* York Seewald; *Rights & Permissions:* Heide Radkowitz
Subjects: History, Politics, Economics, Social Science, High-priced Paperbacks, Books on Wine, Biographies and Memoirs, Education, Philosophy
1978: 30 titles *1979:* 35 titles *Founded:* 1956
ISBN Publisher's Prefix: 3-512

Sellier Verlag GmbH, Postfach 1949, D-8050 Freising Tel: (08161) 2184 Telex: (05) 26511
Man Dir: Kurt Sellier; *Editorial:* Johanna Vogel; *Sales Dir:* Friedrich Otto
Subsidiary Company: Sellier Verlag GmbH, Bahnhofstr 14, D-8050 Freising
Subjects: Juveniles, Secondary & Primary Textbooks, Educational Materials
1977: 340 titles *Founded:* 1702
ISBN Publisher's Prefix: 3-87137

Verlag Jürgen **Sendler***, Sandhoferstr 29, D-6800 Mannheim 31 Tel: (0711) 757763
Shipping Add: Buchvertrieb Hager GmbH, Postfach 5129, Bahnstation Mannheim-Waldhof
Publisher: Jürgen Sendler; *Editorial:* Friedemann Bleicher
Subject: Politics

Siebdruck Süd GmbH, Druck und Verlagshaus*, Hindenburgstr 30, D-7250 Leonberg-Eltringen Tel: (07152) 48053154
Gen Man: Rolf Marxen and Lothar Mittelbach
Subjects: Art Calendars, Original Graphics, Art Books by Peter K Schaav and Elke Sommer
1977: 34 titles projected *Founded:* 1973

Siebert Verlag GmbH, see Siebert und Engelbert Dessart Verlag GmbH

Siebert und Engelbert Dessart Verlag GmbH*, Wildstr 7, Postfach 1240, D-8202 Bad Aibling Tel: (08061) 4045 Telex: 525957
Subjects: Children's Books, Puzzles and Games
1977: 45 titles *Founded:* 1967
ISBN Publisher's Prefixes: 3-8089 (Siebert), 3-920215 (Dessart)

Signal-Verlag Hans Frevert, Balger Hauptstr 8, Postfach 813, D-7570 Baden-Baden Tel: (07221) 61817 Cable Add: Signal-Verlag Baden-Baden
Publisher: Hans-Jürgen Frevert
Subjects: Juveniles, Reference, Encyclopaedias, Dictionaries, Politics
ISBN Publisher's Prefix: 3-7971

S **Simmat***, Twiskenweg 35, D-2900 Oldenburg i. O. Cable Add: Oldenburg i. O. Twiskenweg 35
Publisher: Sigfried Simmat
Subjects: Philosophy, Politics, Scientific Theory

Verlag Ludwig **Simon**, Mozartstr 15, Postfach 247, D-8023 Munich-Pullach Tel: (089) 7930332
Subject: Illustrated Works
ISBN Publisher's Prefix: 3-7972

Skypress International, D-1000 Berlin 41, Grillparzerstr 10-11 Tel: (030) 3238089 Telex: 185275 SCA D

Societäts-Verlag, Frankenallee 71-81, Postfach 2929, D-6000 Frankfurt am Main 1 Tel: (0611) 7501 Cable Add: Zeitung Frankfurtmain Telex: 0411655
Publisher: Heinrich Scheffler; *Sales Manager:* Jörg Emich
Subjects: History, Business, Nonfiction, Literature, Art, Economics
Founded: 1921
Miscellaneous: This company comprises three separate Publishers — Verlag Frankfurter Bücher, Verlag Heinrich Scheffler and Verlag Osterrieth, all taking part in a common catalogue
ISBN Publisher's Prefix: 3-7973

Sonnenweg-Verlag Schäfer und Brandt, Bahnhofstr 4, Postfach 48, D-7442 Neuffen Tel: (07025) 2230/4128
Publisher: Friedrich Schäfer
Subject: Religion
1978: 15 titles
ISBN Publisher's Prefix: 3-7975

Spangenberg, an imprint of Verlag Heinrich Ellermann (qv)

Spectrum Verlag Stuttgart GmbH*, Friedrichstr 16-18, Postfach 1940, D-7012 Fellbach 4 Tel: (0711) 513004 Cable Add: Spectrumverlag Telex: 07254675
Man Dir: Karl O Tritt; *Sales, Publicity, Advertising Dir, Rights & Permissions:* Ulrich Höfker
Subjects: How-to, Reference, Juveniles, Natural Science, Textbooks
Founded: 1963
ISBN Publisher's Prefix: 3-7976

Spee — Buchverlag GmbH+, Fleischstr 61-65, Postfach 3040, D-5500 Trier Tel: (0651) 46171 Telex: 04-72731
Dir: Werner Adrian
Parent Company: Paulinus Druckerei GmbH (at above address)
Associate Company: Paulinus Verlag (qv)
ISBN Publisher's Prefix: 3-87760

W **Spemann** Verlag, Pfizerstr 5-7, Postfach 640, D-7000 Stuttgart 1 Tel: (0711) 21911 Cable Add: Kosmosverlag Stuttgart Telex: 721669 kosm d
Dirs: Claus Keller, R Keller, E Nehmann
Subjects: History, Culture, Art
1978: 25 titles *Founded:* 1873
Miscellaneous: Firm is a subsidiary of Franckh'sche Verlagshandlung W Keller & Co, Federal Republic of Germany (qv)
ISBN Publisher's Prefix: 3-810305

Verlag Volker **Spiess**, Grossgörschenstr 6, Postfach 147, D 1000 Berlin 62 Tel: (030) 7813514
Publisher, Editorial: Volker Spiess; *Production:* Brigitte Mietz, Yvonne Goetz
Associate Companies: Haude & Spener (qv), Bruno Hessling (qv)
Subjects: Library Science, Publishing, Literary Criticism, Mass Media, Education, Social Science, Linguistics, Languages
1977: 40 titles *Founded:* 1967
ISBN Publisher's Prefix: 3-920889

Adolf **Sponholtz** Verlag, Osterstr 19, Postfach 447, D-3250 Hameln 1 Tel: (05151) 200326 Cable Add: Dewezet Telex: 92859

Dir: Erich Schoeneberg
Orders to: Hamburger Kommissionsbuchhandlung GmbH, Libri-Haus, 2 Hamburg 36,
Subjects: General Fiction and Nonfiction, Juveniles, Literature, Animal stories, Hunting, Poetry
Founded: 1894
Miscellaneous: Associate Company of Verlag C W Niemeyer (qv)
ISBN Publisher's Prefix: 3-87766

Verlag für **Sprachmethodik**, Kantering 51-55, D-5330 Königswinter am Rhein Tel: 22771
Man Dir: H Willi Walter
Subjects: University, Secondary & Primary Textbooks, Educational Materials
Founded: 1953
ISBN Publisher's Prefix: 3-8018

Springer-Verlag Berlin-Heidelberg-New York*, Neuenheimer Landstr 28-30, D-6900 Heidelberg Tel: (06221) 4871 Telex: telefacs 06221 43982 and D-1000 Berlin 33, Heidelberger Platz 3 Tel: (030) 822001 Telex: telefacs 030821 4091 Cable Add: Springerbuch
Managing Partners: Dr Heinz Götze, Dr Konrad Springer, Claus Michaletz; *Editorial Dir:* Dr Klaus Peters; *Production Dir:* Heinz Sarkowski; *Sales Dir:* Gunther Holtz; *Advertising Dir:* Edgar Seidler
Parent Company: Springer Verwaltungs GmbH, Berlin
Associate Companies: Springer-Verlag New York – Heidelberg – Berlin, 175 Fifth Ave, New York, NY 10010, United States; Springer-Verlag KG, Vienna, Austria (qv); J F Bergmann, German Federal Republic (qv)
Br Off: Heidelberger Pl 3, D-1000 Berlin 33; Neuenheimer Landstr 28-30, D-6900 Heidelberg 1; Mölkerbastei 5, A-1011 Vienna, Austria
Subjects: Scientific and Technical: especially Medicine, Psychology, Biology; Earth Sciences, Maths, Physics, Chemistry, Computers; Engineering, Economics, Philosophy, Law; Reference Books, Paperbacks, Technical Journals, Technical Journals in English (especially Medical)
Bookshops: Bookselling group comprises: Lange & Springer Wissenschaftliche Buchhandlung, Berlin; Freihofer AG, Zürich, Switzerland; Minerva Wissenschaftliche Buchhandlung GmbH, Vienna, Austria
1977: 641 titles *Founded:* 1842
ISBN Publisher's Prefix: 3-540

Spur Verlag*, Molktestr 1, D-1000 Berlin 45 Tel: 030/8334150
Gen Man: Hellmut Heeger
Orders to: GVA, Gemeinsame Verlagsauslieferung, Postfach 1180, 2919 Strücklingen/Bokelesch Tel: 04498/1629
Founded: 1961
Subjects: Theology, Religious pedagogy, Pedagogy
Miscellaneous: Associate Companies: Bruno Hessling Verlag, Haude & Spener Verlag (qqv)
ISBN Publisher's Prefix: 3-87126

L **Staackmann** Verlag KG+, Leopoldstr 116, D-8000 Munich 40 Tel: (08027) 337 and (089) 342248
Man Dir: Dr Friedrich Vogel
Subjects: General Fiction, Belles Lettres, Poetry, Biography, How-to
1977: 8 titles *1978:* 8 titles *Founded:* 1869

Städte-Verlag, E v Wagner und J Mitterhuber*, Daimlerstr 60, Postfach 501162, D-7000 Stuttgart-Bad Cannstatt (Printing works in Fellbach) Tel: (0711) 561496 Cable Add: staedteverlag
Shipping Add: Postfach 501169, D-7000 Stuttgart 50
Man Dir: J Mitterhuber; *Publicity Dir:* U H Moeller
Subject: Maps, District and Town plans (especially for touring and sightseeing); West German Town Directories
Annually 400 new titles
Founded: 1951

Stähle und Friedel Verlagsgesellschaft mbH und Co, Neue Weinsteige 36, Postfach 492, D-7000 Stuttgart 1 Tel: (0711) 604464/5 Cable Add: Stählefriedel
Man Dir: Willy Klahm
Subjects: Calendars, Travel
ISBN Publisher's Prefix: 3-8116

Verlag **Stahleisen** mbH, Breitestr 27, D-4000 Düsseldorf 1 Tel: (0211) 88941 Cable Add: Stahleisen Düsseldorf Telex: 8587086
Man Dir: Dietrich Schnell; *Sales Dir:* Günther Hecker
Associate Company: Giesserei-Verlag GmbH (Foundry Press) (qv)
Subjects: Scientific and Technical (title denotes 'Iron and Steel Publishing Co')
1977: 15 titles *1978:* 11 titles *Founded:* 1908
ISBN Publisher's Prefix: 3-514

Stalling Verlag GmbH, Druck und Verlagshaus, Ammergaustr 72-78, Postfach 2580, D-2900 Oldenburg Tel: (0441) 34011 Cable Add: Stallingdruck Oldenburgoldb
Man Dir: Joachim Wisotzki; *Editorial:* Hans Jürgen Hansen, Christa Cordes, Rene Rilz; *Sales Dir:* Harry Sticklorat; *Rights & Permissions:* Barbara Zollickhofer
Editorial Offices: Boschstr 8, D-8031 Puchheim-Bahnhof
Subjects: General Nonfiction, Contemporary History, Art, Marine History, Humour, Juveniles
Founded: 1789
ISBN Publisher's Prefix: 3-7979

Stapp Verlag Wolfgang Stapp, Ehrenbergstr 29, D-1000 Berlin 33 Tel: (030) 8313445
Publishers: Wolfgang Stapp
Subjects: Illustrated Books; Books on Mark Brandenburg, Saxony and other areas of the German Democratic Republic; also on Berlin and other Cities and Rural Areas; Monographs on Artists
ISBN Publisher's Prefix: 3-87776

Hanns-Joachim **Starczewski** Verlag/Künstlerhof-Galerie*, Kirchstr 15, Postfach 137, D-5410 Hohr-Grenzhausen Tel: (02624) 2052
Man Dir, Editorial: H-J Starczewski; *Sales:* Birgit Weyers
Subjects: Painting, Sculpture
1977: 15 titles *Founded:* 1964
ISBN Publisher's Prefix: 3-7981

Johannes **Stauda** Verlag*, Heinrich-Schütz-Allee 33, D-3500 Kassel Tel: 30013 Cable Add: Stauda Kassel Telex: 992376
Subjects: Theology, Religious Instruction, Wall Charts for Religious Instruction

Franz **Steiner** Verlag GmbH*, Friedrichstr 24, Postfach 5529, D-6200 Wiesbaden Tel: (06121) 372011 Cable Add: Steinerverlagg Wiesbaden
Man Dirs: Hans Rotta, Vincent Sieveking; *Production:* Gregor Hoppen; *Publicity:* Käthe Schmidt

FEDERAL REPUBLIC OF GERMANY 163

Orders to: Birkenwaldstr 44, Postfach 347, D-7000 Stuttgart 1 Tel: (0711) 294482 Telex: 0723636 daz d
Parent Company: Deutscher Apotheker Verlag Dr Roland Schmiedel GmbH & Co
Associate Companies: Wissenschaftliche Verlagsgesellschaft mbH (qv); S Hirzel Verlag GmbH & Co (qv); Deutscher Apotheker-Verlag Dr Roland Schmiedel GmbH & Co (qv); all in the German Federal Republic
Subjects: Literary Criticism, Archaeology, Art, Music, History, Religion, Classical and Modern Philology, Oriental Studies, Ethnology, Philosophy, Geography, History of Medicine and Science, Sciences; Periodicals
1978: approx 200 titles *1979:* approx 200 titles *Founded:* 1949
ISBN Publisher's Prefix: 3-515

J F **Steinkopf** Verlag GmbH, Herrmannstr 5, Postfach 849, D-7000 Stuttgart 1 Tel: (0711) 626303 Cable Add: Steinkopf Stuttgart
Man Dir: Ulrich Weitbrecht; *Sales:* Lieselotte Haering
Subjects: General Fiction & Nonfiction, Paperbacks, How-to, Religion, Social Science, Secondary & Primary Textbooks
1977: 20 titles *1978:* 24 titles *Founded:* 1792
ISBN Publisher's Prefix: 3-7984

Dr Dietrich **Steinkopff** Verlag, Saalbaustr 12, Postfach 111008, D-6100 Darmstadt 11 Tel: 26538/9 Cable Add: Steinkopf Telex: 419627 stvda d
Man Dir: Jürgen Steinkopff; *Sales Dir:* Luise Eckhardt; *Publicity, Rights & Permissions:* Jürgen Steinkopff; *Advertising Dir:* H Niedermeyer
Subsidiary Company: Uni-Taschenbücher GmbH (qv)
Subjects: Reference, Low- & High-priced Paperbacks, Medicine, Psychology, General & Social Science, University & Secondary Textbooks
1977: 45 titles *1978:* 50 titles *Founded:* 1948
ISBN Publisher's Prefix: 3-7985

Steintor Verlag, Rudolf Jüdes, Postfach 41, D-3167 Burgdorf (Located at: Markstr 36) Tel: (05136) 2110
Subject: Art
1978: 42 titles *Founded:* 1969
Bookshops: Gallerie Steintor Verlag, D-3167 Burgdorf; Gallerie Meiborssen, D-3451 Meiborssen

Stephanus Edition Verlags GmbH, Tüfinger Str 3-5, Postfach 1160, D-7772 Uhldingen 1 Tel: (07556) 6509
Dir: Hans-Martin Braun
Subjects: Religion, Periodicals
ISBN Publisher's Prefix: 3-921213

Carl **Stephenson** Verlag, Gutenbergstr 12, Postfach 291, D-2390 Flensburg Tel: (0461) 28041/7 Tel: 022710
Sales Manager: Klaus Uhse
Subjects: Popular and Erotic Literature, Belles Lettres

Stern-Verlag Janssen und Co, Friedrichstr 24-26, Postfach 7820, D-4000 Düsseldorf 1 Tel: (0211) 373033
Managing Partners: Horst and Klaus Janssen; *Production and Sales:* Oswald Sckaer
Bookshop: Friedrichstr 24-26, D-4000 Düsseldorf 1
Founded: 1900
Subjects: Philosophy, Philology (especially of English)
ISBN Publisher's Prefix: 3-87784

Sternberg-Verlag, see Verlag Ernst Franz

Steyler Verlag, Arnold-Janssen-Str 20-22, D-5205 St Augustin 1 Tel: (02241) 197304
Associate Company: St Gabriel Verlag, Vienna, Austria (qv)
Subjects: Roman Catholic Theology, Novels, Juvenile, Meditations, Scientific Series, Hirarchicus Atlas and Bible

Lothar **Stiehm** Verlag GmbH*, Hausackerweg 16, Postfach 105802, D-6900 Heidelberg 1 Tel: (06221) 21354
Publisher: Lothar Stiehm
Associate Company: Lambert Schneider Verlag GmbH (qv)
Subjects: Classical Philology, German Language & Literature, Bibliography, Literary Criticism
ISBN Publisher's Prefix: 3-7988

Stollfuss Verlag GmbH & Co KG, Dechenstr 7-11, Postfach 2428, D-5300 Bonn 1 Tel: (02221) 631171-76 Cable Add: Stollfussverlag
Man Dir: Wolfgang Stollfuss; *Editorial:* Dr Joachim Lieser; *Sales:* Herbert Rolfsmeyer; *Production:* Werner Hartmann; *Publicity:* Ernst-Wolfgang Bucken
Subjects: Official Publications of German Finance Ministry, Reference Works, Fiscal Law, Administration, Economics, Investment, Taxes, Legal Studies etc.
1978: 25 titles
ISBN Publisher's Prefix: 3-08

Verlag für das **Studium** der Arbeiterbewegung, see VSA

Stürtz Verlag, Beethovenstr 5, D-8700 Würzburg Tel: (0931) 385235 Telex: 068798
Publisher: Rudolf Weiger; *Sales Manager:* Rosemarie Christou
Subjects: Art, Wine, History of Travel, Guidebooks, Scenic photo books, Hobbies, Sports

Stuttgarter Verlagskontor GmbH*, Rotebühlstr 77, Postfach 809, D-7000 Stuttgart Tel: (0711) 66721
Subject: Distribution and Warehousing Services, Nonfiction
ISBN Publisher's Prefix: 3-921138

Südbuch Vertriebsgesellschaft mbH, Mannheim, subsidiary of Bibliographisches Institut AG (qv)

Süddeutsche Verlagsgesellschaft Ulm, Sedelhofgasse 19-21, D-7900 Ulm Tel: (0731) 62447
Man Dir: Robert Abt
Parent Company: Schwabenverlag AG, German Federal Republic (qv)
Subjects: Christian Devotion and Meditation, Theology, Preparation for Sacraments, Juvenile, Religious, Liturgical, Pedagogy, Psychology, Social Problems, Current Affairs
1977: 13 titles *1978:* 14 titles *Founded:* 1898
ISBN Publisher's Prefix: 3-920921

Süddeutscher Verlag Buchverlag*, 43 Goethestrasse, Postfach 780, D-8000 Munich Tel: (089) 530561 Telex: 05/22405
Man Dir: Robert Schäfer; *Editorial:* Dr H-P Rasp; *Sales:* Volker Neumann; *Publicity:* Dr Rolf Cyriax; *Advertising:* Michael Schindler; *Rights & Permissions:* Gabriele Fentzke
Associate Companies: Paul List Verlag KG (qv); Sudwest Verlag GmbH & Co KG (qv)
Subjects: History, How-to, Music, Art, Fiction, Reference, Religion, Nonfiction
1977: 29 titles *Founded:* 1945
ISBN Publisher's Prefix: 3-7991

Südwest Verlag GmbH und Co KG, Goethestr 43, D-8000 Munich 2 Tel: 530561 Telex: 05/22405
Man Dir: Robert Schäfer; *Sales:* Volker Neumann; *Production:* Roger Seitz; *Publicity:* Dr Rolf Cyriax; *Advertising:* Michael Schindler; *Rights & Permissions:* Gabriele Fentzke
Associate Companies: Paul List Verlag KG (qv); Süddeutscher Verlag Buchverlag (qv)
Subjects: History, How-to, Music, Art
1977: 40 titles *1978:* 38 titles *Founded:* 1950
ISBN Publisher's Prefix: 3-517

Suhrkamp Verlag KG*, Lindenstr 29-35, Postfach 4229, D-6000 Frankfurt am Main Tel: (0611) 740231 Cable Add: Suhrkampverlag Telex: 413972
Publisher: Dr Siegfried Unseld; *Man Dir:* Dr Heribert Marré; *Sales:* Dr Gottfried Honnefelder; *Publicity:* Claus Carlé; *Rights & Permissions:* Helene Ritzerfeld
Associate Company: Insel Verlag (qv)
Subjects: General Fiction, Belles Lettres, Poetry, Biography, Philosophy, General Science, High- & Low-priced Paperbacks, Juveniles, Education, Psychology
Founded: 1950
Miscellaneous: Associated imprints include Suhrkamp Taschenbuchverlag and Suhrkamp Verlag Wissenschaft
ISBN Publisher's Prefix: 3-518

Symposion-Verlag GmbH+, Olgastr 25, Postfach 33, D-7300 Esslingen/N Tel: (0711) 311141 Cable Add: Symposion, Esslingen
General Manager: H A Siegler
Associate Company: ER-Verlags GmbH, Postfach 8, D-7300 Esslingen N Tel: (0711) 314702 (Men's Magazine Publisher)
Subjects: Motor Sports, Equestrian Interest, International Model Railways Guide; Periodicals
Founded: 1964 in Stuttgart
ISBN Publisher's Prefix: 3-920877

Syndikat Autoren- und Verlagsgesellschaft, see Autoren- und Verlagsgesellschaft

T B L (Tübinger Beiträge zur Linguistik) Verlag, see Gunter Narr Verlag

T R-Verlagsunion GmbH*, Thierschstr 11, Postfach 5, D-8000 Munich 26
Miscellaneous: Firm is a subsidiary of K G Saur Verlag KG, Federal Republic of Germany (qv)
ISBN Publisher's Prefix: 3-8058

Taylorix Fachverlag Stiegler und Co, Rotebühlstr 72, Postfach 829, D-7000 Stuttgart 1 Tel: (0711) 611773 Telex: 0723810
Dir: Dr Werner Kresse; *Sales Managers:* Dip-Volkswirt Walter Alt, Adolf Göschl
Subjects: Economics, Business, Law
ISBN Publisher's Prefix: 3-7992

Technik Tabellen Verlag Fikentscher und Co*, Eschollbrücker Str 39, Postfach 4135, D-6100 Darmstadt Tel: (06151) 61024 Cable Add: Fikentscher Telex: 419460
Publisher: Christoph Kässner; *Editorial:* Dr Thomas Krist
Subjects: Civil & Mechanical Engineering, Textbooks
ISBN Publisher's Prefix: 3-87807

Telex-Verlag Jaeger Waldmann*, Holzhofallee 38, Postfach 111060, D-6100 Darmstadt 11 Tel: (06151) 84036 Cable Add: Telexverlag
Telex: 419389/419253 *Man Dir:* Heinz Waldmann; *Sales Dir:* Wolfgang Lich; *Advertising Dir:* Ludwig Nicolay
Subjects: International Telex Directories
1977: 6 titles *Founded:* 1953
ISBN Publisher's Prefix: 3-87810

Alf **Teloeken** Verlag KG, see Alba Publikation

Telos series of Paperbacks. This is a series of Bible-based evangelical paperbacks (including works for children), each contributed by one of the following publishers:
Blaukreuz-Verlag Wuppertal (qv), Brendow-Verlag (qv), Verlag der Evangelischer Gesellschaft (qv), Verlag der Francke-Buchhandlung (qv), Hänssler-Verlag (qv), Verlag der Liebenzeller Mission (qv), Verlag der Sankt-Johannis-Druckerei G Schweickhardt (all in Federal Republic of Germany); Verlag der Schweizerischen Schallplattenmission (Swiss gramophone record mission), Evangelischer Schriften-Verlag Schwengeler (all in Switzerland)

Ernst **Tessloff** Verlag*, Bernadottestr 209, D-2000 Hamburg 52 Tel: (040) 8804753, 8801517 Cable Add: Tessloff Hamburg Telex: 0215167
Sales: Moika Leicher, Ursula Seike
Miscellaneous: Associate Company: Neuer Tessloff Verlag (same address)

B G **Teubner** GmbH, Industriestr 15, Postfach 801069, D-7000 Stuttgart 80 Tel: (0711) 733076
Man Dir: Heinrich Krämer; *Sales, Publicity & Advertising Dir:* Walter Hirtz; *Rights & Permissions:* Sophie Penner
Subjects: History, Classical Philology, Reference, High-priced Paperbacks, Mathematics, Physics, Biology, Geography, Engineering, General & Social Science, Secondary & University Textbooks
1979: 80 titles *Founded:* 1811
ISBN Publisher's Prefix: 3-519

Edition **Text und Kritik** GmbH, Levelingstr 6a, Postfach 800529, D-8000 Munich 80 Tel: (089) 432929
Man Dir: Dr Berndt Oesterhelt
Subjects: Contemporary Literature and Criticism, Reference Works, Musical Studies
ISBN Publisher's Prefix: 3-921402 and 3-88377

Konrad **Theiss** Verlag GmbH, Villastr 11, Postfach 730, D-7000 Stuttgart 1 Tel: (0711) 432981 Cable Add: Theissverlag Stuttgart
Dir: Hans Schleuning
Subjects: History, Arts, Nonfiction
1977: 22 titles
ISBN Publisher's Prefix: 3-8062

Theologischer Verlag R Brockhaus, Postfach 110197, 5600 Wuppertal 11 (Located at: Champagne 7, D-5657 Haan 2) Tel: (02104) 6311/12/13
Associate Company: R Brockhaus Verlag (qv)
Subject: Christian Theological Studies and Reference Works, Judeo-Christian Encounter
ISBN Publisher's Prefix: 3-417

Thesen Verlag Vowinckel und Co+, Kittlerstr 34, D-6100 Darmstadt Tel: (06151) 713326

Man Dirs: Heinrich Schirmer, Dr Ilse Vowinckel
Subjects: Literary Criticism, Linguistics, Social Science, University Textbooks, Educational Materials, Book Review *Kritikon Litterarum*
1978: 6 titles *Founded:* 1970
ISBN Publisher's Prefix: 3-7677

Druck- und Verlagshaus **Thiele und Schwarz**, Wilhelmshöher Allee 254-256, Postfach 410160, D-3500 Kassel Tel: (0561) 30076 Cable Add: Thiele & Schwarz Kassel-Wilhelmshöhe Telex: 0992450
Proprietor: Rolf Schwarz; *Editorial:* Claus Reineke
Associate Company: Verlag Schule und Elternhaus, Kassel (qv)
Subjects: General Fiction, Juveniles, Reprints
ISBN Publisher's Prefix: 3-87816

Georg **Thieme** Verlag KG*, Herdweg 63, Postfach 732, D-7000 Stuttgart 1
Tel: (0711) 2148/1 Cable Add: Thiemebuch Telex: 07/21942
Man Dirs: Dr G Hauff, Dr A Greuner; *Sales Manager:* Joachim Hillig; *Publicity:* Dieter Naveau; *Rights & Permissions:* Achim Menge
Subjects: Medicine, Chemistry, Pharmacy, Textbooks, Reference, Paperbacks
1978: approx 190 titles
Founded: 1886
ISBN Publisher's Prefix: 3-13

Verlag Karl **Thiemig** AG+, Pilgersheimerstr 38, Postfach 900740, D-8000 Munich 90 Tel: (089) 662493 Cable Add: Thiemigdruck
Man Dir: Peter Keskari; *Sales & Publicity Dir:* Werner Eyerich; *Advertising Dir:* Peter Schläuss
Subjects: Art, Travel, Natural Science, Technical
1977: 31 titles *1978:* 28 titles
Founded: 1950
ISBN Publisher's Prefix: 3-521

K **Thienemanns** Verlag*, Blumenstr 36, D-7000 Stuttgart 1 Tel: 240641 Telex: 723933 thie d
Dirs: Hansjoerg Weitbrecht, Richard Weitbrecht
Subjects: Juveniles, Children's Picture Books, Theatre, Dietetics
1977: 30 titles *Founded:* 1849
ISBN Publisher's Prefix: 3-522

Jan **Thorbecke** Verlag KG*, Karlstr 10, Postfach 546, D-7480 Sigmaringen
Tel: (07571) 3016 Cable Add: Thorbecke Telex: 732534
Dir, Rights & Permissions: Georg Bensch; *Editorial:* Erna Bensch; *Production, Publicity:* Ulrich Ulrichs; *Sales Dir:* Josef Müller
Subjects: Historical, Geographical, Cultural Accounts of various European Regions, especially in Germany and Switzerland; Art History, European History
1977: 48 titles *1978:* 52 titles *Founded:* 1946
ISBN Publisher's Prefix: 3-7995

Verlag **"Tips für Trips"**, see Friedemann von Engel Verlag

Titania-Verlag+*, Oberer Hoppenlauweg 26, Postfach 1352, D-7000 Stuttgart 1
Tel: (0711) 293551 Cable Add: Titaniaverlag Stuttgart
Publishers: Wolfgang Schroll, Gerdi Schroll
Subjects: General Fiction; Children's Story Books for all ages
1977: 18 titles
ISBN Publisher's Prefix: 3-7996

S **Toeche-Mittler** Verlag*, Hindenburg Str 33, D-6100 Darmstadt Tel: (06151) 81551
Subjects: Nonfiction, Law, Sports, Economics
Miscellaneous: Firm was formerly Mittler & Sohn, Berlin
Founded: 1789
ISBN Publisher's Prefix: 3-87820

Tomus Verlag GmbH, Prinzenstr 7, D-8000 Munich 19 Tel: (089) 132001
Telex: 5215528
General Manager: Claus-Jürgen Frank; *Dir:* Klaus Britting; *Rights & Permissions:* Roswitha Ladwig
Associate Companies: Telelit Verlag AG
Branch Off: Dr Wernerstr 5, D-8031 Gröbenzell
Subjects: Nature, Science, Animals, Hobbies, Travel, Cookery; Exclusive Art Editions; Sale of Co-Publishing Rights
Founded: 1962

P J **Tonger** Musikverlag*, Auf dem Brand 10, D-5000 Cologne 50 Tel: (0221) 392998
Man Dir: P J Tonger; *Sales Dir:* Hans Paul Zimmer; *Publicity Dir:* Hildegard Schneider; *Advertising Dir:* Peter Tonger
Subjects: Music, Art
Founded: 1822
Subsidiary: Carl Engels Musikverlag

Touropa-Urlaubsberater*, Prinzregentenstr 18, Postfach 408, D-8000 Munich 22 Tel: (089) 21011 Cable Add: Touropa Telex: 22857
Subject: Travel

Tradis Verlag und Vertrieb GmbH* Hochaus I an der Feldstr, D-2000 Hamburg 4 Tel: (040) 4394033 Cable Add: Tradisbuch
Man Dir: Klaus Kupfer
Subject: Low-priced Paperbacks
Founded: 1949; 1975 (merger with Distropa)
Miscellaneous: Nationwide distributor of American & British books, especially paperbacks
ISBN Publisher's Prefix: 3-87824

Transatlantik Verlags- und Vertriebsgesellschaft mbH, now known as Tradis Verlag & Vertrieb (qv)

Trautvetter und Fischer Nachf+, Gladenbacher Weg 57, Postfach 546, D-3550 Marburg Tel: (06421) 23309
Owned by: Dr Wilhelm A Eckhardt
Subjects: Local History and Guidebooks; History of Hess and Marburg Districts and their peoples, Church Histories (Protestant), Lyrical Poetry
1978: 2 titles *1979:* 8 titles *Founded:* 1941
ISBN Publisher's Prefix: 3-87822

éditions **trèves**, Postfach 1401, D-5500 Trier 1 Tel: (0651) 78687
Man Dirs: Rainer Breuer, Uschi Dahm; *Chief Reader:* Bernhard Hoffmann
Branch Off: editione trèves Mainz, Postfach 1843, D-6500 Mainz
Subjects: Belles Lettres, Young Literature, Lyrical Poetry, Theatre, Art, Literary Periodicals
1978: 12 titles *Founded:* 1974 (as graphics publishers); in present form, 1976
Miscellaneous: Publishing company for a society for the promotion of artistic activities run by its own (largely young) authors from throughout Europe
ISBN Publisher's Prefix: 3-88081

Trikont Verlag GmbH*, Kistlerstr 1, D-8000 Munich 90 Tel: (089) 6917821
Publisher: Herbert Röttgen; *Editorial:* Achim Bergmann; *Rights & Permission:*

FEDERAL REPUBLIC OF GERMANY 165

Herbert Röttgen; *Production:* Otto Frick
Subjects: General Fiction, History, Public Health, Medicine, Politics, Nonfiction, Social Science, Economics, Biography
ISBN Publisher's Prefix: 3-920385

Tübinger Vereinigung für Volkskunde eV, Schloss, D-7400 Tübingen Tel: (07071) 292374
Man Dir: Utz Jeggle; *Editorial, Production, Sales:* Prof H Bausinger, U Jeggle, M Scharfe, B F Warneken
Orders to: Chr Krämer, Postfach 1851, D-7400 Tübingen 1
Subjects: Low- and High-priced Paperbacks, Reference (Humanities), History, Social Science, University Textbooks
1978: 3 titles *1979:* 3 titles *Founded:* 1963

tuduv Verlagsgesellschaft mbH, Gabelsbergstr 15, D-8000 Munich 2
Tel: (089) 2809095
Subjects: Political Texts, Textbooks, Series connected with Political Science, Economics, Sociology, Jurisprudence, Philology, Literary Criticism, Cultural Arts
1978: 30 titles

Turm-Verlag*, Hindenburgstr 3, Postfach 229, D-7120 Bietigheim Tel: (07142) 44446
Cable Add: Turm, Bietigheim
Miscellaneous: Associate Company: Lorber-Verlag, 3 Hindenburgstr, D-7120 Bietigheim (qv)
Subjects: Health, Religion
ISBN Publisher's Prefix: 3-7999

Turmberg-Verlag*, Sophienstr 21, Postfach 2708, D-6330 Wetzlar Tel: (06441) 45556
Telex: 483794
Subjects: Music

U P N-**Volksverlag**, D-8531 Linden
Tel: (09846) 397
Subjects: Underground Literature — newspapers, periodicals, comics; Picture-Books; Sub-Culture and Life-Reformation
Miscellaneous: The Publishing Company's workers live as a country commune

Verlag Dr Alfons **Ü h l***, Tannhäuser Str 33, D-7094 Unterschneidheim Tel: (07966) 486
Subjects: Architectural and Art History; Graphics and Book Illustration; Art Portfolios

U T B, see Uni-Taschenbücher GmbH

Verlag **Ullstein** GmbH, PO Box 110303, D-1000 Berlin 11 (Located at: Lindenstr 76, D-1000 Berlin 61) Tel: (030) 25911 Cable Add: Ullsteinbuch berlin Telex: vlgul d 183723
Man Dir: W J Freyburg; *Editorial Dirs:* Hans F Erb, Wolfgang Richter; *Marketing and Sales Dir:* Viktor Niemann; *Publicity:* Ingrid Schick
Subsidiary Companies: Propylaen Verlag (qv), Ullstein Taschenbuchverlag
Subjects: Belles Lettres, Poetry, Biography, History, How-to, Music, Art, Juveniles, Low- & High-priced Paperbacks, General & Social Science, Educational Materials, Fiction, Military, Politics
1978: 60 main titles, 300 paperbacks
Founded: 1877
ISBN Publisher's Prefix: 3-550

Verlag Eugen **Ulmer** GmbH & Co*, Gerokstr 19, Postfach 1032, D-7000 Stuttgart 1 Tel: (0711) 246346 Telex: 721774
Man Dir: Roland Ulmer; *Sales Dir:* Gerhard Rentschler; *Advertising Dir:*

Erhard Liebenstein; *Publicity Dir:* Siegfried Hauptfleisch
Subjects: How-to, Reference, General Science, University Textbooks, Agriculture, Horticulture, Veterinary Science; Periodicals, Paperbacks
1977: 56 titles *Founded:* 1868
ISBN Publisher's Prefix: 3-8001

Umschau Verlag Breidenstein GmbH, Stuttgarter Str 18-24, D-6000 Frankfurt am Main 1 Tel: (0611) 26001 Cable Add: Umschau Frankfurtmain Telex: 0411964
Man Dir: Hans Jürgen Breidenstein; *Dir & Editorial Manager:* Dieter Curths; *Sales:* Peter Lugert
Associate Companies: Brönner Verlag Breidenstein GmbH (qv), Brönnersdruckerei Breidenstein GmbH, Sigma Studio Klaus Schlotte GmbH, Dateam Vertriebsgesellschaft mbH & Co KG; all at Stuttgarter Str 18-24, D-6000 Frankfurt am Main 1; also Andres Verlag GmbH, Lenaustr 2, Hamburg (qv)
Subjects: Nonfiction; especially Photographic Travel Books, Art, General Science, Low- & High-priced Paperbacks, Periodicals
Founded: 1850
ISBN Publisher's Prefix: 3-524

Ungarischer Kultureller und Sozialer Fonds eV in der B R D, Zweibrückenstr 2/IV, D-8000 Munich 2 Tel: (089) 294376
Hungarian Social and Cultural Foundation in the Federal Republic of Germany
Man Dir: András Piffkó; *Editorial:* János Röczey; *Rights & Permissions:* János Popovits
Parent Company: Zentralverband Ungarischer Organisationen in der B D R eV, at above address (Central Association of Hungarian Organisations in the Federal Republic of Germany)
Subjects: Works by Hungarian authors
Bookshops: Ungarischer Kultureller und Sozialer Fond in der BRD eV at above address
1978: 35 titles *1979:* 35 titles *Founded:* 1971

Uni-Taschenbücher (UTB) GmbH, Am Wallgraben 129, Postfach 801124, D-7000 Stuttgart 80 Tel: (0711) 734826
Dir: Volkmar Kalki
Orders to: Brockhaus Kommandit-Gesch, Am Wallgraben 127-129, Postfach 800205, D-7000 Stuttgart 80
Subjects: Library Science, Biology, Chemistry, Electrical Engineering, Electronics, Humanities, History, Public Health, Busines Informatics, Data Processing, Engineering, Agriculture, Literary Criticism, Mathematics, Medicine, Education, Philosophy, Physics, Politics, Psychology, Religion, Social Science, Linguistics, Languages, Veterinary Science, Economics; all texts in paperback
Miscellaneous: The company represents a group of 17 publishers producing paperbacks of a general academic/technical/scientific nature

Union Verlag Stuttgart*, Alexanderstr 171, Postfach 326, D-7000 Stuttgart 1 Tel: (0711) 604841/2 Cable Add: Unionverlag
Man Dirs: Dr Heinz Winners, Ulrich Commerell
Subject: Juveniles
Founded: 1890
ISBN Publisher's Prefix: 3-8002

Universitas Verlag Dr Klaus Schweitzer KG*, Welserstr 10-12, Postfach 1443, D-1000 Berlin 30 Tel: (030) 245138
Man Dir: Dr Klaus Schweitzer
Subjects: General Fiction, Biography, History, Low-priced Paperbacks, Cookbooks, Juveniles, Nonfiction
Founded: 1922
Miscellaneous: Firm is a member of Verlagsgruppe Langen-Müller/Herbig (qv)
ISBN Publisher's Prefix: 3-8004

Verlag **Urachhaus** Johannes M Mayer GmbH und Co KG, Urachstr 41, Postfach 131053, D-7000 Stuttgart 1 Tel: (0711) 260589/265939
Dir: Johannes Mayer; *Reader:* Inge Thöns; *Publicity & Marketing:* Winfried Altmann
Orders to: Koch, Neff & Oetinger & Co, Verlagsauslieferung, Am Wallgraben 110, D-7000 Stuttgart 80
Subjects: Fiction, History, Literary Criticism, Philosophy, Religion, Children's Books, Art Books, History of Art
1977: 17 titles *1978:* 27 titles *Founded:* 1924
ISBN Publisher's Prefix: 3-87838

Verlag **Urban und Schwarzenberg** (Medical Publishers)*, Pettenkoferstr 18, Postfach 202440, D-8000 Munich 2 Tel: (089) 530181 Cable Add: Urbanverlag Munich Telex: 0523864
Man Dir: Michael Urban; *Marketing Dir, Rights & Permissions:* Armin Jetter; *Sales:* Lieselotte Meyer; *Promotion:* Gerhard Leibssle
Associate Company: Urban & Schwarzenburg Inc, 7 East Redwood St, Baltimore, Md 21202, USA
Br Offs: Frankgasse 4, Vienna, Austria; Hardenbergstr 11, D-1000 Berlin 12, German Federal Republic
Subjects: Medicine, Psychology, Pedagogics, University Textbooks; also Slides and Journals
1977: 140 titles *1978:* 160 titles *Founded:* 1866
Bookshops: Oscar Rothacker Buchhandlung, Pettenkoferstr 18, D-8000 Munich 2; Oscar Rothacker, Hardenbergstr 11, D-1000 Berlin 12; Oscar Rothacker, Universitätsstr 11, D-2400 Regensburg; Oscar Rothacker, Kerpenerstr 75, D-5000 Cologne 1
ISBN Publisher's Prefix: 3-541

V A P Verlag*, Rösslerstr 10, Postfach 5764, D-6200 Wiesbaden Tel: 06121/302323
Subject: Political Texts

V D E-Verlag GmbH*, Bismarckstr 33, D-1000 Berlin 12 Tel: (030) 3413041 Telex: 0181683 vde d
Sales: Günther Schmiedichen
Orders to: D-6050 Offenbach, Merianstrasse 29
Miscellaneous: This is the publishing company of the Verband Deutscher Elektrotechniker (VDE — Association of German Electro-Technicians) Many specifications may be bought in English
Subjects: Electrical Engineering, Electronics, Technical Specifications
ISBN Publisher's Prefix: 3-8007

V D I-Verlag GmbH (Verlag des Vereins Deutscher Ingenieure), Graf-Recke-Str 84, Postfach 1139, D-4000 Düsseldorf 1 Tel: (0211) 62141 Cable Add: Ingenieurverlag Düsseldorf Telex: 08586525
Man Dir: J Larink; *Publishing Manager:* Klaus D Baldus; *Editorial:* Dr Gerhard Scheuch; *Rights & Permissions:* Marianne Diensthuber; *Sales:* Gunther Bicker; *Exports:* Inge Hanry
Associated Company: Beuth Verlag GmbH (qv), D-1000 Berlin 30 and D-5000 Cologne 1
Subjects: Engineering, Chemistry, Technology, Scientific Reports, Reports of Proceedings, Series of VDI Guidelines, Paperbacks
1977: 24 titles *1978:* 43 titles *Founded:* 1923
Miscellaneous: V D I is German Engineers' Association Publishing Company
ISBN Publisher's Prefix: 3-18

V-Dia-Verlag GmbH*, Heinrich-Fuchs-Str 95-97, Postfach 105980, D-6900 Heidelberg Tel: (06221) 37041 Cable Add: Vaudia Heidelberg
Subjects: Science-Technology, Geography, Astronomy, Biology, Medicine, History, Economics
Founded: 1953

V F P (Verlag Frauenpolitik) GmbH, Hafenweg 2-4, D-4400 Munster Tel: (0251) 60363
Man Dir: Anne Mussenbrock; *Production:* Angelika Müller; *Publicity:* Monika Walther; *Rights & Permissions:* Erika Leuteritz
Subjects: History of Women's Movement, Historical Texts, Women in Fascism, Third World, Sexual and Social Topics; Belles Lettres; Periodical *Die Eule*
1978: 10 titles *1979:* 4 titles *Founded:* 1976
ISBN Publisher's Prefix: 3-88175

V M B, see Verlag Marxistische Blätter

V S A (Verlag für das Studium der Arbeiterbewegung) GmbH, Eiffestr 598, D-2000 Hamburg 26 Tel: (040) 214510
Publishing House for the Study of the Workers' Movement
Manager: Gerd Siebecke; *Sales:* Bernhard Müller; *Rights & Permissions:* Horst Arenz
Orders to: VSA, Eiffestr 598, Postfach 260230, D-2000 Hamburg 26
Subjects: Political and Social Science, Political and Social Movements
1977: 25 titles
ISBN Publisher's Prefix: 3-87975

V W K (Verlag für Wirtschafts-und-Kartographie Publikationen) Ryborsch GmbH, Laubenstr 3, Postfach 2105, D-6053 Obertshausen 2 Tel: (06104) 7839
Dirs: Dipl V Mrs H Ryborsch-Tschinkel, Ing grad Reinhard Ryborsch
Subjects: Economics, Aviation, Geography, Travel
1977: 6 titles *1978:* 6 titles *Founded:* 1975
ISBN Publisher's Prefix: 3-920339

Franz **Vahlen** GmbH*, Wilhelmstr 9, D-8000 Munich 40 Tel: (089) 381891
Sales Dir: Günter Elze; *Publicity Dir:* Erhard Hoppe
Associate Companies: Verlag C H Beck (qv) Q Biederstein Verlag (qv)
Subjects: Law, Social Science, University Textbooks
Founded: 1870
ISBN Publisher's Prefix: 3-8006

Vandenhoeck und Ruprecht, Theaterstr 13, Postfach 77, D-3400 Göttingen Tel: (0551) 54031/3 Cable Add: Vandenhoeck
Dirs: Dr Arndt Ruprecht, Dr Dietrich Ruprecht; *Editorial:* Dr Winfried Hellmann; *Sales and Publicity:* Ursula Nahrgang
Subsidiary Companies: Druckerei Hubert & Co, Robert-Bosch-Breite 6, D-3400

Göttingen (Printers); Ehrenfried Klotz Verlag (qv)
Branch Off: Vandenhoeck & Ruprecht, Badener Str 69, CH-8026 Zürich, Switzerland
Subjects: University Textbooks, Research Monographs and Handbooks, Religion, Philology, History, Economics, Mathematics, Medical Psychology, Periodicals
1978: 240 titles *Founded:* 1735
Bookshop: Deuerlich'sche Buchhandlung, D-3400 Göttingen, Weender Str 33
ISBN Publisher's Prefix: 3-525

Velber Verlag GmbH*, Im Brande 15, D-3016 Seelze 6 Tel: (0511) 482091 Cable Add: Friedrich/Velber Telex: 0922923
Man Dir: Erhard Friedrich
Subjects: Juveniles, Games
Founded: 1972
ISBN Publisher's Prefix: 3-921187

Velhagen und Klasing, Lützowstr 105-106, D-1000 Berlin 30 Tel: (030) 2621071
Man Dir: Franz Cornelsen
Subsidiary Companies: Geographische Verlagsgesellschaft Velhagen & Klasing und Hermann Schroedel GmbH & Co KG (qv); Velhagen & Klasing und Schroedel Geographisch-Kartographische Anstalt GmbH, D-4800 Bielefeld, Düppelstr 21 (all in German Federal Republic)
Subjects: Cartography, Textbooks, Educational
Founded: 1835

Edition **Venceremos**, Verlag G Reinheimer, Postfach 1212, D-6090 Rüsselsheim (Located at: Heinrichstr 15) Tel: (06142) 65280
Man Dir, Sales, Production, Publicity: Wilhelm G Reinheimer; *Editorial, Rights & Permissions:* Heinz Mees
Subjects: German and International Folklore, Songs, Cabaret, Periodical *FOLKmagazin*
1978: 20 titles *1979:* 14 titles *Founded:* 1974
ISBN Publisher's Prefix: 3-88541

Klaus Dieter **Vervuert** Buchhandel und Verlag, Rheinstr 21, D-6000 Frankfurt am Main 1 Tel: (0611) 752256
Combined Bookshop and Publishing House
Subjects: Specialist in books about Latin America, Spain and Portugal
1978: 3 titles
ISBN Publisher's Prefix: 3-921600

Friedr **Vieweg** und Sohn Verlagsgesellschaft mbH, Gustav-Stresemann-Ring 12-16, Postfach 5829, D-6200 Wiesbaden Tel: (06121) 5341 Telex: 4186880 remy d
Orders to: VVA (Vereinigte Verlagsauslieferung), Postfach 7777, D-4830 Gütersloh 1
Man Dir: Dr Frank Lube; *Rights & Permissions:* Angelika Bolisega; *Sales Man:* Heinz Detering
Parent Company: Verlagsgruppe Bertelsmann GmbH (qv)
Subsidiary Company: Deutscher Eichverlag, Burgplatz 1, Postfach 3367, D-3300 Braunschweig
Subjects: Philosophy, Reference, Low- & High-priced Paperbacks, Engineering, General Science, University & Secondary Textbooks, Educational Materials
1977: 120 titles *1978:* 125 titles *Founded:* 1786
ISBN Publisher's Prefix: 3-528

Curt R **Vincentz** Verlag, Schiffgraben 41-43, Postfach 6247, D-3000 Hanover 1 Tel: (0511) 327746 Telex: 923846
Man Dir: Dr L Vincentz; *Sales:* Dr F Vincentz
Subjects: General Science, Commerce
1978: 13 titles *Founded:* 1893
ISBN Publisher's Prefix: 3-87870

Vogel-Verlag KG, Max-Planck-Str 7-9, Postfach 6740, D-8700 Würzburg 1 Tel: (0931) 41021 Cable Add: Vogelverlag Würzburg Telex: 068883
Man Dir: Dr Kurt Eckernkamp
Subjects: Technical texts covering Science, Electrical, Textile & Agricultural Engineering, Electronics, Mass Media, Medicine, Education, Transport; Export Journals in 14 languages
1978: 220 titles, 27 technical journals
Founded: 1891
ISBN Publisher's Prefix: 3-8023

Emil **Vollmer** Verlag, see Vollmer/Löwit Verlagsgruppe

Vollmer/Löwit Verlagsgruppe*, Sonnenberger Str 44, Postfach 4060, D-6200 Wiesbaden Tel: (06121) 39571 Telex: 4182577
Dir: Sylvia Vollmer
Subjects: Art and Artists, Collectors' Books, Mythology, Natural History, Religions, History, Fiction, Belles Lettres, Juveniles, Popular Editions of Classics

Hartfrid **Voss** Verlag*, Lechner Str 27, Postfach 16, D-8026 Ebenhausen bei Munich Tel: (08178) 4857
Subjects: General Fiction, Music
ISBN Publisher's Prefix: 3-87878

Kurt **Vowinckel** Verlag, Assenbucherstrasse 28, 8131 Berg am See Tel: 08151, 51675
Dir: Dr Gert Sudholt; *Sales:* Linda Sudholt
Subjects: Current Affairs, Politics
ISBN Publisher's Prefix: 3-87879

W R S — Verlag (Wirtschaft, Recht, Steuern), Irmgardstr 1, D-8000 Munich 71
Parent Company: Rudolf Haufe Verlag (qv)
Subjects: Economics, Law, Taxes

Karl **Wachholtz** Verlag*, Gänsemarkt 1-3, Postfach 2769, D-2350 Neumünster Tel: (04321) 46161 Cable Add: courier Telex: 299618
Dir: Walter Kardel; *Sales & Publicity Manager:* Hans-Hermann Lipsius
Subjects: Humanities, History, Calendars, Arts, Reference, Encyclopaedias, Dictionaries, Literature, Music, Reprints, Linguistics, Languages, Periodicals
1978: 32 titles
ISBN Publisher's Prefix: 3-529

Verlag Klaus **Wagenbach***, Bamberger Str 6, Postfach 1409, D-1000 Berlin 30 Tel: (030) 2115060/69
Man Dir, Editorial: Dr Klaus Wagenbach; *Sales:* Katia Wagenbach; *Production:* Gabriele Kronenberg; *Publicity, Rights & Permissions:* Barbara Herzbruch
Subjects: General Fiction, Belles Lettres, Poetry, Low- and High-priced Paperbacks, Political and Social Science
1977: 30 titles *Founded:* 1964
ISBN Publisher's Prefix: 3-8031

Walter-Verlag GmbH, Erwinstr 58-60, D-7800 Freiburg-im-Breisgau
Parent Company: Walter Verlag AG, Switzerland (qv)

Ernst **Wasmuth** Verlagsbuchhandlung KG*, Fürststr 133, Postfach 2728, D-7400 Tübingen Tel: (07071) 33658
Man Dir: Sibylle von Bockelberg; *Sales Dir:* Karl H Schattner; *Production:* Manfred Heinrich
Subjects: Architecture, Archaeology, History of Art, Applied Art
Founded: 1872
Bookshop: Wasmuth Buchhandlung & Antiquariat, D-1000 Berlin 12, Hardenbergstr 9A
ISBN Publisher's Prefix: 3-8030

Wehr und Wissen Verlagsgesellschaft mbH, Heilsbachstr 26, D-5300 Bonn 1 (Duisdorf) Tel: (02221) 643066-68 Telex: 8869429 mvkb d
Man Dir: Manfred Sadlowski; *Sales Dir:* Joachim Latka; *Publicity Dir:* Heinz-Jürgen Witzke; *Advertising Dir:* Peter Konietschke; *Rights & Permissions:* J Latka
Subjects: History, How-to, High-priced Paperbacks, Military Manuals, Yearbooks

A **Weichert** Verlag, Tiestestr 14, D-3000 Hanover Tel: (0511) 813068 Cable Add: Buchweichert Telex: 0923872 awv
Man Dir: Alfred Trippo; *Sales:* Harald Droste
Imprint: Karo-Bücher
Branch Off: Hans Feulner, Lindenallee 25, D-1000 Berlin 19
Subject: Juveniles (Story Books for all ages)
1978: 11 titles *1979:* 17 titles *Founded:* 1872
Associate Company: Neuer Jugendschriften-Verlag (qv)
ISBN Publisher's Prefix: 3-483

Wolfgang **Weidlich** Verlag, Savignystr 61, D-6000 Frankfurt am Main Tel: (0611) 746215
Publisher: Wolfgang H Weidlich; *Editorial:* Brigitte Weidlich; *Sales:* Doris Böhler; *Production:* Wilfred Sindt; *Publicity:* Ulrike Karmeier
Subjects: Architecture, General Fiction, History, Maps, Nonfiction
ISBN Publisher's Prefix: 3-8035

Verlag **Weinmann**, Beckerstr 7, D-1000 Berlin 41 Tel: (030) 8554895
Man Dir: Dr Weinmann
Subject: Sport, (especially the martial arts), Instruction books for all ages; Yoga
1978: 10 titles *Founded:* 1961
ISBN Publisher's Prefix: 3-87892

Weismann Verlag-Frauenbuchverlag GmbH, Kreittmayrstr 26, D-8000 Munich 2 Tel: (089) 192970
Man Dir: Peter Weismann; *Editorial:* Frank Göhre, Antje Kunstmann
Orders to: AVS-Verlagsauslieferung Joachim Schäfer, Taunusstr 82, D-6237 Liederbach
Subsidiary Company: Frauenbuchverlag (qv)
Subjects: Literature and Nonfiction for young people; theatrical texts for Juveniles; Politics
1977: 10 titles *Founded:* 1970
ISBN Publisher's Prefix: 3-921040

Gebrüder **Weiss** Verlag*, Hewaldstr 9, D-1000 Berlin 62 Tel: (030) 7817725
Owner: Richard Weiss
Subjects: General Fiction, Juveniles, Popular Science, Nonfiction, Paperbacks
Founded: 1945
ISBN Publisher's Prefix: 3-8036

Weitbrecht GmbH, Blumenstr 36, D-7000 Stuttgart

Verlag **Welsermühl**, Kufsteiner Str 8, D-8000 Munich 80 Tel: (089) 982031 Cable Add: welsermuhldruck Telex: 5216349
Dir, Editorial, Rights & Permissions: Karl Pramendorfer; *Sales:* Friederike Weiss-Füreder; *Production:* Friedrich Spendou; *Publicity:* K Füreder
Orders to: Kufsteinerstr 8, D-8000 Munich 80
Subsidiary Company: Zweimühlen Verlag GmbH, Kufsteinerstr 8, Munich 80
Branch Off: Verlag 'Welsermühl' Fritsch & Dusl KG, Austria (qv)
Subjects: General Non-fiction, Travel, Illustrated Books, Current Events
1977: 26 titles *1978:* 18 titles *Founded:* 1928
ISBN Publisher's Prefix: 3-85339

Weltkreis-Verlags-GmbH+, Brüderweg 16, D-4600 Dortmund 1 Tel: (0231) 572010 Telex: 8227284 wkv el
Man Dir: H W v Oppenkowski; *Editorial:* Dr Rutger Booss; *Publicity & Advertising Dir:* Friedhelm Kuelpmann
Orders to: (Federal Republic of Germany): Brücken Verlag, Postfach 1928, D-4000 Düsseldorf; (West Berlin): Zirk & Ellenrieder, Postfach 3147, D-1000 Berlin 30
Subjects: Belles Lettres, Poetry, Biography, How-to, Juveniles, Low-priced Paperbacks
1977: 24 titles *1978:* 21 titles *Founded:* 1958
ISBN Publisher's Prefix: 3-88142

Karl **Wenschow** GmbH, Munich, see JRO – Verlagsgesellschaft, the subsidiary company which now handles all marketing and distribution

Werner Verlag GmbH, Berliner Allee 11a, D-4000 Düsseldorf 1 Tel: (0211) 320988 Cable Add: Wernerverlag Telex: 8587828
Man Dir: Klaus Werner; *Publicity Dir:* E Dickert
Subjects: University Textbooks, Reference, Engineering, Educational Materials, Law, Social Science, Economics
1977: 60 titles *1978:* 65 titles *Founded:* 1945
ISBN Publisher's Prefix: 3-8041

Westdeutscher Verlag GmbH, Gustav-Stresemann-Ring 12-16, Postfach 5829, D-6200 Wiesbaden Tel: (06121) 5341 Telex: 4186880 remy d
Man Dir: Dr Frank Lube; *Editorial:* Manfred Müller; *Sales, Publicity:* Heinz Detering; *Rights & Permissions:* Angelika Bolisega
Orders to: VVA (Vereinigte Verlagsauslieferung), Postfach 7777, D-4830 Gütersloh 1
Parent Company: Verlagsgruppe Bertelsmann GmbH (qv)
Branch Off: Reuschenberger Str 55, D-5090 Leverküsen 3
Subjects: History, Literature, Social Science, University Textbooks
1977: 60 titles *1978:* 55 titles *Founded:* 1947
ISBN Publisher's Prefix: 3-531

Georg **Westermann** Verlag, Druckerei & Kartographische Anstalt GmbH & Co, Georg-Westermann-Allee 66, D-33 Brunswick Tel: (0531) 7081 Cable Add: Gewebuch Telex: 0952841
Man Dirs: Dr Jürgen Mackensen, Dirck Tebbenjohanns, Gerd Mackensen; *Marketing Dir:* Wolfgang Dick; *Exports:* Wolfgang Mann; *Publicity Dir:* Karl-Heinz Grothe; *Rights & Permissions:* Dr Carl-August Schröder
Subsidiary Companies: Lehrmittelanstalt Richard Herold, Bonn-Bad Godesberg; Lehrmittelhandlung Heinz Vogel, Wilhelmshaven and Bremen; Lehrmittelanstalt Köster, Munich
Subjects: History, Education, Paperbacks, University, Secondary & Primary Textbooks, Educational Materials, Periodicals
1977: 250 titles *1978:* 270 titles *Founded:* 1838
ISBN Publisher's Prefix: 3-14

Erich **Wewel** Verlag, Anzinger Str 1, D-8000 Munich 80 Tel: (089) 403031 Telex: 522504
Sales: Erna Schmidt; *Publicity:* Siegbert Seitz
Subjects: Philosophy, Religion
Miscellaneous: Subsidiary of Manz Verlag (qv)
ISBN Publisher's Prefix: 3-87904

Who's Who — Book & Publishing Company, Hauptstr 1, Postfach 1150, D-8031 Wörthsee/Steinebach Tel: (08153) 8033/8034
General Manager: Georg Otto
Subjects: Encyclopedias; Bibliographical, Arts, Literature, Medicine, Technology, Fashion
1978: 2 titles *1979:* 3 titles
ISBN Publisher's Prefix: 3-921220

Herbert **Wichmann** Verlag, Rheinstr 122, Postfach 210949, D-7500 Karlsruhe Tel: (0721) 555955 Telex: 7825909
Man Dir: Dr Christof Müller-Wirth; *Sales, Publicity:* Winfried Ammon; *Production, Rights & Permissions:* Jochen Schmitt
Subjects: Geodesy, Photogrammetry, Land Registration, Cartography, Estate Evaluation
1977: 5 titles *1978:* 2 titles *Founded:* 1889
ISBN Publisher's Prefix: 3-87907

Willing Verlag GmbH*, Darmstädterstr 11, Postfach 402045, D-8000 Munich 50 Tel: (089) 146724
Subjects: Politics, Juveniles, Literature, Art

Rosa **Winkel** Verlags-und-Versand GmbH, Bülowstr 17, D-1000 Berlin 30 Tel: (030) 2153742
Man Dirs for All Offices: Egmont Fassbinder, Hans Hutt
Subjects: Heterosexual-Homosexual 'Social Norms' Debate, Homosexual Emancipation
1978: 3 titles *1979:* 8 titles *Founded:* 1975
ISBN Publisher's Prefix: 3-921495

Winkler-Verlag, Martiusstr 8, Postfach 26, D-8000 Munich 44 Tel: (089) 348074
Man Dir: Dr Dieter Lutz; *Publicity:* Anita Douat
Subjects: Belles Lettres, Reference, General Science, University Textbooks, Reprints
Founded: 1945
Miscellaneous: Firm is a subsidiary of Artemis und Winkler Verlag (qv)
ISBN Publisher's Prefix: 3-538

Carl **Winter** Universitätsverlag GmbH, Lutherstr 59, Postfach 106140, D-6900 Heidelberg 1 Tel: (06221) 49111 Telex: 0461660
Publisher: Dr Carl Winter; *Sales:* Ruth Wutke
Subject: University Books
1977: 75 titles *1978:* 75 titles
Founded: 1822
ISBN Publisher's Prefix: 3-533

Wirtschaft, Recht, Steuern, see WRS-Verlag

Verlag für **Wirtschafts- und Kartographie-**Publikationen, Ryborsch, see V W K

Verlag für **Wirtschaftsskripten**, Dipl-Kfm C Ölschläger GmbH, Amalienstr 81, D-8000 Munich 40 Tel: (089) 284942
Man Dirs: Claus Ölschläger, Christina Ölschläger
Associate Company: Verlag Ölschläger GmbH (qv)
Subjects: Economics, Business, Management, Law
1978: 35 titles *Founded:* 1974
ISBN Publisher's Prefix: 3-921636

Wirtschaftsverlag*, Hubertusstr 4, D-8000 Munich 19 Tel: (089) 177041 Telex: 215045
Subjects: Business Economics, Work Study and Allied Subjects
Miscellaneous: Firm is a member of Verlagsgruppe Langen-Müller/Herbig (qv)

Wison Verlag GmbH, Weyertal 59, Postfach 410948, D-5000 Cologne 41 Tel: 443031
Subjects: Economic Sciences; Data Processing; Research Reports

Wissen Verlag GmbH*, Gachenaustr 11-13, D-8036 Herrsching Tel: (08152) 1087 Telex: 526493
Dir: Anton Bolza; *Editorial:* Christian Schneider, Dr Barbara Chabrow; *Sales Manager:* Andreas Goëss
Subjects: Reference, Encyclopaedias, Dictionaries
ISBN Publisher's Prefix: 3-8075

Verlag **Wissenschaft und Politik**, see von Nottbeck

Verlag für **Wissenschaft, Wirtschaft und Technik** GmbH und Co KG, An den Weiden 15, D-3388 Bad Harzburg Tel: (05322) 81385 Telex: 957623 DVG
Man Dir: Maria Marschefski; *Dir:* Gisela Böhme
Subjects: Management, Sociology, Social Science, Primary and Secondary Textbooks, Economics
1977: 10 titles *Founded:* 1960
ISBN Publisher's Prefix: 3-8020

Wissenschaftliche Buchgesellschaft, Hindenburgstr 40, Postfach 111129, D-6100 Darmstadt 11 Tel: (06151) 82141
Man Dir: Ernst Knauer; *Chief Reader:* Jürgen Bauer; *Rights & Permissions:* Uwe Lessing
Subjects: History, Music, Art, Philosophy, Reference, Religion, Medicine, Psychology, General & Social Science, Low-priced Paperbacks, Education, Mathematics, Theology, Archaeology, Jurisprudence, Economics
Book Club: Wissenschaftliche Buchgesellschaft
1978: 110 titles *Founded:* 1949
ISBN Publisher's Prefix: 3-534

Wissenschaftliche Verlagsgesellschaft mbH, Birkenwald Str 44, Postfach 40, D-7000 Stuttgart 1 Tel: (0711) 292559 Telex: 0723636 daz d
Man Dirs: Hans Rotta, Dr Hanskarl Hornüng; *Sales Manager:* Karl Hübler; *Publicity Manager:* Barbara Schreck
Associate Companies: Deutscher Apotheker Verlag Dr Roland Schmiedel GmbH & Co (qv); S Hirzel Verlag GmbH & Co (qv); Franz Steiner Verlag GmbH (qv); all in the German Federal Republic
Subjects: Medicine, Pharmacy, Biology, Chemistry, Physics
Founded: 1921
ISBN Publisher's Prefix: 3-8047

Friedrich **Wittig** Verlag, Papenhuder Str 2, D-2000 Hamburg 76 Tel: (040) 221059 Cable Add: Wittigverlag
Man Dir: Friedrich Wittig

Subjects: Religion, Arts, History, Bibliophily
1977: 15 titles *1978:* 5 titles *Founded:* 1946
ISBN Publisher's Prefix: 3-8048

Verlag Konrad **Wittwer** KG, Nordbahnhofstr 16, Postfach 147, D-7000 Stuttgart 1 Tel: 250211 Telex: 723751
Man Dir: Konrad Wittwer; *Editorial:* Gertrud Bernlöhr; *Sales:* U Holland; *Production, Publicity:* Mr Hasler
Subjects: Mathematics (School Textbooks), Geodesy, Building Technology, General Literature
Bookshop: Königstr 30, D-7000 Stuttgart 1
1977: 5 titles *1978:* 4 titles *Founded:* 1867
ISBN Publisher's Prefix: 3-87919

Gerhard **Witzstrock** GmbH, Bismarckstr 9, Postfach 509, D-7570 Baden-Baden Tel: (07221) 2047 Telex: 781162 gewi d
Man Dir: Gerhard Witzstrock; *General Manager:* Lotte Witzstrock
Subsidiary Company: Gerhard Witzstrock Publishing House Inc, New York, 381 Park Ave South, Suite 1123, New York, NY 10016 USA
Subjects: Medicine, Electron Scanning Microscopy
1979: 12 titles *Founded:* 1969
ISBN Publisher's Prefix: 3-87921

Womm-Press*, Mittelstr 51, D-4934 Horn-Bad Meinberg 1 Tel: (05234) 3780
Man Dir: Burkhart Weecke; *Publicity:* Horst Knauf; *Editorial:* Uli Becker; *Production:* W Linnemann
Subjects: General Fiction, Belles Lettres, Poetry, Music, Art, University Textbooks
Founded: 1974
ISBN Publisher's Prefix: 3-88080

Rainer **Wunderlich** Verlag Hermann Leins, Goethestr 6, Postfach 2740, D-7400 Tübingen Tel: (07071) 24354 Cable Add: Wunderlichverlag Telex: 7262891 mepo d
Man Dir: Günther Schweizer; *Sales & Publicity Manager:* Albrecht Karnbach; *Rights & Permissions:* Monika Mölle
Subjects: Belles Lettres, Poetry, Biography, History, Music, Art, Politics
1978: 19 titles *Founded:* 1926
ISBN Publisher's Prefix: 3-8052

Edgar **Wüpper***, Wilh Weber Str 37, D-3400 Göttingen Tel: (0551) 47172
Man Dir: Edgar Wüpper
Subjects: Book Journal, Children's Newspaper, Children's Books, Postcards, Posters
Founded: 1974
Miscellaneous: Associate Company: Verlag Bert Schlender (qv)

Xenos Verlagsgesellschaft mbH & Co, Lottbekheide 17, D-2000 Hamburg 65 Tel: 6049140 Telex: 2174727
Man Dir: Erwin Heimberger; *Sales and Publicity:* Hans Klingenberg; *Sales:* Josef Brauers; *Production:* Frau Rohardt; *Rights & Permissions:* Inge Heimberger
Subjects: Juveniles, Nonfiction, Belles Lettres; Paperbacks
1978: 134 titles *1979:* 109 titles *Founded:* 1975

Dr **Zambon***, Leipziger Str 24, Alte Gasse 38, D-6000 Frankfurt am Main 90 Tel: (0611) 281224
Publisher: Guiseppe Zambon; *Sales:* Johannes Bornheim
Subjects: Juveniles, Foreign-language Teaching, Reprints

Zechner und Hüthig Verlag GmbH, Daimlerstr 9, Postfach 2080, D-6720 Speyer-am-Rhein Tel: (06232) 33076 Cable Add: Zechner Verlag Speyer Telex: 465167
Publisher: Rudolf Zechner
Subject: General Science
ISBN Publisher's Prefix: 3-87927

Verlag Andreas **Zettner** KG+*, Hofweg 12, Postfach 13, D-8702 Würzburg-Veitschöchheim Tel: (0931) 91970 Cable Add: Zettner Würzburg
Man Dir: Andreas Zettner
Subject: General Fiction
Founded: 1955
Book Club: Buchclub 69
Bookshops: Dr Müllers Buchboutique, D-8000 Munich 13, Citta 2000 & D-8500 Nuremberg, Breite Gasse 62; D-8100 Augsburg, Neuburger Str 67; D-854 Schwabach, Neutorstr 1

Verlag Wolfgang **Zimmer**, Haunstetter Str 18, D-8900 Augsburg Tel: (0821) 554135
Publisher: Wolfgang Zimmer
Imprint: Schwarz Bildbücher
Subjects: Hobbies, Maps, Transport, Commerce
Miscellaneous: Formerly Rösler und Zimmer Verlag
ISBN Publisher's Prefix: 3-87987

Verlagsgemeinschaft Friedrich **Zluhan***, Hindenburgstr 3, Postfach 229, D-7120 Bietigheim Tel: (07142) 44446
Subjects: Belles Lettres, Homeopathy; Works of Alice Bailey; Astrosophy

Paul **Zsolnay** Verlag GmbH, Hohe Bleichen 7/Libri Haus, D-2000 Hamburg Tel: (040) 345156 Cable Add: Hakobuch Hamburg Telex: 214900
Dirs: Kurt Lingenbrink, Hans Polak
Parent Company: Heinemann & Zsolnay Ltd, UK (qv)
Associate Company: Paul Zsolnay Verlag GmbH, Austria (qv)
Subjects: General Fiction, Poetry, Nonfiction
Founded: 1948
ISBN Publisher's Prefix: 3-552

Zweipunkt Verlag KG*, Wilhelm-Leuschner-Str 1, D-6078 Neu Isenburg Tel: (06102) 7247
Subjects: Picture Books, Activity Books, Puzzles

Zweitausendeins Versand*, Hahnstr 54-56, Postfach 710249, D-6000 Frankfurt/AM 71 Tel: (0611) 663386
Subjects: New German and International Books; Reprints; Co-operative Works

Literary Agents

Babylon Übersetzungen*, Düsseldorferstr 38, D-1000 Berlin 15 Tel: (03) 8838296
Man Dir: Walter Bengs
Literary, Copyright and Translation Agency

Balkan-Press, D-8000 Munich 70, Schmied-Kochel-Str 20 Tel: 3204450
Specialization: General books, Novels, Short Stories; Theatrical and TV scripts; Education, Psychology, Sociology, Politics; copyright and novel serialisation for newspapers and magazines

Winfried **Bluth** Literary Agency*, D-5630 Remscheid, Augustinusstr 43·

Buchagentur München*, D-8032 Gräfelfing, Maria-Eich-Str 54b
Contact: Dr Hanns Martin Elster

Dr rer pol Dr Julius **Démuth***, Krautgartenweg 22, D-6000 Frankfurt am Main 50 Tel: (0611) 571970

Fralit-F K Albrecht, Brahmsallee 29/1, D-2000 Hamburg 13 Tel: (040) 456073 Cable Add: Fralitagentur

Geisenheyner und Crone, D-7000 Stuttgart 1, Gymnasiumstr 31B Tel: (0711) 293738 Cable Add: Gecelit Telex: 722664
Proprietor: Ernst W Geisenheyner

Gustav **Greve***, D-1000 Berlin 12, Fasanenstr 15

Hans Hermann **Hagedorn**, D-2000 Hamburg 20, Erikastr 142 Tel: (040) 4603232

Dagmar **Henne***, D-8000 Munich 40, Seestr 6

Münchner Verlagsbüro Horst **Hodemacher**-Axel Poldner GmbH & Co KG, D-8000 Munich 19, Barellistr 7 Tel: (089) 171789

Agence **Hoffman**, D-8000 Munich 40, Seestr 6 Tel: (089) 396402 Cable Add: Aghoff München
Contact: Frau Dagmar Henne

Interlita-Literaturagentur Peter Vilimek GmbH*, D-1000 Berlin 31, Paulsborner Str 90, Postfach 150210
Contact: Peter Vilimek

International Literary Agency*, D-2000 Hamburg 39, Zesenstr 16 Tel: (0411) 2791111

Gerhard **Kowalski**, Kurfürstendamm 229, D-1000 Berlin 15 Tel: (030) 8827290 Telex: 0184560
Specialization: Memoirs, Biographies, Reference, Fiction, Theatre
Branches in Paris, New York and Palm Springs, USA
See also: Publishing Company Champion Verlag G Kowalski

Karl Ludwig **Leonhardt**, An der Alster 22, D-2000 Hamburg 1

Rose M **Meerwein**, Literary Scout, Reuterpfad 6-8, D-1000 Berlin 33 Tel (030) 8262039

Münchner Verlagsbüro, Horst Hodemacher-Axel Poldner*, Barellistr 7, D-8000 Munich 19 Tel: (089) 171789

Gerd **Plessl** Agency, Seidlstr 18, D-8000 Munich 2 Tel: (089) 554084/597117
Specialization: Selling rights to South and East European publishers

Axel **Poldner***, D-8000 Munich 21, Rauheckstr 11 Tel: (089) 574824

Quelle Press*, Postfach 1314, D-7800 Freiburg im Breisgau Tel: (0761) 7016 Cable Add: Quellepress Freiburg

Thomas **Schlueck**, Hinter der Wörth 12, D-3008 Garbsen 9 Tel: (05131) 93053 Telex: 923419 litag d

Wilfried Th **Sieber***, D-4973 Viotho 2, Im Königsfeld 5 Tel: (05228) 336
Specialization: Science Fiction

BP **Singer** Features Inc*, Postfach 1314, D-7800 Freiburg im Breisgau Tel: (0761) 7016
US Office: 3164 West Tyler Ave, Anaheim, CA 92801, USA

Skandinavia Verlag, Knesebeckstr 100, D-1000 Berlin 12 Tel: (030) 8137006/8616074
Contact: Marianne Weno, Michael Günther
Specialization: Scandinavian Stage, Radio and TV plays

Herta **Weber-Stumfohl**, D-8035 Gauting, Waldpromenade 32 Tel: (089) 8501241
Specialization: Translations from Swedish; Reviews

Book Clubs

Bertelsmann Lesering*, Carl Bertelmannstr 270, D-4830 Gütersloh Postfach 555
Members: 3 million
Founded: 1950
Owned by: Verlagsgruppe Bertelsmann GmbH

Verlag **Bibliotheca** Christiana*, D-5300 Bonn, Endenicher Str 104, Postfach 415

Bonner Buchgemeinde (BBG)*, Endenicherstr 104, Postfach 1246, D-5300 Bonn

Buchclub 69 GmbH, Hofweg 12, Postfach 13, D-8702 Würzburg-Veitshöchheim
Owned by: Verlag Andreas Zettner KG (qv)

Christlicher Bildungskreis Verlags GmbH*, D-7000 Stuttgart 1, Lindenspürstr 32, Postfach 285

Deutsche Buch-Gemeinschaft C A Koch's Verlag Nachfolger*, Berliner Allee 6, Postfach 4131, D-6100 Darmstadt
Owned by: Deutsche Buch-Gemeinschaft C A Koch's Verlag Nachfolger

Deutsche Hausbücherei GmbH*, D-2000 Hamburg 36, Gr Theaterstr 32

Deutscher Bücherbund GmbH, Libanonstr 3-5, D-7000 Stuttgart 1
Owned by: Georg von Holtzbrinck (at above address)

Deutscher Buchkreis, D-7400 Tübingen, Postfach 1629
Owned by: Grabert-Verlag (Tübingen) (qv)
Tel: (07071) 61206 Telex: 7262863 grav-d

Freundeskreis des **Euphorion** Verlags*, D-6000 Frankfurt am Main 50, Neumannstr 13
Members: 28
Founded: 1976
Owned by: Euphorion Verlag (Frankfurt am Main)

Europäische Bildungsgemeinschaft Verlags GmbH, D-7000 Stuttgart 1, Lindenspürstr 32, Postfach 1069

Europarings der Buch- und Schallplattenfreunde*, D-4830 Gütersloh, Carl-Bertelsmann-Str 270
Owned by: Verlagsgruppe Bertelsmann GmbH

Evangelische Buchgemeinde GmbH*, Libanonstr 3-5, D-7000 Stuttgart 1
Owned by: Georg von Holtzbrinck (at above address)

Fackel-Buchklub, Verlags- und Vertriebs GmbH*, D-7000 Stuttgart 1, Herdweg 29-31, Postfach 442
See Fackelverlag G Bowitz GmbH

Herder Buchgemeinde, Hermann-Herder-Str 4, D-7800 Freiburg im Breisgau
Owned by: Verlag Herder (Freiburg im Breisgau)

Herold Buch-Club*, D-8000 Munich 70, Waldgarten Str 66
Owned by: Vereinigte Herold Verlage (Munich)

Kosmos Gesellschaft*, D-7000 Stuttgart 1, Pfizerstr 5-7, Postfach 640
Owned by: Franckh'sche Verlagshandlung W Keller & Co (Stuttgart)

Kunstkreis für Bibliophile Mappen*, D-665 Homburg-Schwarzenacker/Saar
Owned by: Edition Monika Beck (qv)

Verlag für **Lehr- und Lernmittel**, D-7800 Freiburg im Breisgau, Richard-Strauss-Str 11

Verlag Das Beste GmbH **Reader's Digest***, Augustenstr 1, D-7000 Stuttgart 1 Tel: (0711) 66021 Telex: 0723539

Verlag Wilhelm **Rubsamen***, D-7000 Stuttgart 1, Reinsburgstr 102

Volksverband der Bücherfreunde Verlag GmbH*, Harvestehuder Weg 41, D-2000 Hamburg 13

Wissenschaftliche Buchgesellschaft*, Hindenburgstr 40, Postfach 111129, D-6100 Darmstadt 11
Owned by: Wissenschaftliche Buchgesellschaft (Publisher), Darmstadt (qv)

Major Booksellers

Artibus et Literis, Friedrichstr 26, D-4000 Düsseldorf 1
Worldwide export and import of books and journals
Parent Company: The bookseller Stern-Verlag Janssen & Co (qv)

Buchhandlung G D **Baedeker***, D-4300 Essen 1, Kettwiger Str 33-35, Postfach 128 Tel: (02141) 221381

Blazek und Bergmann*, Inhaber Dr Hans Bergmann, Universitätsbuchhandlung, D-6000 Frankfurt am Main 1, Goethestr 1 Tel: (0611) 288648

Universitätsbuchhandlung **Bouvier** GmbH, D-5300 Bonn 1, Am Hof 32 Tel: (02221) 654445

Buchhandlung **Elwert und Meurer** GmbH, D-1000 Berlin 62, Hauptstr 101 Tel: (030) 784001

F B V Frauenbuchvertrieb GmbH*, Mehringdamm 32-34, D-1000 Berlin 61 Tel: (030) 2511666
Books written by women for women and published by women; subjects relating to women's movements

Buchhandlung Heinrich **Gonski***, D-5000 Cologne 1, Neumarkt 24 Tel: (0221) 210528

Grossohaus Wegner und Co, Conventstr 14, Postfach 102540, D-2000 Hamburg 1 Tel: (040) 25761 Telex: (02) 15096 Cable Add: Grossohaus Hamburg
Wholesaler and Exporter of German books, including those in the English language published in German-speaking countries

Hamburger Kommissionsbuchhandlung GmbH*, D-2000 Hamburg 36, Postfach 303430 Tel: (040) 341061
Wholesaler; branch of Georg Lingenbrink (qv)

Otto **Harrassowitz***, Taunusstr 6, Postfach 2929, D-6200 Wiesbaden Tel: (06121) 521046

Buchhandlung H **Hugendubel**, D-8000 Munich 1, Salvatorpl 2 Tel: (089) 226646

Internationale Presse, Import- und Export GmbH, Borsigallee 17, D-6000 Frankfurt am Main 60 Tel: (0611) 419198 Cable Add: Airedition Frankfurt Telex: 4189645 ip d
Book and Periodical Wholesaler representing companies in France, Italy, Portugal, Spain, United Kingdom, United States
Managing Director and Associate: Gustav Stuekrath
Founded: 1946

Buchhandlung Christian **Kaiser***, D-8000 Munich 2, Marienplatz 8 Tel: (089) 223441
Owned by: Fritz Lempp

Koch, Neff und Oetinger und Co*, Am Wallgraben 110, Postfach 800620, D-7000 Stuttgart 80 Tel: (0711) 78603325/78603352 Telex: 07255684 knov d stgt
Wholesaler

Barsortiment Georg **Lingenbrink** (Wholesale Bookseller)*, D-2000 Hamburg 36, Amelungstr 3-5, Postfach 303430 Tel: (040) 341061 Telex: 0214900 and 0214673 also at D-6000 Frankfurt-Preungesheim; D-5000 Cologne; D-8047 Munich-Karlsfeld; Nüremberg, Stuttgart, Berlin

J A **Mayer'sche** Buchhandlung*, D-5100 Aachen, Ursulinerstr 17-19 Tel: (0241) 22441/5 Cable Add: Mayer Aachen Telex: 832768

Vereinigte Verlagsauslieferung R **Mohn** oHG*, Carl-Bertelsmann Str 161, D-4830 Gütersloh, Postfach 7777 Tel: (05241) 853202 Telex: 0933827
Miscellaneous: Associate Company: Art Reference Reinhard Mohn oHG, Gütersloh

Hans Heinrich **Petersen** Buchimport GmbH, Rugenbarg 250, Postfach 530230, D-2000 Hamburg 53 Tel: (040) 831171-75 Cable Add d: bucHpetersen hamburg Telex: 211401 hhp d
Manager: Egon Schormann
Importer of books, journals, audiovisual material from throughout world (but especially UK, USA, Netherlands)

Pro Media Literaturvertrieb GmbH, Werner Voss Damm 54, D-1000 Berlin 42 Tel: (030) 7855971
This is a wholesale marketing organisation representing small Publishing Houses dealing with the 'Alternative Society'

Martin **Sandkühler**, Verlagsauslieferungen, Paracelsusstr 26, Postfach 720308, D-7000 Stuttgart 72 Tel: (0711) 454723

Stern-Verlag Janssen und Co, Friedrichstr 24-26, D-4000 Düsseldorf 1, Postfach 7820 Tel: (0211) 373033
Managing Partners: Horst and Klaus Janssen
Subsidiary Company: The bookseller Artibus et Literis (qv)
Worldwide export and import of books and journals

V V A (Vereinigte Verlagsauslieferung) Reinhard Mohn*, (United Publishers Deliveries), Carl-Bertelsmann Str 161, D-4830 Gütersloh Tel: (05241) 85 Telex: 0933827
Wholesale Book Supplier

Buchhandlung **Wendelin** Niedlich KG, D-7000 Stuttgart 1, Schmale Str 9 Tel: (0711) 223287

Buchhandlung Konrad **Wittwer** KG, D-7000 Stuttgart 1, Königstr 30 Tel: (0711) 250211 Telex: 723751

Major Libraries

Bayerische Staatsbibliothek, Ludwigstr 16, Postfach 150, D-8000 Munich 34 Tel: (089) 21981
Librarian: Dr F G Kaltwasser

Bibliothek für Zeitgeschichte, Konrad-Adenauer-Strasse 8, D-7000 Stuttgart 1, Postfach 769 Tel: (0711) 244117
Library for Contemporary History
Director: Professor Dr Jürgen Rohwer
Publications: Jahresbibliographie, Schriften der Bibliothek für Zeitgeschichte, Dokumentationen der BfZ, Wehrtechnik im Bild
Miscellaneous: Special Subjects: International Literature on history of wars, revolutions and military sciences; international 20th-century politics
Library is housed in same building as the Württembergische Landesbibliothek (qv) but has separate administration

Bundesarchiv (National Archives), D-5400 Koblenz, Am Wöllershof 12

Deutsche Bibliothek (National Library), D-6000 Frankfurt am Main 1, Zeppelinallee 4-8 Tel: (0611) 75661 Telex: 416643 denbi

Herzog August Bibliothek*, D-3340 Wolfenbüttel, Lessingplatz 1, Postfach 227 Tel: (05331) 5081

Hessische Landes- und Hoch-schulbibliothek Darmstadt, D-6100 Darmstadt, Schloss Tel: (06151) 124420

Ibero-Amerikanisches Institut*, Preussischer Kulturbesitz, Potsdamer Str 37, D-1000 Berlin 30 Tel: (030) 2662500

Bibliothek des **Instituts für Weltwirtschaft** — Zentralbibliothek der Wirtschaftswissenschaften*, Düsternbrooker Weg 120-122, Postfach 4309, D-2300 Kiel 1 Tel: (0431) 8841 Telex: 0292479
Library of the Institute for World Economics — National Library of Economics

Niedersächsische Staats- und Universitätsbibliothek, D-3400 Göttingen, Prinzenstr 1, Postfach 318 Tel: (0551) 395212 (Secretariat)
Librarian: Dir Helmut Vogt

Staats- und Universitätsbibliothek, D-2000 Hamburg 13, Moorweidenstr 40 Tel: (040) 41232213

Staatsbibliothek Bamberg*, D-8600 Bamberg, Neue Residenz, Domplatz 8 Tel: (0951) 53014

Staatsbibliothek Preussischer Kulturbesitz, Potsdamer Str 33, Postfach 1407, D-1000 Berlin 30 Tel: (030) 2661 Telex 183160 staab d
State Library of the Prussian Cultural Foundation
Director: Dr Ekkehart Vesper
Publications: Jahresbericht (irregular); *Mitteilungen* (quarterly); *ZDB — Zeitschriften-Datenbank* (Periodicals' Data Bank), in association with das Deutsche Bibliotheksinstitut and Publisher Otto Harrassowitz (qv)
ISBN Publisher's Prefix: 3-88053

Stadt- und Universitätsbibliothek*, Bockenheimer Landstr 134-138, D-6000 Frankfurt am Main 1 Tel: (0611) 79071 Telex: 414024 stub d
Director: Mr Lehmann

Universitäts- und Stadtbibliothek*, Universitätsstr 33, D-5000 Cologne 41 Tel: (0221) 4702260/4702214

Universitätsbibliothek, Werthmannpl 2, Postfach 1629, D-7800 Freiburg Tel: (0761) 2033901 (management); 2034000 (enquiries); 2033940 (main reading room)

Universitätsbibliothek der Eberhard-Karls-Universität*, D-7400 Tübingen 1, Wilhelmstr 32, Postfach 2620 Tel: (07071) 292577

Universitätsbibliothek Erlangen-Nürnberg, Universitätsstr 4/Schuhstr 1a, D-8520 Erlangen Tel: (09131) 852151

Universitätsbibliothek Heidelberg, Plöck 107-109, Postfach 105749, D-6900 Heidelberg 1 Tel: (06221) 542380

Württembergische Landesbibliothek, Konrad-Adenauer-Str 8, Postfach 769, D-7000 Stuttgart 1 Tel: (0711) 2125424
Württemberg State Library
Director: Dr Hans-Peter Geh
Miscellaneous: The Bibliothek für Zeitgeschichte (Library for Contemporary History) — qv — is housed in same building, but has separate administration

Library Associations

Arbeitsgemeinschaft der Hochschulbibliotheken, c/o Universitätsbibliothek, Olshausenstr 29, D-2300 Kiel
Joint Association of Academic Libraries
Chairman: Dr G Wiegand

Arbeitsgemeinschaft der kirchlichen Büchereiverbände Deutschlands, D-5300 Bonn, Wittelsbacherring 9
Joint Association of Library Associations of the Churches in Germany
Executive Secretary: Erich Hodick

Arbeitsgemeinschaft der Kunstbibliotheken, c/o Bibliothek des Germanischen Nationalmuseums, Kartäusergasse 1, Postfach 9580, D-8500 Nuremberg
Joint Association of Art Libraries

Arbeitsgemeinschaft der Parlaments- und Behördenbibliotheken, Bibliothek des Deutschen Bundestages, Bundeshaus, D-5300 Bonn
Joint Association of Parliamentary and Administration Libraries
Chairman: Wolfgang Dietz; *Executive Secretary:* Heinz-Ottmar Schmidt
Publications: Arbeitshefte (Work Programmes) and *Mitteilungen* (News Sheets)

Arbeitsgemeinschaft der Regionalbibliotheken, Staats- und Stadtbibliothek, Schaezlerstr 25, D-8900 Augsburg
Joint Association of Regional Libraries
President: Josef Bellot

Arbeitsgemeinschaft der Spezialbibliotheken eV, Universitätsbibliothek der Technischen Universität Berlin, Str des 17 Juni 135, D-1000 Berlin 12 (Charlottenburg) Tel: (030) 3143671 Telex: 0183872 ubtu d

Joint Association of Special Libraries
Executive Secretary: Ingeborg Pohle
Publication: Bericht über die Tagung (Conference Report; every 2 years)

Arbeitsgemeinschaft für das Archiv- und Bibliothekswesen in der evangelischen Kirche, Veilhofstr 28, D-8500 Nuremberg
Joint Association for Archives and Libraries in the Evangelical Church
President: Dr Helmut Baier
Publications: Mitteilungen der AABevK (AABevK News Bulletin); *Veröffentlichungen der AABevK* (Publications of the AABevK)

Arbeitsgemeinschaft für juristische Bibliotheks- und Dokumentationswesen, c/o Renate Bellmann, Bibliothek des Juristischen Seminars der Universität, D-7400 Tübingen
Joint Association for Law Libraries and Legal Documentation
Chairperson: Renate Bellman
Publications: Mitteilungen der Arbeitsgemeinschaft für juristisches Bibliotheks- und Dokumentationswesen (3 times yearly) and *Arbeitshefte* (irregularly)

Arbeitsgemeinschaft für medizinisches Bibliothekswesen, c/o Joseph-Stelzmann-Str 9, D-5000 Cologne-Lindenthal
Joint Association for Medical Libraries

Arbeitsgemeinschaft katholischtheologischer Bibliotheken, c/o Bibliothek des Priesterseminars, Postfach 1330, D-5500 Trier
Joint Association of Catholic Theological Libraries
Dir: Dr Franz Rudolf Reichert
Publication: Mitteilungsblatt

Arbeitsstelle für das Bibliothekswesen, see Deutscher Bibliotheksverband

Bundesarbeitsgemeinschaft der katholisch-kirchlichen Büchereiarbeit, Wittelsbacherring 9, D-5300 Bonn
National Joint Association of Library work in the Catholic Church
Executive Secretary: Erich Hodick

Deutsche Gesellschaft für Dokumentation eV, Westendstr 19, D-6000 Frankfurt am Main 1
German Society for Documentation
President: Prof Dip Ing P Canisius
Publication: Nachrichten für Dokumentation (5 a year)

Deutscher Bibliotheksverband eV*, Fehrbelliner Platz 3, D-1000 Berlin 31 Tel: (030) 860245 Telex: 184166 afbbl d
German Library Association — Publications Dept
Manager: Helmut Rösner, Berlin
Publications: Bibliotheksdienst (monthly), *INSPEL* (quarterly), *musikbibliothek aktuel* (quarterly), *schulbibliothek aktuel* (quarterly), *Scandinavian Public Library Quarterly*, several reference books, monographs, bibliographical and statistical services

Deutscher Leihbuchhändler-Verband eV (German Circulating Libraries Federation)*, D-4600 Dortmund-Marten, Martener Str 317 Tel: 614089

Deutscher Verband evangelischer Büchereien eV, Bürgerstr 2, D-3400 Gottingen
German Association of Evangelical (Protestant) Libraries

172 FEDERAL REPUBLIC OF GERMANY

Gesellschaft für Bibliothekswesen und Dokumentation des Landbaues (GBDL), Paracelsusstr 2, D-7000 Stuttgart 70 Tel: (0711) 4701-2111
Society for Librarianship and Documentation in Agriculture
Publication: Mitteilungen der Gesellschaft für Bibliothekswesen und Dokumentation des Landbaues

Gesellschaft für Information und Dokumentation mbH (GID), Sektion für Technik, Postfach 710370, D-6000 Frankfurt am Main 71 (Located at: Herriotstr 5)
This organization continues work previously done by the Zentralstelle für maschinelle Dokumentation

Institut für Dokumentations-wesen (Institute for Documentation Science)*, D-6000 Frankfurt am Main — Niederrad, Herriotstr 5, Postfach 710350
Dir: Dr Martin Cremer

Institut für Jugendbuchforschung der J W Goethe-Universität*, Georg Voigt-Str 10, D-6000 Frankfurt am Main
Institute for Research into Books for the Young

Internationale Vereinigung der Musikbibliotheken, Deutsche Gruppe BRD, Städtische Musikbibliothek, Salvatorpl 1, D-8000 Munich 2
German Section of the International Association of Music Libraries
Secretary-General: Brigitta Kohl

Verband der Bibliotheken des Landes Nordrhein-Westfalen*, c/o Frau Renate Baumhoff, Maischützenstr 57, D-4630 Bochum
Association of Libraries of North Rhine-Westphalia
Secretariat: at above address; *Editorial:* Universitätsbibliothek, D-5300 Bonn
Publication: Mitteilungsblatt (News Sheet)

Verband deutscher Werkbibliotheken eV, c/o BASF Aktiengesellschaft, Werkbücherei, Carl-Bosch Str, D-6700 Ludwigshafen Tel: (0621) 603689
Association of Industrial Libraries of the Federal Republic of Germany
President: Christiane Lüderssen

Verein Angehörige des mittleren und nichtdiplomierten Bibliotheksdienstes eV (Association of Nonprofessional Librarians)*, Bremen, Klattenweg 59
Secretary: Melitta Thomas

Verein der Bibliothekare an öffentlichen Büchereien eV, Roonstr 57, D-2800 Bremen
Association of Public Librarians
President: Dip-Bibl Karl-Heinz Pröve
Publication: Buch und Bibliothek

Verein der Diplom-Bibliothekare an Wissenschaftlichen Bibliotheken eV, Universitätsbibliothek, D-4630 Bochum 1, Postfach 102148 Tel: (0234) 7005200
Association of Certified Librarians at Academic Libraries
Chairman: Ingeborg Sobottke
Publication: Rundschreiben

Verein Deutscher Archivare (VdA), Hessisches Staatsarchiv, Schloss, D-6100 Darmstadt
Association of German Archivists

Chairman: Dr Eckhart G Franz
Publication: Verzeichnis der Archivare (Register of Archivists) — at irregular intervals of several years

Verein deutscher Bibliothekare eV, Universitätsbibliothek Stuttgart, Holzgartenstr 16, D-7000 Stuttgart 1
Association of German Librarians
President: Juergen Hering
Publications: Zeitschrift für Bibliothekswesen und Bibliographie; Jahrbuch der deutschen Bibliotheken

Verein deutscher Dokumentare eV, Postfach 2509, D-5300 Bonn
Association of German Documentalists and Information Officers
Publication: Nachrichten für Dokumentation, D-6000 Frankfurt am Main 1, Westendstr 19

Württembergische Bibliotheksgesellschaft, Postfach 769, D-7000 Stuttgart (Located at: Konrad-Adenauer Str 8)
Society of Friends of the Württemberg State Library
Secretary: Dr Gerhard Römer

Zentralstelle für maschinelle Dokumentation, see Gesellschaft für Information und Dokumentation

Library Reference Books and Journals

Books

Bibliothekswesen in Deutschland (Library Science in Germany), German Publishers' and Booksellers' Association, D-6000 Frankfurt 1, Großer Hirschgraben 17-21

Handbuch des Büchereiwesens (Handbook of Library Science), Verlag Otto Harrassowitz, D-6200 Wiesbaden, Taunusstr 6, Postfach 2929

Jahrbuch der Deutschen Bibliotheken (Yearbook of German Libraries), Verlag Otto Harrassowitz, D-6300 Wiesbaden 1, Taunusstr 6, Postfach 2929

Libraries in the Federal Republic of Germany, Verlag Otto Harrassowitz, D-6200 Wiesbaden 1, Taunusstr 6, Postfach 2929

Sigelverzeichnis für die Bibliotheken der Bundesrepublik Deutschland und West-Berlins (Classification List for the Libraries of the BRD and West Berlin), State Library of Prussian Cultural Foundation, D-1000 Berlin 30, Potsdamer Str 33, Postfach 1407

Verzeichnis der Archivare (Register of Archivists), Verein deutscher Archivare, Hessisches Staatsarchiv, Schloss, D-6100 Darmstadt

Verzeichnis der Spezialbibliotheken in der Bundesrepublik Deutschland einschl West Berlin (List of Special Libraries in the BRD including West Berlin), Friedr Vieweg & Sohn Verlagsgesellschaft mbH, D-6200 Wiesbaden, Gustav-Stresemann-Ring 12-16, Postfach 5829

Journals

Bibliotheksdienst (Library Service), German Library Association — Publications Dept, Fehrbelliner Platz 3, D-1000 Berlin 31

Buch und Bibliothek (Book and Library), K G Saur KG, D-8000 Munich 71, Pössenbacherstr 2

Dokumentation, Fachbibliothek, Werksbücherei (DFW) *Zeitschrift für Allgemein- und Spezial-bibliotheken, Büchereien und Dokumentationsstellen* (Documentation, Technical Libraries, Works Libraries, Journal for General and Special Libraries and Documentation Centres), Nordwestverlag Stephanie Schräpel, D-3000 Hanover-Waldhausen, Güntherstr 21

INSPEL, German Library Association — Publications Dept, Fehrbelliner Platz 3, D-1000 Berlin 31

Musikbibliothek aktuell (Music Library Today), German Library Association — Publications Dept, Fehrbelliner Platz 3, D-1000 Berlin 31

Nachrichten für Dokumentation (News for Documentation), German Society for Documentation, D-6000 Frankfurt am Main 1, Westendplatz 29

das neue buch: book profile for Catholic library work, Borromäusverein, Wittelsbacherring 9, D-5300 Bonn; St Michaelsbund, Herzog-Wilhelmstr 5, D-8000 Munich 2

schulbibliothek aktuell (School Library Today), German Library Association — Publications Dept, Fehrbelliner Platz 31, D-1000 Berlin 3

Zeitschrift für Bibliothekswesen und Bibliographie (Journal of Library Science and Bibliography), Association of German Librarians, Universitätsbibliothek der technischen Universität Braunschweig, Pockelstr 13, D-3300 Braunschweig, Strasse des 17 Juni 135, D-1000 Berlin 12

Zentralblatt für Bibliothekswesen (Central Journal for Library Science), Verlag Otto Harrassowitz, D-6200 Wiesbaden, Taunusstr 6, Postfach 2929

Literary Associations and Societies

Akademie der Wissenschaften und der Literatur (Academy of Sciences, Arts and Literature), D-6500 Mainz, Geschwister-Schollstr 2
Secretary-General: Dr G Brenner
Publications: Jahrbuch, Abhandlungen, Forschungsreihen
Large number of learned studies in fields of Literature, Mathematics, History, and the Sciences and Arts generally; Periodicals

Arbeitsgemeinschaft wissenschaftliche Literatur eV, PO Box 21086, D-6000 Frankfurt am Main
Joint Association for Scientific Literature
Director: Peter Czerwonka

Arbeitskreis für Jugendliteratur eV (Youth Literature Committee) (Section of the International Board on Books for Young People)*, Elisabethstr 15, D-8000 Munich 40
Man Dir: R Majonica

Deutsche Akademie für Sprache und Dichtung, Glückert-Haus, Alexandraweg 23, D-6100 Darmstadt Tel: 44823
German Academy of Language and Poetry. It is responsible for the administration of a number of literary prizes

Deutsche Shakespeare-Gesellschaft West eV, D-4630 Bochum, Rathaus
West German Shakespeare Society
President: Professor Dr Habicht
Publications: Shakespeare Jahrbuch

Deutsches Jugendschriftenwerk (German Children's Writers), Frankfurt, Kurt-Schumacher-Str 1

Gutenberg-Gesellschaft (Gutenberg Society)*, D-6500 Mainz, Liebfrauenplatz 5
Chairman: Professor Dr H Widmann
Publications: Gutenberg-Jahrbuch, Kleine Drucke, Veröffentlichungen

Literarischer Verein in Stuttgart eV, Rosenbergstr 113, Postfach 723, D-7000, Stuttgart 1 Tel: (0711) 638265
Stuttgart Literary Society
Founded: 1839
Publication: Bibliothek des Literarischen Vereins in Stuttgart Vol 1 (1842) — Vol 300 (1978) — ISSN 0340 — 7888: about 1 vol per year
Published by Anton Hiersemann Verlag (qv) at above address
The aim of the Society is to publish the texts of valuable unpublished manuscripts and old printed texts in a new form — especially with regard to old German literature

P E N Zentrum Bundesrepublik Deutschland, Sandstr 10, D-6100 Darmstadt
Secretary-General: Martin Gregor-Dellin

Literary Periodicals

Akzente (Accents); journal for literature, Carl Hanser Verlag, D-8000 Munich 80, Kolberger Str 22, Postfach 860420

Bücherkommentare (Book Commentaries); journal for book criticism, Verlag Rombach, D-7800 Freiburg im Breisgau, Lörracher Str 3, Postfach 1349

Bücherschiff (Book Galley); the German book journal, Verlag Bücherschiff Walter Reutin, D-7500 Karlsruhe 21, Rheinstr 122, Postfach 210947

Bulletin Jugend + Literatur (Youth and Literature Bulletin), Lesen Verlag GmbH, Eulenhof, D-2351 Hardebek

Deutschheft (German Number), Verlag Pohl und Mayer, Postfach 24, Kaufbeuren

Epitaph; young journal for literature, D-8000 Munich 40, Belgradstr 24

Formation, Zur Halle 5, D-6751 Sulybachtal 1, Kaiserlauten-Land

Imprint; the literary journal for German-language literature, Lesen Verlag GmbH, Eulenhof, D-2351 Hardebek

Lektüre (Reading), Lektüre Verlagsgesellschaft mbH, Friedrichstr 13, D-8000 Munich 40

Literarische Hefte (Literary Magazine), Raith Verlag, D-8000 Munich 2, Herzog Heinrich Str 21

Literarische Umschau (Literary Review), Verlag Marie Hemmerle 1, D-8000 Munich 70, Pullacherstr

Literat (Man of Letters); journal for literature and art, Verband deutscher Schriftsteller Hessen, D-6000 Frankfurt am Main, Goethestr 29

Literature, Music, Fine Arts; a review of German-language research contributions on literature, music, and fine arts (text in English), Institut für Wissenschaftliche Zusammenarbeit (Institute for Scientific Co-operation), D-7400 Tübingen, Landhusstr 18

Litfass, Berlin journal for literature, Ostpreussendamm 159, D-1000 Berlin 45 Tel: (030) 7728339

Neue Rundschau (New Review), Fischer Verlag, D-6000 Frankfurt am Main, Mainzer Landstr 10–12

Text und Kritik (Text and Criticism); journal for literature, Edition Text und Kritik, D-8000 Munich 80, Levelingstr 6a

Universitas; journal for science, art and literature (editions in German, English and Spanish), Wissenschaftliche Verlagsgesellschaft mbH, Birkenwald Str 44, Postfach 40, D-7000 Stuttgart 1

Viergroschenbogen ('Four Groschen Sheets'); journal for contemporary literature and art), Relief-Verlag-Eilers, D-8000 Munich 2, Martin Greif Str 3

Wissenschaft-Literaturanzeiger (Scientific Literature Advertiser), Verlag Rombach, Lörracher Str 3, Postfach 1349, D-7800 Freiburg im Breisgau

Wolfenbütteler Notizen zur Buchgeschichte (Wolfenbütteler Notes on Book History), Pöseldorfer Weg 1, D-2000 Hamburg 13

Literary Prizes

Georg Büchner Prize
Founded in 1923 by Volksstaat Hessen, it has been given since 1951 by the Academy to writers who have been especially noteworthy through their work and have contributed to the current cultural scene in Germany. 20,000 DM. Awarded annually. Enquiries to Deutsche Akademie für Sprache und Dichtung, Glückert-Haus, Alexandraweg 23, D-6100 Darmstadt

Konrad Duden Prize
For special achievement in the German language; co-sponsored by the Bibliographical Institute. 10,000 DM. Awarded every two years. Applications are not invited. Enquiries to Stadt Mannheim, Hauptamt, Rathaus E5, D-6800 Mannheim 1

Theodor Fontane Prize
Founded in 1948 and given for a single work or a body of work. 30,000 marks. Awarded every six years. Enquiries to Akademie der Künste, Hanseatenweg 10, D-1000 Berlin 21

Sigmund Freud Prize
For a scientific presentation in prose. 10,000 DM. Awarded annually. Enquiries to Deutsche Akademie für Sprache und Dichtung, Glückert-Haus, Alexandraweg 23, D-6100 Darmstadt

Goethe Prize
Founded in 1927 for work showing the value of, or respect for Goethe's ideals and thoughts. 50,000 marks. Awarded every three years. Enquiries to Amt für Wissenschaft und Kunst, Brückenstr 3-7, D-6000 Frankfurt am Main 70

Friedrich Gundolf Prize for Germanistics abroad
For essays in German. 6,000 DM. Awarded annually. Enquiries to Deutsche Akademie für Sprache und Dichtung, Alexandraweg 23, Glückert-Haus, D-6100 Darmstadt

Immermann Prize*
For the work of a living author or poet born within the borders of Germany since 1937. 20,000 marks awaaarded every three years. Enquiries to Düsseldorf City Cultural Office, D-4000 Düsseldorf, Kaiserstr 44

The Alfred **Kerr** Prize for Literary Criticism
Founded in 1976/77 by the Börsenblatt für den deutschen Buchhandel (German Book Trade Gazette). 5,000 DM plus a Certificate and the reimbursement of expenses incurred by the Presentation Ceremony. Awarded annually. For outstanding continuing literary criticism in a German newspaper, magazine, or TV or radio programme. Won in 1978 by the Literary Editorial of the *Deutsches Allgemeines Sonntagsblatt*. Enquiries to Redaktion Börsenblatt, Chefredakteur Hanns Lothar Schütz, Grosser Hirschgraben 17-21, D-6000 Frankfurt am Main

Lessing Prize
To poets, writers, scholars in German cultural fields who are able to meet the challenge represented by the name of Lessing. 30,000 marks (less 10,000 for foundation fees). Awarded every four years. Enquiries to Kulturbehörde der Freien und Hansestadt Hamburg, Hamburgerstr 45, D-2000 Hamburg 76

Literature Prize
To a poet or writer for his whole work. A monetary prize awarded annually (no award in 1979). Enquiries to Bayerische Akademie der Schönen Künste, Max Joseph Platz 3, D-8000 Munich 22

Thomas Mann Prize
Founded in 1975 in honour of Thomas Mann to celebrate the 100th anniversary of his birth. The prize will be awarded to personalities who have, through their literary work, shown the humanitarian spirit set out in the work of Thomas Mann. 10,000 marks. Awarded every three years. Enquiries to Der Senat der Hansestadt Lübeck, Amt für Kultur, Rathaushof, Postfach, D-2400 Lübeck 1

Johann Heinrich Merck Prize
For literary criticism. 10,000 DM. Awarded annually. Enquiries to Deutsche Akademie für Sprache und Dichtung, Glückert-Haus, Alexandraweg 23, D-6100 Darmstadt

Rheinland-Palatinate Prize
Founded in 1956 for a single work or body of work in literature (as well as fine art and music). Winner should be closely related to the area. 10,000 marks. Enquiries to Rheinland-Palatinate Ministry of Education, Mittlere Bleiche 61, D-6500 Mainz 1

Nelly Sachs Prize
The cultural prize of Dortmund City, instituted by the Dortmund City Council in 1961. Awarded every 2 years: current value

20,000 DM. 1979 winner: Erich Fromm. Enquiries to Kulturamt der Stadt Dortmund, Karl-Marx-Strasse 24, D-4600 Dortmund 1

Schiller Prize
For outstanding achievements in the cultural field. 25,000 DM. Awarded every four years; applications are not invited. Enquiries to Stadt Mannheim, Hauptamt, Rathaus E5, D-6800 Mannheim 1

Johann Heinrich **Voss** Translation Prize
For a single work or life's work in translation. 6,000 DM. Awarded annually. Enquiries to Deutsche Akademie für Sprache und Dichtung, Glückert-Haus, Alexandraweg 23, D-6100 Darmstadt

Carl **Zuckmayer** Medal
Instituted 1978 by the Minister President of Rheinland-Pfalz (Rhineland Palatinate). First award was made in 1979 to Günther Fleckenstein. The award is for those whose services to the German language make them worthy of honour in memory of Carl Zuckmayer, the noted German dramatist and poet. Enquiries to Rheinland-Pfalz Kulturministerium, Mittlere Bleiche 61, D-6500 Mainz 1

Translation Agencies and Associations

Babylon Übersetzungen*. Texts, Copyrights. Düsseldorfer Str 38, D-1000 Berlin 15 Tel: (030) 8838296
Man Dir: Walter Bengs

Bundesverband der Dolmetscher und Übersetzer eV (BDÜ), Schlossallee 9, D-5300 Bonn 2 Tel: (02221) 345000
Federal German Association of Interpreters and Translators
Secretary: Georg Frantz
Publication: Mitteilungsblatt für Dolmetscher und Übersetzer (Interpreters' and Translators' News Sheet), six times per year

Verband deutschsprachiger Übersetzer literarischer und wissenschaftlicher Werke eV (VDÜ), Fürststr 17, D-7400 Tübingen Tel: (07071) 32493
Association of German-speaking translators of Literary and Scientific Works
Dir: Ursula Brackmann
Publication: Der Übersetzer (monthly)

Ghana

General Information

Language: English
Religion: About 40 per cent Christian, remainder follow traditional beliefs
Population: 10.5 million
Bank Hours: 0830-1400 Monday-Thursday; 0830-1500 Friday
Shop Hours: 0800-1200, 1400-1730 Monday-Friday
Currency: 100 pesawas = 1 cedi
Export/Import Information: No tariffs on books; advertising matter over 1 kg gross weight 50%. Import licence required, but single copies of books under Open General Licence. Levy of 10% charged on import licenses required
Exchange controls: Some movement toward centralized control of economy
Copyright: UCC, Florence (see International section)

Book Trade Organizations

Ghana Booksellers' Association*, PO Box 899, Accra

Ghana National Book Development Council, Education Loop, PO Box M430, Accra Tel: 29178 Cable Add: Ghanabook Accra

Book Trade Reference Journal

Ghana National Bibliography, c/o Research Library on African Affairs, PO Box 2970, Accra

Publishers

Advance Publishing Co Ltd*, New Town Rd, PO Box 2317, Accra New Town
Tel: 21577
Man Dir: A O Mills
Subjects: General Nonfiction, Paperbacks

Afram Publications (Ghana) Ltd*, 29 Ring Road East, PO Box M18, Accra
Tel: 74248 Cable Add: Aframbooks
Telex: 2171 SIC Accra
Man Dir, Rights & Permissions: Kwesi Sam-Woode; *Editor:* Akosua Ofori-Mensah; *Sales, Publicity:* Emman A Manful (Marketing Officer); *Production:* Kofi A Duker
The Company is partly owned by the State Insurance Corporation of Ghana
Subjects: General Fiction, Belles Lettres, Poetry, Biography, History, Africana, How-to Study Guides, Religion, General and Social Science, Paperbacks, Secondary and Primary Schools Text Books
1978: 38 titles *Founded:* 1974

Africa Christian Press*, PO Box 30, Achimota Tel: 77553
General Secretary: Donald Banks; *Sales Manager:* P Addo
Subjects: Christian Fiction & Nonfiction, Biography, Paperbacks and Booklets. No Tracts. Priority is given to African writers
Founded: 1964
ISBN Publisher's Prefix: 85352

Anowuo Educational Publications*, 2R McCarthy Hill, PO Box 3918, Accra
Tel: 24910
Man Dir: S A Konadu
Subjects: Africana, How-to, Study Guides, Reference, Juveniles, Books in Ghanaian Languages, Paperbacks, General Science, Secondary Textbooks, General Fiction, Belles Lettres, Poetry, History
Miscellaneous: also Booksellers and Sales Representatives of Overseas Publishing Houses
Founded: 1966

Benibengor Book Agency*, PO Box 40, Aboso
Man Dir: J Benibengor Blay
Subjects: General Fiction, Belles Lettres, Poetry, Biography, Juveniles, Paperbacks

Bureau of Ghana Languages, PO Box 1851, Accra Tel: 64130/65194/65461 ext 513
Cable Add: Velbo, Accra, Ghana
Dir: F S Konu; *Sales Manager:* A A Amartey; *Rights and Permissions:* F S Konu
Br Off: PO Box 177, Tamale, Northern Region, Ghana
Subjects: Fiction, Drama, Poetry, Biography, Science, School Text Books, Dictionaries, Bibliographies, Material for New Literates. Books are published in 11 Ghanaian languages
1977: 63 titles *Founded:* 1951

Editorial and Publishing Services*, PO Box 5743, Accra
Man Dir: M Danquah
Subjects: General, Reference

Encyclopaedia Africana Project*, PO Box 2797, Accra Tel: 77651 Cable Add: Enafsec
Man Dir: L H Ofosu-Appiah
Subject: Reference

Frank Publishing Ltd, PO Box M414, Ministry Branch Post Office, Accra
Tel: 29510 Cable Add: Knowledge
Man Dir, Editorial, Production: Francis K Dzokoto; *Sales, Public Relations:* Moses K Dzokoto
Subjects: Secondary School Textbooks
Founded: 1976

Ghana Publishing Corporation, Publishing Division, PMB, Tema Tel: 4166/2521 (Tema); 66349 (Accra) Cable Add/Telex: Publishing Tema
Man Dir: M W Ofori; *General Manager (Publishing Division):* K B Arkorful; *Chief Editor/Rights & Permissions:* Isaac Dankyi-Mensah; *Sales Manager:* M H K Attah; *Production:* K B Arkaful; *Publicity:* Fidelis D Adzakey
Parent Company: Ghana Publishing Corp, Head Office, PO Box 4348, Accra
Printing Division: see Government Printer
Sales & Distribution Division: PO Box 3632 Accra
Br Off: at Accra, Cape Coast, Ho, Tamale, Koforidua, Hohoe, Sunyani, Bolgatanga, Kumasi, Wa, Swedru
Subjects: General Fiction & Nonfiction; Belles Lettres, Poetry, Biography, History, Africana, Languages, Reference, Juveniles, Books in Various Ghanaian languages, Paperbacks, Science & Technology, General & Social Science; University, Secondary and Primary Textbooks
Bookshops: throughout Ghana
1978: 215 titles *1979:* 228 titles *Founded:* 1965

Ghana Universities Press*, PO Box 4219, Accra Tel: 25032 Cable Add/Telex: Univpress Accra
Dir: N K Adzakey
Subjects: General Nonfiction, Belles Lettres, Poetry, Biography, History, Africana, Philosophy, Religion, Law, Paperbacks, Medicine, Psychology, Science & Technology, General & Social Science, University Textbooks
Founded: 1962

The **Government Printer** (Ghana Publishing Corporation, Printing Division)*, PO Box 124, Accra

Graphic Corporation*, Book Sales Division, Brewery Rd, PO Box 742, Accra
Subject: Reference
Subsidiary: Daily Graphic, Sunday Mirror

Moxon Paperbacks Ltd, Barnes Rd, PO Box M 160, Accra Tel: 66640
Man Dir: Chief James Moxon
Subjects: General Fiction & Nonfiction, Belles Lettres, Poetry, History, Africana, Reference, Juveniles, Guidebooks, Paperbacks
Founded: 1967
Subsidiary: The Atlas Bookshop, Ambassador Hotel Gardens, PO Box M 160, Accra

Presbyterian Book Depot Ltd*, PO Box 195, Accra, see main entry under "Major Booksellers" and range of publications under Waterville Publishing House below

Waterville Publishing House*, PO Box 195, Accra Tel: 63124/62415 Cable Add: Books Accra
Man Dir: F E Y Attipoe; *Publications Officer:* E K Asante
Parent Company: Presbyterian Book Depot Ltd (qv under Major Booksellers)
Subjects: General Fiction & Nonfiction, Belles Lettres, Poetry, Biography, History, Africana, Religion, Juveniles, Paperbacks, General & Social Science, Secondary & Primary Textbooks

Major Booksellers

Astab Books Ltd*, Osu R E, PO Box 346, Accra Tel: 76766

The **Atlas** Bookshop Ltd, Ambassador Hotel Gdns, PO Box M 160, Accra Tel: 66640

Cape Coast University Bookshop*, PMB, Cape Coast Tel: 24409

E P Book Depot* PO Box 42, Ho

Ghana Publishing Corporation, Distribution and Sales Division*, PO Box 124, Accra

Kingsway Stores, Books and Periodicals Department*, PO Box 1638, Accra

Methodist Book Depot Ltd*, Head Off: Atlantis House, Commercial St, PO Box 100, Cape Coast Tel: 2133/4 Branches at Accra, Berekum, Kumasi, Swedru, Takoradi, Tarkwa, Tema

Presbyterian Book Depot Ltd*, Thorpe Rd., PO Box 195, Accra Tel: 63124/62415 Cable Add: Books Accra
Chairman: E H Booheme; *Man Dir:* A Ott
Branches at: Accra, Tudu, Koforidua, Kumasi, Nkawkaw, Tamale, Akim Oda, Odumase, Ada
Founded: 1910
Miscellaneous: The organisation comprises bookselling, stationery supply, printing and publishing activities (see Waterville Publishing House).

Queensway Bookshop and Stores*, Bank Lane, PO Box 4276, Accra Tel: 62707 (Accra) Cable Add: Success Accra
Suppliers of Educational, Library and HMSO Publications

Universal Paper Products and Distributors Ltd*, PO Box 5233, Accra

University Bookshop*, University Post Office, Kumasi Tel: 5351

University Bookshop*, University of Ghana, PO Box 1, Legon, Accra Tel: 75381 extensions 8227, 8827, 9227

Major Libraries

Accra Technical Training Centre Library*, PO Box M 177, Accra Tel: 28344

Advanced Teacher Training College Library*, PO Box 129, Winneba Tel: 139 ext 18

American Center Library, PO Box 2288, Accra Tel: 29179

Armed Forces Library Service*, Ministry of Defence, Burma Camp, Accra Tel: 76111 ext 628

British Council Library, Liberia Road, PO Box 771, Accra Tel: 21766

Central Bureau of Statistics*, Economic Library, PO Box 1098, Accra Tel: 66512

C S I R Central Reference and Research Library*, PO Box M 32, Accra Tel: 77651
Librarian: J A Villars
Publications: Ghana Science Abstracts, Directory of Special and Research Libraries in Ghana; List of Publications by CSIR Staff, 1958-1971; Medical Research Centres in Ghana; Current Research Projects, 1973; Union List of Scientific Periodicals (1976)

Ghana Institute of Management and Public Administration, Library and Documentation Centre*, Greenhill, PO Box 50, Achimota Tel: 77625

Research Library on African Affairs*, PO Box 2970, Accra Tel: 23526, 28402
Librarian: A N deHeer
Publications: Ghana National Bibliography (annual), Current Ghana Bibliography

University of Cape Coast Library*, PMB, Cape Coast Tel: 24409 ext 370
Publication: Bulletin

University of Ghana Library, PO Box 24, Legon Tel: 75381 ext 410
Librarian: J Michael Walpole
Publications: Annual Report, Bulletin

University of Science and Technology Library*, Private Bag, Kumasi Tel: 5351 ext 235

Library Associations

Ghana Library Association*, PO Box 4105, Accra
Secretary: Francis K Dzokoto
Publication: Ghana Library Journal (bi-annual)

Ghana Library Board, Thorpe Rd, PO Box 663, Accra Tel: 62795, 65083, 66337
Publications: Ghana National Bibliography, Annual Reports

Library Reference Books and Journals

Books

Directory of Libraries in Ghana, Department of Library and Archival Studies, University of Ghana, Legon

Directory of Special and Research Libraries in Ghana, CSIR Library, PO Box M 32, Accra

Journals

Ghana Library Journal, Ghana Library Association, PO Box 4105, Accra

Literary Associations and Societies

Ghana Association of Writers*, PO Box 4414, Accra
Holds an annual writers' congress
Publications: Okyeame, Takra

Literary Periodicals

Asemka, c/o French Department, University of Cape Coast, Cape Coast (A new biennial literary magazine published since 1974)

Okyeame, Ghana Association of Writers, PO Box 4414, Accra (This journal has been defunct for some time now, but there are plans to recommence publication shortly. The Association also publishes a newsletter entitled *Takra*)

Pleisure, Moxon Paperbacks, PO Box M 160, Accra (A popular magazine with many literary contributions in each number)

Transition, PO Box 9063, Accra (Most important bi-monthly magazine serving as a forum for free and outspoken intellectual discussion in the areas of art, politics, literature, sociology and economics. Originally published in Uganda, and edited by Rajat Neogy, it is now published from Ghana and edited by the Nigerian writer Wole Soyinka)

Translation Agencies and Associations

Bureau of Ghana Languages, PO Box 1851, Accra
See entry under Publishers

Gibraltar

General Information

Language: English (both English and Spanish used commercially)
Religion: Christian (mainly Catholic) and Jewish predominantly
Population: 30,000
Bank Hours: 0900-1530 Monday-Friday, plus 1630-1800 Friday
Shop Hours: 0900-1300, 1500-2000 Monday-Friday; 0900-1300 Saturday (Jewish shops closed Saturday)
Currency: 100 pence = 1 Gibraltar pound
Export/Import Information: No tariff on books or advertising matter. No import licence. Exchange controls
Copyright: Berne, UCC see International section

Major Booksellers

The **Book Centre***, Church Lane
Junior fiction and non-fiction

Francis **Caruana***, 249 Main St

Gibraltar Bookshop, 300 Main St Tel: 71894
Manager: A Benady

Gibraltar Junior Bookshop*, Governor's Parade
Junior literature

Imperial News Agency and Bookshop*, 291/293 Main St Tel: 4823
Children and adult literature, especially paperbacks

Major Libraries

Gibraltar Garrison Library*, Library Gardens, Governor's Parade Tel: 2418
Librarian: Major (ret) J Halmshaw MBE
Local and military history. Lending service for subscribing members

Gibraltar Library Service*, 310 Main St Tel: 71564
Opened as public library in 1979

John Mackintosh Hall Library*, John Mackintosh Hall, Main St Tel: 4000
Free lending library set up under will of late John Mackintosh. Mainly adult fiction

Greece

General Information

Language: Greek
Religion: Greek Orthodox
Population: 9.28 million
Literacy Rate (1971): 84.4%
Bank Hours: 0800-1300, 1730-1930 Monday-Saturday. Some open 0800-2200 daily
Shop Hours: Vary. Generally 0800-1500 Monday, Wednesday, Saturday; 0800-1330 Tuesday, Thursday, Friday; 1630-2000 Monday-Saturday
Currency: 100 lepta = 1 drachma
Export/Import Information: No tariff on non-Greek books except children's picture books: free from EEC, 13% from other. Foreign-language advertising catalogues free from EEC, 4.2% from other; other advertising matter free from EEC, 9% from other. Children's picture books and advertising matter subject to 3% stamp duty, and books and advertising subject to small additional taxes, 0.50% University Tax and 0.15% Bank Fee, 1% Contribution for Farmer's Social Assistance. Only books printed in Greek need import licence; all advertising matter other than price lists require licence. No special exchange controls
Copyright: UCC, Berne, Florence (see International section)

Book Trade Organizations

Federation of Printing and Bookbinding Enterprises*, Psaromilingoi 22, Athens

Silogos Ecdoton Bibliopolon (Greek Publishers' Association)*, 22-24 Har. Trikoupi St, Athens
President: D Papademas

Book Trade Reference Books and Journals

Books

Greek Bibliography, Ministry to the Prime Minister's Office, General Direction of Press, Research and Cultural Relations Division, Athens

Journals

Bulletin analytique de Bibliographie hellénique (Analytical Bulletin of Hellenic Bibliography), Institut Français d'Athènes, 29-31 Odos Sina, Athens 144

New Books, bibliographic quarterly bulletin, I D Kollaros & Co Corporation 38 Stadiou St, Athens 132

O Kosmos Tou Vivliou (Book World), 43 Stadiou, Athens 141

Publishers

Alkaios-Tropaiatis*, Aristidou 5, Athens
Subjects: Literature, Children's Books

Anglo-Hellenic Publishing, D Harvey & Co, Anapiron Polemou 16, Kolonaki, Athens Tel: 7012240/3631860 Telex: 6850 ADKK
Subjects: In English: all aspects of Greek Life and Culture, General Interest. In Greek: Translations from foreign texts. Specialist in production of Greek copy, Classical or Modern, for Non-Greek Publishers

Angyra Ekdotikos Oikos*, Pireaus 18, Athens 101 Tel: (021) 5223694
Man Dir: D Papadimitriou; *Publicity, Advertising, Rights & Permissions:* Nestor Hounos
Subjects: General Fiction, Belles Lettres, Poetry, History, Religion, Juveniles, Low-priced Paperbacks, Psychology
1977: 56 titles *Founded:* 1932
Bookshop: Bookstore Angyra, Pireaus 18, Athens 101

John **Arsenides** Ekdotis*, Akadimias 57, Athens 143 Tel: (021) 618707/629538
Man Dir: John Arsenides
Subjects: Biography, History, Philosophy, Social Science

Aspioti-Elka SA*, 276 Vouliagmenis St, Athens 459 Tel: (021) 9711021/2/3 Cable Add: Elkasp Telex: 215519 GON GR
Subjects: History, Archaeology, Folklore

Assimakopouli*, 45 Harilaou Trikoupi St, Athens Tel: 611720

Astir*, Papadimitriou, Alexandros, Lycourgou 10, Athens
Subjects: Religion, especially referring to Greek Orthodox Church; Children's and Juveniles

Ekdotike **Athenon** SA, Vissarionos 1, Athens 135 Tel: (01) 3608911
Man Dirs: George A Christopoulos, John C Bastias
Subjects: History, Archaeology, Art, High-priced Paperbacks
Bookshop: Ekdotike Athenon, Omirou 11, Athens 135
1977: 54 titles *1978:* 60 titles *Founded:* 1961

Atlantis-M Pechlivanides & Co SA*, 8 Korai St, Athens 132 Tel: 3222846/3231624
Subjects: General Fiction, Nonfiction, Education, Art, Children's

Atlas-Diagoras*, Ch Trikoupi 13, Athens 142 Tel: (021) 627342

Bergadi Editions, Michel Bergadis, 4 rue Mauromichali, Athens TT 143 Tel: 3614263
Subjects: History, Sociology, Belles Lettres, Juveniles
1978: 1 title

Boukoumanis' Editions*, Ilias Boukoumanis, Mavromichali 1, Athens 143 Tel: 3606313 Cable Add: 214422 RC GR
Man Dir: Elias Boukoumanis; *Rights & Permissions:* Mrs Roee Scaras
Subjects: History, Sociology, Belles Lettres, Children's, Psychology, Education, Politics
1977: 15 titles *Founded:* 1968

Chrissi Penna — Les Editions de la Plume d'Or, 6 Argentinis Dimokratias Sq, Athens 708 Tel: (01) 3618711-2/3618503/8018250-1-2
Man Dir: Dip Eng K Papachrysanthou
Associate Company: Papachrysanthou Chryss SA (qv)
Subjects: Juvenile, Educational, Nonfiction, Political (for adult readers)
1977: 14 titles *1978:* 17 titles *Founded:* 1964

Chryssos Typos*, 28 Harilaou Trikoupi St, Athens Tel: 637945

G **Dardanos** — H Karakatsanis and Co Ltd — Gutenberg, 103 Solonos St, Athens Tel: 3600127/3626684/3624606
Also 55-57 Didotou St, Athens
Man Dir, Editorial, Publicity, Rights & Permissions: George Dardanos; *Sales:* Christos Dardanos; *Production:* Haralambos Karakatsonis
Orders to: 55-57 Didotou St, Athens
Subjects: Art, Chemistry, Physics, Mathematics, Politics, Economics
Bookshop: 103 Solonos St, Athens
1978: 70 titles *1979:* 80 titles *Founded:* 1968

Difros*, Giannis Goudelis, Akademias 57, Athens
Subjects: Modern Greek Literature

Dodoni*, Asklipiou 3, Athens 143
Subjects: Fiction, Nonfiction, Juveniles, Encyclopaedias, History, Maps

Ekdoseis **Domi** AE*, Navarinou 20, Athens 144
Subjects: History, Enycpaedias

Dorikos Makridis*, Z Pigis 4, Athens
Subjects: General Literary

P **Efstathiadis** & Sons SA, Valtetsiou St 14, Athens TT 144 Tel: 3600495/615011 Cable Add: Efbook Athens Telex: 216176
Branch Off: 34 Olympou-Diikitiriou Str, Thessalonica Tel: 511781
Subjects: English language teaching books and courses for Greek students; miscellaneous books connected with English (and some other languages)

G C **Eleftheroudakis** SA, Nikis 4, Athens 126 Tel: (00301) 3222255 Cable Add: Elefbooks Telex: 0219410 Elef GR
Man Dir: Mrs V Eleftheroudakis-Gregos
Branch Off: 2 Sinopis Str, Tower of Athens
Subjects: Greece, Dictionaries, Fiction, Juvenile, Texts in Greek, English
1979: 23 titles *Founded:* 1915
Bookshop: G C Eleftheroudakis SA, Nikis 4, Athens 126 (qv)

Ermis*, Ippokratous 20, Athens
Subjects: Paperbacks, Literary

Eteria Ellinikon Ekdoseon*, Akadimias 84, Athens 142 Tel: 3630282/3631724/3607343
Man Dir: Stavros Tavoularis; *Editorial:* by Committee; *Sales:* Dr Caounis; *Production:* Rodakis Pericles; *Publicity:* Karayannis Nicolaos
Subjects: General Fiction, Belles Lettres, Poetry, History, Philosophy, Primary Textbooks, Educational Materials
1977: 8 titles *Founded:* 1958
Bookshop: Etairia Ellinikon Ekdoseon, Ermou 44, Salonika

Ekdoseis **Filon***, Panepistimiou 10, Athens 135 Tel: (021) 311714
Subjects: Literature, Philosophy, Juveniles

Chr **Fytrakis***, Stadiou 33, Athens
Subjects: Art, Biography

Giovanis*, Zoodochou Pigis 7, Athens 142 Tel: (021) 638572
Subjects: General Science, Reference, Maps, Miscellaneous

Grafia Galaxias*, Sokratous 59, Benaki Library, Odos Anthimou Gazi, Athens

Kassandra M **Grigoris***, Solonos 73, Athens 143
Subjects: Greek History and Archaeology, Literature, Translations
Associate Companies: Imha; Athanassios Karavias; Nikolaos Karavias (qqv) all at above Athens address

Dardanos **Gutenberg**, see Dardanos
Subjects: General

Ikaros Ekdotiki*, Voulis 4, Athens
Subjects: Literature

Imha*, Solonos 73, Athens 143 Tel: 629684
Subjects: Scientific Texts on Medieval and Modern Greek History
Associate Companies: see Kassandra M Grigoris

Athanassios **Karavias***, Solonos 73 Athens 143 Tel: 629684
Subjects: Science, History
Associate Companies: see Kassandra M Grigoris

Nikolaos **Karavias***, Solonos 73, Athens 143 Tel: 629684
Subjects: Catalogues, Bibliographies, Memoirs, Modern and Medieval Greek History
Associate Companies: see Kassandra M Grigoris

Kedros, El Venizelou 44, Athens Tel: (01) 3615783/3603572
Subjects: Literature, Philosophy, Juveniles
1977: 85 titles *1978:* 140 titles

Kentavros Ekdoseis OE*, Ag Konstantinou 14, Athens 101 Tel: (021) 536553
Subjects: Poetry, Juveniles, Maps

I D **Kollaros** & Co Corporation+, 60 Solonos St, Athens 135 Tel: (021) 3635970
Publicity Manager: Evangelos Daskalou
Subjects: Fiction, History, Geography, Juveniles, Literature
1978: 70 titles
Bookshop: Hestia Bookstore, 60 Solonos St, Athens

Koutsoumbos*, 18 Fidiou St, Athens Tel: 633738/606449/601978

Koymantereas*, 83 Mavromihali St, Athens Tel: 3246188

Melissa Publishing House, Panepistimiou 34, Athens 143 Tel: (01) 3611692
Man Dir: George Rayas; *Sales Dir:* Chrys Rayas
Br Off: Tsimiski 41, Salonika
Subjects: History, Art
1978: 1 title *Founded:* 1952

Minoas*, Stadiou 43, Athens 121 Tel: (021) 3217545
Man Dir: Elias Konstantazopoulos
Subjects: General Fiction, Belles Lettres, Poetry, Biography, History, Music, Art, Reference, Juveniles, High-priced Paperbacks
Bookshop: Patission 126, Athens
1977: 10 titles *Founded:* 1948

Nikas*, 102 Solonos and 16 Mavromihali St, Athens Tel: 634686

Papachrysanthou Chryss SA, Graphic Arts and 'Golden Pen' Editions, 5 Mantzarou St, Athens 135 Tel: 3618711/2/8018250/1/2
Man Dir: Dip Eng K Papachrysanthou
Associate Company: Chrissi Penna (qv), Athens
Subjects: General Books, Juveniles, Tourist Guides, Comic Magazines
1977: 14 titles *Founded:* 1888

Papaioannou*, 34 Venizelou St, Athens Tel: 618139

Papazissis Publishers SA*, Nikitara 2, Athens TT 142, Greece
Tel: 3622496/3609150/3638020;
Telex: 219139 HAPSGR
Man Dir: Victor Papazissis;
Sales/Advertising: Marios Haritopoulos;
Rights and Permissions: Costas Sophoulis
Orders to: Papazissis Publishers SA
Parent Company: Corais Ltd, Nikitara 2, Athens TT 142
Subjects: Economics, Sociology, Philosophy, Politics, Law, Education, Environment, Greek Recent History, University Handbooks (especially on economics), School Books
Bookshop: Papazissis Bookshop, Nikitara 2, Athens TT 142
Founded: 1929

Papyros Press*, 17 Voulis St, Athens Tel: 3220013

Grigorios **Parissianos** 'Epistemonikai Ekdoseis'*, Solonos 69, Athens 701 Tel: (021) 610519
Subjects: Science, Medicine

Rayas, 34 Venizelou St, Athens Tel: 611692
1978: 1 title

Siamandas*, Akadimias 61, Athens Tel: (021) 615777/627164
Subjects: General Fiction & Nonfiction, History, Juveniles

J **Sideris** OE Ekdoseis*, Stadiou 44, Athens Tel: (021) 3229638
Subjects: Literature, Science, Linguistics, Juveniles

Skaraveos*, Charilaou Trikoupi 24, Athens Tel: (021) 3612405
Subjects: Belles Lettres, History, General Literature

Costas **Spanos***, Mavromihali 7, Athens 143 Tel: 3614332
Man Dir, Editorial: C Spanos; *Sales:* John Papadakis; *Publicity:* Sofia Tsimogianni
Subsidiary Company: 'Leon' editions
Subjects: Rare Books, Limited Editions, Byzantine and Post-Byzantine
Bookshop: 23 Hippocrates Str, Athens 143

Syropoulos Adelfoi OE Ekdotikos Oikos*, Akadimias 64, Athens Tel: (021) 614146
Subjects: Reference, History

Technical Chamber of Greece*, 4 Kar Servias, Athens 125 Tel: (021) 3222466
General Director: Ath Iatrou
Subjects: Science, Technology, Periodicals
1978: 10 titles *Founded:* 1923
Miscellaneous: The Technical Chamber of Greece (TEE) is a corporate body, under public law, supervised by the Ministry of Public Works

Tegopoulos*, 57 Panepistimiou St, Athens

Typos* 8 Londou St, Athens Tel: 619084

J **Vasiliou** Bibliopoleion*, Ippocratous 15, Athens Tel: (021) 623382
Subjects: Fiction, History, Philosophy

M **Vergadis**, see Bergadi Editions

Frères **Vlasis***, Londou 2, Athens Tel: (021) 639128
Subjects: History, Reference, General Science

Word and Vision Ltd, 42 Trivonianou, Mets, Athens Tel: (021) 9216590 Telex: 215910
Subjects: English Language General and Travel Books, English and Greek Language Teaching Books

Z O E*, Karytsih 14, Athens 124 Tel: (021) 3223560
Man Dir: G Karadzas
Subject: Religion
1977: 34 titles *Founded:* 1907
Bookshops: at Karytsih 14, Athens 124; St Sophia 41, Salonika; and in three other Greek cities

Har **Zolindakis***, Panepistimiou 65, Athens Tel: (021) 314546/316504
Subject: History

Literary Agents

Anglo-Hellenic Agency*, Koumpari 5, Kolonaki Sq, Athens 138
Tel: 3606808/3606807
Specializations: Translations, Medical

Book Clubs

Vivliofilia*, Mavromichali 7, Athens 114

Major Booksellers

American Bookstore*, Amerikis 23, Athens Tel: (021) 3624151
See also A Samouhos Bookstore

P **Efstathiadis** & Sons SA, Valtetsiou Str 14, Athens TT 144 Tel: (021) 615011/3600495
Importers and exporters

G C **Eleftheroudakis** Co Ltd*, International Bookstore, Nikis 4, Athens 126 Tel: (021) 229388

Kass M **Grigoris*** Solonos 71, Athens 143

Hestia Bookstore, 60 Solonos St, Athens 135 Tel: (021) 3635970
Owned by: I D Kollaros & Co Corporation (qv under Publishers)

C **Kakoulides***, International Bookshop, El Venizelos 39, Athens Tel: 231703

GREECE — GUATEMALA

Gr **Kaloudis***, Filonos 31, Piraeus Tel: (021) 479027

Kaufmann*, Stadiou 28, Athens Tel: (021) 3222160

Odysseus S **Klonis***, International Bookshop, Homirou 38, Athens Tel: 621218

John **Mihalopoulos** & Son, Booksellers, Hermou 75, Salonica Tel: 279695/263786

Minoas*, Patission 126, Athens Tel: (021) 815664

Solomon **Molcho***, International Bookshop M Alexandrou 10, Salonica Tel: 275271

Pantelides, Amerikis 11, Athens Tel: (01) 3623673

A **Samouhos** Bookstore*, Aghias Sofias 28, Thessalonica Tel: 239936
Under same management as American Bookstore (qv)

Major Libraries

Athens Academy Library*, Odos Venizelou, Athens

Athens College Library, Athens College, PO Box 5, Psychico, Athens Tel: 6714621

British Council Library*, PO Box 488, Athens 138 Tel: 3633211/5
Librarian: Miss M Lazard ALA

Gennadius Library, American School of Classical Studies at Athens, Souidias 61, Athens 140 Tel: (021) 710536
Acting Librarian: S Papageorgiou

National Library of Greece*, Panepistemiou, Athens Tel: (021) 614413/606495/608597

Library of the **National Technological University** of Athens*, Odos 28, Octovriou 42, Athens

Pan Library ('Circle of the Friends of Progress')*, Odos Giorgios 43, Tripolis, Arcadia

Parliament Library*, Palaia Anactora, Athens Tel: (021) 3235030

Library of the **Technical Chamber** of Greece, Odos Karageorgi Servias 4, Athens Tel: (021) 3226001

Library of the **Three Hierarchs***, Odos Demetriados-Ogl, Volos

Library of the **University of Salonika***, Salonika Tel: 9912218

Library Associations

Enossis Ellenon Bibliothakarion, Skouleniou 4, PO Box 2118, Athens TT 124 Tel: 322625
Greek Library Association
Secretary: Sofia Palamiotou
Publication: Bulletin

Library Reference Books and Journals

Books

Guide to Greek Libraries and Cultural Organizations, National Printing Office, Athens

Journals

Greek Library Association Bulletin, Amerikis 11, Athens 134

Literary Associations and Societies

Association of Arts and Letters, c/o 38 Mitropoleos St, Athens Tel: (021) 3233033
General Secretary: S Xefloudas

The **Circle** of Greek Children's Books, Zalongou 7, Athens 142 Tel: 3602990
Greek National Section of the International Board on Books for Young People (IBBY)
Founded: 1969

Etairia Ellinon Logotechnon, Mitropoleos 38, Athens 126
Society of Greek Writers
Secretary: Phaedra Tamleatha-Pagoulatou

Kentron Ekdoseos Ellinon Syngrafeon*, Academy of Athens, Panepistimiou, Athens
Centre for the Publication of Ancient Greek Authors
Dir: Ch Floratos

P E N Centre*, 60a rue Skoufa, Athens 144
Secretary: Yannis Manglis

Vivliografiki Etaireia tis Ellados (Bibliographical Society of Greece)*, Skoufa 60, Athens 144
General Secretary: J A Thomopoulos

Women's Literary Society*, Evrou 4, Athens 611

Literary Periodicals

Aiolika Grammatia (Aeolian Letters), Hodos Nircos 41, Palaion Phaliron, Athens

Diaghonios (Diagonal), Dinos Christianopoulous, Franklin Roosevelt, Salonika 4

Nea Hestia (text in Greek), G C Eleftheroudakis AE, Nikis 4, Athens 126

Literary Prizes

Circle of Greek Children's Books Prizes*
The Circle awards prizes for the following works: Greek tales for children submitted in manuscript; stories taken from nature; poems taken from nature; plays for children; illustration of Children's Books. Enquiries to the Circle of Greek Children's Books, Zalongou 7, Athens 142

Goulandris Prize*
For the best literary criticism, travel impressions or essay published in Greece. Awarded annually. Enquiries to 'Group of the Twelve', Othonos 10, Athens

Hatzipatera Prize*
For the best collection of poetry published in Greece. Awarded annually. Enquiries to 'Group of Twelve', Othonos 10, Athens

King Paul National Foundation Prize*
For an essay on community development written by an adolescent. Awarded annually. Enquiries to King Paul National Foundation, Philellinon 9, Athens 118

Pourfina Prize*
To the writers who have best depicted Greek civilization. Awarded annually. Enquiries to 'Group of the Twelve', Othonos 10, Athens

Tsakalos Prize*
For prose work, poetry and criticism, published by the members of the Society. 50,000 drachmas. Awarded annually. Enquiries to Society of Greek Writers, Mitropoleos 38, Athens 126

Women's Literary Society Prizes*
Each year the Society awards prizes for the following works for children: historical novel on a subject from Greek history; poems for very young children; poems for older children; a book of short stories; a theatrical play for older children; journeys and excursions within Greece. Enquiries to Women's Literary Society, Evrou 4, Athens 611 Athens 101

Guatemala

General Information

Language: Spanish
Religion: Roman Catholic
Population: 6.44 million
Literacy Rate (1964): 37.9%
Bank Hours: 0900-1500 Monday-Friday
Shop Hours: 0800-1200, 1400-1800 Monday-Friday; 0800-1200 Saturday
Currency: 100 centavos = 1 quetzal
Export/Import Information: Duty on catalogues is $0.03 per gross kilo. No import licences, no exchange control
Copyright: UCC, Buenos Aires, Florence (see International section)

Book Trade Organizations

Gremial de Libreros de Guatemala, Avenida Reforma 13-70, Zona 9, Edificio Real Reforma Interior 13N, Guatemala City Tel: 313326/27505/26478
Association of Booksellers of Guatemala
President: Victor Hugo Granados Gonzalez

Publishers

Editorial del **Ministerio de Educacion** 'Jose de Pineda Ibarra'*, 15° Ave 3-22, zona 1, Guatemala City

Piedra Santa*, 11 Calle 6-50, Guatemala City Tel: 85087
Bookshop: at above address

Seminario de Integración Social Guatemalteca, 11 Calle No 4-31, zona 1, Guatemala City Tel: 29754
Subjects: Sociological, Ecological, Educational, Anthropological texts connected with Guatemala
1977: 2 titles *1978:* 1 title *Founded:* 1956

Universidad de San Carlos*, Departmento de Publicaciones, Ciudad Universitaria, Guatemala City
Printing House: 10 Calle 9-59, Guatemala City 1

Book Clubs

Libroclub de Guatemala, Ave Elena "B" 2-25 Zona 2, El Sauce, Guatemala City Tel: 313326
Man Dir: Victor Hugo G Gonzalez
See also Libreria Cervantes (Bookseller)

Major Booksellers

Librería **'13 Calle'***, 13 Calle 8-69, zona 1, Guatemala City Tel: 81055

Librería **Acrópolis**, 9 Ave 13-20, zona 1, Guatemala City Tel: 80819

Librería **C E E S***, Apdo postal 652, Guatemala City

Libreria **Cervantes** — Libroclub de Guatemala, Ave Reforma 13-70, Zona 9, Edificio Real Reforma Interior 13N, Guatemala City Tel: 313326
Direct Importers and Distributors of books in Spanish, English, Gerand French

Distribuidora de Libros, Rodrigo Galindo, 11 Calle 4-15, zona 1, Guatemala City Tel: 28746

Edelcid Libros Científicos*, 11 Calle 8-66, zona 1, Guatemala City Tel: 20934

Librería **Feria** del Libro*, 6 Ave 15-65, zona 1, Guatemala City

Ediciones **Hispanas***, 13 Calle, 6-77, zona 1, of 408, Guatemala City

Distribuidora Cultural **I G A***, Ruta 1 Via 4, zona 4, Guatemala City

Librería **Universal***, 13 Calle, 4-16, zona 1, Guatemala City

Piedra Santa, 11 Calle 6-50, Guatemala City Tel: 85087

Librería **Tuncho** Granados G*, 10 Calle 6-56, zona 1, Apartado Postal 13, Guatemala City, CA Tel: 24736 and 27269
also at La Plaza del Sol, Calle Montúfar y 2 Ave, zona 9, Guatemala City CA

Major Libraries

Archivo General de Centro*, América, 4a Ave, 7a-8a Calles, zona 1, Guatemala City

Biblioteca Nacional de Guatemala (National Library)*, 5a Ave 7-26, zona 1, Guatemala City

Biblioteca Central de la **Universidad de San Carlos***, Ciudad Universitaria, zona 12, Guatemala City

Library Associations

Asociación Bibliotecologica Guatemalteca (Library Association of Guatemala)*, c/o The Director, Biblioteca Nacional de Guatemala, 5a Avenida 7-26, zona 1, Guatemala, CA

Literary Periodicals

Alero (Eaves), Universidad de San Carlos, Confederacions Universitaria Centroamericana, Guatemala City

Guinea

General Information

Language: French
Religion: Muslim predominantly
Population: 4.65 million
Bank Hours: 0800-1130 Monday-Saturday
Shop Hours: 0730-1230, 1430-1830 Monday-Saturday
Currency: 100 cauris = 1 sily
Copyright: No copyright conventions signed
Export/Import Information: Books imported by State Trading Corporation: LIBRAPORT BP 270, Conakry. Tariffs listed as free for books except children's picture books 15% revenue, 10% customs. 1% ad valorem Statistical Tax; 6% cost price stamp tax. Import licences

Major Booksellers

Libraport*, BP 270, Conakry

Major Libraries

Bibliothèque nationale (National Library)*, Conakry

Institut polytechnique de Conakry*, Bibliothèque, BP 1147, Conakry

International Communication Agency Library*, c/o American Embassy, BP 711, Conakry

Library Associations

Institut national de Recherches et Documentation (National Research and Documentation Institute)*, BP 561, Conakry
Dir: S Bounama Sy

Guyana

General Information

Language: English
Religion: Hinduism, Muslim, Christian
Population: 827,000
Bank Hours: 0800-1200 Monday-Friday; 0800-1100 Saturday
Shop Hours: 0800-1130, 1300-1600 Monday-Friday; 0800-1130 Saturday
Currency: 100 cents = 1 Guyana dollar
Export/Import Information: No tariff on books. Only advertising of commercial value, subject to 45% duty. Guyana National Trading Corporation, Camp and South Rd, Georgetown is sole importer of books. Import licence required. Nominal exchange controls

Publishers

Guyana Printers Ltd*, 18-20 Industrial Estate, Ruimveldt

Peter **Taylor** & Co Ltd*, La Penitence, East Bank, Demerara
Subjects: Literature, Fiction

Major Booksellers

Guyana National Trading Corporation*
Camp and South Rd, Georgetown
Sole importer of books

Major Libraries

Guyana Medical Science Library*, Georgetown Hospital Compound, Georgetown

Guyana Society Library*, Georgetown

National Library*, PO Box 110, Georgetown
Chief Librarian: Joan L Christiani

Library Associations

Guyana Library Association, 76-77 Main St, PO Box 110, Georgetown
Tel: 62690/62699
Secretary: P Hoskanns
Publication: Bulletin

Library Journals

Bulletin, Guyana Library Association, 76-77 Main St, PO Box 110, Georgetown

Literary Periodicals

University of Guyana Language Forum; review of literary, linguistic and educational studies (text in English), University of Guyana, PO Box 841, Georgetown

Haiti

General Information

Language: French and Creole
Religion: Roman Catholic
Population: 4.75 million
Literacy Rate (1950): 10.4%
Bank Hours: 0900-1300 Monday-Friday
Business Hours: Winter: 0800-1700; Summer: 0700-1500
Currency: 100 centimes = 1 gourde
Export/Import Information: Books charged 4% ad valorem, children's picture books 0.20 gourdes per kilo net + 4%. Advertising matter under 1 kilo gross weight duty-free. No import licences or exchange controls, other than occasional exchange rationing, leading to delays
Copyright: UCC (see International section)

Publishers

Deschamps*, Imprimerie, Grand' Rue, PO Box 164, Port-au-Prince
Subjects: History, Religion, Literature, Education, Fiction

F **Joseph***, Editions Caraibes, Lalve, Port-au-Prince

Theodor*, Imprimerie, rue Dantes Destouches, Port-au-Prince
Subjects: History, Literature, Fiction

Major Libraries

Bibliothèque du petit Séminaire*, Port-au-Prince

Bibliothèque nationale d'Haiti (National Library)*, rue Hammerton Killick, Port-au-Prince

Centre de Documentation*, Port-au-Prince

Bibliothèque **Saint Louis de Gonzague***, Port-au-Prince

Literary Associations and Societies

Le **Bibliophile** (The Book Lover)*, Cap Haïtien
Secretary: Louis Toussaint
Publications: La Citadelle (weekly), *Stella* (monthly)

Literary Periodicals

La Citadelle, Le Bibliophile, Cap Haïtien

Stella, Le Bibliophile, Cap Haïtien

Honduras

General Information

Language: Spanish (English on northern coast)
Religion: Roman Catholic
Population: 2.8 million
Literacy Rate (1961): 43.7%
Bank Hours: 0830-1200, 1400-1630 Monday-Friday
Shop Hours: Tegucigalpa: 0800-1200, 1330-1800 Monday-Friday; 0800-1200 Saturday; San Pedro Sula: 0730-1100, 1330-1800 Monday-Friday; 0800-1200 Saturday
Currency: 100 centavos = 1 lempira
Export/Import Information: No tariff on books. Duty on catalogues is $0.03 per kilogram. No import licences. No exchange controls
Copyright: Buenos Aires (see International section)

Book Trade Reference Journal

Bibliografía hondureña (Honduras Bibliography), Banco Central de Honduras, PO Box C-58, 1A Calle, Tegucigalpa

Publishers

Editorial Universitaria*, Universidad de Honduras, Tegucigalpa

Editorial **Nuevo** Continente*, Ave Cervantes, Tegucigalpa Tel: 225073

Major Booksellers

Librería the Bookstore*, Edificio Midence Soto local 108, Apdo Postal 167 C, Tegucigalpa Tel: 226824

Ney's Libros and Revistas*, Apdo 609, Tegucigalpa Tel: 23865

Librería Universitaria Jose T **Reyes***, Universidad Nacional Autónoma de Honduras, Tegucigalpa DC

Major Libraries

Biblioteca Nacional de Honduras (National Library)*, 6a Ave Salvador Mendieta, Tegucigalpa

Sistema Bibliotecario (Librarians' System)*, Ciudad Universitaria, Carretera Suyapa, Tegucigalpa Tel: 229101/229107 ext 212/122/124
Dir: Lic Liliana S Cañadas Mejia

Library Associations

Asociación de Bibliotecarios y Archiveros de Honduras (Association of Librarians and Archivists of Honduras)*, 3 Avenidas, 4 y 5 Calles, No 416 Comayagüela, DC, Tegucigalpa
Secretary-General: Juan Angel Ayes R

Library Journals

Catálogo de Préstamo, Association of Librarians and Archivists of Honduras, 3 Avenidas, 4 y 5 Calles, No 416, Comayagüela, DC, Tegucigalpa

Hong Kong

General Information

Language: English and Cantonese
Religion: Traditional Chinese beliefs, especially Buddhism
Population: 4.51 million
Literacy Rate (1971): 77.3
Bank Hours: Many open 7 days until 2100. Department stores: 0900-1830 Monday-Friday; 0900-1730 Saturday
Currency: 100 cents = 1 Hong Kong dollar
Export/Import Information: No tariffs on books and advertising. No import licences required. No exchange controls
Copyright: No copyright conventions signed

Book Trade Organizations

Anglo-Chinese Textbook Publishers Organization Ltd*, c/o Heinemann Educational Books (Asia) Ltd, KPO Box 6086, Tsim Sha Tsui Post Office, Kowloon
Chairman: L Comber

Hong Kong Booksellers' & Stationers' Association*, Man Wah House, Kowloon Tel: 3882356

Hong Kong Educational Publishers Association Ltd*, 1105 Yau Yue Bldg, 127-131 Des Voeux Rd, C
President: Au Bak Ling

Hong Kong Publishers' & Distributors' Association*, National Bldg, 4th Floor, 240-246 Nathan Rd, Kowloon

Publishers

A D I S Press International Ltd*, Unit 5B, Gardena Court, Kennedy Terrace, Kennedy Rd, Hong Kong
Associate Company: ADIS Press Australasia Ltd (qv)

The **Art** Publisher+*, 166 Java Rd, 2/F, North Point
Subjects: Art; Textbooks

Asia Press Ltd*, 88 Yee Wo St, PO Box 2919, Causeway Bay
President: Chang Kuo-Sin
Subjects: General Fiction, Belles Lettres, General Science, Periodicals
Founded: 1952

Book Marketing Ltd, North Point Industrial Building, Flat A, 17F, 499 King's Rd Tel: 5620121 Cable Add: Marketbook Telex: eking 85987 hx
Man Dir: Bernard Chiu King Sum
Associate Companies: Swindon Book Co, Hong Kong Book Centre Ltd, Kelly and Walsh Ltd
Subjects: Educational books and periodicals
1977: 2 titles *Founded:* 1973
ISBN Publisher's Prefix: 0-962211

Books for Asia+*, 30 Tat Chee St, Yau Yat Chuen, Kowloon
Subsidiary Companies: Books for Asia (M) Sdn Bhd, Malaysia (qv); Books for Asia, Philippines; Books for Asia (S) Pte Ltd, Singapore (qv Booksellers); Books for Asia, Thailand
Subject: Textbooks

Chopsticks Cooking Centre (CCC), Kowloon Central PO Box 3515 (Located at: 122 Waterloo Rd, 3rd Floor, Kowloon) Tel: (3) 015989/015911
Dir, Rights & Permissions: Cecilia J Au-Yeung; *Editor:* Virginia Au-Yeung; *Sales, Production, Publicity:* Wilson Au-Yeung
Subject: Chinese Cuisine
1978: 2 titles *1979:* 1 title *Founded:* 1975
ISBN Publisher's Prefix: 962-7018

The **Educational Publishing** House Ltd+*, 196-8 Tsat Tse Mui Rd, 10th Floor, North Point
Subject: Textbooks

F E P International (HK) Ltd+*, 1204 Odell Ho, 32 Laichikok Rd, Mongkok, Kowloon
Subject: Textbooks

Federal Publications (FE)+*, 5A Evergreen Industrial Mansion, Yip Fat St, Wong Chuk Hang Rd, Aberdeen
Subject: Textbooks

Good Earth Publishing Co+*, c/o Everyman Book Co Ltd, 71A Prince Edward Rd, Chit King Industrial Bldg, 10th Floor, San Po Kong, Kowloon
Subject: Textbooks

Greenwood Press+, 47 Pokfulam Road, G/F
Subject: Textbooks

H K Health Knowledge Publication+*, Flat A, 1st floor, 7 Gough St
Subject: Textbooks

Heinemann Educational Books (Asia) Ltd+, Yik Yin Bldg, 1st Floor, 321-323 To Kwa Wan Rd, Kowloon Tel: 3649221/4 Cable Add: Heinebooks Hong Kong Telex: HK 84463 (answerback — 84463 hebhk hx)
Shipping Add: KPO Box 96086, Tsimshatsui PO, Kowloon

Man Dir: Leon Comber
Branch Offs: 41 Jalan Pemimpin, Singapore 20; Suite 4012-3, The Regent, Jalan Imbi, Kuala Lumpur 06-23, Malaysia
Subjects: Belles Lettres, Poetry, Biography, History, Music, Art, Philosophy, Reference, Religion, Medicine, Engineering, General & Social Science, University & Secondary Textbooks, Educational Materials, Asiatic Studies, Management, Accountancy, English as Second Language
1979: 39 titles *Founded:* 1962

Hong Kong Cultural Press Ltd+*, 8/F Lee Sum Factory Bldg, 23 Sze Mei St, San Po Kong, Kowloon
Subject: Textbooks

Hong Kong Publications+*, Room 801, 748A Nathan Rd, Kowloon
Subject: Textbooks

Hong Kong University Press+, University of Hong Kong, 139 Pokfulam Rd Tel: (05) 502703
Dir: Geoffrey W Bonsall; *Editor:* Y K Fung
Subjects: Archaeology, History, Life Sciences, Physical Sciences; Social Sciences, Economics, Languages (especially Chinese), Literature, Economics, Fine Arts, Geography, Law, Medicine, Philosophy, Seamanship, Paperbacks, Micro-prints
1977: 5 titles *1978:* 4 titles *Founded:* 1956
ISBN Publisher's Prefix: 962-209

Hong Kong Witman Publishing Co+*, 72 Kai Yuen St, G/F, North Point
Subject: Textbooks

Hung Fung Book Co+*, 18 Tsat Tse Mui Rd, G/F
Subject: Textbooks

Jing Kung Educational Press+*, 53 Hollywood Rd
Subject: Textbooks

King Shing Publishing Co+*, 89 Sai Yee St, G/F, Kowloon
Subject: Textbooks

T H Lee & Co Ltd+*, 1-15 Electric St, Upper Ground Floor, Wanchai
Subject: Textbooks

Ling Kee Publishing Co+, Zung Fu Industrial bldg, 1067 King's Rd Tel: (5) 616151/2 Cable Add: Bookland
Man Dir: B L Au; *Sales Dir:* Albert Au
Subjects: Reference, University, Secondary & Primary Textbooks, Educational Materials
Founded: 1949
Bookshops: Ling Kee Book Store, Yau Yue Building, 127-131 Des Voeux Rd Central, and 678 Nathan Rd, Kowloon
Miscellaneous: Firm is a division of Ling Kee Group Ltd

Longman Group (Far East) Ltd+*, Longman House, Tong Chong St, Quarry Bay, PO Box 223 Tel: (05) 618171/5
Man Dir: W S V Shen
Subjects: General Fiction, Belles Lettres, Art, History, General Science, Textbooks, Educational Materials, Juveniles, Languages
Miscellaneous: Firm is an associate company of Longman Group Ltd, UK (qv)

Macmillan Publishers (HK) Ltd+, 19/F Warwick Ho, Taikoo Trading Estate, 28 Tong Chong St, Quarry Bay Tel: (05) 636206/9, 620101/2, 643115 Cable Add: Macpublish, Hong Kong
Man Dir: Nigel Carr

Parent Company: Macmillan Publishers, UK (qv)
Subject: Secondary Textbooks
1978: 27 titles *1979:* 111 titles *Founded:* 1969

Modern Educational Research Society Ltd+*, 10th Floor, Harbour Commercial Bldg, 122-124 Connaught Rd
Subject: Textbooks

Oxford University Press+, 18th Floor, Block F, Taikoo Trading Estate, Quarry Bay Tel: (05) 610221/4, 610138/9 Cable Add: Oxonian Telex: HX 65522
Man Dir: M C Campbell; *Editorial, Rights & Permissions:* C G Riches; *Marketing:* P Tam; *Production:* P Ling; *Publicity:* Mrs R Mak
Parent Company: Oxford University Press, UK (qv)
Subject: Textbooks
1977: 30 titles *1978:* 56 titles *Founded:* 1961
ISBN Publisher's Prefix: 0-19 (OUP UK)

Perfecting Press+*, 233 Lockhart Rd, 20th Floor, Flat A
Publicity Manager: Fung Pui Ming
Subject: Textbooks
1978: 8 titles

Shanghai Book Co Ltd+*, 179 Connaught Rd West, 6th Floor, Flat A
Subject: Textbooks

Times Educational Co Ltd+*, No 6, 7/F, Block E, Sunway Gardens, 989 King's Rd
Subject: Textbooks

Tin Fung Book Co+*, 533 Hennessy Rd, 1st Floor
Subject: Textbooks

Union Press Ltd*, 9 College Road, Kowloon
Subject: Textbooks

Vetch & Lee Ltd*, 1035 Man Yee Bldg, 67-71 Queen's Rd Central Tel: (05) 233886/233585
Man Dir: Henri Vetch; *Dir:* Rupert S C Lee
Subjects: Orientalia of Academic & General Interest: Sinology, Natural History, Language, Arts & Crafts

Major Booksellers

Asia Press Bookstore Ltd*, 88 Yee Wo St, Causeway Bay, PO Box 2919

East Asia Book Co*, 39 Shu Kuk St, North Point

Eastern Book Service Ltd*, 11-C Majestic Bldg, 80 Nathan Rd, Kowloon Tel: 3685645
Publishers' Agents and Stockists

Far East Publications Ltd+, Times Book Centre, 67-71 Chatham Rd South, Oriental Centre, Tsimshatsui Tel: (3) 689276/673194
Subject: Running series of books
Miscellaneous: Also major distributor of books, from Mok Chong St, Kowloon City Rd

Hoi Ming Book Store*, 385A Nathan Rd, Alhambra Bldg, Kowloon

Hong Kong Book Centre, On Lok Yuen Bldg, 25 Des Voeux Rd, C

Howard Book Co*, 74 Argyle St, Kowloon

Jing Kung Book Store*, 53 Hollywood Rd

Kowloon Book Store*, 751-A Nathan Rd, Kowloon

Kwong Hin Bookstore*, 75 Hollywood Rd

Kwong Yick Bookstore*, 22 Taipo Rd, Kowloon

Lam Kee Bookstore*, 184 Queen's Rd West

Ling Kee Bookstore*, 100-102 Percival St, Causeway Bay

Swindon Book Co*, 13-15 Lock Rd, Kowloon

Tai Kuen Book Co*, 323 Queen's Rd West

Times Book Centre, 67-71 Chatham Rd South, Tsimshatsui
Also G31 Hutchison Ho, 10 Harcourt Rd, Hong Kong

University Book Store*, University of Hong Kong, Pokfulam Rd

World Book Co*, 74A Hollywood Rd

Major Libraries

British Council Library, Easey Commercial Bldg 1/F, 255 Hennessy Rd, Wanchai Tel: 5-756501

Chinese University of Hong Kong Library System*, Shatin, New Territories

Hong Kong Junior Chamber of Commerce Libraries*, 24 Ice House St, 4th Floor

Hong Kong Polytechnic Library*, Hung Hom, Kowloon Tel: (3) 638344

Sun Yat-Sen Library*, 172-174 Boundary St, Kowloon

University of Hong Kong Main Library*, University of Hong Kong, Pokfulam Rd Tel: (5) 468161 ext 219

Urban Council Libraries*, City Hall, Edinburgh Pl, Hong Kong Tel: (5) 233688
Librarian: Timothy A Chow

Library Associations

Hong Kong Library Association, c/o University Library, University of Hong Kong, Pokfulam Rd Tel: (5) 468161
Chairman: J O'Halloran; *Honorary Secretary:* K W Foo
Publication: Journal (irregular)

Library Journals

Journal (text in English and Chinese), Hong Kong Library Association, The University of Hong Kong Library, Pokfulam Rd

Literary Associations and Societies

Chinese Language and Literature Association*, Block A1, Fa Po Villa, 1st Floor, Fa Po St, Yau Yat Chuen, Kowloon
Secretary: Leung Nga Mei

Hong Kong Chinese P E N Centre*, Victoria Park Mansion, 15th Floor, Flat A, Paterson St
Secretary: William Hsu
Publication: PEN News (weekly in Chinese)

Hong Kong English P E N Centre, Box 1528, Kowloon Central Post Office
Chairman: Professor Hsu Yu

182 HONG KONG — HUNGARY

Literary Periodicals

Eastern Horizon (text in English), Lee Tsung-ying, 472 Hennessy Rd, 3rd Floor

PEN News (text in Chinese), Hong Kong Chinese PEN Centre, Victoria Park Mansion, 15th Floor, Flat A, Paterson St

Shui Hsing Cha Chi (Mercury Magazine) (text in Chinese, title in Chinese and English), Louise Bao, GPO Box 13154

Wu Hsia Shih Chieh, 7-13 Hsin Chieh, 2nd Floor

Hungary

General Information

Language: Hungarian, or Magyar (German widely known)
Religion: Predominantly Roman Catholic
Population: 10.6 million
Literacy Rate (1971): 98%
Bank Hours: 0800-1300 Monday-Friday; 0900-1100 Saturday
Shop Hours: 0900-1800 Monday-Friday; 0900-1500 Saturday
Currency: 100 fillérs = 1 forint
Export/Import Information: Importation is a state monopoly so licences and tariff not of concern to exporter. Exchange controls. Book importing done through Kultura, H-1389 Budapest, Postafiók 149; atlases through Cartographia, H-1443 Budapest, Postafiók 132. Exporting is through the Hungarian Foreign Trade Organization, H-1389 Budapest 62, Postfiok 149. Magyar Hirdeto, Budapest, is a full service advertising agency
Copyright: UCC, Berne (see International section)

Book Trade Organizations

Magyar Könyvkiadók és Könyvterjesztök Egyesülése (Association of Hungarian Publishers and Booksellers)*, H-1051 Budapest V, Vörösmarty tér IX, Postafiók 130 Tel: 184758
President: György Bernát; *Secretary General:* Ferenc Zöld
Founded: 1969
Publication: Könyvvilag; also 3 quarterly journals published in German, English and French on Hungarian books

Book Trade Journals

Hungarian Book Review (text in English, French and German), Kultura, H-1389 Budapest, Postafiok 149

A Könyv (The Book), Association of Hungarian Publishers and Booksellers, Budapest V, Vörösmarty tér 1, Postafiók 130

Könyv és nevelés (Book and Education), Orszagos pedagógiai könyvtár és múzeum, Budapest V, Honvéd u 19, Postafiók 49

Könyvtájèkoztató (Information on Books), Association of Hungarian Publishers and Booksellers, Budapest V, Vörösmarty tér 1, Postafiók 130

Könyvvilag (Book World), Association of Hungarian Publishers and Booksellers, Budapest V, Vörösmarty tér 1, Postafiók 130

Magyar könyvszemle (Hungarian Bibliographical Journal); review of Book history, Bibliography and Documentation (summaries in English, French, German or Russian), Akadémiai Kiadó, Publishing House of the Hungarian Academy of Sciences, H-1054 Budapest V, Alkotmány u 21

Magyar nemzeti bibliográfia (Hungarian National Bibliography), National Széchényi Library, H-1827 Budapest, Múzeum körút 14-x6

Uj könyvek (New Books), Centre for Library Science and Methodology, H-1827 Budapest, Múzeum u 3

Publishers

Akadémiai Kiadó (Publishing House of the Hungarian Academy of Sciences)+*, Postafiók 24 H-1363 Budapest Tel: 111010 Cable Add: Akadémaiai Kiadó Budapest Telex: 226228 AK NYO H
Man Dir: György Bernát; *Sales & Advertising Dir:* Gyula Kiss; *Publicity Dir:* Péter Rubin; *Rights & Permissions:* Géza Takács
Subjects: Belles Lettres, General & Social Science, Medicine, Biology, Earth Sciences, Engineering, University Textbooks, Archaeology, Book Industry, History, Arts, Reference, Literature, Music, Philosophy, Psychology, Politics, Law, Languages, Veterinary Science, Economics
1977: 638 titles *1978:* 646 titles *Founded:* 1828
Bookshop: Akadémiai Könyvesbolt, H-1052, Budapest V, Váci u 22
ISBN Publisher's Prefix: 963-05

Cärtögraphia, H-1443 Budapest XIV, Bósnyák tér 5, Postfiók 132 Tel: 634639 Cable Add: Cartographia Telex: 226218
Subjects: Maps and Atlases (compiling, drawing, printing), Export-Import

Corvina Press+, H-1364 Budapest V, Vörösmarty tér 1 Tel: 176222 Cable Add: Corvina Budapest
Dir: Jenö Simó; *Asst Dir:* Dr Miklós Tóth; *Production Manager:* István Murányi; *Chief Accountant:* Irma Marticskó; *Sales, Advertising & Publicity Dir:* Gábor Ila; *Editorial Dir:* Karoly Uéber
Subjects: Art in Hungarian & foreign languages, Music, Fiction, Juveniles, Tourist Guides, General Information, Cookery Books, Sports in foreign languages
1978: 208 titles *Founded:* 1955
ISBN Publisher's Prefix: 963-13

Európa Könyvkiadó (Europa Publishing House)+, H-1363 Budapest V, Kossuth Lajos tér 13-15, Postafiók 65 Tel: 312700 Cable Add: Euroliber Telex: 225645
Man Dir: János Domokos; *Editorial:* L Antal; *Sales, Rights & Permissions:* Dr L Sármány; *Production:* Mrs G Andrási; *Publicity:* L Horváth
Branch Off: Magyar Helikon Department, Bibliophile Section, Budapest V, Eötvös Lóránd u 8
Subjects: General Fiction, Belles Lettres, Poetry, Biography, Philosophy, Bibliophile interest
1977: 215 titles *1978:* 214 titles *Founded:* 1945
ISBN Publisher's Prefix: 963-07, 963-207

Gondolat Könyvkiadó+, H-1088 Budapest, Bródy Sándor u 16 Tel: 134840/335560
Man Dir: Dr Margit Siklós
Subjects: Reference, Art, General & Social Science
Founded: 1957
ISBN Publisher's Prefix: 963-280

Képzömüveszeti Alap Kidaóvállalata+*, H-1366 Budapest V, Vörösmarty tér 1, Postafiók 110 Tel: 176222
Manager: László Takács; *Editorial:* M Pásztói; *Sales:* Dr L Csajka; *Production:* G Szedlák; *Publicity:* T Geröly
Subject: Fine Art
Bookshop: Képesbolt, Budapest VI, Deák tér 6
1977: 21 titles *1978:* 21 titles *Founded:* 1954

Kossuth Könyvkiadó+, Steindl u 6, Postafiók 127, 1366 Budapest Tel: 117440 Publishing House of Political Literature
Manager: Gyula Rapai; *Editorial:* György Nonn; *Production:* Sándor Méth; *Rights & Permissions:* Artisjus, Vörösmarty tér 1
Subjects: History, Philosophy, Belles Lettres, Social and Political Science, Psychology, Business; Periodicals
1977: 235 titles *1978:* 251 titles *Founded:* 1944
ISBN Publisher's Prefix: 963-09

Közgazdasági és Jogi Könyvkiadó (Publishing House for Economics & Law)+*, Nagy Sándor u 6, Postafiók 578, 1374 Budapest V Tel: 126430/312327 Telex: 226511
Man Dir: Tibor Keresztes; *Editorial, Publicity:* Dr K Cotel; *Sales:* Mrs Tamás, Alfréd Büchler; *Rights & Permissions:* Artisjus, Budapest
Subsidiary Company: Editor Minerva
Distribution: Artisjus, Budapest
Subjects: Economics, Law, Sociology, Education, Children's Literature
1977: 163 titles *Founded:* 1955
ISBN Publisher's Prefix: 963220, 963223 (Minerva)

Magvetö Könyvkiadó (Publishing House of Belles Lettres)+*, H-1806 Budapest V, Vörösmarty tér 1 Tel: 185109
Man Dir: G Kardos; *Sales, Publicity:* I Matolcsy; *Managing Editors:* M Hegedos, A Bor; *Rights & Permissions:* via Artisjus (qv under Literary Agents)
Subjects: General Fiction, Belles Lettres, Poetry, History, Music, Art, Aesthetics, Philosophy, Low-priced Paperbacks
1977: c 180 titles *1978:* 200 titles *Founded:* 1955
ISBN Publisher's Prefix: 963270

Medicina Könyvkiadó+, H-1361 Budapest, Póstafiók 9 (Located at: H-1054 Budapest, Beloiannisz u 8)
Publishing House of Medical Literature
Man Dir: Dr István Árky; *Editors:* Dr János Brencsán, Márta Kosály, Dr Mihály Berend; *Sales:* Mrs I Kuti; *Production:* Ferenc Fraunhoffer; *Rights & Permissions:* Artisjus (qv under Literary Agents)
Orders to: H-1361 Budapest, Póstafiók 9
Subjects: Medicine, Travel, Sports
1977: 135 titles *Founded:* 1957
ISBN Publisher's Prefix: 963240 (Medical); 963243 (Travel); 963253 (Sports)

Mezögazdasági Könyvkiadó (Vállalat+, Budapest V, Báthory u 10 Tel: 116650/318397
Agricultural Publishing House
Manager: Dr Pál Sárkány
Subjects: Agriculture, Reference, General Science, Textbooks

HUNGARY 183

Book Club: Club for Bibliophiles
Bookshop: Agricultural Bookstore,
Budapest V, Vécsei u 5
1978: 102 titles *Founded:* 1950

Editor **Minerva**, subsidiary of Közgazdasági
és Jogi Könyvkiadó (qv)

Móra Ferenc Ifjúsagi Könyvkiadó+, H-
1073 Budapest VII, Lenin körút 9-11
Tel: 221285
Man Dir: György Szilvásy
Subject: Juveniles
1977: 189 titles *1978:* 166 titles *Founded:*
1950
ISBN Publisher's Prefix: 963-11

Editio **Musica**, see Zeneműkiadó

Müszaki Könyvkiadó Vállalat+, H-1374
Budapest V, Bajcsy Zsilinszky u 22
Tel: 113450 Cable Add: Editechn Telex:
226490 mkh
Publishing House of Technical Literature
Man Dir: Herbert Fischer; *Editorial:* Andras
Kelen
Orders to: Müszaki Könyvkiadó, Postafiók
581, H-1374 Budapest 5
Subjects: Science, Technical, Textbooks,
Yearbooks, Catalogues
Book Club: Müszaki Könyvklub
Bookshops: 100 in Budapest, 154 elsewhere
throughout country
1977: 151 scientific/technical, 397 textbooks
1978: 163 scientific/technical, 380 textbooks
Founded: 1949
ISBN Publisher's Prefix: 96310

Statisztikai Kiadó Vállalat+, H-1300
Budapest, Póstafiók 99 Tel: 688460 Telex:
224308 statiH
Statistical Publishing House
Despatch Add: Budapest III, Kaszás u 10-
12
Man Dir: József Kecskés; *Sales Dir:* András
Tasnádi; *Publicity and Advertising Dir:*
Gyula Timár; *Rights and Permissions:*
Artisjus, Budapest (qv under Literary
Agents)
Subjects: Engineering, General & Social
Science
1977: 100 titles *Founded:* 1954
Bookshop: Statistical and Computing
Bookshop, Budapest II, Keleti Károly u 10
Tel: 158018

Szépirodalmi Kiadó (Publishing House of
Belles Lettres)+*, H-1428 Budapest, Lenin
Körút 9-11, Postfiók 58 Tel: 221285
Man Dir: Endre Illés; *Rights & Permissions:*
Ministry of Culture
Subjects: General Fiction, Belles Lettres,
Poetry, Low- & High-priced Paperbacks,
Educational Materials
Founded: 1950
ISBN Publisher's Prefix: 963-15

Táncsics Szakszervezeti Kiadó (Publishing
House of the Trade Union Movement)+*
H-1139 Budapest, Váci u 69-79
Tel: 141479/335790
Manager: István Kádár
Subjects: Technical, Nonfiction, Reference,
Periodicals

Tankönyvkiadó Vállalat+, H-1055
Budapest V, Szalay u 10-14, Póstafiók 20
Tel: 324915
Textbook Publishing House
Man Dir: András Petró; *Editorial:* Sándor
Hinora; *Sales:* Hugó Dobos; *Production:*
Lajos Lojd; *Rights & Permissions:* Artisjus,
H-1051 Budapest V, Vörösmarty tér 1
Subjects: Textbooks; Educational Literature,
Language Books; Periodicals
1977: 818 titles *1978:* 791 titles *Founded:*
1949
ISBN Publisher's Prefix: 96317

Editio Musica Budapest **Zeneműkiadö**+, H-
1370 Budapest, Póstafiók 322 (Located at:
Budapest V, Vörösmarty tér 1) Tel:
176222/184228 Cable Add: Editiomusica
Man Dir: László Sarlós
Exports: via Kultura (qv under Major
Booksellers)
Subject: Sheet Music, Books on Music
1977: 50 book, 330 sheet music titles *1978:*
46 book, 994 sheet music titles *Founded:*
1950

Zrinyi Katonai Kiadó (Publishing House of
the Hungarian Army)+*, H-1087 Budapest
Kerepesi u 29
Manager: László Bedó
Subjects: Military & Popular Science

Literary Agents

Artisjus, Vörösmarty tér 1, Postafiók 67, H-
1364 Budapest Tel: 184704 Cable Add:
Artisjus Telex: 226527 Arjus H
Agency for Literature, Theatre and Music of
the Hungarian Bureau for Copyright
Protection
Contact: Vera Acs

Book Clubs

Club for Bibliophiles*, Budapest V, Báthory
u 10
Owned by: Mezögazdasagi Könyvkiadó
Vállalat (Agricultural Publishing House)
(Budapest)

Müskaki Könyvklub, Bajczy-Zs ut 22, H-
1051 Budapest V
Owned by: Müszaki Könyvkiadó (qv)

Major Booksellers

Állami könyvterjesztö vállalat, Budapest V,
Déak Ferenc u 15
Hungarian State Book-Distributing
Enterprise. It distributes books to its 112
bookshops

Állami könyvterjesztö vállalat orzágos
antikvár, Budapest V, Múzeum körút 21
Hungarian State Book-Distributing
Enterprise, Department for Antiquarian
Books

Hungarian Foreign Trade Organization*
H-1389 Budapest 62, Postafiók 149
The state exporting organization

Könyvértékesitö Vállalat+, H-1052
Budapest, Petöfi Sandor u 3
Hungarian Wholesale Book Trading
Enterprise
This organization stockpiles and despatches
all editions from Hungarian publishers, and
also imported books for the retail trade. It
also sells books directly for bookshops
owned by co-operatives, and has a Library
Service Dept which supplies the entire
Hungarian Library network

Kultura, H-1389 Budapest, Postafiók 149
Tel: 159450 Cable Add: Kulturpress
Man Dir: A Goenyei
This company is the Hungarian export-
import organization

Müvelt nép könyvterjesztö vállalat
(Hungarian Educated People Book-
Distributing Enterprise)*, Budapest V,
Népköztársaság u 21
Distributes books through all outlets
throughout the country

Major Libraries

Budapesti Müszaki Egyetem Központi
Könyvtára, Budapest XI, Budafoki u 4-6
Budapest Technical University Central
Library

Föszékesegyházi könyvtár*, H-2500
Esztergom, Bajcsy Zsilinszky u 28 Tel:
Esztergom 527
Cathedral Library
Dir: Canon Dr Zoltan Kovách

József Attila Tudományegyetem Központi
Könyvtára, H-6701 Szeged, Dugonics tér 13
Central Library of the Attila József
University
Librarian: Dr Béla Karácsonyi
*Publications: Dissertationes ex Bibliotheca
Universitatis de Attila József Nominatae;
Series Bibliographica Universitatis de Attila
József Nominatae; Acta Universitatis
Szegediensis de Attila József Nominatae;
Acta Bibliothecaria* (all irregular)

Kossuth Lajos Tudományegyetem Egyetemi
Könyvtár (Lajos Kossuth University
Library*, H-4010 Debrecen

Könyvtártudományi és módszertani
központ, H-1827 Budapest, Múzeum u 3
Centre for Library Science and
Methodology
Dir: István Papp
*Publications: Uj könyvek, Könyvtári figyelö,
Magyar könyvtári szakirodalom
bibliográfiája, Hungarian Library and
Information Science Abstracts; Könyvtári és
Dokumentációs Szakirodalom, Referálo Lap*

Központi statisztikai hivatal könyvtár és
dokumentációs szolgálat*, H-1525 Budapest
II, Keleti Károly u 5, Postafiók 10
Library and Documentation Service of the
Central Statistical Office

Egyetemi könyvtár (Central Library),
Loránd Eötvös University*, H-1364
Budapest V Pesti Barnabás u 1 Tel: 180960

Uj **Magyar** Központi Levéltár (New Central
Archives of Hungary)*, H-1014 Budapest,
Hess András tér 4

Magyar országos levéltár (National
Archives)*, H-1250 Budapest I, Bécsikapu
tér 4 Pf 3 Tel: 160656

Magyar Tudományos Akadémia Könyvtára,
H-1361 Budapest V, Akadémia u 2,
Póstafiók 7 Tel: 126779/113400
Library of the Hungarian Academy of
Sciences

Országos Széchényi Könyvtár, H-1827
Budapest, Póstafiók 486 (Located at:
Budapest VIII, Múzeum körút 14/16) Tel:
331714 Telex: biblnathung 224226
(Information Dept: Tel: 341684)
National Széchényi Library
Dir: Dr Magda Jóború
Also a National Centre for Library Science
and Methodology

Fövárosi **Szabó** Ervin Könyvtár (Ervin
Szabó Municipal Library)*, H-1371
Budapest, Szabó Ervin tér 1, Postafiók 487
Tel: 330580; Information Service, 141005

Szent benedekrend (Library of the
Benedictine Abbey)*, Közp Fökönyvtára,
H-9090 Pannonhalma Tel: Pannonhalma
5/Vár/

Tiszáninneni Református Egyházkerület
Nagykönyvtára (Library of the Cistibiscan
Reformed Church District)*, H-3950
Sárospatak, Rákóczy út 1 Tel: Sárospatak
29

Library Associations

Kulturális Minisztévium **Levéltári Osztaly**, H-1014 Budapest, Uri u 54-56
National Board of Archives

Magyar Könyvtárosok Egyesülete (Association of Hungarian Librarians)*, H-1372 Budapest VIII, Szentkirályi u 21, Postafiók 452
Secretary: Dezsö Kovács

Országos Müszaki Könyvtár és Dokumentációs Központ (Hungarian Central Technical Library and Documentation Centre)*, H-1428 Budapest, Reviczky u 6, Postafiók 12 Tel: 340151/139851 Telex: OMKDKH 224944
Director: Dr Péter Lázár

Tájékoztatási tudományos társaság (Information Science Society)*, Budapest VI, Anker köz 1
Deputy General Secretary: Miklós Philip

Library Journals

Hungarian Library and Information Science Abstracts (text in English and Russian), Centre for Library Science and Methodology, H-1827 Budapest, Múzeum u 3

Könyvtári figyelo (Library Review); (summaries in English, German and Russian), Centre for Library Science and Methodology, H-1827 Budapest, Múzeum u 3

Magyar könyvtári szakirodalom bibliográfiája (Hungarian Library Literature), (text in Hungarian, titles and summaries in English), Centre for Library Science and Methodology, H-1827 Budapest, Múzeum u 3

Literary Associations and Societies

Magyar Bibliofil társaság (Hungarian Society of Bibliophiles)*, Budapest VIII, Brody Sándor u 16

Magyar Irodalomtörténeti Társaság, Budapest V, Pesti Barnabás u 1
Society of Hungarian Literary History
President: Gabor Tolnai; *Editor-in-Chief:* Peter Nagy
Publications: Irodalomtörténet

Magyar Írók Szövetsége (Association of Hungarian Writers)*, Budapest VI, Bajza u 18
General Secretary: Imre Dobozi

Magyar Tudományos Akadémia Irodalomtudományi Intézete, H-1118 Budapest XI, Menesi u 11-13
Institute of Literary Studies of the Hungarian Academy of Sciences
Dir: Professor István Sötér
Publications: Irodalomtörténeti Közlemények (quarterly); *Helikon* (quarterly), *Literatura* (quarterly), *Irodalomtörténeti Könyvtár* (monographs), *Irodalomtörténeti Füzetek* (papers); *Neo-Helikon* (quarterly)

Magyar **P E N** Club (Hungarian PEN Club)*, Budapest V, Vörösmarty tér 1,
General Secretary: László Kéry
Publications: The Hungarian PEN, Le PEN hongrois (yearly bulletin)

Literary Periodicals

Kortárs (Contemporary), Kultura, H-1389 Budapest, Postafiók 149

Kritica (Critic) (summaries in French, German and Russian), Kultura, H-1389 Budapest, Postafiók 149

Literatura, Institute of Literary Studies of the Hungarian Academy of Sciences, H-1118 Budapest XI, Menesi u 11-13

Magyar muhely (Hungarian Workshop); literary and artistic review (text in Hungarian), Paul Nagy, 139 ave Jean-Jaurès, F-92120 Montrouge, France

New Hungarian Quarterly (text in English), H-1088 Budapest 8, Rákóczi u 17

Literary Prizes

Jozsef **Attila** Prize
For highly significant work in prose or poetry. Given to writers, poets and critics. Awarded annually. Enquiries to Ministry of Culture of the Hungarian People's Republic, Budapest

Szot Literary Prizes*
For meritorious literary works. Awarded annually. Enquiries to Hungarian Trade Unions Council, Budapest VI, Dozsa György u 84 B

Translation Agencies and Associations

Magyar Írok Szövetsége (Association of Hungarian Writers)*, Budapest VI, Bajza u 18
Has a section of Literary Translators

Iceland

General Information

Language: Icelandic (widespread knowledge of Danish and English)
Religion: Lutheran
Population: 222,000
Bank Hours: 0930-1330 Monday-Friday
Shop Hours: 0900-1800 Monday-Friday; open until 2200 Thursday or Friday, open until noon Saturday
Currency: 100 aurar = 1 krona
Export/Import Information: No tariff on books. Sales Tax of 20% or 22%. No import licences required. No exchange controls for books but they may not be imported on credit
Copyright: UCC, Berne, Florence (see International section)

Book Trade Organizations

Félag Islenskra Bókaútgefenda (Icelandic Publishers' Association), Laufasvegi 12, 101 Reykjavik Tel: 9127820
Chairman: Arnbjörn Kristinsson; *General Manager:* G Ólafsson
Publications: Bókatidindi; Bokaskara Boksalafelags Islands; Íslensk Bókatídindi

Félag Islenzkra Bókaverzlana (Icelandic Booksellers' Association)*, Skólavödustig 2, Reykjavik
Publications: Bóksalafélag Islands Siötíu Og Fimm Ára

Innkaupasamband Boksala (Booksellers' Import Union Ltd)*, Skipholti 7, 105 Reykjavik

Book Trade Reference Books and Journals

Books

Bóksalafélag Islands Sjötíu og Fimm Ára (75 years of the Icelandic Booksellers' Association), Skólavördustig 2, Reykjavik; contains addresses of publishers and booksellers

Journals

Arbók (Year Book), National Library of Iceland, Reykjavik; contains an annual list of Icelandic publications

Bókalisti (Booklist), City Library of Reykjavik, Thingholtsstr 29A, Reykjavik

Bokaskara Boksalafelags Islands, Icelandic Publishers' Association, Laufasvegi 12, 101 Reykjavik

Bókatídindi, Icelandic Publishers' Association, Laufasvegi 12, 101 Reykjavik (annual list of books published in Iceland)

Islensic Bó Kaskrá (The Icelandic National Bibliography), National Library of Iceland, Reykjavik (appears in *Íslensk Bókatídindi*)

Íslensk Bókatídindi (Icelandic Book News), Icelandic Publishers' Association, Laufasvegi 12, 101 Reykjavik

Publishers

Bókaútgáfa **Æskunnar***, Laugavegi 56, 101 Reykjavik

Almenna **Bókafélagid**, Austurstr 18, PO Box 9, 101 Reykjavik Tel: 19707 Cable Add: Bókafélagid Telex: 2046
Man Dir: Brynjólfur Bjarnason; *Editorial:* Eirikur H Finnbogason; *Sales Dir:* Anton Örn Kaernested; *Production:* Kristinn Dagsson
Subjects: General Fiction, Belles Lettres, Poetry, Biography, History, Secondary Textbooks, Juveniles
Bookshop: Bókaverzlun Sigfúsar Eymundssonar (BSE), Reykjavik
Book Club: The AB Book Club (BAB)
1977: 31 titles *1978:* 51 titles *Founded:* 1955

Atlantica*, PO Box 1238, Reykjavik
Subjects: Books on Iceland in English: Travel, Folklore, Literature, Culture

Bókaútgáfa Thórhalls **Bjarnarsonar**, Skemmuvegi 4, 200 Kopavogi

Bókaútgáfan **Björk***, Háholti 7, 300 Akranes

Bokaforlag Odds **Björnssonar**+, Tryggvabraut 18-20, PO Box 558, 600 Akureyri Tel: 22500 Cable Add: Prentverk
Man Dir: Geir S Björnsson; *Advertising Dir:* Kirstjan Kristjansson
Subjects: General Fiction, Belles Lettres, Poetry, Biography, History, How-to, Music, Art, Philosophy, Reference, Religion,

Juveniles, Educational Materials
1977: 16 titles *1978:* 14 titles *Founded:* 1897
Book Club: Heima er Bezt Book Club

Bokas hf*, Adalstr 35, 400 Isafirdi

Bókaútgáfan **Bragi***, Austurstr 17, 101 Reykjavik

Bókaverslun Sigfusar **Eymundssonar***, Austurstr 18, 101 Reykjavik
Subject: Educational Books
Bookshop: Address as above

Bókaútgáfa Gudjóns Ó **Gudjónssonar***, Langholtsvegi 111, Reykjavik Tel: 85433

Haraldur J **Hamar**, PO Box 93, Reykjavik Tel: 81590 Telex: 2121
Subjects: Iceland
1978: 5 titles

Heimskringla*, Laugavegi 18, Reykjavik Tel: 15199
Publicity Manager: Thorleifur Hauksson
General Manager: Thröstur Ólafsson

Bókaútgáfan **Helgafell***, Veghúsastíg 7, Reykjavik Tel: 16837

Bókaútgáfan **Hildur***, Fögrubrekku 47, 200 Kópavogi Tel: 44400

Hladbúd hf*, subsidiary of Idunn (qv)

Bókaútgáfan **Hlidskjálf***, Ingólfsstr 22, 101 Reykjavik Tel: 17520

Iceland Review, PO Box 93, 121 Reykjavik (Located at: Hverfisgötu 54) Tel: 27622 Telex: 2121
Man Dir: Haraldur J Hamar
Associate Company: Saga Publishing Co (qv)
Subjects: The Iceland Review Series (all in English) gives an overall picture of the country of Iceland, its culture and developing society; also History, Folklore, Industrial (in English); Icelandic Literature in Foreign Translation
1978: 5 titles *1979:* 4 titles *Founded:* 1962

Iceland Travel Books, subsidiary of Orn og Orlygur (qv)

Idunn, Braedraborgarstíg 16, PO Box 294, 121 Reykjavik Tel: 19156 Cable Add: 2308 publis is
Owner: Valdimar Jóhannsson; *Man Dir:* J P Valdimarsson; *Rights & Permissions, Production:* S Ragnarsson
Subsidiary Companies: Hladbud (University Textbooks); Skalholt (Icelandic Literature)
Subjects: General Fiction, Juveniles, Educational, Poetry, Law, Psychology, Philology, History, Natural Sciences, Philosophy, Management, Social Sciences, Art
1978: 90 titles *Founded:* 1945

Ísafoldarprentsmidja hf*, Tningholtsstr 5, 101 Reykjavik Tel: 17165

Hid **Íslenzka Bókmenntafélag***, Vonarstr 12, Reykjavik Tel: 21960
Subjects: Law, Linguistics, Literature, Philosophy, Politics, Psychology, Social Science
1977: 65 titles *Founded:* 1945

Snaebjörn **Jonsson** & Co HF (The English Bookshop)*, Hafnarstr 4 & 9, PO Box 1131, 101 Reykjavik Tel: 11936/13133 Cable Add: Books Reykjavik
Man Dir: Steinarr Gudjonsson
Subjects: All Subjects
Founded: 1927
Bookshops: The English Bookshop, Hafnarstr 9, Reykjavik; Bókaverzlun Snaebjarnar, Hafnarstr 4, Reykjavik

Bókaútgáfa Thorsteins M **Jónssonar*** Eskihlíd 21, 105 Reykjavik

Kynning Ltd,*, PO Box 1238, Reykjavik Tel: 38456, 74153
Subjects: Books on Iceland in general and on special subjects such as volcanoes, geology, geography, history, literature etc

Leiftur hf*, Höfdatúni 12, 105 Reykjavik Tel: 17554

Bókagerdin **Lilja***, Amtmannsstíg 2b, 101 Reykjavik

Mál og menning*, Laugavegi 18, Reykjavik Tel: 15199
Publicity Manager: Thorleifur Hauksson; *General Manager:* Thröstur Ólafsson
Bookshop/Bookclub: address as above

Bókaútgáfa **Menningarsjóds** og Thjód vinafélagsins*, Skálholtsstíg 7, 101 Reykjavik Tel: 13652/10282

Örn og Örlygur HF+, Vesturgötu 42, 101 Reykjavik Tel: 25722 Cable Add: Örn og Örlygur Telex: 2197
Owner and Man Dir: Örlygur Hálfdanarson;
Editorial and other offices: Örlygur Hálfdanarson;
Subsidiary Companies: Iceland Travel Books, Vesturgötu 42, Reykjavik
Subjects: General Fiction, Belles Lettres, Poetry, Biography, History, How-to, Reference, Religion, Juveniles, Low- & High-priced Paperbacks, Social Science
Book Club: Hraundragni
1977: 45 titles *1978:* 60 titles *Founded:* 1965

Ríkisútgáfa Námsbóka, Tjarnagötu 10, Reykjavik 101, PO Box 1274 Tel: 10436/20830
State Educational Publishing Department
Dir: Bragi Gudjonsson; *Sales:* Vidar Gunnarsson; *Production/Publicity:* Bogi Indridason; *Rights & Permissions:* Eirikur Grimsson
Subjects: School Textbooks and Supplies
Bookshop: Skólavörubúdin, Tjarnargata 10, Reykjavik
1977: 41 titles *1978:* 48 titles *Founded:* 1937

Rökkur, bókaútgáfan*, Flókagötu 15, Reykjavik Tel: 18768

Saga Publishing Co, PO Box 93, 121 Reykjavik (Located at: Hverfisgotu 54) Tel: 27622 Telex: 2121
Man Dir: Haraldur J Hamar
Associate Company: Iceland Review (qv)
Subjects: General (Adults and Juveniles)
1978: 5 titles *1979:* 4 titles *Founded:* 1971

Setberg*, Freyjugötu 14, 101 Reykjavik Tel: 17667
Subjects: History, Juveniles, General Nonfiction, Fiction

Skalholt, subsidiary of Idunn (qv)

Bókaútgáfan **Skjaldborg** sf*, Hafnarstr 67, 600 Akureyri Tel: 11024

Skuggsja bókaforlag*, Strandgötu 31, 220 Hafnarfirdi Tel: 50045
Subject: General Fiction

Bókaútgáfan **Snaefell***, Alfaskeidi 58, 220 Hafnarfirdi

ICELAND 185

Bókaútgáfan **Sudri***, PO Box 1214, Kleppsvegi 2, 105 Reykjavik Tel: 36384

Bókaútgáfan **Thjódsaga***, Thingholtsstr 27, 101 Reykjavik Tel: 13510
Subjects: General Fiction, Travel, General Science, Juveniles

Bókaútgáfan **Valafell***, Thykkvabae 16, 110 Reykjavik Tel: 84179
Subject: General Fiction

Literary Agents

Sveinbjörn **Jonsson**, Gardastr 21, PO Box 438, Reykjavik Tel: (91) 28110/13206
Specialization: General Fiction and nonfiction, books, magazines, plays, TV scripts

Book Clubs

The **A B** Book Club*, Austurstr 18, PO Box 9, Reykjavik
Owned by: Almenna Bókafélagid (Reykjavik)

Heima er Bezt Book Club, Tryggvabraut 18-20, PO Box 558, 600 Akureyri
Owned by: Bokaforlag Odds Björnssonar (Akureyri)

Hraundragni Book Club, Vesturgötu 42, 101 Reykjavik
Owned by: Örn og Örlygur

The **Icelandic Libertarians'** Book Club, PO Box 1334, 121 Reykjavik (Located at: Háaleitisbraut 1, 105 Reykjavik) Tel: (91) 85298
Members: 210
Owned by: The Icelandic Libertarians' Bookshop and The Freedom Association
Specialization: Economics, History, Philosophy, Political Science, Libertarianism

Mal Og Menning*, Laugavegi 18, Reykjavik Tel: 15199
Bookshop: Bókabúd Máls og Menningar, at same address

Major Booksellers

The **English Bookshop***, Hafnarstr 9, Reykjavik

Bókábudin **Helgafell***, Laugavegur 100, Reykjavik
also Njalsgata 64, Reykjavik

The **Icelandic Libertarians'** Bookshop, PO Box 1334, 121 Reykjavik (Located at: Háaleitisbraut 1, 105 Reykjavik) Tel: (91) 85298 Telex: 2074 europa is
Specializing in History, Politics, Economics, Philosophy with special emphasis on the ideology of Libertarianism

The **International Bookshop***, Bókaverzlun Sigfúsar Eymundsonar, Austurstr 18, Reykjavik Tel: 19707/16997/32620

Bókaverzlun **Ísafoldar***, Austurstr 10, Reykjavik

Bókabúd **Máls og Menningar**, Laugavegi 18, Reykjavik Tel: 24242

Major Libraries

Borgarbókasafn (City Library of Reykjavik)*, Thingholtsstr 29A, Reykjavik

Háskólabókasafn, 101 Reykjavik Tel: 25088 Telex: 2307 isinfo
University Library
Head Librarian: Einar Sigurdsson
Publication: Annual Report

Landsbókasafn Islands (National Library of Iceland)*, Reykjavik Tel: 13375 (Director); 16864 (Staff)

Thjodskjalasafn (National Archives)*, Safnahús, Reykjavik

Library Associations

Bókavardafélag Islands, Box 7050, 127 Reykjavik
Icelandic Library Association
President: Thórdís Thorvaldsdóttir
Secretary: Gunmar Markússon
Publication: Fréttabréf (Newsletter) and Bókasafnid

Deild Bokavarda í Islenskum Rannsoknarbokasofnum*, Landsbokasafn Islands, Reykjavik Tel: 13080
Division of Librarians in Icelandic Research Libraries
Executive Secretary: Kristín Thorsteinsdottir

Library Journals

Fréttabréf (Newsletter), Icelandic Library Association, Box 7050 Reykjavik

Skírnir, Icelandic Literary Society, Reykjavik

Literary Associations and Societies

Íslenzka bókmenntafélag*, Reykjavik
Icelandic Literary Society
Secretary: Óskar Halldórsson
Publication: Annual Journal, Skírnir

International **P E N** Centre*, Fifuhvammsvegi 19, Reykjavik
Secretary: Gisli Astthorsson

Rithöfundasamband Íslands, PO Box 949, 121 Reykjavik
Writers' Association of Iceland
Chairman: Njördur P Njardvík

India

General Information

Language: Hindi, English
Religion: Predominantly Hindu
Population: 626 million
Literacy Rate (1961): 29%
Bank Hours: 1000-1400 (1030-1430 Bombay) Monday-Friday; 1000-1200 Saturday (1030-1230 Bombay)
Shop Hours: Delhi: 0930-1930; Calcutta and Bombay: 1000-1830 Madras: 0900-19330. All effective Monday-Saturday, some open Sunday. Many close 2 hours for lunch
Currency: 100 paise = 1 rupee
Export/Import Information: No tariff on books but advertising matter subject to 100%. Import licences required. Books imported by Established Importers. Exchange transactions restricted.
Copyright: UCC, Berne, Buenos Aires (see International section)

Book Trade Organizations

Ahmedabad Publishers' & Booksellers' Association, 47 Gandhi Rd, Ahmedabad 380001 Tel: 366917
President: C C Vora

Akhil Bhartiya Hindi Prakashak Sangh*, Hindi Book Centre, Asaf Ali Rd, New Delhi 110001
President: K C Berry

All India Booksellers' & Publishers' Association*, 17-L Connaught Circus, PO Box 328, New Delhi 110001 Tel: 42166
President: A N Varma

All India Hindi Publishers' Association*, c/o Rajasthan Prakashan, Tripolia Bazaar, Jaipur (Rajasthan)

Assam Publishers' & Booksellers' Association, Lawyers Book Stall, Gauhati

Association of Publishing Professionals of India*, K-14 Rajouri Garden, New Delhi 27
President: Samuel Israel

Bihar Pustak Vyayasayi Sangh, Bharat Bhawan, Govind Mitra Rd, Patna 4

Bombay Booksellers' and Publishers' Association*, 25 6th Floor Building No 3, Navjivan Co-op Housing Society Ltd, Dr Bhadkamkar Marg, Bombay 400008

Book Industry Council of South India*, Madras 14

Booksellers' and Publishers' Association of South India*, c/o Higginbothams Ltd, Mount Rd, Madras-600002

Chandigarh Booksellers' Association*, SCO No 3 Sector 17-E, Chandigarh Tel: 23594
President: V S Puri

Delhi Educational Publishers' Union*, Nath Market, Nai Sarak, Delhi 110006

Delhi State Booksellers' and Publishers' Association, c/o The Students' Stores, Kashmere Gate, PO Box 1511, Delhi 110006 Tel: 227088/225716
Hon Secretary: Devendra Sharma

Educational Publishers' Association*, 4c Daryaganj, New Delhi

Federation of Indian Publishers, M-138 Aggarwal Bldg, Connaught Circus, New Delhi 110001 Tel: 350811
Executive Secretary: M C Minocha

Federation of Booksellers and Publishers Association in Gujarat, Post Box 334 GPO, Ahmedabad 380001
Honorary Secretary: P D Shevade

Federation of Publishers and Booksellers Associations in India*, 1st Floor, 4833/24 Govind Lane, Ansari Rd, New Delhi 110002
Publications: Directory of Indian Publishers, Recent Indian Publications

Gujarat State English Language Booksellers' Association, Academic Book Centre*, 10 Walkeshwar, Ambawadi, Ahmedabad 380015 Tel: 837883
Honorary Secretary: R N Shah

The **Gujarat Textbook** Publishers' Association*, Balgovind Kuberdas & Co, Gandhi Rd, Ahmedabad

Himachal Publishers' & Booksellers' Association*, Goel Book Depot, Palampur Tel: 43151
President: H K S Goel

The **Hyderabad** & Secunderabad Publishers' & Booksellers' Association*, c/o M/S Booklinks Corporation, 3-4-423/5 Narayanaguda, Hyderabad 500029
Secretary: C Lakshmi Narayana

Indian Association of University Presses, Calcutta University Press*, Calcutta
Organizing Secretary: S Kanjilal

Karnataka Publishers' and Booksellers' Association*, 504 Avenue Rd, Bangalore 560002

Kerala Publishers & Booksellers Association*, Paico Buildings, Jew Street, Ernakulam, Cochin 682011 Tel: 34068
Cable Add: Paico
President: D C Kezhakemuri

Lanka Booksellers' Association*, Kohinoor Bldgs, University Rd, Varanasi Tel: 62771
President: Lalchand Mankhand

Meerut Publishers' Association*, c/o Rastogi Publications, Meerut, Uttar Pradesh

Mysore State Publishers' and Booksellers' Association*, 504 Avenue Rd, Bangalore 2

Poona Booksellers' Association*, c/o Venus Book Stall Ltd, Appa Balwant Chowk, Poona

Publishers' & Booksellers' Association of Andhra Pradesh, Sree Venkateswara Book Depot, Main Rd, Guntur 522003
Secretary: P Narasimha Rao

Publishers' and Booksellers' Association of Bengal*, 93 Mahatma Gandhi Rd, Calcutta 700007
Publication: Granthajagat

Publishers' and Booksellers' Guild, 5A Bhawani Dutta Lane, PO Box 12341/700073, Calcutta 700073
President: S Sarkar; *Secretary:* B K Dhur

Publishers' Association of India*, 14-18 Calicut St, Ballard Estate, Bombay 400038
Chairman: P S Jayasinghe

Publishers' Association of South India*, 3 Kondi Chetty St, Madras 1 Tel: 29402
President: T V S Mani

Punjabi Publishers' Association*, 354 Purani Kutchery, Jullundur City

Rajasthan Pustak Vyavasayee Sangh*, SMS Highway, Jaipur 3
President: J L Jasoria

Ranchi District Publishers' and Booksellers' Association*, Kamal Prakashan, Hindpiri, Ranchi 1 Tel: 20983
President: P N Sharma

Singhbhum District Booksellers' Association*, c/o Sanyal Brothers, Bari Mansion, Jamshedpur

Young Publishers' Association, Munshiram Manoharial Publishers Pvt Ltd*, 54, Rani Jahansi Rd, New Delhi 110055

Book Trade Reference Books and Journals

Books

Bookdealers in India; a directory of antiquarian booksellers in Bangladesh, Bhutan, India, Nepal, Pakistan and Sri Lanka, Sheppard Press Ltd, 15 James St, PO Box 42, London WC2E 8BX, UK

Directory of Book Import Trade in the Indian Sub-Continent, Literary Market Review, 6/77 WEA Karol Bagh, New Delhi 110005

Directory of Book Trade in India, National Guide Books Syndicate, 5c/93 Rohtak Rd, New Delhi 110005

Directory of Foreign Book Trade in India, Lord International, 2/6 Canal Rd, Vijay Nagar, Delhi 110009

Directory of Indian Publishers, Federation of Publishers' and Booksellers' Associations in India, 1st Floor, 4833/24 Govind Lane, Ansari Rd, New Delhi 110002

Directory of the Indian Book Industry, Sterling Publishers Pvt Ltd, AB/9 Safdarjang Enclave, New Delhi 16

Indian Books, Indian Bibliographic Centre, 236 Kot Kishan Chand, Jullundur 4, Punjab (books in English only) (annual)

Indian Books; an annual bibliography, Researchco Publications, 1865 Trinajar, Delhi 35 (books in English only) (annual)

Indian Books in Print, Indian Bureau of Bibliographies, 2153/2 Fountain, Delhi 6

Indian Publishers' Directory, Makherjee & Co Pvt Ltd, 2 Bankim Chatterjee St, Calcutta 700012

Journals

American and British Book News, Kunnuparampil P Punnoose, 6/77 WEA Karol Bagh, New Delhi 110005

BEPI; an annual bibliography of English publications in India, DKF Trust, 74–D Anand Nagar, Delhi 110035

Book Bulletin (monthly), Taraporevala Sons & Co Pvt Ltd, 210 Dr Dadabhai Naoroji Rd, Bombay 400001

Book Reviews in Public Administration, Indian Institute of Public Administration, Indraprastha Estate, Ring Rd, New Delhi 110001

Books from Abroad, 2/6 Canal Rd, Vijay Nagar, Delhi 110009

Books of the Week Bulletin, D K Agencies, 313/74-D Inderlok, Old Rohtak Rd, Delhi 110035

Bulletin of Indian Books, Milap Trust, PO Box 23, Bhavangar 364001

Granthajagat, Publishers' and Booksellers' Association of Bengal, 93 Mahatma Gandhi Rd, Calcutta 700007

India Book House News (text in English), A C Chobe for Mirchandani & Co Pvt Ltd, 29 Wodehouse Rd, Bombay 1

Indian Book Industry, Sterling Publishers Pvt Ltd, AB/9 Safdarjang Enclave, New Delhi 110016

Indian Book Market, B–28/15 Durgakund, Varanasi 221005

Indian Book Reporter; author, subject and title index to new publications, Prabhu Book Service, Gurgaon

Indian Book Review Supplement, Delhi Library Association, PO Box 1270, c/o Hardinge Public Library, Queen's Garden, Delhi 6

Indian Books; an information leaflet, Mukherjee Library, 1 Gopi Mohan Dutta Lane, Calcutta 700003

Indian National Bibliography, Central Reference Library, c/o National Library, Belvedere, Calcutta 27

Indian Publisher and Bookseller, Popular Book Depot, Dr Bhadkamkar Rd, Bombay 400007

Lalvani's Book World, Lalvani Brothers, 4 Darya Ganj, Ansari Rd, Delhi 110006

Literary Market Review, 6/77 WEA Karol Bagh, New Delhi 110005 (quarterly)

Paperbound Books, 6/77 WEA Karol Bagh, New Delhi 110005 (quarterly)

Publishers' Monthly (text in English and Hindi), Ravindra Mansion, Ram Nagar, New Delhi 110055

Publishing News, D K Agencies, 313/74-D Inderlok, Old Rohtak Rd, Delhi 110035

Pustak Parichaya (text in Hindi), 2/35 Ansari Rd, Daryaganj, Delhi 6

Recent Indian Publications, Federation of Publishers' and Booksellers' Associations in India, 1st Floor, 4833/24 Govind Lane, Ansari Rd, New Delhi 110002

Rights and Permissions, Aymanathu-parampil Bldgs, Kurichy PO, Kottayam Distt, Kerala State (for promoting reprint and translation rights of foreign publications)

Publishers

Abhinav Publications+, E-37 Hauz Khas, New Delhi 110016
Dir: Shakti Malik
Subjects: Indian Art & Archaeology, Indology, Humanities, Literature, Social Sciences, Criminology, Politics

Academic Publishers+, 5A Bhawani Dutta Lane, PO Box 12341/700073, Calcutta 7000073 Tel: 340936 Cable Add: Acabooks
Man Dir: Bimal Kumar Dhur; *Sales Dir:* Biren Dutta; *Publicity Dir:* S Das; *Rights & Permissions:* L K Ghosh
Subjects: Accountancy, Commerce, History, Indology, Literature, Management, Medicine, Philosophy, Research
1977: 12 titles *Founded:* 1958

Advaita Ashrama, 5 Dehi Entally Rd, Calcutta 700014 Tel: 44–2898 Cable Add: Vedanta
Subjects: Religion, Philosophy, Yoga, Vedanta, Indian Culture, Education
1977–78: 26 titles

Affiliated East-West Press Pvt Ltd+, 104 Nirmal Tower, 26 Barakhamba Rd, New Delhi 110001 Tel: 44398 Cable Add: Bookmail
Man Dir: K S Padmanabhan; *Editorial Dir:* Kamal Malik
Subjects: Philosophy, Low-priced Paperbacks, Psychology, Engineering, General & Social Science, University Textbooks, Arts
Founded: 1962

Allied Publishers Private Ltd, 15 J N Heredia Marg, Ballard Estate, Bombay 400038
Man Dir: R N Sachdev
Br Offs: 13-14 Asaf Ali Rd, New Delhi 110002; 17 Chittaranjan Ave, Calcutta 700072; 150/B/6 Mount Rd, Madras 600002; Jayadeva Hostel Bldg, 5th Main Rd, Gandhinagar, Bangalore 560009
Subjects: General Fiction, Belles Lettres, Art, History, Philosophy, Education, How-to, Psychology, Law, Social, Political & General Science & Technology
1977: 30 titles *1978:* 45 titles

Alpha-Beta Publications Ltd*, 55-1 College St, 2nd Floor, Calcutta 700012

Amarko Booook Agency*, B-42 Amar Colony, Lajpat Nagar, New Delhi 110024
Man Dir, Production, Publicity, Rights & Permissions: V N Bhardwaj; *Sales:* Sh Ashok Bhardwaj
Subsidiary Company: Weltanschaung Publications, 1263 Ganj Mir Khan, Darya Ganj, New Delhi 110002
Subjects: History, Philosophy, Religion
Bookshop: 1263 Ganj Mir Khan, Darya Ganj, New Delhi 110002
1977: 2 titles *Founded:* 1973

Ambika Publications, B-1/598 Janak Puri, New Delhi 110058 Tel: 591072 Cable Add: Ambika
Man Dir, Editorial, Rights & Permissions: P P Anand; *Sales:* Ms Manmeet Maini; *Production:* Suhas Nimbalkar; *Publicity:* Ms Nirdosh Anand
Associate Companies: Arpan International (at above address); Tagore Trading Co, ED 54 Tagore Gardens, New Delhi 110027
Subjects: Sociology, Politics, Anthropology, Ancient and Medieval History, Art, Religion, Buddhism, Tibetan Studies, Management
1978: 20 titles *1979:* 10 titles *Founded:* 1977

Amerind Publishing Co (P) Ltd, subsidiary of Oxford & IBH Publishing Co (qv)

Anand Paperbacks, an imprint of Orient Paperbacks, India (qv)

Ankur Publishing House, Uphaar Cinema Building, Green Park Extension, New Delhi 110016 Tel: 664611
Man Dir: Mrs Seema Mukerjee
Associate Company: Sanjay Composers and Printers (at above address)
Subjects: Politics, Science, Literature
1978: 5 titles *1979:* 3 titles *Founded:* 1976

Arnold-Heinemann Publishers (India) Pvt Ltd+*, AB/9 Safdarjang Enclave, New Delhi 110016 Tel: 667886 Cable Add: Heinemann
Man Dir: G A Vazirani; *Editorial:* Ms Suhasini Ramaswamy; *Accounts:* C P Grover; *Production:* Padam Prakash Khanna; *Publicity:* Ms Parveen Bhola; *Rights & Permissions:* Ms C R Swarna; *Sales:* Maninder Singh
Associated Companies: Edward Arnold, UK (qv); Heinemann Educational Books, UK (qv)
Imprints: Mayfair Paperbacks; Sanskriti; Zebra Books for Children
Subjects: Art, General Fiction, Belles Lettres, Poetry, Philosophy, Religion, Reference, Literary Criticism, Medicine, Engineering, Social Science, Political

Science, University, Secondary & Primary Textbooks, Low-priced Paperbacks
1977: 72 titles *1978:* 110 titles *Founded:* 1969

Asia Publishing House (P) Ltd+, Calicut St, Ballard Estate, Bombay 400038
Tel: 262631/3 Cable Add: Booklore
Chairman, Man Dir: Ananda Jaisingh; *Editorial Consultant:* Homi Vakeel
Br Offs in India: 67 Ganesh Chandra Ave, Calcutta 700013; Indra Palace, Connaught Circus, New Delhi 110001; 199 Mount Rd, Madras 600002; 18 Purana Quilla, Lucknow 226001
Br Off outside India: 141 East 44th St, New York, NY 10017, USA
Subjects: General Fiction, Belles Lettres, Poetry, Biography, History, Music, Art, Philosophy, Reference, Religion, Low- & High-priced Paperbacks, Medicine, Psychology, Engineering, General & Social Science, University Textbooks, Educational Materials, Business Studies
Founded: 1961

Asian Educational Services*, C–2/15 SDA, PO Box 4534, New Delhi 110016
Tel: 664347 Cable Add: Asia-Books New Delhi 110016
Chief Executive, Editorial, Rights & Permissions: Jagdish Jetley; *Production:* Mrs S Jetley; *Publicity:* S K Mohla
Subjects: Ancient Indian History and Culture, Religion, Philosophy, Sociology, Literature
1977: 40 titles *1978:* 25 titles *Founded:* 1973

Asian Publishers, an imprint of Sterling Publishers Pty Ltd (qv)

Associated Publishing House+, New Market, Karol Bagh, New Delhi 110005
Tel: 563069
Man Dir: Ravinder K Paul; *Editorial Dir:* Ashok K Paul; *Publicity Dir:* Sharda Paul
Subjects: General Fiction, Belles Lettres, Poetry, History, Art, Reference, Social Science, Business, Reprints
1977: 5 titles *1978:* 18 titles *Founded:* 1966

Atma Ram & Sons, Kashmere Gate, PO Box 1429, Delhi 110006 Tel: 223092/228159 Cable Add: Books Delhi 6
Man Dir: Ish Kumar Puri
Br Off: 17 Ashok Marg, Lucknow
Subjects: Belles Lettres, Art, History, Philosophy, Religion, Education, Reference, How-to, Juveniles, Medicine, Engineering, Social Science, Science & Technology, Paperbacks, Textbooks
1978: 29 titles *Founded:* 1909

Sri **Aurobindo** Books Distribution Agency (SABDA), Sri Aurobindo Ashram, Pondicherry 605002 Tel: 980 Cable Add: Sabda c/o Aurobindo
Man Dir: B Poddar; *Sales:* Sri Parasnath; *Rights & Permissions:* Sri Harikant Patel
Branch Off: 'Sahakar' B Rd, Bombay 400020
Subjects: Yoga, Philosophy, Religion, Education, History, Social & Political Science (English, French, German, Sanskrit etc)
1978: 66 titles *1979:* 60 titles *Founded:* 1952
Bookshops: 9B rue de la Marine; 2 rue de la Caserne (both in Pondicherry)

B I Publications, 54 Janpath, New Delhi 1
Tel: 46137/42911 Cable Add: Tripplekey
Telex: 3591
Chairman: R D Bhagat; *General Manager, Rights & Permissions:* K P Churamani
Br Offs: 18 Lansdowne Rd, Bombay 400039;
13 Government Pl East, Calcutta 700069; 13 Daryaganj, Delhi 110006; 150 Mount Rd, Madras 600002
Subjects: History, Religion, Low-priced Paperbacks, Medicine, Technology, University Textbooks, Philosophy, Engineering, Science
Founded: 1935

B R Publishing Corporation*, 461 Vivekananda Nagar, Delhi 110035
Tel: 274819 Cable Add: Dikay Book
Telex: 31-3616-DK-IN
Chief Executive, Editorial, Production: I C Mitral; *Sales, Rights & Permissions:* S K Bhatia; *Publicity:* Praveen Mitaal
Orders to: D K Publishers' Distributors, 1 Ansari Rd, New Delhi 110002
Parent Company: D K Publishers' Distributors (qv)
Subjects: Art, Archaeology, History, Social Sciences, Anthropology
1977: 15 titles *1978:* 20 titles *Founded:* 1974

K P **Bagchi** & Co, 286 B B Ganguli St, Calcutta 700012, West Bengal Tel: 267474
Editorial, Chief Executive, Publicity, Rights & Permissions: P K Bagchi; *Editorial, Sales, Production:* K K Bagchi
Subjects: Anthropology, History, Economics, Political Science, Indology, Sociology, Language and Literature
1977: 27 titles *1978:* 10 titles *Founded:* 1972

P M **Bagchi** & Co (P) Ltd+*, 19 Gulu Ostagar Lane, Calcutta 700006

The **Bangalore** Printing & Publishing Co Ltd+, 88 Mysore Rd, PO Box 1807, Bangalore 560018, Karnataka Tel: 601638, 601027 Cable Add: Mudrashala
Man Dir: H C Ramanna
Br Off: The Bangalore Press, Statue Sq, Mysore
Subjects: Biography, Philosophy, Religion, Psychology, Social Science, University, Secondary & Primary Textbooks, Agriculture, Fiction (in English and Kannada languages), Calendars, Diaries
1977: 13 titles *1978:* 20 titles *Founded:* 1916
Bookshop: Bangalore Press Agencies, Avenue Rd, Bangalore 2

Bansal and Co+, K–16 Naveen Shahdara, Delhi 110032 Tel: 204292
Chief Executive: R S Bansal; *Editorial, Sales, Production, Publicity, Rights & Permissions:* Hari Gupta
Subjects: Bibliography, Indology
1977: 3 titles *Founded:* 1959

K P **Basu** Publishing Co+*, 42 Bidhan Sarani, Calcutta 700006

Better Yourself Books, 28–B Chatham Lines, Allahabad 211002, Uttar Pradesh
Tel: 53728
Man Dir: Mathew Veohoor; *Publicity:* Fr Mark Fonseca
Subjects: Home Life, Self-improvement, Biography, Moral Science, Indology, Fiction, Practical Psychology, Sex Education, Media Education
1977: 40 titles *1978:* 50 titles *Founded:* 1954

Bharat-Bharati+*, Western Kutchery Rd, Meerut (UP)
Owner: Suresh Pandey; *Man Dir:* Ganga Nath Pandey
Subjects: Poetry, History, Music, Art, Philosophy, Religion, Oriental & Indian Studies
Founded: 1968

Bharat Law House, 15 Mahatma Gandhi Marg, Allahabad 211001 Tel: 3797
Chief Executive, Production: D C Puliani; *Sales:* Ashok Puliani; *Publicity:* Ravi Puliani
Subject: Law
1978: 5 titles *1979:* 3 titles *Founded:* 1961

Bharatiya Jnanpith+*, B–45 & 47 2nd Floor, Connaught Pl, New Delhi 110001
Subjects: Documentation, History, Music, Philosophy, Religion, Bibliography, Arts, Literature, Linguistics

Bharatiya Vidya Bhavan, PO Box 4057, Munshi Sadan, Kulapati K M Munshi Marg, Bombay 400007 Tel: 351461 Cable Add: Bhavidya
Man Dir, Editorial, Publicity, Rights & Permissions: S Ramakrishnan; *Sales:* V A Madhavan; *Production:* C K Venkataraman
Branch Off: Ahmedabad, Bangalore, Baroda, Bhopal, Bhubaneswar, Calcutta, Chandigarh, Coimbatore, Dakor, Delhi, Ernakulam, Guntur, Hyderabad, Jammu, Jamnagar, Kakinada, Kanpur, Kashmir, Madras, Madurai, Mangalore, Mukundgarh, Nagpur, Shillong, Trichur, Visakhapatnam (all in India); 4a Castle Town Rd, London W14 UK
Subjects: History, Philosophy, Religion, Art, Literature, Culture, Biography, Gita, Vedas, Upanishads, Gandhiana, Mythology, Fiction, Sociology
1977: 48 titles *1978:* 56 titles *Founded:* 1938

Blackie & Son Private Ltd, 103/5 Walchand Hirachand Marg, PO Box 21, Bombay 400001 Tel: 261410/265469 Cable Add: Blackie
Man Dir: D R Bhagi; *Dir:* A Bhagi
Br Off: Bharat Bldgs, 2/18 Anna Salai, Madras 600002
Subjects: Arts, Social Science, Mathematics, Education, Science, Technical
Founded: 1902

Bookventure+*, 14 Thaninabhalam Chetty Rd, Madras 600017 Tel: 441970
Proprietor: Lakshmi Krushnamurti
Subjects: General Fiction, Belles Lettres, Poetry, Biography, History, Music, Art, Philosophy, General Science
Founded: 1965

Business Promotion Bureau, 376 Lajpat Rai Market, Delhi 110006 Tel: 224666/277147
Proprietor: G C Jain
Subjects: Radio, Electronis Textbooks (in English)
1978: 25 titles *Founded:* 1958

Central Book Depot (Publishers)*, 44 Johnstonganj, Allahabad Tel: 2408/2130/53727
Man Dirs: K L Bhargava, M L Bhargava; *Sales Dir:* B K Chatterji
Subsidiary Company: Indian University Press, 18/C Queens Rd, Allahabad
Br Off: 13 University Rd, Allahabad
Subjects: History, Philosophy, Medicine, Psychology, Engineering, General & Social Science, University & Secondary Textbooks
Founded: 1880

S **Chand** & Co Ltd+, Ravindra Mansion, PO Box 5733, Ram Nagar, New Delhi 110055 Tel: 517531 Cable Add: Eschand, New Delhi Telex: 0312185
Man Dir: S L Gupta; *Editorial, Publicity:* R C Kumar; *Rights & Permissions:* R K Kupta
Associated Companies: Eurasia Publishing House Pvt Ltd, India (qv); Rajendra Ravindra Printers Ltd, New Delhi
Br Offs: in Bombay, Calcutta, Patna,

Lucknow, Jullundur, Hyderabad, Madras, Bangalore, Nagpur, Cochin
Subjects: Art, Philosophy, Economics, Social & Political Science, Science and Technology
Bookshop: 4/16-B Asaf Ali Rd, New Delhi 110002
1977: 100 titles *1978:* 125 titles *Founded:* 1917

Chaukhambha Orientalia, Gokul Bhawan K 37/109, Gopal Mandir Lane, PO Box 32, Varanasi 221001 (UP) Tel: 63022 Cable Add: Gokulotsav
Managing Partner: Braj Bhavan Das Gupta
Br Off: Delhi
Subjects: Indian Classical Literature, Oriental A Art, Science (in Sanskrit, Hindi, English)

Chetana Publications+*, E 180 Greater Kailesh Part II, New Delhi 110048 Tel: 513065
Man Dir: Chetana Kohli; *Sales & Publicity Dir, Rights & Permissions:* Suresh Kohli
Subjects: General Fiction, Biography, History, How-to, Philosophy, Religion, Low-priced Paperbacks, Social Science
Founded: 1974
Subsidiary: India Paperbacks, 11052 East Park Rd, New Delhi 110005

The **Chowkhamba** Sanskrit Series Office, K37/99, Gopal Mandir Lane, PO Chowkhamba, PO Box 8, Varanasi-221001 Tel: 63145 Cable Add: Chowkhamba Series, Varanasi
Man Dir, Publicity, Rights & Permissions: Bithal Das Gupta; *Editorial:* Pandit Ramchandra Jha; *Sales, Production:* Brij Mohan Das Gupta
Associated Company: Chaukhamba Amarabharati Prakashan, K37/118, Gopal Mandir Lane, PO Box 138, Varanasi 221001
Subjects: Juveniles, Educational Materials, Primary, Secondary & University Textbooks, Poetry, Biography, History, Music, Art, Philosophy, Reference, Religion, Oriental, Indology
1977: 103 titles *1978:* 3 titles *Founded:* 1892
Bookshop: Chowkhamba Sanskrit Series Office, Varanasi

College Book House, 46/3 Kanakakunnath veedu, Manacud, Trivandrum 695009 Tel: 4578
Man Dir, Editorial, Production, Rights & Permissions: M Easwaran; *Sales:* M Girija; *Publicity:* R Radhakrishnan
Subjects: Indian Studies, Religion, Philosophy, Education, Economics, Sociology, History, Kerala (South India)
Bookshop: College Book House, Library Division (at above address)
1978: 9 titles *1979:* 20 titles *Founded:* 1973

Concept Publishing Co+, H 13 Bali Nagar, New Delhi 110015 Tel: 563967
Chief Executive: Naurang Rai; *Editorial:* Suhasini Ramaswamy; *Sales, Publicity:* Ashok Kumar
Parent Company: D K Agencies, Delhi 110035
Associate Companies: D K Publishers' Distributors (qv); DKF Trust; University Publishers (qv)
Subjects: Indology, Anthropology, Art, Sociology, Philosophy, Economics, Public Administration, Geography, Bibliography
1977: 30 titles *1978:* 30 titles *Founded:* 1975

Crescent Publishing Co, 4 Abdul Qadir Market, Jail Rd, Aligarh 202001 Tel: 3711 Cable Add: Milestone
Man Dir, Publicity, Rights & Permissions: Amanullah Khan; *Editorial:* T Usama; *Sales:* Zikrullah Khan; *Production:* N R Faruqi
Subjects: Religion, Academic
1978: 2 titles *1979:* 3 titles *Founded:* 1976

Current Technical Literature Co (Pvt) Ltd, India House, PB No 1374, Bombay 400001 Tel: 261045/267616 Cable Add: Cutelico
Chief Executives: K Ramanathan, K Sankaranarayanan; *Man Dir:* R K Murthi
Associate Company: Global Publishers Service P Ltd, A-31 3rd Floor, Shri Ram Industrial Estate, G D Ambekar Road, PO Box 7121, Bombay 400 031, India
Branch Offs: 151 Thambu Chetty St, PB 127, Madras 600001; 22 Chittaranjan Ave, PB 8894, Calcutta 700072; Hosite Blood Bank, Narayanguda, Hyderabad 500029; Jai Kumar Niketan, PB 7008, Ansari Road, New Delhi 110002
Subjects: Medical, Scientific & Technical
Founded: 1946

D K Publishers' Distributors+, 1 Ansari Rd, New Delhi 110002 Tel: 247819 Cable Add: Dekaypub Telex: Dikay ND 3616
Partners: I C Mittal, Praveen Mittal, Pramil Mittal; *Editorial:* I C Mittal; *Sales, Production, Publicity, Rights & Permissions:* S K Bhatia
Parent Company: DK Agencies, 74D Inderlok, Old Rohtak Rd, Delhi 110035
Associated Company: DK Book Organization, 74/D Anand Nagar, Delhi 110035
Subsidiary Companies: BR Publishing Corp, India (qv); Concept Publishing Co, India (qv); Inter-India Publications, India (qv); DK Publications, 29/9 Shakti Nagar, Nangia Park, Delhi 110007
Branch Off: No 4 Gurayoof Appan Mansions, No 28/30 Khana Bagh 3rd Lane, Triplicane, Madras 600005; T C 789 Devivilas Compound, Chenthittal, Trivanorum 23
Subjects: Humanities and Social Sciences
1977: 23 titles *1978:* 30 titles *Founded:* 1974
Miscellaneous: Largest Wholesale House for Indian Publications

Dastane Ramchandra and Co*, 456 Raviwar Peth, Phadke Houd, PO Box 535, Poona 411002 Tel: 48193
Man Dir: R D Dastane; *Editorial, Production:* S R Dastane; *Sales, Publicity, Rights & Permissions:* V R Dastane
Associated Company: Abhang Stores, Printers & Stationers (address as above)
Subjects: Chemistry, Geology, Geography, Botany, Sociology, Economics, Literature, Archaeology
1977: 8 titles *Founded:* 1960

Debooks+, 9 Creek Row, Calcutta 700013
Publicity, Rights & Permissions: Mrs R De; *Marketing, Sales:* Ajoy De; *Accounts:* Asok De
1977: 3 titles *1978:* 4 titles *Founded:* 1975

Deep & Deep Publications, D-1/24 Rajouri Garden, New Delhi 110027
Subjects: Law, Military, History, Politics
1978: 3 titles *1979:* 8 titles
Miscellaneous: Also booksellers and exporters

Diamond Comics, 2715 Darya Ganj, New Delhi 110002
Associate Companies: Diamond Books International, Diamond Pocket Books (both at above address); Punjabi Pustak Bhandar (qv)
Subject: Juveniles (in Hindi and English)

Dini Book Depot, 4160 Urdu Bazar, Jamamasjid, Delhi 110006 Tel: 268632/274855 Cable Add: Dini Book
Man Partner, Sales, Production: Arshad Saeed; *Editorial:* Rashid Saeed; *Publicity:* Shahid Saeed
Subsidiary Company: Saeed International (Regd), 2112 Nahar Khan St, Daryaganj, New Delhi 2
Subjects: Islamic Studies, Textbooks
Bookshop: At above address
1978: approx 65 titles *1979:* approx 65 titles *Founded:* 1945
Miscellaneous: Also importers, exporters and suppliers

Eastern Book Co, 34 Lalbagh, Lucknow 226001 Tel: 43171 Cable Add: Law Book
Chief Executive: C L Malik; *Editorial:* Surendra Malik; *Sales, Rights & Permissions:* P L Malik; *Production:* Kamal Malik; *Publicity:* Vijay Malik
Orders to: Law Times Press, 56 C Singarnagar, Lucknow 226001
Associate Companies: Current Legal Publications, Lucknow; Law Times Press, Lucknow; Manav Law House, Allahabad, Eastern Book Co (Sales), Delhi
Subject: Law
1977: 50 titles *1979:* 89 titles *Founded:* 1947

Eastern Law House Pvt Ltd+, 54 Ganesh Chunder Ave, Calcutta 700013 Tel: 274989 Cable Add: Lauriports, Calcutta
Man Dir: B C De; *Sales Executive:* Asok De; *Marketing Executive:* Ajoy De; *Editorial, Production, Publicity, Rights & Permissions:* A K De
Editorial Off: 11 Raja Subodh Mullick Sq, Calcutta 700013
Br Off: 4833/24 Ansari Rd, Daryaganj, New Delhi 110002
Subjects: Law, Accounting, Political & Social Science
1976: 21 titles *1977:* 26 titles *Founded:* 1918
Bookshops: 54 Ganesh Chunder Ave, Calcutta 700013; 4833/24 Ansari Rd, Daryaganj, New Delhi 110002

Ess Ess Publications, 4837/24 Ansari Rd, New Delhi 110002 Tel: 743401 Cable Add: Ess Ess Publications
Man Dir, Publicity, Rights & Permissions: Mrs Sheel Sethi; *Editorial, Sales, Production:* S K Sethi
Orders to: Ess Ess Publishers' Distributors, KD/6A Ashok Vihar, Delhi 110052
Parent Company: Ess Ess Publishers' Distributors, KD/6A Ashok Vihar, Delhi 110052
Subsidiary Company: Sumit Publications, KD/6A Ashok Vihar, Delhi 110052
Subjects: Humanities, Social Sciences
1978: 13 titles *1979:* 20 titles *Founded:* 1974

Eurasia Publishing House Pvt Ltd+, Ravindra Mansion, Ram Nagar, New Delhi 110055 Tel: 266912 Cable Add: Eschand Telex: 0312185
Man Dir: S L Gupta; *Sales Dir:* R K Gupta
Associated Company: S Chand & Co Ltd, India (qv)
Subjects: Low-priced Paperbacks, Psychology, Engineering, General & Social Science, University, Secondary & Primary Textbooks, Educational Materials
Founded: 1960

Firma KLM Private Ltd (Incorporating Firma KL Mukhopadhyay)*, 257B BB Ganguly St, Calcutta 700012 Tel: 344391 Cable Add: Indology (Calcutta)
Man Dir: K L Mukhopadhyay; *Editorial:* S

P Ghosh; *Sales:* R N Mukherji; *Production:* S Chakraborty; *Publicity:* R N Mukherji; *Rights & Permissions:* K L Mukhopadhyay
Orders to: Firma KLM Private Ltd, 257B, BB Ganguly St, Calcutta 700012
Parent Company: Firma Mukhopadhyay, 2/1 Dr Aksay Pal Rd, Calcutta 700034
Subjects: Humanities, Social Sciences
1977: 45 titles *Founded:* 1950

Frank Bros & Co+*, IV/85 Chandni Chowk, Delhi 110006

Ganesh & Co, 41 Pondy Bazar, Madras 600017 Tel: 444938
Partners: S Ganesh Prasad, S Ranganathan
Subjects: Philosophy, Religion, Nutrition
1977: 4 titles *1978:* 3 titles *Founded:* 1910

Geetha Book House+*, New Statue Circle, Mysore 570001 Tel: 21589 Cable Add: Books
General Manager: M Gopalakrishna; *Sales Manager:* M Gururaja Rao; *Rights & Permissions:* M Sathyanarayana Rao
Subjects: Belles Lettres, Poetry, Biography, History, Philosophy, Reference, Religion, Low- & High-priced Paperbacks, General & Social Science, University Textbooks
Bookshop: Geetha Book House, New Statue Circle, Mysore 570001

Geological Survey of India*, 29 Jawaharlal Nehru Rd, Calcutta 700016 Tel: 232314 Cable Add: Geosurvey
Dir-Gen: V S Krishnaswamy
Subject: Geology

Goel Publishing House+*, Subhash Bazar, Meerut 250002 Tel: 72843
Man Dir, Editorial: B D Rastogi; *Sales:* Atul Krishna; *Production:* K Krishna
Publicity & Advertising Dir: Kamalni Rastogi
Subsidiary: Krishna Prakashan Mandir, 119 Krishna Vihar, Shivaji Road, Meerut 250001
Bookshop: Goel publishing, Krishna Prakashan Mandir, Subhash Bazar, Meerut 250002 UP
Subjects: Mathematics, Chemistry, History, Art, Political Science, Economics, University & College textbooks
Founded: 1948

Hans Publishers*, Kamani Chambers, Ballard Estate, Bombay 400038
Tel: 263516 Cable Add: Bukmel
Chief Executive: Miss M Pereira
Parent Company: Myna Press, India (qv)
Subjects: Great works of the present century and reprints of outstanding books
1977: 8 titles *Founded:* 1963

Hemkunt Publishers Pvt Ltd+*, 1-E/15 Patel Rd, New Delhi 110008 Tel: 584174
Cable Add: Hembooks
Man Dir: Bhagat Singh; *Sales, Publicity, Advertising, Rights & Permissions:* G P Singh
Subjects: Religion, Juveniles, Low-priced Paperbacks, University, Secondary & Primary Textbooks
Founded: 1948

Heritage Publishers+*, M-116 Connaught Circus, New Delhi 110001 Tel: 45316
Man Dir: B R Chawla
Subsidiary Companies: Intellectuals' Rendezvous, M-116, Con Circus, New Delhi 110001
Subjects: Biography, History, Bibliography, Literature, Reference, Religion, Economics, Language, Social Science
1977: 8 titles

Himalaya Prakashan+*, 16 Resthouse Crescent, Bangalore 560001 Tel: 65207
Man Dir: Anand Kundaji
Associated Company: Artha Niti Publications, D390 Defence Colony, New Delhi 110024
Subjects: History, Philosophy, Religion, Mysticism
1977: 5 titles *Founded:* 1973

Himalaya Publishing House+*, 4A-16 Sangeeta, 71 Juhu Rd, Santa Cruz West, Bombay 400054 Tel: 351186, 355798
Chief Executive, Sales, Publicity: D P Pandey; *Editorial:* Madan Joshi; *Production:* Kooverjibhai; *Rights & Permissions:* Mrs Meena Pandey
Show Room: 'Swadeshi Mills' Estate, Girgaon, Bombay 400004
Subjects: Arts, Commerce, Science, Management, Law
1977: 60 titles *1978:* 100 titles *Founded:* 1976

Hind Pocket Books Private Ltd+, GT Rd, Shahdara, Delhi 110032 Tel: 202046/202332 Cable Add: Pocketbook Delhi
Man Dir: Dina N Malhotra; *Editorial:* Mrs Mohini Rao; *Marketing, Rights & Permissions:* Shekhar Malhotra
Associate Companies: Indian Book Company, Clarion Books (both at above address); Saraswati Vihar, 21 Dayanand Marg, Daryaganj, New Delhi 110002
Subjects: General, Fiction, Non-Fiction, Self Improvement, Do-It-Yourself, Biography
1978: 100 titles *1979:* 50 titles *Founded:* 1958
Book Clubs: Gharelu Library Yojna, Clarion Book Club
Bookshop: Saraswati Vihar, 21 Dayanand Marg, Daryaganj, New Delhi 110002

Hindi Book Centre, 4/5-B Asaf Ali Rd, New Delhi 110002 Tel: 274874
Subject: General books in Hindi

Hindustan Publishing Corporation (India)*, 6-U B Jawahar Nagar, Delhi 110007
Tel: 220201
Man Dir: S K Jain; *Editorial, Production, Rights & Permissions:* J K Jain; *Sales:* P C Kumar; *Production:* B B Jain
Subjects: Mathematics, Statistics, Physics, Chemistry, Earth Sciences, Life Sciences, Social Sciences
1977: 8 titles *Founded:* 1960
Subsidiary: Hindustan Book Agency, 17 U B, Jawahar Nagar, Delhi 110007

I B I, an imprint of Sterling Publishers Pty Ltd (qv)

India Book House, Mahalaxmi Chambers, 22 Bhulabhai Desai Rd, Bombay 400026
Tel: 365651, 365652, 365653 Cable Add: Indbook Bombay Telex: 0114060
Man Dir: G L Mirchandani; *Publisher:* H G Mirchandani; *Sales Dir:* Harkin Chatlani
Subjects: Fiction, General Nonfiction, Poetry, Humour, Cookery, Biography, Astrology, Sports, Self-improvement, Children's books
Bookshops: 3-a Rashtrapathi Rd, Secunderabad 500003

India Book House Education Trust, 29 Nathalal Parekh Marg, Bombay 400039
Tel: 240626/240678/240720/240779 Cable Add: Indbook
Managing Trustee: G L Mirchandani; *Trustee:* H G Mirchandani
Subjects: Juveniles, Low-priced Paperbacks, Illustrated Classics, Education
1978: 400 titles *Founded:* 1971

India Book House Private Ltd, Eruchshaw Bldg, 3rd Floor, 249 Dr D N Road, Bombay 400001 Tel: 240626/240678/240779
Cable Add: Indbook
Dir: H G Mirchandani; *Publicity Manager:* Shyam Kapoor
Branch Off: 29 Wodehouse Rd, Bombay 400039
Subjects: Juveniles, Low-priced Paperbacks, Illustrated Classics, Children's Educational
1977: 13 titles *Founded:* 1974

Indian Bibliographic Centre*, 236 Kot Kishan Chand, Jullundur 4, Punjab Tel: 3240
Man Dir: Rohini Sharma; *Sales Dir:* K K Lahir
Branch Off: 76 Chandrika Colony, Sigra, Varanasi 221001, Uttar Pradesh
Subjects: Reference, Library Science

Indian Book Industry, subsidiary of Sterling Publishers Pvt Ltd (qv)

Indian Council for Cultural Relations*, Azad Bhawan, Indraprastha Estate, New Delhi 1 Tel: 272114
Subjects: Literature, Culture, International Relations, Performing and Fine Arts
1977: 7 titles

Indian Council of Agricultural Research*, 26 Rajendra Prasada Rd, New Delhi 1
Man Dir: M G Kamath; *Sales Dir:* M Prasad; *Publicity & Advertising:* K E Sankaran
Subjects: How-to, Agriculture, University Textbooks

Indian Museum*, 27 Jawaharlal Nehru Rd, Calcutta 700016, West Bengal Tel: 239855, 234584, 230742 Cable Add: Imbot
Dir: Dr S C Ray
Subjects: Arts, Archaeology, Anthropology, Botany, Geology, Zoology
1977: 7 titles *Founded:* 1814

Indian Press (Publications) Pvt Ltd*, 36 Pannalal Rd, Allahabad, Uttar Pradesh
Tel: 53190 Cable Add: Publikason
Man Dir: D P Ghosh
Br Off: Indian Publishing House, 22/1 Bidhan Sarani, Calcutta 6
Agencies: Indian Publishing House, 23 Daryaganj, Delhi; Indian Press (Pubs) P Ltd, Wright Town, Jabalpur; Indian Press (Pubs) P Ltd, Nicholson Rd, Ambala; Indian Press (Pubs) P Ltd, Jagatganj, Varanasi; Indian Book Depot, Jhandawala Park, Lucknow; Sahitya Ratnalaya, Shradhanand Park, Kanpur; Pustaksthan, Buxipur, Gorakhpur; Agarwal Bros, Katra, Azamgarh
Subject: Textbooks in Hindi, Bengali & English
Miscellaneous: Also publishes in Gurmukhi, Urdu, Marathi & Nepali languages

Indian Publications, 3 Abdul Hamid (British Indian) St, Calcutta 700069 Tel: 236334/344733
Man Dir: C R Sen; *Editorial, Production, Rights & Permissions:* Sankar Sen Gupta; *Sales:* D Bhownick; *Publicity:* Miss Putul Das
Subsidiary Company: Kalyani Prakashani (at above address)
Subjects: Social Science, Humanities, with special reference to Folklore, Anthropology, Archaeology, Ancient History, Bengali Literature, Mass Communication and Traditional Culture
1977: 8 titles *Founded:* 1957

Inter-India Publications+, 105 Anandnagar, Delhi 110035 Tel: 568445
Chief Executive, Editorial, Rights & Permissions: M C Mittal; *Sales:* Praveen Mittal
Parent Company: DK Publishers' Distributors, India (qv)
Subjects: Indology, Geography, Art, Anthropology, Sociology, Archaeology, Philosophy, Religion
1977: 7 titles *1978:* 5 titles *Founded:* 1977

Interprint, Mehta House, 16 A Naraina II, New Delhi 110028 Tel: 589760, 588305, 584387 Cable Add: Calmakers Telex: 2157 ND
Man Dir, Rights & Permissions: S N Mehta; *Production:* Dalip Tuli; *Publicity:* U Krishna Raj
Parent Company: Calendar Makers Corporation (at above address)
Branch Off: Calendar Makers Corporation, 27 Parsee Bazar St, Victoria Building, Bombay 400001
Subjects: Environmental Biology, Pediatrics, Himalayan Buddhist Art, Indian Art
1978: 6 titles *1979:* 4 titles *Founded:* 1976

Intertrade Publications (India) Pvt Ltd, subsidiary of Roy (Pvt) Ltd (K K) (qv)

Jaico Publishing House+, 125 Mahatma Gandhi Rd, Bombay 400023 Tel: 270621, 270746, 270760 Cable Add: Jaicobooks
Man Dir: Jaman H Shah; *Editorial, Production, Sales, Publicity, Rights & Permissions:* Ashwin J Shah
Subsidiary Company: Jaico Press Pvt Ltd
Branch Offs: Jaico Book House, 14-1 1st Main Rd, 6th Cross, Gandhi Nagar, Bangalore 560009; Jaico Book Distributors, G-2, 16 Ansari Rd, Daryaganj, New Delhi 110002
Subjects: Oriental and Western Classics, Indian and Western Fiction, Palmistry, Astrology, Philosophy, Religion, Biography, Autobiography, Reference, Language, Sex, Marriage, Love, Health, Yoga, Management, Economics, Humour, History, Politics, Cookery, Law, Crime, Psychology, Self-improvement
Bookshop: Jaico's Book Shop, 125 Mahatma Gandhi Rd, Bombay 400023
1977: 40 titles *1978:* 48 titles *Founded:* 1947

Jain Brothers*, PO Box 158, Ratanada Rd, Jodhpur Tel: 20779 Cable Add: Jainbros
Man Dir: R C Jain; *Sales Dir:* M L Jain
Br Off: 873 East Park Rd, New Delhi 5
Subjects: History, Philosophy, Psychology, Engineering, General & Social Science, University Textbooks
Founded: 1950
Bookshops: 256 Bapu Bazar, Udaipur; Vidya Vihar, Pilani; Chaura Rasta, Jaipur

Kalyani Publishers+*, 1/1 Rajinder Nagar, Ludhiana (Punjab)
Bookshop: Lyall Book Depot, Chaura Bazar, Ludhiana

Kapur Publications+*, 2601 Nai Sarak, Delhi 110006
Subject: Educational

Karnataka Cooperative Publishing House Ltd+*, 164 1st Main Rd, Chamarajpet, Bangalore 560018

Khanna Publishers+*, 2-B Nath Market, Nai Sarak, Delhi 110006
Subject: Engineering

Kitab Mahal (W D) Pvt Ltd+*, 56 A Zero Rd, Allahabad, Uttar Pradesh Tel: 50540/2927 Cable Add: Kitab Mahal Allahabad
Man Dir: I K Agarwal; *Sales, Publicity & Advertising Dir:* Naresh Agarwal
Br Offs: Kitab Mahal (W D) Pvt Ltd, Ashokrajpath, Patna 4 (Bihar); Kitab Mahal Distributors, 28 Netaji Subhash Marg, Daryaganj, Delhi 6
Founded: 1936

Kosi Books, an imprint of Vidyarthi Mithram Press (qv)

Kothari Publications, Jute House, 12 India Exchange Pl, Calcutta 700001 Tel: 229563/226572
Man Dir: H Kothari
Associate Company: India-International News Service
Subjects: Technical, Reference
Miscellaneous: Publisher of *Who's Who* series in India

Krishna Prakasman Mandir, subsidiary of Goel Publishing House (qv)

Lakshmi Narain Agarwal, Hospital Rd, Agra 3 Tel: 73160
Man Dir: P N Agarwal
Subjects: Education, Textbooks
1978-79: 41 titles *Founded:* 1916

Lalit Kala Akademi (National Academy of Art)*, Rabindra Bhavan, Ferozeshah Rd, New Delhi 1 Tel: 387241 Cable Add: Arta-Kademie
Chairman: Aram Niwas Mirdha; *Secretary:* A K Dutta
Subject: Art (Monographs, Brochures, Portfolios and Multicolour Reproductions)
Publications: Lalit Kala (Ancient Art), *Lalit Kala Contemporary*

Lalvani Brothers*, PO Box 545, Taj Bldg, 210 Dr Dadabhai Naoroji Rd, Bombay 400001 Tel: 266811/2 Cable Add: Lalbrother Bombay Telex: 0115278
Man Dir: C P Karnire; *Editorial, Sales, Production, Publicity, Rights & Permissions:* S P Lalvani
Associated Company: Indian Lead, Rampart Ho, Rampart Row, Bombay
Br Offs: 4 Darya Ganj, Ansari Rd, Delhi 110006; 8 State Bank Lane, Mount Rd, Madras 2; Globe Bldg, 7-E Lindsey St, Calcutta 16
Subjects: Juvenile, Art, Technical
Founded: 1924
ISBN Publisher's Prefix: 112

Law Books in Hindi Publishers, Vidhi Sahitya Prakashan, Ministry of Law, Justice and Company Affairs, Indian Law Institute Building, Bhagwan Das Rd, New Delhi 110001 Cable Add: Patrika
Sales Man: C B Deogam
Subjects: Law, publications include *Uchchatama Nyayalaya Nirnaya Patrika* and *Uchcha Nyayalaya Nirnaya Patrika*
1978: 1 title

Light & Life Publishers, 2428 Tilak St, Paharganj, New Delhi 110055 Tel: 522455
Managing Partner: N Gopinath; *Sales & Publicity:* P N Nair; *Rights & Permissions:* Kartar Singh
Br Offs: Residency Rd, Jammu Tawi (J & K); Delhi Rd, Model Town, Rohtak (Haryana)
Subjects: Philosophy, Political Science, Indology, Low-priced student editions of textbooks, Religion, History, Geography
1979: 65 titles *Founded:* 1971

The **Little Flower** Co*, 43 Ranganathan St, T Nagar, Madras 600017 Tel: 441538
Cable Add: Lifco
Senior Partner: T N C Varadan
Br Off: Lifco Sales Dept, 17/1 Nandi Koil St, Teppakulam, Tiruchirapalli 620002
Subjects: General Fiction, History, How-to, Music, Art, Philosophy, Reference, Religion, Low-priced Paperbacks, edicine, General Science, University, Secondary & Primary Textbooks
Founded: 1929

Little Swan, an imprint of Orient Longman Ltd (qv)

Lok Vangmaya Griha (Pvt) Ltd*, 190-B Khetwadi Main Rd, Bombay 400004 Tel: 351324 Cable Add: Loksahitya
Man Dir: B D Gujarathi; *Sales:* S K Kulkarni
Parent Company: People's Publishing House Pvt Ltd, Rani Zhansi Rd, New Delhi 110055
Branch Off: Red Flag Building, Bindu Chowk, Kolapur; 5-22-32 Tilak Path, Aurangabad
Subjects: General
Bookshops: PPH Book Stall, S V P Rd, Bombay 400004; People's Book House, Fort, Bombay 400001
1977: 50 titles *Founded:* 1973

Lord International*, 19 Netaji Subhash Marg, Daryaganj, New Delhi 110002
Tel: 277193
Chief Executive, Rights & Permissions: Kamall Dev; *Editorial:* K P Punnoose; *Sales:* Shiv Chaudhry; *Production:* Ramesh Chaudhry; *Publicity:* Rajesh Chaudhry
Subjects: Book Trade, Mailing Lists
Founded: 1971

The **Macmillan** Co of India Ltd+, 4 Community Centre, Naraina Industrial Area Phase I, New Delhi 110028 Tel: 393384/393799 Telex: 3741
Shipping Add: 6 Patullo Rd, Madras 600002
Man Dir: S G Wasani; *Rights & Permissions:* Nirupam Chatterjee
Br Offs: Mercantile House, Magazine St, Reay Rd (East), Bombay 400010; 294 Bepin Behari Ganguly St, Calcutta 700012; 6 Patullo Rd, Madras 600002; 2/10 Ansari Rd, New Delhi 110002
Subjects: Biography, History, Philosophy, Reference, Religion, Medicine, Psychology, Engineering, General & Social Science, University, Secondary & Primary Textbooks, Economics, Management, Political Science, Reference, Fiction
1978: 56 titles *Founded:* 1903
Miscellaneous: Firm is 40 per cent owned by Macmillan Publishers Ltd, UK (qv)

Mahajan Brothers, Super Market Basement, Ashram Rd, nr Natraj Cinema, Ahmedabad 380009 Tel: 79947 Cable Add: Periodical
Man Dir: Dinker Mahajan
Subject: Textiles
1978: 1 title *Founded:* 1953

Manohar Publications, 2 Ansari Rd, Darya Ganj, New Delhi 110002 Tel: 277162
Man Dir, Rights & Permissions: Ramesh C Jain; *Editorial:* N K Jain; *Sales, Production, Publicity:* M Saeed
Subjects: History, Sociology, Politics, Indology
1977: 20 titles *1978:* 25 titles *Founded:* 1969

Marg Publications, 3rd floor, Army and Navy Building, 148 Mahatma Gandhi Rd, Bombay 400023 Tel: 242520
Chief Executive: J J Bhabha; *Editorial:*

Mulk Raj Anand; *Sales, Publicity:* Siddarth Kak; *Production:* Dolly Sahiar; *Rights & Permissions:* Mrs R S Sabavala
Parent Company: Tata Sons Ltd
Subject: Art
1977: 4 titles *Founded:* 1947

Mayfair Paperbacks, an imprint of Arnold-Heinemann Publishers, India (qv)

Meenakshi Prakashan+*, Begumpul, Meerut 250002 Tel: 74133, 75062, 72001
Chief Executive: Shri Chandra Prakash; *Editorial:* Ashok Gupta; *Sales:* V N Bajpal; *Production:* Ashok Kumar; *Publicity:* S N Sharma; *Rights & Permissions:* T C Sharma
Br Off: 4 Ansari Rd, Daryaganj, New Delhi 110002
Subjects: Economics, Education, Commerce, Psychology, Hindi Literature, Physical and Biological Sciences, History, Management, Political Science, Sociology
1977: 24 titles *Founded:* 1964

Minerva Associates (Publications) Pvt Ltd+*, 7–B Lake Pl, Calcutta 700029 Tel: 42-3783
Chairman and Man Dir: Sushil Mukherjea; *Editorial Director:* O K Ghosh
Subjects: Political Science, History, Social Science, Economics, Psychology, Education, Belles Lettres, Philosophy
1977: 16 titles *Founded:* 1973

The **Minerva Publishing** House+*, 32 Halls Rd, Egmore, Madras 8

Ministry of Information & Broadcasting*, Publications Divison, Government of India, Patiala House, New Delhi 110001
Dirs: R P Dhamija, G C Chukervartty; *Business Managers:* S L Jaiswal, R N Tyagi, O P Makar, N Mishra
Br Offs: Super Bazar (2nd Floor), Connaught Circus, New Delhi; Botawala Chambers, Sir P M Rd, Bombay; 8 Esplanade East, Calcutta; Shastri Bhawan, 35 Haddows Rd, Madras
Subjects: Art & Culture, History, Speeches & Writings, Land & People, Flora & Fauna, Biographies, Reference, Juveniles, General & Social Science

Motilal Banarsidass, 41 U A Bungalow Rd, Jawahar Nagar, Delhi 110007
Tel: 228355/221985 Cable Add: Gloryindia
Man Dir: Shantilal Jain; *Sales Dir:* R P Jain; *Publicity Dir:* Narendra Prakash; *Advertising Dir:* Jainendra Prakash
Br Offs: Ashok Rajpath, Opp Patna College, Patna 4; Chowk, Varanasi
Subjects: Religion, Philosophy, History, Linguistics, Sanskrit, Arts, Literature, Medicine
1978: 35 titles *Founded:* 1903
Bookshop: 41 U A Bungalow Rd, Jawahar Nagar, Delhi 110007

Mouj Prakashan Griha*, Khatau Wadi Girgaum, Bombay 400004, Maharashtra
1977: 4 titles

A **Mukherjee** & Co Pvt Ltd+*, 2 Bankim Chatterjee St, Calcutta 700012
Tel: 341606/341499
Dir: B K Chatterjee
Subject: Educational Materials
Founded: 1940

Mukherji Book House, 1 Gopi Mohan Dutta Lane, Calcutta 700003
Subjects: Reference, Bibliography
1977: 2 titles *Founded:* 1963

Munshiram Manoharlal Publishers Pvt Ltd+, PO Box 5715, 54 Rani Jhansi Rd, New Delhi 110055 Tel: 513841/513600/ 261153 Cable Add: Literature
Chairman & Man Dir: Manoharlal Jain; *Sales Dir:* Ashok Jain; *Publicity & Advertising:* Mrs Nirmal Jain; *Editorial Dir, Rights & Permissions:* Devendra Jain
Subjects: Belles Lettres, Poetry, Biography, History, Music, Art, Philosophy, Reference, Religion High-priced Paperbacks, Social Science, Linguistics, Archaeology, Architecture, Dictionaries
1977: 58 titles *1978:* 62 titles *Founded:* 1952
Bookshop: Munshiram Manoharlal, 4416 Nai Sarak, Delhi 6
Subsidiary: Oriental Books Reprint Corporation, 54 Rani Jhansi Rd, New Delhi 110055

Myna Press, PO Box 1526, Bombay 400038 (Located at: 32 R Kamani Marg, Bombay) Tel: 261347 Cable Add: Bukmel
Chief Executive: Mohan
Subsidiary Company: Hans Publishers, India (qv)
Subject: Juveniles
1977: 25 titles *1978:* 14 titles *Founded:* 1970

Nachiketa Publications Ltd+*, Statesman House, Connaught Circus, New Delhi 110001
Dir: V N Chhabra
Subject: English
Founded: 1969

S **Nagin** & Co+*, Pratap Rd, Opp Sitla Mandir, Jullundur City 144008 (Punjab)

Narosa Publishing House+, 2/35 Ansari Rd, Daryaganj, New Delhi 110002 Tel: 260327 Cable Add: Narosa New Delhi
Man Dir: N K Mehra
Subjects: Pure and Applied Science, Medicine
1977: 3 titles *1978:* 13 titles *Founded:* 1977

National Book Trust*, A–5 Green Park, New Delhi 110016 Tel: 664020, 664667, 664540 Cable Add: Nabotrust
Dir: U K Mallya; *Editorial Dir:* Lokenath Bhattacharya; *Sales Executive:* M A Krishnamachary; *Information & Publicity Executive:* D Das Gupta
Br Off: Book Centre, City Central Library, Ashok Nagar, Hyderabad 500020
Subjects: Covering all aspects of human endeavour with particular reference to India; meant for a general readership
Bookshops; Book Centre, National Book Trust, City Central Library, Ashok Nagar, Hyderabad 500020; National Book Trust Book Shop, A-4 Green Park, New Delhi 110016
1977: 198 titles *Founded:* 1957

National Council of Applied Economic Research, Publications Division, Parisila Bhawan 11, Indraprastha Estate, New Delhi 110002 Tel: 273791/273798 Cable Add: Arthsandan Telex: ND 3380
Subject: Economics and allied subjects
1978-79: 2 titles

National Council of Educational Research & Training, Publication Department*, Sri Aurobindo Marg, New Delhi 110016 Tel: 678591/678425/678431 Cable Add: Eduprint
Secretary: V K Pandit; *Business Manager:* U N Jha; *Chief Editor:* Jaipal Nangia; *Chief Production Officer:* C N Rao; *Rights & Permissions:* Head, Publication Department
Subjects: Secondary & Primary Textbooks, Educational Materials
1978: 124 titles *Founded:* 1962

National Publishing House+*, 23 Daryaganj, Delhi 110006

Navajivan Trust, Post Navajivan, Ahmedabad 380014 Tel: 447634/5
Man Dir, Rights & Permissions: Jitendra T Desai; *Editorial:* Balmukund Dave; *Sales, Publicity:* Ratilal Naik; *Production:* Ramanbhai Patel
Br Off: 130 Princess St, Bombay 2
Subjects: Biography, History, Philosophy, Reference, Religion, University, Secondary & Primary Textbooks
1977: 8 titles *1978:* 3 titles *Founded:* 1919

Navyug Publishers+, 9B Pleasure Garden Market, Chandni Chowk, Delhi 110006

Naya Prokash, 206 Bidhan Sarani, Calcutta 700006 Tel: 349566
Man Dir, Production, Rights & Permissions: B Mitra; *Editorial:* S Das Gupta; *Sales:* P S Basu; *Publicity:* R Ghose
Subsidiary Companies: Darbari Udjog; India Book Exchange
Subjects: Indology, Social Science, Management, History, Economics, Politics, Military Studies, Linguistics
Bookshop: 206 Bidhan Sarani, Calcutta 700006
1977: 10 titles *1978:* 12 titles *Founded:* 1962

Nem Chand & Brothers+*, Civil Lines, Roorkee 247667 Tel: 258/752 Cable Add: Nemchand Bros
Warehouse: Opp Dy S P Office, Roorkee 247667
Man Dir, Rights & Permissions: N C Jain; *Sales Dir:* P K Jain; *Publicity & Advertising Dir:* T K Jain
Subject: Engineering
Founded: 1951
Subsidiary: Roorkee Press, Roorkee

New Light Publishers (IBI)+*, 31/1, Rajinder Nagar, New Delhi 110060
Tel: 582037
Partners: A S Chowdhry, R K Chowdhry; *Publicity & Advertising:* R D Chowdhry
Subjects: General Fiction & Nonfiction, Paperbacks
Founded: 1964

New Order Book Co*, Ellis Bridge, Ahmedabad 6 Tel: 79065/45409 Cable Add: Nyuorder
Proprietor: D V Trivedi
Subjects: Humanities, Indology, Antiquarian, Art
Founded: 1939

Orient Longman Ltd+, 3/5 Asaf Ali Rd, New Delhi 110002 Tel: 279256/7/8 Cable Add: Orlong New Delhi
Chairman: J Rameshwar Rao; *Editorial:* Sujit Mukherjee; *Sales:* E Raghavan; *Rights & Permissions:* Kamal Sarkar
Imprints: Sangam Books, Swan, Little Swan
Br Offs: Kamani Marg, Ballard Estate, Bombay 400038; 17 Chittaranjan Ave, Calcutta 700072; 36A Mount Rd, Madras 600002; 1/24 Asaf Ali Rd, New Delhi 110002; 3-5-820 Hyderguda, Hyderabad 500001; 80/1 Mahatma Gandhi Rd, Bangalore 560001; SP Verma Rd, Patna 800001
Subjects: General Nonfiction, Biography, History, Philosophy, Reference, Juveniles, Low- & High-priced Paperbacks, Medicine, Psychology, Engineering, General & Social Science, Technology, University, Secondary & Primary Textbooks, Educational Materials
Bookshops: The Bookpoint, Kamari Marg, Ballard Estate, Bombay 700038
1977: 260 titles *Founded:* 1948

Orient Paperbacks (Division of Vision Books), 36-C Connaught Place, New Delhi 110001 Tel: 352081/312978 Cable Add: Visionbook
Man Dir: Vishwanath; *Editorial, Production:* Kapil Malhotra; *Publicity, Rights & Permissions:* Sudhir Malhotra; *Sales:* Rajendra Malhotra
Orders to: Sales Office, Madrassa Rd, Kashmere Gate, Delhi 110006 Tel: 227011/252267
Parent Company: Vision Books, India (qv)
Associate Companies: Raipal & Sons, Publishers, Madrassa Rd, Kashmere Gate, Delhi 6; Shiksha Bharata, India (qv); Shiksha Bharati Press, G T Rd, Shadara, Delhi 32
Imprints: Anand Paperbacks, Vision Books
Br Off: Vasant, Ground Floor, 3-B Pedder Rd, Bombay 400026
Book Clubs: Orient Book Club
Subjects: International Bestseller Reprints, General Nonfiction, Self-Tuition Series, Indo Anglian Fiction, Indian Culture and Thought, Poetry, Drama, Occult, Palmistry, Astrology, Sports, Adventure, Yoga
1977: 100 titles *1978:* 129 titles *Founded:* 1967

Oriental Books Reprint Corporation, subsidiary of Munshiram Manoharlal Publishers Pvt Ltd (qv)

Oxford & I B H Publishing Co+, 66 Janpath, New Delhi 110001
Tel: 321035/320518 Cable Add: Indamer
Dirs: Gulab Primlani, Mohan Primlani; *Production Manager:* M L Gidwani; *Publicity Manager:* G C Sahajwalla
Subsidiary companies: Amerind Publishing Co (P) Ltd, 66 Janpath, New Delhi 110001; Oxonian Press (P) Ltd, N-56 Connaught Circus, New Delhi 110001
Br Off: 17 Park St, Calcutta 700016
Subjects: Reference, Medicine, Psychology, Engineering, University Textbooks
1977: 50 titles *1978:* 60 titles
Founded: 1962
Bookshop: Oxford Book & Stationery Co, Scindia House, New Delhi 110001

Oxford University Press+, 2/11 Ansari Rd, PO Box 7035, Daryaganj, New Delhi 110002 Tel: 273841/2, 277812 Cable Add: Oxonian Delhi
General Manager: R Dayal
Br Offs: Faraday House, P17 Mission Row Extension, GPO Box 530, Calcutta 700013; Oxford House, Mount Rd, PO Box 1079, Madras 600006; Oxford House, Apollo Bunder, PO Box 31, Bombay 400039
Subjects: Academic & General books for all levels (school, college, University and research), Languages (Arabic, Assamese, Bengali, French, Garo, Gujarati, Hindi, Kannada, Khasi, Malayalam, Marathi, Oriya, Punjabi, Sanskrit, Tamil, Telugu, Urdu)
1977: 449 titles *1978:* 467 titles *Founded:* 1912
ISBN Publisher's Prefix: 19

Oxonian Press (P) Ltd+, N-56 Connaught Circus, New Delhi 110001 Tel: 44957
Cable Add: Indamer
Dir, Rights & Permissions: Gulab Primlani; *Sales Dir:* Dr A M Primlani; *Publicity Dir:* M L Gidwani
Br Offs: 17 Park St, Calcutta 700016; 29 Wodehouse Rd, Bombay
Subjects: Reference, Medicine, Engineering, General Science, University Textbooks
1977: 25 titles *1978:* 30 titles
Bookshops: Oxford Book & Stationery Co, Scindia House, New Delhi 110001; 17 Park St, Calcutta 700016
Miscellaneous: Firm is subsidiary of Oxford & IBH Publishing Co (qv)

Paico Publishing House, PO Box 1150, Paico Buildings, Jew Street, Cochin 682011
Tel: 31020/32723 Cable Add: Paico
Man Dir: S V Pai; *Sales Dir:* Kanchana V Pai
Associate Company: Pai & Company, 35 Mount Road, Madras 2
Subjects: General Fiction, History, General Science, University, Secondary & Primary Textbooks, Childrens Books
Bookshops: Pai & Co, Mount Rd, Madras 2; Paico Books & Arts, M G Road, Cochin 682011
1977: 32 titles *1978:* 42 titles *Founded:* 1955

Panjab University Publication Bureau, Chandigarh Tel: 22782
Secretary: R K Malhotra
Subjects: Belles Lettres, Poetry, Biography, History, Philosophy, Reference, Religion, Social Science, University Textbooks
Bookshop: Panjab University Publication Bureau, Chandigarh 160014
1978: 5 titles *Founded:* 1948

Parimal Prakashan, 'Parimal', Khadkeshwar, Aurangabad 431001 Tel: 4556
Man Dir & Production: A B Dashrathe; *Sales:* K D Danekar
Subjects: Social Sciences & Humanities
Bookshops: Marathwada Book Distributors at Tilak Rd, Aurangabad and Marathwada University Campus, Aurangabad
1977: 8 titles *1978:* 8 titles *Founded:* 1974

People's Publishing House (P) Ltd+*, 5 Rani Jhansi Rd, New Delhi 110055
Tel: 529365/523349/521041 Cable Add: Quamikitab
Chairman: Dr G Adhikari; *General Manager:* Shri M C Acharya; *Sales Manager:* Shri N Pisharodi
Subjects: Belles Lettres, Poetry, Biography, History, Philosophy, Juveniles, Low- & High-priced Paperbacks, Engineering, Social Science, University Textbooks
Founded: 1942
Bookshops: 2 Marina Arcade, Connaught Pl, New Delhi 110001; New Campus, Jawaharlal Nehru University, New Mehrauli Rd, New Delhi

Pilgrim Publishers*, 56 Jatin Das Rd, Calcutta 700029, West Bengal Tel: 464323
Man Dir: S De; *Editorial:* Mrs R Mukherjee; *Sales:* F C Dutta; *Production, Publicity:* T K Mukherjee
Parent Company: Traco, India
Subjects: Literature, History, Art, Archaeology
Bookshop: 18B/1B Tamer Lane, Calcutta 700009
1977: 2 titles *Founded:* 1966

Pitambar Book Depot+*, 888 East Park Rd, Karol Bagh, New Delhi 110005
Tel: 519433/562919/512041/561321/526933
Cable Add: Pitambar New Delhi
Man Dirs: Ved Bhushan, Anand Bhushan, Sushil Bhushan; *Sales:* P C Bhandari; *Publicity:* Anand Bhushan; *Editorial:* S K Arora; *Production, Rights & Permissions:* Sushil Bhushan
Associate Company: Bharat Enterprises, Delhi
Subsidary Companies: Ambar Parkashan; Pitambar Industries; Pitambar Printing Co; Pitambar Publishing Press
Subjects: General Fiction, Reference, University, Secondary & Primary Textbooks
1977: 30 titles *Founded:* 1947

Popular Prakashan Pvt Ltd+, 35-C Tardeo Rd, Bombay 400034 WB Tel: 376294/376295/370656
Man Dir: Ramdas Ganesh Bhatkal; *Dir:* Sadanand Ganesh Bhatkal
Subjects: Anthropology, Sociology, Arts, Crafts, Music, Biography, Economics, Education, History, Literature, Law, Philosophy, Religion, Politics, Administration, Physics, Mathematics, Chemistry
1977: 80 titles *1978:* 60 titles

Pragati Prakashan+, Begum Bridge, PO Box 62, Meerut 250001 Tel: Meerut 73022
Man & Sales Dir: K K Mittal; *Publicity & Advertising Dir:* A K Mittal
Subjects: Physics, Chemistry, Mathematics, General & Social Sciences, University Textbooks
1977: 23 titles *1978:* 20 titles *Founded:* 1955
Bookshop: Pragati Prashan, Lajpat Rai Market, Begum Bridge, Meerut

Prakash Prakashan*, 8 Ram Nagar Colony, Agra 2, Uttar Pradesh

Prentice-Hall of India Pvt Ltd+*, M-97 Connaught Circus, New Delhi 110001
Tel: 44769/43750 Cable Add: Prenhall New Delhi
Dirs: Asoke K Ghosh, Mrs Shanti Laroia
Subject: Textbooks
Founded: 1963
Miscellaneous: Firm is an associate company of Prentice-Hall Inc, Englewood Cliffs, NJ07632, USA

Printox*, J-12 Jangpura Extension, New Delhi 110014 Tel: 693097
Proprietor: S G Nene
Subjects: Politics, Social Science, Literary Criticism, Philosophy, Ancient Indian Literature, Art

Progressive Corporation Pvt Ltd, 3rd floor, Jehangir Wadia Building, 51 Mahatma Gandhi Rd, Flora Fountain, Fort Bombay 400023 Tel: 251634/254813 Cable Add: Progcorp
Man Dir: Dr K D P Madon; *Sales Dirs:* Dr Rustom S Davar, Nanabhoy S Davar
Br Off: 1 Velders St, Mount Rd, Madras 600002
Subjects: Management & Commerce, Accountancy, Business Law, Banking, Economics, Statistics, Marketing, Salesmanship, Advertising
1978: 4 titles *Founded:* 1932

Publication Board+*, Assam, Bamunimaidan, Gauhati 781021

Punjabi Pustak Bhandar, Dariba, Delhi 110006
Associate Companies: Diamond Books International, Diamond Pocket Books, Diamond Comics (all at 2715 Daryaganj, New Delhi 11002)
1978: 34 titles

Kunnuparampil P **Punnoose**+, 6/77 WEA Karol Bagh, New Delhi 110005 Tel: 565843
Man Dir, Rights & Permissions: Mrs Santhamma Punnoose; *Editorial, Sales, Production:* K P Punnoose; *Publicity:* Thomas Cherian
Parent Company: Literary Market Review (at above address)

Subsidiary Companies: IBIC International Book Industry Consultants, Jaffe Books
Subjects: Humanities, Social Sciences
1978: 3 titles *Founded:* August 1978
Miscellaneous: Also Literary Agent

Radha Krishna Prakashan+*, 2 Ansari Rd, Daryaganj, Delhi 110006 Tel: 275851
Cable Add: Lokpriya Delhi
Man Dir: Om Prakash
Subjects: General Fiction, Belles Lettres, Poetry, Biography, Juveniles, High-priced Paperbacks, University Textbooks
Founded: 1965

Radiant Publishers+*, E-155, State Bank of India Building, Kalkaji, New Delhi 110019
Man Dir, Sales, Rights & Permissions: Pradeep Jain; *Editorial:* Rashmi Jain; *Production, Publicity:* V Kumar
Subjects: Politics, International Affairs, Economics, Sociology, History, Philosophy
1977: 10 titles *Founded:* 1973

Rajesh Publications, 1 Ansari Rd, Daryaganj, New Delhi 110002 Tel: 274550
Man Dir: Gupta Mohan Lal
Branch Off: 38 SC Basu Rd, Allahabad 211003
Subjects: History, Geography, Religion, Philosophy, Economics, General
1978: 8 titles *1979:* 10 titles *Founded:* 1970

Rajhans Prakashan Mandir+*, Dharma Alok, Ram Nagar, Meerut, Uttar Pradesh

Rajkamal Prakashan Pvt Ltd+*, 8 Netaji Subhash Marg, Delhi 110006
Subjects: Juveniles, Education, Paperbacks

Rajneesh Foundation Ltd, Shree Rajneesh Ashram, 17 Koregaon Park, Poona 411001 Tel: 28127/20981/20982 Cable Add: Tathata Telex: 0145421 Tao
Man Dir, Sales, Rights & Permissions: Ma Yoga Laxmi; *Publicity:* Swami Krishna Prem
Subjects: Religion, Philosophy, Psychology; the teachings of Bhagwan Shree Rajneesh (English and Hindi)
Bookshop: Shree Rajneesh Ashram, 17 Koregaon Park, Poona 411001
1977: 37 titles *1978:* 54 titles *Founded:* 1969

Rajpal & Sons+, Kashmere Gate, PO Box 1064, Delhi 110006 Tel: 229174, 223904
Cable Add: Rajpalsons Delhi
Man Dir: Mr Vishwanath; *Sales:* Ishwar Chandra; *Editorial:* Mahendra Kulshreshtna; *Production:* Rajendra Sharma; *Publicity, Rights & Permissions:* Kapil Malhotra
Associate Companies: Shiksha Bharati, Delhi (qv); Vision Books (P) Ltd, New Delhi (qv)
Subjects: General Fiction, Literary Criticism, Humanities, Science, Juveniles
Bookshop: Rajpal & Sons, Kashmere Gate, Delhi 110006
1977: 120 titles *1978:* 125 titles *Founded:* 1891

Ram Prasad & Sons, Hospital Rd, Agra 282003 Tel: 72935 Cable Add: Modern
Man Dir: H N Agarwala; *Sales Dir:* R N Agarwala; *Publicity & Advertising:* B N Agarwala
Subjects: Agriculture & Veterinary Science, Commerce & Economics, Education & Psychology, Engineering & Technology, Geography, Mathematics & Statistics, Physics, Political Science, Sociology, Social Work, Criminology, University, Secondary & Primary Textbooks
Founded: 1905
Bookshops: Modern Book Depot, Hospital Rd, Agra 3; Bal Vihar, Hamidia Rd, Bhopal 1
Subsidiaries: Modern Printers, 1153 Bagh Muzaffar Khan, Agra 2; Sanchi Prakashan, Bhopal 1

Sri **Ramakrishna** Math, PO Box 635, Mylapore, Madras 600004 Tel: 71231
President: Sri Ramakrishna Math
Subjects: Religion, Culture, Philosophy
Bookshops: 16 Ramakrishna Math Rd, Mylapore, Madras 4; South Mada St, Mylapore Madras 4
1977: 19 titles *1978:* 12 titles *Founded:* 1897

Ramesh Sondhi, Gitanjali Prakashan, Lajpat Nagar 4, New Delhi 110024 Tel: 621991
Subjects: Economics, Social Science, History, Politics, Humanities
Bookshop: Indian Book Service, Lajpat Nagar 4, New Delhi 110024
1977: 3 titles *1978:* 4 titles *Founded:* 1974

Rastogi Publications+*, Shivaji Rd, Meerut 250002 Tel: 73698, 73132 Cable Add: Rastogico
Editorial: Mrs Prakash Wati; *Sales, Publicity:* H K Rastogi; *Production, Rights & Permissions:* R K Rastogi
Associate Company: Rastogi Associates at above address
Subsidiary Companies: Pioneer Printers, Rastogi & Co, both at above address
Subjects: University Textbooks in Botany, Political Science, Zoology and Education
1977: 80 titles *Founded:* 1966

Ratnabharati+, Ilaco House, Sir Pherozeshah Mehta Rd, PO Box 486, Bombay 400001 Tel: 267906 Cable Add: Pustaken
Editorial, Production: Punit Batra; *Sales, Publicity, Rights & Permissions:* Ranjit Batra
Subject: Illustrated children's books on Indian subjects
1978: 2 titles *Founded:* 1965

Roorkee Press, Roorkee, Subsidiary of Nem Chand & Brothers (qv)

K K Roy (Pvt) Ltd, 55 Gariahat Rd, PO Box 10210, Calcutta 700019 Tel: 474872
Cable Add: Helbell
Man Dir: Dr K K Roy; *Sales Dir:* S Paul; *Publicity Dir:* M Misra; *Advertising Dir:* M S Rajan; *Rights & Permissions:* Dr K K Roy
Subjects: Belles Lettres, Poetry, Biography, History, Philosophy, Reference, Religion, Medicine, University Textbooks
1977: 72 titles *1978:* 80 titles *Founded:* 1954
Subsidiary: Intertrade Publications (India) Pvt Ltd, 55 Gariahat Rd, PO Box 10210, Calcutta 700019

Rupa & Co+, 15 Bankim Chatterjee St, PO Box 12333, Calcutta 700073 Tel: 344821/346305 Cable Add: Rupanco
Man Dir, Editorial, Rights & Permissions: D Mehra; *Sales:* R N Barman; *Production:* N D Mehra; *Publicity:* S K Mehra, C K Mehra
Br Offs: 94 South Malaka, Allahabad 211001; 102 Prasad Chambers, Swadeshi Mills Compound, Opera House, Bombay 400004; 3831 Pataudi House Rd, Daryaganj, New Delhi 110002
Subjects: Art, Education, History, Literature, Fiction, Philosophy, Religion, Sport, Pastimes
1977: 44 titles *1978:* 30 titles *Founded:* 1936

Sahitya Bhawan+*, Hospital Rd, Agra 282003, Uttar Pradesh

Sanchi Prakashan, subsidiary of Ram Prasad & Sons (qv)

Sangam Books, an imprint of Orient Longman Ltd (qv)

Sanskriti, an imprint of Arnold-Heinemann Publishers, India (qv)

Saraswat Library*, 206 Bidhan Sarani, Calcutta 700006 Tel: 345492
Man Partner: B Bhattacharyya
Subjects: Poetry, History, Music, Art, Philosophy, Reference, Religion, Juveniles, General & Social Science, University, Secondary Textbooks
1977: 20 titles *Founded:* 1914
Bookshop: 206 Bidhan Sarani, Calcutta 700006

Sarita Prakashan+*, 175 Nauchandi Grounds, Meerut City Tel: 73515/75075
Cable Add: Prabhatpress Telex: 0594-215
Man Dir, Publicity, Rights & Permissions: K A Rastogi; *Editorial:* Rahul Rastogi; *Sales:* Atul Rastogi; *Production:* Abhay Rastogi
Subsidiary Companies: Prabhat Offset Printers Pvt Ltd; Prabhat Press
Br Off: E-1 Jhandewalan Extn, Rani Jhansi Rd, New Delhi 110055
Subjects: Engineering, Botany, Literature, Reference
1977: 9 titles *Founded:* 1963

M C **Sarkar** & Sons (P) Ltd+*, 14 Bankim Chatterjee St, Calcutta 700073

Sasta Sahitya Mandal+, N-77 Connaught Circus, New Delhi 110001 Tel: 40505
Cable Add: Satsahitya
Secretary: Shri Yashpal Jain
Branch Off: Zero Rd, Allahabad
Subjects: History, Agriculture, Textbooks, Literature, Education, Philosophy, Psychology, Languages, Paperbacks, Economics
1977: 11 titles *1978:* 13 titles *Founded:* 1925

Scientific Book Agency+, 22 Raja Woodmunt St, PO Box 239, Calcutta 700001 Tel: 221500 Cable Add: Argosy Telex: Leo In/0212846
Man Dir: J Sinha; *Editorial:* P Sinha; *Sales Dir:* S P Sinha; *Production:* S Sinha; *Publicity & Advertising:* P L Sinha; *Rights & Permissions:* Swapan Mitra
Br Off: 79/2 Mahatma Ghandi Rd, Calcutta 700009; 56–D Mirza Ghalib St, Calcutta 700016
Subjects: History, Medicine, Economics, Politics, Physics, Chemistry, Biological Sciences, Veterinary, Reference
1978: 9 titles *1979:* 6 titles *Founded:* 1954

Selina Publishers+*, 4725/21A Dayanand Marg, Darya Ganj, New Delhi 110002 Tel: 262369/273292
Man Dir, Editorial, Production: H L Gupta; *Sales:* P C Gupta; *Publicity, Rights & Permissions:* S S Dwivedi
Subsidiary Company: Sanket Paperbacks
Associate Company: Granth Bharati (Printing Press)
Branch Off: 113 Chhatta Bhawani Shanker, Fatehnuri, Delhi 110006
Subjects: Primary textbooks, Juveniles
Book Club: Sanket Library Yojna
1977: 14 titles *Founded:* 1975

R R **Sheth** and Co, PO Box 2517, Bombay 400002 (Located at: 110/112 S Gandhi Marg, Bombay) Tel: 313441 Cable Add: Literature Bombay

Man Dir: Bhagatbhai Bhuralal Sheth; *Other Offices:* Dhirajlal Chunilal Mody
Associate Company: Lokpriya Prakashan, 110 S Gandhi Marg, Bombay 400002
Br Off: Opp Phuvara, Gandhi Rd, Ahmedabad 380001 Tel: 380573
Subjects: Gujarati books on all subjects for all ages and tastes
Bookshops: PO Box 2517, 110–112 S Gandhi Marg, Bombay 400002; opp Phuvara, Gandhi Marg, Ahmedabad 380001
1977: 76 titles *1978:* 92 titles *Founded:* 1926
Miscellaneous: Largest wholesaler of Gujarati and Hindi books

Shiksha Bharati, Madarsa Rd, Kashmere Gate, Delhi 110006 Tel: 223904
Man Dir, Rights & Permissions: D P Sehgal; *Editorial:* Miss Meera Malhotra; *Sales, Publicity:* Mrs Parveen Malhotra; *Production:* Indu Malhotra
Associate Companies: Rajpal & Sons, India (qv); Vision Books Pvt Ltd, India (qv)
Subsidiary Company: Shiksha Bharati Press, 18 G T Rd, Shahdara, Delhi 110032
Subjects: Juveniles, Educational
1977: 60 titles *1978:* 60 titles *Founded:* 1959

Shri Ram Centre for Industrial Relations and Human Resources*, 5 Sadhu Vaswani Marg, New Delhi 110005 Tel: 568261 Cable Add: Sricir
Man Dir, Editorial, Rights & Permissions: Arun Joshi; *Sales, Production, Publicity:* K K Bhargava
Subject: Indian Journal of Industrial Relations
1977: 2 titles *Founded:* 1963

Somaiya Publications Pvt Ltd+, 172 Mumbai Marathi Grantha Sangrahalaya Marg, Dadar, Bombay 400014 Tel: 440030 Cable Add: Bookmark, Bombay
Man Dir, Editorial, Rights & Permissions: Dr G S Koshe; *Education Manager:* P S Warty; *Production:* B H Pujar
Parent Company: The Godavari Sugar Mills Ltd, Fazalbhoy Building, Mahatma Ghandi Road, Bombay 400001
Associate Companies: The Book Centre Ltd (Book Sales Division), Ranade Rd, Dadar, Bombay 400028; The Book Centre Ltd (Printing Press Division), Plot No 103, 6th Rd, Sion, Bombay 400022
Br Office: F-6 Bank of Baroda Bldg, Parliament St, New Delhi 110001
Subjects: Economics, Sociology, Education, Engineering, History, Politics, Civics, Language and Literature, Management, Mathematics, Physics, Chemistry, Psychology, Religion, Philosophy, Logic
1977: 38 titles *1978:* 19 titles *Founded:* 1967

Spectrum Publications, PO Box 45, Pan Bazar, Gauhati 781001, Assam Tel: 24791 Cable Add: Spectrum, Gauhati
Publisher: Krishan Kumar; *Editorial:* Alex P Joseph; *Sales:* R K Das; *Publicity:* Miss Rama Brahma
Subjects: Tourism, Reference, Anthropology, Sociology, Annual Yearbooks and Directories, Children's Books, Journals
1977: 12 titles *1978:* 5 titles *Founded:* 1976

Sree Rama Publishers+*, 4000 Market St, Secunderabad 500025 Tel: 73128 Cable Add: Books, Secunderabad
Man Dir: Shiva Ramaiah Pabba; *Editorial:* Sreenivas Prabhu Pabba; *Sales:* Subash Chandra Sekhar Pabba; *Production:* Shivaramaiah Pabba; *Publicity & Rights & Permissions:* Shivarajaiah Pabba

Orders to: 113 Sarojini Devi Rd, Secunderabad 500003
Parent Company: Sree Rama Book Depot, Market St, Secunderabad
Associate Companies: Popular Book House, Pan Bazaar, Secunderabad; Sree Sita Rama Book Depot, Siddiamber Bazar, Hyderabad
Subjects: Primary & Secondary Textbooks, Theology in local language and English
Bookshops: Sree Rama Book Depot, Gunfoundry, Hyderabad 500001; Sree Rama Book Depot, Siddiamber Bazar, Hyderabad
1977: 6 titles *Founded:* 1916

The **Standard** Book Depot, Avenue Rd, Bangalore 560002 Tel: 26535/72625 Cable Add: Stanbook
Man Dir, Rights & Permissions: B Rajashekar; *Editorial:* B Gurunath; *Sales:* B Ananth; *Production:* R L Narasimhiah; *Publicity:* S Sudhindra
Subjects: Fiction, General Literature, Popular Science, Juveniles
Bookshop: At above address
1978: 12 titles *1979:* 15 titles *Founded:* 1935

Star Publications (P) Ltd, 4/5B Asaf Ali Rd, New Delhi 110002 Tel: 273335/274874
Man Dir, Sales, Production, Publicity: Amar Nath
Associate Companies: Hindi Book Centre, India (qv); Star Book Centre, Delhi 110006
Subsidiary Company: Publications India, 108 Surya Kiran, Kasturba Ghandi Road, New Delhi 110001
Subjects: Paperbacks in Urdu and Hindi
Founded: 1969
Book Club: Star Book Bank, Asaf Ali Rd, New Delhi
Miscellaneous: Largest exporter of Indian books to world libraries

Sterling Publishers Pvt Ltd+, AB/9 Safdarjang Enclave, New Delhi 110016 Tel: 669560 Cable Add: Paperbacks
Man Dir: O P Ghai; *Editorial:* T K Ghosh; *Publicity:* V N Camphor; *Sales, Production, Rights & Permissions:* S K Ghai
Imprints: Asian Publishers; IBI; Sterling Paperbacks; Sterling Publishers
Br Off: 695 Model Town, Jullundur City
Subjects: History, Philosophy, Economics, Reference, Low-priced Paperbacks, Social Science, University Textbooks, Political Science, Agriculture, Art, Autobiography, Education, Fiction, International Relations, Library Science, Management and Administration, Religion, Sociology
Book Club: Sterling Book Club
1977: 112 titles *1978:* 120 titles *Founded:* 1965
Subsidiaries: Indian Book Industry, AB/9 Safdarjang Enclave, New Delhi 110016; Asian Publishers; Sterling Printers (both at L-11 Green Park Ext, New Delhi 110016)

The **Students'** Book Co*, SMS Highway, Jaipur 302003 Tel: 72455 (shop), 74087 (res)
Proprietor, Rights & Permissions: Tara Chand Verma; *Man Dir:* J D Verma; *Editorial, Sales, Production:* Subhash Chandra Verma; *Publicity:* Satish Chandra Verma
Subsidiary Company: United Printers, Radha Damoderji Ki Gali, Chaura Rasta, Jaipur 302003
Subjects: Science, Commerce, Arts, Sanskrit, Hindi, English, Rajasthani
Bookshops: Chinmaya Prakashan, Chaura Rasta, Jaipur 302003; Vaner Prakashan, Chaura Rasta, Jaipur 302003
1977: 25 titles *Founded:* 1939

Sudha Publications Pvt Ltd+*, 604 Prabhat Kiran, Rajpath Pl, New Delhi 110008 Tel: 582898
Man Dir: S K Sachdeva; *Sales Dir:* Amar Nath; *Publicity & Advertising Dir:* Vijay Lakshmi; *Rights & Permissions:* C G Advani
Founded: 1960

Sultan Chand and Sons, 4792-23 Darya Ganj, New Delhi 110002 Tel: 278659, 277843
Man Dir: Prakash Chand; *Editorial, Production:* Pratap Chand; *Sales, Publicity, Rights & Permissions:* Prabhat Chand
Associate Company: SCS Publishers' Distributors (at above address)
Subjects: Management, Business, Accounting, Commerce, Economics, Chemistry, Physics, Maths, Statistics, Public Administration
Bookshop: Premier Book Co, 4792-23 Darya Ganj, New Delhi 110002
1977: 130 titles (including reprints) *1978:* 140 titles (including reprints) *Founded:* 1950

Suman Prakashan (P) Ltd+*, 16/1022 Arya Samaj Rd, 18 Hari Singh Nalwa, New Delhi 110005

Surjeet Book Depot+, 4074 Nai Sarak, PO Box 1425, Delhi 110006 Tel: 265987
1978: 100 titles
Miscellaneous: Also Booksellers and Distributors

Swan, an imprint of Orient Longman Ltd (qv)

Taraporevala Publishing Industries Pvt Ltd*, 'Woodlands', 67 Dr D Deshmukh Marg, Bombay 400026 Tel: 393361 Cable Add: Tarabook, Bombay
Subjects: Management, Computer Technology, Social Science, Chemical Engineering, Natural Sciences, Technology, Reprints
1977: 67 titles

Taraporevala Sons & Co Pvt Ltd+*, 210 Dr Dadabhai Naoroji Rd, Bombay 400001 Tel: 261433/269782 Cable Add: Bookshop, Bombay
Chief Executive: Professor Russi J Taraporevala; *Dirs:* Mrs Manekbai J Taraporevala, Miss Sooni J Taraporevala
Subjects: Indian Art Culture, History, Sociology etc; Secondary & University Textbooks, Reprints of scientific and technical titles
Founded: 1864
Miscellaneous: Publishes *Book Bulletin* (monthly)

Tata McGraw-Hill Publishing Co Ltd+, 12/4 Asaf Ali Rd (3rd Floor), New Delhi 110002 Tel: 273105/271303/278711 Cable Add: Corinthian Telex: ND-2257
Dir: Balan Subramanian; *General Manager:* Ish C Dawar; *Editorial, Production:* Suresh Gopal; *Sales:* Hari Ganesh; *Publicity:* N S Nagan
Subjects: Philosophy, Low- & High-priced Paperbacks, Medicine, Psychology, Engineering, General & Social Science, University Textbooks, Educational Materials, Agriculture, Biological Sciences, Management and Economics, Mathematics, Technology
1977: 44 titles *1978:* 42 titles *Founded:* 1970
Miscellaneous: Firm is a subsidiary of McGraw-Hill International Book Co, 1221 Ave of the Americas, New York, NY 10020, USA

Thacker & Co Ltd, 18–20 Kaikushru Dubash Marg, PO Box 190, Bombay 1 Tel: 242745/242683/242667 Cable Add: Booknotes
Dir: J M Chudasama; *Manager:* Mrs D Puri
Subjects: History, Political & Social Science, Law, Business, University Textbooks
1978: 3 titles

The **Theosophical Publishing** House, Adyar, Madras 600020 Tel: 412904 Cable Add: Theotheca
Chairman of Council: John B S Coats; *Sales, Operations Manager:* C Seshadri; *Publicity & Advertising Manager, Rights & Permissions:* K N Ramanathan
Subjects: Philosophy, Religion, Universal Brotherhood, Occultism, Theosophy
1977: 32 titles *1978:* 26 titles *Founded:* 1910

Thomson Press (India) Ltd+*, 9 K Block, Connaught Circus, New Delhi 110001 Tel: 40246/43818/45723/45995/43416 Cable Add: Thompress Telex: ND 2651
Man Dir: Aroon Purie; *Sales:* S Srinivasan
Br Off: 49 Jolly Maker Chambers II, Nariman Point, Bombay 400021
Subjects: Biography, History, Art, Business, Law, Education, Philosophy, Religion, Juveniles, General & Social Science, Engineering, Agriculture, Anthropology, Chemistry, Fiction, Medical Science, Physics, Poetry, Politics, Sport, Periodicals
Miscellaneous: Associate company of Living Media Ltd, at same address

Today and Tomorrow's Book Agency, 22-B/5 Original Rd, Karol Bagh, New Delhi 110005 Tel: 563987 Cable Add: Periodical Telex: 3717
Man Dir: Rajesh K Jain
Subsidiary Company: Jagmander Book Agency
Subjects: Botany, Geology, Life Sciences, Reference, Indian History and Culture, Reprints
Founded: 1953

Trimurti Publications Pvt Ltd+*, W-152 Greater Kailash-I, New Delhi 10048 Tel: 42015
Man Dir, Sales, Rights & Permissions: S P Kumria; *Publicity Dir:* Sudarshan Kumria
Br Off: D-24, Odeon Bldg, Connaught Pl, New Delhi 11001
Subjects: History, Political Science, Economics, Religion, Philosophy, Reference, Social Science, University Textbooks
1977: 11 titles *Founded:* 1972

N M **Tripathi** Pvt Ltd+, 164 Shamaldas Gandhi Marg, Bombay 400002
Man Dir: Arvind S Pandya; *Executive Manager:* Virendra Majmudar
Subjects: Law, Commerce, Gujarati
1977: 26 titles *1978:* 25 titles *Founded:* 1888

U B S Publishers Dist Pvt Ltd, subsidiary of Vikas Publishing House Pvt Ltd (qv)

University Publishers*, Railway Rd, Jullundur City 144001 Tel: 2645 Cable Add: Best Books
Dirs: A N Chopra, R K Chopra; *Sales Dir:* O P Sharma; *Publicity Dir:* Rajinder Pal; *Advertising Dir:* Budhi Ram
Associate Company: Concept Publishing Co, India (qv)
Subjects: Fiction, History, Political Science, Technology, Educational Materials
Founded: 1947

The **Upper India** Publishing House Pvt Ltd*, Aminabad, Lucknow UP 226001 Tel: 42711 Cable Add: Balance
Man Dir: S Bhargava
Subjects: History, Reference, General & Social Science, Secondary & University Textbooks. (In Hindi & English)
1977: 29 titles *Founded:* 1921

Vakils Feffer & Simons Ltd*, 9 Sprott Rd, Ballard Est, Bombay 38 Tel: 261221 Cable Add: Fleetbooks
Man Dir: G U Mehta
Subjects: Educational, College Textbooks

Vidyarthi Mithram Press+, PO Box 81, Baker Rd, Kottayam 686001, Kerala State Tel: 2313/2316/4713 (after office hours 2616) Cable Add: Vidyarthi
Man Dir: Koshy P John
Parent Company: Vidyarthi Mithram Press & Book Depot
Associate Companies: Auroville Publishers, Kottayam; John Samuel Bros, Main Rd, Trivandrum
Imprint: Kosi Books
Subjects: Fiction, Textbooks, Children's Books
Bookshop: Vidyarthi Book Depot (at above address, and seven other branches)
1977: 170 titles *1978:* 200 titles *Founded:* 1928

Vikas Publishing House Pvt Ltd+, 20/4 Industrial Area, Sahibabad, Dish Graziabad (UP) Tel: 205290
Man Dir: Narendra Kumar
Br Offs: Savoy Chambers, 5 Wallace St, Bombay 400001; 10 First Main Rd, Gandhi Nagar, Bangalore 560009; 8/1-B Chowringhee Lane, Calcutta 700016; 80 Canning Rd, Kanpur 208004
Subjects: Adventure, Mountaineering, Agriculture, Animal Husbandry, Art, Architecture, Travel, Biography, Memoirs, Botany, Chemistry, Cookery, Demography, Economics, Education, Engineering, Fiction, Futurology, Geography, Geology, History, Culture, Library Science, Literature, Management, Commerce, Mass Media, Mathematics, Medicine, Military Affairs, Philosophy, Religion, Physics, Politics, Current Affairs, Psychology, Public Administration, Science, Sociology, Anthropology, Sports, Games, Zoology, Children's Books
Founded: 1969

Vishal Publications*, Adda Hoshiarpur, Jullundur City 144001 Tel: 5177/5388
Man Dir: Pardeep Jain; *Sales Dir:* Rajinder K Jain; *Publicity & Advertising:* Sunil Jain
Br Offs: Vishal Publications, 6 U B Bungalow Rd, Delhi 110007
Founded: 1973

Vision Books Pvt Ltd+, Madarsa Rd, Kashmere Gate, Delhi 110004 Tel: 227011/252267/352081/312978 Cable Add: Vision Book
Chairman: Vishwa Nath; *Man Dir, Rights & Permissions, Publicity:* Sudhir Malhotra; *Publishing Dir:* Kapil Malhotra; *Editor:* Krishna Kumar; *Sales:* Rajendra Malhotra
Subsidiary Company: Anand Paperbacks; Orient Paperbacks (qv)
Branch Off: 3-B Peddar Road, 'Vasant' Ground Floor, Bombay
Subjects: General Fiction, Military Science and History, Sciences, Current Affairs, Indology, Management, Religion, Anthropology, Education, International Relations, Medicine, Mountaineering, Travel
1978: 18 titles *1979:* 27 titles *Founded:* 1975

Book Clubs: Anand Book Club, Madrasa Rd, Kashmere Gate, Delhi 110006; Orient Book Club, Madrasa Rd, Kashmere Gate, Delhi 110006
Allied Companies: Rajpal & Sons, Delhi (qv); Shiksha Bharati, Delhi (qv)

Vora & Co Publishers Pvt Ltd, 3 Round Bldg, Kalbadevi Rd, Bombay 2
Man Dir: Manherlal K Vora; *Publicity:* K K Vora
Subjects: Education, Textbooks, Law, Economics, Banking, Literature, History, Science

Wheeler-Pitman Publishing Co Pvt Ltd+*, 15 Lal Bahadur Shastri Rd, Allahabad 211001

Wilco Publishing House, 33 Ropewalk Lane, Rampart Row, Fort Bombay 400023 Tel: 242574
Man Dir: Jaisukh H Shah
Subjects: Fiction, Reference, Philosophy, Psychology, Business, Management, Inspirational, Self-help
1977: 10 titles *1978:* 10 titles *Founded:* 1958

Wiley Eastern Ltd+*, AB 8 Safdarjang Enclave, New Delhi 110016 Tel: 663806/663972 Cable Add: Wileyeast
Dir & Consultant: Anand R Kundaji; *General Manager:* Vinod Kumar; *Sales:* K K Gulati; *Production:* B Bhattacharya
Subjects: Psychology, Engineering, Social Science, University Textbooks, Indian Art, Science
1977: 37 titles *Founded:* 1966
Bookshop: The Wiley Eastern Book Shop, 4654/21 Daryaganj, New Delhi 110002; The Wiley Bookshop, 16 Resthouse Crescent, Bangalore 560001; Abid House, Dr Bhadkamkar Marg, Bombay 400007
Miscellaneous: Firm is an associate company of John Wiley & Sons Ltd, UK (qv for other associates)

The **World** Press Pvt Ltd*, 37A College St, Calcutta 700073 Tel: 341444/343591/342426 Cable Add: Takshasila
Chairman: J Sinha; *Man Dir, Production:* P C Bhattacharji; *Sales, Editorial:* S Bhattacharyya; *Publicity & Advertising, Rights & Permissions:* L Bhattacharjee
Subjects: Economics, History, Political & Social Science, Business, Law, Mathematics, Geology, Botany, Statistics, Library Science, Reference
1977: 24 titles *Founded:* 1947
Bookshop: 37A College St (First floor), Calcutta 73

Writers Workshop*, 162/92 Lake Gardens, Calcutta 700045 Tel: 468325
Man Dir: P Lal
Subjects: General Fiction, Belles Lettres, Poetry, Philosophy, Reference, Religion, Low- & High-priced Paperbacks
1977: 44 titles *Founded:* 1958

Zebra Books for Children, an imprint of Arnold-Heinemann Publishers, India (qv)

Literary Agents

Intellectuals' Rendezvous*, M-116, Con Circus, New Delhi 110001 Tel: 45316
Man Dir: B R Chawla
Specialization: Sheet deals, books on Social Sciences, translation rights for fiction, co-publication arrangements, printing and reprinting jobs

Kunnuparampil P **Punnoose**, 6/77 WEA Karol Bagh, New Delhi 110005 Tel: 565843
Man Dir: K P Punnoose
Specialization: Hardback rights in various branches of Humanities and Social Sciences, paperback rights in Self Improvement and How-to
Also Publisher (qv)

Book Clubs

Anand Book Club*, Madrasa Rd, Kashmere Gate, Delhi 110006
Owned by: Vision Books (P) Ltd

Clarion Book Club*, G T Rd, Shahdara, Delhi 110032
Owned by: Hind Pocket Books Private Ltd

Gharelu Library Yojna*, G T Rd, Shahdara, Delhi 110032
Owned by: Hind Pocket Books/Private Ltd

Orient Book Club*, G T Rd, Shahdara, Delhi 110032
Owned by: Vision Books (P) Ltd (Delhi)

Radical Book Club*, 6 Bankim Chatterjee St, Calcutta 12

Sanket Library Yojna*, 4725/21A Dayanand Marg, Darya Ganj, New Delhi 110002
Owned by: Selina Publishers (qv)

Star Book Bank, 4/5B Asaf Ali Rd, New Delhi
Owned by: Star Publications (P) Ltd

Major Booksellers

D K Publishers' Distributors, 1 Ansari Rd, Darya Ganj, New Delhi 110002 Tel: 274819 Cable Add: Dekaypub Telex: Dikay ND-3616
Partners: I C Mittal, Praveen Mittal, Pramil Mittal; *Sales:* S K Bhatia
The largest wholesale house for Indian books, exclusive stockists of the publications of more than 500 Indian publishers

Diamond Books International, 2715 Darya Ganj, New Delhi 110002
Leading exporters

English Book Store, 17/L Connaught Circus, New Delhi Tel: 42166/44753
Partners: S D Chowdhari, Bhupinder Chowdhari

E D Galgotia & Sons, PO Box 688, New Delhi 110001 (Located at: 17-B Connaught Pl, New Delhi) Tel: 321844
Technical & Scientific Books

India Book House, 3-a Rashtrapathi Rd, Secunderabad 500003

J K Export House*, 3983/2 Jitendra Paper Market, Chawri Bazar, Delhi 110006
Proprietor: K Jitendra
Exporters of any books published in India

Jaico Book Shop, 125 Mahatma Gandhi Rd, Bombay 400023

Lyall Book Depot*, Chaura Bazar, Ludhiana Tel: 20221; 23 Daryaganj, Ansari Rd, New Delhi 110002

Modern Book Depot, Pan Bazar Main Rd, Gauhati 781001, Assam Tel: 24791 Cable Add: Modbook Gauhati; PO Box 68, G S Rd, Shillong 793001, Meghalaya Tel: 3476/3810 Cable Add: Modbook Shillong

Motilal Banarsidass, 41 U A Bungalow Rd, Jawahar Nagar, Delhi 110007 Tel: 221985/228355
Importers and exporters of Indological books

Oxford Book and Stationery Co, Scindia House, New Delhi 110001; 17 Park St, Calcutta 700016 Tel: 44957 Cable Add: Indamer

Popular Book Depot, Dr Bhadkamkar Rd, Bombay 400007 Tel: 359401

Publications India*, 108 Surya Kiran, Kasturba Ghandi Road, New Delhi 110001 Tel: 385709
Exporters of English books on all subjects covering India

R R Sheth & Co, Princess St, Keshavbag, Bombay 400002 Tel: 313441

Star Publications (P) Ltd, 4/5B Asaf Ali Rd, New Delhi 110002 Tel: 273335/274874
Exporter of Indian books to world libraries

Sterling Publishers Pvt Ltd, AB/9 Safdarjang Enclave, New Delhi 110016 Tel: 669560/660904

N M Tripathi Pvt Ltd, 164 Shamaldas Gandhi Marg, Bombay 400002
Manager: A S Pandya

U B S Publisher's Distributors Ltd*, 5 Ansari Rd, PO Box 7015, New Delhi 110002 Tel: 273601

United Publishers, PO Box 82, Pan Bazar, Gauhati 781001 Assam Tel: 26381 Cable Add: Unipub Gauhati
Wholesaler and exporter

Vidyarthi Book Depot*, Baker Rd, Kottayam 686001, Kerala Tel: 2313/2316/2616 Cable Add: Vidyarthi
Branches at Calicut, Palghat, Ernakulam, Round North Trichur and another at Kottayam

Major Libraries

Bombay University Library, Bombay University, Fort, Bombay 32BR Tel: 254372

British Council Library*, AIFACS Bldg, Rafi Marg, New Delhi 110001
South India: 150A Anna Salai, Madras 600002; *East India:* 5 Shakespeare Sarani, Calcutta 700016; *Western and Central India:* 178 Backbay Reclamation, Bombay 400020

Central Library, Nr Mandvi Bank Rd, Baroda, Gujarat PO Box 216, Pin 39006 Tel: 2932
Librarian: P V Mehta

Central Library, Calcutta University, Calcutta 73 Tel: 34301419/34770104

Central Secretariat Library*, G Block, Shastri Bhavan, New Delhi

Connemara (State Central) Public Library*, Egmore, Madras 8

Delhi Public Library*, S P Mukerji Marg, Delhi 110006 Tel: 264001 (Director) and 263810 (general)

Delhi University Library, University of Delhi, Delhi 110007 Tel: 229888

Gujarat Vidyapith Granthalaya, Ahmedabad 380014 Tel: 446148
(Combined university, state central and public library)
Librarian: K L Shah; *Publications:* Tapas Nibandh Suchi (Gujarati) (Bibliography of Dissertations); Indexing of articles from *Gujarati Journals* (1975), published 1979

Indian Council of World Affairs Library, Sapru House, Barakhamba Rd, New Delhi 110001
Librarian: Ashok Jambhekar
Publication: Documentation on Asia (annually)

Indian Institute of Technology Central Library*, Madras 600036 Tel: 432742 ext 207

Indian National Scientific Documentation Centre (INSDOC)*, Hillside Rd, Delhi 12 Tel: 586301
Publication: Annals of Library Science and Documentation

Madras Literary Society Library*, College Rd, Madras 600006

Maulana Azad Library*, Aligarh Muslim University, Aligarh, Uttar Pradesh

National Archives of India, Janpath, New Delhi 110001
Librarian: J C Srivastava

The **National Library**, Government of India, Belvedere, Calcutta 700027 Tel: 455381
Director: Prof R K Dasgupta

State Central Library*, Hyderabad 12, AP

Library Associations

Delhi Library Association*, PO Box 1270, c/o Hardinge Public Library, Queen's Garden, Delhi 6
Publication: Indian Book Review Supplement (quarterly), *Library Herald* (quarterly), *Indian Press Index* (monthly)

Documentation Research and Training Centre, 31 Church St, Bangalore 560001
Head: G Bhattacharyya
Publications: Annual Seminar, DRTC (annual), *Refresher Seminar, DRTC* (annual), *Library Science with a slant to documentation* (quarterly)

Federation of Indian Library Associations*, Misri Bazar, Patiala, Punjab
President: Professor P N Kaula

Indian Association of Special Libraries and Information Centres*, P 291 CIT Scheme No 6M, PO Kankurgachi, Calcutta 700054 Tel: 359651
General Secretary: S M Ganguly
Publications: Bulletin (4 a year), *Newsletter*

Indian Association of Teachers of Library Science*, Department of Library Science, Banaras Hindu University, Varanasi 221005
President: Professor P N Kaula

Indian Library Association, Delhi Public Library, S P Mukerji Marg, Delhi 110006 Tel: 264001
President: B L Bharadwaja; *Secretary:* O P Trikha
Publication: Bulletin

Library Journals

Annals of Library Science and Documentation, Indian National Scientific Documentation Centre, Hillside Rd, Delhi 12

Bulletin, Indian Association of Special Libraries and Information Centres, P 291 CIT Scheme No 6M, PO Kankurgachi, Calcutta 700054

Bulletin, Indian Library Association, Delhi Public Library, S P Mukerji Marg, Delhi 110006

Herald of Library Science, Banaras Hindu University, c/o Editor P N Kaula, C-1, Varanasi 221005

Indian Librarian, 233 Model Town, Jullundur 3

Indian Library Movement, 148 Allenby Lines, Ambala Cantt

Journal of Indexing and Reference Work, Mukherjee Library, 1 Gopi Mohan Dutta Lane, Calcutta 3

Journal of Library Service, Ravikrupa Trust, 1760 Gandhi Rd, Ahmedabad 1

Karnatak Granthalaya (text in Kannada, contents page in English and Kannada), S R Gunjal, Granthalaya Vijnana Prakashana, Saptapur, Dharwar, Karnatak State

Library Science with a slant to Documentation (text in English), Documentation Research and Training Centre, 31 Church St, Bangalore 560001

Pustakalaya (text in Gujurati), Gujarat Pustakalaya Sahayak Sahkari Mandal Ltd, PO Box 10, Raopura, Baroda

Literary Associations and Societies

Madras Literary Society and Auxiliary of the Royal Asiatic Society*, College Rd, Madras 600006
Honorary Secretary: S V B Row

National Academy of Letters (Sahitya Akademi) Rabindra Bhavan, 35 Ferozeshah Rd, New Delhi 110001
Secretary: Dr R S Kelkar
Publications: Indian Literature (bi-monthly), *Samskrita Pratibha* (twice yearly)

P E N All—India Centre, Theosophy Hall, 40 New Marine Lines, Bombay 400020 Tel: 292175
Founder-Organizer: Sophia Wadia;
Secretary-Treasurer: Nissim Ezekiel
Publications: The Indian PEN (bimonthly), PEN series on Indian literatures, *PEN Conference Proceedings*

Literary Periodicals

Bengali Literature, 53 Bidhan Palli, Jadavpur, Calcutta 32

Contemporary Indian Literature (text in English), H 328 Narayana, New Delhi 28

Dhara; a monthly review of Indian literature, Dhara Publications, 37 D Gupta Colony, Delhi 110009

DK Newsletter, DK Publishers' Distributors, 1 Ansari Rd, Darya Ganj, New Delhi 110002. A journal of news and reviews of Indian publications in English

Indian Book Chronicle, Vivek Trust, G-11 Hauz Khas Market, New Delhi 110016. Book news and reviews (fortnightly)

Indian Literature, National Academy of Letters, Rabindra Bhavan, 35 Ferozeshah Rd, New Delhi

Indian PEN (text in English), PEN All-India Centre, Theosophy Hall, 40 New Marine Lines, Bombay 400020

Indian Writing Today, Nirmala-Sadanand Publishers, 35c Tardeo Rd, Bombay 34 WB

Literary Criterion, Popular Prakashan, 35-C Tardeo Rd, Bombay 400034 WB

Literary Half-Yearly, Literary Press, H H A Gowda, Mysore 9

Literary Studies; a quarterly review of literature and criticism from the Panjab, Razdan House, Sirhindi Darwaza, Patiala, Panjab

Miscellany, Writers Workshop, 162-92 Lake Gardens, Calcutta 700045

Opinion Literary Quarterly, Purnima Bridge Rd, Bombay 6

Samskrita Pratibha; a six-monthly journal in Sanskrit devoted to contemporary writing of creative quality in Sanskrit, National Academy of Letters, Rabindra Bhavan, 35 Ferozeshah Rd, New Delhi 1

Vagartha; critical quarterly of Indian literature, Joshi Foundation, N-3 Panchsheel Park, New Delhi 110017

Literary Prizes

Books for Neoliterates Prizes*
For books and manuscripts in Indian languages by Indian nationals. 1,000 Indian rupees for each book. Awarded annually. Enquiries to Ministry of Education and Social Welfare, Government of India, New Delhi

Certificate of Honour*
To Arabic, Persian and Sanskrit scholars who have made outstanding contributions to Arabic, Persian and Sanskrit study. 3,000 Indian rupees. Awarded annually by the President. Enquiries to Office of the President, Government of India, New Delhi

Commission for Scientific and Technical Terminology Prizes*
For fiction, drama, memoirs, travelogues and poetry in Indian languages except Hindi, Sanskrit, tribal languages and authors' mother tongue. 65 prizes of 1,000 Indian rupees each. Awarded annually. Enquiries to Commission for Scientific and Technical Terminology, Ministry of Education and Social Welfare, West Block VII R K Puram, New Delhi 22

Escorts Book Award*
For books on management principles and practices in India by Indian nationals. 1,000 and 500 Indian rupees each. Awarded annually. Enquiries to Escort Ltd, Delhi Management Association, 1/21 Asaf Ali Rd, New Delhi 1

Geetha Prize*
For a Sanskrit work on Indian philosophy by Indian nationals. 1,000 Indian rupees. Awarded annually. Enquiries to Director of Languages, Government of Haryana, Chandigarh

Hali Prize*
Awarded annually to Indian nationals for poetry in Urdu. 1,000 Indian rupees. Enquiries to Director of Languages, Government of Haryana, Chandigarh

Indian National Academy of Letters (Sahitya Akademi) Awards
For the most literary works written in each of the 22 regional languages of India recognized by the Academy (Sahitya Akademi). 5,000 Indian rupees each. Awarded annually to Indian Nationals only, by the Executive Board of the Academy. Enquiries to Indian National Academy of Letters, Rabindra Bhavan, 35 Ferozeshah Rd, New Delhi 1

Jnanpith Literary Award*
For the best literary work in any Indian language by an Indian national. Awarded annually. Enquiries to Bharatiya Jnanpith, B/45-47 2nd Floor, Connaught Pl, New Delhi 1

Law Books in Hindi Prize
Awarded annually for law books/manuscripts in Hindi. Enquiries to Vidhi Sahitya Prakashan, Ministry of Law, Justice and Company Affairs, Govt of India, Indian Law Institute Bldgs, Bhagwandas Rd, New Delhi 110001

National Prize on Literature on Physical Education*
For books on physical education by Indian nationals. Two prizes of 100 Indian rupees each. Awarded annually. Enquiries to Ministry of Education and Social Welfare, Government of India, New Delhi

Sahitya Akademi Award, see Indian National Academy of Letters (Sahitya Akademi) Awards

Sangeet Natak Akademi Prize*
For books on music, dance and drama by Indian nationals. 1,500 Indian rupees for each language. Awarded annually. Enquiries to Sangeet Natak Akademi, Ravindra Bhavan, New Delhi 1

Shriram Awards*
For works on management by Indian nationals. 250 Indian rupees. Awarded quarterly. Enquiries to Charat Ram Foundation, Delhi Management Association, 1/21 Asaf Ali Rd, New Delhi 1

Soviet Land Nehru Awards
For Indian nationals. For literary works, journalistic works in Indian languages and in English and meritorious work done in creative, cultural and public fields for promoting Indo-Soviet friendship, world peace and international amity.
Three prizes of 10,000 Indian rupees with a fortnight's trip to USSR and three prizes of 5,000 Indian rupees with a fortnight's trip to USSR. Ten prizes of 1,500 Indian rupees each. Five awards for children 10-13 age group for painting competition — a month's holiday at the Artek Young Pioneers Camp, Black Sea Coast, Crimea. Awarded annually. Enquiries to Soviet Land, Embassy of the USSR in India, 25 Barakhamba Rd, New Delhi 1

Sur Prize
Awarded annually to Indian nationals for Hindi poetry. 1,000 Indian rupees. Enquiries to Director, Haryana Sahitya Akademi, Chandigarh

Urdu Akademy Awards*
Awarded annually to Indian nationals for Urdu literature. Enquiries to U P Urdu Akademy, 11 Hazratganj, Lucknow

Major Tek Singh **Virdi** Literary Prizes*
Awarded annually to children under 15 years for short stories, essays and dramas in Punjabi. Three prizes of 100, 75 and 50 Indian rupees. Enquiries to Modern Sahit Academy, 'Gulfashan', East Mohan Nagar, Link Rd, Amritsar

Translation Agencies and Associations

Amerind Publishing Co (P) Ltd, N-56 Connaught Circus, New Delhi 110001 Tel: 44957 Cable: Indamer
Dir: Gulab Primlani
Translating Russian, German, Japanese, Hindi

Indonesia

General Information

Language: Bahasa Indonesia (and English)
Religion: Predominantly Muslim
Population: 143 million
Literacy Rate (1971): 59.6% (79.1% Urban, 55.3% Rural)
Bank Hours: Generally 0800-1400 Monday-Thursday; 0800-1100 Friday; 0800-1300 Saturday
Currency: 100 sen = 1 rupiah
Export/Import Information: Books subject to 40% tariff and 10% import sales tax, but on recommendation of Minister of Basic Education and Culture, partial or total exemption may be granted. Advertising: 50% Duty, 10% tax. All imports subject to margin of Profit Tax (5% with Letter of Credit, 10% without). Exchange control. Books and printed matter using Indonesian languages prohibited. Imports require no licence but are categorized into four groups for credit arrangement controls
Copyright: No copyright conventions signed

Book Trade Organizations

Ikatan Penerbit Indonesia (IKAPI) (Association of Indonesian Book Publishers), Jalan Pengarengan 32, Jakarta Tel: 351907
President: Ismid Hadad
Publication: Bulletin

Book Trade Reference Journals

Berita Bibliografi; Indonesian book news (text in Indonesian), Yayasan Idayu, Jl Dr Abdulrachman Saleh 26, Jakarta

Bibliografi Nasional Indonesia Kumulasi (Cumulative Bibliography of Indonesia), National Scientific Documentation Centre, Jalan Jendral Gatot-Subroto, PO Box 3065/JKT, Jakarta

Bulletin, Association of Indonesian Book Publishers, Jl Pengarengan 32, Jakarta Pusat III/4

Publishers

Akadoma+*, Jl Proklamasi No 61, Jakarta Tel: 882328

B P **Alda**+*, Jl Tambak No 12-A, Jakarta

Alma'Arif+*, Jl Tamblong No 48-50, Bandung Tel: 50708

Alumni Press, Jl Geusanulum 17, PO Box 272, Bandung Tel: (022) 50675/58290
Man Dir & Rights & Permissions: Eddy Damian; *Editorial:* Yayat Ruchiyat; *Sales:* Philipus; *Production:* Samsudin
Branch Offs: PT Tanda Djaya, Jl Tangerang, Jakarta
Subjects: Law, Economics, Social Sciences
Founded: 1966

Angkasa+*, Jl Merdeka No 6, Bandung Tel: 58330

Pustaka **Antara**+*, Jl Majaphit No 28, Jakarta Tel: 341321
Man Dir: H M Joesoef Ahmad
Founded: 1952
Subjects: School Textbooks, Children's books, Politics, Religion, General

Aries Lima, see PT New Aqua Press

Asia Afrika+*, Jl Panggung X No 11, Surabaya Tel: 278175

Balai Pustaka+*, Jl Dokter Wahidin No 1, Jakarta Tel: 365994
President: Drs Soetojo Gondo
Subjects: Literature, Juveniles, Science, Journals, Architecture, History, Engineering, Arts, Maps, Music, Education
Founded: 1908

Bale Bandung — Sumur Bandung+*, Jl Asia Afrika 82, Bandung Tel: 59137/52156
Manager: H Moh Koerdi
Subject: Textbooks

P T **Bhakti** Centra Baru+*, Jl Jend Akhmad Yani No 15, Ujung Pandang Tel: 5192; Jl Lembang 9 Tel: 356374 Cable Add: Bhakti Baru Telex: 7156 Hakalla UP
Man Dir: Drs H M Jusuf Kalla; *Publicity Man:* Alwi Hamu
Subject: Religion
Founded: 1972

Bhratara Karya Aksara+, Jl Oto Iskandarinata 111/29, Jakarta Tel: 811858
Subjects: History, Public Health, Industry, Maps, Agriculture, Textbooks, Reference, Education, Philosophy, Politics, Law, Social Sciences, Economics

Bina Ilmu+*, Jl Genteng Kali 9 (Utara Siola), Surabaya Tel: 472214

Binacipta+, Jl Ganesya 4, Bandung Tel: 84319
1978: 15 titles

Bulan Bintang, Penerbit & Pustake NV+*, Jl Kramat Kwitang I/8, Jakarta Tel: 342883
Manager: Mr Amelz
Subjects: Art, Sociology, Science, Religion
Founded: 1954

Bumi Restu+*, Jl Letjen Haryono M T Persil 23, PO Box 404, Jakarta Tel: 882746

Cemerlang+*, Jl Kesatrian VIII No 30, Jakarta Tel: 591431

Cerdas+*, Jl Palasari No 125, Bandung

Dian Rakyat+*, Jl Rawa Gelam I No 4, PO Box 51, Jakarta Tel: 481809/584845

C V **Diponegoro**+, Publisher, 44 Mohd Toha Bandung Tel: 50395 Cable Add: C V Diponegoro Bandung
Man Dir: A A Dahlan; *Editorial, Sales, Production, Publicity:* M D Dahlan
Subjects: Religion
1978: 45 titles *1979:* 13 titles *Founded:* 1962

P T **Djambatan** Penerbit NV+*, Tromolpos 116, Jakarta Tel: 345131/341678
Manager: Roswitha Pamoentjak
Subjects: Art, Literature, Juveniles, Textbooks, Religion, Philosophy, Sociology, Maps
Founded: 1958

P T **Dunia** Pustaka Jaya+, Jalan Kramat II/31A, Jakarta Pusat Tel: 336245, 367479 Cable Add: Depeje
Man Dir, Editorial, Rights & Permissions: Ajip Rosidi; *Sales Dir, Publicity:* Rachmat M A S; *Production:* Yus Rusamsi
Br Off: Jalan Banteng 37, Bandung Tel: 59597
Subjects: General Fiction, Poetry, Art, Essays, Drama, Culture, Childrens Books
1977: 142 titles *1978:* 77 titles *Founded:* 1971

Eresco+*, Jl Hasanudin No 9, Bandung Tel: (022) 82311 Cable Add: Erescopete
Man Dir: Mrs P Rochmat Soemitro; *Editorial:* Prof Dr Rochmat Soemitro; *Sales:* Mr Amun
Branch Off: Jl Perapatan 22 Pav Jakarta
Subjects: Law, Economics
Bookshops: Jl Hasanudin 9 Bandung; Jl Perapatan 22 Pav Jakarta Tel: (021) 361782
1977: 9 titles *Founded:* 1956

Erlangga+, Jl Kramat IV No 11, Jakarta Tel: 356593
Dir: M Hutauruk S H

P T **Gaya** Favorit Press, Book Division+, Jalan Proklamasi 71, Jakarta Pusat Tel: 882148 Telex: 45734 FEGA IA
Man Dir: Sofjan Alisjahbana; *Editorial:* Mrs Ediati Kamil, Sookanto SA; *Sales:* Irwan SLT; *Production, Publicity, Rights & Permissions:* Mrs Ediati Kamil
Parent Company: P T Gaya Favorit Press, Jalan Kebon Kacang Raya 1, Flat 3, tingkat 3, Jakarta Pusat
Subjects: Juvenile Fiction, Adult Fiction, Homecraft, other Non-fiction
1978: 28 titles *1979:* 54 titles *Founded:* 1975

PT **Gramedia**+*, PO Box 615 Jakarta Pusat, Dak (Located at: Palmerah Selatan 22 lantai 4) Tel: 541962, 541238, 541330 Cable Add: Kompas Jakarta Telex: Kompas JKT 46327
Man Dir: J Adisubrata; *Editorial:* A Haryono, G Sugijanto; *Sales:* E Nuhujanan; *Production:* A Harijadi; *Publicity:* Sabungan Panjaitan; *Rights & Permissions:* Nora Sutadi
Orders to: Jalan Gajah Mada lanti 3, Jakarta Barat, PO Box 615 Dak
Subjects: General Fiction and Nonfiction
Bookshops: Jalan Merdeka 43, Bandung, Jalan Gajah Mada 109, Jakarta, Jalan Pintu

Air 72, Jakarta, Jalan Melawai IV/13, Jakarta, Jalan Basuki Rachmat 95, Surabaya
1977: 148 titles *Founded:* 1973

PT Grip+*, Jl Kawung No 2, PO Box 129, Surabaya Tel: 22564
Man Dir, Editorial: Suripto; *Sales:* F D Praseno; *Production:* S Sawitri; *Publicity:* Satriyo Purwanto
Branch Off: Jl Kembung 22, Jakarta
Subjects: Textbooks, Politics, Social Science
1977: 37 titles *Founded:* 1957

Gunung Agung, PT+, Jl Kwitang 8, PO Box 145, Jakarta Tel: 362909
President: Mr Masagung
Subjects: Librarianship, Juveniles, Textbooks, Science, Biography, Language, Literature
Founded: 1953

B P K Gunung Mulia+*, Jalan Kwitang 22, Jakarta Tel: 343476
Dir: A Simandjuntak

Firma **Harris**+*, Jl Veteran Gedung Olahraga No 6, Medan Tel: 22272

Hidakarya Agung+*, Jl Kebon Kosong F-74, Jakarta Tel: 351074

Ichtiar Baru+*, Jl Mojopahit 6, Jakarta Tel: 341226/41551
Subjects: Textbooks, Reference, Law, Social Sciences, Economics

PD & I **Ikhwan**+*, Jl Bujana Dalam No 10, Blok G, Kebayoran Baru, Jakarta Tel: 772679

P T **Indira**+, Jl Borobudur No 20, Jakarta Pusat Tel: 882754 Cable Add: Indira Jakarta
Man Dir: Wahyudi D
Bookshops: Jl Braga No 10, Bandung; Jl Kornel Simanjuntak No 76A, Jogjakarta; Jl Sam Ratulangi 37, Jakarta Pusat; Jl Gajah Mada 3–5, Duta Merlin Shopping Arcade, Jakarta Pusat; Jl Bulungan 76, Garden Hall, Jakarta Selatan; Jl Braga 111, Bandung; Jl Tunjungan 71, Surabaya; Jl Veteran 3394A, Palembang; Jl Sumatra 37, Den Pasar, Bali
Subjects: Education, Technical
Founded: 1950

Indrajaya+*, Jl Jatibaru No 20, Jakarta Tel: 364372

Institut Dagang Muchtar+*, Jl Embong Wungu 8, Surabaya Tel: 42973

Islamiyah+*, Jl Sutomo P 328–329, Kotakpos 11, Medan Tel: 25421

Yayasan **Jaya Baya**+*, Jl Panghela 2 atas, Surabaya Tel: 41169

Jaya Murni+*, Jl Ir H Juanda 34 Pav, Jakarta Tel: 359200
Manager: Tadjib Ermadi
Subject: Textbooks
Founded: 1945

Yayasan **Kanisius**+*, Jl Pangeran Senopati 24, Jogjakarta Tel: 2309
Subjects: Textbooks, Religion, Engineering, Juveniles, Arts, Education, Economics

Karunia+*, Jl Paneleh 18-A, Surabaya Tel: 44120

Yayasan **Kawanku**+*, Jl Setia Budi Raya, Gg Sumbangsih 11/3A, Jakarta Tel: 583100

Kinta+*, Jl Chik Di Tiro No 54-A, Jakarta Tel: 351394

Kurnia Esa+*, Jl Kramat Raya 7-9, PO Box 3181, Jakarta Tel: 350043/5/6 Telex: 44328

LP3ES (Lembaga Penelitian Pendidikan Dan Penerangan Ekonomi Dan Social)+*, Jl Letjen S Parman 81, Slipi, PO Box 493, Jakarta Tel: 591528/594270
The Institute for Economics and Social Research Education and Information
Manager: Ismid Hadad
Subjects: Academic, Popular Science
Founded: 1971

Madju+*, Jl Sutomo No P 341–342, Medan Tel: 25428

Marfiah+*, Jl Kalibutuh No 131, Surabaya

Masa Baru+*, Jl Gereja 3, Bandung Tel: 52045

Mutiara+*, Jl Salemba Tengah No 36, Jakarta Tel: 882441
Subjects: Juveniles, Maps, Mathematics, Music, Education, Physics, Religion, Economics

P T **New Aqua** Press/Aries Lima+, Jl Rawa Gelam II/4, Jakarta Timur Tel: 482163

Nusa Indah+*, Jl Katedral 5, Ende, Flores Tel: 198

Pelajar+*, Jl Palasari 83–85, Bandung Tel: 57559

Pelita Masa+*, Jl Lodaya No 25, Bandung Tel: 50823

Pembangunan*, Jl Raden Saleh No 2, Jakarta Tel: 342469
Managers: Mr Sumantri, Mr Soewando
Br Offs: in Bandung, Jogjakarta, Madiun and Surabaya
Subjects: Textbooks, Juveniles, Sciences
Founded: 1953

Pembimbing Masa+*, Pusat Perdagangan Senen, Blok I, Lantai IV/2, PO Box 3281, Jakarta Tel: 367645

Pradnya Paramita+*, PO Box 146/Jkt, Jl Kebon Sirih 46, Jakarta Pusat Tel: (021) 360411 Cable Add: Pradnya/Jkt
Man Dir, Rights & Permissions: Sadono Dibyowiroyo SH *Editorial, Publicity:* Thaufik Arifin; *Sales:* A F Julianto; *Production:* Waslan Suriapranata
Subjects: General, Primary, Secondary & University Textbooks
Bookshops: Jl Kebon Sirih 46 pav, Jakarta Pusat; Jl Kiai Maja 2A, Kebayoran Baru, Jakarta Selatan
1977: 19 titles *Founded:* 1963

Remaja Karya+*, Jl Ciateul No 34–36, kotakpos 284, Bandung Tel: 58226

Rosda+*, Jl Raya Cimahi, Padalarang Km 12.5 No 858, Bandung Tel: 56627; Jl Kramat Kwitang II No 4, Jakarta Tel: 354920

Saiful+*, Jl Pelangka Raya Baru 28, Medan Tel: 22384

Sastra Hudaya+*, Jl Proklamasi No 61, Jakarta Tel: 882328

A B **Sitti** Syamsiyah+, Jl Secoyudan No 28, Sala/Surakarta Tel: 4721

Soeroengan+*, Jl Pecenongan No 58, Jakarta Tel: 344460

Pustaka **Star**+*, Jl Moh Toha No 58, Bandung Tel: 58710

Sumatera+*, Jl R Dewi Sartika I No 1, Bandung

Sumur Bandung+*, Jl Asia Afrika 82, Bandung Tel: 59137

Tarate+, Jl Sumatera No 26–30, kotakpos 243, Bandung Tel: 51067
1978: 4 titles

Tintamas Indonesia PT+*, Jl Kramat Raya 60, Jakarta Pusat Tel: 346186
Dir: Ali Audah
Subjects: Biography, History, Philosophy, Reference, Religion, Law, High-priced Paperbacks
Founded: 1947
Bookshop: Jl Kramat Raya 60, Jakarta Pusat

Toko Messir+*, Jl Gudang No 135, Cirebon Tel: 57151

U P Indonesia+*, Jl Jend A Yani No 19, Jogjakarta

Warga+*, Jl Karangmenjangan 61, Surabaya Tel: 472160/472872

Widjaja+*, Jl Pecenongan No 48-C, Jakarta Tel: 363446

C V **Yasaguna**+*, Gg Batik 7, Bendungan Hilir, Jakarta Tel: 581850
Manager: Hilman Madewa
Subjects: Textbooks, Agriculture, Juveniles

Major Booksellers

Effendi Harahap Bookstore*, Jl Abimanyu Raya 17, Semarang

Toko Buku **Gramedia***, Jakarta

P T **Gunung Agung***, Jl Kwitang 6, Jakarta Tel: 44678

Toko Buku BPK **Gunung Mulia***, Jl Kwitang 22, Jakarta Tel: 41768

P T **Indira**, Jl Braga No 10, Bandung
For other addresses see entry under Publishers
Miscellaneous: Importers of General/Trade books and Educational/Scientific/Technical books and textbooks. Library suppliers to foreign libraries of Indonesian printed books

Toko Buku **Malabar***, 347 Oto Iskandardinata Bandung

Toko Buku **Melawai***, Jakarta

Toko Buku **Merbabu***, Semarang

Toko Buku Pustaka **Mimbar***, Medan

P T **Pembimbing** Masa, Pusat Perdagangan Senen, Blok I, Lantai IV No 2, PO Box 3281 Jkt, Jakarta Pusat Tel: 367645
Importer, bookshop, subscription agency

Pradnya Paramita*, Jl Kebon Sirih 46, Jakarta Pusat Tel: (021) 360411
Man: Sadano Dibyowiroyo

Toko Buku **Sari Agung***, Jl Kebon Sinih 94, Jakarta; also in Medan and Surabaya

CV Toko Buku **Tropen***, 113 Jl Pasar Baru, Jakarta Pusat Tel: 362695
Man: James Adam

Major Libraries

Arsip Nasional Republik Indonesia (National Archives)*, Jl Gajah Mada III, Jakarta

Bibliotheca Bogoriensis (Central Library for Biology and Agriculture), Jl Ir Haji Juanda 20, Bogor

Bidang Bibliografi dan Deposit, Pusat Pembinaan Perpustakaan (National Bibliographic and Deposit Centre, Centre for Library Development), Departemen P dan K, Jl Medan Merdeka Selatan 11, Jakarta Tel: 360136
Librarian: Paul Permadi
Publication: Bibliografi Nasional Indonesia (quarterly)

Perpustakaan **Biro** Pusat Statistik (Library of Central Bureau of Statistics)*, Jl Dr Sutomo 7, Jakarta

Perpustakaan **Dewan** Perwakilan Rakjat Gotong Rojong (Library of Indonesian Parliament)*, Senajan Pintu 8, Jakarta

Pusat **Dokumentasi Ilmiah Nasional** (National Scientific Documentation Centre), Jl Jenderal Gatot Subroto, PO Box 3065/JKT, Jakarta Selatan Tel: 583465/6/7, 511063 Telex: 45875 IA
Publications: Directory of Special Libraries in Indonesia (irregular); *Index of Indonesian Learned Periodicals* (annual); *Baca* (Read) (quarterly); *Bibliografi Khusus* (Special Bibliography) (irregular); and lists of acquisitions

Library of **Hasanuddin University***, Jl Sunu, Makassar

Perpustakaan Jajasan **Hatta** (Hatta Foundation Library)*, Malioboro 85, Jogjakarta

Perpustakaan Pusat **Institut** Teknologi Bandung (Central Library, Bandung Institute of Technology), Jl Ganesya 10, Bandung

Perpustakaan **Islam** (Islamic Library)*, Jl P Mangkubumi 38, Jogjakarta

Perpustakaan **Museum** Nasional, Departemen Pendidikan dan Kebudayaan (Library of the National Museum, Ministry of Education and Culture), Merdeka Barat 12, Jakarta Tel: 360551
Librarian: Miss M H Prakoso
Publications: Library Guide, Newspaper catalogue and other subject catalogues

Perpustakaan **Negara** (State Library)*, Malioboro 175, Jogjakarta

Pusat **Pembinaan** Perpustakaan, Departemen P dan K Bidang. Bibliografi dan Deposit, Medan Merdeka Selatan 11, Tromolpos 274 Jakarta-Pusat Tel: 360136 Centre for Library Development, Department of Education and Culture, Deposit Library
Publication: Berita Bulanan, checklist of *Serials in the Libraries of Indonesia*

Library of **Political and Social History***, Medan Merdeka Selatan 11, Jakarta Tel: 360136
Librarian: Mrs Sayangbati-Dengah, WW
Publications: Press index; Index Artikel Tentang Negara (Index of Official Publications); *Index Pemilu* (Index of General Elections)

Tman Batjaan dan Perpustakaan Umum (Public Library Jakarta)*, J Budi Keuliaan 3, Jakarta

Library Associations

Ikatan Pustakawan Indonesia (Indonesian Library Association)*, c/o Centre for Library Development, Medan Merdeka Selatan 11, Belakang, Jakarta Tel: 360136
President: Sukarman Kartosedono
Secretary-General: J P Rompas
Publication: Majalah Ikatan Pustakawan Indonesia

Library Reference Books and Journals

Books

Directory of Special Libraries in Indonesia, National Scientific Documentation Centre, Jalan Jendral Gatot-Subroto, PO Box 3065/JKT, Jakarta

Journals

Baca (Read) (quarterly), PO Box 3065, Jakarta

Berita Bulanan (Bulletin), Centre for Library Development, Department of Education and Culture, Deposit Library, Medan Merdeka Selatan 11, Jakarta

Berita Idayu (Idayu News), Yayasan Idayu, Jl Dr Abdulrachman Saleh 26, Jakarta

Checklist of Serials in the Libraries of Indonesia, Centre for Library Development, Department of Education and Culture, Deposit Library, Medan Merdeka, Selatan 11, Jakarta

Diurnal Perpustakaan (Library Journal) (text in Indonesian or English), Perpustakaan Umum Makassar, Jl Kajaolalidjo 16, PO Box 16, Ujung Pandang

Index Artikel Tentang Negara (Index of Official Publications), Library of Political and Social History, Medan Merdeka Selatan 11, Jakarta

Majalah Ikatan Pustakawan Indonesia (Indonesian Library Association Journal), Indonesian Library Association, c/o Centre for Library Development, Medan Merdeka Selatan 11, Jakarta

Iran

General Information

Language: Persian (Farsi), Turkish in Northwest, Arabic in Southwest (English or French also)
Religion: Muslim (Shi'a sect)
Population: 34.3 million
Literacy Rate (1966): 23%
Bank Hours: Generally Winter: 0800-1300 Saturday-Thursday; 1600-1800 Saturday-Wednesday; Summer: 0730-1300, 1700-1900 Saturday-Wednesday, 0730-1130 Thursday
Shop Hours: Generally Winter: 0800-2000 Saturday-Thursday; 0800-1200 Friday; Summer: 0800-1300, 1700-2100 Saturday-Thursday, 0800-1200 Friday
Currency: rial
Export/Import Information: No tariff on books and advertising but catalogues subject to 6% VAT. Import licences; publications offending public order, official religion or morality prohibited. Exchange controls, with new regulations issued each March
Copyright: No copyright conventions signed

Book Trade Organizations

Iranian Publishers' Association*, PO Box 1030, Tehran

Tehran Book Processing Centre (TEBROC)*, PO Box 11-1126, Tehran (Located at: 46 Shahreza Ave, Tehran) Tel: 662940
Dir: Mrs M Tafazzoli
Publications include: Books Catalogued by TEBROC; Iranian National Union Catalogue; School Libraries; Directory of Iranian Periodicals

Book Trade Reference Journals

Bibliography of Persia; National Bibliography, Book Society of Persia, PO Box 1936, Tehran (annual)

Books Catalogued by Tehran Book Processing Centre, Tehran Book Processing Centre, 46 Shahreza Ave, PO Box 11-1126, Tehran

Iranian National Union Catalogue, Tehran Book Processing Centre, 46 Shahreza Ave, PO Box 11-1126, Tehran

National Bibliography, Iranian Publications, National Library, Ghavamossaltań St, Tehran

Publishers

Amir Kabir Publishing & Distributing Corporation*, Shahabd St, Tehran
Dir: Abdulrahim Ja'fari
Parent company: Amir Kabir, 28 Vessal Shirazi St
Subjects: Textbooks, General
Founded: 1950

Boroukhim*, Ave Ferdowski, Tehran
Subjects: Dictionaries, Reference

Eghbal Co*, Shahabad Ave, Tehran
Dir: Djavad Eghbal
Subject: Juveniles, Fiction

Franklin Book Programs Inc*, 2 Alborz Ave, Tehran
Dir: Farhad Massoudi
Subjects: Encyclopaedias, Textbooks, Fiction, Biology, Chemistry, History, Engineering, Juveniles, Arts, Maps, Mathematics, Medicine, Education, Philosophy, Psychology, Politics, Physics, Social Sciences, Economics
Founded: 1952
Miscellaneous: A non-profit-making organization for International Book Publishing Development. Main office in New York

Ibn-Sina Publishers*, Shah Abad St, Tehran
Subjects: Textbooks, Directories, Multilingual Dictionaries, Fiction, Juveniles, Law, Economics

IRAN — IRAQ

Majlis Press*, Ave Baharistan, Tehran
Subjects: Juveniles, Fiction

Shahrokh **Sabzerou**, PO Box 11/1318 Tehran 15 (Located at: 549 Mosadegh Ave, Tehran 15) Tel: 662692 Cable Add: Sabzerou Telex: 215574 Sbru
Man Dir: Shahrokh Sabzerou
Subjects: Children's Books, Painting and Colouring Books
1977: 20 titles *1978:* 43 titles *Founded:* 1972

Tehran Economist*, 99 Sevom Esfand, Tehran 11 Tel: 374181/5 Cable Add: Economist
Man Dir: Dr Bagher Shariat; *Editorial:* Mohammad Mehdi Fakhrizadeh; *Sales:* Mr Khadem; *Production:* Mr Hosseinpoor; *Publicity:* Mr Tavakoli
Subjects: Mining, Commerce, Agriculture, Food Science, Economics, Industry, Transport, Tourism
1977: 51 (Persian) 51 (English) *1978:* 51 (Persian) 51 (English) *Founded:* 1953

Tehran University Press*, Amirabad Shomali, Tehran Tel: 632062/3, 630060/9
Man Dir: Dr B Farahrashi; *Editorial:* Dr H Erfani; *Editorial, Production:* Dr H Karimi; *Sales, Publicity:* K Esfahanian; *Rights & Permissions:* J Qajarieh
Subjects: University Textbooks
Bookshops: Ave 21 Azar, Tehran; Ave Shahreza (next to Royal Cinema House), Tehran; Amirabad Shomali, Tehran
1977: 125 titles *Founded:* 1944

Towfigh*, Istanbul Ave, Tehran
Dir: Dr Farideh Towfigh
Subjects: HumoGuur, Satire

Major Booksellers

Y **Beroukhim** & Sons, Booksellers*, 331 Ferdowsi Ave, Tehran Tel: 34526

Daneshdjou Bookstore*, 222 Shah Reza St, Tehran Tel: 48365

Iran Literature Association*, PO Box 1505, Tehran
Head Office: 1-7 Qavam Saltaneh St, Tehran Tel: 378750
Branches in Tehran, Isfahan, Rezaiyeh
Publications in English and Persian

Mebso Bookshop*, 466 Naderi St, Tehran Tel: 46822/64091

Major Libraries

Astaneh Razavy Library*, Meshed

British Council Libraries*, 38 Ave Ferdowsi, PO Box 1589, Tehran Tel: 303346, 392571 Telex: 215361
Branches: PO Box 28, Isfahan; PO Box 13, Meshed; PO Box 65, Shiraz; PO Box 5, Tabriz; PO Box 896, Ahwaz

Imperial Library*, Tehran

Iranian Documentation Centre (IRANDOC), Ad 46, Enghelab Ave, Tehran Tel: 662223/662140 Cable Add: Asnad Telex: 2889 TN
Dir: A H Agarang

National Library*, Ghavamossaltané St, Tehran

Pahlavi Library*, 9 Bisotoun Avenue, Aryamehr Sq, Tehran, Iran Tel: 623386/88 Telex: 212323
Managing Director: Shojaeddin Shafa
Publication: Acta Iranica

Pahlavi University Libraries*, Shiraz

Parliament Library*, Ketabkhaneh Majiles Showraie Melli, Tehran

Senate Library (Ketabkhaneh Majles Sena), Tehran

T E B R O C (Tehran Book Processing Centre)*, PO Box 11-1126 Tehran Tel: 662940 Telex: 212889 irdc ir

Central Library and Documentation Centre of **Tehran** University*, Shahreza Ave, Tehran

University of Ferdowsi Library*, PO Box 331, Mashhad Tel: 33075
Librarian: Dr A A M Safa

University of Isfahan Library*, Isfahan

Central Library, **University of Tabriz**, Tabriz
Dir: Asgar Delbaripour

Library Associations

Anjoman-e Ketabdaren-e Iran (Iranian Library Association)*, PO Box 11-1391, Tehran Tel: 622768
Secretary: M Nikham Vazifeh
Publications: Nameh, Monthly News

Association of Registered Archivists of Iran Secretariat*, Avenue Lalezar, Passage Afrashteh, 1st floor, Tehran

Library Journals

Monthly News, Iranian Library Association, PO Box 11-1391, Tehran

Nameh (Bulletin) (text in Persian, summaries in English), Iranian Library Association, PO Box 11-1391, Tehran

Literary Associations and Societies

Book Society of Persia*, PO Box 1936, Tehran
Publication: Bibliography of Persia

P E N Club of Iran*, Ave Pahlavi, 34th St No 9, Tehran 16
Founder and General Secretary: Z Rahnama

Iraq

General Information

Language: Arabic (English is the principal foreign language in Baghdad)
Religion: Muslim
Population: 11.9 million
Literacy Rate (1957): 11%
Bank Hours: Winter: 0900-1300 Saturday-Wednesday; 0900-1200 Thursday; Summer: 0800-1200 Saturday-Wednesday, 0800-1100 Thursday
Shop Hours: Winter: 0830-1430, 1700-1900 Saturday-Wednesday, 0830-1330 Thursday; Summer: 0800-1400, 1700-1900 Saturday-Wednesday, 0800-1300 Thursday
Currency: 1,000 fils = 1 Iraqi dinar
Export/Import Information: No tariffs on books and advertising. Import licences required. Exchange control, influenced by annual foreign exchange budget. Importation by state trading company or established importer. The state trading company is the National House for Publishing, Distributing and Advertising, Aljamhuria St, PO Box 624, Baghdad
Copyright: No copyright conventions signed

Book Trade Journal

Iraqi Bulletin for Publications, National Library, Baghdad

Publishers

Al **Ma'arif** Ltd*, Mutanabi St, Baghdad
Subjects: Books in several Middle-Eastern languages, French and English, Fiction, Politics
Founded: 1929

National House for Distributing and Advertising, Aljamhuria St, PO Box 624, Baghdad Tel: 68391 Cable Add: Donta Telex: 2392
Subjects: Politics, Economics, Education, Agriculture, Sociology, Commerce, General Science, Books in Arabic and other Middle-Eastern languages (also distributor)
Founded: 1972
Miscellaneous: Firm is attached to the Ministry of Information and is the sole importer and distributor of newspapers, magazines, periodicals and books

Major Booksellers

The export of Iraqi books is handled by the National House for Publishing, Distributing and Advertising (qv under Publishers)

Major Libraries

Al-**Awqaf** (Library of Waqfs), PO Box 14146, Baghdad Tel: 66104/65860
Librarian: Jassim Al-Juboori
Branches: Al-Qazzaza Library, Baghdad; Munier Al-Qadhi Library, Baghdad; Adhamiya, Mosul; Main Mosque, Anbar; Amarah; Nasiriyah; Sulaymaniyah; Kerkuk; Diala

College of Agriculture Library, University of Baghdad*, Abu Ghraib

The **Diwan** Library, Ministry of Education*, Baghdad

Library of the **Iraq Museum***, Baghdad

Library of the **Iraq Natural History** Research Centre, Babal-Moudham-Baghdad

Library of the **Mosul Museum***, Mosul

Mosul Public Library*, Mosul

National Centre on Archives*, Waziriah, Amr bin Kalthoom St 15/10/9, Baghdad

National Library*, Baghdad
Publications: The National Bibliography of Iraq

Scientific Documentation Centre*, Aqabba Bin Nafie Sq, Al-Masbah, PO Box 2441, Baghdad

Central Library of the **University of Baghdad***, Safi El-Din Ali-Hilli St, PO Box 12, Baghdad Tel: 64742

Library Association

Iraq Library Association*, PO Box 4081, Baghdad-Adhamya Tel: 27077
Secretary: N Kamalal-Deen

Library Journals

Deposit Bulletin, National Library, Baghdad

The Library, Al-Muthanna Library, Al-Mutanabbi St, Baghdad

Republic of Ireland

General Information

Language: English and Irish
Religion: Roman Catholic
Population: 3.19 million
Bank Hours; 1000-1230, 1330-1500 Monday-Friday. Most open until 1700 one evening
Shop Hours: 0900 or 0930-1730 Monday-Saturday
Currency: 100 pence = 1 Irish pound
Export/Import Information: No tariff on books except 4.8% on prayer and similar books from non-UK, 10.4% on children's picture books from non-EEC Pamphlets dutied 8% from non-EEC. VAT is 10% on books, 20% on other printed matter. No import licences. Exchange controls
Copyright: UCC, Berne (see International section)

Book Trade Organizations

Book Association of Ireland, 21 Shaw St Dublin 2
Honorary Secretary: Eoin O'Keeffe

Booksellers Association of Great Britain and Ireland, 154 Buckingham Palace Rd, London SW1W 9TZ

Cumann Leabharfhoilsitheoirí Éireann (CLÉ) (Irish Book Publishers' Association), Veritas House, 7-8 Lower Abbey St, Dublin 1 Tel: (01) 788177
Contact: Hilary Kennedy

Irish Educational Publishers' Association, C J Fallon Ltd, Lucan Rd, Palmerston, Dublin 20 Tel: 365777
Honorary Secretary: M A Ledwidge

National Federation of Retail Newsagents*, Republic of Ireland District Council, 63 Middle Abbey St, Dublin 1 Tel: 745347

Book Trade Journals

Books Ireland, Kingston House, Ballinteer, Dublin 14

Irish Publishing Record, School of Librarianship, University College, Belfield, Dublin 4

Leabharagan An Aosa Oig (Primary Bookshelf) (text in English and Gaelic), Nessa Ni Mhurchu, 45 St Brendan's Ave, Malahide Rd, Dublin 5

Publishers

A P C K+, Dawson St, Dublin 2

The **Academy** Press, 124 Ranelagh, Dublin 6 Tel: (01) 961133
Publisher: Sean I Browne; *Dir:* Seamus Cashman
Subjects: History, Biography, Scholarly Monographs, Literature, Literary Criticism
1978: 5 titles *1979:* 10 titles *Founded:* 1976
ISBN Publisher's Prefix: 0-906187

Anvil Books Ltd+*, 90 Lower Baggot St, Dublin 2 Tel: 762359 Cable Add: Anvil, Dublin
Man Dir Sales, Production, Publicity, Rights & Permissions: Rena Dardis;
Editorial: Dan Nolan
Imprint: The Geraldine Press
Subjects: Biography, Irish History, Folklore, Sociology
1977: 1 title *1978:* 1 title *Founded:* 1964
ISBN Publisher's Prefix: 0-900068

The **Blackwater** Press+, c/o Folens & Co Ltd, Airton Rd, Tallaght, Co Dublin Tel: 515311
Publisher: T F Turley
Subjects: Non-fiction books of Irish interest, Local History, History
1978: 5 titles
ISBN Publisher's Prefix: 0-905471

An **Clócomhar** TTA+, 13 Gleann Carraig, Baile Átha Cliath 13 Tel: Átha Cliath 324906
1978: 6 titles

Clódhanna Teo+*, Conradh na Gaelige, 6 Sraid an Fhearchair, Atha Cliath 2 Tel: Atha Cliath 757401

Cork University Press+, University College, Cork Tel: (021) 26871 ext 2348
Sales Dir & Executive Secretary: D J Counihan
Subjects: Biography, History, Music, Art, Philosophy, Literature, Reference, Religion, Medicine, Psychology, Engineering, General & Social Science, University Textbooks
1978: 3 titles *1979:* 1 title *Founded:* 1925
Bookshop: Cork University Press (Retail Sales), University College, Cork
ISBN Publisher's Prefix: 0-902561

Cuala Press+, Avalon, Leslie Ave, Dalkey, County Dublin Tel: Dublin 808221
Directors: M B Yeats, Anne Yeats, Thomas Kinsella, Liam Miller, Patrick O'Carroll
Subjects: Books formerly selected by W B Yeats. The press continues the tradition of Irish hand-printing & publishing, and issues first editions of Irish writers, booklets, ballad sheets & hand-coloured prints
Founded: 1908

The **Dolmen** Press Ltd+, North Richmond St, Dublin 1 Tel: Dublin 740324 and 740325
Man Dir: Liam Miller; *Sales, Publicity & Advertising Dir:* William C Browne
Subjects: Belles Lettres, Poetry, Biography, High-priced Paperbacks
1977: 12 titles *1978:* 13 titles *Founded:* 1951
Subsidiary: The Five Lamps Press, North Richmond St, Dublin 1
ISBN Publisher's Prefix: 0-85105

Dublin Institute for Advanced Studies+*, 10 Burlington Rd, Dublin 4 Tel: Dublin 680748
Subjects: Celtic Studies, Physics

Eason & Son Ltd, 65 Middle Abbey St, Dublin 1 Tel: (01) 741161 Telex: 4286
Man Dir: S D Carpenter; *Editorial, Sales, Production, Publicity, Rights & Permissions:* W H Clarke
Associate Companies: Eason & Son (NI) Ltd, 17 Donegall St, Belfast
Imprint: Irish Heritage Series
Subject: Irish interest
Bookshops: Antrim, Belfast, Cork, Craigavon, Dublin, Dun Laoghaire, Limerick, Newtownards
1977: 7 titles *1978:* 14 titles *Founded:* 1886
ISBN Publisher's Prefix: 0-900346

Ecclesia Press, an imprint of Irish Academic Press (qv)

Educational Company of Ireland*, PO Box 43A, Ballymount Rd, Walkinstown, Dublin 12 Tel: (01) 500611 Telex: 5864
Man Dir: W J Connolly; *Sales Dir:* Gerald Carroll
Br Offs: 2 Cook St, Cork; 20-1 Talbot St, Dublin 1
Subjects: History, Religion, Irish, English, Geography, French, Technical, Domestic Sccience
1977: 53 titles *Founded:* 1877
Subsidiary: Talbot Press Ltd, 20 Talbot St, Dublin 1 (qv)
ISBN Publisher's Prefix: 0-901802

C J Fallon Ltd, 77 Marlboro St, Dublin 1 Tel: (01) 46191
Shipping Add: Lucan Rd, Palmerstown, Dublin 20
Sales Dir: Edward J White; *Advertising, Publicity, Rights & Permissions:* Maurice A Ledwidge
Br Off: 36 Marlboro St, Cork
Subjects: Secondary & Primary Textbooks, Business
1977: 27 titles *Founded:* 1927
Bookshops: Fallon's Book Shops, 77 Marlboro St, Dublin 1; 36 Marlboro St, Cork
ISBN Publisher's Prefix: 0-7144

Allen **Figgis** & Co Ltd, The Mall, Donnybrook, Dublin 4 Tel: 760461
Man Dir: Allen Figgis
Subjects: General Fiction & Nonfiction
1977: 2 titles *1978:* 2 titles
ISBN Publisher's Prefix: 0-900372

The **Five Lamps** Press, subsidiary of The Dolmen Press Ltd (qv)

Foilseacháin Náisiúnta Tta+, 29 Sraid Ui Chonaill Iocht, Ath Cliath 1 Tel: Ath Cliath 745314

Folens and Co Ltd+, Airton Rd, Tallaght, Co Dublin Tel: 515311
Man Dir: A Folens; *General Manager:* T F Turley
Subject: Educational
1978: 65 titles
ISBN Publisher's Prefix: 0-86121

An **Foras** Forbartha (National Institute for Physical Planning and Construction Research)*, St Martin's House, Waterloo Rd, Ballsbridge, Dublin 4 Tel: 764211 Cable Add: Foras, Dublin Telex: 30846
Chief Executive Officer: George O'Hara; *Rights & Permissions:* C S Curran
Subject: Environmental Research
1977: 5 titles *Founded:* 1964
ISBN Publisher's Prefix: 906120

Four Courts Press, 3 Serpentine Ave, Dublin 4 Tel: Dublin 688033/688236
Man Dir: Michael Adams

Associate Company: Irish Academic Press Ltd (qv)
Subjects: Irish Studies, Philosophy, Theology
1978: 3 titles *Founded:* 1977
ISBN Publisher's Prefix: 0–906127

The **Gallery** Press+*, 19 Oakdown Rd, Dublin 14 Tel: Dublin 985161
Chief Executive, Editorial: Peter Fallon
Associate Company: The Deerfield Press, Deerfield, Mass 01342, USA
Subjects: Poetry, Plays, Prose, Drawings
1977: 8 titles *1978:* 15 titles *Founded:* 1970
ISBN Publisher's Prefix: 0–902996

The **Geraldine** Press, an imprint of Anvil Books Ltd, Republic of Ireland (qv)

Gifford & Craven+*, 50 Merrion Square, Dublin 2 Tel: (01) 767882

Gill & Macmillan Ltd+, 15–17 Eden Quay, Dublin 1 Tel: (01) 788455 Cable Add: Gillmac Dublin Telex: 4142
Man Dir: M H Gill; *Editorial Director:* H Mahoney; *Sales Dir:* Peter Thew; *Publicity Manager:* Eveleen Coyle; *Production Manager:* Eamon O'Rouke
Subjects: Belles Lettres, Biography, History, Philosophy, Religion, Paperbacks, University, Secondary & Primary Textbooks
1977: 34 titles *1978:* 40 titles *Founded:* 1968 (formerly Gill & Son)
Miscellaneous: Firm is an associate company of Macmillan Publishers Ltd, UK (qv)
ISBN Publisher's Prefix: 0–7171

Golden Eagle Books Ltd, subsidiary of the Mercier Press Ltd (qv)

The **Goldsmith** Press+, Martinstown Rd, The Curragh
Subjects: Literature, Fiction, Poetry, Art, Children's, Cookery
1978: 8 titles *1979:* 8 titles
ISBN Publisher's Prefix: 0904984

Institute of Public Administration+, 59 Lansdowne Rd, Dublin 4 Tel: 686233 Cable Add: Admin Dublin
Dir (Publications): James D O'Donnell; *Manager:* Tony Farmar; *Sales:* James Moraghan
Subjects: Irish Government, Economics, Law, Social Policy and Administrative History, Administration Yearbook & Diary, Administration (journal), Young Citizen
1977: 4 titles *1978:* 8 titles *Founded:* 1957
ISBN Publisher's Prefix: 0–902173

Irish Academic Press+, 3 Serpentine Ave, Dublin 4 Tel: Dublin 688236/688033 Shipping Add: Bay 92, Shannon
Man Dir: Michael Adams
Associate Company: Four Courts Press Ltd (qv)
Imprints: Irish University Press, Ecclesia Press
Subjects: History, Government Documents, Irish Studies
1977: 11 titles *Founded:* 1974
ISBN Publisher's Prefix: 0–7165

Irish Heritage Series, an imprint of Eason & Son Ltd (qv)

Irish Management Institute+*, Sandyford Rd, Dublin 14 Tel: 983911 Telex: 30325
Chief Executive: Ivor E Kenny; *Editorial, Rights & Permissions:* Alex Miller; *Sales, Publicity & Advertising Dir:* Diarmuid O'Broin; *Production:* Eric Carroll
Subjects: Management Training and Education Textbooks, Research Reports
1977: 2 titles *1978:* 3 titles *Founded:* 1952

Irish University Press, an imprint of Irish Academic Press (qv)

The **Irish Times** Ltd+, General Services, 11–15 D'Olier St, Dublin 2 Tel: Dublin 722022 Telex: 5167
Subjects: Reprints, Microfilm
1978: 3 titles

Irish University Press, an imprint of Irish Academic Press (qv)

The **Mercier** Press Ltd+, 4 Bridge St, Cork Tel: 504022
Man Dir: Captain J M Feehan
Subjects: Irish Literature, History, Biography, Folklore, Humour, Theology, Philosophy, Religion, Music, Art, Reference, High-priced Paperbacks, University & Secondary Textbooks, Educational Materials
1978: 45 titles *Founded:* 1946
Bookshops: The Mercier Bookshop Ltd, 4 Bridge St, Cork; The University Bookshop, University College, Cork; Mercier Library Supplies, 24 Lower Abbey St, Dublin 1
Subsidiaries: Mercier Distributors Ltd; Golden Eagle Books Ltd (both at 4 Bridge St, Cork)
ISBN Publisher's Prefix: 0–85342

The **National Press***, 2 Wellington Rd, Ballsbridge, Dublin 4 Tel: (01) 681905
Dir: P Cannon
Subjects: Belles Lettres, Religion, Education, Paperbacks

New Writers' Press+*, 61 Clarence Mangan Rd, Dublin 8
Man Dir: Michael Smith
Subjects: Poetry, Criticism, Hardbacks and Paperbacks
Founded: 1967

O'Brien Educational, 11 Clare St, Dublin 2 Tel: (01) 979598
Editorial, Rights & Permissions: Seamus Cashman; *Sales, Production:* Michael O'Brien
Parent Company: The O'Brien Press (qv)
Subjects: Science, Humanities, English, Celtic Studies, Contrast Studies, Teachers Handbooks
1977: 10 titles *1978:* 8 titles
Miscellaneous: Publishers to the Curriculum Development Unit, Trinity College, Dublin 2
ISBN Publisher's Prefix: 0–905140

The **O'Brien** Press+, 11 Clare St, Dublin 2 Tel: Dublin 979598
Man Dir, Rights & Permissions: Michael O'Brien; *Production, Publicity:* Catheine Boland
Orders to: Irish Bookhandling Ltd, Nth Richmond Industrial Est, Dublin 1
Associate Company: Wolfhound Press, Republic of Ireland (qv)
Subsidiary: O'Brien Educational (qv)
Subjects: General Fiction, Belles Lettres, Poetry, Biography, History, Architecture/Planning, Anthropology, Quality Paperbacks, Ornithology, Natural History, Illustrated Books, Folklore, Children's Books
1977: 12 titles *1978:* 12 titles *Founded:* 1974
ISBN Publisher's Prefix: 0–905140

Poolbeg Press Ltd+, Knocksedan Hs, Forrest Great, Swords, Co Dublin Tel: (01) 401133, 401675, 402681, 401957 Telex: 4639
Man Dirs: Philip Mac Dermott, David Marcus; *Editorial:* D Marcus; *Sales:* P Mac Dermott; *Production, Publicity, Rights & Permissions:* Adrienne Fleming
Subjects: Fiction
1978: 7 titles *1979:* 10 titles *Founded:* 1976

Runa Press+, Monkstown, Dublin Tel: Dublin 801869
Subjects: Poetry, Philosophy, Sociology, Fiction, Psychology

Stationery Office (Oifig an tSolathair)+, St Martin's House, Waterloo Rd, Dublin 4

Talbot Press Ltd+*, PO Box 43A, Ballymount Rd, Walkinstown, Dublin 12 Tel: (01) 500611
Dirs: W J Connolly, G Carroll, F Maguire, John Harrison
Subjects: General Fiction, History, Music, Religion, Juveniles, Political Science, Folklore, Religious & Liturgical
Founded: 1913
Miscellaneous: Firm is a subsidiary of the Educational Co of Ireland (qv)
ISBN Publisher's Prefix: 0–85452

Veritas Publications+, Veritas House, 7–8 Lower Abbey St, Dublin 1 Tel: 788177
Dir: Sean O'Boyle
Parent Company: The Catholic Communications Institute of Ireland
Subjects: Religion, Low- & High-priced Paperbacks, University, Secondary & Primary Textbooks, Educational Materials
1977: 28 titles *1978:* 18 titles *Founded:* 1900
Bookshop: Veritas, 7–8 Lower Abbey St, Dublin 1
Miscellaneous: Veritas Publications is the publishing division of the Catholic Communications Institute of Ireland Inc
ISBN Publisher's Prefix: 0–905092

Wolfhound Press+, 98 Ardilaun, Portmarnock, County Dublin Tel: (01) 452162
Publisher: Seamus Cashman
Subjects: Belles Lettres, Poetry, Biography, History, Juveniles, Fiction, Literary Studies
1978: 6 titles *1979:* 10 titles *Founded:* 1974
ISBN Publisher's Prefix: 0–9503454 & 0–905473

Book Club

Wild Geese*, 19 Clare St, Dublin
Owned by: D Murphy

Major Booksellers

Browne & Nolan*, 56 Dawson St, Dublin 2 Tel: 774754

Eason & Son Ltd*, Patrick St, Cork; 40 Lower O'Connel St, Dublin 1 Tel: 803005; Middle Abbey St, Dublin 1 Tel: 741161

The **Eblana** Bookshop*, 46 Grafton St, Dublin 2 Tel: 770178

Wm **Egan** & Sons, Patrick St, Cork, Co Cork

Greene & Co, 16 Clare St, Dublin 2

Fred **Hanna** Ltd, 27–29 Nassau St, Dublin 2 Tel: 771255/720797

Hodges Figgis & Co Ltd, Stephen Court, St Stephen's Green, Dublin 2 Tel: 760461; The Mall, Donnybrook, Dublin 4 Tel: 760461; Shopping Centre, Dun Laoire Tel: 809917; 56 Dawson St, Dublin 2 Tel: 760461; High St, Kilkenny Tel: (056) 22974; Queen's Old Castle Centre, Cork

The **Kilkenny** Bookshop Ltd*, High St, Kilkenny Tel: (056) 22974 (New retail books); Kieran St, Kilkenny Tel: (056) 22974 (Secondhand and antiquarian books)
Proprietors: Don and Mary Roberts

The **Library** Shop, Trinity College, College St, Dublin 2 Tel: 772941

The **Mercier** Bookshop Ltd*, 4 Bridge St, Cork Tel: 54022

O'Mahony & Co Ltd, 120 O'Connell St, Limerick Tel: 48155 (Educational Dept at 40 Thomas St, Limerick)

Paperback Centre*, 20 Suffolk St, Dublin 2 Tel: 774210; Stillorgan Shopping Centre, Co Dublin Tel: 886341

Willis Bookshops, 36 Dawson St, Dublin 2 Tel: 01-773541
Manager: Miss G Wratt
Also 37 Cook St, Cork Tel: 021-20937
Manager: Miss C Nuttall

Major Libraries

The Chester **Beatty** Library and Gallery of Oriental Art*, 20 Shrewsbury Rd, Dublin 4 Tel: 692386
This library, bequeathed to the Irish nation by Sir Chester Beatty, includes manuscripts and works of art which illustrate the history of mankind from 2700 BC (the Babylonian clay tablets) to the present century
Librarian: P Henchy

Central **Catholic** Library*, 74–75 Merrion Sq, Dublin 2

Dublin Public Libraries, Pearse St, Dublin Tel: 0001-777662
City and County Librarian: Mairin O'Byrne

National Library of Ireland, Kildare St, Dublin 2 Tel: 765521

Oireachtas Library, Leinster House, Dublin 2
(Selective works of parliamentary interest)

Public Record Office of Ireland, Four Courts, Dublin 7 Tel: 725275

Representative Church Body Library, Braemor Park, Rathgar, Dublin 14 Tel: 979979

Royal College of Surgeons in Ireland Library, St Stephen's Green, Dublin 2 Tel: Dublin 780200 Ex 248
Librarian: Professor J B Lyons FRCPI;
Executive Librarian: Mrs K M Bishop

Royal Dublin Society Library, Ballsbridge, Dublin 4

Trinity College Library*, College St, Dublin 2 Tel: 772941 Telex: 5442

University College Cork Library, University College, Cork

University College Dublin Library*, Main building at Belfield, Dublin 4 Tel: 693244 Telex: 4114
Librarian: H J Heaney; *Publication:* Annual Report

University College Galway Library, Galway
Librarian: Christopher Townley

Library Associations

Central **Catholic** Library Association Inc, 74 Merrion Sq, Dublin 2
Honorary Secretary: Anthony J Litton

Cumann Leabharlann na h-Éireann (Library Association of Ireland)*, Thomas Prior House, Merrion Rd, Dublin 4
Honorary Secretary: Nodlaig P Hardiman

Publication: An Leabharlann (The Irish Library) (published jointly with the Northern Ireland Branch, The Library Association) (4 per year)

Cumann Leabharlannaithe Scoile (CLS) (Irish Association of School Librarians)*
Executive Secretary: Sister Monaghan, Irish Schools Library Association, Loreto College, Foxrock, Co Dublin

Irish Association for Documentation and Information Services (IADIS), The National Library of Ireland, Kildare St, Dublin 2
Hon Secretary: Alf MacLochlainn
Publication: Union List of Current Periodicals and Serials in Irish Libraries (periodically)

Irish Society for Archives, 82 Saint Stephen's Green, Dublin 2

National Library of Ireland Society*, Kildare St, Dublin 2

Library Journals

An Leabharlann (The Irish Library), Library Association of Ireland, 46 Grafton St, Dublin 2 (published jointly with Northern Ireland Branch)

Long Room, Trinity College, Friends of the Library, College St, Dublin 2

Literary Associations and Societies

Irish Academy of Letters*, 4 Ailesbury Grove, Dundrum, Dublin 14
Secretary: Evan Boland

Irish **P E N**, 52 Silchester Park, Glenageary, Dun Laoghaire, Co Dublin
Secretary: Alun Llewellyn

Literary Periodicals

Comhar (Cooperation) (text in Irish), 37 Sraid na Bhfinini, Dublin

Dublin Magazine, Irish Academy of Letters, 4 Ailesbury Grove, Dundrum, Dublin 14

Journal of Irish Literature, Proscenium Press, PO Box 361, Newark, DE 19711, USA

Studies; an Irish quarterly review of letters, philosophy and science, Talbot Press Ltd, 20 Talbot St, Dublin 1

Literary Prizes

Allied Irish Banks' Award for Literature
For excellence in creative writing, adjudication by the Irish Academy of Letters. £1,000, awarded annually. Enquiries to Allied Irish Bank Ltd, Development Division, Bankcentre, Ballsbridge, Dublin 4

Denis **Devlin** Memorial Award for Poetry
For the best book of poetry in the English language written by an Irish citizen. £600. Awarded every three years, next awarded 1982. Enquiries to Irish Arts Council, 70 Merrion Sq, Dublin 2

Gregory Medal*
For distinction in letters or outstanding literary work in Irish. Awarded periodically. Enquiries to Irish Academy of Letters, 4 Ailesbury Grove, Dundrum, Dublin 14

Irish Arts Council Award
For the best book of poetry in the Irish language. £600. Awarded every three years, next awarded 1980. Enquiries to Irish Arts Council, 70 Merrion Sq, Dublin 2

Irish Life Drama Award*
To encourage new writing for the theatre in Ireland. £1,000 award. Enquiries to Irish Life Assurance Co Ltd, Irish Life Centre, Abbey St, Dublin 1

Macaulay Fellowships
Awarded in literature every three years to young Irish writers. Value £2,500. Next awarded 1981. Enquiries to Irish Arts Council, 70 Merrion Sq, Dublin 2

Novel Prize*
For the best novel written in Irish. Awarded annually. Enquiries to Irish Academy of Letters, 4 Ailesbury Grove, Dundrum, Dublin 14

George **Russell** (AE) Memorial Award
Awards are made approximately every five years from the Fund on recognition of published or unpublished work, creative or scholarly, which, in the opinion of the Advisory Committee is of a high standard of merit. Awards may also be made for similar work planned, although not yet completed. The Award consists of a cash payment of £100. Candidates must be of Irish birth and ordinarily resident in any part of Ireland, and must not have attained 35 years of age on the 1st day of January of the year in which the Award is made. Enquiries to George Russell (AE) Memorial Fund, Bank of Ireland, Lower Baggot St, Dublin 2

Marten **Toonder** Award
Awarded in literature every three years. Value £2,500. Next award in 1980. Enquiries to Irish Arts Council, 70 Merrion Sq, Dublin 2

Israel

General Information

Language: Hebrew and Arabic (English and German widely known)
Religion: Predominantly Jewish
Population: 3.6 million
Literacy Rate (1967): 83.2% total (85% Jewish, 45.65% non-Jewish)
Bank Hours: 0830-1230 Sunday-Friday
Shop Hours: Usually Sunday 0800-1300, 1600-1800; weekdays 0800-1300, 1600-1900
Currency: 100 agorot = 1 Israel pound
Export/Import Information: Books (except for 27.5% on children's picture books) and advertising duty-free. Books exempt from most additional taxes. No import licence required for books but must apply for importing number; exchange granted automatically
Copyright: UCC, Berne, Florence (see International section)

Book Trade Organizations

Book and Printing Center — Israel Export Institute, 47 Nahlat Benyamin St, PO Box 29732, Tel Aviv Cable Add: Memex Telex: 35613

206 ISRAEL

Dir: Shlomo Erel
Division of the Israel Export Institute.
Publications: Israel Book World (quarterly); *Typeface Catalogue* of the printing industry in Israel; *Israel Book Trade Directory* (biannual); *Science Books Published in Israel* (in languages other than Hebrew); Catalogue of books on the Holyland, Israel, Bible and Religion, *Books from Israel Export Catalog* (annual); *Children's Books from Israel*

Book Publishers' Association of Israel, 29 Carlebach St, PO Box 20123, Tel Aviv 67132 Tel: 284191
Executive Dir: Benjamin Sella
Publication: Book News from Israel (Hebrew); *Katalog Sefarim Kelali*

Economic Council for Israel Printing & Publishing Committee, Michael Ho, Baker St, London W1, UK Tel: (01) 935 4422
Executive Secretary: Cyril Jacobs

The **Institute** for the Translation of Hebrew Literature Ltd, 66 Shlomo Hamelech St, Tel Aviv Tel: 244879
Man Dir: Mrs Nilli Cohen
Publications: Modern Hebrew Literature (quarterly, incorporating Hebrew Book Review); *Bibliography of Modern Hebrew Literature in Translation* (bi-annual)

Israel Book Importers' Association*, c/o Emanuel Brown, 35 Allenby Rd, Tel Aviv

Book Trade Reference Books and Journals

Books

Children's Books from Israel, Book & Printing Center—Israel Export Institute, 47 Nahlat Benyamin St, PO Box 29732, Tel Aviv

Publishers & Printers of Israel, Book & Printing Center—Israel Export Institute, 47 Nahlat Benyamin St, PO Box 29732, Tel Aviv

Science Books Published in Israel in languages other than Hebrew, Book and Printing Center—Israel Export Institute, 47 Nahlat Benyamin St, PO Box 29732, Tel Aviv

Journals

Books from Israel Export Catalog, Book & Printing Center—Israel Export Institute, 47 Nahlat Benyamin St, PO Box 29732, Tel Aviv

Hadashot al Pirsuma Ha-memshala (News about Government Publications), Israel Government Printer, Jerusalem

Hasefer be Yisrael (Book News from Israel) (text in Hebrew), The Book Publishers' Association of Israel, 29 Carlebach St, PO Box 20123, Tel Aviv

Israel Book Trade Directory, Book & Printing Center—Israel Export Institute, 47 Nahlat Benyamin St, PO Box 29732, Tel Aviv

Israel Book World, Book & Printing Center—Israel Export Institute, 47 Nahlat Benyamin St, PO Box 29732, Tel Aviv 61290

Katalog Sefarim Kelali (Israel Books In Print), Book Publishers' Association of Israel, 29 Carlebach St, PO Box 20123, Tel Aviv 67132

Kirjath Sepher (City of the Book); bibliographical quarterly (text in Hebrew), Jewish National and University Library, PO Box 503, Jerusalem

Publishers

'A' Publishing Institute*, PO Box 894, Jersualem
Manager: A Chitov
Subjects: Orthodox Textbooks, Religion

Academon (The Hebrew University Students' Printing and Publishing House)*, The Hebrew University Campus, PO Box 41, Jerusalem Tel: 36253
Man Dir: Yitzhal Tzur; *Sales Manager:* Haim Hazan
Bookshop: Academon, The Hebrew University Campus, Jerusalem
Subjects: Academic
Founded: 1952

Academy of the Hebrew Language, The Hebrew University, PO Box 3449, Jerusalem
Subjects: Hebrew: Linguistics, Dictionaries, Terminology, Periodicals

Achiasaf Publishing House Ltd+, 13 Yosef Hanassi St, PO Box 4810, Tel Aviv Tel: (03) 283339
Man Dir: Schachna Achiasaf
Founded: 1933
Subjects: General Nonfiction, Reference, Juveniles, Popular Science, Textbooks, Fiction, Dictionaries
1978: 12 titles

Achiever+*, 22 Hahistadrut St, Jerusalem Tel: (02) 225740
Managers: H Rolnik, D Kessler, S Atzmon
Subject: Maps

Ad Publishers*, 12 Pijotto St, Tel Aviv Tel: (03) 621254
Subjects: General Science, Technical, Textbooks, Educational Materials

Agudat Harashash+*, 7 Bezalei St, Jerusalem Tel: (02) 226904
Manager: I Hasid
Subjects: Orthodox Textbooks, Religion

Aleph Publishers Ltd+*, 49 Nachmani St, Tel Aviv Tel: (03) 612003
Manager: B Feldenkreis
Subjects: Art, Science, History of Israel, Textbooks, Belles Lettres, Poetry, Juveniles, Reference
Founded: 1962

Am Hasefer+*, 9 Bialik St, PO Box 4055, Tel Aviv Tel: (03) 53040
Man Dir: D Lipetz
Subjects: Belles Lettres, Biography, History, Art, Political Science, Periodicals, Numismatics
1977: 8 titles *Founded:* 1955

Am Oved Publishers Ltd+*, 22 Mazeh St, PO Box 470, Tel Aviv Tel: (03) 291526
Cable Add: Amoved, Telaviv
Man Dir: Dov Garfung
Orders to: Distributor's Centre for Israeli Books Ltd, 22 Nachmani St, PO Box 2811, Tel Aviv
Subjects: General Fiction, Belles Lettres, Poetry, Biography, History, Philosophy, Reference, Juveniles, Low-priced Paperbacks, Psychology, Social Science, University, Secondary & Primary Textbooks, Educational Materials
1977: 85 titles *Founded:* 1942

American-Israel Publishing Co Ltd*, 15 Carlebach St, PO Box 20181, Tel Aviv Tel: (03) 280251 Telex: 605 paper il

Man Dir: Joseph Vardi; *Editorial:* Myrna Pollack
Br Off: 11 West 42 St, New York
Subjects: Art Books, Archaeology, Heavily Illustrated Nonfiction, General Fiction, Juveniles
Founded: 1968

Amichai Publishing House Ltd+*, 5 Josef Ha-Nassi St, Tel Aviv Tel: (03) 284990
Man Dir: Yehuda Orlinsky
Subjects: Reference, General Fiction, Juveniles, Popular Science, Textbooks, Languages
Founded: 1948

Amikam*, 33 Frishman St, Tel Aviv

Amir Publishing-Japheth Press Ltd*, 5 Engel St, Tel Aviv Tel: 615943
Man Dir: Avraham Amir; *Editorial:* Immanuel Blauschild
Subjects: Cartography, Guide Books, Historical and Biblical Subjects, Judaica
Founded: 1965

Armon Publishing House Ltd*, 36 Beit Vegan St, Jerusalem Tel: (02) 533991
Subjects: General Fiction, Languages
Founded: 1965

Arrow Co, 6 Wedgwood St, PO Box 8022, Jerusalem

Bar Ilan University, Book Publishing Committee*, Bar Ilan University, Ramat Gan Tel: 718111
Chairman: Professor Daniel Sperber
Subjects: Judaica, Philosophy, Psychology, Law
Founded: 1958

Bar Urian Publishing House*, Bar Ilan University, Ramat Gan Tel: 756012
Man Dir: Jac J L Engelsman
Founded: 1965
Bookshop: Bar Ilan University
Subject: University Textbooks

Barlevi*, 57 Allenby St, Tel Aviv Tel: 283691
Manager: Mr Barlevi
Subjects: Juveniles, Hobbies, Games, Sports

Bazak Israel Guidebook Publishers Ltd*, 2 Shvil Hatenufa, Kiryat Hamelacha, PO Box 35040, Tel Aviv Tel: 828128/9 Cable Add: Bazakpub, Telaviv
Man Dir: Avraham Levi; *Chief Editor:* Tony Pitch; *Sales Manager:* Avraham Dayan
Br Offs: Jerusalem, New York, Madrid
Subject: Guidebooks
Founded: 1960

Beit Lochamei Hagetha'ot+, Kibbutz Lochamei Hagetha'ot Tel: (04) 920412
Manager: B Anulik
Subject: Holocaust, World War II, Jewish Resistance against Nazism
1978: 4 titles

Prof Shaul Shaked, **Ben-Zvi** Institute*, Abarbanel St, Jerusalem Tel: 39204; Yad Ben-Zvi Tel: 39201/2
Dir: Professor Shaul Shaked
Subject: History of Jewish Communities

The **Bialik** Institute, 3 Ibn Gabirol St, PO Box 92, Jerusalem Tel: (02) 639261
Man Dir: Chaim Milkov
Subjects: Philosophy, Hebrew and Yiddish Literature, Belles Lettres, Palestinology, Archaeology, Jewish Studies, History, Arts
Founded: 1935

Biblos*, 54 Sokolov St, Holon
Miscellaneous: Also an exporter to Latin America

Bitan+*, 8 Mordechai St, Ramat-Hasharon Tel: 484565
Manager: A Bitan
Associate Company: Zmora, Bitan, Modan-Publishers (qv)
Subjects: General

Boostan Publishing House+*, 22 Nachmani St, Tel Aviv Tel: (03) 298883/5 Cable Add: Boostanmod Telaviv
Man Dir: Mordechai Sheingarten; *Sales Dir:* Roni Birkenfield; *Publicity Dir:* Riva Almagor; *Advertising Dir:* Sara Wohlfeiler; *Rights & Permissions:* Dalia Sheingarten
Subsidiary Company: Distributors' Centre for Israeli Books Ltd (address as above)
Subjects: General Fiction, Belles Lettres, Poetry, Biography, History, How-to, Juveniles, High-priced Paperbacks, Medicine Psychology, Educational Materials
Founded: 1969

Bronfman's Agency Ltd+*, 2 Tchelnov St, PO Box 1109, Tel Aviv Tel: 611243
Manager: I Bronfman
Subject: Textbooks
Bookshop: 2 Chelnov St, Tel Aviv

Carta, The Israel Map and Publishing Co Ltd+, Yad Harutzim St, PO Box 2500, Jerusalem Tel: (02) 713536/7
Man Dir: Emanuel Hausman; *Editorial:* Lorraine Kessel, Eviatar Nur; *Sales:* Shay Hausman
Subjects: Cartography, Juveniles, Educational Materials, General, History, Reference (publishes in Hebrew and English)
1977: 28 titles *1978:* 18 titles *Founded:* 1958

Chatam Sofer Institute*, PO Box 836, Jerusalem Tel: 38175
Manager: Mr Leible
Subject: Religion

Davar+*, 45 Sheinkin St, Tel Aviv Tel: 286141
Manager: I Shoham

The **Dvir** Publishing Co Ltd+, 58 Mazeh St, PO Box 149, Tel Aviv Tel: 622991
Man Dir: Alexander Broido
Subsidiary Companies: Amud Ltd; Karni Publishers Ltd; Megiddo Publishing Co Ltd
Subjects: Belles Lettres, Poetry, Biography, History, Art, Philosophy, Reference, Juveniles, Low & High-priced Paperbacks, Psychology, General & Social Science, University, Secondary & Primary Textbooks, Educational Materials
1977: 35 titles *1978:* 10 titles *Founded:* 1924

E S H (English for Speakers of Hebrew), an imprint of Universal Publishing Projects (qv)

Edanim Publishers, 24 Agron St, PO Box 7705, Jerusalem Tel: 224486 Cable Add: Weilpub Jerusalem
Man Dir: Asher Weill
Parent Company: Weill Publishers Ltd (qv) and Yediot Aharonot
Subjects: Contemporary Events, Fiction, Biography, History, Reference
1978–79: 20 titles *Founded:* 1975

Eked Publishing House+*, 29 Bar-Kochba St, Tel Aviv Tel: (03) 283648
Man Dir: Maritza Rosman
Subjects: Belles Lettres, Poetry, Fiction
1977: 63 titles *Founded:* 1959

El-Am Publishing (Israel) Ltd*, PO Box 16495, Tel Aviv Tel: (03) 228964/442918 Cable Add: Elampub, Telaviv
Man Dirs: Eliyahu Amiqam, Moshe Segalovitz; *Editorial:* Rabbi Dr A Zvi Ehrman
Subject: Judaica
Founded: 1966

Encyclopaedia Judaica*, Givat Shaul B, PO Box 7145, Jerusalem Tel: (02) 523261/521201 Telex: 25-275
Man Dir: Eliav Cohen; *Sales Dir:* Nissan Balaban
Subject: Reference
Miscellaneous: Firm is a subsidiary of Keter Publishing House Ltd, Givat Shaul, Industrial Area, Jerusalem

Eshkol-Haifa*, 25 Herzl St, Haifa Tel: 532206
Manager: I Fish
Subject: General Fiction

Eshkol-Jerusalem+*, PO Box 5202, Jerusalem Tel: 285351
Manager: Mr Weinfeld
Subject: Judaica

Feldheim Publishers Ltd+, PO Box 6525, Jerusalem Tel: (02) 533947/8/9
Man Dir: Yaakov Feldheim; *Sales Dir:* Yossie Katzberg
Br Off: P Feldheim, 96 East Broadway, New York, NY
Subjects: Biography, History, Philosophy, Reference, Religion, Juveniles
1978: 13 titles *1979:* 12 titles *Founded:* 1939
ISBN Publisher's Prefix: 0-87306

H Fisher, PO Box 1951, Tel Aviv Tel: 744892
Manager: H Fisher
Subject: Juveniles

Franciscan Printing Press, PO Box 14064, Jerusalem Tel: (02) 286594 Cable Add: Terrasanta Jerusalem
Man Dir: Costantino Baratto (Father Claudio)
Subjects: Religion, Theology, Archaeology, Guide Books, Periodicals

Freund Publishing House Ltd*, 61 Nachmani St, PO Box 35010, Tel Aviv Tel: 615335
Man Dir: Chaim Freund
Subjects: Scientific, Juveniles

S Friedman+, 27 Gruzenberg St, Tel Aviv Tel: 656091/659756
General Manager: Sara Friedman
Subjects: General
1978: 12 titles

Gaalyah Cornfeld, 185 Hayarkon St, Tel Aviv 63453 Tel: 221737 Cable Add: Cornfeld Hayarkon 185
Chief Executive, Editorial: G Cornfeld
Subjects: Bibles, Archaeology, Palestine
1977: 2 titles *1978:* 2 titles *Founded:* 1957

Gazit+*, 8 Zvi Brook St, Tel Aviv Tel: 53730
Manager: G Talpir
Subject: Art

Graphica-Bezalel+*, 12 Ben Avigdor St, PO Box 2529, Tel Aviv Tel: 285815
Manager: Mr Benhar
Subject: Juveniles

Hadar+*, PO Box 17061, Tel Aviv Tel: (03) 417971
Manager: I Amrami
Subjects: General

Hakibbutz Hameuchad Publishing House Ltd+*, PO Box 16040, Tel Aviv Tel: (03) 220402
Man Dir: A Avishai; *Sales Manager:* Moshe Ne'eman
Subjects: General Fiction, Belles Lettres, Poetry, Biography, History, How-to, Music, Art, Philosophy, Reference, Religion, General & Social Science, University, Secondary & Primary Textbooks, Educational Materials, Agriculture, Psychology
Founded: 1940

Hamenorah Publishers Ltd*, 24 Zangwill St, PO Box 6012, Tel Aviv Tel: (03) 230670
Man Dir: Mordechai Sonschein
Subjects: General Fiction, Poetry, Biography, History, Literature (Books in Hebrew, Yiddish and English)
Founded: 1958

Heritage*, 2 Kfar Yona St, Ramat Aviv

Holy Land Map Co Ltd, now Terra Sancta Arts (qv)

Institute for the Talmudic Encyclopaedia and Complete Israeli Talmud+*, Bait-Vagan, PO Box 16066, Jerusalem Tel: 423242
Manager: Rabi Y Hotner

International Science Service*, PO Box 4059, Jerusalem Tel: (02) 34405; and Boston University, Center for Philosophy and History of Science, Boston, Ma 02115 USA Tel: 617-353 2604
Man Dir: Miriam Balaban
Subjects: Science, Technology, Medicine, Social Science, Philosophy, Communications
Founded: 1968

The **Israel Academy** of Sciences & Humanities, 43 Jabotinsky Rd, PO Box 4040, Jerusalem 91040 Tel: 636211
Man Dir: Dr Yehezkel Cohen
Bookshop: Direct sales at the Academy
Subjects: Archaeology, History, Philosophy, Religion, Scholarly Publications in Sciences, Humanities, Judaica

Israel Exploration Society, 3 Shmuel Hanagid St, PO Box 7041, Jerusalem Tel: (02) 227991
Man Dir: J Aviram
Subjects: Archaeology, Ancient History, Geography
1978: 3 titles *Founded:* 1913
Miscellaneous: Publish *Eretz-Israel*, *Qadmoniot* (both in Hebrew) and *Israel Exploration Journal* (quarterly, in English)

Israel Program for Scientific Translations, subsidiary of Keter Publishing House Ltd (qv)

Israel Universities Press*, Givat Shaul B, PO Box 7145, Jerusalem Tel: (02) 523261/521201 Telex: 25-275
Man Dir: Eliav Cohen
Subjects: General & Social Science, Reference, Middle East Studies, University Textbooks, Politics
1977: approx 25 titles
Miscellaneous: Subsidiary of Keter Publishing House Ltd, Givat Shaul, Industrial Area, Jerusalem

Israel Yearbook Publications*, 21 Hasharon St, PO Box 1199, Tel Aviv

Israeli Music Publications Ltd, 105 Ben Yehuda St, PO Box 6011, Tel Aviv 61060 Tel: (03) 23078 Cable Add: Ismusica Tel Aviv
Man Dir: Dr P E Gradenwitz
Subjects: Music
Founded: 1949

Izrael Publishing House Ltd+*, 76 Dizengoff St, Tel Aviv Tel: (03) 285350
Man Dir: Alexander Izrael
Subjects: General Fiction, Belles Lettres, Poetry, Biography, History, Reference, Psychology, Juveniles, University, Secondary & Primary Textbooks, Educational Materials
Founded: 1933 *1974:* 20 titles

Jerusalem Publishing House Ltd, 39 Tchernechovski St, PO Box 7147, Jerusalem Tel: (02) 667744/636511 Cable Add: Pubjer Telex: 26144 ext 7065
Man Dir: Shlomo S Gafni; *Editorial:* Rachel Gilon; *Production:* Ofra Kamar
Subjects: Encyclopaedias, History, Archaeology, Reference, Literature, Politics, Art
1977: 18 titles *1978:* 17 titles *Founded:* 1967

The **Jewish Agency***, Publishing Department, 27 Hillel St, PO Box 7044, Jerusalem Tel: 233271
Man Dir: Asher Bukshpan
Founded: 1945
Subjects: Hebrew & Zionist political thought and education

Karni Publishers Ltd, 58 Mazeh St, PO Box 149, Tel Aviv Tel: (03) 622991
Man Dir: Alexander Broido; *Sales:* Nili Sadeh
Subjects: General Fiction, Belles Lettres, Poetry, Biography, How-to, Juveniles, Secondary & Primary Textbooks, Reference
1977: 5 titles *1978:* 3 titles *Founded:* 1951
Subsidiary: Megiddo Publishing Co (at above address)

Keter Publishing House Ltd+*, Giv'at Shaul Industrial Area, PO Box 7145, Jerusalem Tel: 521201 Cable Add: Matam Telex: 25275
Man Dir: M Shani; *Sales Dir:* Nissan Balaban
Subjects: Philosophy, Reference, Religion, Juveniles, Medicine, Psychology, Engineering, Social Science
1977: 120 titles *Founded:* 1959
Subsidiaries: Israel Program for Scientific Translations, Israel Universities Press, Keter Press Ltd, Keter Publishing Ltd UK, Keter Inc, New York, Encyclopaedia Judaica

Kiryat Sefer Ltd+*, 15 Arlosorof St, PO Box 370, Jerusalem Tel: (02) 521141
Man Dir: Shalom Sivan
Subjects: Poetry, Juveniles, Atlases, Dictionaries, Secondary & Primary Textbooks, Fiction, Religion
Founded: 1933

Koren Publishers, 33 Herzog St, PO Box 4044, Jerusalem Tel: (02) 660188
Man Dirs: Eliahu Koren, Eli Kahn
Subjects: Bibles, Religion
1977: 7 titles *1978:* 5 titles *Founded:* 1962

Ledori+*, 19 Geula St, Tel Aviv Tel: 58662
Manager: B Gefner
Subjects: General Books

The **Van Leer** Jerusalem Foundation, 43 Jabotinsky St, PO Box 4070, Jerusalem Tel: 667141
Executive Editor: Esther Shashar
1977: 4 titles *1978:* 2 titles

Lewin-Epstein Ltd+*, Beit Vegan, PO Box 1020, Jerusalem Tel: (02) 527107
Dirs: J Gerlitz, M Weksler, A Friedman
Subjects: Judaica

A **Lewin-Epstein-Modan** Ltd+*, 17 Mossinson St, PO Box 33316, Tel Aviv Cable Add: Offset
Man Dir: C Modan; *Sales Dir:* Eliezer Ben-Ami
Subjects: General Fiction, Belles Lettres, Poetry, History, How-to, Music, Art, Reference, Juveniles, High-priced Paperbacks, Education, Science
Founded: 1930

Ma'alot+, 29 Carlebach St, Tel Aviv Tel: (03) 284191
Dir: Elazar Goor
Subjects: Secondary & Primary Textbooks
1978: 50 titles *Founded:* 1969
Miscellaneous: Established by the Book Publishers' Association of Israel as a jointly owned publishing house in which most of the members of the Association are shareholders

Ma'arachot, imprint of Ministry of Defence Publishing House (qv)

Ma'ariv Book Guild (Sifriat Ma'ariv)*, 72A Dereh Petah Tikra Rd, PO Box 20208, Tel Aviv Tel: (03) 287211 Cable Add: Ma'ariv Telaviv Telex: 033735
Publisher: Naftali Arbel
Br Off: Room 162, 7 Park Ave, New York, NY, USA
Subjects: Biography, Reference, Education, History, Juveniles, Travel, Politics, Religion, Popular Science, Geography, Children, Encyclopaedias
Founded: 1954

Machbarot lesifrut+*, 5 Gnessin St, PO Box 411, Tel Aviv
Manager: Ohad Zmora
Subjects: Fiction, History, Juveniles, Literature (especially of Middle Ages), Politics, Linguistics

The **Magnes** Press, Hebrew University, Jerusalem Tel: (02) 660341
Man Dir: B Yehoshua
Subjects: Biography, History, Music, Art, Philosophy, Psychology, Archaeology, Oriental Studies, Law, Sciences, Bibliography, University Textbooks
Founded: 1929

Makor Publishing Ltd+*, 14 Nili St, Jerusalem Tel: 717257
Man Dir: I Ravitzki; *Sales Manager:* E Fisher
Subjects: Judaica, Reprints
Founded: 1969

S J **Mansour***, 1 Meyouhas St, Mahane Yehuda, Jerusalem Tel: 02-221650
Manager: S J Mansour
Subject: Judaica

I **Marcus**+*, 6 Ben Yehuda St, Jerusalem Tel: 228281
Manager: I Marcus
Subjects: General

Masout+*, 2 Shonzino St, Tel Aviv Tel: 36898
Manager: Z Lewin
Subject: Textbooks

Rubin **Mass**+, 11 David Marcus St, PO Box 990, Jerusalem Tel: (02) 632565 Cable Add: Rubin Mass Jerusalem
Man Dir: Oren Mass; *Sales:* Aharon Bier
Subjects: Religion, Medicine, Secondary Textbooks, Jewish Studies, Educational Materials, Politics, Philosophy, Psychology, Meteorology, Science
1978: 1,020 titles *Founded:* 1927

Massada Press Ltd+, 21 Jabotinsky Rd, Ramat Gan 52511 Tel: (03) 734202/3 Cable Add: Encylomas Telex: 0335770 COIN IL
Chairman: Alexander Peli; *Man Dir:* Shimshon Klaus; *Sales, Production:* Nathan Regev; *Rights & Permissions:* David Peli
Parent Company: Alexander Peli Ltd (qv)
Br Off: 46 Beth Lehem Rd, Jerusalem Tel: (02) 719441 and 719444
Subjects: Belles Lettres, Poetry, Biography, History, How-to, Cookery, Music, Art, Philosophy, Encyclopaedias, Judaica, Reference, Religion, Juveniles, High-priced Paperbacks, Psychology, General and Social Science, Educational Materials
Book Club: Massada Press Ltd, 46 Beth Lehem Rd, Jerusalem
Bookshops: Ruth Ltd, 2 Herzl Street, Tel Aviv
1977: 31 titles *Founded:* 1932

Massada Publishing Ltd, Pelmas, 11 Alouf Sadeh St, PO Box 842, Givatayim Tel: (03) 740811 Cable Add: Peliprint Givatayim Telex: (03) 35770/1 COIN IL/Att Pelmas Printing
Man Dir: Yoav Barash; *Sales Dir:* Joel Bendel; *Production Dir:* Jaap Leuvenberg
Parent Company: Massada Publishing Ltd, 11-15 Tfutzot Israel St, Givatayim
Subsidiary Companies: Pelmas (the Export Division of Massada Publishing Ltd); Peli Printing Works Ltd (both at 11 Alouf Sadeh St, Givatayim)
Associate Company: Reprocolour Ltd
Subjects: History, Art, Juveniles, Educational, Cookery, General Fiction, Reference, Travel
1978: 328 titles *1979:* 305 titles *Founded:* 1932
ISBN Publisher's Prefix: 965-10

Megiddo Publishing Co, subsidiary of Karni Publishers Ltd (qv)

Merkaz Le-Chinuch Torani, PO Box 18, Zichron Yaakov Tel: (063) 99540 Telex: 35770 COIN IL
Man Dir: Rabbi Shalom Meir Jungerman
Subject: Orthodox Textbooks

Michaelmark Books, 12 Stand St, Tel Aviv Tel: (03) 234144 Telex: 341667 Att MIC
Publisher: Myrna Pollak
Subjects: Fiction, Popular Nonfiction
Founded: 1976

Mifalei Tarbut Vehinuch+*, 53 Weizmann St, Tel Aviv Tel: 254867
Manager: Y Silver
Subjects: Music, Textbooks, Pedagogy

Ministry of Defence Publishing House*, 29 Bet St, Hakiriya, Tel Aviv Tel: (03) 259165/212605
Dir: Shalom Seri; *Sales:* Jacob Bloch; *Production:* Izack Kempler
Subjects: Military Science & History, Israeli Geography & History
1978: 40 titles *Founded:* 1939
Miscellaneous: Firm also publishes under Ma'arachot imprint

M **Mizrachi** Publishers+*, 67 Lewinsky St, Tel Aviv Tel: (03) 625652 Cable Add: Mizedition, Telaviv
Man Dir: Meir Mizrachi
Subjects: Engineering, History, Medicine, Science, Juveniles, Encyclopaedias, Fiction
Founded: 1960

M C **Mor-Carmi** Ltd*, 16 Tiomkin St, Tel Aviv Tel: 623266/7/8
Man Dir, Sales, Rights & Permissions: Ram Carmi; *Editorial, Production, Publicity:* Uri Mor
Subsidiary Companies: Elrad Engineering Planning Ltd; M C Electronics Ltd
Subjects: Technical, Scientific
Founded: 1968

Moreshet*, 166 Ibn Gavirol St, Tel Aviv

Mossad Harav Kook+*, PO Box 642, Jerusalem 91000 Tel: (02) 526231
Man Dir: Dr Yitzchak Raphael; *Editorial:* Rabbi M Katznelbogen
Subject: Judaica
1977: 22 titles *Founded:* 1937

Nateev-Printing and Publishing Enterprises Ltd, by Reading Bridge, PO Box 6048, Tel Aviv Tel: (03) 454135 Cable Add: Nateevpub, Telaviv Telex: 03-2470 Att Nateev
Man Dir: Mordecai Ra'anan
Subjects: Religion, Juveniles, General
Miscellaneous: Associated imprints include Otpaz
1978: 9 titles *Founded:* 1971

Netzach*, PO Box 164, Bnei Brak
Tel: 796413
Manager: Mr Rootenberg
Subject: Judaica

M **Newman**+*, 12 Hasharon St, Tel Aviv
Tel: 30621
Manager: M Newman
Subjects: Judaica, Bible Studies, Fiction, Juveniles, Education

Nitzaninn, an imprint of Zur & Zur Ltd (qv)

Ofer Publishing House+*, 7 Tabenkin St, Petach Tikva Tel: 625483
Manager: S Aluf
Subject: Juveniles

Olamenu*, 7 Frishman St, Tel Aviv

Olive Books of Israel*, Reka-Or Production and Publishing Ltd, 22 Shlom-Zion Hamalka St, PO Box 22305, Tel Aviv
Tel: (03) 448676/455199
Publishers: Yoad Avissar, Yosseph Zetouni
Associate Company: Omanei Offset, Printing Ho, Tel Aviv
Subsidiary Companies: Madim, Limud both publishing and distribution
Subjects: Israeli history, Judaica, Educational
1977: 12 titles *Founded:* 1974
Miscellaneous: Publishers of *Who's Who in World Jewry*

Otpaz, an imprint of Nateev-Printing and Publishing Enterprises Ltd (qv)

Otzar Hamoreh+*, Israel Teachers' Union, 8 Ben Saruk St, PO Box 303, Tel Aviv
Tel: 260211
Man Dir: Menachem Levanon; *Production:* Rachel Uri
Subjects: Education, Pedagogy, Textbooks, Mathematics, Psychology, Didactic Games
1977: 4 titles *Founded:* 1951

Pe'er Hatora+*, 7 Mea Shearim, Jerusalem
Tel: 285997
Manager: Rabbi Weingarten
Subject: Bible

Alexander **Peli** Ltd*, 46 Beth Lehem Rd, Jerusalem
Subsidiary Companies: Alumoth Company Ltd; Encyclopedia Publishing Company; Jewish History Publications 1961 Ltd; Massada Press Ltd (qv); Ruth Ltd
Subjects: General, Judaica, Encyclopaedias, Belle Lettres, Poetry, Biography, History, How-to, Music, Art, Philosophy, Reference, Religion, Juveniles, High-priced Paperbacks, Psychology, General and Social Science, Secondary and Primary Textbooks, Educational Materials

Pelmas, 11 Alouf Sadeh St, PO Box 842, Givatayim Tel: (03) 740811 Cable Add: Peliprint Telex: 03/35770 Coin Il/Att: Massada/Peli
The Export Division of Massada Publishing Ltd and Peli Printing Works Ltd
Man Dir: Yoav Barash; *Sales Dir:* Joel Bendel; *Director:* (production): Jaap Leuvenberg; *Coordinator:* Bridget Lahat
Parent Company: Massada Publishing Ltd
Associate Companies: Peli Printing Works Ltd; Reprocolor Ltd
Subjects: History, Art, Juveniles, Cookery, General Fiction, Reference, Travel
Founded: 1975

Y L **Peretz** Publishing Co+*, 31 Allenby St, Tel Aviv Tel: (03) 595927
Man Dir: Moshe Gershonowitz
Subjects: Books (Poetry, Essays, History, Judaica, Belles Lettres, Philosophy, Sociology, Art) in Yiddish, also some in Hebrew
Founded: 1956

Ramdor Publishing Co Ltd+*, 23 Levanda St, Tel Aviv Tel: 3233222
Man Dir: Uri Shalgi
Founded: 1960
Subject: Mass-market paperbacks

Rav Kook Institute*, PO Box 642, Jerusalem Tel: (02) 526231
Dir: Rabbi M Katzenelenbogen
Subjects: Jewish Studies, History, Philosophy, Midrashic & Halachic Law, Theology
Founded: 1937
Miscellaneous: A non-profit-making public corporation supported by the Jewish Agency, Ministry of Education & Culture and Ministry of Religious Affairs. Also provides financial support for works in above subjects

Reka-Or Production and Publishing Ltd, see Olive Books of Israel

E **Rubinstein**+*, 1 King David St, Jerusalem Tel: 225785
Manager: E Rubinstein
Subject: Textbooks

Sadan Publishing House Ltd+, 1 David Hamelech Blvd, PO Box 16096, Tel Aviv 64-953 Tel: (03) 267543 Cable Add: Sadanbooks Telex: 35770 Coin Il Sadan
Man Dir: David Sadan; *Editorial:* Ronny Stein
Subjects: History, How-to, Orientalia,, Judaica, Art, Religion, Law, Business-management
1977: 43 titles *1978:* 20 titles *Founded:* 1962

Schocken Publishing House Ltd+*, 8 Rothschild Blvd, PO Box 2316, Tel Aviv
Tel: (03) 50961
Man Dir: Racheli Eidelman
Subjects: General Fiction, Belles Lettres, Religion, Literature, Poetry, Philosophy, General Science, Politics, Law
Founded: 1938

Shikmona Publishing Co Ltd+, 33 Herzog St, PO Box 4044, Jerusalem Tel: (02) 660188
Man Dirs: Eli Kahn, Eliyahu Korén
Subjects: History, Art, Politics, Textbooks
1977: 5 titles *1978:* 7 titles *Founded:* 1965

Joseph **Shimoni**+*, 13 Rambam St, Tel Aviv Tel: 611732
Manager: J Shimoni
Subjects: General

Shmulik*, 18 Shivtei Yisrael St, Ramat Hasharon

Sifrait Haminhal+*, 93 Arlozoroff St, Tel Aviv Tel: 261111
Man Dir: D Yohanes
Subject: Texts for Office Workers

Sifriat Poalim Ltd+*, 66 Ahad Ha'am St, PO Box 37068, Tel Aviv Tel: (03) 291535
Dir: Ya'acov Dror; *Editorial:* Nathan Yonathan; *Sales:* Hsak Yagen; *Production:* Efraim Ben-Dor; *Rights & Permissions:* Levavi Bracha
Subjects: General Fiction, Belles Lettres, Art, Juveniles, History, Philosophy, Social Science, Paperbacks
Founded: 1939
Bookshop: 73 Allenby St, Tel Aviv
Miscellaneous: Publishing House of the Labour Zionist Movement

Samuel **Simson** Ltd+*, 100 Yehuda Halevi St, PO Box 14227, Tel Aviv Tel: 280456
Man Dir: Samuel Simson
Subject: Juveniles

Siman Krai, an imprint of University Publishing Projects (qv)

Sinai Publishing Co+*, 72 Allenby St, Tel Aviv Tel: (03) 623622
Man Dir: Akiva Schlesinger; *Editorial, Rights & Permissions:* Moshe Schlesinger
Subject: Judaica
1977: 90 titles *Founded:* 1853
Bookshop: Sinai Bookstore, 72 Allenby St, Tel Aviv
Subsidiary: Sinai Export Co Ltd, 15 Balfour St, Tel Aviv

Spotlight Publications*, 88 Hachashmonaim St, Tel Aviv

J **Sreberk**+*, 16 Balfour St, Tel Aviv
Tel: 293343
Manager: Z Namir
Subject: Textbooks

S **Sreberk**+*, 16 Balfour St, Tel Aviv
Tel: 292438
Manager: I Sreberk

Steimatzky's Agency Ltd+, Citrus House, PO Box 628, Tel Aviv Tel: (03) 622536/7 Cable Add: Steimatzky Beithadar Telaviv Telex: 341118 BXTV IL ext 6409
Man Dirs: Ezekiel Steimatzky, Eri M Steimatzky
Subjects: General Fiction, Music, Art, Juveniles, Reference, Social Science, University, Secondary & Primary Textbooks, Low-priced Paperbacks
Bookshops: 30 bookshops and outlets throughout Israel
1978: 20 titles *Founded:* 1925

Talmudic Encyclopaedia Publications*, Yad Harav Herzog, Beit Vegan, Jerusalem

Tarbut Vehinuch*, 53 Weizmann St, Tel Aviv

Tarshish Books, 14 Hanassi St, PO Box 4130, Jerusalem Tel: (02) 636332
Man Dir: Dr M Spitzer
Subjects: General Fiction, Belles Lettres, History, Art, Philosophy, Religion
Founded: 1940

Tcherikover Publishers Ltd+, 12 Hasharon St, Tel Aviv 66185 Tel: (03) 30621
Manager: B Tcherikover; *Editorial:* S Tcherikover
Subjects: Textbooks, Pedagogy, Education, Children's Books, Handbooks, Psychology,

Economics, Literature, History, Art, Languages, Geography, Criminology, Management, Bibles
1977: 20 titles *1978:* 30 titles

Teachers' Union, see Otzar Hamoreh

Tel Aviv University, Publications Sales Division*, Admin Hill, Bldg H, rooms 22–23, Tel Aviv Tel: 426262 ext 897
Manager: Ya'akov Yariv

Terra Sancta Arts*, PO Box 10009, Zahala, Tel Aviv (Located at: 31 Ehud St) Tel: 473597 Telex: 032470
Man Dir: Nachman Ran
Subjects: Maps, Books on the Holy Land
Founded: 1972
Miscellaneous: Formerly Holy Land Map Co Ltd

University Publishing Co+*, 28 Hanatziv St, Tel Aviv Tel: 259057
Dirs: Mordechai Mass, Nan Tzipkis
Imprints: ESH (English for Speakers of Hebrew), Siman Kria
Subjects: School Texts, Belles Lettres, Academic
1977: 50 titles

Vaad Hayeshivot Be'eretz Israel+*, 4 Havatzelet St, Jerusalem Tel: 225042
Man Dir: A Halevi Sher
Subject: Judaica

Weill Publishers Ltd, 24 Agron St, PO Box 7705, Jerusalem Tel: (02) 224486 Cable Add: Weilpub Jerusalem
Man Dir: Asher Weill
Associated Companies: Edanim Publishers, Israel (qv)
Subjects: Children's Books, Educational, Illustrated Books in English and Hebrew, Hebrew edition of *Book Digest Magazine* (*Rav Sefer*)
Founded: 1975

The **Weizmann** Science Press of Israel, Horkania 8a, PO Box 801, Jerusalem Tel: (02) 663203
Man Dir: Rami Michaeli
Subjects: General Science, General Technology
Founded: 1951
Miscellaneous: Publish nine scientific journals

Yachdav, United Publishers Co Ltd+, 29 Carlebach St, PO Box 20123, Tel Aviv Tel: (03) 284191
Chairman: Mordechai Bernstein; *Man Dir:* Benjamin Sella
Subjects: Philosophy, Psychology, Social Science, Administration
1977–78: 7 titles *Founded:* 1960

Yad Eliahu Chitov+*, PO Box 894, Jerusalem Tel: 285617
Man Dir: H Ben-Arza
Subject: Orthodox Textbooks

Yad Vashem — Martyrs' and Heroes' Remembrance Authority, PO Box 3477, Jerusalem Tel: 531202 Cable Add: YadVashem Jerusalem
Chairman: Dr Yitzhak Arad; *Editorial:* Dr Livia Rothkirchen, Dr Yisrael Gutman; *Sales:* Emmanuel Man; *Production:* Y Gutman; *Secretary General:* Shmuel Spector
Br Off: Heychal Wolyn, 10 Korazin St, PO Box 803, Givatayim, near Tel Aviv
Subject: Nazi Holocaust
1977: 6 titles *1978:* 5 titles *Founded:* 1953

Yavneh Ltd+, 4 Mazeh St, Tel Aviv Tel: (03) 297856
Man Dir: Avshalom Orenstein
Subjects: General Fiction, Reference, Music, Religion, General Science, Juveniles, Textbooks
Founded: 1932

Yedioth Ahronoth Enterprises (Book Dept), 12 Mikveh Yisrael St, PO Box 37744, Tel Aviv Tel: (03) 621065 Telex: 33847
Manager: Moshe Babmerger
Parent Company: Yedioth Ahronoth (The Evening Newspaper of Israel)
Subjects: Nonfiction, Judaica, Childrens Books
1977: 22 titles *1978:* 18 titles *Founded:* 1952

Yeshurun*, Merkaz Le–Sifrut Chareidit, PO Box 511, Jerusalem Tel: 534211
Dir: Mr Pardes
Subject: Orthodox Textbooks

Yesod+*, 16 Mazeh St, Tel Aviv
Tel: 291180
Manager: Y Wachtel
Subject: Textbooks

Yuval+*, 13a Yeffe Nof St, Haifa
Tel: 521564
Manager: I Blachman
Subject: Textbooks

S Zak & Co+*, 2 King George St, Jerusalem Tel: (02) 227819
Man Dirs: D Zak, M Zak
Subjects: Science, Fiction, Philosophy, Reference, Religion, Juveniles, University, Secondary & Primary Textbooks, Educational Materials
Founded: 1930
Bookshop: 2 King George St, Jerusalem

Zelkowitz+*, 6 Mazeh St, Tel Aviv
Tel: (03) 296648
Manager: A Zelkowitz
Subject: Juveniles

Zmora, Bitan, Modan Publishers+, 88 Usishkin St, PO Box 22383, Tel Aviv Tel: (03) 450750, 457165
Editorial, Rights & Permissions: Ohad Zmora; *Editorial, Production:* Asher Bitan; *Sales:* Oded Modan
Associated Companies: Bitan, Israel (qv); Lewin-Epstein-Modan Publishers, Israel (qv); Machbarot-Lesifrut, Israel (qv)
Subsidiary Companies: Bayt–Va'gan; Erez Books; Adar Distribution; Metziuth Books; Levanda Press
Subjects: Fiction, Politics, Middle East Studies, Juveniles, Military, History, Textbooks, Cookery, Nature
1977: 50 titles *1978:* 90 titles *Founded:* 1973

Zur & Zur Ltd, 103 Shlomo Hamelech St, Tel Aviv 64586 Tel: 223764 Cable Add: Zunil Telaviv
Man Dir: Shmuel Zur
Imprint: Nitzanim
Subjects: Pocket guides on Cookery, How-to, Children's Books
1977: 15 titles *1978:* 12 titles *Founded:* 1972

Literary Agents

Bar-David Literary Agency*, 41 Montefiore St, PO Box 1104, Tel Aviv Tel: (03) 294239/40/41 Cable Add: Davidbarco Telex: 33721 Brvid Il
Contact: Mrs Varda Mor

The **Book** Publishers' Association of Israel, International Promotion and Literary Rights Department, 29 Carlebach St, PO Box 20123, Tel Aviv 67132 Tel: 284191
Contact: Lorna Soifer

Moadim*, 144 Hayarkon St, 63451 Tel Aviv Tel: (03) 228449
Play Publishers and Literary Agents
Contact: Lorna Soifer

Barbara **Rogan** Literary Agency, 12 George Elliot St, Tel Aviv Tel: 285589 Cable Add: Overworked

Shalom **Sella***, PO Box 1154, 10 Midbar Sinai St, Jerusalem Tel: 812601, 812671, 812560 Cable Add: Scitrans Telex: 25445

Book Clubs

Massada Press Ltd, 46 Beth Lehem Rd, Jerusalem

Major Booksellers

A B C Bookstore Ltd*, 71 Allenby Rd, PO Box 1283, Tel Aviv Tel: 296058

Librarie **Alcheh***, 55 Nachlat Benyamin St, Tel Aviv Tel: 614173 (Largest Importer of French books in Israel)

Bronfman's Agency Ltd*, 2 Chlenov St, PO Box 1109, Tel Aviv Tel: 611243 (Also exporter)

Emanuel **Brown***, 35 Allenby Rd, PO Box 4101, Tel Aviv Tel: 51049 (Specializes in academic books and is sole distributor for books published by the United Nations and its associated agencies)

Distributors' Centre for Israeli Books Ltd*, 22 Nachmani St, PO Box 2811, Tel Aviv

Educational Book Centre (The Modern Library), PO Box 202, Ramallah Tel: 952122

Israbook*, 13 Blum St, Ramat Aviv
Tel: 416881
Suppliers of books and journals in all languages originating with all publishers and learned institutions in Israel

Lonnie **Kahn** and Co Ltd*, 5 Bachlat Benyamin St, Tel Aviv Tel: 623693 (Also importer)

Ludwig **Mayer** Ltd*, 4 Shlomzion Hamalka St, PO Box 1174, Jerusalem 91000
Tel: 222628

J **Robinson** & Co, 31 Nachlat Benyamin St, PO Box 4308, 61040 Tel Aviv Tel: 615461 (also exporter and antiquarian bookseller)

Sharbain's Bookshop, Salah Eddin St, Jerusalem Tel: 286775

Sifriat Poalim Ltd*, 66 Ahad Haam St, PO Box 37068, Tel Aviv Tel: 291535

Steimatzky's Agency Ltd, Citrus House, PO Box 628, Tel Aviv Tel: (03) 622536/7 Telex: 341118 BXTV IL Ext 6409
Owns the largest chain of bookshops in Israel

Universal Library*, Salah-e-Din St, East Jerusalem Tel: 82624 (Specialises in books on the Middle East and religious books)

ISRAEL — ITALY

Major Libraries

Central Library of **Agricultural Science**, PO Box 12, Rehovot 76100

The Central **Archives** for the History of the Jewish People (formerly Jewish Historical General Archives), Jerusalem University Campus, Sprinzak Bldg, PO Box 1149, Jerusalem Tel: (02) 635716
Director: Dr Daniel J Cohen

Bar-Ilan University Library*, Ramat Gan

Ben-Gurion University of the Negev Library*, PO Box 653, Beersheva 84299 Tel: (057) 64422

'**Dvir Bialik**' Municipal Central Public Library*, Hibat-Zion St 14, Ramat Gan

Elisas Sourasky Central Library, Tel Aviv University*, PO Box 39038, Ramat Aviv, Tel Aviv Tel: (03) 416111

Israel State Archives, Prime Minister's Office, Jerusalem

Jerusalem City (Public) Library*, Betzalel St 11, PO Box 1409, Jerusalem Tel: (02) 226785

Jewish National and University Library, PO Box 503, Jerusalem Tel: 585039
Chief Librarian: P Tishby

Knesset Library*, Hakirya, Jerusalem 91999 Tel: 61211

Municipal Library*, 25 King Saul Blvd, PO Box 32, Tel Aviv

Pevsner Public Library, 54 Pevsner St, PO Box 5345, Haifa 31015 Tel: (04) 667766

Tel Aviv University Library*, PO Box 39038, Ramat Aviv, Tel Aviv

University of Haifa Library, Mount Carmel, Haifa Tel: (04) 254411 Telex: 04660

Weizmann Institute of Science Libraries, Rehovot
Chief Librarian: Alma Rosenheck

Library Associations

Centre for Public Libraries, PO Box 242, Jerusalem 91000
Publications: Leket (reviews of books); *Yad-la-Koré* (The Reader's Aid) (library quarterly), and library monographs

Information Processing Association of Israel*, PO Box 13009, Jerusalem
Secretary: Tuvia Saks
Publication: Ma'ase Cho-shev (6 a year)

Israel Library Association*, PO Box 7067, Jerusalem
Executive Secretary: Ruth Porath

Israel Society of Special Libraries and Information Centres (ISLIC), PO Box 20125, Tel Aviv 61200 Tel: (03) 297781
Executive Secretary: Susane Weil
Publications: Bulletin (3 times a year); *Contributions to Information Science* (irregular)

Library Journals

Bulletin, Israel Society of Special Libraries and Information Centres PO Box 20125, Tel Aviv 61200

Kethavim Benossey Med'a (Contributions to Information Science), Israel Society of Special Libraries and Information Centres, PO Box 20125, Tel Aviv 61200

Leket (Gleaning), Centre for Public Libraries, PO Box 242, Jerusalem 91000

Ma'ase Cho-shev (Action and Thought), Information Processing Association of Israel, PO Box 13009, Jerusalem

Yad-la-Koré (The Reader's Aid), Centre for Public Libraries, PO Box 242, Jerusalem 91000

Literary Associations and Societies

Acum Ltd (Society of Authors, Composers and Music Publishers in Israel), 118–120 Rothschild Blvd, PO Box 11201, Tel Aviv Tel: 240115
Dir-General: M Avidom Fial

Association of Hebrew Writers, PO Box 7111, Tel Aviv
Secretary General: Mordechy Ot-Yakar
Publication: Moznayim (monthly)

Mekise Nirdamin Society*, 22 Hatibonim St, Jerusalem
Secretary: Professor E E Urbach
Publishes Hebrew works of the older classical Jewish literature

Israeli P E N Centre*, 19 Shmaryahu Lewine St, Jerusalem
Secretary: Haim Toren

Literary Periodicals

Caiet Pentru Literatura Si Istoriografie (Journal of Literature and Historiography) (text in Hebrew, Romanian and Yiddish), Cenaclul Literar 'Menora', PO Box 763, Jerusalem

HSL (Hebrew University Studies in Literature) (text in English and French), The Hebrew University of Jerusalem, Institute of Languages and Literatures, Jerusalem

Ha-Sifrut (Literature); theory, poetics, Hebrew and comparative literature (text in Hebrew, summaries in English), Tel Aviv University, Ramat Aviv, Tel Aviv

Image; English literary magazine, The Hebrew University of Jerusalem, Jerusalem

Modern Hebrew Literature (quarterly, incorporating Hebrew Book Review), Institute for the Translation of Hebrew Literature, 8 Modigliani St, Tel Aviv 64687

Siidemot (English Edition); literary digest of the kibbutz movement, Ichud Hakvutzot and Hakibbutzim, Youth Division, 10 Dubnov St, Tel Aviv

Literary Prizes

Bialik Prize for Literature*
The highest literary award in Israel. 3,000 Israeli pounds. Awarded annually. Enquiries to Tel Aviv Municipality, Tel Aviv

Brenner Prize
In recognition of outstanding literary works. 7,500 Israeli pounds. Awarded annually. Enquiries to Hebrew Writers' Association, PO Box 7111, Tel Aviv

Holon Literary Prize*
To encourage literary talent in Israel. 5,000 Israeli pounds. Awarded every year. Enquiries to Holon Municipality, Holon

Israeli Prize in Jewish Studies, Hebrew Literature and Education, see Israeli Prize in Humanities and Social Sciences

Israeli Prize in the Arts, see Israeli Prize in Humanities and Social Sciences

Israeli Prize in Humanities and Social Sciences*
For outstanding contribution to the humanities and social sciences. 30,000 Israeli pounds. Awarded annually in each one of the following areas: (1) Judaica, Modern Hebrew Literature and Education; (2) the Humanities and the Social Sciences; (3) the Arts; (4) Science and Technology; (5) outstanding life-long service to the welfare of Israeli society. Enquiries to Israeli Ministry of Education and Culture, Jerusalem

Shazar Prize*
For outstanding works by immigrant writers. 5,000 Israeli pounds divided between two authors. Awarded annually. Enquiries to Israeli Ministry of Education and Culture, Jerusalem

Tchernichowsky Prize*
For outstanding translations into Hebrew. 4,000 Israeli pounds divided between two translators. Awarded biennially. Enquiries to Tel Aviv Municipality, Tel Aviv

Translation Agencies and Associations

The **Institute** for the Translation of Hebrew Literature Ltd*, 8 Modigliani St, Tel Aviv Tel: (03) 235059

Magal Ltd — Translations & Typeset*, 49 Rehov Sokolov, Tel Aviv Tel: (03) 238732/224573

Scientific Translations International Ltd, 10 Midbar Sinai St, PO Box 1154, Jerusalem Tel: 812601/812671/812731 Cable Add: Scitrans Telex: 25445 intra

Italy

General Information

Language: Italian (English and French understood)
Religion: Roman Catholic
Population: 56.4 million
Literacy Rate (1961): 90.7%
Bank Hours: 0830-1330 Monday-Friday
Shop Hours: Vary locally. Winter: 0900-1300, 1330-1930 Monday-Saturday; Summer: 0900-1300, 1430-2000 Monday-Saturday. Often closed Monday morning
Currency: 100 centesimi = 1 lira
Export/Import Information: No tariff on books except children's picture books 13% from non-EEC; advertising matter not single copies 13%. VAT 6% on books, 12% on advertising matter. No import licence required.
Copyright: UCC, Berne, Florence (see International section)

212 ITALY

Book Trade Organizations

Associazione Italiana Editori, Via delle Erbe 2, I-20121 Milan Tel: (02) 8059244
Rome office: Via Pietro della Valle 13, I-00193 Rome Tel: (06) 6540298
Italian Publishers' Association
Secretary-General: A Ormezzano
Publications: Catalogo dei Libri Italiani in Commèrcio; Editori, Librai, Cartolibrai e Biblioteche d'Italia; Giornale della Libreria

Associazione Librai Antiquari d'Italia, Via Jacopo Nardi 6, I-50132 Florence
Antiquarian Booksellers' Association of Italy
President: Dr Renzo Rizzi, Via Cernaia 4, I-20121 Milan

Associazione Librai Italiani*, Piazza G G Belli 2, I-00153 Rome Tel: 5803844
Italian Booksellers' Association
Publication: Libreria

Circolo dei Librai Antiquari*, Via Monte Napoleone 23, I-20121 Milan Tel: (02) 701582
Circle of Antiquarian Booksellers

Associazione Italiana degli **Editori** di Musica (AIDEM), Piazza del Liberty 2, I-20121 Milan Tel: 796473
Italian Association of Music Publishers

I P L (Istituto Propaganda Libraria), Via Mercalli 23, Milan
Institute of Bookshop Advertising

Istituto Centrale per la Patologia del Libro*, Via Milano 76, I-00184 Rome
Central Institute of Book Pathology
Dir: Dott Maria Di Franco

Sindacàto Italiano Editori*, Via Ripamonti 129, I-20141 Milan
Italian Publishers' Trade Union

Unione Editori di Musica Italiani (UNEMI)*, Via F Sforza 1, I-20122 Milan
Publishing Union of Italian Music

Book Trade Reference Books and Journals

Books

Editori, Librai, Cartolibrai e Biblioteche d'Italia (Publishers, Booksellers, Stationers and Libraries of Italy), Italian Publishers' Association, Foro Buonaparte 24, I-20121 Milan

Gli Editori Italiani (over 2,000 Italian publishers listed), Editrice Bibliografica SRL, Viale Veneto 24, I-20124 Milan

Le Librerie Italiane (Italian Booksellers), Editrice Bibliografica SRL, Viale Veneto 24, I-20124 Milan

Journals

Bibliografia Nazionale Italiana (Italian National Bibliography), Central Institute of the Union Catalogue of Italian Libraries and Bibliographical Information, Viale del Castro Pretorio, Rome

Bollettino (Bulletin), Ufficio della Proprietà Letteraria, Artistica e Scientifica, Rome (monthly)

Bollettino bibliografico, Libreria Seeber, Via dei Tornabuoni 70 r, I-50123 Florence

Catalogo dei Libri Italiani in Commèrcio (Italian Books in Print), Italian Publishers' Association, Foro Buonaparte 24, I-20121 Milan

Il Compratore (The Buyer), Editoriale A-Z, Via P Kolbe 8, I-20317 Milan

Gazzettino Librario (Book Trade Gazette), Piazza Lotario 6, Rome (advertises book wants and offers)

Giornale della Libreria (Book Trade Journal), Italian Publishers' Association, Foro Buonaparte 24, I-20121 Milan

Libreria (The Book Trade), Italian Booksellers' Association, Piazza G G Belli 2, I-00153 Rome

Libri e Riviste d'Italia (Italian Books and Periodicals) (available in Italian edition and international edition in English, French, German and Spanish), Via Boncompagni 15, I-00187 Rome

Libro Cattòlico (The Catholic Book), Union of Italian Catholic Publishers, Via Domenico Silveri 9, I-00165 Rome

Mundus, CP 2236, Rome

Ragguaglio Librario (Book Report), Institute of Bookshop Advertising, Via Mercalli 23, Milan

Publishers

A M Z Editrice sas di Mario Abriani e C+*, Corso di Porta Romana 63, I-20122 Milan Tel: (02) 581071 Cable Add: Editamz Telex: Editamz 31607
Manager: Mario Abriani; *Editorial:* Gioacchino Forte, Elena Fasanella; *Publicity:* Loredana Farina; *Rights & Permissions:* Lucia Calza
Br Off: Largo Cardinale Galamini 7/9, I-00165 Roma Tel: (06) 6377916
Subjects: Books and Albums for Children and Young People
Bookshop: Quartiere Albanova, I-20083 Gaggiano (Milan)
Founded: 1955

Edizioni **A R E S**+, Via Stradivari 7, I-20131 Milan Tel: (02) 209202
Dir: Dr Cesare Cavalleri
Subjects: Philosophy, Theology, Architecture, Psychology
1977: 20 titles *1978:* 24 titles *Founded:* 1957

Adelphi Edizioni SpA+, Via G Brentano 2, I-20121 Milan Tel: (02) 871266/866177
Man Dir: Luciano Foà; *Editorial Dir:* Roberto Calasso; *Publicity:* Piero Bertolucci
Orders to: Edizione Adelphi, Servizio Vendita Libri, c/o Fratelli Fabbri Editori, Via Mecenate 91, I-20138 Tel: 5095
Subjects: General Fiction, Belles Lettres, Biography, Music, Art, Philosophy, Religion, Psychology, General Science
1977: 33 titles *1978:* 34 titles *Founded:* 1962

Giacomo **Agnelli** Editore, see Giunti Publishing Group

Alfa Edizioni e Rappresentanze Editoriali, Via Santo Stefano 13, I-40125 Bologna Tel: (051) 262805
Man Dir: Elio Castagnetti
Subjects: Belles Lettres, Poetry, History, Music, Art, Philosophy
1977: 7 titles *1978:* 10 titles *Founded:* 1954

Alfieri Edizioni d'Arte, Via Goldoni 1, I-20124 Milan Tel: (02) 704023
Dirs: Giorgio Fantoni, Massimo Vitta Zelman; *Editorial:* Carlo Pirovano; *Rights & Permissions:* Mirella V Tenderini
Parent Company: Gruppo Editoriale Electa SpA
Associate Company: Electa Editrice (qv)
Subjects: Modern Art, Venetian Art, Architecture, Periodicals, Numbered Editions
Founded: 1939

Alinari Fratelli SpA Istituto di Edizioni Artistiche+*, Via Nazionale 6, I-50123 Florence Tel: (055) 212105 Cable Add: Idea
Man Dir: Mario Sabbieti
Bookshops: Fratelli Alinari, Via Strozzi 19r, Florence; Fratelli Alinari, Via del Babuino 98, Rome
Subjects: Art, Educational Materials
Founded: 1854

Editrice **Ancora** Milano+, Via Niccolini 8, I-20154 Milan Tel: (02) 3189941
Man Dir: Medici Severino; *Editorial Dir:* Zini Vigilio; *Sales Dir:* Giordani Saverio
Subjects: Religion, Juveniles, Social Science
1978: 25 titles *Founded:* 1937

Franco **Angeli** Editore*, Viale Monza 106, CP 4294, I-20127 Milan Tel: 2827651/2/3/4/5
Man Dir: Dr Franco Angeli; *Editorial:* L Gambi, E Becchi, M Cesa-Bianchi; *Sales:* Livio Casati; *Production:* Marilena Aliata; *Publicity:* Ugo Carutli
Subjects: Anthropology, Architecture, Law of Employment and Labour Relations, Economics, Teaching and Education, Geography, History, Politics, Psychology, Finance, Sociology, Urban and Regional Studies, Physics, Electrical Engineering, Electronics, Data Processing, Mathematics, Science, Management, Marketing, Publicity, Public Relations, Essays
1977: 278 titles *1978:* 292 titles *Founded:* 1955

Ruggero **Aprile**, Via San Quintino 43, I-10121 Turin Tel: (011) 538665/546289
Man Dir: Ruggero Aprile; *Editorial:* Ottaviano Ottaviani; *Sales:* Valerio Aprile
Subjects: Fiction, History, Juveniles, Art
1977: 65 titles *1978:* 50 titles *Founded:* 1973

Arcana Editrice Srl, Via Giulia 167, I-00186, Rome Tel:(06) 6542409
Publicity: Raimondo Biffi
Subjects: Youth Questions, Pop Music, Oriental Thought
1977: 20 titles *1978:* 25 titles

Editore **Armando** Armando, Via della Gensola 60-61, I-00153 Rome Tel: (06) 588441/5894525
Man Dir: Prof Armando Armando
Subjects: Psychology, Philosophy, Social Sciences, Politics, Textbooks, Education, Linguistics, Languages, Children's books, Sociology
1977: 80 titles *1978:* 90 titles *Founded:* 1963

Arti Grafiche della Venezie SpA*, Viale S Agostino 152, I-36100 Vicenza Tel: (02) 563011
Subject: Arts
Miscellaneous: Firm is a subsidiary of Arnoldo Mondadori Editore (qv)

Edizioni Dell'**Ateneo** e Bizzarri SRL*, Via Giovanni Amendola 7, CP 7216, I-00185 Rome Tel: (06) 489965/4751092
Man Dir: Franco Volta; *Sales:* G Santo

Geraci; *Production:* Sergio Petrelli
Orders to: Via Ruggero Bonghi 11/B,
I-00184 Rome
Subjects: Belles Lettres, Poetry, Biography,
History, Music, Art, Philosophy, Classical
Philology, Cinema, Reference, Religion,
High-priced Paperbacks, Psychology,
Engineering, General & Social Science,
Secondary and University Textbooks,
Economics, Medicine, Aeronautics, Navy,
Army
Bookshop: Galleria del Libro, Via
Nazionale 246, I-00184 Rome
1977: 198 titles *Founded:* 1946

Verlagsanstalt **Athesia**, Lauben 41, Postfach
417, I-39100 Bolzano-Bozen Tel: (0471)
41444 Cable Add: Athesia, Verlag, Bozen
Telex: 400161
Man Dir: Dr Toni Ebner; *Production:* Peter
Plattner; *Sales Manager:* Richard Fieg;
Publicity Manager: Gustav Theiner
Subjects: Art, Travel, Periodicals, History,
Maps, Textbooks, Poetry, Mountaineering
Bookshops: in Bozen, Meran, Brixen,
Bruneck, Sterzing, Schlanders
1977: 25 titles *1978:* 28 titles *Founded:*
1907

M d'**Auria**, Editore+, Calata Trinità
Maggiore 52, I-80134 Naples Tel: (081)
328963
Dir: Ugo d'Auria
Subject: Religion
1977: 4 titles *1978:* 2 titles *Founded:* 1887

Baldini e Castoldi*, Via Guercino 10,
I-20154 Milan Tel: (02) 342904
Dir: Dr Enrico Castoldi
Subjects: General Fiction, Juveniles,
Memoirs
Founded: 1896

Giunti **Barbera** Editore, see Giunti
Publishing Group

Edizioni Oreste **Barjes**, see Giunti
Publishing Group

Bertani*, Lungadige Panvinio 37, I-37100
Verona Tel: 32686
Subjects: Theatre, History, Class Warfare,
Wars of Liberation

Edizioni d'Arte Carlo **Bestetti**, Via di San
Giacomo 18, I-00187 Rome Tel: (06)
6790174
Man Dir: Carlo Bestetti
Subjects: Art, Architecture, Industry
1978: 1 title *Founded:* 1947

Del **Bianco** Editore*, Via S Daniele 11,
CP 40, I-33100 Udine Tel: (0432) 22134
Cable Add: Del Bianco Udine
Subjects: Engineering, General Science,
University & Secondary Textbooks, Art,
History

Biblical Institute Press (Pontificio Istituto
Biblico), Piazza della Pilotta 35, I-00187
Rome Tel: (06) 6781567
Subjects: Scientific Studies, Biblical Studies,
Ancient languages, Archaeology
Founded: 1909

Bibliopolis—Edizioni di Filosofia e Scienze
SpA, Via Arangio Ruiz 83, I-80122 Naples
Tel: (081) 664606
Man Dir: Dr Francesco del Franco
Subjects: Science and Philosophy
1978: 6 titles *1979:* 10 titles *Founded:* 1976

Bietti SpA+, Via Crescenzio 58, I-00193
Rome Tel: (06) 6545501
Subjects: Fiction, Foreign Languages,
Humanities, History, Hobbies, Juveniles,
Literature Criticism, Education, Philosophy,
Games, Sports, Theatre

B **Boggero** Editore, see Giunti Publishing
Group

Casa Editrice Valentino **Bompiani** & C
SpA+, Via Mecenate 87/6, I-20138 Milan
Tel: (02) 5095 Cable Add: Bompiani
Milano Telex: 311321
President: Valentino Bompiani; *Man Dir:*
Vittorio Di Giuro; *Editorial:* Franco
Occhetto; *Rights & Permissions:* Nicoletta
Grill
Subjects: General Fiction, Belles Lettres,
History, How-to, Low-priced Paperbacks,
General & Social Science, Secondary
Textbooks
Founded: 1929

Bonacci-Libreria Editrice+, Via Paolo
Mercuri 23, I-00193 Rome Tel: (06)
6565995
Man Dir: Giorgio Bonacci
Subjects: Belles Lettres, Secondary
Textbooks
Bookshop: Bonacci — Libreria Editrice, Via
Paolo Mercuri 23, I-00193 Rome
1977: 6 titles *1978:* 2 titles *Founded:* 1942

Casa Editrice **Bonechi**+, Via Cairoli 18b,
I-50131 Florence Tel: (055) 576841/2
Telex: 571323 CEB
Man Dir: Giampaolo Bonechi; *Editorial:*
Giovanna Magi
Subjects: Art, Travel, Reference
1978: 15 titles

Editore **Boringhieri** SpA+, Corso Vittorio
Emanuele 86, I-10121 Turin Tel: (011)
541371 Cable Add: Edibor
Man Dir: Paolo Boringhieri
Subjects: Philosophy, Science, Psychology,
Economics, Low- & High-priced
Paperbacks, University Textbooks
1978: 55 titles *Founded:* 1957

SIL Srl Edizioni **Borla**, Via delle Fornaci
50, I-00165 Rome Tel: (06) 6381618
Man Dir: Dr Vincenzo D'Agostino
Subjects: Philosophy, Psychology,
Sociology, Anthropology, Education,
History, Religion, Politics, Juveniles,
Periodicals
1978: 40 titles

Bottega d'Erasmo*, Via G Ferrari 9,
I-10124 Turin Tel: (011) 830331/831264
Cable Add: Erasmus Turin
Subjects: Religion, Philosophy, Medieval
Art, Literature, Philology, History

Ugo **Bozzi** Editore*, Via Polonia 2, I-00198
Rome Tel: (06) 862179 Cable Add:
Uberart
Man Dir: Dr Ugo Bozzi
Subject: History of Art (in Italian and
English)
1977: 2 titles *1978:* 2 titles *Founded:* 1965

Bracciodieta Editore, see Editorialebari

Bramante Editrice SpA+, Via G Biancardi
1 bis, I-21052 Busto Arsizio Tel: (0331)
620324
Man Dir: Dr Guido Ceriotti
Subjects: History, Music, Art, General
Science, Military, Architecture
1977: 8 titles *Founded:* 1958

L'Erma di **Bretschneider** SpA+, Via
Cassiodoro 19, CP 6192, I-00193 Rome
Tel: (06) 353259/350765
Man Dir: Erminia Bretschneider Marcucci;
Publisher: Dr Roberto Marcucci; *Bookstore:*
Maria Silvia Marcucci
Subjects: Archaeology, Classical Art,
Classical Philology, Ancient History,
Roman Law

Dr Giorgio **Bretschneider**, Publisher &
Bookseller, Via Crescenzio 43, I-00193
Rome Tel: (06) 659361 Cable Add:
Giobrerom
Man Dir: Dr Giorgio Bretschneider
Subjects: Classical Antiquity-Archaeology,
Philology, Ancient History
1978: 25 titles

Bulzoni Editore SRL*, Via Dei Liburni 14,
I-00185 Rome Tel: (06) 4955207
Man Dir, Editorial: Mario Bulzoni; *Sales:*
Ivana Capitani; *Production:* Paola Bulzoni;
Publicity: Anna Catarinozzi
Subjects: Medicine, Law, Sociology,
Science, Fiction, Engineering, Arts,
Literature, Philosophy, Linguistics,
University Textbooks, Theatre, Cinema,
Essays
Bookshop: Libreria Ricerche, Via Liburni
10/12, I-00185 Rome
1977: approx 200 titles *Founded:* 1969

C E D A M (Casa Editrice Dr A Milani)*,
Via Jappelli 5, I-35100 Padua Tel: (049)
23234/23442
Dirs: Antonio Milani, Carlo Porta
Subjects: Belles Lettres, Philosophy, General
& Social Science, Textbooks, Book
Industry, Engineering, Arts, Literature,
Languages, Fiction, Economics, Politics,
Medicine

C E L I (Edizioni)+, Via Gandino, I-40137
Bologna Tel: (051) 391755/309922
Subjects: Medicine, Civil Engineering,
Electronics, Radio, Television

Edizioni **C E P I M**, Via Buonarroti 38,
I-20145 Milan Tel: (02) 4982129/4694778
Man Dir: Sergio Bonelli; *Editorial:* Decio
Canzio; *Sales:* Liliana Gentini; *Production:*
Luigi Corteggi
Subsidiary Companies: Altamira; Araldo;
Edizioni Daim Press; all in Milan
Subjects: Comic Strip Books, Far West
Stories, Adventure Tales, Stories of
Exploration and Travel
1977: 150 titles *1978:* 150 titles *Founded:*
1968

Edizioni **Calderini**+, Emilia Lev 31, I-40139
Bologna Tel: (051) 492211 Cable Add:
Calderini Telex: 510336
Man Dir: S Perdisa; *Rights & Permissions:*
Luisa Manzoni B; *Publicity:* G Belluzzi
Parent Company: Calderini SRL (at above
address)
Associate Company: Edagricole (qv)
Br Offs: Via Bronzino 14, Milan; Via Puglie
3, Rome
Subjects: Art, Sport, Electronics,
Mechanics, Electrical Engineering,
University & Secondary Textbooks,
Nursing, Veterinary Science, Architecture,
Natural Sciences
1978: 85 titles *1979:* 88 titles *Founded:*
1952
ISBN Publisher's Prefix: 88-7019

Capitol Editrice Dischi CEB, CP 441,
I-40100 Bologna (Located at: Via
Minghetti 17/19, I-40057 Cadriano di
Granarolo Emilia (Bologna)) Tel: (051)
766612/766421/2 Cable Add: Edicapitol
Bologna Telex: 511039 EDCAPI I
Man Dir: Maurizio Malipiero; *Rights &
Permissions:* Raffaele Malipiero; *Production
Manager:* Guiseppe Parini
Subjects: General Fiction, Art, Biography,
Reference, Medicine, Juveniles, Secondary
& Primary Textbooks, Educational
Materials, Audiovisual
1977: 178 titles *Founded:* 1956

Nuova Casa Editrice Licinio **Cappelli** SpA+, Via Marsili 9, CP 385, I-40124 Bologna Tel: (051) 330411 Cable Add: Cappelli Editore Bologna Telex: 510198 PP BO I PER CAPPELLI
Man Dir: Giuseppe Milano; *Editorial:* Dr Cesare Sughi; *Textbooks:* Dr Umberto Magrini; *Publicity, Advertising, Rights & Permissions:* Augusto Magagnoli
Subjects: General Fiction, Belles Lettres, Poetry, Biography, History, Art, Philosophy, Reference, Religion, Juveniles, Low-priced Paperbacks, Medicine, Psychology, General & Social Science, Primary, Secondary and University Textbooks, Filmscripts, Drama, Music, Politics
1977: 83 titles *1978:* 107 titles *Founded:* 1851

Casalini Libri+, Via B da Maiano 3, I-50014 Fiesole (Florence) Tel: (055) 599941 Cable Add: Casalini Fiesole
Man Dirs: Mario Casalini, Gerda Casalini von Grebmer
Subjects: History, Philosophy, Sociology, Musicology
1977: 6 titles *1978:* 6 titles *Founded:* 1968
Miscellaneous: Also a book exporter (address as above)

Celuc Libri, Via Santa Valeria 5, I-20123 Milan Tel: (02) 806976/800113
Man Dir: Giovanni Barbatiello
Subjects: History, Philosophy, Religion, Low-priced Paperbacks, Psychology, Engineering, General & Social Science, University Textbooks
1977: 8 titles *1978:* 8 titles *Founded:* 1969

Centro Di*, Piazza de'Mozzi 1 r, CP 1500, I-50125 Florence Tel: (055) 23222/282729 Cable Add: Centrodi Florence
Man Dir: Dr F Marchi; *Sales Dir:* P Riccetti
Subjects: Art, Reference
Bookshop: Centro Di, Piazza d'Mozzi 1 r, I-50125, Florence; 18 via di San Giacomo, I-00187 Rome Tel: 6786963
1977: 30 titles *Founded:* 1968

Centro Internazionale del Libro, see Giunti Publishing Group

Verlag **Chiessi-Morra***, Via Calabrillo 20, I-8021 Naples Tel: (081) 402025
Dirs: Rosanna Chiessi, Giuseppe Morra

Ciarrapico Editore*, Via Panisperna 203, I-00184 Rome Tel: (06) 4741151/2/3
Publisher: Giuseppe Ciarrapico; *Dir:* Gianni Pirrone; *Publicity Manager:* Maria Teresa Musanti
Subjects: Politics, History, Science, Law, Philology Philosophy

Città Armoniosa+, CP 243, I-42100 Reggio Emilia (Located at: Via Lungocrostalo 1/A, I-42100 Reggio Emilia) Tel: (0522) 25973
Man Dir: Mauro Masini; *Editorial:* Giovanni Riva; *Sales:* Mario Ghinoi; *Production:* Massimo Rocchi; *Publicity:* Gino Ruozzi; *Rights & Permissions:* Paola Leoni
Parent Company: Novastampa di Masini Mauro SNC
Subsidiary Company: Novalito di Persona Francesco E C SNC, Via Cecati 15/A, I-42100 Reggio Emilia
Subjects: Fiction, Poetry, Theatre, Juveniles, Cartoons
1978: 36 titles *1979:* 42 titles *Founded:* 1976

Città Nuova Editrice+, Via degli Scipioni 265, I-00192 Rome Tel: (06) 3595212/310955
Man Dir: Dr Giambattista Dadda
Br Off: Via Degli Scipioni 265, I-00192 Rome
Subsidiary Companies: Argentina: Ciudad Nueva, Ave da Rivadavia 4939, Buenos Aires 24; Austria: Verlag Neue Stadt GmbH, A-6263 Fügen 73 (Zillertal); Brazil: Cidade Nova, Rua Pio XII 274, Paraiso, São Paulo; France: Nouvelle Cité (qv); Federal Republic of Germany: Neue Stadt (qv); Italy: Via Bonvicini 2, Florence; Netherlands: Nieuwe Stad, St Stephanusstr 11, Nijmegen; Philippines: New City, 363 Ycaza St, San Miguel, Manila; Spain: Ciudad Nueva, Luis Cabrera 12, III Dcha, Madrid 2; Switzerland: Verlag Neue Stadt, CH-8032 Zürich, Postfach 218; UK: New City (qv); USA: Living City, 360 East 65th St, 16G, New York, NY 10021
Subjects: Religion, Philosophy, Psychology, Social Science, Reference, Juveniles
1977: 70 titles

Cittadèlla Editrice+, Via Ancajani 3, CP 46, I-06081 Assisi Tel: (075) 813595 Cable Add: Cittadella Editrice
All offices: Nello Giostra, Gabriella Persico, Giuseppina Pompei, Virginia Pagani
Subjects: Biography, Religion, Psychology, Social Science, Social Problems, Theology
1978: 40 titles

Coines Edizioni*, Corso Vittorio Emanuele 337, I-00186 Rome Tel: (06) 657948/6543840
Man Dir: Roberto Miotti; *Editorial:* Pierpaolo Benedetti; *Rights & Permissions:* Roma Eulama
Subjects: History, Education, Politics, Psychology, Religion, Social Science, Economics, Periodicals
1977: 30 titles *Founded:* 1970

Collettivo Editoriale 10/16*, Via Decembrio 26, Milan Tel: 595137
Subjects: Instructional and Documentary Material; the Anti-Fascist Struggle in Italy and Europe; Third World Liberation War; Theoretical Discussion

Edizioni di **Comunità** SpA, Via Manzoni 12, I-20121 Milan Tel: 790957
Man & Sales Dir: Dr S Gallo; *Publicity Dir:* Dr A Scoccimarro; *Advertising & Rights & Permissions:* R Cambiaghi
Subjects: Philosophy, Psychology, Social Science, Architecture, Town Planning
1977: 30 titles *1978:* 25 titles *Founded:* 1946

Controinformazione*, Corso di Porta Ticinese 87, I-20123 Milan
Subjects: Anti-Fascism, International Anti-Capitalist Movement; Alternative Information

Edizioni **Cremonese** SpA+, Via Della Croce 77, I-00187 Rome Tel: (06) 6793995 Cable Add: Edizioni Cremonese
Man Dir: Alberto Stianti
Subjects: History, Reference, Engineering, General Science, University & Secondary Textbooks, Architecture, Mathematics, Aviation
1977: 15 titles *1978:* 35 titles *Founded:* 1930

Edizioni **Curci** SRL, Galleria del Corso 4, I-20122 Milan Tel: (02) 794746 Cable Add: Curcimusic Telex: 332683 CURCI I
Subjects: Music, Arts, Textbooks
1977: 33 titles *1978:* 28 titles *Founded:* 1860

Armando **Curcio** Editore SpA+*, Via Corsica 4, I-00198 Rome Tel: (06) 864351/856041 Cable Add: Curcioroma
Chairman: Dr Alfredo Curcio; *Man Dir:* Dr Luciano Delmirani; *Rights & Permissions:* Anita Lehner
Subjects: Art, Reference, Geography, History, Travel, Encyclopaedias
Founded: 1928

Editoriale **Dado***, Via Mameli 31, I-20100 Milan

Dall'Oglio Editore SpA+, Via Santa Croce 20-2, I-20122 Milan Tel: (02) 8351575
President: Andrea dall'Oglio; *Man Dir:* Bruno Romano
Subjects: General Fiction, Belles Lettres, Poetry, Biography, History, Low-priced Paperbacks
Founded: 1925

Piero **Dami** Editore SpA, Piazza Velasca 5, I-20122 Milan Tel: (02) 802731/866514 Cable Add: Eurostudio Milan Telex: 311499
Subjects: Fiction, Illustrated Children's Books, Animals
1978: 15 titles

De Donato Editore, Lungomare Nazario Sauro 25, I-70121 Bari Tel: 331574/334159
Man Dir, Sales: Diego De Donato; *Editorial:* Giancarlo Aresta; *Production:* Cesare Caleno; *Publicity:* Lalla Martellotti; *Rights & Permissions:* Isidoro Mortellaro
Associate Company: Consorzio del Libro srl, Corso Re Umberto 12, I-10121 Torino (Promotion company for Boringhieri, Dedalo, De Donato and Stampatori, publishers)
Subjects: Politics, Economics, Sociology, Literature, Fiction, Psychology, Archaeology, Philosophy
1978: 41 titles *1979:* 48 titles *Founded:* 1970

Giovanni **De Vecchi** Editore SpA*, Via Vittor Pisani 16, I-20124 Milan Tel: 664851/2/3 Telex: 37081 devedit
Subjects: Archaeology, Astronomy, Psychology, Sports, Hunting and Fishing, Domestic Animals, Humour, Occult Sciences, Gardening and Agriculture, Medicinal Herbs, Medical, Yoga, Legal
Miscellaneous: Associated Companies: Éditions De Vecchi SA, Paris, France (qv); Editorial De Vecchi SA, Barcelona, Spain (qv)

Edizioni **Dedalo**, CP 362, I-70100 Bari (Located at: Traversa de Blasio, Zona Industriale, I-70123 Bari) Tel: 371555/371025/371008
Man Dir: Raimondo Coga
Subjects: Politics, History, Architecture, Urban Studies, Science
1978: 45 titles *1979:* 20 titles *Founded:* 1965

Edizioni **Dehoniane** Bologna (EDB), Via Nosadella 6, I-40123 Bologna Tel: (051) 330301/306812
Shipping Add: Via Dal Ferro 4, I-40138 Bologna
Man Dir: Andrea Tessarolo; *Sales Dir, Rights & Permissions:* Giuseppe Albiero; *Publicity Dir:* Sancini Vittorio
Subjects: Philosophy, Religion, Juveniles, Secondary & Primary Textbooks, Educational Materials
Founded: 1965
Bookshops: Libreria Presbyterium, Padua

Delta Editrice SpA*, Piazza dei Martiri 1, I–40121 Bologna Tel: (051) 228219
Telex: 51524
Subjects: History, Travel, Natural History, Astrology

Diki-Books Srl, Via Della Spiga 1, I–20121 Milan Tel: 784129
Man Dir: Massimo Baletti
Subjects: Children's books, Foreign language texts for infants & primary schools
1978: 9 titles *Founded:* 1975

Domus Editoriale*, Viale del Ghisallo 12, I–20151 Milan Tel: (02) 30707
Subjects: Art, Motorcars, Cooking, Tourism, Architecture, Periodicals

E D B, see Edizioni Dehoniane Bologna

E D I 3*, Corso di Porta Nuova 34, I–20121 Milan Tel: (02) 638873
Man Dir: Paolo Colombo
Subjects: Juveniles, Educational Materials

E R I — Edizioni R A I Radiotelevisione Italiana SpA+, Via Arsenale 41, I–10121 Turin Tel: (011) 57101 Cable Add: Edrad Turin
Man Dir: Dr Alberto Luna
Orders to: Via del Babuino 51, I–00187 Rome
Parent Company: RAI Radiotelevisione It, Viale Mazzini 14, Rome
Associate Companies: Sacis, Via del Babuino 9, Rome; Sipra, Via Bertola 34, Turin; Fonit Cetra, Via Meda 45, Milan; Telespazio, Corso d'Italia 42–43, Rome
Subjects: Art and Collector's editions, Literature and Civilization, Essays, General Culture, Sociology, Classics in Translation, Home and Garden, Children's books; Language courses, Communications, Public opinion polls, Music
Bookshops: Via Arsenale 41, I–10121 Turin; Via del Babuino 51, I–00187 Rome
1977: 27 titles *1979:* 9 titles *Founded:* 1949

Edagricole (Edizioni Agricole), Emilia Lev 31, CP 2202 I–40139 Bologna Tel: (051) 492211 Cable Add: Edagri Telex: 510336
Man Dir: Sergio Perdisa; *Editorial:* Luisa Manzoni; *Sales:* Cesare Perdisa; *Production:* Guido Giorgi; *Publicity:* Giuliano Avoni
Associate Companies: Calderini Industrie Grafiche ed Editoriali; Edizioni Calderini (qv); Gruppo Giornalistico Edagricole
Br Offs and Bookshops: Via Bronzino 14, Milan; Via Boncompagni 73, Rome; Via Zamboni 13, Bologna
Subjects: Agriculture, Veterinary Science, Biology, Directories
1978: 160 titles *1979:* 125 titles *Founded:* 1936
ISBN Publisher's Prefix: 88–206

Edibimbi SRL*, Via Speroni 14, I–21100 Varese Tel: (0332) 287766
Subject: Juveniles

Edipem SpA+*, Corso Della Vittoria 91, Postfach 157, I–28100 Novara Tel: (032) 28694
Subjects: Juridical; Medical; Scientific and Technical; Encyclopaedias; Classical Literature; School Books

Editalia (Edizioni D'Italia)+, Via di Pallacorda 7, I–00186 Rome Tel: (06) 6569537/6541592
Man Dir: Lidio Bozzini; *Rights & Permissions:* Arrigo Pecchioli
Subjects: History, Art
Founded: 1952

Editnemo, Via Telesio 15, I–20145 Milan Tel: (02) 4983375
Man Dir: Sandro Nardini; *Sales Dir:* Alberto Nardini; *Rights & Permissions:* S A Nardini
Subject: Juveniles
Founded: 1972

Editorialebari, Corso Sonnino 8, I–70121 Bari Tel: (080) 540267
Man Dir: Dr Giuseppe Bracciodieta; *Editorial:* Domenico Bracciodieta; *Sales:* Rete Concessionari; *Publicity:* Dr Giuseppe Deliso
Subsidiary Company: Bracciodieta Editore (at above address)
Subjects: Fiction, Culture, Scholarly
1978: 20 titles *Founded:* 1965

Editrice Bibliografica+, Viale Vittorio Veneto 24, I–20124 Milan Tel: (02) 6597950/6597246
Subjects: Bibliographies and Reference Publications for the Book Trade
1977: 10 titles *1978:* 10 titles
ISBN Publisher's Prefix: 88–7075

Giulio **Einaudi** Editore SpA+, Via Umberto Biancamano, CP 245, I–10121 Turin Tel: (011) 533653/545384 Telex: 220344
Subjects: General Fiction, Belles Lettres, Poetry, Biography, History, Music, Art, Philosophy, Juveniles, Low- & High-priced Paperbacks, Psychology, Social Science, University Textbooks
1977: 223 titles *1978:* 178 titles *Founded:* 1933

Eldec SpA Edizioni Pregiate+*, Viale Tiziano 25, I–00196 Rome Tel: (06) 3960041/4
Publisher: Giulio de Cicco; *Dir:* Milko Skofic
Subjects: Art, Encyclopaedias, Facsimile Editions, Bibliophilic Editions

Electa Editrice, Via Goldoni 1, I–20124 Milan Tel: (02) 704023
Dirs: Giorgio Fantoni, Massimo Vitta Zelman; *Editorial:* Carlo Pirovano; *Rights & Permissions:* Mirella V Tenderini
Parent Company: Gruppo Editoriale Electa SpA
Associate Company: Alfieri Edizioni d'Arte (qv)
Subsidiary Company: Electa France, Paris; Electa Mailing, Milan
Subjects: Art, History of Art, Architecture, High-priced Paperbacks, Numbered Editions, Catalogues of major exhibitions, Periodicals
1977: 60 titles *1978:* 100 titles *Founded:* 1945

Emme Edizioni+, Via San Maurilio 13, I–20123 Milan Tel: (02) 865459/865951
Man Dir, Editorial: Rosellina Archinto Marconi; *Rights & Permissions:* Renata Discacciati
Subjects: How-to, Juveniles, High-priced Paperbacks, Educational Materials
1978: 64 titles

Eulama SA*, Via Torino 135, I–00184 Rome Tel: (06) 460636
Man Dir: Harald Kahnemann
Subjects: Fiction, Sociology, Law
Also Literary Agent (qv)

Fabbri Editori SpA+, Via Mecenate 91, I–20138 Milan Tel: (02) 5095 Cable Add: Librifabbri Milan Telex: 311321
Man Dir: Giorgio Manina; *Editorial:* Giorgio Savorelli; *Sales:* Giorgio Paolo Tabacchi
Subjects: General Fiction, History, Music, Art, Philosophy, Juveniles, Reference, Low- & High-priced Paperbacks, Medicine, General Science, Secondary & Primary Textbooks, Educational Materials, Hobbies, Sports, Encyclopaedias
Founded: 1945

Faenza Editrice SpA+, Via Firenze 60, CP 68, I–48018 Faenza Tel: (0546) 43120
Cable Add: Editfaenza
Man Dir: Prof Goffredo Gaeta; *Editorial, Sales, Publicity:* Franco Rossi
Subjects: Architecture, Science, Technology, Industries, Crafts, Arts
Founded: 1965

Giangiacomo **Feltrinelli** SpA+, Via Andegari 6, I–20121 Milan Tel: (02) 808346/7 Cable Add: Fedit Milan
Subjects: General Fiction, Belles Lettres, Poetry, Art, Music, History, General Science, Reference, Paperbacks, University Textbooks, Philosophy, Juveniles
1978-79: 350 titles *Founded:* 1954

Edizioni **Ferro** SpA+, Via Cusani 5, I–20121 Milan Tel: (02) 866272
Man Dir: Pia Ferro
Subjects: Geography, Ethnology, Medicine, Religion, Pedagogy, Fiction, Sociology
1977: 5 titles *1978:* 3 titles *Founded:* 1963

Libreria Editrice **Fiorentina** di Vittorio e Valerio Zani snc, Via Ricasoli 105–107r, I–50122 Florence Tel: (055) 216533
Editorial: Vittorio Zani; *Sales:* Valerio Zani
Subjects: Religion, Social Problems, Education, Local Interest, Architecture
Bookshop: At above address
1978: 43 titles *1979:* 9 titles *Founded:* 1901

S F **Flaccovio** Editore+, Via Ruggiero Settimo 37, I–90139 Palermo Tel: 589442/334249/584268
Subjects: General Science, History
Bookshops: Via R Settimo 37, Palermo; Piazza Orlando 15, Palermo; Via E Basile 136, Palermo; Libreria Dante, Quattro Canti Citta, Palermo
1977: 15 titles *1978:* 22 titles

Il **Formichiere***, Via del Lauro 3, I–20121 Milan Tel: (02) 86693
Subjects: Fiction, Sociology, Politics, Psychology

Editrice **Gammalibri**, Via Poma 4, I–20129 Milan Tel: (02) 718315
Man Dir: Domenico Nodari; *Publicity:* Felice Bassi
Subjects: Music, Sport, Politics, Cinema, Theatre
1978: 12 titles *1979:* 15 titles *Founded:* 1976

Garzanti Editore+*, Via Senato 25, I–20121 Milan Tel: (02) 705721/705741 Cable Add: Garzantieditore Telex: Garzal 31461
Publisher: Dr Livio Garzanti; *Editorial:* Piero Gelli; *Sales Manager:* Francesco Rampini; *Rights & Permissions:* Paola Dala
Subjects: General & Crime Fiction, Literature, Poetry, Art, Politics, Biography, History, Reference, Juveniles, Low- & High-priced Paperbacks, Secondary & Primary Textbooks, Encyclopaedias, Dictionaries
Founded: 1861
Bookshops: Libreria Garzanti, Galleria Vittorio Emanuele 66–68, I–20121 Milan; Libreria Garzanti, Palazzo Dell' Università, Pavia
Subsidiaries: Antonio Vallardi Editore, Via Senato 25, (qv); Centri Garzanti, Via Senato 15; Enciclopedia Europea SaS, Via Senato 25 (all in Milan)

Creazioni **Gensy**, see Giunti Publishing Group

Giorgio **Giappichelli**+, Via Vasco 2, I–10124 Turin Tel: (011) 553140/513346
Subjects: University Publications, Humanities (Economics, Law, Philosophy, Politics, Sociology, Classical and Modern Philology)

216 ITALY

Bookshops: Libreria Editrice Scientifica di G Giappichelli, Via Vasco 2, I-10124 Turin; Libreria della Facolta' Umanistiche, Via Verdi 39 bis, I-10124 Turin
1978: 71 titles *Founded:* 1921

A **Giuffré** Editore SpA+*, Via Statuto 2, I-20121 Milan Tel: (02) 652341/2/3
Br Off: Via V Colonna 40, I-00193 Rome
Subjects: History, Law, Social & Political Science
1977: approx 250 titles *Founded:* 1931

Giunti Publishing Group, Via V Gioberti 34, I-50121 Florence Tel: (055) 670451/5
Cable Add: Marzolib Florence
Telex: 571438 Giunti
Dirs: Dr Renato Giunti, Dr Sergio Giunti
Subjects: Art Books, Essays, Fiction, Psychology, Pedagogy, Mathematics, Chemistry, National Edition of Works of Leonardo da Vinci, Galileo Galilei, Italian publishers of National Geographic Society books, Linguistics, Dictionaries, School Textbooks, Juveniles, Popular Science, History, Guidebooks, Handbooks, Periodicals
Miscellaneous: Group comprises: Editrice Giunti Marzocco, Giunti Barbera Editore, Editrice Universitaria, Edizioni Ofiria, Giunti Nardini Editore, Centro Internazionale del Libro, Giacomo Agnelli Editore, Giunti Martello Editore, Creazioni Gensy, Edizioni Oreste Barjes, ME/DI Sviluppo, Organizzazioni Speciali (qv), B Boggero Editore

Gregorian University Press (Universitá Gregoriana Editrice)*, Piazza della Pilotta 4, I-00187 Rome Tel: (06) 6701
Man Dir: Angelo Damboriena
Subjects: Theology, Philosophy, Canon Law, Sociology, Psychology, Missiology
1977: 12 titles *1978:* 12 titles *Founded:* 1914

Libreria Editrice **Gregoriana***, Via Roma 37, I-35100 Padua Tel: 36133/38869
Man Dir: Clodio Fasolo
Subjects: Religion, Philosophy, Sociology, Psychology
Bookshop: Via Roma 37, I-35100 Padua; Via Vescovado 33, I-35100 Padua
1977: 5 titles *Founded:* 1922

Piero **Gribaudi** Editore+, Corso Galileo Ferraris 67, I-10128 Turin Tel: (011) 500360
Publishers: Piero Gribaudi, Maria Luisa Gribaudi Monferrini
Subjects: Maps, Literature Criticism, Philosophy, Religion, Social Science, Linguistics, Languages
1978: 30 titles

L'Editrice Scientifica SaS di L G **Guadagni**, Via Ariberto 20, I-20123 Milan Tel: (02) 8390274
Dir: Dr Leonarda Guadagni
Subjects: Pharmaceuticals, Chemistry, University Textbooks
1977: 3 titles *1978:* 2 titles *Founded:* 1940

Guanda Editore SRL+, Via Daniele Manin 13, I-20121 Milan Tel: (02) 654628, 650973
Man Dir: Dr Giancarlo Paolini; *Rights & Permissions:* Dr Maria Caronia
Subjects: Poetry, General Fiction
1978: 45 titles *1979:* 50 titles *Founded:* 1933

Guaraldi Editore SpA*, Via Masaccio 268, I-50100 Florence Tel: (055) 573968/573978
Man Dir: Mario Guaraldi; *Editorial:* Sandro Savorelli; *Sales:* Rosiano Sensini; *Production:* Vittorio Giudici; *Publicity:* Andrea Rauch; *Rights & Permissions:*

Eulama SA
Subjects: Sociology, Pedagogy, Psychoanalytics
1977: 60 titles *Founded:* 1970

Guida Editori SRL+, Via Ventaglieri 83, I-80135 Naples Tel: (081) 341843
Publisher: Mario Guida
Subjects: History, Philosophy, Ideology, Sociology, Anthropology, Political Science, Lit Criticism, Linguistics, Periodical *Sigma* (Art Criticism)
1978: 48 titles

Herder Editrice e Libreria, Piazza Montecitorio 117-120, I-00186 Rome
Tel: (06) 6794628
Man Dir: Oriol Schaedel
Subjects: Religion, History, Philosophy, Archaeology, Oriental Studies, Philology and Linguistics, Periodicals, Occasional titles
Founded: 1955

Casa Editrice Libraria Ulrico **Hoepli** SpA+, Via Hoepli 5, I-20121 Milan Tel: (02) 865446 Cable Add: Hoepli Milan
Shipping Add: Via Mameli 13, I-20129 Milan
Man Dirs: Dr Ulrico Hoepli, Dr Gianni Hoepli; *Sales Dir:* Lodovico Colombo; *Rights & Permissions:* Dr Ulrico Carlo Hoepli
Br Off: Via Mameli 13, I-20129 Milan
Subjects: How-to, Music, Art, Philosophy, Reference, Religion, Juveniles, Low- & High-priced Paperbacks, Psychology, Engineering, General & Social Science, University & Secondary Textbooks, Technology
Bookshop: Ulrico Hoepli Libreria Internazionale, Via Hoepli 5, I-20121 Milan
1977: 119 titles *1978:* 103 titles *Founded:* 1870

Idea Editions, Via Cappuccio 21, I-20123 Milan Tel: (02) 807997 Cable Add: Ideabooks Milano
Dirs: Alvise Passigli, Filippo Passigli
Subjects: Visual Arts, Photography, Architecture, Design
Bookshop: Museum Bookshop, Padiglione d'Arte Moderna, Milan
Miscellaneous: Associate company of Idea Books, Amsterdam, Netherlands; Idea Books, Milan (at above address)

Intergest SRL*, Via del Lauro n3, I-20121 Milan Tel: (02) 866393
Subject: Military

Istituto Centrale di Statistica*, Via C Balbo 16, I-00184 Rome Tel: (06) 471666
Subject: Political Economy

Istituto della Enciclopedia Italiana+*, Piazza Paganica 4, CP 717, I-00186 Rome Tel: (06) 6544337 Cable Add: Enciclopedia
Subjects: Encyclopaedias, Dictionaries, Reference, Art

Istituto Editoriale Italiano SpA*, Via Priv Passo Pordoi 21, I-20139 Milan
Subjects: Fine & Applied Arts, Illustrated Books, Encyclopaedias & Dictionaries

Istituto Geografico de Agostini SpA+*, Corso della Vittoria 91, CP 157, I-28100 Novara Tel: (0321) 23691 Cable Add: Geografico Novara Telex: 20020 IGDA NO
Subjects: Belles Lettres, Art, Reference, History, Religion, Juveniles, Textbooks, Geography, Literature

Istituto Italiano D'Arti Grafiche*, Via Zanica 92, I-24100 Bergamo Tel: (035) 246292/243645/249675 Cable Add: Grafiche Bergamo Telex: 30114

Man Dir: Comm Remo Montanari
Subjects: Art, Juveniles, Reference, Textbooks, Religion
Founded: 1873

Istituto Poligrafico e Zecca dello Stato*, Piazza Verdi 10, I-00100 Rome
Subjects: Law, Politics, Linguistics, Literature, Fiction, Arts, Numismatology, Philately
Founded: 1928
Miscellaneous: State Publishing House and Italian State Stationery Office, Mint and School of Medal's Art

Cooperativa Edizioni **Jaca** Book+, Via Aurelio Saffi 19, I-20123 Milan Tel: (02) 8057088/8057055 Telex: 331393
Man Dir: Dr Sante Bagnoli; *Editorial Dir:* Dr Maretta Campi; *Editors:* Dr Elio Guerriero (Theology), Dr Massimo Guidetti (History); *Rights & Permissions:* Laura Geronazzo
Subjects: History, Philosophy, Religion, Psychology, Social & Political Science, Economics, Juveniles, Fiction, Literature, Art
1978: 60 titles *1979:* 65 titles *Founded:* 1966

Casa Editrice Dr Eugenio **Jovene** SpA+, Via Mezzocannone 109, I-80134 Naples Tel: 206518/206575 Cable Add: Jovene
Man Dir: Dr Alessandro Rossi
Subjects: Law, Economics
1978: 50 titles *1979:* 30 titles *Founded:* 1854

Kina Italia SpA*, Piazza Aspromonte 13, Milan Cable Add: 296263, 293284
Subjects: Art, Tourist Publications

Etas **Kompass***, Via Mantegna 6, I-20154 Milan Tel: (02) 347051/314007/341137
Telex: 33152
Man Dir: Aldo Lanza
Subjects: Reference, Law, Medicine, General & Socal Science, Technical, Periodicals

Editrice **Lanterna***, Via Robino 71 a/r, I-16142 Genoa Tel: 881441
Dirs: Lino De Benetti, Dino Galiazzo
Subjects: Religion, Theology, Sociology, Politics, Fminism, Non-violence
1977: 12 titles *Founded:* 1969

Giuseppe **Laterza** & Figli SpA+, Via di Villa Sacchetti 17, I-00197 Rome Tel: (06) 803693/878053
Shipping Add: Via F Zippitelli 3, Zona Industriale, I-70123 Bari
Man Dir: Vito Laterza (Rome); *Editorial Dir:* Enrico Mistretta (Rome); *Sales Dir:* Domenico Scoppio (Bari); *Press, Publicity & Advertising:* Nico Perrone (Bari); *Rights & Permissions:* Eulama Agency, Via Torino 135, Rome
Br Off: Via D Alighieri 51, I-70121 Bari
Subjects: Belles Lettres, Biography, Art, Reference, Religion, Architecture, Classics, History, Economics, Philosophy, Low- & High-priced Paperbacks, Psychology, Social Science, University & Secondary Textbooks
1978: 130 titles *Founded:* 1889
Bookshop: Via Sparano 134, I-70121 Bari

Casa Editrice Felice **Le Monnier**+, Via Scipione Ammirato 100, CP 202, I-50136 Florence Tel: (055) 676201
Subjects: Belles Lettres, Poetry, Biography, History, How-to, Music, Art, Philosophy, Religion, Juveniles, Multilingual Dictionaries, Languages

Leschiera Valerio*, Via Perugino 21, I-21 Cologno Monzese (Milan) Tel: 2546545/2543986

Edizioni **Librex**+*, Via Bellezza 15, I-20136 Milan Tel: (02) 544407/584523 Cable Add: Librex Milan Telex: 34208
General Manager: Antonio Mancia; *Export Manager:* Anna Vanzo; *Production:* Fabiola Ferrario
Subjects: Reference, Juveniles, International Co-productions, Encyclopedias

Etas **Libri** SpA, Via Mecenate 87/6, I-20138 Milan Tel: (02) 5065249/5065223/501101 Telex: Fabbri 32321
Man Dir: Romano Trabucchi
Subjects: General & Social Science, Economics, Technical, Mathematics, Management
1978: 44 titles

Licosa SpA, Via Lamarmora 45, CP 552, I-50121 Florence Tel: 579751/3, 571809 Cable Add: Licosa Firenze Telex: 570466 LICOSA I
Man Dir, Sales, Rights & Permissions: Mirko Zanello; *Editorial:* Barbara Adamska; *Publicity:* Capo Servizio, Barbara Adamska
Branch Off: Via Bartolini 29, I-20155 Milan
Subjects: Philology, Linguistics, Archaeology
Bookshops: Via Lamarmora 45, Florence; Libreria Desi, Via Bartolini 29, Milan
1977: 12 titles *1978:* 18 titles *Founded:* 1954

Liguori Editore SRL+, Via Mezzocannone 19, I-80134 Naples Tel: (081) 203606/206077 Cable Add: Liguori Napoli
Man Dir: Dr Rolando Liguori; *Editorial and Rights & Permissions:* Guido Liguori; *Sales:* Franco Liguori
Subjects: Linguistics, Lit Criticism, Philosophy, History, Sociology, Anthropology, Law, Economics, Mathematics, Astronomy, Natural Sciences, Medicine, Technology, Periodical — *Lo Statuto dei Lavoratori*
1978: 85 titles

Loescher Editore+, Via Vittorio Amedeo 18, I-10121 Turin Tel: (011) 549333
Dir: Maurizio Pavia
Subjects: University & Secondary Textbooks
1977: 70 titles *Founded:* 1867

Longanesi e C+, Via Borghetto 5, I-20122 Milan Tel: (02) 782551/5 Cable Add: Editlong Milan
President: Dr Mario Monti; *Editorial:* Ferruccio Viviani; *Sales:* Dino Calderari; *Production:* Lorenzo Pellizzari; *Publicity:* Mario Biondi; *Rights & Permissions:* Olivia Olivieri, Carla Tanzi
Subjects: General Fiction, Belles Lettres, Poetry, Biography, History, How-to, Music, Art, Philosophy, Religion, Low-priced Paperbacks, Medicine, Psychology, General & Social Science, University Textbooks, Educational Materials
1977: about 200 titles *1978:* 148 titles *Founded:* 1946

Longman Italia SRL+, Via Giovanni Pascoli 55, I-20133 Milan
Associate company of Longman Group Ltd, UK (qv)

Longo Editore, Via Rocca ai Fossi 6, CP 431, I-48100 Ravenna Tel: (0544) 27026
Editorial, Production: Alfio Longo; *Sales:* Angelo Longo
Subjects: Art, Archeology, Bibliography, Philology, Italian Classics, Philosophy, Linguistics, Pedagogy, Critical Literature, Sociology, History, History of Art, Poetry, Fiction

Bookshop: Libreria Longo, Via Diaz 39, I-48100 Ravenna
1977: 68 titles *1978:* 60 titles *Founded:* 1962

M E/D I Sviluppo, see Giunti Publishing Group

Malipiero SpA+*, Viale Liguria 12–14, CP 788, I-40064 Ozzana Emilia (Bologna) Tel: (051) 799264 Cable Add: TLX 51260 Matex, Ozzanoemilia Telex: 51260
Dirs: Dr Pierpaolo Malipiero, Comm Giuseppe Malipiero; *Editorial Dir:* Donato Malipiero
Subjects: Juveniles, Hobbies, Education
Founded: 1969

Marietti Editori SpA+, Via Adam 15, I-15033 Casale Monferrato Tel: (0142) 55181/2 Cable Add: Marietti Editori
Man Dir: Ing Pietro Marietti
Br Off: Largo Card, A Galamini 7, I-00165 Rome
Subjects: Philosophy, Religion, Secondary & Primary Textbooks, History, Psychology, Social Sciences

Alberto **Marotta** Editore SpA*, Via Francesco Giordani 21, I-80122 Naples Tel: (081) 685144 (PBX)
Man Dir: Alberto Marotta; *Editorial:* Dott Giuseppe Maggi; *Sales:* Pasquale Marotta
Br Offs: Via Monte di Pieta 1/A, I-20121 Milan; Via Nizza 45, I-00198 Rome
Subjects: General Fiction, Belles Lettres, Poetry, Biography, Music, Art, Social Science, Dictionaries, Encyclopaedias, History, Neapolitan Studies, Medicine, Science
Bookshops: Via dei Mille 78–80–82; Via Francesco Giordani 46; Via Giuseppe Verdi 46 (all in Naples)
1977: 3 titles *Founded:* 1959

Marsilio Editori*, Fondamenta S Chiara, S Croce 518a, I-30125 Venice Tel: (041) 707188
Man Dir: Professor Cesare de Michelis
Subjects: General Fiction, Architecture, Social & Political Science, Economics, Psychology, Literature, Languages

Giunti **Martello** Editore, see Giunti Publishing Group

Editrice Giunti **Marzocco**, see Giunti Publishing Group

Marzorati Editore SRL+, Via Piero Martinetti 6, I-20147 Milan Tel: (02) 405050
Man Dir: Antonio Marzorati; *Editorial:* Romain Rainero; *Sales:* Franco Faglioni; *Production:* Fiorenza Vittori; *Publicity:* Patrizia Fatigati; *Rights & Permissions:* Elena Maglia
Subjects: Literature, History, Philosophy
1977: 12 titles *1978:* 15 titles *Founded:* 1942

Editrice **Massimo**+, Corso di Porta Romana 122, I-20122 Milan Tel: (02) 544104
Man Dir: Dr Cesare Crespi
Subjects: General Fiction, Biography, History, Religion, Juveniles, Low- & High-priced Paperbacks, Psychology, General & Social Science, Secondary Textbooks
1978: 27 titles *Founded:* 1951
Bookshops: Via dei Pellegrini 1, I-20122 Milan; Agenzia Mescat, Corso di Porta Romana 122, I-20122 Milan

Gabriele **Mazzotta** Editore SpA+, Foro Buonaparte 52, I-20121 Milan Tel: (02) 895803

ITALY 217

Shipping Add: Via Col di Lana 6/a
Man Dir: Gabriele Mazzotta; *Sales Dir:* Alberto Bini; *Publicity Dir:* Nadine Bortolotti; *Rights & Permissions:* Pierrette Coppa
Subjects: Biography, History, Architecture, Art, Low- & High-priced Paperbacks, Psychology, Social Science
1977: 64 titles *1978:* 65 titles *Founded:* 1966

Organizzazione Editoriale **Medico Farmaceutica** SRL+, Via Edolo 42, CP 3580, I-20125 Milan Tel: (02) 600376
Dir: Lucio Marini
Subjects: Medicine, Pharmacy

Edizioni **Mediterranee** SRL, Via Flaminia 158, I-00196 Rome Tel: (06) 3601656
General Manager: Giovanni Canonico; *Editorial:* Romualdo d'Alessandro; *Sales:* Graziella Torre; *Publicity:* Nadia Bocchini; *Rights & Permissions:* Luigi Coppe
Subjects: ESP, Parapsychology, Occult, Magic, Yoga, Zen, Meditation, UFOs, Philosophy, Psychology, Art, Archaeology, Sport
1978: 50 titles *1979:* 45 titles *Founded:* 1953

Milano Libri Edizioni+*, Corso Garibaldi 86, I-20121 Milan Tel: (02) 650518/651597
Subjects: Fiction, Juveniles, Essays, Manuals

Minerva Italica SpA+, Via Maglio del Rame 6, I-24100 Bergamo, CP 216 Tel: (035) 237331/232688/211293
Man Dir: Arnoldi Gianni
Br Offs: Via Alfani 68, I-50121 Florence; Via S Sebastiano is 247a, I-98100 Messina; Via Petrella 6, I-20124 Milan; Via A Emo 162–168, I-00136 Rome; via Lattanzio 90–94, I-70126 Bari (all in Italy)
Subjects: General Fiction, Juveniles, University, Secondary & Primary Textbooks, Educational Materials
1978: 574 titles *Founded:* 1951

Moizzi*, Via Fiori Chiari 12, I-20121 Milan Tel: (02) 886169/873453
Subjects: Art, Politics, Science Fiction, Psychology, Satire

Monas Hierogliphica Inc Cooperativa Editrice*, Via Borghetto 5, I-20122, Milan Telex: 32108 Martemon
Editorial: Nicolas Monti; *Publicity:* Carla Manenti
Subjects: Erotica, Art, Architecture
Founded: 1978

Arnoldo **Mondadori** Editore+, CP 1772, I-20100 Milan (Located at: I-2000 Segrate) Tel: (02) 75421 Cable Add: Mondadori Segrate (MI) Telex: 34457
Man Dir: Sergio Polillo; *Editorial:* Dr Franco Migiarra, Dr Sergio Morando; *Sales:* Gian Paolo Slaviero; *Marketing:* Dr Leonardo Mondadori; *Production:* Bruno Borghini; *Publicity:* Dr Romano Billet; *Rights & Permissions:* Donatella Ciapessoni, Dr Marco Polillo
Associate Companies: Auguri di Mondadori, Sommacampagna, I-37066 Verona; Arti Grafiche della Venezie, Viale S Agostino 152, I-36100 Vicenza (qv); Cartiera di Ascoli, Mariono del Tronto, I-63046 Ascoli Piceno; Arti Grafiche della Lombardia, San Donato, I-20097 Milan; Nuova Stampa Mondadori, I-38023 Trento (all in Italy)
Branch Offs: Mondadori EPEE, France; Arnoldo Mondadori Deutschland GmbH, German Federal Republic; Arnoldo Mondadori Editore, Via Belvedere N1, I-37100 Verona, Italy; Arnoldo Mondadori

218 ITALY

Scandinavia AB, Scandinavia; Arnoldo Mondadori Co Ltd, UK; Mondadori Publishing Co, USA
Subjects: General Fiction, Belles Lettres, Poetry, Biography, History, How-to, Music, Art, Philosophy, Reference, Religion, Juveniles, Low- & High-priced Paperbacks, Medicine, Psychology, General Science, Secondary Textbooks, Educational Materials
Book Club: Club Degli Editori (with Giulio Einaudi Editore)
Bookshops: Branches throughout Italy
1977: 600 titles *Founded:* 1907

Edizioni Scolastiche Bruno **Mondadori**+, Via Archimede 23, CP 1772, I-20122 Milan Tel: (02) 792623/795837/795949 Telex: 34457
Man Dir: Roberta Mondadori; *Dirs:* Roberto Gulli, Mario Candiani
Subjects: Textbooks, Reference, Dictionaries, *Easy Readers*
1977: 20 titles

Mondadori Ragazzi*, Via Zeviani 2, I-37100 Verona Tel: 75421 (Segrate) Telex: 34457 Mondedit

Mondoperaio edizioni Avanti SpA+, Via Tomacelli 146, I-00186 Rome
Editorial: Settimio Cavalli
Subjects: Political and Social Science, Philosophy, History of Labour and the Trade Unions, Workers' Movements in Italy and World-Wide, Periodicals — *Mondoperaio, Economia e territorio, Economia e Politica*

Editrice **Morcelliana** SpA+, Via Gabriele Rosa 71, I-25100 Brescia Tel: (030) 46451
Man Dir: Stephano Minelli
Subjects: History, Philosophy, Religion, Social Science
1978: 18 titles *Founded:* 1925

Verlag **Morra**, Via Calabritto 20, I-80121 Naples Tel: 402025
Man Dir: Giuseppe Morra; *Sales:* Giuseppe Orabona
Subject: Art
1977: 5 titles *1978:* 3 titles *Founded:* 1974

Federico **Motta** Editore+*, Via Branda Castiglioni 7, I-20156 Milan Tel: (02) 390404/367708
Subjects: Encyclopaedias, Dictionaries

Società Editrice Il **Mulino**+, Via Santo Stefano 6, I-40125 Bologna Tel: (051) 233415/6
Man Dir: Giovanni Evangelisti; *Sales Dir:* Marcello Bolognini; *Publicity Dir:* Giuseppe Lovato; *Rights & Permissions:* Luisa Pece
Subjects: History, Philosophy, Linguistics & Literary Criticism, Political Science, Law, Economics, Reference, Low-priced Paperbacks, Psychology, Social Science, University Textbooks, Journals
1977: 138 titles *1978:* 112 titles *Founded:* 1954

Ugo **Mursia** Editore SpA, Via Tadino 29, I-20124 Milan Tel: (02) 209341 Cable Add: Umedizioni Milan
Subsidiary Company: Edizioni Scolastiche APE SpA (qv)
Man Dir: Dr Ugo Mursia; *Editorial:* Dr Piero Bajetta; *Publicity:* Floriana De Martino; *Rights & Permissions:* Dr Flavio Fagnani
Subjects: General Fiction, Belles Lettres, Poetry, Biography, History, Music, Art, Philosophy, Reference, Religion, Juveniles, Low- & High-priced Paperbacks, General & Social Science
1977: 180 titles *1978:* 175 titles *Founded:* 1922

Società Editrice **Napoletana** SRL*, Corso Umberto I 34, I-80138 Naples Tel: (02) 206602
Man Dir: Avv A De Dominicis
Subjects: Belles Lettres, Poetry, History, Art
1977: 40 titles

Nardini Editore — Centro Internazionale del Libro SpA*, Via Scipione Ammirato 37, I-50136 Florence Tel: (055) 670330/679997
Subjects: Juveniles, History, Biography, Art, Essays, Classics, Science, Educational
Founded: 1970
Miscellaneous: Part of Giunti Publishing Group (qv)

New Interlitho SpA*, Via Curiel, I-20090 Trezzano S/N Tel: 4451926/4452753 Telex: 32140
Dir & Sales Manager: Renzo Aimini
Subjects: Juveniles, Encyclopaedias

Newton Compton Editori SRL+, Via Germanico 197, I-00192 Rome Tel: 3580205/3580201
Subjects: Paperbacks on General Fiction, Belles Lettres, Poetry, History, Philosophy, Social & General Science, Anthropology, Mathematics, Psychology, Political Science, Reference, How-to, Archaeology

Editrice **Nord** Sdf, Via Rubens 25, I-20148 Milan Tel: 405708/4042207
Man Dir: Gianfranco Viviani; *Editorial:* Saudro Pergameno
1977: approx 52 titles *1978:* approx 200 titles
Subjects: Fantasy and Science Fiction

Nova Rico SpA, Via Colle Ramole 9 CP 473, I-50029 Tavarnuzze, Florence Tel: (055) 2020141 Cable Add: Rico-Firenze Telex: 570407
Subjects: Geographical Globes, Posters

Edizioni di **Novissima***, Via Civitavecchia 102, I-20132 Milan Tel: (02) 2563141/2563151
Subjects: General Fiction, Belles Lettres, Paperbacks

La **Nuova Foglio** SpA*, Piane di Chienti 12, I-62010 Pollenza (MC) Tel: (0733) 517145 Cable Add: La Nuova Foglio Pollenza
Subject: Art

La **Nuova Italia** Editrice+, Via Antonio Giacomini 8, I-50132 Florence Tel: (055) 2798
Man Dirs: Tristano Codignola, Mario Casalini
Br Offs: Via Dieta di Bari 38/c, I-70121 Bari; Via Brugnoli 7, I-40122 Bologna; Via D Cimarosa 14, I-09100 Cagliari; Via Etnea 688, I-95128 Catania; Corso Italia 158/D, I-87100 Cosenza; Via G Fattori 7-9, I-50132 Florence; Corso Europa 454/A, I-16132 Genoa; Via Boncompagni 51/2, I-20139 Milan; Via G Carducci 15, I-80121 Naples; Via M Buonarroti 4, I-35100 Padua; Via F Cordova 95, I-90143 Palermo; Via P Maroncelli 25, I-65100 Pescara; Viale Carso 44-46, I-00195 Rome; Via Colli 24 (angolo Corso Montevecchio), I-10129 Turin; Via Adigetto 39, I-37100 Verona
Subjects: Biography, History, Art, Philosophy, Reference, Young Adult, Low- & High-priced Paperbacks, Psychology, Social Science, University & Secondary Textbooks
1977: 121 titles *1978:* 75 titles *Founded:* 1926

Nuova Vallecchi Editore SpA, Via Gino Capponi 26, CP 409, I-50121 Florence Tel: (055) 587141/2/3 Cable Add: Nuova Vallecchi Editore, Firenze
Man Dir: Lodovico Bevilacqua
Subjects: Art, Fiction, Classics
1978: 80 titles *1979:* 70 titles *Founded:* 1975

O S (Organizzazioni Speciali SRL)+, Via R Franchi 5, CP 1442, I-50137 Florence Tel: 606290/607555
Subjects: Psychology, Economics, Education
Miscellaneous: Member of Giunti Publishing Group

Edizioni **Ofiria**, see Giunti Publishing Group

Leo S **Olschki**+, CP 66, I-50100 Florence Tel: (055) 687444/5
Shipping Add: Viuzzo del Pozzetto (Viale Europa), I-50126 Florence
Man Dir: Alessandro Olschki
Subjects: Biography, History, Music, Art, Reference, Bibliography, Religion, Paperbacks, Medicine, Social Science, University Textbooks, General Humanities
1978: 102 titles *Founded:* 1886

Olympia Press Italia*, Corso Concordia 9, I-20129 Milan Tel: (02) 780164
Man Dir: Mario Carrillo
Subjects: General Fiction, General Science, Erotica
1977: 13 titles

Edizioni **Omnia** Medica*, Via San Michele degli Schlazi 63, I-56100 Pisa Tel: (050) 570016
Subjects: Science, Medicine

Nuove Edizioni **Operaie** SRL*, Via Crescenzio 58, I-00193 Rome Tel: (06) 314979
Man Dirs: Angelo Ruggieri; Pietro Brugnoli
Subjects: Politics, Sociology, Religion, Culture
1977: 34 titles *Founded:* 1976

Organizzazioni Speciali SRL, see O S

Edizioni **Orientalia Christiana***, Piazza Santa Maria Maggiore 7, I-00185 Rome Tel: (06) 7312254/55
General Dir: Ignacio Ortiz de Urbina
Subjects: Eastern Christianity (History, Theology, Liturgy, Canon Law etc), Periodicals: *Orientalia Christiana Analecta, Concilium Florentinum, Documenta et Scriptores, Anaphorae Syriacae*
1977: 5 titles *Founded:* 1923

Edizioni **Ottaviano***, Via S Croce 2, I-20122 Milan Tel: 8350832
Subjects: Politics, Law
1977: 22 titles *1978:* 25 titles *Founded:* 1974

Paideia Editrice*, Via Corsica 58m, I-25100 Brescia Tel: (030) 342523
Man Dir: Dr Giuseppe Scarpat
Subjects: Belles Lettres, Poetry, Music, Art, Philosophy, Religion, University Textbooks
1978: 33 titles
Miscellaneous: Firm also publishes literary review *Paideia; Annali della Facoltá di Lingue e Letterature straniere di Ca' Foscari; Rivista Biblica* (Biblical Review); *Studi Biblici*

G B **Palumbo** e C Editore SpA+, Via B Ricasoli 59, 90139 Palermo Tel: (091) 588850/334961
Manager: Giovan Battista Palumbo
1978: 27 titles

Panda Press SRL*, Via Curiel 19, I-20090 Trezzano S/N (MI) Tel: 4451926/4452753 Telex: 32140

Man Dir: Renzo Aimini; *Rights & Permissions:* Louise Kissane
Subject: Juveniles
Founded: 1971

Edizioni **Panini** SpA+*, Viale Emilio Po 380, I-41100 Modena Tel: (059) 331133 Cable Add: Edipan Modena Italia Telex: 51650
Publisher: Franco Panini
Subjects: Educational, Sport, Card albums for children

Edizioni **Paoline**, Corso Regina Margherita 1, CP 1333 I-10100 Turin Tel: (011) 836744/5/6/7 Cable Add: Edipaoline
Man Dir, Sales: Gino Pizzeghello; *Editorial:* Valentino Gambi; *Production:* Francesco Chessa; *Publicity:* Lamberto Schiatti
Parent Company: Pia Società, San Paolo
Associated Companies: Edizioni Paoline Dischi — Audiovision; Editrice SAIE, Italy (qv)
Subjects: General Fiction, Belles Lettres, Biography, History, How-to, Music, Art, Philosophy, Reference, Religion, Juveniles, Low- & High-priced Paperbacks, Medicine, Psychology
Bookshops: 98 bookshops throughout Italy
1977: 297 titles *Founded:* 1914

Casa Editrice **Pàtron** SAS, Quarto Inferiore, Via Badini 12–14, I-40127 Bologna Tel: 767003
Man Dir: Adelson Pàtron
Subsidiary Company: Libreria Editrice Universitaria Pàtron, Via Marzolo 28, I-35100 Padua
Subjects: Literature, Linguistics, History, Philosophy, Psychology, Sociology, Art, Medicine, Engineering
Bookshop: Libreria Internazionale Pàtron, Via Zamboni 24, I-40126 Bologna

'**Pensiero Scientifico**' SRL+, Via Panama 48, I-00198 Rome Tel: 863633/859506
Subject: Medicine
1977: 45 titles *1978:* 34 titles

Piccin Editore sas, Via Brunacci 12, I-35100 Padua Tel: (049) 38955/24841/23350
Man Dir, Editorial, Production, Rights & Permissions: Dr Massimo Piccin; *Sales:* Dr Raffello Steccanella
Subjects: Medicine, Chemistry, General Science
Bookshops: Via Festa del Perdono 14, Milan; Via Porciglia 10, Padua; Via Lancisi 37, Rome
1977: c 200 titles *1978:* 200 titles *Founded:* 1954

Editrice **Piccoli** SpA+, Via Rosellini 12, I-20124 Milan Tel: (02) 606341 Cable Add: Lapiccoli Milano
Man Dir, Editorial: Oliviero Dolci; *Sales:* Giuliano Barisone; *Marketing:* Leonardo Vasco
Subject: Children's Books
1978: 50 titles *1979:* 52 titles *Founded:* 1943

La **Pietra**, Via Fulvio Testi 75, I-20126 Milan Tel: (02) 6428440
Man Dir: Enzo Nizza
Subjects: Politics, Anti-Fascism and Resistance, History, Art
1977: 18 titles *1978:* 22 titles *Founded:* 1962

Amilcare **Pizzi** SpA, Via M de Vizzi 86, Cinisello Balsamo, Milan Tel: (02) 6188821 Telex: 330006
Chairman: Rodolfo Pizzi; *Man Dir:* Fulvio G Nembrini; *Sales:* Gilberto Leuci
Associate Company: Silvana Editoriale d'Arte, Via M de Vizzi 86, Cimisello 13, Milan
Subjects: Art, Illustrated Books, Encyclopaedias, Paperbacks, Calendars, Catalogues
Founded: 1920

Neri **Pozza**+, CP 513, I-36100 Vicenza (Located at: Via Gazzolle 6, I-36100 Vicenza) Tel: (0444) 27228/36585 Cable Add: Edipozza
Man Dir: Neri Pozza
Subjects: Ancient and Modern Art, Literary Criticism and History, Politics, Local Interest
1978: 14 titles *Founded:* 1946

Priuli e Verlucca, Editori*, Via Soana 6, I-10015 Ivrea Tel: (0125) 48364 Cable Add: Priuli Verlucca Ivrea
Chairman: Cesare Verlucca; *Dir of Production:* Gherardo Priuli
1977: 24 titles *Founded:* 1971
Subjects: Life and Traditions of the Alpine Region, Mountains and Mountaineering, Photographic Studies of Regional Costume and Culture, Graphic Arts

Quadragono Libri, Viale Diaz 10, I-31015 Conegliano (TV) Tel: (0438) 21240/31840
Man Dir: Vigiak Bugara Mario
Subjects: Illustrated books for children and adults
1977: 7 titles *1978:* 6 titles *Founded:* 1974

Editrice **Queriniana**+, Via Piamarta 6, I-25100 Brescia Tel: (030) 294653
Man Dir: Gianfranco Ransenigo; *Sales:* Ettore Pelati; *Advertising:* Mario de Risio; *Rights & Permissions:* Rosino Gibellini
Br Offs: Rome, Milan, Turin, Verona
Subjects: Philosophy, Religion, Theology
Bookshop: Libreria Queriniana, Via Trieste 13, I-25100 Brescia
1977: 100 titles *Founded:* 1965

R Editore*, Via Larga 9, Ortonovo (LS)
Associate Company: Editions R, France (qv)

Edizioni **R A I** Radiotelevisione Italiana (ERI) SpA, see ERI

Franco Maria **Ricci** Editore+, Via Cino Del Duca 4/8, I-20122 Milan Tel: (02) 798804/793117/780275
Man Dir: Franco Maria Ricci
Associated Companies: Fine Books, 160 East, 92 St, New York, USA; Galerie 12, 12 rue des Beaux Arts, Paris 6, France
Subsidiary Company: Deco Press
Subjects: Art, Graphic Design, Reference
Bookshop: Franco Maria Ricci, 12 rue des Beaux-Arts, Paris 6, France
Book Club: Club dei Bibliofili; Collectors Club of Franco Maria Ricci
1977: 65 titles *1978:* 70 titles *Founded:* 1965
Miscellaneous: Publish limited editions, including Bodoni editions & *Encyclopédie* of Diderot & D'Alembert

Riccardo **Ricciardi** Editore SpA+, Via G Morone 3, I-20121 Milan Tel: (02) 875155/804248
Man Dir: Dr Maurizio Mattioli
Subjects: Italian Classics, History, Philosophy
1977: 4 titles *1978:* 6 titles

Rico SpA*, I-50029 Florence-Certosa Tel: 2020141/2/3 Telex: 57407
Subjects: Art, Scientific, Geography, Posters

Arti Grafiche **Ricordi** SpA*, Via Cortina d'Ampezzo 10, I-20139 Milan Tel: (02) 536355 Telex: 31177 Idrocir Cable Add: Graficordi
Man Dir: Giulio Sala
Parent Company: G & C Ricordi SpA, Via Berchet 2, Milan (qv)
Subject: Fine Art Prints

G e C **Ricordi** SpA+, Via Berchet 2, I-20121 Milan Tel: (02) 8881 Telex: 310177 RICOR I
President: N H Carlo Origoni; *Vice-President:* Eugenio Clausetti; *Man Dir:* Dr Guido Rignano
Subjects: Scholarly, Music, Art
Subsidiaries: Ricordi Dischi SpA & Ricordi Arti Grafiche SpA, Via Cortina d'Ampezzo 10, I-20139 Milan; Gruppo Editoriale Musica Leggera Ricordi, Via Berchet 2, I-20121 Milan
1978: 76 titles

Editori **Riuniti***, Via Serchio 9–11, Rome Tel: (06) 866383
Man Dir: Roberto Bonchio; *Sales Dir:* Marco Rocchi; *Publicity & Advertising:* Franco Bertone; *Rights & Permissions:* Cecilia Fasano
Subjects: General Fiction, Textbooks, Reference, Paperbacks, History, Art, General & Social Science, Religion, Juveniles
Founded: 1953

Rizzoli Editore SpA+*, Via Civitavecchia 102, I-20132 Milan Tel: (02) 2588 Cable Add: Rizzoli Editore, Milan Telex: Rizzoli 33119
Chairman: Andrea Rizzoli; *Man Dir:* Angelo Rizzoli; *Editorial:* Dr Sergio Pautasso; *Marketing:* Dr Romano Zago; *Rights & Permissions:* Anita Calabi, Vera Salvago
Subjects: General Fiction, Belles Lettres, Poetry, Biography, History, Music, Hobbies, Medicine, Art, Religion, Juveniles, Low- & High-priced Paperbacks, Social Science, Reference, Textbooks
Subsidiaries: Rizzoli Film SpA; Cineriz SpA

Litografia A **Romero** SA*, Avenida Angel Romero s/n, Apartado 324, Santa Cruz de Tenerife Tel: 221540-2 Cable Add: Larsa, Tenerife Telex: 92159 Larsa E
Dir: Edgardo Romero
Subjects: Textbooks, Juveniles

Rosenberg e Sellier srl+, Via Andrea Doria 14, I-10123 Turin Tel: (011) 518388 Cable Add: Rosenberg Sellier
Man Dir: Ugo Gianni Rosenberg; *Editorial, Rights & Permissions:* Katie Roggero, Cristina Savio; *Production, Publicity:* Katie Roggero
Subjects: Philology, Social Sciences, Philosophy
Bookshop: Via Andrea Doria, I-10123 Turin
1978: 15 titles *1979:* 24 titles *Founded:* 1883
Miscellaneous: Firm is International import-export bookseller and subscription agent

Edizioni La **Ruota***, Via Arzaga 24, I-20146 Milan Tel: (02) 4158896
Subjects: Encyclopaedias, Education

Rusconi Editore+*, Via Vitruvio 43, I-20124 Milan Tel: (02) 2775 Cable Add: Rusconi Editore Milan
Editor: Alfredo Cattabiani; *Sales Dir:* Giuseppe Zanetti; *Publicity:* Carlo Arditi de Castelvetere; *Advertising Dir:* Domenico Cattaneo; *Rights & Permissions:* Maura Bastiglia
Br Off: Via Leonida Bissolati 76, I-00100 Rome
Subjects: General Fiction, Belles Lettres, Poetry, History, Philosophy, Religion, Low- and High-priced Paperbacks

Founded: 1957
Bookshops: Libreria Internaz Rusconi, Via Vitruvio 43, I-20124 Milan & Via Carlo Porta 1, Milan

S A G E P+, Piazza Merani 1, I-16145 Genoa Tel: (010) 313453 Telex: 211343 SAGEP I
Publisher: Eugenio de Andreis; *Sales Manager:* Carla Bisacchi; *Press Chief:* Carla Costa
Subjects: Architecture, Art, Economy, Ethnography, History, Natural Sciences, Travel and Tourism
1977: 42 titles *1978:* 46 titles *Founded:* 1967

S A I E Editrice*, Corso Regina Margherita 2, I-10153 Turin Tel: (011) 870887
Subjects: Reference, Encyclopaedias, Dictionaries, Literature Criticism, Multimedia, Philosophy, Linguistics, Languages, Economics, Religion, Medicine, History, Earth Sciences, Philosophy, Education, Art, Juveniles

S C O D E+, Via Ampère 28/a, I-20131 Milan Tel: (02) 2360244/5 Cable Add: SCODE Milano
Publisher: Carlo Gandini
Subjects: Architecture, History, Hobbies, Arts, Maps, Literary Criticism, Religion, Encyclopaedias, Linguistics, Educational

S E I (Società Editrice Internazionale)+, Corso Regina Margherita 176, I-10152 Turin Tel: (011) 481604/5/6/7/8 Cable Add: SEI Turin Telex: 221114 CSIND I 114 SEI
Man Dir: Gian Nicola Pivano; *Editorial:* Francesco Meotto; *Sales:* Paolo Bottazzi; *Production:* Enrico Paolucci Delle Rowcole
Branch Off: at Bari, Bologna, Florence, Genoa, Milan, Naples, Palermo, Padua, Rome, Turin, Pescara, Catania
Subjects: General Fiction, Belles Lettres, Biography, History, Art, Philosophy, Religion, Juveniles, Psychology, General & Social Science, Educational Materials, Textbooks, Paperbacks
1977: 109 titles *1978:* 110 titles *Founded:* 1910

S I S A R Edizioni (Società italiana stampati affini reclame) SpA, Via Marco d'Agrate 35, I-20139 Milan Tel: (02) 5393846/5397441/2
Man Dir: Mazio Occhipinti
Subjects: Art, Architecture
1977: 21 titles *1978:* 30 titles *Founded:* 1953

S T E M-Mucchi (Società Tipografica Editrice Modenese)+*, Viale Nicola Fabrizi 15, I-41100 Modena Tel: (059) 222162/214152
Subjects: History, Philosophy, Science, Technical, Textbooks, Hobbies, Literature, Education, Law, Languages
1977: 8 titles *1978:* 6 titles

Saar SRL*, Viale di Porta Vercellina 14, I-20123 Milan Tel: (02) 4696251 Cable Add: Saar Milano
Man Dir: Walter Gurtler; *Sales:* Sergio Balloni
Subject: Juveniles

Il **Saggiatore** SpA+, Via San Senatore 10, I-20122 Milan Tel: (02) 875119/875892
Man Dir: Maria Laura Boselli; *Rights & Permissions:* Elena Panizza
Subjects: History, Philosophy, Economics, Architecture, Mathematics, Social Sciences, Geography, Linguistics, Art, Music, Belles Lettres, Afro-Asian Studies, Latin American Studies, Juveniles
1977: 21 titles *1978:* 40 titles *Founded:* 1958

La **Salamandra**, Via Fabio Filzi 27, I-20124 Milan Tel: (02) 667097
Man Dir, Editorial, all other offices: Giovanni Barbatiello
Subjects: Feminism, Critiques of society, Libertarian thought, Critical Marxism, Sexual freedom, Psychoanalysis, Biography, Autobiography
Bookshop: Celuc, Via Santa Valeria 5, I-20123 Milan
1978: 16 titles *1979:* 12 titles *Founded:* 1975

Salamon e Agustoni Editori, Via Montenapoleone 3, I-20121 Milan Tel: (02) 700832
Man Dir: H Salamon
Subject: Art, *Il Conoscitore di stampe — Print Collector*
Founded: 1970

Adriano **Salani** SpA+, Via Cittadella 7, I-50144 Florence Tel: (055) 472968/9 Cable Add: Salani Editore Florence
Man Dir: Mauro Finardi
Subjects: Juveniles, Religion, Art, History, Fiction, Social Science
Founded: 1862

Casa Editrice G C **Sansoni** SpA+*, Viale Mazzini 46, I-50132 Florence Tel: (055) 677451/667151 Cable Add: Sansedi Telex: 57466 Sansint
Man Dir: Federico Gentile; *General Manager:* Giovanni Gentile; *Publicity & Advertising:* Mario Biondi
Subjects: Belles Lettres, Poetry, Biography, History, How-to, Music, Art, Philosophy, Reference, Religion, Low- & High-priced Paperbacks, Medicine, Psychology, General & Social Science, Secondary & Primary Textbooks, Educational Materials, Juveniles, Law
Founded: 1873
Associates: USES-Utet/Sansoni Edizioni Scientifiche, Via J Nardi 37, I-50132 Florence; SADEA SpA, Viale Mazzini 46, I-50132 Florence
Subsidiaries: Licosa-Libreria Commissionaria Sansoni SpA, Via Lamarmora 45, I-50121 Florence; Industria Grafica L'Impronta SpA, Via di Scandicci Alto 28, I-50018 Scandicci (Florence)
Miscellaneous: Coproduction with Sansoni International

Scala Istituto Fotografico Editoriale+*, Via Chiantigiana 56, I-50011 Antella-Florence Tel: (055) 641541 Cable Add: Scalafoto Telex: Scalapub 58428
Subjects: Textbooks, Multimedia, Illustrated Art Books, Photography, Slides

Salvatore **Sciascia**+, Corso Umberto 111, I-93100 Caltanissetta Tel: 21946
Subjects: Fiction, History, Business, Industry, Arts, Maps, Agriculture, Literature, Mass Media, Medicine, Music, Education, Philosophy, Politics, Psychology, Religion, Social Sciences, Linguistics
Bookshops: Corso Umberto 111, Caltanissetta; Via Liberta 86, Caltanissetta
1977: 32 titles *Founded:* 1946

Libreria **Scientifica** Editrice*, Corso Umberto I 38-40, I-80138 Naples Tel: (02) 206247
Dir: Dr A De Dominicis
Subjects: Belles Lettres, Poetry, History, Philosophy, Low-priced Paperbacks, University & Secondary Textbooks
Bookshop: Corso Umberto I-38-40, I-80138 Naples
Founded: 1944
Miscellaneous: Associate company of Società Editrice Napoletana SRL (qv)

Edizioni **Scientifiche Italiane***, Via Chiatamone 7, I-80121 Naples Tel: (081) 393346/391921/230021
Subjects: General & Social Science, Architecture, History, Arts, Maps, Agriculture, Literature, Medicine, Music, Philosophy, Law, Religion, Languages

Edizioni **Scolastiche** APE SpA, Via Abbondio Sangiorgio 12, I-20145 Milan Tel: (02) 315118/341807
Man Dir: Dr Franco Turri
Subjects: Textbooks
1979: 35 titles *Founded:* 1974
Miscellaneous: Firm is a subsidiary of Ugo Mursia Editore SpA (qv)

Editrice La **Scuola** SpA+, Via Cadorna 11, Brescia Tel: (030) 47461 Cable Add: Lascuola Brescia Telex: 30836 Lascuola
President: Dr Ing Paolo Peroni; *Man Dir:* Dr Ing Adolfo Lombardi; *General Manager:* Dr Prof Giusto Marchese
Associate Companies: E Co S Didaltica SpA, I-10799 Rome, Italy; Morcelliana Editrice, Italy (qv); Edizione Studium (Vita Nova SpA), Italy (qv)
Br Offs: Bari, Bologna, Milan, Naples, Rome
Subjects: Philosophy, Religion, Juveniles, Psychology, Secondary & Primary Textbooks, Educational Materials
1977: 180 titles *1978:* 200 titles *Founded:* 1904

Sellerio Editore, Via Siracusa 50, I-90141 Palermo Tel: (091) 250390/250587
Subjects: Literature, Popular Art, Food and Wine
1978: 21 titles *1979:* 10 titles *Founded:* 1969

Silvana Editoriale Srl+, Via M de Vizzi 86, Cinisello Balsamo, Milan Tel: (02) 6172464
Chairman: Rodolfo Pizzi; *Foreign Rights:* Fulvio G Nembrini
Parent Company: Amilcare Pizzi SpA, Italy (qv)
Subjects: Art, Facsimile books, Photographs, Architecture, Illustrated books
1977: 25 titles *1978:* 13 titles

Sonzogno SpA, Via Mecenate 87/6, I-20138 Milan Tel: (02) 501101/2/3 Telex: 32321
Dir: Vittorio Di Giuro
Subjects: Fiction, Crafts, Nonfiction, Games, Sports, Hobbies, Languages
Founded: 1861

La **Sorgente** Srl*, Via Garofalo 44, I-20133 Milan Tel: (02) 230025 and 230720
Man Dir, Rights & Permissions: Dr Giorgio Vignati
Subject: Juveniles
1977: 70 titles *Founded:* 1936

Sperling e Kupfer Editori SpA+, Via Monte di Pietà 24, I-20121 Milan Tel: 861980/8056407 Cable Add: Kupferedit, Milan
Dirs: Nicola Carraro, Tiziano M Barbieri
Subjects: General Fiction & Nonfiction, Biography, Health, Travel, Sports, How-to
1979: 80 titles *Founded:* 1889

Le **Stelle** SRL+, Via G Vasari 15, I-20135 Milan Tel: (02) 5455641
Subjects: General Fiction, Belles Lettres, Poetry, Biography, History, Religion, Juveniles, Secondary & Primary Textbooks, Educational Materials
1977: 21 titles *1978:* 26 titles *Founded:* 1954

Studio Editoriale*, Via Spiga 1, I-20121 Milan Tel: (02) 784129
Subjects: Textbooks, Juveniles, Flowers, Herbalism, Graphics

Edizioni **Studium** (Vita Nova SpA)+, Via Crescenzio 63, I-00193 Rome Tel: (06) 6565846/655456 Cable Add: Studium Rome
Subjects: Literature, Pedagogy, Psychology, History, Philosophy, Religion, General & Social Science, University Textbooks, Periodical—*Studium*
1977: 34 titles *1978:* 33 titles *Founded:* 1973

Sugarco Edizioni SRL, Viale Tunisia 41, I-20154 Milan Tel: (02) 652192/6570569
Man Dir: Dr Massimo Pini; *Editorial:* Massimo Rondinelli; *Sales:* Vincenzo Nagari; *Production:* Gianni Bagetto
Subjects: General Fiction, Belles Lettres, Biography, History, Philosophy, Guides
Founded: 1956

Tamburini Editore SpA+*, Via Pascoli 55, I-20133 Milan Tel: (02) 292320/296662/ 235740/235772 Cable Add: Tambeditor Milan
Man Dir: Gianni Tamburini; *Sales Dir:* Laura Piatti; *Publicity & Advertising, Rights & Permissions:* Sergio Guida
Subjects: Medicine, Psychology, Engineering, General Science, University & Secondary Textbooks
Founded: 1868
Bookshop: Via Pascole 55, I-20133 Milan

Nicola **Teti** e C Editore SRL+*, Via Enrico Noe 23, I-20133 Milan Tel: (02) 2043597/2043539
Man Dir: Nicola Teti; *Editorial:* Piero Lavatelli; *Sales:* Vincenzo Fracchiolla; *Production:* Rita Vaccari, Vanna Guzzi; *Publicity:* Nino Oppo; *Rights & Permissions:* Rita Vaccari
Subjects: Textbooks, Encyclopaedias, Politics, Marxism, Social Science, Juveniles, Reprints of Socialist documents, Natural History, History, Pedagogy
1977: 50 titles *Founded:* 1971

Trec Edizioni Pregiate, Via Cassia Antica 132, I-00191 Rome Tel: 3288361
Sole Administrator: Antonino Pecora
Subjects: Old Artistic Treasures, Graphics, Reproduction of Antique Manuscripts
1977: 3 titles *Founded:* 1971

Edizioni Il **Tripode** SRL+, Viale Gramsci 12, I-80122 Naples Tel: (081) 683086
Man Dir: Dott Giuseppe Martano

U T E T (Unione Tipografico-Editrice Torinese)+, Corso Raffaello 28, CP 1166 Ferrovia, I-10125 Turin Tel: (011) 688666 Cable Add: UUUTET Turin
President: Dr Gianni Merlini
Subjects: Belles Lettres, History, Art, Architecture, Music, Religion, Philosophy, Reference, Psychology, Law, Veterinary Science, General & Social Science, Juveniles, University Textbooks
Founded: 1795

Unites SRL, Annuario Politecnico Italiano, Via Silvio Pellico 12, I-20121 Milan Tel: (02) 874566/874658
Publicity: Gianola Carlo
Subjects: Year-books, Reference

Editrice **Universitaria**, see Giunti Publishing Group

Società Editrice **Universo**+*, Via G Battista Morgagni 1, I-00161 Rome Tel: (06) 859063/8445243
Subjects: Medicine, Physics, Chemistry, Engineering, Mathematics

Antonio **Vallardi** Editore*, Via Senato 25, I-20121 Milan Tel: (02) 705741/4 Telex: Garzal 31461
Dir: Luciano Schinetti
Subjects: Art, How-to, Reference, Industries, Maps, Juveniles, Textbooks, Literature, Travel, Architecture
Founded: 1822

Vallardi Industrie Grafiche+*, Via Trieste 20, I-20020 Lainate (Milan) Tel: (02) 9370284/5 Cable Add: Valgraf, Lainate
Publisher: Giuseppe Vallardi; *Editorial:* Elisabetta Vallardi
Subjects: Atlases, Juveniles

Augusto **Vallerini** Editore di Alberto Vallerini*, Via Consoli del Mare 15, Pisa Tel: 40604
Orders to: Andrea Vallerini (Libri Esteri e Abbonamenti), Via dei Mille 13, I-56100 Pisa Tel: 40393
Subjects: Pisa — past and present, Italian Scientific and Medical books, Reprints

Società Editrice **Vannini**+, Viale d'Italia 8b, CP 68, I-25100 Brescia Tel: (030) 56272/57089 Cable Add: Vannini Brescia
Subjects: Scholastic, Reference, Law
1977: 11 titles *1978:* 13 titles

Giovanni de **Vecchi** Editore SpA, see De Vecchi

Z I R A L (Zajednica Izdanja Ranjeni Labud)*, Via Merulana 124b, Rome
Dirs: Dr Lucijan Kordic, Professor Dr D Vinko Lasic
Head Off: 4851 Drexel Blvd, Chicago Il, 60515 USA
Subjects: Religion, History, Literature

Nicola **Zanichelli** SpA+*, Via Irnerio 34, I-40126 Bologna Tel: (051) 293111
Chairman: Giovanni Enriques
Subjects: History, Philosophy, Reference, Mathematics, Chemistry, Biology, Engineering, General Science, University & Secondary Textbooks, Law, Psychology, Visual Design, Architecture, Juveniles, Physics, Electronics, Linguistics, Literature, Geography, Earth Sciences, Paperbacks
1977: 105 titles *Founded:* 1859
Bookshop: Libreria Zanichelli, Portici del Pavaglione, CP 227, I-40124 Bologna

Casa Editrice La **Zattera***, Largo C Felice 76, I-09100 Cagliari
Bookshop: Libreria Internazionale Fratelli Cocco, Largo C Felice 76, Cagliari
Subjects: Books on Sardinia

Literary Agents

Agenzia Letteraria Internazionale, Via Manzoni 41, I-20121 Milan Tel: (02) 6572465/6572594/6572596

Maria-Pia D'**Arborio***, Viale Tiziano 5, Rome

Ursula **Caputo**, Via Pisacane 25, I-20129 Milan

Creative Management Associates Ltd*, Via Lazio 9, I-00189 Rome

Dais Literary Agency*, Via Nicotera 7, I-00195 Rome Tel: (06) 353126

Eulama SA, Via Torino 135, I-00184 Rome Tel: (06) 460636
President: Harald Kahnemann
Specializes in social sciences, politics, psychology, education, philosophy, religion, linguistics and literature, mass-media, architecture, urban studies, Latin-American literature and books for young readers

I L A (International Literary Agency)*, I-18015 Terzorio — IM Tel: San Remo (0184) 44111 Cable Add: Friedmann Terzorio (IM) Legal Add: 305 East 75th St, New York, NY 10021, USA
Specializes in handling of foreign language translation rights to multi-volume book and magazine projects, Children's books, Encyclopedias, Best Sellers (in all European languages)

Living Literary Agency Elfriede Pexa, Via E Q Visconti 103, I-00193 Rome Tel: (06) 381720

William **Morris** Organization SpA*, Via Nomentana 60, I-00161 Rome

Natoli and **Stefan** Literary Agency, Galleria Buenos Aires 14, I-20124 Milan

Christa **Pucci***, Largo Generale Gonzaga del Vodicez, I-00195 Rome Tel: (06) 317996

Rizzoli Editore SpA, Via Rizzoli 2, I-20132 Milan

Transafrica*, Via Trieste 34, I-25100 Brescia Tel: (03) 55080/54844
Specialization: African Subjects

Book Clubs

Club Degli Editori, Viale Majno 10, I-20129 Milan
Owned by: Arnoldo Mondadori Editore (Milan)

Club dei Bibliofili and **Collectors Club of Franco Maria Ricci***, Via Santa Sofia 8, I-20122 Milan
Owned by: Franco Maria Ricci Editore (Milan)

Selezione dal **Reader's Digest**: Grandi Opere di Selezione*, Via Alserio 10, I-20159 Milan

Major Booksellers

Casalini Libri, Via B da Maiano 3, I-50014 Fiesole (Florence) Tel: (055) 599941 Cable Add: Casalini Fiesole
Man Dirs: Mario Casalini, Gerda Casalini von Grebmer
General Book Exporter

Libreria Internazionale Fratelli **Cocco***, Largo C Felice 76, I-09100 Cagliari, Sardinia
Also at Via Manno 9, I-09100 Cagliari, Sardinia

Libreria **Feltrinelli***, Via del Babuino 41, Rome Tel: (06) 6793360; Via Carlo Alberto 2 and Piazza Castello 9, Turin; Piazza Porta Ravegnana 1, Bologna; Via Cavour 12-20, I-50129 Florence Tel: (055) 292196

Libreria SF **Flaccovio**, Via Ruggiero Settimo 37, I-90139 Palermo

Libreria G G **Görlich***, Via del Politecnico 5, I-20121 Milan

Libreria **Gregoriana***, Via Roma 37, I-35100 Padua
Also at Via Vescovado 33, I-35100 Padua

Ulrico **Hoepli** Libreria Internazionale, Via Hoepli 5, I-20121 Milan Tel: (02) 865446
Manager: Dr Ulrico Carlo Hoepli

Libreria **Liberma**, Via di Saponara 20A, I-00125 Acilia-Roma, CP 492 (San Silvestro) Roma

Libreria A **Longo**, Via A Diaz 39, I-48100 Ravenna Tel: (0544) 33500

Libreria G **Luna***, I-06034 Foligno

Libreria Editrice **Minerva***, Via Castiglione 13-15, Bologna

Libreria Commissionaria Internazionale di Raffaele **Pancaldi**, Via S Petronio Vecchio 3, I-40125 Bologna Tel: (051) 229466
Man: Raffaele Pancaldi

Libreria Internazionale **Pàtron***, Via Zamboni 24, I-40126 Bologna Tel: (051) 275735

Libreria all' Accademia SNC di **Randi** Pietro, Via S Lucia 1, I-35100 Padua
(The above is the head office address only)
Shops: Libreria Draghi-Randi, Via Cavour 17-19; Libreria Universitaria, Via 8 Febbraio 10; Libraria Accademia, Via Accademia 2-4; Libreria Nuova Moderna, Via Paolotti 5 (all CP 1003, I-35100 Padua Tel: (049) 20425/35976/26676/24525/26648

Libreria **Rizzoli**, Galleria Colonna, Largo Chigi, Rome
Manager: Enrico Di Nappo
Galleria Vittorio Emanuele II 79, I-20121 Milan
Manager: Attilio Pupella

Rosenberg e Sellier Srl, Via Andrea Doria 14, I-10123 Turin
Proprietors: Ugo Gianni Rosenberg, Elvi Rosenberg; International import-export booksellers and subscription agents

Libreria **Rosmini** di R Maly*, Corso Rosmini 30, I-38068 Rovereto

Libreria **Seeber***, Via dei Tornabuoni 70 r, I-50123 Florence

Libreria **Sperling & Kupfer**, Piazza San Babila 1, I-20122 Milan

Major Libraries

Biblioteca **Ambrosiana**, Piazza Pio XI, 2, I-20123 Milan Tel: (02) 800146
Librarian: Angelo Paredi

Biblioteca **Angelica***, Piazza S Agostino 8, I-00186 Rome Tel: (06) 655874

Biblioteca Comunale dell' **Archiginnasio***, Portici del Pavaglione, Piazza Galvani 1, I-40124 Bologna Tel: 225509/279565

Biblioteca dell' **Archivio Storico** Civico e Biblioteca Trivulziana*, Castello Sforzesco, I-20121 Milan Tel: 6236, int 3946/3960/3967

Archivio Centrale dello Stato*, Piazzale degli Archivi, EUR, I-00144 Rome
Tel: (06) 596555
General Dir: Prof Dr Renato Grispo
National Archives

Biblioteca Estense, Biblioteca Universitaria, Largo Porta S Agostino 309, I-41100 Modena Tel: Central (059) 222248; Director 210530

Biblioteca Nazionale **Braidense***, Palazzo di Brera, Via Brera 28, I-20121 Milan
Tel: (02) 872376/808345
Dir: Dr Letitzia Pecorella Vergnano

Biblioteca Nazionale **Centrale***, Piazza Cavalleggeri 1, Florence Tel: 287052; Director 294423

Biblioteca Nazionale **Centrale**, Vittorio Emanuele II, Viale Castro Pretorio, I-00185 Rome Tel: (06) 4989
Dir: Dr Luciana Mancusi

Biblioteca Nazionale **Marciana**, Palazzi della Libreria Vecchia e della Zecca, San Marco 7, I-30124 Venice Tel: (041) 708788
Dir: Dr Gian Albino Ravalli Modoni

Biblioteca Nazionale **Vittorio Emanuele III**, I-80132 Naples (Palazzo Reale) Tel: (081) 407921/40282/425093/416212
Dir: Dr Maria Cecaro

Biblioteca Musicale Governativa del **Conservatorio di Musica** S Cecilia*, Via dei Greci 18, Rome Tel: (06) 6784552/12

European University Institute Library, Badia Fiesolana, Via dei Roccettini 5, I-50016 San Domenico di Fiesole, Florence Tel: (055) 477931 Telex: 58528 ive

Biblioteca Medicea **Laurenziana**, Piazza S Lorenzo 9, I-50123 Florence Tel: (055) 210760/214443
Chief Librarian: Dr Antonietta Morandini

Biblioteca Comunale **Malatestiana**, Piazza Bufalini 1, I-47023 Cesena (Forlì)
Tel: 21297

Biblioteca **Palatina***, Palazzo della Pilotta, Parma Tel: (0521) 22217

Biblioteca **Riccardiana**, Via dei Ginori 10, I-50129 Florence Tel: (055) 212586, 211379
Dir: Dr Maria Jole Minicucci

Università degli Studi di Firenze, Biblioteca della Facolta di Lettere e Filosofia*, Piazza Brunelleschi 4, I-50121 Florence Tel: (55) 260705
Dir: Dott Tomaso Urso

Library Associations

Associazione Italiana Biblioteche, c/o Istituto di Patologia del Libro, Via Milano 76, I-00184 Rome
Italian Library Association
Chairman: Dr Angela Vinay *Secretary:* Dr Attilio Mauro Caproni
Publications: Bollettino d'Informazioni; Quaderni del Bollettino d'Informazione

Associazione Italiana per la Documentazione e Informazione*, Piazza Indipendenza 11 B, I-00185 Rome
Italian Association of Documentation and Information
Secretary: Rag Bruno Fratter
Publications: Documentazione e Informazione (yearly)

Associazione Nazionale Archivistica Italiana*, Viale Trastevere 215, I-00153 Rome
National Associationnn of Italian Archivists
Secretary: Antonio Dentoni-Litta
Publication: Archivi e Cultúra (2 a year)

Ente Nazionale per le Biblioteche Popolari e Scolastiche*, Via Michele Mercati 4, I-00197 Rome
National Organization for Public and Academic Libraries
Publication: La Parola e il Libro (monthly)

Federazione Italiana delle Biblioteche Popolari*, c/o La 'Società Umanitaria', Via Daverio 7, I-20122 Milan
Federation of Italian Public Libraries
General Dir: Marco Cavallotti
Publication: La Cultura Popolare (6 a year)

Istituto Centrale per il Catalogo Unico delle Biblioteche Italiane e per le Informazioni Bibliografiche, Viale del Castro Pretorio, Rome
Central Institute of the Union Catalogue of Italian Libraries and Bibliographical Information
Publications: Bibliografia Nazionale Italiana; Manuale del Catalogatore; Soggettario per i Cataloghi delle Biblioteche Italiane

Library Reference Books and Journals

Books

Almanàcco dei Bibliotecari Italiani (Almanac of Italian Libraries), Fratelli Palombi Editori, Via del Gracchi 181-185, I-00192 Rome

Annuario Bibliografico per Le Biblioteche (Bibliographical Annual for Libraries), Federation of Italian Public Libraries, c/o La 'Società Umanitaria', Via Daverio 7, I-20122 Milan

Annuario delle Biblioteche Italiane (Italian Library Annual), Fratelli Palombi Editore, Via del Gracchi 181-185, I-00192 Rome

Guida delle Biblioteche Italiane (Guide to Italian Libraries), National Organization for Public and Academic Libraries, Via Michele Mercati 4, I-00197 Rome

Journals

Accademie e Biblioteche d'Italia (Academies and Libraries of Italy), Fratelli Palombi Editori, Via del Gracchi 181-185, I-00192 Rome

Archivi e Cultura (Archives and Culture), National Association of Italian Archivists, Viale Trastevere 215, I-00153 Rome

Bollettino d'Informazioni (Information Bulletin), Italian Library Association, c/o Istituto di Patologia del Libro, Via Milano 76, I-00184 Rome

La Cultura Popolare (Popular Culture), Federation of Italian Public Libraries, c/o La 'Società Umanitaria', Via Daverio 7, I-20122 Milan

Manuale del Catalogatore (Cataloguing Manual), Central Institute of the Union Catalogue of Italian Libraries and Bibliographical Information, Viale del Castro Pretorio, Rome

La Parola e il Libro (The Word and the Book), National Organization for Public and Academic Libraries, Via Michele Mercati 4, I-00197 Rome

Soggettario per i Cataloghi delle Biblioteche Italiane (Subject Collections in Italian Libraries), Central Institute of the Union Catalogue of Italian Libraries and Bibliographical Information, Viale del Castro Pretorio, Rome

Literary Associations and Societies

Accademia di Scienze, Lettere ed Arti*, Piazza Indipendenza 17, Palermo
Secretary: Professor Romualdo Giuffrida

Accademia Ligure di Scienze e Lettere*, Via Balbi 10, I-16126 Genoa
Secretary-General: P Scotti

Accademia Nazionale di Scienze, Lettere ed Arti*, Palazzo Coccapani, Corso Vittorio Emanuele II 59, Modena
President: Professor Antonio Pignedoli
Publications: Atti e Memorie

Accademia Petrarca di Lettere, Arti e Scienze, Via dell'Orto Arezzo
Secretary: Dr Guido Goti
Publication: Atti e Memorie della Accademia, Studi Petrarcheschi

Accademia Toscana di Scienze e Lettere la Colombaria*, Via S Egidio 21-23, Florence

Accademia Virgiliana di Scienze, Lettere ed Arti di Mantova*, Via Accademia 47, I-46100 Mantua Tel: (0376) 20314
Secretary: Comm G Amadei
Periodical Publication: Atti e Memorie NS (annual)

Istituto Lombardo Accademia di Scienze e Lettere, Via Brera 28, I-20121 Milan
President: Professor A Giordano
Publications: Rendiconti della Sezione di Scienze Matematiche e Naturali, Rendiconti della Sezione di Scienze Biologiche e Mediche, Rendiconti della Classe di Scienze Morali, Rendiconti-Parte Generale e Atti Ufficiali, Memorie della Classe di Scienze Matematiche e Naturali, Memorie della Classe di Scienze Morali, Proceedings and Symposiums

Keats-Shelley Memorial Association, Piazza di Spagna 26, Rome
Dir: Sir Joseph Cheyne
Publications: Bulletin, Journal, A Room in Rome by Vera Cacciatore

P E N International Centre*, Via Fratelli Ruspoli 2, Rome
President: Maria Bellonci

Società Dante Alighieri, Palazzo di Firenze, Piazza Firenze 27, I-00186 Rome
Secretary-General: G Cota
For the teaching and diffusion of Italian language and culture throughout the world

Società Dantesca Italiana, Via dell'Arte della Lana 1, I-50123 Florence
President: Professor Dr Francesco Mazzoni
Publications: Studi Danteschi, Quaderni degli Studi Danteschi, Edizione Nazionale delle Opere di Dante Alighieri (Library open to public)

Società Letteraria*, Piazzetta Scalette Rubiani 1, Verona
Dir: Avvocato Alfonso Balis Crema
Publication: Bollettino (annually)

Literary Periodicals

Belfagor, Leo S Olschki, CP 66, I-50100 Florence

Bibliofilia (Bibliophily) (text in English, French, German and Italian), Leo S Olschki, CP 66, I-50100 Florence

Il giornale storico della letteratura italiana (Historical Journal of Italian Literature), Loescher Editore, Via Vittorio Amedeo 18, I-10121 Turin

Italia Che Scrive (The Italy That Writes), Ia dei Banchi Vecchi 61, Rome

Lettere Italiane (Italian Letters), Viuzzo del Pozzetto (Viale Europa), I-50126 Florence

Libri Paese Sera (*Paese Sera* book supplement), Società Editrice 'Il Rinnovamento', Via dei Taurini 19, I-00185 Rome

Nuòva Corrènte (New Current) (text in several languages), Via Lattuada 26, Milan

Paideia; literary review with bibliographical information (text in English, French, German and Italian), Via Corsica 58m, I-25100 Brescia

Penarete-Letture d'Italia (Readings from Italy), Via Beruto 7, I-20131 Milan

Pròve di Letteratura (Examinations of Literature), Nino Palumbo, Via Ai Castagneti 4, San Michele di Pagana, Rapallo

Rassegna della Letteratura Italiana (Review of Italian Literature), Casa Editrice GC Sansoni SpA, Viale Mazzini 46, I-50132 Florence

Revue des Etudes italiennes, Librairie Marcel Didier SA, 15 rue Cujas, F-75005 Paris

Rivista di Letteratura Moderne e Comparate (Review of Modern and Comparative Literature) (text in English, French and Italian), Casa Editrice G C Sansoni SpA, Viale Mazzini 46, I-50132 Florence

Uomini e libri (Men and Books), Emme Edizioni, Via San Maurilio 13, I-20123 Milan

Literary Prizes

Andersen Prize*
For a fairy tale for children. 300,000 lire. Awarded annually. Enquiries to Comune di Sestri Levante, CP 60, Genoa

Bagutta Prize*
For the best book of the year, given for several literary forms including the novel, poetry, journalism. Awarded annually. Enquiries to Bagutta Restaurant, Via Bagutta 14, Milan

Bancarellino Prize*
For children's books of high quality and great popular appeal, preferably written by an Italian author. Awarded annually. Enquiries to Unione Librai Pontremolesi, Via Ricci Armani 8, Pontremoli, Massa Carrara

Campiello Prize
For the best Italian prose works. 10,000,000 lire. Awarded annually. Enquiries to Ca' Mocenigo Gambara, Secretariat of the Campiello Prize, Accademia 1056, Venice

Castello-Sanguinetto Prize
For a novel for young readers between 11 and 14. 1,000,000 lire and 500,000 lire. Awarded annually. Enquiries to Castello-Sanguinetto Prize, Community of Sanguinetto, Verona

Critics' Prize for Children's Literature*
For the best critical study in the field of juvenile literature. Enquiries to Institute for Pedagogics, University of Padua, Via VIII Febraio 9, Padua

Golden Book Prize*
To the publisher who has most influenced the public culturally. Awarded annually. Enquiries to Italian Council of Ministers, Via Bancopagni 15, Rome

Golden Pen Prize*
To an author who has made an important contribution to Italian culture. 5,000,000 lire. Awarded annually. Enquiries to Italian Council of Ministers, Via Bancopagni 15, Rome

Laura Orvieto Prize*
For the manuscript of a book of fiction or poetry for children. 1,000,000 lire for a novel and 500,000 lire for poetry. Awarded every other year. Enquiries to Orvieto Prize, Piazza Indipendenza 23, Florence

Strega Prize*
Founded in 1947 by the Strega liquor producer Alberti for the best novel of the year. 1,000,000 lire. Awarded annually. Enquiries to Strega Prize, Via Fratelli Ruspoli 2, Rome

Tormargana Prize*
To outstanding writers, publishers, artists, architects, actors and film makers. Awarded every few months. Enquiries to Angelino Restaurant (Hosteria Angelino a Tormargana), Piazza Margana 37, I-00186 Rome

Viareggio Prizes*
For the best novel, poetry, essay, best first work, occasionally for drama and journalism. Sometimes given to foreign writers and poets. 3,000,000 lire. Awarded annually. Enquiries to Viareggio Prize, Via Lima 28, Rome

Villa Benia Prize*
For the best storybook for young readers. Enquiries to International Institute for the Elimination of Speech Deficiencies, Villa Benia, Rapallo

Olga Visentini Prize
For the best book for young people. 500,000 lire. Awarded biennially. Enquiries to Olga Visentini Foundation, Cerea, Verona

Translation Agencies and Associations

Associazione Itaaliana Traduttori e Interpreti (AITI) (Italian Association of Translators and Interpreters)*, Via Arrigo Boito 126, 00199 Rome Tel: 8393457
Secretary: Anna Bonanome-Via

Eulama*, Via Torino 135, I-00184 Rome Tel: (06) 460636 (also Publisher and Literary Agent)

Transafrica*, Via Trieste 34, I-25100 Brescia Tel: (030) 55080/54844
Specialization: African texts

Ivory Coast

General Information

Language: French
Religion: Animism, Muslim and some Christian
Population: Estimates vary between 5.2 and 6.7 million
Bank Hours: 0800-1130, 1430-1630 Monday-Friday

Shop Hours: 0800-1200, 1430-1830 or 1900 Monday-Friday; 0800-1200, 1430-1730 Saturday
Currency: CFA franc
Export/Import Information: No tariff on books; single copies free but most advertising subject to 5% customs duty, 20% fiscal duty and 20.5% VAT. No import licences required. Exchange controls from non-franc zone
Copyright: Berne, Florence (see International section)

Book Trade Reference Journal

Bibliographie de la Côte-d'Ivoire, Bibliothèque universitaire, BP 8859, Abidjan (the national bibliography, published annually in two volumes since 1969)

Publishers

Centre d'Edition et de Diffusion africaines*, BP 4541, Abidjan Plateau Tel: 222055/228137 Telex: Ediceda 2451
Man Dir: Venance Kacou; *Editorial Dir:* Christian Lescure
Subjects: General Nonfiction, Biography, History, Africana, Philosophy, Reference, Religion, Juveniles, Law, Paperbacks, General & Social Science, Secondary & Primary Textbooks
Bookshop: At above address
1977-78: 21 titles
Miscellaneous: Distributors on behalf of INADES, the National University of the Ivory Coast, and the bibliotheque nationale

Centre de Publications Evangeliques, 08 BP 900, Abidjan 08 Tel: 444805
Dir: Marjorie Shelley; *Administrator:* E T Emmett
Subjects: General Nonfiction, Religion, Christian Tracts, Paperbacks, Periodicals for adults and children
1977: 15 titles *1978:* 22 titles *Founded:* 1970

Government Printer*, Imprimerie nationale, BP V87, Abidjan

I N A D E S — Edition (Institut africain pour le developpement éconnnomique et social), 08 BP 8, Abidjan 08 Tel: 441594
Man Dir, Editorial: Raymond Deniel; *Sales:* Albert Hanrion
Subjects: African studies, Philosophy, Religion, Economics, Agriculture, Sociology, Essays
1978: 2 titles *1979:* 2 titles *Founded:* 1975

Les Nouvelles Editions Africaines, 01 BP 3525, Abidjan 01 (Located at: 15 ave Noguès, Résidence Noguès, 2e etage, Abidjan 01) Tel: 32924/324907
Parent Company: Les Nouvelles Editions Africaines Dakar, Senegal (qv)
Subjects: Bibliography, Fiction, Poetry, Religion, Art, Juveniles, History, Textbooks
1978: 34 titles

Université Nationale de Côte d'Ivoire*, BP V34, Abidjan Tel: 312395 Cable Add: Rectuniv Abidjan Telex: 469
Secretary General in Charge of Publications: Mme Dehaile-Leoni
Subjects: General Nonfiction, History, Africana, Reference, Law, Medicine, General & Social Science, Economics, Geography, Linguistics, Sociology, Journals
1977: 11 titles Founded: 1964
ISBN Publisher's Prefix: 2-7166

Major Booksellers

Librairie **Carrefour**, 09 BP 326, Abidjan 09 Tel: 442370

Centre d'Edition et de Diffusion africaines*, BP 4541, Abidjan Tel: 222055/228137
Manager: Kakou Venance

Librairie de **France***, ave Chardy, BP 228, Abidjan Tel: 322655

Maison des Livres*, 23 blvd de la République, BP 4645, Abidjan Tel: 322887

Librairie **Villepastour**, 01 BP 2461, Abidjan 01 Tel: 353352/355117 Telex: 2454 PASTOUR
Manager: J Villepastour

Major Libraries

Bibliothèque centrale de la Côte d'Ivoire*, BP 6243, Abidjan-Treichville Tel: 22753

Bibliothèque municipale*, Plateau, Abidjan

Bibliothèque nationale (National Library), BP V180, Abidjan Tel: 323872

Bibliothèque de l'Université nationale de Côte d'Ivoire*, BP 8859, Abidjan Tel: 312395
Librarian: Mme N'goran; *Publications enquiries:* Mme Dehail-Leoni
Publications include: Bibliographie de la Côte d'Ivoire

Centre culturel américain*, Bibliothèque, BP 1866, Abidjan

Centre culturel français*, Bibliothèque, ave Noguès, Abidjan

I N A D E S (Institut africain pour le Développement économique et social) Documentation*, BP 8008, Abidjan Tel: 349292
Librarian: Nicole Vial
Publication: 'Le Fichier-Afrique', (bi-monthly)

Library Associations

Association pour le Développement de la Documentation, des Bibliothèques et Archives de la Côte d'Ivoire (ADBACI), c/o Bibliothèque Nationale, BP V180, Abidjan
Secretary General: Cangah Guy

Literary Associations and Societies

P E N Club International Centre de Côte d'Ivoire*, BP 1718, Abidjan
Secretary: Jean Dodo

Jamaica

General Information

Language: English
Religion: Predominantly Protestant
Population: 2 million
Literacy Rate (1960): 80.5%
Bank Hours: 0900-1400 Monday-Thursday; 0900-1200, 1430-1700 Friday
Shop Hours: Downtown Kingston: 0900-1600 Monday and Tuesday, Thursday-Saturday; 0900-1200 Wednesday. Other areas: 0900-1700, with early closing Thursday
Currency: 100 cents = 1 Jamaican dollar
Export/Import Information: No tariff on books, 45% on advertising matter. No import licence required for books; no obscene literature permitted. Exchange restrictions
Copyright: No copyright conventions signed

Book Trade Organizations

Booksellers' Association of Jamaica*, c/o Sangster's Book Stores Ltd, 101 Water Lane, Kingston Tel: 9223640
Secretary: B A Sangster

Book Trade Reference Journal

Jamaican National Bibliography, Institute of Jamaica, 12-16 East St, Kingston

Publishers

Caribbean Universities Press*, PO Box 83, Kingston 7
Subjects: Academic, Education (Spanish and English)

William **Collins** & Sangster (Jamaica) Ltd, PO Box 881, Kingston (Located at: Barclays Building, 54 King St, Kingston) Tel: 9224783
Man Dir: Jan Collins; *Editorial & Production:* G R Luff; *Sales & Publicity:* T D Menzies; *Rights & Permissions:* P M Clark
Parent Company: William Collins Sons & Co Ltd, UK (qv)

Government Printing Office*, 77 Duke St, Kingston
Subject: Law

Jamaica Publishing House Ltd, 97 Church St, Kingston Tel: (0922) 2038
Chairman: Fay E Saunders; *Man:* Thelma E L Pyne
Parent Company: Jamaica Teachers' Association
Subject: Educational
1977: 2 titles *1978:* 2 titles *Founded:* 1969

Kingston Publishers Ltd, 1A Norwood Ave, Kingston 5 Tel: 9265506 Cable Add: Kingbooks
Chairman: L M J Henry
Founded: 1972

Major Booksellers

Bolivar Bookshop*, 1D Grove Rd, Kingston 10 Tel: 9268799

Henderson's Book Store*, 27 St James St, Montego Bay

Kingston Bookshop*, 70b King St, Kingston

Literary Supplies*, 38 Mandeville Plaza, Mandeville

Novelty Trading Co*, 53 Hanover St, Kingston

Readers' Book Shop*, Liguanea Plaza, 134 Old Hope Rd, Kingston 6

Sangster's Book Stores Ltd, PO Box 366, 101 Water Lane, Kingston Tel: 9223640

Shadeed's Educational & General Supplies*, 14 French St, Spanish Town

Stationery & Educational Book Centre*, Silver Slipper Plaza, Kingston 5

Teachers' Book Centre Ltd, 95 Church St, Kingston Tel: (09) 26295/24716/27921

Times Stores Ltd*, 8 King St, Kingston

Major Libraries

Jamaica Archives, Spanish Town

Jamaica Library Service, PO Box 58, 2 Tom Redcam Dr, Kingston 5 Tel: 936 3310
Dir: Leila T Thomas

National Library of Jamaica, Institute of Jamaica, 12-16 East St, Kingston

University of the West Indies Library, Mona, Kingston 7 Tel: Librarian 9276661 ext 294; Reference Desk 9276661 ext 296 or 9270923
Librarian: K E Ingram
Publication: Annual Report

Library Associations

Jamaica Library Association*, PO Box 58, Kingston 5
Honorary Secretary: Ms A Chambers
Publication: Bulletin (annual)

Library Journals

Bulletin, Jamaica Library Association, PO Box 58, Kingston 5

Literary Associations and Societies

P E N Club, 1 Norbrook Rd, Apt 4, Kingston 8
Secretary: George Clough

Japan

General Information

Language: Japanese
Religion: Buddhism and Shinto
Population: 114 million
Literacy Rate (1960): 96.6%
Bank Hours: 0900-1500 Monday-Friday; 0900-1200 Saturday
Shop Hours: No fixed weekly holiday; department stores usually close Wednesday or Thursday, others Sunday. Generally department store hours are 1000-1800
Currency: yen
Export/Import Information: No tariff on books and advertising matter. Only declaration by importer to a foreign exchange bank is required
Copyright: UCC, Berne, Florence (see International section)

Book Trade Organizations

Antiquarian Booksellers' Association of Japan, 29 San-Ei-Cho, Shinjuku-ku, Tokyo 160 Tel: (03) 3571441 Cable Add: Yushodo Tokyo Telex: 0232-4136
President: Ukichi Sakai

Japan Book Importers' Association*, Room 302, Aizawa Bldg, 20-3 Nihonbashi 1-chome, Chuo-ku, Tokyo 103
Secretary: Kazushige Terakubo

Japan Book Publishers' Association, 6 Fukuro-machi, Shinjuku-ku, Tokyo 162 Tel: (03) 2681301 Cable Add: Shosekiyo Tokyo
Secretary General: Shigeshi Sasaki; Dir: Masaaki Shigehisa
Publication: Publishing in Japan, Japanese Books in Print, The Catalogue of Books in the Near Future

Nihon Shoten Kumiai Rengokai*, 1-2 Kanda Surugadai, Chiyoda-ku, Tokyo 101 Tel: (03) 2940388
Japan Booksellers' Federation
Publications: Zenkoku Shoten Meibo (Address Book of Japan Booksellers); Zenkoku Shoten Shinbun

Publishers' Association for Cultural Exchange, 1-2-1, Sarugaku Cho, Chiyoda-ku, Tokyo 101 Tel: (03) 2915685
Cable Add: Publishersasso
President: Mr Shoichi Noma; Man Dir: Shoichi Nakajima
European Rep: c/o Euro-Japanische Gesellschaft eV, Bonifaciusplatz 3, D-6500 Mainz, German Federal Republic
Publications: Guide to Publishers and Related Industries in Japan, Guide to Foreign Publishers, Annotated Catalogue of Books Published in Japan

Textbook Publishers' Association of Japan (Kyokasho Kyokai)*, 20-2 Honshiocho Shinjuku-ku, Tokyo 160
Secretary: Masae Kusaka

Book Trade Reference Books and Journals

Books

Annotated Catalogue of Books Published in Japan, Publishers' Association for Cultural Exchange, 1-2-1, Sarugaku Cho, Chiyoda-ku, Tokyo 101

Directory of Japanese Publishing and Bookselling, British Book and Educational Display Centre, Iwanami Jimbo-Cho Bldg, 1 Jimbo 2 2-chome, Kanda, Chiyoda-ku, Tokyo 101

Guide to Foreign Publishers, Publishers' Association for Cultural Exchange, 1-2-1, Sarugaku Cho, Chiyoda-ku, Tokyo 101

Publishing in Japan, Japan Book Publishers' Association, 6 Fukuro-machi, Shinjuku-ku, Tokyo 162

Journals

Biblia (text in Japanese), Tenri University Press, Tenri Central Library, Tenri City, Nara

The Catalogue of Books in the Near Future, Japan Book Publishers' Association, 6 Fukuro-machi, Shinjuku-ku, Tokyo 162

Guide to Publishers and Related Industries in Japan, Publishers' Association for Cultural Exchange, 1-2-1, Sarugaku Cho, Chiyoda-ku, Tokyo 101

Japan Book News, Publishing Research Associates, c/o Kyowa Book Co, Kanda, PO Box 173, Tokyo

Japanese Books in Print, Japan Book Publishers' Association, 6 Fukuro-machi, Shinjuku-ku, Tokyo 162

Japanese Publications News and Reviews, 3-2-4 Misaki-cho, Chiyoda-ku, Tokyo

Newsletter, Tokyo Book Development Centre, 6 Fukuro-machi, Shinjuku-ku, Tokyo

Seihon Kai (text in Japanese), Tokyodo Co Ltd, 3-5 Kanda-Nishiki-cho, Chiyoda-ku, Tokyo

Shinkan Nyusu (News of New Books), Tokyo Shuppan Hanbai Co Ltd, 53 Higashigoken-cho, Shinjuku-ku, Tokyo

Shuppan Nenkan; information on publishing for the previous year, Shuppan Nyusu-sha, Tokyo (annual)

Suppan Nyusu (Publishers' News), Shuppan Nyusu-sha, 2-4 Misaki-cho 3-chome, Chiyoda-ku, Tokyo 101 (3 times a month)

Zen Nihon Shuppanbutsu Somokuroku (Japanese National Bibliography), National Diet Library, 10-1, 1-chome, Nagata-cho, Chiyoda-ku, Tokyo

Zenkoku Shoten Meibo (address book of Japanese booksellers), Japan Booksellers' Federation, 1-2 Kanda Surugadai, Chiyoda-ku, Tokyo 101

Publishers

A D A Edita Tokyo Co Ltd, 3-12-14 Sendagaya, Shibuya-ku, Tokyo 151 Tel: (03) 4031581
Director: Yukio Futagawa
Subject: Architecture
1978: 5 titles 1979: 3 titles

Akane Shobo Co Ltd*, 3-2-1 Nishikanda, Chiyoda-ku, Tokyo Tel: (03) 2630641
President: Mutsuto Okamoto; Editor-in-Chief: Yoshiaki Ushiro
Subjects: Juveniles, Science, Literature, Picture Books

Akita Shoten Publishing Co Ltd*, 2-10-8 Iidabashi, Chiyoda-ku, Tokyo 102 Tel: (03) 2647011
Man Dir: Sadami Akita; Editorial: Nobumichi Akutsu; Sales: Toshimichi Okubo
Subjects: General Subjects, Juveniles, History, Social Science, Literature, Magazines
1977: 188 titles Founded: 1948

Aoki Shoten Co Ltd*, 60 Kanda Jimbo-cho 1-chome, Chiyoda-ku, Tokyo 101 Tel: (03) 2920481
President: Noboru Yamane; Foreign Trade: Kiyoshi Furukawa; Foreign Rights: Toyoichi Eguchi
Subject: Social Science
1977: 74 titles Founded: 1947

Asakura Publishing Co Ltd*, 2-10 Shinogawama-chi, Shinjuku-ku, Tokyo 162 Tel: (03) 2600141
President: Kozo Asakura; Foreign Trade:

Nobuji Okada; *Foreign Rights:* Akira Hata
Subjects: Medicine, Natural Science, Engineering, Industry, History, Geography, Pedagogy, Sociology
Founded: 1929

Baseball Magazine-Sha, 3-3 Kanda-Nishiki-cho, Chiyoda-ku, Tokyo Tel: (03) 2917901/2917909
President: Tsuneo Ikeda
Subjects: Sports, Physical Education, Psychology, History, Fitness

Bijutsu Shuppan-Sha, 15 Ichigaya Honmura-cho, Shinjuku, Tokyo 162 Tel: (03) 2602151 Cable Add: Fineart Book Tokyo
President: Atsushi Oshita; *Sales Manager:* Koichi Matsumura
Subjects: Art, Architecture, Design
1978: 65 titles *Founded:* 1905
Subsidiary: Bijutsu Shuppan Design Centre, Yamato Bldg, 1-7-4 Yaesu Chuyuo-ku, Tokyo 103

Bungeishunju Ltd*, 3 Kioi-cho, Chiyoda-ku, Tokyo Tel: (03) 2651211
President: Genzo Chiba; *Foreign Trade:* Hisashi Mukaibo; *Foreign Rights:* Itaro Abe
Subjects: General Fiction and Nonfiction, Philosophy, Religion, History, Geography, Social Science, Art, Economics, Politics, Natural Science, Industry, Language, Literature, High- and Low-priced Paperbacks
1977: 199 titles *Founded:* 1923

Centre for Academic Publications Japan, 4-16 Yayoi 2-chome, Bunkyo-ku, Tokyo 113 Tel: (03) 8150416
Man Dir: T Yamada; *Editorial, Sales, Production, Publicity, Rights & Permissions:* K Oshida
Orders to: Business Centre for Academic Societies Japan at above address
Associated Company: Japan Scientific Societies Press, 2-10 Hongo, 6-chome, Bunkyo-ku, Tokyo 113
1977: 6 titles *1978:* 8 titles *Founded:* 1972

Chikuma Shobo Publishing Co Ltd, 8, 2-chome, Kanda Ogawamachi, Chiyoda-ku, Tokyo 101-91 Tel: (03) 2917651
Administrator: Hidesato Sekine; *Editorial, Rights & Permissions:* Mineo Nakajima; *Sales:* Tetsuo Mukaiyama; *Production:* Kazuyoshi Tsunoda; *Publicity:* Toshihiko Ebisawa
Subjects: General Fiction, Belles Lettres, Poetry, Biography, History, Religion, Music, Art, Philosophy, Juveniles, High-priced Paperbacks, Medicine, Psychology, General & Social Science, Secondary Textbooks
1977: 263 titles *1978:* 429 titles *Founded:* 1930

Child-Honsha Inc, c/o Famille Hisakata Bldg 2F, 24-21 Koishikawa 5-chome, Bunkyo-ku, Tokyo 112 Tel: (03) 8133781
President: Shinko Miyata; *Editorial:* Yasuyuki Ouchi; *Sales:* Seiichiroh Shimizu; *Production:* Kotaro Ohasi; *Publicity:* Hirosato Okada; *Rights & Permissions:* Ikuzo Shibasaki
Associate Company: Kyodo Printing Co Ltd
Subsidiary Company: Basic Inc
Imprints: Kyodo Printing Co Ltd
Subjects: Juveniles, Education
1977: 20 titles *1978:* 30 titles *Founded:* 1930

Chuo-Tosho Shuppan-Sha, Aburanokoji-dori, Motoseiganji-sagaru, Kamigyo-ku, Kyoto 602 Tel: 4412174
President: Toshihiko Hirokou; *Foreign Trade:* Keizou Hirotsu; *Foreign Rights:* Takanori Ikeda
Subjects: Language, Literature, Reference Books
1978: 25 titles *Founded:* 1946

Chuokoron-Sha Inc*, 2-8-7 Kyobashi, Chuo-ku, Tokyo 104 Tel: (03) 5615921 Cable Add: Chuokoron Tokyo
President: Hoji Shimanaka; *Man Dir:* Shigeru Takanashi; *International Section Manager:* Yukio Shimanaka
Subjects: General Fiction, Belles Lettres, History, Art, Philosophy, Low-priced Paperbacks, Politics, Economics, Natural Science, Social Science, Religion, Periodicals
1977: 372 titles *Founded:* 1887

Consolidated Labor Institute (Japan)*, 38 Yoyogi 1-chome, Shibuya-ku, Tokyo 151 Tel: (03) 3792281 Cable Add: Sogoroken Tokyo
President: Mrs Fujiko Hongo; *Foreign Trade Executive:* Kenji Hongo; *Foreign Rights Executive:* Chiyoshi Otuka
Subjects: Social Science, Law, Educational, History, Journals
1977: 10 titles *Founded:* 1950

Corona Publishing Co Ltd, 4-46-10 Sengoku, Bunkyo-ku, Tokyo 112 Tel: (03) 9413131
Executive Director and Foreign Rights: Tatsuo Fujita; *Foreign Trade:* Tatsumi Gorai
Subjects: Natural Science, Technology
1978: 70 titles *Founded:* 1927

Daiichi Shuppan Co Ltd, 1-39 Kanda Jimbo-cho, Chiyoda-ku, Tokyo 101 Tel: (03) 2914576
President: Gen Kurita; *Foreign Trade Executive:* Yoshiya Takamatsu; *Foreign Rights Executive:* Yoshiya Takamatsu
Subjects: Medicine, Natural Science, Nutrition, Magazines
1978: 15 titles *Founded:* 1945

Diamond Inc*, 1-4-2 Kasumigaseki, Chiyoda-ku, Tokyo Tel: (03) 5046381 Cable Add: Keizaidia Tokyo
President: Yoshio Tsubouchi; *Editorial:* Hideki Fujishima; *Sales:* Minami Takahashi; *Production:* Kiyoji Ogo; *Publicity:* Kenichiro Iwasaki; *Rights & Permissions:* Katsuyoshi Saito
Associated Company: President KK
Subsidiary Companies: Diamond (weekly economics Journal); Diamond Agency; Diamond Big; Diamond Fund; Diamond Graphics; Diamond Service
Branch Off: Osaka
Subjects: Nonfiction, Business, Economics, Management, Finance, Politics
1977: 143 titles *Founded:* 1913

Froebel-Kan Co Ltd*, 3-1 Kanda Ogawa-machi, Chiyoda-ku, Tokyo 101 Tel: (03) 2927781/9 Cable Add: Froebelkan Tokyo Telex: J24907
General Manager (International Division): Harry H Idichi; *Assistant Manager, International Division:* Tony S Endo
Subjects: Juveniles, Educational Materials
Founded: 1907

Fukuinkan Shoten Publishers, 1-9 Misakicho 1-chome, Chiyoda-ku, Tokyo 101 Tel: (03) 2923401/2303821 Cable Add: Fukuinkanshoten Tokyo
Man Dir: Tadashi Matsui; *Editorial:* Ken Minakuchi; *Sales:* Katsumi Sato, Kishiro Kikuma; *Publicity:* Hiroshi Ishikawa; *Rights & Permissions:* Yumiko Bando, Tamotsu Hozumi
Subjects: Children's books
Book Club: Ehon Library (Picture Book Library)
1977: 35 titles *1978:* 26 titles *Founded:* 1951
Miscellaneous: Publishers of *Children's Companion, Science Companion, Mother's Companion, Children's House* (all monthly)

Fuzambo Publishing Co*, 1-3 Kanda Jimbo-cho, Chiyoda-ku, Tokyo 101 Tel: (03) 2912171
President: Kiichi Sakamoto
Subjects: General Works, Philosophy & Religion, History, Geography, Law, Literature, Language, Art, Juveniles, Dictionaries
Founded: 1886

Gakken Co Ltd*, 4-40-5 Kamiikedai, Ohta-ku, Tokyo 145 Tel: (03) 7201111 Cable Add: Gakkencol Telex: gakkenco J26389
Man Dir: Hiroshi Furuoka; *Foreign Trade Executive:* Shoichi Inagaki; *Foreign Rights:* Ryu Tanaka
Subjects: General Fiction, Art, Dictionaries, Encyclopaedias, Juveniles, Natural & Social Science
Founded: 1946

Gakuseisha Publishing Co Ltd, 2-2-4 Kudan-Minami, Chiyoda-ku, Tokyo 102 Tel: (03) 2632611
President: Masami Tsuruoka; *Foreign Rights Executive:* Atsuo Miki
Subjects: Ancient History, Archaeology, Reference
1978: 55 titles *Founded:* 1952

Hakusui-Sha*, 3-24 Kanda-Ogawamachi, Chiyoda-ku, Tokyo 101 Tel: (03) 2917811
President: Sueo Nakamori; *Foreign Trade Executive:* Souichi Kobayashi; *Foreign Rights Executive:* Tsutomu Izumikawa
Subjects: Science, Languages, Fiction, Literature, Education, Art, Philosophy
Founded: 1915

Hakuyu-Sha*, 9 Ageba-cho, Shinjuku-ku, Tokyo 162 Tel: (03) 2688271
Man Dir: Eiji Takamori; *Foreign Trade Executive:* Montaro Ono; *Publicity & Advertising:* Kazuya Baba; *Foreign Rights:* Eiji Takamori
Subjects: Dictionaries, Natural Science, Industry
Founded: 1948

Hayakawa Publishing Inc, 2-2 Kanda-Tacho, Chiyoda-ku, Tokyo 101 Tel: (03) 2541551 Cable Add: Hayakawashobo Tokyo
Executive Vice-President, Foreign Trade & Rights Executive: Hiroshi Hayakawa
Subjects: Foreign Fiction, Nonfiction, History, Philosophy & Religion, Art, Juveniles, Natural, Social & Political Sciences, Literature, Magazines, Plays, Mysteries, Science Fiction, Fantasy

Heibonsha Ltd, Publishers, 4 Yonbancho, Chiyoda-ku, Tokyo 102 Tel: (03) 2650451 Cable Add: Booksheibonsha
President: Kunihiko Shimonaka; *Dirs:* Masakiyo Nakajima, Tadashi Uemura
Subjects: Encyclopedias, Japanese & Chinese studies, General nonfiction, Art, Reference, Education, History, Philosophy, Social Science, Graphic monthly magazine, *The Sun*
1978: 225 titles *Founded:* 1914

Hikarinokuni Co Ltd*, 3-2 Uehon-machi, Tennoji-ku, Osaka 543 Tel: 7681151
Man Dir: Yotaro Matsumoto; *Editorial & Export Dir:* Masaaki Tsuchiya
Subjects: Juveniles, Education
Founded: 1945

Hirokawa Publishing Co*, PO Box 38 Hongo, Bunkyo-ku, Tokyo 113-91 (Located at: 27-14 Hongo 3-chome, Bunkyo-ku, Tokyo 113) Tel: (03) 8153651 Cable Add: Higesehi Tokyo
President: Genji Hirokawa; *Man Dir (Editor):* Setsuo Hirokawa; *Sales Dir:* Hideo Hirokawa
Subjects: Medicine, Pharmacy, Natural Sciences, Engineering
1977: 349 titles *Founded:* 1926

Hoikusha Publishing Co Ltd, 17-13, 1-Chome Uemachi, Higashi-ku, Osaka 540 Tel: (06) 7621731 Cable Add: Hoikusha
President: Tatsuo Imai; *Man Dir:* Ryoji Nakanishi; *Editorial:* Masao Ikeyama
Br Off: 1-1 Minami-Otsuka, Toshima-ku, Tokyo 170
Subjects: Natural History, Poetry, Biography, History, How-to, Music, Art, High-priced Hard cover books, General Science, Illustrated Nature & Craft Books in English & Japanese
1977: 45 titles *1978:* 46 titlses *Founded:* 1947

Hokuryukan Co Ltd*, Bunkyo Trading Bldg, 2-12-7 Iidabashi, Chiyoda-ku, Tokyo 102 Tel: (03) 2919511
President & Editorial: Kisaburo Fukuda
Subjects: Juveniles, General Science, Reference, Engineering
Founded: 1919

The **Hokuseido** Press*, 12 Nishikicho 3-chome, Kanda, Chiyoda-ku, Tokyo Tel: (03) 2943301 Cable Add: Hokusedpres Tokyo
Dir: Jumpei Nakatsuchi; *Sales, Advertising, Rights & Permissions:* Katsuo Wakiyama
Subjects: Belles Lettres, Poetry, Biography, Philosophy, Religion, University Textbooks
1977: 38 titles *Founded:* 1914

Holp Book Co Ltd, 2-19-13 Shinjuku, Shinjuku-ku, Tokyo 160 Tel: (03) 3566211 Cable Add: Holpbook Tokyo Telex: 2322421
President: Makito Nakamori; *Editorial:* Hiroyoshi Shimizu; *Rights & Permissions:* Minoru Shibuya; *International Trade:* Masumi Misaki
Br Offs: 250 throughout Japan
Subsidiary Companies: Holp Shuppan, Publishers Ltd; Shumi-to-Seikatsu Co Ltd
1979: 76 titles *Founded:* 1964
Subjects: Art, Education, El-Hi Textbooks, Geography, Juveniles, Literature, Mathematics, Music, Reproductions, Science

Hyoronsha Publishing Co Ltd*, 2-16 Kanda Jimbo-cho, Chiyoda-ku, Tokyo 101 Tel: (03) 2651961
President: Mrs Mina Takeshita; *Chief Editor:* Saburo Tsuyama; *Sales Manager:* Zenzo Uchida
Subjects: Philosophy & Religion, Education, History, Social Science, Industry, Language, Juveniles, Reference
1977: 100 titles *Founded:* 1948

Ie-No-Hikari Association*, 11 Funakawara-cho, Ichigaya, Shinjuku-ku, Tokyo 162 Tel: (03) 2603151 Cable Add: IeNoHikari Tokyo Telex: 2322367
Man Dir: Yoshiro Takahashi; *Editorial, Sales:* Mareki Kuruba; *Book Publication Department:* Naomichi Muratani; *Production:* Shinichi Saito; *Publicity:* Yoshiro Takahashi
Subjects: General, Social Science, Industry, Periodicals
1977: 65 titles *Founded:* 1925

Igaku-Shoin Ltd, PO Box 5063, Tokyo International (Located at: 5-24-3 Hongo, Bunkyo-ku, Tokyo 11391) Tel: (03) 8111101 Cable Add: Igakushoin Telex: 272 3334
President, Editor-in-Chief: Isumi Hasegawa; *Vice-President, International Publishing:* Naobumi Ando; *Editorial Manager:* Hideo Okada; *Export Manager:* Makoto Yamamoto; *Imports Managers:* Masayuki Nishizawa (Books), Yasuo Sakaguchi (Journals)
Subsidiary Company: Igaku-Shoin Medical Publishers Inc, New York, USA
Subjects: Medical and Dental Sciences, Nursing
1977: 95 titles *Founded:* 1944
ISBN Publisher's Prefix: 0-89640

The **International Nursing** Foundation of Japan, 1-32 4-chome Kudan Kita, Chiyoda-ku, Tokyo 102 Tel: (03) 2646667 Cable Add: Infurse Tokyo
Man Dirs: Kazuharu Ogura, Mrs Sada Nagano; *Editorial, Rights & Permissions:* Tetsuro Nishizaki; *Publicity & Advertising:* Miss Fujiko Masame
Subjects: Nursing Science (National & International)
1978: 32 titles *1979:* 7 titles *Founded:* 1971

International Society for Educational Information Inc*, Kikuei Bldg 3-5, Shintomi-cho, Chuo-ku, Tokyo Tel: (03) 5529481/2
Executive Director: Michiko Kaya
Subject: Japan

Ishiyaku Publishers Inc*, PO Box 8, Hongo, Tokyo 113-91 (Located at: 7-10 Honkomagome 1-chome, Bunkyo-ku, Tokyo 113) Tel: (03) 9443131 Cable Add: Mepharma Tokyo
Man Dir: Hiroshi Miura; *Sales & Publicity Dir:* Akira Iwase; *Advertising Dir:* Toji Yasue; *Foreign Trade, Rights & Permissions:* Toshi Arisaka
Orders to: Tokyo Mail Service Co Ltd, PO Box 101, Hongo, Tokyo 113-91
Br Off: Suite 602, 12 Shinmeicho, Kita-ku, Osaka 530
Bookshop: Shiensha Ltd, c/o Nakayama Bldg, 8-6 Misakicho 2-chome, Chiyoda-ku, Tokyo 101
Subjects: Medicine, Dentistry, Pharmacology, Nutrition, Veterinary Medicine, University textbooks, Educational materials
1977: 86 titles *Founded:* 1921

Iwanami Shoten, Publishers, 2-5-5 Hitotsubashi, Chiyoda-ku, Tokyo Tel: (03) 2654111 Cable Add: Iwanamipress Tokyo
Chairman: Yujiro Iwanami; *President:* Toru Midorikawa; *Executive Dir, Sales, Publicity & Advertising:* Akira Kigoshi; *Dir, Chief Editor (Natural Sciences):* Yujiro Hayashi; *Dir, Chief Editor (Social Sciences):* Yoshikatsu Nakajima; *Foreign Rights:* Mitsuko Takiguchi, Takao Hori, Takeko Tomita
Subjects: Biography, Economics, History, Reference, Philosophy, Psychology, Art, Juveniles, Social & Natural Science, Paperbacks, University Textbooks, Dictionaries, Periodicals
1977: 337 titles *1978:* 329 titles *Founded:* 1913

Iwasaki Shoten Co Ltd*, 1-9-2 Suido, Bunkyo-ku, Tokyo 112 Tel: (03) 8129131
Man Dir: Koyu Moriyama; *Sales Manager:* Matsutoshi Ohkawa; *Editorial:* Masayasu Konishi
Subjects: Juveniles, Art
Founded: 1934

Japan Broadcast Publishing Co Ltd*, 41-1 Udagawa-cho, Shibuya-ku, Tokyo 150 Tel: (03) 4647311 Cable Add: Nhpublishco Tokyo
President: Kazuo Fujinei; *Foreign Trade Executive:* Tsuguo Mizutani; *Foreign Rights Executive:* Yoshio Nemoto
Subjects: Radio, Television, Philosophy, Religion, History, Geography, Social & Natural Sciences, Politics, Law, Economics, Engineering, Medicine, Technology, Industry, Art, Language, Juveniles, Literature, Reference, Textbooks
1977: 266 titles *Founded:* 1931

Japan Publications Inc, PO Box 5030 Tokyo International, Tokyo 101-31 (Located at: 1-2-1 Sarugaku-cho 1-chome, Chiyoda-ku, Tokyo 101) Tel: (03) 2958411 Cable Add: Shutsubo Tokyo Telex: J 27161
President: Iwao Yoshizaki; *Executive Dir:* Soshichi Toyoshima; *Editor-in-Chief:* Richard L Gage; *Sales Manager:* Akio Takeuchi; *Rights & Permissions:* Masatoshi Sato
Subjects: History, How-to, Reference, Juveniles, Health, High-priced Paperbacks
1977: 37 titles *1978:* 36 titles *Founded:* 1942
Subsidiaries: Japan Publications Trading Co Ltd, PO Box 5030, Tokyo International, Tokyo 101-31; Japan Publications Trading Co (USA) Inc, 1174 Howard St, San Francisco, CA 94103, USA

Japan Times*, Publishing Department, 5-4 Shibaura 4-chome, Minato-ku, Tokyo
Man Dir: Toshio Tojo
Subjects: Nonfiction, Reference, Textbooks

Japan Travel Bureau Inc*, Publishing Division, 8th Floor, OKI Bldg, 3 Kanda Kaji-Cho 3-chome, Chiyoda-ku, Tokyo 101 Tel: (03) 2578320 Cable Add: Jtbbook Tokyo J24418 Telex: 2228020
Man Dir: Shigeo Miyakoshi; *Editorial:* Akito Hiroki; *Foreign Trade, Foreign Rights:* Shoichi Takeuchi
Subsidiary Companies: Densan Process Co; Kotsu Print Co; Kotsu Seihon Co; Toyo Books Co
Br Off: The International Bldg, 45 Rockfeller Plaza, New York, NY 10020, USA; 510 West Sixth St, Los Angeles, Calif, 90014, USA; 402 Qantas Bldg, Union Sq, 360 Post St, San Francisco, Calif 94108, USA; The Royal Exchange Bldg, 56 Pitt St, Sydney, Australia; Waikiki Business Plaza, 2270 Kalakaua Avenue, Honolulu, Hawaii 96815; 77 rue la Boetie, Paris 75008, France; Room 203, Hotel Miramar, Nathan Rd, Kawloon, Hong Kong; 5 Rue Chantepoulet, Geneva, Switzerland; 32 Old Burlington St, London W1X 1LB, UK; c/o Guam Hilton Hotel, Ipao Beach, Guam; Via Emilia 47, Rome, Italy
Subjects: General, Travel Guides, Maps, History, Geography, Language
1977: 10 titles *Founded:* 1945
ISBN Publisher's Prefix: 0-87040-344-3

Kadokawa Shoten, 2-13-3 Fujimi-cho, Chiyoda-ku, Tokyo Tel: (03) 2657111
Man Dir: Haruki Kadokawa; *Editorial:* Sadaharu Mouri; *Sales:* Tsuguhiko Kadokawa; *Production:* Shigeo Nakai; *Publicity:* Akio Baba; *Rights & Permissions:* Hiroshi Tagami

Subjects: General Fiction, Fine Arts, History, Religion, Literature, Dictionaries
1977: 350 titles *1978:* 350 titles *Founded:* 1945

Kaibundo Publishing Co Ltd*, 2-5-4 Suido, Bunkyo-ku, Tokyo 112 Tel: Tokyo 815 3291 Cable Add: Kaibundo Tokyo
President: Yoshiro Okada; *Editorial Dir:* Ichiro Tsubota; *Foreign Trade:* Michiharu Utsonomia; *Foreign Rights:* Shinichi Arihara
Subjects: Engineering, Industry, Natural Science
Founded: 1914

Kairyudo Publishing Co Ltd*, 3-18 Kanda Nishiki-cho Chiyoda-ku, Tokyo 101 Tel: (03) 2931811-9
Man Dir: Takahiro Nakamura; *Editorial:* Masatoshi Yoshinari; *Foreign Trade, Foreign Rights:* Shoju Yoshinari *Sales:* Shoichi Akane; *Production:* Kenji Nakamura; *Publicity:* Mistunobu Okawa
Associated Company: Kairyukan Publishing Co Ltd
Br Off: at Fukuoka, Nagoya, Osaka, Sapporo
Subjects: Textbooks, Natural Science, Art, Language, Reference, Teaching Aids
1977: 1,242 titles *Founded:* 1926

Kaisei-Sha, 3-5 Ichigaya, Sadohara-cho, Shinjuku-ku, Tokyo 162 Tel: (03) 2603221 Cable Add: Kaiseisha
President: Hiroshi Imamura; *Editorial Dir:* Mitsuo Takamori; *Sales Dir:* Rokuroh Isohata; *Editor & Foreign Rights:* Nobuo Kandori
Subject: Juveniles
1978: 120 titles *Founded:* 1936

Kaitaku-Sha*, 2-5 Kanda Jinbo-cho, Chiyoda-ku, Tokyo 101 Tel: (03) 2657641
President: Kunio Naganuma; *Foreign Trade:* Takehito Yamaguchi; *Foreign Rights:* Yasuhiko Yamamoto
Subjects: Reference, Education, Language, Literature
Founded: 1927

Kajima Institute Publishing Co Ltd, 6-5-13 Akasaka, Minato-ku, Tokyo 107 Tel: (03) 5822251
President: Syoichi Kajima; *Foreign Trade:* Tsunesuke Utsumi; *Foreign Rights:* Hiroshi Yamamoto
Subjects: Architecture, Urban Engineering, Civil Engineering
1978: 765 titles *Founded:* 1963
Bookshop: Kasumigaseki Bookstore, 3-2-5 Kasumigaseki, Chiyoda-ku, Tokyo; Shinjuku Mitsui Building Bookstore, 2-1 Nishishinjuku, Shinjuku-ku, Tokyo; Shibuya Tohoseimei Building Bookstore, 2-15 Shibuya, Shibuya-ku, Tokyo

Kanehara & Co Ltd*, 31-14, 2-chome, Yushima, Bunkyo-ku, Tokyo 113, Tel: (03) 8117161 Cable Add: Kaneharaco Tokyo
President and General Manager: Hideo Kanehara; *Director (Foreign Business):* Hiroshi Kohno
Subjects: Medicine, Technology, Industry
1977: 330 titles *Founded:* 1875
Miscellaneous: Publish Ishihara's Tests for Colour-blindness

Kawade Shobo Shinsha*, 95 Sumiyoshi-cho, Shinjuku-ku, Tokyo 162 Tel: (03) 3555311
President: Kozo Sato
Subjects: General Fiction, Natural & Social Science, Art, History, Philosophy
Founded: 1957

Kenkyusha Ltd*, 1-2 Kagurazaka, Shinjuku-ku, Tokyo 162 Tel: (03) 2694521
President: Mutsumi Ogura; *Foreign Trade Executive:* Shiro Nagai; *Foreign Rights Executive:* Yuki Kohno
Subjects: Reference, Languages, Dictionaries
1977: 36 titles *Founded:* 1907

Kinokuniya Bookstore Co Ltd (Publishing Department), 12 Gobancho, Chiyoda-ku, Tokyo 102 Tel: (03) 2634914/5 & 2639006 Cable Add: Kinokuni
General Manager: Toshio Kaneko; *Sales:* Shigeru Yagi
Associated Companies: Kinokuniya Book-Stores of America Co Ltd, 1581 Webster St, San Francisco, CA 94115, USA, 110 S Los Angeles St, Los Angeles, CA 90012, USA; Kinokuniya Publications Service of New York Co Ltd, 633 Third Ave, Suite 1925, New York, NY 10017, USA; Kinokuniya Publications Service of London Co, Radnor House, 93-97 Regent St, London W1, UK
Subjects: Biography, History, Music, Art, Philosophy, Politics, Medicine, Psychology, Engineering, General Science, Social Science, University Textbooks
Bookshops: 17-7 Shinjuku 3-chome, Shinjuku-ku, Tokyo 160, (23 branches throughout Japan)
1977: 47 titles *1978:* 45 titles *Founded:* 1926

Kodansha Ltd*, 2-12-21 Otowa, Bunkyo-ku, Tokyo 112 Tel: (03) 9451111 Cable Add: Kodanshapublish Tokyo Telex: 2722570 Kodanc J
President: Shoichi Noma; *Foreign Trade:* Shoji Nadaya; *Editorial:* Yutaka Kubota; *Sales:* Kanzo Yamaguchi; *Production:* Teikichi Tarusawa; *Publicity:* Tsutomu Matsubayashi; *Rights & Permissions:* Samio Degawa
Subsidiary Companies: Kodansha International, Japan (qv); Kodansha Scientific, Japan (qv)
Br Off: in Fukuoka, Hiroshima, Nagoya, Osaka, Sapporo, Sendai, Takamatsu
Subjects: General Non-fiction, Religion, Philosophy, History, Geography, Art, Politics, Economics, Pedagogy, Sociology, Natural Science, Medicine, Social Science, Engineering, Language, Literature, Juveniles, Reference Books
Book Clubs: Kodansha Disney Children's Book Club
Founded: 1909

Kodansha International Ltd, 2-12-21 Otowa, Bunkyo-ku, Tokyo 112 Tel: (03) 9446491 Cable Add: Kodanshaint Tokyo
Man Dir: Saburo Nobuki; *Editorial:* Kim Schuefftan; *Sales & Rights & Permissions:* Yukimori Akanoma; *Publicity:* Drew Stroud
Br Off: Kodansha International/USA Ltd, 10 East 53rd St, New York, NY 10022, USA; 44 Montgomery St, San Francisco, Calif 94104, USA
Subjects: Specializing in Japan and Asia: General Fiction, Belles Lettres, Art, How-to, History, Philosophy, Reference, Traditional Crafts, Martial Arts, Cooking
1978: 26 titles *1979:* 37 titles *Founded:* 1963
ISBN Publisher's Prefix: 0-87011

Kodansha Scientific Ltd*, 2-12-21 Otowa, Bunkyo-ku, 112 Tokyo Tel: 9434541
Founded: 1970
Subjects: Scientific Texts

Komine Shoten Publishing Co Ltd*, 6 Yotsuya Funa-machi, Shinjuku-ku, Tokyo
Man Dir: Hiroe Komine
Subjects: Education, Juveniles
Founded: 1946

Kosei Publishing Co Ltd, 2-7-1, Wada, Suginami-ku, Tokyo 166 Tel: (03) 3833151 Cable Add: Koseishuppansha Tokyo
President: Tadashi Furukawa; *Foreign Trade Executive:* Hiroshi Nomura; *Foreign Rights Executive:* Masuo Nezu
Subjects: Religion, Juveniles, English Translations, Literature, Magazines
1977: 38 titles *1978:* 26 titles *Founded:* 1950

Koseisha-Koseikaku Co Ltd*, 8 San-ei-cho, Shinjuku-ku, Tokyo 160 Tel: (03) 3597371
President: Hisao Satake; *Editorial Department:* Fukase Simao; *Publishing Department:* Hajime Torizuka; *Business Department:* Masaru Tajima
Subjects: Philosophy, Sociology, Natural Sciences, Technology, Industry, Astronomy
Founded: 1922

Kyo Bun Kwan Inc*, 4-5-1 Ginza, Chuo-ku, Tokyo 104 Tel: (03) 5618446 Cable Add: Kyobunkwan Tokyo
Subject: Religion
Founded: 1885
Bookshop: 4-5-1 Ginza, Chuo-ku, Tokyo 104

Kyoritsu Shuppan Co Ltd*, 6-19 Kobinata, 4-chome, Bunkyo-ku, Tokyo 112 Tel: (03) 9472511
Chief Man Dir: Masataka Takeuchi
Subjects: Natural Science & Technology, Medicine, Industry, Textbooks
1978: 119 titles *Founded:* 1926

Maruzen Co Ltd, PO Box 5050, Tokyo International 10031 (Located at: 3-10 Nihonbashi 2-chome, Chuo-ku, Tokyo 103) Tel: (03) 2727211 Cable Add: Maruya Tokyo Telex: J26517
President: Shingo Iizumi; *Man Dir:* Kumao Ebihara; *Dir (Export and Import):* Yasuo Kanazawa; *General Manager (Publishing Division):* Junji Sekine; *Dir (Import):* Tadashi Fukuda
Subsidiary Companies: Maruzen Asia (Pte) Ltd; Maruzen International Co Ltd, New York, USA
Subjects: Linguistics, Medicine, General & Social Science, Technical, Architecture, Mathematics, Engineering, Economics, Management, Dictionaries
1977: 99 titles *1978:* 63 titles *Founded:* 1869
Bookshops: 3-10 Nihonbashi 2-chome, Chuo-ku, Tokyo 103; also at Fukuoka, Hiroshima, Kobe, Kyoto, Nagoya, Okayama, Osaka, Sapporo, Sendai

Medical Friend Co Ltd, 1-32 4-chome Kudan Kita, Chiyoda-ku, Tokyo 102 Tel: (03) 264 6611
President: Kazuharu Ogura; *Editorial, Publicity & Advertising, Sales, Rights & Permissions:* Yoshihiro Ogura
Br Off: 2-2-1200 1-chome Umeda, Kita-ku, Osaka 530
1978: 254 titles *1979:* 317 titles *Founded:* 1947
Subjects: Medical, Paramedical, Nursing Science & Arts, Expert Publications, Textbooks and Periodicals

Minerva Shobo Co Ltd, 1 Tsutsumidani-cho, Hinooka Yamashina, Yamashina-ku, Kyoto 607 Tel: Kyoto 5815191
President: Nobuo Sugita; *Editorial Dir:* Keiji Nakanishi; *Foreign Trade:* Ichiro Terauchi; *Foreign Rights:* Seiji Miyamoto
Subjects: Philosophy & Religion, History, Social Science, Literature, Reference
1977: 260 titles *1978:* 243 titles *Founded:* 1948

Misuzu Shobo Publishing Co Ltd*, 17–15 Hongo 3-chome, Bunkyo-ku, Tokyo 113 Tel: (03) 8159181
Foreign Trade, Foreign Rights: Toshito Obi; *Sales Dir:* Yoshio Aida
Subjects: General, History, Art, Literature, Philosophy, Religion, High-priced Paperbacks, Psychiatry, Mathematics, Natural Science, General Science, Social Science
1977: 280 titles *Founded:* 1946

Morikita Shuppan Co Ltd, 4-11 Fujimi 1-chome, Chiyoda-ku, Tokyo 102 Tel: (03) 2658341
President: Hajime Morikita; *Foreign Trade Executive:* Kazuo Mori; *Foreign Rights Executive:* Mohachi Yanagisawa
Subjects: Natural Science, Technology, Secondary Textbooks
1977: 50 titles *Founded:* 1940 (as Morikita Shoten)

Nagai Shoten Co Ltd, 21–15, Fukushima 8-chome, Fukushima-ku, Osaka 553 Tel: (06) 4521881
President: Hideichi Nagai; *Man Dir, Editorial:* Tadao Nagai
Subject: Medicine
1977: 16 titles *1978:* 18 titles *Founded:* 1946

Nankodo Co Ltd*, PO Box 5272, Tokyo International, Tokyo 100–31 (Located at: 42–6 Hongo, 3-chome, Bunkyo-ku, Tokyo 113) Tel: (03) 8117234 Cable Add: Booknankodo
President: Takehiko Kodachi; *Dir (Publications):* Kaguhiko Ootomo; *Dir (Foreign Division):* Shoji Sano; *Manager of Planning, Publicity:* Takayuki Izumi; *Sales Dir:* Takashi Ito; *Manager, Imports:* Masao Takahashi
Br Off: Oike-minami Teramachi dori, Nakakyo-ku, Kyoto 604
Subjects: Medicine, Language, Natural Science, Technology
1977: 51 titles *1978:* 45 titles *Founded:* 1879

Nanzando Co Ltd*, 4-1-11 Yushima, Bunkyo-ku, Tokyo 113 Tel: (03) 8117241
Man Dir: Kimio Suzuki
Subjects: Reference, High-priced Paperbacks, Medicine, University Textbooks, Pharmacology
Founded: 1901

Nihon Bunka Kagakusha Co Ltd*, 15–17 Honkomagome 6-chome, Bunkyo-ku, Tokyo 113 Tel: (03) 9463131 Cable Add: Nihonbunkamm Tokyo
President: Mohachi Motegi; *Foreign Trade Executive:* Yoshiteru Furuta; *Foreign Rights Executive:* Yagoro Kojima
Subjects: Education, Natural Science, Medicine, Reference Books
1977: 35 titles *Founded:* 1948

Nihon Vogue (Publishing) Co Ltd*, 34 Ichigaya-Honmuracho, Shinjuku-ku, Tokyo 162 Tel: (03) 2698711 Cable Add: Spinningwheel
Man Dir: M Ajiro; *Foreign Trade:* Shigeo Suzuki; *Rights & Permissions:* Ichiro Murakami
Subjects: Knitting, Crocheting, Embroidery, Handicrafts (in Paperback)
Founded: 1954

Obunsha Co Ltd, 55 Yokodera-cho, Shinjuku-ku, Tokyo 162 Tel: (03) 2666100
President: Yoshio Akao
Subjects: General Fiction, Biography, How-to, Reference, General Science, Secondary & Primary Textbooks, Educational Materials, Cassettes
1978: 300 titles *Founded:* 1931
Affiliates: The Japan Society of English Study; The Society for Testing English Proficiency (both at 55 Yokodera-cho, Shinjuku-ku, Tokyo 162); The Japan LL Education Center, 3-14-16 Shimo-ochiai, Shinjuku-ku, Tokyo 161; Asahi National Broadcasting Co Ltd, 6-4-10 Roppongi, Minato-ku, Tokyo 106

The **Ohm**-Sha Ltd*, 3-1 Kanda-Nishiki-Cho, Chiyoda-ku, Tokyo 101 Tel: (03) 2330641
President: S Mitsui; *Man Dir:* K Tobe; *Foreign Rights:* Kiyokazu Iijima
Subjects: Science and Engineering, Periodicals
1977: 141 titles *Founded:* 1914

Ondori Sha Publishers Co Ltd, 32 Nishi Goken-cho, Shinjuku-ku, Tokyo 162 Tel: (03) 2683101
President: Toshizo Takeuchi; *Editor:* Takeo Sanada; *Sales:* Sigeo Yamamoto
Subjects: Fiction, Hobbies, Art, Mass Media, Juveniles
1977: 58 titles *1978:* 52 titles *Founded:* 1945

Ongaku No Tomo Sha Corporation, 6-30 Kagurazaka, Shinju-ku, Tokyo 161 Tel: (03) 2606271/8 Cable Add: Ongakuno Tomo Tokyo
President: Sunao Asaka; *Rights & Permissions:* Teruaki Kurata
Subsidiary Companies: Toa Music Co, 6-32 Kagurazaka, Shinju-ku, Tokyo; Suiseisha Music Publishers, 3-3 Sanban-cho, Chiyoda-ku, Tokyo; Musica Nova, 1-11-3-108 Sakashita, Itabashi-ku, Tokyo
Subjects: Music, Textbooks
1977: 950 titles *1978:* 148 titles *Founded:* 1941

Oriental Economist Ltd (K K Toyo Keizai Shimposha), 4 Hongoku-cho 1-chome, Nihonbashi, Chuo-ku, Tokyo Tel: (03) 2704111
Man Dir: Iko Furukawa
Subjects: Scholastic, Economics, General Nonfiction, Directories

Pacifica Ltd*, Time-Life Books, PO Box 88, Tokyo 100–91 Tel: (03) 2706611 Cable Add: Publiftim Tokyo Telex: J 22276
Publisher: Mitsuo Honda; *Editor-in-chief:* Masatoshi Takeuchi; *Rights & Permissions:* Chiz Nakao
Parent Company: Time Inc
Subjects: General Fiction and Nonfiction
1977: 24 titles *Founded:* 1977

Poplar Publishing Co Ltd, 5 Suga-cho, Shinjuku-ku, Tokyo 160 Tel: (03) 3572211
President: Tadao Kubota; *Foreign Trade Executive:* Haruo Tanaka; *Foreign Rights Executive:* Hideo Tanaka; *Foreign Rights Editor:* Tetsuo Kubota
Subjects: Juveniles, Textbooks, Fiction, Biography, History, Geography, Natural Sciences, Picture Books
1978: 180 titles *Founded:* 1947

Prentice-Hall of Japan Inc*, Akasaka Mansion Room 405, 12–23 Akasaka 2-chome, Minato-ku, Tokyo 107 Tel: 5832591
Manager (Books & Rights Sales): Tetsuo Fujiyama
Subjects: Engineering, Technology, Sciences, Social Sciences, Business, Economics, Humanities
Miscellaneous: Firm is a affiliate of Prentice-Hall International, Englewood Cliffs NJ 07632, USA (see Prentice-Hall UK for Associated Companies)
Founded: 1961

The **Reader's Digest** of Japan Limited+, 1-1 Hitotsubashi 1-chome, Chiyoda-ku, Tokyo 100 Tel: (03) 2844111 Cable Add: Readigest Tokyo Telex: J23941 Rdtyo
President: Kaoru Ogimi
Subjects: Geography, Education, Natural Science, Art, Language, Literature, Juveniles
1978: 2 titles *Founded:* 1946 (in Japan)

Risosha Ltd*, 46 Akagishita-machi, Shinjuku-ku, Tokyo 162 Tel: (03) 2681306
President: Tetsuo Shimomura; *Foreign Trade:* Tsugumoto Ishii; *Foreign Rights:* Kazumasa Doi
Subjects: Philosophy, Religion, Literature
1978: 11 titles *Founded:* 1927

Ryosho-Fukyu-Kai Co Ltd*, 8-2 Kasuga 1-chome, Bunkyo-ku, Tokyo 112 Tel: (03) 8131251
President & Editor: Ichigaku Kawanaka; *Foreign Trade Executive:* Isao Hiramatsu; *Foreign Rights Executive:* Shigeru Fukuhara; *Man Dir:* Kiyoshi Funakoshi
Subjects: Law, Social & Political Sciences, Public and Local Administration
Founded: 1914

Sangyo Tosho Publishing Co Ltd*, 1-4-21 Soto-Kanda, Chiyoda-ku, Tokyo 101 Tel: (03) 2537821
Man Dir: Katsuhisa Morita; *Editorial:* Takehiko Ezura; *Sales:* Eiji Horino
Subjects: Natural Science, Engineering, Technology, Industry
1977: 18 titles *Founded:* 1925

The **Sankei** Shimbun Shuppankyoku Co*, 3-15 Kanda Nishiki-cho, Chiyoda-ku, Tokyo 101 Tel: (03) 2950911 Telex: J2–2235
Man Dir: Masashi Onoda; *Editorial:* Katsumi Shirai; *Sales:* Hiroshi Ohsato; *Rights & Permissions:* Nobaru Enomoto
Parent Companies: The Sankei Shimbun (Newspaper), Fuji Television Co, Nippon Broadcasting Co
Subjects: History, Social & Political Sciences, Industry, Art, Literature, Juveniles, Journals
1977: approx 100 titles *Founded:* 1950

Sanseido Co Ltd*, 1-1 Kanda-Jimbocho, Chiyoda-ku, Tokyo 101 Tel: (03) 2933441
President: Hisanoli Ueno; *Publishing Dir:* Kiyohide Kato; *Foreign Trade:* Toshio Gomi; *Sales:* Masaaki Moriya; *Production:* Tukaaki Hisasi; *Publicity:* Yasuo Nomura; *Rights & Permissions:* Koji Suzuki
Subjects: History, Geography, Reference, Low- & High-priced Paperbacks, Engineering, General & Social Science, Natural Science, University & Secondary Textbooks, Educational Materials, Dictionaries, Literature, Languages
Founded: 1881
Bookshop: Sanseido Bookstore Ltd, 1-1 Kanda-Jimbocho, Chiyoda-ku, Tokyo

Sansyusya Publishing Co Ltd, 26-11 Hongo 2-chome, Bunkyo-ku, Tokyo 113 Tel: (03) 8134031 Cable Add: Sansyusyapubl Tokyo
Man Dir: Kanji Maeda; *Sales, Publicity, Advertising, Rights & Permissions Dir:* Shohei Ohara
Subjects: Language Textbooks, Educational Materials, Scientific Linguistic Reprints
1978: 79 titles *Founded:* 1938

Sanyo Shuppan Boeki Co Inc*, PO Box 5037, Tokyo International 100-31 Tel: (03) 6693761 Cable Add: Sanyobook Tokyo Telex: 02524435
President: Tsuneo Suzuki; *Editorial:* Toshiaki Ibe; *Foreign Trade:* Masahiro Takeda; *Rights & Permissions:* Makoto Ito
Associated Company: Shinryo Bunko K K (medical bookstore)
Br Off: at Kyoto, Machida, Niihama, Osaka, Tsukuba
Subjects: Food and Cookery, Science, Chemistry
1977: 10 titles *Founded:* 1956
Miscellaneous: Also importers

Seibundo Shinkosha Publishing Co Ltd*, 5 Nishikicho 1-chome, Kanda, Chiyoda-ku, Tokyo 101 Tel: (03) 2921211 Cable Add: Varipubco Tokyo
Man Dir: Shigeo Ogawa; *Editorial:* Teruaki Shimada; *Sales:* Yasushi Muragi; *Publicity:* Kazuhiko Furiya
Subjects: Commerce, Agriculture, Horticulture & Landscaping, Natural Science, Technology, Industry, Juvenile
1977: 344 titles *Founded:* 1912
Miscellaneous: Publish *Idea*, an international advertising art magazine

Seiwa Shoten Co Ltd, 2-5 Kamitakaido, 1-chome, Suginamiku, Tokyo 168 Tel: 3290031 Cable Add: Seiwapublishers
President: Youji Ishizawa; *Editor-in-Chief:* Yoshinori Asanuma; *Sales Manager:* Masaharu Fujiwara; *System Manager:* Yukio Shimura; *Foreign Books Manager:* Yumi Matsuzawa
Subjects: Medicine, Psychiatry, Psychology, Language
Book Club: Bookclub Psyche
Bookshops: 1-11 Kamitakaido, 1-chome, Suginamiku, Tokyo 168; 2-5 Kamitakaido, 1-chome, Suginamiku, Tokyo 168; 1-48 Sengawacho, Chofushi, Tokyo 182
1978: 12 titles *1979:* 14 titles *Founded:* 1976

Seizando-Shoten Publication Co Ltd, 4-51 Minami-motomachi, Shinjuku-ku, Tokyo 160 Tel: (03) 3575861
President: Minoru Ogawa; *Editorial:* Yoshihiro Munekata; *Sales:* Jitsuo Moriyama; *Production:* Yuhei Shibuya, Nobuyuki Tanaka; *Publicity:* Yoshio Kimura; *Rights & Permissions:* Kokichi Shiogi
Subjects: Maritime, Technology, Transport
1977: 130 titles *1978:* 110 titles *Founded:* 1953
ISBN Publisher's Prefix: 3056

Sekai Bunka Publishing Inc*, 4-2-29 Kudan Kita, Chiyoda-ku, Tokyo 102 Tel: (03) 2625111 Cable Add: Sebunpub
President: Tsutomu Suzuki; *Foreign Trade & Rights:* Kazumi Haga
Br Off: 501 Fifth Ave, Suite 2102, New York, NY 10017, USA
Subjects: Art, History, Geography, Juveniles, Educational Materials, Audiovisual
Founded: 1946

Shakai Shiso-Sha*, 25-21 Hongo 1-chome, Bunkyo-ku, Tokyo 113 Tel: (03) 8138101
President: Kazuki Komorida; *Editorial:* Hitoshi Tanaka; *Sales:* Tadashi Kamatsuka
Subjects: General Fiction, Fine Arts, Architecture, Poetry, Music, History, Travel, Social Science, Theatre
1977: 46 titles *Founded:* 1947

Shiko-Sha Co Ltd*, 10-12 Hiroo 2-chome, Shibuya-ku, Tokyo 150 Tel: (03) 4007152/4 Cable Add: LMDECW Tokyo Telex: J24903
Man Dir: Yasoo Takeichi
Subject: Juveniles
1977: 7 titles *Founded:* 1950

Shinchosha Co, 71 Yarai-cho, Shinjuku-ku, Tokyo 162 Tel: (03) 2665110 Cable Add: Shinchosha
President: Ryoichi Sato; *Sales:* Shunichi Sato; *Publishing Department:* Hiroshi Nitta
Subjects: General Fiction, Fine Arts, History, Philosophy, Juveniles, Social Science, Reference, Literature
Founded: 1896

Shindan to Chiryo Co Ltd*, Room 406, Marunouchi Bldg, Marunouchi 2-4-1, Tokyo 100 Tel: (03) 2144957
President: Hiroshi Fujizane; *Editorial:* Takeshi Hisatsugi
Subject: Medicine
1978: 30 titles *Founded:* 1914

Shinkenchiku-Sha Co Ltd, 31-2 Yushima 2-chome, Bunkyo-ku, Tokyo 113 Tel: (03) 8117101 Cable Add: Japanarch Tokyo
President: Yoshio Yoshida; *General Manager:* Masao Nakamura; *Foreign Rights Executive:* Masao Nakamura
Subjects: Architecture, Periodicals
1977: 10 titles *1978:* 16 titles *Founded:* 1925
Subsidiary: The Japan Architect Co Ltd, 31-2, Yushima 2-chome, Bunkyo-ku, Tokyo 113

Shogakukan Publishing Co Ltd, 2-3 Hitotsubashi, Chiyoda-ku, Tokyo 101 Tel: (03) 2305211 Cable Add: Tokyo Shogakukan Telex: 2322191 (Shogak-J)
President: Tetsuo Ohga; *Man Dir:* Shuichi Nozaki; *Editorial:* Kiichi Toyoda; *Sales:* Tokio Ueno; *Production:* Mitsuo Kokubo
Associated Company: Shueisha Publishing Co (qv)
Subjects: Art, How-to, Juveniles, Dictionaries, Geography, History, Encyclopaedias, Travel
1977: 539 titles *1978:* 531 titles *Founded:* 1922

Shokabo Publishing Co Ltd*, 8-1 Yonban-cho, Chiyoda-ku, Tokyo 102 Tel: (03) 2629166
Man Dir: Tatsuji Yoshino
Subjects: Mathematics, Natural Science, Technology
1976: 12 titles *1977:* 11 titles *Founded:* 1897

Shokoku-Sha Publishing Co Ltd, 25 Sakamachi, Shinjuku-ku, J-160 Tokyo Tel: (03) 3593231
President: Genshichi Shimoide; *Sales Dir:* Hideo Shimizu; *Editorial Dir:* Taishiro Yamamoto
Subjects: Fine Arts, Technical, Architecture, Engineering, General Science, University Textbooks, Educational Materials
1977: 100 titles *Founded:* 1932

Shueisha Publishing Co Ltd*, 2-5-10 Hitotsubashi, Chiyoda-ku, Tokyo 101 Tel: (03) 2306111
President: Sueo Horiuchi; *Editorial:* Shusei Suzuki; *Sales:* Hisao Suzuki; *Foreign Trade:* Takeo Hasegawa; *Foreign Rights:* Hajime Kanazawa
Subjects: General Fiction, Nonfiction, Art, Language, Literature, Juveniles, Periodicals
Founded: 1926

Shufu-to-Seikatsu Sha Ltd*, 5-3-chome, Kyobashi, Chuo-ku, Tokyo 104 Tel: (03) 5625951
Man Dir: Tokumitsu Higuchi; *Editor in Chief:* Miss Miyako Kiyohara; *Publishing Department, Foreign Rights:* Shujiro Murakawa
Subjects: Philosophy & Religion, History, Medicine, Technology, Art, Literature, Juveniles
Founded: 1935

Shufunotomo Co Ltd, 6, 1-chome Surugadai, Kanda, Chiyoda-ku, Tokyo 101 Tel: 2941111 Cable Add: Shufunotomo Tokyo Telex: 26925
President: Haruhiko Ishikawa; *Manager of International Department:* Kazuhiko Nagai
Subjects: Cookery, Flower Arrangement, Bonsai, Gardening, How-to, General Fiction
1977: 200 titles *1978:* 180 titles *Founded:* 1916

The **Simul** Press Inc+, Kowa Bldg No 9, 1-8-10, Akasaka, Minato-ku, Tokyo 107 Tel: (03) 5824221 Cable Add: Simulshuppan Tokyo
President and Editor-in-Chief: Katsuo Tamura; *Senior Man Dir:* Eiko Ikuta; *Man Dirs:* Mitsuo Hirano, Yutaka Suzuki; *Dir (overseas affairs):* Masumi Muramatsu; *Secretary (foreign relations):* Masako Miyoshi; *Senior Editor:* Daitaro Suwabe; *Marketing:* Motoo Miyashita; *Publicity:* Koichiro Watanabe
Associate Company: Simul International, Inc
Subjects: General, Philosophy and Religion, Social Sciences, History, Education, Business and Economics, Current Affairs, Language, Literature, English-language books on Japan and Asia
1977: 41 titles *1978:* 40 titles *Founded:* 1967

Sogensha Publishing Co Ltd*, 4-2 1-chome, Nishitenma, Kita-ku, Osaka 530 Tel: (06) 3632531
President: Bunji Yabe
Associate Company: Tokyo Sogensha Co Ltd, Japan (qv)
Subjects: Art, History, Philosophy, Religion, Low-priced Paperbacks, Medicine, University Textbooks, Educational Materials
1977: 43 titles *Founded:* 1925

Syokabo Publishing Co Ltd, 8-1 Yomban-cho, Chiyoda-ku, Tokyo 102 Tel: (03) 2629166
President: Tatsuji Yoshino; *Foreign Trade:* Tatsuji Yoshino; *Foreign Rights:* Kyohei Endo
Subjects: Natural Science and Engineering
1978: 15 titles *Founded:* 1895

Taishukan Publishing Co Ltd (Taishukan Shoten), 3-24 Kanda-Nishiki-cho, Chiyoda-ku, Tokyo 101 Tel: (03) 2942221
Man Dir: Toshio Suzuki; *Sales, Publicity & Advertising:* Shigeo Suzuki; *Rights & Permissions:* Toshio Saeki
Subjects: Reference, High-priced Paperbacks, Language & Linguistics, Sports, Social Science, University & Secondary Textbooks, Educational Materials, Dictionaries, Periodicals
1978: 65 titles *Founded:* 1918

Takahashi Shoten Co Ltd*, 22-13 Otowa 1-chome, Bunkyo-ku, Tokyo 112 Tel: (03) 9434525
President: Kyushiro Takahashi; *Foreign*

Trade Executive: Yukihiko Takahashi
Subjects: Technology, Law Education, Medicine, Language, Juveniles
Founded: 1939 (as Kowado Co Ltd)

Tanko-Sha Publishing Co Ltd*, Tanko Bldg, Horikawa Kuramaguchi-agaru, Kita-ku, Kyoto 603 Tel: Kyoto 4325151
Man Dir: Saburo Iguchi; *Editorial Dir:* Shiro Usui
Subjects: Philosophy & Religion, History, Art, Japanese Culture
Founded: 1945

Teikoku-Shoin Co Ltd, 3-29 Kanda Jinbo-cho, Chiyoda-ku, Tokyo 101 Tel: (03) 2611584 Cable Add: Books Teikoku Telex: 2324921 Tekoku J
President: Kaoru Ohata; *Foreign Trade:* Takashi Saito; *Foreign Rights:* Takashi Goto
Subjects: History, Geography, Maps, Textbooks
1978: 150 titles *Founded:* 1926

Tokai University Press, Tokai Bldg, 3-27-4 Shinjuku, Shinjuku-ku, Tokyo 160 Tel: (03) 3561541
Man Dir: Tatsuro Matsumae; *Editorial:* Yasunosuke Yamamoto; *Sales:* Eizaburo Okada; *Production:* Chimaju Kato; *Publicity:* Wataru Yamada
Orders to: Orion Books, Export Dept of Orion Service & Trading Co Inc, PO Box 5216, Tokyo International
Subjects: Philosophy, Religion, History, Social & Natural Science, Technology, Art, Language, Literature
1977: 45 titles *1978:* 49 titles *Founded:* 1962
Miscellaneous: Tokai University European Center is at Strandvej 476, DK-2950, Vedbæk, Denmark

Tokuma-Shoten, 4-10-1 Shinbashi, Minato-ku, Tokyo Tel: 4336231
President: Yasuyoshi Tokuma; *Editor:* Minoru Hagiwara; *Foreign Trade:* Osamu Okamura
Subjects: General Fiction, Nonfiction, Belles Lettres, How-to, Social Science, Art, Games, Sports
Founded: 1954

Tokyo Kagaku Dozin Co Ltd*, 36-7 Sengoku 3-chome, Bunkyo-ku, Tokyo 112 Tel: (03) 9465311
President: Atsushi Ueki; *Editorial:* Minako Ozawa
Subjects: Natural Science, Medical Science, Chemistry
1978: 63 titles *Founded:* 1961

Tokyo News Service Ltd*, 8-10 Ginza-Nishi, Chuo-ku, Tokyo
President: T Okuyama
Subjects: Social Science, Economics, Business, General Nonfiction, Periodicals
Founded: 1947

Tokyo Sogensha Co Ltd*, 1-16 Shin Ogawa-machi, Shinjuku-ku, Tokyo 162 Tel: (03) 2688201
President: Takao Akiyama; *Editorial:* Jun Atsuki; *Sales:* Ichiro Hiramatsu; *Production:* Haruo Hashimoto; *Publicity:* Nobuko Okubo; *Rights & Permissions:* Yasunobu Togawa
Subjects: Detective Stories, Science Fiction, Social Science, Literature
1977: 70 titles *Founded:* 1925

Tokyo Tosho Co Ltd*, 2-5 Suido, Bunkyo-ku, Tokyo 112 Tel: (03) 8147818
President: Susumu Otake; *Foreign Trade Executive:* Hiroyasu Katayama; *Foreign Rights:* Shigeaki Matsumoto
Subjects: Natural Science, Popular Science, Engineering, Biographies
Founded: 1955

Toppan Co Ltd, Shufunotomo Bldg, 1-6 Kanda Surugadai, Chiyoda-ku, Tokyo 101 Tel: 2953461 Cable Add: Toppan Book Tokyo Telex: J27317
Chief Executive: Kazuo Suzuki; *Man Dir:* Hiroyuki Watanabe; *General Managers:* Moto Sekino, William A Feuillan
Associate Company: Toppan Co (S) Pte Ltd, Singapore (qv)
Subjects: Medicine, Psychology, Engineering, Social Science, Agriculture, Economics, Mathematics, Statistics, Zoology, Chemistry, Physics, Languages and Linguistics in authorized International Student Edition reprints for university students
1977: 34 titles *Founded:* 1963

Toyo Keizai Shinposha Ltd, 4 Hongokucho 1-chome, Nihonbashi, Chuo-ku, Tokyo 103 Tel: (03) 2704111
President: Yoshiyuki Nakai; *Foreign Trade:* Sasuke Takahashi; *Foreign Rights:* Ikuo Inada
Subjects: Economic Science, Industry, Social Science, General
1978: 100 titles *Founded:* 1895

Tsuru-Shobo Co Ltd*, 12-2 Fujimi 2-chome, Chiyoda-ku, Tokyo 102 Tel: (03) 2654781 Cable Add: Bookstsuru Tokyo
Man Dir: Mitsusaburo Sadahira; *Foreign Rights & Permissions:* Hiro Nagano
Subjects: How-to, Juveniles, Art, Reference
Founded: 1926

Charles E **Tuttle** Co Inc, 2-6 Suido 1-chome, Bunkyo-ku, Tokyo 112 Tel: (03) 8117106/9 Cable Add: Tuttbooks Telex: 0272-3170
President, Editorial, Sales, Publicity: Keiko Iwamoto; *Production:* Satoru Iwamoto; *Rights & Permissions:* Keiko Iwamoto
Br Offs: 402 Seki, Tama-ku, Kawasaki-shi 214; 2-7 Showa-cho, Suita-shi, Osaka 564; CPO Box 302, Naha-shi, Okinawa 900-91
Subjects: Japanese & Asian Studies, Art, Domestic & Handicrafts, Fiction, Martial Arts, Poetry, Belles Lettres, Political & Social Science, Juveniles, Languages
Bookshops: Kanda Book Shop, 1-3 Jimbo-cho, Kanda, Chiyoda-ku, Tokyo 101; American Club Book Shop, 4 Mamiana-cho, Azabu, Monato-ku, Tokyo 106
1977: 50 titles *1978:* 52 titles *Founded:* 1948
ISBN Publisher's Prefix: 0-8048

U N A C Tokyo*, 1-4-7 Azabu-da, Minato-ku, Tokyo 106 Tel: (03) 5857069/5853069 Cable Add: Unacprod
Publisher: Masaomi Unagami

University of Tokyo Press, 7-3-1 Hongo, Bunkyo-ku, Tokyo 113-91 Tel: (03) 8110964 Cable Add: Universitypress
Man Dir: Kazuo Ishii; *Associate Dir:* Senzaburo Nakahira; *Sales:* Kazuhiko Kurata; *Publicity, Rights & Permissions:* Masami Yamaguchi
Subsidiary Companies: Centre for Academic Publications Japan; Business Centre for Academic Societies Japan (both at 2-14-16 Yayoi, Bunkyo-ku, Tokyo 113)
Subjects: History, Philosophy, Reference, Religion, Medicine, Psychology, Engineering, Natural & Social Sciences, University Textbooks
Bookshop: Yurinsha Ltd, PO Box 63, Hongo Post Office, Tokyo
1977: 173 titles *1978:* 163 titles *Founded:* 1951

John **Weatherhill** Inc*, 7-6-13 Roppongi, Minato-ku, Tokyo Tel: 4048871 Cable Add: Weatherhill Tokyo Telex: 23424004
Man Dir: Meredith Weatherby; *Sales & Advertising:* Jun'ichiro Minagawa; *Rights & Permissions:* Emile Dubrule, 149 Madison Ave, New York, NY 10016, USA
Subjects: Belles Lettres, Poetry, Biography, History, How-to, Music, Art, Reference, Religion, Juveniles, High-priced Paperbacks — all on Asia
Founded: 1962

Yama-Kei (Publishers) Co Ltd*, 1-1-33 Shiba-Daimon, Minato-ku, Tokyo 105 Tel: (03) 4364021
President: Yoshimitsu Kawasaki; *Foreign Trade:* Susumu Harada; *Foreign Rights:* Naotake Murakami
Br Off: Riverside Bldg, 4-11-12 Kamiji, Higashinari-ku, Osaka
Subjects: Mountaineering, Skiing, Geography, Natural Science
Founded: 1930

Yamada Shoin (Yamada Publishing Co)*, 26 Saka-machi, Shinjuku-ku, Tokyo 160 Tel: (03) 3534331
Chairman: Yonekichi Yamada; *President:* Minoru Yamada; *Sales:* Akira Shimizu
Subjects: Fine Arts, History, Juveniles, Travel, Textbooks
Founded: 1919

Yokendo Ltd*, 5-30-15 Hongo, Bunkyo-ku, Tokyo 113 Tel: (03) 8140911
Chairman: Gomiji Oikawa; *President:* Toshio Oikawa
Subjects: Natural Science, Engineering, Industry
1977: 15 titles *Founded:* 1914

Yuhikaku Publishing Co Ltd, 17 2-chome, Kanda Jinbo-cho, Chiyoda-ku, Tokyo 101 Tel: (03) 2641311 Cable Add: Yuhikakubook
Dirs: Shiro Egusa, Tadaatsu Egusa
Subjects: Law, Economics, Sociology, Psychology, History, Education
1977: 200 titles *1978:* 230 titles *Founded:* 1877

Yushodo Booksellers Ltd, 29 San-ei-cho, Shinjuku-ku, Tokyo 160 Tel: (03) 3571411 Cable Add: Yushodo Tokyo Telex: 0232-4136
President: Mitsuo Nitta; *Editorial:* Toshihiko Ito, Yoshito Yamada
Subsidiary Companies: Publishers International Corp, Yushodo Film Publications Ltd
Br Off: Kansai, Kyoto
Subjects: Political Economics, Japanese Classical Literature
1977: 20 titles *1978:* 24 titles
Miscellaneous: Company are also Booksellers

The **Zauho** Press, Sogo Daiichi Bldg, 3-2 Kojimachi, Chiyoda-ku, Tokyo 102 Tel: (03) 2623661 Cable Add: Zauhopress
President: Shigeki Gotoh; *Foreign Trade Executive:* Yoshiki Gotoh; *Foreign Rights Executive:* Masao Nishida
Subjects: Art, History, Co-editions
1978: 1 title *Founded:* 1925

232 JAPAN

Zoshindo Juken-Kenkyusha, 19-15 2-chome Shinmachi, Nishi-ku Osaka 550
President: Shigetoshi Okamoto
Subjects: Education, Juveniles
1978: 442 titles *Founded:* 1890

Literary Agents

The **English Agency**, 705 Azabu Empire Mansion, 4-11-28 Nishi Azabu, Minato-ku, Tokyo
Dirs: Anthony Blond, Desmond Briggs, William Miller, Peter Thompson
Specialization: English books

Japan Uni Agency Inc, Naigai Bldg, 1-1 Kanda Jimbocho, Chiyoda-ku, Tokyo 101 Tel: (03) 2950301 Cable Add: Uniliterary Telex: J27260
President: Noboru Miyata; *Man Dir:* Kozaburo Yano; *Dirs:* Hideo Aoki (Co-Production); Yoshio Taketomi (Copyrights); *Foreign Rights:* Akiko Kurita

Kern Associates, 5-18 Sakae-cho, Sagamihara-shi Kanagawa-ken 228 Tel: 0427461829/31/32 Cable Add: Kern Machida Telex: 2872408 Kenics
Chairman: Lawrence E Kern; *Dirs:* D Kern, N Kern
Specialization: Fiction, Nonfiction, Academic, Juvenile

Orion Press, 55, 1-chome, Kanda-Jimbocho, Chiyoda-ku, Tokyo 101 Tel: (03) 2951405/2951406 Cable Add: Orionserv Tokyo Telex: J24447 Orionprs
Contact: G G Pompilio

Toppan Co Ltd, Rights Agency Section, Shufunotomo Building, 1-6 Kanda Surugadai, Chiyoda-ku, Tokyo 101 Tel: (03) 295 3461 Cable Add: Toppanbook Tokyo Telex: J27317
Contact: William A Feuillan

Tuttle-Mori Agency Inc*, 2-6 Suido 1-chome, Bunkyo-ku, Tokyo 112 Tel: 816 3286 Cable Add: Tuttbooks Tokyo Telex: 02723170

United Publishers Services Ltd*, Shimura Building, 4-1, Kojimachi, Chiyoda-ku, Tokyo 102 Tel: (03) 2625278 Cable Add: Unitedbooks Tokyo
General Manager: Sumio Saito

Book Clubs

Books-on-Japan-in-English Club, Shin Nichibo Bldg, 2-1 Sarugaku-cho 1-chome, Chiyoda-ku, Tokyo 101
President: Katsuji Yabuki; *Secretary General:* Akio Takeuchi
Founded: 1955
Miscellaneous: Club consists of 36 leading publishers, bookstores, exporters, and printers of English-language books and periodicals dealing with Japan and Orient

Ehon Library*, 1-9 Misaki-cho 1-chome, Chiyoda-ku, Tokyo 101
Owned by: Fukuinkan Shoten Publishers (Tokyo)
Subject: Picture Books

Kodansha Disney Children's Book Club*, 2-12-21 Otowa, Bunkyo-ku, Tokyo
Owned by: Kodansha (Tokyo)
Subject: Children's Books

Bookclub **Psyche**, 2-5 Kamitakaido, 1-chome, Suginamiku, Tokyo 168
Owned by: Seiwa Shoten Co Ltd
Subject: Psychiatry

Major Booksellers

Asahiya Shoten Ltd (Booksellers), Osaka-Fukoku-Seimei Bldg 3F, 2-4 Komatsubara-cho Kita-ku, Osaka 530 Tel: (06) 3150971
Foreign Books Department: c/o Asahi Building, 17-9 Toyosaki 3-chome, Ohyodo-ku, Osaka 531 Tel: (06) 3727251
16 bookstores throughout the country

Goethe Book Dealers Inc*, Room 560, Marunouchi Bldg, Chiyoda-ku, Tokyo 100 Tel: (03) 2117839

Ikubundo Publishers Co*, 30-21 Hongo 5-chome, Bunkyo-ku, Tokyo 113 Tel: (03) 8145571/5

Japan Publications Trading Co Ltd (Import and Export), 2-1, 1-chome, Sarugaku-cho, Chiyoda-ku, Tokyo 101 Tel: (03) 2923751 Telex: J27161

Kinokuniya Bookstore Co Ltd, 17-7 Shinjuku 3-chome, Shinjuku-ku, Tokyo 160-91 Tel: (03) 3540131 (and 37 branches throughout Japan)

Kurita Shuppan Hanbai Co Ltd*, 3-1 Higashisakashita 1-chome, Itabashi-ku, Tokyo 174 Tel: (03) 9652111
Distributor

Maruzen Co Ltd, 3-10 Nihonbashi 2-chome, Chuo-ku, Tokyo 103 Tel: (03) 2727211
Branches: Sapporo, Sendai, Tsukuba, Nagoya, Kyoto, Osaka, Kobe, Okayama, Hiroshima, Fukuoka
Importer/Exporter

Nippon Shuppan Hanbai KK, 3 4-chome, Kanda Surugadai, Chiyoda-ku, Tokyo 101 Tel: (03) 2932111 Cable Add: Honnippan Tokyo Telex: J 25627 Nippan
Distributors

Tokyo Shuppan Hanbai Co Ltd (Distributors)*, 53 Higashigoken-cho, Shinjuku-ku, Tokyo 162 Tel: (03) 2696111 Cable Add: Hontohan Tokyo Telex: 2322141

Charles E **Tuttle** Co Inc, 2-6 Suido 1-chome, Bunkyo-ku, Tokyo 112 Tel: 8117106

United Publishers Services Ltd*, Shimura Bldg, 4-1, Kojimachi, Chiyoda-ku, Tokyo 102 Tel: (03) 2625278 Cable Add: Unitedbooks Tokyo
The largest agent of overseas publishers in the Japanese foreign book market

Yohan Publications Inc, 14-9 Okubo 3-chome, Shinjuku-ku, Tokyo 160 Tel: (03) 2080181

Major Libraries

Hokkaido University Library, Kita-8, Nishi-5, Sapporo 060 Tel: (011) 711-2111
Librarian: Masahiko Takashima
Publication: Yuin (The Hokkaido University Library Bulletin, only in Japanese, quarterly)

Kokuritsu Kobunshokan (National Archives)*, 3-2 Kitanomaru Park, Chiyoda-ku, Tokyo

Kyoto Sangyo University Library*, Kamigamo, Kita-ku, Kyoto Tel: (075) 7012151

Kyushu University Library*, 3576 Hakozaki-machi, Fukuoka City, Fukuoka Prefecture

School of **Library** and Information Science*, Keio University, Mita Minato-ku, Tokyo 108 Tel: (03) 4533920

Nagoya University Library*, Furo-cho, Chikusa-ku, Nagoya

National Diet Library*, 10-1, 1-chome, Nagata-cho, Chiyoda-ku, Tokyo Tel: (03) 5812331
Librarian: Minoru Miyasaka

Osaka Prefectural Nakanoshima Library*, 1-27 Nakanoshima, Kita-ku, Osaka Tel: (06) 2030474

Osaka Gakuin University Library*, Kishibe, Suita City, Osaka

Tenri Central Library, Tenri University, Somanouchi-cho 1050, Tenri City, Nara 632 Tel: (07436) 31511 ext 6750
Chief Librarian: Hidetsugu Ueda

Tohoku University Library*, Kawauchi, Sendai City 980

Tokyo Metropolitan Central Library, 5-7-13 Minami-Azabu, Minato-ku, Tokyo 106

The **Toyo** Bunko, Honkomagome 2-chome, 38-21, Bunko, Tokyo 113 Tel: (03) 9420121
Publications: Findings of the Research Department of the Toyo Bunko
Also Centre of East Asian Cultural Studies for UNESCO, for which publications include various directories, bibliographies, textbooks, etc

University of Tokyo Library*, 3-1 Hongo 7-chome, Bunkyo-ku, Tokyo 113 Tel: (03) 8122111

Waseda University Library*, 6-1 Nishiwaseda 1-chome, Shinjuku-ku, Tokyo 160

Library Associations

Gakujutsu Bunken Fukyu-Kai (Association for Science Documents Information)*, c/o Tokyo Institute of Technology, 2-15-1 O-okayama, Meguro-ku, Tokyo
President: Taku Uemura
Publications: Union Catalog of Books on Japan in Western Languages (English), Reports on Progress in Polymer Physics in Japan (English), Directory of Japanese Scientific Periodicals (English), Aseismic Design and Testing of Nuclear Facilities (English), Union Index of Books in the Field of Documentation (English)

Joho Shori Gakkai (Information Processing Society of Japan), Kikai Shinko-Kai Building No 3-5-8, Shiba-Koen, Minato-ku, Tokyo
President: K Kobayashi
Publications: Journal of Information Processing (English, quarterly), *Joho-shori* (Journal of IPSJ, Japanese, monthly), *Transactions of IPSJ* (Japanese, bi-monthly)

Nippon Dokumentesyon Kyokai (Japan Documentation Society), Sasaki Bldg, 5-7 Koisikawa 2, Bunkyo-ku, Tokyo 112 Tel: (03) 8133791
President: S Hamada
Publication: Documentation Study

Nippon Igaku Toshokan Kyokai (The Japan Medical Library Association), c/o Business Centre for Academic Societies, 4-16 Yayoi 2-chome, Bunkyo-ku, Tokyo 113

Nippon Nogaku Toshokan Kyogikai (Japan Association of Agricultural Librarians and Documentalists) (JAALD), Taiyo Seimei Building, 2-17-2, Shibuya, Shibuya-ku, Tokyo 150 Tel: (03) 4090722
Secretary: Masatada Oyama
Publications: Quarterly Bulletin of JAALD, Japanese Agricultural Sciences Index (monthly with semi-annual indexes)

Nippon Toshokan Gakkai (Japan Society of Library Science)*, c/o National College of Library Science, 1-1 Simouma 4-chome, Setagaya-ku, Tokyo
Executive Secretary: Takaaki Kuriwa
Publication: Toshokangakki Nempo (Annals) (2-4 a year)

Nippon Toshokan Kyokai (Japan Library Association), 1-10, 1-chome, Taishido Setagaya-ku, Tokyo 154
Secretary-General: Hitoshi Kurihara
Publications: Toshokan Zasshi (monthly), *Gendai no Toshokan* (quarterly), *Nippon no Sankotosho Shikiban* (quarterly), *Nippon no Toshokan* (annually)

Nippon Yakugaku Toshokan Kyogikai (Japan Pharmaceutical Library Association), c/o Library, Faculty of Pharmaceutical Sciences, Hongo 7-3-1, Bunkyo-ku, Tokyo 113
Publication: Yakugaku Toshokan (Pharmaceutical Library Bulletin)

Senmon Toshokan Kyogikai (SENTOKYO) (Japan Special Libraries Association), c/o National Diet Library, 1-10-1, Nagata-cho, Chiyoda-ku, Tokyo 100 Tel: (03) 5811364
President: Shigeo Nagano
Publications: Bulletin (quarterly), *Directory of Special Libraries*

Library Reference Books and Journals

Books

Directory of Special Libraries, Special Libraries Association, c/o National Diet Library, 10-1, 1-chome, Nagata-cho, Chiyoda-ku, Tokyo

Nippon no Toshokan (Library of Japan), Japan Library Association, 1-10, 1-chome, Taishido Setagaya-ku, Tokyo

Union Index of Books in the Field of Documentation, Association for Science Documents Information, c/o Tokyo Institute of Technology, 2-15-1 O-okayama, Meguro-ku, Tokyo

Journals

Biburosu Biblos, National Diet Library, 10-1, 1-chome, Nagata-cho, Chiyoda-ku, Tokyo

Bulletin, Special Libraries Association, c/o National Diet Library, 10-1, 1-chome, Nagata-cho, Chiyoda-ku, Tokyo

Dokumentesyon Kenkyu (Documentation Study), Japan Documentation Society, Sasaki Bldg, 5-7 Koisikawa 2, Bunkyo-ku, Tokyo 112

Handbook, Special Libraries Association, c/o National Diet Library, 10-1, 1-chome, Nagata-cho, Chiyoda-ku, Tokyo

Library System (text in Japanese), Medical Library and Information Centre, Keio Unveristy, 35, Shinanomachi, Shinjuku-ku, Tokyo

Nippon no Sakotosho Shikiban (Reference Library Quarterly of Japan), Japan Library Association, 1-10, 1-chome, Taishido Setagaya-ku, Tokyo

Reference, National Diet Library, 10-1, 1-chome, Nagata-cho, Chiyoda-ku, Tokyo

Toshokan-Kai (Library World) (text in Japanese, table of contents in English), Japan Institution for Library Science, Tenri University, Tenri, Nara

Toshokan Zasshi (Library Journal), Japan Library Association, 1-10, 1-chome, Taishido Setagaya-ku, Tokyo

Sendai no Toshokan (Library of Today), Japan Library Association, 1-10, 1-chome, Taishido Setagaya-ku, Tokyo

Literary Associations and Societies

The **Dickens** Fellowship*, Bungei-Gakuba, Seijo University 6-1-20, Seijo Setagaya, Tokyo
Honorary Secretary: Prof Koichi Miyazaki

Japan Contemporary Poets' Society*, c/o Hideki Isomura, 1-14-6 Kamata, Setagaya-ku, Tokyo

Japan Essayists' Club*, c/o Yujiro Chiba, 1-1-1 Shimbashi, Minato-ku, Tokyo

Japan Poet Club*, c/o Showa Joshi University, 1-7 Taishido, Setagaya-ku, Tokyo

Nihon Eibungakkai (English Literary Society of Japan), 18 Nakamachi, Shinjuku-ku, Tokyo 162
President: Yoshiaki Fuhara
Publication: Studies in English Literature (three times yearly)

Nippon Bungaku Kyokai*, 2-17-10 Minami-otsuka, Toshima-ku, Tokyo
Japanese Literature Association
President: Nobutsuna Saigo
Publication: Japanese Literature (monthly)

Nippon Dokubungakkai*, c/o Ikubundo, Hongo 5-30-21, Bunkyo-ku, Tokyo 113
Japanese Society of German Literature
President: Professor Sakae Hamakawa
Publication: Doitsu Bungaku (German Literature) (twice yearly)

Nippon Furansu-go Furansu-bungaku Kai*, c/o La Maison franco-japonaise, 2-3, Kanda-Surugadai Chiyoda-ku, Tokyo
Japanese Society of French Language and Literature
President: Takeo Kuwabara
Publication: Etudes de Langue et Littérature françaises (half-yearly)

Nippon Hikaku Bungakukai*, Aoyamagakuim University, Shibuya-ku, Tokyo
Comparative Literature Society of Japan
General-Secretary: Saburo Ota
Publications: Journal (annually), *Bulletin* (quarterly)

Nippon Romazikai*, Yosida Honmati 27, Kyoto
Japanese Society of Roman Letters
President: Akabori Siro
Publication: Romazi Sekai (The World of Roman Letters)

Nippon Rosiya Bungakkai*, Faculty of Literature Waseda University, Toyama-cho, Shinjuku-ku, Tokyo
Russian Literary Society of Japan
Secretary-General: General K Nakano
Publication: Bulletin

Japan P E N Club*, Room 265, Syuwa Residential Hotel, 9-1-7 Akasaka, Minato-ku, Tokyo 107
Secretary: Yuzo Toki
Publication: Japan PEN News (twice yearly)

Society for the Promotion of Japanese Literature*, c/o Bungei Shunju Publishing Co Ltd, 3 Kioi-cho, Chiyoda-ku, Tokyo

Women Writers' Association*, 17 Yanaka-Shimizucho, Daito-ku, Tokyo

Literary Periodicals

Doitsu Bungaku (German Literature), Japanese Society of German Literature, Hongo 5-30-21, Bunkyo-ku, Tokyo 113

Doshisha Literature; a journal of English literature and philology (text in English), Doshisha University, English Literature Society, Kyoto

Doshisha Studies in Foreign Literature (text in Japanese, English, French or German), Doshisha University, Foreign Literature Society, Kyoto

East-West Review; essays on literature and translations of literary works, Doshisha University, Department of English, Kyoto

Etudes de Langue et Littérature françaises (Studies in French Language and Literature), Japanese Society of French Language and Literature, c/o La Maison franco-japonaise, 2-3, Kanda-Surugadai Chiyoda-ku, Tokyo

Hon: a Book-bin for Scholars, Yushodo Booksellers Ltd, 29 Saneicho, Shinjuku-ku, Tokyo 160

Japan Quarterly, Asahi Shimbun-Sha, Tokyo

Japanese Literature, Japanese Literature Association, 2-17-20 Minami-otsuka, Toshima-ku, Tokyo

Mototachi no Kagaribi (The Little Sister's Watchfire), Kodansha International Ltd, 2-12-21 Otowa, Bunkyo-ku, Tokyo

Outlook (Japan), Yoshidahon-machi, Sakyo-Ka, Kioto

The Sea, Chuokoron-Sha Inc, 2-8-7 Kyobashi, Chuo-ku, Tokyo 104

Studies in English Literature, English Literary Society of Japan, 18 Nakamachi, Shinjuku-ku, Tokyo 162

Literary Prizes

Akutagawa Prize*
In memory of Ryunosuke Akutagawa for works written by unknown authors. One of the most important literary prizes in Japan. 300,000 yen. Awarded twice a year.

Enquiries to The Society for the Promotion of Japanese Literature, c/o Bungei Shunju Publishing Co Ltd, 3 Kioi-cho, Chiyoda-ku, Tokyo

Culture Prize*
For outstanding achievement in the following areas: illustrations, photographs, book designs, juvenile cartoons and picture books. 300,000 yen. Awarded annually to publishers in Japan. Enquiries to Kodansha International Ltd, 2-12-21 Otowa, Bunkyo-ku, Tokyo

Japan Essayists' Club Prize*
For the best essays and criticism including those in book form, especially the work of new authors. 100,000 yen. Awarded annually. Enquiries to Japan Essayists' Club, c/o Yujiro Chiba, 1-1-1 Shimbashi, Minato-ku, Tokyo

Japan Poet Club Prize*
For an author who has contributed significantly to poetry. 50,000 yen. Awarded annually. Enquiries to Japan Poet Club, c/o Showa Joshi University, 1-7 Taishido, Setagaya-ku, Tokyo

Japan Translation Prize for Publisher
For outstanding translations. Awarded annually. Enquiries to Japan Society of Translators, Rm 208, Shiba Mansion, 5-11-6 Toranomon, Minato-ku, Tokyo

Japan Woman Writer Prize*
For the best novel. 500,000 yen. Awarded annually. Enquiries to Chuokoron-Sha Inc, 2-8-7 Kyobashi, Chuo-ku, Tokyo

Japan Women Writers' Literary Prizes*
To encourage women novelists. Awarded annually. Enquiries to Women Writers' Association, 17 Yanaka-Shimizucho, Daito-ku, Tokyo

Kikuchi Prize*
In memory of Hiroshi Kan Kikuchi, awarded annually for significant achievement in Japanese literature, drama, cinema, newspaper or magazine publication and for introducing Japanese literature to foreign countries. Enquiries to The Society for the Promotion of Japanese Literature, c/o Bungei Shunju Publishing Co Ltd, 3 Kioi-cho, Chiyoda-ku, Tokyo

Kishida Prize for Drama*
In commemoration of the playwright Kunio Kishida for an outstanding contribution to theatre. 100,000 yen. Awarded annually. Enquiries to Shin-cho-Sha, 71 Yarai-cho, Shinjuku-ku, Tokyo 162

Mainichi Publishing Culture Prize*
To the authors and publishers of works contributing to human culture. 100,000 yen. Awarded annually. Enquiries to Mainichi Newspapers Publishing Co, 1-1, 1-chome, Hitotsubashi, Chiyoda-ku, Tokyo

Mr H's Prize*
For works by a new poet. 100,000 yen. Awarded annually. Enquiries to Japan Contemporary Poets' Society, c/o Mr Hideki Isomura, 1-14-6 Kamata, Setagaya-ku, Tokyo

Nakamori Prize
Founded 1975 for imported or translated children's books. To be awarded to one work annually. In addition there is a Readers' Prize for the most popular book selected by readers (authors, artists and publishers are eligible for this prize). Enquiries to Holp Publishing Co Ltd, 2-19-13 Shinjuku-ku Tokyo 160

Naoki Prize*
In memory of Sanjugo Naoki, for the most promising writer of light fiction. 300,000 yen. Awarded twice a year. Enquiries to The Society for the Promotion of Japanese Literature, c/o Bungei Shunju Publishing Co Ltd, 3 Kioi-cho, Chiyoda-ku, Tokyo

Noma Prize for Juvenile Novel*
For the best juvenile novel. 500,000 yen. Awarded annually. Enquiries to Kodansha International Ltd, 2-12-21 Otowa, Bunkyo-ku, Tokyo

Noma Prize for Literature*
For the best Japanese novel of the Year. 1,000,000 yen. Awarded annually. Enquiries to Kodansha International Ltd, 2-12-21 Otowa, Bunkyo-ku, Tokyo

Oya Soichi Nonfiction Prize*
To encourage new nonfiction writers. $1,000, plus Round-the-World air ticket. Awarded annually. Enquiries to Bungei Shunju Co Ltd, 3 Kioi-cho, Chiyoda-ku, Tokyo

Sankei Juvenile Literature Prize*
For authors of outstanding works published for children. First prize of 500,000 yen and five prizes of 50,000 yen. Publishers of the works are also recognized. Awarded annually. Enquiries to Sankei Newspaper Co, 1-7-2 Otemachi, Chiyoda-ku, Tokyo

Shincho Prizes*
For the best work published during the preceding year, including stories for children and dramatic works. Jury of authors and editorial staff of the monthly magazine Shincho (New Friends). 500,000 yen. Awarded annually. Enquiries to Shincho-Sha, 71 Yarai-cho, Shinjuku-ku, Tokyo 162

Shogakukan Literary Prize
For the best novel, poem, drama and non-fiction for children published during the preceding year. 500,000 yen. Awarded annually. Enquiries to Shogakukan, 2-3-1 Kanda-Hitotsubashi, Chiyoda-ku, Tokyo 101

Tanizaki Junichiro Prize
To recall the works by Tanizaki and to celebrate the publisher's 80th birthday. 500,000 yen. Enquiries to Chuokoron-Sha Inc, 2-8-7 Kyobashi, Chuo-ku, Tokyo 104

Yomiuri Literature Prize*
For the best work in six categories: novel, essay and travels, drama, literary study and translation, poetry and haiku, critique and biography. 500,000 yen each. Awarded annually. Enquiries to Yomiuri Newspapers Publishing Co, 1-7-1 Otemachi, Chiyoda-ku, Tokyo

Yoshikawa Prize for Popular Novel*
For the most popular novel. 1,000,000 yen. Awarded annually. Enquiries to Kodansha International Ltd, 2-12-21 Otowa, Bunkyo-ku, Tokyo

Translation Agencies and Associations

Japan Society of Translators, Rm 208, Shiba Mansion, 5-11-6 Toranomon, Minato-ku, Tokyo

Jordan

General Information

Language: Arabic (and English)
Religion: Muslim (and large Christian minority)
Population: 2.7 million
Literacy Rate (1961): 39%
Bank Hours: 0800-1330 Saturday-Thursday; cashiers close at 1230
Shop Hours: 0800-1300, 1500-1800 Saturday-Thursday
Currency: 1000 fils = 1 dinar
Export/Import Information: No tariffs on books and advertising matter, but 2% tax applies. No import licences or exchange licences required
Copyright: No copyright conventions signed

Publishers

Jordan Distribution Agency, PO Box 375, Amman Tel: 30191/2 Cable Add: Jodistag Amman Telex: 1497 JO ALRAI
Man Dir: Raja Elissa; *Man:* Mrs Nadia Elissa
Subjects: Jordanian Tourism and History
1977: 1 title *1978:* 2 titles *Founded:* 1951

Jordan Press and Publishing Co Ltd*, Amman
Publishes daily newspaper, *al-Destour*
Founded: 1967
Miscellaneous: 25% of capital held by government

National Press Library*, Amman
Subjects: Education, Politics, Law, Textbooks

Major Booksellers

Joseph I **Bahous** & Co*, Dar-Ul-Kutub, Salt Rd, PO Box 66, Amman

Gibralter Book Store*, Corner Faisal St, Amman

Al **Istiklal** Library*, PO Box 156, Amman

George Y **Koro***, Petra Library, PO Box 1061, Amman

Al **Ma'aref** Library*, PO Box 650, Amman

Youth's Library Mohamad Ahmed Sharareh*, PO Box 180, Amman

Major Libraries

American Library*, Kabarday St, Amman

Amman Public Library*, c/o City Librarian, PO Box 132, Amman

British Council Library, Amman Centre, Jebel Amman, PO Box 634, Amman Tel: 36147/8, 38194

Public Library*, PO Box 348, Irbid

Public Library*, Nablus

University of Jordan Library, PO Box 1682, Amman Tel: 65111/65125 Telex: 1629 unuj jo

Yarmouk University Library*, PO Box 566, Irbid Tel: 582311

Library Associations

Jordan Library Association, PO Box 6289, Amman
President: Mahmoud El-Akhras; *Executive Secretary:* Yousef Kandil
Publications: Rissalat al-Maktaba (The Message of the Library) (quarterly); *Palestinian-Jordanian Bibliography 1900-1970*, 1972; *1971-1975*, 1976; *Directory of Libraries in Jordan 1976*, 1976

Library Journals

Rissalat al-Maktaba (Message of the Library) (text in Arabic, summaries in English), Jordan Library Association, PO Box 6289, Amman

Kampuchea

General Information

Language: French is the commercial language
Religion: Buddhism
Population: 8.6 million
Literacy Rate (1962): 36.1%
Business Hours: 0700-1400 Monday-Saturday
Currency: riel
Export/Import Information: Little current information available; free foreign exchange market arrangements not operating
Copyright: UCC, Florence (see International section)

Publishers

Ministère de l'Education nationale*, Phnom-Penh
Subjects: All academic

Major Booksellers

E K L I P*, 3 rue Kramuon-Sâr, Phnom-Penh Tel: 24733

Tomneub*, BP 381, Phnom-Penh Tel: 444

Major Libraries

Archives et Bibliothèque nationales (National Archives and Library)*, Vithei Daun Penh, BP 4, Phnom-Penh Tel: 22844

Bibliothèque nationale*, Phnom-Penh

Bibliothèque royale*, Phnom-Penh

Bibliothèque du **Centre Culturel Maison de France***, 21 Vithei Kraumuon Sar, Phnom-Penh

Bibliothèque du **Centre royal de Documentation** et d'Edition*, Phnom-Penh

Bibliothèque de l'**Institut Bouddhique***, Phnom-Penh

Bibliothèque du **Ministère de l'Information***, Phnom-Penh

Library Association

Office national de Planification et de Developpement des Bibliotheques (National Office of Planning and Development of Libraries)*, Phnom-Penh

Literary Associations and Societies

Association des Ecrivains khmers (Association of Khmer Writers)*, Phnom-Penh
President: Trinh Hoanh
Publication: Monthly literary review in Khmer

Kenya

General Information

Language: Swahili (also English)
Religion: No dominant religion; both tribal religions and Christianity found
Population: 14.3 million
Bank Hours: 0900-1300 Monday-Friday; 0900-1100 Saturday (except on coast, where banks open and close half an hour earlier)
Shop Hours: 0830-1230, 1400-1630 Monday-Friday; 0830-1200 or 1230 Saturday
Currency: 100 cents = 1 Kenya shilling
Export/Import Information: No tariff on books or advertising matter. Import licences and exchange controls
Copyright: UCC (see International section)

Book Trade Organizations

Kenya Booksellers' and Stationers' Association*, PO Box 26, Murang'a

Kenya Publishers' Association*, c/o PO Box 72532, Nairobi Tel: 336377
Secretary: R G Houghton

Book Trade Reference Books and Journals

Books

Catalogue of Government Publications, Government Printing Press, PO Box 30128, Nairobi

Journals

Bookshop Bulletin, Kijabe St, PO Box 47540, Nairobi

Publishers

Comb Books*, PO Box 20019, Nairobi Tel: 332270
(Distributed by the Text Book Centre Ltd, PO Box 47540, Nairobi)
Man Dir: David Maillu
Subjects: General Fiction, Social & Sexual Problems, Paperbacks
Founded: 1972

East African Directory Co*, PO Box 41237, Nairobi Tel: 24151
Man Dir: T A Bhatt
Parent Company: United Africa Press Ltd (qv)
Subject: Reference
Founded: 1947

East African Literature Bureau, see Kenya Literature Bureau

East African Publishing House, Lusaka Close, PO Box 30571, Nairobi Tel: 557417 Cable Add: Afrobooks Nairobi
Man Dir: E N Wainaina; *Editorial:* P Njoroge; *Editorial, Rights and Permissions:* Richard Ntiru; *Marketing, Publicity, Sales, Distribution:* J J Atunga; *Production:* John Mwazo
Parent Company: E A Cultural Trust
Subsidiary Company: Afropress Ltd, PO Box 30502, Nairobi
Br Off: PO Box 3209, Dar es Salaam, Tanzania
Subjects: General Fiction & Nonfiction, Belles Lettres, Poetry, Biography, History, Africana, How-to, Study Guides, Reference, Religion, Juveniles, Books in Kiswahili and other East African languages, Paperbacks, Medicine, Science & Technology, General & Social Science, University, Secondary & Primary Textbooks
1977: 70 titles *1978:* 30 titles *Founded:* 1965

Equatorial Publishers*, PO Box 47973, Nairobi Tel:337529
Man Dir: Y N Okal
Subjects: Belles Lettres, Poetry, Biography, History, Africana, Paperbacks, Social Science, Secondary Textbooks

Evangel Publishing House*, PO Box 28963, Nairobi Tel: 27070 Cable Add: Evangelit Nairobi
Man Dir, Editorial, Rights and Permissions: Rev A Labrentz; *Sales, Publicity:* Rev Cal R Bombay; *Production:* Bruce Brandt
Subjects: General Nonfiction, Reference, Religion, Christian Tracts, Paperbacks, Children's Books
Bookshop: PO Box 1015, Kisumu

Foundation Books+, NCM House, Tom Mboya St, PO Box 73435, Nairobi Tel: 26333
Man Dir: F O Okwanya; *Editorial:* Mary Akinyi Ojienda; *Sales Manager:* C R Ojienda; *Production:* Sophia Wanjiku Ojienda
Subjects: Belles Lettres, Poetry, Biography, History, Africana, Juveniles, Books in Kiswahili, Paperbacks, Social Science, Secondary & Primary Textbooks
Founded: 1974

Gaba Publications, AMECEA Pastoral Institute, PO Box 908, Eldoret
(Formerly at PO Box 4165, Kampala, Uganda)
Manager: Peter Dougherty
Subjects: Religion, Anthropology, Scripture, Third World Theology, Religious Education
1977: 11 titles *1978:* 11 titles

Heinemann Educational Books (East Africa) Ltd, International House, Mama Ngina St, PO Box 45314, Nairobi Tel: 22057/338642 Cable Add: Hebooks Nairobi
Man Dir, Rights and Permissions: Henry Chakava; *Editorial:* Ben Ole Mollel; *Sales:* Johnson K Mugweru
Subjects: General Fiction & Nonfiction, Belles Lettres, Poetry, Biography, History, Africana, Study Guides, Juveniles, Swahili Language & Literature, Paperbacks, General

KENYA

& Social Science, University, Secondary & Primary Textbooks
1977: 20 titles *1978:* 20 titles *Founded:* 1967
Miscellaneous: Firm is a subsidiary of Heinemann Educational Books Ltd, UK (qv)

Kenya Literature Bureau, PO Box 30022, Nairobi Tel: 26411 Cable Add: Literature Nairobi
Man Dir: N G Ngulukulu; *Managing Editor:* Rose Mwangi; *Sales:* A R Minja
Br Offs: Branches in Dar es Salaam and Kampala
Subjects: General Fiction & Nonfiction, Belles Lettres, Poetry, Biography, History, Africana, Reference, Religion, Juveniles, Books in numerous East African Languages, Paperbacks, Medicine, Psychology, Science & Technology, General & Social Science, University, Secondary and Primary Textbooks
Founded: 1947

The Jomo **Kenyatta** Foundation*, PO Box 30533, Nairobi Tel: 20704 Cable Add: Foundation
Man Dir: S C Lang'at; *Production Man:* Len M Fernandes
Subjects: Secondary & Primary Textbooks

Longman Kenya Ltd+, 6th Floor, Kenya Commercial Bank, PO Box 18033, Nairobi Tel: 555477/555530
Man Dir: T J Openda; *Publishing Manager:* Charlotte Rolfe; *Sales Manager:* T Kamuyu; *Rights and Permissions:* Longman Group, UK (qv)
Associate Company: Longman Group Ltd, UK (qv)
Subjects: General Fiction & Nonfiction, Belles Lettres, Poetry, Biography, History, Africana, Reference, Juveniles, Books in 14 Kenyan languages, Paperbacks, General & Social Science, Secondary & Primary Textbooks
Founded: 1965

Newspread International, PO Box 46854, Nairobi Tel: 331402 Cable Add: Newspread
Man Dir: Kul Bhushan; *Publishing Manager:* Ashok Kumar; *Production Manager:* Benedict Nzomo
Subjects: Reference
Founded: 1971

Njogu Gitene Publications*, PO Box 72989, Nairobi
Subjects: Belles Lettres, Poetry, Juveniles, Books in Kiswahili, Secondary & Primary Textbooks
Founded: 1970

Oxford University Press, Eastern Africa Branch, PO Box 72532, Nairobi (Located at: First Floor, Science House, Monrovia St, Nairobi) Tel: 336377 Cable Add: Oxonian Nairobi
General Manager: Abdilahi Nassir; *Man Editor:* Jonathan Kariara; *Production:* Godfrey Nyerwanire; *Publicity:* Sam Mbure; *Rights & Permissions:* Abdilahi Nassir; *Sales:* A K Ismaily; *Administration:* E M Nyang'aya
Br Off: Dar es Salaam
Subjects: General Fiction & Nonfiction, Belles Lettres, Poetry, Biography, History, Africana, Reference, Juveniles, Books in 12 East African languages, Paperbacks, General & Social Science, Secondary & Primary Textbooks
1977-78: 25 titles *Founded:* 1963
ISBN Publisher's Prefix: 0-19
Miscellaneous: Firm is a branch of Oxford University Press, UK (qv)

Salama Publications Ltd*, PO Box 48009, Nairobi
Subjects: How-to, Study Guides, Secondary Textbooks

Success Publications*, PO Box 10893, Nairobi
Subjects: How-to, Study Guides

Text Book Centre Ltd*, Kijabe St, PO Box 47540, Nairobi Tel: 337337/8
Man Dir: M J Rughani; *Sales Manager:* C D Shah
Subjects: Belles Lettres, Poetry, Juveniles, Books in Kiswahili, Paperbacks, Secondary & Primary Textbooks
Bookshop: Kijabe St, PO Box 47540, Nairobi

Transafrica Book Distributors*, Kenwood House, Kimathi St, PO Box 49421, Nairobi Tel: 861253
Man Dir: John Nottingham
Subjects: General Fiction & Nonfiction, Belles Lettres, Poetry, Biography, History, Africana, How-to, Study Guides, Reference, Religion, Juveniles, Books in Kiswahili, Paperbacks, Social Science, Secondary & Primary Textbooks
1977-78: 30 titles

United Africa Press Ltd*, Victoria Ho, Victoria St, PO Box 41237, Nairobi Tel: 24151
Man Dir: T A Bhatt
Subjects: General, Educational, Reference, Animals
Founded: 1952
Subsidiary: East African Directory Co (qv)

University Press of Africa Ltd*, Bank Ho, Government Rd, PO Box 3981, Nairobi Tel: 26060
Man Dir: R R Ryan
Subjects: Reference, Travel Guides, Medicine, Science & Technology, General & Social Science

Uzima Press Ltd+, PO Box 48127, Nairobi Tel: 20239
Man Dir: Rev Horace Etemesi
Subjects: Religion, Fiction
1977: 12 titles *1978:* 60 titles *Founded:* 1974

Vipopremo Agencies*, Koinange St, PO Box 47717, Nairobi Tel: 27189
Subjects: How-to, Study Guides

Government Printer*, Government Printing Press, PO Box 30128, Nairobi

Literary Agents

Africa Educational Representatives*, PO Box 20521, Nairobi Cable Add: Afragency Tel: 26543
Head Office: Africa Educational Reps, 639 Massachusetts Ave, Suite 335, Cambridge, Mass, 02139, USA

Major Booksellers

The **Bookshop** Ltd, Esso Ho, Kaunda St, PO Box 30247, Nairobi Tel: 23364

The **Catholic** Bookshop Ltd, Kaunda St, PO Box 30249, Nairobi Tel: 25172

Dhanani's Ltd*, Kimasi St, Corner Ho, PO Box 72399, Nairobi Tel: 27049

E S A Bookshop*, Church Ho, Government Rd, PO Box 30167, Nairobi Tel: 20158

Keswick Book Society*, Portal Ho, Banda St, PO Box 10242, Nairobi Tel: 26047

Macdonald's*, Kimathi St, PO Box 49240, Nairobi Tel: 21979

S J **Moore** Ltd, Moi Ave, PO Box 30162, Nairobi Tel: 22213

Mount Kenya Bookshop*, PO Box 281, Nyeri Tel: 2513; PO Box 47772, Nairobi Tel: 337883; PO Box 659, Nakuru Tel: 2806; PO Box 10, Kakamega Tel: 63; PO Box 29, Meru Tel: 36

Patwa (Embakasi) Ltd*, PO Box 19200, Nairobi Airport, Embakasi, Nairobi

Prestige Booksellers*, Prudential Assurance Bldg PO Box 45425, Nairobi Tel: 23515

The **Textbook** Centre Ltd*, Kijabe St, PO Box 47540, Nairobi Tel: 337337/335205/24672/24308 Cable Add: Text books

University of Nairobi Bookshop, PO Box 30197, Nairobi Tel: 334244 ext 2111 Cable Add: Varsity
Manager: N J Patel

Wanyee Bookshop Ltd*, Wabera St, PO Box 46815, Nairobi Tel: 331769

Major Libraries

East African Statistical Department Library*, PO Box 30462, Nairobi Tel: 26411 ext 425

Egerton College Library, PO Njoro Tel: 27/44/47

Kabete Library*, University of Nairobi, PO Box 29053, Kabete

Kenya National Archives*, Jogoo House 'A', PO Box 30520, Nairobi

Kenya National Library Service, Ngong Rd, PO Box 30573, Nairobi Tel: 27871/29186
Librarian: Apollo R Oluoch
Publications: Annual Audit Report; Quarterly Accession; List of Adult Books

Kenya Polytechnic Library*, PO Box 52428, Nairobi

Kenya Technical Teachers' College Library*, PO Box 44600, Nairobi Tel: 520211
Librarian: Mary Pat Kraemer

Kenyatta University College Library, PO Box 43844, Nairobi Tel: Kahawa 356/7/8/9; 247/249/346/421/442/459
Librarian: James Mwangi Nganga
Publications: Directory of Research in the College; Annual Report; Directory of Libraries in Kenya; Occasional Bibliographies

McMillan Memorial Library*, Banda St, PO Box 40791, Nairobi Tel: 21844
Chief Librarian: R G Opondo

Mombasa Polytechnic Library*, Tom Mboya Ave, PO Box 90420, Mombasa

University of Nairobi Library, PO Box 30197, Nairobi Tel: 334244

Library Associations

Kenya Library Association*, PO Box 46031 Nairobi
Secretary: Rosemary Kiathe
Publication: Maktaba

Library Reference Books and Journals

Books

Directory of Libraries in Kenya, Kenyatta University College Library, PO Box 43844, Nairobi

Journals

Maktaba, Kenya Literature Bureau, PO Box 30022, Nairobi (The official, biannual, journal of the Kenya Library Association)

Literary Periodicals

Busara, Kenya Literature Bureau, PO Box 30022, Nairobi (biannual literary magazine published under the auspices of the Department of Literature, University of Nairobi)

Dhana, Kenya Literature Bureau, PO Box 30022, Nairobi (The Makerere University, Department of Literature, journal of creative writing; twice yearly)

Joe; Africa's entertainment monthly, Joe Publications Ltd, PO Box 30362, Nairobi (a lively and well-put-together popular magazine with regular literary contributions, review of new books and plays, etc. Edited by Terry Hirst; enjoys a very substantial circulation)

Joliso (East African Journal of Literature and Society), Kenya Literature Bureau, PO Box 30022, Nairobi (new literary and cultural magazine edited by Chris Wanjala and published twice yearly since 1973)

Umma, Kenya Literature Bureau, PO Box 30022, Nairobi (The University of Dar es Salaam, Department of Literature, journal of creative writing; twice yearly)

Translation Agencies and Associations

Kenya Literature Bureau*, PO Box 30022, Nairobi

Democratic People's Republic of Korea

General Information

Language: Korean
Religion: Confucianism and Buddhism
Population: 16.7 million
Currency: 100 jun = 1 won
Export/Import Information: No tariff information; all importation must go through Korea Publications Export and Import Corporation, Pyongyang

Publishers

Academy of Sciences Publishing House*, Central District Nammundong, Pyongyang
Subjects: Science, Chemistry, Geology, Metallurgy, Physics, Biology, History, Maps, Mathematics, Meteorology, Education, Economics
Founded: 1953

Academy of Social Sciences Publishing House*, Pyongyang
Subject: Social Sciences

Agricultural Books Publishing House*, Pyongyang
President: Li Hyun U
Subjects: Agriculture, Industry

Economic Publishing House*, Pyongyang
Subject: Economics

Educational Books Publishing House*, Pyongyang
Subject: Education, Textbooks

Foreign Languages Publishing House*, Pyongyang
President: L Ryang Hun
Subject: Books on Korea, Periodicals (English language)

Publishing House of the **General Federation of Literary and Art Unions***, Pyongyang
Subjects: Fiction, Arts

Higher Educational Books Publishing House*, Pyongyang
Acting President: Shin Jong Sung
Subjects: Education, Academic, Mathematics, Physics

Industry Publishing House*, Pyongyang
Subjects: Trade, Industry

Korean Workers' Party Publishing House*, Pyongyang
Subjects: Fiction, Politics

Mass Culture Publishing House*, Pyongyang

Medical Science Publishing House*, Pyongyang
Subject: Medicine, Psychology, Veterinary Science

Transportation Publishing House*, Pyongyang
Acting Editor: Paek Jong Han
Subject: Transport
Founded: 1952

Major Booksellers

Korea Publications Export and Import Corporation*, Pyongyang
The sole importing organization

Major Libraries

State Central Library*, Pyongyang

Library Associations

Library Association of the Democratic People's Republic of Korea*, State Central Library, Pyongyang Tel: 3-8741
Executive Secretary: Li Geug

Republic of Korea

General Information

Language: Korean (English also spoken in business)
Religion: Animism, Buddhism, Confucianism and Protestant
Population: 36.4 million
Literacy Rate (1970): 87.6% (94.3% Urban, 82.2% Rural)
Bank Hours: 0930-1600 Monday-Friday; 0930-1300 Saturday
Shop Hours: 0930-1200, 1300-1700 Monday-Friday; 0930-1300 Saturday
Currency: won
Export/Import Information: No tariffs on books and advertising matter. 2.5% Defence Tax. No import licences required. Exchange controls; prior deposits required at present
Copyright: No copyright conventions signed

Book Trade Organizations

Korean Publishers Association, 105-2 Sagan-dong, Chongno-ku, Seoul 110 Tel: (72) 5904 Cable Add: Bookhouse Seoul
Secretary: Kyung-hoon Lee
Publications: Korean Books Journal (monthly); *Korean Publication Yearbook* (annual); *Books from Korea (biennial)*

Book Trade Reference Books and Journals

Books

Books from Korea, Korean Publishers Association, 105-2 Sagan-dong, Chongno-ku, Seoul 110

Catalogue of Government Publications (including University publications), National Assembly Library, Taepyong-ko, Chung-ku, Seoul

Korean Publication Yearbook, Korean Publishers Association, 105-2 Sagan-dong, Chongno-ku, Seoul 110

Journals

Ch'ulp'an Munhwa (Korean Books Journal) (text in Korean), Korean Publishers' Association, 105-2 Sagan-dong, Chongno-ku, Seoul 110 *Han-gug Chulpanyungam* (Korean Publication Yearbook) (text in Korean), Korean Publishers' Association, 105-2 Sagan-dong, Chongno-ku, Seoul 110
Korean National Bibliography (text in Korean), Central National Library, 6 Sokong-dong, Chung-ku, Seoul

Publishers

Bak Yung Sa*+, 184 Kwanchul-dong, Chongno-ku, Seoul 110
President: Won Ok Ahn
Subjects: Philosophy, Literature, Social Science
Founded: 1952

Beupmun Sa Publishing Co +, 1-48 Cheung-dong, Chung-Ku, Seoul 100 Tel: (75) 6317/6318/6319
President: Sung Soo Kim; *Man Dir:* Byeong

Cheol Park; *Sales:* Hyo Seon Bae; *Editorial:* Bok Hyun Chok; *Publicity:* Myeong Hwan Kim
Subjects: Law, Economics, Management, Politics, Public Administration, Education, Psychology
1977: 32 titles *1978:* 58 titles *Founded:* 1952

Changjak Kwa Pipyung Sa+, 3 Kongpyong-dong, Chongno-ku, Seoul 110
President: Yom Hong-gyong
Subjects: Literature and other subjects of general interest
Founded: 1974

Changjo Sa+*, 92 Sinmun-ro 2-ka, Chongno-ku, Seoul 110
President: Deok Kyu Choi
Subjects: Literature, Linguistics, History
Founded: 1963

The **Christian Literature** Society of Korea+*, 84-8 Chongno, 2-ka, Chongno-kuSeoul 110 Tel: 74-3092, 1792, 5981 Cable Add: Chlisoofko
General Secretary: Rev Sun Chool Chough
Subjects: Religion, Theology, Sociology
1977: 42 titles

Dongwha Publishing Co+*, 130-4 Wonhyo-ro, Yongsan-ku, Seoul 100
President: In Kyu Lim
Subjects: Literature, Fine Arts, Philosophy
Founded: 1968

Encyclopaedia Britannica (Korea) Inc*, 58-14 Sinmun-ro 1 ka, Chongno-ku, Seoul
Mailing Add: CPO Box 690, Seoul
President: Changgi Hahn
Subject: Reference Books
Publication: The Deep Rooted Tree (monthly)
Miscellaneous: Firm is an associate company of Encyclopaedia Britannica International Ltd, UK (qv)

Eulyoo Publishing Co Ltd+, PO Box 362 Gwanghwa-Mun, 46-1 Susong-dong, Jongro-gu, Seoul 110 Tel: (73) 8150, (74) 3515 Cable Add: Eulyoo
President: Chin Sook Choung; *Man Dir:* Pil Young Choung; *Editorial, Production:* Il Joon Park; *Sales:* Chin Il Choung
Subjects: General
1977: 200 titles *1978:* 300 titles *Founded:* 1945

Ewha Woman's University Press+*, 11-1 Daehyun-dong, Seodaemun-ku, Seoul 120
President: Ok Kil Kim
Subjects: General, Literature, History, Linguistics
Founded: 1954

Hak Won Sa+*, 147 Chongno-3-ka, Chongno-ku, Seoul 110
President: Ik Tal Kim
Subjects: General, Juveniles, Educational Materials, Encyclopaedias
Founded: 1945

Hollym Corporation+*, 14-5 Kwanchul-dong, Chongno-ku, Seoul 110 Tel: (75) 7551/4
Man Dir: In Soo Rhimm; *Sales Dir:* Yong Kwon Kim; *Publicity Dir:* Shin Won Zoo; *Advertising Dir:* Tae Hong Jeong
Subjects: General Fiction, Belles Lettres, Poetry, Biography, History, Juveniles, High-priced Paperbacks
1977: 28 titles *Founded:* 1963
Book Club: Korea Book Club

Hwimoon Publishing Co+*, 30 Kyunji-dong, Chongno-ku, Seoul 110
Tel: (72) 4897
Man Dir: Myong Hui Yi
Subjects: General Fiction, Belles Lettres, Poetry, Biography, History, Philosophy, Religion, Juveniles
Founded: 1961

Hyangmun Sa+*, 39-16 Kyunji-dong, Chongno-ku, Seoul 110
President: Mal Sun Na
Subjects: Agriculture, Science
Founded: 1957

Hyun Am Sa+*, 1 Chongno 5-ka, Chongno-ku, Seoul 110 Tel: (75) 5421
Man Dir: Sang Won Cho
Subjects: History, Philosophy, Literature, Religion
Founded: 1951

Il Cho Kak*+, 9 Gongpyung-dong, Chongno-ku, Seoul 110 Tel: (73) 5430/1
Cable Add: Ichopublico Seoul
Man Dir: Man-Nyun Han; *Sales Dir:* L J Kim; *Publicity Dir:* J Y Choi
Subjects: History, High-priced Paperbacks, Medicine, Psychology, Engineering, General & Social Science, Secondary & University Textbooks, Educational Materials, Law, Philosophy
Founded: 1953

Il Ji Sa+*, 46-1 Chunghak-dong, Chongno-ku, Seoul 110
Man Dir: Sung Jae Kim; *Publicity Dirs:* Byungki Yoo, Donhong Cho
Subjects: General Fiction, Belles Lettres, Criminology, Poetry, History, Reference, Low- & High-priced Paperbacks, University & Secondary Textbooks, Educational Materials
Founded: 1956

Il Shinsa*+, 22-1 Samkak-dong, Chung-ku, Seoul 100 Tel: 749005/736948/736980
Man Dir: Kwang-mo Yun; *Editorial:* Ryun So; *Sales:* Jong-sun Ahn; *Production:* Sang-kap La
Subjects: Philosophy, Law, Politics, Economics, Literature, Natural Science
1977: 130 titles *Founded:* 1959

Jeongeumsa Publishing Co+*, PO Box 7, 22-5 Chungmu-ro 5-ka, Chung-ku, Seoul 100 Tel: (27) 9580/3 & (25) 5681/2
Cable Add: Jeongeumsa
President: Yong Hae Choi; *Sales Dir:* Young-tek Yoon; *Publicity & Advertising:* Dae-hee Park
Subjects: General Fiction, Belles Lettres, Philosophy, Social Science
Bookshop: 22-5, 5-ka, Chungmu-Ro, Jung-Gu, Seoul
Founded: 1928

Jisik Sanup Sa+*, 18-8 Kwanchul-dong, Chongno-ku, Seoul 110
President: Kyung Hee Kim
Subjects: Fine Arts, Social Sciences, History, Literature, Technical and Scientific
Founded: 1969

Junpa Kwahak Sa+*, 156-10 Dongkyo-dong, Mapo-ku, Seoul 121
President: Yung Soo Shon
Subjects: Sciences, Engineering
Founded: 1956

Korea Directory Co+*, 12-20 Chungmuro 2-ka, Chung-ku, Seoul
President: Saeung Tae Kim
Subject: Directories

Korea University Press+*, 1 Anam-dong 5-ka, Sungbuk-ku, Seoul 132
President: Sang Hyop Kim
Subjects: Philosophy, History, Literature, Sociology, Language, Education Psychology, Social Science, Natural Science, Engineering, Agriculture
Founded: 1956

Kwan Dong Publishing Co+*, 195-11 Yeongun-dong, Chongno-ku, Seoul 110
Tel: 29-6517, 99-4638
President: Seung Woo Kim; *Editorial:* Hyo Ja Kim; *Sales:* Heung Jo Choi; *Production:* Ki Dong Park; *Publicity:* Ill Kyoun Oh; *Rights & Permissions:* Hyong Sook Park
Subjects: Literature, Textbooks, Monthly magazines
1977: 48 titles *Founded:* 1964

Kwangmyong Printing & Publishing Co Ltd+*, CPO Box 3785, Seoul (Located at: 62 Manri-dong 1-ka, Chung-ku, Seoul) Tel: (23) 0671/9, 6584 Cable Add: Kwangmyong, Seoul
President: Kim Hak-Jin; *Dirs:* Hwang Tong-Kyu, Yoon Yun-Bai
Subsidiary Companies: Korea Textbook Co; Kwangmyong Toppan Moore Printing Co; Kwangmyong Toppan Printing Co
Subject: Korean Art (ancient and contemporary)
1977: 14 titles *1978:* 15 titles *Founded:* 1951

Kyemong-sa+*, 128-1 Kwanchul-dong, Chongno-ku, Seoul
President: Chun Sik Kim
Subjects: Children's Books

Kyohak Sa+*, 92 Sunhwa-dong, Seodaemun-ku, Seoul
Man Dir: Cheol U Yang
Subjects: Educational Materials, Industry, Nonfiction

Kyung In Munwha Sa+*, 86-2 Yunhee-dong, Seodaemun-ku, Seoul 120
President: Sang Ha Han
Subjects: General, History, Philosophy
Founded: 1969

Min Eum Sa+*, 44-1 Kwanchul-dong, Chongno-ku, Seoul 110
President: Maeng Ho Pak
Subjects: Literature, Philosophy, Engineering, Social Science
Founded: 1966

Minjungseogwan+*, 35 Tongeu-dong, Chongno-ku, Seoul 110
President: Byung Jun Lee
Subjects: General Fiction, Belles Lettres, Music, Reference, Medicine, Agriculture, Business, Law, Political Science, Science & Technology, Textbooks
Bookshop: 35 Tongeui-dong, Chongno-ku, Seoul
Founded: 1946

Moonye Publishing Co+*, 115 Doryum-dong, Chongno-ku, Seoul 110
President: Byung Suk Jun
Subjects: Literature, Fine Arts, Philosophy, Social Science, Psychology
Founded: 1966

Mun Woon Dang+*, 45-3 Myongryun-dong, Chongno-ku, Seoul
President: Sung Bum Lee
Subjects: Engineering, Science
Founded: 1962

Omun Kak+*, 39-1 Ankuk-dong, Chongno-ku, Seoul 110
President: Yung Whan Kim
Subjects: Literature, Korean Language, Social Science, Children's Books
Founded: 1960

Panmun Book Co Ltd+*, PO Box 1016, 40 Chongno 1-ka, Seoul 110 Tel: (73) 8688, (72) 5131/3 Cable Add: Panmuse Seoul
Man Dir: I H Liu; *Sales Dir:* H B Choi
Subjects: Medicine, General & Social Science, University Textbooks
Bookshops: 40 Chongro 1-ka, Seoul; 16 Kwangbok-dong 1-ka, Pusan
Founded: 1956

Pochinjae*, 8 Dangsan-dong 5-ka, Yungdeungpo-ku, Seoul
President: Jun Ki Kim

Pomso Publishers*, 3-2 Kwansu-dong, Chongno-ku, Seoul
President: So Yong Yi

Pyungwha Press*, 91-4 Sinmun Ro, 2-ka, Chongno-ku
President: Chang Song Ho

Sam Joong Dang Publishing Co+*, 244-5 Huam-dong, Yongsan-ku, Seoul 140
President: Kun Suk Seo
Subjects: Literature, History, Philosophy, Social Science
Founded: 1946

Sam-sung Publishing Co+*, 43-7 Kwanchul-dong, Chongno-ku, Seoul 110
President: Bong Kyu Kim
Subjects: Literature, Dictionaries, History, Children's Books
Founded: 1952

Samwha Publishing Co+*, 15 Eulji-ro 2-ka, Chung-ku, Seoul 100
President: Kon Su Yu
Subjects: Children's Books, Social Science, Linguistics, Fine Arts
Founded: 1962

Se Kwang Musical Publication Co+*, 232-32 Sogye-dong, Yongsan-ku, Seoul Tel: (25) 3616/8
President: Jin Joon Pak; *Sales Dir:* Chun Chae Ho; *Publicity Dir:* Ban Kwang Sik
Subject: Music
Founded: 1953

Sejong Daewang Kinyom Saophoe*, 1-57 Chongryangli-dong, San, Dondaemun-ku, Seoul
President: Gwan Ku Yi
Subjects: Religion, Classical Literature, Modern History

Seomun Dang+*, 94-97 Yongdeungpo, 3-dong, Yongdeungpo-ku, Seoul
President: Suk Ro Choi
Subjects: Philosophy, Ancient History, Literature, Fine Arts
Founded: 1973

Seonjin Publishing Co+*, 35-5 Supyo-dong, Chung-ku, Seoul
President: Gon Haeng Yi
Subject: Literature

Si-Sa-Yong-O-Sa+*, 5-3 Kwanchul-dong, Chongno-ku, Seoul 110
President: Yung Bin Min
Subject: Linguistics
Founded: 1964

Singu Munwha Sa+*, 68-2 Susong-dong, Chongno-ku, Seoul
President: Yong Ik Yi
Subjects: Literature, History, Linguistics, Children's Books
Founded: 1952

Taeguk Publishing Co+*, 47-11 Cho-dong, 2-ka, Chung-ku, Seoul 110
President: Yoon Hee Hong
Subjects: Dictionaries, Literature, History, Science, Fine Arts
Founded: 1969

Tamgu Dang Book Centre+*, 101-1 Kyungwoon-dong, Chongno-ku, Seoul 110 Tel: (72) 2004/5
Shipping Add: PO Box 240, Kwang-hwa-mun, Seoul
President: Suk Woo Hong; *Sales Dir:* Jean Byong-hun; *Publicity Dir:* Kim Chang-su; *Advertising Dir:* Lee Chung-rim
Subjects: History, Classics, Art, Reference, Low- & High-priced Paperbacks, University & Secondary Textbooks
Founded: 1950

Universal Publications Agency Ltd*, UPA Building, 54 Kyonjindong, Chongno, Seoul
Man: C Y Park
Miscellaneous: Also booksellers and distributors

Yonsei University Press+, 134 Shinchon-dong, Seodaemun-ku, Seoul 120
President: Pong-Kook Lee
Subjects: General, Philosophy, Religion, Social Science, Natural Science, Literature, Art, Technical Science
Founded: 1955

Yulwha Dang+*, 3-3 Chungjin-dong, Chongno-ku, Seoul 110
President: Ki Woong Lee
Subjects: Fine Arts, History, Literature
Founded: 1971

Book Clubs

Korea Book Club*, 145 Kwanchul-dong, Chongno-ku, Seoul
Owned by: Hollym Corporation Publishers (Seoul)

Major Booksellers

Airport Bookshop*, Civil International Airport, Seoul

Hyun Dae Mun Hak*, 130 Chongro-ku, Hyojedong, Seoul Tel: (72) 7319
Wholesaler

Panmun Book Co Ltd*, CPO Box 1016, Seoul
Also 16 Kwangbok-dong 1-ka, Pusan Tel: (73) 8688

Science Publications Centre, 21 1-ka, Chongno, Chongno-ku, Seoul

Seungmun-gak*, 155-12 Kwanhun-dong, Chongno-gu, Seoul Tel: (73) 6148
Specialise in second-hand and antiquarian books

Universal Publications Agency Ltd*, UPA Building, 54 Kyonjindong, Chongno, Seoul
Man: C Y Park
Also distributors

Major Libraries

Dongguk University Library*, 263-ka, Pil-dong, Seoul

Ewha Woman's University Library*, 11-1 Daehyon-dong, Sudaemun-ku, Seoul 120

International Communication Agency Library*, 63 1-ka, Ulchiro, Choung-ku, Seoul

Korea University Library*, 1 Anam-dong, Sungbuk-ku, Seoul

Kyungpook National University Library*, 1370 Sankyuck-dong, Pukku, Taegu

National Assembly Library*, Yoi-dong 1, Yeongdeungpo-gu, Seoul
Publication: Review

Central **National Library***, 100-171 1-ga, Hoe-hyeon-dong, Jung-gu, Seoul

Seoul National University Library*, San 56-1 Sinlim-Dong, Gwanag-gu, Seoul 151

Transport Library*, Seoul

United Nations Depository Library*, Korea University, 1 An-Am-Dong, Sungbuk-ku, Seoul

Yonsei University Library, Yonsei University, 134 Sinchon-dong, Sudaemoon-ku, Seoul 120

Library Associations

Hanguk Seoji Hakhoe (Korean Bibliographical Society)*, c/o National Assembly Library, 1-ka Taepyung, Chung-ku, Seoul

Hanguk Tosogwan Hakhoe (Korean Library Science Society)*, c/o Department of Library Science, Yonsei University, 134 Shinchon-dong, Seodaemun-ku, Seoul 120
Publication: Tosogwan Hak (Korean with English abstracts)

Korean Library Association, 100-177, 1-ka, Hoehyun-dong, Choong-Ku, Seoul
Executive Director: Dae Kwon Park
Publication: KLA Bulletin (monthly)

Korean Micro-Library Association*, Central National Library Bldg, 6 Sokong-dong, Chung-ku, Seoul
Publication: Micro-Library Bulletin

Library Reference Books and Journals

Books

Bibliography of Korean Bibliographies, Kyong'in Munwha Sa, 86-2 Yonhi-dong, Seodaemun-ku, Seoul

Journals

KLA Bulletin, Korean Library Association, 100-177, 1-Ka, Hoehyun-Dong, Choong-Ku, Seoul (monthly)

Micro-Library Bulletin, Korean Micro-Library Association, Central National Library Bldg, 6 Sokong-dong, Choong-Ku, Seoul

National Assembly Library Review (test in Korean), National Assembly Library, Processing and Reference Bureau, Yoi-dong 1, Yeongdeungpo-gu, Seoul

Tosogwan Hak (Journal of the Korean Library Science Society) (text in Korean with English abstracts), c/o Ewha Woman's University Library, 11-1 Daehyon-dong, Seodaemun-Ku, Seoul 120

Literary Associations and Societies

National Academy of Arts*, no 1 Sejongro Chongro-gu, Seoul
Head of Literature Section: Yeom-Hyeom Cho

Korean P E N Centre*, 163 Ankuk-dong, Jongno-ku, Seoul 110
Secretary-General: Dr Jung-kee Lee
Publications: The Korean PEN, Asian Literature

Literary Prizes

Literary Prize*
In recognition of an outstanding literary work. $5,000. Awarded annually. Enquiries to Korean National Academy of Arts, 1 Seajong Ro Chongro-gu, Seoul

Samil Cultural Award*
For the best novel. 2,000,000 hwan. Awarded annually. Enquiries to Pacific Cement Co, 1-ka, Ulchi-ro, Chung-ku, Seoul

Kuwait

General Information

Language: Arabic (English used also)
Religion: Muslim
Population: 1.13 million
Literacy Rate (1970): 55%
Bank Hours: Winter: 0730-1330 Saturday-Wednesday: 0730-1130 Thursday. Summer: 0700-1300 Saturday-Wednesday; 0700-1030 Thursday
Shop Hours: 0800-1300, 1600-2000 Saturday-Thursday; 0800-1200 Friday (markets and shopping centres open 1600-2000)
Currency: 1000 fils = 1 Kuwaiti dinar
Mailing Information: Weight limits: books, 5 kg (11 lb); printed matter, 2 kg (4 lb); parcel post, 20 kg (44 lb); air parcel post, 20 kg (44 lb)
Export/Import Information: No tariffs on books or advertising in reasonable quantity; all immoral and seditious publications prohibited. Import licence required. No exchange permit required
Copyright: No copyright conventions signed

Publishers

Kuwait Publishing House*, PO Box 5209 Tel: 510188

Ministry of Information, PO Box 193, Kuwait
Subjects: Art, Geography, History, Physics, Sociology, Textbooks, Maps, Literature, Mathematics, Education, Linguistics

Press Agency*, PO Box 1019, Kuwait Tel: 432269/411495 Cable Add: Matboat
Man Dir: Abdullah M N Harami; *Editorial:* K A Harami
Subjects: General (in Arabic and English)
Bookshops: in Kuwait and Salmiayit
1977: 103 titles *Founded:* 1954

Wkallat Matbouat*, PO Box 1019
Subject: Travel, Maps

Major Booksellers

Tahseen S **Khaya***, Gulf Union Co, Qubla Bldg, Al Soor St, Apt No 10, PO Box 2911, Safat Tel: 411688/411880 Cable Add: Florya Kuwait

Major Libraries

Kuwait Central Library*, Kuwait City

Kuwait University Central Library*, Kuwait City Tel: 813182

Library Association

Kuwait University Libraries Department* Chief Librarian's Office, PO Box 5969

Library Journals

The Library Bulletin, Kuwait University Central Library, Kuwait City

The University Library, Kuwait University Libraries Department, PO Box 5969, Kuwait

Laos

General Information

Language: Laotian and French
Religion: Buddhism
Population: 3.3 million
Bank Hours: 0800-1200, 1400-1700 Monday-Friday
Shop Hours: 0800-2200 Monday-Friday
Currency: 100 ats = 1 kip
Export/Import Information: No tariff on books (except children's picture books, 15%), none on most advertising matter. No import licences required for books. Exchange controls

Publishers

Lao-phanit*, Vientiane Ministère de l'Education nationale, Comité littéraire, Bureau des Manuels scolaires, Vientiane
Subjects: Education, Physics, Sociology, Economics, History, Cookery, Arts, Geography, Music, Fiction

Pakpassak Kanphin*, 9-11 quai Fa-Hguun, Vientiane

Vieng Krung*, Khoualuang Rd, Vientiane

Major Booksellers

Gumekong*, Vientiane

M **Jumsai***, Manich Bookshop, BP 28, Vientiane

Kaye Ando Technical Services*, 3-8 Villa Khamsouk, Sethathirath St, Vientiane Tel: 2760 Cable Add: Kaye Ando

M **Nicolai***, Casa Lao, Vientiane

Major Libraries

Direction des **Archives nationales** (National Archives)*, Présidence du Conseil des Ministres, BP 59, Vientiane

Bibliothèque nationale (National Library)*, BP 704, Vientiane

Centre national de Documentation (National Documentation Centre)*, Vientiane

Bibliothèque de l'**Ecole** royale de Médecine*, BP 131, Vientiane

Library Associations

Association des Bibliothécaires Laotiens (Association of Laos Librarians)*, c/o Direction de la Bibliothèque nationale, Ministry of Education, BP 704, Vientiane

Library Journals

Journal officiel (Official Journal), Centre national de Documentation, Vientiane

Lebanon

General Information

Language: Arabic (French and English also used)
Religion: Half Christian, with Maronites predominant, half Muslim
Population: 3.1 million
Bank Hours: 0830-1230 Monday-Friday; 0830-1200 Saturday
Shop Hours: Vary. Generally 0900-1900 in winter, 0800-1500 in summer
Currency: 100 Lebanese piastres = 1 Lebanese pound
Copyright: UCC, Berne (see International section)

Publishers

Dar al **Adab***, Beirut
Subject: Fiction

Arab Institute for Research and Publishing*, Syria St and Samadi Bldg, 5th Floor, PO Box 5460, Beirut
Subjects: Works in Arabic and English

Dar **Assayad***, BP 1038, Beirut
Man Dir: Bassam Freiha
Subjects: Politics, Periodicals and Newspapers
Founded: 1943

Dar **Beirut***, Librairie Beyrouth, Immeuble Lazarieh, rue Amir Bechir, Beirut Tel: 232504/301984
Proprietor: M Safieddine
Subjects: History, Islamic Books, Poetry, Encyclopedias (Arabic), Old Arabic Languages
Founded: 1936

Geoprojects Sàrl, PO Box 113, 5294 Beirut
Tel: 344346 Telex: 22661 Khayat le
Man Dirs: Mac Purcell, Tahseen Khayat
Associate Companies: Gulf Union Co, PO Box 2911 Safat, Kuwait; All Prints Bookshop, PO Box 857, Abu Dhabi, UAE; Uncle Sam's Bookshop, PO Box 8375, Beirut
Subjects: Tourist Maps & Guides Series, Arabic books
1978: 2 titles *1979:* 8 titles *Founded:* 1978

Dar el-**Ilm** Lilmalayin, PO Box 1085, Beirut (Located at: rue de Syrie, Beirut) Tel: 224502/291027 Cable Add: Malayin
Owners: Munir Ba'albaky, Bahij Osman
Subjects: Textbooks, Islamic Studies, Dictionaries, History, Mathematics, Physics, Law, Children, Health, Languages, Literature, Philosophy, Education, Psychology, Biographies
1977: 50 titles *Founded:* 1945

Institute for Palestine Studies, Publishing and Research Organization, Institute Bldg, Anis Nsouli St, PO Box 11-7164, Beirut
Tel: 319627/301599/ 301941/301089 Cable Add: Dirasat
Executive Secretary: Prof Walid Khalidi; *Editorial:* Miss Ghada Malki; *Sales:* Ghazi Khorshid
Subjects: Palestine and the Arab-Israeli conflict
1977: 16 titles *1978:* 21 titles *Founded:* 1963

The **International Documentary** Centre of Arab Manuscripts*, Darwish Bldg, rue de Syrie, BP 2668, Beirut
Proprietor: Zouhair Baalbaki
Subjects: Reprints, Facsimiles
Founded: 1965

Dar al **Kash'shaf**, Assad Malhamee St, PO Box 112091, Beirut Tel: 296805 Cable Add: Dakashaf Beirut
Proprietor: M Fathallah
Subjects: Scouting, Atlases, Maps
Founded: 1930

Khayat Book and Publishing Co SAL*, 90-94 rue Bliss, Beirut
Man Dir: Paul Khayat
Subjects: Fiction, History, Juveniles, Arts, Maps, Medicine, Education, Law, Religion, Social Sciences, Games, Sports, Economics, Books on the Middle East, Islam, Arabic, Reprints

Dar al-**Kitab** Al Jadid*, rue Hamra, Hindi Bldg, BP 1284, Beirut
Owner: Fuad Badr
Subject: Politics

Librairie du Liban*, Riad Al-Solh Sq, PO Box 945 Beirut Tel: 258259/295735 Cable Add: Librairie du Liban, Beirut Telex: 21037
Man Dirs: Khalil and George Sayegh; *Editorial:* Ahmad Khatib; *Sales:* Suhail Berjawi; *Production:* Albert Mutlag; *Publicity:* George Sayegh; *Rights and Permissions:* Khalil Sayegh
Subjects: Textbooks, Fiction, Linguistics, Travel, Islam, Dictionaries, Children's Books
Bookshops: Lebanon Bookshop, Bliss St, Beirut; Librairie du Liban, Hamra St, Beirut; Librairie sayegh, Damascus, Syria; Sphinx Bookshop, Cairo, Egypt
1977: 35 titles *Founded:* 1944

Longman Arab World Centre*, PO Box 945, Beirut
Miscellaneous: Firm is an associated company of Longman Group Ltd, UK (qv)

Dar Al-**Maaref** Liban SAL*, Esseily Bldg, sq Riad Al-Solh, PO Box 11-2320, Beirut
Tel: 223574/294064/383621 Cable Add: Damaref Beirut
Man Dir: Dr Fouad Ibrahim; *General Manager:* Joseph Nachou; *Sales:* Joseph Ibrahim
Parent Company: Dar Al Maaref, Egypt (qv)
Subjects: Juveniles, Textbooks in Arabic
Founded: 1959

Mac Purcell*, PO Box 1135294, Beirut

Dar al-**Makshouf***, rue Amir Beshir, Beirut
Owner: Sheikh Fuad Hobeish
Subjects: Science, Textbooks, Culture

Dar-el **Mashreq**, Imprimerie catholique, rue Huvelin 30, BP 946, Beirut Tel: 234942/326469 Cable Add: Cathopress
Man Dir: Paul Brouwers; *Rights & Permissions:* Paul Brouwers
Orders to: Librairie orientale, BP 1986, Beirut
Subjects: Archaeology, Geography, Educational, History, Dictionaries, Religion, Art, Literature, Languages, Science, Philosophy, Periodicals
1977: 15 titles *1978:* 30 titles *Founded:* 1853
ISBN Publisher's Prefix: 2-7214

Middle East Publishing Co*, rue G Picot, Imm El Kaissi, Beirut
Man Editor: Elie Sawaf
Subjects: Medicine, Periodicals
Medical Index, Revue Immobilière
Founded: 1954

New Book Publishing House*, Beirut

Rihani Printing & Publishing House*, Selim Jazairi, Beirut
Manager: Daoud Stephan
Subjects: Geography, History, Juveniles, Maps, Law, Encyclopaedias, Fiction, Agriculture, Mathematics, Physics
Founded: 1963

Major Booksellers

Librairies **Antoine***, Rue Patriarche Hoyek, Beirut Tel: 229745

Esquire*, Rue Sidani, Beirut Tel: 348074

Help Bookshop*, Rue Jeanne d'Arc, Im Saghiri, Beirut Tel: 341679

Tahseen S **Khayat***, Uncle Sam's Bookshop, PO Box 8375 Beirut Tel: 344346

Lebanon Bookshop*, Bliss St, Beirut

Librairie du **Liban***, Hamra St, Beirut

Georges **Murr***, Rue Ahmed Chawki, Beirut Tel: 233810

Major Libraries

Library of **American University** of Beirut*, Beirut Tel: 340740 Telex: amunob 20801 le

Library of **Beirut Arab University***, PO Box 5020, Beirut

Bibliothèque nationale du Liban (National Library)*, à la pl de l'Etoile, Imm du Parlement, Beirut Tel: 256160/256161

Bibliothèque orientale (Oriental Library), rue de l'Université St Joseph, BP 293, Beirut

Bibliothèque de l'**Ecole** supérieure des Lettres*, rue de Damas, Beirut

Library of the **Faculty** of Law*, Université St Joseph, BP 293, Beirut

Library of the **French Faculty of Medicine***, Pharmacy and Dentistry, Université St Joseph, BP 5076, Beirut

Library of the **Higher School** of Engineering*, Université St Joseph, BP 1514, Beirut

Bibliothèque de l'**Institut** français d'Archéologie*, rue Omar Daouk, BP 11-1424, Beirut

Nami C **Jafet** Memorial Library*, American University of Beirut, Beirut Tel: 340740 ext 2205

Librairie du Liban*, Imm Esseily, pl Riad Solh, BP 945, Beirut

Library of the **Monastery of St-Saviour** (Basilian Missionary Order of St-Saviour)*, Saïda

Library of the **Near East School** of Theology, PO Box 7424, Beirut

Library of the **Syrian Patriarchal Seminary***, Seminary of Charfet, Daroon-Harissa

Library Associations

The **Lebanese Library** Association, c/o National Library, pl de l'Etoile, Beirut Tel: 256160
Executive Secretary: Linda Sadaga
Publication: Newsletter

Library Journals

Bulletin bibliographique (Bibliographic Bulletin), Bibliothèque nationale du Liban, à la pl de l'Etoile, Imm du Parlement, Beirut

Newsletter, The Lebanese Library Association, c/o National Library, pl de l'Etoile, Beirut

Literary Associations and Societies

Lebanese **P E N** Club*, c/o M Camille Aboussouan, 12 ave Marie Curie, Beirut
Secretary: Zakaria Nsouli

Lesotho

General Information

Language: Sesotho (and English)
Religion: Roman Catholic and Protestant
Population: 1.2 million
Literacy Rate (1966): 58.6%
Bank Hours: 0830-1300 Monday-Friday; 0830-1100 Saturday
Shop Hours: Winter: 0830-1630 Monday-Friday; 0830-1300 Saturday; Summer: 0800-1630 Monday-Friday; 0800-1300 Saturday. Usually closed weekdays 1300-1400
Currency: South African

Export/Import Information: No tariffs on books or advertising matter. No import licence required; no obscene literature permitted. Exchange controls being relaxed

Publishers

Mazenod Institute, PO Box 18, Mazenod 160 (Railhead: Maseru Station) Tel: 0502224
Manager: Father B Mohlalisi
Subjects: History, Africana, Religion, Sotho Language & Literature, Secondary & Primary Textbooks
Founded: 1933

Morija Sesuto Book Depot*, PO Box 4, Morija
Man Dir: G L Richard
Subjects: Belles Lettres, Poetry, History, Africana, Religion, Juveniles, Southern Sotho Language, Paperbacks, General Science, Secondary & Primary Textbooks
Founded: 1862

Saint Michael's Mission*, The Social Centre, PO Box 25, Roma
Man Dir: Rev Father M Ferrange;
Production: Peter Ntsaoana
Subjects: Biography, History, Africana, Religion, Social Science, Secondary & Primary Textbooks, Anthropology
1977: 5 titles *1978:* 5 titles *Founded:* 1968

Government Printer*, Mazenod Printing Press, PO Mazenod, Maseru

Major Booksellers

Catholic Book Depot*, PO Box MS 78, Maseru Tel: 2634

Lesotho Book Centre*, PO Box MS 608, Maseru Tel: 3783

Mazenod Book Centre, PO Box 39, Mazenod (Located at: Mazenod Railhead, Maseru Station) Tel: 0502224 Cable Add: Books Mazenod Lesotho

Morija Sesuto Book Depot*, PO Box MJ 4, Morija Tel: 204

Major Libraries

British Council Library, PO Box 429, Maseru 100 Tel: 22609

Lesotho National Library Service, PO Box 985, Maseru 100

National University of Lesotho Library*, PO Roma Tel: 201

Liberia

General Information

Language: English and local dialects
Religion: Officially Christian but most practise traditional religions (only about 8% are Christian)
Population: 1.7 million
Literacy Rate (1962): 8.6%
Bank Hours: 0800-1200 Monday-Thursday; 0800-1400 Friday
Shop Hours: 0730-1200, 1400-1600 or longer
Currency: 100 cents = 1 Liberian dollar
Export/Import Information: No tariff on books and advertising matter. 5% FOB Public Fund Levy. No import licence or exchange control
Copyright: UCC (see International section)

Publishers

Cole & Yancy*, PO Box 286, Monrovia
Man Dir: Henry B Cole
Subjects: General, Reference, Annuals, Paperbacks
Bookshop: PO Box 286, Monrovia

Liberian Literary & Educational Publications*, PO Box 2387, Monrovia
Man Dir: S Henry Cordor
Subjects: General, Educational, Belles Lettres, Poetry

Government Printer*, Government Printing Office, Department of State, Monrovia

Major Booksellers

Wadih M Captan Bookstores*, Randall St, PO Box 414, Monrovia Tel: 21393

Cole and Yancy Bookshop Ltd*, PO Box 286, Monrovia

Liberian Educational Materials Supply Corporation*, New Port St, PO Box 2088, Monrovia Tel: 22356
Man: N Chandru

University Bookstore*, University of Liberia, Monrovia Tel: 22515 ext 225

Major Libraries

College of Our Lady of Fatima Library*, Harper

Cuttington College and Divinity School Library*, PO Box 277, Monrovia Tel: 21065

Government Public Library*, Ashmun St, Monrovia

International Communication Agency Library*, Broad St, Monrovia

University of Liberia Libraries*, PO Box 9020, Monrovia Tel: 22537
Dir: Dr C Wesley Armstrong
Publication: Newsletter

Literary Associations and Societies

Literary Club of Monrovia*, Monrovia

Literary Prizes

Edward Wilmot **Blyden** Prize*
For literary achievement. Awarded annually. Enquiries to Literary Club of Monrovia, Monrovia

Libya

General Information

Language: Arabic
Religion: Muslim
Population: 2.5 million
Literacy Rate (1964): 21.7%
Bank Hours: Generally Winter: 0900-1300; Summer: 0800-1230 Saturday-Thursday
Shop Hours: Vary greatly. Friday is weekly holiday but some Christian shops closed Sunday. Many are open 0830-1230, 1500-1730 Saturday-Thursday (slightly earlier hours in summer months)
Currency: 1,000 dirhams = 1 Libyan dinar
Export/Import Information: No tariff on books; advertising dutied 15%. Charity Tax of 5% and Municipal Tax of 5% levied on dutiable goods. Open General Licence for books. Exchange permit, liberally granted, required. Import and export of books is handled by the General Company for Publishing, Advertising and Distribution, Tripoli
Copyright: Berne (see International section)

Publishers

Dar Libya Publishing House*, PO Box 2487, Benghazi
Subject: Literature

General Press Corporation*, General Publication and Advertising Co, PO Box 959, Tripoli Tel: 45773/77/45537
Publicity: Moustafa A Elmasri
Subjects: General Books; Educational and Academic Books

Government Printer*, Agency for Development of Publication and Distribution, PO Box 34/35, Tripoli

Major Booksellers

General Company for Publishing, Advertising and Distribution*, Suf el Mahmudi, PO Box 959, Tripoli Tel: 457736777 Telex: 20235

Major Libraries

Al-Fateh University, The Central Library*, PO Box 398, Tripoli Tel: 39101 ext 2465

American Cultural Center Library*, Al Qayrawaan St, Tripoli

Arts and Crafts School Library*, Shar'a 24 December, Tripoli

Government Library*, 14 Shar'a al-Jazair, Tripoli

Institut Culturel Français Bibliothèque*, 15–17 Sciara Karachi, PO Box 683, Tripoli Tel: 35567
Librarian: Mme Bianciotto
Publication: Bulletin (monthly)

National Archives*, Castello, Tripoli

National Library*, Secretariat of Information and Culture, PO Box 9127, Benghazi Tel: 90509, 96379, 96380
Librarian: Mohammed O Fannoush

Public Library*, Shar'a 'Umar al-Mukhtar, Benghazi

Qurinna Library*, Mukhtar St, Benghazi

University of Garyounis Library*, Central Library Benghazi Tel: 87633
Librarian: Ahmed M Gallal

University of Libya*, Library, Benghazi

University of Tripoli*, Central Library, PO Box 398, Tripoli Tel: 39101 ext 236

Literary Associations and Societies

Intellectual Society of Libya*, 136 Shar'a Baladia, PO Box 1017, Tripoli

Liechtenstein

General Information

Language: German
Religion: Roman Catholic
Population: 25,000
Bank Hours: 0800-1200, 1330-1600 Monday-Friday
Shop Hours: 0800-1200, 1330-1830 Monday-Friday; 0800-1600 Saturday
Currency: Swiss
Export/Import Information: No tariff on books. Most books exempt from Turnover Tax. Advertising matter usually dutiable, some exempt from Turnover Tax. No import licences required. No exchange controls
Copyright: UCC, Berne, Florence (see International section)

Publishers

Alpenland Verlag*, FL-9494 Schaan
Subjects: Geography, Travel

Baltic Verlag und Verwaltungsges GmbH*, FL-9490 Vaduz, Im Städtle 22
Publications: Internationale Börsen-Vorschau, Spiegel der Wirtschaft
Founded: 1931

Buch und Verlagsdruckerei AG*, FL-9490 Vaduz, Im Städtle 32

A R **Gantner** Verlag KG, FL-9490 Vaduz, Postfach 225 (Located at: Beckagässle 4)
Subjects: Art, Literature, Botany

Kraus Reprint, FL-9491 Nendeln Tel: (075) 71155 Cable Add: Kraus Nendeln Telex: 77800
Dir: Ulfa von den Steinen
Associate Companies: Kraus Periodicals, KTO Press, KTO Microform
Br Off: Route 100, Millwood, New York, NY 10546, USA
Subjects: Scholarly publications and reference works in all subjects and languages
Founded: 1956
ISBN Publisher's Prefix: 3-262

K T O Press, FL-9491, Nendeln Tel: (075) 71155 Cable Add: Kraus Nendeln Telex: 77800
Dir: Ulfa von den Steinen
Parent Company: Kraus-Thomson Organization Ltd (at above address)
Associate Companies: Kraus Periodicals, Kraus Reprint, KTO Microform

Branch Off: KTO Press, Route 100, Millwood, New York, NY 10546 USA
Subjects: Scholarly publications and reference works in all subjects and languages
Founded: 1976
ISBN Publisher's Prefix: 3-262

Liechtenstein Verlag AG*, FL-9490 Vaduz, Schwefelstr 33 Tel: (075) 23925 Telex: 77826
Man Dir: Albart Piet Schiks
Subjects: Belles Lettres, Poetry, History, Educational Materials
1977: 1 title *Founded:* 1945
Miscellaneous: Firm is also a literary agency

Literarische Agentur und Verlagsgesellschaft, Litag Etablissement, FL-9490 Vaduz, Beckägassle 4
Dir: Dr Anton Gantner

Park & Roche Establishment*, 256 Kirchenstrasse, FL-9494 Schaan
Subjects: Music, Art, Architecture, History

Quarto Press, Postfach 143, Beckagässli 8, FL-9490 Vaduz Tel: (075) 24855 Telex: 77030
Man Dir: Elmar Bissig
Subjects: Art, Architecture, Orientalia
1977: 2 titles *Founded:* 1976
ISBN Publisher's Prefix: 3-85851

Topos Verlag AG*, Aeulestrasse 74, Postfach 668, FL-9490 Vaduz Tel: (075) 21711 Cable Add: Topos Vaduz Telex: 77817
Man Dir: Graham A P Smith
Subjects: Law, Economics, Social Science, Periodicals
1977: 40 titles *Founded:* 1977
ISBN Publisher's Prefix: 3-289

Literary Agents

Liechtenstein Verlag AG*, FL-9490 Vaduz, Schwefelstr 33 Tel: (075) 23925 Telex: 77826
Firm is also a publisher (qv)

Major Booksellers

Buchhandlung im Stadtle*, FL-9490 Vaduz

Kraus-Thomson Organization Ltd*, FL-9491 Nendeln Tel: 31805/060708

Major Libraries

Liechtensteinische Landesbibliothek (National Library)*, Offentliche Stiftung, Postfach 385, FL-9490 Vaduz Tel: (075) 66111
Director: Dr Alois Ospelt

Literary Associations and Societies

P E N Centre*, Postfach 416, FL-9490 Vaduz
Secretary: Manfred Schlapp

Luxembourg

General Information

Language: Mainly French, but also German. Also Luxembourg dialect, Letzeburgesch
Religion: Roman Catholic
Population: 356,000
Bank Hours: 0900-1200, 1400-1430 Monday-Friday
Shop Hours: 0800-1200, 1400-1800 Monday-Saturday
Currency: 100 centimes = 1 Luxembourg franc
Export/Import Information: No tariff on books except children's picture books, 13% from non-EEC; advertising other than single copies 9%. VAT 5% on books and advertising. No import licence required
Copyright: UCC, Berne, Florence (see International section)

Book Trade Organizations

Fédération des Commerçants, Groupement Papetiers-Libraires, Journaux, Editeurs et Galeries d'Art (Federation of Retailers Group for Stationers and Booksellers, Journals, Publishers and Art Galleries)*, 21 allée Scheffer, Luxembourg Tel: 473125
Dir: Victor Delcourt

Fédération luxembourgeoise des Travailleurs du Livre (Luxembourg Federation of Workers in the Book Trade)*, 38 rue Goethe, Luxembourg
President: Mathias Warny
Secretary: Nicolas Weber

Book Trade Reference Journal

Bibliographie luxembourgeoise (Luxembourg Bibliography), National Library, 37 blvd F D Roosevelt, Luxembourg

Publishers

Christian **Butterbach**, BP 516, Luxembourg Tel: 26926/26927/22022 Cable Add: Interferences
Owner and Manager: Christian Butterbach
Subjects: Literature, Periodical *Interferences*, Postcards
1978: 1 title *Founded:* 1959
ISBN Publisher's Prefix: 3-921400

Hasso **Ebeling** Verlag*, 4 rue Pierre de Coubertin, Luxembourg Tel: 488348 Telex: 1354
Man Dir: Hasso Ebeling
Subsidiary company: Ebeling Publishing Ltd, 63 Kings Rd, Windsor, Berkshire, UK Tel: 56 966 Telex: 848516; Ebeling Verlag, German Federal Republic (qv)
Subjects: Art, Architecture
Founded: 1974

Maison **Krippler-Muller**, 52 blvd G-D Charlotte, Luxembourg Tel: 470339/42709
Man Dir: J-P Krippler
Subjects: Belles Lettres, History, Maps, Regional Literature, Law, Languages
Bookshop: address as above
1977: 4 titles *1978:* 3 titles *Founded:* 1949

Edouard **Kutter**, 17 rue des Bains, Luxembourg
Subjects: Art, Photography, Facsimile editions on Luxembourg
1978: 4 titles

Imprimerie **Saint-Paul** SA, 2 rue Christophe-Plantin
Publicity: Charles Jourdain
Subject: Literature
1978: 19 titles
Miscellaneous: Publishes newspaper *Luxemburger Wort*

Verlag-Buchhandlung Joseph **Thielen**, 222 route de Thionville, Luxembourg
Owner and Manager: Joseph Thielen
Founded: 1950

Literary Agents

Hasso **Ebeling***, 4 rue Pierre de Coubertin, Luxembourg Tel: 488348 Telex: 1354

Major Booksellers

Librairie De **Bourcy** Lucien, 49 blvd Royal, Luxembourg

Librairie Paul **Bruck***, 22 Grand-rue, Luxembourg

Librairie du **Centre**, 49 blvd Royal, Luxembourg Tel: 45255/27999
Proprietor: L de Bourcy

Librairie R **Daman**, 4 rue de Brabant, Diekirch

Librairie J-Cl **Diderich**, 2 rue Victor-Hugo, Esch/Alzette Tel: 52695
Manager: J-Cl Diderich

Librairie Pierre **Ernster***, 27 rue du Fossé, Luxembourg

Librairie **Française***, 1 pl d'Armes, Luxembourg

Librairie des Messageries Paul **Kraus***, 5 rue de Hollerich, Luxembourg

Librairie **Lenners***, succ M Altwies, 30 rue Notre-Dame, Luxembourg

Librairie **Muller-Groff***, 4a ave Pasteur, Luxembourg

Librairie Armand **Peiffer***, ave Monterey, Luxembourg

Librairie **Promoculture**, BP 1142, 14 rue Duchscher, Luxembourg Tel: 480691
Manager: Albert P Daming

Librairie Jos **Wilwers**, 68 Grand-rue, Luxembourg

Major Libraries

Archives de l'Etat (National Archives)*, Plateau du St-Esprit, BP 6, Luxembourg 2

Bibliothèque de la Ville*, 26 rue Emile Mayrisch, Esch-sur-Alzette
Librarian: Fernand Roeltgen

Bibliothèque de Gouvernement, 37 blvd F D Roosevelt, Luxembourg

Bibliothèque nationale du Grand-Duché de Luxembourg (National Library), 37 blvd F D Roosevelt, Luxembourg Tel: 26255

Macao

General Information

Language: Portuguese (English used in business)
Religion: Chinese, the majority of population are Buddhist and Catholic is religion of Europeans
Population: 279,000
Literacy Rate (1960): 67.4%
Bank Hours: 1000-1500 Monday-Friday; 0930-1200 Saturday
Shop Hours: 0900-1730 Monday-Saturday
Currency: 100 cents = 1 Macao dollar (Hong Kong dollars also acceptable)
Export/Import Information: Macao is a free port

Major Booksellers

The **World** Book Company*, PO Box 201, 68 Rua Dos Mercadores Tel: 3591 Cable Add: Libiblioteca

Major Libraries

Biblioteca Nacional de Macao (National Library)*, Edificio do Leal Senado, Macao

Biblioteca **Sir Robert Ho Tung** (Sir Robert Ho Tung's Chinese Library)*, Largo do Sto Agostinho, Macao

Democratic Republic of Madagascar

General Information

Language: French and Malagasy
Religion: Roman Catholic and Protestant
Population: 8.52 million
Bank Hours: 0815-1100, 1400-1600 Monday-Friday. Closed afternoon preceding a holiday
Shop Hours: 0800-1200, 1400-1800 Monday-Saturday
Currency: Malagasy franc
Export/Import Information: For book, 5% customs duty, 22% import duty, 10% unique tax. For advertising matter, 5%, (31%) and 10%. Import licence required
Copyright: Berne, Florence (see International Section)

Book Trade Organization

Office du Livre Malagasy, BP 617, Tananarive Tel: 25872
Secretary-General: Juliette Ratsimandrava

Book Trade Reference Journal

Bibliographie annuelle de Madagascar, Bibliothèque universitaire de Madagascar, BP 908, Tananarive (The national bibliography, published annually since 1964)

Publishers

Maison d'Edition Protestante '**Antso**', Imarivolanitra, BP 660, Tananarive Tel: 20886 Cable Add: Fijekrima Tfbpi
Man Dir: Hans Andriamampianina;
Editorial: Charles Ramaniraka
Subjects: Religion, Sociology, Politics, Economics, Journals
Bookshop: Lot IIB 18, Tohatohabato Ranavalona 1, Antananarivo
1978/79: 18 titles *Founded:* 1966

Société de Presse et d'Edition de Madagascar*, BP 1570, Tananarive
Man Dir: Mme Rajaofera-Andriambelo
Subjects: General Nonfiction, Reference, General Science, University Textbooks

Société Malgache d'Edition*, BP 659, Ankorondrano, Tananarive Tel: 22635
Man Dir: Rahaga Ramaholimihaso;
Publicity: Daniel Ramanandraibe
Subjects: University & Secondary Textbooks
Bookshop: address as above
Founded: 1959

Société Nouvelle de l'Imprimerie Centrale*, BP 1414, Tananarive
Man Dir: M Hantzberg
Subjects: Paperbacks, General Science, University, Secondary & Primary Textbooks
Founded: 1959

Imprimerie **Takariva***, 4 rue Radley, BP 1029, Antanimena, Tananarive Tel: 22128
Man Dir: Paul Rapatsalahy
Subjects: General Fiction, Malagasy Languages, Paperbacks, Secondary Textbooks
Founded: 1933

Trano Printy Loterana-Trano Printy Fiangonana Loterana Malagasy (TPFLM)- (Imprimerie Luthérienne), 9 ave Grandidier, BP 538, Antsahamanitra, Tananarive Tel: 24569
Man Dir: Abel Arnesa; *Editorial:* Pastor Rasolofomanana; *Production:* Razafind-ramanitra Georges
Subjects: General Fiction, Religion, Paperbacks, Secondary & Primary Textbooks
Bookshop: address as above
Founded: 1875

Government Printer, Imprimerie nationale, BP 38, Tananarive

Major Booksellers

Bibliomad, 11 rue de Nice, BP 602, Tananarive Tel: 23280
Manager: Ramaromandray Amedée

Librairie de Madagascar*, 38 ave de l'Indépendance, BP 402, Tananarive Tel: 22454

Librairie lutherienne*, ave Grandidier, BP 538, Tananarive Tel: 23340

Librairie mixte Sàrl, 37 bis Ave du 26 Juin 1960, Analakely, BP 3204, Tananarive Tel: 25130

Librairie universitaire*, 26 rue Amiral Pierre, Tananarive

Société Malgache d'Edition*, BP 659, Ankorondrano, Tananarive

Librairie 'Tout pour l'Ecole'*, Immeuble Vitasoa, rue de Nice, BP 1099, Tananarive Tel: 23521

Trano Printy Loterana*, 9 ave Grandidier, BP 538, Antsahamanitra, Tananarive Tel: 24569

Major Libraries

Archives de Madagascar*, BP 3384, Tananarive
Dir: Mme Razoharinoro-Randriam-Boavonjy

Bibliotheque municipale*, ave 18 Juin, BP 729, Tananarive Tel: 21176

Bibliotheque nationale (National Library), BP 257, Antaninarenina, Tananarive Tel: 20511
Publications include: Ny Boky loharanom-pandrosoana (Le Livre Source de Progrès)

Bibliothèque universitaire*, Campus universitaire, BP 908, Tananarive Tel: 26000
Librarian: Mlle de Nuce
Publication: Bibliographie annuelle

Bibliothèque du Centre culturel 'Albert **Camus**'*, 11 ave Grandidier, Isoraka, Tananarive

Collège rural d'Ambatobe*, Bibliothèque, BP 1629, Tananarive

International Communication Agency Library*, 26 rue Paul Dussac, Tananarive Tel: 20238

Library Journals

Ny Boky loharanom-pandrosoana (Le Livre Source du Progrès) (The Book, Source of Progress) National Library, Antaninarenina, BP 257, Tananarive

Literary Periodicals

Fanasina, BP 1574, Analakely-Tananarive (literary and current affairs weekly edited by Paul Rakotovololona)

Literary Prizes

Literature Prize*
For an outstanding novel. 130,000 Malagasy francs. Awarded every two years. Enquiries to Malagasy Ministry of Cultural Affairs, Anosy-Tananarive

Malawi

General Information

Language: English and Chichewa
Religion: Mohammedanism and Christian (Church of Central Africa, Presbyterian, Roman Catholic and Anglican)

Population: 5.5 million
Literacy Rate (1966; African Population): 22.1%
Bank Hours: 0800-1230 Monday, Tuesday, Thursday, Friday; 0800-1130 Wednesday; 0800-1030 Saturday
Shop Hours: 0730 or 0800-1600 or 1700 Monday-Friday (with some closing for lunch); until midday Saturday
Currency: 100 tambala = 1 kwacha
Export/Import Information: No tariff on books; some advertising matter subject to 30%. No import licence required. Exchange controls

Book Trade Reference Journal

Malawi National Bibliography, c/o National Archives of Malawi, PO Box 62, Zomba

Publishers

Christian Literature Association in Malawi, PO Box 503, Blantyre Tel: 635046
Subjects: General Fiction, Poetry, Biography, History, Africana, Religion, Juveniles, Christian Tracts, Paperbacks
Bookshop: CLAIM, at above address
1977: 2 titles *Founded:* 1968

Government Printer (Imprimerie National)*, Government Printing Department, Office of the President and Cabinet, PO Box 37, Zomba

Popular Publications*, PO Box 5592, Limbe Tel: 651139/651833 Telex: 4130
General Manager: John Kleinpenning; *Editorial, Production, Rights & Permissions:* A E Ulanga; *Sales, Publicity:* Z D Mullewa
Subsidiary Company: Montfort Press, PO Box 5592, Limbe
Subjects: Belles Lettres, Poetry, Paperbacks, Biography, Plays, Religion, *MONI-Magazine*
Bookshop: Moni Bookshop, PO Box 5592, Limbe
1977: 2 titles *Founded:* 1975

Major Booksellers

C L A I M Bookshop, PO Box 503, Blantyre Tel: 635046

Central Bookshop Ltd*, PO Box 264, Blantyre Tel: 635447
Man: A. Hamid Sacranie

Malawi Book Service, PO Box 30044, Chichiri, Blantyre 3
Branches in Zomba, Lilongwe, Kasungu, Mzuzu

Times Bookshop Ltd, Victoria Ave, Private Bag 39, Blantyre Tel: 636355
Man: Shaibu Itimu

Major Libraries

British Council Library, Victoria Rd, PO Box 456, Blantyre Tel: 636500
Also Taurus House, PO Box 30222 Area 40/4, Capital City, Lilongwe 3 Tel: 30484/30266

Malawi National Library Service, PO Box 30314, Lilongwe 3
Dir: R S Mabomba

The **Malawi Polytechnic** Library*, PMB 303, Chichiri, Blantyre 3 Tel: Blantyre 32144
Acting Librarian: Paul Kanthambi
Publications: Accessions List, Annual Report

National Archives of Malawi, PO Box 62, Zomba Tel: 2478/9
Librarian: D D Najira
Publication: Malawi National Bibliography

University of Malawi Library, PO Box 280, Zomba Tel: 2791
Librarian: S A Patchett

Library Associations

The **Malawi Library Association***, c/o National Archives of Malawi, PO Box 62, Zomba Tel: 2478/9
Secretary: S S Mwiyeriwa

Literary Associations and Societies

The **Writers'** Group*, PO Box 280, Zomba
Publication: Odi

Literary Periodicals

Odi, The Writers' Group, PO Box 280, Zomba

Malaysia

General Information

Language: Many languages. National language is Malay and English is used commercially
Religion: Predominantly Muslim (Islam is the official religion) and large Buddhist group
Population: 12.6 million
Literacy Rate (1970): Sabah 44.3% total (69.1% Urban, 38.9% Rural); Sarawak 38.3% (64.1% Urban, 32.6% Rural); West Malaysia 60.8% (68.2% Urban, 57.6% Rural)
Bank Hours: (some states observe Muslim weekly holiday) Peninsula: 1000-1500 Monday-Friday; 0930-1130 Saturday. Sabah: 0800-1200, 1400-1500 Monday-Friday; 0900-1100 Saturday. Sarawak: 1000-1500 Monday-Friday; 0930-1130 Saturday
Shop Hours: Peninsula varies; average 0830-1830 Monday-Saturday. Sabah: 0830-1830 Monday-Saturday. Sarawak: 0900-1800 Monday-Friday; 0900-1300 Saturday
Currency: 100 cents = 1 Malaysian dollar (or ringgit)
Export/Import Information: No tariff on books. Advertising matter dutied at 25 cents per lb, subject to 5% CIF surtax. No obscene literature allowed. Import licences required only in Sabah, for books not having on first or last printed page the name and address of printer and publisher. No exchange controls
Copyright: Florence (see International section)

Book Trade Organizations

Malaysian Book Publishers' Association, PO Box 335, Kuala Lumpur Tel: 941344 Cable Add: Bukumal, Kuala Lumpur
Honorary Secretary: J B Ho

Book Trade Reference Journals

Berita Oxford (text in English and Malay), Oxford University Press, East Asian Branch, Bangunan Loke Yew, Jalan Belanda, Kuala Lumpur

Bibliografi Negara Malaysia (Malaysian National Bibliography), National Library of 1st Floor, Wisma Thakurdas, Jalan Raja Laut, Kuala Lumpur

Publishers

Academia Publications P Ltd+*, 10 Jalan 217, Petaling Jaya, Selangor

Pustaka **Aman** Press Sdn Bhd+*, 4200–A Simpang Tiga-Telipot, Jalan Pasir Puteh, Kota Bharu, Kelantan

Pustaka **Antara**+*, 399A Jalan Tuanku Abdul Rahman, Kuala Lumpur 02-01 Tel: 24622
Bookshop: 399A Jalan Tuanku Abdul Rahman, Kuala Lumpur 02-01

Anthonian Stores Sdn Bhd+*, 235 Jalan Brickfields, Kuala Lumpur 09-08 Tel: 205088
Man Dir, Publicity: Soh Boon Chuan; *Editorial, Production, Rights & Permissions:* Francis C K Lee; *Sales:* Y S Tan
Associate Company: Anthonian Store Sdn Bhd, Ipoh
Subsidiary Company: Anthonian (Pte) Ltd, Singapore
Subjects: Educational, General
Bookshops: in 108 schools
1977: 14 titles *1978:* 21 titles *Founded:* 1953

Book Distributors Sdn Bhd+*, 8-1/8-2 Jalan Batai, PO Box 944, Kuala Lumpur 01-02

Books for Asia (M) Sdn Bhd*, 103 Jalan Bungsar, Kuala Lumpur
Parent Company: Books for Asia, Hong Kong (qv)

The **Cultural Supplies** Co*, 8-1 Pater Bldg, Jalan Brunei off Jalan Pudu, Kuala Lumpur

Dewan Bahasa dan Pustaka, PO Box 803, Kuala Lumpur 08-08 Tel: 481169 Cable Add: Bahasa
Director General: Datuk Hj Hassan Ahmad; *Editorial:* Baha Zain, Noor Azam; *Sales:* Mokhtar Mohamad; *Production:* Rahmat Ramly; *Publicity:* A Rahim Esa; *Rights & Permissions:* Ariffin Siri
Br Off: Kota Kinabalu, Sabah; Kuching, Sarawak
Subjects: Textbooks in Malay Language, Literature, General Books, Children's Books
Bookshop: address as above
1977: 100 titles *1978:* 200 titles *Founded:* 1956

Eastern Cultural Organizations Sdn Bhd*, 27-9 Jalan Loke Yew, Kuala Lumpur

Eastern Universities Press+, No 134 Jalan Kasah, Damansara Heights, Kuala Lumpur Tel: 942604
Manager: Ong Kim Chuan
Parent Company: Hodder & Stoughton, Sevenoaks, Kent, UK (qv)
Subjects: Primary and Secondary Schoolbooks, Art, Archaeology, Architecture, Biography, Botany, Customs and Usage, Economics and Politics, Languages, Sociology, Religion, Travel, Topography
1978: 50 titles

F E P International (M) Sdn Bhd (Far Eastern Publishers)+*, 8246 Jalan 225, PO Box 1091, Petaling Jaya, Selangor Tel: 560976/772828 Cable Add: Bookmark
Man Dir: Lim Mok Hai
Subjects: Reference, General Nonfiction, Secondary & Primary Textbooks
1977: 26 titles

Penerbit **Fajar** Bakti Sdn Bhd+, 3 Jalan 13/3, PO Box 1050, Jalan Semangat, Petaling Jaya, Selangor Tel: 563111 Cable Add: Oxonian Petaling Jaya Telex: 37578
Regional Manager: J A Nicholson; *General Manager:* M Sockalingam; *Publishing Manager:* Mohd Yusoff Shamsuddin; *Sales:* Koh Seng Hwi; *Production:* Yap Kok Hoong; *Publicity:* Thor Gim Lock
Parent Company: Oxford University Press (qv)
Imprint: PFB
Subjects: Malay Language Teaching, Dictionaries, Reference, Secondary Textbooks, General
Bookshop: at same address
1977: 76 titles *1978:* 92 titles *Founded:* 1969
ISBN Publisher's Prefix: 019

Federal Publications Sdn Bhd+*, Lot 8238, Jalan 222, Petaling Jaya, Selangor
General Manager: H S Koh
Subject: Education

M S Geetha Publishers*+, 13A Jalan Kovil Hilir, Batu 2½, Jalan Ipoh, Sentul, Kuala Lumpur 13-05
Man Dir: Mr Sethu
Subjects: History, Education, How-to, Reference, Textbooks, Bibliography, Book Industry

Heinemann Educational Books (Asia) Ltd+, No 2, Jalan 20/16A, Paramount Garden, Petaling Jaya, Selangor
Miscellaneous: Firm is a subsidiary of Heinemann Educational Books Ltd, UK (qv)

Penerbit **Jaya***, PO Box 6103, Pudu PO, Kuala Lumpur
Subjects: Dictionary (*English–Bahara Malaysia Idiomatic Phrases*)
1978: 1 title

Longman Malaysia Sdn Bhd+, PO Box 63, Kuala Lumpur Tel: 941344/941461 Cable Add: Freegrove Kualalumpur
Dir: J B Ho
Subjects: Educational Materials, Textbooks
1977: 67 titles *1978:* 35 titles
Miscellaneous: Firm is an associate company of the Longman Group Ltd, UK (qv)

Macmillan Malaysia+*, Rm 805, 8th Floor, Selangor Complex, Jalan Sultan, Kuala Lumpur 01-26 Tel: 299194/5

Pustaka **Mahligai** Press*, 4591 Jalan Pasir Puteh, Kota Bharu, Kelantan

Malaya Books Suppliers Co+*, 183 Lebuh Carnarvon, Pulau Pinang

Malaya Educational Supplies Sdn Bhd+*, 48 Jalan Raja Laut, Kuala Lumpur
Subject: Education

The **Malaya Press** Sdn Bhd*+, 24B Jalan Bukit Bintang, Kuala Lumpur Tel: (03) 428831/425764
Man Dir: Yu Nan Shen; *Editorial:* Yiu Hong; *Sales:* Chong Tek Seng
Parent Company: Union Cultural Organization Sdn Bhd, 10 Jalan 217, Petaling Jaya, Malaysia
Associated Companies: Hong Kong Cultural Press Ltd, 9 College Rd, Kowloon, Hong Kong; Singapore Press (Pte) Ltd, 303 North Bridge Rd, Singapore 7
Subject: School Textbooks
Bookshops: Ipoh Book Co, 75 Market St, Ipoh, Perak; Malaya Book Co, 22–24 Jalan Bukit Bintang, Kuala Lumpur
1977: 34 titles *Founded:* 1958

Pustaka **Melayu** Baru+*, 1015 Selangor Mansion, Jalan Masjid India, Kuala Lumpur

Oxford University Press+, 3 Jalan 13/3, PO Box 1050, Jalan Semangat, Petaling Jaya, Selangor Tel: 563111 Cable Add: Oxonian Petaling Jaya Telex: 37578
Regional Manager: J A Nicholson; *General Manager:* M Sockalingham; *Sales:* Koh Seng Hwi; *Production:* Yap Kok Hoong; *Publicity:* Thor Gim Lock
Parent Company: Oxford University Press, UK (qv)
Subsidiary Company: Penerbit Fajar Bakti Sdn Bhd (qv)
Subjects: Educational, English Language Teaching, General, Dictionaries, Reference, Malaysiana
Book Club: Triple Crown Club
Bookshop: address as above
1977: 33 titles *1978:* 40 titles *Founded:* 1957
ISBN Publisher's Prefix: 019

P F B, an imprint of Penerbit Fajar Bakti Sdn Bhd (qv)

Pan Malayan Publishing Co Sdn Bhd+*, 211 Jalan Bandar, Kuala Lumpur 01-30

Penerbitan Buku **Panther** (Panther Books Malaysia)*, 135A Jalan Abdul Samad, Brickfields, Kuala Lumpur 09-02 Tel: 21406/206687
Chief Executive, Publicity: R Vijesurier; *Editorial, Production:* Bella Mary Peters; *Sales:* Inche Mustapha Aziz
Branch Off: 8 Cambridge Rd, Singapore 10
Subjects: School Textbooks, Revision Guides, Travel Books, Street Guides
1977: 12 titles *Founded:* 1972

Pustaka **Pendidekan** Sdn Bhd*, 19 Jalan Ismail, Kluang, Johore

Preston Corporation Ltd+, 18 Jalan 19/3, Petaling Jaya, Selangor Tel: 563734/5 Telex: Prest MA 37433
Associate Companies: Preston Publications Ltd, & Vista Productions Ltd, 1 & 6, 7th Floor Block E, Sunway Gardens, 989 King's Rd, North Point, Hong Kong; Preston Corporation (Pte) Ltd, 9 Irving Place, Singapore 13

Preston-Times Printing & Publishing*, Lots 2, 4 & 6 Kawasan MIEL, Phase 3, Shal Alam Industrial Estate, Selangor, Malaysia

Associated Company: Preston Corporation (Pte) Ltd, 9 Irving Place, Singapore 13
Subjects: General Nonfiction, Reference Books, Primary and Secondary Textbooks, Library Books

Sino-Malay Publishing Co+*, 183 Lebuh Carnarvon, Pulau Pinang

Pustaka **Sistem** Pelajaran+*, 4 Jalan Angsoka, Kuala Lumpur 05-11
Subjects: School Textbooks, Children's Books

Pustaka **Sri Jaya** Sdn Bhd+, 273 Ampang Park Shopping Centre, Kuala Lumpur
Subjects: Juveniles, Textbooks

Syarikat Cultural Supplies Sdn Bhd+*, 8-1 Pater Bldg, Jalan Brunei, Off Jalan Pudu, Kuala Lumpur 06-18

Syarikat Dian Sdn Bhd+*, 97A Jalan Raja Abdullah, Kampung Baru, Kuala Lumpur

Syarikat United Book Sdn Bhd+*, 187-189 Lebuh Carnarvon, Pulau Pinang

Text Books Malaysia Sdn Bhd+*, Peti Surat 30, Segamat, Johore (Located at: 39 Jalan Buloh Kasap, Segamat, Johore)

Times Educational Co Ltd+, 22 Jalan 19/3, Petaling Jaya, Selangor Tel: 51194 Cable Add: Timesbooks Telex: Prest MA 37433
Orders to: Preston Corporation Ltd, 18 Jalan 19/3, Petaling Jaya Selangor
Parent Company: Times Educational Co Ltd, 1 & 6, 7th Floor, Block E, Sunway Gardens, 989 King's Road, North Point, Hong Kong
Subjects: Textbooks (Primary & Secondary), Library books, General & Reference books
1978: 198 titles
Miscellaneous: Associate Company of Preston Corporation Ltd, Petaling Jaya Selangor, Malaysia; Preston-Times Printing & Publishing, Selangor, Malaysia; Preston Corporation (Private) Ltd, Singapore

Penerbit **Titiwangsa** Sdn Bhd+*, 199 Jalan Imbi, Kuala Lumpur

Uni-Text Book Co*, 50 Jalan 552/61, SEA Park, Petaling Jaya Tel: 560197
Dir: E S Lim
Subject: Malay Books
Bookshop: address as above
1977-78: 154 titles

United Publishers Services (M) Sdn Bhd+, 134 Jalan Kasah, Damansara Heights, Kuala Lumpur Tel: 942604
Man Dir, Sales, Publicity: Johnny K C Ong; *Editorial, Production, Rights & Permissions:* Goh Kee Seah
Associated Companies: United Publishers Service Hong Kong Ltd; United Publishers Services Tokyo Ltd, Japan (qv)
Subsidiary Company: Eastern Universities Press Sdn Bhd
Br Off: No 8, 1st Floor, Leboh Naning, Penang; 112F Boon Keng Rd, Block 5, Singapore 12
Subjects: Educational, General, Paperbacks
Founded: 1968

United Publishing House and Stationers Sdn Bhd+*, 21-23 Jalan Taiping, Off Jalan Pahang, Kuala Lumpur 02-14, Kuala Lumpur

Universal Publications Sdn Bhd+*, 6 Jalan 13/6, Petaling Jaya, Selangor Tel: 773630
Subjects: School textbooks

University of Malaya Press Ltd*, University of Malaya, Pantai Valley, Kuala Lumpur 22-11 Tel: (03) 774361 Cable Add: Vasitipres Kuala Lumpur
Man Dir, Publicity, Rights & Permissions: Harun Haji Abdullah; *Editorial:* Syed Zulflida Shahabuddin; *Sales:* Yang Sharifah Baharuddin; *Production:* Kamar Bidin
Subjects: General Fiction, Belles Lettres, Poetry, History, Politics, Economics, General & Social Science, Medicine, Bahasa Malaysia
1977: 18 titles *Founded:* 1954

Utusan Publications and Distributions Sdn Bhd+*, 5 Medan Tuanku, Kuala Lumpur

Yayasan Buku*, 143 C Jalan Sungai Besi, Kuala Lumpur
Subjects: How-to, Reference, Juveniles, Nonfiction, Bibliography, Book Industry

Book Clubs

Triple Crown Club, 3 Jalan 13/3, PO Box 1050, Jalan Semangat, Petaling Jaya, Selangor
Owned by: Oxford University Press (Selangor)

Major Booksellers

Anthonian Store Sdn Bhd*, 235 Jalan Brickfields, Kuala Lumpur 09-08
Tel: 205088

Cosdel (Singapore) Pte Ltd, PO Box 6073, Jalan Pudu, Kuala Lumpur 06-10 (Located at: 23-25 Jalan Jejaka 7, Taman Maluri; Batu 3, Jln Cheras, Kuala Lumpur) Distributors

Eastern Book Service Sdn Bhd (wholesalers)*, 10-A Jalan Telawi 4, Bangsar Baru, Kuala Lumpur Tel: 80445

Johore Central Store*, 55-56 Jalan Ibrahim, Johor Bahru Tel: 2637

Kwang Hwa Bookstore Pte Ltd, 26 Carpenter St, PO Box 326, Kuching, Sarawak Tel: 22968
Man: Francis Hsu Cheng Loo

M P H Distributors Sdn Bhd*, Peti Surat 1076, Jalan Semangat, Petaling Jaya

Marican & Sons (M) Sdn Bhd, 321 Jalan Tuanku Abdul Rahman, Kuala Lumpur 02-01 Tel: 981133/981218; 211 Ampang Park Shopping Centre, Jalan Ampang, Kuala Lumpur Tel: 485172; Weld Supermarket (First Floor), Jalan Raja Chulan, Kuala Lumpur Tel: 27994

Nabco Pendidekan Sdn Bhd, 24 Market St, Ipoh, Perak Tel: (05) 78456/518439; 44 Jln Persiaran Ipoh Satu, Ipoh Garden, Ipoh, Perak (formerly New Asia Book Co)

Parry's Book Center, KL Hilton Hotel, PO Box 960, Kuala Lumpur Tel: 422631, 922329, 924985

Rex Book Store*, 40-2 K L Arcade, Jalan Masjid India, Kuala Lumpur

Times Distributors Sdn Bhd, NZI Building, 2 Jalan 52/10, Petaling Jaya, Selangor
Also 1 New Industrial Rd, Singapore 1953

University of Malaya Co-operative Bookshop Ltd, PO Box 1127, Jalan Pantai Bahru, Kuala Lumpur Tel: 54058/51425

Major Libraries

British Council Library*, PO Box 539, Jalan Bukit Aman, Kuala Lumpur 01-02
Branches in Penang (PO Box 595) and Kota Kinabalu (PO Box 746)

Kuala Lumpur Public Library*, Sam Mansion, Jalan Tuba, Kuala Lumpur

Mara Institute of Technology Library*, Shah Alam, Selangor

Ministry of Agriculture Library*, Swettenham Rd, Kuala Lumpur 10-02
Librarian: Beatrice Lip

National Archives of Malaysia, Federal Government Building, Jalan Sultan, Petaling Jaya
Publications: Annual Report of the National Archives, Siri Ucapan Perdan Menteri Tun Abdul Razak (Speeches of Tun Abdul Razat, Prime Minister of Malaysia), inventories and lists of archives groups

National Library of Malaysia*, 1st Floor, Wisma Thakurdas, Jalan Raja Laut, Kuala Lumpur
Deputy Director General: D E K Wijasuriya
Publications: Malaysian National Bibliography (quarterly, annually); *Malaysian Periodicals Index* (annually)

Rubber Research Institute of Malaysia Library, PO Box 150, Kuala Lumpur 16-03 Tel: 467033
Librarian: J S Soosai

Sabah State Library*, PO Box 1136, Kota Kinabalu, Sabah Tel: 54333

Sarawak State Library*, Jalan Jawa, Kuching

Selangor Public Library*, 21 Jalan Raja, Kuala Lumpur 01-02 Tel: (03) 85370
Librarian: Mrs Shahaneem Mustafa
Publication: Annual Report; Accession List (quarterly)

Tun Razak Library, Jalan Club, Ipoh, Perak

University of Malaya Library*, Pantai Valley, Kuala Lumpur 22-11

Library Associations

Persatuan Perpustakaan Malaysia (Library Association of Malaysia)*, Peti Surat 2545, Kuala Lumpur Tel: 564287
Honorary Secretary: Noor Aini Osman
Publication: Majalah Perpustakaan Malaysia

Library Reference Books and Journals

Books

Directory of Libraries in Malaysia, University of Malaya Library, Pantai Valley, Kuala Lumpur

Journals

Library Industry, No 19, Road 22/7, Kampong Tunku, Petaling Jaya, Jayathissa

Majalah Perpustakaan Malaysia (Official Journal) (text in English and Malay), Library Association of Malaysia, Peti Surat 2545, Kuala Lumpur

Literary Associations and Societies

Dewan Bahasa dan Pustaka (Language and Literary Agency of the Ministry of Education), PO Box 803 Jalan Lapangan Terbang, Kuala Lumpur 08-08
Dir General: Datuk Haji Hassan bin Ahmad
Publications: Dewan Bahasa, Dewan Masyarakat, Dewan Pelajar, Dewan Sastera (monthly); *Dewan Budaya, Dewan Siswa* (monthly); *Tenggara* (half-yearly)

Literary Periodicals

Tenggara (text in English and Malay, (half-yearly)). Dewan Behasa dan Pustaka, PO Box 803 Jl Lapangan Terbang, Kuala Lumpur 08-08

Literary Prizes

National Literary Awards*
Panel established in 1971 by the late Tun Abdul Razak to award prizes. Enquiries to Dewan Bahasa dan Pustaka, PO Box 803, Kuala Lumpur 08-08

Mali

General Information

Language: French
Religion: Muslim
Population: 6 million
Literacy Rate (1960): 2.2%
Working Hours: normally 0800 or 0900-1200, 1500-1800 Monday-Friday; 0800 or 0900-1200 Saturday
Currency: Malian franc
Export/Import Information: No tariff on books but subject to 10% VAT; children's picture books 20% VAT; atlases 10% VAT. Advertising matter (more than single copy): 5% tariff, 25% import tax, 20% VAT. All goods subject to local tax of 3% customs value. Import licence required. Importation is either by private importers or state enterprises. Exchange controls for non-franc zone

Publishers

Government Printer (Imprimerie Nationale)*+, ave Kasse Keita, BP 21, Bamako

Editions Imprimeries du **Mali***, ave Kasse Keita, BP 21, Bamako Tel: 22041
Man Dir: Barthélémy Koné
Subjects: General Fiction & Nonfiction, Belles Lettres, Poetry, Biography, History, Africana, Religion, Paperbacks, Social Science, University, Secondary & Primary Textbooks
Founded: 1972
Subsidiaries: Editions populaires; Imprimerie Kasse Keita; Imprimerie nationale

Major Booksellers

Librairie **Deves et Chaumet***, BP 64, Bamako

Librairie populaire de Mali*, ave Kasse Keita, BP 28, Bamako Tel: 23403

Major Libraries

Archives nationales du Mali*, Institut des Sciences Humaines, BP 159, Koulouba, Bamako
Dir: A Gamby N'Diaye

Bibliothèque municipale*, Bamako

Bibliothèque nationale (National Library)*, Institut de Sciences humaines, BP 159, Koulouba, Bamako

Centre français de Documentation*, Ambassade de France, BP 1547, Bamako Tel: 24019

Ecole normale supérieure*, Bibliothèque, BP 241, Bamako

Library Associations

Inspection des **Archives***, Musées et Bibliothèques du Mali (Inspectorate of Archives, Museums and Libraries of Mali), BP 241, Bamako

Malta

General Information

Language: Maltese (English second language)
Religion: Roman Catholic
Population: 332,000
Literacy Rate (1948): 56%
Bank Hours: 0830-1230 Monday-Friday; 0830-1200 Saturday
Shop Hours: 0900-1300, 1500-1800 Monday-Friday; most shops open Saturday at least half day
Currency: 100 cents (1,000 mils) = 1 Maltese pound
Export/Import Information: No tariff on books or advertising. No import licence required. Exchange control by Central Bank

Publishers

A C **Aquilina** & Co, 58D Republic St, Valletta
Subjects: Literature, History
Bookshop: At above address

Lux Press*, St Joseph St, Hamrun
Subject: Literature

Progress Press, PO Box 328, Valetta (Located at: Strickland Ho, 341 St Paul St, Valletta) Tel: 24031 Cable Add: Progress Telex: MW341
Man Dir: W B Asciak
Subjects: Literature, Malta
1978: 4 titles *Founded:* 1957

A **Vassallo** and Sons Ltd*, 49 Main Gate St, Victoria, Gozo Tel: 76609
Subjects: School Textbooks, Maps, Guides
Bookshop: The Ideal Bookshop

Major Booksellers

A C **Aquilina** & Co, 58D Republic St, Valletta Tel: 624774

D C **Cortis***, 324/325 Prince of Wales Rd, Shema Tel: 34633

Hamrun Library*, The, 673 St Joseph Rd, Hamrun Tel: 28542

The **Ideal** Bookshop*, 49 Main Gate St, Victoria, Gozo Tel: 76609
Owned by: A Vassallo and Sons Ltd

Merlin Library Ltd, Mountbatten St, Blata I-Bajda Tel: 625838 (also Wholesalers and Remainder Dealers)

Giov **Muscat** & Co Ltd, 213 St Ursola St, Valletta Tel: 27668; 48 Merchants St, PO Box 348, Valletta
Manager: A de Domenico

Sapienza's Library*, 26 Republic St, Valletta Tel: 625621

Major Libraries

British Council Library*, Pjazza Indipendenza, Valletta

Gozo Public Library, Vajringa St, Victoria, G Gozo6 Tel: 556200

National Library of Malta, 36 Old Treasury St, Valletta Tel: Central 26585
Librarian: Dr Vincent A Depasquale
Publication: Annual Report

University of Malta Library, Msida Tel: 36451
Librarian: Paul Xuereb
Publications: Malta, Official Statistical Publications 1975; The Maltese Woman; Il-Poezija bil-Malti 1964-74; Liberty to Print: Catalogue of an exhibition of Street Literature 1976; A Bibliography of Maltese Bibliographies 1978

Library Associations

Malta Library Association (Ghaqda Bibljotekarji), c/o Din-l-Art Helwa, 133 Britannia St, Valletta
Secretary: Margaret R Psaila
Publications: Malta Library Association Newsletter; Malta Library Association Yearbook; Bibliography of Children's Literature in Malta

Library Reference Books and Journals

Books

A Bibliography of Maltese Bibliographies, University of Malta Library, Msida

Yearbook Malta Library Association, c/o Ms Nora Sammut, Old University of Malta Library, Msida

Journals

Newsletter, Malta Library Association, c/o Ms Nora Sammut, Old University of Malta Library, Msida

Martinique

General Information

Language: French
Population: 374,000
Literacy Rate (1967): 87.8%
Currency: French
Export/Import Information: Tariff same as France. 7% overseas tax and reduced VAT on books, 3.5%. Small quantity of advertising free. No import licences required. Exchange restrictions as in France

Major Booksellers

A **Jean-Charles***, 32 & 47 rue Schoelcher, Fort de France Tel: 4155
Branches: 4

Société de Distribution et de Culture*, 7 rue Ernest-Renan, Fort de France Tel: 5885

Major Libraries

Archives départementales de la Martinique*, Tartenson, Route de la Clairière, BP 649, 97262 Fort de France

Bibliothèque Victor **Schoelcher***, Fort de France, Martinique

Mauritania

General Information

Language: Arabic and French
Religion: Muslim
Population: 1.5 million
Literacy Rate (1965): 11.1%
Bank Hours: 0800-1115, 1430-1630 Monday-Saturday
Shop Hours: Vary. Generally 0800-1200, 1430-1800 Monday-Saturday. Some closed Monday morning, some open Sunday morning
Currency: 1 ouguiya = 5 khoums
Export/Import Information: No tariff on books, Advertising matter (other than single copies) 10% fiscal, 5% customs duty and added tax of 12%. Import licences and exchange controls apply to imports outside of EEC and franc zone
Copyright: Berne (see International section)

Publishers

Government Printer (Imprimerie Nationale)*, BP 618, Nouakchott

Imprimerie Commerciale et Administrative de Mauritanie*, BP 164, Nouakchott
Subjects: Education, Textbooks

Major Booksellers

Librairie-Papeterie **Mauritanie** Nouvelle*, BP 61, Nouakchott

Major Libraries

Arab Library*, Chinguetti

Bibliothèque nationale (National Library)* BP 20, Nouakchott Tel: 24-35 or 278

Bibliothèque publique centrale*, BP 77, Nouakchott

Mauritius

General Information

Language: English and French
Population: 909,000
Bank Hours: Banks close 1130 on Saturday
Currency: 100 cents = 1 Mauritius rupee
Export/Import Information: No tariff on books and advertising but 25% special levy. No import licence required

Book Trade Journals

Mauritius Archives, Memorandum of Books Printed in Mauritius, Mauritius Archives, Sir William Newton St, Port Louis

Publishers

Editions **Croix** de Sud*, 1 Barracks St, Port Louis
Subjects: General, Educational

Government Printer (Imprimerie National)* Government Printing Office, Elizabeth II Ave, Port Louis

Editions **Nassau***, rue Barclay, Rose Hill
Man Dir: R A Y Vilmont
Subjects: General Fiction, Paperbacks

Major Booksellers

Librairie **Allot**, Botanical Gardens St, Curepipe Tel: 61253

Librairie **Bonanza***, Corner of Virgile Naz and Monsignor Gonin Sts, Port Louis Tel: 5179

Librairie **Bourbon***, 28 Bourbon St, Port Louis Tel: 21467
Manager: Mrs M Allagapen

Librairie Le **Colibri***, St Jean Rd, Quatre Bornes Tel: 2445; Arcades Atchia, Royal Rd, Rose Hill Tel: 1126

Librairie Le **Cygne***, Royal Rd, Rose Hill Tel: 2444

Librairie Nationale*, 25 Bourbon St, Port Louis Tel: 0748

Librairie des **Mascareignes**, 5 Queen St, Rose Hill Tel: 42748 Cable Add: Manjoo Rose Hill

Nalanda Co Ltd*, 30 Bourbon St, Port Louis Tel: 0160

Librairie du **Trèfle***, Royal St, Port Louis Tel: 1106; Les Arcades, Curepipe Tel: 25

Major Libraries

British Council Library, PO Box 111, Royal Rd, Rose Hill Tel: 42034/5

Carnegie Library, Queen Elizabeth II Terrace, Curepipe Tel: 86-4041/44
Librarian: Madeleine Philippe

City Library*, City Hall, Municipality of Port Louis, PO Box 422, Port Louis Tel: (2) 0831 Cable Add: Cerne/Port Louis
Librarian: Gaetan Benoit
Publication: Annual Report

Mauritius Archives, Sunray Hotel, Coromandel
Dir: Dr P H Sooprayen
Publication: Annual Report of the Archives Department (including a bibliographical supplement), *Quarterly Memorandum of Books Printed in Mauritius and Registered in the Archives*

Mauritius Institute Public Library, PO Box 54, Port Louis Tel: 20639
Librarian: S Jean-Francois

University of Mauritius Library*, Reduit Tel: 41041
Librarian: Jean de Chantal
Publication: Vice-Chancellor's Annual Report

Library Associations

Mauritius Library Association*, c/o The British Council, Rose Hill
Secretary: Ms M C Benoit
Publication: Mauritius Library Association Bulletin

Literary Associations and Societies

Académie mauricienne de Langue et de Littérature*, Curepipe
Secretary: C de Rauville
Publication: Oeuvres et Chroniques de l'Océan indien

Mexico

General Information

Language: Spanish
Religion: Roman Catholic
Population: 64.6 million
Literacy Rate (1970): 74.2%
Bank Hours: 0900-1330 Monday-Friday
Shop Hours: 1000-1900 Monday, Tuesday, Thursday, Friday; 1100-2000 Wednesday and Saturday
Currency: 100 centavos = 1 peso
Export/Import Information: Foreign language books and textbooks generally dutied at 38 pesos per kg legal weight, children's picture books 65% ad valorem or 14 pesos per kg, whichever greater and require import licence. Three copies of non-Spanish advertising catalogues free but all others require licence and dutied 35% ad valorem. Customs request from Bank of Mexico all necessary information to decide cases of tariff
Copyright: UCC, Berne, Buenos Aires (see International section)

250 MEXICO

Book Trade Organizations

Cámara Nacional de Comercio, Sección de Librerías (National Trade Association, Booksellers' Section)*, Paseo de la Reforma 42, México 1, DF

Cámara Nacional de la Industria Editorial (Mexican Publishers' Association)*, Calle Vallarta 21, 3° piso, México 4, DF
Secretary General: R S Arroyo

Instituto Mexicano del Libro, AC (Mexican Book Institute)*, Paseo de la Reforma 95, Depto 1024, México 7, DF
Secretary-General: Isabel Ruiz González

Book Trade Reference Journals

Anuario Bibliográfico (Bibliographical Yearbook), National Library, República de El Salvador 70, México 1, DF

Bibliografía Mexicana (Mexican Bibliography), National Library, República de El Salvador 70, México 1, DF

Boletín Bibliográfico Mexicano (Mexican Bibliographical Bulletin), Editorial Porrúa SA, Argentina 15, 5° piso, México 1, DF

Recent Books in Mexico, Mexican Authors' Centre, San Francisco 12, Col Del Valle, México 12, DF

Publishers

Aconcagua Edic y Pub SA, Blvd Adolfo López Mateos 235, Periferico, Col Mixcoac, México 19, DF Tel: 5635480
Man Dir: Julio Sanz Crespo; *Sales Dir:* Hector Delgado Narvaez
Subjects: Literature, History, How-to, Religion, Technology, Juveniles, Low-priced Paperbacks, University Textbooks, Educational Materials

M **Aguilar** Editor SA+*, Ave Universidad 757, México Tel: 5755511 Cable Add: Guilarditor
Man Dir: Antonio Ruano Fernández
Parent Company: Aguilar SA de Ediciones, Spain (qv)
Subject: General Literature
Founded: 1965

Alianza Editorial Mexicana*, José Morán 93-1A, México 18, DF
Associated Companies: See under Alianza Editorial SA, Spain

Editorial **Azteca** SA, Calle La Luna 225–227, México 3, DF Tel: 5261157 Cable Add: Edasa
Man Dir: Alfonso Alemón Jalomo; *Sales Dir:* Juan Alemón Jalomo
Subjects: General Literature, Technical, Popular Science
1978: 15 titles *Founded:* 1956

Editorial **Banca y Comercio** SA, Reforma 202, México 6, DF Tel: 5353587
Man Dir: Luis Ruiz de Velasco; *Assistant Manager:* Antonio Zelleil Guaida
Subjects: Business & Administration, Mathematics, Law
1978: 40 titles *Founded:* 1934

Libreria y Ediciones **Botas** SA*, Justo Sierra 52, Apdo 941, México 1, DF Tel: 5223896/5224717
Man Dir: Andres Botas Arredondo; *Sales Dir:* Everado Jiménez Martínez
Subjects: Art, History, Economics, General Fiction, Philosophy, Law, General Science, Medicine, Reference
Founded: 1910

Editorial **Bruguera** Mexicana SA*, Ave Popacatapetl, 421 Colonia General Amaya, México B
Parent Company: Editorial Bruguera SA, Spain (qv)

Buena Prensa AC*, Orozco y Berra 180, Apdo 2181, México 1, DF Tel: 5357304
Man Dir: Wilfredo Guinea
Subjects: Religion, Education
Founded: 1936

Editorial **Cajica***, 19 Sur 2501, Apdo 336, Puebla, Pue
Manager: José M Cajica
Subject: Law

Centro de Estudios Monetarios Latinoamericanos (CEMLA), Durango 54, México 7, DF Tel: 5330300 Cable Add: Cemla, Mexico Telex: 1771229
Man Dir: Jorge González del Valle; *Editorial, Rights & Permissions:* Juan Manuel Rodriguez; *Sales:* Genoveva de Mária y Campos de Gil; *Production, Publicity:* Cristina Conde
Subjects: Economics, Finance
1977: 7 titles *Founded:* 1952

El **Colegio** de México, Depto de Publicaciones, Apdo 20–671, México 20, DF (Located at: Camino al Ajusco 20, México 20, DF) Tel: 5840585/5848663 Cable Add: Colmex
Man Dir: Alberto Dallal
Subjects: Literature, Social Science, History, International Relations, Demography, Economy
Bookshop: Librería de El Colegio de México, Camino al Ajusco 2000, México 20, DF
1978: 150 titles *Founded:* 1940

Compañia General de Ediciones SA*, Schiller 227D, México 5, DF Tel: 5437016
Man Dir: Santiago Sanz
Subjects: Textbooks, Fiction

Editorial **Concepto** SA, Av Cuachtémoc 1434, México 13, DF Tel: 5594631
Man Dir, Rights & Permissions: Gerardo Gally; *Editorial:* Francisco Javier Fonseca; *Production:* Margara Clavé
Subjects: Architecture, Psychology, Pedagogy, Children's books, Alternative Technology, How-to
1979: 78 titles *Founded:* 1977
ISBN Publisher's Prefix: 968-405

Ediciones **Contables y Administrativas**, SA, H Frías 1451-101, México 12, DF Tel: 5590443
Man Dir: Pedro Gasca Rocha; *Sales Dir:* Gustavo Gasca Bretón
Br Off: Zaragoza 39-106, Guadalajara, Jalisco, Mexico
Subjects: Technical, Accounting & Management
1977: 7 titles *1978:* 11 titles *Founded:* 1967

Cía Editorial **Continental** SA (CESCA)*, Calzada de Tlalpan 4620, Apdo 22022, México 22, DF Tel: 5732300 Cable Add: Ediconti
Man Dir: Elena Ocampo de Lanz; *Sales Manager:* Eduardo A Tappan
Subjects: Science & Technology, Textbooks
Founded: 1954

Editorial **Cosmos**, España 396, México 13, DF Tel: 5829928
Man Dir: Cesar Macazaga Ordoño; *Editorial:* Cesar Macazaga; *Sales, Publicity:* Raul Macazaga; *Production:* Carlos Macazaga
Subject: Mexican history, Directories
1977: 30 titles *1978:* 35 titles *Founded:* 1956
ISBN Publisher's Prefix: 968-440

Publicaciones **Cosmos**, Bajio 335-604, México 7, DF Tel: 5646039
Man Dir: Catalina Ramirez de Arellano; *Editorial:* Cesar Macazaga; *Sales, Publicity:* Raul Macazaga; *Production:* Carlos Macazaga
Subjects: Technical dictionaries (Spanish-English)
1977: 5 titles *1978:* 6 titles *Founded:* 1963
ISBN Publisher's Prefix: 968-7095

B **Costa Amic***, Editor, Mesones 14, Apdo 29-188, Mexico 1, DF Tel: 5124810
Man Dir: Bartolome Costa Amic; *Editorial, Production:* Bartomeu Costa L; *Sales, Publicity:* Jordi Costa L; *Rights & Permissions:* Bartolome Costa Amic, Bartomeu Costa L
Subjects: Fiction, Literature, Biography, History, Psychology, Social Science, Low-priced Paperbacks, University & Secondary Textbooks
Bookshop: Bolivar 55, México 1, DF
1977: 98 titles *Founded:* 1941

Ediciones de **Cultura** Popular SA*, San Juan de Letrán 37, desp 401-407, México 1, DF Tel: 5185928 Cable Add: Edipop
Man Dir: Salvador González Marín; *Sales Dir:* Eduardo Goicochea
Subjects: General Literature, Technical, Economics, Political Science
Founded: 1969

Editorial **Diana**, SA Roberto Gayol 1219, Apdo 44-986, México 12, DF Tel: 5750711 Cable Add: EDISA Telex: 1777618 DIME
Man Dir: José Luis Ramírez Junior; *Assistant General Manager:* Homero Gayosso Animas; *Sales:* Iván García; *Production:* Manuel Landavede
Subjects: Fiction, Juveniles, General Nonfiction
Bookshop: address as above
1977: 146 titles *Founded:* 1946

Editorial **Diogenes**, SA*, Apdo 82-016, Contadero Cuajimalpa, México 18, DF (Located at: Arteaga y Salazar 21, Lonbolero Lusjimalpa, México 18, DF) Tel: 9158120046
Subjects: Belles Lettres, History, Social & Political Science, Medicine
1977: 12 titles

E D A M E X, see Editores Asociados Mexicanos SA

Editora Nacional*, Dr Erazo 42, Mexico 7, DF Tel: 5782353
Subject: General Literature

Editores Asociados SA, Angel Urraza 1322, México 12, DF Tel: 5757035
Man Dir: Octavio Colmenares; *Editorial, Rights & Permissions:* Mrs Ella de Gedovius; *Sales:* Miss Noemi Chavez; *Production, Publicity:* Manuel Colmenares
Associate Company: Editorial Meridiano SA
Subjects: Social Sciences, Economics, Politics, Literature, Communications, Recreation, Humour
1977: 64 titles *Founded:* 1973
ISBN Publisher's Prefix: 968-409

Editores Asociados Mexicanos SA (EDAMEX), Angel Urraza 1322, Mexico 12 DF Tel: 5591566/5591499
Man Dir: Manuel Colmenares Grunberger
Subjects: General Fiction & Nonfiction, Social Sciences, Sports, Music, How-to
Founded: 1963
ISBN Publisher's Prefix: 968-409

Empresas Editoriales SA*, Río Nazas 55, Dto 1 & 2, Apdo 5-188, México 5, DF Tel: 5144303
President: Martín Luis Guzmán; *Technical Dir:* Rafael Giménez Siles
Subject: General Fiction
Founded: 1944

Editorial **Epoca** SA*, Emperadores 185, Apdo 69-647, México 13, DF Tel: 5328163 Cable Add: Epocasa
Subject: General Literature

Ediciones **Era** SA, Avena 102, Col Granjas Esmeralda, Apdo 74-092, México 13, DF Tel: 5820344 Cable Add: Liberamex
Man Dir: Mrs Nieves Espresate Xirau
Subjects: General Fiction, Art, Belles Lettres, Social & Political Science, Economics, *Cuadernos Políticos* (quarterly reviews)
1978: 28 titles *Founded:* 1960

Editorial **Esfinge** SA, Colima 220-503, México 7, DF Tel: 5112771/5142823
Man Dir: Agustín Mateos Muñoz; *Sales Dir:* Eduardo Mateos Gay
Subjects: Literature, Law, Science, University, Secondary & Primary Textbooks
1978: 60 titles *Founded:* 1957

Ediciones **Euroamericanas**, Perugino 35-1, México 19, DF Tel: 5632063
Man Dir: Klaus Thiele; *Sales:* Ma del Rocío Sánchez Vega
Subjects: History and Anthropology of the Americas, Practical Technology, Languages
1978: 2 titles *1979:* 7 titles *Founded:* 1971
ISBN Publisher's Prefix: 968-414

Editorial **Extemporaneos** SA*, Poniente 126-A, No 400 Col Residencial Vallejo, Apdo 78-048, México 14, DF Tel: 5875424/5878785 Cable Add: Ediextempo México
Director General, Editorial: Lautaro Gondalez Porcel; *Sales, Publicity:* Humberto Reyes Ordoñez; *Production:* Eduardo Peña Alfaro; *Rights & Permissions:* Eva Somlo
Associated Companies: Librerias Extemporaneos SA
Subjects: Anthropology, Architecture, Art, Economics, Philosophy, Humour, Literature, Pedagogy, Politics, Sociology, Theatre
Book Club: Club de Lectores Extemporaneos
Bookshops: Condesa, Tamaulipas 203-A, México 11, DF; Del Valle, Ave Coyoacán 512-A, México 12, DF; Santa Maria, Amado Nervo 47-B, México 4, DF; Jaurez, Hamburgo 260, México 6, DF
1977: 21 titles *Founded:* 1970
ISBN Publisher's Prefix: 968-415

Fernández Editores SA*, calzada México Coyoacán 321, Col General Anaya, México 13, DF Tel: 5244600
Man Dir: Luis Fernández González; *Assistant Man Dir, Sales Manager:* Luis Gerardo Fernández; *Production Manager:* Luis Ramón Fernandez
Subjects: Textbooks, Education, Technical Subjects
Founded: 1943

Fondo de Cultura Económica, Ave Universidad 975, Apdo 44975 México 12, DF Tel: 5244376 Cable Add: Doraca
Man Dir: José Luis Martínez; *Assistant Dir, Editorial:* Jaime García Terrés; *Senior Editor:* Alí Chumacero; *Business Manager:* Jorge Farías Negrete; *Production:* Felipe Garrido; *Sales:* Hero Rodríguez Toro; *Publicity:* Alba Rojo; *Rights & Permissions:* Alicia Hammer
Branch Offs:
Argentina: Suipacha 617, Buenos Aires; Colombia: Av Jiménes 8-39, Bogotá; Peru: Berlín 238, Miraflores, Lima; Spain: Vía de los Poblados s/n, Edif Indulbuilding Goico 4-15, Hortaleza, Madrid 33; Venezuela: Edif Polar, planta baja, Plaza Venezuela, Caracas
Subjects: Social Sciences, Humanities, Literature, University Textbooks, Periodicals
Bookshop: Ave Universidad 975
Founded: 1934

Fondo Educativo Interamericano*, Apdo 19188, México 19, DF
Parent Company: Addison-Wesley Publishing Co Inc, Reading Mass 01867, USA (see Addison-Wesley UK for associate companies)
Subjects: School and University Textbooks in Spanish

Librería **Font**, SA*, López Cotilla 440, Guadalajara, Jalisco Tel: 140820 Telex: 0682715
Man Dir: Leopoldo Font Hernández; *Sales Dir:* Leopoldo Font Solana
Subjects: Literature, History, Art, Philosophy, University & Secondary Textbooks
Bookshop: López Cotilla 440, Guadalajara, Jalisco
Founded: 1908

Editorial Gustavo **Gili** de Mexico Sa*, Tácatas 218, México 12, DF
Parent Company: Editorial Gustavo Gili SA, Spain (qv)

Editorial **Grijalbo** SA*, Apdo 17-568, México 17, DF (Located at: Ave Granjas 82, México 16, DF) Tel: 3520688 Cable Add: Grijalmex
Editorial: Andrés Léon Quintanar; *Sales:* Joaquín Pérez Cuéllar; *Production:* Rogelio Carvajal; *Publicity:* Lucy Marcías
Parent Company: Ediciones Grijalbo SA, Spain (qv)
Subsidiary Companies: Grijalbo SA, Argentina (qv); Grijalbo Bolivia, Ltda, Bolivia (qv); Distribuidora exclusivo Grijalbo, Colombia (qv); Grijalbo y Cía Ltda, Chile (qv); Distribuidora exclusiva Grijalbo SA, Perú (qv); Grijalbo SA, Venezuela (qv); Grijalbo Centroamerica y Panamá SA, Costa Rica (qv); Editorial Grijalbo Ecuatoríana Ltda, Ecuador
Subjects: General Fiction & Nonfiction
1977: 42 titles *Founded:* 1954

Harla, SA de CV, see Harper & Row Latinoamericana

Harper & Row Latinoamericana-Harla, SA de CV*, Antonio Caso 142, Apdo 30-546, México 4, DF Tel: 5664589/5668860 Cable Add: Harpemex Telex: 1777235
Dir General: Francisco Gutiérrez F; *Manager:* Jaime Arvizu; *Sales:* Marco Antonio Trujillo A
Parent Company: Harper & Row Publishers Inc, 10 East 53rd St, New York, NY 10022, USA

MEXICO 251

Associate Companies: Harper & Row (Australasia) Ltd, Australia; Harper & Row Ltd (UK) (qqv)
Subsidiary Companies: Editora Harper & Row do Brasil Ltda, Brasil (qv); Editorial Sec Cien Ltda, Bogota, Columbia
Subjects: University & Secondary Textbooks, Science & Technology, Medicine, Psychology, Engineering
1977: 7 titles *Founded:* 1970
ISBN Publisher's Prefix: 968-006

Editorial **Hermes** SA, Castilla 229-A, México 13, DF Tel: 5790468 Cable Add: Editermes
Man Dir: Antonio López Rivero
Subjects: General Fiction, Belles Lettres, History, Art
Founded: 1945

Editorial **Herrero** SA*, Río Amazonas 44, Apdo 2404, México 5, DF Tel: 5664900
General Dir: Donato Elías Herrero
Manager: Ricardo Arancón L
Subjects: Art, Technical, Textbooks
Founded: 1945

Herrero Hermanos Sucesores SA*, Comonfort 44, Apdo 671, México 2, DF Tel: 5299235
Man Dir: Jorge Rodríguez Fernandez
Subjects: Belles Lettres, Psychology, Economics, Social Science, Business
Founded: 1883

Impulso, Tehuantepec 170, Apdo 27-718, México 7, DF Tel: 5644100 Cable Add: IEELM, México Telex: 01776359
Director General, Editorial: Rafael Giménez Navarro; *Sales:* Gerardo Sánchez; *Production:* Marta Carpio
Parent Company: Libreros Mexicanos SA de CV, Mexico
Subjects: Children's Books, Literature, Technical and Scientific
1977: 2 titles *Founded:* 1976
ISBN Publisher's Prefix: 968-17

Editorial **Innovacion** SA, Bajio 335-603, México 7, DF Tel: 5644214
Man Dir: Catalina Ramirez de Arellano; *Editorial:* Cesar Macazaga; *Sales, Publicity:* Raul Macazaga; *Production:* Carlos Macazaga
Subjects: Camping, Touring, Mexican History, Suppliers' Directories
1977: 11 titles *1978:* 18 titles *Founded:* 1971

Instituto de Investigaciones Sociales — Universidad Nacional Autonoma de Mexico*, Torre de Humanidades 5° piso, Ciudad Universitaria, México 20, DF Tel: 5486500 ext 196
Man Dir: Raúl Benítez Zenteno; *Sales Dir:* Armida Vazquez A
Subjects: Social Science
Founded: 1939

Instituto Indigenista Interamericano*, Niños Héroes No 139, Mexico 7, DF Tel: 5786101/5786210 Cable Add: Indigeni
Man Dir, Rights & Permissions: Oscar Arze Quintanilla; *Sales:* Raquel Mendez de Hoyle
Subjects: Social Studies, Anthropology, Periodicals
1977: 5 titles *Founded:* 1940

Instituto Nacional de Antropologia e Historia, Córdoba 45, Mexico 7, DF Tel: 5144222
Subjects: Mexican Archaeology & Anthropology, History
Founded: 1822

Instituto Nacional de Bellas Artes*, Oficina de ventas de publicaciones, Palacio de Bellas Artes, México 1, DF Tel: 5123811
Subjects: Art, Biography, Literature, Philosophy, Reference, Educational Materials

Instituto Panamericano de Geografía e Historia, Ex-Arzobispado 29, México 18, DF Tel: 2775888
Secretary General: José A Sáenz G; *Editorial Dir:* Lea Salinas
Subjects: Geography, Cartography, History, Anthropology, Geophysics, Folklore, Periodicals
1978: 9 titles

Editorial **Iztaccihuatl** SA*, Miguel Schultz No 21, Apdo 2343, México 4, DF Tel: 5352321 Cable Add: Eiztamexa
President: Orlando Vieyra Legorreta
Subject: General Literature
Founded: 1946

Editorial **Jus** SA*, Plaza de Abasolo 14, Col Guerrero, México 3, DF Tel: 5629959/5260616/5260540/5260538
Man Dir: Armando Avila Sotomayor; *Sales Manager:* Dalila Farias Godinez
Subjects: General Fiction, Law, Textbooks, History, Political & Social Sciences
Founded: 1941

Lasser Press Mexicana, SA*, Praga 56, Apdo 6-791, México 6, DF Tel: 5142215 Cable Add: Laspresa
Subjects: General Fiction & Nonfiction
Founded: 1972

Editora **Latino** Americana SA*, Guatemala 10-220, México 1, DF Tel: 5211909
Dir: Roger Orellana Gallardo
Subject: Popular Literature

Editorial **Letras** SA*, Ave Morelos 37, 4° piso, México 1, DF
Man Dir: Manuel Dávalos
Subjects: General Fiction & Nonfiction
Founded: 1957

Editorial **Limusa** SA*, Arcos de Belén 75, México 1, DF Tel: 5854255 Cable Add: Elimusa
Man Dir: Carlos Noriega Milera; *Executive Vice-President:* Francisco Trillas Mercader; *Assistant Executive Manager:* Juan Antonio Hernández Zamudio
Subjects: Science & Technology, Social Science, History, Psychology, University & Secondary Textbooks
Founded: 1962
Miscellaneous: Firm is an associate company of John Wiley & Sons Ltd, UK (qv for other associates)

Logos Consorcio Editorial, SA*, General Molinos del Campo 64, Col San Miguel Chapultepec, México 18, DF Tel: 5151633
Man Dir: Fernando Rodriguez Diaz
Subject: General

Libros **McGraw-Hill** de Mexico SA de CV, Atlacomulco 499, San Andrés Atoto, Apdo 5-237, México 5, DF Tel: 5769044 Cable Add: Limcoramex Telex: 01774284
Director General: Raymundo Cruzado; *Publishers:* Guillermo Hernández, Luis Castañeda, Rafael Sainz; *Production:* Oscar Alvarez; *Publicity:* Ignacio Arce; *Rights & Permissions:* Ramón Cortés
Parent Company: McGraw-Hill Inc, 1221 Ave of the Americas, New York, NY 10020, USA
Associated Companies: See McGraw-Hill UK Co
Imprint: Ediciones Pegaso
Br Offs: Monterrey, N L; Guadalajara, Jal

Subjects: Natural Sciences, Technology, Textbooks, Education, Business, General
1977: 13 titles *1978:* 34 titles *Founded:* 1967

El **Manual** Moderno, SA, Ave Sonora 206, México 11, DF Tel: 5740333/5746646
Man Dir: Gustavo Setzer; *Editorial:* Armando Soto; *Sales:* Juan Sánchez Villarreal; *Production:* Felipe Vaquez; *Rights & Permissions:* Lourdes Reyes
Parent Company: Elsevier-NDU nv, Netherlands (qv)
Subjects: Medicine, Psychology, Nursing, Veterinary Science, Chemistry, Economics
1977: 36 titles *Founded:* 1958
ISBN Publisher's Prefix: 968-426

Masson Editores*, Dakota 383, Colonia Napoles, México 18, DF
Associate Companies: Masson Editeur, Paris, France (qv); Masson do Brasil, Rua da Quitanda 20, Sala 301, 20011 Rio de Janeiro, Brazil; Toray-Masson, Spain (qv); Masson Publishing USA Inc, 111 West 57th St, New York, NY, USA

Editorial **Mexicana***, S de RL, Orizaba 115 y 119, Apdo 7-852, México
Parent Company: Editorial Labor, Spain (qv)

Editores **Mexicanos** Unidos (Edimex)*, L González Obregón 5-B, Apdo 45-671, México 1, DF Tel: 5217596/5125552/5210925
Man Dir & Editorial: Fidel Miro Solanes; *Sales:* Roque Laclau; *Production, Publicity and Rights & Permissions:* Sonia Miro de Laclau
Subjects: General Fiction & Nonfiction
Bookshops: Libro-Mex Editores SRL, Argentina 23, Mexico 1, DF
1977: 400 titles *Founded:* 1954
ISBN Publisher's Prefix: 968-15

Galeria de Arte **Misrachi** SA*, Génova 20, Mexico 6, DF Tel: 5334551
Manager: Alberto J Misrachi; *Editorial, Sales, Production, Rights & Permissions:* Enrique Beraha; *Publicity:* Amelie Beraha de Esquenazi
Subject: Art
Bookshops: Génova 20, Mexico 6, DF; Central de Publicaciones SA, Juárez 4, Mexico 1, DF
1977: 4 titles *Founded:* 1961
ISBN Publisher's Prefix: 968-7047

Editorial Joaquín **Mortiz** SA, Tabasco 106, Apdo 7-832 México 7, DF Tel: 5331250 Cable Add: Morditor
Man Dir, Editorial: Joaquín Diez-Canedo; *Sales, Rights & Permissions:* Elisabeth Rojas; *Production, Publicity:* Bernardo Giner de Los Rios
Subjects: General Fiction & Nonfiction, History, Psychology, Social Science
1977: 38 titles *1978:* 72 titles *Founded:* 1962
ISBN Publisher's Prefix: 968-27

Organización Editorial **Novaro** SA*, Donata Guerra 9, Apdo 10500, México, DF Tel: 5760155 Cable Add: Novaromex
President: Richard Small; *Dirs:* Armando Arrendondo Zertuche, Ernesto Duhart Meade
Subjects: Juveniles, Popular Paperbacks
Founded: 1950

Nueva Editorial Interamericana SA de CV*, Cedro 512, Apdo 26370, México 4, DF Tel: 5413155 Cable Add: Tusmexa
President: Lic. Juan Manuel Martinez Parente
Subjects: Medicine and Health Sciences,

General Science and Technology, Textbooks
1977: 43 titles *Founded:* 1944
Miscellaneous: Firm is an associate company of CBS Publishing Group (see Holt-Saunders UK for other associates)

Editorial **Nueva Imagen** SA, PO Box 600, México 1, DF (Located at: Sacramento 109, México 12, DF) Tel: 5361015/5361055/5237373 Telex: 01771427 Enime
Administrative Dir: Enrique Sealtiel Alatriste L.; *Editorial Dir:* Guillermo J. Schavelzon; *Sales Man:* Roberto Espinoza Rocco
Subjects: General Fiction, History, Psychology, Economics, Art, Science, Social Science, Anthropology, Sociology, Humour, Linguistics, Mass Communication, Latin American problems
1977: 80 titles *1978:* 120 titles *Founded:* 1976
ISBN Publisher's Prefix: 968-429

Ediciones **Oasis** SA*, Oaxaca 28, Apdo 24-416, México 7, DF Tel: 5259171/2
Man Dir: Ruben Rizo Lopez *Sales Dir:* Ricardo Rizzo Lavarino
Subjects: General Fiction, Belles Lettres, History, Education
Founded: 1954

Editorial **Orion***, Sierra Mojada 325, Lomas de Chapultepec, México 10, DF Tel: 5200224
Man Dir: Silvia Hernandez Vda de Cárdenas; *Sales Dir, Rights & Permissions:* Laura Hernandez Baltazar; *Publicity Dir:* Silvia Hernandez Baltazar; *Advertising:* Mariaelena Molina
Subsidary Companies: Edit Vila; Edit Cuzamil
Subjects: Literature, Philosophy, Religion, Mysticism, Yoga, Astrology, Theosophy, Psychology, & Parapsychology
1977: 37 titles *Founded:* 1942
ISBN Publisher's Prefix: 968-6053

Editorial **Patria**, SA*, Uruguay 25, 2° piso, Apdo 784, México 1, DF Tel: 5127651/5184509
Man Dir: Isabel Lasa de la Mora; *Deputy Manager & Administrator:* Rafael Guerrero; *Sales Dir:* Santiago Hernández; *Publicity Dir:* José Vega; *Rights & Permissions:* José l Mantecón
Subjects: Literature, Biography, History, Philosophy, How-to, Secondary & Primary Textbooks
Founded: 1933

Libreria **Patria** SA, 5 de Mayo No 43, Apdo 2055, México 1, DF Tel: 5852099
Man Dir: Florian Trillas Rafols; *Sales:* Francisco Majewski M.
Orders to: Belisario Dominguez 53, México 1, DF
Subsidiary Company: Samara, Cia Papelera SA, Av. 5 de Mayo 29-C, México 1, DF
Subjects: Textbooks, Literature, General
Bookshop: Av 5 de Mayo 43, Belisario Dominguez 53
Founded: 1940

Ediciones **Paulinas** SA, Ave Taxqueña 1792, México 21, DF Tel: 5491454
General Manager: Ricardo Rojas Sarmiento
Subjects: Religion, Education
Bookshop: Librería San Pablo, Ave Madero 61-A, México 1, DF
1978: 40 titles *Founded:* 1948

Editorial **Pax** México*, Rep Argentina 9, Apdo 45-009, México 1, DF Tel: 5425890
Man Dir: Humberto Gally Grivé

MEXICO 253

Subjects: Technical, Psychology, Education
Founded: 1920
Bookshop: Librería Carlos Cesarman SA, Rep Argentina 9, México 1, DF

Ediciones **Pegaso**, an imprint of McGraw-Hill de Mexico (qv)

Editorial **Pomaire** SA*, Manuel M Ponce 143, México 20, DF
Parent Company: Editorial Pomaire SA, Spain (qv)

Editorial **Porrúa** SA*, Argentina 15, 5° piso, México 1, DF Tel: 5224866 Cable Add: Porruas Mexico
Man Dir: José Antonio Pérez Porrúa; *Sales Dir:* Francisco Pérez Porrúa
Subject: General Literature
Founded: 1944
Bookshop: Librería de Porrúa Hnos y Cía, Argentina 15, México 1, DF

Librería de Manuel **Porrúa***, 5 de Mayo 49, Apdo 45-590, México 1, DF Tel: 5102634
Manager: Manuel Porrúa
Subject: University Textbooks

La **Prensa Editora** de Periodicos SCL*, Basilio Vadillo 40, Apdo 947, México 4, DF Tel: 5120851
Subjects: Popular Literature, Juveniles

La **Prensa Médica** Mexicana, Paseo de Las Facultades 26, Fraccionamiento Copilco-Universidad, Apdo 20-413, México 20, DF Tel: 5504500 Cable Add: Laprememex
Man Dir: Carolina Amor de Fournier; *Assistant Manager:* Guadalupe Arias de Gutiérrez; *Medical Editor:* Dr Jorge Avendaño Inestrillas; *Sales Dir:* Juan de Dios Díaz Salgado
Subjects: Medicine, Social Science
Founded: 1947

Editorial **Progreso** SA*, Naranjo 248, Apdo 26-372, México 4, DF Tel: 5477304
Subjects: Secondary & Primary Textbooks

Publicaciones Cultural SA, Lago Mayor 186, Colonia Anáhuac, México 17, DF Tel: 5456860/1/2
President: Gustavo González Lewis; *Man Dir:* Carlos Frigolet Lerma; *Assistant Manager:* Pedro de Andres Romero; *Sales:* Javier Saavedra; *Rights & Permissions:* Abelardo Fabrega Esteba
Subjects: University, Secondary and Primary Textbooks, Educational Materials
Founded: 1965
ISBN Publisher's Prefix: 968-6058

Queromón Editores SA*, Bucareli 59-A, Apdo M-7914, México 6, DF Tel: 5356040
Cable Add: Queromón
Man Dir: Manuel Mallén Sangüesa
Subject: Juveniles
Founded: 1951

Editorial **Renacimiento** SA*, Blvd Xola 1408, Apdo 1506, México 12, DF Tel: 5309404/5 Cable Add: Edirensa
Man Dir: Juan Sapiña Camaro
Subjects: General Fiction, Belles Lettres
Founded: 1958

Representaciones y Servicios de Ingeniería SA*, Apdo 70-180, México 20, DF (Located at: Av San Antonio No 62-2 Col Napoles, Mexico 18) Tel: 5634740/5635721/0
Man Dir, Editorial: Enrique Reyes Morfín; *Production, Publicity:* Gonzalo Ferreyra

Cortes; *Rights & Permissions:* Baltazar Feregrino Paredes
Subject: Engineering
1977: 4 titles *Founded:* 1965
ISBN Publisher's Prefix: 968-6062

Editorial **Reverté** Mexicana SA*, Río Pánuco 141-A, México 5, DF Tel: 5335658
Man Dir: Pedro Reverté Planells
Associated Companies: See under Editorial Reverté SA, Spain
Subjects: Science, Technical
Founded: 1955

Revista Mexicana de Seguros, Temixco 33, Bosque Echegaray, México Tel: 5103910
Man Dir: Augusto Escalante Bates
Subject: Insurance
Founded: 1948

Riomar Editores y Distribuidores S de CV (see Emecé Editores SA, Argentina)

Ediciones **Rusbet***, Apdo 12-621, Pitagoras 25-101, Mexico 12, DF Tel: 5233655
Man Dir: Frederick A Clark
Subject: Self-improvement
1977: 1 title *Founded:* 1977
ISBN Publisher's Prefix: 968-7190

Ediciones **S E P** Setentas (Secretaria de Educacion Publica*, Direccion General de Educacion Audiovisual y Divulgacion, Sur 124, No 3006, México 13, DF Tel: 5797115/5791478
Dir: María del Carmen Mellón
Subjects: General Literature & Culture of Mexico

Siglo XXI Editores SA, Ave Cerro del Agua 248, Apdo 20626, Mexico 20 DF Tel: 5503011 Cable Add: Sigloedit
Man Dir, Editorial: Arnaldo Orfila R; *Administrative Man:* Concepción Zea; Production: Mart Soler V; *Publicity:* M de García; *Rights & Permissions:* Carmen Simón
Parent Company: Siglo XXI de España Editores, Spain (qv)
Associate Company: Siglo XXI de Colombia Ltda, Colombia (qv)
Subjects: General Fiction, History, Psychology, Economics, Arts, Science & Technology, Social Science, Anthropology, Architecture, Philosophy, Languages, Latin-American Politics
1977: 90 titles *Founded:* 1966
ISBN Publisher's Prefix: 968-23

Editorial V **Siglos**, SA, Av Miguel Angel de Quevedo 1020, México 21, DF Tel: 5447514/5495949/5440172
Man Dir: Guillermo Garavito Escobar; *Editorial:* Amapola Garavito López; *Production:* Georgina Greco; *Sales:* Roberto Ibarra Rivera; *Publicity:* Amapola G de Velarde; *Rights & Permissions:* Georgina Greco H.
Subjects: General Fiction & Nonfiction, How-to
Bookshop: at same address
1977: 15 titles *1978:* 69 titles *Founded:* 1973

Editorial **Sopena** Colombiana SA*, Ave Chapultepec 153, Mexico City 6
Parent Company: Ramón Sopena SA, Spain (qv)

Time — Life International de México, SA*, Paseo de la Reforma 195, Apdo 5-592, México 5, DF Tel: 5469000 Cable Add: Tlimsa Telex: (017) 71358
General Manager: Koos H Siewers
Subject: Nonfiction
Founded: 1962

Editorial **Trillas**, SA, Ave 5 de Mayo 43-105, Apdo 10534 México 1, DF Tel: 5850222 Cable Add: Etrillasa
Man Dir: Francisco Trillas Mercader; *Editorial, Rights & Permissions:* Gonzalo Godínez; *Sales:* Jesús Galera; *Production:* Alfonso Durán; *Publicity:* Marina Trillas Salazar
Associated Companies: Cía Editorial Carmex SA, Argentina; Cía Editorial Comex SA, Colombia; Alamex SA, Spain
Subjects: Psychology, Education, Mathematics, General & Social Science, Technical, University & Secondary Textbooks, Business
1977: 80 titles *1978:* 92 titles *Founded:* 1954

Unión Tipográfica Editorial Hispanoamericana (UTEHA)*, Ave Universidad 767, México 12, DF Tel: 5755311
Subjects: General Literature, Reference, Technical, General Science
Founded: 1937

Universidad Nacional Autónoma de México (UNAM), Depto de Distribucion de Libros Universitarios, Ave Insurgentes Sur 299, México 11, DF Tel: 5845511
Subjects: University Textbooks, Scholarly
Founded: 1935

Book Clubs

Círculo Mexicano de Lectores*, Chiapas 207, Esq Manzanillo, México 7, DF

Club de Lectores Extemporaneos*, Poniente 126-A, No 400 Col Residencial Vallejo, Apdo 78-048, México 14
Owned by: Editorial Extemporaneos SA (México)

Libro Club de Nuevo Léon SA*, Padre Mier 167 Pte, Monterrey

Major Booksellers

American Book Store SA, Ave Madero No 25, Apdo 79 Bis, México 1, DF Tel: 5127279/5127284/5120306/5852576/5126350
Branches: Circuito Médicos No 3, Ciudad Satélite, Edo de México Tel: 3930682/3930843

Librería **Bellas Artes**, Ave Juárez No 18, México 1, DF Tel: 5182917
Man: Carlos Noriega M.

Central de Publicaciones*, Ave Juárez 4, Apdo 2430, México 1, DF Tel: 5104331

Cia Internacional de Publicaciones SA de CV*, (Libreria Anglo Americana), Serapio Rendon 125, Apdo Postal 30-528, Mexico 4, DF Tel: 5666400. Branches

Librería **Cosmos***, Ave Padre Mier 474 Oriente, Monterrey Tel: 431074

Librerías de **Cristal***, Calle del Rio 10, México, DF Tel: 5762530 (Centre for reception and distribution). Many branches in Mexico City and other cities

Librería **Font***, López Cotilla 440, Guadalajara, Jalisco Tel: 140820

Librerías **Gonvill** de Guadalajara*, Ave Chapultepec Sur No 146, Guadalajara Tel: 163060

Librería **Hamburgo** Antonio Navarrete*, Insurgentes Sur No 58, México 6, DF Tel: 5287316/5145086; Ribera de San Cosme 133, Mexico 4, DF Tel: 5464736; Insurgentes Sur 317, Mexico 11, DF Tel: 5744015

Librerías **Iztaccihuatl*,** Miguel Schultz No 21, México 4, DF Tel: 5352321 (and several provincial addresses)

Librería **Letrán***, Ave San Juan de Letrán 5–C, México, DF Tel: 5123232

Librería **Intercontinental** SA*, Actopan No 3, Esq Monterrey, Col Roma Sur, México 7, DF Tel: 5641718

Librería **Internacional** SA*, Ave Sonora 206, México 11, DF Tel: 5330905
Owned by: Elsevier-NDU nv, Netherlands (qv)

Librería **Tecnológico**, Ave Tecnológico No 2440, Monterrey Tel: 583812

Librería **Universitaria***, Insurgentes Sur No 299, México, DF Tel: 5646637 (and several branches)

Librolandia del Centro SA, Matamoros 83, Hermosillo, Sonora Tel: 37491/37492
Telex: Liceme 058788
Dir: Gerardo Cantú
60 bookshops located in 33 cities throughout México

Librería Editorial Gerardo **Mayela***, Emiliano Zapata 60–B, México 1, DF Tel: 5225556

Editores **Mexicanos** Unidos*, Luis González Obregón 5–B, México, DF Tel: 5217596

Librería **Patria**, Ave 5 de Mayo 43, México 1, DF Tel: 5852099

Librería de **Porrúa** Hnos y Cía*, Argentina 15, México 1, DF Apdo M–7990 Tel: 5228800

Librería del **Sotano***, Ave Juárez 64, México, DF Tel: 5217044

Librería **Studio***, Benjamin Franklin 44, México, DF Tel: 5167486

Major Libraries

Archivo General de la Nación (National Archives)*, Tacuba 8–20 Piso, Apdo 1999, México 1, DF Tel: 5851833
Librarian: Alejandra Moreno Toscano

Archivos Históricos y Bibliotecas (Historical and Library Archives)*, Instituto Nacional de Antropología e Historia, Calzada M Gandi y Paseo de la Reforma, México 5, DF Apdo Postal M20–29 Tel: 5536342/5536231

Biblioteca Central*, Ciudad Universitaria, Villa Obregón, AP 70–219 México 20, DF Tel: 5489780
Librarian: Q F B Margarita Almada de Ascencio
Publications: Informe de actividades; Directorio de Bibliotecas UNAM; Informes Técnicos, Catálogo de Publicaciones Periódicas

Biblioteca de México*, Plaza de la Ciudadela 6, México 1, DF

Biblioteca Nacional de Agricultura (National Library of Agriculture), Biblioteca Central, Escuela Nacional de Agricultura, Universidad Autónoma de Chapingo, Chapingo, Texcoco, Est de México

Biblioteca Nacional de Antropología e Historia (National Library of Anthropology and History)*, Paseo de la Reforma y Calzada Gandhi, México, DF

Biblioteca Nacional de México (National Library)*, República de El Salvador 70, México 1, DF Tel: 5129316/5103161/5121771

Biblioteca del **Colegio de México***, Guanajuato 115, México 7, DF

Biblioteca del **Congreso de la Unión** (Congress Library)*, Tacuba 29, México, DF

Biblioteca '**Benjamin Franklin**' (USICA)*, Calle Londres 16, México 6, DF Tel: 5910244

Hemeroteca Nacional de México (National Periodicals Library)*, Calle del Carmen 31, México 1, DF
Publication: Hemerografía Literaria (monthly)

Biblioteca del **Instituto Anglo-Mexicano de Cultura** (British Council Library), Calle M Antonio Caso 127, México 4, DF

Biblioteca del **Instituto Panamericano de Geografía** e Historia (Pan American Institute of Geography and History), Ex-Arzobispado 29, México 18, DF

Biblioteca del **Instituto Tecnológico** y de Estudios Superiores de Monterrey, Sucursal de Corres 'J'*, Monterrey, NL, México

Biblioteca de la **Universidad Iberoamericana***, Cerro de las Torres 395, Mexico City 21 Tel: 5444183

Library Associations

Asociación de Bibliotecarios de Instituciones de Enseñanza Superior e Investigación (ABIESI) (Association of Librarians of Higher Education and Research Institutions), Apdo Postal 5–611, México 5, DF

Asociación Mexicana de Bibliotecarios AC (AMBAC) (Mexican Association of Librarians)*, Apdo 27–132, México 7, DF Tel: 5489780
Secretary: N Pérez Paz
Publication: Noticiero (Bulletin); *Memorias de Congreso*

Departamento de Biblioteca y Publicaciones (Department of Libraries and Publications)*, Ave Cuauhtemoc y Dr Liceaga, México, DF

Escuela Nacional de Biblioteconomía y Archivonomía (National School of Librarianship and Archives)*, Viaducto Miguel Alemán 155, México 13, DF
Dir: Professor Eduardo Salas Estrada
Publication: Bibliotecas y Archivos

Instituto de Investigaciones Bibliográficas (Institute of Bibliographical Research)*, c/o Biblioteca Nacional de México, República de El Salvador 70, México 1, DF and Hemeroteca Nacional de México, Calle del Carmen 31, México 1, DF
Dir: María del Carmen Ruiz Castañeda
Publications: Boletin; Bibliografía Mexicana; Anuario Bibliográfico

Library Reference Books and Journals

Books

Anuario Bibliográfico, Instituto de Investigaciones Bibliograficas, c/o Biblioteca Nacional de Mexico, Republica de El Salvador 70, México 1, DF

Anuario de Bibliotecología Archivología Informática (Annual of Library Science, Archives, and Information Science), Universidad Nacional Autónoma de México, Ciudad Universitaria, Villa Obregón, México 20, DF

Bibliografía Mexicana, Instituto de Investigaciones Bibliograficas, c/o Biblioteca Nacional de Mexico, República de El Salvador 70, México 1, DF

Directorio de Bibliotecas de la Ciudad México (Directory of Libraries of the City of Mexico), Universidad de las Américas, Biblioteca, 16 Carretera Mexico-Toluca, México 10, DF

Journals

Bibliotecas y Archivos (Libraries and Archives), Escuela Nacional de Biblioteconomía y Archivonomía, Viaducto Miguel Alemán 155, México 13, DF

Boletín (Bulletin), Institute of Bibliographical Researches, c/o National Library, República de El Salvador 70, México 1, DF

Boletín (Bulletin), National Archives, Palacio Nacional, México, DF

Boletín (Bulletin), National Library, República de El Salvador 70, México 1, DF

Noticiero (News), Mexican Association of Librarians, Apdo 27–132, México 7, DF

Literary Associations and Societies

Centro Mexicano de Escritores AC (Mexican Authors' Centre)*, San Francisco No 12, Col del Valle, México 12, DF
Secretary of Executive Committee: Felipe Garcia Beraza
Publication: Recent Books in Mexico

Mexican **P E N** Club*, Filomeno Mata 8, Mexico City 1, DF
Secretary: Marco Antonio Montes de Oca

Sociedad Mexicana de Bibliografía (Mexican Bibliographical Society)*, Hemeroteca Nacional, Carmen 31, México 1, DF
Dir: Dr Agustín Millares Carlo
Publication: Boletin (quarterly)

Literary Periodicals

Comunidad (Community), Universidad Iberoamericano, Cerro de las Torres 395, México 21, DF

Cuadernos Americanos (American Notebooks), Ave Coyocán 1035, Apdo Postal 965, México, DF

El Cuento (The Story); magazine of imagination, Ave División del Norte 521–101, México 12, DF

Lectura (Readings), Apdo 545, Bolivar 23–4, México, DF

Letras (Letters); literary and bibliographical publication, Libreria y Ediciones Botas SA, Justo Sierra 52, Apdo 941, Mexico 1, DF

Mexico Quarterly Review (text in English and Spanish), University of the Americas, 15 Sta Catavina Martir, via Puebla, Ruebla México

Plural, Cía Editorial Excelsior, SCL, Reforma 18, México, DF

Salamandra (Salamander), Editorial Alfonso Reyes, Adolfo Prieto 2407 Oriente, Monterrey, NL

Literary Prizes

Manuel Avila **Camacho** Prize*
For an author's total work, either poetry or prose. Awarded periodically. Enquiries to Mexican Book Institute, Paseo de la Reforma 95, Depto 1024, México 1, DF

Miguel Lanz **Duret** Prize*
Founded in 1941 for the best novel written by a young author. Awarded annually. Enquiries to El Universal, Bucareli 8, México, DF

National Prize for Literature*
For the best literary works in the fields of the novel, poetry, essay, biography, drama and motion picture scriptwriting. 100,000 Mexican pesos. Awarded annually. Enquiries to Mexican Ministry of Public Education, Brazil 21, México 1, DF

Villaurrutia Prize*
For poetry, prose, drama or essays by a new author. Awarded annually. Enquiries to Society of Friends of Xavier Villaurrutia, Paseo de la Reforma 18, Galeria Excelsior, México 1, DF

Monaco

General Information

Language: French
Religion: Roman Catholic
Population: 25,000
Bank Hours: 0830-1730 Monday-Friday
Shop Hours: 0830-1300, 1600-1930 Monday-Friday
Currency: French franc

Publishers

Académie Internationale de Tourisme*, 4 rue des Iris, Monte-Carlo Tel: 309768
President: Guido Ricci
Subjects: Travel Literature, Dictionary of Tourism
Founded: 1951

Editions de l'**Oiseau-Lyre**, Les Remparts Tel: (93) 300944
Man Dir: Margarita M Hanson
Subject: Music

Editions **Regain***, Palais Miami, 10 blvd d'Italie, Monte-Carlo
Subjects: Poetry, Literature

Les Editions du **Rocher***, 28 Rue du Comte Félix Castaldi, Monaco
Subject: General Literature

Editions du Livre André **Sauret***, SA, 8 quai Antoine 1er, BP 48, Monte-Carlo Tel: 306884
Subjects: Art, Fiction
ISBN Publishers Prefix: 2-85051

Union Continentale d'Editions SA*, 17 rue de Millo, Monte-Carlo
Subject: Literature

Major Booksellers

Les **Beaux Livres***, 4 rue des Iris, Monte Carlo Tel: 307390

Quartier-Latin*, 26 blvd Princess-Charlotte, Monte Carlo Tel: 302621

Sainte-Devote*, 19 blvd Princess-Charlotte, Monte Carlo Tel: 302279

Major Libraries

Bibliothèque de Monaco (National Library), 8 rue de la Poste Tel: 309509
Director: Pierre Fénart

Literary Associations and Societies

P E N Club*, Musée d'Anthropologie Préhistorique, blvd du Jardin Exotique
Secretary: Louis Barral

Mongolian People's Republic

General Information

Language: Mongolian
Religion: None (Tibetan Buddhist Lamaism suppressed in 1930's)
Population: 1.5 million
Bank Hours: Vary. 0800-1700 or 1800 with lunch closing
Shop Hours: Generally 0900-1500
Currency: 100 mongo = 1 tugrik

Publishers

Mongolgoskinigotorg*, Ulan-Bator
Function: Distributor

State Press*, Ulan-Bator
Subjects: Geography, Politics, Law

Major Booksellers

State Book Trading Office*, Leniny gudamch 41, Ulan-Bator Tel: 22312 Cable Add: Mongolbook

Major Libraries

State Archives*, Ulan-Bator State Public Library of the Mongolian People's Republic, Lenin Prospekt, Ulan-Bator Tel: 22396
Dir: M Bayaizul

Montserrat

General Information

Language: English
Religion: Anglican and other Protestant denominations and Catholic
Population: 13,000
Bank Hours: 0800-1200 Monday-Thursday; 0800-1200, 1500-1700 Friday
Shop Hours: 0800-1200, 1300-1600 Monday-Thursday; 0800-1200, 1300-1700 Friday; 0800-1300 Saturday
Currency: 100 cents = 1 East Caribbean dollar
Export/Import Information: No tariffs on books and advertising catalogues. Parcel Tax of 15 cents on each postal parcel. No import licences required
Copyright: Berne, UCC (see International section)

Major Bookseller

Empire Shop, George St, Plymouth Tel: Montserrat 2400

Major Libraries

Montserrat Public Library*, Plymouth, Montserrat
Librarian: V J Grell

Morocco

General Information

Language: Moroccan Arabic spoken, classical Arabic written (commercially, French used in the south and Spanish and French in the north)
Religion: Muslim
Population: 18.2 million
Literacy Rate (1971): 21.4% (49.5% Urban, 11.5% Rural)
Bank Hours: Winter: 0815-1130, 1415-1630 Monday-Friday; Summer: 0830-1130, 1500-1700 Monday-Friday
Shop Hours: Tangiers: 0900-1200, 1600-2000; rest: 0900-1200, 1500-1800 or 1900
Currency: 100 centimes = 1 Dirham
Export/Import Information: No tariff on books; most advertising dutiable. 5% Special Tax and Stamp Duty of 2% of amount of import duty. No import licences required. Exchange controls but permission liberally granted
Copyright: UCC, Berne (see International section)

256 MOROCCO — MOZAMBIQUE

Book Trade Organizations

Syndicat des Editeurs du Maroc (Federation of Moroccan Publishers)*, rue de Vesoul, Casablanca

Syndicat des Librairies du Moroc*, 10 ave Dar el Maghzen, Rabat

Book Trade Journals

Bibliographie nationale marocaine, Bibliothèque générale et Archives du Maroc, ave Moulay Chérif, Rabat (national bibliography published monthly)

Publishers

Government Printer (Imprimerie Officielle)*, ave Jean Mermoz Rabat-Chellah, Rabat

Dar El **Kitab**, pl de la Mosqueé, Quartier des Habous, BP 4018, Casablanca Tel: 23381 Telex: 22620 Darki; Foreign Department: 18 rue Marechal, Casablanca Tel: 241168/246326
Dir: Boutaleb Abdou Abdelhay; *Manager:* Mme Soad Kadiri; *Publicity Manager:* Mounjedine Abdel-Ghani
Subjects: History, Africana, Philosophy, General & Social Science
Founded: 1948

Editions La **Porte***, 281 Ave Mohammed-V, Rabat Tel: 24977
Man Dir: Paul Souchon; *Sales:* Mohamed Rafii
Subsidiary Companies: Librairie aux Belles Images (Bookshop)
Subjects: Law — Constitutional, Social, Labour etc; Economics, Ministry of Justice Publications (in French and Arabic), Morocco Tourist Guides, Arab and French Language Teaching, Religion — the Koran, Islam
Bookshops: Librairie aux Belles Images (qv), address as above

Les Editions **Maghrebines***, 5–13 rue Soldat Roch, Casablanca Tel: 245148 Telex: Edima 22994 M
Subjects: General Nonfiction, History, Africana, Reference, Law, Science & Technology, General Science, Medicine
Founded: 1962

Major Booksellers

Librairie '**Aux Belles Images**'*, 281 ave Mohammed V, Rabat Tel: 24977
Parent Company: Editions La Porte (Publisher — qv)

Librairie des **Colonnes**, 54 Ave Pasteur, BP 352, Tangier Tel: 36955
Director: Mrs R Muyal
Parent Company: Sté Atlantique d'Edition

Cultura-Maroc*, 10 rue Bendahan, Casablanca Tel: 275990

Librairie des **Ecoles***, 12 ave Hassan II, Casablanca Tel: 66741

Librairie des **Etudes***, rue Allal B Abdallah, Rabat

Librairie **Farairre***, 43 rue de Foucauld, Casablanca Tel: 220388

Librairie de **France***, 4 rue Chenier, Casablanca Tel: 26534

Librairie **internationale***, 36 rue de Limousin, Rabat

Librairie **nationale***, 2 ave Mers Sultan, Casablanca Tel: 23678

Maghreb Livres*, 57 rue Oved Ziz, BP 725, Rabat Tel: 70340

Major Libraries

Bibliothèque générale et Archives*, BP 41, Tetuan

Bibliothèque générale et Archives du Maroc (National Archives)*, ave Moulay Chérif, Rabat Tel: 71890/72152
Publication: Bibliographie nationale marocaine

Bibliothèque municipale*, 142 ave de l'Armeé Royales, Casablanca Tel: 274170/223798
Dir: Haj Mohamed Bouzid

British Council Library, 22 Ave Moulay Youssef, BP 427, Rabat Tel: 20314

Centre Africain de Formation et de Recherche administrative pour le Développement*, Centre de Documentation, BP 300, Tangier Cable Add: Cafrad Tangier Telex: 33664 M
Librarian: Mrs Touria Temsamani

Centre national de Documentation (National Documentation Centre), Charii Maa El Ainain, BP 826, Rabat Tel: 74944 Telex: 31052M

Ecole Mohammedia d'Ingénieurs*, Bibliothèque, BP 765, Rabat Tel: 72647

Institut scientifique chérifien*, Bibliothèque, ave Moulay Chérif, Rabat
Publication: Travaux

International Communication Agency Library*, rue Emile Duploye angle rue Pegoud, Casablanca

Bibliothèque de l'**Université Al Quarawiyin***, 27 rue St Pierre et Miquelon, Rabat

Bibliothèque de l'**Université Mohammed V***, ave Moulay Chérif, Rabat

Mozambique

General Information

Language: Portuguese (English is used in business)
Religion: Predominantly Roman Catholic
Population: 9.7 million
Literacy Rate: Civilized Population, 1955, 87.5%; Noncivilized, 1950, 1.3%
Bank Hours: 0800-1100 Monday, Tuesday, Thursday, Friday; 0800-1000 Wednesday and Saturday
Shop Hours: 0800-1130, 1400-1700 Monday-Friday; 0800-1200 Saturday
Currency: 100 centavos = 1 Mozambique escudo
Export/Import Information: Children's picture books dutied at 20 escudos per kg net weight, otherwise books and advertising matter duty-free. No additional taxes apply. Import licences and strict exchange controls; authorities have classified books and advertising as List 3 in priorities

Book Trade Organization

Instituto Nacional do Livro e do Disco*, CP 4030, Avda 24 de Julho 1921/27, Maputo
Director: João Correia

Publishers

Empresa Moderna Lda*, 13 Ave da Republica, CP 473, Maputo
Man Dir: Louis Galloti
Subjects: General Fiction & Nonfiction, History, Africana, University & Secondary Textbooks
Founded: 1937

Government Printer (Impressa Nacional de Moçambique)*, CP 275, Maputo

Instituto de Investigação Cientifica de Moçambique*, CP 1780, Lourenço Margues Tel: 741135
Subjects: Social Sciences (especially Mozambique history), Ecology, Rural Development, Natural Resources
1977: 3 titles

Editora **Minerva** Central*, 84 Rua Consigliere Pedroso, CP 272, Maputo
Man Dir: J A Carvalho
Subjects: Medicine, General Science, University & Secondary Textbooks
Founded: 1908
Subsidiary: J A Carvalho & Co Ltd

Major Booksellers

Academica Lda*, 47 rua Joaquim Lapa, Maputo Tel: 3576

Armazens Distribuidores Lta*, CP 1215, Maputo

A W **Bayly** & Co Lda*, CP 185, Maputo

Cooperative das Casas*, 32 rua Major Araujo, Maputo

Minerva Central*, J A Carvalho & Co Lda, CP 212, Maputo

Major Libraries

Arquivo Historico de Moçambique*, CP 2033, Maputo
Director: A Lobato

Biblioteca Municipal*, Maputo

Biblioteca Nacional de Moçambique (National Library)*, CP 141, Maputo

Centro de Documentação Cientifica de Moçambique (Centre of Scientific Documentation of Mozambique)*, Instituto de Investigação Cientifica de Moçambique, CP 1780, Maputo

Centro de Documentação e Informação do Ensino (Centre of Documentation and Information on Education)*, CP 1406, Maputo
Publication: Humus e Seiva

Universidade Eduardo Mondlane, Centro Coordenador da Documentação, CP 257, Maputo Tel: 24426

NAMIBIA — NETHERLANDS 257

Namibia

General Information

Language: Afrikaans, German and English
Religion: Christian (Europeans and many Africans)
Population: Estimates vary between 852,000 and 1.2 million (for 1974)
Literacy Rate: 35%
Currency: South African

Book Trade Reference Book

Namibische National Bibliographie 1971-75, contact Nordiska Afrikaininstitutets Bibliotek, BP 2126, S-750 02 Uppsala, Sweden

Publishers

Gamsberg Publishers, PO Box 22830, Windhoek 9100 (Located at: 21 Post St, Windhoek) Tel: 28714/27669
Man Dir, Editorial: J J Hans Viljden; *Sales:* Anne Buys; *Production:* Herman van Wyk; *Publicity:* Cecelia Blom; *Rights & Permissions:* Petrus Amakali
Subjects: School Textbooks (in eight indigenous languages of Namibia, English and Afrikaans), Fiction, Poetry, Non-fiction
Bookshop: Gamsberg Bookshop, at above address
1978: 22 titles *1979:* 45 titles *Founded:* 1977
ISBN Publisher's Prefix: 86848

Native Language Bureau*, Department of Bantu Education, PMB 13236, Windhoek 9100 Tel: 24601 Cable Add: Imfundo Windhoek Telex: 3178
Head: W Zimmermann; *Rights & Permissions:* Department of Bantu Education, Pretoria, South Africa
Subjects: Primary and Secondary School Textbooks in indigenous languages, Nama, Ndonga, Kwanyama, Kwangali, Mbukushu, Herero
1977: 16 titles *Founded:* 1964
ISBN Publisher's Prefix: 0-621

Major Booksellers

The **Bookshop**, PO Box 119, 9020 Keetmanshoop Tel: (0631) 2309
Owner and Manager: Th Prahl-Andresen

Central News Agency*, PO Box 2104, Windhoek

Educmeds Pty Ltd, PO Box 2961, Windhoek 9100

Nasionale Boekhandel (SWA) (Pty) Ltd*, PO Box 1099, Windhoek 9100 Tel: 22711
Miscellaneous: Subsidiary of Nasionale Boekhandel Ltd, South Africa (qv)

Major Libraries

Government Archives, Department of National Education, PB 13250, Windhoek Tel: 22108

Library Services for South West Africa*, Huegel St, PB 13186, Windhoek Tel: 24528
Librarian: Dr N J Pienaar

Technical High School Library, PMB 12014, Windhoek 9111

Windhoek Public Library, PO Box 3180, Windhoek 9100 Tel: 30295

Translation Agencies and Associations

Native Language Bureau*, PMB 13236, Windhoek 9100

Nepal

General Information

Language: Nepali
Religion: Sanátan or Pauranic (traditional) Hinduism and Buddhism
Population: 13.1 million
Literacy Rate (1971): 12.5%
Bank Hours: 1000-1700 Sunday-Friday
Shop Hours: 1000-1700 Sunday-Friday
Currency: 100 pice = 1 Nepalese rupee
Export/Import Information: No tariff on books and advertising. Import licences required. Exchange controls

Publishers

Department of Publicity*, Ministry of Communications, Katmandu

Educational Enterprise*, Mahankalsthan, Katmandu Tel: 13749
Subject: Education

Lakoul Press*, Palpa-Tanben
Subjects: Education, Physical Sciences

Mahabir Singh Chiniya Main*, Makhan Tola, Katmandu

Mandas Sugatdas*, Kamabachi, Katmandu

Nepal Academy*, Ganabahal Dharhara, Katmandu
Subjects: Science, Literature, History, Art, Social Science

Ratna Pustak Bhandar*, Bhotahity, Katmandu

Sajha Prakashan, Co-operative Publishing Organization*, Pulchowk lalitpur, Katmandu Tel: 21023/21118 Cable Add: Sajha Prakashan Katmandu
Chairman: Shri Kshetra Pratap Adhikary; *Gen Man:* Mr K C S Pradhan
Br Offs: 40 branches and sub-offices throughout Nepal
Subjects: Literary, Educational Textbooks, General (published in English and Nepali)
1977: 70 titles *Founded:* 1966

Major Booksellers

Educational Enterprises (Pte) Ltd*, Kingsway, Kanthopath, Katmandu

International Progressive Books and Periodicals Store, Centre for General Selling, Distribution and Publication, PO Box 2131, Katmandu
General Manager: Sugat Dass Tuladhar

Januka Pustak Bhandar*, Budhhat Chowk, Biratnagar (Morang) Tel: 226 Cable Add: Januka Biratnagar

Nepal Booksellers*, 6/78 Dharmapath, Katmandu Tel: 14603

Ratna Pustak Bhandar*, Bhotahity, Katmandu

Sahayogi Prakashan*, Tripureshwar, Katmandu

Major Libraries

American Library*, Katmandu

Bir Library*, Ranipolhari, Katmandu

British Council Library, PO Box 640, Kanthi Path, Katmandu Tel: 11305/13796

National Library*, Katmandu

Nepal-Bharat Sanskritik Kendra Pustakalay*, Ganga Path, Katmandu

Tribhuvan University Library*, Kirtipur, Katmandu
Plays the leading role in library development

Library Associations

Nepal Library Association*, PO Box 207 GPO, Asan Tole, Katmandu

Netherlands

General Information

Language: Dutch (English widely spoken)
Religion: Roman Catholic and Protestant
Population: 13.9 million
Bank Hours: 0900-1500 Monday-Friday
Shop Hours: 0830-1800 Monday-Saturday. Half day one day a week
Currency: 100 cents = 1 Netherlands gulden or guilder
Export/Import Information: No tariff on books except children's picture books, 13% from non-EEC; advertising other than single copies 9%; VAT, 18% on books except children's picture books, 4%; 18% on advertising matter. Import licences required for certain countries (not US or UK)
Copyright: UCC, Berne, Florence (see International section)

Book Trade Organizations

Centraal Boekhuis BV*, Erasmusweg 10, Postbus 125, Culemborg Tel: (03450) 4841/4208
Dir: Ir R H Smedema

Collectieve Propaganda van het Nederlandse Boek (CPNB) (Commission for the Collective Promotion of the Netherlands Book)*, Langestr 61, Postbus 10576 , Amsterdam C Tel: (020) 264971
Dirs: Dick Ouwehand, Wim Berbers
Publications: Boekenmolen (quarterly); *Premium Bookweek* (booklet); *Children's Bookweek* (booklet); *Books of the Month*

NETHERLANDS

Koninklijke Nederlandse Uitgeversbond (Royal Dutch Publishers' Association), N Z Voorburgwal 44, 1012 SB-Amsterdam Tel: (020) 222779/257039
Secretary: R M Vrij
Founded: 1880

Nederlandsche Vereniging van Antiquaren (Netherlands Association of Antiquarian Booksellers), Nieuwe Spiegelstraat 40, 1017 DG Amsterdam

Nederlandsche Vereeniging voor Druk- en Boekkunst (Netherlands Society for the Art of Printing and Book Production), Bestevaerstr 10, Haarlem
Secretary: F Mayer
Publications: Mededelingen (irregular) and books

Nederlandse Boekverkopersbond (Dutch Booksellers' Association), Waalsdorperweg 119, 2597 HS The Hague Tel: (070) 244395
President: H Nelissen
Publication: De Boekverkoper (quarterly)

Stichting Bibliotheek en Documentatieacademies (Foundation for Library and Documentation Academies)*, Keizersgracht 225, Postbus 10895, 1001 EW Amsterdam 2 Tel: (020) 265155
Secretary: P den Hoed

Stichting Speurwerk betreffende het Boek (Book Research Foundation), Keizersgracht 144, 1015 CX Amsterdam Tel: (020) 264974
Secretary: A A Herpers

Vereeniging ter bevordering van de belangen des Boekhandels (Association for the Promotion of the Interests of Booksellers and Publishers), Lassusstr 9, Postbus 5475, 1007 AL Amsterdam
Secretary: Mrs M van Vollenhoven

Vereniging van Uitgeversvertegenwoordigers (Association of Publishers' Representatives)*, Westerstr 62, Wormerveer
Publication: Vertegenwoordiger

Book Trade Reference Books and Journals

Books

Bibliografie van in Nederland verschenen Officiële en Semi-officiële Uitgaven (Bibliography of Official and Semi-official Publications), Royal Library, Lange Voorhout 34, The Hague

Lystenboek (List of Dutch Booksellers), Nieuwsblad voor de Boekhandel, Postbus 5475, Amsterdam Z

Journals

Boeken-kijkboek (Book Review), Commission for the Collective Promotion of the Netherlands Book, N Z Voorburgwal 44, Amsterdam C

Boekenband (The Bond of Books), Christelijke Blindenbibliotheek (Evangelical Library for the Blind), Putterweg 140, Ermelo

De Boekverkoper (The Bookseller), Dutch Booksellers' Association, Waalsdorperweg 119, NL-2019 The Hague

Book Mill, Netherlands Graphic Export Centre, Prinsengracht 668, Amsterdam Tel: (020) 234283

Brinkman's Cumulatieve Catalogus (Brinkman's Cumulative Book Catalogue), A W Sijthoff International Publishing Co BV, Schuttersveld 9, Postbus 9, Leiden

Buitenlandse Boek (The Foreign Book), Prinsengracht 1083, Amsterdam

Duitse Boek (The German Book), (text in Dutch and German), Editions Rodopi NV, Keizersgracht 302-304, Amsterdam

Gouden Uren (Golden Hours), Netherlands Book Club, Prinsevinkenpark 2, The Hague

Nieuwe Pockets en Paperbacks (New Pocket-books and Paperbacks), Nederlandse Boek, Prinsengracht 1083, Amsterdam

Nieuwsblad voor de Boekhandel (Newssheet for the Book Trade), Vereniging ter Bevordering van de Belangen des Boekhandels, Lassusstr 9, Postbus 5475, Amsterdam Z

Nijhoff Information; books and periodicals from the Netherlands in foreign languages, Martinus Nijhoff FB, Lange Voorhout 9-11, Postbus 269, The Hague

Prisma; book reviews for public libraries, Protestant Foundation for the Promotion of Librarianship and Reading Information in the Netherlands, Parkweg 20a, Voorburg

Spectrum Boekengids, Uitgeverij Het Spectrum BV, Park Voorn 4, De Meern

De Uitgever (The Publisher), Royal Dutch Publishers' Association, N Z Voorburgwal 44, Amsterdam C

Vertegenwoordiger (The Representative), Association of Publishers' Representatives, Westerstr 62, Wormer

Publishers

A P A (Academic Publishers Associated)+*, Postbus 1850, NL-1000 BW Amsterdam
Man Dir: G van Heusden
Orders to: Postbus 122, NL-3600 AC Maarssen Tel: (030) 445700, (020) 240536
Subsidiary Companies: Fontes Pers (qv); Holland University Press BV (qv); Oriental Press BV (qv); Philo Press/Van Heusden/Hissink & Co CV (qv); University Press Amsterdam BV (qv)
Subjects: Academic Books in the Arts, Humanities and Sciences
1978: 15 titles *Founded:* 1963
ISBN Publisher's Prefix: 90-302, 90-6022, 90-6023, 90-6024, 90-6025, 90-6037, 90-6039, 90-6042
Miscellaneous: Formerly Associated Publishers Amsterdam

Academic Publishers Associated, see APA

Addison-Wesley Publishing Group, de Lairessestr 90, 1071 PJ Amsterdam Tel: (020) 764044/45 Cable Add: Adiwes Amsterdam Telex: 14046 wss nl
Marketing Manager: Frans Gianotten; *Rights & Permissions:* S B Warren, Addison-Wesley, USA; *Operations:* Jan Fleere
Parent Company: Addison-Wesley Publishing Co Inc, Reading, Mass 01867, USA
Subsidiary Companies: Addison-Wesley Publishers BV; Inter-European Editions *Associate Companies:* see Addison-Wesley UK
Subjects: Humanities, Reference, Juveniles, General & Social Science, Technology, Economics, University, Secondary & Primary Textbooks, Educational Materials,

General, EFL, Business, Management
Founded: 1942
Miscellaneous: Firm is an associate company of Addison-Wesley Publishers Ltd, UK (qv)
ISBN Publisher's Prefix: 0-201/0, 8465, 8053

Agathon+*, Nieuwe S'Gravenlandseweg 17-19, Postbus 17, Bussum Tel: (02159) 34241 Cable Add: Unieboek, Bussum
Subjects: Fiction, Poetry, Politics
Miscellaneous: Firm is a member of the Unieboek Group, Netherlands (qv)

Agon Elsevier BV+*, Rivierstaete, Amsteldijk 166, Postbus 70707, Amsterdam Tel: (020) 5413413 Cable Add: Elsbook Telex: 14481
Publisher: Dr Arnold Escher; *Dir:* Dr Jacques F Remarque; *Editorial:* Peter Fiedeldij Dop
Subjects: Education, Science, Medicine, General nonfiction

Uitgeverij **Ambo** BV+, Parkstraat 33, PO Box 308, 3740 AH Baarn Tel: (02154) 18441 Telex: 43272
Publisher: H Pijfers; *Editorial:* Dr Willem Reindert Kuipers
Imprints: Basis
Subjects: Religion, Philosophy, Psychiatry, Sociology, Psychology
Miscellaneous: Firm is a member of the Combo Group, Netherlands (qv)
1978: 49 titles
ISBN Publishers Prefix: 90-263

Amsterdam Boek BV+, now incorporated in Uitgeverij Het Spectrum BV (qv)

Ankh-Hermes BV*+, Menstr 17-21, Postbus 125, Deventer Tel: (05700) 14043
Man Dir, Rights & Permissions: Paul Kluwer
Subjects: History, Philosophy, Religion, Juveniles, Psychology, Archaeology, Astrology, Occult, Yoga, Sport
Founded: 1949
ISBN Publishers Prefix: 90-202

BV Uitgeverij de **Arbeiderspers**+, Singel 262, Postbus 3879, 1016 AC Amsterdam Tel: (020) 239326 Telex: 11556 Apqwu
Man Dir: Theo A Sontrop; *Editorial:* Martin Ros; *Sales Manager:* Arthur Dekker; *Publicity:* Gert-Jan Hemmink
Subjects: General Fiction & Nonfiction, Paperbacks
Miscellaneous: Firm is an associate company of Em Querido's Uitgeverij BV (qv) and Wetenschappelijke Uitgeverij BV (qv) (both in the Netherlands)
1977: 60 titles *1978:* 120 titles
ISBN Publishers Prefix: 90-295

Argus Elsevier BV+*, Rivierstaete, Amsteldijk 166, Amsterdam
Parent Company: Elsevier NDU nv (qv)

A **Asher** & Co, BV*, Keizersgracht 526, Amsterdam Tel: (020) 222255 Cable Add: Asherbooks Telex: 14070 ashni-nl
Man Dir: Nico Israel; *Sales Dir:* Julius W Steiner
Subjects: General & Natural Science, Reference
1978-79: 10 titles *Founded:* 1830
Miscellaneous: Associate company of Nico Israel (qv); and Theatrum Orbis Terrarum (qv), both Amsterdam

Associated Publishers Amsterdam, renamed APA (Academic Publishers Associated) (qv)

B R E S*, Madoerastr 10, 2585 VB The Hague Tel: (070) 656592
Editorial: A Gabrielli, J Klautz
Subjects: Comparative Religion, Parapsychology, Metaphysics, Philosophy, Alternative Medicine, Fantastic Art, Archaeology

Bert **Bakker** BV+, Herengracht 406, Amsterdam C Tel: (020) 241934
Man Dir: Bert Bakker; *Editorial:* Harko Keijzer, Harold Ytsma; *Rights & Permissions:* Marijke Bartels
Subjects: Dutch and Foreign Literature, Psychology, Social Science, Handicrafts, Cookery, Family Interest
1977: 120 titles *Founded:* 1893
Miscellaneous: Firm is an associate company of Kluwer NV, Netherlands (qv)
ISBN Publishers Prefix: 90-6019

A A **Balkema**+, PO Box 1675, 3000 BR Rotterdam Tel: (010) 666861
Man Dir: A T Balkema; *Rights & Permissions:* G Balkema-Pieterse
Br Offs: Lisplein 11, 3037 AR Rotterdam; PO Box 3117, Cape Town, South Africa
Subjects: Philosophy, Religion, Social, General and Applied Sciences, Medicine, Arts, Sport, Languages, Literature, Geography, History (esp South African)
1978: 10 titles *1979:* 15 titles *Founded:* 1932
ISBN Publisher's Prefix: 90-6191

H J W **Becht's** Uitgeversmij bv/Uitgeverij H J de Bussy BV+, Keizersgracht 810, PO Box 162, NL-1000 AD Amsterdam Tel: 242449 Telex: 18069 bebus nl
Dirs: J J F Aleva, M de Metz, J Schilt
Subjects: General Fiction and Non-fiction, Juveniles, Hobbies, Leisure Activities, History, Arts and Crafts, Health, General and Social Science, Textbooks

John **Benjamins** BV, Postbus 52519, 1007 HA Amsterdam (Located at: Amsteldijk 44, Amsterdam) Tel: (020) 738156 Cable Add: Benper, Amsterdam Telex: 15798 jbds
Man Dir: John L Benjamins
Subjects: Linguistics, Literature, Philosophy, Reference, Social Science, Educational Materials, Reprints of Backfile-Periodicals
1977: 18 titles *1978:* 30 titles *Founded:* 1964
ISBN Publishers Prefix: 90-272

De **Bezige** Bij+, Van Miereveldstr 1, Postbus 5184, Amsterdam Z Tel: (020) 735731 Cable Add: Beebook
Man Dirs: G Lubberhuizen, J L Witteman
Subjects: General Fiction, Belles Lettres, Poetry, Children's Books, Low-priced Paperbacks
1978: 120 titles *1979:* 120 titles *Founded:* 1945
ISBN Publishers Prefix: 90-234

Bigot en Van Rossum BV, Bloemlandseweg 6, Postbus 10, 1260 AA Blaricum Tel: (02153) 82548
Dir: Mrs M H van Rossum-Berg; *Sales Dir:* E L Westra-Sillevis
Subjects: General Fiction, Paperbacks
1978: 14 titles *Founded:* 1934
Subsidiary: Mulder & Co, Bloemlandseweg 6, Blaricum (qv)
ISBN Publishers Prefix: 90-6134

Erven J **Bijleveld**+, Janskerkhof 7, Utrecht Tel: (030) 317008
Man Dir: J B Bommeljé Jr
Subjects: Philosophy, Religion, Medicine, Psychology, Social Science, History
1977: about 20 titles *1978:* about 20 titles
Founded: 1864

Andries **Blitz** BV+*, Oud Blaricummerweg 31, Postbus 3, Laren Tel: (02153) 2401
Subjects: General Fiction, Belles Lettres, Poetry, Biography, History, Music, Art
Founded: 1929
ISBN Publishers Prefix: 90-6081

H W **Blok** Uitgeverij BV, Schiedamsevest 51, 3012 BD Rotterdam Tel: (010) 137997
Subjects: Medical Year Books, Dutch for Spanish-speaking and Portuguese for Dutch-speaking persons, *Handbook gymnastics*
ISBN Publishers Prefix: 90-70008

Boekencentrum BV+, Scheveningseweg 72, Postbus 84176, 2508 AD The Hague Tel: (070) 512111
Subjects: Education, Theology, Religion

De **Boekerij** BV+*, Parkstr 7, Postbus 239, Baarn Tel: (02154) 17247
Man Dirs: A M Beumer, J Verweij
Subjects: General Fiction, Sports
Founded: 1945
Subsidiary: NV De Verkenner Publishers
Miscellaneous: Firm is a member of the Edicom Group, Netherlands (qv)
ISBN Publisher's Prefixes: 90-225 (De Boekerij), 90-70016 (De Verkenner), 90-224 (Meulenhoff)

Uitgeverij De **Boer**+*, Nieuwe Maritiem S'Gravenlandseweg 17-19, Postbus 17, Bussum Tel: (02159) 34241 Cable Add: Unieboek, Bussum
Subject: Maritime
Miscellaneous: Firm is a member of the Unieboek Groep, Netherlands (qv)

Bohn, Scheltema & Holkema+, Wetenschappelijke Uitgevers, Emmalaan 27, Utrecht Tel: (030) 511274
Man Dirs: Fons Drabbe, Jan van Geelen
Subjects: University Textbooks (Medicine, Biology, Linguistics)
Founded: 1899
Miscellaneous: Firm is a member of the Kluwer Group, Netherlands (qv)
ISBN Publishers Prefix: 90-313

Boom-Pers Boeken-En Tijdschriftenuitg BV*, Kromme Elleboog 2, Postbus 58, Meppel Tel: (05220) 54306 Editorial & Directors' Off: Sarphatistr 9, Amsterdam Tel: (020) 226107 Cable Add: Boompers
Man Dirs: H L Bouman, J H Boom
Subjects: Philosophy, Philosophy of Science, Psychology, General, Social & Political Science, Periodicals
1977: 48 titles *Founded:* 1842
Bookshops: Kamper Boekhandel, Oude Str 82, Kampen; Elburger Boekhandel, Beekstr 26, Elburg; De Brunte, Snijderstr 11, Lelystad; Boekhandel Boom, Winkelcentrum Gordinan, Lelystad; Boekhandel v/h G Taconis, Hoofdstraat West 10, Wolvega (all in Netherlands)
ISBN Publishers Prefix: 90-6009

Born NV Uitgeversmaatschappij*, Esstr 10, Postbus 22, Assen
Man Dir: H Born
Subjects: General Fiction, How-to, Philosophy, Textbooks, Reference, Juveniles, Medicine, Engineering, Social Science, Low- & High-priced Paperbacks
Founded: 1885
ISBN Publishers Prefix: 90-283

Bosch en Keuning NV+*, Bremstr, Postbus 1, Baarn Tel: (02154) 8241 Telex: beka-43272
Man Dir: Aize de Visser
Subjects: Biography, History, Music, Art, Religion, Low- & High-priced Paperbacks, Medicine, Primary Textbooks, Educational Materials, Popular Science (Sesam Pocketbooks)
Founded: 1925
Miscellaneous: Firm is a member of the Combo Group, Netherlands (qv)
ISBN Publishers Prefix: 90-246

Paul **Brand**+*, Uitgeverij en Drukkerij, Nieuwe S'Gravendseweg 17-19, Postbus 17, Bussum Tel: (02159) 34241 Cable Add: Unieboek, Bussum
Subjects: Sociology, Psychology, Educational
Miscellaneous: Firm is a member of the Unieboek Group, Netherlands (qv)

Redactie **Bres***, Madoerastraat 10, 2585 VB The Hague Tel: 070-656592
Subjects: Fantastic Art, Metaphysics, Religion, Natural Medicine, Psychology

NV Boekhandel & Drukkerij voorheen E J **Brill**+, Oude Rijn 33a, Leiden Tel: (071) 146646 Cable Add: Brill Leiden Telex: 39296
Manager: T A Edridge
Br Offs: Orient Buchhandlung am Friesenplatz, E J Brill GmbH, D-5000 Cologne 1, Antwerpener Str 6-12, German Federal Republic; E J Brill London Ltd, 41 Museum St, London WC1A 1LX, UK
Subjects: Classical, Mediaeval and Renaissance Studies, Religion, Oriental & Islamic Studies, University Textbooks
Founded: 1683
ISBN Publishers Prefix: 90-04

Ten **Brink-Meppel** BV AFD Uitgeverij+, Stationsweg 44, Postbus 56, 7940 AB-Meppel Tel: (05220) 51947
Man Dir: B G Ten Brink
Subject: Educational books for 6-18 year olds
Founded: 1848
ISBN Publishers Prefix: 90-248

A W **Bruna** & Zoon's Uitgeversmaatschappij BV+, Postbus 8181, 3503 RD Utrecht (Located at: Hollantlaan 2, 3526 AM Utrecht) Tel: 884233 Cable Add: Brunazoon Telex: 47518
Dirs: H Bruna, H M Bruna; *Man Dir:* J Buis; *Assistant Man Dir:* J C Bloemsma; *Sales:* K Eksteen; *Rights & Permissions:* Ellen-C van der Ploeg
Br Off: Antwerpse Steenweg 29A, B-2630 Aartselaar, Belgium
Subjects: General Fiction, Belles Lettres, History, Philosophy, Children's Picturebooks, Juveniles, Low- & High-priced Paperbacks, Psychology, General & Social Science
1977: 150 titles *1978:* 180 titles *Founded:* 1868
ISBN Publishers Prefix: 90-229

Buijten & Schipperheijn BV Drukkerij en Uitg Mij v/h+, Valkenburgerstr 106, NL-1001 Amsterdam Tel: (020) 236612
Subject: Philosophy, Religion, History, Literature
1977: 15 titles *1978:* 20 titles *Founded:* 1902
Miscellaneous: Associated imprints include Repro Holland, Alphen aan den Rijn
ISBN Publisher's Prefix: 90-6064

Uitgeverij G F **Callenbach** BV+, Hoogstr 24, Postbus 86, Nijkerk Tel: (03494) 1241 Telex: beka-43722
Man Dir: G F Callenbach; *Rights & Permissions:* Mrs P van Elven-Scholtes
Subjects: General Fiction, Belles Lettres, Poetry, Religion, Juveniles, Low- & High-priced Paperbacks, Psychology, Psychiatry,

260 NETHERLANDS

Medicine, Sociology, Hobbies
1979: 500 titles *Founded:* 1854
Miscellaneous: Firm is a member of the Combo Group, Netherlands (qv)
ISBN Publisher's Prefix: 90-266

Uitgeverij Cantecleer BV+, PO Box 24, 3730 AA De Bilt (Located at: Dorpsstraat 74, De Bilt) Tel: (030) 764014
Man Dir: K J Bekkers; *Publisher:* J A J Jungerhans; *Editors:* H Stenfert, M Nauta, G G van Schaik
Subjects: Art, Juveniles, Handicrafts, Travel Guides, Paperbacks
Founded: 1947
Miscellaneous: Firm is a member of the Combo Group, Netherlands (qv)
ISBN Publishers Prefix: 90-213

Castrum Peregrini Presse, Herengracht 401, Postbus 645, 1000 AP Amsterdam
Tel: (020) 235287
Man Dir: M R Goldschmidt; *Editorial:* Th Karlauf
Subjects: History of Literature, Art, History of Art, Belles Lettres, Poetry, Biography, History, Archaeology, Philology, History of Ideas, Reference
1977-78: 5 titles *Founded:* 1950
ISBN Publishers Prefix: 90-6034

D B Centen+*, Nieuwe S'Gravenlandseweg 17-19, Bussum

Combo Uitgeversgroep+, Bremstr 11, Baarn Tel: (02154) 18241
Miscellaneous: Members of the Combo Group in the Netherlands include: Uitgeverij Ambo BV (qv), Uitgeverij Bekadidact (qv), Bosch & Keuning NV (qv), Uitgeverij Callenbach BV (qv), Uitgeverij Cantecleer BV (qv), Uitgeverij De Fontein BV (qv), Uitgeverij ten Have (qv), Uitgeverij Market Books BV (qv), Uitgeverij 'In den Toren' (qv), Uitgeverij Van Walraven (qv)
ISBN Publishers' Prefixes: 90-263 (Ambo), 90-321 (Bekadidact), 90-246 (Bosch & Keuning), 90-266 (Callenbach), 90-213 (Cantecleer), 90-261 (De Fontein), 90-259 (ten Have), 90-6049 (Van Walraven)

Uitgeverij Contact BV, now fully integrated in Bert Bakker BV (qv)

Stichting D J O (de jonge onderzoekers)+*, Groesbeekseweg 70, Nijmegen Tel: (080) 229549

Davaco Publishers*, Varenstraat 41, Soest, Holland Tel: 02155-18099 Cable Add: Millbooks
Subjects: Art History, Monographs on Painters, Architecture, Sculpture, Archaeology (Greek/Roman)

Dekker en Van de Vegt+, Fransestr 30, 6524 JC Nijmegen Tel: (080) 232765 Cable Add: Dekkervegt Nijmegen
Man Dir: K W J van Rossum
Subjects: Religion, High-priced Paperbacks, Medicine, Social Sciences, Psychology, Secondary Textbooks
Bookshop: Plein 1944 129-131, Nijmegen
1977: 25 titles *1978:* 23 titles *Founded:* 1856
Miscellaneous: Firm is a subsidiary of Van Gorcum BV, Netherlands (qv)
ISBN Publishers Prefix: 90-255

Delft University Press, Mijnbouwplein 11, 2628 RT Delft, PO Box 5 Tel: (015) 783254
Dir: Ir P A M Maas; *Editorial:* Lydia tes Horst-ten Wolde
1977: 7 titles *1978:* 15 titles *Founded:* 1972

Uitgeverij Didier Nederland BV*, Amstel AB 134, Postbus 5530, Amsterdam Tel: (020) 244339
Man Dir: Mrs M E Eikhoudt
Subject: Textbooks

Jacob Dijkstra's Uitg Mij BV+*, Helperoostsingel 20, Postbus 284, Groningen Tel: (050) 262866

Dijkstra's Uitgeverij Zeist BV+, Dijnselburgerlaan 9, Postbus 48, 3700 AA Zeist Tel: (03404) 21021

Diligentia BV+*, Tesselschadestr 18-22, NL-1013 Amsterdam Tel: (020) 211911
Cable Add: Publipress Amsterdam
Telex: 14407
Dir: C van der Sluys
Subjects: Directories, Trade Journals

C A'J van Dishoeck+*, Nieuwe S'Gravenlandseweg 17-19, Postbus 17, Bussum Tel: (02159) 34241 Cable Add: Unieboek, Bussum
Subjects: Cookery, Crafts
Miscellaneous: Firm is a member of the Unieboek Group, Netherlands (qv)

Djambatan BV+, Postbus 43110, 2504 AC The Hague Tel: (070) 299180 Cable Add: Djambatan Den Haag
Man Dir: E G Niessen
Parent Company: NV Falkplan/CIB
Subjects: History, Reference, Geography, Cartography, Educational Materials (Atlases, Wall Maps)
Founded: 1949

Uitgeversmaatschappij Ad Donker NV, Koningin Emmaplein 1, Rotterdam 2
Tel: (010) 362851
Dir: Ad Donker
Subjects: General Fiction, Belles Lettres, Poetry, Biography, History, Music, Art, Juveniles, High-priced Paperbacks
Founded: 1938
ISBN Publishers Prefix: 90-6100

Dragon's Dream, Postbus 212, AE 3340 Hendrik Ido Ambacht Tel: (01858) 7070
Telex: 28856
Editorial: Roger Dean; *Sales:* Evert Chevalier; *Production:* Linda Korpel
Subjects: Speculative art in the fields of science fiction, fantasy, prophecy, past, future and other worlds
1978: 12 titles *Founded:* 1975
ISBN Publisher's Prefix: 90-6332

De Driehoek BV, Keizersgracht 756, 1017 EZ Amsterdam Tel: (020) 246426
Director: H J Heule
Subjects: Medicine, Health, Yoga, Herbs, Nutrition, Vegetarianism, Mysticism, Buddhism etc, Astrology

East-West Publications Fonds BV, Anna Paulownastraat 78, POB 85617, 2508 CH-The Hague Tel: (070) 461594 Telex: 16384
Subjects: Books on Sufism, Religions, Mysticism, Symbolism, Middle East Culture, Medieval Art & Iconography
1978: 6 titles

Edicom NV+*, Frankenslag 173, Postbus 290, The Hague Tel: (070) 512601
Presidents: Dr P A F van Veen, J H Docter Edicom; *Rights & Permissions:* Henk Drijvers; *Contracts & Subsidiary Rights Dept:* 27 Torenlaan, Postbus 44, Laren, Noord Holland Tel: (02153) 87075
Subjects: General Fiction, Belles Lettres, Poetry, Biography, History, How-to, Philosophy, Reference, Religion, Juveniles, High-priced Paperbacks, Medicine,
Psychology, General & Social Science, Secondary & Primary Textbooks, Educational Materials
Members of the Edicom Group in the Netherlands: De Boekerij BV (qv), De Brug Ad M C Stok-Zuid-Hollandsche Uitgeversmaatschappij BV (qv)
Foreign Group Members: A Manteau NV, Belgium (qv); Ikhtiar, Indonesia (qv)
Bookshop: Co-libri BV (wholesaler), Frankenslag 173, Postbus 290, The Hague
Miscellaneous: Firm is a holding company
ISBN Publisher's Prefixes: 90-225 (De Boeke), 90-6006 (Paris), 90-224 (Meulenhoff), 90-235 (Stok-Zuid-Hollandsche)

Educaboek BV+*, Industrieweg 1, Postbus 48, Culemborg
Miscellaneous: Firm is a member of the Kluwer Group, Netherlands (qv)

Eindhovensche Drukkerij BV, Cederlaan 2, Postbus 382, Eindhoven Tel: (040) 513620
Telex: 51476
Dir: Peter Smeets; *Export Manager:* Willem Ambaum
Subjects: Juveniles, Activity Books, Board Books

Elmar BV, Delftweg 147, 2289 BD Rijswijk (Z.H) Tel: (015) 125067
Man Dir: A C Roodnat
Subjects: Biography, History, How-to, Reference, Medicine & General Science, Sci-Fic, Sport
1977: 27 titles *1978:* 41 titles *Founded:* 1961

Elsevier-NDU nv+, Jan van Galenstr 335, Amsterdam Tel: (020) 5159111 (Internal and External Relations Tel: (020) 5152350)
Cable Add: Elsevier Telex: 16479 epc nl
Presidents: W Pluygers, Prof P J Vinken; *Other members of Executive Board:* H N Appel, Dr A J Bindenga, D P van de Merwe, J H Verleur
Dutch Subsidiaries: Elsevier Books International BV, Elsevier International Projects Ltd, W van Hoeve BV, Elsevier Nederland BV, BV Uitgeversmaatschappij Elsevier Argus, BV Uitgeversmaatschappij Elsevier Boekerij, BV Uitgeversmaatschappij Elsevier Focus, Edicom BV (all at Rivierstaete, Amsteldijk 166, Amsterdam); Multiboek BV, Pruimendijk 104, Ridderkerk; Nederlandse Dagbladunie BV, NRC BV (both at Westblaak 180, Rotterdam); De Courant Het Vaderland BV, Parkstr 25-27, The Hague; Dagblad van Rijn en Gouwe BV, P Doelmanstr 8, Alphen a/d Rijn; BV De Dordtenaar, Johann de Wittstr 17-19, Dordrecht; Elsevier-NDU Grafische Groep BV, Van Boekhoven-Bosch BV (both at Europalaan 12, Utrecht); Boom-Ruygrok BV, Hulswitweg 15, Haarlem; Henkes-Senefelder BV, Van IJsendijkstraat 150, Purmerend; Krips Repro BV, Industrieweg 5, Meppel; Misset Grafische Bedrijven BV, Uitgeversmaatschappij C Misset BV (both at IJsselkade 32, Doetinchem); Periodieken Service Holland BV, Keppelseweg 15, Doetinchem; Vlasveld & Co's Drukkerij BV, Parmentierplein 31, Rotterdam; Zetterij Holland BV, Kontekst Groep BV (both at Nw Zijds Voorburgwal 303, Amsterdam); Elsblad BV, Prof J H Bavincklaan 5, Amstelveen; BV Uitgevermaatschappij Bonaventura, Spuistr 110-112, Amsterdam; BV Uitgeversmaatschappij Annoventura, Kloveniersburgwal 51, Amsterdam; Folio Groep BV, Welboom Bladen BV, Herengracht 362, Amsterdam; Fonorama BV, Kon Wilhelminalaan 12, Amersfoort; Jongerenmedia BV, IJselstraat 20-24,

Amsterdam; Koninklijke PBNA NV, Velperbuitensingel 6, Arnhem; Elsevier Detailhandel BV, Kring van Boekspecialisten BV (both at Vredenburg 139, Utrecht); Dekker & Nordemann's Wetenschappelijke Boekhandel BV, Meulenhoffbruna BV (both at Beulingstr 2, Amsterdam); Elsevier Science Publishers BV, Overschiestr 55–57, Amsterdam; Elsevier's Wetenschappelijke Uitgeverij BV, BV Noord-Hollandsche Uitgeversmaatschappij, Elsevier/North-Holland Biomedical Press BV (all at Jan van Galenstraat 335, Amsterdam); Northprint BV, Industrieweg 1b, Meppel; Excerpta Medica International BV, Excerpta Medica BV (both at Keizersgracht 305–311, Amsterdam); Het Vrije Volk BV (50%), W de Withstraat 25, Rotterdam; Infonet BV (50%), Nwe Prinsengracht 75, Amsterdam
Foreign Subsidiaries: American Elsevier Publishers Inc, Elsevier-Dutton Inc, Education & Economic Systems Inc, D & N (USA) Library Services Inc, Elsevier North-Holland Inc, Excerpta Medica Inc, Medical Examination Publishing Company Inc (all in USA); Elsevier Publishing Projects SA, Elsevier Sequoia SA, Excerpta Medica SA (all in Switzerland); Elsevier International Projects Ltd, Elsevier (UK) Ltd, Phaidon Publishers Ltd, Phaidon Press Ltd, Applied Science Publishers Ltd, Elsevier Editorial Services Ltd, Elsevier-IRCS Ltd (all in UK); Elsevier Sequoia SA, Elsevier Sequoia NV, Librico NV, A Manteau NV, Elsevier Business Press NV, International Equipment News Europe NV (50%), Computer Product News Europe NV (50%) (all in Belgium); Editions Elsevier Sequoia SARL, France; Selecciones Editoriales SA, Spain; Elsevier Zeitschriften-Verlag GmbH, Krausskopf Verlag GmbH, Ingenieur Digest Verlag GmbH (all in Federal Republic of Germany); Dekker en Nordemann Ireland Ltd, Elsevier/North-Holland Scientific Publishers Ltd, Irish Elsevier Printers Ltd (all in Republic of Ireland); Libreria Internacional SA, El Manual Moderno SA (both in Mexico); Editora Campus Ltda, Brazil
Subjects: Archaeology, Art, Agricultural/Environmental Sciences, Biochemistry, Biology, Chemistry, Computer and Information Sciences, Dictionaries, Earth Sciences, Economics, History, Law, Linguistics, Literature, Medicine, Neurology, Philosophy, Physics (Atomic, General & History), Psychology, Religion, Management Sciences, Mathematics, Social Sciences, Space Sciences, Metallurgy, Engineering, Reference Works, Handbooks, Paperbacks, Juveniles, Textbooks, Illustrated Books, Atlases, Newspapers, Periodicals, Audiovisual and Educational Materials
Bookshops: Elsevier Retailers Group; Dekker en Nordemann BV, Sims
Miscellaneous: Elsevier-NDU nv is holding company which was formed in 1979 by a merger of NV Uitgeversmaatschappij Elsevier and Nederlandse Dagbladunie NV. Elsevier Books International BV, Nederlandse Dagbladunie BV, Elsevier-NDU Grafische Groep BV, Elsblad BV, Elsevier Detailhandel BV, Elsevier Science Publishers BV and American Elsevier Publishers Inc are subholdings
1978: 1349 titles *Founded:* 1979 (NV Uitgeversmaatschappij Elsevier 1880)
ISBN Publishers' Prefixes: 90–10 (NV Uitgeversmaatschappij Elsevier), 90–444 (Elsevier Wetenschappelijke Uitgeverij BV)

Uitgeversmaatschappij **Elsevier Boekerij** BV, Riverstaete, Amsteldijk 166, Postbus 70707, Amsterdam Tel: (020) 5413413 Cable Add: Elsbook Telex: 14481
Publishers: Tj Dijkstra, Wim Hazeu; *Man Dirs:* J C de Graaff, C van der Sluys; *Sales:* H Betzema
Parent Company: Elsevier-NDU nv (qv)
Subjects: Fiction (adult and children's)

Elsevier/North Holland Biomedical Press+, PO Box 1527 Amsterdam Tel: (515) 9222 Cable Add: Elspubco Telex: 16479
Man Dir/Editorial: Dr J Franklin; *Production:* H Ostendorf; *Publicity:* M Boswood
Orders to: PO Box 211, Amsterdam
Parent Company: Elsevier-NDU nv (qv)
Subjects: Life Sciences, Biochemistry, Biological Sciences, Neurosciences, Pharmaceutics
1978: 80 titles *1979:* 90 titles *Founded:* 1974
ISBN Publisher's Prefix: 0–444 or 0–7204

Elsevier's Wetenschappelijke Uitgeverij (Elsevier Scientific Publishing Co) BV+, Jan van Galenstr 335, Postbus 330, 1000 AH Amsterdam
Dir: Dr V M Atkins
Parent Company: Elsevier-NDU nv (qv)
Subjects: Social Science, Technology, Chemistry, Earth Sciences, Agricultural Sciences, Multilingual Dictionaries
1977: 114 titles *1978:* 85 titles

Enschede en Zonen Grafische Inrichting BV+*, Klokhuisplein 5, Postbus 114, 2000 AC Haarlem Tel: (023) 319240 Telex: 41049

Eska*, Lijnmarkt 41–43, Utrecht Tel: (030) 328411 Telex: 47188
Publisher: Cees Smaling
Subjects: Periodicals, Hobbies

Europese Bibliotheek Uitgeverij Boekhandel Antiquariaat*, Gasthuisstr 12, Zaltbommel Tel: (04180) 3144
Man Dir: J C Lissenberg; *Assistant Dir:* M Uijthaven
Orders to: Korte Steigerstr 12–14, Zaltbommel
Subjects: History, Topography
Founded: 1963
Bookshop: Europese Bibliotheek, Gasthuisstr 12, Zaltbommel
ISBN Publishers Prefix: 90–288

Uitgeverij **F E D** BV, part of the Kluwer Group (qv)

Facsimile Uitgaven Nederland BV (FUN), subsidiary of Theatrum Orbis Terrarum (qv)

NV **Falkplan**/CIB+, Zichtenburglaan 52, Postbus 43107, 2504 AC The Hague Tel: (070) 299180 Cable Add: falkplan den haag Telex: 33290
Publisher: Edmond Gerrit Niessen; *Sales Manager:* Aad Kistemaker; *Editorial:* Martinus de Smit
Subsidiary Company: Djambatan BV (qv)
Subject: Maps

Frank **Fehmers** Productions+, Herengracht 487, Amsterdam Tel: (020) 238766 Cable Add: Intpubcon Telex: 16740 fepro nl
Man Dir: Frank Fehmers; *Rights & Permissions:* Nancy Patricia Lund
Associated Companies: FFP Licensing North America, FFV Licensing Latin America
Subject: Juveniles
1977: 25 titles *1978:* 25 titles
Miscellaneous: Firm arranges for international book & film coproductions
ISBN Publishers Prefix: 90–6151

Fibula-Van Dishoeck+*, Nieuwe S'Gravenlandseweg 17–19, Postbus 17, Bussum Tel: (02159) 34241 Cable Add: Unieboek
Man Dir: H Dijkstra
Subjects: Art, History, Social Science
Miscellaneous: Firm is a member of the Unieboek Group, Netherlands (qv)

Focus Elsevier BV+*, Rivierstaete, Amsteldijk 166, Amsterdam, Postbus 70707 Tel: (020) 5413413 Cable Add: Elsbook Telex: 14481
Man Dir: J Schilt
Parent Company: Elsevier-NDU nv (qv)

Uitgeverij De **Fontein** BV+, Parkstr 33, Postbus 308, 3740 AH Baarn Tel: (02154) 18441 Telex: beka-43272
Man Dir: H Pijfers
Subjects: General Fiction & Nonfiction, Juveniles, High-priced Paperbacks
1977: 30 titles *Founded:* 1946
Miscellaneous: Firm is a member of the Combo Group, Netherlands (qv)
ISBN Publishers Prefix: 90–261

Fontes Pers (APA)*, Postbus 1850, NL-1000 BW Amsterdam
Parent Company: APA (Academic Publishers Association) (qv)
Subjects: Maritime History, History of Law
ISBN Publisher's Prefix: 90–302; 90–6039

Foris Publications, Postbus 509, 3300 AM Dordrecht (Located at: Nijverheidsweg 65, HI Ambacht) Tel: (01858) 2622 Cable Add: Intergraph Dordrecht Telex: 29337 icg nl
Man Dir: Henk J La Porte; *Sales:* Mrs E C Ijsselsijn-Oosterling
Parent Company: Intercontinental Graphics Holland BV
Subsidiary Companies: Interset Holland, ICG Printing BV
1978: 2 titles *1979:* 10 titles *Founded:* 1978
ISBN Publisher's Prefix: 90–701

W **Gaade** BV+, Postbus 10, 3958 ZT Amerongen Tel: (03434) 1044
Man Dir: Marinus Beck
Subjects: Art, Biology, Cultural History, General Science, Nature, Illustrated books, Co-productions
1977: 15 titles *1978:* 15 titles *Founded:* 1954
ISBN Publishers Prefix: 90–6017

Van **Gennep** Ltd+, Nes 128, Amsterdam C Tel: (020) 247033
Man Dirs: R O van Gennep, J H Jansen; *Foreign Rights:* Ms. Annelies de Korver
Bookshops: Van Gennep Nieuwezijds, Nieuwe Zijds Voorburgwal 330, Amsterdam C; Boekhandel Van Gennep, Nes 128, Amsterdam C; Boekhandel Van Gennep, Grimburgwal 1–5, Amsterdam C; Boekhandel Van Gennep, Oude Binnenweg 131b, Rotterdam
Subjects: Belles Lettres, Poetry, History, Philosophy, Political Science, Economics, Marxist Publications
1977: 29 titles *1978:* 35 titles *Founded:* 1969
ISBN Publishers Prefix: 90–6012

BV Uitgeversbedryf Het **Goede Boek**, Koningin Wilhelminastr 8, Postbus 122, 1270 AC Huizen Tel: (02152) 53508
Dir: W E J Rikmans; *Advertising Dir:* F Rikmans
Subject: Children's Books
1977: 21 titles *1978:* 29 titles
ISBN Publishers Prefix: 90-240

De **Gooise** Uitgeverij+*, Nieuwe S'Gravenlandseweg 17-19, Postbus 17, Bussum Tel: (02159) 34241 Cable Add: Unieboek, Bussum
Subjects: Sports, Games
Miscellaneous: Firm is a member of the Unieboek Group, Netherlands (qv)
ISBN Publishers Prefix: 90-616

G B van **Goor** Zonen's Uitgeversmaatschappij BV+*, Riverstaete, Amsteldijk 166, Amsterdam Tel: (020) 5412333
Manager: H de Bruijn
Subjects: History, Music, Medicine, Secondary & Primary Textbooks, Educational Materials
Founded: 1839
ISBN Publishers Prefix: 90-00

Van **Gorcum** BV+, Industrieweg 38, NL-8500 Assen Tel: (05920) 15647 Cable Add: Vangorcum Telex: 77101
Man Dirs: H M G Prakke, G Vlieghuis; *Dirs:* J W Meijer (General & Academic Books), K W J van Rossum (Dekker & Van de Vegt, Nijmegen); H Ijzerman (Secondary & Primary Textbooks & School supply); *Sales:* A W J Rousseau; *Rights & Permissions:* D. Bakkes
Orders to: Van Gorcum, PO Box 43, Assen
Subjects: Social Science, Anthropology, Medicine, History, Language & Literature, Law, Philosophy, Psychology, Economics, Religion, Geography, Education, University Textbooks, Educational Materials
1977: 93 titles *1978:* 100 titles *Founded:* 1800
Subsidiary: Dekker en Van de Vegt, Netherlands (qv)
ISBN Publisher's Prefixes: 90 232 (Van Gorcum BV), 90-255 (Dekker en Van de Vegt)

J H **Gottmer** Publishers+*, Postbus 555, Haarlem, NL-1542 (Located at: Prof van Vlotenweg 1a, Bloemendaal) Tel: (023) 257150 Telex: 41856
Dir: Mrs H V M Gottmer; *Editorial:* J F Schoolenaar; *Publicity:* M P Gottmer
Subjects: General Fiction, Religion, Juveniles, Educational, General Nonfiction
1977: 100 titles *Founded:* 1937
ISBN Publisher's Prefix: 90-257

BV v/hB **Gottmer's** Uitgeversbedrijf*, Sint Annastraat 167, Postbus 103, 6500 AC Nijmegen Tel: (080) 231098
Man Dir: B Gottmer
Subjects: Religion, Humour, Cartoons, Scientific Works, Mysticism, Poetry
1977: 12 titles *Founded:* 1950
ISBN Publisher's Prefix: 90-6075

S **Gouda** Quint+, Postbus 1148, 6801 MK Arnhem (Located at: Willemsplein 2, Arnhem) Tel: (085) 454762
Man Dir: K H Mulder
Parent Company: Kluwer Group (qv)
Subjects: Textbooks, Law, Taxation, Periodicals
1978: 15 titles *Founded:* 1739
Miscellaneous: 77 new instalments to publications published in 1978
ISBN Publisher's Prefix: 90-6000

De **Graaf** Publishers, Zuideinde 40, Postbus 6, NL-2420 AA Nieuwkoop Tel: (01725) 1461 Cable Add: Degraaf Nieuwkoop
Man Dir: Bob de Graaf
Subjects: Reference, Religion, University Textbooks
1978: 350 titles *Founded:* 1959
Subsidiary: Miland Publishers, Postbus 6, NL-2420 AA Nieuwkoop (qv)
ISBN Publishers Prefix: 90-6004

B R **Grüner** BV, Nieuwe Herengracht 31, 1011 RM Amsterdam Tel: (020) 264371 Cable Add: Veriditas
Publisher: Bruno Roland Grüner
Subjects: Philosophy, Religion, Social Science, Periodicals, Poetry, Politics, Classical history
1977: 16 titles *1978:* 18 titles

Uitg Mij W de **Haan**+*, Nieuwe S'Gravenlandseweg 17-19, Postbus 17, Bussum Tel: (02159) 34241 Cable Add: Unieboek, Bussum
Subjects: Art, Geography
Miscellaneous: Firm is a member of the Unieboek Group, Netherlands (qv)

Ten **Hagen** BV+*, Carnegiepl 5, Postbus 34, The Hague Tel: (070) 924311
Subjects: Fiction, Periodicals
Miscellaneous: Firm is a member of the Kluwer Group, Netherlands (qv)

Adolf M **Hakkert** BV*, Spuistr 90A, Amsterdam C Tel: (020) 64359
Dir: A M Hakkert
Subjects: Classical Philology, Archaeology
ISBN Publishers Prefix: 90-256

De **Harmonie**, Postbus 3547, 1016 AJ Amsterdam (Located at: Singel 390, Amsterdam) Tel: (20) 245181
Man Dir: Jaco Groot; *Rights & Permissions:* Dieneke Corvers
Associate Company: Gaberbocchus Press
Subjects: Modern Dutch and International Literature, Illustrated Books, Juveniles, Humour
1978: 15 titles *1979:* 15 titles *Founded:* 1972
ISBN Publisher's Prefix: 90-6169

Uitgeverij ten **Have** NV*+, Bremstr 11, Postbus 1, Baarn Tel: (02154) 18241 Telex: beka-43272
Man Dir: Ton van der Worp
Subjects: History, Religion, Paperbacks, Maps
Founded: 1831
Miscellaneous: Firm is a member of the Combo Group, Netherlands (qv)
ISBN Publishers Prefix: 90-259

R **Hazewinkel** Jnz's Uitg Mij BV+*, Gedempte Zuiderdiep 24, Groningen Tel: (050) 188111

Helmond*+, Churchil-laan 107, Postbus 23, Helmond Tel: (04920) 39802 Telex: 51337
Man Dir: Dr M H J Hendriks Jr
Subjects: How-to, Juveniles, Low- & High-priced Paperbacks, Primary Textbooks, Reference
1978: 200 titles *Founded:* 1913
ISBN Publishers Prefix: 90-252

Alexander **Herzen** Foundation*, 268 Amstel, Amsterdam Tel: (020) 225343
Subject: Russian Fiction & Nonfiction
Founded: 1969

Uitgeverij **Heuff**+*, Postbus 40, 2420 AA Nieuwkoop (Located at: Bachstr 24, 2421 TS Nieuwkoop) Tel: (01725) 1649 Cable Add: Heuff/Nieuwkoop
Man Dir: H Heuff
Subjects: Music, Art, History, Illustrated Books, Juveniles
1977: 12 titles *1978:* 21 titles *Founded:* 1970
ISBN Publisher's Prefix: 90-6141

Uitgeverij **Heureka**+, Postbus 40, 2420 AA Nieuwkoop (Located at: Bachstr 24, 2421 TS Nieuwkoop) Tel: (01725) 1649
Man Dir: F H B Cladder
Subjects: History (Political, Social & Cultural)
1977: 5 titles *1978:* 6 titles *Founded:* 1976
ISBN Publisher's Prefix: 90-6262

Gérard Th van **Heusden** (APA)*, Postbus 1850, NL-1000 BW Amsterdam
Parent Company: APA (Academic Publishers Associated) (qv)
Subjects: Bibliography, Typography, History of Printing
ISBN Publisher's Prefix: 90-6024

Hippoboek/Studio de Zuid, see Zuidgroep BV

G W **Hissink** & Co (APA)*, Postbus 1850, NL-1000 BW Amsterdam
Parent Company: APA (Academic Publishers Associated) (qv)
Subjects: History of the Fine and Graphic Arts
ISBN Publishers Prefix: 90-6025

Van **Holkema** en Warendorf+*, Nieuwe S'Gravenlandseweg 17-19, Postbus 17, Bussum Tel: (02159) 34241 Cable Add: Unieboek, Bussum
Subjects: Fiction, Juveniles
Miscellaneous: Firm is a member of the Unieboek Group, Netherlands (qv)

Holland+, Spaarne 110, 2011 CM Haarlem Tel: (023) 323061
Man Dir: Rolf van Ulzen; *Sales Dir:* Mike de Wijs; *Permissions:* Rolf van Ulzen
Subjects: General Fiction, Belles Lettres, Poetry, Reference, Religion, Juveniles, High-priced Paperbacks, General Science
Founded: 1922
ISBN Publishers Prefix: 90-251

Holland University Press BV (APA)*, Postbus 1850, NL-1000 BW Amsterdam
Parent Company: APA (Academic Publishers Associated) (qv)
Subjects: Academic Books on the Humanities, European Studies
ISBN Publisher's Prefix: 90-302

Hollandia BV, Beukenlaan 16-20, Postbus 70, Baarn Tel: (02154) 18941 Cable Add: Hollandia, Baarn Telex: 43776 incom attn Hollandia
Man Dir: J Muntinga
Subjects: General (by Dutch and translated foreign authors), Nautical, Water Sports
1977: 60 titles *1978:* 68 titles *Founded:* 1899
Bookclub: (part-owner) Nederlandse Lezerskring
ISBN Publisher's Prefix: 90-6045

NV **I C U** (Informatie en Communicatie Unie NV)+, Burg Van Royensingel 19, Postbus 1115, Zwolle Tel: (05200) 15910
Miscellaneous: Members of the ICU Group: Samsom Uitgeverij BV (qv), A W Sijthoff International Publishing Co BV (qv), A W Sijthoff's Uitg Mij BV (qv), H D Tjeenk Willink BV (qv), Wolters Noordhoff BV (qv) (all Netherlands); Groner Publications Ltd, UK (qv); Aspen Systems Corporation, USA
ISBN Publisher's Prefixes: 90-14 (Samsom), 90-6092 (Tjeenk Willink), 90-01 (Wolters Noordhoff)

Stichting **I V I O**+, Maerlanthuis, Maerlant 2, Postbus 37, 8200 AA Lelystad Tel: (03200) 26514
Subject: Educational
1978: 10 titles

Icob, an imprint of Septuaginta BV Uitgeverij (qv)

Ideeboek BV, Cronenburg 75, 1081 GM Amsterdam
Parent Company: Meijer Pers BV (qv)

Uitgeverij **In den Toren**+*, Bremstr 11, Postbus 1, Baarn Tel: (02154) 8241 Telex: 43272
Man Dir: Aize de Visser
Subjects: History, Social Sciences, Politics
Miscellaneous: Firm is a member of the Combo Group (qv)

Inter-European Editions, De Lairessestr 90, Amsterdam 1007 Tel: 764044/45 Cable Add: Adiwes Amsterdam Telex: 1406 wssnl
Operations: Jan Fleere; *Marketing:* Frans Gianotten
Parent Company: Addison-Wesley BV (qv)
Subsidiary Company: Inter-Editions, Paris, France
Subjects: General Science, University Textbooks, General Reading
ISBN Publisher's Prefix: 0–201

B M Israel BV, NZ Voorburgwal 264, 1012 LS Amsterdam Tel: 247040 Cable Add: Isrealbook
Subjects: Reference, History of Medicine, Sciences, Arts

Nico **Israel***, Keizersgracht 526, 1017 EK Amsterdam Tel: (020) 222255 Cable Add: Ennibook Telex: 14070 ashni nl
Man Dir: Nico Israel
Subjects: History, Reference, University Textbooks, Geography, Cartography, Bibliography, Travel, Periodicals
1977–78: 5 titles *Founded:* 1950
Miscellaneous: Associate Company of A Asher & Co BV (qv); and Theatrum Orbis Terrarum (qv), both Amsterdam
ISBN Publishers Prefix: 90–6072

Stichting De **Jonge** Onderzoekers, see Stichting DJO

Dr W **Junk** BV+, Publishers, Lange Voorhout 9, Postbus 13713, 2501 ES-The Hague Tel: (070) 463256
Publisher: Wil R Peters
Subjects: Natural Science, Medicine
1977: 43 titles *1978:* 40 titles *Founded:* 1899
Miscellaneous: Firm is a member of the Kluwer Group, Netherlands (qv)

K B S, see Katholieke Bijbelstichting

Uitgeverij Van **Kampen** BV+, Nassaulaan 10, Postbus 4, Baarn Tel: (02154) 13480/16646 Cable Add: Stanu nl Telex: 43580
Miscellaneous: Firm is a subsidiary of Standaard Uitgeverij en Distributie BV, Netherlands (qv)

PN Van **Kampen & Zoon** BV, Nassaulaan 10, Baarn Tel: (02154) 13480
Subjects: Belles Lettres, How–to, Art, History, Literature, Popular Science, Fiction, Architecture, Maps, Games, Sports
Founded: 1841

Katholieke Bijbelstichting, Baroniestraat 43, PB 27, 5280 AA Boxtel Tel: 04116 73537
Subjects: Religious literature on practical aspects of Catholic Bible work in Belgium and the Netherlands
1978: 15 titles

Uitgeverij **Kluitman** Alkmaar BV, Postbus 123, 1800 AC Alkmaar (Located at: Kelvinstraat 20, Heerhugowaard) Tel: (02207) 17326
Dirs: P Kluitman, W Gerla
Subject: Juveniles
1977: 405 titles *Founded:* 1864
ISBN Publishers Prefix: 90–206

Kluwer Group, Stromarkt 8, Deventer Tel: (05700) 74411 Telex: 49295
Man Dirs: B Zevenbergen, A M Resius, J Somerwil
Members of the Kluwer Group in the Netherlands: Publishing Houses: Bert Bakker (qv); Bohn, Scheltema & Holkema (qv); Uitgeversmij. Born (qv); Contact, Educaboek (qv); Eska (qv); FED, Gouda Quint (qv); Ten Hagen (qv); ID-Tijdschriften; Dr W Junk (qv); Kluwer Algemene Boeken (qv); Kluwer's Couranten Bedrijf (qv); Kluwer Fiscaal Juridisch (qv); Kluwer Publiekstijdschriften; Kluwer Sociaal-Wetenschappelijk (qv); Kluwer Technische Boeken (qv); Kluwer Technische Tijdschriften; Kluwerpers; Kosmos (qv); Libresso; Van Loghum Slaterus (qv); Nederlandse Bouw-Dokumentatie; Martinus Nijhoff (qv); Noorduijn (qv); Oosthoek (qv); Reidel Publishing (qv); Scheltens & Giltay; Schoolpers (qv); Stam/Robijns (qv); Stam Technische Boeken (qv); Stam Tijdschriften (qv); Stenfert Kroese; Tjeenk Willink/Noorduijn (qv); W E J Tjeenk Willink (qv); L J Veen (qv); Zomer & Keuning Boeken (qv); Z & K Tijdschriften
Members outside the Netherlands: Eskabel; Heideland-Orbis; Uitgeverij Kluwer (qv); Plantyn (qv) (all in Belgium); Hulton Educational Publications; Kluwer Publishing Ltd; Van Leer; Stanley Thornes/Stam Press (qv) (all in UK); Kommentator (qv); Metzner (qv); Verlag Schubert; Verlag H Stam; Thalhammer Verlags GmbH (all in Federal Republic of Germany); Delta, Spès SA, Switzerland (qqv); Kluwer Boston Inc; Nijhoff Boston (both in USA)
Affiliate Company: Succes (qv)
Subjects: Law and Taxation, Academic Publications in various fields, Education, Technical, Encyclopaedias, Trade Books, Graphic Industries, Newspapers and Periodicals
Bookshops: Broese Kemink, Utrecht; Dekker Van de Vegt, Nijmegen; De Gelderse Boekhandel, Arnhem; Boekhandel Gianotten, Tilburg — Breda; Praamstra, Deventer; Scheltema Holkema Vermeulen, Amsterdam — Haarlem; Stamboekhandel, Eindhoven — Venlo; Verwijs & Stam, The Hague; Wetenschappelijke Boekhandel Rotterdam, Rotterdam
Founded: 1889
ISBN Publisher's Prefixes: 90–6117 (Kluwer NV), 90–313 (Bohn, Scheltema & Holkema), 90–11 (Educaboek), 90–267 (Kluwer Soc-Wet), 90–201 (Kluwer Tec), 90–6001 (Van Loghum Slaterus), 90–247 (Martinus Nijhoff), 90–207 (Stenfert-Kroese), 90–6117 (Kluwer Algemene Boeken), 90–200 (Kluwer Fiscale en Juridische Boeken), 90–6019 (Bert Bakker), 90–254 (Uitgeverij Contact), 90–204 (Veen), 90–210 (Zomer & Keuning)

Kluwer Algemene Boeken BV+, Postbus 235, 6710 BE Ede (Located at: Kernhemseweg 7, Ede) Tel: (08380) 19031 Cable Add: Zkede Telex: 45836 Zkede
Man Dir: J J Mons; *Editorial:* Bert Onnink, Martin van Huijstee, Benno von Lochem, Rien Meyer, Piet Terlouw; *Permissions:* Kees van der Sloot; *Marketing:* Hans de Snoo
Subjects: How–to, General Science, Atlases, Domestic, Countryside, Needlework, Novels, Human Relations, Religion
Founded: 1970
Miscellaneous: Firm is a member of the Kluwer Group, Netherlands (qv)
ISBN Publishers Prefix: 90–6117

Kluwer Fiscale en Juridische Boeken en Tijdschriften+, Staverenstr 13, Postbus 23, 7400 GA Deventer Tel: (05700) 91911 Telex: 49295
Man Dir: J H Brouwer; *Sales/Publicity:* M Nieuwenhuis; *Production:* G J Hupse
Subsidiary Companies: Alfred Metzner, Kommentator Verlag – both in German Federal Republic
Br Offs: Antwerp, Belgium; Boston, USA
Subjects: Law, Taxation, Labour Law and Industrial Relations, Social Security; Periodicals
Bookshops: 10 associated bookshops
1977: 200 titles
Miscellaneous: Firm is an Associate Company of Kluwer Group (qv), Netherlands
ISBN Publisher's Prefixes: 90–268, 90–200, 90–312

Kluwer Sociaal-Wetenschappelijke Boeken en Tijdschriften+, Postbus 23, 7400 GA Deventer Tel: (05700) 20577 Telex: 49774
Publisher: Wouter van Zeytveld
Subjects: Business, Economics, Periodicals
Miscellaneous: Firm is a member of the Kluwer Group, Netherlands (qv)
1978: 60 titles
ISBN Publishers Prefix: 90–267

Kluwer Technische Boeken BV+, Brink 25, Postbus 23, 7400 GA Deventer Tel: (05700) 74411 Telex: 49295 Kluwer dv
Man Dir: Noud H L van Herk; *Editorial:* Wim van Oosten-John Smal; *Foreign Rights:* Oeble Hoekstra; *Sales:* Jan Willems; *Production:* Dick Laus
Subsidiary Companies: Kluwer Technische Boeken; Santvoortbeeklaan, Deurne (both Belgium)
Subjects: Electronics, Motor Engineering, Hobbies, Do-it-yourself, Engineering, Dictionaries
1977: 52 titles
Miscellaneous: Firm is a member of the Kluwer Group, Netherlands (qv)
ISBN Publishers Prefix: 90–2010

Kluwers Couranten Bedrijf+*, Assenstr 8–14, Deventer
Dir: H J van den Beld
Miscellaneous: Firm is a member of the Kluwer Group, Netherlands (qv)

F **Knuf** Publishers, Postfach 720, 4116 ZJ Buren Tel: 034471691
Subjects: Musicology and Musical Theory, Biography and Musical History, Periodicals
1978: 16 titles

Uitgeversmaatschappij J H **Kok** BV+, Gildestraat 5, 8263 AH Kampen Tel: (05202) 13545 Cable Add: Kok Kampen Telex: 42721 jh kok nl
Man Dir: W E Steunenberg; *Assistant Man Dir:* A C Van Dam; *Editorial:* Gerrit Brinkman, Rien Ipenburg; *Rights & Permissions:* Tineka Bouma
Subjects: General Fiction, Belles Lettres, Poetry, Biography, History, How-to, Art Philosophy, Religion, Textbooks, Educational Materials, Reference, Juveniles, Psychology, General & Social Science, Low- & High-priced Paperbacks
1977: 300 titles *Founded:* 1894
Book Club: VCL (series of novels) (qv)

Subsidiaries: J N Voorhoeve, The Hague (Religion, Educational Materials, Juveniles); Uitgeverij Omniboek, The Hague (Juveniles, Belles Lettres, General Nonfiction)
ISBN Publishers Prefix: 90-242

Kooyker Scientific Publications BV, Postbus 23096, 3016 AA Rotterdam (Located at: Koningin Emmaplein 1, Rotterdam) Tel: (010) 363009
Man Dir: W A Donker; *Sales and Publicity:* W A Donker
Subjects: Medicine, Psychology, Sociology, Education
1977: 16 titles *1978:* 18 titles *Founded:* 1975
ISBN Publishers Prefix: 90-6212

Kosmos BV+, Keizersgracht 133, 1015 CJ Amsterdam Tel: (020) 240897
Publisher: S P Bakker; *Editorial:* Willem G Benthem, P Smulders, J Vonk, M Both
Subjects: Children, Juveniles, Crafts and Hobbies, Natural History, Plants and Gardening, Dogs, Travelling, Psychology
Miscellaneous: Firm is an associated company of Kluwer Group (qv), Netherlands

Kugler Medical Publications BV*, PO Box 516, 1180 AM Amstelveen Tel: (3120) 412340 Cable Add: Medpub Amstelveen Telex: 18180
Man Dir: Shimon Kugler
Subject: Medical

Allert de **Lange** BV+, Damrak 62, 1012 LM Amsterdam Tel: (020) 246744

Uitgeverij **Lannoo**, Lichttorenhoofd 28-30, Postbus 1009, Etten-Leur (N-Br) Tel: (01608) 13750 Telex: 54202 stadi NL
Subjects: General Nonfiction covering Travel, Philosophy, Genetics, Reference, Children's, Religious
Miscellaneous: Firm is a subsidiary of Standaard Uitgeverij en Distributie BV, Netherlands (qv)
1978: 48 titles
ISBN Publishers Prefix: 90-209

Leiden University Press, c/o Martinus Nijhoff, PO Box 566, Lange Voorhout 9-11, 2501 CN The Hague Tel: (070) 469460 Telex: 34164 Cable Add: Books Hague
Subjects: History, Languages, Law, Social Sciences, Biology, Medicine
1978: 16 titles
ISBN Publishers Prefix: 90-6021

Lemniscaat+, Vijverlaan 48, Postbus 4066, Rotterdam Tel: 141744 Cable Add: Lemniscaat Rotterdam
Man Dir: J L Boele van Hensbroek; *Editorial:* Dr Marijke Boele van Hensbroek-Ressink; *Rights & Permissions:* Els Pikaar
Subjects: Juveniles, Picture Books, Psychology, Social Science
1979: 30 titles *Founded:* 1963
ISBN Publishers Prefix: 90-6069

Uitgeverij **Leopold** BV+, Badhuisweg 232, The Hague Tel: (070) 549604
Man Dir: Liesbeth ten Houten; *Permissions:* Jacolien Kingmans
Subjects: General Fiction, Juveniles, History, Philosophy, High-priced Paperbacks
1977: 40 titles *1978:* 40 titles *Founded:* 1923
Miscellaneous: Firm is a subsidiary of BV Uitgeverij Nijgh & Van Ditmar, Netherlands (qv)
ISBN Publishers Prefix: 90-258

Littera Scripta Manet*, Joppelaan 60, PO Box 20, 7213 ZG- Gorssel Tel: (05759) 1950
Man Dir: A Rutgers; *Editorial:* Mrs R L Rutgers-Schiff; *Other Offices:* A Rutgers
Subject: General Science
Bookshop: International Hobby-Bookshop, Gorssel
1977: 8 titles *Founded:* 1947
ISBN Publishers Prefix: 90-6036

Uitg Mij van der **Loeff** BV+, Getfertsingel 41, Postbus 28, Enschede Tel: (053) 320420
Subjects: Newspapers, Free Sheets

Van **Loghum** Slaterus+, Geert Grootestr 4, Postbus 23, NL-6600 Deventer Tel: (05700) 10811 Telex: 49295
Publisher: Fons Drabbe
Subjects: Humanities, Public Health, Education, Psychology, Social Science, Linguistics, Languages, Periodicals
Miscellaneous: Firm is a member of the Kluwer Group, Netherlands (qv)
1978: 46 titles
ISBN Publishers Prefix: 90-6001

Luctor Publishing — Stadler & Sauerbier BV*, Weegbreestr 11, Postbus 33017, NL-3012 Rotterdam Tel: (010) 180081 Cable Add: Sensoffset Telex: 23411
Subjects: Juveniles, Educational, Calendars

Uitgeverij **Luitingh** BV, Hilversumseweg 16, 1251 EX-Laren, Noord Holland Tel: (02153) 87214/86567 Cable Add: Luitingh Laren Telex: 730 96 luiti nl
Man Dir: Peter J Houbolt
Subsidiary Companies: Uitgeverij Skarabee BV; Boek Promotions BV; Novapres BV
Subjects: General Fiction and Nonfiction, Science Fiction, Games and Pastimes, History, How-to, Reference, Religion, Juveniles, Low- & High-priced Paperbacks, General Science, Educational Materials; Sponsored Books, Homecrafts (cookery, gardening etc)
1977: about 150 titles *1978:* 150 titles *Founded:* 1946
ISBN Publisher's Prefix: 90-245

Otto **Maier** Benelux BV*, Heliumweg 16, Amersfoort Tel: (03490) 11445 Telex: 47991
Subjects: Architecture, Hobbies, Juveniles, Nonfiction

Malmberg BV+, Leeghwaterlaan 16, Postbus 233, 's-Hertogenbosch Tel: (073) 215565 Cable Add: Malmberg 's-Hertogenbosch Telex: 50058
Man Dir: Dr O O Gorter; *Manager, International Department:* Joh J Arends; *Publishers:* F Geurts (Primary Education), Dr M J van Dalen (Secondary Education), G Struyk (Educational Magazines)
Subjects: Pre-school, Primary & Secondary Textbooks, Educational Materials, Educational Juveniles, Teaching Equipment for Physics, Chemistry and Biology
1978: 100 titles *Founded:* 1885
Miscellaneous: Firm is a member of VNU NV Group, Netherlands (qv)
ISBN Publishers Prefix: 90-208

Meijer Pers BV, PO Box 7897, 1008-AB Amsterdam (Located at: Cronenburg 75, 1081 GM-Amsterdam) Tel: (020) 441066
Man Dir: J J Woudt; *Permissions:* Miss Berty Bakker
Parent Company: Meijer Wormerveer NV, Wormerveer
Subsidiary Companies: Ideeboek BV (qv), Amsterdam

Subjects: Do-it-yourself Books, Cookery and Sponsored Books Generally
1977: 50 titles *1978:* 45 titles *Founded:* 1966
Book Club: Librah

Meinema/Waltman+, Hippolytusbuurt 4, Postbus 3150, Delft Tel: (015) 125915
Subject: Textbooks

Educatieve Uitgeverij **Meulenhoff** Educatief BV+, Postbus 100, 1000 AC Amsterdam (Located at: Herengracht 507, 1017 BV Amsterdam) Tel: (020) 235707 Cable Add: Manuscript Telex: 16234
Man Dirs: D van Foeken, Cl W Suermondt, AC van Hoek; *Editorial:* R Nouwen, T A vd Veen, W ten Oever, T Scheffer
Parent Company: Meulenhoff en Co BV (at above address)
Associate Companies: Meulenhoff Informatief BV, Meulenhoff International BV, Meulenhoff Nederland BV (qqv)
Subjects: Educational Materials, Textbooks
1979: 106 titles
ISBN Publishers Prefix: 90-280

Meulenhoff Informatief BV+, Postbus 100, 1000 AC Amsterdam (Located at: Herengracht 507, 1017 BV Amsterdam) Tel: (020) 235707 Cable Add: Manuscript Telex: 16234
Editorial Dir: Mrs E van Unen
Parent Company: Meulenhoff en Co BV (at above address)
Associate Companies: Educatieve Uitgeverij Meulenhoff Educatief BV, Meulenhoff International BV, Meulenhoff Nederland BV (qqv)
Subjects: Informative Non-fiction, Reference
1979: 25 titles
ISBN Publisher's Prefix: 90-290

Meulenhoff International BV+, Postbus 100, 1000 AC Amsterdam (Located at: Herengracht 507, 1017 BV Amsterdam) Tel: (020) 235707/241611 Cable Add: Intart Telex: 16234
Man Dir: W J van Hoorn; *Editorial Dir:* B van Dobbenburgh
Parent Company: Meulenhoff en Co BV (at above address)
Associate Companies: Educatieve Uitgeverij Meulenhoff Educatief BV, Meulenhoff Informatief BV, Meulenhoff Nederland BV (qqv)
Subjects: Coproductions, General Nonfiction, Art
Miscellaneous: Firm's main activity is selling foreign rights internationally

Meulenhoff Nederland BV+, Postbus 100, 1000 AC Amsterdam (Located at: Herengracht 507, 1017 BV Amsterdam) Tel: (020) 235707 Cable Add: Manuscript Telex: 16234
Man Dir: Laurens van Krevelen; *Financial Dir:* Wim van der Wilk; *Editorial:* Wouter Donath Tieges; *Rights & Permissions:* Sarely Bourdrez
Parent Company: Meulenhoff & Co BV (at above address)
Associate Companies: Educatieve Uitgeverij Meulenhoff Educatief BV, Meulenhoff International BV, Meulenhoff Informatief BV (qqv)
Subjects: Dutch and translated foreign literature, Science Fiction, Detective Stories, Nonfiction
1978: 100 new titles, 60 reprints *Founded:* 1895
ISBN Publishers Prefix: 90-290

Miland Publishers, Zuideinde 40, Postbus 6, NL-2420 AA Nieuwkoop
Miscellaneous: Firm is a subsidiary of De Graaf Publishers, at same address (qv)
ISBN Publishers Prefix: 90-6003

Mirananda Publishers BV*, Zijdeweg 5A, Wassenaar 2270 Tel: (01751) 78471
Man Dir: Carolus Vehulst;
General Manager: Manda Plettenburg
Orders to: Centraal Boekhuis, Erasmusweg 10, Culemborg
Subjects: Art (Western and Oriental), Religion, Mysticism, Yoga, Theosophy, Astrology, Popular Science, Psychology, Philosophy, Quality Paperbacks, Linguistics, Education, Literature, Outstanding Children's Books
1977: 36 titles *Founded:* 1976
ISBN Publishers Prefix: 90-6271

Moussault's Uitgeverij BV+, Nassaulaan 10, Postbus 4, 3740 AA-Baarn Tel: (02154) 13480/16646 Cable Add: Stanu NL
Telex: 43580
Dir/Editorial/Permissions: I Gay;
Production: G Priem
Orders to: Standaard Uitgeverij en Distributie bv, Postbus 1009, 4870 BA-Etten-Leur
Subjects: Primary Textbooks, Horticulture, Hobbies, Illustrated Nature Guides, Antiques and Collecting
1979: 115 titles *Founded:* 1941
Miscellaneous: Firm is a subsidiary of Standaard Uitgeverij en Distributie BV, Netherlands (qv)
ISBN Publishers Prefix: 90-226

Mouton Publishers, Noordeinde 41, 2514 GC The Hague Tel: (070) 649910/11/12/13 Telex: 33630 mopub nl
Man Dir: A Bornkamp
Parent Company: (since 1977) Walter de Gruyter und Co, Federal Republic of Germany (qv)
Branch Offs: Editions Mouton & Cie, 7 rue Dupuytren, F-75006 Paris, France; Mouton Publishers, Walter de Gruyter Inc, 200 Saw Mill River Rd, Hawthorne, NY 10532, USA
Subjects: Anthropology, Art, Economics, Education, Geography, History, Law, Linguistics, Belles Lettres, Mathematics, Philosophy, Psychology, Religion, Social Science
Founded: 1954
ISBN Publishers Prefix: 90-279

De **Muiderkring** BV*, Nijverheidswerf 17-21, Postfach 10, NL-1351 Bussum 1400 AA Tel: 02159-31851 Telex: 15171
Man Dir: R Bayards; *Sales Dept:* P Oosterlaak
Subjects: Specialist Literature connected with Electronics, Hobbies

Mulder en Co, subsidiary of Bigot & Van Rossum NV (qv)

Mulder Holland BV, Transformatorweg 35, Postbus 8064, Amsterdam Tel: (020) 824805 Cable Add: Emzet Amsterdam
Telex: 14627
Subject: Juveniles
1979: 32 titles

J **Muusses** BV+, Kerkstr 20-3013, 1440 AA Purmerend Tel: (02990) 23746
Man Dir: D Struving
Subjects: History, Education, Music, How-to, General Science, Textbooks
1977: 18 titles *1978:* 18 titles *Founded:* 1873
ISBN Publisher's Prefix: 90-231

Uitgeverij **N I B**+, Postbus 144, Zeist (Located at: Wilhelminalaan 7, Zeist) Tel: (03404) 15631
Man Dir: Dr H C van Hummel; *Editorial:* H W J Jonker, A J W Boks
Bookseller: Netherlands Importing Booksellers, PO Box 144, Zeist
Subjects: Textbooks for Secondary Education on: Chemistry, Biology, Modern Languages, History
1977: 47 titles *1978:* 25 titles
ISBN Publishers Prefix: 0075-4

Nederland's Boekhuis BV*, Erasmusweg 10, Culemborg Tel: (03450) 4841
Dir: Ir R J Smedema
Subjects: General Fiction, Belles Lettres, Religion, Juveniles
Founded: 1919
ISBN Publishers Prefix: 90-6070

Nederlandsche Zondagsschool Vereeniging, Bloemgracht 65, NL-1016 KG Amsterdam
Tel: (020) 239121
Subjects: Religion, Juveniles
1978: 24 titles

Nederlandse Lezerskring Boek en Plaat BV+, Postbus 2201, 1000 EK Amsterdam (Located at: Wildenborch 2, 1112 XB Diemen) Tel: (020) 906911 Telex: 16188

Uitgeverij H **Nelissen** BV+, Duinlustweg 36, 2051 AB Overveen Tel: (023) 245481
Man Dir/Editorial/Permissions: R M M Nelissen; *Sales/Publicity:* Dick Boer; *Production:* Net Ekering
Subjects: General Fiction, Religion, Sociology, Politics, Education, Philosophy, High-priced Paperbacks
1978: 14 titles *Founded:* 1922
ISBN Publishers Prefix: 90-244

BV Uitgeverij **Nijgh en Van Ditmar**+, Badhuisweg 232, 2597 JS The Hague
Tel: (070) 512711
Man Dir: A J J Siebelink; *Editorial:* N D Dekker, A E Blatter, J D M Mulder, Miss J. Waerebeek; *Permissions:* Miss J Waerebeek
Subjects: General Fiction, Belles Lettres, Poetry, Biography, History, Juveniles, High-priced Paperbacks, Engineering, Secondary Textbooks, Home Economics
Founded: 1837
Subsidiaries (all in Netherlands): Uitgeverij Leopold BV (qv); Rotterdam University Press (qv)
ISBN Publishers Prefix: 90-236

Martinus **Nijhoff** Publishers+, Postbus 566, 2501 CN The Hague (Located at: Lange Voorhout 9-11, The Hague) Tel: (070) 469460 Cable Add: Books Hague
Dir: F H van Eysinga; *Production:* Mrs S Oostenrijk
Subjects: Biography, History, Music, Art, Philosophy, Religion, Textbooks, Reference, Psychology, Social Science, Medicine, Applied Sciences, Veterinary Sciences, Agriculture
Bookshop: Postbus 269, The Hague
Founded: 1853
Miscellaneous: Firm is a member of the Kluwer Group, Netherlands (qv)
ISBN Publishers Prefix: 90-247

Noord-Hollandsche Uitgeversmaatschappij BV (North Holland Publishing Company)+, Jan van Galenstraat 335, Amsterdam
Tel: (020) 5159222 Cable: nohum amsterdam Telex: 16479 epc nl
Dir: Dr W H Wimmers; *Deputy Dirs:* Dr P S H Bolman, Dr E H Fredriksson, Dr K Michielsen

Subjects: Mathematics, Information Processing, Management Science & Operation Research, Physics, Chemical Physics, Economics, Accountancy, Law, Linguistics, History, Humanities, Psychonomy
1978: 103 titles
Parent Company: NV Uitgeversmaatschappij Elsevier, The Netherlands (qv)

Noordhoff International Publishing, see Sijthoff & Noordhoff

Noorduijn BV+, Postbus 1148, 6801 MK Arnhem (Located at: Willemsplein 2, Arnhem) Tel: (085) 454762
Man Dir: K H Mulder
Parent Company: Kluwer Group (qv)
Subjects: Law and Taxation
1977: 3 titles *1978:* 3 titles *Founded:* 1819
Miscellaneous: 32 new instalments to publications published in 1978
ISBN Publisher's Prefix: 90-203

Omega Boek BV, Postbus 20072, 1000 HB Amsterdam (Located at: Sarphatistraat 13, 1017 WS Amsterdam) Tel: (020) 231969/245284
Orders to: Centraal Depot Culemborg
Imprints: De Centaur, Nieuwe Wieken, Triton Pers, Omega Jeugdboekerij, Oisterwijk
Subjects: General Fiction and Nonfiction, War Stories, Thrillers, Art, Children's Books, Gift Books
1977: 55 titles *1978:* 60 titles *Founded:* 1968
ISBN Publisher's Prefix: 90-6057, 90-6142, 90-70015

Uitgeverij **Omniboek**, subsidiary of Uitgeversmaatschappij J H Kok BV (qv)

Oosthoek*, Domstraat 5-13, Utrecht
Tel: (030) 334464
Man Dirs: H Smit, K Booden
Subject: Encyclopedia Publishers
ISBN Publishers Prefix: 90-6046

Orbit NV, Keisersgracht 526, Amsterdam, subsidiary of Theatrum Orbis Terrarum (qv)

Oriental Press BV (APA)*, Postbus 1850, NL-1000 BW Amsterdam
Parent Company: APA (Academic Publishers Associated) (qv)
Subjects: Oriental Studies, Text editions
ISBN Publisher's Prefix: 90-6023

Philo Press-van Heusden-Hissink & Co CV (APA)*, Postbus 1850, NL-1000 BW Amsterdam
Parent Company: APA (Academic Publishers Associated) (qv)
Subjects: Academic Books on the Arts and Humanities, History of Sciences, Oriental Studies
ISBN Publishers Prefix: 90-6022, 90-6024, 90-6025

Uitgeverij **Ploegsma**+*, Postbus 19857, 1000 GW Amsterdam (Located at: Keizersgracht 616, 1017 ER Amsterdam) Tel: (020) 262907
Man Dir: Paul Brinkman
Subjects: Children's books, Juveniles, How-to, Natural Science, Handicraft, Leisure
ISBN Publishers Prefix: 90-216

Polak en Van Gennep Uitg Mij BV+, Keizersgracht 608, 1017 EP-Amsterdam Tel: (020) 226288
Man Dir: B M Hosman
Subjects: Scientific Literature, General Literature
1977: 25 titles *1978:* 235 titles *Founded:* 1964
ISBN Publisher's Prefix: 90-253

NETHERLANDS

Pudoc, Centre for Agricultural Publishing and Documentation+, Marijkeweg 17, Postbus 4, 6700 AA Wageningen Tel: (08370) 19146 Telex: 45015
Man Dir: A Rutgers; *Sales Dir:* J Vermeulen
Subjects: Natural Science, Agriculture
1977: 30 titles *1978:* 30 titles *Founded:* 1957
ISBN Publishers Prefix: 90-220

Putsj Publications Antwerpen*, 86 Alice Hahonlei, NL-2120 Shoten Tel: (031) 589272 Telex: 32432
Subjects: Original-style colouring and reading books for infants (3–7 yrs)

Em **Querido's** Uitgeverij BV+, Singel 262, 1016 AC Amsterdam Tel: (020) 237195
Man Dir: Ary T Langbroek
Subjects: General Fiction, Belles Lettres, Poetry, Biography, History, Music, Art, Juveniles, Low-priced Paperbacks
1977: 143 titles *1978:* 124 titles *Founded:* 1915
Miscellaneous: Firm also publishes under Salamander Paperbacks imprint, and is an associate company of Uitgeverij De Arbeiderspers BV (qv) and Wetenschappelijke Uitgeverij BV (qv) (both in the Netherlands)
ISBN Publishers Prefix: 90-214

van **Reemst***, Nieuwe's Gravelandseweg 17–19, Postbus 17, Bussum
Tel: 02159/34241 Cable Add: Unieboek Bussum Telex: 43064
Subjects: Educational Books and Toys for very young children

D **Reidel** Publishing Co, Postbus 17, Dordrecht (Located at: Voorstraat 479–483, Dordrecht) Tel: (078) 135388 Cable Add: Reipubco Telex: 29245
Publisher: B Vance; *Sales and Promotion Manager:* J F Hattink; *Production:* R Doornebal; *Permissions:* J F Hattink
Parent Company: Kluwer Group (qv)
Subsidiary Companies: D Reidel, 160 Old Derby St, Hingham, Mass 02034, USA
Subjects: Philosophy, Humanities, General & Social Science, Technology, Linguistics, Mathematics, Astronomy, Chemistry, Environmental Sciences
1977: 80 titles *1978:* 73 titles
ISBN Publisher's Prefix: 90-277

Peter de **Ridder** Press BV*, Postbus 168, 2160 AD-Lisse (Located at: 8 Johan Vermeerstr, 2162 BJ Lisse) Tel: 15239
Dir: Peter de Ridder
Subjects: Semiotics, Linguistics, Literary Theory, Anthropology
1977: 20 titles *1978:* 32 titles *Founded:* 1974
ISBN Publishers Prefix: 90-316

Editions **Rodopi** NV*, Keizersgracht 302–304, Amsterdam Tel: (020) 227507
Dir: Fred van der Zee
Subjects: History, Philosophy, Religion, High-priced Paperbacks, University Textbooks, Languages and Literature, Classical Antiquity, Communications
1977: 36 titles *Founded:* 1966
ISBN Publisher's Prefix: 90-6203

Romen+*, Nieuwe S'Gravelandseweg 17–19, Bussum
Miscellaneous: Firm is a member of the Unieboek Group, Netherlands (qv)

Rotterdam University Press, Badhuisweg 232, The Hague Tel: (070) 512711
Man Dir: J Dijkema
Subjects: Economics, Development Planning, Social Science, University Textbooks

Founded: 1964
Miscellaneous: Firm is a subsidiary of BV Uitgeverij Nijgh en Van Ditmar, Netherlands (qv)
ISBN Publishers Prefix: 0-90237

Uitgeverij **S M D** BV (Spruyt, Van Mantgem en De Does)+, Postbus 63, 2300 AB Leiden (Located at: Langebrug 87, 2311 TJ Leiden) Tel: (071) 146541
Subjects: Medical, Educational, Technical
1977: 57 titles *1978:* 36 titles

S U N socialistische Uitgeverij, Bijleveldsingel 9, Nijmegen Tel: (080) 221700
Publicity/Permissions: Wilfried Nitterhoere
Subjects: Marxism, Culture, Philosophy, History of the Workers' Movements, Architecture, Periodicals — *Te Elfder Ure, Recht en Kritiek*
1977: 26 titles *1978:* 25 titles *Founded:* 1969
ISBN Publisher's Prefix: 90-6168

Samsom Uitgeverij BV+, Postbus 4, Alphen aan den Rijn Tel: (01720) 66633 Cable Add: Samsom Alphenrijn Telex: 39682
Dirs: Dr W P N Schrijver, C Verweij; *Editorial:* H J Demoet, F Gorter; *Rights & Permissions:* José van der Meer
Imprint: H D Tjeenk Willink BV
Subjects: Business, Fiscal Law, Management, Textbooks, Social Science, Computer Science, Administration, Public Health
1977: 146 titles *1978:* 120 titles *Founded:* 1882
Miscellaneous: Firm is a member of NV ICU (Informatie en Communicatie), Netherlands (qv)
ISBN Publishers Prefix: 90-14

Boekhandel **Scheltema Holkema Vermeulen** BV, Spui 10, 1012 WZ Amsterdam Tel: (020) 267212 Telex: 17193
Man Dir: M Bakker; *Commercial Man:* A E Harteveld
Subjects: Art, Economics, General & Social Science, History, Law, Medicine, Psychology
Founded: 1853
Bookshops: Spui 10, 1012 WZ Amsterdam; Santpoorterstr 70, 2023 DD Haarlem
Miscellaneous: Firm is a member of Kluwer Group Bookstores

Schipper*, Printers/Publishers BV, Klaaskampen 36, Postbus 141, Laren, Noord-Holland Tel: (02153) 15754 Cable Add: Printhouse Laren Telex: 43776 Inco nl att spp
Dir: C C Schipper
Subjects: Juveniles, Calendars

Schoolpers+*, PO Box 48, Culemborg
Subject: Textbooks
Miscellaneous: Firm is a member of the Kluwer Group, Netherlands (qv)

Schuyt en Co CV, Postbus 563, 2003 RN Haarlem (Located at: Gedempte Oude Gracht 35, 2011 GL Haarlem) Tel: (023) 325440 Telex: 41532 sco nl
General Manager: K C Schuyt; *Sales:* W G Kok
Subsidiary Company: Schuyt en Co nv, Hansahuis, Suikerrui 5, 2000 Antwerp, Belgium
Subjects: Juveniles, Art, History, Railways
1977: 18 titles *Founded:* 1953
ISBN Publisher's Prefix: 90-6097

Uitgeverij Gary **Schwartz**, Herengracht 22, Postbus 162, 3600 AD Maarssen Tel: (03465) 62778 Telex: 39556 habla

Dir & Other Offices: Gary Schwartz
Subjects: Fine Art Books
1977: 4 titles *1978:* 3 titles *Founded:* 1972
ISBN Publisher's Prefix: 90-6179

Semic Press, Brouwersgracht 97–99, Amsterdam Tel: 226341 Telex: 15558 semic nl
Man Dir: Hierro Guillermo
Subjects: Comic Magazines, Colouring Books, Albums, Pocket Books

Uitgeverij **Semper** Agendo BV+*, Prins Willem Alexanderlaan 601, Postbus 327, Apeldoorn Tel: (055) 773232

Septuaginta BV Uitgeverij, Postbus 392, 2400 AJ Alphen aan den Rijn (Located at: Ondernemingsweg 60, Alphen aan den Rijn) Tel: (01720) 23202 Telex: 39700 icob nl
Man Dir: Hans Meijer; *Editorial:* Peter Albarda
Parent Company: I C O B CV (at above address)
Imprint: Icob
Subjects: Art, Natural History, Reference, Illustrated
1978: 25 titles *1979:* approx 25 titles
Founded: 1969
ISBN Publisher's Prefix: 90-6113

Servire BV Uitgevers, Secr Varkevisserstr 52, 2225 LE Katwijk aan Zee Tel: (01718) 16741
Associate Companies: Momenta Publishing Ltd, UK (qv); Qalandar Verlag GmbH, Sauerbruchstr 8, D-708 Aalen 9, Federal Republic of Germany
Subsidiary Company: Hunter House Inc, Publishers, 748 East Bonita Ave, Suite 105, Pomona, CA 91767, USA
Subjects: Books in Dutch, German, English on Human Endeavour and Creativity, Mysticism, Alternative Living, Education, Psychology
Founded: 1932

Sijthoff & Noordhoff International Publishers+, Postbus 4, 2400 MA Alphen aan den Rijn (Located at: Stadhoudersplein 1, 2400 MA Alphen aan den Rijn) Tel: (1720) 62270 Telex: 39682
Man Dir/Editorial: Arne Visser; *Sales:* Rafael Grasso
Parent Company: ICU (qv)
Associate Companies: Samson Uitgeverij, Wolters-Noordhoff (qqv)
Branch Off: 20010 Century Boulevard, Germantown, Md 20767, USA
Subjects: International Law, International Political and Economic Relations, Pure and Applied Mechanics and Mathematics, Applied Science
1977: 70 titles *1978:* 90 titles *Founded:* 1839
Miscellaneous: The company combines two firms which formerly operated separately as A W Sijthoff International Publishing Co and Noordhoff International Publishing
ISBN Publisher's Prefix: 90-286

A W **Sijthoff's** Uitg Mij BV+, Postbus 4, 2400 MA- Alphen aan den Rijn
Tel: (01720) 62465 Cable Add: Sijthoff Alphen aan den Rijn Telex: 39682
Dir: Frans Pruyt; *Editorial:* Willemien Hoogendijk
Parent Company: Firm is a member of NV ICU (Informatie en Communicatie Unie) (qv)
Subjects: How-to, Fiction (Detective), Nonfiction, History, Illustrated books
1977: 60 titles *1978:* 55 titles *Founded:* 1851
ISBN Publisher's Prefix: 90-218

Uitgeverij **Skarabee** BV, subsidiary of Uitgeverij Luitingh BV (qv)

Smeets Illustrated Projects, Molenveldstr 90, Postbus 17, Weert Tel: (04950) 38055 Telex: 51101
Manager: A de Jong
Subject: Art

Uitgeverij Het **Spectrum** BV+, Park Voorn 4, 3454 JR De Meern Tel: (03406) 3737 Cable Add: Het Spectrum BV, De Meern Telex: 4677
Dir: R A J Huyzer
Orders to: Postbus 2073, 3500 GB Utrecht Amsterdam Boek Division: Wibautstr 129, Amsterdam Tel: (020) 934933 Telex: 15033 (Orders to: Postbus 543, Amsterdam)
Br Off: Bijkhoevelaan 12, B-2110 Wijnegem, Belgium
Subjects: General Fiction, Encyclopaedias, Religion, Science & Technical, Textbooks, Paperbacks, Juveniles, Partworks
1977: 350 titles *1978:* 450 titles *Founded:* 1935
Miscellaneous: Firm is a member of the VNU NV Group, Netherlands (qv)
ISBN Publishers Prefix: 90-274

Spectrum Amsterdam, International Publishing, Wibautstr 129, Postbus 107, Amsterdam Tel: (020) 926927 Telex: 15033
Man Dir: R Emmelkamp
Subjects: Encyclopaedias, Reference
1977: 4 titles *1978:* 4 titles

Spruyt, van Mantgem en de Does BV, see SMD

Staatsdrukkerij en Uitgeverijbedrijf*, Chr Plantijnstr 1, The Hague Tel: 814511
Man Dir: H J A M van Haaren
Subjects: Government Publications
ISBN Publishers Prefix: 90-9012

Stafleu's Wetenschappelijke Uitgeversmaatschappij BV+, and Stafleu en Tholen BV, Postbus 4, 2400 MA Alphen aan den Rijn (Located at: Stadhoudersplein 1, 2404 MA Alphen aan den Rijn) Tel: (01720) 62371 Cable Add: Stafleu Publishers Alphen aan der Rijn
Man Dirs: C L Stafleu, J B Oonk
Subjects: Medicine, Psychology, General Science, Nursing, Dental Science
1977: 35 titles *1978:* 32 titles *Founded:* 1947
ISBN Publisher's Prefixes: 90-6016/90-6065

Stam/Robijns+, Industrieweg 1, Postbus 48, 4100 AA Culemborg Tel: (03450) 3143 Telex: 47306
Dirs: Bob Balder, Andries Snoek
Subjects: Education, Educational Materials
Miscellaneous: Firm is a member of the Kluwer Group, Netherlands (qv)

Stam Technische Boeken+, Industrieweg 1, Postbus 48, 4100 AA Culemborg Tel: (03450) 3143 Telex: 47306
Publisher: Bob Balder
Subjects: Architecture, Chemistry, Electrical Engineering, Electronics, Earth Sciences, Industries, Crafts, Civil & Mechanical Engineering, Agriculture, Literary Criticism, Aviation, Mathematics, Physics, Law, Linguistics, Languages, Transport, Economics
Miscellaneous: Firm is a member of the Kluwer Group, Netherlands (qv)

Stam Tijdschriften BV+, PO Box 375, 2501 BG The Hague Tel: (070) 646814
Subjects: Engineering, Chemistry, Economics, Computers, Periodicals
Miscellaneous: Firm is a member of the Kluwer Group, Netherlands (qv)
1978: 5 titles

Standaard Uitgeverij en Distributie BV+, Lichttorenhoofd 28-30, Etten-Leur (N-Br) Tel: (01608) 13750
Subjects: Juveniles, Religion, Paperbacks
Subsidiaries: D A P-Reinaert Uitgaven, De Nederlandse Boekhandel, Standaard Uitgeverij (all in Belgium) (qqv); Uitgeverij Van Kampen BV, Uitgeverij Lannoo, Moussault's Uitgeverij BV, Het Wereldvenster BV Internationale Uitg Mij (all in The Netherlands) (qqv)
ISBN Publisher's Prefixes: 90-02 (Standaard), 90-266 (Moussault), 90-293 (Wereldvenster), 90-6091 (Van Kampen), 90-209 (Lanoo), 90-310 (Dap-Reinaert), 90-289, 90-292, 90-616 (Nederlandse Boekhandel)

Uitgeverij M **Stenvert** en Zoon BV+, Postbus 70, 7300 AB Apeldoorn (Located at: Sutton 10, Apeldoorn) Tel: (055) 414644

Uitgeverij W P Van **Stockum** en Zoon NV*, Noorderbeekdwarsstr 45-47, Postbus 6032, The Hague Tel: (070) 180721
Dir: H Sloterdijk
Subjects: General Fiction, Belles Lettres, Philosophy, Juveniles, General Science, Chemistry, History
Founded: 1833
ISBN Publishers Prefix: 90-6059

Ad M C **Stok**-Zuid-Hollandsche Uitgeversmaatschappij BV+*, Parkstr 7, Baarn, PO Box 245 Tel: (02154) 17247
Man Dirs: A M Beumer, J Verweij
Subjects: General Fiction, Belles Lettres, Poetry, Biography, History, How-to, Music, Art, Philosophy, Juveniles, General & Social Science
Founded: 1881
Book Club: Member of Europaclub International
Miscellaneous: Firm is a member of the Edicom Group, Netherlands (qv)
ISBN Publisher's Prefix: 90-235

A J G **Strengholt's** Boeken Anno 1928 BV*, Hofstede 'Oud Bussem', Flevolaan 41, Naarden Tel: (02159) 46266 Telex: 43191 (Shipping Add: Postbus 338, Bussum)
Man Dir: F E Breitenstein; *Rights & Permissions:* Céline Gockinga
Subjects: General Fiction, Belles Lettres, Biography, History, How-to, Music, Art, Textbooks, Reference, High-priced Paperbacks
1978-79: 75 titles *Founded:* 1928
ISBN Publisher's Prefix: 90-6010

Succes BV*, Uitgeversmaatschappij, Prinsevinkenpark 2, PO Box 16, The Hague Tel: 514351 Cable Add: Success Denhaag
Man Dir/Sales: P Schreuder;
Editorial/Permissions: J Kasander; *Production:* J Verhoef; *Publicity:* R Wentholt
Parent Comapny: Kluwer (50%); Buhrmann-Tetterode (50%)
Subsidiary Companies: Succes NV, Belgium, Success Verlag GmbH, German Federal Republic
Imprints: Nederlandse Boekenclub, Baedeker voor de Vrouw, Uitgeverij Archipel, Universiteit voor Zelfstudie
Subjects: General
Book Clubs: Nederlandse Boekenclub
1977: 40 titles *Founded:* 1928
Miscellaneous: Firm is an affiliate member of the Kluwer Group, Netherlands (qv)

Swets en Zeitlinger BV, Heereweg 347B, 2160 AH-Lisse Tel: (02521) 19113 Cable Add: Swezeit-Lisse Telex: 41325 slzis nl
Dirs: A Swets, C Schuurman;
Editorial/Permissions: K J Plasterk;
Sales/Production/Publicity: J Lammerts
Subsidiary Companies: Swets North America Inc, PO Box 517, Berwyn, Pa 19312, USA; Europeriodiques SA, 31 ave de Versailles, F-78170 La Celle St Cloud, France; Swets-Servicos para Bibliotecas Ltda, Rua Olimpio Machado 58, Ilha do Governador, 21911 Rio de Janeiro, RJ, Brazil
Subjects: Music, Medicine, Child Psychology, Engineering, Life Sciences, Education, English Language, Psychological Tests
Bookshop: Swets Book Service, Heereweg 347B, 2160 AH Lisse
1977: 29 titles *1978:* 38 titles *Founded:* 1901
ISBN Publisher's Prefix: 90-265

Theatrum Orbis Terrarum*, Keizersgracht 526, 1017 EK Amsterdam Tel: (020) 222255 Cable Add: Toterra Telex: 14070 ashni nl
Publisher: Nico Israel
Subsidiaries: Orbit BV, Keizersgracht 526, Amsterdam; Facsimile Uitgaven Nederland NV (FUN) Amsterdam (both in Netherlands)
Subjects: Biography, History, Cartography, Music, Art, Philosophy, Reference, Religion, High-priced Paperbacks, Medicine, General Science, University Textbooks
1977-78: 130 titles *Founded:* 1963
Miscellaneous: Associate company of A Asher & Co (qv); and Nico Israel (qv), both Amsterdam
ISBN Publishers Prefix: 90-221

BV Uitgeverij en Boekhandel W J **Thieme** & Cie+, Industrieweg 85, Postbus 7, 7200 AA Zutphen Tel: (05750) 10566 Cable Add: Thieme Zutphen
Dirs: L Groenendijk, K Schillemans
Subjects: General Science, Biology, Schoolbooks
1978: 204 titles *Founded:* 1863
ISBN Publishers Prefix: 90-03

NV Uitgeversmaatschappij de **Tijdstroom**+, Bagijnestr 11, Postbus 14, Lochem Tel: (05730) 3651 Telex: 49642
Man Dir: B Mathis
Subjects: Art, Antiques, Medicine, Nursing, Hospital Sciences
1978: 48 titles *Founded:* 1924
Subsidiary: Tijdstroom-Amsterdam
ISBN Publishers Prefix: 90-6087

Tilburg University Press*, 112 Heemraadssingel, Postbus 1474, Rotterdam Tel: (010) 765804
Man Dirs: H M J Broekhuis, H Kok;
Permissions: Mrs L van Oostveen-de Haan
Subjects: High-priced Paperbacks, Economics, Social Science, University Textbooks

Time-Life Books*, Ottho Heldringstr 5, NL-1066 AZ Amsterdam Tel: (020) 157551 Cable Add: Time Inc Amsterdam Telex: 14288
Editorial: George Constable; *Sales:* George Gillespie; *Production:* T Maloney; *Rights & Permissions:* Wendy Dolleman (Eastern Europe and Scandinavia); Richard Stollenwerck (Southern Europe)
Br Offs: Time & Life Bldg, New Bond St, London W1Y 0AA, UK; 17 ave Matignon, F-75008 Paris, France; Stievestrasse 17, Munchen, D8000, Germany

Subjects: Art, Cookery, Gardening, General, Social & Political Science, History, How-to, Photography
ISBN Publishers Prefix: 90-6182

H D Tjeenk Willink BV+, an imprint of Samson Uitgeverij BV (qv)

W E J Tjeenk Willink BV+, Koestr 8, Postbus 25, 8000 AA Zwolle
Publicity: M Nieuwenhuis
Subjects: Textbooks and Periodicals on Law
Miscellaneous: Firm is a member of the Kluwer Group, Netherlands (qv)

Tjeenk Willink-Noorduijkn BV+, Industrieweg 1, Postbus 48, Culemborg Tel: (03450) 3143 Telex: 47306
Man Dirs: A Snoek, J Th Timmer
Br Off: Educaboek BV, Industrieweg 1, Culemborg
Subjects: Belles Lettres, Poetry, Secondary & Primary Textbooks, Educational Materials
Founded: 1970
Miscellaneous: Firm is a member of the Kluwer Group, Netherlands (qv)

Uitgeverij De **Toorts**+, Nijverheidsweg 1, Postbus 576, 2003 RN Haarlem Tel: (023) 319360 Cable Add: Gradus Haarlem Telex: 41494
Man Dir: J Hesseling; *Editorial:* Mrs M Klis; *Sales:* C Klemann; *Production:* R Leideritz; *Publicity:* C Klemann, Mrs M Klis, R Leideritz; *Permissions:* Mrs W Gaus
Subjects: Humanities, Religion, Medicine, Music, Psychology
1977: 21 titles *1978:* 24 titles *Founded:* 1936
ISBN Publishers Prefix: 90-6020

Unieboek NV+*, Nieuwe S'Gravenlandseweg 17-19, Postbus 17, Bussum Tel: (02159) 34241 Cable Add: Unieboek
Man Dirs: C A J van Dishoeck, H Dijkstra, A E Stheeman, P J Zwaan; *Editorial:* Henny Bodenkamp, W de Bruyn, B G J Elias, C J Goossens, N H Witteman, W R Wybrands Marcussen; *Sales Dir:* C A J van Dishoeck; *Permissions:* Jane Baird
Subjects: General Fiction, History, Reference, Religion, Nautical, Juveniles, High-priced Paperbacks, Medicine, General & Social Science, Secondary & Primary Textbooks
Founded: 1890
Miscellaneous: The Unieboek group includes the following publishing houses — Maritiem de Boer (qv); Pauld Brand (qv); van Dishoeck (qv); Fibula Van Dishoeck (qv); de Haan (qv); Van Holkema & Warendorf (qv); Agathon (qv); De Gooise Uitgeverij (qv); Romen (qv) (all located at Nieuwe S'Gravenlandseweg 17-19, Bussum)
ISBN Publisher's Prefixes: 90-228, 90-269 (Unieboek) 90-616 (De Gooise Uitgeverij)

Universitarie Pers Leiden, see Leiden University Press

University Press Amsterdam BV (APA)*, Postbus 1850, NL-1000 BW Amsterdam
Parent Company: APA (Academic Publishers Associated) (qv)
Subjects: History of Law, Political Studies
ISBN Publisher's Prefix: 90-6042

Stichting **V A M**+*, Papelaan 85, Voorschoten Tel: (01717) 4141

V N U (Verenigde Nederlandse Uitgeversbedrijven) NV+*, Azieweg 1, Postbus 4028, Haarlem Schalkwijk Tel: (023) 339000/339040

Subsidiary Company: VNU Business Press Group (qv)
Miscellaneous: Members in the Netherlands include Malmberg BV (qv), Uitgeverij Het Spectrum BV (qv)
ISBN Publisher's Prefixes: 90-208 (Malmberg), 90-274 (Het Spectrum)

V N U Business Press Group, NZ Voorburgwal 225, 1012 RL Amsterdam Tel: (020) 249465 Telex: 14407 Publi NL
Man Dir: F X I Koot
Parent Company: VNU (qv)
Subsidiary Companies: Intermediar and Diligentia; in Amsterdam and Brussels, Belgium
1977: 30 titles *1978:* 25 titles

De **Vaar** bv Dordrecht*, Voorstraat 149, POB 427, Dordrecht Tel: 44567, 44066
Subjects: Sexual Education, Multilingual Sexual Periodicals

Uitgeverij L J **Veen** BV+, Mariaplaats 3, 3511 L H Utrecht Tel: (030) 331484
Man Dir: A de Groot; *Editorial:* Bert Onnink
Subjects: General Fiction, Belles Lettres, Poetry, History, How-to, Low- & High-priced Paperbacks, Sports, Cookery
1978: 38 titles *Founded:* 1887
Miscellaneous: Firm is a member of the Kluwer Group, Netherlands (qv)
ISBN Publishers Prefix: 90-204

Uitgeverij De **Verkenner** NV+*, Parkstr 7, Baarn Tel: (02154) 17247
Subjects: Fiction, Paperbacks
Miscellaneous: Firm is a subsidiary of De Boekerij BV, Netherlands (qv)
ISBN Publishers Prefix: 90-70016

W **Versluys'** Uitg Mij BV+, Postbus 4037, 1009 AA-Amsterdam (Located at: 2e Oosterparkstr 221-223, 1092 BL-Amsterdam) Tel: (020) 650817/947588
Man Dir: H M A Bakker; *Sales Manager:* J H Goedheer; *Editor:* W L Miner
Subject: Textbooks
1977: 160 titles *1978:* 139 titles *Founded:* 1875
ISBN Publishers Prefix: 90-249

J N **Voorhoeve**, The Hague, subsidiary of Uitgeversmaatschappij J H Kok BV (qv)

De **Walburg** Pers+, PO Box 222, Zaadmarkt 84a-86, Zutphen Tel: 05750/10522
Man Dir, Publicity, Rights & Permissions: C F J Schriks; *Editorial Dir:* Dr W R Wybrands Marcussen; *Sales:* R Postma; *Production:* J van 't Leven, R Postma
Subjects: History, Culture, Monuments, Architecture, Theatre
1978: 40 titles *1979:* 40 titles *Founded:* 1961
ISBN Publisher's Prefix: 90-6011

Uitgeverij Van **Walraven** BV+*, Emmalaan 1, Apeldoorn Tel: (055) 218959
Miscellaneous: Firm is a member of the Combo Group, Netherlands (qv)
ISBN Publishers Prefix: 90-6049

Wereldbibliotheek BV, Keizersgracht 810, PO Box 162, 1000 AD Amsterdam Tel: 242449 Telex: 18069 bebus nl
Man Dirs: J J F Aleva, J Schilt
Subjects: High quality Fiction and Non-fiction, Belles Lettres, Juveniles

Het **Wereldvenster** BV Internationale Uitg Mij, Nassaulaan 10, Postbus 4, 3740 AA-Baarn Tel: (02154) 13480/16646 Telex: 43580 Stanu nl Cable Add: Stanu nl
Dir/Editorial/Permissions: J Gay;

Production: G Priem
Orders to: Standaard Uitgeverij, Postbus 1009, 470 BA-Etten-Leur
Parent Company: Standaard Uitgeverij en Distributie BV, Etten-Leur, Netherlands (qv)
Subjects: Philosophy, Religion, Natural History, Travel, Paperbacks, Social Science, Political Science, Environment, Biography etc.
1979: 240 titles *Founded:* 1947
ISBN Publishers Prefix: 90-293

Uit-Mij **'West-Friesland'**+, Kleine Noord 7-9, Postbox 45, 1620 AA- Hoorn Tel: (02290) 18941 Cable Add: Westfriesland
Man Dir: Mevr J C Jonkers-Butter; *Editorial:* A M J C Ripken
Subjects: General Fiction, Juveniles, General Science, Low- & High-priced Paperbacks
1977: 83 titles *1978:* 77 titles *Founded:* 1918
ISBN Publishers Prefix: 90-205

Uitgeverij **Westers**+*, Hammarskjöldhof 7, Utrecht Tel: (030) 931043/932859 Cable Add: Westers Utrecht
Man Dir and other offices: R J N M Westers Sr.
Subjects: Children's Books, Novels
Bookshop: at above address
1977: 10 titles *1978:* 12 titles *Founded:* 1967
ISBN Publisher's Prefix: 90-6107

Wetenschappelijke Uitgeverij+, Singel 262, 1016 AC Amsterdam Tel: (020) 247674 Cable Add: Scientpublish
Man Dir: Th A Sontrop; *Publicity:* Gert-Jan Hemmink
Subjects: Biography, History, Music, Art, Philosophy, Religion, High-priced Paperbacks, Medicine, Psychology, General & Social Science, Secondary & University Textbooks
1978: 15 titles *Founded:* 1948
Miscellaneous: Firm is an associate company of Uitgeverij De Arbeiderspers BV (qv) and Em Querido's Uitgeverij BV (qv) (both in Netherlands)
ISBN Publishers Prefix: 90-214

Uitgeverij **Wever** BV+*, Zilverstr 12-16, Franeker Tel: (05170) 3147
Subjects: History, Philosophy, Politics

Wolters-Noordhoff BV+, Oude Boteringestr 22, Postbus 58, 9700 MB Groningen Tel: (050) 162911 Telex: 53443
Man Dir: J de Groot, J Buiring; *Rights & Permissions:* P G A Geenen
Orders to: PO Box 567, 9700 A N Groningen
Parent Company: NV ICU (qv)
Associate Company: Wolters-Noordhoff Longman BV (qv)
Subjects: Secondary, Primary & Tertiary Textbooks, Educational Materials, *Easy Readers*, Maps, Atlases
1978: 261 titles *Founded:* 1836, 1858
ISBN Publishers Prefix: 90-01

Wolters Noordhoff Longman BV, Postbus 58, 9700 MB Groningen (Located at: Oude Boteringestraat 22, 9700 MB Groningen) Tel: (050) 162236 Telex: 53443/53529
General Executive: Aloys Doodkorte
Associate companies: Wolters-Noordhoff BV, Netherlands (qv); the Longman Group Ltd, UK (qv)
Subjects: Texts connected with English Language Teaching

Zomer en Keuning Boeken BV+, Postbus 235, 6710 BE Ede (Located at: Kernhemseweg 7, 6718 ZB Ede) Tel:

(08380) 19031 Cable Add: Zkede Telex: 45836 Zkede
Man Dir: J J Mons; *Editors:* B H van Lochem, M van Huijstee, P Terlouw, B Onnink, R Meyer; *Marketing:* Hans de Snoo; *Permissions:* Kees van der Sloot
Subjects: General Fiction, How-to, Reference, Religion (Protestant), Bibles, High-priced Paperbacks, Nature, Gardening, Cookery, Handicrafts
1977: 65 titles *1978:* 80 titles *Founded:* 1919
Book Club: Spiegelserie
Miscellaneous: Firm is a member of the Kluwer Group, Netherlands (qv)
ISBN Publishers Prefix: 90–210

Zuidgroep BV (formerly Hippobook/Studio de Zuid)*, Postbus 245, 2501 CE The Hague (Located at: Koninginnegracht 49 2514 AE The Hague) Tel: (070) 637950
General Dirs: A L van Ingen Schenau, J H Bartels; *Publisher, Sales, Foreign Rights:* D J Rog
Imprints: Zuidboek, Hippoboek, Bresboek, Rekreaboek
Subjects: Pets, Equestrian, Nature Study, Gardening, Plants and Flowers, Sports, Crafts, Hobbies, Travel, Cookery, Games, Photography, Film
1977: 40 titles *1978:* 68 titles *Founded:* 1975
ISBN Publisher's Prefix: 90–6248

Uitgeverij **Zwijsen** BV+, Gasthuisring 58, Postbus 805, Tilburg Tel: (013) 353635
Man Dirs: J N A Verwielen, G M Janssen
Subjects: Juveniles, Primary Textbooks
Founded: 1846
ISBN Publishers Prefix: 90–276

Literary Agents

Auteursbureau Greta **Baars-Jelgersma**, Den Heuvel 73, NL–6881 VD–Velp Tel: (85) 635017 Telex: Incom 43776/11000
Specialization: International co-printing of illustrated books; mediation of copyrights; translations from Scandinavian and German languages into Dutch

Alexander **Gans***, Witte de Withstr 20, Noordwijk aan Zee Tel: (01719) 13133

International Bureau voor Auteursrecht BV, Goudestein 1, 2352 JX Leiderdorp Tel: (071) 891056
Contact: Hans Keuls

International Literatuur Bureau BV, Koninginneweg 2A, 1217 KW Hilversum Tel: (035) 13500 Cable Add: ILB Telex: 73201 ILB
Contact: Hein and Menno Kohn

Prins en Prins, De Lairessestr 6, Postbus 5400, NL–1007 Amsterdam Tel: (020) 761001 Cable Add: prinsrights

Servire BV Uitgevers, Secr Varkerisserstr 52, Katwijk aan Zee Tel: (01718) 16741

Book Clubs

E C I voor Boeken en Grammofoonplaten BV, Gebouw Cranenborch, Jaarbeursplein 17, 3521 AN Utrecht Tel: (030) 910911 Telex: 47449

English Book Club, Leidestr 52, 1017 PC, Amsterdam
The above address is for Netherlands enquiries. Head office is Book Club Associates, UK (qv under UK Book Clubs)
Owned by: W H Smith & Son Ltd (London) and Doubleday & Co Inc (New York)

Librah, Postbus 123, 1520 AC Wormerveer
Owned by: Meijer Wormerveer BV (Wormerveer)

Nederlandse Boekenclub (Netherlands Book Club), Prinsevinkenpark 2, The Hague
Manager: P Schreuder
Subject: General
Members: 325,000
Owned by: Succes BV (The Hague)

Uitgeversmaatschappij, **Reader's Digest** NV*, Postbus 7300, Amsterdam

Spiegelserie, Postbus 6710 BE Ede (Located at: Huis Kernhem, Kernhemseweg 7, 6718 ZB Ede)
Owned by: Zomer en Keuning Boeken BV (Wageningen)

V C L, Gildestraat 5, 8263 AH Kampen
Owned by: Uitgeversmaatschappij J H Kok BV (Kampen)

Major Booksellers

Athenaeum Boekhandel*, Spui 14–16, Amsterdam
Manager: G Schut

Broese-Kemink BV, Stadhuisbrug 5, Postbus 38, 3511 KP Utrecht Tel: (030) 313804

H **Coebergh**, Gedempte Oude Gracht 74, Postbus 98, Haarlem Tel: (023) 319198
Manager: J B I M Kat

Dekker en Nordemann BV, O Z Voorburgwal 239, 1012 EZ Amsterdam (Located at: Lippynstr 4, Amsterdam) Tel: (020) 220635
Modern and antiquarian books.
Subscription Agency. Founded 1928
A Division of Elsevier

Dekker en Van de Vegt*, Plein 1944 129–131, Nijmegen Tel: (080) 221010

Boekhandel **Gianotten** BV*, Heuvel 43, Tilburg
Orders to: Jac Oppenheimstr 15, 5042 NM–Tilburg Tel: (013) 682991 (two branches in Tilburg and one in Breda)

Ginsberg Univ Boekhandel, Schuttersveld 9, Postbus 9003, 2300 PA Leiden Tel: (071) 124642, 141773
Manager: Mrs C Bos-Vink

C **Kooyker** BV*, Nieuwe Rijn 15–16, Postbus 24, 2312 JC Leiden Tel: (071) 144146
Man Dir: Fj Arkenau

Mensing en Visser BV*, Calandplein 4, Postbus 1480, The Hague Tel: (070) 469213/462786

Meulenhoff Bruna BV*, Beulingstr 2–4, Postbus 197, Amsterdam Tel: (020) 240885
Manager: J van Seggelen
International bookseller and subscription agency

Rudolf **Müller** International Booksellers BV, Overtoom 487, Postbus 9016, 1006 AA Amsterdam Tel: (020) 165955
Managers: R Muller, Mrs C M Griffioen

Martinus **Nijhoff** BV, Postbus 269, 2501 AX The Hague Tel: (070) 469460 Cable Add: books hague Telex: 34164 nijbu nl

Boekhandel **Scheltema**, Holkema Vermeulen BV, Spui 10, Amsterdam

Scholtens en Zoon BV, Grote Markt 43–44, Postbus 1, 9700 AA–Groningen Tel: (050) 139788

Universitaire Boekhandel Nederland*, Oosterstr 11, 9711 NN Groningen

Major Libraries

Bibliotheek van het **Centraal Bureau** voor de Statistiek (Library of the Netherlands Central Bureau of Statistics), Prinses Beatrixlaan 428, Postbus 959, 2270 AZ Voorburg

Bibliotheek- en Documentatie-centrum van de **Economische Voorlichtingsdienst** (Library and Documentation Centre of the Economic Information Service)*, Bezuidenhoutseweg 151, The Hague

Gemeentebibliotheek Rotterdam (Rotterdam Municipal Library), Nieuwe Markt 1, Rotterdam

Bibliotheek van het **International Instituut** voor Sociale Geschiedenis (Library of the International Institute of Social History)*, Herengracht 262-266, Amsterdam C Tel: (020) 246671
Dir: Rein van der Leeuw

Koninklijke Bibliotheek (Royal Library) (National Library)*, Lange Voorhout 34, The Hague Tel: (070) 644920
Publication: (in co-operation with others) Dutch Bibliography= Brinkman's Cumulatieve Catalogus; Centrale Catalogus voor Periodieken (Union Catalogue of Periodicals, in book form)

Bibliotheek der **Koninklijke Nederlandse Akademie** van Wetenschappen (Library of Royal Netherlands Academy of Arts and Sciences), Kloveniersburgwal 29, 1011 JV Amsterdam

Bibliotheek der **Landbouwhogeschool** (Library of the Agricultural University), Postbus 9100, 6700 HA Wageningen Tel: (08370) 82006 Telex: 45015

Openbare Bibliotheek (Public Library), Bilderdijkstr 1–3, 2513 CM The Hague Tel: (070) 469235

Rijksmuseum Meermanno-Westreenianum/ Museum van het Boek (Book Museum), Prinsessegracht 30, 2514 AP The Hague Tel: (070) 462700

Bibliotheek der **Rijksuniversiteit**, Wittevrouwenstr 9–11, Utrecht Tel: (030) 333116 Telex: NL 47103

Bibliotheek der **Rijksuniversiteit te Groningen***, Oude Kijk in't Jatstr 5, Postbus 559, 9700 AN Groningen

Bibliotheek der **Rijksuniversiteit te Leiden***, Rapenburg 70–74, 2311 EZ–Leiden
And Postbus 9501, 2300 RA–Leiden Tel: (071) 148333 ext 7501 Telex: 31513

Universiteitsbibliotheek van Amsterdam*, Singel 425, Amsterdam Tel: (020) 5252333

Library Associations

Algemene Nederlandse Bond van Leesbibliotheekhouders (Netherlands Association of Reference Librarians)*, Litslaan 14, Santpoort-Zuid Tel: 7566

270 NETHERLANDS

Centrum voor Literatuuronderzoekers (Centre for Literature Research), Debijeweg 82, Rotterdam
A section of the Dutch Librarians' Association

Convent van Universiteitsbibliothekarissen in Nederland (Association of University Librarians in the Netherlands), see UKB

Federatie van Organisaties van Bibliotheek-, Informatie-, Dokumentatiewezen (FOBID) (Federation of Library Information and Documentation Organizations), Taco Scheltemastr 5, The Hague Tel: (070) 264351
Co-ordinating Officer: F H J Buijs

Nederlands Bibliotheek en Lektuurcentrum (NBLC = Netherlands Centre for Public Libraries and Literature), Taco Scheltemastr 5, Postbus 93054, 2509 AB The Hague Tel: (070) 264351 Telex: 32102 nblc nl
Executive Dir: D Reumer
Publication: Bibliotheek en Samenleving; Open (published jointly with 2 other associations: Nederlandse Vereniging van Bedrijfsarchivarissen and Nederlandse Vereniging van Bibliothekarissen)

Nederlandse Vereniging van Bedrijfsarchivarissen (Netherlands Association of Business Archivists), Aalsburg 2526, 6602 WD Wijchen
Publication: Open (published jointly with 2 other associations: Nederlands Bibliotheek en Lektuurcentrum and Nederlandse Vereniging van Bibliothekarissen)

Nederlandse Vereniging van Bibliothecarissen, Documentalisten en literatuuronderzoekers (NVB) (Netherlands Librarians' Society), pa Provinciale Bibliotheek van Zeeland, Abdij 9, 4331 BK Middelburg Tel: (01180) 28055
Secretary: G van Dijk
(Publication: Open (published jointly with 2 other associations: Nederlands Bibliotheek en Lektuurcentrum and Nederlandse Vereniging van Bedrijfsarchivarissen)

Protestantse Stichting tot Bevordering van het Bibliotheekwezen en de Lectuurvoorlichting in Nederland (Protestant Foundation for the Promotion of Librarianship and Reading Information in the Netherlands)*, Parkweg 20a, Voorburg
Publication: Prisma

U K B (Samenwerkingsverband van de Universiteits- en Hogeschoolbibliotheken en de Koninklijke Bibliotheek), c/o J L M van Dijk, Librarian, State University Limburg, Postbus 616, 6200 MD Maastricht
President: W R H Koops
Secretary: Dr J L M van Dijk

Vereniging van Archivarissen in Nederland (Association of Archivists in the Netherlands)*, Ter Pelkwykpark 21, Zwolle
Executive Secretary: Casper van Heel
Publication: Archievenblad

Vereniging voor het Theologisch Bibliothecariaat (Association for Theological Librarianship)*, Secretariat: Doddendaal 20, Nijmegen
Executive Secretary: R van Dijk
Publication: Mededelingen van de VTB

Library Reference Books and Journals

Books

Bibliotheek-en Documentatiegids (Library and Documentation Guide), NOBIN, Van Karnebeeklaan 19, The Hague

Brinkman's Cumulatieve Catalogus (Dutch Bibliography), Koninklijke Bibliotheek, Lange Voorhout 34, The Hague

Journals

Archievenblad (Archive News), Association of Archivists in the Netherlands, Ter Pelkwykpark 21, Zwolle

Bibliotheek en Samenleving (Library and Social Life), Netherlands Centre for Public Libraries and Literature, Central Bureau, Taco Schetemastr 5, Postbus 2054, The Hague

Mededelingen (Communications), Association for Theological Librarianship, Doddendaal 20, Nijmegen

Open, professional journal for librarians, researchers, archivists and documentalists, Netherlands Librarians' Society, Abel Tasmankade 9, Haarlem (published jointly with Netherlands Centre for Public Libraries and Literature and Netherlands Association of Business Archivists)

Literary Associations and Societies

The **Dickens** Fellowship*, Banstr 60, Amsterdam Z
Honorary Secretary: Frank H Keene

Foundation for the Promotion of Translation of Dutch Literary Works*, Singel 450, Amsterdam C Tel: (020) 231056/257189
Dir: Joost de Wit
Publication: Writing in Holland and Flanders

Maatschappij der Nederlandse Letterkunde (Society of Netherlands Literature), Secretariat: Universiteitsbibliotheek, Rapenburg 74, Leiden
Publication: Tijdschrift voor Nederlandse Taal- en Letterkunde, Jaarboek der Maatschappij (annually)

Netherlands Centre of the International **P E N**, Van Tuldenstraat 24, 5688 DB Oirschot
Secretary: (internal business) Jan-Willem Overeem; (foreign business) Dr Mineke Schipper; Wevelaan 39, 3571 XS Utrecht

Literary Periodicals

Amsterdamer Publikationen zur Sprache und Literatur (Amsterdam Publication on Language and Literature), Editions Rodopi NV, Keizersgracht 302–304, Amsterdam

Boeken-Zoekblad (Hard-to-Find Books), 'Stabo/All-Round' BV, Oosterweg 68, Groningen

Castrum Peregrini; journal for literature and art (text in German), Castrum Peregrini Presse, Herengracht 401, Postbus 645, Amsterdam

Forum der Letteren (Forum of Letters), Smits NV, Westeinde 135, 15 The Hague

Gids (Guide), Meulenhoff Nederland NV, Prinsengracht 468, Amsterdam

Hemelspleet (Poles Apart), Bilderdijksstr 45a, Rotterdam

Hollands Maandblad (Holland Monthly), Drukkeij Trio, Nobelstr 27, The Hague

Kentering (The Turning-point) literary review, Nijgh & Van Ditmas, Badhuisweg 232, The Hague

Lezen om te Leven (Reading as a Life Style), 'Stabo/All-Round' BV, Oosterweg 68, Groningen

Quaerendo; a quarterly journal from the Low Countries devoted to manuscripts and printed books (text mainly in English, occasionally in French and German), Theatrum Orbis Terrarum, Keizersgracht 526, Amsterdam

Revisor (The Inspector), Keizersgracht 608, Amsterdam

Trotwaer (The Pavement), (text in Frisian), Miedema Pers, Nieuweburen 97–103, Postbus 45, Leeuwarden

Writing in Holland and Flanders (text in English), Foundation for the Promotion of Dutch Literary Works, Singel 450, Amsterdam C

Literary Prizes

Amsterdam Prizes*
For the best drama, novel, poetry, essay, novella and short story. Awarded annually. Enquiries to Amsterdam City Government, Town Hall, O Z Voorburgwal 197, Amsterdam

Bayle Prize (also known as Netherlands Critics' Prize)*
For outstanding criticism in such fields as architecture, film, music, theatre and fine arts. Awarded annually. Enquiries to Rotterdam Art Foundation, Rotterdam

F **Bordewijk** Prize
For the best Dutch novel. 4,000 Dutch florins. Awarded annually. Enquiries to Jan Campertstichting, Burg de Monchyplein 9, The Hague

Jan **Campert** Prize
For outstanding Dutch poetry. 4,000 Dutch florins. Awarded annually. Enquiries to Jan Campertstichting, Burg De Monchyplein 9, The Hague

Dutch Prize for the Best Children's Book
For the best Dutch children's books (maximum 3). 3,000 Dutch florins. For foreign, translated books (maximum 9, minimum 7), silver slate pencils. Awarded annually. Enquiries to the Commission for the Collective Promotion of the Netherlands Book, Langestr 61, Amsterdam C

J **Greshoff** Prize
For the best Dutch essay. 4,000 Dutch florins. Awarded every two years. Enquiries to Jan Campertstichting, Burg de Monchyplein 9, The Hague

Nienke van **Hichtum** Prize
For the best Dutch children's book. 4,000 Dutch florins. Awarded every two years. Enquiries to Jan Campertstichting, Burg de Monchyplein 9, The Hague

Lucy B en C W van der **Hoogt**-prijs
To an outstanding Dutch writer. 1,000 Dutch florins and a medal. Awarded annually. Enquiries to Maatschappij der Nederlandse Letterkunde (Society of Netherlands Literature), Rapenburg 74, Leiden

Constantijn **Huygens** Prize
To a distinguished Dutch author for all his works. 8,000 Dutch florins. Awarded annually. Enquiries to Jan Campertstichting, Burg De Monchyplein 9, The Hague

Reina **Prinsen-Geerlings** Prize*
Established by the parents of Reina Prinsen-Geerlings to commemorate her execution by the Germans and awarded to a young Dutch author. 200 Dutch florins. Awarded annually. Enquiries to Reina Prinsen-Geerlings Foundation, Koninginneweg 141, Amsterdam

State Prize for **Children's** and Youth Literature
For the best author's work for children and young people. 6,500 Dutch florins. Awarded triennially. Enquiries to Netherlands Ministry of Culture, Recreation and Social Welfare (CRS), Postbus 5406, 2280 HK Rijswijk

State Prize for **Literature** (also known as Pieter Cornelisz Hooft Prize)
For important and original literary works in Dutch. 10,000 Dutch florins. Awarded annually where possible: one year for poetry, the next year for prose, the next year for literary essay. Enquiries to Netherlands Ministry of Culture, Recreation and Social Welfare (CRS), Postbus 5406, 2280 HK Rijswijk

Vijverberg Prize*
For the best Dutch novel or play. 3,000 Dutch florins. Awarded annually. Enquiries to Jan Campertstichting, Burg De Monchyplein 9, The Hague

Netherlands Antilles

General Information

Language: Dutch (and English)
Religion: Roman Catholic
Population: 252,000
Bank Hours: 0830-1130, 1400-1600 Monday-Friday. St Maarten: 0800-1300 Monday-Friday (also 1600-1700 on Friday)
Shop Hours: 0800-1200, 1400-1800 Monday-Saturday
Currency: 100 cents = 1 Netherlands Antilles florin or guilder
Export/Import Information: No tariff on books or advertising. No import licences. No exchange controls

Publishers

Curaçaosche Drukkerij en Uitgevers Maatschappij*, Pietermaaiweg, Willemstad, Curaçao
Subjects: Geography, Travel

Van **Dorp** Aruba NV*, Nassaustr 77, PO Box 596, Oranjestad, Aruba

Van **Dorp** Eddine NV*, Book Department, PO Box 200, Willemstad, Curaçao

Drukkerij de Stad NV*, Compagniestr 41, Willemstad, Curaçao
Dir: Ronald Yrausquin
Subject: Law

Ediciones **Populares***, Compagniestr 41, Willemstad, Curaçao
Dir: Ronald Yrausquin
Subjects: Popular Sciences, Literature
Founded: 1929

Tipografia Nacional*, Bitterstr 3, Curaçao
Subject: Law

Volksdrukkerij NV*, Van Swietenstr 8, Curaçao

De **Wit** Stores NV*, VAD Bldg, L G Smith Blvd 110, Oranjestad, Aruba
Man Dir: F Olmtak

Major Booksellers

Casa **America***, Madurostraat 3, Curaçao

Aruba Boekhandel*, Nassaustraat 94, Oranjestad, Aruba

El **Curaçao***, Hotel Curaçao, Curaçao

Hollandsche Boekhandel*, Breedestraat (P) 22 Curaçao

Major Libraries

Openbare Leeszaal en Bibliotheek (Public Reading Room and Library)*, Johan van Walbeeckplein 6-13, Willemstad, Curaçao

Openbare Leeszaal en Boekerij (Public Reading Room and Library), Eilandgebied, Aruba
Librarian: Alice van Romondt

Stichting Wetenschappelijke Bibliotheek (Scientific Library Foundation)*, Drukkerijstr 4, Willemstad, Curaçao
Librarian: Maritza F Eustatia

Library Associations

Asociation di Biblioteka i Archivo di Korsow (Carbidor) (Association of Libraries and Archives)*, Drukkerijstr 4, Willemstad, Curaçao Tel: 23434
President: Maritza F Eustatia

New Caledonia

General Information

Language: French
Population: 136,000
Literacy Rate (1963): 83.8%
Currency: CFP franc
Export/Import Information: No tariff on books except luxury bindings, 15%, and children's picture books, 10%. Advertising matter generally dutiable at 10%. Special Tax of 0.5% on all. No import licences required

Major Booksellers

Barrau*, 16 et 18 rue Anatole-France, Nouméa Tel: 3093

J-P **Layraud***, rue de la République, Nouméa Tel: 2197

Modernix*, 7 ave du Maréchal-Foch, BP 129 Tel: 2001 Nouméa

Montaigne*, 24 rue de Sébastopol, BP 267 Tel: 3488 Nouméa

Pentecost*, 24 rue de l'Alma, Nouméa Tel: 2114
Importer/Exporter

A **Ragot**, ave de la Victoire, Nouméa

Major Libraries

Bibliothèque **Bernheim**, Bibliothèque territoriale de la Nouvelle-Caledonie (Bernheim Library), Route 13, BP G 1, Nouméa
Librarian: Hélène Colombani

South Pacific Commission Library, South Pacific Commission, PO Box D5, Nouméa Cedex

New Zealand

General Information

Language: English
Religion: Predominantly Protestant
Population: 3.1 million
Bank Hours: 1000-1600 Monday-Friday
Shop Hours: 0900-1730 Monday-Friday (open until 2100 either Thursday or Friday). Some local shops open Saturday
Currency: 100 cents = 1 New Zealand dollar
Export/Import Information: No tariffs on books and advertising. No import licences, but literature 'indecent' or 'advocating violence, lawlessness, disorder or seditiousness' prohibited. No special exchange controls
Copyright: UCC, Berne, Florence (see International section)

Book Trade Organizations

Book Publishers Association of New Zealand, Box 78071, Grey Lynn, Auckland 2 (Located at: 180 Surrey Cres, Grey Lynn, Auckland 2) Tel: 767251
President: D J Heap; *Dir:* Gerard Reid
Publication: Book Publishers Directory of New Zealand

Booksellers Association of New Zealand (Inc), PO Box 11-377, Wellington Tel: (04) 728678
Dir: Harold T White

Christian Booksellers' Association (NZ Chapter), 21 Glenwood Ave, Birkenhead, Auckland 10
Secretary: R A Woodhams

New Zealand Book Council, PO Box 11377, Wellington
Secretary: Kate Fortune

New Zealand Book Trade Organization, PO Box 78071, Auckland 2 (Located at: 180 Surrey Cres, Auckland 2) Tel: (01) 767251
Chairman: R Ross; *Secretary:* G E Reid

Book Trade Reference Books and Journals

Books

Book Publishers Directory of New Zealand, Book Publishers Association of New Zealand, Box 78071, Grey Lynn, Auckland 2

Journals

New Zealand Book World; journal of the New Zealand book trade, PO Box 9405, Courtenay Pl, Wellington

New Zealand National Bibliography, National Library of New Zealand, PMB, Wellington 1

Spotlight; on the book, stationery, magazine, greeting cards, and toys trades in New Zealand, PO Box 3911, Auckland

Publishers

A B P (NZ) Ltd, see Associated Book Publishers (NZ) Ltd

Action Publications+*, PO Box 5160, Christchurch (Located at: 49 Hudson St, Christchurch) Tel: 516460
Man Dir: Desmond Sewell; *Sales:* Pamela Sewell
Subjects: Secondary Textbooks, Geography, Social Studies
1977: 3 titles *1978:* 5 titles *Founded:* 1971
ISBN Publisher's Prefix: 0-908586

H J **Ashton** Co Ltd+, PO Box 12328, Auckland
1978: 1 title

Asia Pacific Research Unit Ltd+*, PO Box 3978, Wellington Tel: (04) 850237 Cable Add: Haaspress
Man Dir: Anthony Haas; *Editorial:* Toshio Toshimura; *Sales:* Pam Brown; *Production:* Rex Evans
Associated Companies: Oriental Press Service, Central Postbox 1226, Tokyo 100-91, Japan; Thompson, Roberts, 13 The Crescent, Vaucluse, Sydney, New South Wales, Australia
Br Offs: Auckland, New Zealand; Bangkok, Thailand; Palmerston, New Zealand; Sydney, Australia; Tokyo, Japan
Subjects: Economics, Geography
1977: 1 title *Founded:* 1970
ISBN Publisher's Prefix: 0-908583

Associated Book Publishers (NZ) Ltd+, CPO Box 4439, Auckland (Located at: 61 Beach Rd, Auckland) Tel: 796369 Cable Add: Methlisps Telex: CPO AK NZ 2553 Methlisps
Man Dir: A D Mackie; *Publishing Dir:* E Ann Mallinson; *Sales Manager:* Kenneth W Shearman
Parent Company: Associated Book Publishers Ltd, London, UK (qv)
Subsidiary Companies: Methuen New Zealand, Sweet and Maxwell (NZ) Ltd (both at above address)
Associated Company: Associated Book Publishers (Aust) Ltd, Australia (qv)
Subjects: General, Educational (School), Tertiary (Social Sciences, Management), Legal
Bookshop: Sweet and Maxwell (NZ) Ltd, 54 The Terrace, Wellington
1978: 30 titles *1979:* 30 titles
ISBN Publisher's Prefix: 0-456/0457

Auckland University Press+, University of Auckland, PMB, Auckland Tel: (09) 792300
Man Editor: R D McEldowney
Subjects: Education, History, Literature, Social Sciences, Textbooks
1977: 7 titles *1978:* 4 titles *Founded:* 1966

Thomas **Avery** & Sons Ltd*, PO Box 442, New Plymouth, North Island Tel: (067) 78122 Cable Add: Avery New Plymouth
Man Dir: D V Avery
Subjects: History, Secondary & Primary Textbooks
Founded: 1882
Bookshop: Thomas Avery & Sons Ltd, 79 Devon St, New Plymouth, North Island

Beaux Arts Ltd+*, PO Box 28017, Auckland 5 Tel: 771774 Cable Add: Beauxarts
Man Dir: R Innes; *Sales:* Mrs M Dunkley
Subjects: Arts, Crafts, History
Bookshop: N W Wheeler Ltd
1977: 2 titles *1978:* 2 titles *Founded:* 1975

Black Apple, PO Box 23, Port Chalmers Tel: 739885
Man Dir and all offices: H Scott
Orders to: More than 10 copies: to above address; less than 10 copies: Macmillan Publishers Ltd, PO Box 33570, Takapuna, Auckland
Subjects: Children's Books, Dual Language Books (Japanese and English, Arabic and English, etc)
1978: 2 titles *Founded:* 1977
ISBN Publisher's Prefix: 0-908589

Butterworths of New Zealand Ltd+, PO Box 472, T & W Young Building, 77-85 Custom House Quay, Wellington 6001 Tel: 722021 Cable Add: Butterwort Wellington Telex: 31306
Man Dir: D A Day
Parent Company: Butterworth & Co (Publishers) Ltd, UK (qv)
Subjects: Legal, Medical, Scientific, Technical
1977: 8 titles *Founded:* 1914
ISBN Publisher's Prefix: 0-409

Cambridge University Press+, PO Box 33055, Takapuna, Auckland 9 Tel: 451609
Man Dir: R M Ross
Parent Company: Cambridge University Press, UK (qv)

Cape Catley Ltd+, PO Box 199, Picton
Man Dir: Christine C Catley
Subject: Fiction
1977: 3 titles *1978:* 2 titles

Capper Press Ltd, PO Box 1388, Christchurch Cable Add: Avonprint Christchurch
Bookshops: The Bookshop in Campbell Grant, 196 Hereford St, Christchurch
Subjects: Reprints of rare and out-of-print New Zealand, Australian and Pacific books
1977: 13 titles *1978:* 12 titles
Miscellaneous: Associate Company of Avon Fine Prints Ltd

Cassell Ltd+, 46 Lake Rd, PO Box 36013, Northcote Central, Auckland 9 Tel: 484055/371 Cable Add: Caspeg Auckland Telex: NZ 2244
Manager: Margaret Gibson
1978: 3 titles *1979:* 5 titles
ISBN Publisher's Prefix: 0-908572
Miscellaneous: Firm is a registered branch in New Zealand of Cassell Ltd UK (qv) and Collier Macmillan International Inc, USA

Caveman Publications Ltd+, PO Box 1458, Dunedin (Located at: 2nd Floor, OSB Building, 106 George St, Dunedin) Tel: 772326, 772461
Subjects: Poetry, Fiction, Nonfiction
1977: 3 titles

The **Caxton** Press+*, 113 Victoria St, PO Box 25088, Christchurch Tel: 68516 Cable Add: Imprint
Man Dir: E B Bascand
Subjects: General Fiction, Belles Lettres, Poetry, Biography, History, Music, Art, High-priced Paperbacks, Juveniles, Education
Miscellaneous: Publishers of literary periodical, *Landfall*

William **Collins** Publishers Ltd+, PO Box 1, Auckland (Located at: 31 View Rd, Glenfield) Tel: 447299 Cable Add: Folio Telex: 21685
Man Dir: B D Phillips; *Marketing Manager:* B J Davies
Br Offs: 175 The Terrace, PO Box 3737, Wellington; 234 Barbados St, PO Box 2162, Christchurch
Subjects: Fiction, History, Juveniles, Arts, Maps, Reference, Natural Science, Paperbacks, Educational, New Zealand titles
Founded: 1870
Miscellaneous: Firm is a branch of William Collins Sons & Co Ltd, UK (qv)

Cranwell Publishing Co Ltd, 419a Queen St, Auckland Tel: 74139 Cable Add: Crancat
Man Dir: R G Riddell; *Editorial & Sales:* G A Tait; *Production:* D Reddaway
Br Off: 32 Burton St, Milsons Point, New South Wales, Australia
Subjects: Building, Architecture, Reference, New Zealand Export, Commercial Fishing
1977: 12 titles *1978:* 3 titles *Founded:* 1947

Doubleday New Zealand Ltd+, 8 Taylors Rd, Morningside, Auckland 3
Manager: Keith Paterson
Parent Company: Doubleday Australia Pty Ltd, Australia (qv)
Book Club: See Doubleday New Zealand Ltd, Book Club Associates Division in Book Club section for individual clubs.

Dunmore Press Ltd+, PO Box 5115, Palmerston North (Located at: 661 Main St, Palmerston North) Tel and Cable Add: 79242
Man Dir: John Dunmore; *Sales:* Joyce Dunmore; *Editorial, Publicity, Rights & Permissions:* Patricia Chapman
Subjects: History, Fiction, General, Academic, Political, Book of New Zealand Records
1978: 10 titles *1979:* 14 titles *Founded:* 1975
ISBN Publishers Prefix: 0-908564

Forum, an imprint of Sevenseas Publishing Pty Ltd (qv)

Fourth Estate Books Ltd+, PO Box 9344, Wellington Tel: 736876 Cable Add: Natbus
General Manager: Ian F Grant
Subjects: Business, History, Law, Politics, Sociology
1977: 3 titles *1978:* 3 titles *Founded:* 1976

Leonard **Fullerton** Ltd+, PO Box 316, Auckland (Located at: 5-7 Shaddock St, Auckland) Tel: 371674

Man Dir, Sales: D L Hart
Founded: 1967
ISBN Publisher's Prefix: 0-903680

Golden Press Pty Ltd+, Private Bag, Rosebank, Auckland 7 Tel: 8845889 Cable Add: Gold Press Auckland
Imprints: Golden Press, Whitman
Br Off: 35 Osborne St, Christchurch
1978: 22 titles

William **Heinemann** (New Zealand) Ltd+, PO Box 36020, Northcote, Auckland 9 Tel: 487193 Cable Add: Sunlocks
Man Dir: M G Dowthwaite; *Sales, Production & Publicity:* E D Bland
Parent Company: William Heinemann Ltd, UK (qv)
Subjects: Fiction, General, Children's, Medical, Religious, Technical
1977: 3 titles *1978:* 3 titles *Founded:* 1974

Heinemann Educational Books (New Zealand) Ltd+, PO Box 36064, Northcote Central, Auckland 9 Tel: (09) 489153 Cable Add: Hebooks Telex: NZ 2244 Alptrau
Shipping Add: 26 Kilham Ave, Auckland 9
Man Dir, Rights & Permissions: D J Heap; *Financial Dir:* A G Wernham; *Publicity, Advertising, Sales:* Peter Fowler; *Editorial:* David Ling
Subjects: University & Secondary Textbooks, Fiction, Hobbies, Technical, Children's
1977: 27 titles *1978:* 21 titles *Founded:* 1969
ISBN Publisher's Prefix: 0-86863
Miscellaneous: Firm is a subsidiary of Heinemann Educational Books Ltd, UK (qv)

Hodder & Stoughton Ltd+, PO Box 3858, Auckland 1 (Located at: 44-46 View Rd, Glenfield, Auckland 10) Tel: 445049 Cable Add: Expositor Auckland Telex: NZ 21422
Editorial Dir: N C Robinson
Subjects: Fiction, Nonfiction, Education, Children's books
1977: 15 titles *1978:* 15 titles
Miscellaneous: Firm is a subsidiary of Hodder & Stoughton Ltd, UK (qv)

Holt-Saunders Pty Ltd+, 10 Moa Street, PO Box 22-245, Otahuhu, Auckland 6 Tel: 62087 Cable Add: Aytcholt, Auckland
Manager: Ian C Swallow
Miscellaneous: Firm is an associate of Holt-Saunders Ltd, UK

Hutchinson Group (NZ) Ltd+, 32-34 View Rd, Glenfield, PO Box 40086, Auckland 10 Tel: 447197/524
Man Dir: K C Pounder; *General Manager:* N G Sturt
Associate Company: Hutchinson Publishing Group Ltd, UK (qv)
Subjects: General & Academic
1978: 12 titles

Jacaranda Wiley Ltd+*, PO Box 2259, Auckland (Located at: 32 Nikau St, Mt Eden, Auckland)
Miscllaous: Firm is a branch of Jacaranda Wiley, Australia (qv)

Jason Publishing Co Ltd*, PO Box 9390, Newmarket, Auckland (Located at: Kingdon House, Kingdon St, Newmarket, Auckland 1) Tel: 546-091 Cable Add: Jasonpub
Man Dir, Editorial, Rights & Permissions: John Sandford; *Sales:* Peter Alford; *Production:* Johan Newby; *Publicity:* Daphne Trask
Subjects: Sports, Agriculture, Periodicals
1977: 2 titles *Founded:* 1969

Lancaster Publishing*, PO Box 6134, Auckland
Man Dir: Sir Bruce Henderson; *Editorial:* Olive L Rance; *Sales:* Michael Sinclair; *Rights & Permissions:* Red Parsons
Orders to: PO Box 1706, Palmerston North
Subsidiary Company: Dharma Press
Br Off: PO Box 1706, Palmerston North
Subjects: Art, Radical Politics, Children's, General
1977: 4 titles *Founded:* 1976
ISBN Publisher's Prefix: 0-908576

Longman Paul Ltd+, CPO Box 4019, Auckland 1 (Located at: 182-190 Wairau Rd, Takapuna, Auckland 10) Tel: (09) 446183 Cable Add: Freegrove Telex: NZ 21041
Publisher: Rosemary Stagg; *Editors:* John Barnett, David Pointon, Anne Else
Subjects: General Fiction, Primary, Secondary & Tertiary Textbooks
1977: 15 titles *1978:* 12 titles *Founded:* 1968
Miscellaneous: Firm is an associate company of Longman Group Ltd, UK (qv)

Thomas C **Lothian** Pty Ltd+*, 88 Lelson St, PO Box 68220, Auckland Tel: 373692 Cable Add: Lothwell
Manager: D H Forrester
Head Office: Thomas C Lothian Pty Ltd, 4-12 Tattersalls Lane, Melbourne, Victoria, Australia
Subjects: General Nonfiction, Educational, Children's
1977: 3 titles *Founded:* 1954
ISBN Publisher's Prefix: 0-85091

McGraw-Hill Book Co, New Zealand Ltd+, 28 Airedale St, CPO Box 85, Auckland 1 Tel: 779368
Man Dir: Richard J A Bird; *Promotion:* Margaret Railton
Associate Company: McGraw-Hill Book Co (UK) Ltd, UK (qv)
Subjects: Educational
1977: 1 title *1978:* 1 title *Founded:* 1974

John **McIndoe** Ltd+*, PO Box 694, Dunedin Tel: 70355
Shipping Add: 51 Crawford St, Dunedin
Man Dir: J H McIndoe; *Advertising, Publicity, Rights & Permissions:* B L Turner
Subjects: General Fiction, Belles Lettres, Poetry, Biography, History, How-to, Music, Art, Reference, High-priced Paperbacks, Medicine, General Science, University Textbooks
1977: 13 titles *Founded:* 1893
ISBN Publisher's Prefix: 0-908565

Methuen New Zealand, a subsidiary of Associated Book Publishers (New Zealand) Ltd (qv)

Millwood Press Ltd+, 19 Ottawa Rd, Ngaio, Wellington 4 Cable Add: Siersprod
Dirs: Jim and Judy Siers
Subjects: New Zealand & Pacific

Minerva Bookshop Ltd+*, 13 Commerce St, PO Box 2597, Auckland 1 Tel: (09) 30863 Cable Add: Minerva
Man Dir: Esther Porsolt; *Dir:* Nigel Faigan
Subjects: General Nonfiction, Textbooks, Education
Founded: 1946

Moa Publications+, 23 Orakau Ave, PO Box 26092, Auckland Tel: 655306 Cable Add: Moabooks
Man Dir: John G Blackwell
Subjects: Sport
1978: 8 titles *1979:* 8 titles *Founded:* 1971
ISBN Publisher's Prefix: 0-908570

G W **Moore** Ltd, PO Box 26-222, Epsom, Auckland (Located at: 69 Great South Rd, Remuera, Auckland) Tel: 548283
Man Dir: G W Moore; *Manager:* John G Paton; *Sales:* Graham O Walker

N Z E I, see New Zealand Educational Institute

New Zealand Council for Educational Research+*, PO Box 3237, Wellington Tel: 847939 Cable Add: Edsearch
Dir: John E Watson; *Sales Dir:* Llewelyn M Richards; *Publicity Dir, Rights & Permissions:* Alistair T A Campbell
Subject: Educational Materials
Founded: 1934

New Zealand Educational Institute (NZEI), West Block, Education House, 178 Willis St, PO Box 466, Wellington Tel: 849689 Cable Add: Edistute
National Secretary: J E Smith
Orders to: Education House Ltd, Publications Division, PO Box 466, Wellington
Subject: Educational
1978: 4 titles *1979:* 3 titles *Founded:* 1883
ISBN Publisher's Prefix: 0-908579

New Zealand Government Printing Office+*, Private Bag, Wellington

Newrick Associates Ltd+, PO Box 820, Wellington Tel: 728231/843676 Cable Add: Backgam
Man Dir: Henry P Newrick
Associated Companies: Medici Galleries Ltd, Professional Publications (qv)
Subjects: Art, Antiques, Reference
1977: 2 titles *1978:* 2 titles *Founded:* 1967

Nexus Books+*, PO Box 67-008, Mount Eden, Auckland 3
Manager: A J C Begg
Subject: Mathematics
1977: 1 title *1978:* 1 title *Founded:* 1973
ISBN Publisher's Prefix: 0-85912

Outrigger Publishers Ltd+, PO Box 13049, Hamilton Tel: 85602
Man Dir: Sefulu Ioane; *Editorial:* Norman Simms; *Sales:* Vera Robinson; *Circulation Manager:* L E Scott
Subjects: Literature, Criticism, Folklore, Periodical Arts reviews: *Pacific Quarterly, Journal of Criminal Literature Studies* and others
ISBN Publisher's Prefix: 0-908571

Oxford University Press+, 2nd Floor, McKenzies Bldg, 222-236 Willis St, Wellington, C1 Tel: (04) 843723 Cable Add: Oxonian, Wellington
Shipping Add: PO Box 27344, Wellington, C1
Manager: J W B Griffin
Subjects: Belles Lettres, Poetry, History, Social Science, University & Primary Textbooks, New Zealand
1978: 8 titles *1979:* 14 titles *Founded:* 1947
Miscellaneous: Branch of Oxford University Press, UK (qv)

Pegasus Press Ltd+, 14 Oxford Terrace, PO Box 2244, Christchurch 1 Tel: 64509
Man Dir: Albion Wright; *Editor:* Robin Muir; *Sales Dir:* D H Wallace; *Rights & Permissions:* Pamela Rogers
Subjects: General Fiction, Poetry, Biography, History, Sports, Library and Paperback editions
1978: 13 titles *1979:* 14 titles *Founded:* 1948
ISBN Publishers Prefix: 0-908568

Penguin Books (NZ) Ltd+*, PO Box 4019, Auckland 1 (Located at: 183 190 Wairau Rd, Auckland 10) Tel: 448396 Cable Add: Penguinook Auckland Telex: 21041
Man Dir: Graham Beattie; *Sales & Publicity:* Margaret Greer
Founded: 1973
Miscellaneous: Firm is an associate company of Penguin Books Ltd, UK (qv)

M **Peryer** Ltd+*, 93-97 Cambridge Terrace, PO Box 833, Christchurch 1 Tel: 64733
Cable Add: Medico
Br Offs: Cnr John St & Adelaide Rd, PO Box 7389, Wellington; PO Box 8542, Symonds St, Auckland; 8 Park Ave, Grafton, Auckland
Subjects: Medical, Educational
1977: 5 titles *Founded:* 1932
ISBN Publisher's Prefix: 0-85185

Pitman Publishing NZ Ltd+*, PO Box 38688, Petone, Wellington
1978: 2 titles
Miscellaneous: Firm is an associate company of Pitman Publishing Ltd, UK (qv)

Price Milburn & Co Ltd+, Suite 4, Book House, Boulcott St, PO Box 2919, Wellington Tel: 727533/758838/285254
Cable Add: Mice Wellington
Man Dir: Hugh Price; *Secretary:* Sidney Heppleston; *Sales Manager:* Barbara Milburn; *Editor, Permissions:* Beverley Price
Parent Company: Education House Ltd (NZEI), Wellington
Subjects: Juveniles, Social Science, University, Secondary & Primary Textbooks, particularly junior readers
Bookshop: Bilbo's Book Centre, 2 Whiteman Rd, Silverstream
1979: 90 titles *Founded:* 1957
Miscellaneous: Publishes for New Zealand Institute of International Affairs, New Zealand University Press, Victoria University Press, New Zealand Council for Civil Liberties and Kea Press imprints
ISBN Publishers Prefix: 0-7055

Professional Publications, PO Box 820, Wellington Tel: 728231/843676 Cable Add: Backgam
Man Dir: Henry P Newrick
Associate Companies: Medici Galleries Ltd, Newrick Associates Ltd (qv)
Subjects: Business, Economics, Taxation
1979: 2 titles *Founded:* 1979

A H & A W **Reed** Ltd Publishers+, 65-67 Taranaki St, Wellington Tel: (04) 858849
Cable Add: Reedkiwi Telex: NZ 31489
Chairman, Man Dir: J M Reed; *Executive Dir (Overseas):* Murray McL Humphries
Subsidiary Company: A H & A W Reed Pty Ltd (Australia) (qv)
Br Offs: 16 Beresford St, Auckland; 85 Thackeray St, Christchurch (both in New Zealand); 11 Southampton Row, London WC1B 5HA, UK
Bookshop: Reed Books Ltd, 65-67 Taranaki St, Wellington
Subjects: General Fiction, Belles Lettres, Poetry, Biography, History, How-to, Music, Art, Reference, Juveniles, High-priced Paperbacks, Social Science, Agriculture
1977: 126 titles *Founded:* 1907

Richards Publishing+, PO Box 31285, Milford, Auckland 9 (Located at: 49 Aberdeen Rd, Castor Bay, Auckland 9) Tel: 469681
Man Dir: Ray Richards; *Editorial:* Barbara Richards; *Production:* Don Sinclair
Associate Company: Richards Publishing Consultants (qv)
Branch Off: 54 Ranui Terrace, Linden, Wellington
Subjects: New Zealand Biography, History, Art, Adventure
1978: 4 titles *1979:* 3 titles *Founded:* 1978
ISBN Publisher's Prefix: 0-908596

Sevenseas Publishing Pty Ltd, 5-7 Tory St, PO Box 1431, Wellington 1 Tel: 859759
Cable Add: Vikseven
Man Dir, Editorial, Production, Rights & Permissions: Murdoch Riley; *Sales, Publicity Dir:* K Southern
Imprints: Forum, Viking Sevenseas
Br Off: ANZ Bank Bldg, 68 Pitt St, Sydney, Australia
Subjects: How-to, Music, Art, South Pacific, Health, Nutrition, General
1978: 6 titles *1979:* 3 titles *Founded:* 1963
Associates: Viking Record Co Ltd, Delta Trading Co Ltd
ISBN Publishers Prefix: 0-85467

Shortland Educational Publications+*, PO Box 56113, Auckland Tel: 689959
Cable Add: Newspress
Managing Editor: Wendy Pye; *Editor:* Miss Jo Noble; *Sales:* Bruce Denny
Parent Company: NZ Newspapers Ltd, PO Box 1409, Auckland
Br Offs: Newspaper House, Wellington; Christchurch Star, Christchurch
Subjects: Gardening, Cookery, Sports, Children's Activities, General
1977: 7 titles *Founded:* 1977
ISBN Publisher's Prefix: 0-86867

Stockton House+*, Box 46, Albany Tel: GNH 528
Man Dir: R S Witter
Subjects: Educational, General
1977: 3 titles *Founded:* 1974

Sweet and Maxwell (NZ) Ltd, a subsidiary of Associated Book Publishers (New Zealand) Ltd (qv)

Alister **Taylor** Publishers+, Waiura, PO Box 87, Martinborough Tel: Featherston 69847 Cable Add: Taylor, Martinborough
Subjects: Fiction, Poetry, New Zealand, Art, Photography, General, Limited Editions
1979: 15 titles *Founded:* 1971
ISBN Publisher's Prefix: 0-908578

University of Canterbury Publications, PMB, Christchurch Tel: 482009 Cable Add: Canterbury University
Secretary: The Registrar
Subjects: Fine Art, History, Literature, Physics, Chemistry, Social Sciences
1977: 1 title *1978:* 2 titles *Founded:* 1960
ISBN Publishers Prefix: 0-900392

University of Otago Press+, PO Box 56, Dunedin Tel: 40109
Orders to: John McIndoe Ltd, PO Box 694, Dunedin
Subjects: Scholarly Monographs, Biography, Music, Poetry, Literature, History, Medicine
1977: 3 titles *Founded:* 1959
ISBN Publisher's Prefix: 0-908569

Viking Sevenseas Ltd+, an imprint of Sevenr Publishing Pty Ltd (qv)

Whitcoulls Ltd+, Private Bag, Christchurch Tel: 794580 Cable Add: Whitcoulls
Man Dir: P E Bourne; *Manager, Publishing Division:* Max Rogers; *Gen Man, Merchandising Division:* K Shore; *Senior Editor:* R S Gormack; *Advertising Manager:* E A Walker
Subsidiary Company: Whitcombe & Tombs Pty Ltd, Australia
Subjects: Educational, Fiction, Nonfiction, New Zealand, General
Bookshops: Throughout New Zealand
1977: 25 titles *1978:* 19 titles *Founded:* 1882
ISBN Publisher's Prefix: 0-7233

Whitman, an imprint of Golden Press Pty Ltd (qv)

Wilson & Horton Ltd+, PO Box 32, Auckland
1978: 14 titles

Literary Agents

Richards Publishing Consultants, PO Box 31285, Milford, Auckland (Located at: 49 Aberdeen Rd, Castor Bay, Auckland 9) Tel: 469681
Contact: Ray Richards, Barbara Richards
Also at 54 Ranui Terrace, Linden, Wellington

Book Clubs

20th Century Classics, see Doubleday New Zealand Ltd, Book Club Associates Division

Doubleday Book Club, see Doubleday New Zealand Ltd, Book Club Associates Division

Doubleday History Book Club, see Doubleday New Zealand Ltd, Book Club Associates Division

Doubleday New Zealand Ltd, Book Club Associates Division, 8 Taylors Rd, Morningside, Auckland 3
Includes: Doubleday Book Club, Doubleday History Book Club, The Literary Guild, 20th Century Classics

The **Literary Guild**, see Doubleday New Zealand Ltd, Book Club Associates Division

Major Booksellers

A B C Bookshop*, 284 Trafalgar St, Nelson

G H Bennett & Co Ltd, 38-42 Broadway, PO Box 138, Palmerston North

Dorothy **Butler** Ltd*, Children's Book Specialists, Cnr Sunnybrae & Archers Rds, Takapuna, Auckland

Goddard's Bookshop Ltd*, 21 Devonport Rd, PO Box 41, Tauranga
Man Dir: Ray Goddard

Horizon Bookshop Ltd, T & G Bldg, Queens Drive, Lower Hutt, Wellington

London Bookshops Ltd, 106 Cuba St, PO Box 6143, Wellington 1
also St Luke's Shopping Centre, Mount Albert, Auckland; Shore City, Takapuna, Auckland; Downtown Mall, Queen St, Auckland; 99 Cashels St, Christchurch; 239 George St, Dunedin; Hartham Pl, Porirua; Maidstone Mall, Upper Hutt; 326 Lambton Quay, Wellington; Manners Plaza, Wellington (Educational Division); Kirkcaldies, Brandon St, Wellington

Roy **Parsons***, Massey House, 126 Lambton Quay, Wellington 1

Pauls University Bookshop Ltd, 211 Victoria St, PO Box 928, Hamilton Tel: 80379
Manager: A N Kerby

School Supplies Ltd*, 6 Gordon Rd, Morningside, PO Box 41-163, Auckland 3
also 5 Wall Pl, Linden, Wellington 1; PO Box 50-384 Porirua; Rathbone St, PO Box 224, Whangarei

Gordon **Tait**, Bookseller Ltd*, 79 Cashel St, Christchurch 1

Unity Books Ltd, 42 Willis St, PO Box 3676, Wellington
Manager: A H Preston

University Book Shop (Auckland) Ltd, Student Union Bldg, 34 Princes St, Auckland 1

University Book Shop (Canterbury) Ltd, University Drive, University of Canterbury, Christchurch Tel: 488579 Cable Add: Unibooks
Also at: The Book Shop in the Arts Centre, Arts Centre, Christchurch Tel: 60568

University Book Shop (Otago) Ltd, 378 Great King St, PO Box 6060, Dunedin North Tel: 776976

Whitcoulls Ltd, 111 Cashel St, PMB, Christchurch 1
and 35 branches throughout New Zealand

Wholesale Book Distributors, Box 4149, New Plymouth Telex: DCS NZ 3939
Publishers Representatives; Paperback Specialists
Also Novdit Books, PO Box 40047, Wenfield, Auckland
Publishers Representatives; Hardcover Specialists

Major Libraries

Auckland Public Library*, Lorne St, PO Box 4138, Auckland 1 Tel: 70209
Telex: NZ2750
Librarian: Robert Duthie

Canterbury Public Library*, 109 Cambridge Terrace, Christchurch

Canterbury University Library, Private Bag, Christchurch

Dunedin Public Library, PO Box 906, Moray Place, Dunedin
City Librarian: Michael Wooliscroft

General Assembly Library*, Parliament House, Wellington 1 Tel: 738288

National Archives*, 129–141 Vivian St, Box 6162, Te Aro, Wellington Tel: 738699
Chief Archivist: Miss J S Hornabrook
Publication: A Summary of Work (annually)

National Library of New Zealand, Private Bag, Wellington 1 Tel: 722101 Telex: nz 3076

Otago University Library, PO Box 56, Dunedin
Librarian: W J McEldowney
Publication: Annual Report

Palmerston North Public Library, PO Box 1948, Palmerston North
Librarian: I W Malcolm

Alexander **Turnbull** Library, 44 The Terrace, PO Box 12349, Wellington Tel: 722107

University of Auckland Library, PB, Auckland Tel: Auckland 792-300 Telex: NZ 21480

Wellington Public Library, PO Box 1992, Wellington
Librarian: B K McKeon

Library Associations

Bibliographical Society of Australia and New Zealand, see Australia

International Association of Music Libraries, Australia/New Zealand Branch, see Australia

New Zealand Library Association, 10 Park St, PO Box 12212, Wellington 1
Tel: 735834
Executive Officer: H Stephen-Smith
Publications: Library Life (11 a year), *New Zealand Libraries* (4 a year)

Library Reference Books and Journals

Books

Special Libraries and Collections: A New Zealand Directory, New Zealand Library Association, 10 Park St, PO Box 12212, Wellington 1

Who's Who in New Zealand Libraries, New Zealand Library Association, 10 Park St, PO Box 12212, Wellington 1

Journals

Library Life (11 times yearly), New Zealand Library Association, 10 Park St, PO Box 12212, Wellington 1

New Zealand Libraries (quarterly), New Zealand Library Association, 10 Park St, PO Box 12212, Wellington 1

Literary Associations and Societies

The **Dickens** Fellowship*, 237 Hereford St, Christchurch 1
Honorary Secretary: Hilda Wilson
Branches also in Dunedin and Wellington

New Zealand Women Writers' Society*, 37A Maida Vale Rd, Roseneath, Wellington 3
Secretary: Hestia Quinn

P E N International New Zealand Centre*, 30 Verviers St, Karori, Wellington
Secretary: Gillian Shadbolt
Publication: PEN Gazette (quarterly)

Literary Periodicals

Arena; a literary magazine, Noel Farr Hoggard, PO Box 6188, Te Aro, Wellington

Islands; a New Zealand quarterly of arts and letters, Robin Dudding, 4 Scaly Rd, Torbay, Auckland 10

Landfall, Caxton Press, 113 Victoria St, PO Box 25088, Christchurch

Mate; a magazine of New Zealand writing, Wellesley St, PO Box 5670, Auckland

New Quarterly Cave; an international magazine of arts and ideas, Outrigger Publishers Ltd, 1 Von Tempsky St, Hamilton

Northland, Northland Magazine Inc, PO Box 694, Whangarei

Literary Prizes

A H I Literary Research Award
An award of $7,000 (New Zealand) to enable an established writer to undertake research towards the publication of literary, historical or critical works. Enquiries to Secretary, New Zealand Literary Fund Advisory Committee, c/o Department of Internal Affairs, Private Bag, Wellington

Achievement Award
For a contribution to literature. $500 (New Zealand). Awarded annually. Enquiries to New Zealand Literary Fund, c/o Department of Internal Affairs, Private Bag, Wellington

Bank of New Zealand Young Writers' Awards*
For unpublished short stories written by young people in two age groups: Senior (under 25 years); and Junior (school age). $250 and $150 (NZ). A grant of $150 is given to the library of the secondary school attended by the Junior awardee. Awarded every other year. Enquiries to New Zealand Women Writers' Society, 37A Maida Vale Rd, Roseneath, Wellington 3

Best First Book of Poetry Award
(incorporating the Jessie Mackay Award)*
For the best first book of published poetry. $600 (New Zealand). Awarded annually. Enquiries to PEN International New Zealand Centre, PO Box 2283, Wellington

Best First Book of Prose Award
(Incorporating the Hubert Church Award)*
For the best first book of prose. $600 (New Zealand). Awarded annually. Enquiries to PEN International New Zealand Centre, PO Box 2283, Wellington

Buckland Literary Award*
Founded in 1966 by the late Freda M Buckland for the work of the highest literary merit by a New Zealand Writer. Awarded annually. The winner in 1976 was Joy Cowley for *The Mandrake Root*. Enquiries to Buckland Literary Award, Trustees Executors and Agency Company of New Zealand Ltd, 24 Water St, PO Box 760, Dunedin

Choysa Bursary for Children's Writers
A bursary of $5,000 (New Zealand) to enable an author of imaginative work for children to work full-time for a period of up to one year on an approved project(s) which will reach book form. Enquiries to Secretary, New Zealand Literary Fund Advisory Committee, c/o Department of Internal Affairs, Private Bag, Wellington

Esther **Glen** Award*
For the best children's book. $50 (New Zealand). Awarded annually. Enquiries to New Zealand Library Association, 10 Park St, Wellington 1

I C I Writing Bursary
An annual award of $5,000 is made to one or more writers (not necessarily of repute) with potential to work full-time for one year on an approved project. Enquiries to The Secretary, New Zealand Literary Fund, Advisory Committee, c/o Department of Internal Affairs, Private Bag, Wellington

Katherine **Mansfield** Memorial Award*
For an unpublished short story. Sponsored by the Bank of New Zealand. $500 (NZ) awarded in 1977. Awarded biennially. Enquiries to New Zealand Women Writers' Society, 37A Maida Vale Rd, Roseneath, Wellington 3

New Zealand Book Awards
Annual awards of $2,000 for the best book published each year in the categories of poetry, fiction and non-fiction. Enquiries to The Secretary, New Zealand Literary Fund, Advisory Committee, c/o Department of Internal Affairs, Private Bag, Wellington

New Zealand Literary Fund
In addition to awards specifically mentioned, various grants are made from time to time by the above Fund to writers, publishers of creative literature and literary magazines. Enquiries to The Secretary, New Zealand Literary Fund, Advisory Committee, c/o Department of Internal Affairs, Private Bag, Wellington

Professor J C Reid Award for Excellence in Arts Criticism*
For arts criticism. $150 (New Zealand). Awarded annually. Enquiries to New Zealand Journalists' Union, PO Box 6545, Wellington

The Scholarship in Letters
An award of $6,000 to enable an established writer to work full-time for one year on an approved project. Enquiries to The Secretary, New Zealand Literary Fund, Advisory Committee, c/o Department of Internal Affairs, Private Bag, Wellington

James Wattie Award for the New Zealand Book of the Year
For the best books written by New Zealanders and published by members of the Book Publishers Association of New Zealand. $2000, $1000 and $500 (New Zealand). Awarded annually. Enquiries to Book Publishers Association of New Zealand, PO Box 78071, Grey Lynn, Auckland 2

Young Writers' Incentive Awards*
For prose and poetry by New Zealanders under 20. $100 and $50 (New Zealand). Enquiries to PEN International New Zealand Centre, PO Box 2283, Wellington

Nicaragua

General Information

Language: Spanish
Religion: Roman Catholic
Population: 2.3 million
Literacy Rate (1963): 49%
Bank Hours: 0900-1500 Monday-Friday; 0900-1130 Saturday
Shop Hours: 0800-1200, 1430-1730 or longer Monday-Saturday
Currency: 100 centavos = 1 córdoba
Export/Import Information: Catalogues dutied at $0.03 per gross kilo. 10% Compensatory Tax on advertising. No import licences or exchange controls
Copyright: UCC, Buenos Aires, Florence (see International section)

Publishers

Academia Nicaragüense de la Lengua*, Biblioteca Nacional, Managua
Subject: Languages

Editorial **Alemana***, 2A Calle SO 108, Managua

Editorial **Chile***, 8 Ave, Calle SE 604, Managua

Editorial **Nicaragüense***, Calle del Triunfo, Managua
Dir: Mario Cajina Vega

Editorial **Lacayo***, 2A Avda SE 507, Managua
Subject: Religion

Editorial **Nuevos Horizontes***, Calle de Candelaria, Managua
Dir: María Teresa Sánchez

Editorial **San José***, Calle Central Este 607, Managua

Club del Libro Nicaragüense, Librería y Editorial **Siglo XX***, Apdo 2173, Managua
Dir: Dr Fernando Centeno Zapata
Subject: Law

Editorial **Unión***, Avda Central Norte, Managua
Subject: Travel

Librería y Editorial, **Universidad Nacional** de Nicaragua*, León
Subjects: Education, History, Mathematics, Law, Philology, Economics, Sciences, Politics, Literature

Major Booksellers

Librería **América***, Bosques de Altamira, Managua Tel: 80895

Centro Cultural **Bautista**, Apdo 5776, Managua Tel: 24714

Librería **Blandon***, Apdo 2206, Managua

Librería **Club** de Lectores*, Centro Comercial Módulo 9, Managua Tel: 82240

Librería Recinto 'Ruben **Dario'***, Universidad Nacional Autonoma de Nicaragua, Apdo 663, Managua

Librería **Cultural Nicaraguense***, Apdo 807, Managua Tel: 6663

Librería **Tecnológica Universitaria***, Universidad Centroamericana, Apdo 69, Managua Tel: 80351

Librería **Universitaria***, Universidad Nacional Autónoma de Nicaragua, León Tel: 2612

Librería **Recalde***, Apdo 666, Managua Tel: 81156/61239

Major Libraries

Archivo General de la Nación (National Archives)*, 6a Calle 402, Managua

Biblioteca Nacional (National Library)*, Calle del Triunfo 302, Managua

Biblioteca Central del **Universidad Nacional** de Nicaragua*, León

Library Associations

Asociación de Bibliotecas Universitarias y Especializadas de Nicaragua (Association of University and Special Libraries of Nicaragua)*, Apdo 68, León
Publication: Boletín

Asociación Nicaraguense de Bibliotecarios (ASNIBI) (Nicaraguan Association of Librarians)*, Biblioteca Nacional, Ministerio de Educacion Publica, Barrio 'La Fuente', Managua
Executive Secretary: Susana Morales Hernández

Library Journals

Boletín (Bulletin), Association of University and Special Libraries of Nicaragua, Apdo 68, León

Niger

General Information

Language: French
Religion: Catholic and Muslim
Population: 4.9 million
Currency: CFA franc
Export/Import Information: No tariff on books; advertising matter subject to 10% Fiscal and 5% Customs Duty (EEC members pay 50% of Customs Duty). 2.5% Statistical Tax. Import licence for goods from non-franc zone. Exchange controls for non-franc zone

Publishers

Church World Service*, BP 624, Niamey Tel: 2449 Cable Add: Le Sahel
Telex: 5232NI
Man Dir: Jon Otto
Subjects: Reference, Religion, Paperbacks

Government Printer (Imprimerie Générale du Niger)*, BP 61, Niamey

Major Booksellers

Librairie **Fellicelli & Poli***, BP 331, Niamey

Librairie **Mauclert***, BP 868, Niamey Tel: 722778

Major Libraries

Archives nationales*, Présidence de la République, Niamey

Centre d'Enseignement supérieur de Niamey (University Education Centre)*, Bibliothèque, BP 237, Niamey

Centre de Documentation*, Commission du Fleure Niger, BP 933, Niamey Tel: 723101/723102 Cable Add: Comfleuniger Niamey
Dir: Dr I Insa
Parent organization: Commission du fleure Niger
Publications (1 in 1976; 1 in 1977) are concerned with development of the natural resources of the River Niger Basin
Founded: 1971

Bibliothèque de l'**Université de Niamey***, BP 237, Niamey Tel: 732713

Library Associations

River Niger Commission, Documentation and Analysis Centre*, PO Box 729, Niamey
Publication: Bulletin of Bibliographic Descriptions and Abstracts

Library Journals

Bulletin of Bibliographic Descriptions and Abstracts, River Niger Commission, Documentation and Analysis Centre, PO Box 729, Niamey

Nigeria

General Information

Language: English
Religion: Muslim predominantly
Population: estimates vary between 66.6 million and 80.6 million
Bank Hours: 0800-1500 Monday; 0800-1300 Tuesday-Friday
Shop Hours: Vary locally. 0800-1230, 1400-1630 Monday-Friday; 0800-1230 Saturday
Currency: 100 kobo = 1 naira
Export/Import Information: No tariffs on books or advertising matter. Open general licence. Obscene literature prohibited. Exchange controls
Copyright: UCC, Florence (see International section)

Book Trade Organizations

Nigerian Booksellers' Association, PO Box 3168, Ibadan
President: 'Wunmi Adegbonmire; *Secretary:* Sam Olaniyan

Nigerian Publishers' Association, c/o PMB 5164, Ibadan Tel: 462972
President: Chief Gabriel Adeleke Alawode
Publication: Book Publishing Process

Book Trade Reference Books and Journals

Books

Publishing in Nigeria, Ethiope Publishing Corporation, PMB 1192, Benin City (Contains several informative articles on the publishing scene in Nigeria)

Serials in Print in Nigeria, National Library of Nigeria, 4 Wesley St, PMB 12626, Lagos

Journals

National Bibliography of Nigeria, National Library of Nigeria, 4 Wesley St, PMB 12626, Lagos (Published annually since 1950. Cumulations before 1971 published by the Ibadan University Press. Also available as a weekly service)

New Nigeriana, University of Ife Bookshop Ltd, Ile-Ife (Bi-annual checklist, available free of charge from the Ife bookshop)

Nigerian Books in Print, National Library of Nigeria, 4 Wesley St, PMB 12626, Lagos

Northern Nigerian Publications, Ahmadu Bello University Library, Zaria (annual)

Publishers

A B I C Publishers, PMB 1161, Oshodi, Lagos
Branch Off: 6 Old Cemetry Rd, Onitsha
Subjects: Reference, Dictionaries
ISBN Publisher's Prefix: 978-2269

Academy Press Ltd, subsidiary of West African Book Publishers Ltd (qv)

African Resources Publishing Co*, PMB 5398, Ibadan
Subjects: General Fiction & Nonfiction, Belles Lettres, Poetry, Biography, History, Africana, How-to, Study Guides, Secondary Textbooks

African Universities Press+, Pilgrim Books Ltd, PMB 5617, Ibadan (Located at: 9 First Rd, Oluyole Estate, Ring Rd, Ibadan) Cable Add: Pilgrim Ibadan Telex: 31530
Man Dir: John E Leigh; *Sales Manager:* J A Kilanko
Parent Company: Pilgrim Books Ltd (qv)
Subjects: Primary, Secondary and Tertiary Textbooks
Miscellaneous: Depots at 305 Herbert Macaulay St, PO Box 3560, Lagos; 74 Oguta Rd, PO Box 21, Onitsha; 17 Ciroma St, Gellesu, Zaria

Africana Educational Publishers Co, PMB 1639, Onitsha (Located at: 13B Oguta Rd, Onitsha)
Man Dir: P N C Omabu; *Editorial:* K B C Onwubiko; *Marketing:* Frank Morebike
Br Off: 49 Zik's Ave, Uwani, Enugu
Subjects: How-to, Study Guides, General Science, Secondary & Primary Textbooks, *At a Glance* series
Founded: 1971

Africani Agency*, 98 Emir's Rd, PO Box 38, Ilorin
Subjects: General Nonfiction, History, Africana, How-to, Study Guides, Paperbacks, Secondary Textbooks

Ahmadu Bello University Press Ltd, PMB 1094, Zaria Tel: 2054 Cable Add: Unibello Press Zaria Telex: 75241 Zarabu Ng
Man Dir: Mrs Modupe Adeogun
Subjects: Biography, History, Africana, Reference, Social Science, University Textbooks
1977: 2 titles *1978:* 5 titles *Founded:* 1974
ISBN Publisher's Prefix: 978-125

Alliance West African Publishers & Co*, Orindingbin Estate, New Aketan Layout, PMB 1039, Oyo Tel: Oyo 124
Manager: Chief M O Ogunmola BA; *Editorial:* Poju Amori BA; *Sales:* L Oyeniji; *Publicity/Permissions:* Kehinde Ogunmola
Subjects: Biography, History, Africana, How-to, Study Guides, Nigerian Languages, General Science, Secondary & Primary School Textbooks
1978: 1 title *Founded:* 1971

Aowa Press & Publications*, PO Box 3090, Ibadan
Subjects: How-to, Study Guides, Primary & Secondary Textbooks

Aromolaran Publishing Co Ltd, PO Box 1800, Ibadan Tel: 410529 Telex: 31158 Arbook Nigeria
Man Dir: Adekunle Aromolaran; *Sales:* Mrs V M Aromolaran
Subjects: Belles Lettres, Poetry, Biography, How-to, Study Guides, Religion, Juveniles; Arts, Science and General Books for Primary and Secondary Schools and Universities
1978: 20 titles *Founded:* 1970

Black Academy Press*, PO Box 255, Owerri, Imo State Cable Add: Bapress
Man Dir: Dr S Okechukwu Mezu
Subjects: General Nonfiction, Belles Lettres, Poetry, Biography, History, Africana
Miscellaneous: Publishers of *Black Academy Review* (quarterly of the Black World)

C S S Bookshops, Agency and Publishing Division+*, 50 Broad St, PO Box 174, Lagos Tel: 25517/9 Cable Add: Bookshops
Man Dir: Akin O Shenbanjo; *Publicity:* 'Dele Oladuiyuye
Subjects: General Nonfiction, Biography, History, Africana, Religion, General Science, Law, Medicine, Secondary & Primary Textbooks
Subsidiary: CSS Bookshops, PO Box 174, Lagos (and regional offices at Ibadan, Zaria, Port Harcourt)

Conch Magazine Ltd*, Publishers, 113 Douglas Rd, Owerri
Man Dir: Sunday Anozie
Subjects: General Nonfiction, Belles Lettres, Poetry, History, Africana, Paperbacks, Social Science
Subsidiary: Conch Magazine Ltd, 65 Jenkenstown Rd, New Paltz, NY 12561, USA

Cross Continent Press Ltd*, 226 Murtala Muhammed Way, PO Box 282, Yaba, Lagos Tel: 31828 Cable Add: Croconpres Lagos
Man Dir: T C Nwosu; *Editorial, Publicity:* O A Achonu; *Marketing:* P C Echeruo; *Financial:* L O Oshin
Subsidiary Company: Editorial Consultancy & Agency Services (Authors' and Publishers' Agents and Consultants) GPO Box 4573, Lagos
Subjects: General Fiction & Nonfiction, Belles Lettres, Poetry, Biography, How-to, Study Guides, Juveniles, Paperbacks, Primary, Secondary & Tertiary Textbooks
Founded: 1974
ISBN Publisher's Prefix: 978-134

Daily Times of Nigeria Ltd+*, Book Sales Division, 3-7 Kakawa St, PO Box 139, Lagos Tel: 26611 Telex: 21333
Chief Executive: Dr P D Cole; *Editorial:* Peter Osugo; *Sales:* J Tan Olu; *Production:* E A Cole
Subsidiary Company: Times Press Ltd
Subjects: Reference, Nigerian *Who's Who*
Book Club: Times Book Club
Founded: 1925

Daystar Press (Publishers)+*, Daystar Ho, PO Box 1261, Ibadan Tel: 23230
Man Dir/Editorial/Permissions: Modupe Oduyoye; *Production:* Emmanuel Olodun; *Trade:* Lazarus Akidi; *Publicity:* A Osuji
Subjects: Christian Religions, Health, Home & Family Life, Nigerian Culture
1977: 7 titles *Founded:* 1962
ISBN Publisher's Prefix: 978-122

E C W A Productions Ltd+*, PMB 10, Jos
Man Dir: G D H Stanley; *Editorial Dir:* Rev J K Bolarin
Subjects: General, Educational, Religion
Bookshops: Challenge Bookshops (qv)
1977: 32 titles

Educational Research Institute*, PO Box 277, Ibadan
Man Dir: Areoye Oyebola

Subjects: General Nonfiction, Biography, History, Africana, How-to, Study Guides, Religion, General & Social Science, Secondary & Primary Textbooks
Founded: 1970
Subsidiary: Also at 116 Denton St, Lagos

Elizabethan Publishing House*, 41 Ogunlena Drive, Surulere, Lagos Tel: 45305
Man Dir: C A Kogbe
Subjects: Academic, Geology

Emotan Publishing Co (Nigeria) Ltd*, 152nd Ire St, Benin City
Man Dir: P O Onaghise
Subjects: General Fiction, Belles Lettres, Poetry, Paperbacks

Ethiope Publishing Corporation+*, Ring Road, PMB 1332, Benin City Tel: 467 Cable Add: Mass Comm Telex: 41104 MNCBEN
Man Dir: Sunday Olaye; *Senior Editor, Rights & Permissions:* Chris Ghomorrai
Subjects: General Fiction, & Nonfiction, Belles Lettres, Poetry, Biography, History, Africana, How-to, Study Guides, Philosophy, Reference, Juveniles, Paperbacks, Science & Technology, General & Social Science, Law, University & Secondary Textbooks
Founded: 1970

Evans Brothers (Nigeria Publishers) Ltd+, Jericho Rd, PMB 5164, Ibadan Tel: 462970/71/72 Cable Add: Edbooks Ibadan Telex: 31104 Edbook
Man Dir: B O Bolodeoku; *Publishing Director:* C T McGregor; *Trade Director:* R A Oyewole; *Publishing Manager:* Valentine Olayemi, *Marketing Manager:* S A Oke
Associated Company: Evans Bros Ltd, London (qv)
Br Offs: Kaduna, Onitsha and Osogbo
Subjects: Educational generally; General Nonfiction, Belles Lettres, Poetry, Biography, History, Africana, Reference, Juveniles, Paperbacks, Science & Technology, General & Social Science, Secondary & Primary Textbooks
Founded: 1966
ISBN Publisher's Prefix: As for Evans UK (qv)

Olaiya **Fagbamigbe** Ltd (Publishers)*, 11 Methodist Church Rd, Akure Tel: 2075 Cable Add: Fagbamigbe Akure
Man Dir: O Fagbamigbe; *Editorial:* Dr K Omotoso; *Publicity:* G Bolagade Adesina; *Rights & Permissions:* O Fagbamigbe
Orders to: PO Box 14, Akure
Br Offs: Abayonin Estate, Old Ife Rd, PO Box 1176, Ibadan
Subjects: Educational and General
Bookshop: Universal Book Co Ltd, PO Box 136, Akure
1977: 13 titles *1978:* 25 titles *Founded:* 1976
ISBN Publisher's Prefix: 978-164

Grassroots Books, an imprint of Third World First Publications

Heinemann Educational Books (Nigeria) Limited+*, Ighodaro Road, Jericho, PMB 5205, Ibadan Tel: 62060/1/21167 Cable Add: Hebooks Ibadan Telex: 31113 Hebook NG
Man Dir: Aigboje Higo; *Publishing Dir and Rights & Permissions:* Akin Thomas; *Sales & Publicity Dir:* Joe Osadolor
Associated Companies: Heinemann Educational Books Ltd, London (qv) and other Heinemann Educational Books worldwide

Br Offs: 17 Sherikin Ruwa St, Gyelesu, Via Institute of Administration, Zaria, Kaduna State; PMB 2156, Jos, Plateau State; PRB 5648, Port Harcourt, Rivers State; 112 New Hospital Rd, Akure, Ondo State
Subjects: Educational (Primary, Post-Primary and Tertiary), Law, Medicine
1977: 14 titles *Founded:* 1960
ISBN Publisher's Prefix: 978-129

I C I C (Directory Publishers) Ltd*, PMB 3204, Surulere, Lagos (Located at: Directory House, 28 Tauridi St, opp Census Office, Surulere, Lagos) Tel: 41909 Cable Add: ICIC
Man Dir: Olu Adeyemi
Subjects: General, Reference, Telephone and Business Directories
Founded: 1965

Ibadan University Press+, Ibadan Tel: 62550 ext 1244 Cable Add: Univpress Ibadan
Subjects: Biography, History, Africana, Philosophy, Reference, Paperbacks, Medicine, Psychology, Science & Technology, General & Social Science, Law, University & Secondary Textbooks
Founded: 1952
ISBN Publisher's Prefix: 978-121

Ilesanmi Press & Sons (N) Ltd+*, B61, Okesha St, PO Box 204, Ilesha Tel: 2062/2017 Cable Add: Ilesanmi Press Ilesha
Man Dir/Rights & Permissions: G E Ilesanmi; *Editorial:* A Omowaiye; *Sales:* D Ayeni; *Production:* M Adedipe; *Publicity:* Mrs M Ilesanmi
Br Offs: Uyo, Kano, Ibadan, Lagos, Akure, Jos, Calabar, Enugu
Subjects: Educational Books generally; Biography, History, Africana, How-to, Study Guides, Books in Yoruba Language, Teacher Training Manuals, General & Social Science
Bookshop: Faji, Ilesha
1977: 26 titles *Founded:* 1956
ISBN Publisher's Prefix: 157

Islamic Publications Bureau*, 39 Payne Crescent, PO Box 3881, Apapa, Lagos Tel: 48097 Cable Add: Islambureu
Man Dir: Ahmad Patel
Subjects: Islamic and Arabic Language and Literature
Founded: 1969

Kolasanya Publishing Enterprise+*, PO Box 252, Ijebu-Ode
Man Dir: Kola Osunsanya
Subjects: General Nonfiction, How-to, Study Guides, General Science, Secondary & Primary Textbooks

Longman Nigeria Ltd+*, 52 Oba Akran Ave, PMB 1036, Ikeja, Lagos Tel: 33007/33176 Cable Add: Longman Ikeja
Man Dir: Felix A Iwerebon; *Marketing Manager:* O Bankole; *Publishing Manager:* D Royle; *Production:* A W Amaeshi
Subjects: General Fiction & Nonfiction, Belles Lettres, Poetry, Biography, History, Africana, Reference, Religion, Juveniles, Books in Nigerian Languages (various), Paperbacks, Psychology, Science & Technology, General & Social Science, University, Secondary & Primary Textbooks
Founded: 1961
Miscellaneous: Firm is an associate company of Longman Group Ltd, UK (qv)

Macmillan Nigeria Publishers Ltd+, Lagos-Ibadan Expressway Link, PO Box 1463, Ibadan Tel: 413917 Cable Add: Macbooks Ibadan Telex: Mabook 31141

Man Dir: Olu Anulopo; *Publishing:* A Amori; *Marketing:* S Asere, E Ohuka, I Ademokun; *Production:* K Adekogbe; *Publicity:* D Obisesan
Orders to: PO Box 264, Yaba
Parent Company: (40% owner): Macmillan Education Ltd, UK (qv)
Associate Company: Northern Nigerian Publishing Co Ltd (qv)
Branch Offs: Onitsha; Benin City; PO Box 264, Yaba
Subjects: Educational and General Fiction & Non-fiction: Biography, History, Africana, Religion, Juveniles, Books in various Nigerian Languages, Paperbacks, General & Social Science, University, Secondary, Primary and Nursery Textbooks
1977: 12 titles *Founded:* 1965
ISBN Publisher's Prefix: 978-132

Thomas **Nelson** (Nigeria) Ltd+, Nelson Ho, 8 Ilupeju By-Pass, PMB 21303, Ikeja, Lagos Tel: 931452 Cable Add: Thonelson Ikeja
Man Dir: Chief Gabriel Alawode; *Publishing Manager:* S Mabogunje; *Marketing Dir:* Ezekiel Iyekolo
Subjects: General Nonfiction, History, Africana, Books in various Nigerian Languages, General & Social Science, Secondary & Primary Textbooks
1976-78: 18 titles
Miscellaneous: Company is in the Thomson Books Ltd group, a part of International Thomson Organization Ltd (Canada)

New Horn Press Ltd*, PO Box 4138, Ibadan
Man Dir: Dr Abiola Irele; *Senior Editor, Rights & Permissions:* Kole Omotoso
Subjects: General Fiction & Nonfiction, Belles Lettres, Poetry, How-to, Study Guides, Paperbacks
Founded: 1974

Nigerian Trade Review, PO Box 603, Lagos
Man Dir: P A Dawodu
Subjects: General, Business Directories
Founded: 1958
Miscellaneous: Publish *General Trade Directory of Nigeria*

Northern Nigerian Publishing Co Ltd+* Gaskiya Bldg, PO Box 412, Zaria Tel: 2087 Cable Add: Gasmac
Man Dir: Malam Amfani Joe; *Publishing Executive:* Ian Taylor
Associate Company: Macmillan Nigeria Ltd (qv)
Subjects: General Nonfiction, Belles Lettres, Poetry, Biography, History, Africana, Religion, Juveniles, Books in Hausa and other Nigerian Languages, Paperbacks, Secondary & Primary Textbooks

Nwamife Publishers Ltd*, 10 Ibiam St, Uwani, PO Box 430, Enugu Tel: (042) 254566 Cable Add: Nwamife Enugu
Chairman: Alex I Ekwueme; *Sales/Production/Publicity:* Samuel Umesike; *Editorial/Rights & Permissions:* Mrs Nina Mba
Subjects: General Fiction & Nonfiction; Belles Lettres, Poetry, Biography, History, Africana, How-to, Study Guides, Juveniles, Igbo Language & Literature, General Science, Law; University, Secondary & Primary Textbooks; Paperbacks
1977: 10 titles *Founded:* 1970
ISBN Publisher's Prefix: 978-124

Ogunsanya Press, Publishers and Bookstores Ltd+, PO Box 95, Ibadan (Located at: SW9/1133 Orita Challenge, Ibadan) Tel: Ibadan 410619 Cable Add: Pombapress

Man Dir, Editorial, Rights & Permissions: Lucas Justus Popo-Ola Ogunsanya; *Sales, Publicity:* J P F Adeyoju; *Production:* S B O Folayan
Branch Off: Popo-Ola Jubilee Lodge, Oke Imoru, PO Box 155, Ijebu Ode, Ogun State
Subjects: History, Geography, Mathematics, English, Science, Social Studies, Arabic
Bookshop: 64 Agbeni St (opp Foko Junction), Ibadan
1977: 9 titles *1978:* 27 titles *Founded:* 1970

Onibonoje Press & Book Industries (Nigeria) Ltd+*, SW8/77 Oke-Ado, PO Box 3109, Ibadan Tel: 24326
Man Dir: Gabriel Onibonoje; *Sales Manager:* E A Onibonoje; *Senior Editor, Rights & Permissions:* J Olu Onibonoje
Subjects: General Fiction & Nonfiction, Belles Lettres, Poetry, Biography, History, Africana, How-to, Study Guides, Religion, Juveniles, Yoruba Language & Literature, Paperbacks, General & Social Science, Secondary & Primary Textbooks
Book Club: Onibonoje Book Club
Bookshop and Showroom: SW8/77 Oke-Ado, Ibadan
Founded: 1958

Orisun Editions*, PO Box 3079, Ibadan
Man Dir: Bola Ige
Subjects: General, Belles Lettres, Poetry

Paico Ltd*, 46 Commercial Ave, PO Box 3944, Yaba, Lagos
Man Dir: A S Ette
Subjects: General Nonfiction, How-to, Study Guides, General Science, Secondary & Primary Textbooks
Founded: 1971

People's Publishing Co Ltd*, PO Box 3121, Lagos
Subjects: General Nonfiction, Socialism

Pilgrim Books Ltd, 305 Herbert Macauley St, PO Box 3560, Lagos Tel: 45939 Cable Add: Pilgrim Lagos
Man Dir: John E Leigh; *Sales Manager:* J O Awodiran
Subjects: General Nonfiction, Belles Lettres, Poetry, Biography, History, Africana, Juveniles, Paperbacks, General & Social Science, Secondary & Primary Textbooks
Subsidiary: African Universities Press (qv)

Publications International (Nigeria) Ltd*, PMB 5097, Ibadan
Man Dir: 'Bisi Talwo
Subjects: General, Secondary & Primary Textbooks
Founded: 1971

Scholar Publications International (Nigeria) Ltd*, PO Box 5097, Ibadan
Subjects: Government, Economics, English, Religion, Chemistry
1977: 6 titles *Founded:* 1972
ISBN Publisher's Prefix: 978-138

Sketch Publishing Co Ltd*, Sketch Bldgs, New Court Rd, PMB 5067, Ibadan Tel: 25191/93 Cable Add: Sketch
Man Dir: Felix A Adenaike; *Editorial:* 'Tola Adeniyi
Subjects: General Books, Reference Books
Founded: 1964

Third World First Publications, 10–14 Calcutta Crescent, PO Box 610, Apapa, Lagos
Man Dir: Naiwu Osahon; *Senior Editor, Rights & Permissions:* Bakin Kunama; *Advertising:* L Williams
Imprints: Grassroots Books

Subjects: General Fiction and Nonfiction, Belles Lettres, Poetry, Black Power, Paperbacks (quarterly publication, *Third World First*)
1977-78: 12 titles *Founded:* 1971

Town & Gown Press*, 4 Kajew St, Akoka, PMB 5073, Yaba, Lagos
Man Dir: J E Adetoro
Subjects: General Nonfiction, Belles Lettres, Poetry, Biography, History, Africana, Paperbacks, Secondary Textbooks

University of Ife Press+, Ile-Ife Tel: 2291 ext 308 Cable Add: Press Ifevarsity
Acting Executive Editor: 'Gbemi Sodipo
Subjects: Biography, History, Africana, Philosophy, Reference, Religion, Law, Social Science, University Textbooks
1977-78: 50 titles *Founded:* 1968

University of Lagos Press*, Yaba, Lagos
Secretary: E Bejide Bankole
Orders to: Evans Brothers (Nigeria Publishers) Ltd, PMB 5164, Ibadan
Subjects: Biography, History, Africana, Law, Social Science, University Textbooks

University of London Press*, PO Box 62, Ibadan

University Press Ltd+, Oxford House, Iddo Gate, PMB 5095, Ibadan Tel: 23066/7 & Warehouse, PMB 5142 Jericho, Ibadan Tel: 24117 Cable Add: Oxonian Ibadan Telex: Ibadan 31121
Man Dir: Michael O Akinleye; *Publishing Services Manager:* T J Benbow; *Editorial:* B O Adeleke; *Production Manager:* G O Abegunde; *Sales Manager:* M A Akpan
Associate Company: Oxford University Press, UK (qv)
1977-78: 40 titles *Founded:* 1949
Subjects: General Fiction & Nonfiction, Poetry, Biography, History, Africana, Reference, Religion, Juveniles, Books in various Nigerian Languages, Paperbacks, Medicine, Science & Technology, General & Social Science, University, Secondary & Primary Textbooks

University Publishing Co, 11 Central School Rd, PO Box 386, Onitsha Tel: 223 Onitsha Cable Add: Varsity Box 386 Onitsha
Dirs: F C Ogbalu, W C Ifezue; *Editorial:* J U Eburne; *Sales:* D O Orakwue; *Production:* I Nweke; *Publicity:* Christian Ogbalu; *Permissions:* Cecilia Ogbalu
Orders to: Varsity Bookshop, 64 New Market Rd, Onitsha
Associate Companies: Cynako International Press, Aba; Thomas Nelson (Nigeria) (qv); African Literature Bureau, Aba
Br Offs: Varsity Bookshop/Press, Eke-Oyibo, Abagana, Njikoka, LGA; 64 New Market Rd, Onitsha
Subjects: General Nonfiction, Belles Lettres, Poetry, Biography, History, Africana, Philosophy, Religion, Juveniles, Igbo Language & Literature, Quality Paperbacks, Primary & Secondary Textbooks, Periodicals, Books in Vernacular and Dialect
Bookshops: Varsity Bookshop/Press at: Oye-Agu, Abagana, Njikoka LGA; Eke-Amawbia, Amawbia, Awka LGA; Abiriba, Ohafia LGA
1977: 10 titles *Founded:* 1959
ISBN Publisher's Prefix: 978-160

Varsity Industrial Press, 11 Central School Rd, Onitsha
Man Dir: Walter Ifezue
Subjects: Igbo Language & English, Primary & Secondary Textbooks

John **West** Publications Ltd, 212 Broad St, PO Box 2416, Lagos Tel: 24388/20558 Cable Add: Jakpress
Man Dir: L K Jakande; *Manager:* Bayo Fadoju
Subjects: General Nonfiction, Biography, How-to, Study Guides, Reference, Annuals, Paperbacks
Founded: 1962

West African Book Publishers Ltd*, PO Box 3445, Ilupeju Industrial Estate, Lagos Tel: 34555/6 Cable Add: Acadpress
Man Dir: B A Idris Animashaun; *Sales Manager:* J O A Onifade; *Editorial:* Laoye Egunjobi
Subjects: Reference, Guide Books, Paperbacks, Health, General Science
Founded: 1967
Subsidiary: Academy Press Ltd, PO Box 3445, Lagos

Literary Agents

Africa Agency*, PO Box 3810, Lagos

Editorial Consultancy & Agency Services*, PO Box 4573, Lagos (Located at: 226 Murtala Muhammed Way) Tel: 931828 Cable Add: Edicanses Lagos
Authors' & Publishers' Agents & Consultants
Editorial Director: T C Nwosu
Special Interests: Africana/Nigeriana, Fiction, Plays, Educational Books at all levels
Parent Company: Cross Continent Press Limited, Lagos, Nigeria (qv)

F C **Ogbalu**, PO Box 386, Onitsha

Book Clubs

Onibonoje Book Club*, PO Box 3109, Ibadan
Owned by: Onibonoje Press & Book Industries (Nigeria) Ltd (Ibadan)
Subjects: Fiction, Drama

Times Book Club*, 3–7 Kakawa St, PO Box 139, Lagos
Owned by: Daily Times of Nigeria

Varsity Book Club, 11 Central School Rd, Onitsha
Organized by: Varsity Press

Major Booksellers

Ahmadu Bello University Bookshop*, Zaria

Benin University Bookshop*, University of Benin, PMB 1154, Benin City Tel: 343 ext 33

The **Bestseller**, Universal Distributors Ltd, PO Box 7036, Falomo Shopping Centre, SW Ikoyi, Lagos Tel: 22407 (subsidiary of Nigerian Book Suppliers Ltd)
Manager: Mrs B Bot
Also at Durbar Hotel, Kaduna

Book Representation Co Ltd*, PMB 5349, E9/806B Ife Rd, Agodi Area, Ibadan

C S S (Nigeria) Bookshops Ltd*, 50 Broad St, PO Box 174, Lagos Tel: 25517 (branches throughout the country)

Challenge Bookshops, Agege Motor Rd, PMB 12256, Lagos Tel: 847690 30 branches throughout the country, and several wholesale outlets

NIGERIA

Edekes Bookshop Stores Ltd, 2 Falolu Rd, PO Box 974, Surulere, Lagos

Hart Mossman & Co Ltd*, PMB 2283, Lagos

Kingsway Stores*, PO Box 652, Lagos
Major department store with book department — branches throughout the country

Kwaratech Bookshop*, Kwana State College of Technology, PMB 1375, Ilorin Tel: 2440 ext 14

Mabrochi International Co, PO Box 1572, Lagos
Specializes in mail order services

Morison Arnold Ltd*, 63 Hadejia Rd, PO Box 251, Kano

Niger (Acada) Bookshop Ltd*, 90 Ojuelagba Rd, Surulere, Lagos Tel: 44016

Nigerian Baptist Book Stores*, Lagos By-Pass, PMB 5070, Ibadan

Nigerian Book Suppliers Ltd, PO Box 3870, 20 Akinremi St, Ikeja, Lagos Tel: 22407
General Manager: Mrs O Williams
Library Suppliers specializing in Legal and Academic Books
(Retail Shop: The Bestseller (qv))

Odusote Bookstores Ltd, 68 Lagos Bye-Pass, Oke-Ado, PO Box 244, Ibadan Tel: 414419 Cable Add: Odbook, Ibadan Telex: 31215 (Odbook NG)
Also at 177 Herbert Macaulay St, Yaba, Lagos State Tel: 844015
Man Dir: Ola Odusote

Rational Bookshops (Nigeria)*, Rational Bldgs, Oke-Bola, PO Box 3162, Ibadan

University Bookshop (Nigeria) Ltd, University of Ibadan, Ibadan Tel: 62550 ext 1208 (branches in Ilorin, Port Harcourt, Calabar, and Maiduguri)
General Manager: Simon Walton

University of Ife Bookshop Ltd, University of Ife, Ile-Ife Tel: Ife 2291 ext 2145 and 2146 Cable Add: Bookshop Ifevarsity
Branches at Ondo and Uyo

University of Lagos Bookshop*, Yaba, Lagos Tel: 41361/9

University of Nigeria Bookshop, Nsukka Tel: 6251 ext 7
Manager: K K Oyeoku

Major Libraries

Agricultural Library, PMB 1044, Samaru, Zaria Tel: 2091
Librarian: Malam R Salami
Publications include: *Library Accession List* (monthly), *List of Current Serials in the Library* (annually), *KWIC Index to the Abstracting & Indexing Publications currently being received by the IAR Library*, 2nd edition 1976

Ahmadu Bello University Library*, Samaru-Zaria Tel: 06322553
Publication: Northern Nigerian Publications

Benin University Library, PMB 1191, Benin City Tel: 240115
University Librarian: O O Ogundipe;
Publications: Annual Report, Library News, List of Serials, Current Awareness Bulletin of the Medical Sub-library

Ibadan University Library, Ibadan Tel: 462550 ext 1424-26
Librarian: T Olabisi Odeinde
Publications: Library Record (m); *Annual Report, 1976/77; Humanities: A Guide to Reference Sources in the Library* (1976) (Library Guide No 3); *Biological Sciences: A Guide to Reference Sources in the Library* (1976) (Library Guide No 4); *Education: A Guide to Reference Sources in the Library* (1978) (Library Guide No 5)

International Institute of Tropical Agriculture Library, PMB 5320, Ibadan Tel: 413440 Cable Add: Tropfound Ikeja Telex: 31417 Tropic NG

Library Board of **Kaduna** State, PMB 2061, Bida Rd, Kaduna Tel: 242590/210322
Dir: Inuwa Diko
Publications: Annual Report, New Additions to Stock (monthly)

Kano State Library*, PMB 3094, Kano

Lagos City Council Libraries*, 48 Broad St, PMB 2025, Lagos Tel: 50246

Midwest Library Board*, Bendel State Library, PMB 1127, Benin City Tel: 537/1350
Dir: Mrs W Onyeonwu

National Archives of Nigeria Library*, PMB 4, University of Ibadan Post Office, Ibadan
Library Officer: O A Momoh
Publications: Catalogues; Bibliographies; Handlists; Guides

National Library of Nigeria*, 4 Wesley St, PMB 12626, Lagos Tel: 56547 Cable Add: Biblios
Publication: National Bibliography of Nigeria

Nnamdi Azikiwe Library, University of Nigeria, Nsukka Tel: 6251 ext 59
Librarian: S C Nwoye
Publication: Nsukka Library Notes

University of Ife Library*, Ile-Ife Tel: 2290

University of Lagos Library*, Akoka, Yaba, Lagos Tel: 41361/2

Library Associations

Anambra/Imo States School Libraries Association*, c/o Enugu Campus Library, University of Nigeria, Enugu Tel: 252080 Cable Add: Nigersity Enugu
Hon Sec: Dr Dorothy S Obi

Nigerian Library Association*, PMB 12655, Lagos Tel: 56590
Secretary: Inuwa Diko
Publications: Nigerian Libraries (3 a year), *NLA Newsletter*
(There are also regional associations in the various states under the umbrella of the Nigerian Library Association)

Library Reference Books and Journals

Books

Directory of Lagos Libraries, Oceana Publications Inc, Dobbs Ferry, NY 10522, USA

Libraries in Nigeria. A Directory, National Library of Nigeria, 4 Wesley St, PMB 12626, Lagos

Nominal List of Practising Librarians in Nigeria, National Library of Nigeria, 4 Wesley St, PMB 12626, Lagos (Useful listing providing names and addresses of practising librarians at 59 libraries in Nigeria. To be published annually in the future)

Journals

ECS School Libraries Bulletin, East Central State School Libraries Association, c/o Enugu Campus Library, University of Nigeria, Enugu

Library Record, Ibadan University Library, Ibadan

NLA Newsletter, Nigerian Library Association, PMB 12655, Lagos

Nigerian Libraries, Nigerian Library Association, PMB 12655, Lagos (the official publication of the Nigerian Library Association; the Association also publishes a mimeographed newsletter)

Literary Associations and Societies

There is no national literary association or professional body of writers, but small literary societies and writers' circles, etc are attached to the English departments at the various universities

Literary Periodicals

Afriscope, Pan Afriscope (Nigeria) Ltd, 45 Saibu St, PMB 1119, Yaba, Lagos (An influential and widely circulated monthly current affairs, political, economic, and cultural magazine edited by Uche Chukumerije. Contains a regular 'Literary Scene' column edited by the Nigerian writer Kole Omotoso, which features book reviews and gives extensive coverage to cultural and literary events throughout Africa)

The Benin Review, Ethiope Publishing Corporation, PMB 1192, Benin City (Impressive new magazine edited by Abiola Irele and Pius Olehe, the first number of which was published late in 1974. The journal's scope covers all the arts in Africa, both traditional and modern, and is also concerned with cultural life in the Black World generally.)

The Muse; literary journal of the English Association at Nsukka, University of Nigeria, Nsukka (An irregularly published literary magazine. Another literary magazine, *Okike*, originally published from Nsukka and edited by Chinua Achebe, is now published in the USA)

Nigeria Magazine, Cultural Division, Federal Ministry of Information, PMB 12524, Lagos (Bi-monthly cultural and literary magazine published since 1932 and currently edited by Frank Aig-Imoukhuede)

Oduma, Rivers State Council for Arts and Culture, 74-76 Bonny St, PMB 5049, Port Harcourt (A well produced new magazine published since 1973 and edited by Theo Vincent. Covers a wide spectrum of the arts, history, languages and philosophy)

Note: There are several more 'little magazines', largely in mimeographed form, published by English departments and writers' groups at the various universities

Literary Prizes

Ife Book Fair Prizes
For children's books in the age groups up to 6, and 7 to 12. Awarded annually. Enquiries to University of Ife Bookshop Ltd, Ile-Ife

Nigerian Broadcasting Corporation
Various literary and drama competitions are sponsored by the Nigerian Broadcasting Corporation, Lagos, from time to time. Enquiries to Nigerian Broadcastng Corporation, Broadcasting Ho, Ikoyi, Lagos

Translation Agencies and Associations

Igbo Language Translation Agency, c/o University Publishing Co Ltd, 11 Central School Rd, PO Box 386, Onitsha

The **Nigeria Educational Research** Council, PO Box 8058, Lagos (Located at: 17 James Robertson St, Surulere, Lagos) Tel: 843209/841593 Cable Add: Edusearch, Lagos
The Research Council has a Translation Bureau attached to it

Norway

General Information

Language: Norwegian (English widely spoken)
Religion: Lutheran
Population: 4 million
Bank Hours: 0845–1615 Monday-Wednesday and Friday; 0845–1800 Thursday
Shop Hours: 0830–1700 Monday-Friday; 0830–1400 Saturday
Currency: 100 øre = 1 Norwegian krone
Export/Import Information: No tariff on books except children's picture books, normally 12% but EFTA free, EEC 4.8% and preferential to long list of 'developing countries'. Books exempt from VAT. No duty on advertising. No import licence required. Nominal exchange controls
Copyright: UCC, Berne, Florence (see International section)

Book Trade Organizations

Norsk Antikvarbokhandlerforening (Norwegian Antiquarian Booksellers' Association)*, Ullevålsveien 1, Oslo 1

Norsk Bokhandler Medhjelper Forening (Norwegian Book Trade Employees' Association)*, Ovre Vollgate 15, Oslo 1
Publications: Norsk Bokhandler Matrikel, Krebsen, Norsk Boknøkkel

Norsk Bokhandlersamband (Norwegian Christians Booksellers' Union), Kirkegt 32, Oslo 1
Chairman: Odd Løver

Norsk Bokimport A/S*, Ovre Vollgate 5, Oslo 1 Tel: (02) 417050

Norsk Forleggersamband (Norwegian Christians Publishers' Union), Kirkegt 32, Oslo 1
Secretary: Per Johnsen

Norsk Musikkforleggerforening (Norwegian Music Publishers' Association)*, c/o Musikk-Huset, Karl Johansgate 45, Oslo 1 Tel: 334897

Norske Bokhandlerforening (Norwegian Booksellers' Association)*, Ovre Vollgate 15, Oslo 1 Tel: (02) 410760
Publications: Bokcentralens Fortegnelse Over Bokhandlere, Norsk Bokfortegnelse, Norsk Bokhandlertidende

Den **Norske Forleggerforening** (Norwegian Publishers' Association)*, Ovre Vollgate 15, Oslo 1 Tel: (02) 422285/411858
Dir: T Solumsmoen

Sentral Bokhandel A/S, Gml Drammensvei 48, Postboks 170, N-1321 Stabekk Tel: (02) 532376
Dir: Cathrine Holst

Book Trade Reference Books and Journals

Books

Bibliografi over Norges Offentlige Publikasjoner (Bibliography of Norwegian Government Publications), The Royal University Library, Drammenesveien 42, N-1302, Oslo

Bokcentralens Fortegnelse over Bokhandlere (The Book Centre's List of Booksellers), Norwegian Booksellers' Association, Ovre Vollgate 15, Oslo 1

Norsk Bokhandler Matrikel (Norwegian Booksellers Membership List), Norwegian Book Trade Employees' Association, Ovre Vollgate 15, Oslo 1

Journals

Krebsen (The Crab); Norwegian journal for booksellers, Norwegian Book Trade Employees' Association, Övre Vollgate 15, Oslo 1

Norsk Bokfortegnelse (Norwegian National Bibliography), Norwegian Booksellers' Association, Ovre Vollgate 15, Oslo 1

Norsk Bokhandlertidende (Norwegian Booksellers' News), Norwegian Booksellers' Association, Ovre Vollgate 15, Oslo 1

Publishers

Ansgar Forlag A/S+*, Møllergate 26, Oslo 1 Tel: (02) 208518
Manager: Edvin Tinnesand
Subjects: Fiction, General, Religion
ISBN Publishers' Prefix: 82-503

H **Aschehoug** & Co (W Nygaard) A/S+, Sehestedsgate 3, Oslo 1 Tel: (02) 337990 Cable Add: Aco Oslo
Man Dir: William Nygaard; *Editorial:* Oivind Blom, Harald Horjen, Leif Rosse, Ivar Havnevik; *Rights & Permissions:* Harald Horjen
Subsidiary Company: Kunnskapsforlaget (jointly owned with Gyldendal Norsk Forlag) (qv)
Book Club: Den Norske Bokklubben A/S, Bokklubben Nye Bøker (with three other Norwegian publishers)
Subjects: General Fiction and Nonfiction, Reference, Juveniles, Quality Paperbacks, General & Social Science, Secondary & Primary Textbooks
1977: 600 titles *1978:* 600 titles *Founded:* 1872
ISBN Publisher's Prefix: 82-03

Bladkompaniet A/S+, Stålfjæra 5, Oslo 9 Tel: (02) 257190
Man Dir: Claus Huitfeldt; *Sales Dir:* Reidar Myhre; *Advertising:* Ole Wågenes; *Rights & Permissions, Editor-in-Chief:* Finn Arnesen
Subjects: General Fiction, Paperbacks
1979: 105 titles *Founded:* 1915
ISBN Publisher's Prefix: 82-509

F **Bruns** Bokhandels Forlag A/S+*, Kongensgate 10, Postboks 476, N-7001 Trondheim Tel: (075) 20625
Dir: Finn Brun
Subjects: Science, Technology
Founded: 1873
Bookshop: Kongensgate 10, Postboks 476, N-7000 Trondheim
ISBN Publisher's Prefix: 82-7028

J W **Cappelens** Forlag A/S+*, Kirkegaten 15, Oslo 1 Tel: (02) 336280 Cable Add: Cappelen
Man Dirs: Sigmund Strømme, Jan Wiese; *Editorial:* Per Glad, Aase Gjerdrum, Egil A, Kristoffersen, Ola Haugen; *Sales:* Per Pedersen; *Production:* Erik Pettersen; *Rights & Permissions:* Marie L Holm
Subjects: General Fiction, Nonfiction, Textbooks, Reference, Maps, Religion, Juveniles, Low- & High-priced Paperbacks, Encyclopaedias
Founded: 1829
Book Club: Den Norske Bokklubben A/S (with three other Norwegian publishers)
Antiquarian Booksellers: J W Cappelens Antikvariat, Kirkegate 15, Oslo 1
Subsidiaries: Wennergren-Cappelen A/S, Nedre Vollgate 4, Oslo 1; Cappelen Musikk, Kirkegaten 15, Oslo 1
ISBN Publishers Prefix: 82-02

N W **Damm** og Søn A/S+, Tvetenveien 32, Postboks 6140 Etterstad, Oslo 6 Tel: (02) 687406 Cable Add: Damson
Dirs: Arne Damm, Niels Wilhelm Damm, Per Støkken
Subjects: How-to, Children's Books, Textbooks, Dictionaries, Guidebooks
1977: 90 titles *1978:* 85 titles *Founded:* 1843
ISBN Publishers Prefix: 82-517

Dreyers Forlag+, (B A Butenschøn A/S & Co), Arbiensgate 7, Oslo 2 Tel: (02) 443810 Cable Add: Dreyerbok
Man Dir: Halfdan Kielland; *Editorial:* Anton Fr Andresen, Oistein Parmann; *Sales & Publicity:* Ulla Løhren; *Production:* Bjørn Pedersen
Imprint: Perspektiv
Subjects: General Fiction, Belles Lettres, Poetry, Music, Art, Low- & High-priced Paperbacks, Secondary & Primary Textbooks, Educational Materials, Atlases
1978: 56 titles *Founded:* 1942
ISBN Publishers Prefix: 82-09

J W **Eide** Forlag A/S+, Fosswinckelsgate 8, Postboks 146, N-5001 Bergen Tel: (05) 215801 Cable Add: Eidebok
Man Dir: Sigvald Flataker
Subjects: General Fiction, History, Music, Art, University, Secondary & Primary Textbooks, Educational Materials, Juveniles
ISBN Publishers Prefix: 82-514

Elingaard Forlag A/S+, now Nå Forlag (qv)

Fabritius Forlagshus, Brobekkveien 80, Alnabru, Oslo 5 Tel: (02) 220354
Man Dir: Öyvind Skarlund; *Sales:* Laila Jensen
Subjects: General Nonfiction, Technical, Textbooks, Educational Materials
Founded: 1844
ISBN Publishers Prefix: 82-07

Fonna Forlag L/L+, St Olavs Plass 3, Boks 6912 Oslo 1 Tel: (02) 201303/201201
Chief Executive: Bergitt Villesvik
Subjects: General Fiction, Poetry, Biography, Magazines, Juveniles
1977: 7 titles *1978:* 7 titles *Founded:* 1940
ISBN Publishers Prefix: 82-513

E **Greens** Forlag+*, Sverdrupsgaten 8, Oslo 5 Tel: (02) 376602
Subjects: General Fiction, Belles Lettres, Juveniles
ISBN Publishers Prefix: 82-01

John **Griegs** Forlag+, Vaskerelven 8, Postboks 248, N-5001 Bergen Tel: (05) 233900 Cable Add: Bokgrieg
Man Dir: Rolf Moe Nilssen
Subjects: Non-fiction, Fiction for Children, Co-editions
1978: 17 titles *Founded:* 1721
ISBN Publishers Prefix: 82-533

Grøndahl og Søn Forlag A/S+, Munkedamsveien 35, Oslo 2 Tel: (02) 419740 Cable Add: Bokgrøndahl
Man Dir: Finn P Nyquist; *Editor:* Sølvi Foseide
Subjects: General Nonfiction, Reference, Crime, Textbooks, Illustrated Books, Fiction
Founded: 1812
Bookshop: Grøndahl & Søn Bokhandel A/s, Slottsgate 12, Oslo 1
ISBN Publishers Prefix: 82-504

Gyldendal Norsk Forlag+, Universitetsgaten 16, Postboks 6860 St Olavs Plass, Oslo 1 Tel: (02) 200710 Cable Add: Gyldendal
Man Dir: Dr Brikt Jensen
Subsidiary Company: Kunnskapsforlaget (jointly owned with H Aschehoug og Co A/S) (qv)
Subjects: General Fiction, Science Fiction, Belles Lettres, Poetry, Art, Music, Biography, History, How-to, Politics, Philosophy, Psychology, Reference, Religion, Juveniles, Low-priced Paperbacks, Social Science, Secondary & Primary Textbooks, Easy Readers, Encyclopaedias, Periodicals
1977: approx 660 titles *1978:* approx 730 titles *Founded:* 1925
Book Club: Den Norske Bokklubben A/S and Bokklubben Nye Bøker (with three other Norwegian publishers)
ISBN Publishers Prefix: 82-05

Henny's Forlag, Hagalivegen 1, N-1342 Jar-Oslo
Man Dir: Mrs Henny Andenäs
Subjects: General Fiction, Biography, History, How-to, Philosophy, Religion
Founded: 1962

Hjemmenes Forlag A/S+*, Postboks 1739, Vika, Oslo 1 Tel: (02) 143151
Publisher: Yngve Woxholth
Subject: Cultural and Historical Books (mainly in colour)

Hjemmet A/s*, Kristian den 4des Gate 13, Oslo 1
Parent Company: Gutenberghus Group, Denmark
Associate Companies: Ehapa-Verlag GmbH, German Federal Republic; Gutenberghus Publishing Service, Denmark; Hemmets Journal AB, Sweden (qqv)
Subjects: Juveniles, Business, Periodicals
Founded: 1969

Kunnskapsforlaget, Postboks 6736, Oslo 1 (Located at: Sehestedsgt 4, Sankt Olavs Plass, Oslo 1) Tel: (02) 205215
Administration Dir: Lars Bucher

Johannessen; *Chief Editor:* Egil Tveterås; *Marketing Dir:* Reidar Bøe; *Production:* Rolf Andersson; *Sales Manager:* Tom Thorsteinsen
Parent Companies: H Aschehoug og Co A/S, Gyldendal Norsk Forlag (qqv)
Subjects: Encyclopaedias, Dictionaries
1979: 10 titles *Founded:* 1975
ISBN Publisher's Prefix: 573

Lunde Forlag og Bokhandel A/S+*, Grensen 19, Oslo 1 Tel: (02) 332525 Cable Add: Norskluth
Man Dir: Torbjørn Grønvik; *Rights & Permissions:* Jan Bøe
Subjects: General Fiction, Belles Lettres, Poetry, Biography, Music, Art, Religion, Juveniles, High-priced Paperbacks, Secondary & Primary Textbooks, Educational Materials
1977: 71 titles *Founded:* 1905
Bookshop: Lunde Forlag og Bokhandel A/S, C Sundtsgate 2, N-5000 Bergen, Norway
ISBN Publishers Prefix: 82-520

Luther Forlag A/S+, Kirkegaten 32, Oslo 1 Tel: (02) 332180
Man Dir: Nils Tore Andersen
Subjects: General Fiction, Biography, History, Religion, Juveniles, Low- & High-priced Paperbacks, Dictionaries
1977: approx 120 titles *1978:* approx 140 titles
Miscellaneous: Firm is a merger of Nomi Forlag & Luther Forlag A/S, Kirkegate 32, Oslo 1
ISBN Publishers Prefix: 82-531

Harald **Lyche** og Co A/S+*, N Storgaten 2, Postboks 1102, N-3000 Drammen Tel: (02) 837970
Subjects: General Fiction & Nonfiction, Textbooks
ISBN Publishers Prefix: 82-7008

Minerva Forlag A/S+*, Hansteensgate 12, Oslo 2 Tel: (02) 564548
Publisher: Kjell Stahl Johannessen
Subjects: Nonfiction, Politics, Social & Culture
ISBN Publishers Prefix: 82-528

Ernst G **Mortensens** Forlag+, Sørkedalsveien 10A, Oslo 3 Tel: (02) 603090 Cable Add: Pressmort Telex: 17626
Man Dir: Arne Bonde; *Editorial:* Asbjørn Andresen, Rigmor Foss, Solveig Høysaeten; *Sales:* O E Grønaker; *Administration:* E Werner Hansen; *Book Publishing:* Halvor Pedersen; *Information:* Knut-Jørgen Erichsen; *Advertising:* R Marthinsen; *Rights & Permissions:* Per R Mortensen, Jr
Parent Company: Ernst G Mortensen & Co A/S
Subsidiary Companies: NPs/AssP (Norsk Presseservice/Associated Press A/s, Oslo; Forenede Trykkerier A/s, Oslo; Centralfilm A/s, Oslo
Subjects: General (Publish three weekly magazines and one quarterly)
Founded: 1933
ISBN Publisher's Prefix: 82-527

N K I-forlaget, Professor Kohts vei 108, Postboks 10, N-1321 Stabekk Tel: (472) 122950
Publisher: Jan Lien; *Sales:* Kjell G Rosland; *Publicity:* Bjørn Ribsskog
Subjects: Primary & Secondary Textbooks, Technical Textbooks, General Nonfiction
1977: 60 titles *1978:* 65 titles *Founded:* 1967
ISBN Publisher's Prefix: 82-562

Nå Forlag A/S (formerly Flingaard Forlag)+, Postboks 7058 H, Oslo 3 (Located at Oscarsgate 55, Oslo 2) Tel: (02) 565070
Parent Company: Libertas, Oscarsgate 55, Oslo 2
Subjects: Politics, Marketing, Economy, Crime
1977: 15 titles *1978:* 8 titles
ISBN Publisher's Prefix: 82-505

Norges Boklag+*, Kr Augustgate 14, Oslo 1 Tel: (02) 202823
Manager: Per Roar Öian
Subjects: Plays, Poetry, Biography, Music, Juveniles
Founded: 1925
ISBN Publishers Prefix: 82-522

Olaf **Norlis** Forlag A/S, see Tanum-Norli

Norsk Kunstforlag A/S+*, Arbiensgate 13, Oslo 2 Tel: (02) 566180
Man Dir: Arne Dahl; *Sales Dir:* Simon Gundhus
Subjects: General, Art, Atlases
ISBN Publishers Prefix: 82-90069

Det **Norske Samlaget**+, Postboks 4672 Sofienberg, Oslo 5 (Located at: Trondheimsvegen 15, Oslo 5) Tel: (02) 687600
Man Dir: Olav Vesaas; *Editorial:* Olav Hr Rue; *Sales:* Roar Hauge
Subjects: General Fiction, Belles Lettres, Poetry, Biography, History, Philosophy, Religion, Textbooks, Reference, Juveniles, High-priced Paperbacks
1977: 159 titles *1978:* 138 titles *Founded:* 1868
Miscellaneous: Publish periodicals *Syn og Segn*, *Vår Samtid*, & *Maal og Minne*
ISBN Publishers Prefix: 82-521

Novus Forlag A/S+, Postboks 748, Sentrum, Oslo 1
Man Dir: Olav Røsset
Subjects: Education, General
1977: 4 titles *1978:* 3 titles *Founded:* 1972
ISBN Publisher's Prefix: 82-7099

Pax Forlag A/S+, Gøteborggt 8, Oslo 5 Tel: (02) 379082
Man Dir: Bjørn Einarsen; *Editorial:* Paul Hedlund; *Editorial (Pax leksikon: encyclopaedias):* Irene Iversen; *Sales:* Asmund Lindal; *Production:* Aage-H Hansen; *Publicity:* Haagen Sund
Imprint: Unipax
Bookshop: Thranes Konditori, Gøteborggt 8, Oslo 5
Subjects: Radical and Alternative Publications on Politics, History, Philosophy, Social science, Women in society, Education, Children's books, Modern Classics, General literature, Quality paperbacks
1977: 72 titles *1978:* 50 titles *Founded:* 1964
ISBN Publishers Prefix: 82-530

Pedagogisk Forlag A/S*, Dronningensgaten 23, Oslo 1 Tel: (02) 414927
Subjects: Textbooks, Educational Materials

Rune Forlag+*, Postboks 1202, N-7001 Trondheim Tel: (075) 32362
Publisher: Erling Skjølberg
Subject: General
ISBN Publishers Prefix: 82-523

Chr **Schibsteds** Forlag+, Kristian IV's Gate 1, Postboks 1178, Sentrum, Oslo 1 Tel: (02) 205060 Telex: 11230
General Manager: Ola Veigaard; *Editorial:* Kirsti Schei; *Sales Dir:* Odd Firing; *Rights & Permissions:* Ola Veigaard

Orders to: Forlagsentralen, Postboks 6005, Oslo 6
Parent Company: Schibsted-gruppen, Postboks 1178, Sentrum, Oslo 1
Subjects: How-to, Reference, Juveniles
1977: 55 titles *1978:* 49 titles *Founded:* 1839
ISBN Publishers Prefix: 82-516

Snøfugl Forlag+, Postboks 95, N-7084 Melhus Tel: (074) 70743
Chief Executive, Editorial: Åsmund Snøfugl; *Sales:* Johan Snøfugl
Associate Company: A/s Bygdetrykk, 7084 Melhus
Subjects: General
1977: 16 titles *1978:* 12 titles *Founded:* 1972
ISBN Publisher's Prefix: 82-7083

Solum Forlag A/S+*, Asveien 5, 1324 Lysaker Tel: 534692
Subject: General
ISBN Publishers Prefix: 82-560

Stabenfeldt Forlag+, Tanke Svilandsgate 55, Postboks 189, N-4001 Stavanger Tel: (045) 21553 Cable Add: Bokorm
Man Dir: Hugo Stabenfeldt; *Publishing Dir, Publicity:* Tor Tjeldflåt
Subjects: General Fiction & Nonfiction, Biography
1977: 6 titles *1978:* 11 titles *Founded:* 1920
ISBN Publishers Prefix: 82-532

P F **Steensballes** Boghandels Eftg+, Postboks 130, N-2261 Kirkenaer Tel: (066) 47588
Publisher: Bjarne H Reenskaug
Subjects: General, Schoolbooks
ISBN Publishers Prefix: 82-7004

Tanum-Norli (Johan Grundt Tanum Forlag og Olaf Norlis Forlag A/S)+*, Kr Augustsgate 7A, Oslo 1 Tel: (02) 110260 Cable Add: Tanumlag
Man Dir: Ingar Tanum; *Editorial:* Birger Huse, Helge G Simonsen
Subjects: General Nonfiction, Reference, Textbooks, Education
Bookshops: Tanum/Cammermeyer, Karl Johansgate 41-43, Oslo 1; Tanum bøker Bekkestua, Ringeriksvei 31, N-1340 Bekkestua; Tanum bøker Oppegård, Kolbotnveien 5, N-1410 Kolbotn; Tanum bøker Oppsal, Haakon Tveters Vei 96, Oslo 6; Karl P Thorstensen A/S, Storgt 19, N-2000 Lillestrøm; Alida Waaler Bok- og Papirhandel, Bogstadvn 43, Oslo 6
1977: 80 titles
ISBN Publishers Prefix: 82-518

Teknologisk Forlag, Enebakkveien 117, Oslo 6 Tel: (02) 679690
Man Dir: Rudolf Jenssen; *Sales Dir:* Karl H Ormen; *Rights & Permissions:* Rudolf Jenssen
Subjects: How-to, Philosophy, Textbooks, Reference, Engineering, General Science
1978: 25 titles *Founded:* 1958
ISBN Publishers Prefix: 82-512

Tiden Norsk Forlag+, Postboks 8326, Hammersborg (Located at: Youngstorget 2, Oslo 1) Tel: (02) 335380 Cable Add: Tiden
Man Dir: Trygve Johansen; *Sales & Publicity:* Kåre Myhr; *Financial Man:* Hans Raastad; *Editorial and Rights & Permissions:* Miss Signe Bakken; *Production:* Jakob Rask Arnesen
Subsidiary Companies: Tiden Finans A/S, Aktuell Kunst, Læremiddelhuset
Subjects: General Fiction & Nonfiction, Textbooks, Reference, Paperbacks, Juveniles
Book Clubs: Den Norske Bokklubben A/S; Bokklubben Nye Bøker (with three other Norwegian publishers)
Bookshop: Arbeidernes Bok- og Papirhandel, Youngstorget 4, Oslo 1
1977: 225 titles *Founded:* 1933
ISBN Publishers Prefix: 82-10

Unipax, an imprint of Pax Forlag A/S (qv)

Universitetsforlaget, Postboks 7508, Skillebekk, Oslo 2 Tel: (02) 447900 Cable Add: Universitypress Telex: 18610 Ubook N
Man Dir: Tor Bjerkmann; *Editorial:* Fredrik Lund; *Sales Manager:* Jon Oestboe; *Rights & Permissions:* Vibeke Siegwarth
Orders to: Postboks 2997, Tøyen, Oslo 6
Subjects: Technical, Reference, Science, Paperbacks, Textbooks, Educational Materials (Publishers to the Norwegian Universities)
1977: 400 titles *Founded:* 1935
Miscellaneous: Publishers for the University of Oslo, The University of Bergen, the University of Tromsø, and other institutions of higher learning
ISBN Publishers Prefix: 82-00

Literary Agents

E M B L A, see Pat Shaw Associates

Carlota **Frahm** Literary Agency, Valkyriegaten 17, Postboks 5385, Majorstua, Oslo 3 Tel: (02) 463002 Cable Add: Frahmbook
Dirs: Carlota Frahm, Suzanne Palme

Edith **Kiilerich***, Fiolstr 12, DK-1171 Copenhagen K, Denmark
Miscellaneous: This Danish literary agency also acts for Finnish, Norwegian and Swedish writers

Hanna-Kirsti **Koch***, Postboks 3043, Oslo 2
Contact: Eilif Koch

Kvinner og Klaer*, Allers, Postboks 250, Okern, Oslo 6

Pat **Shaw** Associates (formerly EMBLA)*, Fredbosvei 61, N-1370 Asker Tel: (02) 782829

Book Clubs

Bokklubbens **Barn**, see Den Norske Bokklubben A/S
Subject: Juveniles

Det **Beste** A/S*, Postboks 726-Sentrum, Oslo 1

Bokklubbens **Lyrikkvaennene***, see Den Norske Bokklubben
Subject: Poetry

Den **Norske Bokklubben** A/S*, Ensjoveien 12b, Oslo 6
Includes: Bokklubbens Lyrikkvenner, Bokklubbens Barn, Nye Bøker
Members: 215,000
Owned by: H Aschehoug & Co (W Nygaard) A/S (Oslo), J W Cappelens Forlag A/S (Oslo), Gyldendal Norsk Forlag (Oslo), Tiden Norsk Forlag (Oslo)
Subjects of Den Norske Bokklubben: Fiction, Biography, Travel

Nye Bøker (New Book Club), see Den Norske Bokklubben

Major Booksellers

F **Beyer** Bok-Og Papirhandel A/S*, Strandgate 4, N-5000 Bergen Tel: (05) 215020

F **Bruns** Bokhandel*, Kongensgate 10, Postboks 476, N-7000 Trondheim

Gardum, Søregate 22, N-4000 Stavanger Tel: (045) 20200/20400

Ed B **Giertsen** A/S*, Småstrandgate, Postboks 217, N-5001 Bergen Tel: (05) 219680

Lyngs Bokhandel A/S, Postboks 328, N-7001 Trondheim (Located at: Olav Trygvasonsgate 26, N-7000 Trondheim) Tel: (075) 28616
Manager: Ragnvald C Knudsen

Olaf **Norlis** Bokhandel A/S*, Universitetsgaten 24, Oslo 1 Tel: (02) 336190
Specialists in school books, medical and maritime literature, antiquarian books. Also exporters.

Norsk Bokimport A/S*, Ovre Vollgate 15, Postboks 784, Oslo 1 Tel: (02) 417050

Erik **Qvist** Bokhandel A/S*, Drammensveien 16, Oslo 2 Tel: (02) 445269
Manager: Erik Chr Qvist

Sellevolds Bokhandel A/S, Nedre Slottsgate 8, Oslo 1 Tel: 425258/414150/421529

Sentral Bokhandel a/s, Gml Drammensvei 48, Postboks 170, N-1321 Stabekk Tel: (02) 532376

H **Sundems** Bokhandel A/S, Storgate 12, N-8000 Bodø Tel: (081) 20154
Manager: Carl August Veigård

Tanum/Cammermeyer*, Karl Johansgate 41-43, Oslo 1 Tel: (02) 332980

Tapir*, Universitet i Trondheim, N-7034 Trondheim NTH

Universitetsbokhandeln*, PO Box 307, Blindern, Oslo 3
Manager: Tom Vister

Major Libraries

Bergen offentlige Bibliotek Horda land Fylkesbibliotek (Municipal and County Library)*, Bergen

Deichmanske Bibliotek (City Library of Oslo), Henrik Ibsens gate 1, Oslo 1 Tel: (02) 204335

Drammen Folkebibliotek (Public Library of Drammen), Gamle Kirkeplass 7, Postboks 1136, N-3001 Drammen

Styret for det **Industrielle Rettsvern** Bibliotek (Library of the Norwegian Patent Office), Middelthunsgate 15b, Postboks 8160 Oslo-Dep, Oslo 1

Kristiansand Folkebibliotek (Municipal Library), Kristiansand S

Norges Landbrukshøgskoles Bibliotek (Library of the Agricultural University of Norway), N-1432 Ås-NLH

Norges Tekniske Høgskole, Biblioteket (Library of the Norwegian Institute of Technology, affiliated to the University of Trondheim), N-7034 Trondheim-NTH Tel: (075) 95110 Telex: 55186 nthhb n

Riksarkivet (National Archives of Norway), Folke Bernadottes veg 21, Oslo 8

Statistisk Sentralbyras Bibliotek (Library of the Central Bureau of Statistics), Postboks 8131 Dep, Oslo 1

Stavanger Bibliotek (Stavanger Municipal Library)*, N-4000 Stavanger

Universitetsbiblioteket i Bergen (The University Library of Bergen), Möhlenprisbakken 1, N-5000 Bergen

Universitetsbiblioteket i Oslo (The Royal University Library) (National Library)*, Drammenesveien 42, N Oslo 2 Tel: (02) 564980

Universitetsbiblioteket i Trondheim, Avd B(Kongelige Norske Videnskabers Selskab Biblioteket), Erling Skakkes Gt 47C, N-7000 Trondheim Tel: 92204
University of Trondheim, Library of the Royal Norwegian Society of Sciences and Letters

Library Associations

Arkivarforeningen (The Association of Archivists), Riksarkivet, Folke Bernadottes vei 21, Kringsjå, Oslo 8

Kommunale Bibliotekarbeiderers Forening (Municipal Librarians' Association)*, c/o Kari Hjelde, Oppegårdbibliotekene, N-1410 Kolbotn
Publication: Kontakten (6 a year)

Norsk Bibliotekarlag (Norwegian Librarians' Association)*, Notodden Bibliotek, N-3670 Notodden
Executive Secretary: Helge Laerum
Publications: Meldinger (12 a year)

Norsk Bibliotekforening (Norwegian Library Association)*, Malerhaugveien 20, Oslo 6
Tel: (02) 688576
Secretary-Treasurer: Gro Langeland

Norsk Dokumentasjonsgruppe (Norwegian Documentation Society, Postboks 350, Blindern, Oslo 3

Norske Deitidsbibliotekarers Yrkeslag (Norwegian Association for Part-Time Librarians)*, c/o Norsk Bibliotekforening, Malerhaugveien 20, Oslo 6

Norske Forskningsbibliotekarers Forening (Norwegian Research Librarians' Association)*, Malerhaugveien 20, Oslo 6
Tel: (02) 688576
Executive Secretary: Gro Langeland

Riksbibliotektjenesten (National Office for Research and Special Libraries), Postboks 2439, Solli, Oslo 2 (Located at: Drammensveien 42, Oslo 2) Tel: (02) 550880
Director: Gerhard Munthe
Publications: Report series (irr.), *Synopsis* (6 per year), *Annual Report*

Library Reference Books and Journals

Books

Bibliothek og Forskning (Library and Research), The University Library of Bergen, Fastings Minde, N-5000 Bergen

Journals

Bok og Bibliotek (Book and Library), Statens Bibliotektilsyn, Munkesdamsveien 62, N-1301 Oslo

Meldinger (Announcements), Norwegian Librarians' Association, Notodden Bibliotek, N-3670 Notodden

Literary Associations and Societies

Norske Akademi for Sprog og Litteratur (Norwegian Academy for Language and Literature)*, Oslo
Secretary: L R Langslet

Norske Forfatterforening (Norwegian Authors' Association)*, Rådhusgata 7, Oslo 1
Secretary: Hjørdis Baartvedt

Det **Norske Videnskaps-Akademi** (The Norwegian Academy of Science and Letters), Drammensveien 78, Oslo 2
Secretary-General: Professor Dr A Semb-Johansson; *Executive Secretary:* Kjell Herlofsen
Publications: Skrifter, Avhandlinger, Årbok

Norwegian Association of Children's and Young Peoples' Authors, Rådhusgata 7, Oslo 1

Den Norske **P E N-Klubb** (Norwegian Centre of International PEN)*,
President: Professor Johan Vogt, Faculty of Social Science, Oslo University, Oslo 3

Literary Periodicals

Edda (Scandinavian); literary research, Universitetsforlaget, Postboks 307, Blindern, Oslo 3

Norseman, Nordmanns-Forbundet, Raadusgate 23b, Oslo

Samtiden (The Age); journal for politics, literature and social questions, H Aschehoug (W Nygaard), Sehestedsgate 3, Oslo 1

Syn og Segn (Vision and Tradition), Norske Samlaget, Trondheimsveien 15, Oslo 5

Vinduet (The Window), Gyldendale Norsk Forlag, Universitetsgate 16, Oslo 1

Literary Prizes

Bastian Prize*
Awarded annually for an outstanding translation by one of the members of the Norwegian Association of Translators. Enquiries to Norwegian Association of Translators, Rådshugata 7, Oslo 1

Children's Book Prize
For the best books for children by Norwegian authors for illustrations by Norwegian artists in books for children, and for picture-books. Awarded annually. Enquiries to Royal Norwegian Ministry of Education and Ecclesiastical Affairs, Oslo 1

Hartvig **Lassens** Gold Medal
For the best work on the history of Norwegian literature. Swedes and Danes also eligible. Awarded biennially. Enquiries to Oslo University, Postboks 1071, Blindern, Oslo 3

Den **Monradske** Medal
For a philosophical essay. Awarded every three years. Enquiries to Oslo University, Postboks 1071, Blindern, Oslo 3

Rolf **Stenersen** Prize*
For the best drama by a young playwright. Awarded every two years. Enquiries to Norwegian Authors' Association, Rådhusgata 7, Oslo 1

Translation Prize
For translations from foreign literature. 15,000 Norwegian kroner. Awarded annually. Enquiries to Norwegian Cultural Council, Rosenkrantzgate 11, Oslo 1

Tarjei **Vesaas** Debutant Prize*
To a writer under 30 for the best first book of prose or poetry. 3,000 Norwegian kroner. Awarded annually. Enquiries to Norwegian Authors' Society, Fr Nansensplass 6, Oslo 1

Translation Agencies and Associations

Norwegian Association of Translators*, Rådhusgata 7, Oslo 1

Pakistan

General Information

Language: Urdu is national language but English is used commercially
Religion: Muslim
Population: 75.3 million
Literacy Rate (1960): 21.8%
Bank Hours: 0900-1300 Saturday-Thursday
Shop Hours: 0930-1300, 1500-2000 Monday-Saturday
Currency: 100 paisa = 1 rupee
Export/Import Information: No tariff on books, magazines and advertising matter. Import licence issued freely if required. Anti-Islamic and obscene literature prohibited. Exchange controls
Copyright: UCC, Berne, Buenos Aires, Florence (see International section)

Book Trade Organizations

National Book Council of Pakistan*, Theosophical Hall, MA Jinnah Rd, Karachi
Dir General: Mr S H R Rizvi
Publications: Kitab (Urdu, monthly), trade directories, manuals, bibliographies

Pakistan Publishers' and Booksellers' Association*, YMCA Bldg, Shahra-e-Quaid-e-Azami, Lahore

Book Trade Reference Books and Journals

Books

Books from Pakistan, National Book Council of Pakistan, Theosophical Hall, Bunder Rd, Karachi

Karachi Book Trade Directory, National Book Council of Pakistan, Theosophical Hall, Bunder Rd, Karachi

Journals

Kitab (text in Urdu), National Book Council of Pakistan, 126 Riwaz Garden, Lahore

Pakistan National Bibliography, Directorate of Libraries, National Bibliographical Unit, c/o Liaquat Library, Stadium Rd, Karachi (annual)

Publishers

Aane-Adab, Anarkali, Lahore Tel: 67504
Proprietor: Sh Abdul Salam

Ahsan Brothers*, Chowk Anarkali, Lahore
Proprietor: Mohammad Ahsan
Subjects: Literature, Education

Shaikh Muhammad **Ashraf**, Kashmiri Bazar, Lahore 8 Tel: 53171 Cable Add: Islamiclit Lahore
Chief Literary Adviser: M Ashraf Darr
Subjects: Books about Islam, Islamic history, biography, in English
Bookshop: address as above
1977: 5 titles *1978:* 6 titles *Founded:* 1923

Azim Publishing House*, Khyber Bazar, Peshawar Tel: 3313
Subjects: History, Literature

Barque & Co*, Barque Chambers, Barque Sq, 87 Shahrah-e-Liaquat Ali Khan, PO Box 201, Lahore
Man Dir: A M Barque
Br Off: Karachi
Subjects: Trade Directories, Journals, Who's Who
Founded: 1930

Bisat-e-Adab*, Circular Rd, Lahore Tel: 65621
Proprietor: Sana-Ullah Bhutta
Subjects: Politics, Islamic Studies

The **Book** House*, PO Box 734, Lahore 2 (Located at: 8 Trust Building, Urdu Bazar, Lahore 2) Tel: 61212 Cable Add: Bookhouse
Proprietor: Muhammad Saeed; *General Manager:* Muhammad Hamid Saeed
Subjects: Religion, Library, Textbooks
Founded: 1951
Miscellaneous: Exporters of English and Urdu books

Carvan Book House*, Kutcher Rd, Lahore Tel: 52296
Proprietor: Ch Abdul Hameed
Subjects: General, Textbooks

Classic*, 42 Shahrah-e-Quaid-e-Azam, Lahore Tel: 61830 Cable Add: Classic 42 Mall Lahore
Man Dir/Editorial/Production/Permissions: Agha A Hussain; *Sales/Publicity:* S Akbar Zaidi
Orders to: Classic, 42 The Mall Lahore
Subsidiaries: Shish Mahal Kitab Ghar, Classic Bookshop (both in Lahore)
Associate Company: Menarva Publications, Lahore
Subjects: The Arts, National Topics, Fiction
Bookshop: 42 The Mall, Lahore
1977: 2 titles *Founded:* 1956

Crescent Publications*, Urdu Bazar, Lahore

East and West Publishing Co*, 22 Corner Chambers, Chundrigar Rd, Karachi-0102 Tel: 212036 Cable Add: Goodbooks
Publisher: Rafique Akhtar
Subjects: Pakistan, Research Material, *Pakistan Year Book 1977*
1977: 2 titles *Founded:* 1971

Economic and Industrial Publications, Al-Masiha, 47 Abdullah Haroon Rd, PO Box 7843, Karachi 3
Subjects: Economics, Industrial Development, Finance; Periodical journals and reports on economics and investment
Founded: 1965

Ferozsons Ltd, 60 Shahrah-e-Quaid-e-Azam, Lahore Tel: 65196/65197/65198 Cable Add: Ferozsons
Man Dir, Publicity: A Salam; *Editorial:* A Hameed Khan; *Sales:* Major N H Wankadia; *Production:* M Javeed Khan
Br Offs: 150 outlets throughout Pakistan
Subjects: Maps, Atlases, Journals
Bookshop: Address as above
Founded: 1894

Frontier Publishing Co*, Urdu Bazar, Lahore

Sh **Ghulam** Ali & Sons*, Chowk Urdu Bazar, Lahore
Proprietor: Sh Niaz Ahmed
Br Offs: Jinnah Rd, Karachi; Hospital Rd, Hyderabad
Subjects: Islamic Studies, General Books

Government Publications*, Manager of Publications, Central Publications Branch, Government of Pakistan, Stationery and Forms Building, University Rd, Karachi

Hamdard National Foundation, Nazimabad, Karachi 18
President: Hakim Mohammed Said
Subjects: Health, Medicine (Traditional), Islam
1977: 5 titles *1978:* 6 titles

Idara-e-Faroghe-Undu*, Aibak Rd, Lahore
Proprietor: Mohammad Tufail
Subjects: Literature, Education

Idara Siqafat-e-Islamia*, Club Rd, Lahore

Ilmi Kitab Khana*, Urdu Bazar, Lahore Tel: 62833
Proprietor: Ch Sardar Mohammad
Subjects: Textbooks, Educational

Islami Kitab Khana*, Sadar Bazar, Mianwali, Punjab
Subject: Law

Islamic Book Centre*, 25B Masson Rd, PO Box 1625, Lahore 3 Tel: 66272 Cable Add: Islamibook
Man Dir: Rozina Saeed; *Sales Dir:* Muhammad Bashir; *Publicity Dir:* Muhammad Sajid Saeed; *Advertising Dir:* Muhammad Hamid Saeed
Br Off: J M Malik, 35 Cawdor Rd, Fallowsfields, Manchester M14 6LS, UK
Subjects: Religion, University, Secondary & Primary Textbooks, Reference
1977: 35 titles *1978:* 24 titles

Institute of **Islamic Culture***, Club Rd, Lahore Tel: 53908 Cable Add: ICULT
Subject: Islamic ideology
Founded: 1950

Islamic Publications Ltd*, 13-E Shahalam Market, Lahore 7 Tel: 68341 Cable Add: Alilm
Man Dir: Ashfaque Mirza; *Manager:* Abdul W Khan
Subjects: Standard Islamic literature on current topics
1977: 88 titles *Founded:* 1960

Islamic Research Institute, PO Box 1035, Islamabad
Circulation Manager: Mumtaz Liaqat
Subjects: History, Law, Religion, Periodicals (in English, Arabic and Urdu)
1978: 5 titles

Kitabi Dunya*, Mcleod Rd, Lahore
Proprietor: Ch Sultan Ahmed
Subject: Detective Fiction

Maktaba Jadeed*, PO Box 456, Lahore
Proprietor: Ch Rasheed Ahmed
Subject: Fiction

Maktaba Meri Library*, Chowk Urdu Bazar, Lahore
Proprietor: Basheer Ahmed
Subject: Paperbacks

Maktaba Shahkar*, Chowk Urdu Bazar, Lahore Tel: 354103
Proprietor: S Qasim Mahmud
Subjects: Encyclopedias, Paperbacks

Malik Din Mohammad & Sons*, Bull Rd, Lahore Tel: 54315, 52621
Proprietor: Malik Mohammad Arif
Br Off: Chundrigar Rd, Karachi
Subject: Islamic Studies

Malik Siraj ud Din & Sons, Kashmiri Bazar, Lahore 8 Tel: 52169/311498/65539/67832 Cable Add: Serajco, Lahore
Man Dir: M S Ud Din; *Editorial:* S A Malik; *Sales:* S ud Din Malik; *Production:* A A Malik; *Publicity/Permissions:* M A Rouf
Subsidiary Company: Siraj Mohammadi Press, Lahore 7
Subject: Religion
1977: c 200 titles *1978:* 100 titles

Maqbool Academy*, Adabi Market, Chowk Anarkali, Lahore Tel: 64740
Proprietor: Maqbool Ahmed Malik
Subject: Fiction

Mercantile Guardian Press and Publishers*, 81-83 Shahra-e-Quaid-e-Azami, Lahore
Subject: Trade Directories
Founded: 1949

Nafees Academy*, Blassis St, Karachi Tel: 232956
Proprietor: Saleem Gahandri
Subject: History

Nairoshni*, Nicol Rd, Karachi 2

The **Oriental & Religious** Publishing Corp Ltd, Rabwah
Subjects: The Holy Qur'an in Arabic and English; Commentaries on the Qur'an; Books on Islam

Orientalia Publishers*, Lahore
Subject: Islamic literature

Oxford University Press, GPO Box 442, Karachi 1 (Located at: 2nd floor, Haroon House, Dr Ziauddin Ahmed Rd, Karachi)
Manager: C H Lewis
Subjects: Textbooks, Reference Books, Educational, Economics, History, Islamic Studies
Bookshop: address as above
1977: 5 titles *1978:* 5 titles

Pak Publishers*, Urdu Bazar, Lahore

Pakistan Law Times Publications*, Kabir St, Urdu Bazar, Lahore

Pakistan Publications*, Shahrah Iraq, PO Box 183, Karachi 1
Subjects: Books about Pakistan in Urdu, Arabic and English

Pakistan Publishing Co Ltd*, 56-N Gulberg Industrial Colony, Lahore
Man Dir: S M Shah
Subject: Textbooks
Founded: 1932
Miscellaneous: Government Printers

Pakistan Publishing House*, Victoria Chambers 2, A Haroon Rd, Karachi
Dir: M Noorani
Subjects: Politics, Law, Religion, Economics
Founded: 1959

People's Publishing House, PO Box 862, Lahore (Located at: 26 Shahrah-e-Quaid-e-Azam, Lahore) Tel: 54512
Man Dir, Publication: Abdur Rauf Malik; *Sales:* G Mustafa; *Publicity:* M Siddique
Subject: Social Science
1978: 20 titles *Founded:* 1947

Publishers International*, Bandukwala Bldg, 4 McLeod Rd, Karachi
Man Dir: Kamaluddin Ahmad
Subjects: Advertising, Reference, Science, Technical, Textbooks
Founded: 1948

Publishers United Ltd, PO Box 1689, Lahore (Located at: 176 Anarkali, Lahore) Tel: 52238 Cable Add: Pubun (Warehouse: 9 Rattigan Rd, Lahore Tel: 53423)
Man Dir: Mohammad Amin
Subjects: Religion, Economics, Technical, Reference
1977: 10 titles *1978:* 7 titles *Founded:* 1942

Qaumi Kutab Khana*, Railway Rd, Lahore
Tel: 53810
Proprietor: Mohammad Ahsan & Bros

'Rast Gufter' Press*, Bhawana Bazar, Lyallpur
Manager & Proprietor: Shamshar Ali Baskhshi
Founded: 1889

Royal Book Co, PO Box 7737, Karachi 3 (Located at: 232 Saddar Cooperative Market, Abdullah Haroon Rd, Karachi 3) Tel: 514244
Proprietor: Jamshed Mirza
Subjects: Politics, Economics, Banking, General History, Asian Historical Reprints
Bookshop: At above address
1978: 7 titles *1979:* 6 titles *Founded:* 1963

H M Saeed Co, Dr Ziauddin Ahmad Rd, Pakistan Chowk, Karachi
Proprietor: Mohammad Zaki
Subject: Islamic Studies, Literature (in Arabic, Urdu, Persian)

Sang-e-Meel Publications*, Chowk Urdu Bazar, Lahore
Proprietor: Niaz Ahmed
Subjects: History and Islamic Studies

Taj Co Ltd, Manghopir Rd, PO Box 530, Karachi Tel: Karachi 292021/292648 Cable Add: Kalampak
Man Dir: Sheikh Enayat Ullah
Br Offs: Rawalpindi, Lahore
Subject: Religion
Founded: 1929
Bookshop: Agency Taj Co, M A Jinnah Rd, Karachi

Taxation*, 6 Liaquat Rd, Lahore 6

University Book Agency*, Khyber Bazar, Peshawar Tel: 2534
Br Off: Abbatabad
Subjects: General, Textbooks

Urdu Academy Sind*, Jinnah Rd, Karachi
Tel: 73730
Proprietor: Ala-ud-Din Khalid
Br Offs: Lahore, Hyderabad
Subjects: General, Textbooks

West Pakistan Publishing Co Ltd*, 56-N Gulberg, Lahore Tel: 80409
Proprietor: Mohammad Shah
Subject: Textbooks

Writers' Guild Publishing House*, Strachan Rd, Karachi
Subject: Literature

Major Booksellers

Bookcentre*, Lakshmi Mansion, Shahrah-e-Quaid-e-Azam, Lahore

Ferozsons Ltd*, 60 Shahrah-e-Quaid-e-Azam, Lahore

S I Gillani, 65 Shahrah-e-Quaid-e-Azam, Lahore 3

Liberty Bookstall*, PO Box 7427, Karachi 3

Maktaba Ishaat-e-Adab*, Anarkali, Lahore

S M Mir, 40 Chartered Bank Chambers, Talpur Rd, Karachi 2
Also Publishers' Agent

Mirza Book Agency, 65 Shahrah-e-Quaid-e-Azam, PO Box 729, Lahore 3 Tel: 66839
Cable Add: Knowledge

Oxford University Press, 2nd floor, Haroon Ho, Dr Ziauddin Ahmed Rd, GPO Box 442, Karachi 1
Man: C H Lewis

Pak American Commercial Inc*, Zaibunnisa St, Karachi 3

Pak Book Corporation, 37 Commercial Bldg, Shahrah-e-Quaid-e-Azam (The Mall), Lahore Tel: 55166 Cable Add: Magbookco
Dir: M Iqbal Cheema; *Man Dir:* M A Khan Akter

Paradise Book Stall*, Shambu Nath Rd, Karachi

Paramount Book Stall*, Preedy St, Saddar, Karachi 3
Branches at Lahore, Peshawar
Also wholesaler

Petiwala and Co, Ismail Mansion, Strechen Rd, Pakistan Chowk, Karachi 1
Tel: 218643

Royal Book Co, 232 Saddar Cooperative Market, Abdullah Haroon Rd, Karachi 3

Major Libraries

Agriculture University Library*, Lyallpur
Head Department of Library: Najif Ali Khan

British Council Libraries, 32 Mozang Rd, PO Box 88, Lahore Tel: 52755/6
Also Tilak Incline, Jacob Rd, PO Box 126 Hyderabad; 14 Civic Centre, Ramna 6, PO Box 1135, Islamabad; 20 Bleak House Rd, PO Box 146, Karachi 4; 35 The Mall, PO Box 49, Peshawar; Lansdowne Gardens, The Mall, PO Box 1135, Rawalpindi; Chartered Bank Building, Shahrah-e-Quaid-e-Azam, PO Box 88, Lahore

Central Secretariat Library*, Government of Pakistan, Islamabad

Ewing Memorial Library*, Forman Christian College, Lahore 11

Government College Library*, Lahore

Islamabad University Library*, PO Box 1190, Islamabad

Islamic Research Institute Library, PO Box 1035, Islamabad

Karachi University Library*, Karachi 32
Tel: 418227, 419291/43, 419291/46

Liaquat Memorial Library*, Stadium Rd, Karachi 5

National Archives of Pakistan*, Secretariat Block-D, Islamabad

National Library*, Islamabad

Pakistan Forest Institute, Central Forest Library, PO Forest Institute, Peshawar

Pakistan Institute of Nuclear Science & Technology Library*, PO Nilore, Rawalpindi

Pakistan Scientific and Technological Information Centre (PASTIC)*, 435 F-6/3 Islamabad

Planning Commission Library*, Government of Pakistan, 'P' Block, Pakistan Secretariat, Islamabad

Punjab Public Library*, Lahore

Punjab University Library*, 1 Kutchery Rd, Lahore 2/12 Tel: 52262

Sind University Central Library*, University of Sind, New Campus, Jamshoro, Sind
Librarian: Moinuddin Khan

University of Baluchistan Library*, Quetta, Baluchistan

University of Engineering and Technology*, Lahore
Acting Librarian: Mohammad Ramzan

University of Peshawar Library, Peshawar
Librarian: I U Khan

Library Associations

Directorate of Libraries*, National Bibliographical Unit, Karachi
Director: Hafiz Akhtar
Publication: Pakistan National Bibliography

Federal Library Association*, Pakistan National Centre, 169 Sawar Rd, Rawalpindi
Publication: Federal Librarian

Karachi University Library Science Alumni Association*, c/o Dept of Library Science, University of Karachi, Karachi 32
Publication: Newsletter

Library Promotion Bureau*, Old Students' Lodge, Karachi University, Karachi 32
Tel: 418227
Executive Secretary: M Adil Usmani
Publications: Pakistan Library Bulletin (quarterly); Pakistan Book Trade Directory; Who's Who in librianship in Pakistan

Library Science Society*, c/o Department of Library Science, Karachi University, Karachi 32

Mehran Library Association*, PO Box 126, Hyderabad
Secretary: I A S Bokhari MA
Publication: Newsletter

Pakistan Library Association*, c/o University of Peshawar, Peshawar
Publications: PLA Newsletter, Proceedings

Society for the Promotion and Improvement of Libraries*, 54 M A Jinah Rd, Hameed Manzil, Karachi 5
Publications: Karachi Public Library: A Scheme; Report of the School Library Workshop; School Library Handbook; Newsletter and others

Library Journals

Federal Librarian, Federal Library Association, Pakistan National Centre, 169 Sawar Rd, Rawalpindi

Newsletter, Karachi University Library Science Alumni Association, Karachi 32

Newsletter, Pakistan Library Association, c/o University of Peshawar, Peshawar

Pakistan Library Bulletin (international edition in English, domestic edition in English and Urdu), Library Promotion Bureau, Old Students' Lodge, University Campus, Karachi 32

Literary Associations and Societies

Anjuman Taraqqi-e-Urdu Pakistan, Baba-e-Urdu Rd, Karachi 1
For the promotion of the Urdu language and literature
President: Akhter Husain; *Secretary:* Jamiluddin A'Ali
Publications: Urdu (quarterly), *Qaumi Zaban* (monthly); various books

Pakistan Board for Advancement of Literature*, Narsing Das Garden, Club Rd, Lahore

Pakistan Writers' Guild*, B-16 Sindhi Muslim Housing Society, Karachi
Secretary-General: Mahbub Jamal Zahedi
Publication: Ham Qalam (monthly)

Punjab Text Board*, 21/E-11, Gulberg 111, Lahore
Similar Text Boards exist in Sind at Karachi, Baluchistan at Quetta, NWFP at Peshawar

Sindhi Adabi Board*, Sind University Campus, Jamshoro, Hyderabad, Sind
To promote the language, literature and culture of the Sind region

Literary Periodicals

Ham Qalam, Pakistan Writers' Guild, B-16 Sindhi Muslim Housing Society, Karachi 3

Perspective, Pakistan Publications, Shahrah Iraq, PO Box 183, Karachi

Literary Prizes

Adamjee Prize*
Founded in 1960 for the best book of creative and progressive poetry, novel, short story, drama, travelogue or biography. 20,000 rupees. Awarded annually.
Administered by the Pakistan Writers' Guild in Karachi. Enquiries to Pakistan Writers' Guild, B-16 Sindhi Muslim Housing Society, Karachi 3

Book Production Award*
For the best produced books of the year, to publishers, artists and illustrators. Awarded annually. Enquiries to National Book Council of Pakistan, Theosophical Hall, MA Jinnah Rd, Karachi

Dawood Prize for Literature*
Founded in 1963 for the best books on literary research, literary history, literary criticism; for research works on the Pakistan movement; and for the best translation. 25,000 rupees. Sponsored by the Dawood Foundation. Awarded annually. Enquiries to the Pakistan Writers' Guild, B-16 Sindhi Muslim Housing Society, Karachi 3

Habib Bank Prize for Literature*
Founded in 1968 for the best translation or adaptation of the year (into English or a Pakistani language) of a modern or classical work in any Pakistani language, 25,000 rupees. Awarded annually. Enquiries to Pakistan Writers' Guild, B-16 Sindhi Muslim Housing Society, Karachi 3

National Bank of Pakistan Prize for Literature*
Founded in 1964 for the best books on economics and scientific, technical and professional subjects. 25,000 rupees. Awarded annually. Enquiries to Pakistan Writers' Guild, B-16 Sindhi Muslim Housing Society, Karachi 3

Pakistan Board for Advancement of Literature Awards*
For academic works in Urdu, and for articles and poems published in Pakistan journals. Awarded annually. Enquiries to Pakistan Board for Advancement of Literature, Narsing Das Garden, Club Rd, Lahore

President's Award for Pride of Performance*
For notable achievements in literature. Awarded annually. Enquiries to Pakistan Ministry of Education, Islamabad

Prizes for Manuscripts for Juveniles*
Six prizes for creative writing in the field of children's literature in the Urdu language. Awarded annually. Enquiries to Pakistan Writers' Guild, B-16 Sindhi Muslim Housing Society, Karachi 3

Punjab Advisory Board for Books Prizes*
For books of high educational and literary value in the Urdu language. Awarded annually. Enquiries to the Secretary, Punjab Advisory Board for Books, Lahore

Regional Literature Awards*
For the best literary works, including the novel, short story, drama, poetry, biography, travel, literary criticism or research work, in each of the four regional languages of Punjabi, Pushto, Sindhi and Gujrati. Awarded annually. Enquiries to Pakistan Writers' Guild, c/o Regional Secretary, Princess Hotel, Montgomery Rd, Lahore

United Bank Prize for Literature*
Founded in 1967 for books in Urdu and Bengali in the following categories: for children up to 15 years of age; and poetry or prose, fiction or nonfiction, for young children. 20,000 rupees. Awarded annually. Enquiries to Pakistan Writers' Guild, B-16 Sindhi Muslim Housing Society, Karachi 3

Panama

General Information

Language: Spanish (English widely used)
Religion: Roman Catholic
Population: 1.8 million
Literacy Rate (1970): 78.3%
Bank Hours: 0800-1300 or 1330 Monday-Friday
Shop Hours: 0700 or 0800-1800 or 1900 Monday-Saturday, with 2-hour lunch closing
Currency: 100 cents = 1 Balboa
Export/Import Information: No tariffs on books and advertising matter. No import licences or exchange controls
Copyright: UCC, Buenos Aires (see International section)

Publishers

Dirección de Estadística y Censo, Contraloría General de la República, Apdo 5213, Panamá 5 Tel: 640777 Cable Add: Estadicen-Contraloría Panama
Man Dir: D Castillo; *Editorial:* J M Caballero; *Sales/Production/Publicity:* R Tapia
Subjects: Statistics, *Panamá en cifras* (annual); *Supplement of Panamanian Statistics: special report*
1977: 22 titles *1978:* 30 titles *Founded:* 1941

Ediciones Instituto Nacional de Cultura*, Apdo 662, Panamá 1 Tel: 220880/84 Cable Add: Inac
President: Jaime Ingram; *Editorial, Sales:* Juan A Hochberg; *Production:* Pedro Montañez; *Publicity:* Ricardo Ledezma; *Legal:* Raul Moreno
Subjects: Literature in general, History, Anthropology, Archaeology, Folklore, Sociology
1977: 19 titles *Founded:* 1976

Ediciones **Librería Cultural Panameña** SA, Apdo de Correos 2018, Panamá 1 Tel: 235628/236267 Cable Add: Culpasa
Man Dir/Editorial: A J Fraguela R; *Sales:* F M Fraguela Ruiz
Subjects: University, Secondary & Primary Textbooks, Antiquaria, Reference Works
Bookshop: Vía España 16, Apdo 2018, Panama 1 (and 2 other branches)
1977: 12 titles *1978:* 32 titles *Founded:* 1955

Editorial Universitariá, Estafeta Universitariá, Universidad de Panamá Tel: 23-0210 ext 11 Cable Add: Cuidad Universitariá
Man Dir/Editorial: Dr Carlos M Gasteazoro; *Sales:* Carlos Castro Jr; *Production:* Prof C A Araúz; *Publicity:* H Muñoz
Subjects: History, Philosophy, Geography, Sciences, Law, Literature, Art, Architecture, Social Sciences, Technical, Education
Bookshop: University Bookshop
1977: 9 titles *Founded:* 1969

Editorial **McGraw-Hill** Latino-Americana SA*, Apdo 2036, Colón Tel: 474900 Cable Add: Books-Panama
Man Dir: Daniel Waingart; *Editorial/Permissions:* M Bates; *Sales:* J Fischer; *Production:* G Rodriguez; *Publicity:* Gloria Angel
Parent Company: McGraw-Hill Inc, USA
Associate Companies: see McGraw-Hill UK

Subsidiary Companies: McGraw-Hill Latin-Americano (Puerto Rico); Editorial McGraw-Hill Latin-Americano (Colombia)
Br Off: Ave 65 de Infantería Kml, Hml Rio Piedras, San Juan, Puerto Rico
Subjects: Scholarly, Reference, University, Secondary & Primary Textbooks
Founded: 1966

Major Booksellers

Librería **Argosy***, Vía Argentina, Edificio Pancho Verde, and Vía España, Apdo 6620, Panamá 5 Tel: 235344

Librería **Athenea***, Ave M Espinosa Batista 13-50, Apdo 2755, Panamá Tel: 238350

Librería **Cultural Panameña**, SA*, Apdo de Correos 2018, Panamá 1 Tel: 235628 (and 2 other branches) Cable Add: Culpara

Librería **Menéndez**, Ave 5a, 11-33, Panamá Tel: 223199
Also at: Galerías Obarrio, Via Brasil, Panamá; Ave Justo Arosemena y Calle 36, Panamá; Aeropuerto Tocumen, Panamá And Librería Santa Ana, Plaza Santa Ana, Panamá; Librería La Escolar SA, Plaza Cervantes, David

Servicio Continental de Publicaciones, Calle 29 Este 5-70, Apdo 1379, Panamá Tel: 250614 (and 2 other branches)

Servicio de Lewis*, Calle 26 y Ave Balboa, Apdo 1634, Panamá 1 Tel: 627000

Major Libraries

Biblioteca Nacional (National Library)*, Apdo 3435, Panamá

Gorgas Memorial Laboratory Bio-Medical Research Library (Biblioteca Bio-Médica del Laboratorio Conmemorativo Gorgas)*, Apdo 6991, Panamá 5 (Located at: Ave Justo Arosemena, No 35-30, Panamá 5) Tel: Panama 256550 Cable Add: Gomela Telex: Gml pa 3480333
Also at Box 2016, Balboa Heights, Panama Canal Zone Tel: Panama Canal Zone 525064
Dir: Dr Abram Benenson
Medical librarian: Professor M Víctor De Las Casas
Publications: Annual Report, Bibliography of Papers Emanating from the Gorgas Memorial Laboratory; El Laboratorio Conmemorativo Gorgas; su Historia y su Labor; 40 Years of Tropical Medicine Research

Biblioteca de la **Universidad** de Panamá*, Estafeta Universitaria, Panamá

Library Associations

Asociación de Bibliotecarios Graduados del Istmo de Panamá (Association of Graduate Librarians of the Isthmus of Panama)*, c/o Director, Biblioteca de la Universidad de Panamá, Estafeta de la niversidad, Universidad, Panamá 3 Tel: 238786
Secretary (Spanish): Ana B de Forero;
Secretary (English): Nancy Dail Claridge

Asociación Panameña de Bibliotecarios (Panama Library Association)*, Apdo 3435, Panamá
President: Lic Nuria F De Gonzalez
Publication: Boletín

Universidad de Panama, Escuela de Bibliotecología (University of Panama, School of Library Science)*, Estafeta Universitaria, Panamá 3
Publication: Boletín

Library Journals

Boletín (Bulletin), Panama Library Association, c/o Inés María Herrera, President, Apdo 3435, Panamá

Boletín (Bulletin), University of Panama, School of Library Science, Apdo 3277, Panamá 3

Papua New Guinea

General Information

Language: English is one of official languages, as is pidjin English or neo-Melanesian, and 700 distinct languages are in use
Population: 2.9 million
Literacy Rate (1966): 29.4%
Banks close 1100 Saturday
Currency: 100 toca = 1 kina
Export/Import Information: No tariff on books and advertising but 5% import tax on non-educational books. No import licence for books, but no obscene literature permitted. No exchange controls

Publishers

Robert **Brown** & Associates Pty Ltd, PO Box 3395, Port Moresby Tel: 254551/254855 Cable Add: Brownbooks Port Moresby Telex: RBA POM NE 22263
General Manager: Rex P Lingard
Parent Company: Gordon and Gotch (Australia) Pty Ltd
Subsidiary Companies: Waigani Enterprises, New Guinea Book Depot, Taurama Newsagency, Gerehu Newsagency
Subjects: Travel, Natural History, Languages, Cookery, New Guinea History, Art and Folklore
1977: 6 titles *1978:* 7 titles

The **Christian Book** Centre*, PO Box 222, Madang
Subjects: Literature, Religion

Isopang Publishing Pty Ltd*, Cnr Wards Rd and Mango St, Hohola, Port Moresby

Major Booksellers

Bougainville Copper Pty Ltd*, Arawa, Bougainville (and other branches)

Burns Philp (NG) Ltd*, Kieta, Bougainville (and other branches)

New Guinea Book Depot, PO Box 5495, Boroko
Manager: Don Smith

Rabaul Newsagency, c/o Bali Merchants Pty Ltd, PO Box 390, Rabaul

Steamships Trading Co*, PO Box 30, Goroka

University Book Shop*, PO Box 4614, University PO

Major Libraries

University of Papua New Guinea Library*, PO Box 4819, University Post Office, Waigani Tel: 53900 Port Moresby

Library Associations

Papua New Guinea Library Association*, PO Box 5368, Boroko Tel: 424999, ext 270
Executive Secretary: Ms W Avosa

School Library Association of Papua New Guinea*, c/o School Library Officer, Department of Education, Konedobu Tel: 56358
Executive Secretary: S Rauka

Literary Periodicals

Kovave; journal of New Guinea literature, Jacaranda Press Pty Ltd, 65 Park Rd, Milton, Queensland 40664, Australia

Papua New Guinea Writing, Literature Bureau, Office of Information, PO Box 2312, Konedobu

Paraguay

General Information

Language: Spanish (Guarani, an aboriginal Indian tongue, is universally spoken)
Religion: Roman Catholic
Population: 2.8 million
Literacy Rate (1962): 74.6%
Bank Hours: 0730-1100 Monday-Friday
Shop Hours: 0700 or 0730-1200, 1500-1800 Monday-Friday; open until noon Saturday
Currency: 100 centimos = 1 guarani
Export/Import Information: Children's picture books: 10% ad valorem, 7.5% added tax, 12% compensatory tax, Atlases: 11% ad valorem, 15% added tax, 24% compensatory tax. Advertising catalogues subject to 15% added tax and compensatory tax of 24%. Additional taxes on all goods totalling $6^1/_2$% VAT C & I + 20%; also Consular Fee 5% VAT FOB. No import licences required. Exchange controls; foreign exchange surcharge is 36%, VAT C & I + 20%
Copyright: UCC, Buenos Aires (see International section)

Book Trade Organizations

Cámara Paraguaya del Libro (Paraguayan Publishers' Association)*, Librería Internacional, Estrella 380, Asunción

Publishers

La **Colmena**, SA*, Presidente Franco 328, Casilla 302, Asunción
Dir: Daumas Ladouce

Editorial **Comuneros***, Presidente Franco 480, CC980, Asunción Tel: 46176
Subjects: Social History, Poetry

Ediciones **Diálogo***, Calle Brasil 1391, Asunción
Manager: Miguel Angel Fernández
Subjects: Fine Arts, Literature, Poetry, Criticism, History, Science
Founded: 1957

Ediciones **Nizza***, Estrella 721, Asunción Tel: 9634
Subject: Medicine
Bookshop: Agencia de Librerías Nizza, Estrella 721, Asunción

Major Booksellers

Librería El **Ateneo***, General Diaz 347, Asunción Tel: 43668

El **Colegio** SA*, Estrella 372, Asunción Importer/Exporter, Wholesaler

Librería **Comuneros***, Presidente Franco 480, CC980 Asunción Tel: 46176

Librería La **Cultura***, Palma esq Montevideo, Asunción Tel: 45093

Librería **Internacional***, Estrella 380, Casilla de Correo 991, Asunción Tel: 41423

Librería **Universal**, Palma 519, Casilla de Correo 432, Asunción

Agencia de Librerías **Nizza**, Tacuari 144, Asunción Tel: 47160

Selecciones SA Comercial*, Iturbe 436, Asunción Tel: 41588

Major Libraries

Biblioteca y Archivo Nacionales (National Library and Archives)*, Mariscal Estigarriba 95, Asunción

Biblioteca de la **Sociedad Científica** del Paraguay (Library of the Paraguayan Scientific Society)*, Ave España 505, Asunción

Library Associations

Asociación de Bibliotecarios del Paraguay (Association of Paraguayan Librarians)*, Calle Casilla de Correo 1505, Asunción
Secretary: Mafalda Cabrerar
Publication: Revista de Bibliotecologia y Documentación Paraguaya

Asociación de Bibliotecarios Universitarios del Paraguay (Paraguayan Association of University Librarians)*, c/o Professor Yoshiko M de Freundorfer, Head, Escuela de Bibliotecologia, Universidad Nacional de Asunción, Asunción
Secretary: Maria Cristina Recalde Blanco

Comisión Paraguaya de Documentación e Información (Paraguayan Committee of Documentation and Information)*, c/o Instituto de Ciencias, Universidad Nacional, Ave España 1098, Asunción
Executive Secretary: Luis Fernando Meyer

Library Journals

Revista de Bibliotecologia y Documentación Paraguaya (Review of Paraguay Library Science and Documentation), Association of Paraguay Librarians, Calle Casilla de Correo 1505, Asunción

Peru

General Information

Language: Spanish
Religion: Roman Catholic
Population: 16.4 million
Literacy Rate (1961): 57.8%
Bank Hours: January-March: 0830-1130 Monday-Friday; April-December: 0830-1200 Monday-Friday
Shop Hours: January-March: 0930-1245, 1615-1900 Monday-Saturday; April-December: 0900-1245, 1515-1900 Monday-Saturday (some close Saturday afternoon)
Currency: 100 centavos = 1 sol
Export/Import Information: Children's picture books 6 soles KG + 82% VAT. Advertising matter 5 soles KG+ 82% VAT. 5% sales tax applies. No freight tax on books but there is 1% wholesalers' tax. Import licences required. Exchange controls
Copyright: UCC, Buenos Aires (see International section)

Book Trade Organizations

Cámara Peruana del Libro (Peruvian Publishers' Association)*, Calle Washington 1206, Of 508, Apdo 3744, Lima 1 Tel: 325694
Secretary: A Carbone

Book Trade Reference Journal

Anuario Bibliográfico Peruano (Peruvian National Bibliography), National Library, Ave Abancay, Apdo 2335, Lima 1

Publishers

Librerías **A B C** SA, Las Magnolias 841, Of 201, San Isidro, Apdo 5595, Lima Tel: 413712 Cable Add: Molagent
Man Dir: H H Moll; *Editorial:* Eduardo Nugent V
Associate Companies: Florida 725, Cordoba 685, Martinez, Argentina; Librerias Galax, Pl las Americas, Loc 59, Caracas; Centro Iñaquito, Quito
Subjects: History, Peruvian Art & Archaeology
Bookshops: Colmena 725; Hotel Bolivar, Lima; Centro Comercial Todos, San Isidro; Centro Comercial Galax, Chacarilla del Estanque; Edificio El Pacífico, Miraflores; Aeropuerto Jorge Chavez, Callao
Founded: 1956

Aguilar Peruana de Ediciones SA*, Ave Inca Garcilaso de la Vega 1156, Lima
Parent Company: Aguilar SA de Ediciones, Spain (qv)

Editorial **Arica**, SA*, Paseo de la República 3285, San Isidro, Lima Tel: 401670
Man Dir: Boris Romero Accinelli; *Sales Manager:* Angélica Li; *Editorial Dir:* Benjamin Romero Accinelli
Br Off: Casilla 3537, Lima 1
Subjects: Literature, Technical, Textbooks, Educational Materials, Law, History
Founded: 1958

Asociación Editorial **Bruño***, Ave Arica 751, Breña, Apdo 1759, Lima Tel: 244134
Man Dir: Hno Francisco Alvarez Penelas
Subjects: University, Secondary & Primary Textbooks and Educational Materials
Founded: 1950

Editorial **Desarrollo**, SA, Lampa 921, 2° piso, Apdo 3824, Lima Tel: 285380 Cable Add: Edidesa
Man Dir: Luis Sosa Núñez; *Assistant Manager:* Bertha de Berrospi
Bookshop: Librería de Editorial Desarrollo, Lampa 921, 2° piso, Lima
Subjects: Business, Accounting, General Reference, Industrial Engineering
1978: 29 titles *1979:* 34 titles *Founded:* 1965

Editorial **Ecoma** SA*, Ave Arequipa 4168 'B', Miraflores 18, Lima Tel: 473017 Cable Add: Ecoma
Man Dir: Eduardo Congrains Martin; *Sales Dir:* Ramón Lalupu Lazaro
Subjects: Paperbacks, Literature, Biography, History, Philosophy, Juveniles
Founded: 1970

Distribuidora exclusivo **Grijalbo** SA*, Apdo 4978, Lima
Parent Company: Editorial Grijalbo SA, Mexico (qv)

Editorial **Horizonte***, Jirón Camaná 878, Lima Tel: 279364
Man Dir: Humberto Damonte Larraín
Subject: Literature in general
Bookshop: Jirón Camaná 878, Lima

Promotion Editorial **Inca** SA*, Emilio Althaus 442, Lince, Lima Tel: 718201
Man Dir: José Muñoz Rodríguez; *Sales Dir:* José López Angulo
Subject: Peruvian Literature

Instituto de Estudios Peruanos, Horacio Urteaga 694, Jesus Maria, Lima 11 Tel: 323070/244658 Cable Add: Ieperu
Man Dir: José Matos Mar; *Sales Manager:* Ursula Lizarraga
Subjects: Peruvian studies in Agriculture, Archaeology, Economics, History, Anthropology
1977: 6 titles *1978:* 12 titles *Founded:* 1964

Librería-Editorial Juan **Mejía** Baca, Jirón Azángaro 722, Lima Tel: 274067
Man Dir: Juan Mejía Baca
Subjects: Peruvian Literature & History
Founded: 1945

Mosca Azul Editores, SRL, La Paz 651, Lima 18 Tel: 470655
Dirs: Mirko Lauer, Abelardo Oquendo
Subjects: Fiction & Nonfiction, Social Science, University Textbooks
1977: 10 titles *1978:* 9 titles *Founded:* 1972

Ediciones **Peisa***, Emilio Althaus 442, Lince, Lima Tel: 718201
Subjects: Literature, History

Editorial **Plata** SA, Casilla 5595, Lima Tel: 413712
Man Dir: Herbert H Moll
Subjects: South America — History, Art, Guidebooks, Juveniles, Maps
1977: 11 titles *Founded:* 1971 (in Venezuela)

Librería **Studium** SA, Pl Francia 1164, Apdo 2139, Lima Tel: 326278 Cable Add: Studium
Man Dir: Andrés Carbone O; *Assistant Manager:* Andrés Carbone Montes; *Exports:* José Córdova C
Subjects: Textbooks & General Culture
Founded: 1936
Bookshops: At above address and Jiron de la Union 560, Lima; Colmena 626, Lima; Ave Larco 720, Miraflores; Saenz Peña 625, Callao; Francisco Pizarro 533, Trujillo; General Morán 123, Arequipa; Calle Moral

107A-107B, Arequipa; Elías Aguirre 251, Chiclayo; Calle Real 377, Huancayo; Calle Arequipa 110, Ayacucho; Tacna 216, Piura; Mesón de la Estrella 144, Cuzco (all in Peru)

Fondo Editorial de la **Universidad Católica**, Apdo 12514, Lima 21 (Located at: Fundo Pando, Pueblo Libre, Lima 21) Tel: 622540 ext 128
Man Dir: Dr F Pease G Y
Subjects: Humanities, Social Sciences, Mathematics, Engineering, Periodicals
1977: 3 titles *1978:* 6 titles

Universidad Nacional Mayor de San Marcos*, Apdo 454, Lima (Located at: Direccion Universitaria de Biblioteca y Publicaciones, Ave República de Chile 295, of 508) Apdo 454, Lima Tel: 319689
Man Dir: Juan de Dios Guevara, Rector de la Universidad
Subjects: Medicine, Law, Science, General Literature, Engineering, Textbooks
Founded: 1952

Editorial **Universo** SA, Ave Nicolás Arriola 2285, La Victoria, Apdo 241, Lima 30 Tel: 241639/233190
Man Dir: Augusto Sandoval Valcárcel;
Executive Manager: Paulino Advíncula Rios
Subjects: Social Science, Textbooks
Founded: 1967

Major Booksellers

Librerías **A B C** SA, Las Magnolias 841, Of 201, San Isidro, Apdo 5595, Lima
also Colmena 725; Hotel Bolivar, Lima; Centro Comercial Todos, San Isidro; Centro Comercial Galax, Chacarilla del Estanque; Edificio El Pacifico, Miraflores; Aeropuerto Jorge Chavez, Callao

Librería **Arica***, Paseo de la República 3285, San Isidro, Lima, Casilla 3537, Lima 1 Tel: 401670

Editorial Interamericana SA, Apdo 76, Lima 1 (Located at: Av 28 de Julio 787, Lima 1) Tel: 233471/241944/241845
General Manager: Dr José de la Riva-Agüero

Librería **Epoca***, Jirón Unión 1042, Apdo 4703, Lima Tel: 249545

Librerías La **Familia***, Ave Nicolás de Pierola 346, Lima Tel: 243544

Librería **Galería** Castro Soto*, Miguel Dasso 200, San Isidro, Lima Tel: 401343

Editorial **Horizonte***, Jirón Camaná 878, Lima Tel: 279364

Librería Internacional del Perú, Casilla 1417, Boza 892, 2° piso, Lima Tel: 288611

Librería Juan **Mejía** Baca, Jirón Azángaro 722, Lima Tel: 274067

Librería **Studium** SA, Pl Francia 1164, Apdo 2139, Lima Tel: 326278 (for branches see Publisher entry)

Librería de la **Universidad Nacional Mayor** de San Marcos*, Jirón Unión (Belén) 1098, Lima 1 Tel: 2894255

Librería 'La **Universidad**', Nicholas Ojeda Fierro e Hijos, SCR Ltda*, Ave Nicolás de Piérola 639, Lima Tel: 282461/282036
Branch Off: Ave Nicolás de Piérola 515, Lima Tel: 275408

Major Libraries

Archivo General de la Nación (National Archives)*, Calle Manuel Cuadros, s/n, Palacio de Justicia, Apdo 3124, Lima

Biblioteca Nacional (National Library)*, Ave Abancay, Apdo 2335, Lima 1 Tel: 277331/287690
Dir: María C Bonilla de Gaviria
Publications: Anuario Bibliográfico Peruano (Bibliographical Annual of Peru); *Boletín de la Biblioteca Nacional* (Bulletin of the National Library); *Revista Fénix* (Phoenix Magazine); *Gaceta Bibliotecaria* (Library Gazette)

Biblioteca Central de la **Pontificia Universidad Nacional** Católica del Perú, Final de la Ave Bolivar s/n, Apdos 1761-5729, Lima

Biblioteca Central de la **Universidad Nacional de Cuzco***, Apdo 167, Cuzco

Biblioteca Central de la **Universidad Nacional de San Agustín***, Apdo 23, Arequipa

Biblioteca Central de la **Universidad Nacional Mayor de San Marcos**, Apdo 454, Lima

Library Associations

Agrupación de Bibliotecas para la Integración de la Información Socio-Económica (ABIISE) (Library Group for the Integration of Socio-economic Information)*, Apdo 2874, Lima 100 Tel: 351760
Dir: Isabel Olivera Rivarola
Publications: Directorio de Bibliotecas Especializadas del Perú

Asociación de Bibliotecas Agricolas (Association of Agricultural Librarians)*, c/o Library, Universidad Nacional Agraria, La Molina, Lima

Asociación Peruana de Archiveros (Peruvian Association of Archivists)*, Archivo General de la Nación, Calle Manuel Cuadros s/n, Palacio de Justicia, Apdo 1802, Lima

Asociación Peruana de Bibliotecarios (Peruvian Association of Librarians)*, Apdo 3760, Lima
Publication: Carta Informativa (Newsletter)
Executive Secretary: Amparo Geraldino de Orban

Library Reference Books and Journals

Books

*Directorio de Bibliotecas Especializadas del Perú**, Library Group for the Integration of Socio-economic Information, Apdo 2874, Lima 100

Journals

Boletín (Bulletin)*, National Library, Ave Abancay, Apdo 2335, Lima 1

Boletín Bibliografico (Bibliographical Bulletin)*, Universidad Nacional Mayor de San Marcos, Ave República de Chile 295, Apdo 454, Lima

Fénix (Phoenix): review of Peruvian libraries*, National Library, Ave Abancay, Apdo 2335, Lima 1

Gaceta Bibliotecaria del Peru (Peruvian Library Gazette)*, National Library, Ave Abancay, Apdo 2335, Lima 1

Literary Associations and Societies

Asociación Nacional de Escritores y Artistas (ANEA) (National Association of Writers and Artists)*, Jirón de la Unión Belén 1054, Lima
President: Dr Pedro Ugarteche

Centro del **P E N** Internacional (International PEN Centre)*, Santa Teresita 327, San Isidor, Lima
Secretary: Blanca Varela

Literary Periodicals

Después (Afterwards), Roca y Boloña 633, Lima 18

Revista Peruana de Cultura (Peruvian Review of Culture), Institute Nacional de Cultura, Ancash 390, Lima 1

Textual, Instituto Nacional de Cultura, Ancash 390, Lima 1

Literary Prizes

Premio José María **Arguedas***
For the best novel, under auspices of the Goodyear del Perú. Awarded every other year. Enquiries to Goodyear del Perú, Casio de la Republic 959, La Victoria, Apdo 1690, Lima

Premio **Universo***
For the best novel. Awarded every other year. Enquiries to Editorial Universo SA, Ave Nicolás Arriola 2285, San Luis, Apdo 241, Lima 30

Philippines

General Information

Language: Pilipino (English also used)
Religion: Predominantly Roman Catholic
Population: 45 million
Literacy Rate (1970): 83.3%
Bank Hours: 0800-2000 Monday-Friday; some open Saturday
Shop Hours: Vary. Many open 0900-1200, 1400-1930 Monday-Saturday (some close 1730; some open Sunday)
Currency: 100 centavos =1 peso
Export/Import Information: 10% duty on books except those which are philosophical, historical, economic, scientific, technical or vocational, approved by Department of Education for use of certain institutions (not exceeding 10 copies for an institution, or 2 for an individual) or for encouragement of sciences or fine arts; no tariffs on Bibles and similar religious books. No duty on advertising matter. No import licences, but no obscene or immoral literature permitted. Release certificate issued on behalf of

Central Bank required to clear goods. Imports subject to 7% sales tax. No formal exchange controls but most imports need Letter of Credit (over $100 in any month, for example)
Copyright: Berne, Buenos Aires, Florence (see International section)

Book Trade Organizations

Philippine Book Dealers' Association*, c/o Philippine Education Co, Quezon Ave, Corner Banawe St, Quezon City, Metro Manila
President: Jose Benedicto

Philippine Educational Publishers' Association, 315 Quezon Blvd Extension, Quezon City   Tel: 991682
President: Jesus Ernesto Sibal

Publishers

Abiva Publishing House Inc, 851-881 G Araneta Blvd, Quezon City   Tel: 615403/4
Man Dir: Luis Q Abiva Jr; *Sales Dir:* Arturo V Austria; *Publicity Dir:* Mila S Precioso; *Advertising Dir:* Felicito Q Abiva; *Rights & Permissions:* Milagros R Arceo
Subjects: History, Reference, Religion, General Science, Primary Textbooks, Educational Materials
1978: 10 titles   *Founded:* 1963
Subsidiary Company: Hiyas Press Inc

Addison-Wesley Publishing Co Inc*, PO Box 1802, Manila   Cable Add: Adiwes Manila
General Manager: Ricardo M Hizon
Miscellaneous: Firm is a branch of Addison-Wesley Publishing Co Inc, USA. See Addison-Wesley Publishers Ltd, UK for associated companies and ISBNs

Alemar-Phoenix Publishing House Inc*, 927 Quezon Ave, Quezon City 3008   Tel: 991682/993897/997647
President: Jesus Ernesto R Sibal; *Advertising/Marketing Dir:* Pilar R Sibal; *Editor-in-Chief:* Dr Máximo D Ramos; *Associate Editor:* Avelina J Gil
Orders to: Alemar's, 769 Rizal Ave, Manila
Subjects: Educational and Non-Fiction Books
1976-78: 261 titles
Bookshops: Alemar's, 769 Rizal Ave, Metro Manila; 526-8 United Nations Ave, Ermita, Metro Manila; 927 Quezon Ave, Quezon City; Makati Arcade, Makati; Commercial Center, Makati, Metro Manila; Corner General Roxas Ave, Times Sq St, Araneta Center, Cubao, Quezon City; Harrison Plaza Commercial Center, Malete, Metro Manila; Corner CM Recto and Nicanor Reyes Sts, Metro Manila

Alip & Sons Publishing Inc*, 1306 Dos Castillas St, Manila
Man Dir: Dr E M Alip; *Sales Dir:* Ella B Ortega; *Publicity Dir:* Miss Bellen A Alip; *Advertising Dir:* Rita A Aramil
Subjects: Textbooks, Reference
Founded: 1946

Associated Publishers Inc*, 63 Quezon Blvd Extension, Quezon City, PO Box 449, Manila
President: J V Roxas
Subjects: Medicine, Education, Law
Founded: 1952

Bookman Publishing House*, PO Box 709, Manila (Located at: 373 Quezon Ave, Quezon City)   Tel: 614631/621706/62187   Cable Add: Bookman
President: Ceferino M Picache; *Sales Dir:* Soriano Seda; *Editorial Dir:* Mrs Patrocinio S Picache
Subsidiary Companies: Bookman Printing House, Mission Publishing Co (both at 373 Quezon Ave, Quezon City)
Subjects: Textbooks & Reference for Elementary, Secondary & Collegiate Schools, Educational Materials
1978: 183 titles   *Founded:* 1945

Bustamente Press Inc*, 155 Panay Ave, Quezon City
President: Pablo N Bustamente Jr
Subjects: Textbooks on English, Sciences, Mathematics
Founded: 1949

Capitol Publishing House Inc*, 54 Don Alejandro A Roces Ave, Quezon City

Communication Foundation for Asia*, PO Box SM-434, Manila 2806   Tel: 602689/607659   Cable Add: Socomter Manila   Telex: 7527854 SCC PH
Man Dir: G V Ong Jr; *Editorial:* Fr P Diaz, J Ballesteros; *Publicity:* Rosario D Nolasco
Subjects: Pastoral and Human Interests/Educational Materials
Book Clubs: Foundation Book Club
1977: 10 titles   *Founded:* 1968

Erehwon Publishing House*, 569 Padre Faura, Ermita, Manila
Subjects: General Fiction, Belles Lettres, How-to
Bookshop: 569 Padre Faura, Ermita, Manila

Filipino Publishing House Inc*, Scout Reyes St, Quezon City

R M Garcia Publishing House*, 903 Quezon Ave, Quezon City   Tel: 999847/993286   Cable Add: Romgar
Orders to: PO Box 1860, Manila
Man Dir: Rolando M Garcia; *Editorial:* Ms J Cruz; *Sales:* R M Garcia Jr; *Publicity:* R G Garcia; *Permissions:* Ms B Gutierrez
Parent Company: R P Garcia Publishing & Printing Co
Subjects: College Textbooks for Philippine Schools; Elementary and Secondary Textbooks
1977: 10 titles   *Founded:* 1951

Industry & Trade Publishers*, 5 Martelino St, Quezon City
Subjects: Business, Industry

Jonef Publications*, 1137 Looban, Paco, Manila   Tel: 598910/502702/597647
Man Dir: J N Francisco
Subjects: Reference, Primary & Intermediate Textbooks
Founded: 1950

Lawin Publishing House*, 1227 M H del Pilar, Ermita, Manila   Tel: 583958
President: Amado Lagdameo Jr; *Manager & Sales Dir:* Maria Paz Diaz Lagdameo; *Publicity & Advertising:* Maria Esperanza Diaz; *Rights & Permissions:* Amado Lagdameo Jr
Subjects: Belles Lettres, Poetry, Reference, Textbooks
Founded: 1971
Bookshop: L C Books and Raggs, 1227 M H del Pilar, Ermita, Manila
Miscellaneous: Firm is primarily a distributor

Lawyers' Co-operative Publishing Co (Philippines) Inc*, Quezon Blvd Extension 63, PO Box 449, Quezon City, Manila
President: Jaime V Roxas
Subjects: Law, Medicine, Educational
Founded: 1913
Miscellaneous: Firm is an affiliate of Lawyers' Co-operative Publishing Co, New York, NY 14603

M C S Enterprises Inc*, 1835-B Recto Ave, PO Box 3667, Manila
President: Mar C Sanchez Sr; *Man Dir:* Constancia P Puno
Subjects: Art, Anthropology, History, Political Science
Bookshop: 1835-B Recto Ave, Manila

Macaraig Publishing Co*, 1144 Vermont St, Manila
President: Serafin E Macaraig
Subjects: Social Science, Textbooks
Founded: 1926

Manor Press*, 715 Evangelista Sq, Quiapo, Manila

Roberto **Martinez** & Sons*, 3 España, Quezon City

Modern Book Company Inc*, 926 Rizal Ave, PO Box 632, Manila   Tel: 274318   Cable Add: Moboco
Man Dir: Exequiel Villacorta
Subjects: History, Social Science, Secondary & Primary Textbooks
1978: 1 title   *Founded:* 1945
Bookshop: 926 Rizal Ave, Manila

Mutual Books Inc, 425 Shaw Blvd, Mandaluyong, Metro Manila (Shipping Add: PO Box 245, Greenhills, San Juan, Metro Manila)   Tel: 797538/796050   Cable Add: Mubinc
President: Alfredo S Nicdao Jr; *Sales:* F F Gonzalez IV
Associate Company: Alfredo S Nicdao Jr Inc
Subjects: Business, Economics, Management, Accounting, Mathematics, Secretarial
1977: 35 titles   *1978:* 36 titles   *Founded:* 1959

National Book Store*, 701 Rizal Ave, Manila   Tel: 494306/07/08/09   Cable Add: Nabost Manila   Telex: 7890 NBS-PH
Man Dir: Benjamin R Ramos; *Sales Dir:* Mitto Licauco; *Publicity & Advertising:* Mrs Socorro C Ramos; *Rights & Permissions:* Alfredo C Ramos
Subjects: General Fiction & Nonfiction, How-to, Music, Art, Juveniles, Low-priced Paperbacks, University, Secondary & Primary Textbooks
Founded: 1945
Bookshops: 701 Rizal Ave, Manila; C M Recto Ave, near Morayta, Manila; Araneta Coliseum Bldg, Cubao, Quezon City; The Quad, Makati; Harrizon Plaza, Mabini
Miscellaneous: Firm reprints over 300 titles annually for foreign publishers

New City, 363 Ycaza St, San Miguel, Manila, subsidiary of Città Nuova Editrice, Rome (qv)

Philippine Arts and Architecture*, 1346 UN Ave, Ermita, Manila
Subjects: Art, Architecture

Philippine Book Co*, 851 Orouieta St, Sta Cruz, Manila   Tel: 274337
Subjects: General Fiction, Belles Lettres, School texts
Bookshop: Address as above

PHILIPPINES

Philippine Education Co Inc*, PO Box 706, Makati Commercial Center, Manila (Located at: Banawe St, corner Quezon Ave, Quezon City) Tel: 603041/42/43 Cable Add: Pecoi Manila Telex: 7222321
General Manager: Jose C Benedicto
Subjects: General Fiction, Belles Lettres, Art, Social Science, Textbooks, Educational Materials
Bookshops: Araneta Center, Cubao, Quezon City; Makati Commercial Center, West Drive Arcade, Makati; Broadway Centrum, Doña Juana Rodriguez and Aurora Blvd, Quezon City; Banawe St, corner Quezon Ave, Quezon City
1977: 50 titles

Philippine International Publishing Co*, 1789 A Mabini St, Ermita, Manila

Regal Publishing Co, 1729 J P Laurel St, San Miguel, Manila 2804 Tel: 498196/8 Cable Add: Repress Manila
Man Dir/Editorial/Publicity: Corinna B Mojica; *Sales:* Ms C B Benipayo; *Production:* L B Benipayo; *Permissions:* A B Benipayo
Associate Companies: Benipayo Press Inc, 1131 Quezon Ave, Heroes Hills, Quezon City 3008
Subjects: Philippine Writings, Philippine and English Translations of German Books
1977: 4 titles *1978:* 2 titles *Founded:* 1958

Sinag-Tala Publishers Inc, Greenhills, PO Box 536, Manila 3113 (Located at: 2506 Taft Ave, Manila 2801) Tel: 582966/581524/505215 Cable Add: Sinapub Manila
Man Dir: P M Hernandez; *Editorial:* F L Tupas; *Sales:* M R De La Cruz; *Production:* E Q Laureola; *Permissions:* E Q Laureola
Subjects: Business, Economics, Educational Textbooks, Home & Family, Religion
1978: 15 titles *1979:* 16 titles *Founded:* 1969

Solidaridad Publishing House, 531 Padre Faura, Ermita, Manila Tel: 586581/591241 Cable Add: Soldad
Man Dir: F Sionil Jose
Subjects: Biography, Fiction, History, Reference
Founded: 1965
Bookshop: Solidaridad Bookshop, 531 Padre Faura, Ermita, Manila
Miscellaneous: Publish monthly journal, *Solidarity*

Tamaraw Publishing Co*, Cebu Ave, Quezon City

University of the Philippines Press*, Gonzalez Hall, Diliman, Quezon City 3004
Acting Dir, Rights & Permissions: Luis D Beltran; *Editorial:* Renato Correa; *Sales, Publicity:* Pilar E Tongson; *Production:* Francisco Felix
Subjects: General Fiction, Belles Lettres, Art, Music, Religion, Philosophy, How-to, Medicine, Business, Law, Psychology, Political & Social Science, Science & Technology, Educational Materials

University Publishing Co*, Central Office, 1128 Washington, Sampaloc, Manila
Dirs: Dr José M Aruego and Constancia E Aruego
Subjects: Business, Law, Educational Materials
Founded: 1936

Vera-Reyes Inc*, 40 Valencia St, Quezon City 3008 Tel: 783976 Cable Add: Verareyes Manila Telex: Verareyes c/o 3199 Etpimo pn
Man Dir: L O Reyes
Subjects: Arts & Culture
1977: 6 titles *Founded:* 1964

Vision Publishing Corporation*, Room 305, B Jalandoni Bldg, Mabini, Cor. Romero Salas Sts, Ermita, Manila Tel: 571234/571225
Man Dir: Anacleto del Rosario; *Advertising Dir:* Betty B Tipon
Br Off: L & S Bldg, 1414 Roxas Blvd, Manila
Founded: 1962

Book Club

Foundation Book Club*, PO Box 5M-434, Manila 2806
Owned by: Communication Foundation for Asia (Manila)

Major Booksellers

Alemar's, PO Box 2119, Manila (Located at: 769 Rizal Ave, Manila) Tel: 475502 Telex: 27634 ALE PH and several others, see entry for Alemar-Phoenix Publishing House under Publishers)

Bookmark Inc*, 357 T Pinpin, Escolta, Manila Tel: 497939; Ayala Arcade, Makati Commercial Center, Makati, Rizal

Eastern Book Service Corp, UPO Box 10, Diliman, Quezon City (Located at: 3 Malamig St, UP Village, Quezon City 3004) Tel: 994388 Cable Add: Eastbook Manila
Manager: Fiorello Rifareal
Publishers' Agents and Stockists

Goodwill Trading Co Ltd*, Goodwill Book Store, 711-715 Rizal Ave, Manila Tel: 477211/12/13/14

G Miranda & Sons*, 1887 C M Recto Ave, Manila Tel: 274867

Modern Book Co Inc*, 926 Rizal Ave, PO Box 632, Manila 2800

National Book Store*, 701 Rizal Ave, Manila Tel: 494306/07/08/09; and four other branches (see entry under Publishers)

Philippine Book Co*, 851 Oroquieta St, Sta Cruz, Manila Tel: 274337

Philippine Education Co Inc*, PO Box 620, Manila (Located at: 245 Banawe St, cnr Quezon Blvd, Quezon City) Tel: 603041/42/43
General Manager: Jose C Benedicto

Popular Bookstore, 1572 Doroteo Jose, PO Box 2855, Manila Tel: 274762

Major Libraries

Ateneo de Manila University Libraries*, PO Box 154, Loyola Heights, Quezon City; Padre Faura, Manila

Far Eastern University Library*, PO Box 609, Manila 2806 Manila City Library, Kamaynilaan Bldg, Arroceros St, Manila 10401

National Library*, T M Kalaw St, PO Box 2926 Ermita, Manila Tel: Filipiniana 485519; Reference 485588; Public Documents 491114

Silliman University Library*, Dumaguete City 6501
Librarian: Professor Gorgonio D Siega
Publications: Selected Philippine Periodical Index; Student's Library Manual (revised annually); *Occasional Library Bulletin*

Ramona S **Tirona** Memorial Library*, The Philippine Women's University, Taft Ave, Manila 2801 Tel: 503277
Librarian: Esperanza A Sta Cruz
Publications: Philippine Educational Forum, Administrative Bulletin, The Philwomenian, Research Abstracts

University of Manila Central Library*, 546 Dr M V de los Santos, Sampaloc, Manila

University of San Carlos Library*, P del Rosario St, Cebu City 6401
Dir: Mrs Marilou P Tadlip

University of Santo Tomas Library*, España, Manila 2806 Tel: 210081 local 234

University of the East Library*, Claro M Recto Ave, Manila ZC 2806

University of the Philippines Library, Gonzalez Hall, Diliman, Quezon City 3004 Tel: 976061/8, local 284

Library Associations

Association of Special Libraries of the Philippines (ASLP)*, PO Box 4118, Manila
President: Potenciana D David
Publications: ASLP Bulletin (quarterly), *Directory of Special Library Resources in the Philippines*

Bibliographical Society of the Philippines*, c/o National Archives, National Library Bldg, T M Kalaw, Ermita, Manila
Secretary-Treasurer: Leticia R Maloles
Publications: Newsletter

Division of Documentation, **National Institute** of Science and Technology — see Scientific Library and Documentation Division

Philippine Library Association*, c/o National Library, T M Kalaw St, Manila 2801 Tel: 590177
Secretary: Ms H Ll Carpio
Publication: PLAI Bulletin (irregular); *PLAI Newsletter* (bi-monthly)

Scientific Library and Documentation Division, National Science Development Board, Bicutan, Taguig, PO Box 3596, Manila
Chief: Dr Irene D Amores

University of the Philippines, Institute of Library Science, Diliman, Quezon City 3004 Tel: 976061 ext 249
Dir: Ursula Picache (Dean)
Publications: Journal of Philippine Librarianship, Newsletter

Library Reference Books and Journals

Books

Bibliography of Philippine Bibliographies, Ateneo de Manila University Press, PO Box 154, Manila

Directory of Special Library Resources in the Philippines Association of Special Libraries of the Philippines, PO Box 4118, Manila

Philippine Bibliography, University of the Philippines Library, Gonzalez Hall, Diliman, Quezon City 3004

Journals

Bulletin, Association of Special Libraries of the Philippines (ASLP), PO Box 4118, Manila

Bulletin, Philippine Library Association, c/o National Library, T M Kalaw, Ermita, Manila

Journal of Philippine Librarianship (text in English), University of the Philippines, Institute of Library Science, Diliman, Quezon City

Newsletter, Bibliographical Society of the Philippines, c/o National Archives, National Library Bldg, T M Kalaw, Ermita, Manila

Newsletter, University of the Philippines, Institute of Library Science, Diliman, Quezon City

Literary Associations and Societies

Kawika (Society of Tagalog Writers)*, 1655 Soler, Santa Cruz
Secretary: Gemiliane Pinade
Publication: Liwayway (weekly)

International **P E N** Centre, Solidaridad Publishing Ho, 531 Padre Favra, Ermita, Manila
Secretary: F Sionil José

Literary Periodicals

Balthazar, Balthazar Publishing House, 1782 M Adriatico, Malate, Manila

Diliman Review, University of the Philippines, College of Arts and Sciences, Diliman, Quezon City D-505

Far Eastern University Journal, Far Eastern University, PO Box 609, Manila 2806

Manila Review (text in English); Philippines journal of literature and the arts, Bureau of National and Foreign Information, Department of Public Information, PO Box 3396, Manila

Philippine Studies, Ateneo de Manila University Press, PO Box 154, Manila

Literary Prizes

Cultural Centre of the Philippines Literary Awards
For the best volume of verse and best play written in English and in Pilipino languages, including fiction (novel), epic poetry, criticism and biography once every five years marking the special inaugurations of the Centre, with correspondingly bigger prizes. Open to Filipino citizens, resident or non-resident. Prizes 5,000 Philippine pesos for best verse volume, 7,000 Philippine pesos for best play. Prizes also for 2nd and 3rd places. Awarded annually. Enquiries to Cultural Centre of the Philippines, Roxas Blvd, Manila

Carlos **Palanca** Memorial Awards for Literature*
For short stories, poems and plays written in English and in Pilipino languages. 10,000 Philippine pesos for the best work in three-act plays both in English and in Pilipino; 5,000 pesos for the best work in short stories, poems and one-act plays also in English and in Pilipino. Awarded annually. Enquiries to Carlos Palanca Senior Memorial Foundation, 453 C Palanca St, Quiapo, Manila

Poland

General Information

Language: Polish (German and Russian used, English especially among young people)
Religion: Roman Catholic
Population: 34.7 million
Literacy Rate (1970): 97.8% (98.8% Urban, 96.5% Rural)
Bank Hours: 0900-1300 Monday-Friday; 0800-1300 Saturday
Shop Hours: 1100-1900 Monday-Saturday
Currency: 100 groszy = 1 zloty
Export/Import Information: Book importation done by the Foreign Trade Enterprise Ars Polona, ul Krakowskie Przedmieście 7, PO Box 1001, 00-068 Warsaw, which pays any duties applicable. Advertising may be placed through AGPOL Foreign Trade Advertising agency, Kierbedzia 4, PO Box 7, 00-957 Warsaw, or through its London agent, Albert Milhado & Co Ltd. No import licences as such required. All overseas trade is conducted in foreign currency. Small quantities of advertising materials duty free
Copyright: Berne, UCC (see International section)

Book Trade Organizations

A G P O L (Przedsiebiorstwo Reklamy i Wydawnictw Handlu Zagranicznego) (Foreign Trade Publicity and Publishing Enterprise)*, ul Kierbedzia 4, PO Box 7, 00-957 Warsaw Tel: 416061 Telex: 813364 agpol pl Cable Add: Agpol Warszawa
Dir: Tadeusz Polanowski
Offers Publicity services abroad for Polish foreign trade and in Poland for foreign companies
Founded: 1956

Editorial Office for **Polish Bibliography** (formerly Karol Estreicher Republication Centre of Polish 19th Century Bibliography)*, ul Jagiellońska 15, Cracow
Dir: Professor Dr Karol Estreicher

Polskie Towarzystwo Wydawców Ksiazek (Polish Publishers' Association)*, ul Mazowiecka 2-4, 00-048 Warsaw Tel: 260735
Publication: Przeglad Ksiegarski i Wydawniczy (jointly with Zjednoczenie Ksiegarstwa (United Booksellers, qv under Major Booksellers)

R S W (Robotnicza Spóldzielnia Wydawnicza)*, 'Prasa-Ksiazka-Ruch' (Workers' Publishing Cooperative), ul Bagatela 14, 00-950 Warsaw Tel: 28851. Includes 'Ksiazka i Wiedza' (qv), Interpress (qv), Krajowa Agencja Wydawnicza (qv), Agencja Wydawnicza (qv) and Wydawnictwo Artystyczno-Graficzne; also the Foreign Trade Enterprise Ars Polona (qv under Booksellers)

Stowarzyszenie Ksiegarzy Polskich (Association of Polish Booksellers)*, ul Mokotowska 4-6, 00-641 Warsaw Tel: 252874
President: Tadeusz Hussak
Social organization for State book trade employees
Publication: Ksiegarz

Zjednoczenie Przedsiebiorstw Wydawniczych Naczelny Zarzad Wydawnictw (United Publishers — Central Publishing Board)*, ul Krakowskie Przedmieście 15-17, 00-071 Warsaw Tel: 268830

Book Trade Reference Books and Journals

Books

Bibliografia Bibliografii i Nauki o Ksiazce. Bibliografia Poloniae Bibliographica (Bibliography of Bibliographies and Library Science), National Library, ul Hankiewicza 1, 00-973 Warsaw

Polish Publishers and Booksellers (text in English), Państwowy Instytut Wydawniczy, ul Foksal 17, 00-372 Warsaw

Journals

Biuletyn (Bulletin), Bibliographical Institute, National Library, ul Hankiewicza 1, 00-973 Warsaw

Books in Polish or Relating to Poland, Polish Library, 9 Princes Gardens, London SW7, UK

Ksiegarz (The Bookseller), Association of Polish Booksellers, ul Mokotowska 4-6, 00-641 Warsaw

New Books (editions in English and Polish), Ossolineum, Rynek 9, PO Box 70, 50-106 Wroclaw

New Polish Publications; a monthly review of Polish books (editions in English, German and Russian), Ars Polona-Ruch, ul Krakowskie Przedmieście 7, 00-068 Warsaw

Przeglad Ksiegarski i Wydawniczy (Publishing and Bookselling Review), United Booksellers, ul Jasna 26, 00-950 Warsaw (published jointly with the Polish Publishers' Association)

Przewodnik Bibliograficzny. Urzedowy wykaz druków wydanych w Polskiej Rzeczypospolitej Ludowej (Bibliographical Guide. Official List of Publications Issued in Poland), National Library, ul Hankiewicza 1, 00-973 Warsaw

Rocznik Literacki (The Literary Yearbook), Państwowy Instytut Wydawniczy, ul Foksal 17, 00-372 Warsaw

Soon to Appear (French, German and Russian editions), Foreign Trade Publicity and Publishing Enterprise, ul Kierbedzia 4, PO Box 7, 00-957 Warsaw

Zapowiedzi Wydawnicze (Publishing Announcements), United Booksellers, ul Jasna 26, 00-950 Warsaw

Publishers

Agencja Autorska (Authors' Agency Ltd), ul Hipoteczna 2, 00-092 Warsaw Tel: 278396
Subjects: Contemporary Polish writers; Periodicals
Also Literary Agency (qv)

Arkady Publishing House*, ul Sienkiewicza 14, PO Box 169, 00-950 Warsaw Tel: 269316
Man Dir: Eugeniusz Piliszek; *Rights & Permissions:* Ewa Luboiedea
Subjects: Art, Architecture, Building
1977: 105 titles *Founded:* 1957

Ars Christiana*, ul Ogrodowa 37, PO Box 471, 00-873 Warsaw Tel: 204738
Subjects: Religion Problems, Periodicals
Founded: 1951

Wydawnictwa **Artystyczne i Filmowe**, ul Pulawska 61, 02-595 Warsaw Tel: 455301/455584
Man Dir: Jerzy Wittlin; *Editorial:* Edward Rylukowski; *Editorial, Publicity:* Barbara Olszańska; *Production:* Jerzy Mika
Orders to: Ars Polona, Krakowskie Przedmieście 7, 00-068, Warsaw
Subjects: Art, Film, Theatre, Reprints of old books and engravings
1978: 52 titles *Founded:* 1959

Instytut Wydawniczy **Centralnej Rady Związków Zawodowych** (Publishing House of the Central Council of Trade Unions)*, ul W Spasowskiego 1-3, 00-389 Warsaw Tel: 279011
Dir: Tadeusz Lipski
Subjects: Health and Safety at Work, Workers' Education, Sociology
Founded: 1950
Bookshop: Ksiegarnia Skladowa, Marienształ 8, 00-302 Warsaw

Spóldzielnia Wydawnicza **'Czytelnik'**, ul Wiejska 12a, Warsaw Tel: 281441 Cable Add: Czytelnik Warsaw
Man Dir: Stanislaw Bebenek; *Publicity & Advertising:* Zenon Skuza
Subjects: General Fiction, Belles Lettres, Poetry, Juveniles, Low-priced Paperbacks, Social Science, Memoirs, Journalism
Founded: 1944

Drukarnia Narodowa, an imprint of Polskie Wydawnictwo Muzyczne (qv)

Państwowe Wydawnictwo **Ekonomiczne** (State Economic Publishers), ul Niecala 4a, 00-098 Warsaw Tel: 278001 Cable Add: Pewue
Man Dir: Zbigniew Gajczyk
Imprint: PWE
Subjects: Scholarly, Reference, Economics, Social Science, Business
Bookshop: address as above
1977: 119 titles *1978:* 122 titles *Founded:* 1949

Wydawnictwo **'Epoka'**, ul W Hibnera 11, PO Box 393, 00-018 Warsaw Tel: 278081 Cable Add: Wydawnictwo Epoka Warszawa
Subjects: Publications of the Central Committee of the Democratic Party, Periodicals
Founded: 1957

Wydawnictwa **Geologiczne**, ul Rakowiecka 4, PO Box 72, 00-975 Warsaw Tel: 495081
Dir: Franciszek Szejgis
Subjects: Academic and professional books on Geology, Surveying
1977: 90 titles *1978:* 85 titles *Founded:* 1953

Zarzad Wydawnictw **Głównego Urzedu Statystycznego** (Publishers of the Central Statistical Office)*, ul Wawelska 1-3, 02-034 Warsaw Tel: 253454
Subject: Statistics
Founded: 1966

Wydawnictwo Harcerskie **'Horyzonty'**, incorporated in new organization Mlodziezowa Agencja Wydawnicza (qv)

Państwowy **Instytut** Wydawniczy (State Publishing Institute)*, ul Foksal 17, 00-950 Warsaw Tel: 260201 Cable Add: Piw
Man Dir: Andrzej Wasilewski; *Editorial Dir:* Jerzy Skórnicki
Subjects: General Fiction, Belles Lettres, Poetry, Biography, History, History of Culture, Essays, Memoirs
1977: 227 titles
Founded: 1946

Wydawnictwo **'Interpress'**, ul Bagatela 12, PO Box 388, 00-585 Warsaw Tel: 219325 Cable Add: Interpress Warszawa Telex: 814481/814775 pai pl
Editor-in-Chief: Lubomir Mackiewicz; *Sales:* Roman Kochánski; *Rights & Permissions:* Miroslawa Wernik
Subjects: Contemporary and Historical Poland, Popular Science, Tourist Guides
1978: 87 titles *1979:* 116 titles *Founded:* 1967
Miscellaneous: Member of RSW (see under Book Trade Organizations)

Państwowe Wydawnictwo **'Iskry'**, ul Smolna 11-13, PO Box 897, 00-375 Warsaw Tel: 276001/3 (Central) 279415 (Director) Cable Add: Iskry
Man Dir: Lukasz Szymański
Subjects: General Fiction, Belles Lettres, Poetry, Biography, Travel-Adventure books, How-to, Religion, Juveniles, Low- & High-priced Paperbacks, Social Science
1977: 119 titles *1978:* 95 titles *Founded:* 1952

Państwowe Przedsiebiorstwo Wydawnictw **Kartograficznych**, ul Solec 18, 00-410 Warsaw Tel: 283251 Cable Add: Pepewuka, Warszawa
Dir: Jan Rzedowski (Tel: 280236)
Subjects: Geographical, Historical, Maps and Atlases; Geodetic, Cartographic books
1979: 122 titles *Founded:* 1951

Wydawnictwo **Katalogów i Cenników** (Catalogue and Price List Publishers)*, ul Wiejska 12a, 00-490 Warsaw Tel: 291396 Cable Add: Wukace Warszawa
Subject: Catalogues, Price Lists, Handbooks, Guidebooks
Founded: 1962

Wydawnictwa **Komunikacji i Laczności** (Transport and Communications Publishers), ul Kazimierzowska 52, PO Box 71, 02-546 Warsaw Tel: 492751
Dir: Czeslaw Kulesza
Subjects: Mechanical Engineering, Aeronautics, Electronics, Radio, Communications, Transport
1977: 142 titles *1978:* 212 titles *Founded:* 1949

Krajowa Agencja Wydawnicza (KAW), ul Wilcza 46, PO Box 179, 00-679 Warsaw Tel: 286481/286485 (5 lines) Telex: 813487 KAW PL
Man Dir, Editor-in-Chief: Dobroslaw Kobielski
Subjects: Culture, Science, Educational material, Juveniles, Politics, Guides, Belles Lettres, Sport, Science and Detective Fiction

Founded: 1974
Miscellaneous: Member of RSW 'Prasa-Ksiazka-Ruch' (qv under Book Trade Organizations)

Wydawnictwo **'Ksiazka i Wiedza'**, ul Smolna 13, PO Box 476, 00-375 Warsaw Tel: 275401 Cable Add: KiW Warszawa
Subjects: History, Politics, Sociology, Philosophy
Founded: 1948
Miscellaneous: Member of RSW (see under Book Trade Organizations)

Państwowy Zaklad Wydawnictw **Lekarskich** (Polish Medical Publishers), Dluga 38-40, PO Box 379, 00-238 Warsaw Tel: 314281 Cable Add: Wydlek Warszawa
Dir: Benedykt Nowakowski; *Chief Editor:* Andrzej Wiczynski; *Editorial Secretary:* Ewa Cierniak
Subjects: Medicine, Biology, Biochemistry, Pharmacy, Psychology, Textbooks, Monographs, Dictionaries, Periodicals, Audio-Visual Materials
1978: 200 titles *Founded:* 1945

Wydawnictwo **Literackie**, ul Dluga 1, 31-147 Cracow Tel: 25423/24644/24761
Dir: Andrzej Kurz; *Editorial:* Katarzyna Krzemuska, Jan Pieszczachowicz, Ireneusz Maślarz
Subjects: Polish Classical and Contemporary Literature and Translations, History of Literature and Art
1977: 201 titles *1978:* 206 titles *Founded:* 1953

Wydawnictwo **Lodzkie** (Lodz Publishing House)*, ul Piotrkowska 171-173, PO Box 372, 90-447 Lodz Tel: 60331
Editorial Dir: Jacek Zaorski; *Sales & Publicity:* Janina Sobczak; *Production:* Pawel Marchewka; *Rights & Permissions:* Jerzy Badowski
Subjects: Socio-Political Literature, Belles Lettres, Memoirs, Translations of modern Yugoslav and Soviet Union Literature
1977: 48 titles *Founded:* 1957

Wydawnictwo **Lubelskie** (Lublin Publishers)*, ul Okopowa 7, 20-022 Lublin Tel: 27344
Dir and Editor-in-Chief: Pawel Dabek
Subjects: Social & Political Sciences, Humanities, Belles-Lettres, Juveniles, Poetry, Ukrainian Literature
1977: 48 titles *Founded:* 1957

Ludowa Spóldzielnia Wydawnicza, ul Grzybowska 4, 00-131 Warsaw Tel: 200251 Cable Add: LSW, Warszawa People's Publishing Cooperative
Chairman, Editor-in-Chief: Leon Janczak
Subjects: Polish Literature, History, The Peasant Movement, Agricultural Problems
1978: 150 titles *Founded:* 1946

Wydawnictwo **Ministerstwa Obrony Narodowej** (Publishing House of the Ministry of National Defence)*, ul Grzybowska 77, 00-844 Warsaw Tel: 201261
Dir: Lech Szymański; *Editorial:* Zdzislaw Korys, Renata Wojciechowska
Subject: Military (History, Memoirs, Technical Literature)
1977: 170 titles *Founded:* 1947

Mlodziezowa Agencja Wydawnicza (Youth Publishing Agency and Publishing Co-operative)*, ul Koszykowa 6A, PO Box 188, 01-564 Warsaw
Agency Editor-in-Chief: Zygmunt Konopka (Tel: 280973); *Books Editor-in-Chief:* Irena Kuźniewska (Tel: 289030); *Publicity Manager:* Beata Wójcikiewicz (Tel: 288720)

Subjects: Literature for young people; Instructions and Programmes of Activity of Polish Socialist Youth Organizations; Belles Lettres, Sociology, Politics, Popular Science; Handbooks
1978: 163 titles *Founded:* 1974
Miscellaneous: This organization replaces the former Wydawnictwo Harcerskie 'Horyzonty'. It is also a Workers' Publishing Co-operative, allied to R S W (see under Book Trade Organizations). Mlodziezowa acts as both Agency and Publisher for Polish youth

Wydawnictwo **Morskie**, ul Szeroka 38-40, 80-835 Gdansk Tel: 311031
Man Dir: Edward Mazurkiewicz; *Editorial:* Stanislaw Ludwig; *Sales, Publicity:* Jerzy Szulczewski; *Production:* Wladyslaw Kawecki; *Rights & Permissions:* Magdalena Tomsio
Subjects: Maritime, Technical, Economics, Popular Science, Belles Lettres, History
Book Club: Publisher's Club, address as above
Bookshop: Publisher's Bookshop, address as above
1977: 77 titles *1978:* 86 titles *Founded:* 1951
ISBN Publisher's Prefix: 83-215

Polskie Wydawnictwo **Muzyczne** (Polish Music Publishers), Al Krasińskiego 11a, PO Box 115, 31-111 Cracow Tel: 27044 Cable Add: PWM
Man Dir: Mieczyslaw Tomaszewski; *Editorial:* Stanislaw Haraschin; *Sales:* Wladyslaw Duda; *Production:* Henryk Wiśniewski; *Publicity:* Halina Czubinska; *Rights & Permissions:* Jan Paździora
Orders to: Biuro Handlu Zagranicznego, ul Krak Przedmieście 7, Warszawa
Associate Company: Agencja Autorska, ul Hipoteczna 2, Warszawa (qv)
Subsidiary Company: Centralna Biblioteka Muzyczna-Nutowa, ul Senatorska 13/15, Warsaw
Imprint: Drukarnia Narodowa
Branch Off: 'Synkopa', ul Senatorska 13/13 Warsaw
Subject: Music
Book Clubs: Skladnica Ksiegarska, ul Smoleńsk 33, Cracow; Dom Ksiazki, ul Smoleńsk, Cracow
Bookshop: Skladnica Ksiegarska, ul Smoleńsk, Cracow
1977: 362 titles *1978:* 359 titles *Founded:* 1945

Instytut Wydawniczy '**Nasza Ksiegarnia**', ul W Spasowskiego 4, PO Box 380, 00-389 Warsaw Tel: 262431 Cable Add: Nasza Ksiegarnia
Man Dir: Ignacy Gajewski
Subjects: Juveniles, General Science, Education, Periodicals
1978: 205 (including 56 translations) *1977:* 171 (including 54 translations) *Founded:* 1921

Państwowe Wydawnictwo **Naukowe***, ul Miodowa 10, PO Box 391, 00-251 Warsaw Tel: 262291 Cable Add: Pewuen Warszawa
Man Dir: Stanislaw Puchala; *Sales Dir:* Jerzy Kozlowski; *Rights & Permissions:* Zygmunt Gebethner
Branch Offs: ul Wieckowskiego 13, 90-721 Lódź; ul Smoleńsk 14, 31-112 Cracow; ul Ratajczaka 35, 61-816 Poznań; ul Wierzbowa 15, 50-056 Wroclaw
Orders to: Ars Polona-Ruch, Importers & Exporters, Krakowskie Przedmiescie 7,00-68 Warsaw Cable Add: Arspolona-Ruch Warsaw
Subjects: History, Philosophy, Sociology, Psychology, Pedagogics, Economy, Law, Linguistics, Literary Studies, Geography, the Arts, Biology, Mathematics, Physics, Chemistry, Engineering, Agricultural Sciences, Political Science, Information on Warsaw, University Textbooks, Popular Scientific Works, Encyclopaedias, Dictionaries, Scientific Periodicals
Annual Production of approximately 1,200 titles, including reprints and scientific periodicals (about 100 such periodicals, 40 being in other languages)
Founded: 1951
Miscellaneous: Poland's major Scientific Publishing House. It publishes books in foreign languages and co-operates with foreign publishers

Wydawnictwa **Naukowo-Techniczne**, ul Mazowiecka 2-4, PO Box 359, 00-950 Warsaw Tel: 267271 Cable Add: Ente Warszawa
Man Dir: Ryszard Pogonowski; *Foreign Dept, Rights & Permissions:* Zofia Kochanowicz
Subjects: Applied Sciences, Engineering, many fields of Technology; Management; Technical Reference works; Bi- and Multi-lingual Technical Dictionaries at student, graduate, post-graduate and research levels
1978: 143 titles *Founded:* 1949

Wydawnictwa **Normalizacyjne** (Standardization Publishers)*, ul Nowogrodzka 22, PO Box 206, 00-375 Warsaw Tel: 287261 Cable Add: Wuen Warszawa
Subject: Standardization
Founded: 1956

Zaklad Narodowy im **Ossolińskich** Wydawnictwo Polskiej Akademii Nauk, Rynek 9, PO Box 911, 50-106 Wroclaw Tel: 38625 Cable Add: Ossolineum Wroclaw Telex: 0712771
Ossolineum-Publishing House of the Polish Academy of Sciences
Man Dir: Eugeniusz Adamczak
Branch Offs: ul Dluga 26, 00-238 Warsaw; Manifestu Lipcowego 19a, 31-110 Cracow; ul Lagiewniki 56, 80-855 Gdansk
Subjects: Bibliographies, History, Art, Philosophy, Psychology, Physical Sciences, Life Sciences, Earth Sciences, Law, Politics, Literature, Pedagogy/Education, Sociology, Technology, Geography, Economics, Languages, Ethnology; University Textbooks, Educational Materials
1977: 602 titles *Founded:* 1817

P W N (Panstwowe Wydawnictwo Naukowe), see Naukowe

'**Pallottinum**' Wydawnictwo Stowarzyszenia Apolstolstwa Katolickiego (Publishers of the Catholic Apostolate Association)*, PO Box 1095, 60-959 Poznan (Located at: Al S Przybyszewskiego 30, Poznan) Tel: 47212
Manager: Stefan Dusza
Subjects: Catholic Philosophy and Theology
1977: 14 titles *Founded:* 1948

Instytut Wydawniczy **Pax***, ul Chocimska 8-10, 00-791 Warsaw Tel: 499517
Dir: Zbigniew Czajkowski; *Chief Editor:* Antoni Kapliński;
Subjects: Contemporary trends in Christian Theology, Philosophy and Literature
Founded: 1949

Wydawnictwo Stowarzyszenia Spoleczno-Kulturalnego '**Pojezierze**', ul Zwyciestwa 32, 10-578 Olsztyn Tel: 22352/22285
Subjects: Belles Lettres, Popular Science, Art
1977: 40 titles

Wydawnictwo **Poznańskie** (Poznań Publishers)*, ul A Fredry 8, PO Box 63, 60-967 Poznań Tel: 58534
Man Dir: Dr Jerzy Ziolek; *Publicity Dir:* Miss Mag Krystyna Woźniak
Subjects: History of Great Poland and Polish culture, Modern Polish and Foreign Fiction, Science Fiction
Founded: 1956
Miscellaneous: Specializes in translations from the literature of Scandinavian and German-speaking countries

Wydawnictwo **Prawnicze** (Law Publishers)*, ul Wiśniowa 50, 02-520 Warsaw Tel: 496151-53
Subject: all aspects of Law and Criminology
1977: 50 titles *Founded:* 1952

Wydawnictwo **Radia i Telewizji** (Radio and Television Publishers), ul Chelmska 9, 00-724 Warsaw Tel: 412264
Subjects: Radio and Television
Founded: 1968

Państwowe Wydawnictwo **Rolnicze i Leśne** (State Agricultural and Forestry Publishers), Al Jerozolimskie 28, PO Box 374, 00-024 Warsaw Cable Add: Pewril Warszawa Tel: 266451
Man Dir: Mr Marian Bajorek
Subjects: Textbooks, Reference, Agriculture, Forestry, Food Science, Veterinary Science
Founded: 1947

Zaklad Wydawnictw CRS '**Samopomoc Chlopska**' (Publishing Institute of the 'Samopomoc Chlopska' — Peasant Cooperative)*, ul Jasna 1, PO Box 38, 00-013 Warsaw Tel: 271529 Cable Add: Zetwuceres Warszawa Telex: 81622
Subjects: Books and Periodicals for the Peasant Cooperative
Founded: 1957

Wydawnictwo '**Slask**', ul Armii Czerwonej 51, PO Box 67, 40-161 Katowice Tel: 583220
'Silesia' Publishing House
Dir and Editor-in-Chief: Jeremi Gliszczynski
Subjects: Mining and Metallurgy, Polish Literature, Translations from Czech and Slovak, Social and Political Literature
1977: 74 titles *1978:* 70 titles *Founded:* 1954

Slaska kjiegarnia Techniczna, ul Zwirki i Wigury 33, 40-063 Katowice
Subjects: Metallurgy, Technical
Book Club: Klub Czytelników Literatury Hutniczej

Wydawnictwo **Sport i Turystyka** (Sport and Tourism Publishers)*, ul H Rutkowskiego 7-9, 00-021 Warsaw Tel: 262451 Cable Add: Sportur Warszawa
Dir: Alfred Górny; *Editor-in-Chief:* Engeniusz Skrzypek
Subjects: Sport, Travel
Book Club: Klub Czytelników Literatury Gorniczej
Founded: 1953

Statistical Publications and Printing Board of the Central Statistical Office, al Niepodleglosci 208, 00-925 Warsaw Tel: 259545/254886 Cable Add: GUS Telex: 814581
Man Dir: Jerzy Sufin-Suliga; *Editorial:* Jozef Gluzinski
Subject: State statistics
1977: 31 titles *1978:* 24 titles *Founded:* 1966

Ksiegarnia **Św Wojciecha** (St Adalbert's Bookshop), pl Wolności 1, PO Box 288, 60-967 Poznan Tel: 59186/7 Cable Add:

Albertinum Poznan
Man Dir: Ludwik Bielerzewski
Branch Off: ul Królewska 15, Lublin; ul Freta 48, Warsaw
Subjects: Biblical Texts, Theology; Periodicals
Bookshops: Plac Wolności 1, Poznań; ul Królewska 15, Lublin; ul Freta 48, Warsaw
1977: 19 titles *1978:* 16 titles *Founded:* 1895

Wydawnictwa **Szkolne i Pedagogiczne** (The Publishing House for School and Pedagogical Books), pl H Dabrowskiego 8, 00-950 Warsaw, PO Box 480 Tel: 265451/55 Cable Add: Wuesipe Warszawa
Man Dir: Jerzy Loziński; *Rights & Permissions:* Janina Marczak; *Advertising and Head of Foreign Department:* Krystyna Górecka
Orders to: Ars Polona-Ruch, ul Krakowskie Przedmieście 7, Warsaw (qv under Book Trade Organizations)
Branch Off: Delegatura WSiP, Basztowa 15, 31-143 Cracow
Subjects: Primary, Secondary and Vocational Textbooks, Education, Pedagogics, Psychology, Pedagogical Periodicals
Founded: 1945

Towarzystwo Przyjaciól Ksiazki (TPK) (Society of Friends of Books)*, ul Hipoteczna 2 ZAIKS, 00-092 Warsaw Tel: 277304
Man Dir: Alexandre Bochenski
Br Off: Rynek Gl 35, 31-011 Kraków; Plac Wolnosci 12, 40-078 Katowice; uk św Jadwigi 3/4, 50-266 Wroclaw; ul Slowackiego 9, Rzeszów
Subject: Book Collecting
1977: 13 titles *Founded:* 1957

Wydawnictwa Kultura Zycia Codziennego '**Watra**', PO Box 17, 02-001 Warsaw (Located at: Aleje Jerozdimskie 87) Tel: 212241-8
Subjects: Health, Domestic Science, Food, Family Life, Periodicals
Founded: 1954

Wydawnictwa Przemyslu Maszynowego '**Wema**', ul Danitowiczowska 18, PO Box 90, 00-950 Warsaw Tel: 275456
Subjects: Mechanical Engineering
1977: 1,372 titles *1978:* 1,295 titles
Founded: 1967

'**Wiedza Powszechna**' Państwowe Wydawnictwo, ul Jasna 26, PO Box 162, 00-054 Warsaw Tel: 277651
Orders to: Ars Polona
Man Dir & Editor-in-Chief: Tadeusz Kosmala
Subjects: Encyclopaedias, Dictionaries, General Reference, Language Handbooks, Popular Science
1977: 91 titles *1978:* 85 titles *Founded:* 1952

Wydawniczo Oświatowa Spóldzielnia Inwalidów '**Wspólna Sprawa**' (Educational Publishing Cooperative of the Disabled)*, ul Zelazna 40, 00-838 Warsaw Tel: 209071
Subjects: Graphic art textbooks for primary and nursery schools; Periodicals for foreign language sessions; Games
Founded: 1956

Spoleczny Instytut Wydawniczy '**Znak**' (Social Publishing Institute)*, ul Wiślna 12, 31-007 Cracow Tel: 50162
Man Dir: Jacek Wosniakowski
Subjects: Religious Subjects, Belles Lettres
Founded: 1959

Literary Agents

Agencja Autorska, ul Hipoteczna 2, 00-950 Warsaw Tel: 278396
Contact: Wladyslaw Jakubowski, Andrzej Mierzejewski
Also Publisher (qv)

Mlodziezowa Agencja Wydawnicza — Polish Youth Publishing Agency, see main entry under Publishers

Book Clubs

Club of Mining and Metallurgical Books, Wydawnictwo 'Slask' ('Silesia' Publishing House), ul Armii Czerwonej 51, PO Box 67, 40-161 Katowice

Club of Twentieth Century Poetry*, Horizons of Technology Club of Popular Science Books, ul Nowolipie 4, 00-950 Warsaw

Dom Ksiazki*, ul Smoleńsk, Cracow
Owned by: Polskie Wydawnictwo Muzyczne (Cracow)

Klub Czytelnikow **Literatury Gorniczej**, ul Armii Czerwonej 51, 40-161 Katowice
Owned by: Wydawnictwo Slask (qv)

Klub Czytelnikow **Literatury Hutniczej**, ul Zwirki i Wigury 33, 40-063 Katowice
Owned by: Slaska Ksiegarnin Techniczna (qv)

New Countryside Book Club*, ul Nowolipie 4, 00-950 Warsaw

Publisher's Club, ul Szeroka 38/40, 80-835, Gdańsk
Owned by: Wydawnictwo Morskie (Gdansk)

Sktachnica Ksiegarska*, ul Smoleńsk 33, Cracow
Owned by: Polskie Wydawnictwo Muzyczne (Cracow)

Major Booksellers

Ars Polona*, ul Krakowskie Przedmieście 7, PO Box 1001, 00-068 Warsaw Tel: 261201 Cable Add: Ars Polona Warszawa Telex: 813498
Foreign Trade Enterprise
Miscellaneous: Member of RSW (see under Book Trade Organizations)

Dom Ksiazki, ul Jasna 26, 00-950 Warsaw Tel: 277651
Collective name for the State-owned Polish book-retailing enterprises. There are 18, each controlling 50-250 bookshops throughout Poland, subordinate to Zjednoczenie Ksiegarstwa (qv)

Orpan Export*, Palac Kultury, 00-901 Warsaw

Publisher's Bookshop, ul Szeroka 38/40, 80-835, Gdańsk

Powszechna Ksiegarnia Wysylkowa (General Delivery Bookshop) (mail order)*, ul Nowolipie 4, 00-950 Warsaw Tel: 310021 (subordinate to Zjednoczenie Ksiegarstwa qv)

Państwowe, Przedsiebiorstwo '**Skladnica Ksiegarska**'*, ul Mazowiecka 9, 00-950 Warsaw
Organization for wholesale book trade, subordinate to Zjednoczenie Ksiegarstwa (qv)

Zjednoczenie Ksiegarstwa, PO Box 48, 00-950 Warsaw (Located at: ul Jasna 26)
Dir: Kazimierz Majerowicz Tel: 268393 (Dir) or 277651
National organization for the sale of books; subordinate to the Minister of Culture and Art and controlling Skladnica Ksiegarska (wholesale), Dom Ksiazki (retail), and Powszechna Ksiegarnia Wysylkowa (mail order) (qqv under 'Major Booksellers')
Publication: Przeglad Ksiegarski i Wydawniczy (jointly with the Polish Publishers' Association)

Major Libraries

Naczelna Dyrekcja **Archiwów Państwowych** (Main Directorate of the Polish State Archives)*, Dluga St 6, Warsaw

Archiwum Akt Nowych (Centre for Recent Documents)*, Al Niepodleglości 162, 02-554 Warsaw

Archiwum Glówne Akt Dawnych (Central Archives for Historical Documents), Dluga 7, 00-263 Warsaw
Dir: Dr Mieczyslaw Motas

Biblioteka Jagiellońska, Aleja Mickiewicza 22, 30-059 Cracow Tel: 33505/33500/36377; Secretary 30903; Director 31971 Telex 0325682 bj pl
Dir: Professor Dr Stanislaw Grzeszczuk
Publication: Biuletyn Biblioteki Jagiellońskiej (Biannual)

Biblioteka Narodowa, ul Hankiewicza 1, 00-973 Warsaw Tel: Main Bldg 224621; Special Collections: 313241 Telex: 813702 bn pl
This is the National Library, Warsaw. See also Instytut Bibliograficzny
Dir: Professor Witold Stankiewicz

Biblioteka Publiczna m st Warszawy (Public Library), ul Koszykowa 26, 00-553 Warsaw Tel: 283147
Librarian: Stefan Durmaj
Publication: Prace Biblioteki Publicznej m st Warszawy

Biblioteka Śląska, ul Francuska 12, 40-015 Katowice Tel: 516441 Telex: 0312534 bsk pl
Silesian Library
Dir: Doc dr Andrzej Szefer
Miscellaneous: A major Polish library. Specializes in scientific publications, but has many special collections covering Literature, History, Law and Religion and especially Silesian Interest

Centrum Informacji Naukowej, Technicznej i Ekonomicznej (National Centre for Scientific, Technical and Economic Information)*, al Neipodleglości 186, 00-931 Warsaw
Publication: Aktualne Problemy Informacji i Dokumentacji

Glówna Biblioteka Lekarska, Chocimska 22, 00-791 Warsaw
Central Medical Library

Biblioteka **Glówna Politchniki** Warszawskiej, plac Jedności Robotniczej 1, 00-662 Warsaw
Library of the Technical University of Warsaw

Biblioteka **Glówna Uniwersytetu** im Adama Mickiewicza (Library of Adam Mickiewicz University)*, ul Ratajczaka 38-40, Poznan

Instytut Bibliograficzny, National Library, ul Hankiewicza 1, 00-973 Warsaw
Bibliographical Institute. The Institute is a Division of the National Library (see Biblioteka Narodowa above)

Zaklad Narodowy im **Ossolińskich Biblioteka** Polska Akademia Nauk (Library of the Ossoliński National Institute of the Polish Academy of Science)*, ul Szewska 37, Wroclaw Tel: 44471/44472; Director 34304

Biblioteka **Uniwersytecka w Toruniu**, Gagarina 13, 87-100 Toruń
Library of the University of Toruń
Librarian: Dr Bohdan Ryszewski

Biblioteka **Uniwersytecka w Warszawie**, Krakowskie Przedmieście 26-28 and 32, 00-927 Warsaw Tel: Chief Librarian 264155; Department of Scientific Information 264047
Library of the University of Warsaw
Chief Librarian: Jan Baculewski
Publications: Prace Biblioteki Uniwersyteckiej w Warszawie (Irregular); *Uniwersytet Warszawski Materialy bibliograficzne* (annually) in *Roczniki Uniwersytetu Warszawskiego*

Biblioteka **Uniwersytecka w Wrocławiu** (Library of the University of Wroclaw)*, Szajnochy 10, Wroclaw

Library Associations

Polish Academy of Sciences*, Documentation and Scientific Information Centre, ul Nowy Swiat 72, 00-330 Warsaw

Stowarzyszenie Bibliotekarzy Polskich, ul Konopczyńskiego 5/7, 00-953 Warsaw Tel: 275296/270847
Polish Librarians Association
Chairman: Witold Stankiewicz; *Secretary-General:* Tadeusz Zarzebski
Publications: Przegląd Biblioteczny, Bibliotekarz, Poradnik Bibliotekarza, Informator Bibliotekarza i Ksiegarza

Library Reference Books and Journals

Books

Informator Bibliotekarza i Ksiegarza (Guide for the Librarian and Bookseller), Polish Librarians Association, ul Konopczyńskiego 5-7, 00-953 Warsaw

National Library Yearbook (covers scientific library science) (text in Polish with English summaries), National Library, ul Hankiewicza 1, 00-973 Warsaw

Journals

Aktualne Problemy Informacji i Dokumentacji (Current Problems in Information and Documentation) (summaries in English, French, Polish and Russian), National Centre for Scientific, Technical and Economic Information, ul Niepodległości 186, 00-931 Warsaw

Bibliotekarz (The Librarian) (text in Polish, summaries in English and Russian), Polish Librarians Association, ul Konopczyńskiego 5-7, 00-953 Warsaw

Poradnik Bibliotekarza (The Librarian's Handbook), Polish Librarians Association, ul Konopczyńskiego 5-7, 00-953 Warsaw

Przeglad Biblioteczny (Library Review) (summaries in English), Polish Librarians Association, ul Konopczyńskiego 5-7, 00-953 Warsaw

Studia o Ksiazce (Studies on the Book), Ossolineum, Rynek 9, PO Box 70, 50-106 Wroclaw

Literary Associations and Societies

Instytut Badań Literackich, Nowy Świat 72, Palac Staszica, 00-330 Warsaw Tel: 265231/269945
Institute of Literary Research
Acting Dirs: Prof Mieczyslaw Klimowicz, Doc Stefan Treugutt, Ryszard Górski
Publications: Pamiętnik Literacki (Literary Journal quarterly); *Biuletyn Polonistyczny* (Bulletin of Polish Literary Scholarship, quarterly); *Teksty* (Texts, fortnightly); *Kwartalnik Historii Prasy Polskiej* (Quarterly of the History of Polish Journalism); and other Literary Study series
Founded: 1948

Polish **P E N** Club, Palac Kultury i Nauki, 00-901 Warsaw
Secretary: Wladyslaw Bartoszewski

Stowarzyszenie Autorów Zaiks, 2 rue Hipoteczna, 00-092 Warsaw Tel: 277577 Telex: 812470 zaikz pl
Polish Society of Authors
Foreign Dept Manager: Wlodzimierz Lalak

Towarzystwo Literackie im Mickiewicza (The Mickiewicz Literary Society)*, Nowy Świat 72, Warsaw
President: Julian Krzyzanowski
Publication: Rocznik (Yearbook)

Towarzystwo Przyjaciól Ksiazki (Society of Friends of Books)*, ul Hipoteczna 2, 00-092 Warsaw

Towarzystwo Przyjaciól Nauk w Przemyślu, ul Orzechowskiego 2, 37-700 Przemyśl
Society of Science and Letters of Przemyśl
Chairman: Mgr A Kunysz; *Secretary:* Mgr Z Felczyński
Publications: include *Rocznik Przemyski* (21 vols), *Biblioteka Przemyska* (7 vol), *Sprawozdania z działalności towarzystw naukowych miasta Przemyśla* (5 vol); *Rocznik Nauk Medycznych* (2 vols)

Związek Literatów Poliskich (Union of Polish Writers)*, Krakowskie Przedmieście 87-89, Warsaw
President: Jaroslaw Iwaszkiewicz

Literary Periodicals

Literatura (Literature), RSW, ul Bagatela 14, 00-950 Warsaw

Literatura na świecie (World Literature), Ars Polona, ul Krakowskie Przedmieście 7, PO Box 1001, 00-068 Warsaw

MKL (Miesiecznik Kulturalny Litery) (Monthly Journal of Literary Culture), Targ Drzewny 3-7, 80-886 Gdansk

Miesiecznik Literacki (Monthly Review of Literature), Ars Polona, ul Krakowskie Przedmieście 7, PO Box 1001, 00-068 Warsaw

Nowy Wyraz (New Expression), Ars Polona, ul Krakowskie Przedmieście 7, PO Box 1001, 00-068 Warsaw

Pamietnik Literacki (Literary Diary) (contents page in English, Polish and Russian), Institute of Literary Research, Nowy Świat 72, Palac Staszica, 00-330 Warsaw

Poezja (Poetry), Ars Polona, ul Krakowskie Przedmieście 7, PO Box 1001, 00-068 Warsaw

Polish Literature (text in English and French), Agencja Autorska, ul Hipoteczna 2, 00-092 Warsaw

Ruch Literacki (The Literary Movement), Polish Academy of Sciences, Historico-Literary Commission, ul Slawkowska 17, Cracow

Teksty (Texts), Institute of Literary Research, Nowy Świat 72, Palac Staszica, 00-330 Warsaw

Teksty (Texts), RSW, ul Bagatela 14, 00-950 Warsaw

Twórczość (Literary monthly), Ars Polona, ul Krakowskie Przedmieście 7, PO Box 1001, 00-068 Warsaw

Zycie Literackie (Literary Life), ul Wislna 2, Cracow

Literary Prizes

Cracow City Literary Prize*
For the entire work of an author whose life and writings were connected with Cracow. Awarded annually. In 1978 the winner was Feliks Konopka. Enquiries to Cracow City Council and Cracow Section of the Union of Polish Writers, ul Krupnicza 22, Cracow

Polish Ministry of National Defence Prize*
For the best book dealing with the history of the Polish Armed Forces and with the defence of the country. Awarded annually. Enquiries to Polish Ministry of National Defence Publishing House, ul Grzybowska 77, Warsaw

Polish Prime Minister Award for Literature for Children and Youth*
For the entire work of an author of books for children and young people. Awarded annually. Enquiries to Polish Prime Minister's Office, ul Ujazdowskie 113, Warsaw

Polish Union of Socialist Youth Prose Award*
For the best novel by an author under 30. Awarded annually. Enquiries to Polish Union of Socialist Youth and the Daily Paper 'Sztandar Mlodych', ul Wspolna 61, Warsaw

Poznan Poetical November Prize*
For the book judged the best first work of the year by a young poet. Awarded annually. Enquiries to Poznan City Council, ul Stalingradska 18, Poznan

Warsaw City Prize*
For the entire work of a distinguished author writing for children and young people. Awarded annually. Enquiries to Warsaw Municipal Council, Department of Culture, pl Dzierzynskiego 3-5, Warsaw

Warsaw City Prize for Young Poets*
For best poetry written by a young author. Co-sponsored by the Warsaw Creative Youth Club of the Polish Union of Writers

and the Students' Club 'Hybrydy'. Awarded annually. Enquiries to Warsaw Municipal Council, Department of Culture, pl Dzierzynskiego 3-5, Warsaw

Mariusz **Zaruski** Literary Prize*
For the authors of best books about the sea. Awarded annually. Enquiries to Marine Club of the League of the Friends of Soldiers, ul Chocimska 14, Warsaw

'Zycie Literackie' Prize*
For literary criticism, journalism and essays. Awarded annually. Enquiries to Zycie Literackie, ul Wislna 2, Cracow

Portugal

General Information

Language: Portuguese
Religion: Roman Catholic
Population: 9.7 million
Bank Hours: 0900-1200, 1400-1530 Monday-Friday
Shop Hours: 0900-1300, 1500-1900 Monday-Friday (some open continuously); 0900-1300 Saturday. Generally closed Monday morning October-November
Currency: 100 centavos = 1 Portuguese escudo
Export/Import Information: Foreign language books from most countries dutied at 0.08 escudos per kg (free from UK and reduced from EEC); atlases and children's picture books have higher tariff rate and children's picture books have 30% import surcharge. Small quantity of advertising duty-free. No import licence required for goods not exceeding 5,000 escudos, otherwise licence including permission to transfer foreign exchange required. Deposit scheme: importer must deposit 50% value in non-interest bearing account for 180 days
Copyright: UCC, Berne (see International section)

Book Trade Organizations

Associação Portuguesa dos Editores e Livreiros, Largo de Andaluz, 16-1° Esq°, 1000 Lisbon Tel: 546182 Cable Add: Apel
Portuguese Association of Publishers and Booksellers
President: Alvaro de Moura Bessa; *Secretary-General:* Dr Jorge de Carvalho Sá Borges; *Admin Chief:* José N Vieira

Book Trade Reference Books and Journals

Books

O Mundo do Edição Luso-Brasileira (The World of Publishing, Portugal and Brazil), Publicações Europa-Americana, Apdo 8, Mem Martins

Journals

Boletim de Bibliografia Portuguesa (Portuguese Bibliographical Bulletin), National Library, Rua Ocidental do Campo Grande 83, Lisbon 5

Livros de Portugal (Portuguese Books), Portuguese Association of Publishers and Booksellers, Largo de Andaluz, 16-1°, Esq°, Lisbon 1

Publishers

Edições **70** Lda*, Ave Duque d'Ávila 69 R/C Esq, Lisbon 1 Tel: 556898/572001
Man Dir: J J Soares da Costa; *Editorial, Rights & Permissions:* Carlos Araújo; *Copy Editor:* João R Nunes; *Production Dir:* Rui Oliveira; *Sales:* Alfredo Sarmento; *Publicity Manager:* Alceu S Coutinho
Subjects: General Fiction, Literature, Biography, History, Philosophy, Psychology, Social Science, Politics, Economics, Educational, Occult, Leisure Pursuits; University Textbooks
1977: 28 titles *Founded:* 1970

A E I International+*, Rua Sampaio e Pina, 7-1° Fte, Lisbon 1 Tel: 654664/680628 Telex: 16423 aei p
Firm is also a Literary Agency

Edições **A O V**+*, Rua Formosa, 189 Oporto Tel: 28756/22058 Cable Add: Olival-Porto
Man Dir and other offices: Dr José Rebelo
Subjects: History of World War II, Reportage, Politics, Fiction
Founded: 1925

Edições **Acrópole***, Rua Alberto Aldim, Alfragide, Damaia, Lisbon Tel: 971379/972302/972433
Man Dir: Neves Ramos
Subjects: General Fiction, Belles Lettres, Poetry, Biography, History, Philosophy, Juveniles, Low- & High-priced Paperbacks, Psychology, General & Social Science
Founded: 1974
Bookshop: Edições Acrópole, Rua Alberto Aldim, Alfragide, Damaia, Lisbon

Ediçoes **Afrontamento**, Rua Costa Cabral 859, Apartado 1309, Oporto Tel: 489271
Man Dir, Editorial, Production: Jose Sousa Ribeiro; *Sales, Publicity:* Marcela Figueiredo Torres; *Rights & Permissions:* Arnaldo Fleming
Subjects: General Literature, Social Sciences, Urbanism, Politics, Cinema
1977: 16 titles *1978:* 14 titles *Founded:* 1965

Arménio **Amado** Editor Suc, Ceira, Coimbra
Man Dir: Simões Pereira
Subjects: Philosophy, Religion, Psychology, Social Science, Law, Architecture, History, Politics, Languages
Founded: 1929

Livraria **Apostolado** da Imprensa+, Rua da Boavista 591, Oporto Tel: 27875
Man Dir, Editorial: José Maria de Azeredo, Luiz Archer; *Publicity:* A Nunes da Rocha
Branch Off: Rua da Lapa 111, Lisbon 2
Subjects: General Fiction, Belles Lettres, Poetry, Biography, Philosophy, Religion, Juveniles, Secondary Textbooks
Bookshop: address as above
1977: 5 titles *Founded:* 1922

Editora **Arcádia** Sarl*, Campo de Santa Clara 160, Lisbon 2 Tel: 863151/3 Cable Add: Arcádia
Shipping Add: Ave Camilo Castelo Branco, 9-A, Buraca-Damaia
Dirs: Ricardo F Martins, Dr João Rodrigues Martins, Dr Alberto dos Santos Antonio; *Sales Dir:* Alvaro A F Ferreira

Subjects: General Fiction, Belles Lettres, Biography, History, How-to, Music, Art, Philosophy, Religion, Juveniles, Paperbacks, Medicine, Psychology, Engineering, General & Social Science
Founded: 1957

Livraria **Arnado** Lda+*, Rua Joao Machado 9-11, Coimbra Tel: 27573
Man Dir: José Fernandes de Almeida
Parent Company: Porto Editora Lda (qv)
Subsidiary Company: Empresa Literária Fluminense Lda
Subjects: Scholarly, Scientific, Legal, Literary
1976: 25 titles *1977:* 30 titles *Founded:* 1966

Editorial **Aster**+*, Largo D Estefânia 8-1° Esq°, Lisbon 1 Tel: 534611/532973
Man Dir, Sales, Publicity, Rights & Permissions: Fernando de Souza; *Editorial:* Dr H Barrilaro Ruas; *Production:* Carlos A Lopes
Br Offs: Praça Guilherme Gomes Fernandes 24-2° Esq°, Oporto; Rua de Santa Margarida, 2-A, 1°, Braga
Subjects: General Fiction, Belles Lettres, Poetry, Biography, History, Music, Art, Philosophy, Religion, Psychology, How-to, Juveniles, Paperbacks, Secondary and University Textbooks
1977: 52 titles *Founded:* 1954

Livraria Editora **Atlântida** Ltda+*, Rua Ferreira Borges 103, Coimbra
Dir: Afonso Queiró
Subject: Law

Editorial **'Avante!'**+, Ave Santos Dumont 57-3°, Lisbon 1 Tel: 76972/3/4/5
Man Dir: Francisco Melo
Orders to: C D L (Central Distribuidora Livreira) SARL, Ave Santos Dumont 57-4° Lisbon
Subjects: Politics, Economics, Philosophy, Sociology, Literature
1977: 52 titles *Founded:* 1974

Livraria **Bertrand** SARL+, Rua João de Deus, Venda Nova, Amadora Tel: 974571 Cable Add: Libertran Telex: 12709
Man Dirs: António B Monteiro, Ferreira Filipe; *Editorial, Rights & Permissions:* Piedade Ferreira, Pina Mendes; *Sales:* Fausto Amaro; *Production:* Antero Branco; *Publicity:* Ferreira da Cruz
Subjects: General Portuguese and Foreign Literature, Social Sciences, Juveniles (all ages), Dictionaries, School Books, Cartoon Strips
Bookshops: (Lisbon) Rua Garrett 73/75, Ave Roma 13-B, Rua Dr J Soares 4-A, Rua D Estefânea 46-C/D, Rua Latino Coelho 12A-12B; (Coimbra) Largo da Portagem 9; (Oporto) Rua de Santo António 43, 45, 65, Shopping Center, Brasilia; (Aveiro) Ave Dr L Peixinho 87-B; (Vian do Castelo) Rua Sacadura Cabral 32; (Tomar) Rua Alexandre Herculano 21; (Castelo Branco) Av D Nuno Alvares Pereira 4-B; (Faro) Rua D Francisco Gomes 27; (Villa Moura) Centro Comercial da Marina
1977: 195 titles *1978:* 187 titles *Founded:* 1732

Brasília Editôra (J Carvalho Branco & Cia Lda), Rua José Falcão 173, CP 101 Oporto Tel: 315854 Cable Add: Brasiliaeditora
Man Dir: J Carvalho Branco; *Editorial, Rights & Permissions:* Dr Zulmira C Branco; *Sales, Publicity:* Dr Isabel C Branco; *Production:* J Silvo Couto
Associate Company: Livraria Leitura — Fernandes & Branco Lda, Rua de Ceuta 88, Oporto

Subsidiary Company: Livraria Boa Leitura, Av Almirante Reis 256, Lisbon
Subjects: Portuguese and Foreign Literature; Belles Lettres, Fiction, Poetry, Biography, How-to, Philosophy, Religion, Psychology, Social Science, Politics, Yoga, Sex, Occult
Bookshops: Livraria Leitura, Ave Almirante Reis 256B, Lisbon; Livraria Leitura, Rua de Ceuta 88, Oporto
1977: 21 titles *1978:* 26 titles *Founded:* 1961

Editorial **Caminho** SARL+*, Rua Cidade de Quelimane 3-A, Lisbon Tel: 766402
Man Dir: Zeferino Antas de Sousa Coelho
Orders to: C D L — see 'Major Booksellers'
Subjects: General Fiction (especially Crime Thrillers, Sci-Fic, Romantic), Socio-Political, Juveniles
1977: 26 titles *Founded:* 1977

Centro do Livro Brasileiro+, Rua Almirante Barroso 13-2°, Lisbon 1000 Tel: 560165/6/7/8 Cable Add: Celbrasil
Man Dir, Editorial: Alvaro Conçalves Pereira; *Sales:* Henrique Caetano Cordo; *Production:* Alvaro Martins Parreira; *Publicity:* A Gonçalves Pereira; *Rights & Permissions:* Mario Relvas
Associate Companies: Vasco Luso Brasileira
Branch Off: Rua De Ceuta 79, Oporto
Subjects: Philosophy, Religion, Social Science, Philology, Pure and Applied Science, Art, History, Geography, General
Bookshops: Rua do Ouro 160, Lisbon; Rodrigues Sampaio 30B, Lisbon; Rua de Sao Antonio 146, Oporto; Rua de Ceuta 79, Oporto; Rua Luis de Camoès 125, Luanda, Angola
1977: 49 titles *Founded:* 1963

Livraria **Civilização** (Américo Fraga Lamares 8 Ca Lda)+*, Rua Alberto Aires de Gouveia 27, Oporto 1 Tel: 22286/7/32382 Cable Add: Alamares
Man Dir: Arquitecto Moura Bessa; *Rights & Permissions:* Maria Alice Moura Bessa
Branch Off: Ave Almirante Reis 102 r/c-Dt°, Lisbon
Subjects: Social and Political Science, Economics, History, Art, Fiction, Juveniles
1977: 62 titles *1978:* 52 titles *Founded:* 1921

Editorial **Confluência**+*, Rua Fernandes Tomás 13, Lisbon 2 Tel: 690391
Subjects: Philology, Reference, Textbooks, Literature, Languages

Edições **Cosmos**+, Rua da Emenda 111-2°, Lisbon 2 Tel: 322050 Cable Add: Cosmos-Lisboa
Man Dir: Manuel R de Oliveira
Subjects: Music, Sociology, History
1977: 7 titles *1978:* 9 titles *Founded:* 1938

Sá da Costa Editora+, Praça Luís de Camões 22 4, Lisbon 1294 codex Tel: 360721 Cable Add: Livrosacosta
Man Dir, Editorial: João Sá da Costa; *Sales, Publicity:* Manuel Sá da Costa; *Production:* Idalina Sá da Costa
Subjects: Textbooks, History, Philosophy, Literature, Classics, Essays
Bookshop: Rua Garrett 100-102, Lisbon 1294 codex
Founded: 1913

Didáctica Editora, Avenida da Ilha da Madeira 26, 1400 Lisbon Tel: 611731/611209/614887
Subject: Education
Founded: 1945

Publicações **Dom Quixote**, Rua Luciano Cordeiro 119, 1098 Lisbon codex Tel: 40250/538079/538088 Cable Add: Quixote Telex: 14331 Quixot P
Man Dir: Snu Abecassis; *Sales:* Fernando Silva; *Production:* Virginia Caldeira; *Rights & Permissions:* Cristina Potier
Subjects: General Fiction, Belles Lettres, Poetry, History, Education, Philosophy, Social Science, Reference
1977: 60 titles *1978:* 56 titles *Founded:* 1965

Editorial **Enciclopédia** Lda+*, Rua António Maria Cardoso 33, Lisbon 2 Tel: 326452/33330
Subjects: Encyclopaedias, Fiction, History, Art, Technical
Founded: 1934

Livraria **Escolar** Infante*, Manuel Ferreira & Gomes Lda, Rua de Santa Teresa 20-22, Oporto Tel: 26281/37098
Subjects: History, Religion, Juveniles, Paperbacks, General & Social Science, Secondary & Primary Textbooks, Educational Materials, Law
Founded: 1962
Bookshop: Livraria Escolar Infante, Rua de Santa Teresa 22, Oporto

Editorial **Estúdios** Cor Sarl*, Rua João Pereira da Rosa 20-A, Lisbon 2 Tel: 328889/362146
Subjects: Belles Lettres, Biography, History, Music, Art, Philosophy, Politics, Juveniles, General Science, Translations; General Fiction; Paperbacks
Founded: 1949

Publicações **Europa-America** Lda+, Apdo 8, Estrada Lisbon-Sintra Km 14, Mem Martins Tel: 2911461/2/3 Cable Add: Europamérica
Man Dir: Francisco Lyon de Castro; *Sales Dir:* Tito Lyon de Castro
Subsidiary Companies: Publicações Forum, Publicações Trevo
Branch Offs: Delegação de Lisbon, Rua da Flores, 45-2°, Lisbon; Delegação do Pôrto, Rua 31 de Janeiro, 221 Oporto
Subjects: General Fiction, Biography, History, How-to, Music, Art, Philosophy, Reference, Medicine, Psychology, General & Social Science, Nursery books, Juveniles, Low- & High-priced Paperbacks, University Textbooks, Educational Materials, Belles Lettres, Poetry, Engineering, Technical
Bookshops: Lojas Europa-America, Ave Marquês de Tomar 1-B, Rua das Flores 45, 1°, Lisbon; Ave António Enes 14-B, Ave Elias Garcia 104-B, Queluz; Ave 1 de Maio 61, Castelo Branco; Ave 31 de Janeiro 221, Alameda Eça de Queirós 32, Oporto; Pr Ferreira de Almeida 21-22, Faro; Av 25 de Abril 48, Almada
1977: 97 titles *1978:* 104 titles *Founded:* 1945

Familia 2000, Rua 5 de Outubro, 484-488, Porto
Man Dir: Adriano Correia Pinho

Livraria **Ferin** Lda+, Rua Nova do Almada 70-74, Lisbon 1200 Tel: 324422
Man Dir: Margarida dias Pinheiro; *Sales:* Isabel Carvalho
Subjects: Law
Bookshop: Rua Nova do Almada 70-74, Lisbon
1977: 3 titles *1978:* 3 titles *Founded:* 1840

Livraria Editora **Figueirinhas** Lda+, Praça da Liberdade 67, Oporto 1 Tel: 24985/25751/317698
Man Dir: João Pimenta; *Editorial, Sales,*

PORTUGAL 299

Production, Publicity, Rights & Permissions: Mario Figueirinhas
Subjects: General Literature
1977: 23 titles *Founded:* 1944

Forja Editora SARL+*, Rua da Emenda 30 3° C, Lisbon 2 Tel: 322334 Cable Add: Ediforja
Man Dir, Editorial, Production, Rights & Permissions: Anibal Telo; *Sales:* João Sá; *Publicity:* Aida Soeiro
Subjects: Fiction, Juveniles, Theatre, Cinema
1977: 8 titles *Founded:* 1974

Editorial **Franciscana**+, Montariol, Apartado 17, Braga 4701 codex Tel: 22490
Man Dir: António Pedro da Anunciação
Branch Off: Apartado 17, Braga 4701 codex
Subjects: Biography, History, Music, Art, Philosophy, Religion, Juveniles, Theology
Bookshop: Livraria Editorial Franciscana, Rua de Cedofeita 350, Oporto; Montariol, Braga
1977: 10 titles *1978:* 29 titles *Founded:* 1922

Editorial **Futura**+, Ave 5 de Outubro 317-1°, Lisbon 1600 Tel: 779114
Man Dir: José Chaves Ferreira
Subjects: General Literature
Founded: 1970

G E C T I (Gabinete de Especialização e Cooperacão Tecnica Internacional L)+*, Ave Republica 47-6D, PO Box 1918, Lisbon 1 Tel: 768877/771940/772154
Man Dir, Editorial: A Almeida Teixeira; *Sales:* Ester Malafaia
Subjects: Business, Administration, Marketing, Professional Training, Programmed Learning
Founded: 1963

Gabinete de Especialização e Cooperacão Tecnica Internacional, see G E C T I

Livros **Horizonte** Lda+*, Rua das Chagas 17-1° Dt, Apdo 2818, Lisbon 2 Tel: 366917/368505 Cable Add: Livroshorizonte
Man Dir, Rights & Permissions: Rog Mendes de Moura; *Sales:* Francisco Ramos Vasquez; *Production:* Henrique Grácio; *Publicity:* M C Ribeiro da Silva; *Foreign Rights:* M H Fernandes
Subjects: Pedagogy, Philosophy, Sociology, Art
1977: 72 titles *Founded:* 1953

Edições **I T A U** (Instituto Tecnico de Alimentaçao Humana) Lda, Ave da República 46-A r/c Esq, Lisbon 1 Tel: 733307/733482/733245/733019/733265
Man Dir: Júlio Roberto; *Editorial, Sales, Production, Publicity:* José Maria Paula
Orders to: Ave Elias Garcia 87-A, Lisbon 1
Parent Company: Instituto Tecnico de Alimentação Humana Lda
Subjects: Human Nutrition, Pedagogy, Poetry, Literature, Sociology, Juvenile Literature
Bookshop: Galerias Itau, Rua de Entrecampos 66-A
1977: 7 titles *1978:* 7 titles *Founded:* 1969

Imprensa Nacional-Casa da Moeda*, Rua D Francisco Manuel de Melo No 5, Lisbon 1 Tel: 685684 Cable Add: INCM
Man Dir: Humberto Fernando de Matos; *Editorial, Sales & Publicity:* Dr Américo Farinha de Carvalho
Br Offs: 4 in Lisbon, 1 each in Oporto and Coimbra
Subjects: Political and Civil Administration, Archeology, Arts, Economics, Ethnography, Ethnology, Pharmacy, Philology, Philosophy, History, Memoirs, Religion

300 PORTUGAL

Bookshops: Livraria Camões, Rua Bittencourt da Silva 12C, Rio de Janeiro, Brazil; Gabinete Portugues de Lectura, Rua do Imperador 290, Recife, Brazil
Founded: 1768

Editorial **Inicio**+*, Distribuidora de Publicações Lda*, Ave Almirante Reis 21-2° Esq, Lisbon 1 Tel: 40092
Subjects: General Fiction, Biography, History, Religion, Juveniles, Paperbacks, University Textbooks
Founded: 1965

Editorial **Inquérito** Lda+*, Travessa da Queimada 23, 1° D, Lisbon 2 Tel: 328659
Subjects: General Fiction, Belles Lettres, History, Philosophy, Juveniles, Social Science, Law
Founded: 1938

Instituto Tecnico de Alimentaçao Humana, see I T A U

Americo Fraga **Lamares** & Ca Lda, see Livraria Civilizacao

Lello e Cia Lda+*, Rua Conde de Vizela 12, Oporto 1 Tel: 23209
Dir: J Pinto Mesquita Lello
Subjects: Fine Arts, Education, Textbooks

Lello e Irmão+*, Rua das Carmelitas 144, Oporto 4000 Tel: 22037/318170 Cable Add: Jolello
Man Dir: Edgar Pinto Da Silva Lello
Subjects: General Literature, Juveniles, History, Dictionaries
Founded: 1868

Editora **Livros** do Brasil Sarl, Rua dos Caetanos 22, PO Box 2953, Lisbon 2 Tel: 362621/323170/326113 Cable Add: Librasil
Man Dir, Rights & Permissions: Antonio de Souza-Pinto; *Editorial, Publicity:* Mascarenhas Barreto; *Sales:* José Manuel Lopes Filipe
Associate Company: Editores Associados Lda
Branch Off: Rua de Ceuta 80, Oporto
Subjects: General and Science Fiction, Politics, History, Biography, Philosophy, Scientific Research
1977: 72 titles *Founded:* 1944

Livraria **Lopes Da Silva**-Editôra de M Moreira Soares Rocha+, Rua Chã 101-103, Oporto Tel: 21678/26017
Man Dir: Mário Moreira Soares Da Rocha
Subjects: Medicine, Science, Technical
1977: 117 titles *Founded:* 1870

Livraria **Luso-Espanhola** Lda+*, Rua Nova do Almada 86-90, Lisbon 2 Tel: 324917/367667 Cable Add: Livraluso
Man Dir: Inocencio Casimiro Araujo
Br Off: Livraria—Médica do Porto, Rua do Carmo 14, Oporto; Livraria Luso-Espahola, Rua da Sofia 121-1°, Coimbra
Subjects: Medicine, Technical, Textbooks, Law, Economics
Founded: 1941
Bookshops: Livraria Luso-Espanhola e Brasileira Lda, Ave 13 Maio 23-4°, Rio de Janeiro, Brasil; Livraria Cientifico Médico do Porto, Rua do Carmo 14, Oporteeo

Fernando **Machado** e Co Ltd+, Rua das Carmelitas 15, Oporto Tel: 25718
Man Dir: Manuel Correia Vieira
Branch Off: Rua dos Clérigos 23, Oporto
Founded: 1922
Bookshop: Livraria Fernando Machado, Rua das Carmelitas 15, Oporto

Livraria Tavares **Martins**+, Rua dos Clérigos 14, Oporto Tel: 23459
Man Dir: Américo Tavares Martins
Subjects: Drama, Poetry, Biography, History, Art, Philosophy, Religion, Juveniles
Founded: 1934

Meribérica — Editorial e Comercialização de Direitos Lda*, Rua Dona Filipa de Vilhena 8-3° Dt°, Lisbon 1 Tel: 58433/578485/577947/576085
Man Dirs: Adriano Eliseu, Telmo Protásio; *Editorial:* Adriano Eliseu; *Production:* Branca Protásio
Subjects: Children's Books
Book Club: Clube Walt Disney

Editorial **Minerva**+*, Rua Luz Soriano 31-33, 1°, Lisbon 2 Tel: 322535
Dir: Leonor Dias Rodrigues
Subjects: General Fiction, Juveniles, Paperbacks, Reference
Founded: 1927

Moraes Editores*, Rua do Século 34-2°, Lisbon 2 Tel: 325391/327717/320636
Man Dir, Editorial, Rights & Permissions: Nelson De Matos; *Sales:* Carlos Mendonça
Subjects: General Fiction, Belles Lettres, Poetry, Biography, Philosophy, Reference, Juveniles, High-priced Paperbacks, Psychology, History, Religion, Law, General & Social Science
Bookshop: Livraria Moraes, Largo do Picadeiro 11, Lisbon 2
1977: 45 titles *1978:* 56 titles *Founded:* 1955

Livraria Editora **Pax** Lda+, Rua do Souto 73-77, Braga 4700 Tel: 22604 Cable Add: pax
Man Dir and other offices: José Moreira
Subjects: Fiction, Belles Lettres, Poetry, History, Ethnography, Travel, Spiritual Life, Theatre, Education
1977: 15 titles *1978:* 25 titles *Founded:* 1928

Parceria A M **Pereira** Lda+*, Rua Augusta 44-54, Lisbon 2 Tel: 361730/361710 Cable Add: Parcepereira
Subjects: General Fiction, Belles Lettres, Biography, History, How-to, Juveniles, Social Science, Technical, Primary Textbooks
Founded: 1848

Editorial **Perpétuo** Socorro+*, Rua Dr Alves da Veiga 207, Oporto Tel: 564251
Subject: Religion, Education
Founded: 1946

Platano Editora SARL+*, Ave de Berna, 31-2° Esq, Lisbon 1 Tel: 774250/779278 Telex: 13659 platan p
Editorial: Francisco Prata Ginja
Subsidiary Companies: Alicerce Editora Lda, Oporto; Paralelo Editora Lda, Lisbon
Associate Companies: Alicerce Editora SARL, Rio de Janeiro, Brazil
Subjects: Primary, Secondary and Technical School Books, Theatre, Poetry, Juveniles
Bookshop: Alicerce Editora Lda, Rua Guerra Junqueiro 456, Oporto

Editorial **Portico**, Rua Dr Julio Dantas 4, Lisbon 1

Porto Editôra Lda, Rua da Restauração 365, Oporto Tel: 25813
Dir: Vasco Teixeira
Man Dir: Mario Trindade
Associated Companies: Empresa Literaria Fluminense Lda, Rua de S João Nepomuceno 8-A, Lisbon; Livraria Arnado Lda, Rua João Machado 9, Coimbra
Subjects: University, Secondary & Primary Textbooks, Educational Materials, Foreign Language Teaching and Dictionaries, Law, General Nonfiction
Bookshops: Rua da Fabrica 90, Oporto; Praça D Filipa de Lencastre 42, Oporto
Founded: 1944

Portugalia Editôra Lda, Rua Luciano Cordeiro 81-C, Lisbon 2 Tel: 535741
Man Dir: Diniz Gandon da Nazareth Fernandes
Branch Off: Rua da Condessa 74-78, Lisbon
Subjects: General Fiction, Belles Lettres, Poetry, Biography, History, Philosophy, Juveniles, Low- & High-priced Paperbacks, Psychology
Bookshop: Rua Luciano Cordeiro 81C, Lisbon 1100
1977: 1 title *1978:* 18 titles *Founded:* 1942

Prelo Editora Sarl*, Alameda de Sto Antonio dos Capuchos 6B, Lisbon 1 Tel: 572224
Man Dir: Viriato Camilo
Subjects: Portuguese Fiction, Theatre, Belles Lettres, History, Social Science, Political Science, Economics
Bookshop: at above address
1977: 17 titles *Founded:* 1960

Editorial **Presença***, Rua Augusto Gil 35-A, Lisbon 1 Tel: 766912/763060 Cable Add: Editorial Presença Lisboa
Man Dir, Editorial: Francisco Espadinha; *Sales:* Francisco Santos; *Production:* Manuel Aquino; *Publicity:* Wanda Ramos; *Rights & Permissions:* Carlos Grifo
Subjects: Sociology, Politics, Philosophy, History, Children's Books, Hobbies, School Textbooks
1977: 114 titles *Founded:* 1960

Edições António **Ramos**+, Rua Padre Luis Aparício 9-1° F, Lisbon 1 Tel: 577205
Man Dir, Editorial: António Ramos; *Sales:* Jorge Peralta; *Production:* Margarida Fonseca; *Publicity:* Nuno Vasco
Orders to: C L B, Rua Almirante Barroso, 13-2° Lisbon 1
Subjects: General Fiction and Nonfiction
1977: 20 titles *1978:* 45 titles *Founded:* 1977

Realizações Artis Lda*, Rua das Taipas 12, r/c Esq, Lisbon 2 Tel: 363796
Man Dirs: Rogério de Freitas, Leão Penedo
Subjects: Belles Lettres, Poetry, Biography, Music, Art
Founded: 1950

A **Regra** do Jogo+*, Rua Sousa Martins 5, 2° Dto, Lisbon Tel: 571631
Man Dir: Jose Leal de Loureiro; *Rights & Permissions:* Antonio de Vasconcelos
Subjects: Fiction, Poetry, Music, History, Juveniles, Anthropology, Philosophy, Economy
1977: 11 titles *Founded:* 1974

Edições **Rotep***, Rua de São Bento 39, Lisbon 2 Tel: 601501
Man Dir: João Camacho Pereira
Subjects: Iconography, Reproductions of Ancient Engravings, Ideographic Maps of Portugal
1977: 3 titles *Founded:* 1944

Editorial **Ruiz** Romero, — see A E I International (Publisher), Lisbon

Edições **Salesianas**, Rua Dr Alves da Veiga 128, Oporto Tel: 565750
Man Dir: João António Machado; *Editorial, Sales, Production, Publicity:* Elías de Jesus
Br Off: Rua Saraiva de Carvalho 275, Lisbon

Subjects: Biography, Religion, Juveniles, Paperbacks, Psychology, Technical, Educational Materials
Bookshops: Livraria Salesiana, Largo Luis de Camões 6-9, Evora; Livraria Salesiana, Rua Sanaiva de Carvalho 375, Lisbon
1977: 17 titles *1978:* 20 titles *Founded:* 1947

Empresa de Publicidade **Seara** Nova SARL+, R Bernardo Lima, 42-r/c 1199 Lisbon codex Tel: 530869/571302
Man Dir, Editorial, Sales: Dr Ulpiano Nascimento; *Production, Publicity, Rights & Permissions:* Costa Marques
Subjects: Fiction, Sociology, Politics, Economics, History, Pedagogics, Juveniles, Belles Lettres
Bookshop: Livraria Seara Nova, R Conde Redondo 38-A, 1100 Lisbon
1977: 47 titles *Founded:* 1921

A M Teixeira e Cia (Filhos) Lda (Livraria Classica Editora)+*, Praça dos Restauradores 17, Lisbon Tel: 321229/321391/321286 Cable Add: Classica
Editorial, Rights & Permissions: Antonio B Teixeira; *Production, Publicity:* Jose F Teixeira
Subjects: General Fiction, Belles Lettres, Poetry, History, Reference, Religion, Juveniles, General and Social Science, Psychology, University and Primary Textbooks, Agriculture, Philology, Electronics, Economics, Management
1977: 40 titles *1978:* 37 titles *Founded:* 1903

João Romano Torres & Cia Lda+*, Livraria Romano Torres, Largo de Sao Mamede 3-A, Lisbon 2 Tel: 601244
Man Dir: Amelia Lucas Torres Farinia; *Editorial, Publicity, Rights & Permissions:* Francisco de Noronha e Andrade; *Sales, Production:* Osorio Marques Martius
Subjects: Historical Works, World Classics, Romantic Fiction, Juvenile Adventure Stories
1977: 32 titles *Founded:* 1885

União Gráfica Sarl*, Rua de Santa Marta 48, Lisbon 2 Tel: 44191/2, 46174/5 Cable Add: Novidades
Dir: Carlos M Castelo Gonçalves
Subjects: General Fiction, Belles Lettres, Poetry, Biography, History, Philosophy, Religion, Juveniles, Low- & High-priced Paperbacks, Psychology, Social Science
Founded: 1923

Verbo Sarl, Rua Carlos Testa 1, Lisbon Tel: 562131 Cable Add: Verbo
Man Dir: Fernando Guedes; *Sales Dirs:* Edmundo Pereira, David Duarte
Subjects: History, Juveniles, General Science, Secondary and Primary Textbooks, Educational Materials
1977-78: 185 titles *1978-79:* 193 titles
Founded: 1959
Book Club: Companhia Editoria de Livros e Discos Sarl

Livraria Verdade e Vida Editora*, Cava da Tria, Fatima Tel: 97417
Subjects: Biography, History, Philosophy, Religion, Juveniles, Fiction, Education
Founded: 1945
Bookshop: Livraria Verdade & Vida, Cava da Tria, Fátima

Literary Agents

A E I International*, Rua Sampaio e Pina, 7-1° Fte, Lisbon 1 Tel: 654664/680628 Telex: 16423 aei p
Firm is also a Publisher

Ilidio da Fonseca Matos*, Rua de S Bernardo, 68-3 Lisbon 2 Tel: 669780 Cable Add: Ilphoto
Man Dir: Ilidio Matos

Book Clubs

Amigos do Livro*, Ave Sidónio Pais, 16-1° Dto, Lisbon 1

Círculo de Leitores, Rua Eng° Paulo de Barros, 22-1599 Lisbon codex Tel: 709215/709221/709224 Telex: 18343 cilecl p
Dir: Manuel Dias de Carvalho
Subjects: Fiction, Biography, Juvenile, Encyclopedias, Scientific, Historical
Owned by: Bertelsmann AG, German Federal Republic (qv)

Companhia Editora de Livros e Discos Sarl*, Rua Carlos Testa 1, Lisbon
Owned by: Verbo Sarl (Lisbon)

Clube do Livro-**Curado** Ribeiro*, Ave Casal Ribeiro 17-A, Lisbon 1

Clube **Walt Disney***, Rua Filipa de Vilhena, 8-3° Dt° Lisbon 1
Owned by: Meribérica-Editorial e Comercializaçao de Directos Lda (Lisbon)

Major Booksellers

Livraria **Bertrand***, Rua Garrett 73-75, Apdo 2078, Lisbon 2

Biblarte Lda, Rua de Sao Pedro de Alcantara 71, Lisbon 1200
Manager: Ernesto Martins

Livraria **Bucholz***, Rua Duque de Palmela 4, Lisbon

C D L (Central Distribuidora Livreira) SARL, Ave Santos Dumont 57-2°, 1100 Lisbon

Livraria **Castro e Silva**, Rua da Rosa 31, Lisbon 1200

Livraria **Sá da Costa**, Rua Garrett 100-102, Lisbon 1294 codex
Manager: Manuel F da Costa

D I G Ldá (Distribuidora Geral de Informação), Rua Vitor Cordon 45 (Páteo Bragança, porta B), Lisbon 2

Expresso*, Sarl, Apdo 21, Buraca/Damaia, Lisbon

Livraria **Nunes***, Rua de S Domingos de Benfica 5-A, Lisbon 4

Livraria **Portugal**, Dias &\Andrade Lda, Apdo 681, Rua do Carmo 70, Lisbon 1117 codex

Regimprensa*, Sarl, Ave D José 1, lote 12, Reboleira (Amadora), Lisbon

Livraria **Sam Carlos***, Largo de S Carlos 11, Lisbon

Editorial o **Século***, Rua do Século 73, Lisbon 2

Livraria **Sousa** e Almeida, Rua da Fabrica 42, Oporto

Major Libraries

Biblioteca da **Academia** das Ciências de Lisboa (Library of the Academy of Sciences)*, Rua da Academia das Ciências 19, Lisbon 2

Biblioteca da **Ajuda***, Palácio da Aejuda, Lisbon 3 Tel: 638592

Arquivo Nacional da Torre do Tombo, Palácio de S Bento, Lisbon 1200
National Archives of Torre do Tombo
Dir: Pereira da Costa

Biblioteca **Municipal Central** (Central Town Library)*, Palácio Galveias, Largo do Campo Pequeno, Lisbon

Biblioteca **Nacional** de Lisboa (National Library)*, Rua Ocidental do Campo Grande 83, Lisbon 5 Tel: 767786/7/8/9/0

Biblioteca **Popular** de Lisboa*, Rua Ivens 35 and Rua de Academia das Ciências 19, Lisbon

Biblioteca **Pública de Ponta Delgada** (Public Library)*, The Azores

Biblioteca **Pública e Arquivo Distrital de Braga** (Public Library and District Archives)*, Braga

Biblioteca **Pública e Arquivo Distrital de Évora** (Public Library and District Archives)*, Évora

Biblioteca **Pública Municipal** do Porto, Oporto
Dir: M F de Brito
Municipal Library of Oporto

Centro de Documentacão Científica e Técnica, Ave Prof Gama Pinto 2, Lisbon 1699 codex Tel: 772886/762891/765622/731300/731350 Telex: 18428 educa p
Dir: Eng Carlos Pulido
Centre of Scientific and Technical Documentation. The Library is a branch of the Instituto Nacional de Investigação Científica (National Scientific Research Institute)

Biblioteca do **Palácio** Nacional de Mafra*, Terreiro de João V, Mafra Tel: 52398

Biblioteca Geral da **Universidade** de Coimbra*, Coimbra Tel: 23015/25541

Library Associations

Associação Portuguesa de Bibliotecários Arquivistas e Documentalistas (Portuguese Association of Librarians, Archivists and Documentalists)*, Edificio da Biblioteca Nacional, Campo Grande 83, Lisbon 5 Tel: 767786
President: Dr L F Abreu Nunes

Library Reference Books and Journals

Books

Lista das Bibliotecas Portuguesas (List of Portuguese Libraries), Centre of Scientific Documentation, Campo dos Mártires da Pátria 130, Lisbon

Journals

Boletim de Bibliografia Portuguesa (Portuguese Bibliographical Bulletin), National Library, Rua Ocidental do Campo Grande 83, Lisbon 5

Cadernos de Biblioteconomia, Arquivistica e Documentacao (Library Management, Archives and Documentation) (summaries in English), Apdo 103, Coimbra

Literary Associations and Societies

Instituto Português da Sociedade Científica de Goerres (Portuguese Institute of the Goerres Research Society)*, Rua Visconde de Seabra 2-3, Lisbon 5
Researches into the language and literature of the 16th and 17th centuries
Secretary: Dr Helga Bauer
Publication: Portugiesische Forschungen (Researches in Portuguese)

Portuguese **P E N** Centre*, Rua Tomas da Anunciaçao 58-5° Esq, Lisbon 3
Secretary: Ana Hatherly

Literary Periodicals

Coloquio-Letras (Dialogue-Literature), Empresa Nacional de Publicidade, Ave da Liberdade 266, Lisbon 2

Jornal de Letras e Artes (Journal of Letters and Arts), Rua Vitor Bastos 14A, Lisbon 1

Ocidente (The West); Portuguese review of culture, Antonio H de Azevedo Pinto and Amelia de Azevedo Pinto, Rua de S Felix 41D

Peninsula, Agencia Internacional de Livraria e Publicações Lda, R S Pedro de Alcantara, 63-1 D, Lisbon

Seara Nova (New Harvest), Empresa de Publicidade 'Seara Nova' Sarl, R Bernardo Lima, 23-1 Esq, Lisbon

Literary Prizes

Children's and Juvenile Literature Prize*
For the best book written for readers between four and sixteen. 15,000 escudos. Awarded annually. Enquiries to Portugal State Secretariat for Information and Tourism, Palacio Foz, Lisbon 2

National Award for Poetry and the Novel*
Two prizes, one for the best book of poetry and the other for the best novel or book of short stories. 50,000 escudos each. Awarded annually. Enquiries to Portugal State Secretariat for Information and Tourism, Palacio Foz, Lisbon 2

National Essay Award*
For the best essay written by a Portuguese author and printed in Portuguese. 50,000 escudos. Awarded every other year. Enquiries to Portugal State Secretariat for Information and Tourism, Palacio Foz, Lisbon 2

Revelation Awards (Poetry and Prose)*
Four prizes, two given for the best unpublished manuscript of poetry and two for prose. 5,000 escudos. Awarded annually. Enquiries to Portugal State Secretariat for Information and Tourism, Palacio Foz, Lisbon 2

Puerto Rico

General Information

Language: English and Spanish
Religion: Roman Catholic
Population: 3.3 million
Literacy Rate (1970): 89.2%
Export/Import Information: No tariff on books and advertising matter. No import licences required

Book Trade Reference Journal

Anuario bibliográfico puertorriqueño (Puerto Rican Annual Bibliography), Estado Libre Asociado de Puerto Rico, Dept de Instrucción Pública, Río Piedras

Publishers

Distribuidora **Cima** Inc*, PO Box G-2172, San Juan, PR 00936 (Located at: Calle O'Neill 177, Hato Rey, PR 00919) Tel: 7676188/7647635 Cable Add: CIMA
President: Héctor E Serrano; *Vice-President:* Miguel A Serrano
Subjects: General Literature, Textbooks, Technical Books
Founded: 1969

Editorial **Club** de la Prensa*, Apdo 4692, San Juan, PR 00903
Subjects: Fiction, Maps, Folklore

Editorial **Cordillera** Inc*, Calle O'Neill 177, Hato Rey, PR 00918 Tel: 7676188/7647635 Cable Add: Cordillera
Man Dir, Editorial, Production: Héctor E Serrano; *Sales, Publicity:* Isaac Serrano
Subjects: General Literature, Social Studies, Spanish
1977: 10 titles *Founded:* 1962
ISBN Publisher's Prefix: 0-88495

Editorial **Edil** Inc, Apdo 23088, Universidad de Puerto Rico, Río Piedras, PR 00931 Tel: 7643740 Cable Add: Edil
Man Dir: Norberto Lugo Ramírez; *Sales Dir:* Eunice Lugo Frank; *Publicity Dir:* George E Frank
Subjects: General Literature, Puerto Rican Books, Textbooks, History
1978: 200 titles *Founded:* 1967

Editorial Cultural, Apdo 21056, Rio Piedras Station, PR 00928 Tel: 7663234
Man Dir: Francisco Vázques; *Sales Dir:* Aida Vázquez; *Publicity Dir:* F V Alumo
Imprint: Editorial Antillana
Branch Off: Editorial Antillana, Roble 51, Rio Piedras, PR 00925
Subjects: Literature, Biography, History, University and Secondary Textbooks
Bookshop: Librería Cultural, Roble 51, Río Piedras, PR 00925
1977: 32 titles *Founded:* 1949

Instituto de Cultura Puertorriqueña, Apdo 4184, San Juan, PR 00905 Tel: 7232115/7251988 Telex: 3453096
Man Dir, Editorial, Rights & Permissions: Luis M Rodríguez Morales; *Sales:* Jeana Colon de Barreto
Orders to: San Francisco 305, San Juan, PR 00901
Subjects: General Literature, History, Music, Poetry, Anthropology
Bookshop: Librería del Instituto de Cultura Puertorriqueña, San Francisco 305, San Juan, PR 00901
Founded: 1958

Editorial **McGraw-Hill** Latinoamerica SA, Apdo 20712, Rio Piedras, Puerto Rico 00928
Subjects: Primary, Secondary & University Textbooks, Reference
Miscellaneous: Branch office of Editorial McGraw-Hill Latino-Americana SA, Panama (qv)

Editorial y Librería La **Reforma**, Calle El Roble 54, Río Piedras, PR 00925 Tel: 7651635
Man Dir: Germán Stevenson
Parent Company: Fortress Church Supply Stores
Subject: Religion
1977: 3 titles *1978:* 5 titles *Founded:* 1954

University of Puerto Rico Press (UPRED), Apdo X, Estacion UPR, Río Piedras, PR-00931 Tel: 7651924/7643670/7643770 Cable Add: UPRED
Dir: Carmelo Delgado-Cintrón; *Subdirector:* Pablo Vincenty; *Chief Editor:* Juan Martínez-Capó; *Publicity:* María Teresa Flórez
Subjects: General Fiction, Belles Lettres, Poetry, History, Art, Philosophy, Reference, Low- & High-priced Paperbacks, Medicine, Psychology, Engineering, General & Social Science, University Textbooks, Educational Materials
Founded: 1932
ISBN Publisher's Prefix: 0-8477

Major Booksellers

Librería **Alma Mater** Inc*, 867 Cabrera St, Santa Rita, Río Piedras, PR 00925 Tel: 7646752

Distribuidora de Libros Inc*, Calle Norte 52, Apdo 1669, Río Piedras

Librería **Escorial***, Recinto Sur 313, San Juan, PR 00901 Tel: 7250972

Librería **Hispanoamericana**, Ave Ponce de León 1013, Apdo 20830, Río Piedras, PR 00928 Tel: 7633415

Librería **Contemporanea***, Ave González 1054, Río Piedras, PR 00925

Librería **Cultural**, Roble 51, Río Piedras, PR 00925 Tel: 7659767

Librería **Cultural Puertorriqueña** Inc, Ave Fernandez Junco 1406 — Parada 20, Apdo 8863, Santurce, PR 00910

Librería **Universitaria** de Puerto Rico*, Apdo B J Estación UPR, Río Piedras

Librería La **Tertulia***, Amalia Marin esq Ave González, Río Piedras, PR 00928 Tel: 7651148

Librería **Thekes***, Plaza las Américas, San Juan Tel: 7651539

Major Libraries

Agricultural Experiment Station Library*, Box H, Río Piedras

PUERTO RICO — ROMANIA 303

Archivo General de Puerto Rico, Instituto de Cultura Puetorriqueña, Apdo 4184, San Juan 00905 Tel: 7220331/7222113
National Archives of Puerto Rico
Dir: Miguel Angel Nieves

Biblioteca General de Puerto Rico (General Library)*, Instituto de Cultura Puertorriqueña, Apdo 4184, San Juan PR 00905 Tel: 7242680
Dir: Lcdo Roberto Beascoechea Lota

Caribbean Regional Library*, University Station, Apdo 21927, San Juan 00931 Tel: 7640000 ext 3319

Inter American University of Puerto Rico Library*, San Germán

University of Puerto Rico, General Library, Mayaguez Campus*, Mayaguez

University of Puerto Rico, General Library, Río Piedras Campus, Box C, UPR Station 00931 Tel: (809) 7640000
Dir: Rafael R Delgado
Specialist collections in all fields of knowledge

University of Puerto Rico, Medical Sciences Campus Library*, Apdo 5067, San Juan 00936 00936

Library Associations

Sociedad de Bibliotecarios de Puerto Rico (Society of Librarians of Puerto Rico), Apdo 22898, Universidad de Puerto Rico, Rio Piedras, PR 00931 Tel: 7640000 ext 2211
President: Carmencita León; *Executive Secretary:* Belsie I C de Pinero
Publications: Boletín, Informa (News Letter), *Cuadernos Bibliotecologicos, Cuadernos Bibliograficos*

Library Journals

Boletín (Bulletin) (text in English and Spanish), Society of Librarians of Puerto Rico, Apdo 22898, Universidad de Puerto Rico, Río Piedras, PR 00931

Informa (Newsletter), Society of Librarians of Puerto Rico, Apdo 22898, Universidad de Puerto Rico, Rio Piedras, PR 00931

Literary Associations and Societies

Congreso de Poesia de Puerto Rico (Puerto Rican Congress of Poetry)*, c/o Colegio de Agricultura y Artes Mecánicas, Mayaguez
President: Francisco Lluch Mora

P E N Club de Puerto Rico*, Cordero SS Santurce, San Juan, PR 00903
President: Nilita Vientes Gaston

Sociedad Puertorriqueña de Escritores (Puerto Rican Society of Writers)*, Apdo 4692, San Juan
President: Ernesto Juan Fonfrías

Literary Periodicals

Asomante, Asociación de Graduadas de la Universidad de Puerto Rico, Apdo 1142, San Juan, PR 00902

Atenea (text in Spanish, English, French and Italian), University of Puerto Rico at Mayaguez, College of Arts and Sciences, Mayaguez, PR 00708

Sin Nombre (Anonymous), Sin Nombre Inc, 55 Cordero St, Santurce, Pr 00911

Zona Carga y Descarga (Loading and Unloading Area), Apdo 3871, San Juan, PR 00903

Qatar

General Information

Language: Arabic (English used commercially)
Religion: Wahabi Muslim, officially
Population: 98,000
Bank Hours: 0730-1130 Saturday-Thursday
Shop Hours: 0730-1200, 1430-1800 Saturday-Thursday (some open few hours Friday morning)
Currency: 100 dirhams = 1 Qatar riyal
Export/Import Information: No tariff on books or advertising matter. No import licence; no obscenity permitted. Exchange authorization required for value over 50,000 Qatari

Major Booksellers

Abdulla **Abdulghani** & Sons Co*, PO Box 111, Doha

Codco Est*, PO Box 1990, Doha Tel: 26573/25867

Family Bookshop*, PO Box 1990, Doha Tel: 24148

Major Libraries

Qatari Public Library (National Library)*, PO Box 205, Doha

Réunion

General Information

Language: French
Religion: Predominantly Roman Catholic
Population: 489,000
Literacy Rate (1967): 62.9%
Business Hours: Generally 0800-1200, 1400-1800
Currency: 1 French franc = 100 centimes
Export//Import Information: No tariff on books and advertising. Books have reduced VAT of 3.5%. No import licence. Nominal exchange control over 1,500 franc value. For imports over 50,000 francs documents must be 'domiciliated' before any other transaction occurs

Major Booksellers

Librairie **Daude***, 97400 St-Denis

Firmin **Pause***, 2 rue Sadi-Carnot, Le Port

Librairie Universitaire de la Réunion*, 13 ave de la Victoire Tel: 210758

Major Libraries

Archives départementales de la Réunion, 97487 St-Denis cedex Tel: 212829

Bibliothèque centrale de Prêt*, pl Joffre, 97400 St-Denis Tel: 210324
Librarian: Yves Drouchet

Bibliothèque départementale*, rue Roland Garros, 97400 St-Denis

Bibliothèque municipale*, rue Rodier, 97410 St-Pierre

Bibliothèque universitaire*, Campus universitaire du Chaudron, 97400 Ste-Clotilde Tel: 215910

Rhodesia

See **Zimbabwe**

Romania

General Information

Language: Romanian, French, German and English
Religion: Romanian Orthodox
Population: 21.7 million
Literacy Rate (1956): 85.8%
Bank Hours: 0900-1200, 1300-1500 Monday-Friday; 0900-1200 Saturday
Shop Hours: 0900-1900 Monday-Friday; early closing Saturday
Currency: 100 bani = 1 leu
Export/Import Information: Book import and export co-ordinated by the Publishing Centre, Piata Scînteii 1, R-71350 Bucharest, 1. The commercial operations are carried out by the Foreign Trade Enterprise ILEXIM, Str 13 Decembrie 3, PO Box 136-137, Bucharest. Import licences required. Exchange controls: terms of payment established in the sales contract made with the Romanian enterprise
Copyright: Berne (see International section)

Book Trade Organizations

Centrala Cartii (Book Centre)*, Str Biserica Amzei 5-7, Bucharest

Centrala Editoriala (Publishing Centre)*, Piata Scînteii 1, R-71350 Bucharest Tel: 183520
The state body which co-ordinates the whole book publishing and selling activity
General Dir: Gheorghe Trandafir

ROMANIA

Book Trade Reference Journals

Bibliografia Republicii Populare Romîne (Romanian National Bibliography), Central State Library, Str Ion Ghica 4, Bucharest

Carti Noi (New Books), Book Centre, Str Biserica Amzei 5-7, Bucharest

Romanian Books; a quarterly bulletin (text in English or French), Publishing Centre, Foreign Relations Department, Piata Scînteii 1, 7000 Bucharest

Romanian Books in Foreign Languages, Book Centre, Str Biserica Amzei 5-7, Bucharest

Publishers

Editura **Academiei** Republicii Socialiste România, Calea Victoriei 125, Bucharest 71021 Tel: 507680 Cable Add: Edacad Publishing House of the Academy of the Socialist Republic of Romania
Man Dir: C Busuioceanu; *Editorial:* D Trifu; *Production:* F Stoenescu
Subjects: Scientific Works, Monographs, Documents, General Science, Social Science, Mathematics, Technical, Economics, Philology, Physics, Chemistry, Biology, Medicine; Periodicals
1977: 129 titles *1978:* 90 titles *Founded:* 1948
Miscellaneous: Publish 66 specialized periodicals in Romanian and foreign languages

Editura **Albatros**, Piata Scînteii 1, 71341 Bucharest Tel: 180448
Man Dir: Mircea Sântimbreanu
Subject: Juveniles
1977: 130 titles *1978:* 119 titles *Founded:* 1969

Editura **'Cartea Românesca'** (Publishing House of 'The Romanian Book')*, Str Nuferilor 41, Bucharest Tel: 149352
Dir: Marin Preda
Subject: Romanian Contemporary Literature
Founded: 1969

Editura **Ceres***, Piata Scînteii 1, 7000 Bucharest Tel: 176010
Man Dir: Gabriel Manoliu
Subjects: Agriculture, Veterinary Medicine, Textbooks
Founded: 1953

Editura Ion **Creangă***, Piata Scînteii 1, Sector 1, R-71341 Bucharest Tel: 182525/182566/176010/176020
Man Dir: Tiberiu Utan; *Editor-in-Chief:* Alexandru Georgescu; *Sales, Production, Publicity:* Jenica Panaitescu
Subjects: Poetry, Biography, History, Music, Art, Belles Lettres, Literature, Fiction — all for Juvenile appeal only
1977: 151 titles *1978:* 163 titles *Founded:* 1969

Editura **Dacia**, Str 1, Mai 23, R-3400, Cluj-Napoca Tel: (951) 145-48 and 11665
Dir: Alexandru Caprariu
Subjects: Literature, Art, Science (in Romanian, Hungarian, German)
1977: 144 titles *1978:* 129 titles *Founded:* 1969

Editura **Didactica si Pedagogica**, Str Spiru Haret 12, Cod 70738, Sectorul 7, Bucharest Tel: 333440 Telex: 011352
Man Dir: Dr Ion Stanciu; *Editorial:* Roman Mihai; *Sales, Publicity, Rights & Permissions:* Stelian Galos; *Production:* Trifan Onoriu
Subjects: History, Philosophy, Juveniles, Medicine, Psychology, Engineering, General & Social Science, University, Secondary & Primary Textbooks (in various languages), Educational Materials
1977: 980 titles *Founded:* 1951

Editura **Eminescu***, Piata Scînteii 1, 7000 Bucharest Tel: 177380
Man Dir: Valeriu Rîpeanu
Subjects: Romanian Classical & Contemporary Literature, Poetry, History (all in various languages)

Editura **Facla**, J-H Pestalozzi Str 14, Timisoara
Dir: Simion Dima
Subjects: Socio-Political, Poetry, Fiction, Humour, Art and Music, Literary Criticism, Medicine, Scientific; Publications in Romanian, Hungarian, German, Serbo-Croat
1977: 50 titles *1978:* 55 titles *Founded:* 1972

Editura **Junimea**, 1 rue Gh Dimitroff, R-6600 Iassy Tel: 17290
Dir: Mircea Radu Iacoban
Subjects: Original and Translated Works in Literary and Technical fields, Literary Theory and Criticism
Founded: 1969

Editura **Kriterion***, Piata Scînteii 1, 7000 Bucharest Tel: 176010/174060
Dir: Géza Domokos
Subjects: General Fiction, Classical & Contemporary Literature, How-to, Poetry, Music, Art, General Science, Education, Translations
Founded: 1969

Editura **Medicala** (Medical Publishing House)*, Str Smîrdan 5, Bucharest
Man Dir: Dr Ghoerghe Panaitescu
Subjects: Medical & Pharmaceutical Literature, Textbooks
Founded: 1954
Miscellaneous: Specialize in reviews in Romanian and foreign languages

Editura **Meridiane***, Piata Scînteii 1, 71341 Bucharest Tel: 181087
Man Dir: George Sorin Movileanu; *Editor-in-Chief:* Modest Morariu
Subjects: Fine Arts, Folk Art, Theatre, Cinema, Architecture, Economic, Social, Political and Cultural Information on Romania
1977: approx 115 titles *Founded:* 1952

Editura **Militara**, Str Izvor 137, Bucharest Tel: 310852
Man Dir: Tudor Tamas
Subjects: Belles Lettres, Poetry, Biography, History, Medicine, Psychology, Engineering, Social Science, Military, Fiction
Founded: 1950

Editura **Minerva**, Piata Scînteii 1, 71341 Bucharest Tel: 176010/176020
Subjects: Literary (especially Classical and Foreign), Bilingual Editions, Poetry, Folklore, Various Series
Founded: 1969

Editura **Muzicala***, Str Poiana Narciselor no 6 sector 7, Cod 70718 Bucharest Tel: 164099
Man Dir: Aurel Popa
Subjects: Scores, Musicology
1977: 100 titles *Founded:* 1958

Editura **Politica**, Piata Scînteii 1, 7000 Bucharest Tel: 176010/172987
Man Dir: Valter Roman
Subjects: Biography, History, Philosophy, Reference, Political & Social Science, Economics, International Relations, University Textbooks
1977: 260 titles *1978:* 240 titles *Founded:* 1944

Editura **'Scrisul Românesc'** ('Romanian Writing' Publishing House)*, Str Paltinis 4, Craiova Tel: 13717
Dir: Ilarie Hinoveanu
Subjects: Social & Political Science, Literature, Technical
Founded: 1972

Editura **Stadion** (Sports and Tourism Publishing House)*, Str Vasile Conta 16, Bucharest Tel: 124170
Editor: Ionel Simion
Subjects: Sports, Travel Guides
Founded: 1950

Editura **Stiintifica si Enciclopedica**, Piata Scînteii 1, R-71341 Bucharest Tel: 175168
Man Dir: Dr Mircea Mâciu; *Production Manager, Sales Dir:* Alexandru Banciu
Subjects: Encyclopaedias, Encyclopaedic Dictionaries, Reference, General & Social Sciences, Dictionaries, Biography, History, How-to, Music, Art, Philosophy, High- & Low-priced Paperbacks, Medicine, Psychology, Engineering
1977: 113 titles *1978:* 135 titles *Founded:* 1975 (by amalgamation of Romanian Encyclopaedic Publishing House and Scientific Publishing House)

Editura **Tehnica**, Piata Scînteii 1, 7000 Bucharest Tel: 176010
Man Dir: Mihai Condruc
Subjects: Engineering, General Science, Dictionaries, Reference
1979: 140 titles *Founded:* 1950

Editura **Univers**, Piata Scînteii 1, R-71341 Bucharest Tel: 181762
Man Dir: Professor Dr Romul Munteanu; *Sales Dir:* Emil Idriceanu; *Publicity, Advertising:* N Alexe
Subjects: Translations of Fiction, Poetry, Drama, Biography, Literary Criticism, Low-priced Paperbacks
Founded: 1961

Major Booksellers

I L E X I M — Foreign Trade Enterprise*, Str 13 Decembrie 3, PO Box 136-137, Bucharest Tel: 504095
Carries out all the commercial operations connected with book import and export

Major Libraries

Biblioteca Centrala, **Academia de Studii Economice***, Piata Romana 6, sector 7, Bucharest

Biblioteca **Academiei Republicii Socialiste Romania***, Calea Victoriei 125, Bucharest Tel: 503043

Biblioteca Filialei Cluj a **Academiei Republicii Socialiste România** (The Library of the Cluj Branch of the Academy of the RSR)*, Blvd Lenin 9, Cluj

Archivele Statului (National Archives), Bul Gheorghe, Gheorghe-Dej 29, Bucharest

Biblioteca Centrala de Stat a Republicii Socialiste România (Central State Library)*, Str Ion Ghica 4, R-70018 Bucharest Tel: 161260/507063/140746

Biblioteca Centrala Universitara*, Str Onesti 1, Sectorul 1, Bucharest 1 Tel: 132557

Biblioteca Centrala Universitara*, Str Clinicilor 2, 3400 Cluj-Napoca Tel: 21092

Biblioteca Centrala Universitara 'Mihail Eminescu', Str Pacurari 4, Jassy Tel: 40709

Biblioteca Judeteana Mures*, Str Enescu 2, Tîrgu-Mures

Biblioteca Judeteana Timis*, Piata Libertatii 3, Timisoara

Biblioteca **Facultatii** de Medicina din Bucuresti (Library of the Medical Faculty)*, Blvd Dr Petru Groza 8, Bucharest 35, sector 6
Dir: Prodan Iraian

Biblioteca Institutului Politehnic **'Gheorge Gheorghiu-Dej'** Bucuresti*, Calea Grivitei 132, Bucharest

I N I D, see Institutul National de Informare si Documentare

Institutul National de Informare si Documentare (INID), Str Cosmonautilor 27–29, 70141 Bucharest 1 Tel: 134010 Telex: 11247
National Institute for Information and Documentation
Dir: eng Gheorghe Anghel
Publications: Reviste de sumare ale periodicelor intrate in biblioteca INID (Current Contents Reviews of Periodicals in INID Library); *Abstracts of Romanian Scientific and Technical Literature* (in English, French, Russian and Romanian); *Information and Documentation Problems* (in English and Romanian)

Oficiul de Informare Documentara in Stiintele Sociale si Politice (Office of Information and Documentation in Social and Political Sciences)*, Str Mihail Moxa 3–5, Bucharest
Dir: M Ioanid
Publication: Romanian Scientific Abstracts (2 a year)

Biblioteca Municipala 'Mihail **Sadoveanu'***, Str Nikos Beloiannis 4, Bucharest

Library Associations

Asociatia Bibliotecarilor din RSR (Librarians' Association of Romania)*, Biblioteca Centrala de Stat, Str ion Ghica 4, 70018 Bucharest Tel: 503765
Executive Secretary: St Gruia
Publication: Revista Bibliotecilor (Library Review) (monthly)

Library Reference Books and Journals

Books

Ghidul Bibliotecilor din România (Guide to Libraries in Romania), Editura Enciclopedică Româna, Calea Victoriei 126, Bucharest

Journals

Buletinul de Informare în Bibliologie (Librarianship Information Bulletin), Central State Library, Str Ion Ghica 4, Bucharest

Fise Signaletice ale Articolelor din Domeniul Bibliologiei (Indicative Cards for Articles in the Field of Librarianship), Central State Library, Str Ion Ghica 4, Bucharest

Information and Documentation Problems (text in English and Romanian), National Institute for Information and Documentation, Str Cosmonautilor 27–29, Bucharest 1

Revista Bibliotecilor (Library Review), Librarians' Association of Romania, Biblioteca Centrala de Stat, Str ion Ghica 4, 70018 Bucharest

Revista de Referate in Bibliologie (Librarianship Abstracts Review), Central State Library, Str Ion Ghica 4, Bucharest

Revista de Titluri: Informare Documentare (Review of Titles: Information and Documentation), National Institute for Information and Documentation, Str Cosmonautilor 27–29, Bucharest 1

Literary Associations and Societies

Institutul de Istorie si Teorie Literara 'George **Calinescu'***, Bul Republicii 73, Bucharest
Dir: Professor Dr Zoe Dumitrescu-Busulenga
Publication: Revista de Istorie si Teorie Literara (quarterly)

Centrul de Lingvistica Istorie Literara si Folclor*, Aleea Mihail Sadoveanu 12, Jassy
Dir: A Teodorescu
Publication: Anuar de Linguisticasi Istorie Literară

Comitetul National pentru Literatura Comparata (National Committee for Comparative Literature)*, Str Onesti 2, Bucharest
Secretary: Dr Alexandru Dutu
Publication: Synthesis (annual)

P E N Club, Casa Scriitorilor Mihail Sadoveanu, Calea Victoriei 115, Bucharest
Vice Presidents: Eugen Jebeleanu, Horia Lovinescu; *Secretary:* Geo Dumitrescu

Romanian Society of Bibliophiles*, Sos Kiseleff 10, Bucharest

Uniunea Scriitorilor din Republica Socialista România, Calea Victoriei 115, 71102 Bucharest
Writers' Union of the Socialist Republic of Romania
President: George Macovescu
Publications: România Literara, Luceafarul, Viata Românească, Secolul XX, Steaua, Orizont, Vatra, Convorbiri literare, Utunk, Igaz Szó, Neue Literatur, Knijevni Jivot

Literary Periodicals

Cahiers roumains d'Etudes Littéraires (Romanian Literary Studies) (text in French and English, occasionally German, Russian, Spanish, Italian), Editura Univers, Piatu Scînteii 1, R-71341 Bucharest

Convorbiri Literare (Literary Conversations), Writers' Union of the Socialist Republic of Romania (Jassy branch), Palatul Culturii, Jassy

Manuscriptum (Manuscripts), Muzeul Literaturii Romane, Central State Library, Str Ion Ghica 4, Bucharest

Orizont (Horizon), Writers' Union of the Socialist Republic of Romania (Timisoara branch), Pta Vasile Roaita 3, Timisoara

Revista de Istorie si Teorie Literara (Review of Literary History and Theory) (summaries in Franch and Russian), Publishing House of the Academy of the Socialist Republic of Romania, Str Gutenberg 3 bis, Bucharest

Romania Literara (Literary Romania), Writers' Union of the Socialist Republic of Romania, Sos Kiseleff 10, Bucharest

Romanian Review (texts in English, French, German and Russian), Foreign Languages Press, Str Ion Ghica 5, Bucharest

Secolul XX (Twentieth Century) Writers' Union of the Socialist Republic of Romania, Sos Kiseleff 10, Bucharest

Steaua (The Star), Writers' Union of the Socialist Republic of Romania, Sos Kiseleff 10, Bucharest

Viata Romineasca (Romanian Life) Writers' Union of the Socialist Republic of Romania, Sos Kiseleff 10, Bucharest

Literary Prizes

'Book Salon' Award*
For typographical and editorial presentation of books, outstanding layout, illustration, binding, etc. Awarded annually. Enquiries to Romanian Council for Culture and Socialist Education, Piata Scînteii 1, 7000 Bucharest

Literary Award*
For literary works reflecting humanistic and democratic ideals. Awarded annually. Enquiries to Romanian Union of Communist Youth, Bucharest

National Award for Book Design*
For the best designed book. Awarded annually. Enquiries to Romanian Society of Bibliophiles, Sos Kiseleff 10, Bucharest

National Prize of Bibliophily*
For a well printed literary masterpiece. Awarded annually. Enquiries to Romanian Society of Bibliophiles, Sos Kiseleff 10, Bucharest

Perpessicius Prize*
Awarded annually by *Manuscriptum* Review for the best edition of a classic writer. Enquiries to Dr Al Oprea, Romanian Literature Museum, Str Fundatiei 4, Bucharest

Romanian Literature Museum Award, see Perpessicius Prize

Writers' Union Prize
For an outstanding contribution to Romanian literature, For poetry, prose, drama, literary criticism, history of literature, literary reportage, literature for children and youth, translations from world literature, and for a promising new literary work by a young writer. Awarded annually. Enquiries to Writers' Union of the Socialist Republic of Romania, Calea Victoriei 115, Bucharest.

(Separate prizes are awarded by Bucharest, Cluj, Jassy, Timisoara, Craiova, Sibiu, Brasov and Tirgu-Mures Writers' Associations. Awarded annually. For further information contact the appropriate Associations of the Writers' Union of the Socialist Republic of Romania)

Rwanda

General Information

Language: Kinyarwanda (a Bantu tongue) but French and Ki-Swahili spoken widely
Religion: Half the population is animist; sizeable minority of Muslim
Population: 4.37 million
Bank Hours: 0830-1130 Monday-Friday for cash transactions; other business 1400-1700 Monday-Friday
Shop Hours: Dawn to dusk
Currency: Rwanda franc
Export/Import Information: No tariff on books and advertising, but Statistical Tax of 3%. Import licence, for statistical purposes, and Foreign Exchange Licence required. Application to National Bank, through authorized bank

Publishers

Government Printer (Imprimerie de Kabgayi)*, BP 9, Gitarama

Government Printer (Imprimerie National du Rwanda)*, BP 114, Kigali

Editions **Rwandaises***, Caritas Rwanda, BP 124, Kigali Tel: 5786
Man Dir: Abbé Cyriaque Munyansanga; *Editorial:* Albert Nambaje
Subjects: Religion, Kinyarwanda language, General, Educational, Children's Paperbacks
Bookshop: address as above
Subsidiary: Caritas

Major Booksellers

Librairie **Caritas***, BP 124, Kigali Tel: 5786

Somec-Rwanda*, BP 628, Kigali Tel: 5378/5497

Major Libraries

Ecole Technique officielle **Don Bosco** Bibliothèque*, BP 80, Kigali

Bibliothèque de l'**Université** Nationale du Rwanda*, BP 54, Butare Tel: 3071
Librarian: Emmanuel Serugendo

Saudi Arabia

General Information

Language: Arabic (English widely understood)
Religion: Muslim (officially)
Population: 9.52 million
Bank Hours: 0830-1200 Saturday-Thursday. Varies during month of Ramadan
Shop Hours: Vary greatly. Generally (except during Ramadan): Jedda: 0900-1330, 1630-2000. Riyadh: 0830-1200, 1630-1930. Eastern Province: 0730-1200, 1430-1700 Saturday-Thursday
Currency: 100 halalah = 1 Saudi Riyal
Export/Import Information: No tariffs on books; advertising matter subject to 3% ad valorem but if total duty on one consignment is less than 50 riyals, matter can enter free. Catalogues distributed gratis, usually admitted free. All printed matter except textbooks subject to censorship. No import licences required
Copyright: No copyright conventions signed

Publishers

Al **Jazirah** Organization for Press, Printing, Publishing*, Ap 88, Municipality Bldg, Safat, PO Box 354, Riyadh
Dir-Gen: Saleh Al-Ajroush; *Editor-in-Chief:* Khalid el Malek
Subject: Politics, Law
Founded: 1964

Saudi Publishing and Distributing House*, Al-Jauhara Bldg, Flats 7 and 12, PO Box 2043, Baghdadia
Man Dir: Muhammed Salahuddin; *General Manager:* Adnan K Salah
Subjects: Arabic and English publications

Major Booksellers

Al-**Adab** Bookshop*, Riyadh Tel: 27865

Dabbous Stores*, King St, Jeddah

Abdullah **Dawood***, El-Jilani, El-Ashaf Bldg, King St, Jeddah

Dar al-**Ilm** Bookshop*, Riyadh Tel: 29947

Mohamed Noor Salah **Jamjoom & Bros***, PO Box 12, Jeddah

Al-**Maktaba***, King St, Jeddah

Riyadh Modern Bookshop*, Riyadh Tel: 27993

Al-**Sha'b** Bookshop*, Riyadh Tel: 22635

Ali **Wahbah** Bookshop*, Riyadh Tel: 67654

Major Libraries

Educational Library*, General Directorate of Broadcasting, Press and Publications, Jeddah

Institute of Public Administration Library*, PO Box 205, Riyadh

Islamic University Library*, Medina Munawarah

King Abdul Aziz University Library*, c/o Dr Abbass Tashkandi, Dean, Library Affairs, PO Box 1540, Jeddah Tel: 27033

Dar al **Kutub** al-Wataniya*, King Faisal St, Riyadh

National Library*, King Faisal St, Riyadh
Publication: Bulletin

Saudi Library*, Riyadh

University Libraries*, University of Riyadh, PO Box 2454, Riyadh Tel: 21722
Dean: Dr A M Al-Dhubaib
Publications: Riyadh University Periodicals (Bulletins published by the Arts, Science, Agricultural Research and Education Depts; Journals of the Agricultural College, Engineering Science and Commerce Depts); *Abstracts of and Indexes to Riyadh University Periodicals; Abstracts and Proceedings of Conferences held by or in collaboration with Riyadh University;* Manuals, Textbooks, Directories and other Reference Works connected with Riyadh University; *Information Bulletin; Union Lists; Accession List;* Bibliographies; *Riyadh University Council Resolution Indexes*

Library Journals

Bulletin, National Library, King Faisal St, Riyadh

Senegal

General Information

Language: French
Religion: Muslim predominantly, also Roman Catholic
Population: 5 million
Literacy Rate (1961): 5.2%
Bank Hours: Generally 0800-1115, 1430-1630 Monday-Saturday
Shop Hours: Vary, and some open Sunday morning, some close Monday morning. Generally are 0800-1200, 1430-1800 Monday-Saturday
Currency: CFA franc
Export/Import Information: No tariff on books except atlases. Added taxes apply to atlases. Advertising matter (more than one copy) subject to 10% fiscal and 5% customs duty plus added taxes of 4% + 22% + 13.5%. Import licences and exchange controls apply for imports outside EEC and franc zone

Book Trade Journals

Bibliographie du Sénégal, Archives du Sénégal, Immeuble administratif, ave Roume, Dakar

Publishers

Africa Editions, 12 rue Bourgi Dr Theze, BP 1926, Dakar Tel: 22222
Man Dir: Joel Decuper
Subjects: General Literature, Reference Works, Annuals, Telephone Directory, Periodicals
Founded: 1958

Edition **Afrique-Levant***, 50 rue de Grammont, Dakar Tel: 36372
Man Dir: Mroueh Brahum
Subjects: General, Religion, Islam
Founded: 1974

Agence de Distribution de Presse*, BP 374, Dakar Tel: 23522
Man Dir: Michel Bedoux
Subjects: General, Reference
Miscellaneous: Affiliated to Librairie Hachette, Paris

Centre Sénégalaise d'Editions et de Diffusion*, 31 rue Wagane Diouf, BP 1745, Dakar Tel: 26994
Man Dir: Jacques Coudon Jaefus
Subjects: General Fiction, Law, Medicine, Paperbacks, Secondary Textbooks
Founded: 1974

Government Printer (Imprimerie du Gouvernement)*, rue Fisque, BP 1, Dakar

Les **Nouvelles Editions** Africaines*, 10 rue Thiers, BP 260, Dakar Tel: 23876/77
General Manager: Mamadou Seck;
Editorial: Roger Dorsinville; *Production:* Sanhivian Diop; *Publicity:* Rosalie Diop
Subjects: General Fiction & Nonfiction, Belles Lettres, Poetry, Biography, History, Africana, Philosophy, Religion, Juveniles, Paperbacks, Psychology, General & Social Science, University & Secondary Textbooks
Founded: 1972
Subsidiary: NEA, ave Noguès, BP 20615, Abidjan

Société Africaine d'Edition*, 16 bis rue de Thiong, BP 1877, Dakar Tel: 32216
Man Dir: Pierre Biarnes
Branch Off: 32 rue de l'Echiquier F-75010 Paris, France
Subjects: African Political and Economic mainly
1978: 20 titles *Founded:* 1961

Société d'Edition d'Afrique Nouvelle*, 9 rue Paul Holle, BP 283, Dakar Tel: 26575
Man Dir: Paul Fondeur; *Senior Editor/Rights & Permissions:* Alcino Louis da Costa
Subjects: Information, statistics and analyses of African affairs, Religion, Magazines

Editions des **Trois Fleuves***, 18 blvd de la République, Dakar Tel: 23001
Man Dir: Roland de Boistel
Subjects: General Nonfiction, Luxury Editions
Founded: 1972

Major Booksellers

Afrique-Levant*, 60 rue de Grammont, Dakar Tel: 36372

Agence de Distribution de Presse*, 4 rue Carnot, BP 374, Dakar

Librairie afrique*, 58 ave William Ponty, BP 1240, Dakar Tel: 23618

Librairie clairafrique*, pl de l'Indépendance, BP 2005, Dakar

Librairie nouvelle de l'Ouest Africain (LINOA)*, Bldg Maginot, 43 ave Maginot, BP 2039, Dakar Tel: 26450

Librairie universitaire et technique*, BP 396, Dakar

La **Maison** du Livre*, 13 ave Roume, BP 2060, Dakar

Mamadou Traoré Ray Autra*, BP 2380, Dakar

Librairie du **Point d'Interrogation***, BP 437, Dakar

Librairie **Sankore***, 25 ave William Ponty, BP 7040, Dakar Tel: 22105

Major Libraries

L'**Alliance** française*, Bibliothèque, 10 rue Colbert, BP 1777, Dakar Tel: 20105

Archives de Sénégal, Immeuble administratif, ave Roume, Dakar Tel: 215072
National Archives of Senegal
Dir: Saliou Mbaye
Publication: Bibliographie du Sénégal

Centre culturel américain*, Bibliothèque, pl de l'Indépendance, BP 49, Dakar Tel: 26146

Centre culturel français, Bibliothèque, 96 rue Blanchot, BP 4003, Dakar Tel: 211821/216427

Centre de Recherches et de Documentation du Sénégal (CRDS)*, rue Neuville, Pointe Sud, BP 382, St-Louis Tel: 71050
Dir: Mohamed Fadel DIA

Lycée technique Maurice **Delafosse***, Bibliothèque, BP 4004, Dakar Tel: 33897

Lycée Blaise **Diagne***, Bibliothèque, Canal IV, BP 12003, Dakar-Colobane Tel: 33535

Lycée de Jeunes Filles Ameth **Fall***, Bibliothèque, BP 1, St-Louis Tel: 71000

Institut africain de Développement économique et de Planification, Bibliothèque, rue de 18 Juin, BP 3186, Dakar Tel: 22577 Telex: 579 Dakar

Institut fondamental d'Afrique noire*, Bibliothèque, Université de Dakar, BP 206, Dakar-Fann Tel: 34002

Université de Dakar, Bibliothèque*, BP 2006, Dakar-Fann Tel: 32918/19/20

Library Associations

A N B A D S, see Association nationale des Bibliothécaires, Archivistes et Documentalistes sénégalais

Association nationale des Bibliothécaires, Archivistes et Documentalistes sénégalais*, Ecole de Bibliothécaires, Archivistes et Documentalistes de Dakar (EBAD), PO Box 3252, Dakar Tel: 24039
Executive Secretary: Theodore Ndiaye

Commission des Bibliothèques de l'ASDBAM (Association Senegalaise pour le Développement de la Documentation, des Bibliothèques, des Archives et des Musées)*, BP 375, Dakar Tel: 34139
Commission of the Libraries of the Senegal Association for the Development of Documentation, Libraries, Archives and Museums

Library Reference Books

Répertoire des Bibliothèques et Organismes de Documentation au Sénégal (Catalogue of the Libraries and Documentation Centres of Senegal), Ecole de Bibliothécaires, Archivistes, et Documentalistes, BP 3252, Dakar-Fann (Information on 124 libraries, archives and documentation centres throughout Senegal)

Literary Associations and Societies

Senegal **P E N** Centre*, Presidential Residence, Dakar
President: HE Leopold Senghor

Translation Agencies and Associations

Provincial Literature Bureau*, PO Box 28, Bo

Seychelles

General Information

Language: English and French
Population: 62,000
Literacy Rate (1971): 57.7%
Export/Import Information: No tariffs on books and advertising. Books on Open General Licence

Major Booksellers

Chez Nanon*, Royal St, Victoria

Newservice Ltd*, Seychelles News Service, PO Box 131, Kingsgate House, Mahe Tel: 22309 Cable Add: Legal Seychelles
Man Dir: Paul B Chow

Sierra Leone

General Information

Language: English
Religion: Muslim and Christian
Population: 3.47 million
Literacy Rate (1963): 6.7%
Bank Hours: 0800-1300 Monday-Friday; 0800-1100 Saturday
Shop Hours: 0800-1200 or 1230, 1400-1630 or 1700 Monday-Friday; 0800-1230 Saturday
Currency: 100 cents = 1 Leone
Export/Import Information: No tariff on books except children's picture books 40%. Advertising matter 40%. Open general licence. Exchange controls

Book Trade Reference Journal

Sierra Leone Publications, Sierra Leone Library Board, PO Box 326, Freetown (the national bibliography, published annually since 1962)

Publishers

Government Printer, Government Printing Department, George St, Freetown

Njala University Publishing Centre*, Njala University, PMB, Freetown
Subjects: Science & Technology, University Textbooks
Miscellaneous: UNESCO sponsored

Sierra Leone University Press*, Fourah Bay College, PO Box 87, Freetown Tel: 27300/23494/27399/27323 Cable Add: Fourahbay
Chairman, Honorary Editor: Professor Eldred Jones; *Honorary Secretary, Rights & Permissions:* Dr W S Marcus Jones
Subjects: General Nonfiction, History, Africana, Religion, Social Science, University Textbooks
1977: 1 title *Founded:* 1968

United Christian Council Literature Bureau*, Bunumbu Press, Bo
Subjects: Books in Mende, Temne, Susu

Major Booksellers

Fourah Bay College Bookshop Ltd, University of Sierra Leone, Freetown Tel: 27351/25307

Njala University College Bookshop, PMB, Freetown Tel: Njala exchange: ext 26, 71
Manager: Prof D R G Gwynne-Jones

The **Sierra Leone** Diocesan Bookshop*, PO Box 104, Freetown Tel: 22302

Major Libraries

Public **Archives** of Sierra Leone*, c/o Fourah Bay College Library, PO Box 87, Freetown

British Council Library, PO Box 124, Freetown Tel: 22223

Fourah Bay College Library, University of Sierra Leone, Freetown Tel: 27337
Librarian: Gladys M Jusu-Sheriff
Publications include: Annual Report; List of New Accessions to the Sierra Leone Collection; Printed Catalogue of the Sierra Leone Collection; Report on Visits to Francophone University Libraries in West Africa

Milton **Margai** Teachers' College Library, Goderich, PMB, Freetown Tel: 024305

Njala University College Library (University of Sierra Leone), Private Mail Bag, Freetown Tel: 00412
Librarian: Mrs M O Akinsulure
Publication: Library Bulletin; Occasional Papers; Annual Report

Sierra Leone Library Board, PO Box 326, Freetown Tel: 23848
Acting Chief Librarian: Mrs G E Dillsworth
Publications: Annual Report; Sierra Leone Publications (annual)

U S I S Library*, American Embassy, Walpole St, Freetown

Library Associations

Sierra Leone Library Association*, c/o Sierra Leone Library Board, PO Box 326, Freetown Tel: 23848
Secretary: Ms M A Roberts

Publications: Sierra Leone Library Journal (biannual), *Directory of Libraries and Information Services*

Library Reference Books and Journals

Books

Directory of Libraries and Information Services, Sierra Leone Library Association, c/o The Secretary, High Court Library, Siaka Stevens St, Freetown

Journals

Sierra Leone Library Journal, Sierra Leone Library Association, c/o The Secretary, High Court Library, Siaka Stevens St, Freetown

Republic of Singapore

General Information

Language: English
Religion: All major religions, especially Confucianism, Muslim, Buddhism, Taoism
Population: 2.3 million
Bank Hours: 1000-1500 Monday-Friday; 0930-1130 Saturday
Shop Hours: 0900-1800 Monday-Saturday
Currency: 100 cents = 1 Singapore dollar
Export/Import Information: No tariffs on books and advertising. Import licences; no seditious publications permitted. Nominal exchange control
Copyright: Florence (see International section)

Book Trade Organizations

Book Publishers' Association*, M/S Eastern Universities Press Sdn Bhd, 112F, Block 5, 6th Floor Boon Keng Rd, Singapore 12 Tel: 2582077
Secretary-General: C Nair

National Book Development Council of Singapore, c/o National Library, Stamford Rd, Singapore 0617
Publication: Singapore Book World

Singapore Booksellers' Association*, 428-429 Katong Shopping Centre, Singapore 15 Tel: 401495
President: N T S Chopra

Singapore Chinese Booksellers' Association*, 19b Carpenter St, Singapore 1

Book Trade Reference Books and Journals

Books

Books in Singapore; a survey of publishing, printing, bookselling and library activity in the Republic of Singapore, Chopmen Enterprises, 428-429 Katong Shopping Centre (4th Floor), Singapore 15

Journals

The Memoranda of Books Registered in the 'Catalogue of Books Printed at Singapore under the Provisions of the Printer's and Publisher's Ordinance', National Library, Stamford Rd, Singapore 6

Singapore Book World, National Book Development Council of Singapore, c/o National Library, Stamford Rd, Singapore 6

Singapore National Bibliography (SNB), National Library, Stamford Rd, Singapore 6

Publishers

Addison-Wesley Singapore (Pte) Ltd, Room 456 4th Floor, Peoples Park Centre, 101 Upper Cross St, Singapore 1 Cable Add: Adiwes Singapore
Manager: Benjamin Kong Tan Ho
Miscellaneous: Firm is an associate company of Addison-Wesley Publishers Ltd, UK (qv)

Angus & Robertson (South-East Asia) Ltd, 159 Boon Keng Rd, Block 2, Ground Floor, Singapore 12 Tel: 2582663/2582889 Cable Add: Austbook Singapore Telex: RS 24297
Man Dir, Editorial, Rights & Permissions: Richard Walsh; *Dir:* Janet Theseira; *Sales Rep:* Patrick Tan; *Publicity:* Bessie Tay, Ng Kheng Chuan
Parent Company: Angus & Robertson Publishers, Australia (qv)
Associate Company: Angus & Robertson (UK) Ltd, UK (qv)
Branch Offs: Angus & Robertson (Publishers) Pty Ltd, Philippines; PO Box 1072, MCC Makati, Metro Manila, Philippines (Miss M Mariano)
Subjects: Educational, Business Management, Academic, Library Science, General, Medical, Children's Books
Founded: 1968

Apa Productions (Pte) Ltd, Suite 1021 10th Floor, International Plaza, 10 Anson Rd, Singapore 2 Tel: 2205288/2205323 Cable Add: Apaproduct Telex: rs 23660 delite
Publisher: Hans Hoefer; *Marketing Dir:* Leo Haks; *Production:* Wong Kum Chiew; *Rights & Permissions:* Leo Haks
Associate Company: Apa Productions (HK) Ltd, South China Bldg, One Wyndham St, Hong Kong
Subjects: Travel Guides, Culture, History, Religion, Photography
1977: 8 titles *Founded:* 1971

M/S **Asia** Pacific Press, Pte, Ltd*, Liat Towers, 541 Orchard Rd, Singapore 9 Tel: 379364
Man Dir: John Ede
Subjects: General Fiction, Biography, How-to, Religion, Economics, Cookery, Travel, Politics
Founded: 1969

Graham **Brash** Pte Ltd+, see Literary Agents

Chopmen Enterprises*, 428-429 Katong Shopping Centre (4th Floor), Singapore 15 Tel: 401495 Cable Add: Nirmalji Singapore
Man Dir: N T S Chopra
Subjects: Reference, Social & General Science, Fiction, General, Religion, Poetry, Asiatic Studies, University & Secondary Textbooks, Paperbacks, Educational Materials
1977: 12 titles *Founded:* 1966

Eastern Universities Press Sdn Bhd, 112F, Block 5, Boon Keng Rd, PO Box 1742, Singapore 12 Tel: 2582077 Cable Add: Eastup
Man Dir: Goh Kee Seah; *Editorial:* Anne Marie Nalpon; *Production:* Violet Phoon
Orders to: United Publishers Services Sdn Bhd, 112-F Boon Keng Rd, Block 5, 6th Floor, Singapore 12
Subsidiary Company: Eastern Universities Press (Malaysia) Sdn Bhd (qv)
Subjects: Biography, History, English Language, Cookery, Juvenile Fiction, Economics; Primary, Secondary and University Textbooks
1977: 27 titles *1978:* 54 titles *Founded:* 1958

F E P International Private Ltd*, Jalan Boon Lay, Jurong, Singapore 22 Cable Add: bookmark Telex: rs 2560
Man Dir: David Chew; *Executive Dir:* Cho Jock Min
Br Offs: Accra, Hong Kong, Karachi, Kingston, Lagos, London, Manila, Maseru, Mbabana, Nairobi, Petaling Jaya, Port-of-Spain, Singapore, Sydney
1977: 45 titles

Federal Publications (S) Pte Ltd, No 1 New Industrial Road, Singapore 1953 Tel: 2848844 Cable Add: Fedpubs, Singapore Telex: rs 25713
General Manager: H H Chiam; *Sales Manager:* L H Teo *Publishing Manager:* Y H Mew
Associate Companies: Federal Publications (HK) Ltd, 5A Evergreen Industrial Mansion, Wong Chuk Hang Rd, Aberdeen, Hong Kong; Federal Publications Sdn Bhd, 8238 Jalan 222, Petaling Jaya, Selangor
Subsidiary Companies: Home Studies Division, 1307 International Plaza, Singapore 0207; (publishers of *Yippee*, a magazine for children)
Subjects: Secondary and Primary Textbooks, Teaching and Study Aids, Reference Works, Juvenile Story Books; also *Asia Pacific* series (socio-political on SE Asia), *Tangent* series (popular knowledge about current topics)
1977: 500 titles *1978:* 74 titles *Founded:* 1957

Institute of Southeast Asian Studies, Cluny Rd, Singapore 10 Tel: 514211/2/2528088 Cable Add: ISEAS
Man Dir: Kernial S Sandhu; *Editorial, Sales, Production, Publicity, Rights & Permissions:* Christine Tan
Subjects: Modernization in Southeast Asia, Social and Political Change
1977: 14 titles *1978:* 18 titles *Founded:* 1968

Longman Malaysia Sdn Bhd, 25 First Lokyang Rd, Jurong Town, Singapore 2262 Tel: 2682666
Man Dir: James B Ho
Subjects: Textbooks, Medical, Science and Technology
1977: 73 titles *1978:* 14 titles
Miscellaneous: Firm is an associate company of Longman Group Ltd, UK (qv)

McGraw-Hill International Book Co, 348 Jalan Boon Lay, Jurong, Singapore 22 Tel: 654633/654156 Cable Add: McGrawbook Singapore
Man Dir: Harry B Engelander; *Sales:* John Lim
Parent Company: McGraw-Hill Inc, New York, USA
Subject: Educational Materials
Founded: 1969

Macmillan Southeast Asia Pte Ltd*, 41 Jalan Pemimpin, Singapore 20 Tel: 2521337 Cable Add: Publish Singapore Telex: RS 23196
Dir: Loh Mun Wai
Miscellaneous: Firm is a subsidiary of Macmillan Holdings Ltd, UK

Malayan Law Journal (Pte) Ltd, 1302-1305 (13th Floor), Shenton Ho, 3 Shenton Way, Singapore 0106 Tel: 2203684 Cable Add: Malool
Man Dir, Editorial, Production, Rights & Permissions: Al-Mansor Adabi; *Sales, Publicity:* Amir Mallal
Branch Off: 4th Floor Bangunan Ming, Jalan Bukit Nanas, Kuala Lumpur 04-01, Malaysia
Subjects: Law, Accountancy, Tax
Bookshops: 1302-1305 (13th Floor) Shenton Ho, Shenton Way, Singapore 1; 4th Floor Bangunan Ming, Jalan Bukit Nanas, Kuala Lumpur 04-01, Malaysia
1977: 2 titles *1978:* 8 titles *Founded:* 1932

Malaysia Press Sdn Bhd, 745-747 North Bridge Rd, Singapore 0719 Tel: 2933454
Man Dir: Omar Bin Ally; *Sales Dir:* Abu Talib Bin Ally; *Publicity and Advertising:* Abdullah Bin Ally
Subsidiary Company: Pustaka Melayu, 745-747 North Bridge Rd, Singapore 0719
Subjects: School Textbooks, Educational Books etc, in the Malay language
Founded: 1950

Maruzen Asia (Pte) Ltd, 6th Floor, Block 7, Ayer Rajah Industrial Estate, Singapore 0513 Tel: 7759844-6 Telex: Mapore RS26521 Cable Add: Maruzen Singapore
Man Dir: Minoru Taguchi
Associate Company: Maruzen Co Ltd, Japan (qv)
Subjects: Technical, Social and Medical Sciences
1978: 5 titles *Founded:* 1978

Medical World Book Co Pte Ltd*, Newton PO Box 96, Singapore 11
Man Dir: Andrew Lee
Associate Company: University Education Press, Singapore (qv)
Subjects: Medical, Scientific and Technical books

Pustaka **Nasional** Pte Ltd, Suite 1211, Shaw Towers Beach Rd, Singapore 0718 Tel: 2941917/8
Subjects: Malay books
Bookshop: 40 Kandahar St (also Distributors)
1979: 2 titles

Oxford University Press, Unit 4-2 Block A, 4th Floor, Tong Lee Bldg, 35 Kallang Pudding Rd, Singapore 13 Tel: 2840566/2840567 Cable Add: Oxonian Singapore
Regional Manager: J A Nicholson; *Representative:* Goh Teow Huat
Subjects: Education, History, Low- and High-priced Paperbacks, General and Social Sciences, Secondary Textbooks, Educational Materials
Miscellaneous: Firm is a branch of Oxford University Press, UK (qv)

P G Medical Books, 413 Tanglin Shopping Centre, 19 Tanglin Rd, Singapore 10 Tel: 235006
Man Dir: Chan Poh Geok; *Editorial:* A S M Lim
Parent Company: P G Lim (Pte) Ltd
Subsidiary Company: P G Books (Pte) Ltd
Branch Off: 227 Tanglin Shopping Centre, 19 Tanglin Rd, Singapore 10
Subject: Medical
1978: 1 title *1979:* 1 title *Founded:* 1974

Pan Pacific Book Distributors (S) Pte Ltd, 597 Havelock Rd (Teck Huat Chambers), Singapore 0316 Tel: 436411/981526 Cable Add: Pacolmac
Man Dir: Seow Kui Lim
Editorial Off: Rooms 1011 & 1013, 10th Floor, Manhattan Ho, 151 Chin Swee Rd, Singapore 0316 Tel: 915530/431961
Subjects: Secondary and Primary Textbooks, Reference, General Literature
Bookshop: Pacific Book Centre, 597 Havelock Rd (Teck Huat Chambers), Singapore 0316
1977: 25 titles *1978:* 35 titles *Founded:* 1971

Prentice-Hall of Southeast Asia Pte Ltd, 4, 4B, Block 1, Ayer Rajah Industrial Estate, Singapore 5
Tel: 7759085/7759086/7753269 Cable Add: Prenhall Singapore
Man Dir: Joseph Hang; *Marketing Manager:* K C Ang
Parent Company: Prentice-Hall International Inc, Englewood Cliffs, NJ 07632, USA
Associate Companies: See entry for Prentice-Hall, UK
Subjects: Belles Lettres, Poetry, History, How-to, Music, Art, Philosophy, Reference, Religion, Medicine, Psychology, Engineering, Computer Textbooks, General and Social Science, University Textbooks, Educational and Audio-Visual Materials

Singapore University Press Pte Ltd, University of Singapore, Kent Ridge, Singapore 5 Tel: 673443/50451 ext 453 Cable Add: Singpress
Manager, Editor: Marian Pan
Subjects: Scholarly studies relating to all aspects of life in SE Asia and/or Singapore; Sociology, Law, the Arts and Sciences, Medicine, Politics, Pedagogy,
Bibliographies; Journals: Journal of SE Asian Studies, SE Asia Ethnicity & Development Newsletter, Contemporary SE Asia
1977: 11 titles *Founded:* 1971

Southeast Asian Ministers of Education Organization (SEAMEO), Regional Language Centre (RELC), 30 Orange Grove Rd, Singapore 1025 Tel: 7379044 Cable Add: Relcentre
Subjects: Language Teaching and Research, Linguistics, English for Special Purposes
1979: 27 titles *Founded:* 1968

Stamford College Publishers, 218 Queen St, Singapore 0718 Tel: 323144/8
Man Dir, Publicity: L P Nicol; *Editorial:* L Thomas; *Sales:* J Dennis; *Production:* Mr Arangasamy
Branch Off: Stamford Executive Bookshop, Petaling Jaya, Malaysia
Subjects: Educational Books
Bookshop: 218 Queen St, Singapore 0718
1977: 7 titles *1978:* 9 titles *Founded:* 1970

Toppan Co (Singapore) Private Ltd, PO Box 22, Jurong Town Post Office, Singapore 2262 (Located at: 38 Liu Fang Rd, Jurong, Singapore 2262) Tel: 656105 Cable Add: Toppan Singapore Telex: RS 21596
Man Dir: Naomi Yoshikawa; *Sales:* Chu Bong; *Production:* Y Yamamoto
Parent Company: Toppan Co Ltd, Japan (qv)
Associate Company: Froebel-Kan Ltd, Tokyo, Japan

Subjects: Agriculture, Biochemistry, Biology, Botany, Chemistry, Civil, Electrical and Industrial Engineering, Earth Sciences, Economics, Mathematics, Mechanics, Medicine, Physiology, Physics, Statistics, Zoology

University Education Press*, Newton, PO Box 96, Singapore 11
Manager: Yeo Teo Kong
Associate Company: Medical World Book Co, Singapore (qv)
Subjects: East and South-East Asia, Humanities, Social Sciences, History of Singapore

Literary Agents

Graham **Brash** Pte Ltd, Prinsep House, 36-C Prinsep St, Singapore 0718 Tel: 332497/333705 Cable Add: Bookscout Singapore
Manager: K C Campbell
This Company acts mainly as an Agency, but also engages in occasional minor publishing

Chopmen Enterprises*, 428-429 Katong Shopping Centre (4th Floor), Singapore 15

Major Booksellers

Asia Book Co, 155 Cross St, Singapore 1

Books for Asia (Singapore) Pte Ltd, c/o 65 Crescent Rd, Singapore 15 Tel: 4462903/4462377 Cable Add: Asiabooks (Wholesalers)

Chopmen Bookshop*, B-72 Katong Shopping Centre (Lower Ground Floor), Singapore 15 Tel: 401606

Eastern Book Service Pte Ltd, 11 Irving Place, Singapore 13 Tel: 801077 Cable Add: Eastbook, Singapore Telex: RS 23163
Group Dir: Jack Sherman; *Executive Dir:* Brian Lim
Publishers' Agents and Stockists

Educational Aids Production Co Pte Ltd*, 33 Beo Crescent, Singapore 3

Educational Book Centre*, 69 Stamford Rd, Singapore 6 Tel: 327731

Far East Book Co*, 17 Goldhill Plaza, Newton Rd, Singapore 11
Also 161 Thomson Rd, Singapore 11

Haji Hashim bin Haji Abdullah*, 134 Arab St, Singapore 7

M P H Pte Ltd, 71-77 Stamford Rd, GPO Box 347, Singapore 6 Tel: 363633

Michael's Bookshop*, 22 Orchard Rd, Singapore 9 Tel: 361327

Modern Book Store*, 34 Bras Basah Rd, Singapore 7

Pustaka **Nasional***, 40 Kandahar St, Singapore 7 Tel: 2937791
(Booksellers and Distributors)

National Book Store*, 72 Bras Basah Rd, Singapore 7 Tel: 321165

Pacific Book Centre, 597 Havelock Rd, (Teck Huat Chambers) Singapore 3 Tel: 436411, 981526 Cable Add: Pacolmac

S T P Distributors Sdn Bhd, B4 International Bldg, Orchard Rd, Singapore 9 Tel: 379522

Shanghai Book Co Pte Ltd, 81 Victoria St, Singapore 0718 Tel: 360144 Cable Add: Shoobook

Singapore Book Store*, 66 Bras Basah Rd, Singapore 7

University Bookstore*, 13 Orchard Rd, Singapore 9 Tel: 326311

World Book Co Ltd*, 205-207 South Bridge Rd, Singapore 7

Major Libraries

American Library Resource Center, American Embassy, 30 Hill St, Singapore 6

Nanyang University Library, Upper Jurong Rd, Singapore 2263

National Archives and Records Centre*, 16-18 Lewin Terrace, Singapore 7

National Library, Stamford Rd, Singapore 0617 Tel: 327355/8 Cable Add: Natlib Singapore Telex: RS 26620
Dir: Mrs Hedwig Anuar

University of Singapore Library, Bukit Timah Rd, Singapore 1025 Tel: 2560451/2560454
Librarian: Peggy W C Hochstadt
Publications: Catalogue of Singapore/Malaysia Collection and Supplements; Checklist of Current Serials; Accessions List (monthly); Library Handbook; Dissertations, Theses and Academic Exercises, 1947-1976, 1977; Annual Report

Library Associations

Library Association of Singapore, c/o National Library, Stamford Rd, Singapore 0617
Honorary Secretary: Isabel Tang
Publications: Singapore Libraries (annual), *Directory of Libraries in Singapore*, 2nd edition, *Who's Who in Singapore Librarianship, LAS newsletter* (irregular)

Library Reference Books and Journals

Books

Directory of Libraries in Singapore, Library Association of Singapore, c/o National Library, Stamford Rd, Singapore 6

Singapore Libraries, Library Association of Singapore, c/o National Library, Stamford Rd, Singapore 6

Journals

Newsletter, Library Association of Singapore, Stamford Rd, Singapore 6

Literary Associations and Societies

Chinese Language and Literary Society*, Jurong Rd, Singapore 22
Publication: Hsin Sheng

Literary Periodicals

Hsin Sheng (New Life), Chinese Language and Literary Society, Jurong Rd, Singapore 22

Literary Prizes

National Book Development Council of Singapore Book Awards*
For outstanding works of creative and non-creative writing by local authors in any of the four official languages (Malay, English, Chinese, and Tamil). The awards are for fiction, poetry, drama, non-fiction, and children's and young people's books. Up to fifteen prizes of 500 to 1,000 Singapore dollars. Awarded every three years (or annually if there are sufficient works of merit). Enquiries to National Book Development Council of Singapore, c/o National Library, Stamford Rd, Singapore 0617

Somalia

General Information

Language: Somali is the national language; Arabic, Italian and English are official languages and widely spoken
Religion: Muslim
Population: 3.35 million
Bank Hours: 0800-1130 Saturday-Thursday
Currency: Somali or Samli shilling
Export/Import Information: No tariff on books; advertising matter distributed gratis is free, otherwise 40% Revenue and 10% Customs Duty. Administration Tax, 10%; Wharfage Tax, 1.5%. Exchange controls

Publishers

Government Printer*, Ministry of Information, Mogadishu

Somalia d'Oggi*, Piazzale della Garesa, PO Box 315, Mogadishu
Subjects: Law, Economics

Major Booksellers

New Africa Booksellers*, PO Box 897, Mogadishu Tel: 30087

Major Libraries

National Library of Higher Education and Culture*, Ministry of Higher Education and Culture, Mogadishu

Biblioteca dell' Universita Nazionale della Somalia*, PO Box 15, Magadishu Tel: 2535

Republic of South Africa

General Information

Language: English and Afrikaans
Religion: White population predominantly Protestant
Population: 26.1 million
Literacy Rate (1960): 57% Total (50% Bantu, 98% White, 74% Asiatic, 69% Coloured)
Bank Hours: 0900-1530 Monday-Tuesday, Thursday, Friday; 0900-1300 Wednesday; 0830-1100 Saturday
Shop Hours: Vary province to province. Often 0830-1700 Monday-Friday; 0830-1230 Saturday
Currency: 100 cents = 1 rand
Mailing Information: Weight limits: books, 5 kg (11 lb); printed matter, 2 kg (4 lb); parcel post, 10 kg (22 lb); air parcel post, 10 kg (22 lb)
Export/Import Information: No tariffs on books or advertising matter. No import licence required. No obscene literature permitted. Exchange controls being relaxed
Copyright: Berne (see International section)

Book Trade Organizations

Associated Booksellers of Southern Africa Ltd, 1 Meerendal, Nightingale Way, Pinelands 7405 Tel: 533952
Secretary: P G van Rooyen

Book Trade Association of South Africa*, PO Box 724, Pretoria

Directorate of Publications*, Private Bag 9069, Cape Town 8000 Tel: 211000 Telex: 570165
Dir: D Vosloo
See also Publications Appeal Board below

Overseas Publishers' Representatives Association of Southern Africa, PO Box 8879, Johannesburg Tel: (838) 2147
Secretary: P Hardingham

Publications Appeal Board*, Private Bag X114, Pretoria 001 Tel: 36353 Telex: 53668
Subsidiary to the Directorate of Publications (qv)

South African Publishers' Association, PO Box 123, Kenwyn 7790
Secretary: P G van Rooyen

Book Trade Reference Books and Journals

Books

Catalogue of Books (English) Published in Southern Africa, Still in Print (1970), C Struik, Corner Wale and Loop Sts, PO Box 1144, Cape Town (useful compilation produced by the prominent firm of booksellers)

Journals

Central News, Central News Agency Ltd, PO Box 9, Cape Town 8000 (trade organ published by CNA, the large bookselling chain with branches throughout the country)

South African National Bibliography (text in Afrikaans, Bantu languages and English), The State Library, Vermeulen St, PO Box 397, Pretoria (published since 1933; annual volume and quarterly cumulations; also available as a weekly card service)

Publishers

Africana Book Society (Pty) Ltd*, PO Box 1071, Johannesburg
Man Dir: L W Bolze; *Editorial:* P T Joyce
Parent Company: Books of Rhodesia Publishing Co (Pvt) Ltd, Rhodesia (qv)
Subjects: General Academic, Biography, History, Africana, Hunting, Wildlife, Illustrated & Fine Editions, Reprints
Founded: 1975
ISBN Publisher's Prefix: 0-994971

B L A C Publishing House*, PO Box 17, Athlone, Cape Town
Man Dir: James Matthews
Subjects: General Fiction, Belles Lettres, Poetry, Paperbacks
Founded: 1974

A A Balkema Publishers+, 93 Keerom St, PO Box 3117, Cape Town Tel: (021) 229009/431935 Cable Add: Balkema Cape Town
Man Dir: A A Balkema
Head Office: A A Balkema, Postbus 1675, 3000 BR Rotterdam, Netherlands
Subjects: Texts of scientific nature covering Anthropology, African and Oriental Studies, Palaeontology, Archaeology, Botany, Zoology, Ecology, Agriculture, Soil Engineering
1977: 15 titles *1978:* 10 titles *Founded:* 1930
ISBN Publisher's Prefix: 0-86961

Bateleur Press, c/o Ravan Press (Pty) Ltd, PO Box 31910, Braamfontein 2193 (Located at: 416-419 Dunwell, 35 Jorissen St, Braamfontein) Tel: 397832/5 and 7252094/6
Subjects: General Fiction and Nonfiction
Founded: 1975

Black Community Programmes Ltd*, 86 Beatrice St, Durban Tel: 67558
Executive Dir: B A Khoapa; *Senior Editor:* Thoko Mbajwa
Br Off: 15 Leopold St, King Williams Town
Subjects: General Nonfiction, Community Development, Reference, Annuals, Paperbacks
Founded: 1972

Books of Africa, now incorporated in T V Bulpin (qv)

T V Bulpin (Pty) Ltd, 1004 Cape of Good Hope Bldg, 117 George St, PO Box 1516, Cape Town 8000 Tel: 227921
Man Dir, Rights & Permissions: T V Bulpin; *Sales:* M Bulpin, Ray Howell; *Production, Publicity:* R Handler, H Rennie
Subsidiary Company: Books of Africa (Pty) Ltd
Subjects: Biography, History, Africana, Art
1978: 3 titles *Founded:* 1947
ISBN Publisher's Prefix: 0-949956

Butterworth & Co (SA) (Pty) Ltd+, PO Box 792, Durban 4000 (Located at: 152/154 Gale St, Durban 4001) Tel: (031) 66516/68070 Cable Add: Butterlaw Durban
Man Dir, Rights & Permissions: A McAdam; *Editorial:* J B Talbot; *Sales:* J Destombes; *Production:* K Prinsloo; *Publicity:* Miss Muller

Parent Company: Butterworth & Co (Publishers) Ltd, UK (qv)
Branch Off: PO Box 27711, Sunnyside 0132
Subjects: Law, Medicine, Science & Technology, General Science, University Textbooks
1977: 21 titles *1978:* 41 titles *Founded:* 1935
ISBN Publisher's Prefix: 0-409

C N A, see Central News Agency Ltd

C U M, an imprint of Christian Publishing, Co — Newman Art (qv)

Killie **Campbell** Africana Library, see University of Natal Press

Central News Agency Ltd*, Laub St, New Centre, PO Box 10799, Johannesburg 2000 Tel: (011) 8361711
Subjects: Children's Books, Paperbacks
Bookshops: Retail outlets throughout the country (see under Booksellers)

Christian Publishing Co — Newman Art+, PO Box 132, Roodepoort 1725 (Located at: Baanbreker Avenue 2, Helderkruin, Roodepoort 1725) Tel: (011) 7642460 Cable Add: Chrispub Telex: 84667
Man Dir: Timo Crous (Chrispub), Ray Parsons (Newman Art); *Editorial:* Jan du Plessis; *Sales:* Mr N Delport; *Production, Publicity, Rights & Permissions:* Pieter Joubert
Imprint: C U M
Subjects: Religion, Juveniles, Paperbacks
1978: 60 titles *1979:* 67 titles *Founded:* 1939

Church Publishing Trust, see Interkerklike Uitgewerstrust

College of Careers (Pty) Ltd*, PO Box 2081, Cape Town 8000 (Located at: 4th Floor, Garmar Ho, 121-127 Plein St, Cape Town 8001) Tel: 452041 Cable Add: Colcareers
Man Dir: Cyril Kemp; *Production:* Ivor Furman
Subjects: Educational
1977: 49 titles *Founded:* 1946

Collier-Macmillan South Africa (Pty) Ltd, PO Box 17, Kempton Park 1620, Transvaal (Located at: 51 Forge Rd, Spartan Industrial Township, Kempton Park) Tel: 9701827/8/9 Cable Add: Pachamac
Man Dir: L James Armstrong
Parent Company: Macmillan Inc, New York, USA
Allied and Subsidiary Companies: Cassell Australia (qv); Cassell & Co, New Zealand (qv); Cassell Ltd, Collier Macmillan Ltd, UK (qqv); Collier Macmillan Australia (qv); Collier Macmillan Canada Ltd; Collier Macmillan International, Philippines; Collier Macmillan International, USA

Ad Donker (Pty) Ltd+, PO Box 41021, Craighall 2064 (Located at: Hyde Park Corner, Jan Smuts Ave, Hyde Park, Johannesburg 2196) Tel: 7885030 Cable Add: Reppub
Man Dir, Rights & Permissions: Adriaan Donker; *Sales:* Karen Lubisch; *Editorial:* Christine Susman; *Publicity:* Gillian Sellers
Associate Company: International Publishers' Representatives (SA) (Pty) Ltd
Subjects: General Fiction & Nonfiction, Poetry, Africana, Academic
1978: 14 titles *1979:* 14 titles *Founded:* 1973
ISBN Publisher's Prefix: 0-949937

REPUBLIC OF SOUTH AFRICA

Dutch Reformed Church Publishers, PO Box 4539, Cape Town 8000 Tel: 221376 Cable Add: D R C Publishers Telex: 76922
Man Dir: W J van Zijl; *Editorial, Rights and Permissions:* Mrs B Smit; *Sales:* A Peens; *Production:* W Theron; Mrs M Volschenk
Parent Company: N G Kerk-Uitgewers en Boekhandel (qv)
Associate Company: Verenigde Protestantse Uitgewers (qv)
Branch Off: PO Box, Kempton Park, South Africa
Subjects: Christian Literature (Educational and General)
Bookshops: 20 Bookshops throughout South Africa
1978: 52 titles *1979:* 29+ titles *Founded:* 1818
ISBN Publisher's Prefix: 0-86991

Educum Uitgewers Beperk+*, Posbus 87, King Williams Town 5600

Erudita Publications (Pty) Ltd+*, PO Box 25111, Ferrairas Town 2048, Transvaal
Subjects: Reference, Directories

Flesch Financial Publications (Pty) Ltd+, 58 Burg St, PO Box 3473, Cape Town Tel: (021) 436625 Cable Add: Fairlead Telex: 577826
Man Dir: W J Flesch; *Editorial:* C G Thompson; *Sales Manager:* Derek Wood
Br Off: SARB Ho, 80 Commissioner St, PO Box 3473, Johannesburg
Subjects: Reference, Finance
1978: 2 titles *Founded:* 1966
ISBN Publisher's Prefix: 0-949989

Da **Gama** Publishers (Pty) Ltd, 311 Locarno Ho, Loveday St, Johannesburg
Man Dir: Daphne de Freitas
Subjects: General Nonfiction, Educational, Reference, Travel Books

Government Printer*, Bosman St, Pretoria

T W **Griggs** & Co (Pty) Ltd+, PO Box 466, Durban 4000 (Located at: 341 West St, Durban, 4001) Tel: 328571/2 Cable Add: Adamsco
Dir, Editorial, Sales, Production, Publicity: E G Rabjohn; *Rights & Permissions:* P B Harvey
Parent Company: Adams & Company Ltd, 341 West St, Durban, 4001 (qv)
Subsidiary Companies: Adams & Griggs Educational Suppliers; Thirty Three Victory Street (Pty) Ltd; both at 33 Victoria St, Durban 4001
Subjects: Africana

H & R Academica, subsidiary of Human & Rousseau Publishers (Pty) Ltd (qv)

H A U M (Hollandsch Afrikaansche Uitgevers Maatschappij)+, 58 Long St, PO Box 1371, Cape Town 8000 Tel: (021) 435008 Cable Add: Haum
Manager, Publisher: A A J van Niekerk; *Editorial:* Elsa Naudé
Associate Companies: Interkerklike Uitgewerstrust (qv); N G Kerk-Uitgewers en Boekhandel (qv); N G Kerkboekhandel Transvaal (qv); Pro Rege Press (qv)
Subjects: General Fiction & Nonfiction, Belles Lettres, Poetry, Biography, History, Juveniles, Books in Afrikaans, Science and Technology, General Science, University Textbooks
Bookshops: 480 Paul Kruger St, PO Box 460, Pretoria 001; HAUM Akademiese Boekhandel, Trust Bank Centre, Stellenbosch 7600

1978: 45 titles *Founded:* 1894
ISBN Publisher's Prefix: 0-7986

Human & Rousseau Publishers (Pty) Ltd+, State House, 3-9 Rose St, PO Box 5050, Cape Town Tel: (021) 410625 Cable Add: Persdiens Telex: 570294
General Manager: J J Human; *Publicity:* D Saayman
Parent Company: Nasionale Boekhandel Ltd (qv)
Subsidiary Company: H & R Academica, PO Box 558, Pretoria 0001
Branch Offs: 607 Southern Life Building, 239 Pretorius St, Pretoria Tel: (012) 37588 Cable Add: Hurou
Subjects: General Fiction & Nonfiction, Belles Lettres, Poetry, Biography, History, Africana, Philosophy, Reference, Religion, Juveniles, Books in Afrikaans, General Science, University and Secondary Textbooks
1977: 137 titles *1978:* 138 titles

Hutchinson Group (SA) (Pty) Ltd, PO Box 337, Bergvlei 2012 Tel: (786) 2983 Cable Add: Hutchbooks
Man Dir: John F Banks; *Sales (Educational):* Cory Voigt
Associate Company: Hutchinson Publishing Group Ltd, UK (qv)
Subjects: General Fiction & Nonfiction, Belles Lettres, Poetry, University & Secondary Textbooks
Founded: 1966

Interkerklike Uitgewerstrust+, PO Box 2744, Pretoria 0001
Church Publishing Trust
Secretary: I B Kasselman
Associate Companies: H A U M (qv); Pro Rege Press (qv); N G Kerkboekhandel Transvaal (qv); N G Kerk-Uitgewers en Boekhandel (qv)
Subjects: Religious handbooks for Schools, Universities and Churches; also Visual Aids

Juta & Co Ltd+, PO Box 123, Kenwyn 7790 (Located at: Mercury Cres, Hillstar Industrial Township, Wetton) Tel: (021) 711181 Cable Add: Juta
Man Dir: J D Duncan; *Sales Manager:* L Massella; *Senior Editor, Rights & Permissions:* J Pottgieter, J D Duncan
Branch Off: PO Box 403, Umtata, Transkei
Subjects: Reference, Law, Medicine, Science and Technology; General School, University & Educational Textbooks
Bookshops: Church St, PO Box 30, Cape Town 8000; Cnr Pritchard & Loveday Sts, PO Box 1010, Johannesburg 2000; Suite 5b, Mangrove Beach Centre, 91 Somtseu Rd, Durban 4001
1977: 96 titles *Founded:* 1853
ISBN Publisher's Prefix: 0-7021

Die **Kinderpers** Van SA, PO Box 2652, Cape Town 8000
Subject: Children's Books
1977: 36 titles *1978:* 29 titles

Kosmo Uitgewery Beperk+*, Posbus 178, Stellenbosch 7600

Longman Penguin Southern Africa (Pty) Ltd+*, Marine Drive, Paarden Eiland, PO Box 1616, Cape Town 8000 Tel: (021) 517324/5 and 515758 Cable Add: Freegrove Capetown Telex: 570841
Man Dir: M A Peacock; *Publishing Manager:* R Cornford; *Sales Manager Schools Division:* G F Visser; *Sales Manager Higher Education:* J H Collyer; *Trade Sales Manager:* J H Allen; *Publicity and Advertising by Sales Managers; Rights & Permissions:* D van der Horst

Parent Company: Longman Group Ltd, Harlow, Essex, England
Subsidiary Company: Willem Gouws (Pty) Ltd, c/r Vrystaat St and Marine Drive, Paarden Eiland, South Africa
Subjects: Primary, Secondary and Tertiary Textbooks, General Nonfiction, History and Africana, Juveniles, Books in Zulu, Xhosa, Tswana & other Southern African languages, Paperbacks, General & Social Science, University, Secondary & Primary Textbooks
1977: 11 titles *Founded:* 1960

Lovedale Press+*, PO Lovedale, 5702 Cape Province Tel: Alice 167/278
Man Dir: R B Raven
Subjects: General Fiction and Nonfiction, Belles Lettres, Poetry, Biography, History, Africana, Books in various Southern African languages
Bookshop: PO Lovedale, 5702 Cape Province; Butterworth, Transkei; Alice Bookshop, Main St, Alice 5700
Founded: 1841

M S A, an imprint of Purnell & Sons (SA) (Pty) Ltd (qv)

McGraw-Hill Book Co (South Africa) (Pty) Ltd+, Hulley Rd, PO Box 371, Isando 1600 Tel: (011) 361181 Cable Add: McGraw-Hill Isando Telex: 89272
Man Dir, Rights & Permissions: Rolf Pakendorf; *Editorial:* Basil van Rooyen; *Sales:* Charles Grobler; *Publicity:* Monica Nelson
Parent Company: McGraw-Hill International Book Co, New York
Subjects: General Nonfiction, Medicine, Science and Technology, General Science, University Textbooks
1977: 13 titles *1978:* 24 titles *Founded:* 1966
ISBN Publisher's Prefix: 0-007

Macmillan South Africa Publishers (Pty) Ltd+, Braamfontein Centre, PO Box 31487, Braamfontein 2017 Tel: 396761 Cable Add: Macbooks Telex: 87280
Man Dir: David Mitchell; *Marketing Dir:* F A Low
Subjects: General Fiction and Nonfiction, Belles Lettres, Poetry, Biography, History, Africana, Reference, Social Science; University, Secondary and Primary Textbooks; Paperbacks
Founded: 1966
Miscellaneous: Firm is a subsidiary of Macmillan Publishers Ltd, UK (qv)
ISBN Publisher's Prefix: 0-86954

John **Malherbe** (Pty) Ltd, Sanso Centre, 8 Adderley St, PO Box 1207, Cape Town 8001 Tel: (021) 431485 Telex: 570261
Man Dir: John Malherbe, A Ashworth (Brit)
Subjects: General Fiction & Nonfiction, Belles Lettres, Poetry, Biography, History, Africana, Philosophy, Juveniles, Paperbacks
Book Club: Pluim Book Club
Founded: 1963
ISBN Publisher's Prefix: 0-86966

Maskew **Miller** Ltd+*, 7-11 Burg St, PO Box 396, Cape Town 8000 Tel: (021) 457731 Cable Add: Maskewmiller Capetown Telex: 576053
Man Dir: J Schoeman; *Editorial Manager:* G J Kruger
Subjects: General Fiction & Nonfiction, Juveniles, Books in Afrikaans and in the African languages, Paperbacks, General Science, Secondary Textbooks
Bookshops: 7-11 Burg St, PO Box 396, Cape Town

Br Offs: Trust Bank Centre, George St, Kimberley; Constantia Centre, 31 Lavinia St, Port Elizabeth; PO Box 11430, Johannesburg
Founded: 1893
ISBN Publisher's Prefix: 0–623

The **Methodist** Publishing House and Book Depot, 52 Burg St, PO Box 708, Cape Town 8000 Tel: (021) 220527 Cable Add: Methodist
Book Steward: M Fearns
Subjects: Religion, Books in Xhosa and Zulu
1978: 8 titles
ISBN Publisher's Prefix: 0–949942

N G Kerk-Uitgewers en Boekhandel*, PO Box 4539, Cape Town 8000
Associate Companies: HAUM (qv); Interkerklike Uitgewerstrust (qv); N G Kerkboekhandel Transvaal (qv); Pro Rege Press (qv)
Subsidiary Companies: Dutch Reformed Church Publishers (qv); Verenigde Protestantse Uitgewers (qv)

N G Kerkboekhandel Transvaal (DRC Publishers), Schoemanstr 260, PO Box 245, Pretoria 0001 Tel: 38401
Man Dir: I B Kasselman; *General Manager:* J Olivier; *Publication Manager:* Dr F A H van Staden MPC
Associate Companies: Interkerklike Uitgewerstrust (qv); HAUM (qv); N G Kerk-Uitgewers en Boekhandel (qv); Pro Rege Press (qv)
Branch Offs: 11 branches in Transvaal and Natal
Subjects: Religion
1978: 21 titles *1979:* 58 titles
Bookshop: Schoemanstr 260, Pretoria

Nasionale Boekhandel Ltd, 386 Voortrekker Rd, PO Box 122, Parow 7500 Tel: 987021 Cable Add: Nasboek
Group Man Dir: H G Jaekel
Subsidiary and Associate Companies: Cape Booksellers Ltd; Drakensberg Boekhandel; Human & Rousseau (qv); Nasionale Boekhandel (SWA) (Pty) Ltd, Namibia (qv); Nasionale Boekwinkels Ltd (qv under Booksellers); Nasou Ltd (qv); Natal Booksellers Ltd, Durban; Oudiovista Productions (Pty) Ltd (qv); Tafelberg Publishers Ltd (qv); Via Afrika Ltd (qv); Via Afrika (Botswana) Ltd, PO Box 332, Gaborone; Via Afrika (Ciskei) Ltd, King Williamstown; Via Afrika (Transkei) Ltd, Umtata; Via Afrika (Kwazulu) Ltd, Umlazi, Durban; Via Afrika (Lebowa) Ltd, Pietersburg; Rygill's Educational Suppliers, Pinetown; Heer Printers (Pty) Ltd, Pretoria
Subjects: General, Educational, Academic, Medicine
Founded: 1950

Nasou Ltd+*, 386 Voortrekker Rd, PO Box 105, Goodwood, Parow 7500 Tel: (021) 987021 Cable Add: Nasou Cape Town Telex: 7751
Man Dir: H G Jaekel; *General Manager, Rights & Permissions:* W R van der Vyer; *Publicity & Advertising Manager:* F Potgieter
Parent Company: Nasionale Boekhandel Ltd (qv for Associated Companies)
Br Offs: PO Box 361, Pietermaritzburg 3200; PO Box 11231, Johannesburg 2000; PO Box 1058, Bloemfontein 9300
Subjects: Reference, University, Secondary & Primary Textbooks
1977: 34 titles *Founded:* 1963
ISBN Publisher's Prefix: 0–625

New World Publications (Pty) Ltd*, 7 Church St, PO Box 4429, Cape Town Tel: (021) 433682 Cable Add: Nucomix Capetown
Man Dir: J Marks; *Sales Manager:* I D Creighton
Subjects: General Nonfiction, Secondary Textbooks

Newman Art, see Christian Publishing Company

Rebecca **Ostrowiak** School of Reading+, PO Box 4106, Germiston South 1411 Tel: 514262
Principals: Rebecca Ostrowiak, Edna Freinkel
Subjects: Remedial reading teaching for children (Series *Teach Any Child to Read*)
Founded: 1965

Oudiovista Productions (Pty) Ltd+, PO Box 122, Parow 7500 Tel: 987021 Cable Add: Oudiovista
Man Dir: H G Jaekel; *Manager:* G J Bezuidenhout
Parent Company: Nasionale Boekhandel Ltd (qv)
Subjects: Educational, Audio-Visual Aids
Founded: 1969

Oxford University Press Southern Africa+, PO Box 1141, Cape Town 8000 (Located at: Top Floor, Harrington Ho, 37 Barrack St, Cape Town 8001) Tel: (021) 457266/7/8/9 Cable Add: Oxonian Capetown
General Manager: N C Gracie; *Editorial:* P Branford; *Sales Manager:* Peter Hyde
Parent Company: Oxford University Press, UK (qv)
Branch Offs: PO Box 41390 Craighall 2024; PO Box 37166, Overport 4067; PO Box 3892, Salisbury, Rhodesia
Subjects: General Fiction and Nonfiction, Belles Lettres, Poetry, Biography, History, Africana, Juveniles; Books in Xhosa, Zulu, Sotho, Tswana, Shona and Afrikaans; General & Social Science, Educational, Textbooks, Music, Prayer Books; Paperbacks
1977: 29 titles *Founded:* 1915
ISBN Publisher's Prefix: 0–19

P S A, an imprint of Purnell & Sons (SA) (Pty) Ltd (qv)

Perskor Books (Pty) Ltd+, 28 Height St, Doornfontein, PO Box 845, Johannesburg 2000 Tel: 285460 Cable Add: Vaderland Telex: 83561, 87483/4
Man Dir: D S van der Merwe; *Editorial, Rights & Permissions:* P V Heerden; *Sales:* N P Fourie; *Production:* A Bothma; *Publicity:* S J Fourie
Orders to: Perskor-Boekwinkel, 4 Banfield Rd, Industria North (Postal Add: PO Box, Maraisburg, 1700)
Subsidiary Company: Perskor Publishers (at above address)
Subjects: Education, Law, General
Bookclubs: Klub 707; Dagbreek-Boekkring; Voortrekker-Boekklub; all at PO Box 4892, Johannesburg 2000
Bookshops: PO Box 102, Maraisburg 1700; PO Box 309, Kroonstad 9500; PO Box 133, Bellville 7530; PO Box 15531 Lynn East 0039; Johannesburgse Boekwinkel, PO Box 91119, Aucklandpark 2006
1977: 300 titles *Founded:* 1940
ISBN Publisher's Prefix: 0–628

David-**Philip** Publisher (Pty) Ltd+, PO Box 408, Claremont, Cape 7735 (Located at: 217 Werdmuller Centre, Claremont, Cape Province Tel: Cape Town 654968/653046 Cable Add: Philipub, Cape Town

Man Dir: David Philip; *Marketing Manager:* Murray Coombes; *Rights and Permissions Dir:* Marie Philip
Subjects: General Fiction & Nonfiction, Belles Lettres, Poetry, Biography, History, Africana, Philosophy, Juveniles, Social Science, Politics, University Textbooks, Reference Books, Paperbacks
1977: 15 titles *1978:* 15 titles *Founded:* 1971
ISBN Publisher's Prefix: 0–908396

Pitman Publishing Co SA (Pty) Ltd, PO Box 41021 Craighall 2024 (Located at: Hyde Park Corner, Jan Smuts Ave, Hyde Park, Johannesburg 2196) Tel: 7885030 Cable Add: Reppub
Man Dir: Adriaan Donker
Associate Company: Pitman Ltd, UK (qv)
Subjects: Reference, Commercial and Business Studies, Secondary Textbooks, Shorthand
1978: 6 titles *1979:* 4 titles
ISBN Publisher's Prefix: 0–273

President Publishers+*, PO Box 488, Krugersdorp 1740
Subjects: General Fiction, Books in Afrikaans

Pretoria Boekhandel Ltd+*, Ben Swartstraat 894, Villieria, Pretoria 0002

Pride, an imprint of Purnell & Sons (SA) (Pty) Ltd (qv)

Pro Rege Press Ltd+*, PO Box 343, Potchefstroom 2520
Associate Companies: N G Kerkboekhandel Transvaal (qv); HAUM (qv); Interkerklike Uitgewerstrust (qv); N G Kerk-Uitgewers en Boekhandel (qv)
Subjects: General Fiction & Nonfiction, Religion, Secondary Textbooks
ISBN Publisher's Prefix: 0–949988

Purnell & Sons (SA) (Pty) Ltd+*, 97 Keerom St, PO Box 4501, Cape Town 8000 Tel: (021) 432662 Cable Add: Purprint Capetown Telex: 575010
Man Dir: J St Clair Whittall; *Sales Manager:* N Hargreaves; *Production:* J B Head
Parent Company: British Printing Corporation, UK (qv)
Associate Companies: Futura Publications Ltd, UK (qv); Macdonald & Jane's Publishers Ltd, UK (qv); Macdonald Educational Ltd, UK (qv); Macdonald Raintree Inc, USA; Phoebus Publishing Co, UK (qv); Purnell Books, UK (qv)
Imprints: MSA, PSA, Pride
Br Off: PO Box 10021, Johannesburg
Subjects: Nonfiction (South African interest), Botany, Natural History
1977: 31 titles *Founded:* 1948
ISBN Publisher's Prefix: 0–86843

Ravan Press (Pty) Ltd+, PO Box 31910, Johannesburg (Located at: 409–416 Dunwell, 35 Jorissen St, Braamfontein 2017 Johannesburg) Tel: 397832/5
Man Dir: Mike Kirkwood
Associate Company: Bateleur Press (qv), Braamfontein
Branch Off: 105 Corbett Pl, PO Box 31910, Braamfontein 2017, Johannesburg
Subjects: Specializes in Socio-Political problems of Southern Africa; also General Fiction & Nonfiction, Belles Lettres, Poetry, Biography, History, Africana, Philosophy, Reference, Religion, Juveniles, Paperbacks, Periodicals
1978: 11 titles *Founded:* 1973
ISBN Publisher's Prefix: 0–86975

314 REPUBLIC OF SOUTH AFRICA

S A Cultural Holdings (Pty) Ltd+, PO Box 9019, Johannesburg 2000 Tel: 219211 Telex: J83031
Man Dir: Arnold Feinstein
Parent Company: Calan Ltd
Subsidiary Companies: Die Kinderkultuurvereniging (Edms) Bpk; Encyclopaedia Britannica (SA) (Pty) Ltd; Ensiklopedie Afrikana (Edms) Bpk; Systems for Education (SA) (Pty) Ltd

S A Kultuurbeleggings, see S A Cultural Holdings Ltd

J L van Schaik (Pty) Ltd+, Libri Bldg, Church St, PO Box 724, Pretoria Tel: (012) 412441 Cable Add: Bookschaik Pretoria
Man Dir: J van Schaik
Subjects: General Fiction & Nonfiction, Belles Lettres, Poetry, Biography, History, Africana, How-to, Study Guides, Reference, Religion, Juveniles, Books in Afrikaans and Southern African languages, Psychology, General & Social Science, University & Secondary Textbooks
Bookshop: Libri Bldg, Church St, Pretoria
1978: 27 titles *Founded:* 1914
ISBN Publisher's Prefix: 0-627

Shuter & Shooter (Pty) Ltd+, 230 Church St, PO Box 109, Pietermaritzburg 3200, Natal Tel: (0331) 28121 Cable Add: Shushoo
Man Dir: M N Prozesky; *Editorial:* L van Heerden; *Sales, Publicity:* J A Wilken; *Production:* J Sharpe; *Rights & Permissions:* Mary Monteith
Parent Company: The Natal Witness (Pty) Ltd
Associate Company: Kwa-Zulu Booksellers (Pty) Ltd, PO Box 100, Imbali
Subsidiary Company: Shuter & Shooter (Transkei) (Pty) Ltd, PO Box 648, Umtata, Transkei
Branch Off: E G Castle, 703/704 Gilhove Chambers, 57 Villiers St, Johannesburg; M Bonga, PO Box 723, King William's Town
Subjects: General Nonfiction, Biography, History, Africana, Books in Zulu and Xhosa, Science and Technology, General and Social Sciences, Primary and Secondary Textbooks
Bookshop: 230 Church St, Pietermaritzburg
1978: 40 titles *1979:* 41 titles *Founded:* 1925
ISBN Publisher's Prefix: 0-86985

Simondium Publishers (Pty) Ltd*, Old Mill Rd, PO Box 3737, Cape Town Tel: (021) 532011 Cable Add: Labels Capetown
Man Dir: W P Loubser
Subjects: General Fiction & Nonfiction

Sondagskool Boekhandel+*, Posbus 396, Bloemfontein 9300

South African Natural History Publications Co*, PO Box 61, Blouberg 7436 Tel: 561598
Man Dir, Editorial, Rights & Permissions: A V Bird; *Sales, Production, Publicity:* H Lutzeyer
Subjects: Flowers, Birds
1977: 1 title *Founded:* 1957
ISBN Publisher's Prefix: 0-620

Ernest **Stanton** Publishers (Pty) Ltd+, PO Box 25803, Denver 2027, Transvaal (Located at: Keartland Press Bldg, Nicholson St, Denver, Transvaal) Tel: 6162100/16 Cable Add: Lithocraft Johannesburg Telex: 80309 Johannesburg
Man Dir: Ernest Stanton; *Sales:* Norman Barber; *Publicity:* Vyn Stanton; *Rights and Permissions:* M V Stanton
Subsidiary Company: (Associated) Professional Book Services (Pty) Ltd
Subjects: South African interest, Biography, Wild Life and Nature Conservation, Gardening, General Literature
1977: 5 titles *Founded:* 1964
ISBN Publisher's Prefix: 0-949997

Struik (Pty) Ltd+*, Corner Wale & Loop Sts, PO Box 1144, Cape Town 8000 Tel: (021) 224204/227456 Cable Add: Dekena Capetown
Man Dir: J W Struik; *Sales Manager:* G Struik; *Publicity/Promotion/Advertising Manager:* G Struik; *Production:* Pieter Struik
Bookshop: Corner Wale & Loop Sts, PO Box 1144, Cape Town 8000
Subjects: Biography, History, Africana, Reprints, Travel
Founded: 1957
ISBN Publisher's Prefix: 0-86977

Tafelberg Publishers Ltd+, 28 Wale St, PO Box 879, Cape Town 8000 Tel: (021) 410127 Cable Add: Boeknuus Cape Town
Man Dir: H G Jaekel; *General Manager, Rights & Permissions:* D J van Niekerk; *Publicity/Promotion/Advertising Manager:* D Saayman
Parent Company: Nasionale Boekhandel Ltd, Parow (qv)
Subjects: General Fiction & Nonfiction, Belles Lettres, Poetry, Biography, History, Africana, How-to, Study Guides, Reference, Religion, Juveniles, Books in Afrikaans, Paperbacks
1978: 105 titles *Founded:* 1950
ISBN Publisher's Prefix: 0-624

Target Publishers (Edms) Bpk*, PO Box 910, Klerksdorp 2570

Technitrain (Pty) Ltd*, 117 Everite Ho, 20 de Korte St, PO Box 31648, Braamfontein Tel: 7242465
Man Dir: W M Smith
Subjects: Vocational Guidance, Science & Technology, University & Secondary Textbooks
Founded: 1974
Miscellaneous: Affiliated with the Argus Group of Newspapers; Eastern Province Herald; SABC

Thomson Publications South Africa (Pty) Ltd, Marcuson Centre, Park & Menton Rds, PO Box 8308 Richmond, Johannesburg 2000 Tel: (011) 7263100
Man Dir: W Corry
Subjects: Reference, Daily/Monthly Bulletins and Journals, Annual/Biennial Buyers' Guides
1977: 7 titles *1978:* 1 title
Miscellaneous: Affiliated to Thomson Newspaper Group

Howard B **Timmins** (Pty) Ltd+, PO Box 94, Cape Town 8000 (Located at: Sanso Centre, 8 Adderley St, Cape Town 8001) Tel: (021) 411228/431485 Telex: 570261
Chairman: Howard B Timmins; *Man Dir:* John Malherbe; *Dirs:* A Ashworth, P Jooste
Subjects: General South African Nonfiction, Biography, History, Books in Afrikaans, Travel, Medicine, Gardening, Cookery
Founded: 1937

Torpis Publishing Co, PO Box 1275, Bloemfontein Tel: (051) 71506
Man Dir: D Pistor

Treffer Uitgewers (Edms) Ltd+*, Posbus 3599, Pretoria 0001

United Protestant Publishers (Pty) Ltd, see Verenigde Protestantse Uitgewers

University of Natal Press, PO Box 375, Pietermaritzburg 3201 Tel: (0331) 63320
Man Dir: Ms M P Moberly
Imprints: Killie Campbell Africana Library (Durban)
Subjects: South African History, Politics, Botany; Natal and Zulu Studies, Africana; General Literature, Reprints
1977: 3 titles *1978:* 4 titles *Founded:* 1947
ISBN Publisher's Prefix: 0-86980

University of South Africa, PO Box 392, Pretoria 0001 Tel: 4402202 Cable Add: Unisa Telex: 3777
Publishing Officer: E van Heerden
Subjects: General Nonfiction, Belles Lettres, Anthropology, Accountancy, Botany, Chemistry, Communications, Criminology, Economics, Education, Fine Arts, Poetry, Biography, History, Africana, Philosophy, Reference, Religion, Theology, Psychology, Science & Technology, Social Science, Geography, Geology, Academic Journals, Library Science, Linguistics, Literature, Law, Mathematics, Music, Physics, Politics, Statistics, University Textbooks
1977: 6 titles *1978:* 15 titles (also large number of textbooks, not for sale to booksellers)
ISBN Publisher's Prefix: 0-86981

University Publishers & Booksellers (Pty) Ltd+, PO Box 29, Stellenbosch 7600 Tel: (02231) 4811/4851 Cable Add: Biblia Stellenbosch
Man Dir: B B Liebenberg
Subjects: General Nonfiction, Juveniles, University & Secondary Textbooks

Valiant Publishers (Pty) Ltd+*, Sandton City, PO Box 78236, Sandton 2146 Tel: 7835012/5 Telex: 83023
Man Dir: F R Metrowich; *General Manager, Rights & Permissions:* A N Keevy
Subjects: General Nonfiction, History, Africana, Reference, Religion, TFH Pet Books
1977: 17 titles *1978:* 9 titles *Founded:* 1975

Varia Books*, PO Box 3868, Alrode 1451 Tel: 8693609 Cable Add: Varia, Alberton
Man Dir: P J Lubbe
Subjects: Educational, Academic
Founded: 1968

Verenigde Protestantse Uitgewers (Edms) Bpk+*, Posbus 1822, Cape Town 8000 Tel: 437618
Man Dir: W J van Zijl
Parent Company: N G Kerk-Uitgewers en Boekhandel (qv)
Associate Company: Dutch Reformed Church Publishers (qv)
Subject: Christian Literature
1977: 8 titles *1978:* 4 titles *Founded:* 1956
ISBN Publisher's Prefix: 0-86997

Via Afrika Ltd+*, PO Box 114, Parow 7500 Tel: (021) 987021 Cable Add: Via Afrika
Manager: G J J Rousseau; *Production Manager:* E R Arnold; *Marketing Manager:* T Priem
Subjects: General Fiction, Belles Lettres, Poetry, Books in Zulu, Xhosa and other Southern African Languages, Science and Technology, General & Social Science, Secondary & Primary Textbooks
1977: 31 titles *Founded:* 1970
Bookshops: Several retail outlets (see under Booksellers)
Miscellaneous: Firm is a subsidiary of Nasionale Boekhandel Ltd (qv)
ISBN Publisher's Prefix: 0-7994

J P van der **Walt** & Seun (Pty) Ltd+*, 80 Bosman St, PO Box 123, Pretoria 0001 Tel: (012) 32341
Man Dir: D H van der Walt; *Sales Manager:* A Christie; *Editorial:* I van der Westhuizen
Subjects: General Fiction & Nonfiction, Philosophy, Reference, Religion, Law, Juveniles, Books in Afrikaans, Paperbacks, University Textbooks
Founded: 1947
Book Clubs: Eike-Boekklub, Keurbiblioteek, Treffer-Boekklub
ISBN Publisher's Prefix: 0-7993

Who's Who of Southern Africa, 47 Sauer St, PO Box 8620, Johannesburg Tel: 8363388
Subjects: Reference, Annuals
Parent Company: Argus Group, Johannesburg

Witwatersrand University Press, 1 Jan Smuts Ave, Johannesburg 2001 Tel: (011) 394011 ext 794
Chairman of Publications Committee: Professor Desmond T Cole; *Publications Officer:* Mrs N H Wilson
Subjects: General Nonfiction, Belles Lettres, Poetry, Biography, History, Philosophy, Reference, Religion, Medicine, Psychology, Science & Technology, Social Science, University Textbooks, Africana, Books in Zulu, Xhosa and other Southern African Languages
1977: 3 titles *1978:* 3 titles *Founded:* 1923
ISBN Publisher's Prefix: 0-85494

Literary Agents

The **International Press** Agency (Pty) Ltd, PO Box 682, Cape Town 8000 (Located at: 44 Howard Centre, Pinelands, Cape Province) Tel: (021) 531926 Cable Add: Inpra Howard Place South Africa
Man Dir: Dr Ursula A Barnett

Book Clubs

Africana Book Society Ltd*, Shop 149, Blue Route, Carlton Centre, PO Box 1071, Johannesburg
Owned by: Books of Rhodesia Publishing Co (Pvt) Ltd, Rhodesia
Subjects: Africana, Hunting, Wildlife

Associated Book Clubs*, PO Box 9909, Johannesburg
Managers: D B Mackenzie, R L Nathan
Subjects: General Books & Records
Members: 130,000

Dagbreek-Boekkring, PO Box 4892, Johannesburg 2000
Owned by: Perskor Books (Pty) Ltd, Johannesburg (qv)
Subject: Fiction

Eike-Boekklub*, 80 Bosman St, PO Box 123, Pretoria
Owned by: J P van der Walt en Seun (Edms) Bpk (Pretoria)
Subject: Children's Books

Keurbiblioteek*, 80 Bosman St, PO Box 123, Pretoria
Owned by: J P van der Walt en Seun (Edms) Bpk (Pretoria)
Subject: Fiction

Klub 707, PO Box 4892, Johannesburg 2000 Tel: 285460
Owned by: Perskor Books (Pty) Ltd, Johannesburg (qv)

Subjects: Fiction: especially Suspense, Espionage, Whodunnits, Thrillers (in Afrikaans)
1978: 12 titles *1979:* 12 titles

Pluim Book Club, PO Box 1207, Cape Town 8000 (Located at: Sanso Centre, 8 Adderley St, Cape Town 8001)
Owned by: John Malherbe (Pty) Ltd (Cape Town)
Subject: Children's Books

Treffer-Boekklub*, 80 Bosman St, PO Box 123, Pretoria
Owned by: J P van der Walt en Seun (Edms) Bpk (Pretoria)
Subject: Fiction

Voortrekker-Boekklub, PO Box 4892, Johannesburg 2000
Owned by: Perskor Books (Pty) Ltd, Johannesburg (qv)
Subject: Fiction

Major Booksellers

Adams & Co Ltd*, 341 West St, PO Box 466, Durban 4000 Tel: (031) 69381/328571/2

Central News Agency Ltd, PO Box 1033, Johannesburg 2000 Tel: (011) 8361711; PO Box 9, Cape Town 8000; PO Box 938, Durban 4000 (and further 200 branches throughout the country)

Exclusive Books (Pty) Ltd, 48 Pretoria St, PO Box 17554, Hillbrow 2038, Transvaal Tel: (011) 6425068 Telex: 8-6579 SA; PO Box 4628, Cape Town 8000 (Located at: Southern Life Arcade, 101 St Georges St, Cape Town 8000) Tel: (021) 226860 Telex: 57-6078 SA

Fogarty's Bookshop*, Main St at Market Sq, Port Elizabeth Tel: (041) 21035

H A U M Academic Bookshop, PO Box 343, Stellenbosch 7600 (Located at: Trust Bank Centre, Andringa Street) Tel: 70385/70315

H A U M Booksellers, 480 Paul Kruger St, PO Box 460, Pretoria 0001 Tel: 36417

Johanesburgse Boekwinkel, PO Box 91119, Aucklandpark 2006

Juta & Co Ltd, PO Box 30, Cape Town 8000 (Located at: Regis Ho, Church St, Cape Town 8001) Tel: (021) 224571; Cnr Pritchard/Loveday Sts, PO Box 1010, Johannesburg 2000 Tel: (011) 8336113; Suite 5b, Mangrove Beach Centre, 91 Somtseu Rd, Durban 4001

Literary Services (Pty) Ltd, PO Box 31361, Braamfontein Tel: 391711

Logans University Bookshop (Pty) Ltd, 227–229 Francois Rd, Durban
Office & Warehouse: 622 Umbilo Rd, Durban 4001 Tel: 354111

Maskew Miller Ltd*, 7–11 Burg St, PO Box 396, Cape Town Tel: (021) 24151; Trust Bank Centre, George St, Kimberley; Constantia Centre, 31 Lavinia St, Port Elizabeth; PO Box 11430, Johannesburg

N G Kerkboekhandel Transvaal, Schoemanstr 260, PO Box 245, Pretoria 0001 Tel: 38401
Subjects: Religion, Books in Afrikaans and English

Nasionale Boekwinkels Bpk, PO Box 122 and 119, Parow 7500 Tel: 987021; PO Box 912, Kimberley; PO Box 2063, Cape Town; PO Box 9898, Johannesburg; PO Box 1715 & 95, Port Elizabeth; 78 Maitland St, PO Box 1047 & 1058, Bloemfontein; Noordstr 11, PO Box 279, East London

Ulrich **Naumann***, Park Gerou 303, Durban Rd/Weg 49, Bellville 7530
Academic and Scientific Booksellers

Perskor Bookshop*, PO Box 102, Maraisburg
Also at: PO Box 309, Kroonstad 9500; PO Box 133, Bellville 7530; Burnettstraat 1072, Hattfield, Pretoria 0083

Pilgrims Booksellers (Pty)*, Old Mutual Centre and Cavendish Sq, PO Box 3559, Cape Town

Van **Schaik's** Bookstore (Pty) Ltd*, Church St, PO Box 724, Pretoria 0001

Shuter and Shooter (Pty), Church St, PO Box 109, Pietermaritzburg Tel: (0331) 28121

C **Struik** Booksellers*, Corner Wale & Loop Sts, PO Box 1144, Cape Town 8000; Shop 2, Norwich Union Ho, 91 Commissioner St, Johannesburg

United Book Distributors (Pty) Ltd, PO Box 17294, Hillbrow 2038 (Located at: Permad House, 28 Betty St, Jeppe, Johannesburg 2094) Tel: (614) 6431/2/3 Telex: 86579 SA
Wholesalers and Distributors

Universitas Books (Pty) Ltd, PO Box 1557, 0001 Pretoria

Via Afrika Book Store, PO Box 9898, Johannesburg
Also PO Box 248, Pietersburg; PO Box 380, Pietermaritzburg; PO Box 107, King William's Town; PO Box 259, Umtata

Major Libraries

Cape Town City Libraries, 30 Chiappini St, Cape Town Tel: 2102036

Central Agricultural Library*, Department of Agriculture & Technical Services, Private Bag X116, Pretoria 0001 Tel: 413111

Centre for Scientific and Technical Information, PO Box 395, Pretoria 0001 Tel: (74) 9111 Telex: 3630 Cable Add: Navorslig
Publicity Dir: J F Herbst
A department of the Council for Scientific and Industrial Research (CSIR), at the same address. Library stock covers Science and Technology

Department of National Education Library, Oranje-Nassau Bldg, Schoeman St, PB X122, Pretoria Tel: 482901
Librarian: Miss J Burrows
Publication: Library News

Durban Municipal Library, PO Box 917, Durban 4000 Tel: 320111
Publications: Annual Report; Accessions List; Booklist; Bookworm (Staff Quarterly Magazine)

Government Archives, Cape Archives Depot, Library*, Queen Victoria St, PB X9025, Cape Town 8000 Tel: 411888 (Branch of Department of National Education)
Archivist: F S van Rensburg

316 REPUBLIC OF SOUTH AFRICA

Government Archives, Natal Archives Depot, Library, 231 Pietermaritz St, PB X9012, Pietermaritzburg 3200 Tel: 24712
Archivist: F Nel

Government Archives, Orange Free State Archives Depot, Library*, 37 Elizabeth St, PB X20504, Bloemfontein 9300 Tel: 72840
Archivist: J W Cronje

Government Archives, Transvaal Archives Depot, Library*, Union Bldgs, Church St, PB X236, Pretoria 0001 Tel: 24971
Archivist: Dr M H Buys

Johannesburg Public Library, Market Sq, Johannesburg 2001 Tel: 8363787
Librarian: Miss L Kennedy
Publications: Annual Report; Municipal Reference Library Bulletin (monthly); Index to South African Periodicals (annual)

Library of Parliament, PO Box 15, Cape Town 8000 Tel: 458165
Chief Librarian: J C Quinton

Royal Society of South Africa Library, University of Cape Town Libraries, Rondebosch 7700 Tel: (021) 698531
Publications: Transactions of the Royal Society of South Africa (irregular)

South African Library, Queen Victoria St, Cape Town 8001 Tel: 431132/433829/432486
Dir: Dr A M Lewin Robinson
Publications: Quarterly Bulletin; Grey Bibliographies; Reprint series

State Library*, Vermeulen St, PO Box 397, Pretoria 0001 Tel: 483920 Telex: SA 3778
Publications: South African National Bibliography; Reprint series; Micrographic series; Contribution to Library Science; Bibliographic series

University of Cape Town Libraries*, Private Bag, Rondebosch 7700 Tel: (021) 698531
Librarian: Jean I Laurenson
Publications: Bibliographical series (irregular); Varia series (irregular)

University of Natal Library*, King George V Ave, Durban 4001 Tel: (031) 352461

University of Pretoria, Merensky Library, Brooklyn, Pretoria Tel: (012) 746071

University of South Africa Library*, PO Box 392, Pretoria Tel: (012) 424011

University of the Witwatersrand Library, 1 Jan Smuts Ave, Johannesburg 2001 Tel: (011) 394011

Library Associations

African Library Association of South Africa, c/o Library, University of the North, Private Bag X5090, Pietersburg
Secretary-Treasurer: Mrs A N Kambule
Publication: Newsletter (quarterly)

South African Indian Library Association*, 7 Ascot St, Durban
Executive Secretary: G H Haffajee

South African Library Association, c/o Ferdinand Postma Library, Potchefstroom University, Potchefstroom 2520
Publications: South African Libraries, Newsletter

Library Reference Books and Journals

Books

Handbook of South African Libraries, The State Library, Vermeulen St, PO Box 397, Pretoria

Journals

Bookworm, Durban Municipal Library, PO Box 917, Durban 4000

The Cape Librarian (text in Afrikaans and English), Cape Provincial Library Service, Hospital and Chiappini Sts, PO Box 2108, Cape Town

Free State Libraries, Orange Free State Provincial Library, PO Box X0606, Bloemfontein

Library News, Department of National Education Library, Oranje-Nassau Bldg, Schoeman St, PB X122, Pretoria 0001

Mousaion II, Department of Library Science, University of South Africa, PO Box 392, Pretoria

Newsletter, South African Library Association, c/o Ferdinand Postma Library, Potchefstroom University, Potchefstroom

Quarterly Bulletin of the South African Library, South African Library, Queen Victoria St, Cape Town 8001

South African Libraries, South African Library Association, c/o Ferdinand Postma Library, Potchefstroom University, Potchefstroom (the official publication of the South African Library Association, published quarterly)

Literary Associations and Societies

Afrikaans Literature Society (ALV)*, PO Box 11422, Johannesburg 2000

Artists' and Writers' Guild of South Africa*, 37-17th St, Parkhurst, Johannesburg 2001

South African **P E N** Centre (Cape)*, Apartment C, 2 Scott Rd, Claremont 7700 Cape Province
Secretary: Adele Naudé

Literary Periodicals

Contrast: South African literary journal (text in English and Afrikaans), South African Literary Journal Ltd, 3 Scott Rd, PO Box 3841, Claremont, Cape Town

Dialogue: a literary annual for young writers, PO Box 102, Wynberg 7824

New Classic, Ravan Press (Pty) Ltd, 508 Diakonia Ho, 80 Jorissen St, PO Box 31134, Braamfontein 2017 (important quarterly literary and cultural magazine, originally published as *The Classic*, edited by Sydney Sipho Sepamla)

Ophir, Ravan Press (Pty) Ltd, 508 Diakonia Ho, 80 Jorissen St, PO Box 31134, Braamfontein (biannual poetry magazine)

Literary Prizes

Afrikaans Literature Society Prize*
To encourage Afrikaans authors, artists and research workers. 300 British pounds. Awarded annually. Enquiries to Afrikaans Literature Society (ALV), PO Box 11422, Johannesburg 2000

Stephen **Black** Prize for Drama, see Department of National Education Literary Prizes

Jochem van **Bruggen** prys vir Prosa, see Department of National Education Literary Prizes

C N A Literary Award*
Established in 1961 for the best original works, one in English and one in Afrikaans, published for the first time during the calendar year of the competition. 2,500 rand each plus a bronze plaque. Awarded annually. Authors must be South African citizens or registered permanent residents of South Africa. Enquiries to Central News Agency Literary Award, PO Box 10799, Johannesburg

Roy **Campbell** Prize for Poetry, see Department of National Education Literary Prizes

Department of National Education Literary Prizes
In the English Section, the names of the prizes awarded are as follows: Stephen Black Prize for Drama; Roy Campbell Prize for Poetry; Pauline Smith Prize for Prose. In the Afrikaans Section, the names of the prizes are as follows: J W F Grosskopf prys vir Drama; Louis Leipoldt prys vir Poesie; Jochem van Bruggen prys vir Prosa. Prizes of 750 and 500 rand are awarded to the authors of the two best entries in each of the two sections. Awarded annually. Enquiries to Secretary for National Education, Private Bag X122, Pretoria 0001

English Association (South African Branch) Literary Prize
For an original unpublished manuscript by a South African citizen or permanent resident of South Africa. Subject, literary form and amount of award vary from year to year. Usually awarded annually. Enquiries to English Association, PO Box 81, Rondebosch 7700

Percy **Fitzpatrick** Medal
For outstanding books for children written in English. Awarded annually. Enquiries to South African Library Association, c/o Ferdinand Postma Library, Potchefstroom University, Potchefstroom 2520

J W F **Grosskopf** prys vir Drama, see Department of National Education Literary Prizes

Katrine **Harris** Award
For outstanding illustrations in South African children's books, regardless of language. Awarded annually. Enquiries to South African Library Association, c/o Ferdinand Postma Library, Potchefstroom University, Potchefstroom 2520

Hertzog Prize
A Prestige Prize for Afrikaans Literature. Prizes are awarded in rotation for Poetry, Drama and Prose. 1,500 rand. Awarded annually. Enquiries to South African Academy of Science and Arts, PO Box 538, Pretoria 0001

W A Hofmeyr Prize
Awarded annually for the best book of a belletristic nature published by Tafelberg, Human & Rousseau, Nasou and Via Afrika; 1000 rand. Enquiries to Nasionale Boekhandel, Voortrekker Rd, PO Box 122, Parow 7500

C P Hoogenhout Award
To encourage the production of outstanding Afrikaans children's books. Awarded annually. Enquiries to South African Library Association, c/o Ferdinand Postma Library, Potchefstroom University, Potchefstroom 2520

Ingrid Jonker Prize*
For the best first volume of poetry in English or Afrikaans written during the two previous years. Awarded alternately for English and Afrikaans poetry. 50 rand. Awarded annually by the panel of critics appointed by the Funds Board of Trustees. Enquiries to Funds Board of Trustees, Pretoria

C J Langenhoven Prize
For outstanding work in field of Afrikaans linguistics. 250 rand. Awarded every three years. Enquiries to South African Academy of Science and Arts, PO Box 538, Pretoria 0001

Louis Leipholdt prys vir Poesie, see Department of National Education Literary Prizes

H R Malan Prize
Awarded annually for the best nonfiction book published by Tafelberg, Human & Rousseau, Nasou and Via Afrika, 1000 rand. Enquiries to Nasionale Boekhandel, Voortrekker Rd, PO Box 122, Parow 7500

Eugène Marais Prize
For a first, or early, work of belles lettres in Afrikaans. 250 rand. Awarded annually. Enquiries to South African Academy of Science and Arts, PO Box 538, Pretoria 0001

Mofolo-Plomer Prize
Initiated by Nadine Gordimer for a South African writer resident in Southern Africa or elsewhere. For a novel or a collection of short stories in English. Enquiries to Mofolo-Plomer Prize Committee, c/o Ravan Press (Pty) Ltd, 409/416 Dunwell, 35 Jorissen St, Braamfontein 2017, Johannesburg

Samuel Edward Mqhayi Prize*
For an original literary work in a South African Bantu language. 100 rand donated by Shell Company. Awarded irregularly. Enquiries to South African National Council for Adult Education, 211 Skinner St, Sunny Side, Pretoria 0002

Perskor Prize for Literature
For the best literary work published in Afrikaans by Perskor. R3,000. Awarded biennially. Enquiries to Perskor Publishers, PO Box 845, Johannesburg 2000

Perskor Prize for Youth Literature
For the best youth work published in Afrikaans by Perskor Press. 3,000 rand. Awarded every second year. Enquiries to Perskor Publishers, PO Box 845, Johannesburg 2000

Reina **Prinsen**-Geerlings Prize for South Africa*
For an outstanding new literary contribution by an Afrikaans author between 20 and 30. 350 guilders. Awarded every three years. Enquiries to Algemeen Nederlands Verbond, PO Box 4543, Cape Town

Radio Plays Prize*
Awarded in alternate years for the best English and Afrikaans play or feature programme written for the radio. 500 rand. Awarded annually. Enquiries to South African National Council for Adult Education, 211 Skinner St, Sunny Side, Pretoria 0002

Scheepers Prize
For the best books written for children. 250 rand. Awarded every three years. Enquiries to South African Academy of Science and Arts, PO Box 538, Pretoria 0001

Olive **Schreiner** Prize for English Literature
For original literary work in English by a promising South African writer and published in South Africa. 250 rand. Awarded annually in one of the following categories: Prose, Poetry, Drama. Enquiries to English Academy of Southern Africa, Ballater House, 35 Melle Str, Braamfontein, Johannesburg 2001, South Africa

Pauline **Smith** Prize for Prose, see Department of National Education Literary Prizes

South African Academy of Science and Arts Prizes
The Academy awards a number of prizes for works in Afrikaans; the following are noted in this section: Hertzog Prize; C J Langenhoven Prize; Eugène Marais Prize; Scheepers Prize; Translation Prize. See individual entries for details. Enquiries to South African Academy of Science and Arts, PO Box 538, Pretoria 0001

Translation Prize
For translation of Belles Lettres from any language into Afrikaans. 250 rand (donated by Nederlandse Bank). Awarded annually. Enquiries to South African Academy of Science and Arts, PO Box 538, Pretoria 0001

Spain

General Information

Language: Spanish (Castilian), Basque and Catalan
Religion: Roman Catholic
Population: 36.7 million
Literacy Rate (1970): 90.1%
Bank Hours: Vary. Generally 0900-1300 or 0900-1600 Monday-Friday; half day Saturday
Shop Hours: Generally 0900-1300, 1700-2000 Monday-Saturday
Currency: 100 centimos = 1 peseta
Export/Import Information: Varying tariffs on books, related to type, binding, language, etc; children's picture books 13% duty, 11% tax; 10% compensatory tax on books in general
Note: Temporary increases of duty effective 30.8.76 (e.g. 13% increased by 6%) and all import duties increased with 20% import surcharge
Most advertising matter free of tariff but have 11% tax. Import licence required; foreign books subject to censorship. Exchange controls
Copyright: UCC, Berne, Florence (see International section)

Book Trade Organizations

Comisión Asesora de Editores de Musica del INLE (Advisory Commission of Music Publishers)*, Apdo 5447, Barcelona 9

Gremio Sindical de Libreros de Barcelona (Association of Barcelona Booksellers)*, Calle Mallorca 272-276, Barcelona 9
Publication: Librería

Instituto Nacional del Libro Español*, Calle Santiago Rusiñol 8, Madrid 3 Tel: (01) 2330802/2330902/2334502
Spanish Publishers' and Booksellers' Association
Secretary: Eduardo Nolla López
Publications: El Libro Español (monthly); Libros Españoles ISBN (annual); Libros y Material de de Enseñanza (annual); Libros Infantiles y Juveniles (biannual); Llibres en Catalá (annual)

Instituto Nacional del Libro Español, Delegación de Barcelona, Calle Mallorca 272-276, Barcelona 3 Tel: (03) 2155650
Barcelona Section of the Spanish Publishers' and Booksellers' Association
Executive Delegate: S Olives Canals
Publications: Guía de Editores de España, Catálogo ISBN, Catalogo de Libros de Ensenanze

Spanish Book Center, Milanesado 21-23, Barcelona 17 Tel: (03) 2039916 Telex: 54675 contb-e
Export organization for all books published in Spain

Book Trade Reference Books and Journals

Books

Guía de Editores de España (Guide to the Publishers of Spain), Spanish Publishers' and Booksellers' Association, Calle Santiago Rusiñol 8, Madrid 3

Guía de Libreros y Distribuidores de España (Guide to the Booksellers and Distributors of Spain), Spanish Publishers' and Booksellers' Association, Calle Santiago Rusiñol 8, Madrid 3

Indice Cultural Español (Spanish Cultural Index), Dirección General de Relaciones Culturales, Ministerio de Asuntos Exteriores, Plaza de la Provincia 1, Madrid 12

Indice de la Producción Editorial Española (Index of Spanish Book Production), Spanish Publishers' and Booksellers' Association, Calle Santiago Rusiñol 8, Madrid 3 (four-year cumulation of *El Libro Español*)

Libros en Venta (Books for Sale); annual supplements including Spanish language book production of the year from all countries. Turner Ediciones Chile 1441, 1° piso, of 3, Buenos Aires

SPAIN

Libros Españoles ISBN (Spanish Books assigned ISBNs), Spanish Publishers' and Booksellers' Association, Calle Santiago Rusiñol 8, Madrid 3

Llibres en Català (Books in Catalan), Spanish Publishers' and Booksellers' Association, Calle Santiago Rusiñol 8, Madrid 3

Journals

Bibliografía Española (Spanish Bibliography), Hispanic Bibliographical Institute, Calle de Atocha 106, Madrid 12

Cuadernos de Bibliografía Española (Notebook of Spanish Bibliography), Hispanic Bibliographical Institute, Calle de Atocha 106, Madrid 12

Librería (Bookselling), Association of Barcelona Booksellers, Calle Mallorca 272-276, Barcelona 9

El Libro Español (The Spanish Book), Spanish Publishers' and Booksellers' Association, Calle Santiago Rusiñol 8, Madrid 3

Publishers

Ediciones **29**, Mandri 41, Barcelona 22 Tel: (93) 2123836
Man Dir: Alfredo Lloreme Diez
Subjects: Fiction, Literature, General Nonfiction
1978: 22 titles *Founded:* 1968
ISBN Publishers Prefix: 84-7175

Ediciones **62** SA, Provenza 278 1°-1a, Barcelona 8 Tel: (93) 2160062
Dir: Romà Cuyàs Sol; *Editorial:* Josep M Castellet; *Production:* Ramon Bastardes; *Publicity:* Eliseu Gil
Associate Company: Ediciones Peninsula (qv)
Subsidiary Company: Distribuciones de Enlace SA
Subjects: General (in Catalan)
1977: 78 titles *1978:* 101 titles *Founded:* 1963
ISBN Publishers Prefix: 84-297

Ediciones **99** SA*, Calle General Martínez Campos 42-Bajo, Madrid 10
Part of Grupo Editorial Guadiana (qv)

Editorial **A E D O S**, Consejo de Ciento 391, Barcelona 9 Tel: (03) 3170141/3012845 Cable Add: Aedos
Man Dir: Juan Badosa
Subjects: Agriculture, Veterinary Science, Sports, How-to, Biography
1977: 16 titles *Founded:* 1939
ISBN Publishers Prefix: 84-7003

Publicacions de l'**Abadia** de Montserrat*
Abadia de Montserrat, Barcelona Tel: 2450303
Shipping Add: Ausias March, 92-98, Barcelona 13
Man Dir: Josep MaassotMuntaner; *Sales, Advertising & Publicity:* Jordi Ubeda; *Rights & Permissions:* Bernabé Dalmau
Subjects: Religion, History, Geography, Biography, Literature, Juveniles, Travel (mostly in Catalán)
1977: 40 titles *Founded:* 1915
ISBN Publishers Prefix: 84-7202

Ediciones **Acervo**, Julio Verne 5-7, Apdo 5319, Barcelona 6 Tel: (93) 212264/2474425
Man Dir: José A Llorens
Subject: General Literature
1978: 23 titles *Founded:* 1954
ISBN Publishers Prefix: 84-70002

Editorial **Acribia**, C Royo 23, Apdo 466, Saragggos Tel: 232089
Man Dir: Pascual López Lorenzo; *Sales, Publicity & Advertising:* Mercedes Marcen
Subjects: Veterinary Science, Agriculture, General Science, Medicine, Oceanography, Marine Biology
1977: 23 titles *1978:* 36 titles *Founded:* 1957
ISBN Publishers Prefix: 84-200

Afha Internacional SA*, Maestro Nicolau 4, Apdo 75, Barcelona 21 Tel: (93) 2507912/3 Cable Add: Afhinter Telex: 52743
Man Dir: José Ma Llovet; *Editorial:* Diego de Herrera; *Sales:* Ramón Bertrand; *Production, Rights & Permissions:* Ulisses Farreras; *Publicity:* Pedro Richard
Parent Company: Ediciones Afha
Subsidiary Company: Editorial Columna
Imprint: Emograph
Subjects: Juveniles, Education
1977: 25 titles *Founded:* 1951
ISBN Publishers Prefix: 84-201

Aguilar SA de Ediciones*, Juan Bravo 38, Madrid 6 Tel: (91) 2763800 Cable Add: Guilarditor
Man Dir: Carlos Aguilar; *Sales Dir:* Jaime Lejarraga; *Rights & Permissions:* Manuel Aguilar
Br Offs:
Argentina (qv); Aguilar Chilena de Ediciones, Santiago, Chile; Colombia (qv); Mexico (qv); Peru (qv); Venezuela (qv)
Subjects: General Fiction, Belles Lettres, Poetry, Biography, History, Music, Art, Philosophy, Reference, Religion, Juveniles, Paperbacks, Medicine, Psychology, Engineering, General & Social Science, Law, Technical, Educational Materials
Bookshops: M Aguilar, Librería General, Serrano 24; Goya 18; Ave Generalísimo 44-46 (all in Madrid)
ISBN Publishers Prefix: 84-03

Editorial '**Alas**', Valencia 234, Apdo 707, Barcelona 7 Tel: (93) 2537506
Subjects: Sports, How-to, Para-psychology, Crosswords, Martial Arts, Periodicals
1977: 42 titles *1978:* 31 titles
ISBN Publishers Prefix: 84-203

Ediciones **Alfaguara** SA, Ave de América 37, Madrid 2 Tel: (91) 4160900/4160860 Cable Add: Guara Madrid Telex: 27575
Man Dir: Jaime Salinas; *Editor-in-Chief:* Casto Fernandez; *Sales:* Libresa SA, Barcelona; *Production:* Antonio Sama; *Publicity:* Ymelda Navajo; *Rights & Permissions:* Helene Couzinie
Subjects: General Fiction, History, Psychology, Social Science, Literature, Art, Architecture, Economics, Sociology, Anthropology, Sciences, Children's Books
1977: 44 titles *1978:* 60 titles *Founded:* 1964
ISBN Publishers Prefix: 84-204

Editorial **Alhambra** SA, Claudio Coello 76, Madrid 1 Tel: (91) 2764209 Cable Add: Edimbrasa
Man Dir: Erich Ruiz Albrecht; *Editorial:* José Ma Esteban Bermúdez; *Sales:* Jose Paulino Perona; *Production:* José Francisco Zambrana; *Publicity:* María Teresa Esteban Fernández; *Rights & Permissions:* Ana Ma Sampedro
Branch Offs: Enrique Granados 61, Barcelona 8; Doctor Albiñana 12, Bilbao 14; Pasadizo de Pernas 13, La Coruña; La Regente 5, Málaga; Avda del Cristo 9, Oviedo; Reina Mercedes 35 (entrada pr Marqués de Luca de Tena), Sevilla 12; General Porlier, SY, Santa Cruz Se Tenerife; Cabillers 5, Valencia 3; Concepcion Arenal, 25 Zaragoza
Subjects: Medicine, General Science, Literature, History, Philosophy, Reference, University, Secondary and Primary Textbooks, Audiovisual Aids, Languages
1977: 72 titles *1978:* 39 titles *Founded:* 1952
ISBN Publishers Prefix: 84-205

Alianza Editorial SA, Milán 38, Apdo 9107, Madrid 33 Tel: (91) 2000045
President: Jose Vergara Doncel; *Editorial:* Javier Pradera; *Sales:* Faustino Linares; *Marketing:* Enrique Folch; *Production:* Ascension Vazquez; *Publicity:* Salvador Navajo; *Rights & Permissions:* Monica Acheroff
Associated Companies: Alianza Editorial Mexicana, Mexico (qv); Distasa, Argentina (qv); Revista de Occidente SA, Madrid (qv)
Branch Off: Mariano Cubí 92, Barcelona 21
Subjects: General Fiction, Belles Lettres, Poetry, History, Music, Art, Philosophy, Political and Social Science, High-priced Paperbacks, Mathematics, General Science
1977: 75 titles *1978:* 81 titles *Founded:* 1959
ISBN Publishers Prefix: 84-206

Ediciones **Altea** SA, General Mola 84, Madrid 6 Tel: (91) 2625300 Cable Add: Edialtea Telex: 43879
Man Dir: Miguel Azaola; *Sales:* Carlos Martínez; *Publicity:* Arturo Gonzalez; *Co-productions:* Juan Ramón Azaola
Subjects: Activity books, Children's Books, Picture Books
1977: 34 titles *1978:* 16 titles *Founded:* 1973
ISBN Publishers Prefix: 84-372

Editorial **Anagrama***, Calle La Cruz 44, Barcelona 17 Tel: (93) 2037652
Man Dir: Jorge de Herralde Grau
Subjects: Literature, Philosophy, Psychology, Social Science, Anthropology
1977: 70 titles *Founded:* 1968
ISBN Publishers Prefix: 84-339

Ediciones **Anaya** SA, Calle Iriarte 4, Madrid 28 Tel: (91) 2468604/5/6 Cable Add: Edinaya Telex: 26825 Edaya E
President: Germán Sánchez Ruiperez; *Man Dir:* Ambrosio María Ochoa Vázquez; *Editorial:* Ramiro Sánchez Sanz; *Rights & Permissions:* José M Delgado de Luque
Br Off: Iriarte 3-4, Madrid 28
Subjects: University, Secondary & Primary Textbooks, Educational Materials
Founded: 1959
ISBN Publishers Prefix: 84-207

Editorial **Aranzadi**, Carlos III, 34, Pamplona Tel: 243112/249950
Man Dir: Estanislao de Aranzadi; *Sales Dir:* Javier de Epalza y Aranzadi
Subject: Law
1978: 18 titles *Founded:* 1929
ISBN Publishers Prefix: 84-7018

Editorial **Argos** Vergara SA, Aragón 390, Barcelona 13 Tel: (03) 2457600 Cable Add: Leargos

President: Enrique Moyá; *Man Dir:* Mario Lacruz; *Editor-in-Chief:* Anne-Marie Comert
Subjects: Fiction, Nonfiction, Reference, Art Books
Bookshop: Librería Editorial Argos, Paseo de Gracia 30, Barcelona 7
ISBN Publisher's Prefix: 84-7017

Editorial **Ariel** SA, Tambor del Bruch s/n, Sant Joan Despi, Barcelona Tel: (93) 3731409
Man Dir: Antonio Comas Baldellou; *Editorial, Rights & Permissions:* Alejandro Argullós Marión; *Sales:* Luis Carlos Sanchez Montoya; *Production & Publicity:* Angel Jasanada París
Associate Company: Editorial Seix Barral SA (qv for subsidiary companies). The two Companies constitute the organization Ariel/Seix Barral Editoriales
Subjects: General and Social Sciences, Psychology, Philosophy, Religion, Economics, History, Literature, Texts in Catalan, Geography, Biography, University Textbooks
1978: 45 titles *1979:* 52 titles *Founded:* 1941
ISBN Publisher's Prefix: 84-344

Asesoría Técnica de Ediciones SA*, Ronda General Mitre 90, Barcelona 90 Tel: (93) 2479133/2477066
Man Dir, Editorial: José Dalmau Salvia; *Sales:* Antonio Dalmau Salvia; *Production:* José Luis Arribas; *Rights & Permissions:* Carmen Eulate Echague
Subsidiary Company: Libroexpress
Subjects: Fiction, Communications, Science Fiction, Classics, Microbiology
1977: 48 titles
ISBN Publisher's Prefix: 84-7442

Asociación para el Progreso de la Dirección (APD)*, Montalban 3, Madrid 14 Tel: (91) 2325487
Dir of Publications: Vidal Pérez Herrero
Subject: Business Administration
ISBN Publishers Prefix: 84-7019

Sociedad de Educación **Atenas** SA, Mayor 81, Apdo 1096, Madrid 13 Tel: (91) 2480127
Subjects: Religion, Education, Psychology, Biography
Miscellaneous: Firm is a subsidiary of Ediciones Sigueme (qv)
ISBN Publishers Prefix: 84-7020

Atika SA*, Fuencarral 138, Madrid 10 Tel: (91) 4485361
Man Dir: Mr Thermolle
Subjects: Technical, How-to, Automobile Manuals
Founded: 1964
ISBN Publishers Prefix: 84-7022

Biblioteca de **Autores** Cristianos*, Mateo Inurria 15, Madrid 16 Tel: 2592800
Editorial: José L García; *Sales:* Eduardo M de Sequera; *Publicity:* Bartolomé P Galmes
Subjects: Theology, Philosophy, History, the Scriptures, Liturgical
1977: 33 titles
ISBN Publisher's Prefix: 84-220

Aymá SA Editora (& Edicions Proa), Tuset 333°, Barcelona 6 Tel: (93) 2000933/200576 Cable Add: Aymol
President: Joan B Cendrós Carbonell
Subjects: General Fiction, Belles Lettres, Poetry, Biography, History, How-to, Music, Art, Philosophy, Religion, Low- and High-priced Paperbacks, Juveniles
1977: 58 titles *1978:* 46 titles *Founded:* 1952
ISBN Publishers Prefix: 84-209

Editorial **Ayuso***, San Bernardo 34, Madrid 8
Subject: Social Sciences
ISBN Publishers Prefix: 84-336

Barral Editores SA, Calabria 235, Barcelona 29 Tel: (93) 3220551
Subjects: General Fiction, Belles Lettres, Poetry, Art, Theatre, Paperbacks
Founded: 1970
ISBN Publishers Prefix: 84-211

Ediciones **Bellaterra** SA*, Felipe de Paz 12, Barcelona 28 Tel: (93) 3390511
Man Dir: Felio Riera Domenech; *Editorial:* Jeannine Rochefort; *Sales:* Angeles Galán Gallego
Subjects: Science & Technology, Social Sciences
1977: 3 titles *Founded:* 1972
ISBN Publishers Prefix: 84-7290

Ediciones **Betis**, Calle Bot 4 bis, Barcelona 2 Tel: (93) 3175844
Man Dir, Editorial, Rights & Permissions: Santiago Subirana; *Sales:* Eugenio Subirana
Subjects: Juveniles, Popular Science, History, Philosophy, Infants
1977: 28 titles *1978:* 28 titles *Founded:* 1939
ISBN Publishers Prefix: 84-7160

Editorial **Biblioteca** Nueva SL, Almagro 38, Madrid 4 Tel: (91) 4100436
Man Dir: Miguel Ruiz-Castillo; *Sales Dir:* José Ruiz-Castillo
Subjects: Belles Lettres, Poetry, Biography, History, Psychology
Founded: 1920
ISBN Publishers Prefix: 84-7030

Editorial **Bibliograf** SA*, Calle de Bruch 151, Barcelona 9 Tel: (93) 2571304/2573158 Cable Add: Biblograf
Man Dir: Antonio Mercadé Olíu
Subjects: Dictionaires, Philology
Founded: 1952
ISBN Publishers Prefix: 84-7153

Editorial **Blume**, Calle Milanesado 21-23, Barcelona 17 Tel: (93) 2042300/04/08 Cable Add: Ediblume Telex: 54675 Contbe; also H Blume Ediciones, Rosario 17, Madrid 5 Tel: (91) 2659200
Man Dir: Siegfried Blume; *Editorial:* José Maria Riaño; *Rights and Permissions:* Rita Blume
Imprints: Ed R Torres, Floraprint, Galaxis SA
Founded: 1965
Subjects: Architecture and Building Construction, Art, History, Politics, Technology, Ecology, Nature Study, Physical and Life Sciences, books in English and Catalan
ISBN Publishers Prefix: 84-7031

Al-**Borak** SA*, Calle General Martínez Campos, 42-Bajo, Madrid 10
Part of Grupo Editorial Guadiana (qv)

Bosch Casa Editorial SA, Calle Urgel 51 bis, Barcelona 11 Tel: (93) 2548437
Man Dir: Agustín Bosch Domenech; *Madrid Representative:* Iber-Amer Madrid
Subjects: Law, Economics, Science & Technology, Philology, General Literature
1978: 40 titles *Founded:* 1934
ISBN Publishers Prefix: 84-7162

Editorial **Bruguera** SA, Camps y Fabrés 5, Barcelona 6 Tel: (93) 2282107 Cable Add: Brugueditor Telex: 52551
Man Dirs: Guillermo Molinas Bruguera, Joaquin Miñano, Consuelo Bruguera; *Editorial:* Jorge Gubern, Ricardo Rodrigo, Miguel Pellicer; *Sales:* Emilio Martinez; *Production:* Guillermo Molinas Carreño; *Rights & Permissions:* Ute Kórner de Moya
Associated Company: Nueva Linea
Subsidiary Companies: Argentina; Colombia; Mexico; Venezuela (qqv)
Branch Offs: Ave del Mediterráneo 7, Madrid 7; Canarias 2-A, Bilbao 14; Luis Oliag 71-73, Valencia 6; Elda 44, Alicante; Juan M Rodríguez Correas 3-9, Seville; Durán y Borrell 24-26, Barcelona 6
Subjects: General Fiction, Belles Lettres, Biography, History, How-to, Juveniles; Paperbacks
Bookshop: Librería Proa SL, Rambia Cataluña 72, Barcelona
1977: 310 titles *1978:* 380 titles *Founded:* 1954
ISBN Publishers Prefix: 84-02

Editorial **Bruño***, Marqués de Mondéjar 32, Madrid 28 Tel: (91) 2460607/06/05
Man Dir: Juan Santaeulalia
Subjects: Secondary & Primary Textbooks, Education, Communication
1977: 58 titles *Founded:* 1882
ISBN Publishers Prefix: 84-216

Burulan, SA de Ediciones*, Avenida de Francia 4, POB 754, San Sebastian Tel: (93) 426220, (93) 416829 Cable Add: Burulan Telex: 36228 Camino-E Ref Burulan
Subjects: Encyclopedias, Various Publications for Children and Juveniles

Editorial **C E D E L** (Centro de Difusión del Libro)+, Mallorca 257, Barcelona 8 Tel: (93) 2156039
Man Dir: Jose O Avila Monteso
Subjects: Hygiene, Health and Body Culture, Psychology, Magic and the Occult, Radio, Television, Electronics, Electroplating; General Technical; General Literature
Bookclub: Club de Amigos del Libro (qv)
1978: 50 titles *Founded:* 1959
ISBN Publisher's Prefix: 84-352

Editorial **Cantabrica** SA*, Plaza Conde de Aresti 51°, Bilbao Tel: (044) 217197
Man Dir: Mrs Rosario Fernandez Urcelay
Br Offs: Calle Marqués de Sentemenat 55-57, Barcelona; Calle O'Connell, 43 bajo, Madrid
Subject: Juveniles
Founded: 1960
ISBN Publishers Prefix: 84-221

Luis de **Caralt** Editor SA, Rosellón 246, Barcelona 8 Tel: (93) 2156516 Cable Add: Edinoguer Barcelona Telex: 52534
Man Dir: Emilio Ardévol; *Editorial:* José Mas Godayol; *Sales:* Ignacio Medrano; *Production:* Manuel Tort; *Publicity:* Ramón Hervás; *Rights & Permissions:* María A de Miquel
Orders to: Norildis (qv under Major Booksellers)
Associate Company: Editorial Noguer (qv)
Subjects: General Fiction and Nonfiction, History, Art, Medicine, Geography, Paperbacks
1977: 117 titles *1978:* 70 titles *Founded:* 1942
ISBN Publishers Prefix: 84-217

Casamajo-Lappas*, Avenida Carlos III 94 5° 4a, Apdo 12050, Barcelona 14 Tel: 8703908/62
Subjects: High class Books, Calendars etc

Editorial **Castalia***, Zurbano 39, Madrid 10 Tel: (91) 4198940/4195857
Man Dir: Amparo Soler; *Sales Dir:* Federico Ibáñez

320 SPAIN

Subjects: Literature, Criticism, Classics, Philology
Founded: 1941
Miscellaneous: Specializes in editions of the classics
ISBN Publishers Prefix: 84-7039

Ediciones **Cátedra** SA, Don Ramón de la Cruz, Apdo 50512, Madrid Tel: (91) 4011200 Cable Add: Grupedi
Man Dir: José Luis Torres; *Rights & Permissions:* Gustavo Dominguez
Orders to: Grupo Editorial SA, Don Ramón de la Cruz 67, Madrid 1
Subjects: Literature, Criticism, Humanities, Linguistics, Art
1977: 24 titles *Founded:* 1974
ISBN Publisher's Prefix: 84-376

La Editorial **Católica** SA*, Mateo Inurria 15, Madrid 16 Tel: (91) 2592800 Cable Add: Edica
Dirs: Mariana de Rioja, Fernández de Mesa; *Sales Manager:* Eduardo Masip; *Advertising & Publicity:* Vicente Lasheras
Subjects: Philosophy, Religion, Theology
Founded: 1912
ISBN Publishers Prefix: 84-720

Ediciones **Ceac** SA*, Via Layetana 17, Barcelona 3 Tel: (93) 3197400 Cable Add: Ediceac
Man Dirs: Juan Martí, José Menal; *Advertising & Publicity Dir:* J M Quesada; *Foreign Sales:* J L Martin
Subjects: Technical, Arts & Crafts, Homecrafts & Domestic Science
Founded: 1954
ISBN Publishers Prefix: 84-329

Editorial **Científico Médica***, Vía Layetana 53, Barcelona 3 Tel: (93) 3186832
Man Dir: Eugeniano Barrera San Martín; *Chief Editor:* Dr Enrique Sierra Ruiz
Distributor: Científico Médica Dossat SA, Plaza de Santa Ana 9, 1°, Madrid 12
Subjects: Medicine, Psychology, Veterinary Science, Engineering, Architecture, Technical Subjects
Founded: 1915
ISBN Publishers Prefix: 84-224

Ciudad Nueva*, Luis Cabrera 12, III Dcha, Madrid 2
Parent Company: Città Nuova Editrice, Rome (qv)
Associate Companies: Nouvelle Cité, France (qv); Neue Stadt, Federal Republic of Germany (qv); Niewe Stad, St Stephanusstraat 11, Nijmegen, Netherlands; Cidade Nova, Rua Pio xii, 274 Paraiso Sao Paulo, Brazil; New City, UK (qv)

Compañía Bibliográfica Española SA*, Sánchez Pacheco 52-54, Madrid 2 Tel: (91) 4155300
Man Dir: Rafael Agulló
Subjects: Biography, History, Music, Art, Philosophy, Religion, Reference, Linguistics, Juveniles, Social Science, Textbooks, Educational Materials
Founded: 1951
ISBN Publisher's Prefix: 84-326

Alberto **Corazón** Editor*, Roble 22, Madrid 15 Tel: (91) 2704378
Man Dir: Alberto Corazón; *Sales Dir:* José Miguel García
Subjects: Literature, History, Philosophy, Social Sciences, University Textbooks
Founded: 1969
ISBN Publisher's Prefix: 84-7053

Ediciones **Cristiandad***, Huesca 30, Madrid 20 Tel: (91) 2701636
Subjects: Religion, History
ISBN Publisher's Prefix: 84-7057

Editorial **Crítica** SA, Calle de la Cruz 58 1° 1a, Barcelona 34 Tel: 2049311
Man Dir: Xavier Folch y Gonzalo Pontón
Orders to: Deu y Mata 98, Barcelona
Parent Company: Ediciones Grijalbo (qv)
Subjects: Social Sciences, Politics, Current Affairs, Marxism, Philosophy
1977: 26 titles *1978:* 40 titles *Founded:* 1976
ISBN Publisher's Prefix: 84-7423

Ediciones **Cultura** Hispánica*, Ave de los Reyes Católicos 4, Madrid 3 Tel: (91) 2440600 (287, 285)
Subjects: Literature, Biography, History, Art, Economics, Law, Philology, Social Science
ISBN Publisher's Prefix: 84-7232

Editorial **D O P E S A** (Documentacion Periodistica SA)*, Cardenal Reig s/n, Edificio Grupo Mundo, Barcelona 28 Tel: (93) 3342000
Man Dir: Juan Agut; *Editorial:* Mauricio Waquez; *Sales, Publicity:* Pablo Bordona BA; *Production:* Manuel Gallego; *Rights & Permissions:* José Planas
Subjects: General
Bookshop: Libreria Grop, Ave infanta Carlota 37, Barcelona 15
1977: 50 titles *1978:* 180 titles *Founded:* 1969
ISBN Publisher's Prefix: 84-7235

Ediciones **Daimon** — Manuel Tamayo*, Provenza 284, Barcelona 8
Subjects: Art, History, How-to, Reference, Medicine, Cinematography, Photography, Sexology, Astrology, Philosophy, Science
1977: 60 titles
ISBN Publisher's Prefix: 84-231

Ediciones **Danae** SA*, Calle Muntaner 81, Barcelona 11 Tel: (93) 2543700
Sales: José Maria Minguet; *Production:* Julieu Bermelle; *Rights & Permissions:* Antonio Balagne
Subjects: Belles Lettres, History, Geography, Social Science, Art, Religion, Technical, Encyclopaedias, Juveniles, General Culture
Founded: 1963
ISBN Publisher's Prefix: 84-7060

Editorial **De Vecchi** SA, Balmes 247, Barcelona 6 Tel: (93) 2171854/217858 Cable Add: Deveditor Telex: 51042 Deve E
Man Dir: Giovanni de Vecchi
Branch Off: Hermosilla 114, Madrid 9
Subjects: How-to and Practical Books generally, Animals, UFO investigation
Founded: 1967
ISBN Publisher's Prefix: 84-315

Editorial de **Derecho Financiero**, see EDERSA

Editorial Revista de **Derecho Privado**, see EDERSA

Ediciones **Destino** SL, Consejo de Ciento 425, Barcelona 9 Tel: (93) 2462305
Man Dir: José Vergés
Subjects: General Fiction, Art Books, History
Bookshop: Libreria Ancora y Delfín, Ave Generalísimo Franco 564, Barcelona 11
Founded: 1942
ISBN Publisher's Prefix: 84-233

Diafora SA*, Lauria 118, Barcelona Tel: (93) 2577889
Subjects: Cartographic Studies; Audio-Visual aids; Geography

Didactronia SA*, Programmed Learning Systems, General Moscardó 5, Madrid 20 Tel: (91) 2333175

Man Dir: Raúl Rispa Marquez
Subject: Educational Materials
Founded: 1973
ISBN Publishers Prefix: 7336

Dilagro SA*, Editorial-Librería, Comercio 40, Apdo 114, Lérida Tel: 233480
Man Dir: Jorge Marimón; *Sales Dir:* Antonio Miñano
Subjects: Agriculture, History and Customs of the region of Lérida
Bookshops: Librería Ténica, Gral Brito 1; Librería Universitaria, Ave Cataluña 7
1977: 2 titles *1978:* 3 titles
ISBN Publishers Prefix: 84-7234

Grupo Editorial **Distein**–CEAC–Timun Mas, see Timun

Ediciones **Don Bosco***, Paseo San Juan Bosco 62, Barcelona 17 Tel: (93) 2037408
Subjects: Technical works on Printing, Graphics, Typography, Technical Drawing, Computers and Electronics
ISBN Publishers Prefix: 84-236

Doncel*, Perez Ayuso 20, Madrid 2 Tel: (91) 4257400 Cable Add: Edidoncel
Man Dir: Juan Van Halen Acedo
Subjects: Juveniles, Secondary & Primary Textbooks
Founded: 1959
Bookshops: Librería Doncel, Ave Calvo Sotelo 7, Zaragoza and José Ortega y Gasset 71, Madrid 6
ISBN Publishers Prefix: 84-325

Editorial **Dossat** SA, Plaza de Santa Ana 9°, Madrid 12 Tel: (91) 4334000 Telex: 42572 DOATE
Man Dir, Sales and Other Offices: Eugeniano B San Martín
Branch Off: Via Layetana 53, Barcelona 3
Subjects: Medicine, Engineering, Science in General, University Textbooks
ISBN Publishers Prefix: 84-237

E D E R S A (Editoriales de Derecho Reunidas SA)*, Caracas 21, Apdo 4032, Madrid 4 Tel: (91) 4101862/4199623 Cable Add: Revipriv
Man Dir: Narciso Amorós Rica
Imprint: Ediciones Pegaso
Subjects: Biography, History, Philosophy, Social Science, Law, Technical, University Textbooks
Founded: 1900
ISBN Publishers Prefix: 84-7130
Miscellaneous: Company comprises Editorial Revista de Derecho Privado; Editorial de Derecho Financiero; Ediciones Pegaso

E D H A S A (Editora y Distribuidora Hispano-Americana SA), Diagonal 521, 2°, Barcelona 29 Tel: (93) 2395104
Man Dir: Jaime Rodrigué
Subjects: Literature, History, Essays
1978: 50 titles
ISBN Publishers Prefix: 84-350

E U N S A (Ediciones Universidad de Navarra SA)*, POB 396, Pamplona (Located at: Plaza de los Sauces, 1 & 2 Barañain, Pamplona) Tel: (948) 256850 Cable Add: EUNSA Pamplona
Man Dir: Francisco Salvadó; *Administrator:* José M Echalare; *Editorial:* Rosario Ruiz; *Sales:* Robert Kimball; *Production:* Luis Ma Echeverría; *Publicity:* Luis Felipe Bansá; *Rights & Permissions:* Eugenia Puyales
Subjects: Architecture, Business Administration, Economics, Education, History, Journalism, Law, Literary Criticism, Medicine, Natural Sciences, Nursing, Paperbacks (Biblioteca NT), Philosophy, Religion, Social Science, Social

Work, Theology
1977: 100 titles *Founded:* 1967
ISBN Publishers Prefix: 84–313

Edaf Ediciones y Distribuciones SA, Jorge Juan 30, Madrid 1 Tel: (91) 2263500
Bookshop: Librería Edaf, Jorge Juan 30, Madrid 1
Subjects: History, Philosophy, Juveniles, Reference, Textbooks
ISBN Publishers Prefix: 84–7166

Edica SA, Calle Mateo Inurria 15, Apdo 466, Madrid 16 Tel: (91) 2592800 Cable Add: Edica Telex: 27727
Dir: Dr José Luis Gutierrez Garcia; *Sales:* Dr Eduardo Masip de Sequera
Subjects: Theology, Asceticism, Mysticism, History, Philosophy, Hagiography, Pocket Editions
1978: 46 titles

Ediciones Iberoamericanas SA (EISA)*, Oñate 15, Madrid 20 Tel: (91) 2795804 Cable Add: Asepe
Dir: Rafael Ordoñez Miranda
Subjects: Social Sciences, Medicine, Biography, Religion, Psychology, Law, others
Founded: 1949
ISBN Publishers Prefix: 84–7084

Edigraf, Editorial Vilcar y Gráficas Hamburg SA*, Tamarit 130, Barcelona 15 Tel: (05) 3255550
Man Dir: Francisco Vilar
Subject: Juveniles
ISBN Publishers Prefix: 84–7066

Editora Nacional, Calle Torregalindo 10, Madrid 16 Tel: (91) 2508600
Man Dir: Tomas Zamora Rodriguez
Subjects: Poetry, History, Art, Essays, Literature, Law
1977: 54 titles *1978:* 53 titles *Founded:* 1937
ISBN Publishers Prefix: 84–276

Emograph, an imprint of Afha Internacional SA (qv)

Editorial **Espasa-Calpe** SA, Apdo 547, Madrid 34 (Located at: Carretera de Irún, km 12,200 (variante de Fuencarral))
Tel: (91) 7343800 Cable Add: Espacalpe
Man Dir: Fermín Vargas Lázaro
Branch Offs: Espasa-Calpe SA, Diputación 251, Barcelona 7; Espasa-Calpe SA, General Salazar 1, Bilbao 12 (both in Spain); Espasa-Calpe Argentina SA, Tacuarí 328, Buenos Aires, Argentina; Espasa-Calpe Mexicana SA, Pitágoras 1139, Mexico City 12, Mexico; Espasa Calpe Ecuatoriana CA, Manuel Larrea y Asunción 239, Quito, Ecuador; Espasa Calpe Colombiana Ltda, Calle 40 num 21-23, Bogota DE, Colombia
Subjects: General Fiction, Belles Lettres, Biography, History, How-to, Music, Art, Philosophy, Reference, Religion, Juveniles, Paperbacks, Medicine, Psychology, Law, Technical, University Textbooks
Founded: 1925
Bookshops: Casa del Libro, Ave José Antonio 29, Madrid 13; Material de Enseñanza, Barquillo 23, Madrid 4
ISBN Publishers Prefix: 84–233

Editorial **Espaxs** SA*, Calle Rosellón 132, Barcelona 36 Tel: (93) 2530706 Cable Add: Editespaxs
Subject: Medicine
Bookshops: Librería Espaxs, Calle Rosellón 132, Barcelona 36; Librería Espaxs, Calle Fernando el Católico 57, Zaragoza; Libreria Espaxs, Calle Zaragoza 5, Cadiz
ISBN Publishers Prefix: 84–7179

Editorial **Everest** SA*, Apdo 339, León (Located at: Carretera León-Coruña, Km 5 León) Tel: (987) 235904 Cable Add: Everest León Telex: 89916
Man Dir: José Antonio López Martínez; *Administrative Dir:* Rafael Siguienza Benaquero
Subsidiary: Everest Libros SA, Apdo 339, León-España
Subjects: Belles Lettres, History, How-to, Juveniles, Engineering, Technical, Secondary & Primary Textbooks, Tourist Guides, Paperbacks, Educational Materials
Founded: 1958
ISBN Publishers Prefix: 84–241

Editorial **Fher** SA*, Gordoniz 44, 6a planta, Apdo 362, Bilbao 2 Tel: (044) 4318000/4325090 Cable Add: Gerfu Telex: 32195
Man Dir: Juan José Fuentes; *Editorial:* José Luis Ayarzagüena
Subject: Juveniles
Founded: 1941
ISBN Publishers Prefix: 84–243

Editorial **Fontanella** SA, Escorial 50, Barcelona 24 Tel: (93) 2131731
Man Dir: F Fortuny Comaposada; *Permissions:* C Lopez
Subjects: Social and Political Science, Education, Psychology, Sexology, Religion, Philosophy, History, Economy, Biography
1977: 39 titles *1978:* 32 titles *Founded:* 1962
ISBN Publishers Prefix: 84–244

Heraclio **Fournier** SA*, Heraclio Fournier 19, POB 94, Vitoria Tel: 251100 Cable Add: Fournier Telex: 35510
Subjects: High Quality Illustrated Books in Fields of Art, History, Science, General Knowledge etc

Fragua Editorial*, Gaztambide 77 & Andres Mellado 64, Madrid 15 Tel: (91) 2442430/4497315/2431595
Man Dir: Mariano Muñoz Alonso
Subjects: Linguistics, Philosophy, Communications, Political Science
Bookshop: Librería Augustinus
Founded: 1971
ISBN Publishers Prefix: 84–7074

Editorial **Fundamentos**, Caracas 15, Madrid 4 Tel: (91) 4199619/4195584
Man Dir: Juan Serraller Ibañez; *Permissions:* Cristina Vizcaino
Subjects: Social Sciences, Philosophy, Psychology, Psychiatry, Sexology, History, Theatre, Literature, Cinema, Low-priced Paperbacks
1977: 38 titles *1978:* 30 titles
ISBN Publishers Prefix: 84–245

Ediciones **Gaisa** SL*, Gran Via Marques del Turia 64, Valencia Tel: (96) 3339321/3333976 Cable Add: Gaisa
Man Dir: Manuel Mas Santacreu
Subjects: Juveniles, Encyclopaedias, Multi-volume Collections
Founded: 1960
ISBN Publishers Prefix: 84–7077

La **Galera** SA Editorial, Ronda del Guinardó 38, Barcelona 25 Tel: (93) 2557991/2360203
Man Dir: Roman Doria Forcada
Subjects: Pre-School and Infant Teaching texts, Children's Books, Education
1977: 26 titles *1978:* 51 titles *Founded:* 1965
ISBN Publishers Prefix: 84–246

Ediciones **Garriga** SA, París 143, Barcelona 36 Tel: (93) 2306825/2393547
Man Dir: Xavier Garriga Jové

Subjects: Art, Archaeology, Ancient History, Religion, Technical (Nautical)
Founded: 1957
ISBN Publishers Prefix: 84–7079

Geocolor SA, Travesera de Gracia 15 3°-2°, Barcelona 21 Tel: 2009489
Man Dir, Editorial: Enric Gras P; *Sales:* Matt Areny; *Production:* Lidia Beltran; *Publicity:* Xavier Gras S
Subjects: Tourism, Art, Archaeology, Biography, Cookery, Magic
1978: 21 titles *1979:* 20 titles *Founded:* 1977
ISBN Publisher's Prefix: 84–7424

Editorial Gustavo **Gili** SA, Rosellón 87–89, Barcelona 29 Tel: (93) 2591400 Cable Add: Gusto Barcelona
Man Dir: Gustavo Gili; *Sales:* Ramón Pascual; *Production:* Andres Martinez
Associate Companies: Ediciones G Gili SA Argentina (qv); Editorial Gustavo Gili Ltda, Chile (qv); Editorial Gustavo Gili Ltda, Colombia (qv); Editorial Gustavo Gili de Mexico SA, Mexico (qv)
Branch Offs: Alcántara 21, Madrid 6; Marqués de Valladares 47, 1, Vigo; Colón de Larreátegui 14, 2, Bilbao 1; Madre Rafols 17, Seville 11 (all in Spain)
Subjects: Architecture, Art, Communication and Technology in general
Founded: 1902
ISBN Publishers Prefix: 84–252

Editorial **Gredos** SA, Sánchez Pacheco 81, Apdo 2076, Madrid 2 Tel: (91) 4157408/4156836
Man Dirs: Mr Calonge, Mr Escolar, Mr Yebra, Mr Oliveira
Subjects: Philology, Criticism, Classical Literature, Literary History, Dictionaries
ISBN Publishers Prefix: 84–249

Ediciones **Grijalbo** SA, Deu y Mata 98, Barcelona 29 Tel: 3223753 Cable Add: Edigrijalbo Telex: 53940 egri e
President: Juan Grijalbo Serres; *General Manager:* José M Vives; *Rights & Permissions:* Ana Dexeus
Subsidiary Companies and Branch Offs: Ediciones Junior, Editorial Critica — both in Barcelona; Editorial Grijalbo, Mexico; Distrib. Exclusiva Grijalbo, Peru; Juan Grijalbo, Editor, Uruguay; Grijalbo SA, Venezuela; Grijalbo SA, Argentina; Grijalbo Boliviana Ltda, Bolivia; Distrib. Exclusiva Grijalbo, Colombia; Grijalbo Centroamericana y Panama, Costa Rica; Grijalbo & Cia Ltda, Chile; Editorial Grijalbo Ecuatoriana Ltda, Ecuador
Subjects: General Fiction & Nonfiction, Biography, Philosophy, History, Politics, Religion, Psychology, Technology, Art, Social Science
1978: 96 titles *1979:* 80 titles *Founded:* 1962
ISBN Publishers Prefix: 84–253

Artes Gráficas **Grijelmo** SA*, Uribitarte 4, Bilbao 1 Tel: (344) 4239628 Telex: 31209 aggc e
Man Dir, Rights & Permissions: Federico Guillermo Grijelmo Ribechini; *Editorial:* Amancio Gerardo Grijelmo Ribechini; *Sales:* Juan Santiago Grijelmo Ribechini
Subsidiary Companies: Ediciones Deusto SA (qv); Urmo SA de Ediciones (qv); Ediciones Moreton (qv)
Br Off: Barcelona, Madrid
Subjects: Art Books, Appointment Diaries

Ediciones **Guadarrama**, Alcalá 144, Madrid 9 Tel: (91) 4021642 Cable Add: Edirrama
Man Dir: Francisco Gracia Guillen;

Advertising Dir: Silverio Ruiz Daimiel
Subjects: General Fiction, Nonfiction, Belles Lettres, Music, Art, Philosophy, Paperbacks
1978: 14 titles *Founded:* 1955
ISBN Publishers Prefix: 84–250

Grupo Editorial **Guadiana** SA*, Calle General Martínez Campos 42–Bajo, Madrid 10 Cable Add: Guadisa
Man Dir: Gabriel Camuñas
Subjects: Social Science, History, Business Administration
Founded: 1967
Miscellaneous: Firm is a holding company of Guadiana de Publicaciones SA, Al-Borak SA & Ediciones 99 SA
ISBN Publishers Prefix: 84–251

Editorial **Herder** SA, Provenza 388, Barcelona 25 Tel: (93) 2577700 Cable Add: Herder
Man Dir: Antonio Valtl Friedl
Branch Offs: Editorial y Librería Herder, AveCallao 565, Buenos Aires, Argentina; Herder Editorial y Librería, Calle 12, No 6/89, Apdo Aereo 6855, Bogotá, Colombia
Subjects: Philosophy, Theology, Religion, Medicine, Psychology, Social Science, Reference Works, Economics, Languages, University & Secondary Textbooks, Atlases
Bookshop: Librería Herder, Balmes 26, Barcelona 7
1978: 81 titles *Founded:* 1943
ISBN Publishers Prefix: 84–254

Editorial **Hispano Europea***, Bori y Fontestá 6, Barcelona 6 Tel: (93) 2397023
Man Dir, Editorial, Publicity: J Prat Ballester; *Sales:* J Carrió Sarrato; *Production:* J Madneño Machado
Subjects: Business Management, Sports, Social Science, Industrial Processes, General Technology
1977: 26 titles *Founded:* 1956
ISBN Publishers Prefix: 84–255

Hrvatska Revija*, San Juan Bosco 62, Apartado Correos 14030, Barcelona 17 Tel: 2037408
Man Dir, Editorial: Vinko Nikolić
Subjects: Politics, History, Literature, Sociology, Memoirs; Periodical — *Hrvatska Revija* (in Croatian)
1977: 4 titles *Founded:* 1951
ISBN Publisher's Prefix: 84–399

Publicaciones **I C C E***, Calle Eraso 3, Madrid 28 Tel: (91) 2557200
Man Dir: E Olcina
Subjects: Education, Psychology, Tests, History, Religion, Social Sciences
1977: 18 titles *Founded:* 1970
ISBN Publishers Prefix: 84–7278

Ibérico Europea de Ediciones SA, Serrano 44–3°, Madrid 1 Tel: (91) 2253527/2261578/2754492
Subjects: Biography, How–to, Music, Art, Social Science, Business Management
Founded: 1966
ISBN Publishers Prefix: 84–256

Iberlibros — Unidad de Exportación*, Magallanes 25, Madrid 15 Tel: (91) 2764391
Publisher: Angel Orbegozo
Subjects: Human Sciences, Religion, Technical, School Texts, Dictionaries

Editorial **Index** (Tormes, SL), Comandate Zorita 13–6°, Madrid 20 Tel: 2349150/2544980
Man Dir: R L Ortueta
Orders to: Hernani 17/19, Madrid 20 Tel: 234376
Subjects: Science & Technology
1977: 25 titles *Founded:* 1965
ISBN Publishers Prefix: 84–7087

Instituto de Estudios de Administración Local, Publicaciones, Joaquín García Morato 7, Madrid 10
Dir: Gregorio Burgueño Alvarez
Subjects: Public Administration, Urbanism, City Planning, Periodicals
ISBN Publishers Prefix: 84–7088

Instituto de Estudios Politicos*, Plaza Marina Española 8, Madrid 13 Tel: (91) 2415000, 2418300/09
Distributor: LESPO, Calle Arriza 16
Subjects: Law, Politics, History, Social Science, Philosophy
Founded: 1939
ISBN Publishers Prefix: 84–259

Ediciones **Instituto Pontificio** San Pío X*, Ave Cardenal Herrera Oria 242, Apdo 54027, Madrid 35 Tel: (91) 7399151
Man Dir: Eduardo Malvido Miguel; *Editorial:* Serafín Tapia Nevado; *Sales:* José Luis Peralta García; *Production:* Rafael Pascual
Subjects: Theology, Pedagogy, Psychology, Religion
Bookshop: Librería La Salle, Bocángel 15, Madrid 28
1977: 13 titles *Founded:* 1964
ISBN Publishers Prefix: 84–7221

Ediciones y Publicaciones de **Insula**, Benito Gutiérrez 26, Madrid 8 Tel: (91) 2435415
Man Dir: Enrique Canito Barrera; *Publicity:* A Muñoz Canito
Subjects: Fiction, Poetry, Literary Studies, Criticism, Essays
Bookshop: Insula, Librería de Ciencias y Letras, Benito Gutiérrez 26, Madrid 8
1977: 10 titles *1978:* 20 titles *Founded:* 1944
ISBN Publishers Prefix: 84–7185

Ediciones **Istmo**, General Pardiñas 26, Madrid 1 Tel: (91) 2263127
Man Dir: José Antonio Llardent Viciana; *Sales Dir:* Deogracias González; *Publicity Dir:* Leoncio Martín
Subjects: History, Reference, Social Science, Philosophy, Literature, University Texts
1978: 6 titles *Founded:* 1969
ISBN Publishers Prefix: 84–7090

Editorial **Jims**, Calle Regás 7–9, Barcelona 6 Tel: (93) 2188800 Cable Add: EDITOJIMS
Man Dir, Editorial, Publicity: Antonio Jimenez Sánchez; *Sales:* Teresa Jimenez Sayo; *Production:* Luis Jimenez Sayo
Subject: Medicine
1977: 25 titles *1978:* 17 titles *Founded:* 1956
ISBN Publishers Prefix: 84–7092

Editorial **Jover** SA, San Pedro Matir 18, Barcelona 12 Tel: (93) 2185216
Subjects: Educational Materials
ISBN Publishers Prefix: 84–7093

Editorial **Juventud** SA, Provenza 101, Apdo 3, Barcelona 29 Tel: (93) 2392950/3212100/2398383 Cable Add: Juventud
Man Dirs: Pablo Zendrera, José María Zendrera
Associated Company: Distr del Pacifico, Jiron Camaná 953, Lima, Peru
Subsidiary Companies: Editorial Juventud Argentina (qv); Editorial Juventud Ltda, Colombia (qv)
Subjects: General Fiction, Biography, History, How–to, Music, Art, Nautical, Travel, Pocketbooks, Textbooks, Reference, Juveniles, Paperbacks
1977: 148 titles *1978:* 119 titles *Founded:* 1923
ISBN Publishers Prefix: 84–261

Editorial **Kairos** SA, Numancia 110, Barcelona 29 Tel: (93) 2303746/2505166
Man Dir: Salvador Pániker; *Editorial, Rights & Permissions:* Carmen Tord; *Sales:* José Miralles; *Production, Publicity:* Pilar Tomás
Subjects: Philosophy, Religion, Psychology, Reference, General and Social Science
1977: 12 titles *Founded:* 1966
ISBN Publishers Prefix: 84–7245

L E D A (Las Ediciones de Arte), Riera San Miguel 37, Barcelona 6 Tel: (93) 2284029
Man Dir: Daniel Basilio Bonet
Subjects: Art and Craft techniques, Technical drawing
1977: 3 titles *1978:* 2 titles *Founded:* 1942
ISBN Publishers Prefix: 84–7095

Editorial **Labor** SA, Calabria 235–239, Barcelona 15 Tel: (93) 3220551 Cable Add: Edilabor Telex: (51130) 1600091
Man Dir: Francisco Gracia Guillen
Branch Offs: Argentina; Brazil; Colombia; Ecuador; Mexico; Venezuela (qqv)
Subjects: General Fiction & Nonfiction, Reference, Art, Law, Medicine, Science & Technology
Founded: 1915
ISBN Publishers Prefix: 84–335

Editorial **Laia**, Calle Constitucion 18–20, Barcelona 14 Tel: (93) 3328408
Man Dir: Josep Verdura Tenas; *Editorial:* Alfonso Carlos Comin Ros; *Sales:* Frederic Pagès; *Production:* Montserrat Corral; *Publicity:* Àngels Jové; *Rights & Permissions:* Pilar Esteve
Orders to: Itaca, SA Distribuciones Editoriales, Lopez de Hoyos 141, 5°, Madrid 2
Subjects: General Nonfiction, Social Sciences, Politics, Literature, Essays, Psychology, Pedagogy
1977: 95 titles *1978:* 77 titles *Founded:* 1972
ISBN Publishers Prefix: 84–7222

Editorial **Linosa-Linomonograph** SA*, Calle Riera de San Miguel 9, Barcelona 6 Tel: (93) 2285504/03/02
Man Dir: José Chimenos Reig; *Sales Dir:* José Antonio Chimenos Calderon; *Publicity Dir:* Ma Mercedes Chimenos Calderon; *Advertising Dir:* Elena Isabel Gil Fornas
Subjects: Fiction, Literature, History, How–to, Reference, Social Science, Juveniles
Founded: 1968
ISBN Publishers Prefix: 84–7097

Editorial **Lumen***, Ramón Miquel y Planas 10, Barcelona 17 Tel: (93) 2043496/2042139
Man Dir: Esther Tusquets
Subjects: General Fiction, Belles Lettres, Biography, History, Music, Art, Juveniles, Social Science, Paperbacks
Founded: 1939
ISBN Publishers Prefix: 84–264

Editorial **Magisterio** Español SA, Calle de Quevedo 1, Madrid 14 Tel: (91) 2287900 Cable Add: Magisterio Telex: 44259 EM E
Man Dir: Juliana Congosto Gonzalez; *Editorial:* José María Díez Manteca; *Rights & Permissions:* Ma del Carmen Núñez Amador
Subjects: Education, Fiction, Essays, Philosophy, Pedagogy
Bookshop: Calle Cervantes 18, Madrid 14; Calle Ecuador 3, Barcelona 29
Founded: 1866
ISBN Publishers Prefix: 84–265

Editorial **Marbán***, Hilarión Eslava 55,
Madrid 15 Tel: (91) 2433767/2444673
Man Dir, Editorial: Jose Marban Gonzalez;
Sales, Production, Publicity: Jose M
Marban Corral
Subjects: Medicine, Physiology
1977: 10 titles *Founded:* 1949
ISBN Publishers Prefix: 84-7101

Marcombo SA de Boixareu Editores+, Ave
José Antonio 594-1°, Barcelona 7 Tel: (93)
3180079
Dir: Josep Ma Boixareu Vilaplana;
Editorial: José Ma Boixareu Ginesta; *Sales:*
Juan Plans Comas; *Production:* José Costa
Ardiaca; *Publicity:* José Romero González;
Rights & Permissions: José Deckler Martí
Subsidiary Company: Boixareu Editores
SA, Ave José Antonio 594-2°, Barcelona 7
Branch Off: Marcombo-Boixareu Editores,
Plaza de la Villa 1, Madrid 12
Subjects: Technology, Science, Automation,
Economics, Accounting, How-to, University
and Secondary Textbooks, Electronics,
Mathematics
Bookshop: Librería Hispano Americana,
Ave José Antonio 594
1977: 88 titles *1978:* 56 titles *Founded:*
1949
ISBN Publishers Prefix: 84-267

Editorial **Marfil** SA, Plaza de Emilio Sala 3,
Alcoy Tel: 541746/540233 Cable Add:
Marfil
Sales: Rafael Ortiz Botí
Parent Company: Papeleras Reunidas SA
Subjects: Secondary & Primary Textbooks
Founded: 1947
ISBN Publishers Prefix: 84-268

Editorial **Marin** SA, Calle Nicaragua 85-95,
Barcelona 29 Tel: (93) 3216800 Cable Add:
Marinedi
Man Dirs: Manuel Marin Correa, Luis
Marin Correa; *Editorial, Rights &
Permissions:* Manuel Marin Correa; *Sales:*
Luis Marin Correa; *Production:* Manuel
Marin Bruna
Associate Company: Durvan SA de
Ediciones, Colón de Larreátegui 13, Bilbao
Branch Offs: Ave Belgrano 3715, 1210
Buenos Aires, Argentina; Carrera 15
no 32-41, Bogota DE, Colombia;
Anaxágoras 1400, Mexico 13 DF, Mexico;
San Rafael 1400, Santurce, PR 00909,
Puerto Rico
Subjects: Art Books, Reference, Medicine,
Nonfiction, Encyclopedias, Children's Books
Founded: 1900
ISBN Publishers Prefix: 84-7102

Ediciones **Marova** SL, Viriato 55,
Madrid 10 Tel: (91) 4486856/4487355
Man Dir: Germán Alonso Fernández;
Publicity & Advertising Manager: Mariano
Moreno
Subjects: Religion, Psychology, Education
1977: 40 titles *Founded:* 1956
ISBN Publishers Prefix: 84-269

Editorial **Marsiega** SA, E Jardiel Poncela 4,
Madrid 16 Tel: (91) 2598364
Parent Company: Propaganda Popular
Católica (PPC) (qv)
1978: 10 titles

Ediciones **Martínez** Roca SA, Ave José
Antonio 774, 7a planta, Barcelona 13
Tel: (93) 2251576
Man Dirs: Francisco Martínez Roca,
Manuel Martínez Roca; *Production:* Sergio
Puyol; *Permissions:* Manuel Martínez
Alsinet
Subjects: General Fiction & Nonfiction,
Science & Technology, Human & Social
Sciences, Chess, Occult Sciences, Science
Fiction
1977: 90 titles *1978:* 98 titles *Founded:*
1965
ISBN Publishers Prefix: 84-270

Ediciones **Mensajero**, Ave de las
Universidades 13, Apdo 73, Bilbao 7
Tel: (044) 4454261 Cable Add: Mensajero
Man Dir: José Velasco; *Editorial,
Production:* Jesús Leguina; *Sales:* Juan
Aguirre; *Publicity:* Alvaro Sánchez
Branch Offs: Templarios 12, Barcelona 2;
EAPSA, Velázquez 28, Madrid 1
Subjects: Social Science, Religion,
Philosophy, Education, How-to,
Psychology, Juveniles
1977: 73 titles *1978:* 62 titles *Founded:*
1915
ISBN Publishers Prefix: 84-271

Editorial Luis **Miracle** SA*, Calle
Sicilia 402, Barcelona 25 Tel: (93)
2581800/9 Cable Add: Micle
Editorial: Josefina Vera Vera
Subjects: Anthropology, Philosophy,
Education, Economics, Social Science,
Business, Psychology, History, Religion,
Encyclopedia
Founded: 1929
ISBN Publishers Prefix: 84-7109

Editorial **Molino**, Calabria 166,
Barcelona 15 Tel: (343) 2434769 Cable
Add: Molino Barcelona
Man Dir: Luis del Molino Mateus; *Sales &
Advertising Dir:* Pablo del Molino Sterna;
Permissions: L A del Molino
Subjects: Juveniles, Popular Paperbacks,
Cookery, Children's books, Education
1978: 64 titles *Founded:* 1933
ISBN Publishers Prefix: 84-272

Editorial **Moll**, Torre del Amor 4, Apdo
142, Palma de Mallorca Tel: (071)
971224176/971224472
Man Dir: Francisco Moll
Subjects: Fiction, Literature, Biography,
History, Art, Reference, Social Sciences,
Secondary & Primary Textbooks, Natural
Science
Bookshop: Libros Mallorca, Fortuny 5,
Palma de Mallorca
1977: 36 titles *1978:* 56 titles *Founded:*
1934
ISBN Publishers Prefix: 84-273

Montaner y Simon SA, Aragón 255, Apdo
322, Barcelona 7
Subjects: General Literature, History, Belles
Lettres, Reference, Dictionaries,
Encyclopedias, Geography, Scientific and
Technical
ISBN Publishers Prefix: 84-274

José **Montesó** — Editor*, Vía Augusta
251-253, Barcelona 17 Tel: (93) 2301739
Man Dir: José M Montesó
Br Off: Calle Paraná 480, Buenos Aires,
Argentina
Subjects: How-to, Engineering, Technical,
University Textbooks
Founded: 1928
ISBN Publishers Prefix: 84-7186

Ediciones **Morata** SA, Mejía Lequerica 12,
Madrid 4 Tel: (91) 4480926 Cable Add:
Moratedi
Man Dir: Flora Morata
Subjects: Psychology, Medicine, Pedagogy,
Philosophy, Psychiatry, Sexology,
Sociology, Politics, Mathematics, University
Textbooks
1977: 14 titles *1978:* 16 titles *Founded:*
1920
ISBN Publishers Prefix: 84-7112

Ediciones **Moreton** SA*, Espartero 10,
Bilbao 9 Tel: (094) 4239169
Man Dir: C Moretón; *Sales:* Victoria Peña;
Publicity & Advertising: Maria Saturnina
Abón
Subjects: Literature, Biography, History,
Music, Art, Reference (in luxury and multi-
volume editions)
Founded: 1964
ISBN Publishers Prefix: 84-7113

Mundi-Prensa Libros SA, Castelló 37,
Apdo 1223, Madrid 1 Tel: (91)
2754655/2760253 Cable Add: Mundipren
Man Dir: Pedro Hernández; *Editorial,
Publicity:* José Ma Hernández; *Sales:*
Alfonso Hernández
Subjects: Agriculture, Technology, Ecology,
Livestock, University & Secondary
Textbooks
Bookshops: Librería Mundi-Prensa, Castelló
37, Apdo 1223, Madrid 1; Librería Agrícola,
Fernando VI, 2, Madrid 4
1977: 10 titles *1978:* 10 titles *Founded:*
1948
ISBN Publishers Prefix: 84-7114

Editorial La **Muralla**, Constancia 33,
Madrid 2 Tel: (91) 4161371/4153687/
4159148
Man Dir: Lidio Nieto; *Sales Dir:* Pilar
Jiménez; *Publicity, Permissions:* Ma
Antonia Casanova
Subjects: Art, Literature, Geography,
History, Religion, Technology, Life and
Culture, Biology, all in books with slides for
visual education, Primary and University
Textbooks
1979: 286 titles *Founded:* 1968
ISBN Publishers Prefix: 84-7133

Editorial **Musica** Moderna, Antonio
Carmona Reverte, Calle Marqués de Cubas
6, Madrid 14 Tel: (91) 2215593
Editor and Dir: Antonio Carmona Reverte
Subject: Music
1978: 2,000 titles *Founded:* 1935

Ediciones **Naranco** SA*, Sta Susana 4-6,
Apdo 542, Oviedo Tel: 215768
Subjects: Photo-strip Editions of Don
Quixote and The Bible; Animals; Art;
Scientific Guides to Spanish Provinces;
Juveniles; La Fauna Europea (European
fauna) (8 vols); weekly parts editions of
major collections

Narcea SA de Ediciones, Dr Federico Rubio
89 & 91, Madrid 20 Tel: (91) 2546484
Subjects: Education, Psychology, Pedagogy,
Religion, Juveniles, Textbooks
1978: 66 titles
ISBN Publishers Prefix: 84-277

Ediciones **Nauta** SA, Loreto 16,
Barcelona 29 Tel: (343) 2392204 Cable
Add: Edinauta Telex: 54495 sele e
Man Dir: José Luis Ruiz de Villa Macho
Subjects: General Fiction and Nonfiction,
Classics, Art Books, Reference
1977: 12 titles *1978:* 15 titles *Founded:*
1962
ISBN Publishers Prefix: 84-278

Neguri Editorial SA (Editorial
Cartográfica), Juan Ajuriaguerra 10-1°,
Bilbao 9 Tel: (94) 4233070
Man Dir: José Ignacio Zarza Stuyk
Subjects: Atlases, Agendas, Plans of
Spanish Cities

Bookshop: Librería Deusto, Calle O'Donnell 43, Madrid 9
1979: 17 titles *Founded:* 1960
ISBN Publishers Prefix: 84-85085

Editorial **Noguer** SA, Paseo de Gracia 96, Barcelona 8 Tel: (93) 2156516 Cable Add: Edinoguer Barcelona Telex: 52534
Man Dir: Emilio Ardevo; *Editorial:* José Mas Godayol; *Sales:* Ignacio Medrano; *Publicity:* Ramon Hervas; *Rights & Permissions:* Maria A de Miquel; *Production:* Claudio Gancho
Orders to: Norildis (qv under Major Booksellers)
Associate Company: Luis de Caralt Editor SA (qv)
Subjects: General Fiction and Nonfiction, Belles Lettres, Biography, History, Encyclopaedias, Art, Juveniles, Paperbacks
1977: 128 titles *1978:* 50 titles *Founded:* 1949
ISBN Publishers Prefix: 84-279

Nostromo Editores SA*, Antonio Arias 15, Madrid 9 Tel: (91) 2747485
Man Dir: Mauricio d'Ors; *Sales Dir:* J A Molina Foix; *Publicity & Advertising:* Diego Lara; *Permissions:* Mauricio d'Ors
Subjects: Fiction, Literature, Literary Studies, Biography
Founded: 1974

Editorial **Nova Terra***, Canalejas 65, Barcelona 14 Tel: (93) 3342350
Man Dir: Antonio Munné
Subjects: Religion, Philosophy, Psycholoy, Sex Education, Juveniles, Social Science
1977: 23 titles *Founded:* 1963
ISBN Publishers Prefix: 84-280

Oikos-Tau SA Ediciones, Montserrat 12-14, Vilassar de Mar, Apdo 5347, Barcelona Tel: (93) 7590791
Man Dir, Editorial: Jordi Garcia-Bosch; *Sales:* Climent Garcia-Bosch; *Production, Rights & Permissions:* Jordi Garcia-Jacas
Subjects: Scientific and Technical, Economics, Marketing and Management, Agriculture, Geography, Education, History, Politics, Psychology, Architecture, Town Planning
1977: 21 titles *1978:* 25 titles *Founded:* 1963
ISBN Publishers Prefix: 84-281

Ediciones **Omega** SA*, Casanova 220, Barcelona 11 Tel: (93) 2392328
Man Dir: Gabriel Paricio Fonts
Subjects: Science & Technology, Agriculture, Business Administration, University textbooks
ISBN Publishers Prefix: 84-282

Alfredo **Ortells** Ferriz, Sagunto 5, Valencia 9 Tel: (06) 3651549/3650786
Man Dir: Alfredo Ortells Ferriz
Subjects: Infants and Juvenile, Children's Classics, Popular Knowledge series
1977: 12 titles *1978:* 14 titles *Founded:* 1952
ISBN Publishers Prefix: 84-7189

P P C (Propaganda Popular Católica)*, E Jardiel Poncela 4, Apdo 19049, Madrid 16 Tel: (91) 2592300 Cable Add: Pepece
Man Dir: José Ma Burgos; *Sales Dir:* Catalina Jaume; *Publicity & Advertising:* Pedro Candanedo
Subsidiary Company: Editorial Marsiega SA, Jardiel Poncela 4, Madrid 16
Subjects: Religion, Philosophy, Textbooks
Founded: 1955
Bookshops: Retail outlets throughout Spain (see under Booksellers)
ISBN Publishers Prefix: 84-288

Pala SA, Paseo de los Olmos 5 (Parque Bidebieta), San Sebastian Tel: 398780
Subjects: Children's, Juvenile, Comics, Reference Works, Cinema, Parapsychology

Editorial **Paraninfo** SA, Magallanes 25, Madrid 15 Tel: (91) 4463350
Man Dir: Alfonso Mangada Sanz; *Sales Dir:* Manuel Montalbán Beltrán
Subjects: Science & Technology, Data Processing & Computation, Business Administration, How-to, Secondary & University Textbooks
Bookshops: Librería Paraninfo, Magallanes 25; Meléndez Valdés 65, Madrid 15
1977: 80 titles *1978:* 93 titles *Founded:* 1948
ISBN Publishers Prefix: 84-283

Instituto **Parramon**, Ediciones, Calle Lepanto 264, Apdo 2001, Barcelona 13 Tel: (93) 2457002/3
Man Dir: José Ma Parramón; *Sales:* José Mira del Rio
Subjects: Art, Photography, Drawing (Instruction), Languages, Reference
1977: 12 titles *1978:* 30 titles *Founded:* 1958
ISBN Publishers Prefix: 84-342

Ediciones **Partenon**, Paseo de la Habana 56, Madrid 16 Tel: (91) 2505498 Cable Add: Partenón Madrid
Man Dir: Rafael Torres Gorriz
Subjects: Literature, Language and Philology, Social Science, University Textbooks
Founded: 1969
ISBN Publishers Prefix: 84-7119

Ediciones **Paulinas***, Carretera de La Coruña, Km 16 800, Las Rozas, Madrid Tel: (91) 6371000
Subjects: Biography, Philosophy, Psychology, Education, Religion
ISBN Publishers Prefix: 84-285

Editorial **Paz** Montalvo, Jorge Juan 127, Madrid 9 Tel: (91) 4019722
Man Dir: José Fernando de Paz; *Advertising:* José Luis Fernández
Subject: Technical literature on all aspects of medicine, ophthalmology, psychiatry, pediatrics, biochemistry and associated fields
1977: 7 titles *1978:* 6 titles *Founded:* 1947
ISBN Publishers Prefix: 84-7121

Editorial **Pediátrica***, Mayor de Gracia 102, Barcelona 12 Tel: (93) 2174996
Man Dir: Anselmo Garrido
Subject: Medicine
1978: 8 titles *Founded:* 1969
ISBN Publishers Prefix: 84-7193

Ediciones **Pegaso**, see EDERSA

Ediciones **Peninsula**, Provenza 278 1°-1a, Barcelona 8 Tel: (93) 2160062
Dir: Romà Cuyàs Sol; *Editorial:* Josep M Castellet; *Production:* Ramon Bastardes; *Publicity:* Eliseu Gil
Associate Company: Edicions 62 SA (qv)
Subsidiary Company: Distribuciones de Enlace SA
Subjects: General (in Castilian)
1977: 27 titles *1978:* 34 titles *Founded:* 1963
ISBN Publisher's Prefix: 84-297

Ediciones **Pirámide** SA, Don Ramón de la Cruz 67, Apdo 50512, Madrid 1 Tel: (91) 4011200 Cable Add: Grupedi
Man Dir: Jose Luis Torres; *Rights & Permissions:* Esther Rincón Quemada, Sergio Pelaez, Maurico S Arrabal
Orders to: Grupo Editorial SA, Don Ramón de la Cruz 67, Madrid 1

Subjects: Economics, Business, Science and Technology, Law
1979: 120 titles *Founded:* 1974
ISBN Publisher's Prefix: 84-368

Editorial **Planeta** SA*, Córcega 273, Barcelona 8 Tel: (93) 217550 Cable Add: Ediplan
Man Dir, Editorial: José Manuel Lara Hernández; *Sales:* José Miguel García Piriz; *Production:* José Grasa; *Publicity:* Rafael Abella
Br Offs: Editorial Planeta Argentina SAIC, Viamonte 1451, Buenos Aires, Argentina; Planeta Colombiana, Editorial, Carrera 7-A, No 13-41 Mezzanine, Bogotá, Colombia; Editorial Planeta Chilena, Bombero Augusto Salas 1361-5, Santiago, Chile; Editorial Planeta Mexicana SA, Vallarta 21, 1er piso, Mexico City 4, Mexico; Planeta Venezolana, Edif Pigalle, Ave Leonardo da Vinci, Colinas de B Monte, Apdo 51285, Caracas, Venezuela
Subjects: General Fiction & Nonfiction
Founded: 1958
ISBN Publishers Prefix: 84-320

Playor, Santa Polonia 7, Madrid 14 Tel: (91) 2306097 Telex: 42252 IVSAE
Subjects: Art, Linguistics, Literature, Spanish and Cuban Studies, Illustrated Juvenile
1977: 37 titles *1978:* 48 titles
ISBN Publishers Prefix: 84-359

Plaza y Janés SA, Editores, Virgen de Guadalupe 21-33, Esplugas de Llobregat, Barcelona Tel: (93) 3710200
Man Dir: Carlos Plaza de Diego
Subjects: General Fiction & Nonfiction, Classics, Paperbacks
ISBN Publishers Prefix: 84-01

Ediciones **Poligrafa** SA*, Balmes 54, Barcelona 7 Tel: (93) 2220794
Sales: Juan P Cortina, Juan de Muga
Subject: Art Books, mainly of the works of Spanish artists, with text in several languages
ISBN Publishers Prefix: 84-313

Editorial **Pomaire** SA, Ave Infanta Carlota 114, Barcelona 29 Tel: (93) 2501363
Man Dir: José Manuel Vergara
Br Offs: Argentina; Chile; Colombia; Mexico; Uruguay; Venezuela (qqv)
Subjects: General Fiction & Nonfiction
1977: 40 titles *Founded:* 1957
ISBN Publishers Prefix: 84-286

Ediciones José **Porrúa** Turanzas SA*, Cea Bermúdez 10, Madrid 3 Tel: (91) 2542344/2541466
Man Dir, Editorial: José Porrúa Venero; *Sales:* Mauricio Maroto Maroto; *Production:* Constantino García Garvía; *Rights & Permissions:* Enrique Porrúa Venero
Subsidiary Company: North American Division, 1383 Kersey Lane, Potomac, MG 20854, USA
Subjects: History of Mexico and Latin America, Literature
Bookshop: Cea Bermúdez 10, Madrid 3
1977: 14 titles *1978:* 16 titles *Founded:* 1958
ISBN Publishers Prefix: 84-7317

Editorial **Pórtic**, Ave Marqués de Argentera 17, Barcelona 3 Tel: 3196684
Man Dir: Jordi Fornas; *Administration and Sales:* Salvador Lhimona
Subjects: Religion, Politics, Essays, Poetry & Prose-poetry, Novels, Memoirs (in Catalan)

Bookshops: Llibreria Claris, Vía Layetana 82, Barcelona 10
1977: 15 titles *1978:* 23 titles
ISBN Publishers Prefix: 84-7306

Editorial **Prensa** Española*, Serrano 61, Apdo 43 and 6004, Madrid 6 Tel: (91) 2758148
Dir: Rogelio González-Ubeda
Subjects: General Fiction & Nonfiction
Founded: 1905
ISBN Publishers Prefix: 84-287

Ediciones **Prometeo***, Universidad 3, Valencia 3 Tel: (96) 3213012
Man Dir: Pilar Tortosa Domingo; *Sales Dir:* Ma Luisa Sagreras
Subjects: Fiction, Literature, Geography & Travel, Philosophy
Founded: 1966
ISBN Publishers Prefix: 84-7199

Ediciones de **Promoción** Cultural SA*, Rocafort 256-258, Barcelona 15 Tel: (93) 2590140 Cable Add: Edsprocusa
Man Dir: J Ma Mas Solench
Subjects: Social Sciences, Education, General Science & Technology, University Textbooks
Founded: 1972

Selecciones del **Reader's Digest** (Iberia) SA, Calle Telémaco 3, Madrid 27 Tel: (91) 7420011 Cable Add: Readigest Telex: 27407
Director General: Mario A Freude; *Editorial, Rights & Permissions:* Joaquín Amado; *Sales:* Ivo Duchacek; *Production:* Alfredo Latour; *Publicity:* Xavier Muntañola
Parent Company: The Reader's Digest Association Inc, 750 Third Ave, New York, NY 10017, USA
Branch Off: Barcelona
Subjects: Education, Pocket editions, General Interest, Atlases
Book Club: Biblioteca de Selecciones
1977: 8 titles *Founded:* 1952
ISBN Publisher's Prefix: 84-7142

Editorial **Reus** SA*, Preciados 23, Madrid Tel: (91) 2213619/2223054
Man Dir: Rafael Martinez Reus
Subjects: Law and General Culture
Bookshop: Librería Reus, Calle de Preciados 6, Madrid
Founded: 1852
ISBN Publishers Prefix: 84-290

Editorial **Reverté** SA, Calle Encarnación 86-88, Apdo 1237, Barcelona 24 Tel: (93) 2194353 Cable Add: Edirever
Dirs: Pedro Reverté Gil, Felipe Reverté Planells; *Editorial:* Juan Sala Inglabaga; *Sales:* Magin Hortal Samsó; *Rights & Permissions:* Andres Doria Dexeus
Associate Companies: Editora Reverté Ltda, Brazil (qv); Editorial Reverté Colombiana SA, Colombia (qv); Editorial Reverté Mexicana SA, Mexico (qv); Editorial Reverté Venezolana SA, Venezuela (qv)
Branch Offs: Ave Angel Gallardo 613, Buenos Aires 5, Argentina
Subjects: Engineering, General Science, University & Secondary Textbooks
Founded: 1947
ISBN Publishers Prefix: 84-291

Revista de Occidente SA, Milán 38, Madrid 33
Man Dir: José V Doncel
Associate Company: Alianza Editorial SA, Madrid (qv)

Subjects: History, Philosophy, Political & Social Science
Founded: 1923
ISBN Publishers Prefix: 84-292

Ediciones **Rialp** SA*, Preciados 34, Madrid 13 Tel: (91) 2311004
Subjects: Belles Lettres, Poetry, History, Music, Art, Philosophy, Religion, Textbooks, Engineering, General & Social Science, High-priced Paperbacks
Founded: 1945
ISBN Publishers Prefix: 84-321

Ediciones **Rodas** SA*, Donoso Cortés 39, Madrid 15 Tel: (91) 2548641 Telex: 42710
Man Dir: José Manuel Zañartu; *Literary Agent:* International Editors' Co, Rambla Cataluña 39, Barcelona
Subjects: General Fiction, Essays, Juveniles, How-to
1977: 7 titles *Founded:* 1972
ISBN Publishers Prefix: 84-347

Victor **Sagi** Servicios Editoriales, Av Generalisimo 614, Barcelona 29 Tel: (93) 3220053 Telex: 54254
Man Dir: C H Knapp; *Sales:* Eva Alsina
Parent Company: Victor Sagi Communications Group
Subjects: Cinema, Art, Photography, Health, General Interest
1977: 2 titles *1978:* 2 titles *Founded:* 1977
ISBN Publisher's Prefix: 84-85186

Sagitario SA*, De Ediciones y Distribuciones, Vía Layetana 180 4°, Barcelona 9 Tel: (93) 2154942
Man Dir: Bernardo Almenar Ibarra
Subjects: Literature, Science, Technology
Founded: 1960
ISBN Publishers Prefix: 84-7136

Editorial **Sal Terrae**, Geuvara 20, Apdo 77, Santander Tel: 212617
Man Dir: Manuel Gutiérrez
Subjects: Religion, Philosophy, Parapsychology, Essays, Biography, History, Juveniles, Textbooks
1977: 31 titles *1978:* 24 titles *Founded:* 1919
ISBN Publishers Prefix: 84-293

Salvat Editores SA*, Mallorca 41-49, Barcelona 15 Tel: (93) 2303607 Telex: 53132
Man Dir: Manuel Salvat; *Sales Dir:* Juan José Deiros García; *Permissions:* Julián Viñuales Solé
Br Offs: Salvat Editores Argentina SA; Salvat Editores Mexicana SA; Salvat Editores Venezuelana SA, Edif Arauca, Gran Avenida, Apdo 51106-105, Caracas, Venezuela
Subjects: Reference, History, Art, Music, Literature, Medicine, Veterinary Science, Agriculture, Science, Technology, Geography, Paperbacks
Founded: 1869
ISBN Publishers Prefix: 84-345

Salvat SA de Ediciones*, Arrieta 25, Pamplona Tel: 231304 Telex: 36739 saaae
Subjects: Encyclopedias, Dictionaries, Art, History
ISBN Publishers Prefix: 84-7137

Editorial Miguel A **Salvatella**, Santo Domingo 5, Barcelona 12 Tel: (93) 2189026
Subjects: Primary Textbooks, Educational Materials
Founded: 1922
ISBN Publishers Prefix: 84-7210

Editorial **San Martin***, Puerta de Sol 6, Apdo 97, Madrid 14 Tel: (91) 2214292/2216897

Man Dir: Jorge Tarazona
Subjects: History, Aviation, Military
Bookshop: Librería San Martin, Puerta del Sol 6, Madrid 14
1977: 15 titles *Founded:* 1854
ISBN Publishers Prefix: 84-7140

Santillana SA de Ediciones*, Calle Elfo 32, Madrid 27 Tel: (91) 4034000 Cable Add: Santillana Telex: 43879
President: Jesús de Polanco Gutérrez; *Vice-Presidents:* Francisco Pérez González, Ricardo Díez Hochleitner; *Man Dir:* Emiliano Martinez Rodriguez; *Editorial:* Antonio Ramos Perez; *Sales:* Jose Muñoz Juan; *Production:* Francisco Jerez Vazquez; *Publicity:* Jose Manuel Lopez Bottiglieri; *Rights & Permissions:* Gloria Roldan Perez
Associate Companies: Editorial Santillana, Argentina; Edyca SA, Dominican Republic; Nutesa, Mexico; Santillana del Pacifico SA, Chile; Santillana Publishing Co, USA; Teduca, Venezuela (qv)
Br Offs: Capitán Segarra 41, Alicante; Rambla de Cataluña 81, Barcelona 7; Ave del Ejército 3, Deusto (Vizcaya); Julián Romero Brionez 4, Las Palmas; Placentines 2, Sevilla; Jacinto Benavente 19, Valencia 5; Almirante Carrero Blanco 91 (bloque 3), Granada; Av del Mar 7, Oviedo; Polígono Industrial Portazgo, Bloque B, Nave 105, Cra de Logroño Km 6,600, Zaragoza; Polígono BENS parcela S-1-B, La Coruña; Conde de Ribadeo 4, 2°-C, Valladolid (all in Spain)
Subjects: Textbooks, Educational Materials for Kindergarten, Primary and Secondary, Teachers and Educational Specialists
1977: 255 titles *Founded:* 1960
ISBN Publishers Prefix: 84-294

Sedmay Ediciones SA*, Dr Fleming 51, Madrid Tel: 4161200 Telex: 43239
Man Dir: José Mayá Rius; *Export Manager:* Dr Sabine Kleinhaus
Subjects: Novels, Biography, Essays, Politics, Cinema, Juveniles

Editorial **Seix** Barral SA, Apdo de Correos 31, Tambor del Bruch s/n, Sant Joan Despi, Barcelona Tel: 3731409/3731652/3731208 Cable Add: Seibarh Telex: 53066 seix e
Man Dir: Antonio C Baldellou; *Editorial:* Alejandro A Marimón; *Sales:* Luis Carlos S Montoya; *Production, Publicity, Rights & Permissions:* Angel Jasanada Paris
Associate Company: Editorial Ariel SA (qv). The two companies constitute the organization Ariel/Seix Barral Editoriales
Subsidiary Companies: Formentor Argentina, Argentina (qv); Formentor Ltda, Chile; Ariel Seix Barral Ltda, Ecuador (qv); Ed Ariel-Seix Barral, Colombia; Ariel-Seix Barral, Mexico; Ediciones Andinas SA, Peru; Ediciones Formentor SRL, Venezuela
Subjects: Stories from Spanish, Latin-American, German, French, English, Italian, Soviet Russian, North American, Oriental and other literatures; Poetry, Drama, the Classics, Literary Criticism, Linguistics, Economics, Philosophy, Science, Politics, History, Psychology, Sociology, the Arts, Memoirs, Travel
1978: 41 titles *1979:* 21 titles *Founded:* 1945
ISBN Publisher's Prefix: 84-332

Selecciones Editoriales SA, Rita Bonnat 9, Barcelona Telex: 54495 Sele e Barcelona 29
Miscellaneous: Firm is a subsidiary of NV Uitgeversmaatschappij Elsevier, Netherlands (qv)

Siglo XXI Editores de España SA, Plaza 5, Apdo 48023, Madrid 33 Tel: (93) 7594809 Cable Add: Sigloedit

Man Dir: Faustino Lastra; *Sales:* Eduardo Rivas; *Production, Publicity:* Javier Abasolo
Subsidiary Companies: Siglo XXI de Colombia Ltda (qv); Siglo XXI Editores SA, Mexico (qv)
Subjects: Anthropology, Psychology, Sociology, History, Philosophy, Politics, Literature and Criticism
Bookshop: address as above
1977: 39 titles *Founded:* 1966
ISBN Publisher's Prefix: 84-323

Ediciones **Sigueme**, García Tejado 3, Apdo 332, Salamanca Tel: 218203 Cable Add: Sigueme Salamanca
Man Dir, Editorial: Germán González; *Sales:* Primitivo Fernández; *Production:* Francisco Lansac; *Publicity:* Leandro Cuadrado
Associate Company: Editorial Patria Grande, Argentina
Subsidiary Company: Sociedad de Educación Atenas SA, Madrid
Subjects: Philosophy, Religion, Juveniles, Psychology, Social Science, University Textbooks, Cinema, Education
Bookshop: Librería Sigueme, García Tejado 3, Salamanca
1977: 42 titles *1978:* 49 titles *Founded:* 1958
ISBN Publishers Prefix: 84-301

Silex*, Cid 4, Of 502, Madrid 1 Tel: (91) 2255534
Man Dir: E Domínguez; *Sales Dir:* Sra de Cruz; *Publicity, Advertising, Permissions:* P S Parrent
Subjects: Art & Artists of Spain, Slides for audiovisual education
Founded: 1972
ISBN Publishers Prefix: 84-85041

Ediciones **Sima***, Apdo 1317, Bilbao Tel: (044) 4312135
Man Dir: Victoria Inunciaga
Subject: Juveniles
Founded: 1975

Editorial **Sintes** SA, Apdo 1078, Barcelona Tel: (93) 3182838
Man Dirs, Editorial: Luis Sintes Pros, Jorge Sintes Pros
Orders to: Ronda Universidad 4, Barcelona 7
Subjects: Sports, Technical, Health
Bookshop: Librería Sintes, Ronda Universidad 4, Barcelona
1977: 38 titles *1978:* 45 titles *Founded:* 1968
ISBN Publishers Prefix: 84-302

Ramón **Sopena** SA, Provenza 93-95, Barcelona 15 Tel: (93) 2303809 Cable Add: Sopenar Telex: 52195 Sopec E
Man Dir: Dr Ramón Sopena Rimblas; *Sales:* Javier Egusquiza Trabudua; *Permissions:* Domingo Castellar Andreu; *Production:* Antonio Bometon Garcés
Subjects: History, How-to, Art, Reference, Juveniles, Paperbacks, General Science, Languages, Dictionaries, Children's books
Founded: 1894
Subsidiaries: Editorial Ramon Sopena del Río de la Plata SAIC, Argentina (qv); Editorial Sopena Colombiana SA, Colombia (qv); Editorial Sopena Mexicana SA, Mexico (qv); Editorial Ramón Sopena Venezolana SA, Venezuela (qv)
ISBN Publishers Prefix: 84-303

Studium Ediciones*, Bailén 19, Madrid 13 Tel: (91) 2485921
Distribution: Difusora del Libro, Bailén 19, Apdo 5018, Madrid 13
Man Dir: José Guerrero Carrasco

Subjects: Religion, Philosophy, Psychology, Education, Juveniles
Founded: 1949
ISBN Publishers Prefix: 84-304

Ediciones **Susaeta** SA*, Km 11 Carretera de Barcelona, Madrid 22 Tel: (91) 2051642/4 Cable Add: Susaeta
Sales Dir: José Luis Mejias Cubero
Subject: Juveniles
ISBN Publishers Prefix: 84-305

Taller Ediciones JB*, Ambrós 8, Apdo 9129, Madrid 28 Tel: (91) 2551266
Man Dir: J Betancor; *Sales Dir:* I Izquierdo; *Publicity Dir:* M Padorno; *Permissions:* J Betancor
Subjects: General Literature, Fiction, Philosophy, Psychology, Social Sciences, Art, Cinema
Founded: 1972

Editores **Ténicos** Asociados SA*, Maignón 26, Barcelona 24 Tel: (93) 2144178/2144266
Man Dir: Carlos Palomar Llovet; *Sales, Publicity & Advertising:* Juan Cuenca Martínez
Subjects: Engineering, Technical, Construction, Computers, Organization, How-to, University Textbooks
1977: 18 titles *Founded:* 1963
ISBN Publishers Prefix: 84-7146

Editorial **Tecnos** SA, O'Donnell 27, Apdo 18, Madrid 9 Tel: (91) 2262923
Man Dir, Editorial: Gabriel Tortella; *Sales:* Pilar Lagarma; *Production:* Julio Sanchez; *Publicity, Rights & Permissions:* Fernando Valesco
Branch Off: Brusi 46, Barcelona 6
Subjects: Social Sciences, History, Art, Philology, Science and Technology, Psychology, Philosophy, Literature
1977: 52 titles *1978:* 34 titles *Founded:* 1947
ISBN Publishers Prefix: 84-309

Editorial **Teide** SA*, Calle Viladomat 291, Barcelona 15 Tel: (93) 2504507 Cable Add: Editeide
Man Dir, Rights & Permissions: Federico Rahola de Espona; *Editorial, Sales:* Federico Rahola Aguade; *Production:* Christian Rahola Aguade; *Publicity:* Francisco Queraltó
Subsidiary Companies: Editorial Varazen, Monterrey 70-101, Mexico 7, DF; Teide Ltda, Apdo 53694, Bogota 2, Colombia
Subjects: University, Secondary & Primary Textbooks, Pedagogy, Art, Educational Materials, Navigation, Dictionaries, Languages, Mathematics, Literature, Geography, History, Philosophy
1977: 300 titles *Founded:* 1940
ISBN Publishers Prefix: 84-307

Ediciones **Telstar***, Consejo de Ciento 257-1° 1a, Barcelona 11 Tel: (93) 2534670
Man Dirs: Miguel Boladeras Cucurella, José Nin Catalá; *Sales:* José Nin Catalá; *Production:* Boladeras Cucurella
Subjects: Tourist Guidebooks & Maps
Founded: 1967
ISBN Publishers Prefix: 84-7237

Editorial **Timun** Mas SA, Via Layetana 17-3 3a, Barcelona Tel: (93) 3103714
Dirs: Juan Capdevila Font, José Menal
Subjects: Children's, Juveniles, Teaching Manuals
1978: 22 titles

Ediciones **Toray** SA, Duero 6, Barcelona 31 Tel: (93) 3577550 Cable Add: Toray
Dirs: Mariano Torrecilla, Miguel Vilanova

Branch Off: Cea Bermúdez, 44, Madrid 3; Junín 925, Buenos Aires, Argentina
Subjects: General Fiction, Art, Juveniles, Medicine, Psychology, University Textbooks
1977: 725 titles *1978:* 942 titles *Founded:* 1945
ISBN Publishers Prefix: 84-310

Toray-Masson SA*, Balmes 151, Barcelona 8 Tel: (93) 2179954 Cable Add: Massonsa
Man Dir: Nestor Bereciartu
Associate Companies: Masson SA, France (qv); Masson Publishing USA Inc, 111 West 57th St, New York NY USA
Subjects: Medicine, Science
ISBN Publishers Prefix: 84-311

G del **Toro** Editor*, Hortaleza 81, Madrid 4 Tel: (91) 4190486/4199518/4190139/4190184
Subjects: Fiction & Nonfiction, Juveniles, Secondary Textbooks
ISBN Publishers Prefix: 84-312

Instituto Eduardo **Torroja***, Costillares, Chamartín, Apdo 19002, Madrid 33 Tel: (91) 2020440
Subjects: Construction, Engineering
ISBN Publishers Prefix: 84-7292

Tucar Ediciones SA*, Calle Almagro 44, Madrid 4 Tel: (91) 4197669
Man Dir: Andrés de Blas Guerrero
Subjects: Social Sciences
1976: 11 titles *1977:* 12 titles *Founded:* 1975
ISBN Publisher's Prefix: 84-85199

Tusquets Editores, Calle Iradier 24 bajos, Barcelona 17 Tel: (93) 2474170
Man Dirs: Beatriz de Moura, Antonio López Lamadrid; *Sales:* Josefa Valero; *Production, Rights & Permissions:* Lía Nouguès; *Publicity:* Pep Albanell
Subjects: Fiction, Literature in general, Biography, History, Philosophy, Art, Social Science
1977: 21 titles *1978:* 23 titles *Founded:* 1969
ISBN Publishers Prefix: 84-7223

Editorial **Txertoa***, Plaza de las Armerías 4, Apdo 767, San Sebastian Tel: 459757/460941
Man Dir: Luis Aberasturi
Subjects: Literature, Biography, History and Art of the Basque Region
1978: 43 titles *Founded:* 1968
ISBN Publishers Prefix: 84-7148

Ultramar Editores SA*, Mallorca 49, Barcelona 29 Tel: 3212400
Above is address for all matters relevant to sales and administration
Man Dirs: José Sedó, Emilio Teixidor
Head Office: Hermosillo 63, Madrid 1
Subjects: General Literature, Fiction, Science Fiction, Paperbacks, Juveniles
Founded: 1973

Universidad de Granada, Secretariado de Publicaciones, Hospital Real, Granada Tel: (958) 234397
Subjects: Literature, History, Law, Art, Sciences, Philosophy, Social Sciences, Philology, Biology, Geology, Botany, Anthropology, Archaeology, Medicine, Geography, Music
1978: 52 titles

Universidad de Malaga, Avda del Generalísimo 23, Malaga Tel: (952) 213314
Subjects: Sociology, Philosophy

Ediciones **Universidad de Navarra** SA, see EUNSA

Urmo SA de Ediciones, Espartero 10, Apdo 1506, Bilbao 9 Tel: (94) 4245307
Man Dir: José Angel Grijelmo Ribechini
Branch Offs: Librería Deusto, Madrid; Urmo SA de Ediciones, Barcelona
Subjects: Engineering, General Science, University Textbooks
1977: 15 titles *1978:* 9 titles *Founded:* 1963
ISBN Publishers Prefix: 84-314

Editorial **Vasco** Americana SA (EVA)*, Ave de Castilla 79, Apdo 731, Bilbao Tel: (044) 4333700
Subject: Juveniles and Children's books
ISBN Publishers Prefix: 84-319

Editorial De **Vecchi**, see De Vecchi

Editorial **Verbo** Divino*, Carretera de Pamplona 41, Estella, Navarra Tel: 550449
Cable Add: Verbodivino
Man Dir: Father Miguel Angel Gimeno; *Sales Dir:* Angel Egurza; *Advertising, Permissions:* Angel Beltran
Subjects: Religion, Biography, Social Science, Educational Materials
Founded: 1957
ISBN Publishers Prefix: 84-7151

Veron Editor, Ronda del General Mitre 163, Barcelona 22 Tel: (93) 2121599/(93) 2119300
Man Dir, Sales: Climent Luis Veron; *Editorial, Publicity:* Jane Luis Veron; *Production, Rights & Permissions:* Rafael Zendrera Pijoan
Subjects: Escapist Literature, Juvenile, Ancient & Modern Classics
Bookshops: Libreria Scriba at above address Tel: (93) 2477124
1978: 6 titles *1979:* 8 titles *Founded:* 1965
ISBN Publisher's Prefix: 84-7255

Editorial **Vicens-Vives***, Ave de Sarriá 132–136, Barcelona 17 Tel: (93) 2034400
Man Dirs: Roser Rahola, Pere Vicens
Subjects: General Literature, Belles Lettres, Art, History, Biography, Geography, General Science, Mathematics, Secondary Textbooks, Education
ISBN Publishers Prefix: 84-316

Editorial Luis **Vives** (Edelvives)+, Carretera de Zaragoza, Km 315 7, Apdo 387, Saragossa Tel: 344100 Cable Add: Edelvives
Man Dir: David Sebastián; *Sales Dir:* Luis Fernández
Br Offs: Barcelona, Bilbao, Madrid, Seville, Valencia, Valladolid, Vigo, Saragossa
Subjects: Secondary & Primary Textbooks, Educational Materials
1977: 68 titles *1978:* 40 titles *Founded:* 1932
ISBN Publishers Prefix: 84-263

Xarait Editorial, Juan Vigon 3, Madrid 3
Owned by: Miguel Ortiz Martinez
Bookshop: Xarait Libros (qv)
1978: 3 titles
ISBN Publisher's Prefix: 84-85434

Zero SA, now Zero-Zyx SA (qv)

Editorial **Zero-Zyx** SA, Lérida 80, Madrid 20 Tel: (91) 2796591
Man Dir: Jesús Carrascosa; *Sales:* Jose Lozano; *Publicity & Advertising:* Manuel Irusta; *Rights & Permissions:* Teresa Garcia-Abad
Subjects: Belles Lettres, Poetry, Biography, History, Philosophy, Religion, Juveniles, Paperbacks, Psychology, Social Science
1978: 48 titles *Founded:* 1963

Literary Agents

A C E R*, Bolonia 5, Madrid 28, Contact: Marcel Laignoux Tel: (91) 2559943 Cable Add: Teleacer
Specialization: General Literature, Social Sciences, Philosophy, History, Biography, Documents and Memoirs, Encyclopedias (Rights negotiated in all Spanish and Portuguese speaking countries)

Carmen **Balcells** Agencia Literaria, Diagonal 580, Barcelona 21 Tel: (93) 2008565/2008933 Cable Add: Copyright Barcelona Telex: 50459 copy e (Barcelona)
Manager: Carmen Balcells
Branch Off: Rio de Janeiro, Brazil (qv)

Cecilio **Cardeñoso**, Juan Güell 74–76, Barcelona 28 Tel: (93) 3303416
Specializations: Philosophy, Psychology, Politics, Sociology, General Interest, General Spanish and Latin-American language Fiction

International Editors' Co SA*, Rambla de Cataluña 39, Barcelona 7 Tel: (93) 3188980
Cable Add: Lifeplay
Also office in Argentina (qv)

Elisabeth **Jowers**, Recoletos 11 3°B, Madrid 1 Tel: 2756252
Specializations: Fiction, Nonfiction, Religious, Encyclopedias, Gift Books

Andrés de **Kramer***, Castello 30, Madrid 1

José **Moya** und Ute Körner de Moya*, Ronda Guinardo 32, 5°, 5a, Barcelona 13

J F **Yañez**, Agencia Literaria (Universitas), Marco Aurelio 5, 5° 3a, Barcelona 6
Tel: 2479360 Cable Add: Agenliter
Dirs: Julio F Yañez and Mrs Mayte Yañez

Book Clubs

Círculo de Amigos de la Historia*, Conrado del Campo 9 & 11, Madrid 27

Círculo de Lectores SA*, O'Donnell 19, Madrid 30
Owned by: Círculo de Lectores SA (Madrid)

Club de Amigos del Libro, Mallorca 257, Barcelona 8 Tel: (93) 2156088
Secretary: Amparo Antiga
Owned by: Editorial C E D E L, Barcelona (qv)
Subjects: Radio, Television, Metallurgy, Yoga, Naturism, Chemistry, Industrial Studies

Biblioteca de **Selecciones*** (Selections from the Reader's Digest) (Iberia) SA, Calle Telémaco 3, Madrid 27 Tel: (91) 7420011

Major Booksellers

M **Aguilar***, Goya 18, Madrid
also: Serrano 24, Madrid; Ave Generalísimo 44–46, Madrid

Librería **Ancora y Delfín***, Diagonal 564, Barcelona 21 Tel: (93) 2000746

Librería Editorial **Argos** SA*, Paseo de Gracia 30, Barcelona 7 Tel: (93) 3014558

Librería **Augustinus***, Gaztambide 75, Madrid 15 Tel: (91) 2442430

Librería **Bastinos**, Pelayo 52, Barcelona 1 Tel: (93) 3018474

Librería **Bosch***, Ronda de la Universidad 11, Barcelona 7 Tel: (93) 3175308

Casa del Libro SA*, Ronda de San Pedro 3, Barcelona 10 Tel: (93) 3182640

Cinc d'Oros — Jaime Farrás Solé*, Diagonal 462, Barcelona 8

Delsa, Importadora de Publicaciones SA, Serrano 80, Madrid 6 Tel: 2268880

Librería **Díaz** de Santos, Lagasca 95, Madrid 6 Tel: (91) 2255697

Casa del Libro **Espasa-Calpe** SA*, Ave José Antonio 29, Madrid 13 Tel: (91) 2216657

Librería **Francesa***, Paseo de Gracia 91, Barcelona 8 Tel: (93) 2151417/2151426/2156618

Librería **Herder**, Balmes 26, Barcelona 7
Tel: (93) 3170578
Manager: Hermann Nahm

Librería **Hispano Americana***, Ave de José Antonio 594, Barcelona 7 Tel: (93) 3175337/3180079
Manager: José M B Ginesta

Hogar del Libro, Vergara 3, Barcelona 2
Tel: (93) 3182700
Manager: Sebastián Fábregues
Also Major Distributor

Insula, Librería de Ciencias y Letras, Benito Gutiérrez 26, Madrid 8 Tel: (91) 2435415

H F **Martínez** de Murguía, Valverde 30, Madrid 13 Tel: (91) 2226634
Universal supplier and distributor of books published in Spain

Librería **Mediterranea***, Ave Generalísimo Franco 403, Barcelona 9

Miessner Libreros*, José Ortega y Gasset 14, Madrid 6 Tel: (91) 2250978/2250998
Subjects: General Literature, Classics, Language, Philosophy, Archaeology, Art

Librería **Mundi-Prensa**, Castelló 37, Apdo 1223, Madrid 1 Tel: (91) 2754655
Man Dir: Pedro Hernández
Subsidiary: Libreria Agricola, Fernando VI, no 2, Madrid
Specializations: Economics, Life Sciences, Agriculture, Engineering, Technology
Founded: 1948

N R L — **Norildis**, Paseo de Gracia 96, Barcelona 8 Tel: 2156516
Spanish-American Distributor of Books and Periodicals: branches in Madrid, Bilbao, Gijon, Seville, Valencia

Librerías **P P C** (Propaganda Popular Católica)*, San Mateo 30, Madrid 1 Tel: (91) 4190034/4190906; E Jardiel Poncela 4, Madrid 16 Tel: (91) 4582335; Librería PPC, Canuda 9, Barcelona Tel: (93) 3172939; Librería Remel, Carrer Badal 144, Barcelona Tel: (93) 2578652 (and 13 other branches of PPC throughout Spain)

Librería **Passim**, Bailén 134, Barcelona 9
Tel: (93) 2574757 Cable Add: Passim
Publishes catalogues of new and out of print books about Spain and Latin America published in Spain. Specializes in export sales to foreign Universities and Libraries

Librería José **Porrúa** Turanzas SA, Cea Bermúdez 10, Madrid 3 Tel: (91) 2542344
Manager: José P Veriero

328 SPAIN

Libros **Porter***, Ave Puerta del Angel 9, Barcelona 2 Tel: (93) 2226437

Praxis Libros, now Xarait Libros (qv)

Librería Pedro **Pueyo***, Arenal 16, Madrid 13 Tel: (91) 2213344

Xarait Libros, San Francisco de Sales 32, Madrid 3

Major Libraries

Archivo General de la **Administracion** Civil del Estado (General Archives of the Civil Administration of the State), Ronda Fiscal 1, Alcalá de Henares, Madrid
Documents on administration no longer of current relevance

Archivo General de Indias (Archives of the Indies)*, Queipo de Llano 3, Seville

Archivo Historico Nacional (National Historical Archives), Calle Serrano 115, Madrid
Director: Dr Sanchez Belda

Archivo y Biblioteca Capitulares (Archives and Library of the Cathedral Chapter)*, Cathedral of Toledo, Toledo
Dir: Ramón Gonzálvez

Biblioteca del **Ateneo de Barcelona** (Library of the Athenaeum of Barcelona)*, Calle Canuda, Barcelona

Biblioteca del **Ateneo de Madrid** (Library of the Madrid Athenaeum)*, Prado 21, Madrid

Biblioteca del **Ateneo Mercantil** Valenciano (Library of the Mercantile Athenaeum of Valencia)*, Plaza del Generalísimo, Valencia

Biblioteca Nacional (National Library)*, Paseo de Calvo Sotelo 20, Madrid 1 Tel: (91) 2756800

Biblioteca del **Consejo** Superior de Investigaciones Científicas (Library of the Council for Scientific Research)*, Medinaceli 4, Madrid

Archivo de la **Corona** de Aragon (Royal Archives of Aragon)*, Conde de Barcelona 2, Barcelona

Biblioteca Central de la **Diputación** de Barcelona (Biblioteca de Cataluña y Central de Bibliotecas Populares) (Catalan Library and Central Public Library)*, Calle del Carmen 47, Apdo 1077, Barcelona 1 Tel: Director 217086; General 214639

Hemeroteca Municipal de Madrid (Madrid Periodical Library)*, Plaza de la Villa 3, Madrid

Biblioteca del **Instituto de Cultura** Hispánica (Library of the Institute of Hispanic Culture)*, Madrid

Biblioteca del **Instituto Nacional** del Libro Español (Library of the Spanish Publishers' and Booksellers' Association), Calle Mallorca 272-276, Barcelona 37

Biblioteca de **Menéndez Pelayo***, Rubio 6, Santander

Biblioteca del **Ministerio de Información y Turismo** (Library of the Ministry of Information and Tourism)*, Ave Generalísimo 39, Planta 2, Madrid 16

Biblioteca del **Palacio** Real (Library of the Royal Palace), Plaza de Oriente Madrid 13

Real Biblioteca de San Lorenzo de El Escorial (Escorial Library)*, El Escorial

Biblioteca General, **Universidad Autónoma** de Barcelona, Campus Universitario, Bellaterra (Barcelona)
Dir: M Mundó Marcet
Tel: 6920200

Biblioteca Central, **Universidad Complutense** de Madrid*, Ciudad Universitaria, Madrid 3

Biblioteca de la **Universidad Complutense de Madrid**, Ciudad Universitaria, Madrid 3

Biblioteca Universitaria, **Universidad Pontificia** de Salamanca*, Calle de Libros, Salamanca Tel: 213964

Biblioteca **Universitaria de Barcelona**, Gran Vía de las Cortes Catalanas 585, Barcelona 7
Librarian: Rosalia Guilleumas Brosa

Library Associations

Associació de Bibliotecàries*, Via Augusta 120, Pl Baixa Local G, Barcelona 6 Tel: 2181997
Secretary: N Ventura

Asociación Nacional de Bibliotecarios, Archiveros y Arqueólogos, (National Association of Librarians, Archivists and Archaeologists, Paseo Calvo Sotelo 22, Madrid 1 Tel: (91) 2756800
Chief Executive: Dr Justo García Morales
Secretary: Celina Iñiguez Galíndez
Section for Catalonia and the Balearics: Apdo 1868, Barcelona
President: Mercé Rossell
Publications: Include *Boletín* (which has bibliography section), *Inspección General de Archivos*

Instituto Bibliográfico Hispánico, Calle de Atocha 106, Madrid 12 Tel: (91) 2283878
Dir: Vicente Sánchez Muñoz
Hispanic Bibliographical Institute
Publications: Bibliografía Española (monthly), *Indices de Revistas de Bibliotecología* (3 a year)

Servicio de Bibliotecas de la Diputación Provincial de Barcelona*, Carmen 47, Barcelona 1 Tel: 3185996

Library Reference Books and Journals

Books

Bibliotheca Hispana (Spanish Library), Consejo Superior de Investigaciones Científicas, Serrano 117, Madrid

Inspección General de Archivos (Report on Spanish Archives), General Directorate of Archives and Libraries, Paseo Calvo Sotelo 22, Madrid 1

Journals

Boletín (Bulletin), General Directorate of Archives and Libraries, Paseo Calvo Sotelo 22, Madrid 1

Boletín (Bulletin), National Association of Librarians, Archivists and Archaeologists, Paseo Calvo Sotelo 22, Madrid 1

Indices de Revistas de Bibliotecología (Indexes to Library Science Periodicals), Spanish Bibliographical Institute, Paseo Calvo Sotelo 22, Madrid 1

Informacion Librera (Library Information), Javier Romani Sopena, Pelayo 11, 4, Barcelona

Revista de Archivos, Bibliotecas y Museos (Review of Archives, Libraries and Museums), Ministerio de Educación y Ciencia, Servicio de Publicaciónes, Ciudad Universitaria, Madrid 3

Literary Associations and Societies

Academia de Buenas Letras de Barcelona (Barcelona Academy of Belles Lettres)*, Calle Obispo Cassador 3, Barcelona 22
Secretary: José Alsina Clota
Publications: Boletín, Memorias

Asociación de Escritores y Artistas Españoles (Spanish Writers' and Artists' Association)*, Calle de Leganitos 10, Madrid 13
Secretary: José G Manrique de Lava

Ateneo Científico, Literario y Artístico (Scientific, Literary and Artistic Athenaeum)*, Calle del Prado 2¹ Apdo 272, Madrid
President: José María de Cossío
Publication: Hoja del Ateneo

Ateneo Científico, Literario y Artístico (Scientific Literary and Artistic Athenaeum)*, Calle Cifuentes 25, Mahón, Minorca, Balearic Islands
Secretaries: Calixto Martín Neé, María Esther Sebastian Sandino
Publication: Revista de Menorca (quarterly)

Mutualidad Laboral de Escritores de Libros (Book Writers' Friendly Society)*, General Mola 34, 2° izqda, Madrid 1 Tel: 2756192

Spanish **P E N** Club*, Librería Turner, Génova 3, Madrid
Secretary: José Antonio Gabriel y Galan

Spanish **P E N** Club (Cataluña)*, Apdo 2502, Central de Correos, Barcelona
Secretary: A Artis-Gener, c/o Josep Paulau i Fabre at above address

Real Academia de Ciencias, Bellas Letras y Nobles Artes (Royal Academy of Science, Literature and Fine Arts)*, Madrid
Secretary: Juan Gómez Crespo
Publications: Boletín (half-yearly), scientific, historical and literary works

Real Academia Sevillana de Buenas Letras (Seville Royal Academy of Belles Lettres)*, Plaza del Museo 8, Seville
Secretary: Dr Ildefonso Camacho Baños
Publication: Boletín de Buenas Letras (quarterly)

Sociedad de Ciencias, Letras y Artes (Scientific, Literary and Art Society)*, Dr Chil 33, Las Palmas, Canary Islands
Secretary: Juan Rodríguez Doreste
Publication: El Museo Canario (quarterly)

Sociedad General de Autores de España, Fernando VI 4, Apdo 484, Madrid 4
General Society of Spanish Authors
Secretary-General Carlos Galiano de Prados

Literary Periodicals

Camp de l'Arpa, Valencia 72, Entlo 4a, Barcelona 15

Destino (Destiny), Ediciones Destino SL, Consejo de Ciento 425, 5, Barcelona 9

La Estafeta Literaria (The Literary Courier), Editora Nacional, Ave del Generalísimo 29, Madrid 16

Insula (Island); bibliographical review of sciences and letters, Ediciones y Publicaciones de Insula, Benito Gutiérrez 26, Madrid 8

Litoral; monthly poetry review, Visor-Libros, Calle del Roble 22, Madrid 20

Nuestro Tiempo (Our Time), Ediciones Universidad de Navarra SA, Plaza de los Sauces, 1 & 2 Barañain, Pamplona

Razon y Fe; Spanish-American review, Pablo Aranda 3, Madrid 6

Revista de Literatura (Review of Literature), Libreria Cientifico Medinaceli del CSIC, Madrid

Revista de Occidente (Review of the West), Revista de Occidente SA, General Mola 11, Madrid 1

Revista Literaria Azor (The Goshawk — a Literary Review), C Borell 128, 1 2A Barcelona 15

Serra d'Or, Publicaciones de l'Abadia de Montserrat, Abadia de Montserrat, Barcelona

El Urogallo (The Capercailzie), Matias Montero 24, Madrid 6

Literary Prizes

Adonais Prize*
For the best poetry. Awarded annually. Enquiries to Ediciones Rialp SA, Preciados 34, Madrid 13

Miguel de **Cervantes** Prize*
For the best novel published during the year. 200,000 pesetas. Awarded annually. In 1976 the prize was awarded to Jorge Guillen. Enquiries to Ministry of Information and Tourism, Ave Generalísimo 39, Madrid 16

Duke of Alba Prize
Established 1905 for original, unpublished works in Spanish. 48,000 pesetas. Awarded once every nine years. Enquiries to Royal Spanish Academy, Felipe IV, 4, Madrid 14

Manuel **Espinosa** y Cortina Prize
Established 1891 for the best dramatic work performed for the first time. 4,000 pesetas. Awarded once every five years. Enquiries to Royal Spanish Academy, Felipe IV, 4, Madrid 14

Fastenrath Prize
Established 1909 for works of excellence written in the Spanish language. 6,000 pesetas. Awarded annually in rotation for the following categories of writing: poetry; essays, criticism; novel or story; history, biography; drama. Enquiries to Royal Spanish Academy, Felipe IV, 4, Madrid 14

Lope de Vega Prize*
This is a Villa de Madrid prize for the best play. 500,000 pesetas. Awarded annually. Enquiries to Ayuntamiento de Madrid, Madrid

Marques of Cerralbo XVII Prize
Established 1922 for the best original, unpublished work related to Spanish language and literature. 40,000 pesetas. Awarded once every four years. Enquiries to Royal Spanish Academy, Felipe IV, 4, Madrid 14

Eugenio **Nadal** Prize
For the best novel, preferably by a young writer. 200,000 pesetas. Awarded annually. Enquiries to Ediciones Destino SL, Consejo de Ciento 425, 5, Barcelona 9

Alvarez **Quintero** Prize
Established 1949 for the best work in two categories alternately: novel or story collection and theatrical works. 5,000 pesetas. Awarded biennially. Enquiries to Royal Spanish Academy, Felipe IV, 4, Madrid 14

Rivadeneyra Prizes
Established 1940 for the best work on Spanish literature and linguistics. Two prizes, of 30,000 pesetas and 20,000 pesetas. Awarded annually. Enquiries to Royal Spanish Academy, Felipe IV, 4, Madrid 14

Sri Lanka

General Information

Language: Sinhalese and Tamil (also English)
Religion: Buddhism
Population: 14 million
Literacy Rate (1969): 81% (88.3% Urban, 79.3% Rural)
Bank Hours: 0900-1330 Monday-Friday
Shop Hours: 0900-1700 Monday-Friday
Currency: 100 cents = 1 Sri Lanka/Ceylon rupee
Export/Import Information: No tariff on books or advertising. Import licence required for most book importation. Exchange controls.
Copyright: Berne, Florence (see International section)

Book Trade Organizations

Booksellers' Association of **Sri Lanka***, PO Box 25, Colombo 1 Tel: 22675/7
Secretary: R J Faber

Sri Lanka Publishers' Association*, 61 Sangaraja Mawatha, Colombo 10
Secretary-General: Eamon Kariyakarawana

Book Trade Journals

Ceylon National Bibliography (text in English, Sinhalese and Tamail), Sri Lanka National Library Services Board, 72 Bauddhaloka Mawatha, Colombo 4

Publishers

Architecture & Arts Publications Co*, 75 Ward Pl, Colombo 7
Subjects: Art, Architecture

W E **Bastian** & Co, 23 Canal Row, Fort, PO Box 10, Colombo 1
Man Proprietor: W D E Bastian
Subjects: Literary, Technical
Founded: 1904

H W **Cave** & Co, 81 Sir Baron Jayatilaka Mawatha, PO Box 25, Colombo 1 Tel: 22675/6/7 Cable Add: Cave Telex: 1241

Man Dir: B J L Fernando; *Dirs:* K Prabachandran, C J S Fernando; *Dir/General Manager:* J R W Rerera
Subjects: History, Archaeology, Juveniles, Literature, Law, Management, Medicine, Engineering, Economics, Education, Psychology, Environmental Studies
Founded: 1876

Ceylon Printers Ltd*, Parsons Rd, Colombo
Subject: Belles Lettres

Colombo Catholic Press, 956 Gnanartha Pradipaya Mawatha, Colombo 8 Tel: 95984
Dir and Manager: Rev Father Benedict Joseph
Founded: 1865

Cultural Council of Sri Lanka, 135 Dharmabala Mawatha, PO Box 307, Colombo 7 Tel: 27505/26125 Cable Add: Sanskriti
Dir: R L Wimaladharma; *Editorial:* Prof D E Hettiaratchi, Prof J D Dheerasekera, D P Ponnamperuma
Subjects: Literature, Religion, Art, Culture
Book Club: Book Club of the Cultural Council of Sri Lanka
Bookshop: Jayanti Bookshop, 135 Dharmapala Mawatha, Colombo 7
1977: 15 titles *1978:* 15 titles *Founded:* 1971

M D **Gunasena** & Co Ltd*, 217 Olcott Mawatha, PO Box 246, Colombo 11 Tel: 23981/4 Cable Add: emdeegee Colombo Telex: 1306 a/b Davasa Colombo
Subjects: University & School Books on all subjects
Founded: 1915
Miscellaneous: Associated imprints include Ananda Books, Sirisara Vidyalaya

Hansa Publishers Ltd*, Hansa Ho, Clifford Ave, Colombo 3
Subjects: General and Children's Fiction, Biographical, Politics, Law, Economics, Children's Science

J K G **Jayawardena** & Co*, BTS Bldg, 203, 1/13 Olcott Mawatha, Colombo 11

Karunaratne & Co*, 145 Olcott Mawatha, Colombo 11

Lake House Investments Ltd*, 41 WAD Ramanayake Mawatha, PO Box 1453, Colombo 2 Tel: 33271/2/3
Chairman: R S Wijewardene; *Dir:* G B S Gomes; *Editorial, Production, Publicity, Rights & Permissions:* H Amarasinghe (Tel: 35175); *Sales:* V L C Walatara (Tel: 27316)
Orders to and Bookshop: The Manager, Lake House Bookshop, 100 Sir Chittampalam Gardiner Mawatha, PO Box 244, Colombo 2
Subjects: Education, Law, General Fiction, Children's Books, Dictionaries, Medicine (in English and Sinhala)
1977: 22 titles *Founded:* 1965

Department of **National Museums**, PO Box 854, Sir Marcus Fernando Mawata, Colombo 7 Tel: 94767
Subjects: Publications relating to Sri Lanka's Antiquities, Anthropology, Natural History, *Spolia Zeylanica* (Journal of the National Museums of Sri Lanka)
See also: National Museum Library (under Major Libraries)

Ratnakara Press Ltd*, 74 Dam St, Colombo 12

Saman Publishers Ltd*, 49/16 Iceland Bldgs, Colombo 3

Sandesa Ltd*, 44A Alfred House Gardens, Colombo 3
Br Off: 185 Grandpass Rd, Colombo 14

K V G De Silva & Sons (Kandy), 44/9 YMBA Bldg, Fort, Colombo Tel: 083254
Cable Add: Silco
Man Dir: K V N De Silva; Sales Dir: Miss D De Silva; Publicity & Advertising Dir: Mrs K V N De Silva; Permissions: K V N De Silva
Shipping Add: 86 D S Senanayake Veediya, Kandy
Subjects: History, Religion
Founded: 1898
Bookshops: 86 D S Senanayake Veediya, Kandy; 44/9 YMBA Bldg, Fort, Colombo

Sri Lanka Publishing Co*, 209 Norris Rd, Colombo 11

The Union Press, 169 Union Pl, PO Box 362, Colombo 2 Tel: 20485/35912 Cable Add: Unionpress
Managing Proprietor: A H Dhas
Founded: 1942

Book Club

Book Club of the Cultural Council of Sri Lanka, 135 Dharmabala Mawatha, PO Box 307, Colombo 7
Owned by: Cultural Council of Sri Lanka (Colombo)

Major Libraries

British Council Libraries, PO Box 753, 154 Galle Rd, Colombo 3
Branch Library: Dalada Vidiya, Kandy

Ceylon Institute of Scientific and Industrial Research Library, 363 Bauddhaloka Mawatha, Colombo 7
Librarian: Clodagh Nethsingha
Publications: Current Technical Literature (quarterly; bibliographical series; state-of-the-art surveys of spices, essential oils

Colombo Public Library System, 18 Sir Marcus Fernando Mawatha, Colombo 7
Tel: 95156/96530/91968
Librarian: Mrs Ishvari Corea
Publications: Libraries and People; A Manual for Public Libraries in Sri Lanka

National Archives*, 7 Reid Ave, Colombo 7

National Museum Library, Department of National Museums PO Box 854, Sir Marcus Fernando Mawatha, Colombo 7 Tel: 93314
Librarian: C I Karunanayake
Publications: Sri Lanka Periodicals Index; Ceylon Periodicals Directory (Annual Supplements)
See also Department of National Museums (Publisher)

University of Peradeniya Library, University Park, Peradeniya
Acting Librarian: S Murugaverl
Publications (on exchange): Modern Ceylon Studies, A Journal of the Social Sciences, Sri Lanka Journal of Humanities, Ceylon Journal of Science (Biological Sciences), Library Handbook

Library Associations

Sri Lanka Library Association, University of Sri Lanka*, Colombo Campus, PO Box 1698, Colombo 3 (Located at: Reid Avenue, Colombo 7)
Secretary: Jayasiri Lankage
Publication: Sri Lanka Library Review (biannual)

Sri Lanka National Library Services Board, 3rd Floor, New Secretariat, Maligawatte, Colombo 10 Tel: 31332
Director/Secretary: N Amarasinghe

Library Journals

Library News, Sri Lanka National Library Services Board, 72 Bauddhaloka Mawatha, Colombo 4

Sri Lanka Library Review, Sri Lanka Library Association, University of Sri Lanka, Colombo Campus, PO Box 1698, Colombo 3

Literary Associations and Societies

Afro-Asian Writers' Bureau*, 73 Castle St, Colombo 8
Publication: Call

The Dickens Fellowship*, University of Ceylon, Thurston Rd, Colombo
Honorary Secretary: M M Aryrtane

Literary Periodicals

Call (Editions in English and French), Afro-Asian Writers' Bureau, 73 Castle St, Colombo 8

New Ceylon Writing; creative and critical writing of Sri Lanka, Macquarie University, School of English and Linguistics, North Ryde, NSW 2113, Australia

Vidyodaya; journal of arts, science and letters (text in English, Sinhalese and Tamil), University of Sri Lanka, Vidyodaya Campus Library, Nugegoda

Literary Prizes

Literary Prizes for Sinhala Literature
For the best books published in the previous year in the Sinhala language in the following categories: novels, short stories, poetry, translations, children's literature, scientific literature, drama; also three awards in miscellaneous literary areas and awards for original works in Pali, Sanskrit and Arabic. 1,000 Sri Lanka rupees each. Awarded annually. Enquiries to Sri Lanka Cultural Council and the Department of Cultural Affairs, 135 Dharmapala Mawatha, Colombo 7

Literary Prizes for Tamil Literature
For the best books of the year in Tamil in the following categories: novels, short stories, poetry (plus three prizes in miscellaneous literary areas). 1,000 Sri Lanka rupees. Awarded annually. Enquiries to Sri Lanka Cultural Council and the Department of Cultural Affairs, 135 Dharmapala Mawatha, Colombo 7

Don Pedrick Memorial Literary Award*
For the best original literary work in Sinhala. 1,000 Sri Lanka rupees. Awarded annually. Enquiries to Don Pedrick Memorial Literary Award Committee, 79 Dharmapala Mawata, Colombo 7

Sudan

General Information

Language: Arabic (English also used)
Religion: Muslim (Sunni sect) in north, pagan in south
Population: 17 million
Literacy Rate (1956): 9.6%
Bank Hours: 0830-1200 Saturday-Thursday
Shop Hours: 0800-1300, 1700-2000 Saturday-Thursday
Currency: 100 piastres (1,000 milliemes) = 1 Sudanese pound
Export/Import Information: No tariff on books; some advertising matter may be dutied at 40% and 5% ad valorem. Import licences required. Exchange controls; annual foreign exchange budget

Publishers

Al-Ayam Press Co Ltd*, Aboul Ela Bldgs, United Nations Sq, PO Box 363, Khartoum
Man Dir: Beshir Muhammad Said
Subjects: General Fiction & Nonfiction, Belles Lettres, Poetry, Reference, Magazines, Books in Arabic, Paperbacks
Founded: 1953

Khartoum University Press*, PO Box 321, Khartoum Tel: 80558/81806/81869/73222
Man Dir: El-Fatih Mahgoub; Sales Manager: Abdel Raham Ibrahim; Editorial, Rights & Permissions: Ali El-Mak
Subjects: General Fiction and Nonfiction, Belles Lettres, Poetry, Biography, History, Africana, Philosophy, Reference, Religion, Books in Arabic, Paperbacks, Science & Technology, General & Social Science, University & Secondary Textbooks
Bookshop: PO Box 321, Khartoum
Founded: 1968

Government Printer Government Printing Press*, PO Box 38, Khartoum

Major Booksellers

Al Bashir Bookshop*, PO Box 1118, Khartoum

The Church Bookshop*, PO Box 110, Juba

The Khartoum Bookshop, PO Box 968, Khartoum Tel: 77594/74425

The Sudan Bookshop*, PO Box 156, Khartoum Tel: 2089

University of Khartoum Bookshop*, PO Box 321, Khartoum Tel: 72271

Major Libraries

American Cultural Center Library*, Qasr Ave, Khartoum

British Council Library, 45 Sharia Gama'a, PO Box 1253, Khartoum Tel: 70159/70308/73454/76607/80269
Houses both books and periodicals

Higher Teachers' Training Institute Library*, PO Box 406, Omdurman

Khartoum Polytechnic Library*, PO Box 407, Khartoum Tel: 78922

University of Cairo*, Khartoum Branch Library, PO Box 1055, Khartoum

University of Khartoum Library*, PO Box 321, Khartoum Tel: 72271

Library Associations

Sudan Library Association*, PO Box 32, Khartoum North Tel: 33804
Secretary: Mohd Abashar
Publication: Sudan Library Journal

Library Journals

Sudan Library Journal (Text in Arabic and English), Sudan Library Association, PO Box 32, Khartoum North

Suriname

General Information

Language: Dutch (and English)
Religion: Hinduism, Roman Catholic, Muslim, Protestant
Population: 448,000
Literacy Rate (1964): 83.6%
Bank Hours: 0800-1230 Monday-Friday; 0800-1100 or 1200 Saturday
Shop Hours: Generally 0700-1300, 1600-1800 Monday-Friday; 0700-1300, 1600-1900 Saturday
Currency: 100 cents = 1 Surinam guilder
Export/Import Information: No tariff on books except children's picture books, 20% ad valorem; none on small quantities of advertising matter. Added taxes of 1½ + ½%. Import licences liberally granted. Exchange controls
Copyright: Berne

Book Trade Organization

Surinam Publishers' Association, PO Box 1841, Paramaribo Tel: 72545

Publishers

Lionarons Drukkerij NV*, Dr J F Nassylaan 107-109, Paramaribo

Vaco NV+, PO Box 1841, Paramaribo Tel: 72545 Cable Add: Vaco Telex: 123 Incosme (Located at: Domineestraat 26, Paramaribo)
Man Dir: E Hogenboom
Subjects: History, Low-priced Paperbacks, Primary and Secondary Textbooks, Maps
1977: 12 titles 1978: 5 titles Founded: 1952
Bookshop: Vaco NV, Domineestr 26, Paramaribo

Leo Victor*, Gemenlandsweg 4, Paramaribo

Major Booksellers

Vaco NV, Domineestr 26, Paramaribo

Major Libraries

Bibliotheek CCS, see Cultural Centre

Library of the Cultural Centre Surinam (Bibliotheek CCS), Gravenstr 112-114, PO Box 1241, Paramaribo
Librarian: Mrs C Carrilho-Fazal Alikhan

Swaziland

General Information

Language: English and Afrikaans
Religion: Tribal religions, some Christianity
Population: 507,000
Banks close 1100 Saturday
Currency: 100 cents = 1 lilangeni; South African currency also legal tender
Export/Import Information: Same as South Africa

Major Booksellers

Swaziland News Agency*, PO Box 171, Manzini

Major Libraries

Swaziland National Library Service*, PO Box 652, Manzini Tel: Manzini 2433
Acting Dir: D Simelane

University College of Swaziland Library*, PB Kwaluseni Tel: 52111 (Manzini)
Librarian: A W Z Kuzwayo

Sweden

General Information

Language: Swedish (English widely known)
Religion: Protestant
Population: 8.26 million
Bank Hours: 0930-1500 Monday-Friday
Shop Hours: 0900-1800 (later Friday) Monday-Friday; early closing Saturday
Currency: 100 ore = 1 Swedish krona
Export/Import Information: No tariff on books, Advertising Tax is 10%. 17.65% VAT on most imported goods. No import licences. No exchange controls
Copyright: UCC, Berne, Florence (see International section)

Book Trade Organizations

Bok-, Pappers- och Kontorsvaruförbundet, Skeppargatan 27, S-11452 Stockholm Tel: Växel (08) 630205
Swedish Federation of Book, Stationery and Office Supplies Dealers

Bokbranschens Finansierings-institut AB (Book Trade Finance Institute)*, Klara Norra Kyrkogata 34, S-111 22 Stockholm

Bokbranschens Marknadsinstitut AB, Sveavägen 52, S-111 34 Stockholm
Book Trade Marketing Institute

Bokhandelsrådet, c/o Svenska Bokförläggareföreningen, Sveavägen 52, S-111 34, Stockholm
Book Trade Council

Kristna Bokförläggareföreningen*, Tegnérgatan 34, S-113 59 Stockholm Tel: (08) 340290
Christian Publishers' Association
Secretariat: Tony Goldbranzén

Svenska Antikvariatföreningen*, Birger Jarlsgatan 32, S-114 29 Stockholm
Swedish Antiquarian Booksellers' Association

Svenska Bokförläggareföreningen, Sveavägen 52, S-111 34 Stockholm Tel: (08) 231800
Association of Swedish Publishers
Secretary: Jonas Modig
Publication: Svensk Bokhandel (jointly with the Swedish Booksellers' Association)

Svenska Bokhandels-Medhjälpare-Föreningen, Luntmakargatan 15, S-111 37 Stockholm Tel: 109698
Swedish Booksellers' Assistants' Association

Svenska Bokhandlareföreningen, Skeppargatan 27, S-114 52 Stockholm Tel: (08) 630205
Secretary: Per Nordenson
Swedish Booksellers' Association
Publication: Svensk Bokhandel (jointly with the Swedish Publishers' Association)

Svenska Musikförläggareföreningen (Swedish Music Publishers' Association)*, Höglandstorget 2, S-161 40 Bromma Tel: (08) 250799

Sveriges B-Bokhandlareförbund (Swedish Association of Smaller Booksellers)*, S-280 10 Sösdala Tel: (0451) 60096

Book Trade Reference Books and Journals

Books

Boksverige, Författare, Förlag, Bokhandel, Bibliotek (The Book in Sweden: Author, Publisher, Bookshop, Library), Albert Bonniers Förlag AB, Sveavägen 56, S-111 34 Stockholm

Svenska Bokförläggareföreningens Matrikel över dess Medlemmar och Kommissionärer samt Bokhandelns Föreningar och Organisationer (Swedish Publishers' Association. List of Members and Agents, together with Book Trade Associates and Organizations), Swedish Publishers' Association, Sveavägen 52, S-111 34 Stockholm

Journals

Bokrevy (Book Review), Bibliotekstjänst AB, Tornvägen 9, Fack, S-221 01 Lund

Bokvännen (The Bibliophile), Sällskapet Bokvännera, Ulvsatervagen 18, S-191 43 Sollentuna 3

Svensk Bokförteckning (Swedish National Bibliography), Royal Library, Bibliographical Institute, Box 5039, S-102 41 Stockholm 5 Cumulates into the Svensk Bokkatalog

Svensk Bokhandel (Swedish Book Trade), Swedish Publishers' Association, Sveavägen 52, S-111 34 Stockholm
Published jointly with the Swedish Booksellers' Association

Text: Swedish bibliographical journal (text in English and Swedish), Centre for Bibliographical Studies, Uppsala

Publishers

Acta Universitatis Gothoburgensis, Box 5096, S-402 22 Göteborg 5 Tel: (031) 810400 Telex: 20896 (UBGBG S)
Man Dir: Paul Hallberg

Parent Company: Göteborgs Universitetsbibliotek (qv)
Subjects: Scholarly works in the humanities and the social sciences (monograph series)
1977: 17 titles *1978:* 17 titles
ISBN Publisher's Prefix: 91-7346

Akademiförlaget, Fack S-400 10 Göteborg 3 Tel: 031/179600
Manager: Gunnar Jedenius
Order Department: Esselte Studium AB, S-112 85 Stockholm Tel: (08) 520660
Subjects: Languages, Medicine, Technical Economics, Textbooks
1977: 35 titles *1978:* 30 titles *Founded:* 1835
Miscellaneous: Firm is a part of Esselte Studium AB (qv)

Akademilitteratur Förlaget AB+, PO Box 50016, S-104 05 Stockholm Tel: (08) 152182 Cable Add: stockacademic Telex: 13115 Akademi S
Man Dir: Hanserik Tönnheim
Parent Company: Förlagsbokhandelsaktiebolaget Akademibokhandeln AB, PO Box 50016, S-104 05 Stockholm (a student-owned, non-profit-making chain of bookshops)
Subjects: Academic textbooks and essays: mainly in Economics, the Humanities, Foreign Languages
1978: 41 titles *1979:* 50 titles *Founded:* 1976
ISBN Publisher's Prefixes: 91-7410, 91-7200

Alba AB+, Karlavägen 86, Box 10041, S-100 55 Stockholm Tel: (08) 600050 Telex: 11620 Bonbook
Man Dir & Editorial: Dr Daniel Hjorth; *Rights & Permissions:* Ann-Mari Torstensson
Parent Company: Albert Bonniers Förlag AB, Sweden (qv)
Associate Companies: Bokforlaget Forum, Bonniers Juniorförlag (qqv)
Subjects: General Fiction and Nonfiction
1977: 34 titles *1978:* 54 titles *Founded:* 1977
ISBN Publisher's Prefix: 91-7458

Allhems Förlag AB+, Norra Bulltoftavägen 65, S-212 20 Malmö Tel: (040) 934060 Cable Add: Allhem
Man Dir: Einar Hansen; *Editorial:* S Arthur Svensson
Subjects: Classics, Biography, Natural History, Art, Reference, Guide Books, Marine, Naval and Aviation Interest, Swedish/Scandinavian Culture, Illustrated works
1978: 16 titles *Founded:* 1932
ISBN Publisher's Prefix: 91-7004

AB **Allmänna** Förlaget, see LiberFörlag

Almqvist och Wiksell Förlag AB+, Brunnsgränd 4, POB 2120, S-103 13 Stockholm Tel: (08) 245290 Cable Add: AWE/Gebers
Man Dir: Göran Ahlberg; *Editorial Dir:* Karl-Åke Kärnell
Subjects: General Fiction, Biography, Medicine, Reference, Juveniles, Low- and High-priced Paperbacks, Psychology, Engineering, General and Social Science, University Textbooks
Founded: 1878
Miscellaneous: Firm is one of the companies comprising Esselte Förlag AB (qv)
ISBN Publishers Prefix: 91-20

Almqvist och Wiksell International, Gamla Brogatan 15-17, PO Box 62, S-101 20 Stockholm Tel: (08) 237990 Cable Add: Almqvistbook Telex: 12430 Almqwik S
Dir: F Davids Thomsen; *Sales Manager:* Bengt Sjöström
1977: 212 titles *1978:* 232 titles
Subjects: Scientific & Technical books and periodicals
Miscellaneous: Publishers to the universities of Stockholm, Uppsala and Lund
ISBN Publishers Prefix: 91-22

Almqvist och Wiksell Läromedel AB+, Gamla Brogatan 26, Box 159, S-10122 Stockholm 1 Tel: (08) 229180 Cable Add: AWEDUC
Man Dir: Lars-G Ståhl; *Editorial Dir:* E Edman; *Sales:* Claes Witthoff
Subjects: Schoolbooks and Educational Aids (all levels), Foreign Languages, Music, Pre-school Material
1977: 85 titles *1978:* 81 titles

Apoteksbolaget AB+, Humlegårdsgatan 20, S-105 14 Stockholm Tel: (08) 240800 Telex: 11553 apobol s
Man Dir: Åke Nohrlander
Subject: Special Pharmaceutical Textbooks
1977: 2 titles

Förlagsaktiebolaget **Arbetarkultur**+*, Kungsgatan 84, S-112 27 Stockholm Tel: (08) 543882
Man Dir: Claes-Göran Jönsson
Subjects: Fiction, Political Science, Social Sciences
ISBN Publishers Prefix: 91-7014

AB **Arcanum**+*, Box 14116, S-400 12 Gothenburg Tel: (031) 871516
Man Dir: Bo Ramme

Askild och Kärnekull Förlag AB+, Banérgatan 37, Box 10148, S-100 55 Stockholm Tel: (08) 140880 Cable Add: Timjan Telex: 12475
Man Dir: Timo Kärnekull; *Sales:* Jerker Wennhag; *Production:* Stella Åkerstedt; *Publicity:* Love Kellberg; *Rights & Permissions:* Monica Stein
Subjects: Fiction & Nonfiction, Science Fiction Memoirs, Guidebooks
1977: 70 titles *Founded:* 1969
ISBN Publisher's Prefix: 91-7008

Bokförlaget **Atlantis** Peterson & Co AB+, Västra Trädgårdsgatan 11 B, S-111 53 Stockholm Tel: (08) 200350 Cable Add: Atlantisbooks
Man Dir: Kjell Peterson; *Dir:* Lars Falk, Ove Pihl; *Production:* Lennart Rolf; *Rights & Permissions:* Maj-Britt Jonsson
Subjects: Quality Non-fiction, Illustrated Books, Swedish and Foreign Fiction, including Classics
1979: 40 titles *Founded:* 1977
ISBN Publisher's Prefix: 91-7486

Beckmans Bokförlag AB, see Liber Grafiska AB

Berghs Förlag AB+, Box 17049, S-200 10 Malmö 17 Tel: (040) 231333 Cable Add: Sebergh Malmö
Chairman: Sven-Erik Bergh MA; *Production Man:* Ingrid Bergh; *Executive Editor:* Liselotte Weiss; *Foreign Rights:* Karin Bergh
Orders to: Seelig och Co, Stockholm (qv under Booksellers)
Subsidiary Companies: Edition Sven Erik Bergh, Federal Republic of Germany (qv); Edition Sven Erik Bergh in Europabuch AG, Switzerland (qv)
Subjects: General Fiction, Belles Lettres, Poetry, History, Music, Art, Juveniles, Religion, Low- and High-priced Paperbacks, Medicine, Psychology, General Science, Educational Materials, Mysteries, Thrillers, Books in German
Book Club: Berghs Bokklubb
1977: 90 titles *Founded:* 1954

Bernces Forlag AB+, Erikslustvägen 21, POB 20058, S-200 74 Malmö 20 Tel: (040) 77265 Cable Add: Beobolag
Man Dir: Arvid Bernce; *Editorial:* Margaret Bernce; *Sales:* Gudmund Hamrelius, Gregor Lindgren
Subjects: General Fiction and Non-fiction, Biography, Cookery, History, Reference, Art, Illustrated Books
ISBN Publishers Prefix: 91-500

Biblioteksförlaget AB+, PO Box 7514, S-103 92 Stockholm (Located at: Smålandsgatan 4, Box 7514, S-103 92 Stockholm) Tel: (08) 143460 Cable Add: Universitypress Telex: 11785 Unpress S
Executive Chairman: Lars E Frieberg; *Man Dir:* Sven Hartman
Subjects: Reference, University and Secondary and Primary Textbooks, Maps and Atlases, Physics, Chemistry, Social Sciences, Children's Books
1977: 45 titles *1978:* 50 titles *Founded:* 1923
Associate Company: Unicart Kartografisk Produktion AB, Sweden (qv)
ISBN Publishers Prefix: 91-542

Bibliotekstjänst AB+, Tornavägen 9, Fack, S-221 01 Lund Tel: (046) 140480 Telex: 32200 btjlund s
Subjects: Library Science, Reference
1977: 20 titles *Founded:* 1951
ISBN Publishers Prefix: 91-7018

Albert **Bonniers** Förlag AB+, Sveavägen 56, Box 3159, S-103 63 Stockholm Tel: (08) 229120 Cable Add: Bonniers Telex: 11620 Bonbook S
Man Dir: Olle Måberg
Subsidiary Companies: Bokförlaget Forum (qv), Bokforlaget Alba (qv), Bonniers Juniorförlag (qv), Ahlen & Akerlund (Periodical publishers)
Subjects: General Fiction, Nonfiction, Medical & Technical, Paperbacks, Reference, Juveniles, Young Adult
1978: 300 titles *Founded:* 1837
Book Clubs: Bokklubben, Svalan, Bonniers Bokklubb, Stora Romanklubben Underhållningsbokklubben, part-owner of Månadens Bok
ISBN Publishers Prefix: 91-0

Bonniers Juniorverlag AB+, Kammakargatan 9A, Box 3159, S-103 63 Stockholm Tel: (08) 229120
Parent Company: Albert Bonniers Förlag (qv)
Subject: Children's Books

Bokförlaget **Bra Böcker** AB, Södra vägen, S-263 00 Höganäs Tel: (042) 39000 Cable Add: Bebebooks Telex: 72643 S BBBOOKS
Man Dir: Bengt Revin; *Publicity:* Rolf G Jansing; *Editorial, Rights & Permissions:* Sven Gunnar Särman; *Production:* Lars Danielsson
Subjects: General Fiction, History, Geography, Classics, Crime novels, Illustrated Books, Encyclopaedia, Art Reproductions
1977: 65 titles *1978:* 68 titles *Founded:* 1965
Book Clubs: Bokklubben Bra Böcker, Bra Deckare (detective novels); Bra Klassiker (classics); Bra Konst (Art Reproduction Club)

Brombergs Bokförlag Scientia+, östra
Ågatan 39, Box 23052, S-750 23 Uppsala
Tel: (018) 121880
Man Dir, Editorial, Sales & Publicity:
Dorotea Bromberg, MA; *Production, Rights
& Permissions:* Dr Adam Bromberg
Subjects: Fiction, Politics, Science, Popular
Science, Medicine
1977: 12 titles *1978:* 25 titles *Founded:*
1975
ISBN Publisher's Prefix: 91-85342

Carlsen/if AB+, Bredgrand 2, S-111 30
Stockholm Tel: (08) 246880
Man Dir: Arne Mossberg; *Sales:* Bengt
Stagman
Parent Company: Carlsen/if A/S,
Copenhagen, Denmark
Associate Company: Carlsen Verlag GmbH,
Hamburg, Federal Republic of Germany
Subjects: Children's Picture-books
1979: 125 titles *Founded:* 1968
ISBN Publishers Prefix: 91-510

Bo **Cavefors** Bokförlag AB+*, Box 1047,
S-221 04 Lund Tel: (046) 151504/140764
Man Dir: Bo Cavefors
Subjects: General Fiction, Belles Lettres,
Poetry, Biography, History, Music, Art,
Philosophy, Psychology, Low- & High-
priced Paperbacks, General & Social
Science, University Textbooks
1977: 80 titles *Founded:* 1959
ISBN Publishers Prefix: 91-504

René **Coeckelberghs** Bokförlag AB+,
Saltmätargatan 3B, Box 45059, S-104 30
Stockholm Tel: (08) 248245/113180
Man Dir: René Coeckelberghs
Subjects: Fiction, Nonfiction, Poetry,
Political Science, Social Sciences, High-
priced Paperbacks
1978: 15 titles
ISBN Publishers Prefix: 91-7250

Combi International AB, Box 5315, S-102
46 Stockholm Tel: (08) 432860
Man Dir: Tord Pramberg
Subjects: Reference, Knowledge Books,
Educational Materials
Founded: 1963
Subsidiaries: Förlagshuset Norden AB
ISBN Publishers Prefix: 91-548

Edition **Corniche** AB, a subsidiary of Bengt
Forsbergs Förlag AB (qv)

Bokforlaget **Corona** AB+, Nobelvägen 135,
Box 5, 201 20 Malmö Tel: (040) 189480
Publisher: Nils-Åke Janséus; *Dir:* Lars
Welinder
Subjects: Juveniles, Textbooks, Education,
Fiction, Non-fiction

Tidnings AB **Dagen**, S-105 36 Stockholm
(Located at: Gammelgårdsvägen 38, Stora
Essingen) Tel: (08) 130340 Cable Add:
Dagen Telex: 10888 dagen
*Man Dir, Production, Rights &
Permissions:* Sverre Larsson; *Editorial:* Olof
Djurfeldt; *Sales:* David Edström; *Publicity
Dir:* Rune Flygg; *Advertising Dir:* Gunnar
Forsberg
Subsidiary Companies: Förlaget Filadelfia
AB (qv), Normans Förlag AB (qv)
Subjects: Biography, History, Music, Art,
Religion, Juveniles, Low-priced Paperbacks,
Educational Materials
Book Club: Den Kristna Bokringen,
Dagenhuset, S-105 36 Stockholm
Bookshops: Gospel Center, Kungsgatan 62,
S-111 22 Stockholm; Filadelfias Bokhandel,
Bråvallagatan 11, S-113 36 Stockholm
1978: about 40 titles *1979:* 30-35 titles
Founded: 1945

Dahlia Books*, International Publishers and
Booksellers, Box 23037, S-75023
Uppsala 23 Tel: (018) 100525 Cable Add:
Dahlia, Uppsala
Man Dir: Gun-Britt Du Rietz
Subjects: Botany, Zoology, Australiana,
Bibliography, Publications of the Royal
Swedish Academy of Science
Founded: 1973

Delta Förlags AB+*, Fack,
Nyängsvägen 87, S-161 16 Bromma 16
Tel: (08) 254781
Man Dir: Sam J Lundwall
Subjects: General Fiction, High-priced
Paperbacks
Founded: 1973
Book Club: Delta Science Fiction Bok
Klubb
ISBN Publishers Prefix: 91-7228

Ehrlingförlagen AB+, PO Box 5268,
S-102 45 Stockholm (Located at:
Linnégatan 9-11) Tel: (08) 630760 Cable
Add: Ehrlingmusik
Man Dir: Staffan Ehrling
Associate Company: Belwin-Mills Nordiska
AB
Subsidiary Companies: Thore Ehrling
Musik AB, Nils-Georgs Musikförlags AB,
Edition Sylvain AB; all at above address
Subject: Music
1978: 22 titles *1979:* 10 titles *Founded:*
1952

Elkan och Schildknecht+, Emil Carelius,
Västmannagatan 95, S-113 43 Stockholm
Tel: (08) 338463/338464
Man Dir: Bengt Carelius
Subject: Music

Esselte Förlag AB+, Tryckerigatan 2, S-103
12 Stockholm 2 Tel: (08) 228040
Man Dir: Göran Ahlberg
Book Clubs: Vår Bok, Familje Bokklubben
1978: 300 titles
Miscellaneous: Esselte Förlag is the name of
the Publishing Divison within the Esselte
Group.It consists of four independent
houses, namely Almqvist och Wiksell Förlag
AB (qv), Focus Uppslagsböcker AB (qv),
AB P A Nordstedt och Söners Förlag (qv),
Wëzata Forlag (qv)

Esselte Herzogs AB+*, Box 155, S-131 06
Nacka Tel: (08) 7162680 Cable Add:
Herzogs Telex: 12297
Man Dir: Rune Sirvell
Parent Company: Esselte AB, Sturegatan
11, Stockholm
Subjects: Bibles, Hymnals, Religion
Founded: 1862

Esselte Map Service, Garvargatan 9, POB
22069, S-104 22 Stockholm Tel: (08)
541920 Cable Add: Esseltemap Telex:
120 84 EMS S
General Manager: Lars Brenner;
Cartographic Manager: Rune Hermansson;
Marketing Manager: Bo Gramfors;
Editorial: Pian Boalt
Imprint of Generalstabens Litografiska
Anstalts Forlag (qv)
Subjects: Atlases, Travel Guides, Reference
Books

Esselte Studium AB+, Scheelegatan 24,
S-112 85 Stockholm Tel: (08) 520660
Cable Add: Esseltestudium Telex: 11681
Studium S
Man Dir: Göran Digmar; *Sales Dir:* Bo
Peterson (International Trade); *Foreign
Rights:* Henny Björklund
Subjects: Juveniles, Languages, Arts,
Medicine, Psychology, Engineering, General
& Social Science, University, Secondary &
Primary Textbooks, Technical & Scientific
Management, Furnishings, Educational
Materials, *Easy Readers*
1977: 225 titles
Miscellaneous: A merger of Akuma,
Gumperts Skolmateriel, Incentive Learning
Systems, Läromedelsförlagen, Norstedts
School Department, Skrivrit, the activities
of A S E A Education and L M Ericsson
Instruktionsteknik. See also
Akademiförlaget
ISBN Publishers Prefix: 91-24

Evangeliska Fosterlands-Stiftelsens Förlag+,
Tegnérgatan 34, S-113 59 Stockholm
Tel: (08) 340290 Cable Add: Stiftelsen
Man Dir: Tony Guldbranzén
Subjects: General Fiction and Non-fiction,
Poetry, Reference, Religion, Juveniles,
Young Adult, High-priced Paperbacks
1978: 27 titles *Founded:* 1856
ISBN Publishers Prefix: 91-7080

Förlaget **Filadelfia** AB, Dagen-huset,
S-105 36 Stockholm Tel: (08) 130340
Cable Add: Dagen Telex: 10888 dagen
*Man Dir, Editorial, Production, Rights &
Permissions:* Sverre Larsson; *Sales:* David
Edström; *Publicity:* Rune Flygg
Parent Company: Tidnings AB Dagen (qv)
Associate Companies: Den Kristna
Bokringen (Book Club), Normans Förlag
(qv)
Subjects: Christian religious
1978: 40 titles *1979:* 33 titles *Founded:*
1915
ISBN Publisher's Prefix: 91-536

Focus Uppslagsböcker AB (Focus
International Book Production AB)*,
Brunnsgränd 4, Stockholm Tel: (08) 245290
Man Dir: Lars Almgren
Subject: Reference (Encyclopaedias)
Miscellaneous: Firm is one of the companies
comprising Esselte Förlag AB (qv)

Bengt **Forsbergs** Förlag AB+, Södra
Tullgatan 4, S-211 40 Malmö Tel: (040)
76320 Cable Add: Godbok
Man Dir: Bengt Forsberg; *Sales Dirs:*
Jörgen Forsberg, Claës Forsberg, Mets
Forsberg
Subjects: General Non-fiction; especially
Biography, History, Medicine, General
Science, Politics, Pornography
Founded: 1943
Subsidiary: Edition Corniche AB (qv)
Miscellaneous: Produces films
ISBN Publishers Prefix: 91-7046

Förskolans Förlag i Stockholm+*,
Vastmannagatan 48, 113 25 Stockholm
Tel: (08) 328747
Man Dir: Börje Dahl
Subjects: Pre-School Materials
Founded: 1976

Bokförlaget **Forum** AB+, Tegnérgatan 40,
S-113 59 Stockholm Tel: (08) 311064
Cable Add: Bokforum
Man Dir: Bertil Käll; *Editorial:* Sven Olof
Sundborg; *Sales Manager:* Jan-Olof
Westrell; *Production Manager:* Majbritt
Hagdahl; *Permissions:* Monica Heyum
Parent Company: Albert Bonniers Förlag
AB, Sweden (qv)
Associate Companies: Bokförlaget Alba,
Bonniers Junior verlag (qqv)
Shipping Add: Malmvägen 80-82, S-191 47
Sollentuna
Subjects: General Fiction, Biography,
Popular History, How-to, Music, Art,
Science, High- & Low-priced Paperbacks
1977: 106 titles *Founded:* 1944
ISBN Publishers Prefix: 91-37

AB Carl Gehrmans Musikförlag+,
Apelbergsgatan 58, Box 505, S-101 26
Stockholm 1 Tel: (08) 103004 Cable Add:
Musikgehrman
Man Dir: Kettil Skarby
Subject: Music
1978: 50 titles *Founded:* 1893

Generalstabens Litografiska Anstalts
Förlag+, Garvargatan 9, Box 22069, S-104
22 Stockholm Tel: (08) 541920 Cable Add:
Esseltemap Telex: 12084 EMS S
Man Dir: Lars Brenner
Imprint: Esselte Map Service (qv)
Subjects: Geography, Travel, Politics,
General Science
Founded: 1872

Gidlunds Förlag+, PO Box 120 16, 10221
Stockholm (Located at: Karlsviksgatan 16,
S-112 41 Stockholm) Tel: (08)
549985/540180
Man Dir: Krister Gidlund; *Sales Dir:*
Gertrud Gidlund; *Editorial:* Ylva Holm,
Ayreri Karabuda; *Literary Agent:* Lennart
Sane Agency
Subjects: General Fiction, Belles Lettres,
Poetry, Biography, History, Music, Art,
Philosophy, Juveniles, High-priced
Paperbacks, Psychology, Social Science
1978: 60 titles *Founded:* 1968
ISBN Publishers Prefix: 91-7021

AB C W K Gleerup Bokförlag, see Liber
Grafiska AB, Sweden

Gullers International AB, Kungsgatan 30xv,
S-111 35 Stockholm Tel: (08) 230585
Telex: 13437 Cable Add: Gullersfoto
Publisher: Karl Werner Gullers; *Man Dir:*
Claes Jugård
Subjects: Health, Industrial, Crafts

Gummessons Bokförlag+, Tegnérgatan 8,
Box 6302, S-113 81 Stockholm Tel: (08)
151830 Cable Add: Förbundet
Man Dir: David Englund
Subjects: General Fiction, Religion
1977: 20 titles *1978:* 30 titles *Founded:*
1895
ISBN Publishers Prefix: 91-7070

Harriers Bokforlag AB+, PO Box 143,
S-162 12 Vällingby Tel: (08) 380335
Man Dir, Rights & Permissions: Kjell-Erik
Sellin; *Editorial, Production:* Bertil
Almebäck; *Sales:* Birgit Hellbom, Daniel
Lindberg; *Publicity:* Els-Marie Norrby;
Juliane Elven
Subjects: General Fiction and Nonfiction,
Biography, Documentaries, Juvenile,
Religious
Book Club: Önskeboken
1978: 25 titles *1979:* 25 titles *Founded:*
1932
ISBN Publisher's Prefix: 91-7068

Förlags AB Hem i Sverige+*, Box 6507,
S-113 83 Stockholm Tel: (08) 151910
Man Dir: Rolf Bergholm
Subjects: Houses & Cottages (including
How-to, Hobbies)
1976: 10 titles *Founded:* 1927
ISBN Publishers Prefix: 91-85020

Hemmets Journal AB, Fack, S-212 05
Malmö
Parent Company: Gutenberghus Group,
Denmark
Associate Companies: Ehapa-Verlag GmbH,
Federal Republic of Germany;
Gutenberghus Publishing Service, Denmark
(qv), Hjemmenes Forlag A/S, Norway (qv)
Subjects: Juveniles, Fiction, Human Interest
Founded: 1927

Hermods Publishing House, see Liber
Grafiska AB

Hermods, Correspondence School,
Slottsgatan 24, S-205 10 Malmö Tel: (040)
76900 Cable Add: Libergraph
Rights & Permissions: Alva Jansson
Subjects: Educational Materials for School
and Adult Education
1978: 50 titles
Miscellaneous: Division of Liber Grafiska
AB (qv)
ISBN Publishers Prefix: 91-23

Lars **Hökerbergs** Bokförlag+, Box 8071,
S-104 20 Stockholm (Located at:
Fleminggatan 21) Tel: (08) 244360
Man Dir: Rolf Hökerberg
Subjects; Nonfiction, Technical, Textbooks,
Educational Materials, Vocational Training
by Correspondence
1977: 45 titles *1978:* 50 titles *Founded:*
1882
Subsidiary: I T K-skolan
ISBN Publishers Prefix: 91-7084

I C A-Förlaget AB+, Stora Gatan 41,
S-721 85 Västerås Tel: (021) 110440
Telex: 19435 ICA S Cable Add: Icaförlaget
Man Dir: Erik Rydholm; *Publisher:* Birgitta
O'Nils; *Sales:* Ulf Åberg; *Production:* Stig
Osterlund
Branch Off: Grev Turegatan 19, Box 5273,
S-102 46 Stockholm
Subjects: Cookery; How-to on Handicrafts,
Hobbies, Gardening, Domestic Animals,
Antiques
1978: 35 titles *1979:* 34 titles *Founded:*
1947
Miscellaneous: Firm also publishes five
periodicals
ISBN Publishers Prefix: 91-534

Ingenjörsvetenskapsakademien (I V A)+,
Grev Turegatan 14, Box 5073, S-102 42
Stockholm 5 Tel: (08) 220760 Cable Add:
Ivacademi
Royal Swedish Academy of Engineering
Sciences
Man Dir: Gunnar Hambraeus; *Editorial:*
Peter Wilhelm
Subjects: Science, Technology
1977: 24 titles
ISBN Publisher's Prefix: 91-7082

Interpublishing AB Rahm and Stenström,
Taptogatan 4, S-115 28 Stockholm
Tel: (08) 637601/02 Cable Add:
Interpublishing
Mans: Anders Rahm, Bengt Stenström
Subjects: Biography, History, Hobby,
Engineering, General Science, Reference
Miscellaneous: Previously Interbook
Publishing AB

Interskrift Publishing House, PO Box 135,
S-527 00 Herrljunga Tel: (0513) 11930
Telex: Startex S 42109
Man Dir: Per-Ove Lannerö; *Editorial,
Production:* Nils Erik Karlsson; *Rights &
Permissions:* Rigmor Andersson
Parent Company: Tyndale House Publisher,
336 Gondersen Drive, Wheaton, Illinois
60187 USA
Associate Company: Living Bibles
International, PO Box 155, S-52700
Herrljunga, Sweden
Subjects: Bibles, General Religious
Book Clubs: Info Book
1978: 30 titles *1979:* 35 titles *Founded:*
1974
ISBN Publisher's Prefix: 91-7336

Jannersten Förlag AB+, Box 45, S-744 01
Avesta Tel: (0226) 52045
Man Dir: Eric Jannersten
Subject: Books on Bridge

Kometförlaget AB, subsidiary of
B Wahlströms Bokförlag AB (qv)

L Ts Förlag AB+, Vasagatan 12, S-105 33
Stockholm Tel: (08) 141620 Cable Add:
Lantförbundet Telex: 12396 land s
Man Dir, Editorial: Uno Larsson; *Sales Dir:*
Bo Norberg; *Production Manager:* Harry
Krieg; *Permissions:* Elly Widell
Subjects: Specialize in books used in the
agricultural schools of Sweden; also
Ethnology, Politics, Adult Education,
General Fiction, Biography, History,
How-to, Economics, General Science,
Handicrafts
Founded: 1935
ISBN Publishers Prefix: 96-36

Bokförlaget Robert **Larson** AB+, Box 3063,
S-183 03 Täby Tel: (08) 7565640 Cable
Add: Larson books
Dirs: Birgitta and Robert Larson
Subjects: General Fiction and Nonfiction:
especially Psychology, Philosophy, Current
Events, Animals and Nature, Leisure
Pursuits, Astrology, Photography, Ecology,
Alternative Medicine
1977: 5 titles *1978:* 8 titles
ISBN Publishers Prefix: 91-514

Liber Grafiska AB+, Sorterargatan 23,
S-162 89 Vällingby Tel: (08) 890200 Cable
Add: Libergraph
Man Dir: Karl-Axel Swedérus; *Dirs:* Bertil
Almgren (general publishing), Etna Prior
(tele-education), Olle Hedbom (maps), Nils
Zetterberg (educational publishing)
Divisions: LiberFörlag, (qv) (formed by
amalgamation of AB Allmänna Förlaget
and Beckmans Bokförlag AB);
LiberHermods (formed by Hermods Skola);
LiberLäromedel (qv) (formed by
amalgamation of AB C W K Gleerup
Bokförlag, Svenska Utbildningsförlaget
Liber AB and Hermods Läromedel);
LiberKartor (Svensk Kartjänst AB, Swedish
Map Service) (qv)
Orders to: Liber Distribution, 162 89
Vällingby
Imprints: Publica
Bookshops: AB C E Fritzes Kungl
Hovbokhandel, Regeringsgatan 12,
Stockholm (qv)
ISBN Publisher's Prefix: 91-23, 91-38,
91-40, 91-47

Liber Tryck, an imprint of LiberLäromedel
(qv)

LiberFörlag+, S-162 89 Vällingby Tel: (08)
890200 Cable Add: Libergraph Telex:
12801
Man Dir: Karl-Axel Swedérus; *Publishing:*
Bertil Almgren; *Sales:* Per Lidberg;
Production: Ingemar Johansson;
Permissions: Alva Jansson
Orders to: Liber distribution, Förlagsorder,
S-162 89 Vällingby
Parent Company: Liber Grafiska AB (qv) of
which LiberFörlag is General Publishing
Division
Associate Company: Allmänna Förlaget
Subjects: Government Publications, High-
priced Paperbacks, Marketing, Social
Science, University Textbooks
Bookshops: AB C E Fritzes Kungl
Hovbokhandel, Regeringsgatan 12, Box
16356, S-103 27 Stockholm
Miscellaneous: LiberFörlag is official
publisher for the Government authorities
1978: 500 Government, 110 other titles
Founded: 1969
ISBN Publishers Prefix: 91-38

LiberKartor (Svensk Karttjänst AB, Swedish Map Service), Sorterargatan 23, S-16289 Vällingby Tel: (08) 890200 Cable Add: Libergraph
Division for Map Services of Liber Grafiska AB (qv)
Subjects: Maps and charts of all kinds for Sweden (especially) and world

LiberLäromedel, Sorterargatan 23, S-162 89 Vällingby Tel: (08) 890200 Cable Add: Libergraph
Divisional Man Dir: Nils Zetterberg; *Sales Dir, Publicity:* Karl Glansborg; *Rights & Permissions:* Alva Jansson (Malmö office)
Parent Company: Liber Grafiska AB (qv)
Associated Companies: See Liber Grafiska AB
Imprint: Liber Tryck
Branch Offs: Slottsgatan 24, S-205 10 Malmö, Öresundsvägen 1, S-221 05 Lund
Subjects: Official Swedish Educational Publisher: Textbooks and Educational Aids for Pre-school, Primary, Secondary, University and Adult Education, Management
1978: 500 titles *Founded:* 1969
Book Clubs: Bättre Ledarskap (qv), LiberLäromedel; Lärarbokklubben, LiberLäromedel, S-205 10 Malmö
Bookshop: Fritzes Kungl Hovbokhandel, Regeringsgatan 12, Box 16356, S-103 27 Stockholm
ISBN Publisher's Prefixes: 91-23/91-40/91-47

Libris Publishing House, PO Box 1623, Skolgatan 11, S-701 16 Örebro Tel: (019) 119360
Man Dir, Rights & Permissions: Björn-Ingvar Olsson; *Editorial:* Gunnar Jonsson; *Sales:* Erik Westling; *Production:* Arnold Segerlund; *Publicity:* Kenneth Pettersson
Subjects: General Interest, Theological
Bookshops: Libris Bookshop, Storgatan 23, Box 1623, S-701 16 Örebro
1978: 30 titles *1979:* 40 titles *Founded:* 1916
ISBN Publisher's Prefix: 7194

Lidman Production, Karlavägen 71, Box 5098, S-102 72 Stockholm
Publisher: Sven Lidman
Subjects: Educational, Encyclopaedias

J A Lindblads Bokförlag AB+, Warfvinges väg 30, S-112 51 Stockholm Tel: (08) 534640 Cable Add: Bookjal Telex: 17174 (Wahlströms)
Man Dir: Bo Wahlström; *Sales:* Bertil Wahlström; *Production:* Tord Pramberg; *Permissions:* Eva Melin
Shipping Add: c/o B Wahlströms Bokindustri AB, Lövåsvägen 24, S-791 00 Falun
Subjects: General Fiction and Non-fiction; Juvenile
1977: 14 titles *1978:* 18 titles *Founded:* 1894
Miscellaneous: Firm is a subsidiary of B Wahlströms Bokförlag AB (qv)
ISBN Publishers Prefix: 91-32

Lindqvist Förlag AB*, Torkel Knutssonsgatan 27, Box 17037, S-104 62 Stockholm Tel: (08) 840415 Cable Add: Boklind
Man Dir: Jan Askild; *Sales Dir:* Erik Ahlenius; *Editorial Dir:* Jörgen Peterzén; *Editor of the series Bulldog:* K Arne Blom; *Editor of the series Hedman Thriller:* Iwan Hedman
Subjects: General Fiction, Biography, Art, Philosophy, Juveniles, Science Fiction, Paperbacks, Thrillers & Detective Novels
Founded: 1922
Book Club: Läsklubben Fyrklövern
ISBN Publishers Prefix: 91-7090

Abr Lundqvists Musikförlag AB+*, Katarina Bangatan 17, S-116 25 Stockholm Tel: (08) 436767
Man Dir: Helge Roundqvist; *Editorial:* Anders Roundqvist
Subject: Music
Founded: 1838

Månadens Bok+, Box 2255, S-103 16 (Located at: Skeppsbron 20) Stockholm Tel: (08) 232310
Man Dir: Erik Hyllner
Founded: 1973

Bokförlaget **Medium** AB+*, Fack, S-162 10 Vällingby Tel: (08) 380340
Man Dir: Bo Pederby
Subject: School Textbooks
ISBN Publishers Prefix: 91-512

Gustav **Melins** AB+*, Box 5057, S-402 22 Gothenburg Tel: (031) 400140 Cable Add: Wezätamelins
Man Dir: Jonas Forssman
Subjects: Bibles, Hymn Books, Juvenile
Founded: 1898

Bokförlaget **Natur och Kultur**+, Torsgatan 31, Box 6408, S-113 82 Stockholm Tel: 46 8 34 06 60 Cable Add: Naturkultur
Man Dir: Lars Almgren; *Deputy Man Dir:* Per Ivarsson; *Editorial:* Harriet Alfons; *Publicity and Sales Manager:* Ini Ljung (General Books), P G Mohss (Educational); *Rights and Permissions:* Britta Svensson
Orders to: Gårdsvägen 6, S-171 52 Solna
Subjects: General Non-fiction: Biography, History, Medicine, Psychology, General Science, University, Secondary & Primary Textbooks, Audiovisual Materials
1978: 150 titles *Founded:* 1922
ISBN Publishers Prefix: 91-27

AB **Nautic**+*, Skeppsbron 3, S-411 21 Gothenburg Tel: (031) 111200/111500 Cable Add: Nautic
Man Dir: Björn Traung
Subjects: Nautical Literature, Sea Charts
Miscellaneous: Agent for International Hydrographic publications
Founded: 1953

Nautiska Förlaget Sjökortshallen AB+*, Box 19059, S-104 32 Stockholm Tel: (08) 345493/345682 Cable Add: Namco
Manager: S Hiljding
Subjects: Shipping Publications, Sea Charts, Navigational Literature
Miscellaneous: Agent for International Hydrographic publications

Bokforlaget **Niloe** AB+, Box 45, S-451 01 Uddevalla (Located at: N Drottninggatan 15-17) Tel: (0522) 10708
Man Dir: Olof Ericson; *Editorial:* Harry Lundin; *Sales:* Sture Marcusson
Subjects: Classical Literature, Reference
1978: 7 titles *1979:* 12 titles *Founded:* 1953
ISBN Publisher's Prefix: 91-7102

AB **Nordbok**, PO Box 7095, S-40232 Gothenburg (Located at: Pusterviksgatan 13, Gothenburg) Tel: (031) 171085 Cable Add: Nordbokab Telex: 21782
Publisher: Einar Engelbrektson; *Man & Sales Dir:* Gunnar Stenmar; *Editorial Dir:* Turlough Johnston
Subjects: History, Reference, Engineering, Educational Materials, How-to
1977: 8 titles *1978:* 2 titles *Founded:* 1974

SWEDEN 335

Förlagshuset **Norden** AB, subsidiary of Combi International AB (qv)

AB **Nordiska Bokhandeln**+*, Box 7, S-101 20 Stockholm Tel: (08) 227380 Cable Add: Nordbok
Man Dir: Hans Molander
Subjects: Medicine, Psychology, Social Science, University Textbooks
Founded: 1851
Bookshop: Drottninggatan 7, Fack, S-101 10 Stockholm
ISBN Publishers Prefix: 91-516

AB **Nordiska Musikförlaget** (Edition Wilhelm Hansen Stockholm), Drottninggatan 37, Box 745, S-101 30 Stockholm Tel: (08) 249430 Cable Add: Musicalia
Man Dir: Bengt Edwardsson
Subject: Music

AB P A **Nordstedt** och Söners Förlag+, Tryckerigatan 2, Box 2052, S-103 12 Stockholm 2 Tel: (08) 228040 Cable Add: Norstedts
Man Dir: Göran Ahlberg; *Editorial Dir:* Lasse Bergström; *Rights & Permissions:* Agneta Markas
Subjects: General Fiction, Belles Lettres, Poetry, Biography, History, How-to, Music, Art, Philosophy, Reference, Religion, High-priced Paperbacks, Medicine, Psychology, Engineering, General and Social Science, Law
Book Club: part-owner of Månadens Bok
1977: 200 titles *1978:* 200 titles *Founded:* 1823
Miscellaneous: Firm is one of the companies comprising Esselte Förlag AB (qv)
ISBN Publisher's Prefix: 91-1

Normans Förlag AB, Gammelgårdsvägen 38-42, Dagenhuset, S-105 36 Stockholm Tel: (08) 130340 Cable Add: Normanbok
Man Dir: Sverre Larsson
Parent Company: Tidnings AB Dagen (qv)
Subject: Religion
ISBN Publishers Prefix: 91-536

Nybloms Förlag+*, Lästmakargatan 1E, Box 154, S-751 04 Uppsala 1 Tel: (018) 257350 Cable Add: Nybloms
Man Dir: Carl-G Swanström
Subjects: Archaeology, Popular Science, Hobbies, Technology, Biography, General Non-fiction
Founded: 1939
ISBN Publishers Prefix: 91-85040

AB Håkan **Ohlssons** Förlag+, see S K E A B Forlag

Oktoberförlaget AB+, PO Box 5398, S-102 46 Stockholm (Located at: Nybrogatan 25) Tel: (08) 600043 Cable Add: Oktbook
Man Dir: Karl Hägglund; *Editorial:* Ulf Sörenson
Orders to: Oktober Centrallager, PO Box 3144, S-103 62 Stockholm
Subjects: General Fiction and Non-fiction, Journalism, Juveniles, Social Science, Politics
Bookshops: Bokhandeln Oktober, Holländargatan 9A, S-111 36 Stockholm; also fifty further bookshops throughout Sweden
1978: 25 titles *1979:* 40 titles *Founded:* 1966
ISBN Publisher's Prefix: 7242

Bokforlaget **Opal** AB+, Tegelbergsvägen 31, S-161 70 Bromma Tel: (08) 282179
Joint Publishers: Bengt Christell, Valborg Segerhjelm

Subject: Juveniles
1977: 40 titles *1978:* 50 titles *Founded:* 1973
ISBN Publisher's Prefix: 91-7270

Ordfront tryckeri & förlag AB+, Fack, S-104 32 Stockholm Tel: (08) 341925/160335
Man Dir: Tom Carlsson; *Editorial, Rights and Permissions:* Dan Israel
Subjects: Fiction, Home and International Politics, Social Science, History, Juveniles; Quality Paperbacks
1978: 27 titles *1979:* 23 titles *Founded:* 1969
ISBN Publisher's Prefix: 91-7324

Bokförlaget **Plus**+*, Skt Eriksgatan 48, S-11234 Stockholm Tel: (08) 547408
Man Dir: Bengt Svensson
Subjects: General Fiction and Non-fiction, Juvenile
Founded: 1976

Bokförlaget **Prisma** AB+, Apelbergsgatan 56, Box 3192, S-103 63 Stockholm Tel: (08) 237280 Cable Add: Prismabok
Man Dir: Stig Edling
Subjects: General Fiction, Quality Paperbacks, Politics, Social Science, Dictionaries, Handbooks, Reference, University Textbooks, General Science
1978: 60 titles *Founded:* 1963
ISBN Publishers Prefix: 91-518

Psykologiförlaget AB+, Störtloppsvägen 40, Box 461, S-12604 Hägersten Tel: (08) 970395
Managing Editor: Lars Lindquist
Subjects: Psychology, Education
1978: 6 titles *Founded:* 1957

AB **Rabén och Sjögren** Bokförlag+, Tegnérgatan 28, Box 45022, S-104 30 Stockholm 45 Tel: (08) 349960 Cable Add: Rosbook Stockholm
Man Dir: Per A Sjögren; *Sales Dir:* Björn Englund; *Rights & Permissions:* Kerstin Kvint
Subjects: Speciality: Juveniles; also General Fiction, Belles Lettres, Poetry, Biography, History, How-to, Music, Art, Philosophy, Reference, Paperbacks, Psychology, Social Science, University Textbooks; Book Club
1977: approx 300 titles *1978:* approx 300 titles *Founded:* 1942
ISBN Publishers Prefix: 91-29

Bokförlaget **Rediviva**, Facsimileförlaget+, Fack, S-104 32 Stockholm 19 Tel: (08) 157271
Man Dir: Greta Helms
Subjects: Speciality: Reprints generally; also Bibliography, Topography, Facsimile Reprints of old Swedish books of travel, Dictionary of Anonymous and Pseudonymous Swedish Literature
Founded: 1968
ISBN Publishers Prefix: 91-7120

S A M — förlaget, PO Box 615, S-551 02 Jönköping Tel: (46036) 119130 Cable Add: SAM
Man Dir and other offices: Ragnwald Ahlnér
Subjects: Religious
1978: 8 titles *1979:* 9 titles
ISBN Publisher's Prefix: 91-7484

S E M I C Förlags AB+, PO Box 74, Landsvägen 57, S-172 22 Sundbyberg Tel: (46-8) 981140 Cable Add: semicpress, Stockholm Telex: 173 70 semic s
Man Dir: Kurt Björkman; *Editorial:* Agneta Hyllén (books), Ebbe Zetterstad (magazines); *Rights & Permissions:* Leif Kronbladh
Parent Company: Bonnier Magazine Group
Associate Company: Interpresse A/S, Bagsvaerd, Denmark
Subsidiary Companies: Kustannus Oy SEMIC, Tampere, Finland; SEMIC/Norge, Oslo, Norway
Subjects: Comic Magazines, Comic Albums, Comic Books, Knitting, Sports, Children's Books, Christmas Publications
Book Club: Serie-pocket-klubben
1977: about 110 titles *1978:* about 160 titles *Founded:* 1950
ISBN Publisher's Prefix: 91-552

S K E A B Förlag AB+, PO Box 1504, S-125 25 Älvsjö
Man Dir: Lars Kamlin; *Sales Dir:* Torbjörn Wetterö; *Publicity:* John Frederik Ivarsson
Orders to: Box 907, Jakobsdalsvagen 13-15, S-126 09 Hägersten Tel: (08) 188430
Branch Off: Box 1025, Sankta Annegatan 4, S-221 04 Lund Tel: (046) 124240
Subjects: Biography, Music, Religion, Reference, Juveniles, High-priced Paperbacks, Psychology, Textbooks, Educational Materials, Philosophy
Founded: 1910
Miscellaneous: This Company results from the merger of the two former independent Publishing Companies Verbum and Håkan Ohlssons

Förlaget **Sanctus**+, Sibyllegatan 18, Box 5020, S-102 41 Stockholm Tel: (08) 670155
The Publishing House of the United Methodist Church in Sweden
Man Dir: Karin Hellberg
Orders to: Sibyllegatan 18, S-114 42 Stockholm
Subjects: Theology and Christian Devotional

Bokförlaget **Settern**+, Drakabygget, S-286 00 Örkelljunga Tel: (0435) 80050/80070
Man Dir: Magdalena Rönneholm; *Sales, Publicity & Advertising Dir:* Christer Rönneholm
Orders to: Seeling & Co, Stockholm (qv under Booksellers)
Subjects: General Fiction and Nonfiction, High-priced Paperbacks
1978: 26 titles *1979:* 37 titles *Founded:* 1974
ISBN Publisher's Prefix: 7586

Skolförlaget Gävle AB+, Box 646, S-801 27 Gävle 1 Tel: (026) 115335 Cable Add: Skolförlaget
Man Dir: Barbro Larsson; *Editorial:* Jan-Olov Molin, Eva Winkler
Subjects: School Textbooks (especially Languages & Mathematics), Educational Materials
1977: 110 titles
ISBN Publishers Prefix: 91-42

Smålänningens Forlag AB+*, Sveavägen 98, S-113 50 Stockholm Tel: (08) 344296
Man Dir: Bengt-Ola Söder
Founded: 1964
Subjects: Hunting, Fishing, Hobbies
ISBN Publisher's Prefix: 91-7132

Sohlmans Förlag AB, Tegnérgatan 4, Box 45054, S-10430 Stockholm Tel: (08) 349890 Telex: 13434
Dir: Hans Hedström
Subjects: Music, Encyclopaedias, Sport
Founded: 1975

Sparfrämjandet, Förlagsaktiebolag+, Fack, Drottninggatan 29, S-103 20 Stockholm 16 Tel: (08) 141020
Man Dir: Torbjörn Hessling
Subjects: School Textbooks, Handbooks
Founded: 1925
ISBN Publishers Prefix: 91-7208

Bokförlaget **Spektra** AB+, Box 7024, S-300 07 Halmstad 7 Tel: (035) 36030 Cable Add: Comprint
Man Dirs: Åke Hallberg, Solveig Hallberg; *Literary Agent:* Lennart Sane Agency
Subjects: General Fiction, How-to, Music, Arts & Crafts, Reference, General Science
ISBN Publishers Prefix: 91-7136

Språkförlaget Skriptor AB+*, Södermalmstorg 8, S-10465 Stockholm Tel: (08) 7430555 Telex: 10393 Kval S
Man Dir: Jan Olsson
Founded: 1976

Leif **Stegeland** Förlag AB+, Box 446, Södra Hamngatan 45, S-40126 Gothenburg Tel: (031) 192540 Cable Add: Stegeland Telex: 27172 Stebook S
Man Dir: Leif Stegeland; *Sales Dir:* Gunnar Gärdhagen; *Rights & Permissions:* Agnita R-Birjesson
Subjects: General Fiction and Nonfiction, Juveniles, Educational Materials
Founded: 1967

Frank **Stenvalls** Förlag, Malmgatan 3, S-211 22 Malmö Tel: (040) 127703
Man Dir: Frank Stenvall
Subsidiary Company: Distrirail, Ave J B Sluysmans 135, B-4030, Liège, Belgium
Subjects: Railway, Maritime, Motoring Interest
1978: 10 titles *1979:* 12 titles *Founded:* 1966
ISBN Publisher's Prefix: 91-7266

Studentlitteratur AB+, PO Box 1719, S-221 01 Lund 1 Tel: (046) 307070 Cable Add: Studlitt Telex: 33345 educate s
Man Dir: Bertil Bratt; *Marketing Man:* Anders Regnér; *Publicity and Advertising:* Elisabeth Karlsson; *Rights and Permissions:* Inge Helander
Orders to: Åkergränden 1, S-222 39 Lund
Subjects: School and University Textbooks, covering Data Processing, Technology, Medicine, Social Sciences, Economics, Humanities
1977-78: 112 titles *Founded:* 1963
ISBN Publishers Prefix: 91-44

Svensk Kartjänst AB, Swedish Map Service, see Liber Grafiska AB

Svenska Utbildningsförlaget Liber AB, see Liber Grafiska AB

Sveriges Exportrads Förlag+, Storgatan 19, PO Box 5513, S-11485 Stockholm Tel: (08) 630580 Cable Add: Export Stockholm Telex: 19620 export a
Publishing Department of the Swedish Export Council
Man Dir: Lars Åkerman
Associate Company: Språkjänst (Translation and Interpreting Services)
Subjects: International Marketing, Customs, Shipping & Export Laws, Market Reports
Bookshop: at above address
1978: 72 (incl 64 Marketing Reports) *1979:* about 65 titles (incl 55 Marketing Reports)
Founded: 1887
ISBN Publisher's Prefix: 91-7548

Sveriges Radios Förlag, S-105 10 Stockholm Tel: (08) 7840000 Cable Add: Broadcast Telex: 100 00
Man Dir: Karl-Vilhelm Holne
Subjects: Educational Materials, Juveniles, Paperbacks
Founded: 1947
ISBN Publishers Prefix: 91-522

Teknografiska Institutet AB*,
Apelbergsgatan 56, Box 611, S–10128
Stockholm Tel: (08) 235675
Man Dir: Bertil Silwer
Subject: Technical books
Founded: 1946
ISBN Publishers Prefix: 91-7172

Bokförlags AB **Tiden**+, Torsgatan 2, Box
130, S–101 21 Stockholm 30 Tel: (08)
237640 Cable Add: Tidenbok
Man Dir: Anders Ferm; *Editorial:* Ulla
Freidh, Sten Dahlstedt, Henry Rolfner
Subjects: General Fiction and Non-fiction;
Juveniles, Politics, Social Science,
Psychology, Memoirs, Poetry, Illustrated
Books, High-priced Paperbacks
1977: 90 titles *Founded:* 1912
ISBN Publishers Prefix: 91-550

Tidnings AB Dagen, see Dagen

Tomas Förlag AB+*, Mälarlunden 4, S–152
00 Strängnäs Tel: (0152) 109 31
Man Dir: Alrik Hummel-Gumælius
Subject: Fiction
ISBN Publishers Prefix: 91-85070

Bokförlaget **Trevi** AB+, Barnhusgatan 3,
S–111 23 Stockholm Tel: (08)
101850/101590 Cable Add: Bok Trevi
Owners: Adam Helms, Solveig Nellinge
Subjects: General Fiction & Non-fiction,
Biography, How-to, Illustrated Books,
Feminism
1977: 60 titles *Founded:* 1971
ISBN Publishers Prefix: 91-7160

Unicart Kartografisk Produktion AB, PO
Box 7514, S–103 92 Stockholm (Located at:
Smålandsgatan 4, Box 7514, S–103 92
Stockholm) Tel: (08) 143460 Cable Add:
Universitypress Telex: 11785 Unpress S
Executive Chairman: Lars E Frieberg; *Man
Dir:* Sven Hartman
Subjects: Atlases, Wall Maps, Textbooks
Founded: 1973
Associate Company: Biblioteksförlaget AB,
Sweden (qv)

Utbildningsbolaget M M AB+, Box 4092,
S–171 04 Solna Tel: (08) 7302848
Man Dir: Mats Myrén
Subject: Teaching Aids

Vår Skola Förlag AB+, Grev
Magnigatan 11, S–114 55 Stockholm
Tel: (08) 623351
Man Dir: C O Sjögren
Subjects: School Textbooks, Magazines for
teachers and pupils

Förlagsaktiebolaget **Västra** Sverige+, Box
10238, S–434 01 Kungsbacka Tel: (0300)
11570 Cable Add: Printer
Telex: 21234 eba s
Man Dir: Per Elander; *Sales Dir,
Permissions:* Otto Elander; *Advertising Dir:*
Lars Henriksson
Subjects: General Non-fiction, especially
How-to, Hobbies, Hunting and Fishing,
Paperbacks
Founded: 1912
Book Club: Jaktjournalens Bokklubb
Subsidiary: Elanders Boktryckeri AB

Verbum, see S K E A B

AB **Wahlström** och **Widstrand**+, Tysta
Gatan 10, S–115 24 Stockholm Tel: (08)
679815 Cable Add: Wahlwid s Telex:
12757
Man Dir: Per I Gedin; *Sales Dir:* Sigvard
Olsson; *Rights & Permissions:* Ulla Asplund

Subjects: General Fiction & Non-fiction,
Handbooks, University & Quality
Paperbacks
1977: 110 titles *Founded:* 1884
ISBN Publishers Prefix: 91-46

B **Wahlströms** Bokförlag AB+*, Warfvinges
väg 30, S–112 51 Stockholm Tel: (08)
244600 Cable Add: Wahlbook, Stockholm
Telex: 17174
Man Dir: Bo Wahlström; *Editorial:* Karl-
Rune Östlund, Britt-Marie Jonsson; *Sales:*
Bertil Wahlström; *Publicity:* Pierre Roten;
Production: Tord Pramberg; *Permissions:*
Eva Melin
Subjects: General Fiction, Juveniles, Low-
priced Paperbacks
1977: 601 titles *Founded:* 1911
Subsidiaries: J A Lindblads Bokförlag
AB (qv); Kometförlaget AB (both at
Warfvinges Väg 30, S–112 51 Stockholm)
ISBN Publishers Prefix: 91-32

AB **Waldia** Förlag*, Brogatan 41, Box 35,
57100 Nässjö Tel: (038) 016200
Man Dir: Ernst Wallin

Ernst **Westerbergs** Förlags AB+,
Norrtullsgatan 10, Fack, S–102 30
Stockholm Tel: (08) 241650 Cable Add:
Baptistförlaget
Man Dir: Bengt Sjöblom
Subjects: Education, Juveniles, Music,
Religion, Philosophy
Founded: 1897

Wezäta Förlag, Grafiska Vägen, Box 5057,
S–402 22 Gothenburg Tel: (031) 400140
Cable Add: Wezätamelins Telex: 20872
Man Dir: Claes Lundgren; *Publicity
Manager:* Arne Arvidsson
Subject: How-to
Founded: 1886
Miscellaneous: Firm is one of the
independent houses within the Esselte
Förlag AB Group (qv)
ISBN Publishers Prefix: 91-85074

Zindermans Förlag+, Götgatan 13, Box
310, S–401 25 Gothenburg 1 Tel: (031)
136890/137832 Cable Add: Zindermans
Man Dir: Sune Stigsjöö
Subjects: General Fiction and Non-fiction,
especially Belles Lettres, Poetry, Biography,
History, How-to, Medicine, Psychology,
Social & Political Science
1978: 50 titles *Founded:* 1960
ISBN Publisher's Prefix: 91-528

Literary Agents

Arlecchino Teaterförlag, Gränsvägen 14,
S–131 71 Nacka Tel: (08) 7181717

D Richard **Bowen**, Box 30037, S–200 61
Malmö 30
Contact: D Richard Bowen Tel: (040)
161200/30

Gösta **Dahl** och Son AB*, Aladdinsvägen
14, S–161 38 Bromma/Stockholm Tel: (08)
256235 Cable Add: Literarius

Teaterförlag Arvid **Englind** AB*,
Karlavägen 56, Box 5124, S–102 43
Stockholm 5
Contact: Christer Englind

Mrs Lena I **Gedin***, Linnégatan 38, S–114
47 Stockholm Tel: 606067

Folmer **Hansen** Teaterförlag, Lundagatan 4,
S–171 63 Solna Tel: (08) 279838 Cable
Add: Folmerhansen Stockholm
Dir: Gerd Widestedt-Ericsson;

Dramaturgist: Peter Böök; *Public Relations:*
Annika Ånnerud
Specialization: Foreign Plays in
Scandinavia, Scandinavian Plays in
Scandinavia and Abroad, Children's Plays

Edith **Kiilerich**, Fiolstr 12, DK–1171
Copenhagen K, Denmark
This Danish literary agency also acts for
Finnish, Norwegian and Swedish writers

Nordiska Teaterförlaget/Edition Wilhelm
Hansen*, Norrlandsgatan 16, S–111 43
Stockholm Tel: (08) 104613 Cable Add:
Hammersmidt
Head Office: Gothersgade 9–11, DK–1123
Copenhagen, Denmark

Lennart **Sane** Agency, Holländerplan 9,
S–292 00 Karlshamn Tel: (0454) 12356
Cable Add: Saneagency Karlshamn
Dir: Lennart Sane; *Assistant Dir:* Elisabeth
Cederholm
Branch Off: Norra Vallgatan 98, S–211 22
Malmö Tel: (040) 123440
Founded: 1968

Book Clubs

Bättre Ledarskap, S–205 10 Malmö
Owned by: LiberLäromedel (Malmö);
Contact: Ingemar Ternbo
Subject: Management

Berghs Bokklub*, Box 17049, S–200 10
Malmö 17
Owned by: Berghs Forlag AB (Malmö)

Bonniers Bokklubb, Sveavägen 56, S–111 34
Stockholm
Owned by: Albert Bonniers Förlag AB
(Stockholm)

Bokklubben **Bra** Böcker, Södra Vägen,
S–263 00 Höganäs
Owned by: Bokförlaget Bra Böcker AB
(Höganäs)

Delta Science Fiction Bok Klubb*, Fack,
S–161 16 Bromma 16
Owned by: Delta Förlags AB (Bromma)

Familje Bokklubben, Fack, S–103 10
Stockholm 2
Owned by: Esselte Forlag AB (Stockholm)

Info Book, PO Box 135, S–527 00
Herrljunga
Owned by: Interskrift Publishing House
Subject: Religion

Jaktjournalens Bokklubb, Box 10238,
S–434 01 Kungsbacka Tel: 0300/11570
Cable Add: Printer, Kungsbacka
Telex: 21234
Owned by: Elanders Boktryckeri AB, Box
10238, S–434 01 Kungsbacka (a printing
company and a subsidiary of
Förlagsaktiebolaget Västra Sverige, qv)

Den **Kristna** Bokringen, Dagenhuset,
S–105 30 Stockholm
Owned by: Tidnings AB Dagen (Stockholm)

Lärarbokklubben*, LiberLäromedel, S–205
10 Malmö
Owned by: LiberLäromedel, Malmö (qv)
Subject: Education (Book Club for
Teachers)

Läsklubben Fyrklövern*, Torkel
Knutssonsgatan 27, Box 17037, S–104 62
Stockholm
Owned by: Lindqvist Forlag AB
(Stockholm)

SWEDEN

Månadens Bok, Box 2255, S-103 16
Stockholm (Located at: Skeppsbron 20)
Tel: (08) 232310
Man Dir: Erik Hyllner
Owned by: Albert Bonniers Förlag AB and
AB P A Nordstedt och Söners Förlag (both
Stockholm)

Readers' Digest AB, Box 6064, S-102 31
Stockholm 6 Tel: (08) 340780 Telex: 11689

Bokklubben Svalan*, Sveavägen 56, S-111
34 Stockholm
Owned by: Albert Bonniers Förlag AB
(Stockholm)

Vår Bok AB*, Tryckerigatan 2, Box 2052,
S-103 12 Stockholm 2
Subjects: Classics, Current Affairs,
Dictionaries, Encyclopedias, Detective
fiction, Periodicals
Owned by: Esselte Forlag AB (Stockholm)

Major Booksellers

Johan Åkerbloms Universitetsbokhandel*,
Östra Rådhusgatan 6, Box 83, S-901 03
Umeå Tel: (090) 125770

Almqvist och Wiksell Bokhandel AB,
Gamla Brogatan 26, Box 62, S-101 20
Stockholm Tel: (08) 237990

Eckersteins Universitetsbokhandel AB*,
Grönsakstorget, Box 3050, S-400 10
Gothenburg 3 Tel: (031) 171100

AB C E Fritzes Kungl Hovbokhandel,
Regeringsgatan 12, Box 16356, S-103 27
Stockholm Tel: (08) 238900 Cable Add:
Bokfritze Telex: 123 87 S Fritzes
Man Dir: Eide Segerbäck
Parent Company: Liber Grafiska AB (qv)
Founded: 1837

AB Gleerupska Universitetsbokhandeln*,
Fack, S-221 01 Lund Tel: (046) 117260

Gumperts Universitetsbokhandel AB, Norra
Hamngatan 26, Box 346, S-401 25
Gothenburg Tel: (031) 235480 Telex: 21178

Söderbokhandeln **Hansson och Bruce** AB,
Götgatan 37, S-116 21 Stockholm Tel: (08)
405432
Manager: T Fredriksson

AB Lundequistska Bokhandeln, Östra
Ågatan 31, Box 610, S-751 25 Uppsala 1
Tel: (018) 139830

AB Edvin **Lundgrens** Bokhandel,
Södergatan 3, S-211 34 Malmo Tel: (040)
76660

AB Nordiska Bokhandeln*, Kungsgatan 4,
Fack, S-101 10 Stockholm Tel: (08) 227380

AB Sandbergs Bokhandel*, Humlegårds-
gatan 12, Box 5518, S-114 85 Stockholm
Tel: (08) 236480
Manager: Ann-Mari Ericson

AB Seelig och Co*, Karlsrogatan 2,
S-17120 Solna Tel: 08850300 Telex: 12081
Cable Add: Seelig
(Book Importers)

Wettergrens Bokhandel AB, Västra
Hamngatan 22, S-41117, Gothenburg
Tel: (031) 170090

Major Libraries

Göteborgs Stadsbibliotek (City Library and
County Library)*, Götaplatsen, Gothenburg

Göteborgs Universitetsbibliotek, Central-
biblioteket, Renströmsgatan 4, Box 5096,
S-402 22 Gothenburg 5 Tel: (031) 810400
Librarian: Paul Hallberg
Publications: Årsberättelse (Annual Report);
*Acta Bibliothecae Universitatis
Gothoburgensis* (irregular)

Kungliga Biblioteket, Box 5039, S-102 41
Stockholm 5 Tel: (08) 241040
Royal Library of Stockholm
Secretary: Eva Andersson

Kungliga Svenska Vetenskapsakademiens,
S-106 91 Stockholm
Library of the Royal Swedish Academy of
Sciences. It constitutes the Mathematics and
Natural Sciences division of Stockholm
University Library (Stockholm Universitets
Bibliotek, qv)
Librarian: Dr Wilhelm Oldberg

Lund Universitetsbibliotek, Box 1010,
S-221 03 Lund Tel: (046) 124620 Telex:
322 08 LUB LUND
Librarian: Björn Tell

Malmö Stadsbibliotek, Regementsgatan 3,
S-21142 Malmö Tel: (040) 77810
Telex: 32577
City Library, County Library and Loan
Centre for South Sweden
Librarian: Bengt Holmström
*Publications: Annual Report; Catalogue of
Annual Acquisition; Bibliographies*

Riksarkivet (National Record Office)*,
Fyrverkarbacken 13-17, Fack, S-100 26
Stockholm 34

Statistiska Centralbyråns Bibliotek, Fack,
S-102 50 Stockholm
Library of the National Central Bureau of
Statistics

Stiftelsen Svenska Barnboksinstitutet,
Tjärhovsgatan 36, S-116 21 Stockholm Tel:
446355
Swedish Institute for Children's Books

Stockholm Universitets Bibliotek
(Stockholm University Library)*, S-106 91
Stockholm
This Library now also incorporates the
Library of the Royal Swedish Academy of
Sciences (Kungliga Svenska Vetenskapsa-
kademiens) (qv) covering Humanities, Law,
Social Sciences, Mathematics and Science

Stockholms Stadsbibliotek, Box 6502,
S-113 83 Stockholm
City Library of Stockholm

Sveriges Lantbruksuniversitets Bibliotek
(Libraries of the Swedish University of
Agricultural Sciences)*, Central Library
Ultunabiblioteket, S-750 07 Uppsala Tel:
(18) 102000
Dir: Lars-Erik Sanner

Uppsala Universitetsbibliotek, Box 510,
S-751 20 Uppsala Tel: (018) 139440 Telex:
76076 ubupps
Librarian: Thomas Tottie

Library Associations

Svenska Arkivsamfundet (Swedish
Association of Archivists)*, c/o Riksarkivet,
Fack S-100 26 Stockholm

Svenska Bibliotekariesamfundet, Sveriges
Lantbruksuniversitets Bibliotek,
Ultunabiblioteket, S-750 07 Uppsala Tel:
018-102000
Swedish Association of University and
Research Librarians
Executive Secretary: Birgit Nilsson
*Publication: Bibliotekariesamfundet
Meddelar*

Svenska Folkbibliotekarieförbundet,
Secretarial Office: Box 36, S-13106 Nacka
Union of Swedish Public Librarians
President: Barbro Forsberg

Sveriges Allmänna Biblioteksförening
(Swedish Library Association)*, Tornavägen
9, Fack, S-221 01 Lund
Acting Secretary: Jan Nyberg
Publication: Biblioteksbladet

Sveriges Vetenskapliga Specialbiblioteks
Förening (Association of Special Research
Libraries)*, c/o Statens Psykologisk-
Pedagogiska Bibliothek, Box 23099, S-104
35 Stockholm 23 Tel: (08) 228160/232
Secretary: I Bjorkman

Tekniska Litteratursällskapet (Swedish
Society for Technical Documentation)*, Box
5073, S-102 42 Stockholm 5
Secretary: Birgitta Levin
Publications: Tidskrift för Dokumentation
(6 a year)

Vetenskapliga Bibliotekens Tjänstemanna-
förening VBT, c/o D I K-förbundet, Box
36, S-131 06 Nacka
Association of Research and University
Librarians
President: Bo Stenström, Library of
Parliament, S-100 12 Stockholm

Library Journals

Bibliotekariesamfundet Meddelar (Reports
of the Librarians' Association), Swedish
Association of University and Research
Librarians, c/o Linköping University
Library, Fack, S-581 83 Linköping

Biblioteket Presenterar Nya Boecker (The
Library Presents News Books),
Bibliotekstjänst AB, Tornavägen 9, Fack,
S-221 01 Lund

Biblioteksbladet (Library Journal) (text in
Scandinavian languages, summaries in
English), Swedish Library Association,
Tornavägen 9, Fack, S-221 01 Lund

Tidskrift för Dokumentation (Scandinavian
Documentation Journal) (text in Swedish,
occasionally in English, summaries in
English), Tekniska Litteratursällskapet, Grev
Turgatan, S-114 35 Stockholm

Literary Associations and Societies

Författares Bokmaskin*, Box 2126, S-75002
Uppsala
Writers' Book Machine

Kungl Vitterhets Historie och Antikvitets
Akademien (Royal Academy of Letters,
History and Antiquities), Villagatan 3,
S-114, 32 Stockholm
Secretary: Örjan Lindberger
Publications: Fornvännen (journal),
Handlingar (memoirs), *Arkiv* (archives),
Årsbok (Yearbook), monographs, Library
and Archives

Litteraturfrämjandet, Bellmansgatan 30, S–116 47 Stockholm Tel: (08) 449175
Foundation for Promotion of Literature

Svenska Pennklubben (Swedish Centre of International P E N), AB P A Nordstedt & Söners Förlag, Tryckerigatan 2, Box 2052, S–103 12 Stockholm 2
President: Thomas von Vegesack; *Secretary:* Kerstin M Lundberg

Samfundet de Nio, c/o Anders Öhman, Smålandsgatan 14, S–111 46 Stockholm
Nine Swedish Authors' Society
Secretary: Anders R Öhman (lawyer)
Publication: Svensk Litteraturtidskrift (quarterly)

Svenska Österbottens Litteraturförening, c/o Olof Haegerstrand, Fasanvaegen 4, S–775 00 Krylbo
Swedish Österbottens Literary Association
Publication: Horisont

Sveriges Författarförbund, Linnégatan 10, Box 5252, S–102 45 Stockholm
Swedish Union of Writers
Secretary: Sonja Thunborg
Publication: Författaren

Literary Periodicals

BLM (Bonniers Litteraera Magasin) (Bonniers Literary Magazine), Albert Bonniers Förlag AB, Sveavägen 56, S–111 34 Stockholm

Horisont (Horizon), Svenska Österbottens Litteraturförening, c/o Harry Jarv, Fyreerkarbacken 32, S–112 60 Stockholm

Ord och Bild (Word and Picture), Stiftelsen Ord och Bild, Box 15116, S–104, 65 Stockholm

Svensk Litteraturtidskrift (Swedish Journal of Literature), Almqvist och Wiksell Förlag AB, Gamla Brogatan 26, S–101 20 Stockholm

Tulimuld (Scorched Earth); literary and cultural magazine of Estonian exiles (text in Estonian), Bernard Kangro, Skördevägen 1, S–222 38 Lund

Literary Prizes

Ida **Bäckman** Prize, see Swedish Academy Prizes

Bellmans Prize
For poetry. 50,000 Swedish crowns. Awarded annually. Enquiries to Swedish Academy, Börshuset, S–111 29 Stockholm

Beskow Prize, see Swedish Academy Prizes

Blom Prize, see Swedish Academy Prizes

The **Dalén-Engqvists** Prize
Annual award for Swedish Literature and Cultural Journalism. 13,000 Swedish crowns. This prize cannot be applied for. Enquiries to Swedish Academy, Börsuhet, Källargränd 4, S–111 29 Stockholm

Dobloug Prize, see Swedish Academy Prizes

Signe **Ekblad-Eldhs** Prize
To a famous Swedish writer. 25,000 Swedish crowns. Enquiries to Swedish Academy, Börshuset, S–111 29 Stockholm

The Lydia and Herman **Erikssons** Prize
Annual award to a Swedish writer for a work of prose or poetry. 14,000 Swedish crowns. This prize cannot be applied for. Enquiries to Swedish Academy, Börsuhet, Källargränd 4, S–111 29 Stockholm

Karin **Gierows** Prizes, see Swedish Academy Prizes

Grand Prize
For outstanding literary work. 50,000 Swedish crowns. Awarded annually. Enquiries to The Foundation for Promotion of Literature, Bellmansgatan 30, S–116 47 Stockholm

Grand Prize for a Book of Poetry
For the best original collection of new poems by a single author. 25,000 Swedish crowns. Awarded annually. Enquiries to Foundation for the Promotion of Literature, Bellmansgatan 30, S–116 47 Stockholm

Grand Prize for a Novel
For the best novel. 25,000 Swedish crowns. Awarded annually. Enquiries to The Foundation for Promotion of Literature, Bellmansgatan 30, S–116 47 Stockholm

Kalleberger Foundation — The Tekla **Hanssons** and Gösta Ronnströms Prize
Annual award in memory of Tekla Hansson to a Swedish writer for a work of prose or poetry. 3,000 Swedish crowns. This prize cannot be applied for. Enquiries to Swedish Academy, Börsuhet, Killärgränd 4, S–111 29 Stockholm

Axel **Hirsch** Prize, see Swedish Academy Prizes

Nils **Holgersson** Plaque*
The highest award for children's literature in Sweden. Awarded annually. Enquiries to Swedish Library Association, Tornavägen 9, Fack, S–22101 Lund

Kalleberger Foundation, see Hanssons

Ilona **Kohrtz** Prize, see Swedish Academy Prizes

The **Nine** Prize
For an author of established reputation for outstanding literary work. 20,000 Swedish crowns. Awarded annually. Enquiries to Nine Swedish Authors' Society, Smålandsgatan 14, S–111 46 Stockholm

Royal Prize, see Swedish Academy Prizes

Birger **Schöldström** Prize, see Swedish Academy Prizes

Henrik **Schück** Prize, see Swedish Academy Prizes

Swedish Academy Prizes
In addition to those fully listed individually, the Swedish Academy awards the following prizes — all of a literary nature:
Royal Prize (Cultural/Literary: annual);
Beskow Prize (Literary: biennial); *Blom Prize* (Swedish Language: annual); *Ida Bäckman Prize* (Literature/Journalism: biennial); *Dobloug Prize* (Swedish Literature: annual); *Karin Gierows Prizes* (1 Cultural Information: annual; 2 Promotion of Knowledge: annual); *Axel Hirsch Prize* (Biographic/Historic: biennial); *Ilona Kohrtz Prize* (Prose/Poetry: annual); *Henrik Schück Prize* (Literary History: annual); *Birger Schöldström Prize* (Literary History/Biography: every 4 years); *Swedish Linguistics Prize* (annual); *Swedish into Foreign Language Translation Prize* (annual); *Translation into Swedish Prize* (annual); *Zibet Prize* (Literary/Historic referring to reign of Gustav III: irregular); miscellaneous prizes for work in literary or linguistic fields.
Enquiries to The Swedish Academy, Börshuset, Källargränd 4, S–111 29 Stockholm

Swedish into Foreign Language Translation Prize, see Swedish Academy Prizes

Swedish Linguistics Prize, see Swedish Academy Prizes

Translation into Swedish Prize, see Swedish Academy Prizes

Zibet Prize, see Swedish Academy Prizes

Zorn Prize
For outstanding literary work. 20,000 Swedish crowns. Awarded annually. Enquiries to Swedish Academy, Börhuset, S–111 29 Stockholm

Translation Agencies and Associations

Språktjänst, PO Box 5513, S–114 85 Stockholm (Located at: Storgatan 19)
Translating and Interpreting Service of the Swedish Export Council (See Sveriges Exportråds Förlag under Publishers)

Switzerland

General Information

Language: German, French and Italian
Religion: Protestant and Catholic
Population: 6.33 million
Bank Hours: Vary. Often 0800-1230, 1330-1630 Monday-Friday
Shop Hours: 0800-1200, 1330-1830 Monday-Friday; in most cities, closed Monday morning; 0800-1200, 1330-1600 or 1700 Saturday
Currency: 100 centimes = 1 Swiss franc
Export/Import Information: No tariff on books. Most books exempt from Turnover Tax. Advertising matter usually dutiable, some exempt from Turnover Tax. No import licences required. No exchange controls
Copyright: UCC, Berne, Florence (see International Section)

Book Trade Organizations

Angestellten Verein des schweizer Buchhandels (Association of Swiss Book Trade Employees)*, CH–3110 Münsingen, Aeschistr 5, Postfach 144 Tel: 920477
Publication: Der Buchhändler

SWITZERLAND

Association romande du Personnel de la Librairie et de l'Edition (Swiss Association of Bookshop and Publishing Personnel), Les Saules en Mordagne, CH-1462 Yvonand Tel: 311393

Association suisse des Editeurs de Langue française, 2 ave Agassiz, CH-1001 Lausanne Tel: (021) 202811
Swiss Publishers' Association (French Language)
Secretary General: Robert Junod

Association suisse des Libraires de Langue française, 2 ave Agassiz, CH-1001 Lausanne Tel: (021) 202811
Association of Swiss French-language Bookshops

Association suisse romande des Diffuseurs de Livres, 2 ave Agassiz, CH-1001 Lausanne Tel: (021) 202811
Association of Book Distributors of French-speaking Switzerland

Associazione del Librai della Svizzera Italiana (ALSI) (Association of Bookshops of Italian-speaking Switzerland)*, CH-6948 Porza Tel: (091) 519688
Secretary: Luigi Rusconi

S B I, see Schweizer Buchwerbung und Information

Schweizer Buchwerbung und –Information (S B I), CH-8245 Feuerthalen Tel: (053) 44877
Swiss Book Publicity and Information Service
Dir: Gottfried Bürgin
Publications: Bucherkatalog des Schweizer Buchhandels, Schweizer Buchspiegel; also Wir Lesen — Sie auch? (a twice-yearly publication distributed to every household in German-speaking Switzerland)

Schweizer Buchzentrum, Hägendorf, POB 522, CH-4600 Olten 1
Swiss Book Centre

Schweizer Verband der Musikalienhändler und Verleger, Secretariat: Dr A Huber, Buchhaltungs und Revisions AG, Treudhandgesellschaft, CH-6301 Zug, Neugasse 29, Postfach
Swiss Association of Music Sellers and Publishers

Schweizerischer Adressbuchverleger-Verband, c/o Verlag für Wirtschaftsliteratur GmbH, Birmendorferstr 421, Postfach 271, CH-8055 Zurich Tel: (01) 335030/36
Swiss Association of Directory Publishers
President: Chr Laemmel

Schweizerischer Buchhändler- und Verleger-Verband (SBVV), Postfach 408, CH-8034 Zurich (Located at: Bellerivestr 3, CH-8008 Zürich) Tel: (01) 323345
Swiss Booksellers' and Publishers' Association – German language
Secretary: Peter Oprecht
Publications: Der Schweizer Buchhandel (bi-monthly) (official organ of this association, also its French equivalent (SLESR), and its Italian equivalents SESI and ALSI; also publishes Das Schweizer Buch, Adressbuch des Schweizer Buchhandels, Schweizer Bücherverzeichnis; see also similar publications by the SBI (above)

Schweizerischer Bühnenverleger-Verband (Association of Swiss Publishers for the Stage)*, Steinentorstr 13, CH-4010 Basel Tel: 231352
President: Dr R Corrodi (at Utoquai 41, CH-8008 Zurich)

Societa Editori della Svizzera Italiana (SESI), Viale Portone 4, POB 282, CH-6501 Bellinzona Tel: (092) 258555/56
Telex: 79018 ASEG
Association of Publishers for Italian-speaking Switzerland
Dir: Romano Montalbetti

Société des Librairies et Editeurs de la Suisse romande (SLESR), 2 ave Agassiz, CH-1001 Lausanne Tel: (021) 202811
Booksellers' and Publishers' Association of French-speaking Switzerland
Secretary General: Robert Junod
Publications: La Librairie suisse (bi-monthly) official organ of this association, its German equivalent (SBVV), its Italian equivalent (SESI)

Syndicat de la Librairie ancienne et du Commerce de l'Estampe en Suisse (Vereinigung der Buchantiquare und Kupferstichhändler in der Schweiz), CH-8001 Zurich, Trittligasse 19
Association of Antiquarian Book and Print Sellers in Switzerland

Verband evangelischer Buchhandlungen und Verlage der Schweiz, Badenerstr 69, CH-8026 Zurich Tel: (01) 2428155
Association of Swiss Protestant Booksellers and Publishers
Dir: Mr Voemel

Verband schweizerischer Antiquare und Kunsthändler (Association of Swiss Secondhand Booksellers and Art Dealers)*, CH-3011 Bern, Gerechtigkeitsgasse 30 Tel: (031) 221104

Verband schweizerischer Zeitungsagenturen und Büchergrossisten (Union d'Agences suisses de Journaux et Livres en Gros) (Association of Swiss Newspaper Distributors and Book Wholesalers)*, CH-4002 Basle, St Jakobsstr 25 Tel: (061) 225500

Vereinigung der Schweizerischen Buchgemeinschaften (Association of Swiss Book Clubs)*, CH-8048 Zurich, Hermetschloostr 77 Tel: 625100

Vereinigung katholischer Buchhändler und Verleger der Schweiz, c/o Leobuchhandlung, Galusstr 20, CH-9001 St Gallen Tel: 222917
Association of Swiss Catholic Booksellers and Publishers

Book Trade Reference Books and Journals

Books

Adressbuch des schweizer Buchhandels, Schweizerischer Buchhändler- und Verleger-Verband, CH-8008 Zurich, Bellerivestr 3
Directory of the Swiss Book Trade, containing Lists of Publishers, Booksellers, Distributors, Trade Organizations and Cross-Reference Indices.

Adressbuch für den deutschsprachigen Buchhandel. This Directory of the German-speaking Book Trade lists all Swiss, Austrian and German publishers. See Book Trade Reference Books, Federal Republic of Germany.

Schweizer Buchspiegel (Swiss Book Mirror), Swiss Booksellers' and Publishers' Association, CH-8008 Zurich, Bellerivestr 3

Wir Lesen — Sie Auch? (We are Readers — You, too?), Swiss Book Publicity and Information Service, CH-8245 Feuerthalen

Journals

Bibliographie analytique des Bibliographies suisses courantes (Analytical Bibliography of Current Swiss Bibliographies), Swiss National Library, CH-3003 Berne, Hallwylstr 15

Bibliographie des Publications officielles suisses (Bibliography of Swiss Official Publications), Swiss National Library, CH-3003 Berne, Hallwylstr 15

Der Buchhändler (The Bookseller), Association of Swiss Book Trade Employees, CH-3110 Münsingen, Aeschistr 5, Postfach 144

Edition, Stauffacher Verlag AG, CH-8055 Zürich 3, Birmensdorfer Str 318 (book advertiser)

Guilde du Livre (Book Guild), 5 rue de l'Ecole Supérieure, CH-1005 Lausanne

Librarium (text in German and French), Schweizerische Bibliophilen-Gesellschaft, CH-8001 Zurich, Zwingliplatz 3

Das schweizer Buch (The Swiss Book); bibliographical bulletin, Swiss Booksellers' and Publishers' Association, CH-8008 Zurich, Bellerivestr 3

Schweizer Bücherverzeichnis (Swiss Book Catalogue), Swiss Booksellers' and Publishers' Association, CH-8008 Zurich, Bellerivestr 3

Der Schweizer Buchhandel (La Librairie suisse) (The Swiss Bookseller), Swiss Booksellers' and Publishers' Association, CH-8008 Zurich, Bellerivestr 3

Publishers

Editions **24 Heures**+, 33 ave de la Gare, CH-1001 Lausanne Tel: (021) 203111
Telex: CH 24495
Man Dir: P Ruckstuhl; *Advertising, Permissions:* L R Pisler
Subjects: Belles Lettres, History, Music, Art, Juveniles, Educational Materials
1978: 10 titles *Founded:* 1969
Miscellaneous: Associated imprints include Imprimeries Réunies SA (qv)

A B C Verlag+, Rüdigerstr 12, Postfach, CH-8021 Zurich Tel: (01) 2013671 Cable Add: ABC Verlag Zurich
Man & Sales Dir: Konrad Baumann
Subjects: Graphic Design, Art
1977: 5 titles *1978:* 4 titles *Founded:* 1936
ISBN Publishers Prefix: 3-85504

A L A Verlag, Klosbachstr 46, CH-8032 Zurich Tel: (01) 320890
Man Dir and other offices: Berta Rahm
Subjects: Human Rights (and especially Women's Emancipation); Social Science, Biography, History
1978: 1 title *1979:* 1 title *Founded:* 1968
ISBN Publishers Prefix: 3-85509

Aare-Verlag+*, see Schweizer Jugend-Verlag

Aargauer Tagblatt Verlag AG+, CH-5001 Aarau 5, Postfach 225, Bahnhofstr 39 Tel: (064) 251133
Dir: Walter Widmer
Subjects: Technical, Reference
Founded: 1847
ISBN Publishers Prefix: 3-85502

Editions **Adversaires**, now known as Francois Grounauer (qv)

Aesopus Verlag GmbH, Grellingerstr 95, CH–4058 Basel Tel: (061) 423373
Man Dir: Nicolaus M Fisch
Branch Off: Munich
Subjects: Health, Sports, Accident Prevention
Miscellaneous: Publish in 9 languages

Editions L'**Age d'Homme** — La Cité+*, 10 Métropole, PO Box 263, CH–1003 Lausanne Tel: (021) 220095
Man Dir: Vladimir Dimitrijevic
Parent Company: Alfred Eibel, Editeur, France (qv)
Subjects: General Fiction, Belles Lettres, Poetry, Biography, Music, Art, Philosophy, Religion, Psychology, Social Science, Futurism and Esoterica, Slavica, Sci-Fic, Cinema, Literary Criticism, Reprints
Bookshops: Librairie la Proue, Escaliers du Marché 17, CH–1000 Lausanne
1977: approx 60 titles *1978:* approx 60 titles *Founded:* 1966
ISBN Publishers Prefix: 2-8251

Albanus Verlag*, J H Göhre, Hulfteggstr 10, Postfach, CH–8401 Winterthur 1 Tel: (052) 293503
ISBN Publisher's Prefix: 3-85510

Albatros Verlag AG, Lenzenwiesstr 2, CH–8702 Zollikon Tel: (01) 340866
Subjects: Illustrated Reference Books, Animals and Plants, Technical, Culture
1978: 9 titles

Amadeus Verlag, Germaniastr 64, CH–8006 Zurich
Subjects: Music Books, Records

Ansata-Verlag*, Paul A Zemp, 'Helfenstein', CH–3150 Schwarzenburg Tel: (031) 931586 Cable Add: Ansata, Schwarzenburg Tel: (031) 931586
Subjects: Occultism, Astrology, Folklore, History of Culture and Science

Editions **Anthroposophiques Romandes**+, 13 rue Verdaine, CH–1204 Geneva Tel: (022) 285150
Subjects: Anthroposophical/Rosicrucian Literature in French
1979: 25 titles

Antonius-Verlag*, CH–4500 Solothurn, Gärtnerstr 7 Tel: (065) 223912
Subjects: Psychology, Therapeutics, Pedagogy
ISBN Publisher's Prefix: 3-85520

Verlag der **Arche** Peter Schifferli AG+, Rosenbühlstr 37, CH–8044 Zurich Tel: (01) 342154 Cable Add: Archeverlag
Owner: Peter Schifferli
Orders to: Erikastr 11, CH–8003 Zurich
Branch Offs: Zurich (2), Konstanz (1), Berlin (1), Vienna (2)
Associate Companies: Sanssouci Verlag AG, Zürich (qv); Dr Franz Hain, Austria (qv); E Pfister GmbH, German Federal Republic (qv)
Subjects: General Fiction, Belles Lettres, Scholarly
1977-78: 40 titles *Founded:* 1944
ISBN Publishers Prefix: 3-7160

Archimedes Verlag, Rolf Christiani, Marktweg 7, Postfach 180, CH–8280 Kreuzlingen Tel: (072) 722672
Subjects: Geodesy, Electronics, Mechanical Engineering; Periodical *Technik Heute*
ISBN Publishers Prefix: 3-85525

Ariston Verlag (formerly Ramòn F Keller)+, 39 rue Peillonnex, PO Box 82, CH–1225 Chêne-Bourg, Geneva Tel: (022) 481262/3 Cable Add: Ariston CH–1225 Chêne-Bourg
Man Dir/Editorial: Dr Heinz Bundschuh; *Sales/Rights & Permissions:* Mrs A Bundschuh; *Production:* U Lerf; *Publicity:* C Chenevard
Imprints: Ariston Verlag Genf
Subjects: How-to, Psychology, Nature Medicine, Parapsychology, Hypnosis, Yoga, Self-Help, General Fiction
1979: 86 titles *Founded:* 1964
ISBN Publisher's Prefix: 3-7205

Art-CC A G*, Peter Merian Str 49, CH–4052 Basle Tel: (061) 237030 Telex: 63487
Publisher: Christoph Czwiklitzer
Br Offs: Christoph Czwiklitzer, D–7570 Baden-Baden, Federal German Republic; Czwiklitzer — Le Gall, F–75016 Paris, France
Subject: Art

Art Edit AG, Drusbergstr 1, CH–8703 Erlenbach ZH
Subsidiary Company: Edition Cicero Verlagsgesellschaft mbH, German Federal Republic (qv)
Subject: Art

Artemis Verlags AG+, CH–8024 Zurich, Limmatquai 18 Tel: (01) 341100/02 Cable Add: Artemis Zurich Telex: 59477
Man Dir: Dr Bruno Mariacher; *Rights & Permissions:* Ingrid Parge
Branch Off: Verlag für Architektur Artemis, Federal Republic of Germany (qv)
Subjects: General Fiction, Philosophy, Art, Architecture, Encyclopaedias, Juveniles
1977: 59 titles *1978:* 54 titles *Founded:* 1943
ISBN Publishers Prefix: 3-7608

Athenaeum Verlag AG, Via Miravalle 23, CH–6900 Lugano-Massagno Tel: (091) 571536 Cable Add: athenag
Man Dir: J-E Nussbaumer; *Administration:* I Wolfensberger; *Editorial:* Dr von Zschinski, J Steiner
Branch Off: Buchauslieferung, Schweizer Buchzentrum, Olten
Subjects: General Nonfiction: Art, History, Science, Literature, Biography, Politics
1977: 3 titles *1978:* 1 title *Founded:* 1972
ISBN Publisher's Prefix: 3-85532

Atlantis Verlag AG+, Zürichbergstr 66, Postfach 200, CH–8044 Zürich Tel: (0411) 325343
Man Dir: Dr Max Mittler
Branch Off: Atlantis Verlag KG, D–7800 Freiburg im Breisgau, Erwinstr 58-60, Postfach 11127, Federal Republic of Germany (qv)
Subjects: Pictorial Geography and Travel, Art, Literature, History, Colonialism, Music and Theatre, Juveniles
1977: 40 titles *1978:* 25 titles *Founded:* 1930
ISBN Publishers Prefix: 3-7611

Atrium Verlag AG+*, Rütistr 4, CH–8030 Zürich Tel: (01) 479006
Subjects: Fine & Applied Arts, Illustrated Books, Juveniles, Belles Lettres, Fiction
Founded: 1936
ISBN Publishers Prefix: 3-85535

Augustin-Verlag*, Schlatterweg 11, CH–8240 Thayngen Tel: (053) 67131
Subjects: Geography, History, Textbooks — especially series of anatomical booklets for schoolchildren (*Unser Korper* = Our Body)
ISBN Publisher's Prefix: 3-85540

Editions de la **Baconnière** SA+, 7 ave du Collège, BP 185, CH–2017 Boudry-Neuchâtel Tel: (038) 421004 Cable Add: Baconnière Boudry
Man Dir, Editorial, Publicity, Production, Sales: Dr Hermann Hauser; *Rights & Permissions:* Miss Marie-Christine Hauser
Orders to: Diffusion Payot (Booksellers), rue des Côtes de Montbenon, CH–1002 Lausanne
Subjects: Belles Lettres, Poetry, Biography, History, Music, Art, Philosophy, Reference, Psychology, Social Science, University Textbooks
1977: 31 titles *Founded:* 1927
Miscellaneous: Publish the international periodical *Cultures*
ISBN Publisher's Prefix: 2-8252-0800

Balmer AG Verlag, Neugasse 12, CH–6301 Zug Tel: (042) 214141 Telex: 78812
Man Dir: Christoph Balmer
Subjects: Local History, Literature, Psychology, Pedagogics
Bookshop: Neugasse 12, CH–6301 Zug
Miscellaneous: Associate Co: Klett & Balmer GmbH Verlag, Landesgemeindepl 4, CH–6301 Zug (qv)
ISBN Publisher's Prefix: 3-85548

U **Bär** Verlag*, CH–8008 Zurich, Hufgasse 17 Tel: (01) 472377
Man Dir: Dr Ulrich Bär; *Permissions:* Marianne Widmer
Associate Company: A S Börsen Verlag AG, Switzerland (qv)
Subjects: How-to, Art, Reference

Librairie **Barblan et Saladin**+, 10 rue de Romont, CH–1701 Fribourg Tel: (037) 226065
Bookshop: Address as above
Founded: 1954

Bargezzi-Verlag AG, Wasserwerkgasse 17-19, Postfach 1199, CH–3001 Berne Tel: (031) 221380 Cable Add: Bargezzi Bern
Man Dir/Editorial/Sales/Publicity/Rights & Permissions: Josef Grübel; *Production:* Hugo Tanner
Subjects: Novels, Religious Literature
1977: 4 titles *1978:* 3 titles *Founded:* 1948

Basileia Verlag, CH–4003 Basel, Missionsstr 21 Tel: (061) 251766
Man Dir: Rudolf Kellenberger
Subject: Religion
ISBN Publishers Prefix: 3-85555

Basilius Presse+, Güterstr 86, Postfach 153, CH–4002 Basel Tel: (061) 228000 Cable Add: Basiliuspresse Telex: 62652
Man Dir: Josef Felix
Orders to: Karger Libri AG, CH–4011 Basel, Petersgraben 31
Subjects: General Fiction, Nonfiction, Juveniles, Music, Art (Paintings), High-priced Paperbacks, General Science
Founded: 1959
ISBN Publishers Prefix: 3-85560

Baufachverlag AG+, Schöneggstr 102, Postfach 6721, CH–8953 Dietikon Tel: (01) 7407673 Telex: 52702 impagch
Dir: Wolfgang R Felzmann
Subject: Building Trade and Architecture (Technical and Specialist Books)
1977: 4 titles *Founded:* 1970
ISBN Publishers Prefix: 3-85565

Beltz+*, Rittergasse 20, Postfach 227, CH–4051 Basle Tel: (061) 239470
Owner: Dr Manfred Beltz Rübelmann
Subject: Textbooks, Psychology, Juveniles
ISBN Publisher's Prefix: 3-407

Benteli Verlag+, Gerechtigkeitsgasse 6, Postfach 102, CH-3000 Berne 8 Tel: (031) 228866 Cable Add: Bag 3000 Berne 8
Man Dir: Ted Schaap (Scapa)
Subjects: General Fiction, Belles Lettres, Poetry, History, Art, Textbooks, Reference, *1977:* 32 titles *1979:* 35 titles *Founded:* 1899
ISBN Publishers Prefix: 3-7165

Benziger AG+, Bellerivestr 3, CH-8008 Zurich Tel: (01) 347050 Cable Add: Benzigerverlag Zurich Telex: 004554545
Man Dir: Dr Oscar Bettschart; *Editorial:* Dr Renate Nagel, Willy Walker, Anton Scherer; *Sales and Rights & Permissions Dir:* Robert E Oehler; *Production:* Walter Eberle; *Advertising Dir:* Heinrich Flüeler
Branch Off: Benziger Verlag, Federal Republic of Germany (qv)
Subjects: General Fiction, Belles Lettres, Poetry, Religion, Juveniles, Educational Materials
1978: 85 titles *1979:* 95 titles *Founded:* 1792
Bookshops: Buchhandlung Benziger, Martinstr 16, D-5000 Cologne; Carolus, Kunst- und Bücherstube, Neue Kräme 21, D-6000 Frankfurt am Main (both in the German Federal Republic)
ISBN Publishers Prefix: 3-545

Berchtold-Haller-Verlag, Nägeligasse 9, Postfach 15, CH-3000 Berne 7 Tel: (031) 222583 Cable Add: BEG Berne
Manager and Sales Dir: Peter Schranz
Branch Offs: Buchhandlung der Evangelischen Gesellschaft, Nägeligasse 9, CH-3000 Berne 7; Evangelische Buchhandlung, CH-3400 Burgdorf, Schmiedengasse 26; Evangelische Buchhandlung, CH-4900 Langenthal, Melchstr 8 (all in Switzerland)
Subjects: Religion, Juveniles
1977: 3 titles *1978:* 4 titles *Founded:* 1848
ISBN Publishers Prefix: 3-85570

Edition Sven Erik **Bergh** im Europabuch AG, Erlenweg 6, CH-6314 Unterägeri, Zug Tel: (042) 723077 Telex: 862112
Man Dir: Dr S E Bergh; *Editorial:* Liselotte Bergh; *Rights & Permissions:* Karin Bergh
Parent Company: Berghs Förlag AG, Sweden (qv)
Associate Company: Edition Sven Erik Bergh, Federal Republic of Germany (qv)
Subjects: General Fiction, Belles Lettres, Picture Books, Juveniles
1977: 17 titles *1978:* 16 titles *Founded:* 1976

Berichthaus Verlag, Dr Conrad Ulrich+*, Voltast, 43, CH-8044 Zurich Tel: (01) 346349
Subjects: History, Theology
Founded: 1730
ISBN Publishers Prefix: 3-85572

Editions **Berlitz** SA+, 1 ave des Jordils, CH-1000 Lausanne 6 Tel: (021) 277561 Cable Add: Berledit Lausanne Telex: 25492 CH
Man Dir: Marshall D Mascott; *Editorial:* Konrad Fuchs; *Production Manager:* Jean-Paul Minder
Parent Company: Macmillan Publishing Co, USA
Subjects: Travel, Tourism, Language-learning
1977: 100 titles *1978:* 100 titles (figures approx) *Founded:* 1970
ISBN Publisher's Prefix: According to distributor

Beyeler Editions Basel+*, Bäumlcingasse 9, CH-4001 Basel Tel: (061) 235412
Owner: Ernst Beyeler
Subject: Art
Founded: 1967
ISBN Publishers Prefix: 3-85575

The **Bhaktivedanta** Book Trust*, 94 rue de Lausanne, CH-1202 Geneva Tel: (022) 326368
Subjects: Indian Philosophy, Religion & Culture
Miscellaneous: Firm is also a distributor

Bibliographisches Institut AG+*, Hardturmstr 76, Postfach 130, CH-8021 Zurich Tel: (01) 446642 Telex: 58480 bilag
Man Dir: Rudolf Hans Fürrer; *Production:* B Mannheim
Parent Company: Bibliographisches Institut AG, Mannheim
Subjects: Philosophy, Linguistics, General Science, Reference Works
Founded: 1967
ISBN Publishers Prefix: 3-411

Verlag **Bibliophile Drucke** von Josef Stocker AG, Hasenbergstr 7, CH-8953 Dietikon-Zurich Tel: (01) 7404444
Man Dir: Mr Stocker
Parent Company: Verlag Stocker-Schmid AG (qv)
Associate Company: Urs Graf-Verlag GmbH (qv)
Subjects: Belles Lettres, Poetry, Reference, Historical Manuscript facsimiles
Bookshop: Buchhandlung Stocker-Schmid, CH-8953 Dietikon, Hasenbergstr 7
ISBN Publishers Prefix: 3-85577

Birkhäuser Verlag+, Elisabethenstr 19, Postfach 34, CH-4010 Basle Tel: (061) 231810 Cable Add: Edita Telex: 63475
Man Dir: Carl Einsele; *Sales Dir:* H Jo Pfeiffer
Subjects: Art, Architecture, Engineering, Mathematics, Natural Science, Psychology, Pharmacy, Railway Interest, General & Social Science, University Textbooks, Paperbacks, 22 scientific journals
1977: 91 titles *1978:* 68 titles *Founded:* 1879
Subsidiaries: 'Interavia' SA, Geneva, Switzerland (qv); Birkhäuser Verlag GmbH, Federal Republic of Germany (qv); Birkhaeuser Boston Inc, 380 Green St, PO Box 2007, Cambridge, MA 02139, USA
ISBN Publishers Prefix: 3-7643

Blaukreuz-Verlag Bern+, Postfach 1196, Lindenrain 52, CH-3001 Berne Tel: (031) 235866 Cable Add: Blaukreuzverlag
Man Dir: Eduard Müller
Parent Company: Blaues Kreuz der deutschen Schweiz
Subjects: Belles Lettres, Poetry, Biography, Religion, Juveniles; Addiction Problems (Alcohol, Drugs, Tobacco)
1978: 10 titles *1979:* 8 titles *Founded:* 1884
ISBN Publishers Prefix: 3-85580

Les Editions de la Fondation Martin **Bodmer**, CP 7, CH-1223 Cologny-Geneva Tel: (022) 362370
Subjects: Philology, Papyrus Editions
ISBN Publisher's Prefix: 3-85682

Bohem Press Kinderbuchverlag, Asylstr 67, CH-8007 Zürich Tel: (01) 347714
Dir: O Bozejowsky v Rawennoff; *Art Dir:* S Zavrel
ISBN Publishers Prefix: 3-85581

A S **Börsen** Verlag AG, Hufgasse 17, CH-8008 Zurich Tel: (01) 473329
Dirs: Dr Ulrich Bar, Marianne Widmer
Associate Company: U Bar Verlag, Zurich (qv)
Subject: Industrial Management
1977: 1 title *Founded:* 1977

Brain Anatomy Institute, Untere Zollgasse 71, CH-3072 Ostermundigen/BE Tel: (031) 512411
Dir/Rights & Permissions: Prof G Pilleri
Subjects: Biology of Marine Animals, Comparative Anatomy, Investigations on Cetacea
1977: 3 titles *Founded:* 1969

Brunnen-Verlag+, Spalenberg 20, CH-4001 Basle Tel: (061) 254407
Man Dir: Hans-Peter Züblin
Publishers Represented: MFB Phono- und Schriftenmission, German Federal Republic (qv)
Subject: Religion
Bookshops: Buchhandlung Pilgermission, CH-4001 Basel, Spalenberg 20; CH-9500 Wil/SG, Utere Bahnhofstr 20
Miscellaneous: Firm is branch office of Brunnen-Verlag GmbH, Pestalozzistr 1, D-6300 Giessen, Federal Republic of Germany (qv)
Founded: 1920
ISBN Publishers Prefix: 3-7655

Bubenberg Verlag AG, Postfach 2736, CH-3007 Berne (Located at: Monbijoustr 61) Tel: (031) 455941
Subjects: Belles Lettres, Poetry, How-to, Reference
Founded: 1951
ISBN Publisher's Prefix: 3-85585

Verlag der **Buchdruckerei** Ostschweiz AG*, CH-9001 St Gallen, Hintere Poststr 2 Tel: (071) 208585 Telex: 77393
Man & Sales Dir: Dr Hans Schmid
Subjects: Belles Lettres, Poetry, History, Music, Art, Social Science
Bookshop: Thorbecke Verlag KG, Sigmaringen, German Federal Republic
1977: 3 titles *Founded:* 1892
ISBN Publisher's Prefix: 3-85837

Verlag Alfred **Bucheli***, CH-6301 Zug, Baarerstr 61, Postfach 281 Tel: 211247 Telex: 78737
Subjects: Car and Motor Cycle Engineering, Flying

Verlag C J **Bucher** AG+, Zürichstr 3, CH-6002 Lucerne Tel: (041) 391111 Cable Add: Cibag Luzern Telex: 65245 edbuch
Publishing Dir: Hans Peter Renner; *Editorial:* Axel Schenck; *Sales:* Eduard Gogel; *Rights & Permissions:* Maryam Sauer; *Production:* Hans Blender; *Publicity:* Rolf Gaensslen
Subjects: Natural History, Animals, Cities and Countries, Art, Cultural History, Photography, Reference, Film Book Series, General Non-fiction
1978: 25 titles *1979:* 27 titles *Founded:* 1870
Subsidiary: C J Bucher GmbH, D-6000 Frankfurt am Main 1, Hanauer Landstr 11 (qv)
ISBN Publishers Prefix: 3-7658

Buchhaus AG, see Office du Livre SA

Büchler-Verlag+*, Rämistr 50, Postfach, CH-8028 Zurich Tel: (01) 342034/342347 Telex: 32697
Man Dirs: Marc F Büchler, Urs Gresly; *Advertising:* Bücherpick-Werbung AG; *Permissions:* Urs Gresly

Parent Company: Büchler & Co AG, Printers and Publishers, CH-3084 Wabern-Bern
Subjects: How-to, Reference, Guidebooks, Art, Educational Materials
1977: 3 titles *Founded:* 1886
ISBN Publishers Prefix: 3-7170

Hugo **Buchser** SA+, 4 Tour de l'Ile, CH-1211 Geneva Tel: (022) 288155 Telex: 289469 HB8A CH
Subjects: Management, Directories, Periodicals
Founded: 1927

C E E L (Centre Expérimental pour l'Enseignement des Langues), Palais Wilson, 52 rue des Pâquis, 1211 Geneva 14 Tel: (022) 325893/325612
Centre for Experimentation and Evaluation of Language Learning Techniques
Man Dir: Nicolas Ferguson
Orders to: Sistemas Educativos SA, Mexico DF (for Mexico); CEEL Finland, Albertinkatu 6B 30, SF-00150 Helsinki, Finland (for Finland, Norway, Sweden); Geneva address above for rest of world
Subjects: Applied Linguistics, English, French, German, Spanish, Italian, Russian, Greek and Finnish as Foreign Languages
1977: 8 titles *1978:* 6 titles *Founded:* 1972
ISBN Publisher's Prefix: 2-88047

C V B Buch und Druck, CH-8026 Zurich, Badenerstr 69 Tel: (01) 2428155
Associate Company: Gotthelf Verlag (qv) at same address
Bookshop: Company owns 6 bookshops in Switzerland
Founded: 1892
ISBN Publishers Prefix: 3-85628

Cahiers de la Renaissance Vaudoise+*, 18 rue du Petit-Chêne, CH-1003 Lausanne Tel: (021) 221914
President: Marcel Regamey; *Dir:* Olivier Delacrétaz
Subjects: Belles Lettres, History, Secondary Textbooks, Politics, Militaria
ISBN Publishers Prefix: 2-88017

Camera-Verlag*, CH-6002 Lucerne, Zürichstr 3-7 Tel: (041) 223385 Cable Add: Cibag Telex: Innch 78122
Subject: Photography (in separate editions in English, French, German)
ISBN Publishers Prefix: 0008-2074

Edizioni del Prof Mario Agliati **Cantonetto**+*, CH-6900 Lugano, Via Greina 2

Caritas-Verlag*, Löwenstr 3, Postfach 902, CH-6002 Lucerne Tel: (041) 235676
Subject: Religion
ISBN Publisher's Prefix: 3-85592

Carta, Lüthi & Ramseier, Haslerstr, CH-3000 Bern Tel: (031) 259548 Cable Add: Zeilerag Telex: 32391 (Zeiler AG)
Man Dir/Rights & Permissions: Lüthi Heinz; *Sales:* Volders Viktor; *Production:* Ramseier Ulrich
Orders to: Zeiler AG, Gartenstadstr 5, Postfach 32, Dept Geo-Carta, CH-3098 Köniz-Bern
Subjects: Maps of Europe and World in various scales and layouts, Atlases, Street Maps, Local Area Maps
Founded: 1964

Edizioni **Casagrande** SA+, Via del Bramantino, Postfach 489, CH-6501 Bellinzona Tel: (092) 256622 Telex: 73131
Man Dir: Libero Casagrande; *Sales:* Giampiero Casagrande
Associate Companies: Istituto Grafico Casagrande SA, Bellinzona; Gianni Casagrande SA, Bellinzona
Subjects: Literature, Art, Academic, History, Art History
1977: 25 titles *1978:* 24 titles *Founded:* 1969
ISBN Publisher's Prefix: 3-85897

Caux Verlag-, Theater- & Film-AG+, Postfach 218, CH-6002 Lucerne Tel: (021) 614241
Subsidiary Company: Editions de Caux, CH-1824 Caux (qv)
Subjects: Theatre and Film, Social Science, Biography, Religion
ISBN Publisher's Prefix: 3-85601

Editions de **Caux**+, CH-1824 Caux Tel: (021) 614241 Telex: 24278
Man Dir, Editorial, Production, Publicity: Chas Piguet; *Sales, Rights and Permissions:* B Utzinger
Parent Company: Caux Verlag AG, Lucerne (qv)
Subjects: Moral Rearmament, Social Sciences, Religion, Theatre, Biographies
Bookshop: Librairie de Caux, CH-1824 Caux
1977: 2 titles *1978:* 1 title
ISBN Publisher's Prefix: 2-88037

Centre Expérimental pour l'Enseignement des Langues (Centre for the Experimentation and Evaluation of Language Learning Techniques), see C E E L

Christiana-Verlag+*, CH-8260 Stein am Rhein Tel: (054) 86820/86847
Man Dir: Arnold Guillet
Subject: Religion
Founded: 1948
ISBN Publishers Prefix: 3-7171

Werner **Classen** Verlag+, Splügenstr 10, Postfach 683, CH-8027 Zurich Tel: (01) 2015606 Cable Add: Classenverlag Zurich
Dir: Werner Classen
Subjects: Belles Lettres, Poetry, Music, Juveniles, Psychology, Humour, Technical Paperbacks
1978: 12 titles *Founded:* 1945
ISBN Publishers Prefix: 3-7172

De **Clivo** Press+*, Dr Walter Amstutz, Usterstr 126, PO Box, CH-8600 Duebendorf, Zurich Tel: (01) 8201224/8201216 Cable Add: declivopress Duebendorf Telex: CH 55256 Serco
Proprietor: Dr Walter Amstutz
ISBN Publishers Prefix: 3-85634

Imprimerie La **Concorde**+*, PO Box 330, CH-1010 Lausanne (Located at: 6 ch des Croisettes CH-1066 Epalinges) Tel: (021) 33141
Dir: Paul Perrin
Subjects: Religion, Science, Art
Founded: 1910
ISBN Publishers Prefix: 2-88000

Manesse-Verlag, **Conzett und Huber**+, CH-8021 Zurich, Morgarten-Str 29 Tel: (01) 2424455
Man Dir: Dr Hans Conzett
Subsidiary Company: Manesse und Morgarten Verlag (qv), at same address
Subjects: Belles Lettres, Art, Classics (Manesse-Bibliothek der Weltliteratur)
Founded: 1886
ISBN Publishers Prefix: 3-7175

Imprimerie **Corbaz** SA+*, 22 ave des Planches, CH-1820 Montreux Tel: (021) 624762/4
Dir: Jean-Paul Corbaz
Subjects: Typographic Illustrations, Brochures
Founded: 1899

Cosmos-Verlag AG+, Postfach 2637, CH-3001 Berne (Located at: Oberer Wehrliweg 5, CH-3074 Muri bei Bern) Tel: (031) 526611
Man Dir: H R Aeberli
Subjects: Tax and Finance Laws; High-priced Paperbacks, including publications on behalf of the Swiss Institute of Business Management (Sch. Inst für Unternehmungsführung im Gewerbe)
1978: 8 titles *1979:* 9 titles *Founded:* 1926

Cratander AG*, Druckerei, Petersgraben 34, CH-4051 Basel Tel: (061) 258166
Subjects: Civil Engineering, General Technology
ISBN Publisher's Prefix: 3-85622

Edizioni Armando **Dadò**, Tipografia Stazione+, CP 229, CH-6601 Locarno (Located at: Via Bramantino 6) Tel: (093) 314802
Man Dir: Armando Dado
Subjects: Books in Italian on Art, History, Literature, Photography, Swiss Italian Costume

Daphins-Verlag*, J Fischlin, Rainweg 2, CH-8704 Herrliberg Tel: (01) 9153639
Man Dir: J Fischlin
Subjects: Belles Lettres, Poetry, Limited Editions
1977: 1 title *Founded:* 1959
ISBN Publisher's Prefix: 3-85631

Editions **Delachaux et Niestlé** SA+*, 4 rue de l'Hôpital, CH-2001 Neuchâtel Tel: (021) 203651 Telex: 25822
Man Dir: David Perret; *Sales, Advertising Dir:* Gabriel Audemars; *Permissions:* Robert Ros Bioley
Subjects: Biography, How-to, Philosophy, Reference, Religion, Juveniles, Medicine, Pedagogy, Psychology, General & Social Science, Natural Sciences, Educational Materials
Founded: 1860
Bookshops: Librairie Spes, 2 rue St-Pierre, CH-1000 Lausanne; Librairie Delachaux, 4 rue de l'Hôpital, CH-2000 Neuchâtel
Subsidiary: Delachaux & Niestlé, 32 rue de Grenelle, F-75007 Paris
ISBN Publisher's Prefix: 2-603
Miscellaneous: Associate Company: Spes SA, 2 rue St-Pierre, CH-1002 Lausanne (qv)

Delphin Verlag+, Postfach 157, CH-8031 Zurich (Located at: Limmatstr 111) Tel: 440733/6 Cable Add: Delphinverlag Zürich Telex: 53815
Man Dir: Oswald Boxer
Subject: Juveniles, Non-fiction, Paperbacks
Founded: 1962
ISBN Publishers Prefix: 3-7735

Delta SA+, 2 rue du Château, BP 20, CH-1800 Vevey 2 Tel: (021) 510526 Telex: 25792 edelt
Publisher: André Delcourt; *Man Dir:* René Galimont
Subjects: History, Sociology, Art, Engineering, General Science, University, Secondary & Primary Textbooks, Educational Materials
1978: 30 titles *1979:* 30 titles *Founded:* 1963
Miscellaneous: Firm is a member of the Educagroep, Netherlands

Desertina Verlag, CH-7180 Disentis
Tel: (086) 7544142 Cable Add: Desertina Disentis
Man Dir, Rights & Permissions, Editorial, Production, Publicity: P Condrau; *Sales:* L Huonder
Subjects: Belles Lettres of Romance Literature, Art Reproductions
Bookshop: Condrau, Disentis
Founded: 1953

Verlag **Deutsch**+, Riedstr 2, CH-3600 Thun Tel: (033) 223975
Man Dir: Harri Deutsch
Parent Company: Verlag Harri Deutsch, Federal Republic of Germany (qv)
Subjects: Maths, Physics, Chemistry, Other Natural Sciences, Technology, Economics
ISBN Publisher's Prefix: 3-87144

Diana-Verlag AG*, Hadlaubstr 131, CH-8006 Zurich Tel: (01) 264850 Cable Add: Dianaverlag
Dir: Dr S Menzel
Subjects: Belles Lettres, Psychology, Religion, Law
Founded: 1946
ISBN Publishers Prefix: 3-87158

Diogenes Verlag AG, CH-8032 Zurich, Sprecherstr 8 Tel: (01) 478947 Cable Add: Diogenesverlag Zurich Telex: 52810
Man Dirs & Owners: Daniel Keel (Publisher), Rudolf C Bettschart (Administration & Finance); *Editorial Dir:* Gerd Haffmans; *Sales Dir:* Hartmut Radel; *Rights & Permissions:* Anne Elisabeth Suter
Subjects: Fiction, Art, Paperbacks, Pocket Books, Children's Books
1977: 220 titles *Founded:* 1953
ISBN Publishers Prefix: 3-257

Drei Eichen Verlag AG+, Mühlematt 11, CH-6390 Engelberg Tel: (041) 941129
Cable Add: Dreieichen Engelberg
Dirs: Hermann Kissener, Hans Rudi Marti, Josef Waser
Subjects: Comparative Religion, Popular Medicine, Education, Philosophy, Yoga Instruction
1978: 8 titles *Founded:* 1931
ISBN Publisher's Prefix: 3-7699

Drei Eidgenossen Verlag*, Rottmannsbodenstr 77, CH-4102 Binningen Tel: (061) 475166
Man Dir: Mr Hosch
Subject: Juveniles
Founded: 1936
ISBN Publisher's Prefix: 3-85643

Droemersche Verlagsanstalt AG*, CH-8021 Zurich, Stauffacherquai 46, Postfach 670 Tel: (00411) 394214
Subjects: Fiction, Nonfiction, Natural Sciences

Librairie **Droz** SA+, 11 rue Massot, CP 389, CH-1211 Geneva 12 Tel: (022) 466666
Man Dir: A Dufour; *Sales Dir:* Miss Gueguen; *Rights & Permissions:* A Dufour
Subjects: French language publisher of Belles Lettres, Poetry, History, Literature Reference, Religion, Social Science, University Textbooks
1977: 60 titles *Founded:* 1924
ISBN Publishers Prefix: 2-600

Henry-Robert **Dufour**+*, 7 ave de Rumine, CH-1005 Lausanne Tel: (021) 233062/233070
Subjects: French language publisher of General Non-fiction, Fine Arts, Technical, Industrial, Belles Lettres, Education

Gottlieb **Duttweiler** Institute for Economic & Social Studies, CH-8803 Rueschlikon-Zurich Tel: (01) 7240020 Cable Add: Green Meadow Telex: 55699
Subjects: Reference, Social Science, Economics
Bookshop: Verlagsbuchhandlung GDI, CH-8803 Rueschlikon-Zurich
Founded: 1963
Miscellaneous: Specialists in distributive trades, management education, economic growth and new forms of organization

Dynamis Verlag, Postfach 256, CH-8280 Kreuzlingen Tel: (072) 727781 Cable Add: Dynamis
Man Dir: Peter Weber
Subject: Religion
1977: 5 titles *1978:* 4 titles *Founded:* 1973
Bookshop: Christliche Buchhandlung, CH-8280 Kreuzlingen, Konstanzerstr 17

Ecart Publications, 6 rue Plantamour, PO Box 253, CH-1211 Geneva 1 Tel: 457395/288803/313473
Man Dirs: John M Armleder, Patrick Lucchini; *Editorial:* John Armleder
Subsidiary Companies: Leathern Wing Scribble Press, The Geneva Pund Bubbles
Associate Companies: Centre d'Art Contemporain, 16 rue d'Italie, CH-1204 Geneva
Subjects: Art (especially New Trends), Photography, Video, Cinema
Bookshops: Ecart Books, Librairie, 14 rue d'Italie, PO Box 253, CH-1211 Geneva
1978: 10 titles *1979:* 10 titles *Founded:* 1969

Edita SA+, 3 rue de la Vigie, CP 121, CH-1000 Lausanne 9 Tel: (021) 205631 Telex: 26296 Cable Add: Editasa Lausanne
Man Dir: Ami Guichard; *Editorial:* Joseph Jobé, Tim Chilvers; *Production:* Charles Riesen
Subjects: Art, Social and Military Popular Historical, Transport Popular Historical (especially Automobile), How-to, General Science
1977: 20 titles *Founded:* 1952
ISBN Publishers Prefix: 2-88001

Editeurs Associes SA+*, 5 rue César-Soulié, PO Box 84, CH-1260 Nyon Tel: (022) 612676 Telex: Buco 22886 Nyon
Man Dir: F Gendreau
Subjects: Fiction, History
1977: 50 titles *Founded:* 1966
ISBN Publisher's Prefix: 2-8291

Editions Universitaires (Universitätsverlag), 36 Pérolles, CH-1700 Fribourg Tel: (037) 226802
Man Dir, Publicity: Dr Martin Nicoulin
Subjects: Literature, History, Music, Art, Philosophy, Reference, Religions, Theology, Psychology, Economic and Political Sciences, Secondary and University Textbooks, Medicine, Ethnology, Law
Bookshops: Librairie et Edition de la Suisse Romande
1978: 33 titles *1979:* 21+ titles
ISBN Publisher's Prefixes: 3-7278 (German books), 2-8271 (French books)

Edito-Service SA+*, 9 ter chemin de Roches, BP 307, CH-1211 Geneva 6 Tel: (022) 357233 Cable Add: Editoservice Geneva
Man Dir: Gaston Burnand; *Publisher:* Yvonne Rosso; *Marketing Manager:* Julian Trunkfield; *Permissions:* Anne Hauser
Subjects: General Fiction, Belles Lettres, Poetry, Biography, Reference, History, How-to, Music, Art, Religion, Juveniles, Medicine, Psychology, Engineering, General Science, Educational Materials, Co-editions in all languages
1977: 200 titles

Alfred **Eibel** Editeur+, 7 rue de Genève, CH-1002 Lausanne
Subsidiary Company: Alfred Eibel Editeur, Montparnasse Diffusion, France (qv for full list of Associate Companies etc)

Eidgenössische Landestopographie, Seftigenstr 264, CH-3084 Wabern
Subject: Maps (Switzerland)

André **Eiselé**+*, Editeur, 17 route de Cossonay, BP 19, CH-1008 Prilly/Lausanne Tel: (021) 256324
Subjects: Arts, Education, Popular Science, Juveniles, Belles Lettres, Textbooks
ISBN Publishers Prefix: 2-88002

Verlag **Eisenbahn***, Gut Vorhard, CH-5234 Villigen Tel: (056) 982595 Cable Add: Verlageisenbahn Villigen
Owner: Claude Jeanmarie-dit-Quartier
Subjects: Railway, Tramcar and Model Rail Literature; Model Railways; Toys of the Past
Bookshops: Eisenbahnbücherecke, CH-5234 Villigen AG
1977: 6 titles *Founded:* 1961
ISBN Publisher's Prefix: 3-85649

Elektrowirtschaft, Schweizerische Gesellschaft für Elektrizitätsverwertung, CH-8023 Zurich, Bahnhofplatz 9, Postfach 2272 Tel: (01) 2110355
Swiss Electricity Marketing Association
Subject: Electrical Engineering
ISBN Publisher's Prefix: 3-85651

Elsevier Sequoia SA+, 50 ave de la Gare, BP 851, CH-1001 Lausanne 1 Tel: (021) 207381 Cable Add: Elsevier Lausanne
Man Dir, Rights & Permissions: Louk Bergmans; *Editorial:* E Vogelezang, I Holmes; *Sales, Publicity:* P Schafer; *Production:* E Vogelezang
Parent Company: NV Uitgeversmaatschappij Elsevier, Netherlands (qv)
Associate Companies: Thomond Books, Republic of Ireland; Elsevier's Wetenschappelijke Uitgeverij, Noord-Hollandsche Uitgeversmaatschappij, Elsevier/North Holland Biomedical Press (all in Netherlands, qqv); Applied Science Publishers, UK (qv); Elsevier North Holland Inc, USA
Subjects: Chemistry, Technology, Energy; Biological, Medical, Environmental and Social Sciences, Psychology; Periodicals
1977: 13 titles *1978:* 5 titles *Founded:* 1967

'**Elvetica**' Edizioni SA+, CP 694, CH-6830 Chiasso Tel: (091) 435056 Telex: 73254
Subjects: Works of Piero Scanziani (in Italian), Swiss Financial Year Book
1978: 2 titles *Founded:* 1967

Emmentaler Druck AG, Postfach 2502, Dorfstr 5, CH-3550 Langnau Tel: (035) 21911 Cable Add: Emmentalerdruck Langnau Telex: 32187 (915100)
Man Dir: P Gerber; *Editorial:* N Stuber; *Sales:* H R Bodenmann; *Production:* L Martin; *Publicity:* P Blaser
Subjects: Novels and Art Books
1977: 3 titles *1978:* 5 titles *Founded:* 1845
ISBN Publisher's Prefix: 3-85654

Erker-Galerie AG+*, Franz Larese und Jürg Janett, Gallustr 32, CH-9000 St Gallen Tel: (071) 227979/233607
Subject: Modern Art, Literature
Founded: 1964

Edition **Etcetera***, Postfach 572, CH-4001, Basel Tel: (061) 380570
Subjects: Theory of Socialism, Third World, Near East, Switzerland, The Media and Mass Communications
Miscellaneous: Company has common interests with the Z-Verlag (qv) and Lenos Press (qv)

Eulenburg Edition GmbH+, Grütstr 28 CH-8134 Adliswil-Zürich Tel: (01) 7103681
Subjects: Instrumental Sheet Music; Books on Music and Musicians
Founded: 1945
ISBN Publishers Prefix: 3-85662

Europa-Verlag AG+*, CH-8001 Zurich, Rämistr 5 Tel: (01) 471629 Cable Add: Europaverlag Zurich Telex: 55210 feren ch
Man Dir: Emmie Oprecht
Associate Company: Verlag Oprecht, Zurich (Theatrical)
Subjects: History, Politics, Philosophy, Art, Belles Lettres
Founded: 1933
Miscellaneous: Distributor for UNESCO, Paris
ISBN Publishers Prefix: 3-85665

Europabuch AG, see Edition Sven Erik Bergh im Europabuch AG

Evangelischer Schriften Verlag Schwengler, see Schwengler (Switzerland) and Telos (German Federal Republic)

Ex Libris*, Hermetschloostr 77, CH-8023 Zürich
Subjects: Belles Lettres, Children's Books, Reference Books

Pierre Marcel **Favre**+, rue de Bourg 29, PO Box 3569, CH-1002 Lausanne Tel: (021) 221717 Cable Add: Favrepublisa Lausanne
Man Dir: P M Favre
Subjects: Current Affairs, Politics, Sport, Ecology, Illustrated Editions, Fiction
1978: 9 titles *1979:* 11 titles *Founded:* 1975
ISBN Publisher's Prefix: 2-8289

Fehr'sche Buchhandlung AG+*, Schmiedgasse 16, CH-9001 St Gallen Tel: (071) 221152/231381 Telex: 77588
Subjects: History, Law, Political Economy, Textbooks
Founded: 1780
Bookshop: Address as above
ISBN Publishers Prefix: 3-85674

François **Feij**+*, pl de l'Eglise, CH-1166 Perroy Tel: (021) 752777

Ferenczy Verlag AG, CH-8024 Zurich, Rämistr 5 Tel: 326054 Cable Add: Ferenczyverlag Zürich Telex: 55210

Flamberg Verlag+, Brauerstr 60, Postfach, CH-8026 Zurich Tel: (01) 2413938/2412863
Man Dir: Werner Blum
Orders to: Auwiesenstr 1, Postfach, CH-8406 Winterthür
Parent Company: Theologischer Verlag (qv) at above address
Subject: Juvenile
1977: 3 titles *1978:* No titles *Founded:* 1957
ISBN Publishers Prefix: 3-7179

Maurice & Pierre **Foetisch** SA+*, CP 2793, CH-1002 Lausanne (Located at: 6 rue de Bourg, CH-1002 Lausanne) Tel: (021) 239444/5 Telex: 24227
Man Dir and other offices: Jean-Claude Foetisch
Associate Company: Disco SA

Subjects: Music, Records, Pianos, TV, Educational, Textbooks (especially ASSIMIL Language Teaching Courses)
Founded: 1947

Editions **Foma** SA+, Ave de Longemalle 5, CP 226, CH-1020 Renens Tel: (021) 351361 Telex: CH-Cedil 25416
Man Dir, Editorial: J-L Peverelli; *Sales:* M Sculati; *Rights & Permissions:* J-L Berthoud
Subsidiary Company: Cedilivre SA
Subjects: Philosophy, Psychology, Secondary and Primary Textbooks, Yoga
Bookshop: Didax
1977: 2 titles *Founded:* 1948
ISBN Publisher's Prefix: 2-88003

Editions de **Fontainemore**+, 5 chemin du Port, CH-1094 Paudex Tel: (021) 392716
Man Dir: René Creux
Subjects: Biography, History, Sailing, Art and Folk Art
1977: 2 titles *1978:* 1 title *Founded:* 1962
ISBN Publisher's Prefix: 2-88004

Fortuna-Verlag W Heidelberger*, Postfach, CH-8172 Niedergiatt/ZH Tel: (01) 8503586
Man Dir: W Heidelberger
Imprints: Fortuna Verlag, W Heidelberger
Subject: Financial Publications
1977: 2 titles *Founded:* 1950
ISBN Publisher's Prefix: 3-85684

Foto und Schmalfilm-Verlag+, subsidiary of Gemsberg-Verlag (qv)

Francke Verlag+, Hochfeldstr 113, CH-3000 Berne 26 Tel: (031) 237469 Cable Add: Frankeverlag Bern
Man Dir: Dr Carl L Lang; *Production:* K Gschwend; *Publicity:* Mrs B Bieri
Parent Company: Francke Verlag GmbH, German Federal Republic (qv)
Subjects: Germanic, Romanic and Anglian Language Studies, History, Philology, Philosophy, Psychology, Textbooks, Reference; Paperbacks
Bookshop: Buchhandlung A Francke AG, CH-3001 Berne, Neuengasse 43
1977: 45 titles *1978:* 58 titles *Founded:* 1831
ISBN Publisher's Prefix: 3-7720

Freihofer AG, Weinbergstr 109, Postfach, CH-8033 Zurich Tel: (01) 3634282 Telex: 57305 frbk
Man Dir: R Gösken; *Sales:* E K Jansen; *Publicity:* A Fröhlich
Parent Company: Springer-Verlag (qv), Berlin-Heidelberg-New York
Subsidiary Company: Freihofer AG Inc, 175 Fifth Ave, New York NY 10010
Subjects: Medicine, Natural Sciences
Bookshops: Universitätsstr 11, Rämistr 37 (Medicine/Psychology), Sonneggstr 21 (all in Zürich)
Founded: 1957

Gebrüder **Fretz** Verlag AG+, CH-8008 Zurich, Mühlebachstr 54, Postfach 8032 Tel: (01) 341444
Subjects: Fine and Applied Arts, Illustrated Books, Belles Lettres, Fiction
Founded: 1860
ISBN Publishers Prefix: 3-85692

Fretz und Wasmuth Verlag AG+*, Bellerivestr 5, CH-8008 Zurich Tel: (01) 323585
Subjects: Archaeology, Architecture, Civil Engineering, Fine & Applied Arts, Illustrated Books
Founded: 1927
ISBN Publisher's Prefix: 3-7180

Frobenius AG+*, Spalenring 31, CH-4012 Basle Tel: (061) 437610
Subjects: History, Law, Literature (especially local)
ISBN Publishers Prefix: 3-85695

G S Verlag Basle+, Postfach 55, CH-4003 Basel (Located at: Petersgraben 29, CH-4003 Basle) Tel: (061) 253514
Man Dir: Hugo Weibel
Branch Offs: Falkenplatz 22, CH-3012 Berne Tel: (031) 235651; Wiesenstr 48, BP 47, CH-8703 Erlenbach Tel: (01) 9105313
Subjects: General Fiction, Belles Lettres, Biography, History, Music, Art, Juveniles, Low-Priced Paperbacks
1977: 5 titles *Founded:* 1889
ISBN Publishers Prefix: 3-7185

Editions Bertil **Galland**+*, 29 rue du Lac, CH-1800 Vevey Tel: (021) 511732
Proprietor: Bertil Galland
Subject: Modern Literature
Founded: 1972
ISBN Publisher's Prefix: 2-88015

Rudolf **Geering** Verlag, see Philosophisch-Anthroposophischer/Rudolf Geering Verlag

Gemsberg-Verlag, Foto+Schmalfilm-Verlag, Garnmarkt 10, Postfach 778, CH-8401 Winterthür Tel: (052) 857171 Cable Add: Gemsberg-Verlag Telex: 76417
Sales: Hans Egli; *Production:* Hans Ziegler
Parent Company: Ziegler Druck- und Verlags-AG (Proprietors)
Subsidiary Company: Foto Schmalfilm-Verlag (Winterthur)
Subjects: Amateur Photography and Filmmaking
1977: 8 titles *1978:* 9 titles *Founded:* 1838
ISBN Publishers Prefix: 3-85701

Genfer Bibelgesellschaft, Das Haus der Bibel, 11 rue de Rive, CH-1211 Geneva 3 German title of the Société biblique de Genève (qv under Maison de la Bible)

Pierre **Genillard**+, Editeur, 9 ch de Primerose, CH-1007 Lausanne Tel: (021) 264632
Subjects: Religion, Philosophy, Psychology, Naturism, Esotericism, Rosicrucian Thought
Founded: 1949
ISBN Publishers Prefix: 2-88005

Georg et Cie SA+, Librairies-Editeurs, 5 rue de la Corraterie, CH-1211 Geneva 11 Tel: (022) 216633 Telex: 23985
Man Dir: Henri Longchamp
Subjects: Medical Science, Administration, Law, Secondary & Primary Textbooks, Religion, Philosophy, Psychology, Economics, Statistics, Social & Natural Sciences, Politics, Military Subjects, Languages, Literature, Geography, Ethnology, Travel, History
Bookshop: 5 rue de la Corraterie, CH-1211 Geneva 11
Founded: 1857

Georgi Publishing Company/Editions Georgi+, CH-1813 St-Saphorin Tel: (021) 529508
Owner/President: Heinz Georgi
Imprint: Georgi
Subjects: Scientific and technical books and journals in Computer Science, Engineering, Electrical Engineering and Electronics, Metallurgy, Human Ecology, Environment, Social and Political Sciences (publications may be in English, French or German, or a combination of 2 or 3 languages)
Founded: 1975
ISBN Publishers Prefix: 2-604

Gesellschaft für Volkskunde, associated imprint of G Krebs Buchdruckerei AG (qv)

Gesellschäftsstelle der Schweiz, associated imprint of G Krebs Buchdruckerei AG (qv)

Globi Verlag AG+, Eichstr 23, CH-8045 Zurich Tel: (01) 354135 Cable Add: Globiverlag Zürich Telex: 52791
Man Dir: Emil M Herzog
Subject: Juveniles, especially Illustrated Books
Founded: 1935
ISBN Publishers Prefix: 3-85703

Viktor **Goldschmidt** Verlagsbuchhandlung+*, Mostackerstr 17, CH-4051 Basel Tel: (061) 236565
Subjects: German-Judaica, Hebraica
Founded: 1902
ISBN Publishers Prefix: 3-85705

André et Pierre **Gonin**+, Editions d'Art, 2 rue Etraz, CH-1003 Lausanne Tel: (021) 226492/229996
Subject: Art
Founded: 1902
ISBN Publishers Prefix: 2-88016

Gotthelf-Verlag+, CH-8026 Zurich, Badenerstr 69 Tel: (01) 2428155
Man Dir: Max Hirt; *Sales Dir:* Paul Hauser
Associate Company: CVB Buch & Druck (qv) at same address
Subjects: Religion, Juveniles
1978: 8 titles *Founded:* 1928
ISBN Publishers Prefix: 3-85706

Editions du **Grand-Pont**+*, Jean-Pierre Laubscher, 2 pl Bel-Air, CH-1003 Lausanne Tel: (021) 223222

The **Graphis** Press (Walter Herdeg)*, 107 Dufourstr, CH-8008 Zurich Tel: (01) 329211 Cable Add: Graphispress
Man Dir/Editorial: Walter Herdeg; *Sales/Publicity:* Walter Danzer; *Production:* Gerhard Ruoss
Orders to: Permedia, Hirschmattstr 36, CH-6002 Lucerne
Subjects: Art and Graphics generally: especially Advertising Art, Packaging Design, Film and TV Graphics; Diagrams etc, Record Sleeves, Technical/Scientific Illustration, Children's Book Illustration; Annuals – *Art Directors, Graphis, Graphis Posters, Photographis* etc; Periodical – *Graphis*
1977: 4 titles *Founded:* 1944
ISBN Publisher's Prefix: 3-85709

Editions du **Griffon**+, 17 Faubourg du Lac, BP 545, CH-2001 Neuchâtel Tel: (038) 252204
Chairman: Dr Marcel Joray
Subject: Modern Art (especially sculpture and the plastic arts generally)
Founded: 1944
ISBN Publishers Prefix: 2-88006

Editions François **Grounauer**, 1 rue du Belvédère, CH-1203 Geneva 1 Tel: (022) 311595
Subjects: History, Politics, Social Sciences
1977: 5 titles *1978:* 3 titles *Founded:* 1972

Th **Gut** & Co Verlag*, Seestr, CH-8712 Stäfa Tel: (01) 9281101 Telex: Seeztg Stafa 75668
Subjects: Politics, Swiss and Regional History
ISBN Publisher's Prefix: 3-85717

Gute Schriften Verein, Basel, see GS Verlag

Verlag **Habegger** AG+, Gutenbergstr 1, CH-4552 Derendingen-Solothurn Tel: (065) 411151 Telex: 43744
Dir: Gerda Raschendorfer; *Production Manager:* Werner Stucki
Subjects: Sports, Photography and Films, Texts in Dialect, Juvenile, Medical, Archaeology
1977: 18 titles *1978:* 14 titles *Founded:* 1900
ISBN Publishers Prefix: 3-85723

F **Haeschel-Dufey**, Comptoir du Livre — now Editions Novos SA (qv)

Berchtold **Haller** Verlag, see Berchtold-Haller

Hallwag Verlag AG+*, CH-3000 Berne, Nordring 4 Tel: (031) 423131 Cable Add: Hallwag Berne Telex: 32460
President: Otto Erich Wagner; *Dir:* Dr U P Thoenen; *Editorial, Permissions:* Dr K Weibel; *Sales:* Jürg Burri, Klaus Wolfgramm
Br Off: Hallwag Verlagsgesellschaft GmbH, D-7301 Kemnat bei Stuttgart, Marco-Polo-Str 1, German Federal Republic
Subjects: General Nonfiction, Travel, History, How-to, Music, Art, General Science
1977: 23 titles *Founded:* 1912
ISBN Publishers Prefix: 3-444

Harwood Academic Publishers GmbH, Poststr 22, CH-7000 Chur
Man Dir: A Theus; *Editorial:* M B Gordon; *Sales:* Patricia Bardi; *Production:* Bernard J Yates; *Publicity:* Lila Henry; *Rights & Permissions:* Francoise Chantrel-Riols
Branch Off: Harwood Academic Publishers, 7-9 rue Emile Dubois, F-75014 Paris, France
Subjects: Astronomy and Astrophysics, Chemical & Nuclear Engineering, Chemical & Chemical Technology, Civil Engineering, Computers, Systems & Control Engineering, Earth & Extraterrestrial Sciences, Economics, Electronics & Electrical Engineering, Life Sciences & Medicine, Management Science & Business, Mathematics & Statistics, Mechanical Engineering, Metallurgy & Materials Science, Physics, Social Sciences, Space Science & Technology, Learned Journals
1978: 1 title *1979:* 10 titles *Founded:* 1978
ISBN Publisher's Prefix: 3-786

Paul **Haupt** Bern+, CH-3001 Berne, Falkenplatz 14 Tel: (031) 232425 Cable Add: Hauptbern Telex: 23561 haupt ch
Man Dir: Dr Max Haupt; *Production:* Kurt Thönnes; *Sales, Publicity, Advertising Dir:* Ulrich Dodel; *Permissions:* Wilhelm Jost
Subjects: How-to, Music, Art, Philosophy, Psychology, General & Social Science, University, Secondary & Primary textbooks, Educational Materials, Pedagogy, Business Economics, Handicraft
Bookshops: Falkenpl 14 and Triangel, Länggass Str 8 (both Bern); Höheweg 11, Interlaken
1977: 119 titles *Founded:* 1906
ISBN Publishers Prefix: 3-258

Haus der Bibel+, see Maison de la Bible

Helbing & Lichtenhahn Verlag AG+, 13 Steinentorstr, Postfach, CH-4010 Basel Tel: (061) 231116 Cable Add: jaeb 63873
Dir: H Helbing; *Procuring Editor:* Beat A Jenny
Subjects: History, Law, Textbooks
Founded: 1822
ISBN Publishers Prefix: 3-7190

Arts Graphiques **Héliographia** SA+*, 2 ave de Tivoli, BP 1060, CH-1001 Lausanne Tel: (021) 204151 Telex: 24060
Man Dir: Philippe Luquiens

Helvetica Chimica Acta-Verlag, CH-4002 Basel, Postfach Tel: (061) 376652
Subject: Chemistry
ISBN Publisher's Prefix: 3-85727

Walter **Herdeg**: The Graphis Press, see Graphis Press

Herder AG+, Malzgasse 18, 4002 Basel 21 Tel: 230818 Telex: 64358
Miscellaneous: Company is an Associate of Verlag Herder GmbH & Co KG, Federal Republic of Germany (qv); of Verlag Herder & Co, Austria (qv); of A G Ploetz KG and of Herder & Herder GmbH, both in Federal Republic of Germany (qqv)

Rolf **Heyne** Verlag+*, CH-8832 Woolerau/SZ, Bächerstr Tel: (01) 7841722 Telex: 75113
Man Dir: Rolf Heyne
Subjects: Reference, Pocket Books

Verlag für Psychologie Dr C J **Hogrefe**, Zeltweg 6, CH-8032 Zurich
Parent Company: Verlag für Psychologie, Göttingen, Federal Republic of Germany (qv)
Subjects: All aspects of general and applied Psychology; Handbooks, Conference Reports, Directories

Van **Hoorick** Verlag*, Postfach, CH-8805 Richterswil Tel: (01) 764272
Subjects: Books and Cards for Meditation Practice, Christmas Cards etc; Colour Slide Library

Verlag **Huber** & Co AG+, Promenadenstr 16, Postfach 83, CH-8500 Frauenfeld Tel: (054) 73739/73737 Telex: 76383
Man Dir, Publisher: Dr Peter Keckeis; *Sales, Publicity:* Hansrudolf Frey; *Production:* Bruno Furrer; *Rights & Permissions:* Silvia Fust
Subjects: Belles Lettres, Biography, History, Politics, Folklore, Linguistics, Art, Juveniles, Social Science, Forestry, Agriculture, Thurgau Canton Interest, Educational Books and Materials
Bookshop: Buchhandlung Huber & Co AG, CH-8500 Frauenfeld, Freiestr 8
1977: 27 titles *1978:* 31 titles *Founded:* 1809
ISBN Publisher's Prefix: 3-7193

Hans **Huber Medical** Publisher+, Länggasstr 76 & Marktgasse 9, Postfach, CH-3000 Berne 9 Tel: (031) 242533 Cable Add: Huberverlag Telex: 32516
Man Dir: Walter Jäger; *Sales Dir:* Max Pauli; *Publicity & Advertising:* Fritz Hochuli
Branch Off: Verlag Hans Huber, Am Wallgraben 127-131, D-7000 Stuttgart-Vaihingen, Federal Republic of Germany
Subjects: Medicine, Psychology, Pedagogy, Sociology
1977: 110 titles *Founded:* 1927
Bookshops: CH-3000 Berne 9, Länggasstr 76 & Marktgasse 9; Buchhandlung für Medizin und Psychologie, CH-8032 Zurich, Zeltweg 6
ISBN Publishers Prefix: 3-456

Humata Verlag Harold S Blume+*, CH-3000 Berne 6, Dufourstr 7 Tel: (031) 444600
Man Dir: Harold S Blume
Shipping Add: CH-3000 Berne, BP 74

Subjects: How-to, Philosophy, Medicine, Psychology
Founded: 1951
ISBN Publishers Prefix: 3-85120

Huthig & Wepf Verlag+, Eisengasse 5, CH-4001 Basel Tel: (061) 256379 Cable Add: Wepfco Telex: 0045-62027
Associate Companies: Verlag Wepf, Basel (qv); Dr A Hüthig Verlag, Heidelberg, Federal Republic of Germany (qv)
Subsidiary Company: Hüthig & Wepf Verlag, 13 East 16th St, New York, NY 10003, USA
Branch Off: Hüthig & Wepf, Wilckensstr 3-5, D-6900 Heidelberg, Federal Republic of Germany
Subjects: Macromolecular Chemistry and Related Subjects
Miscellaneous: Publishes two Scientific Journals
ISBN Publisher's Prefix: 3-85739

Idéa Editions*, BP 424, CH-2300 La Chaux-de-Fonds Tel: (039) 236725
Sales Dir: Claude Garino
Subjects: General Fiction, Music, Art, Juveniles, University Textbooks
Founded: 1974

Ides et Calendes SA+, 19 Evole, CH-2001 Neuchâtel Tel: (038) 253861 Cable Add: Idecal
Man Dir: André Rosselet; *Administration Chief:* Fred Uhler; *Editorial:* Joan Rosselet
Subjects: Art, Belles Lettres, Law, University Textbooks
1978: 7 titles *Founded:* 1941
ISBN Publishers Prefix: 2-8258

Imba Verlag+, 4 ave de Beauregard, BP 1052, CH-1701 Friburg Tel: (037) 241341 Cable Add: Kanisiuswerk Friburg
Man Dir: Martin Stieger; *Production Manager:* Rudolf Studer
Subjects: Social Science, Religion
Associate Company: Kanisius Verlag, Fribourg (qv)
ISBN Publishers Prefix: 3-85740

Impressum Verlag AG*, CH-8953 Dietikon, Schöneggstr 102 Tel: (01) 7407673
ISBN Publishers Prefix: 3-7200

Editions **Imprimerie** Fédérative SA Berne, see Verbandsdruckerei

Verlag **Industrielle Organisation**+, CH-8028 Zurich, Zürichbergstr 18 Tel: (01) 470802
Man & Publicity Dir: Dr Roland Scheuchzer; *Sales, Advertising Dir:* Fritz Dedial
Subjects: Management and Organisation, Personnel Studies, Problem-Solving Activities, Product Planning, Marketing, EDP
Publication: Management-Zeitschrift Industrielle Organisation (Industrial Organisation Management Magazine)
1977: 4 titles *1978:* 6 titles
ISBN Publishers Prefix: 3-85743

Institut für Heilpädagogik Verlag, (Therapeutic Pedagogy Institute Publishing House)*, CH-6000 Lucerne, Löwenstr 5
Subjects: Education, Diagnostic Therapy Publications

Institut Universitaire de Hautes Etudes Internationales+*, 132 rue de Lausanne, CH-1211 Geneva 21 Tel: (022) 311730
Subject: Politics

Inter Documentation Co AG, Poststr 14, Zug Tel: (42) 214974 Cable Add: INDOCO ZUG Telex: 78819 Zugal
President: Dr L Vieli

Subsidiary Companies: Inter Documentation Co BV, Uiterste Gracht 45, Leiden, Netherlands; Inter Documentation Co Ltd, 351 Richmond Rd, Twickenham, England, UK
Subjects: Microfiche/microfilm editions of rare scholarly publications, especially in connection with Slavic and Oriental studies, African, Latin American, Middle Eastern and Jewish Studies, Development Plans, Musicology, Anthropology, Natural Sciences, Art, Social Sciences, Religion
Total Published Titles: 500,000 *Founded:* 1957
ISBN Publishers Prefix: 38575

'Interavia' SA (Société anonyme d'Editions aéronautiques internationales)+, 86 Ave Louis Casaï, CH-1216 Cointrin, Geneva Tel: (022) 980505 Telex: 22122 itav ch
Dirs: K Regelin, P Russak, R H Gasser
Subjects: World Directory of Aviation and Astronautics (Interavia ABC-Annual); periodicals connected with Aeronautics, Astronautics, Avionics, Defence
Founded: 1933
Miscellaneous: Firm is a subsidiary of Birkhäuser Verlag, Basel (qv)
ISBN Publishers Prefix: 3-85749

Edition **Interfrom** AG+, Hügelstr 44, Postfach 169, CH-8022 Zürich Tel: (01) 2020900
Publisher: Leo V Fromm; *Man Dir:* Annette Harms-Hunold; *Sales Manager:* Annegret Busch; *Public Relations:* Ursula Malzahn
Associate Companies: Verlag A Fromm, Federal Republic of Germany (qv); Fromm International Publishing Corp, 1212 Ave of the Americas, New York, NY 10036, USA (German into English Literary Translation)
Subjects: Authoritative Texts by celebrated German-speaking Authors on Politics, Economics, Culture/Education, Society, Nature and the Environment
ISBN Publisher's Prefix: 3-7201

Iris Verlag AG+*, CH-3177 Laupen Tel: (031) 947744
ISBN Publishers Prefix: 3-85751

J H Jeheber SA+*, 3 chemin du Vallon, CH-1224 Chênes-Bougeries Tel: (022) 493543
Manager: Jean H Jeheber
Subjects: History, Religion, Juveniles, Sports and Games
Founded: 1797

Johannesverlag Einsiedeln+, Arnold Böcklinstr 42, CH-4051 Basel
Chairman: Dr Hans Urs von Balthasar
Orders to: Bücherdienst, Kornhausstr 23, CH-8840 Einsiedeln
Shipping Add: Benziger Buchzentrum, CH-8840 Einsiedeln
Subjects: Philosophy, Religion
1977: 8 titles *1978:* 7 titles *Founded:* 1947
ISBN Publishers Prefix: 3-265

Juris Druck & Verlag AG+, Basteiplatz 5, Postfach, CH-8039 Zurich Tel: (01) 2117727
Man Dir: Dr H Christen
Subjects: History, Music, Art, Philosophy, Religion, Medicine, Psychology, Engineering, General & Social Science
Bookshop: Juris Druck & Verlag AG, Buchhandlung, Postfach, CH-8039 Zurich
1977: 170 titles *Founded:* 1945
ISBN Publisher's Prefix: 3-260

Kanisius Verlag+, 4 ave du Beauregard, CH-1701 Fribourg Tel: (037) 241341 Cable Add: Kanisiuswerk Freiburg
Man Dir: Martin Stieger; *Production*

Manager: Rudolf Studer
Subjects: Religion
Founded: 1898
Miscellaneous: Associate Company: Imba Verlag, Fribourg (qv)
ISBN Publishers Prefix: 3-85764

S Karger AG, Medical and Scientific Publishers+, Allschwilerstr 10, CH-4000 Basle Tel: (061) 390880 Cable Add: Kargermed Basle Telex: CH 62652
Man Dir: Dr Thomas Karger
Subsidiary Company: Karger Libri AG (Library), Petersgraben 31, CH-4011 Basle
Imprints: S Karger (Basle, Munich, Paris, London, New York, Sydney)
Branch Off: S Karger GmbH, Munich, Federal Republic of Germany (qv)
Subjects: Medical and Scientific Publications (Series and Journals); Reference Works, Medicine, Psychology, University Textbooks
1978: about 150 titles *Founded:* 1890
Bookshop: Karger Libri AG, Petersgraben 31, CH-4011 Basle
ISBN Publisher's Prefix: 3-8055

Verlag Ramon F **Keller**+, now known as Ariston Verlag (qv)

Kinderbuchverlag Reich Luzern AG, see Reich

Kindler Verlag AG+*, Nelkenstr 20, CH-8006 Zurich Tel: (00411) 603007 Cable Add: Kindlerverlag Zurich Telex: 0045 57608
Publishers: Helmut Kindler, Nina Kindler
Subjects: Encyclopedias (modern Psychology)

Editions **Kister** SA+*, 33 quai Wilson, CH-1211 Geneva 1 Tel: (022) 315000
Subjects: General Non-fiction, Mathematics, Physics, Music, Games and Sports, Reference Books
ISBN Publisher's Prefix: 3-463

Dr **Klein** SA+*, 3 rue de la Concorde, PO Box 1, CH-1341 L'Orient Tel: (021) 856640
Man Dir: Dr R F Klein
Imprints: DKSA
Br Off: 19 Ave Villamont, CH-1005 Lausanne
Subjects: Medicine, Psychology, Geographical
Founded: 1977

Klett & Balmer Verlag GmbH+, Chamerstr 12a, Postfach 287, CH-6300 Zug Tel: (042) 214131/32
Man Dir: Chr Balmer, Dr Thomas Klett; *Editorial, Sales, Publicity, Production, Rights & Permissions:* H Egli
Parent Company: Ernst Klett Verlag, Federal Republic of Germany (qv)
Associate Company: H R Balmer AG, Zug, Switzerland (qv)
Subjects: School Textbooks, Teachers' Training, Educational Politics in Switzerland, Adult Education, fringe areas of Science, Philosophy, Theology
1977: 13 titles *1978:* 5 titles *Founded:* 1967
ISBN Publisher's Prefix: 3-264

Kober'sche Verlagsbuchhandlung AG+, Maulbeerstr 10, Postfach 2481, CH-3001 Berne Tel: (031) 251648
Man & Publicity Dir: Harald F Blum; *Sales Dir:* Roland Triet
Subject: Religious/Philosophical, especially the teaching texts of Bô Yin Râ
1977: 50 titles *1978:* 4 titles by Bô Yin Râ
Founded: 1926
ISBN Publishers Prefix: 3-85767

Kolumbus-Verlag, Muhlebuhl 248, CH–5737 Menziken Tel: (064) 711370 Cable Add: Vdb Menziken
Man Dir: Dr G van den Bergh
Subjects: Schoolbooks (ref languages)

Kornfeld & Klipstein+, Nachfolger Kornfeld & Co, Laupenstr 49, CH–3008 Berne Tel: (031) 254673 Cable Add: Artus
Proprietor: Eberhard W Kornfeld
Subjects: Fine Arts, 19th–20th Century Illustrated Books
Founded: 1864
ISBN Publishers Prefix: 3–85773

Kossodo Verlag AG*, 27a chemin des Hutins, CH–1247 Anières/Geneva Tel: (022) 512247
Dir: Martha Düssel
Orders to: above address (direct supply only)
Subjects: Art Books, De Luxe Limited Editions
Founded: 1956
ISBN Publishers Prefix: 3–7208

Verlag Karl **Krämer** & Co, Spiegelgasse 14, CH–8001 Zurich
Associate Company: Karl Krämer Verlag GmbH und Co, Federal Republic of Germany (qv)
ISBN Publisher's Prefix: 3–85774

Verlag René **Kramer** AG, Strada di Gandria 48, PO Box 90, CH–6976 Lugano-Castagnola Tel: (091) 518941 Cable Add: Edikramer
Man Dir, Publicity: René Kramer
Subjects: Gastronomy and the Culinary Arts, Pastry-Cookery

Verlag G **Krebs** AG+, CH–4006 Basel, St Alban-Vorstadt 56 Tel: (061) 239723
Orders to: Gesellschaft für Volkskunde, CH–4006 Basel, Postfach
Dirs: Franz Käser, Willy Kohler
Subjects: Folklore Studies, Swiss Handicrafts, Song Books; Periodicals
1977: 6 titles *1978:* 8 titles *Founded:* 1897
Miscellaneous: Associated imprints include Geschäftsstelle der Schweiz, Schweizerische Gesellschaft für Volkskunde (Swiss Folklore Society)
ISBN Publishers Prefix: 3–85775

Kümmerly & Frey (Geographischer Verlag)+, Hallerstr 6–10, CH–3001 Berne Tel: (031) 235111 Cable Add: Kümmerlyfrey Telex: 32860
Man Dir: W Frey; *Dirs:* P Etzweiler, Toni Kaufman
Associate Company: J Fink-Kümmerley & Frey Verlag GmbH, Federal Republic of Germany (qv)
Subjects: Geography, Maps, Topography, Photobooks
Founded: 1852
ISBN Publishers Prefix: 3–259

Imprimerie Albert **Kündig** SA+*, 10 rue Vieux-Collège, CH–1204 Geneva Tel: (022) 285188
Manager: André Kundig
Founded: 1828

Kunstkreis AG*, Alpenstr 5, CH–6004 Lucerne
Subject: Art
Book Club: address as above

Labor et Fides+, 1 rue Beauregard, CH–1204 Geneva Tel: (022) 291134
Man Dir, Sales, Production, Rights & Permissions, Editorial, Publicity: Pierre Gisel
Subjects: Religion, Theology and General Subjects

Bookshops: Librairie Labor et Fides SA, 1 rue Beauregard, CH–1204 Geneva
1977: 9 titles *1978:* 8 titles *Founded:* 1924
ISBN Publishers Prefix: 2–8259

Herbert **Lang** & Cie AG+, Münzgraben 2, PO Box 82, CH–3000 Berne 7 Tel: (031) 228871 Cable Add: Librilang Telex: 33173
President: Christoph H Lang PhD
Subject: Science
Founded: 1813 (re-formed 1921)
Bookshop: Münzgraben 2, CH–3011 Berne
Miscellaneous: Agents for libraries throughout the world
ISBN Publishers Prefix: 3–261

Verlag Peter **Lang** AG, Münzgraben 2, Postfach, CH–3000 Berne 7 Tel: (031) 228781 Cable Add: Pelag Bern Telex: 32420 verl ch
Subjects: Liberal Arts, Sciences

Langenscheidt AG+*, CH–8021 Zurich, Hardturmstr 76
Parent Company: Langenscheidt KG, German Federal Republic (qv)
Subjects: Linguistics, Languages
ISBN Publishers Prefix: 3–269

Franz **Larese** und Jürg Janett, see Erker-Galerie AG

Larousse (Suisse) SA+, BP 120, 1211 Geneva 6 Tel: (022) 369140
Man Dir: Jean-Claude Viatte
Subjects: Reference Works, Dictionaries
ISBN Publisher's Prefix: 28276

Lector-Verlag GmbH, Höhgaden, CH–8852 Altendorf Tel: (055) 633729 Cable Add: lectorverlag altendorfschwyz Telex: 75257 lecv ch
Man Dir and Other Offices: Walter E Krüttner
Subjects: Belles Lettres, Nonfiction, Art
1979: 26 titles *Founded:* 1978
ISBN Publisher's Prefix: 3–272

Leemann AG, Buchdruckerei und Verlag+*, CH–8034 Zurich, Arbenzstr 20 Tel: (01) 346650/1
Dir: Emil Kappeler
Subjects: Metallurgy, Physics
Founded: 1853
ISBN Publishers Prefix: 3–85786

Lenos (Lenos-Presse/Z–Verlag), Postfach 794, CH–4002 Basle
Subjects: Belles Lettres, Pedagogics, Politics, Literary Periodical — drehpunkt
Miscellaneous: Company has common interests with the Z–Verlag (qv) and Edition Etcetera (qv)

Leobuchhandlung, Verlag der Quellenbändchen+, Gallusstr 20, CH–9001 St Gallen Tel: (071) 222917/228475 Telex: 77452
Man Dir: Walter Gnägi
Associate: Vereinigung Katholischer Buchhändler (qv under Book Trade Organizations)
Founded: 1918
Bookshop: Leobuchhandlung, at above address
ISBN Publishers Prefix: 3–85788

Leonis Verlag+, Villa Meridiana, Titlisstr 14, 8032 Zurich
Sales and distribution: PO Box 952, CH–8034 Zurich (Located at: Klausstr 49) Tel: (01) 327560/(01) 475565 Cable Add: Leonisverlag Zurich
Owner & Man Dir: Dr Wolfgang M Metz
Subjects: Biography, Politics, Social Science; Paperbacks
1977: 2 titles *1978:* 3 titles *Founded:* 1976
ISBN Publisher's Prefix: 3–721

Ligia Romontscha (Lia Rumantscha), Via Plessur 47, CH–7001 Cuera Tel: (081) 224422/224448
Subjects: Publishers of books in the Romantsch language of Switzerland; dictionaries, grammar, linguistics, background and history of Romantsch; Biography, Belles Lettres, Poetry, Music and Songs, Religion, Periodicals
1979: 20 titles
Miscellaneous: Company also gives financial support to publications in Romantsch

Limmat Verlag Genossenschaft+, Wildbachstr 48, Postfach, CH–8034 Zürich Tel: (01) 556300
Subjects: Academic and Popular Texts on the Worker's Movement and Associated Socialist-orientated Organisations, Socialism in Switzerland, Socio-Political Studies

Logos-Verlag+*, CH–8021 Zurich, Witikonerstr 368 Tel: (01) 530340
Subject: Textbooks
1977: 4 titles *Founded:* 1932
ISBN Publishers Prefix: 3–85790

E **Löpfe-Benz** AG Rorschach+, Graphische Anstalt und Verlag (Graphical Institute and Publisher), Signalstr 7, CH–9400 Rorschach Tel: (071) 414341
Dirs: Emil Enderle, Dieter Mildenberger; *Editorial:* Franz Mächler; *Sales:* Peter Kruijsen; *Advertising:* Theo Walser, Hans Schöbi, Peter Bick
Orders to: above address
Subsidiary Company: Nebelspalter Verlag (qv)
Subjects: Topical Works, Humour, Satire, Juvenile, Poetry, History; Periodical *Der Nebelspalter* (qv under Nebelspalter Verlag)
1978: 4 titles *Founded:* 1875
ISBN Publishers Prefix: 3–85819

Lüdin AG+*, Buchhandlung und Verlagsdruckerei, CH–4410 Liestal Tel: (061) 912211 Telex: 63243
Man Dir: Hugo Lüdin
Subject: Medical
Founded: 1833
Subsidiary: Verlag Ars Medici Lüdin AG (Liestal)
ISBN Publishers Prefix: 3–85792

Hans-Rudolf **Lutz**, Lessingstr 11, CH–8002 Zurich Tel: 2017672
Man Dir and other offices: H–R Lutz
Subjects: Visual Communication, Art, Architecture, Revolutionary Art
1977: 1 title *Founded:* 1966

McGraw-Hill Book Co, Co Publishing Office, Museggstr 7, CH–6004 Lucerne
Editorial Dir: Emil Bührer; *Art Dir:* Robert Tobler; *Managing Editor:* Francine Peeters; *Editor:* David Baker; *Production Manager:* Franz Gisler
Subjects: Illustrated General Literature, Reference Works
Miscellaneous: Firm is a Co-Publishing Office of the McGraw-Hill Book Co, 1221 Ave of the Americas, New York, NY 10020 See McGraw-Hill (UK) for Associate Companies etc

La **Maison** de la Bible+, Société Biblique de Genève, 11 rue de Rive, CH–1211 Geneva Tel: (022) 285259
Subjects: Religion, Juveniles, Educational
Bookshop: La Maison de la Bible, at above address
1977: 2 titles *1978:* 4 titles *Founded:* 1917
Miscellaneous: Also known as Das Haus der Bibel (Genfer Bibelgesellschaft)
ISBN Publishers Prefix: 2–8260

Manesse-Verlag, see Conzett und Hubert

Manesse und Morgarten Verlag, Morgartenstr 29, Postfach, CH-8021 Zurich Tel: (01) 2424455 Cable Add: Cozetthuber
Man Dir: Dr Hans Conzett; *Editorial, Rights & Permissions:* Dr F Hindemann; *Sales, Publicity:* Alex Aepli; *Production:* Kurt Oggier
Parent Company: Manesse-Verlag, Conzett und Huber; see Conzett und Huber
Subjects: Literary Works in German and from other worldwide languages in translation; the Classics, Fables and Legends; Religion, Music; Presentation Editions
1977: 10 titles *Founded:* 1886
ISBN Publisher's Prefix: 3-7175

Librairie-Editions J **Marguerat**+*, 2 pl St François, CH-1003 Lausanne 2 Tel: (021) 237717
Dir: Jean Marguerat
Subjects: Belles Lettres, History, Travel, Music, Geography, Ethnology
Founded: 1940
ISBN Publishers Prefix: 2-88008

Anna Marie **Mariani** – Wagenkampfverlag*, Haldenstr 579, CH-8955 Aetwil Tel: (01) 7480227 Cable Add: a m mariani 8955 oetwil
Man Dir and all offices: Anna Marie Mariani
Subjects: Topical Criticism in Prose and Verse
1977: 4 titles *Founded:* 1976

Marva, route des Acacias, BP 254, CH-1211 Geneva 26 Tel: 925671 Cable Add: Marva Geneva 26
Publisher: Hennecke Kardel and Dietrich Bronder
Subject: Modern History (especially European and Nazi-related)
1977: 1 title *1978:* 2 titles

Editions la **Matze**+, Case Postale, CH-1951 Sion (Located at: Bellevue B, CH-1964 Chateauneuf-Conthey Tel: 363232
Man Dir: Guy Gessler; *Sales Dir:* Nelly Tanner
Subjects: General Fiction, Military and General History, Archaeology, Swiss Painters series
Founded: 1975

Verlag A & G de **May***, 6 chemin des Sorbiers, BP 52, CH-1012 Lausanne Tel: (021) 289608
Subjects: History, Arts, Archaeology

Médecine & Hygiène+, BP-229, 78 Ave de la Roseraie, CH-1211 Geneva 4 Tel: 469355
Man & Sales Dir: J P Balavoine; *Publicity and Advertising Dir:* P Y Balavoine
Subjects: Medicine, Psychology, General Science, University Textbooks
1977: 9 titles *Founded:* 1943

Peter **Meili** & Co+*, CH-8200 Schaffhausen, Fronwagplatz 13 Tel: (053) 54144/5
Subjects: History, Literature about the Schaffhausen area, Dialect Stories
Founded: 1838
ISBN Publishers Prefix: 3-85805

Christoph **Merian** Verlag*, St Alban-Vorstadt 5, CH-4052 Basle Tel: (061) 221288
Subjects: Basle and Area
ISBN Publisher's Prefix: 3-85616

Henri **Messeiller**+, 11 rue St Nicolas, CH-2000 Neuchâtel Tel: (038) 251296
Subjects: Textbooks, Education, Art, Belles Lettres, Religion, Psychology, Law, Administration
Founded: 1887
ISBN Publishers Prefix: 2-8261

Max S **Metz** Verlag AG*, CH-8022 Zurich, Limmatquai 36 Tel: (01) 325357
Man Dir: Max S Metz
Subjects: Culture, Politics, Economics, Technical, History, Maps
Founded: 1946
ISBN Publishers Prefix: 3-85807

Editions **Minkoff** Reprint+*, 46 chemin de la Mousse, CH-1225 Chêne-Bourg, Geneva Tel: (022) 485568
Dir and all offices: Youval Minkoff, Sylvie Minkoff
Subjects: Music and Musicology, Musical Iconography, Theatre, Fine Arts, Japanese Art, General History of Socialism
1977: 32 titles *1978:* 25 titles *Founded:* 1972
ISBN Publishers Prefix: 2-8266

Moderne Industrie AG+*, Dörflistrasse 73, 8050 Zürich Tel: (01) 468140 Telex: 57547
Subjects: Technical, Data Processing, Personnel, Marketing, Sales
ISBN Publishers Prefix: 3-478

Alfred **Mohler** Verlag+*, CH-8800 Thalwil, Seestr 1 Tel: (01) 7207691
Founded: 1970
ISBN Publishers Prefix: 3-85808

Editions **Mon Village** SA, CH-1099 Vulliens, Vaud Tel: (021) 931363
Man Dir, Sales, Production, Publicity, Rights & Permissions: Albert-Louis Chappuis; *Editorial:* André Plomb
Subjects: Novels of rural life
Book Club: Club Mon Village SA
1978: 4 titles *1979:* 4 titles *Founded:* 1953

Mondo SA+, 18 ave Reller, 1800 Vevey Tel: (021) 528021
Man Dir: P Mayor

Les Editions du **Mont-Blanc** SA+, 72 rue de Lausanne, CH-1200 Geneva Tel: (022) 315210
Man Dir: Bernard Steele
Subjects: Philosophy, Religion, Medicine, Psychology, Social Science
1977: 5 titles *Founded:* 1942

Morgarten-Verlag+, see Manesse und Morgarten Verlag

Verlag Rudolf **Mühlemann**+*, Haus Z Wolfau, CH-8570 Weinfelden Tel: (072) 50888
Founded: 1949
ISBN Publishers Prefix: 3-85809

Jacques **Muhlethaler***, 5 rue du Simplon, CH-1211 Geneva 6 Tel: (022) 364451/2
Subjects: Fine & Applied Arts, Illustrated Books, Belles Lettres, Dietary, Handicrafts
Founded: 1945

Albert **Müller** Verlag AG+, CH-8803 Rüschlikon/Zürich, Bahnhofstr 69, Postfach 150 Tel: (01) 7241760 Cable Add: Müllerverlag Rüschlikon Telex: 56320 AMV CH
Man Dir: Adolf Recher-Vogel; *Editorial:* Dr Marta Jacober-Züllig; *Sales, Rights & Permissions:* Dr Bernhard Recher; *Production:* R Kleinschnittger
Subjects: Specializes in books on a variety of domestic and pet animals; also Juvenile Animal Stories and Science Fiction,
How-to, Music, Reference, Sports, Recreation, Cookery, Self-Help, Health, Yoga, Homecrafts
1977: 80 titles *1978:* 80 titles *Founded:* 1938
ISBN Publisher's Prefix: 3-275

Multiling Verlag AG, subsidiary of U Bär AG (qv)

N Z N-Buchverlag AG+, Zeltweg 71, Postfach A25, CH-8032 Zurich Tel: (01) 474951
Man Dir: Trottmann Alphons
Subjects: Art, Religion, Architecture, History
1977: 2 titles *1978:* 5 titles *Founded:* 1972
ISBN Publishers Prefix: 3-85827

Les Editions **Nagel** SA*, 5-5 bis rue de l'Orangerie, CH-1211 Geneva 7 Tel: (022) 341730/9 Cable Add: Nageledit Geneva
Man Dir: Louis Nagel
Subjects: Philosophy, Politics, Archaeology, Art, Travel Guides
Founded: 1952
Miscellaneous: Publishes 'Who's Who in Switzerland'
ISBN Publishers Prefix: 2-8263

Natura-Verlag+, Pfeffingerweg 1, CH-4144 Arlesheim Tel: (061) 721011
Subjects: Nature Cure, Philosophy, Therapeutic Pedagogy texts
1978: 2 titles *1979:* 2 titles
ISBN Publishers Prefix: 3-85817

Naville & Cie SA+, 5-7 rue Lévrier, CH-1201 Geneva Tel: (022) 322400 Telex: navico 28469
President: Marc Payot; *General Manager:* Gilles Martin
Founded: 1877

Nebelspalter Verlag, CH-9400 Rorschach Tel: (071) 414341
Parent Company: E Löpfe-Benz AG, CH-9400 Rorschach (qv)
Subjects: Humour, Satire, Cartoons, Texts in Schweizerdialekt, Juvenile
Publication: Periodical *Der Nebelspalter*
1978: 4 titles
ISBN Publishers Prefix: 3-85819

Neptun-Verlag+* Ing H Frei, CH-8280 Kreuzlingen 1, Postfach 307 Tel: (072) 727262 Telex: Nept ch 77414
Manager: H Frei-Gmür
Subjects: Contemporary History, Art Reproductions, Travel
Founded: 1946
ISBN Publishers Prefix: 3-85820

Neue Diana Press AG+, Splügenstr 10, CH-8002 Zurich Tel: (01) 2027441 and 2016370
Man Dirs: Dr Rolf Zollikofer, Dr Richard Bechtle
Subjects: General Fiction, Biography, History
1977: 10 titles *Founded:* 1973
ISBN Publisher's Prefix: 3-87158

Verlag **Neue Stadt**, Postfach 218, CH-8032 Zürich (Located at: Seestr 426, CH-8038 Zurich)
Parent Company: Verlag Neue Stadt, Federal Republic of Germany (qv)
Associate Company: Verlag Neue Stadt, Austria (qv)

Neue Zürcher Zeitung, Buchverlag, CH-8021 Zürich, Postfach
Subject: Textbooks

Neufeld Verlag und Galerie, PO Box, CH-9434 Au/SG Tel: (071) 712977 Cable Add: neufeld
Man Dir: K G Löpfe; *Editorial and other offices:* Kurt Prantl
Orders to: Lustenau, A-6890 Austria
Parent Company: Löpfe KG, Lustenau, A-6890 Austria
Subject: Art
1977: 2 titles *1978:* 2 titles *Founded:* 1962

Verlag Arthur **Niggli** AG+*, CH-9052 Niederteufen Tel: (071) 331772 Cable Add: Niggliverlag, Niederteufen Appenzell
Man Dir: Arthur Niggli
Shipping Add: c/o Danzas und Co, St Gallen
Subjects: Visual Arts, Architecture, Fine Arts
1978: 25 titles *Founded:* 1950
Bookshop: Buchhandlung Niggli, Abt Versandbuchhandlung, CH-9052 Niederteufen
Subsidiaries: Gallery Ida Niggli Ltd, CH-9052 Niederteufen; CH-8057 Zurich, Ringstr 76
ISBN Publishers Prefix: 3-7212

Nord-Süd Verlag+, CH-8617 Mönchaltorf Tel: (01) 9480617/9481057 Cable Add: nordsued
Dir, Editorial: Brigitte Sidjanski-Hanhart; *Sales, Production, Publicity, Rights & Permissions:* Davy Sidjanski
Orders to: Sauerländer AG, Postfach, CH-5001 Aarau Tel: (064) 221264 Telex: 68736 (for Switzerland)
Subjects: Children's Picture Books, Picture Calendars, Posters
Book Clubs: Punktum (in co-operation with Walter Verlag)
1979: 13 titles *Founded:* 1961
ISBN Publishers Prefix: 3-85825

Nova-Press International Publishers Ltd*, Hallwylstr 71, Postfach 275, CH-8036 Zurich Tel: (01) 2418117 Telex: 53094 npz
Man Dir, Rights & Permissions: Marcel H Huber; *Editorial:* H P Elermann; *Sales:* Hans Wiederkehr; *Production:* D Weimar; *Publicity:* J W Geisen
Imprints: Nova-Press International, Zurich, Munich, Vienna, Paris, London
Subjects: Popular texts on Economics, Politics, History, Factual Reportage, Art and Picture Books, 30-vol Musical Encyclopaedia with records
Book Club: International Classical Music Ltd: Zurich, Munich, Vienna, Paris, London
1977: 15 titles *Founded:* 1976
ISBN Publisher's Prefix: 3-85826

Novalis Verlag AG+*, 8200 Schaffhausen, Vordergasse 58 Tel: (053) 88111
Subjects: Arts, Social Sciences, Educational
ISBN Publishers Prefix: 3-7214

Editions **Novos** SA+, 4 ave Ruchonnet, CH-1001 Lausanne Tel: (021) 226372
Dir: Gabrielle Philippin
Subjects: Fiction, Calendars, Desk Calendars, Art

Emil **Oesch** Verlag AG+*, CH-8800 Thalwil, Zürich, Seestr 3 Tel: 7201333 Cable Add: Oesch
Man Dir & Sales, Publicity & Advertising: Marianna K Moebis
Subjects: General Fiction, How-to, Philosophy, Religion, Psychology, General & Social Science, Educational Materials
Founded: 1935
ISBN Publishers Prefix: 3-85833

L'**Oeuvre Gravée**, Münstergasse 36, Postfach 205 (CH-3000 Berne 8), CH-3011 Berne Tel: (031) 225071 Cable Add: Schindlerart
Editorial, Publicity: Werner Schindler

Office du Livre SA (Buchhaus AG)+, 101 route de Villars, CP 1061, CH-1701 Fribourg Tel: (037) 240744 Cable Add: LIVREOFFICE Telex: 36227
Man Dir: Jean Hirschen; *Editorial:* Didier Coigny; *Sales Manager:* Pierre Engel
Subjects: Art, Architecture, Arts and Crafts, Golf
1977: 60 titles *1978:* 60 titles *Founded:* 1947
ISBN Publishers Prefix: 37215

Edition **Olms** AG, Postfach 159, CH-8033 Zurich (Located at: Haldenbachstr 17) Tel: (01) 691160
Man Dir and Other Offices: Manfred Olms
Subjects: First Editions, Facsimile Reprints (especially of illustrated Travel Works), Bibliophile, Myth and Legend, Magic, Helvetica, Humour, Chess, Toy Catalogues
1978: 10 titles *1979:* 14 titles *Founded:* 1977
ISBN Publisher's Prefix: 3-283

Inigo von **Oppersdorff** Verlag, Waldschulweg 5, CH-8032 Zurich Tel: (01) 551140
Man Dir: B Lennier
Subjects: Belles Lettres, Poetry, History, Music, Art, Religion
1977: 2 titles *1978:* 5 titles *Founded:* 1966
ISBN Publisher's Prefix: 3-85834

Orell Füssli Verlag+*, CH-8022 Zurich, Nüschelerstr 22 Tel: (01) 2113630 Cable Add: Orellverlag Zurich Telex: 54021 orlag ch
Man Dir: Max Hofmann; *Editorial:* Ernst Halter, Armin Ochs; *Sales & Advertising Dir:* Walter Köpfli; *Publicity:* Hanne Piccot; *Rights & Permissions:* Walter Köpfli
Parent Company: Orell Füssli Graphische Betriebe AG, Dietzingerstr 3, CH-8036 Zürich
Subjects: Belles Lettres, Biography, History, How-to, Music, Art, Juveniles, Educational Materials, Railways and Aircraft
Bookshops: Pelikanstr 10, CH-8022 Zurich; City-Buchhandlung, Nüschelerstrasse 31, CH-8022 Zurich
1977: 32 titles *Founded:* 1519
ISBN Publishers Prefix: 3-280

Verlag **Organisator** AG+, Löwenstr 16, CH-8021 Zurich Tel: (01) 2118155 Cable Add: orga/ch Telex: 813834
Man Dir, Editorial: Dr V Bataillard; *Sales, Publicity:* V A Bataillard; *Production:* K Raggenbach
Subjects: Swiss Law and Taxes, International Taxes, Industrial Management; Monthly Management Periodical *Der Organisator*
Bookshops: In Basle, Lucerne, St Gallen, Schaffhausen, Winterthur, Zurich and many other Swiss towns
1977: 4 titles *1978:* 12 titles *Founded:* 1919
ISBN Publisher's Prefix: 3-7220

Origo-Verlag, Rathausgasse 30, CH-3011 Berne Tel: (031) 224480 Cable Add: Wildbuch
Man Dir: Alexander Wild (owner)
Associate Company: Verlag Alexander Wild, at same address
Subjects: Philosophy and Religion of East and West
1977: 7 titles *1978:* 8 titles *Founded:* 1947
ISBN Publisher's Prefix: 3-282

Orte-Verlag, Postfach 2028, CH-8006 Zurich (Located at: Ekkehardstr 14) Tel: (01) 600234, 477070
Man Dir: Werner Bucher
Subjects: Poetry, Belles Lettres

Ott Verlag AG Thun+, CH-3600 Thun 7, Länggasse 57 Tel: (033) 221622 Cable Add: Ottpubl Thun Telex: 33991
Man Dir: Walter Knecht; *Publicity & Advertising:* Hans M Ott; *Sales Manager:* Nino D'Andrea
Subsidiary Company: Verlags und Versandbuchhandlung Thun AG, Thun
Subjects: General Nonfiction, Lexicons, Earth Sciences, Military, Sports, Industry/Commerce
1978: 5 titles *Founded:* 1923
ISBN Publishers Prefix: 3-7225

Editions du **Panorama**+, CP 38 CH-2500 Bienne 3 Tel: (032) 224240
Man Dir: Paul Thierrin
Subjects: General Fiction, History, Dance, Philosophy, Commerce, Secondary, Textbooks, Law, Social Science, Languages, Belles Lettres, Music, Theatre, Geography, Travel, Transport
1978: 6 titles *Founded:* 1951

Edizioni **Pantarei**+*, CH-6900 Lugano, Via Sempione 2
Subjects: Music, Belles Lettres

Park and Roche Establishment+*, 11 rue Général Dufour, CH-1211 Geneva 11 Tel: 282744
Editorial, Permissions: Peter Bellew, Canto Lou Vent, Route de la Colle, 06570 St Paul de Vence, France Tel: (93) 329338
Subjects: Illustrated books on Art, Architecture, Cookery, Cultural History, Music, General Knowledge: published in international co-editions

Paulusverlag+, 36 Pérolles, CH-1700 Fribourg Tel: (037) 226802
Dir: Martin Nicoulin
Subjects: Religion, Philosophy, History, Anthropology, Theology
Miscellaneous: Firm also publishes *Anthropos*, a multi-lingual review of ethnology and linguistics and *Monumenta Serica* (Oriental Studies)

Librairie **Payot** SA+, Case Postale 3212, CH-1002 Lausanne (Located at: 4 pl Pépinet, CH-1003 Lausanne) Tel: (021) 203331 Cable Add: Payotco Telex: 24961
Manager: Jean Hutter
Associated Company: Editions Payot, France (qv)
Branch Offs: 107 Freiestr, CH-4051 Basle; 16 Bundesgasse, CH-3011 Berne; 2 rue Vallin, PO Box 381, CH-1211 Geneva 11; 14 Grand-Rue, CH-1820 Montreux; 8a rue du Bassin, CH-2000 Neuchâtel; 51 rue d'Italie, CH-1800 Vevey; 9 Bahnhofstr, CH-8001 Zurich
Subjects: Belles Lettres, Poetry, History, Music, Art, General and Natural Sciences, Philosophy, Psychology, Law, Commerce, Regional, University, Secondary & Primary Textbooks, Transport, Agriculture, Domestic, Sport
1977: 60 titles *Founded:* 1835
Bookshops: Librairie Payot SA, 1 rue de Bourg, CH-1003 Lausanne; 4 pl Pépinet, CH-1003 Lausanne; Tel: (021) 203331
Telex: 24961 for both shops
See also list of Branch Offices above
ISBN Publishers Prefix: 2-601

Carlo **Pedrazzini**+*, Via B Varenna 7, CH-6600 Locarno Tel: (093) 317734 35
Man Dir and other offices: Carlo Pedrazzini
Subjects: Scholastic, Historical, Church Historical, Literary
1977: 14 titles *Founded:* 1880

Pendo-Verlag*, Gemeindestr 25, CH-8032 Zürich Tel: (01) 346814
Subjects: Travel, Religion, International Co-operation
ISBN Publisher's Prefix: 3-85842

Pharos-Verlag+*, Hansrudolf Schwabe AG, CH-4002 Basel, Postfach 917 Tel: (061) 395671
Man Dir: Hansrudolf Schwabe; *Advertising Dir:* Heiner Hartmann
Subjects: Belles Lettres, Poetry, Juveniles
Founded: 1958
Bookshop: Buchhandlung Münsterberg, CH-4000 Basel, Münsterberg 13
ISBN Publishers Prefix: 3-7230

Philosophisch-Anthroposophischer Verlag+, Goetheanum, Hügelweg 63, Postfach, CH-4143 Dornach Tel: (061) 721116
Orders to: Martin Sandkühler, Paracelsusstr 26, Postfach 720308, D-7000 Stuttgart 72, Federal Republic of Germany (qv)
Subsidiary Company: Rudolf Geering-Verlag, at above address
Subjects: Philosophy, Anthroposophy, Nature Study, Eurhythmics, Music, Literature, Medicine etc; all subjects especially in connection with the thought of Rudolf Steiner
Bookshop: at above address
ISBN Publishers Prefix: 3-7235

Phoebus-Verlag GmbH+*, CH-4052 Basle, Malzgasse 7
Subject: Arts
ISBN Publishers Prefix: 3-85841

Phoenix Verlag AG, see Scherz Verlag AG

Editions **Pierrot** SA+*, 51 ave de Rumine, CH-1005 Lausanne Tel: (021) 220753

R **Piper** & Co Verlag GmbH+*, CH-4654 Lostorf, Zehntenweg 146 Tel: (062) 482181
Parent Company: R Piper & Co Verlag (qv), Munich, German Federal Republic
Subjects: Belles Lettres, Juveniles, Politics, Social Science, Psychology, Education, Natural Sciences
ISBN Publisher's Prefix: 3-7236

Polana AG*, Postfach 1173 CH-8036 Zürich
Subjects: Belles Lettres, Poetry, Politics

Populaires*, Ave Tivoli 2, Lausanne Tel: (022) 332600
Man Dir: Philippe Luquiens

Presses Centrales Lausanne SA+*, 7 rue de Genève, CH-1003 Lausanne Tel: (021) 205901
Dir: Gilbert Rohrer
Subject: Art

Les **Presses de la Connaissance***, c/o Weber SA d'Editions, 13 rue de Monthoux, BP 385, CH-1211 Geneva 2 Tel: 326450
Cable Add: Livrart
Parent Company: Les Presses de la Connaissance, Paris, France
Subjects: Mythology; Witnesses and Testimonies

Pro Juventute Verlag+, Seefeldstr 8, Postfach, CH-8022 Zürich Tel: (01) 2517244
Subjects: Children's Education and Welfare generally; covers Family, Playgroups, Playgrounds, Pedagogy, Teaching Media etc; Texts in German, French, Italian and English
1977: 2 titles

Editions **Pro Schola**+, 29 rue des Terreaux, CH-1003 Lausanne Tel: (021) 236655
Cable Add: Dirbenedict
Man Dir: Dr Jean J Bénédict
Orders to: BP 298, CH-1000 Lausanne 9
Subjects: Language: Textbooks, Reference; especially, language teaching by the "Bénédict Direct Progressive Method"
Founded: 1928
ISBN Publishers Prefix: 2-88009

Problem-Verlag*, CH-6000 Lucerne, Hirschmattstr 1, Postfach 834
Subject: Hobbies

edition **proTHESE**, Stegstr 791, CH-8912 Obfelden Tel: (01) 998822
Man Dirs, Editorial, Rights & Permissions: Jürg Moser, Werner Zogg; *Sales:* W Zogg; *Production:* Rene Pulfer; *Publicity:* J Moser, W Zogg, R Pulfer
Subjects: Early literature in German, Graphic Art; Periodical *proTHESE*
1977: 2 titles *Founded:* 1973

Verlag fur **Psychologie** Dr C J Hogrefe, see Hogrefe

Psychosophische Gesellschaft*, CH-8021 Zurich, Postfach 204
Subjects: Psychology, Philosophy, Theology, Pedagogy, Mysticism and Magic, the Works of Aleister Crowley

R A Verlag*, CH-8640 Rapperswil, Postfach 120
Subjects: Art, Education, Games

Rabe Verlag Zurich+, Oberdorfstr 23, CH-8001 Zurich Tel: (01) 478540; Depot at: CH-8608 Bubikon Zurich Tel: (055) 382383; Cable Add: rabeverlag Zurich
Man Dir, Sales: Dr J Kanitz; *Editorial, Rights & Permissions:* Dr Elsa Kanitz; *Production, Publicity:* Dr P Portmann
Subjects: Art Books, Cards; Large-format graphics on old/modern art; Art Prints
Bookshop: rabe verlag, at above address
1977: 1 title and 26 prints *Founded:* 1962
ISBN Publisher's Prefix: 3-85852

Raeber AG Luzern*, CH-6002 Lucerne, Frankenstr 7-9 Tel: (041) 227422/3/4
Telex: 72381
Man Dir: B L Raeber
Imprint: Edition Galerie Raeber
Subjects: General Fiction, Belles Lettres, Poetry, History, Music, Art, Juveniles, Secondary Textbooks, Religion
1977: 4 titles *1978:* 8 titles *Founded:* 1825
Bookshops: Raeber Buchhandlung, CH-6002 Lucerne, Frankenstr; Taschenbuchladen Kornmärt, Lucerne, Kornmarktgasse 7
ISBN Publishers Prefix: 3-7239

Verlag für **Recht und Gesellschaft** AG+, Postfach 1004, CH-4002 Basel (Located at: 15 Bundesstr, CH-4054 Basel) Tel: (061) 396600 Cable Add: Regesverlag
Man Dir: Berta Hess
Subject: Law, Taxation
Founded: 1933
ISBN Publishers Prefix: 3-7242

Regenbogen-Verlag*, Postfach 240, CH-8025 Zurich Tel: (01) 475860
Gen Man: Theo Ruff
Orders to: Neue Bücher AG, Gotthardtstr 49, CH-8027 Zürich Tel: 257474
Subjects: Art Books, Swiss Literature, Objets d'Art in the 'Edition Regenbogen'
ISBN Publishers Prefix: 3-85862

Kinderbuchverlag **Reich** Luzern AG+, Zinggentorstr 4, CH-6000 Lucerne 6 Tel: (041) 228871 Telex: 72508 reic ch
Man Dir: Jürgen Braunschweiger; *Editorial:* Heidrun Diltz; *Sales, Admin, Publicity:* Verlag Sauerländer, CH-5001 Aarau (qv)
Parent Company: Reich Verlag AG (qv), from which this Company has taken over the Children's List
Subjects: Juvenile Fiction and Non-fiction with photographic illustrations
1979: 10 titles *Founded:* 1979
ISBN Publisher's Prefix: 3-7941

Reich Verlag AG+, CH-6000 Lucerne 6, Zinggentorstr 4, Tel: (041) 220721 Telex: 72508 reic ch
Man Dir: Jürgen Braunschweiger; *Sales & Administration:* Alfons Wüest; *Editorial and Publicity:* Heidrun Diltz
Subsidiary Company: Kinderbuchverlag Reich Luzern AG (qv)
Subjects: Photographic Picture Books (terra magica), Hippology Books (terra hippologica), Belles Lettres (Edition Reich)
1979: 15 titles *Founded:* 1974
ISBN Publishers Prefix: 3-7243

Ernst **Reinhardt** Verlag AG+, Sommergasse 46, CH-4000 Basel 12 Tel: (061) 430336
Parent Company: Ernst Reinhardt GmbH & Co Verlag, Federal Republic of Germany (qv)
Orders to: Munich address of parent company
Man Dir: H Jungck
Subjects: Humanities, Psychology, Education, Psychotherapy
1977: 14 titles *1978:* 25 titles *Founded:* 1945
ISBN Publishers Prefix: 3-497

Verlag Friedrich **Reinhardt** AG+, CH-4012 Basel, Missionstr 36 Tel: (061) 253390
Cable Add: Freinhardt Basel
Man Dir, Rights & Permissions: Dr Ernst Reinhardt
Subjects: General Fiction, Belles Lettres, Biography, History, How-to, Religion, Juveniles, General Science, University Textbooks, Educational Materials
1978: 19 titles
ISBN Publishers Prefix: 3-7245

Editions **Rencontre** SA*, 29 chemin d'Entre-Bois, CH-1018 Lausanne Tel: (021) 323841
Cable Add: Rencontre Lausanne
Telex: 24876
Subjects: General Fiction, Belles Lettres, Poetry, Biography, History, Music, Art, Philosophy, Reference, Religion, Juveniles, Medicine, General Science, Educational Materials
Founded: 1950

Eugen **Rentsch** Verlag AG+, Wiesenstr 48, Postfach 47, CH-8703 Erlenbach-Zurich Tel: (01) 9100133 Telex: CH 59784 Revag
Man Dir, Rights & Permissions: Dr Eugen Rentsch; *Publicity Dir:* Dr Leonore Rentsch
Subjects: Biography, History, Biology, Psychology, Economy, Social Science, Environmental, Political, Educational Books and Materials, Children's Books
1977: 26 titles *1978:* 20 titles *Founded:* 1910
ISBN Publisher's Prefix: 3-7249

Imprimeries **Réunies** SA+, ave de la Gare, CH-1003 Lausanne Tel: (021) 203111
Telex: 24495
Subjects: Art, Belles Lettres, Natural Sciences, Geography, Travel
Miscellaneous: Associated imprints include Editions 24 Heures (qv)

Rex-Verlag+, CH-6000 Lucerne 5, St Karliquai 12, Postfach 161 Tel: (041) 224914
Man Dir: Dr Zeno Inderbitzin
Subjects: Belles Lettres, Education, Juveniles, Religion (Catholicism)
1977: 35 titles *Founded:* 1931
Bookshop: Rex Buchladen, St-Karliquai 12, CH-6000 Lucerne 5
ISBN Publishers Prefix: 3-7252

Edizioni Raimondo **Rezzonico**+*, CH-6600 Locarno, Via Luini

Ringier & Co AG+*, Graphisches Institut und Verlagsanstalt, CH-4800 Zofingen, Florastr Tel: (062) 510101
President: Hans Ringier; *Executive President:* Dr Hch Oswald
Subjects: Fashion, Directories
Founded: 1833
ISBN Publishers Prefix: 3-85859

Editiones '**Roche**', F Hoffmann – La Roche & Co, Aktiengesellschaft, Postfach CH-4002 Basle Tel: 271122 Cable Add: Roche Basel Telex: 62922 a roch ch
Man Dir, Sales, Production, Publicity: Martin Schneider; *Editorial:* Dr W Kolditz
Orders to: H Huber, Länggassstrasse 76, CH-3000 Berne 9 (for Editiones 'Roche'); F Hoffmann – La Roche & Co, Postfach, CH-4002 Basel (for Rocom Publications)
Imprint: Rocom
Subjects: Medical
1977: 4 titles *Founded:* 1971

Rocom, imprint of Editiones 'Roche' (qv)

Rodana Verlag, see Schweizer Spiegel Verlag AG

Hans **Rohr**, Oberdorfstr 5, CH-8024 Zurich 1 Tel: (01) 2513636 Telex: 56385
Man Dir: H Rohr
Subjects: Tourist Interest, Swiss History, Swiss Dialect, Classical Antiquity, Books on Films and the Cinema
Bookshops: Buchhandlung Hans Rohr, Oberdorfstr 5, CH-8024 Zurich; Filmbuchhandlung Hans Rohr, Oberdorfstr 3, CH-8024 Zurich (Films and Cinema)
1977: 2 titles *1978:* 6 titles *Founded:* 1921
ISBN Publisher's Prefix: 3-85865

Rosepierre SA+*, 10 ch Rieu, 1211 Geneva 11 Tel: (022) 353225
Man Dir: Pierre Bouffard

Rotapfel-Verlag AG+, Frankengasse 6, CH-8024 Zurich Tel: (01) 470388
Dir: Dr Paul Toggenburger
Subjects: Textbooks, Juveniles, Beaux-arts, Belles Lettres
Founded: 1919
ISBN Publishers Prefix: 3-85867

Roth et Sauter SA+*, à l'Enseigne du Verseau, La Pâle, CH-1026 Denges/Lausanne Tel: (021) 717561
Man Dirs: Michel Logoz, Pierre Sauter
Imprints: Include Editions du Verseau
Subjects: Art, Belles Lettres, General
Founded: 1890

Rotten-Verlags AG, Terbinerstr 2, CH-3930 Visp Tel: (028) 462252

Editions **Roulet** & Cie+*, 2 bis blvd des Promenades, CH-1227 Carouge Tel: (022) 425560
ISBN Publishers Prefix: 2-88010

Librairie **Rousseau***, 36 rue Rousseau, CH-1201 Geneva Tel: (022) 325622
Proprietor: Roland Audéoud
Founded: 1954
Subjects: Slav studies, Politics

Rütten und Loening Verlag GmbH+, see Scherz Verlag AG

Verlag **S O I** (Schweizerisches Ost-Institut)+, CH-3000 Berne 6, Jubiläumsstr 41 Tel: (031) 431212 Cable Add: Schweizost Telex: 32728
Man Dir: Peter Sager; *Sales Manager:* Bea Sager; *Production Manager:* Peter Dolder
Subjects: History, Politics, Social Science, especially with respect to the Eastern Bloc countries
Bookshop: Buchhandlung SOI, CH-3000 Berne 6, Jubiläumsstr 41
1977: 4 titles *1978:* 5 titles *Founded:* 1958
ISBN Publisher's Prefix: 3-85913

Librairie **Saint-Albert** le Grand+*, 1 rue du Temple, BP 1057, CH-1701 Fribourg Tel: (037) 220151
Bookshop: As above

Société de l'Oeuvre **Saint-Augustin**+*, 1890 St-Maurice Tel: (025) 36022
Man Dirs: Germaine Mauron, Elise Lenherr

Saint-Paul+, Imprimerie et Librairie, Pérolles 38-40, CH-1700 Fribourg Tel: (037) 811121
Dir: Dr Hugo Baeriswyl
Subjects: Philosophy, Religion, Educational
Founded: 1873

Salvioni & Co+*, CH-6500 Bellinzona, Via Franscini

Sanssouci Verlag+, Rosenbühlstr 37, CH-8044 Zurich Tel: (01) 342154 Cable Add: Archeverlag
Owner: Peter Schifferli
Orders to: Erikastr 11, CH-8003 Zurich
Associate Companies: Verlag der Arche, Zurich (qv); E Pfister GmbH, German Federal Republic (qv); Dr Franz Hain, Austria (qv)
Subjects: General Fiction, Humour, How-to, Cookery
1978-79: 30 titles
ISBN Publishers Prefix: 3-7254

Säntis Verlag*, CH-9107 Urnäsch

Sauerländer AG+*, Laurenzenvorstadt 89, Postfach 570, CH-5001 Aarau Tel: (064) 221264 Telex: 68726
Man Dir: Hans Christof Sauerländer; *Editorial:* Rolf Inhauser, Jitka Bodlakova, Dörthe Binkert; *Sales and Publicity:* Peter Streit; *Production:* Albert Steinmann, Fritz Gebhard; *Rights & Permissions:* Renate Fischer
Subsidiary Companies: H R Sauerländer & Co, Frankfurt-am-Main, German Federal Republic; Verlag Sauerländer, Salzburg, Austria
Associate Companies: SABE-Verlag für Lehrmittel, CH-8001 Zurich
Subjects: Belles Lettres, Poetry, Biography, History, Reference, Juveniles, Medicine, General & Social Science, University, Secondary & Primary Textbooks, Educational Materials
1977: 80 titles *Founded:* 1807
ISBN Publishers Prefix: 3-7941

Scherz Verlag AG+, Marktgasse 25, CH-3000 Berne Tel: (031) 226831 Cable Add: Scherzedit Telex: 32552 sherz d
President, Man Dir: Rudolf Streit-Scherz; *Sales Dirs:* Elmar Send (Switzerland and Austria); *Editorial Department:* Ursula Ibler, Jürgen Lütge; *Subsidiary Rights & Permissions:* Ursula Griessel
Subsidiary Companies: Otto Wilhelm Barth-Verlag KG, Federal Republic of Germany (qv); Phoenix, Rütten & Loening; Spectrum
Branch Off: Scherz Verlag GmbH, Federal Republic of Germany (qv)
Subjects: General Fiction & Nonfiction, Biography, History, Psychology, Parapsychology, Philosophy; Paperback series of Crime Thrillers
Bookshop: Marktgasse 25, CH-3011 Berne
1977: 112 titles *1978:* 114 titles *Founded:* 1939
ISBN Publishers Prefix: 3-502

Verlag der Arche Peter **Schifferli**, see Arche

Otto **Schlaefli** Verlag+*, CH-3800 Interlaken, Bahnhofstr 15 Tel: (036) 221312/3
Subjects: Belles Lettres, Fiction
Founded: 1930
ISBN Publishers Prefix: 3-85884

Schläpfer & Co AG*, CH-9100 Herisan 1 Tel: (071) 513131 Telex: 77147
Man Dir: P Schläpfer
Br Off: Schläpfer & Co AG, CH-9043 Trogen
Subjects: Books on the Home
1977: 3 titles *1978:* 3 titles *Founded:* 1974

Schnell und Steiner, CH-8260 Stein-am-Rhein
Parent Company: Verlag Schnell und Steiner GmbH und Co, Munich, Federal Republic of Germany (qv)

Verlag fur **Schöne** Wissenschaften (Belles Lettres Publishing Co — Albert Steffen Foundation), Unterer Zielweg 36, CH-4143 Dornach
Subjects: Poetry, Art, Anthroposophic Literature, Cultural History, Philosophy, Pedagogy, Therapeutics, Literary Criticism; specialises in Editions of the Works of the Swiss poet Albert Steffen (1884-1963), covering novels, stories, memoirs, verse, drama, essays, paintings and sketches
Publication: Therapeutische Dichtung (Therapeutic Poetry)
1977: 2 titles *1978:* 2 titles
ISBN Publishers Prefix: 3-85889

Hermann **Schroedel** Verlag AG, Hardstr 95, CH-4020 Basel Tel: (061) 423330
Associate Company: Hermann Schroedel Verlag KG, Federal Republic of Germany (qv)
Subsidiary Companies: Bilderbuch-Studio Neugebauer, Austria (qv); Neugebauer Press Verlag für Bibliophile, Austria (qv)
Subjects: Artistic Picture Books for Nursery Children and Adults (won many awards); Bibliophile Volumes; Facsimiles and Graphics
1977: 22 titles
ISBN Publisher's Prefix: 3-285

Schubiger Verlag AG+*, Mattenbachstrasse 2, 8400 Winterthur Tel: (052) 297221
Man Dir: E R Benz; *Sales, Publicity:* A Jaermann; *Production:* A Keller
Subject: Educational

F **Schuler**+*, CH-7002 Chur, Postplatz Tel: (081) 221160
Bookshop: As above
ISBN Publishers Prefix: 3-85894

Schulthess Polygraphischer Verlag AG+, CH-8022 Zurich, Zwingliplatz 2 Tel: (01) 2519336 Cable Add: Buchschulthess
Man Dir, Advertising, Permissions: Dr Charlotte Mark-Hürlimann; *Sales Dir:* Bruno Waldburger

Subjects: Law, Commerce, Social Science, University Textbooks, Schoolbooks
1978: 73 titles *Founded:* 1791
ISBN Publishers Prefix: 3-7255

Schwabe & Co Ltd+, Steinentorstr 13, Postfach 190, CH-4010 Basel Tel: (061) 235523 Cable Add: Schwabeco Basel
Man Dirs: Drs Christian Overstolz Sr & Jr, Hans Reimann, Josef A Niederberger, Marc Götz
Subjects: History, Art, Philosophy, Medicine, Psychology, University and Secondary Textbooks
1977: 23 titles *1978:* 20 titles *Founded:* 1494
ISBN Publisher's Prefix: 3-7965

Schweiz Verlag Arbeitsgemeinschaft für die Bergbevölkerung (SAB)*, CH-5200 Brugg, Laur-Str 10, Postfach 174

Aare-Verlag/**Schweizer Jugend**-Verlag+*, Kapuzinerstr 6, CH-4502 Solothurn Tel: (065) 229458; *Publishing Man:* Felix Furrer
Subsidiary Company: Eulen-Verlag, Postfach 1164, D-7000 Stuttgart 1, German Federal Republic
Subjects: Reference, Juveniles, Primary Textbooks, Educational Materials
Miscellaneous: Aare-Verlag and Schweizer Jugend-Verlag are divisions of the one company, and are under the same management
ISBN Publishers Prefix: 3-7260

Schweizer Spiegel Verlag AG & Rodana Verlag+, Rämistr 18, Postfach 5837, CH-8024 Zurich 1 Tel: (01) 472195
Dir: Dr P Huggler
Subjects: Belles Lettres, Poetry, Music, Art, Philosophy, Juveniles, Psychology, Social Science
Founded: 1925
ISBN Publisher's Prefixes: 3-85900 (Schweizer Spiegel), 3-85863 (Rodana)

Schweizer Verlagshaus AG+, CH-8008 Zurich, Klausstr 10, Tel: (01) 349134 Cable Add: svzuerich Telex: 53514
Dirs: Dr Armin Meyer, Walter Meyer; *Editorial, Rights & Permissions:* Dr A Meyer
Subjects: General Fiction, Biography, Art, Music, How-to, History, Travel, Juveniles, General Science, Textbooks, Medicine, Entertainment, Reference etc
1978: 19 titles *Founded:* 1907
ISBN Publishers Prefix: 3-7263

Schweizerische Stiftung für Alpine Forschungen (Swiss Foundation for Alpine Research), Binzstr 17, CH-8045 Zurich Tel: (01) 660147/48
Subjects: Alpine Research Publications

Schweizerische Zentralstelle für Stahlbau, CH-8034 Zurich, Seefeldstr 25 Tel: (01) 478980
Man Dir: Urs Wyss
1979: 6 titles

Verlag der **Schweizerischen Schallplattenmission**, member of the Telos group (qv in German Federal Republic), publishing evangelical paperbacks

Schweizerisches Jugendschriftenwerk+*, CH-8008 Zürich, Seehofstr 15, Postfach 8022 Tel: (01) 327244
Subjects: Literature for Juveniles in the four Swiss languages — French, German, Italian and Romansch
Founded: 1931
ISBN Publishers Prefix: 3-7269

Verlag **Schweizerisches katholisches Bibelwerk**, Institut Biblique de l'Université, CH-1700 Freiburg Tel: (037) 219385
Subjects: Religious Literature (Roman Catholic) on biblical subjects
Miscellaneous: Company is a member of AMB (qv under Federal Republic of Germany)

Schweizerisches Ost-Institut, see Verlag SOI

Schwengler-Verlag*, Postfach 262, CH-9435 Heerbrugg Tel: (071) 721232 and (071) 724358
Br Off: Schwengelg-Verlag, CH-8400 Winterthür
Subjects: Christian Literature
Founded: 1969
Miscellaneous: Member of the Telos group (qv in German Federal Republic), publishing evangelical paperbacks
ISBN Publisher's Prefix: 3-85666

Schwitter Edition GmbH, Allschwilerstr 90, Postfach 312, CH-4000 Basel 9 Tel: 061381230 Telex: 62934
Subjects: Art Books, Calendars, Art Reproductions, Facsimiles

F P **Schwitter** Holding Inc, PO Box 636, CH-8065 Zurich Tel: (01) 8101166 Telex: 58178 swint (Publishing Division located at: Talackerstr 9, Glattbrugg, Postfach 101, CH-8052 Zurich Tel: (057) 52555)
Man Dir: Fridolin Schwitter; *Editorial Dir:* Norma Schwitter
Subjects: Reference Works and Encyclopedias, Science and Technology, Medicine, Countries and Peoples, Natural History, Art, Juveniles
Founded: 1972
ISBN Publisher's Prefix: 3-284

Scrépel*, c/o Weber SA d'Editions, 13 rue de Monthoux, Postf 385, CH-1211 Geneva 2 Tel: 326450 Cable Add: Livrart
Subjects: Books on Painting and Painters, Art Reproductions
Miscellaneous: Associated Company: Scrépel, Paris, France

Editions **Scriptar** SA+, 23 ave de la Gare, CH-1003 Lausanne Tel: (021) 202351 Cable Add: Orlog Telex: Green 25587
Subjects: Watches and Jewellery, Gemmology; Art productions connected with these interests
1978: 3 titles *Founded:* 1946
ISBN Publishers Prefix: 2-88012

Edition **Seefeld**+, Minervastr 33, CH-8032 Zurich Tel: (01) 344717
Man Dir: T P A Flueler
Subjects: Facsimile Reprints of Old MS; Art Books with Original Prints
Bookshop: Galerie Edition Seefeld, at address above
1977: 2 titles *1978:* 5 titles *Founded:* 1976

Sinwel-Buchhandlung Verlag, Lorrainestr 10, CH-3000 Bern 22
Subjects: Belles Lettres, Current Affairs
1978: 6 titles
ISBN Publisher's Prefix: 3-85911

Editions D'Art Albert **Skira** SA+, 89 route de Chêne, CH-1208 Geneva Tel: (022) 495533 Cable Add: Edart Geneva
Subjects: Art, Art History, Art Reference, Low- & High-priced Paperbacks, Educational Materials

Slatkine Reprints+*, 5 rue des Chaudronniers, CH-1211 Geneva 3 Tel: (022) 200476/762551

Scherz Taschenbuch Verlag **Spectrum**, see Scherz Verlag AG

Speer-Verlag+, R Römer, CH-8044 Zurich, Hofstr 134 Tel: (01) 321203 Cable Add: Speerverlag
Man Dir: R Römer
Subjects: General Fiction, Belles Lettres, Philosophy, Juveniles, Poetry
Founded: 1944
ISBN Publisher's Prefix: 3-85916

Spes SA+, BP 20, CH-1800 Vevey (Located at: 2 rue du Château) Tel: (021) 510527 Telex: 451165 dlta
Man Dir: René F Galimont; *Publisher:* André Delcourt
Subjects: Scientific and Technical textbooks, Primary and Secondary textbooks, Mathematics, Physics, Chemistry, Mechanics, Automobile, Electronic technology, Civil Engineering, Horticulture
Founded: 1917
ISBN Publishers Prefix: 2-602
Miscellaneous: Member of the Kluwer Group, Netherlands (qv)

Sphinx Verlag, Spalenberg 37, CH-4003 Basel Tel: (061) 258583
Dir: D A Hagenbach
Orders to: Neue Bücher AG, Zürich
Subjects: Fantasy, Magic, Philosophy, Religion, Art, Picture Books, General Fiction
Bookshops: Sphinx, D A Hagenbach, Nadelberg 47 and Spalenberg 38, CH-4051 Basel Tel: 259292
1977: 6 titles *1978:* 6 titles *Founded:* 1975
ISBN Publisher's Prefix: 3-85914

Sport Verlags AG+*, Zweierstrasse 138, 8003 Zürich Tel: (01) 355683
Dirs: J Stemmle, Max Frey, H Brunner, G Furrer
Subject: Sport
ISBN Publishers Prefix: 3-85917

Verlag **Stämpfli** & Cie AG+, Haller-Str 7-9, Postfach 2728, CH-3001 Berne Tel: (031) 232323 Cable Add: Buchstaempfli Bern Telex: 32950
Man Dir, Rights & Permissions: Dr Jakob Stämpfli; *Sales & Advertising Dir:* K Zeller
Subjects: Jurisprudence, Political Science, Economics, History, Social Science, University Textbooks
1977: 32 titles *1978:* 30 titles *Founded:* 1799
ISBN Publishers Prefix: 3-7272

Rudolf **Steiner** Verlag+, Haus Duldeck, Postfach 135, CH-4143 Dornach Tel: (061) 722240
Man Dir, Editorial, Sales: Benedikt Marzahn; *Publicity:* Kurt Lüthi; *Production:* B Marzahn, K Lüthi; *Rights & Permissions:* Administrators of the Rudolf Steiner Literary Estate
Subjects: All branches of the Arts and Sciences in the context of anthroposophical (Rudolf Steiner) world conception
Bookshops: Duldeck, CH-4143 Dornach
1977: 40 titles *1978:* 30 titles *Founded:* 1956
ISBN Publishers Prefix: 3-7274

Josef **Stocker** AG*, CH-6002 Lucerne, Kapellgasse 5 Tel: (041) 224948
Subjects: Fiction, Law, Politics, Philosophy, Religion
Bookshop: As above
ISBN Publishers Prefix: 3-85922

Verlag **Stocker**-Schmid AG+, CH-8953 Dietikon-Zurich, Hasenbergstr 7 Postfach 66 Tel: (01) 7404444
Man Dir: Mr Stocker

Subsidiary Companies: Verlag Bibliophile Drucke von Josef Stocker AG, Dietikon (qv); Urs Graf-Verlag GmbH, Dietikon (qv)
Bookshop: Buchhandlung Stocker-Schmid, CH-8953 Dietikon, Hasenbergstr 7
Subjects: Modern and Historical Weapons and Equipment of the Swiss Army, subjects of Swiss Interest, especially Bibliophile Editions, Facsimiles of Incunabula, Old Maps, MSS
ISBN Publisher's Prefix: 3-7276

Strom-Verlag*, E Kobelt-Schultze, Staffelhof 21, CH-8055 Zurich 3 Tel: (01) 357415
Man Dir: Ernst Kobelt
Subjects: General Fiction, Art, Philosophy, High-priced Paperbacks, Psychology, Social Science, Poetry
1977: 14 titles
ISBN Publishers Prefix: 3-85921

Sumus Verlag Jutta Gütermann, Höschstr 19, Postfach 2, CH-8706 Feldmeilen Tel: (01) 9230259 Cable Add: Sumus
Editorial: Jutta Gütermann
Subject: Belles Lettres in Large Print, Swiss Literature
Titles: 1 per year *Founded:* 1976
ISBN Publisher's Prefix: 385926

Swan Productions AG*, Baarer Str, CH-6300 Zug Tel: (01) 257850
Subjects: Volumes of Pictures, Calendars, Posters etc; participant in International Co-Editions

Swedenborg Institut, c/o Dr P Stamm, Lautengartenstr 12, CH-4052 Basel
President: Björn Holmström (resident at PO Box 99 MC, Principality of Monaco)
Subject: Religion
Founded: 1952
ISBN Publishers Prefix: 3-85925

Tages-Nachrichten+*, 3110 Münsingen
Founded: 1884
Subjects: Belles Lettres, Juveniles

Theologischer Verlag AG+, Postfach, CH-8026 Zurich
Dir, Editorial, Production, Rights & Permissions: Werner Blum; *Sales:* C Salden; *Publicity:* E Gutmann
Consignment Add: Brauerstr 60, CH-8004 Zurich Tel: (01) 2413938
Orders to: Auwiesenstr 1, Postfach CH-8406 Winterthür
Subsidiary Company: Flamberg Verlag, Zurich (qv)
Subjects: Religion; Theology, emphasising Scriptural Knowledge and Reformation History; Works of Barth and Brunner; Popular Religious Works; Illustrated Books, Art Prints
Bookshops: Nova Buchhandlung — Sihlstr 33, Zurich; Nansenstr 4, Zurich; Freiestr 5, Uster; Bahnhofstr 12, Wetzikon
1977: 18 titles *1978:* 14 titles *Founded:* 1934
ISBN Publisher's Prefix: 3-290

Theseus Verlag AG, Freudwilerweg 7, CH-8044 Zürich
Subject: Eastern Religions

Thomas-Verlag+*, CH-8000 Zurich, Rennweg 14
Subjects: Belles Lettres, Religion
ISBN Publisher's Prefix: 3-85938

Verlags und Versandbuchhandlung **Thun** AG, subsidiary of Ott Verlag AG Thun (qv)

Tipografia Stazionne SA+*, see under Edizioni Armando Dado

Edizioni Giulio **Topi**+*, CH-6900 Lugano, Cso Elvezia 9

Editions **Townson**, Townson Publishing Co Ltd, PO Box 859, CH-1211 Geneva 3
Subjects: Books in French and English languages
ISBN Publisher's Prefix: 0-920822

Traber Verlag*, Bollwerk 19, 3011 Bern Tel: (031) 227121
Man Dir: Markus Traber
Subjects: Belles Lettres, Humour, Psychology
ISBN Publishers Prefix: 3-85941

Trachsel Verlag, CH-3714 Frutigen Tel: (033) 711407
Man Dir: Pauli Ernst Trachsel; *Editorial, Production, Rights & Permissions:* Ernst Trachsel; *Sales, Publicity:* Walter Trachsel
Imprints: TVF, Trachsel Verlag
Subjects: Christian Religious
Bookshop: At CH-3714 Frutigen
1978: 4 titles *1979:* 8 titles *Founded:* 1946
ISBN Publisher's Prefix: 3-7271

Tradexim SA+*, 10 rue du Prince, CH-1204 Geneva Tel: (022) 213444 Telex: 23947 Dexim ch

Trans Tech Publications SA*, CH-4711 Aedermannsdorf Tel: (062) 741379
Subjects: Materials Science, Physics, Technology for Heavy Industry, Mining Engineering, Geology

Translegal AG+, CH-6300 Zug, Loebern-Str 5 Tel: (042) 213044
Subjects: Multi-lingual Legal/Financial/Commercial Dictionaries
Founded: 1955
ISBN Publishers Prefix: 3-85942

Edizioni **Trelingue**, Luigi Rusconi+*, CH-6948 Porza-Lugano
Subjects: Philosophy, Religion

Tribune Editions, PO Box 434, CH-1211 Geneva 11 Tel: (022) 212121 Telex: 23381 trib ch
Man Dir, Rights & Permissions: Drago Arsenijevic; *Literary Dir:* Jean Vuilleumier; *Sales:* Christiane Lançon
Parent Company: La Tribune de Genève SA
Subjects: Current Affairs, History, Documentaries, Series on Health, also on Television, Illustrated Books, Juveniles
1978: 16 titles *1979:* 19 titles *Founded:* 1977

Editions du **Tricorne***, 5 route des Jeunes, CH-1211 Geneva 26, PO Box 228 Tel: (022) 431600 Cable Add: Studerprint Geneve Telex: 22406 Press ch
Man Dir: Serge Kaplun
Subjects: Art (Tapestry); Pedagogy (Maths); Poetry, Local Interest
1977: 4 titles *Founded:* 1976

Editions des **Trois Collines**+*, 1 rue de la Cité, BP 470, CH-1211 Geneva Tel: (022) 561309
Dir: François Lachenal
Subjects: Art, Politics, Belles Lettres, Philosophy, Psychology
Founded: 1936

Editions des **Trois Continents**, 3 rue de la Vigie, CP 121, CH-1000 Lausanne 9 Tel: (021) 205631 Cable Add: editasa Telex: 26296 edita ch
Chairman: Ami Guichard; *Man Dir:* Stéphane Hobeika
Subjects: History, Ethnology, Politics, Religion, Philosophy, General and Social Science, Art, Photography, Biography, Guide Books, Facsimile Editions; Co-Editions in all languages (including Mid- and Far-Eastern), especially books on Arab and Moslem world
Founded: 1976
ISBN Publisher's Prefix: 288042

U Bar Verlag, see Bar

Union dals Grischs*, CH-7505 Celerina

Union Helvetia Fachbuchverlag, Adligenswilerstr 22, Postfach 1115, CH-6002 Lucerne Tel: (041) 235454
Orders to: Postfach 1115, CH-6002 Lucerne
Subjects: Hotel and Catering trades (including Foreign Language Instruction)
Bookshops: Adligenswilerstr 22, Lucerne; Freigutstr 10, Zurich; 16 ave des Acacias, Lausanne
Miscellaneous: Publishing branch of the Schweizerischer Zentralverband der Hotel- und Restaurant-Angestellten (Swiss Industrial Union of Hotel and Restaurant Employees)

Union Verlagsvereinigung, Postfach 3348, CH-8048 Zurich Tel: (01) 640078
Man Dir: Josef Wandeler; *Editorial:* Lucien Leitess; *Publicity:* Alex Wick
Subjects: Labour Movement, Swiss Stories, Folk Literature
1978: 2 titles *1979:* 5 titles *Founded:* 1976
ISBN Publisher's Prefix: 3-293

Universitätsverlag, see Editions Universitaires

Uranium Verlag*, Postfach 42, CH-6317 Oberwil Tel: (042) 217744 Telex: Topaz 58280
Man Dir, Sales: L Young; *Editorial:* Mrs Young
Br Off: Atzelbergstr 22, D-6000 Frankfurt-am-Main
Subjects: Children's Books (Picture Story Books and Nonfiction)
1977: 66 titles *Founded:* 1976
ISBN Publisher's Prefix: 294

Urs Graf-Verlag GmbH, CH-8953 Dietikon, Hasenbergstr 7 Tel: (01) 7404444
Man Dir: Mr Stocker
Parent Company: Verlag Stocker-Schmid AG (qv)
Associate Company: Verlag Bibliophile Drucke Von Josef Stocker AG (qv)
Subjects: University Textbooks, Facsimile Editions of Old Maps and MSS
ISBN Publisher's Prefix: 3-85951

Verband schweizerischer Schreinermeister und Möbelfabrikanten Verlag und Fachbüchervertrieb+*, Postfach 134, CH-8044 Zurich (Located at: Schmelzbergstr 56, CH-8044 Zurich) Tel: (01) 473540 Cable Add: VSSM
General Secretary and all offices: Dr Josef Kaufmann
Subjects: Specialist Literature for the Joinery Trade
1978: 1 title *1979:* 1 title *Founded:* 1889

Buchverlag der **Verbandsdruckerei**/Editions Imprimerie Fédérative SA Berne+, Maulbeerstr 10, Postfach 2/41, CH-3001, Berne Tel: (031) 252911 Cable Add: verbandsdruck bern Telex: 32255
Man Dir: Roland Triet
Parent Company: Verbandsdruckerei AG, Berne
Subjects: Specialist Agricultural Texts, Belles Lettres, Travel, Swiss and Berne Regional Interest, General Nonfiction
1977: 20 titles *Founded:* 1919
Miscellaneous: Book publishing branch of Verbandsdruckerei/Imprimerie Fédérative (Printers' Federation)
ISBN Publisher's Prefix: 3-7280

Verkehrshaus der Schweiz, Lidostr 3-7, CH-6006 Lucerne
Subjects: Transport, Traffic, Communications, Tourism, Planetarium, Cosmorama
ISBN Publisher's Prefix: 3-85954

Verlagsgenossenschaft*, Lessingstr 11, Postf 157 8059 Zürich, CH-8002 Zürich Tel: 367672
Subjects: Socially-orientated Literature on Current Problems, especially connected with Switzerland

Editions du **Verseau**, an imprint of Roth et Sauter SA (qv)

Verlag Alfred F **Vetter**, Schifflande 22, CH-8001 Zürich
ISBN Publisher's Prefix: 3-85956

Viktoria Verlag*, CH-3072 Ostermundigen, Obere Zollgasse 69e Tel: (031) 514283
Subjects: Belles Lettres, Books on Berne, Dialect Texts, Humour
ISBN Publisher's Prefix: 3-85958

Vogt-Schild AG Druck & Verlag+, CH-4501 Solothurn 1 Tel: (065) 214131
Subjects: Vehicles (Utility), Chemistry, Pharmacy, Plastics, Environment, Hospital, Nursing, Horology
Founded: 1906
ISBN Publishers Prefix: 3-85962

Verlag Die **Waage**, Zurich und Hamburg*, Dorfstr 90, CH-8802 Kilchberg, Zurich Tel: (01) 7155569
Publisher and all offices: Felix M Wiesner
Subjects: Old Chinese Fiction and Folktales in their original translations into German; also other Nonfiction and Belles Lettres, Poetry etc from other countries; Paperback series
1977: 1 title *Founded:* 1951
ISBN Publishers Prefix: 3-85966

Gebrüder **Wagner** & Co Verlag+*, CH-4024 Basel, Meyer-str 14
Subject: Textbooks
ISBN Publisher's Prefix: 3-85969

Walter Verlag AG+, CH-4600 Olten, Amthausquai 21 Tel: (062) 217621 Cable Add: Walterverlag Olten Telex: 68226
Man Dir: Guido Elber; *Editorial:* I Buhofer, B Jentzsch, K Baumann; *Sales:* C Götz; *Production:* T Frey; *Publicity:* B Dähnert, R Wolfstädter; *Rights & Permissions:* Niedieck Linder AG
Subsidiary Company: Walter-Verlag GmbH D-7800 Freiburg im Breisgau, Erwinstr 58-60, German Federal Republic
Subjects: Literature, Cultural History, Travel Guides, Psychology, Religion, Picture Books, Children's Fiction
Book Club: Punktum (in co-operation with Nord-Sud Verlag)
1977: 45 titles *1978:* 45 titles *Founded:* 1921
ISBN Publishers Prefix: 3-530

Weber SA d'Editions+*, 13 rue de Monthoux, CP 385, CH-1211 Geneva 2 Tel: (022) 326450/59 Cable Add: Livrart, Geneva
Man Dir: Marcel Weber; *All other offices:* Marcel and Hilde Weber
Subjects: Books on Art and Architecture; Photographic, Bibliophile, Practical Living
1977: 6 titles *Founded:* 1951
ISBN Publisher's Prefix: 3-295

v **Wehrenalp** & Co*, Sevogelstr 34, CH-4002 Basel Tel: (061) 421290

Weltrundschau Verlag AG*, Via Trevano 7a, CP 230, CH-6904 Lugano Tel: (091) 27801 Cable Add: Worldreview Telex: 79682
Man Dir: G Braun; *Editorial:* E Gysling; *Rights & Permissions:* Jeanese Verlagsanstalt, Kirchstr 1, FL-9490 Vaduz, Liechtenstein
Founded: 1962

Verlag **Wepf** & Co+, Eisengasse 5, CH-4001 Basel Tel: 256377 Cable Add: Wepfco Basel Telex: 62027
Dir: Robert Wepf
Associate Company: Huthig & Wepf Verlag, Basel (qv)
Subsidiary Companies: Wepf GmbH, Obere Schanzstr 18, Postfach 1610, D-7858 Weil am Rhein; Wepf & Co, Booksellers, 13 East 16th St, New York, NY 10003, USA
Subjects: Geology, Mineralogy, Natural Sciences, Helvetica
Bookshops: Eisengasse 5, CH-4001 Basel; Marktgasse 42, CH-4310 Rheinfelden
1977: 1 title *1978:* 5 titles *Founded:* 1902
ISBN Publisher's Prefix: 3-85977

Werner & **Bischoff** AG+*, CH-4001 Basel, Kanonengasse 32, Postfach Tel: (061) 220690
President & Co-Dir: Karlmartin Werner; *Co-Dir:* Ch Bischoff
Subjects: Fine & Applied Arts, Illustrated Books
Founded: 1862
ISBN Publishers Prefix: 3-85979

Buchverlag der Druckerei **Wetzikon** AG, CH-8620 Wetzikon
Subjects: Nature Protection, Belles Lettres
ISBN Publisher's Prefix: 3-85981

Richard Rudolf **Wieland***, Postfach 24, CH-8135 Gattikon Tel: (01) 7201666 Cable Add: rrwieland Zurich
Man Dir: R R Wieland
Imprints: R R Wieland Autor & Selbst Verlag
Subjects: Books by Hans B Wieland: Drawings, Letters, Memoirs etc
1977: 1 title *Founded:* 1977
ISBN Publisher's Prefix: 3 85984 0010

Verlag Alexander **Wild**, Rathausgasse 30, CH-3011 Berne
Associate Company: Origo-Verlag (qv)

Verlag für **Wissenschaft**, Technik und Industrie AG+*, CH-4000 Basel, Schützenmattstr 43 Tel: (061) 238560
Subject: Technical
Founded: 1942
ISBN Publisher's Prefix: 3-85985

Verlag der **Wolfsbergdrucke**+*, J E Wolfensberger AG, CH-8059 Zurich, Bederstr 109 Tel: (01) 362777
Dir: Ulla Wolfensberger
Subjects: Fine & Applied Arts, Illustrated Books, Juveniles
Founded: 1899
ISBN Publishers Prefix: 3-85987

K J **Wyss** Erben AG+, CH-3001 Berne, Effingerstr 17 Tel: (031) 253715
Dir: Christoph Wyss
Subjects: History, Jurisprudence, Art, Agriculture, Food Science
1977: 4 titles *1978:* 5 titles *Founded:* 1849
ISBN Publishers Prefix: 3-7285

Genossenschaft **Z-Verlag***, Postfach 6, CH-4020 Basle
Subjects: Problems connected with the Workers' Movement and Politics generally;

socio-political literature and current affairs commentary
Miscellaneous: Has common interests with Edition Etcetera (qv) and Lenos Press (qv)

Zbinden Druck und Verlag AG+*, St Albanvorstadt 16, CH-4006 Basle Tel: (061) 232105
Man Dir: Kurt Krause
Subjects: Belles Lettres, Poetry, Biography, Educational, Anthroposophical Literature
1977-8: 8 titles
ISBN Publisher's Prefix: 3-85989

Zodiaque, La Pierre-qui-Vire*, c/o Weber SA d'Editions, 13 Rue de Monthoux, Postf 385, CH-1211 Geneva 2 Tel: 326450 Cable Add: Livrart
Subjects: Collected Editions (various)

Zollikofer Fachverlag AG, Fürstenlandstr 122, Postfach 805, CH-9001 St Gallen Tel: (071) 292222 Telex: 77537
Man Dir, Rights & Permissions: Peter Kleiner; *Marketing Dir:* P Kleiner; *Marketing Assistant, Production, Publicity:* Roger Albert
Subjects: Travel Guides, Miscellaneous
1977: 7 titles *1978:* 8 titles *Founded:* 1977
ISBN Publishers Prefix: 3-85993

Zumstein & Cie, Zeughausgasse 24, CH-3001 Berne
Owned by: Hertsch & Co
Subject: Philately (specialist catalogues and texts)
1978: 4 titles *1979:* 3 titles
ISBN Publisher's Prefix: 3-85994

Zwei-Bären Verlag der VDB+, CH-3001 Berne, Maulbeerstr 10, Postfach 2741
Man Dir: Hans Erpf
Parent Company: Buchverlag der Verbandsdruckerei (qv)
Subjects: Fiction, Juveniles, Mass Media

Zytglogge Verlag, Eigerweg 20, Postfach 118, CH-3073 Gümligen Tel: (031) 522030
Programme Dir: Beat Brechbühl; *Sales Dir:* Rolf Attenhofer; *Reader:* Willi Schmid; *Publicity:* Thomas Baer
Subjects: Belles Lettres, Pedagogy, Theatre, Art, Songs, Cabaret
1977: 10 titles, 12 LPs *1978:* 25 titles, 10 LPs *Founded:* 1964
ISBN Publishers Prefix: 3-7296

Literary Agents

Boxerbooks Inc*, Limmatstr 111, POB 157, CH-8031, Zürich Tel: 440733 Cable Add: Boxerbooks Zurich Telex: 53815
Representatives of British, American and Japanese Publishing Cos

Gesellschaft für Verlagswerte GmbH, CH-8280 Kreuzlingen, Hafenstr 38

Dr Ruth **Liepman**, CH-8044 Zurich, Maienburgweg 23 Tel: (01) 477660 Cable Add: Litagent Telex: Litag 56739

Linder AG Literary Agency, Postfach, CH-8032 Zurich (Located at: Jupiterstr 1, CH-8032 Zurich) Tel: (01) 534140 Cable Add: Linderag Zürich Telex: 55123 Linag ch
Man Dirs: Paul Fritz, Peter S Fritz
Founded: 1962
Specialization: Representation of American and English Authors/Agents/Publishers in German-language areas

Litpress, Rudolf Streit & Co, Amtshausgässchen 3, CH-3011 Berne
Associated with the Scherz Verlag Publishing Co (qv)

Mohrbooks Literary Agency*, CH-8030 Zurich, Klosbachstr 110 Tel: (01) 321610
Contact: Rainer Heumann

Neue Presse Agentur, (NPA)*, Haus am Herterberg, Haldenstr 5 CH-8500 Frauenfeld-Herten
Contact: René Marti
Specialization: Edits Women's Interest and Education Interest Correspondence; markets fiction, features, exclusive articles

Niedieck Linder AG, Holzgasse 6, CH-8039 Zurich Tel: (01) 2021450 Cable Add: Linderag Zürich Telex: 55123 Linag ch
General Manager: Gerda Niedieck
Founded: 1975
Specialization: Representation of German language authors on a world-wide basis

rabe verlag zürich, Oberdorf str 23, CH-8001 Zürich Tel: (01) 478540

Book Clubs

Europaring der Buch- & Schallplattenfreunde*, Worblentalstr 33, 3063 Papiermühle-Bern

Ex Libris, Hermetschloostrasse 77, CH-8048 Zürich

Büchergilde Gutenberg*, Kasernenstr 25, CH-8004 Zürich
Owned by: Büchergilde Gutenberg (Frankfurt am Main, German Federal Republic)

Edition Kunstkreis im Ex Libris Verlag, Postfach, CH-8023 Zurich
Subject: Art

Club **Mon Village** SA, CH-1099 Vulliens, Vaud
Owned by: Editions Mon Village SA
Subjects: Novels on rural life

Neue Schweizer Bibliothek*, Schweizer Verlagshaus AG, Klausstr 10, CH-8008 Zürich

Punktum, CH-8617 Monchaltorf Tel: (01) 9481057
Owned by: Nord-Sud Verlag (Monchaltorf) and Walter Verlag (Olten)
This club deals exclusively with children's books, intended as gifts. Six titles are sent annually to members (3 at Christmas, 3 at Easter)

Schweizer Volksbuchgemeinde AG, Habsburgerstr 44, CH-6003 Lucerne

Major Booksellers

Athena-Verlag AG*, Langmattweg 36, CH-4123 Allschwil 3 Tel: (061) 380343
Wholesaler

Librairie **Barblan et Saladin**+*, 10 Rue de Romont, CH-1701 Fribourg
See also entry under Publishers

Buchhandlung zum **Elsässer** AG, Postfach, CH-8022 Zurich (Located at: Limmatquai 18, CH-8001 Zurich) Tel: (01) 321612 Telex: 57268

Fehr'sche Buchhandlung AG, CH-9001 St Gallen, Schmiedgasse 16 Tel: (071) 221152

Film buchhandlung Hans Rohr, Oberdorfstr 3, CH-8024 Zurich Tel: (01) 2513636

Buchhandlung A **Francke** AG, Neuengasse 43, Von Werdt-Passage, CH-3001 Berne Tel: (031) 221715 Telex: 32326

Georg & Cie SA, Librairie de l'Université, 5 rue de la Corraterie, CH-1211 Geneva 11 Tel: (022) 216633

Hans **Huber**, Zeltweg 6, CH-8032 Zurich Tel: (01) 343426/343360
Specializes in books on Medicine and Psychology

Buchhandlung **Jäggi** AG, CH-4001 Basel, Freiestr 32 Tel: (061) 255200

Leobuchhandlung, Gallusstr 20, CH-9001 St Gallen Tel: 222917

Buchhandlung **Meili** & Co*, CH-8200 Schaffhausen, Fronwagpl 13

Orell Füssli, Pelikanstr 10, CH-8022 Zurich 1 Tel: (01) 2118011

Librairie **Payot** SA, 1 rue de Bourg, CH-1003 Lausanne Tel: (021) 203331 Telex: 24961; (See entry for Librairie Payot under Publishers for other addresses)
Wholesale Supplier: Librairie Payot SA, 30 rue des Côtes de Montbenon, CH-1003 Lausanne Tel: (021) 205221 Telex: 24953

Buchhandlung Hans **Rohr**, Oberdorfstr 5, CH-8024 Zurich Tel: (01) 2513636 (from 19.3.1980) Telex: 56385

Dr A **Scheidegger***, Kaltackerstr 32, Postfach 4, CH-8908 Hedingen Tel: (01) 995234/993188
Wholesaler

Buchhandlung **Scherz** AG*, CH-3000 Berne, Marktgasse 25 Tel: (031) 226837

Buchhandlung Kurt **Stäheli** & Co*, CH-8001 Zurich, Bahnhofstr 70 Tel: (01) 237662

Theologischer Verlag (wholesaler)+, Auwiesenstr 1, Postfach, CH-8406 Winterthur Tel: (052) 221138

Buchhandlung W **Vogel***, CH-8400 Winterthur, Marktgasse 41-43 Tel: (052) 226588 Telex: 74622 vogel ch

Wepf & Co Buchhandlung und Antiquariat, Eisengasse 5, Postfach, CH-4001 Basle Tel: (061) 256377 Telex: 62027

Major Libraries

Archives fédérales (Federal Archives)*, 24 rue des Archives, CH-3003 Berne

Bibliothèque cantonale et universitaire (Kantons- und Universitätsbibliothek)*, 16 rue St-Michel, CH-1701 Fribourg

Bibliothèque cantonale et universitaire de Lausanne*, 6 Pl de la Riponne, CH-1005 Lausanne Tel: (021) 228831

Bibliothèque de la Ville, 3 Place Numa-Droz, CH-2000 Neuchâtel Tel: (038) 251358
Librarian: Jacques Rychner
Publications: Ville de Neuchâtel: Bibliothèques et Musées (annual); Musée Neuchâtelois (qtly)

Bibliothèque Nationale Suisse+, CH-303 Berne Tel: (031) 618911 Telex: 32526 slbbe ch

Bibliothèque publique et universitaire de Genève*, Promenade des Bastions, CH-1211 Geneva 4 Tel: (022) 208266
Director: Paul Chaix
Publication: Compte rendu (annual)

Fondation Martin **Bodmer**, Bibliotheca Bodmeriana, BP 7, CH-1223 Cologny/Geneva Tel: (022) 362370
Dir: Dr Hans E Braun

Bureau International du Travail, see International Labour Office Library

E T H Bibliothek (Eidgenössische Technische Hochschule Bibliothek), Rämistr 101, CH-8092 Zürich Tel: (01) 326211 Telex: 53178 (ethbich)
Library of the Swiss Federal Institute of Technology

International Labour Office Library (ILO)*, 4 rte des Morillons, CH-1211 Geneva 22
Librarian: Geo K Thompson
Publication: International Labour Documentation (bi-monthly)

Schweizerische Landesbibliothek (Bibliothèque nationale suisse) (Swiss National Library), CH-3003 Berne, Hallwylstr 15 Tel: Secretary (031) 618921; Lending Department (031) 618931

Schweizerisches Wirtschaftsarchiv (Archives économiques suisses) (Swiss Economic Archives), Kollegienhaus der Universität, Basel, Petersgraben
Founded: 1910

Stadt- und Universitätsbibliothek, CH-3000 Berne 7, Münstergasse 61

Stiftsbibliothek*, CH-9000 St Gallen, Klosterhof 6 Tel: (071) 225719 (library of former Benedictine abbey of St Gall)

United Nations Library*, Palais des Nations, Geneva

Öffentliche Bibliothek der **Universität Basel***, CH-4056 Basel, Schönbeinstr 18-20 Tel: (061) 252250

Zentralbibliothek Zürich, Kantons- Stadt- und Universitätsbibliothek, CH-8025 Zurich, Zähringerplatz 6, Postfach Tel: (01) 477272

Library Associations

Association des Bibliothécaires suisses (Vereinigung schweizerischer Bibliothekare), Bibliothèque nationale suisse, Hallwylstr 15, CH-3003 Berne Tel: (031) 618911
Association of Swiss Librarians
Secretary: W Treichler
Publication: Nouvelles (jointly with Swiss Association for Documentation) (6 times a year)

Association suisse de Documentation (Schweizerische Vereinigung für Dokumentation)*, CH-8032 Zurich, Postfach A158
Swiss Association for Documentation
Secretary: K Zumstein
Publication: Nouvelles (jointly with Association of Swiss Librarians) (6 a year)

Association suisse des Bibliothèques d'Hôpitaux (Association of Swiss Hospital Libraries), c/o Mme J Schmid-Schädelin, Executive Director, Hirschengraben 22, CH-8001 Zurich

Kantonale Kommission für Jugend- und Volksbibliotheken, Zurich, Am Züriweg, CH-8906 Bonstetten Zürich Tel: (01) 7000304
Cantonal Commission for Juvenile and Public Libraries
President: Dr Felix Wendler
Publications: Numerous handbooks, catalogues etc relating to library procedures and practice

Leihbücherei-Gewerbeverband der Schweiz (Swiss Lending Library Association)*, CH-8004 Zurich, Zweierstr 53 Tel: 237477

Vereinigung Schweizerischer Archivare (Association of Swiss Archivists), Bundesarchiv, Archivstr 24, CH-3003 Berne Tel: (031) 618389
Secretary: Dr Christoph Graf
Publication: Mitteilungen (News Sheet)
Founded: 1922

Library Journals

Mitteilungen (News), Association of Swiss Archivists, Bundesarchiv, Archivstr 24, CH-3003 Berne

Nouvelles (News), Association of Swiss Librarians, Swiss National Library, CH-3003 Berne (jointly with Swiss Association for Documentation)

Literary Associations and Societies

Gesellschaft für deutsche Sprache und Literatur in Zürich, Deutsches Seminar der Universität Zürich, Postfach 147, CH-8028 Zürich
Society for German Language and Literature in Zurich
Secretary: J Etzensperger

P E N Club de Suisse romande*, 4 rue Mont de Sion, CH-1206 Geneva
Secretary: Juliette Monnin-Hornung

P E N Club di Italian Romansch*, Via Signore in Croce 12, CH-6612 Ascona
Secretary: Maddalena Kerenyi

Schweizerische Bibliophilen-Gesellschaft*, c/o Herrn K Kahl, Wolfbachstr 17, CH-8032 Zurich
Swiss Society of Bibliophiles
President: Dr Conrad Ulrich
Publications: Stultifera Navis, published 1944-1957; *Librarium,* published 3 times a year since 1958

Schweizerischer Schriftsteller-Verband, CH-8001 Zürich 1, Kirchgasse 25
Society of Swiss Writers
Secretary: Otto Böni

Literary Periodicals

Cenobio (text in French and Italian), Dr Pier-Riccardo Frigeri, CP 6655, CH-6901 Lugano

drehpunkt, CH-4002 Basel, Postfach 794

Ecriture (Writing), Editions Bertil Galland, 29 rue du Lac, CH-1800 Vevey

Etudes de Lettres (Literary Studies), Université de Lausanne, Faculté des Lettres, Lausanne

Niemo Press; topical press and literature references with commentary (text in German), Emil Rahm, CH-8215 Hallau

Revue de Belles-Lettres (Review of Belles Lettres) (text in French), Société de Belles-Lettres de Lausanne, 4 Plainpalais, BP 216, CH-1211 Geneva

Schweizer Monatshefte (Swiss Monthly Magazine), Gesellschaft Schweizer Monatshefte, CH-8034 Zurich, Postfach 86

Translation Agencies and Association

Association suisse des Traducteurs et Interprètes (Swiss Association of Translators and Interpreters)*, c/o M D Perret, 20 Poudrières, Neuchâtel

Syria

General Information

Language: Arabic (French and English used)
Religion: Sunni Muslim
Population: 8 million
Literacy Rate (1970): 40%
Bank Hours: 0800-1400 Saturday-Thursday
Shop Hours: Vary greatly. Closed Friday. Generally long lunch closinggg
rrency: 100 piastre = 1 Syrian Pound
Export/Import Information: No tariffs on books except children's picture books 15%, with additional taxes of 26.80%; most advertising matter dutied at 15%. State organization for control and execution of publicity and advertising within Syria is Arab Advertising Organization, Damascus. The General Advertising Institute, PO Box 2842, must get samples of commercial advertising and promotional materials before distribution permitted. Import licence must be submitted to Commercial Bank of Syria in order to obtain exchange licence
Copyright: No copyright conventions signed

Publishers

Arab Advertising Organization, 28 Moutanabbi St, PO Box 2842 & 3034, Damascus Tel: 225219/225220/1 Cable Add: Arador Damascus Telex: Arador 77923 SY
Dir-General: George Khoury; *Publicity:* Haitham Basheer
Imprint: Arador
Br Off: Aleppo, Hama, Homs, Lattakia
Subject: Directories
Founded: 1963

Damascus University Press*, Damascus
Subjects: Education, History, Geography, Engineering, Medicine, Law, Sociology, School Textbooks

Office Arabe de Presse et de Documentation, 67 pl Chahbandar, PO Box 3550, Damascus Tel: 559166/559892
President: Samir A Darwich
Subjects: Periodical and non-periodical publications about Economics, Politics, Syria and the Arab World
Founded: 1964
Miscellaneous: Associated imprints include Bureau des Documentations Syriennes et Arabes, PO Box 3550, Damascus

Syrian Documentation Papers*, PO Box 2712, Damascus
Dir-General: Louis Farés
Subjects: Reference, Directories, Politics, Economics, Sociology, Law
Founded: 1968

al-Tawjih Press*, Palestine St, PO Box 3320, Damascus
Subject: Literature

Major Booksellers

Dar Dimashk (Adib Tunbakji) Bookshop*, Port Said St Tel: 111048

Dummar & Mowakadeh & Co*, Tajhiz St, PO Box 2456 Tel: 112911

Dar Al-Fikr (Salem & Zu'bi) Bookshop*, Saadallah Al-Jabiri St, PO Box 962 Tel: 111041

Kutubi Moh'd Nihad Hashem*, Souk Al-Asrounieh Tel: 110512

Dakr Abdul **Wahab***, Port Said St Tel: 115486

Major Libraries

Damascus University Library*, Damascus

Dar al-Kutub al-Wataniah (National Library)*, Homs

Al Maktabah Al Wataniah (National Library)*, Bab El-Faradj, Aleppo

National Library of Latakia*, Latakia

Al Zahiriah (National Library)*, Bab el Barid, Damascus

Library Journals

Damascus University Library Review, Damascus University Library, Damascus

Literary Periodicals

Al-Mawgif Al-Adabi, Ittihad al-Kuttab al-Arab, Shari Murshid Khatir, Damascus

Tanzania

General Information

Language: Swahili (and English)
Religion: Predominantly Muslim
Population: 16.1 million
Bank Hours: Mainland Tanzania: 0900-1200 Monday-Friday; 0900-1100 Saturday. Zanzibar: 0830-1130 Monday-Friday; 0830-1000 Saturday
Shop Hours: 0800-1200, 1400-1715 or 1800 Monday-Saturday
Currency: 100 cents = 1 Tanzania shilling
Export/Import Information: No tariff on

books or advertising matter. Import licence and exchange controls
Copyright: Florence (see International section)

Book Trade Reference Journals

Government and Tanu Publications List, Government Publications Agency, PO Box 1801, Dar es Salaam

Tanzania National Bibliography, Tanzania Library Service, PO Box 9283, Dar es Salaam (the national bibliography, published annually since 1969)

Publishers

Central Tanganyika Press, PO Box 15, Dodoma
Manager: Alexander Chibehe
Subject: Religion
1978: 2 titles *Founded:* 1954

Dar es Salaam University*, PO Box 35091, Dar es Salaam Tel: 53611 Cable Add: University Dar es Salaam
University Publications Officer: Z K Rigby
Subjects: History, Africana, Reference, Religion, Medicine, Psychology, Science & Technology, Social Science, University Textbooks
1978/79: 90 titles

East African Literature Bureau*, PO Box 1408, Dar es Salaam
(see under Kenya for full information)

Inland Publishers*, Africa Inland Church Literature Department, PO Box 125, Mwanza Tel: 40064
Dir: S M Magesa
Subjects: General Nonfiction, Religion, Books in Kiswahili, Paperbacks

Longman Tanzania Ltd, Independence Ave, PO Box 3164, Dar es Salaam Tel: 29748 Cable Add: Longman Dar es Salaam
Man Dir: A B Moshi
Subjects: General Nonfiction, Belles Lettres, Poetry, Biography, History, Africana, Juveniles, Books in Kiswahili, General Science, Secondary & Primary Textbooks, Science & Technology
Founded: 1965
Miscellaneous: Firm is an associate company of Longman Group Ltd, UK (qv)

Ndanda Mission Press*, Ndanda PO Box 1004, Ndanda via Lindi
Subject: Religion
1977: 4 titles *1978:* 7 itles

Oxford University Press, Maktaba Rd, PO Box 5299, Dar es Salaam Tel: 29209 Cable Add: Oxionian
Sales: Anthony Theobald
Subjects: General Nonfiction, Literature, Poetry, Biography, History, Africana, Reference, Books in Kiswahili, General & Social Science, Secondary & Primary Textbooks
Founded: 1969
Miscellaneous: Firm is a branch of Oxford University Press, Eastern Africa, Nairobi, Kenya (qv)

T M P Book Department, PO Box 550, Tabora
Subject: Religion

Tanzania Library Service*, PO Box 9283, Dar es Salaam Tel: 26121
Parent Company: The Ministry of National Education, Dar es Salaam
Associate Company: Transafrica (1976)
1977: 8 titles *Founded:* 1963

Tanzania Mission Press, see T M P Book Department

Tanzania Publishing House, 47 Independence Ave, PO Box 2138, Dar es Salaam Tel: 32164 Cable Add: Publish Dar es Salaam
General Manager: Walter Bgoya; *Sales Manager:* S Nkini
Subjects: General Fiction & Nonfiction, Belles Lettres, Poetry, Biography, History, Africana, Philosophy, Juveniles, Paperbacks, Social Science, University & Secondary Textbooks (in Kiswahili and English)
Founded: 1966

Government Printer*, Government Publications Agency, PO Box 1801, Dar es Salaam

Major Booksellers

The **Cathedral** Bookshop*, Mansfield St, PO Box 2381, Dar es Salaam Tel: 22873

The **Dar es Salaam Bookshop***, Makunganya St, PO Box 9030, Dar es Salaam Tel: 23416

Dar es Salaam University Bookshop*, PO Box 35091, Dar es Salaam Tel: 53137

International Bookshop, PO Box 21341, Dar es Salaam Tel: 21930/27458 Cable Add: Safina, Dar es Salaam
Wholesale, Distribution: International Publishers Agencies (at above address)
Retail Outlet: International Bookshop (at above address)

The **Standard** Bookshop*, Independence Ave, PO Box 9402, Dar es Salaam Tel: 23126

T M P Book Department, PO Box 550, Tabora

Tanzania Elimu Supplies*, Book Division, IPS Bldg, PO Box 20873, Dar es Salaam

Tanzania Mission Press, see T M P Book Department

Major Libraries

Arusha Public Library*, PO Box 1273, Arusha

British Council Library, Independence Ave, Ohio St, PO Box 9100, Dar es Salaam Tel: 22726

Dar es Salaam Technical College Library*, Morogoro Rd, PO Box 20571, Dar es Salaam Tel: 23231

Faculty of Agriculture, Forestry and Veterinary Science, University of Dar es Salaam, PO Box 704, Morogoro Tel: 2511
Librarian: J K Chirwa

Faculty of Medicine Library*, University of Dar es Salaam, PO Box 20693, Dar es Salaam Tel: 27081 ext 266

International Communication Agency Library*, PO Box 9170, Dar es Salaam Tel: 26611

Kibaha Public Library*, PO Box Kibaha, Kibaha Tel: 258

Marangu College of National Education Library*, PO Box 3080, Moshi Tel: 16 Himo

National Archives of Tanzania*, India St, PO Box 2006, Dar es Salaam Tel: 23954

Tanzania Library Service*, PO Box 9283, Dar es Salaam Tel: 26121
Publication: Tanzania National Bibliography

University of Dar es Salaam Library, PO Box 35092, Dar es Salaam Tel: 53162

Zanzibar Government Archives*, PO Box 116, Zanzibar

Library Associations

Tanzania Library Association*, PO Box 2645, Dar es Salaam Tel: 26121
Secretary: T E Mlaki
Publications: Someni (journal); *Matukio* (newsletter)

Tanzania Library Service*, PO Box 9283, Dar es Salaam
Publication: Printed in Tanzania, Directory of Libraries in Tanzania

Library Reference Books and Journals

Books

Directory of Libraries in Tanzania, Tanzania Library Service, PO Box 9283, Dar es Salaam (comprehensive annotated listing)

Journals

Matukio, Tanzania Library Association, PO Box 2645, Dar es Salaam

Someni (text in English), Tanzania Library Association, PO Box 2645, Dar es Salaam

Literary Periodicals

Umma, East African Literature Bureau, PO Box 1408, Dar es Salaam (or PO Box 30022, Nairobi, Kenya) (a biannual literary magazine published under the auspices of the Department of Literature, University of Dar es Salaam)

Translation Agencies and Associations

East African Literature Bureau*, PO Box 1408, Dar es Salaam

Thailand

General Information

Language: Thai (also English)
Religion: Buddhism
Population: 44 million
Literacy Rate: (1970) 78.6% (87.7% Urban, 77.1% Rural)

Bank Hours: 0830-1530 Monday-Friday
Shop Hours: Vary. Those catering for tourists generally open 0830-1800 or later
Currency: 100 satang = 1 baht
Export/Import Information: No tariff on books but 5% Standard Profit Tax and 1.5% Business Tax apply (also a Municipal Tax of 10% of Business Tax). Advertising subject to same taxes and 3% ad val import duty. No import licences for books, but special permit required by importer for orders over 3,000 bahts (approx $150). Certificate of payment (from Exchange Control Authority) required
Copyright: Berne, Florence (see International section)

Book Trade Organizations

Publishers' and Booksellers' Association of Thailand*, 108 Sukhumvit Soi 53 (Madee Paidee), Bangkok Tel: 528759
Secretary: Mr M Jusai
President: M L M Jumsai, Chalermnit Press, 1-2 Erawan Arcade, Bangkok Tel: 528759

Publishers

Aksorn Charerntat+*, 142 Praengsanpasart, Tanao Rd, Bangkok Tel: 214587
Subjects: Textbooks, Industry, Arts, Maps, Literature, Mathematics, Education, Physics, Linguistics

Aksorn Charoen Tasna Ltd*, 195 Bamrung Muang Rd, Bangkok
Subject: Textbooks

Bandarnsarn+*, 136-138 Nakorn Sawan Rd, Bangkok Tel: 82551
Subject: Thai books

Banmai+*, 1 Soi Prasanmit, Sukhumvit, Bangkok

Barnakarn+*, 236 Nakern Kashem, Bangkok Tel: 227796
Subject: Thai books

Barnakieh Trading+*, 34 Nakorn Sawan Rd, Bangkok Tel: 825520
Subject: Thai books

Barnasilpa+*, 1 Soi Praengsanpasart, Asdang Rd, Bangkok Tel: 220060
Subject: Thai books

Chalermnit Press+*, 108 Sukhumvit Soi 53, Bangkok Tel: 2528759
Managers: M L M Jumsai, Mrs Jumsai
Subjects: Books on Thailand, Pocket books and Children's books in English, French & German, Magazines, Dictionaries
Founded: 1957
Bookshop: 1-2 Erawan Arcade, Bangkok

Chiangmai Book Centre+*, 2 Kochasam Rd, Suriya Cinema, Chiangmai
Bookshop: Address as above

Chokechai Tewet+*, 63t Teetorng Rd, Bangkok

Dhammabucha+*, 5/1-2 Asdang Rd, Bangkok Tel: 223549/850010
Subject: Thai books on Buddhism

Duang Kamol+*, 244-246 Siam Sq Soi 2, Patumwan, Bangkok Tel: 2516335/6
Subjects: English, French and Thai books

Hor Samut Klang +*, 5 Soi Praeng Sanpasart, Asdang Rd, Bangkok Tel: 219751
Subject: Thai books

Klang Vidhya+*, 742 Wang Burapa, Bangkok Tel: 224546
Subject: Thai books
Bookshops: 742 Wang Burapa, Bangkok; 3931/26-29 Chumpol Rd, Nakorn Rajsima; 197/2 Srichan Rd, Tambon Wat Mai, Chantaburi

Languages School+*, Wat Phra Singha, Chiangmai

Narongsarn+*, 647/14 Charernrat Rd, (Big Circle), Dhonburi, Bangkok

Nibondh+*, 40-42 New Rd, Bangkok Tel: 212611
Subjects: English and Thai books
Bookshop: 40-42 New Rd, Bangkok; 975/4 Gaysorn Rd, Bangkok

Niyom Vidhya+*, 192 Bamrungmuang Rd, Bangkok Tel: 217661
Subject: Thai Technical Textbooks

Norn+*, 1/1 Boonsiri, Sukhumvit Rd, Paknam Tel: 90130
Subject: Thai books

Odeon Store LP+*, 862 Wang Burapa, Bangkok Tel: 2210742/2216567 Cable Add: Odeonstore
Man Dir: Vichai Praepanich
Br Off: Siain Sq soi 1, Bangkok
Subjects: Textbooks, Nonfiction, Paperbacks
1977: 24 titles *Founded:* 1947

Parnfah Pittaya+*, 440-2 Nakornsawan Rd, Bangkok
Subjects: Thai books, Comics

Pikkhanet+*, 99 Praeng Sanpasart, Tanao Rd, Bangkok Tel: 222850
Subject: Thai pocket books

Pittayakarn+*, 226 Nakorn Kashem, Bangkok Tel: 221501
Subject: Thai books

Pra Cha Chang & Co Ltd*, 816/3 Talad Noi, New Rd, Bangkok
Subject: Academic

Prae Pittaya Ltd+*, 716-718 Burapa Palace, PO Box 914, Bangkok Tel: 2214283/221286
Manager: Chitt Praepanich
Subjects: Fiction, Juveniles
Bookshop: as above

Pramuansarn Publishing House*, 703/15-16 Petchaburi Rd, Bangkok
Manager: Lime Taechatada
Subjects: Guidebooks, Popular Sciences, Juveniles
Founded: 1955

Praphansarn Book Centre+*, 236/6-7 Beside Lido Theatre, Siam Square Soi 2, Rama I Rd, Bangkok Tel: 2512342/3
Man Dir: Suphol Taechatada

Prasarnmitr+*, 3382 New Petchaburi Rd, Bangkok Tel: 915387/925230
Subject: Textbooks

Progress+*, 882 Wang Burapa, Bangkok Tel: 226541
Subject: Thai books, English occasionally

Religious Revival Organization+*, 176 Sukhumvit, Santikam Soi 1, T Samrong North, Samutprakarn

Ruamsarn(1977) Co Ltd+, Part, 864 Burapa Palace, Bangkok 2 Tel: 2216483
Man Dir: Bumrung Tawewatanasarn; *Sales Dir:* Nongyao Tawewatanasarn; *Publicity Dir:* Piya Tawewatanasarn; *Advertising Dir:* Piti Tawewatanasarn

Subjects: General Fiction, Belles Lettres, Poetry, Biography, History, How-to, Music, Art, Philosophy, Reference, Religion, Low-priced Paperbacks, General Science, University & Secondary Textbooks
Founded: 1951
Bookshops: Ruamsarn (1977) Co Ltd, 864 Burapa Palace, Bangkok 2; Dheerasarn Ltd, Part, 326-8 Siam Sq 4, Bangkok 5; Tawesarn, 89/51 Near President Theatre, Bangkok 5
Subsidiary: Bumrungsarn Ltd, Part, 864 Burapa Palace, Bangkok 2

Rungvit Sawarn-Apichorn+*, Chiengmai Book Centre, 2 Kochasarn Rd, opposite Suriya Cinema, Chiengmai

Sangna Vuddhichai Saranonda+*, Prabhasarn, 130 Nakornsauran Rd, Bangkok

Sayam Paritat+*, 14-6 Nakorn Lane, Taprachand, Maharat Rd, Bangkok Tel: 219108
Subject: Thai books

Sermwit Barnakarn+*, 222 Nakorn Kashem, Bangkok Tel: 214541
Subject: Thai books

Siam Directory*, 2 Mansion, 96 Rajdamnern Ave, Bangkok
Subjects: History, Politics, Technical

Sinpattana+*, 74 Pra Atit Rd, Bangkok Tel: 824357/816917
Subject: Thai books

Social Science Association Press*, 2 Chula Soi, Phya Thai Rd, Bangkok
Manager & Editor: Sulak Sivaraksa
Subject: Textbooks
Founded: 1961

Sommai Press+*, 90-18 Ekkachai Rd, Bangkok Tel: 30037
Subject: Thai books

Suksapan Panich (Business Organization of Teachers' Institute)+*, 9 Mansion, Rajdamnern Ave, Bangkok Tel: 816543
Manager: Kamthon Sathirakul
Subjects: Juveniles, Textbooks, Dictionaries
Founded: 1950

Suksit Siam Co Ltd+*, 1715 Rama IV Rd, Samyan, Bangkok 5 Tel: 511630
Subjects: Mainly Thai books on Social Science & Politics
Bookshop: 1715 Rama IV Rd, Bangkok

Suriyaban Publishers+, 14 Pramuan Rd, Bangkok Tel: 2347991/2
Publicity Manager: Philip Tsang
Subjects: Religious, Educational, General, Children's Books, Dictionaries (in Thai language), Buddhism, Cultural and Historical studies (in English)
Bookshops: The Christian Bookstore, 14 Pramuan Rd, Bangkok; Suriyaban Bookstore, 124/1 Silom Rd, Bangkok 5
1978: 20 titles

Sutpaisarn+*, 638 Somdet Chaopaya Rd, Bangkok Tel: 664392
Subject: Thai books on Law

Thai Commercial Printing Press*, Bangkok
Subjects: Law, Management

Thai Inc*, 96 Mansion, 2 Rajdamnern Ave, Bangkok
Subjects: Politics, History, Religion

Thai Watana Panich+*, 599 Maitrijit Rd, Bangkok Tel: 210111
Subject: School books in Thai (occasionally English)

Tong-In Sunsawat+*, Wat Prasing, Chiengmai
Subject: English books

Vadhana Panich+*, 216-220 Bumrungmuang Rd, Bangkok
Subject: School Textbooks

Vajarindra+*, 364 Sumeru Rd, Bangkok Tel: 816207

Viratham+*, 141 St Louis Soi 2, Sathorn Tai Rd, Bangkok Tel: 866848
Subjects: English, French and English-Thai books

Wattana Panich+*, 216-220 Bumrungmuang Rd, Bangkok
Subjects: Textbooks, Fiction, Maps

Major Booksellers

Asia Books Co Ltd, 6/1 Soi Chidlom, Ploenchit Rd, PO Box 2776, Bangkok Tel: 2526400/2520064 Cable Add: ASIABOOKS Telex: TH2189 (ASIABOOKS)
Showroom: 221 Sukhumvit Rd, between Soi 15 and 17, Bangkok Tel: 2527277
Man Dir: Mr Vinai Suttharoj
Also publishers' agent, distributor and retailer of English books

Bangkok Central Book Depot*, Sikak Phya Sri, Bangkok

Central Department Store, 306 Silom Rd, Bangkok
Manager: Mrs Ratana Norabhanlobh
Largest distributor and wholesaler for magazines, paperbacks, trade books, textbooks and childrens books

Chalermnit Bookshop*, 1-2 Erawan Arcade, Bangkok Tel: 528759
Also importers

Christian Bookstore*, 14 Pramuan Rd, Bangkok

Dheerasarn Ltd*, Part, 326-8 Siam Sq, Bangkok 5
Also at: Tawesarn 89/51 Near President Theatre, Bangkok 5

International Book Distributors Co Ltd*, 1035-4 Pleonchit Shopping Centre, Pleonchit Rd, PO Box 5-59, Bangkok

Klang Vidhya*, 742 Wang Burapa, Bangkok
Also at: 3931/26-29 Chumpol Rd, Nakorn Rajsima; 197/2 Srichan Rd, Tambon Wat Mai, Chantaburi

Nibondh (Gaysorn)*, 975/4 Gaysorn Rd, Bangkok
English books at the above address
English, Thai books and magazines at Nibondh (Sikak), 40-42 New Rd, Bangkok

Praepittaya Ltd*, 716-718 Burapa Palace, PO Box 914, Bangkok
(also importers and wholesaler)

Pramual Sarn Book Centre Ltd*, Partnership, 678 Chalerm Khetr Bldg, Bangkok

Ruamsarn (1977) Co Ltd, 864 Burapa Palace, Bangkok 2 Tel: 2216483
Manager: Nongyao Tawewatanasarn

Siam Book House*, 11 Silom Rd, Corner Saladeng, Bangkok

Suksit Siam Co Ltd*, 1715 Rama IV Rd, Samyan, Bangkok 5 Tel: 2511630
Also importers and library suppliers

Suriwongs Book Centre*, Suriyong Cinema Arcade, Chiengmai
Manager: Miss J Jittidecharaks

Major Libraries

British Council Library, 428 Rama I Rd, 2 Siam Sq, Bangkok 5 Tel: 2526136

Chulalongkorn University Library*, Phya Thai Rd, Bangkok 5

Department of Science Library*, Rama VI St, Bangkok 4

Main Library, **Kasetsart University**, Bangkok 9 Tel: 5790113/20
Librarian: Miss Daruna Somboonkun

National Archives Division*, Fine Arts Department, Samsen Rd, Bangkok 3

National Library*, Ta-Vasukri Tel: 815449/810263

Siriraj Medical Library*, Mahidol University, Bangkok 7

Sri Nakharinwirot University Library*, Sukhumvit 23, Bangkok 11

Thai National Documentation Centre (TNDC)*, 196 Phahonyothin Rd, Bang Khen, Bangkok 9

Thammasat University Library*, Bangkok

United Nations, Economic and Social Commission for Asia and the Pacific Library, United Nations Bldg, Rajadamnern Ave, Bangkok 2
Librarian: Mrs Zerrin Polite

Library Associations

Thai Library Association*, c/o National Library, Ta-Vasukri Tel: 825928
Secretary: N Puakpong
Publication: Bulletin (6 a year)

Library Reference Books and Journals

Books

An Annotated Bibliography of Librarianship in Thailand, Department of Library Science, Chulalongkorn University, Faculty of Arts, Phya Thai Rd, Bangkok 5

List of Scientific Libraries in Thailand, Thai National Documentation Centre, 196 Phahonyothin Rd, Bangkhen, Bangkok 9

Journals

Bulletin, Thai Library Association, 241 Prasumaeru Rd, Bangkok 2

Literary Associations and Societies

P E N International-Thailand Centre, 56/21-22 Rama I Rd, Bangkok 5
Secretary: K Direk

The **Siam** Society, Soi Asoke, Bangkok Tel: 3914401
President: HSH Prince Supedrahdis Disku;
Editorial: Mr Kim Atkinson; *Rights & Permissions:* Mr F Martin
Subjects: Art and Culture of South East Asia
Founded: 1904

Literary Prizes

Bangkok Bank Prize
For prose or poetry in Thai concerning history, art, culture, religion, social affairs, philosophy or new creative ideas. 50,000 baht each for prose and poetry. Awarded annually. Enquiries to Bangkok Bank, Public Relations Department, Suriwong Branch, PO Box 95, Bangkok

Kennedy Prize*
For promoting understanding of Thailand, the Thai people or Thai culture, using the Thai language. 30,000 baht each for prose and poetry. Awarded annually. Enquiries to John F Kennedy Foundation of Thailand, Ministry of Foreign Affairs, Bangkok 2

Togo

General Information

Language: French is the commercial language
Religion: Animism or fetishism; Muslim in north; Catholicism is most active Christian religion
Population: 2.35 million
Bank Hours: 0730-1130, 1430-1530 Monday-Friday
Shop Hours: 0800-1200, 1430 or 1500-1730 or 1800 Monday-Friday; 0730-1230 Saturday
Currency: CFA franc
Export/Import Information: No tariff on books; advertising catalogues 10%. Additional taxes: 18% Tax Forfaitaire, 2% Statistical Tax, and Customs Stamp Tax of 4% of duties and added taxes. Small Wharfage Tax. Import licence required for goods from non-franc zones (except under 12,500 CFA francs); from franc zone, need authorization of Togolese Government Office. Exchange controls on non-franc zone.
Copyright: Berne (see International section)

Publishers

Ecole Professionelle de la Mission Catholique*, BP 341, Lomé
Subjects: Religion, Secondary & Primary Textbooks

Editogo*, BP 891, Lomé
Subjects: General and Educational
Founded: 1962

Major Booksellers

Librairie du **Bon Pasteur***, rue du Commerce, BP 1164, Lomé Tel: 3628

Librairie **Evangélique***, 1 rue du Commerce, BP 378, Lomé Tel: 2967

Nouvelle Librairie **Togolaise***, BP 2096, Lomé

Major Libraries

American Cultural Center Library*, BP 852, Lomé

Bibliothèque de l'Université du Benin*, BP 1515, Lomé Tel: 2748

Bibliothèque nationale (National Library), BP 1002, Lomé Tel: 6367
Dir: Kanaoua Bekoutare

Centre culturel français, Bibliothèque*, BP 2090, Lomé Tel: 7232/3442
Librarian: Mme Lacrampe

Library Associations

Association togolaise pour le Développement de la Documentation, des Bibliothèques, Archives et Musées, c/o Bibliothèque de l'Université du Bénin, BP 1515, Lomé Tel: 4843
Secretary: E E Amah

Trinidad and Tobago

General Information

Language: English
Religion: Roman Catholic and Anglican
Population: 1 million
Literacy Rate (1946): 71.1%
Bank Hours: 0800-1230 Monday-Thursday; 0800-1200, 1500-1700 Friday
Shop Hours: 0800-1630 Monday-Friday; 0800-1200 Saturday
Currency: 100 cents = 1 Trinidad and Tobago dollar
Export/Import Information: No tariff on books; 45% duty and 25 cents postal fee on advertising matter. No import licence required for books; no obscene literature permitted. Exchange controls

Book Trade Organizations

Booksellers' Association of Trinidad and Tobago, Metropolitan Book Suppliers, Time Plaza, Henry St, Port of Spain
Secretary: Terry Cassim

Book Trade Journals

Trinidad and Tobago and West Indian Bibliography, Central Library of Trinidad and Tobago, West Indian Reference Section, 20 Queens Park East, Port of Spain

Publishers

Charran's Educational Publishers, 58 Western Main Rd, St James
Bookshop: Charran's Bookshop (1978) Ltd (at above address)
Subject: Textbooks

Columbus Publishers Ltd*, 64 Independence Sq, PO Box 140, Port of Spain Tel: (62) 53615
Dir: P A Headley
Subjects: General, Books for Students
1977: 3 titles *Founded:* 1969
ISBN Publisher's Prefix: 0-85643

Longman Caribbean Ltd*, 79 Belmont Circular Rd, Port of Spain
Dir: Percy Cezair
Subject: General
Miscellaneous: Firm is an associate company of Longman Group Ltd, UK (qv)

Trinidad Publishing Co*, 22-26 St Vincent St, Port of Spain
Subjects: Law, Political Economy

Major Booksellers

Abercromby Bookshop*, 22 Abercromby St, Port of Spain Tel: 6237752

Asgar Ali Book Centre*, 90 Duke St, Port of Spain

Campus Corner Ltd*, 72 Pembroke St, Port of Spain

Cassia House Bookshop*, Corner Pembroke and Oxford Sts, Port of Spain Tel: 6235156

Charran's Bookshop (1978), 58 Western Main Rd, St James
Caribbean educational distributors, wholesale and retail

F W M Books Ltd*, PO Box 6, Port of Spain

Hobby Centre*, 86 Frederick St, Port of Spain

The Ideal Leather Store Ltd*, Jermingham St, Scarborough, Tobago

Jeffers Bookstore*, 28 Independence Square, Port of Spain

Victor Manhin Ltd*, 49 High St, San Fernando

Muir Marshall Ltd*, 64a Independence Square, Port of Spain

Metropolitan Book Suppliers Ltd, 17 Time Plaza, 26/28 Henry St, Port of Spain

J C Sealy*, The Bookshop, 111 Frederick St, Port of Spain
Also at 111 Belmont Circular Rd, Belmont, Port of Spain

Stephens Book Department*, 8/10 Frederick St, Port of Spain

Major Libraries

Carnegie Free Library*, Harris Promenade, San Fernando

National Archives*, The Government Archivist, Whitehall, 29 Maraval Rd, Port of Spain

Central Library of Trinidad and Tobago (County Library Department of the Government)*, PO Box 547, Port of Spain

Trinidad Public Library*, Knox St, Port of Spain

University of the West Indies Library, St Augustine

Library Associations

Library Association of Trinidad and Tobago*, c/o PO Box 1177, Port of Spain
Secretary: Ms L Elliott
Publication: Blatt (Bulletin of the Library Association of Trinidad and Tobago) (annual)

Library Journals

Blatt (Bulletin of the Library Association of Trinidad and Tobago), Library Association of Trinidad and Tobago, c/o PO Box 1177, Port of Spain

Tunisia

General Information

Language: Arabic (also French)
Religion: Muslim (Sunni)
Population: 6.07 million
Literary Rate (1956): 15.7% (Muslim Population)
Bank Hours: Winter: 0800-1100, 1400-1600 Monday-Friday; Summer: 0730-1130 Monday-Friday
Shop Hours: Generally 0800-1200, 1500-1800 Monday-Saturday
Currency: 1,000 millimes = 1 Tunisian dinar
Export/Import Information: Tunisia has preferential tariffs and EEC agreement but most books are dutied 26%, children's picture books 6%, and advertising free. Customs Formalities Tax of 40 millimes per 1,000 kg or less gross weight, with minimum rate of 2.5%. Consumption Tax on duty and tax paid for books: 46% if importer is merchant, 36.5% if importer is manufacturer; for advertising matter, 28.5% or 23%. Advertising matter subject to Production Tax of 26% of duty and tax paid if importer merchant, 20.5% if importer a manufacturer. Imports liberalized but in practice licences granted dependent on foreign exchange position
Copyright: UCC, Berne (see International section)

Book Trade Organizations

Syndicat des Librairies de Tunisie (Tunisian Booksellers' Association)*, 10 ave de France, Tunis

Book Trade Journals

Bibliographie nationale de la Tunisie (Tunisian National Bibliography), National Library, 20 Souk-el-Attarine, Tunis

Publishers

Ceres Productions, BP 56 Tunis Belvedere, Tunis Tel: 282033 LG Cable Add: Cerepro Telex: CERESP 12363 TN
Man Dir: Mohamed Ben Smail; *Editorial:* Moncef Guellaty
Orders to: Demeter, 2 rue de la Coté d'Ivoire, Tunis Tel: 283579
Subsidiary Company: Demeter (address as above)
Associate Company: Sud Editions, 9 bis rue de la Nouvelle Delhi, Tunis

Dar Arabia Lil Kitab, 43 bis, avenue Jugurtha, BP 1104, Tunis Tel: 288688
Man Dir: Mohamed Ahmed En Neifer
Branch Off: Immeuble 'Wafa', avenue Ghouma Mahmoudi, BP 3185, Tripoli, Libya Tel: 47287

Subjects: General Literature, Biography, Bibliography, Linguistics, Pedagogy, Religion, History, Economics, Children's Books
1978: 104 titles *Founded:* 1975

En-Najah*, Editions Hedi Ben Abdelgheni, 11 ave de France, Tunis
Bookshop: Address as above

Faculté des Lettres et Sciences Humaines de Tunis*, Service des Publications et Echanges, 94 blvd du 9 Avril 1938, BP 1128, Tunis Tel: 260858
Secretary: O Bchini
Subjects: History, Africana, Philosophy, Paperbacks, Social Science, University Textbooks
1977: 13 titles

Government Printer (Imprimerie Officielle de la République Tunisienne)*, Route de Rades Km2, Chouchet Radès, Tunis Tel: 295 124/014
Publication: Journal Officiel de la République Tunisienne

Maison Tunisienne d'Edition*, 54 ave de la Liberté, Tunis Tel: 285873 Cable Add: Matédition
Man Dir: Azouz Rebai
Subsidiary Company: Imprimerie de la MTE, Rue du 2 Mars 34, Tunis
Subjects: General Fiction & Nonfiction, Belles Lettres, Poetry, Biography, History, Africana, Philosophy, Reference, Religion, Juveniles, Paperbacks, Social Science, University & Secondary Textbooks, Law, Medicine, Literature, Sciences
1977: 47 titles *Founded:* 1966

Imprimerie/Librairie Al Manar*, BP 121, Tunis Tel: 243224 Cable Add: Manar
Man Dir: T El M'Hamdi
Subsidiary Company: Librairie Al Manar, 60 ave Bab Djedid, Tunis
Subjects: History, Africana, Religion, Arabic Language, Islam

Société nationale d'Edition et de Diffusion*, 5 ave de Carthage, BP 440, Tunis Tel: 255000 Cable Add: Studiffusion
Bookshop: address as above

Sud Editions, 9 bis rue de la Nouvelle Delhi, Tunis Tel: 280400/281994 Telex: 12363 TN
Man Dir: Mohamed Masmoudi; *Editorial:* Abderrazak Khadraoui; *Sales:* Moncef Guellaty
Orders to: Demeter, rue de la Coté d'Ivoire, Tunis
Associate Company: Ceres Productions, 6-8 avenue Montplaisir, Tunis
Subjects: Art, Art History
1979: 2 titles *Founded:* 1976
ISBN Publisher's Prefix: 86444

Major Booksellers

Librairie orientale Ahmed **Belkhodja***, 15 blvd Bab Menara, Tunis

La **Caravelle** Librairie*, 8 ave H Bourguiba, Sfex

Cité des Livres*, 7 rue d'Alger, Tunis

Librairie **En-Najah***, 11 ave de France, Tunis

Librairie **moderne***, 21 ave de la Liberté, Tunis

Librairie Al **Manar***, 60 ave Bab Djedid, PO Box 121, Tunis Tel: 243224

Société Librairie nouvelle*, 15 ave de France, Bizerte

Société nationale d'Edition et de Diffusion*, 5 ave de Carthage, BP 440, Tunis Tel: 255000

Major Libraries

Archives nationales (National Archives)*, Présidence de la République, Pl du Gouvernment, Tunis

Bibliothéque nationale (National Library), 20 Souk-el-Attarine, BP 42, Tunis Tel: 245338
Librarian: M A Guellouz
Publications: Bibliographie nationale; Informations bibliographiques; le catalogue des manuscrits

Bibliothéques publiques*, 10 rue de Russie, Tunis
(branches throughout the country)

British Council Library*, c/o British Embassy, 5 pl de la Victoire, Tunis Tel: 245100/259053

Ecole nationale d'Administration Bibliothèque*, 24 ave Docteur Calmette, Mutuelleville, Tunis

Bibliothèque de l'**Université de Tunis***, 94 blvd du 9 Avril 1938, Tunis Tel: 260858

Library Associations

Association tunisienne de Documentalistes, Bibliothécaires et Archivistes, 43 Rue de laa Liberté, le Bardo
President: M Abdeljaoued
Tunisian Association of Record-Keepers, Librarians and Archivists
Publication: Bulletin ATD (4 a year)

Library Journals

Bulletin, Association tunisienne des Documentalistes, Bibliothécaires et Archivistes, BP 575, Tunis

Literary Associations and Societies

Institut des Belles Lettres arabes, 12 rue Jamâa el Haoua, Tunis Tel: 260133
Institute of Arab Belles Lettres
Publication: Revue IBLA (biannual study of cultural problems in the Arab-Moslem world)

Union tunisienne des Ecrivains (Tunisian Writers' Union)*, rue dar Jeld, Tunis

Turkey

General Information

Language: Turkish (English spoken by many)
Religion: Predominantly Muslim
Population: 42.1 million
Literacy Rate (1970): 51.4%

Bank Hours: 0900-1200, 1400-1730 Monday-Friday
Shop Hours: 0900-1200, 1330-1900 Monday-Saturday
Currency: 100 kurus = 1 Turkish lira (or pound)
Export/Import Information: No tariffs on books and advertising matter. Advertising matter subject to 15% Expenditure Tax. Books on liberalized list, so import licences are granted freely, but textbooks must be imported with permission of Ministry of Education. Exchange controls
Copyright: Berne, Florence (see International section)

Book Trade Organizations

Türk Editörler Birligi*, Ankara Cad 60, Istanbul
Turkish Publishers' Association

Book Trade Reference Books and Journals

Books

T C Devlet Yayinlarl Bibliyografyasi (Bibliography of Turkish Government Publications), National Library, Yenisehir, Ankara

Journals

Turkiye Bibliyografyasi (Turkish National Bibliography), National Library, Bibliographical Institute, Yenisehir, Ankara

Publishers

Arkin Kitabevi, Ankara Cad 60, Istanbul Tel: 750734/750600/1 Cable Add: Birarkinlar Istanbul
Man Dir, Rights & Permissions: Ramazan Gökalp Arkın;
Br Offs: Arkın Dagıtım Ltd, Sti, Ankara Cad 60, Istanbul; Arkin Ofset Basimevi, Merter Sitesi Yol Sokak No 7, Bayrampasa, Istanbul
Subjects: Juveniles, Maps, Educational Materials, Reference, General Science, Secondary & Primary Textbooks
Bookshop: Arkın Kitabevi, Ankara Cad 60, Istanbul
Founded: 1957

Artel Publishing & Commercial Organization Co Ltd*, Halaskârgazi Cad 214/4, Osmanbey, Istanbul Tel: 486040
Man Dir: Engin Serozan
Subjects: Reference, High-priced Paperbacks, Educational Materials
1978: 1 title

Aydınlık Yayinlari*, PO Box 242, Arksaray, Istanbul (Located at: Nuruosmaniye Caddesi 34/204, Cagaloglu, Istanbul)
Man Dir, Rights & Permissions: Mrs Leyla Yurdakul; *Editorial:* Dogan Yurdakul; *Sales:* Hüseyin Göçer; *Production:* Alp Hamuroglu; *Publicity:* Leyla and Dogan Yurdakul
Parent Company: Aydınlık Dergisi
Subjects: Marxism, Turkey and World Affairs
1977: 16 titles *Founded:* 1974

Dergâh Yayinlari AS, see Kara

Dogan Kardes Matbaacilik SAS*, Türbedar Sok 22, Istanbul
Subjects: Juveniles, Educational Materials, Weekly Magazines

Elif Kitabevi*, Sahaflar Çarsisi 4, Beyazit, Istanbul Tel: 222096
Man Dir: Arslan Kaynardag; *Sales Dir:* Gani Yener
Subjects: Belles Lettres, Poetry, History, Music, Art, Philosophy, Social Science
Founded: 1957
Bookshop: Sahaflar Çarsisi 4, Beyazit, Istanbul
Miscellaneous: Firm distributes Turkish publications. Associated imprints include Elif Yayinlari

Gelisim Publishing, Safak sokak No 2, Nisantasi, Istanbul Tel: 486182/486183/475445 Cable Add: Gelbay
Chairman and Man Dir: Ercan Arikli
Associate Company: Süreli Yayinlar AS (Periodical Press, Inc), Dr Sevkibey sokak No 6, Divanyolu, Istanbul Tel: 286478/276817
Subjects: Encyclopaedias, Reference, Nonfiction

Hürriyet Yayinlari (Hür Yayin)*, Cemal Nadir Sokak 7-Cagaloglu, 1183 Istanbul Tel: 222038, 271502 Telex: 22276 HA TR, 22277 HA TR
Dir: Ali Z Oraloglu
Parent Company: Hürriyet Holding
Subjects: Fiction, History, Classics, Poetry, TV Series, Yearbooks, General Reference
1977: 50 titles

Inkilap Ve Aka Kitabevleri*, Ankara Cad 95, Istanbul Tel: 222851
Man Dir: Nazar Fikri; *Sales Manager:* Aka Eren
Subjects: General Fiction & Nonfiction, Cartography, Politics, Religion, Literature, History, Juveniles

Ismail **Kara**/Dergâh Yayinlari AS Müessese Müdürü, PO Box 1240 Sirkeci, Istanbul (Located at: Nuruosmaniye Cad 3/1 Cagaloglu, Istanbul) Tel: 265370
Man Dir: Ezel Erverdi; *Editorial:* Mustafa Kutlu; *Sales:* Fatih Gokdag; *Production:* Ahmet Debbagoglu; *Publicity:* Mustafa Modanlioglu
Subsidiary Companies: Dergâh kitapcilk AS, Ankara Cad 85 Cagaloglu, Istanbul; Emek matbaacilik ve ilancilik Ltd sti; Derya Dagitim AS, Babiali Cad 52 Cagaloglu, Istanbul
Subjects: Encyclopedias, Islamic Classics, History, Books of 'Hareket', Modern Turkish Philosophy, Modern Turkish Policy, Culture, Islamic Thought, Western Thought, Education, Turkish Literature
Book Clubs: Dergâh kitabevi, Istanbul; Dergâh kitabevi, Erzurum
Bookshops: Dergâh kitabevi, Istanbul; Dergâh kitabevi, Erzurum
1978: 11 titles *Founded:* 1977

Altin **Kitaplar** Publishing Co, Altin Kitaplar, Cagaloglu, Istanbul Tel: 224045/268012 Telex: 23382 mudo TR
Man Dir: Mr Fethi Ul; *Editorial:* Dr Turhan Bozkurt; *Sales:* Mr Mursit Ul; *Production:* Mr Ugur Gergin; *Publicity:* Mr Ferhan Filiztekin
Associate Companies: Ders Kitaplari SA, Babiali Cad 39, Istanbul; Bozkurt Publishing Co, Ticarethane Sokak Sultanahmet, Istanbul
Subjects: Fiction, Non-fiction, Memoirs, Textbooks, Children's Books, Classics, History, Crime, Holy Koran
Bookshop: Altin Kitaplar, Cagaloglu, Istanbul
1978: 119 titles *1979:* 70 titles *Founded:* 1959

Milliyet Yaynlari AS, Basın Sarayı Cagaloglu, Istanbul Tel: 270034 Cable Add: Mlliyet-Yayn Telex: 22251
Man Dir: Ülkü Tamer; *Editorial:* Gul Onet; *Production:* Ulvi Okar; *Publicity:* Ismet Istinyeli
Parent Company: Milliyet Holding AS
Subjects: General Fiction, Literature, History, Reference, Philosophy, Dictionaries, Encyclopaedias, Children's Books, Magazines
Bookshop: Basın Sarayı Cagaloglu, Istanbul
1977: 105 titles *1978:* 98 titles *Founded:* 1970

Redhouse Press, PK 142, Istanbul
Editor: Robert Avery
Subjects: Turkish-English Dictionaries, Guidebooks in English, Cookery (in English and Turkish), General
Bookshop: Redhouse Kitabevi, Rizapasa Yokusu 48, Sultanhaman, Istanbul
1977: 5 titles *1978:* 15 titles

Remzi Kitabevi, Selvilimescit Sokak No 8, Cagaloglu, Istanbul Tel: 220583/227248 Cable Add: Remzi Kitabevi
Man Dir: Erol Erduran; *Sales, Rights & Permissions:* Erol Erduran; *Publicity & Advertising:* Nejat Ebcioglu
Subsidiary Company: Evrim Matbaacılık Ltd, Sirketi Cagaloglu, Istanbul
Subjects: General Fiction, Biography, History, Philosophy, Reference, Low-priced Paperbacks, Medicine, Psychology, General & Social Science, Secondary & Primary Textbooks, Educational Materials
Bookshop: Ankara Cad 93, Istanbul
1978: 22 titles *Founded:* 1931

Sander Yayınları*, Kırağı Sok 78, Osmanbey, Istanbul Tel: 408475/483209
Man Dir, Production, Rights & Permissions: Necdet Sander; *Editorial:* Nuran Ücok; *Sales:* Ali Unver Tatlici; *Publicity:* Allegra Mitrani
Parent Company: Sander Kitabevi
Subjects: Literature, Fiction, Poetry, Essays, Political History, Sport, Education, Tourist Guides (of Turkey)
Bookshops: Sander Kitabevi, Halaskargazi Cad 275-277, Osmanbey, Istanbul; Istiklal Cad 178, Beyogıu, Istanbul
1977: 4 titles

Literary Agents

Hür Yayin ve Ticaret*, Cemai Nadir Sokak 7, Cagaloglu, Istanbul Tel: 222038/262000 Cable Add: PK 1183 Istanbul

Nurcihan **Kesim***, Basinkoy Ahmet Ihsan No 6, Istanbul
Branch Office; Nuruosmaniye Caddesi No 8, Cagaloglu, Istanbul Tel: 790222/285800/285394 Cable Add: Nurcihan Kesim, Basinkoy, Istanbul
Man Dir: Nurcihan Kesim; *Sales:* Ertugrul Kesim; *Rights & Permissions:* Oya Alpar
Specialization: Fiction, Nonfiction, Art Works, Serials, Encyclopaedias

O N K Copyright Agency*, Ankara Cad 40, PO Box 983, Istanbul Tel: 267074/275345 Cable Add: Copyright Istanbul
Dir: Osman N Karaca
Specialization: Serials, Plays, TV Programmes

Book Clubs

Dergâh kitabevi, Istanbul
Owned by: Ismail Kara (qv)

Dergâh kitabevi, Erzurum
Owned by: Ismail Kara (qv)

Major Booksellers

Bilgi Yayinevi*, Tuna Cad, Kizilay, Ankara

Gençlik Kitabevi*, Muvakkithane Cad, 35 Kadiköy, Istanbul Tel: 363017

Hakki Bigeç*, Baskeny Yayinevi, Izmir Cad 55/22, Ankara

Haset Kitabevi AS*, Istiklal cad 469, Beyoğlu, Istanbul Tel: 449470/1
Branches at Cumhuriyet Bulvari 143/G, Izmir; Ziya Gökalp cad 14/E, Yenisehir, Ankara
Formerly Hachette Kitabevi

Nejat Yalki Kitabevi*, Valikonagi Cad, Nisantasi, Istanbul

Orhan Özsisman*, Datiç AS, 452 Sokak, No 5, Konak, Izmir

Redhouse Kitabevi*, Rizapasa Yokusu 48, Sultanhamam, Istanbul Tel: 223905

Sander Kitabevi*, Halaskârgazi Cad 275–277, Osmanbey, Istanbul Tel: 483209; Istiklal Cad 178, Beyoglu, Istanbul Tel: 440134

Major Libraries

Ankara University Library*, Ankara

Beyazit Library*, Istanbul

Bogaziçi University Library (formerly Robert College Library)*, Bebek, PK 2, Istanbul Tel: 653400
Acting Librarian: Mary Beeley

Library of the **Grand National Assembly***, Palais de la Grande Assemblée Nationale, Ankara Tel: 251352

Il **Halk Kütüphanesi** (Provincial Public Library*, formerly the Vatan Library), Balikesir

Istanbul Üniversitesi Merkez Kütüphanesi (Istanbul University Central Library), Takvimhane Caddesi 15, Beyazit, Istanbul Tel: 222180

Izmir General Library*, Millî Kütüphane Cad 39, Izmir

Middle East Technical University Library*, Ankara

Millet Library*, Fatih, Istanbul

Millî Kütüphane (National Library)*, Yenisehir, Ankara Tel: 253498
Dir: Mrs Esin Karaaslan

Library of the **Mineral Research and Exploration Institute***, Ismet Inönü Bulvari, Ankara Tel: 234255
Librarian: Sevim Özertan;
Publication: Selected list of New Publications in *MTA News* (Monthly)

Selimiye Library*, Edirne

Süleymaniye Kütüphanesi Müdürlüğü (Library of the Süleymaniye), Süleymaniye Mahallesi, Ayse Kadin Sokak 30; 35, Beyazit-Istanbul Tel: 220186/278708

Technical University Library*, Istanbul Teknık Üniversitesi, Merkez Kütüphane Müdürlüğü, Gümüssuyu Cad 87, Beyoglu

Library Journals

Bülteni (Bulletin), Turkish Librarians' Association, Necatibey Cad, PK 175, Yenisehir, Ankara
Turkish Librarians' Association
Secretary: M N Seferioğlu
Publication: Bülteni (4 a year)

Library Journals

Bülteni (Bulletin), Turkish Librarians' Association, Necatibey Cad, PK 175, Yenisehir, Ankara

Literary Associations and Societies

P E N Yazarlar Dernegi*, Cagoglu Yokusu 40, Istanbul
President: Yasar Nabi Nayir
PEN-Turkish Centre

Literary Periodicals

Orta Dogu (Middle East), Celal Tevfik Karasapan, Tunali Hilmi Cad 121-5, Kavaklidere, Ankara

Varlik (Existence), Varlik Yayinevi, Cagaloglu Yokusu, Ankara Cad, Istanbul

Literary Prizes

Award for Literature and Scientific Publications*
To encourage the use of the Turkish language. Five prizes of 5,000 Turkish liras each for literature and one prize of 5,000 liras for scientific publication. Awarded annually. Enquiries to Turkish Language Society, Kavaklidere, Ankara

Sait **Faik** Prize*
For the best short story. 5,000 Turkish liras. Awarded annually. Enquiries to Darussafaka Association, Halaskargazl Cad 231, Istanbul

Orhan **Kemal** Award*
To encourage publication of novels which reflect the views of Orhan Kemal. Awarded annually. Enquiries to Orhan Kemal Family and Associates, c/o Turkish Language and History Society, Kavaklidere, Ankara

Fikret **Madarali** Prize*
For the best novel. Three prizes of 10,000, 5,000 and 3,000 Turkish liras. Awarded annually. Enquiries to Fikret Madarali Family and Associates, c/o Turkish Language and History Society, Kavaklidere, Ankara

Uganda

General Information

Language: Luganda (English also used)
Religion: Muslim, Hindu and Christian
Population: 12.4 million
Literacy Rate (1959 African Population): 20%

Bank Hours: 0830-1230 Monday-Friday; 0800-1100 Saturday
Shop Hours: 0800-1230, 1400-1630 or longer Monday-Friday; 0800-1230 Saturday
Currency: 100 cents = 1 Uganda shilling
Export/Import Information: No tariff on books or advertising matter but subject to 10% sales tax. Import licence and exchange controls (granted automatically with import license)

Book Trade Journals

The Uganda Journal, PO Box 4980, Mapala (published by the Uganda Society and includes an annual bibliography of books published in or about Uganda)

Publishers

East African Literature Bureau*, Uganda Branch, PO Box 1317, Kampala
For full information see under Kenya

Government Printer*, PO Box 33, Entebbe

Longman Uganda Ltd*, PO Box 3409, Kampala Tel: 42940/32914 Cable Add: Longman Uganda
Manager: M K L Mutyaba
Subjects: Biography, History, Africana, Juveniles, Books in Luganda & other Ugandan Languages, General Science, Secondary & Primary Textbooks
Founded: 1965
Miscellaneous: Firm is an associate company of Longman Group Ltd, UK (qv)

Uganda Publishing House*, UTA Ho, Bombo Rd, PO Box 2923, Kampala Tel: 59601/42362
Man Dir: G Rugege; *Sales Manager:* John B Bugembe
Subjects: General Fiction & Nonfiction, Belles Lettres, Poetry, Biography, History, Africana, Reference, Juveniles, General & Social Science, Secondary & Primary Textbooks
Founded: 1966

Major Booksellers

E S A Bookshop*, PO Box 2515, Kampala

Makerere University Bookshop*, PO Box 7062, Kampala

Saint Paul Book Centre*, PO Box 4392, Kampala Tel: 56346

Uganda Bookshop*, Colville St, PO Box 7145, Kampala Tel: 43756

Major Libraries

Albert **Cook** Library, Makerere University, Makarere Medical School, PO Box 7072, Kampala Tel: 58731
Medical Librarian: Leonard Ssennyonjo
Publications: East African Medical Bibliography (bi-monthly); *Bulletin and Accession List* (monthly) *Annual Report*

International Communication Agency Library*, PO Box 7186, Kampala Tel: 54351

Kabarole Public Library*, PO Box 28, Fort Portal Tel: 2255

Makerere Institute of Social Research Library, PO Box 16022, Kampala Tel: 54582
Librarian: Dorcas Kigozi

Makerere University Library*, PO Box 16002, Kampala Tel: 31041/2
Librarian: T K Lwanga
Publication: Library Bulletin (quarterly)

National Institute of Education Library* Makerere University, PO Box 7062, Kampala
Publication: Journal

Public Libraries Board*, Buganda Rd, PO Box 4262, Kampala Tel: 54661 Cable Add: Library, Kampala
Dir: P K Birungi
Publications: Annual Report, Accessions List (quarterly) and occasional publications

Uganda Technical College Library, PO Box 1991, Kampala Tel: 65211 ext 37 Cable Add: Technical
Senior Librarian: R Nganwa

Library Associations

Uganda Library Association, PO Box 5894, Kampala Tel: 54661
Executive Secretary: I M N Kigongo-Bukenya
Publication: Ugandan Libraries

Uganda Schools Library Association*, PO Box 7014, Kampala
Executive Secretary: J W Nabembezi
Publication: Newsletter (quarterly)

Uganda Special Library Association*, c/o PO Box 9, Entebbe
Secretary: M D'Mello

Library Journals

Newsletter, Uganda Schools Library Association, PO Box 7014, Kampala

Ugandan Libraries, Uganda Library Association, PO Box 5894, Kampala

Literary Periodicals

Dhana, East African Literature Bureau, PO Box 1317, Kampala (or PO Box 30022, Nairobi) (biannual literary magazine published on behalf of the Department of Literature at Makerere University)

Translation Agencies and Associations

East African Literature Bureau*, PO Box 1317, Kampala

Union of Soviet Socialist Republics

General Information

Language: Russian (second language varies from one republic to another)
Religion: Atheistic state
Population: 259 million
Literacy Rate (1970): 99.7%
Bank Hours: 0900-1600 Monday-Friday
Shop Hours: 0830-1800 Monday-Saturday
Currency: 100 kopeks = 1 rouble
Export/Import Information: Foreign trade is state monopoly and duties and licences only the concern of the corporation Mezhdunarodnaya Kniga, Smolenskaya Sennaya 32-34, Moscow G-200. The State Bank of USSR or its subsidiary, USSR Bank for Foreign Trade, is only organization handling foreign currency matters
Copyright: UCC (see International section)

Book Trade Organizations

Komitet po pechati pri Sovete Ministrov SSSR*, Petrovka 26, Moscow K-51
Committee for Publishing and the Press under the Council of Ministers of the USSR
Foreign Trade Dir: I V Shamraev

Publishing Council of the Academy of Sciences of the USSR*, Leninsky prospekt 13, Moscow

Vsesoyuznaya Knichnaya Palata*,
Kremlevskaya naberezhnaya 1-9, Moscow
All-Soviet Book Chamber
Publications: Knizhnaya Letopis'
All books and publications are registered and described

Book Trade Reference Books and Journals

Books

Knizhnaya Moskva: Putevoditel'-Spravochnik (Books in Moscow: A Guide and Handbook), 'Reklama', Moscow

Spravochnik Normativnykh Materialov dlya Rabotnikov Knizhnoi Torgovli (Handbook of Rules and Precedents for Book Trade Workers), Izdatelstvo 'Kniga', Nezhdanovoi pereulok 8-10, Moscow K-9

Journals

Ezhegodnik Knigi SSSR (USSR National Bibliography), Izdatelstvo 'Kniga', Nezhdanovoi pereulok 8-10, Moscow K-9

Index to Forthcoming Russian Books; English translation of bibliographic entries from *Novye Knigi*, Scientific Information Consultants Ltd, 661 Finchley Rd, London W2 2HN, UK
(*Editor:* Eugene Gros)

Knizhnaya Letopis' (Book Chronicle) (weekly bulletin), All-Soviet Book Chamber, Kremlevskaya naberezhnaya 1-9, Moscow

Knizhnaya Letopis' — Dopolnitel'nyi Vypusk; monthly supplement to *Knizhnaya Letopis',* quoting 'restricted' publications, small imprints, 'not-for-sale' or institutional items etc, All-Soviet Book Chamber, Kremlevskaya naberezhnaya 1-9, Moscow

Knizhnaya Torgovlya (Book Trade), Mezhdunarodnaya Kniga, Smolenskaya Sennaya pl 32-34, Moscow G-200

Knizhnoe Obozrenie (Book Reviews), USSR Library Council, The Lenin State Library of the USSR, Prospect Kalinina 3, Moscow 101 000

Letopis' Pechati BSSR (Byelorussian National Bibliography), Godudarstvennaya Biblioteka BSSR im V I Lenina, Knizhnaya Palata BSSR, Minsk

Letopis' Periodicheskikh i Prodolzhaiushchikhsya Izdanii (Periodicals and Continuations), Mezhdunarodnaya Kniga, Smolenskaya Sennaya pl 32-34, Moscow G-200

Novye Knigi (New Books); announcements of forthcoming books, Mezhdunarodnaya Kniga, Smolenskaya Sennaya pl 32-34, Moscow G-200

Sovetskaya Bibliografia (Soviet Bibliography), USSR Library Council, The Lenin State Library of the USSR, Prospect Kalinina 3, Moscow 101 000

Ukrainska Knyha (Ukrainian Book) (text in Ukrainian), Association of Book Lovers, Kyiw Publishing, 4800 North 12th St, Philadelphia, PA 19141, USA

Publishers

Atomizdat, ul Zhdanova 5, 103031 Moscow K-31 Tel: 2942228/2959993
Publishing House for Atomic Literature
Dir: V A Kulyamin
Subjects: Nuclear Science and Technology (peaceful use of nuclear energy)

Aurora Art Publishers, 7-9 Nevsky prospekt, 191065 Leningrad Tel: 2151924
Cable Add: Exportizdat Aurora Leningrad
Telex: 81562
President, Rights & Permissions: Boris Pidemsky; *Editor-in-Chief:* Alla Slizhevskaya; *Production:* Anatoly Peshkov
Subject: Art
1977: 950 titles *Founded:* 1969
Miscellaneous: Publishes in foreign languages

Detskaya Entsiklopediya*, Khokhlovskii pereulok 16, Moscow
Children's Encyclopaedia

Izdatelstvo **Detskaya Literatura**, Malyi Cherkaskii pereulok 1, Moscow
Children's Literature Publishing House
Dir: G K Peshekhodova
Subject: Juveniles

Znak Pochyota Order **Dosaaf** Publishing House*, Novo-Ryazanskaya 26, Moscow 107066
Voluntary Society for the Promotion of the Army, Air Force and Navy
Subject: Military

Izdatelstvo '**Ekonomika**'*, Berezhovskaya naberezhnaya 6, Moscow
Economics Publishing House
Dir: K V Grechishnikov
Subjects: Economics, Industry, Agriculture, Textbooks
Founded: 1963

Izdatelstvo '**Energiya**'*, Shlyuzovaya naberezhnaya 10, Moscow Z-114
Energy Publishing House
Dir: S P Rozanov
Subject: Scientific and technical literature on Power Engineering, Radio Engineering

Izdatelstvo '**Finansy**'*, Chernyshevskogo ul 7, Moscow K-142
Finances Publishing House
Dir: V I Vinogradov
Subjects: Banking, Taxation, Accounts

Izdatelstvo '**Fizkultura i Sport**'*,
Kalyaevskaya ul 27, Moscow 103006
Physical Culture & Sport Publishing House
Man Dir: Yurii Metaev
Subjects: Sport Games

Gidrometeorizdat*, Moskovskoe Otdelenie, Gor'kovo ul 18a, Moscow
Hydrometeorology

Izdatelstvo **Iskusstvo***, Tsvetnov bul'var' 25, Moscow K-51
Publishing House for Art Literature
Dir: E Y Savostianov
Subjects: Fine Arts, Music, Theatre

Izvestiya Publishing House*, Pushkinskaya pl 5, Moscow K-6
Dir: L P Grachev
Subjects: Izvestiya, Official Publications of USSR and RSFSR Supreme Soviets

Izdatelstvo '**Khimiya**' (Publishing House for Chemistry)*, Strominka ul 23, Moscow B-76
Dir: Ya S Mashkevich
Subject: Chemistry

Izdatelstvo '**Khudozhestvennaya Literatura**'*, Novo-Basmannaya ul 19, Moscow B-66
Publishing House for Fiction & Poetry
Dir: V S Somov
Subjects: Fiction, Literature

Khudozhnik RSFSR Publishers*, Bolsheokhtinsky Pereulok 6, Block 2, Leningrad 195027
Subjects: General, Catalogues

Izdatelstvo '**Kniga**', Nezhdanovoi ul 8-10, Moscow K-9
Dir: V F Kravchenko
Subjects: Bibliography, Printing, Publishing, Bibliology, Bibliophilism, Miniature and Facsimile Editions

Izdatelstvo '**Kolos**'*, Sadovaya-Spasskaya ul 18, Moscow I-139
Dir: I P Khramkov
Subjects: Agriculture, Veterinary Science

Izdatelstvo '**Legkaya Industriya**', Kuznetskii most 22, Moscow K-31
Light Industry Publishing House
Dir: T G Gromova; *Publicity:* Y Y Gosenpoud
Subject: Light Industry

Izdatelstvo '**Lenizdat**'*, Fontanka 59, Leningrad D-23
Leningrad Publishing House
Subjects: Politics, Technical, Agriculture, Fiction, Juveniles, Art, Popular Science, Folklore

Izdatelstvo '**Lesnaya Promyshlennost**', Kirova ul 40a, Moscow
Forest Industry Publishing House
Dir: B S Oreshkin
Subjects: Forestry, Wood & Paper Products, Logging, Woodworking, Dendrochemistry, Nature Conservation
1978: 130 titles

Izdatelstvo **'Malysh'***, Butyrskii val 68, Moscow A-55
Children's World Publishing House
Dir: I N Boronetsky
Subject: Pre-school Publications

Izdatelstvo **'Mashinostroenie'***, Pervyi Basmannyi pereulok 3, Moscow
Publishing House for Mechanical Engineering
Dir: A V Astakhov
Subject: Mechanical Engineering

Izdatelstvo **'Meditsina'***, Petroverigskii pereulok 6-8, Moscow K-142
Publishing House for Medicine
Dir: V I Maevsky
Subjects: Medicine, Health
Founded: 1918

Izdatelstvo **'Metallurgiya'**, 2-oi Obydenskii pereulok 14, Moscow G-34, 119034
Publishing House for Metallurgy
Dir: M A Kovalevskiy
Subject: Metallurgy
1978: 246 titles

Izdatelstvo **'Mezhdunarodnye Otnosheniya'***, Kuznetskii most 24, 103031 Moscow K-31
International Relations Publishing House
Dir: S P Emelyanikov
Subjects: International Information, Translations for UN Textbooks

Leidykla **'Mintis'**, Sierakausko 15, Vilnius
Tel: 632943
Dir: Algimantas Garliauskas
Subjects: Politics, Law, Philosophy, Tourism, Sport Directories, Economics, History, Hobbies, Social Sciences, Textbooks, Juveniles, Periodicals, Calendars
1978: 148 titles *Founded:* 1949

Izdatelstvo **Mir**, 129820, 2 Pervy Rizhskii pereulok, Moscow I-110, GSP Telex: 411466 MIR SU
Dir: S G Sosnovsky; *Editor-in-Chief:* Dr G B Kurganov
Orders to: Mezhdunarodnaya Kniga, Moscow
Subject: Translations from and into Russian of technical and scientific works
1977: 386 titles *1978:* 431 titles *Founded:* 1946

Izdatelstvo **Molodaya Gvardiya**, Sushchevskaya ul 21, Moscow K-30 Tel: 2511145
Young Guard Publishing House of All-Union Leninist Young Communist League
Dir: Vladimir Desyaterik
Subjects: Political Science, Social Science, History, Biography, Art, Science Fiction, Juveniles
1978: 340 titles *Founded:* 1922

Izdatelstvo **'Moskovskii Rabochiy'***, Kuibysheva ul 21, Moscow
Moscow Worker Publishing House
Dir: N H Eselyek
Subjects: General Fiction & Nonfiction

Izdatelstvo **Moskovskogo Universiteta***, Gertzena ul 5-7, Moscow K-9
Moscow University Press
Dir: Dr A K Avelitchev; *Rights & Permissions:* VAAP, Bolshaya Bronnaya 6a, Moscow
Subject: Science
Founded: 1926

Izdatelstvo **'Muzyka'***, Neglinnaja ul 14, Moscow
Music Publishing House
Subject: Music
1978: 615 titles

Izdatelstvo **Mysl***, Leninsky prospekt 15, Moscow V-71
Thought Publishing House
Dir: A P Porivaev
Subjects: Science, Economics, Geography, Philosophy, History

Izdatelstvo **'Nauka'***, Podsosenskii pereulok 21, Moscow K-62
Science Publishing House
Dir: G D Komkov
Subjects: General & Social Science, Mathematics, University Textbooks, Educational Materials
Founded: 1964

Izdatelstvo **'Nedra'***, Tret'yakovskii pereulok 1-19, Moscow K-12
Natural Resources Publishing House
Dir: M S Lvov
Subjects: Meteorology, Geology, Energy

Agentstvo Pechati **'Novosti'** (Apn), 13/5 Podkolokolny pereulok, Moscow 109028
Tel: 2971953 Telex: 7581, 7582
Novosti Press Agency Publishing House
Dir: N I Efimov; *Editorial:* Yu S Fantalov; *Sales, Publicity:* S G Mishchenko; *Production:* R S Vakhitova; *Rights & Permissions:* M B Krupkin
Subjects: History, Philosophy, Social Science, Politics, Economics, International Affairs, General Informative Books, Low- & High-priced Paperbacks
1977: 732 titles *1978:* 760 titles *Founded:* 1964

Pedagogika*, Pogodinskaya 8, Moscow
Dir: Mr Razumny
Subject: Pedagogics

Izdatelstvo **'Pishchevaya Promyshlennost'***, 1 Kadashevskii pereulok 12, Moscow
Publishing House for the Food Industry
Dir: N A Zarin
Subjects: Food Science & Technology
1977: 160 titles

Planeta Publishers*, Petrovka 8/11, Moscow 103031
Subjects: Guidebooks, Illustrated books

Politizdat, Myusskaya pl 7, Moscow D-47
Publishing House for Political Literature
Dir: H B Tropkin
Subjects: Political Literature, History
1978: 381 titles

Pravda Publishing House*, Pravdy ul 24, Moscow
Dir: B A Feldman

Profizdat, Kirova ul 13, Moscow
Publishers for Trade-union Literature
Dir: Vladimir A Boldyzev
Subjects: Economics, Sociology, Psychology of Work, Trade Union Movement, Literature, Fiction, Prose
Miscellaneous: Publishers for the All-Union Central Council of Trade Unions

Progress Publishers, Zubovsky Boulevard 17, Moscow 119021 Tel: 2469032
Dir: Volf Nikolayevich Sedykh; *Editor-in-Chief:* Viktor Ivanovich Neznanov; *Production:* Mikhail Pavlovich Kryakovkin
Subjects: Scientific Socialism, Marxism-Leninsim, Philosophy, Political Economy, International Relations, International Communist and Workers Movement, History, Sociology, Law, Russian Classics and Modern Soviet Literature, Russian Translations of Fiction, Social and Political Literature, Art, Children's Books
1977: 1157 titles *1978:* 1161 titles *Founded:* 1931

Izdatelstvo **'Prosveshchenie'**, 3-ii proezd Marinoi Roshchi 41, Moscow 129846
Dir: D D Zuev
Subjects: Education, Textbooks

Russky Yazyk*, Luchnikov Pereulok 5, Moscow 101000
Russian Language Publishing House
Subjects: Textbooks, Reference, Dictionaries

Izdatelstvo **'Sovetskaya Entsiklopediya'**, Pokrovskii bul'var' 8, Moscow 109817 Tel: 2973562/2977483
Soviet Encyclopaedia Publishing House
Chairman of Editorial Council: A Prokhorov
Founded: 1925

Izdatelstvo **'Sovetskaya Rossiya'***, Suapnova Proezd 13-15, Moscow K-12
Soviet Russia Publishing House
Dir: E A Petrov

Izdatelstvo **'Sovetskii Khudozhnik'**, Chernyahovskogo ul 4a, Moscow 125319
Soviet Artist Publishing House
Dir: V Goryainov
Subject: Art, Reference
1978: 1583 titles

Izdatelstvo **'Sovetskii Kompozitor'**, 14-12 Sadovaya-Triumfalnaya St, Moscow 103006 Tel: 2092384
Soviet Composer Publishing House
Dir: M Y Kunin
Subject: Music
Founded: 1957
Bookshop: Magazin-Salon Sovetskaya Muzyka (at above address)

Izdatelstvo **Sovietskii Pisatel**, 121069 Moscow 69, ul Vorovskovo 11
USSR Writer's Union Publishing House
Dir: V N Eramenko
Founded: 1934
Subjects: Belles Lettres, Art History, Literary History, Poetry, Literary Criticism, Literary Translations
Founded: 1935
Miscellaneous: Publishes monthly magazine *Soviet Motherland* in Yiddish

Izdatelstvo **'Sovetskoe Radio'** Glavnyi Pochtamt p/ya693*, Moscow
Dir: N G Zabolotsky
Subjects: Radio, TV

Sovremennik Publishers*, Yartsevskaya 4, Moscow 121351
Subjects: Fiction, Literary Criticism, Drama

Znak Pochyota Order Izdatelstvo **Standartov***, Novopresnensky Pereulok 3, Moscow 123022
Subject: Official Standards

Statistika, Kirova ul 39, Moscow
Dir: E I Kobzar
Subjects: Statistics on economics, on demography and on computers in the national economy
1978: 113 titles

Stroyizdat Publishing House*, Kalyayevskaya 23a, Moscow 102006
Subjects: Building Sciences, Machinery, Urban Development, Architecture, Geology, Hydrogeology

Izdatelstvo **'Sudostroenie'***, 8 Gogolya St, Leningrad 191065 Tel: 2153048
Publishing House for Shipbuilding
Man Dir: V Iv Lapin; *Editor-in-Chief;* A L Mitrofanov; *Sales, Publicity:* Mrs T M Goolkova; *Production:* V Iv Pashko; *Rights & Permissions:* Yu V Popov
Subjects: Shipbuilding, Ship Repairing, Ship Installations Equipment and Devices,

Navigation, Underwater Exploration, University and Secondary Textbooks on these subjects
Bookshop: Shipbuilding, 40 Sadovuja St, Leningrad
1977: 81 titles *1978/9:* 86 titles *Founded:* 1940

Izdatelstvo **'Svyaz'***, Chistoprudnyi bul'var' 2, Moscow
Communications Publishing House
Dir: G Rodin
Subject: Communications (postal, telegraphic and wireless, television, Hi-Fi equipment), Philately

Izdatelstvo **'Transport'***, Basmannyi Tupik 6a, Moscow B-174
Dir: A L Golovanov
Subject: Transport

Vsesoyuznoe Obyedineniye **'Vneshtorgizdaf'***, 1 Fadyeev St, Moscow 107207 Tel: 2505162 Telex: 7238 VTI SU
Foreign Trade Publishing House
President: Rostislav V Morolov; *Editorial:* Boris V Lensky; *Sales:* Leonid G Koftov; *Production:* Wladimir Mitin
Subject: Foreign Trade
Founded: 1925
Miscellaneous: Publish Catalogues, Prospectuses and Advertising Material in Russian and Foreign Languages on Soviet exports. Execute orders of foreign organizations for translation and publishing in Russian of maintenance and other documents

Voyenizdat*, Upravleniye Voyennogo Izdateltsva, Moscow K-160
Chief: A I Kopytin
Subject: Military

Izdatelstvo **'Vysshaya Shkola'***, Neglinnaya ul d29/14, Moscow
Higher School Publishing House
Dir: V G Panov
Subject: Textbooks (Secondary Education)

Izdatelstvo **'Yuridicheskaya Literatura'***, Chkalova 38-40, Moscow
Law Literature Publishing House
Dir: V G Yuzbashev
Subject: Law

Znanie*, Novaya ploshchad 3-4, Moscow K-12
Knowledge Publishing House
Dir: V Belyakov
Subjects: General Science, Education, Culture

Literary Agents

V A A P, see entry below

Vsesoyuznoe agentstvo po avtorskim pravam (VAAP), Bolshaya Bronnaya ul 6a, Moscow K-104 Tel: 2034599 Cable Add: Moscow AVTOR Telex: 7627AVTOR SU
Copyright Agency of the USSR
Contact: B Pankin, Chairman; or M Shisigin, Vice-Chairman

Major Booksellers

Mezhdunarodnaya Kniga*, Smolenskaya sennaya pl 32-34, Moscow G-200 Tel: 2441022 Cable Add: Mezhkniga Moscow
(The sole organization in the USSR through which foreign purchasers can obtain books)

The leading agent for distribution of USSR books and periodicals abroad is Les Livres Etrangers SA, 10 rue Armand-Moisant, F-75737 Paris cedex 15 Tel: (01) 7342727/5665680; retail bookshop Maison du Livre Etranger ('Dom Knigi'), 9 rue de l'Eperon, F-75006 Paris Tel: (01) 3261060

Major Libraries

Fundamental Library of the **Academy** of Medical Sciences*, Baltiyskaya ul 8, Moscow

Biblioteka **Akademii Nauk SSSR***, Birzhevaya liniya 1, Leningrad V-164 Tel: Director's Office 183592 and 184091; Information and Bibliographical Department 183991
Library of the Academy of Sciences of the USSR

Gosudarstvennaya publichnaya nauchno-tekhnicheskaya biblioteka Sibirskogo otdeleniya **Akademii Nauk SSSR***, Voskhod ul 15, 630200 Novosibirsk Tel: Director 661860; Reference and Bibliography Department 661991; Reader Registration 668071
State Public Scientific and Technical Library of the Siberian Department of the Academy of Sciences of the USSR

Institut nauchnoy informatsii po obschestvennym naukam **Akademii Nauk SSSR***, Krasikova ul 28/45, 117418 Moscow V-418 Tel: 1288930
Institute of Scientific Information in the Social Sciences of the Academy of Sciences of the USSR

Tsentral'nava nauchnaya biblioteka **Akademii Nauk USSR***, Vladimirskaya ul 62, 252601 Kiev 601 Tel: Director 243126; Reference/Bibliography Section 213231
Central Scientific Library of the Academy of Sciences of the Ukrainian SSR

All-Union Patent and Technical Library*, Berezhkovskaya naberezhnaya 24, Moscow

Central State **Archives of Early Russian Historical Records**, Bolshaya Pirogovskaya ul 17, Moscow

Central State **Archives of the October Revolution** and Higher State Bodies, Bolshaya Pirogovskaya ul 17, Moscow

Central State **Archives of the RSFSR***, Berezhkovskaya naberezhnaya 26, Moscow

Central State Historical **Archives of the USSR***, Naberezhnaya Krasnogo Flota 4, Leningrad

Central State Literature and Art **Archives of the USSR***, Leningradskoe chausee 50, Moscow
Dir: N B Volkova

Azerbaidzhanskaya gosudarstvennaya respublikanskaya biblioteka im. M F Akhundova*, Tsentr ul Khagani 29, 37061 Baku Tel: 936801; Reference and Bibliography Department 936004
M F Akhundov State Republic Library of Azerbaizhan

Nauchnaya biblioteka im A M **Gor'kovo** Leningradskovo gosudarstvennovo universiteta im A A Zhdanova*, Universitetskaya naberezhnaya 7-9, Leningrad 199164 Tel: Director 2-182741; Reference and Information Department 2-189555
A M Gor'kii Scientific Library of the A A Zhdanov State University of Leningrad
Dir: Mrs K M Romanovskaya

Nauchnaya biblioteka im A M **Gor'kogo Moskovskogo** gos universiteta im M V Lomonosova*, Marx prospekt 20, Moscow K-9 Tel: Director's Office 2036525; Service Department 2033751
Gor'kii Scientific Library of The Lomonosov State University of Moscow

Vsesoyuznaya **gosudarstvennaya ordena Trudovogo Krasnogo Znameni biblioteka** inostrannoi literatury*, Ulyanovskaya 1, Moscow 109240 Tel: 2972839
All-Union State Library of Foreign Literature

Gosudarstvennaya publichnaya istoricheskaya biblioteka RSFSR*, 101839 Moscow, Bogdana Khmel'nitskogo ul, Starosadskii per d 9 Tel: Director 2956514; Information 2280582
State Public Historical Library of the RSFSR

Gosudarstvennaya publichnaya nauchno-tekhnicheskaya biblioteka SSSR*, Kuznetskii most 12, Moscow K-31 Tel: Director K59288; Reference-Bibliography B87379
State Public Scientific and Technical Library of the USSR

Gosudarstvennaya ordena Lenina biblioteka SSSR imeni V I **Lenina***, Prospect Kalinina 3, Moscow 101000 Tel: 2024056 Telex: 7167 wgbibl su
V I Lenin State Library of the USSR
Secretary: G A Semenova

Gosudarstvennaya Respublikanskaya biblioteka Gruzinskoi SSR im K **Marksa***, Ketskhoveli ul 5, Tbilisi 380007 Tel: Director's Office 931233/999286
State Republican Karl Marx Library of the Georgian SSR

Gosudarstvennaya biblioteka UzSSR im Alishera **Navoi***, Alleya paradov 5, Tashkent 700000 Tel: 398658/394341/394440/394450
Alisher Navoi State Public Library of the Uzbek SSR

Gosudarstvennaya publichnaya biblioteka im M E **Saltykova-Schedrina***, Sadovaya ul 18, Leningrad D-69 Tel: 152856
M E Saltykov-Shchedrina State Public Library

Tartu Riikliku Ulikooli Teaduslik Raamatukogu*, Toomemägi, 202400 Tartu, Estonian SSR Tel: Tartu 34121/286 Telex: 208010 Nauka
Scientific Library of Tartu State University
Librarian: Laine Peep
Publication: Publicationes bibliothecae universitatis litterarum Tartuensis; Raamataeg-restaureerimine; Teadusliku Raamatukogu töid (serials); Eksliibris TRÜ Teaduslikus Raamatukogus

The Scientific Library of the **Vilnius** Vincas Kapsukas State University*, Universiteto gatve 3, 232633 Vilnius Tel: 26787/26389

Library Associations

Council on Libraries of the **Academy** of Sciences of the USSR*, Prospect Leninsky 14, Moscow
Academy Chairman: P N Fedoseev

U S S R Library Council*, The Lenin State Library of the USSR, Prospect Kalinina 3, Moscow 101000 Telex: 7167 wgbibl su Tel: 2024656/2228551
President: Professor N M Sikorsky;

Executive Secretary: G A Semenova
Publications: Bibliotekar (Librarian);
Sovetskoje bibliotekovedonie (Former:
Biblioteki SSSR) (Soviet Library Science);
Nauchnye i tekhnicheskie biblioteki SSSR
(Scientific and Technical Libraries of the
USSR); *Nauchnaya i tekhnicheskaya
informatsiya* (Scientific and Technical
Information) *Seriya I:* Organizatsiya i
metodika informatsionnoi raboty
(Organisation and Methodology of
Information Work) *Seriya 2:*
Informatsionnye processy i systemy
(Information Processes and Systems);
Sovetskaya Bibliografia (Soviet
Bibliography); *Bibliotekovedenie i
bibliografiya za rubezhom* (Librarianship
and Bibliography Abroad); *Kniga
Issledovaniya i materialy* (Book Studies and
Materials); *V mire knig* (In the World of
Books); *Knizhnoe obozrenie* (Book
Reviews); *Informatika* (Information Science)
Bibliotekovedenie i Bibliografovedenie
Bibliograficheskaya informatsiya
(a) Sovetskaya literatura (b) Inostrannaya
literatura (Library Science and Theory of
Bibliography, Bibliographic Information
(a) Soviet Literature (b) Foreign
Literature;Bibliotekovedenie i
Bibliografovedenie (Library Science and
Theory of Bibliography) (a) Nauchnyi
Referativnyi Sbornik (Abstracts Collection)
(b) Obzornaya informatsiya (Survey
Information) (c) Express-informatsiya
(Express-Information)

Library Reference Books and Journals

Books

*Bibliotekovedenie i bibliografiya za
rubezhom* (Librarianship and Bibliography
Abroad), USSR Library Council, The Lenin
State Library of the USSR, Prospect
Kalinina 3, Moscow 101 000

*Bibliotekovedenie i Bibliografovedenie,
Bibliograficheskaya informatsiya* (Library
Science and Theory of Bibliography,
Bibliographie Information), USSR Library
Council, The Lenin State Library of the
USSR, Prospect Kalinina 3, Moscow 101
000

Libraries in the USSR, Clive Bingley Ltd,
16 Pembridge Rd, London W11, UK

Nauchnye i tekhnicheskie biblioteki SSSR
(Scientific and Technical Libraries of the
USSR), USSR Library Council, The Lenin
State Library of the USSR, Prospect
Kalinina 3, Moscow 101 000

Journals

Bibliotekar (The Librarian), USSR Library
Council, The Lenin State Library of the
USSR, Prospect Kalinina 3, Moscow 101
000

Sovetskoje bibliotekovedenie (Soviet Library
Science), USSR Library Council, The Lenin
State Library of the USSR, Prospect
Kalinina 3, Moscow 101 000

Literary Associations and Societies

U S S R Union of Writers*, Vorovskogo ul
52, Moscow
First Secretary of the Board: Professor K A
Fedin

Publications: Voprosy Literatury (jointly
with the Institute of World Literature of the
USSR Academy of Sciences); *Soviet
Literature, Literaturnaya Gazeta,
Literaturnaya Rossiya, Neva, Novyi Mir*

Literary Periodicals

Culture and Life (text in English, French,
German, Russian and Spanish), Union of
Soviet Societies for Friendship and Cultural
Relations with Foreign Countries, proezd
Sapunova 13-15, Moscow-Centre

Litaratura i Mastatstva (Literature and Art),
Ministerstva Kul'tury i Sayuz Pismennikaw
BSSR, Zakharava ul 19, Minsk

Literaturnaya Gazeta (Literary Newspaper),
USSR Union of Writers, Vorovskogo ul 52,
Moscow

Literaturnaya Rossiya (Literary Russia),
USSR Union of Writers, Vorovskogo ul 52,
Moscow

Molodaya Gvardiya (The Young Guards),
Vsesoyuznyi Leninskii Kommunisticheskii
Soyuz Molodozhi, Tsentral'nyi Komitet,
Sushchevskaya ul 21, Moscow A-55

Moskva; literary magazine, Arbart 20,
Moscow

Neva, USSR Union of Writers, Vorovskogo
ul 52, Moscow

Novyi Mir (New World); literary, artistic
and socio-political journal, USSR Union of
Writers, Vorovskogo ul 52, Moscow

Radyans'ke Literaturoznavstvo (Soviet
Literary Studies), Akademiya Nauk
Ukrayinskoyi SSR, Instytut Literatury im T
H Shevchenka ta Spilka Pys'mennykiv
Ukrayiny, Kirova 4, Kiev

Russian Literature, North-Holland
Publishing Co, PO Box 211, Amsterdam,
Netherlands

Russian Literature Triquarterly, Ardis
Publishers, 2901 Heatherway, Ann Arbor,
Mich 48104, USA

Russkaya Literatura (Russian Literature),
Nauka (Science Publishing House),
Podsosenskii pereulok 21, Moscow K-62
(journal of the Institute of Russian
Literature of the USSR)

Soviet Literature (editions in English,
German, Polish, Spanish, Japanese and
Czech), USSR Union of Writers,
Vorovskogo ul 52, Moscow

V Mire Knig (In the World of Books),
USSR Library Council, The Lenin State
Library of the USSR, Prospect Kalinina 3,
Moscow 101 000

Voprosy Literatury (Questions of
Literature), USSR Union of Writers,
Vorovskogo ul 52, Moscow

Literary Prizes

Belinsky Prize*
For the best works of literary criticism and
theory and history of literature. Awarded
annually. Enquiries to Academy of Sciences
of the USSR, Division of Literature and
Linguistics, Volkhonka 1812, Moscow

United Arab Emirates

General Information

Language: Arabic (English used in business)
Religion: Muslim
Population: 236,000
Bank Hours: Abu Dhabi: 0800-1200
Saturday-Wednesday; 0800-1100 Thursday.
Northern Emirates: 0800-1200 Saturday-
Thursday
Shop Hours: Abu Dhabi: Summer: 0800-
1300, 1600-dusk Saturday-Thursday; Winter:
0800-1300, 1530-1900 Saturday-Thursday.
Northern Emirates: Summer: 0900-1300,
1630-2000 or 2100 Saturday-Thursday;
Winter: 0900-1300, 1600-2000 or 2100
Saturday-Thursday
Currency: 100 fils = 1 dirham
Export/Import Information: No tariff on
books or advertising matter, except 3% duty
on imports by sea, 2% by air in Dubai; 1%
ad valorem in Ras al Khaimah and 2% ad
valorem in Sharjah. No import licence
required except for obscene publications in
Dubai

Major Booksellers

Family Bookshop*, PO Box 956 Abdu
Dhabi Tel: 45702 Cable Add: Fambooks

Tahseen S **Khayat***, PO Box 857, Abdu
Dhabi Tel: 41853

Major Libraries

Centre for Documentation and Research*,
Old Palace, PO Box 2380, Abu Dhabi
Dir: Mohammad Morsi Abdullah PhD
Publication: Arabian Gulf Research Review
(quarterly)

United Kingdom

General Information

Language: English
Religion: Protestant
Population: 56 million
Bank Hours: 0930-1530 Monday-Friday
Shop Hours: Generally 0900-1730 Monday-
Saturday. Early closing one day week
usually.
Currency: 100 pence = 1 pound sterling
Export/Import Information: No tariffs on
books; advertising matter dutiable over $2^{1}/_{4}$
lb gross weight. No import licences required;
nominal exchange controls. Advertising in
UK is regulated by statutes and voluntary
codes; for information contact Advertising
Standards Authority Ltd, 15 Ridgmount St,
London WC1
Copyright: UCC, Berne, Florence (see
International section)

Book Trade Organizations

Advisory Committee on the Selection of Low-Priced Books for Overseas, c/o The British Council, 10 Spring Gardens, London SW1A 2BN Tel: (01) 930 8466
Secretary: J C Bayliss

Antiquarian Booksellers' Association, 154 Buckingham Palace Rd, London SW1 Tel: (01) 730 9273
Secretary: Cynthia Bonham-Carter

Association of Authors' Agents, 10 Buckingham Street, London WC2N 6BU Tel: (01) 839 2556
President: Michael Sissons
Secretary: Deborah Rogers

Association of British Directory Publishers, Windsor Court, East Grinstead Ho, East Grinstead, West Sussex RH19 1XA
Chairman: John Dawson *Hon Secretary:* R Duncombe

Association of Learned & Professional Society Publishers, c/o R J Millson, Institution of Mechanical Engineers, 1 Birdcage Walk, London SW1H 9JJ Tel: (01) 839 1211

Association of Mail Order Publishers, 1 New Burlington St, London W1X 1FD Tel: (01) 437 0706
Dir: D R Vickers

Association of Publishers' Educational Representatives
Secretary: John Sayer, 7 Westbury Rd, St Ives, Cambs Tel: St Ives 68364 (STD code 0480)

B A S H, see Booksellers' Association Service House

B O D, see Booksellers' Orders Distribution

Book Centre*, Southport PR9 8LA Tel: Southport 26881/24331 (STD code 0704) Telex: 67457
London Sales Office, North Circular Rd, London NW10 0JE Tel: (01) 459 1222
Man Dir: Anthony del Tufo

The **Book Marketing** Council, 19 Bedford Sq, London WC1B 3HJ Tel: (01) 580 6321/5
Chairman: Charles Clark
Dir: Nigel Sisson
A new home trade division of the Publishers Association, working to promote and expand sales of books in the home market

Book Publishers' Representatives' Association
Honorary Secretary: David Oliphant, 74a Grosvenor Rd, Caversham, Reading RG4 0ES Tel: Reading 475254 (STD code 0734)

Book Tokens Ltd, 152 Buckingham Palace Rd, London SW1W 9TZ
Secretary: J S Crowe

Book Trade Benevolent Society*, Dillon Lodge, The Booksellers Retreat, Kings Langley, Herts WD4 8LT Tel: Kings Langley 63128
Secretary: Ann Brown

Booksellers Association of Great Britain and Ireland, 154 Buckingham Palace Rd, London SW1W 9TZ Tel: (01) 730 8214
Membership Secretary: M J Bedford
Publications: List of Members, Directory of British Publishers, Directory of Book Wholesalers (temporarily out of print), *Trade Reference Book, Charter Group Economic Survey, Opening a Bookshop,* and other books, lists and directories relating to the bookselling trade

Booksellers Association Service House Ltd (BASH), is the distribution and marketing agency of the Booksellers' Association (at the same address)

Booksellers' Order Distribution Ltd (BOD), 4 Grosvenor Rd, Aldershot, Hants GU11 1DS Tel: Aldershot 20697 (STD Code 0252)

Educational Publishers' Council, 19 Bedford Sq, London WC1B 3HJ Tel: (01) 580 6321/5
Dir: John R M Davies

I B I S, see International Book Information Services

Independent Publishers Guild
Secretary: Rosemary Pettit, 52 Chepstow Rd, London W2 Tel: (01) 727 0919

International Book Information Services*, Waterside, Lowbell Lane, London Colney, St Albans, Herts AL2 1DX Tel: St Albans 25209 (STD code 0727)
Operates a questionnaired computerized mailing list of academics, schools, libraries, booksellers, worldwide

National Federation of Retail Newsagents, 2 Bridewell Pl, London EC4 6AR Tel: (01) 353 6816

P I C S (Publishers' Information Card Services), IBIS Ltd, Waterside, Lowbell Lane, London Colney, St Albans, Herts AL2 1DX Tel: St Albans 25209 (STD code 0727)
Man Dir: Philip J Sturrock
Direct mail promotion for publishers

Printing and Publishing Industry Training Board, Merit Ho, Edgware Rd, London NW9 5AG Tel: (01) 205 0162
Secretary: George Reid

Publishers Association, 19 Bedford Sq, London WC1B 3HJ Tel: (01) 580 6321/5
Chief Executive: C Bradley

Publishers/Booksellers Delivery Service (PBDS)*, PO Box 30, North Circular Rd, London NW10 0JE Tel: (01) 459 1222

Publishers' Overseas Circle
Chairman: Nicholas Battle, Octopus Books, 59 Grosvenor St, London W1

Publishers Publicity Circle, c/o J M Dent & Sons Ltd, Aldine Ho, 33 Welbeck St, London W1M 8LX
Publications: Directory of members

Retail Book, Stationery and Allied Trades Employers' Association*, 7 Grape St, London WC2 Tel: (01) 836 4897

Retail Bookselling and Stationery Wages Council (Great Britain), 12 St James's Square, London SW1Y 4LL Tel: (01) 214 6573

School Bookshop Association, 7 Albemarle St, London W1X 4BB Tel: (01) 493 9001
School Bookshop Officer: Angie Gibbons
Publication: School Bookshop News

Scottish General Publishers' Association, 25a South West Thistle St La, Edinburgh EH2 1EW Tel: (031) 225 5795
Administrative Executive: Janis G Fox

Chairman: Norman Wilson; *Secretary:* Bill Campbell
Publications: New Books from Scottish Publishers (quarterly)

Society of Authors, 84 Drayton Gardens, London SW10 9SD
General Secretary: David Machin
Publication: The Author (quarterly)

The **Society of Indexers***
Secretary: J Ainsworth Gordon, 28 Johns Ave, London NW4 4EN Tel: (01) 203 0929
Publication: The Indexer

Society of Young Publishers, c/o Sarah Rae-Scott, The Bookseller, 12 Dyott St, London WC1A 1DF
Membership Secretary: John Doyle, ITV Books Ltd, 247 Tottenham Court Rd, London W1P 0AU Tel: (01) 636 3666
Publication: Inprint (monthly)

Standard Book Numbering Agency Ltd, 12 Dyott St, London WC1A 1DF Tel: (01) 836 8911
Parent Company: J Whitaker & Sons Ltd, UK (qv)

Union of Welsh Publishers and Booksellers*, c/o Welsh Books Council, Queen's Sq, Aberystwyth, Dyfed, Wales

Welsh Books Council (Cyngor Llyfrau Cymraeg), Queen's Sq, Aberystwyth, Dyfed, Wales Tel: Aberystwyth 4151/3 (STD code 0970)

Book Trade Reference Books and Journals

Books

The British Book Trade, a Bibliographical Guide, André Deutsch Ltd, 105 Great Russell St, London WC1B 3LJ

The British Library General Catalogue of Printed Books to 1975 (first volumes of total estimated 360 published 1979, completion due 1984); Clive Bingley Ltd, 1-19 New Oxford St, London WC1A 1NE

British Official Publications, Pergamon Press Ltd, Headington Hill Hall, Oxford OX3 0BW

Cassell's Directory of Publishing in Great Britain, the Commonwealth, Ireland and South Africa, Cassell & Co Ltd, 35 Red Lion Sq, London WC1R 4SG

Current British Directories; a guide to the directories published in Great Britain, Ireland, the British Commonwealth and South Africa, CBD Research Ltd, 154 High St, Beckenham BR3 1EA

Dealers in Books: a Directory of Dealers in Secondhand and Antiquarian Books in the British Isles, Sheppard Press Ltd, 15 James St, London WC2E 8BX

Directory of Book Wholesalers, Booksellers Association of Great Britain and Ireland, 154 Buckingham Palace Rd, London SW1W 9TZ

Paperbacks in Print, J Whitaker & Sons Ltd, 12 Dyott St, London WC1A 1DF

Picture Research Handbook, Samuel Smiles Ho, 11 Granville Park, London SE13 7DY

Publishing and Bookselling, Jonathan Cape Ltd, 30 Bedford Sq, London WC1B 3EL

UNITED KINGDOM

Trade Reference Book, Booksellers Association of Great Britain and Ireland, 154 Buckingham Palace Rd, London SW1W 9TZ

Writer's and Artist's Yearbook, A & C Black Ltd, 35 Bedford Row, London WC1R 4JH

Journals

Antiquarian Book Monthly Review, 3 Brayfield Ho, Cold Brayfield, Nr Olney, Bucks

The Author, Society of Authors, 84 Drayton Gardens, London SW10 9SD

Book Exchange, Fudge & Co Ltd, Sardinia Ho, 52 Lincolns Inn Fields, London WC2A 3NW

Book Market; for antiquarian and out-of-print books, Clique Ltd, 75 World's End Rd, Handsworth Wood, Birmingham B20 2NS Tel: (021) 554 7308

Bookdealer, Fudge & Co Ltd, Sardinia Ho, 52 Lincolns Inn Fields, London WC2A 3NW

Books from Scotland, Scottish General Publishers' Association, 25 London St, Edinburgh EH3 6LY

Books of the Month and Books To Come, J Whitaker & Sons Ltd, 12 Dyott St, London WC1A 1DF

Bookseller, J Whitaker & Sons Ltd, 12 Dyott St, London WC1A 1DF

Bookselling News, Booksellers' Association of Great Britain and Ireland, 154 Buckingham Palace Rd, London SW1W 9TZ

British Book News, British Council, 65 Davies St, London W1Y 2AA

British Book Production, National Book League, 7 Albemarle St, London W1X 4BB

British Books in Print, J Whitaker & Sons Ltd, 12 Dyott St, London WC1A 1DF

British National Bibliography, British Library, Bibliographic Services Division, 7 Rathbone St, London WC1E 7DG

Children's Books of the Year, National Book League, 7 Albemarle St, London W1X 4BB

Clique; the antiquarian booksellers' medium, Clique Ltd, 75 World's End Rd, Handsworth Wood, Birmingham B20 2NS Tel: (021) 554 7308 *Editor:* Margaret Pamphilon

Directory of British Publishers and their Terms, Booksellers Association of Great Britain and Ireland, 154 Buckingham Palace Rd, London SW1W 9TZ

Gee Report, 15 Hanover Sq, 3rd Floor, London W1

Good Book Guide (quarterly), Braithwaite & Taylor Ltd, PO Box 28, London SW11 4BT

The Indexer, Journal of British, Australian and American Societies of Indexers *Honorary Editor:* Hazel K Bell, 139 The Ryde, Hatfield, Herts AL9 5DP Tel: Hatfield 65201 (STD code 070 72)

List of Members, Booksellers Association of Great Britain and Ireland, 154 Buckingham Palace Rd, London SW1W 9TZ

Llais Llyfrau, Cyngor Llyfrau Cymraeg, Queen's Sq, Aberystwyth, Wales (list of all books published in Welsh during previous 6 months and list of books to be published)

National Newsagent, Bookseller, Stationer (weekly), National Newsagent Ltd, Lennox Ho, Norfolk St, London WC2

Publishers in the United Kingdom and their Addresses, J Whitaker & Sons Ltd, 12 Dyott St, London WC1A 1DF

Publishing News, 37-49 Brick St, London W1A 1AN

School Book Review, (half-yearly) Europa Publications Ltd, 18 Bedford Sq, London WC1B 3JN

School Bookshop News, School Bookshop Association, 7 Albermarle St, London W1X 4BB

Smith's Trade News, W H Smith & Son Ltd, Strand Ho, Portugal St, London WC2A 2HS

Whitaker's Cumulative Book List, J Whitaker & Sons Ltd, 12 Dyott St, London, WC1A 1DF

Publishers

A B C D Group, 18 Brewer St, London W1R 4AS Tel: (01) 734 1985/6900
Sales: Michael Hayes
This is the marketing organization for Allison & Busby, Marion Boyars, John Calder, Davis Poynter (see individual entries for further details)

Abacus, an imprint of Sphere Books Ltd, (qv)
ISBN Publisher's Prefix: 0-349

Abacus Press+, Abacus Ho, Speldhurst Rd, Tunbridge Wells, Kent TN4 0HU Tel: Tunbridge Wells 29783/27237 (STD code 0892) Cable Add: Abacus Tunbridge Wells Telex: 95652
Man Dir, Publisher: N A Jaysekera; *Editorial:* C J Rivington; *Sales, Rights & Permissions:* Mrs J M White; *Publicity:* Mrs A Terry
Associate Company: Abacus Kent Ltd
Subjects: Medicine, Science, Technology, Engineering, Mathematics, Computer Sciences, Architecture, Design, Travel Guides, Agriculture, Environmental Sciences, Health Books for Lay Readers, Crafts
1977: 22 titles *1978:* 14 titles *Founded:* 1971
ISBN Publisher's Prefix: 0-85626

Abbey, an imprint of Murrays Remainder Books (qv)

Abelard-Schuman Ltd+, Furnival Ho, 14/18 High Holborn, London WC1 Tel: (01) 242 5832
Man Dir: R Michael Miller; *Editorial:* Rosemary Creek, Olga Norris, A D Mitchell; *Sales Manager:* Geoff Meakin; *Publicity:* Patsy Irwin; *Rights & Permissions:* Roseanne Holme
Parent Company: Blackie & Son Ltd (qv)
Imprints: include Grasshopper Books
Subjects: Children's Books
1978: 31 titles *1979:* 39 titles *Founded:* 1958
ISBN Publisher's Prefix: 0-200

Aberdeen University Press Ltd, see Pergamon Press Ltd

Abson Books+, Abson, Wick, Bristol BS15 5TT Tel: Abson 2446 (STD code 027582)
Partners: Anthea Bickerton, Pat McCormack
Subjects: Language Glossaries, Cookery, Regional Eating Out Guides, Sports, Humour, Gardening, Local Bristol & Bath books
ISBN Publisher's Prefix: 0-902920

Academic Press Inc (London) Ltd+, 24-28 Oval Rd, London NW1 7DX Tel: (01) 267 4466 Cable Add: Acadinc London NW1 Telex: 25775
Shipping Add: High St, Footscray, Sidcup, Kent
Man Dir & Editorial: R A Farrand; *Marketing Dir:* A J Cornwall; *Promotions Manager:* D C Sanderson; *Advertising Manager, Rights & Permissions:* P A Spencer
Parent Company: Academic Press Inc, 111 Fifth Ave, New York, NY 10003, USA
Subsidiary Companies: Johnson Reprint Co Ltd, UK; Harcourt Brace Jovanovich Ltd, UK (qv)
Associate Companies: Harcourt Brace Jovanovich Group (Australia) Pty Ltd, Australia (qv); Grune & Stratton Inc and Johnson Reprint Corporation (both at 111 Fifth Ave, New York, NY 10003)
Subjects: Reference, Scientific, Technical, Medicine, Psychology, Social Science, University Textbooks, Educational Materials
1978: 565 titles
ISBN Publisher's Prefixes: 0-12 (Academic Press), 0-15 (Harcourt Brace Jovanovich), 0-8089 (Grune & Stratton), 0-384 (Johnson Reprint).

Academic Publications+, Highfield, Dane Hill, Haywards Heath, Sussex RH17 7EX Tel: Dane Hill 214 (STD code 082573) Cable Add: Copen Telex: 95246 (COPEN-G)
Subjects: University Textbooks, Technical & Scientific, Medical, Philosophy, General Literature
Founded: 1974
ISBN Publisher's Prefix: 0-900307

Academy Editions+, 42 Leinster Gardens, London W2 Tel: (01) 402 2141 Telex: 896928
Man Dir: Dr Andreas C Papadakis; *Sales Manager:* John Rule; *Rights & Permissions, Publicity:* Solveig Williams; *Production:* Richard Kelly
Orders to: Academy Editions, 7/8 Holland St, London W8 Tel: (01) 937 6996
Parent Company: Academy Art Books Ltd (at above address)
Subsidiary Companies: Academy Editions, France (qv); Architectural Design, 42 Leinster Gardens, London W2
Imprint: Alec Tiranti (firm also publishes *Architectural Design* and *Architectural Monographs*)
Subjects: Architecture, Fine and Applied Arts, Photography
Bookshops: Academy Bookshop & London Art Bookshop, 7/8 Holland St, London W8
1977: 50 titles *Founded:* 1967
ISBN Publisher's Prefixes: 0-85670, 0-85458, 0-902620

Actinic Press Ltd, 129 St John's Hill, London SW11 1TD Tel: (01) 228 8091
Subjects: Technical & Scientific, Medical
ISBN Publisher's Prefix: 0-900024

Addison-Wesley Publishers Ltd+, West End Ho, 11 Hills Pl, London W1R 2LR
Tel: (01) 439 2541 Cable Add: Adiwes London W1 Telex: 8811948
Man Dir: Paul R Chapman; *Sales Dir:* Stanley B Malcolm; *Rights & Permissions:* Samuel B Warren
Parent Company: Addison-Wesley Publishing Co Inc, Mass 01867, USA
Associate Companies: Addison-Wesley Publishing Co, Australia (qv); Addison-Wesley (Canada) Ltd, 36 Prince Andrew Pl, Don Mills, Ontario, Canada; Addison-Wesley Publishing Group, Netherlands (qv); Intereditions, Paris, 7 rue Sarrette, 75014, Paris; Addison-Wesley (Singapore) Private Ltd, Singapore (qv); Addison-Wesley Publishing Co Inc, Philippines (qv); Benjamin/Cummings Publishing Co Inc, 2727 Sand Hill Rd, Menlo Park, Calif 94025; Fondo Educativo Interamericano CA, Venezuela (qv); Fondo Educativo Interamericano de Mexico SA, Mexico (qv); W A Benjamin Inc, UK (qv)
Subjects: Reference, Business, Juveniles, Humanities, General & Social Sciences, Textbooks, Educational Materials, Medicine
Founded: 1942
ISBN Publisher's Prefixes: 0-201 (Addison-Wesley), 0-8053 (Benjamin), 0-8465 (Cummings)

Adkinson Parrish Ltd, 49 Great Marlborough St, London W1V 1DB Tel: (01) 434 2617 Cable Add: Macjan Telex: 23168
Chairman: Ronald Whiting; *Man Dir:* Robert Adkinson; *Managing Editor:* Clare Howell
Associate Company: Macdonald & Jane's Publishing Group (qv)
Subjects: General Nonfiction, Biography, History, How-to, Music, Art, Reference, Religion
Miscellaneous: Editorial and production organization producing books for international co-editions

Adlard Coles Ltd, see Granada Publishing

Alex **Aiken**+, 48 Merrycrest Ave, Glasgow G46 6BJ Tel: (041) 637 2438
Principal: Alex Aiken
Subjects: Military and Naval History, Biography, Natural Sciences
1977: 1 *Founded:* 1971
ISBN Publisher's Prefix: 0-9502134

Airlife Publications (Shrewsbury) Ltd, 7 St John's Hill, Shrewsbury, Salop SY1 1JE Tel: Shrewsbury 3651 (STD code 0743)
Man Dir, Rights & Permissions: A D R Simpson; *Editorial, Sales:* C A Nelson
Associate Company: Anthony Nelson Ltd (address as above)

Akros Publications+, Albert Ho, 21 Cropwell Rd, Radcliffe-on-Trent, Nottingham, NG12 2FJ Tel: Radcliffe-on-Trent 4802 (STD code 06073)
Man Dir, Editorial, Production, Publicity, Rights & Permissions: Duncan Glen; *Sales:* Margaret Glen
Subjects: Scottish Poetry and Literary Criticism
1977: 12 titles *1978:* 6 titles *Founded:* 1965

Albyn Press Ltd+, 2 & 3 Abbeymount, Edinburgh EH8 8JH Tel: (031) 661 9339
Man Dir: Charles Skitton
Subjects: Scottish, General, Prints
Miscellaneous: Firm is an allied company of Charles Skilton Ltd, UK (qv)
ISBN Publisher's Prefix: 0-284

Alden & Mowbray Ltd, see A R Mowbray & Co Ltd

Aldine Paperbacks, an imprint of J M Dent & Sons Ltd (qv)

Aldus Books Ltd+*, Aldus Ho, 17 Conway St, London W1P 6BS Tel: (01) 387 2811 Cable Add: Alday London W1 Telex: 261675
Chairman: John T Sargent; *Man Dir:* Wolfgang Foges; *Dirs:* Nelson Doubleday, Miss Frame-Smith, D H Bekhor; *Editorial:* John Mason; *European Sales Manager:* Florence Robbins
Subject: General Nonfiction
1977: approx 17 titles
ISBN Publisher's Prefix: 0-490

Aldwych Press, 3 Henrietta St, London WC2E 8LU Tel: (01) 240 0856
Man Dir, Rights & Permissions: Danny Maher; *Editorial:* Robert Haggelstein; *Sales, Publicity:* Jessica Kingsley
Associate Company: Eurospan Ltd (at above address)
Subjects: Academic, Library Science, Sociology, Economics, Politics
1979: 4 titles *Founded:* 1979
ISBN Publisher's Prefix: 0-86172

Alison Press, an associate of Secker & Warburg (qv)

Ian **Allan** Ltd+, Terminal Ho, Shepperton, Middx TW17 8AS Tel: Walton-on-Thames 28950 (STD Code 09322) Cable Add: Ianallanshepp Telex: 929806
Chairman & Man Dir: Ian Allan; *Editorial:* A Hollingsworth; *Sales:* Richard Fagge; *Production:* R Dymott; *Rights & Permissions:* Richard Fagge, R Dymott
Parent Company: Ian Allan (Group) Ltd
Associated Companies: A Lewis (Masonic Publishers) Ltd; Locomotive Publishing Co Ltd; Modern Transport Publishing Co Ltd; Railway Publications Ltd; Railway World Ltd
Imprints: Ian Allan, A Lewis, Modern Transport
Subjects: Transport, Travel, Aviation, Militaria
1977: 93 titles *1978:* 98 titles *Founded:* 1945
ISBN Publisher's Prefix: 0-7110

Philip **Allan** Publishers Ltd+, Market Pl, Deddington, Oxford OX5 4SE Tel: Deddington 38652 (STD code 0869)
Man Dir, Editorial: Philip Allan
Subjects: University & College Textbooks in Economics, Accounting and Business Studies
1977: 6 titles *1978:* 6 titles *Founded:* 1973
ISBN Publisher's Prefix: 0-86003

J A **Allen** & Co Ltd+, 1 Lower Grosvenor Pl, London SW1W 0EL Tel: (01) 834 5606/7 Cable Add: Allenbooks London
Sales Dir: C Kendall; *Publicity & Advertising:* Mrs E Martyn; *Rights & Permissions:* J A Allen
Associated Company: Sporting Book Centre Inc, New York, USA
Br Off: D M S Bldg, Sheldon Way, New Hythe Lane, Larkfield, Maidstone, Kent
Subject: Horsemanship, Horses & Horse Sports
Book Club: Horseman's Bookclub

Bookshop: The Horseman's Bookshop, 1 Lower Grosvenor Pl, London SW1
Subsidiary: The Caduceus Press, Sporting Book Services, Both as 1 Lower Grosvenor Pl, London SW1
1977: 22 titles *1978:* 15 titles *Founded:* 1926
ISBN Publisher's Prefix: 0-85131

W H **Allen** & Co Ltd+, 44 Hill St, London W1X 8LB Tel: (01) 493 6777 Cable Add: Wyndhoward London Telex: 28117
Man Dir: Francis Bennett; *Marketing Dir:* Gordon Rae; *Sales Dir:* Michael Beattie; *Editorial:* Judith Burnley, Robert Postema; *Publicity & Advertising:* Robert Dirskovski; *Rights & Permissions:* Robert Harvey
Orders to: Tiptree Book Services Ltd, Tiptree, Colchester, Essex CO5 0SR
Parent Company: Howard & Wyndham Ltd
Associate Companies: Brown Watson Ltd; Murrays Remainder Books; The Grant Educational Co Ltd
Subsidiary Companies: Allan Wingate (Publishers) Ltd (qv), Wyndham Publications Ltd (qv), Tandem Publishing Ltd (qv)
Imprints: W H Allen, Made Simple Books, Star, Target, Wingate
Br Offs: W H Allen & Co Ltd, 20 Upper Merrion St, Dublin; W H Allen Publishing Inc, 260 Madison Ave, New York, NY 10016
Subjects: Belles Lettres, Poetry, Biography, History, How-to, Reference, Juveniles, Paperbacks, Social Science, Primary & Secondary Textbooks
1977: 400 titles *1978:* 350 titles *Founded:* 1780
ISBN Publisher's Prefixes: 0-352 (Star), 0-491 (W H Allen), 0-85523 (Allan Wingate), 0-426 (Target)

George **Allen** & Unwin (Publishers) Ltd+, 40 Museum St, London WC1A 1LU Tel: (01) 405 8577 Cable Add: Deucalion London WC1
Shipping Add: United Cargo Containers, Thameside Industrial Estate, Silvertown, London E16
Chairman: Rayner Unwin; *Publicity Manager:* Christine King; *Home Sales Manager:* Colin Robb; *Sales Development Manager:* Martin Blackman; *College Sales Manager:* Mike Clancy; *Export Sales Manager:* Mark Streatfeild; *Production:* Laurie Pine; *Foreign Rights Manager:* Alina Dadlez
Sales, Distribution, Accounts & Publicity Off: PO Box 18, Park Lane, Hemel Hempstead, Herts Tel: Hemel Hempstead 3244 (STD Code 0442) Telex: 826261
Subsidiary Companies: George Allen & Unwin (Australia) Ltd; Allen & Unwin Inc, USA; Thomas Murby Ltd (qv)
Subjects: Belles Lettres, Biography, History, Art, Philosophy, Oriental Religions, Juveniles, Psychology, Natural & Social Science, Economics, Management, Travel, University & Secondary Textbooks
1977: 130 titles *1978:* 150 titles *Founded:* 1914
ISBN Publisher's Prefix: 0-04

Allison & Busby Ltd+, 6a Noel St, London W1V 3RB Tel: (01) 734 1498
Dirs: Clive Allison, Margaret Busby
Subjects: General Fiction, Belles Lettres, Music, Art, Biography, History, Political & Social Science, Economics, Juveniles
1978: approx 40 titles *1979:* approx 50 titles *Founded:* 1968
Imprints: Alternative Editions, Motive
ISBN Publisher's Prefix: 0-85031

Allman & Son (Publishers) Ltd, see Mills & Boon Ltd

Almark Publishing Co Ltd*, 49 Malden Way, New Malden, Surrey KT3 6EA Tel: (01) 942 9241
Subjects: Military, Naval, Railway, Transport History, Reference
ISBN Publisher's Prefix: 0-85524

Alphabet & Image Ltd, Manor Farm, Caundle Marsh, Sherborne, Dorset DT9 5LX Tel: Bishop's Caundle 588 (STD Code 096 323) Cable Add: Alphabook Sherborne Telex: 46534 Alphab G
Man Dir, Production: A E Birks-Hay; *Editorial:* M L Birks-Hay
Subsidiary Company: Alphabooks (illustrated co-editions)
Imprint: Alphabooks
Br Off: 63a Lancaster Grove, London NW3
Subjects: Co-editions on Crafts, Fine Arts, Architecture, Horticulture, Archaeology, History, Sport
1977: 12 titles *1978:* 10 titles *Founded:* 1972

Alpine Books, an imprint of Everest Books Ltd (qv)

Alternative Editions, an imprint of Allison & Busby Ltd (qv)

Althea's Pet Series, an imprint of Dinosaur Publications Ltd (qv)

American University Publishers Group Ltd, 1 Gower St, London WC1 E6HA Tel: (01) 580 3994 Cable Add: Amunpress
Man Dir: John Dawson; *Sales Manager:* P Chapman; *Publicity:* J Browning
Subjects: Belles Lettres, Poetry, Biography, History, Music, Art, Philosophy, Reference, Religion, High-priced Paperbacks, Medicine, Psychology, General & Social Science
Founded: 1965
Miscellaneous: Group includes University of Alabama Press, University of Illinois Press, Indiana University Press, University of Missouri Press, University of Nebraska Press, University of Notre Dame Press, Pennsylvania State University Press, Texas A & M University Press, University of Texas Press, University of Washington Press, University of Wisconsin Press

Ampersand Ltd*, 504 Victoria Ho, Southampton Row, London WC1 Tel: (01) 242 3202
Subjects: Politics, Political Economy, Sociology, Questions of the Day
ISBN Publisher's Prefix: 0-903328

Anchor, an imprint of Doubleday & Co Inc (qv)

Andersen Press Ltd, 3 Fitzroy Sq, London W1P 6JD Tel: (01) 387 2888 Cable Add: Literarius London W1 Telex: 261212
Man Dir, Editorial: Klaus Flugge; *Sales:* Robert Hyde; *Publicity, Rights & Permissions:* Audrey Adams
Associated Company: Hutchinson Publishing Group
Subjects: Children's Books
1977: 25 titles *1978:* 26 titles *Founded:* 1975
ISBN Publisher's Prefix: 0-905478

Andrew Publishing Co+*, 61 St John St, London EC1M 2AN Tel: (01) 251 3494/3531
Man Dir: John Philipps; *Editorial, Sales, Production, Promotion, Rights & Permissions:* E Kent
Parent Company: Henderson Philipps & Partners Ltd

Associate Company: Cobham Numismatic Ltd
Subject: Numismatics
1976: 3 titles *1977:* 9 titles *Founded:* 1967
ISBN Publisher's Prefix: 0-903681

Angus & Robertson (UK) Ltd+, 10 Earlham St, London WC2H 9LP Tel: (01) 240 2935 Cable Add: Ausboko Telex: 897284 arpubg
Man Dir: David Harris; *Sales Manager:* Bob Siwecki; *Publicity and Promotions Manager:* Alan Greene; *Rights & Permissions:* Gwenda Jarred
Orders to: Tiptree Book Services Ltd, Tiptree, Colchester, Essex CO5 0SR
Parent Company: Angus & Robertson Publishers, Australia (qv)
Subjects: General Fiction & Nonfiction, Biography, Beauty & Health, Autobiography, Cookery, Craft, Natural History, Poetry, Sports & Outdoor Games, Children's Books
1978: 50 titles *Founded:* 1884
ISBN Publisher's Prefix: 0-207

The **Appletree** Press Ltd+, 7 James St South, Belfast BT2 7DL Tel: Belfast 43074 (STD code 0232)
Man Dir: J D Murphy; *Publicity Dir:* D Marshall; *Rights & Permissions:* D Webster
Subjects: Belles Lettres, Poetry, History, Music, Art, Juveniles, Low- & High-priced Paperbacks, Educational Materials, Photography, Fishing, Guide Books
1977: 9 titles *1978:* 8 titles *Founded:* 1974
ISBN Publisher's Prefix: 0-904651

Applied Science Publishers Ltd+, Ripple Rd, Barking, Essex Tel: (01) 595 2121 Cable Add: Elsbark Barking
Man Dir, Overseas Sales: Leslie E Rayner; *Editorial, Rights & Permissions:* George Olley; *Production:* Alan Chesterton; *UK Sales:* Clive Rayner; *Promotions Manager:* Robert Young
Parent Company: NV Uitgeversmaatschappij Elsevier, Netherlands (qv)
Imprints: Include C R Books, MacLaren & Sons Ltd
Subjects: Agriculture, Architectural Science, Building, Civil Engineering, Bakery, Materials Science, Chemistry, Chemical Engineering, Mechanical Engineering, Environmental Science, Food Technology, Petroleum Technology, Plastics & Rubber, Dictionaries
1977: 46 titles *1978:* 50 titles *Founded:* 1936
Miscellaneous: Publish journals covering agriculture, food technology, applied energy, conservation, pollution, plastics, acoustics, material science associates, mechanical engineering
ISBN Publisher's Prefix: 0-85334

Aquaran Press Ltd, an imprint of Thorsons Publishers Ltd (qv)

Aquila Publishing+, PO Box 1, Portree, Isle of Skye IV51 9BT Tel: Sligachan 257 (STD code 047 852)
Chairman, Man Dir, Editorial, Production: James Green; *Sales:* A Johnston; *Publicity, Rights & Permissions:* A Green
Associate companies: Johnston Green & Co (Publishers) Ltd, 27 Hamilton Dr, Glasgow G12; Wayzgoose Press
Subsidiary Company: The Phaethon Press; Prospice
Imprints: Aquila/The Phaethon Press, Prospice, Aquila/The Wayzgoose Press
Subjects: Literature, Cookery, Ecology, Poetry, Critical Studies

Bookshop: address as above
1977: 47 titles *1978:* 12 titles *Founded:* 1968
ISBN Publisher's Prefixes: 0-903226, 0-7275

Architectural Press Ltd+*, 9 Queen Anne's Gate, London SW1H 9BY Tel: (01) 930 0611 Cable Add: Buildable London SW1
Book Publishing Dir: Godfrey Golzen; *Man Dir:* Michael Regan; *Senior Editor:* Alexandra Artley; *Trade Manager:* Alan Mason; *Marketing Manager:* Janet Pilch; *Production:* Keith Kneebone; *Rights & Permissions:* Caroline Nelson
Subsidiary Company and Imprint: Astragal Books
Subjects: Architecture, High-priced Paperbacks, Urban Planning, Reference, University Textbooks, Energy Conservation
1976: 30 titles *1977:* 35 titles *Founded:* 1895
ISBN Publisher's Prefix: 0-85139

The **Archon** Press Ltd, 70 Old Compton St, London W1V 5PA Tel: (01) 734 5186 Cable Add: Archon London Telex: 21115
Man Dir: Charles V Nicholas; *Production Manager:* Sue Glover; *Foreign Rights:* Lynn Lockett
Parent Company: Grampian Holdings Ltd
Subjects: Juveniles, Co-editions
1977: 21 titles *1978:* 23 titles *Founded:* 1973

Arena, an imprint of Inter-Varsity Press (qv)

Argus Books Ltd*, Argus Ho, 14 St James Rd, Watford, Herts Tel: Watford 47281/2 (STD code 0923)
Man & Sales Dir: H Ricketts
Associate Company: Wayland Publishers Ltd (qv)
Imprints: Fountain Press; Model & Allied Publications; Harleyford Publications; Bellona Publications
Subjects: Hobbies, Photography, Technical
Miscellaneous: Firm is a subsidiary of Argus Press Ltd
ISBN Publisher's Prefixes: 0-85242, 085344

Argus Communications (UK Division)*, Plumpton Ho, Plumpton Rd, Hoddesdon, Herts EN11 0LB Tel: Hoddesdon 43434/5 (STD code 09924) Telex: 262284
General Manager: Richard De Rosa; *Marketing Manager:* James Forman
Parent Company: DLM Inc, 7440 Natchex Ave, Niles, Illinois 60648, USA
Subjects: Religion, Popular Psychology, Education
1977: 48 titles *Founded:* (UK) 1975
ISBN Publisher's Prefix: 0-913592

Aris & Phillips Ltd*, Teddington Ho, Warminster, Wilts BA12 8PQ Tel: Warminster 213409 (STD CCooode 0985)
Shipping Add: Obelisk Ho, Church St, Warminster, Wilts
Man Dir: Adrian Phillips; *Editorial:* John Aris; *Sales, Publicity, Rights & Permissions:* Lucinda Phillips; *Production:* Michael Coultas
Associate Companies: La Haule Books Ltd, West Lodge, La Haule, Jersey, Channel Islands; Serindia Publications, 10 Parkfields, Putney, London SW15
Br Off: Anthony Aris, 10 Parkfields, Putney, London SW15 Tel: (01) 788 1966; John Aris, 11 Halkin Place, London SW1
Subjects: Ancient History, Oriental, Classical, Middle East, Archaeology
1977: 8 titles *Founded:* 1972
ISBN Publisher's Prefix: 0-85668

Ark, an imprint of Scripture Union (qv)

Arlington Books (Publishers) Ltd, 3 Clifford St, Mayfair, London W1X 1RA Tel: (01) 439 1688
Chairman, Man Dir: Desmond Elliott; *Rights & Permissions Dir:* Christine Lunness; *Sales Dir:* Dallas Manderson; *Production and Editorial:* Angela Dahms
Trade Dept: Biblios Ltd, Glenside Industrial Estate, Partridge Green, Horsham, West Sussex Tel: Horsham 710971 (STD Code 0403)
Subjects: General Fiction and Nonfiction, Health, Biography, Secondary & Primary Textbooks
1977: 20 titles *1978:* 20 titles *Founded:* 1960
ISBN Publisher's Prefix: 0-85140

Armada Books, see William Collins Sons & Co Ltd

Arms & Armour Press, an imprint of Lionel Leventhal Ltd, (qv)

E J **Arnold** & Son Ltd+, Butterley St, Leeds LS10 1AX Tel: Leeds 442944 (STD Code 0532) Cable Add: Arnold Leeds
Telex: 556347
Man Dir: E M Arnold; *Editorial:* S D L Keating; *Sales, Rights & Permissions:* Brian Green; *Production:* D R Shenton; *Publicity:* Mrs P Jackson
Subjects: Primary & Secondary Educational Books, Language kits, Audio Visual Material, Educational Supplies
1977: 18 titles *Founded:* 1863
ISBN Publisher's Prefix: 0-560

Edward **Arnold** (Publishers) Ltd+, 41 Bedford Sq, London WC1B 3DQ Tel: (01) 637 7161 Cable Add: Scholarly London W1
Chairman & Man Dir: Anthony Hamilton; *Sales:* George Davies, Peter Moran; *Production:* Robin Smeeton; *Publicity:* Jane Oakley; *Rights & Permissions:* Arlene Seaton
Subsidiary Company: Edward Arnold (Australia) Pty Ltd, Australia (qv)
Br Off: Woodlands Park Ave, Woodlands Park, Maidenhead, Berks (Trade)
Subjects: Humanities, General & Science, Medicine, University & Secondary Textbooks, Technical, Education
1977: 180 titles *1978:* 195 titles
ISBN Publisher's Prefix: 0-7131

Arrow Books Ltd+, 3 Fitzroy Sq, London W1P 6JD Tel: (01) 388 7601
Chairman: R A A Holt; *Man Dir:* Roger Lloyd-Taylor; *Sales:* Richard Tucker; *Editorial:* Terence Blacker
Orders to: Tiptree Book Services, Church Rd, Tiptree, Nr Colchester, Essex
Subjects: General Fiction & Nonfiction, Paperbacks
Founded: 1948
Miscellaneous: Arrow Books is a Division of The Hutchinson Publishing Group Ltd (qv)
ISBN Publisher's Prefix: 0-09

Artemis Press Ltd, Sedgwick Park, Horsham, Sussex Tel: Lower Beeding 369 (STD code 040376) Cable Add: Artemis Horsham
Man Dir: M T Bizony; *Sales Manager:* A B Simmons
Subsidiary Companies: Riband Books, Sedgwick Park, Horsham, Sussex; New Educational Press (imprint)
Subjects: General Fiction, Belles Lettres, Poetry, History, Music, Art, Philosophy, Reference, High-priced Paperbacks, General Science, Technical, University, Secondary & Primary Textbooks, Educational Materials, Large-type Reprints
Founded: 1955
ISBN Publisher's Prefix: 0-85141

Artists House, an imprint of Mitchell Beazley Marketing Ltd (qv)

Ascent Books Ltd, 49-51 Bedford Row, London WC1V 6RL Tel: (01) 242 7866
Telex: 28413
Man Dir, Editorial, Sales, Production, Rights & Permissions: Christopher Foster; *Publicity:* Louise Hudson
Orders to: George Philip & Son, PO Box 1, Littlehampton, Sussex BN17 7EN
Subject: European History
ISBN Publisher's Prefix: 0-906407

Ashmolean Museum Publications, Ashmolean Museum, Beaumont St, Oxford OX1 2PH Tel: Oxford 511281/57522 (STD code 0865)
Publications Officer: R I H Charlton
Subjects: European & Oriental Art & Archaeology, Numismatics, Classical Studies, Egyptology
1977: 7 titles *1978:* 10 titles
ISBN Publisher's Prefix: 0-900090

Aslan Publishing Services Ltd, see Lion Publishing

Associated Book Publishers Ltd+, 11 New Fetter Lane, London EC4P 4EE Tel: (01) 583 9855 Cable Add: Elegiacs London EC4P 4EE Telex: 263398
Shipping Add: North Way, Andover, Hants
President: M W Maxwell; *Chairman:* P H B Allsop; *Sales Dir:* C H Shirley
See subsidiary company individual entries for further details
Subsidiary Companies: Associated Book Publishers (Aust) Ltd, Australia (qv); Associated Book Publishers (New Zealand) Ltd, New Zealand (qv); Associated Book Publishers (UK) Ltd; Associated Book Publishers (Services) Ltd; Chapman & Hall Ltd (qv); Current Law Publishers Ltd; Eyre & Spottiswoode (Publishers) Ltd (qv); W Green & Son Ltd (qv); Magnum Books (imprint only) (qv); Methuen & Co Ltd (qv); Methuen Children's Books Ltd (qv); Eyre Methuen Ltd; Methuen Educational Ltd; Methuen Paperbacks Ltd; Momentum Licensing Ltd; Police Review Publishing Co Ltd; E & F N Spon Ltd (qv); Stevens & Sons Ltd (qv); Sweet & Maxwell Ltd (qv); Sweet & Maxwell Spon (Booksellers) Ltd; Tavistock Publications Ltd (qv)
Subjects: Legal, Periodicals, Academic & Scientific, Children's, General
Bookshops: Hammicks Bookshops Ltd at Alton, Farnham, Basingstoke, Horsham, London, Southampton, Windsor
1977: 523 titles *1978:* 641 titles *Founded:* 1958

Associated Business Press*, Ludgate Ho, 107-111 Fleet St, London EC4A 2AB Tel: (01) 353 3851 Telex: 917036
Publishing Director: Nicholas Chapman
Subject: Management

Associated University Presses, associate company of Thomas Yoseloff Ltd (qv)

Antony **Atha** Publishers Ltd, Hillmorton Rd, Rugby, Warwickshire CV22 5AN Tel: Rugby 72755 (STD code 0788)
Man Dir: C A Atha
Subjects: Sporting Books, Limited Editions, Educational Materials
1977: 1 title *1978:* 5 titles *Founded:* 1975
ISBN Publisher's Prefix: 0-904475

Athene Publishing Co, an imprint of Thorsons Publishers Ltd (qv)

The **Athlone** Press+, 90-91 Great Russell St, London WC1B 3PY Tel: (01) 580 9535/6 (Shipping Add: Tiptree Book Services Ltd, Tiptree, Colchester, Essex)
Sales Manager: P N Marks; *Rights & Permissions:* Miss S Fairbairn
Parent Company: Bemrose UK Ltd (qv for associate companies)
UK Trade Representation: Constable & Co Ltd, 10 Orange St, London WC2
Subjects: Architecture, Archaeology, Bibliography, Biological Sciences, Chemistry, Ecology, Physics, Astronomy, Computer Science, Economics, Modern & Classical Languages, Belles Lettres, Poetry, Biography, History, Music, Art, Philosophy, Religion, High-priced Paperbacks, Medicine, Engineering, General & Social Science, University & Secondary Textbooks, Law
1977: 16 titles *1978:* 20 titles *Founded:* 1949
ISBN Publisher's Prefix: 0-485

Atlantic, an imprint of Ramboro Enterprises Ltd, UK (qv)

Atlantic Communications Ltd*, 19 Coalecroft Rd, London SW15 Tel: (01) 7892740
Subjects: Contemporary History, Current Affairs, Ecology & the Environment

Augener, an imprint of Stainer & Bell Ltd (qv)

Autobooks Ltd, Golden Lane, Brighton BN1 2QJ Tel: Brighton 721721 (STD code 0273)
Man Dir, Publisher: Kenneth Ball; *Sales Dir:* Stuart C Forbes
Parent Company: Siemssen Hunter Ltd
Subjects: Do-it-Yourself, Car Workshop Manuals
1977: 13 titles *Founded:* 1958
ISBN Publisher's Prefix: 0-85147

Automobile Association+, Fanum Ho, Basingstoke RG21 2EA Tel: Basingstoke 62929 (STD Code 0256) Telex: 858538
Editorial: T E G Davies; *Sales:* Victor Press
Subjects: Tourist Guides, Guidebooks, Maps, Atlases
1978: 12 titles
ISBN Publisher's Prefix: 0-901088

Avebury Publishing Co Ltd, Olympic Ho, 63 Woodside Rd, Amersham, Bucks HP6 5AA Tel: Amersham 22121 (STD code 02403)
Man Dir: J M Dening
Orders to: The Distribution Centre, Blackhorse Rd, Letchworth, Herts SG6 1HN
Imprints: Avebury, Gregg International
Subjects: Scholarly Monographs and Reprints in Humanities, Languages, Philosophy; Business/Professional (publishes some titles in microfiche)
Founded: 1976
ISBN Publisher's Prefixes: 0-86127 (Avebury), 0-576 (Gregg)

B B C Publications, 35 Marylebone High St, London W1M 4AA Tel: (01) 580 5577 Cable Add: Broadcasts London
Telex: 265781
General Manager: J G Holmes; *Head of Exports, Rights:* John Hore; *Circulation Manager:* P G Shaw; *Advertising Dir:* K G Hurst
Orders to: 144/152 Bermondsey St, London SE1 3TH

Subjects: General Fiction, History, How-to, Music, Art, Reference, Religion, Juveniles, Low- & High-priced Paperbacks, Medicine, Engineering, General & Social Science, Secondary Textbooks, Adult Education
Founded: 1925
Bookshops: 35 Marylebone High St, London W1M 4AA; Broadcasting House, Portland Pl, London W1A 1AA; BBC Television Centre, Wood Lane, London W12 7RJ
ISBN Publisher's Prefix: 0-563

B C W Publishing Ltd+, 177A High St, Ryde, Isle of Wight, PO33 2HW Tel: Ryde 67427/8 (STD Code 0983) Cable Add: Filmbooks, Ryde
Chairman: John Williams; *Editorial:* Lisa Dewson; *Publicity, Publishers Representative:* John Williams
Subjects: Cinema, Theatre, Art, Isle of Wight
1977: 19 titles *1978:* 68 titles *Founded:* 1970
ISBN Publisher's Prefix: 0-904159

B H R A Fluid Engineering, Cranfield, Bedford MK43 0AJ Tel: Bedford 750422 (STD code 0234) Telex: 825059
Subjects: Reviews, Bibliographies, Conference Proceedings and Abstracts Journals on Fluid Engineering
1978: 10 titles *1979:* 8 titles
ISBN Publisher's Prefix: 0-906085

B P C Ltd (formerly British Printing Corporation Ltd), 44 Great Queen St, London WC2B 5AS Tel: (01) 240 3411 Cable Add: Britprint Telex: 262725
Supervising Dir: A M Alfred
Subjects: General Fiction, Belles Lettres, Poetry, Biography, History, How-to, Music, Art, Philosophy, Reference, Low-priced Paperbacks & Part-works, Primary & Secondary Textbooks
Miscellaneous: BPC is a holding company which controls Adkinson Parrish Ltd (qv); Arben Publishing Co Ltd; The Caxton Publishing Co Ltd (qv); Futura Publications Ltd (qv); Macdonald & Janes (qv); Macdonald Educational (qv); New Caxton Library Service Ltd (qv); Phoebus Publishing Co (qv); Waterlow (London) Ltd (qv)
Overseas Subsidiaries: Novalit (ANZ) Pty Ltd, Australia; IPA Produktion AS, Denmark; International Learning Systems (Japan) Ltd, Tokyo, Japan; Purnell & Sons (SA) Pty Ltd, South Africe (qv); Novalit (Books) Ltd, New Zealand; IPA Distributusjon Als, Norway; KG Bertmarks Förlag AB, Sweden; Delphin Verlag GmbH, Switzerland (qv); Macdonald Middle East rl, Lebanon; Macdonald & Janes (Australia) Pty Ltd

B S C Books Ltd, 33 Maiden Lane, London WC2 Tel: (01) 836 3341
Man Dir: Bill Smith
Imprint: The Booksmith
Bookshops: Booksmith chain
Miscellaneous: Firm is also a wholesaler and remainder dealer
1978: 10 titles
ISBN Publisher's Prefix: 0-900123

Bernard **Babani** (Publishing) Ltd, The Grampians, Shepherds Bush Rd, London W6 7NF Tel: (01) 603 2581/7296 Cable Add: Radiobooks London W6 (Formerly Babani Press and Bernards (Publishers) Ltd)
Man Dir, Editorial: M H Babani; *Sales, Rights & Permissions:* S Babani; *Production, Publicity:* P Pragnell
Associate Companies: Babani Press;

Bernards (Publishers) Ltd
Subjects: Low-priced Paperbacks, Radio & Electronics
1977: 13 titles *1978:* 11 titles *Founded:* 1977 (Babani Press 1974, Bernards Publishers 1942)
ISBN Publisher's Prefixes: 0-85934, 0-900162

Bachman & **Turner** Ltd+, The Old Hop Exchange, 1/3 Central Bldgs, 24 Southwark St, London SE1 1TY Tel: (01) 403 3366
Man Dir: Simon Bott; *Chairman:* Cecil Turner; *Director:* Marta Bachman
Subjects: General Fiction, Biography, History, Music, Art, Philosophy
1978: 9 titles *Founded:* 1972
ISBN Publisher's Prefix: 0-85974

Samuel **Bagster** & Sons Ltd+, 1 Bath St, London EC1V 9LB Tel: (01) 251 2925
Subjects: Religious, Reference, Bibles, Prayer & Hymn Books
Founded: 1794
Miscellaneous: Firm is a subsidiary of Marshall, Morgan & Scott Publications Ltd (qv)
ISBN Publisher's Prefix: 0-85150

Bailey Brothers & Swinfen Ltd+, Warner Ho, Folkestone, Kent Tel: Folkestone 56501 (STD code 0303) Cable Add: Forenbuks Telex: 96328
Man Dir: J R Bailey; *Publicity, Advertising, Rights & Permissions:* Malcolm Maclean
Subsidiary Companies: Bailey Bros & Swinfen Exports Ltd; Bailey Subscription Agents Ltd
Imprints: Fantasy Library, Ghost Hunters' Library, Hour-Glass Press
Subjects: General Fiction, History, How-to, Reference, Engineering
Book Clubs: Bailey's German, French, Italian & Spanish Book Clubs
1977: 18 titles *Founded:* 1929
ISBN Publisher's Prefix: 0-561

Baillière Tindall+, 35 Red Lion Sq, London WC1R 4SG Tel: (01) 831 6100 Telex: 28648 CASMAC-G
Divisional Dirs: S A Reynolds, D H Tindall, N J Mendelson
Subjects: Medical, Veterinary, Nursing, Pharmaceutical
Founded: 1826
Miscellaneous: Division of Cassell Ltd, UK (qv)
ISBN Publisher's Prefix: 0-7020

John **Baker** (Publishers) Ltd, 35 Bedford Row, London WC1R 4JH Tel: (01) 242 0946 Cable Add: Biblos, London WC1 Telex: 21792 ref 2546
Dirs: A A G Black, C A A Black
Subjects: Art, Archaeology, History, General & Social Science, Biography
1978: 3 titles *Founded:* 1897
Miscellaneous: Firm is a subsidiary of A & C Black Ltd (qv)
ISBN Publisher's Prefix: 0-212

Balding & **Mansell**, Park Works, Wisbech, Cambs PE13 2AX Tel: Wisbech 2011 (STD code 0945) Cable Add: Mansell Wisbech Telex: 32162
Dir: Alan Dickenson; *Sales Managers:* Guy Dawson, Robert Hatch
Subject: Primary Education, Art books for young people, Museum Guides

Ballantine, an imprint of Futura Publications (qv)

Arthur **Barker** Ltd+, 91 Clapham High St, London SW4 7TA 7TA Tel: (01) 622 9933 Cable Add: Nicobar London SW4 1XA Telex: 918066
Man Dir: Christopher Falkus; *Sales Dir:* D Livermore; *Publicity & Advertising:* Rosalind Lewis; *Rights & Permissions:* Miss B J Maclennan
Subjects: Biography, How-to, Reference, Military History, Crime, Sport
Founded: 1946
Miscellaneous: Firm is a subsidiary of George Weidenfeld & Nicolson Ltd (qv)
ISBN Publisher's Prefix: 0-213

Barrie & **Jenkins**, an imprint of Hutchinson General Books Ltd (qv)

John **Bartholomew** & **Son** Ltd+, 12 Duncan St, Edinburgh EH9 1TA Tel: (031) 667 9341 Cable Add: Bartholomew Edinburgh
Man Dir: D A Ross Stewart; *Editorial:* J C Bartholomew; *Marketing:* M J Chittleburgh; *Production:* R G Bartholomew; *Rights & Permissions:* J M Shillingford
Subsidiary Company: T & T Clark Ltd (qv)
Br Off: Bartholomew Books, 216 High St, Bromley, Kent BR1 1PW
Subjects: Maps, Atlases, Leisure Books
1977: 50 titles *1978:* 50 titles *Founded:* 1826
ISBN Publisher's Prefix: 0-7028

Bartholomew Books, 216 High St, Bromley, Kent BR1 1PW Tel: (01) 460 3239 Cable Add: Bartholomew Bromley Telex: 896521
Man Dir: David Ross Stewart; *Editorial:* Christopher Wheeler; *Sales Dir:* Michael J Chittleburgh; *Production:* John M Shillingford; *Rights & Permissions:* Christine Pott
Parent Company: John Bartholomew & Son Ltd, UK (qv)
Subsidiary Company: T & T Clark Ltd, UK (qv)
Head Off: 12 Duncan St, Edinburgh EH9 1TA
Subjects: Biography, History, How-to, Reference, Educational Materials, Guidebooks, Architecture, History of Art, Cooking, Hobbies, Natural History, Atlases
1977: 21 titles *1978:* 15 titles *Founded:* 1972
ISBN Publisher's Prefixes: 0-7028, 0-85152

The **Basilisk** Press Ltd, 32 England's Lane, London NW3 1YB Tel: (01) 722 2142
Man Dir: Charlene B Garry
Subjects: Literature, Botany, Architecture, Landscape Gardening
Bookshop: address as above
1978: 1 title *1979:* 1 title *Founded:* 1973

B T Batsford Ltd+, 4 Fitzhardinge St, London W1H 0AH Tel: (01) 486 8484 Cable Add: Batsfordia London Shipping Add: PO Box 4, Braintree, Essex CM7 7QY
Man Dir: Peter Kemmis Betty; *Editorial Dir, Rights & Permissions:* William Waller; *Editorial:* Samuel Carr, Thelma M Nye, Paula Shea, Pauline Stride; *Sales Manager:* Robert Beard; *Publicity Manager:* Richard Coltart
Subjects: History, How-to, Music, Art & Craft, Juveniles, Psychology, Engineering, Social Science, Educational Materials, Topography, Needlecraft, Sports, Hobbies, Cookery, Costumes
1978: 150 titles *Founded:* 1843
ISBN Publisher's Prefix: 0-7134

Beaver Books, an imprint of The Hamlyn Publishing Group Ltd (qv)

Bedford Square Press of the National Council of Social Service*, 26 Bedford Sq, London WC1B 3HU Tel: (01) 636 4066
Subjects: Secondary and University Textbooks, Legal, Reference, Social Policy, Local History, Music Education, Sociology, Social Services
1977: 9 titles
Miscellaneous: Bedford Square Press also publish outside the National Council of Social Service
ISBN Publisher's Prefix: 0-7199

Bell & Hyman Ltd+, Denmark Ho, 37-39 Queen Elizabeth St, London SE1 2QB Tel: (01) 407 0709/5237 Cable Add: Bellhyman London SE1 Telex: 886245
Chairman, Man Dir: R P Hyman; *Marketing Dir:* N C Britten
Subjects: Secondary Textbooks, Collecting and Crafts, Chess, Pepys
1977: 19 titles *1978:* 40 titles *Founded:* 1838
ISBN Publisher's Prefix: 0-7135

Bellona Publications, an imprint of Argus Books Ltd (qv)

Belton Books, an imprint of Stainer & Bell Ltd (qv)

Bemrose UK Ltd, Publishing Division, 39 Great Russell St, London WC1
Firm is not itself a publishing company, but parent company of The Athlone Press (qv), Grant McIntyre Ltd, Mansell Publishing (qv), Jill Norman Ltd (qv), Scolar Press Ltd (qv)

Benjamin Cummings Inc+, West End Ho, 11 Hills Pl, London W1R 2LR Tel: (01) 439 2541 Cable Add: Adiwes London W1 Telex: 8811948
Manager: Paul R Chapman; *Rights & Permissions:* Samuel B Warren
Subjects: Reference, Science, Technology, University Textbooks
Founded: 1960
Miscellaneous: Firm is a member of the Addison-Wesley Publishing Group (qv)
ISBN Publisher's Prefix: 0-8053

Ernest **Benn** Ltd+, 25 New Street Sq, London EC4A 3JA Tel: (01) 353 3212 Telex: 27844
Chairman & Man Dir: Timothy Benn; *Deputy Man Dir:* John Beer; *Sales Dir:* Anthony Llewellyn; *Publicity & Advertising:* Sarah Groom; *Editors:* John Collis (Academic), Michael Gale (Fishing & Technical), Paul Langridge (Juveniles and Blue Guides)
Orders to: Sovereign Way, Tonbridge, Kent TN9 1RW Tel: Tonbridge 364422 (STD Code 0732)
Parent Company: Benn Brothers Ltd
Associated Company: Benn Publications Ltd
Subsidiary Company: Charles Knight Publications, 25 New Street Sq, London EC4A 3JA
Imprints include: Tolley Publishing Co, Charles Knight Ltd
Subjects: History, Music, Art, Archaeology, Reference, Juveniles, High-priced Paperbacks, General Science, Technology, Political Science, Law
1977: 55 titles *1978:* 58 titles *Founded:* 1925
ISBN Publisher's Prefixes: 0-510 (Ernest Benn), 0-85314 (Charles Knight)

Bergström & Boyle Books Ltd, 31 Foubert's Place, London W1 Tel: (01) 437 4825 Cable Add: Berbo London
Dir: Alexandra Boyle; *Editorial:* Veronica Pratt
Subjects: Art, Architecture, Design (photographic and graphic)
1977: 3 titles *1978:* 2 titles *Founded:* 1973
ISBN Publisher's Prefix: 0-903767

Bernards (Publishers) Ltd, see Bernard Babani (Publishing) Ltd

Better Books, 11 Springfield Pl, Lansdown Rd, Bath BA1 5RA Tel: Bath 28010 (STD code 0225)
Proprietor: H Welchman; *Publicity Manager:* Pip Mason
Subject: Remedial Education
1977: 2 titles *1978:* 8 titles *Founded:* 1974
ISBN Publisher's Prefix: 0-904700

Big O Publishing Ltd*, 219 Eversleigh Rd, London SW11 5UY Tel: (01) 228 3392 Telex: 914549
Man Dir: Peter Ledeboer; *Sales Manager:* Paul Henderson; *Marketing:* Ron Ford; *Production:* Alice Lindsay
Parent Company: Big O Posters Ltd
Associated Companies: Big O Inc, Charlottesville Va, USA; Big O Verlag GmbH, Munich, German Federal Republic
Subjects: Illustrated Books, Art
1977: 6 titles *1978:* 11 titles *Founded:* 1975
ISBN Publisher's Prefix: 0-905664

Clive **Bingley** Ltd+, 1-19 New Oxford St, London WC1A 1NE Tel: (01) 404 4818 Telex: 24902 bingle g
Warehouse: Wentworth Book Co, Pindar Rd, Hoddesdon, Herts
Man Dir: Bruce Coward
Parent Company: K G Saur Verlag KG, Federal Republic of Germany (qv)
Subjects: Library Science, Textbooks, Technical, Science, Reference, Music, Hotels, Catering
Miscellaneous: Associated imprints include Anne Bingley, New University Education
1978: 17 titles
ISBN Publisher's Prefix: 0-85157

Birmingham Museums and Art Gallery+, Publications Unit, Chamberlain Sq, Birmingham B3 3DH Tel: (021) 235 4051
Publications Manager: Trevor Jones
Subjects: Fine & Applied Arts, Archaeology, Natural History
1977: 8 titles *1978:* 7 titles
ISBN Publisher's Prefix: 0-903504

Bison Books Ltd, 4 Cromwell Pl, London SW7 Tel: (01) 584 9597/8 Telex: 888014 Bison G
Sydney L Mayer
1978: 21 titles *Founded:* 1975
Subjects: Military and Modern History, Animals, Cookery, Transport

A & C **Black** (Publishers) Ltd+, 35 Bedford Row, London WC1R 4JH Tel: (01) 242 0946 Cable Add: Biblos London WC1 Telex: 21792 ref 2546
Shipping Add: Howard Rd, Eaton Socon, Huntingdon, Cambs PE19 3EZ
Man Dirs: Charles Black, David Gadsby; *Editorial:* Paul White
Subjects: History, Music, Art, Sports, Reference, Religion, Juveniles, University & Primary Textbooks
1977: 73 titles *1978:* 75 titles *Founded:* 1807
Subsidiaries: John Baker (Publishers) Ltd (qv); F Lewis (Publishers) Ltd (qv)
ISBN Publisher's Prefixes: 0-7136 (Black), 0-212 (Baker), 0-85317 (Lewis)

Black Pig Press, Higher Wick Farm, Glastonbury, Somerset Tel: Glastonbury 31321 (STD code 0458)
Man Dir, Rights & Permissions: R F Plewes; *Editorial:* John Anthony West; *Sales:* O Caldicott; *Production:* R Clarke
Subjects: Autobiography, Mystery, Facsimiles
1978: 3 titles *Founded:* 1977
ISBN Publisher's Prefix: 0-906180

Blacker Calmann Cooper Ltd, see Calmann & Cooper Ltd

Blackie & Son Ltd+, Bishopbriggs, Glasgow G64 2NZ Tel: (041) 772 2311 Cable Add: Blackie Glasgow
Man Dir: R Michael Miller; *Editorial:* A D Mitchell, Rosemary Creek, Olga Norris (Children's); Dr A G MacKintosh (Academic); *Sales Managers:* Geoff Meakin (Children's), Barry Richards (Educational), Bill Baird (Academic), John Drummond (Export); *Publicity:* Patsy Irwin (Children's), Russell Watt (Educational), Bill Baird (Academic); *Rights & Permissions:* Roseanne Holme
Br Off: Furnival Ho, 14-18 High Holborn, London
Subjects: School Textbooks, Reference, Juveniles, Scientific & Engineering, General & Social Science, Quality Paperbacks
1977: 120 titles *1978:* 177 titles *Founded:* 1809
Subsidiaries: Abelard-Schuman Ltd (qv); International Textbook Co Ltd (qv); Leonard Hill (qv); Surrey University Press (qv)
ISBN Publisher's Prefix: 0-216

Blacklock Farries & Sons*, Church Crescent, Dumfries Tel: Dumfries 4288 (STD code 0387)
ISBN Publisher's Prefix: 0-900173

Blackstaff Press Ltd+, 255A Upper Newtowards Rd, Belfast BT4 3JF Tel: Belfast 652829 (STD Code 0232)
Man & Sales Dir: Jim Gracey; *Publicity & Advertising Dir, Rights & Permissions:* Anne Tannahill
Subjects: General Fiction, Belles Lettres, Poetry, Biography, History, Reference, Paperbacks, General & Social Science, Art, Music, Photography, Children's Books, Natural History, Folklore, Sport
1978: 21 titles *1979:* 40 titles *Founded:* 1971
ISBN Publisher's Prefix: 0-85640

Basil **Blackwell Publisher** Ltd+, 5 Alfred St, Oxford OX1 4HB Tel: Oxford 722146 (STD Code 0865) Cable Add: Books Oxford
Shipping Add: 108 Cowley Rd, Oxford OX1 4JF
Man Dir: David Martin; *Sales Dir:* Norman Drake; *Education Dept Dir:* Angus Doulton; *Publicity:* Joana Dodsworth; *Rights and Permissions:* Stella Welford
Allied Company: Blackwell Scientific Publications Ltd, UK (qv)
Subsidiary Companies: Blackwell Press Ltd, Osney Mead, Oxford; Martin Robertson & Co Ltd (qv)
Imprints: Basil Blackwell, Shakespeare Head Press
Subjects: Economics and Industrial Relations, History, Philosophy, Politics, Languages, Linguistics, History, Geography, Children's Books, Reference, Religion, Academic Paperbacks, Social Science, Primary and Secondary Textbooks, Journals
1977-78: 65 titles *Founded:* 1921
Miscellaneous: Member of the Blackwell Group (qv B H Blackwell Ltd under Major Booksellers)
ISBN Publisher's Prefix: 0-631

Blackwell Scientific Publications Ltd+, Osney Mead, Oxford OX2 0EL Tel: Oxford 40201 (STD code 0865) Cable Add: Research Oxford Telex: 83118
Man, Editorial Dir and Rights & Permissions: Per Saugman; *Sales Dir:* Keith Bowker; *Production:* John Robson; *Publicity:* Andrew Bax
Allied Company: Basil Blackwell Publisher Ltd, UK (qv)
Br Offs: 9 Forrest Rd, Edinburgh EH1 2QH; 8 John St, London WC1; PO Box 9, North Balwyn, Victoria 3104, Australia
Subjects: Medicine, Dentistry, Veterinary Medicine, Botany, Biology, University Textbooks
1977: 57 titles *1978:* 53 titles *Founded:* 1939
ISBN Publisher's Prefix: 0-632

William **Blackwood** & Sons Ltd+, 32 Thistle St, Edinburgh EH2 1HA Tel: (031) 225 3411/3
Man Dir, Rights & Permissions: J M D Blackwood; *Publishing Director and Editor of Blackwood's Magazine:* D J Fletcher
Subjects: Monographs of Scottish Subjects
1978: 8 titles *Founded:* 1804
Miscellaneous: Publishers of *Blackwood's Magazine*
ISBN Publisher's Prefix: 0-85158

Jones **Blakey** Publishing*, 14 Monteith Crescent, Boston, Lincs PE21 9AX Tel: Boston (Lincs) 63437 (STD code 0205)
Man Dir: P Jones Blakey; *Senior Editor:* John Jonas; *Rights & Permissions:* Blanche Wise
Subjects: Biography, History
ISBN Publisher's Prefix: 0-903546

Blandford Books Ltd+, Robert Rogers Ho, New Orchard, Poole, Dorset BH15 1LU Tel: Poole 71171 (STD code 02013)
Man Dir: R G Dingwall; *Joint Man Dir, General Manager:* R B Erven; *Publishing Dir:* T Goldsmith; *Managing Editor:* Stuart Booth; *Sales and Marketing Manager:* Christopher Lloyd; *Publicity:* Pauline Jaffray; *Rights & Permissions:* Lindsay MacLeod
Parent Company: Link House Publications Ltd, Robert Rogers Ho, New Orchard, Poole BH15 1LU
Subjects: History, Religion, Music, Art, Archaeology, Biology, Crafts, Education, Geography, Horticulture, Militaria, Natural History, Riding, Space, Astronomy, Transport
1977: 50 titles *Founded:* 1919
ISBN Publisher's Prefix: 0-7137 (Blandford)

Geoffrey **Bles**, an imprint of Garnstone Press Ltd (qv)

Blond & Briggs Ltd, an imprint and subsidiary company of Frederick Muller Ltd (qv)

The **Bodley Head** Ltd+, 9 Bow St, London WC2E 7AL Tel: (01) 836 9081 Cable Add: Bodleian London WC2
Man Dir: Max Reinhardt; *Home Sales:* Norman Askew; *Overseas Sales:* Quentin Hockliffe; *Publicity Dir:* Euan Cameron; *Rights & Permissions:* Ms Reet Nelis, Guido Waldman
Subsidiary Companies: Max Reinhardt, UK (qv); Hollis & Carter; T Werner Laurie; The Nonesuch Library; Putnam & Co Ltd, UK (qv); (all at 9 Bow St, London WC2E 7AL)
Subjects: General Fiction, Belles Lettres, Poetry, Biography, History, Juveniles
1978: 73 titles *Founded:* 1887

Miscellaneous: Firm is a member of the Chatto, Bodley Head & Jonathan Cape Ltd Group (qv)
ISBN Publisher's Prefix: 0-370

Book Sales Ltd+, 78 Newman St, London W1P 3LA Tel: (01) 636 9033 Telex: 21892 Musicsales
A division of Music Sales Ltd
Man Dir: Robert Wise; *Sales:* Ken Denham
Subjects: Music (Learning and Biography), General Books
ISBN Publisher's Prefix: 0-86001

The **Booksmith**, an imprint of BSC Books Ltd (qv)

Boosey & Hawkes Music Publishers Ltd*, 295 Regent St, London W1A 1BR Tel: (01) 580 2060 Cable Add: Sonorous London W1
Man Dir: Robert A Fell
Subjects: Music, Secondary & Primary Music Textbooks
ISBN Publisher's Prefix: 0-85162

Bowes & Bowes (Publishers), 9 Bow St, London WC2E 7AL Tel: (01) 836 9081 Cable Add: Bodleian London WC2

Bowker and Bertram Ltd (Marine Publishers), Whitewalls, Harbour Way, Old Bosham, Sussex PO18 8QH
Subjects: Marine (Literary and Technical)
1978: 4 titles *1979:* 6 titles

Bowker Publishing Co, Xerox Publishing Group Ltd, PO Box 5, Epping, Essex CM16 4BU (Located at: Erasmus Ho, 58-62 High St, Epping) Tel: Epping 77333 (STD Code 0378) Telex: 81410
Shipping Add: H Kent Ltd, 135 South St, Bishop's Stortford, Herts
Man Dir and Rights & Permissions: David Collischon; *Marketing Manager:* Patrick Wynne-Jones; *Publicity:* Charles Arthur
Parent Company: R R Bowker Co, 1180 Ave of the Americas, New York, NY 10036, USA. Ultimate holding company Xerox Corporation
Subjects: Works of Bibliography, Reference, and Library Science handbooks for Libraries and the Book Trade
1978: 2 titles *1979:* 3 titles
ISBN Publisher's Prefixes: 0-8352, 0-85935

Marion **Boyars** Publishers Ltd, 18 Brewer St, London W1R 4AS Tel: (01) 439 7827/8 Cable Add: Bookdom
Man Dir, Editorial, Rights & Permissions: Marion Boyars; *Editorial:* Arthur Boyars; *Sales:* Michael Hayes; *Publicity:* Tim Binding
Associate Company: Marion Boyars Inc, 99 Main St, Salem, New Hampshire 03079, USA
Subjects: General Fiction, Belles Lettres, Poetry, Literary Criticism, Plays, Music, Philosophy, Sociology, Psychology
Series: Open Forum, Ideas in Progress, Signature, Critical Appraisals
1977: 30 titles *1978:* 35 titles *Founded:* 1975
ISBN Publisher's Prefix: 0-715

Boydell & Brewer Ltd, PO Box 9, Woodbridge IP12 3DF Tel: Woodbridge 411320 (STD code 0394)
Chairman: R W Barber
Imprints: Boydell Press, D S Brewer
Distributors for: Suffolk Record Society, Royal Historical Society, Folklore Society, Horn Book Inc
Subjects: Medieval and Renaissance Literature and History, General Non-fiction, Sport
1977: 12 titles *1978:* 25 titles
ISBN Publisher's Prefix: 0-85115 (Boydell), 0-85991 (Brewer)

Bradt Enterprises, Overmead, Monument Lane, Chalfont St Peter, Bucks SL9 0HY Tel: Chalfont St Giles 3865 (STD Code 024 07)
Man Dir: Mrs Hilary Bradt; *Editorial:* George Bradt, Hilary Bradt
Imprint: Backpacker's Guides Series
Br Off: Yugilbar, Rankine's Rd, St Andrews, Victoria 3761, Australia; 409 Beacon St, Boston, Mass 02115, USA
Subjects: Trekking and Backpacking
1978: 1 title *1979:* 2 titles *Founded:* 1975
ISBN Publisher's Prefix: 0-9505797

Branch Line, an imprint of The Harvester Press Ltd (qv)

Brassey's Publishers Ltd, 10 Upper Berkeley St, Nr Portman Sq, London W1H 7PE Tel: (01) 262 7448
Publisher: A H Begg
Orders to: Croom Helm Ltd, 2-10 St John's Rd, London SW11
Subjects: Defence & Military Books
1978/9: 15 titles *Founded:* 1886
ISBN Publisher's Prefix: 0-904609

D S **Brewer** Ltd, see Boydell & Brewer Ltd

Brimax Books, 347U Cherry Hinton Rd, Cambridge CB1 4DH Tel: Cambridge 44914/5 (STD code 0223) Cable Add: Brimax Cambridge Telex: 817625
Man Dir: A G Rogers; *Editorial:* Marjorie Rogers; *Rights & Permissions:* Brimax Rights Ltd, Long Ace, Newmarket Rd, Moulton, Newmarket, Suffolk
Subjects: General Children's Books, Toy Books
1977: 202 titles
ISBN Publisher's Prefixes: 0-900195, 0-904494, 0-86112

British & Foreign Bible Society+*, 146 Queen Victoria St, London EC4V 4BX Tel: (01) 248 4751 Cable Add: Testaments, London ECV 4BX
Gen Dir: N B Cryer; *Executive Dir:* T Houston; *Publishing Dir:* R Worthing-Davies
Subjects: Bibles, Testaments
Founded: 1803
ISBN Publisher's Prefix: 0-564

The **British Council**, Printing and Publishing Department, 65 Davies St, London W1Y 2AA Tel: (01) 499 8011 Ext 3363/7
Director: B A Cracknell
HQ: 10 Spring Gardens, London SW1A 2BN Tel: (01) 930 8466
Subjects: Those related to the promotion of a wider knowledge of Britain and the English language abroad and developing closer cultural relations with other countries. Co-publishers for some titles including: Writers & their Work Series: Longman Group Ltd (qv) *Journals: British Book News, British Medical Bulletin, British Medicine, Educational Broadcasting International* (published by Peter Peregrinus), *English Language Teaching Journal* (published by OUP), *ELT Documents, English Teaching & Linguistic Abstracts* (published by CUP)
ISBN Publisher's Prefix: 0-900229

The **British Horse** Society+, The British Equestrian Centre, Kenilworth, Warwickshire CV8 2LR Tel: Coventry 52241 (STD code 0203) Cable Add: Brithorse, Kenilworth
Subjects: Equestrian Reference Books and Training Aids
1978: 3 titles
ISBN Publisher's Prefix: 0-900226

British Library, Bibliographic Services Division+, Store St, London WC1E 7DG Tel: (01) 636 1544 Telex: 21462
Subjects: Bibliographies, Indexes, *British National Bibliography, British Education Index, British Catalogue of Music, Books in English*
Founded: 1973
ISBN Publisher's Prefix: 0-900220

British Museum (Natural History)+, Cromwell Rd, London SW7 5BD Tel: (01) 589 6323
Head of Publications: Robert Cross; *Editorial:* Chris Owen, Myra Givens; *Sales, Publicity:* J Abraham; *Production:* M Gilmartin, Eric Dent; *Rights & Permissions:* V Campbell
Subjects: Natural History, Scientific, Popular, Periodicals
Bookshops: Museum Bookshop (address as above); Museum Bookshop at Tring Museum
1977: 6 titles *Founded:* 1963
ISBN Publisher's Prefix: 0-0565

British Museum Publications Ltd+, 6 Bedford Sq, London WC1B 3RA Tel: (01) 323 1234
Man Dir, Rights & Permissions: M J Hoare; *Editorial:* Celia Clear; *Sales, Publicity:* Irene Fekete; *Production:* Nicholas Russell
Orders to: Thames & Hudson Ltd, Farnborough
Imprints: British Museum Publications, Colonnade
Subjects: Reference Books, Art & Architecture, Archaeology, Oriental, General Guides to British Museum
Bookshop: Bernard Shaw Bookshop, British Museum, Great Russell St, London WC1
1977: 45 titles *1978:* 49 titles *Founded:* 1973
ISBN Publisher's Prefix: 0-7141

British Printing Corporation Ltd, see B P C

James **Brodie** Ltd, 15 Queen Sq, Bath, Avon BA1 2HW Tel: Bath 22110 (STD code 0225)
Subjects: Primary & Secondary Education, *Notes on Chosen Texts* series (which are produced by Brodie and published by Pan Books Ltd (qv))
ISBN Publisher's Prefix: 0-7142

Brodies Notes, an imprint of Pan Books Ltd (qv)

Broomsleigh Press, an imprint of Fudge & Co Ltd (qv)

Brown Watson Ltd & Brown Watson Juvenile*, 143 Gt Windmill St, London W1 Tel: (01) 734 7394 Cable Add: Bookstocks London Telex: 21996
Man Dirs: Brian D Babani, Peter Babani; *Sales, Rights & Permissions:* Bernhardt Marcus
Subject: Juveniles
Miscellaneous: Firm is an associate company of Murrays Remainder Books (qv), parent company of Murrays Childrens Books (at above address) and a subsidiary of Howard & Wyndham Ltd (qv)
Imprint: Rainbow Books
ISBN Publisher's Prefixes: 0-7027, 0-85175 (Brown Watson), 0-7239 (Juvenile)

Bunch Books*, 14 Rathbone Place, London W1 Tel: (01) 637 7991/2/3 Cable Add: Bunch Books, London Telex: 943763
Man Dir: Felix Dennis; *Editorial, Rights & Permissions:* Andrew Fisher; *Production:* Richard Pountain
Parent Company: H Bunch Associates Ltd
Subsidiary Company: Sportscene Publishers Ltd
Subjects: Sport, Martial Arts, Film, TV, Biography, Leisure, General Interest
1977: 35 titles *Founded:* 1974

Burke Publishing Co Ltd+, Pegasus Ho, 116-120 Golden Lane, London EC1Y 0TL Tel: (01) 253 2145/6 Cable Add: Burkebooks London WC1
Chairman: H Starke; *Man Dir, Sales, Editorial, Rights & Permissions:* Miss N Galinski; *Production:* C Tuthill; *Publicity:* Mrs W Wilson
Orders to: The Barn, Northgate, Beccles, Suffolk
Subsidiary Company: Harold Starke Ltd (qv)
Br Off: Burke Publishing (Canada) Ltd, 91 Station St, Ajax, Ontario, Canada L1S 3H2
Subjects: Juveniles, Secondary & Primary Textbooks, Educational Materials
1977: 21 titles *1978:* 21 titles *Founded:* 1934
ISBN Publisher's Prefix: 0-222

Burke's Peerage Ltd, 56 Walton St, London SW3 1RB Tel: (01) 584 1106 Telex: 916851
Man Dir: Jeremy G Norman
Subjects: Genealogy, Heraldry, Architectural, Biographical, and Social History
1978: 1 title *Founded:* 1826
ISBN Publisher's Prefix: 0-85011

Burns & Oates Ltd, a subsidiary company of Search Press Ltd (qv)

Business Books Ltd, 24 Highbury Crescent, London N5 1RX Tel: (01) 359 3711 Cable Add: Hutchbiz Telex: 21373
Orders to: Tiptree Book Services, Church Rd, Tiptree, Nr Colchester, Essex
Man Dir: Mark Cohen; *Sales Dir:* John Fulford; *Editorial:* Vivien James
Subjects: Management, Advertising, Marketing, Technical & Industrial, Directories
1978: 23 titles *1979:* 18 titles
Miscellaneous: Business Books Ltd is an imprint of Hutchinson Educational (qv)
ISBN Publisher's Prefix: 0-220, 0-85015 (for pre-1979 publications), 0-09 (for 1979 onwards)

Butterworth & Co (Publishers) Ltd+, Borough Green, Sevenoaks, Kent TN15 8PH Tel: Borough Green 884567 (STD code 0732) Cable Add: Butterwort Sevenoaks Kent TN15 8PH Telex: 95678
Chairman and Chief Executive: W Gordon Graham; *Dirs:* Simon Partridge (Law), David Summer (Scientific, Technical and Medical), Don Saville (Financial), George Norton (Administrative); Colin Whurr (Marketing); *Export Sales Manager:* K W Maclennan; *International Sales Manager:* Phillip Woods; *Marketing Administrative Manager:* Geoff Hill; *Production:* R N G Harrison (Law), J Carruthers (Scientific, Technical and Medical); *Publicity:* Sue Henderson; *Rights & Permissions:* R J Hedley-Jones (UK), Betty Cottrell (Foreign Rights)
London Off: 88 Kingsway, London WC2 6AB Tel: (01) 405 6900 Cable Add: Butterwort London WC2
Parent Company: International Publishing Corporation Ltd, UK (qv)
Subsidiary Companies: Butterworths Pty Ltd, Australia (qv); Butterworth & Co (Canada) Ltd, 2265 Midland Ave, Scarborough, Ontario M1P 4S1, Canada; Butterworths of New Zealand Ltd, New Zealand (qv); Butterworth & Co (South Africa) (Pty) Ltd, South Africa (qv); Butterworth (Publishers) Inc, 10 Tower Office Park, Woburn, Mass 01801, USA
Imprints: Newnes-Butterworths, Newnes Technical
Bookshop: 9-12 Bell Yard, Temple Bar, London WC2
Subjects: Law, Medicine, Engineering, Technology, Science, Social Science, Business Studies
1977: approx 200 titles *1978:* approx 180 titles *Founded:* before 1905
ISBN Publisher's Prefixes: 0-0406/7/8/9, 0592, 06004

Buzby Books Ltd, an imprint of Severn House Publishers Ltd (qv)

C B D Research Ltd, 154 High St, Beckenham, Kent BR3 1EA Tel: (01) 650 7745
Man Dir: G P Henderson
Subject: Reference
1977: 3 titles *1978:* 4 titles *Founded:* 1961
ISBN Publisher's Prefix: 0-900246

C R Books, imprint of Applied Science Publishers Ltd (qv)

Caffrey, Smith Publishing Co+, 8 Forres Street, Edinburgh EH3 8BJ Tel: (031) 226 6680 Cable Add: Bookhouse Edinburgh Telex: 25264
Orders to: Caffrey, Smith Publishing Co, Station Ho, Darkes Lane, Potters Bar, Herts EN6 1AT
Subject: Educational (Primary & Secondary)
1978: 7 titles
ISBN Publisher's Prefix: 0-7024

John **Calder** (Publishers) Ltd, 18 Brewer St, London W1R 4AS Tel: (01) 734 3786 Cable Add: Bookdom London
Man, Publishing Dir: John Calder; *Sales:* Michael Hayes; *Production:* Chris Davidson; *Editorial, Promotion:* Bill Swainson; *Rights & Permissions:* Alice Watson
Associate Company: Calder & Boyars Ltd (distributors — at above address)
Subjects: Modern Literature, Classics, Belles Lettres, Poetry, Biography, History, Music, Art, Philosophy, Reference, High-priced Paperbacks, Psychology, Social Science, University Textbooks
1978: 50 titles *Founded:* 1950
ISBN Publisher's Prefix: 0-7145

John **Calmann & Cooper** Ltd, 7 Cleveland Square, London W2 6DH Tel: (01) 262 9870/9389 Telex: 298246
Man Dir, Sales, Rights & Permissions: John Calmann; *Editorial:* Elisabeth Ingles; *Production:* Andrew Ivett
Founded: 1976
Miscellaneous: Designers and producers of high quality illustrated books, and specialists in international co-editions

Cambridge Information and Research Services Ltd, School Ho, Heydon, Royston, Herts SG8 8PW Tel: Royston 83615 (STD code 0763)
Orders to: Sussex Ho, Hobson St, Cambridge CB1 1NJ
Dir: A R Buckley
Subsidiary Company: The Clavering Press Ltd
Subjects: Reference, Energy Management, Regional Locations, Social Science
1977: 2 titles *1978:* 4 titles *Founded:* 1975
ISBN Publisher's Prefix: 0-905332

Cambridge University Press+, PO Box 110, Cambridge CB2 3RL Cable Add: Unipress, Cambridge
The above are the postal and cable

addresses for all departments. See below for individual telephone and Telex numbers
Editorial, Journals, Rights: Tel: Cambridge 64122 (STD Code 0223) Telex: 817256
Trade Orders, Enquiries, Home Sales: Tel: Cambridge 312393 Telex: 817342
Export Sales, Publicity, Bibles, English Language Teaching: Tel: Cambridge 65546 Telex: 817256
Warehouse, Distribution, Shipping, Stock Control: Tel: Cambridge 880735 Telex: 817342
Chief Executive: G A Cass; *Man Dir (Publishing Division):* P E V Allin; *Publisher:* M H Black; *Marketing:* D A Knight; *Sales Dirs:* Joan Bunting, Dennis Stanton; *Publicity:* John Adamson; *Rights & Permissions:* Sarah Chapman, Irena Jeziorska
Br Off: Cambridge University Press (Australia) Pty Ltd, Australia (qv); Cambridge University Press (American Branch), 32 East 57th St, New York; NY 10022, USA, and 510 North Ave, New Rochelle, NY 10801, USA; Cambridge University Press, New Zealand (qv)
Subjects: Anthropology, Archaeology, Architecture, Drama, Classical Studies, Economics, History, Philosophy, Politics, Bibles, Prayer Books, Psychology, Sociology, Engineering, Demography, Geography, Urban Studies, Area Studies, Law, Languages, Literature, Linguistics, Mathematics, Secondary & University Textbooks, Physical & Biological Science, Music, Art, Medicine, Bibliography, Education, English Language Teaching, Theology, Learned Journals, Examination Papers
1977: 350 titles *1978:* 460 titles *Founded:* 1534
ISBN Publisher's Prefix: 0-521

Cameron & Tayleur (Books) Ltd, 25 Lloyd Baker St, London WC1X 9AT Tel: (01) 837 7126/7 Cable Add: Garamond London WC1
Dirs: Ian A Cameron, Bettina Tayleur
Subjects: Nonfiction, Illustrated Reference Books, Encyclopedias, Cinema, Cookery, Decorative Arts, Collecting
1977: 2 titles *1978:* 2 titles
ISBN Publisher's Prefix: 0-7153

Canongate and Southside+, 17 Jeffrey St, Edinburgh EH1 1DR Tel: (031) 556 0023
Man Dirs: Stephanie Wolfe Murray, Charles Wild; *Sales Manager:* Stephanie Wolfe Murray
Subjects: Biography, Fiction, Poetry, Current Affairs
ISBN Publisher's Prefixes: 0-903937 (Canongate), 0-900025 (Southside)

Jonathan **Cape** Ltd+, 30 Bedford Sq, London WC1B 3EL Tel: (01) 636 5764 Cable Add: Capajon London WC1
Shipping Add: 9 Bow St, London WC2
Man Dir: Graham C Greene; *Sales:* Quentin Hockliffe (Export), Norman Askew (Home); Gaye Poulton (Continental), Jean Mossop (American)
Subsidiary Companies: Cape Goliard Press Ltd; Jackdaw Publications Ltd
Subjects: General Fiction, Belles Lettres, Poetry, Biography, History, Music, Art, Philosophy, Juveniles, High-priced Paperbacks, Social Science, Educational Materials
Founded: 1921
Miscellaneous: Firm is a member of the Chatto, Bodley Head & Cape Ltd Group (qv)

Carcanet Press Ltd, 330-332 Corn Exchange Bldgs, Manchester M4 3BG Tel: (061) 834 8730
Shipping Add: Noonan Hurst Ltd, 131 Trafalgar Rd, London SE10 9TX
Man Dir: Peter Jones; *Editorial Dir:* Michael Schmidt; *Sales Dir:* Helen Lefoy
Subjects: Belles Lettres, Poetry, Religion, Low-priced Paperbacks
1977: 25 titles *1978:* 40 titles *Founded:* 1969
ISBN Publisher's Prefixes: 0-85635, 0-902145

Carter Nash Cameron Ltd, 25 Lloyd Baker St, London WC1X 9AT Tel: (01) 837 7126/7 Cable Add: Garamond London WC1
Directors: Ian A Cameron, Bettina Tayleur
Subjects: Nonfiction, Reference, Encyclopaedias, Decorative Arts, Crafts, Collecting

Frank **Cass** & Co Ltd, Gainsborough Ho, 11 Gainsborough Rd, London E11 1HT Tel: (01) 530 4226 Cable Add: Simfay London Telex: 897719
Shipping Add: Macdonald & Evans Ltd, Purdeys Way, Sutton Rd, Rochford, Essex SS4 1LX
Man Dir: Frank Cass; *Editorial:* Murray Mindlin; *Production:* Kenneth Cowell; *Publicity:* Suzzette Reed; *Trade Manager:* Jeremy Quy
Associate Companies: The Woburn Press (qv); Vallentine Mitchell & Co Ltd (qv)
Subjects: Third World Studies, Economics, Economic History, Social History, Politics, History, Africana, Middle East Studies
1977: 10 titles *1978:* 20 titles *Founded:* 1957
Bookshop: Frank Cass (Books) Ltd, 10 Woburn Walk, London WC1
ISBN Publisher's Prefixes: 0-7146 (Frank Cass), 0-7130 (Woburn Press), 0-85303 (Vallentine Mitchell)

Cassell Ltd+, 35 Red Lion Sq, London WC1R 4SG Tel: (01) 831 6100 Cable Add: Caspeg, London WC1 Telex: 28648 CASMAC-G
Man Dir: Marshall D Mascott
Trade Division: *Editorial:* J J Greenwood; *Sales:* B Holmes; *Production:* G S Mitchell; *Publicity:* M Felgate-Catt; *Rights & Permissions:* June Badcock
Balliere Tindall Division: S A Reynolds; Educational Division: D Napier
International Division: F Kobrak
Orders to: 8 Trident Way, Brent Rd, Southall, Middlesex
Parent Company: Cassell & Collier Macmillan Ltd, London
Subsidiary Company: Cassell Australia Ltd, Australia (qv)
Divisions: Studio Vista, Geoffrey Chapman, Balliere Tindall, Johnston & Bacon (qqv)
Imprints: As under Divisions
Br Offs: Cassell Ltd, New Zealand (qv)
Subjects: General, Biography, Fiction, Music, Nonfiction, Medical, Educational, Technical
1977: 260 titles *Founded:* 1848
ISBN Publisher's Prefix: 0-304

Castle, an imprint of Murrays Remainder Books (qv)

Cathay, an imprint of Octopus Books Ltd (qv)

Caxton Publications Ltd+, Holywell Ho, 72-90 Worship St, London EC2A 2HR Tel: (01) 247 8492 Cable Add: Interknow London EC2 Telex: 886048
Shipping Add: Gatehouse Rd, Aylesbury, Buckinghamshire
Man Dir: D Rodrigues; *Editorial:* Georgiana Balfour; *Sales Dir:* E La Frenais; *Editorial Dir (Rights & Permissions):* J F Skilling
Subjects: Encyclopaedias, Education, Yearbooks, History, Reference, Juveniles
Company's main works: The New Caxton Encyclopedia, Chamber's Encyclopedia
Miscellaneous: Firm is part of the Caxton Publishing Group, and a member company of B P C Ltd (qv)
Founded: 1966
ISBN Publisher's Prefix: 0-7014

Cedar Books, an imprint of World's Work Ltd (qv)

Celtic Educational Ltd+*, Celtic Ho, St James's Gardens, Swansea SA1 6EA Tel: Swansea 59398 (STD code 0792)
Subjects: Education, Science, Commerce, Management, Law, Wales, Scotland

Cement & Concrete Association, Wexham Springs, Slough, Bucks SL3 6PL Tel: Fulmer 2727 (Std code 02816) Cable Add: Advicret Slough Telex: 848352
Subjects: Engineering, Concrete, Cement
Miscellaneous: Associated imprints include Viewpoint
ISBN Publisher's Prefix: 0-7210

Centaur Press Ltd, Fontwell, Arundel, Sussex Tel: Eastergate 3302 (STD code 024368)
Shipping Add: 11-14 Stanhope Mews West, London SW7
Man Dir: T J L Wynne-Tyson
Subsidiary Company: The Linden Press, Fontwell, Arundel, Sussex
Literary Agent: Howard Moorepark, 444 East 82nd St, New York, NY 10028, USA
Subjects: General, Fiction, Biography, Philosophy, Social Science, Textbooks, Reference
1978: 2 titles *Founded:* 1954
ISBN Publisher's Prefixes: 0-900000 (Centaur), 0-900001 (Linden Press)

Centre for Investment Studies, an imprint of Teakfield Ltd (qv)

Chadwyck-Healey Ltd+, 20 Newmarket Rd, Cambridge CB5 8DT Tel: Cambridge 311479 (STD code 0223)
Dirs: Charles E Chadwyck-Healey, A M Chadwyck-Healey, H Fellner
Subjects: Reference, Nonfiction, Art, Economics, History, Literary History, Bibliography, Radio and TV

W & R **Chambers** Ltd+, 11 Thistle St, Edinburgh EH2 1DG Tel: (031) 225 4463 Cable Add: Chambers Edinburgh
Chairman, Sales Dir: A S Chambers; *Man Dir, Rights & Permissions:* I Gould; *Sales Manager:* David Mill
Subjects: General Textbooks, Reference, Juveniles, Educational Materials, Mathematical Tables, Low-priced Paperbacks
1977: 23 titles *1978:* 28 titles *Founded:* 1820
ISBN Publisher's Prefix: 0-550

Chancerel Publishers Ltd, 40 Tavistock St, London WC2E 7PB Tel: (01) 240 2811
Man Dir: J M Idé; *General Manager:* D Prowse; *Marketing Manager:* R Littman; *Serial Rights:* Chr de la Roche
Associate Company: Chancerel Editions SA, France (qv)
Subjects: Leisure Activities (Sports, Hobbies, Homecraft) Picture Strips,

Illustrated How-to, Paperbacks
1977: 30 titles *1978/9:* 20 titles *Founded:* 1976
ISBN Publisher's Prefix: 0–905703

Geoffrey **Chapman**+, 35 Red Lion Sq, London WC1R 4SG Tel: (01) 831 6100 Telex: 28648 CASMAC-G
Editorial: John Ainslie; *Publicity:* John Miller
Subjects: Religion, Religious Educational, Specialized African Publishing
1977: 3 titles *1978:* 10 titles *Founded:* 1957
Miscellaneous: Division of Cassell Ltd, UK (qv)
ISBN Publisher's Prefix: 0–225

Chapman & Hall Ltd+, 11 New Fetter Lane, London EC4P 4EE Tel: (01) 583 9855 Cable Add: Elegiacs London EC4P 4EE Telex: 263398
Man Dir: R Stileman; *Marketing:* Peter F Shepherd; *Production:* B West; *Publicity:* L Williams; *Rights & Permissions:* J V Anderson
Orders to: Northway, Andover, Hants SP10 5BE
Parent Company: Associated Book Publishers Ltd, UK (qv)
Subjects: Science, Technology, Medicine
1978: 61 titles *Founded:* 1830
ISBN Publisher's Prefix: 0–412

Chatto, Bodley Head & Jonathan Cape Ltd+, 9 Bow St, London WC2E 7AL Tel: (01) 379 6831
Parent company of Chatto & Windus, Jonathan Cape, The Bodley Head

Chatto & Windus Ltd+, 40–42 William IV St, London WC2 Tel: (01) 836 0127 Cable Add: Bookstore London WC2
Chairman & Man Dir: Nora Smallwood; *Deputy Man Dir:* John Charlton; *Home Sales:* Roger Kirkpatrick; *Export Sales:* Quentin Hockliffe; *Publicity & Advertising:* Rosalind Bell; *Rights & Permissions:* Jane Gregory
Subsidiary and Associate Companies: The Hogarth Press Ltd, UK (qv)
Subjects: General Fiction, Belles Lettres, Poetry, Art, Biography, History, Philosophy, Juveniles, Psychology, Travel, High-priced Paperbacks
Founded: 1855
Miscellaneous: Firm is a member of Chatto, Bodley Head & Jonathan Cape Ltd Group (qv)
ISBN Publisher's Prefix: 0–7011

The **Chemical Society**, Burlington Ho, London W1V 0BN Tel: (01) 734 9864 Telex: 268001
Dir, Information Services: Dr A K Kent; *Sales & Marketing Manager:* Dr A Kabi; *Advertising Manager:* Jill Gunsell
Orders to: The Chemical Society, Distribution Centre, Blackhorse Rd, Letchworth, Herts SG6 1HN
Subjects: General Science, University Textbooks
Founded: 1841
ISBN Publisher's Prefixes: 0–85186, 0–85404, 0–85990

Child's Play (International) Ltd+, Restrop Manor, Purton, Swindon, Wilts Tel: Swindon 770389 (STD code 0793) Telex: 449391
Man Dir: Michael Twinn; *Sales:* D Anthony Finnigan; *Editorial, Publicity:* Alex Webb
Subsidiary Companies: D A Finnigan Ltd, Aylesbury, UK; Child's Play Inc, Chicago, USA
Associate Company: F X Schmid (UK) Ltd, Swindon

Subject: Juveniles (pre- and Primary School ages)
1977: 12 titles *1978:* 9 titles *Founded:* 1972
ISBN Publisher's Prefix: 0–85953

Chivers Press Publishers, 93–100 Locksbrook Rd, Bath BA1 3HB Tel: Bath 316872 (STD code 0225) Telex: 449897
Man Dir: C A Coles (to whom all correspondence)
Associate Companies: Chivers Book Sales Ltd; Firecrest Publishing Ltd (qv); Lythway Press (qv)
Imprints: New Portway Large Print, New Portway Facsimile Editions
Subjects: General Fiction and Nonfiction
ISBN Publisher's Prefixes: 0–85594 (Chivers), 0–85997 (Portway)

The **Christian Community** Press, see Floris Books

Christian Journals Ltd+, 2 Bristow Park, Upper Malone Rd, Belfast BT9 6TH Tel: Belfast 668268 (STD code 0232)
Man Dir: W G Forker; *Rights & Permissions:* Miss P Lovegrove
Subject: Religion
1977: 15 titles *1978:* 16 titles *Founded:* 1974
ISBN Publisher's Prefix: 0–904302

Church Book Room Press, now Vine Books Ltd (qv)

Church Pastoral Aid Society, see Falcon Books

Churchill Livingstone+, Robert Stevenson Ho, 1–3 Baxter's Pl, Leith Walk, Edinburgh EH1 3AF Tel: (031) 556 2424 Cable Add: Churchliv Telex: 727511 Longman G (Edin)
Shipping Add: Longman Group Ltd, Pinnacles, Harlow, Essex
Man Dir: R G B Duncan; *Sales, Publicity & Advertising:* A J Smith; *Production:* A D Lewis; *Rights & Permissions:* Sheena Gibb
Br Off: 5 Bentinck St, London W1M 5RN Tel: (01) 935 0121
Subjects: Medicine, Dentistry, Nursing
1977: 90 titles *1978:* 97 titles *Founded:* 1863
Miscellaneous: Firm is a division of Longman Group Ltd, UK (qv)
ISBN Publisher's Prefix: 0–443

Citadel, an imprint of L S P Books Ltd (qv)

Clarendon Press, see Oxford University Press

Robin **Clark** Ltd, The Pines, Aspley Guise, Milton Keynes MK17 8JX Tel: Milton Keynes 583257 (STD code 0908) Telex: 919034
Chairman & Man Dir: J C Reynolds; *Sales Dir:* D Elliott; *Production Dir:* R J Reilly; *Editorial:* Ann Gosling; *Publicity:* Sheila Turnbull
Associate Company: Quartet Books Ltd (qv)
Subjects: Non-fiction Paperbacks: Originals and Reprints; Biography, Social History, Humour, County Guides, Animal Books, Practical Handbooks including Cookery and Gardening
1977: 8 titles *1978:* 8 titles *Founded:* 1976
Miscellaneous: Firm is a member of the Namara Group, Namara Ho, 45–46 Poland St, London W1
ISBN Publisher's Prefix: 0–86072

T & T **Clark** Ltd+*, 36 George St, Edinburgh EH2 2LQ Tel: (031) 225 4703 Cable Add: Dictionary Edinburgh
Man Dir: T G Ramsay D Clark; *Editorial, Sales, Production, Publicity, Rights &*

Permissions: Geoffrey F Green
Subjects: Philosophy, Theology, History, Law
Parent Company: John Bartholomew & Son Ltd (qv)
1977: 20 titles *Founded:* 1821
ISBN Publisher's Prefix: 0–567

Anthony **Clarke** Books*, 16 Garden Court, Wheathampstead, Herts AL4 8RF Tel: Wheathampstead 2460 (STD code 058283) Cable Add: Clarkbook St Albans
Shipping Add: 27 Brewhouse Hill, Wheathampstead, Herts AL4 8AN
Proprietor: Anthony Clarke
Subject: Religion
Bookshop: All Saints Bookshop, All Saints, London Colney, Herts
1977: 5 titles *Founded:* 1970
ISBN Publisher's Prefix: 0–85650

James **Clarke** & Co Ltd+, 7 All Saints' Passage, Cambridge CB2 3LS Tel: Cambridge 350865 (STD code: 0223) Telex: 817570
Man Dir: A C Brink
Subjects: Librarianship, Religion, Textbooks, Reference, Technical
1978: 15 titles *1979:* 9 titles *Founded:* 1859
Subsidiary: Allenson & Co Ltd, 7 All Saints Passage, Cambridge
ISBN Publisher's Prefix: 0–227

E W **Classey**, Park Rd, Faringdon, Oxfordshire SN7 7DR Tel: Faringdon 20911 (STD code 0367)
Publisher: E W Classey
Orders to: George Philip & Son, PO Box 1, Littlehampton, Sussex BN17 7EN
Subjects: Entomology, Cats
ISBN Publisher's Prefix: 0–900848

Clematis Press Ltd*, 18 Old Church St, London SW3 5DQ Tel: (01) 352 8755 Cable Add: Clematis London
Man Dir: Mrs Clara Waters
Trade Counter: Wentworth Book Co Ltd, Pindar Rd, Hoddesdon, Herts EN11 0HF
Founded: 1950
Subjects: Art, Architecture, Sport, Cookery
ISBN Publisher's Prefix: 0–568

William **Clowes** (Publishers) Ltd+*, 31 Newgate, Beccles, Suffolk NR35 9QP Tel: Beccles 712884 (STD code 0502)
Manager: Gordon Knights
Subjects: General, Religion, Hymn Books
ISBN Publisher's Prefix: 0–85194

Club Leabhar+, 91 Cromwell St, Stornoway, Isle of Lewis Tel: Stornoway 3812 (STD code 0851)
Subjects: Books in Gaelic, Juveniles, Fiction in English
1977: 2 titles *1978:* 1 title
ISBN Publisher's Prefix: 0–902796

Co-chuideachd Leabhneachean Gaidhlig, an imprint of Volturna Press (qv)

Cohen & West, an imprint of Routledge & Kegan Paul Ltd (qv)

Collet's Holdings Ltd+, Denington Estate, Wellingborough, Northants NN8 2QT Tel: Wellingborough 224351 (STD code 0933) Cable Add: Colholdin Wellingborough
Man Dir: Joan Birch; *Advertising:* Philip Taylor
Subjects: Music, Art (History), Textbooks, Reference (Modern Language, Audiovisual), Engineering, General & Social Science, Low- & High-priced Paperbacks
Bookshops: Collet's Chinese Bookshop, 40 Great Russell St, London WC1; Collet's London Bookshop, 66 Charing Cross Rd,

London WC2; Collet's International Bookshop, 129/131 Charing Cross Rd, London WC2; Collet's Penguin Bookshop, 52 Charing Cross Rd, London WC2; Collet's Record Shop, 180 Shaftesbury Ave, London WC2
Founded: 1934
Miscellaneous: Specialists in Russian language teaching materials
ISBN Publisher's Prefix: 0-569

Collier Macmillan Ltd, Stockley Close, Stockley Rd, West Drayton, Middx UB7 9BE Tel: West Drayton 40651 (STD code 089 54) Cable Add: Pachamac West Drayton Telex: 28648 CASMAC-G
Man Dir: Brian J Collins; *Sales, Marketing Manager:* Alastair Gordon; *Publicity, Promotion:* R Bower
Parent Company: Cassell & Collier Macmillan Ltd, London
Subjects: Academic, Primary and Secondary Textbooks, Trade, Professional Reference, English as a second Language
1977: 250 titles *1978:* 192 titles *Founded:* 1964
ISBN Publisher's Prefix: 0-02

Collingridge, an imprint of The Hamlyn Publishing Group Ltd (qv)

Rex **Collings** Ltd*, 69 Marylebone High St, London W1M 3AQ Tel: (01) 487 4201
Man Dir: Rex Collings
Orders to: Noonan Hurst Ltd, 131 Trafalgar Rd, London SE10
Subjects: General, Poetry, Juveniles, Africana, Biography, Drama, Reference
1978: 30 titles
Miscellaneous: Distributor for Anvil Press Poetry
ISBN Publisher's Prefix: 0-86036, 0-901720

William **Collins** Sons & Co Ltd+, 14 St James's Pl, London SW1A 1PS Tel: (01) 493 7070 Cable Add: Herakles London SW1 Telex: 25611
Chairman: W J Collins; *Marketing Dir:* M Hyde; *Man Dirs:* S A M Collins (Fontana), C E Allen (Childrens, Reference, Bibles), A R House (General Trade Publishing), T R Ballard (International Div); *Rights:* Miss I Bossy (Adult), Miss L Pooley (Children)
Subsidiary Companies: Fontana Books (Collins), Armada Books (Collins), Angus Hudson Ltd (division handling co-edition rights and arrangements for publishers worldwide) (all at 14 St James's Pl, London SW1); Collins Liturgical Books Ltd, 187 Piccadilly, London W1; Harvill Press Ltd (qv); Hatchards Ltd, 187 Piccadilly, London W1
Br Offs: Westerhill Rd, Bishopbriggs, Glasgow; Wm Collins Publishers Pty Ltd, Australia (qv); Wm Collins Sons & Co (Canada) Ltd, 100 Lesmil Rd, Don Mills, Ontario, Canada; Wm Collins Sons & Co (New Zealand) Ltd, PO Box 1, Auckland, New Zealand; Wm Collins (Africa) (Pty) Ltd, PO Box 8879, Johannesburg, South Africa; Wm Collins & World Publishing Co Inc, 2080 West 117th St, Cleveland, Ohio 44111, USA
Subjects: General Fiction & Nonfiction, Belles Lettres, Biography, History, How-to, Art, Archaeology, Philosophy, Reference, Religion, Bibles, Low- & High-priced Paperbacks, General & Natural Sciences, University, Secondary & Primary Textbooks, Educational Materials, Juveniles, Technical, Military, Sports, Travel
Bookshops: Hatchards Ltd, 187 Piccadilly, London W1; Hatchards at Harvey Nichols, Knightsbridge, London SW1; The Ancient House, Ipswich, Suffolk; Hanningtons, 53 Market St, Brighton, Sussex; The Deben Bookshop, Woodbridge, Suffolk
Founded: 1819
Miscellaneous: Collins-Longman Atlases, Westerhill Rd, Bishopbriggs, Glasgow G64 2PW distributes atlases for Wm Collins and the Longman Group
ISBN Publisher's Prefixes: 0-00 (Collins), 0-01 (Fontana, Armada, Harvill)

Colonnade, an imprint of British Museum Publications (qv)

Columbia University Press, see University Presses of Columbia and Princeton

Common Ground, an imprint of Longman Group Ltd (qv)

Compton Press Ltd, The Old Brewery, Tisbury, Wiltshire SP3 6NH Tel: Tisbury 870619 (STD code 0747) Cable Add: Bearpress, Salisbury
Man Dir: Julian Berry
Subjects: Art History, Guides, Energy Sciences, Limited Editions and Packaging
1977: 10 titles *1978:* 12 titles *Founded:* 1969
ISBN Publisher's Prefix: 0-900193

Concertina Publications Ltd, 11-13 Broad Court, Covent Garden, London WC2B 5QJ Tel: (01) 836 1758/2929
Subjects: Illustrated Nonfiction, Reference

Condor Books, an imprint of Souvenir Press Ltd (qv)

The **Connoisseur**, an imprint of National Magazine Co Ltd (qv)

Conservative Political Centre+, 32 Smith Sq, London SW1P 3HH Tel: (01) 222 9000 Cable Add: Constitute, London, SW1P 3HH
Subjects: Reference Books, Politics, Political Economy, Sociology, Questions of the Day
1978: 20 titles
ISBN Publisher's Prefix: 0-85070

Constable & Co Ltd+, 10 Orange St, London WC2H 7EG Tel: (01) 930 0801 Cable Add: Dhagoba London WC2H 7EG
Man Dir: B K Glazebrook; *Editorial:* Elfreda Powell; *Sales:* Paul Marks; *Publicity & Editorial:* Miles Huddleston; *Rights & Permissions:* Christine Senior
Orders to: Tiptree Book Services Ltd, Tiptree, Colchester, Essex Tel: (0621) 816362 Cable Add: Literarius Tiptree Telex: 99487
Subjects: General Fiction, Literature, Biography, Memoirs, History, Politics, Current Affairs, Food, Travel & Guidebooks, Social Sciences, Psychology & Psychiatry, Counselling, Social Work, Sociology, Mass Communications
1977: 48 titles *1978:* 47 titles *Founded:* 1896
ISBN Publisher's Prefix: 0-09

Construction Press Ltd+*, Lunesdale Ho, Hornby, Lancaster LA2 8NB Tel: Hornby 21888 (STD code 0468) Telex: 81259
Man Dir & Publicity: P J Horrobin; *Editorial:* Shirley Crabtree; *Sales:* Michael Wymer; *Production:* Terry Mann; *Rights & Permissions:* Lynette Owen
Orders to: Longman Group Ltd, Fourth Ave, Harlow, Essex
Parent Company: Longman Group Ltd
Subjects: Architecture, Building, Civil Engineering
1977: 13 titles *1978:* 24 titles *Founded:* 1974
ISBN Publisher's Prefix: 0-904406 & 0-86095

Continua Productions Ltd, see Macdonald & Evans Ltd

Conway Maritime Press Ltd, 2 Nelson Rd, Greenwich, London SE10 9JB Tel: (01) 858 7211
Man Dir: W R Blackmore; *Editorial Dir:* Robert Gardiner
Orders to: Marston Book Services Ltd, PO Box 87, Marston St, Oxford OX4 1LB
Associate Company: Paul Popper Ltd, 24 Bride Lane, Fleet St, London EC4Y 8DR
Subjects: Naval, Maritime
Bookshop: Meridian Books, 2 Nelson Rd, Greenwich, London SE10 9JB
1978: 20 titles *1979:* 20 titles *Founded:* 1968
ISBN Publisher's Prefix: 0-85177

Leo **Cooper** Ltd, 196 Shaftesbury Ave, London WC2H 8JL Tel: (01) 836 6225 Cable Add: Tomatkins
Shipping Add: 81A Endell St, London WC2H 8JL
Man Dir: Leo Cooper; *Editorial Dir:* T R Hartman; *Publicity, Rights & Permissions:* Alison Gordon
Subsidiary Company: Seeley Service & Co Ltd, UK (qv)
Subjects: Military History, Biography
1977: 9 titles *1978:* 8 titles *Founded:* 1969
ISBN Publisher's Prefix: 0-85052

Trewin **Copplestone** Publishing Ltd, Advance Ho, 101-109 Ladbroke Grove, London W11 1PG Tel: (01) 229 8861/3 Cable Add: Trewcop London W11 Telex: 25766
Man Dir: Trewin Copplestone
Subjects: History, Rock Music, Art, Reference, Regional Encyclopedias, Low- & High-priced Paperbacks, General Science
1977: 9 titles *1978:* 8 titles *Founded:* 1972
Miscellaneous: Firm originates, designs and produces books for co-edition publication
ISBN Publisher's Prefix: 0-85674

Corgi Books, an imprint of Transworld Publishers Ltd (qv)

Cornell University Press+*, 2-4 Brook St, London W1Y 1AA Tel: (01) 493 5061, (01) 499 4688
Warehouse: International Book Distributors, 66 Wood Lane End, Hemel Hempstead, Herts
Man Dir: J Trevor Brown
Subjects: Academic
Miscellaneous: Firm is a subsidiary of Cornell University Press, 124 Roberts Pl, Ithaca, NY 14850
ISBN Publisher's Prefix: 0-8014

Coronet, an imprint of Hodder & Stoughton Ltd (qv)

Cotman Colour and **Cotman House**, imprints of Jarrold Colour Publications (qv)

Country Life Books, an imprint of Hamlyn Group Ltd (qv)

Coventure Ltd+, 1 Prince of Wales Passage, 117 Hamstead Rd, London NW1 3EE Tel: (01) 388 5389 Cable Add: Coventure
Man Dir, Editorial: Ian Fenton; *Sales:* David Harrison; *Production:* Felicity Clarke; *Rights & Permissions:* Ian Fenton
Subjects: Juveniles, Psychology, Sociology, International Co-editions
1977: 15 titles *1978:* 10 titles *Founded:* 1973
ISBN Publisher's Prefix: 0-904576

Coverdale House Publishers Ltd+, an imprint of Kingsway Publications Ltd (qv)

The **Crafts** Council, 12 Waterloo Pl, London SW1Y 4AU Tel: (01) 839 1917
Publications Officer: Marigold Coleman
Bookshop: Crafts Council Gallery, 12 Waterloo Pl, London SW1Y 4AU
1977: 6 titles *Founded:* 1971
Subjects: Arts & Fine Crafts
Miscellaneous: Government-financed body promoting Britain's artist craftsmen
ISBN Publisher's Prefix: 0-903798

Cressrelles Publishing Co Ltd+, Kestrels Ho, Peppard Common, Henley-on-Thames, Oxon RG9 5EP Tel: Kidmore End 3165 (STD code 073525)
Man Dir: Leslie Smith
Subjects: Juveniles, Pre-school Education, Fiction, General
1977: 8 titles *1978:* 5 titles *Founded:* 1972
ISBN Publisher's Prefix: 0-85956

Paul H **Crompton** Ltd, 638 Fulham Rd, London SW6 Tel: (01) 736 2551
Publicity & Sales: Paul Crompton; *Subscription Enquiries:* B Crompton; *Shop Enquiries:* C Hanson
Orders to: (Private) above address; (Trade) IBD, 66 Wood Lane End, Hemel Hempstead, Herts
Subjects: Oriental Martial Arts and Survival
Miscellaneous: Publish magazine *Karate & Oriental Arts* (bi-monthly)

Croner Publications Ltd, 46-50 Coombe Rd, New Malden, Surrey Tel: (01) 942 9615
Man Dir: A S Brode; *Marketing Dir:* D E Sleat
Subject: Business Reference Books
1978: 1 title
Miscellaneous: Firm is member of NV I C U Group, Netherlands (qv)
ISBN Publisher's Prefix: 0-900319

Croom Helm Ltd+, 2-10 St John's Rd, London SW11 Tel: (01) 228 9343/4
Man Dirs: Christopher Helm, David Croom; *Editorial:* Melanie Crook; *Sales:* Graham Harris; *Production:* John Saunders; *Publicity:* Richard Welsh
Subjects: Technical & Scientific, Legal & Parliamentary, Medical, Commercial & Professional, Naval & Military, Reference Books, Art & Architecture, Sports, Games & Pastimes, History, Archaeology, Biography & Memoirs, Politics, Political Economy, Sociology, Questions of the Day, Philosophy, Oriental, Directories & Guidebooks, General Literature
1978: 135 titles
ISBN Publisher's Prefixes: 0-85664, 0-7099

Crosby Lockwood Staples Ltd, see Granada Publishing Ltd

Curzon Press Ltd+, 88 Gray's Inn Rd, London WC1 Tel: (01) 405 1865 and 9325
Shipping Add: Interbook Ltd, 52 Manchester St, London W1
Man Dir: J F Standish
Subjects: Oriental and African Studies
1978: 18 titles *1979:* 21 titles *Founded:* 1970
ISBN Publisher's Prefix: 0-7007

Cut & Colour Books, an imprint of Dinosaur Publications Ltd (qv)

D P Publications+, 4 Amport Close, Winchester, Hants SO22 6LP Tel: Winchester 881806 (STD code 0962)
Orders to: 69 Harford Drive, Cassiobury, Watford, Herts Tel: Watford 31754 (STD code 0923)
Subjects: Finance, Law, Accountancy, Quantitative Techniques, Management, Data Processing
1978: 8 titles
ISBN Publisher's Prefix: 0-905435

The C W **Daniel** Co Ltd, 1 Church Path, Saffron Walden, Essex CB10 1JP Tel: Saffron Walden 21909 (STD code 0799)
Man Dir: Ian Miller; *Editorial:* Mrs Jana Garai; *Sales:* Sebastian Hobnut; *Production:* Barnaby Miller; *Publicity:* Ida Honorofe; *Rights & Permissions:* Jenne Miller
Associate Company: Health Science Press (qv)
Subjects: Natural Healing, Homoeopathy
ISBN Publisher's Prefix: 0-85207

Alan **Darby** Publications Ltd, now Lotus Press Ltd (qv)

Darton, Longman & Todd Ltd+, 89 Lillie Rd, London SW6 1UD Tel: (01) 385 2341
Cable Add: Librabook London SW6 1UD
Dirs: Robin Baird-Smith, J M Tood, Miss E A C Russell; *Publicity & Advertising:* Miss A Hornby
Subjects: History, Philosophy, Reference, Religion, Bibles, High-priced Paperbacks, Medicine, Psychology, Secondary Textbooks, Travel Guides, Gardening
1977: 35 titles *Founded:* 1959
ISBN Publisher's Prefix: 0-232

Darwen Finlayson Ltd, Shopwyke Hall, Chichester, West Sussex Tel: Chichester 787636 (STD code 0243)
Chairman & Man Dir: Philip Harris; *Editorial Director:* Noel H Osborne
Subjects: History, Historical Biography, Company Histories, Family Histories
Miscellaneous: Firm is subsidiary of Phillimore & Co Ltd (qv)
ISBN Publisher's Prefix: 0-85208

David & Charles+, Brunel Ho, Forde Rd, Newton Abbot, Devon TQ12 4PU
Tel: Newton Abbot 61121 (STD code 0626)
Cable Add: Books Nabbot Telex: 42904
Chairman: David St John Thomas; *Man Dir:* J Angell; *Sales Dir:* Colin Macleod; *Publicity Dir:* Nicholas Loasby; *Rights & Permissions:* Dieter L Klein
Parent Company: David & Charles (Holdings) Ltd
Subsidiary Company: David & Charles Inc, North Pomfret, Vermont 05053, USA
Subjects: History, How-to, Architecture, Archaeology, Reference, Engineering, General Science, Technical, Marine & Railway Transport
Book Club: Readers Union Ltd
Bookshop: St John Thomas, The Baker St Book & Record Shop, 33 Baker St, London W1M 1AE
1977: 145 titles *Founded:* 1960
ISBN Publisher's Prefix: 0-7153

Christopher **Davies** Publishers Ltd, 52 Mansel St, Swansea, West Glamorgan SA1 5EL Tel: Swansea 41933 (STD code 0792)
Joint Man Dirs: John M Phillips, Christopher Davies
Subjects: Literature, Belles Lettres, Poetry, Biography, History, Religion, Sport, Welsh Language Publications
1977: 15 English titles *1978:* 17 English titles *Founded:* 1941
ISBN Publisher's Prefixes: 0-7154, 0-85339

Peter **Davies** Ltd+, 10 Upper Grosvenor St, London W1X 9PA Tel: (01) 493 4141
Cable Add: Pedebooks London W1
Chairman: C S Pick; *Dir:* Nigel Hollis; *Rights:* Caroline Ball
Parent Company: Heinemann Group of Publishers Ltd, UK (qv)
Br Offs: The Windmill Press, Kingswood, Tadworth, Surrey; 11a Gower Mews, London WC1
Subjects: General Fiction, Biography, History, Religion, Travel, Seafaring,

Theatre, Countryside, Cookery
1978: 20 titles *1979:* 16 titles *Founded:* 1925
ISBN Publisher's Prefix: 0-432

Davis & Moughton Ltd+, Ludgate Ho, 23 Waterloo Pl, Leamington Spa, Warwickshire CV32 5LA Tel: Leamington Spa 24003 (STD code 0926)
Man Dir: W Edward Moughton
Subjects: Secondary & Primary Textbooks, Educational Materials
Founded: 1883
ISBN Publisher's Prefix: 0-85209

Davis-Poynter Ltd+, 20 Garrick St, London WC2E 9BJ Tel: (01) 240 3144 Cable Add: Deepeebook, London WC2E 9BJ
Orders to: George Philip & Son Ltd, PO Box 1, Arndale Rd, Lineside Industrial Estate, Littlehampton, Sussex BN17 7EN
Man Dir Editorial, Publicity: R G Davis-Poynter; *Sales, Production, Rights & Permissions:* Susan Herbert
Subjects: Fiction, History, Politics, Naval & Military, Music, Poetry & Drama, Biography, Memoirs, Politics, Sociology, Travel, Gardening, Folklore
1978: 8 titles *1979:* 8 titles *Founded:* 1970
ISBN Publisher's Prefix: 0-7067

Davison Publishing Ltd, 109 Southampton Row, London WC1B 4HH Tel: (01) 637 2541
Dirs: Thomas Tessier, Phil Edwards; *Editorial:* Jane Dixon
Imprint: Millington Books
Subjects: Science Fiction, Gothic/Romance Fiction, Biography, History, General Non-fiction, High-priced Paperbacks
1979: 21 titles *Founded:* 1973
ISBN Publisher's Prefix: 0-86000

Dawson Publishing+, Cannon Ho, Folkestone, Kent CT19 5EE
Tel: Folkestone 57421 (STD code 0303)
Cable Add: Dawbooks Folkestone
Telex: 96392
Man Dir: D A Brewer; *Publishing Dir:* Ian Williams; *Rights & Permissions:* Linda Webb
Subjects: Music, Art, Geography, University Textbooks, Biography, History, Reference, Medicine, General & Social Science, Cartography
Bookshops: Dawson Book Service, 10-14 Macklin St, London WC2B 5NG; Cannon Ho, Folkestone, Kent CT19 5EE; Dawson-France SA, BP 40, F-91121 Palaiseau, France (all three general sales); Dawson Rare Books, 16-17 Pall Mall, London SW1Y 5WB; Bow Windows Book Shop, 128 High St, Lewes, East Sussex BN7 1XL; Deighton, Bell & Co and Frank Hammond, both at 13 Trinity St, Cambridge CB2 1TD (all antiquarian sales)
1978: 53 titles *Founded:* 1809
ISBN Publisher's Prefix: 0-7129

Dean & Son, an imprint of The Hamlyn Publishing Group (qv)

Delightful Books, an imprint of Ramboro Enterprises Ltd (qv)

Delta Books, an imprint of Phillimore & Co Ltd (qv)

Dempsey & Squires Publishers Ltd*, 8 Berwick St, London W1V 3RG Tel: (01) 734 6571
Man Dir: Michael Dempsey; *Sales:* Martin Squires
Subjects: Fiction, Non-fiction illustrated books & large format paperbacks

Denholm House Press, see National Christian Education Council

J M **Dent** & Sons Ltd+, Aldine Ho, 33 Welbeck St, London W1M 8LX Tel: (01) 486 7233 Cable Add: Malaby London W1 Telex: 825751
Chairman: Piers Raymond; *Man Dir:* Peter Shellard; *Editorial:* Malcolm Gerratt, Peter Shellard (General), Vanessa Hamilton (Juvenile), Jocelyn Burton (Everyman); *Marketing Dir:* Peter Collins; *Production:* David Rye; *Publicity Manager:* Elizabeth Newlands; *Contracts & Permissions:* John Sundell; *Rights:* Maggie Hemingway (General), Clarissa Cridland (Juvenile)
Orders to: J M Dent (Distribution) Ltd, Dunhams Lane, Letchworth, Herts SG6 1LF
Parent Company: J M Dent & Sons (Holdings) Ltd
Associated Companies: J M Dent (Distribution) Ltd; J M Dent (Sales) Ltd; J M Dent & Sons (Letchworth) Ltd (Printers and Bookbinders)
Subsidiary Companies: J M Dent Pty Ltd, 604 City Rd, South Melbourne, Victoria 3205, Australia; J M Dent & Sons (Canada) Ltd, Don Mills, Ontario
Imprints: Aldine Paperbacks, Malaby Press, Dent Dolphins, Everyman's Library
Subjects: Belles Lettres, Biography, History, Natural History, Music, Reference, Juveniles, Low- & High-priced Paperbacks, Social Science, University Textbooks, Regional, Topography, Archaeology, Cookery, Gardening, Popular Science
1978: 100 titles *Founded:* 1888
Miscellaneous: Publishers of *Everyman's Encyclopaedia*, Everyman's Reference Library, Everyman's Library, Everyman's University Library
ISBN Publisher's Prefix: 0–460

Design Council Publications, The Design Centre, 28 Haymarket, London SW1Y 4SU Tel: (01) 839 8000 Telex: 8812963
Publications Manager: Terry Bishop; *Editorial:* Nicola Hamilton, Jane Sykes; *Promotion, Sales & Rights:* Pam Solomon
Orders on general trade books to: Macdonald & Jane's, 8 Shepherdess Walk, London N1
Orders on professional and educational books to: Heinemann Educational Books, 22 Bedford Sq, London WC1
Parent Company: Design Council, 28 Haymarket, London SW1Y 4SU
Imprints: Design Centre Books, Design Council
Bookshops: The Design Centre Bookshop and The Design Centre Bookshop Mail Order, 28 Haymarket, London SW1Y 4SU
1977: 8 titles *1978:* 11 titles *Founded:* 1974
Subjects: Design in the Home, Design Books for the General Public, Design Education and Design in General Education, Professional Design Books, Management Books, Educational Visual Aids, Design History Books
ISBN Publisher's Prefix: 0–85072

André **Deutsch** Ltd+, 105 Great Russell St, London WC1B 3LJ Tel: (01) 580 2746 Cable Add: Adlib, London WC1
Man Dir: André Deutsch; *Sales Dir:* W J McCreadie; *Publicity & Advertising Dir:* Sheila Murphy; *Rights & Permissions:* Piers Burnett, Anne-Louise Fisher
Subsidiary Companies: Rapp & Whiting Ltd (qv), Grafton Press
Subjects: General Fiction, Belles Lettres, Poetry, Biography, History, Music, Art, Philosophy, Reference, Juveniles, High-priced Paperbacks, Psychology, General & Social Science
Founded: 1951
ISBN Publisher's Prefixes: 0–233 (Deutsch), 0–85391 (Rapp & Whiting)

Diagram Visual Information Ltd*, 22 Chenies St, London WC1E 7EX Tel: (01) 637 4646
Dirs: Bob Chapman, Bruce Robertson, Trevor Bounford
Subjects: Reference, Juveniles

Dinosaur Publications Ltd+, Beechcroft Ho, Over, Cambridge CB4 5NE Tel: Swavesey 30324 (STD code 0954)
Man Dir: Bruce Graham-Cameron; *Managing Editor:* Althea Braithwaite; *Marketing Dir:* Mike Graham-Cameron; *Rights & Permissions:* Bruce Graham-Cameron, Sarah Allen
Associate Companies: Polyhedron Printers Ltd; Graham Cameron & Braithwaite, Advertising Consultants
Imprints: Althea, Cut & Colour Books, Dinosaur's Althea Books, National Trust Children's Series, Dinosaur's Action Books, Althea's Pet Series, Wingate Series
Subjects: Juveniles, Educational Materials, Sponsored Books
1978: 24 titles *1979:* 23 titles *Founded:* 1968
ISBN Publisher's Prefix: 0–85122

'Discovering' Books, see Shire Publications Ltd

Dennis **Dobson** (Dobson Books Ltd)+, 80 Kensington Church St, London W8 4BZ Tel: (01) 229 0225/6022
Shipping Add: 186 Campden Hill Rd, London W8
Man Dir: Margaret Dobson; *Sales:* Arthur Presland; *Publicity:* Vicky Carne
Subjects: General Fiction, Belles Lettres, Poetry, Biography, History, Music, Art, Theatre, Juveniles, General & Social Science, Economics, Political Science
1978: 26 titles
ISBN Publisher's Prefix: 0–234

Dolphin, an imprint of Doubleday & Co Inc (qv)

Dolphin Press, see Blandford Press Ltd

The **Dolphin Publishing** Co Ltd, At the Sign of the Dolphin, Milton Rd, Aylesbury, Buckinghamshire HP21 7TH Tel: Aylesbury 23211 (STD code 0296) Telex: 837216
Chairman: P G Medcalf
Subjects: Sponsored Publishing, Specialist Production & Distribution Services
Miscellaneous: A publishing division of Hunt Barnard & Co Ltd (same address)
ISBN Publisher's Prefix: 0–85940

John **Donald** Publishers Ltd+, 138 Stephen St, Edinburgh EH3 5AA
Man Dir: D M Morrison; *Editorial, Rights & Permissions:* J B Tuckwell; *Sales, Production, Publicity:* J E Bruce
Subjects: Academic, Scottish
1978: 8 titles *1979:* 14 titles *Founded:* 1973
ISBN Publisher's Prefix: 0–85976

Ad **Donker** Ltd*, 1 Prince of Wales Passage, 117 Hampstead Rd, London NW1 3EE
Man Dir: David Harrison
Parent Company: Ad Donker (Pty) Ltd, PO Box 41021, Craighall Park, Johannesburg 2001, South Africa (qv)
Subjects: General Fiction & Nonfiction, Belles Lettres, Poetry, Biography, Reference
Founded: 1976

Dorling Kindersley Ltd+, 9 Henrietta St, Covent Garden, London WC2E 8PS Tel: (01) 240 5151 Telex: 8954527 Deekay G
Man Dirs: Christopher Dorling, Peter Kindersley; *Foreign Sales:* Caroline Oakes; *Editorial:* Christopher Davis; *Design:* Roger Bristow
Subjects: Illustrated Reference Books for the International Market on Photography, Gardening, Cookery, Crafts, Family Health, Child Care, History, Sport, DIY
1978: 3 titles *Founded:* 1974

Doubleday & Co Inc, 100 Wigmore St, London W1H 9DR Tel: (01) 935 1269 Cable Add: Doubco Telex: 264676
Editorial: Margaret Pringle; *Sales, Rights & Permissions:* Gloria Ferris
Orders to: Transatlantic Book Service
Parent Company: Doubleday & Co, Inc, 245 Park Ave, New York, NY 10017, USA
Associated Companies: Doubleday Canada Ltd; Doubleday-France, Paris
Imprints: Anchor, Dolphin, Image
Subjects: General
Book Clubs: Book Club Associates (qv)
Founded: 1897
ISBN Publisher's Prefix: 0–385

Dragon Books, see Granada Publishing

Dragon's World Ltd*, High St, Limpsfield, Surrey RH8 0DY Tel: Oxted 5044 (STD code 08833) Telex: 95631
Dir, Publisher, Sales, Rights & Permissions: H A Schaafsma; *Dir, Publisher:* R Dean; *Editorial Manager:* D Lehmkuhl; *Production:* Martyn Dean; *Publicity:* Irene Howells
Orders to: PHIN Distributors Ltd, Churchill Rd, Cheltenham, Glos
Imprint: Paper Tiger
Br Off: 33 Portland Rd, London W11 4LH
Subjects: Illustrated Science Fiction, Art, Children's Books
1977: 3 titles *1978:* 14 titles *Founded:* 1976
ISBN Publisher's Prefix: 0–905895

Gerald **Duckworth** & Co Ltd, The Old Piano Factory, 43 Gloucester Crescent, London NW1 Tel: (01) 485 3484 Cable Add: Platypus
Man Dir: Colin Haycraft; *Sales Manager:* David Lines; *Publicity Advertising Manager, Rights & Permissions:* Isolde Simmonds
Subjects: Fiction, General, Academic
1977: 71 titles *Founded:* 1898
ISBN Publisher's Prefix: 0–7156

E P Publishing Ltd, Bradford Rd, East Ardsley, Wakefield, West Yorkshire WF3 2JN Tel: Wakefield 823971 (STD code 0924) Cable Add: Edpro, Wakefield Telex: 917963 Solomon, London
Man Dir, Rights & Permissions: Brian Lewis; *Sales:* Brian Lewis; *Production:* John Oldham
Parent Company: Siemssen, Hunter Ltd
Subsidiary Companies: Educational Productions Ltd, E P Microform Ltd, Tabard Press Ltd
Br Off: 10 Snow Hill, London EC1A 2EB Tel: (01) 236 6479
Subjects: Sport, History, Health, Reprints
1977: 29 titles *1978:* 30 titles
ISBN Publisher's Prefixes: 0–7158 (Educational Productions), 0–85409 (SRP), 0–85948 (Tabard)

E S A Creative Learning Ltd+, PO Box 22, Pinnacles, Harlow, Essex CM19 5AY Tel: Harlow 21131 (STD code 0279)
Dir: Michael Bodman
Subject: Primary Education
Miscellaneous: Publish reprints of GCE Examination Papers
ISBN Publisher's Prefix: 0–7159

East-West Publications (UK) Ltd+, 120 Charing Cross Rd, London WC2H 0JR Tel: (01) 379 6838
Man Dir: L W Carp
Subjects: Far & Middle East Culture & Religion, Children's & Adults Reference Books
1979: 10 titles
Miscellaneous: Associate company of Words & Music Ltd, Words & Music (Wholesale) Ltd
ISBN Publisher's Prefix: 0–85692

Ebury Press, an imprint of National Magazine Co Ltd (qv)

The **Economist** Newspaper Ltd, 25 St James's St, London SW1A 1HG Tel: (01) 839 7000 Cable Add: Mistecon Ldn Telex: 919555
Man Dir: Ian Trafford; *Rights & Permissions:* David McGill
Subsidiary Companies: Economist Intelligence Unit Ltd (UK); The Economist Newspaper Inc, 75 Rockefeller Plaza, NY 10019, USA
Br Off: 75 Rockefeller Plaza, New York, NY 10019, USA
Subjects: Economic Reference Books, Diaries, Educational Materials
1977: 4 titles *Founded:* 1843
ISBN Publisher's Prefix: 0–85058

Eddison Press Ltd, 58 North Hill, Colchester, Essex CO1 1PX Tel: Colchester 44526/7 (STD code 0206)
Dirs: R Rayner, Roger W G Curtis
Orders to: c/o Melrose Press Ltd, 17/21 Churchgate St, Soham, Ely, Cambs CB7 5DS
Imprints: Eddison Bluesbooks, Eddison Musicbooks
Subjects: Reference, Music
1977: 1 title
ISBN Publisher's Prefix: 0–85649

Edinburgh University Press+, 22 George Sq, Edinburgh EH8 9LF Tel: (031) 667 1011 Cable Add: Edinpress
Man Dir, Rights & Permissions: A R Turnbull; *Sales Manager:* J G Angus; *Assistant Secretary & Production Manager:* J McI Davidson
Subjects: Belles Lettres, Poetry, Biography, History, Music, Art, Philosophy, Religion, Textbooks, Reference, Medicine, Psychology, General & Social Science
1977: 21 titles *Founded:* 1948
ISBN Publisher's Prefix: 0–85224

Edinburgh University Student Publications Board+, 1 Buccleuch Pl, Edinburgh EH8 9LW Tel: (031) 667 1011/5718
Subjects: Politics, Sociology, Fiction, Poetry, History, all with special regard to Scotland
1978: 3 new titles *1979:* 8 new titles

Educational Book Promotions, see Macdonald & Evans Ltd

Educational Explorers Ltd+*, 40 Silver St, Reading, Berkshire RG1 2SU Tel: Reading 83103 (STD code 0734)
Man Dir: Dr Caleb Gattegno; *Editorial:* Rachel Bleackley; *Sales:* Jackie House
Parent Company: Educational Solutions (UK) Ltd of Reading
Associated Companies: Educational Solutions Inc, 80 Fifth Ave, New York, NY 10011; The Cuisenaire Co Ltd, and Educational Explorers Film Co Ltd, both of 40 Silver St, Reading, Berkshire RG1 2SU
Subjects: Primary & Secondary Textbooks and Teachers Guides, Mathematics, Reading, Foreign Languages, Educational Psychology, Career Biographies, Library Science, Humanities, Public Health, Social Science, Military History
ISBN Publisher's Prefix: 0–85225

Educational Productions Ltd, see E P Publishing Ltd

Educational Systems Ltd+, Waverley Rd, Yate, Bristol BS17 5RB Tel: Chipping Sodbury 316774 (STD code 0454)
Man Dir: N Whalley; *Publications Manager:* R E Smith
Parent Company: ESL Bristol Ltd
Subjects: Secondary & Primary Textbooks, Nautical, Management and Industrial Training Manuals, Audio-visual Aids
1977: 40 titles *1978:* 10 titles *Founded:* 1964
ISBN Publisher's Prefix: 0–900737

Paul **Elek** Ltd, see Granada Publishing Ltd

Elliot Right Way Books, Kingswood Bldgs, Lower Kingswood, Tadworth, Surrey KT20 6TD Tel: Mogador 2202 (STD code 073783)
Man Dir: Andrew G Elliot; *Sales Dir:* A Clive Elliot
Imprints: Paperfronts, Right Way Books
Subjects: How-to, Reference, Juveniles, Low-priced Paperbacks, Sport, Technical, Education
1978: 18 titles *1979:* 24 titles *Founded:* 1945
ISBN Publisher's Prefix: 0–7160

Aidan **Ellis** Publishing Ltd, Cobb Ho, Nuffield, Henley-on-Thames, Oxfordshire RG9 5RU Tel: Nettlebed 641496 (STD code 0491) Cable Add: Aidanellis Henley-on-Thames
Man Dir: Aidan Ellis
Orders to: Tiptree Book Services Ltd, Tiptree, Colchester, Essex
Subjects: Fiction, General, Children's, Sport
1977: 15 titles *1978:* 12 titles *Founded:* 1971
ISBN Publishers Prefix: 0–85628

Elm Tree Books Ltd, see Hamish Hamilton Ltd

Elmfield Press, see Severn House Publishers Ltd

Elron Press Ltd, 20 Garrick St, London WC2E 8BJ Tel: (01) 836 0670/0771
Dirs: Tim Jenns, Viv Whiteley, Alan Smith
Subjects: General Nonfiction, Illustrated Adult Reference
Miscellaneous: Provides editorial, design and production services for other publishers
ISBN Publisher's Prefix: 0–904499

Elsevier Publishing Projects (UK) Ltd, Mayfield Ho, 256 Banbury Rd, Oxford OX2 7DH Tel: Oxford 511151 (STD code 0865) Telex: 837484
Man Dir: George Riches; *Publisher:* Herman Friedhoff; *Editorial Dir:* Ben Lenthall; *Chief Editor:* Michael Desebrock
Associated Companies: E P Dutton & Co Inc, New York; Elsevier Sequoia, Paris and Brussels (qv); Phaidon Press, UK (qv); Selecciones Editoriales, Spain (qv)
Subjects: Reference, Illustrated Nonfiction
Founded: 1969 as Elsevier International Projects Ltd
Miscellaneous: Firm is a subsidiary of NV Uitgeversmaatschappij Elsevier, Netherlands (qv)

Elsevier-Phaidon, see Phaidon Press Ltd

Emblem, an imprint of Mitchell Beazley Ltd (qv)

Embryo, an imprint of William Maclellan (qv)

Encyclopaedia Britannica International Ltd+*, Mappin Ho, 156–162 Oxford St, London W1N 0HJ Tel: (01) 637 3371 Cable Add: Knowingly London W1 Telex: 23866
Man Dir & Head of Sales: Joe D Adams; *Advertising Manager:* A Tebbutt; *Publicity:* Derek Snoxall; *Rights & Permissions:* Robin Sales
Associate Companies: Encyclopaedia Britannica (Australia) Inc, Australia (qv); Encyclopaedia Britannica Publications Ltd, Two Bloor St West, Toronto 5, Ontario, Canada; Encyclopaedia Britannica, German Federal Reublic (qv); Encyclopaedia Britannica (Korea) Inc, Korea (qv); G & C Merriam Co, 47 Federal St, Springfield, Mass 01101, USA
Subject: Reference
Miscellaneous: Firm is a subsidiary of Encyclopaedia Britannica Inc, 425 North Michigan Ave, Chicago, Ill 60611, USA
ISBN Publishers Prefix: 0–85229

Epworth Press, an imprint of Methodist Publishing House (qv)

Ethnographica Ltd*, 19 Westbourne Rd, London N7 8AN Tel: (01) 607 3074
Managing Editor: Stuart Hamilton; *Sales, Publicity, Rights & Permissions:* John L Smith; *Production:* Roger Davies
Subjects: Anthropology, Archaeology, Ethnography
1977: 4 titles *1978:* 4 titles *Founded:* 1976
ISBN Publisher's Prefix: 0–905788

Eurobook Ltd, 49 Uxbridge Rd, London W5 Tel: (01) 840 4411 Cable Add: Beurok London W5 Telex: 934610
Shipping Add: PDAS Ltd, Unit 18, Denham Studios Estate, North Orbital Rd, Denham, Bucks
Man Dir: Peter S Lowe; *Sales, Publicity & Advertising:* Kim P Richardson; *Rights and Permissions:* Elizabeth Marks
Imprint: Peter Lowe
Subjects: Natural History, Illustrated Information Books, International Co-productions
Founded: 1968
ISBN Publishers Prefix: 0–85654

Europa Publications Ltd, 18 Bedford Sq, London WC1B 3JN Tel: (01) 580 8236 Cable Add: Europub London
Chairman: C H Martin; *Man Dir:* Walter Simon; *Editorial:* P A McGinley; *Business Manager:* H J Wombill; *Sales, Publicity & Advertising:* Peter G C Jackson
Subjects: Reference, History, International Affairs, Business
1977: 15 titles *1978:* 10 titles *Founded:* 1928
ISBN Publisher's Prefix: 0–905118

European Schoolbooks Ltd+, 122 Bath Rd, Cheltenham, Gloucestershire GL53 7LW Tel: Cheltenham 45252 (STD code 0242) Cable Add: Eurobooks, Cheltenham Telex: 43658
Man Dir: F A Preiss; *Sales Manager:* D Young
Imprint: European Schoolbooks Hatier Ltd
Subjects: Educational, Modern Languages
1977: 23 titles *1978:* 11 titles
ISBN Publishers Prefix: 0–85048

Evans Brothers Ltd+, Montague Ho, Russell Sq, London WC1B 5BX Tel: (01) 637 1466 Cable Add: Byronitic London WC1 Telex: 8811713
Chairman, Man Dir: L J Browning; *Deputy*

Man Dir: R C Chesher; *Dirs:* (Trade Books, Rights, Export) Miss A F White; (Educational, Overseas) F J Austin; (Periodicals) D S Dyerson; *Rights & Permissions:* Jennifer Leigh-Bramwell
Associate Company: Evans Brothers (Nigeria Publishers) Ltd, Nigeria (qv)
Subsidiary Companies: Evans Brothers (Africa) Ltd; Evans Brothers (Periodicals) Ltd (both at Montague Ho, Russell Sq, London WC1B 5BX); Rivingtons (Publishers) Ltd, UK (qv)
Subjects: Craft, ELT, How-to, General Non-fiction, Juveniles, Pre-school, Primary & Secondary Textbooks, Educational Periodicals, Plays
1977: 150 titles *1978:* 120 titles *Founded:* 1905
ISBN Publishers Prefix: 0–237

Hugh **Evelyn** Ltd, 53 Charlbert St, St John's Wood, London NW8 6JN Tel: (01) 586 5108/9 Cable Add: Bookstreet
Man & Sales Dir: Hugh Street; *Rights & Permissions:* Barbara Mills
Subsidiary Company: Hugh Evelyn Prints Ltd
Subjects: Architecture, Transport History, Military, Nautical
Founded: 1958
ISBN Publishers Prefix: 0–238

Everest Books Ltd+, 4 Valentine Pl, London SE1 8QH Tel: (01) 261 1536
Man Dir: Robin McGibbon; *Sales Manager:* Gillian Schofield; *Publicity, Rights & Permissions:* Rita Fenn
Imprints: Alpine Books, Everest Books
Subjects: Biography
1977: 40 titles *1978:* 4 titles *Founded:* 1973
ISBN Publishers Prefix: 0–905018

Everymans Library, see J M Dent & Sons Ltd

Exley Publications Ltd, 63 Kingsfield Rd, Watford, Herts, WD1 4PP Tel: Watford 43892/36961 (STD code 0923) Telex: 261234 Ref: H/5753L
Man Dir: Richard Exley; *Editorial Dir:* Helen Exley
Orders to: Noonan Hurst Ltd, 131 Trafalgar Rd, E Greenwich, London SE10
Subjects: Anthologies of Children's Work, Directories, Humour, Travel, General Trade Books, Old Age
1977: 9 titles *1978:* 5 titles *Founded:* 1976
ISBN Publishers Prefix: 0–905521

Express Logic Ltd+*, Foley Estate, Hereford HR1 2SJ Tel: Hereford 4516 (STD code 0432)
Man Dir: C B Tannatt Nash; *Dir:* Miss J L Craig
Parent Company: Business Management Promotions Ltd
Subjects: General Literature
1977: 1 title *Founded:* 1970
ISBN Publisher's Prefix: 0–904464

Eyre & Spottiswoode (Publishers) Ltd+, 11 New Fetter Lane, London EC4P 4EE Tel: (01) 583 9855 Cable Add: Exaltedly London EC4P 4EE Telex: 263398
Shipping Add: North Way, Andover, Hampshire
Chairman: Charles Shirley; *Man Dir:* Austin Holder; *Marketing Dir:* David Ross; *Dir:* Charles Friend
Parent Company: Associated Book Publishers Ltd, UK (qv)
Subjects: Bibles, Book of Common Prayer, Summa Theologiae, Religion
1978: 11 titles *Founded:* 1769
ISBN Publishers Prefix: 0–413

Eyre Methuen Ltd+, 11 New Fetter Lane, London EC4P 4EE Tel: (01) 583 9855
Cable Add: Elegiacs London EC4
Telex: 263398
Shipping Add: North Way, Andover, Hampshire
Chairman: Allen Miles; *Man Dir:* Geoffrey Strachan; *Editorial:* Nicholas Hern; *Marketing Dir:* David Ross; *Publicity Manager:* Jan Hopcraft; *Rights & Permissions:* Ann Mansbridge
Subjects: General Fiction, Belles Lettres, Poetry, Biography, History, Low- & High-priced Paperbacks, Current & Social Affairs, Plays, Humour, Film
1978: 100 titles
Miscellaneous: Subsidiary of Associated Book Publishers Ltd (qv)
ISBN Publishers Prefix: 0–413

Faber & Faber Ltd+, 3 Queen Sq, London WC1N 3AU Tel: (01) 278 6881 Cable Add: Fabbaf London WC1
Shipping Add: Elizabeth Way, Harlow, Essex
Man Dir: Matthew Evans; *Export Sales Manager:* Michael McLennan; *Publicity Manager:* John Bodley; *Rights & Permissions:* Judith Fiennes
Branch Off: Faber & Faber Inc, 99 Main St, Salem, New Hampshire 03079, USA
Subjects: General Fiction, Belles Lettres, Poetry, Biography, History, How-to, Music, Art, Philosophy, Religion, Juveniles, Paperbacks, Medicine, Psychology, Social Science, University & Secondary Textbooks
1977: 190 titles *1978:* 207 titles *Founded:* 1929
ISBN Publishers Prefix: 0–571

The **Faith** Press Ltd+*, 17 Wing Rd, Leighton Buzzard, Bedfordshire LU7 7NQ Tel: Leighton Buzzard 3365 (STD code 05253)
Subject: Religion
ISBN Publishers Prefix: 0–7164

Falcon Books*, Falcon Court, 32 Fleet St, London EC4Y 1DB Tel: (01) 353 0751
Cable Add: Pastoral London EC4
Publications Secretary: Rev Gavin Reid; *Marketing Manager:* James Fraser; *Editorial:* Eileen Thompson; *Design & Production:* Derek Keeling
Subjects: Religion, Low-priced Paperbacks, Educational Materials
Founded: 1960
Miscellaneous: Imprint for books published by Church Pastoral Aid Society
ISBN Publishers Prefix: 0–85491

Fantasy Library, an imprint of Bailey Brothers & Swinfen Ltd (qv)

Feminist Books Ltd*, PO Box HP5, Leeds LS6 1LM Tel: (053) 36765
Collective Management: A Sebestyen, S Allen, L Sanders, J Wallis
Subjects: Fiction, Non-fiction, Drama, Juveniles
ISBN Publishers Prefix: 0–904426

Fernstyle Ltd, see Books for Your Children Club (Book Clubs)

The **Financial Times** Ltd*, Business Publishing Division, Minster Ho, Arthur St, London EC4R 9AX Tel: (01) 623 1211
Telex: 8814734
Man Dir: John Prime
Yearbooks: Managing Editor: Pamela Jenkins; *Business Manager:* Don Nelson; *Sales Manager:* John Suffolk
Business Studies: Books Editor: Wilfrid Pickard
Diaries: Diary Manager: Geoffrey Phillips
Subjects: International Yearbooks & Directories, Financial & Company Information, Specialized Business Studies, Fairplay Publications
ISBN Publishers Prefix: 0–900671

Financial Training Publications Ltd, 136–142 Bramley Rd, London W10 6SR Tel: (01) 960 4486
Man Dir: John Gibbs
Parent Company: Park Place Investments Ltd
Subjects: Accountancy, Finance, Management, also publishes professional examination study manuals for students
1977: 25 titles *1978:* 20 titles *Founded:* 1976
ISBN Publisher's Prefix: 0–906322

Finax Publications+, 31 Curzon St, London W1 Tel: (01) 499 8241 Telex: 262570
Man Dir: Noel Fox
Parent Company: Tax Management Inc, 1231 25th St NW, Washington DC 20037, USA
Subjects: Tax, Finance, Investment
1978: 4 titles *1979:* 6 titles *Founded:* 1976

Findhorn Publications+, The Park, Forres IV 36 0TZ Tel: Forres 582
Man Dir: Stephen Clark; *Editorial:* Dennis Evanson; *Sales:* Edward Bickford
Parent Company: Findhorn Foundation (address as above)
Subjects: Spiritual Philosophy, Metaphysics, Inspirational Alternative Lifestyles
Bookshop: Cluny Hill Bookshop, Cluny Hill College, Forres IV 36 0RD
1978: 8 titles *1979:* 7 titles *Founded:* 1965
ISBN Publisher's Prefix: 0–905249

Firecrest Publishing Ltd, 93–100 Locksbrook Rd, Bath BA1 3HB Tel: Bath 316872 (STD code 0225) Telex: 449897
Man Dir: C A Coles (to whom all correspondence)
Associate Companies: Chivers Book Sales Ltd; Lythway Press Ltd (qv); Chivers Press Publishers (qv)
Imprint: Firecrest Large Print
Subjects: Contemporary Fiction and Nonfiction
1977: 9 titles *1978:* 16 titles *Founded:* 1977
ISBN Publisher's Prefix: 0–85119

Fishing News Books Ltd+, 1 Long Garden Walk, Farnham, Surrey GU9 7HX Tel: Farnham 726868 (STD code 0252)
Editorial, Production: W E Redman; *Sales, Publicity, Rights & Permissions:* Vivien M Heighway
Subjects: Commercial Fisheries, Aquaculture, Marine Engineering, Scientific Angling
1977: 3 titles *1978:* 7 titles *Founded:* 1953
ISBN Publisher's Prefix: 0–85238

Fitzwilliam Museum, Trumpington St, Cambridge CB2 1RB Tel: Cambridge 69501 (STD code 0223)
Dir: Prof A M Jaffé; *Bookshop Manager:* R Maddicott
Subjects: Antiquities, Coins Medals & Gems, Applied Arts, Medieval Manuscripts, Early Printed Books, Music & Letters, Paintings, Drawings & Miniatures, Prints
Bookshop: Fitzwilliam Museum Enterprises Ltd
1977: 5 titles *1978:* 6 titles *Founded:* 1816
ISBN Publisher's Prefix: 0–521216206

Flare Books, an imprint of The Harvester Press Ltd (qv)

Floris Books+, 77 Morningside Rd, Edinburgh EH10 4AY Tel: (031) 447 5145
Editorial: Michael Jones; *Sales, Production, Publicity, Rights & Permissions:* Christian Maclean
Subsidiary Company: The Christian Community Press
Subjects: Religion, Children's Books, General
1979: 8 titles *Founded:* 1976
ISBN Publisher's Prefixes: 0–903540 (Floris), 0–900285 (Christian Community Press)

Focal Press Ltd+, 31 Fitzroy Sq, London W1P 6BH Tel: (01) 387 0711 Cable Add: Focalpres London W1
Shipping Add: c/o Thomas Meadows & Co Ltd, Dale Ho, Kirkdale Rd, Leytonstone, London E11
Chairman: Nicholas Thompson; *Man Dir:* Colin Ancliffe; *Sales Dir:* R W Dear; *Production:* Finn Jensen; *Editorial:* Paul Petzold; *Marketing:* Terry Ackroyd; *Rights:* V A Talbot
Orders to: Book Centre, Rufford Rd, Crossens, Southport, Merseyside PR9 8LA
Associated Company: Focal Press Inc, Suite 3705, 10 East 40th St, New York, NY 10016, USA
Subjects: Audiovisual Methods, Graphic Arts, Textbooks, Reference, Technical & Scientific Books on Photography, Cinematography, Television, Sound, Printing Technology, How-to, Low-priced Paperbacks, Secondary & Further Education
1977: 27 titles *1978:* 41 titles *Founded:* 1938
Miscellaneous: Member of the Pitman Group of companies
ISBN Publishers Prefix: 0–240

The **Folio** Society Ltd, see Book Clubs

Fontana Books, see William Collins Sons & Co Ltd

Forbes Publications Ltd+, Hartree Ho, 151a Queensway, London W2 4SH Tel: (01) 229 9322
Man Dirs: Rosemary Crellin, Joan Forbes
Subjects: Secondary, University, Commercial & Technical Education, Educational & Scientific, Reference Books
ISBN Publishers Prefix: 0–901762

Foreign Affairs Publishing Co Ltd*, 139 Petersham Rd, Richmond, Surrey TW10 7AA Tel: (01) 948 4833
Subject: Politics

Fortune Press, an imprint of Charles Skilton Ltd (qv)

Foulis Books, an imprint of The Haynes Publishing Group (qv)

Foulsham & Co Ltd+*, Yeovil Rd, Slough, Berkshire SL1 4JH Tel: Slough 26769/30956 (STD code 0753) Cable Add: Bariebooks Slough Bucks
Man Dir: R S Belasco; *Editorial Dir:* B A R Belasco; *Editorial Controller:* Marion Harris; *Financial Dir:* G M Kitchen; *Sales & Marketing Manager:* Nigel Stovin-Bradford; *Production Manager:* Roy Mantel
Subjects: General, Technical, Educational
1977: 24 titles *Founded:* 1819
Subsidiary Company: W Foulsham & Co (Canada) Ltd, 184 Front St E, Toronto, Canada
ISBN Publisher's Prefix: 0–572 (W Foulsham)

The **Foundational** Book Co Ltd+, 29 Pinfold Rd, Streatham, London SW16 2SL Tel: (01) 584 1053
Man Dir: Peggy M Brook
Subject: Religion
1978: 1 title *Founded:* 1946
ISBN Publishers Prefix: 0–85241

Fountain Press, an imprint of Argus Books Ltd (qv)

Foxcub, an imprint of Foxwood Publishing Ltd (qv)

Foxwood Publishing Ltd+*, 27 Chancery Lane, London WC2A 1NF Tel: (01) 242 9826 Telex: 21451
Chairman: J P Howitt; *Man Dir:* Brian Thompson; *Editorial:* Gillian Schwab; *Production:* Claudia Wondrausch
Parent Company: J Howitt & Son Ltd
Imprints: Foxcub, Foxwood
Subjects: Children's Books
1977: 34 titles *1978:* 22 titles *Founded:* 1977 (under new ownership)
ISBN Publisher's Prefixes: 0–861070, 0–904897

W & G **Foyle** Ltd & John Gifford Ltd, 119–125 Charing Cross Rd, London WC2H 0EB Tel: (01) 437 0216 Cable Add: Foylibra London WC2 Telex: 261107
Chairman & Man Dir: Christina Foyle; *Man Dir:* (John Gifford Ltd): C Batty; *Editorial, Sales, Publicity, Rights & Permissions:* Alistair MacQueen
Subjects: Crafts, Antiques, Reference, Gardening, Natural History
1977: 15 titles *1978:* 15 titles *Founded:* 1904
Book Clubs: The Book Club, Thriller Book Club, Romance Book Club, Western Book Club, Travel Book Club, Catholic Book Club, Children's Book Club, Quality Book Club, Garden Book Club, Scientific Book Club
Bookshop: W & G Foyle, 119–125 Charing Cross Rd, London WC2H 0EB
Miscellaneous: Firm is owned by W & G Foyle Ltd
ISBN Publisher's Prefixes: 0–7071 (Foyle), 0–7072 (Gifford)

Gordon **Fraser** Gallery Ltd+, Fitzroy Rd, London NW1 8TP Tel: (01) 722 0077 Cable Add: Frasercard London NW1 Telex: 25848
Dirs: Gordon Fraser, Ian G Fraser; *General Manager:* Peter Guy; *Editorial (Art):* Michele Mason; *Promotion:* Shelley Bourne
Orders to: Eastcotts Rd, Bedford MK42 0JX
Subsidiary Company: The Roundwood Press Ltd (qv)
Subjects: Photography, Film, Art, Architecture, Graphic Arts, High-priced Paperbacks
1977: 17 titles *1978:* 17 titles *Founded:* 1936
ISBN Publisher's Prefixes: 0–900406, 0–86092

Freeland Press Ltd, see The Technical Press Ltd

W H **Freeman** & Co Ltd, 58 Kings Rd, Reading RG1 3AA Tel: Reading 583250 (STD code 0734)
Dirs: Sir Jonathan Backhouse, A Kudlacik, S Schaefer, R Warrington
Subjects: University Textbooks & Monographs in Pure & Applied Science
1977: 42 titles *1978:* 71 titles *Founded:* 1959

ISBN Publisher's Prefix: 0–7167
Miscellaneous: Subsidiary of W H Freeman & Co, 660 Market St, San Francisco, Calif 94104

Samuel **French** Ltd+, 26 Southampton St, Strand, London WC2E 7JE Tel: (01) 836 7513 Cable Add: Dramalogue London WC2
Chairman: Abbott van Nostrand; *Man Dir:* John Laurence Hughes; *Editorial Dir:* Lionel Noel Woolf; *Dirs:* John Bedding, Harold Pumfrett
Associate Companies: Samuel French (Australia) Pty Ltd, Dominie Pty Ltd, 8 Cross St, Box 33 PO Brookvale, NSW 2100, Australia; Samuel French (Canada) Ltd, 80 Richmond St East, Toronto, Canada; Samuel French Inc, 25 West 45th St, New York, NY 10036 and 7623 Sunset Blvd, Hollywood, Calif 90046, USA
Subjects: Drama, Reference (Theatre)
Bookshop: French's Theatre Bookshop, 26 Southampton St, Strand, London, WC2E 7JE
Founded: 1830
ISBN Publishers Prefix: 0–573

Julian **Friedmann** Publishers Ltd+, 4 Perrins Lane, London NW3 Tel: (01) 794 0061
Man Dir: Julian Friedmann; *Sales:* Andrew Jarvis
Associated Companies: Julian Friedmann Books, Julian Friedmann Literary Agency Ltd
Subjects: Fiction, Politics, History, African Studies, Gardening and General Trade Books
1978: 8 titles *1979:* 10 titles *Founded:* 1974
ISBN Publishers Prix: 0–904014

Fudge & Co Ltd+, Sardinia Ho, 52 Lincoln's Inn Fields, London WC2A 3NW Tel: (01) 242 8258
Man Dir: B K Shaw
Imprints: Research Publishing Co, Broomsleigh Press, Skilton & Shaw
Subjects: Fiction, Biography, History, Spirituality, Juvenile, General
Miscellaneous: Firm is an associate company of Charles Skilton (qv)
ISBN Publishers Prefix: 0–7050

Futura Publications Ltd+, 110 Warner Rd, Camberwell, London SE5 9HQ Tel: (01) 737 2431 Cable Add: Futurapub London SE5 Telex: 916042
Man Dir, Editorial: Anthony Cheetham; *Editorial:* Nick Chapman; *Production:* David Edwards; *Publicity:* Judy Dobias
Parent Company: B P C (qv)
Associate Company: Macdonald & Jane's Publishing Group (qv)
Imprints: Ballantine, Future, Omega, Orbit, Troubadour
Subjects: General Fiction and Nonfiction
1977: 183 titles *1978:* 186 titles *Founded:* 1973
ISBN Publisher's Prefix: 0–8600

Gaberbocchus Press Ltd+, All correspondence (except orders from UK) to de Harmonie Publishers (Gaberbocchus Books), Singel 390, 1016 AJ Amsterdam, Netherlands. Orders from UK to Big O (Gaberbocchus Books), 228 Fulham Rd, London SW10 9NB

Gall & Inglis+, 12 Newington Rd, Edinburgh EH9 1RB Tel: (031) 667 2791 Cable Add: Reckoners, Edinburgh
Man Dir: J Horsburgh
Subjects: Technical & Scientific, Commercial & Professional, Directories & Guidebooks
ISBN Publishers Prefix: 0–85248

Galliard, an imprint of Stainer & Bell Ltd (qv)

Garnstone Press Ltd, Barlavington Farm Ho, Barlavington, Nr Petworth, West Sussex Tel: Sutton, West Sussex 349 (STD code 07987)
Man & Sales Dir: Michael Balfour
Associated Imprint: Geoffrey Bles
Subjects: Nonfiction, Guides, Information, Hobbies, Prehistory, Ancient Science and Mysteries
1979: 10 titles *1980:* 12 titles *Founded:* 1966
ISBN Publisher's Prefixes: 0–900391, 0–85511 (Garnstone Press), 0–7138 (Geoffrey Bles)

Gemini Publishing*, 8 Herrick Rd, London N5 2JX Tel: (01) 226 0639
Dir: Cliff Hopkinson
Subjects: Games, Educational Materials

Gentry Books Ltd, 16 Regency St; London SW1P 4DD Tel: (01) 821 8206
Chairman: Lord Montagu of Beaulieu; *Man Dir:* C F Burness; *Editorial Dir:* Lorna Gentry
Subjects: Motoring, Travel, Business History
1978: 6 titles *1979:* 9 titles *Founded:* 1971
ISBN Publishers Prefix: 0–85614

Geographia Ltd+, 93 St Peter's St, St Albans, Hertfordshire AL1 3EH Tel: St Albans 30121 (STD code 0727) Telex: 261212
Man Dir: Dennis Stevenson; *Sales & Marketing Dir:* Colin Tagg
Associate Company: Hutchinson Publishing Group (qv)
Subsidiary Company: Robert Nicholson Publications Ltd (qv)
Subjects: Maps & Atlases, Directories & Guide Books
ISBN Publishers Prefix: 0–09

Ghost Hunters' Library, an imprint of Bailey Brothers & Swinfen Ltd (qv)

Stanley **Gibbons** (Publications) Ltd+, 391 Strand, London WC2R 0LX Tel: (01) 836 8444 Cable Add: Philatelic, London WC2R 0LX Telex: 28883
Trade Department: Stangib Ho, Sarehole Rd, Birmingham B28 8EE Tel: (021) 777 7255
Subject: Philately
ISBN Publishers Prefix: 0–85259

John **Gifford** Ltd, see W & G Foyle Ltd

Ginn & Co Ltd+, Elsinore Ho, Buckingham St, Aylesbury, Buckinghamshire HP20 2NQ Tel: Aylesbury 88411 (STD code 0296) Cable Add: Ginnbooks Aylesbury Telex: 83535
Shipping Add: Unit 1, Block H, Long Eaton Industrial Estate, Acton Grove, Long Eaton, Nottingham NG10 1GG
Man Dir: D Blunt; *Marketing Dir:* E F Keartland; *Publishing Manager:* W Shepherd; *Production:* D Miller; *Art & Design Manager:* A Miller; *Publicity:* R T Tadman; *International Manager:* A G Pittam
Parent Company: Thomas Tilling Ltd, UK (also parent company of Heinemann Group (qv))
Subjects: Primary & Secondary Textbooks
1978: approx 150 titles *Founded:* USA — 1862; London — 1920
ISBN Publishers Prefix: 0–602

Mary **Glasgow** Publications Ltd+, 140 Kensington Church St, London W8 4BN Tel: (01) 229 9531 Telex: MGP KNT 31440
Man Dir: B J Clifton; *Marketing:* C A Bayne; *Sales & Distribution:* D J Raggett; *Publicity:* Mrs J Falla
Subjects: Educational Magazines and Audio Visual Materials in EFL, Modern Languages, English, Geography
1977: 60 titles, 20 magazines, 16 films
Founded: 1956
Subsidiary: Sound Communication (Publishers) Ltd
ISBN Publisher's Prefixes: 0–900400, 0–905999, 0–86158

Glaven, an imprint of Jarrold Colour Publications (qv)

Gleniffer Press+*, 11 Low Rd, Castlehead, Paisley, PA2 6AQ Tel: (041) 889 9579
Man Dir: Ian Macdonald
Subjects: Poetry, History, Short Stories, Essays, Art, Specialists in Miniature Books
1977: 2 titles *1978:* 3 titles *Founded:* 1968
ISBN Publisher's Prefixes: 0–9502177, 0–906005

Global Book Resources Ltd, 109 Great Russell St, London WC1B 3NA Tel: (01) 580 4011 Cable Add: Globooks, London WC1
Man Dir: John Walter; *Publicity:* Jane Price
Subjects: Academic, Scientific

Felix **Gluck** Press Ltd, 72 Northcote Rd, Twickenham, Middx TW1 1PA Tel: (01) 892 3834 Telex: 21792/2886
Man Dir: Felix Gluck
Subjects: Nature, Classics, Juvenile, Reference, Children's Books, High quality Paperbacks
1977: 8 titles *1978:* 10 titles

George **Godwin** Ltd+*, Builder Ho, 1–3 Pemberton Row, Red Lion Court, Fleet St, London EC4P 4HL Tel: (01) 353 2300 Telex: 25212
Dir: John L Brooks; *Editorial:* Julia Burden
Parent Company: The Builder Ltd
Subjects: Architecture, Planning, Design Building, Technology & Crafts, Chemical & Process Engineering, Manufacturing Chemistry, Arts & Crafts, Educational
ISBN Publisher's Prefix: 0–7114

Golden Cockerel, associate company of Thomas Yoseloff Ltd (qv)

Golden Pleasure Books Ltd, Astronaut Ho, Hounslow Rd, Feltham, Middx TW14 9AR Tel: (01) 890 1480 Cable Add: Pleasbooks Fletham Telex: 25650
Dirs: Hugh Campbell, Douglas Dring
Subjects: Juveniles, Reference
Founded: 1961
Miscellaneous: Firm is a member of The Hamlyn Publishing Group Ltd (qv)
ISBN Publishers Prefix: 0–601

Goldex, an imprint of Murrays Remainder Books (qv)

Victor **Gollancz** Ltd+, 14 Henrietta St, Covent Garden, London WC2E 8QJ Tel: (01) 836 2006 Cable Add: Vigollan London WC2
Man Dirs: Livia Gollancz, John Bush; *Sales Dir:* Kenneth Kemp
Subjects: General Fiction, Belles Lettres, Biography, History, Music, Art, Architecture, Philosophy, Juveniles, Travel, Mountaineering, General & Social Science
1977: 137 titles *1978:* 130 titles *Founded:* 1928
ISBN Publishers Prefix: 0–575

Gomer Press (J D Lewis & Sons Ltd), Llandysul, Dyfed SA44 4BQ Tel: Llandysul 2371 (STD code 055932) Cable Add: Gomerian Llandysul
Man Dir: J H Lewis; *Editorial, Rights & Permissions:* Miss M Scourfield; *Sales, Publicity:* John H Lewis; *Production:* J Huw Lewis
Parent Company: J D Lewis & Sons Ltd
Imprint: Gwasg Gomer
Subjects: Welsh Language Publications, Books on Wales
Bookshop: Gomerian Press, Llandysul, Dyfed
1977: 47 titles *1978:* 50 titles *Founded:* 1892
ISBN Publishers Prefix: 0–85088

Good Reading Ltd+, 69 Fleet St, London EC4Y 1EU Tel: (01) 353 4781
Manager: Peter Daffron; *Production Editor:* Jane Jenkins; *Publicity and Marketing Manager:* Elizabeth Perkins
Parent Company: Southern Newspapers Ltd, Southampton
Imprint: Good Reading
Subject: Educational Materials
1978: 10 titles *Founded:* 1973

Gordon and Breach Science Publishers Ltd+, 41–42 William IV St, London WC2N 4DE Tel: (01) 836 5125 Cable Add: Sciencepub, London WC2 Telex: 23258
Dirs: Martin B Gordon (USA), J A Levene; *Editorial:* B J Yates, Alison Lovejoy; *Promotions:* Gill Speirs; *Rights:* Françoise Chantrel-Riols (7–9 rue Emile Dubois, Paris F-75014)
Parent Company: Gordon and Breach Science Publishers Inc, 1 Park Ave, New York, NY 10016, USA
Subjects: Astronomy and Astrophysics, Chemistry & Nuclear Engineering, Chemistry & Chemical Technology, Civil Engineering, Computers, Systems & Control Engineering, Earth & Planetary Sciences, Economics, Electronics & Electrical Engineering, Languages & Dictionaries, Life Sciences & Medicine, Management Science & Business, Mathematics & Statistics, Mechanical Engineering, Metallurgy & Materials Science, Physics, Social Sciences, Space Science & Technology, Learned Journals
1978: 35 titles *1979:* 35 titles
ISBN Publishers Prefix: 0–677

Gordon & Cremonesi, New River Ho, 34 Seymour Rd, London N8 0BE Tel: (01) 348 7042 Cable Add: Cremones London N8
Man Dirs: Gilles Cremonesi, Heather Gordon
Subjects: Biography, History, High-priced Paperbacks, Social Science
1977: 17 titles *1978:* 17 titles *Founded:* 1975
ISBN Publishers Prefix: 0–86033

Henry **Goulden** Ltd, 22 High St, East Grinstead, Sussex Tel: (0342) 22669
Man Dir: L H Goulden
Subjects: Rudolf Steiner
ISBN Publishers Prefix: 0–904822

Gower Press, 1 Westmead, Farnborough, Hampshire GU14 7RU Tel: Farnborough 519221 (STD code 0252)
An imprint of Gower Publishing Co Ltd (qv), details as for Gower Publishing except as follows:
Editorial: Malcolm Stern
Subjects: Practical management and business information
1978: 15 titles
ISBN Publisher's Prefixes: 0–7161 (pre-1976 titles), 0–566

Gower Publishing Co Ltd, 1 Westmead, Farnborough, Hampshire GU14 7RU Tel: Farnborough 519221 (STD code 0252) Cable Add: Gregg-Press Fnbro Telex: 858193
Man Dir, Sales, Rights & Permissions: N Farrow; *Marketing Manager:* C Simpson
Imprints: Gower Press (qv), Saxon House (qv), Wilton House Publications (qv) and English-language programme of Rotterdam University Press
Subjects: See under individual imprint
1977: 90 titles *1978:* 60 titles *Founded:* 1967
Miscellaneous: Gower Publishing Co Ltd is owned by Teakfield Ltd
ISBN Publisher's Prefix: 0–566

Grafton, an imprint of André Deutsch Ltd (qv)

Graham & Trotman Ltd+, Bond St Ho, 14 Clifford St, London W1X 1RD Tel: (01) 493 6351 Telex: 21879/25247
Man Dir: A Graham; *Editorial:* G Bricault, M Lawn, J Alban-Davies; *Sales:* G Raphael; *Marketing Dir:* I Pulley; *Production:* J Hodgson; *Marketing:* G Steddy
Subjects: Business Reference, Business Management, Business Law, Applied Technology, Earth Sciences, Energy Resources, Pollution Control
1979: 36 titles *Founded:* 1974
ISBN Publisher's Prefix: 0–86010

Granada Publishing Ltd+, PO Box 9, 29 Frogmore, St Albans, Herts AL2 2NF Tel: St Albans 72727 (STD code 0727) Cabe Add: Granada St Albans Telex: 262802
Man Dir: A R H Birch; *Sales Dir:* T J Kitson; *Editorial:* Mark Barty-King (Paperback), Roger Schlesinger (Hardback); *Production Managers:* M Lee (Paperback), J Parsons (Hardback); *Publicity:* H Wesolowski (Paperback), K O'Connor (Hardback); *Rights & Permissions:* M Brozicevic; *Managers:* D Fulton (Crosby Lockwood Staples Div), K Hills (Education Div), T Lacey (Children's Div)
Subsidiary Companies controlled by Granada Publishing: (Hardcover) Hart-Davis, MacGibbon Ltd; Hart-Davis Educational Ltd; Crosby Lockwood Staples Ltd; Adlard Coles Ltd; Paul Elek Ltd; (Paperback) Panther Books Ltd; Mayflower Books Ltd; Dragon Books, Paladin Books
Br Offs: 3 Upper James St, London W1R 4PB; Granada Publishing Ltd, 117 York St, Sydney, NSW 2000, Australia; Granada Publishing Canada Ltd, 100 Skyway Ave, Toronto, Ontario M9W 3A6, Canada; Granada Publishing Ltd, 110 Northpark Centre, Cnr 3rd & 7th Aves, Parktown North, 2193, Johannesburg South Africa; Granada Publishing Ltd, CML Centre, Queen & Wyndham St, Auckland 1, New Zealand; Granada Publishing Ltd, Suite 405, 4th Floor, 866 United Nations Plaza, New York, NY 10017, USA
Subjects: Agriculture, Architecture, Building, Fiction, Leisure & Hobbies, Nautical and Sailing, Biography, History, Mathematics, Nonfiction, Physics, Science, Technology, Music, Art, Philosophy, Reference, Juveniles, Low- & High-priced Paperbacks, Engineering, General & Social Science, University, Primary & Secondary Textbooks
1977: 350 titles *1978:* 400 titles
ISBN Publisher's Prefixes: 0–7053 (Granada), 0–229 (Adlard Coles), 0–258 (Grosby Lockwood Staples), 0–247 (Hart-Davis Educational), 0–246 (Hart-Davis MacGibbon), 0–586 (Panther Books), 0–583 (Mayflower Books)

Grasshopper Books, an imprint of Abelard-Schuman Ltd (qv)

W **Green** & Son Ltd+*, St Giles St, Edinburgh EH1 1PU Tel: (031) 225 4879 Cable Add: Viridis Edinburgh
Subject: Law
Parent Company: Associated Book Publishers Ltd (qv)
ISBN Publishers Prefix: 0–414

Gregg International, an imprint of Avebury Publishing Co Ltd (qv)

John **Gresham**, an imprint of Robert Hale Ltd (qv)

Charles **Griffin** & Co Ltd, Charles Griffin Ho, Crendon St, High Wycombe, Buckinghamshire HP13 6LE Tel: High Wycombe 36341 (STD code 0494) Cable Add: Explanatus High Wycombe
Man Dir, Rights & Permissions: James R Griffin; *Sales, Publicity & Advertising Manager:* Kathleen Mansfield
Br Off: Finance: 87 Chancery Lane, PO Box 63, London WC2A 1DW
Subjects: High-priced Paperbacks, Engineering, General & Social Science, University & Secondary Textbooks especially Statistics
1977: 5 titles *1978:* 7 titles *Founded:* 1820
ISBN Publishers Prefix: 0–85264

Grisewood & Dempsey Ltd, Grosvenor Ho, 141–3 Drury Lane, London WC2B 5TG Tel: (01) 379 7333 Cable Add: Greatbooks, London Telex: 27725 Gridem
Man Dir: D Grisewood; *Editorial:* M Dempsey; *Sales:* D Risner
Subjects: Children's Colour Information Books, Adult Reference
1977: 70 titles *1978:* 70 titles *Founded:* 1973
Miscellaneous: Firm is an editorial and production organization producing books for other publishers

Grosvenor Books (The Good Road Ltd)+, 54 Lyford Rd, London SW18 3JJ Tel: (01) 870 2124
Manager: J H V Nowell; *Production Manager:* Michael Smith; *Rights & Permissions:* Ronald Plumstead
Subjects: Biography, Music, Art, Philosophy, Religion, Non-Fiction, Education, Children's Books
1977: 9 titles *1978:* 9 titles
ISBN Publishers Prefix: 0–901269

The **Gubblecote** Press, an imprint of Shire Publications Ltd (qv)

Guinness Superlatives Ltd+, 2 Cecil Court, London Rd, Enfield, Middx EN2 6DJ Tel: (01) 367 4567 Cable Add: Mostest Telex: 23573 Enfield
Man Dir: D F Hoy; *Marketing Manager:* M J Hodge (Home); *Sales Manager:* P J Lynn (Home)
Subject: Reference
1979–80: 57 titles *Founded:* 1954
Miscellaneous: Firm is a subsidiary of Arthur Guinness Son & Co (Park Royal) Ltd, Park Royal, London NW10
ISBN Publisher's Prefixes: 0–900424, 0–85112

H F L (Publishers) Ltd+, 9 Bow St, London WC2E 7AL Tel: (01) 836 9081 Cable Add: Fimexted, London WC2
Man Dir: J R Hews; *Sales Dir:* Quentin Hockliffe
Subjects: Commercial & Technical Education, Legal & Parliamentary, Commercial & Professional
ISBN Publishers Prefix: 0–372

H M & M Publishers Ltd+, Milton Rd, Aylesbury, Buckinghamshire Tel: Aylesbury 5781 (STD code 0296) Telex: 837216
Chairman: P G Medcalf; *General Manager:* Mary Sketch; *Editor:* Patrick West
Subjects: Medicine, Nursing
1978: 5 titles *1979:* 6 titles *Founded:* 1971
ISBN Publisher's Prefix: 0–85602

H M S O, see Her Majesty's Stationery Office

Peter **Haddock** Ltd*, Pinfold Lane, Bridlington YO16 5BT Tel: Bridlington 78121 (STD code 0262) Cable Add: Bridbooks Telex: 52180
Man Dir: Peter Haddock
Subjects: Low-priced Children's Painting, Activity and Story Books

Robert **Hale** Ltd, Clerkenwell Ho, 45–47 Clerkenwell Green, London EC1R 0HT Tel: (01) 251 2661 Cable Add: Barabbas London EC1
Shipping Add: 4 Vestry Rd, Vestry Estate, Sevenoaks, Kent
Man Dir: John Hale; *Editorial:* Gordon Chesterfield; *Marketing Dir:* Martin Kendall; *Production:* Eric Restall; *Advertising:* John Gittens; *Publicity:* Nella Bevan; *Rights & Permissions Dir:* Betty Weston
Imprints: Include John Gresham
Subjects: General Fiction, Belles Lettres, Poetry, Biography, History, How-to, Music, Art, Sport, Philosophy, Reference, Religion, Low- & High-priced Paperbacks
1977: 592 titles *1978:* 641 titles *Founded:* 1936
ISBN Publishers Prefix: 0–7091

Hamish **Hamilton** Ltd+, Garden Ho, 57–59 Long Acre, London WC2E 9JL Tel: (01) 836 7733 Cable Add: Hamisham Westcent London Telex: 298265
Chairman: Hamish Hamilton; *Man Dir, Editorial:* Christopher Sinclair-Stevenson; *Marketing Dir:* Andrew Connel; *Production Dir:* Peter Kilborn; *Publicity Dir:* Juliet Nicolson; *Rights & Permissions Dir:* Jane Turnbull
Subsidiary Companies: Hamish Hamilton Children's Books Ltd; Elm Tree Books Ltd
Subjects: General Fiction, Biography, History, Music, Art, Juveniles
1977: 233 titles *Founded:* 1931
Miscellaneous: Company is a member of the Thomson Books Ltd group, a part of International Thomson Organization Ltd (Canada)
ISBN Publishers Prefix: 0–241

The **Hamlyn** Publishing Group Ltd+, Astronaut House, Hounslow Rd, Feltham, Middlesex TW14 9AR Tel: (01) 890 1480 Cable Add: Pleasbooks Feltham
Shipping Add & Trade Office, Sanders Lodge Industrial Estate, Rushden, Northamptonshire
Chief Executive: Hugh Campbell; *Man Dir:* Barry Rowland; *Sales:* William Dancer, David Foster, David Burbage; *Distribution:* Ron Chopping; *Publicity:* John Bradshaw; *Rights & Permissions:* Terence Cross, Patrick Hawkey, Margaret Jappe
Associated Companies: The Hamlyn Publishing Group (Canada) Ltd, 50 Prince Andrew Pl, Don Mills, Ontario, Canada; A & W Promotional Book Corporation, 95 Madison Ave, New York, NY 10016, USA
Subjects: General Nonfiction, History, How-to, Music, Art, Reference, Juveniles, Paperbacks
Book Club: Companion Book Club
Founded: 1947

Miscellaneous: Firm is a subsidiary of IPC Ltd (qv)
Publish also under following Imprints: Beaver Books, Collingridge, Country Life, Dean & Son, Golden Pleasure Books (qv), Paul Hamlyn, Newnes, Odhams, Pearson, Spring Books, Temple Press
ISBN Publisher's Prefixes: 0–600 (Beaver Books, Collingridge, Country Life, Hamlyn, Newnes, Odhams, Pearson, Spring, Temple), 0–601 (Golden Pleasure), 0–603 (Dean & Son)

Hampton House Productions Ltd, 9 York Rd, Maidenhead, Berks SL6 1SQ Tel: Maidenhead 70014 (STD code 0628) Telex: 847295
Subjects: Juveniles, General

Heinrich **Hanau** Publications Ltd*, 59 Old Compton St, London W1V 5PN Tel: (01) 734 4353 Telex: 28604 Ref 909
Man Dir: John Hanau
Associate Company: Heinrich Hanau Publications Ltd, Suite 460, 230 Park Ave, New York, NY10017, USA
Subjects: Non-fiction, High Quality Juveniles in International Co–publications
ISBN Publishers Prefix: 0–902826

The **Handsel** Press, 33 Montgomery St, Edinburgh EH7 5JX Tel: (031) 556 2796
Man Dir, Editorial, Rights & Permissions: Douglas Grant; *Sales, Publicity:* H Whittaker
Subject: Theology
1978: 2 titles *1979:* 2 titles *Founded:* 1976
Miscellaneous: Associated with Sussex University Press and The Scottish Academic Press (qqv)
ISBN Publisher's Prefix: 0–905312

Hansen House (London) Ltd, 64 Dean St, London W1 Tel: (01) 439 7797
Publisher: Charles Hansen
Subject: Music

Harcourt Brace Jovanovich Ltd+*, 24–28 Oval Rd, London NW1 7DU Tel: (01) 485 7074/5 Cable Add: Harbrex London NW1 Telex: 25775
Man Dir: C M Hutt; *Sales Manager:* J Cornwall
Subjects: Fiction, Educational, Religious, Technical & Scientific, Medical, Commercial & Professional, Music, Art & Architecture, Children's Books, Sports, Games & Pastimes, Poetry & Drama, History, Archaeology, Biography & Memoirs, Sociology, Philisophy, Encyclopaedias
Miscellaneous: Firm is a subsidiary of Harcourt Brace Jovanovich Inc, 757 Third Ave, New York NY 10017, and of Academic Press Inc (London) Ltd, UK (qv)
ISBN Publishers Prefix: 0–15

Harley & Jones, 24 Quentin Rd, London SE13 5DF Tel: (01) 852 1490
Partners: Rosemary Harley, Humphrey Jones
Subjects: General Non-fiction
Founded: 1978
Miscellaneous: Consultant editors, designers, publishers, printers. Co-publishers and packagers

Harleyford Publications, an imprint of Argus Books Ltd (qv)

Harper & Row Ltd+, 28 Tavistock St, London WC2E 7PN Tel: (01) 836 4635 Cable Add: Harprow, London WC2E 7PN Telex: 267331
Publisher: Michael Forster; *Rights & Permissions:* New York Office
Subjects: Business, Education, Chemistry

Subsidiary Companies: Barnes & Noble; Basic Books; Beacon Press; Bussell Sage Foundation; Canfield Press; T Y Crowell; Dodd-Head; Quadrangle/New York Times Book Co
Miscellaneous: Firm is a subsidiary of Harper & Row Inc, 10 East 53rd St, New York, NY 10022, USA, and an associate company of Harper & Row Latinoamericana-Harla, SA de CV, Mexico (qv), and Harper-Row (Australasia) Ltd, PO Box 226, Artamon, NSW 2067, Australia
ISBN Publishers Prefix: 0–06

George G **Harrap** & Co Ltd+, 182 High Holborn, London WC1V 7AX Tel: (01) 405 9935, 405 0941/2, 405 2853/5 Cable Add: Harrapbook London WC1 Telex: 28673 consol g
Hon President: R Olaf Anderson; *Chairman, Joint Man Dir & General Books Publisher:* G Paul Harrap, CBE; *Joint Man Dir:* M W Berry; *Publicity Dir:* C R Butterworth; *Educational & Dictionary Publisher:* P H Collin; *UK Sales Dir:* M P Hills; *Home Sales Manager:* M B Armstrong; *Overseas Marketing Manager:* M Allen; *Rights & Permissions:* Martin Lee
Associate Company: Nautical Publishing Co Ltd (qv)
Subjects: Modern Language Dictionaries, General Fiction, Biography, History, Howto, Music, Art, Reference, Juveniles, Highpriced Paperbacks, Psychology, Engineering, Sports, General & Social Science, University, Secondary & Primary Textbooks, Educational Materials
1978: 95 titles *Founded:* 1901
ISBN Publishers Prefix: 0–245

Paul **Harris** Publishing+, 25 London St, Edinburgh EH3 6LY Tel: (031) 556 9696
Man Dir: Paul Harris; *Production:* Robert Wishart; *Publicity:* J Geddes Wood
Parent Company: ARG Investments Ltd
Subjects: General Non-fiction, Novels, Maritime, Fine Arts
1977: 18 titles *1978:* 20 titles *Founded:* 1974
ISBN Publishers Prefix: 0–904505

Harrow House Editions Ltd, 7a Langley St, Covent Garden, London WC2H 9JA Tel: (01) 836 6072/6041/6031/6069 Telex: 8813235
Man Dirs: Graham D Sadd, Nicholas J Eddison; *Editorial:* Victor Stevenson; *Sales, Rights & Permissions:* Graham D Sadd, Ruth Sandys; *Production:* Kenneth D Cowan
Parent Company: Time Life International Ltd
Subjects: Music, Arts, Natural History, General, Reference
1978: 4 titles *Founded:* 1976
ISBN Publisher's Prefix: 0–905663

Hart-Davis Educational Ltd, see Granada Publishing Ltd

Hart-Davis, MacGibbon Ltd, see Granada Publishing Ltd

Harvard University Press, see The MIT Press

The **Harvester** Press Ltd+, 16 Ship St, Brighton, Sussex Tel: Brighton 723031 (STD code 0273) Cable Add: Harvester Brighton
Chairman and Man Dir, Rights & Permissions: John Spiers; *Sales, Marketing, Advertising:* Mark Holland
Imprints: Harvester Press, Flare Books, Branch Line
Subjects: History, Politics, Economics, Philosophy, Psychology, Reference,

Literature, Fiction, also Microform Publications
1978: 92 titles *1979:* 86 titles *Founded:* 1969
ISBN Publisher's Prefixes: 0–901759, 0–85527

Harvill Press Ltd+, 30a Pavilion Rd, London SW1X 0HJ Tel: (01) 589 1096/1631 Cable Add: Harvill Western Union Telex: 25611
Parent Company: William Collins Sons & Co Ltd, UK (qv)
1978: 8 titles

Haynes Publishing Group, Sparkford, Yeovil, Somerset BA22 7JJ Tel: North Cadbury 635/6/7 (STD code 09634) Telex: 46212
Chairman & Chief Executive: John H Haynes; *Man Dir:* Frank Day; *Marketing Dir:* Terry Egan; *Editorial Dir, Public Relations Officer and Rights & Permissions:* J R Clew
Associated Company: Haynes Publications Inc, California, USA
Imprint: Foulis Books
Subjects: Motoring History, Motorcar Tuning & Overhaul, Motor Sport, Touring, Aviation, Motorcycle Histories, Automobile Engineering
1978: 60 titles *Founded:* 1960
ISBN Publisher's Prefixes: 0–85696, 0–900550, 0–85429 (Foulis)

Health Science Press (Leslie J Speight Ltd), Hengiscote, Bradford, Holsworthy, Devon EX22 7AP Tel: Shebbear 469
Dirs: Leslie J Speight, Phyllis M Speight, Ian Miller
Orders to: The C W Daniel Co Ltd, 1 Church Path, Saffron Walden, Essex CB10 1JP
Subjects: Homoeopathy, Acupuncture, Radionics, Radiesthesia, Nature Cure, Biochemistry, Diet and Health
ISBN Publishers Prefix: 0–85032

Heatherbank Press+, 163 Mugdock Rd, Milngavie, Glasgow G62 6BR Tel: (041) 956 2687
Editorial: Colin Harvey; *Sales, Marketing & Public Relations:* Rosemary Harvey
Subjects: History of Social Work & Welfare, Topography (Glasgow), Occupational Costume, Community Publishing (Also publish Film Strips & Slides)
1977: 5 titles *1978:* 6 titles *Founded:* 1974
ISBN Publishers Prefix: 0–905192

William **Heinemann** Ltd+, 10 Upper Grosvenor St, London W1X 9PA Tel: (01) 493 4141 Cable Add: Sunlocks London W1 Shipping Add: The Windmill Press, Kingswood, Tadworth, Surrey
Chairman & Man Dir: Charles Pick; *Deputy Man Dirs:* T R Manderson, N M Viney; *Publicity Dir:* Nigel Hollis; *Rights & Permissions:* Anne Garwood, Elizabeth Wright
Parent Company: The Heinemann Group of Publishers, UK (qv)
Subsidiary Companies: William Heinemann Australia Pty Ltd, Australia (qv); William Heinemann South Africa (Pty) Ltd, South Africa (qv); William Heinemann (NZ) Ltd, New Zealand (qv)
Subjects: General Fiction, Belles Lettres, Poetry, Biography, History, Music, Art, Philosophy, Religion, Juveniles, Psychology, Engineering, General & Social Science
1977: 123 titles *Founded:* 1890
ISBN Publishers Prefix: 0–434

UNITED KINGDOM 389

Heinemann Educational Books Ltd+, 22 Bedford Sq, London WC1B 3HH Tel: (01) 637 3311 Cable Add: Hebooks London W1 Telex: 261888
Orders to: The Windmill Press, Lower Kingswood, Tadworth, Surrey Tel: Mogador 3511 (STD code 073783)
Chairman: Alan J W Hill; *Man Dir:* A R Beal; *Publicity Manager:* Robert Creffield
Parent Company: Heinemann Educational Books (International) Ltd, UK (qv)
Subjects: Belles Lettres, History, Music, Engineering, General & Social Science, Economics, Political Science, University, Secondary & Primary Textbooks, Education
1978: 230 titles *Founded:* 1961
ISBN Publishers Prefix: 0-435

Heinemann Educational Books (International) Ltd+, 22 Bedford Sq, London WC1B 3HH Tel: (01) 637 3311 Cable Add: Hebooks London W1 Telex: 261888
Chairman & Man Dir: Alan Hill
Parent Company: The Heinemann Group of Publishers Ltd, UK (qv)
Subsidiary Companies: Heinemann Educational Books Ltd, UK (qv); Heinemann Educational Australia Pty Ltd, Australia (qv); Heinemann Educational Books (Asia) Ltd, Hong Kong (qv); Heinemann Educational Books (East Africa) Ltd, Kenya (qv); Heinemann Educational Books (New Zealand) Ltd, New Zealand (qv); Heinemann Educational Books (Nigeria) Ltd, Nigeria (qv); Heinemann Educational Books (Caribbean) Ltd, Jamaica; Heinemann Educational Books Inc, USA

The **Heinemann Group** of Publishers Ltd+, 22 Bedford Sq, London WC1B 3HH Tel: (01) 637 3311 Cable Add: Hebooks London W1 Telex: 261888
Shipping Add: Heinemann Publishers Ltd, Lower Kingswood, Tadworth, Surrey
Chairman: Douglas Manser; *Man Dir:* Alan Hill
Parent Company: Thomas Tilling Ltd
Subsidiary Companies: William Heinemann Ltd (qv), Heinemann Educations Books (International) Ltd (qv), William Heinemann Medical Books Ltd (qv), Martin Secker & Warburg Ltd (qv), Peter Davies Ltd (qv), World's Work Ltd (qv), all UK; Heinemann & Zsolnay Ltd (see Paul Zsolnay Verlag GmbH, Austria and German Federal Republic)

William **Heinemann Medical Books** Ltd+, 23 Bedford Sq, London WC1B 3HH Tel: (01) 580 0641 Cable Add: Heinmed, London WC1B 3HH
Man Dir: Richard S Emery; *Sales Manager:* Michael Pearman
Parent Company: The Heinemann Group of Publishers, UK (qv)
Subjects: Biology, Medicine, Dentistry, Veterinary Science
ISBN Publishers Prefix: 0-433

Heinemann/Octopus, an imprint of Octopus Books Ltd (qv)

Helicon Press, Knight St, Sawbridgeworth, Herts CM21 9AX Tel: Bishop's Stortford 722318 (STD code 0279)
Man Dir, Editorial: Candida Tobin; *Sales, Production, Publicity, Rights & Permissions:* Christopher Dell
Orders to: Wentworth Book Co, Pindar Rd, Hoddesdon, Herts EN11 0HF
Associated Company: Hesperus Music Co,

28 South Main St, Newtown, Conn 06470, USA
Imprint: Tobin Music Books
1977: 6 titles *1978:* 4 titles *Founded:* 1973
ISBN Publisher's Prefix: 0-905684

Ian **Henry** Publications Ltd, 38 Parkstone Ave, Hornchurch, Essex RM11 3LW Tel: Hornchurch 42042 (STD code 04024)
Man Dir: Ian Wilkes; *Sales Dir:* William G S Oliver
Orders to: Wentworth Book Co Ltd, Pindar Rd, Hoddesdon, Herts EN11 0HF
Subjects: Plays, Natural History, Travel, History, Fiction Reprints, Sport, Automobile Engineering
1977: 37 titles *1978:* 35 titles *Founded:* 1975
ISBN Publishers Prefix: 0-86025

Her Majesty's Stationery Office, Sovereign Ho, Botolph St, Norwich NR3 1DN Tel: Norwich 22211 (STD code 0603) Telex: 97301 hemstenory
Publishing Group: Saint Crispin's Ho, Duke St, Norwich Tel: Norwich 22211 (STD code 0603)
Dir: B C E Lee
London Office: Atlantic Ho, Holborn Viaduct, London EC1P 1BN Tel: (01) 583 9876 ext 6386 Cable Add: Hemstenory London EC1 Telex: 22805
Subjects: General Nonfiction, Government Publications
1978: approx 8000 titles
Bookshops: 49 High Holborn, London WC1V 6HB (counter sales); Cornwall Ho, Stamford St, PO Box 569, London SE1 9NH (trade & mail orders); 13A Castle St, Edinburgh EH2 3AR; 258 Broad St, Birmingham B1 2HE; 41 The Hayes, Cardiff CF1 1JW; Southey Ho, Wine St, Bristol BS1 2BQ; 80 Chichester St, Belfast BT1 4JY; Brazennose St, Manchester M60 8AS
ISBN Publisher's Prefixes: 0-10, 0-11, 0-337

The **Herbert** Press Ltd, 65 Belsize Lane, London NW3 5AU Tel: (01) 794 5965
Man Dir: David Herbert
Subjects: Art, Design, Crafts, Music, Literature, Biography, and General Illustrated Books
1978: 4 titles *1979:* 3 titles *Founded:* 1975
ISBN Publisher's Prefix: 0-273

Heyden & Son Ltd, Spectrum Ho, Hillview Gardens, London NW4 2JQ Tel: (01) 203 5171 Cable Add: Heyspectra London Telex: 28303
Man Dir: K G Heyden; *Editorial:* K G Heyden, P M Williams; *Production:* M Moran; *Publicity:* T Barnett; *Rights & Permissions:* P M Williams
Subsidiary Companies: Heyden & Son GmbH, Münsterstrasse 22, 4440 Rheine, German Federal Republic; Heyden & Son Inc, 247 South 41st St, Philadelphia, Pa 19104, USA
Subjects: Secondary, University, Commercial & Technical Education, Technical & Scientific, Medical
ISBN Publishers Prefix: 0-85501

Adam **Hilger** Ltd, Techno Ho, Redcliffe Way, Bristol BS1 6NX Tel: Bristol 297481 (STD code 0272) Telex: 449149
Man Dir: Cecil I Pedersen; *Editorial:* Ken J Hall; *Sales, Publicity, Rights & Permissions:* Martin Beavis
Parent: Institute of Physics (qv)
Subjects: Scientific and Technical
1977: 16 titles *1978:* 12 titles *Founded:* 1967
ISBN Publishers Prefix: 0-85274

Leonard **Hill**, a subsidiary of Blackie & Son (qv)

Hobsons Press (Cambridge) Ltd+, Bateman St, Cambridge CB2 1LZ Tel: Cambridge 69811 (STD code 0223) Telex: 81546
Man Dir: Adrian Bridgewater; *Sales:* Alison Peasson
Subject: Education
ISBN Publishers Prefix: 0-86021

Hodder & Stoughton Children's Books, see Hodder & Stoughton Ltd

Hodder & Stoughton Ltd+, Mill Rd, PO Box 700, Dunton Green, Sevenoaks, Kent TN13 2YA Tel: Sevenoaks 50111 (STD code 0732) Cable Add: Expositor Sevenoaks Telex: 95122
Company is organized in divisions with the following divisional managing directors: Hodder & Stoughton: Eric Major; Hodder & Stoughton Educational: L M H Timmermans; Hodder & Stoughton Paperbacks: Michael Attenborough; Hodder & Stoughton Children's Books: Ronald Read
Rights & Permissions: Clare Bristow
London Off: 47 Bedford Sq, London WC1B 3DP Tel: (01) 636 9851
Subjects: General Fiction, Religion and Theology, Educational, Children's (Fiction & Nonfiction), Medical, Dictionairies, Guidebooks, Travel, Sports & Games, Co-editors (Reader's Digest and Consumer Association)
Subsidiary Companies (UK): Hodder & Stoughton Dunton Green Ltd, Hodder & Stoughton Storage Ltd, Hodder & Stoughton Overseas Ltd, The Lancet Ltd
Subsidiary Companies (Outside UK): Hodder & Stoughton (Australia) Pty Ltd, Australia (qv); Hodder & Stoughton Ltd New Zealand (qv); Hodder & Stoughton (Pty) Ltd, 45 Shortmarket St, PO Box 94, Cape Town, South Africa; Hodder & Stoughton Ltd, 30 Lesmill Rd, Don Mills, Ontario M3B 2T6, Canada
Associated Company: Hodder Fawcett Ltd
Imprints: include Coronet and Teach Yourself Books
Founded: 1838
ISBN Publishers Prefix: 0-340

Alison **Hodge**, 5 Chapel St, Penzance, Cornwall Tel: Penzance 5444 (STD code 0736)
Man Dir: Alison Hodge
Subjects: Social and Regional History, Traditional and Contemporary Crafts, Collections of Photographs
1979: 2 titles *Founded:* 1979

Francis **Hodgson**, see Longman Group Ltd

The **Hogarth** Press Ltd+, 40-42 William IV St, London WC2 Tel: (01) 836 0127 Cable Add: Hogarth London WC2
Chairman & Man Dir: Norah Smallwood; *Deputy Man Dir:* John Charlton; *Home Sales:* Roger Kirkpatrick; *Export Sales:* Quentin Hockliffe; *Publicity & Advertising:* Rosalind Bell; *Rights & Permissions:* Jane Gregory
Parent Company: Chatto & Windus Ltd, UK (qv)
Subjects: General Fiction, Belles Lettres, Poetry, History, Art, Architecture, Philosophy, Juveniles, Travel, Psychology, Psychoanalysis, Social Science
Founded: 1917
ISBN Publishers Prefix: 0-7012

390 UNITED KINGDOM

The **Holland** Press, 37 Connaught St, London W2 2AZ Tel: (01) 262 6184, (01) 723 1623
Subjects: Reference, Music, Travel, Bibliography, Art, Cartography
1979: 30 titles *Founded:* 1956
ISBN Publishers Prefix: 0-900470

Hollis & Carter, see The Bodley Head Ltd

Holmes McDougall Ltd+, Allander Ho, 137-141 Leith Walk, Edinburgh EH6 8NS Tel: (031) 554 9444 Cable Add: Educational
Man Dir: H G Bennett; *Editorial Dir:* I M Christie; *Sales & Publicity Manager:* T A Maher
Subsidiary Companies: W & R Holmes; Harold Hill & Son; Blacklock, Farries & Sons (qv); Pace/Minerva Posters; Scottish Field; Climber and Rambler; Business Scotland; Scottish Farmer; The Scottish Gardener; Horse and Pony; The Great Outdoors
Bookshop: Holmes McDougall Ltd, Barnton St, Stirling
Subjects: Secondary & Primary Textbooks
1978: 56 titles *Founded:* 1870
ISBN Publishers Prefix: 0-7157

Holt-Blond Ltd, now Holt-Saunders Ltd (qv)

Holt-Saunders Ltd+, 1 St Anne's Rd, Eastbourne, East Sussex BN21 3UN Tel: Eastbourne 638221 (STD code 0323) Cable Add: Volumists Eastbourne Telex: 877503 Volmist
Shipping Add: Unit 5B, Edison Rd, Highfield Industrial Estate, Lottbridge Drove, Hampden Park, Eastbourne
Man Dir: Robert Kiernan; *Professional Division Dir:* David S B Inglis; *College Division Dir:* Stephen White; *Publicity Manager:* Eoin MacGillivray
Parent Company: CIP, (a division of Columbia Broadcasting System Inc), 385 Madison Ave, New York, NY 10017, USA
Associate Companies: Editorial Interamericana de Argentina SACel, Argentina (qv); Holt-Saunders Pty Ltd, Australia (qv); Holt, Rinehart & Winston of Canada Ltd, 55 Horner Ave, Toronto, Ontario, Canada; Holt, Rinehart et Winston Ltée, 8305 est, rue Jarry Anjou, Montreal, PQ, Canada; Editorial Interamericana de Colombia SA, Colombia (qv); Editorial Interamericana del Ecuador SA, Ecuador (qv); Nueva Editorial Interamericana SA de CV, Mexico (qv); Holt, Saunders (NZ) Pty Ltd, New Zealand (qv); Editorial Interamericana de Peru SA, Peru (qv); Distribuidora Interamericana de España SA, Spain; Editorial Interamericana del Uruguay SA, Uruguay (qv); Editorial Interamericana de Venezuela CA, Venezuela (qv); Holt, Rinehart & Winston Inc, 383 Madison Ave, New York, NY 10017, USA; W B Saunders Co, West Washington Sq, Philadelphia, Pa 19105, USA
Subsidiary Companies: Holt, Rinehart & Winston Co Ltd
Subjects: Medicine, Nursing, Veterinary, Dentistry, Biology, Mathematics, Physics, Chemistry, University Textbooks, Education, Business Studies
1977: 182 titles *Founded:* 1900
ISBN Publisher's Prefixes: 0-03 (Holt, Rinehart & Winston); 0-7216 (Saunders)

Home Health Education Service+, 653 St Albans Rd, Garston, Watford, Hertfordshire WD2 6JP Tel: Garston (Herts) 71635 (STD code 09273)
Man Dir: Roland Fidelia
Subjects: Secondary & Primary Education, Religion, Medical, Juveniles
ISBN Publisher's Prefix: 0-900703

Ellis **Horwood** Ltd*, Coll Ho, Market Cross Ho, 1 Cooper St, Chichester, West Sussex PO19 1EB Tel: Chicester 89942 (STD code 0243) Cable Add: Horwood Chichester
Editorial: Ellis Horwood; *Sales, Production:* Clive Horwood; *Publicity:* Sue Gibson; *Rights & Permissions:* Christine Burbridge
Orders to: John Wiley & Sons Ltd, Baffins Lane, Chichester, West Sussex
Distributor: John Wiley (worldwide)
Subjects: Advanced Scientific Technology, Environmental Science, Engineering, Geology
1977: 18 titles *Founded:* 1973
ISBN Publisher's Prefix: 0-85312

Hour-Glass Press, an imprint of Bailey Brothers & Swinfen Co Ltd (qv)

How & Why Books, imprint of Transworld Publishers Ltd (qv)

Howard & Wyndham Ltd*, 44 Hill St, London W1 Tel: (01) 629 7335
Firm is not itself a publisher, but the parent company of: W H Allen & Co Ltd (qv), Brown Watson Ltd (qv), Grant Educational Co Ltd, Murrays Remainder Books Ltd (qv), Wyndham Publications Ltd (qv)

Hugo's Language Books Ltd, 104 Judd St, London WC1H 9NF Tel: (01) 278 6136
Dirs: Mrs V Lock, Mrs J Lock, R J Batchelor-Smith; *Sales, Publicity, Rights & Permissions:* R J Batchelor-Smith
Subjects: How-to, Reference, Secondary Textbooks, Courses on disc, tape & cassette
1977: 2 titles (cassettes) 4 titles (discs)
Founded: 1875
ISBN Publishers Prefix: 0-85285

Hulton Educational Publications Ltd+, Raans Rd, Amersham, Buckinghamshire HP6 6JJ Tel: Amersham 4196 (STD code 02403) Cable Add: Hulted Amersham Bucks Telex: 837916
Dirs: L G Marsh, J van der Veen, Stanley Thornes
Subjects: History, Religion, Juveniles, General & Social Science, University, Secondary & Primary Textbooks, Educational Materials
1977: 15 titles *1978:* 20 titles *Founded:* 1954
ISBN Publishers Prefix: 0-7175

C **Hurst** & Co (Publishers) Ltd+, 1-2 Henrietta St, London WC2E 8PS Tel: (01) 240 2666
Shipping Add: J M Dent & Sons Ltd, Dunhams Lane, Letchworth, Herts SG6 1LF
Man Dir: Christopher Hurst; *Editorial:* Antony J Mason; *Rights & Permissions:* Julia Hogg
Subjects: Area Studies (Politics, Economic Development, Anthropology)
1977: 25 titles *Founded:* 1968
ISBN Publisher's Prefixes: 0-838905, 0-903983

Hutchinson Educational, 24 Highbury Crescent, London N5 1RX Tel: (01) 359 3711
Man Dir: Mark Cohen; *Sales:* John Fulford; *Export:* David Lester
Orders to: Tiptree Book Services, Church Rd, Tiptree, Nr Colchester, Essex
Imprints: Hutchinson Technical Books, Hutchinson University Library, Business Books Ltd (qv)
Subjects: School Books, Technical & Academic
Miscellaneous: Hutchinson Educational is a Division of The Hutchinson Publishing Group Ltd (qv)

Hutchinson General Books Ltd, 3 Fitzroy Sq, London W1P 6JD Tel: (01) 387 2888
Man Dir: Brian Perman; *Editorial:* James Cochrane; *Sales:* David Roy; *Export:* Robert Hyde; *Marketing:* Jeremy Cox
Orders to: Tiptree Book Services, Church Rd, Tiptree, Nr Colchester, Essex
Imprints: Barrie & Jenkins, Hutchinson Junior Books, Popular Dogs Publishing Co Ltd, Rider & Co, Stanley Paul & Co Ltd
Subjects: General Fiction, Crime & Non-fiction, Biography, Memoirs, Travel, Reference, Juvenile, Fine Arts & Collecting, Dog Breeds, Eastern Philosophy and Mysticism, Sports & Hobbies
Miscellaneous: Hutchinson General Books is a Division of The Hutchinson Publishing Group Ltd (qv)

Hutchinson Junior Books, an imprint of Hutchinson General Books Ltd (qv)

The **Hutchinson Publishing Group** Ltd+, 3 Fitzroy Sq, London W1P 6JD Tel: (01) 387 2888 (Sales: (01) 388 7601) Cable Add: Literarius London W1 Telex: 261212
Man Dir: Charles Clark; *Rights & Permissions:* Susanna Yager
Orders to: Tiptree Book Services, Church Rd, Tiptree, Nr Colchester, Essex
The Hutchinson Publishing Group operates three publishing divisions:
Hutchinson General Books Ltd, Hutchinson Educational Books, Arrow Books Ltd (qqv for details)
Associate Companies: Andersen Press Ltd, UK (qv), Hutchinson Group (Australia) Pty Ltd, Australia (qv), Hutchinson Group (NZ) Ltd, New Zealand (qv) and Hutchinson Group (SA) (Pty) Ltd, South Africa (qv), Geographia Ltd, UK (qv)
Subjects: General Fiction & Nonfiction, Juveniles, Paperbacks, Science & Technical, Textbooks, Biography, Memoirs, Travel, Reference
Founded: 1887
ISBN Publishers Prefix: 0-09

Hutchinson Technical Books, an imprint of Hutchinson Educational (qv)

Hutchinson University Library, an imprint of Hutchinson Educational (qv)

Hylton Lacy Publishers, an imprint of Profile Books Ltd (qv)

I C Magazines Ltd, 63 Long Acre, London WC2E 9JH Tel: (01) 836 8731 Cable Add: MACHRAK London WC2 Telex: 8811757 ARABY G
Chairman: Afif Ben Yedder; *Editorial:* Richard Synge; *Sales:* Nejib Ben Yedder; *Production:* Kevin Pearce; *Publicity:* Christian Digby-Firth; *Rights & Permissions:* Jean Norton
Subsidiary Companies: I C Publications Ltd, Room 1121, 122 East 42nd St, New York, NY 10017, USA; I C Expo
Subjects: Economics, Political History, Regional Affairs, Business & Tourist Guides
1978: 5 titles *1979:* 5 titles *Founded:* 1974
ISBN Publisher's Prefix: 0-905268

I P C, see International Publishing Corporation Ltd

Idea Books*, 49 Endell St, London WC2H 9AJ Tel: (01) 836 8266/7
Man Dir, Rights & Permissions: Anthony Mathews; *Sales Dir:* Christopher Gates; *Publicity, Advertising Manager:* Ian Shipley
Associate Companies: Idea Books, 104-108 Sussex St, Sydney, NSW 2000, Australia;

Idea Books, France (qv); Idea Books, Italy (qv)
Subjects: Biography, Music, Art, High-priced Paperbacks
ISBN Publishers Prefix: 0-85988

Igloo Promotions Ltd*, 8 Northington St, London WC1 N2JG Tel: (01) 242 4808
Telex: 21407
Subjects: Children's Leieure, Educational

Image, an imprint of Doubleday & Co Inc (qv)

Initial Teaching Publishing Co, 39 Parker St, London WC2B 5PB Trade: c/o Pitman Publishing Ltd, UK (qv)
Subject: Primary Education
ISBN Publishers Prefix: 0-254

Institute of Personnel Management+, Central Ho, Upper Woburn Pl, London WC1 0HX Tel: (01) 387 2844
Editorial, Rights & Permissions: Sally Herbert; *Sales & Publicity:* David Grieves; *Production:* Marcella Randall
Orders to: IPM Distribution Centre, The Technical Press Ltd, Freeland, Oxford OX7 2AP
Subjects: Management, Personnel Management
1977: 14 titles *1978:* 12 titles
ISBN Publishers Prefix: 0-85292

Institute of Petroleum, imprint of Applied Science Publishers Ltd (qv)

The **Institute of Physics**+, Techno Ho, Redcliffe Way, Bristol BS1 6NX Tel: Bristol 297481 (STD code 0292) Telex: 449149
Publishing Dir: C I Pedersen; *Editorial:* Ken J Hall; *Sales, Publicity, Rights & Permissions:* M J S Beavis
Orders to: Adam Hilger Ltd, Techno Ho, Redcliffe Way, Bristol BS1 6NX
Subsidiary Company: Adam Hilger Ltd (qv)
Subjects: Physics, General Science. Publishes 9 journals and 3 magazines
1977: 13 titles *1978:* 12 titles *Founded:* 1874
ISBN Publishers Prefix: 0-85498

Institute of Pyramidology, 31 Station Rd, Harpenden, Herts AL5 4XB Tel: Harpenden 64510 (STD code 05827) Telex: 826957 INSTITUTE OF PYRAMIDOLOGY
Vice President: James Rutherford
Associated Company: Top Stone Books, 29 Station Rd, Harpenden, Herts AL5 4XB
Subject: Pyramidology
Founded: 1940
ISBN Publisher's Prefix: 0-903402

The **Institution of Civil Engineers** (Publications Division), see Thomas Telford Ltd

Institution of Electrical Engineers, Publishing Dept, PO Box 8, Southgate Ho, Stevenage, Herts SG1 1HQ Tel: Stevenage 3311 (STD code 0438) Cable Add: Voltampere Stevenage Telex: 261176
Publishing Dir: D H Barlow; *Editor in Chief:* J D St Aubyn; *Marketing Manager:* O Ball
Orders to: Publication Sales Dept, Institution of Electrical Engineers, PO Box 26, Hitchin, Herts SG5 1SA Tel: Hitchin 53331 (STD code 0462) Telex: 825962
Br Off & Bookshop: Savoy Pl, London WC2R 0BL
Subjects: (Periodicals) Electrical & Electronic Engineering, Power & Control & Science, Computer Technology, IEE Conference Publication, Colloquium

Digests, Technical Regulations, Vacation Schools
1977: 58 titles *1978:* 100 titles *Founded:* 1871
Miscellaneous: Represented by Association of Learned & Professional Society Publishers (qv under Book Trade Organizations)
ISBN Publishers Prefix: 0-85296

Inter-Varsity Press+, 38 De Montfort St, Leicester LE1 7GP Tel: Leicester 551700 (STD code 0533) Cable Add: Unifell
Man Dir: F R Entwistle; *Editorial:* D R W Wood; *Marketing, Publicity:* J S Hey; *Production:* M R Sims; *Rights & Permissions:* Miss M K Gladstone
Orders to: IVP, Norton St, Nottingham NG7 3HR
Parent Company: UCCF
Imprints: Arena; Tyndale Press
Subject: Religion
Bookshops: UCCF Bookcentre, Norton St, Nottingham
1977: 15 titles *1978:* 20 titles *Founded:* 1928
ISBN Publishers Prefix: 0-85110

Intercontinental Book Productions, Berkshire Ho, Queen St, Maidenhead, Berkshire SL6 1NF Tel: Maidenhead 34433 (STD code 0628) Telex: 848036
Man Dir: Michael J Morris; *Publishing Dir:* Desmond Marwood *Production Dir:* David Wescott
Subjects: Full colour co-edition packages, General Nonfiction, How-to, Juveniles, Paperbacks, Educational Aids and Toys
1977: 125 titles *1978:* 60 titles *Founded:* 1972
ISBN Publishers Prefix: 0-85047

International Bible Reading Association, see National Christian Education Council

International Biographical Centre, an imprint of Melrose Press, (qv)

International Book Export Group (IBEG) Ltd*, 2-4 Brook St, London W1Y 1AA Tel: (01) 493 5061/499 4688
Warehouse: International Book Distributors, 66 Wood End Lane, Hemel Hempstead, Hertfordshire
Man Dirs: James Clark, Roger Howley, J E Goellner; *Man Dir:* Trevor Brown; *Sales Manager (Exports):* Jurgen Hahn; *Promotions:* Ian Eastment
Miscellaneous: Firm is the London office of University of California Press (qv), Cornell University Press (qv) and the Johns Hopkins University Press (qv)
ISBN Publisher's Prefixes: 0-520 (California), 0-8014 (Cornell), 0-8018 (Johns Hopkins)

International Communications, see I C Magazines Ltd

International Correspondence Schools Ltd+*, Intertext Ho, Stewart's Rd, London SW8 Tel: (01) 622 9911 Cable Add: Intertext, London SW8
Subjects: Commercial & Technical Education, Commercial & Professional, Art & Architecture, Leisure
ISBN Publishers Prefix: 0-7002

International Publishing Corporation Ltd*, King's Reach Tower, Stamford St, London SE1 9LF Tel: (01) 261 5000
This firm is the holding company for Butterworth & Co (Publishers) Ltd, UK (qv), and the Hamlyn Publishing Group Ltd, UK (qv)

International Textbook Co Ltd+, Bishopbriggs, Glasgow G64 2NZ Tel: (041) 772 2311
London office: Furnival Ho, 14-18 High Holborn, London Tel: (01) 242 5832
Shipping Add: J & M Dent (Distribution) Ltd, Dunhams Lane, Letchworth SG16 1LF
Dir: Dr G MacKintosh
Subjects: Chemistry, Physics, Mathematics, Computing, Engineering, Environmental Sciences, Business Studies, Hotel and Catering
Founded: 1902
Miscellaneous: Firm is a subsidiary of Blackie & Son Ltd (qv)
ISBN Publisher's Prefix: 0-7002

Jackdaw Publications Ltd, see Jonathan Cape Ltd

Arthur **James** Ltd+, The Drift, Greenhill Park Rd, Evesham, Worcs WR11 4NW Tel: Evesham 6566 (STD code 0386) Cable Add: James Evesham
Man Dir: F A Russell; *Editorial:* M MacQueen
Subjects: Religion, Psychology
1977: 7 titles *1978:* 5 titles *Founded:* 1935
ISBN Publisher's Prefix: 0-85305

Jane's Publishing Co, an imprint of Macdonald & Jane's Publishing Group (qv)

Jane's Yearbooks, an imprint of Macdonald & Jane's Publishing Group (qv)

Jarrold Colour Publications, Barrack St, Norwich NR3 1TR Tel: Norwich 60211 (STD code 0603) Cable Add: Jarrolds Telex: 97497
Man Dir, Rights & Permissions: Antony Jarrold; *Sales Manager (Home):* B D Clements
Imprints: Cotman House, White Horse Books, Cotmancolour, Glaven, Walsingham
Subjects: Topography, Travel, Natural History, Gardening, Hobbies
Bookshop: Jarrold & Sons Ltd, Barrack St, Norwich
1978: 43 titles *Founded:* 1770
ISBN Publishers Prefix: 0-85306

The **Johns Hopkins** University Press+, 2-4 Brook St, London W1Y 1AA Tel: (01) 493 5061, (01) 499 4688
Warehouse: International Book Distributors, 66 Wood Lane End, Hemel Hempstead, Herts
Man Dir: J Trevor Brown; *Publicity Manager:* Andrew Nolan
Parent Company: The Johns Hopkins University Press, Baltimore, Maryland 21218, USA
Subjects: Humanities & Social Sciences
1978: 95 titles
ISBN Publisher's Prefix: 0-8018

Johnson Publications Ltd+, 55 Langley Park Rd, Sutton, Surrey Tel: (01) 642 6530 (Trade: 11-14 Stanhope Mews West, London SW7 Tel: (01) 373 8543)
Subjects: Medicine, History, Archaeology, Biography, Memoirs, Politics, Political Economy, Sociology, Questions of the Day, Travel & Adventure, Directories & Guidebooks, General Literature
ISBN Publishers Prefix: 0-85307

Johnston & Bacon Publishers+, 35 Red Lion Sq, London WC1R 4SG Tel: (01) 831 6100
Editorial: A G Sanders
Subjects: Road & Tourist Maps, Atlases, Scottish Publications, Books of General Leisure Interest

1977: 6 titles *1978:* 12 titles *Founded:* 1825
Miscellaneous: Division of Cassell Ltd, UK (qv)
ISBN Publishers Prefix: 0-7179

Join-in Books, an imprint of Latimer New Dimensions Ltd (qv)

John **Jones** Cardiff Ltd+*, 41 Lochaber St, Cardiff CF2 3LS Tel: Cardiff 41267 (STD code 0222)
Man Dir: John Idris Jones
Subjects: Books on Wales, Quality Paperbacks to Welsh and West Country Tourist Trade
1977: 6 titles

Jordan & Sons Ltd+, PO Box 260, 15 Pembroke Rd, Bristol BS99 7DX Tel: Bristol 32861 (STD code 0272) Telex: 449119
Man Dir: Dennis Lloyd; *Editorial/Sales Dir:* Patrick Lockstone; *Marketing Dir:* Andrew Kampe
Subsidiary Company: Oswalds of Edinburgh Ltd, 54 Queen St, Edinburgh EH2 3NY Tel: (031) 225 7308/9
London Off: Jordan Ho, 47 Brunswick Pl, London N1 6EE Tel: (01) 253 3030
Br Offs: 3 Victoria St, Liverpool L2 5QF Tel: (051) 227 4064; 44 Whitchurch Rd, Cardiff CF4 3UQ Tel: Cardiff 371901 (STD code 0222)
Subjects: Secondary, University, Commercial & Technical Education, Legal & Parliamentary, Commercial & Professional
Bookshops: 20 Clothier Rd, Brislington, Bristol (Warehouse); Tower Chambers, 19 Athol St, Douglas, Isle of Man
ISBN Publishers Prefix: 0-85308

Michael **Joseph** Ltd+, 44 Bedford Sq, London WC1 3EF Tel: (01) 323 3200 Cable Add: Emjaybuks London WC1 Telex: 21322
Shipping Add: TBL Book Service Ltd, 17-23 Nelson Way, Tuscam Trading Estate, Camberley, Surrey
Man Dir: Victor Morrison; *Marketing Dir:* Richard Douglas-Boyd; *Publicity & Advertising:* Karen Geary; *Editorial Dir:* Alan Brooke; *Rights & Permissions:* Diana Mackay
Associate Company: Pelham Books, UK (qv)
Subjects: General, Fiction, Biography, History, How-to, Reference, Young Adult, High-priced Paperbacks, Music
1978: 200 titles *Founded:* 1936
Miscellaneous: Company is in the Thomson Books Ltd Group, a part of International Thomson Organization Ltd (Canada)
ISBN Publisher's Prefixes: 0-7181, 0-7207

The **Journeyman** Press, 97 Ferme Park Rd, Crouch End, London N8 9SA Tel: (01) 348 9261 Cable Add: Journeyrad, London N8 Telex: 25247
Man Dir: Peter Sinclair
Orders to: Central Books Ltd, 14 The Leather Market, London SE1 3ER
Imprints: Journeyman Press, Radical Reprints
Subjects: Politics, Socialist and Marxist History, Fiction, Biography, Art, Poetry
1977: 4 titles *1978:* 8 titles *Founded:* 1975
ISBN Publisher's Prefix: 0-904526

Jupiter Books (London) Ltd*, 167 Hermitage Rd, London N4 1LZ Tel: (01) 800 6601
Man Dir, Rights & Permissions: S H Austen; *Editorial Dir:* Anthony Frewin
Subjects: History, Music, Art, Juveniles
Founded: 1973
ISBN Publishers Prefix: 0-904041

K & R Books Ltd, Edlington Hall, Edlington, Horncastle, Lincolnshire LN9 5RJ Tel: Horncastle 3383 (STD code 065 82)
Editorial Dir: D Kelsey-Wood; *Dir:* E Kelsey-Wood
Subjects: Natural History, Pets
1978: 8 titles *1979:* 15 titles

Kaye & Ward Ltd+, 21 New St, London EC2M 4NT Tel: (01) 283 7495/6/7 Cable Add: Kayebooks London EC2
Shipping Add: The Windmill Press, Kingswood, Tadworth, Surrey
Man Dir: S H Pickard; *Editorial:* Diane Burston, Rosemary Debham; *Sales & Publicity Dir:* Austen Smith; *Production:* Ian MacFarlen
Subjects: Novels, Belles Lettres, Biography, History, How-to, Juveniles, Sport, Hobbies, Handicrafts
1977: 68 titles *1978:* 35 titles *Founded:* 1942
ISBN Publishers Prefix: 0-7182

Kelly's Directories Ltd, Windsor Court, East Grinstead Ho, East Grinstead, West Sussex RH19 1XB Tel: East Grinstead 26972 (STD code 0342)
Man Dir: R Haddrell; *Publishing Dir:* T J Ulrick
Parent Company: IPC Business Press Information Services Ltd
Subject: Directories
1977/78: approx 10 titles *Founded:* 1799
ISBN Publishers Prefix: 0-610

Kemps Group (Printers & Publishers) Ltd+, 1-5 Bath St, London EC1V 9QA Tel: (01) 253 4761 Cable Add: Kemptory London EC1
Man Dir: M J Barber; *Sales & Publicity Dir:* X Pullen
Subsidiary Companies: Kemps Specialist Media Ltd; Halesworth Press Ltd
Br Off: 2309 Coventry Rd, Sheldon, Birmingham B26 3PG
Subject: Reference and General
1977: 15 titles *Founded:* 1946
ISBN Publishers Prefix: 0-905255

Kershaw Publishing Co Ltd+*, 109 Gt Russell St, London WC1B 3ND Tel: (01) 580 1862 Cable Add: European London WC2
Shipping Add: International Book Distributors Ltd, 66 Wood Lane End, Hemel Hempstead, Hertfordshire
Man Dir: Peter K Taylor; *Sales, Publicity, Advertising, Rights & Permissions:* Janet Buttery
Br Off: Bolholt, Walshaw Rd, Bury, Lancs
Subjects: Mathematics, Business, Social Sciences, Scholarly Reprints
1977: 3 titles *Founded:* 1969
ISBN Publishers Prefix: 0-901665

Kestrel Books, an imprint of Penguin Books Ltd (qv)

Keswick, an imprint of Marshall Morgan & Scott (Publications) Ltd (qv)

William **Kimber** & Co Ltd+, Godolphin Ho, 22a Queen Anne's Gate, London SW1H 9AE Tel: (01) 222 7684/6
Man Dir: William Kimber; *Editorial, Rights & Permissions:* Amy Howlett; *Sales:* W L Vaughan; *Production:* O J Colman; *Publicity:* C A Stuart-Hunt
Orders to: 72-74 Paul St, London EC2
Subjects: Biography, History, General, Fiction, Current Affairs, Travel, Memoirs, Naval, Military, Aviation
1977: 36 titles *1978:* 36 titles *Founded:* 1950
ISBN Publishers Prefix: 0-7183

Henry **Kimpton** (Publishers) Ltd+, 7 Leighton Pl, Leighton Rd, London NW5 2QL Tel: (01) 267 5483
Man Dir: Ronald Deed; *Editorial, Rights & Permissions:* Pat Pembroke; *Production:* G McMahon; *Publicity:* Ann Mear
Subject: Medicine
Bookshops: Kimptons, 205 Great Portland St, London W1N 6LR; Kimptons, 49 Newman St, London W1P 4BB
1977: 5 titles *1978:* 1 title *Founded:* 1900
Miscellaneous: Associate company, with Lepus Books (qv), of Henry Kimpton Ltd
ISBN Publishers Prefix: 0-85313

Kingfisher Books, an imprint of Scripture Union (qv)

Kingsmead Press+, Rosewell Ho, Kingsmead Sq, Bath BA1 2AD Tel: Bath 64474 (STD code 0225)
Man Dir: B W Frost
Imprints: Kingsmead Press, Kingsmead Reprints
Subjects: Art Reference, Illustrated Reference Books of Towns etc
Bookshops: Rosewell Ho, Kingsmead Sq, Bath; 18 Old St, Clevedon, Avon
1977: 12 titles *1978:* 14 titles *Founded:* 1969
ISBN Publisher's Prefixes: 0-901571, 0-906230

Kingsway Publications Ltd+*, Lottbridge Drove, Eastbourne, East Sussex BN23 6NT Tel: Eastbourne 27454/5 (STD code 0323) Telex: 877415
Chairman: Dr J Hywel-Davies; *Man Dir:* Hugh D Fuller; *Sales Dir:* Charles Henshall; *Sales Manager:* Geoff Booker
Subjects: Religion, High- & Low-priced Paperbacks
Miscellaneous: Firm was formed in 1977 by the merger of Coverdale House Publishers Ltd and Victory Press
1977: 12 titles *1978:* 27 titles
ISBN Publisher's Prefixes: 0-86065 (Kingsway) 0-902088 (Coverdale), 0-85476 (Victory)

Kluwer Publishing Ltd+, Harlequin Ave, Gt West Rd, Brentford, Middx TW8 9EW Tel: (01) 568 6441
Shipping Add: As above
Man Dir: W E Porter; *Marketing Dir:* J G Paul; *Editorial, Rights & Permissions:* J P H Connell
Parent Company: Kluwer BV, Netherlands
Imprints: Kluwer Business Handbooks, Kluwer Medical Handbooks
Subjects: Business, Management, Law, Taxation, Insurance, Finance, Medicine, Farming (Mostly loose-leaf)
1977: 8 titles *1978:* 8 titles *Founded:* 1972
Miscellaneous: Firm was created by Kluwer BV, Netherlands (qv) and George G Harrap & Co, UK (qv)

Knight, an imprint of Hodder & Stoughton Ltd (qv)

Charles **Knight**, see Ernest Benn Ltd

Kogan Page Ltd+, 120 Pentonville Rd, London N1 9JN Tel: (01) 837 7851
Man Dir, Editorial, Rights & Permissions: Philip Kogan; *Marketing Dir:* Peter Newman; *Production:* Janson Woodall; *Publicity, Advertising Manager:* Jane Tatam
Associate Company: Nichols Publishing Co, PO Box 96, New York, NY 10024, USA
Subjects: Business Reference, General Management, Personnel Management, Industrial Relations, Training, Energy and Energy Exploration, Educational Technology and Innovation, Careers,

Transport, Journals
1978: 35 titles *1979:* 60 titles *Founded:* 1967
ISBN Publishers Prefix: 0–85038

L S P Books Ltd, 8 Farncombe St, Farncombe, Surrey GU7 3AY Tel: Godalming 28622 (STD code 04868) Cable Add: Litserve, Godalming Telex: 919101 Video-Teknik
Man Dir: C P de Laszlo; *Rights & Permissions:* B Jafrato
Imprints: Citadel, Lorrimer Books
Subjects: Art, Cinema, Reference, Paperbacks
1977: 5 titles *Founded:* 1964
Bookshop: 8 Farncombe St, Farncombe, Surrey GU7 3AY
ISBN Publisher's Prefixes: 0–85321 (LSP), 0–8065 (Citadel), 0–8184 (Lorrimer)

Ladybird Books Ltd+, Beeches Rd, PO Box 12, Loughborough, Leicestershire LE11 2NQ Tel: Loughborough 68021 (STD code 0509) Cable Add: Ladybird, Loughborough Telex: 341347
Man Dir: M P Kelley; *Editorial Dir:* V Mills; *Works Dir:* C W Hall; *Art Dir:* R Smith; *Sales Dir:* B Cotton; *Sales Managers:* E Whitehouse (UK), G Duncan (Export)
Subjects: Children's Books, Educational (Infants, Primary, Secondary), Educational Materials
1977: 34 titles *1978:* 42 titles *Founded:* 1924
Miscellaneous: Formerly Wills & Hepworth Ltd. Associated companies include Longman Group (qv) and Penguin Books Ltd (qv)
ISBN Publishers Prefix: 0–7214

Lakeland Paperbacks, an imprint of Marshall, Morgan & Scott (Publications) Ltd (qv)

Jay **Landesman** Ltd, 159 Wardour St, London W1V 3AT Tel: (01) 439 1644/734 3233 Telex: 935163
Man Dir, Publicity: Jay Landesman; *Editorial:* Cosmo Landesman; *Sales:* Stan Stunning; *Production, Rights & Permissions:* Pam Hardyment
Orders to: Kogan Page, 120 Pentonville Rd, London N1
Imprint: Polytantric Press
Subjects: Satire, Sociology, Poetry, Fiction
1978: 4 titles *1979:* 5 titles *Founded:* 1977
ISBN Publisher's Prefix: 0–905150

Allen **Lane**, 536 Kings Rd, London SW10 0UH Tel: (01) 351 2393 Cable Add: Penguinook West Drayton Telex: 263130 Penbok g
Chief Executive: Peter Mayer; *Joint Editors-in-Chief:* Peter Carson, Philippa Harrison; *Man Editor:* Eleo Gordon; *Sales:* Alan Wherry (UK), Mike Hogben (Export); *Production:* Richard Keller; *Marketing:* David Brown; *Publicity:* Susan Meddows-Taylor; *Rights & Permissions:* Carol Heaton
Orders to: Penguin Books, Bath Road, Harmondsworth, Middx
Parent Company: Penguin Books Ltd (Allen Lane is hardcover imprint)
Associated Company: Longman Group (qv)
Br Off: See Penguin Books Ltd
Subjects: Fiction, General Non-fiction, Biography, Travel, Cookery, History, Art, Social Science
1977: 55 titles *1978:* 60 titles *Founded:* 1969
ISBN Publishers Prefix: 0–7139

T Werner **Laurie**, see The Bodley Head Ltd

Lawrence & Wishart+*, 39 Museum St, London WC2 Tel: (01) 405 0103 Cable Add: Interbook London WC1
Man Dir: J Skelley; *Sales Dir:* K Waddington
Subjects: Biography, History, Philosophy, High-priced Paperbacks, Social Science
Founded: 1936
ISBN Publishers Prefix: 0–85315

Leicester University Press+, Fielding Johnson Bldg, University of Leicester, University Rd, Leicester LE1 7RH Tel: Leicester 551860/555510 (STD code 0533)
Secretary to the Press: P L Boulton
Subjects: Archaeology, History, Literature, International Relations
1977: 15 titles *1978:* 13 titles *Founded:* 1951
ISBN Publisher's Prefix: 0–7185

Leisure Arts Ltd*, 18 St Ann's Crescent, London SW18 2LX Tel: (01) 874 0441 Cable Add: Cohallclub London Telex: 25881
Dirs: Leonard Joseph (USA), L Phillips, Lord Redesdale
Subsidiary Companies: International Art Club Editions, The Corsano Co (both at 18 St Ann's Crescent, London SW18 2LX)
Subjects: General Fiction, History, Art, Reference, Cooking, How-to, Philosophy, Poetry, Sport
Book Club: Heron Books
ISBN Publisher's Prefix: 0–900948

Lepus Books, 7 Leighton Pl, Leighton Rd, London NW5 2QL Tel: (01) 267 5483
Man Dir: R G Deed; *Editorial:* Pat Pembroke; *Publicity:* Ann Mear
Subjects: Philosophy, Psychology, Social Science, University Textbooks, Educational Materials, Sport
1977: 4 titles *1978:* 4 titles
Miscellaneous: Associate company, with Henry Kimpton Publishing (qv), of Henry Kimpton Ltd
ISBN Publishers Prefix: 0–86019

Charles **Letts** & Co Ltd+, Diary Ho, Borough Rd, London SE1 1DW Tel: (01) 407 8891 Cable Add: Diarists London Telex: 884498
Chairman: A A Letts; *Marketing Dir:* J A Kearns; *General Manager:* T M Green
Subjects: Guide Books, Travel, Education, General Non-fiction
1978: 21 titles *Founded:* 1796
ISBN Publishers Prefix: 0–85097

Lionel **Leventhal** Ltd, 2–6 Hampstead High St, London NW3 1QQ Tel: (01) 794 0246 Cable Add: Armsbooks Ldn NW3 Telex: 896691
Man Dir: Lionel Leventhal
Imprint: Arms & Armour Press
Subjects: Military and Illustrated Reference
Bookshop: Ken Trotman Arms Books, 2–6 Hampstead High St, London NW3 1QQ
1977: 26 titles *Founded:* 1966
ISBN Publishers Prefix: 0–85368

Leviathan House Ltd+*, 11 John Prince's St, London W1M 9HB Tel: (01) 629 6953
Man Dir: George Gremin; *Rights & Permissions:* Mrs M Broderick
Parent Company: W Dummer Ltd, Zurich, Switzerland
Associated Company: Verlag Moderne Industrie, Munich, German Federal Republic
Subjects: Management, Marketing
1977: 1 title *Founded:* 1971
ISBN Publishers Prefix: 0–900537

A **Lewis**, an imprint of Ian Allan Ltd (qv)

F **Lewis** (Publishers) Ltd+*, The Tithe Ho, 1461 London Rd, Leigh on Sea, Essex SS9 2SD Tel: Southend on Sea 78163 (STD code 0702)
Chairman: Charles A A Black; *Man Dir:* Frank Lewis
Parent Company: A & C Black (Publishers) Ltd (qv)
Subjects: Fine & Applied Art, Ceramics, Textiles
1978: 6 titles *Founded:* 1932
ISBN Publisher's Prefix: 0–85317

H K **Lewis** & Co Ltd+, 136 Gower St, London WC1E 6BS Tel: (01) 387 4282 Cable Add: Publicavit, London WC1E 6BS
Subjects: Technical & Scientific, Medical, Foreign Languages, Dictionaries
ISBN Publishers Prefix: 0–7186

J D **Lewis** & Sons Ltd, see Gomer Press

Frances **Lincoln** Publishers Ltd, 37–41 Mortimer St, London W1N 7RJ Tel: (01) 580 4965
Man Dir: Frances Lincoln; *Sales (UK):* David Livermore; *Production:* Richard Hussey; *Publicity:* Rosalind Lewis
Orders to: Weidenfeld & Nicolson, Heinemann Group Services, Windmill Press, Kingswood, Tadworth, Surrey KT20 6TG
Associate Company: George Weidenfeld & Nicolson Ltd (qv)
Subjects: High quality illustrated books for international co-editions
1979: 4 titles *Founded:* 1978
ISBN Publisher's Prefix: 0–906459

Linden Press, see Centaur Press Ltd

Linguaphone Institute Ltd+, Linguaphone Ho, 207–209 Regent St, London W1R 8AU Tel: (01) 741 1655 Cable Add: Linguafone, London W6 Telex: 266181
Chairman: Lord Evans of Hungershall; *Editorial, Rights & Permissions:* K Rawson-Jones; *Sales, Publicity:* L J Goodwin; *Production:* S Evans
Parent Company: Westinghouse Learning Corporation, USA
Subsidiary Company: Language Tuition Centre Ltd
Subject: English and Foreign Language Courses
Founded: 1922
ISBN Publisher's Prefix: 0–85320

Lion Publishing+, Aslan Publishing Services Ltd, Icknield Way, Tring, Herts Tel: Tring 5151 (STD code 044 282)
Man Dir: David S Alexander; *Editorial:* Pat Alexander; *Rights & Permissions:* Tony Wales; *Marketing Manager:* David Vesey
Subjects: Religion, Educational Materials
1977: 17 titles *1978:* 20 titles *Founded:* 1972
ISBN Publishers Prefix: 0–85648

Litor Publishers, 45 Grand Parade, Brighton, East Sussex BN2 2QA Tel: Brighton 603254 (STD code 0273) Telex: 87369
Dir: Bengt Christiansen
Parent Company: Editions Lito, France (qv)
Subjects: Albums, Encyclopaedias
ISBN Publishers Prefix: 0–85322

Liverpool University Press+, 123 Grove St, Liverpool L7 7AF Tel: (051) 709 3630/7303 Cable Add: Cormorant
Chairman of the Board: A M Bourn; *Man Dir:* J G O'Kane; *Assistant Secretary, Sales & Promotion:* Miss R P Meek
Subjects: Architecture, Archaeology, Oriental Studies, Economics, Education, Philosophy, General & Social Science,

Politics, History, Literature, Environmental Sciences, University Textbooks
1977: 5 titles *Founded:* 1899
ISBN Publishers Prefix: 0-85323

Lloyd-Luke (Medical Books) Ltd+, 49 Newman St, London W1P 4BX Tel: (01) 580 4255
Man Dir, Editorial, Production, Rights & Permissions: Douglas Luke; *Sales, Publicity:* Susan H Luke
Subject: Medical
1977: 7 titles *1978:* 5 titles *Founded:* 1951
ISBN Publishers Prefix: 0-85324

London Editions Ltd*, 30 Uxbridge Rd, London W12 8ND Tel: (01) 749 3926/7/8/9 Cable Add: Lonedit London W12 Telex: 933855 Lonedi G
Chairman: David St John Thomas; *Man Dir:* Hugh Begg; *Sales Dir:* John Turner
Subjects: Art, Anthropology, Reference, Sports, History, Natural History
Founded: 1973
Miscellaneous: Firm is a subsidiary of David & Charles (Holdings) Ltd, UK (qv). Firm designs and produces books for publication by other firms

London Magazine Editions*, 30 Thurloe Pl, London SW7 Tel: (01) 589 0618/584 9682
Man Dir: Alan Rose; *Sales Dir, Rights & Permissions:* Oliver Low
Subjects: General Fiction, Belles Lettres, Poetry, Biography
Founded: 1965
Subsidiary: London Magazine, a monthly review of the contemporary arts

Longbow, an imprint of W H Allen & Co Ltd (qv)

Longman Group Ltd+, Longman Ho, Burnt Mill, Harlow, Essex Tel: Harlow 26721 (STD code 0279) Cable Add: Longman Harlow Telex: 81259
Shipping Add: Pinnacles, Harlow, Essex
Chairman: C R E Brooke; *Chief Exec:* T J Rix; *Sales Dir:* M G P Wymer; *Publicity:* B Ullstein; *Foreign Rights:* Lynette Owen; *Rights & Permissions:* C Nelson
Br Off: 5 Bentinck St, London W1M 5RN
Associate Companies: Longman Cheshire Pty Ltd, Australia (qv); Armand Colin-Longman, France (qv); Langenscheidt-Longman GmbH, German Federal Republic (qv); Longman Group (Far East) Ltd, Hong Kong (qv); Longman Italia Srl, Italy (qv); Longman Caribbean Ltd, Jamaica and Trinidad (qv); Longman Kenya Ltd, Kenya (qv); Longman Arab World Center, Lebanon (qv); Longman Malaysia Sdn Bhd, Malaysia (qv) and Singapore (qv); Wolters Noordhoff Longman BV, Groningen, Postbus 58, Netherlands; Longman Paul Ltd, New Zealand (qv); Longman Nigeria Ltd, Nigeria (qv); Longman Rhodesia (Pvt) Ltd, Rhodesia (qv); Longman Tanzania Ltd, Tanzania (qv); Longman Uganda Ltd, Uganda (qv); Ladybird Books Ltd, UK (qv); Penguin Books Ltd, UK (qv); Longman Inc, 19 West 44th St, New York, NY 10036, USA; Churchill Livingstone, UK (qv); Francis Hodgson and Oliver & Boyd, UK (qv) are Divisions of Longman Group Ltd; Collins-Longman Atlases, Glasgow, distributes atlases.
Subjects: Biography, History, Children's Books, Dictionaries, Sociology, Education, Sciences, Geography, Travel, Educational Books
1978: 400 titles *Founded:* 1724
ISBN Publisher's Prefix: 0-582

Lorrimer Books, an imprint of L S P Books Ltd (qv)

Lotus Press Ltd, 8 Stourbridge Rd, Bromsgrove, Worcs B61 0AB Tel: Bromsgrove 71979 (STD code 0527) Cable Add: Lotus Bromsgrove Telex: 335497
Miscellaneous: Formerly Alan Darby Publications Ltd
ISBN Publisher's Prefix: 0-903865

Peter **Lowe**, an imprint of Eurobook Limited (qv)

Robson **Lowe** Ltd, 50 Pall Mall, London SW1Y 5JZ Tel: (01) 839 4034 Cable Add: Stamps London SW1 Telex: 915410
Man Dir: Alan Bosworth; *Publicity & Advertising:* Anne Lyon
Br Offs: The Auction House, 39 Poole Hill, Bournemouth BH2 5PX, Dorset; Robson Lowe International, Via Dell'Orso 7a, Milan, Italy; Robson Lowe (Bermuda) Ltd, Harrington Sound, PO Box 88, Bermuda
Subjects: Philately, Postal History
1977: 3 titles *1978:* 4 titles *Founded:* 1920
ISBN Publishers Prefix: 0-85397

Lucis Press Ltd+, Suite 54, 3 Whitehall Court, London SW1A 2EF Tel: (01) 839 4512
Dirs: Mary Bailey, Jack Albert (both NY), J J G Bourne, Winifred H Brewin (both UK)
Subjects: Educational, Religious, Politics, Political Economy, Sociology, Questions of the Day, Philosophy
Associated Company: The Lucis Publishing Co, 866 United National Plaza, Suite 356-7, New York NY 10017, USA
ISBN Publishers Prefix: 0-85330

Lund Humphries Publishers Ltd+, 26 Litchfield St, London WC2H 9NJ Tel: (01) 836 4243 Cable Add: Lundhumpub London WC2
Parent Company: A Zwemmer Ltd, UK (qv) who also distribute for Lund Humphries
Subjects: Art, Architecture, Graphic Arts, Languages
1977: 10 titles *1978:* 12 titles
ISBN Publishers Prefix: 0-85331

William **Luscombe**, an imprint of Mitchell Beazley Marketing Ltd, UK (qv)

Lutterworth Press+, Luke Ho, Farnham Rd, Guildford, Surrey Tel: Guildford 77536/0 (STD code 0483) Cable Add: Lutteric Guildford Telex: 858623 TELBURG
Man Dir: M E Foxell; *Sales Manager:* F T Childs; *Publicity Manager:* L J Folkes; *Rights & Permissions:* J Bunn
Subjects: Biography, History, How-to, Music, Philosophy, Reference, Religion, Juveniles, Paperbacks, General Science, Garden and Craft, Sport
1977: 38 titles *1978:* 35 titles *Founded:* 1932
ISBN Publishers Prefix: 0-7188

Luxor Press, an imprint of Charles Skilton Ltd (qv)

Lyle Publications Ltd, Glenmayne, Galashiels, Selkirkshire TD1 3PT Tel: Galashiels 2005 (STD code 0896)
Dirs: T Curtis, Annette Hogg
Subjects: How-to, Reference, Art, Directories, Antiques
ISBN Publishers Prefix: 0-902921

Lythway Press Ltd, 93-100 Locksbrook Rd, Bath BA1 3HB Tel: Bath 316872 (STD code 0225) Telex: 449897
Man Dir: C A Cole (to whom all correspondence)
Associate Companies: Chivers Book Sales Ltd; Firecrest Publishing Ltd (qv); Chivers Press Publishers (qv)
Imprint: Lythway Large Print
Subjects: General Fiction, Mystery, Crime, Romance
1977: 62 titles *1978:* 52 titles *Founded:* 1972
ISBN Publisher's Prefix: 0-85046

M & J Raven, an imprint of Macdonald & Jane's Publishing Group (qv)

The **M I T** Press, 126 Buckingham Palace Rd, London SW1W 9SD Tel: (01) 730 9208/9 Cable Add: Chibooks Telex: 23933 Chibooks Ldn
Man Dir: Graham K Voaden; *Sales Dir:* Warren Bertram
Subjects: Biograaphy, History, Music, Art, Philosophy, Reference, Paperbacks, Medicine, Psychology, Engineering, General & Social Science, Education
1977: 100 titles *1978:* 90 titles
Miscellaneous: Branch of MIT Press, Cambridge, Mass, USA
Associated Companies: University of Chicago Press Ltd, Harvard University Press (both at 126 Buckingham Palace Rd, London SW1W 9SD)
ISBN Publisher's Prefixes: 0-262 (MIT), 0-226 (University of Chicago), 0-674 (Harvard University Press)

M R P, see Motor Racing Publications Ltd

M T P Press Ltd, Falcon Ho, Cable St, Lancaster LA1 1PE Tel: Lancaster 68765 (STD code 0524) Telex: 65212
Man Dir: D G T Bloomer; *Sales Dir:* C K Timms
Subjects: Medicine, Psychology
1977: 23 titles *1978:* 35 titles *Founded:* 1969
ISBN Publishers Prefix: 0-85200

M W H London Publishers, 233 Seven Sisters Rd, London N4 2DA Tel: (01) 272 5170 Cable Add: Muslimdar London N4 Telex: 8812176 Muslim G
Man Dir: Ashur A Shamis
Associate Company: Muslim Information Services, UK
Subjects: Islamic and Arabic Studies
Bookshop: address as above
1978: 5 titles *1979:* 9 titles *Founded:* 1970
ISBN Publisher's Prefix: 0-906194

Macdonald & Evans Ltd, Estover, Plymouth, Devon PL6 7PZ Tel: Plymouth 705251 (STD code 0752) Cable Add: MacEvans, Plymouth Telex: 45635
Man Dirs: G B Davis, R B North; *Editorial:* D A F Sutherland; *Sales & Publicity:* G J Marshall
Subsidiary Companies: Continua Productions Ltd; Macdonald & Evans (Publications) Ltd; Educational Book Promotions; Macdonald & Evans Distribution Services Ltd (all at Estover, Plymouth)
Subjects: Commercial, Professional & Business Studies, Dance & Movement, Geography, Language & Literature, Law, Science & Technology, Social Studies
1978: 85 titles *1979:* 76 titles *Founded:* 1907
ISBN Publishers Prefix: 0-7121

Macdonald & Jane's Publishing Group+, 8 Shepherdess Walk, London N1 7LW Tel: (01) 251 1666 Cable Add: Macjan Telex: 23168
Chairman: A M Alfred; *Man Dir:* Ronald Whiting; *Marketing Dir:* David Rivers; *Editorial:* Penelope Hoare (General), Sidney Jackson (Jane's/Military), Alan Smith (Queen Anne Press); *Publicity:* Gilly Vincent; *Rights & Permissions:* Pat James

The Publishing Group consists of two companies:
Macdonald General Books/Queen Anne Press: Personnel as above
Jane's Publishing Company: *Chairman:* Ronald Whiting; *Man Dir:* Sidney Jackson; *Rights & Permissions:* Pat James; *Publicity:* Andrea Pomroy
Orders to: Macdonald Publishing Services (Paulton) Ltd, Nr Bristol, Avon BS18 5LQ; Jane's Yearbooks, orders to London office
Parent Company: B P C (qv)
Associate Companies: Futura Publications (qv); Macdonald Educational Ltd (qv); Phoebus Publishing Co (qv); Purnell Books (qv), Adkinson Parrish Ltd (qv)
Imprints: Macdonald General Books, Queen Anne Press, Jane's Publishing Co, Raven Books, M & J Raven, Playfair, Troubador (Hardback)
Subjects: General Fiction & Nonfiction, Naval, Military, Aviation, Juveniles, Jane's Yearbooks, Sport
1978: approx 160 titles *1979:* approx 180 titles *Founded:* 1973
ISBN Publisher's Prefixes: 0-354, 0-356

Macdonald Educational Ltd+, Holywell Ho, Worship St, London EC2A 2EN Tel: (01) 247 5499 Cable Add: Maced Ldn EC2 Telex: 885233
Man Dir: T V Boardman Jr; *Deputy Man Dir & Editorial Dir:* Stephen Pawley; *Sales & Marketing Dir:* Barrie Knight; *Sales Dir, Export:* K E Pickett; *Rights & Permissions:* Jane Cholmeley; *Production Dir:* Philip Hughes; *Marketing Manager:* Derek Cross
Orders to: Macdonald Publishing Services (Paulton) Ltd, Paulton, Bristol, Avon BS18 5LQ
Parent Company: B P C Ltd (qv)
Associate Companies: Macdonald & Jane's Publishing Group (qv for other UK associate companies); Macdonald (Middle East) Sarl, Holywell Ho, Worship St, London EC2; Macdonald Raintree Inc, 205 West Highland Ave, Milwaukee, Wisconsin 53203, USA; Macdonald Educational Australia Pty Ltd, 203 Drummond St, Carlton, Victoria 3053, Australia
Imprints: Macdonald, Macdonald Guidelines, Macdonald Starters
Subjects: Colour Information and Reference Books for pre-School, Primary, Middle and Secondary Schools; Adult Reference Books
1978: 107 titles *1979:* 129 titles *Founded:* 1971
ISBN Publisher's Prefix: 0-356

Macdonald General Books, an imprint of Macdonald & Jane's Publishing Group (qv)

Macdonald Publishers+*, Edgefield Rd, Loanhead, Midlothian EH20 9SY Tel: (031) 440 0246
Subjects: Scottish Poetry, Biography

McGraw-Hill Book Co (UK) Ltd+, Shoppenhangers Rd, Maidenhead, Berkshire SL6 2QL Tel: Maidenhead 23431 (STD code 0628) Cable Add: McGrawHill Telex: 848484
Vice President: Derek Speake; *Publishing Dir:* Margaret Tilling; *Rights & Permissions:* Lena Armstrong; *Marketing Dir:* Ian McIntyre
Associate Companies: McGraw-Hill Book Co Australia Pty Ltd, Australia (qv); McGraw-Hill Ryerson Ltd, Canada; Editôra McGraw-Hill do Brasil Ltda, Brazil (qv); McGraw-Hill Inc, France (qv); McGraw-Hill Book Co GmbH, Federal Republic of Germany (qv); Tata McGraw-Hill Publishing Co Ltd, India (qv); McGraw-Hill Kogakusha Ltd, Japan; Libros McGraw-Hill de Mexico SA de CV, Mexico (qv); McGraw-Hill Book Co, New Zealand, Ltd, New Zealand (qv); Editorial McGraw-Hill Latinoamericana SA, Panama (qv); McGraw-Hill International Book Co, Singapore (qv); McGraw-Hill Book Co (SA) (Pty) Ltd, South Africa (qv); McGraw-Hill Book Co, Switzerland; McGraw-Hill de Espana SA, Spain; Editora McGraw-Hill, Portugal
Subjects: Reference, Medicine, Psychology, Engineering, General & Social Science, University, Secondary Textbooks, Educational Materials, Gregg Shorthand, Further Education
1978: 40 titles *1979:* 50 titles *Founded:* 1899
Miscellaneous: Firm is a subsidiary of McGraw-Hill Inc, 1221 Ave of the Americas, New York, NY 10020, USA
ISBN Publishers Prefix: 0-07

MacLaren & Sons Ltd, an imprint of Applied Science Publishers Ltd (qv)

William **Maclellan**+*, 104 Hill St, Glasgow G3 6UA Tel: (041) 332 0727
Imprint: Embryo
Subjects: Art, Folklore, Poetry, Music, Travel, Philosophy, all with particular reference to Scotland
ISBN Publishers Prefix: 0-85335

Macmillan Education Ltd+, Houndmills, Basingstoke, Hampshire RG21 2XS Tel: Basingstoke 29242 (STD code 0256) Cable Add: Publish Basingstoke Telex: 858493
Chairman: N G Byam Shaw; *Man Dir:* S A Josephs; *Publishing Dirs:* (Primary Schools & Educational Media) R S Balkwill; (Secondary Schools) A S Feldmann; (Overseas Schools) M J Thorrowgood; (Children's Books) M Wace; *Marketing Dir:* D Fothergill; *Dir (Special Education):* W S D Jollands; *Dir (West Africa):* C R Harrison
Subjects: Reference, Juveniles, Secondary & Primary Textbooks, Educational Materials
Miscellaneous: Firm is a subsidiary of Macmillan Publishers Ltd, UK (qv)
ISBN Publishers Prefix: 0-333

Macmillan London Ltd+, 4 Little Essex St, London WC2R 3LF Tel: (01) 836 6633 Cable Add: Publish London WC2 Telex: 262024
Shipping Add: Houndmills, Basingstoke, Hampshire RG21 2XS
Chairman: A D Maclean; *Man Dir:* Robert McKay; *Publishing Dirs:* (Crime & Suspense) Lord Hardinge; (Popular Illustrated) Julian Ashby; *Publicity Dir:* J Hadfield; *Rights & Permissions:* Tess Sacco
Subjects: General Fiction, Belles Lettres, Poetry, Biography, History, How-to, Reference, Juveniles, High-priced Paperbacks
Miscellaneous: Firm is a subsidiary of Macmillan Publishers Ltd, UK (qv)
ISBN Publishers Prefix: 0-333

The **Macmillan Press** Ltd+, 4 Little Essex St, London WC2R 3LF Tel: (01) 836 6633 Cable Add: Publish London WC2 Telex: 262024
Shipping Add: Houndmills, Basingstoke, Hampshire RG21 2XS
Man Dir: A Soar; *Sales:* Barry Turner; *Publicity Manager:* M Horsfield; *Publishing Dirs:* T M Farmiloe, T J Jackman; *European Sales:* J M Arnhard Aretz; *Rights Manager:* N Piggot
Parent Company: Macmillan Publishers Ltd, UK (qv)
Subjects: College and University Textbooks, Monographs and Reference Books in Science, Technology, Medicine, Humanities, Social Sciences, English as a Foreign Language
1978: 306 titles
ISBN Publishers Prefix: 0-333

Macmillan Publishers Ltd+, 4 Little Essex St, London WC2R 3LF Tel: (01) 836 6633 Cable Add: Publish London WC2 Telex: 262024
Man Dir: N G Byam Shaw
Orders to: Macmillan Administration Ltd, Houndmills, Basingstoke, Hants
Miscellaneous: Firm is a holding company
Associate Companies: Gill & Macmillan Ltd, Republic of Ireland (qv); Northern Nigeria Publishing Co Ltd, Nigeria
Subsidiaries in the UK: Macmillan Education Ltd (qv); Macmillan London Ltd (qv); The Macmillan Press Ltd (qv); Macmillan Journals Ltd
Subsidiaries outside the UK: Grove's Dictionaries of Music Inc, USA; The Macmillan Co of Australia Pty Ltd, Australia (qv); Macmillan Publishers (HK) Ltd, Hong Kong (qv); The Macmillan Co of India Ltd, India (qv); Macmillan Shuppan, Japan; Macmillan Books for Africa, Kenya; Macmillan Nigeria Publishers Ltd, Nigeria (qv) (previous two entries only 40% owned from 1978–79); Macmillan South East Asia Ltd, Singapore (qv); Macmillan South Africa (Publishers) Pty Ltd, South Africa (qv); Macmillan Shuppan KK, Japan; Peninsula Publishers Ltd, Hong Kong; St Martin's Press Inc, 175 Fifth Ave, New York, NY 10010, USA; The Macmillan Co of New Zealand Ltd, New Zealand
Branch Office outside the UK: PO Box 10722 Off Link Rd, Accra, Ghana

Made Simple Books, an imprint of W H Allen & Co Ltd (qv)

Magna Print Books+, Skirden, Bolton-by-Bowland, Nr Clitheroe, Lancs BB7 4NZ Tel: Bolton-by-Bowland 243 (STD code 02007)
Man Dir, Production: Derek Cressey; *Sales:* Margaret Cressey
Parent Company: Library Magna Books Ltd
Imprint: Magna Large Print Series
Subjects: Fiction, Nonfiction, Handicrafts & Pastimes in Large Print
1977: 38 titles *1978:* 53 titles *Founded:* 1973
ISBN Publishers Prefix: 0-86009

Magnum Books*, 11 New Fetter Lane, London EC4P 4EE Tel: (01) 583 9855 Cable Add: Elegiacs London EC4 Telex: 263398
Man Dir: Charles Shirley; *Editorial Dir:* Ms Chris Holifield; *Marketing Dir:* Graham Lane; *Production Dir:* Chris Holgate; *Publicity:* Nichola Wilson; *Rights & Permissions:* Ann Mansbridge
Miscellaneous: An imprint of Associated Book Publishers Ltd (qv)
ISBN Publisher's Prefix: 0-417

Mainstream Publishing Co (Edinburgh) Ltd+, 28 Barony St, Edinburgh EH3 6NY Tel: (031) 556 9913
Dirs: Bill Campbell, Peter Mackenzie
Branch Off: 5 Glen St, Edinburgh EH3 9JD
Subjects: Literature, History, Current Affairs, Politics, General
1978: 3 titles *1979:* 4 titles *Founded:* 1978
ISBN Publisher's Prefix: 0-906391

Malaby Press, an imprint of J M Dent & Sons Ltd, UK (qv)

Manchester University Press+, Oxford Rd, Manchester M13 9PL Tel: (061) 273 5539
Publisher: J M N Spencer; *Editorial:* Ray Offord; *Marketing:* Clive Luhrs; *Rights & Permissions:* Miss S A Lawrence
Subjects: English Language and Literature, Modern Languages, History, Philosophy, Religion, Medicine, Psychology, Engineering, General & Social Science, Economics, Geography, University Textbooks
1977: 45 titles *Founded:* 1912
ISBN Publishers Prefix: 0-7190

Mansell Publishing+, 3 Bloomsbury Pl, London WC1A 2QA Tel: (01) 580 6784 Cable Add: Infoman London Telex: 28604 ref 1647
Man Dir: John E Duncan; *Editorial, Rights & Permissions:* Murray Mindlin; *Sales Manager:* June S Eaton; *Publicity & Advertising:* Catherine Johnston
Parent Company: Bemrose UK Ltd (qv for associate companies)
Subjects: Bibliographic Reference
1977: 31 titles *1978:* 26 titles *Founded:* 1966
ISBN Publisher's Prefix: 0-7201 (Mansell)

Manxman Publications, an imprint of Shearwater Press Ltd, Isle of Man (qv)

Map Productions Ltd, see George Philip & Son Ltd

Marshall Cavendish Ltd, 58 Old Compton St, London W1V 5PA Tel: (01) 734 6710 Cable Add: Quicken London Telex: 23880
Chairman: George Amy; *Man Dir:* Robin Vivian; *Marketing Dir:* Frank Marvin; *International Marketing Dir, Books:* Tony Grabrovaz
Reference Set Rights: Tim Wilton-Steer; *Single Volume Book Rights:* Philip Costick, Nick Kennedy
Subjects: How-to, Reference, Partworks, General Science
1978: 90 titles *1979:* 120 titles *Founded:* 1967
Subsidiary: Marshall Cavendish Corporation, 575 Lexington Ave, New York, NY 10022
ISBN Publisher's Prefixes: 0-462, 0-85080, 0-85685

Marshall Editions Ltd, 71 Eccleston Sq, London SW1V 1PJ Tel: (01) 834 0785 Cable Add: Marsheds Telex: 22847 Marsh G
Man Dir & Editorial: Bruce Marshall; *Sales:* Barbara Anderson; *Production:* Hugh Stancliff
Subjects: Highly-illustrated Non-fiction including Cookery, Travel, Wild Life, Photography, Interior Design, Home-making, Music
1978: 3 titles *1979:* 5 titles

Marshall, Morgan & Scott Publications Ltd+, 1 Bath St, London EC1V 9LB Tel: (01) 251 2925
Shipping Add: Unit 14, Trident Industrial Estate, Pindar Rd, Hoddesdon, Herts EN11 0LD
Chairman: Michael Raeburn; *Man Dir:* David A Payne; *Sales, Publicity & Advertising:* Noël Halsey; *Rights & Permissions:* Noël Halsey, David A Payne
Subsidiary Company: Samual Bagster & Sons Ltd (qv), Pilgrim Records
Imprints include Lakeland Paperbacks, Oliphants
Subjects: Religion, Hymns
1978: 32 titles *Founded:* 1859
Miscellaneous: Holding company is Pentos Ltd (qv)
ISBN Publishers Prefix: 0-551

Marsland Press, an imprint of Volturna Press (qv)

Martin Books, an imprint of Woodhead-Faulkner (Publishers) Ltd (qv)

Martin Robertson & Co Ltd+, 108 Cowley Rd, Oxford OX4 1JF Tel: Oxford 49104 (STD code 0865) Cable Add: Marcobooks Oxford
Production: Rachel Douglas; *Sales:* Norman Drake; *Editorial:* Edward Elgar; *Promotion:* Polly Woodward
Orders to: Marston Book Services, PO Box 87, Oxford OX4 1LB
Subjects: Social Sciences at Degree Level, Sociology, Politics, Public Administration, Economics, Social Policy, Criminology, Education, International Affairs
1977: 22 titles *1978:* 26 titles
ISBN Publishers Prefix: 0-85520

Kenneth **Mason** Publications Ltd+, Homewell, Havant, Hampshire PO9 1EE Tel: Havant 486262 (STD code 0705)
Man Dir: Kenneth Mason; *Dir:* Robert Anderson
Distributor: Heinemann
Subjects: Nautical, Leisure Activities, Licensing, Slimming Paperbacks
1977: 12 titles *1978:* 22 titles
ISBN Publisher's Prefixes: 0-85937, 0-900534

Mathews Miller Dunbar*, 51 Endell St, London WC2H 9AJ Tel: (01) 836 0912
Man Dir: Barry Miller; *Art Dir:* Peter Dunbar
Orders to: PDAS (Cowley) Ltd, Bldg No 18, Denham Studios Estate, North Orbital Rd, Denham, Bucks
Subjects: Visual Arts, Documentary Photography
Founded: 1972
ISBN Publishers Prefix: 0-903811

Mayflower Books Ltd, see Granada Publishing Ltd

Kevin **Mayhew** Ltd, 55 Leigh Rd, Leigh-on-Sea, Essex SS9 1JP Tel: Southend-on-Sea 76425 (STD code 0702)
Man Dir, Production: Kevin Mayhew; *Editorial, Rights & Permissions:* Hugh McGinlay; *Sales, Publicity:* Anthony P Castle
Subjects: Popular Religious Liturgy, Music, Theology, Educational
1978: 20 titles *1979:* 25 titles *Founded:* 1976
ISBN Publisher's Prefix: 0-905725

Mayhew-McCrimmon Ltd, 10-12 High St, Great Wakering, Essex Tel: Southend-on-Sea 218956 (STD code 0702)
Man Dir: Joan McCrimmon; *Sales & Promotion Manager:* Mike Wade
Associate Companies: Celebration Records; Rainbow Books; Mayhew McCrimmon (Printers) Ltd
Subjects: Religion, Primary & Secondary Textbooks, Educational Materials, Music, Prayer Books, Liturgy
1978: 200 titles *Founded:* 1968
ISBN Publisher's Prefix: 0-85597

Meadowfield Press Ltd, ISA Bldg, Dale Rd Industrial Estate, Shildon, Co Durham DL4 2QZ Tel: Morpeth 55860 (STD code 0670)
Man Dir: J Gordon Cook
Associate Company: Merrow Publishing Co Ltd (qv)
Subjects: Technical, Scientific, Academic

The **Medici** Society Ltd, 34-42 Pentonville Rd, London N1 9HG Tel: (01) 837 7099 Cable Add: Medici N1
Man Dir: J Gurney; *Rights & Permissions, Art Dir:* H B Jane
Subjects: Art, Juveniles
1978: 5 titles *Founded:* 1908
Bookshops: The Medici Galleries, 7 Grafton St, London W1 3LA; 26 Thurloe St, London SW7 2LT; 63 Bold St, Liverpool L1 4HP
ISBN Publishers Prefix: 0-85503

Melbourne House (Publishers) Ltd, 24 Red Lion St, London WC1R 4PX Tel: (01) 405 6347 Telex: 28257 OCTABS
Dir & Publisher: Alfred Milgrom; *Editorial:* Sheila Thompson; *Publicity Manager:* Ms Leigh Jackson; *Rights & Permissions:* Naomi Besen
Orders to: Pandemic Ltd (address as above)
Associate Company: Outback Press Pty Ltd, Australia (qv)
Subjects: General Fiction and Non-fiction
1978: 2 titles *1979:* 20 titles *Founded:* 1978
ISBN Publisher's Prefix: 0-86161

Melrose Press Ltd, 17/21 Churchgate St, Soham, Ely, Cambs CB7 5DS Tel: Ely 721091 (STD code 0353) Cable Add: Melrosepres Ely Telex: 81584
Man Dir: Richard A Kay; *Sales:* Roger W G Curtis; *Production:* Nicholas S Law
Imprint: International Biographical Centre
Subject: Reference
1977: 6 titles *1978:* 6 titles *Founded:* 1969
ISBN Publishers Prefix: 0-900332

Mentor, an imprint of New English Library Ltd (qv)

The **Merlin** Press Ltd, 3 Manchester Rd, London E14 Tel: (01) 987 7959
Man Dir: Martin Eve
Imprint: Seafarer Books
Subjects: History, Economics, Philosophy, Political & Social Science
Founded: 1956
Book Club: Merlin Book Club
ISBN Publishers Prefix: 0-85036

Charles E **Merrill** Publishing Co, Alperton Ho, Bridgewater Rd, Wembley, Middlesex Tel: (01) 902 8812 Cable Add: Behow Wembley Telex: 261378
Sales, Advertising, Publicity, Rights & Permissions: Paul Poynton
Parent Company: Charles E Merrill Publishing Co, 1300 Alum Creek Drive, Columbus, Ohio, USA
Subjects: Education, Educational Psychology, Special Education, Technology, Social Sciences, Business & Economics, Science, Communication & Speech, Mathematics, Multi-media Programmes
1977: 80 titles *1978:* 80 titles *Founded:* 1842
ISBN Publisher's Prefix: 0-675

The **Merrion** Press+, 16 Groveway, London SW9 0AR Tel: (01) 735 7791 & 733 5173
Partners: Montague & Susan Shaw
Subjects: Finely produced books on English Literature, Printing, Calligraphy, Fine Arts
ISBN Publishers Prefix: 0-903560

Merrow Publishing Co Ltd+, ISA Bldg, Dale Rd Industrial Estate, Shildon, Co Durham DL4 2QZ Tel: Morpeth 55860 (STD code 0670)
Man Dir: J Gordon Cook
Associate Company: Meadowfield Press Ltd (qv)
Subjects: Technical, Scientific, Academic
ISBN Publisher's Prefixes: 0-900541, 0-904095

Metal Bulletin Books Ltd, Park Ho, Park Terrace, Worcester Park, Surrey KT4 7HY Tel: (01) 330 4311 Cable Add: Metalbul Worcester Park Telex: 21383 Metbul-G
Man Dir: T J Tarring; *Sales & Advert Dir:* B R Orbell; *Editorial Dir:* R P Cordero
Br Offs: 45/46 Lower Marsh, London SE1 7RG; 708 Third Ave, New York, NY 10017, USA
Subjects: Steel and Metal Industries, Industrial Minerals
1977: 5 titles *1978:* 9 titles *Founded:* 1937

Methodist Publishing House+, Wellington Rd, Wimbledon, London SW19 8EU Tel: (01) 947 5256/9 Cable Add: Metodico, London SW19 8EU
General Manager, Rights & Permissions: Albert M Jakeway; *Sales Manager:* P J Derry; *Publicity Manager:* David W Hirst
Imprint: Epworth Press
Subjects: Religion, History, Archaeology, Biography, Memoirs, Philosophy, Directories
1977: 13 titles *1978:* 16 titles *Founded:* 1733
ISBN Publisher's Prefixes: 0-7150, 0-7162, 0-7192, 0-901027

Methuen & Co Ltd+, 11 New Fetter Lane, London EC4P 4EE Tel: (01) 583 9855 Cable Add: Elegiacs London EC4 Telex: 263398
Man Dir: John Naylor; *Editorial:* Janice Price; *Sales:* Peter Shepherd; *Production:* Carol Somerset; *Publicity:* Lyndsay Williams; *Rights & Permissions:* Vicki Anderson
Orders to: North Way, Andover, Hampshire SP10 5BE
Parent Company: Associated Book Publishers Ltd (qv)
Subjects: Academic
ISBN Publisher's Prefix: 0-416

Methuen Children's Books Ltd+, 11 New Fetter Lane, London EC4P 4EE Tel: (01) 583 9855 Cable Add: Elegiacs, London EC4P 4EE Telex: 263398
Chairman: Charles Shirley; *Man Dir:* Marilyn Malin; *Sales:* David Ross; *Production:* Christopher Holgate; *Publicity:* John Mason; *Rights & Permissions:* Rosalind Nell
Orders to: Associated Book Publishers Ltd, Andover, Hampshire SP10 5BE Tel: Andover 62141 (STD code 0264) Cable Add: APT Andover Telex: 47214
Parent Company: Associated Book Publishers Ltd, UK (qv)
Subjects: Juveniles, Fiction & Nonfiction
1978: 80 titles approx *1979:* 80 titles approx
ISBN Publishers Prefix: 0-416

Maurice **Michael**, Partridge Green, Horsham, West Sussex Tel: Horsham 710412 (STD code 0403) Cable Add: Bartolo Horsham
Publisher: Maurice Michael
Subjects: Military, Gardening, Sport, Cookery, Co-editions, Illustrated History
1978: 4 titles

Michelin Tyre Co Ltd, Maps & Guides Dept, 81 Fulham Rd, London SW3 6RD Tel: (01) 589 1460 Cable Add: Pneumilin London Telex: 919071
Sales Manager: E G Whiston
Associate Company: Michelin et Cie (Services de Tourisme), France (qv)
Subjects: Guides (Tourist, Hotel & Restaurant), Maps
1978: 1 guide, 1 map *1979:* 1 guide, 2 maps
ISBN Publisher's Prefixes: 0-206, 0-392

Midas Books+, 12 Dene Way, Speldhurst, Tunbridge Wells, Kent TN3 0NX Tel: Langton 2860 (STD code 089286)
Man Dir: Ian Morley-Clarke; *Editorial:* Kathleen Morley-Clarke, Robert Hardcastle; *Production:* Raymond Green
Subsidiary Company: Buildtay Ltd, address as above
Subjects: Militaria, Leisure, Sport, Social History, Biography, Music, Guides, Collectors' Library Series, Art, Craft Library Series
1978: 24 titles *1979:* 22 titles *Founded:* 1973
ISBN Publisher's Prefix: 0-85936

J Garnet **Miller** Ltd+, 129 St John's Hill, London SW11 1TD Tel: (01) 228 8091
Man Dir: J G F Miller
Subjects: Music, Drama, Juveniles, General Science
Founded: 1951
Subsidiary: Steele's Play Bureau
ISBN Publishers Prefix: 0-85343

Harvey **Miller** Publishers+, 20 Marryat Rd, London SW19 5BD Tel: (01) 946 4426
Publishers: Mrs Elly Miller, Harvey Miller
Subject: History of Art
1977: 1 title *1978:* 2 titles
Miscellaneous: Publishers of *Courtauld Institute Illustration Archives*
ISBN Publishers Prefix: 0-905203

Millington Books, an imprint of Davison Publishing Ltd

Mills & Boon Ltd+, 17-19 Foley St, London W1A 1DR Tel: (01) 580 9074/0 Cable Add: Millsator London W1 Telex: 24420
Chairman: J T Boon; *Man Dir:* P J Scherer; *Editorial:* Alan Boon, Heather Jeeves, Michael Stephenson, Frances Whitehead; *Export:* N S Boon; *Publicity & Advertising:* G Britton; *Rights & Permissions:* Deborah Burgess
Subsidiary Companies: Allman & Son (Publishers) Ltd, 17-19 Foley St, London W1A 1DR, UK; Mills & Boon Pty Ltd, Suite 404, 282 Victoria Ave, Chatswood, NSW 2067, Australia
Subjects: General Fiction, History, How-to, Music, Art, Reference, Religion, Low-priced Paperbacks, General Science, Secondary & Primary Textbooks
1977: 109 titles *Founded:* 1908
Miscellaneous: Distribution by Distribution & Management Services, Sheldon Way, Larkfield, Kent. Imprints include Owlet
ISBN Publishers Prefix: 0-263

The **Minerva** Press Ltd+*, 44 Great Russell St, London WC1B 3PA Tel: (01) 580 7200
Subjects: Natural History, Art & Architecture, General Children's Books, Oriental, Travel & Adventure, General Literature
ISBN Publisher's Prefix: 0-85636

Mirror Books Ltd, Athene Ho, 66-73 Shoe Lane, London EC4P 4AB Tel: (01) 353 0246 Cable Add: Mirror London EC1 Telex: 27286
Man Dir: Peter K Robins; *Editorial, Rights & Permissions:* Michael Glover, Anthony Finn; *Sales:* Gerry Bolt; *Production:* Bernard Smith; *Publicity:* James Hole
Parent Company: Mirror Group Newspapers Ltd
Subjects: General
1978: 50 titles *1979:* 50 titles
ISBN Publisher's Prefix: 0-85939

Mitchell Beazley Marketing Ltd+, Artists Ho, 14-15 Manette St, London W1V 5LB Tel: (01) 434 1694 Telex: 24892
Man Dir, Rights & Permissions: Ken Banerji; *Marketing Dir:* David Hight; *Publicity:* Chris Kirby
Imprints: Emblem, William Luscombe, Artists House
Subjects: General Books, Encyclopaedias, Dictionaries, Atlases, Practical Books, High-priced Paperbacks
1978: 88 titles *1979:* approx 50 titles
Founded: 1969
ISBN Publisher's Prefixes: 0-85533 (Mitchell Beazley), 0-86002 (William Luscombe), 0-86134 (Artists House)

Model & Allied Publications*, 13-35 Bridge St, Hemel Hempstead, Hertfordshire HP1 1EE Tel: Hemel Hempstead 41221 (STD code 0442)
Subjects: Technical, Transport
Miscellaneous: An imprint of Argus Books Ltd (qv)
ISBN Publisher's Prefixes: 0-85076, 0-85242, 0-85344

Modern Transport, an imprint of Ian Allan Ltd (qv)

The **Molendinar** Press+, 73 Robertson St, Glasgow G2 Tel: (041) 221 2512 Cable Add: Greenleaf Glasgow
Rights & Trade Enquiries: Simon Berry
Subjects: Leisure, Current Affairs, History, Fiction, Scottish
1979: 3 titles

Momenta Publishing, 23 East St, Farnham, Surrey GU9 7SD Tel: Farnham 721879 (STD code 0252)
Orders to: Biblios Publishers' Distribution Services Ltd, Glenside Industrial Estate, Partridge Green, Horsham, Sussex RH13 8RA Tel: Partridge Green 710971 (STD code 0403)
Subjects: Psychology, Sociology, Art, Communication
1979: 6 titles *Founded:* 1979
Miscellaneous: Momenta is an associate of the Servire Group which includes Servire BV, Netherlands (qv), Hunter House Inc, USA, and Qalandar Verlag GmbH, Federal Republic of Germany. Several Momenta titles are co-produced with the US affiliate, Hunter House
ISBN Publisher's Prefix: 0-86164

Monthly Review Press, 47 Red Lion St, London WC1R 4PF Tel: (01) 242 3501
Publisher: Jules Geller
Subjects: University, Commercial & Technical Education, Politics, Social Science
1978: 25 titles
ISBN Publishers Prefix: 0-85345

Moonraker Press, 26 St Margarets St, Bradford-on-Avon, Wiltshire Tel: Bradford-on-Avon 3469 (STD code 02216)
Man Dir, Sales, Publicity & Advertising, Rights & Permissions: Anthony Adams
Subjects: Biography, History, Reference
Founded: 1975
ISBN Publishers Prefix: 0-239

Moorland Publishing Company Ltd+, PO Box 2, Ashbourne, Derbyshire DE6 1DE Tel: Ashbourne 5086 (STD code 03355)
Editorial Dir, Production: Dr J A Robey; *Sales, Publicity, Rights & Permissions:* C L M Porter
Subjects: History, Geography, General Nonfiction, Railways, Natural History, Architecture
1977: 11 titles *1978:* 11 titles *Founded:* 1972
ISBN Publisher's Prefix: 0-903485

398 UNITED KINGDOM

Morgan-Grampian Book Publishing Co Ltd*, 30 Calderwood St, Woolwich, London SE18 6QH Tel: (01) 855 7777
Subjects: Reference, Directories
ISBN Publisher's Prefix: 0-900865

Motive, an imprint of Allison & Busby Ltd (qv)

Motor Racing Publications Ltd, 28 Devonshire Rd, Chiswick, London W4 2HD Tel: (01) 994 6783
Man Dir, Editorial, Production, Publicity, Rights & Permissions: John Blunsden; *Sales:* Ken Gard
Associate Company: Connoisseur Carbooks (address as above)
Imprint: MRP
Branch Off: (Editorial, Production and Promotion) 56 Fitzjames Ave, Croydon, Surrey CR0 5DD
Subjects: Motor Racing and Rallying, Racing Car Design, Motoring History including Cars, Trucks and Motorcycles
1978: 3 titles *1979:* 5 titles *Founded:* 1948
ISBN Publisher's Prefix: 0-900549

A R **Mowbray** & Co Ltd+, St Thomas Ho, Becket St, Oxford OX1 1SJ Tel: Oxford 42507 (STD code 0865)
Shipping Add: Dent Distribution Ltd, Dunhams Lane, Letchworth, Herts SG6 1LF
Man Dir: K B Baker; *Sales Dir:* Eva Jesse; *Rights & Permissions:* L Harris
Subjects: History, Philosophy, Reference, Religion, Juveniles, Low- & High-priced Paperbacks, Social Science, University Textbooks
1977: 45 titles *1978:* 37 titles *Founded:* 1858
Bookshops: 28 Margaret St, Oxford Circus, London W1N 7LB; 8-10 Cambridge Terrace, Oxford; 14 King's Parade, Cambridge; St Martins, The Bull Ring, Birmingham
ISBN Publishers Prefix: 0-264

Frederick **Muller** Ltd+, Victoria Works, Edgware Rd, London NW2 6LE Tel: (01) 450 2566 Cable Add: Efmull London NW2
Man & Marketing Dir: V Andrews; *Dir:* M A A Baig; *Editorial, Rights & Permissions Dir:* Andrew Mylett (*Foreign Rights* (Blond & Briggs): Rosemarie Buckman, Ryman's Cottage, Little Tew, Oxon); *Publicity:* Johanna Fawkes
Subsidiary Companies and Imprints: Muller Educational; Blond & Briggs Ltd
Subjects: Biography, History, How-to, Reference, Juveniles, Science & Technology, University, Secondary & Primary Schoolbooks, Fiction, Collectors, General, Natural History, Occult
1978: 34 titles *1979:* 40 titles
Founded: 1933
ISBN Publisher's Prefixes: 0-584 (Muller), 0-85634 (Blond & Briggs)

Munch Bunch, an imprint of Studio Publications (Ipswich) Ltd (qv)

Thomas **Murby** & Co*, 40 Museum St, London WC1A 1LU Tel: (01) 405 8577 (3 lines) Cable Add: Deucalion, London WC1A 1LU
Orders to: Park Lane, Hemel Hempstead, Hertfordshire HP2 4TE Tel: Hemel Hempstead 3244 (STD code 0442)
Parent Company: George Allen & Unwin (Publishers) Ltd, UK (qv)
Subjects: Technical & Scientific, Geology
ISBN Publishers Prefix: 0-04

Donald **Murray** (Ramboro Books), 6 Highbury Corner, London N5 1RD Tel: (01) 609 3091/2
Subjects: Children's Books, Dictionaries, Art, Cookery
Miscellaneous: Also Remainder Dealers

John **Murray** (Publishers) Ltd+, 50 Albemarle St, London W1X 4BD Tel: (01) 493 4361 Cable Add: Guidebook London W1 Telex: 21312 Murray G
Shipping Add: 20 Onslow St, London EC1
Man Dir: Kenneth Foster; *Editorial:* John G Murray, Simon Young, Roger Hudson, Mrs Leeston; *Educational Marketing Dir:* Nick Perren; *Sales Dir:* John R Murray; *Sales Manager:* John Harbour; *Publicity & Advertising:* John Gammons; *Rights & Permissions:* Valerie Ripley
Subjects: General Fiction, Travel, Aviation, Nautical, Poetry, Biography, History, Architecture, Music, Art, Craft, Philosophy, Religion, Reference, Juveniles, Low- & High-priced Paperbacks, General Science, Textbooks, *Easy Readers*, *Success Study Books* series
1977: 81 titles *1978:* 93 titles *Founded:* 1768
ISBN Publishers Prefix: 0-7195

Murrays Childrens Books, a subsidiary of Brown Watson Ltd (qv)

Murrays Remainder Books Ltd, 146-152 Holloway Rd, London N7 Tel: (01) 609 1234 Cable Add: Goldex London N7 Telex: 261670
Shipping Add: 11 Benwell Rd, London N7
Man Dir: Peter Kite
Parent Company: Howard & Wyndham Ltd (qv)
Associate Companies: Brown Watson Ltd (qv); Murrays Childrens Books
Imprints: Abbey, Castle, Goldex, Rex
Subjects: Belles Lettres, Poetry, Music, Art, Reference, Juveniles, 'Treasure Hour' Books
1977: 6 titles *Founded:* 1954
Miscellaneous: Firm's main activity is as Remainder Dealer

Music Sales Ltd, see Book Sales Ltd

Muslim Welfare House, see M W H London Publishers

N A G Press, an imprint of Northwood Books (qv)

N C C Publications+, The National Computing Centre Ltd, Oxford Rd, Manchester M1 7ED Tel: (061) 228 6333 Telex: 668962
Man Dir: G E Hall; *Publicity:* M Bridge
Orders to: J M Dent & Sons (Distribution) Ltd, Dunhams Lane, Letchworth, Herts SG6 1LF
Subjects: Primary, Secondary & University Textbooks, Educational Materials on Computing and allied subjects
1978: 88 titles *Founded:* 1971
ISBN Publisher's Prefix: 0-5012

N E L, an imprint of New English Library (qv)

N F E R Publishing Co Ltd+*, Darville Ho, 2 Oxford Rd East, Windsor, Berkshire SL4 1DF Tel: Windsor 69345 (STD code 07535)
Man Dir: A Yates; *Manager, Publications Dept:* J K Sansom
Subjects: Education, Special Education, Social Sciences, Psychology, Educational Materials
1977: 28 titles *1978:* approx 22 titles
Founded: 1970
ISBN Publisher's Prefixes: 0-85633, 0-901225

National Christian Education Council+, Robert Denholm Ho, Nutfield, Redhill, Surrey RH1 4HW Tel: Nutfield Ridge 2411 (STD code 073 782)
General Secretary: Rev G R Chapman; *Publicity:* Eric A Thorn
Subjects: Primary, Secondary, Education, Religion, Maps & Atlases, Music, Bible Reading Guides, Pictures
1977: 17 titles
Subsidiaries: Denholm House Press, International Bible Reading Association
ISBN Publisher's Prefixes: 0-7197 (National Christian Council), 0-85213 (Denholm House)

National Computing Centre, see NCC

National Council of Social Services, see Bedford Square Press

National Foundation for Educational Research in England & Wales, see NFER

National Magazine Co Ltd+, National Magazine Ho, 72 Broadwick St, London W1V 2BP Tel: (01) 437 7833 Cable Add: Shanmag, London W1 Telex: 263879
Man Dir: Marcus Morris; *Publisher:* Roger Barrett; *Editorial:* Isabel Sutherland; *Advertising, Rights & Permissions:* Tim Whale
Orders to: Michael Joseph Limited, 44 Bedford Sq, London WC1
Subjects: General Non-fiction, How-to, Reference
1978: 15 titles
Miscellaneous: Books are published under the imprints of The Connoisseur and Ebury Press
ISBN Publisher's Prefixes: 0-85223 (Ebury Press), 0-900305 (The Connoisseur)

National Trust Children's Series, an imprint of Dinosaur Publications Ltd (qv)

Natural History Museum, see British Museum (National History)

Nautical Publishing Co Ltd, Nautical House, Lymington, Hampshire SO4 9BA Tel: Lymington 72578 (STD code 0590) Telex: 47674
Man & Sales Dir: Commander Erroll Bruce; *Publicity Dir:* Richard Creagh-Osborne; *Advertising Dir:* Sir Peter Johnson Bt
Associate Companies: United Nautical Publishers SA, Basle, Switzerland; George Harrap & Co Ltd, UK (qv)
Subjects: Sailing, Nautical Subjects, Maritime History, Pilotage, Navigation, Design and Construction
1977: 12 titles *1978:* 12 titles *Founded:* 1967
ISBN Publisher's Prefix: 0-245

Thomas **Nelson** & Sons Ltd+, Lincoln Way, Windmill Rd, Sunbury on Thames, Middlesex TW16 7HP Tel: Sunbury on Thames 85681 (STD code 09327) Cable Add: Thonelson Sunbury on Thames Telex: 929365
Man Dir: John G Jermine; *Executive Publisher:* David R Worlock; *Marketing Dirs:* Michael E Thompson (Home), Geoffrey Wright (Export); *Rights & Permissions:* Allan Ramsay
Subjects: History, Reference, Religion, High-priced Paperbacks, Engineering, General & Social Science, Medicine, Psychology, University, Secondary & Primary Textbooks, Educational Materials
1977: 150 titles *1978:* 288 titles *Founded:* 1798
Subsidiaries: Thomas Nelson (Australia) Ltd, Australia (qv); Thomas Nelson & Sons (Canada) Ltd, 81 Curlew Dr, Don Mills, Ontario, Canada;

Thomas Nelson (Nigeria) Ltd, Nigeria (qv)
Miscellaneous: Company is in the Thomson Books Ltd group, a part of International Thomson Organization Ltd (Canada)
ISBN Publisher's Prefix: 0–17

New Cavendish Books+*, 65 Marylebone High St, London W1M 3AH Tel: (01) 486 7063
Publisher: Allen Levy
Subjects: Toys (history & collection), Mechanical Antiquities, Models
Founded: 1973

New Caxton Library Service Ltd+*, Premier Ho, 150 Southampton Row, London WC1 Tel: (01) 837 4145
Man Dir: A H Windrum
Subjects: University, Secondary & Primary Textbooks, English Dictionaries, Reference Books, Maps & Atlases, Juveniles, History, Archaeology, Biography & Memoirs, Encyclopaedias
Miscellaneous: Firm is a subsidiary of Caxton Publications Ltd (qv)
ISBN Publisher's Prefix: 0–903322

New City, London, 57 Twyford Ave, London W3 9PZ Tel: (01) 992 7666
Chairman, Editorial: D Bregant; *Sales, Production, Publicity, Rights & Permissions:* R van Geffen
Associate Company: Citta Nuova Editrice, Italy (qv for other Associates)
Subjects: Christian Concerns, Spirituality, Witness, Ecumenism
1978: 3 titles *1979:* 4 titles *Founded:* 1958
ISBN Publisher's Prefix: 0–904287

New Educational Books, an imprint of Artemis Press Ltd (qv)

The **New English Library** Ltd+, Barnard's Inn, Holborn, London EC1N 2JR Tel: (01) 242 0767 Cable Add: Nelpublish Telex: 21924
(Trade Counters: (Hardcover) The Airfield, Norwich Rd, Mendlesham, Suffolk; (Paperbacks) Fulham Wharf, Townmead Rd, London SW6)
Man Dir: T R D'Cruz; *Sales Dirs:* D F Morse, J B O'Leary; *Rights & Permissions:* M Pachnos
Subjects: General Fiction & Nonfiction, Art, Biography, Classics, Paperbacks
Founded: 1957
Miscellaneous: Subsidiary of The Times Mirror Co, Times Mirror Sq, Los Angeles, Calif 90053, USA
Associated Companies: New American Library Inc; Harry N Abrams Inc (both New York, USA)
Imprints: NEL, Mentor
ISBN Publisher's Prefix: 0–450

New Leaf Books Ltd, 38 Camden Lock, Chalk Farm Rd, London NW1 8AF Tel: (01) 267 6183 Cable Add: Nuleaf London NW1 Telex: 261507 Ref 3228
Man Dir: Michael Wright
Subjects: Highly Illustrated Practical, Reference and General Books (International Co-editions)
Founded: 1973

New Left Books+, 7 Carlisle St, London W1 Tel: (01) 437 3546
also Verso Editions
Orders to: IBD, 66 Wood Lane End, Hemel Hempstead, Herts HP2 4RG
Subjects: Philosophy, History, Economics, Politics, Aesthetics, Psychology, Sociology
1977: 6 titles *1978:* 16 titles
ISBN Publisher's Prefixes: 0–902308, 0–86091

New Portway, an imprint of Chivers Press Publishers (qv)

New University Education, an imprint of Clive Bingley Ltd (qv)

Newnes Books, an imprint of Hamlyn Publishing Group Ltd (qv)

Newnes-Butterworths, an imprint of Butterworth & Co (qv)

Newnes-Technical, an imprint of Butterworth & Co (qv)

Robert **Nicholson** Publications Ltd, 93 St Peter's St, St Albans, Hertfordshire AL1 3EH Tel: St Albans 30121 (STD code 0727) Telex: 261212
Man Dir: Dennis Stevenson; *Sales & Marketing Dir:* Colin Tagg
Parent Company: Geographia Ltd (qv)
Subjects: Maps and Guides
ISBN Publisher's Prefix: 0–900568

Nile & Mackenzie Ltd+*, 43 Dover St, London W1 Tel: (01) 493 0351 Cable Add: Nilemac Telex: 268312 Nilemac/Westcham
Man Dir: D S Sehbai; *Rights & Permissions:* Penelope Carreau
Subjects: Reference, Juveniles, Educational Materials
Founded: 1974

James **Nisbet** & Co Ltd*, Digswell Pl, Welwyn, Hertfordshire AL8 7SX Tel: Welwyn Garden 25491/3 (STD code 096) Cable Add: Stebsin, Welwyn Garden City
Chairman: G H B McLean
Subjects: Dictionaries, Economics, Philosophy, Religion, University, Secondary & Primary Textbooks, Education
Founded: 1810
ISBN Publisher's Prefix: 0–7202

The **Nonesuch** Library, see The Bodley Head Ltd

Norfolk Press+, 52 Manchester St, London W1M 6DR Tel: (01) 935 3441/3481
Man Dir: Raymond Holdsworth
Subjects: Religion, Philosopy, History, Literature, Outdoor Life
Founded: 1969
ISBN Publisher's Prefix: 0–85211

Jill **Norman** Ltd, 90 Great Russell St, London WC1B 3PY Tel: (01) 631 4141 Telex: 28604 Ref 1647
Man Dir: Jill Norman
Parent Company: Bemrose UK Ltd (qv for associate companies)
Subjects: Politics, History, Social History, Medicine, Psychology, Travel, Cookery, Handbooks
Founded: 1979
ISBN Publisher's Prefix: 0–906908

Northwood Books, 93–99 Goswell Rd, London EC1V 7QA Tel: (01) 253 9355 Telex: 21746
Man Dir: William Heaps; *Publisher, Sales, Rights & Permissions:* Douglas Westland; *Editorial:* Diana Briscoe; *Production:* Helen McKay; *Publicity:* Susan Hunt
Parent Company: Thomson Organization Ltd, Elm Ho, Elm St, London WC1X 0BP
Associate Companies: Northwood Publications Ltd; N A G Press Ltd (at above address)
Imprint: N A G Press
Subjects: Horology, Gemmology, Precious Metals, Catering and Hotel Management, Brewing, Building and Construction, Electronics, Medicine, Printing and Graphic Arts, Meat Trades
1978: 18 titles *1979:* 25 titles *Founded:* 1954
ISBN Publisher's Prefix: 0–7198

Van **Nostrand Reinhold** Co Ltd+, Molly Millar's Lane, Wokingham, Berkshire RG11 2PY Tel: Wokingham 789456 (STD code 0734) Telex: 847798 BORDS-G
Man Dir: R S R Hutchison; *Sales Manager:* Harry Robinson
Associate Company: Van Nostrand Reinhold, Australia (qv)
Subjects: Art, Reference, Professional, General & Social Science, University Textbooks, Educational Materials, High-priced Paperbacks, Medicine, Psychology, Engineering, Practical, Crafts
Miscellaneous: Firm is a subsidiary of Litton Educational Publishing Co Inc, 450 West 33rd St, New York, NY 10001, USA
ISBN Publisher's Prefix: 0–442

Nova Hrvatska Ltd, 30 Fleet St, London EC4Y 1AJ Tel: (01) 947 0498 Telex: 896616 Sendit G Nova Hrvatska
Man Dir: J Kusan; *Sales Dir:* G Saganic
Subjects: Joint publishers with Hrvatska Revija of Munich and Barcelona of: Secondary Textbooks, Educational Materials, Memoirs. Also *Hrvatska Revija* (quarterly literary review), *Nova Hrvatska* (Fortnightly current affairs magazine)
1978: 15 titles *Founded:* 1959
Miscellaneous: Publishers of reprinted *Croatian Orthography* and *Croatian Grammar* (Zagreb editions)

Novello & Co Ltd+, Borough Green, Sevenoaks, Kent TN15 8DT Tel: Borough Green 883261 (STD code 0732) Cable Add: Novellos Sevenoaks
Man Dir: G Rizza; *Sales Manager:* S W Freeman; *Publicity & Advertising Manager:* J Woodmason; *Rights & Permissions:* B Axcell
Subject: Music
1978: 4 titles

Oasis Books, 12 Stevenage Rd, London SW6 6ES Tel: (01) 736 5059
Man Dir: Ian Robinson
Subjects: General Fiction, Poetry, Literature, Periodical *Oasis*
1978: 10 titles *1979:* 10 titles *Founded:* 1969
ISBN Publisher's Prefix: 0–903375

Ocean Interpol Publishing Ltd*, 17 Oakley Road, London N1 3LL Tel: (01) 226 0573/226 6171, Oxted (988) 5044 Telex: 95631
Subjects: Juvenile hardcover books

The **Octagon** Press Ltd*, 14 Baker St, London W1M 1DA Tel: (089 286) 2045 Cable Add: Octapress London W1
Man Dir: Sally Mallam
Subjects: General Fiction, Philosophy, Religion, Psychology
1977e 37 titles *1978:* 37 titles
ISBN Publisher's Prefix: 0–900860

Octopus Books Ltd, 59 Grosvenor St, London W1X 9DA Tel: (01) 493 5841 Cable Add: Octobooks
Chairman: Paul Hamlyn; *Man Dir:* Timothy Clode; *Marketing Dir:* Peggy Singleton; *Rights & Permissions:* Gerd Seeber
Branch Offs: Octopus Pty Ltd, 107 Moray St, Melbourne, Victoria, Australia; Octopus Books Inc, The Olympic Towers, 645 Fifth Ave, New York, NY 10022, USA
Subjects: Children's Classics, Cookery, Handicrafts, Gardening, Natural History, Militaria, Transport, Entertainment, Art, Antiques, Adult Fiction

400 UNITED KINGDOM

Founded: 1971
Imprints: Cathay, Sundial, Heinemann/Octopus
ISBN Publisher's Prefix: 0-7064

Odeon, an imprint of Lorrimer Publishing Ltd (qv)

Odhams Books an imprint of Hamlyn Publishing Group Ltd (qv)

The **Oleander** Press, 17 Stansgate Ave, Cambridge CB2 2QZ Tel: Cambridge 44688 (STD code 0223)
Office for USA & Canada: 210 Fifth Ave, New York, NY 10010
Subjects: Middle East & Far East, Cambridge, Arabic, Language & Literature, Libya, Poetry, Drama, Travel
1977: 13 titles *1978:* 15 titles *Founded:* 1960
ISBN Publisher's Prefixes: 0-900891, 0-902675

Oliphants, an imprint of Marshall, Morgan & Scott (Publications) Ltd (qv)

Oliver & Boyd+, Robert Stevenson Ho, 1/3 Baxter's Pl, Edinburgh EH1 3BB Tel: (031) 556 2424 Cable Add: Almanac Edinburgh Telex: 727511
Shipping Add: Pinnacles, Harlow, Essex
Man Dir: Roger Watson; *General Manager:* A A Dunnett; *Man Editor:* A Paulin; *Sales Manager:* Rhys Edwards; *Publicity:* Russell Bruce
Subjects: Secondary & Primary Textbooks, Educational Materials
1977: 62 titles *1978:* 78 titles *Founded:* 1778
Miscellaneous: Division of Longman Group Ltd, UK (qv)
ISBN Publisher's Prefix: 0-05

Omega, an imprint of Futura Publications Ltd (qv)

Omnibus Book Service*, 25 East St, Farnham, Surrey GU9 7SD Tel: Farnham 26009 (STD code 02513) Telex: 858193
Man Dir: Fazal Inayat-Khan; *Editorial, Sales:* David Barnes; *Production:* Owen Stroebel; *Publicity:* Cyohn Reinhart
Parent Company: Servire Uitgeverij, Netherlands (qv)
Subjects: Religion, Psychology, Art, Health Cookery, Alternative Medicine, Music

Open Books Publishing Ltd+, West Compton Ho, Shepton Mallet, Somerset Tel: Pilton 264 (STD code 074 989)
Man Dir: Patrick Taylor
Subjects: Social Sciences & Humanities
1977: 15 titles *1978:* 10 titles *Founded:* 1974
ISBN Publisher's Prefix: 0-7291

The **Open University** Press (Open University Educational Enterprises Ltd)+, 12 Cofferidge Close, Stony Stratford, Milton Keynes MK11 1BY Tel: Milton Keynes 566744 (STD code 0908) Telex: 826147
Man Dir: J E Cox; *Sponsoring Editor:* Anthony Seward; *General Manager, Marketing and Product Development:* Donald M Hill; *Media Development Manager:* Nicholas J Freethy
Subjects: Books, Films and Audiotapes in the fields of Arts, Education, Mathematics, Science, Social Science, Technology, Adult Education
1977: 120 titles *1978:* 133 titles
ISBN Publisher's Prefix: 0-335

Orbis Publishing Ltd+, 20-22 Bedfordbury, London WC2N 4BT Tel: (01) 379 6711 Cable Add: Orbooks London WC2 Telex: 22725
Man Dir: Martin Heller; *Editorial:* Stephen Adamson; *Sales:* Geoffrey Howard; *Publicity:* Penny Pilch; *Rights & Permissions:* Charles Merullo
Subjects: Ancient History and Archaeology, Architecture, Aviation, Cookery, Educational, English Literature, Fine Arts, Gardening, General Nonfiction, Military History, Motoring, Nautical, Ornithology, Practical Crafts, Sociology, How-to, Music, Reference, Juveniles, Medicine, General Science, Natural History
1978: 39 titles *1979:* 48 titles
ISBN Publisher's Prefix: 0-85613

Orbit, an imprint of Futura Publications Ltd (qv)

Ordnance Survey, British Government Map Publishers, Romsey Rd, Maybush, Southampton SO9 4DH Tel: Southampton 775555 (STD code 0703) ext 305 Cable Add: Ordsurvey, Southampton
Deputy Dir: Allan Marles; *Publishing Manager:* Arthur Wood
Subject: Maps
1978-9: 21 titles

Oresko Books*, 30 Notting Hill Gate, London W11 Tel: (01) 727 3188
Director & Editor: Robert Oresko
Subjects: Art, Pictorial Biographies

Oriel Press Ltd+, Stocksfield Studio, Branch End, Stocksfield, Northumberland NE43 7NA Tel: Stocksfield 3065 (STD code 06615)
Man Dir: Bruce Allsopp; *Sales Manager:* David O'Connor
Orders to: Routledge & Kegan Paul Ltd (qv)
Subjects: Religious, Technical & Scientific, Reference Books, Art & Architecture, History, Archaeology, Biography & Memoirs, Politics, Political Economy, Sociology, Questions of the Day, Philosophy, Oriental, Directories & Guidebooks
Miscellaneous: Firm is a subsidiary of Routledge & Kegan Paul Ltd (qv)
ISBN Publisher's Prefix: 0-85362

Osprey Publishing Ltd+, 12-14 Long Acre, London WC2E 9LP Tel: (01) 836 7863 Cable Add: Osprey London WC2E 9LP Telex: 21667
Man Dir: M A Bovill; *Export Sales Manager:* Rex Knott; *Rights & Permissions:* Tony Bovill
Associate Company: George Philip & Son Ltd (qv)
Subjects: History, Militaria, Motoring, Aviation, Reference
ISBN Publisher's Prefix: 0-85045

Overseas Publications Interchange Ltd, 40 Elsham Rd, London W14 8HB Tel: (01) 994 4723
Subjects: Publish and distribute books in Russian and East European languages — especially Soviet and Polish dissident literature

Peter **Owen** Ltd+, 73 Kenway Rd, London SW5 0RE Tel: (01) 373 5628
Man Dir, Sales & Advertising, Publicity, Rights & Permissions: Peter Owen
Subjects: General Fiction, Belles Lettres, Biography, Music, Art, Sociology
1979: 26 titles *Founded:* 1950
ISBN Publisher's Prefix: 0-7206

Owlet, an imprint of Mills & Boon Ltd (qv)

Oxford Illustrated Press Ltd+, Shelley Close, Headington, Oxford OX3 8HB Tel: Oxford 63739 (STD code 0865)
Man Dir: John Webb
Parent Company: Oxford Illustrators Ltd
Subjects: Illustrated Leisure, Transport, Local History
1977: 10 titles *1978:* 8 titles
ISBN Publisher's Prefix: 0-902280

Oxford Microform Publications Ltd, 19A Paradise St, Oxford OX1 1LP Tel: Oxford 46252 (STD code 0865) Telex: 83118
Subjects: Out-of-print books, Scholarly & Scientific Journals, Collections, Serial Publications in Economics, Colour Microfiche, Art, Science

The **Oxford Railway** Publishing Co, 8 The Roundway, Headington, Oxford OX3 8DH Tel: Oxford 66215 (STD code 0865)
Man Dir: C W Judge
Subsidiary Company: The Railway Book Centre, 8 The Roundway, Headington, Oxford OX3 8DH
Subject: Railways
1978: 64 titles *1979:* 74 titles
ISBN Publisher's Prefixes: 0-902888, 0-86093

Oxford University Press+, Walton St, Oxford OX2 6DP Tel: Oxford 56767 (STD code 0865) Cable Add: Clarendon Press Oxford Telex: (Clarpress) 837330
Secretary to the Delegates and Chief Executive: G B Richardson; *Academic Publisher:* R A Denniston; *General Publisher:* Sir John Brown; *Educational Publisher:* R E Brammah; *Rights & Permissions:* Judith Haworth
Orders to: Press Rd, Neasden, London NW10 0DD
London Off and Music Departments: Ely Ho, 37 Dover St, London W1X 4AH Tel: (01) 629 8494
Associate Companies: Cornelsen & Oxford University Press GmbH, Federal Republic of Germany (qv); University Press Ltd, Nigeria (qv)
Br Offs: Oxford University Press, Australia (qv); Oxford University Press, 70 Wynford Dr, Don Mills 403, Toronto, Ontario, Canada; Oxford University Press, Hong Kong (qv); Oxford University Press, India (qv); Oxford University Press, Gedung Gunung Mulia, Kwitang 22, Jakarta, Indonesia; Oxford University Press KK, Enshu Bldg, 3-3 Otsuka, 3-chome, Bunkyo-ku, Tokyo, Japan; Oxford University Press, Kenya (qv); Oxford University Press, Malaysia (qv); Oxford University Press, New Zealand (qv); Oxford University Press, 2nd Floor, Haroon Ho, Dr Ziauddin Ahmed Rd, Karachi 4, Pakistan; Oxford University Press, Rhodesia (qv); Oxford University Press, Singapore (qv); Oxford University Press, South Africa (qv); Oxford University Press, Tanzania (qv); Oxford University Press, Shawfield Industrial Estate, Rutherglen Rd, Rutherglen, Glasgow G73 1UL, UK; Oxford University Press, 200 Madison Ave, New York, NY 10016, USA, Oxford University Press, c/o Intersaf Co Ltd, 140 Wireless Rd, 11th Floor, Shell Ho, Bangkok, Thailand. Branches also in Beirut, Cairo and Mexico City
Subjects: Belles Lettres, Poetry, Biography, History, English Language Teaching, Music, Art, Classics, Language, Law, Philosophy, Reference, Bibles, Religion, Juveniles, High-priced Paperbacks, Medicine, Psychology, Engineering, General & Social Science,

Atlases, University, Secondary & Primary Textbooks, Educational Materials, Journals
1978: 650 titles *Founded:* 1478
ISBN Publisher's Prefix: 0–19

Oyez Publishing Ltd, Norwich Ho, 11/13 Norwich St, London EC4A 1AB Tel: (01) 404 5721/8 Telex: 8812079
Man Dir: J F Platt; *Sales Publicity Manager:* C E Marshall
Orders to: Riverside Way, Northampton NN1 5AR
Parent Company: The Solicitors Law Stationery Society Ltd, UK
Subsidiary Company: Vander-Oyez SA, France (qv)
Subjects: Commercial & Technical Education, Law, Commercial & Professional
1977: 11 titles *1978:* 38 titles
ISBN Publisher's Prefixes: 0–85120, 0–85121

Packard Publishing Ltd, 16 Lynch Down, Funtingdon, Chichester, Sussex PO18 9LR Tel: West Ashling 621 (STD code 024 358)
Man Dir: Michael Packard
Subjects: Biology, Environmental Studies, Applicable Mathematics

Paddington Press Ltd+, 21 Bentinck St, London W1M 5RL Tel: (01) 935 3738 Telex: 27604
Dirs: Janet Marqusee, John Marqusee, Anthony White; *Editorial:* J Marqusee; *Sales Dir:* Heather Dean; *Right & Permissions:* Janet Marqusee (foreign), Anthony White (domestic)
Subjects: General Fiction and Nonfiction
1978: 48 titles *Founded:* 1971
ISBN Publisher's Prefixes: 0–7092, 0–8467

Paintaway, an imprint of Ramboro Enterprises Ltd (qv)

Paladin Books, see Granada Publishing Ltd

Pan Books Ltd+, 18/21 Cavaye Pl, London SW10 9PG Tel: (01) 373 6070 Cable Add: Pandition London Telex: 917466
Shipping Add: Brunel Rd, Basingstoke, Hampshire
Man Dir: R Vernon-Hunt; *Deputy Man Dir:* T W V McMullan; *Sales Dirs:* (Home) R J Williams, (Export) N S Potts; *Publicity Dir:* M Cheyne; *Publishing Dir:* S H Master; *Editorial Dir:* A S Mehta
Subjects: Low-priced Paperbacks, General Fiction & Non-fiction
Founded: 1947
Imprints: Pan, Piccolo, Picador, Brodies Notes
ISBN Publisher's Prefix: 0–330 (Pan)

Panther Books Ltd, see Granada Publishing Ltd

Paper Tiger, an imprint of Dragon's World Ltd (qv)

Paperfronts, an imprint of Elliot Right Way Books (qv)

Walter **Parrish** Ltd, see Adkinson Parrish Ltd

The **Paternoster** Press Ltd+, Paternoster House, 3 Mount Radford Crescent, Exeter, Devon, EX2 4JW Tel: Exeter 50631 (STD Code 0392)
Chairman and Man Dir: Jeremy H L Muddit; *Editorial, Rights and Permissions:* P E Cousins; *Sales/Publicity/Advertising:* Jeremy H L Muddit
Subjects: History, Philosophy, Religion, Paperbacks
1977: 16 titles *Founded:* 1934
ISBN Publisher's Prefix: 0–85364

Stanley **Paul** & Co Ltd, an imprint of Hutchinson General Books Ltd (qv)

Pelham Books Ltd, 44 Bedford Sq, London WC1B 3EF Tel: (01) 323 3200 Cable Add: Emjaybuks London WC1 Telex: 21322
Man Dir: Eric T L Marriott; *Sales Dir:* R Douglas-Boyd; *Publicity & Advertising:* Susan Palmer; *Rights & Permissions:* Jean Aserappa
Subjects: Biography, How-to, Reference, Juveniles, Sports, Crafts
1977: 80 titles *1978:* 80 titles
Associate Company: Michael Joseph Ltd (qv)
Miscellaneous: Company is in the Thomson Books Ltd group, a part of International Thomson Organization Ltd (Canada)
ISBN Publisher's Prefix: 0–7207

Pelican, an imprint of Penguin Books Ltd (qv)

Pemberton Publishing Co Ltd*, 88 Islington High St, London N1 8EN Tel: (01) 226 7251 Cable Add: Ratiopres London N1 4EN
Managing Editor, Rights & Permissions: Nicolas Walter
Parent Company: Rationalist Press Association (same address)
Subjects: Philosophy, Religion, Low-priced Paperbacks, Psychology, General & Social Science, University Textbooks
1977: 4 titles *Founded:* 1960
ISBN Publisher's Prefix: 0–301

Penguin Books Ltd+, 536 King's Rd, London SW10 0UH Tel: (01) 351 2392 Cable Add: Penguinook SW10
Warehouse & Accounts: Bath Rd, Harmondsworth, West Drayton, Middlesex UB7 0DA Tel: (01) 759 1984 Cable Add: Penguinook West Drayton Telex: 263130
For further details see Penguin Publishing Co Ltd

Penguin Publishing Co Ltd+, 536 King's Rd, London SW10 0UH Cable Add: Penguinook SW10
Warehouse & Accounts: Bath Rd, Harmondsworth, West Drayton, Middlesex UB7 0DA Tel: (01) 759 1984 Cable Add: Penguinook West Drayton Telex: 263130
Chairman: E J B Rose; *Man Dirs:* R J E Blass, R Maskery; *Chief Executive:* P Mayer; *Editorial Dirs:* Peter Carson (Non-fiction), Philippa Harrison (Fiction); *Sales:* Alan Wherry; *Rights & Permissions:* Carol Heaton; *Publicity Dir:* Patrick Wright; *Press Officer:* Jenny Wilford
Associate Companies: Viking Penguin Inc, 625 Madison Ave, New York, NY 10022, USA; Longman Group, UK (qv); Ladybird Books Ltd, UK (qv)
Subsidiary Companies: Penguin Books Australia Ltd, Australia (qv); Penguin Books Canada Ltd, 41 Steelcase Rd West, Markham, Ontario L3R 1B4, Canada; Penguin Books New Zealand Ltd, New Zealand (qv)
Book Clubs: Puffin Book Club; Junior Puffin Club
Subjects: Low- & High-priced Paperbacks (General Fiction, General Nonfiction, Juveniles, Technical, Educational)
1978: 4000 titles *1979:* 4000 titles
Miscellaneous: Hardcover imprints of firm are Allen Lane (qv), Kestrel Books (qv). Other imprints include Pelican Books, Peregrine Books, Puffin Books
ISBN Publisher's Prefixes: 0–14 (Penguin), 0–7139 (Allen Lane), 0–7226 (Kestrel)

Pentos Ltd, New Bond Street Ho, 1–5 New Bond St, London W1Y 0SB Tel: (01) 499 0386
Firm is (non-publishing) ultimate holding company of group of subsidiaries owned by (non-publishing) Pentos Publishing Group Ltd
General Publishing: Hollen Street Press Ltd; Ward Lock Ltd (qv); Ward Lock Educational Ltd (qv); Marshall Morgan & Scott Publications Ltd (qv)
Popular Publishing: Sandle Brothers Ltd; Whitman Publishing (UK) Ltd; World Distributors (Manchester) Ltd (qv)
The company owns Dillon's University Bookshop Ltd, Hudsons Bookshops Ltd and Hodges Figgis & Co Ltd, Dublin, Republic of Ireland (qqv under Major Booksellers), also Sisson & Parker Ltd and F F Allsopp & Co Ltd

Pergamon Press Ltd+, Headington Hill Hall, Oxford OX3 0BW Tel: Oxford 64881 (STD code 0865) Cable Add: Pergapress Telex: 83177
Chairman & Publisher: I R Maxwell; *Joint Man Dirs:* C R Ellis and G F Richards; *Group Marketing Dir:* M Kermian; *Sales Manager:* J G Ennals; *Publicity Manager:* Graham Jones; *Rights & Permissions:* Anna Moon
Associate and Subsidiary Companies: The Aberdeen University Press Ltd, UK (qv); Pergamon Press (Australia) Pty Ltd, Australia (qv); Pergamon Press Canada Ltd, Toronto, Canada; Pergamon Press Sarl, Paris, France; Pergamon Press GmbH, Kronberg, German Federal Republic; Bumpus, Haldane & Maxwell, UK; Religious Education Press, UK (qv); A Wheaton & Co, UK (qv); Pergamon Press Inc, Elmsford, New York, USA
Subjects: Philosophy, Religion, Music, Art, Biography, History, How-to, General Science, Life Sciences & Medicine, Veterinary Sciences, Physical Sciences, Engineering, Psychology, Social & Behavioural Sciences and Liberal Arts, Business Management, University, Secondary & Primary Textbooks, Educational Materials
1977: 300 titles *1978:* 350 titles *Founded:* 1949
ISBN Publisher's Prefix: 0–08

Permanent Press, 52 Cascade Ave, London N10 Tel: (01) 444 8591
Man Dir: Robert Vas Dias
Br Off: 1040 Park Ave, New York, NY 10028, USA
Subject: Poetry
1978: 2 titles *1979:* 2 titles *Founded:* 1972
ISBN Publisher's Prefix: 0–905258

The **Phaethon** Press, an imprint of The Aquila Publishing Co Ltd (qv)

Phaidon Press Ltd+, Littlegate Ho, St Ebbe's St, Oxford OX1 1SQ Tel: Oxford 46681 (STD code 0865) Cable Add: Phaidon Oxford Telex: 83308
Man Dir: George Riches; *Editorial Dirs:* Simon Haviland, Jean-Claude Piessel; *Marketing Dir:* Robert Sarsfield; *Rights & Permissions:* Alice Hammond
Orders to: Unit B, Ridgeway Trading Estate, Iver, Buckinghamshire
Subjects: Art, Art History, Music, Natural History, Illustrated Reference Books
1978: 70 titles *1979:* 80 titles *Founded:* 1925
Miscellaneous: Firm is a subsidiary of NV Uitgeversmaatschappij Elsevier, Netherlands (qv)
Imprints: Phaidon, Elsevier Phaidon
ISBN Publisher's Prefixes: 0–7148 (Phaidon), 0–7290 (Elsevier Phaidon)

George **Philip Alexander** Ltd+, Norfolk Ho, Smallbrook Queensway, Birmingham B5 4LT Tel: (021) 643 8641/4
Man Dir: A Alexander; *Sales Manager:* R Bond
Subject: Education
Miscellaneous: Firm is an associate company of George Philip & Son Ltd (qv)

George **Philip** & Son Ltd+, 12–14 Long Acre, London WC2E 9LP Tel: (01) 836 7863 Telex: 21667
Shipping Add: Lineside Industrial Estate, Littlehampton, Sussex
Man Dir: R J Shattock; *Export Sales Manager:* Rex Knott; *Rights & Permissions:* D C Yeoman
Associate Companies: George Philip Son Ltd; George Philip Printers; E Stanford Ltd; Stanford Maritime Ltd; Map Productions Ltd; Osprey Publishing Ltd, UK (qv); George Philip Alexander Ltd (qv)
Subjects: Atlases and Maps, Textbooks, Educational Materials
Founded: 1834

Philip & Tacey Ltd, see Philograph Publications Ltd

Phillimore & Co Ltd, Shopwyke Hall, Chichester, West Sussex PO20 6BQ Tel: Chichester 787636 (STD code 0243)
Cable Add: Phillimore Chichester
Honorary President: Lord Darwen; *Chairman & Man Dir:* Philip Harris; *Editorial Dir:* Noel H Osborne
Subjects: History, Historical Biography, Architectural History, Archaeology, Genealogy, Heraldry
Founded: 1875 *Incorporated:* 1897
Subsidiary: Darwen Finlayson Ltd (qv)
Bookshop: The Phillimore Bookshop, Shopwyke Hall, Chichester
Imprint: Delta Books
ISBN Publisher's Prefix: 0-900592, 0-85033

Philograph Publications Ltd+*, North Way, Andover, Hampshire SP10 5BA Tel: Andover 61171 (STD code 0264)
Telex: 47496
Man Dir: Jon Tacey
Subjects: Primary Education, Teaching Aids
Associated Company: Philip & Tacey Ltd, Andover
ISBN Publisher's Prefix: 0-85370

Phoebus Publishing Co, 52 Poland St, London W1A 2JX Tel: (01) 734 9132
Cable Add: Phoebus Ldn Telex: 23451
Chief Executive: Peter Morrison; *Deputy Chief Executive:* Philip Nugus; *Editorial Dir:* Nicolas Wright; *Production Dir:* Mike Emery; *Sales Dir:* Richard Ganson; *Rights & Permissions:* Roberta Bailey
Parent Company: B P C, UK (qv)
Associate Company: Macdonald & Jane's Publishing Group, UK (qv)
Subjects: Naval & Military, Cookery, Social Science, Reference Books, Encyclopaedias
ISBN Publisher's Prefix: 0-7026

Piatkus Books, 17 Brook Rd, Loughton, Essex Tel: (01) 508 7362
Man Dir: Judy Piatkus
Orders to: George Philip & Son Ltd, PO Box 1, Littlehampton, Sussex BN17 7EN
Parent Company: Judy Piatkus (Publishers) Ltd (address as above)
Subjects: Fiction, Cookery, Leisure, Arts, History, Biography
1979: 12 titles *Founded:* 1979
ISBN Publisher's Prefix: 0-86188

Picador, an imprint of Pan Books Ltd (qv)

Piccolo, an imprint of Pan Books Ltd (qv)

Pickering & Inglis Ltd+, 26 Bothwell St, Glasgow G2 6PA Tel: (041) 552 5044
Man Dir: Andrew Gray; *Sales Dir:* Albert G Glover; *Publicity & Advertising:* Andrew Kerr; *Marketing and Sales Manager:* Nicholas Gray
Subjects: Religion, Juveniles
1977: 31 titles *1978:* 21 titles *Founded:* 1870
Bookshops: 1 Creed Lane, London EC4V 5BR; 26 Bothwell St, Glasgow G2 6PA
ISBN Publisher's Prefix: 0-7208

Pied Piper, an imprint of World Book-Childcraft International Inc (qv)

Pierrot Publishing Ltd, 17 Oakley Rd, London N1 3LL Tel: (01) 226 0573/6171
Managing: Philip Dunn; *Editorial:* Jane Dunn, Karen Thesen
Orders to trade distribution: New English Library, Barnard's Inn, Holborn, London EC1
Subjects: Large format Colour Paperbacks/Originals, Science Fiction, Non-fiction, General, Reference. Co-editions
Founded: 1975
ISBN Publisher's Prefix: 0-905310

James **Pike** Ltd (EJP Publications), Consols Ho, St Ives, Cornwall Tel: St Ives (Cornwall) 6363 (STD code 073670) Cable Add: Piktorial St Ives Cornwall
Man Dir: E J Pike
Subjects: Juveniles, Education, Games, Sports, Commercial & Technical Textbooks, Guidebooks
ISBN Publisher's Prefixes: 0-85932, 0-900850

Frances **Pinter** Ltd+, 5 Dryden St, Covent Garden, London WC2E 9NW Tel: (01) 240 2430
Subjects: International Relations, Political Economy, Social Policy, Socio-legal Studies, Technology
1978: 12 titles
ISBN Publisher's Prefix: 0-903804

Pitkin Pictorials Ltd*, 11 Wyfold Rd, London SW6 6SG Tel: (01) 385 4351/3
Cable Add: Pitkins London SW6
Subjects: Architectural History, and Guides for the Tourist Industry
ISBN Publisher's Prefixes: 0-85372, 0-904234

Pitman Medical Publishing Co Ltd+, PO Box 7, Tunbridge Wells TN1 1XH Tel: Tunbridge Wells 38488 (STD code 0892)
Subjects: Medical Texts, Reference, Monographs, Symposia
1978: 40 titles
Miscellaneous: Associate company of Pitman Publishing Ltd (qv)

Pitman Publishing Ltd+, 39 Parker St, Kingsway, London WC2B 5PB Tel: (01) 242 1655 Cable Add: Ipandsons London WC2 Telex: 261367
Chairman: Nicolas Thompson; *Man Dir:* Navin Sullivan; *Marketing Dir:* Martin Marix Evans; *Home Sales Dir:* Kenneth Welham; *Trade Marketing Manager:* Michael Evans; *Educational Marketing Manager:* David Smith; *Editorial Dirs:* Phoebe Phillips (Trade), F I S McKendrick (Schools and Further Education), Alfred Waller (University/College), John Hindley (Advanced Publishing Programme); *Rights & Permissions:* Andrew Hall; *International Sales Dir:* Neill Ross
Associates & Br Offs: Pitman Publishing Pty Ltd, Australia (qv); Copp Clark Pitman Publishing Co, 517 Wellington St West, Toronto 135, Ontario, Canada; Pitman Publishing New Zealand Ltd, New Zealand (qv); Pitman Publishing Co SA (Pty) Ltd, South Africa (qv); Focal Press Ltd, UK (qv); Pitman Medical Publishing Co Ltd, UK (qv); Fearon-Pitman Publishers Inc, 6 Davis Dr, Belmont, California 94002, USA
Subjects: Art, Craft, Cookery, Hobbies, How-to, Theatre, Technical, Business, University, Technical & Professional Textbooks, Advanced Monographs & Reference Works, Shorthand
ISBN Publisher's Prefix: 0-273

Playfair, an imprint of Macdonald & Jane's Publishing Group, UK (qv)

Plexus Publishing Ltd, 30 Craven St, London WC2N 5NT Tel: (01) 839 1315
Sales, Production: Terence Porter; *Editorial, Publicity, Rights & Permissions:* Sandra Wake, Nicola Hayden
Subjects: Illustrated Books on Films, Rock, Folk, Biography, Popular Culture and Art
1977: 3 titles *1978:* 3 titles *Founded:* 1973
ISBN Publisher's Prefix: 0-85965

Plough Publishing House+, Darvell, Robertsbridge, East Sussex TN32 5DR Tel: Robertsbridge 880626 (STD code 0580)
Man Dir, Rights & Permissions: Peter P Cavanna; *Sales, Publicity & Advertising Dir:* Mrs Cavanna
Subjects: Biography, Reference, Religion, Juveniles
1977: 3 titles *1978:* 3 titles *Founded:* 1937
Miscellaneous: Firm is the publishing house of the Hutterian Society of Brothers
ISBN Publisher's Prefix: 0-87486

Plume, an imprint of New English Library Ltd (qv)

Pluto Press+, Unit 10, Spencer Court, 7 Chalcot Rd, London NW1 8LH Tel: (01) 722 0141
Editorial: Michael Kidron, Richard Kuper
Subjects: Biography, History, Workers' Handbooks, Politics, Social Sciences, Plays, Literature, Low- & High-priced Paperbacks, Popular Culture
1977: 32 titles *1978:* 42 titles *Founded:* 1970
ISBN Publisher's Prefixes: 0-902818, 0-904383

Policy Studies Institute+*, 1/2 Castle Lane, London SW1E 6DN Tel: (01) 828 7055
Subjects: Politics, Economics, Sociology
ISBN Publisher's Prefix: 0-85374

Polybooks Ltd, an imprint of Charles Skilton Ltd (qv)

Polytantric Press, an imprint of Jay Landesman Ltd (qv)

Pond Press*, 5 Norbreck Parade, North Circular Rd, London NW10 7HR Tel: (01) 997 7425
Subjects: University, Secondary & Primary Education, Reference Books, Poetry & Drama, Directories & Guidebooks
ISBN Publisher's Prefix: 0-85375

Popular Dogs Publishing Co Ltd, an imprint of Hutchinson General Books Ltd (qv)

H **Pordes***, 529b Finchley Rd, London NW3 7BH Tel: (01) 435 9878/9
Man Dir: H Pordes; *Sales & Publicity Dir:* W H Gardner
Subjects: History, Reference
Founded: 1947

Book Club: The Jewish Book Club
(R Pordes)
Miscellaneous: See also under Remainder Dealers
ISBN Publisher's Prefix: 0–85376

T & A D Poyser Ltd, 281 High St, Berkhamsted, Hertfordshire HP4 1AJ
Tel: Berkhamsted 4158 (STD code 044 27)
Man Dir: Trevor Poyser
Subjects: Ornithology, Aviation
1977: 4 titles *1978:* 3 titles *Founded:* 1972
ISBN Publisher's Prefix: 0–85661

Pre-School Publishing Co*, 116–120 Golden Lane, London EC17 0TL Tel: (01) 253 2145
Editorial, Rights & Permissions: Miss N Galinski; *Sales:* H Starke; *Production:* C Tuthill; *Publicity:* Mrs W Wilson
Orders to: The Barn, Northgate, Beccles, Suffolk
Subject: Pre-school books

Prentice-Hall International, 66 Wood Lane End, Hemel Hempstead, Hertfordshire HP2 4RG Tel: Hemel Hempstead 58531 (STD code 0442) Cable Add: Prenhall Hemel Telex: 82445
Vice President: Donald Deeks; *Sales Managers:* Haydn Jenkins (UK/Middle East, Africa excl south), Gary Utterson (Western Europe), Tony Murray (Eastern Europe), Roy Jones (UK Trade), Jeremy Dicks (UK Academic); *Rights & Permissions:* Tony Murray
Associated Companies: Prentice-Hall Inc, Englewood Cliffs, NJ 07632, USA; Prentice-Hall of Australia Pty Ltd, Australia (qv); Prentice-Hall of Canada Ltd, 1870 Birchmount Rd, Scarborough, Ontario, Canada; Prentice-Hall of India Pvt Ltd, India (qv); Prentice-Hall of Japan Inc, Japan (qv); Goodyear Publishing Co Inc, 15113 Sunset Blvd, Pacific Palisades, Calif 90272, USA; Institute for Business Planning Inc, IBP Plaza, 320 Hudson Terrace, Englewood Cliffs, NJ 07632, USA; Parker Publishing Co, West Nyack, NY 10994, USA; Reston Publishing Co, Box 547, Reston, Va 22090, USA; Winthrop Publishers Inc, 17 Dunster St, Cambridge, Mass 02138, USA; International Book Distributors Ltd, UK
Division: Appleton-Century-Crofts (US)
Subjects: History, Music, Art, Philosophy, Religion, Medicine, Psycoogy, University Textbooks and Postgraduate Material in Science and Technology, Sociology, Education, Business, Economics, English, English as a Second language, Political Science, Speech, Drama, Trade Books
1978: 748 titles *Founded:* 1913
Miscellaneous: Firm is a branch of Prentice-Hall International Inc, Englewood Cliffs, NJ 07632, USA
ISBN Publisher's Prefixes: 0–13 (Prentice-Hall and Parker), 0–87620 (Goodyear), 0–87624 (Institute for Business Planning), 0–87909 (Reston), 0–87626 (Winthrop), 0–8385 (Appleton-Century-Crofts)

Princeton University Press, see University Presses of Columbia and Princeton

George **Prior** Associated Publishers Ltd, 37–41 Bedford Row, London WC1R 4JH
Tel: (01) 405 6603/6626
Shipping Add: Biblios, Glenside Industrial Estate, Partridge Green, Horsham, West Sussex RH13 8RA Tel: Horsham 710971 (STD code 0403)
Man Dir, Rights & Permissions: George Prior; *Editorial:* Stephen Dobell; *Publicity & Advertising Dir:* Brian O'Cathain
Subjects: General Fiction, History, Music, Art, Philosophy, Reference, High-priced Paperbacks, Social Science
1977: 26 titles *1978:* 42 titles *Founded:* 1972
Subsidiaries: George Prior Publishers; Book Mail International
ISBN Publisher's Prefix: 0–904000, 0–86043

Priory Press Ltd, see Wayland Publishers Ltd

Prism Press, Stable Court, Chalmington, Dorchester, Dorset DT2 0HB Tel: Maiden Newton 524 (STD code 03002)
Dirs: Julian King, Colin Spooner
Subjects: Alternative Technology, Self-Sufficiency, Philosophy, Politics, Literature
Miscellaneous: Distributed by George Philip & Co, PO Box 1, Littlehampton, Sussex
ISBN Publisher's Prefix: 0–904727

Profile Books Ltd*, Dial Ho, 6 Park St, Windsor, Berks SL4 1UU Tel: Windsor 69777
Dirs: P E Butler, H B Jones; *Mail Order:* P Bridgeman
Imprints: Profile Publications, Hylton Lacy Publishers
Subjects: Aircraft, Cars, AFVs, Warships, Small Arms, Locomotives

Prospice, an imprint of Aquila Publishing (qv)

Proteus (Publishing) Ltd, Bremar Ho, Sale Pl, London W2 1PT Tel: (01) 402 7360 Telex: 21969
Man Dir, Editorial, Rights & Permissions: Michael Brecher; *Sales, Publicity:* George Loucaides; *Production:* Sharon Barnfield
Subsidiary Company: Proteus Publishing Co, 502 East John St, Carson City, Nevada, USA
Subjects: General Non-fiction, Fiction, Travel and Professional Guides, Juveniles
1977: 2 titles *1978:* 4 titles *Founded:* 1977
ISBN Publisher's Prefix: 0–906071

Psychic Press Ltd+*, 23 Great Queen St, London WC2B 5BB Tel: (01) 405 2914/5 Cable Add: Psychic London WC2
Man Dir: Maurice Barbanell; *Advertising Dir:* Ronald Baker; *Rights & Permissions:* Gordon Adams
Subjects: Philosophy, Reference
Founded: 1932
Bookshops: Psychic News Bookshop, 23 Great Queen St, London WC2B 5BB
ISBN Publisher's Prefix: 0–85384

Purnell Books, Berkshire Ho, Queen St, Maidenhead, Berkshire SL6 1NF
Tel: Maidenhead 37171 (STD code 0628)
Telex: 847747
General Manager: Charles Harvey;
Editorial: Susan Hook; *Sales:* R T Wroe;
Production: Martyn Lewis; *Publicity:* Fiona Lock; *Rights & Permissions:* Lesley Willcock
Orders to: Purnell Books, Paulton, Bristol BS18 5LQ
Associate Companies: Sampson Low (qv), Macdonald & Jane's Publishing Group (qv)
Subjects: Reference, Juveniles
1977: 172 titles
ISBN Publisher's Prefixes: 0–361, 0–430

Putnam & Co Ltd+, 9 Bow St, London WC2E 7AL Tel: (01) 836 9081 Cable Add: Bodleian London WC2
Parent Company: The Bodley Head, UK (qv for further details)

Q Press Ltd+, 58 Queen St, Edinburgh EH2 3NS Tel: (031) 226 6572
Man Dir: Peter Chiene
Subjects: Politics, Economics, International Affairs, History, Philosophy
1977: 1 titles *1978:* 3 titles *Founded:* 1975
ISBN Publisher's Prefix: 0–905470

Q E D Publishing Ltd, 32 Kingly Court, London W1 Tel: (01) 734 4611 Telex: 298844
Man Dir: Laurence F Orbach; *Art Dirs:* Alastair Campbell, Edward Kinsey;
Editorial Dir: Jeremy Harwood
Subjects: International Co-editions, Reference, Education

Quartet Books Ltd, 27–29 Goodge St, London W1P 1FD Tel: (01) 636 3992, (01) 636 0968 Telex: 919034
Dirs: Naim Attallah (Chairman), John Boothe (Managing), David Elliott, Alan Stafford, Stephen Cockburn, Herbert Nagourney (USA); *Sales:* David Elliott;
Production: Gary Grant; *Publicity:* Sheila Turnbull; *Rights & Permissions:* John Boothe
Associate Company: Robin Clark Ltd (qv)
Subsidiary Companies: Quartet Books Australia Pty Ltd, 10 Hyland St, South Yarra, Victoria 3141, Australia; Quartet Books Inc, 12 East 69th St, New York, NY 10021, USA; Namara Publications, Namara Ho, 45–46 Poland St, London W1
Subjects: Fiction, Biography, Music, History, Philosophy, Politics, Social Science, Trade Paperbacks, Psychology, The Arab World, Sexual Politics
1977: 98 titles *1978:* 74 titles *Founded:* 1972
Miscellaneous: Firm is a member of the Namara Group, Namara Ho, 45–46 Poland St, London W1
ISBN Publisher's Prefix: 0–7043

Quarto Publishing Ltd, 32 Kingly Court, Beak St, London W1 Tel: (01) 734 4611 Telex: 298844
Man Dir: Laurence F Orbach; *Editorial Dir:* Jim Mallory; *Art Dir:* Robert J Morley
Parent Company: Quarto Ltd, 666 Fifth Ave, New York, NY 10019, USA
Associate Company: QED Publishing Ltd (qv)
Subjects: International Co-editions, Illustrated books on Wine & Food, History, Militaria, Transport, Natural History, Reference
1977: 10 titles *1978:* 12 titles
ISBN Publisher's Prefix: 0–906286

Queen Anne Press Ltd, now part of Macdonald & Jane's Publishing Group (qv)

Quentin Press Ltd, 11–12 West Stockwell St, Colchester, Essex CO1 1HN
Tel: Colchester 65151 (STD code 0206)
Cable Add: Paterson, Colchester Telex: 896616 MP Sendit G, Markit 987562 Cochac
Man Dir: Mark Paterson
Subjects: High-class Illustrated Books
Founded: 1978
Miscellaneous: Packagers of books for other publishers

R I B A Publications Ltd*, Finsbury Mission, Moreland St, London EC1
Tel: (01) 251 0791 Cable Add: Ribazo London
Man Dir: R H McKie; *Production:* M Stribbling
Parent Company: Royal Institute of British Architects
Associated Company: RIBA Services Ltd
Subjects: Architecture and Design

Bookshop: RIBA Bookshop, 66 Portland Place, London W1N 4AD
1977: 6 titles *Founded:* 1967
Miscellaneous: Represented by Association of Learned & Professional Society Publishers (qv under Book Trade Organisations)
ISBN Publisher's Prefix: 0-900630

Radical Reprints, an imprint of The Journeyman Press (qv)

The **Rainbird** Publishing Group+, 36 Park St, London W1Y 4DE Tel: (01) 491 4777 Cable Add: Rainmac London Telex: 261472
Man Dir: Michael Rainbird; *Editorial:* Michael O'Mara; *Sales:* Colin West; *Production:* Peter Phillips; *Publicity:* Annette Denniff; *Rights & Permissions:* Valerie Reuben
Subsidiary Companies: George Rainbird Ltd; Rainbird Reference Books Ltd
Subjects: Art, Archaeology, Architecture, History, Travel, Hobbies, Leisure, Sport, Natural History, Crafts, Medical
1977: 15 titles *1978:* 23 titles *Founded:* 1951
Miscellaneous: Company is in the Thomson Books Ltd group, a part of International Thomson Organization Ltd (Canada)
ISBN Publisher's Prefix: 0-902935

Ramboro Enterprises Ltd, 6 Highbury Corner, London N5 1RD Tel: (01) 609 3091/2 Cable Add: Dons Bar Telex: 24224 ref 1297
Man Dir, Sales: Donald Murray; *Rights & Permissions:* E Lacher
Associated Company: Number One Publishing Co Ltd
Imprints: Atlantic, Delightful Books, Paintaway, Ramboro, University, Varsity
Subjects: Children's Books, Art, Cookery, Dictionaries
1977: 18 titles *Founded:* 1960
Miscellaneous: Also Remainder Dealers

The **Ramsay** Head Press+, 36 North Castle St, Edinburgh EH2 3BN Tel: (031) 226 6692
Editorial Dir: Norman Wilson
Subjects: Biography, Literature, Poetry, Art, Architecture, Reference, New Assessments series (critical studies of outstanding figures in literature and arts)
1977: 11 titles *1978:* 8 titles *Founded:* 1971
ISBN Publisher's Prefix: 0-902859

Ranelagh Editions, 82 Hurlingham Court, Ranelagh Gardens, London SW6 3UR Tel: (01) 736 0189
Man Dir: Raymond Holdsworth
Subject: Limited Editions
Founded: 1975
ISBN Publisher's Prefix: 0-904862

Rapp & Whiting Ltd*, 105 Great Russell St, London WC1B 3LJ Tel: (01) 580 2746 Cable Add: Rappidly, London WC1B 3LJ
Subjects: Fiction, University Education, Art & Architecture, Children's Books, Poetry & Drama, History, Archaeology, Biography & Memoirs, Politics, Economics, Sociology, Directories & Guidebooks
Miscellaneous: Firm is a subsidiary of André Deutsch (qv)
ISBN Publisher's Prefix: 0-85391

Rationalist Press Association, see Pemberton Publishing Co Ltd

Raven Books, an imprint of Macdonald & Jane's Publishing Group (qv)

The **Reader's Digest** Association Ltd+*, 25 Berkeley Sq, London W1X 6AB Tel: (01) 629 8144 Cable Add: Readigest London W1X 6AB Telex: 264631
Distributors: Hodder & Stoughton Ltd (qv)
Subjects: Fiction, English Dictionaries, References, Maps & Atlases, Travel, Encyclopaedias, Directories, Guidebooks
1977: 4 titles
ISBN Publisher's Prefix: 0-276

Reference International Publishers Ltd, 21 Soho Sq, London W1V 5FD Tel: (01) 437 7624/5 Telex: 22635
Director: Martin Self
Subjects: Encyclopaedias, Dictionaries, General Reference

Max **Reinhardt** Ltd, 9 Bow St, London WC2E 7AL Tel: (01) 836 9081 Cable Add: Bodleian London WC2
Subsidiary Company: The Bodley Head (qv for further details)

Religious Education Press+, Hennock Rd, Exeter, Devon EX2 8RP Tel: Exeter 74121 (STD code 0392) Telex: 42749
Publishing Dir: John Halsall; *Editorial:* Ian Aitken; *Marketing:* Don Bibey
Subjects: Religion, Juveniles, Secondary & Primary Textbooks, Educational Materials
1977: 9 titles *1978:* 15 titles *Founded:* 1921
Miscellaneous: Subsidiary of Pergamon Press Ltd (qv)
ISBN Publisher's Prefix: 0-08

Reprographia, an imprint of Gordon Wright Publishing (qv)

Research Publishing Co, an imprint of Fudge & Co Ltd (qv)

Rex, an imprint of Murrays Remainder Books (qv)

Riband Books, see Artemis Press

The **Richmond** Publishing Co Ltd, Orchard Rd, Richmond, Surrey Tel: (01) 876 1091
Subjects: Reprints, History, Social Sciences, Botany, Limited & De Luxe Editions
ISBN Publisher's Prefix: 0-85546

Rider & Co, an imprint of Hutchinson General Books Ltd (qv)

Right Way Books, an imprint of Elliot Right Way Books (qv)

Rivers Press, an imprint of Writers and Readers Publishing Co-operative (qv)

Rivingtons (Publishers) Ltd+, Montague Ho, Russell Sq, London WC1B 5BX Tel: (01) 637 1466 Cable Add: Byronitic, London WC1B 5BX
Subjects: Classics
Miscellaneous: Firm is a subsidiary of Evans Brothers Ltd (qv)
ISBN Publisher's Prefix: 0-280

Robinson & Watkins Books Ltd+, see Watkins Publishing

Robson Books Ltd+, 28 Poland St, London W1V 3DB Tel: (01) 734 1052 Cable Add: Robsobook London W1
Man Dir: Jeremy Robson; *Sales Manager:* Martin Hanks; *Editorial Dir:* Elizabeth Rose; *Rights, Publicity:* Katie Walsh
Subjects: General, Literature, Children's Books, Biography, Music, Humour
1977: 35 titles *1978:* 40 titles *Founded:* 1973
ISBN Publisher's Prefix: 0-903895, 0-86051

George **Ronald**+, 46 High St, Kidlington, Oxford OX5 2DN Tel: Oxford 5273 (STD code 08675) Cable Add: Talisman Oxford
Man Dir: Russell Busey
Subjects: Biography, Religion, High-priced Paperbacks
1977: 6 titles *1978:* 6 titles *Founded:* 1947
ISBN Publisher's Prefix: 0-85398

Barry **Rose** (Publishers) Ltd, Little London, Chichester, Sussex PO19 1PG Tel: Chichester 783637 (STD code 0243)
Chairman and Man Dir: Barry Rose; *Sales & Publicity:* R S Childs
Parent Company: Justice of the Peace (Holdings) Ltd
Associate Company: Professional Training Consultants Ltd
1976: 32 titles *1977:* 17 titles *Founded:* 1971
ISBN Publisher's Prefixes: 0-85992, 0-900500

The **Roundwood** Press (1978) Ltd, Kineton, Warwick CV35 0JA Tel: Kineton 640400 (STD code 0926)
Man Dir: Gordon Norwood; *Sales, Publicity, Rights & Permissions:* Neil Gordon
Parent Company: Gordon Fraser Gallery Ltd (qv)
Subjects: History, Social History, Biography, General
ISBN Publisher's Prefixes: 0-900093, 0-906418

Routledge & Kegan Paul Ltd+, 39 Store St, London WC1E 7DD Tel: (01) 637 7651 Cable Add: Columnae London WC1
Shipping Add: Broadway Ho, Newtown Rd, Henley-on-Thames, Oxfordshire RG9 1EN Tel: Henley-on-Thames 78321 (STD code 04912)
Man Dir: Norman Franklin; *Sales Dir:* Richard Bailey; *Publicity Dir:* Terence Lucas; *Advertising:* Heather Moss; *Permissions & Foreign Rights:* Gela Jacobson
Br Off: Routledge & Kegan Paul of America, 9 Park St, Boston, Mass 02108, USA
Subjects: General Fiction, Belles Lettres, Biography, History, Education, Occult, Art, Philosophy, Reference, Religion, High-priced Paperbacks, Psychology, Social Science, University & Secondary Textbooks
1977: 220 titles *1978:* 243 titles *Founded:* 1834
Subsidiary Company: Oriel Press Ltd (qv)
Bookshop: Kegan Paul, Trench, Trubner & Co, 39 Store St, London WC1E 7DD
ISBN Publisher's Prefix: 0-7100

Roxby Press Ltd, 98 Clapham Common North Side, London SW4 9SG Tel: (01) 228 2558
Dir: Hugh Elwes; *Rights & Permissions:* Grania Kearsley
Subjects: Illustrated Reference Books, Encyclopaedias
1979: 10 titles *Founded:* 1973

S A G E Publications Ltd, 28 Banner St, London EC1Y 8QE Tel: (01) 253 1516 Cable Add: SAGEPub London
Man Dir: David Brooks; *Editorial, Production, Rights & Permissions:* Carole Sutherland; *Marketing Manager:* Philip Glover
Associate Company: SAGE Publications Inc, 275 South Beverly Dr, Beverly Hills, California 90212, USA
Subjects: Social Sciences (Sociology, Political Science, Methodology,

International Relations, Human Services)
1978: 10 titles *1979:* 10 titles *Founded:* 1971
ISBN Publisher's Prefix: 0-8039

S C M Press Ltd+, 56-58 Bloomsbury St, London WC1B 3QX Tel: (01) 636 3841/4 Cable Add: Torchpres London WC1
Man Dir: The Rev John Bowden; *Production:* Mark Hammer; *Rights & Permissions:* Margaret Lydamore
Subjects: Religion, Theology, Religious Education
Bookshop: SCM Bookroom, 58 Bloomsbury St, London WC1B 3QX
1978: 40 titles *1979:* 45 titles *Founded:* 1929
ISBN Publisher's Prefix: 0-334

S P C K (The Society for Promoting Christian Knowledge)+, Holy Trinity Church, Marylebone Rd, London NW1 4DU Tel: (01) 387 5282 Cable Add: Futurity London NW1
Man Dir: Patrick Gilbert; *Publishers:* Robin Brookes, Darley Anderson; *Sales Manager:* Alan Goodworth; *Promotion:* Walter Petchey
Subjects: Philosophy, Religion, Specialist Paperbacks
1978: 70 titles *Founded:* 1698
Miscellaneous: A division of this Society is Sheldon Press (qv)
ISBN Publisher's Prefix: 0-281

S T L Books, PO Box 48, 9 London Rd, Bromley, Kent BR1 1BY Tel: (01) 464 1191 Cable Add: Mobiliser Bromley Telex: 896706 EBE G
Dir: G M Davey; *General Manager:* Dave Brown
Orders to: S T L Distributors, 1 Sherman Rd, Bromley, Kent BR1 3JH
Parent Company: Send the Light Trust, address as above
Subjects: Religion, Juveniles, Bibles
Bookshops: Bromley Christian Supply Centre, 9 London Rd, Bromley, Kent; Christian Bookshop, 17 Lordship Lane, London SE22; Bolton Christian Bookshop, 204 St Georges Rd, Bolton, Lancs; Coventry Christian Bookshop, 21 City Arcade, Coventry CV1 3HX
1977: 12 titles *1978:* 10 titles *Founded:* 1963
ISBN Publisher's Prefix: 0-903843

Saint Andrew Press+, 121 George St, Edinburgh EH2 4YN Tel: (031) 225 5722 Cable Add: Free, Edinburgh
Publisher: C L Rawlins
Subjects: Religion, Juveniles, Theology, Scottish Affairs, Current Issues
1978: 27 titles
Miscellaneous: Parent body is The Church of Scotland Committee on Publications
ISBN Publisher's Prefix: 0-7152

Saint James Press+*, 3 Percy St, London W1P 9FA Tel: (01) 580 4155
Man Dir: George Walsh
Subject: Reference
Founded: 1968
ISBN Publisher's Prefixes: 0-900997, 0-86066

Salamander Books Ltd, 27 Old Gloucester St, London WC1N 3AF Tel: (01) 242 6693 Cable Add: Salamander London WC1 Telex: 261113
Chairman: J Proost; *Joint Man Dirs:* Jeremy Westwood, Malcolm Little; *Editorial:* Ray Bonds; *Sales:* Jeremy Westwood; *Production:* Malcolm Little; *Publicity, Rights & Permissions:* Janet Pilch
Orders to: New English Library Ltd,
Barnard's Inn, Holborn, London EC1N 2JR
Parent Company: Henri Proost & Cie, Belgium (qv)
Subjects: Illustrated Reference Books: Military, Natural History, Music
1977: 7 titles *1978:* 10 titles *Founded:* 1974
ISBN Publisher's Prefix: 0-86101

Salesian Publications & Don Bosco Film Strips+, Blaisdon Hall, Longhope, Gloucestershire GL17 0AQ Tel: Longhope 830247 (STD code 0452)
Subject: Religion

The **Saltire** Society+, Saltire Ho, 13 Atholl Crescent, Edinburgh EH9 2AP Tel: (031) 228 6621
Subsidiary Company: New Saltire Ltd (at above address)
Imprint: Saltire Classics
Subjects: Scottish Art, Literature, Law, Music
Founded: 1936
Miscellaneous: Associated with The Scottish Civic Trust, 24 George Sq, Glasgow, in publishing *The Scottish Review*
ISBN Publisher's Prefix: 0-85411

Salvationist Publishing & Supplies Ltd+, 117-121 Judd St, King's Cross, London WC1H 9NN Tel: (01) 387 1656 Cable Add: Savingly, London WC1H 99
Sales: T W Carey; *Rights & Permissions:* Lt Col B Sylvester
Associated Company: Campfield Press, St Albans
Subjects: Religion, Music, Juveniles
1978: 5 titles
ISBN Publisher's Prefix: 0-85412

Sampson Low, Berkshire Ho, Queen St, Maidenhead, Berkshire SL6 1NF Tel: Maidenhead 37171 (STD code 0628) Telex: 847747
General Manager: Charles Harvey; *Editorial:* Carole Edwards; *Sales:* R T Wroe; *Production:* Martyn Lewis; *Publicity:* Fiona Lock; *Rights & Permissions:* Lesley Willcock
Subjects: Reference, Juveniles, Leisure
Miscellaneous: Firm is a division of Purnell Books, UK (qv)
ISBN Publisher's Prefix: 0-562

Satellite Books Publishers*, Kendall Ho, 9 Kendall Rd, Isleworth, Middlesex Tel: (01) 568 4506
Man Dir, Rights & Permissions: Charles Ejiofar; *Editorial:* Jeremy Hudson, Bernadette Deacon; *Publicity:* Audrey Holmwood
Subjects: General Fiction, Biography, Occult, Politics, Humour
1977: 5 titles *1978:* 6 titles *Founded:* 1976
ISBN Publisher's Prefix: 0-905186

W B **Saunders** Co Ltd, see Holt-Saunders Ltd

Saxon House, 1 Westmead, Farnborough, Hampshire GU14 7RU Tel: Farnborough 519221 (STD code 0252)
An imprint of Gower Publishing Co Ltd (qv), with details as for Gower Publishing except as follows:
Editorial: John Irwin
Subjects: Sociology, Economics, Politics, Law, Medicine, Psychology, Engineering, Public Administration, Environment
ISBN Publisher's Prefixes: 0-347 (pre-1976 titles), 0-566

Schofield & Sims Ltd, 35 St John's Rd, Huddersfield HD1 5DT Tel: Huddersfield 30684 (STD code 0484) Cable Add: Schosims Huddersfield

UNITED KINGDOM 405

Deputy Chairman & Man Dir: John S Nesbitt; *Sales Dir:* Jack Brierley
Subjects: Secondary & Primary Textbooks, Educational Materials
1977: 22 titles *1978:* 30 titles *Founded:* 1901
ISBN Publisher's Prefix: 0-7217

Scholastic Publications+, 161 Fulham Rd, London SW3 6SW Tel: (01) 581 0241/3 Cable Add: Scholastic, London SW3 Telex: 22281
Man Dir: David Kidd; *Editorial Dir:* Dorothy Wood
Subjects: Primary Education, Juvenile Fiction and Non-fiction
Book Clubs: Lucky, See-saw, Chip, Scene, Criterion
1978: 10 titles
ISBN Publisher's Prefix: 0-590

School of Oriental & African Studies, Malet St, London WC1E 7HP Tel: (01) 637 2388 Cable Add: Soasul London WC1
Publications Officer: M J Daly
Subjects: Oriental and African Language, Literature, History, Religion, Bibliography, Art
1977: 6 titles *1978:* 10 titles *Founded:* 1917
ISBN Publisher's Prefix: 0-901877, 0-7286

Schoolmaster Publishing Co Ltd+, Derbyshire Ho, Lower St, Kettering, Northamptonshire NN16 8BB Tel: Kettering 518407 (STD code 0536)
ISBN Publisher's Prefix: 0-900642

Science Research Associates Ltd+, Newtown Rd, Henley-on-Thames, Oxfordshire RG9 1EW Tel: Henley-on-Thames 5959 (STD code 04912) Cable Add: Sciresuk, Henley-on-Thames RG9 1EW Telex: 848454
Man Dir & Editorial: David M Neale; *Sales/Advertising/Publicity:* B Preston; *Rights & Permissions:* K L Turner
Associate Companies: Science Research Associates Pty Ltd, Australia (qv); Science Research Associates (Canada) Ltd, 707 Gordon Baker Rd, Willowdale, Ontario, Canada; Société de Recherche Appliquée à l'Education, 92 blvd de Latour-Maubourg, F-75007 Paris, France
Subjects: University, Secondary & Primary Textbooks, Commercial & Technical Education, Academic & Vocational Guidance Publications, Educational & Industrial Tests
Miscellaneous: Firm is a subsidiary of Science Research Associates Inc, 155 North Wacker Dr, Chicago, Ill 60606 (Science Research Associates Inc is a subsidiary of IBM)
ISBN Publisher's Prefix: 0-574

Scientechnica (Publishers) Ltd, see John Wright & Sons Ltd

Scolar Press+, 90 Great Russell St, London WC1 Tel: (01) 631 4141
Chairman: J E Commander: *Man Dir:* James Price; *Sales Manager:* Ann Sexsmith
Parent Company: Bemrose UK Ltd (qv for associate companies)
Subjects: English Literature, History, Music, Art, Children's Books, Social Sciences, Facsimile and Limited Editions
1978: 80 titles *Founded:* 1966
Bookshop: Scolar Book-room, 90 Great Russell St, London WC1
ISBN Publisher's Prefixes: 0-85417, 0-85967

Scorpion Publications Ltd, 377 High St, Stratford, London E15 4QZ Tel: (01) 555 3339 Telex: 261547
Editorial: L Harrow; *Sales:* A Grangelin; *Production, Publicity, Rights &*

Permissions: Colin Larkin
Associate Company: Dark Star Magazine, 58 Islip Manor Rd, Northolt, Middlesex UB5 5EA
Subjects: Art, Architecture, Photography, Music, Juveniles, Oriental Carpets, General Non-fiction
1978: 8 titles *1979:* 8 titles *Founded:* 1977
ISBN Publisher's Prefix: 0-905906

Scottish Academic Press Ltd+, 33 Montgomery St, Edinburgh EH7 5JX Tel: (031) 556 2796
Dirs: J Steven Watson, Douglas Grant, Christopher Blake, W N Everitt, Matthew Black, P Mc L D Duff, Ronald Crawford
Subjects: Scholarly, Scottish interest
1977: 80 titles *Founded:* 1970
Miscellaneous: Owned jointly by the Universities of St Andrews, Dundee and Strathclyde, and associated with Sussex University Press and The Handsel Press (qqv)
ISBN Publisher's Prefix: 0-7073

Scripture Union+, 47 Marylebone Lane, London W1M 6AX Tel: (01) 486 2561
Publishing Dirs: Paul Marsh and Robert Hicks; *Rights & Permissions:* John Hunt
Subsidiary Companies: Frontier Youth Trust; Inter School Christian Fellowship; Bibellesebund eV, Federal Republic of Germany (qv)
Imprints: Kingfisher, Tiger
Subjects: Music, Religion, Juveniles, Educational Materials
Bookshops: 5 Wigmore St, London W1H 0AD; 77 Bridge St, Manchester M3 2RH; 16 Park St, Croydon CR0 1YE; 3 King Edward St, Leeds LS1 6AX; 3 Suffolk Rd, Cheltenham, Gloucestershire; 280 St Vincent St, Glasgow C2; 30 Cow Wynd, Falkirk, Stirlingshire; 21 Rutland Sq, Edinburgh; 8 Kings Rd, Brighton, Sussex BN1 1NE; 22 Fisher St, Carlisle, Cumbria CA3 8RH; 14 North Bridge St, Sunderland, Tyne and Wear SR5 1LD; 14 Eton St, Richmond, Surrey TW9 1EE; 29 Woodthrope Rd, Ashford, Middx; 22 Lower Hillgate, Stockport, Cheshire SK1 1JE; 18 Slater St, Liverpool L1 4BS; 12 Wellington Pl, Belfast BT1 6JB; 38 Ardconnel, Inverness; 68 Princes St, Perth; 4 Peterborough Rd, Harrow, Middx HA1 2BQ
Founded: 1867
ISBN Publisher's Prefix: 0-85421

Seafarer Books, an imprint of The Merlin Press Ltd (qv)

Search Press Ltd and Burns & Oates Ltd, 2-10 Jerdan Pl, Fulham, London SW6 5PT Tel: (01) 385 6261
Man Dir, Sales, Publicity: Charlotte de la Bedoyere; *Editorial, Rights & Permissions:* John Cumming, David Lewis; *Production:* John Cleary; *Publicity:* Diana Dubens
Associated Companies: Burns & Oates Ltd; Search for Leisure Ltd (both at above address)
Subjects: Philosophy, Theology, Literature and Literary Criticism, Poetry, History, Biography, Religion, General, Moral Education, Mysticism, Third World, Children's, Arts and Crafts
1977: 29 titles *1978:* 31 titles *Founded:* 1962
ISBN Publisher's Prefix: 0-85532

Martin **Secker & Warburg** Ltd+, 54 Poland St, London W1V 3DF Tel: (01) 437 2075 Cable Add: Psophidian London W1
Man Dir: T G Rosenthal; *Sales Dir:* T R Manderson; *Production Dir:* P Ireland; *Publicity Manager:* Chris Holmes; *Rights & Permissions:* Gillian Vale
Orders to: The Windmill Press, Kingswood, Tadworth, Surrey KT20 6TG Tel: Mogador 3511 (STD code 073783)
Parent Company: Heinemann Group of Publishers Ltd, UK (qv)
Associate Company: Alison Press, 5 Harley Gardens, London SW10 9SW
Subjects: General Fiction, Belles Lettres, Poetry, Biography, History, Music, Cinema, Art, Philosophy, Reference, Psychology, Social Science, High-priced Paperbacks, Criticism, Photography, Judaica, Political Science
1977: 91 titles *1978:* 82 titles *Founded:* 1910
ISBN Publisher's Prefix: 0-436

Seeley, Service & Co Ltd, 196 Shaftesbury Ave, London WC2H 8JL Tel: (01) 836 6225 Cable Add: Tomatkins
Shipping Add: 81A Endell St, London WC2 8JL
Man Dir: Leo Cooper; *Editorial Dir:* T R Hartman; *Publicity, Rights & Permissions:* Alison Gordon
Subsidiary Company: Leo Cooper Ltd, UK (qv)
Subjects: Sport, Naval History
1977: 6 titles *1978:* 6 titles *Founded:* 1744
ISBN Publisher's Prefix: 0-85422

Severn House Publishers Ltd, 144-46 New Bond St, London W1Y 9FD Tel: (01) 499 3784
Man Dir: Edwin Buckhalter; *Editorial Manager:* Ian Jackson; *Sales Manager:* Philip Cotterell; *Production Manager:* Louisa Lazarus; *Rights & Permissions:* Barbara Levy
Orders to: Tiptree Book Services Ltd, St Luke's Chase, Tiptree, Colchester, Essex CO5 0SR
Parent Company: Severn House Books (Holdings) Ltd, 144-46 New Bond St, London W1Y 9FD
Subsidiary Companies: Severn House Paperbacks Ltd (address as above); Buzby Books Ltd (address as above)
Associate Companies: Elmfield Press Ltd (qv), White Lion Publishers Ltd
Imprint: Buzby Books Ltd
Subjects: Thrillers, Romance, War, Historical, Science Fiction, Westerns, Film and TV tie-ins, Juveniles, Natural History, Cookery, Biography
1978: 84 titles *1979:* 124 titles *Founded:* 1974
ISBN Publisher's Prefixes: 0-7278 (Severn House), 0-7284 (White Lion), 0-7057 (Elmfield Press)

Shakespeare Head Press, an imprint of Basil Blackwell & Mott Ltd (qv)

Shearwater Press Limited+, Welch Ho, Church Rd, Onchan, Isle of Man Tel: Douglas 3598 (STD code 0624)
Man Dir: Ian Faulds; *Editorial:* Clare Faulds; *Sales:* Susan Quayle
Imprint: Manxman Publications
Subjects: History, Local History, Topography, Fine Art, Fiction, Isle of Man
Bookshop: Glebe Books, Welch Ho, Church Rd, Onchan
1977: 6 titles *1978:* 5 titles *Founded:* 1973
ISBN Publisher's Prefix: 0-904980

Sheed & Ward Ltd, 6 Blenheim St, London W1Y 0SA Tel: (01) 629 0306 Cable Add: Stanza London W1
Dirs: M T Redfern, K G Darke
Subjects: Biography, History, Philosophy, Reference, Religion
Founded: 1926
ISBN Publisher's Prefix: 0-7220

Sheldon Press+, SPCK Bldg, Marylebone Rd, London NW1 4DU Tel: (01) 387 5282 Cable Add: Futurity London NW1
General Secretary: P N G Gilbert; *Editorial Dir:* Darley Anderson; *Sales Dir:* Alan Goodworth; *Advertising Dir:* Walter Petchey
Subjects: Biography, Philosophy, Religion, High-priced Paperbacks, Social & Political Science, Psychology, Animals
1977: 27 titles *1978:* 24 titles
Miscellaneous: Division of SPCK (qv)
ISBN Publisher's Prefix: 0-85969

Shepheard-Walwyn (Publishers) Ltd+, 51 Vineyard Hill Rd, London SW19 7JL Tel: (01) 946 0437 Cable Add: Shepwyn, London SW19
Man Dir: A R A Werner
Subjects: General Nonfiction
1978: 5 titles *Founded:* 1971
ISBN Publisher's Prefix: 0-85683

Sheppard Press Ltd, PO Box 42, Russell Chambers, Covent Garden, London WC2E 8AX Tel: (01) 240 0406 Cable Add: Iffcass London WC2
Man Dir: T Rendall Davies
Subjects: Book Trade Reference
1977: 3 titles *1978:* 3 titles *Founded:* 1944
ISBN Publisher's Prefix: 0-900661

Shire Publications Ltd, Cromwell Ho, Church St, Princes Risborough, Aylesbury, Buckinghamshire Tel: Princes Risborough 4301 (STD code 08444)
Man Dir: John W Rotheroe
Subsidiary Companies: The Gubblecote Press; Cadbury Lamb
Subjects: Biography, History, How-to, Low- & High-priced Paperbacks. Publishers of 'Discovering' Books, 'Lifelines' and Shire Albums
1977: 60 titles *1978:* 45 titles *Founded:* 1966
ISBN Publisher's Prefix: 0-85263

Sidgwick & Jackson Ltd+, 1 Tavistock Chambers, Bloomsbury Way, London WC1A 2SG Tel: (01) 242 6081/3 Cable Add: Watergate Westcent London
Chairman: The Earl of Longford; *Man Dir:* William Armstrong; *Sales Dir:* Stephen du Sautoy; *Rights & Permissions:* William Armstrong; *Editorial:* Margaret Willes; *Publicity:* Victoria Stace
Subjects: General Fiction, Belles Lettres, Poetry, Biography, History, Music, Art, Philosophy, Religion, Juveniles, General & Social Science, High-priced Paperbacks, Science Fiction
1978: 70 titles *Founded:* 1908
ISBN Publisher's Prefix: 0-283

Charles **Skilton** Ltd+, 2 & 3 Abbeymount, Edinburgh EH8 8JH Tel: (031) 661 9339
Man Dir: Charles Skilton; *Editorial:* Jean Desebrock
Associate Company: Fudge & Co (qv)
Subsidiary Companies: Albyn Press Ltd, Luxor Press Ltd, Tallis Press Ltd, Fortune Press, Polybooks Ltd (all at 2 & 3 Abbeymount, Edinburgh 8)
Br Off: 115 Old St, London EC1
Subjects: Art, Graphic Arts, Reference, Biography, Antiquarian, Cookery, Sexology, Scottish Fiction
Founded: 1943
ISBN Publisher's Prefixes: 0-284 (Skilton, Albyn, Luxor, Tallis), 0-85240 (Fortune), 0-7050 (Fudge)

Skilton & Shaw, an imprint of Fudge & Co Ltd (qv)

UNITED KINGDOM 407

Thomas Skinner Directories, Windsor Court, East Grinstead Ho, East Grinstead, West Sussex RH19 1XE Tel: East Grinstead 26972 (STD code 0342)
Man Dir: R Haddrell; *Publishing Dir:* R J E Dangerfield
Parent Company: IPC Business Press Information Services Ltd
Subject: Directories
ISBN Publisher's Prefixes: 0-611, 0-900808

Colin Smythe Ltd, PO Box 6, Gerrards Cross, Buckinghamshire SL9 7AE Tel: Gerrards Cross 86000 (STD code 02813) Cable Add: Smythebooks Gerrards Cross Bucks
Man Dir: Colin Smythe
Subjects: Belles Lettres, Poetry, Biography, History, Music, Art, Philosophy, Reference, Religion, Parapsychology, High-priced Paperbacks, English and Anglo-Irish Literature & Criticism
1977: 14 titles *1978:* 19 titles *Founded:* 1966
ISBN Publisher's Prefixes: 0-900675, 0-901072, 0-86140

The **Society** for Promoting Christian Knowledge, see SPCK

Soncino Press Ltd*, Audley Ho, North Audley St, London W1Y 2EU Tel: (01) 629 6506 Cable Add: Soncino London W1
Man Dir: S M Bloch
Br Off: 100 Park Ave, New York, NY 10017
Subject: Religion (Jewish)
Founded: 1929
ISBN Publisher's Prefix: 0-900689

Sotheby Parke Bernet Publications, an imprint of Philip Wilson Publishers (qv)

Southside, see Canongate and Southside

Souvenir Press Ltd+, 43 Great Russell St, London WC1B 3PA Tel: (01) 580 9307/8 & 637 5711/2/3 Cable Add: Publisher London WC1 Telex: 24710
Shipping Add: Tiptree Book Services, Tiptree, Colchester, Essex
Man Dir & Rights & Permissions: Ernest Hecht; *Editorial:* Rosalynde de Lanerolle; *Sales:* T E Wiseman; *Production:* Rodney King; *Publicity & Advertising Manager:* Tessa Harrow
Associated Company: Souvenir Press (Australia) Pty Ltd
Subsidiary Companies: Souvenir Press (Educational & Academic) Ltd; Euro-Features Ltd; Pictorial Presentations Ltd; Pop-Universal Ltd; Condor Books
Imprints: Condor Books, Souvenir Press
Br Off: 311 Singel, Amsterdam, Netherlands
Subjects: General Fiction, Belles Lettres, Poetry, Biography, History, How-to, Music, Art, Philosophy, Religion, Juveniles, Large-format Paperbacks, Medicine, Psychology, Social Science
Bookshop: Souvenir Press Bookshop, 43 Great Russell St, London WC1B 3PA
1978: 63 titles *1979:* 50 titles *Founded:* 1954
ISBN Publisher's Prefix: 0-285

Neville **Spearman***, The Priory Gate, 57 Friars St, Sudbury, Suffolk Tel: Sudbury 71818 (STD code 07873)
Dirs: Neville Armstrong, M J Armstrong
Subjects: Specialists in the Occult, Metaphysical and Unorthodox
Subsidiary: Neville Spearman (Jersey) Ltd, Normandy Ho, PO Box 75, St Helier, Jersey, Channel Islands
ISBN Publisher's Prefixes: 0-85435, 0-85978 (Jersey)

Sphere Books Ltd+, 30-32 Gray's Inn Rd, London WC1X 8JL Tel: (01) 405 2087
Cable Add: Spherbooks London
Telex: 858846
Shipping Add: High St, Sandhurst, Camberley, Surrey. Export orders to London address
Imprints: include Abacus, Sphere
Subjects: General Fiction and Nonfiction, Biography, History, How-to, Music, Art, Philosophy, Reference, Low- & High-priced Paperbacks, Medicine, Psychology, General & Social Science
1977: 212 titles *1978:* 262 titles *Founded:* 1967
Miscellaneous: Company is in the Thomson Books Ltd group, a part of International Thomson Organization Ltd (Canada)
ISBN Publisher's Prefixes: 0-7221 (Sphere), 0-349 (Abacus)

E & F N **Spon** Ltd+, 11 New Fetter Lane, London EC4P 4EE Tel: (01) 583 9855
Cable Add: Fenspon London EC4
Shipping Add: North Way, Andover, Hampshire
Editorial: Phillip Read; *Marketing:* Peter F Shepherd; *Production:* Brian West; *Rights & Permissions:* Vikki Anderson
Parent Company: Associated Book Publishers Ltd, UK (qv)
Subjects: Reference, Engineering, Building
1977: 7 titles *1978:* 10 titles *Founded:* 1830
ISBN Publisher's Prefix: 0-419

Sporting Handbooks Ltd+, 12 Dyott St, London WC1A 1DF Tel: (01) 836 8911
Subjects: Sports, Games & Pastimes
Miscellaneous: Firm is a subsidiary of J Whitaker & Sons Ltd (qv)
ISBN Publisher's Prefix: 0-85020

Spring Books, an imprint of The Hamlyn Publishing Group (qv)

Springwood Books Ltd, 49-51 Bedford Row, London WC1V 6RL Tel: (01) 242 7866/7 Telex: 28413
Man Dir, Editorial, Sales, Production, Rights & Permissions: Christopher Foster; *Publicity:* Louise Hudson
Orders to: George Philip & Son, PO Box 1, Littlehampton, Sussex BN17 7EN
Subjects: Fiction, Poetry, Biography, Children's Books, History, Finance, Music, Archeology, Art, Cookery
1978: 20 titles *1979:* 40 titles *Founded:* 1976
ISBN Publisher's Prefix: 0-905947

Spurbooks Ltd+*, 6 Parade Court, Bourne End, Bucks Tel: Bourne End 25350 (STD code 06285) Cables: Spurbooks Bourne End Bucks
Man Dir: Robin Neillands; *Editorial Dir:* Estelle Huxley; *Publicity:* Margaret Feldon
Subjects: Venture Sports, Outdoor Leisure, History
1977: 23 titles *Founded:* 1968
ISBN Publisher's Prefix: 0-902875, 0-904978

Stacey International, 128 Kensington Church St, London W8 4BH Tel: (01) 727 5627 Cable Add: Staceybook London W8 Telex: 298768
Man Dir: T Stacey; *Editorial:* Charlotte Odgers; *Sales:* Rhona Hanbury; *Production:* Anthony Nelthorpe; *Publicity:* Anna Dowson; *Rights & Permissions:* Anthony Lejeune
Subjects: General, Middle East
1977: 10 titles *1978:* 11 titles *Founded:* 1974
ISBN Publisher's Prefix: 0-905743

Stage 1, 47 Red Lion St, London WC1R 4PF Tel: (01) 405 7780
Publisher: Richard Handyside
Subjects: University & Secondary Education, Politics, Economics, Social Sciences
1978: 5 titles
ISBN Publisher's Prefix: 0-85035

Stainer & Bell Ltd+, 82 High Rd, London N2 9PW Tel: (01) 444 9135
Man Dir: Bernard A Braley; *Marketing Dir:* Keith Robinson; *Executive Chairman & Editorial Dir:* Allen Percival
Subjects: Music, Education, Drama, Humour, Religion, Biography, Sociology, Travel
Imprints include: Augener, Belton Books, Galliard, A Weekes, Joseph Williams
ISBN Publisher's Prefix: 0-85249

Stam Press Ltd+, Educa House, Liddington Estate, Leckhampton Rd, Cheltenham, Glos GL53 0DN Tel: Cheltenham 42127/42451 (STD code 0242) Telex: 43592
Man Dir: Stanley Thornes; *Production Dir:* Roy Kendall; *Trade Manager:* Margot van de Weyer
Parent Company: The Kluwer Group, Netherlands
Associate Company: Stanley Thornes (Publishers) Ltd
Subjects: Technical & Scientific

Stanford Maritime Ltd+*, 12-14 Long Acre, London WC2E 9LP Tel: (01) 836 7863 Cable Add: Philip London WC2
Telex: 21667
Man Dir: M A Bovill; *Export Sales Manager:* Rex W Knott; *Rights & Permissions:* Phoebe Mason
Orders to: George Philip & Son Ltd, Arndale Rd, Lineside Industrial Estate, Littlehampton, Sussex BN17 7EN
Subjects: Nautical books and charts for yachtsmen and professional seamen
Miscellaneous: Firm is an associate company of George Philip & Son Ltd (qv)
ISBN Publisher's Prefix: 0-540

Star Books, see Wyndham Publications Ltd

Harold **Starke** Ltd+, Pegasus Ho, 116-120 Golden Lane, London EC1Y 0TL Tel: (01) 253 2145/6
Editorial, Rights & Permissions: Miss N Galinski; *Sales:* H Starke; *Production:* C Tuthill; *Publicity:* Mrs W Wilson
Orders to: The Barn, Northgate, Beccles, Suffolk
Parent Company: Burke Publishing Co Ltd (qv)
Subjects: General Nonfiction, Reference, Medical
1977: 1 title *Founded:* 1960
ISBN Publisher's Prefix: 0-287

Rudolf **Steiner** Press+, 35 Park Rd, London NW1 6XT Tel: (01) 723 9514
Man Dir, Sales, Rights & Permissions: U Babbel; *Editorial:* J Collis; *Production, Publicity:* J Playfoot
Subjects: Art & Architecture, Philosophy, Education, Religion, Social Sciences, Natural Sciences, Agriculture
Bookshops: 35 Park Rd, London NW1; 38 Museum St, London WC1
1979: 25 titles *Founded:* 1920
ISBN Publisher's Prefix: 0-85440

Patrick **Stephens** Ltd+, Bar Hill, Cambridge CB3 8EL Tel: Crafts Hill 80010 (STD code 0954) Cable Add: Peeselpubs, Cambridge
Telex: 817677
Man Dir: Patrick Stephens; *Deputy Man & Editorial Dir:* Darryl Reach; *Sales Manager:*

Peter Townsend; *Production:* Ian Heath; *Managing Editor & Rights & Permissions:* Bruce Quarrie
Subjects: How-to, Maritime, Military, Modelling, Motoring, Motorcycling, Aviation, Art, Photography, Wargaming, Crafts, Railways, Angling, Boating & Sailing, Commercial Vehicles
1977: 32 titles *1978:* 39 titles *Founded:* 1967
ISBN Publisher's Prefix: 0–85059

Stevens & Sons Ltd+, 11 New Fetter Lane, London EC4P 4EE Tel: (01) 583 9855 Cable Add: Subjicio London EC4
Shipping Add: North Way, Andover, Hampshire
Man Dir: C D O Evans
Parent Company: Associated Book Publishers Ltd, UK (qv)
Subjects: Reference books for lawyers and solicitors, Textbooks for law students and law teachers
1978: 25 titles *Founded:* 1888
ISBN Publisher's Prefix: 0–420

Stillitron+, 72 New Bond St, London W1Y 0QY Tel: (01) 493 1177 Cable Add: Stillitron, Ldn Telex: 23475
President: Gerald B Stillit
Subject: Modern Languages
1978: 11 titles
ISBN Publisher's Prefix: 0–288

Stobart & Son Ltd+, 67/73 Worship St, London EC2A 2EL Tel: (01) 247 0501
Publicity: B J Davies
Subjects: Woodwork, Timber, Forestry, Handicrafts
1979: 8 titles
ISBN Publisher's Prefix: 0–85442

Student Christian Movement Press, see S C M Press Ltd

Studio Publications (Ipswich) Ltd, 32 Prince St, Ipswich, Suffolk IP1 1RJ Tel: Ipswich 217127 (STD code 0473)
Man Dir: Barrie John Henderson; *Publicity:* Elizabeth Henderson
Imprints: Munch Bunch, Studio Publications
Subjects: Sports, Children's
1977: 10 titles *1978:* 8 titles *Founded:* 1975
ISBN Publisher's Prefix: 0–904584

Studio Vista+, 35 Red Lion Sq, London WC1R 4SG Tel: (01) 831 6100
Dirs: See Cassell Ltd, UK
Subjects: Art, Applied Art, Design, Crafts, Architecture, Interior Decoration, Theatre, Dance, Cinema
1977: 50 titles
Miscellaneous: Division of Cassell Ltd, UK (qv)
ISBN Publisher's Prefix: 0–289

Sufi Publishing Co Ltd+*, 25 East St, Farnham, Surrey Tel: Farnham 26439 (STD Code 025 13)
Man Dir: Fazal Inayat-Khan; *Editorial:* K Rana; *Sales:* I D Francis; *Rights & Permissions:* A Evans
Branch Off: Secr Varkevisserstraat 52, Katwikj aan Zee, The Netherlands
Subjects: Sufism and related subjects
1977: 1 title *Founded:* 1933
ISBN Publisher's Prefix: 0–217

Sundial, an imprint of Octopus Books (qv)

Surrey University Press, Bishopbriggs, Glasgow G64 2NZ Tel: (041) 772 2311
London Off: Furnival Ho, 14–18 High Holborn, London Tel: (01) 242 5832
Dir: Dr G MacKintosh
Parent Company: Blackie & Son (qv)

Subjects: Engineering, Microbiology, Biomedicine, Chemistry, Physics, Hotel & Catering Studies
1977: 4 titles *Founded:* 1972
ISBN Publisher's Prefix: 0–903384

Sussex University Press*, Sussex Ho, Falmer, Brighton, East Sussex BN1 9RH Tel: Brighton 606755 (STD code 0273)
Publications Committee: Professors G F A Best, R J Blin-Stoyle, D F Pocock, A K Thorlby
Subjects: Scholarly
1977: 5 titles *Founded:* 1971
Miscellaneous: Associated with The Scottish Academic Press and The Handsel Press (qqv)
ISBN Publisher's Prefix: 0–85621

Sweet & Maxwell Ltd+, 11 New Fetter Lane, London EC4P 4EE Tel: (01) 583 9855 Cable Add: Subjicio London EC4
Shipping Add: North Way, Andover, Hampshire
Man Dir: C D O Evans
Parent Company: Associated Book Publishers Ltd, UK (qv)
Subjects: Law (Reference & University Textbooks), Business
1978: 81 titles *Founded:* 1799
ISBN Publisher's Prefix: 0–421

Systems Publications Ltd, now Caxton Publications Ltd (qv)

Tabard Press Ltd, see E P Publishing Ltd

Tabor Publications, 3–5 Valentine Pl, London SE1 Tel: (01) 928 4468
Publisher: Colin Heard

Tallis Press Ltd, an imprint of Charles Skilton Ltd (qv)

Talmy, Franklin Ltd*, 29 Rupert Ho, Nevern Sq, London SW5 Tel: (01) 584 7545 Cable Add: Franklit, London
Man Dir: Mike Franklin; *Sales, Publicity, Advertising, Rights & Permissions:* Madeleine Morel
Br Off: 170 Philip St, Sydney, Australia
Subjects: General Fiction, Belles Lettres, Biography, History, How-to, Philosophy
ISBN Publisher's Prefix: 0–900735

Tandem Publishing Limited, see Wyndham Publications Ltd

Tantivy Press, associate company of Thomas Yoseloff (qv)

Target, an imprint of Wyndham Publications Ltd (qv)

Tate Gallery Publications, Millbank, London SW1P 4RG Tel: (01) 834 5651/2 Telegrams: Tategal London
Publications Manager: Iain Bain; *Sales Manager:* Brian Lawler; *Rights & Permissions:* Sarah Jacobs; *Shop Manager:* Stanley Bennett
Retail Shop: Tate Gallery, Millbank, London SW1P 4RG
1978: 6 titles *Founded:* 1931
Subjects: Art books and catalogues
ISBN Publisher's Prefix: 0–900874, 0–905005

Tattoo, an imprint of Wyndham Publications Ltd (qv)

Tavistock Publications Ltd+, 11 New Fetter Lane, London EC4P 4EE Tel: (01) 583 9855 Cable Add: Subjicio London
Shipping Add: Associated Book Publishers Ltd, North Way, Andover, Hampshire
Ed Dir: Gill Davies; *Marketing Dir:* Peter Shepherd; *Advertising:* Lyndsay Williams; *Rights & Permissions:* V Anderson
Parent Company: Associated Book Publishers Ltd (qv)
Subjects: Sociology, Anthropology, Psychiatry, Psychology, Philosophy, Social Medicine, Paperbacks, Reference
1977: 18 titles *Founded:* 1947
Bookshop: Sweet & Maxwell Spon Booksellers, North Way, Andover, Hampshire
ISBN Publisher's Prefix: 0–422

Taylor & Francis Ltd+, 10–14 Macklin St, London WC2B 5NF Tel: (01) 405 2237 Telex: 858540
Man Dir: S A Lewis
Book Publishing Dir: N Hughes; *Sales & Marketing Manager:* K R Courtney
Br Off: Trade, Publicity, Warehouse
Orders to: Taylor & Francis Ltd, Rankine Rd, Basingstoke, Hampshire RG24 0PR
Subsidiary Companies: Wykeham Publications (London) Ltd (qv); Taylor & Francis (Printers) Ltd; Taylor & Francis (Filmsetting) Ltd
Subjects: Physics, Medicine, Psychology, Engineering, General Science, University Textbooks, International Affairs
1977: 18 titles *1978:* 21 titles *Founded:* 1798
ISBN Publisher's Prefix: 0–85066

Teach Yourself Books, an imprint of Hodder & Stoughton Ltd (qv)

Teakfield Ltd, see Gower Publishing Co Ltd

The **Technical Press** Ltd+*, Freeland, Oxford OX7 2AP Tel: Freeland 881788 (STD code 0993) Cable Add: Tecpreslon Oxford
Man Dir, Rights & Permissions: Paul Stobart
Subjects: How-to, Reference, High-priced Paperbacks, Engineering, General Science, University & Secondary Textbooks
1977: 2 titles *Founded:* 1933
Associate Company: Freeland Press Ltd (details as for The Technical Press)
ISBN Publisher's Prefixes: 0–291 (Technical), 0–900363 (Freeland)

Thomas **Telford** Ltd*, Telford Ho, PO Box 101, 26–34 Old St, London EC1P 1JH Tel: (01) 253 9999 Telex: 21792 ref 966
Man Dir: Sydney Lenssen; *Director of Publications:* Paul Thompson; *Marketing:* John Fisher (Books), Derek Tehan (Serials)
Parent Company: The Institution of Civil Engineers
Subjects: Engineering, Transportation, Hydraulics, Hydrology and Public Health, Soil Mechanics & Foundations, Structures and Buildings, Education & Training, Nuclear Engineering, Journals
Bookshop: 26–34 Old St, London EC1P 1JH
1977: 30 titles *1978:* 40 titles *Founded:* 1973
ISBN Publisher's Prefix: 0–91948, 0–7277

Temple Press, an imprint of The Hamlyn Publishing Group (qv)

Maurice **Temple Smith** Ltd, 37 Great Russell St, London WC1 3PP Tel: (01) 636 9810
Man Dir: Maurice Temple Smith
Subjects: Biography, History, Philosophy, Religion, High-priced Paperbacks, Psychology, Social Science
Founded: 1970
ISBN Publisher's Prefix: 0–85117

Teredo Books Ltd+, 19 Waldegrave Rd, Brighton, East Sussex BN1 6GR Tel: (0273) 505432
Man Dir: Alex A Hurst; *Trade Manager:* R M Cookson
Orders to: PO Box 430, Brighton, East Sussex BN1 6BT
Subjects: High-quality Nautical, Marine Art
1977: 1 title *1978:* 1 title
ISBN Publisher's Prefix: 0-903662

Tetrad Press*, 103 Grove Park, London SE5 8LE Tel: (01) 274 6305
Subject: Art

Thames & Hudson Ltd+, 30-34 Bloomsbury St, London WC1B 3QP Tel: (01) 636 5488 Cable Add: Thameshuds London WC1 Telex: 25992/3
Shipping Add: 44 Clockhouse Rd, Farnborough, Hampshire
Dirs: Thomas Neurath, Eva Neurath; *Editorial:* Stanley Baron; *Sales:* Trevor Craker; *Production:* Werner Guttmann; *Rights & Permissions:* Ian Middleton
Associate Companies: Thames & Hudson (Australia) Pty Ltd, 86 Stanley St, West Melbourne, Victoria 3003, Australia; Thames & Hudson Inc, 500 Fifth Ave, New York, NY 10036, USA
Subjects: Art, Architecture, History, Archaeology, High-priced Paperbacks
ISBN Publisher's Prefix: 0-500

A **Thomas**, imprint of Thorsons Publishers Ltd (qv)

Henry **Thompson** Ltd, London Rd, Sunningdale, Berks SL5 0EP Tel: Ascot 24615
Man Dir: G C Thompson; *Marketing Services Manager:* Mrs P M Cooper; *Sales:* E C M Brown, G E Scoffin

Thomson Book Ltd+, Elm Ho, 10-16 Elm St, London WC1X 0BP Tel: (01) 278 2345 Telex: 21746
Man Dir: J C Fleming
Parent Company: Thomson Publications Ltd a member of the International Thomson Organization (Canada) group
Group Companies' Imprints:
Paperback: Abacus; Sphere Books
General Trade: Elm Tree; Hamish Hamilton; Hamish Hamilton Children's Books; Michael Joseph; Pelham; Rainbird
Educational: Thomas Nelson
Overseas Companies: Thomas Nelson (Canada); Read-Way Books (Canada); Thomas Nelson (Nigeria—40 per cent holding); Thomas Nelson (Australia); Bowmar/Noble Publishers (USA)
Founded: 1977
Miscellaneous: See separate group company entries for further information. T B L Book Service Ltd, 17-23 Nelson Way, Tuscan Trading Estate, Camberley, Surrey GU15 3EU, is the warehousing and distribution subsidiary of the company

Stanley **Thornes** (Publishers) Ltd+, Educa Ho, Liddington Estate, Leckhampton Rd, Cheltenham, Glos GL53 0DN Tel: Cheltenham 42127/42451 (STD code 0242)
Man Dir: Stanley Thornes; *Production Dir:* Roy Kendall; *Trade Manager:* Margot van de Weyer
Parent Company: The Kluwer Group, Netherlands
Associate Company: Stam Press Ltd
Subjects: Mathematics, Engineering, Chemistry, Biology, Business Studies, Modern Languages
1978: 22 titles
ISBN Publisher's Prefix: 0-85950

Thornhill Press Ltd, 24 Moorend Rd, Cheltenham, Glos GL53 0AU Tel: Cheltenham 519137 (STD code 0242)
Man Dir: D Badham-Thornhill
Subjects: Horticulture, Poetry, Medical, Juveniles, Topographical Guides
1978: 6 titles *Founded:* 1972
ISBN Publisher's Prefix: 0-904110

Thornton Cox Ltd, 45 Flood St, London SW3 Tel: (01) 589 2620
Man Dir: Richard Cox
Orders to: Geographia Ltd, 93 St Peter's St, St Albans, Herts
Subjects: Travel Guides
Founded: 1966
ISBN Publisher's Prefix: 0-902726

F A **Thorpe** (Publishing) Ltd, The Green, Bradgate Rd, Anstey, Leicester LE7 7FU Tel: Anstey 4325 (STD code 053721)
Man Dir: F A Thorpe
Subjects: Fiction, Travel & Adventure, Nonfiction
1978: 132 titles
Miscellaneous: Publishers of Ulverscroft Large Print Books
ISBN Publisher's Prefixes: 0-85456, 0-7089

Thorsons Publishers Ltd+, Denington Estate, Wellingborough, Northamptonshire NN8 2RQ Tel: Wellingborough 76031/4 (STD code 0933)
Man Dir: J A Young; *Sales Dir:* D J Young; *Rights & Permissions:* Janet Winslow; *Editorial Dir:* J R Hardaker; *Production Dir:* D C J Palmer; *Marketing Dir:* A J Procter
Subjects: Health and healing embracing Nature cure and Diet Reform, Natural Foods & Cookery, Herbalism, Acupuncture, Homoeopathy, Yoga, Self-sufficiency and Gardening, Occultism, Self-improvement, Guides to Practical Management Techniques, Psychology
1978: 75 titles *Founded:* 1930
Imprints: Aquarian Press Ltd, Athene Publishing Co, A Thomas, *Psychologist Magazine*
ISBN Publisher's Prefixes: 0-7225, 0-85030, 0-85454, 0-85385

The **Thule** Press+, Compass Ho, Sandwick, Shetland Tel: Sandwick 204 (STD code 095 05)
Editorial: John Button; *Sales:* Martine Robertson
Bookshop: Compass Ho, Sandwick, Shetland
Subjects: History, Topography and Literature of Scotland and Scandinavia
1978: 6 titles *1979:* 11 titles *Founded:* 1973

Tiger, an imprint of Scripture Union

Times Books Ltd*, 18 Ogle St, London WC1P 7LG Tel: (01) 637 5724 Telex: 264971
Chairman: Derek Jewell; *Man Dir:* B Winkleman; *Senior Editor:* P Middleton; *Assistant Editor:* A Hudson; *Production Manager:* D Osler
Orders to: Hamish Hamilton, 90 Great Russell St, London WC1B 3PT
Subjects: Atlases, General Nonfiction, Reference
ISBN Publisher's Prefix: 0-7230

Alec **Tiranti** Ltd, an imprint of Academy Editions (qv)

Tobin Music Books, an imprint of Helicon Press (qv)

Tolly Publishing Co, an imprint of Ernest Benn Ltd (qv)

Top Stone Books+, 29 Station Rd, Harpenden, Herts AL5 4XB Tel: Harpenden 64510 (STD code 05827) Telex: 826957 Top Stone
Manager: James Rutherford
Subjects: Esoteric, Religion
1978: 2 titles *Founded:* 1976

Topaz Publishing Ltd, 67 High St, Gt Missenden, Bucks Tel: Gt Missenden 4161/2/3/4 (STD code 02406) Cable Add: Rosco Gt Missenden Telex: Delray G 847777 Attn Topazco 431
Man Dir, Editorial & Sales: Colin Rose; *Rights & Permissions:* Diana Rose
Subjects: Nonfiction, Popular Science, Psychology, Humour
1977: 5 titles *Founded:* 1975
ISBN Publisher's Prefix: 0-905553

Transworld Publishers Ltd+, Century Ho, 61-63 Uxbridge Rd, Ealing, London W5 5SA Tel: (01) 579 2652 Cable Add: Transcable London W5 Telex: 267974
Shipping Add: Sanders Rd, Wellingborough, Northamptonshire
Chairman: Patrick Newman; *Man Dir:* Philip Flamank; *Editorial Dir:* Alan Earney; *Publicity Dir:* Wendy Tury; *Rights & Permissions:* Lavinia Trevor, Jane Smith
Br Off: PO Box 1872, Johannesburg, South Africa
Subjects: General Fiction, Low-priced Paperbacks. Publish How and Why books, Wonder Why Books, Storychair, Carousel Children's Books
1978: 450 titles *Founded:* 1950
Subsidiary: Corgi Books Ltd
Miscellaneous: Firm is a subsidiary of Bantam Books Inc, 666 Fifth Ave, New York, NY 10019, USA
Associate Companies: Transworld Publishers (Australia) Pty Ltd, Australia (qv); Bantam Books of Canada Inc, 888 Dupont St, Toronto, Ontario, Canada; Transworld Publishers (Pty) Ltd, South Africa
ISBN Publisher's Prefix: 0-552

Travel Aid Services Ltd, 7A Belsize Park, London NW3 Tel: (01) 794 2647
Trading as Travelaid Publishing
Man Dir: M Von Haag
Orders to: PO Box 28, Southwater Industrial Estate, Southwater, Sussex Tel: Southwater 731174 (STD code 0403) Telex: 87493
Subjects: Travel
1978: 3 titles *1979:* 5 titles *Founded:* 1969
ISBN Publisher's Prefix: 0-902743

Trophy, an imprint of Wyndham Publications Ltd (qv)

Troubador, an imprint of (paperback) Futura Publications Ltd (qv) and (hardback) Macdonald & Jane's Publishing Group, UK (qv)

Turnstone Books+, 37 Upper Addison Gardens, London W14 8AJ Tel: (01) 602 6885 Cable Add: Perception W14
Man Dir: Alick Bartholomew
Subjects: Alternative Lifestyles and Philosophies, Radical Psychology, Holistic Medicine, Prehistory
1978: 8 titles *Founded:* 1971
ISBN Publisher's Prefix: 0-85500

Tyndale Press, an imprint of Inter-Varsity Press

Ulverscroft Large Print Books Ltd, see F A Thorpe (Publishing) Ltd

Uni Books, an imprint of Volturna Press (qv)

Universal, an imprint of Wyndham Publications Ltd (qv)

University Microfilms International, Xerox Publishing Group Ltd, 18 Bedford Row, London WC1R 4EJ Tel: (01) 242 9485 Telex: 8811363
International Marketing Dir: Timothy Smartt; *Sales Development Manager:* Kim Deshayes
Parent Company: Ultimate holding company Xerox Corporation
Subjects: Multi-disciplinary materials in microfilm and hardcopy at tertiary & professional levels including dissertations and periodicals
1978: 35,000 Dissertations, 7000 serials in microform *Founded:* 1938 (USA); 1952 (UK)

University of Chicago Press Ltd, see The MIT Press

University of London Press Ltd (now Hodder & Stoughton Educational), see Hodder & Stoughton

University of Wales Press, 6 Gwennyth St, Cathays, Cardiff CF2 4YD Tel: Cardiff 31919 (STD code 0222)
Dir: John Rhys
Subjects: History, Music, Art, Reference, Religion, Science, Humanities, Social Sciences, University, Secondary & Primary Textbooks (Welsh & English), Journals
1977: 23 titles *1978:* 31 titles *Founded:* 1922
ISBN Publisher's Prefixes: 0-7083, 0-900768

University Presses of Columbia and Princeton, 15A Epsom Rd, Guildford, Surrey GU1 3JT Tel: Guildford 68364 (STD code 0483)
Man Dir: Wolfgang Wingerter
Parent Companies: Columbia University Press, New York, USA and Princeton University Press, Princeton, New Jersey, USA
Subjects: Academic Books and Paperbacks in the Humanities, Social and Natural Sciences
1978: 210 titles *1979:* 190 titles
ISBN Publisher's Prefixes: 0-231 (Columbia), 0-691 (Princeton)

University Tutorial Press Ltd+, Bateman St, Cambridge CB2 1NG Tel: Cambridge 50949 (STD code 0223)
Man Dir: R R Briggs; *Trade Dir:* R E Everard
Subjects: University & Secondary Textbooks
1978: 9 titles *Founded:* 1901
ISBN Publisher's Prefix: 0-7231

Laurence **Urdang** Associates Ltd, Market Ho, Market Sq, Aylesbury, Bucks HP20 1TN Tel: Aylesbury 84911 (STD code 0296) Telex: 83635
Chairman: A Isaacs; *Dirs:* G J Morse, T H Long, J Daintith, L Urdang; *Production:* B D Evans
Associated Company: Laurence Urdang Inc, Essex, Conn 06426, USA
Founded: 1969
Miscellaneous: Firm compiles reference books (dictionaries, encyclopaedias, etc) and provides editorial services for publishers

Usborne Publishing Ltd*, 20 Garrick St, London WC2E 9BJ Tel: (01) 836 1806/1470 Cable Add: Uspub, London Telex: 27950 Ref 864
Man Dir: Peter Usborne; *Production, Rights & Permissions:* David Lowe
Subjects: Children's Books (Nonfiction)
1978: 100 titles *Founded:* 1973
ISBN Publisher's Prefix: 0-86020

Vallentine, Mitchell & Co Ltd, Gainsborough Ho, 11 Gainsborough Rd, Leytonstone, London E11 1RS Tel: (01) 530 4226 Cable Add: Valmico London Telex: 897719
Warehouse: Macdonald & Evans Ltd, Estover Rd, Estover, Plymouth PL6 7PZ
Man Dir: Frank Cass; *Editorial:* Murray Mindlin; *Trade:* Jeremy Guy; *Production:* Kenneth Cowell; *Publicity:* Suzette Reed
Subjects: Jewish Studies, Literature, History, Politics
1977: 1 title *Founded:* 1950
Miscellaneous: Firm is a subsidiary of Frank Cass & Co Ltd (qv), and an associate company of The Woburn Press (qv)
ISBN Publisher's Prefix: 0-85303

Variorum Reprints+, 21a Pembridge Mews, London W11 3EQ Tel: (01) 727 5492
Proprietor: Mrs E Turner
Subjects: Directories, Architecture, History, Arts, Reference, Education, Politics, Religion, University Textbooks, Dictionaries, Archaeology, Biography, Economics, Sociology, Oriental, Travel, Encyclopaedias, General Literature
1977: 16 titles *1978:* 17 titles
ISBN Publisher's Prefixes: 0-902080, 0-86078

Ventura Publishing Ltd, 44 Uxbridge St, London W8 7TG Tel: (01) 221 6395 Telex: 8953658 venpub G
Man Dir, Rights & Permissions: Robin Ellis
Subjects: Art, Cookery, Fashion, Practical Reference, How-to, *Namesake* Books (with Seymour Press)
1978: 24 titles (own imprint) *Founded:* 1977
Miscellaneous: Firm is mainly an editorial and production organization producing books for other publishers
ISBN Publisher's Prefix: 0-906284

Verso Editions, see New Left Books

Victory Press, an imprint of Kingsway Publications Ltd (qv)

Vikas Publishing Co Ltd+*, c/o UBS Publishers Distributors Ltd, 71 Mount Dr, North Harrow, Middlesex
Subjects: Humanities, Social Sciences
ISBN Publisher's Prefix: 0-7069

Vine Books Ltd, Dean Wace Ho, 7 Wine Office Court, Fleet St, London EC4 Tel: (01) 583 1484
Subjects: Religious, Hymn Books, History
1978: 2 titles
ISBN Publisher's Prefix: 0-85190

Virago Ltd+, Fourth Floor, 5 Wardour St, London W1V 3HE Tel: (01) 734 4608/9 Cable: Caterwaul London W1
Man Dir, Publicity Dir and Rights & Permissions: Carmen Callil; *Editorial Dir:* Ursula Owen; *Sales Dirs:* Harriet Spicer, Carmen Callil
Orders to: (UK orders only) Wildwood House, 1 Prince of Wales Passage, 117 Hampstead Rd, London NW1 3EE Tel: (01) 388 5389
Overseas orders to Virago
Subjects: Fiction, Biography, History, Philosophy, Education, Politics, Social Science & History, Women's Studies, Education, Health, Reference, Feminist Books
1978: 23 titles *1979:* 30 titles *Founded:* 1973
ISBN Publisher's Prefix: 0-86068

Virtue & Co Ltd, 25 Breakfield, Coulsdon, Surrey CR3 2UE Tel: (01) 668 4632 Cable Add: Virtutis Croydon Telex: 261507
Man Dir: Michael Virtue; *Sales Dir:* R S Cook
Br Offs: London, Bristol, Dublin
Subjects: Reference, Religion, Educational Materials
1978: 3 titles *1979:* 4 titles *Founded:* 1819
ISBN Publisher's Prefix: 0-900778

Vision Press Ltd, 11-14 Stanhope Mews West, London SW7 5RD Tel: (01) 589 9773
Man Dir: Alan Moore
Subjects: Belles Lettres, Biography, History, Music, Art, Philosophy, Religion, Psychology
1978/79: 14 titles *Founded:* 1947
ISBN Publisher's Prefix: 0-85478

Voltaire Foundation, Taylor Institution, St Giles, Oxford OX1 3NA Tel: Oxford 512931 (STD code 0865)
1977: 11 titles *1978:* 6 titles

Volturna Press+, 52 Ormonde Rd, Hythe, Kent Tel: Hythe (Kent) 69465 (STD code 0303)
Sole Partner: Dr D M C MacEwan
Imprints: Marsland Press, Uni Books, Co-chuideachd Leabhneachean Gaidhlig
Branch Off: Peterhead, Aberdeenshire
Subjects: Religion, Conservation, Biographies, Family Memoirs; All types of books in minor languages including Scottish Gaelic
1978: 3 titles *Founded:* 1968
ISBN Publisher's Prefix: 0-85606

Wales Tourist Board+, Sales and Distribution Centre, Davis St, Cardiff CF1 2FU Tel: Cardiff 372685 (STD code 0222) Telex: 497269
Subjects: Maps, History, Archaeology, Accommodation & Travel Guides, Angling, Guides & Posters
ISBN Publisher's Prefix: 0-900784

Walsingham, an imprint of Jarrold Colour Publications (qv)

Henry E **Walter** Ltd+, 26 Grafton Rd, Worthing, West Sussex Tel: Worthing 204567 (STD code 0903)
Subjects: Religious, Children's Books (Rewards), Bibles, Prayer & Hymnbooks
ISBN Publisher's Prefix: 0-85479

The **Warburg** Institute+* (University of London), Woburn Sq, London WC1 Tel: (01) 580 9663
All enquiries about publications: Elsie H Horstead, Assistant Secretary
Subjects: Art, History
1977: 2 titles *Founded:* (The Institute) 1921
Miscellaneous: The Institute is a non-commercial organization

Ward Lock Educational Ltd, subsidiary of Ward Lock Ltd (qv)

Ward Lock Ltd+, 116 Baker St, London W1 Tel: (01) 486 3271 Cable Add: Warlock London W1 Telex: 262364
Shipping Add: Unit 14, Trident Estate, Pindar Rd, Hoddesdon, Herts EN11 0LD
Chairman: T A Maher; *Man Dir:* Peter Lock; *Rights & Permissions Dir:* Timothy Evans
Subjects: Equestrian, Sailing, Crafts, Yoga, Sports, Antiques, Specialist Colour Illustrated International Co-editions, How-to, Children's Information Books, Sport, Paperbacks, Reference, Cookery, Gardening
1978: 70 titles *Founded:* 1854
Miscellaneous: Holding company is Pentos Ltd (qv for associated publishing companies)
ISBN Publisher's Prefix: 0-7063

Frederick **Warne** & Co Ltd+,
40 Bedford Sq, London WC1B 3HE
Tel: (01) 580 9622 Cable Add: Warne
London WC1 Telex: 859635
Man Dir, Rights & Permissions: C W
Stephens; *Editorial Dir:* D W Bisacre; *Sales
Dir:* R D Traube
Orders to: Warne Ho, Vincent Lane,
Dorking, Surrey RH4 3FW Tel: Dorking
5081 (STD code 0306)
Subsidiary Company: Frederick Warne &
Co Inc, 101 Fifth Ave, New York
NY 10003, USA
Subjects: How-to, Music, Art, Reference,
Religion, Juveniles, Natural History,
University, Secondary & Primary
Textbooks, Educational Materials
1978: 66 titles *Founded:* 1865
ISBN Publisher's Prefix: 0-7232

Waterlow (London) Ltd, Holywell Ho,
Worship St, London EC2A 2EN Tel: (01)
247 5400 Telex: 888804
Man Dir: E Carter; *Publishing:*
V Williamson
Parent Company: British Printing
Corporation Ltd (qv)
Subjects: Banking, Legal, General Business
ISBN Publisher's Prefix: 0-9007791

Watkins Publishing+*, Bridge St,
Dulverton, Somerset Tel: Dulverton 23395
(STD code 0398)
Man Dir: Richard Robinson
Subjects: Religion, Technical, Science,
Medicine, Music, History, Archaeology,
Biography, Memoirs, Philosophy, Oriental,
Travel & Adventure, General Literature
Subsidiary: Robinson & Watkins Books Ltd
ISBN Publishing Prefix: 0-7724

W **Watson** & Co+*, St Ann's Hill, Carlisle,
Cumbria
Subject: Religion

Franklin **Watts** Ltd+*, 8 Cork St,
London W1 Cable Add: Frawatts
London W1
Shipping Add: J M Dent & Sons
(Distribution) Ltd, Dunhams Lane,
Letchworth, Hertfordshire SG6 1LF
Man Dir: David Howgrave-Graham;
Marketing Dir: W E Bloodworth; *Editorial
Director:* Margaret Crush; *Rights &
Permissions:* Elizabeth Hamilton
Subjects: Reference, Juveniles
1977: 76 titles *Founded:* 1969
ISBN Publisher's Prefix: 0-85166

Wayland Publishers Ltd+*, 49 Lansdowne
Pl, Hove, East Sussex BN3 1HS
Tel: Brighton 722561 (STD code 0273)
Cable Add: Bookwright Hove Telex: 23961
Shipping add: Book Centre Ltd, Rufford
Rd, Crossens, Southport, Merseyside
PR9 8LA
Man Dir, Editorial: Roger Ferneyhough;
Man Dir, Sales, Publicity & Advertising:
John Lewis; *Rights & Permissions:* Roger
Ferneyhough
Associate Company: Argus Books Ltd (qv)
Subsidiary Company: Priory Press
Subjects: Illustrated School library Books,
Biography, History, Natural History,
Science, Crafts, Careers, General, Socio-
medicine, Mass Market Tourist Guides
1978: 60 titles *Founded:* 1969
ISBN Publisher's Prefixes: 0-85340
(Wayland), 0-85078 (Priory Press)

The **Wayzgoose** Press, an imprint of Aquila
Publishing (qv)

Webb & Bower (Publishers) Ltd,
33 Southernhay East, Exeter, Devon
EX1 1NS Tel: 35362/3 (STD code 0392)
Cable Add: Webbower Exeter Telex: 21792
(844)
Man Dir: Richard Webb; *Editorial Dir:*
Delian Bower; *Publishing Dir:* Nicholas
Facer
Subjects: General Non-fiction
1978: 6 titles *1979:* 12 titles *Founded:* 1975
Miscellaneous: Editorial, design and
production organization specializing in
producing illustrated books for the UK,
USA and the international co-edition
market

A **Weekes**, an imprint of Stainer & Bell
Ltd (qv)

George **Weidenfeld & Nicolson** Ltd+, 91
Clapham High St, London SW4 7TA Tel:
(01) 622 9933 Cable Add: Nicober London
SW11 1XA Telex: 918066
Shipping Add: The Windmill Press,
Kingswood, Tadworth, Surrey KT20 6TG
Chairman, Chief Executive and Man Dir:
Lord Weidenfeld; *Joint Deputy Man Dirs:*
Ray Compton, Richard Hussey; *Sales Dir:*
David Livermore; *Publicity & Advertising:*
Rosamund Lewis; *Rights & Permissions:*
Miss B J MacLennan
Associate Company: Frances Lincoln
Publishers Ltd (qv)
Subsidiary Company: Arthur Barker Ltd
(qv)
Imprints: Include World University Library
Subjects: General Fiction, Belles Lettres,
Poetry, Biography, History, Music, Art,
Philosophy, Reference, Religion, High-
priced Paperbacks, Psychology, General &
Social Science, University Textbooks
ISBN Publisher's Prefix: 0-297

A **Wheaton** & Co Ltd+*, Hennock Rd,
Exeter, Devon EX2 8RP Tel: Exeter 74121
(STD code 0392) Telex: 42749
Man Dir: John Halsall; *Publicity:* Don
Bibey
Subjects: Juveniles, Secondary & Primary
Textbooks, Educational Materials
1977: 114 titles *Founded:* 1780
Miscellaneous: Subsidiary of Pergamon
Press Ltd, UK (qv)
ISBN Publisher's Prefix: 0-08

J **Whitaker** & Sons Ltd+, 12 Dyott St,
London WC1A 1DF Tel: (01) 836 8911
Cable Add: Whitmanack London WC1
Man Dir: Haddon Whitaker
Subjects: Textbooks, Reference
1978: 6 titles *Founded:* 1841
Subsidiaries: Sporting Handbooks Ltd (qv);
The Standard Book Numbering Agency Ltd;
Whitaker's Book Listing Services Ltd (all at
12 Dyott St, London)
ISBN Publisher's Prefixes: 0-85021
(Whitaker), 0-949999 (Standard Book
Numbering Agency)

White Eagle Publishing Trust+, New Lands,
Liss, Hampshire GU33 7HY Tel: Liss 3300
(STD code 073082)
Man Dir: Mrs Y G Hayward; *Sales, Rights
& Permissions:* G R H Dent; *Publicity &
Advertising:* Colum Hayward
Subjects: Religion, Astrology, Vegetarian
Cookery
1977: 1 title *1978:* 2 titles *Founded:* 1953
Miscellaneous: Publishing house of the
White Eagle Lodge, an undenominational
Christian church
ISBN Publisher's Prefix: 0-85487

White Horse Books, an imprint of Jarrold
Colour Publications (qv)

White Lion Publishers Ltd, see Severn
House Publishers Ltd

G **Whizzard** Publications Ltd, 11A Camden
High St, London NW1 7JE Tel: (01) 388
7411/2 Cable Add: Whizzkids London
Telex: Whizzard 896691
Man Dirs: Douglas Maxwell, Graham
Tarrant; *Production:* David Bann; *Publicity:*
Susan Robinson; *Sales, Rights &
Permissions:* Alison Browne
Orders to: André Deutsch Ltd, 105 Great
Russell St, London WC1
Associate Company: André Deutsch Ltd
(address as above)
Subjects: Children's Fiction and Non-fiction,
Natural History, Adult Non-fiction
1978: 15 titles *1979:* 12 titles *Founded:*
1975
ISBN Publisher's Prefix: 0-233

Wildwood House Ltd, 1 Prince of Wales
Passage, 117 Hampstead Rd, London
NW1 3EE Tel: (01) 388 5389 Cable Add:
Wildwood London NW1
Shipping Add: Wentworth Book Co,
Pindar Rd, Hoddesdon, Hertfordshire
EN11 0HF
Editorial Dirs: Oliver Caldecott, Dieter
Pevsner; *Sales Dir:* David Harrison; *Rights
& Permissions:* Oliver Caldecott
Subjects: General Nonfiction, Biography,
History, How-to, Music, Art, Philosophy,
Reference, Religion, Medicine, Psychology,
General & Social Science, Occasional
Fiction
1977: 35 titles *1978:* 27 titles *Founded:*
1972
ISBN Publisher's Prefix: 0-7045

John **Wiley** & Sons Ltd, Baffins Lane,
Chichester, West Sussex PO19 1UD Tel:
Chichester 784531 (STD code 0243) Cable
Add: Wilebook Chichester Telex: 86290
Warehouse: John Wiley & Sons Ltd,
Southern Cross Trading Estate, Distribution
Centre, Shripney Rd, Bognor Regis, West
Sussex PO22 9SA
Man Dir: J A E Higham; *Marketing Dir:*
M B Foyle; *Sales Manager:* A A L Durrant;
Publicity: J D E Lea
Parent Company: John Wiley & Sons Inc,
605 Third Ave, New York, NY 10016, USA
Associate Companies: Jacaranda Wiley Ltd,
Australia (qv); Livros Técnicos e Científicôs
Editôra SA, Brazil (qv); John Wiley & Sons
Canada Ltd, 22 Worcester Rd, Rexdale,
Ontario, Canada; Wiley Eastern Ltd,
India (qv); Editorial Limusa SA,
Mexico (qv); Halsted Press, 605 Third Ave,
New York, NY 10016, USA; Hamilton
Publishing Co, 1129 State St, Santa
Barbara, Calif 93101, USA; The Ronald
Press Co, 79 Madison Ave, New York,
NY 10016, USA
Subjects: Chemistry, Physics, Life Sciences,
Earth Sciences, Mathematics, Medicine,
Psychology, Engineering, Reference, Social
Science, University Textbooks, Educational
Material
1978: 1000 titles
ISBN Publisher's Prefixes: 0-471 (Wiley),
0-470 (Halsted)

Wilfion Books Publishers+, 12 Townhead
Terrace, Paisley, Renfrewshire PA1 2AX
Tel: (041) 887 1241 Ext 264
Dirs: Konrad Hopkins, Ronald van Roekel
Subjects: Poetry, Philosophy
1978: 1 title *Founded:* 1975

Joseph **Williams**, an imprint of Stainer &
Bell Ltd (qv)

Williams & Norgate, see Ernest Benn Ltd

Philip **Wilson** Publishers, Russell Chambers, Covent Garden, London WC2E 8AA Tel: (01) 240 1091/2 Telex: 22158
Man Dir: Philip Wilson
Imprint: Sotheby Parke Bernet Publications (*USA office:* 81 Adams Drive, Totowa, NJ 07512, USA)
Subjects: Art, Antiques, Reference
1977: 6 titles *1978:* 14 titles *Founded:* 1975
ISBN Publisher's Prefix: 0–85667

Wilton Publications, 1 Westmead, Farnborough, Hampshire GU14 7RU Tel: Farnborough 519221 (STD code 0252)
An imprint of Gower Publishing Co Ltd (qv), with details as for Gower Publishing except as follows:
Editorial: John Irwin
Subjects: Business, Finance, Economics
ISBN Publisher's Prefixes: 0–904655 (pre-1978 titles), 0–566

Wine & Spirit Publications Ltd*, Harling Ho, 47–51 Gt Suffolk St, London SE1 Tel: (01) 261 1604
Man Dir: T J Straker
Subjects: General Nonfiction, Wine, Travel, Entertaining
Founded: 1958

Allan **Wingate** (Publishers) Ltd*, 44 Hill St, London W1X 8LB Tel: (01) 493 6777
For personnel see W H Allen & Co Ltd
Subjects: General Fiction, Nonfiction, Juveniles
Miscellaneous: Firm is a subsidiary of W H Allen & Co Ltd (qv), and an associate company of Tandem Publishing Ltd (qv)
ISBN Publisher's Prefix: 0–85523

Wingate Series, an imprint of Dinosaur Publications Ltd (qv)

H F & G **Witherby** Ltd and Witherby & Co Ltd+*, 5 Plantain Pl, Crosby Row, London SE1 1YN Tel: (01) 407 1801
Man Dirs: Antony Witherby (H F & G Witherby), Alan Witherby (Witherby & Co Ltd)
Subjects: Biography, History, How-to, Secondary & University Textbooks, Reference, Natural Science, Insurance & Banking
ISBN Publisher's Prefixes: 0–85493 (H F & G Witherby), 0–900886 (Witherby & Co)

The **Woburn** Press, Gainsborough Ho, 11 Gainsborough Rd, Leytonstone, London E11 1RS Tel: (01) 530 4226 Cable Add: Simfay London Telex: 897719
Warehouse: Macdonald & Evans Ltd, Estover Rd, Estover, Plymouth PL6 7PZ
Man Dir: Frank Cass; *Editorial:* Murray Mindlin; *Trade:* Jeremy Guy; *Production:* Kenneth Cowell; *Publicity:* Suzzette Reed
Subjects: Literature Criticism, Educational Studies, Social Science, General Literature
1978: 11 titles *1979:* 6 titles *Founded:* 1969
Miscellaneous: Firm is a subsidiary of Frank Cass & Co Ltd (qv), and an associate company of Vallentine, Mitchell & Co Ltd (qv)
ISBN Publisher's Prefix: 0–7130

Wolfe Medical Publications Ltd, 10 Earlham St, London WC2H 9LP Tel: (01) 240 2935 Cable Add: Wolfebooks London
Chairman & Man Dir: Peter Wolfe; *Deputy Man Dir:* Peter Heilbrunn; *Editorial:* Patrick Daly; *Home Sales:* George Hayward; *Export Sales:* Stuart Binns; *Publicity:* Evanna Morris; *Rights & Permissions:* Fiona Aretz
Subjects: Medical, Dental, Veterinary
1977: 6 titles *1978:* 8 titles *Founded:* 1969
ISBN Publisher's Prefix: 0–7234

Wolfe Publishing Ltd, see Wolfe Medical Publications Ltd

Oswald **Wolff** (Publishers) Ltd+, 52 Manchester St, London W1M 6DR Tel: (01) 935 3481 Cable Add: Bookwolff
Man & Sales Dir, Rights & Permissions: Mrs I R Wolff; *Editorial Dir:* R W Last
Subjects: Biography, History, Music, Art, Literary Criticism, German Studies, High-priced Paperbacks
1977: 5 titles *Founded:* 1958
ISBN Publisher's Prefix: 0–85496

The **Women's** Press Ltd, 124 Shoreditch High St, London E1 6JE Tel: (01) 729 5257 Cable Add: Namara London SW1 Telex: 919034
Man Dir: Stephanie Dowrick; *Editorial, Rights & Permissions:* Stephanie Dowrick, Christine Muirhead; *Design:* Suzanne Perkins
Orders to: Quartet Books Ltd, 27 Goodge St, London W1
Parent Company: Namara Ltd, 18b Wellington Court, Knightsbridge, London SW1
Subjects: Fiction, Literature and Criticism, Art History, Politics, Physical and Mental Health (all women writers)
1978: 12 titles *Founded:* 1977
ISBN Publisher's Prefix: 0–7043

Woodhead-Faulkner (Publishers) Ltd, 8 Market Passage, Cambridge CB2 3PF Tel: Cambridge 66733 (STD code 0223)
Man Dir: Martin J Woodhead; *Editorial:* Ian C Faulkner; *Sales:* Gilmour Drummond
Imprint: Martin Books
Subjects: Business Investment and Finance, Social Welfare and Rehabilitation, Careers, Popular Nonfiction
1978: 18 titles *1979:* 25 titles *Founded:* 1972
ISBN Publisher's Prefix: 0–85941

Word Books (Word (UK) Ltd)+*, Park Lane, Hemel Hempstead, Hertfordshire HP2 4TD Tel: Hemel Hempstead 50132/3 (STD code 0442)
Man Dir: W T Hamilton
Subjects: Religion, Music
Miscellaneous: Firm is a subsidiary of Word Inc, Waco, Texas, USA
ISBN Publisher's Prefix: 0–85009

Workshop Press Ltd, 2 Culham Court, Granville Rd, London N4 4JB Tel: (01) 348 4054
Subjects: Poetry
1978: 2 titles
ISBN Publisher's Prefix: 0–902705

World Book-Childcraft International Inc+, Canterbury Ho, Sydenham Rd, Croydon, Surrey CR9 2LR Tel: (01) 686 6421 Cable Add: World Book Int, Croydon Telex: 946314
Man Dir: J R Threlfall; *Editorial, Publicity:* Howard Timms
Imprint: Pied Piper
Subjects: Primary & Secondary Education, English Dictionaries, Reference Books, Juveniles, Encyclopaedias
Miscellaneous: Firm is a subsidiary of World Book-Childcraft International, Inc, Merchandise Mart Plaza, Chicago, Illinois, USA
1977: 7 titles *1978:* 10 titles
ISBN Publisher's Prefix: 0–7166

World Distributors (Manchester) Ltd, PO Box 111, Manchester M60 1TS Tel: (061) 228 3841 Cable Add: Sydpem Manchester Telex: 668609

Shipping Add: Victoria Mills, Pollard St, Manchester M4 7AU
Acting Man Dir: Barry McKenzie; *Sales:* Ian Watson; *Publisher:* Roger Lewis; *Production Manager:* David Sheldrake
Subjects: Children's Books and Annuals
Miscellaneous: Holding company is Pentos Ltd (qv)
ISBN Publisher's Prefix: 0–7235

World Microfilms Publications Ltd, 62 Queen's Grove, London NW8 6ER Tel: (01) 586 3092 Cable Add: Microworld
Man Dir: Stephen Albert; *Technical:* Michael J Gunn
Subjects: Research Collections in Microform, Periodical Reprints in Microform
1977: 20 titles *1978:* 30 titles *Founded:* 1969

World of Islam Festival Trust, 1 Adam Court, Gloucester Rd, London SW7 4SS Tel: (01) 370 6002/3/4 Cable Add: Islamtrust London SW7
Dir: Alistair Duncan
Orders to: Thorsons Publishers Ltd, Dennington Estate, Wellingborough, Northants
Subjects: Islamic Art, Culture and Civilisation
1977: 1 title *1978:* 2 titles *Founded:* 1974
ISBN Publisher's Prefix: 0–905035

World Reporting Ltd+*, 51A Carfax, Horsham, West Sussex Tel: Horsham 5511/5516 (STD code 0403)
Subjects: Primary & Secondary Education, Juveniles, Politics, Sociology
ISBN Publisher's Prefix: 0–900826

World University Library, an imprint of Weidenfeld & Nicolson Ltd (qv)

World's Work Ltd+, The Windmill Press, Kingswood, Tadworth, Surrey
Tel: Mogador 3511 STD code 073 783 Cable Add: Sunlocks Tadworth
Man Dir: C Forster; *Deputy Man Dir & Foreign Rights:* D Elliot; *Export Sales Manager:* M Percival; *Trade Manager:* Daphne Mallard; *Publicity Manager:* Peggy Lince
Parent Company: Heinemann Group of Publishers Ltd, UK (qv)
Imprint: Cedar Books
Subjects: Business, How-to, Religion, Juveniles, Sport, Archaeology, Fiction, Low- & High-priced Paperbacks
1977: 86 titles *1978:* 79 titles
ISBN Publisher's Prefix: 0–437

Gordon **Wright** Publishing+, 55 Marchmont Rd, Edinburgh EH9 1HT Tel: (031) 229 8566
Proprietor: Gordon Wright
Imprints: Reprographia
1977: 2 titles *1978:* 6 titles *Founded:* 1969
Subjects: General, Scottish Literature, Nonfiction and Fiction
ISBN Publisher's Prefix: 0–903065

John **Wright** & Sons Ltd+, 42–44 Triangle West, Bristol BS8 1EX Tel: Bristol 23237 (STD code 0272) Cable Add: Wright Publishers Bristol Telex: 449752
Chairman: C N Clarke; *Publishing Dir:* D Kingham; *Editorial:* J Gillman; *Executive Sales Dir, Rights & Permissions:* Miss J M Eales; *Production:* R Lamb; *Publicity:* R Pitt
Orders to: 823–825 Bath Rd, Bristol BS4 5NU
Associate Company: Scientechnica (Publishers) Ltd
Subsidiary Company: Henry Ling Ltd, Dorchester, Dorset

Subjects: Medicine, Veterinary Medicine, Dentistry, Psychology, Science, University Textbooks
Bookshop: John Wright & Sons Ltd, 44 Triangle West, Bristol BS8 1EX
1977: 34 titles *1978:* 35 titles *Founded:* 1825
ISBN Publisher's Prefixes: 0-7236 (Wright), 0-85608 (Wright-Scientechnica)

Writers and Readers Publishing Co-operative, 9-19 Rupert St, London W1V 7FS Tel: (01) 437 8942/8917
Man Dir: Glenn Thompson; *Editorial Dir:* Richard Appignanesi; *Sales Dir:* Siân Williams; *Publicity & Advertising Dir:* Gary Pulsifer; *Rights & Permissions Dir:* Lisa Appignanesi
Subsidiary Company: Rivers Press
Subjects: Education, Primary, Secondary & University Textbooks, Feminism, General Literature, Fiction, Poetry, Juveniles, Politics, Sociology, Humour, Biography, Art
1977: 15 titles *1978:* 21 titles *Founded:* 1974
Miscellaneous: Firm is a collective publishing model, member of Industrial Common Ownership Movement
ISBN Publisher's Prefixes: 0-904613, 0-906386, 0-906495

Wykeham Publications (London) Ltd+, 10-14 Macklin St, London WC2B 5NF Tel: (01) 405 2237/9
Distributors: Taylor & Francis Ltd, Rankine Rd, Basingstoke, Hampshire RG24 0PR
Man Dir: Stanley A Lewis; *Sales & Marketing:* Keith R Courtney; *Director of Book Publishing:* Noel Hughes
Parent Company: Taylor & Francis Ltd, UK (qv)
Subjects: Secondary, University, Commercial & Technical Textbooks, Technical, Science
1977: 6 titles *1978:* 7 titles *Founded:* 1969
ISBN Publisher's Prefix: 0-85109

Wyndham Publications Ltd, 44 Hill St, London W1X 8LB Tel: (01) 493 6777 Telex: 937943
Man Dir: Henry Kitchen; *Editorial:* Mike Bailey; *Sales:* Stephen Howe, Colin Gower; *Production:* Deryck Cheyne; *Publicity:* Margaret Douglas; *Rights & Permissions:* Robert Harvey
Orders to: Tiptree Book Services, Tiptree, Essex
Parent Company: W H Allen & Co Ltd, UK (qv)
Imprints: Star, Tandem, Target, Tattoo, Trophy, Universal
1978: 144 titles *Founded:* 1976

Xerox Publishing Group Ltd, see Bowker Publishing Co and University Microfilms International

Yale University Press+, 13 Bedford Sq, London WC1B 3JF Tel: (01) 580 2693 Cable Add: Yalepress London WC1
Manager: Stephanie Sutton; *Publicity:* Christina Logan; *Rights & Permissions:* Kathleen Yorke
Subject: Scholarly Books
1977: 83 titles *1978:* 85 titles
Miscellaneous: Firm is the British office of Yale University Press, 302 Temple St, New Haven, Conn 06511, USA
ISBN Publisher's Prefix: 0-300

Thomas **Yoseloff** Ltd, Magdalen Ho, 136-148 Tooley St, London SE1 2TT Tel: (01) 407 7566 Cable Add: Tantivy London SE1
Man Dir, Rights & Permissions: Peter Cowie; *Editorial:* Allen Eyres; *Sales:* Peter Cowie; *Publicity:* Juliet Shepherd
Subject: General Nonfiction
1977: 112 titles
Miscellaneous: Firm is an associate company of The Tantivy Press, Associated University Presses, The Golden Cockerel
ISBN Publisher's Prefix: 0-498

Zed Press+, 57 Caledonian Rd, London N1 9DN Tel: (01) 837 4014
Sales, Publicity, Rights & Permissions: Roger van Zwanenberg; *Editorial:* Robert Molteno
Subjects: Third World Social Science, Africa, Middle East, Asia, Imperialism
1978: 8 titles *1979:* 16 titles *Founded:* 1976
ISBN Publisher's Prefix: 0-905762

Hans **Zell** (Publishers) Ltd, PO Box 56, 14A St Giles, Oxford, OX1 3EL Tel: Oxford 512934 (STD code 0865)
Man Dir, Editorial, Rights & Permissions: Hans M Zell; *Sales, Publicity:* Elizabeth Scarratt
Subjects: Reference, Africana, Periodicals
1979: 2 titles *Founded:* 1975
ISBN Publisher's Prefixes: 0-86070, 0-905450

Zeno Booksellers & Publishers, 6 Denmark St, London WC2H 8LP Tel: (01) 836 2522 Cable Add: Zengreek London WC2
Man Dir: M P Zographos
Bookshop: 6 Denmark St, London WC2H 8LP (specializing in Greek books, Books on Greece, The Balkans, Middle East, Antiquarian and Modern)
Subjects: Belles Lettres, Poetry, History, Art, Travel
Founded: 1944
ISBN Publisher's Prefixes: 0-900834, 0-7228

A **Zwemmer** Ltd+, 26 Litchfield St, London WC2H 9NJ Tel: (01) 836 1749 Cable Add: Zwemmera Lesquare London WC2H 9NJ Warehouse: Unit 27, Bermondsey Trading Estate, Rotherhithe New Rd, London SE16
Man Dir: D Zwemmer
Subsidiary Company: Lund Humphries Publishers Ltd, UK (qv), for whom Zwemmer Ltd is also distributor
Subjects: Art, Architecture
Bookshops: Zwemmers Bookshop, 76-80 Charing Cross Rd, London WC2H 0BH; Zwemmers OUP Bookshop, 72 Charing Cross Rd, London WC2H 0BE

Remainder Dealers

B S C Books Ltd, 33 Maiden Lane, London WC2 Tel: (01) 836 3341 (Owners of the Booksmith chain of bookshops)
Sales: Bill Smith

Roy **Bloom** Ltd*, 45 Camden High St, London NW1 Tel: (01) 388 7485 Telex: 24224
Sales: Paul White

Bridge Book Co Ltd*, 34 Grange Rd, New Haw, Weybridge, Surrey KT15 3RQ Tel: Weybridge 47976 (STD code 0932) Remainder paperback book merchants, importers and exporters in bulk

Donald **Murray** (Ramboro Books), 6 Highbury Corner, London N5 1RD Tel: (01) 609 3091/2
See also under Publishers

Murrays Remainder Books*, 146-152 Holloway Rd, London N7 Tel: (01) 609 1234
See also under Publishers

H **Pordes***, 529b Finchley Rd, London NW3 7BH Tel: (01) 435 9878/9
Subjects: Remainders of all types, learned, reference and scientific reprints, antiquarian periodicals and back issues
See also under Publishers

Ramboro Enterprises Ltd, 6 Highbury Corner, London N5 1RD Tel: (01) 609 3091/2 Telex: 24224
See also under Publishers

Literary Agents

Bolt & Watson Ltd, 8-12 Old Queen St, London SW1 Tel: (01) 222 5378 Cable Add: Bandwag London SW1
Dirs: David Bolt, Sheila Watson

E J **Carnell** Literary Agency, Rowneybury Bungalow, Nr. Old Harlow, Essex CM20 2EX Tel: Harlow 29408 (STD code 0279)
Specialization: Science-Fiction, Fantasy

Curtis Brown Academic Ltd*, 1 Craven Hill, London W2 3EW Tel: (01) 262 1011
Man Dir: Andrew Best

Curtis Brown Group Ltd, 1 Craven Hill, London W2 3EW Tel: (01) 262 1011
Chairman: Graham Watson

John **Farquharson** Ltd, Bell House, 8 Bell Yard, London WC2A 2JU Tel: (01) 242 2445 Cable Add: Jofachad London WC2
Contact: George Greenfield, Vanessa Holt or Vivienne Schuster

David **Grossman** Literary Agency Ltd*, 12-13 Henrietta St, London WC2

A M **Heath** & Co Ltd*, 40-42 William IV St, London WC2N 4DD Tel: (01) 836 4271 Cable Add: Script London WC2
Man Dir: Mark Hamilton

David **Higham** Associates Ltd*, 5-8 Lower John St, Golden Sq, London W1R 4HA Tel: (01) 437 7888 Cable Add: Highlit London W1 Telex: 28910

Hughes Massie Ltd, 31 Southampton Row, London WC1B 5HL Tel: (01) 405 8137 Cable Add: Litaribus London Telex: 298391
Dirs: Edmund Cork, Patricia Cork, J E Lunn, N E Cork, Brian Stone

London Independent Books Ltd, 1a Montagu Mews North, London W1H 1AJ Tel: (01) 935 8090 Cable Add: Trifem London W1
Dirs: Carolyn Whitaker, Patrick Whitaker

M B A Literary Agents Ltd, 118 Tottenham Court Rd, London W1P 9HL Tel: (01) 387 2076/4785
Dirs: Diana Tyler, Janet Freer

Andrew **Nurnberg** Associates Ltd, Clerkenwell Ho, 45-47 Clerkenwell Green, London EC1R 0HT Tel: (01) 251 0321 Cable Add: Nurnbooks London Telex: 23353
Specialization: Translation Rights

Mark **Paterson** & Associates, 11 & 12 West Stockwell St, Colchester, Essex CO1 1HN Tel: Colchester 65151 (STD code 0206) Cable Add: Paterson Colchester Telex:

896616MP Sendit G or markit 987562 Cochac
Specialization: Psychoanalysis, Psychiatry, Sigmund Freud copyrights, but other subjects also handled
Founded: 1955

Peterborough Literary Agency, The Daily Telegraph, 135 Fleet St, London EC4P 4BL Tel: (01) 353 4242 ext 529
Cable Add: Telenews London EC4
Telex: 22874 Telesyndic
Executive Managers: Ewan MacNaughton, Andrea Whittaker

A D **Peters** & Co Ltd*, 10 Buckingham St, London WC2N 6BU Tel: (01) 839 2556
Man Dir: Michael Sissons; *Dirs:* Anthony Jones, Pat Kavanagh

Laurence **Pollinger** Ltd, 18 Maddox St, London W1R 0EU Tel: (01) 629 9761
Cable Add: Laupoll London W1
Man Dir: Gerald J Pollinger; *Foreign Rights:* Yvonne Muller

Deborah **Rogers** Ltd, 5-11 Mortimer St, London W1H 7RH Tel: (01) 580 0604/5
Cable Add: Deborgers London W1

Sheri **Safran** Associates Ltd, 4 Prince's Mews, Hereford Rd, London W2 Tel: (01) 229 7819
Also office at 866 United Nations Plaza, New York, NY 10017, USA Tel: (212) 752 7734
Representing agents in France, Federal Republic of Germany, Latin America, Scandinavia, Spain, and agents and publishers in USA with a general list, but specializing in women's books

Patrick **Seale** Books Ltd, 2 Motcomb St, Belgrave Sq, London SW1X 8JU Tel: (01) 235 0934 Cable Add: Obseale London SW1

Anthony **Sheil** Associates Ltd, 2-3 Morwell St, London WC1B 3AR Tel: (01) 636 2901 Cable Add: Novelist
Man Dir: Anthony Sheil

A P **Watt** Ltd, 26-28 Bedford Row, London WC1R 4HL Tel: (01) 405 1057 Cable Add: Longevity London WC1
Contact: Michael Horniman, Hilary Rubinstein, Maggie Noach or Caradoc King

Book Clubs

20th Century Classics, see Book Club Associates

Ancient History Book Club, see Book Club Associates

The **Artists'** Book Club, PO Box 244, London WC2B 5PB
Owned by: Pitman Publishing Division Ltd

Arts Book Society, see Readers Union Ltd

Arts Guild, see Book Club Associates

Best of Books International Ltd*, 3 Queens Gate Pl, London SW7 5NT
Owned by: Chapman, Morris, Williams Ltd (London)

Biography Book Club, see Book Club Associates

The **Book Club**, see Foyles Book Clubs

Book Club Associates, 87-91 Newman St, London W1P 4EN Tel: (01) 637 0341
Telex: 24359
Chief Executive: S T Remington; *General Manager (Books):* M Lawson; *General Manager (Editorial and Creative):* J Goehr
Monthly Book Clubs: Ancient History Book Club; Biography Book Club; Book of the Month Club; Family Book Club; History Guild; Literary Guild; Master Storytellers; Military Book Society; Mystery Book Club; Skylark Children's Book Club; World Books
Quarterly Book Clubs: Arts Guild; British Heritage; Encounters; English Book Club (Netherlands); Home & Garden Guild; Military Guild; The Railway Book Club; Readers Choice; World of Nature
Book Series: 20th Century Classics, Kings & Queens of England, Great English Classics
Owned by: W H Smith & Son Ltd (London) and Doubleday & Co Inc (New York)

Book of the Month Club, see Book Club Associates

Books for Children, Premier Ho, 150 Southampton Row, London WC1B 5AL Tel: (01) 278 2817
Chairman: R P Cope; *Man Dir:* John Smith; *Editorial Manager:* Sally Grindley
Owned by: Fernstyle Ltd

The **Bookworm** Club*, Napier Pl, Cumbernauld, Glasgow G69 0DN
Owned by: W Heffer & Sons Ltd (Cambridge) and E J Arnold & Son Ltd (Leeds)
Subject: Paperbacks for 5-12-year-olds

British Heritage, see Book Club Associates

Business Leaders Book Club*, 18 St Ann's Crescent, London SW18
Owned by: Heron Books Ltd

Catholic Book Club, see Foyles Book Clubs

Children's Book Club, see Foyles Book Clubs

Chip Book Club*, 161 Fulham Rd, London SW3 6SW
(Junior and low senior school)
Owned by: Scholastic Publications

Collectors' Editions Book Club, see Heron Books

Companion Book Club, Hamlyn Group, Mail Order Division, Wellingborough Rd, Rushden, Northants
Subjects: Fiction, Biographies, True Adventure
Members: 25,000
Owned by: The Hamlyn Group (Feltham)

Country Book Society, see Readers Union Ltd

Craft Book Society, see Readers Union Ltd

Criterion: Teachers' Book Shelf Book Club, 161 Fulham Rd, London SW3 6SW
Owned by: Scholastic Publications

Encounters, see Book Club Associates

Family Book Club, see Book Club Associates

The **Folio** Society Ltd, 202 Great Suffolk St, London SE1 1PR Tel: (01) 407 7411 Cable Add: Folios Telex: 8951460
Man Dir: H Lynner; *Sales, Publicity, Advertising, Rights & Permissions:* J Letts
Subjects: General Fiction, Belles Lettres, Poetry, Biography, History
1979: 123 titles *Founded:* 1947
Subsidiaries: Folio Press, UK; Folio Fine Editions, UK; Folio Books Ltd New York, at 575 Lexington Avenue, New York, NY 10022, USA
Bookshop: Folio Gallery, 5 Royal Arcade, 28 Old Bond St, London W1
Miscellaneous: Firm publishes finely produced editions of the classics and eye-witness accounts of historical events; for sale to members only

Foyles Book Clubs*, 119-125 Charing Cross Rd, London WC2H 0EB
Owned by: W & G Foyle & John Gifford Ltd (London)
Includes: The Book Club, Catholic Book Club, Children's Book Club, Garde Book Club, Quality Book Club, Romance Book Club, Scientific Book Club, Thriller Book Club, Travel Book Club, Western Book Club

French Book Club, Warner Ho, Folkestone, Kent
Owned by: Bailey Brothers & Swinfen Ltd (Folkestone)

Garden Book Club, see Foyles Book Clubs

Gardeners Book Society, see Readers Union Ltd

German Book Club, Warner Ho, Folkestone, Kent
Owned by: Bailey Brothers & Swinfen Ltd (Folkestone)

Great English Classics, see Book Club Associates

Heron Books*, 18 St Ann's Crescent, London SW18 2LX
Includes: Collectors' Editions Book Club, The History of Art, The Nobel Prize Library
Miscellaneous: Also publishes finely bound, illustrated reprints, including Literary Heritage (English classics), Russian Classics, Women Who Made History, Books That Have Changed Man's Thinking, Explorer's Bookshelf, Immortal Moderns; and collected works of individual authors
Owned by: Leisure Arts Ltd

History Guild, see Book Club Associates

The **History of Art**, see Heron Books

Home and Garden Guild, see Book Club Associates

Horseman's Bookclub, 1 Lower Grosvenor Pl, London SW1
Owned by: J A Allen & Co Ltd (London)

Italian Book Club, Warner Ho, Folkestone, Kent
Owned by: Bailey Brothers & Swinfen Ltd (Folkestone)

The **Jewish Book Club***, 529b Finchley Rd, London NW3 7BH
Owned by: R Pordes

Junior Puffin Club, Penguin Books Ltd, Bath Rd, Harmondsworth, Middlesex UB7 0DA
Owned by: Penguin Publishing Co Ltd

Kings & Queens of England, see Book Club Associates

The **Leisure Circle** Ltd, York Ho, Empire Way, Wembley, Middx HA9 0PF Tel: (01) 903 3161 Telex: 8951315
Man Dir: Dr M Herriger; *Publishing:* C Goulden; *Sales:* D M Cripps; *Marketing:* H Bickon; *Member Service:* L Grothues
Subjects: General Fiction, Nonfiction, Biography, History, Children's Books
Owned by: Bertelsmann Group, (German Federal Republic)

Literary Guild, see Book Club Associates

Lucky Book Club, 161 Fulham Rd, London SW3 6SW
(Infants, low juniors)
Owned by: Scholastic Publications

Mainstream Book Club, 108 Cowley Rd, Oxford Tel: Oxford 724041 (STD code 0865)
Owned by (majority share): B H Blackwell Ltd (qv under Major Booksellers)
Subject: Middle-of-the-road political books

Maritime Book Society, see Readers Union

Master Storytellers, see Book Club Associates

Merlin Book Club, 3 Manchester Rd, London E14
Owned by: Merlin Press Ltd

Military Book Society, see Book Club Associates

Military Guild, see Book Club Associates

Mystery Guild, see Book Club Associates

The **New Fiction** Society, 196 Shaftesbury Ave, London WC2H 8JL Tel: (01) 240 2967
Sponsored by the Arts Council and the National Book League

The **Nobel Prize** Library, see Heron Books

Phoenix Book Society, see Readers Union Ltd

Poetry Book Society, 8–9 Long Acre, London WC2E 9LH Tel: (01) 379 6597
Publications: Bulletin (quarterly); Checklist of New Poetry 1977; Poetry Supplement 1978

The **Puffin** Club, Penguin Books Ltd, Bath Rd, Harmondsworth, Middlesex UB7 0DA
Owned by: Penguin Publishing Co Ltd

Quality Book Club, see Foyles Book Clubs

The **Railway** Book Club, see Book Club Associates

Readers Choice, see Book Club Associates

Readers Union Ltd, PO Box 6, Newton Abbot, Devon TQ12 2DW
Man Dir: E A Howes; *Marketing Dir:* M Deane; *Product Dir:* S Margrett; *Sales Dir:* B Bailey; *Literary Dir:* R Allen
Includes: Arts Book Society, Country Book Society, Craft Book Society, Gardeners Book Society, Maritime Book Society, Phoenix Book Society, Readers Union, Science Fiction Book Club, Sportsman's Book Club
Founded: 1937
Owned by: David & Charles (Holdings) Ltd (Devon)

Romance Book Club, see Foyles Book Clubs

Scene Book Club, 161 Fulham Rd, London SW3 6SW
Secondary school and top juniors
Owned by: Scholastic Publications

Science Fiction Book Club, see Readers Union Ltd

Scientific Book Club, see Foyles Book Clubs

See-saw Book Club, 161 Fulham Rd, London SW3 6SW
Nursery and infants
Owned by: Scholastic Publications

Skylark Children's Book Club, see Book Club Associates

Spanish Book Club, Warner Ho, Folkestone, Kent
Owned by: Bailey Brothers & Swinfen Ltd (Folkestone)

Sportsman's Book Club, see Readers Union Ltd

Thriller Book Club, see Foyles Book Clubs

Travel Book Club, see Foyles Book Clubs

Western Book Club, see Foyles Book Clubs

The **Wine** Book Club, Woodlands, Hazel Grove, Hindhead, Surrey GU26 6BJ

World Books, see Book Club Associates

World of Nature, see Book Club Associates

Major Booksellers

Austick's Headrow Bookshop*, 64 The Headrow, Leeds LS1 8EH Tel: Leeds 39607 (STD code 0532)

B H **Blackwell** Ltd, 48–51 Broad St, Oxford Tel: Oxford 49111 (STD code 0865)
Book Club: Mainstream Book Club

Bowes & Bowes Books*, 1 Trinity St, Cambridge CB2 1SX Tel: Cambridge 55488 (STD code 0223)

Dillon's University Bookshop Ltd, 1 Malet St, London WC1E 7JB Tel: (01) 636 1577

W & G **Foyle** Ltd, 119–125 Charing Cross Rd, London WC2H 0EB Tel: (01) 437 5660

William **George's** Sons Ltd*, 89 Park St, Bristol BS1 5PW Tel: Bristol 26602 (STD code 0272)

Grant Educational Co Ltd*, 91 Union St, Glasgow (Home and Export)

Haigh & Hochland Ltd*, 11 Whitworth St, Manchester 1 Tel: (061) 236 9950; The Precinct Centre, Oxford Rd, Manchester M13 9QZ Tel: (061) 273 4156

Hammicks Wholesale*, 16 Newman Lane, Alton, Hants GU34 2PJ Tel: Alton 85822 (STD code 0420) (wholesalers)

Harrods Ltd*, Knightsbridge, London SW1 Tel: (01) 730 1234

Hatchards Ltd, 187 Piccadilly, London W1V 9DA Tel: (01) 439 9921

W **Heffer** & Sons Ltd, 20 Trinity St, Cambridge CB2 3NG Tel: Cambridge 358351 (STD code 0223)

Hudsons Bookshops Ltd, 116 New St, Birmingham B2 4JJ Tel: (021) 643 8311

John **Menzies** (Holdings) Ltd*, Villiers Ho, 40 Strand, London WC2 Tel: (01) 930 0033 (many branches throughout the United Kingdom)

Parker & Son Ltd, 27 Broad St, Oxford OX2 6AQ Tel: Oxford 54156 (STD code 0865)

Sherratt & Hughes (Bowes & Bowes), 17 St Ann's Sq, Manchester M2 7PD Tel: (061) 834 7055

John **Smith** & Son (Glasgow) Ltd, 577–61 St Vince St, Glasgow G2 5TB Tel: (041) 221 7472

W H **Smith** & Son Ltd*, 11 Kingsway, London WC2B 6YA Tel: (01) 836 5951;
W H Smith & Son Ltd (Wholesale), Strand Ho, 10 New Fetter Lane, London EC4A 1AD Tel: (01) 353 0277 (many branches throughout the United Kingdom)

James **Thin**, Bookseller*, 53–59 South Bridge, Edinburgh Tel: (031) 556 6743

W H **Willshaw** Ltd*, 16 John Dalton St, Manchester M2 6HS Tel: (061) 834 8734

Major Libraries

Belfast Public Library, Central Library, Royal Ave, Belfast, Northern Ireland

Birmingham Public Libraries, Central Library, Paradise, Birmingham B3 3HQ Tel: (021) 235 4511 Telex: 337655
Librarian: B H Baumfield

Bodleian Library, Oxford OX1 3BG Tel: Oxford 44675 (STD code 0865) Telex: 83656
Secretary and Deputy Librarian: E J S Parsons

British Library, Bibliographic Services Division, Store St, London WC1E 7DG
Publications: British National Bibliography; British Education Index; British Catalogue of Music; Books in English 'ultrafiche)

British Library Lending Division, Boston Spa, Wetherby, West Yorkshire LS23 7BQ Tel: Boston Spa 843434 (STD code 0937) Telex: 557381
Publications: Interlending Review; Current Serials Received; Index of Conference Proceedings Received
The Lending Division lends only to libraries and organizations, not to individual members of the public

British Library Reference Division, Great Russell St, London WC1B 3DG Tel: (01) 636 1544
Publications: British Library Journal (twice yearly); Catalogue of Additions to the Manuscripts in the British Museum; General Catalogue of Printed Books, supplements, 1971–5; Catalogue of the Newspaper Collections in the British Library; Subject Index of Modern Books; Guide to the Department of Oriental Manuscripts and Printed Books; numerous catalogues of special types of material and of books in different languages; exhibition catalogues; facsimiles, slides, postcards, etc. Full list obtainable from British Library, Reference Division Publications, Great Russell St, London WC1B 3DG

British Library, Science Reference Library, 25 Southampton Bldgs, Chancery Lane, London WC2A 1AW Tel: (01) 405 8721 Telex: 266959
and 10 Porchester Gardens, Queensway, London W2 4DE Tel: (01) 727 3022 Telex: 22717
Lists of publications available on request

British Library of Political and Economic Science*, 10 Portugal St, London WC2A 2AE Tel: (01) 405 7686

Cambridge University Library, West Rd, Cambridge CB3 9DR Tel: Cambridge 61441 (STD code 0223) Telex: 81395

The **Dean and Chapter** Library, The College, Durham Tel: Durham 62489 (STD code 0385)
Deputy Librarian: R C Norris

Durham University Library, Palace Green, Durham DH1 3RN Tel: Durham 61262/3 (STD code 0385)
Librarian: A M McAulay

Edinburgh University Library, George Sq, Edinburgh EH8 9LJ Tel: (031) 667 1011 Telex: 727442 Unived G

Guildhall Library, Aldermanbury, London EC2P 2EJ Tel: (01) 606 3030
Librarian: Godfrey Thompson
Publications: Guildhall Studies in London History (twice a year), various handlists of Library material

India Office Library and Records, Orbit Ho, 197 Blackfriars Rd, London SE1 8NG Tel: (01) 928 9531
Director: B C Bloomfield

Leeds University Library, Leeds LS2 9JT Tel: Leeds 31751 (STD code 0532)

Liverpool City Libraries*, William Brown St, Liverpool L3 8EW Tel: (051) 207 2147 Telex: 62500

Llyfrgell Genedlaethol Cymru (National Library of Wales), Aberystwyth, Dyfed SY23 3BU Tel: Aberystwyth 3816/9 (STD code 0970) Telex: 35165
Librarian: David Jenkins; *Librarian Designate:* R Geraint Gruffydd
Publications: The National Library of Wales Journal (semi-annual); *Handlist of Manuscripts in the National Library of Wales* (annual); *Bibliotheca Celtica* (annual)

The **Mitchell** Library (Glasgow District Libraries), North St, Glasgow G3 7DN Tel: (041) 248 7121 (12 lines) Telex: 778732
Librarian: R A Gillespie

National Library of Scotland, George IV Bridge, Edinburgh EH1 1EW Tel: (031) 226 4531 Telex: 72638 nlsedi g; Map Room, NLS Annexe, 137 Causewayside, Edinburgh EH9 1PH Tel: (031) 667 7848

Oxford University, Taylor Institution Library, St Giles, Oxford OX1 3NA Tel: Oxford 57917 (STD code 0865)

P R O N I (Public Record Office of Northern Ireland), 66 Balmoral Ave, Belfast BT9 6NY

Public Record Office, Ruskin Ave, Kew, Richmond, Surrey TW9 4DU and Chancery Lane, London WC2A 1LR (national archives of the United Kingdom)

John **Rylands** University Library of Manchester, Oxford Rd, Manchester M13 9PP Tel: Main Library Bldg (061) 273 3333; Deansgate Bldg (061) 834 5343

School of Oriental and African Studies Library, Malet St, London WC1E 7HP Tel: (01) 637 2388

Scottish Record Office, PO Box 36, HM General Register Ho, Edinburgh EH1 3YY

Trinity College Library, Cambridge CB2 1TQ Tel: Cambridge 58201 (STD code 0223)

University of London Library*, Senate Ho, Malet St, London WC1E 7HU Tel: (01) 636 4514 Telex: 269400 senlib g

Wellcome Institute for the History of Medicine Library, 183 Euston Rd, London NW1 2BP Tel: (01) 387 4477

Westminster City Libraries, Central Administration, Marylebone Rd, London NW1 5PS Tel: (01) 828 8070 Telex: 263305
City Librarian: K C Harrison MBE, FLA

Library Associations

A R L I S (The Art Libraries Society), c/o Kingston upon Thames Polytechnic Library, Knights Park, Kingston upon Thames, Surrey
Secretary: Mrs G Varley
Publications: Art Libraries Journal (quarterly), *ARLIS News-sheet* (six a year), *Directory* (annually)

Aslib, 3 Belgrave Sq, London SW1X 8PL
Dir: Basil Saunders
Incorporating the Association of Special Libraries and Information Bureaux and the British Society for International Bibliography
Publications: Index to Theses accepted for Higher Degrees in the Universities of Great Britain and Ireland (half-yearly), *Journal of Documentation* (quarterly), *Aslib Proceedings* (monthly), *Aslib Information* (monthly), *Aslib Book List* (monthly), *Program* (quarterly), *Forthcoming International Scientific and Technical Conferences* (quarterly), *Audiovisual Librarian*, handbooks, reports, directories and membership list

Association of Assistant Librarians
Honorary Secretary: K Cranshaw, Mobile and Special Services, Sheffield City Libraries, 443 Handsworth Rd, Sheffield S13 9DD

Association of British Library and Information Studies Schools (ABLISS), c/o E P Dudley, Chairman, ABLISS School of Librarianship, Polytechnic of North London, 207-25 Essex Rd, London N1 3PN
Chairman: E P Dudley

Association of British Theological and Philosophical Libraries, King's College Library, Strand, London WC2R 2LS
Honorary Secretary: Miss E M Elliott
Publication: Bulletin

Association of London Chief Librarians,
Honorary Secretary: K A Doughty, Southwark Library Services, 20-22 Lordship Lane, East Dulwich, London SE22 8HN
Publications: Directory of London Public Libraries

Association of Scottish Health Sciences Librarians*, Mrs E A Ferro, General Library, Royal Infirmary of Edinburgh, Edinburgh EH3 9YW

Bibliographical Society, British Academy, Burlington Ho, London W1V 0NS
Honorary Secretaries: R J Roberts, Mrs Mirjam Foot
Publications: The Library (quarterly), various books on bibliographical subjects

British and Irish Association of Law Librarians, c/o Harding Law Library, University of Birmingham, PO Box 363, Birmingham B15 2TT
Honorary Secretary: Miss D M Blake
Publication: The Law Librarian

Cambridge Bibliographical Society, University Library, Cambridge CB3 9DR
Honorary Secretary: F R Collieson
Publications: Transactions (annually), *Monographs* (irregular)

Circle of State Librarians*,
Honorary Secretary: Mrs D C Scott, c/o Royal Botanic Gardens, Kew, Richmond, Surrey TW9 3AE Tel: (01) 940 1171 Ext 222
Publication: State Librarian (3 a year)

Classification Research Group,
Honorary Secretary: D J Foskett, School of Library, Archive and Information Studies, University College, London WC1

Committee for Postgraduate Awards in Librarianship and Information Work, c/o Department of Education and Science, Elizabeth Ho, 39 York Rd, London SE1 7PH Tel: (01) 928 9222
Secretary: K L R English

Edinburgh Bibliographical Society, c/o National Library of Scotland, George IV Bridge, Edinburgh EH1 1EW
Honorary Secretary: I C Cunningham
Publication: Transactions (irregular — for Members only)

Friends of the National Libraries*, c/o The British Library, Great Russell St, London WC1B 3DG
Honorary Secretary: Sir Edward Warner
Publication: Annual Report

Institute of Information Scientists*, 657 High Rd, Tottenham, London N17
Honorary Secretary: M Howes
Publication: Information Scientist

Institute of Reprographic Technology*, PO Box 101, Witham, Essex CM8 1QS
Secretary: Mrs J C Odell

International Association of Music Libraries (UK Branch), c/o Miss S M Clegg, Birmingham School of Music, Paradise Circus, Birmingham B3 3HG Tel: (021) 359 6851
General Secretary: Miss S M Clegg
Publication: Brio (twice yearly)

Library Advisory Council for England, c/o Department of Education and Science, Elizabeth Ho, York Rd, London SE1 7PH Tel: (01) 928 9222
Secretary: K L R English

Library Advisory Council for Wales, General I Division, Welsh Office, Cathays Park, Cardiff Tel: Cardiff 825111 (STD code 0222) ext 5322
Secretary: Peter G Smith

The **Library Association**, 7 Ridgmount St, London WC1E 7AE Tel: (01) 636 7543 Telex: 21897
Secretary: K Lawrey
Publications: include *Library Association Record, British Technology Index* (both monthly), *British Humanities Index, Journal of Librarianship* (both quarterly), *Library and Information Science Abstracts* (bi-monthly), *Radials Bulletin* (2 a year), *Year Book, Student's Handbook* (annually), books and pamphlets on librarianship and bibliography, including *Guide to Reference Material, Libraries in the United Kingdom and the Republic of Ireland:* a complete list of public library services and a select list of academic and other library addresses; *A Librarian's Handbook:* documentary and statistical material; *British Librarianship and Information Science*

Microfilm Association of Great Britain*,
8 High St, Guildford, Surrey GU2 5AJ
Tel: Godalming 6653
Executive Secretary: P A Baker

Oxford Bibliographical Society, Bodleian
Library, Oxford
Secretary: Mrs G I Hampshire
Publications: First Series, Vols I-VII,
1923-46, *New Series*, Vol I, 1948-,
Occasional Publications, No 1, 1967-

School Library Association, Victoria Ho,
29-31 George St, Oxford OX1 2AY
Tel: Oxford 722746 (STD code 0865)
Secretary: Miriam Curtis; *Honorary
Secretary:* C A Waite
Publication: The School Librarian
(quarterly)

Scottish Library Association, c/o Secretary,
M C Head, Department of Librarianship,
Robert Gordon's Institute of Technology,
St Andrew St, Aberdeen AB1 1HG
Tel: Aberdeen 574511 ext 564 (STD code 0224)
Publications: SLA News (every two months); Scottish Library Studies Series

Society of Archivists, Lancashire Record
Office, Bow Lane, Preston, Lancashire
Secretary: K Hall
Publication: Journal of the Society of Archivists

Society of County Librarians, County
Library Headquarters, Princes St,
Huntingdon, Cambridgeshire Tel:
Huntingdon 52181 (STD code 0480) ext 22
Secretary: R Brown

**Society of Metropolitan & County Chief
Librarians**, County Library Headquarters,
44 St Anne's Crescent, Lewes, East Sussex
BN7 1SQ

Standing Conference of National and
University Libraries (SCONUL),
102 Euston St, London NW1 2HA Tel: (01) 387 0317
Executive Secretary: A J Loveday

Welsh Library Association, Gwynedd
County Council, County Library
Headquarters, Maesincla, Caernarvon
LL55 1LH Tel: Caernarvon 4441 ext 87 (STD code 0286)
Honorary Secretary: Geoffrey Thomas

Library Reference Books and Journals

Books

*Address List of Public Library Authorities
in the United Kingdom and the Republic of
Ireland*, The Library Association,
7 Ridgmount St, London WC1E 7AE

Aslib Directory, Association of Special
Libraries and Information Bureaux,
3 Belgrave Sq, London SW1X 8PL

Aslib Membership List, Association of
Special Libraries and Information Bureaux,
3 Belgrave Sq, London SW1X 8PL

*British Librarianship and Information
Science*, The Library Association,
7 Ridgmount St, London WC1E 7AE

British Library General Catalogue, Clive
Bingley Ltd, 1-19 New Oxford St,
Commonwealth Ho, London WC1A

Guide to Reference Material, The Library
Association, 7 Ridgmount St, London
WC1E 7AE

A Librarians's Handbook; documentary and
statistical material, The Library Association,
7 Ridgmount St, London WC1E 7AE

*Libraries, Museums and Art Galleries Year
Book*, James Clarke & Co Ltd, 7 All Saints
Passage, Cambridge CB2 3LS

*Libraries in the United Kingdom and the
Republic of Ireland: a complete list of
public library services and a select list of
academic and other library addresses*, The
Library Association, 7 Ridgmount St,
London WC1E 7AE

Library Association Year Book, The Library
Association, 7 Ridgmount St, London
WC1E 7AE

*Who's Who in Librarianship and
Information Science*, Abelard-Schuman Ltd,
450 Edgware Rd, London W2 1EG

Journals

Archives, British Records Association,
Indian Office Records, 197 Blackfriars Rd,
London SE1 8NG

Art Libraries Journal, ARLIS (The Art
Libraries Society)
Secretary: Mrs G Varley, Kingston upon
Thames Polytechnic Library, Knights Park,
Kingston upon Thames, Surrey

*Aslib Information, Aslib Journal of
Documentation, Aslib Proceedings, Aslib
Book List*, Association of Special Libraries
and Information Bureaux, 3 Belgrave Sq,
London SW1X 8PL

Assistant Librarian, Association of Assistant
Librarians, c/o Editor, Brian Arnold,
Central Library, Southgate, Stevenage
Hertfordshire SG1 1HD

BLL Review, British Library, Lending
Division, Boston Spa, Wetherby, West
Yorkshire LS23 7BQ

Bibliotheck; a Scottish journal of
bibliography and allied topics, Library
Association, Scottish Group, University
College & Research Section, c/o Editor,
Douglas S Mack, University Library,
Stirling FK9 4LA

Brio, International Association of Music
Libraries (UK Branch), Music Department,
Town Hall, Green Lanes, Palmers Green,
London N13 4XD

British Library Journal, British Library,
Reference Division, Great Russell St,
London WC1B 3DG

Information Scientist, Institute of
Information Scientists, 657 High Rd,
Tottenham, London N17

Journal of Documentation, Association of
Special Libraries and Information Bureaux,
3 Belgrave Sq, London SW1X 8PL

Journal of Librarianship, The Library
Association, 7 Ridgmount St, London
WC1E 7AE

Journal of the Society of Archivists, Society
of Archivists, c/o Editor, Mrs F Strong,
South Cloister, Eton College, Windsor,
Berkshire SL4 6DB

The Law Librarian, British and Irish
Association of Law Librarians, c/o Harding
Law Library, University of Birmingham,
PO Box 363, Edgbaston, Birmingham
B15 2TT

The Library, Bibliographical Society, British
Academy, Burlington Ho, London
W1V 0NS

Library and Information Science Abstracts,
The Library Association, 7 Ridgmount St,
London WC1E 7AE

Library Association Record, The Library
Association, 7 Ridgmount St, London
WC1E 7AE

Library Review, W & R Holmes (Book),
30 Clydeholm Rd, Glasgow G14 0BJ

New Library World, Clive Bingley
(Journals) Ltd, 16 Pembridge Rd,
London W11

Private Library, Private Libraries
Association, Ravelston, South View Rd,
Pinner, Middlesex

SLA News, Scottish Library Association,
c/o M C Head, Department of
Librarianship, Robert Gordon's Institute of
Technology, St Andrew's St, Aberdeen
AB1 1HG

State Librarian, c/o Editor, Mrs B Howard,
Civil Service Department Library,
Whitehall, London SW1A 2AZ

Literary Associations and Societies

Yr **Academi** Gymreig (The Welsh
Academy), Swyddfa'r Academi Gymreig,
4 Llawr, Adeilad Cory, Heol Bute,
Caerdydd/Cardiff CF1 6QP
Secretary: Ann Beynon
English Language Section Secretary: Mrs
Sue Harries, 4th Floor, Cory Bldg, Bute St,
Cardiff CF1 6QP

Association for Scottish Literary Studies,
Department of English, University of
Aberdeen, Aberdeen AB9 2UB
Secretary: K Buthay, Department of
Scottish Literature, the University of
Glasgow
Publications: Scottish Literary Journal
(twice yearly plus survey of past year's work
and review supplements); an edited work of
Scottish literature (annually)

Association of British Science Writers*, c/o
21 Albemarle St, London W1X 4BS
Secretary: Sally Owen

Association of Yorkshire Bookmen,
28 Crawshaw Rd, Pudsey, West Yorkshire
Honorary General Secretary: Miss W M
Heap Tel: Pudsey 567977 (STD code 0532)

Authors' Club, 40 Dover St, London W1
Honorary Secretary: Mrs Lesley
Weissenborn

Francis **Bacon** Society Inc, Canonbury
Tower, Islington, London N1
President: Commander Martin Pares
Publication: Baconiana (periodically),
Jottings (periodically)

Books Across the Sea, The English-
Speaking Union, Dartmouth Ho,
37 Charles St, London W1X 8AB Tel: (01) 408 0013
Librarian: Jean Huse
Publication: Ambassador Booklist
(quarterly)

The **British Science Fiction** Association Ltd,
18 Gordon Terrace, Blantyre G72 9NA
Membership Secretary: Sandy Brown

The Incorporated **Brontë** Society, The Brontë Parsonage, Haworth, nr Keighley, West Yorkshire BD22 8DR Tel: Haworth 42323 (STD code 0535)
Honorary Secretary: A H Preston, 4 Mytholmes Lane, Haworth, Keighley, West Yorkshire BD22 8EZ
Publication: Brontë Society Transactions (annually)

Bulwer-Lytton Circle, 125 Markyate Rd, Dagenham, Essex
Publication: The Lytton Record (annual)

Children's Writers' Group, The Society of Authors, 84 Drayton Gardens, London SW10 9SD
Secretary: Diana Shine

Crime Writers' Association, c/o National Book League, 7 Albemarle St, London W1

The **Dickens** Fellowship, Dickens Ho, 48 Doughty St, London WC1N 2LF Tel: (01) 405 2127
Honorary Secretary: Ian Watts
Publication: The Dickensian (four-monthly)

Early English Text Society, Lady Margaret Hall, Oxford
Honorary Dir: Professor Norman Davis FBA
Publications: texts (annually)

East Anglian Writers*, The Old Post Office, Burgh-Next-Aylsham, Norfolk
Honorary Secretary: P Somerset Fry

Educational Writers' Group, 84 Drayton Gardens, London SW10 9SD
Secretary: Philippa MacLiesh

Edwardian Studies Association, 125 Markyate Rd, Dagenham, Essex
Publication: Edwardian Studies

English Association, 1 Priory Gardens, London W4 1TT
Secretary: Lt-Col R T Brain
Publications: English (3 times yearly), *Essays and Studies, The Year's Work in English Studies, Guide to Degree Courses in English*

Federation of Children's Book Groups*, 30 Sennelys Park Rd, Northfields, Birmingham B31 1AL
Chairman: David Blanch

Guild of Travel Writers*, 20 Great Chapel St, London W1V 3AQ
Honorary Secretary: Gerry Brenes

Thomas **Hardy** Society Ltd, The Rectory, Mells, Frome, Somerset BA11 3PY
Secretary: Rev J M C Yates Tel: Mells 812320 (STD code 0373)

The Sherlock **Holmes** Society of London*, 5 Manor Close, Warlingham, Surrey CR3 9SF
Honorary Secretary: Captain W R Michell

The **Hopkins** Society, 162 Turkey St, Enfield, Middx EN1 4NW
Chief Executive: Dr A Thomas
Publications: Hopkins Research Bulletin, Annual lecture, Annual sermon

Johnson Society of London, 72 Fairfield Rd, East Grinstead, West Sussex
Honorary Secretary: Miss S B S Pigrome
Publication: The New Rambler (annually)

Kipling Society, 18 Northumberland Ave, London WC2N 5BJ
Honorary Secretary: John Shearman Tel: (01) 930 6733
Publication: The Kipling Journal (quarterly)

Charles **Lamb** Society*, Charles Lamb's House, 64 Duncan Terrace, London N1 8AG
Honorary Secretary: A D G Cheyne
Publication: The Charles Lamb Bulletin (quarterly)

Lancashire Authors' Association, 8 Whitefield Rd East, Penwortham, Preston PR1 0XJ
General Secretary: Celia Harvey
Publication: The Record (quarterly)

London Writer Circle, 308 Lewisham Rd, London SE13 7PA
Honorary Secretary: Miss M E Harris

The **National Book** League, Book Ho, East Hill, Wandsworth, London SW18 Tel: (Old number — new number not available at time of going to press) (01) 493 9001 (Book enquiries (01) 493 3501)
Dir: Martyn Goff
Libraries: Reference library of current British children's books; The Mark Longman Library on books and the book trade
Publications: Booknews, British Book Design and Production, Children's Books of the Year

P E N English Centre*, 7 Dilke St, Chelsea, London SW3 4JE Tel: (01) 352 6303
Secretary: Miss Josephine Pullein-Thompson
Publication: Broadsheet (biannually)

P E N Scottish Centre*, 18 Crown Terrace, Glasgow G12 9ES
Hon Secretary: Miss Mary Baxter

Poetry Society, 21 Earls Court Sq, London SW5 Tel: (01) 373 7861
General Secretary: Brian Mitchell
Publication: The Poetry Review

Romantic Novelists' Association, Hillfoot, Brookfield Crescent, Ramsey, Isle of Man
Treasurer: Beatrice Taylor

Royal Literary Fund*, 11 Ludgate Hill, London EC4M 7AE

Royal Society of Literature of the United Kingdom, 1 Hyde Park Gardens, London W2 2LT Tel: (01) 723 5104
Secretary: Mrs P M Schute
Publications: Transactions, Report, Special Editions

Shakespearean Authorship Society, 10 Uphill Grove, Mill Hill, London NW7 4NJ
Honorary Secretary: Dr D W Thomson Vessey

Bernard **Shaw Centre**, 125 Markyate Rd, Dagenham, Essex
Publications: Shaw Centre Series

Bernard **Shaw Society**, 125 Markyate Rd, Dagenham, Essex
Secretary: Eric Ford
Publications: The Shavian, etc

Society for the Study of Medieval Languages and Literature,
Treasurer: Dr D G Pattison, Magdalen College, Oxford
Publications: Medium Aevum, Medium Aevum Monographs (new series)

The **Tolkien** Society, 11 Regal Way, Harrow, Middlesex HA3 0RZ
Secretary: Mrs Jessica Yates
Publications: Amon Hen (bi-monthly), *Mallorn* (occasional magazine)

Jules **Verne** Circle, 125 Markyate Rd, Dagenham, Essex
Publication: Voyages

H G **Wells** Society, 24 Wellin Lane, Edwalton, Nottingham
Secretary: J R Hammond
Publications: Newsletter (quarterly), *The Wellsian* (annually)

Wellsiana—The World of Wells, 125 Markyate Rd, Dagenham, Essex
Publication: Wellsiana

Writers' Guild of Great Britain*, 430 Edgware Rd, London W2 1EH
General Secretary: Elaine Steel

Literary Periodicals

Bananas (quarterly), 60 Elgin Crescent, London W11

Blackwood's, William Blackwood & Sons Ltd, 32 Thistle St, Edinburgh EH2 1HA

Book Collector, Collector Ltd, 58 Frith St, London W1V 6BY

Books, National Book League, Book Ho, East Hill, London SW18

Books and Bookmen, 2-4 Old Pye St, off Strutton Ground, Victoria St, London SW1

Critical Quarterly, Manchester University Press, Oxford Rd, Manchester M13 9PL

Encounter, Encounter Ltd, 59 St Martins Lane, London WC2N

The Literary Review, 7 Northumberland St, Edinburgh EH3 6LI

The London Review of Books (contained within *New York Review of Books*), 1 Malet St, London WC1

New Statesman, Statesman & Nation Publishing Co, 10 Great Turnstile, London WC1V 7HJ

Notes and Queries; for readers and writers, collectors and librarians, Oxford University Press, Press Rd, Neasden, London NW10 0DD

Oasis Magazine, 12 Stevenage Rd, London SW6 6ES, 6 times a year, each issue devoted to work by one author

Phoenix; a magazine for writers, Phoenix Publications, 60 Abbey Ho, 2 Victoria St, London SW1

Poetry Review, Poetry Society, 21 Earls Court Sq, London SW5

Quarto, 20 Fitzroy Sq, London W1

Review of English Studies; a quarterly journal of English literature and the English language, The Clarendon Press, Walton St, Oxford OX2 6DP

Scottish Literary Journal, Association for Scottish Literary Studies, Department of English, University of Aberdeen, Aberdeen AB9 1FX

Spectator, Spectator Ltd, 99 Gower St, London WC1E GAE

Taliesin; the Welsh literary journal, Garth Martin, Ffordd Llysonnen, Carmarthen

Times Literary Supplement, Times Newspapers Ltd, Gray's Inn Rd, PO Box 7, London WC1X 8EZ

Transatlantic Review, 33 Ennismore Gardens, London SW7

Literary Prizes

Authors' Club First Novel Award
For the most promising first novel published in English in the UK in the preceding year. Award consists of a silver-plated quill presented to the author at a dinner. Awarded annually. Last award was to Barbara Benson for *The Underlings* (Constable). Enquiries to the Honorary Secretary, Authors' Club, 40 Dover St, London W1X 3RB

Benson Medal
Founded 1916 by Dr A C Benson. For meritorious work in poetry, fiction, history, biography and belles lettres. A silver medal given at the discretion of the Council of the Royal Society of Literature. Applications are not invited. Last awarded in 1975 to Philip Larkin. Enquiries to Royal Society of Literature, 1 Hyde Park Gardens, London W2 2LT

Besterman Medal
The Library Association awards this medal annually for an outstanding bibliography or guide to the literature first published in the United Kingdom during the preceding year. Recommendations for the award are invited from members of The Library Association. Among criteria for the award are the authority of the work, quality of articles and entries, accessibility of information, scope and coverage, up-to-dateness, and originality. Awarded in 1977 to E W Padwick for *A Bibliography of Cricket* (Library Association for the Cricket Society). No award was made in 1978. Enquiries to The Library Association, 7 Ridgmount St, London WC1E 7AE

James Tait **Black** Memorial Prizes
These literary prizes were founded by the late Mrs Janet Coats Black in memory of her husband, a partner in the publishing house of A & C Black Ltd, London. Mrs Black set aside £11,000 to be used for two prizes of whatever income the fund would produce after paying expenses. The prizes, supplemented by the Scottish Arts Council, now amount annually to approximately £1,000 each. One prize is given to the author of the best biography in the English language first published in the United Kingdom during the year and the other to the author of the best novel. The choice is made in the spring for books of the preceding year by the Regius Professor of English Literature at the University of Edinburgh, preferably, or the Professor of English at the University of Glasgow. Awarded in 1979 for 1978 to Maurice Gee for *Plumb* and Robert Gittings for *The Older Hardy*. Enquiries to Department of English Literature, David Hume Tower, George Sq, Edinburgh EH8 9JX

Arnold Vincent **Bowen** Competition
Awarded annually for the best single lyric poem in English of up to thirty lines. Prize of £10. Enquiries to the General Secretary, The Poetry Society, 21 Earls Court Sq, London SW5

British Science Fiction Award
Awarded annually for the best science fiction book published in a paperback edition in Britain for the first time in the previous year. The award for 1978 was to Philip K Dick for *A Scanner Darkly*. Enquiries to Alan Dorey (BSFA Chairman), 20 Hermitage Woods Crescent, St John's, Woking, Surrey GU21 1UE

Carnegie Medal
First awarded 1936. Instituted by The Library Association to commemorate the centenary of Andrew Carnegie's birth in 1835. Annual award for an outstanding book for children written in English and first published during the preceding year in the UK. Recommendations for the award are made by members of The Library Association. The 1978 Carnegie Medal was awarded to David Rees for *The Exeter Blitz* (Hamish Hamilton). Enquiries to The Library Association, 7 Ridgmount St, London WC1E 7AE

Sid **Chaplin** Literary Award
Established in 1977 to encourage the writing of short stories. £100 and a scroll to be awarded annually. The 1978 award was won jointly by Marc Svetov for *A Businessman* and Eamon McDonnell for his writing in *New World for Old*. Enquiries to Public Relations Department, Aycliffe Development Corporation, Churchill Ho, Newton Aycliffe, Co Durham

John **Creasey** Memorial Award
Founded 1973. Magnifying glass with onyx handle and inscribed plate for best first crime-fiction novel. Awarded annually by a panel of reviewers. The 1978 award was made to Paula Gosling for *A Running Duck* (Macmillan). Enquiries to Crime Writers' Association, c/o The National Book League, Book Ho, East Hill, Wandsworth, London SW18

Eleanor **Farjeon** Award
The Eleanor Farjeon Award was established in 1965 to commemorate the work of the late children's author. The Children's Book Circle makes an annual award of £75 which may be given to a librarian, teacher, author, artist, publisher, reviewer or television producer who, in the judgment of the Awards Committee, is considered to have done outstanding work for children's books. Awarded in 1979 to Joy Whitby. Enquiries to Mrs Elizabeth Attenborough, Kestrel Books, 536 Kings d, London SW10

Prudence **Farmer** Poetry Prize
Founded 1974. Awarded annually for the best poem printed in the *New Statesman*. In 1978 the prize was awarded to Craig Raine. Enquiries to Literary Editor, 10 Great Turnstile, London WC1V 7HJ

John **Florio** Prize
Established in 1963 under the auspices of the Italian Institute and the British-Italian Society, and named after John Florio. For the best translation into English of a twentieth-century Italian work of literary merit and general interest, published by a British publisher during the preceding year. No Prize was awarded for books published in 1977 — this was included in the entries for 1978. The award subsequently presented was to Quintin Hoare for his translation of *Selected Political Writings 1921-26* by Antonio Gramsci (Lawrence & Wishart). Enquiries to Secretary, Translators' Association, 84 Drayton Gardens, London SW10 9SD

Glaxo Travelling Fellowships for Science Writers
Founded 1966. Two awards annually to anyone writing popular scientific material published in English, in national papers or magazines, regional papers or magazines, radio or TV, and trade, technical or house magazines. The major criterion in judging is that the entrants must have significantly improved the quality of science journalism. The 1978 winners were David Fishlock, Science Editor, *The Financial Times*; Barry Paine, Television Producer, Natural History Unit, BBC Bristol; and Dr Michael O'Donnell, Editor, *World Medicine*. The awards are sponsored by Glaxo Holdings Ltd and administered by the Association of British Science Writers. Enquiries to Association of British Science Writers, c/o 21 Albemarle St, London W1X 4BS

Gold Dagger Award
Inaugurated 1956, revised 1970. A gilded dagger for the best crime-fiction novel of the year awarded annually by a panel of reviewers. The 1978 fiction award was made to Lionel Davidson for *The Chelsea Murders* (Cape). The non-fiction Gold Dagger (inaugurated 1978) went to Audrey Williamson for *The Mystery of the Princes* (Alan Sutton). Enquiries to Crime Writers' Association, c/o The National Book League, Book Ho, East Hill, Wandsworth, London SW18

Kate **Greenaway** Medal
First awarded 1955. Offered annually by The Library Association for the most distinguished work in the illustration of children's books first published in the UK during the preceding year. Recommendations for the award are made by members of The Library Association. The 1978 medal was awarded to Janet Ahlberg for illustrating *Each Peach, Pear, Plum* (Kestrel Books) to a text by her husband Alan Ahlberg. Enquiries to The Library Association, 7 Ridgmount St, London WC1E 7AE

Eric **Gregory** Trust Fund Awards
A number of awards are made each year to encourage young poets. Candidates for awards must be British subjects by birth, ordinarily resident in the UK and under the age of 30 on 31 March in the year of the award. Candidates must submit a published or unpublished volume of belles lettres, poetry or drama-poems. In 1979 awards were made to Stuart Heuson, Alan Hollinghurst, Michael Jenkins, Peter Thabit Jones, James Lindesay, Brian Moses, Jean O'Brien and Walter Perrie. Enquiries to Society of Authors, 84 Drayton Gardens, London SW10 9SD

Hawthornden Prize
Founded in 1919 by Miss Alice Warrender and administered now by the Society of Authors. It is awarded annually in June to a British subject under 41 for the best work of imaginative literature. In 1978 it was increased to £500 through the generosity of the Arts Council of Great Britain. It is especially designed to encourage young authors, and the word 'imaginative' is given a broad interpretation. Biographies are not excluded. Books do not have to be submitted for the prize; it is awarded without competition. A panel of judges chooses the winner. In 1978 the prize was awarded to David Cook for *Walter* (Secker and Warburg). Enquiries to Society of Authors, 84 Drayton Gardens, London SW10 9SD

Heinemann Award for Literature
A foundation was established in 1944 through a bequest in the will of the late William Heinemann, eminent British publisher. The Royal Society of Literature

administers the annual foundation award which is 'primarily to reward those classes of literature which are less remunerative, namely, poetry, criticism, biography, history, etc' and 'to encourage the production of works of real merit'. The amount of the award is not definitely specified. Submitted works must have been written originally in English. A reading committee decides on the winner, whose name is announced in April or May; the prize is presented at a meeting of the Royal Society of Literature in June or July. The 1978 awards were made to Frank Tuohy for *Live Bait* and Robert Gittings for *The Older Hardy*. Enquiries to Royal Society of Literature, 1 Hyde Park Gardens, London W2 2LT

Felicia **Hemans** Prize for Lyrical Poetry
For a lyrical poem by past and present members and students of the University of Liverpool. Books or cash awarded annually. Enquiries to Registrar, University of Liverpool, PO Box 147, Liverpool L69 3BX

Winifred **Holtby** Memorial Prize
Founded in 1966 by Vera Brittain in memory of Winifred Holtby. An annual award for the best regional novel of its year. Submissions by publishers, not by individual authors. Awarded in 1978 to Richard Herley for *The Stone Arrow*. Enquiries to Secretary, Royal Society of Literature, 1 Hyde Park Gardens, London W2 2LT

Keats (£2,000) Poetry Prize Competition*
Instituted in 1971 to encourage poets and raise the standard of writing, especially of poetry in English. The prize poems are published by the organizer, London Literary Editions Ltd. Enquiries to London Literary Editions Ltd, 29 Ave Chambers, Vernon Pl, London WC1

Martin Luther **King** Memorial Prize
Inaugurated 1968. For a literary work reflecting the ideals to which Dr King devoted his life. It may be given for a novel, story, poem, play, television, radio or film script published or performed in the UK during the preceding year. Prize of £100 awarded annually, augmented in 1979 to £250 by generosity of the Arts Council. 1978 prize awarded to Amrit Wilson for *Finding a Voice* (Virago). Enquiries to Martin Luther King Memorial Prize, c/o National Westminster Bank, 7 Fore St, Chard, Somerset TA20 1PJ.
No enquiries answered without stamped and addressed envelope

McColvin Medal
This annual award is given for an outstanding reference book first published in the United Kingdom. Encyclopaedias, dictionaries, biographical dictionaries, annuals, year-books and directories, handbooks and compendia of data, and atlases are eligible. Recommendations are invited from members of The Library Association who are asked to submit a preliminary list of not more than three titles. No awards were made in 1977 or 1978. Enquiries to The Library Association, 7 Ridgmount St, London WC1E 7AE

Arthur **Markham** Memorial Prize
Instituted 1927. For a poem, short story, first chapter of a novel or a one-act play by a manual worker in coal-mining. There are specified themes and strict limits on length. Prize of £125 annually. Enquiries to Registrar and Secretary, The University, Sheffield S10 2TN

Somerset **Maugham** Award
Founded 1946 by Somerset Maugham to encourage young writers to travel abroad. Given to a promising author of a published work of poetry, fiction, criticism, biography, history, philosophy, belles lettres or travel. Candidates must be British subjects by birth and ordinarily resident in the UK and under 35. Awards of £1,000 must be used for foreign travel. The 1979 awards were to Helen Hodgman for *Jack and Jill* and to Sara Maitland for *Daughter of Jerusalem*. Enquiries to Society of Authors, 84 Drayton Gardens, London SW10 9SD

Netta **Muskett** Award
Established 1960. For an unpublished romantic novel by an author who has not previously had a romantic novel published. A trophy is awarded annually and the winning novel is guaranteed publication. Enquiries to Beatrice Taylor, Romantic Novelists' Association, Hillfoot, Brookfield Crescent, Ramsey, Isle of Man

Sir Roger **Newdigate** Prize for English Verse
The Newdigate Prize Foundation was established in 1806 by Sir Roger Newdigate who had been a member of Parliament for Oxford University from 1750 to 1780. This foundation was the first one founded solely to award a literary prize. The sum of £1,000 was bequeathed by Sir Roger with the stipulation that £21 of the income should be awarded each year to a member of Oxford University for 'a copy of English verse of fifty lines and no more, in recommendation of the study of the ancient Greek and Roman remains of architecture, sculpture, and painting'. Later, with the consent of the Newdigate heirs, these restrictions were modified. The award, increased to about £80, is now open to undergraduate members of the University of Oxford who have not exceeded four years from their matriculation. It is given for a poem of no more than 300 lines on a given subject. Three judges award the prize. Announcement is made by Oxford University annually in May or early June; the winner recites part of the poem at commemoration in June. The award was not given during the war, but was resumed again in 1947. In 1979 the prize was not awarded. Enquiries to Head Clerk, University of Oxford, University Offices Wellington Sq, Oxford OX1 2JD

Frederick **Niven** Literary Award
Founded in 1950 by Pauline, widow of the Scottish novelist Frederick Niven. For the best novel by a Scotsman or Scotswoman published during the preceding three years. £100 awarded every three years. The 1977 award was to John Quigley for *Queen's Royal* (Hamish Hamilton). Enquiries to Honorary Secretary, PEN Scottish Centre, 18 Crown Terrace, Glasgow G12 9ES

North West Arts Publication Awards
For writers, editors and publishers of original creative written material. Enquiries to North West Arts, 12 Harter St, Manchester M1 6HY Tel: (061) 228 3062

George **Orwell** Memorial Prize
Founded 1975. For an article, essay or a series of articles commenting on current cultural, social or political issues anywhere in the world and published in the UK. The judges will look for originality, literary merit and expressive power. £750 awarded annually. In 1978 the award was made to Paul Bailey for his article 'The Limitations of Despair'. Submissions must be made by the editor of the publication in which articles appeared or the organization which commissioned a pamphlet. Enquiries to Penguin Books Ltd, 536 Kings Rd, London SW10 0UH

The **Other** Award
Commendation by the Children's Rights Workshop of a number of books a year as non-biased works of literary merit. In 1979 the chosen books were Dick Cate's *Old Dog, New Tricks*, Sue Wagstaff's *Two Victorian Families*, Roger Mills' *A Comprehensive Education* and Farrukh Dhondy's *Come to Mecca*. Enquiries to Children's Rights Workshop, 4 Aldebert Terrace, London SW8

Provincial Booksellers Fairs Association Annual Book Awards*
Two awards of £250 each are made annually covering different types of books. The 1978 awards were for an illustrated book and a bibliography. Enquiries to Mrs Edna Whiteson Ltd, 343 Bowes Rd, London N11

The **Queen's** Gold Medal for Poetry
Instituted in 1933 by King George V, at the suggestion of the Poet Laureate, John Masefield, this Medal is given for a book of verse, on the recommendation of a committee of eminent men and women of letters headed by the Poet Laureate. The Medal is usually given for a book by a British subject writing in the English language, but an exceptional translation may also be considered. The Medal is not necessarily awarded every year. Awarded in 1977 to Norman Nicholson. Enquiries to the Press Secretary to the Queen, Buckingham Palace, London SW1

R N A Major Award
Established 1960. For the best romantic novel (modern or historical) published during the year. Trophy awarded annually, open to non-members. The 1978 award was to Josephine Edgar for *Countess*. Enquiries to Beatrice Taylor, Romantic Novelists' Association, Hillfoot, Brookfield Crescent, Ramsey, Isle of Man

Rogers Prize
For an essay or dissertation on an appointed medical or surgical subject by a person whose name is on the Medical Register of the UK. Prize of £100 awarded whenever there is enough money in the prize fund. Next award will be in 1980 when the topic is 'Advance in Medicine'. Enquiries to Secretary to the Scholarships Committee, University of London, Senate Ho, London WC1E 7HU

Schlegel-Tieck Prize
Established in 1964 under the auspices of the Translators Association, a subsidiary organization of the Society of Authors, to be awarded annually for the best translation published by a British publisher during the previous year. Only translations of German twentieth-century works of literary merit and general interest will be considered. The work should be entered by the publisher and not the individual translator. In 1978 a first prize of £1,000 was awarded to Ralph Mannheim for his translation of *The Flounder* by Gunter Grass (Secker and Warburg). A runner-up prize of £600 was awarded to John Brownjohn for his translation of *People & Politics* by Willy Brandt (Collins). Enquiries to Secretary, The Translators Association, 84 Drayton Gardens, London SW10 9SD

Scott-Moncrieff Prize
Established in 1964 under the auspices of the Translators Association of the Society of Authors to be awarded annually for the best translation published by a British publisher during the previous year. Only translations of French twentieth-century works of literary merit and general interest will be considered. The work should be entered by the publisher and not the individual translator. The £1000 prize for books published in 1978 was divided equally between Richard Mayne for his translation of *Memoirs* by Jean Monnet (Collins), and John and Doreen Weightman for their translation of *The Origin of Table Manners* by Claude Lévi-Strauss (Cape). Enquiries to Secretary, Translators Association, 84 Drayton Gardens, London SW10 9SD

Scottish Arts Council Book Awards*
A limited number of Awards, value £400 each, are made each year by the Scottish Arts Council to published books of literary merit written by Scots or writers resident in Scotland. The Awards fall into two categories: Scottish Arts Council New Writing Awards for first books, and Scottish Arts Council Book Awards for established authors. All types of books are eligible for consideration and the closing date is the 31 October of each year. Books are submitted by the author's publisher. Enquiries to Literature Department, The Scottish Arts Council, 19 Charlotte Sq, Edinburgh EH2 4DF

Silver Dagger Award
Inaugurated 1956, revised 1970. A silvered dagger for the runner-up crime-fiction novel of the year (see Gold Dagger Award). Awarded annually by a panel of reviewers. The 1978 fiction award was made to Peter Lovesay for *Waxwork* (Macmillan). The non-fiction Silver Dagger (inaugurated 1978) went to Harry Hawkes for *The Capture of the Black Panther* (Harrap). Enquiries to Crime Writers' Association, c/o The National Book League, Book Ho, East Hill, Wandsworth, London SW18

W H Smith & Son Children's Literary Competition
Established in 1958 and previously backed by the *Daily Mirror*, the competition aims to encourage expression in the written word. Open to all children up to the age of 16 years and of British nationality. Sixty-three awards totalling £2,150 will be made and the award-winning work will be published in book form. Enquiries to Public Relations Department, W H Smith & Son Ltd, Strand Ho, 10 New Fetter Lane, London EC4A 1AD

W H Smith & Son Literary Award
Established 1959 to encourage and bring international esteem to authors of the Commonwealth. Given to an author whose book, written in English and published in the UK, makes the most significant contribution to Literature. Award of £2,500 annually. The award for 1979 was made to Mark Girouard for *Life in the English Country House* (Yale University Press). Enquiries to W H Smith & Son Ltd, Strand Ho, 10 New Fetter Lane, London EC4A 1AD

Bertrand Stewart Prize*
Under the will of the late Captain Bertrand Stewart, killed in the battle of the Marne, 1914, this Prize is given for the best essay on some military problem, the study and discussion of which would tend to increase the efficiency of the British Army as a fighting force. Open to any British subject who has served, or is serving, in any of the fighting services. The Prize of at least £80 is given annually. Enquiries to *The Army Quarterly and Defence Journal*, 1 West St, Tavistock, Devon

Reginald **Taylor** Prize
Instituted 1932. For the best unpublished essay, not exceeding 7,500 words, on any subject of archaeological, art historical, or antiquarian interest within the period from the Roman era to AD 1830. Prize of £30 awarded annually. Enquiries to the Honorary Editor, British Archaeological Association, c/o County Planning Department, County Offices, Newland, Lincoln

Tom-Gallon Trust Award
Founded 1943. Given to short-story writers of limited means. Entrants must submit a list of already published fiction, one published or unpublished short story, and a brief statement of their financial position and willingness to devote substantial time to writing fiction as soon as they are financially able. It is awarded every other year. The award in 1978 was made to Michael Morrissey and was increased to £500 through the generosity of the Arts Council of Great Britain. Enquiries to Society of Authors, 84 Drayton Gardens, London SW10 9SD

Welsh Arts Council Awards to Writers
Since 1968, the Welsh Arts Council has given awards to authors whose books are of exceptional literary merit or which make an important contribution to the literature of Wales. The books must be written in English or Welsh. The prize is awarded to recognize achievement, to draw attention to writers of promise and to encourage the writing of creative literature in English and Welsh. Cash prizes of £300 to £500 awarded annually. Bursaries of up to £5,000 each are awarded to enable writers to devote themselves, for periods of up to one year, to their writing. Enquiries to Welsh Arts Council, Museum Pl, Cardiff CF1 3NX

Wheatley Medal
Instituted 1961. Presented by The Library Association, after consultation with The Society of Indexers, for a book published in the UK during the preceding three years which sets an outstandingly high standard in the quality of its index. The 1977 medal was awarded to T Rowland Powel for the index to *Archaeologia Cambrenois, 1901-1960* (Cambrian Archaeological Association). No award was made for 1978. Enquiries to The Library Association, 7 Ridgmount St, London WC1E 7AE

Whitbread Literary Awards
Instituted 1971. Annual awards of £1,500 each to acknowledge outstanding published books in each of three categories of literature: best novel; best biography or autobiography; best children's book. Authors must be domiciled in the UK or the Republic of Ireland. 1979 awards were made to Jennifer Johnston for *The Old Jest* (Hamish Hamilton), Penelope Mortimer for *About Time* (Allen Lane) and Peter Dickinson for *Tulku* (Gollancz). Enquiries to the Booksellers Association of Great Britain and Ireland, 154 Buckingham Palace Rd, London SW1W 9TZ

Francis **Williams** Book Illustration Award*
This award is given every five years to practising book illustrators, professional or student, for books published in Great Britain in which illustration is a major element. Books privately printed or in limited editions are excluded. Books to be submitted by their publishers. Illustrations of a purely technical nature and photographs are excluded. The first Exhibition was held at the Victoria and Albert Museum in 1972 and the second in 1977. Enquiries to The Victoria and Albert Museum Library, South Kensington, London SW7 2RL
or The National Book League, Book Ho, East Hill, Wandsworth, London SW18

Griffith John **Williams** Memorial Prize
(Gwobr Goffa Griffith John Williams) Awarded to non-members of the Welsh Academy for the best literary work in Welsh produced in the previous year. About £50 awarded annually. Enquiries to Yr Academi Gymreig, 4 Llawr, Adeilad Cory, Heol Bute, Cardiff CF1 6QP

Wolfson History Awards
Founded 1972. Two awards are made annually to authors of published works on history. A first prize is given for an author's published body of work culminating with the particular work for which the award is given. In 1978 £7,000 was awarded to H M Colvin for his outstanding contribution to the study of architectural history, exemplified by his greatly enlarged new edition of the *Dictionary of British Architects* (John Murray). A second prize of £5,000 to encourage the writing of scholarly history for the general public was awarded in 1978 to Alistair Horne for *A Savage War of Peace* (Macmillan). Enquiries to Paisner & Co (Solicitors), Bouverie Ho, 154 Fleet St, London EC4A 2DQ

Yorkshire Arts Association Literary Awards
The Association offers a number of biennial awards, together worth £2,000 for published books of poetry, drama, novels or works of nonfiction, having strong literary connections with Yorkshire. Some of the awards are usually made to new writers (ie with only one work in print) whilst the others are for more established authors (with two or more books published). Enquiries to The Director, Yorkshire Arts Association, Glyde Ho, Glydegate, Bradford, West Yorkshire BD5 0BQ

Translation Agencies and Associations

Tek Translation & International Print Ltd, 11 Uxbridge Rd, London W12 8LH

Thames Translations, 65-67 Kingston Rd, New Malden, Surrey Tel: (01) 949 5711

Translators Association, 84 Drayton Gardens, London SW10 9SD Tel: (01) 373 6642

Translators' Guild, Institute of Linguists, 24a Highbury Grove, London N5 2EA Tel: (01) 359 7445

Upper Volta

General Information

Language: French, officially
Religion: Muslim, tribal religions, Catholicism
Population: 6.3 million
Bank Hours: 0800-1200 Monday-Friday
Currency: CFA franc
Export/Import Information: No tariff on books except children's picture books and atlases, 52%; single advertising catalogues sent as printed matter free but otherwise 64%. Statistical Tax 1%; Customs Stamp Tax 6%. No import licences required. Exchange controls outside franc zone
Copyright: Berne (see International section)

Publishers

Les **Presses** Africaines*, BP 90, Ouagadougou
Man Dir: M Armand
Subjects: General Fiction, Religion, Secondary & Primary Textbooks
Bookshop: Librairie Jeunesse d'Afrique, BP 90, Ouagadougou
Book Club: Librairie 'Jeunesse et Afrique'

Government Printer, Imprimerie Nationale*, BP 7040, Ouagadougou

Book Clubs

Librairie **'Jeunesse et Afrique'***, BP 90, Ouagadougou
Owned by: Les Presses Africaines (Ouagadougou)

Major Booksellers

Librairie **Attié***, BP 64, Ouagadougou

Librairie **Evangélique***, BP 29, Ouagadougou

Librairie de **France***, BP 73, Ouagadougou

Librairie **Jeunesse d'Afrique***, BP 90, Ouagadougou

Major Libraries

American Cultural Center Library, BP 539, Ouagadougou

Bibliothèque universitaire*, Université de Ouagadougou, BP 7021, Ouagadougou Tel: 3310/11

Library Associations

Association voltaique pour le Développement des Bibliothèques, des Archives et de la Documentation (AVDBAD)*, BP 1140, Ouagadougou
Voltan Association for the Development of Libraries, Archives and Documentation
Executive Secretary: Louis Aristide Rouamba

Uruguay

General Information

Language: Spanish
Religion: Roman Catholic
Population: 2.8 million
Literacy Rate (1963): 90.4%
Bank Hours: 1300-1700 Monday-Friday
Shop Hours: 0900-1200, 1400-1900 Monday-Friday; 0900-1230 Saturday
Currency: 100 centesimos = 1 peso
Export/Import Information: No tariffs on books or single copies catalogues but 75% surcharge on advertising matter. 7% Additional Surcharge on all imports, plus 18% VAT CIF, plus Stamp Tax of 5% total invoice value. No Import licences. No exchange controls
Copyright: Berne, Buenos Aires (see International section)

Book Trade Organizations

Asociación de Libreros del Uruguay*, Ave Uruguay 1325, Montevideo
Uruguayan Booksellers' Association

Cámara Uruguaya del Libro*, Carlos Roxlo 1446 piso 1°, Apdo 2, Montevideo Tel: 411860
Uruguayan Publishers' Association
Secretary: Arnaldo Medone

Book Trade Reference Journals

Anuario bibliográfico uruguayo (Uruguayan Bibliographical Annual), National Library, Calle Guayabo 1793, Montevideo

Bibliografía uruguaya (Uruguayan Bibliography), Library of the Legislative Power, Palacio Legislativo, Ave Agradiada, Montevideo

Publishers

Editorial **Alfa** SA*, Cuidadela 1393, Montevideo Tel: 981244/80417
Man Dir: Leonardo Milla
Subjects: General Fiction, Poetry, Belles Lettres, History, Social Science
Founded: 1960

Editorial **Arca** SRL+, Andes 1118, Montevideo
Man Dir: Alberto Oreggioni
Subjects: General Literature, History, Social Science

Ediciones de la **Banda** Oriental SRL*, Yi 1364, Montevideo Tel: 982810
Man Dir: Heber Raviolo
Subjects: Literature, Fiction, History, Education, Social Science
Founded: 1961

Barreiro y **Ramos** SA, Juan Carlos Gómez 1436, Casilla de Correo 15, Montevideo Tel: 919202 Cable Add: Bareiramos
Man Dir: Gaston Barreiro Zorrilla; *Sales Dir:* Raúl Catelli
Subjects: General Literature, Textbooks Reference
Founded: 1871
Bookshops: Juan Carlos Gómez 1436; (For branches see under Booksellers)

Editorial y Librería Juridica Amalio M **Fernández**, 25 de Mayo 477, planta baja, Of 11, Montevideo Tel: 916384
Man Dir: Amalio M Fernández; *Editorial:* Carlos W Deamestoy Perez; *Sales:* Andrés Paz López
Subjects: Law, Sociology
1977: 10 titles *1978:* 7 titles *Founded:* 1951

Fundación de Cultura Universitaria*, 25 de Mayo 537, Montevideo Tel: 913385
Man Dir: Román Delgado; *Sales Dir:* Ignacio Sanz; *Editorial Dir:* José Moura
Br Offs: Artigas 1251, Salto; Zorrilla 975, Paysandú
Subjects: Social Science, Law
Founded: 1946

Editorial **Interamericana** del Uruguay SA*, Casilla de Correos 357, Montevideo
Manager: Mirta Gaidos
Miscellaneous: Firm is an associate company of Holt-Saunders Ltd, UK (qv for other associates)

Editorial **Medina** SRL*, Gaboto 1521, Montevideo Tel: 44100/45800
Man Dir: Marcos Medina Vidal
Subject: Low-priced Paperbacks
Founded: 1933

A **Monteverde** y Cia SA, 25 de Mayo 577, Casilla de Correo 371, Montevideo Tel: 902473
Man Dir: Héctor Mussini; *Sales Dir:* Néstor Barón; *Production:* Leandro Mendaro
Subjects: Literature, Primary & Secondary Textbooks, Educational Materials
Founded: 1879
Bookshop: Palacio del Libro- 25 de Mayo 577, Montevideo

Mosca Hnos SA*, Ave 18 de Julio 1578, Montevideo Tel: 404131 Cable Add: Moscaher
Man Dir: Miguel Angel Mosca; *Sales Dir:* Raúl Mosca
Subjects: General Literature, Religion, Textbooks
Founded: 1888
Bookshop: Ave 18 de Julio 1578, Montevideo

Editorial **Nuestra Tierra***, Cerrito 566, Montevideo Tel: 916217
Man Dir: Daniel Aljanati; *Editorial Dir:* Jaime D Aljanati
Subject: General Literature
Founded: 1968

Ediciones **Papacito***, Andes 1346, Montevideo Tel: 987250
Bookshop: Librerías Papacito, Andes 1340, Montevideo
Subject: Essays

Editorial **Pomaire** SA*, Somme 1612, Montevideo
Parent Company: Editorial Pomaire SA, Spain (qv)

Major Booksellers

Albe Soc Com*, Cerrito 566, Montevideo Tel: 85692

America Latina*, 18 de Julio 2089, Montevideo Tel: 415127

Librería Los **Apuntes***, Eduardo Acevedo 1490, Montevideo Tel: 43651

Barreiro y **Ramos** SA, Juan Carlos Gómez 1430, Montevideo Tel: 986621
Branches at: Ave 18 de Julio 941 and 1777; Ave General Flores 2426; Ave 8 de Octubre

3728; Ave Agraciada 3945; Ave Rivera 2684; Calle 21 de Setiembre 2753 (all in Montevideo); Ave General Artigas 714, Las Piedras

Feria del Libro*, Ave 18 de Julio 1308, Montevideo Tel: 902070

Librería Amalio M **Fernández**, 25 de Mayo 477 planta baja ofic 11, Montevideo Tel: 916384

Ibana, SA*, Paysandú 876, Montevideo Tel: 94738

Librería Inglesa*, Sarandi 530, Montevideo Tel: 81955

Librería Adolfo **Linardi**, Juan Carlos Gomez 1418, Montevideo Tel: 912749 Cable Add: Linbooks

Mosca Hnos*, Ave 18 de Julio 1578, Montevideo Tel: 404131

Palacio del Libro, Casilla de Correo 371, Montevideo Tel: 902473

Librerías **Papacito***, Andes 1340/46, Montevideo Tel: 82872/987250

Major Libraries

Archivo General de la Nación (National Archives)*, Calle Convención 1474, Montevideo

Biblioteca **Artigas-Washington** (ICA), Calle Paraguay 1217 Tel: 917423

Biblioteca Central de Educación básica, secundaria y superior*, Eduardo Acevedo 1419, Montevideo
Central Library of Primary, Secondary and Higher Education
Dir: David Yudchak

Biblioteca Nacional del Uruguay (National Library)*, 18 de Julio 1790, Casilla de Correo 452, Montevideo Tel: 45030/496011

Centro Nacional de Información y Documentación (National Information and Documentation Centre)*, Plaza de Cagancha 1175, Montevideo
Dir: Sra Mercedes Fitz-Patrick
Publications: Anales, Enciclopedia de educación, Legislación escolar

Departamento de Documentación y Biblioteca*, Faculted de Humanidades y Ciencias, Universidad de la República, Piedras S/N Montevideo

Biblioteca del **Instituto Cultural** Anglo-Uruguayo (Anglo-Uruguayan Cultural Institute Library)*, San José 1426, Montevideo

Biblioteca del **Museo** Histórico Nacional (Library of the National Historical Museum)*, Casa Lavalleja, Zaballa 1469, Montevideo

Biblioteca del **Poder** Legislativo (Library of the Legislative Power)*, Palacio Legislativo, Ave Agradiada, Montevideo

Biblioteca Municipal 'Dr Joaquín de **Salterain'***, Palacio Municipal, Ave 18 de Julio, Santiago de Chile

Library Associations

Agrupación Bibliotecológica del Uruguay, Cerro Largo 1666, Montevideo Tel: 405740
Uruguayan Library and Archive Science Association
President: Luis Alberto Musso
Publications: Bibliografía uruguaya sobre Brasil, Aportes para la historia de la bibliotecología en el Uruguay, Bibliografía y documentación en el Uruguay, La estrella del sur-Indice, Bibliografía bibliográfica y bibliotecologca, Uruguay-Brasil y sus medallas, Bibliografía de numismática uruguaya, Anales del Senado del Uruguay, El Río de la Plata en el Archivo General de Indias de Sevilla, Legislación uruguaya sobre Brasil

Asociación de Bibliotecarios del Uruguay*, N/D Ibicuy, 1276-Esc-No 3, Casilla de Correo 1415, Montevideo
Uruguayan Library Association
President: Hortensia Braceras

Library Reference Books

Bibliografía bibliográfica y bibliotecología del Uruguay (Bibliography of Bibliography and Library Science in Uruguay), Uruguayan Library and Archive Science Association, Cerro Largo 1666, Montevideo

Bibliografía y documentación en el Uruguay (Bibliography and Documentation in Uruguay), Uruguayan Library and Archive Science Association, Cerro Largo 1666, Montevideo

Literary Associations and Societies

Academia Nacional de Letras*, Calle Solís 1446, (Palacio Taranco), Montevideo
Secretary: Celia Mieres

Asociación Uruguaya de Escritores*, Bartolomé Mitre 1260, Montevideo
Uruguayan Writers' Association

Literary Periodical

Revista de la Biblioteca Nacional (National Library Review), National Library, Calle Guayabo 1793, Montevideo

Literary Prizes

Concurso Literario Municipal (Municipal Literary Competition)
Three prizes are awarded in each of the following four groups: prose, fiction, essay, and biography and history. The most recent first-prize awards in each group were to Sara Bollo for *Mundo Secreto*, Julio Ricci for *El Grongo*, Fernando Assunçao for *Pilchas Criollas*, and Saúl D Cestau for *Historia del Notariado Uruguayo desde la época Colonial hasta la sanción de la Ley Nº 1421*. Enquiries to Intendencia Municipal de Montevideo (Palacio Municipal), 18 de Julio 1360, Montevideo

Gran Premio Nacional de Literatura*
For the total work of an author. Awarded every three years. Enquiries to Ministerio de Educación y Cultura, Sarandi 444, Montevideo

Premio de Remuneraciones Literarias*
Four prizes: poetry; fiction, juveniles or biography; essays; science and technology, sociology, history, education or philosophy. Awarded annually. Enquiries to Ministerio de Educación de Cultura, Sarandi 444, Montevideo

Premio Nacional de Literatura*
For a book in the field of culture. Awarded every two years. Enquiries to Ministerio de Educación y Cultura, Sarandi 444, Montevideo

Vatican City State

General Information

Language: Italian
Religion: Roman Catholic
Population: 1,000

Publishers

Tipografia Poliglotta Vaticana*, Vatican City
Dir: Very Rev Angelo Vedani
Subjects: Juveniles, Education, Natural & Social Science

Libreria Editrice **Vaticana**, I-00120 Vatican City Tel: 6983345/6984834
Dir: Rag Brenno Bucciarelli
Subjects: Religion, Philosophy, Literature, Art, Latin Philology, Theology, History, Works of Karol Wojtyla
Bookshop: I-00120 Vatican City
1977: 25 titles *1978:* 26 titles *Founded:* 1926

Major Libraries

Biblioteca Apostolica Vaticana, I-00120 Vatican City Tel: (06) 6983323
Vatican Apostolic Library

Venezuela

General Information

Language: Spanish
Religion: Roman Catholic
Population: 12.7 million
Literacy Rate (1971): 82.4%
Bank Hours: 0830-1130, 1400-1630 Monday-Friday
Shop Hours: 0900-1300, 1500-1900 Monday-Saturday
Currency: 100 centimos = 1 bolivar
Export/Import Information: Hardcover children's picture books and atlases pay 1% duty 200% duty on catalogues. 3½% VAT CIF Customs Service Tax (1% for parcel

424 VENEZUELA

post) 2% VAT FOB Air Cargo Tax (excluding postal packets)
No import licences or exchange controls
Copyright: UCC (see International section)

Book Trade Organizations

Cámara de Editores*, Puente Yanes a Tracabordo 80–82, Edificio Belvel, Of 4-3, Apdo 14234, Caracas 101
Publishers' Association

Cámara Venezolana del Libro, Torre Lincoln, Ave Lincoln, Sabana Grande, Apdo 51858, Caracas 105 Tel: 7812809
Venezuelan Publishers' Association
Secretary: J B Orraca

Book Trade Journals

Bibliografía venezolana (Venezuelan Bibliography), National Library, San Francisco a Bolsa, Apdo 6525, Caracas 101

Indice bibliográfico (Bibliographical Index), National Library, San Francisco a Bolsa, Apdo 6525, Caracas 101

Publishers

Aguilar Venezolana SA de Ediciones*, Ave San Juan Bosco, Qta Pasecita (entre 3a y 5a Altamira), Apdo 1768, Caracas Tel: 324177/78/327376
Man Dir: José Luis Inés
Parent Company: Aguilar SA de Ediciones, Spain (qv)

Ernesto **Armitano***, Editor, Cuarto Transversal de la Ave Principal de Boleita, Edificio Centro Industrial, 2° piso, Apdo 50853, Sabana Grande, Caracas Tel: 342565/68 Cable Add: Armitpress
Man Dir: P Salazar; *Sales Dir:* E Armitano
Subjects: Venezuelan Painters, Venezuelan Studies (some titles also in English and German)

Biblioteca **Ayacucho**, AP 14413, Caracas 101 (Located at: Edificio JA p/1° Ave Universidad, de Corazón de Jesús a Coliseo, Caracas) Tel: 454507/454411 Cable Add: Biayacucho Telex: 23420 WPSV
President of Editorial Commission: Dr José Ramón Medina; *Editorial, Rights & Permissions:* Prof Ángel Rama; *Sales, Publicity:* Dr Daniel Divinsky; *Production:* Andrés Eloy Romero
Subjects: Latin-America, Classic and Contemporary Literature, Belles Lettres, Politics, History, Art
1978: 25 titles *1979:* 28 titles *Founded:* 1975
ISBN Publisher's Prefix: 84-660

Editorial **Bruguera** Venezolana SA*, Ave Andrés Bello esq Ave de las Acacias, La Florida, Caracas
Parent Company: Editorial Bruguera SA, Spain (qv)

Colegial Bolivariana CA*, Ave Principal de Los Ruices, Edificio Co-Bo, Apdo del Corres 70324, Caracas 107 Tel: 364755 Cable Add: Colegial
Man Dir: José Juzgado C
Subjects: Primary & Secondary Textbooks, Juveniles
Founded: 1961

Ediciones y Distribuciones **E D I M E***, Apdo 51666, Caracas 105 (Located at: Prolong Ave Sur Las Acacias, Qta Provi, Urb San Antonio, Caracas) Tel: 7824510/7826943 Cable Add: Agedime
Man Dir: Nils Koehler; *Sales Dir:* Dietrich Sellhorn; *Publicity & Advertising:* E Mascaraque; *Permissions:* Juan Agero
Subjects: Literature, Biography, History & Art of Venezuela, Low-priced Paperbacks, Secondary & Primary Textbooks
Founded: 1948

Ediciones de la **Biblioteca** (EBCV)*, Servicio de Distribución de Publicaciones, Biblioteca, 1er piso, Universidad Central de Venezuela, Caracas Tel: 622811/619811 ext 2130
Editorial Dir: Marcio S Meléndez
Subjects: Belles Lettres, History, Philosophy, Paperbacks, Medicine, Psychology, Engineering, General & Social Science, Law, University Textbooks
Founded: 1961

Fondo Editorial Común SC*, Ave Abraham Lincoln, Apdo de Correos 50992, Caracas 105 Tel: 726705/723921/5 Cable Add: Editcomun
Man Dir: Rolando Grooscors; *Director:* Peter Neumann
Subjects: Social Science, Communication, Urban Planning, Law

Fondo Educativo Interamericano CA, Apdo del Este 62361, Caracas (Located at Calle Madariaga, Qta El Lago, Los Chaguaramos, Caracas) Tel: 6612356 Cable Add: Adiwes Caracas
Vice-President: Jorge José Giannetto
Subjects: Mathematics, Biology, Engineering, Business, Textbooks
Miscellaneous: Editorial department functions in Bogotá. Firm is an associated company of Addison-Wesley Publishers Ltd, UK (qv)

Grijalbo SA*, Apdo 62260, Caracas (Located at: Edificio Palmira, piso 1-D, Esq B Campo, Ave Fco Miranda, Caracas) Tel: 316746/316721
Man Dir: Manuel de los Reyes
Parent Company: Editorial Grijalbo SA, Mexico (qv)

Grolier de Venezuela*, Apdo 50930, Caracas (Located at: Edificio Continental, Esq Jabillos, S Grande) Tel: 762659/7828609
Man Dir: Gilberto Livay
Associate Companies: See under the Grolier Society of Australia

Editorial **Interamericana** de Venezuela CA*, Apdo 50785, Caracas Tel: 729492/723720
General Manager: Pedro Alvarez
Miscellaneous: Firm is an associate company of Holt-Saunders Ltd, UK (qv for other associates)

Editorial **Kapelusz** Venezolana SA+*, Apdo 14234, Caracas (Located at: Ave Urdaneta, Animas a Platanal, Edificio Camoruco, Caracas) Tel: 5629177/5629188 Cable Add: Kapelusz
Man Dir: Horacio Perotti Beraldo
Subject: Secondary & Primary Textbooks
Founded: 1963

Editorial **Labor** de Venezuela SA*, Apdo 14165, Caracas (Located at: Ave Andrés Bello, Edificio Garten) Tel: 7811398/7815819
Man Dir: Lorenzo Nasarre
Parent Company: Editorial Labor, Spain (qv)

Editorial **Libertador**, Apdo 1331, Maracaibo Tel: 228804/228806
Man Dir, Rights & Permissions and Production: Jake Zondag; *Sales Dir:* John Cornell; *Publicity Dir:* Robert Tuttle
Subjects: History, Religion, How-to, Juveniles, Bible Textbooks
1979: 60 titles *Founded:* 1966

Monte Avila Editores CA*, Apdo 70712, (zona 107), Caracas (Located at: Ave Principal los Cortijos de Lourdes, Edificio los Hermanos, 3°, piso, (zona 107) Caracas) Tel: 359107/358817
Man Dir: Benito Milla; *Editorial, Rights & Permissions:* Juan Liscano; *Sales:* Ricardo Lozano; *Publicity:* Olga González; *Production:* Hugo García Robles
Subjects: Fiction, Literature, Biography, History, How-to, Art, Philosophy, Medicine, Psychology, General Science, Social Science, University Textbooks
1977: 120 titles *Founded:* 1968

Editorial **Natura** SRL*, Ave Boyaca (Cota Mil), Edificio Fundación La Salle, PB 3, Apdo 8150, Caracas 101 Tel: 727145/74767
Man Dir: Serafín Mazparrote
Orders to: Distribuciones Maytex SRL, Ave Norte-Sur 4, No 154 (Pilita a Mamey), Caracas
Subjects: Primary & Secondary Textbooks, Science

Editorial **Plata** SA, now in Peru

Pomaire Venezuela*, Apdo 51960-105, Caracas (Located at: Ave El Cafetal, Qta La Mora, Chuao, Caracas) Tel: 924658
Man Dir: Jorge Barros
Parent Company: Editorial Pomaire SA, Spain (qv)

Editorial **Reverté** Venezolana SA*, Apdo 68685, Caracas (Located at: Peligro a Pele el Ojo, Edif Torre Carabobo, PB, Caracas 106) Tel: 5726670
Associate Companies: See under Editorial Reverté SA, Spain

Editorial Ramón **Sopena** Venezolana SA*, Apdo 14267, Caracas (Located at: Alcabala a Puente Anauco, Edificio AN-VI, 1er piso, Caracas) Tel: 5729709/5728368
Man Dir: A García Sánchez
Miscellaneous: Firm is a subsidiary of Ramón Sopena SA, Barcelona, Spain (qv)

Teduca Tecnicas Educativas*, 4a Ave No 30, Qta Mi Iata, Altamira, Caracas Tel: 337529
Man Dir: Hugo Manzanilla
Parent Company: Santillana SA de Ediciones, Spain (qv)
Subject: Education

Editorial **Tiempo** Nuevo SA*, Calle San Antonio, Edificio Hotel Royal, Apdo 50304, Sabana Grande, Caracas Tel: 729073
Man Dir: Benito Milla Navarro; *Sales Dir:* Ricardo Lozano
Subject: General Literature
Founded: 1970

Ediciones **Vega** SRL+*, Calle Sorbona, Edificio Saturno, Colinas de Bello Monte, Apdo Postal: 51662, Caracas Tel: 763068 Cable Add: Edivega
Man Dir: Fernando Vega Alonso
Subjects: Secondary & University Textbooks
Founded: 1965
Bookshop: Librería Técnica Vega, Plaza Las Tres Gracias, Los Chaguaramos, Caracas

Major Booksellers

Librería Anibal **Alvárez***, Apdo 13462, Caracas

El **Amigo** de Todos*, Madrices a Ibarras, Loc 7, Edificio Bergantín, Caracas Tel: 815580

Librería del **Este***, Ave Miranda 52, Edificio Galipán, Apdo 60–337, Caracas 106 Tel: 332604/322301

Librería **Lectura**, Centro Comercial Chacaito, local 129, Caracas Tel: 717861

Librería Cultural*, Ave 77 no 17–31, Maracaibo Tel: 73993

Librería Cultural Venezolana*, Santa Capilla a Mijares 26, Caracas Tel: 813306

Librería **Medica** Paris*, Gran Ave, Edif Caroni, Apdo 60681, Caracas 106 Tel: 7812709 Telex: 21420 Cable Add: Libmedica

Librería **Mundial***, Véroes a Jesuitas, 16, Caracas Tel: 820337

Organización Bienestar Estudiantes (OBE)*, Universitaria Central de Venezuela, Ciudad Universitaria, Caracas

El **Palacio** del Libro*, Bloque 3, loc 4, El Silencio, Caracas Tel: 452854

Librería **Politécnica Moulines***, Calle Villaflor, Apdo 50738, Sabana Grande, Caracas 105 Tel: 710692/729370

Publicaciones Españolas SA*, Pele el Ojo a Puente Brion, Ave Mexico, Caracas Tel: 5715943/5727302/5725224

Distribuidora "**Rango**" de Publicaciones*, Calle 88, No 13A–89, Maracaibo

Librería **Selecta***, Ave 3, 231-23, Apdo 111, Mérida Tel: 23609

Librería **Suma***, Real Sabana Grande 90, Apdo del Este 5346, Caracas Tel: 724449

Tecni Ciencia Libros*, Torre Phelps, Mezz, Central, Plaza Venezuela, Caracas Tel: 552091

Librería Técnica **Vega**, Plaza Tres Gracias, Edificio Odeón, Apdo 3093, Caracas Tel: 624779
Manager: Lucia Ribas
Owned by: Fernando Vega, Ediciones Vega SRL (qv)

Major Libraries

Archivo General de la Nación (National Archives)*, Santa Capilla a Carmelitas 5, Caracas

Biblioteca de la Universidad Catolica 'Andres **Bello**'*, Urb Montalban, La Vega, Apdo 29068, Caracas

Biblioteca del Congreso*, Plaza del Capitolio, Caracas

Biblioteca Nacional (National Library)*, San Francisco a Bolsa, Apdo 6525, Caracas 101 Tel: 422814/4832058

Biblioteca Central 'Tulio Febres **Cordero**', Edificio Administrativo de la ULA 2° piso, Ave Tulio Febres Cordero, Mérida Tel: (074) 35555 ext 312/553 Telex: 74173 CDCHULA

Director: Dra Francisca Rodríguez C
Publications: Boletín Bibliográfico; Catálogo de Publicaciones Periódicas; Catálogo de Tesis de Grado; Catálogo de Obras Editadas en los Talleres Gráficos de la Universidad de los Andes

Biblioteca del **Instituto** Venezolano de Investigaciones Científicas (Library of the Venezuelan Institute for Scientific Research)*, Altos de Pipe, Km 11 Carretera Panamericana, Apdo 1827, Caracas

Biblioteca Central de la **Universidad Central** de Venezuela*, Ciudad Universitaria, Caracas Tel: 619811

Biblioteca Central de la **Universidad de Zulia***, Grano de Oro Apdo 526, Maracaibo Tel: 515390
Librarian: Margarita Alvárez
Publication: Boletín (biennial)

Library Associations

Colegio de Bibliotecólogos y Archivólogos de Venezuela, Apdo 6283, Caracas Tel: 7816533
Venezuelan College of Librarians and Archivists
President: Celmira Tirado E

Library Journal

Codex, Boletin de la Escuela de Biblioteconomia y Archivos (Bulletin of the School of Librarianship and Archives), Universidad Central de Venezuela, Facultad de Humanidades y Educación, Escuela de Biblioteconomia y Archivos, Ciudad Universitaria, Caracas

Literary Associations and Societies

Asociación Nacional de Escritores Venezolanos*, Velázquez a Miseria 22, Apdo 429, Caracas
National Association of Venezuelan Writers
General Secretary: Angel Mancera Galetti
Publication: Cuadernos

Galaxia*, Canje al Apdo 4023, Carmelitas 101, Caracas
Venezuelan Writers' Group
Director-Editor: Modesto Vargas Lopez
Publications: Galaxia 71;
Books by Venezuelan Authors

International **P E N** Centre*, Biblioteca Ayacucho, Apdo 14–413, Caracas (Located at: Edificio Banco Exterior, Of 322, Ave Urdaneta–Esq Urapal, Caracas)
President: José Ramon Medina

Literary Periodicals

Cuadernos (Notebooks), National Association of Venezuelan Writers, Velázquez a Miseria 22, Apdo 429, Caracas

Galaxia 71, Venezuelan Writers' Group, Canje al Apdo 4023, Carmelitas 101, Caracas

Literary Prizes

Municipal Prize for Prose and Poetry*
For the best prose or poetry work published in the Federal District or an unpublished work from any part of Venezuela. 5,000 bolivares. Awarded annually. Enquiries to Caracas Municipal Council of Federal District, Caracas

El **Nacional** Annual Story Award*
For the best story by a Venezuelan or foreign resident in Venezuela. Awarded annually. Enquiries to Edificio El Nacional, Puente Nuevo a Puerto Escondido, Apdo 209, Caracas

National Prize for Literature*
Awarded annually to the best Venezuelan author. 1977 winner was Ida Gramcko (poetry) 30,000 bolivares. Also includes contestants in narrative prose and essays. Enquiries to Concejo Nacional de la Cultura (CONAC), Apdo 50995, Caracas 105

Socialist Republic of Viet Nam

General Information

Language: French and English as well as Vietnamese
Religion: Taoism predominantly
Population: 47.9 million
Currency: 100 xu = 1 dong (Vietnamese piastre)
Export/Import Information: None available at present.
Copyright: Florence (see International section)

Book Trade Organizations

Syndicat des Libraires*, 185 rue Catinat, Hô Chí Minh City
Union of Booksellers

Book Trade Journals

Thu-tich Quôc-gia Viet Nam (National Bibliography of Viet Nam), The Archives Service of the Prime Minister's Office of the Socialist Republic of Viet Nam, 72 Nguyên–Du, PO Box 15, Hô Chí Minh City

Publishers

Foreign Languages Publishing House, Hanoi
Chief Editor: Nguyen Huu Ngoc
Subjects: Books and Periodicals from Viet Nam (English language)

Giao Duc Publishing House*, 81 Tran Hung Dao, Hanoi
Dir: Nguyen Si Ty
Subjects: Education, School Books
Founded: 1957

Khoa Hoc (Social Sciences) Publishing House*, Hanoi
Subject: Social Science

Lao Dong (Labour) Publishing House*, Hanoi

Nha Xuat Ban Van Hoc (Literature Publishing House)*, 49 Tran Hung Dao, Hanoi
Dir: Nhu Phong
Subject: Literature
1978: 46 titles

Pho Thong (Popularization) Publishing House*, Hanoi

Popular Army Publishing House*, Hanoi
Subject: Military

Sa Tu-Thu Dich-Thuat Va An-Loat*, Le Văn Duyệt, Hô Chí Minh City
(Service de Traduction et de Publication des Manuels scolaires)
Subjects: All Academic, Textbooks

Scientific Publishing House*, Hanoi
Subject: Scientific

Su Hoc (Historical) Publishing House*, Hanoi
Subjects: Politics, Philosophy, Marxist Classics

Su That (Truth) Publishing House*, Hanoi
(Controlled by the Government)
Subjects: Marxist Classics, Politics, Philosophy, Social Science

Trung-Tam San Xuat Hoc-Lieu*, Tran-binh-Trong 240, Hô Chí Minh City 5
Subjects: Textbooks, Audiovisual, Instruction Materials

Vietnamese Publishing House*, Hanoi
Subjects: Politics, Law

Y Hoc Publishing House*, Hanoi
Subject: Medical

Major Booksellers

Xunhasoba*, 32 Hai Ba Trung, Hanoi
Distributor for foreign orders

Major Libraries

The **Archives Service** of the Prime Minister's Office of the Socialist Republic of Viet Nam*, South Viet Nam Branch, 72 Nguyên-Du, Hô Chí Minh City

Central Library of the **Department of Information***, Hô Chí Minh City

Municipal Library*, 22 Yersin St, Dalat

National Institute of Administration Library*, 10 Tran Quoc Toan, Hô Chí Minh City

Social Sciences Library*, 34 Ly tu Trong, Ho Chi Minh City

Thu Viên Quóc Gia Viet Nam*, 31 Tràng Thi, Hanoi Tel: 2643
National Library of the Socialist Republic of Viet Nam

Library Associations

Hôi Thu-Viên Viet Nam*, 8 Le Qui Don, Hô Chí Minh City
Vietnamese Library Association
Secretary: Nguyen Van Thu
Publication: Thư'-Viên Tâp-san (Library Bulletin)

Library Journals

Thư'-Viên Tâp-san (Library Bulletin), Vietnamese Library Association, 8 Le Qui Don, Hô Chí Minh City

Literary Periodicals

Van Hoc, c/o Phan Kim Thinh, 449 Bhai Ba Trung, Q3 Hô Chí Minh City

Western Samoa

General Information

Language: English
Population: 153,000
Literacy Rate (1966): 97.4%
Currency: 100 sene = 1 tala
Export/Import Information: No tariff on most books, printed advertising generally free but some subject to 52%. No import licence or exchange controls

Major Libraries

Avele College Library*, Avele

Nelson Memorial Public Library*, PO Box 598, Apia

People's Democratic Republic of Yemen

General Information

Language: English and Arabic both used commercially
Religion: Muslim
Population: 1.8 million
Bank Hours: 0745-1400 Saturday-Wednesday; 0745-1330 Thursday
Currency: 1,000 fils = 1 Yemeni dinar
Export/Import Information: 14th October Corporation has sole right to import and distribute books. Import licences required. Exchange controls

Major Booksellers

14th October Corporation, PO Box 4227, Crater, Aden
Sole importer and distributor of books

Major Libraries

Miswat Library*, Aden
(Previously called Lake Library. Administration by Aden Municipality)

Teachers' Club Library*, Aden

Yemen Arab Republic

General Information

Language: Arabic (English and Russian common foreign languages)
Religion: Muslim
Population: 7.1 million
Bank Hours: 0800-1200 (1130 Thursday) Saturday-Thursday
Shop Hours: 0800-1300, 1600-2100 Saturday-Thursday
Currency: 100 fils = 1 Yemeni riyal
Export/Import Information: No tariff on books except 10% on children's picture books. Advertising matter dutied at 20%. 5% Defence Tax, 2% Statistical Tax; Cooperation Tax is 15% CIF. Small Welfare Tax. Import licence required; no pornography permitted. Exchange control approval readily available, generally

Major Libraries

British Council Library*, PO Box 2157, Sana'a (Located at: Beit 41, Mottahar, Harat Handhal, Sana'a) Tel: 3179

Library of the **Great Mosque of Sana'a***, Sana'a

Yugoslavia

General Information

Language: Serbo-Croatian most common; Macedonian (German, in north and west, and English spoken)
Religion: Eastern Orthodox and Roman Catholic
Population: 21.8 million
Literacy Rate (1971): 83.5% (92.3% Urban, 77.7% Rural)
Bank Hours: 0730-1200 Monday-Friday
Shop Hours: 0800-1200, 1700-2000 Monday-Friday; 0800 or 0900-1400 Saturday. Some open weekdays continuously and early Sunday morning
Currency: 100 para = 1 new dinar
Export/Import Information: No tariffs on books except 28% on publications of

Yugoslav publishers printed abroad. Advertising catalogues for such books dutied at 27%, otherwise free; non-Yugoslavian language advertising materials dutied at 18%. 5% special equalization tax, 1% Customs Clearance Charge and 10% import surcharge when goods are subject to duty. No import licences required. Exchange controls. The basic commercial unit is known as an enterprise but there are no state monopolies

Book Trade Organizations

Association of Yugoslav Publishers and Booksellers*, YU-11000 Belgrade, Kneza Milosa 25/I, Poštanski fah 883 Tel: (011) 642533/642248
Dir: Jelenko Bučevac
Publications: Knjiga i svet (The Book and the World); *Catalogue of Book Fair in Belgrade; Directory of Members of the Association of Yugoslav Publishers and Booksellers; Publishing Plans of the Publishing Houses in Yugoslavia* (annual); *Books Published by Yugoslav Publishers* (annual)

Book Trade Reference Journals

Bibliografija domace i strane literature (Bibliography of Native and Foreign Literature) (text in Serbo-Croatian), Centralna Biblioteka JNA, Belgrade, Balkanska 53a

Bibliografija Jugoslavije (Yugoslavia Bibliography), Yugoslav Bibliographic Institute, YU-11000 Belgrade, Terazije 26

Books Published by Yugoslav Publishers. Association of Yugoslav Publishers and Booksellers, YU-11000 Belgrade, Kneza Milósa 25/I, Póstanski fah 883

Directory of Members, Association of Yugoslav Publishers and Booksellers, YU-11000 Belgrade, Kneza Milósa 25/I, Poštanski fah 883

Katalog Medunarodnog Sajma Knjige u Beogradu (Catalogue of the International Book Fair at Belgrade), Association of Yugoslav Publishers and Booksellers, YU-11000 Belgrade, Kneza Milósa, Póstanski fah 883

Knjiga i svet (The Book and the World), Association of Yugoslav Publishers and Booksellers, YU-11000 Belgrade, Kneza Miloša 25/I, Poštanski fah 883

Publishing Plans of the Publishing Houses in Yugoslavia, Association of Yugoslav Publishers and Booksellers, YU-11000 Belgrade, Kneza Milósa 25/I, Póstanski fah 883

Slovenska Bibliografija (Slovene Bibliography), Državna Založba Slovenije, YU-61000 Ljubljana, Mestni trg 26, Poštanski fah 50-1

Publishers

A L F A — Radna organizacija za izdavačku djelatnost, YU-41000 Zagreb, Čerinina 9a, Póstanski fah 32 Tel: (041) 217614
Manager: Stjepan Martinović
Subjects: Geography, Maps, Art

August Cesarec*, YU-41000 Zagreb, Braće Oreški 18 Tel: (041) 576615/576651
Dir: Mirko Andrić
Subjects: Belles Lettres, Politics, Science, Fiction

Beogradski Izdavačko-Grafički Zabod*, YU-11000 Belgrade, blvd vojode Mišića 17, Poštanski fah 340 Tel: 651666 Cable Add: BEOGRAF Telex: 11855 yu bigz
Man Dir: Dušan Popović; *Editorial Dir, Permissions:* Uglješa Krstić
Br Offs: BIGZ-OOUR, Zagreb, Ilica 132 BIGZ-OOUR, Sarajevo, Stjepana Radića 10a
Subjects: General Fiction, Belles Lettres, Poetry, How-to, Philosophy, Juveniles, Low-priced Paperbacks, Social Science, University Textbooks

Birografika*, YU-24000 Subotica, Put Moše Pjade 72 Tel: (024) 26215 Cable Add: YU BIGRAF 15111
Director: Andrija inž Bukvić

Borba*, YU-11000 Belgrade, trg Marksa i Engelsa 7, Poštanski fah 629 Tel: (011) 334531/344201
Dir: Novica Dukić

Bratsvo-Jedinstvo*, YU-21000 Novi Sad, Arse Teodorovića 11, Poštanski fah 274 Tel: 42633/42302
Dir: Srbislav Bojović
Subjects: Textbooks in Serbo-Croat, Belles Lettres

C D D (Centar društvenih djelatnosti Saveza socijalističke omladine Hrvatska)+*, YU-41001 Zagreb, Opaticka 10, Poštanski fah 99 Tel: (041) 419026/443809/447055/415659/449817
General Manager: Josip Čondić; *Publishing Manager:* Inoslav Bešker; *Art Manager:* Zoran Pavlović
Subjects: Fiction, Marxism, Philosophy, Social Sciences, Political Journalism, Science Journalism; *Pitanja* (Scientific and Cultural Review); *Polet* (Youth Weekly)
1977: 22 titles

Cankarjeva Založba*, YU-61001 Ljubljana, Kopitarjeva 2, Poštanski fah 201/IV Tel: 323841
Man Dir: Miloš Mikeln
Subjects: Belles Lettres, Poetry, General Fiction, Biography, History, How-to, Philosophy, Reference, Social Science, Psychology
Founded: 1945
Bookshops: Kopitarjeva 2, Wolfova 5, Titova 15, Miklošičeva 16, Tržaška 59, Založka 35 (all in Ljubljana), Trbovlje, 1 junija 27

Dečje Novine*, YU-32300 Gornji Milanovac, Takovska 6 Tel: (032) 81527/81073/81195 Telex: 13731 YU DNGRM
Subjects: Juveniles, Picture-books, Albums

Delta Press+, YU-11000 Belgrade, Draže Pavlovića 14, Poštanski fah 467 Tel: (011) 333969
Dir: Jovan Janićijević
Subjects: Reference Material, Juveniles and Young People, Social Sciences
1977: 9 titles *1978:* 35 titles *Founded:* 1969

Državna Založba Slovenije*, YU-61000 Ljubljana, Mestni trg 26, Poštanski fah 50-1 Tel: (061) 24695 Cable Add: DZS Ljubljana
Man Dir: Ivan Bratko
Subjects: General Fiction, Belles Lettres, Poetry, Biography, History, Music, Art, Philosophy, Reference, General & Social Science, University, Secondary & Primary Textbooks, Educational Materials
1977: 188 titles *Founded:* 1945
Bookshops: DZS at Bled, C Svobode 15; Brežice, C Prvih borcev 37; Celje, trg V Kongresa 3; Ljubljana, Mestni trg 26; Ljubljana, Šubičeva 1a; Foreign Dept, Ljubljana, Titova 25; Ljubljana, Čopova 3

NiP Edit*, YU-51000 Rijeka, bulevar Marxa i Engelsa 20, Poštanski fah 137-138 Tel: 22516/22443/22646 Telex: 24247
Director: Ennio Machia
Subjects: Books, Papers, Periodicals in Italian
Bookshop: YU-51000 Rijeka, Korzo Narodne Revolucije 37

Forum*, YU-21000 Novi Sad, vojvode Mišića 1, Poštanski fah 200 Tel: 57207 Telex: 14199
Director: Kálmán Petkovics
Subjects: Periodicals, Fiction, Politics in Hungarian and Serbo-Croatian

Glas*, YU-11000 Belgrade, Vlajkovićeva 8 Tel: (011) 335380
Director: Radojko Mrlješ
Provides complete printing services to other publishers

Globus, YU-41000 Zagreb, Ilica 12, Poštanski pretinac 232 Tel: (041) 447300/447500 Cable Add: Globus Zagreb
Editors: V Ogrizović, I Sor
Parent Company: ČGP Delo, YU-61000 Ljubljana, Titova Cesta 35
Subjects: Politics, History, Sociology, Philosophy, General Fiction, Handbooks
1977: 40 titles *Founded:* 1948

Izdavačka ustanova **Gradina***, YU-18000 Niš, ul Pobede br 38/I, Poštanski fah 242 Pobede 38/I Tel: 25864
Dir: Dobrivoje Jevtić
Subjects: Belles Lettres, Science, Art, Periodicals
Bookshops: (all at Niš) ul Pobede br 38; Pobede 113; Voždova 74; 12 februar 56a; Obilićev venac 50

Gradjevinska Knjiga*, YU-11000 Belgrade, trg Marksa i Engelsa 8, Poštanski fah 798 Tel: (011) 333565
Man Dir: Ljubica Jurela; *Sales Dir:* Radovan Vuković
Subjects: Technical, Engineering & University Textbooks
Bookshops: Gradjevinska Knjiga, Narodnog fronta 14 & bulevar Revolucije 84; Student, 27 marta 78 (all in Belgrade)

Grafički zavod Hrvatske, YU-41000 Zagreb, Frankopanska 26, Poštanski fah 227 Tel: (041) 418600 Cable Add: GZH Zagreb Telex: 21606 YUGZH
Man Dir: Zlatko Jeličić; *Commercial Manager:* Boris Brekalo; *Publishing Manager:* Vladimir Štokalo
Subjects: Belles Lettres, Art, Tourism, Dictionaries
1977: 82 titles *Founded:* 1874
Bookshop: GZH, YU-41000 Zagreb, Frankopanska 26

Grafos*, YU-11000 Belgrade, Simina 9A, Poštanski fah 459 Tel: 623980 Cable Add: Grafos Belgrade
Dir: Vito Marković
Subjects: Lexicography, Rare Publications, Fiction, Science, Juveniles, Periodicals

I C S Izdavačko Informativni Centar Studenata*, YU-11000 Belgrade, Balkanska 4/III Tel: 325854
Dir: Aleksandar Urdarević

Bookshops: Novi Belgrade: Studentski grad, II Blok & Dom kultur Studenski grad, bulevar Avnoja 152a; Belgrade: Fakultet političkih nauka, Jove Ilića 165 & Arhitektonski fakultet, bulevar Revolucije 73

Informator*, Izdavački i Birotehnički Zavod, YU-41001 Zagreb, Masarykova ul 1, Poštanski fah 794 Tel: 442222 Cable Add: YU INF Telex: 21264
General Dir: Nikola Šaranović
Subjects: Dictionaries, Law

Jedinstvo*, YU-38000 Priština, Dom Štampe bb, Poštansk: pregradak 81 Tel: (038) 27549/29090 Cable Add: Jedinstvo Pristina
Director: Milan Śeślija
Subjects: Belles Lettres, Social & Political Science, History, Philosophy, Medicine

Jugoreklam*, YU-61000 Ljubljana, Moše Pijade 5, Poštanski fah 142 Tel: 316075
Dir: Hinko Urbanc
Br Offs: YU-11000 Belgrade: Nebojšina 2 & Dure Dakovića 88; YU-41000 Zagreb, Petretičev trg 4; YU-63320 Velenje, Celjska 27
Subjects: Juveniles, Economics

Jugoslovenska Revija*, YU-11000 Belgrade, Terazije 31 Tel: 332625
Dir: Nebojša Tomašević
Subjects: Art, Tourism, Periodicals

Izdavački Zavod **Jugoslavenske Academije** Znanosti i Umjetnosti (Publishing House of the Yugoslav Academy of Sciences and Arts)*, YU-41000 Zagreb, Gundulićeva 24, Poštanski fah 1017 Tel: 449099
Man Dir: Josip Hanževački
Subjects: History, Philosophy, Medicine, Technical, General & Political Science, Education
Miscellaneous: Publishing department of the Yugoslav Academy of Arts & Sciences
Founded: 1918

Jugoslavenski Leksikografski Zavod*, YU-41000 Zagreb, Strossmayerov trg 4, Poštanski fah 410 Tel: 36743/36871
Director: Miroslav Krieža
Subjects: Encyclopaedias, Bibliography
Founded: 1951
Bookshop: Poslovnica Zagreb Masarykova 26

Jugoslavija, Izdavački Zavod, YU-11000 Belgrade, Nemanjina 34, Poštanski fah 52 Tel: 643870/643852 Cable Add: Pubzavod Belgrade Telex: 11265
Shipping Add: c/o Transjug-Split, YU-11000 Belgrade, Pop Lukina 12
Dir, Editor-in-Chi: Živislav-Žika Bogdanović
Subjects: Art, Travel Guides, Reference, How-to, General Non-fiction, Juveniles, Science Fiction & Epic Fantasy
Founded: 1948

Izdavački Centar **Komunist***, Belgrade, trg Marksa i Engelsa 11, Poštanski fah 233 Tel: 335061/334189
Dir: David Atlagić
Subjects: Communism, Marxism, Literary Criticism
Bookshop: Klub Citalaca 70, Belgrade, trg Marksa i Engelsa 9

Krścanska sadašnjost*, YU-41000 Zagreb, Marulićev trg 14, Postf 02748 Tel: 444102
Subjects: Bible, Liturgy, Theology, Art History, Church History, Fine Arts, Periodicals
Miscellaneous: Company also acts as a press agency

Kultura (Izdavačko Pretprijatie)*, YU-91000 Skopje, bulevar JNA 68A, Poštanski fah 298 Tel: 35361/23437 Cable Add: Kultura
Man Dir: Dušan Crvenkovski
Subjects: Art, Philosophy, Political Science, Economics, Juveniles
Founded: 1945
Bookshops: 32 bookshops throughout Yugoslavia

Sveučilišna Naklada **Liber***, YU-41000 Zagreb, Savska cesta 16, Poštanski fah 493 Tel: (041) 415602
Dir: Slavko Goldstein
Subjects: Croatian culture and scientific heritage, Literature, *Povijesti, Temelji, Znanstven Radovi* and *Razlog* collections
Miscellaneous: Publishing service of Zagreb University

Libertatea*, YU-26000 Pančevo, Žarka Zrenjanina br 7, Poštanski fah 27 Tel: 3401/3351 Cable Add: Libertatea Pančevo
Dir: Todor Gilezan
Subjects: Textbooks, Periodicals, Rare Publications, Reprints, Romanian Language publications

Makedonska Knjiga (Knigoizdatelstvo)*, YU-91000 Skopje, 11 Oktomvri bb, Poštanski fah 349 Tel: (091) 235524 Cable Add: Makedonska Kniga
Man Dir: Slavko Janevski
Subjects: General Fiction, Belles Lettres, Art, Juveniles
Bookshops: 26 bookshops

Medicinska Knjiga, YU-11000 Belgrade, Mata Vidakovića 24, Poštanski fah 681 Tel: (011) 458135/458165
Dir: Jovan Duletić; *Editor-in-Chief:* Mile Medić; *Sales Dir:* Milojko Gajić
Subjects: Medicine, Pharmacy, Stomatology, Textbooks, Popular literature
1978: 23 titles *Founded:* 1946

Medicinska Naklada*, YU-41000 Zagreb, Šalata bb, Poštanski fah 517 Tel: (041) 33630
Dir: Mirko Madjor

'Minerva'*, YU-24000 Subotica, trg 29 novembra br 3, Poštanski fah 116 Tel: (024) 25701 Cable Add: Minerva Subotica
Dir: Josip Prčić
Subjects: Textbooks, Dictionaries, Scientific and Children's Literature
Bookshops: YU-24000 Subotica: ul oktobra 4; Maksima Gorkog 20; Put M Pijade 25

Misla*, YU-91000 Skopje, Gradski zid, Blok 2, Poštanski fah 460 Tel: 23336 Cable Add: Misla Skopje
Dir: Božin Pavlovski; *Head of Sales:* Vančo Spasovski

Mladinska Knjiga, YU-61000 Ljubljana, Titova 3, Poštanski fah 36/1 Tel: (060) 24851 Telex: 31345 yu emka
Director General: Karel Trplan; *Publishing Dir:* Ivan Bizjak; *Editor-in-Chief:* Borut Ingolič; *Sales:* Joze Wagner; *Production:* Marjan Cerne; *Co-production:* Ciril Treek; *Publicity:* Nace Borštnar
Br Off: YU-11000 Belgrade, 27 Merte; YU-41000 Zagreb, Ilica 30
Subjects: Children's books, General Fiction, Art, Popular Science, Geography, How-to
Book Club: Svet Knjige, Ljubljana, Nazorjeva 6
Bookshops: 23 throughout Yugoslavia
1977: 310 titles *Founded:* 1945

Mladost*, YU-11000 Belgrade, Maršala Tita 2, Poštanski fah 252 Tel: (011) 323390
Dir: Borisav Džuverović
Subjects: Marxist literature, Philosophy, Fiction, Periodical *Mladost*
Founded: 1956

Mladost, Izdavačka i knjižarska radna organizacija, YU-41000 Zagreb, Ilica 30, Poštanski fah 1028 Tel: (041) 440211 Cable Add: Ikape Zagreb Telex: 21263
Man Dir: Branko Juričević; *Import-Export Dir:* Viktor Mučnjak; *Publisher:* Ante Marjanović *Production Manager:* Josip Fruk; *Publicity* & *Advertising:* Lidija Grabúsnik
Subjects: General Fiction, Belles Lettres, Poetry, History, How-to, Music, Art, Philosophy, Reference, Juveniles, General & Social Science, Sports
1977: 80 titles *1978:* 83 titles *Founded:* 1948
Book Club: Mladost's Book Fans Club, Zagreb, Radićeva 37
Bookshops: 20 in Zagreb, 2 in Rijeka, 1 in Osijek, 1 in Belgrade, 1 in Zadar, 1 in Split, 1 in Pula, 1 in Banja Luka

Muzička Naklada*, Zagreb, Nikole Tesle 10/I, Poštanski fah 543
Dir: Albert Trinki
Subject: Music
Founded: 1952

Nakladni Zavod Matice Hrvatske, YU-41000 Zagreb, ul Matice Hrvatske 2, Poštanski fah 515 Tel: (041) 33573/ 33359/33967/35325/6
Man Dir, Rights and Permissions: Pero Badak; *Editorial:* Zane Turtko; *Sales:* Jakov Curić; *Production:* Anton Galic; *Publicity:* Luka Roić
Br Offs: YU-71000 Sarajevo, Maršala Tita 22; YU-11000 Belgrade, Trščanska 5
Subjects: General Fiction, Reference, Art, Literature, Political & General Science, Biography, History, Dictionaries
Bookshops: 41000 Zagreb, Ilica 62 & Dure Salaja 3; YU-50000 Dubrovnik, Poljana Paska Miličevića bb; Dakova, ul Jna 15; YU-47000 Karlorac, Autobusni kolodvor; YU-54500 Našice, Radićeva 23; YU-51270 Senj, Obala Maršala Tita 2; YU-79000 Mostar, Bracé Brkića 8; YU-51000 Rijeka, Dure Dakovića 20
1977: 41 titles *Founded:* 1960

Naprijed*, YU-41000 Zagreb, Palmotićeva 30, Poštanski fah 1029 Tel: 442001/442400/442283 Cable Add: Izdavacko Naprijed Telex: 21449 yu ikpnzg
Man Dir: Autun Žvan; *Sales:* Dragiša Marković
Subjects: General Fiction, History, Art, General Science, Psychology, Political & Social Science, Economics

Narodna Biblioteka Srbije*, YU-11000 Belgrade, Skerlićeva 1 Tel: 451242/9
Dir: Svetislav Durić
Subjects: Bibliography, Reference, History

Narodna Knjiga*, YU-11000 Belgrade, Safarikova 11, Poštanski fah 241 Tel: (011) 328610
Dir: Vidak Perić
Subjects: Politics, Encyclopaedias, Dictionaries, Textbooks, Science, Juveniles, Belles Lettres

Narodne Novine*, YU-41000 ZRreb, Ratkajev prolaz 4, Poštanski fah 557 Tel: 411611/411666
Dir: Ilija Dautović
Subjects: Science, Textbooks, Careers
Bookshops: 21 throughout Yugoslavia

Naša Djeca*, YU-41000 Zagreb, Gajeva 25, Poštanski fah 563 Tel: (041) 447077 Cable Add: Násadjeca
Dir: Petar Butković
Subject: Juveniles

Naša Knjiga*, YU-91000 Skopje, Partizanski odred 17, Poštanski fah 132 Tel: (091) 228066/237014
Dir: Vlado Popovski
Subjects: Textbooks, Sociology, Politics, Agriculture, Literature

Naučna Knjiga*, YU-11000 Belgrade, Uzun Mirkova 5, Poštanski fah 690 Tel: 637230 Cable Add: Naučna Knjiga
Man Dir: Dragoslav Joković
Subjects: Reference, Medicine, Engineering, Science, University Textbooks, Educatial Materials, Maps, Atlases
Founded: 1947
Bookshops: 'Znanje', Belgrade, Gračanička br 16; 'Naučna knjiga', Belgrade, Knez Mihailova br 19

Naučno Delo*, Izdavačka Ustanova, YU-11000 Belgrade, Vuka Karadžića 5, Poštanski fah 201 Tel: 637615
Man Dir: Ljubiša Stokić; *Sales Dir:* Jovan Generalović
Subjects: Archaeology, Architecture, Education, Ethics, Ethnology, Law, Literature, Linguistics, Biology, History, Philosophy, Psychology, Political & General Science, Medicine, Mathematics, Music, Geography, Publications of the Serbian Academy of Sciences & Arts and other science institutes
Bookshop: Naučno Delo, YU-11000 Belgrade, Kneza Milhaila 35

Nolit Publishing House*, YU-11000 Belgrade, Terazije 27/II, Poštanski fah 369 Tel: 332357 Cable Add: Nolit BGD Telex: 11603 nolit bgd
Man Dir: Dragoljub Gavaric; *Editorial:* Miloš Stambolić; *Sales:* Milorad Mojsilović; *Production:* Nicola Kandić
Subjects: General Fiction, Philosophy, Psychology, Sociology, Agriculture, History, Art, Juveniles
Bookshops: 50 bookshops throughout Yugoslavia
Founded: 1928

Mip Nota*, YU-19350 Knjaževac, Karadordeva 15/I, Poštanski fah 63 Tel: 84375/84516 Cable Add: Nota-Knjaževac
Dir: Nenad Živković; *Editorial:* Stojanović Ljubomir; *Sales:* Jovanovic Negica; *Production:* Nikolić Alexsandar; *Rights & Permissions:* Simić Dura
Br Off: YU-11000 Belgrade, Balkanska 9
Subject: Music
1976: 120 titles *1977:* 160 titles *Founded:* 1970

Nova Knjiga*, Obrenovac, Maršala Tita

Obod*, YU-81250 Cetinje, Njegoševa 3, Poštanski fah 59 Tel: 22020 Cable Add: Obod Cetinje
Dir: Slobodan Koljević
Br Off: Belgrade, Dobračina 32
Subjects: Belles Lettres, Fiction, Textbooks, Dictionaries
Bookshop: Belgrade, Njegoševa 11

Obzor*, YU-21000 Novi Sad, bulevar 23, Oktobra 31/V, Poštanski fah 267 Tel: 21555 Cable Add: Obzor, Novi Sad
Dir: Anna Makanová
Bookshop: Bački Petrovac Bodviš Jan

NIP Oslobodenje*, YU-71000 Sarajevo, Maršala Tita 13, Poštanski fah 663 Tel: 35177/34233 Telex: 41148/41136
Dir: Ivica Lovrić

Otokar Keŕsovani-Rijeka*, YU-51410 Opatija, Maŕsala Tita 65, Poštanski fah 13 Tel: 711099/711922 Cable Add: Otakar Kerósvani
Man Dir, Rights & Permissions: Drago Crnčević; *Sales:* Vladimir Bakotić
Branch Offs: Zagreb, Biankinijeva 11; Belgrade, Zrmanjska 2/a; Sarajevo, Mehmed paš Sokolovića 24
Subjects: Fiction, Horticulture, Picture Books
Bookshop: Pančevo 26000, Borisa Kidriča 6
1977: 36 titles *Founded:* 1954

'Petar Kočić'*, YU-11000 Belgrade, Nevesinjska 2 Tel: (011) 432477 Cable Add: 'Petar Kočić'

Pobjeda*, YU-81000 Titograd, Bulevar revolucije 11 Tel: 45955
Dir: Ljubo Burić
Br Off: Zemun, Karadordev trg 7
Subjects: Belles Lettres, Popular Scientific Literature and Lexicography

Pomurski Tisk*, YU-69000 Murska Sobota, Kidriceva 4/I, Poštanski fah 136 Tel: 21374/21061
Dirs: Franc Kolarić, Jože Vild
Subject: Tourist publications

Izdavačko **Preduzeće Matice Srpske***, YU-21000 Novi Sad, trg Svetozara Markovića 2 Tel: (021) 29777/43040 (director)
Dir: Sava Josić
Subjects: Belles Lettres, Science, Politics, Juveniles, Textbooks, Encyclopaedias, Dictionaries
Bookshops: Belgrade, Studentski trg 5; Backa Palanka, Maršala Tita 40 and others

Izdavačko **Preduzeće Sloboda***, YU-11000 Belgrade, Vojvode Stepe 315 Tel: 462131/461721/462341 Cable Add: Sloboda Belgrade
Dir: Streten Hrkalović
Subjects: Belles Lettres, Juveniles, Reference

Primorski Tisk*, YU-66000 Koper, Muzejski trg 7, Poštanski fah 132 Tel: 23291
Dir: Črtomir Kolenc
Br Off: Studenski servis, Ljubljana, Borstnikov trg 25
Subject: Fiction
Bookshops: 9 throughout Yugoslavia

Privredni Pregled*, YU-11000 Belgrade, Maršala Birjuzova 3, Poštanski fah 903 Tel: 623399/625662 Cable Add: Privredni Pregled Bgd Telex: 11509 yu pp
Dir: Toma Marković
Br Offs: Zagreb, Moše Pijade 21; Ljubljana, Hala 'Tivoli'; Skopje, Orce Nikolova 79; Sarajevo, Maršala Tita 86
Subject: Production Reference Books

Prosveta*, YU-11000 Belgrade, Čika Ljubina 11/IV Tel: (011) 631566/632672 Cable Add: Prosveta Belgrade
Dir: Jordan Živković
Subjects: General Fiction, History, Music, Art, Reference, Paperbacks, Juveniles, Textbooks

Prosvetno Delo*, YU-91000 Skopje, Ulica Ivo Lola Ribar, bb, Gradski zid, Blok IV, Poštanski fah 6 Tel: 33675/31398
Man Dir: Mihajlo Korveziroski

Subjects: Reference, Textbooks, Educational Materials, Juveniles
Bookshop: Br 1 Skopje, bulevar Kočo Racin, kula B-20

Prosvjeta*, YU-41000 Zagreb, Berislavićeva 10, Poštanski fah 634 Tel: 445450/444664 Cable Add: Prosvjeta Zagreb
Dir: Branislav Ćelap
Subjects: Journalism, Business Books
Bookshop: Zagreb, trg Bratstva i Jedinstva 5

Prosvjeta (Novinsko-izdavačko i Štamparsko)*, Bjelovar, Vladimira Nazora 25 Tel: 3150 Cable Add: Nišp Prosvjeta Bjelovar
Dir: Branimir Premužić; *Production:* Ivan Ninić
Br Off: Zagreb, Moše Pijade 31

Prva Književna Komuna*, YU-79000 Mostar, trg 14 februar 3/III Tel: 25798 Cable Add: PKK Mostar
Man Dir: Ico Mutevelić
Subjects: Bibliophile Editions, Tourist Publications
Bookshop: Mostar, ul Stari most 3

Izdavačka Organizacija **Rad**, YU-11000, Belgrade, Moše Pijade 12, Poštanski fah 881 Tel: (011) 330923/339758/338994
Man Dir: Milenko Kovačević; *Sales Dir:* Milovan Vlahović
Subjects: Belles Lettres, Poetry, Biography, Philosophy, Low-priced Paperbacks, Engineering, Social Science, Politics, Economics, University Textbooks
Bookshops: Papirus, Belgrade, Terazije 26; Zagreb, Frankopanska 5 and 20 other bookshops throughout Yugoslavia
Miscellaneous: Publishes critical magazine *Književna kritika*

Radnička Štampa*, YU-11000 Belgrade, trg Marksa i Engelsa 5, Poštanski fah 995 Tel: (011) 330927 Cable Add: Radnička štampa Belgrade
Dir: Života Kamperelić; *Sales Manager:* Dragan Kreclović
Subjects: Social, Political and Economic Sciences, Textbooks, Encyclopedias, *Rad* newspaper

Republički Zavod za Unapredivanje Školstva*, YU-81000 Titograd, Novaka Miloševa 36 Tel: (081) 24168, 24126 (Director)
Subjects: Primary and Secondary Textbooks, Education
Miscellaneous: This is the Republic Bureau for the Advancement of Education

Rilindja*, YU-38000 Priština, Dom Štampe, Poštanski fah 27 Tel: (038) 23868/28611/28411
Dir: Rexhep Zogaj
Subjects: Textbooks, Belles Lettres (in Albanian), Periodicals, *Rilindja* newspaper

Savez Inženjera i Tehničara Jugoslavije*, 11000 Belgrade, Kneza Mološa 9, Poštanski fah 187 Tel: 343653/335816/332924
Secretary: Dr Petar Radičević
Founded: 1945
Miscellaneous: Union of Engineers and Technicians of Yugoslavia

Savremena Administracija*, YU-11001 Belgrade, Knez Mihajlova 6/V, Poštanski fah 479 Tel: 648567/647436/687913
Dir: Živorad Jevtić
Subjects: Literature, Law, Work Study, Economics, Reference
Founded: 1954

Škola za Strane Jezike, YU-41000 Zagreb, Varšavska 14 Tel: (041) 419895
Subjects: Language textbooks and teaching materials

'Školska knjiga'+, YU-41000 Zagreb, Masarykova 28, Poštanski fah 1039 Tel: 449505/448111 Cable Add: Školska knjiga Zagreb
Man Dir: Professor Josip Malić; *Sales Manager:* Dr Ivo Bekić; *Production Dir:* Mira Krizmanić
Subjects: University, Secondary & Primary Textbooks, Educational Materials, History, Music, Art, Philosophy, Refeeeence, Juveniles, Low- & High-priced Paperbacks, Medicine, Psychology, Engineering, General & Social Science, Belles Lettres, Poetry, Biography, How-to
1978: 132 titles *Founded:* 1950
Bookshop: Knjižara 'Školske knjige', YU-41000 Zagreb, Bogovićeva 1/a; Knjižara 'Studentski trg', YU-11000 Belgrade, Studentski trg 6

Sloboda+*, YU-11040 Belgrade, Vojvode Stepe 315 Tel: (011) 462131/461721/462341 Cable Add: Sloboda Beograd
Dir: Miroslav Marković
Subjects: Historical Literature, Belles Lettres, Juveniles, Encyclopaedias

Slovo Ljubve*, YU-11000 Belgrade, Mutapova 12 Tel: (011) 436360/492128
Dir: Ljubiša Pantić

Službeni List*, YU-11000 Belgrade, Jovana Ristića 1, Poštanski fah 226 Tel: 650155
Telex: 11756 yu slist
Dir: Dušan Mašović
Subjects: Službeni List (Official Register) in languages of peoples and nationalities of Yugoslavia; collections of court decisions, university textbooks, federation regulations, handbooks for applying regulations, comments on codes, special and periodical publications
Bookshops: Belgrade: Prodavnica 1, Brankova 16; Prodavnica 2, 29 Novembra 1a

Sportska Knjiga*, YU-11000 Belgrade, Makedonska 19, Poštanski fah 720 Tel: 25361 Cable Add: Sportska Knjiga
Dir: Miloš Petronić; *Editor:* Dušan Cvetković
Subject: Sport
Founded: 1949
Bookshop: Belgrade, Makedonska 19

Srpska Književna Zadruga*, YU-11000 Belgrade, Maršala Tita 19 Tel: 330305/334977
President: Risto Tošović
Subjects: History, Belles Lettres
Founded: 1892
Bookshop: Belgrade, Maršala Tita 19

Stručna Štampa*, YU-11000 Belgrade, Francuska 24, Poštanski fah 618 Tel: 335483

Stvarnost*, YU-41000 Zagreb, Frankopanska 11, Poštanski fah 734 Tel: 413808
Man Dir: Petar Majstorović; *Editorial:* Marijan Sinković; *Sales:* Miroslav Mišković
Subjects: General Fiction, Biography, History, How-to, Music, Art, Philosophy, Reference, Juveniles, High-priced Paperbacks, Medicine, General & Social Science
Book Club: Klub 42, Zagreb, Leskovačka 18
Bookshop: Zagreb: Knjizara Stvarnost, Savska 1; Jlica 163b; Rooseveltov trg 4
Founded: 1952

Svjetlost*, YU-71000 Sarajevo, Petra Preradovića 3, Poštanski fah 129 Tel: (071) 512144/31100 Cable Add: Svjetlost Sarajevo Telex: 41326 yu lkpres
Man Dir: Abdulah Jesenković; *Sales Dir:* Rizvanbegović Enver; *Editorial:* Miodrag Bogićević
Branch Offs: Belgrade, Obilićev venac 10; Zagreb, Subićeva 65
Subjects: Belles Lettres, Reference, Science, Juveniles, Business, Textbooks, Business Directories, Encyclopaedias, Periodicals
Bookshops: At above address, and 42 branches throughout the country

Tehnička Knjiga*, YU-11000 Belgrade, ul 7 jula br 26/I, Poštanski fah 307 Tel: (011) 626046
Man Dir: Prvoslav Trajković
Subjects: General Science, Engineering, Secondary & Primary Textbooks

Tehnička Knjiga*, YU-41000 Zagreb, Jurišićeva 10, Poštanski fah 816 Tel: 35097 Cable Add: Tehnoknjiga
Man Dir: Kuzman Ražnjević
Subjects: Science, Technical Engineering, Periodicals
Founded: 1947

Tehnika, formerly publishing house of Savez Inženjera i Tehničara Jugoslavije (qv)

Tiskarna Ljudske Pravice*, Kopitarjeva 2, YU-61000 Ljubljana Tel: 323841
Telex: 31177 ljudne
Subjects: Children's and Juvenile Books; Periodicals and Newspapers

Turistička Štampa*, YU-11000 Belgrade, Knez Mihajlova 21/II, Poštanski fah 606 Tel: (011) 621080
Man Dir: Dragan Nikolić
Subjects: Art, Tourist Guides
Bookshop: Belgrade, Obilićev venac 26

Veselin Masleša*, YU-71000 Sarajevo, Sime Milutinovića 4, Poštanski fah 237 Tel: (071) 34633/24634 Cable Add: Vesmas Masleša Telex: 41154 ju vesmas
Man Dir, Editorial, Rights and Permissions: Ahmed Hromadžić
Br Offs: in Zabreb, Belgrade, Skoplje
Subjects: General Fiction, General & Political Science, Reference, Philosophy, Juveniles
Bookshops: Sarajevo, Maksima Gorkog 2 & Pavla Goranina 2; Belgrade, Terazije 38. Also over 30 group bookshops throughout Yugoslavia
1977: 111 titles *Founded:* 1950

Vesti*, YU-31000 Titovo Užice, 4 jula br 14 Tel: 21262
Dir: Mihajlo Rebić

Vojnoizdavački Zavod*, YU-11002 Belgrade, Balkanska 53 Tel: (011) 641586
Subject: Military

Vuk Karadžic, YU-11000 Belgrade, Kraljevića Marka 9, Poštanski fah 762 Tel: (011) 628066/628043/620024 (Director) Cable Add: Vuk Karadžić Belgrade
Man Dir: Slobodan Durić
Br Offs: Zagreb, Nikole Tesle 14/III; Sarajevo, Sime Milutinovića 10; Novi Sad, Laze Kostića 22; Svetozarevo, Slavke Durdević bb zgr B-3
Subjects: Encyclopedias and Reference, Art, Popular Science, History, Criticism, Psychology, Sociology, Philosophy, Children's books, Education, Periodicals
Founded: 1956

Založba Obzorja*, YU-62000 Maribor, Partizanska 5, Poštanski fah 135 Tel: 25681/21086
Dir: Drago Simončič
Subjects: Professional, Science, Journalism

Zavod za Izdavanje Udžbenika*, YU-71000 Sarajevo, Otokara Keršovanija 3, Poštanski fah 262 Tel: 33728
Man Dir: Dr Ljubomir Berberović
Subjects: Education, Textbooks

Zavod za obrazovanje kadrova za administrativne poslove SR Srbije*, Izdavačko-Stamparska OOUR Stručna Knjiga, YU-11000 Belgrade, ul Lole Ribara 48 Tel: 341332/342512/342514 Cable Add: Stručna knjiga
Dir: Mrs V Brgulan
Subjects: Textbooks, Business, Management

Zavod za udžbenike i nastavna sredstva*, YU-11000 Belgrade, Obilićev Venac 5, Poštanski fah 312 Tel: 335337
Dir: Zdavko Vuković
Subjects: Textbooks, Educational Materials
Bookshop: YU-11000 Belgrade, Kosovska 45

Zavod za Udžbenike i Nastavna Sredstva Sap Kosovo*, YU-38000 Priština, Beogradska 29, Poštanski fah 112 Tel: (038) 24752
Dir: Ramuš Rama
Subjects: Textbooks, Educational Materials
Founded: 1958
Bookshop: Priština, Lenjinova 66

Nakladni Zavod 'Znanje'*, YU-41000 Zagreb, Socijalističke revolucije 17, Pretinac 955 Tel: (041) 411500/411483/411474 Cable Add: Znanje Zagreb
Man Dir: Dragntin Brenčun
Br Offs: Sarajevo, A Šenoe 14; Belgrade, M Kovačevića 2-4
Subjects: General Fiction, Popular Science, Agriculture
Founded: 1946
Bookshops: August Šenoa, Socijalističke revolucije 17; Nakladni, Trg Republike 17, 'Ivan Goran Kovacic', Marticeva 12; Antikvarijat, Tin Vjević, Zrinjevac 17 (all in Zagreb)

Zora*, Zagreb, Prilaz JNA 2/II, Poštanski fah 117 Tel: 419285/419093/418830
Dir: Nasko Frndič
Subjects: Art, Dictionaries, Belles Lettres, Periodicals
Founded: 1950

Literary Agents

Jugoslovenska Autorska Agencija*, Belgrade, Majke Jevrosime 38

V P A (Vjesnikova Press Agencija)+*, YU-41000 Zagreb, Ave bratstva i jedinstva 4 Tel: (041) 515555 Telex: 21121

Book Clubs

Klub 42*, Zabreb, Leskovacka 18
Owned by: Stvarnost (Zagreb)

Mladost's Book Fans Club*, YU-41000 Zagreb, Ilica 30, Poštanski fah 1028
Owned by: Mladost (Zagreb)

Svet Knjige*, Ljubljana, Nazorjeva 6
Owned by: Mladinska Kujiga (Ljubljana)

Major Booksellers

Cankarjeva Zalozba*, YU-61001 Ljubljana, Kopitarjava 2, Poštni predal 201-IV Tel: (061) 323841
Importer/Exporter

Državna Založba Slovenije*, YU-61000 Ljubljana, Mestni trg 26, Postanski fah 50/1 Tel: 24695/310736
Importer/Exporter

Export-Press*, YU-11000 Belgrade, Francuska 27, Poštanski fah 358 Tel: (011) 625363
Importer/Exporter (the latter particularly as supplier to various US libraries, and UK and US Slavic departments)

Forum*, YU-21000 Novi Sad, Vojvode Mišića 1, Poštanski fah 200 Tel: (021) 57207
Importer/Exporter

Jugoslovenska Knjiga*, Trg Republike 5/VIII, Postf 36, YU-11000 Belgrade Tel: 621992 Cable Add: Jugoknjiga Beograd Telex: 12466 yu jkbdg
Import and Export of Books, Periodicals and Newspapers

Kultura*, YU-91000 Skopje, JNA 68a, Postanski fah 298 Tel: 35361
32 bookshops throughout Yugoslavia

Makedonska Knjiga*, YU-91000 Skopje, 11 Oktomvri bb, Poštanski fah 349 Tel: (091) 33710
26 bookshops in Skopje and in all major towns in Macedonia

Mladinska Knjiga*, YU-61000 Ljubljana, Titova 3, Poštanski fah 36/1 Tel: (061) 24851/6
Importer/Exporter (Children's Books)

Mladost, YU-41000 Zagreb, Ilica 30, Poštanski fah 1028 Tel: (041) 440211 Telex: 21263 YU MLADZG
Importer/Exporter

Nolit*, YU-11000 Belgrade, Terazije 27/II, Poštanski fah 369 Tel: (011) 332257/332258/333353
Importer/Exporter

Prosveta*, YU-11000 Belgrade, Terazije 16/I Tel: (011) 320566
Importer/Exporter

Svjetlost*, YU-71000 Sarajevo, Radojke Lakić 3 Tel: (071) 38678
Importer/Exporter

Tehnička Knjiga, YU-41000 Zagreb, Jurišićeva 10, Poštanski fah 816 Tel: (041) 35097
Importer/Exporter (Technical Books)

Veselin Masleša*, YU-71000 Sarajevo, Sime Milutinovića 4 i 2 Tel: (071) 24634
Importer/Exporter

Vuk Karadžic, YU-11000 Belgrade, Kraljevića Marka 9, Poštanski fah 762 Tel: (011) 628066/628043
Importer/Exporter

Major Libraries

Arhiv Hrvatske*, YU-41000 Zagreb, Marulićev trg 21
Archives of Croatia

Arhiv na SR Makedonija*, Skopje, Kej Dimitar Vlahov bb, Poštanski fah 496
Archives of Macedonia

Arhiv SR Slovenije*, YU-61000 Ljubljana, Zvezdarska 1 Tel: 21436
Dir: Marija Oblak-Čarni

Arhiv Srbije, YU-11000 Belgrade, Karnedžijeva 2
Librarian: Mrs L Mirković
Archives of Serbia

Institute for Scientific and Technical Documentation and Information*, Belgrade, Kataniceva 15
Publication: Yugoslav Research Guide

Jugoslovenski centar za tehničku i naučnu dokumentaciju, Belgrade, S Peneziča-Krcuna 29, Poštanski fah 724
Dir: Aleksić Miodrag
Yugoslav Centre for Technical and Scientific Documentation
Publications: Bulletin of Documentation (24 series abstracts from technical literature), *Informatika* (periodical for theory and practice of documentation and information), *Bibliography on Automatic Data Processing, Scientific and Professional Meetings in Yugoslavia and Foreign Countries, MF-Technique* (journal on applying microfilm)

Univerzitetska biblioteka 'Svetozar **Marković'**, YU-11000 Belgrade, Bulevar revolucije 71 Tel: (011) 342116/341446
University Library 'Svetozar Markovič' *1978-79:* 7 titles

Nacionalna i Sveučilišna Biblioteka*, YU-41001 Zagreb, Marulićev trg 21, Poštanski fah 550 Tel: Director 445440; Secretariat 446725; Information Office 446525
National and University Library

Narodna biblioteka NR Bosne i Hercegovine*, YU-71000 Sarajevo, Obala 42
National Library of Bosnia and Herzegovina

Centralna **narodna biblioteka** SR Crne Gore*, Cetinje, Njegoševa 100
Central National Library of Montenegro

Narodna biblioteka SR Srbije*, YU-11000 Belgrade, Skerlićeva 1 Tel: 451242/9
National Library of Serbia

Narodna in univerzitetna knjižnica (Ljubljana), YU-61001 Ljubljana pp 259, Turjaška 1 Tel: Central (061) 23197; Information (061) 22045
National and University Library

Narodna in univerzitetna knjižnica (Zagreb), Marulićev trg 21, YU-41001 Zagreb pp 550 Tel: 446725

Naučna biblioteka, Rijeka, Dolac 1
Research Library

Narodna i univerzitetska biblioteka 'Kliment **Ohridski'*,** YU-91000 Skopje, ul 'Goce Delčev' bb Tel: 34360/50301/50303
'Kliment Ohridski' National and University Library

Biblioteka **Srpske** Akademije Nauka i Umetnosti, YU-11001 Belgrade, Knez Mihailova 35
Library of the Serbian Academy of Sciences and Arts

Library Associations

Društvo bibliotekara Bosne i Hercegovine* YU-71000 Sarajevo, Obala 42 Tel: 36047
Library Association of Bosnia and Herzegovina
Executive Secretary: Kalender Fahrudin
Publication: Bibliotekarstvo (quarterly)

Društvo bibliotekarjev Slovenije, YU-61000 Ljubljana, Turjaška 1 Tel: 23197/8
Library Association of Slovenia
Executive Secretary: Majda Armeni
Publications: Knjižnica (quarterly)

Društvo na arhivskite rabotnici i arhivite na SRM*, YU-91000 Skopje
Society of Archivists of Macedonia
Secretary: Zvonko Janevski
Publication: Makedonski arhivist

Društvo na bibliotekarite na Makedonija*, 'Kliment Ohridski' National and University Library, YU-91000 Skopje, ul 'Goce Delčev' bb
Librarians' Society of Macedonia
Secretary: Kiro Dojčinovski
Publication: Bibliotekarska iskra

Hrvatsko bibliotekarsko društvo*, YU-41000 Zagreb Marulićev trg 21
Croatian Library Association
Secretary: Nada Gomerčić
Publications: Vjesnik bibliotekara Hrvatske (quarterly), *Knjiga i čitaoci* (six per year)

Jugoslovenski bibliografski institut*, YU-11000 Belgrade, Terazije 26, Poštanski fah 20 Tel: 328513
Yugoslav Bibliographic Institute
Dir: Miodrag Džuverović
Publishes the *Yugoslavia Bibliography*, which includes books, pamphlets, music scores and articles of literary, scientific interest, philology, art and sport; also publishes *Biblioteke u Jugoslaviji*

Savez biblioteckih radnika Srbije*, YU-11000 Belgrade, Skerlićeva 1 Tel: 451242
Union of Library Workers of Serbia
Executive Secretary: Branka Popović
Publication: Bibliotekar (bimonthly)

Savez društava bibliotekara Jugoslavije (Serbo-Croatian), see Zveza društev bibliotekarjev Jugoslavije

Sojuz na društvata na bibliotekarite na Jugoslavija (Macedonian), see Zveza društev bibliotekarjev Jugoslavije

Zveza društev bibliotekarjev Jugoslavije (Slovene)*, Belgrade, YU-71000 Sarajevo, Obala 42 1
League of the Librarians' Associations of Yugoslavia: official titles rotate every two years among Zveza društev bibliotekarjev Jugoslavije (Slovene), Savez društava bibliotekara Jugoslavije (Serbo-Croatian) and Sojuz na društvata na bibliotekarite na Jugoslavija (Macedonian)
Secretary: Ljubica Glumac

Library Reference Books and Journals

Books

Biblioteke u Jugoslaviji (Libraries in Yugoslavia), Yugoslav Bibliographic Institute, YU-11000 Belgrade, Terazije 26

Biblioteke u SR Srbiji (Libraries in Serbia), National Library of Serbia, YU-11000 Belgrade, Skerlićeva 1

Journals

Bibliotekar (The Librarian), Union of Library Workers of Serbia, YU–11000 Belgrade, Skerlićeva 1

Bibliotekarska iskra (The Librarian's Spark), Librarians' Society of Macedonia, 'Kliment Ohridski' National and University Library, YU–91000 Skopje, ul 'Goce Delčev' bb

Bibliotekarstvo (Librarianship), Library Association of Bosnia and Herzegovina, YU–71000 Sarajevo, Obala 42

Knjiga i čitaoci (Book and Readers), Croatian Library Association, YU–41000 Zagreb, Marulićev trg 21

Knjižnica (The Library) (text in Slovenian, summaries in English) Library Association of Slovenia, YU–61000 Ljubljana, Turjaška 1

Makedonski arhivist (Macedonian Archivist) (text in Macedonian, summaries in French), Society of Archivists of Macedonia, YU–91000 Skopje

Viesnik bibliotekara hrvatske (Croatian Librarians' Bulletin), Croatian Library Association, YU–41000 Zagreb, Marulićev trg 21

Literary Associations and Societies

Društvo na pisatelite na SRM*, YU–91000 Skopje, Maksim Gorki 18
Society of Writers of Macedonia
Secretaries: Adem Gajtani, Eftim Manev

Društvo za srpski jezik i književnost*, Belgrade University, Belgrade
Society of Serbian Language and Literature
Secretary: D Pavlović
Publication: Pritozi za književnost, jezik, istorija i folklor

Literary Club **'Oktobar'***, Kraljevo, Mire Cukulica 2
Publication: Oktobar

Yugoslav **P E N Club***, Serbian Centre, YU–11000 Belgrade, 7 Francuska St
Publication: Literary Quarterly

Pedagoško-književni zbor, pedagoško društvo SR Hrvatske (Pedagogical and Literary Union of Croatia)*, Zagreb

Sojuz na društvata za makedonski jazik i literatura*, Institute for the Macedonian Language 'Krste Misirkov', YU–91000 Skopje, Grigor Prlicev 5
Federation of Societies for Macedonian Language and Literature
Secretary: Olga Ivanova
Publication: Literaturen zbor (Literary Door)

Literary Periodicals

Bagdala; literature, art and culture (text in Serbo-Croatian), Književni Klub, Krusevac, Obilićeva 20

Brazde (Furrows); journal for literature and culture, Narodni Univerzitet, Bijeljina, Vase Pelagica 1

Bridge; literary review, Zagreb, trg Republike 7

Delo (The Literary Work) (text in Serbo-Croatian), Nolit Publishing House, YU–11000 Belgrade, Terazije 27/II, Poštanski fah 369

Forum; journal of the Section for Contemporary Literature of the Yugoslav Academy of Sciences and Arts (Text in Serbo-Croatian), Zagreb 1, Zrinski trg 11

Izraz (Expression); journal of literary and artistic criticism, Sarajevo, Radojke Lakio Broj 3–1, Poštanski fah 322

Knjizevne novine (Literary News) (text in Serbo-Croatian), Novinsko Izdavačko Preduzeće 'Književne Novine', Belgrade, Francuska 7

Literary Quarterly (text in English and French), Yugoslav PEN Club, Belgrade Centre, Jugoslavenska Knjiga, Belgrade, Poštanski fah 36

Literaturen zbor (Literary Door) (text in Macedonian); journal of the Federation of Societies for Macedonian Language and Literature, Institute for the Macedonian Language, 'Krste Misirkov', YU–91000 Skopje, Grigor Prličev 5

Lumina (Light); literary and cultural review, Panciova, Zarka Zrenjanina 7

Macedonian Review; history, culture, literature, arts, Cultural Life, Skopje, Poštanski fah 85

Oktobar (October); review of literature, art and culture, Literary Club 'Oktobar', Kraljevo, Mire Cukulica 2

Pregled naših i stranih knjiga i članaka (Review of Domestic and Foreign Books and Articles), Centralna biblioteka JNA, Belgrade, Balkanska 53a

Razgledi (Perspectives), review of literature, art and culture (text in Macedonian), Maršala Tita Iv Baraka, Skopje, Maršala Tita 4, Poštanski fah 345

Savremenik (Contemporary); literary monthly (text in Serbo-Croatian), Beogradski Izdavačko-Grafički Zavod, YU–11000 Belgrade, bulevar vojode Mišića 17, Poštanski fah 340

Stremez (Aspiration); journal for literature and culture (text in Macedonian), Prilep, Joska Jordanovski 2

Stremliena; literary review published every two months, Jedinstvo, YU–38000 Priština, Dom Štampe bb, Postanski, pregradak 81

Stvaranje (Creation); journal for literature and culture, Cedo Vukovic, Titograd, Marka Miljanova 11A

Translation Agencies and Associations

Društvo na literaturnite preveduvači na SRM*, YU–91000 Skopje
Society of Literary Translators of Macedonia
Secretary: Taško Širilov

Zaire

General Information

Language: Officially French, but there are 200 ethnic groups, each with own language or dialect. Main vernacular such as Lingala, Kikongo, Kiswahili, widely spoken and largest foreign groups are Belgian, Portuguese and Greek
Religion: Liberty of worship. There are Catholic and Protestant churches, as well as synagogues and mosques
Population: 26.4 million
Bank Hours: 0800-1130 Monday-Friday
Shop Hours: 0800-1200, 1500-1800 Monday-Saturday; generally early closing Wednesday
Currency: 100 makutu (singular likuta) = 1 zaïre; 100 sengi = 1 likuta
Export/Import Information: No tariff but for books not of educational, scientific or cultural use, revenue tax of 25%; children's picture books and atlases, 10% tax. Small quantities of advertising matter free. 3% Statistical Tax on all imports. Goods subject to duty also subject to Turnover Tax of $8^3/_4\%$ CIF value + customs + statistical tax. No import licences for books. Exchange controls
Copyright: Berne, Florence (see International section)

Book Trade Journal

Bibliographie nationale (National Bibliography), Bibliothèque nationale, 10 blvd Tshatshi, BP 3090, Kinshasa-Gombe

Publishers

Bureau d'Etudes et de Recherches pour la Promotion de la Sante*, BP 1977, Kangu-Mayombe
Man Dir, Rights & Permissions: J Courtejoie
Subject: Health Education

C E E B A Publications, BP 19, Bandundu
Cable Add: CEEBA Bandundu
Man Dir, Editorial: Dr Hermann Hochegger; *Sales:* P J Dufraing
Orders to: Steyler Verlag, D–5202 St Augustin, German Federal Republic
Parent Company: Anthropos Institut
Subjects: Social Anthropology, Ethnology, Myths, Rituals, Sociology, Linguistics, Arts, Agriculture, History, Religion
1977: 10 titles *1978:* 11 titles *Founded:* 1965
ISBN Publisher's Prefix: 84–399

Centre International de Sémiologie*, Ave Pruniers 109, Zone de Kampemba, BP 1825, Campus de Lubumbashi
Secretary: Dr V Y Mudimbe
Publications: Bulletins on Medical Anthropology, Religious Syncretisms, Culture-contact, Africanisms

Centre Protestant d'Editions et de Diffusion (CEDI)*, 209 ave Kalemie, BP 11398, Kinshasa I Tel: 22202
Man Dir: Volker Gscheidle
Bookshops: CEDI Bookshop, 209 ave Kalemie, BP 11398, Kinshasa 1
Subjects: General Fiction, Belles Lettres, Poetry, Biography, Religion, Juveniles, Christian Tracts, Books in Kikongo, Lingala and other Zaïre languages, Paperbacks
Founded: 1935

Commission de l'Education chrétienne*, BP 3258, Kinshasa-Gombe Tel: 30087 Telex: 203 DIA
Man Dir: Abbé Dibalu-Didi
Subjects: Educational, Academic, Religion

Government Printer (Imprimerie du Gouvernement Central)*, BP 3021, Kinshasa-Kalina

Editions **Lokole**, BP 5085 Kinshasa X (Located at: Ave Colonel Ebeya no 1082, Kinshasa/Gombe) Tel: 22559
Dir: Yoka Lye Mudaba
Miscellaneous: State organization charged with the promotion of literature in Zaïre

Editions du **Mont Noir***, BP 1944, Lubumbashi
Man Dir: V Y Mudimbe; *Sales:* Pierre Detienne; *Secretary and Publicity:* Mukala Kadima Nzuji
Subjects: General Fiction, Belles Lettres, Poetry, Reference
Founded: 1971

Les **Presses Africaines***, pl du 27 Octobre, BP 12924, Kinshasa I
Man Dir: Mwamba-di-Mbuyi
Subjects: General Nonfiction, Belles Lettres, Poetry, Paperbacks

Presses universitaires du Zaïre et l'Office du Livre (PUZ)*, BP 1682 Kinshasa I Tel: 31380/30652/24786 Cable Add: PUZ Rectorat Unaza Telex: 331
Man Dir, Rights & Permissions: Makanda Mpinga Shambuyi; *Editorial:* Kabukala Mulowayi; *Sales:* Ngalahvlume Kanku; *Production:* Memvanga Kanza; *Publicity:* Wiluwilu Mabanza
Br Off: Lubumbashi
Subjects: Belles Lettres, Poetry, Biography, History, Africana, Philosophy, Reference, Religion, Paperbacks, Psychology, Medicine, Science & Technology, Agronomy, Social Science, University Textbooks, Economics, Law, Literature, Education
1977: 30 titles *Founded:* 1972
Bookshop: Librairie des Presses universitaires, BP 1682, Kinshasa I

Editions **Saint Paul***, ave du Commerce 76, BP 8505, Kinshasa Tel: 25544
Dir: Sister Lucia d'Agosto
Subjects: General Fiction & Nonfiction, Belles Lettres, Poetry, Religion, Juveniles, Christian Tracts, Paperbacks
Bookshop: Firm has bookshop outlets in Kinshasa (BP 8505) and Lubumbashi (BP 2447)

Librairie Les **Volcans***, 22 ave Président Mobuto, BP 400, Goma (Kivu) Tel: 366
Man Dir: Ruhama Mukandoli; *Sales Manager:* Pierre Mangez
Subjects: Reference, Social Science
Bookshop: 22 ave President Mobuto, BP 400, Goma (Kivu)

Major Booksellers

C E D I Bookshop*, 209 ave Kalemie, BP 11398, Kinshasa I

Librairie **Declés***, BP 224, Kinshasa

Diffusion de la Presse*, BP 505, Kisangani

La **Générale des Carrières et des Mines** (GECAMINES)*, BP 450, Lubumbashi Telex: 234
and BP 8714, Kinshasa Telex: 21207

Librairie de l'**Institut national** d'Etudes politiques*, BP 2307, Kinshasa

Librairie **évangélique***, BP 123, Kinshasa

Okapi Centre de Diffusion*, BP 908, Kinshasa

Librairie des **Presses** universitaires*, BP 1682, Kinshasa I Tel: 24786

Procure scolaire*, BP 70, Kanaga

Librairie **Saint Paul***, 76 ave du Commerce, BP 8505, Kinshasa
and BP 2447, Lubumbashi

Librairie **Salutiste***, 249 ave du Plateau, BP 8905, Kinshasa

Librairie **Sarma***, BP 7098, Kinshasa

Librairies **Sodimca***, BP 2700, Kinshasa

Librairie Les **Volcans***, 22 ave Président Mobutu, BP 400, Goma

Librairie du **Zaïre***, 12 ave des Aviateurs, BP 2100, Kinshasa I Tel: 26748

Major Libraries

Alliance française*, Bibliothèque, BP 5237, Kinshasa

Archives nationales du Zaïre*, 42 ave Valcke, BP 3428, Kinshasa

Bibliothèque nationale (National Library), 10 blvd Tshatshi, BP 3090, Kinshasa-Gombe Tel: 30834
Publication: Bibliographie nationale

Bibliothèque publique*, 2 ave Bawaboli, BP 1741, Kisangani Tel: 2617

Centre culturel français, Bibliothèque*, BP 5236, Kinshasa

Institut pédagogique national*, Bibliothèque, BP 8815, Kinshasa I Tel: 80573

Bibliothèque centrale de l'**Université nationale, Campus de Kinshasa***, BP 125, Kinshasa XI Tel: 77920 ext 161
Librarian: Tubomeshi Milambo
Publication: Chronique des Bibliothèques

Bibliothèque centrale de l'**Université nationale, Campus de Kisangani***, BP 2102, Kisangani Tel: 2153
Chief Librarian: Lelo Mamosi

Bibliothèque centrale de l'**Université nationale, Campus de Lubumbashi***, BP 2896, Lubumbashi Tel: 4479

Library Associations

Association Zaïroise des Archivistes, Bibliothécaires et Documentalistes*, BP 805, Kinshasa XI Tel: 30123/4
Zaire Association of Archivists, Librarians and Documentalists
Executive Secretary: E Kabeba-Bangasa
Publication: Mukanda

Library Reference Books and Journals

Book

Liste des bibliothèques publiques (List of Public Libraries), Ministère de la culture et des arts, Bibliothèque centrale, Kinshasa-Kalina

Journal

Mukanda; archives, libraries and documentation bulletin, Zaire Association of Archivists, Librarians and Documentalists, BP 805, Kinshasa XI

Literary Periodicals

Cahiers de Littérature et de Linguistique appliqué (Journal of Literature and Applied Linguistics), Université nationale du Zaïre, Faculté des Lettres, BP 1825, Campus de Lubumbashi

Dombi; Congolese review of letters and the arts, BP 3498, Kinshasa-Kalina (bi-monthly 'little magazine' edited by Philippe Masegabio)

Zambia

General Information

Language: English
Religion: Christian
Population: 5.3 million
Literacy Rate (1969): 47.3%
Bank Hours: 0815-1245 Monday, Tuesday, Wednesday, Friday; 0815-1200 Thursday; 0815-1100 Saturday
Shop Hours: Generally 0800-1700 Monday-Friday; 0800-1300 Saturday
Currency: 100 ngwee = 1 kwacha
Export/Import Information: No tariffs on books but all imports subject to sales tax (10% of duty value + 20%). Single copies of advertising free. Import licence required. Exchange controls

Book Trade Organizations

Booksellers' Association of Zambia*, PO Box 139, Ndola
Secretary: D J P White

Publishers

Africa Literature Centre*, PO Box 1319, Kitwe Tel: 84712/3 Cable Add: Mincen
Man Dir: E C Makunike
Subjects: General, Educational, Religion, Books in Zambian Languages
Bookshop: address as above

Directory Publishers of Zambia Ltd, PO Box 1659, Ndola (Located at: Rooms 101-103 First Floor, Security Ho, Buteko Ave, Ndola) Tel: 4882
Man Dir, Rights & Permissions: D E Smith; *Editorial & Publicity:* Mrs D E Bell; *Sales:* Mrs J M Maxwell
Subjects: Reference, Directories
1977: 10 titles *Founded:* 1958

Government Printer*, PO Box 136, Lusaka

Multimedia Zambia*, PO Box 8199, Lusaka Tel: 53864
Man Dir: Mr Chimfwamba
Parent Company: Christian Council of Zambia
Subjects: Biography, Africana, Religion, Juveniles, Drama, Law, Physiotherapy
1977: 12 titles *Founded:* 1970

National Educational Company of Zambia Ltd+, Chishango Rd, PO Box 2664, Lusaka Tel: 75121/3 Cable Add: Neczam Lusaka
General Manager: Christopher Chirwa; *Editorial:* M J Phirl; *Production:* G K Simanwe; *Sales:* H Chisulo
Bookshop: Chishango Rd, PO Box 2664, Lusaka
Subjects: General Fiction & Nonfiction, Belles Lettres, Poetry, Biography, History, Africana, Reference, Juveniles, Books in numerous Zambian languages, Paperbacks, General & Social Science, Secondary & Primary Textbooks
1977-78: 150 titles *Founded:* 1967
Miscellaneous: Firm is subsidiary of the Kenneth Kaunda Foundation

Prometheus Publishing Co*, PO Box 1850, Lusaka
Subjects: General Nonfiction, Biography, History, Africana, Social Science

Temco Publishing Ltd*, No 10 Kabelenga Rd, PO Box 886, Lusaka Tel: 73746 Cable Add: Longman Telex: ZA 45250
Man Dir, Editorial, Production, Publicity, Rights & Permissions: S V Tembo; *Sales:* Sylvia Sakala
Subjects: Educational, General
Founded: 1977

Major Booksellers

The **Bookshelf***, Caravelle Ho, Buteko Ave, PO Box 977, Ndola Tel: 3438

Christian Bookshop*, PO Box 1206, Kitwe

Christian Council of Zambia*, Farmers Ho, PO Box 315, Lusaka Tel: 73287

Kingstons (Zambia) Ltd*, PO Box 977, Ndola (Department store with book department) (5 other branches)

Malsa Book Service Ltd*, Cairo Rd, PO Box 1700, Lusaka Tel: 81155

Standard Books Ltd, PO Box 94, Lusaka

University Bookshop*, PO Box 2379, Lusaka Tel: 54755

Zambia Catholic Bookshop, PO Box 1581, Ndola

Zambia Educational Distributors Ltd*, PO Box 1917, Lusaka

Major Libraries

Evelyn **Hone** College Library*, PO Box 29, Lusaka Tel: 72961

Kitwe Public Library*, PO Box 70, Kitwe Tel: 2367

Lusaka City Libraries, PO Box 1304, Katondo Rd, Lusaka Tel: 81762
City Librarian: P C Kulleen
Publications: Annual Report; New Additions List (quarterly)

Mindolo Ecumenical Foundation, Hammarskjold Memorial Library, PO Box 1493, Kitwe Tel: 215198/214572
Librarian: Nyambe Namushi
Publications: Annual Report; Mindolo Newsletter (occasional); various reports of conferences and seminars

National Archives of Zambia*, PO Box RW 10, Ridgeway, Lusaka Tel: 51677

Natural Resources Development College Library*, PO Box CH 99, Lusaka Tel: 73046
Senior Librarian: Edward Tankersley

Ndola Public Library, PO Box 388, Ndola Tel: 4049/2637/8

Nkrumah Teachers' College Library*, PO Box 404, Kabwe Tel: 3221

Northern Technical College Library*, PO Box 1563, Ndola Tel: 6210 ext 18

University of Zambia Library, PO Box 2379, Lusaka Tel: 54755

Zambia Institute of Technology Library*, PO Box 1993, Kitwe
Librarian: M C Banda
Publications: ZIT Library Catalogue (quarterly); *Annual Report; ZIT Prospectus* (annual)

Zambia Library Service*, PO Box 802, Lusaka Tel: 74206

Library Associations

Zambia Library Association*, PO Box 2839, Lusaka
Executive Secretary: F G Tembo
Publication: Journal (quarterly)

Library Reference Books and Journals

Book

Directory of Libraries in Zambia, Zambia Library Association, PO Box 2839, Lusaka (provides details on all the major libraries in the country)

Journal

Zambia Library Association Journal, PO Box 2839, Lusaka

Literary Associations and Societies

Mphala Creative Society*, c/o International House 5-13, University of Zambia, PO Box 2379, Lusaka
Publication: The Jewel of Africa

The **New Writers'** Group*, PO Box 1889, Lusaka
Publication: New Writing from Zambia

Literary Periodicals

The Jewel of Africa, Mphala Creative Society, c/o International House 5-13, University of Zambia, PO Box 2379, Lusaka (literary and cultural quarterly edited by Steven May and published since 1968)

New Writing from Zambia, The New Writers' Group, PO Box 1889, Lusaka

Zimbabwe

General Information

Language: English and native dialects
Population: 6.7 million
Currency: 100 cents = 1 Rhodesian dollar
Mailing Information: Weight limits: books, 5 kg (11 lb); printed matter, 2 kg (4 lb); parcel post, 10 kg (22 lb); air parcel post, 10 kg (22 lb)
Export/Import Information: No tariff on books. Advertising matter in bulk has 30% duty and VAT. No import licence required for books or advertising matter

Book Trade Organizations

Booksellers' Association of Rhodesia, PO Box 1934, Salisbury (Located at: Equity House, Rezende St, Salisbury) Tel: 708611
Secretary: Mrs L Craven

Book Trade Reference Journal

Rhodesia National Bibliography, National Archives of Rhodesia, Causeway, PMB 7729, Salisbury

Publishers

B & T Directories (Rhodesia) (Pvt) Ltd*, PO Box 2119, Bulawayo
Subject: Directories

Books of Rhodesia Publishing Co (Pvt) Ltd*, 137A Rhodes St, PO Box 1994, Bulawayo Tel: 61135
Man Dir & Editor: L W Bolze; *Rights & Permissions:* Joan Hopcroft
Orders to: Books of Rhodesia Publishing Co, PO Box 1994, Bulawayo
Subsidiary Company: Africana Book Society (Pty) Ltd, PO Box 1071, Johannesburg, 2000 RSA (qv)
Subjects: Rhodesiana Reprints & New Works, Fine Prints, Antique Maps of Africa, General Fiction and Nonfiction, Biography, History, Colour-plate Fine editions, Education, Visual Aids
Book Clubs: Books of Rhodesia Book Club, 137A Rhodes St (14th 15th Aves), PO Box 1994, Bulawayo (qv); Africana Book Society, Shop 149, Blue Route, Carlton Centre, PO Box 1071, Johannesburg, RSA (qv)
Founded: 1968
ISBN Publisher's Prefix: 0-86920

A C **Braby** (Rhodesia) (Pvt) Ltd*, PO Box 1027, Bulawayo
Subjects: Reference, Directories, Telephone Books

Burke Enterprises (Pvt) Ltd*, PO Box 550, Gatooma

M O **Collins** (Pvt) Ltd, PO Box 3094, Dublin Ho, Victoria St/Albion Rd, Salisbury Tel: 704719
Man Dir: Brig M O Collins
Subjects: Science & Technology, General Science, Textbooks, History, Biography, Atlases, Children's Books
1977: 3 titles *1978:* 3 titles *Founded:* 1965
ISBN Publishers Prefix: 0-86919

Peter **Dearlove** Publishers*, PO Box UA 106, Salisbury
Man Dir: Peter Dearlove
Subjects: General Nonfiction, Biography, History, Africana, Paperbacks, Social Science

Dominion Press (Pvt) Ltd*, PO Box 1160, Salisbury

Flame Lily, an imprint of Rhodesia Literature Bureau (qv)

Galaxie Press (Pvt) Ltd, PO Box 3041, Salisbury

Government Printer, PO Box 8062, Causeway, Salisbury

The **Literature Bureau**, Ministry of Education, PO Box 8137, Causeway, Salisbury   Tel: 26929   Cable Add: Rholitburo
Dir: E W Krog;   *Asst Dir:* David Hlazo;   *Editorial:* P Mashiri (Shona); P Mpofu (Ndebele)
Imprint: Flame Lily
Branch Off: PO Box 857, Bulawayo
Subjects: General Fiction & Nonfiction, Belles Lettres, Poetry, Biography, History, Africana, How-to, Study Guides, Books in Shona, Ndebele and English
Book Club: Shona Readers' Book Club; Ndebele Readers' Book Club; both at Box 8137, Causeway, Salisbury
Bookshop: Electra Ho, Jameson Ave, Salisbury
1977: 21 titles   *1978:* 280 titles   *Founded:* 1954
ISBN Publisher's Prefix: 0-86926

Lomagundi Printing (Pvt) Ltd*, PO Box 110, Sinoia

Longman Publishers (Pvt) Ltd, PO Box ST125, Southerton, Salisbury   Tel: 62711/2/3/4   Cable Add: Freegrove Salisbury
Man Dir: Ben Gingell;   *General Manager:* D R Mackenzie;   *Marketing Manager:* S G Mpofu;   *Senior Editor, Rights & Permissions:* Marilyn Poole;   *Publicity:* Mia Sullivan
Subjects: General Fiction & Nonfiction, Belles Lettres, Poetry, Biography, History, Africana, Juveniles, Books in Shona and Ndebele, Paperbacks, General & Social Science, Secondary & Primary Textbooks
1978-79: 18 titles   *Founded:* 1964
Miscellaneous: Firm is an associate company of Longman Group Ltd, UK (qv)
ISBN Publisher's Prefix: 0-582

Mambo Press, PO Box 779, Gwelo   Tel: 4016
Man Dir: Albert Plangger;   *Sales Manager:* James Amrein
Branch Off: 51 Stanley Ave, PB 6602, Kopje, Salisbury   Tel: 705899; Fort Victoria, PB 9213, Gokomere   Tel: 2519-12
Subjects: General Fiction & Nonfiction, Poetry, Religion, Books in Shona, Ndebele and English, Secondary & Primary Textbooks
Bookshop: Mambo Press Bookshop, 51 Stanley Ave, PB 6602, Kopje, Salisbury; PO Box 779, Gwelo
1978: 36 titles   *Founded:* 1958
ISBN Publishers Prefix: 0-86922

Mercantile Publishing House (Pvt) Ltd*, PO Box 1561, Salisbury

Oxford University Press Southern Africa*, Rooms 57-58, Roslin Ho, Baker Ave, PO Box 3892, Salisbury   Tel: 27848   Cable Add: Oxonian
General Manager: N C Gracie;   *Publicity:* C Rambanepasi
Subjects: General Nonfiction, Belles Lettres, Poetry, Biography, History, Africana, Books in Shona & other Rhodesian Languages, Secondary Textbooks, Music, Prayer Books
1977: 1 title   *Founded:* 1915
Miscellaneous: Firm is a branch office of Oxford University Press Southern Africa qv under Republic of South Africa
ISBN Publisher's Prefix: 0-19

Publications Central Africa*, PO Box 1027, Bulawayo
Subjects: Reference, Annuals

R C P (Private) Ltd*, Bulawayo
(formerly Rhodesian Christian Press)

Rhodesian Christian Press, see R C P (Private) Ltd

Rhodesian Publications*, PO Box 1210, Salisbury
Founded: 1969

University of Rhodesia, Publications Officer, PO Box MP45, Mount Pleasant, Salisbury   Tel: 303211   Cable Add: University   Telex: 4152 RH
Subjects: Biography, History, Africana, Philosophy, Reference, Religion, Medicine, Science & Technology, General & Social Science, University Textbooks
1977: 2 titles   *1978:* 1 title (further volume in *Zambezia* series)

Book Clubs

Books of Rhodesia Book Club*, 137A Rhodes St (14th 15th Aves), PO Box 1994, Bulawayo
Founded: 1968
Owned by: Books of Rhodesia Publishing Co (PVT) Ltd, Bulawayo (qv)
Subjects: Reproductions of scarce early Rhodesiana/Africana

Ndebele Readers' Book Club, Box 8137, Causeway, Salisbury
Sponsored by: The Literature Bureau (qv)
Subject: Ndebele Literature

Shona Readers' Book Club, Box 8137, Causeway, Salisbury
Sponsored by: The Literature Bureau, Salisbury (qv)
Subject: Shona literature

Major Booksellers

Adventist Book Centre, 114 Jameson St, PO Box 573, Bulawayo   Tel: 61845

African Book Centre*, PO Box 2020, Bulawayo   Tel: (19) 65919

Alpha Books, PO Box 1056, Salisbury   Tel: 22553
Manager: L Craven

Archibald Brothers*, PO Box 280, Gwelo   Tel: (154) 2871

Baptist Book Centre, PO Box 831, Gwelo (Located at: 5th Street, Mandis Bldg, Gwelo)   Tel: (154) 4242
Manager: Shayne T Masimira

Belmont Press, PO Box 31, Fort Victoria   Tel: 2633
Also printers, stationers, office suppliers

Book Centre*, PO Box 3799, Salisbury (Located at: Gordon Ave and Union Ave, Salisbury)   Tel: 704621   Cable Add: textbook
Miscellaneous: This bookshop is associated with Books of Africa (qv under Publishers, Republic of South Africa)

The **Book Exchange***, 57 Stanley Ave, Salisbury   Tel: 22468

The **Book Mart***, 4-10 Berkeley Bldgs, 61 Speke Ave, PO Box 503, Salisbury

Evans Shepherd*, PO Box 36, Salisbury   Tel: 702531

Kingstons Ltd, PO Box 2374, Salisbury   Tel: 700526 (Wholesaler, also retailer with 7 branches)

The **Literature Bureau**, PO Box 8137, Causeway, Salisbury   Tel: 26929; Electra Ho, Jameson Ave, Salisbury   Cable Add: Rholitburo
Wholesale and retail distributors

Mambo Press Bookshop*, 51 Stanley Ave, PB 6602, Kopje, Salisbury   Tel: 705899

Matopo Book Centre, PO Box 554, Bulawayo   Tel: (19) 71152

Philpott & Collins (1978) (Pvt) Ltd, PO Box 1977, Salisbury   Tel: 705441

Townsend & Co (Pvt) Ltd*, PO Box 3281, Salisbury   Tel: 24611/26679
Manager: M D Evans

Major Libraries

Bulawayo Public Library, PO Box 586, Bulawayo   Tel: Bulawayo 60966
Librarian: R W Doust
Publications: Triennial Report; Spectrum: Quarterly Guide to new books

National Archives of Rhodesia, Pvt Bag 7729, Causeway   Tel: 792741
Publication: Rhodesia National Bibliography

National Free Library Service, Twelfth Ave, PO Box 1773, Bulawayo   Tel: 62359   Telex: 3128
Publication: Shelfmark

Nyatsime College Library*, Seke

Queen Victoria Memorial Library*, PO Box 1087, Salisbury   Tel: 704921

Salisbury Polytechnic Library*, Causeway, PO Box 8074, Salisbury   Tel: 705951
Librarian: Mrs D M Thorpe

Turner Memorial Library*, Queen's Way Civic Complex, PO Box 48, Kingsway, Umtali   Tel: 3412

University of Rhodesia Library, PO Box MP45, Mount Pleasant, Salisbury   Tel: 303211   Cable Add: University   Telex: 4152 rh

Library Associations

Rhodesia Library Association*, PO Box 3133, Salisbury
Publication: The Rhodesian Librarian

Library Reference Books and Journals

Books

Directory of Rhodesian Libraries, National Archives of Rhodesia, Pvt Bag 7729, Causeway, Salisbury

Journals

The Rhodesian Librarian, Rhodesia Library Association, PO Box 3133, Salisbury

Literary Associations and Societies

P E N Centre of Zimbabwe-Rhodesia, PO Box 1900, Salisbury
Secretary: Nora S Kane, 4 Avonfriars, Oxford Rd, Avondale, Salisbury

Shona/Ndebele Writers' Association*
Secretary: Mrs J G Sibanda, PO Box 7009, Mzilikazi

Literary Periodicals

Moto, PO Box 779, Gwelo (A political, cultural and religious weekly published by Mambo Press since 1958, with contributions in English and Shona. It has however been banned in recent years)

Literary Prizes

Kingston's Literary Awards
The awards are for outstanding published works in English, Shona and Sindebele. Three awards, each of 500 Rhodesian dollars, one in respect of each language. Enquiries to P E N International, Zimbabwe-Rhodesia Centre, PO Box 1900, Salisbury

The **Literature Bureau** Annual Literary Award
300 Rhodesian dollars for the best works in Shona and Ndebele. Most genres, including translations, qualify for entry. Enquiries to The Literature Bureau, PO Box 8137, Causeway, Salisbury

Two Tone Poetry Awards
Two Tone is published quarterly. A prize of fifteen Rhodesian dollars is awarded for the best poem in each issue, with a further prize of fifty Rhodesian dollars for the poet who has sent in the best contributions to be published throughout the year. Winners of the latter award will not be eligible to compete for awards in the following two years. Enquiries to PO Box MP 79, Mount Pleasant, Salisbury

International Section

Copyright Conventions

The Universal Copyright Convention was sponsored by UNESCO in 1952. It states that 'Each signatory country extends to foreign works covered by UCC the same protection which such country extends to works of its own nationals published within its own borders'.

The Berne Convention is a system of international copyright which is maintained among countries which have become signatories to the International Copyright Union for the Protection of Literary and Artistic Works. This Union plan, which was first agreed upon at Berne, Switzerland, in 1888, has been subject to revisions every 20 years. The basic principle of the agreement is that any work properly copyrighted in its country of origin has protection in every Union country. Any work originating in a non-Union country, if it is simultaneously published in a Union country has the same standing as it would if it had originated in a Union country. Since different countries have different relationships under one or more of the revisions (Paris, 1896; Berlin, 1908; Rome, 1928; Brussels, 1948; and Stockholm, 1968), persons interested in obtaining information, including application of the various provisions to territorial areas, should consult the Bureau de l'union internationale pour la protection des oeuvres littéraires et artistiques, 32 chemin des Colombettes, Geneva, Switzerland.

The Florence Agreement, also known as the 'free flow of books', is a UNESCO-sponsored international agreement aimed at easing the flow of books and other scientific, educational and cultural materials, through the elimination or reduction of tariffs and other barriers.

The Buenos Aires Convention: In most Latin-American countries, compliance with the copyright law of the country of first publication protects the work in other countries of the Buenos Aires Convention, 1910. To secure copyright, each work must carry a notice to the effect that any use of the book or article will not be permitted without the consent of the copyright owner, and that copyright is reserved in English or any other language; for complete safety it is advised to add 'All rights reserved'. A later revision of the Buenos Aires Convention was made at the Washington Conference (Pan-American Copyright Convention) of 1946 which goes into greater detail than the Buenos Aires Convention. This Convention has been ratified by Argentina, Bolivia, Brazil, Chile, Costa Rica, Cuba, Dominican Republic, Ecuador, Guatemala, Haiti, Honduras, Mexico, Nicaragua and Paraguay

International Organizations

International Book Trade, Literary and Library Organizations

A C U R I L (Association of Caribbean University, Research and Institutional Libraries), Box S, University Station, San Juan, Puerto Rico 00931
General Secretary: Oneida R Ortiz;
President: (1978–79) Maritza F Eustatia (Librarian, University of the Netherlands Antilles, Jan Noorduynweg z/n, Curacao, Netherlands Antilles)
Publications: ACURIL Newsletter; Proceedings of Annual Conference

Afro-Asian Writers' Permanent Bureau*, 104 Kasr el-Aini St, Cairo, Egypt
Secretary-General: Youssef El-Sebai
Publications: Lotus (magazine of Afro-Asian writing in English, French and Arabic), Afro-Asian Literature Series

Arab Regional Branch of the International Council on Archives*, Dr E M El Sheneti, President, c/o The National Library, Midan Ahmed Maher (Post Office), Bab El-Khalq, Cairo, Arab Republic of Egypt
Secretary General: M J Abdusalim (Sudan)

Arab University Library Association*, c/o Chief Librarian, Kuwait University, Kuwait

Asociación Interamericana de Bibliotecarios y Documentalistas Agrícolas (Inter-American Association of Agricultural Librarians and Documentalists), IICA-CIDIA, Turrialba, Costa Rica
Secretary-Treasurer: Ana María Paz de Erickson
Publications: Bibliografía Agrícola Latinoamericana (up to 1975); *Boletín Informativo, Boletín Técnico* (up to 1979), *Boletín Especial* (these three bulletins sent free to members); *Informe RIBDA; Revista Aibda* (twice yearly, starting 1980)

Asociación Interamericana de Escritores (Inter-American Association of Writers)*, Casilla de Correo 4852, Humberto I, No 431, Buenos Aires, Argentina
Secretary: Maria E Pardo M de Gomis
Publications: Hoja Informativa; Biblioteca Interamericana

Asociación Latinoamericana de Escuelas de Bibliotecología y Ciencias de la Información (ALEBCI) (Latin American Association of Schools of Library and Information Science)*, Colegio de Bibliotecología, Universidad Nacional Autónoma de México, México 20 DF, Mexico
President: Judith Licea de Arenas
Publications: ALEBCI; Boletín Informativo

Association des Bibliothèques Internationales (Association of International Libraries)*, c/o Library, United Nations, CH-1211 Geneva, Switzerland
President: Th Dimitrov
Publication: Newsletter

Association des Ecrivains d'Expression française de la Mer et de l'Outre-Mer (Associāton of Writers in French in France and Abroad)*, 41 rue de la Bienfaisance, F-75008 Paris, France

Association européenne des Editeurs de Publications pour la Jeunesse (EUROPRESS-JUNIOR) (European Association of Publishers of Publications for Young People)*, 99 ave de la Brabançonne, B-1040 Brussels, Belgium
Tel: (02) 341276

Association for the Promotion of the International Circulation of the Press (Association pour la Promotion de la Diffusion Internationale de la Presse), Vereinigung zur Förderung des internationalen Pressevertriebes, CH-8002 Zürich, Beethovenstrasse 20, Switzerland
This is Distripress

Association internationale de Bibliophilie, c/o Bibliothèque nationale, 58 rue de Richelieu, F-75084 Paris cedex 02, France
This is a book collectors' association
Secretary-General: Jacques Guignard
Publication: Le Bulletin du Bibliophile (quarterly)

Association internationale des Documentalistes et Techniciens de l'Information AID (International Association of Documentalists and Information Officer)*
General Secretary: Dr Jacques Samain, 74 rue des Saints-Pères, F-75007 Paris, France

Association internationale pour le Développement de la Documentation, des Bibliothèques et des Archives en Afrique*, BP 375, Dakar, Senegal Tel: 34139 (International Association for the Development of Documentation, Libraries and Archives in Africa)
Secretary: E K W Dadzie

Association littéraire et artistique internationale (ALAI) (International Literary and Artistic Association)*, Cercle de la Librairie, 117 blvd St-Germain, F-75279 Paris cedex 06, France
Permanent Secretary: André Françon, 55 rue des Mathurins, F-75008 Paris, France
Founded: 1878

Association of Libraries of Judaica and Hebraica in Europe, Bibliothèque de l'Alliance Israelite Universelle, 45 rue La Bruyère, F-75425 Paris, France
Chairman: Mr Georges Weill
Librarian Publications: Chairman issues an occasional newsletter

Association of South-East Asian Publishers (ASEAP)*, c/o University of Malaysia Press, Pantai Valley, Kuala Lumpur, Malaysia
President: Encik Ghazali Yunua; *Secretary-General:* R Narayana Menon

Bibliographical Society of Australia and New Zealand (BSANZ)*, Department of English, Monash University, Clayton, Victoria 3168, Australia
Executive Secretary: Ivan Page
Publication: Bulletin of the Bibliographical Society of Australia and New Zealand

Books in Progress, Register of Literary and Technical Research, National Book League, Book House, East Hill, London SW18, UK
Administrator: Yolanta May
Confidential (i.e. not open for inspection) register of works in progress. Writers planning to start work on a book or research project may contact the register to elicit whether subject already covered by another writer. The fee for an enquiry is £3. There is no charge for writers registering works for inclusion.

Cámara Latinoamericana del Libro (CIAL) (Latin-American Book Association)*, Rafael Cañas 16, Dp 1, Santiago, Chile Tel: 40055

Centre de Documentation economique et sociale africaine (CEDESA) (Centre for African Economic and Social Documentation)*, 7 pl Royale, B-1000 Brussels, Belgium
Secretary-General: J-B Cuyvers
Publications: Bibliographical Enquiries, Documentary monographs

Centre international de documentation classique*, 14 rue Paul Deroulede, Bois Colombes, France
Publications: Bulletin des sommaires des 700 periodiques mondiaux et des livres reçus à la bibliothèque du centre

Centre régional de Promotion du Livre en Afrique (Regional Centre for Book Promotion in Africa)*, BP 1646, Yaoundé, Cameroun
Secretary: William Moutchia
Publication: Bulletin

Centro Di (International Documentation Centre), see under Italian publishers

Centro Regional para el Fomento del Libro en América Latina y el Caribe (CERLAL) (Regional Centre for Encouragement of Books in Latin America and Carribbean), Calle 70 No 9-52, Apdo Aereo 17438, Bogotá, Colombia
Director: Gonzalo Canal Ramirez; *Secretary General:* Lucila de Jiménez
Publications: CERLAL; noticias sobre el Libro y Bibliografía (news on books and bibliographies); *Boletín Bibliográfico del CERLAL* (current Latin-American bibliography)

Commonwealth Library Association, 2a Ruthven Rd, PO Box 534, Kingston 10 Jamaica Tel: 9264929
Secretary: Mrs C P Fray
Publication: COMLA Newsletter (quarterly)

Congress of South-East Asian Librarians IV (CONSAL IV), c/o National Library, Samsen Road, Bangkok 3, Thailand
Chairman: Mrs Maenmas Chavalit
Publications include: Proceedings of Congresses

Conseil International des Associations de Bibliothèques de Théologie (International Council of Theological Library Associations), Gereonstr 2, Cologne 1, Federal Republic of Germany
Secretary: J A Cervelló-Margalef

Distripress, see Association for the Promotion of the International Circulation of the Press

East and Central Africa Regional Branch of the International Council of Archives (ECARBICA)*, c/o Kenya National Archives, Jogoo House 'A', PO Box 30520, Nairobi, Kenya
Publication: ECARBICA Journal

European Association of Directory Publishers, (Association Européenne des Editeurs d'Annuaires) (Europäischer Adressbuchverleger — Verband), rue Antoine Dansaert 42, B-1000 Brussels, Belgium Tel: 5124499
President: Konrad Bryde; *Secretary-General:* Jean Lerat

F I D, see International Federation for Documentation

Fédération Internationale des Libraires (FIL), see International Booksellers' Federation

Fédération Internationale des Traducteurs (FIT) (International Federation of Translators)*, Heiveldstr 269, B-9110 Sint-Amandsberg, Belgium
Secretary-General: Dr Rene Haeseryn

Fundación Interamericana de Bibliotecología Franklin (Franklin Inter-American Foundation of Library Science)*, Buenos Aires, Argentina

Groupe des Editeurs de Livres de la CEE (EEC Book Publishers Group), 111 ave du Parc, B-1060 Brussels, Belgium Tel: (02) 5382167

Intergovernmental Copyright Committee, Copyright Division, UNESCO, pl de Fontenoy, F-75700 Paris, France
Chairman: André Kerever

International Association for Mass Communication Research (Association internationale des etudes et recherches sur l'information), c/o Professor J D Halloran, Centre for Mass Communication Research, University of Leicester, 104 Regent Road, Leicester LE1 7LT, UK
Secretary-General: Emil Dusiska

International Association of Agricultural Librarians and Documentalists — IAALD, Library, Ministry of Agriculture Fisheries and Food, Central Veterinary Laboratory, New Haw, Weybridge, Surrey KT15 3NB, UK
(Association Internationale des Bibliothécaires et Documentalistes Agricoles)
Secretary-Treasurer: D E Gray
Publications: Quarterly Bulletin; Current Agricultural Serials; Primer for Agricultural Libraries

International Association of Law Libraries (IALL) (Association internationale des bibliothèques de droit), c/o Vanderbilt Law Library, Nashville, Tennessee 37203, USA
Secretary-Treasurer: Professor Arno Liivak; *President:* Professor Igor I Kavass
Publications: International Journal of Law Libraries; IALL Newsletter; Directory

International Association of Literary Critics (Association internationale des critiques littéraires), 38 rue du Faubourg-St-Jacques, F-75014 Paris, France
President: M R André
Publication: Revue

International Association of Metropolitan City Libraries (INTAMEL)*, Hamburger Offentliche Bücherhallen, Gertrudenkirchhof 9, Hamburg, German Federal Republic
Secretary-Treasurer: F Andrae

International Association of Music Libraries (Association internationale des bibliothèques musicales), c/o Svenskt Musikhistoriskt Arkiv, Sibyllegatan 2, S-11451 Stockholm, Sweden
President: Prof Barry S Brook (City University of New York); *Secretary-General:* Anders Lönn
Publication: Fontes artis musicae

International Association of Orientalist Librarians*
Secretary-Treasurer: John E Leide, c/o Asian Studies Program, University of Hawaii at Manoa, 315 Moore Hall, 1890 East-West Road, Honolulu, Hawaii 96822, USA

International Association of School Librarianship, School of Librarianship, Western Michigan University, Kalamazoo, Michigan 49008, USA
Publications: Newsletter of the International Association of School Librarianship (quarterly to members); *Annual Conference Proceedings; Directory of National School Library Associations; People to Contact for Visiting School Libraries/Media Centers*

International Association of Sound Archives*, Imperial War Museum, Lambeth Road, London SE1 6HZ, UK
Publication: Phonographic Bulletin

International Association of Technological University Libraries (IATUL), c/o Bibliotheek Technische Hogeschool Twente, Campus Drienerlo, Postbus 217, Enschede, Netherlands
(Association internationale des bibliothèques d'universités polytechniques)
President: Dr G A Hamel; *Secretary:* Dr Sven Westberg, Chalmers Tekniska Høgskolas Bibliotek, Fack, Gothenburg, Sweden
Publications: IATUL Proceedings; IATUL Conference Proceedings

International Board on Books for Young People (IBBY), CH-4051 Basel, Leonhardsgraben 38a, Switzerland
Secretary: Mrs Leena Maissen
Publications: Bookbird (quarterly); *20 Years of IBBY; IBBY's International Guide to Sources of Information about Children's Literature, Congress Reports*

International Booksellers' Federation (IBF), Grünangergasse 4, A-1010 Vienna, Austria (Federation Internationale des Librairies (FIL), Internationale Buchhändler-Vereinigung (IBV))
General Secretary: Dr Gerhard Prosser

International Comparative Literature Association (Association internationale de littérature comparée), Institut de littératures modernes comparées, 17 rue de la Sorbonne, Paris 5e, France

Secretaries-General: Douwe W Fokkema, 31 Ramstr, Utrecht, Netherlands; Frederick Garber, State University of New York, Binghampton, NY 13901, USA
Founded: 1954

International Confederation of Societies of Authors and Composers (Confédération internationale des sociétés d'auteurs et compositeurs)*, 11 rue Keppler, F-75116 Paris, France
Secretary-General: Jean-Alexis Ziegler
Publication: Interauteurs

International Council of Theological Library Associations, see Conseil International des Associations de Bibliothèques de Théologie

International Council on Archives (Conseil international des archives)*, 60 rue des Francs-Bourgeois, 75003 Paris, France
General Secretary: Dr Carlos Wyffels
Publications: Archivum; ADPA/Archives and Automation; Bulletin of the Microfilm Committee; Bulletin of the ICA

International Federation for Documentation (Fédération internationale de documentation), PO Box 30115, 2500 GC, The Hague, Netherlands
Publications: FID News Bulletin; International Forum on Information and Documentation; R & D Projects in Documentation and Librarianship; FID Directory; Annual Report; Extensions and Corrections to the UDC (annual) Proceedings of Congresses and Seminars, UDC editions in several languages, Studies on Information Science, Manuals, Bibliographies and Directories

International Federation of Film Archives (Fédération internationale des archives du film), 74 galerie Ravenstein, B-1000 Brussels, Belgium Tel: (02) 5111390
Executive Secretary: Brigitte van der Elst

International Federation of Library Associations and Institutions IFLA (Fédération internationale des associations de bibliothécaires et des Bibliothèques), Netherlands Congress Building, Postbus 82128, 2508 EC, The Hague, Netherlands
Secretary-General: Miss M Wijnstroom
Publications: IFLA Journal including IFLA News, IFLA Annual, IFLA Directory, IFLA Publications (series of monographs, published by K G Saur, Munich)

International Fiction Association, Department of German and Russian, University of New Brunswick, Fredericton, New Brunswick, Canada
Publication: The International Fiction Review (biannual)

International Group of Scientific, Technical and Medical Publishers (STM), Keizersgracht 462, 1016 GE Amsterdam, Netherlands Tel: (020) 225214
Secretary-General: P Nijhoff Asser

International Institute for Children's Literature and Reading Research, UNESCO category C (Institut International de Littérature pour Enfants et de Recherches sur la Lecture)*, Fuhrmannsgasse 18A, A-1080 Vienna, Austria Tel: 433543
Director: Dr Richard Bamberger
Publications include: Bookbird; Jugend und Buch; PA-Kontakte

International Institute of Iberoamerican Literature, 1312 CL, University of Pittsburgh, Pa 15260, USA
Secretary-Treasurer: Bruce Stiehm
Publications: Revista Iberoamericana; Memorias

International League of Antiquarian Booksellers*, 5 Bloomsbury St, London WC1B 3QE, UK Tel: (01) 580 3976
President: Stanley Crowe (at above address); *General Secretary:* Dr Maria Conradt, Poststr 14-16, D-2000 Hamburg 36, German Federal Republic Tel: (040) 343236

International Publishers Association, 3 ave de Miremont, CH-1206 Geneva, Switzerland
Secretary-General: J Alexis Koutchoumow
Publication: IPA Publishing News
Founded: 1896

International Reading Association*, 800 Barksdale Rd, Newark, Delaware 19711, USA

International Scientific Film Library (ISFL) (Cinémathèque scientifique internationale), 31 rue Vautier, B-1040 Brussels, Belgium
Director-Curator: P Bormans
Publications: Catalogue of Films Deposited; The Pioneers of the Scientific Cinema (series)
Founded: 1961

International Study Group of Restorers of Archives, Libraries and Graphic Reproductions (Internationale Arbeitsgemeinschaft der Archiv-, Bibliotheks-und Grafikrestauratoren), Geschäftsstelle der IADA, Postfach 540, 3550 Marburg, German Federal Republic
Publications: IADA-Mitteilungen, in: Maltechnik

International Translations Centre, Doelenstr 101, 2611 NS Delft, Netherlands
The object of the Centre is to encourage, improve and facilitate the use of literature published in less accessible languages and of interest to science and industry, and also to promote international co-operation in this field.
Director of Centre: D van Bergeijk
Publications: World Transindex, Journals in Translation

International Youth Library (Internationale Jugendbibliothek), D-8000 Munich 22, Kaulbachstr 11a, German Federal Republic
Director: Walter Scherf
Publications: Catalogues of various exhibitions; *Prize Book Catalogue; The Best of the Best; Bewältigung der Gegenwart? Das Porträt der Frau in der zeitgenössischen Jugendliteratur*

Internationale Buchhändler-Vereinigung (IBV), see International Booksellers' Federation

Ligue des Bibliothèques Européennes de Recherche (LIBER) (League of European Research Libraries), c/o The Library, European University Institute, Badia Fiesolana, 50016 San Domenico di Fiesole, Italy
President: Dr K W Humphreys
Publication: LIBER Bulletin

Middle East Librarians Association, Room 032, Main Library, Ohio State University, 1858 Neil Avenue Mall, Columbus, Ohio 43210, USA Tel: (614) 4228389
Secretary and Treasurer: Marsha McClintock
Publication: MELA Notes (three times a year)

Nordisk Musikforleggerunion (Nordic Music Publishers Union), Gothersgade 9-11, DK-1123, Copenhagen, Denmark Postboks 1499, Vika, Oslo, Norway

Nordiska Vetenskapliga Bibliotekarieförbundet (Scandinavian Association of Research Librarians)*, Aalborg University Library, Postboks 8200, DK-9220 Aalborg OEst, Denmark
Secretary-Treasurer: Lizzi Kirkegaard

P E N, International (A World Association of Writers), 7 Dilke St, London SW3 4JE, UK Tel: (01) 352 9549
General-Secretary: Peter Elstob
Publications: Broadsheet; New Poetry (in collaboration with Arts Council) (English Centre); *Bulletin of Selected Books* (in English and French, with the assistance of UNESCO); various regional bulletins

The **Penman** Club, 175 Pall Mall, Leigh-on-Sea, Essex SS9 1RE, UK Tel: Southend-on-Sea 74438 (STD Code 0702)
Secretary: Leonard G Stubbs
Literary advice, criticism

Private Libraries Association (PLA), Ravelston, South View Rd, Pinner, Middlesex, UK
Executive Secretary: Frank Broomhead
Publications include: The Private Library (official journal); *Newsletter;* other publications: *Engraved Bookplates, European Ex Libris, 1950-1970; Cock-a-hoop* (vol 4 of the Bibliography of the Golden Cockerel Press); *Private Press Books* (annual bibliography of the work of private presses throughout the world)

S T M, see International Group of Scientific, Technical and Medical Publishers

Seminar on the Acquisition of Latin American Library Materials (SALALM)*, SALALM Secretariat, Benson Latin American Collection, The University of Texas at Austin, Austin, Texas 78712, USA Tel: 512 4715056
Executive Secretary: Anne H Jordan
Publications: Newsletter; Final Report and Working Papers; Microfilming Projects Newsletter; Bibliography Series

Société africaine de Librairie-Papeterie (African Society of the Stationery and Book Trade)*, (SALP), BP20, Libreville, Gabon

Société internationale de Bibliographie classique, 11 ave René Coty, F-75014, Paris, France
General Secretary: Juliette Ernst Tel: 3276790
Publications: L'Année philologique (Bibliographie de l'antiquité grécolatine 1923 ss)

Société internationale des Bibliothèques-Musées des Arts du Spectacle (SIBMAS) (International Society of Libraries and Museums for the Performing Arts)*, 1 rue de Sully, 75004 Paris, France Tel: 277 4421
Publications: L'Information du Spectacle, Bibliotheques et Musées des Arts du Spectacle dans le Monde (both France)

South East Asian Regional Branch of the International Council on Archives (SARBICA), c/o National Archives of Malaysia, Jalan Sultan, Petaling Jaya, Malaysia Tel: 551814/5
Chairman: Zakiah Hanum Nor (Malaysia)

Standing Conference of African Library Schools (SCALS)*, c/o School of Librarians, Archivists and Documentalists, University of Dakar, BP 3252 Dakar, Senegal
Publications: SCALS Newsletter

Standing Conference of African University Libraries (SCAUL)*, c/o E Bejide Bankole, University Librarian, University of Lagos, Yaba, Lagos, Nigeria
Publication: SCAUL Newsletter

Standing Conference on Library Materials on Africa (SCOLMA), c/o Institute of Commonwealth Studies, 27 Russell Sq, London WC1B 5DS, UK Tel: (01) 580 5876
Publication: African Research and Documentation (Subscriptions to Mrs P Naish, Centre for West African Studies, University of Birmingham, Birmingham B15 2SD, UK)

Union des Editeurs de Langue française (Union of French-language Publishers)*, 117 blvd St-Germain, F-75279 Paris cedex 06, France

Union of Writers of the African Peoples (Union des Ecrivains Negro-Africains)*, c/o Ghana Association of Writers, PO Box 4414, Accra, Ghana.
Among its objectives: to operate a writers' publishing co-operative; to encourage the use of Swahili as the common language of all black African peoples
Secretary-General: Wole Soyinka, Dept of Literature, University of Ife, Ife-Ife, Nigeria
Publication: African World Alternatives

West African Library Association (WALA)*, c/o Ghana Library Association, PO Box 4105, Accra, Ghana
Publications: West African Libraries Newsletter

United Nations Agencies with Publishing Activities

Food and Agriculture Organization of the United Nations (FAO), Via delle Terme di Caracalla, I-00100 Rome, Italy Tel: (06) 5797 Cable Add: Foodagri Rome
Director-General: E Saouma; *Chief Editor:* D J Grossman; *Sales, Advertising & Publicity Dir:* C Beauchamp
Subjects: Agriculture, World Food Situation, Economics & Statistics, Fisheries, Forestry & Forest Products, Nutrition, Legislation, Educational Materials
Founded: 1945
A specialized agency of the United Nations, the Food and Agriculture Organization was created in 1945. Since the purpose of FAO is to increase world agricultural production and raise the standard of living, all its publications are directed toward that goal. The FAO titles consist of monographs, periodicals, official records of the work of FAO, yearbooks and annuals — in sum, what the FAO describes as a 'world intelligence service on production, price and trade that covers almost every commodity used to feed, clothe and house people throughout the world'. Unsolicited manuscripts are automatically rejected. Technical articles of no more than 2,500 words on international aspects of the animal industry, forestry, and food and nutrition are occasionally accepted; no payment is made
ISBN Publishers Prefix: 92-5 (publications by Headquarters), 92-851 (African Regional Office), 92-852 (Regional Office for Asia and Far East), 92-853 (European Regional Office), 92-854 (Latin American Regional Office), 92-855 (Near East Regional Office)

Inter-Governmental Maritime Consultative Organization (IMCO), 101 Piccadilly, London W1, UK Tel: (01) 499 9040 Cable Add: Inmarcor Telex: 04423588
Subjects: Texts of International Maritime Treaties concluded under its auspices, Maritime Technical Publications
1978: 17 titles
ISBN Publisher's Prefix: 92-801

International Atomic Energy Agency (IAEA), Vienna International Centre, Wagramerstr 5, Postfach 100, A-1400 Vienna, Austria Tel: 23600 Cable Add: Inatom Vienna
Subjects: Nuclear Sciences, Safeguards, Safety Codes, Technical Assistance, Information Exchange, Energy Data Bank, Medicine, Food and Agriculture, Feasibility Studies, Market Studies, Training
Founded: 1957
The International Atomic Energy Agency is an international organization within the United Nations family, having the general purpose of seeking 'to accelerate and enlarge the contribution of atomic energy to peace, health and prosperity throughout the world'. The Agency's publications result, almost exclusively, from its own activities; published material is of intense interest only to a relatively small group of scientists and technicians and, therefore, unlikely to be published commercially.
ISBN Publishers Prefix: 92-0

International Institute for Educational Planning (IIEP), 7–9 rue Eugène-Delacroix, F-75016 Paris, France Tel: (01) 5042822 Cable Add: Eduplan Paris Telex: 620074
Dir: Michel Debeaurais
Publications Officer: John Hall
Subjects: Economics of education, costs and financing; administration and management of education (including statistics, methodologies, techniques and models); curriculum development and evaluation (including the qualitative aspects of education); manpower and employment; educational technology; etc
1979: 30 titles *Founded:* 1963
Established by UNESCO in 1963, IIEP is an international centre for advanced training and research in educational planning. The Institute's aim is to contribute to the development of education by expanding both knowledge and the supply of competent professionals in the field of educational planning. In this endeavour the Institute cooperates with interested training and research institutions throughout the world. IIEP is financed by UNESCO and by voluntary contributions from individual member states. The programme and budget of the Institute is approved by its own Governing Board.
ISBN Publishers Prefix: 92-803

International Labour Organisation (ILO), International Labour Office, ILO Publications, 4 route des Morillons, CH-1211 Geneva 22, Switzerland Tel: (022) 996111 Cable Add: Interlab Geneva Telex: 22271
Director-General: Francis Blanchard; *Chief, Editorial Services:* R P Payró; *Chief, Sales, Marketing & Foreign Rights Services:* I M C S Elsmark
Br Offs: 87-91 New Bond St, London W1Y 9LA, UK; 1750 New York Ave NW, Washington, DC 20006, USA
Subjects: Conditions of Work and Welfare, Cooperatives, Developing Countries & Technical Cooperation, Economics, Employment and Employment Creation, Holidays & Weekly Rest, Human Rights, Labour & Discrimination, Standards & Administration, Migration of Workers & Popular Questions, Productivity & Management Development & Training, Occupational Safety & Health, Statistics, Social Security, Trade Unions, Unemployment, Vocational Guidance & Training, Wages & Hours of Work, Worker's Education & Vocational Training, etc
Founded: 1919
Miscellaneous: Publishes periodicals: *International Labour Revue, Official Bulletin, Legislative Series, Social and Labour Bulletin, Bulletin of Labour Statistics, Year Book of Labour Statistics, Documents & Proceedings of the International Labour Organisation & the International Labour Conference, Labour Management Relations Series, International Labour Documentation, Occupational Safety and Health Series, Management Development Series*
From the creation of the ILO in 1919, publishing has formed an important part of its activities. The publishing work falls into six main categories: international exchange of factual information; analysis of trends in social affairs; issuing the results of ILO research, including comparative studies as a basis for international cooperation in solving economic and social problems; issuing the required reports for the discussions of international labour conferences leading to the adoption of international labour standards; providing government officials, employers and workers with practical information and guidance; and issuing official records.
This substantial publishing programme has over 1,300 titles in print which cover not only studies, monographs, handbooks and periodicals, but also reports on conditions and practices in different countries prepared for the General Conference, regional conferences and meetings for special industries and subjects.
ISBN Publishers Prefix: 92-2

International Telecommunication Union (ITU)*, pl des Nations, CH-1211 Geneva 20, Switzerland
Secretary-General: Mohamed Mili
The ITU was founded in 1865 as the International Telegraphic Union. It became the International Telecommunication Union in 1934 and a specialized agency of the UN in 1947. Structure: 4 permanent organs – General Secretariat, International Telegraph and Telephone Consultative Committee (CCITT), International Radio Consultative Committee (CCIR) and the International Frequency Registration Board (IFRB). It encourages world cooperation for the improvement and rational use of telecommunications.
ISBN Publishers Prefix: 92-61, 92-71

U N E S C O, see United Nations Educational, Scientific and Cultural Organization

U N E S C O Institute for Education (UIE), Feldbrunnenstr 58, D-2000 Hamburg 13, German Federal Republic
The UIE was created in 1951 with the financial support of UNESCO and a number of member states. It is funded by the German Federal Republic, UNESCO and other donors, and housed in premises provided by the City of Hamburg. It is a research centre which has enabled more than 2,000 scholars to participate in international cooperative research projects and has developed a particular interest in lifelong education. Major areas of the current research programme include the

relation of lifelong education to national systems of education, to school curriculum, to basic education, teacher training, evaluation and research. Publications include over 120 titles and the quarterly *International Review of Education*.
1977: 11 titles *1978:* 7 titles
ISBN Publishers Prefix: 92-820

United Nations, Sales Section, Publishing Service, 801 United Nations Plaza, New York, NY 10017, USA Tel: (212) 754 1234
Chief of Section: Bjorn Hafgren
European Office: Palais des Nations, Geneva, Switzerland
Chief of Unit: Roland Furstenberg
Subjects: Reference, Economics, International Trade, International Law, Social Science
Founded: 1945
Since 1946, United Nations has published more than 2,000 reports, studies, annual surveys, yearbooks, and monthly and quarterly periodicals in addition to the United Nations official records.
Reflecting the varied work of the Organization, the subjects include international trade, world and regional economic questions, international law, social questions, atomic energy, public administration, and literature concerning the role and activities of the United Nations.
ISBN Publishers Prefix: 92-1

United Nations Educational, Scientific and Cultural Organization (UNESCO)*, pl de Fontenoy, F-75700 Paris, France Tel: (01) 5771610 Cable Add: UNESCO Paris
Director-General: Amadou-Mahtar M'Bow; *Director of Publications:* Ramon Nieto; *Deputy Director of Publications:* E Wegman; *Programme Coordinator:* P Esway; *Programming of Publications:* G Provenchère; *Commercial Services:* D Kraatz; *Rights & Permissions:* Miss S Adlung
Subjects: Education, Culture, Reference, Communications, General & Social Science, Scientific Maps, Periodicals
Founded: 1946
Miscellaneous: Co-publish with commercial publishers under joint imprint.
The work of UNESCO, a specialized agency of the United Nations, is primarily concerned with programs in the scientific, educational and cultural fields. It provides assistance to its member nations for programs which develop and improve educational facilities, stimulate scientific research, encourage the exchange of ideas and the free flow of information and bring about mutual understanding of cultures. UNESCO now has more than 1,000 titles in print, intended for specialists in the fields of libraries, culture and art, international exchange, education, mass communications, museums and monuments, social sciences, and science and technology
UNESCO publishes eight periodicals and three series (issued irregularly) in the fields of social science, of mass communications and statistics.
ISBN Publishers Prefix: 92-3

United Nations Institute for Training and Research (UNITAR), 801 United Nations Plaza, New York, NY 10017, USA Tel: (212) 7541234 Cable Add: Uninstar
Subjects: Peaceful Settlement of Disputes, Transfer of Technology, Environment, Communications, Economic Development, UN Functions

Universal Postal Union (UPU), CP, CH-3000 Berne 15, Switzerland Tel: (031) 432211
Director-General: Mohamed Ibrahim Sobhi
1978: 38 titles *Founded:* 1874
ISBN Publishers Prefix: 92-62

World Health Organization (WHO)*, 20 ave Appia, CH-1211 Geneva 27, Switzerland Tel: (022) 346061 Cable Add: Unisante Geneva Telex: 27821
Chief, Distribution & Sales Section: E S Annaheim
Subjects: Reference, Medicine, Psychology, Social Science, Textbooks
The pattern of WHO publications derives, in part, from the work of earlier and similar organizations — the Office International d'Hygiène Publique, and the Health Organization of the League of Nations, from which WHO inherited certain functions.
The main purpose of WHO's publications programme is to convey information relating to the various aspects of medicine and public health.
1977: 135 titles (62 English, 38 French, 35 Spanish)
ISBN Publishers Prefix: 92-4

World Meteorological Organization (WMO), CP 5, CH-1211 Geneva 20, Switzerland
In early 1951, the WMO took over the work of the 73-year-old International Meteorological Organization; later that year, it became a specialized agency of the United Nations. It promotes world-wide cooperation in weather science by establishing a network of observation stations, helps to bring about the development of service centres, sets up systems of rapid exchange of information, standardizes statistics and observations, furthers the application of meteorology to aviation, shipping, water problems, agriculture and other human activities and encourages research and training
The publications of WMO include the records and reports of the World Meteorological Congresses; cloud atlases; manuals on nomenclature; weather reporting; and guides to regulations and instrumentation.
ISBN Publishers Prefix: 92-63

Other International Organizations with Publishing Activities

Association des Universités Partiellement ou Entièrement de Langue Française (AUPELF), Université de Montréal, BP 6128, Montréal, Canada H3C 3J7
Secretary-General: Maurice-Etienne Beutler
Publications: Journals Review, Directories
Founded: 1961

Association of African Universities (Association des Universités africaines), PO Box 5744, Accra North, Ghana
Secretary-General: L Mackany
Publications: Bulletin (twice yearly); *List of Staff Vacancies in African Universities* (monthly); *Creating the African University*; *Newsletter* (quarterly)
Founded: 1967

Association of Arab Universities, Scientific Computation Centre, Tharwat St, Orman Post Office, Giza, Egypt
Secretary-General: Dr M Mursi Ahmed
Publications: Bulletin (2 a year); *Directory of Arab Universities*; *Directory of Teaching Staff of Arab Universities*; *Proceedings of Seminars*

Association of Commonwealth Universities, John Foster House, 36 Gordon Square, London WC1H 0PF, UK
Secretary-General: Sir Hugh W Springer
Publications: Commonwealth Universities Yearbook; *ACU Bulletin of Current Documentation*; lists of scholarships, courses and entrance requirements etc (20 titles)
1977: 5 titles *1978:* 9 titles *Founded:* 1913
ISBN Publishers Prefix: 0-85143

Association of Information and Dissemination Centers*, PO Box 8105, Athens, GA 30603, USA
USA Secretary: D Wilde
Publication: ASIDIC Newsletter (quarterly — available only to members)
Founded: 1968

Center for Inter-American Relations, 680 Park Ave, New York, NY 10021, USA Tel: (0212) 249 8950
Publication: Review (English language journal devoted to Latin American/Caribbean literature and art)

Centre international de Documentation Concernant les Expressions Plastiques (CIDEP)*, Clinique des Maladies mentales et de l'Encéphale, 100 rue de la Santé, Paris 14e, France
Director: Dr C Wiart
Founded: 1963

Commonwealth Agricultural Bureaux, Farnham House, Farnham Royal, Slough, Berkshire SL2 3BN, UK Tel: Farnham Common 2281 Cable Add: Comag Slough Telex: 847964
Executive Director: N G Jones
Subjects: Agricultural Science, Applied Biology
Founded: 1929
ISBN Publishers Prefix: 0-85198

Council for International Organizations of Medical Sciences (CIOMS) (Conseil des Organisations internationales des Sciences medicales), Secretariat: c/o WHO, ave Appia, CH-1211 GenevaSwitzerland
Executive Secretary: Dr Z Bankowski
Publications: Calendar of International and Regional Congresses (annual); *Proceedings of Symposia*; *International Nomenclature of Diseases*
Founded: 1949

Council of Europe, Publications Section, Palais de l'Europe, F-67006 Strasbourg-cedex, France Tel: 614961 Telex: 870943
Secretary-General: Georg Kahn-Ackermann
Subjects: Economics, Sociology, Demography, Law, Conservation, Education, Culture
1978: 79 titles *1979:* 85 titles *Founded:* 1949

E U R O D I D A C (European Association of Manufacturers and Distributors of Educational Materials), Jägerstr 5, CH-4058 Basle, Switzerland
Director: Christine Ryffel

European Broadcasting Union (EBU), Ancienne Route 17A, CP 193, CH-1211 Geneva 20, Switzerland Tel: (022) 987766 Telex: 289193
Secretary-General: Dr Régis de Kalbermatten
Founded: 1950

European Organization for Nuclear Research (CERN) (Organisation européenne pour la recherche nucléaire), CH-1211 Geneva 23, Switzerland
Directors-General: Dr J B Adams, Professor L van Hove
Publications: CERN Courier (monthly in English and French), *Annual Report*, scientific and technical reports, articles in scientific periodicals, conference proceedings, press releases

European Space Agency, 8-10 rue Mario-Nikis, 75738 Paris Cedex 15, France
Director-General: Roy Gibson
Publications: Annual Report; Bulletin; Journal; Conference Proceedings; Scientific and Technical Reports and Memoranda; Procedures Standards and Specifications Series; Space Brochures
Founded: 1964

Intergovernmental Bureau for Informatics (Bureau Intergouvernemental pour l'Informatique) (Oficina Intergubenamental para la Informática)*, CP 10253, EUR, I-00144 Rome, Italy (Located at: Viale della Civilta del Lavoro 23, Rome)
Director: Professor F A Bernasconi
Publications: Quarterly newsletter
Founded: 1951

International Academic Union (Union académique internationale)*, Palais des Académies, 1 rue Ducale, B-1000 Brussels, Belgium
Administrative Secretary: M Leroy
Publications: Corpus Vasorum Antiquorum; Catalogue des Manuscrits alchimiques; Œuvres de Grotius; Dictionnaire du Latin médiéval; Tabula Imperii Romani et Forma Orbis Romani; Documents historiques inédits concernant le Japon; Corpus Philosophorum Medii Aevi; Etudes Islamiques; Monumenta Musicae Byzantinae; Catalogus translationum et commentariorum; Dictionnaires assyriens; Corpus Vitrearum; Dictionnaire Pâli; Corpus des Troubadours; Corpus des Antiquités précolombiennes; OEuvres d'Érasme; Fontes Historiae Africanae; Dictionnaires; Civilisations de l'Asie Centrale; Sylloge Nummorum Graecorum; Corpus Inscriptionum Iranicarum; Lexique Iconographique; Lexique de Codicologie; Corpus Constitutionnel; Atlas Linguarum Europae; Répertoires de l'Art; Inventaire critique du Ramayana; Oeuvres de Voltaire

International African Institute, 210 High Holborn, London WC1V 7BW, UK
Tel: (01) 405 0351
Director: David Dalby
Subjects: Africa and its societies: the application of research to practical needs in agriculture, nutrition, social anthropology, language, education, geography, history, the arts. Journal *Africa*
Founded: 1926
Miscellaneous: 2,500 institutions and individuals are subscribing members and the governing body includes representatives from 50 countries, 30 in Africa

International Association for the History of Religions (Association internationale pour l'Histoire des Religions)*, Hebrew University of Jerusalem, Jerusalem, Israel
Secretary-General: Professor Z Werblowsky
Founded: 1950

International Association of Universities (IAU), 1 rue Miollis, F-75732 Paris cedex 15, France
Founded: 1950
ISBN Publishers Prefix: 92-9002

International Astronomical Union (Union astronomique internationale), 61 ave de l'Observatoire, F-75014 Paris, France
General Secretary: Professor P A Wayman
Publications: Transactions of the International Astronomical Union and Symposia organized by the International Astronomical Union
Founded: 1919

International Audio-Visual Technical Centre (Centre Technique Audio-Visuel International)*, Foundation-Lamoriniérestr 236, B-2000 Antwerp, Belgium
Secretary-General: A J Salesse-Lavergne
Publications: Bibliographical References; Studies and Reports

International Bureau of Fiscal Documentation, Sarphatistr 124, PO Box 20237, 1000 HE Amsterdam, Netherlands
Tel: (020) 267726 Telex: 13217
Man Dir: Prof J van Hoorn, Jr
Subject: Taxation
Founded: 1938

International Centre for African Economic and Social Documentation (Centre International de Documentation économique et sociale africaine — CIDEAS)*, 7 pl Royale, Brussels 1, Belgium
Secretary-General: Dr J B Cuyvers
Subjects: Bibliographical index-cards; bulletin of information on current research on human sciences concerning Africa (all publications in both English and French)
Founded: 1961

International Committee for Social Science Documentation (Comité international pour la documentation des sciences sociales)*, 27 rue Saint-Guillaume, Paris 7e, France
Secretary-General: Jean Meyriat
Subjects: Bibliographies, Directories, *International Political Science Abstracts*
Founded: 1950

International Committee of Historical Sciences (Comité international des Sciences historiques), Union Bank of Switzerland, Lausanne, Switzerland
Secretary-General: Michel François, 270 blvd Raspail, F-75014 Paris, France
Publications: Congress Reports; Bulletin d'Information (1953-76); *Bibliographies*
Founded: 1926

International Committee on the History of Art (Comité international d'histoire de l'art), Institut d'Art et d'Archéologie, 3 rue Michelet, F-75006 Paris, France
Secretary-General: Professor Jacques Thuillier
Publications: Bulletin du CIHA; Corpus international des vitraux du Moyen Age; Repertoire d'Art et d'Archéologie (quarterly)
Founded: 1930

International Congress of Africanists (Congrès International des Africanistes)*, c/o Haile Selassie University, Addis Ababa, Ethiopia
Secretary-General: Dr Nicholas Otieno (Kenya)
Publication: Proceedings of the Third International Congress of Africanists (in English and French)
Founded: 1900

International Council for Philosophy and Humanistic Studies (ICPHS) (Conseil international de la Philosophie et des Sciences humaines), Maison de l'UNESCO, 1 rue Miollis, F-75732 Paris cedex 15, France
Secretary-General: Jean D'Ormesson
Publications: Bulletin of Information (biennially); *Diogenes* (quarterly)
Founded: 1949

International Council of Scientific Unions (Conseil international des Unions scientifiques)*, 51 blvd de Montmorency, F-75016 Paris, France
Secretary-General: Sir John Kendrew
Publications: ICSU Year Book; ICSU Bulletin
Founded: 1931

International Federation of Modern Languages and Literatures (Fédération internationale des Langues et Littératures modernes), University of Provence, 13100 Aix-en-Provence, France
Secretary-General: Professor André M Rousseau
Publications: Répertoire chronologique des Littératures modernes; Acts of the Triennial Congresses
Founded: 1928

International Federation of Philosophical Societies (Fédération internationale des Sociétés de philosophie, FISP), Universitat Bern, Institut für exakte Wissenschaften, Sidlersstr 5, CH-3012 Berne, Switzerland
Secretary-General: André Mercier
Publications: Under the auspices of FISP: *Proceedings of the International Congresses of Philosophy; An International Bibliography of Philosophy; Chroniques de Philosophie; Philosophers on their own work*
Founded: 1948

International Federation of the Societies of Classical Studies (Fédération internationale des Associations d'Etudes classiques), c/o Professor F Paschoud, 26 rue de Vermont, CH-1202 Geneva, Switzerland
Secretary: Professor F Paschoud
Publications: L'Année philologique; Thesaurus Linguae Latinae; other reference works
Founded: 1948

International Food Information Service, Editorial Office, Lane End House, Shinfield, Reading, Berkshire, RG2 9BB, UK
Joint Man Dirs: E J Mann, U Schützsack
Publication: Food Science and Technology Abstracts (monthly)
Founded: 1968

International Geographical Union (IGU) (Union geographique internationale), c/o Prof Dr W Manshard, United Nations University, 29th Floor Toho Seimei Bldg, 15-1 Shibuya 2-chome, Shibuya-ku, Tokyo 150, Japan
Secretary General: Professor Dr Walther Manshard
Publication: IGU Bulletin (twice yearly)
Founded: 1923

International Hospital Federation (Fédération internationale des Hôpitaux), 126 Albert Street, London NW1 7NX, UK
Director-General: M C Hardie
Publications: World Hospitals (quarterly; English with French and Spanish supplements)
Founded: 1947

International Mathematical Union*, Collège de France, F-75231 Paris, France
Secretary General: J-L Lions
Founded: 1952

International Music Council-IMC (Conseil international de la musique), UNESCO, 1 rue Miollis, F-75732 Paris cedex 15, France
Secretary-General: Dimiter Christoff;
Executive Secretary: Jack Bornoff
Publication: The World of Music (quarterly)
Founded: 1949

International Musicological Society, CP 1561, CH-4001 Basel, Switzerland
Secretary-General: Rudolf Hausler
Publications: An International Repertory of Musical Sources; *Acta Musicologica; Documenta Musicologica; Catalogus Musicus; RILM; RIDIM*
Founded: 1927

International Organization for Standardization (Organisation internationale de normalisation), 1 rue de Varembe, CP 56, CH-1211 Geneva 20, Switzerland
Secretary-General: O Sturen
Publication: International Standards
Founded: 1947

International Permanent Committee of Linguists (Comité international permanent des Linguistes)*, Stationsplein 10 (910A), Leiden, Netherlands
Secretary General: E M Uhlenbeck
Publication: Linguistic Bibliography (annual)
Founded: 1928

International Society for Music Education, The School of Music, The University of Canterbury, Christchurch 1, New Zealand
Secretary-General: John Ritchie
Publications: ISME Year Book; Reports of ISME Conferences and Seminars
Founded: 1953

International Statistical Institute (Institut international de statistique), Prinses Beatrixlaan 428, 2270 AZ Voorburg, Netherlands
Secretary-Treasurer/Director: E Lunenberg
Publications: Glossaries; Bibliographies, Journals
Founded: 1885

International Union for Conservation of Nature and Natural Resources (Union internationale pour la Conservation de la Nature et de ses Ressources), CH-1196 Gland, Switzerland
Director-General: David A Munro
An independent nongovernmental organization with membership in 105 countries, comprised of 51 States, 115 government agencies, 284 nongovernmental organizations and several hundred individuals
Publications: Bulletin (monthly); Annual Report; IUCN books on conservation and development, land and freshwater animals, marine and coastal ecology and management, national parks and other protected areas, and regional conservation; Environmental Policy and Law Papers; *Red Data Book; United Nations List of National Parks and Equivalent Reserves; World Directory of National Parks and Other Protected Areas*
Founded: 1948

International Union of Anthropological and Ethnological Sciences (Union internationale des Sciences anthropologiques et ethnologiques)*, Freie Universität Berlin, Berlin, German Federal Republic
Secretary-General: Professor Dr L Krader
Founded: 1948

International Union of Biochemistry (Union internationale de biochimie), c/o Department of Biochemistry, University of Miami, School of Medicine, PO Box 016129, Miami, Florida 33101, USA
Secretary-General: Professor William J Whelan
Founded: 1955

International Union of Biological Sciences (Union internationale des sciences biologiques), 51 blvd de Montmorency, F-75016 Paris, France
Secretary-General: Professor E Ayensu;
Executive Secretary: Dr P-H Bonnel
Founded: 1919

International Union of Crystallography (Union internationale de cristallographie), 5 Abbey Sq, Chester CH1 2HU, UK
General-Secretary and Treasurer: Professor S E Rasmussen (Aarhus, Denmark);
Executive Secretary: Dr J N King
Publications: Acta Crystallographica, Journal of Applied Crystallography, Structure Reports, International Tables for X-ray Crystallography, Molecular Structures and Dimensions, World Directory of Crystallographers, Index of Crystallographic Supplies, Symmetry Aspects of MC Escher's Periodic Drawings, Early Papers on Diffraction of X-rays by Crystals, Fifty Years of X-ray Diffraction, others

International Union of Geodesy and Geophysics (Union géodésique et géophysique internationale)*, Geophysics Laboratory, University of Toronto, Toronto 5, Canada
General-Secretary: G D Garland
Publications: IUGG Chronicle (bi-monthly); *IUGG Monographs* (irregular); *Proceedings of Assemblies*
Founded: 1919

International Union of Geological Sciences (Union Internationale des Sciences géologiques), c/o Geological Survey of Canada, 601 Booth St, Ottawa, Canada K1A 0E8
Secretary-General: W W Hutchison
Publications: Episodes, geological newsletter of IUGS (quarterly); short scientific articles and reports of current geological events
Founded: 1961

International Union of Nutritional Sciences (IUNS) (Union Internationale des Sciences de la Nutrition)*, c/o Professor J C Somogyi, Ruschlikon, Switzerland
Secretary-General: Professor J C Somogyi
Founded: 1946

International Union of Physiological Sciences, c/o Professor A G B Kovách, Experimental Research Department, Semmelweis Medical University, Üllöi út 78/A, H-1082 Budapest, Hungary
Member Union of ICSU (International Council of Scientific Unions, Paris)
Secretary: Professor A G B Kovách
Publication: Newsletter (biannual); *World Directory of Physiologists* (triannual)
Founded: 1953

International Union of Prehistoric and Protohistoric Sciences (Union internationale des Sciences préhistoriques et protohistoriques)*, Mosegaard, Højbjerg, Denmark
Secretary-General: O Klindt-Jensen
Publications: Inventaria archaeologica; Archaeologia urbium, etc
Founded: 1931

International Union of Pure and Applied Biophysics*, Physiological Laboratory, Cambridge CB2 3EG, UK
Secretary-General: R Keynes
Publication: Quarterly Reviews of Biophysics
Founded: 1961

International Union of Pure and Applied Chemistry (IUPAC) (Union internationale de Chimie pure et appliquée), Bank Court Chambers, 2-3 Pound Way, Cowley Centre, Oxford OX4 3YF, UK Tel: (0865) 770125/772834
Secretary-General: Professor G Ourisson;
Executive Secretary: Dr M Williams
Publications: Pure and Applied Chemistry (1 vol of 12 issues each year); *Information Bulletin* (3 issues 1979, 6 issues 1980)
Founded: 1919

International Union of Pure and Applied Physics (Union internationale de Physique pure et appliquée)*, Université Laval, Quebec G1K 7P4, PQ, Canada
Secretary-General: Prof Larkin Kerwin
Founded: 1922

International Union of Radio Science (Union radio-scientifique internationale), 81 rue de Nieuwenhove, B-1180 Brussels, Belgium
Secretary-General: Prof P Hontoy
Publications: Proceedings of General Assemblies of the URSI; Information Bulletin (quarterly); *Review of Radio Science* (triennial); *International Reference Ionosphere 1978*
Founded: 1919

International Union of the History and Philosophy of Science*, Division of the History of Science, Science Museum, London SW7, UK
Secretary-General: Dr F Greenaway;
Division of the History of Logic, Methodology and Philosophy of Science, University of Pittsburgh, Pittsburgh, Pa, USA
Secretary: Professor N Rescher
Founded: 1954

International Union of Theoretical and Applied Mechanics (Union internationale de Mécanique théorique et appliquée), c/o Professor Jan Hult, Chalmers University of Technology, Fack, S-40220 Gothenburg, Sweden
Secretary-General: Professor Jan Hult
Founded: 1947

Organisation for Economic Cooperation and Development (OECD), 2 rue André Pascal, F-75775 Paris, cedex 16, France
Secretary-General: Emile van Lennep
Founded: 1961
ISBN Publishers Prefix: 92-64

Stockholm International Peace Research Institute (SIPRI), Sveavägen 166, S-11346 Stockholm, Sweden
Director: Frank Barnaby; *Press Secretary:* Jean-Louis Sainz
Publications: SIPRI Yearbook; Monographs; occasional Research Reports
Founded: 1966
ISBN Publishers Prefixes: 91-85114 and 0-85066

Union of International Associations*, 1 rue aux Laines, B-1000 Brussels, Belgium
Publications: Yearbook of International Organizations (English and French editions); *Yearbook of World Problems and Human Potential; Transnational Associations International Congress Calendar* (monthly journal)

World Academy of Art and Science*, 50 Rockefeller Centre, 1009, New York, NY 10020, USA
President: Harold D Lasswell
Founded: 1960

World Council of Churches (WCC), 150 route de Ferney, CP 66, CH-1211 Geneva 20, Switzerland Tel: (022) 989400
General Secretary: Dr Philip A Potter
Founded: 1948

World Federation for Mental Health (Fédération mondiale pour la Santé mentale)*, University of the West Indies, Department of Psychiatry, Mona, Kingston 7, Jamaica
Administrative Secretary: Elaine Brooks
Publications: Bulletin (quarterly); *Annual Report*
Founded: 1948

World Intellectual Property Organization (WIPO) (Organisation Mondiale de la Propriété Intellectuelle), 34 Chemin des Colombettes, 1211, Geneva 20, Switzerland
Director-General: Dr Arpad Bogsch
Publications: Le Droit d'Auteur; Copyright; Noticias de la OMPI

World Medical Association (Association médicale mondiale)*, 1841 Broadway, New York, NY 10023, USA
Secretary-General: Sir William Refshauge
Publications: World Medical Journal; International News Items
Founded: 1947

World Psychiatric Association (Association mondiale de Psychiatrie)*, Psychiatrische Universitätsklinik, Währinger Gürtel 74-76, A-1090 Vienna, Austria
Secretary-General: Professor Peter Berner
Founded: 1961

World Veterinary Association (Association mondiale Vétérinaire), 70 route du Pont-Butin, Petit-Lancy/Ge, Switzerland
Secretary-Treasurer: Dr M Leuenberger
Publications: News Items (twice a year); *News Letters* (5 times a year); 1975 World Catalogue of Veterinary Films and Films of Veterinary Interest
Founded: 1959, as the continuation of the Permanent Committee for the International Veterinary Congresses (first Congress, 1863)

International Bibliography

Books

The African Book World and Press: A Directory, Hans Zell Publishers Ltd, PO Box 56, Oxford OX1 3EL, UK

African Books in Print, Mansell Information/Publishing Ltd, 3 Bloomsbury Pl, London WC1A 2QA, UK

Asian Book Trade Directory, Nirmala Sadanand Publishers, 35c Tardeo Rd, Bombay 34 WB

Australian and Pacific Book Prices Current, OP Books Pty Ltd, PO Box 591, Brookvale, NSW 2109, Australia

Author's and Writer's Who's Who, Burke's Peerage Ltd, 56 Walton St, London SW3 1BB, UK

Bibliographie nationale courante de l'Année ... des pays d'Afrique d'expression française (National Bibliography for the Year ... of Francophone African Countries), annual bibliography covering books and other materials, published in Francophone Africa since 1967, Ecole de Bibliothécaires, Archivistes, et Documentalistes, Université de Dakar, BP 2006, Dakar, Senegal

Bibliography of the Middle East; A complete and classified list of all the books published in about ten Middle Eastern countries, Damascus University Library, Damascus

Bibliothèques et Musées des Arts du Spectacle dans le Monde (Performing Arts Libraries and Museums of the World), Société internationale des Bibliothèques et Musées des arts du Spectacle, c/o President, 1 rue de Sully, F-75004 Paris, France

Book-Auction records, Dawsons of Pall Mall, Cannon Ho, Folkestone, Kent CT19 5EE, UK

The Book Revolution; a detailed examination and analysis of book production and distribution throughout the world, George G Harrap & Company Ltd, 182-184 High Holborn, London WC1V 7AX, UK

The Book Trade of the World, Verlag für Buchmarktforschung, D-2000 Hamburg 1, Beim Strohhause 34, German Federal Republic. André Deutsch Ltd, 105 Great Russell St, London WC1B 3LJ; R R Bowker Co, 1180 Ave of the Americas, New York, NY 10036, USA

Bookdealers in India, Pakistan and Sri Lanka, Sheppard Press, PO Box 42, Russell Chambers, Covent Garden, London WC2E 8AX, UK

The Bowker Annual of Library and Book Trade Information, Bowker Publishing Company, Erasmus House, Epping, Essex, CM16 4BU, UK

British Library Catalogue of Printed Books to 1975 (first volumes, of estimated total of 360, published in 1979), Clive Bingley Ltd, 1-19 New Oxford St, London WC1

Cassell's Directory of Publishing, Cassell & Co Ltd, 35 Red Lion Sq, London WC1R 4SG, UK

Catalogue général des ouvrages parus en langue française (Catalogue of Books Published in the French Language), Cercle de la Librairie, 117 blvd St-Germain, F-75279 Paris cedex 06, France

Clegg's Directory of the World's Book Trade, James Clarke & Co Ltd, 7 All Saints Passage, Cambridge CB2 3LS, UK

Cumulative Book Index, H W Wilson Co, 950 University Ave, New York, NY 10452, USA (world index of English language books)

Current African Directories; incorporating *African Companies,* a guide to directories published in or concerned with Africa, and to sources of information on business enterprises in Africa. CBD Research Ltd, 154 High St, Beckenham, Kent BR3 1EA, UK

Current European Directories; annotated guide to international, national, city and specialised directories and similar reference works for all countries of Europe, CBD Research Ltd, 154, High St, Beckenham, Kent BR3 1EA, UK

Dictionarium bibliothecarii praticum (ad usum internationalem in XXII linguis). (The Librarian's practical dictionary in 22 languages), Akadémiai Kiadó, H-1054 Budapest V, Alkotmány u 21, Hungary; and K G Saur KG, D-8000 Munich 71, Pössenbacherstr 2, Postfach 711009, German Federal Republic

Directory of East African Libraries, Makerere University Library, Kampala, Uganda

Directory of Government Printers and Prominent Bookshops in the African Region, Economic Commission for Africa, Africa Hall, PO Box 3001, Addis Ababa, Ethiopia

La Empresa del Libro en América Latina (Companies in the Book Trade in Latin America), R R Bowker Co, 1180 Ave of the Americas, New York, NY 10036, USA

Ensemble; international literary yearbook (Text in English, French, German) Verlagsgruppe Langen-Müller Herbig, D-8000 Munich 19, Hubertusstr 4, German Federal Republic

European Bookdealers: A Directory of Dealers in Secondhand and Antiquarian Books on the Continent of Europe, Sheppard Press Ltd, PO Box 42, Russell Chambers, Covent Garden, London WC2E 8AX, UK

European Law Libraries Guide (Guide européen des bibliothèques de droit), Morgan-Grampian Book Publishing Co Ltd, 30 Calderwood St, Woolwich, London SE18 6QH

European Library Directory, Geographical and Bibliographical Guide Leo S Olschki, Viuzzo del Possetto, I-50126 Florence, Italy

Guia de Bibliografia Especializada (Guide to Specialist Libraries), Brazilian Library Association, Ave General Justo 171, 4° anolar, Rio de Janeiro, Brazil (covers all Latin America)

Guide du Livre Ancien et du Livre d'occasion (Guide to Antiquarian and Second-Hand Books), Association of Antiquarian and Modern Booksellers, 117 Blvd St Germain, F-75279 Paris cedex 06

IFLA Directory (annual), International Federation of Library Associations, Netherlands Congress Bldg, Postbus 9128, 2508 EC The Hague, Netherlands

IFLA Standards for Public Libraries, International Federation of Library Associations, Netherlands Congress Bldg, Postbus 9128, 2508 EC The Hague, Netherlands

International Academic and Specialist Publishers' Directory, Bowker Publishing Co, Erasmus House, High St, Epping, Essex CM16 4BU, UK

International Authors and Writers Who's Who; information on 10,000 of world's leading writers, including index of pseudonyms and literary agents, Melrose Press Ltd, International Biographical Centre, Cambridge CB2 3QP, UK

International Bibliography of Reprints/Internationales Verzeichnis der Reprints, K G Saur KG, D-8000 Munich 71, Pössenbacherstr 2, Postfach 711009, German Federal Republic

International Book Trade Directory, Bowker Publishing Co, Erasmus House, High St, Epping, Essex CM16 4BU, UK Listing details of booksellers world-wide

International Books in Print, K G Saur KG, D-8000 Munich 71, Postfach 711009, Federal Republic of Germany; Clive Bingley Ltd, 1-19 New Oxford St, London WC1A, UK
Listing titles published in the English language outside the UK and USA

International Directory of Antiquarian Booksellers, International League of Antiquarian Booksellers, Poststr 14-16, D-2000 Hamburg 36

International Directory of Booksellers, K G Saur KG, Postfach 711009, Federal Republic of Germany

International Librarianship, UNESCO, pl de Fontenoy, F-75700 Paris, France

International Library Directory: A World Directory of Libraries, A P Wales Organization, 18 Charing Cross Rd, London WC2H 0HR, UK

International Literary Market Place, Bowker Publishing Co, Erasmus House, Epping, Essex CM16 4BU, UK (covers the world apart from the North American continent, which is covered by *Literary Market Place*)

International Maps and Atlases in Print, Bowker Publishing Co, Erasmus House, High St, Epping, Essex CM16 4BU, UK

International Publishers, Imprints, Agents and Distributors Directory, R R Bowker Co, 1180 Ave of the Americas, New York, NY 10036, USA

International Who's Who in Poetry, International Biographical Centre, Cambridge CB2 3QP, UK

Irregular Serials and Annuals: An International Directory, Bowker Publishing Co, Erasmus House, High Street, Epping, Essex CM16 4BU, UK

Jahrbuch der Auktionspreise (Yearbook of Auction Prices), Hauswedell & Co, D-2000 Hamburg 13, Pöseldorfer Weg 1, German Federal Republic (book auction prices in Germany, Austria, Switzerland and the Netherlands)

Libros en Venta (Books for Sale) annual supplements including Spanish language book production of the year from all countries, Turner Ediciones SRL, Alsina 1535, 8° piso, of 803, 1088 Buenos Aires, Argentina

Literary and Library Prizes, Bowker Publishing Co, Erasmus House, Epping, Essex CM16 4BU, UK

Literary Market Place, R R Bowker Co, 1180 Ave of the Americas, New York, NY 10036, USA (covers North American continent — rest of world covered by *International Literary Market Place*)

Major Libraries of the World: A Selective Guide, Bowker Publishing Co, Erasmus House, High St, Epping, Essex CM16 4BU, UK

A Manual of European Languages for Librarians, Bowker Publishing Co, Erasmus House, High St, Epping, Essex CM16 4BU, UK

Mason's Publishers, Kenneth Mason Publications Ltd, 13-14 Homewell, Havant, Hampshire PO9 1EF, UK

Private Press Books; an annual bibliography of the work of private presses throughout the world, Private Libraries Association, Ravelston, South View Rd, Pinner, Middlesex, UK

Publishers' International Directory/Internationales Verlagsadressbuch, K G Saur KG, D-8000 Munich 71, Pössenbacherstr 2, Postfach 711009, German Federal Republic

Publishing in Africa in the Seventies, University of Ife Press, Ile-Ife, Nigeria

Reference Resources on South Asia, Indian Librarian, 233 Model Town, Jullundur 3, India

Répertoire international des Editeurs et Diffuseurs de Langue française (International List of French-Language Publishers and Distributors), Syndicat national de l'Edition, 117 blvd St-Germain, F-75279 Paris cedex 06, France

Répertoire international des Libraires de Langue française (International List of French Language Bookshops), Cercle de la Librairie, 117 blvd Saint-Germain, F-75006 Paris, France

Subject Collections in European Libraries, Bowker Publishing Co, Erasmus House, High St, Epping, Essex CM16 4BU, UK

Ulrich's International Periodicals Directory, Bowker Publishing Co, Erasmus House, High St, Epping, Essex CM16 4BU, UK

Who's Who at the Frankfurt Book Fair: An International Publishers' Guide, K G Saur KG, D-8000 Munich 71, Pössenbacherstr 2, Postfach 711009, German Federal Republic

Who's Who in African Literature, Horst Erdmann Verlag für Internationalen Kulturaustausch, D-7400 Tübingen, Hartmeyerstr 117, Postfach 1380, German Federal Republic

Willings Press Guide, Thomas Skinner Directories, 41-43 Perrymount Rd, Haywards Heath, West Sussex RH16 3BS, UK

World Guide to Libraries, K G Saur KG, D-8000 Munich 71, Pössenbacherstr 2, Postfach 711009, German Federal Republic

World Guide to Library Schools and Training Courses in Documentation (Guide mondial des écoles de bibliothecaires et documentalists), Clive Bingley Ltd, Commonwealth Ho, 1-19 New Oxford St, London W1, UK

The Writers' & Artists' Year Book, Adam & Charles Black Ltd, 35 Bedford Row, London WC1R 4JH, UK

The Writers Directory, St James Press, 3 Percy St, London W1P 9FA, UK

Journals

African Book Publishing Record (text occasionally in French), Hans Zell Publishers Ltd, PO Box 56, Oxford OX1 3EL, UK

African Books Newsletter; a checklist of recent books published in English, arranged according to subject, K K Roy (Private) Ltd, 55 Gariahat Rd, PO Box 10210, Calcutta 700019, India

African Research and Documentation, Standing Conference on Library Materials on Africa, c/o Institute of Commonwealth Studies, 27 Russell Sq, London WC1B 5DS, UK

L'Afrique littéraire et artistique, Société Africaine d'Edition, 6 Passage Leblanc, BP 1877, Dakar, Senegal

Anales de Literatura Hispanoamericana (Annals of Spanish-American literature); Universidad Complutense de Madrid, Cátedra de Literatura Hispanoamericana, Ciudad Universitaria, 3, Madrid, Spain

Asian Book Development, Asian Cultural Centre for Unesco, 6 Fukuro-machi, Shinjuku-ku, Tokyo, Japan

Asian Books Newsletter; a checklist of recent books published in English, arranged according to subject, K K Roy (Private) Ltd, 55 Gariahat Rd, PO Box 10210, Calcutta 700019, India

Babel (International Journal of Translation), D-6000 Frankfurt am Main, Wolfsgangstr 148, German Federal Republic

Bibliografía actual de Caribe (Current Caribbean Bibliography) Caribbean Regional Library, Ponce de León 452, Hato Rey, Puerto Rico 00919

Bibliographie Documentation, Terminologie (Bibliography, Documentation, Terminology) (Editions in English, French, Russian and Spanish), UNESCO, Département de la Documentation des Bibliothèques et des Archives, 7 pl de Fontenoy, F-75700 Paris, France

Bibliophilie (text in English, French and German), Association Internationale de Bibliophilie, 58 rue de Richelieu, F-75084, Paris cedex 02, France

Bibliotheca Orientalis; international bibliographical and reviewing bi-monthly for Near Eastern and Mediterranean Studies (text in English, French and German), Nederlands Instituut voor Het Nabije Oosten, Noordeindplein 4-6, Leiden, Netherlands

Boletim Internacional de Bibliografia Luso-Brasileira, Calouste Gulbenkian Foundation, 98 Portland Pl, London W1, UK

Boletín Bibliográfico del CERLAL (current Latin-American bibliography), CERLAL, Calle 70 No 9–52, Apdo Aereo 17438, Bogota, Colombia

Bookbird, literature for children and young people, news from all over the world, recommendations for translation, International Institute for Children's Literature and Reading Research, Karl Werner, Bandgasse 34, A–1071 Vienna, Austria

Bulletin, Bibliographical Society of Australia and New Zealand, Department of English, Monash University, Clayton, Victoria 3168, Australia

Bulletin de l'Association internationale des Documentalistes et Techniciens de l'Information (Bulletin of the International Association of Documentalists and Information Officers), 74 rue des Saints-Pères, F–75007 Paris, France

CERLAL; noticias sobre el Libro y Bibliografia (news on books and bibliographies), CERLAL, Calle 70 No 9–52, Apdo Aereo 17438, Bogota, Colombia

Caribbean Quarterly, Department of Extra-Mural Studies, University of the West Indies, Mona, Kingston 7, Jamaica

Cumulative Book Index; a world list of books in the English language, H W Wilson Co, 950 University Ave, Bronx, NY 10452 USA

Edition; international book advertiser (text in English, French and German), Stauffacher-Verlag AG, CH–8055 Zurich 3, Birmensdorfer Str 318, Switzerland

Fichero Bibliográfico Hispanoamericano; monthly review of librarians, booksellers, distributors and publishers, Turner Ediciones SRL, Alsina 1535, 8° piso, of 803, 1088 Buenos Aires, Argentina

Francophonie-Edition, France Expansion, 336–340 rue St-Honoré, F–75001 Paris, France (review of French-language publishing throughout the world)

Germanistik, Internationales Referatenorgan mit bibliographischen Hinweisen (German Language and Literature: International Review Journal with Bibliographical References), Max Niemeyer Verlag, D–74 Tübingen, Pfrondorfer Str 4, German Federal Republic

Helikon Vilagirodalmi Figyelo. (Helikon Review of World Literature) (summaries in French and Russian), Akademiai Kiadó, H–1054 Budapest V, Alkotmány u 21, Hungary

Index translationum. International bibliography of translations, UNESCO, pl de Fontenoy, F–75700 Paris, France

International Cataloguing, IFLA Committee on Cataloguing, Longman Group Ltd, Journals Division, 43/45 Annandale St, Edinburgh EH7 4AT, UK

International Fiction Review, (bi-annually) Dr S Elkhadem, Dept of German and Russian, University of New Brunswick, Federicton, NB, Canada

International Library Review (quarterly), Academic Press Inc (London) Ltd, 24–28 Oval Rd, London NW1 7DX, UK

International PEN Bulletin of Selected Books (issued with the assistance of UNESCO) (text and title in English and French), International PEN, 7 Dilke St, London SW3 4JE, UK

Journal, East and Central Africa Regional Branch of the International Council on Archives, c/o Kenya National Archives, Jogoo House 'A', PO Box 30520, Nairobi, Kenya

Jugend und Buch (Youth and Books) (International Institute for Children's Literature and Reading Research), Karl Werner, A–1071 Vienna, Bandgasse 34, Austria (Co-Sponsor: Österreichischer Buchklub der Jugend)

LIBER Bulletin (text in English and French), Ligue des Bibliothèques européenes de Recherche, c/o The Library, European University Institute, Badia Fiesolana, Florence, Italy

Library & Information Science Abstracts (LISA), The Library Association, 7 Ridgmount St, London WC1E 7AE, UK

Newsletter, West African Library Association, c/o Ghana Library Association, PO Box 4105, Accra, Ghana

Nordisk Tidskrift för Bok- och Biblioteksväsen (Scandinavian Journal for Bibliography and Librarianship), Almqvist & Wiksell, Gebers Förlag AB, Gamla Brogatan 26, Box 159, S–10122 Stockholm 1, Sweden

Review; journal on contemporary Latin American literature in English translation, Center for Inter-American Relations, 680 Park Ave, New York, NY 10021, USA

Revista Interamericana de Bibliografía (Inter-American Review of Bibliography), Department of Cultural Affairs, Pan American Union, Washington, USA

SCALS Newsletter, c/o School of Librarians, Archivists and Documentalists, University of Dakar, BP 2006, Dakar, Senegal (official publication of the Standing Conference of African Library Schools)

SCAUL Newsletter, c/o E Bejide Bankole, University Librarian, University of Lagos, Yaba, Lagos, Nigeria (official publication of the Standing Conference of African University Libraries)

Scandinavian Public Library Quarterly, German Library Association — Publications Dept, Fehrbelliner Platz 3, D–1000 Berlin 31

South Asia: Library Notes and Diaries, University of Chicago Library, 5801 Ellis Ave, Chicago, Illinois 60637, USA

South Asian Book News, Duke University, Program in Comparative Studies on Southern Asia, Durham, NC 27706, USA (Co-sponsor: Duke University Library)

South-East Asian Archives, South-East Regional Branch of the International Counciil on Archives, c/o National Archives and Library of Malaysia, Jalan Sultan, Petaling Jaya, Malaysia

Third World First (a bi-monthly journal of arts, culture and letters of Africa), 10–14 Calcutta Crescent, PO Box 610, Apapa, Lagos, Nigeria

UNESCO Book Promotion News (text in English and French), UNESCO, Bureau of Documents and Publications, 7 pl de Fontenoy, F–75700 Paris, France

International Literary Prizes

Jane **Addams** Children's Books Award Established 1953. To the publisher and the author of books for children which are of literary merit and contain themes on brotherhood and peace. Awarded annually. Enquiries to Women's International League for Peace and Freedom, United States Section, 1213 Race St, Philadelphia, Pennsylvania 19107, USA

Afriscope/University of Ife Bookshop Ltd Prize*
For (1) the best piece of creative writing by an African author and published in Africa, (2) for an outstanding contribution in the field of African literature. Enquiries to Dr K Omotoso, Department of Arabic and Islamic Studies, University of Ibadan, Ibadan, Nigeria

Aleko International Competition Awards in Comic Short Story
Gold and Silver medals. No more than six first and second prizes are awarded annually. Enquiries to 'Narodna Mladez' (National Youth) Newspaper, Lenin 47, Blvd Sofia, Bulgaria

Alexander Prize*
For an essay in English on a historical subject; must be a genuine work of original research, not hitherto published, and not awarded any other prize. Silver medal, awarded annually. Enquiries to Secretary, Royal Historical Society, University College London, Gower St, London WC1E 6BT, UK

Hans Christian **Andersen** Awards
The International Board on Books for Young People (IBBY) awards this prize every two years to a living author and a living illustrator who, through their life's work, have made a distinguished contribution to international children's and young adult literature. (Until 1966 the prize was awarded for a specific book and to an author only.)
A jury of ten members, appointed by the Executive Committee of IBBY, makes the decision from selections submitted from member countries all over the world. Awarded in 1978 to Paula Fox, USA (author) and Svend Otto S, Denmark (illustrator). Enquiries to IBBY Secretariat, CH-4051 Basel, Leonhardsgraben 38a, Switzerland

Argentine Authors Society Medal of Honour*
For a contribution to literature. Honorary recognition. Awarded annually. Enquiries to Association of Argentine Writers, Uruguay 1371, 1016 Buenos Aires, Argentina

Arts Council Awards and Bursaries
Full details of the help given to playwrights is available on request. Enquiries to Drama Director, Arts Council of Great Britain, 105 Piccadilly, London W1V 0AU, UK

Austrian State Prize for European Literature*
A prize of 150,000 Austrian schillings and testimonial, established in 1964, are presented by the Austrian Minister of Education to a renowned European author for the sum of his work. Awarded annually. The 1978 winner was Simone de Beauvoir for her contribution to European literature. Enquiries to Bundesministerium für Unterricht, Postfach 65, A-1014, Vienna, Austria

Alice Hunt **Bartlett** Prize
To the poet the society most wishes to honour. In the case of poems translated into English, the prize of £200 will be divided equally between the poet and translator. The original poet must be living. Awarded annually. Closing date for entries each year is 31st December. Enquiries to The Secretary, The Poetry Society, 21 Earls Court Sq, London SW5, UK

Charles **Baudelaire** Poetry Prize*
To discover and encourage a poet under 21 years of age. $500. Awarded irregularly. Enquiries to International Who's Who in Poetry, International Biographical Centre, Cambridge CB2 3QP, UK

Bennett Award
For a writer of substantial achievement whose work has not received full recognition, or who is at a critical stage. $12,500, biennially. No applications or nominations accepted. The 1978 winner was Andrei Singavsky. Enquiries to The Hudson Review, 65 East 55 St, New York, NY 10022, USA

Anton **Bergmann** Prize
For the author of a historical account or monograph, written in Dutch and relating to a Flemish town or community in Belgium. 50,000 francs. Awarded every five years for a work appearing in print or (provisionally) in manuscript form, during the period. Foreign authors may also compete, provided work is in Dutch and is published in Belgium or the Netherlands. Winner for 16th period (1970–1975), Guy Vande Putte. Enquiries to Académie Royale de Belgique, Palais des Académies, Brussels, Belgium

David **Berry** Prize
For an essay in English on any subject dealing with Scottish history within the reigns of James I to James VI inclusive. Awarded every 3 years. Enquiries to Secretary, Royal Historical Society, University College London, Gower St, London WC1E 6BT, UK

Best Book of the Sea Award*
Established 1971. For a nonfiction book about the sea judged to have made the most valuable contribution to the knowledge and enjoyment of those interested in sailing. £250 and a gold medal. Awarded annually. Enquiries to John Coote FFPA, Nascreno House, 27 Soho Sq, London W1V 6QE, UK

Biennial International Art Book Prize
To promote the publication of fine illustrated books on archaeology, fine arts, architecture and applied arts, including photography. Prize consists of silver medals, free hotel accommodation in Jerusalem during the Jerusalem International Book Fair for the publisher and designer of the winning entry. Three to four books will also be awarded silver medals. All entries to be exhibited as a special exhibit of the International Book Fair. Awarded every two years. Enquiries to The Public Affairs Department, The Israel Museum, Jerusalem, Israel

James **Blish** Award
Awarded biennially for excellence in science fiction criticism which has been published in the English language. The prize is a bronze plaque and a small sum of money. First awarded in 1977 to Brian Aldiss for general criticism in 1975/76. Enquiries to Science Fiction Foundation, North East London Polytechnic, Longbridge Road, Barking, Essex RM8 2AS, UK

Bologna Fair Budding Critics' Prize
Awarded by jury of children on the basis of geographic requisites, originality of presentation and impression made by the work on the child reader. 1979 award to *Ein Tag im Leben der Dorothea Wutz* by Tatjana Hauptmann, published by Diogenes Verlag (Switzerland). Enquiries to Fiera del Libro per Ragazzi-Ente Autonomo per le Fiere di Bologna, Piazza Costituzione 6, I-40128 Bologna, Italy

Bologna Fair Graphic Prize for Children and Youth
Awarded for typographical, artistic and technical merit or innovation at the Bologna Children's Book Fair, by a Committee of experts made up of the G B Bodoni Study Centre in Parma. The prizes, consisting of golden plates, are awarded to the publishers of the winning works. The graphic prize for children was awarded in 1979 to *Histoire du Petit Stephen Girard* by Mark Twain, translated by Alphonse Allais, illustrated by Jean Michel Nicollet and published by Gallimard (France). The graphic prize for youth was awarded in 1979 to *Avrora* by Adela Turin and Annie Goetzinger, published by Dalla Parte delle Bambine (Italy). Enquiries to Fiera del Libro per Ragazzi — Ente Autonomo per le Fiere di Bologna, Piazza Costituzione 6, I-40128 Bologna, Italy

Booker McConnell Prize
Instituted in 1969. £10,000 donated by Booker McConnell Ltd and administered by The National Book League, for any full-length novel, written in English by a citizen of the British Commonwealth, Eire, Pakistan or South Africa. Any United Kingdom publisher who publishes works of fiction may enter not more than four full-length novels, with scheduled publication dates between 1 January and 30 November. Awarded in 1979 to Penelope Fitzgerald for *Offshore* (Collins). Enquiries to The National Book League, Book House, East Hill, London SW18, UK

Books Abroad/English-Speaking Union of the United States Best Book of Belles Lettres*
Instituted 1973, to foster creative writing by African and Asian writers in the English language. $2000. Awarded annually. Won in 1974 by R K Narayan for *My Days*. Enquiries to Professor Charles R Larson, 3600 Underwood St, Chevy Chase, Md 20015, USA

Juan **Boscan** Prize*
To the best Spanish and Hispano-American poets writing in Castilian language. 50,000 pesetas. Awarded annually. Enquiries to Barcelona Institute of Hispanic Culture, Calle de Valencia 231, Barcelona, Spain

Christo **Botev** International Prize for Revolutionary Poetry*
To distinguished authors. Gold medal and 2,000 leva. Awarded every five years. Enquiries to Bulgarian People's Republic State Council, Sofia, Bulgaria

Brasilia Prize for Poetry*
For poets writing in Italian, Spanish, French and Portuguese. Monetary prize and medal 'Amicia Italo-Braziliana'. Awarded annually. Enquiries to Brasilia City Government, Brasilia, Brazil

Brazil Theatre Prize*
For the best play written by a Latin American author. Enquiries to Brazilian Ministry of Foreign Affairs, Cultural Division, Brasilia, Brazil

Bremen Literature Encouragement Prize
5,000 DM awarded annually. Won in 1978 by Maria Erlenberger (Austria) for *Der Hunger nach Wahnsinn*; in 1979 by Uwe Timm for *Morenga*. Enquiries to Senator für Wissenschaft und Kunst, Freie Hansestadt Bremen, D-2800 Bremen 1, Federal Republic of Germany

Bremen Literature Prize
Given by Rudolf-Alexander-Schröder Foundation to German-speaking poets and writers in order to encourage literature. 10,000 DM awarded annually. Won in 1978 by Christa Wolf (German Democratic Republic) for *Kindheitsmuster*; in 1979 by Dr Alexander Kluge for *Unheimlichkeit der Zeit*. Enquiries to Senator für Wissenschaft und Kunst, Freie Hansestadt Bremen, D-2800 Bremen 1, Federal Republic of Germany

John W **Campbell** Memorial Award*
Founded 1973, for the best science-fiction novel in any language. First prize $600. Enquiries to the Secretary, T A Shippey, St John's College, Oxford OX1 3JP, UK

Caorle City Prize*
For the best published or unpublished book for young people which reflects the principles of modern European education. Must be written by a European. 1,000,000 liras. Awarded biennially. Enquiries to Istituto de Pedagogia, University of Padua, I-35100 Padua, Italy

Carducci Prize*
Established 1950. For poetry, monographs and essays on poetry and poets. 1,000,000 liras. Awarded annually. Enquiries to Bologna University, Bologna, Italy

Pierre **Chauveau** Medal
Established 1952. In recognition of an outstanding contribution to literature. Gold medal and $1,000. Awarded biennially. Enquiries to Royal Society of Canada, 344 Wellington St, Ottawa, Ontario, K1A 0N4 Canada

Cheltenham Festival of Literature Competition
An annual competition in association with the Cheltenham Festival of Literature which takes place between September and November. The closing date is in April or May. Enquiries to Festival Organizer, Cheltenham Festival of Literature, Town Hall, Imperial Sq, Cheltenham, Glos GL5 1QA, UK

Children's Book Award
Established 1974. For a new author who shows unusual promise. Awarded annually. Enquiries to International Reading Association, 800 Barksdale Rd, PO Box 8139, Newark, Delaware 19711, USA

Cholmondeley Award for Poets
Established by the Marchioness of Cholmondeley in 1965 for 'the benefit and encouragement of poets of any age, sex or nationality'. The non-competitive award is for work generally, *not* for a specific book and submissions are not required. Approximately £2,000 awarded annually. 1979 award to Alan Brownjohn, Charles Tomlinson and Andrew Motion. Enquiries to Society of Authors, 84 Drayton Gardens, London SW10, UK

Collins Religious Book Award
Founded 1969 to commemorate the 150th anniversary of the publisher William Collins Sons & Co Ltd. For the book which has made the most distinguished contribution to the relevance of Christianity in the modern world on one of the following subjects: science, ethics, sociology, philosophy, psychology and other religions. Open to living citizens of the UK, the Commonwealth, the Republic of Ireland and South Africa. Prize of £1,000 awarded every two years. Awarded in 1979 to W H Vorstone for *Love's Endeavour, Love's Expense* (Darton, Longman & Todd). Enquiries to William Collins Sons & Co Ltd, 14 St James's Pl, London SW1A 1PS, UK

Commonwealth Poetry Prize
Instituted 1972. For a first published book of poetry (in English) by an author from a Commonwealth country other than Britain. £500 awarded annually. Enquiries to Librarian, Commonwealth Institute, Kensington High Street, London W8 6NQ, UK

Albert **Counson** Prize*
For a scholarly work on romance languages. Monetary prize. Awarded every five years. Enquiries to Royal Academy of French Language and Literature, Palais de Académies, 1 rue Ducale, Brussels, Belgium

Count of Cartagena Prizes
Established 1929. For unpublished works by Spaniards or Latin-Americans written in Spanish on a theme to be decided for each competition. 90,000 pesetas. Awarded annually. Enquiries to Royal Spanish Academy, Filipe IV 4, Madrid, Spain

The Rose Mary **Crawshay** Prizes
Founded 1888. Awarded by the Council of the British Academy to women writers of any nationality for an historical or critical work of value on any subject relating to English literature. Preference is given to works on Byron, Shelley or Keats. One or more prizes awarded annually. 1979 winners: Elizabeth Murray for *Caught in the Web of Words* and Joan Rees for *Shakespeare and the Story*. Enquiries to Secretary, British Academy, Burlington House, Piccadilly, London W1V 0NS, UK

Franz **Cumont** Prize
For a work by a Belgian or foreign author dealing with the history of religion or science in antiquity, i.e. in the Mediterranean area prior to the time of Mohammed. No application necessary. The prize cannot be divided, except where one or more authors have acted in collaboration. 90,000 francs. Awarded every three years. Winner for 2nd period (1973–1975) Mr M J Vermaseren. Enquiries to Académie Royale de Belgique, Palais des Académies, Brussels, Belgium

Cyril and Methodius Prize*
For original research in the field of old Bulgarian literature, linguistics and art. 2,000 leva. Awarded annually. Enquiries to Bulgarian Academy of Sciences, 7th November 1, Sofia, Bulgaria

Isaac **Deutscher** Memorial Prize
Instituted 1968. For a work published or in typescript in any of the main European languages which contributes to the development of Marxist thought. £100 awarded annually. Enquiries to Isaac Deutscher Memorial Prize, c/o Lloyds Bank Ltd, 68 Warwick Sq, London SW1, UK

Ernest **Discailles** Prize
Alternates between the best work on the history of French literature and on contemporary history. Open to (1) Belgians, (2) Foreigners who are studying or have studied at the University of Ghent. 40,000 francs. Awarded every five years. Enquiries to Royal Academy of Belgium, Division of Letters and Moral and Political Sciences, Palais des Académies, Brussels, Belgium

Dobloug Prize
For outstanding literary work by one Norwegian and one Swedish writer 25,000 Swedish crowns. Awarded annually. Enquiries to Swedish Academy, Börshuset 11129, Stockholm, Sweden

Duff Cooper Memorial Prize
First awarded 1956. For a nonfictional literary work published in English or French. The Prize is the interest from a Trust Fund. Awarded annually. 1978 winner: Mark Girouard for *Life in the English Country House*. Enquiries to Lord Norwich, 24 Blomfield Rd, London W9, UK

Dutch (Flemish) Literature Grand Prizes
Established 1956. To the most outstanding prose writer or poet in the Netherlands and in Belgium writing in Dutch. 18,000 Dutch florins. Awarded annually. Enquiries to Netherlands Government, c/o Ministry of Culture, Recreation and Social Welfare, Postbus 5406, 2280 HK Rijswijk Z-H, Netherlands or Belgian Government, Ministry of Culture, Brussels, Belgium

The **Dutton** Animal Book Award
Inspired by the great success of Gavin Maxwell's *Ring of Bright Water*, the story of two otters, E P Dutton & Company, New York, in 1962 established an international literary prize of $7,500, to be given as an advance on publication to the author of the manuscript judged by the editors of Dutton to be the best book-length work of adult fiction or nonfiction relating to animals. In 1967 the award was raised to $10,000 and it has now been raised to $15,000. The contest is open to new authors and to previously published authors throughout the world, but manuscripts must be submitted in English. No manuscripts of fewer than 35,000 words are eligible. The contest is annual. The opening date is January 1, and the closing date is December 31. Enquiries to E P Dutton, 2 Park Avenue South, New York, NY 10016, USA

Mary **Elgin** Prize
For the encouragement of gifted new writers of fiction. £50, annual. Enquiries to Hodder & Stoughton Ltd, 7 Bedford Square, London WC1, UK

Camille **Engelman** Prize*
For the outstanding literary work of the year (published or unpublished) written in French. Monetary prize. Awarded annually. Enquiries to Royal Academy of French Language and Literature, Palais des Académies, 1 rue Ducale, Brussels, Belgium

English-Speaking Union Book Award
For the best non-technical work published in the English language by an author whose native language is not English. $2,000, annual. Enquiries to the English-Speaking Union, 16 East 69 St, New York, NY 10021, USA

Etna-Taormina International Poetry Prize*
Established 1951. To one or more poets. Awarded annually. Enquiries to Ente Provinciale Turismo, Largo Paisiello 5, Catania, Italy

European Cortina-Ulisse Prize
Instituted 1949 for a work of popular science on a set subject, first published in Europe during the 5 years prior to the year of award. A work published in a language other than Italian, English, French, German or Spanish must be accompanied by a printed or typed translation into one of these languages. 1,000,000 lire. Awarded annually. Enquiries to the Editor, *Rivista Ulisse*, Sezione Premio Europeo Cortina-Ulisse, Via Po 11, I-00198, Rome, Italy

Christopher **Ewart-Biggs** Memorial Prize
Established in 1977 to commemorate Christopher Ewart-Biggs, the British Ambassador to Ireland, who was assassinated in Dublin in 1976. This award is to be made annually to the writer of any nationality whose published work contributes most to peace and understanding in Ireland, closer ties between the peoples of Britain and Ireland, or to cooperation between the partners of the European Community. Entries should be in English and the prize is £1,500. In 1978 the award was to Dervla Murphy for *A Place Apart* (John Murray). Enquiries to Janet Riddell, The National Book League, Book House, East Hill, London SW18, UK

The Geoffrey **Faber** Memorial Prize
Established in 1963 by Faber and Faber Ltd as a memorial to the founder and first Chairman of the firm, this prize of £500 is awarded annually. It is given, in alternate

years, for a volume of verse and for a volume of prose fiction. It is given to that volume of verse or prose fiction first published originally in this country during the two years preceding the year in which the Award is given which is, in the opinion of the judges, of the greatest literary merit. To be eligible for the prize the volume of verse or prose fiction in question must be by a writer who is: (a) not more than forty years old at the date of publication, (b) a citizen of the United Kingdom and Colonies, of any other Commonwealth state, of the Republic of Ireland or of the Republic of South Africa. There are three judges, who are reviewers of poetry or fiction as the case may be, and they are nominated each year by the editors or literary editors of newspapers and magazines which regularly publish such reviews. Faber and Faber invite nominations from such editors and literary editors. No submissions for the prize are to be made. The 1979 prize was awarded to Timothy Mo for *The Monkey King* (Deutsch). Enquiries to Faber & Faber Ltd, 3 Queen Sq, London WC1N 3AU, UK

Antonio **Feltrinelli** Prize
Each year the Lincei Academy (the National Italian Academy of Sciences) awards Antonio Feltrinelli prizes for accomplishment in the various branches of sciences, humanities, and literature. These prizes were instituted by an Italian businessman who died in 1942 and bequeathed his fortune to the Academy for the purpose of 'rewarding toil, study, intelligence..those men who with greater success distinguished themselves with high achievements in art and science, since they are the true benefactors of their own country as well as of all humanity'. The literature award is granted every five years and the amount varies — the 1977 prize was approximately $30,000. Enquiries to Accademia Nazionale dei Lincei, Via della Lungara 10, I-00165 Rome, Italy

City of **Florence** International Poetry Prize*
Established 1955. For an outstanding book of poetry. 1,000,000 liras and Dante Alighieri Medal. The Medal of the Community of Florence (Comune di Firenze) to the publisher of the award-winning poetry. Awarded annually. Enquiries to Florence City Prize, c/o Nuovo Cenacolo Fiorentino, Piazza Pietro Leopoldo 11, Florence, Italy

Foreign Poetry Prize*
Monetary Prize. Enquiries to Recontres Poetiques du Mont-Saint-Michel, rue Saint Michel, Granville (Manche), France

Formentor Prize*
For fiction sponsored by publishers from 14 nations. Enquiries to Nuovo Cenacolo Fiorentino, Piazza Pietro Leopoldo II, Florence, Italy

Franco-German Friendship Prize*
For any work of literature, theatre, sociology, art or psychology that furthers good relations between France and Germany. Monetary prize. Awarded annually. Enquiries to Franco-German Association, 168 Quai de Javel, Paris 15, France

French Academy, Foreigner's Book Award*
For the best book written in French by an author of any nationality other than French. Medal. Enquiries to French Academy, Institut de France, 23 Quai de Conti, F-75006 Paris, France

French Language Prize*
Established 1914. For work done abroad in the best interests of the French language. 50 francs; two prizes of 20 francs and medals. Awarded annually. Enquiries to French Academy, Institut de France, 23 Quai de Conti, F-75006 Paris, France

Rómulo **Gallegos** International Novel Prize
The prize was established in 1965 by the National Institute of Culture and Fine Arts of the Republic of Venezuela. Originally instituted to mark the 80th anniversary of the birth of the illustrious author Rómulo Gallegos, which was celebrated in August 1964, the first award was made in 1967, the 400th anniversary of the founding of Caracas — birthplace of the novelist. Competition is open to any writer from Latin America, Spain or the Philippines whose novel is written in Spanish and has been published originally in one of the countries of the above designated areas. The amount of the prize is approximately $22,223 and will be granted every five years — the next award to be in 1982. Enquiries to Consejo Nacional de la Cultura, Premio Internacional de Novela 'Rómulo Gallegos', Apdo de Correos 50995, Caracas 105, Venezuela
or from Centro de Estudios Latinoamericanos 'Rómulo Gallegos', Apdo 75667, Caracas 107, Venezuela

German Peace Prize
The Peace Prize of the German Book Trade (Friendenspreis des Deutschen Buchhandels) is awarded annually during the Frankfurt Book Fair. The prize is supported by the Boersenverein des Deutschen Buchhandels (organization of the German Book Trade) and is awarded without regard to nationality, race or creed. Prize of DM 25,000 since 1979 (DM 10,000 up to 1978). 1977 award to Leszek Kolakowski (Poland, living in Oxford). Enquiries to Boersenverein des Deutschen Buchhandels, Friedenspreisarchiv, Grosser Hirschgraben 17-21, D-6000 Frankfurt am Main, Federal Republic of Germany

The **German Youth** Book Award
The German Youth Book Award is given by the Federal Ministry for Youth, Family and Health. The selection of the books and the arrangements for granting the award are in the hands of the Arbeitskreis für Jugendliteratur eV, a body in which the organizations concerned with promoting good books for the young in Germany are represented. The selection is restricted to books published in the German language, primarily books from the Federal Republic of Germany, Austria and Switzerland (translations included). The rules for the award have been altered periodically. Since 1971 the award consists of a total of five prizes, each DM 7,500 which can be awarded for picture books, fiction, nonfiction and for appreciation of outstanding achievement. 1979 prizes to Janosch for *Oh, wie schön ist Panama* (Verlag Beltz und Gelberg), Tormod Haugen for *Die Nachtvögel* (Benziger Verlag), Virginia Allen Jensen and Dorcas Woodbury Haller for *Was ist das?* (Verlag Sauerländer), Peter Parks for *Das Leben unter Wasser* (Tessloff Verlag), Rosemarie Wildermuth for *Heute — und die 30 Jahre davor* (Ellermann Verlag). Enquiries to Arbeitskreis für Jugendliteratur eV, Elisabethstr 15, 8 Munich 40, Federal Republic of Germany

Golden Eagle Award of the Festival International du Livre
This festival, held in Nice, annually awards the Golden Eagle Prize, worth 30,000 francs, to an author of any nationality for his total literary work. The recipient of the award is selected by an international jury consisting of well-known authors and literary critics. In 1979 the award went to Octavio Paz. Enquiries to Festival International du Livre, 5 rue Stanislas, 75006 Paris, France

Grand Prize for Children's Literature*
For an unpublished children's book in the French language. Monetary prize. Awarded annually. Enquiries to Association 'Salon de l'Enfance', 11 rue Anatole de la Forge, Paris 17, France

Grand Prize for the Dissemination of the French Language*
For work contributing to the dissemination of the French language. Monetary prize. Enquiries to French Academy, Institut de France, 23 Quai de Conti, F-75006 Paris, France

The **Guardian Award** for Children's Fiction
The Guardian's annual prize of £150 (subject to revision) for an outstanding work of fiction for children by a British or Commonwealth writer, instituted in 1967. In 1979 the award went to Andrew Davies for *Conrad's War* (Blackie). Enquiries to Literary Editor, The Guardian, 119 Farringdon Rd, London EC1R 3ER, UK

The **Guardian Fiction** Prize
Instituted in 1965 and awarded annually. The prize of £500 is given for a novel published by a British or Commonwealth writer and is intended to encourage ambitious and original work by British writers. The judges are the Literary Editor and fiction reviewers of *The Guardian*. In 1979 the prize was awarded jointly to D Marechera for *House of Hunger* (Heinemann Educational) and Neil Jordan for *Light in Tunisia* (Writers and Readers Publishing Co-operative). Enquiries to Literary Editor, The Guardian, 119 Farringdon Rd, London EC1R 3ER, UK

Heredia Prize*
Given in alternate years to (1) a Latin American writer for a piece of prose or poetry written in French; (2) the author of a collection of sonnets (printed or typed). Monetary award. Awarded annually. Enquiries to French Academy, Institut de France, 23 Quai de Conti, F-75006 Paris, France

The Georgette **Heyer** Historical Novel Prize
Established in 1977 for previously unpublished outstanding historical novel written in English. Annual award of £1,500. Awarded in 1980 to Lynn Guest for *Children of Hachiman* (The Bodley Head). Enquiries to The Bodley Head, 9 Bow St, Covent Garden, London WC2E 7AL, UK or Transworld Publishers Ltd, Century Ho, 61-63 Uxbridge Rd, Ealing W5 5SA, UK

David **Higham** Prize for Fiction
Founded 1975. For the best first novel or book of short stories, in the opinion of the judges, written in English by a citizen of the Commonwealth, Republic of Ireland or Republic of South Africa. Prize of £500 awarded annually. Awarded in 1978 to Leslie Norris for *Sliding* (J M Dent). Enquiries to Janet Riddell, The National Book League, Book House, East Hill, London SW18, UK

The **Hugo** Awards
Established 1953, for the best science fiction writing in several categories. Chrome-plated rocket ship. Awarded annually. Enquiries to c/o Howard DeVore, 4705 Weddel St, Dearborn Heights, Michigan 48125, USA

International Grand Prize for Poetry*
For poetry by a living author. Monetary prize. Awarded every two years. Enquiries to International House of Poetry, 147 Chaussée de Maecht, Brussels, Belgium

International Literary Braille Competition Awards*
Established 1940. To an individual who is legally blind. Cash prizes in the categories of fiction, nonfiction and poetry. Awarded every five years. Enquiries to Jewish Braille Institute of America Inc, 110 East 30th St, New York, NY 10016, USA

International Literary Peace Prize*
For the best literary work or collection of works which reflect the idea of peace in the world. Monetary prize. Awarded annually. Enquiries to Administrative Council of the International Peace Prize, Palais des Congres, Esplanade de l'Europe, Liège, Belgium

International Prize for the First Novel*
For a novel written in, or translated into French. Monetary prize and publication of the book by the Julliard Publishing House. Awarded annually. Enquiries to International Prize for the First Novel, Selection Committee, 34 rue de l'Universite, Paris 7, France

International Prize of French Friendship
For poetry written in French by a foreigner. Awarded biennially. Last awarded in 1979. Enquiries to Society of French Poets, 38 rue du Faubourg St Jacques, F-75014 Paris, France

International Publication Cultural Award*
Awarded for the book published in Japan in English or with a summary in English which has made the most outstanding achievement in the presentation of Japanese culture to people abroad. Enquiries to Secretary, Publishers Association for Cultural Exchange, 2-1 Sarugaku-cho, 1-chome, Chiyoda-ku, Tokyo, Japan

International Publications Cultural Prize
Established 1965. To stimulate the development of Japanese publications in foreign languages, and to promote cultural exchange between Japan and other countries. Awarded irregularly. Enquiries to Japanese Ministry of Foreign Affairs and Publishers Association for Cultural Exchange, Shin Nichi-Bo Building, 1-2-1 Sarugaku-cho, Kanda, Chiyoda-Ku, Tokyo, Japan

International Who's Who in Poetry Awards*
To discover new poets and to encourage existing poets. Prizes total $2,500; First prize: $1,000. Awarded irregularly. Enquiries to International Who's Who in Poetry, International Biographical Centre, Cambridge CB2 3QP, UK

Irish-American Cultural Institute Literary Awards
Established 1967. For writers in the Irish or English language. Three prizes: $5,600, $2,800, and $1,400. Awarded for each language in alternate years. Awarded in 1976 to Breandán Ó hEithir and in 1977 to John Montague, poet. Enquiries to Irish-American Cultural Institute, 683 Osceola Ave, St Paul, Minnesota 55105, USA

Japan Translation Prize
To encourage translation from and into Japanese language. Honorary recognition and trophy. Awarded annually. Enquiries to Japan Society of Translators, Room 208, Shiba Mansion, 5-11-6, Toranomon, Minato-Ku, Tokyo, Japan

The **Jerusalem** Prize
This international prize of $3,000 is awarded during the Jerusalem International Book Fair which is held every two years. The award is made to an author or philosopher whose life's work has been devoted to the ideal of man's freedom in society. In 1979 the winner was Sir Isaiah Berlin. Enquiries to Mr Gershon Polak, Executive Director, Book Fair, 22 Jaffa Rd, Jerusalem 91000, Israel

Jewish Chronicle — Harold H Wingate Book Awards
Instituted in 1977 by the *Jewish Chronicle* and the Wingate Foundation, and administered by the National Book League. Awards of £1,000 each are made annually for a work of fiction and of nonfiction which stimulate an interest in Jewish themes. They are aimed equally at encouraging writers and scholars to handle Jewish themes and stimulating an awareness of these subjects among the reading public. Awarded in 1978 to Dan Jacobson for *Confessions of Josef Baisz* (fiction) and Lionel Kochen for *The Jew and His History* (nonfiction). Enquiries to Janet Riddell, The National Book League, Book House, East Hill, London SW18, UK

Stanislas **Julien** Prize
For the best work related to China. Monetary prize. Awarded annually. Enquiries to Academy of Inscriptions and Belles-Lettres, 23 Quai de Conti, F-75006 Paris, France

Kalinga Prize
This prize, awarded annually by UNESCO, was established in 1951 by the Kalinga Foundation Trust, for the dual purpose of recognizing outstanding interpretation of science to the general public and of strengthening scientific and cultural links between India and other nations. The recipient of the prize is selected by an international jury and may be anyone who has contributed to the promotion of the public understanding of science and technology. The winner receives a cash prize of £1,000 sterling. The award takes its name from an ancient empire of the Indian subcontinent, which was conquered in the third century BC by the Emperor Asoka, who was so appalled by the cost of his conquest in terms of human life and suffering that he swore never to wage war again. Awarded in 1977 to Fernand Seguin (Canada). Enquiries to UNESCO SC/SER/SCW, 7 pl de Fontenoy, F-75700 Paris, France

Jomo **Kenyatta** Prize for Literature*
For the most outstanding work of literature in English or Swahili published in the preceding year (July-June) and written by a citizen of Kenya, Uganda or Tanzania. Prize of 10,000 Kenya shillings (half each for the best English and the best Swahili books). Awarded annually. Enquiries to Kenya Publishers' Association, PO Box 72532, Nairobi, Kenya

The **Lanchester** Prize
Since 1954, The Operations Research Society of America has awarded an annual prize (now $2,000) for the best paper in English on operations research. Occasionally, it is awarded to a book. The prize commemorates the work of Frederick W Lanchester (1868-1946), an automotive and aeronautical pioneer. Enquiries to Business Manager, Operations Research Society of America, 428 East Preston St, Baltimore, Md 21202, USA

Latin Friendship Prize*
Established 1958. For the work of a French, or Latin-American, writer which expresses solidarity of Latin countries and Latin culture of Europe or America. Monetary prize. Enquiries to Amitiés Latines, Impasse Truillot, Paris 9, France

Lazarillo Prize*
To Spanish and Latin-American candidates in the following categories: (1) to the author of the best book for children and teenagers; (2) for the best illustration of a book for children; (3) to a publishing house. Monetary prizes and honorary citations. Awarded annually. Enquiries to Spanish Ministry of Information and Tourism, Ave del Generalisimo 39, Madrid 16, Spain

Pierre **Lecomte** du Nouy Award*
Established 1954. For an outstanding essay, biography, autobiography, or other work concerning the spiritual life of our epoch, and the defence of human dignity. Silver medal and $2,000. Awarded annually alternately for works written in French or translated into French, and for similar literary works published in English. Enquiries to Lecomte du Nouy Association, United States Trust Co, 45 Wall St, New York, NY 10005, USA

Manchester Odd Fellows Social Concern Annual Book Awards
Established 1977. Two prizes of £500 ech are awarded for the book, or pamphlet of not less than 10,000 words, that provides the most stimulating impetus for the improvement in living conditions within fields of social concern (to be specified each year). Entries must first have appeared in English and been written by citizens of the UK, Commonwealth, Republic of Ireland, Pakistan or South Africa. The 1978 winners were Gill Brason for *The Ungreen Park* and Ruth Lister and Frank Field for *Wasted Labour*, and the 1979 winners were Merren Parker and David Mauger for *Children with Cancer: A Handbook for Families and Helpers* (Cassell), and Michael Rutter, Barbara Maugham, Peter Mortimer, Janet Austin with Alan Smith for *Fifteen Thousand Hours: Secondary Schools and their Effects on Children* (Open Books). Enquiries to Janet Riddell, The National Book League, Book House, East Hill, London SW18, UK

Mandat des Poètes Prize*
Founded in 1950 by Pierre Béarn, to aid a French-language poet of talent, young or old, in time of need. Awarded annually. Enquiries to Pierre Béarn, 60 rue Monsieur-le-Prince, F-75006 Paris, France

The **Man in His Environment** Book Award
In February 1969, E P Dutton & Company established The Man in His Environment Book Award. This prize is offered annually for an unpublished manuscript written in English dealing with the past, present or future of man in his environment, natural or manmade. Dutton guarantees a minimum of $10,000 advance on publication against all earnings. The contest is open to new authors and to authors whose work has already been published, to authors in the United States and abroad. Enquiries to Man in His Environment Book Award, E P Dutton, 2 Park Ave South, New York, NY 10016, USA

Katherine Mansfield Menton Memorial Prize
Instituted 1959. Two prizes awarded for published short stories, one English and one French. Just over £100 each. Awarded triennially (next award 1981). Enquiries to The Secretary, English PEN Centre, 7 Dilke St, London SW3 4JE, UK (Enquiries regarding the French short story to Monsieur Dimitri Stolypine, General Secretary, Maison Internationale des PEN Clubs, 6 rue François Miron, Paris IV, France – marked Prix Menton)

Medicis Foreign Prize*
For the best foreign novel appearing in French during the preceding year. Monetary prize. Awarded annually. In 1976 the prize was awarded to Doris Lessing for *The Golden Notebook*. Enquiries to Medicis Prize, c/o Francine Mallet, 25 rue Dombasle, Paris 15, France

Ramón Menéndez Pidal Prize
For an outstanding work in the fields of Spanish linguistics or Spanish literature. 30,000 pesetas. Awarded biennially. Enquiries to Royal Spanish Academy, Felipe IV No 6, Madrid, Spain

Monceau Prize*
For a novel by a French-speaking author of any nation except metropolitan France. Monetary prize. Awarded annually. Enquiries to Centre of Expansion of the French Culture, 1 pl Raynouard, Paris 16, France

National Tourism Prize*
To writers and journalists whose works contribute to the development of tourism in Spain. 50,000 pesetas. Enquiries to Spanish Ministry of Information and Tourism, Ave del Generalisimo 39, Madrid 16, Spain

Neustadt International Prize for Literature
World Literature Today, an international literary quarterly, established in 1969 an award for distinguished and continuing artistic achievement in the fields of poetry, drama or fiction. A new international jury of twelve is appointed for each successive award by the editor in consultation with the editorial board. Each juror presents one candidate for the prize. A majority (7) of the jury must be present for the deliberations and the final voting. Representative selections of a candidate's work must be available to the jury in either French or English translation.
Announcement of the winner is made in February, and the award is officially presented at The University of Oklahoma, Norman, Oklahoma, every other year. The prize is an award certificate, a replica of an eagle's feather in silver, and $10,000. *World Literature Today* dedicates one issue to the recipient. The University of Oklahoma Press will seriously consider the publication of a book by or on the winner. In 1978 the prize was awarded to Czeslaw Milosz (Polish poet). Prize not open to application. Enquiries to World Literature Today, 630 Parrington Oval, Room 110, Norman, Oklahoma 73019, USA

Martinus Nijhoff Prize
Established 1953. For translation of literary work into and from Dutch. 7,500 Dutch florins. Awarded annually. Enquiries to Prince Bernhard Fund, Leidsegracht 3, Amsterdam, Netherlands

Nobel Prize for Literature*
Of all the literary prizes, the Nobel Prize for literature is the highest in value and in honour bestowed. It is one of the five prizes founded by Alfred Bernhard Nobel (1833–1896); the other four awards are for physics, chemistry, physiology or medicine, and peace. By the terms of Nobel's will, the prize for literature is to be given to the person 'who shall have produced in the field of literature the most distinguished work of an idealistic tendency'. It consists of a gold medal, a diploma and a sum of money; the amount in 1977 was about $147,000. The award is administered by the Swedish Academy in Stockholm and official presentation is made on December 10, the anniversary of Nobel's death. No one may apply for the Nobel Prize; there is no competition. It is awarded to an author usually for his total literary output and not for any single work. Awarded in 1979 to Odysseus Elytis. Enquiries to Nobel Foundation, Swedish Academy, Sturegatan 14, S-11436 Stockholm, Sweden

Nordic Council Literary Prize
Established 1962. To an individual author for a current work of literature in one of the Scandinavian Languages. 75,000 Danish crowns. Awarded annually. Enquiries to Nordic Council, Box 7765, 10396 Stockholm, Sweden

Leopoldo Panero Prize*
For poetry. 100,000 pesetas. Awarded annually. Enquiries to Madrid Institute of Hispanic Culture, Ave Reyes Catolicos, Ciudad Universitaria, Spain

Yugoslav P E N Club Award
For the translation of a book from and into languages spoken or used in Yugoslavia. Monetary prize. Enquiries to Yugoslav PEN Club, Serbian Centre, YU-11000 Belgrade, 7 Francuska St, Yugoslavia

Hungarian P E N Club Medal*
For translation of Hungarian literary work into foreign languages. Awarded when merited. Enquiries to Hungarian PEN Club, Vörösmarty ter 1, Budapest V, Hungary

Polish P E N Club Prizes
For best translations of foreign poetry and prose into Polish, and of Polish literature into foreign languages. Three awards 20,000 zlotys each. Awarded annually. Enquiries to Polish PEN Club, Palac Kultury i Nauki, Warsaw, Poland

Lorne Pierce Medal
Established 1926. For achievement and conspicuous merit in the field of imaginative or critical literature, in English or French. Gold medal and $1,000. Awarded biennially. Enquiries to Royal Society of Canada, 344 Wellington St, Ottawa, Ontario K1A ON4, Canada

Pilgrim Award
Established 1970 and awarded annually by a committee of the Science Fiction Research Association for outstanding contributions made over a period of time to scholarship relating to the study of science fiction and modern fantasy. Enquiries to Science Fiction Research Association Inc, Box 3186, The College of Wooster, Wooster, Ohio 44691, USA

Planeta Prize*
Established 1952. For the best unpublished novel. Open to writers of Spanish speaking countries. 4,000,000 pesetas, and publication by Planeta Publishing House. Awarded annually. Enquiries to Planeta Publishing House, Corcega 273-277, Barcelona, Spain

Edgar Poe Prize*
To the best foreign poet writing in the French language. 100 francs. Awarded annually. Enquiries to Maison de Poèsie, 11 bis rue Ballu, F-75009 Paris, France

Poetry in Irish Award
Established 1962. To the author of best book of poetry in the Irish language. £600 Irish. Awarded triennially. Enquiries to Irish Arts Council, 70 Merrion Sq, Dublin 2, Republic of Ireland

Polish Authors' Prizes
For best translations of Polish literature into foreign languages. Three prizes, 20,000 zlotys each. Awarded annually. Enquiries to Society of Authors ZAiKS, ul Hipoteczna 2, Warsaw, Poland

Prince Pierre de Monaco Prize for Literature
Restricted to French-speaking writers. For the entirety of the literary work of one author. 30,000 French francs. Awarded annually. Enquiries to Prince Pierre de Monaco Foundation, Ministère d'Etat, Monaco

Prix Internationale des Editeurs
Radical literature prize established in 1977 by the below-mentioned 7 publishers. $5,000 to be awarded for a work already accepted for publication by one of them (to be subsequently published by each in the appropriate language). The most recent (1977) award was to Erich Fried for *100 Poems Without a Country* and a special award was made to Breyten Breytenbach for *In Africa even the Flies are Happy*. The 8 publishers are: Christian Burgois (France), Verlag Klaus Wagenbach (Germany), G Feltrinelli SpA (Italy), Van Gennep Ltd (Netherlands), Publições Dom Quixote (Portugal), Editorial Anagrama (Spain), John Calder (Publishers) Ltd (UK), Urizen Press (USA). Enquiries to John Calder (Publishers) Ltd, 18 Brewer Street, London W1R 4AS, UK

Putnam Awards
Established 1960. For outstanding manuscripts in the English language already under contract to the house, fiction or nonfiction, not previously published by Putnam's. Advance of $7,500 against royalties and $7,500 for advertising and promotion. Not more than three awarded annually. Enquiries to G P Putnam's Sons, 200 Madison Ave, New York, NY 10016, USA

Regina Medal
Established 1959. For recognition of continued distinguished contributions to children's literature. Silver medal. Awarded annually. Won in 1979 by Morton Schindel; won in 1978 by Scott O'Dell. Enquiries to Catholic Library Association, 461 West Lancaster Ave, Haverford, Pennsylvania 19041, USA

Remembrance Award
Established 1964. To an author of a literary work of high merit that was inspired by the experience of the Nazi holocaust and which most effectively presents this experience for the benefit of the present and future generations. $2,500. Awarded annually. Awarded in 1975 to Andre Ne'her for *Collected Philosophical Works*. Enquiries to World Federation of the Bergen-Belsen Associations, PO Box 333, Lenox Hill Station, New York, NY 10021, USA

Felix Restrepo Prize
For distinguished contributions to philology. 100,000 Colombian pesos and publication of the work. Awarded annually. Enquiries to Academia Colombiana, Bogotá, Colombia

John Llewelyn **Rhys** Memorial Prize
Established in 1941 by the widow of an airman killed on active service who was awarded the Hawthornden Prize posthumously. For a 'memorable work' by a Commonwealth citizen who was under 30 at the time of its publication. Prize of £300 awarded annually for a book published the previous year. Entries should be received by 30 April of the year of the award. 1979 prize awarded to Peter Boardman for *The Shining Mountain* (Hodder & Stoughton). Enquiries to Janet Riddell, The National Book League, Book House, East Hill, London SW18, UK

Rose of French Poets Prize
Established 1949. For a foreign poet who has celebrated France in his verse. Medal. Enquiries to Society of French Poets, 38 rue du Faubourg St Jacques, F-75014 Paris, France

'La **Sonrisa** Vertical' Prize
Founded in 1978 in homage to Lorenzo Barbadillo. Awarded to the best erotic novel written in Spanish or another language of the Spanish State. The first winner was Susana Constante (Argentinian) for *La educación sentimental de la Señorita Sonia*. Enquiries to *La sonrisa vertical*, Tusquets Editores, Calle Iradier 24 bajos, Barcelona 17, Spain

The '**Times Educational Supplement**'
Information Book Awards
Instituted 1972. For outstandingly good information books originating in Britain or the Commonwealth. Two awards are offered for a book for children up to the age of 9 and for a book for those aged between 10 and 16, both awards for £150. The judges may award a further £150 to the illustrator of either or both books. Won in 1979 by George Bernard (Oxford Scientific Films) for a photographic study *The Common Frog* (G Whizzard/André Deutsch) (Junior Award) and by Jane Cousins for *Make It Happy* (Virago) (Senior Award). Enquiries to Literary Editor, Times Educational Supplement, Times Newspapers Ltd, New Printing House Square, Gray's Inn Rd, London WC1X 8EZ, UK

Translation Prize*
For the best translation of a literary, scientific or cultural work written by a Portuguese author which is published in the form of a book. 30,000 escudos. Awarded biennially. Enquiries to Portugal State Secretariat for Information and Tourism, Palacio Foz, Lisbon 2, Portugal

Triennial Prize for Bibliography
The International League of Antiquarian Booksellers (ILAB) awards a prize, every three years, of $1000 to the author of the best work, published or unpublished, of learned bibliography, of research into the history of the book or typography, or a book of general interest on the subject. The competition is open, without restriction, but entries must be submitted in a language which is universally read. An already published work is eligible only if it has an imprint bearing a date within the three years preceding the closing date for submission. Enquiries to Dr Frieder Kocher-Benzing, Rathenaustr 21, D-7000 Stuttgart 1, Federal Republic of Germany

Walmap Prize*
Created by Waldomiro Magalhães Pinto for unpublished literary works in the Portuguese language. Prizes total $13,000. Awarded biennially. Enquiries to Antônio Olinto, 34 Landward Ct, Harowby St, London W1, UK

John Rowan **Wilson** Award
An annual award made by *World Medicine* in memory of John Rowan Wilson — surgeon, novelist, journalist — to a doctor for a piece of writing of fiction or fact, or to a lay person writing on a medical subject. The prize is £500 and a silver goblet. Awarded in 1979 to Jonathan Miller for *The Body in Question* (Jonathan Cape). Enquiries to The Editor, World Medicine, Clareville Ho, 26 Oxendon St, London SW1Y 4EL, UK

World Festival of Negro Arts Literary Prizes*
For the following works in English or French: a novel by a Negro author; a collection of poetry by a Negro author; an essay by a Negro writer; a work on the subject of Negro art, whoever the author; a scientific or historical essay by a Negro author; a piece of reporting on the Negro world, whoever the author; a play by a negro playwright. Monetary prizes. Awarded every 4 years (next 1981). Enquiries to Secretariat, World Black and African Festival of Arts and Culture, PMB 12568, Ikoyi, Lagos, Nigeria

Abraham **Woursell** Prize (University of Vienna)*
Instituted 1965. For young creative writers. 200,000 Austrian schillings annually for 5 years. Enquiries to Selection Committee Chairman, Faculty of Philosophy, University of Vienna, Austria

'**Yorkshire Post**' Book of the Year Award
Instituted 1964. First prize of £400 and runner-up prize of £250 for the best books published each year. Translations and works of a strictly scientific or technical nature are excluded. If the first prize is awarded to a non-fiction work, the runner-up prize goes to a fiction work and vice versa. Awarded in 1978 to Gavin Kennedy for *Bligh* (Duckworth) (first prize) and Sian James for *Yesterday* (Collins) (fiction). In addition there are Best First Work Awards to new authors in 1978. £300 first prize went to Edna Healey for *Lady Unknown — The Life of Angela Burdett-Coutts* (Sidgwick & Jackson) and the runner-up prize of £200 went to Jane Dunn for *Moon In Eclipse — A Life of Mary Shelley* (Weidenfeld & Nicolson). There are special annual awards of £350 each for the book selected to advance the popular appreciation of Art: the 1978 award went to Hilary Taylor for *James McNeil Whistler* (Studio Vista); and the best book selected to further the better appreciation of Music: the 1978 award went to Julian Budden for *The Operas of Verdi* (Cassell). Enquiries to Secretary, Book of the Year Awards, Yorkshire Post Newspapers Ltd, PO Box 168, Wellington St, Leeds LS1 1RF, UK

Young People's Book Prize*
For an outstanding book or the collected works of a writer or illustrator in the field of juvenile literature. 3,000 Swiss francs or more. Awarded annually. Enquiries to Swiss Teachers Association, Ringstrasse 54, 8057 Zurich, Switzerland

The ISBN System

Background

The question of the need and feasibility of an international numbering system for books was first discussed at the third international Conference on Book Market Research and Rationalization in the Book Trade held in November 1966 in Berlin. At that time a number of publishers and book distributors in Europe were considering the use of computers in order processing and inventory control and it was evident that a pre-requisite of an efficient machine system was a unique and simple identification number for a published item.
The system which fulfilled this requirement and which became known as the International Standard Book Number (ISBN) System developed out of the book numbering system introduced into the United Kingdom in 1967.
In a report to the British Publishers Association, Professor F G Foster of the London School of Economics stated that there was '... a clear need for the introduction into the book trade of standard numbering ... and substantial benefits would accrue to all parties therefrom'. After further study and deliberation, a detailed plan for standard numbering was produced. At the same time, the Technical Committee Documentation of the International Organization for Standardization (ISO/TC 46) set up a working party (with the British Standards Institution acting as secretariat) to investigate the possibility of adapting the British system for international use.
A meeting was held in London in 1968 with representatives from Denmark, France, Federal Republic of Germany, Eire, the Netherlands, Norway, the United Kingdom, the United States of America and an observer from UNESCO. Other countries contributed written suggestions and expressions of interest. A report of the meeting was circulated to all countries belonging to the ISO. Comments on this report and subsequent proposals were considered at meetings held in Berlin and Stockholm in 1969.
As a result of these meetings there emerged ISO Recommendation 2108 which sets out

the principles and procedure for international standard book numbering. The purpose of the ISO Recommendation is to coordinate and standardize internationally the use of book numbers so that an International Standard Book Number (ISBN) identifies one title or edition of a title from one specific publisher and is unique to that edition.
The ISBN applies in the main to books — for which the system was originally created — but, by extension, it may be used for any item produced by publishers or collected by libraries.

How the International Standard Book Number (ISBN) is Built Up

Every International Standard Book Number (ISBN) consists of ten digits and whenever it is printed it is preceded by the letters ISBN. (Note: In those countries where the Latin alphabet is not used, an abbreviation in the characters of the local alphabet may be used in addition to the Latin letters ISBN). The ten-digit number is divided into four parts of variable length, each part when printed being separated by a hyphen or space. (Note: Experience suggests that the hyphen is preferable to the space.)
The four parts are as follows:

Part 1. Group Identifier
This part identifies the national, geographic or other similar grouping of publishers.

Part 2. Publisher's Prefix
This part identifies a particular publisher within a group.

Part 3. Title Identifier
This part identifies a particular title or edition of a title published by a particular publisher.

Part 4. Check Digit
This is a single digit at the end of the ISBN which provides an automatic check on the correctness of the ISBN.

Group identifier
Group identifiers are allocated by the International ISBN Agency and a publisher wishing to participate in the ISBN system must belong to a recognized ISBN group. Groups are determined by national, geographic, language or other pertinent considerations. Experience has shown that groups based on national or geographic considerations are the most satisfactory. The following group identifiers are in use at present:

0 and 1	Australia, Canada, Republic of South Africa, UK, USA, Zimbabwe
2	France, French-speaking Belgium, French-speaking Switzerland
3	Austria, Federal Republic of Germany, German-speaking Switzerland
5	Union of Soviet Socialist Republics
82	Norway
84	Spain, Spanish-speaking South America (partly)
85	Brazil
87	Denmark
88	Italy
90	Netherlands, Dutch-speaking Belgium
91	Sweden
92	United Nations
951	Finland
962	Hong Kong
963	Hungary
965	Israel
968	Mexico
977	Egypt
978	Nigeria

Publisher's Prefix
The publisher's prefix designates the publisher of a given book. Publishers with a large output of books are assigned a short publisher's prefix; publishers with a small output of books are assigned a longer publisher's prefix.

Title identifier
The title identifier is assigned to a particular title or edition of a title by the publisher from within the range of numbers assigned to him and which will depend upon the length of his publisher's prefix. Title identifiers are normally assigned by the publisher himself. Publishers who assign their own title identifiers may use them to identify titles in the publishing house throughout the planning stages.

Check digit
The 'check digit' is the last digit in an ISBN and is computed as the result of an elaborate calculation on the other nine digits.
This calculation is performed almost instantaneously by an electronic computing device, and is a means of detecting incorrectly transcribed numbers. The check digit is calculated on a modulus 11 with weights 10-2, using X in lieu of 10 where ten would occur as a check digit.
This means that each of the first nine digits of the ISBN — ie excluding the check digit itself — is multiplied by a number ranging from 10 to 2 and the sum of the products thus obtained, plus the check digit, must be divisible, without remainder, by 11. For example:

	Group Identifier			Publisher's Prefix		
ISBN			0	8	4	3 6
Weight			10	9	8	7 6
Products			0+72+32+21+36+			

	Title Number			Check Digit
ISBN	1	0	7	2 7
Weight	5	4	3	2
Products	5 + 0+21 + 4			+ 7

Total: 198

As 198 can be divided by 11 without remainder 0 8436 1072 7 is a valid International Standard Book Number.

The number of digits in each part; and how to recognize them in an ISBN
The number of digits in each of the identifying parts 1, 2 and 3 is variable, though the total number of digits contained in these parts is always 9. These nine digits together with the check digit bring the total number of digits in an ISBN to ten.
The number of digits in the group identifier will vary according to the likely output of books in a group. Thus groups with an expected large output will get numbers of one or two digits and publishers with an expected large output will get numbers of two or three digits.
Exceptionally, a one-digit number may be assigned to a publisher but it will be appreciated that the assignment of one-digit publisher identifiers greatly reduces the range of possible identifiers in the group.
For ease of reading, the four parts of the ISBN are divided by spaces or hyphens. These spaces or hyphens, however, are not retained in a computer which depends upon the special distribution of ranges of numbers for the recognition of the parts.

Scope of the ISBN

For the purposes of the ISBN system books and other items to be numbered include:

Printed books and pamphlets

Microform publications

Braille publications

Mixed media publications

Machine-readable tapes designed to produce readable printout

Other similar media

Except:
Ephemeral printed materials such as diaries, calendars, advertising matter and the like

Art prints and art folders without title page and text

Sound recordings

Serial publications

Application of ISBN

General
A separate ISBN must be assigned to every different edition of a book, but NOT to an unchanged impression or unchanged reprint of the same book in the same format and by the same publisher. Price changes do not need new ISBN.

Facsimile reprints
A separate ISBN must be assigned to a facsimile reprint produced by a different publisher.

Books in different formats
A separate ISBN must be assigned to the different formats in which a particular title is published. For example: a hardback edition and a paperback edition each receives a separate ISBN. On the same principle, a microform edition receives a separate ISBN.

Multi-volume works
An ISBN must be assigned to the whole set of volumes of a multi-volume work as well as to each individual volume in the set.

Back stock
A publisher is required to number his back stock and publish the ISBN in his catalogues.
He must also print the ISBN in the first available reprint of an item from his back stock.

Collaborative publications
A publication issued as a coedition or joint imprint with other publishers is assigned an ISBN by the publisher in charge of distribution.

Books sold or distributed by agents
According to the principles of the ISBN

system, a particular edition, published by a particular publisher receives only one ISBN and this ISBN must be retained no matter where or by whom the book is distributed or sold.

A book imported by an exclusive distributor or sole agent from an area not yet in the ISBN system and for which therefore no ISBN has been assigned, may be assigned an ISBN by the exclusive distributor.

A book imported by an exclusive distributor, or sole agent to which a new title-page, bearing the imprint of the exclusive distributor, has been added in place of the title page of the original publisher, is to be given a new ISBN by the exclusive distributor or sole agent. The ISBN of the original publisher is also to be given as a related ISBN.

A book imported by several distributors from an area not yet in the ISBN system and for which, therefore, no ISBN has been assigned, may be assigned an ISBN by the group agency responsible for those distributors.

Publishers with more than one place of publication
A publisher operating in a number of places which are listed together in the imprint of a book will assign only one ISBN to the book.

A publisher operating separate and distinct offices or branches in different places may have a publisher identifier for each office or branch. Nevertheless, each book published is to be assigned only one ISBN, the assignment being made by the office or branch responsible for publication.

Register of ISBNs
Every publisher must keep a register of ISBNs that have been assigned to published and forthcoming books. The register is to be kept in numerical sequence giving ISBN, author, title and edition (where appropriate).

ISBN not to be re-used under any circumstances
An ISBN once allocated must not under any circumstances be re-used. This is of the utmost importance to avoid confusion. It is recognized that, owing to clerical errors, numbers will be incorrectly assigned. If this happens, the number must be deleted from the list of usable numbers and must not be assigned to another title. Every publisher will have sufficient numbers in his range for the loss of these numbers to be insignificant. Publishers should advise the group agency of the numbers thus deleted and of the titles to which they were erroneously assigned.

Printing of the ISBN

General
The ISBN must appear on the item itself. This is essential for the efficient running of the system.

Printing of ISBN on books
In the case of books, the ISBN must appear whenever possible: On the reverse of the title-page, or, if this is not possible, on the base of the title-page, or, if this too is not possible, at some other conspicuous location in the book. On the base of the spine. On the back of the cover in 9-point type or larger.
On the back of the dust-jacket, and on the back of any other protective case or wrapper.
The ISBN should always be printed in type large enough to be easily legible (eg not smaller than 9 point).

Administration of the ISBN System

General
The administration of the ISBN system is carried on at three levels. These are the international, group and publisher levels.

International administration
The international administration of the system is in the hands of the International Standard Book Number Agency which has an Advisory Panel representing the ISO and the publishing and library world. The address of the International Agency is:

The International Standard Book Number Agency,
Staatsbibliothek Preussischer Kulturbesitz,
Potsdamer Str 33, Postfach 1407,
D-1000 Berlin 30, Federal Republic of Germany

The principal functions of the International Agency are:

To supervise the use of the system

To approve the definition and structure of groups

To allocate identifiers to groups

To advise groups on the setting up and functioning of group agencies

To advise group agencies on the allocation of publisher identifiers

To promote the world-wide use of the system

In addition, the International Agency also offers the following services. It will:

Provide a group agency with lists of ISBNs (with computergenerated check digits) for the use of publishers in the group.

Provide international registers of publishers, prefixes and publishers' names.

Provide from information supplied by group agencies a computer printout of lists of publishers' prefixes, names and locations.

Provide from information supplied by group agencies a computer printout of invalid or duplicate ISBNs.

Group administration
Groups are administered by Group Agencies. Within the group there may be several national agencies, eg group 0/1 has separate agencies in USA, United Kingdom, Canada, Australia etc. with the main agency for the whole group in the UK.

The functions of a group agency are:

To manage and administer the affairs of the group.

To handle relations with the International ISBN Agency on behalf of all the publishers in the group.

To decide, in consultation with trade organizations and publishers, the publisher identifier ranges required.

To allocate publishers' prefixes to publishers eligible to join the group and to maintain a register of publishers and their prefixes.

To decide, in consultation with trade organizations and publishers, which publishers shall assign numbers to their own titles and which publishers shall have numbers assigned to their titles by the group agency.

To provide technical advice and assistance to the publishers and to ensure that standards and approved procedures are observed in the group.

To make available a manual of instruction for publishers.

To make available computer printouts of ISBNs to publishers numbering their own books with check digits already calculated. (Such printouts may be obtained from the International Agency on request.)

To validate all ISBNs assigned by publishers numbering their own books and keep a register of them.

To inform publishers of any invalid or duplicate ISBNs assigned by them.

To assign numbers to all publications from those publishers who do not assign their own ISBNs and advise the publishers concerned of ISBNs assigned upon request.

To achieve, thereby, total numbering in the group.

To arrange with book listing and bibliographic agencies for the publication of ISBNs with the titles to which they refer.

To arrange with publishers for the numbering of their back lists and for the publication of these in appropriate trade lists and bibliographies.

To maintain liaison with all elements of the book trade and introduce new publishers to the system.

To assist the trade in the use of the ISBN in computer systems.

The national agencies are:

Australia
Ms Cornell Platzer, National Library of Australia, Parkes Pl, Canberra, ACT 2600

Austria
Dr G Prosser, Hauptverband des Österreichischen Buchhandels, A-1010 Vienna I, Grunangergasse 4

Belgium (Dutch-speaking)
Netherlands agency

Belgium (French-speaking)
French agency

Brazil
Biblioteca Nacional, Agência Brasileira do ISBN, Av Rio Branco 219/39, 20000 Rio de Janeiro, RJ

Canada (English-speaking)
Paul McCormick, National Library of Canada, 395 Wellington St, Ottawa, Ontario K1A 0N4

Canada (French-speaking)
J Z Leon Paternaude, Conseil supérieur du Livre, 3405 rue Saint-Denis, Montreal 130, Quebec

Denmark
Karen Lunde Christensen, Bibliothekscentralen Dansk Bogfortegnelse, Telegrafvej 5, DK-2750 Ballerup

Egypt
Dr S M El Sheniti, General Egyptian Book Organization, Boulac, Cairo

Finland
Dr Thea Aulo, Finnish ISBN Numbering Agency, Helsinki University Library, PL 312, SF-00170 Helsinki 17

Federal Republic of Germany
Wilfried H Schinzel, Buchhändler-
Vereinigung GmbH, Postfach 2404, D-6000
Frankfurt am Main 1

France
Cécile Renault, Agence francophone pour la
Numérotation internationale du Livre
(AFNIL-ISBN), 117 blvd St-Germain,
F-75279 Paris cedex 06

Hong Kong
Timothy A Chow, Books Registration Unit,
City Hall Library 6/F, Edinburgh Place,
Hong Kong

Hungary
Dr Susánszky Zoltánné, Országos Széchényi
Könyvtár Magyar ISBN Iroda, Pollack
Mihálytér 10, H-1827 Budapest

Israel
Israel ISBN Group Agency, c/o Center for
Public Libraries, PO Box 242, Jerusalem

Italy
Gianni Merlini, Assoziacione Italiana
Editori, Agenzia per l'Area di Lingua
Italiana ISBN, Via delle Erbe 2, I-20121
Milan

Mexico
Direccion General del Derecho de Autor
Centro Nacional de Informacion, Mariano
Escobedo 438, 5° piso, Mexico 5 DF

Netherlands
J van Leeuwan, Bureau ISBN, Centraal
Boekhuis, Postbus 125, Culemborg

New Zealand
D C McIntosh, National Library of New
Zealand, Private Bag, Wellington 1

Nigeria
Mrs O Omolayole, National Library of
Nigeria, 4 Wesley St, PMB 12626, Lagos

Norway
May Ruth Novakowski, Norsk
Boknummerkontor, Universitetsbiblioteket i
Oslo, Drammensvegen 42, Oslo 2

Republic of South Africa
Dr H J Aschenborn, State Library, PO Box
397, Pretoria 0001

Spain
José M Garcia Diéguez, Instituto Nacional
del Libro Español, Santiago Rusiñol 8,
Madrid 3

Sweden
Folke Hermanson-Snickars, Swedish
National ISBN-Centre, Bibliographical
Institute, Royal Library, PO Box 5039,
S-10241 Stockholm 5

Switzerland (French-speaking)
French agency

Switzerland (German-speaking)
Herr Oprecht, Schweizerischer Buchhandler-
und Verleger-Verband, CH-8008 Zurich,
Bellerivestr 3

Union of Soviet Socialist Republics
Ju I Fartunin, Bibliografičeskij Institut
SSSR, Kremlevskaja nab 1/9, 119816
Moscow G-19

UK
James Coates, Standard Book Numbering
Agency Ltd, 12 Dyott St, London
WC1A 1DF

United Nations
Lionel Tzod, Book & International Cultural
Exchange Promotions Division, UNESCO,
7 pl de Fontenoy, F-75700 Paris

USA
Emery Koltay, Standard Book Numbering
Agency, 1180 Ave of the Americas, New
York, NY 10036

Zimbabwe
E E Burke, National Archives of Rhodesia,
Private Bag 7729, Causeway, Salisbury

ISBN and ISSN

In addition to the International Standard
Book Number System, a complementary
numbering system for serial publications has
also been established.
A serial is defined as any publication issued
in successive parts, usually bearing
numerical or chronological designations and
intended to be continued indefinitely. Serials
include periodicals, yearbooks and
monographic series.
The International Standard Serial Number
(ISSN) is administered by the International
Center for the Registration of Serials
(ISDS), whose address is:

International Serial Data System,
20 rue Bachaumont, F-75002 Paris, France

Publishers of serials should apply to the
International Serials Data System or to
their National Serials Data Centre, if there
is one, for ISSNs for their serial
publications.
Certain publications, such as yearbooks,
annuals, monographic series, etc., should be
assigned an ISSN for the serial title (which
will remain the same for all the parts or
individual volumes of the serial) and an
ISBN for each individual volume.
Both ISSN and ISBN where they are
assigned must be given on the publication
and clearly identified.

(The above information is from the ISBN
Users' Manual, compiled by the
International ISBN Agency,
Staatsbibliothek Preussischer Kulturbesitz,
Berlin, Federal Republic of Germany.)

Book Trade Calendar

DATE	EVENT	CONTACT
1980		
January 20–25	American Library Association: Midwinter Meeting. Chicago, Illinois, USA	American Library Association, 50 East Huron St, Chicago, Illinois 60611, USA
January 24–February 4	12th Cairo International Book Fair. Cairo, Egypt	General Egyptian Book Organization, Corniche El Nil, Boulac, Cairo, Egypt
February 29–March 9	4th World Book Fair. New Delhi, India	National Book Trust, A5 Green Park, New Delhi 110016, India
March 2–6	5th Ife Book Fair. Ile-Ife, Nigeria	The Fair Director, Ife Book Fair, University of Ife Bookshop Ltd, University of Ife, Ile-Ife, Nigeria
March 5–15	Leipzig Spring Fair. Leipzig, German Democratic Republic	Leipziger Messeamt, Markt 11–15, Postfach 720, DDR-701 Leipzig, German Democratic Republic
March 6	Book Print Fair. London, UK	Book Print Fair, 8-9 Giltspur St, London EC1A 9DE, UK
March 15–23	Brussels International Book Fair. Brussels, Belgium	International Book Fair, 111 Ave du Parc, B-1060 Brussels, Belgium
March 23–26	EURIM 4. Brussels, Belgium	The Conference Organiser, Aslib, 3 Belgrave Sq, London SW1X 8PL, UK
March 27	The Publishers Association: Annual General Meeting. London, UK	The Publishers Association, 19 Bedford Sq, London WC1, UK
March 27–30	17th Children's Book Fair and 14th Exhibition for Illustrators. Bologna, Italy	Fiera del libro per ragazzi, Piazza della Constituzione 6, I-40128 Bologna, Italy
March 29–April 6	9th Annual Book Fair. Bangkok, Thailand	Publishers' and Booksellers' Association of Thailand, 108 Sukhumvit Soi 53 (Madee Paidee), Bangkok, Thailand
April 2	International Children's Book Day (1980 sponsor: Poland)	IBBY Secretariat, Leonhardsgraben 38a, CH-4051 Basle, Switzerland
April 9–12	Montreal International Book Fair. Montreal, Canada	Montreal International Book Fair, 436 est, rue Sherbrooke, Montreal, Quebec, Canada H2L 1J6
April 13–19	National Library Week. USA	American Library Association, 50 East Huron St, Chicago, Illinois 60611, USA
April 18–21	The Booksellers Association of Great Britain & Ireland: Annual Conference and Trade Exhibition. Bristol, UK	Conference Secretary, The Booksellers Association of Great Britain & Ireland, 154 Buckingham Palace Rd, London SW1W 9TZ
April 23	London Academic Book Fair. London, UK	The London Book Fair, 16 Pembridge Rd, London W1, UK

DATE	EVENT	CONTACT
1980 (Cont'd)		
April 26–29	Book Publishers Association of New Zealand: Annual Conference. New Zealand	Book Publishers Association of New Zealand, PO Box 78-071, Grey Lynn, Auckland 2, New Zealand
April 26–29	New Zealand Booksellers Conference. Rotorua, New Zealand	Booksellers Association of New Zealand (Inc), PO Box 11-377, Wellington, New Zealand
April 26–May 3	Cape Town Book Festival. Cape Town, Republic of South Africa	Associated Booksellers of Southern Africa, 1 Meerendal, Nightingale Way, Pinelands 7405, Republic of South Africa
May 5–9	International Reading Association: Annual Convention. St Louis, Missouri, USA	International Reading Association, 800 Barksdale Rd, PO Box 8139 Newark, Delaware 19711, USA
May 8–10	Union internationale des industries graphiques de reproduction: Congress. Paris, France	Union internationale des industries graphiques de reproduction, 142 Blvd St-Germain, F-75278 Paris Cedex 06, France
May 9–14	International Book Festival. Nice, France	Festival International du Livre, Palais des Expositions, F-06300 Nice, and 5 rue Stanislas, F-75006 Paris, France
May 21–26	25th International Book Fair. Warsaw, Poland	Ars Polona, Sekretariat Międzynarodowych Targów Książki, PO Box 1001, 00-068 Warsaw, Poland
June 7–10	American Booksellers Association: Annual Convention. Chicago, USA	American Booksellers Association, 122 East 42nd St, New York, NY 10017, USA
June 23–26	International Association of Literary Critics: Annual Congress. Helsinki, Finland	Association internationale des critiques litteraires, 38 rue du Faubourg St-Jaques, F-75014 Paris, France
June 29–July 5	American Library Association: Annual Conference. New York City, USA	American Library Association, 50 East Huron St, Chicago, Illinois 60611, USA
August 1–10	São Paulo VI Bienal Internacional do Livro. São Paulo, Brazil	Administrative Secretary, Câmara Brasileira do Livro, Av Ipiranga 1267, 10° andar, 01039 São Paulo 2, Brazil
August 3–7	The International Association of Printing House Craftsmen, Inc: Annual Convention. Las Vegas, USA	The International Association of Printing House Craftsmen, Inc, 7599 Kenwood Rd, Cincinnati, Ohio 45236, USA
August 5–7	International Reading Association: 8th World Congress. Manila, Philippines	International Reading Association, 800 Barksdale Rd, PO Box 8139, Newark, Delaware 19711, USA
August 12–23	Book Fair and Annual General Meetings of: South African Publishers Association Associated Booksellers of Southern Africa Overseas Publishers Representatives Book Trade Association. East London, Republic of South Africa	Associated Booksellers of Southern Africa, 1 Meerendal, Nightingale Way, Pinelands 7405, Republic of South Africa
August 16–22	32nd Writers' Summer School. Swanwick, Derbyshire, UK	The Secretary, Writers' Summer School, 308 Lewisham Rd, London SE13 7PA, UK

DATE	EVENT	CONTACT
1980 (Cont'd)		
August 18–23	Federation Internationale de Documentation (FID): 40th Conference and Congress. Lyngby, Denmark	Federation Internationale de Documentation, Hofweg 7, The Hague, Netherlands
August 30–September 4	Distripress Annual Congress. San Francisco, USA	Distripress, Beethovenstr 20, CH-8002 Zurich, Switzerland
September	New Zealand Book Week. New Zealand	Book Publishers Association of New Zealand, PO Box 78-071, Grey Lynn, Auckland 2, New Zealand
September 15–19	Aslib/Institute of Information Scientists/Library Association: Joint Conference. Sheffield, UK	Aslib/IIS/LA Joint Conference Organizer, 3 Belgrave Sq, London SW1X 8PL, UK
September 18–24	13th Sofia International Book Fair. Sofia, Bulgaria	International Book Fair, 11 Slaveikov Sq, Sofia, Bulgaria
September 21–24	The International League of Antiquarian Booksellers: International Congress. New York, USA	The International League of Antiquarian Booksellers, Poststr 14-16, 2 Hamburg 36, Federal Republic of Germany
September 25–28	International Antiquarian Book Fair. New York, USA	The International League of Antiquarian Booksellers, Poststr 14-16, 2 Hamburg 36, Federal Republic of Germany
September 28–October 3	International Board on Books for Young People: Biennial Congress. Prague, Czechoslovakia	IBBY Secretariat, Leonhardsgraben 38a, CH-4051 Basle, Switzerland
October 4–11	National Children's Book Week. UK	Children's Book Officer, The Publishers Association, 19 Bedford Sq, London WC1, UK
October 5–7	The London Book Fair. London, UK	The London Book Fair, 16 Pembridge Rd, London W11, UK
October 8–13	32nd Frankfurt Book Fair. Frankfurt am Main, Federal Republic of Germany	Ausstellungs-und Messe-GmbH des Börsenvereins des Deutschen Buchhandels, Postfach 2404, Kleiner Hirschgraben 10/12, D-6000 Frankfurt am Main 1, Federal Republic of Germany
October 24–29	25th International Book Fair. Belgrade, Yugoslavia	International Book Fair, Association of Yugoslav Publishers and Booksellers, YU-11000 Belgrade, Kenza Miloša 25/I, Yugoslavia
October 26–29	Book Manufacturers' Institute: Annual Conference. Rancho Mirage, California, USA	Book Manufacturers' Institute Inc, 111 Prospect St, Stamford, Connecticut 06901, USA
November 1–6	Interdidacta '80. Cairo, Egypt	Eurodidac, Jägerstr 5, CH-4058 Basle, Switzerland
November 2–December 2	The Jewish Book Month. USA	The Jewish Book Council of the National Jewish Welfare Board, 15 East 26th St, New York, NY 10010, USA

DATE	EVENT	CONTACT
1980 (Cont'd)		
November 17–23	National Children's Book Week. USA	The Children's Book Council, 67 Irving Pl, New York, NY 10003, USA
November 28–29	4th Socialist Book Fair. London, UK	Evelyn Barker, 265 Seven Sisters Rd, London N4, UK
December 27–30	Modern Language Association of America: Annual Convention. Houston, USA	Modern Language Association of America, 62 Fifth Ave, New York, NY 10011, USA
1981		
January or February	10th National Book Fair. India	National Book Trust, A5 Green Park, New Delhi 110016, India
February 1–6	American Library Association: Midwinter Meeting. Washington DC, USA	American Library Association, 50 East Huron St, Chicago, Illinois 60611, USA
March	Book Print Fair. London, UK	Book Print Fair, 8-9 Giltspur St, London EC1A 9DE, UK
March 14–22	Brussels International Book Fair. Brussels, Belgium	International Book Fair, 111 Ave du Parc, B-1060 Brussels, Belgium
March 24–28	18th Didacta Eurodidac. Basle, Switzerland	Eurodidac, Jägerstr 5, CH-4058 Basle, Switzerland
March or April	Leipzig Spring Fair. Leipzig, German Democratic Republic	Leipziger Messeamt, Markt 11-15, Postfach 720, DDR-701 Leipzig, German Democratic Republic
March or April	Publishers Association: Annual General Meeting. London, UK	The Publishers Association, 19 Bedford Sq, London WC1, UK
March or April	18th Children's Book Fair and 15th Exhibition for Illustrators. Bologna, Italy	Fiera del libro per ragazzi, Piazza della Constituzione 6, I-40128, Bologna, Italy
April 2	International Children's Book Day (1981 sponsor: Federal Republic of Germany)	IBBY Secretariat, Leonhardsgraben 38a, CH-4051 Basle, Switzerland
April 5–10	10th Jerusalem International Book Fair. Jerusalem, Israel	The Jerusalem International Book Fair, 22 Jaffa Rd, Jerusalem 91000, Israel
April 24–27	The Booksellers Association of Great Britain & Ireland: Annual Conference. Eastbourne, UK	Conference Secretary, The Booksellers Association of Great Britain & Ireland, 154 Buckingham Palace Rd, London SW1W 9TZ, UK
April (end)	Book Publishers Association of New Zealand: Annual Conference. New Zealand	Book Publishers Association of New Zealand, PO Box 78-071, Grey Lynn, Auckland 2, New Zealand
April 27–May 1	International Reading Association: Annual Convention. New Orleans, Louisiana, USA	International Reading Association, 800 Barksdale Rd, PO Box 8139 Newark, Delaware 19711, USA

DATE	EVENT	CONTACT

1981 (Cont'd)

DATE	EVENT	CONTACT
May (beginning)	International Book Festival. Nice, France	Festival International du Livre, Palais des Expositions, F-06300 Nice, and 5 rue Stanislas, F-75006 Paris, France
May 20–25	26th International Book Fair. Warsaw, Poland	Ars Polona, Sekretariat Miedzynarodowych Targów Książki, PO Box 1001, 00-068 Warsaw, Poland
May 23–26	American Booksellers Association: Annual Convention. Atlanta, USA	American Booksellers Association, 122 East 42nd St, New York, NY 10017, USA
June 28–July 4	American Library Association: Annual Conference. San Francisco, California, USA	American Library Association, 50 East Huron St, Chicago, Illinois 60611, USA
August	Book Fair and Annual General Meetings of: South African Publishers Association Associated Booksellers of Southern Africa Overseas Publishers Representatives Book Trade Association. Cape Town, Republic of South Africa	Associated Booksellers of Southern Africa Ltd, 1 Meerendal, Nightingale Way, Pinelands 7405, Republic of South Africa
August 2–5	The International Association of Printing House Craftsmen, Inc: Annual Convention. Boston, Mass, USA	The International Association of Printing House Craftsmen, Inc, 7599 Kenwood Rd, Cincinnati, Ohio 45236, USA
August 28–September 8	International Federation for Modern Languages and Literature: XVth International Congress. Phoenix, Arizona, USA	Professor Peter Horwath, Department of Modern Languages, Arizona State University, Tempe, Arizona, USA
September	P E N 45th International Congress. France	International PEN, 7 Dilke St, London SW3 4JW, UK
September	New Zealand Book Week. New Zealand	Book Publishers Association of New Zealand, PO Box 78-071, Grey Lynn, Auckland 2, New Zealand
September 22–25	Aslib 54th Annual Conference. Oxford, UK	Conference Organizer, Aslib, 3 Belgrave Sq, London SW1X 8PL, UK
October	Distripress Annual Congress. Rome, Italy	Distripress, Beethovenstr 20, CH-8002 Zurich, Switzerland
October 14–19	33rd Frankfurt Book Fair. Frankfurt am Main, Federal Republic of Germany	Ausstellungs-und Messe-GmbH des Borsenvereins des Deutschen Buchhandels, Postfach 2404, D-6000 Frankfurt am Main 1, Federal Republic of Germany
November 1–4	Book Manufacturers' Institute: Annual Conference. Marco Island, Florida, USA	Book Manufacturers' Institute Inc, 111 Prospect St, Stamford, Connecticut 06901, USA
November 16–22	National Children's Book Week. USA	The Children's Book Council, 67 Irving Pl, New York, NY 10003, USA
December 27–30	Modern Language Association of America: Annual Convention. Los Angeles, USA	Modern Language Association of America, 62 Fifth Ave, New York, NY 10011, USA

DATE	EVENT	CONTACT
1981 (Cont'd)		
Second half 1981	UNESCO Intergovernmental Copyright Committee: 4th Session. New Delhi, India	Copyright Division, UNESCO, 7 Pl de Fontenoy, F-75700 Paris, France
Date unknown at time of going to press	International Association of Literary Critics: Annual Congress. Warsaw, Poland	Association internationale des critiques litteraires, 38 rue du Faubourg St-Jaques, F-75014 Paris, France
1982		
March 14-21	Leipzig Spring Fair, Leipzig, German Democratic Republic	Leipziger Messeamt, Markt 11-15, Postfach 720, DDR-701 Leipzig, German Democratic Republic
April 2	International Children's Book Day	IBBY Secretariat, Leonhardsgraben 38a, CH-4051 Basle, Switzerland
April 26-30	International Reading Association: Annual Convention. Chicago, Illinois, USA	International Reading Association, 800 Barksdale Rd, PO Box 8139, Newark, Delaware 19711, USA
May (beginning)	International Book Festival. Nice, France	Festival International du Livre, Palais des Expositions, F-06300 Nice, and 5 rue Stanislas, F-75006 Paris, France
May 19-24	27th International Book Fair. Warsaw, Poland	Ars Polona, Sekretariat Miedzynarodowych Targów Ksiazki, PO Box 1001, 00-068 Warsaw, Poland
May 29-June 1	American Booksellers Association: Annual Convention. Anaheim, CA, USA	American Booksellers Association, 122 East 42nd St, New York, NY 10017, USA
October 6-11	34th Frankfurt Book Fair. Frankfurt am Main, Federal Republic of Germany	Ausstellungs-und Messe-GmbH des Börsenvereins des Deutschen Buchhandels, Postfach 2404, Kleiner Hirschgraben 10/12, D-6000 Frankfurt am Main 1, Federal Republic of Germany
November 15-21	National Children's Book Week. USA	The Children's Book Council, 67 Irving Pl, New York, NY 10003, USA
December 27-30	Modern Language Association of America: Annual Convention. New York, USA	Modern Language Association of America, 62 Fifth Ave, New York, NY 10011, USA
Date unknown at time of going to press	International Board on Books for Young People: Biennial Congress: London, UK	British IBBY, Ms B Mathias, National Book League, Book House, East Hill, Wandsworth, London SW18, UK
Date unknown at time of going to press	P E N 46th International Congress. Japan or Yugoslavia (Belgrade)	International PEN, 7 Dilke St, London SW3 4JE, UK

Index

The order of the index is word by word so that, for example, Alpha Literatur comes before Alphabet & Image.

Some words at the beginning of names are ignored when indexing. These include initials and forenames of personal names (so Jonathan Cape Ltd is listed under C) and words which simply mean 'publisher', 'bookseller' or 'company' (so Editions Arcade is listed under A). In the text the first word of a name that is counted when the indexing is printed in bold type.

Names which start with numbers written as numerals are put before A in the index (so Edition der 2 is the first entry in the index, while Les Editions des Deux Coqs d'Or is listed under D).

2, Edition der, (Federal Republic of Germany) 123
'8' Nentori Publishing House (Albania)
'13 Calle', Librería, (Guatemala) 179
14th October Corporation (People's Democratic Republic of Yemen) 426
20th Century Classics (New Zealand) 274
20th Century Classics (United Kingdom) 414
24 Heures, Editions, (Switzerland) 340
29, Ediciones, (Spain) 318
62, Ediciones, SA (Spain) 318
70, Edições, Lda (Portugal) 298
99, Ediciones, SA (Spain) 318

A B, The, Book Club (Iceland) 185
A B C, Editions, Jeunesse SARL (Belgium) 34
A B C, Librería, (Argentina) 8
A B C, Librerías, SA (Peru) 290
A B C, Librerías, SA (Peru) 289
A B C (Aurelia Book Club) (Belgium) 44
A B C Bookshop (New Zealand) 274
A B C Bookstore Ltd (Israel) 210
A B C Buchklub GmbH & Co KG (Austria) 29
A B C D Group (United Kingdom) 370
A B C Verlag (Switzerland) 340
A B G R A (Asociación de Bibliotecarios Graduados de la República Argentina) (Argentina) 8
A B I C Publishers (Nigeria) 277
A B M, Librairie, (Benin) 46
A B M, Librairie-Papeterie, (Benin) 47
A B P (NZ) Ltd (New Zealand) 272
A C E R (Spain) 327
A C U R I L (Association of Caribbean University, Research and Institutional Libraries) (International Organizations) 437
A D A C Verlag (Federal Republic of Germany) 123
A D A Edita Tokyo Co Ltd (Japan) 225
A D I S Press Australasia Pty Limited (Australia) 10
A D I S Press International Ltd (Hong Kong) 180
A D L A F (Federal Republic of Germany) 123
A E D O S, Editorial, (Spain) 318
A E G - Telefunken Zentralabteilung Firmenverlag (Federal Republic of Germany) 123
A E I International (Portugal) 298
A E I International (Portugal) 301
A G I R (Artes Graficas Industrias Reunidas SA) (Brazil) 49
A G P O L (Przedsiebiorstwo Reklamy i Wydawnictw Handlu Zagranicznego) (Foreign Trade Publicity and Publishing Enterprise) (Poland) 293
A H I Literary Research Award (New Zealand) 275
A L A Verlag (Switzerland) 340
A L F A — Radna organizacija za izdavačku djelatnost (Yugoslavia) 427
A M B (Arbeitsgemeinschaft mitteleuropäischer Bibelwerke), Association of Mid-European Biblical Presses (Federal Republic of Germany) 123

A M Z Editrice sas di Mario Abriani e C (Italy) 212
A N B A D S (Senegal) 307
A N Z Local History Award (Australia) 21
A O V, Edições, (Portugal) 298
A P A (Academic Publishers Associated) (Netherlands) 258
A P C K (Republic of Ireland) 203
A P C O L (Australia) 10
'A' Publishing Institute (Israel) 206
A R E D I P (Agence Recherches Droits Internationaux et Promotion) (France) 89
A R E S, Edizioni, (Italy) 212
A R L I S (The Art Libraries Society) (United Kingdom) 416
Aane-Adab (Pakistan) 285
Aar- Verlag (Federal Republic of Germany) 123
Aare-Verlag (Switzerland) 340
Aarestrup, Emil, Prize (Denmark) 79
Aargauer Tagblatt Verlag AG (Switzerland) 340
Abaco, Editorial, de Rodolfo Depalma SRL (Argentina) 3
Abacus (United Kingdom) 370
Abacus Press (United Kingdom) 370
Abadia, Publicacions de l', de Montserrat (Spain) 318
Abakon Verlagsgesellschaft mbH (Federal Republic of Germany) 123
Abakus Schallplatten Barbara Fietz (Federal Republic of Germany) 123
Abbaye, Edition de l', d'Encalcat (France) 89
Abbey (United Kingdom) 370
Abbey's Bookshop (Australia) 19
Abdulghani, Abdulla, & Sons Co (Qatar) 303
Abelard-Schuman Ltd (United Kingdom) 370
Abeledo, Editorial, Perrot SAEeI (Argentina) 3
Abercromby Bookshop (Trinidad and Tobago) 361
Aberdeen University Press Ltd (United Kingdom) 370
Abhinav Publications (India) 187
Abiva Publishing House Inc (Philippines) 291
Abril SA Cultural e Industrial (Brazil) 49
Abson Books (United Kingdom) 370
Abtour, Georges, SA, Librairie-Papeterie (Chad) 62
Academi, Yr, Gymreig (The Welsh Academy) (United Kingdom) 417
Academia (Czechoslovakia) 70
Academia, Biblioteca da, das Ciências de Lisboa (Library of the Academy of Sciences) (Portugal) 301
Academia Amazonense de Letras (Brazil) 56
Academia Argentina de Letras (Argentina) 9
Academia Cachoeirense de Letras (Brazil) 56
Academia Catarinense de Letras (Brazil) 56
Academia Cearense de Letras (Brazil) 57
Academia de Buenas Letras de Barcelona (Barcelona Academy of Belles Lettres) (Spain) 328
Academia de Ciencias de la República de Cuba (Cuba) 68
Academia de Letras (Brazil) 57
Academia de Letras da Bahia (Brazil) 57
Academia de Letras de Piauí (Brazil) 57
Academia de Studii Economice, Biblioteca Centrala,. (Romania) 304
Academia Feminina Espirito Santense de Letras (Brazil) 57
Academia Matogrossense de Letras (Brazil) 57
Academia Mineira de Letras (Brazil) 57
Academia Nacional de Letras (Uruguay) 423
Academia Nicaragüense de la Lengua (Nicaragua) 276
Academia Paranaense de Letras (Brazil) 57
Academia Paulista de Letras (Brazil) 57
Academia Pernambucana de Letras (Brazil) 57
Academia Publications P Ltd (Malaysia) 246
Academia Riograndense de Letras (Brazil) 57
Academia Sinica, The Library of, (People's Republic of China) 63
Academic Press Inc (London) Ltd (United Kingdom) 370
Academic Publications (United Kingdom) 370
Academic Publishers (India) 187
Academic Publishers Associated (Netherlands) 258
Academica Lda (Mozambique) 256
Académie, L', du Livre SA (Belgium) 44
Académie des Lettres et des Arts (France) 112
Académie Goncourt, Société des Gens de Lettres (France) 112
Académie Internationale de Tourisme (Monaco) 255

Académie mauricienne de Langue et de Littérature (Mauritius) 249
Académie Montaigne (France) 112
Académie royale de Langue et de Littérature françaises (Belgium) 45
Académie royale des Sciences, des Lettres et des Beaux-Arts de Belgique (Belgium) 45
Academiei, Editura, Republicii Socialiste România (Romania) 304
Academiei Republicii Socialiste România, Biblioteca, (Romania) 304
Academiei Republicii Socialiste România, Biblioteca Filialei Cluj a, (The Library of the Cluj Branch of the Academy of the RSR) (Romania) 304
Academon (The Hebrew University Students' Printing and Publishing House) (Israel) 206
Academy, Council on Libraries of the, of Sciences of the USSR (Union of Soviet Socialist Republics) 367
Academy, Fundamental Library of the, of Medical Sciences (Union of Soviet Socialist Republics) 367
Academy, The, Press (Republic of Ireland) 203
Academy Editions (France) 89
Academy Editions (United Kingdom) 370
Academy of Sciences Publishing House (Democratic People's Republic of Korea) 237
Academy of Social Sciences Publishing House (Democratic People's Republic of Korea) 237
Academy of the Hebrew Language (Israel) 206
Academy of Thirteen Prize (France) 112
Academy Press Ltd (Nigeria) 277
Accademia di Scienze, Lettere ed Arti (Italy) 222
Accademia Ligure di Scienze e Lettere (Italy) 222
Accademia Nazionale di Scienze, Lettere ed Art (Italy) 223
Accademia Petrarca di Lettere, Arti e Scienze (Italy) 223
Accademia Toscana di Scienze e Lettere la Colombaria (Italy) 223
Accademia Virgiliana di Scienze, Lettere ed Arti di Mantova (Italy) 223
Accidentia Druck- und Verlagsgesellschaft mbH (Federal Republic of Germany) 123
Acco SV (Belgium) 34
Accra Technical Training Centre Library (Ghana) 175
Acervo, Ediciones, (Spain) 318
Achberger Verlag GmbH (Federal Republic of Germany) 124
Achenbach, Verlag Andreas, (Federal Republic of Germany) 124
Achiasaf Publishing House Ltd (Israel) 206
Achievement Award (New Zealand) 275
Achiever (Israel) 206
Ackermanns, F A, Kunstverlag (Federal Republic of Germany) 124
Acme, Editorial, SA (Argentina) 3
Acme Books (Australia) 10
Aconcagua Edic y Pub SA (Mexico) 250
Acribia, Editorial, (Spain) 318
Acrópole, Edições, (Portugal) 298
Acrópolis, Librería, (Guatemala) 179
Acta Medica Belgica ASBL (Belgium) 34
Acta Universitatis Gothoburgensis (Sweden) 331
Actinic Press Ltd (United Kingdom) 371
Action Publications (New Zealand) 275
Actualquarto (Belgium) 34
Acum Ltd (Society of Authors, Composers and Music Publishers in Israel) (Israel) 211
Ad Publishers (Israel) 206
Adab, Al-, Bookshop (Saudi Arabia) 306
Adab, Dar al, (Lebanon) 240
Adam, R P, (Denmark) 78
Adamjee Prize (Pakistan) 287
Adams & Co Ltd (Republic of South Africa) 315
Addams, Jane, Children's Books Award (International Literary Prizes) 446
Addis Ababa University Library (Ethiopia) 84
Addis Ababa University Press (Ethiopia) 84
Addison-Wesley Publishers Ltd (United Kingdom) 371
Addison-Wesley Publishing Co (Australia) 10
Addison-Wesley Publishing Co Inc (Philippines) 291
Addison-Wesley Publishing Group (Netherlands) 258
Addison-Wesley Singapore (Pte) Ltd (Republic of Singapore) 308

INDEX 463

Adelaide University Union Press (Australia) 10
Adelphi Edizioni SpA (Italy) 212
Adeyle Brothers (Bangladesh) 32
Adeylebros & Co (Bangladesh) 32
Adkinson Parrish Ltd (United Kingdom) 371
Adlard Coles Ltd (United Kingdom) 371
Administracion, Archivo General de la, Civil del Estado (General Archives of the Civil Administration of the State) (Spain) 328
Adonais Prize (Spain) 329
Adressbuchausschuss der deutschen Wirtschaft (German Trade Directory Committee) (Federal Republic of Germany) 121
Advaita Ashrama (India) 187
Advance Publishing Co Ltd (Ghana) 174
Advanced Teacher Training College (Ghana) 175
Adventist Book Centre (Zimbabwe) 435
Adversaires, Editions, (Switzerland) 341
Advisor Editions (France) 89
Advisory Committee on the Selection of Low-Priced Books for Overseas (United Kingdom) 369
Adyar-Verlag (Austria) 24
Æskunnar, Bókaútgáfa, (Iceland) 184
Aesopus Verlag GmbH (Switzerland) 341
Affiliated East-West Press Pvt Ltd (India) 187
Afghan Kitab (Afghanistan) 1
Afha Internacional SA (Spain) 318
Afram Publications (Ghana) Ltd (Ghana) 174
Africa Agency (Nigeria) 279
Africa Christian Press (Ghana) 174
Africa Editions (Senegal) 306
Africa Educational Representatives (Kenya) 236
Africa Literature Centre (Zambia) 433
African Book Centre (Zimbabwe) 435
African Library Association of South Africa (Republic of South Africa) 316
African Resources Publishing Co (Nigeria) 277
African Universities Press (Nigeria) 277
Africana Book Society (Pty) Ltd (Republic of South Africa) 311
Africana Book Society Ltd (Republic of South Africa) 315
Africana Educational Publishers Co (Nigeria) 277
Africani Agency (Nigeria) 277
Afrikaans Literature Society (ALV) (Republic of South Africa) 316
Afrikaans Literature Society Prize (Republic of South Africa) 316
Afrique-Levant (Senegal) 307
Afrique-Levant, Edition, (Senegal) 307
Afriscope/University of Ife Bookshop Ltd Prize (International Literary Prizes) 446
Afro-Asian Writers, Permanent Bureau of, (Egypt) 83
Afro-Asian Writers' Bureau (Sri Lanka) 330
Afro-Asian Writers' Permanent Bureau (International Organizations) 437
Afrontamento, Edições, (Portugal) 298
Agathon (Netherlands) 258
'Age' Book of the Year (Australia) 21
Age d'Homme, Editions L', — La Cité (Switzerland) 341
Agence belge des grandes Editions SA (Belgium) 34
Agence belge des grandes Editions SA (Belgium) 44
Agence de Distribution de Presse (Senegal) 307
Agence de Distribution de Presse (Senegal) 307
Agence Parisienne de Distribution Sarl (France) 89
Agencja Autorska (Poland) 296
Agencja Autorska (Authors' Agency Ltd) (Poland) 294
Agents Editores Ltda (Brazil) 49
Agenzia Letteraria Internazionale (Italy) 221
Agir, Livraria, (Brazil) 55
Agis Verlag GmbH (Federal Republic of Germany) 124
Agnelli, Giacomo, Editore (Italy) 212
Agon Elsevier BV (Netherlands) 258
Agora-Verlag (Federal Republic of Germany) 124
Agricultural Books Publishing House (Democratic People's Republic of Korea) 237
Agricultural Experiment Station Library (Puerto Rico) 302
Agricultural Library (Nigeria) 280
Agricultural Science, Central Library of, (Israel) 211
Agriculture University Library (Pakistan) 286
Agrupación Bibliotecológica del Uruguay (Uruguay) 423
Agrupación de Bibliotecas para la Integración de la Información Socio-Económica (ABIISE) (Library Group for the Integration of Socio-economic Information) (Peru) 290
Agudat Harashash (Israel) 206
Aguilar, Editora Nova, S/A (Brazil) 49
Aguilar, M, (Spain) 327
Aguilar, M, Editor SA (Mexico) 250
Aguilar Argentina SA de Ediciones (Argentina) 3
Aguilar Chilena de Ediciones (Chile) 62
Aguilar Colombiana de Ediciones (Colombia) 65
Aguilar Peruana de Ediciones SA (Peru) 289
Aguilar SA de Ediciones (Spain) 318
Aguilar Venezolana SA de Ediciones (Venezuela) 424
Aguirre, Librería, (Colombia) 66

Ahd, Al, Al Gadeed Bookstore (Egypt) 82
Ahmadu Bello University Bookshop (Nigeria) 279
Ahmadu Bello University Library (Nigeria) 280
Ahmadu Bello University Press Ltd (Nigeria) 277
Ahmedabad Publishers' & Booksellers' Association (India) 186
Ahnert, L B, -Verlag (Federal Republic of Germany) 124
Ahora, Publicaciones, C por A (Dominican Republic) 80
Ahram, Al-, Establishment (Egypt) 82
Ahram, Al-, Establishment (Egypt) 82
Ahsan Brothers (Pakistan) 285
Aiken, Alex, (United Kingdom) 371
Airlife Publications (Shrewsbury) Ltd (United Kingdom) 371
Airport Bookshop (Republic of Korea) 239
Ajuda, Biblioteca da, (Portugal) 301
Akadémiai Kiadó (Publishing House of the Hungarian Academy of Sciences) (Hungary) 182
Akademie der Wissenschaften und der Literatur (Academy of Sciences, Arts and Literature) (Federal Republic of Germany) 172
Akademie-Verlag (German Democratic Republic) 117
Akademiförlaget (Sweden) 332
Akademii Nauk SSSR, Biblioteka, (Union of Soviet Socialist Republics) 367
Akademii Nauk SSSR, Gosudarstvennaya publichnaya nauchno-tekhnicheskaya biblioteka Sibirskogo otdeleniya, (Union of Soviet Socialist Republics) 367
Akademii Nauk SSSR, Institut nauchnoy informatsii po obschestvennym naukam, (Union of Soviet Socialist Republics) 367
Akademii Nauk USSR, Tsentral'naya nauchnaya biblioteka, (Union of Soviet Socialist Republics) 367
Akademilitteratur Förlaget AB (Sweden) 332
Akademische Druck- und Verlagsanstalt (Austria) 24
Akademische Verlagsgesellschaft (Federal Republic of Germany) 124
Akademische Verlagsgesellschaft Athenaion (Federal Republic of Germany) 124
Akademisk Boghandel (Denmark) 78
Akademisk Forlag (Denmark) 74
Akadia, Librería, Editorial (Argentina) 3
Akadoma (Indonesia) 199
Akane Shobo Co Ltd (Japan) 225
Akateeminen Kirjakauppa (Finland) 87
Akateeminen Kustannusliike Oy (Finland) 85
Åkerbloms, Johan, Universitetsbokhandel (Sweden) 338
Akhil Bhartiya Hindi Prakashak Sangh (India) 186
Akita Shoten Publishing Co Ltd (Japan) 225
Akros Publications (United Kingdom) 371
Aksorn Charerntat (Thailand) 359
Aksorn Charoen Tasna Ltd (Thailand) 359
Aktuell-Verlag (Austria) 24
Akutagawa Prize (Japan) 233
Al-Aadab Bookshop (Bahrain) 32
Al-Fateh University, The Central Library (Libya) 242
'Alas', Editorial, (Spain) 318
Alba AB (Sweden) 332
Alba Buchverlag GmbH und Co KG (Federal Republic of Germany) 124
Alba Publikation Alf Teloeken GmbH und Co KG (Federal Republic of Germany) 124
Albanus Verlag (Switzerland) 341
Albatros (Czechoslovakia) 70
Albatros, Editorial, SRL (Argentina) 3
Albatros, Editura, (Romania) 304
Albatros Verlag AG (Switzerland) 341
Albe Soc Com (Uruguay) 422
Albér, Verlag Karl, GmbH (Federal Republic of Germany) 124
Albin, Editions, Michel (France) 89
Albino Jose de Magalhes Lda (Angola) 2
Albrecht, Emil, (Austria) 30
Albyn Press Ltd (United Kingdom) 371
Alcheh, Librarie, (Israel) 210
Alda, B P, (Indonesia) 199
Alden & Mowbray Ltd (United Kingdom) 371
Aldine Paperbacks (United Kingdom) 371
Aldus Books Ltd (United Kingdom) 371
Aldwych Press (United Kingdom) 371
Aleko International Competition Awards in Comic Short Story (International Literary Prizes) 446
Alemana, Editorial, (Nicaragua) 276
Alemany, Juan Max, (Dominican Republic) 80
Alemar-Phoenix Publishing House Inc (Philippines) 291
Alemar's (Philippines) 292
Aleph Publishers Ltd (Israel) 206
Alexander Prize (International Literary Prizes) 447
Alexandria Municipal Library (Egypt) 83
Alfa, Editorial, Argentina SA (Argentina) 3
Alfa, Editorial, SA (Uruguay) 422
Alfa — Vydavateľstvo technickej a ekonomickej literatury (Czechoslovakia) 70
Alfa Edizioni e Rappresentanze Editoriali (Italy) 212
Alfa y Omega, Editora, (Dominican Republic) 80
Alfaguara, Ediciones, SA (Spain) 318
Alfieri Edizioni d'Arte (Italy) 212

Algamiia Almasriia Lilmaktabat Almadrasiia (Egypt) 83
Algemene Nederlandse Bond van Leesbibliotheekhouders (Netherlands Association of Reference Librarians) (Netherlands) 269
Algemene Vlaamse Boekverkopersbond (Belgium) 33
Algona Publications Pty Ltd (Australia) 10
Alhambra, Editorial, SA (Spain) 318
Ali Publications (Bangladesh) 32
Alianza Editorial Mexicana (Mexico) 250
Alianza Editorial SA (Spain) 318
Alinari Fratelli SpA Istituto di Edizioni Artistiche (Italy) 212
Alip & Sons Publishing Inc (Philippines) 291
Alison Press (United Kingdom) 371
Alkaios-Tropaiatis (Greece) 176
All India Booksellers' & Publishers' Association (India) 186
All India Hindi Publishers' Association (India) 186
All-Union Patent and Technical Library (Union of Soviet Socialist Republics) 367
Állami könyvterjesztő vállalat (Hungary) 183
Állami könyvterjesztő vállalat orzágos antikvár (Hungary) 183
Allan, Ian, Ltd (United Kingdom) 371
Allan, Philip, Publishers Ltd (United Kingdom) 371
Allara Publishing (Australia) 10
Allen, J A, & Co Ltd (United Kingdom) 371
Allen, W H, & Co Ltd (United Kingdom) 371
Allen & Unwin, George, (Publishers) Ltd (United Kingdom) 371
Allen & Unwin, George, Australia Pty Ltd (Australia) 10
Allhems Förlag AB (Sweden) 332
Alliance, L', française (Senegal) 307
Alliance française (Zaire) 433
Alliance West African Publishers & Co (Nigeria) 277
Allied Irish Banks' Award for Literature (Republic of Ireland) 205
Allied Publishers Private Ltd (India) 187
Allison & Busby Ltd (United Kingdom) 371
Allman & Son (Publishers) Ltd (United Kingdom) 371
Allmänna, AB, Förlaget (Sweden) 332
Allot, Librairie, (Mauritius) 249
Alma Mater, Libreria, Inc (Puerto Rico) 302
Alma'Arif (Indonesia) 199
Almark Publishing Co Ltd (United Kingdom) 372
Almenna Bókafélagid (Iceland) 184
Almonde (France) 89
Almqvist och Wiksell Bokhandel AB (Sweden) 338
Almqvist och Wiksell Förlag AB (Sweden) 332
Almqvist och Wiksell International (Sweden) 332
Almqvist och Wiksell Läromedel AB (Sweden) 332
Alonso, Editorial Rodolfo, SRL (Argentina) 3
Alpenland Verlag (Liechtenstein) 243
alpha 9 GmbH (Federal Republic of Germany) 124
Alpha-Beta Publications Ltd (India) 187
Alpha Books (Australia) 11
Alpha Books (Zimbabwe) 435
Alpha Editions (France) 89
Alpha Literatur Verlag (Federal Republic of Germany) 124
Alphabet & Image Ltd (United Kingdom) 372
Alphonsiana, Bibliotheca, VZW (Belgium) 34
Alpina, Editions, (France) 89
Alpine Books (United Kingdom) 372
Alsatia SA (France) 89
Alta, Editions, (France) 89
Altea, Ediciones, SA (Spain) 318
Alternative Editions (United Kingdom) 372
Alternative Publishing Co-operative Ltd (Australia) 11
Alternative Verlag GmbH (Federal Republic of Germany) 124
Althea's Pet Series (United Kingdom) 372
Altiora NV (Belgium) 34
Alumni Press (Indonesia) 199
Alvárez, Librería Anibal, (Venezuela) 425
Alves, Livraria Francisco, Editôra SA (Brazil) 49
Alviella, Goblet d', Prize (Belgium) 45
Am Hasefer (Israel) 206
Am Oved Publishers Ltd (Israel) 206
Amadeus (Switzerland) 341
Amado, Arménio, Editor Suc (Portugal) 298
Amalthea-Verlag (Austria) 24
Aman, Pustaka, Press Sdn Bhd (Malaysia) 246
Amarko Book Agency (India) 187
Amazonen Frauenverlag GmbH (Federal Republic of Germany) 124
Ambassadors' Prize (France) 112
Ambika Publications (India) 187
Ambo, Uitgeverij, BV (Netherlands) 258
Ambrosiana, Biblioteca, (Italy) 222
America, Casa, (Netherlands Antilles) 271
América, Librería, (Nicaragua) 276
América, Librería, (Colombia) 66
America Latina (Uruguay) 422
América Norildis Editores SA (Argentina) 3
Américalee, Editorial, SRL (Argentina) 3
American Book Store SA (Mexico) 253

464 INDEX

American Books (Argentina) 8
American Bookstore (Greece) 177
American Center Library (Ghana) 175
American Cultural Center Library (Libya) 242
American Cultural Center Library (Upper Volta) 422
American Cultural Center Library (Sudan) 330
American Cultural Center Library (Togo) 360
American-Israel Publishing Co Ltd (Israel) 206
American Library (Ethiopia) 84
American Library (Jordan) 234
American Library (Nepal) 257
American Library Resource Center (Republic of Singapore) 310
American University, Library of, of Beirut (Lebanon) 241
American University in Cairo Library (Egypt) 83
American University in Cairo Press (Egypt) 82
American University Publishers Group Ltd (United Kingdom) 372
Americana, Editorial, (Argentina) 3
Américas, Casa de las, (Cuba) 68
Amerind Publishing Co (P) Ltd (India) 199
    Amerind Publishing Co (P) Ltd (India) 187
Amharic Literature Award (Ethiopia) 84
Amichai Publishing House Ltd (Israel) 206
Amigo, El, de Todos (Venezuela) 425
Amigos, Editorial Los, del Libro (Bolivia) 47
Amigos, Librería Los, del Libro (Bolivia) 47
Amigos del Libro, Ediciones los, (Bolivia) 47
Amigos do Livro (Portugal) 301
Amikam (Israel) 206
Amir Kabir Publishing & Distributing Corporation (Iran) 201
Amir Publishing-Japheth Press Ltd (Israel) 206
Amis, Les, de Franco Maria Ricci (France) 110
Amis, Les, de Milosz (France) 90
Amitié, Editions de l', (France) 90
Amitié, L', par le Livre (France) 110
Amman Public Library (Jordan) 234
Amorrortu Editores SA (Argentina) 3
Ampersand Ltd (United Kingdom) 372
Amphora, Editions, SA (France) 90
Amsterdam Boek BV (Netherlands) 258
Amsterdam Prizes (Netherlands) 270
Anabas-Verlag Günter Kämpf KG (Federal Republic of Germany) 124
Anael (France) 90
Anagrama, Editorial, (Spain) 318
Anambra/Imo States School Libraries Association (Nigeria) 280
Anand Book Club (India) 197
Anand Paperbacks (India) 187
Anaya, Ediciones, SA (Spain) 318
Anceau, Annuaires Ravet, (France) 90
Anchor (United Kingdom) 372
Ancient History Book Club (United Kingdom) 414
Ancora, Editrice, Milano (Italy) 212
Ancora y Delfin, Librería, (Spain) 327
Andersen, Hans Christian, Awards (International Literary Prizes) 447
Andersen, Hans Christian, Prize (Denmark) 80
Andersen Press Ltd (United Kingdom) 372
Andersen Prize (Italy) 223
Andreas, Jörn, Verlag (Austria) 24
Andreas und Andreas Verlagsbuchhandel (Austria) 24
Andrei, Organização, Editora SA (Brazil) 49
Andres Kalender und Buch Verlag GmbH (Federal Republic of Germany) 124
Andrew Publishing Co (United Kingdom) 372
Andromeda, Ediciones, (Argentina) 3
Angelet (Belgium) 34
Angeli, Franco, Editore (Italy) 212
Angelica, Biblioteca, (Italy) 222
Angestellten Verein des schweizer Buchhandels (Association of Swiss Book Trade Employees) (Switzerland) 339
Angkasa (Indonesia) 199
Anglo American, Al-, Bookshop (Egypt) 82
Anglo-Chinese Textbook Publishers Organization Ltd (Hong Kong) 180
Anglo Egyptian, Al-, Bookshop (Egypt) 82
Anglo-Hellenic Agency (Greece) 177
Anglo-Hellenic Publishing (Greece) 176
Angolana, Nova Editorial, SARL (Angola) 2
Angst, Verlag Roland, (Federal Republic of Germany) 124
Angus & Robertson (South-East Asia) Ltd (Republic of Singapore) 308
Angus & Robertson (UK) Ltd (United Kingdom) 372
Angus & Robertson Bookshops (Head Office) (Australia) 19
Angus & Robertson Publishers (Australia) 11
Angus & Robertson Writers' Fellowship (Australia) 21
Angyra Ekdotikos Oikos (Greece) 176
Anjoman-e Ketabdaren-e Iran (Iranian Library Association) (Iran) 202
Anjuman Kitab-Khana-I-Afghanistan (Afghan Library Association) (Afghanistan) 1

Anjuman Taraqqi-e-Urdu Pakistan (Pakistan) 287
Ankara University Library (Turkey) 363
Ankh-Hermes BV (Netherlands) 258
Ankur Publishing House (India) 187
Anowuo Educational Publications (Ghana) 174
Anrich, Neithard, Verlag (Federal Republic of Germany) 124
Ansata-Verlag (Switzerland) 341
Ansay Pty Ltd (Australia) 11
Ansgar Forlag A/S (Norway) 281
Antara, Pustaka, (Malaysia) 246
Antara, Pustaka, (Indonesia) 199
Antarès Editions d'Art (France) 90
Antenna Edições Técnicas Ltda (Brazil) 49
Anthonian Store Sdn Bhd (Malaysia) 247
Anthonian Stores Sdn Bhd (Malaysia) 246
Anthropos, Editions, SA (France) 90
Anthroposophiques Romandes, Editions, (Switzerland) 341
Antipodean Publishers Pty Ltd (Australia) 11
Antiquarian Booksellers' Association (United Kingdom) 369
Antiquarian Booksellers' Association of Japan (Japan) 225
Antoine, Editions Jacques, SPRL (Belgium) 34
Antoine, Librairies, (Lebanon) 241
Antonius-Verlag (Switzerland) 341
'Antso', Maison d'Edition Protestante, (Democratic Republic of Madagascar) 244
Antwerpse Lloyd NV (Belgium) 34
Anvil Books Ltd (Republic of Ireland) 203
Anwari Publications (Bangladesh) 32
Ao Livro Técnico (Brazil) 55
Ao Livro Técnico SA Indústria e Comércio (Brazil) 49
Aoki Shoten Co Ltd (Japan) 225
Aowa Press & Publications (Nigeria) 277
Apa Productions (Pte) Ltd (Republic of Singapore) 308
Apec Editôra SA (Brazil) 49
Apollinaire, Guillaume, Prize (France) 112
Apostolado, Livraria, da Imprensa (Portugal) 298
Apoteksbolaget AB (Sweden) 332
Apple Paperbacks (Australia) 11
Appletree, The, Press Ltd (United Kingdom) 372
Applied Science Publishers Ltd (United Kingdom) 372
Aprile, Ruggero, (Italy) 212
Apuntes, Librería Los, (Uruguay) 422
Aquaran Press Ltd (United Kingdom) 372
Aquarius Editora e Distribuidora de Livros Ltda (Brazil) 49
Aquila Publishing (United Kingdom) 372
Aquilina, A C, & Co (Malta) 248
Aquilina, A C, & Co (Malta) 248
Arab, Al, Bookshop (Egypt) 82
Arab Advertising Organization (Syria) 357
Arab Institute for Research and Publishing (Lebanon) 240
Arab Library (Mauritania) 249
Arab Publishing, Al, House (Egypt) 82
Arab Regional Branch of the International Council on Archives (International Organizations) 437
Arab University Library Association (International Organizations) 437
Arango, Biblioteca Luis-Angel, (Colombia) 66
Aranha, Graca, Prize (Brazil) 57
Arani-Verlag GmbH (Federal Republic of Germany) 124
Aranzadi, Editorial, (Spain) 318
Ararat Verlag GmbH (Federal Republic of Germany) 124
Arbalète, L', (France) 90
Arbeiderspers, BV Uitgeverij de, (Netherlands) 258
Arbeiterbewegung und Gesellschaftswissenschaft, Verlag, (Federal Republic of Germany) 124
Arbeitsgemeinschaft Buchgemeinschaften und verwandte Unternehmen im Börsenverein des Deutschen Buchhandels (Federal Republic of Germany) 121
Arbeitsgemeinschaft der Hochschulbibliotheken (Federal Republic of Germany) 171
Arbeitsgemeinschaft der kirchlichen Büchereiverbände Deutschlands (Federal Republic of Germany) 171
Arbeitsgemeinschaft der Kunstbibliotheken (Federal Republic of Germany) 171
Arbeitsgemeinschaft der Parlaments- und Behördenbibliotheken (Federal Republic of Germany) 171
Arbeitsgemeinschaft der Regionalbibliotheken (Federal Republic of Germany) 171
Arbeitsgemeinschaft der Spezialbibliotheken eV (Federal Republic of Germany) 171
Arbeitsgemeinschaft der Vertriebsfachverbände (Federal Republic of Germany) 121
Arbeitsgemeinschaft Deutsche Lateinamerika-Forschung (ADLAF) (Federal Republic of Germany) 124
Arbeitsgemeinschaft für das Archiv- und Bibliothekswesen in der evangelischen Kirche (Federal Republic of Germany) 171
Arbeitsgemeinschaft für juristische Bibliotheks- und Dokumentationswesen (Federal Republic of Germany) 171

Arbeitsgemeinschaft für medizinisches Bibliothekswesen (Federal Republic of Germany) 171
Arbeitsgemeinschaft katholischtheologischer Bibliotheken (Federal Republic of Germany) 171
Arbeitsgemeinschaft Literarische und Sachbuchverlage (Federal Republic of Germany) 121
Arbeitsgemeinschaft mitteleuropäischer Bibelwerke (Federal Republic of Germany) 124
Arbeitsgemeinschaft rechts- und staatswissenschaftlicher Verleger (Economics and Legal Publishers Alliance) (Federal Republic of Germany) 121
Arbeitsgemeinschaft sozialistischer und demokratischer Verleger und Buchhändler (Co-operative of Socialist and Democratic Publishing Houses and Bookshops) (Federal Republic of Germany) 124
Arbeitsgemeinschaft von Jugendbuchverlegern in der Bundesrepublik Deutschland eV (Federal Republic of Germany) 122
Arbeitsgemeinschaft wissenschaftliche Literatur eV (Federal Republic of Germany) 172
Arbeitskreis für Jugendliteratur eV (Youth Literature Committee) (Section of the International Board on Books for Young People) (Federal Republic of Germany) 172
Arbeitsstelle für das Bibliothekswesen (Federal Republic of Germany) 171
Arbeitswelt, Verlag Die, GmbH (Federal Republic of Germany) 125
Arbetarkultur, Förlagsaktiebolaget, (Sweden) 332
Arbó SACeI (Argentina) 3
Arborio, Maria-Pia D', (Italy) 221
Arca, Editorial, SRL (Uruguay) 422
Arcade-Fonds Mercator, Editions, (Belgium) 34
Arcádia, Editora, Sarl (Portugal) 298
Arcana Editrice Srl (Italy) 212
Arcane Bookshop (Cyprus) 69
Arcanum, AB, (Sweden) 332
Archbishopric, Library of the, (Cyprus) 69
Arche, Verlag der, Peter Schifferli AG (Switzerland) 341
Archibald Brothers (Zimbabwe) 435
Archiginnasio, Biblioteca Comunale dell', (Italy) 222
Archimedes Verlag (Switzerland) 341
Architectural Press Ltd (United Kingdom) 372
Architecture & Arts Publications Co (Sri Lanka) 329
Architektur, Verlag für, (Federal Republic of Germany) 125
Archiv der Universität Wien (Austria) 30
Archival Institution (Bahamas) 32
Archivele Statului (National Archives) (Romania) 304
Archives, Central, of the People's Republic of Bulgaria (Bulgaria) 58
Archives, Central Historical, (Bulgaria) 58
Archives, Direction des, de France (France) 111
Archives, Inspection des, (Mali) 248
Archives, Public, of Sierra Leone (Sierra Leone) 308
Archives, The Central, for the History of the Jewish People (formerly Jewish Historical General Archives) (Israel) 211
Archives de l'Etat (National Archives) (Luxembourg) 244
Archives de Madagascar (Democratic Republic of Madagascar) 245
Archives de Sénégal (Senegal) 307
Archives départementales de la Martinique (Martinique) 249
Archives départementales de la Réunion (Réunion) 303
Archives et Bibliothèque nationale (National Library and Archives) (Gabon) 116
Archives et Bibliothèque nationales (National Archives and Library) (Kampuchea) 235
Archives fédérales (Federal Archives) (Switzerland) 356
Archives générales du Royaume (Belgium) 44
Archives nationales (Algeria) 2
Archives nationales (Niger) 276
Archives nationales (France) 111
Archives nationales, Direction des, (National Archives) (Laos) 240
Archives nationales (National Archives) (Tunisia) 362
Archives nationales de la République Populaire du Benin (Benin) 47
Archives nationales du Cameroun (United Republic of Cameroon) 61
Archives nationales du Mali (Mali) 248
Archives nationales du Zaïre (Zaire) 433
Archives of Early Russian Historical Records, Central State, (Union of Soviet Socialist Republics) 367
Archives of the October Revolution, Central State, and Higher State Bodies (Union of Soviet Socialist Republics) 367
Archives of the RSFSR, Central State, (Union of Soviet Socialist Republics) 367
Archives of the USSR, Central State Historical, (Union of Soviet Socialist Republics) 367
Archives of the USSR, Central State Literature and Art, (Union of Soviet Socialist Republics) 367
Archives Service, The, of the Prime Minister's Office of the Socialist Republic of Viet Nam (Socialist Republic of Viet Nam) 426

Archivio Centrale dello Stato (Italy) 222
Archivio Storico, Biblioteca dell', Civico e Biblioteca Trivulziana (Italy) 222
Archivo General de Centro (Guatemala) 179
Archivo General de Indias (Archives of the Indies) (Spain) 328
Archivo General de la Nación (Dominican Republic) 81
Archivo General de la Nación (National Archives) (Mexico) 254
Archivo General de la Nación (National Archives) (Nicaragua) 276
Archivo General de la Nación (National Archives) (Peru) 290
Archivo General de la Nación (National Archives) (Venezuela) 425
Archivo General de la Nación (National Archives) (Uruguay) 423
Archivo General de Puerto Rico (Puerto Rico) 303
Archivo Histórico Municipal de la Habana (Municipal Archives of Havana) (Cuba) 68
Archivo Historico Nacional (National Historical Archives) (Spain) 328
Archivo Nacional de Colombia, Biblioteca Nacional (Colombia) 66
Archivo Nacional de Historia (Ecuador) 81
Archivo y Biblioteca Capitulares (Archives and Library of the Cathedral Chapter) (Spain) 328
Archivos Históricos y Bibliotecas (Historical and Library Archives) (Mexico) 254
Archiwów Państwowych, Naczelna Dyrekcja, (Main Directorate of the Polish State Archives) (Poland) 296
Archiwum Akt Nowych (Centre for Recent Documents) (Poland) 296
Archiwum Główne Akt Dawnych (Central Archives for Historical Documents) (Poland) 296
Archon, The, Press Ltd (United Kingdom) 372
Aredit, Publications, (France) 90
Arena (United Kingdom) 372
Arena-Verlag Georg Popp (Federal Republic of Germany) 125
Argente, Sentos & Cia Lda (Angola) 2
Argentine Authors Society Medal of Honour (International Literary Prizes) 447
Argentine National Prize for Literature (Argentina) 9
Argos, Editorial, Vergara SA (Spain) 318
Argos, Librería Editorial, SA (Spain) 327
Argosy, Librería, (Panama) 288
Arguedas, Premio José María, (Peru) 290
Argus Books Ltd (United Kingdom) 372
Argus Communications (UK Division) (United Kingdom) 372
Argus Elsevier BV (Netherlands) 258
Arhiv Hrvatske (Yugoslavia) 431
Arhiv na SR Makedonija (Yugoslavia) 431
Arhiv SR Slovenije (Yugoslavia) 431
Arhiv Srbije (Yugoslavia) 431
Århus Kommunes Biblioteker (Denmark) 78
Arica, Editorial, SA (Peru) 289
Arica, Librería, (Peru) 290
Ariel, Editorial, SA (Spain) 319
Ariel Ltda (Ecuador) 81
Aries Lima (Indonesia) 199
Arinos, Afonso, Prize (Brazil) 57
Aris & Phillips Ltd (United Kingdom) 372
Ariston Verlag (formerly Ramòn F Keller) (Switzerland) 341
Ark (United Kingdom) 372
Arkady Publishing House (Poland) 294
Arkana-Verlag (Federal Republic of Germany) 125
Arkin Kitabevi (Turkey) 362
Arkistoyhdistys ry (Finland) 87
Arkivarforeningen (The Association of Archivists) (Norway) 284
Arkivforeningen (Denmark) 79
Arlecchino Teaterförlag (Sweden) 337
Arlington Books (Publishers) Ltd (United Kingdom) 373
Armada Books (United Kingdom) 373
Armando, Editore Armando, (Italy) 212
Armazens Distribuidores Lta (Mozambique) 256
Armed Forces Library Service (Ghana) 175
Armée, Editions Populaires de l', (Algeria) 2
Armitano, Ernesto, (Venezuela) 424
Armon Publishing House Ltd (Israel) 206
Arms & Armour Press (United Kingdom) 373
Arnado, Livraria, Lda (Portugal) 298
Arndt, Ernst-Moritz-, Universität Universitatsbibliothek (German Democratic Republic) 120
Arnkrone Forlaget A/S (Denmark) 74
Arnold, Edward, (Australia) Pty Ltd (Australia) 11
Arnold & Son, E J, Ltd (United Kingdom) 373
Arnold (Publishers), Edward, Ltd (United Kingdom) 373
Arnold-Heinemann Publishers (India) Pvt Ltd (India) 187
Aromolaran Publishing Co Ltd (Nigeria) 277
Arquivo Historico de Moçambique (Mozambique) 256
Arquivo Nacionaal (Brazil) 56
Arquivo Nacional da Torre do Tombo (Portugal) 301

Arrow (Australia) 19
Arrow Books Ltd (United Kingdom) 373
Arrow Co (Israel) 206
Ars, Verlag, Sacra Josef Müller (Federal Republic of Germany) 125
Ars Christiana (Poland) 294
Ars Polona (Poland) 296
Arscia, Editions, SA (Belgium) 34
Arsenal, Bibliothèque de l', (France) 111
Arsenides, John, Ekdotis (Greece) 176
Arsip Nasional Republik Indonesia (National Archives) (Indonesia) 201
Art, The, Publisher (Hong Kong) 180
Art Address Verlag Müller GmbH und Co KG (Federal Republic of Germany) 125
Art-CC A G (Switzerland) 341
Art Edit AG (Switzerland) 341
Art et Valeur (France) 90
Arte, Editorial, y Literatura (Cuba) 68
Arted (Editions d'Art) (France) 90
Artel Publishing & Commercial Organization Co Ltd (Turkey) 362
Artemis Press Ltd (United Kingdom) 373
Artemis und Winkler Verlag (Federal Republic of Germany) 125
Artemis Verlags AG (Switzerland) 341
Artenova, Editôra, SA (Brazil) 49
Artes, Livraría Editôra, Medicas Ltda (Brazil) 49
Arthaud, Editions, SA (France) 90
Arti Grafiche della Venezie SpA (Italy) 212
Artia (Czechoslovakia) 70
Artia (Czechoslovakia) 72
Artibus et Literis (Federal Republic of Germany) 170
Artigas-Washington, Biblioteca, (ICA) (Uruguay) 423
Artis-Historia, SC, (Belgium) 34
Artisan du Livre (Guérin et Cie) (France) 90
Artisjus (Hungary) 183
Artists', The, Book Club (United Kingdom) 414
Artists' and Writers' Guild of South Africa (Republic of South Africa) 316
Artists House (United Kingdom) 373
Artrey, Editions d', (France) 90
Arts & Science University Library (Burma) 59
Arts and Crafts School Library (Libya) 242
Arts Book Society (United Kingdom) 414
Arts Council Awards and Bursaries (International Literary Prizes) 447
Arts et Métiers Graphiques (France) 90
Arts et Voyages, Editions, (Belgium) 34
Arts Graphiques, Compagnie Française des, SA (France) 90
Arts Guild (United Kingdom) 414
Artystyczne i Filmowe, Wydawnictwa, (Poland) 294
Aruba Boekhandel (Netherlands Antilles) 271
Arusha Public Library (Tanzania) 358
Arvi A Karisto Oy (Finland) 85
Asahiya Shoten Ltd (Booksellers) (Japan) 232
Asakura Publishing Co Ltd (Japan) 225
Ascent Books Ltd (United Kingdom) 373
Aschehoug, H, & Co (W Nygaard) A/S (Norway) 281
Aschehoug Dansk Forlag A/S (Denmark) 74
Aschendorffsche Verlagsbuchhandlung (Federal Republic of Germany) 125
Asesoría Técnica de Ediciones SA (Spain) 319
Asgar Ali Book Centre (Trinidad and Tobago) 361
Asher, A, & Co, BV (Netherlands) 258
Ashmolean Museum Publications (United Kingdom) 373
Ashraf, Shaikh Muhammad, (Pakistan) 285
Ashton, H J, Co Ltd (New Zealand) 272
Ashton Scholastic (Australia) 11
Asia, M/S, Pacific Press, Pte, Ltd (Republic of Singapore) 308
Asia Afrika (Indonesia) 199
Asia Book Co (Republic of Singapore) 310
Asia Books Co Ltd (Thailand) 360
Asia Pacific Research Unit Ltd (New Zealand) 272
Asia Press Bookstore Ltd (Hong Kong) 181
Asia Press Ltd (Hong Kong) 180
Asia Publishing House (P) Ltd (India) 188
Asian Educational Services (India) 188
Asian Publishers (India) 188
Asiathèque, L', (France) 90
Askild och Kärnekull Förlag AB (Sweden) 332
Aslan Publishing Services Ltd (United Kingdom) 373
Aslib (United Kingdom) 416
Asmara Public Library (Ethiopia) 84
Asociación Argentina de Bibliotecas y Centros de Información Cientificos y Tecnicos (Argentina) 8
Asociación Bibliotecologica Guatemalteca (Library Association of Guatemala) (Guatemala) 179
Asociación Boliviana de Bibliotecarios (A B B) (Bolivia) 48
Asociación Colombiana de Bibliotecarios (Colombia) 66
Asociación Costarricense de Bibliotecarios (Costa Rica) 68
Asociación de Bibliotecarios de El Salvador (El Salvador) 84

Asociación de Bibliotecarios de Instituciones de Enseñanza Superior e Investigación (ABIESI) (Association of Librarians of Higher Education and Research Institutions) (Mexico) 254
Asociación de Bibliotecarios del Paraguay (Association of Paraguayan Librarians) (Paraguay) 289
Asociación de Bibliotecarios del Uruguay (Uruguay) 423
Asociación de Bibliotecarios Graduados del Istmo de Panamá (Association of Graduate Librarians of the Isthmus of Panama) (Panama) 288
Asociación de Bibliotecarios Universitarios del Paraguay (Paraguayan Association of University Librarians) (Paraguay) 289
Asociación de Bibliotecarios y Archiveros de Honduras (Association of Librarians and Archivists of Honduras) (Honduras) 180
Asociación de Bibliotecas Agricolas (Association of Agricultural Librarians) (Peru) 290
Asociación de Bibliotecas Universitarias y Especializadas de Nicaragua (Association of University and Special Libraries of Nicaragua) (Nicaragua) 276
Asociación de Escritores de Colombia (Colombia) 67
Asociación de Escritores y Artistas Españoles (Spanish Writers' and Artists' Association) (Spain) 328
Asociación de Ex-Alumnos de la Escuela Nacional de Bibliotecarios (Argentina) 9
Asociación de Libreros del Uruguay (Uruguay) 422
Asociación Dominicana de Bibliotecarios (ASODOBI) (Dominican Republic) 81
Asociación Ecuatoriana de Bibliotecarios (AEB) (Ecuador) 81
Asociación General de Archivistas de El Salvador (El Salvador) 84
Asociación Interamericana de Escritores (Inter-American Association of Writers) (International Organizations) 437
Asociación Latinoamericana de Escuelas de Bibliotecologia y Ciencias de la Información (ALEBCI) (Latin American Association of Schools of Library and Information Science) (International Organizations) 437
Asociación Mexicana de Bibliotecarios AC (AMBAC) (Mexican Association of Librarians) (Mexico) 254
Asociación Nacional de Autores de Obras Didacticas (AUCOLDI) (Colombia) 67
Asociación Nacional de Bibliotecarios, Archiveros y Arqueólogos, (National Association of Librarians, Archivists and Archaeologists) (Spain) 328
Asociación Nacional de Escritores Venezolanos (Venezuela) 425
Asociación Nacional de Escritores y Artistas (ANEA) (National Association of Writers and Artists) (Peru) 290
Asociación Nicaraguense de Bibliotecarios (ASNIBI) (Nicaraguan Association of Librarians) (Nicaragua) 276
Asociación Panameña de Bibliotecarios (Panama Library Association) (Panama) 288
Asociación para el Progresso de la Dirección (APD) (Spain) 319
Asociación Peruana de Archiveros (Peruvian Association of Archivists) (Peru) 290
Asociación Peruana de Bibliotecarios (Peruvian Association of Librarians) (Peru) 290
Asociación Uruguaya de Escritores (Uruguay) 423
Asociatia Bibliotecarilor din RSR (Librarians' Association of Romania) (Romania) 305
Asociation di Biblioteka i Archivo di Korsow (Carbidor) (Association of Libraries and Archives) (Netherlands Antilles) 271
Aspekte Verlag GmbH (Federal Republic of Germany) 125
Aspioti-Elka SA (Greece) 176
Assam Publishers' & Booksellers' Association (India) 186
Assayad, Dar, (Lebanon) 240
Assimakopouli (Greece) 176
Assimil, Editions, SA (France) 90
Assimil, Uitgaven Nelis PVBA (Belgium) 34
Assimil-Verlag KG (Federal Republic of Germany) 125
Asso Verlag Anneliese Althoff (Federal Republic of Germany) 125
Associação Brasileira de Bibliotecarios (Brazil) 56
Associação Brasileira de Livreiros Antiquarios (Brazilian Association of Antiquarian Booksellers) (Brazil) 48
Associação Brasileira do Livro (Brazil) 48
Associação dos Arquivistas Brasileiros (Brazil) 56
Associação Paulista de Bibliotecarios (Brazil) 56
Associação Portuguesa de Bibliotecários Arquivistas e Documentalistas (Portuguese Association of Librarians, Archivists and Documentalists) (Portugal) 301
Associação Portuguesa dos Editores e Livreiros (Portugal) 298
Associação Riobrandense de Bibliotecarios (Brazil) 56
Associació de Bibliotecàries (Spain) 328
Associated Book Clubs (Republic of South Africa) 315
Associated Book Publishers (Aust) Ltd (Australia) 11

Associated Book Publishers (NZ) Ltd (New Zealand) 272
Associated Book Publishers Ltd (United Kingdom) 373
Associated Booksellers of Southern Africa Ltd (Republic of South Africa) 311
Associated Business Press (United Kingdom) 373
Associated Publishers Amsterdam (Netherlands) 258
Associated Publishers Inc (Philippines) 291
Associated Publishing House (India) 188
Associated University Presses (United Kingdom) 373
Association, Verlag, GmbH & Co (Federal Republic of Germany) 125
Association belge de Documentation (Belgium) 44
Association belge des Editeurs de Langue française (ABELF) (Belgium) 33
Association de l'Ecole nationale supérieure de Bibliothécaires (France) 111
Association de l'Institut national des Techniques de la Documentation (Association of the National Institute for Information Sciences) (France) 111
Association des Amis du Livre (Association of Book Lovers) (French Guiana) 116
Association des Archivistes et Bibliothécaires de Belgique (Belgium) 44
Association des Archivistes français (France) 111
Association des Bibliothécaires, Archivistes, Documentalistes et Muséographes du Cameroun (ABADCAM) (United Republic of Cameroon) 61
Association des Bibliothécaires-Documentalistes de l'Institut d'Etudes sociales de l'Etat (Belgium) 44
Association des Bibliothécaires et du Personnel des Bibliothèques des Ministères de Belgique (Belgium) 44
Association des Bibliothécaires français (France) 111
Association des Bibliothécaires Laotiens (Association of Laos Librarians) (Laos) 240
Association des Bibliothécaires suisses (Vereinigung schweizerischer Bibliothekare) (Switzerland) 356
Association des Bibliothèques ecclésiastiques de France (ABEF) (France) 111
Association des Bibliothèques Internationales (Association of International Libraries) (International Organizations) 437
Association des Consommateurs, Editions de, ASBL (Belgium) 34
Association des Diplômés de l'Ecole de Bibliothécaires-Documentalistes (Association of Graduates of the School of Librarians and Documentalists) (France) 111
Association des Ecrivains belges de langue française (Belgium) 45
Association des Ecrivains combattants (Association of Combatant Writers) (France) 112
Association des Ecrivains d'Expression française de la Mer et de l'Outre-Mer (Association of Writers in French in France and Abroad) (International Organizations) 437
Association des Ecrivains khmers (Association of Khmer Writers) (Kampuchea) 235
Association des Sociétés scientifiques médicales belges (ASBL) (Belgium) 34
Association des Universités Partiellement ou Entièrement de Langue Française (AUPELF) (International Organizations) 441
Association européenne des Editeurs de Publications pour la Jeunesse (EUROPRESS-JUNIOR) (European Association of Publishers of Publications for Young People) (International Organizations) 437
Association for Scottish Literary Studies (United Kingdom) 417
Association for the Promotion of the International Circulation of the Press (Association pour la Promotion de la Diffusion Internationale de la Presse) (International Organizations) 437
Association française des Documentalistes et Bibliothécaires spécialisés (French Association of Information Scientists and Special Librarians) (France) 111
Association internationale de Bibliophilie (International Organizations) 437
Association internationale des Documentalistes et Techniciens de l'Information AID (International Association of Documentalists and Information Officer) (International Organizations) 437
Association internationale pour le Développement de la Documentation, des Bibliothèques et des Archives en Afrique (International Organizations) 437
Association littéraire et artistique internationale (ALAI) (International Literary and Artistic Association) (International Organizations) 437
Association nationale des Bibliothécaires, Archivistes et Documentalistes sénégalais (Senegal) 307
Association nationale des Bibliothécaires d'Expression française (Belgium) 44
Association nationale des Bibliothécaires Municipaux (National Association of Municipal Librarians) (France) 111
Association nationale des Poètes et Ecrivains camerounais (APEC) (United Republic of Cameroon) 61

Association of African Universities (Association des Universités africaines) (International Organizations) 441
Association of Arab Universities (International Organizations) 441
Association of Arts and Letters (Greece) 178
Association of Assistant Librarians (United Kingdom) 416
Association of Australian University Presses (Australia) 9
Association of Authors' Agents (United Kingdom) 369
Association of British Book Publishers Representatives in Australia (Australia) 9
Association of British Directory Publishers (United Kingdom) 369
Association of British Library and Information Studies Schools (ABLISS) (United Kingdom) 416
Association of British Science Writers (United Kingdom) 417
Association of British Theological and Philosophical Libraries (United Kingdom) 416
Association of Commonwealth Universities (International Organizations) 441
Association of Hebrew Writers (Israel) 211
Association of Information and Dissemination Centers (International Organizations) 441
Association of Learned & Professional Society Publishers (United Kingdom) 369
Association of Libraries of Judaica and Hebraica in Europe (International Organizations) 438
Association of London Chief Librarians (United Kingdom) 416
Association of Mail Order Publishers (United Kingdom) 369
Association of Publishers' Educational Representatives (United Kingdom) 369
Association of Publishing Professionals of India (India) 186
Association of Registered Archivists of Iran Secretariat (Iran) 202
Association of Scottish Health Sciences Librarians (United Kingdom) 416
Association of South-East Asian Publishers (ASEAP) (International Organizations) 438
Association of Special Libraries of the Philippines (ASLP) (Philippines) 292
Association of Translators (Denmark) 80
Association of Yorkshire Bookmen (United Kingdom) 417
Association of Yugoslav Publishers and Booksellers (Yugoslavia) 427
Association pour la Médiathèque publique (AMP) (France) 111
Association pour le Développement de la Documentation, des Bibliothèques et Archives de la Côte d'Ivoire (ADBACI) (Ivory Coast) 224
Association romande du Personnel de la Librairie et de l'Edition (Swiss Association of Bookshop and Publishing Personnel) (Switzerland) 340
Association suisse de Documentation (Schweizerische Vereinigung für Dokumentation) (Switzerland) 356
Association suisse des Bibliothèques d'Hôpitaux (Association of Swiss Hospital Libraries) (Switzerland) 356
Association suisse des Editeurs de Langue française (Switzerland) 340
Association suisse des Libraires de Langue française (Switzerland) 340
Association suisse des Traducteurs et Interprètes (Swiss Association of Translators and Interpreters) (Switzerland) 357
Association suisse romande des Diffuseurs de Livres (Switzerland) 340
Association togolaise pour le Développement de la Documentation, des Bibliothèques, Archives et Musées (Togo) 361
Association tunisienne de Documentalistes, Bibliothécaires et Archivistes (Tunisia) 362
Association voltaique pour le Développement des Bibliothèques, des Archives et de la Documentation (AVDBAD) (Upper Volta) 422
Association Zaïroise des Archivistes, Bibliothécaires et Documentalistes (Zaire) 433
Associazione del Librai della Svizzera Italiana (ALSI) (Association of Bookshops of Italian-speaking Switzerland) (Switzerland) 340
Associazione Italiana Biblioteche (Italy) 222
Associazione Italiana Editori (Italy) 212
Associazione Italiana per la Documentazione e Informazione (Italy) 222
Associazione Italiana Traduttori e Interpreti (AITI) (Italian Association of Translators and Interpreters) (Italy) 223
Associazione Librai Antiquari d'Italia (Italy) 212
Associazione Librai Italiani (Italy) 212
Associazione Nazionale Archivistica Italiana (Italy) 222
Astab Books Ltd (Ghana) 175
Astaneh Razavy Library (Iran) 202

Aster, Editorial, (Portugal) 298
Ästhetik und Kommunikation Verlags-GmbH (Federal Republic of Germany) 125
Astir (Greece) 176
Astrea, Editorial, de Alfredo y Ricardo Depalma SRL (Argentina) 3
ASTRID (Belgium) 34
Astrolabe, L', (France) 90
Atelier (Egypt) 83
Atelier-Handpresse Verlag H Hoffmann (Federal Republic of Germany) 125
Atelier im Bauernhaus, Verlag, (Federal Republic of Germany) 125
Atelier Verlag Andernach (AVA) (Federal Republic of Germany) 125
Atenas, Sociedad de Educación, SA (Spain) 319
Ateneo, Editorial El, (Argentina) 3
Ateneo, Edizioni Dell', e Bizzarri SRL (Italy) 212
Ateneo, El, (Argentina) 8
Ateneo, Librería El, (Paraguay) 289
Ateneo Cientifico, Literario y Artistico (Scientific, Literary and Artistic Athenaeum) (Spain) 328
Ateneo Cientifico, Literario y Artistico (Scientific Literary and Artistic Athenaeum) (Spain) 328
Ateneo de Barcelona, Biblioteca del, (Library of the Athenaeum of Barcelona) (Spain) 328
Ateneo de Madrid, Biblioteca del, (Library of the Madrid Athenaeum) (Spain) 328
Ateneo de Manila University Libraries (Philippines) 292
Ateneo Mercantil, Biblioteca del, Valenciano (Library of the Mercantile Athenaeum of Valencia) (Spain) 328
Atha, Antony, Publishers Ltd (United Kingdom) 373
Athena-Verlag AG (Switzerland) 356
Athenaeum Boekhandel (Netherlands) 269
Athenaeum Verlag AG (Switzerland) 341
Athenaion (Federal Republic of Germany) 125
Athenäum Verlag GmbH (Federal Republic of Germany) 125
Athene Publishing Co (United Kingdom) 373
Athenea, Librería, (Panama) 288
Atheneu, Livraria, Ltda (Brazil) 49
Athenon, Ekdotike, SA (Greece) 176
Athens Academy Library (Greece) 178
Athens College Library (Greece) 178
Athesia, Verlagsanstalt, (Italy) 213
Athlone, The, Press (United Kingdom) 373
Atica, Editora, SA (Brazil) 49
Atika SA (Spain) 319
Atlanta NV (Belgium) 44
Atlantic (United Kingdom) 373
Atlantic Communications Ltd (United Kingdom) 373
Atlantica (Iceland) 184
Atlántida, Editorial, SA (Argentina) 3
Atlântida, Livraria Editora, Ltda (Portugal) 298
Atlantis, Bokförlaget, Peterson & Co AB (Sweden) 332
Atlantis-M Pechlivanides & Co SA (Greece) 176
Atlantis NV (Belgium) 34
Atlantis Verlag AG (Switzerland) 341
Atlantis-Verlag GmbH & Co Kg (Federal Republic of Germany) 125
Atlas, Editions, (France) 90
Atlas, Editôra, SA (Brazil) 49
Atlas, The, Bookshop Ltd (Ghana) 175
Atlas-Diagoras (Greece) 176
Atma Ram & Sons (India) 188
Atomizdat (Union of Soviet Socialist Republics) 365
Atrium Verlag AG (Switzerland) 341
Attié, Librairie, (Upper Volta) 422
Attila, Jozsef, Prize (Hungary) 184
Atual Editora Ltda (Brazil) 49
Au Messager (Central African Republic) 61
Au Ping-Pong, Librairie, (French Polynesia) 116
Aubanel Ed (France) 90
Aubier-Montaigne, Editions, SA (France) 90
Auckland Public Library (New Zealand) 275
Auckland University Press (New Zealand) 272
Audiffred, Francois-Joseph, Prize (France) 112
Audivox (Belgium) 44
Audivox (Belgium) 34
Auer, Verlag Ludwig, (Federal Republic of Germany) 125
Aufbau-Verlag Berlin und Weimar (German Democratic Republic) 117
Augener (United Kingdom) 373
August Cesarec (Yugoslavia) 427
Augustin-Verlag (Switzerland) 341
Augustinus, Librería, (Spain) 327
Aujourd'hui, Editions d', (France) 90
Aujourd'hui Prize (France) 113
Aulis Verlag Deubner & Co KG (Federal Republic of Germany) 125
Aurelia Books (Belgium) 34
Auria, M d', Editore (Italy) 213
Aurobindo, Sri, Books Distribution Agency (SABDA) (India) 188
Aurora, Asociación Ediciones La, (Argentina) 3
Aurora, Gráfica Editôra, Ltda (Brazil) 50

Aurora Art Publishers (Union of Soviet Socialist Republics) 365
Aurum Verlag GmbH & Co KG (Federal Republic of Germany) 125
Aussaat Verlag GmbH (Federal Republic of Germany) 126
Aussenhandels-Ausschuss (Federal Republic of Germany) 122
Austick's Headrow Bookshop (United Kingdom) 415
Australasian Book Society Ltd (Australia) 11
Australasian Book Society Ltd (Australia) 19
Australasian Publishing Co Pty Ltd (Australia) 11
Australia & New Zealand Book Co Pty Ltd (Australia) 11
Australia Archives (Australia) 20
Australian Academy of Science (Australia) 11
Australian Advisory Council on Bibliographical Services (AACOBS) (Australia) 20
Australian Book Publishers Association (Australia) 9
Australian Booksellers Association (Australia) 10
Australian Copyright Council (Australia) 10
Australian Council for Educational Research (Australia) 11
Australian Encyclopaedia Pty Ltd (Australia) 11
Australian Government Publications (Australia) 19
Australian Government Publishing Service (Australia) 11
Australian Independent Publishers' Association (Australia) 10
Australian Industry Awards for Young Writers (Australia) 21
Australian Institute of Aboriginal Studies (Australia) 11
Australian Institute of Criminology (Australia) 11
Australian Jewish Book Club Ltd (Australia) 19
Australian Law Librarians' Group (Australia) 20
Australian Library Promotion Council (Australia) 20
Australian Library Technicians' Association (Australia) 20
Australian Literature Society (Australia) 21
Australian Literature Society Gold Medal (Australia) 21
Australian National University Library (Australia) 20
Australian National University Press (Australia) 11
Australian Natives' Association Literature Award (Australia) 21
Australian School Library Association (Australia) 20
Australian Society of Archivists (Australia) 20
Australian Society of Authors (Australia) 21
Australian Society of Indexers (Australia) 10
Australian Universities Press Pty Ltd (Australia) 12
Australian Writers' Guild (Australia) 21
Austrian State Prize for European Literature (International Literary Prizes) 447
Authors' Club (United Kingdom) 417
Authors' Club First Novel Award (United Kingdom) 419
Autobooks Ltd (United Kingdom) 373
Automobile Association (United Kingdom) 373
Autoren, Verlag der, GmbH & Co KG (Federal Republic of Germany) 126
Autoren-und Verlagsgesellschaft, Syndikat, (Federal Republic of Germany) 126
Autores, Biblioteca de, Cristianos (Spain) 319
Autran, Joseph, Prize (France) 113
'Aux Belles Images', Librairie, (Morocco) 256
'Aux Frères Réunis', Librairie, (United Republic of Cameroun) 61
Auxilium Verlag (Federal Republic of Germany) 126
Auzou, Editions Philippe, (France) 90
Ava Bookshop (Government Bookshop) (Burma) 59
Avant-Scène, L', Théâtre, Cinéma et Opéra (France) 90
'Avante!', Editorial, (Portugal) 298
Avebury Publishing Co Ltd (United Kingdom) 373
Avele College Library (Western Samoa) 426
Avery, Thomas, & Sons Ltd (New Zealand) 272
Avicenum, zdravotnické nakladatelství (Czechoslovakia) 70
Award for Literature and Scientific Publications (Turkey) 364
Awgie Awards (Australia) 21
Awqaf, Al-, (Library of Waqfs) (Iraq) 202
Axel-Juncker Verlag Jacobi KG (Federal Republic of Germany) 126
Ayacucho, Biblioteca, (Venezuela) 424
Ayam, Al-, Press Co Ltd (Sudan) 330
Aydınlık Yayinlari (Turkey) 362
Aymá SA Editora (& Edicions Proa) (Spain) 319
Ayuso, Editorial, (Spain) 319
Azerbaidzhanskaya gosudarstvennaya respublikanskaya biblioteka im. M F Akhundova (Union of Soviet Socialist Republics) 367
Azevedo, Arthur, Prize (Brazil) 57
Azhar, Al-, University Library (Egypt) 83
Azim Publishing House (Pakistan) 285
Azteca, Editorial, SA (Mexico) 250

B & T Directories (Rhodesia) (Pvt) Ltd (Zimbabwe) 434
B A E S A (Buenos Aires Edita SA) (Argentina) 3
B A G Buchhändler-Abrechnungs-Gesellschaft mbH (Federal Republic of Germany) 122
B A S H (United Kingdom) 369
B B C Publications (United Kingdom) 373
B C W Publishing Ltd (United Kingdom) 374
B H R A Fluid Engineering (United Kingdom) 374
B I Publications (India) 188
B L A C Publishing House (Republic of South Africa) 311
B L V Verlagsgesellschaft mbH (Federal Republic of Germany) 126
B N V (Bohmann-Noltemeyer Verlag) (Federal Republic of Germany) 126
B O D (United Kingdom) 369
B P C Ltd (formerly British Printing Corporation Ltd) (United Kingdom) 374
B P I. Editions, (Bureau de Presse et d'Informations) (France) 90
B R E S (Netherlands) 259
B R G M. Editions, (France) 90
B R Publishing Corporation (India) 188
B S C Books Ltd (United Kingdom) 374
B S C Books Ltd (United Kingdom) 413
B S-Verlag Manfred Kerler (Federal Republic of Germany) 126
B V B (Federal Republic of Germany) 126
Baars-Jelgersma, Auteursbureau Greta, (Netherlands) 269
Babani, Bernard, (Publishing) Ltd (United Kingdom) 374
Babylon Übersetzungen (Federal Republic of Germany) 174
Babylon Übersetzungen (Federal Republic of Germany) 169
Bacchus Books (Australia) 12
Bachem, J P, Verlag GmbH (Federal Republic of Germany) 126
Bachman & Turner Ltd (United Kingdom) 374
Backer, De, Publishers PVBA (Belgium) 34
Bäckman, Ida, Prize (Sweden) 339
Bacon, Francis, Society Inc (United Kingdom) 417
Bacon, S John, Pty Ltd (Australia) 12
Baconnière, Editions de la, SA (Switzerland) 341
Baedeker, Buchhandlung G D, (Federal Republic of Germany) 170
Baedeker, Karl, (Federal Republic of Germany) 126
Baedekers Autoführer-Verlag GmbH (Federal Republic of Germany) 126
Baekelmans, Lode, Prize (Belgium) 45
Baensch, Hans A, (Federal Republic of Germany) 126
Bagchi, K P, & Co (India) 188
Bagchi, P M, & Co (P) Ltd (India) 188
Bagster, Samuel, & Sons Ltd (United Kingdom) 374
Bagutta Prize (Italy) 223
Baha'i Verlag GmbH (Federal Republic of Germany) 126
Baha'ies, Maison d'Editions, ASBL (Belgium) 34
Bahamas Anglo American Book Store (Bahamas) 32
Bahamas Book & Bible House (Bahamas) 32
Bahn, Friedrich, Verlag GmbH (Federal Republic of Germany) 126
Bahous, Joseph I, & Co (Jordan) 234
Bahrain Bookshop (Bahrain) 32
Bahrain Writers and Literators Association (Bahrain) 32
Baihaqi Book Publishing Institute (Afghanistan) 1
Bailey Brothers & Swinfen Ltd (United Kingdom) 374
Baillière, Editions J-B, (France) 90
Baillière Tindall (United Kingdom) 374
Bak Yung Sa (Republic of Korea) 237
Bakalov, Knigoizdatelstvo 'Georgi,' (Bulgaria) 58
Baker, John, (Publishers) Ltd (United Kingdom) 374
Bakker, Bert, BV (Netherlands) 259
Balai Pustaka (Indonesia) 199
Balcells, Carmen, Agencia Literaria (Spain) 327
Balcells, Carmen, Agencia Literaria (Brazil) 55
Balding & Mansell (United Kingdom) 374
Baldini e Castoldi (Italy) 213
Bale Bandung — Sumur Bandung (Indonesia) 199
Balkan-Press (Federal Republic of Germany) 169
Balkema, A A, (Netherlands) 259
Balkema, A A, Publishers (Republic of South Africa) 311
Balland, André, (France) 90
Ballantine (United Kingdom) 374
Balmer AG Verlag (Switzerland) 341
Baltic Verlag und Verwaltungsges GmbH (Liechtenstein) 243
Banana Press NV (Belgium) 34
Banca y Comercio, Editorial, SA (Mexico) 250
Bancarellino Prize (Italy) 223
Banco, Biblioteca del, Central de la República Argentina (Argentina) 8
Banda, Ediciones de la, Oriental SRL (Uruguay) 422
Bandarnsarn (Thailand) 359
Banga Sahitya Bhavan (Bangladesh) 32
Bangalore, The, Printing & Publishing Co Ltd (India) 188
Bangkok Bank Prize (Thailand) 360
Bangkok Central Book Depot (Thailand) 360

Bangladesh Books International Ltd (Bangladesh) 32
Bangladesh Granthagar Samity (Bangladesh) 33
Bangladesh Institute of Development Studies Library (Bangladesh) 33
Bangladesh Pustak Prokashak o Bikreta Samity (Bangladesh Publishers' & Booksellers' Association) (Bangladesh) 32
Bank of New Zealand Young Writers' Awards (New Zealand) 275
Banmai (Thailand) 359
Bansal and Co (India) 188
Baptist Book Centre (Zimbabwe) 435
Bär, U, Verlag (Switzerland) 341
Bar-David Literary Agency (Israel) 210
Bar Ilan University, Book Publishing Committee (Israel) 206
Bar-Ilan University Library (Israel) 211
Bar Urian Publishing House (Israel) 206
Barbera, Giunti, Editore (Italy) 213
Barbiaux (Drukkerij G — Uitgeverij de Garve) PVBA (Belgium) 35
Barblan et Saladin, Librairie, (Switzerland) 341
Barblan et Saladin, Librairie, (Switzerland) 356
Bardet, René, Prize (France) 113
Bärenreiter Verlag, Karl Vötterle KG (Federal Republic of Germany) 126
Bargezzi-Verlag AG (Switzerland) 341
Barjes, Edizioni Oreste, (Italy) 213
Barker, Arthur, Ltd (United Kingdom) 374
Barlevi (Israel) 211
Barn, Bokklubbens, (Norway) 283
Barnakarn (Thailand) 359
Barnakieh Trading (Thailand) 359
Barnasilpa (Thailand) 359
Barque & Co (Pakistan) 285
Barr Smith, The, Library (Australia) 20
Barral Editores SA (Spain) 319
Barrau (New Caledonia) 271
Barre, André, Prize (France) 113
Barreiro y Ramos SA (Uruguay) 422
Barreiro y Ramos SA (Uruguay) 422
Barrie & Jenkins (United Kingdom) 374
Barry, Editorial Com Ind, SRL (Argentina) 3
Bartels und Wernitz, Verlag, KG (Federal Republic of Germany) 126
Barth, Johann Ambrosius, Verlagsbuchhandlung (German Democratic Republic) 117
Barth, Otto Wilhelm, -Verlag KG (Federal Republic of Germany) 126
Bartholomew & Son, John, Ltd (United Kingdom) 374
Bartholomew Books (United Kingdom) 374
Barthou, Alice Louis, Prize (France) 113
Barthou, Louis, Prize (France) 113
Barthou, Max, Prize (France) 113
Bartlett, Alice Hunt, Prize (International Literary Prizes) 447
Barudio & Hess Verlag (Federal Republic of Germany) 126
Baschet, Les Editions de l'Illustration, et Cie (France) 90
Baseball Magazine-Sha (Japan) 226
Bashir, Al, Bookshop (Sudan) 330
Basileia Verlag (Switzerland) 341
Basilisk, The, Press Ltd (United Kingdom) 374
Basilius Presse (Switzerland) 341
Basis-Verlag (Federal Republic of Germany) 126
Bassermann'sche Verlagsbuchhandlung, Friedrich, im Falken-Verlag Erich Sicker KG (Federal Republic of Germany) 126
Bastei-Verlag Gustav H Lübbe (Federal Republic of Germany) 126
Bastian, W E, & Co (Sri Lanka) 329
Bastian Prize (Norway) 284
Bastilla, Ediciones la, (Argentina) 3
Bastinos, Librería, (Spain) 327
Basu, K P, Publishing Co (India) 188
Bataille, Agence, (France) 110
Bateleur Press (Republic of South Africa) 311
Batsford, B T, Ltd (United Kingdom) 374
Battenberg, Ernst, Verlag (Federal Republic of Germany) 126
Bättre Ledarskap (Sweden) 337
Baudelaire, Charles, Poetry Prize (International Literary Prizes) 447
Bauer, Hermann, Verlag KG (Federal Republic of Germany) 126
Baufachverlag AG (Switzerland) 341
Bautista, Asociacion, Argentina de Publicaciones (Argentina) 3
Bautista, Centro Cultural, (Nicaragua) 276
Bauverlag GmbH (Federal Republic of Germany) 126
Bauwesen, VEB Verlag für, (German Democratic Republic) 118
Baxters (Bermuda) 47
Bayard-Presse SA (France) 90
Bayerische Staatsbibliothek (Federal Republic of Germany) 171

Bayerische Verlagsanstalt Bamberg (B V B) (Federal Republic of Germany) 127
Bayerischer Schulbuch-Verlag (Federal Republic of Germany) 127
Bayle Prize (also known as Netherlands Critics' Prize) (Netherlands) 270
Bayly, A W, & Co Lda (Mozambique) 256
Bazak Israel Guidebook Publishers Ltd (Israel) 206
Beatrice-Nauwelaerts, Editions, (Belgium) 35
Beatty, The Chester, Library and Gallery of Oriental Art (Republic of Ireland) 205
Beauchesne, Editions, (France) 91
Beaufort, Mme, (French Guiana) 116
Beaux Arts Ltd (New Zealand) 272
Beaux Livres, Les, (Monaco) 255
Beaver Books (United Kingdom) 374
Becher, Institut für Literatur Johannes R. (Johannes R Becher Institute for Literature) (German Democratic Republic) 121
Bechtle (Federal Republic of Germany) 127
Becht's, H J W, Uitgeversmij bv/Uitgeverij H J de Bussy BV (Netherlands) 259
Beck, Edition Monika, (Federal Republic of Germany) 127
Beck, Verlag C H, (Federal Republic of Germany) 127
Becker, Reinhard, Verlag (Federal Republic of Germany) 127
Beckers Groep (Belgium) 35
Beckers NV Uitgeverij (Belgium) 44
Beckers SA Editions (Belgium) 35
Beckmans Bokförlag AB (Sweden) 332
Bedford Square Press of the National Council of Social Service (United Kingdom) 375
Bedout, Editorial, SA (Colombia) 65
Beernhaert Prize (Belgium) 45
Behzad Bookshop (Afghanistan) 1
Behzad Bookstore (Afghanistan) 1
Beijing Tushuguan (People's Republic of China) 63
Beirut, Dar, (Lebanon) 240
Beirut Arab University, Library of, (Lebanon) 241
Beit Lochamei Hagetha'ot (Israel) 206
Belaieff, M P, (Federal Republic of Germany) 127
Belfast Public Library (United Kingdom) 415
Belfond, Editions Pierre, (France) 91
Belgian Government Prizes for Literature (Ministry of Flemish Culture) (Belgium) 45
Belgian Government Prizes for Literature (Ministry of French Culture) (Belgium) 45
Belgisch Instituut voor Voorlichting en Documentatie (INBEL) (Belgium) 35
Belier-Prisma, Editions le, SA (France) 91
Belin, Librairie Classique Eugène, (France) 91
Belinsky Prize (Union of Soviet Socialist Republics) 368
Belis-Vinck, Boekhandel, (Belgium) 44
Belize Book Shop (Belize) 46
Belize Library Association (Belize) 46
Belkhodja, Librairie orientale Ahmed, (Tunisia) 362
Bell, SA Editorial, (Argentina) 3
Bell & Hyman Ltd (United Kingdom) 375
Bellas Artes, Librería, (Mexico) 253
Bellaterra, Ediciones, SA (Spain) 319
Belle, Uitgeverij van, PVBA (Belgium) 35
Bellens, Librairie, (Belgium) 44
Belles Images, Editions Les, (France) 91
Belles Lettres, Société d'Edition 'Les,' (France) 91
Bellmans Prize (Sweden) 339
Bello, Biblioteca de la Universidad Catolica 'Andres,' (Venezuela) 425
Bello, Editorial Andrés, /Juridica de Chile (Chile) 62
Bello, Librería Andrés, (Chile) 62
Bellona Publications (United Kingdom) 375
Belmont Press (Zimbabwe) 435
Belser, Chr, AG für Verlagsgeschäfte und Co KG (Federal Republic of Germany) 127
Belton Books (United Kingdom) 375
Beltz (Switzerland) 341
Beltz Verlag (Federal Republic of Germany) 127
Bemrose UK Ltd (United Kingdom) 375
Ben-Gurion University of the Negev Library (Israel) 211
Ben-Zvi, Prof Shaul Shaked, Institute (Israel) 206
Benediktinerklosters, Bibliothek des, (Austria) 30
Bengali Academy Literary Awards (Bangladesh) 33
Benibengor Book Agency (Ghana) 174
Benin University Bookshop (Nigeria) 279
Benin University Library (Nigeria) 280
Benjamin Cummings Inc (United Kingdom) 375
Benjamins, John, BV (Netherlands) 259
Benn, Ernest, Ltd (United Kingdom) 375
Bennett, G H, & Co Ltd (New Zealand) 274
Bennett Award (International Literary Prizes) 447
Benson Medal (United Kingdom) 419
Benteli Verlag (Switzerland) 342
Benziger AG (Switzerland) 342
Benziger Verlag (Federal Republic of Germany) 127
Beogradski Izdavačko-Grafički Zabod (Yugoslavia) 427
Berchmans, Johannes, Verlag GmbH (Federal Republic of Germany) 127

Berchtold-Haller-Verlag (Switzerland) 342
Berg International Editeurs (France) 91
Bergadi Editions (Greece) 176
Bergen offentlige Bibliotek Horda land Fylkesbibliotek (Municipal and County Library) (Norway) 283
Berger, Ferdinand, und Söhne (Austria) 24
Berger-Levrault (France) 91
Bergh, Edition Sven Erik, (Federal Republic of Germany) 127
Bergh, Edition Sven Erik, im Europabuch AG (Switzerland) 342
Berghaus Verlag (Federal Republic of Germany) 127
Berghs Bokklub (Sweden) 337
Berghs Förlag AB (Sweden) 332
Bergland-Buch, Verlag 'Das,' (R Kiesel & Co) (Austria) 24
Bergland Verlag (Austria) 24
Bergmann, Anton, Prize (International Literary Prizes) 447
Bergmann, J F, (Federal Republic of Germany) 127
Bergs, H M, Forlag ApS (Denmark) 74
Bergström & Boyle Books (United Kingdom) 375
Bergverlag Rudolf Rother GmbH (Federal Republic of Germany) 127
Berhan Bookshop and Stationery (Ethiopia) 84
Berichthaus Verlag, Dr Conrad Ulrich (Switzerland) 342
Berlin Verlag (Federal Republic of Germany) 127
Berliner Handpresse Wolfgang Joerg und Erich Schoenig (Federal Republic of Germany) 127
Berliner Stadtbibliothek (German Democratic Republic) 120
Berliner Union GmbH (Federal Republic of Germany) 127
Berliner Verleger- und Buchhändlervereinigung eV (Federal Republic of Germany) 122
Berlingske Forlag A/S (Denmark) 74
Berlitz, Editions, SA (Switzerland) 342
Berlitz, Société Internationale des Ecoles, SA (France) 91
Bermuda Archives (Bermuda) 47
Bermuda Book Store Ltd (Bermuda) 47
Bermuda Library (Bermuda) 47
Bermuda Press Ltd (Bermuda) 47
Bermudian Publishing Co (Bermuda) 47
Bernard, Librería Claudio, (El Salvador) 83
Bernard & Graefe Verlag (Federal Republic of Germany) 127
Bernards (Publishers) Ltd (United Kingdom) 375
Bernces Forlag AB (Sweden) 332
Bernhardt, Verlag Alexander, (Austria) 24
Bernheim, Bibliothèque, Bibliothèque territoriale de la Nouvelle-Caledonie (Bernheim Library) (New Caledonia) 271
Beroukhim, Y, & Sons, Booksellers (Iran) 202
Berry, David, Prize (International Literary Prizes) 447
Bertani (Italy) 213
Bertelsmann, C, Verlag (Federal Republic of Germany) 127
Bertelsmann GmbH, Verlagsgruppe, (Federal Republic of Germany) 128
Bertelsmann Lesering (Federal Republic of Germany) 170
Bertelsmann Lexikon-Verlag (Federal Republic of Germany) 128
Bertelsmann München, Verlagsgruppe, (Federal Republic of Germany) 128
Bertrand, Livraria, (Portugal) 301
Bertrand, Livraria, SARL (Portugal) 298
Beskow Prize (Sweden) 339
Best Book of the Sea Award (International Literary Prizes) 447
Best First Book of Poetry Award (incorporating the Jessie Mackay Award) (New Zealand) 275
Best First Book of Prose Award (Incorporating the Hubert Church Award) (New Zealand) 275
Best of Books International Ltd (United Kingdom) 414
Beste, Det, A/S (Norway) 283
Bestetti, Edizioni d'Arte Carlo, (Italy) 213
Bestseller, The, Universal Distributors Ltd (Nigeria) 279
Beta, Editorial, SRL (Argentina) 4
Betis, Ediciones, (Spain) 319
Beton-Verlag (Concrete Publishing) GmbH (Federal Republic of Germany) 128
Better Books (United Kingdom) 375
Better Yourself Books (India) 188
Betz, Annette, Verlag (Federal Republic of Germany) 128
Betz, Verlag Annette, (Austria) 24
Betzel, Elke, Verlag (Federal Republic of Germany) 128
Beuhler's Shoppe (Belize) 46
Beupmun Sa Publishing Co (Republic of Korea) 237
Beuroner Kunstverlag GmbH (Federal Republic of Germany) 128
Beurs, De, NV (Belgium) 35
Beuth Verlag GmbH (Federal Republic of Germany) 128
Beyaert, Editions, (Belgium) 35
Beyazit Library (Turkey) 363
Beyeler Editions Basel (Switzerland) 342
Beyer, Atelier, (France) 91

Beyer, F, Bok–Og Papirhandel A/S (Norway) 283
Bezige, De, Bij (Netherlands) 259
Bhakti, P T, Centra Baru (Indonesia) 199
Bhaktivedanta, The, Book Trust (Switzerland) 342
Bharat-Bharati (India) 188
Bharat Law House (India) 188
Bharatiya Jnanpith (India) 188
Bharatiya Vidya Bhavan (India) 188
Bhratara Karya Aksara (Indonesia) 199
Bialik, The, Institute (Israel) 206
Bialik Prize for Literature (Israel) 211
Bianchi, Alfredo A, Essay Prize (Argentina) 9
Bianco, Del, Editore (Italy) 213
Bias (Société Nouvelle des Editions) SA (France) 91
Bias Editora (Argentina) 4
Bias Editora (Libros Jurídicos) (Argentina) 8
Bibellesebund eV (Federal Republic of Germany) 128
Biblarte Lda (Portugal) 301
Bible, The, Churchmen's Missionary Society (Ethiopia) 84
Bible Churchman's Society (Ethiopia) 84
Bible Churchmen's Missionary Society (Ethiopia) 84
Biblical Institute Press (Pontificio Istituto Biblico) (Italy) 213
Bibliofiilien Seura (Finland) 87
Bibliographical Society (United Kingdom) 416
Bibliographical Society of Australia and New Zealand (New Zealand) 275
Bibliographical Society of Australia and New Zealand (Australia) 20
Bibliographical Society of Australia and New Zealand (Australia) 21
Bibliographical Society of Australia and New Zealand (BSANZ) (International Organizations) 438
Bibliographical Society of the Philippines (Philippines) 292
Bibliographisches Institut, VEB, (German Democratic Republic) 118
Bibliographisches Institut AG (Federal Republic of Germany) 128
Bibliographisches Institut AG (Switzerland) 342
Bibliographisches Institut GmbH (Austria) 24
Bibliomad (Democratic Republic of Madagascar) 244
Bibliophile, Le, (The Book Lover) (Haiti) 180
Bibliophile Drucke, Verlag, von Josef Stocker AG (Switzerland) 342
Bibliopolis—Edizioni di Filosofia e Scienze SpA (Italy) 213
Biblioteca, Editorial, Nueva SL (Spain) 319
Biblioteca Apostolica Vaticana (Vatican City State) 423
Biblioteca Central (Mexico) 254
Biblioteca Central de Educación básica, secundaria y superior (Uruguay) 423
Biblioteca Centrala de Stat a Republicii Socialiste România (Central State Library) (Romania) 304
Biblioteca Centrala Universitara (Romania) 305
Biblioteca Centrala Universitara (Romania) 305
Biblioteca Centrala Universitara 'Mihail Eminescu' (Romania) 305
Biblioteca de la Associación Argentina de Cultura Inglesa (Argentina) 8
Biblioteca de México (Mexico) 254
Biblioteca del Congreso (Venezuela) 425
Biblioteca del Instituto de Cultura Hispánica (Library of the Institute of Hispanic Culture) (Spain) 328
Biblioteca dell' Universita Nazionale della Somalia (Somalia) 310
Biblioteca Dominicana (Dominican Republic) 81
Biblioteca Ecuatoriana 'Aurelio Espinosa Pólit' (Ecuador) 81
Biblioteca Estadual (Brazil) 56
Biblioteca Estense, Biblioteca Universitaria (Italy) 222
Biblioteca General de Puerto Rico (General Library) (Puerto Rico) 303
Biblioteca Histórica Cubana y Americana (Cuban and American Historical Library) (Cuba) 68
Biblioteca Judeteana Mures (Romania) 305
Biblioteca Judeteana Timis (Romania) 305
Biblioteca Municipal (Mozambique) 256
Biblioteca Municipal Central (Central Town Library) (Portugal) 301
Biblioteca Municipal Mário de Andrade (Brazil) 56
Biblioteca Nacional (Brazil) 56
Biblioteca Nacional (Costa Rica) 68
Biblioteca Nacional (Chile) 63
Biblioteca Nacional (Dominican Republic) 81
Biblioteca Nacional (El Salvador) 83
Biblioteca Nacional (National Library) (Argentina) 8
Biblioteca Nacional (National Library) (Spain) 328
Biblioteca Nacional (National Library) (Peru) 290
Biblioteca Nacional (National Library) (Panama) 288
Biblioteca Nacional (National Library) (Nicaragua) 276
Biblioteca Nacional (National Library) (Venezuela) 425
Biblioteca Nacional de Agricultura (National Library of Agriculture) (Mexico) 254
Biblioteca Nacional de Angola (National Library) (Angola) 2
Biblioteca Nacional de Colombia (Colombia) 66

Biblioteca Nacional de Guatemala (National Library) (Guatemala) 179
Biblioteca Nacional de Honduras (National Library) (Honduras) 180
Biblioteca Nacional de Lisboa (National Library) (Portugal) 301
Biblioteca Nacional de Macao (National Library) (Macao) 244
Biblioteca Nacional de Maestros (Argentina) 8
Biblioteca Nacional de México (National Library) (Mexico) 254
Biblioteca Nacional de Moçambique (National Library) (Mozambique) 256
Biblioteca Nacional del Ecuador (Ecuador) 81
Biblioteca Nacional del Uruguay (National Library) (Uruguay) 423
Biblioteca Nacional José Martí (National Library) (Cuba) 68
Biblioteca Nazionale Braidense (Italy) 222
Biblioteca Nazionale Centrale (Italy) 222
Biblioteca Nazionale Centrale (Italy) 222
Biblioteca Nazionale Marciana (Italy) 222
Biblioteca Nazionale Vittorio Emanuele III (Italy) 222
Biblioteca Popular de Lisboa (Portugal) 301
Biblioteca Pública de Ponta Delgada (Public Library) (Portugal) 301
Biblioteca Publica do Estado do Rio de Janeiro (Brazil) 56
Biblioteca Pública e Arquivo Distrital de Braga (Public Library and District Archives) (Portugal) 301
Biblioteca Pública e Arquivo Distrital de Évora (Public Library and District Archives) (Portugal) 301
Biblioteca Pública Municipal do Porto (Portugal) 301
Biblioteca Publico Central (Argentina) 8
Biblioteca Universitaria Departamento de Bibliotecas Universidad Boliviana Tomás Frías (Bolivia) 47
Biblioteca y Archivo Nacionales (National Library and Archives) (Paraguay) 289
Biblioteca y Centro Nacional de Documentación Pedagógica, Sección de Servicios Bibliotecarios (Colombia) 66
Biblioteca ye Archivo Nacional de Bolivia (National Library and Archives) (Bolivia) 48
Bibliotecarios Agricolas Colombianos (Colombia) 66
Biblioteka Jagiellońska (Poland) 296
Biblioteka Kombëtare (National Library) (Albania) 1
Biblioteka Narodowa (Poland) 296
Biblioteka Publiczna m st Warszawy (Public Library) (Poland) 296
Biblioteka Śląska (Poland) 296
Bibliotekarforbundet (Denmark) 79
Bibliotekarforbundet for Forsknings- og Fagbiblioteker (Denmark) 79
Biblioteksboghandelen ApS (Denmark) 78
Bibliotekscentralen (Denmark) 79
Bibliotekscentralens Forlag (Denmark) 74
Biblioteksförlaget AB (Sweden) 332
Bibliotektjänst AB (Sweden) 332
Bibliotheca, Verlag, Christiana (Federal Republic of Germany) 170
Bibliotheca Bogoriensis (Central Library for Biology and Agriculture) (Indonesia) 201
Bibliotheek CCS (Suriname) 331
Bibliothek für Zeitgeschichte (Federal Republic of Germany) 171
Bibliotheksverband der Deutschen Demokratischen Republik (Bibliotheksverband der DDR) (German Democratic Republic) 120
Bibliothèque, Centre, d'Information (Gabon) 116
Bibliothèque cantonale et universitaire (Kantons- und Universitätsbibliothek) (Switzerland) 356
Bibliothèque cantonale et universitaire de Lausanne (Switzerland) 356
Bibliothèque centrale de la Côte d'Ivoire (Ivory Coast) 224
Bibliothèque centrale de Prêt (Réunion) 303
Bibliothèque de Gouvernement (Luxembourg) 244
Bibliothèque de la Ville (Luxembourg) 244
Bibliothèque de la Ville (Switzerland) 356
Bibliothèque de l'Université du Benin (Togo) 361
Bibliothèque de l'Université nationale de Côte d'Ivoire (Ivory Coast) 224
Bibliothèque de Monaco (National Library) (Monaco) 255
Bibliothèque départementale (Réunion) 303
Bibliothèque du petit Séminaire (Haiti) 180
Bibliothèque Franconie (French Guiana) 116
Bibliothèque générale et Archives (Morocco) 256
Bibliothèque générale et Archives du Maroc (National Archives) (Morocco) 256
Bibliothèque Interuniversitaire de Médecine (France) 111
Bibliothèque Interuniversitaire de Pharmacie (France) 111
Bibliothèque mazarine (France) 111
Bibliothèque municipale (France) 111
Bibliothèque municipale (Mali) 248
Bibliothèque municipale (Morocco) 256

Bibliothèque municipale (Ivory Coast) 224
Bibliothèque municipale (Democratic Republic of Madagascar) 245
Bibliothèque municipale (Réunion) 303
Bibliothèque municipale (Algeria) 2
Bibliothèque municipale de la Ville de Lyon (France) 111
Bibliothèque nationale (France) 111
Bibliothèque nationale (Kampuchea) 235
Bibliothèque nationale (National Library) (Laos) 240
Bibliothèque nationale (National Library) (Democratic Republic of Madagascar) 245
Bibliothèque nationale (National Library) (Ivory Coast) 224
Bibliothèque nationale (National Library) (Mali) 248
Bibliothèque nationale (National Library) (Mauritania) 249
Bibliothèque nationale (National Library) (Guinea) 179
Bibliothèque nationale (National Library) (Algeria) 2
Bibliothèque nationale (National Library) (Benin) 47
Bibliothèque nationale (National Library) (Tunisia) 362
Bibliothèque nationale (National Library) (Togo) 361
Bibliothèque nationale (National Library) (Zaire) 433
Bibliothèque nationale d'Haiti (National Library) (Haiti) 180
Bibliothèque nationale du Cameroun (United Republic of Cameroun) 61
Bibliothèque nationale du Grand-Duché de Luxembourg (National Library) (Luxembourg) 244
Bibliothèque nationale du Liban (National Library) (Lebanon) 241
Bibliothèque nationale et universitaire de Strasbourg (France) 111
Bibliothèque nationale populaire (Popular Republic of Congo) 67
Bibliothèque Nationale Suisse (Switzerland) 356
Bibliothèque orientale (Oriental Library) (Lebanon) 241
Bibliothèque paroissiale (Parochial Library) (Chad) 62
Bibliothèque Publique (Burundi) 60
Bibliothèque publique (Zaire) 433
Bibliothèque publique centrale (Mauritania) 249
Bibliothèque publique et universitaire de Genève (Switzerland) 356
Bibliothèque royale (Kampuchea) 235
Bibliothèque royale Albert Ier (Koninklijke Bibliotheek Albert I) (Belgium) 44
Bibliothèque universitaire (Democratic Republic of Madagascar) 245
Bibliothèque universitaire (Réunion) 303
Bibliothèque universitaire (Upper Volta) 422
Bibliothèque universitaire, Université d'Alger (Algeria) 2
Bibliothèque universitaire, Université Marieu N Gouabi (Popular Republic of Congo) 67
Bibliothéques publiques (Tunisia) 362
Biblique, Société, Française (France) 91
Biblograf, Editorial, SA (Spain) 319
Biblos (Israel) 206
Bidang Bibliografi dan Deposit, Pusat Pembinaan Perpustakaan (National Bibliographic and Deposit Centre, Centre for Library Development) (Indonesia) 201
Biederstein Verlag (Federal Republic of Germany) 128
Bielmas Librairie-Papeterie (Chad) 62
Biennial International Art Book Prize (International Literary Prizes) 447
Bierman & Bierman (Denmark) 78
Bierman og Bierman A/S (Denmark) 74
Bietti SpA (Italy) 213
Big O Publishing Ltd (United Kingdom) 375
Bigot en Van Rossum BV (Netherlands) 259
Bihar Pustak Vyayasayi Sangh (India) 186
Bijleveld, Erven J, (Netherlands) 259
Bijutsu Shuppan-Sha (Japan) 226
Bilac, Olavo, Prize (Brazil) 57
Bilderbuchstudio Neugebauer (Austria) 24
Bilgi Yayinevi (Turkey) 363
Billeret, Librairie, (Chad) 62
Bina Ilmu (Indonesia) 199
Binacipta (Indonesia) 199
Bingley, Clive, Ltd (United Kingdom) 375
Biography Book Club (United Kingdom) 414
Bir Library (Nepal) 257
Birkhäuser Verlag (Switzerland) 342
Birkhäuser Verlag (Federal Republic of Germany) 128
Birmingham Museums and Art Gallery (United Kingdom) 375
Birmingham Public Libraries (United Kingdom) 415
Biro, Perpustakaan, Pusat Statistik (Library of Central Bureau of Statistics) (Indonesia) 201
Birografika (Yugoslavia) 427
Bisat-e-Adab (Pakistan) 285
Bison Books Ltd (United Kingdom) 375
Biswakosh (Bangladesh) 32
Bitan (Israel) 207
Bitter, Georg, Verlag (Federal Republic of Germany) 128
Bjarnarsonar, Bókaútgáfa Thórhalls, (Iceland) 184
Björk, Bókaútgáfan, (Iceland) 184
Björnssonar, Bokaforlag Odds, (Iceland) 184

Black, A & C, (Publishers) Ltd (United Kingdom) 375
Black, James Tait, Memorial Prizes (United Kingdom) 419
Black, Stephen, Prize for Drama (Republic of South Africa) 316
Black Academy Press (Nigeria) 277
Black Apple (New Zealand) 272
Black Community Programmes Ltd (Republic of South Africa) 311
Black Pig Press (United Kingdom) 375
Blacker Calmann Cooper Ltd (United Kingdom) 375
Blackie & Son Ltd (United Kingdom) 375
Blackie & Son Private Ltd (India) 188
Blacklock Farries & Sons (United Kingdom) 375
Blackstaff Press Ltd (United Kingdom) 375
Blackwater, The, Press (Republic of Ireland) 203
Blackwell, B H, Ltd (United Kingdom) 415
Blackwell Publisher, Basil, Ltd (United Kingdom) 375
Blackwell Scientific Publications Ltd (United Kingdom) 376
Blackwood, William, & Sons Ltd (United Kingdom) 376
Bladkompaniet A/S (Norway) 281
Blakey, Jones, Publishing (United Kingdom) 376
Blanc, Charles, Prize (France) 113
Blanchart, Editions Gérard, & Cie SA (Belgium) 35
Blandford Books Ltd (United Kingdom) 376
Blandon, Librería, (Nicaragua) 276
Blanvalet Verlag (Federal Republic of Germany) 128
Blas de la Rosa (Dominican Republic) 80
Blaukreuz-Verlag (Federal Republic of Germany) 128
Blaukreuz-Verlag Bern (Switzerland) 342
Blazek und Bergmann (Federal Republic of Germany) 170
Bleicher Verlags-KG (Federal Republic of Germany) 128
Blémont, Emile, Prize (France) 113
Bles, Geoffrey, (United Kingdom) 376
Blewett, Dorothy, Associates (Australia) 19
Blish, James, Award (International Literary Prizes) 447
Blitz, Andries, BV (Netherlands) 259
Bloch, Dr J E, and Mrs Karin Schindler (Brazil) 55
Bloch Editores SA (Brazil) 50
Blok, H W, Uitgeverij BV (Netherlands) 259
Blok, Nakladatelství, (Czechoslovakia) 70
Blom Prize (Sweden) 339
Blond & Briggs Ltd (United Kingdom) 376
Blondel La Rougery SA (France) 91
Bloom, Roy, Ltd (United Kingdom) 413
Blotzheim, P Stephan, Ostasiatischer Kunstverlag (Federal Republic of Germany) 128
Bloud et Gay (Librairie) SA (France) 91
Blücher Ltda, Editôra Edgard, (Brazil) 50
Blume, Editorial, (Spain) 319
Bluth, Winfried, Literary Agency (Federal Republic of Germany) 169
Blyden, Edward Wilmot, Prize (Liberia) 242
Boccard, Editions E de, (France) 91
Bodleian Library (United Kingdom) 415
Bodley Head, The, Ltd (United Kingdom) 376
Bodmer, Fondation Martin, Bibliotheca Bodmeriana (Switzerland) 356
Bodmer, Les Editions de la Fondation Martin, (Switzerland) 342
Boeck, Maison d'Edition A de, SA (Belgium) 35
Boekencentrum BV (Netherlands) 259
Boekerij, De, BV (Netherlands) 259
Boer, Uitgeverij De, (Netherlands) 259
Boesen, Borge, (The English Bookshop) (Denmark) 78
Bog- og Papirbranchens Kreditor-Udvalg (Denmark) 74
Bogans Forlag (Denmark) 74
Bogaziçi University Library (formerly Robert College Library) (Turkey) 363
Bøger, Clemens, og Papir I/S (Denmark) 78
Boggero, B, Editore (Italy) 213
Boghallen (Denmark) 78
Bogvennerne (Denmark) 79
Bohem Press Kinderbuchverlag (Switzerland) 342
Böhlau-Verlag GmbH (Federal Republic of Germany) 128
Böhlaus, Hermann, Nachfolger (German Democratic Republic) 118
Böhlaus, Verlag Hermann, Nachf GmbH (Austria) 24
Bohmann Druck und Verlag AG (Austria) 25
Bohn, Scheltema & Holkema (Netherlands) 259
Boighar (Bangladesh) 32
Boje-Verlag (Federal Republic of Germany) 128
Bok-, Pappers- och Kontorsvaruförbundet (Sweden) 331
Bokas hf (Iceland) 185
Bókavardafélag Islands (Iceland) 186
Bokbranschens Finansierings-institut AB (Book Trade Finance Institute) (Sweden) 331
Bokbranschens Marknadsinstitut AB (Sweden) 331
Bokhandelsrådet (Sweden) 331
Boldt, Harald, Verlag KG (Federal Republic of Germany) 128
Bolivar Bookshop (Jamaica) 224
Bolivian Grand Prize for Literature (Bolivia) 48
Bollmann-Bildkarten-Verlag GmbH & Co Kg (Federal Republic of Germany) 129

Bologna Fair Budding Critics' Prize (International Literary Prizes) 447
Bologna Fair Graphic Prize for Children and Youth (International Literary Prizes) 447
Bolt & Watson Ltd (United Kingdom) 413
Bombay Booksellers' and Publishers' Association (India) 186
Bombay University Library (India) 197
Bompiani, Casa Editrice Valentino, & C SpA (Italy) 213
Bon Pasteur, Librairie du, (Togo) 360
Bonacci-Libreria Editrice (Italy) 213
Bonanza, Librairie, (Mauritius) 249
Bond Alleenverkopers van Nederlandstalige Boeken (BANB) (Belgium) 33
Bonechi, Casa Editrice, (Italy) 213
Bonetti, Pascal, Grand Prize (France) 113
Bongers, Verlag Aurel, KG (Federal Republic of Germany) 129
Bonn Aktuell GmbH (Federal Republic of Germany) 129
Bonne, Editions André, (France) 91
Bonner Buchgemeinde (BBG) (Federal Republic of Germany) 170
Bonniers, Albert, Förlag AB (Sweden) 332
Bonniers Bokklubb (Sweden) 337
Bonniers Juniorverlag AB (Sweden) 332
Bonum, Librería, SACI (Argentina) 4
Bonz, Verlag Adolf, GmbH (Federal Republic of Germany) 129
Book, The, House (Pakistan) 285
Book, The, Publishers' Association of Israel, International Promotion and Literary Rights Department (Israel) 210
Book and Printing Center — Israel Export Institute (Israel) 205
Book Association of Ireland (Republic of Ireland) 203
Book Centre (United Kingdom) 369
Book Centre (Zimbabwe) 435
Book Centre, The, (Gibraltar) 175
Book Club, The, (United Kingdom) 414
Book Club Associates (United Kingdom) 414
Book Collectors' Society of Australia (Australia) 21
Book Design Awards (Australia) 21
Book Distributors Sdn Bhd (Malaysia) 246
Book Exchange, The, (Zimbabwe) 435
Book Industry Council of South India (India) 186
Book Marketing, The, Council (United Kingdom) 369
Book Marketing Ltd (Hong Kong) 180
Book Mart, The, (Zimbabwe) 435
Book Mart, The, (Bermuda) 47
Book of the Month Club (United Kingdom) 414
Book People of Australia P/L (Australia) 12
Book People of Australia P/L (Australia) 19
Book Production Award (Pakistan) 287
Book Publishers' Association (Republic of Singapore) 308
Book Publishers' Association of Israel (Israel) 206
Book Publishers Association of New Zealand (New Zealand) 271
Book Publishers' Representatives' Association (United Kingdom) 369
Book Publishing Institute (Afghanistan) 1
Book Representation Co Ltd (Nigeria) 279
Book Sales Ltd (United Kingdom) 376
'Book Salon' Award (Romania) 305
Book Society of Persia (Iran) 202
Book Tokens Ltd (United Kingdom) 369
Book Trade Association of South Africa (Republic of South Africa) 311
Book Trade Benevolent Society (United Kingdom) 369
Book Trade Group (New South Wales) (Australia) 10
Book Trade Group (Queensland) (Australia) 10
Book Trade Group Secretary (Victoria) (Australia) 10
Bookcentre (Pakistan) 286
Booker McConnell Prize (International Literary Prizes) 447
Bookman, A/S, (Denmark) 78
Bookman of the Year Award (Australia) 21
Bookman Publishing House (Philippines) 291
Bookmark Inc (Philippines) 292
Books Abroad/English-Speaking Union of the United States Best Book of Belles Lettres (International Literary Prizes) 447
Books Across the Sea (United Kingdom) 417
Books for Asia (Hong Kong) 180
Books for Asia (M) Sdn Bhd (Malaysia) 246
Books for Asia (Singapore) Pte Ltd (Republic of Singapore) 310
Books for Children (United Kingdom) 414
Books for Neoliterates Prizes (India) 198
Books for Pleasure (Australia) 12
Books in Progress (International Organizations) 438
Books of Africa (Republic of South Africa) 311
Books of Rhodesia Book Club (Zimbabwe) 435
Books of Rhodesia Publishing Co (Pvt) Ltd (Zimbabwe) 434
Books-on-Japan-in-English Club (Japan) 232
Booksellers' and Publishers' Association of South India (India) 186

Booksellers Association of Great Britain and Ireland (Republic of Ireland) 203
Booksellers Association of Great Britain and Ireland (United Kingdom) 369
Booksellers' Association of Jamaica (Jamaica) 224
Booksellers Association of New Zealand (Inc) (New Zealand) 271
Booksellers' Association of Rhodesia (Zimbabwe) 434
Booksellers' Association of Trinidad and Tobago (Trinidad and Tobago) 361
Booksellers' Association of Zambia (Zambia) 433
Booksellers Association Service House Ltd (BASH) (United Kingdom) 369
Booksellers' Order Distribution Ltd (BOD) (United Kingdom) 369
Bookshelf, The, (Zambia) 434
Bookshop, The, (Namibia) 257
Bookshop, The, Ltd (Kenya) 236
Booksmith, The, (United Kingdom) 376
Bookventure (India) 188
Bookwise (Australia) Pty Ltd (Australia) 12
Bookworm, The, Club (United Kingdom) 414
Boom-Pers Boeken-En Tijdschriftenuitg BV (Netherlands) 259
Boosey & Hawkes (France) 91
Boosey & Hawkes Music Publishers Ltd (United Kingdom) 376
Boostan Publishing House (Israel) 207
Booth, Michael, Publications (Australia) 12
Borak, Al-, SA (Spain) 319
Borba (Yugoslavia) 427
Bordas, Editions, (France) 91
Bordas-Dunod Bruxelles SA (Belgium) 35
Bordewijk, F, Prize (Netherlands) 270
Bordin Prize (France) 113
Borgarbókasafn (City Library of Reykjavik) (Iceland) 186
Borgens Forlag A/S (Denmark) 74
Boringhieri, Editore, SpA (Italy) 213
Borla, SIL Srl Edizioni, (Italy) 213
Born NV Uitgeversmaatschappij (Netherlands) 259
Bornemann, Editions, (France) 91
Borntraeger, Gebrüder, Verlagsbuchhandlung (Federal Republic of Germany) 129
Borotha-Schoeler, Verlag Dr Gerda, (Austria) 25
Boroukhim (Iran) 201
Börsen, AS, Verlag AG (Switzerland) 342
Børsen Forlaget A/S (Denmark) 74
Börsenverein der Deutschen Buchhändler zu Leipzig (Association of German Democratic Republic Publishers and Booksellers in Leipzig) (German Democratic Republic) 117
Börsenverein des deutschen Buchhandels eV (Federal Republic of Germany) 122
Boscan, Juan, Prize (International Literary Prizes) 447
Bosch, Librería, (Spain) 327
Bosch Casa Editorial SA (Spain) 319
Bosch en Keuning NV (Netherlands) 259
Boscher-Chapron (France) 91
Bosco, Jean-Pierre, (France) 110
Bosse, Gustav, Verlag (Federal Republic of Germany) 129
Botas, Librería y Ediciones, SA (Mexico) 250
Botella, Ediciones, al Mar (Argentina) 4
Botev, Christo, International Prize for Revolutionary Poetry (International Literary Prizes) 447
Botswana Book Centre (Botswana) 48
Botswana National Archives (Botswana) 48
Botswana National Library Service (Botswana) 48
Bottega d'Erasmo (Italy) 213
Boubée, Editions N, et Cie (France) 91
Bougainville Copper Pty Ltd (Papua New Guinea) 288
Boukoumanis' Editions (Greece) 176
Bourbon, Librairie, (Mauritius) 249
Bourcy, Librairie De, Lucien (Luxembourg) 244
Bourdeaux-Capelle SA (Belgium) 35
Bourgeois, Christian, (France) 91
Bourrelier, Editions Colin, (France) 91
Boutique, La, Bleue (French Guiana) 116
Bouvier, Universitätsbuchhandlung, GmbH (Federal Republic of Germany) 170
Bouvier-Parviliez, Ernest, Prize (Belgium) 45
Bowen, Arnold Vincent, Competition (United Kingdom) 419
Bowen, D Richard, (Sweden) 337
Bowes & Bowes (Publishers) (United Kingdom) 376
Bowes & Bowes Books (United Kingdom) 415
Bowker and Bertram Ltd (Marine Publishers) (United Kingdom) 376
Bowker Publishing Co (United Kingdom) 376
Boxerbooks Inc (Switzerland) 355
Boyars, Marion, Publishers Ltd (United Kingdom) 376
Boydell & Brewer Ltd (United Kingdom) 376
Bozzi, Ugo, Editore (Italy) 213
Bra, Bokförlaget, Böcker AB (Sweden) 332
Bra, Bokklubben, Böcker (Sweden) 337
Braby, A C, (Rhodesia) (Pvt) Ltd (Zimbabwe) 434
Bracciodieta Editore (Italy) 213
Bradley, Mrs W A, (France) 110

Bradt Enterprises (United Kingdom) 376
Bragi, Bókaútgáfan, (Iceland) 185
Brain Anatomy Institute (Switzerland) 342
Bramante Editrice SpA (Italy) 213
Branch Line (United Kingdom) 376
Brand, Paul, (Netherlands) 259
Branding, De, NV (Belgium) 35
Brandstetter, Oscar, Verlag (Federal Republic of Germany) 129
Branner og Korch's Forlag A/S (Denmark) 74
Brash, Graham, Pte Ltd (Republic of Singapore) 308
Brash, Graham, Pte Ltd (Republic of Singapore) 310
Brasil, Editôra do, SA (Brazil) 50
Brasília, Editora, / Rio Ltda (Brazil) 50
Brasília Editôra (J Carvalho Branco & Cia Lda) (Portugal) 298
Brasília Editôra Ltda (Brazil) 50
Brasilia Prize for Poetry (International Literary Prizes) 447
Brasiliense, Editôra, SA (Brazil) 50
Brasiliense, Editôra, SA (Brazil) 55
Brassey's Publishers Ltd (United Kingdom) 376
Bratislava Literary Prize (Czechoslovakia) 73
Bratsvo-Jedinstvo (Yugoslavia) 427
Braumüller, Wilhelm, Universitätsverlag GmbH (Austria) 25
Braun, Literarischer Verlag Helmut, KG (Federal Republic of Germany) 129
Braun, Verlag G, GmbH (Federal Republic of Germany) 129
Braun und Schneider, Verlag, (Federal Republic of Germany) 129
Braunkohle, Verlag die, (Federal Republic of Germany) 129
Brazil Theatre Prize (International Literary Prizes) 447
Bréa Éditions (France) 91
Bread and Cheese Club (Australia) 21
Breitenbrunn, Galerie und Werkstatt, (Austria) 25
Breitenbrunn, Werkstatt und Galerie, (Federal Republic of Germany) 129
Breitkopf und Härtel (Federal Republic of Germany) 129
Breitkopf und Härtel, VEB, Musikverlag (German Democratic Republic) 118
Breitschopf, Julius, KG (Federal Republic of Germany) 129
Breitschopf, Verlagsbuchhandlung Julius, (Austria) 25
Breklumer Verlag (Federal Republic of Germany) 129
Bremen Literature Encouragement Prize (International Literary Prizes) 447
Bremen Literature Prize (International Literary Prizes) 447
Brendow-Verlag (Federal Republic of Germany) 129
Brenner Prize (Israel) 211
Brentano's (France) 110
Brepols, Editions, SA (France) 91
Brepols IGP (Belgium) 35
Bres, Redactie, (Netherlands) 259
Bretschneider, Dr Giorgio, Publisher & Bookseller (Italy) 213
Bretschneider, L'Erma di, SpA (Italy) 213
Brewer, D S, Ltd (United Kingdom) 376
Bridge Book Co Ltd (United Kingdom) 413
Brigg Verlag GmbH (formerly Verlag die Brigg) (Federal Republic of Germany) 129
Bright Advertising and Publishing Ltd (Bahamas) 32
Brill, NV Boekhandel & Drukkerij voorheen E J, (Netherlands) 259
Brimax Books (United Kingdom) 376
Brink-Meppel, Ten, BV AFD Uitgeverij (Netherlands) 259
British & Foreign Bible Society (United Kingdom) 376
British and Irish Association of Law Librarians (United Kingdom) 416
British Council, The, (United Kingdom) 376
British Council Libraries (Sri Lanka) 330
British Council Libraries (Pakistan) 286
British Council Libraries (Iran) 202
British Council Library (India) 197
British Council Library (Ethiopia) 84
British Council Library (Hong Kong) 181
British Council Library (Greece) 178
British Council Library (Ghana) 175
British Council Library (Malaysia) 247
British Council Library (Mauritius) 249
British Council Library (Malta) 248
British Council Library (Morocco) 256
British Council Library (Nepal) 257
British Council Library (Lesotho) 242
British Council Library (Malawi) 245
British Council Library (Jordan) 234
British Council Library (Sudan) 330
British Council Library (Sierra Leone) 308
British Council Library (Tanzania) 358
British Council Library (Tunisia) 362
British Council Library (Thailand) 360
British Council Library (Yemen Arab Republic) 426
British Council Library (Bangladesh) 33

INDEX 471

British Council Library (Cyprus) 69
British Council Library (Colombia) 66
British Council Library (United Republic of Cameroun) 61
British Heritage (United Kingdom) 414
British Horse, The, Society (United Kingdom) 376
British Library (United Kingdom) 377
British Library, Bibliographic Services Division (United Kingdom) 415
British Library, Science Reference Library (United Kingdom) 415
British Library Lending Division (United Kingdom) 415
British Library of Political and Economic Science (United Kingdom) 415
British Library Reference Division (United Kingdom) 415
British Museum (Natural History) (United Kingdom) 377
British Museum Publications Ltd (United Kingdom) 377
British Printing Corporation Ltd (United Kingdom) 377
British Science Fiction, The, Association Ltd (United Kingdom) 417
British Science Fiction Award (United Kingdom) 419
Brno Literary Prize (Czechoslovakia) 73
Brockhaus, F A, (Federal Republic of Germany) 129
Brockhaus, R, Verlag (Federal Republic of Germany) 129
Brockhaus, VEB F A, Verlag (German Democratic Republic) 118
Brodie, James, Ltd (United Kingdom) 377
Brodies Notes (United Kingdom) 377
Broele, Vanden, PVBA (Belgium) 35
Broese-Kemink BV (Netherlands) 269
Brombergs Bokförlag Scientia (Sweden) 333
Bronfman's Agency Ltd (Israel) 210
Bronfman's Agency Ltd (Israel) 207
Brönner Verlag Breidenstein KG (Federal Republic of Germany) 129
Brontë, The Incorporated, Society (United Kingdom) 418
Bronze Swagman Award (Australia) 22
Broomsleigh Press (United Kingdom) 377
Broquette-Gonin Grand Prize (France) 113
Broschek Druck GmbH & Co KG (Federal Republic of Germany) 129
Broschek Verlag (Federal Republic of Germany) 129
Broutta, Michèle, Oeuvres Graphiques Contemporaines (France) 92
Brown, Emanuel, (Israel) 210
Brown, Robert, & Associates Pty Ltd (Papua New Guinea) 288
Brown Watson Ltd & Brown Watson Juvenile (United Kingdom) 377
Browne & Nolan (Republic of Ireland) 204
Bruck, Librairie Paul, (Luxembourg) 244
Brücken-Verlag GmbH Literaturvertrieb Import-Export (Federal Republic of Germany) 129
Bruckmann, Verlag F, KG (Federal Republic of Germany) 130
Bruckmann Kunst, Studio, im Druck Fine Art GmbH (Federal Republic of Germany) 130
Bruggen, Jochem van, prys vir Prosa (Republic of South Africa) 316
Bruguera, Editorial, Argentina (Argentina) 4
Bruguera, Editorial, Colombiana Ltda (Colombia) 65
Bruguera, Editorial, Mexicana SA (Mexico) 250
Bruguera, Editorial, SA (Spain) 319
Bruguera, Editorial, Venezolana SA (Venezuela) 424
Bruna, A W, & Zoon NV (Belgium) 35
Bruna, A W, & Zoon's Uitgeversmaatschappij BV (Netherlands) 259
Brunei, The, Press (Brunei) 57
Brunnen-Verlag (Switzerland) 342
Brunnen-Verlag GmbH (Federal Republic of Germany) 130
Brunner, Ing Johann, (Austria) 29
Brunner Verlagsgesellschaft (Federal Republic of Germany) 130
Brunnquell-Verlag der Bibel-und Missions-Stiftung Metzingen (Federal Republic of Germany) 130
Bruño, Asociación Editorial, (Peru) 289
Bruño, Editorial, (Spain) 319
Bruns, F, Bokhandel (Norway) 283
Bruns, F, Bokhandels Forlag A/S (Norway) 281
Bruylant, Etablissements Emile, SA (Belgium) 35
Bubenberg Verlag AG (Switzerland) 342
Buch- und Bibliothekswesen, VEB Verlag für, (German Democratic Republic) 118
Buchagentur München (Federal Republic of Germany) 169
buchclub 65 (German Democratic Republic) 120
Buchclub 69 GmbH (Federal Republic of Germany) 170
Buchdruckerei, Verlag der, Ostschweiz AG (Switzerland) 342
Bucheli, Verlag Alfred, (Switzerland) 342
Bücher, C J, GmbH (Federal Republic of Germany) 130
Bucher, Verlag C J, AG (Switzerland) 342
Bücherbund Buch- und Schallplattenhandel Verlagsgesellschaft mbH (Austria) 29
Buchet/Chastel, Editions, (France) 92

Buchexport — Volkseigener Aussenhandelsbetrieb der Deutschen Demokratischen Republik, (GDR Peoples' Export Undertaking) (German Democratic Republic) 117
Buchhandlung b Theater a d Wien (Austria) 29
Buchhandlung im Stadtle (Liechtenstein) 243
Buchhaus AG (Switzerland) 342
Buchholz, Librería, (Colombia) 66
Buchholz Verlag (Federal Republic of Germany) 130
Buchklub der Schüler (German Democratic Republic) 120
Büchler-Verlag (Switzerland) 342
Büchner, Georg, Prize (Federal Republic of Germany) 173
Buchner, Rudolf, (Austria) 29
Büchner, Selbstverlag Walter, (Federal Republic of Germany) 130
Bucholz, Livraria, (Portugal) 301
Buchser, Hugo, SA (Switzerland) 343
Buckland Literary Award (New Zealand) 275
Budapesti Müszaki Egyetem Központi Könyvtára (Hungary) 183
Buena Prensa AC (Mexico) 250
Buenos Aires Literary Prizes (Argentina) 9
Buijten & Schipperheijn BV Drukkerij en Uitg Mij v/h (Netherlands) 259
Bulan Bintang, Penerbit & Pustake NV (Indonesia) 199
Bulawayo Public Library (Zimbabwe) 435
Bulgarian Academy of Sciences, Central Library, (Bulgaria) 59
Bulgarian Academy of Sciences, Institute of Literature (Bulgaria) 59
Bulgarian Publishing Award (Bulgaria) 59
Bulgarian Union of Public Libraries (Bulgaria) 59
Bulgarskata Akademia, Izdatelstvo na, na Naukite (Bulgaria) 58
Bulgarskata Komunisticheska Partiya, Izdatelstvo na, (Bulgaria) 58
Bulgarski Houdozhnik (Bulgaria) 58
Bulgarski Pissatel (Bulgaria) 58
Bulgarskiya Zemedelski Naroden Suyuz, Izdatelstvo na, (Bulgaria) 58
Bulpin, T V, (Pty) Ltd (Republic of South Africa) 311
Bulwer-Lytton Circle (United Kingdom) 418
Bulzoni Editore SRL (Italy) 213
Bumi Restu (Indonesia) 199
Bunch Books (United Kingdom) 377
Bund-Verlag GmbH (Federal Republic of Germany) 130
Bundesarbeitsgemeinschaft der katholisch-kirchlichen Büchereiarbeit (Federal Republic of Germany) 171
Bundesarchiv (National Archives) (Federal Republic of Germany) 171
Bundesgremium des Handels mit Büchern, Kunstblättern und Musikalien, Zeitungen und Zeitschriften (Austria) 23
Bundeskanzeramt, Administrative Bibliothek und österreichische Rechtsdokumentation im, (Austria) 30
Bundesverband der deutschen Verlagsvertreter eV (National Association of German Publishers' Representatives) (Federal Republic of Germany) 122
Bundesverband der deutschen Versandbuchhändler eV (National Federation of German Mail-order Booksellers) (Federal Republic of Germany) 122
Bundesverband der Dolmetscher und Übersetzer eV (BDÜ) (Federal Republic of Germany) 174
Bundesverband des werbenden Buch- und Zeitschriftenhandels eV (National Federation of the Promotional Book and Periodical Trade) (Federal Republic of Germany) 122
Bungeishunju Ltd (Japan) 226
Burckhardthaus-Laetare Verlag GmbH (Federal Republic of Germany) 130
Burda, Verlag Aenne, (Federal Republic of Germany) 130
Bureau de Presse et d'Information (France) 92
Bureau de Recherches Géologiques et Minières (France) 92
Bureau d'Etudes et de Recherches pour la Promotion de la Sante (France) 92
Bureau International du Travail (Switzerland) 356
Bureau of Ghana Languages (Ghana) 175
Bureau of Ghana Languages (Ghana) 174
Bureau of Statistics, Central, (Ghana) 175
Burgert Handpresse (Federal Republic of Germany) 130
Burke Enterprises (Pvt) Ltd (Zimbabwe) 434
Burke Publishing Co Ltd (United Kingdom) 377
Burke's Peerage Ltd (United Kingdom) 377
Burma Library Association (Burma) 60
Burmese Publishers' Union (Burma) 59
Burns & Oates Ltd (United Kingdom) 377
Burns Philp (NG) Pty Ltd (Papua New Guinea) 288
Büro für Urheberrechte (German Democratic Republic) 120
Burulan, SA de Ediciones (Spain) 319
Busche, Kartographischer Verlag, GmbH (Federal Republic of Germany) 130
Buschmann, J E, PVBA (Belgium) 35

Busck, Arnold, International Boghandel A/S (Denmark) 78
Busck, Nyt Nordisk Forlag Arnold, A/S (Denmark) 74
Bushatsky, Livraría e Editôra Juridica José, Ltda (Brazil) 50
Business Books Ltd (United Kingdom) 377
Business Information Establishment SA (Belgium) 35
Business Leaders Book Club (United Kingdom) 414
Business Promotion Bureau (India) 188
Business Publications Ltd (China (Taiwan)) 64
Busse Kunstdokumentation GmbH (Federal Republic of Germany) 130
Bussesche Verlagshandlung GmbH (Federal Republic of Germany) 130
Bustamente Press Inc (Philippines) 291
Butler, Dorothy, Ltd (New Zealand) 274
Butterbach, Christian, (Luxembourg) 243
Butterworth & Co (Publishers) Ltd (United Kingdom) 377
Butterworth & Co (SA) (Pty) Ltd (Republic of South Africa) 311
Butterworths of New Zealand Ltd (New Zealand) 272
Butterworths Pty Ltd (Australia) 12
Butzon und Bercker, Verlag, GmbH (Federal Republic of Germany) 130
Buzby Books Ltd (United Kingdom) 377

C A L (Culture Art Loisirs SA) (France) 110
C A L/Retz (France) 92
C B D Research Ltd (United Kingdom) 377
C D D (Centar društvenih djelatnosti Saveza socijalističke omladine Hrvatske) (Yugoslavia) 427
C D L (Central Distribuidora Livreira) SARL (Portugal) 301
C D R (France) 92
C E D A M (Casa Editrice Dr A Milani) (Italy) 213
C E D A R, The, Press (Barbados) 33
C E D E L, Editorial, (Centro de Difusión del Libro) (Spain) 319
C E D I Bookshop (Zaire) 433
C E D I L (Centro Distribuidor de Libros) (Chile) 62
C E D S (France) 92
C E D-Samsom NV (Belgium) 35
C E E B A Publications (Zaire) 432
C E E L (Centre Expérimental pour l'Enseignement des Langues) (Switzerland) 343
C E E S, Librería, (Guatemala) 179
C E F A, Editions, (Centre d'Éducation à la Famille et à l'Amour) (Belgium) 35
C E F A G (France) 92
C E L I (Edizioni) (Italy) 213
C E L S E (Compagnie d'Editions Libres, Sociales et Economiques SA) (France) 92
C E P A (Brazil) 50
C E P A D (France) 92
C E P I M, Edizioni, (Italy) 213
C E P L (Centre d'Etude et de Promotion de la Lecture) (France) 92
C I E S P A L, Fondo Editorial de, (Centro Internacional de Estudios Superiores de Comunicación para América Latina) (Ecuador) 81
C K P (Clenská knižnica Pravdy) (Czechoslovakia) 72
C L A I M Bookshop (Malawi) 245
C L D (France) 92
C L E, Editions, (Centre de Littérature Evangélique) (United Republic of Cameroun) 60
C L E International (France) 92
C N A (Republic of South Africa) 311
C N A Literary Award (Republic of South Africa) 316
C N R S, Editions du, (Centre National de la Recherche Scientifique) (France) 92
C N R S, Laboratoire Intergeo (France) 92
C O R, Ediciones, (Cuba) 68
C R Books (United Kingdom) 377
C R E R (France) 92
C S I R Central Reference and Research Library (Ghana) 175
C S I R O (Commonwealth Scientific and Industrial Research Organization) (Australia) 20
C S I R O (Commonwealth Scientific and Industrial Research Organization) (Australia) 12
C S S (Nigeria) Bookshops Ltd (Nigeria) 279
C S S Bookshops, Agency and Publishing Division (Nigeria) 277
C U M (Republic of South Africa) 311
C V B Buch und Druck (Switzerland) 343
Caann Verlag GmbH (Federal Republic of Germany) 130
Cadernos Didáticos, Livros Cadernos Ltda (Brazil) 50
Caffrey, Smith Publishing Co (United Kingdom) 377
Cahiers d'Art, Editions, (France) 92
Cahiers de la Renaissance Vaudoise (Switzerland) 343
Cahiers Les, Européens Sàrl (France) 92
Cairo University Press (Egypt) 82
Cajica, Editorial, (Mexico) 250
Calder, John, (Publishers) Ltd (United Kingdom) 377

Calderini, Edizioni, (Italy) 213
Calicanto, Editorial, (Argentina) 4
Calinescu, Institutul de Istorie si Teorie Literara 'George, (Romania) 305
Callenbach, Uitgeverij G F, BV (Netherlands) 259
Callwey, Verlag Georg D W, (Federal Republic of Germany) 130
Calmann & Cooper, John, Ltd (United Kingdom) 377
Calmann-Lévy, Editions, Sàrl (France) 92
Calozet, Editions, SPRL (Belgium) 35
Calwer Verlag (Federal Republic of Germany) 130
Calypso Distributors Ltd (Bahamas) 32
Camacho, Manuel Avila, Prize (Mexico) 255
Cámara, Biblioteca de la, Oficial de Comercio, Agricultura e Industria del Distrito Nacional (Dominican Republic) 81
Cámara Argentina de Editores de Libros (Argentina) 3
Cámara Argentina de Editoriales Tecnicas (Argentina) 3
Cámara Argentina de Publicaciones (Argentina) 3
Cámara Argentina del Libro (Argentina) 3
Cámara Boliviana del Libro, Librería Selecciones (Bolivia) 47
Câmara Brasileira do Livro (Brazil) 48
Cámara Chilena del Libro (Chile) 62
Cámara Colombiana de la Industria Editorial (Colombia) 65
Cámara Colombiana del Libro (Colombia) 65
Cámara de Editores (Venezuela) 424
Cámara Latinoamericana del Libro (CIAL) (Latin-American Book Association) (International Organizations) 438
Cámara Nacional de la Industria Editorial (Mexican Publishers' Association) (Mexico) 250
Cámara Paraguaya del Libro (Paraguayan Publishers' Association) (Paraguay) 288
Cámara Peruana del Libro (Peruvian Publishers' Association) (Peru) 289
Cámara Uruguaya del Libro (Uruguay) 422
Cámara Venezolana del Libro (Venezuela) 424
Cambridge Bibliographical Society (United Kingdom) 416
Cambridge Information and Research Services Ltd (United Kingdom) 377
Cambridge University Library (United Kingdom) 416
Cambridge University Press (United Kingdom) 377
Cambridge University Press (New Zealand) 272
Cambridge University Press (Australia) Pty Ltd (Australia) 12
Camera-Verlag (Switzerland) 343
Cameron & Tayleur (Books) Ltd (United Kingdom) 378
Cameroun Book Centre (United Republic of Cameroun) 61
Caminho, Editorial, SARL (Portugal) 299
Campbell, John W, Memorial Award (International Literary Prizes) 447
Campbell, Killie, Africana Library (Republic of South Africa) 311
Campbell, Roy, Prize for Poetry (Republic of South Africa) 316
Campert, Jan, Prize (Netherlands) 270
Campiello Prize (Italy) 223
Campos, Academia de Letras 'Humberto de, ' (Brazil) 57
Campus, Editora, Ltda (Brazil) 50
Campus Corner Ltd (Trinidad and Tobago) 361
Campus Verlag GmbH (Federal Republic of Germany) 130
Camugli (France) 92
Camus, Bibliothèque du Centre culturel 'Albert, ' (Democratic Republic of Madagascar) 245
'Canberra Times' Short Story Award (Australia) 22
Cangallo, Editorial, SACI (Argentina) 4
Cankarjeva Zalozba (Yugoslavia) 431
Cankarjeva Založba (Yugoslavia) 427
Canongate and Southside (United Kingdom) 378
Cantabrica, Editorial, SA (Spain) 319
Cantecleer, Uitgeverij, BV (Netherlands) 260
Canterbury Public Library (New Zealand) 275
Canterbury University Library (New Zealand) 275
Cantonetto, Edizioni del Prof Mario Agliati, (Switzerland) 343
Cantor, Editio, (Federal Republic of Germany) 130
Canuto, Livraria, Ltda (Brazil) 55
Caorle City Prize (International Literary Prizes) 448
Cape, Jonathan, Ltd (United Kingdom) 378
Cape Catley Ltd (New Zealand) 272
Cape Coast University Bookshop (Ghana) 175
Cape Town City Libraries (Republic of South Africa) 315
Capendu, Editions, (France) 92
Capitol Editrice Dischi CEB (Italy) 213
Capitol Publishing House Inc (Philippines) 291
Cappelens, J W, Forlag A/S (Norway) 281
Cappelli, Nuova Casa Editrice Licinio, SpA (Italy) 214
Capper Press Ltd (New Zealand) 272
Caputo, Ursula, (Italy) 221
Caralt, Luis de, Editor SA (Spain) 319
Caravelle, La, Librairie (Tunisia) 362
Carcanet Press Ltd (United Kingdom) 378
Cardeñoso, Cecilio, (Spain) 327

Carducci Prize (International Literary Prizes) 448
Caribbean Regional Library (Puerto Rico) 303
Caribbean Universities Press (Jamaica) 224
Caribbean Universities Press (Barbados) 33
Caribe, Editora El, (Dominican Republic) 80
Caribe Grolier Inc (Dominican Republic) 80
Carinthia, Verlag, (Austria) 25
Carit Andersens Forlag I/S (Denmark) 75
Caritas, Librairie, (Rwanda) 306
Caritas-Verlag (Switzerland) 343
Carl, Verlag Hans, KG (Federal Republic of Germany) 131
Carlsen if (Denmark) 75
Carlsen Verlag GmbH (Federal Republic of Germany) 131
Carlsen/if AB (Sweden) 333
Carmelitana VZW ('De Karmelieten') (Belgium) 35
Carnegie Free Library (Trinidad and Tobago) 361
Carnegie Library (Mauritius) 249
Carnegie Medal (United Kingdom) 419
Carnell, E J, Literary Agency (United Kingdom) 413
Caro y Cuervo, Instituto, (Colombia) 65
Carrefour, Librairie, (Ivory Coast) 224
Carroll's Pty Ltd (Australia) 12
Carson-Gold, Ronald, Memorial Short Story Competition (Australia) 22
Carta, Lüthi & Ramseier (Switzerland) 343
Carta, The Israel Map and Publishing Co Ltd (Israel) 207
Cartago, Editorial, (Argentina) 4
'Cartea Românesca', Editura, (Publishing House of 'The Romanian Book') (Romania) 304
Carter Nash Cameron Ltd (United Kingdom) 378
Cartographia (Hungary) 182
Caruana, Francis, (Gibraltar) 175
Carto PVBA (Belgium) 35
Carvajal SA (Colombia) 65
Carvan Book House (Pakistan) 285
Casa de la Cultura Ecuatoriana, Biblioteca de la, (Ecuador) 81
Casa del Libro, Librería, (Colombia) 66
Casa del Libro SA (Spain) 319
Casagrande, Edizioni, SA (Switzerland) 343
Casalini Libri (Italy) 221
Casalini Libri (Italy) 214
Casamajo-Lappas (Spain) 319
Casavalle, Carlos, Prize (Argentina) 9
Cass, Frank, & Co Ltd (United Kingdom) 378
Cassell Australia Ltd (Australia) 12
Cassell Ltd (United Kingdom) 378
Cassell Ltd (New Zealand) 272
Cassia House Bookshop (Trinidad and Tobago) 361
Castaigne, Librairie, (Belgium) 44
Castalia, Editorial, (Spain) 319
castellla, editions andré, (France) 92
Castello-Sanguinetto Prize (Italy) 223
Casterman (Belgium) 35
Casterman, Editions, (France) 92
Castex, Louis, Prize (France) 113
Castiau, Adelson, Prize (Belgium) 45
Castle (United Kingdom) 378
Castro e Silva, Livraria, (Portugal) 301
Castrum Peregrini Presse (Netherlands) 260
Cat and Fiddle Press (Australia) 12
Catalanes, Editions, de Paris (France) 92
Catalogue de l'Edition Française (France) 92
Cátedra, Ediciones, SA (Spain) 320
Cátedra, Livraria Editôra, Ltda (Brazil) 50
Catenacci, Hercule, Prize (France) 113
Cathasia (France) 92
Cathay (United Kingdom) 378
Cathedral, The, Bookshop (Tanzania) 358
Cathedral Bookshop (Belize) 46
Catholic, Central, Library (Republic of Ireland) 205
Catholic, Central, Library Association Inc (Republic of Ireland) 205
Catholic, The, Bookshop Ltd (Kenya) 236
Catholic Book Club (United Kingdom) 414
Catholic Book Depot (Lesotho) 242
Católica, La Editorial, SA (Spain) 320
Caux, Editions de, (Switzerland) 343
Caux Verlag-, Theater- & Film-AG (Switzerland) 343
Cave, H W, & Co (Sri Lanka) 329
Cavefors, Bo, Bokförlag AB (Sweden) 333
Caveman Publications Ltd (New Zealand) 272
Caxton, The, Press (New Zealand) 272
Caxton Publications Ltd (United Kingdom) 378
Caymi, Editorial, (Argentina) 4
Ceac, Ediciones, SA (Spain) 320
Cedar Books (United Kingdom) 378
Cedibra Editora Brasileira Ltda (Brazil) 50
Cedic, Editions, (France) 92
Cèdre, Editions, (France) 92
Celcius — J J Vallory (Argentina) 4
Celtic Educational Ltd (United Kingdom) 378
Celuc Libri (Italy) 214
Cement & Concrete Association (United Kingdom) 378
Cemerlang (Indonesia) 199

Centaur Press Ltd (United Kingdom) 378
Centen, D B, (Netherlands) 260
Center for Inter-American Relations (International Organizations) 441
Centraal Boekhuis BV (Netherlands) 257
Centraal Bureau, Bibliotheek van het, voor de Statistiek (Library of the Netherlands Central Bureau of Statistics) (Netherlands) 269
Central Agricultural Library (Republic of South Africa) 315
Central Book Depot (Publishers) (India) 188
Central Bookshop Ltd (Malawi) 245
Central de Publicaciones (Mexico) 253
Central Department Store (Thailand) 360
Central Library (India) 197
Central Library (India) 197
Central Medical Library (Bulgaria) 58
Central News Agency (Namibia) 257
Central News Agency Ltd (Republic of South Africa) 315
Central News Agency Ltd (Republic of South Africa) 311
Central Secretariat Library (Pakistan) 286
Central Secretariat Library (India) 197
Central Tanganyika Press (Tanzania) 358
Centrala Cartii (Book Centre) (Romania) 303
Centrala Editoriala (Publishing Centre) (Romania) 303
Centrale de l'Industrie du Livre (Belgium) 33
Centralnej Rady Zwiazków Zawodowych, Instytut Wydawniczy, (Publishing House of the Central Council of Trade Unions) (Poland) 294
Centre, Librairie du, (Luxembourg) 244
Centre Africain de Formation et de Recherche administrative pour le Développement (Morocco) 256
Centre belge de Traduction (Belgium) 46
Centre culturel américain (Ivory Coast) 224
Centre culturel américain (Senegal) 307
Centre culturel américain (Gabon) 116
Centre culturel américain, Bibliothèque (Chad) 62
Centre culturel américain, Bibliothèque (United Republic of Cameroun) 61
Centre culturel du Burundi (Burundi) 60
Centre culturel français (Central African Republic) 61
Centre culturel français (Senegal) 307
Centre culturel français (Ivory Coast) 224
Centre culturel français, Bibliothèque (Togo) 361
Centre culturel français, Bibliothèque (United Republic of Cameroun) 61
Centre culturel français, Bibliothèque (Popular Republic of Congo) 67
Centre culturel français, Bibliothèque (Chad) 62
Centre culturel français, Bibliothèque (Zaire) 433
Centre culturel français St-Exupéry (Gabon) 116
Centre Culturel Maison de France, Bibliothèque du, (Kampuchea) 235
Centre d'Archives et de Documentation politiques et sociales (Centre for Political and Social Archives and Documentation) (France) 111
Centre de Documentation (Haiti) 180
Centre de Documentation (Niger) 276
Centre de Documentation économique et sociale africaine (CEDESA) (Centre for African Economic and Social Documentation) (International Organizations) 438
Centre de Documentation Pédagogique, Bibliothèque (Chad) 62
Centre de Documentation Universitaire et Société d'Edition d'Enseignement Supérieur Réunis (CDU & SEDES) (France) 93
Centre de Géographie, Bibliothèque (France) 111
Centre de la Productivité du Livre (Book Research Centre) (France) 88
Centre de Littérature Chrétienne (Benin) 46
Centre de Littérature Evangélique (Gabon) 116
Centre de Publications Evangeliques (Ivory Coast) 224
Centre de Recherches et de Documentation du Sénégal (CRDS) (Senegal) 307
Centre d'Edition et de Diffusion africaines (Ivory Coast) 224
Centre d'Edition et de Diffusion africaines (Ivory Coast) 224
Centre d'Edition et de Production de Manuels et d'Auxiliaires de l'Enseignement (United Republic of Cameroun) 60
Centre d'Edition et de Production de Manuels scolaires de l'UNESCO (United Republic of Cameroun) 61
Centre d'Education à la Famille et à l'Amour (Belgium) 35
Centre d'Enseignement supérieur de Niamey (University Education Centre) (Niger) 276
Centre d'Etude et de Promotion de la Lecture (France) 92
Centre d'Etude et d'Edition Conjugale et Familiale ASBL (Belgium) 35
Centre d'Etudes et de Documentation, Editions du, Scientifiques (CEDS Editions) (France) 92
Centre d'Etudes et Fabrication Arts Graphiques (CEFAG) (France) 93
Centre Expérimental pour l'Enseignement des Langues (Centre for the Experimentation and Evaluation of Language Learning Techniques) (Switzerland) 343

INDEX 473

Centre for Academic Publications Japan (Japan) 226
Centre for Documentation and Research (United Arab Emirates) 368
Centre for Investment Studies (United Kingdom) 378
Centre for Pedagogical Information and Documentation (Bulgaria) 58
Centre for Public Libraries (Israel) 211
Centre for Scientific and Technical Information (Republic of South Africa) 315
Centre français de Documentation (Mali) 248
Centre international de documentation classique (International Organizations) 438
Centre international de Documentation Concernant les Expressions Plastiques (CIDEP) (International Organizations) 441
Centre International de Sémiologie (Zaire) 432
Centre international d'Etudes de la Formation religieuse Lumen Vitae ASBL (Belgium) 35
Centre national d'Art et de Culture Georges Pompidou (France) 93
Centre national de Documentation (National Documentation Centre) (Morocco) 256
Centre national de Documentation (National Documentation Centre) (Laos) 240
Centre national de Documentation scientifique et technique (Belgium) 44
Centre national de la Recherche Scientifique (France) 93
Centre national de Recherches 'Primitifs Flamands' ASBL (Belgium) 35
Centre national des Académies et Associations littéraires et savantes des Provinces françaises (National Centre of the Literary and Learned Academies and Associations of the French Provinces) (France) 112
Centre national des Lettres (France) 112
Centre national d'Etudes et de Recherches socio-économiques (CERSE) ASBL (Belgium) 35
Centre Protestant d'Editions et de Diffusion (CEDI) (Zaire) 432
Centre Publications (Australia) 12
Centre régional de Promotion du Livre en Afrique (Regional Centre for Book Promotion in Africa) (International Organizations) 438
Centre royal de Documentation, Bibliothèque du, et d'Edition (Kampuchea) 235
Centre Sénégalaise d'Editions et de Diffusion (Senegal) 307
Centro, Biblioteca del, Cultural Costarricense-Norteamericano (Costa Rica) 68
Centro, Fundación, de Investigación ed Educación Popular (CINEP) (Colombia) 65
Centro de Documentação Científica de Moçambique (Centre of Scientific Documentation of Mozambique) (Mozambique) 256
Centro de Documentacão Científica e Técnica (Portugal) 301
Centro de Documentação e Informaçao da Camara dos Deputados (Brazil) 56
Centro de Documentação e Informação do Ensino (Centre of Documentation and Information on Education) (Mozambique) 256
Centro De Documentación Bibliotecológica (Argentina) 9
Centro de Estudios Monetarios Latinoamericanos (CEMLA) (Mexico) 250
Centro de Investigação e Documentação (Brazil) 56
Centro Di (Italy) 214
Centro Di (International Documentation Centre) (International Organizations) 438
Centro do Livro Brasileiro (Portugal) 299
Centro Editor de America Latina SA (Argentina) 4
Centro Editor de Psicologia Aplicada Ltda (CEPA) (Brazil) 50
Centro Filosófico-Literario (Colombia) 67
Centro Internazionale del Libro (Italy) 214
Centro Latinoamericano de Demografía (CELADE) (Chile) 62
Centro Mexicano de Escritores AC (Mexican Authors' Centre) (Mexico) 254
Centro Nacional de Documentación Científica y Tecnológica (Bolivia) 48
Centro Nacional de Documentación e Información Educativa (Bolivia) 48
Centro Nacional de Información y Documentación (CENID) (Chile) 63
Centro Nacional de Información y Documentación (National Information and Documentation Centre) (Uruguay) 423
Centro Regional para el Fomento del Libro en América Latina y el Caribe (CERLAL) (Regional Centre for Encouragement of Books in Latin America and Carribbean) (International Organizations) 438
Centrul de Lingvistica Istorie Literara si Folclor (Romania) 305
Centrum Informacji Naukowej, Technicznej i Ekonomicznej (National Centre for Scientific, Technical and Economic Information) (Poland) 296
Centrum voor Literatuuronderzoekers (Centre for Literature Research) (Netherlands) 270

Centurion, Editions du, (France) 93
Cepadues Editions (C E P A D) SA (France) 93
Cercle Belge de la Librairie (Belgium) 33
Cercle d'Art, Editions, SA (France) 93
Cercle de la Librairie (Syndicat des Industries et Commerces du Livre) (France) 88
Cercle du Bibliophile (France) 110
Cerdas (Indonesia) 199
Ceres (Belgium) 35
Ceres, Editura, (Romania) 304
Ceres Productions (Tunisia) 361
Ceres-Verlag Rudolf-August Oetker KG (Federal Republic of Germany) 131
Cerf, Editions du, (France) 93
Certificate of Honour (India) 198
Cervantes, Librería, (Ecuador) 81
Cervantes, Libreria, — Libroclub de Guatemala (Guatemala) 179
Cervantes, Miguel de, Prize (Spain) 329
České socialistické republiky, Státni knihovna, (Czechoslovakia) 72
Českého fondu, Výtvarná služba, výtvarných umělcu, sekce krásné knihy a grafiky (Czechoslovakia) 73
Československý spisovatel (Czechoslovakia) 70
Ceylon Institute of Scientific and Industrial Research Library (Sri Lanka) 330
Ceylon Printers Ltd (Sri Lanka) 329
Chadwyck-Healey Ltd (United Kingdom) 378
Chaix, Editions R, (France) 93
Chalantika (Bangladesh) 32
Chalermnit Bookshop (Thailand) 360
Chalermnit Press (Thailand) 359
Chalet, Editions du, (France) 93
Challenge Bookshops (Nigeria) 279
Chambers, W & R, Ltd (United Kingdom) 378
Chambre syndicale des Editeurs d'Annuaires et de Publications similaires (Association of Publishers of Directories and Similar Publications) (France) 88
Champ Libre, Editions, (France) 93
Champion Verlag G Kowalski (Federal Republic of Germany) 131
Champs-Elysées, Librairie des, SA (France) 93
Chancerel Editions SA (France) 93
Chancerel Publishers Ltd (United Kingdom) 378
Chand, S, & Co Ltd (India) 188
Changjak Kwa Pipyung Sa (Republic of Korea) 238
Changjo Sa (Republic of Korea) 238
Chanlis (Belgium) 36
Chantecler, Editions, (Belgium) 36
Chantereine, Les Editions, (France) 93
Chaplin, Sid, Literary Award (United Kingdom) 419
Chapman, Geoffrey, (United Kingdom) 379
Chapman & Hall Ltd (United Kingdom) 379
Charran's Bookshop (1978) (Trinidad and Tobago) 361
Charran's Educational Publishers (Trinidad and Tobago) 361
Charte, La, NV (Belgium) 36
Charter Books Pty Ltd (Australia) 19
Chatam Sofer Institute (Israel) 207
Chateauneuf-du-Pape Grand Prize (France) 113
Chatto, Bodley Head & Jonathan Cape Australia Pty Ltd (Australia) 12
Chatto, Bodley Head & Jonathan Cape Ltd (United Kingdom) 379
Chatto & Windus Ltd (United Kingdom) 379
Chauveau, Pierre, Medal (International Literary Prizes) 448
Chavée, Honoré, Prize (France) 113
Chekiang Library (People's Republic of China) 63
Cheltenham Festival of Literature Competition (International Literary Prizes) 448
Chemical Society, The, (United Kingdom) 379
Chemie, Verlag, GmbH (Federal Republic of Germany) 131
Chêne, Editions du, (France) 93
Cheng Chung Book Co (China (Taiwan)) 64
Cherche-Midi, Le, Éditeur (France) 93
Cheshire (Australia) 12
Chetana Publications (India) 189
Chevalier Press (Australia) 12
Chez Nanon (Seychelles) 307
Chiangmai Book Centre (Thailand) 359
Chiendent, Editions du, Sarl (France) 93
Chiessi-Morra, Verlag, (Italy) 214
Chikuma Shobo Publishing Co Ltd (Japan) 226
Child-Honsha Inc (Japan) 226
Childerset Pty Ltd (Australia) 12
Children's and Juvenile Literature Prize (Portugal) 302
Children's Book Award (International Literary Prizes) 448
Children's Book Club (United Kingdom) 414
Children's Book Council of Australia (Australia) 10
Children's Book of the Year Awards (Australia) 22
Children's Book Prize (Norway) 284
Children's Writers' Group (United Kingdom) 418
Child's Play (International) Ltd (United Kingdom) 379

Chile, Editorial, (Nicaragua) 276
Ch'in-hua ta hsueh t'u shu kuan (Tsinghua University Library) (People's Republic of China) 64
China National Association of Literature and the Arts (China (Taiwan)) 65
China Youth Publishing House (People's Republic of China) 63
Chindwin Book Distributors (Burma) 59
Chinese Language and Literary Society (Republic of Singapore) 310
Chinese Language and Literature Association (Hong Kong) 181
Chinese University of Hong Kong Library System (Hong Kong) 181
Chip Book Club (United Kingdom) 414
Chiré, Éditions de, (France) 93
Chiron, Editions, (France) 93
Chivers Press Publishers (United Kingdom) 379
Chokechai Tewet (Thailand) 359
Cholmondeley Award for Poets (International Literary Prizes) 448
Chopmen Bookshop (Republic of Singapore) 310
Chopmen Enterprises (Republic of Singapore) 308
Chopmen Enterprises (Republic of Singapore) 310
Chopsticks Cooking Centre (CCC) (Hong Kong) 180
Chotard et Associés (France) 93
Chowkhamba, The, Sanskrit Series Office (India) 189
Choysa Bursary for Children's Writers (New Zealand) 275
Chrissi Penna — Les Editions de la Plume d'Or (Greece) 176
Christian Book, The, Centre (Papua New Guinea) 288
Christian Book Shop (Bahamas) 32
Christian Booksellers' Association (NZ Chapter) (New Zealand) 271
Christian Bookselling Association of Australia (Australia) 10
Christian Bookshop (Zambia) 434
Christian Bookstore (Thailand) 360
Christian Community, The, Press (United Kingdom) 379
Christian Council of Zambia (Zambia) 434
Christian Journals Ltd (United Kingdom) 379
Christian Literature (Belize) 46
Christian Literature, The, Society of Korea (Republic of Korea) 238
Christian Literature Association in Malawi (Malawi) 245
Christian Literature Crusade (Barbados) 33
Christian Publishing Co — Newman Art (Republic of South Africa) 311
Christian-Verlag (Federal Republic of Germany) 131
Christiana-Verlag (Switzerland) 343
Christians, Hans, Druckerei und Verlag (Federal Republic of Germany) 131
Christliche Verlagsanstalt GmbH (Federal Republic of Germany) 131
Christliche Verlagsgessellschaft mbH (Federal Republic of Germany) 131
Christlicher Bildungskreis Verlags GmbH (Federal Republic of Germany) 170
Christliches Verlagshaus GmbH (Federal Republic of Germany) 131
Christophorus-Verlag Herder GmbH (Federal Republic of Germany) 131
Chronique, Editions de la, des Lettres Françaises (France) 93
Chryssos Typos (Greece) 176
Chulalongkorn University Library (Thailand) 360
Chung Hua Book Co (People's Republic of China) 63
Chung Hwa Book Co Ltd (China (Taiwan)) 64
Chung-kuo k'o hsueh yuan t'u shu kuan (Central Library of the China Academy of Sciences) (People's Republic of China) 64
Chungking Library (People's Republic of China) 64
Chungshan Library of Kwangtung Province (People's Republic of China) 64
Chuo-Tosho Shuppan-Sha (Japan) 226
Chuokoron-Sha Inc (Japan) 226
Chur, Verlag Ernst, (Federal Republic of Germany) 131
Church, The, Bookshop (Sudan) 330
Church Book Room Press (United Kingdom) 379
Church Pastoral Aid Society (United Kingdom) 379
Church Publishing Trust (Republic of South Africa) 311
Church World Service (Niger) 276
Churchill Livingstone (United Kingdom) 379
Churchill-Livingstone (Australia) 12
Cia Internacional de Publicaciones SA de CV (Mexico) 253
Ciarrapico Editore (Italy) 214
Cicero verlagsgesellschaft mbH (Federal Republic of Germany) 131
Cid, El, (Argentina) 4
Ciencias Sociales, Editorial, (Cuba) 68
Científica Argentina, Editorial, (Argentina) 4
Científica Técnica, Livraría, (Brazil) 55
Científico, Editorial, Técnica (Cuba) 68
Científico Médica, Editorial, (Spain) 320
Cima, Distribuidora, Inc (Puerto Rico) 302
Cima, Librería, (Ecuador) 81

Cinc d'Oros — Jaime Farrás Solé (Spain) 327
Ciordia, Editorial, SRL (Argentina) 4
Circle, The, of Greek Children's Books (Greece) 178
Circle of Greek Children's Books Prizes (Greece) 178
Circle of State Librarians (United Kingdom) 416
Circolo dei Librai Antiquari (Italy) 212
Círculo de Amigos de la Historia (Spain) 327
Círculo de Lectores (Colombia) 66
Círculo de Lectores Argentina SA (Argentina) 8
Círculo de Lectores SA (Spain) 327
Círculo de Leitores (Portugal) 301
Círculo do Livro SA (Brazil) 55
Círculo Mexicano de Lectores (Mexico) 253
Circus Books (Australia) 12
Citadel (United Kingdom) 379
Cité des Livres (Tunisia) 362
Città Armoniosa (Italy) 214
Città Nuova Editrice (Italy) 214
Cittadèlla Editrice (Italy) 214
City, The, Bookshop (Ethiopia) 84
City Library (Mauritius) 249
Ciudad Nueva (Spain) 320
Civilização, Editôra, Brasileira SA (Brazil) 50
Civilização, Livraria, (Américo Fraga Lamares 8 Ca Lda) (Portugal) 299
Civilização, Livraría, Brasileira (Brazil) 55
Claassen-Verlag GmbH (Federal Republic of Germany) 131
Clarendon Press (United Kingdom) 379
Claretiana, Editorial, (Argentina) 4
Claridad, Editorial, SA (Argentina) 4
Clarion Book Club (India) 197
Clark, Robin, Ltd (United Kingdom) 379
Clark, T & T, Ltd (United Kingdom) 379
Clarke, Anthony, Books (United Kingdom) 379
Clarke, James, & Co Ltd (United Kingdom) 379
Clasicos Roxsil (El Salvador) 83
Classen, Werner, Verlag (Switzerland) 343
Classey, E W, (United Kingdom) 379
Classic (Pakistan) 285
Classification Research Group (United Kingdom) 416
Claudius Verlag GmbH (Federal Republic of Germany) 131
Clausens, J Fr, Forlag (Denmark) 75
Clauwaert, Boekengilde de, (Belgium) 44
Clauwaert, De, (Belgium) 36
Clearway Textbooks (Australia) 12
Cleary, R J, Pty Ltd (Australia) 12
Clematis Press Ltd (United Kingdom) 379
Clifford, The, Press (Australia) 13
Clivo, De, Press (Switzerland) 343
Clócomhar, An, TTA (Republic of Ireland) 203
Clódhanna Teo (Republic of Ireland) 203
Cloister Book Store Ltd (Barbados) 33
Close Up, Editora, SA (Argentina) 4
Clowes, William, (Publishers) Ltd (United Kingdom) 379
Club, Editorial, de la Prensa (Puerto Rico) 302
Club, Librería, de Lectores (Nicaragua) 276
Club Bibliophile de France SA (France) 110
Club de Amigos del Libro (Spain) 327
Club de Lectores (Argentina) 4
Club de Lectores Extemporaneos (Mexico) 253
Club Degli Editori (Italy) 221
Club dei Bibliofili and Collectors Club of Franco Maria Ricci (Italy) 221
Club del Libro Nuevo (Argentina) 8
Club des Amis du Livre (France) 110
Club des Aventures de Guerre (France) 110
Club du Livre d'Art (France) 110
Club du Livre SA (France) 110
Club du Livre technique (France) 110
Club du Roman féminin (France) 110
Club 'El Libro del Mes' (Argentina) 8
Club for Bibliophiles (Hungary) 183
Club Français des Bibliophiles (France) 110
Club Français du Livre (France) 110
Club Leabhar (United Kingdom) 379
Club of Mining and Metallurgical Books (Poland) 296
Club of Twentieth Century Poetry (Poland) 296
Club of Young Readers (Czechoslovakia) 72
Co-chuideachd Leabhneachean Gaidhlig (United Kingdom) 379
Cocco, Libreria Internazionale Fratelli, (Italy) 221
Codco Est (Qatar) 303
Codices Selecti (Austria) 25
Coebergh, H, (Netherlands) 269
Coeckelberghs, René, Bokförlag AB (Sweden) 333
Cogedi SA (Belgium) 36
Cohen & West (United Kingdom) 379
Coines Edizioni (Italy) 214
Cole & Yancy (Liberia) 242
Cole and Yancy Bookshop Ltd (Liberia) 242
Cole Publications (Australia) 13
Colegial Bolivariana CA (Venezuela) 424
Colegio, El, de México (Mexico) 250
Colegio, El, SA (Paraguay) 289
Colegio, Librería del, SA (Argentina) 4

Colegio de Abogados, Biblioteca del, (Library of the College of Advocates) (Cuba) 68
Colegio de Belén, Biblioteca del, (Library of the Belén Jesuit College) (Cuba) 68
Colegio de Bibliotecarios Colombianos (Colombia) 66
Colegio de Bibliotecarios de Chile (Chile) 63
Colegio de Bibliotecarios de Costa Rica (Costa Rica) 68
Colegio de Bibliotecarios de la Provincia de Buenos Aires (Argentina) 9
Colegio de Bibliotecólogos y Archivólogos de Venezuela (Venezuela) 425
Colegio de México, Biblioteca del, (Mexico) 254
Colegio Nacional de Bibliotecarios Universitarios (Cuba) 69
Colibrant-Uitgaven (Belgium) 36
Colibri, Librairie Le, (Mauritius) 249
Colin, Librairie Armand, (France) 93
Collectieve Propaganda van het Nederlandse Boek (CPNB) (Commission for the Collective Promotion of the Netherlands Book) (Netherlands) 257
Collectors' Editions Book Club (United Kingdom) 414
College Book House (India) 189
Collège camerounais des Arts, des Sciences et de la Technologie, Bibliothèque (United Republic of Cameroun) 61
Collège Jésus Marie (Gabon) 116
College of Agriculture Library, University of Baghdad (Iraq) 202
College of Careers (Pty) Ltd (Republic of South Africa) 311
College of Our Lady of Fatima Library (Liberia) 242
College of the Bahamas Library (Bahamas) 32
Collège rural d'Ambatobe (Democratic Republic of Madagascar) 245
Collet's Holdings Ltd (United Kingdom) 379
Collettivo Editoriale 10/16 (Italy) 214
Collier Macmillan Australia (Australia) 13
Collier Macmillan Ltd (United Kingdom) 380
Collier-Macmillan South Africa (Pty) Ltd (Republic of South Africa) 311
Collingridge (United Kingdom) 380
Collings, Rex, Ltd (United Kingdom) 380
Collins, M O, (Pvt) Ltd (Zimbabwe) 434
Collins, Tom, Poetry Prize (Australia) 22
Collins, William, & Sangster (Jamaica) Ltd (Jamaica) 224
Collins, William, Pty Ltd (Australia) 13
Collins, William, Publishers Ltd (New Zealand) 272
Collins, William, Sons & Co Ltd (United Kingdom) 380
Collins Booksellers Pty Ltd (Head Office) (Australia) 19
Collins Religious Book Award (International Literary Prizes) 448
Colloquium Verlag Otto H Hess (Federal Republic of Germany) 131
Colmegna SA (Argentina) 4
Colmena, La, SA (Paraguay) 288
Colomb, Verlag W A, (Federal Republic of Germany) 131
Colombian Novel Contest Awards (Colombia) 67
Colombo Catholic Press (Sri Lanka) 329
Colombo Public Library System (Sri Lanka) 330
Colonial, Editora, (Dominican Republic) 80
Colonnade (United Kingdom) 380
Colonnes, Librairie des, (Morocco) 256
Columba, Editorial, SA (Argentina) 4
Columbia University Press (United Kingdom) 380
Columbus Publishers Ltd (Trinidad and Tobago) 361
Columbus Verlag, Paul Oestergaard GmbH (Federal Republic of Germany) 131
Comb Books (Kenya) 235
Combat Prize (France) 113
Combi International AB (Sweden) 333
Combined Literary Societies (Australia) (Australia) 21
Combo Uitgeversgroep (Netherlands) 260
Comindus, Editions, (France) 93
Comisión Asesora de Editores de Musica del INLE (Advisory Commission of Music Publishers) (Spain) 317
Comisión Paraguaya de Documentación e Información (Paraguayan Committee of Documentation and Information) (Paraguay) 289
Comissao Brasileira de Documentaçao Agricola (CBDA) (Brazil) 56
Comitetul National pentru Literatura Comparata (National Committee for Comparative Literature) (Romania) 305
Commercial Press (People's Republic of China) 63
Commission belge de Bibliographie (Belgium) 45
Commission de l'Education chrétienne (Zaire) 433
Commission des Bibliothèques de l'ASDBAM (Association Senegalaise pour le Développement de la Documentation, des Bibliothèques, des Archives et des Musées) (Senegal) 307
Commission for Scientific and Technical Terminology Prizes (India) 198
Committee for Postgraduate Awards in Librarianship and Information Work (United Kingdom) 416
Common Ground (United Kingdom) 380

Commonwealth Agricultural Bureaux (International Organizations) 441
Commonwealth Archives Offices (Australia) 20
Commonwealth Library Association (International Organizations) 438
Commonwealth Patents, Trade Marks and Designs Offices Library (Australia) 20
Commonwealth Poetry Prize (International Literary Prizes) 448
Communication Foundation for Asia (Philippines) 291
Community Language Children's Books (Australia) 13
Compagnie belge d'Editions (Belgium) 36
Compagnie d'Editions Libres, Sociales et Economiques (France) 93
Compagnie Française d'Editions SA (France) 93
Companhia Editora de Livros e Discos Sarl (Portugal) 301
Compañía Bibliográfica Española SA (Spain) 320
Compañía General de Ediciones SA (Mexico) 250
Compañía Impresora Argentina SA (Argentina) 4
Companion Book Club (United Kingdom) 414
Compass Verlagsgesellschaft Rudolf Hanel und Sohn (Austria) 25
Compendium Pty Ltd (Australia) 13
Complexe, Editions, (Diffusion—Promotion—Formation) (Belgium) 36
Compton Press Ltd (United Kingdom) 380
Comuneros, Editorial, (Paraguay) 289
Comuneros, Librería, (Paraguay) 289
Comunità, Edizioni di, SpA (Italy) 214
Concept Publishing Co (India) 189
Concepto, Editorial, SA (Mexico) 250
Concertina Publications Ltd (United Kingdom) 380
Conch Magazine Ltd (Nigeria) 277
Concordia, Imprimerie La, (Switzerland) 343
Concordia SA—Artes Gráficas e Embalagens (Brazil) 50
Concours, Le, Médical (France) 94
Concurso Literario Municipal (Municipal Literary Competition) (Uruguay) 423
Condor Books (United Kingdom) 380
Confluência, Editorial, (Portugal) 299
Confraria dos Amigos do Livro Ltda (Brazil) 50
Congreso, Biblioteca del, de la Nación (Argentina) 8
Congreso, Biblioteca del, Nacional (Bolivia) 48
Congreso, Biblioteca del, Nacional (Chile) 63
Congreso de la Unión, Biblioteca del, (Congress Library) (Mexico) 254
Congreso de Poesia de Puerto Rico (Puerto Rican Congress of Poetry) (Puerto Rico) 303
Congress of South-East Asian Librarians IV (CONSAL IV) (International Organizations) 438
Conjunta, Editorial, SRL (Argentina) 4
Connemara (State Central) Public Library (India) 197
Connoisseur, The, (United Kingdom) 380
Conradi-Reiseführer oHG (Federal Republic of Germany) 131
Conradi-Verlagsgellschaft mbH (Federal Republic of Germany) 132
Conseil International des Associations de Bibliothèques de Théologie (International Council of Theological Library Associations) (International Organizations) 438
Conseil national des Bibliothèques d'Hôpitaux (Belgium) 44
Consejo Nacional de Cultura (Cuba) 68
Conselho Federal de Biblioteconomia (CFB) (Federal Council of Librarianship) (Brazil) 56
Conservative Political Centre (United Kingdom) 380
Conservatorio di Musica, Biblioteca Musicale Governativa del, S Cecilia (Italy) 222
Consolidated Labor Institute (Japan) (Japan) 226
Constable & Co Ltd (United Kingdom) 380
Construction Press Ltd (United Kingdom) 380
Contabilidad, Ediciones, Moderna SACIC (Argentina) 4
Contables y Administrativas, Ediciones, SA (Mexico) 250
Contact, Uitgeverij, BV (Netherlands) 260
Contact NV (Belgium) 36
Contempa Publications (Australia) 13
Contempora, Editorial, SRL (Argentina) 4
Continental, Cía Editorial, SA (CESCA) (Mexico) 250
Continental Publications (Bangladesh) 32
Continua Productions Ltd (United Kingdom) 380
Controinformazione (Italy) 214
Convent van Universiteitsbibliotekarissen in Nederland (Association of University Librarians in the Netherlands) (Netherlands) 270
Conway Maritime Press Ltd (United Kingdom) 380
Conzett und Huber, Manesse-Verlag, (Switzerland) 343
Cook, Albert, Library (Uganda) 364
Cook, James, Australian Literary Studies Award (Australia) 22
Cooper, Leo, Ltd (United Kingdom) 380
Cooperativa del Libro (Chile) 63
Cooperative das Casas (Mozambique) 256
Coopérative Régionale de l'Enseignement Religieux (CRER) (France) 94
Copernic (France) 94

INDEX 475

Coppée, François, Prize (France) 113
Copplestone, Trewin, Publishing Ltd (United Kingdom) 380
Copress-Verlag (Federal Republic of Germany) 132
Copro International Verlagsgesellschaft mbH (Austria) 29
Copyright Agency Ltd (Australia) 10
Coquito, Ediciones, (Dominican Republic) 80
Corazón, Alberto, Editor (Spain) 320
Corbaz, Imprimerie, SA (Switzerland) 343
Cordero, Biblioteca Central 'Tulio Febres, (Venezuela) 425
Cordillera, Editorial, Inc (Puerto Rico) 302
Cordoba Stories Prizes (Colombia) 67
Core Libraries (Australia) 13
Corgi Books (United Kingdom) 380
Cork University Press (Republic of Ireland) 203
Cornell University Press (United Kingdom) 380
Cornelsen & Oxford University Press GmbH (Federal Republic of Germany) 132
Cornelsen-Velhagen & Klasing GmbH & Co Verlag für Lehrmedien KG (Federal Republic of Germany) 132
Cornelsen-Velhagen & Klasing Verlagsgesellschaft (Federal Republic of Germany) 132
Corniche, Edition, AB (Sweden) 333
Corona, Archivo de, de Aragon (Royal Archives of Aragon) (Spain) 328
Corona, Bokforlaget, AB (Sweden) 333
Corona Publishing Co Ltd (Japan) 226
Corona Verlag KG (Federal Republic of Germany) 132
Coronet (United Kingdom) 380
Corporan, Rafael, de los Santos (Dominican Republic) 80
Correa, Viriato, Prize (Brazil) 57
Corregidon, Ediciones, SAICI & E (Argentina) 4
Cortez e Moraes Ltda (Brazil) 50
Cortis, D C, (Malta) 248
Corvina Press (Hungary) 182
Corvus Verlag (Federal Republic of Germany) 132
Cosdel (Singapore) Pte Ltd (Malaysia) 247
Cosmopolita SRL (Argentina) 4
Cosmos, Edições, (Portugal) 299
Cosmos, Editora, (Dominican Republic) 80
Cosmos, Editorial, (Mexico) 250
Cosmos, Librería, (Mexico) 253
Cosmos, Publicaciones, (Mexico) 250
Cosmos Bookshop (Ethiopia) 84
Cosmos-Verlag AG (Switzerland) 343
Costa, Livraria Sá da, (Portugal) 301
Costa, Sá da, Editora (Portugal) 299
Costa Amic, B, (Mexico) 250
Costa Rica, Editorial, (Costa Rica) 67
Cotman Colour and Cotman House (United Kingdom) 380
Coulouma, L'Imprimerie, (United Republic of Cameroun) 61
Council for International Organizations of Medical Sciences (CIOMS) (Conseil des Organisations internationales des Sciences medicales) (International Organizations) 441
Council of Europe, Publications Section (International Organizations) 441
Council of Libraries (Albania) 1
Counson, Albert, Prize (International Literary Prizes) 448
Count of Cartagena Prizes (International Literary Prizes) 448
Country Book Society (United Kingdom) 414
Country Life Books (United Kingdom) 380
Courrier du Livre Sàrl (France) 94
Courteline Prize (France) 113
Courtille, Editions de la, (France) 94
Coventure Ltd (United Kingdom) 380
Coverdale House Publishers Ltd (United Kingdom) 380
Cracow City Literary Prize (Poland) 297
Craft Book Society (United Kingdom) 414
Crafts, The, Council (United Kingdom) 381
Cramer, J, (Federal Republic of Germany) 132
Cranwell Publishing Co Ltd (New Zealand) 272
Cratander AG (Switzerland) 343
Crawshay, The Rose Mary, Prizes (International Literary Prizes) 448
Crea SA (Argentina) 4
Creadif (Belgium) 36
Creangǎ, Editura Ion, (Romania) 304
Creasey, John, Memorial Award (United Kingdom) 419
Creative Management Associates Ltd (Italy) 221
Crédit Communal de Belgique—Centre Culterel (Belgium) 36
Cremers (Schoollandkaarten) PVBA (Belgium) 36
Cremonese, Edizioni, SpA (Italy) 214
Crépin-Leblond, Editeurs, et Cie SA (France) 94
Crescent Publications (Pakistan) 285
Crescent Publishers (Bangladesh) 32
Crescent Publishing Co (India) 189
Crespillo, Editorial, SA (Argentina) 4
Cressrelles Publishing Co Ltd (United Kingdom) 381
Crime Writers' Association (United Kingdom) 418
Crisp (Belgium) 36
Cristal, Librerías de, (Mexico) 253

Cristiandad, Ediciones, (Spain) 320
Criterion: Teachers' Book Shelf Book Club (United Kingdom) 414
Critica, Editorial, SA (Spain) 320
Critics' Prize for Children's Literature (Italy) 223
Croft Press (Australia) 13
Croix, Editions, de Sud (Mauritius) 249
Cromograf SA (Ecuador) 81
Cromphout, Van, Frères & Soeurs Imprimerie (Belgium) 36
Crompton, Paul H, Ltd (United Kingdom) 381
Croner Publications Ltd (United Kingdom) 381
Croom Helm Ltd (United Kingdom) 381
Crosby Lockwood Staples Ltd (United Kingdom) 381
Cross Continent Press Ltd (Nigeria) 277
Crouch, Colonel, Gold Medal (Australia) 22
Cuadernos de Historia de la Salud Publica, Ministerio de Salubridad y Asistencia Social (Cuba) 68
Cuala Press (Republic of Ireland) 203
Cuban Book Institute (Cuba) 68
Cuello, Casa, (Dominican Republic) 80
Cujas, Editions, (France) 94
Cultrix, Editôra, (Brazil) 50
Cultura, Casa de la, Ecuatoriana (Ecuador) 81
Cultura, Ediciones, Hispánica (Spain) 320
Cultura, Ediciones de, Popular SA (Mexico) 250
Cultura, Fondation, -Stichting Cultura (Belgium) 36
Cultura, Librería La, (Paraguay) 289
Cultura, Librería y Editorial, (Chile) 63
Cultura, Premio Nacional de, (Bolivia) 48
Cultura 70 Livraria e Editora S/A (Brazil) 55
Cultura-Maroc (Morocco) 256
Cultura Médica, Editora, Ltda (Brazil) 50
Cultural, Librería, Salvadoreña SA de CV (El Salvador) 83
Cultural Centre, Library of the, Surinam (Bibliotheek CCS) (Suriname) 331
Cultural Centre of the Philippines Literary Awards (Philippines) 293
Cultural Colombiana Ltda (Colombia) 65
Cultural Council, Book Club of the, of Sri Lanka (Sri Lanka) 330
Cultural Council of Sri Lanka (Sri Lanka) 329
Cultural Supplies, The, Co (Malaysia) 246
Culture Art Loisirs/Retz (France) 94
Culture et Civilisation, Editions, (Belgium) 36
Culture Prize (Japan) 234
Cumann Leabharlann na h-Éireann (Library Association of Ireland) (Republic of Ireland) 205
Cumann Leabharlannaithe Scoile (CLS) (Irish Association of School Librarians) (Republic of Ireland) 205
Cumont, Franz, Prize (International Literary Prizes) 448
Cura Verlag GmbH (Austria) 25
Curaçao, El, (Netherlands Antilles) 271
Curaçaosche Drukkerij en Uitgevers Maatschappij (Netherlands Antilles) 271
Curado, Clube do Livro-, Ribeiro (Portugal) 301
Curci, Edizioni, SRL (Italy) 214
Curcio, Armando, Editore SpA (Italy) 214
Currawong Press Pty Ltd (Australia) 13
Currency Press Pty Ltd (Australia) 13
Current Technical Literature Co (Pvt) Ltd (India) 189
Currey, John, O'Neil Publishers Pty Ltd (Australia) 13
Curriculum Development Centre (Australia) 13
Curtis Brown (Australia) Pty Ltd (Australia) 19
Curtis Brown Academic Ltd (United Kingdom) 413
Curtis Brown Group Ltd (United Kingdom) 413
Curzon Press Ltd (United Kingdom) 381
Cuspide, Distribuidora, (Argentina) 8
Cut & Colour Books (United Kingdom) 381
Cuttington College and Divinity School Library (Liberia) 242
Cygne, Librairie Le, (Mauritius) 249
Cynthia, J. Co Ltd (China (Taiwan)) 64
Cypress Books (Australia) 13
Cyprus Booksellers Association (Cyprus) 69
Cyprus Library Association (Cyprus) 69
Cyprus Museum, Library of the, (Cyprus) 69
Cyril and Methodius National Library (Bulgaria) 58
Cyril and Methodius Prize (International Literary Prizes) 448
Czwiklitzer, Editions d'Art — Christophe, (France) 94
'Czytelnik', Spółdzielnia Wydawnicza, (Poland) 294

D A F S A (France) 94
D A P Reinaert Uitgaven (Belgium) 44
D B V-Verlag (Federal Republic of Germany) 132
D E B Verlag (Das Europäische Buch) (Federal Republic of Germany) 132
D I G Ldá (Distribuidora Geral de Informação) (Portugal) 301

D I L I A (Czechoslovakia) 72
D J O, Stichting, (de jonge onderzoekers) (Netherlands) 260
D K Publishers' Distributors (India) 189
D K Publishers' Distributors (India) 197
D O P E S A, Editorial, (Documentacion Periodistica SA) (Spain) 320
D P Publications (United Kingdom) 381
D R W-Verlag Weinbrenner-KG (Federal Republic of Germany) 132
D T V (Federal Republic of Germany) 132
D und C, Verlag, (Federal Republic of Germany) 132
D V A (Federal Republic of Germany) 132
Dabbous Stores (Saudi Arabia) 306
Dacca Book Mart (Bangladesh) 32
Dacca University Library (Bangladesh) 33
Dacia, Editura, (Romania) 304
Dacosta, Les Editions Roger, (France) 94
Dado, Editoriale, (Italy) 214
Dadò, Edizioni Armando, Tipografia Stazione (Switzerland) 343
Dagbreek-Boekkring (Republic of South Africa) 315
Dagen, Tidnings AB, (Sweden) 333
Dageraad, De, PVBA (Belgium) 36
Dahl, Gösta, och Son AB (Sweden) 337
Dahlia Books (Sweden) 333
Daiichi Shuppan Co Ltd (Japan) 226
Daily Times of Nigeria Ltd (Nigeria) 277
Daimon, Ediciones, — Manuel Tamayo (Spain) 320
Dais Literary Agency (Italy) 221
Dalén-Engqvists Forlag, The, (Sweden) 339
Dall'Oglio Editore SpA (Italy) 214
Dalloz, Jurisprudence Générale, (France) 94
Daman, Librairie R, (Luxembourg) 244
Damascus University Library (Syria) 357
Damascus University Press (Syria) 357
Dami, Piero, Editore SpA (Italy) 214
Damm, N W, og Søn A/S (Norway) 281
Damnitz Verlag GmbH (Federal Republic of Germany) 132
Danae, Ediciones, SA (Spain) 320
Daneshdjou Bookstore (Iran) 202
Dangles, SA (France) 94
Daniel, The C W, Co Ltd (United Kingdom) 381
Danish Academy Prize for Literature (Denmark) 80
Danish Authors' Colleagues Prize (Denmark) 80
Danish Authors' Lyric Prize (Denmark) 80
Danish Critics Literary Prize (Denmark) 80
Danish Prize for Children's Literature (Denmark) 80
Danish Translations Centre (DTC) (Denmark) 80
Danmark, Forlaget, A/S (Denmark) 75
Danmarks Biblioteksforening (Denmark) 79
Danmarks Forskningsbiblioteksforening (Denmark) 79
Danmarks Skolebibliotekarforening (Denmark) 79
Danmarks Skolebiblioteksforening (Denmark) 79
Danmarks Tekniske Bibliotek (Denmark) 78
Danov, Darzhavno Izdatelstov 'Christo G, ' (Bulgaria) 58
Dansk Bibliofil-Klub (Denmark) 79
Dansk Boghandlermedhjaelperforening (Denmark) 74
Dansk Bogtjeneste (Denmark) 74
Dansk Central-Boghandel (Denmark) 78
Dansk Exlibris Selskab (Denmark) 79
Dansk Forfatterforening (Denmark) 79
Dansk Historisk Haandbogsforlag (Denmark) 75
Dansk Litteraturselskab, Nyt, (Denmark) 79
Dansk Musikbiblioteksforening (Denmark) 79
Dansk Teknisk Litteraturselskab (Denmark) 79
Dansk Videnskabs Forlag ApS (Danish Science Press Ltd) (Denmark) 75
Danske Antikvarboghandlerforening (Denmark) 74
Danske Boghandleres Bogimport A/S (Denmark) 74
Danske Boghandleres Importørforening (DANBIF) (Denmark) 74
Danske Boghandleres Kommissionsanstalt (DBK) (Denmark) 74
Danske Boghandlerforening, Den, (Denmark) 74
Danske Bogsamleres Klub (Denmark) 78
Danske Forlaeggerforening (Denmark) 74
Danske Forlag, Det, (Denmark) 75
Danske Sprog-og Litteraturselskab (Denmark) 79
Danubia (Austria) 25
Dap-Reinart, Uitgeverij, SV (Belgium) 36
Daphne, Editions, (Belgium) 36
Daphins-Verlag (Switzerland) 343
Daphne Diffusion SPRL (Belgium) 36
Dar al-Kutub al-Wataniah (National Library) (Syria) 357
Dar Arabia Lil Kitab (Tunisia) 361
Dar es Salaam Bookshop, The, (Tanzania) 358
Dar es Salaam Technical College Library (Tanzania) 358
Dar es Salaam University (Tanzania) 358
Dar es Salaam University Bookshop (Tanzania) 358
Dar Libya Publishing House (Libya) 242
Dar-ul-Kutub (Egypt) 83
Darby, Alan, Publications Ltd (United Kingdom) 381
Dardalet, Editions, SA (France) 94
Dardanos, G, — H Karakatsanis and Co Ltd — Gutenberg (Greece) 176

476 INDEX

Dargaud Editeur (France) 94
Dario. Librería Recinto 'Ruben,' (Nicaragua) 276
Darmstädter Blätter. Verlag. Schwarz und Co (Federal Republic of Germany) 132
Darton, Longman & Todd Ltd (United Kingdom) 381
Darwen Finlayson Ltd (United Kingdom) 381
Darzhavno Obedinenie 'Bulgarska Kniga' (Bulgaria) 58
Dastane Ramchandra and Co (India) 189
Daude. Librairie, (Réunion) 303
Daudy, SEF Philippe, (France) 94
Dauguet, Constant, Endowment (France) 113
Dauphin. Editions du, (France) 94
Dausien, Werner, (Federal Republic of Germany) 132
Dauzat, Albert, Prize (France) 113
Davaco Publishers (Netherlands) 260
Davar (Israel) 207
David & Charles (United Kingdom) 381
Davidsfonds VZW (Belgium) 36
Davies, D J, (Australia) 13
Davies. Peter, Ltd (United Kingdom) 381
Davies Publishers, Christopher, Ltd (United Kingdom) 381
Davis & Moughton Ltd (United Kingdom) 381
Davis-Poynter Ltd (United Kingdom) 381
Davison Publishing Ltd (United Kingdom) 381
Dawood, Abdullah, (Saudi Arabia) 306
Dawood Prize for Literature (Pakistan) 287
Dawson Publishing (United Kingdom) 381
Daystar Press (Publishers) (Nigeria) 277
De Donato Editore (Italy) 214
De Vecchi, Éditions, SA (France) 94
De Vecchi, Editorial, SA (Spain) 320
De Vecchi, Giovanni, Editore SpA (Italy) 214
De Wit Stores NV (Netherlands Antilles) 271
Dean & Son (United Kingdom) 381
Dean and Chapter, The, Library (United Kingdom) 416
Dearlove. Peter, Publishers (Zimbabwe) 435
Debard. Editions, (France) 94
Debooks (India) 189
Debresse, Nouvelles Editions, (France) 94
Dečje Novine (Yugoslavia) 427
Decker's, R v. Verlag G Schenck GmbH (Federal Republic of Germany) 132
Declés. Librairie, (Zaire) 433
Decomble. Librairie Générale de l'Enseignement Mme, (France) 94
Dedalo, Edizioni, (Italy) 214
Deep & Deep Publications (India) 189
Défense de l'Occident (France) 94
Dehoniane, Edizioni, Bologna (EDB) (Italy) 214
Deichmanske Bibliotek (City Library of Oslo) (Norway) 283
Deild Bokavarda i Islenskum Rannsoknarbokasofnum (Iceland) 186
Dejaie, Maison d'Editions Cl, (Belgium) 36
Dekker en Nordemann BV (Netherlands) 269
Dekker en Van de Vegt (Netherlands) 269
Dekker en Van de Vegt (Netherlands) 260
Delachaux et Niestlé. Editions, SA (France) 94
Delachaux et Niestlé, Editions, SA (Switzerland) 343
Delacroix, Eve, Prize (France) 113
Delafosse, Lycée technique Maurice, (Senegal) 307
Delagrave, Librairie, Sàrl (France) 94
Delarge, Jean-Pierre, SA (France) 94
Delattre, Mlle Sabine, (France) 110
Deldebat de Gonzalva Prize (France) 113
Delft University Press (Netherlands) 260
Delhi Educational Publishers' Union (India) 186
Delhi Library Association (India) 197
Delhi Public Library (India) 197
Delhi State Booksellers' and Publishers' Association (India) 186
Delhi University Library (India) 197
Delightful Books (United Kingdom) 381
Delius, Klasing und Co (Federal Republic of Germany) 132
Delmas, Editions J, et Cie (France) 94
Delmas, Imprimeries, (France) 94
Delphin Verlag (Switzerland) 343
Delphin Verlag GmbH (Federal Republic of Germany) 132
Delpire. Editions Robert, SA (France) 94
Delp'sche Verlagsbuchhandlung (Federal Republic of Germany) 132
Delsa, Importadora de Publicaciones SA (Spain) 327
Delta, Editions, (Belgium) 36
Delta Books (United Kingdom) 381
Delta Editrice SpA (Italy) 215
Delta Förlags AB (Sweden) 333
Delta Press (Yugoslavia) 427
Delta SA (Switzerland) 343
Delta Science Fiction Bok Klubb (Sweden) 337
Dempsey & Squires Publishers Ltd (United Kingdom) 381
Démuth, Dr rer pol Dr Julius, (Federal Republic of Germany) 169
Denayer, Felix, Prize (Belgium) 46

Denholm House Press (United Kingdom) 382
Denis, Firma, & Co PVBA (Belgium) 44
Denis & Co PVBA (Belgium) 36
Dennis, C J, Award (Australia) 22
Denoël, Editions, Sàrl (France) 94
Dent, J M, & Sons Ltd (United Kingdom) 382
Denzel Verlag Auto-und Wander Führer (Austria) 25
Depalma SRL (Argentina) 4
Departamento de Biblioteca y Publicaciones (Department of Libraries and Publications) (Mexico) 254
Departamento de Bibliotecas (Colombia) 66
Departamento de Documentación y Biblioteca (Uruguay) 423
Department of Information, Central Library of the, (Socialist Republic of Viet Nam) 426
Department of National Education Library (Republic of South Africa) 315
Department of National Education Literary Prizes (Republic of South Africa) 316
Department of Publicity (Nepal) 257
Department of Science Library (Thailand) 360
der 2. edition, Gerald Fritsch und Stefan Fritsch Buchverlag GmbH (Federal Republic of Germany) 132
Derecho Financiero, Editorial de, (Spain) 320
Derecho Privado, Editorial Revista de, (Spain) 320
Dergâh Yayinlari AS (Turkey) 362
D'Erlanger Prize (France) 113
Desai Bookshops (Fiji) 85
Desarrollo, Editorial, SA (Peru) 289
Desbordes-Valmore, Marceline, Prize (France) 113
Deschamps (Haiti) 179
Desclée, De Brouwer SA (France) 95
Desclée, Editeurs (Belgium) 37
Desclée, Editions, et Cie (France) 95
Desclée de Brouwer SA (Belgium) 36
Desertina Verlag (Switzerland) 344
Desforges, Librairie, (France) 95
Design Council Publications (United Kingdom) 382
Desmet-Huysmans PVBA (Belgium) 37
Desoer, Editions, SA (Belgium) 36
Dessain NV, H, (Belgium) 37
Dessain SPRL, F, (Belgium) 36
Dessart, Engelbert, Verlag KG (Federal Republic of Germany) 132
Destino, Ediciones, SL (Spain) 320
Desvigne, Librairie André, (France) 95
Detskaya Entsiklopediya (Union of Soviet Socialist Republics) 365
Detskaya Literatura, Izdatelstvo, (Union of Soviet Socialist Republics) 365
Deubner, Dr Peter, Verlag GmbH (Federal Republic of Germany) 132
Deuticke, Verlag Franz, (Austria) 25
Deutsch, André, Ltd (United Kingdom) 382
Deutsch, Verlag Harri, (Switzerland) 344
Deutsch, Verlag Harri, (Federal Republic of Germany) 132
Deutsche Akademie für Sprache und Dichtung (Federal Republic of Germany) 173
Deutsche Bibelstiftung (German Bible Foundation) (Federal Republic of Germany) 133
Deutsche Bibliothek — Goethe Institut Brüssel (Belgium) 44
Deutsche Bibliothek (National Library) (Federal Republic of Germany) 171
Deutsche Buch-Gemeinschaft C A Koch's Verlag Nachfolger (Federal Republic of Germany) 170
Deutsche Buch-Gemeinschaft C A Koch's Verlag Nachfolger (Federal Republic of Germany) 133
Deutsche Buch-Gemeinschaft C A Koch's Verlag Nachfolger (Austria) 29
Deutsche Bücherei (German Library) (German Democratic Republic) 120
Deutsche Gesellschaft für Dokumentation eV (Federal Republic of Germany) 171
Deutsche Hausbücherei GmbH (Federal Republic of Germany) 170
Deutsche Jugend-Presse-Agentur KG (Federal Republic of Germany) 133
Deutsche Philips GmbH (Federal Republic of Germany) 133
Deutsche Shakespeare-Gesellschaft West eV (Federal Republic of Germany) 173
Deutsche Staatsbibliothek (German Democratic Republic) 120
Deutsche Verlags-Anstalt GmbH (Federal Republic of Germany) 133
Deutscher, Isaac, Memorial Prize (International Literary Prizes) 448
Deutscher Apotheker Verlag Dr Roland Schmiedel GmbH und Co (Federal Republic of Germany) 133
Deutscher Betriebswirte-Verlag GmbH (Federal Republic of Germany) 133
Deutscher Bibliotheksverband eV (Federal Republic of Germany) 171

Deutscher Bücherbund GmbH (Federal Republic of Germany) 170
Deutscher Buchkreis (Federal Republic of Germany) 170
Deutscher Eichverlag (Federal Republic of Germany) 133
Deutscher Fachschriften-Verlag Braun GmbH & Co KG (Federal Republic of Germany) 133
Deutscher Fachverlag GmbH (Federal Republic of Germany) 133
Deutscher Gemeindeverlag GmbH (Federal Republic of Germany) 133
Deutscher Instituts-Verlag GmbH (Federal Republic of Germany) 133
Deutscher Kunstverlag GmbH (Federal Republic of Germany) 133
Deutscher Landwirtschaftsverlag, VEB, (German Democratic Republic) 118
Deutscher Leihbuchhändler-Verband eV (German Circulating Libraries Federation) (Federal Republic of Germany) 171
Deutscher Taschenbuch Verlag GmbH & Co KG (Federal Republic of Germany) 133
Deutscher Verband evangelischer Büchereien eV (Federal Republic of Germany) 171
Deutscher Verlag der Wissenschaften, VEB, (German Democratic Republic) 118
Deutscher Verlag für Grundstoffindustrie, VEB, (German Democratic Republic) 118
Deutscher Verlag für Kunstwissenschaft GmbH (Federal Republic of Germany) 133
Deutscher Verlag für Musik, VEB, (German Democratic Republic) 118
Deutscher Wirtschaftsdienst John von Freyend GmbH (Federal Republic of Germany) 133
Deutsches Jugendschriftenwerk (German Children's Writers) (Federal Republic of Germany) 173
Deux Coqs d'Or, Les Editions des, (France) 95
Deux Magots Prize (France) 113
Deves et Chaumet, Librairie, (Mali) 248
Devlin, Denis, Memorial Award for Poetry (Republic of Ireland) 205
Dewallens, A, (Belgium) 37
Dewan, Perpustakaan, Perwakilan Rakjat Gotong Rojong (Library of Indonesian Parliament) (Indonesia) 201
Dewan Bahasa dan Pustaka (Malaysia) 246
Dewan Bahasa dan Pustaka (Language and Literary Agency of the Ministry of Education) (Malaysia) 248
Dhammabucha (Thailand) 359
Dhanani's Ltd (Kenya) 236
Dheerasarn Ltd (Thailand) 360
Diafora SA (Spain) 320
Diagne, Lycée Blaise, (Senegal) 307
Diagram Visual Information Ltd (United Kingdom) 382
Diálogo, Ediciones, (Paraguay) 289
Diamond Books International (India) 197
Diamond Comics (India) 189
Diamond Inc (Japan) 226
Dian Rakyat (Indonesia) 199
Diana, Editorial, (Mexico) 250
Diana-Verlag AG (Switzerland) 344
Díaz, Librería, de Santos (Spain) 327
Dickens, The, Fellowship (Sri Lanka) 330
Dickens, The, Fellowship (Japan) 233
Dickens, The, Fellowship (Netherlands) 270
Dickens, The, Fellowship (New Zealand) 275
Dickens, The, Fellowship (Belgium) 45
Dickens, The, Fellowship (Australia) 21
Dickens, The, Fellowship (Argentina) 9
Dickens, The, Fellowship (United Kingdom) 418
Dictionnaire. La Maison du, (France) 95
Didáctica Editora (Portugal) 299
Didactica si Pedagogica, Editura, (Romania) 304
Didactronia SA (Spain) 320
Diderich, Librairie J-Cl, (Luxembourg) 244
Diderot, Livre Club, (France) 110
Didier, Editions Marcel, SA (Belgium) 37
Didier, John, Editions (France) 95
Didier, Librairie Marcel, SA (France) 95
Didier, Uitgeverij, Nederland BV (Netherlands) 260
Didier et Richard, Editions, (France) 95
Didot-Bottin, Société, SA (France) 95
Diederichs, Eugen, Verlag (Federal Republic of Germany) 133
Diesterweg, Verlag Moritz, / Otto Salle Verlag (Federal Republic of Germany) 133
Dieterich'sche Verlagsbuchhandlung (German Democratic Republic) 118
Dietz, Verlag J H W, Nachf GmbH (Federal Republic of Germany) 133
Dietz Verlag (German Democratic Republic) 118
Diffusion de la Pensée Française (France) 95
Diffusion de la Presse (Zaire) 433
Difros (Greece) 176
Difusão Editorial SA (DIFEL) (Brazil) 50
Difusión, Editorial, (Bolivia) 47
Difusión, Editorial, SA (Argentina) 4
Difusión, Librería, (Bolivia) 47
Dijkstra's Uitg Mij, Jacob, BV (Netherlands) 260

INDEX 477

Dijkstra's Uitgeverij Zeist BV (Netherlands) 260
Diki-Books Srl (Italy) 215
Dilagro SA (Spain) 320
Diligentia BV (Netherlands) 260
Diligentia-Uitgeverij (Belgium) 37
Dillon's University Bookshop Ltd (United Kingdom) 415
Dimashk, Dar, (Adib Tunbakji) Bookshop (Syria) 357
Dimitrov' Academy, Central Agricultural Library of the 'G. of Agricultural Sciences (Bulgaria) 58
Dini Book Depot (India) 189
Dinosaur Publications Ltd (United Kingdom) 382
Diogenes,, Editorial, SA (Mexico) 250
Diogenes Verlag AG (Switzerland) 344
Dipa-Verlag und Druck GmbH & Co (Federal Republic of Germany) 134
Diponegoro, C V, (Indonesia) 199
Diputación, Biblioteca Central de la, de Barcelona (Biblioteca de Cataluña y Central de Bibliotecas Populares) (Catalan Library and Central Public Library) (Spain) 328
Dirección de Bibliotecas Municipales (Argentina) 9
Dirección de Cultura, Biblioteca de la, (Library of Cultural Affairs Administration) (Bolivia) 48
Dirección de Estadística y Censo (Panama) 287
Directorate of Archives and Libraries (Bangladesh) 33
Directorate of Libraries (Pakistan) 286
Directorate of Publications (Republic of South Africa) 311
Directory Publishers of Zambia Ltd (Zambia) 433
Direkt Verlag (Federal Republic of Germany) 134
Discailles, Ernest, Prize (International Literary Prizes) 448
'Discovering' Books (United Kingdom) 382
Disesa (Dominican Republic) 80
Dishoeck, C A'J van, (Netherlands) 260
Distasa (Argentina) 4
Distein-, Grupo Editorial, CEAC-Timun Mas (Spain) 320
Distri BD SPRL (Belgium) 37
Distribuidora de Libros (Guatemala) 179
Distribuidora de Libros Inc (Puerto Rico) 302
Distribuidora Escolar SA (Dominican Republic) 80
Distributors' Centre for Israeli Books Ltd (Israel) 210
Distripress (International Organizations) 438
Diwan, The, Library, Ministry of Education (Iraq) 202
Djambatan, P T, Penerbit NV (Indonesia) 199
Djambatan BV (Netherlands) 260
Doblinger, Ludwig, (Bernard Herzmansky) Musikverlag (Austria) 25
Dobloug Prize (International Literary Prizes) 448
Dobloug Prize (Sweden) 339
Dobson, Dennis, (Dobson Books Ltd) (United Kingdom) 382
Documentário, Editora, Ltda (Brazil) 50
Documentation, Bibliothèque de, Internationale Contemporaine (France) 111
Documentation, La, Cistercienne (Belgium) 37
Documentation et d'Analyses, Société de, Financières (France) 95
Documentation Française, La, (Published by the Government General Secretary's Office) (France) 95
Documentation Research and Training Centre (India) 197
Dodoni (Greece) 176
Dogan Kardes Matbaacilik SAS (Turkey) 362
Doin Editeurs (France) 95
Dokumentasi Ilmiah Nasional, Pusat, (National Scientific Documentation Centre) (Indonesia) 201
Dokumentation, Verlag, Saur KG (Federal Republic of Germany) 134
Dokumentationsstelle für neuere österreichische Literatur (Austria) 30
Dollar Books (Australia) 13
Dolmen, The, Press Ltd (Republic of Ireland) 203
Dolphin (United Kingdom) 382
Dolphin Press (United Kingdom) 382
Dolphin Publishing, The, Co Ltd (United Kingdom) 382
Dom Ksiazki (Poland) 296
Dom Ksiazki (Poland) 296
Dom Quixote, Publicações, (Portugal) 299
Domi, Ekdoseis, AE (Greece) 176
Dominion Press (Pvt) Ltd (Zimbabwe) 435
Domino (France) 95
Domus Editoriale (Italy) 215
Don Bosco, Ecole Technique officielle, Bibliothèque (Rwanda) 306
Don Bosco, Ediciones, (Spain) 320
Don Bosco, Editorial y Librería, (Bolivia) 47
Don Bosco, Librería, (Bolivia) 47
Don Bosco Verlag der Gesellschaft der Salesianer (Federal Republic of Germany) 134
Donald, John, Publishers Ltd (United Kingdom) 382
Donauland, Buchgemeinschaft, (Austria) 29
Doncel (Spain) 320
Dongguk University Library (Republic of Korea) 239
Dongwha Publishing Co (Republic of Korea) 238
Donker, Ad, (Pty) Ltd (Republic of South Africa) 311
Donker, Ad, Ltd (United Kingdom) 382

Donker, Uitgeversmaatschappij Ad, NV (Netherlands) 260
Dopravy, Nakladatelství, a spoju (Czechoslovakia) 70
Dorikos Makridis (Greece) 176
Dorling Kindersley Ltd (United Kingdom) 382
Dorp Aruba, Van, NV (Netherlands Antilles) 271
Dorp Eddine, Van, NV (Netherlands Antilles) 271
Dosaaf, Znak Pochyota Order, Publishing House (Union of Soviet Socialist Republics) 365
Dossat, Editorial, SA (Spain) 320
Dossche, Editions Irène, SPRL (Belgium) 37
Dossiers politiques (Belgium) 37
Doubleday & Co Inc (United Kingdom) 382
Doubleday Australia Pty Ltd (Australia) 13
Doubleday Australia Pty Ltd, Book Club Associates Division (Australia) 19
Doubleday Book Club (Australia) 19
Doubleday Book Club (New Zealand) 274
Doubleday-France (France) 95
Doubleday History Book Club (New Zealand) 274
Doubleday History Book Club (Australia) 19
Doubleday New Zealand Ltd (New Zealand) 272
Doubleday New Zealand Ltd, Book Club Associates Division (New Zealand) 274
Doucet, Bibliothèque d'Art et d'Archéologie Fondation Jacques, (France) 111
Doucet, Bibliothèque littéraire Jacques, (France) 111
Dove Communications Pty Ltd (Australia) 13
Draeger Editeur (France) 95
Dragon Books (United Kingdom) 382
Dragon's Dream (Netherlands) 260
Dragon's Dream Ltd (France) 95
Dragon's World Ltd (United Kingdom) 382
Drammen Folkebibliotek (Public Library of Drammen) (Norway) 283
Drei Eichen Verlag AG (Switzerland) 344
Drei Eidgenossen Verlag (Switzerland) 344
Dreisam-Verlag (Federal Republic of Germany) 134
Dreiseitel, Galerie, (Federal Republic of Germany) 134
Drejtoria Quëndrore e Përhapjes dhe e Propagandimit të Librit (Central Administration for the Dissemination and Propagation of the Book) (Albania) 1
Dressler, Cecilie, Verlag (Federal Republic of Germany) 134
Dreyers Forlag (Norway) 281
Driehoek, De, BV (Netherlands) 260
Droemersche Verlagsanstalt AG (Switzerland) 344
Droemersche Verlagsanstalt Th Knaur Nachf (Federal Republic of Germany) 134
Droguet et Ardant (France) 95
Droit et de Jurisprudence, Librairie Générale de, (France) 95
Dronte, Ediciones, Argentina SRL (Argentina) 4
Droste Verlag GmbH (Federal Republic of Germany) 134
Drouot, Librairie, (Ets Robert Drouot) (Benin) 47
Droz, Librairie, SA (Switzerland) 344
Druckenmüller Verlag (Federal Republic of Germany) 134
Druffel-Verlag (Federal Republic of Germany) 134
Drukarnia Narodowa (Poland) 294
Drukkerij de Stad NV (Netherlands Antilles) 271
Drummond Publishing (Australia) 13
Društvo bibliotekara Bosne i Hercegovine (Yugoslavia) 431
Društvo bibliotekarjev Slovenije (Yugoslavia) 431
Društvo na arhivskite rabotnici i arhivite na SRM (Yugoslavia) 431
Društvo na bibliotekarite na Makedonija (Yugoslavia) 431
Društvo na literaturnite preveduvači na SRM (Yugoslavia) 431
Društvo na pisatelite na SRM (Yugoslavia) 432
Društvo za srpski jezik i književnost (Yugoslavia) 432
Državna Založba Slovenije (Yugoslavia) 427
Državna Založba Slovenije (Yugoslavia) 431
Duang Kamol (Thailand) 359
Duas Cidades, Livraria, (Brazil) 55
Duas Cidades, Livraria, Ltda (Brazil) 50
Dublin Institute for Advanced Studies (Republic of Ireland) 203
Dublin Public Libraries (Republic of Ireland) 205
Duckworth, Gerald, & Co Ltd (United Kingdom) 382
Duculot, Editions J, SA (Belgium) 37
Duculot, Jules, Prize (Belgium) 46
Duden, Konrad, Prize (Federal Republic of Germany) 173
Duff Cooper Memorial Prize (International Literary Prizes) 448
Dufour, Henry-Robert, (Switzerland) 344
Duke of Alba Prize (Spain) 329
Dülk, Monika, Verlag (Federal Republic of Germany) 134
Dumas-Millier Prize (France) 113
Dumjahn, Horst-Werner, Verlag (Federal Republic of Germany) 134
Dummar & Mowakadeh & Co (Syria) 357

Dummer, Wolfgang, und Co (Federal Republic of Germany) 134
Dümmlers, Ferd, Verlag (Federal Republic of Germany) 134
Dumreicher, Edition, (Austria) 25
Duncker und Humblot (Federal Republic of Germany) 134
Dunedin Public Library (New Zealand) 275
Dunia, P T, Pustaka Jaya (Indonesia) 199
Dunmore Press Ltd (New Zealand) 272
Dunod (France) 95
Dupuch, Etienne, Jr Publications Ltd (Bahamas) 32
Dupuis, Editions Jean, SA (Belgium) 37
Dupuis, Maison d'Editions J, Fils et Cie SA (France) 95
Durassié, G, et Cie Sàrc (France) 95
Durban Municipal Library (Republic of South Africa) 315
Duret, Miguel Lanz, Prize (Mexico) 255
Durham University Library (United Kingdom) 416
Dustri-Verlag Dr Karl Feistle (Federal Republic of Germany) 134
Dutch (Flemish) Literature Grand Prizes (International Literary Prizes) 448
Dutch Prize for the Best Children's Book (Netherlands) 270
Dutch Reformed Church Publishers (Republic of South Africa) 312
Dutens, Alfred, Prize (France) 113
Dutton, The, Animal Book Award (International Literary Prizes) 448
Duttweiler, Gottlieb, Institute for Economic & Social Studies (Switzerland) 344
Duvivier, Charles, Prize (Belgium) 46
Dvir, The, Publishing Co Ltd (Israel) 207
'Dvir Bialik' Municipal Central Public Library (Israel) 211
Dwyer, E J, (Australia) Pty Ltd (Australia) 13
Dymock's Book Arcade Ltd (Australia) 19
Dynamis Verlag (Switzerland) 344

E C A (Ediciones Culturales Argentinas) (Argentina) 4
E C A Bookshop Co-op Society (Ethiopia) 84
E C I voor Boeken en Grammofoonplaten BV (Netherlands) 269
E C W A Productions Ltd (Nigeria) 277
E D A M E X (Mexico) 250
E D B (Italy) 215
E D E R S A (Editoriales de Derecho Reunidas SA) (Spain) 320
E D H A S A (Editora y Distribuidora Hispano-Americana SA) (Spain) 320
E D I 3 (Italy) 215
E D I M E, Ediciones y Distribuciones, (Venezuela) 424
E K L I P (Kampuchea) 235
E M B L A (Norway) 283
E O S Verlag, Erzabtei Sankt Ottilien (Federal Republic of Germany) 134
E P A (France) 95
E P Book Depot (Ghana) 175
E P O (Belgium) 37
E P Publishing Ltd (United Kingdom) 382
E P U (Brazil) 50
E R B (Czechoslovakia) 72
E R I — Edizioni R A I Radiotelevisione Italiana SpA (Italy) 215
E R Verlags GmbH (Federal Republic of Germany) 134
E S A Bookshop (Kenya) 236
E S A Bookshop (Uganda) 364
E S A Creative Learning Ltd (United Kingdom) 382
E S D U C K (Egypt) 82
E S F, Editions, (Editions Sociales Françaises) (France) 96
E S H (English for Speakers of Hebrew) (Israel) 207
E T H Bibliothek (Eidgenossische Technische Hochschule Bibliothek) (Switzerland) 356
E T P (Editions Techniques Professionnelles et Régies Audiovisuelles) (France) 96
E T S F (France) 96
E U D E B A (Editorial Universitaria de Buenos Aires) (Argentina) 4
E U N S A (Ediciones Universidad de Navarra SA) (Spain) 320
E U R O D I D A C (European Association of Manufacturers and Distributors of Educational Materials) (International Organizations) 441
Early English Text Society (United Kingdom) 418
Eason & Son Ltd (Republic of Ireland) 203
Eason & Son Ltd (Republic of Ireland) 204
East African Directory Co (Kenya) 235
East African Literature Bureau (Kenya) 235
East African Literature Bureau (Tanzania) 358
East African Literature Bureau (Uganda) 364
East African Literature Bureau (Uganda) 364
East African Literature Bureau (Tanzania) 358
East African Publishing House (Kenya) 235

478 INDEX

East African Statistical Department Library (Kenya) 236
East and Central Africa Regional Branch of the International Council of Archives (ECARBICA) (International Organizations) 438
East and West Publishing Co (Pakistan) 285
East Anglian Writers (United Kingdom) 418
East Asia Book Co (Hong Kong) 181
East-West Publications (UK) Ltd (United Kingdom) 383
East-West Publications Fonds BV (Netherlands) 260
Eastern Book Co (India) 189
Eastern Book Service Corp (Philippines) 292
Eastern Book Service Ltd (Hong Kong) 181
Eastern Book Service Pte Ltd (Republic of Singapore) 310
Eastern Book Service Sdn Bhd (wholesalers) (Malaysia) 247
Eastern Cultural Organizations Sdn Bhd (Malaysia) 246
Eastern Law House Pvt Ltd (India) 189
Eastern Publishing Co Ltd (China (Taiwan)) 64
Eastern Universities Press (Malaysia) 246
Eastern Universities Press Sdn Bhd (Republic of Singapore) 309
Ebeling, Hasso, (Luxembourg) 244
Ebeling, Hasso, Verlag (Luxembourg) 243
Ebeling Verlag (Federal Republic of Germany) 134
Eblana, The, Bookshop (Republic of Ireland) 204
Ebraesp Editorial Ltda (Brazil) 50
Ebury Press (United Kingdom) 383
Ecart Publications (Switzerland) 344
Ecclesia Press (Republic of Ireland) 203
Echevarria', Biblioteca 'José Antonio, (Cuba) 68
Echeverria, Aquileo T, Prize (Costa Rica) 68
Echter-Seelsorge Verlag (Federal Republic of Germany) 134
Eckersteins Universitetsbokhandel AB (Sweden) 338
Ecole, Bibliothèque de l', royale de Médecine (Laos) 240
Ecole, Bibliothèque de l', supérieure des Lettres (Lebanon) 241
Ecole, L', /L'Ecole des Loisirs (France) 96
Ecole Mohammedia d'Ingénieurs (Morocco) 256
Ecole nationale d'Administration Bibliothèque (Tunisia) 362
Ecole nationale polytechnique, Bibliothèque (Algeria) 2
Ecole normale supérieure (Mali) 248
Ecole normale supérieure (Gabon) 116
Ecole normale supérieure, Bibliothèque (Burundi) 60
Ecole normale supérieure de l'Afrique centrale, Bibliothèque (Popular Republic of Congo) 67
Ecole Professionnelle de la Mission Catholique (Togo) 360
Ecoles, Librairie des, (Morocco) 256
Ecoma, Editorial, SA (Peru) 289
Econ-Verlag GmbH (Austria) 25
Econ Verlagsgruppe (Federal Republic of Germany) 134
Economic and Industrial Publications (Pakistan) 285
Economic Council for Israel Printing & Publishing Committee (Israel) 206
Economic Publishing House (Democratic People's Republic of Korea) 237
Economische Voorlichtingsdienst, Bibliotheek- en Documentatie-centrum van de, (Library and Documentation Centre of the Economic Information Service) (Netherlands) 269
Economist, The, Newspaper Ltd (UK) 383
Edaf Ediciones y Distribuciones SA (Spain) 321
Edagricole (Edizioni Agricole) (Italy) 215
Edanim Publishers (Israel) 207
Edart (São Paulo Livraria Editôra Ltda) (Brazil) 50
Eddison Press Ltd (United Kingdom) 383
Edekes Bookshop Stores Ltd (Nigeria) 280
Edelcid Libros Científicos (Guatemala) 179
Edhis (France) 96
Edi-Art (Belgium) 37
Edibimbi SRL (Italy) 215
Edica SA (Spain) 321
Edicient SAIC (Argentina) 4
Ediciones de la Biblioteca (EBCV) (Venezuela) 424
Ediciones Iberoamericanas SA (EISA) (Spain) 321
Ediciones Instituto Nacional de Cultura (Panama) 287
Ediciones Pedagógicas Dominicanas, C por A (Dominican Republic) 80
Ediciones Populares (Netherlands Antilles) 271
Edicom NV (Netherlands) 260
Edigraf, Editorial Vilcar y Gráficas Hamburg SA (Spain) 321
Edil, Editorial, Inc (Puerto Rico) 302
Edilec, Les Editions, SA (France) 96
Edinburgh Bibliographical Society (United Kingdom) 416
Edinburgh University Library (United Kingdom) 416
Edinburgh University Press (United Kingdom) 383
Edinburgh University Student Publications Board (United Kingdom) 383
Edinorma Ltda y Cía SCA (Colombia) 65
Edipem SpA (Italy) 215
Ediscience (France) 96
Edisud (France) 96
Edit, NiP, (Yugoslavia) 427
Edita SA (Switzerland) 344

Editalia (Edizioni D'Italia) (Italy) 215
Editart, Société, Quatre Chemins (France) 96
Editeurs Associes SA (Switzerland) 344
Editeurs de Litterature Biblique (Belgium) 37
Editeurs Français, Les, Réunis (France) 96
Editeurs Réunis, Les, (France) 96
Editions Internationales, Les, (France) 96
Editions interuniversitaires (Belgium) 37
Editions Maritimes et d'Outre-Mer SA (France) 96
Editions Modernes Média (France) 96
Editions Mondiales, Les, SA (France) 96
Editions Sociales, Les, (France) 96
Editions Sociales Françaises (France) 96
Editions Techniques et Scientifiques Françaises (France) 96
Editions techniques et scientifiques SPRL (Belgium) 37
Editions Techniques Professionnelles (France) 96
Editions Techniques, SA (France) 96
Editions Universelles, Les, Sàrl (France) 96
Editions universitaires, Les, d'Egypte (Egypt) 82
Editions Universitaires (Universitätsverlag) (Switzerland) 344
Éditions Universitaires-Éditions du Jour SA (France) 96
Editions universitaires SA (Belgium) 37
Editnemo (Italy) 215
Edito-Service SA (Switzerland) 344
Editogo (Togo)
Editôra Americana, Cía, (Brazil) 51
Editora Cultural Dominicana (Dominican Republic) 80
Editora Educativa Dominicana (Dominican Republic) 80
Editôra Interamericana do Brasil Ltda (Brazil) 51
Editora Internacional (Dominican Republic) 80
Editôra Moderna Ltda (Brazil) 51
Editora Nacional (Spain) 321
Editora Nacional (Mexico) 250
Editôra Nacional, Cía, (Brazil) 51
Editôra Pedagogica e Universitaria Ltda (EPU) (Brazil) 51
Editora y Distribuidora Nacional de Libros (Dominican Republic) 80
Editorama, SA (Dominican Republic) 80
Editores Asociados Mexicanos SA (EDAMEX) (Mexico) 251
Editores Asociados SA (Mexico) 250
Editori, Associazione Italiana degli, di Musica (AIDEM) (Italy) 212
Editorial and Publishing Services (Ghana) 174
Editorial Consultancy & Agency Services (Nigeria) 279
Editorial Cultural (Puerto Rico) 302
Editorial Interamericana del Ecuador CA (Ecuador) 81
Editorial Interamericana SA (Colombia) 65
Editorial Interamericana SA (Peru) 290
Editorial Librería Dominicana (Dominican Republic) 80
Editorial Nicaragüense (Nicaragua) 276
Editorial Sudamericana SA (Argentina) 5
Editorial Universidad SRL (Argentina) 5
Editorial Universitaria (Chile) 62
Editorial Universitariá (Panama) 287
Editorial Universitaria (Honduras) 180
Editorial Universitaria Centroamericana (EDUCA) (Costa Rica) 67
Editorial Universitaria de Buenos Aires (Argentina) 5
Editorial Universitaria de la Universidad de El Salvador (El Salvador) 83
Editorialebari (Italy) 215
Editrice Bibliografica (Italy) 215
Educaboek BV (Netherlands) 260
Education et Culture (France) 110
Educational Aids Production Co Pte Ltd (Republic of Singapore) 310
Educational Book Centre (Republic of Singapore) 310
Educational Book Centre (The Modern Library) (Israel) 210
Educational Book Promotions (United Kingdom) 383
Educational Books Publishing House (Democratic People's Republic of Korea) 237
Educational Company of Ireland (Republic of Ireland) 203
Educational Enterprise (Nepal) 257
Educational Enterprises (Pte) Ltd (Nepal) 257
Educational Explorers Ltd (United Kingdom) 383
Educational Library (Saudi Arabia) 306
Educational Material Aid (Australia) 13
Educational Productions Ltd (United Kingdom) 383
Educational Publishers' Association (India) 186
Educational Publishers' Council (United Kingdom) 369
Educational Publishing, The, House Ltd (Hong Kong) 180
Educational Research Institute (Nigeria) 277
Educational Systems Ltd (United Kingdom) 383
Educational Writers' Group (United Kingdom) 418
Educmeds Pty Ltd (Namibia) 257
Educum Uitgewers Beperk (Republic of South Africa) 312
Eduskunnan Kirjasto (Finland) 87
Edwardian Studies Association (United Kingdom) 418
Edwards & Shaw Pty Ltd (Australia) 13

Effendi Harahap Bookstore (Indonesia) 200
Efstathiadis, P, & Sons SA (Greece) 177
Efstathiadis, P, & Sons SA (Greece) 176
Egan, Wm, & Sons (Republic of Ireland) 204
Egerton College Library (Kenya) 236
Eghbal Co (Iran) 201
Egoist-Verlag (Federal Republic of Germany) 134
Egyptian Association for Archives and Librarianship (Egypt) 83
Egyptian Society, The, for the Dissemination of Universal Culture and Knowledge (ESDUCK) (Egypt) 83
Egyptian Society, The, for the Dissemination of Universal Culture and Knowledge (ESDUCK) (Egypt) 82
Egyptian Society, The, for the Dissemination of Universal Culture and Knowledge (ESDUCK) (Egypt) 82
Ehapa Verlag GmbH (Federal Republic of Germany) 134
Ehon Library (Japan) 232
Ehrenwirth Verlag GmbH (Federal Republic of Germany) 134
Ehresmann, Verlag Rena, (Federal Republic of Germany) 134
Ehrlingförlagen AB (Sweden) 333
Eibel, Alfred, (France) 96
Eibel, Alfred, Editeur (Switzerland) 344
Eide, J W, Forlag A/S (Norway) 281
Eidgenössische Landestopographie (Switzerland) 344
Eike-Boekklub (Republic of South Africa) 315
Einaudi, Giulio, Editore SpA (Italy) 215
Eindhovensche Drukkerij BV (Netherlands) 260
Eiselé, André, (Switzerland) 344
Eisenbahn, Verlag, (Switzerland) 344
Ejlers', Christian, Forlag A/S (Denmark) 75
Ekblad-Eldhs, Signe, Prize (Sweden) 339
Eked Publishing House (Israel) 207
Ekenäs Tryckeri AB (Finland) 85
Ekonomiczne, Państwowe Wydawnictwo, (State Economic Publishers) (Poland) 294
'Ekonomika', Izdatelstvo, (Union of Soviet Socialist Republics) 365
El-Am Publishing (Israel) Ltd (Israel) 207
Eldec SpA Edizioni Pregiate (Italy) 215
Elder, Anne, Poetry Fund Award (Australia) 22
Eldorado, A Casa do Livro, Ltda (Brazil) 55
Eldra Taschenbuchverlag (Federal Republic of Germany) 135
Electa Editrice (Italy) 215
Eleftheroudakis, G C, Co Ltd (Greece) 177
Eleftheroudakis, G C, SA (Greece) 176
Elek, Paul, Ltd (United Kingdom) 383
Elektrowirtschaft (Switzerland) 344
Eletrônicas Editôra, Seleções, Ltda (Brazil) 51
Elgin, Mary, Prize (International Literary Prizes) 448
Elif Kitabevi (Turkey) 363
Elingaard Forlag A/S (Norway) 281
Elisas Sourasky Central Library, Tel Aviv University (Israel) 211
Elitera-Verlag GmbH (Federal Republic of Germany) 135
Elizabethan Publishing House (Nigeria) 278
Elkan och Schildknecht (Sweden) 333
Ellenberg Verlag (Federal Republic of Germany) 135
Ellermann, Verlag Heinrich, KG (Federal Republic of Germany) 135
Elliot Right Way Books (United Kingdom) 383
Ellis, Aidan, Publishing Ltd (United Kingdom) 383
Elm Tree Books Ltd (United Kingdom) 383
Elmar BV (Netherlands) 260
Elmfield Press (United Kingdom) 383
Elron Press Ltd (United Kingdom) 383
Elsässer, Buchhandlung zum, AG (Switzerland) 356
Elsevier, Editions, Séquoia Sàrl (France) 96
Elsevier Boekerij, Uitgeversmaatschappij, BV (Netherlands) 260
Elsevier-NDU nv (Netherlands) 260
Elsevier-Phaidon (United Kingdom) 383
Elsevier Publishing Projects (UK) Ltd (United Kingdom) 383
Elsevier Séquoia (Belgium) 37
Elsevier Sequoia SA (Switzerland) 344
Elsevier/North Holland Biomedical Press (Netherlands) 261
Elsevier's Wetenschappelijke Uitgeverij (Elsevier Scientific Publishing Co) BV (Netherlands) 261
Elsner, Otto, Verlagsgesellschaft mbH & Co KG (Federal Republic of Germany) 135
'Elvetica' Edizioni SA (Switzerland) 344
Elwert, N G, Verlag (Federal Republic of Germany) 135
Elwert und Meurer GmbH (Federal Republic of Germany) 135
Elwert und Meurer GmbH, Buchhandlung, (Federal Republic of Germany) 170
Emblem (United Kingdom) 383
Embryo (United Kingdom) 383
Emecé, Premio, Annual Prize (Argentina) 9
Emecé Editores SA (Argentina) 5
Eminescu, Editura, (Romania) 304
Emmaus-Desclée de Brouwer NV (Belgium) 37

Emme Edizioni (Italy) 215
Emmentaler Druck AG (Switzerland) 344
Emograph (Spain) 321
Emotan Publishing Co (Nigeria) Ltd (Nigeria) 278
Empire Shop (Montserrat) 255
Emporium, The, (Belize) 46
Empresa Moderna Lda (Mozambique) 256
Empresas Editoriales SA (Mexico) 251
En-Najah (Tunisia) 362
En-Najah, Librairie, (Tunisia) 362
Enciclopédia, Editorial, Lda (Portugal) 299
Encounters (United Kingdom) 414
'Encouragement Prize' (Austria) 31
'Encouragement Prizes' for Books for Children and Young People (Austria) 31
Encyclopaedia Africana Project (Ghana) 174
Encyclopaedia Britannica (Federal Republic of Germany) 135
Encyclopaedia Britannica (Australia) Inc (Australia) 13
Encyclopaedia Britannica (Korea) Inc (Republic of Korea) 238
Encyclopaedia Britannica de Venezuela SA (Dominican Republic) 80
Encyclopaedia Britannica International Ltd (United Kingdom) 383
Encyclopaedia Judaica (Israel) 207
Encyclopaedia Universalis (Belgium) 37
Encyclopaedia Universalis France SA (France) 96
'Energiya', Izdatelstvo, (Union of Soviet Socialist Republics) 365
Engel, Friedemann von, Verlag (Federal Republic of Germany) 135
Engelbert-Verlag (Federal Republic of Germany) 135
Engelman, Camille, Prize (International Literary Prizes) 448
Englind, Teaterförlag Arvid, AB (Sweden) 337
Englisch, F, Verlag GmbH (Federal Republic of Germany) 135
English Agency, The, (Japan) 232
English Association (United Kingdom) 418
English Association (South African Ban Literary Prize (Republic of South Africa) 316
English Book, The, Club (Denmark) 78
English Book Club (Netherlands) 269
English Book Store (India) 197
English Bookshop, The, (Iceland) 185
English Bookshop, The, (Denmark) 78
English-Speaking Union Book Award (International Literary Prizes) 448
Enke, Ferdinand, Verlag (Federal Republic of Germany) 135
Ennsthaler, Wilhelm, (Austria) 25
Enossis Ellenon Bibliothakarion (Greece) 178
Enriquillo, Editora, (Dominican Republic) 80
Enschede en Zonen Grafische Inrichting BV (Netherlands) 261
Enseignement, Librairie Générale de l', Sàrl (France) 96
Ensslin und Laiblin Verlag GmbH & Co KG (Federal Republic of Germany) 135
Ente Nazionale per*le Biblioteche Popolari e Scolastiche (Italy) 222
Entente, Editions, (France) 96
Entreprise Moderne d'Edition (France) 97
Enzyklopädie, VEB Verlag, (German Democratic Republic) 118
Epargne, Les Editions de l', (France) 97
Epi SA Editeurs (France) 97
Epoca, Editorial, SA (Mexico) 251
Epoca, Librería, (Peru) 290
'Epoka', Wydawnictwo, (Poland) 294
Eppinger, Hans P, (Federal Republic of Germany) 135
Epworth Press (United Kingdom) 383
Equatorial Publishers (Kenya) 235
Equatoriale, La Librairie L', (United Republic of Cameroun) 61
Era, Ediciones, SA (Mexico) 251
Erasme, Editions, (NV Scriptoria) (Belgium) 37
Erdmann, Horst, Verlag für Internationalen Kulturaustausch (Federal Republic of Germany) 135
Erehwon Publishing House (Philippines) 291
Erel (Belgium) 37
Eremiten-Presse und Verlag (Huelsmanns und Reske GmbH) (Federal Republic of Germany) 135
Eres, Edition, Horst Schubert Musikverlag (Federal Republic of Germany) 135
Eresco (Indonesia) 199
Erhvervsarkivet-Statens Erhvervshistoriske Arkiv (Denmark) 78
Erichsens, Chr, Forlag A/S (Denmark) 75
Erikssons, The Lydia and Herman, Prize (Sweden) 339
Erker-Galerie AG (Switzerland) 344
Erlangga (Indonesia) 199
Ermis (Greece) 177
Ernst, Wilhelm, und Sohn Verlag für Architektur und Technische Wissenschaften (Federal Republic of Germany) 135
Ernster, Librairie Pierre, (Luxembourg) 244

Erota-Press (Federal Republic of Germany) 135
Erster Linzer Lesezirkel Heinrich Auer & Co (Austria) 29
Erster Moderner Lesezirkel Kreith & Schram (Austria) 29
Erster Wiener Lesezirkel Gebrüder Kreith (Austria) 29
Erudita Publications (Pty) Ltd (Republic of South Africa) 312
Escobo (Dominican Republic) 80
Escolar, Livraria, Infante (Portugal) 299
Escorial, Librería, (Puerto Rico) 302
Escorts Book Award (India) 198
Esfinge, Editorial, SA (Mexico) 251
Eshkol-Haifa (Israel) 207
Eshkol-Jerusalem (Israel) 207
Eska (Netherlands) 261
Española, Librería, (Argentina) 8
Espasa-Calpe, Casa del Libro, SA (Spain) 327
Espasa-Calpe, Editorial, SA (Spain) 321
Espaxs, Editorial, SA (Spain) 321
Espinosa, Manuel, y Cortina Prize (Spain) 329
Espiritualista, Editôra, (Brazil) 51
Esquire (Lebanon) 241
Ess Ess Publications (India) 189
Esselte Förlag AB (Sweden) 333
Esselte Herzogs AB (Sweden) 333
Esselte Map Service (Sweden) 333
Esselte Studium AB (Sweden) 333
Est-Ouest, Editions, (Belgium) 37
Este, Librería del, (Venezuela) 425
Estoup et Roy, Publications, Sàrl (France) 97
Estrada, Angel, y Cia EICIEI & ASA (Argentina) 5
Estúdios, Editorial, Cor Sarl (Portugal) 299
Etablissements Généraux d'Imprimerie SA (Belgium) 37
Etairia Ellinon Logotechnon (Greece) 178
Etcetera, Edition, (Switzerland) 345
Etelä-Suomen Kustannus Oy (Finland) 85
Eteria Ellinikon Ekdoseon (Greece) 177
Ethiope Publishing Corporation (Nigeria) 278
Ethiopian Library Association (Ethiopia) 84
Ethiopian Manuscript Microfilm Library (Ethiopia) 84
Ethnographica Ltd (United Kingdom) 383
Etna-Taormina International Poetry Prize (International Literary Prizes) 448
Etudes, Librairie des, (Morocco) 256
Etudes Augustiniennes (France) 97
Eulama (Italy) 223
Eulama SA (Italy) 221
Eulama (Italy) 215
Eulenburg Edition GmbH (Switzerland) 345
Eulenspiegel Verlag für Satir und Humor (German Democratic Republic) 118
Eulyoo Publishing Co Ltd (Republic of Korea) 238
Euphorion, Freundeskreis des, Verlags (Federal Republic of Germany) 170
Euphorion Verlag (Federal Republic of Germany) 135
Eurasia Publishing House Pvt Ltd (India) 189
Eurédif (Société Européenne d'Edition et de Diffusion) (France) 97
Euroamericanas, Ediciones, (Mexico) 251
Eurobook Ltd (United Kingdom) 383
Europa (Belgium) 37
Europa-America, Publicações, Lda (Portugal) 299
Európa Könyvkiadó (Europa Publishing House) (Hungary) 182
Europa-Lehrmittel, Verlag, Nourney, Vollmer & Co OHG (Federal Republic of Germany) 136
Europa Publications Ltd (United Kingdom) 383
Europa-Verlag AG (Switzerland) 345
Europa Verlags-GmbH (Austria) 25
Europabuch AG (Switzerland) 345
Europäische Bildungsgemeinschaft Verlags GmbH (Federal Republic of Germany) 170
Europäische Buch, Das, (Federal Republic of Germany) 136
Europäische Gemeinschaften (European Communities) (Federal Republic of Germany) 136
europäische Ideen, Verlag, (Federal Republic of Germany) 136
Europäische Verlagsanstalt GmbH (Federal Republic of Germany) 136
Europaring der Buch- & Schallplattenfreunde (Switzerland) 356
Europarings der Buch- und Schallplattenfreunde (Federal Republic of Germany) 170
European Association of Directory Publishers (International Organizations) 438
European Broadcasting Union (EBU) (International Organizations) 441
European Cortina-Ulisse Prize (International Literary Prizes) 448
European Organization for Nuclear Research (CERN) (Organisation européenne pour la recherche nucléaire) (International Organizations) 442
European Press Scientific Publisher (Belgium) 37
European Schoolbooks Ltd (United Kingdom) 383
European Space Agency (International Organizations) 442
European University Institute Library (Italy) 222

Europese Bibliotheek Uitgeverij Boekhandel Antiquariaat (Netherlands) 261
Europress NV (Belgium) 37
Europrisma-Verlag (Federal Republic of Germany) 136
Evangel Publishing House (Kenya) 235
Evangélique, Librairie, (Upper Volta) 422
Evangélique, Librairie, (Togo) 360
Evangelisch Lutherische Mission, Verlag der, (Federal Republic of Germany) 136
Evangelische Buchgemeinde GmbH (Federal Republic of Germany) 136
Evangelische Verlagsanstalt GmbH (German Democratic Republic) 118
Evangelischer Gesellschaft, Verlag und Schriftenmission der, für Deutschland GmbH (Federal Republic of Germany) 136
Evangelischer Missionsverlag (Federal Republic of Germany) 136
Evangelischer Presseverband für Bayern eV (Federal Republic of Germany) 136
Evangelischer Pressverband in Österreich (Austria) 25
Evangelischer Schriften Verlag Schwengler (Switzerland) 345
Evangelisches Verlagswerk GmbH (Federal Republic of Germany) 136
Evangeliska Fosterlands-Stiftelsens Förlag (Sweden) 333
Evans Brothers (Nigeria Publishers) Ltd (Nigeria) 278
Evans Brothers Ltd (United Kingdom) 383
Evans Shepherd (Zimbabwe) 435
Evelyn, Hugh, Ltd (United Kingdom) 384
Everest, Editorial, SA (Spain) 321
Everest Books Ltd (United Kingdom) 384
Everymans Library (United Kingdom) 384
Ewald, Johannes, Prize (Denmark) 80
Ewart-Biggs, Christopher, Memorial Prize (International Literary Prizes) 448
Ewha Woman's University Library (Republic of Korea) 239
Ewha Woman's University Press (Republic of Korea) 238
Ewing Memorial Library (Pakistan) 286
Ex Libris (Switzerland) 345
Ex Libris (Switzerland) 356
Exclusive Books (Pty) Ltd (Republic of South Africa) 315
Exley Publications Ltd (United Kingdom) 384
Expanded Media Editions (Federal Republic of Germany) 136
Expansion, L', Scientifique Française (France) 97
Exped-Expansaõ Editorial Ltda (Brazil) 51
Export-Press (Yugoslavia) 431
Express Logic Ltd (United Kingdom) 384
Expresso (Portugal) 301
Extemporaneos, Editorial, SA (Mexico) 251
Eymundssonar, Bókaverslun Sigfusar, (Iceland) 185
Eyre & Spottiswoode (Publishers) Ltd (United Kingdom) 384
Eyre Methuen Ltd (United Kingdom) 384
Eyrolles, Éditions, (France) 97

F A D L Forlag (Foreningen af danske Laegestuderendes Forlag) (Denmark) 75
F A W-Barbara Ramsden Award (Australia) 22
F A W-John Shaw Neilson Poetry Award (Australia) 22
F A W Regional Branch Awards (Australia) 22
F B V Frauenbuchvertrieb GmbH (Federal Republic of Germany) 170
F E D , Uitgeverij, BV (Netherlands) 261
F E N A M E—Fundação Nacional de Material Escolar (Brazil) 51
F E P International (HK) Ltd (Hong Kong) 180
F E P International (M) Sdn Bhd (Far Eastern Publishers) (Malaysia) 246
F E P International Private Ltd (Republic of Singapore) 309
F I D (International Organizations) 438
F N A C (France) 110
F T D, Editôra, SA (Brazil) 51
F W M Books Ltd (Trinidad and Tobago) 361
Fabbri Editori SpA (Italy) 215
Faber, The Geoffrey, Memorial Prize (International Literary Prizes) 448
Faber & Faber Ltd (United Kingdom) 384
Fabien Prize (France) 113
Fabril Editora SA (Argentina) 5
Fabritius Forlagshus (Norway) 281
Fachbuchverlag, VEB, (German Democratic Republic) 118
Fackel-Buchklub, Verlags- und Vertriebs GmbH (Federal Republic of Germany) 170
Fackelträger-Verlag Schmidt-Küster GmbH (Federal Republic of Germany) 136
Fackelverlag G Bowitz GmbH (Federal Republic of Germany) 136

Fackelverlag G Bowitz KG (Austria) 25
Facla, Editura, (Romania) 304
Facsimile Uitgaven Nederland BV (FUN) (Netherlands) 261
Facultas Verlag (Austria) 25
Facultatii, Biblioteca, de Medicina din Bucuresti (Library of the Medical Faculty) (Romania) 305
Faculté de Droit, Bibliothèque de la, (France) 111
Faculté des Lettres et Sciences Humaines de Tunis (Tunisia) 362
Faculty, Library of the, of Law (Lebanon) 241
Faculty of Agriculture, Forestry and Veterinary Science (Tanzania) 358
Faculty of Medicine Library (Tanzania) 358
Fællesekspeditionen (Denmark) 74
Faenza Editrice SpA (Italy) 215
Fagbamigbe, Olaiya, Ltd (Publishers) (Nigeria) 278
Faglitteratur, Forlaget for, A/S (Denmark) 75
Faik, Sait, Prize (Turkey) 364
Faith, The, Press Ltd (United Kingdom) 384
Fajar, Penerbit,akti Sdn Bhd (Malaysia) 246
Falcon Books (United Kingdom) 384
Falk- Verlag für Landkarten & Stadtpläne Gerhard Falk GmbH (Federal Republic of Germany) 136
Falken-Verlag Erich Sicker KG (Federal Republic of Germany) 136
Falkplan, NV, /CIB (Netherlands) 261
Fall, Lycée de Jeunes Filles Ameth, (Senegal) 307
Fallon, C J, Ltd (Republic of Ireland) 203
Faltermaier, Dr Martin, (Federal Republic of Germany) 136
Familia, Librerías La, (Peru) 290
Familia 2000 (Portugal) 299
Familia et Patria PVBA (Belgium) 37
Familje Bokklubben (Sweden) 337
Family Book Club (United Kingdom) 414
Family Bookshop (Qatar) 303
Family Bookshop (United Arab Emirates) 368
Family Bookshop (Bahrain) WLL (Bahrain) 32
Fantasia Prize (France) 113
Fantasy Library (United Kingdom) 384
Far East Book Co (Republic of Singapore) 310
Far East Book Co (China (Taiwan)) 64
Far East Publications Ltd (Hong Kong) 181
Far Eastern University Library (Philippines) 292
Farairre, Librairie, (Morocco) 256
Farandole, Editions La, (France) 97
Farjeon, Eleanor, Award (United Kingdom) 419
Farmer, Prudence, Poetry Prize (United Kingdom) 419
Farquharson, John, Ltd (United Kingdom) 413
Fastenrath Prize (Spain) 329
Fausto, Ediciones Librerías, (Argentina) 5
Fausto, Librerías, (Argentina) 8
Favorit-Verlag Huntemann & Co (Federal Republic of Germany) 136
Favre, Jules, Prize (France) 113
Favre, Pierre Marcel, (Switzerland) 345
Fayard, Librairie Arthème, (France) 97
Fazer, Edition, (Finland) 85
Federação Brasileira de Associações de Bibliotecários — Comissão Brasileira de Documentação Jurídica (FEBAB/CBDJ) (Brazil) 56
Federação Brasileira de Associações de Bibliotecários (FEBAB) (Brazilian Federation of Library Associations) (Brazil) 56
Federación Argentina de Librerías, Papelerías y Actividades Afines (Argentina) 3
Federal Library Association (Pakistan) 286
Federal Publications (FE) (Hong Kong) 180
Federal Publications (S) Pte Ltd (Republic of Singapore) 309
Federal Publications Sdn Bhd (Malaysia) 246
Federatie van Organisaties van Bibliotheek-, Informatie-, Dokumentatiewezen (FOBID) (Federation of Library Information and Documentation Organizations) (Netherlands) 270
Fédération des Amicales de Documentalistes et Bibliothécaires de l'Education nationale (Federation of Friends of Documentalists and Librarians of National Education) (France) 111
Fédération des Commerçants, Groupement Papetiers-Libraires, Journaux, Editeurs et Galeries d'Art (Federation of Retailers Group for Stationers and Booksellers, Journals, Publishers and Art Galleries) (Luxembourg) 243
Fédération des Editeurs belges (Belgium) 33
Fédération française des Syndicats de Libraires (French Booksellers' Association) (France) 88
Fédération Internationale des Libraires (FIL) (International Organizations) 438
Fédération Internationale des Traducteurs (FIT) (International Federation of Translators) (International Organizations) 438
Fédération luxembourgeoise des Travailleurs du Livre (Luxembourg Federation of Workers in the Book Trade) (Luxembourg) 243

Fédération nationale des Bibliothèques Catholiques (Belgium) 44
Federation of Booksellers and Publishers Association in Gujarat (India) 186
Federation of Children's Book Groups (United Kingdom) 418
Federation of Indian Library Associations (India) 197
Federation of Indian Publishers (India) 186
Federation of Printing and Bookbinding Enterprises (Greece) 176
Federation of Publishers and Booksellers Associations in India (India) 186
Federazione Italiana delle Biblioteche Popolari (Italy) 222
Federspiel, Librería Universal Carlos, (Costa Rica) 68
Fehling, Willy F P, GmbH (Federal Republic of Germany) 136
Fehmers, Frank, Productions (Netherlands) 261
Fehr'sche Buchhandlung AG (Switzerland) 345
Fehr'sche Buchhandlung AG (Switzerland) 356
Feij, François, (Switzerland) 345
Félag Islenskra Bókaútgefenda (Icelandic Publishers' Association) (Iceland) 184
Félag Islenzkra Bókaverzlana (Icelandic Booksellers' Association) (Iceland) 184
Feldheim Publishers Ltd (Israel) 207
Fellicelli & Poli, Librairie, (Niger) 276
Fellowship of Australian Writers NSW (Australia) 21
Feltrinelli, Antonio, Prize (International Literary Prizes) 449
Feltrinelli, Giangiacomo, SpA (Italy) 215
Feltrinelli, Libreria, (Italy) 221
Fémina Prize (France) 113
Feminist Books Ltd (United Kingdom) 384
Femmes, Des, (France) 97
Femmes dans la Vie (France) 110
Femmes d'aujourd'hui, Groupe, (France) 97
Fenêtre, La, Ouverte SA (France) 97
Fénéon Prize (France) 113
Ferenczy Verlag AG (Switzerland) 345
Ferguson, John, Pty Ltd (Australia) 13
Feria, Librería, del Libro (Guatemala) 179
Feria Chilena del Libro (Chile) 63
Feria del Libro (Uruguay) 423
Ferin, Livraria, Lda (Portugal) 299
Fernández, Editorial y Librería Juridica Amalio M, (Uruguay) 422
Fernández, Librería Amalio M, (Uruguay) 423
Fernández Editores SA (Mexico) 251
Fernstyle Ltd (United Kingdom) 384
Ferozsons Ltd (Pakistan) 286
Ferozsons Ltd (Pakistan) 285
Ferraris, Librairie, (Algeria) 2
Ferro, Edizioni, SpA (Italy) 215
Fersobe, Papeleria, Hnos (Dominican Republic) 80
Festungsverlag (Austria) 29
Feu, Editions du, Nouveau (France) 97
Feuervogel-Verlag GmbH (Federal Republic of Germany) 136
'Feuilles familiales', Les, ASBL (Belgium) 37
Fher, Editorial, SA (Spain) 321
Fibula-Van Dishoeck (Netherlands) 261
Fierro', Librería 'Martín, (Argentina) 8
Fietkau, Wolfgang, Verlag (Federal Republic of Germany) 136
Figgis, Allen, & Co Ltd (Republic of Ireland) 203
Figueirinhas, Livraria Editora, Lda (Portugal) 299
Fiji Library Association (FLA) (Fiji) 85
Fikr, Dar Al-, (Salem And Zu'bi) Bookshop (Syria) 357
Filadelfia AB, Förlaget, (Sweden) 333
Filipacchi, Editions, (France) 97
Filipino Publishing House Inc (Philippines) 291
Filon, Ekdoseis, (Greece) 177
Financial Times, The, Ltd (United Kingdom) 384
Financial Training Publications Ltd (United Kingdom) 384
'Finansy', Izdatelstvo, (Union of Soviet Socialist Republics) 365
Finax Publications (United Kingdom) 384
Findhorn Publications (United Kingdom) 384
Fine Arts Press Pty Ltd (Australia) 13
Fink, Emil, Verlag (Federal Republic of Germany) 136
Fink, Wilhelm, Verlag KG (Federal Republic of Germany) 136
Fink-Kümmerly & Frey, J, Verlag GmbH (Federal Republic of Germany) 136
Finken-Verlag (Federal Republic of Germany) 136
Finlands Svenska Författareförening (Finland) 87
Finot, Jean, Prize (France) 113
Fiorentina, Libreria Editrice, di Vittorio e Valerio Zani snc (Italy) 215
Firecrest Publishing Ltd (United Kingdom) 384
Firma KLM Private Ltd (Incorporating Firma KL Mukhopadhyay) (India) 189
Firmin-Didot et Cie (France) 97
First Book Prize (Argentina) 9
Fiscado, Editions, (France) 97

Fischbacher, Librairie, International Art Book Distribution (import-export) (France) 97
Fischer, Gustav, Verlag (Federal Republic of Germany) 137
Fischer, Rita G, Verlag (Federal Republic of Germany) 137
Fischer, S, Verlag GmbH (Federal Republic of Germany) 137
Fischer, VEB Gustav, Verlag (German Democratic Republic) 118
Fischer, W, Verlag (Federal Republic of Germany) 137
Fischer Taschenbuch Verlag GmbH (Federal Republic of Germany) 137
Fisher, H, (Israel) 207
Fishing News Books Ltd (United Kingdom) 384
Fitzpatrick, Percy, Medal (Republic of South Africa) 316
Fitzwilliam Museum (United Kingdom) 384
Five Lamps, The, Press (Republic of Ireland) 203
Fix, Verlag Johannes, (Federal Republic of Germany) 137
'Fizkultura i Sport', Izdatelstvo, (Union of Soviet Socialist Republics) 365
Flaccovio, Libreria SF, (Italy) 221
Flaccovio, S F, Editore (Italy) 215
Flamberg Verlag (Switzerland) 345
Flame Lily (Zimbabwe) 435
Flammarion (France) 110
Flammarion et Cie (France) 97
Flare Books (United Kingdom) 384
Flat, Paul, Prize (France) 113
Fleischhauer und Spohn Verlag (Federal Republic of Germany) 137
Flensteds Forlag (Denmark) 75
Flesch Financial Publications (Pty) Ltd (Republic of South Africa) 312
Fleurus, Editions, SA (France) 97
Fleury, Ernest, Prize (France) 113
Fleuve, Editions, Noir (France) 97
Flor, Ediciones de la, SRL (Argentina) 5
Florence, City of, International Poetry Prize (International Literary Prizes) 449
Florio, John, Prize (United Kingdom) 419
Floris Books (United Kingdom) 385
Focal Press Ltd (United Kingdom) 385
Foch, Marshal, Prize (France) 113
Focus Elsevier BV (Netherlands) 261
Focus Uppslagsböcker AB (Focus International Book Production AB) (Sweden) 333
Focus-Verlag (Federal Republic of Germany) 137
Foetisch, Maurice & Pierre, SA (Switzerland) 345
Fogarty's Bookshop (Republic of South Africa) 315
Fogtdal, Palle, A/S (Denmark) 75
Foilseacháin Náisiúnta Tta (Republic of Ireland) 203
Folens and Co Ltd (Republic of Ireland) 203
Folio, The, Society Ltd (United Kingdom) 385
Folio, The, Society Ltd (United Kingdom) 414
Folklore Prize (Brazil) 57
Foma, Editions, SA (Switzerland) 345
Fondeur d'Aujourd'hui (France) 97
Fondo de Cultura Económica (Mexico) 251
Fondo Editorial Común SC (Venezuela) 424
Fondo Educativo Interamericano (Mexico) 251
Fondo Educativo Interamericano CA (Venezuela) 424
Fondo Educativo Interamericano SA (Colombia) 65
Fonds, Bibliothèque, Quetelet (Belgium) 44
Fonds Mercator SA (Belgium) 38
Fonna Forlag L/L (Norway) 282
Font, Librería, (Mexico) 253
Font, Librería, SA (Mexico) 251
Fontainemore, Editions de, (Switzerland) 345
Fontana Books (United Kingdom) 385
Fontane, Theodor, Prize (Federal Republic of Germany) 173
Fontanella, Editorial, SA (Spain) 321
Fontein, Uitgeverij De, BV (Netherlands) 261
Fonteintje, Het, (Belgium) 38
Fontes Pers (APA) (Netherlands) 261
Fonteyn Medical Books NV (Belgium) 38
Food and Agriculture Organization of the United Nations (FAO) (International Organizations) 440
Foras, An, Forbartha (National Institute for Physical Planning and Construction Research) (Republic of Ireland) 203
Forbes Publications Ltd (United Kingdom) 385
Foreign Affairs Publishing Co Ltd (United Kingdom) 385
Foreign Language Bookshop (Australia) 19
Foreign Languages Press (People's Republic of China) 63
Foreign Languages Publishing House (Soalist Republic of Viet Nam) 425
Foreign Languages Publishing House (Democratic People's Republic of Korea) 237
Foreign Poetry Prize (International Literary Prizes) 449
Forening for Boghaandvaerk (Denmark) 74
Forening for Forlagsfolk (Denmark) 74
Forense, Editôra, —Universitaria Ltda (Brazil) 51
Författares Bokmaskin (Sweden) 338
Förg, Alfred, GmbH & Co KG (Federal Republic of Germany) 137

INDEX 481

Foris Publications (Netherlands) 261
Forja Editora SARL (Portugal) 299
Forkel-Verlag GmbH (Federal Republic of Germany) 137
Formar, Editôra e Encadernadora, Ltda (Brazil) 51
Formentor, Ediciones, SRL (Argentina) 5
Formentor Prize (International Literary Prizes) 449
Formgebung, Rat für, (Federal Republic of Germany) 137
Formichiere, Il, (Italy) 215
Forsamlingsforbundets Forlags AB (Finland) 85
Forsbergs, Bengt, Förlag AB (Sweden) 333
Förskolans Förlag i Stockholm (Sweden) 333
Fortschritt für Alle-Verlag (Federal Republic of Germany) 137
Fortuna-Verlag W Heidelberger (Switzerland) 345
Fortune Press (United Kingdom) 385
Fortuny, Pascal, Prize (France) 113
Forum (New Zealand) 272
Forum (Yugoslavia) 427
Forum (Yugoslavia) 431
Forum, Bokförlaget, AB (Sweden) 333
Forum littéraire camerounais (United Republic of Cameroun) 61
Forum Publishers Ltd (Denmark) 75
Forum Verlag GmbH (Austria) 25
Főszékesegyházi könyvtár (Hungary) 183
Foto und Schmalfilm-Verlag (Switzerland) 345
Fotokinoverlag, VEB, (German Democratic Republic) 118
Foucher, Les Editions, (France) 98
Foulis Books (United Kingdom) 385
Foulsham & Co Ltd (United Kingdom) 385
Foundation Book Club (Philippines) 292
Foundation Books (Kenya) 235
Foundation for the Promotion of Translation of Dutch Literary Works (Netherlands) 270
Foundational, The, Book Co Ltd (United Kingdom) 385
Fountain Press (United Kingdom) 385
Four Courts Press (Republic of Ireland) 203
Fourah Bay College Bookshop Ltd (Sierra Leone) 308
Fourah Bay College Library (Sierra Leone) 308
Fouraignan Prize (France) 114
Fournier, Heraclio, SA (Spain) 321
Fourth Estate Books Ltd (New Zealand) 272
Fox produktionen traude Aubeck (Federal Republic of Germany) 137
Foxcub (United Kingdom) 385
Foxwood Publishing Ltd (United Kingdom) 385
Foyer, Editions, Notre-Dame (Belgium) 38
Foyle, W & G, Ltd (United Kingdom) 415
Foyle, W & G, Ltd & John Gifford Ltd (United Kingdom) 385
Foyles Book Clubs (United Kingdom) 414
Fragua Editorial (Spain) 321
Frahm, Carlota, Literary Agency (Norway) 283
Fralit-F K Albrecht (Federal Republic of Germany) 169
Française, Librairie, (Luxembourg) 244
France, Librairie de, (Morocco) 256
France, Librairie de, (Ivory Coast) 224
France, Librairie de, (Upper Volta) 422
France Empire, Editions, (France) 98
France Expansion (France) 98
France-Loisirs (France) 98
Francesa, Librería, (Spain) 327
Franciscaines, Les Editions, SA (France) 98
Franciscan Printing Press (Israel) 207
Franciscana, Editorial, (Portugal) 299
Francité, Editions de la, (Imprimeries Havaux) (Belgium) 38
Francke, A, GmbH (Federal Republic of Germany) 137
Francke, Buchhandlung A, AG (Switzerland) 356
Francke Buchhandlung, Verlag der, GmbH (Federal Republic of Germany) 137
Francke Verlag (Switzerland) 345
Franckh'sche Verlagshandlung W Keller & Co (Federal Republic of Germany) 137
Franco-German Friendship Prize (International Literary Prizes) 449
François, Le, (France) 98
Franjas Prizes (Bolivia) 48
Frank Bros & Co (India) 190
Frank Publishing Ltd (Ghana) 174
Frankfurter Bücher, Verlag, (Federal Republic of Germany) 137
Frankfurter Fachverlag Michael Kohl GmbH & Co KG (Federal Republic of Germany) 137
Frankfurter Kinderbücher, Verlag, GmbH (Federal Republic of Germany) 137
Fränkische Gesellschafts-Druckerei Würzburg/Echter Verlag (Federal Republic of Germany) 137
Franklin, Biblioteca 'Benjamin,' (USICA) (Mexico) 254
Franklin, Miles, Award (Australia) 22
Franklin Book Programs Inc (Afghanistan) 1
Franklin Book Programs Inc (Egypt) 82
Franklin Book Programs Inc (Iran) 201
Frankonius Verlag GmbH (Federal Republic of Germany) 137

Franz, Verlag Ernst, und Sternberg-Verlag (Federal Republic of Germany) 137
Franzis-Verlag (Federal Republic of Germany) 138
Fraser, Gordon, Gallery Ltd (United Kingdom) 385
Fraternité Prize (France) 114
Frau, Verlag für die, (German Democratic Republic) 118
Frau und Mutter Verlag (Austria) 29
Frauen-Selbstverlag (Federal Republic of Germany) 138
Frauenbuchverlag (Federal Republic of Germany) 138
Frauenkalender Selbstverlag (Federal Republic of Germany) 138
Frauenoffensive, Verlag, (Federal Republic of Germany) 138
Frauenpolitik, Verlag, (Federal Republic of Germany) 138
Fréal, Editions, (France) 98
Frech, Verlag, (Federal Republic of Germany) 138
Freelance Writing, Committee for, (Australia) 10
Freeland, Editorial, (Argentina) 5
Freeland Press Ltd (United Kingdom) 385
Freeman, W H, & Co Ltd (United Kingdom) 385
freies Geistesleben, Verlag, (Federal Republic of Germany) 138
Freihofer AG (Switzerland) 345
Freitas, Livraria, Bastos (Brazil) 56
Freitas, Livraria, Bastos SA (Brazil) 51
Fremad (Denmark) 75
French, Samuel, Ltd (United Kingdom) 385
French Academy, Foreigner's Book Award (International Literary Prizes) 449
French Book Club (United Kingdom) 414
French Catholic Grand Prize for Literature (France) 114
French Critics' Prize (France) 114
French Faculty of Medicine, Library of the, (Lebanon) 241
French Grand Prize for Humour (France) 114
French Language Prize (International Literary Prizes) 449
French Poets' Grand Prize (France) 114
Fretz, Gebrüder, Verlag AG (Switzerland) 345
Fretz und Wasmuth Verlag AG (Switzerland) 345
Freud, Sigmund, Prize (Federal Republic of Germany) 173
Freund Publishing House Ltd (Israel) 207
Freytag-Berndt und Artaria, Kartographische Anstalt (Austria) 25
Frías, Universidad Boliviana Tomás, Div de Extensión Universitaria (Bolivia) 47
Fricke, Verlag Dieter, GmbH (Federal Republic of Germany) 138
Friedenauer Presse (Federal Republic of Germany) 138
Friedman, S, (Israel) 207
Friedmann, Julian, Publishers Ltd (United Kingdom) 385
Friedrich, Erhard, Verlag (Federal Republic of Germany) 138
Friends of Antiquity (Czechoslovakia) 72
Friends of the National Libraries (United Kingdom) 416
Frimodts, J, Forlag (Denmark) 75
Frisia-Verlag GmbH (Federal Republic of Germany) 138
Fritsch, Edition der 2 Gerald, und Stephan Fritsch (Federal Republic of Germany) 138
Fritzes, AB C E, Kungl Hovbokhandel (Sweden) 338
Frobenius AG (Switzerland) 345
Froebel-Kan Co Ltd (Japan) 226
Fromm, Verlag A, GmbH & Co (Federal Republic of Germany) 138
Frommann-Holzboog (Federal Republic of Germany) 138
Fromme, George, und Co (Austria) 25
Frontier Publishing Co (Pakistan) 285
Frost, Robert, Award (Australia) 22
Fu-Hsing Book Co (China (Taiwan) 64
Fu Ssu-Nien Library Institute of History and Philology (China (Taiwan)) 64
Fuchs, Dr Heinrich, (Austria) 25
Fuchsbichler, Reinfried, (Austria) 29
Fudge & Co Ltd (United Kingdom) 385
Fukuinkan Shoten Publishers (Japan) 226
Fullerton, Leonard, Ltd (New Zealand) 272
Fundação Instituto Brasileiro de Geografia e Estatística (Brazil) 51
Fundação Nacional de Material Escolar (Brazil) 51
Fundación de Cultura Universitaria (Uruguay) 422
Fundamentos, Editorial, (Spain) 321
Fundepar Prize (Brazil) 57
'Furet du Nord', Librairie, (France) 110
Fürstelberger, Hans, (Austria) 30
Futura, Editorial, (Portugal) 299
Futura Publications Ltd (United Kingdom) 385
Fuzambo Publishing Co (Japan) 226
Fytrakis, Chr, (Greece) 177

G E C T I (Gabinete de Especializacão e Cooperacão Tecnica Internacional L) (Portugal) 299
G I A SA (Belgium) 98

G M T, Forlaget, (Denmark) 75
G S Verlag Basle (Switzerland) 345
Gaade, W, BV (Netherlands) 261
Gaalyah Cornfeld (Israel) 207
Gaba Publications (Kenya) 235
Gabalda, J, et Cie (Librairie Lecoffre) SA (France) 98
Gaber, Verlag Franz-Joachim, (Federal Republic of Germany) 138
Gaberbocchus Press Ltd (United Kingdom) 385
Gabinete de Especializacão e Cooperacão Tecnica Internacional (Portugal) 299
Gabler, Betriebswirtschaftlicher Verlag Dr Theodor, (Federal Republic of Germany) 138
Gads, G E C, Dansk og Udenlandsk Boghandel A/S (Denmark) 78
Gads, G E C, Forlag (Denmark) 75
Gaehme, Verlag, (Federal Republic of Germany) 138
Gaisa, Ediciones, SL (Spain) 321
Gakken Co Ltd (Japan) 226
Gakujutsu Bunken Fukyu-Kai (Association for Science Documents Information) (Japan) 232
Gakuseisha Publishing Co Ltd (Japan) 226
Galaxia (Venezuela) 425
Galaxie Press (Pvt) Ltd (Zimbabwe) 435
Galera, La, SA Editorial (Spain) 321
Galería, Librería, Castro Soto (Peru) 290
Galerna, Editorial, SA (Argentina) 5
Galgotia, E D, & Sons (India) 197
Galilée, Editions, (France) 98
Gall & Inglis (United Kingdom) 385
Galland, Editions Bertil, (Switzerland) 345
Gallegos, Rómulo, International Novel Prize (International Literary Prizes) 449
Gallery, The, Press (Republic of Ireland) 204
Galley Club of Sydney (Australia) 10
Galliard (United Kingdom) 386
Gallimard, Editions, (France) 98
Gama, Da, Publishers (Pty) Ltd (Republic of South Africa) 312
Gambia, The, Methodist Bookshop Ltd (The Gambia) 117
Gambia National Library (The Gambia) 117
Gamma, Editions, (France) 98
Gamma, Editions, (Belgium) 38
Gammalibri, Editrice, (Italy) 215
Gamsberg Publishers (Namibia) 257
Ganesh & Co (India) 190
Gans, Alexander, (Netherlands) 269
Gantner, A R, Verlag KG (Liechtenstein) 243
Gantrelle, Joseph, Prize (Belgium) 46
García, Librería y Papelería Casa, SA (Argentina) 5
Garcia, R M, Publishing House (Philippines) 291
García Cambeiro, Fernando, (Argentina) 5
Garden Book Club (United Kingdom) 414
Gardeners Book Society (United Kingdom) 414
Gardet, Imprimerie Librairie, (France) 98
Gardum (Norway) 283
Garnier, Éditions, Frères (France) 98
Garnstone Press Ltd (United Kingdom) 386
Garriga, Ediciones, Argentinas SA (Argentina) 8
Garriga, Ediciones, SA (Spain) 321
Garve, De, PVBA (Belgium) 38
Garzanti Editore (Italy) 215
Gauthier-Villars, Société, (France) 98
Gautier-Languereau, Les Editions, (France) 98
Gaya, P T, Favorit Press, Book Division (Indonesia) 199
Gazelle Publications Pty Ltd (Australia) 13
Gazit (Israel) 207
Gebühr, Verlag Werner, (Federal Republic of Germany) 138
Gedalge, Librairie, (France) 98
Gedin, Mrs Lena l, (Sweden) 337
Gedit SA (Belgium) 38
Geering, Rudolf, Verlag (Switzerland) 345
Geest und Portig, Akademische Verlagsgesellschaft, KG (German Democratic Republic) 118
Geetha, M S, Publishers (Malaysia) 246
Geetha Book House (India) 190
Geetha Prize (India) 198
Gegner Prize (France) 114
Gehlen, Dr Max, Verlagsbuch-handlung (Federal Republic of Germany) 138
Gehrmans, AB Carl, Musikförlag (Sweden) 334
Geisenheyner und Crone (Federal Republic of Germany) 169
Gelisim Publishing (Turkey) 363
Gemeentebibliotheek Rotterdam (Rotterdam Municipal Library) (Netherlands) 269
Gemini Awards (Australia) 22
Gemini Publishing (United Kingdom) 386
Geminis, Editorial, SRL (Argentina) 5
Gemsberg-Verlag (Switzerland) 345
Gençlik Kitabevi (Turkey) 363
General Assembly Library (New Zealand) 275
Géneral Company for Publishing, Advertising and Distribution (Libya) 242

General Egyptian Book Organization (Egypt) 82
General Egyptian Book Organization (Egypt) 82
General Federation of Literary and Art Unions, Publishing House of the, (Democratic People's Republic of Korea) 237
General Organization, The, for Government Press Affairs (Egypt) 82
General Press Corporation (Libya) 242
Générale des Carrières et des Mines, La, (GECAMINES) (Zaire) 433
Generalstabens Litografiska Anstalts Förlag (Sweden) 334
Genfer Bibelgesellschaft (Switzerland) 345
Genillard, Pierre, (Switzerland) 345
Genin, Editions M Th, (France) 98
Gennadius Library (Greece) 178
Gennep, Van, Ltd (Netherlands) 261
Gennotte, Librairie A. & Fils (Burundi) 60
Gensy, Creazioni, (Italy) 215
Gente Nueva, Editorial, (Cuba) 68
Gentofte Kommunebibliotek (Denmark) 78
Gentry Books Ltd (United Kingdom) 386
Geo Center Internationales Landkartenhaus GmbH (Federal Republic of Germany) 138
Geocolor SA (Spain) 321
Geographia Ltd (United Kingdom) 386
Geographische Verlagsgesellschaft Velhagen und Klasing und Hermann Schroedel GmbH und Co KG (Federal Republic of Germany) 138
Geological Survey of India (India) 190
Geologiczne, Wydawnictwa, (Poland) 294
Geoprojects Sàrl (Lebanon) 241
Georg & Cie SA (Switzerland) 356
Georg et Cie SA (Switzerland) 345
Georges, Félix, Prize (France) 114
George's, William, Sons Ltd (United Kingdom) 415
Georgi, Verlag Dr Rudolf, (Federal Republic of Germany) 138
Georgi Publishing Company/Editions Georgi (Switzerland) 345
Georgian House Pty Ltd (Australia) 13
Geraldine, The, Press (Republic of Ireland) 204
Gérard, Editions, & Co SPRL (Belgium) 38
Gerber, Carl, Verlag (Federal Republic of Germany) 138
Gerhardt Verlag (Federal Republic of Germany) 138
Gerlach & Wiedling Buch und Kunstverlag (Austria) 25
Germain, Mme Françoise, (France) 110
German Book Club (United Kingdom) 414
German Peace Prize (International Literary Prizes) 449
German Youth, The, Book Award (International Literary Prizes) 449
Gerold & Co (Austria) 25
Gerold & Co (Austria) 30
Gerstenberg Verlag (Federal Republic of Germany) 138
Geschichte und Politik, Verlag für, (Austria) 25
Gesellschaft für Bibliothekswesen und Dokumentation des Landbaues (GBDL) (Federal Republic of Germany) 172
Gesellschaft für deutsche Sprache und Literatur in Zürich (Switzerland) 357
Gesellschaft für Information und Dokumentation mbH (GID) (Federal Republic of Germany) 172
Gesellschaft für Verlagswerte GmbH (Switzerland) 355
Gesellschaft für Volkskunde (Switzerland) 346
Geschäftsstelle der Schweiz (Switzerland) 346
Geuthner, Librairie Orientaliste Paul, SA (France) 98
Ghana Association of Writers (Ghana) 175
Ghana Booksellers' Association (Ghana) 174
Ghana Institute of Management and Public Administration, Library and Documentation Centre (Ghana) 175
Ghana Library Association (Ghana) 175
Ghana Library Board (Ghana) 175
Ghana National Book Development Council (Ghana) 174
Ghana Publishing Corporation (Ghana) 174
Ghana Publishing Corporation, Distribution and Sales Division (Ghana) 175
Ghana Universities Press (Ghana) 174
Gharelu Library Yojna (India) 197
Gheorghiu-Dej, Biblioteca Institutului Politehnic 'Gheorge, Bucuresti (Romania) 305
Ghost Hunters' Library (United Kingdom) 386
Ghulam, Sh, Ali & Sons (Pakistan) 285
Gianotten, Boekhandel, BV (Netherlands) 269
Giao Duc Publishing House (Socialist Republic of Viet Nam) 425
Giappichelli, Giorgio, (Italy) 215
Gibbons, Stanley, (Publications) Ltd (United Kingdom) 386
Gibert, Librairie Joseph, (France) 110
Gibert Jeune Sàrl (France) 98
Gibraltar Bookshop (Gibraltar) 175
Gibraltar Garrison Library (Gibraltar) 176
Gibraltar Junior Bookshop (Gibraltar) 176
Gibraltar Library Service (Gibraltar) 176
Gibralter Book Store (Jordan) 234
Gidlunds Förlag (Sweden) 334

Gidrometeorizdat (Union of Soviet Socialist Republics) 365
Gierows, Karin, Prizes (Sweden) 339
Giertsen, Ed B, A/S (Norway) 283
Gieseking, Verlag Ernst und Werner, (Federal Republic of Germany) 138
Giesserei-Verlag GmbH (Federal Republic of Germany) 139
Gifford, John, Ltd (United Kingdom) 386
Gifford & Craven (Republic of Ireland) 204
Gigord, Editions De, (France) 98
Gilbert, Girault, SPRL (Belgium) 38
Giles Prize (France) 114
Gili, Ediciones G, SA (Argentina) 5
Gili, Editôra Gustavo, do Brasil SA (Brazil) 51
Gili, Editorial Gustavo, de Mexico Sa (Mexico) 251
Gili, Editorial Gustavo, Ltda (Chile) 62
Gili, Editorial Gustavo, Ltda (Colombia) 65
Gili, Editorial Gustavo, SA (Spain) 321
Gill & Macmillan Ltd (Republic of Ireland) 204
Gillani, S I, (Pakistan) 286
Gillardon Verlag GmbH (Federal Republic of Germany) 139
Gilles und Francke Verlag (Federal Republic of Germany) 139
Gilmore, Mary, Award (Australia) 22
Ginn & Co Ltd (United Kingdom) 386
Ginsberg Univ Boekhandel (Netherlands) 269
Giovanis (Greece) 177
Girardet, Verlag W, (Federal Republic of Germany) 139
Gisbert y Cía SA (Bolivia) 47
Gisbert y Cía SA, Comercio 1270-80 (Bolivia) 47
Giuffrè, A, Editore SpA (Italy) 216
Giunti Publishing Group (Italy) 216
Gjellerup, Jul, Forlagsaktieselskab (Denmark) 75
Gjellerups, Jul, Boghandel ApS (Denmark) 78
Glas (Yugoslavia) 427
Glasgow, Mary, Publications Ltd (United Kingdom) 386
Glaven (United Kingdom) 386
Glaxo Travelling Fellowships for Science Writers (United Kingdom) 419
Gleerup, AB C W K, Bokförlag (Sweden) 334
Gleerupska, AB, Universitetsbokhandeln (Sweden) 338
Glem, Editorial, SACIF (Argentina) 5
Glen, Esther, Award (New Zealand) 275
Gleniffer Press (United Kingdom) 386
Global Book Resources Ltd (United Kingdom) 386
Global Editora e Distribuidora Ltda (Brazil) 51
Globetrotter-Verlag (Federal Republic of Germany) 139
Globi Verlag AG (Switzerland) 346
Globo, Editôra, SA (Brazil) 51
Globo, Livraria do, (Brazil) 56
Globus (Yugoslavia) 427
'Globus' Zeitungs-, Druck- und Verlagsanstalt GmbH (Austria) 25
Glock und Lutz Verlag Heroldsberg (Federal Republic of Germany) 139
Glombig, PR Verlag Kurt, (Federal Republic of Germany) 139
Glöss, Verlagsgesellschaft R. und Co (Federal Republic of Germany) 139
Glówna Biblioteka Lekarska (Poland) 296
Glówna Politchniki, Biblioteka, Warszawskiej (Poland) 296
Glówna Uniwersytetu, Biblioteka, im Adama Mickiewicza (Library of Adam Mickiewicz University) (Poland) 296
Glównego Urzedu Statystycznego, Zarzad Wydawnictw, (Publishers of the Central Statistical Office) (Poland) 294
Gluck, Felix, Press Ltd (United Kingdom) 386
Goddard's Bookshop Ltd (New Zealand) 274
Godwin, George, Ltd (United Kingdom) 386
Goede Boek, BV Uitgeversbedrijf Het, (Netherlands) 262
Goel Publishing House (India) 190
Goethe Book Dealers Inc (Japan) 232
Goethe Prize (Federal Republic of Germany) 173
Gold Dagger Award (United Kingdom) 419
Golden Book House (Bangladesh) 32
Golden Book Prize (Italy) 223
Golden Cockerel (United Kingdom) 386
Golden Eagle Award of the Festival International du Livre (International Literary Prizes) 449
Golden Eagle Books Ltd (Republic of Ireland) 204
Golden Feather of the Figaro littéraire (France) 114
Golden Pen Prize (Italy) 223
Golden Pleasure Books Ltd (United Kingdom) 386
Golden Press Pty Ltd (New Zealand) 273
Golden Press Pty Ltd (Australia) 14
Goldex (United Kingdom) 386
Goldmann, Wilhelm, Verlag GmbH (Federal Republic of Germany) 139
Goldschmidt, Viktor, Verlagsbuchhandlung (Switzerland) 346
Goldsmith, The, Press (Republic of Ireland) 204
Goldstadtverlag (Federal Republic of Germany) 139

Gollancz, Victor, Ltd (United Kingdom) 386
Gomer Press (J D Lewis & Sons Ltd) (United Kingdom) 386
Gómez, P A, (Dominican Republic) 80
Goncourt, Editorial y Librería, (Argentina) 5
Goncourt Prize (France) 114
Gondolat Könyvkiadó (Hungary) 182
Gondrom Verlag GmbH & Co Kg (Federal Republic of Germany) 139
Gondu (Burma) 59
Gonin, André et Pierre, (Switzerland) 346
Gonski, Buchhandlung Heinrich, (Federal Republic of Germany) 170
Gonthier, Société Nouvelle des Editions, Sàrl (France) 98
Gonvill, Librerías, de Guadalajara (Mexico) 253
Good Earth Publishing Co (Hong Kong) 180
Good Reading Ltd (United Kingdom) 386
Goodwill Trading Co Ltd (Philippines) 292
Gooise, De, (Uitgeverij) (Netherlands) 262
Goor, G B van, Zonen's Uitgeversmaatschappij BV (Netherlands) 262
Gorachek, V, KG (Federal Republic of Germany) 139
Gorcum, Van, BV (Netherlands) 262
Gordon & Cremonesi (United Kingdom) 386
Gordon and Breach Science Publishers Ltd (United Kingdom) 386
Gorgas Memorial Laboratory Bio-Medical Research Library (Biblioteca Bio-Médica del Laboratorio Conmemorativo Gorgas) (Panama) 288
Gor'kogo Moskovskogo, Nauchnaya biblioteka im A M, gos universiteta im M V Lomonosova (Union of Soviet Socialist Republics) 367
Gor'kovo Leningradskovo, Nauchnaya biblioteka im A M, gosudarstvennovo universiteta im A A Zhdanova (Union of Soviet Socialist Republics) 367
Görlich, Libreria G G, (Italy) 221
Görner, Lutz, (Federal Republic of Germany) 139
Göschl, Alois, & Co (Austria) 25
gosudarstvennaya ordena Trudovogo Krasnogo Znameni biblioteka, Vsesoyuznaya, inostrannoi literatury (Union of Soviet Socialist Republics) 367
Gosudarstvennaya publichnaya istoricheskaya biblioteka RSFSR (Union of Soviet Socialist Republics) 367
Gosudarstvennaya publichnaya nauchno-tekhnicheskaya biblioteka SSSR (Union of Soviet Socialist Republics) 367
Göteborgs Stadsbibliotek (City Library and County Library) (Sweden) 338
Göteborgs Universitetsbibliotek (Sweden) 338
Gotthelf-Verlag (Switzerland) 346
Gottlob, Adam, Oehlenschläger Prize (Denmark) 80
Gottmer Publishers, J H, (Netherlands) 262
Gottmer's, BV v/hB, Uitgeversbedrijf (Netherlands) 262
Gouda, S, Quint (Netherlands) 262
Gouden, Uitgeverij het, Spoor (Belgium) 38
Goudvink, De, NV (Belgium) 38
Goulandris Prize (Greece) 178
Goulden, Henry, Ltd (United Kingdom) 386
Government Archives (Namibia) 257
Government Archives, Cape Archives Depot, Library (Republic of South Africa) 315
Government Archives, Natal Archives Depot, Library (Republic of South Africa) 316
Government Archives, Orange Free State Archives Depot, Library (Republic of South Africa) 316
Government Archives, Transvaal Archives Depot, Library (Republic of South Africa) 316
Government College Library (Pakistan) 286
Government Library (Libya) 242
Government Press (Afghanistan) 1
Government Press, The, (The Gambia) 116
Government Printer (Egypt) 82
Government Printer (Ethiopia) 84
Government Printer (Finland) 86
Government Printer (Algeria) 2
Government Printer (Chad) 61
Government Printer (Burundi) 60
Government Printer (Popular Republic of Congo) 67
Government Printer (United Republic of Cameroun) 61
Government Printer (Benin) 46
Government Printer (Botswana) 48
Government Printer (Democratic Republic of Madagascar) 244
Government Printer (Libya) 242
Government Printer (Lesotho) 240
Government Printer (Kenya) 236
Government Printer (Liberia) 242
Government Printer (Ivory Coast) 224
Government Printer (Somalia) 310
Government Printer (Republic of South Africa) 312
Government Printer (Tanzania) 358
Government Printer (Uganda) 364
Government Printer (Sierra Leone) 308
Government Printer (Zimbabwe) 435
Government Printer (Zambia) 433
Government Printer, Imprimerie Nationale (Upper Volta) 422

Government Printer, The, (Ghana Publishing Corporation, Printing Division) (Ghana) 174
Government Printer (Impressa Nacional de Moçambique) (Mozambique) 256
Government Printer (Imprimerie Centrale d'Afrique) (Gabon) 116
Government Printer (Imprimerie Centrale d'Afrique) (Central African Republic) 61
Government Printer (Imprimerie de Kabgayi) (Rwanda) 306
Government Printer (Imprimerie du Gouvernement Central) (Zaire) 433
Government Printer (Imprimerie du Gouvernement) (Senegal) 307
Government Printer (Imprimerie Générale du Niger) (Niger) 276
Government Printer (**Imprimerie National du Rwanda**) (Rwanda) 306
Government Printer (Imprimerie National) (Mauritius) 249
Government Printer (Imprimerie National) (Malawi) 245
Government Printer (Imprimerie Nationale) (Mali) 248
Government Printer (Imprimerie Nationale) (Mauritania) 249
Government Printer (Imprimerie Officielle de la République Tunisienne) (Tunisia) 362
Government Printer (Imprimerie Officielle) (Morocco) 256
Government Printer Government Printing Press (Sudan) 330
Government Printing Office (Jamaica) 224
Government Public Library (Liberia) 242
Government Publications (Pakistan) 285
Gower Press (United Kingdom) 386
Gower Publishing Co Ltd (United Kingdom) 387
Goyanarte Editor SA (Argentina) 5
Gozo Public Library (Malta) 248
Graaf, De, Publishers (Netherlands) 262
Graal, Edições, Ltda (Brazil) 51
Graal, Ordem do, na Terra (Brazil) 51
Grabert-Verlag (Federal Republic of Germany) 139
Gradina, Izdavačka ustanova, (Yugoslavia) 427
Gradjevinska Knjiga (Yugoslavia) 427
Gräfe und Unzer GmbH (Federal Republic of Germany) 139
Grafia Galaxias (Greece) 177
Grafički zavod Hrvatske (Yugoslavia) 427
Grafisk Forlag A/S (Denmark) 75
Grafos (Yugoslavia) 427
Grafton (United Kingdom) 387
Graham & Trotman Ltd (United Kingdom) 387
Grahame Book Co Pty Ltd (Australia) 19
Gralsbotschaft, Verlag der Stiftung, GmbH (Federal Republic of Germany) 139
Gram Editora (Argentina) 5
Gramedia, PT, (Indonesia) 199
Gramedia, Toko Buku, (Indonesia) 200
Gran América, Editorial, (Colombia) 65
Gran Colombia, Librería La, (Colombia) 66
Gran Premio Nacional de Literatura (Uruguay) 423
Granada Publishing Australia Pty Ltd (Australia) 14
Granada Publishing Ltd (United Kingdom) 387
Grancher, Jacques, Editeur (France) 98
Grand Franco-Belgian Literary Prize (France) 114
Grand Franco-Belgian Literary Prize (Belgium) 46
Grand National Assembly, Library of the, (Turkey) 363
Grand-Pont, Editions du, (Switzerland) 346
Grand Prize (Sweden) 339
Grand Prize for a Book of Poetry (Sweden) 339
Grand Prize for a Novel (Sweden) 339
Grand Prize for Children's Literature (International Literary Prizes) 449
Grand Prize for Literature (France) 114
Grand Prize for Mystery Stories (France) 114
Grand Prize for Poetry Criticism (France) 114
Grand Prize for the Dissemination of the French Language (International Literary Prizes) 449
Grand Prize of French Poets (France) 114
Granda, Editorial Juan Carlos, (Argentina) 5
Grange Batelière SA (France) 98
Granica Editor SA (Argentina) 5
Grant Educational Co Ltd (United Kingdom) 415
Graphic Corporation (Ghana) 174
Graphica-Bezalel (Israel) 207
Graphis, The, Press (Walter Herdeg) (Switzerland) 346
Grasset et Fasquelle, Société des Editions, (France) 98
Grasshopper Books (United Kingdom) 387
Grassin, Jean, Editeur (France) 98
Grassroots Books (Nigeria) 278
Gratien, Emilio, (French Guiana) 116
Graziano, Librería & Editorial Alfa, SACI (Argentina) 5
Graziano, Librería Alfa, (Argentina) 8
Great Austrian State Prize (Austria) 31
Great China Book Corporation (China (Taiwan)) 64
Great English Classics (United Kingdom) 414
Great Mosque of Sana'a, Library of the, (Yemen Arab Republic) 426

Great Publications Co Ltd (China (Taiwan)) 64
Gredos, Editorial, SA (Spain) 321
Green, W, & Son Ltd (United Kingdom) 387
Green Book House Limited (Bangladesh) 32
Greenaway, Kate, Medal (United Kingdom) 419
Greene & Co (Republic of Ireland) 204
Greenhouse Publications (Australia) 14
Greens, E, Forlag (Norway) 282
Greenwood Press (Hong Kong) 180
Gregg International (United Kingdom) 387
Gregorian University Press (Universitá Gregoriana Editrice) (Italy) 216
Gregoriana, Libreria, (Italy) 221
Gregoriana, Libreria Editrice, (Italy) 216
Gregory, Eric, Trust Fund Awards (United Kingdom) 419
Gregory Medal (Republic of Ireland) 205
Gremial de Libreros de Guatemala (Guatemala) 178
Gremio Sindical de Libreros de Barcelona (Association of Barcelona Booksellers) (Spain) 317
Grenfell 'Henry Lawson' Festival Prizes (Australia) 22
Gresham, John, (United Kingdom) 387
Greshoff, J, Prize (Netherlands) 270
Grevas Forlag (Denmark) 75
Greve, Gustav, (Federal Republic of Germany) 169
Greven Verlag Köln (Federal Republic of Germany) 139
Gribaudi, Piero, Editore (Italy) 216
Griegs, John, Forlag (Norway) 282
Griff, Ukvary, Verlag Kiado (Federal Republic of Germany) 139
Griffin, Charles, & Co Ltd (United Kingdom) 387
Griffon, Editions du, (Switzerland) 346
Griggs, T W, & Co (Pty) Ltd (Republic of South Africa) 312
Grigoris, Kass M, (Greece) 177
Grigoris, Kassandra M, (Greece) 177
Grijalbo, Distribuidora exclusivo, SA (Peru) 289
Grijalbo, Ediciones, SA (Spain) 321
Grijalbo, Editorial, Ltda (Brazil) 51
Grijalbo, Editorial, SA (Mexico) 251
Grijalbo Bolivia Ltda (Bolivia) 47
Grijalbo Centroamerica y Panamá SA (Costa Rica) 67
Grijalbo SA (Argentina) 5
Grijalbo SA (Venezuela) 424
Grijalbo y Cía Ltda (Chile) 62
Grijelmo, Artes Gráficas, SA (Spain) 321
Grip, PT, (Indonesia) 200
Grisewood & Dempsey Ltd (United Kingdom) 387
Grolier, The, Society of Australia Pty Ltd (Australia) 14
Grolier de Venezuela (Venezuela) 424
Grøndahl og Søn Forlag A/S (Norway) 282
Grønlandske Forlag, Det, (Denmark) 75
Groos, Julius, Verlag KG (Federal Republic of Germany) 139
Grösschen, Verlag und Landkartenhaus W, KG (Federal Republic of Germany) 139
Grosskopf, J W F, prys vir Drama (Republic of South Africa) 316
Grossman, David, Literary Agency Ltd (United Kingdom) 413
Grossohaus Wegner und Co (Federal Republic of Germany) 170
Grosvenor Books (The Good Road Ltd) (United Kingdom) 387
Groszer, Altberliner Verlag Lucie, (German Democratic Republic) 118
Grote'sche Verlagsbuch-handlung KG (Federal Republic of Germany) 139
Grounauer, Editions François, (Switzerland) 346
Groupe des Editeurs de Livres de la CEE (EEC Book Publishers Group) (International Organizations) 438
Groupe Expansion (France) 99
Gründ, Librairie, (France) 99
Grundlagen, Verlag, und Praxis GmbH & Co (Federal Republic of Germany) 139
Grüner, B R, BV (Netherlands) 262
Grünewald, Matthias-, -Verlag (Federal Republic of Germany) 139
Grupo Bibliografico Nacional de la Republica Dominicana (Dominican Republic) 81
Gruyter, Walter de, & Co, Mouton Publishers (Federal Republic of Germany) 139
Gryphius-Verlag (Federal Republic of Germany) 140
Gryphon Books Pty Ltd (Australia) 14
Guadagni, L'Editrice Scientifica SaS di L G, (Italy) 216
Guadalupe, (Argentina) 5
Guadarrama, Ediciones, (Spain) 321
Guadiana, Grupo Editorial, SA (Spain) 322
Guanabara, Editôra, Koogan SA (Brazil) 51
Guanda Editore SRL (Italy) 216
Guaraldi Editore SpA (Italy) 216
Guardian Award, The, for Children's Fiction (International Literary Prizes) 449
Guardian Fiction, The, Prize (International Literary Prizes) 449
Guazzelli, Livraria Pioneira Editora Enio Matheus, e Cia Ltda (Brazil) 51
Gubblecote, The, Press (United Kingdom) 387

Gudjónssonar, Bókaútgáfa Gudjóns Ó, (Iceland) 185
Guénégaud, Librairie, (France) 99
Guérin et Cie (France) 99
Guhl, Verlag Klaus, (Federal Republic of Germany) 140
Guida Editori SRL (Italy) 216
Guild of Travel Writers (United Kingdom) 418
Guildhall Library (United Kingdom) 416
Guillot, Editions d'Art Albert, (France) 99
Guinness Superlatives Ltd (United Kingdom) 387
Gujarat State English Language Booksellers' Association, Academic Book Centre (India) 186
Gujarat Textbook, The, Publishers' Association (India) 186
Gujarat Vidyapith Granthalaya (India) 197
Gullers International AB (Sweden) 334
Gumekong (Laos) 240
Gummeruksen Kirjakauppa (Finland) 87
Gummerus, K J, Osakeyhtiö (Finland) 86
Gummessons Bokförlag (Sweden) 334
Gumperts Universitetsbokhandel AB (Sweden) 338
Gunasena, M D, & Co Ltd (Sri Lanka) 329
Gundert, D, Verlag (Federal Republic of Germany) 140
Gundolf, Friedrich, Prize for Germanistics abroad (Federal Republic of Germany) 173
Gunung Agung, P T, (Indonesia) 200
Gunung Agung, PT (Indonesia) 200
Gunung Mulia, B P K, (Indonesia) 200
Gunung Mulia, Toko Buku BPK, (Indonesia) 200
Guozi Shudian, China Publications Centre (People's Republic of China) 63
Güse, Verlag August, (Federal Republic of Germany) 140
Gut, Th, & Co Verlag (Switzerland) 346
Gute Schriften Verein, Basel (Switzerland) 346
Gutenberg (Belgium) 38
Gutenberg, Büchergilde, (Switzerland) 356
Gutenberg, Büchergilde, Verlagsgesellschaft mbH (Federal Republic of Germany) 140
Gutenberg, Dardanos, (Greece) 177
Gutenberg-Gesellschaft (Federal Republic of Germany) 140
Gutenberg-Gesellschaft (Gutenberg Society) (Federal Republic of Germany) 173
Gutenberghus Publishing Service (Denmark) 75
Gütersloher Verlagshaus Gerd Mohn (Federal Republic of Germany) 140
Guttentag, Premio de Novela 'Erich, ' (Bolivia) 48
Guyana Library Association (Guyana) 179
Guyana Medical Science Library (Guyana) 179
Guyana National Trading Corporation (Guyana) 179
Guyana Printers Ltd (Guyana) 179
Guyana Society Library (Guyana) 179
Guyra Publishing Co Pty Ltd (Australia) 14
Gyldendal, Søren, Prize (Denmark) 80
Gyldendal Norsk Forlag (Norway) 282
Gyldendals Bogklub (Denmark) 78
Gyldendals Børnebogklub (Denmark) 78
Gyldendalske Boghandel — Nordisk Forlag A/S (Denmark) 75

H & R Academica (Republic of South Africa) 312
H A D U – Hagemann Lehrmittel und Verlagsgesellschaft mbH (Federal Republic of Germany) 140
H A U M (Hollandsch Afrikaansche Uitgevers Maatschappij) (Republic of South Africa) 312
H A U M Academic Bookshop (Republic of South Africa) 315
H A U M Booksellers (Republic of South Africa) 315
H F L (Publishers) Ltd (United Kingdom) 387
H K Health Knowledge Publication (Hong Kong) 180
H M & M Publishers Ltd (United Kingdom) 387
H M S O (United Kingdom) 387
H U C I T E C Ltda—Editora de Humanismo, Ciência e Tecnologia (Brazil) 51
Haack, VEB Hermann, (German Democratic Republic) 118
Haag und Herchen Verlag (Federal Republic of Germany) 140
Haan, Uitg Mij W de, (Netherlands) 262
Haase, P, & Søns Forlag A/S (Denmark) 76
Habbel, Verlag Josef, (Federal Republic of Germany) 140
Habegger, Verlag, AG (Switzerland) 346
Habelt, Rudolf, Verlag GmbH (Federal Republic of Germany) 140
Habib Bank Prize for Literature (Pakistan) 287
Hachette, Groupe International, (France) 99
Hachette, Librairie, (France) 99
Hachette, Librairie, (Egypt) 82
Hachette, Librairie, (Gabon) 116
Hachette, Librairie, (Popular Republic of Congo) 67
Hachette, Librairie, (Central African Republic) 61
Hachette, Librairie, SA do Brasil (Brazil) 56

INDEX

Hachette, Librería, (Argentina) 8
Hachette, Librería, SA (Argentina) 5
Hachette, Livraria, do Brasil SA (Brazil) 52
Hachette, Société congolaise, (Popular Republic of Congo) 67
Hachette — Réalités (France) 99
Hachette (Département International) (Belgium) 38
Hachette Guides Bleus (France) 99
Hachette-Jeunesse (France) 99
Hachette-Littérature (France) 99
Hachette Pratique (France) 99
Hachette/Enseignement (Hachette Educational) (France) 99
Hadar (Israel) 207
Haddock, Peter, Ltd (United Kingdom) 387
Hädecke, Walter, Verlag (Federal Republic of Germany) 140
Hadwiger, Anna, (Austria) 30
Haeschel-Dufey, F. (Switzerland) 346
Hagedorn, Hans Hermann, (Federal Republic of Germany) 169
Hageland, A van, (Belgium) 44
Hagemann, Lehrmittelverlag Wilhelm, (Federal Republic of Germany) 140
Hagen, Ten, BV (Netherlands) 262
Hager, Buchvertrieb, GmbH (Federal Republic of Germany) 140
Hagerups, H. Forlag (Denmark) 76
Hahns, Mary, Kochbuchverlag (Federal Republic of Germany) 140
Haigh & Hochland Ltd (United Kingdom) 415
Hain, Dr Franz, (Austria) 30
Hain, Dr Franz, (Austria) 25
Hain, Verlag Anton, KG (Federal Republic of Germany) 140
Haji Abdullah Jan Barban & Co (Afghanistan) 1
Haji Hashim bin Haji Abdullah (Republic of Singapore) 310
Hak Won Sa (Republic of Korea) 238
Hakibbutz Hameuchad Publishing House Ltd (Israel) 207
Hakkert, Adolf M, BV (Netherlands) 262
Hakki Biçeç (Turkey) 363
Hakkim's Bookshop (Bangladesh) 32
Hakusui-Sha (Japan) 226
Hakuyu-Sha (Japan) 226
Halbart, Librairie, (Belgium) 44
Hale, Robert, Ltd (United Kingdom) 387
Halévy, Editions Dominique, (France) 99
Hali Prize (India) 198
Halk Kütüphanesi, Il, (Provincial Public Library (Turkey) 363
Haller, Berchtold, Verlag (Switzerland) 346
Hallwag Verlag (Federal Republic of Germany) 140
Hallwag Verlag AG (Switzerland) 346
Hamar, Haraldur J, (Iceland) 185
Hamburger Fremdenblatt Broschek und Co (Federal Republic of Germany) 140
Hamburger Kommissionsbuchhandlung GmbH (Federal Republic of Germany) 170
Hamburger Lesehefte Verlag Iselt und Co Nfl mbH (Federal Republic of Germany) 140
Hamburgo, Librería, Antonio Navarrete (Mexico) 254
Hamdard National Foundation (Pakistan) 285
Hameau, Le, Editeur (France) 99
Hamenorah Publishers Ltd (Israel) 207
Hamidia Library (Bangladesh) 32
Hamilton, Hamish, Ltd (United Kingdom) 387
Hamlyn, Paul, Pty Ltd (Australia) 14
Hamlyn, The, Publishing Group Ltd (United Kingdom) 387
Hammer, Peter, Verlag GmbH (Federal Republic of Germany) 140
Hammicks Wholesale (United Kingdom) 415
Hampton House Productions Ltd (United Kingdom) 388
Hampton Press Features Syndicate (Australia) 19
Hamrun Library (Malta) 248
Hanau, Heinrich, Publications Ltd (United Kingdom) 388
Handsel, The, Press (United Kingdom) 388
Hanguk Seoji Hakhoe (Korean Bibliographical Society) (Republic of Korea) 239
Hanguk Tosogwan Hakhoe (Korean Library Science Society) (Republic of Korea) 239
Hanna, Fred, Ltd (Republic of Ireland) 204
Hans Publishers (India) 190
Hansa Publishers Ltd (Sri Lanka) 329
Hansa Verlag Heinz W Hass (Federal Republic of Germany) 140
Hansen, Bjorn, (Denmark) 78
Hansen, Edition Wilhelm, (Denmark) 76
Hansen House (London) Ltd (United Kingdom) 388
Hansen Teaterförlag, Folmer, (Sweden) 337
Hanser, Carl, Verlag (Federal Republic of Germany) 140
Hänssler-Verlag (Federal Republic of Germany) 141
Hansson och Bruce, Söderbokhandeln, AB (Sweden) 338
Hanssons, Kalleberger Foundation — The Tekla, and Gösta Ronnströms Prize (Sweden) 339

Hanstein, Peter, Verlag GmbH (Federal Republic of Germany) 141
Hanthawaddy Book House (Burma) 59
Hanthawaddy Bookshop (Burma) 59
Haraucourt, Edmond, Prize (France) 114
Harbra (Brazil) 52
Harcourt Brace Jovanovich Group (Australia) Pty Ltd (Australia) 14
Harcourt Brace Jovanovich Ltd (United Kingdom) 388
Hardy, Thomas, Society Ltd (United Kingdom) 418
Hargreen Publishing Co (Australia) 14
Harla (Brazil) 52
Harla (Mexico) 251
Harlekin-Presse (Federal Republic of Germany) 141
Harley & Jones (United Kingdom) 388
Harleyford Publications (United Kingdom) 388
Harmonie, De, (Netherlands) 262
Harper & Row, Editora, do Brasil Ltda (Brazil) 52
Harper & Row (Australasia) Pty Ltd (Australia) 14
Harper & Row Latinoamericana-Harla, SA de CV (Mexico) 251
Harper & Row Ltd (United Kingdom) 388
Harrach und Sabrow (Federal Republic of Germany) 141
Harrap, George G, & Co Ltd (United Kingdom) 388
Harrassowitz, Otto, (Federal Republic of Germany) 170
Harrassowitz, Verlag Otto, (Federal Republic of Germany) 141
Harriers Bokforlag AB (Sweden) 334
Harris, Firma, (Indonesia) 200
Harris, Katrine, Award (Republic of South Africa) 316
Harris, Paul, Publishing (United Kingdom) 388
Harrods Ltd (United Kingdom) 415
Harrow House Editions Ltd (United Kingdom) 388
Hart-Davis, MacGibbon Ltd (United Kingdom) 388
Hart-Davis Educational Ltd (United Kingdom) 388
Hart Mossman & Co Ltd (Nigeria) 280
Hartmann, Verlag Karlheinz, (Federal Republic of Germany) 141
Harvard, John, Lending Library (Bahamas) 32
Harvard University Press (United Kingdom) 388
Harvester, The, Press (United Kingdom) 388
Harvill Press Ltd (United Kingdom) 388
Harwalik, Verlag, KG (Federal Republic of Germany) 141
Harwood Academic Publishers GmbH (Switzerland) 346
Hasanuddin University, Library of, (Indonesia) 201
Hasbach, A L, (Austria) 30
Haset Kitabevi AS (Turkey) 363
Háskólabókasafn (Iceland) 186
Hatchards Ltd (United Kingdom) 415
Hatier, Librairie, SA (France) 99
Hatje, Verlag Gerd, GmbH (Federal Republic of Germany) 141
Hatta, Perpustakaan Jajasan, (Hatta Foundation Library) (Indonesia) 201
Hatzipatera Prize (Greece) 178
Haude und Spener Verlag (Federal Republic of Germany) 141
Haufe, Rudolf, Verlag (Federal Republic of Germany) 141
Haug, Karl F, Verlag GmbH und Co (Federal Republic of Germany) 141
Haupt, Paul, Bern (Switzerland) 346
Hauptverband der graphischen Unternehmungen Österreichs (Austria) 23
Hauptverband des österreichischen Buchhandels (Austria) 23
Haus, Volksbuchhandlung, des Buches (German Democratic Republic) 120
Haus der Bibel (Switzerland) 346
Hauschild, Verlag H M, GmbH (Federal Republic of Germany) 141
Hauswedell, Dr Ernst, und Co (Federal Republic of Germany) 141
Hautot, Pierre, SA (France) 99
Havaux, Imprimeries, (Belgium) 38
Have, Uitgeverij ten, NV (Netherlands) 262
Havez-Planque, Marie, Prize (France) 114
Hawthorn, The, Press Pty Ltd (Australia) 14
Hawthornden Prize (United Kingdom) 419
Hayakawa Publishing Inc (Japan) 226
Hayez, Imprimerie, SPRL (Belgium) 38
Haynes Publishing Group (United Kingdom) 388
Hazan, Fernand, Editeur SA (France) 99
Hazewinkel, R, Jnz's Uitg Mij BV (Netherlands) 262
Health Science Press (Leslie J Speight Ltd) (United Kingdom) 388
Heath, A M, & Co Ltd (United Kingdom) 413
Heatherbank Press (United Kingdom) 388
Heckners Verlag (Federal Republic of Germany) 141
Heenemann, H, Verlagsgesellschaft mbH (Federal Republic of Germany) 141
Heering-Verlag GmbH (Federal Republic of Germany) 141
Heffer, W, & Sons Ltd (United Kingdom) 415
Heibonsha Ltd, Publishers (Japan) 226
Heibrand (Belgium) 38

Heideland, Boekhandel, (Belgium) 44
Heideland NV (Belgium) 38
Heideland-Orbis NV (Belgium) 38
Heideland PVBA (Belgium) 38
Heidmük-Verlag Günther U Müller (Federal Republic of Germany) 141
Heidrich, Leopold, (Austria) 30
Heima er Bezt Book Club (Iceland) 185
Heimatland Verlag (Austria) 25
Heimeran, Ernst, Verlag (Federal Republic of Germany) 141
Heimskringla (Iceland) 185
Heinemann,, Verlag Egon, Chronik der Seefahrt (Federal Republic of Germany) 141
Heinemann, William, (New Zealand) Ltd (New Zealand) 273
Heinemann, William, Australia Pty Ltd (Australia) 14
Heinemann, William, Ltd (United Kingdom) 388
Heinemann Award for Literature (United Kingdom) 419
Heinemann Educational Australia Pty Ltd (Australia) 14
Heinemann Educational Books (Asia) Ltd (Malaysia) 246
Heinemann Educational Books (Asia) Ltd (Hong Kong) 180
Heinemann Educational Books (East Africa) Ltd (Kenya) 235
Heinemann Educational Books (International) Ltd (United Kingdom) 389
Heinemann Educational Books (New Zealand) Ltd (New Zealand) 273
Heinemann Educational Books (Nigeria) Limited (Nigeria) 278
Heinemann Educational Books Ltd (United Kingdom) 389
Heinemann Group, The, of Publishers Ltd (United Kingdom) 389
Heinemann Medical Books, William, Ltd (United Kingdom) 389
Heinemann/Octopus (United Kingdom) 389
Heinrichshofen's Verlag (Federal Republic of Germany) 141
Heintz, Verlag Georg, (Federal Republic of Germany) 141
Heinzle's, Gebhard, Erben (Austria) 30
Helbing & Lichtenhahn Verlag AG (Switzerland) 346
Helgafell, Bókábudin, (Iceland) 185
Helgafell, Bókaútgáfan, (Iceland) 185
Helicon Press (United Kingdom) 389
Héliographia, Arts Graphiques, SA (Switzerland) 346
Hellenic Distribution Agency (Cyprus) Ltd (Cyprus) 69
Helmond (Netherlands) 262
Help Bookshop (Lebanon) 241
Helsingin Kaupunginkirjasto (Finland) 87
Helsingin Teknillisen Korkeakoulun Kirjasto (Finland) 87
Helsingin Yliopiston Kirjasto (Finland) 87
Helsinki Prize (Finland) 88
Helvetica Chimica Acta-Verlag (Switzerland) 346
Hem i Sverige, Förlags AB, (Sweden) 334
Hemans, Felicia, Prize for Lyrical Poetry (United Kingdom) 420
Hemeroteca Municipal de Madrid (Madrid Periodical Library) (Spain) 328
Hemeroteca Nacional de México (National Periodicals Library) (Mexico) 254
Hemisferio, Editorial, Sur SA (Argentina) 5
Hemkunt Publishers Pvt Ltd (India) 190
Hemma, Editions, (Belgium) 38
Hemmets Journal AB (Sweden) 334
'Hemus' Foreign Trade Company (Bulgaria) 58
Hemus-Livraria Editora Ltda (Brazil) 52
Henderson's Book Store (Jamaica) 224
Henle, G, Verlag (Federal Republic of Germany) 141
Henne, Dagmar, (Federal Republic of Germany) 169
Henny's Forlag (Norway) 282
Henriksens, Edvard, Forlag (Denmark) 76
Henry, Ian, Publications Ltd (United Kingdom) 389
Henschelverlag Kunst und Gesellschaft (German Democratic Republic) 118
Henssel Verlag (Federal Republic of Germany) 141
Her Majesty's Stationery Office (United Kingdom) 389
Herbert, The, Press Ltd (United Kingdom) 389
Herbig, F A, Verlagsbuchhandlung (Federal Republic of Germany) 141
Herdeg:, Walter, The Graphis Press (Switzerland) 346
Herder, Editorial, SA (Spain) 322
Herder, Librería, (Spain) 327
Herder, Verlag, GmbH & Co, KG (Federal Republic of Germany) 142
Herder, Verlag, und Co (Austria) 25
Herder AG (Switzerland) 346
Herder Buchgemeinde (Federal Republic of Germany) 142
Herder Editrice e Libreria (Italy) 216
Herder und Co (Austria) 30
Herder und Herder GmbH (Federal Republic of Germany) 142
Heredia Prize (International Literary Prizes) 449
Hering, Bert, Verlag (Federal Republic of Germany) 142

INDEX 485

Heritage (Israel) 207
Heritage Publishers (India) 190
Hermann (Editeurs des Sciences et des Arts) SA (France) 99
Hermes, Editorial, SA (Mexico) 251
Hermes Prize (France) 114
Hermods (Sweden) 334
Hermods Publishing House (Sweden) 334
Herne, Editions de l', (France) 99
Hernieuwen-Uitgaven PVBA (Belgium) 38
Hernovs Book Club (Denmark) 78
Hernovs Forlag (Denmark) 76
Herold Buch-Club (Federal Republic of Germany) 170
Herold Druck- und Verlagsgesellschaft mbH (Austria) 26
Herold Neue Verlagsgesellschaft GmbH (Federal Republic of Germany) 142
Herold Verlag Brück KG (Federal Republic of Germany) 142
Herold Verlage, Vereinigte, GmbH (Federal Republic of Germany) 142
Heron Books (United Kingdom) 414
Herrera, Casa, (Dominican Republic) 81
Herrera, Febio, (Dominican Republic) 81
Herrero, Editorial, SA (Mexico) 251
Herrero Hermanos Sucesores SA (Mexico) 251
Hertoghs, Drukkerij-Uitgeverij, (Belgium) 38
Hertzog Prize (Republic of South Africa) 316
Herzen, Alexander, Foundation (Netherlands) 262
Herzmansky, Bernhard, (Austria) 26
Herzog August Bibliothek (Federal Republic of Germany) 171
Hessische Landes- und Hoch-schulbibliothek Darmstadt (Federal Republic of Germany) 171
Hessischer Verleger- und Buchhandler-Verband eV (Hessen Publishers' and Booksellers' Federation) (Federal Republic of Germany) 122
Hessling, Bruno, Verlag (Federal Republic of Germany) 142
Hestia Bookstore (Greece) 177
Hestia-Verlag GmbH (Federal Republic of Germany) 142
Heuff, Uitgeverij, (Netherlands) 262
Heureka, Uitgeverij, (Netherlands) 262
Heures Claires, Editions d'Art Les, SA (France) 99
Heusden, Gérard Th van, (APA) (Netherlands) 262
Heyden & Son Ltd (United Kingdom) 389
Heyer, The Georgette, Historical Novel Prize (International Literary Prizes) 449
Heymann, B, Verlag (Federal Republic of Germany) 142
Heymanns, Carl, Verlag KG (Federal Republic of Germany) 142
Heyn, Johannes, (Austria) 26
Heyn, Johannes, (Austria) 30
Heyne, Rolf, Verlag (Switzerland) 346
Heyne, Wilhelm, Verlag (Federal Republic of Germany) 142
Hichtum, Nienke van,van, Prize (Netherlands) 270
Hicks Smith & Sons Pty Ltd (Australia) 14
Hidakarya Agung (Indonesia) 200
Hier et Demain, Editions, (France) 99
Hiersemann, Anton, Verlag (Federal Republic of Germany) 142
High Council of Arts & Literature (Egypt) 83
High Court of Australia Library (Australia) 20
Higham, David, Associates Ltd (United Kingdom) 413
Higham, David, Prize for Fiction (International Literary Prizes) 449
Higher Educational Books Publishing House (Democratic People's Republic of Korea) 237
Higher School, Library of the, of Engineering (Lebanon) 241
Higher Teachers' Training Institute Library (Sudan) 330
Hikarinokuni Co Ltd (Japan) 227
Hilal, Dar Al-, Publishing House (Egypt) 82
Hildur, Bókaútgáfan, (Iceland) 185
Hilger, Adam, Ltd (United Kingdom) 389
Hilger, Edition E, (Austria) 26
Hill, Leonard, (United Kingdom) 389
Hill of Content Publishing Co Ltd (Australia) 14
Himachal Publishers' & Booksellers' Association (India) 186
Himalaya Prakashan (India) 190
Himalaya Publishing House (India) 190
Hind Pocket Books Private Ltd (India) 190
Hinder und Deelmann, Verlag, (Federal Republic of Germany) 142
Hindi Book Centre (India) 190
Hindustan Publishing Corporation (India) (India) 190
Hinstorff, VEB, Verlag (German Democratic Republic) 118
Hinterhaus, Gruppe, (Federal Republic of Germany) 142
Hinzelin, Emile, Prize (France) 114
Hippoboek/Studio de Zuid (Netherlands) 262
Hippokrates Verlag GmbH (Federal Republic of Germany) 142
Hirmer Verlag, Gesellschaft für Wissenschaftliches Lichtbild GmbH (Federal Republic of Germany) 142
Hirokawa Publishing Co (Japan) 227

Hirsch, Axel, Prize (Sweden) 339
Hirsch, Carlos, SRL (Argentina) 8
Hirschsprungs, H, Forlag (Denmark) 76
Hirt, Ferdinand, (Federal Republic of Germany) 142
Hirt, Ferdinand, mbH & Co KG (Austria) 26
Hirzel, S, Verlag GmbH und Co (Federal Republic of Germany) 142
Hispanas, Ediciones, (Guatemala) 179
Hispano Americana, Librería, (Spain) 327
Hispano Europea, Editorial, (Spain) 322
Hispanoamericana, Librería, (Puerto Rico) 302
Hissink, G W, & Co (APA) (Netherlands) 262
Histoire et d'Art, Editions d', J & R Wittman (France) 99
Histoire Sociale, Editions d', EDHIS (France) 99
Historical Society of Afghanistan (Afghanistan) 1
History Guild (United Kingdom) 414
History of Art, The, (United Kingdom) 414
Hjemmenes Forlag A/S (Norway) 282
Hjemmet A/s (Norway) 282
Hjorts Forlag ApS (Denmark) 76
Hladbúd hf (Iceland) 185
Hlidskjálf, Bókaútgáfan, (Iceland) 185
Hna Lon Hla (Burma) 59
Hobby, Editorial, (Argentina) 5
Hobby Centre (Trinidad and Tobago) 361
Hobsons Press (Cambridge) Ltd (United Kingdom) 389
Hoch-Verlag (Federal Republic of Germany) 143
Hodder & Stoughton (Australia) Pty Ltd (Australia) 14
Hodder & Stoughton Children's Books (United Kingdom) 389
Hodder & Stoughton Ltd (United Kingdom) 389
Hodder & Stoughton Ltd (New Zealand) 273
Hodemacher, Münchner Verlagsbüro Horst, -Axel Poldner GmbH & Co KG (Federal Republic of Germany) 169
Hodge, Alison, (United Kingdom) 389
Hodges Figgis & Co Ltd (Republic of Ireland) 204
Hodgson, Francis, (United Kingdom) 389
Hoepli, Casa Editrice Libraria Ulrico, SpA (Italy) 216
Hoepli, Ulrico, Libreria Internazionale (Italy) 221
Hoernle, Volksbuchhandlung Edwin, (German Democratic Republic) 120
Hofacker Ing W GmbH Verlag (Federal Republic of Germany) 143
Hofbauer, Buchhandlung Karl, (Austria) 30
Hoffman, Agence, (France) 110
Hoffman, Agence, (Federal Republic of Germany) 169
Hoffmann, Dieter, Verlag (Federal Republic of Germany) 143
Hoffmann, Julius, Verlag (Federal Republic of Germany) 143
Hoffmann und Campe Verlag (Federal Republic of Germany) 143
Hofmann, Verlag Karl, (Federal Republic of Germany) 143
Hofmeister, VEB Friedrich, Musikverlag (German Democratic Republic) 118
Hofmeyr, W A, Prize (Republic of South Africa) 317
Hogar del Libro (Spain) 327
Hogarth, The, Press Ltd (United Kingdom) 389
Hogrefe, Verlag für Psychologie Dr C J, (Switzerland) 346
Hohenloher Druck- und Verlagshaus (Federal Republic of Germany) 143
Hohenstaufen Verlag Schumann KG (Federal Republic of Germany) 143
Hohmann, Grafikverlag, (Federal Republic of Germany) 143
Hoi Ming Book Store (Hong Kong) 181
Hôi Thu-Viên Viet Nam (Socialist Republic of Viet Nam) 426
Hoikusha Publishing Co Ltd (Japan) 227
Hökerbergs, Lars, Bokförlag (Sweden) 334
Hokkaido University Library (Japan) 232
Hokuryukan Co Ltd (Japan) 227
Hokuseido, The, PreP (Japan) 227
Holberg Medal (Denmark) 80
Holgersson, Nils, Plaque (Sweden) 339
Holkema en Warendorf, Van, (Netherlands) 262
Hölker, Verlag Wolfgang, (Federal Republic of Germany) 143
Holland (Netherlands) 262
Holland, The, Press (United Kingdom) 390
Holland University Press, BV (APA) (Netherlands) 262
Hollandia BV (Netherlands) 262
Hollandsche Boekhandel (Netherlands Antilles) 271
Holle Verlag GmbH (Federal Republic of Germany) 143
Hollinek, Brüder, und Co GmbH (Austria) 26
Hollis & Carter (United Kingdom) 390
Hollriegl, Eduard, (Austria) 30
Hollym Corporation (Republic of Korea) 238
Holmes, The Sherlock, Society of London (United Kingdom) 418
Holmes McDougall Ltd (United Kingdom) 390
Holon Literary Prize (Israel) 211
Holp BJ Co Ltd (Japan) 227
Holsten Verlag GmbH und Co KG (Federal Republic of Germany) 143

Holt-Blond Ltd (United Kingdom) 390
Holt-Saunders Ltd (United Kingdom) 390
Holt-Saunders Pty Ltd (New Zealand) 273
Holt-Saunders Pty Ltd (Australia) 14
Holtby, Winifred, Memorial Prize (United Kingdom) 420
Holy Land Map Co Ltd (Israel) 207
Holzapfel, Verlag Gebr, (Federal Republic of Germany) 143
Holzboog, Gunther, GmbH & Co (Federal Republic of Germany) 143
Holzbein, Hans, Verlag (Federal Republic of Germany) 143
Holzmann, Hans, Verlag GmbH und Co KG (Federal Republic of Germany) 143
Home and Garden Guild (United Kingdom) 414
Home Health Education Service (United Kingdom) 390
Home Products Ltd (Fiji) 85
Hommes et Techniques, Editions, (France) 100
Hone, Evelyn, College Library (Zambia) 434
Hong Kong Book Centre (Hong Kong) 181
Hong Kong Booksellers' & Stationers' Association (Hong Kong) 180
Hong Kong Cultural Press Ltd (Hong Kong) 181
Hong Kong Educational Publishers Association Ltd (Hong Kong) 180
Hong Kong Junior Chamber of Commerce Libraries (Hong Kong) 181
Hong Kong Library Association (Hong Kong) 181
Hong Kong Polytechnic Library (Hong Kong) 181
Hong Kong Publications (Hong Kong) 181
Hong Kong Publishers' & Distributors' Association (Hong Kong) 180
Hong Kong University Press (Hong Kong) 181
Hong Kong Witman Publishing Co (Hong Kong) 181
Hönsetryk, Forlaget, (Denmark) 76
Hoogenhout, C P, Award (Republic of South Africa) 317
Hoogt, Lucy B en C W van der, -prijs (Netherlands) 271
Hoorick, Van, Verlag (Switzerland) 346
Hopkins, The, Society (United Kingdom) 418
Hor Samut Klang (Thailand) 359
Horatio-verlag und Agentur (Federal Republic of Germany) 143
Horay, Pierre, Editeur (France) 100
Horizon Bookshop Ltd (New Zealand) 274
Horizons, Editions, de France (France) 100
Horizonte, Editorial, (Peru) 289
Horizonte, Editorial, (Peru) 290
Horizonte, Livros, Lda (Portugal) 299
Horizontes, Editora, de América (Dominican Republic) 80
Hörnemann, Werner, Verlag (Federal Republic of Germany) 143
Horseman's Bookclub (United Kingdom) 414
Horst-Werner Dumjahn Verlag (Federal Republic of Germany) 143
Horwitz Group Books Pty Ltd (Australia) 15
Horwood, Ellis, Ltd (United Kingdom) 390
'Horyzonty', Wydawnictwo Harcerskie, (Poland) 294
Høst og Søns Forlag (Denmark) 76
Hour-Glass Press (United Kingdom) 390
Hove, M van, DPN (Belgium) 38
Hövrings, Birgitte, Biblioteksforlag (Denmark) 76
How & Why Books (United Kingdom) 390
Howard & Wyndham Ltd (United Kingdom) 390
Howard Book Co (Hong Kong) 181
Hraundragni Book Club (Iceland) 185
Hrvatska Revija (Spain) 322
Hrvatsko bibliotekarsko društvo (Yugoslavia) 431
Hsinhua New China Book Agency (People's Republic of China) 63
Hua Kuo Publishing Co (China (Taiwan)) 64
Huber, Edition Volker, (Federal Republic of Germany) 143
Huber, Hans, (Switzerland) 356
Huber, Verlag, & Co AG (Switzerland) 346
Huber Medical, Hans, Publisher (Switzerland) 346
Hudsons Bookshops Ltd (United Kingdom) 415
Hueber, Max, Verlag (Federal Republic of Germany) 143
Hueber-Holzmann, Verlag (Federal Republic of Germany) 143
Huemul, Editorial, SA (Argentina) 5
Huemul, Librería, (Argentina) 5
Huemul, Librería, (Argentina) 8
Hugendubel, Buchhandlung H, (Federal Republic of Germany) 170
Hughes Massie Ltd (United Kingdom) 413
Hugo, The, Awards (International Literary Prizes) 450
Hugo's Language Books Ltd (United Kingdom) 390
Hugues, Clovis, Prize (France) 114
Hulsmanns Reske GmbH (Federal Republic of Germany) 143
Hulton Educational Publications Ltd (United Kingdom) 390
Human & Rousseau Publishers (Pty) Ltd (Republic of South Africa) 312
Humanismo, Editora de, Ciência e Tecnologia (Brazil) 52
Humanitas, Editorial, (Argentina) 6
Humanoïdes, Les, Associés (France) 100
Humata Verlag Harold S Blume (Switzerland) 346

486 INDEX

Humboldt, Volksbuchhandlung Alexander von, (German Democratic Republic) 120
Humboldt-Buchhandlung (German Democratic Republic) 120
Humboldt-Taschenbuchverlag Jacobi KG (Federal Republic of Germany) 143
Humboldt Universität zu Berlin (German Democratic Republic) 120
hundertmark, edition, (Federal Republic of Germany) 143
Hune, La, (France) 100
Hune, Librairie La, (France) 110
Hung Fung Book Co (Hong Kong) 181
Hungarian Foreign Trade Organization (Hungary) 183
Hür Yayin ve Ticaret (Turkey) 363
Hürriyet Yayinlari (Hür Yayin) (Turkey) 363
Hurst, C. & Co (Publishers) Ltd (United Kingdom) 390
Husum Druck- und Verlagsgesellschaft mbH und Co KG (Federal Republic of Germany) 143
Hutchinson Educational (United Kingdom) 390
Hutchinson General Books Ltd (United Kingdom) 390
Hutchinson Group (Australia) Ltd (Australia) 15
Hutchinson Group (NZ) Ltd (New Zealand) 273
Hutchinson Group (SA) (Pty) Ltd (Republic of South Africa) 312
Hutchinson Junior Books (United Kingdom) 390
Hutchinson Publishing Group, The, Ltd (United Kingdom) 390
Hutchinson Technical Books (United Kingdom) 390
Hutchinson University Library (United Kingdom) 390
Hüthig, Dr Alfred, Verlag GmbH (Federal Republic of Germany) 144
Hüthig & Wepf Verlag (Switzerland) 347
Hüthig und Pflaum Verlag GmbH & Co KG (Federal Republic of Germany) 144
Hutten, Ulrich v, Volksbuchhandlung (German Democratic Republic) 120
Huygens, Constantijn, Prize (Netherlands) 271
Hviezdoslavova knižnica (Czechoslovakia) 72
Hwimoon Publishing Co (Republic of Korea) 238
Hyangmun Sa (Republic of Korea) 238
Hyderabad, The, & Secunderabad Publishers' & Booksellers' Association (India) 186
Hyfte, Van, -De Coninck (Belgium) 38
Hylton Lacy Publishers (United Kingdom) 390
Hyoronsha Publishing Co Ltd (Japan) 227
Hyun Am Sa (Republic of Korea) 238
Hyun Dae Mun Hak (Republic of Korea) 239

I B A M (Brazil) 52
I B I (India) 190
I B I S (United Kingdom) 369
I B R A S A (Institução Brasileira de Difusão Cultural SA) (Brazil) 52
I B R E X- Distribuidora de Livros e Material de Escritório Ltda (Brazil) 56
I C A-Förlaget AB (Sweden) 334
I C C E, Publicaciones, (Spain) 322
I C I C (Directory Publishers) Ltd (Nigeria) 278
I C I Writing Bursary (New Zealand) 275
I C Magazines Ltd (United Kingdom) 390
I C S Izdavačko Informativni Centar Studenata (Yugoslavia) 427
I C U, NV, (Informatie en Communicatie Unie NV) (Netherlands) 262
I C U — Belgie, NV (Belgium) 38
I d W₂Verlag GmbH (Federal Republic of Germany) 144
I G A, Distribuidora Cultural, (Guatemala) 179
I L A (International Literary Agency) (Italy) 221
I L E X I M — Foreign Trade Enterprise (Romania) 304
I L S (Institut für Lernsysteme) GmbH (Federal Republic of Germany) 144
I N A D E S — Edition (Institut africain pour le developpement économique et social) (Ivory Coast) 224
I N A D E S (Institut africain pour le Développement économique et social) Documentation (Ivory Coast) 224
I N I D (Romania) 305
I P C (United Kingdom) 390
I P E A (Instituto de Planejamento Econômico e Social) Servico Editorial (Brazil) 52
I P L (Istituto Propaganda Libraria) (Italy) 212
i-Punkt (Federal Republic of Germany) 144
I S P-Verlag (Internationale Sozialistische Publikationen) (Federal Republic of Germany) 144
I T A U, Edições, (Instituto Tecnico de Alimentação Humana) Lda (Portugal) 299
I V A C SA (Belgium) 38
I V A Verlag Bernd Polke GmbH (Federal Republic of Germany) 144
I V I O, Stichting, (Netherlands) 263
Ibadan University Library (Nigeria) 280
Ibadan University Press (Nigeria) 278
Ibana, SA (Uruguay) 423
Ibérico Europea de Ediciones SA (Spain) 322
Iberlibros — Unidad de Exportación (Spain) 322

Ibero-Americano, Livro, (Brazil) 56
Ibero-Americano, Livro, Ltda (Brazil) 52
Ibero-Amerikanisches Institut (Federal Republic of Germany) 171
Ibn-Sina Publishers (Iran) 201
Ibnassus Presse (Federal Republic of Germany) 144
Iceland Review (Iceland) 185
Iceland Travel Books (Iceland) 185
Icelandic Libertarians', The, Book Club (Iceland) 185
Icelandic Libertarians', The, Bookshop (Iceland) 185
Ichtiar Baru (Indonesia) 200
Icob (Netherlands) 263
Icon (Belgium) 45
Icthus, Librería, (Bolivia) 47
Idara-e-Faroghe-Undu (Pakistan) 285
Idara Siqafat-e-Islamia (Pakistan) 285
Idea Books (United Kingdom) 390
Idea Books Distribution SA (France) 100
Idéa Editions (Switzerland) 347
Idea Editions (Italy) 216
Ideal, The, Bookshop (Malta) 248
Ideal Leather, The, Store Ltd (Trinidad and Tobago) 361
Ideeboek BV (Netherlands) 263
Ides et Calendes SA (Switzerland) 347
Idion Verlag (Federal Republic of Germany) 144
Idunn (Iceland) 185
Ie-No-Hikari Association (Japan) 227
Ife Book Fair Prizes (Nigeria) 281
Igaku-Shoin Ltd (Japan) 227
Igbo Language Translation Agency (Nigeria) 281
Igloo Promotions Ltd (United Kingdom) 391
Ikaros Ekdotiki (Greece) 177
Ikatan Penerbit Indonesia (IKAPI) (Association of Indonesian Book Publishers) (Indonesia) 199
Ikatan Pustakawan Indonesia (Indonesian Library Association) (Indonesia) 201
Ikhwan, PD & I, (Indonesia) 200
Ikubundo Publishers Co (Japan) 232
Il Cho Kak (Republic of Korea) 238
Il Ji Sa (Republic of Korea) 238
Il Shinsa (Republic of Korea) 238
Ilesanmi Press & Sons (N) Ltd (Nigeria) 278
Ilidio da Fonseca Matos (Portugal) 301
Illustration, Éditions de l', (France) 100
Ilm, Dar al-, Bookshop (Saudi Arabia) 306
Ilm, Dar el-, Lilmalayin (Lebanon) 241
Ilmi Kitab Khana (Pakistan) 285
Image (United Kingdom) 391
Imba Verlag (Switzerland) 347
Imha (Greece) 177
Immermann Prize (Federal Republic of Germany) 173
Impact (Australia) 15
Impacto, Editôrial e Serviços Ltda (Brazil) 52
Imparudi (Burundi) 60
Imperial Library (Iran) 202
Imperial News Agency and Bookshop (Gibraltar) 176
Imprensa Nacional-Casa da Moeda (Portugal) 299
Impressum Verlag AG (Switzerland) 347
Imprimerie, Editions, Fédérative SA Berne (Switzerland) 347
Imprimerie Commerciale et Administrative de Mauritanie (Mauritania) 249
Imprint Society (Australia) 10
Impulso (Mexico) 251
In, Uitgeverij J van, (Belgium) 38
In den Toren, Uitgeverij, (Netherlands) 263
Inca, Promotion Editorial, SA (Peru) 289
Independent Publishers Guild (United Kingdom) 369
Index, Editorial, (Tormes, SL) (Spain) 322
Index eV (Federal Republic of Germany) 144
India Book House (India) 197
India Book House (India) 190
India Book House Education Trust (India) 190
India Book House Private Ltd (India) 190
India Office Library and Records (United Kingdom) 416
Indian Association of Special Libraries and Information Centres (India) 197
Indian Association of Teachers of Library Science (India) 197
Indian Association of University Presses, Calcutta University Press (India) 186
Indian Bibliographic Centre (India) 190
Indian Book Industry (India) 190
Indian Council for Cultural Relations (India) 190
Indian Council of Agricultural Research (India) 190
Indian Council of World Affairs Library (India) 197
Indian Institute of Technology Central Library (India) 197
Indian Library Association (India) 197
Indian Museum (India) 190
Indian National Academy of Letters (Sahitya Akademi) Awards (India) 198
Indian National Scientific Documentation Centre (INSDOC) (India) 197
Indian Press (Publications) Pvt Ltd (India) 190
Indian Printing and Publishing Co (Fiji) 85
Indian Publications (India) 190

Indira, P T, (Indonesia) 200
Indira, P T, (Indonesia) 200
Indrajaya (Indonesia) 200
Industrias ABC (Angola) 2
Industrias ABC (Angola) 2
Industrielle Organisation, Verlag, (Switzerland) 347
Industrielle Rettsvern, Styret for det, Bibliotek (Library of the Norwegian Patent Office) (Norway) 283
Industry & Trade Publishers (Philippines) 291
Industry Publishing House (Democratic People's Republic of Korea) 237
Info Book (Sweden) 337
Infoboek (Belgium) 38
Inform-Verlag (Federal Republic of Germany) 144
Información, La, (Dominican Republic) 80
Information Processing Association of Israel (Israel) 211
Informations Forlag ApS (Denmark) 76
Informations-Zentrum Buch (Book Information Centre) (Federal Republic of Germany) 122
Informator (Yugoslavia) 428
Ingeniero, Librería del, (Colombia) 66
Ingenjörsvetenskapsakademien (I V A) (Sweden) 334
Inicio, Editorial, (Portugal) 300
Initial Teaching Publishing Co (United Kingdom) 391
Inkata Press Pty Ltd (Australia) 15
Inkilap Ve Aka Kitabevleri (Turkey) 363
Inland Publishers (Tanzania) 358
Inn-Verlag (Austria) 26
Innkaupasamband Boksala (Booksellers' Import Union Ltd) (Iceland) 184
Innovacion, Editorial, SA (Mexico) 251
Inquérito, Editorial, Lda (Portugal) 300
Insel (Federal Republic of Germany) 144
Insel-Verlag Anton Kippenberg (German Democratic Republic) 118
Instituição Brasileira de Difusão Cultural SA (Brazil) 52
Institut, Bibliothèque de l', français d'Archéologie (Lebanon) 241
Institut, Perpustakaan Pusat, Teknologi Bandung (Central Library, Bandung Institute of Technology) (Indonesia) 201
Institut africain de Développement économique et de Planification (Senegal) 307
Institut belge d'Information et de Documentation (INBEL) (Belgium) 44
Institut Bouddhique, Bibliothèque de l', (Kampuchea) 235
Institut Culturel Français Bibliothèque (Libya) 242
Institut Dagang Muchtar (Indonesia) 200
Institut de Bibliothéconomie et des Sciences Documentaires (Institute of Library Management and Documentary Science) (Algeria) 2
Institut de France, Bibliothèque de l', (France) 111
Institut d'Egypte Library (Egypt) 83
Institut des Belles Lettres arabes (Tunisia) 362
Institut fondamental d'Afrique noire (Senegal) 307
Institut français d'Archéologie orientale (Egypt) 83
Institut für Dokumentations-wesen (Institute for Documentation Science) (Federal Republic of Germany) 172
Institut für Heilpädagogik Verlag, (Therapeutic Pedagogy Institute Publishing House) (Switzerland) 347
Institut für Jugendbuchforschung der J W Goethe-Universität (Federal Republic of Germany) 172
Institut für Lernsysteme (ILS) (Federal Republic of Germany) 144
Institut für Marxistische Studien und Forschungen eV (IMSF) Frankfurt/AM (Institute for Marxist Studies and Research) (Federal Republic of Germany) 144
Institut Murundi d'Information et de Documentation (IMIDOC) (Burundi) 60
Institut national, Bibliothèque de l'. des Langues et Civilisations orientales (France) 111
Institut national, Librairie de l', d'Etudes politiques (Zaire) 433
Institut national de Recherches et Documentation (National Research and Documentation Institute) (Guinea) 179
Institut national de Sténodactylographie (Belgium) 38
Institut pédagogique national (Zaire) 433
Institut polytechnique de Conakry (Guinea) 179
Institut polytechnique de l'Afrique centrale (Gabon) 116
Institut royal des Relations internationales (Koninklijk Instituut voor Internationale Betrekkingen) (Belgium) 38
Institut royal des Sciences naturelles de Belgique, Service de Documentation (Belgium) 44
Institut scientifique chérifien (Morocco) 256
Institut Universitaire de Hautes Etudes Internationales (Switzerland) 347
Institute, Central, for Scientific and Technical Information (of the State Committee for Science, Technical Progress and Higher Education) (Bulgaria) 58
Institute, The, for the Translation of Hebrew Literature Ltd (Israel) 211
Institute, The, for the Translation of Hebrew Literature Ltd (Israel) 206

INDEX 487

Institute for Palestine Studies, Publishing and Research Organization (Lebanon) 241
Institute for Scientific and Technical Documentation and Information (Yugoslavia) 431
Institute for the Talmudic Encyclopaedia and Complete Israeli Talmud (Israel) 207
Institute of Arab Research & Studies Library (Egypt) 83
Institute of Economics Library (Burma) 59
Institute of Education Library (Burma) 59
Institute of Education Library, Kabul University (Afghanistan) 1
Institute of Information Scientists (United Kingdom) 416
Institute of Personnel Management (United Kingdom) 391
Institute of Petroleum (United Kingdom) 391
Institute of Physics, The, (United Kingdom) 391
Institute of Public Administration (Republic of Ireland) 204
Institute of Public Administration Library (Saudi Arabia) 306
Institute of Pyramidology (United Kingdom) 391
Institute of Reprographic Technology (United Kingdom) 416
Institute of Southeast Asian Studies (Republic of Singapore) 309
Institute of Technology Library (Burma) 60
Institution of Civil Engineers, The, (Publications Division) (United Kingdom) 391
Institution of Electrical Engineers (United Kingdom) 391
Instituto, Biblioteca del, Chileno-Británico de Cultura (Chile) 63
Instituto Anglo-Mexicano de Cultura, Biblioteca del, (British Council Library) (Mexico) 254
Instituto Bibliográfico Hispánico (Spain) 328
Instituto Brasileiro de Administraçao Municipal (IBAM) (Brazil) 52
Instituto Brasileiro de Edições Pedagógicas (IBEP) (Brazil) 52
Instituto Brasileiro de Geografia, Fundação, e Estatística (Brazil) 52
Instituto Brasileiro de Informação em Ciência e Tecnologia (IBICT) (Brazilian Institute for Information in Science and Technology) (Brazil) 56
Instituto Brasileiro de Informação em Ciência e Tecnologia (IBICT) (Brazilian Institute for Information in Science and Technology) (Brazil) 52
Instituto Campineiro de Ensino Agrícola e Comércio Ltda (Brazil) 52
Instituto Centro Americano de Administración Pública (ICAP) (Costa Rica) 67
Instituto Cubano del Libro (Cuba) 68
Instituto Cultural, Biblioteca del, Anglo-Uruguayo (Anglo-Uruguayan Cultural Institute Library) (Uruguay) 423
Instituto de Bibliográfia del Ministerio de Educación de la Provincia de Buenos Aires (Argentina) 9
Instituto de Cultura Puertorriqueña (Puerto Rico) 302
Instituto de Estudios de Administración Local, Publicaciones (Spain) 322
Instituto de Estudios Peruanos (Peru) 289
Instituto de Estudios Politicos (Spain) 322
Instituto de Investigação Cientifica de Moçambique (Mozambique) 256
Instituto de Investigaciones Bibliográficas (Institute of Bibliographical Research) (Mexico) 254
Instituto de Investigaciones Sociales — Universidad Nacional Autonoma de Mexico (Mexico) 251
Instituto de Literatura (Argentina) 9
Instituto de Literatura, Biblioteca del, y Linguistica (Cuba) 68
Instituto de Planejamento Económico e Social (IPEA) (Brazil) 52
Instituto de Publicaciones Navales (Argentina) 6
Instituto Indigenista Interamericano (Mexico) 251
Instituto Interamericano de Ciencias Agricolas (IICA) (Costa Rica) 67
Instituto Mexicano del Libro, AC (Mexican Book Institute) (Mexico) 250
Instituto Nacional, Biblioteca del, del Libro Español (Library of the Spanish Publishers' and Booksellers' Association) (Spain) 328
Instituto Nacional de Antropologia e Historia (Mexico) 251
Instituto Nacional de Bellas Artes (Mexico) 252
Instituto Nacional del Libro Español (Spain) 317
Instituto Nacional del Libro Español, Delegación de Barcelona (Spain) 317
Instituto Nacional do Livro (Brazil) 48
Instituto Nacional do Livro e do Disco (Mozambique) 256
Instituto Panamericano de Geografia e Historia (Mexico) 252
Instituto Pontificio, Ediciones, San Pío X (Spain) 322
Instituto Pre-universitario, Biblioteca del, de la Habana (Library of the Pre-University Institute of Education) (Cuba) 68
Instituto Tecnico de Alimentaçao Humana (Portugal) 300

Instituto Tecnológico, Biblioteca del, y de Estudios Superiores de Monterrey, Sucursal de Corres 'J' (Mexico) 254
Instituts für Weltwirtschaft, Bibliothek des, — Zentralbibliothek der Wirtschaftswissenschaften (Federal Republic of Germany) 171
Institutul National de Informare si Documentare (INID) (Romania) 305
Instytut, Państstwowy, Wydawniczy (State Publishing Institute) (Poland) 294
Instytut Badań Literackich (Poland) 297
Instytut Bibliograficzny (Poland) 297
Insula (Spain) 327
Insula, Ediciones y Publicaciones de, (Spain) 322
Intellectual Society of Libya (Libya) 243
Intellectuals' Rendezvous (India) 196
Inter American University of Puerto Rico Library (Puerto Rico) 303
Inter Documentation Co AG (Switzerland) 347
Inter-European Editions (Netherlands) 263
Inter-Governmental Maritime Consultative Organization (IMCO) (International Organizations) 440
Inter-India Publications (India) 191
Inter-Kunst und Buch GmbH (Federal Republic of Germany) 144
Inter-Médica, Editorial, SAICI (Argentina) 6
Inter-Varsity Press (United Kingdom) 391
Interallié Prize (France) 114
Interamericana de Venezuela, Editorial, CA (Venezuela) 424
Interamericana del Uruguay, Editorial, SA (Uruguay) 422
'Interavia' SA (Société anonyme d'Editions aéronautiques internationales) (Switzerland) 347
Interbankendienst, Uitgaven van, NV (Belgium) 38
Interbooks (Belgium) 44
Interciencia, Livraría, Ltda (Brazil) 52
Intercontinental Book Productions (United Kingdom) 391
Interéditions (Belgium) 39
InterEditions Paris (France) 100
Interessengemeinschaft Musikwissenschaftlicher Herausgeber und Verleger (IHMV) (Federal Republic of Germany) 122
Interfrom, Edition, AG (Switzerland) 347
Intergéo, CNRS Laboratoire, (Intergéo Laboratory of the French National Scientific Research Centre — CNRS) (France) 100
Intergest SRL (Italy) 216
Intergovernmental Bureau for Informatics (Bureau Intergouvernemental pour l'Informatique) (Oficina Intergubenamental para la Informática) (International Organizations) 442
Intergovernmental Copyright Committee (International Organizations) 438
Interkerklike Uitgewerstrust (Republic of South Africa) 312
Interlita-Literaturagentur Peter Vilimek GmbH (Federal Republic of Germany) 169
International Academic Union (Union académique internationale) (International Organizations) 442
International African Institute (International Organizations) 442
International Association for Mass Communication Research (Association internationale des etudes et recherches sur l'information) (International Organizations) 438
International Association for the History of Religions (Association internationale pour l'Histoire des Religions) (International Organizations) 442
International Association of Agricultural Librarians and Documentalists — IAALD (International Organizations) 438
International Association of Law Libraries (IALL) (Association internationale des bibliothèques de droit) (International Organizations) 438
International Association of Literary Critics (Association internationale des critiques littéraires) (International Organizations) 438
International Association of Metropolitan City Libraries (INTAMEL) (International Organizations) 438
International Association of Music Libraries, Australia/New Zealand Branch (New Zealand) 275
International Association of Music Libraries, Australia/New Zealand Branch (IAMLANZ) (Australia) 20
International Association of Music Libraries (Association internationale des bibliothèques musicales) (International Organizations) 438
International Association of Music Libraries (UK Branch) (United Kingdom) 416
International Association of Orientalist Librarians (International Organizations) 438
International Association of School Librarianship (International Organizations) 438
International Association of Sound Archives (International Organizations) 438
International Association of Techhnoological University Libraries (IATUL) (International Organizations) 438

International Association of Universities (IAU) (International Organizations) 442
International Astronomical Union (Union astronomique internationale) (International Organizations) 442
International Atomic Energy Agency (IAEA) (International Organizations) 440
International Audio-Visual Technical Centre (Centre Technique Audio-Visuel International) (International Organizations) 440
International Bible Reading Association (United Kingdom) 391
International Biographical Centre (United Kingdom) 391
International Board on Books for Young People (IBBY) (International Organizations) 438
International Book Distributors Co Ltd (Thailand) 360
International Book Export Group (IBEG) Ltd (United Kingdom) 391
International Book Information Services (United Kingdom) 369
International Booksellers' Federation (IBF) (International Organizations) 438
International Bookshop (Tanzania) 358
International Bookshop, The, (Iceland) 185
International Bureau of Fiscal Documentation (International Organizations) 442
International Bureau voor Auteursrecht BV (Netherlands) 269
International Centre for African Economic and Social Documentation (Centre International de Documentation économique et sociale africaine — CIDEAS) (International Organizations) 442
International Children's Book Service (Denmark) 78
International Committee for Social Science Documentation (Comité international pour la documentation des sciences sociales) (International Organizations) 442
International Committee of Historical Sciences (Comité international des Sciences historiques) (International Organizations) 442
International Committee on the History of Art (Comité international d'histoire de l'art) (International Organizations) 442
International Communication Agency Library (Morocco) 256
International Communication Agency Library (Republic of Korea) 239
International Communication Agency Library (Democratic Republic of Madagascar) 245
International Communication Agency Library (Liberia) 242
International Communication Agency Library (Guinea) 179
International Communication Agency Library (Tanzania) 358
International Communication Agency Library (Uganda) 364
International Communications (United Kingdom) 391
International Comparative Literature Association (Association internationale de littérature comparée) (International Organizations) 442
International Confederation of Societies of Authors and Composers (Confédération internationale des sociétés d'auteurs et compositeurs) (International Organizations) 439
International Congress of Africanists (Congrès International des Africanistes) (International Organizations) 442
International Correspondence Schools Ltd (United Kingdom) 391
International Council for Philosophy and Humanistic Studies (ICPHS) (Conseil international de la Philosophie et des Sciences humaines) (International Organizations) 442
International Council of Scientific Unions (Conseil international des Unions scientifiques) (International Organizations) 442
International Council of Theological Library Associations (International Organizations) 439
International Council on Archives (Conseil international des archives) (International Organizations) 439
International Documentary, The, Centre of Arab Manuscripts (Lebanon) 241
International Editors' Co (Brazil) 55
International Editors' Co (Argentina) 8
International Editors' Co SA (Spain) 327
International Federation for Documentation (Fédération internationale de documentation) (International Organizations) 439
International Federation of Film Archives (Fédération internationale des archives du film) (International Organizations) 439
International Federation of Library Associations and Institutions IFLA (Fédération internationale des associations de bibliothécaires et des Bibliothèques) (International Organizations) 439
International Federation of Modern Languages and Literatures (Fédération internationale des Langues et Littératures modernes) (International Organizations) 442

International Federation of Philosophical Societies (Fédération internationale des Sociétés de philosophie, FISP) (International Organizations) 442
International Federation of the Societies of Classical Studies (Fédération internationale des Associations d'Etudes classiques) (International Organizations) 442
International Fiction Association (International Organizations) 439
International Food Information Service (International Organizations) 442
International Geographical Union (IGU) (Union geographique internationale) (International Organizations) 442
International Grand Prize for Poetry (International Literary Prizes) 450
International Group of Scientific, Technical and Medical Publishers (STM) (International Organizations) 439
International Hospital Federation (Fédération internationale des Hôpitaux) (International Organizations) 442
International Institute for Children's Literature and Reading Research, UNESCO category C (Institut International de Littérature pour Enfants et de Recherches sur la Lecture) (International Organizations) 439
International Institute for Educational Planning (IIEP) (International Organizations) 440
International Institute of Advanced Buddhistic Studies Library (Burma) 60
International Institute of Iberoamerican Literature (International Organizations) 439
International Institute of Tropical Agriculture Library (Nigeria) 280
International Instituut, Bibliotheek van het, voor Sociale Geschiedenis (Library of the International Institute of Social History) (Netherlands) 269
International Labour Office Library (ILO) (Switzerland) 356
International Labour Organisation (ILO) (International Organizations) 440
International League of Antiquarian Booksellers (International Organizations) 439
International Literair Agentschap (Belgium) 44
International Literary Agency (Federal Republic of Germany) 169
International Literary Braille Competition Awards (International Literary Prizes) 450
International Literary Peace Prize (International Literary Prizes) 450
International Literatuur Bureau BV (Netherlands) 269
International Mathematical Union (International Organizations) 442
International Music Council-IMC (Conseil international de la musique) (International Organizations) 442
International Musicological Society (International Organizations) 443
International Nursing, The, Foundation of Japan (Japan) 227
International Organization for Standardization (Organisation internationale de normalisation) (International Organizations) 443
International Permanent Committee of Linguists (Comité international permanent des Linguistes) (International Organizations) 443
International Press, The, Agency (Pty) Ltd (Republic of South Africa) 315
International Press Agency (Ethiopia) 84
International Prize for the First Novel (International Literary Prizes) 450
International Prize of French Friendship (International Literary Prizes) 450
International Progressive Books and Periodicals Store (Nepal) 257
International Publication Cultural Award (International Literary Prizes) 450
International Publications Cultural Prize (International Literary Prizes) 450
International Publishers' Aid (IPA) (Belgium) 39
International Publishers Association (International Organizations) 439
International Publishing Corporation Ltd (United Kingdom) 391
International Reading Association (International Organizations) 439
International Science Service (Israel) 207
International Scientific Film Library (ISFL) (Cinémathèque scientifique internationale) (International Organizations) 439
International Society for Educational Information Inc (Japan) 227
International Society for Music Education (International Organizations) 443
International Statistical Institute (Institut international de statistique) (International Organizations) 443
International Study Group of Restorers of Archives, Libraries and Graphic Reproductions (Internationale Arbeitsgemeinschaft der Archiv-, Bibliotheks-und Grafikrestauratoren) (International Organizations) 439
International Telecommunication Union (ITU) (International Organizations) 440
International Textbook Co Ltd (United Kingdom) 391
International Translations Centre (International Organizations) 439
International Union for Conservation of Nature and Natural Resources (Union internationale pour la Conservation de la Nature et de ses Ressources) (International Organizations) 443
International Union of Anthropological and Ethnological Sciences (Union internationale des Sciences anthropologiques et ethnologiques) (International Organizations) 443
International Union of Biochemistry (Union internationale de biochimie) (International Organizations) 443
International Union of Biological Sciences (Union internationale des sciences biologiques) (International Organizations) 443
International Union of Crystallography (Union internationale de cristallographie) (International Organizations) 443
International Union of Geodesy and Geophysics (Union géodésique et géophysique internationale) (International Organizations) 443
International Union of Geological Sciences (Union Internationale des Sciences géologiques) (International Organizations) 443
International Union of Nutritional Sciences (IUNS) (Union Internationale des Sciences de la Nutrition) (International Organizations) 443
International Union of Physiological Sciences (International Organizations) 443
International Union of Prehistoric and Protohistoric Sciences (Union internationale des Sciences préhistoriques et protohistoriques) (International Organizations) 443
International Union of Pure and Applied Biophysics (International Organizations) 443
International Union of Pure and Applied Chemistry (IUPAC) (Union internationale de Chimie pure et appliquée) (International Organizations) 443
International Union of Pure and Applied Physics (Union internationale de Physique pure et appliquée) (International Organizations) 443
International Union of Radio Science (Union radio-scientifique internationale) (International Organizations) 443
International Union of the History and Philosophy of Science (International Organizations) 443
International Union of Theoretical and Applied Mechanics (Union internationale de Mécanique théorique et appliquée) (International Organizations) 443
International Who's Who in Poetry Awards (International Literary Prizes) 450
International Youth Library (Internationale Jugendbibliothek) (International Organizations) 439
Internationale Buchhändler-Vereinigung (IBV) (International Organizations) 439
Internationale Pers, De, (Belgium) 39
Internationale Presse, Import- und Export GmbH (Federal Republic of Germany) 170
Internationale Solidarität, Verlag, Verlagsgesellschaft mbH (Federal Republic of Germany) 144
Internationale Vereinigung der Musikbibliotheken, Deutsche Gruppe BRD (Federal Republic of Germany) 172
'Interpress', Wydawnictwo, (Poland) 294
Interpresse, A/S, (Denmark) 76
Interprint (India) 191
Interpublishing AB Rahm and Stenström (Sweden) 334
Intersea (Argentina) 6
Interskrift Publishing House (Sweden) 334
Intertrade Publications (India) Pvt Ltd (India) 191
Iran Literature Association (Iran) 202
Iranian Documentation Centre (IRANDOC) (Iran) 202
Iranian Publishers' Association (Iran) 201
Iraq Library Association (Iraq) 203
Iraq Museum, Library of the, (Iraq) 202
Iraq Natural History, Library of the, Research Centre (Iraq) 202
Iris Verlag AG (Switzerland) 347
Irish Academic Press (Republic of Ireland) 204
Irish Academy of Letters (Republic of Ireland) 205
Irish-American Cultural Institute Literary Awards (International Literary Prizes) 450
Irish Arts Council Award (Republic of Ireland) 205
Irish Association for Documentation and Information Services (IADIS), The National Library of Ireland (Republic of Ireland) 205
Irish Educational Publishers' Association, C J Fallon Ltd (Republic of Ireland) 203
Irish Heritage Series (Republic of Ireland) 204
Irish Life Drama Award (Republic of Ireland) 205
Irish Management Institute (Republic of Ireland) 204
Irish Society for Archives (Republic of Ireland) 205
Irish Times, The, Ltd (Republic of Ireland) 204
Irish University Press (Republic of Ireland) 204
Irish University Press (Republic of Ireland) 204
Irisiana Druck und Verlag (Federal Republic of Germany) 144
Ísafoldar, Bókaverzlun, (Iceland) 185
Ísafoldarprentsmidja hf (Iceland) 185
Ishiyaku Publishers Inc (Japan) 227
'Iskry', Państwowe Wydawnictwo, (Poland) 294
Iskusstvo, Izdatelstvo, (Union of Soviet Socialist Republics) 365
Islam, Perpustakaan, (Islamic Library) (Indonesia) 201
Islam, Verlag der, (Federal Republic of Germany) 144
Islamabad University Library (Pakistan) 286
Islami Kitab Khana (Pakistan) 285
Islamia Library (Bangladesh) 32
Islamic Book Centre (Pakistan) 285
Islamic Cultural Bookshop (Bahrain) 32
Islamic Culture, Institute of, (Pakistan) 285
Islamic Publications Bureau (Nigeria) 278
Islamic Publications Ltd (Pakistan) 285
Islamic Research Institute (Pakistan) 285
Islamic Research Institute Library (Pakistan) 286
Islamic University Library (Saudi Arabia) 306
Islamiyah (Indonesia) 200
Island, The, Shop (Bahamas) 32
Island Press (Australia) 15
Íslenzka bókmenntafélag (Iceland) 186
Íslenzka Bókmenntafélag, Hid, (Iceland) 185
Isopang Publishing Pty Ltd (Papua New Guinea) 288
Israbook (Israel) 210
Israel, B M, BV (Netherlands) 263
Israel, Nico, (Netherlands) 263
Israel Academy, The, of Sciences & Humanities (Israel) 207
Israel Book Importers' Association (Israel) 206
Israel Exploration Society (Israel) 207
Israel Library Association (Israel) 211
Israel Program for Scientific Translations (Israel) 207
Israel Society of Special Libraries and Information Centres (ISLIC) (Israel) 211
Israel State Archives, Prime Minister's Office (Israel) 211
Israel Universities Press (Israel) 207
Israel Yearbook Publications (Israel) 207
Israeli Music Publications Ltd (Israel) 207
Israeli Prize in Humanities and Social Sciences (Israel) 211
Israeli Prize in Jewish Studies, Hebrew Literature and Education (Israel) 211
Israeli Prize in the Arts (Israel) 211
Istanbul Üniversitesi Merkez Kütüphanesi (Istanbul University Central Library) (Turkey) 363
Istiklal, Al, Library (Jordan) 234
Istituto Centrale di Statistica (Italy) 216
Istituto Centrale per il Catalogo Unico delle Biblioteche Italiane e per le Informazioni Bibliografiche (Italy) 222
Istituto Centrale per la Patologia del Libro (Italy) 212
Istituto della Enciclopedia Italiana (Italy) 216
Istituto Editoriale Italiano SpA (Italy) 216
Istituto Geografico de Agostini SpA (Italy) 216
Istituto Italiano D'Arti Grafiche (Italy) 216
Istituto Lombardo Accademia di Scienze e Lettere (Italy) 223
Istituto Poligrafico e Zecca dello Stato (Italy) 216
Istmo, Ediciones, (Spain) 322
Istra, Librairie, Sàrl (France) 100
Italian Book Club (United Kingdom) 414
Ittihad, Al, Bookstore (Egypt) 82
Iwanami Shoten (Japan) 227
Iwasaki Shoten Co Ltd (Japan) 227
Izmir General Library (Turkey) 363
Izrael Publishing House Ltd (Israel) 208
Iztaccihuatl, Editorial, SA (Mexico) 252
Iztaccihuatl, Librerías, (Mexico) 254
Izvestiya Publishing House (Union of Soviet Socialist Republics) 365

J A, Groupe, (Editions J A) (France) 100
J K Export House (India) 197
J R O-Kartografische Verlagsgesellschaft mbH (Federal Republic of Germany) 144
Jaca, Cooperativa Edizioni, Book (Italy) 216
Jacaranda Wiley Ltd (New Zealand) 273
Jacaranda Wiley Ltd (Australia) 15
Jackdaw Publications Ltd (United Kingdom) 391
Jacob, Max, Prize (France) 114
Jacobi Verlag GmbH (Federal Republic of Germany) 144
Jaeger, H-K de, Publications (ASTRID) (Belgium) 39
Jafet, Nami C, Memorial Library (Lebanon) 241

Jäggi, Buchhandlung, AG (Switzerland) 356
Jahreszeitenverlag (Federal Republic of Germany) 144
J'ai Lu, Editions, (France) 100
Jaico Book Shop (India) 197
Jaico Publishing House (India) 191
Jain Brothers (India) 191
Jakobsohn, Verlag Eduard, (Federal Republic of Germany) 144
Jaktjournalens Bokklubb (Sweden) 337
Jal-Verlag/Jal-Reprint Arnulf Liebing (Federal Republic of Germany) 144
Jamaica Archives (Jamaica) 225
Jamaica Library Association (Jamaica) 225
Jamaica Library Service (Jamaica) 225
Jamaica Publishing House Ltd (Jamaica) 224
James, Arthur, Ltd (United Kingdom) 391
Jamjoom, Mohamed Noor Salah, & Bros (Saudi Arabia) 306
Jane's Publishing Co (United Kingdom) 391
Jane's Yearbooks (United Kingdom) 391
Jannersten Förlag AB (Sweden) 334
Janssen, Stern-Verlag, und Co (Federal Republic of Germany) 144
Janssens, J. (Belgium) 39
Januka Pustak Bhandar (Nepal) 257
Japan Book Importers' Association (Japan) 225
Japan Book Publishers' Association (Japan) 225
Japan Broadcast Publishing Co Ltd (Japan) 227
Japan Contemporary Poets' Society (Japan) 233
Japan Essayists' Club (Japan) 233
Japan Essayists' Club Prize (Japan) 234
Japan Poet Club (Japan) 233
Japan Poet Club Prize (Japan) 234
Japan Publications Inc (Japan) 227
Japan Publications Trading Co Ltd (Import and Export) (Japan) 232
Japan Society of Translators (Japan) 234
Japan Times (Japan) 227
Japan Translation Prize (International Literary Prizes) 450
Japan Translation Prize for Publisher (Japan) 234
Japan Travel Bureau Inc (Japan) 227
Japan Uni Agency Inc (Japan) 232
Japan Woman Writer Prize (Japan) 234
Japan Women Writers' Literary Prizes (Japan) 234
Jarrold Colour Publications (United Kingdom) 391
Jasomirgott-Verlag (Austria) 26
Jason Publishing Co Ltd (New Zealand) 273
Jaspert, Reinhard, (Federal Republic of Germany) 144
Jaya, Penerbit, (Malaysia) 246
Jaya Baya, Yayasan, (Indonesia) 200
Jaya Murni (Indonesia) 200
Jayawardena, J K G, & Co (Sri Lanka) 329
Jazirah, Al, Organization for Press, Printing, Publishing (Saudi Arabia) 306
Jean-Charles, A, (Martinique) 249
Jean-Christophe Prize (France) 114
Jecta (Belgium) 39
Jedinstvo (Yugoslavia) 428
Jeffers Bookstore (Trinidad and Tobago) 361
Jeheber, J H, SA (Switzerland) 347
Jeng's Bookshop (The Gambia) 117
Jeongeumsa Publishing Co (Republic of Korea) 238
Jerusalem, The, Prize (International Literary Prizes) 450
Jerusalem City (Public) Library (Israel) 211
Jerusalem Publishing House Ltd (Israel) 208
Jespersen og Pios Forlag (Denmark) 76
Jeune Afrique, Editions, (France) 100
Jeune France Prize (France) 114
Jeunesse d'Afrique, Librairie, (Upper Volta) 422
'Jeunesse et Afrique', Librairie, (Upper Volta) 422
Jeunesses littéraires de France (French Literary Youth) (France) 112
Jewish Agency, The, (Israel) 208
Jewish Book Club, The, (United Kingdom) 414
Jewish Chronicle — Harold H Wingate Book Awards (International Literary Prizes) 450
Jewish National and University Library (Israel) 211
Jims, Editorial, (Spain) 322
Jing Kung Book Store (Hong Kong) 181
Jing Kung Educational Press (Hong Kong) 181
Jisik Sanup Sa (Republic of Korea) 238
Jnanpith Literary Award (India) 198
Joannides, A, & Co (Cyprus) 69
Johanesburgse Boekwinkel (Republic of South Africa) 315
Johannesburg Public Library (Republic of South Africa) 316
Johannesverlag Einsiedeln (Switzerland) 347
Johns Hopkins, The, University Press (United Kingdom) 391
Johnson Publications Ltd (United Kingdom) 391
Johnson Society of London (United Kingdom) 418
Johnston & Bacon Publishers (United Kingdom) 391
Joho Shori Gakkai (Information Processing Society of Japan) (Japan) 232
Johore Central Store (Malaysia) 247

Joie, La, par les Livres (Joy Through Books) (France) 112
Join-in Books (United Kingdom) 392
Jonckheere, Tobie, Prize (Belgium) 46
Jonef Publications (Philippines) 291
Jones, John, Cardiff Ltd (United Kingdom) 392
Jonge, Stichting De, Onderzoekers (Netherlands) 263
Jonker, Ingrid, Prize (Republic of South Africa) 317
Jonsson, Snaebjörn, & Co HF (The English Bookshop) (Iceland) 185
Jonsson, Sveinbjörn, (Iceland) 185
Jónssonar, Bókaútgáfa Thorsteins M, (Iceland) 185
Jordan & Sons Ltd (United Kingdom) 392
Jordan Distribution Agency (Jordan) 234
Jordan Library Association (Jordan) 235
Jordan Press and Publishing Co Ltd (Jordan) 234
Joseph, F, (Haiti) 179
Joseph, Michael, Ltd (United Kingdom) 392
Journal des Notaires et des Avocats SA (France) 100
Journeyman, The, Press (United Kingdom) 392
Jourpart Redaktionsbüro und Verlagsgesellschaft mbH (Federal Republic of Germany) 144
Jovene, Casa Editrice Dr Eugenio, SpA (Italy) 216
Jover, Editorial, SA (Spain) 322
Jowers, Elisabeth, (Spain) 327
József Attila Tudományegyetem Központi Könyvtára (Hungary) 183
Jubilee Library Association (Burma) 60
Judia, Biblioteca Popular, (Argentina) 6
Judogi, Edition, (France) 100
Juelner, Georg, (Denmark) 78
Jugend und Volk GmbH (Federal Republic of Germany) 144
Jugend und Volk Verlagsgesellschaft mbH (Austria) 26
Jugenddienst-Verlag (Federal Republic of Germany) 144
Jugoreklam (Yugoslavia) 428
Jugoslavenske Academije, Izdavački Zavod, Znanosti i Umjetnosti (Publishing House of the Yugoslav Academy of Sciences and Arts) (Yugoslavia) 428
Jugoslavenski LekSlkografski Zavod (Yugoslavia) 428
Jugoslavija (Yugoslavia) 428
Jugoslovenska Autorska Agencija (Yugoslavia) 430
Jugoslovenska Knjiga (Yugoslavia) 431
Jugoslovenska Revija (Yugoslavia) 428
Jugoslovenski bibliografski institut (Yugoslavia) 431
Jugoslovenski centar za tehničku i naučnu dokumentaciju (Yugoslavia) 431
Julien, Stanislas, Prize (International Literary Prizes) 450
Julliard, Editions René, (France) 100
Jumsai, M, (Laos) 240
Juncker, Axel-, -Verlag Nachfolger Jacobi KG (Federal Republic of Germany) 144
Jungbrunnen, Verlag, (Austria) 26
Junge Welt, Verlag, (German Democratic Republic) 119
Junimea, Editura, (Romania) 304
Junior International (Federal Republic of Germany) 144
Junior Puffin Club (United Kingdom) 414
Junk, Dr W, BV (Netherlands) 263
Junpa Kwahak Sa (Republic of Korea) 238
Junta de Educação Religiosa e Publicações da Convenção Batista Brasileira (Brazil) 52
Jupiter, Editions, Sàrl (France) 100
Jupiter Books (London) Ltd (United Kingdom) 392
Jurídica, Ediciones & Librería, (Argentina) 6
Juridica-Verlag GmbH (Austria) 26
Jurif (Société d'Etudes Juridiques Internationales et Fiscales) (France) 100
Juris Druck & Verlag AG (Switzerland) 347
Jus, Editorial, SA (Mexico) 252
Jusautor (Bulgaria) 58
Just, Gertraude, (Austria) 29
Juta & Co Ltd (Republic of South Africa) 312
Juta & Co Ltd (Republic of South Africa) 315
Juteau-Duvigneaux Prize (France) 114
Juventa Verlag, Dr Martin Faltermaier (Federal Republic of Germany) 144
Juventud, Editorial, Argentina (Argentina) 6
Juventud, Editorial, Ltda (Colombia) 65
Juventud, Editorial, SA (Spain) 322
Juventud, Librería, (Bolivia) 47
Juventud, Librería y Editorial, (Bolivia) 47
Jyväskylän Yliopiston Kirjasto (Finland) 87

K & R Books Ltd (United Kingdom) 392
K B S (Netherlands) 263
K M C — Young Readers' Club (Czechoslovakia) 72
K M P (Kruh milovníkov poézie) (Czechoslovakia) 72
K T O Press (Liechtenstein) 243
Kabarole Public Library (Uganda) 364
Kabete Library (Kenya) 236
Kabul University, Institute of Geography (Afghanistan) 1
Kadokawa Shoten (Japan) 227
Kaduna, Library Board of, State (Nigeria) 280

Kaffke, Verlag Gerhard, (Federal Republic of Germany) 145
Kahn, Lonnie, and Co Ltd (Israel) 210
Kaibundo Publishing Co Ltd (Japan) 228
Kairos, Editorial, SA (Spain) 322
Kairyudo Publishing Co Ltd (Japan) 228
Kaisei-Sha (Japan) 228
Kaiser, Buchhandlung Christian, (Federal Republic of Germany) 170
Kaiser, Chr, Verlag (Federal Republic of Germany) 145
Kaiser, Eduard, (Austria) 29
Kaitaku-Sha (Japan) 228
Kajima Institute Publishing Co Ltd (Japan) 228
Kakoulides, C, (Greece) 177
Kalinga Prize (International Literary Prizes) 450
Kalleberger Foundation (Sweden) 339
Kaloudis, Gr, (Greece) 178
Kalyani Publishers (India) 191
Kamp, Verlag Ferdinand, (Federal Republic of Germany) 145
Kampen, Uitgeverij Van, BV (Netherlands) 263
Kampen & Zoon, PN Van, BV (Netherlands) 263
Kanehara & Co Ltd (Japan) 228
Kanisius, Yayasan, (Indonesia) 200
Kanisius Verlag (Switzerland) 347
Kano State Library (Nigeria) 280
Kantonale Kommission für Jugend- und Volksbibliotheken, Zurich (Switzerland) 357
Kapelusz, Editorial, SA (Argentina) 6
Kapelusz, Editorial, Venezolana SA (Venezuela) 424
Kapur Publications (India) 191
Kara, Ismail, /Dergâh Yayinlari AS Müessese Müdürü (Turkey) 363
Karachi University Library (Pakistan) 286
Karachi University Library Science Alumni Association (Pakistan) 286
Karas-Sana Oy (Finland) 86
Karavias, Athanassios, (Greece) 177
Karavias, Nikolaos, (Greece) 177
Karger, S, AG, Medical and Scientific Publishers (Switzerland) 347
Karger, S, GmbH (Federal Republic of Germany) 145
Karilas, Tauno, Prize (Finland) 88
Karl-Marx-Universität (German Democratic Republic) 120
Karl Wenschow GmbH (Federal Republic of Germany) 168
Karnataka Cooperative Publishing House Ltd (India) 191
Karnataka Publishers' and Booksellers' Association (India) 186
Karni Publishers Ltd (Israel) 208
Karo-Bücher (Federal Republic of Germany) 145
Kartograficznych, Państwowe Przedsiebiorstwo Wydawnictw, (Poland) 294
Kartografie NP (Czechoslovakia) 70
Karunaratne & Co (Sri Lanka) 329
Karunia (Indonesia) 200
Kasetsart University, Main Library, (Thailand) 360
Kash'shaf, Dar al, (Lebanon) 241
Katalogów i Cenników, Wydawnictwo, (Catalogue and Price List Publishers) (Poland) 294
Katholieke Bijbelstichting (Netherlands) 263
Katholieke Universiteit Leuven (Belgium) 44
Katholisches Bibelwerk, Verlag, GmbH (Federal Republic of Germany) 145
Katzmann-Verlag KG (Federal Republic of Germany) 145
Kaufmann (Greece) 178
Kaufmann, Verlag Ernst, (Federal Republic of Germany) 145
Kawade Shobo Shinsha (Japan) 228
Kawanku, Yayasan, (Indonesia) 200
Kawika (Society of Tagalog Writers) (Philippines) 293
Kaye & Ward Ltd (United Kingdom) 392
Kaye Ando Technical Services (Laos) 240
Keats (£2,000) Poetry Prize Competition (United Kingdom) 420
Keats-Shelley Memorial Association (Italy) 223
Kedros (Greece) 177
Keesing — Internationale Drukkerij en Uitgeverij NV (Belgium) 39
Keimer, Verlag und Buchvertrieb E, (Federal Republic of Germany) 145
Keip, Verlag, KG Antiquariat (Federal Republic of Germany) 145
Keller, Franckh'sche Verlagshandlung, W , & Co (Federal Republic of Germany) 145
Keller, Verlag Ramon F, (Switzerland) 347
Kelly Books (Australia) 15
Kelly's Directories Ltd (United Kingdom) 392
Kemal, Orhan, Award (Turkey) 364
Kemps Group (Printers & Publishers) Ltd (United Kingdom) 392
K'enkyusha Ltd (Japan) 228
Kennedy Prize (Thailand) 360
Kent-Segep SA (France) 100
Kentavros Ekdoseis OE (Greece) 177
Kentron Ekdoseos Ellinon Syngrafeon (Greece) 178

490 INDEX

Kenya Booksellers' and Stationers' Association (Kenya) 235
Kenya Library Association (Kenya) 236
Kenya Literature Bureau (Kenya) 237
Kenya Literature Bureau (Kenya) 236
Kenya National Archives (Kenya) 236
Kenya National Library Service (Kenya) 236
Kenya Polytechnic Library (Kenya) 236
Kenya Publishers' Association (Kenya) 235
Kenya Technical Teachers' College Library (Kenya) 236
Kenyatta, Jomo, Prize for Literature (International Literary Prizes) 450
Kenyatta, The Jomo, Foundation (Kenya) 236
Kenyatta University College Library (Kenya) 236
Keppe, Norberto R. (Brazil) 52
Képzőművészeti Alap Kiadóvállalata (Hungary) 182
Kerala Publishers & Booksellers Association (India) 186
Kerle, Verlag F H. (Federal Republic of Germany) 145
Kern Associates (Japan) 232
Kerr, The Alfred, Prize for Literary Criticism (Federal Republic of Germany) 173
Kershaw Publishing Co Ltd (United Kingdom) 392
Kesim, Nurcihan (Turkey) 363
Kestrel Books (United Kingdom) 392
Keswick (United Kingdom) 392
Keswick Book Society (Kenya) 236
Keter Publishing House Ltd (Israel) 208
Keurbiblioteek (Republic of South Africa) 315
Keure, Die, NV (Belgium) 39
Keysersche Buchhandlung (German Democratic Republic) 120
Keysersche Verlagsbuchhandlung GmbH (Federal Republic of Germany) 145
Khanna Publishers (India) 191
Khartoum, The, Bookshop (Sudan) 330
Khartoum Polytechnic Library (Sudan) 330
Khartoum University Press (Sudan) 330
Khaya, Tahseen S. (Kuwait) 240
Khayat, Tahseen S. (Lebanon) 241
Khayat, Tahseen S. (United Arab Emirates) 368
Khayat Book and Publishing Co SAL (Lebanon) 241
'Khimiya', Izdatelstvo, (Publishing House for Chemistry) (Union of Soviet Socialist Republics) 365
Khoa Hoc (Social Sciences) Publishing House (Socialist Republic of Viet Nam) 426
'Khudozhestvennaya Literatura', Izdatelstvo, (Union of Soviet Socialist Republics) 365
Khudozhnik RSFSR Publishers (Union of Soviet Socialist Republics) 365
Kibaha Public Library (Tanzania) 358
Kibu-Verlag GmbH (Federal Republic of Germany) 145
Kiefel, Johannes, Verlag (Federal Republic of Germany) 145
Kiehl, Friedrich, Verlag GmbH (Federal Republic of Germany) 145
Kienreich, Jos A. (Austria) 30
Kienreich, Jos A. (Austria) 30
Kiepenheuer, Gustav, Verlag (German Democratic Republic) 119
Kiepenheuer und Witsch, Verlag, (Federal Republic of Germany) 145
Kier, Editorial, SACIFI (Argentina) 6
Kier, Librería, (Argentina) 8
Küilerich, Edith, (Denmark) 78
Küilerich, Edith, (Finland) 86
Küilerich, Edith, (Sweden) 337
Küilerich, Edith, (Norway) 283
Kikuchi Prize (Japan) 234
Kilda Verlag (Federal Republic of Germany) 145
Kilkenny, The, Bookshop Ltd (Republic of Ireland) 204
Kimber, William, & Co Ltd (United Kingdom) 392
Kimpton, Henry, (Publishers) Ltd (United Kingdom) 392
Kina Italia SpA (Italy) 216
Kinderbuchverlag, Der, Berlin (German Democratic Republic) 119
Kinderbuchverlag Reich Luzern AG (Switzerland) 347
Kinderpers, Die, Van SA (Republic of South Africa) 312
Kindler Verlag AG (Switzerland) 347
Kindler Verlag GmbH (Federal Republic of Germany) 145
King, Martin Luther, Memorial Prize (United Kingdom) 420
King Abdul Aziz University Library (Saudi Arabia) 306
King Paul National Foundation Prize (Greece) 178
King Shing Publishing Co (Hong Kong) 181
Kingfisher Books (United Kingdom) 392
Kings & Queens of England (United Kingdom) 414
Kingsmead Press (United Kingdom) 392
Kingston Bookshop (Jamaica) 224
Kingston Publishers Ltd (Jamaica) 224
Kingstons (Zambia) 434
Kingston's Literary Awards (Zimbabwe) 436
Kingstons Ltd (Zimbabwe) 435
Kingsway Publications Ltd (United Kingdom) 392
Kingsway Stores (Nigeria) 280
Kingsway Stores, Books and Periodicals Department (Ghana) 175

Kinokuniya Bookstore Co Ltd (Japan) 232
Kinokuniya Bookstore Co Ltd (Publishing Department) (Japan) 228
Kinta (Indonesia) 200
Kipling Society (United Kingdom) 418
Kirja-ja Paperikauppiasliitto (Finland) 85
Kirjallisuudentutkijain Seura (Finland) 88
Kirjaneliö, Kustannusliike, (Finland) 86
Kirjapalvelu (Book Service) (Finland) 85
Kirjastonhoitajien Keskusliitto-Bibliothekariers Centralforbund ry (Finland) 87
Kirjastopoliittinen Yhdistys-Bibliotekspolitiska Föreningen (Finland) 87
Kirjastovirkailijat-Biblioteksanstallda ry (Finland) 87
Kirjayhtymä Oy (Finland) 86
Kiryat Sefer Ltd (Israel) 208
Kishida Prize for Drama (Japan) 234
Kister, Editions, SA (Switzerland) 347
Kitab, Dar al-, Al Jadid (Lebanon) 241
Kitab, Dar El, (Morocco) 256
Kitab Mahal (W D) Pvt Ltd (India) 191
Kitabi Dunya (Pakistan) 285
Kitabistan (Bangladesh) 32
Kitaplar, Altin, Publishing Co (Turkey) 363
Kitwe Public Library (Zambia) 434
Klang Vidhya (Thailand) 360
Klang Vidhya (Thailand) 359
Klasing und Co GmbH (Federal Republic of Germany) 145
Klein, Dr. SA (Switzerland) 347
Klein, Kunstverlag Woldemar, (Federal Republic of Germany) 145
Klein, Preben, (Denmark) 78
Klemmer und Muller, Buchverlag, (Federal Republic of Germany) 145
Klens Verlag GmbH (Federal Republic of Germany) 145
Klett, Ernst, (Federal Republic of Germany) 145
Klett & Balmer Verlag (Switzerland) 347
Klett Cotta Verlag (Federal Republic of Germany) 146
Klima, Librairie, (French Polynesia) 116
Klincksieck, Editions, (France) 100
Klinkhardt und Biermann Richard Carl Schmidt KG (Federal Republic of Germany) 146
Klonis, Odysseus S. (Greece) 178
Klopp, Erika, Verlag GmbH (Federal Republic of Germany) 146
Klostermann, Vittorio, (Federal Republic of Germany) 146
Klotz, Ehrenfried, Verlag (Federal Republic of Germany) 146
Klub 42 (Yugoslavia) 430
Klub 707 (Republic of South Africa) 315
Klub čtenářů technické literatury (Czechoslovakia) 72
Klub přátel poézie (Czechoslovakia) 72
Kluitman, Uitgeverij, Alkmaar BV (Netherlands) 263
Kluwer, NV Uitgeverij, (Belgium) 39
Kluwer Algemene Boeken BV (Netherlands) 263
Kluwer Fiscale en Juridische Boeken en Tijdschriften (Netherlands) 263
Kluwer Group (Netherlands) 263
Kluwer Publishing Ltd (United Kingdom) 392
Kluwer Sociaal-Wetenschappelijke Boeken en Tijdschriften (Netherlands) 263
Kluwer Technische Boeken BV (Netherlands) 263
Kluwer's, Maarten, Internationale Uitgeversonderneming NV (Belgium) 39
Kluwers Courantan Bedrijf (Netherlands) 263
Knapp, Fritz, Verlag GmbH (Federal Republic of Germany) 146
Knapp, Wilhelm, Verlag (Federal Republic of Germany) 146
Knaus, Albrecht, Verlag (Federal Republic of Germany) 146
Knecht, Verlag Josef, -Carolus Druckerei GmbH (Federal Republic of Germany) 146
Knesset Library (Israel) 211
'Kniga', Izdatelstvo, (Union of Soviet Socialist Republics) 365
Knight (United Kingdom) 392
Knight, Charles, (United Kingdom) 392
Kniha (The Book) (Czechoslovakia) 72
Knihovna Národniho muzea (Czechoslovakia) 72
Knorr und Hirth Verlag GmbH (Federal Republic of Germany) 146
Knowledge Book House (Burma) 59
Knowledge International Marketing (France) 100
Knowledge Printing & Publishing House (Burma) 59
Knuf, E. Publishers (Netherlands) 263
Københavns Kommunes Biblioteker (Denmark) 78
Københavns Stadsarkiv (Denmark) 78
Kober'sche Verlagsbuchhandlung AG (Switzerland) 347
Koch, Hanna-Kirsti, (Norway) 283
Koch, Neff und Oetinger und Co (Federal Republic of Germany) 170
Koch, Verlagsanstalt Alexander, GmbH (Federal Republic of Germany) 146

Koch, Volksbuchhandlung Robert, (German Democratic Republic) 120
Kochbuchverlag Heimeran KG (Federal Republic of Germany) 146
Koch's, C A, Verlag Nachfolger (Federal Republic of Germany) 146
Kodansha Disney Children's Book Club (Japan) 232
Kodansha International Ltd (Japan) 228
Kodansha Ltd (Japan) 228
Kodansha Scientific Ltd (Japan) 228
Koehler, K F, Verlag (Federal Republic of Germany) 146
Koehler und Amelang (VOB) (German Democratic Republic) 119
Koehlers Verlagsgesellschaft (Federal Republic of Germany) 146
Koerner, Verlag Valentin, GmbH (Federal Republic of Germany) 146
Kogan Page Ltd (United Kingdom) 392
Kohlhammer, Unternehmensgruppe Verlag W. GmbH (Federal Republic of Germany) 146
Kohl's Technischer Verlag Erwin Kohl GmbH & Co KG (Federal Republic of Germany) 146
Kohrtz, Ilona, Prize (Sweden) 339
Kok, Uitgeversmaatschappij J H, BV (Netherlands) 263
Kokuritsu Kobunshokan (National Archives) (Japan) 232
Kolasanya Publishing Enterprise (Nigeria) 278
Kolibri-Verlag (Federal Republic of Germany) 146
Kollaros, I D, & Co Corporation (Greece) 177
'Kolos', Izdatelstvo, (Union of Soviet Socialist Republics) 365
Kolumbus-Verlag (Switzerland) 348
Komar (Federal Republic of Germany) 146
Kometförlaget AB (Sweden) 334
Komine Shoten Publishing Co Ltd (Japan) 228
Komitet po pechati pri Sovete Ministrov SSSR (Union of Soviet Socialist Republics) 365
Komitet za Izkustvo i Koultoura, (Committee for Arts and Culture) (Bulgaria) 59
Kommentator, Verlag, GmbH (Federal Republic of Germany) 146
Kommunale Bibliotekarbeiderers Forening (Municipal Librarians' Association) (Norway) 284
Kompass, Etas, (Italy) 216
Komunikacji i Łączności, Wydawnictwa, (Transport and Communications Publishers) (Poland) 294
Komunist, Izdavački Centar, (Yugoslavia) 428
Kongelige Bibliotek, Det, (Denmark) 78
Kongelige Danske Videnskabernes Selskab (Denmark) 79
Koninklijk Instituut voor Internationale Betrekkingen (Belgium) 39
Koninklijke Academie voor Nederlandse Taal- en Letterkunde (Belgium) 45
Koninklijke Academie voor Wetenschappen, Letteren en Schone Kunsten van België (Belgium) 45
Koninklijke Bibliotheek (Royal Library) (National Library) (Netherlands) 269
Koninklijke Nederlandse Akademie, Bibliotheek der, van Wetenschappen (Library of Royal Netherlands Academy of Arts and Sciences) (Netherlands) 269
Koninklijke Nederlandse Uitgeversbond (Royal Dutch Publishers' Association) (Netherlands) 258
Konkordia AG für Druck und Verlag (Federal Republic of Germany) 147
Konrad, Anton H. Verlag (Federal Republic of Germany) 147
Könyvértékesítő Vállalat (Hungary) 183
Könyvtártudományi és módszertani központ (Hungary) 183
Kookaburra Technical Publications Pty Ltd (Australia) 15
Kooyker, C. BV (Netherlands) 269
Kooyker Scientific Publications BV (Netherlands) 264
Korea Book Club (Republic of Korea) 239
Korea Directory Co (Republic of Korea) 238
Korea Publications Export and Import Corporation (Democratic People's Republic of Korea) 237
Korea University Library (Republic of Korea) 239
Korea University Press (Republic of Korea) 238
Korean Library Association (Republic of Korea) 239
Korean Micro-Library Association (Republic of Korea) 239
Korean Publishers Association (Republic of Korea) 237
Korean Workers' Party Publishing House (Democratic People's Republic of Korea) 237
Koren Publishers (Israel) 208
Kornfeld & Klipstein (Switzerland) 348
Koro, George Y. (Jordan) 234
Korsch, A. Verlag (Federal Republic of Germany) 147
Kosei Publishing Co Ltd (Japan) 228
Koseisha-Koseikaku Co Ltd (Japan) 228
Kösel-Verlag GmbH & Co (Federal Republic of Germany) 147
Kosi Books (India) 191
Koska, Verlag A F, (Austria) 26
Kosmo Uitgewery Beperk (Republic of South Africa) 312
Kosmos, Livraria, (Brazil) 56
Kosmos, Livraria, Editôra (Brazil) 52

Kosmos BV (Netherlands) 264
Kosmos Gesellschaft (Federal Republic of Germany) 170
Kossodo Verlag AG (Switzerland) 348
Kossuth Könyvkiadó (Hungary) 182
Kossuth Lajos Tudományegyetem Egyetemi Könyvtár (Lajos Kossuth University Library (Hungary) 183
Kothari Publications (India) 191
Koutsoumbos (Greece) 177
Kowalski, G. (Federal Republic of Germany) 147
Kowalski, Gerhard, (Federal Republic of Germany) 169
Kowloon Book Store (Hong Kong) 181
Koymantereas (Greece) 177
Közgazdasági és Jogi Könyvkiadó (Publishing House for Economics & Law) (Hungary) 182
Központi statisztikai hivatal könyvtár és dokumentációs szolgálat (Hungary) 183
Kraft Prize (Argentina) 9
Krajowa Agencja Wydawnicza (KAW) (Poland) 294
Kral, Frano, Prize (Czechoslovakia) 73
Kramer, Andrés de, (Spain) 327
Kramer, Dr Waldemar, Verlagsbuchhandlung (Federal Republic of Germany) 147
Kramer, Karin, Verlag (Federal Republic of Germany) 147
Krämer, Karl, Verlag GmbH und Co (Federal Republic of Germany) 147
Krämer, Verlag Karl, & Co (Switzerland) 348
Kramer, Verlag René, AG (Switzerland) 348
Kraus, Librairie des Messageries Paul, (Luxembourg) 244
Kraus Reprint (Liechtenstein) 243
Kraus-Thomson Organization Ltd (Liechtenstein) 243
Krausskopf Verlag GmbH (Federal Republic of Germany) 147
Krebs, Verlag G, AG (Switzerland) 348
Kremayr und Scheriau, Verlag, (Austria) 26
Kreuz Verlag (Federal Republic of Germany) 147
Krieg, Walter, (Austria) 30
Kriegsarchivs Wien, Bibliothek des, (Austria) 30
Kriminalistik Verlag GmbH (Federal Republic of Germany) 147
Krippler-Muller, Maison, (Luxembourg) 243
Krishna Prakasman Mandir (India) 191
Kristiansand Folkebibliotek (Municipal Library) (Norway) 283
Kristna Bokförläggareföreningen (Sweden) 331
Kristna Bokringen, Den, (Sweden) 337
Kritak uitgeverij (Belgium) 39
Kriterion, Editura, (Romania) 304
Kronen-Verlag Erich Cramer (Federal Republic of Germany) 147
Kröner, Alfred, Verlag (Federal Republic of Germany) 147
Kršćanska sadašnjost (Yugoslavia) 428
Krüger, Helmut, (Federal Republic of Germany) 147
Kruger, Wolfgang, Verlag (Federal Republic of Germany) 147
Kruh (Czechoslovakia) 70
Kruh priatelov detskej knihy (Czechoslovakia) 73
'Ksiazka i Wiedza', Wydawnictwo, (Poland) 294
Kuala Lumpur Public Library (Malaysia) 247
Kübler Verlag GmbH (Federal Republic of Germany) 147
Kubon & Sagner (Federal Republic of Germany) 147
Kugler Medical Publications BV (Netherlands) 264
Kühl KG, Verlagsgesellschaft (Federal Republic of Germany) 147
Kultura (Hungary) 183
Kultura (Yugoslavia) 431
Kultura (Izdavačko Pretprijatie) (Yugoslavia) 428
Kumm, Wilhelm, Verlag (Federal Republic of Germany) 147
Kümmerly & Frey (Geographischer Verlag) (Switzerland) 348
Kündig, Imprimerie Albert, SA (Switzerland) 348
Kungl Vitterhets Historie och Antikvitets Akademien (Royal Academy of Letters, History and Antiquities) (Sweden) 338
Kungliga Biblioteket (Sweden) 338
Kungliga Svenska Vetenskapsakademiens (Sweden) 338
Kunnskapsforlaget (Norway) 282
Kunst, VEB Verlag der, (German Democratic Republic) 119
Kunst und Wissen Erich Bieber OHG (Federal Republic of Germany) 147
Kunstkreis, Edition, im Ex Libris Verlag (Switzerland) 356
Kunstkreis AG (Switzerland) 348
Kunstkreis für Bibliophile Mappen (Federal Republic of Germany) 170
Kuomintang Central Committee Library (China (Taiwan)) 64
Kupferberg, Florian, Verlag (Federal Republic of Germany) 147
Küpper, Verlag Helmut, (formerly Georg Bondi) (Federal Republic of Germany) 147
Kurita Shuppan Hanbai Co Ltd (Japan) 232
Kurnia Esa (Indonesia) 200

Kutter, Edouard, (Luxembourg) 244
Kutub, Dar Al, Al Hadeetha (Egypt) 82
Kutub, Dar al, al-Wataniya (Saudi Arabia) 306
Kutubi Moh'd Nihad Hashem (Syria) 357
Kuwait Central Library (Kuwait) 240
Kuwait Publishing House (Kuwait) 240
Kuwait University Central Library (Kuwait) 240
Kuwait University Libraries Department (Kuwait) 240
Kvinner og Klaer (Norway) 283
Kwan Dong Publishing Co (Republic of Korea) 238
Kwang Hwa, Sharikat Toko Buku, (Brunei) 57
Kwang Hwa Bookstore Pte Ltd (Malaysia) 247
Kwangmyong Printing & Publishing Co Ltd (Republic of Korea) 238
Kwaratech Bookshop (Nigeria) 280
Kwong Hin Bookstore (Hong Kong) 181
Kwong Yick Bookstore (Hong Kong) 181
Kyemong-sa (Republic of Korea) 238
Kyi-Pwar-Ye Book House (Burma) 59
Kynning Ltd, (Iceland) 185
Kyo Bun Kwan Inc (Japan) 228
Kyohak Sa (Republic of Korea) 238
Kyoritsu Shuppan Co Ltd (Japan) 228
Kyoto Sangyo University Library (Japan) 232
Kyriakou, K P, Books & Stationery (Cyprus) 69
Kyrios-Verlag GmbH (Federal Republic of Germany) 147
Kyung In Munwha Sa (Republic of Korea) 238
Kyungpook National University Library (Republic of Korea) 239
Kyushu University Library (Japan) 232

L & S Publishing Co Pty Ltd (Australia) 15
L E D A (Las Ediciones de Arte) (Spain) 322
L E R, Livraria, (Brazil) 56
L I S A (Livros Irradiantes SA) (Brazil) 52
L I T A (Czechoslovakia) 72
L I T E C-Livraria Editora Técnica Ltda (Brazil) 56
L J Productions (France) 100
L K G (German Democratic Republic) 120
L N-Verlag Lübeck, Lübecker Nachrichten GmbH (Federal Republic of Germany) 147
L S P Books Ltd (United Kingdom) 393
L T r Editora Ltda (Brazil) 52
L Ts Förlag AB (Sweden) 334
La Diffusion Scientifique, Editions, (France) 95
La Fontaine Prize (France) 114
La Paz, Librería, (Bolivia) 47
Lääketieteellinen Keskuskirjasto (Finland) 87
Labbé-Vauquelin, Paul, Prize (France) 114
Labor, Editions, (Belgium) 39
Labor, Editorial, Argentina SA (Argentina) 6
Labor, Editorial, Colombiana Ltda (Colombia) 65
Labor, Editorial, de Venezuela SA (Venezuela) 424
Labor, Editorial, del Ecuador SA (Ecuador) 81
Labor, Editorial, do Brasil SA (Brazil) 52
Labor, Editorial, SA (Spain) 322
Labor et Fides (Switzerland) 348
Lacayo, Editorial, (Nicaragua) 276
Laconti, Imprimerie, SA (Belgium) 39
Lademann Ltd, Publishers (Denmark) 76
Ladybird Books Ltd (United Kingdom) 393
Laetare (Federal Republic of Germany) 147
Lafenestre, Georges, Prize (France) 114
Laffitte, Librairie, (France) 110
Laffont, Editions Robert, (France) 100
Lafite, Elisabeth, (Austria) 26
Lafolye et Lamarzelle Editeurs Sàrl (France) 100
Laget, Librairie Léonce, (France) 100
Lagos City Council Libraries (Nigeria) 280
Lahden Akateeminen Kirjakauppa (Finland) 87
Lahn-Verlag (Federal Republic of Germany) 147
Lahumière, Editions, (France) 100
Laia, Editorial, (Spain) 322
Lake House Investments Ltd (Sri Lanka) 329
Lakeland Paperbacks (United Kingdom) 393
Lakoul Press (Nepal) 257
Lakshmi Narain Agarwal (India) 191
Lalit Kala Akademi (National Academy of Art) (India) 191
Lalvani Brothers (India) 191
Lam Kee Bookstore (Hong Kong) 181
Lamares, Americo Fraga, & Ca Lda (Portugal) 300
Lamarre-Poinat, Editions, SA (France) 100
Lamb, Charles, Society (United Kingdom) 418
Lambert Prize (France) 114
Lambertus Verlag GmbH (Federal Republic of Germany) 148
Lameere, Eugène, Prize (Belgium) 46
Lampe, Editions, d'Or ASBL (Belgium) 39
Lamy SA (France) 100
Lancashire Authors' Association (United Kingdom) 418
Lancaster Publishing (New Zealand) 273
Lanchester, The, Prize (International Literary Prizes) 450

Landbouwhogeschool, Bibliotheek der, (Library of the Agricultural University) (Netherlands) 269
Landbuch-Verlag GmbH (Federal Republic of Germany) 148
Landesgremium Kärnten des Handels mit Büchern, Kunstblättern, Musikalien, Zeitungen und Zeitschriften (Austria) 23
Landesgremium Niederösterreich des Handels mit Büchern, Kunstblättern, Musikalien, Zeitungen und Zeitschriften (Austria) 23
Landesgremium Oberösterreich des Handels mit Büchern, Kunstblättern, Musikalien, Zeitungen und Zeitschriften (Austria) 23
Landesgremium Salzburg des Handels mit Büchern, Kunstblättern, Musikalien, Zeitungen und Zeitschriften (Austria) 23
Landesgremium Steiermark des Handels mit Büchern, Kunstblättern, Musikalien, Zeitungen und Zeitschriften (Austria) 23
Landesgremium Tirol des Handels mit Büchern, Kunstblättern, Musikalien, Zeitungen und Zeitschriften (Austria) 23
Landesgremium Vorarlberg des Handels mit Büchern und Musikalien (Austria) 24
Landesgremium Wien des Handels mit Büchern, Kunstblättern, Musikalien, Zeitungen und Zeitschriften (Austria) 24
Landesman, Jay, Ltd (United Kingdom) 393
Landesverband der Buchhändler und Verleger in Niedersachsen eV (Provincial Federation of Booksellers and Publishers in Lower Saxony) (Federal Republic of Germany) 122
Landesverband der Verleger und Buchhändler Bremen-Unterweser eV (Bremen Provincial Federation of Publishers and Booksellers) (Federal Republic of Germany) 122
Landesverband der Verleger und Buchhändler Rheinland-Pfalz eV (Rhineland-Palatinate Provincial Federation of Publishers and Booksellers) (Federal Republic of Germany) 122
Landesverband der Verleger und Buchhändler Saar eV (LVBS) (Saar Provincial Federation of Publishers and Booksellers) (Federal Republic of Germany) 122
Landesverband des werbenden Buch- und Zeitschriftenhandels von Südwestdeutschland eV (Provincial Federation of the Book and Periodical Trade of South-west Germany) (Federal Republic of Germany) 122
Landsberger Verlagsanstalt Martin Neumeyer (Federal Republic of Germany) 148
Landsbókasafn Islands (National Library of Iceland) (Iceland) 186
Landwirtschaftliche Zentralbibliothek (Agricultural Central Library) (German Democratic Republic) 120
Landwirtschaftlicher Staatsverlag (Agricultural State Publishers) (Czechoslovakia) 70
Landy, Livraria D, (Brazil) 56
Lane, Allen, (United Kingdom) 393
Lang, Herbert, & Cie AG (Switzerland) 348
Lang, Verlag Peter, AG (Switzerland) 348
Lange, Allert de, BV (Netherlands) 264
Langen, Albert, -Georg Müller Verlag (Federal Republic of Germany) 148
Langen-Müller, Verlagsgruppe, / Herbig (Federal Republic of Germany) 148
Langenhoven, C J, Prize (Republic of South Africa) 317
Langenscheidt AG (Switzerland) 348
Langenscheidt Group, The, (Federal Republic of Germany) 148
Langenscheidt-Hachette GmbH (Federal Republic of Germany) 148
Langenscheidt KG (Federal Republic of Germany) 148
Langenscheidt-Longman GmbH (Federal Republic of Germany) 148
Langenscheidt-Verlag GmbH (Austria) 26
Langewiesche, Karl Robert, Nachfolger Hans Koester KG (Federal Republic of Germany) 148
Langewiesche-Brandt KG (Federal Republic of Germany) 148
Langlois Prize (France) 114
Language and Literature Bureau Library (Brunei) 57
Language Book Centre (Australia) 19
Languages School (Thailand) 359
Lanka Booksellers' Association (India) 186
Lannoo (Belgium) 39
Lannoo, Uitgeverij, (Netherlands) 264
Lanore, Editions J, C L T (France) 101
Lanore, Librairie Fernand, Sàrl (France) 101
Lansdowne Editions (Australia) 15
Lanterna, Editrice, (Italy) 216
Lao Dong (Labour) Publishing House (Socialist Republi of Viet Nam) 426
Lao-phanit (Laos) 240
Lapautre, Mme Michelle, (France) 110
Lappeenrannan Kirjakauppa Oy (Finland) 87
Lärabokklubben (Sweden) 337
Larcier, Maison Ferdinand, SA (Belgium) 39

Larese, Franz, und Jürg Janett (Switzerland) 348
Larousse, Ediciones, Argentina SA (Argentina) 6
Larousse, Librairie, (France) 101
Larousse, Librairie, Centrafrique (Burundi) 60
Larousse (Suisse) SA (Switzerland) 348
Larson, Bokförlaget Robert, AB (Sweden) 334
Läsklubben Fyrklövern (Sweden) 337
Lassens, Hartvig, Gold Medal (Norway) 284
Lasser Press Mexicana, SA (Mexico) 252
Lasserre, Luis, y Cía, SACIFI (Argentina) 6
Lasten Keskus Oy (Finland) 86
Laterna Magica, Verlag, Joachim F Richter (Federal Republic of Germany) 148
Laterza, Giuseppe, & Figli SpA (Italy) 216
Latin Friendship Prize (International Literary Prizes) 450
Latina SCA (Argentina) 6
Latino Americana, Editora, SA (Mexico) 252
Latomus ASBL (Belgium) 39
Lattès, Editions Jean-Claude, (France) 101
Laudes, Editôra, SA (Brazil) 52
Laupp'sche, H, Buchhandlung (Federal Republic of Germany) 148
Laurens, Editions Henri, Successeurs Sàrl (France) 101
Laurenziana, Biblioteca Medicea, (Italy) 222
Laurie, T Werner, (United Kingdom) 393
Lavauzelle, Charles, (France) 101
Lavigerie, Les Presses, (Burundi) 60
Laville, Diffusion Bernard, (France) 101
Law, The, Book Co Ltd (Australia) 15
Law Books in Hindi Prize (India) 198
Law Books in Hindi Publishers (India) 191
Lawin Publishing House (Philippines) 291
Lawrence & Wishart (United Kingdom) 393
Lawyers' Co-operative Publishing Co (Philippines) Inc (Philippines) 291
Lax, August, (Federal Republic of Germany) 148
Layraud, J-P, (New Caledonia) 271
Lazarillo Prize (International Literary Prizes) 450
Le Bayon, Alice, (France) 110
Le Moël, Eugène, Prize (France) 114
Le Monnier, Casa Editrice Felice, (Italy) 216
Le Prat, Editions Guy, (France) 101
Lebanese Library, The, Association (Lebanon) 241
Lebanon Bookshop (Lebanon) 241
Lechevalier, Editions, Sàrl (France) 101
Lechner, Rudolf, & Sohn (Austria) 30
Lecomte, Pierre, du Nouy Award (International Literary Prizes) 450
Leconte, Sébastien-Charles, Prize (France) 114
Lector-Verlag GmbH (Switzerland) 348
Lectura, Librería, (Venezuela) 425
Ledori (Israel) 208
Lee, T H, & Co Ltd (Hong Kong) 181
Leeds University Library (United Kingdom) 416
Leemann AG, Buchdruckerei und Verlag (Switzerland) 348
Leer, The Van, Jerusalem Foundation (Israel) 208
Lee's Book Centre (Bahamas) 32
Lefebvre, Francis, (France) 101
Léger, Editions Robert, et Cie (France) 101
Legislación Económica Ltda (Colombia) 65
'Legkaya Industriya', Izdatelstvo, (Union of Soviet Socialist Republics) 365
Legrain, Editions Paul, (Belgium) 39
Legrand, Editions, (Belgium) 39
Lehmann, Librería Imprenta y Litografía, SA (Costa Rica) 68
Lehmann, Librería Imprenta y Litografía, SA (Costa Rica) 67
Lehmanns, J F, Verlag (Federal Republic of Germany) 148
Lehnert & Landrock (Egypt) 82
Lehr- und Lernmittel, Verlag für, (Federal Republic of Germany) 170
Leibnitz-Volksbuchhandlung (German Democratic Republic) 120
Leicester University Press (United Kingdom) 393
Leiden University Press (Netherlands) 264
Leiftur hf (Iceland) 185
Leihbücherei-Gewerbeverband der Schweiz (Swiss Lending Library Association) 357
Leins, Verlag Hermann, (Federal Republic of Germany) 148
Leipholdt, Louis, prys vir Poesie (Republic of South Africa) 317
Leipzig, Edition, (German Democratic Republic) 119
Leipziger Kommissions- und Grossbuchhandel (LKG) (German Democratic Republic) 120
Leisure Arts Ltd (United Kingdom) 393
Leisure Circle, The, Ltd (United Kingdom) 414
Leitfadenverlag Dieter Sudholt (Federal Republic of Germany) 148
Lekarskich, Państwowy Zakład Wydawnictw, (Polish Medical Publishers) (Poland) 294
Lekha Prokashani (Bangladesh) 32
Lello & Cia Lda (Angola) 2
Lello & Cia Lda (Angola) 2

Lello e Cia Lda (Portugal) 300
Lello e Irmão (Portugal) 300
Lembeck, Verlag Otto, (Federal Republic of Germany) 148
Lemniscaat (Netherlands) 264
Lenclud, Anne, (France) 110
Lenina, Gosudarstvennaya ordena Lenina biblioteka SSSR imeni V I, (Union of Soviet Socialist Republics) 367
'Lenizdat', Izdatelstvo, (Union of Soviet Socialist Republics) 365
Lenners, Librairie, (Luxembourg) 244
Lenos (Lenos-Presse/Z-Verlag) (Switzerland) 348
Lensing, Verlag Lambert, GmbH (Federal Republic of Germany) 148
Lentz, Georg, Verlag (Federal Republic of Germany) 148
Lentz og Jenssens Forlag ApS (Denmark) 76
Leo, Franz, & Comp KG (Austria) 30
Leobuchhandlung (Switzerland) 348
Leobuchhandlung, Verlag der Quellenbändchen (Switzerland) 348
Leonardo da Vinci, Livraria, (Brazil) 56
Leong Brothers (Brunei) 57
Leonhardt, Albrecht, ApS (Denmark) 78
Leonhardt, Karl Ludwig, (Federal Republic of Germany) 169
Leonis Verlag (Switzerland) 348
Leopold, Uitgeverij, BV (Netherlands) 264
Lepus Books (United Kingdom) 393
Lerberghe, Van, Prize (France) 114
Lerner, Ediciones, Ltda (Colombia) 65
Lerner, Librería, (Colombia) 66
Lerú, Editorial Victor, SA (Argentina) 6
Leschiera Valerio (Italy) 216
Lesigne, Editions, (Belgium) 39
Leske Verlag und Budrich GmbH (Federal Republic of Germany) 149
'Lesnaya Promyshlennost', Izdatelstvo, (Union of Soviet Socialist Republics) 365
Lesoil, Uitgavenfonds Leon, V Z W (Belgium) 39
Lesot, Editions André, Sàrl (France) 101
Lesotho Book Centre (Lesotho) 242
Lesotho National Library Service (Lesotho) 242
Lesourd, Editions Olivier, (France) 101
Lessing Prize (Federal Republic of Germany) 173
Letouzey, Société Nouvelle des Editions, et Ané Sàrl (France) 101
Letrán, Librería, (Mexico) 254
Letras, Editorial, SA (Mexico) 252
Letras Cubanas, Editorial, (Cuba) 68
Lettres Modernes Minard (France) 101
Letts, Charles, & Co Ltd (United Kingdom) 393
Leuchter-Verlag AG (Federal Republic of Germany) 149
Leuchtturm-Verlag (Federal Republic of Germany) 149
Leuven University Press (Belgium) 39
Levéltári Osztaly, Kulturális Minisztévium, (Hungary) 184
Leven, The Grace, Prize for Poetry (Australia) 22
Leventhal, Lionel, Ltd (United Kingdom) 393
Leviathan House Ltd (United Kingdom) 393
Lewin-Epstein Ltd (Israel) 208
Lewin-Epstein-Modan, A, Ltd (Israel) 208
Lewis, A, (United Kingdom) 393
Lewis, F, (Publishers) Ltd (United Kingdom) 393
Lewis, H K, & Co Ltd (United Kingdom) 393
Lewis, J D, & Sons Ltd (United Kingdom) 393
Lex Editora SA (Brazil) 52
Lexika-Verlag Hablitzel & Wippler KG (Federal Republic of Germany) 149
Ley, La, SA Editora e Impresora (Argentina) 6
Leykam AG (Austria) 26
Liaoning Library (People's Republic of China) 64
Liaquat Memorial Library (Pakistan) 286
Liban, Librairie du, (Lebanon) 241
Liber, Sveučilišna Naklada, (Yugoslavia) 428
Liber Grafiska AB (Sweden) 334
Liber Tryck (Sweden) 334
Liber Verlag GmbH (Federal Republic of Germany) 149
LiberFörlag (Sweden) 334
Liberian Educational Materials Supply Corporation (Liberia) 242
Liberian Literary & Educational Publications (Liberia) 242
LiberKartor (Svensk Karttjänst AB, Swedish Map Service) (Sweden) 335
LiberLäromedel (Sweden) 335
Liberma, Libreria, (Italy) 221
Libertador, Editorial, (Venezuela) 424
Libertatea (Yugoslavia) 428
Liberty Bookstall (Pakistan) 286
Libra Books (Australia) 15
Librah (Netherlands) 269
Librairie afrique (Senegal) 307
Librairie clairafrique (Senegal) 307
Librairie Commerciale et Technique (Licet) Sàrl (France) 101
Librairie de Madagascar (Democratic Republic of Madagascar) 244

Librairie du Liban (Lebanon) 241
Librairie du Liban (Lebanon) 241
Librairie encyclopédique, Editions de la, (Belgium) 39
Librairie évangélique (Chad) 62
Librairie évangélique (Central African Republic) 61
Librairie évangélique (Zaire) 433
Librairie Générale de Droit et de Jurisprudence (France) 101
Librairie Générale Française SA (France) 101
Librairie générale SA (Belgium) 39
Librairie internationale (Morocco) 256
Librairie luthérienne (Democratic Republic of Madagascar) 244
Librairie mixte Sàrl (Democratic Republic of Madagascar) 244
Librairie moderne (Tunisia) 362
Librairie Nationale (Mauritius) 249
Librairie nationale (Morocco) 256
Librairie nouvelle de l'Ouest Africain (LINOA) (Senegal) 307
Librairie-Papeterie Moderne (United Republic of Cameroun) 61
Librairie-Papeterie Protestante CEBEC (United Republic of Cameroun) 61
Librairie-Papeterie Universelle (French Guiana) 116
Librairie Populaire (Popular Republic of Congo) 67
Librairie populaire de Mali (Mali) 248
Librairie universitaire (Democratic Republic of Madagascar) 245
Librairie Universitaire de la Réunion (Réunion) 303
Librairie universitaire et technique (Senegal) 307
Librairies Techniques SA (France) 101
Libraport (Guinea) 179
Library, School of, and Information Science (Japan) 232
Library, The, Shop (Republic of Ireland) 205
Library Advisory Council for England (United Kingdom) 416
Library Advisory Council for Wales (United Kingdom) 416
Library Association, The, (United Kingdom) 416
Library Association of Australia (Australia) 20
Library Association of Barbados (Barbados) 33
Library Association of China (China (Taiwan)) 64
Library Association of Singapore (Republic of Singapore) 310
Library Association of the Democratic People's Republic of Korea (Democratic People's Republic of Korea) 237
Library Automated Systems, The, Information Exchange (LASIE) (Australia) 20
Library Board and the State Reference Library of Western Australia, The, (Australia) 20
Library of Parliament (Republic of South Africa) 316
Library Promotion Bureau (Pakistan) 286
Library Science Society (Pakistan) 286
Library Science Society (China (Taiwan)) 64
Library Service of Fiji (Fiji) 85
Library Services for South West Africa (Namibia) 257
Librería Central (Colombia) 66
Librería Científica (Ecuador) 81
Librería Contemporanea (Puerto Rico) 302
Librería Continental (Colombia) 66
Librería Cultural (Puerto Rico) 302
Librería Cultural (Venezuela) 425
Librería Cultural Colombiana (Colombia) 66
Librería Cultural Nicaraguense (Nicaragua) 276
Librería Cultural Panameña, Ediciones, SA (Panama) 287
Librería Cultural Panameña, SA (Panama) 288
Librería Cultural Puertorriqueña Inc (Puerto Rico) 302
Librería Cultural Venezolana (Venezuela) 425
Librería Española (Ecuador) 81
Librería Inglesa (Uruguay) 423
Librería Intercontinental SA (Mexico) 254
Librería Internacional (Paraguay) 289
Librería Internacional del Perú (Peru) 290
Librería Internacional SA (Mexico) 254
Librería Nacional (Colombia) 66
Librería Tecno-Ciencia (Chile) 63
Librería Tecnológica Universitaria (Nicaragua) 276
Librería Tecnológico (Mexico) 254
Librería the Bookstore (Honduras) 180
Librería Universal (Guatemala) 179
Librería Universal (Paraguay) 289
Librería Universitaria (Mexico) 254
Librería Universitaria (Nicaragua) 276
Librería Universitaria (Chile) 63
Librería Universitaria (Ecuador) 81
Librería Universitaria de Puerto Rico (Puerto Rico) 302
Librex, Edizioni, (Italy) 217
Libri, Etas, SpA (Italy) 217
Libris Publishing House (Sweden) 335
Libro Club de Nuevo Léon SA (Mexico) 253
Libroclub de Guatemala (Guatemala) 179
Librolandia del Centro SA (Mexico) 254
Licet (France) 101
Lichtenberg Verlag GmbH (Federal Republic of Germany) 149

INDEX 493

Lichtkreis Christi (Federal Republic of Germany) 149
Licorne, Editions de la, (France) 101
Licosa SpA (Italy) 217
Lidador, Editôra, Ltda (Brazil) 53
Lidis, Editions, SA (France) 101
Lidis, Libraire, (France) 110
Lidman Production (Sweden) 335
Lidové nakladatelství (Czechoslovakia) 70
Liebenzeller Mission, Verlag der, (Federal Republic of Germany) 149
Liebing, Arnulf, (Federal Republic of Germany) 149
Liebing, Rudolf, (Federal Republic of Germany) 149
Liechtenstein Verlag AG (Liechtenstein) 243
Liechtenstein Verlag AG (Liechtenstein) 243
Liechtensteinische Landesbibliothek (National Library) (Liechtenstein) 243
Liepman, Dr Ruth, (Switzerland) 355
Lietzow, Edition/Galerie, (Federal Republic of Germany) 149
Ligel, Editions, (France) 101
Light & Life Publishers (India) 191
Ligia Romontscha (Lia Rumantscha) (Switzerland) 348
Ligue des Bibliothèques Européennes de Recherche (LIBER) (League of European Research Libraries) (International Organizations) 439
Liguori Editore SRL (Italy) 217
Lile, Editions Michel de, et Philippe Azou (France) 101
Lilja, Bókagerdin, (Iceland) 185
Lima, Waldyr, Editora (Brazil) 53
Limes Verlag (Federal Republic of Germany) 149
Limmat Verlag Genossenschaft (Switzerland) 348
Limonad, Editora Max, Ltda (Brazil) 53
Limpert Verlag (Federal Republic of Germany) 149
Limusa, Editorial, SA (Mexico) 252
Linardi, Librería Adolfo, (Uruguay) 423
Lincoln, Biblioteca, (Argentina) 8
Lincoln, Frances, Publishers Ltd (United Kingdom) 393
Lindblads, J A, Bokförlag AB (Sweden) 335
Linden Press (United Kingdom) 393
Linder AG Literary Agency (Switzerland) 355
Lindhardt og Ringhof (Denmark) 76
Lindqvist Förlag AB (Sweden) 335
Ling, H C, Book Store & Co Ltd (China (Taiwan)) 64
Ling Kee Bookstore (Hong Kong) 181
Ling Kee Publishing Co (Hong Kong) 181
Lingen Verlag (Federal Republic of Germany) 149
Lingenbrink, Barsortiment Georg, (Wholesale Bookseller) (Federal Republic of Germany) 170
Linguaphone Institute Ltd (United Kingdom) 393
Linosa-Linomonograph, Editorial, SA (Spain) 322
Lion Publishing (United Kingdom) 393
Lionarons Drukkerij NV (Suriname) 331
Lisieux, Office Central de, SA (France) 101
List, Paul, Verlag (German Democratic Republic) 119
List, Paul, Verlag KG (Federal Republic of Germany) 149
Listín, Editora, Diario (Dominican Republic) 80
Litchfield, Jessie, Memorial Award (Australia) 22
Literackie, Wydawnictwo, (Poland) 294
Literar-Mechana, Wahrnehmungsgesellschaft für Urheberrechte mbH (Austria) 24
Literarische Agentur und Verlagsgesellschaft (Liechtenstein) 243
Literarischer Verein in Stuttgart eV (Federal Republic of Germany) 173
Literarisches Colloquium Berlin (Federal Republic of Germany) 149
Literary Award (Romania) 305
Literary Club of Monrovia (Liberia) 242
Literary Critics' Grand Prize (France) 114
Literary Guild (United Kingdom) 415
Literary Guild, The, (New Zealand) 274
Literary Guild, The, (Australia) 19
Literary Prize (Republic of Korea) 240
Literary Prize of the Resistance (France) 114
Literary Prizes for Sinhala Literature (Sri Lanka) 330
Literary Prizes for Tamil Literature (Sri Lanka) 330
Literary Services (Pty) Ltd (Republic of South Africa) 315
Literary Supplies (Jamaica) 224
Literature Board of the Australia Council (Australia) 21
Literature Board of the Australia Council (Australia) 22
Literature Bureau, The, (Zimbabwe) 435
Literature Bureau, The, (Zimbabwe) 435
Literature Bureau, The, Annual Literary Award (Zimbabwe) 436
Literature Prize (Democratic Republic of Madagascar) 245
Literature Prize (Federal Republic of Germany) 173
Literatury Gorniczej, Klub Czytelnikow, (Poland) 296
Literatury Hutniczej, Klub Czytelnikow, (Poland) 296
Lito, Editions, (France) 101
Litolff's, Henry, Verlag (Federal Republic of Germany) 149
Litor Publishers (United Kingdom) 393
Litpress (Switzerland) 355
Littera Scripta Manet (Netherlands) 264
Littérature, Editeurs de, biblique (Biblical Publications) (Belgium) 39

Litteraturfrämjandet (Sweden) 339
Little Flower, The, Co (India) 191
Little Swan (India) 191
Liverpool City Libraries (United Kingdom) 416
Liverpool University Press (United Kingdom) 393
Living Literary Agency Elfriede Pexa (Italy) 221
Livraria Editora Tecnica Ltda (LITEC) (Brazil) 53
Livre, Editions, Club de Libraire (France) 110
Livre de Paris, Le, (France) 101
Livre de Poche, Le, (France) 101
Livres de France (Egypt) 83
Livro Científico, Estante do, (Brazil) 55
Livro Politico, Clube do, (Brazil) 55
Livros, Editora, do Brasil Sarl (Portugal) 300
Lloyd, Editions du, Anversois SA (Antwerpse Lloyd NV) (Belgium) 39
Lloyd-Luke (Medical Books) Ltd (United Kingdom) 394
Llyfrgell Genedlaethol Cymru (National Library of Wales) (United Kingdom) 416
Lobato, Monteiro, Prize (Brazil) 57
Löcker Verlag (Austria) 26
Lodzkie, Wydawnictwo, (Lodz Publishing House) (Poland) 294
Loeff, Uitg Mij van der, BV (Netherlands) 264
Loescher Editore (Italy) 217
Loewes Verlag KG (Federal Republic of Germany) 149
Lofler, Paul, Prize (France) 115
Logans University Bookshop (Pty) Ltd (Republic of South Africa) 315
Loghum, Van, Slaterus (Netherlands) 264
Logos Consorcio Editorial, SA (Mexico) 252
Logos-Verlag (Switzerland) 348
Logosófica, Editora, (Brazil) 53
Lohlé, Ediciones Carlos, SA (Argentina) 6
Lohses Forlag (Denmark) 76
Lok Vangmaya Griha (Pvt) Ltd (India) 191
Lokole, Editions, (Zaire) 433
Lomagundi Printing (Pvt) Ltd (Zimbabwe) 435
Lombard SA (Belgium) 39
London Bookshops Ltd (New Zealand) 274
London Editions Ltd (United Kingdom) 394
London Independent Books Ltd (United Kingdom) 413
London Magazine Editions (United Kingdom) 394
London Writer Circle (United Kingdom) 418
Lonely Planet Publications (Australia) 15
Longanesi e C (Italy) 217
Longbow (United Kingdom) 394
Longman Arab World Centre (Lebanon) 241
Longman Caribbean Ltd (Trinidad and Tobago) 361
Longman Cheshire Pty Ltd (Australia) 15
Longman Group (Far East) Ltd (Hong Kong) 181
Longman Group Ltd (United Kingdom) 394
Longman Italia SRL (Italy) 217
Longman Kenya Ltd (Kenya) 236
Longman Malaysia Sdn Bhd (Malaysia) 246
Longman Malaysia Sdn Bhd (Republic of Singapore) 309
Longman Nigeria Ltd (Nigeria) 278
Longman Paul Ltd (New Zealand) 273
Longman Penguin Southern Africa (Pty) Ltd (Republic of South Africa) 312
Longman Publishers (Pvt) Ltd (Zimbabwe) 435
Longman Tanzania Ltd (Tanzania) 358
Longman Uganda Ltd (Uganda) 364
Longo, Libreria A, (Italy) 222
Longo Editore (Italy) 217
Lope, Librería y Papeleria, de Vega (Dominican Republic) 81
Lope de Vega Prize (Spain) 329
Lopes, Julia, de Ameida Prize (Brazil) 57
Lopes Da Silva, Livraria, -Editôra de M Moreira Soares Rocha Lda (Portugal) 300
López Libreros Editores (Argentina) 6
Löpfe-Benz, E, AG Rorschach (Switzerland) 348
Loránd, Egyetemi könyvtár (Central Library),, Eötvös University (Hungary) 183
Lorber-Verlag (Federal Republic of Germany) 149
Lorch-Verlag GmbH (Federal Republic of Germany) 149
Lord International (India) 191
Lorrimer Books (United Kingdom) 394
Losada, Editorial, SA (Argentina) 6
Lothian, Thomas C, Pty Ltd (New Zealand) 273
Lothian Publishing Company Pty Ltd (Australia) 15
Lotu Pasifika Productions (Fiji) 85
Lotus, Uitgeverij, /Editions Lotus (Belgium) 39
Lotus Press Ltd (United Kingdom) 394
Lovedale Press (Republic of South Africa) 312
Lowden Publishing Co (Australia) 16
Lowe, Peter, (United Kingdom) 394
Lowe, Robson, Ltd (United Kingdom) 394
Loyola, Edições, SA (Brazil) 53
LP3ES (Lembaga Penelitian Pendidikan Dan Penerangan Ekonomi Dan Social) (Indonesia) 200
Lübbe, Gustav, Verlag GmbH (Federal Republic of Germany) 149
Lubelskie, Wydawnictwo, (Lublin Publishers) (Poland) 294

Luchterhand, Hermann, Verlag GmbH & Co KG (Federal Republic of Germany) 149
Lucis Press Ltd (United Kingdom) 394
Lucky (Australia) 19
Lucky Book Club (United Kingdom) 415
Luctor Publishing — Stadler & Sauerbier BV (Netherlands) 264
Lüdin AG (Switzerland) 348
Ludowa Spóldzielnia Wydawnicza (Poland) 294
Ludwig, Verlag W, (Federal Republic of Germany) 149
Luitingh, Uitgeverij, BV (Netherlands) 264
Lumen, Editions, Vitae (International centre for Religious Education) ASBL (Belgium) 40
Lumen, Editorial, (Spain) 322
Lumen Christi, Edicoes (Brazil) 53
Lumiere Biblique (France) 101
Luna, Libreria G, (Italy) 222
Lund Humphries Publishers Ltd (United Kingdom) 394
Lund Universitetsbibliotek (Sweden) 338
Lunde Forlag og Bokhandel A/S (Norway) 282
Lundequistska Bokhandeln, AB, (Sweden) 338
Lundgrens, AB Edvin, Bokhandel (Sweden) 338
Lundqvists, Abr, Musikförlag AB (Sweden) 335
Lusaka City Libraries (Zambia) 434
Luscombe, William, (United Kingdom) 394
Luso-Espanhola, Livraria, Lda (Portugal) 300
Luther Forlag A/S (Norway) 282
Luther-Verlag GmbH (Federal Republic of Germany) 149
Lutherisches Verlagshaus (Federal Republic of Germany) 149
Lutterworth Press (United Kingdom) 394
Lutz, Hans-Rudolf, (Switzerland) 348
Lux Press (Malta) 248
Luxor Press (United Kingdom) 394
Lyall Book Depot (India) 197
Lyche, Harald, og Co A/S (Norway) 282
Lydecken, Arvid, Prize (Finland) 88
Lyle Publications Ltd (United Kingdom) 394
Lyngs Bokhandel A/S (Norway) 283
Lyrikkvaennene, Bokklubbens, (Norway) 283
Lythway Press Ltd (United Kingdom) 394

M & J Raven (United Kingdom) 394
M A M (Cyprus) 69
M A M (Cyprus) 69
M B A Literary Agents Ltd (United Kingdom) 413
M C A (Australia) 16
M C L (France) 101
M C S Enterprises Inc (Philippines) 291
M D I, Editions, (La Maison des Instituteurs) (France) 101
M E/D I Sviluppo (Italy) 217
M F B (Phono- und Schriftenmission des Missionstrupps Frohe Botschaft eV) (Federal Republic of Germany) 149
M I M (Belgium) 40
M I T, The, Press (United Kingdom) 394
M P H Distributors Sdn Bhd (Malaysia) 247
M P H Pte Ltd (Republic of Singapore) 310
M R P (United Kingdom) 394
M S A (Republic of South Africa) 312
M T P Press Ltd (United Kingdom) 394
M W H London Publishers (United Kingdom) 394
Ma'alot (Israel) 208
Ma'arachot (Israel) 208
Ma'aref, Al, Library (Jordan) 234
Maaref, Dar Al, (Egypt) 82
Maaref, Dar Al-, Liban SAL (Lebanon) 241
Ma'arif, Al, Ltd (Iraq) 202
Ma'ariv Book Guild (Sifriat Ma'ariv) (Israel) 208
Maatschappij der Nederlandse Letterkunde (Society of Netherlands Literature) (Netherlands) 270
Mabrochi International Co (Nigeria) 280
Mac Purcell (Lebanon) 241
Macaraig Publishing Co (Philippines) 291
Macaulay Fellowships (Republic of Ireland) 205
Macchi, Ediciones, (Argentina) 6
Macdonald & Evans Ltd (United Kingdom) 394
Macdonald & Jane's Publishing Group (United Kingdom) 394
Macdonald Educational Ltd (United Kingdom) 395
Macdonald General Books (United Kingdom) 395
Macdonald Publishers (United Kingdom) 395
Macdonald's (Kenya) 236
Mace, Jean, Prize (France) 115
Machado, Fernando, e Co Ltd (Portugal) 300
Machado de Assis Prize (Brazil) 57
Machbarot Iesifrut (Israel) 208
MacKern, Librerías, SA (Argentina) 8
Mackey's Variety Stores (Bahamas) 32
Mackintosh Hall, John, Library (Gibraltar) 176
MacLaren & Sons Ltd (United Kingdom) 395
Maclellan, William, (United Kingdom) 395

Macmillan, The, Co of Australia Pty Ltd (Australia) 16
Macmillan, The, Co of India Ltd (India) 191
Macmillan Education Ltd (United Kingdom) 395
Macmillan London Ltd (United Kingdom) 395
Macmillan Malaysia (Malaysia) 246
Macmillan Nigeria Publishers Ltd (Nigeria) 278
Macmillan Press, The, Ltd (United Kingdom) 395
Macmillan Publishers (HK) Ltd (Hong Kong) 181
Macmillan Publishers Ltd (United Kingdom) 395
Macmillan South Africa Publishers (Pty) Ltd (Republic of South Africa) 312
Macmillan Southeast Asia Pte Ltd (Republic of Singapore) 309
Madáh (Czechoslovakia) 70
Madarali, Fikret, Prize (Turkey) 364
Made Simple Books (United Kingdom) 395
Madju (Indonesia) 200
Madras Literary Society and Auxiliary of the Royal Asiatic Society (India) 198
Madras Literary Society Library (India) 197
Maeght Editeur (France) 102
Magal Ltd — Translations & Typeset (Israel) 211
Magasin du Nord A/S (Denmark) 78
Maghreb Livres (Morocco) 256
Maghrebines, Les Editions, (Morocco) 256
Magisterio, Editorial, Español SA (Spain) 322
Magna Print Books (United Kingdom) 395
Magnard, Les Editions, Sàrl (France) 102
Magnes, The, Press (Israel) 208
Magnum Books (United Kingdom) 395
Magnus Verlag (Federal Republic of Germany) 150
Magvető Könyvkiadó (Publishing House of Belles Lettres) (Hungary) 182
Magwe College Library (Burma) 60
Magyar Bibliofil társaság (Hungarian Society of Bibliophiles) (Hungary) 184
Magyar Irodalomtörténeti Társaság (Hungary) 184
Magyar Írok Szövetsége (Association of Hungarian Writers) (Hungary) 184
Magyar Írók Szövetsége (Association of Hungarian Writers) (Hungary) 184
Magyar Könyvkiadók és Könyvterjesztők Egyesülése (Association of Hungarian Publishers and Booksellers) (Hungary) 182
Magyar Könyvtárosok Egyesülete (Association of Hungarian Librarians) (Hungary) 184
Magyar Központi Levéltár, Uj, (New Central Archives of Hungary) (Hungary) 183
Magyar országos levéltár (National Archives) (Hungary) 183
Magyar Tudományos Akadémia Irodalomtudományi Intézete (Hungary) 184
Magyar Tudományos Akadémia Könyvtára (Hungary) 183
Mahabir Singh Chiniya Main (Nepal) 257
Mahajan Brothers (India) 191
Mahligai, Pustaka, Press (Malaysia) 246
Maier, Otto, Benelux BV (Netherlands) 264
Maier, Otto, Verlag (Federal Republic of Germany) 150
Maille-Latour-Landry Prize (France) 115
Mainichi Publishing Culture Prize (Japan) 234
Mainstream Book Club (United Kingdom) 415
Mainstream Publishing Co (Edinburgh) Ltd (United Kingdom) 395
Mairs Geographischer Verlag (Federal Republic of Germany) 150
Mai's Reiseführer Verlag (Federal Republic of Germany) 150
Maison, La, de la Bible (Switzerland) 348
Maison, La, du Livre (Senegal) 307
Maison, La, du Livre (Benin) 47
Maison, La, Rustique SA (France) 102
Maison, Librairie '. des Livres' (Algeria) 2
Maison de la Presse, Société congolaise Hachette (Popular Republic of Congo) 67
Maison de Poésie (House of Poetry) (Fondation Emile Blémont) (France) 112
Maison des Instituteurs, La, (France) 102
Maison des Livres (Ivory Coast) 224
Maison du Dictionnaire, La, (France) 102
Maison Tunisienne d'Edition (Tunisia) 362
Maisondieu Prize (France) 115
Maisonneuve et Larose, Editions G P, (France) 102
Maisonneuve-Librairie d'Amérique et d'Orient, Adrien, (France) 102
Máj (Czechoslovakia) 72
Majerove, Marie, Prize (Czechoslovakia) 73
Majlis Press (Iran) 202
Makedonska Knjiga (Yugoslavia) 431
Makedonska Knjiga (Knigoizdatelstvo) (Yugoslavia) 428
Makerere Institute of Social Research Library (Uganda) 364
Makerere University Bookshop (Uganda) 364
Makerere University Library (Uganda) 364
Makor Publishing Ltd (Israel) 208
Makshouf, Dar al-, (Lebanon) 241
Maktaba, Al-, (Saudi Arabia) 306

Maktaba Ishaat-e-Adab (Pakistan) 286
Maktaba Jadeed (Pakistan) 285
Maktaba Meri Library (Pakistan) 285
Maktaba Shahkar (Pakistan) 285
Maktabah, Al, Al Wataniah (National Library) (Syria) 357
Mal Og Menning (Iceland) 185
Mál og menning (Iceland) 185
Malabar, Toko Buku, (Indonesia) 200
Malaby Press (United Kingdom) 395
Maladá Fronta Award (Czechoslovakia) 73
Malan, H R, Prize (Republic of South Africa) 317
Malatestiana, Biblioteca Comunale, (Italy) 222
Malawi Book Service (Malawi) 245
Malawi Library Association, The, (Malawi) 245
Malawi National Library Service (Malawi) 245
Malawi Polytechnic, The, (Malawi) 245
Malaya Books Suppliers Co (Malaysia) 246
Malaya Educational Supplies Sdn Bhd (Malaysia) 246
Malaya Press, The, Sdn Bhd (Malaysia) 246
Malayan Law Journal (Pte) Ltd (Republic of Singapore) 309
Malaysia Press Sdn Bhd (Republic of Singapore) 309
Malaysian Book Publishers' Association (Malaysia) 246
Malherbe, John, (Pty) Ltd (Republic of South Africa) 312
Mali, Editions Imprimeries du, (Mali) 248
Malik Din Mohammad & Sons (Pakistan) 285
Malik Siraj ud Din & Sons (Pakistan) 285
Malipiero SpA (Italy) 217
Malmberg BV (Netherlands) 264
Malmö Stadsbibliotek (Sweden) 338
Maloine, Librairie, (France) 102
Malpertuis Prize (Belgium) 46
Máls og Menningar, Bókabúd, (Iceland) 185
Malsa Book Service Ltd (Zambia) 434
Malta Library Association (Ghaqda Bibljotekarji) (Malta) 248
'Malysh', Izdatelstvo, (Union of Soviet Socialist Republics) 366
Mamadou Traoré Ray Autra (Senegal) 307
Mambo Press (Zimbabwe) 435
Mambo Press Bookshop (Zimbabwe) 435
Mame, Nouvelles Editions, (France) 102
Man in His Environment, The, Book Award (International Literary Prizes) 450
Månadens Bok (Sweden) 338
Månadens Bok (Sweden) 335
Manar, Imprimerie/Librairie Al, (Tunisia) 362
Manar, Librairie Al, (Tunisia) 362
Manchester Odd Fellows Social Concern Annual Book Awards (International Literary Prizes) 450
Manchester University Press (United Kingdom) 396
Mandas Sugatdas (Nepal) 257
Mandat des Poètes Prize (International Literary Prizes) 450
Manesse und Morgarten Verlag (Switzerland) 349
Manesse-Verlag (Switzerland) 348
Mangold, Paul, Verlag (Austria) 26
Manhin, Victor, Ltd (Trinidad and Tobago) 361
Mann, Gebr, Verlag (Federal Republic of Germany) 150
Mann, Thomas, Prize (Federal Republic of Germany) 173
Mann, Volksbuchhandlung Thomas, (German Democratic Republic) 120
Manohar Publications (India) 191
Manole, Editora, Ltda (Brazil) 53
Manor Press (Philippines) 291
Mansell Publishing (United Kingdom) 396
Mansfield, Katherine, Memorial Award (New Zealand) 275
Mansfield, Katherine, Menton Memorial Prize (International Literary Prizes) 451
Mansour, S J, (Israel) 208
Manteau, Uitgeversmaatschappij A, NV (Belgium) 40
Manual, El, Moderno, SA (Mexico) 252
Manutiuspresse Wulf Stratowa Verlag (Austria) 26
Manxman Publications (United Kingdom) 396
Manz Verlag (Federal Republic of Germany) 150
Manz'sche Verlags- und Universitätsbuchhandlung (Austria) 26
Manz'sche Verlags und Universitätsbuchhandlung (Austria) 30
Map Productions Ltd (United Kingdom) 396
Mapa Fiscal Editora Ltda (Brazil) 53
Maqbool Academy (Pakistan) 285
Mara Institute of Technology Library (Malaysia) 247
Marabout, Les Nouvelles Editions, SA (Belgium) 40
Marais, Eugène, Prize (Republic of South Africa) 317
Marangu College of National Education Library (Tanzania) 358
Marbán, Editorial, (Spain) 323
Marchal, Joseph-Edmond, Prize (Belgium) 46
Marcombo SA de Boixareu Editores (Spain) 323
Marcus, I, (Israel) 208
Marczell, Tibor, (Federal Republic of Germany) 150
Mardaga, Pierre, SA (Belgium) 40
Maredsous ASBL (Belgium) 40

Marfiah (Indonesia) 200
Marfil, Editorial, SA (Spain) 323
Marg Publications (India) 191
Margai, Milton, Teachers' College Library (Sierra Leone) 308
Marguerat, Librairie-Editions J, (Switzerland) 349
Marhold, Carl, Verlagsbuchhandlung (Federal Republic of Germany) 150
Maria-Verlag (Federal Republic of Germany) 150
Mariani, Anna Marie, Wagenkampfverlag (Switzerland) 349
Marican & Sons (M) Sdn Bhd (Malaysia) 247
Marie-Médiatrice, Editions, ASBL (Belgium) 40
Marietti Editori SpA (Italy) 217
Marin, Editorial, SA (Spain) 323
Maritim, Edition, (Federal Republic of Germany) 150
Maritime Book Society (United Kingdom) 415
Markham, Arthur, Memorial Prize (United Kingdom) 420
Markovič, Univerzitetska biblioteka 'Svetozar, (Yugoslavia) 431
Marksa, Gosudarstvennaya Respublikanskaya biblioteka Gruzinskoi SSR im K, (Union of Soviet Socialist Republics) 367
Markus, Editions, (Belgium) 40
Maro Verlag (Federal Republic of Germany) 150
Marotta, Alberto, Editore SpA (Italy) 217
Marova, Ediciones, SL (Spain) 323
Marques de Cerralbo XVII Prize (Spain) 329
Marrimpouey, Éditions, Jeune et Cie (France) 102
Marshall, Alan, Award (Australia) 22
Marshall, Morgan & Scott Publications Ltd (United Kingdom) 396
Marshall, Muir, Ltd (Trinidad and Tobago) 361
Marshall Cavendish Ltd (United Kingdom) 396
Marshall Editions Ltd (United Kingdom) 396
Marsiega, Editorial, SA (Spain) 323
Marsilio Editori (Italy) 217
Marsland Press (United Kingdom) 396
Martello, Giunti, Editore (Italy) 217
Martin Books (United Kingdom) 396
Martin Educational (Australia) 16
Martin Robertson & Co Ltd (United Kingdom) 396
Martindale Press (Australia) 16
Martínez, Ediciones, Roca SA (Spain) 323
Martínez, H F, de Murguía (Spain) 327
Martínez, H F, de Murguía (Argentina) 8
Martínez, Roberto, & Sons (Philippines) 291
Martins, Livraria, Editôra SA (Brazil) 53
Martins, Livraria Tavares, (Portugal) 300
Martins Forlag (Denmark) 76
Martinsart, Editions, (France) 102
Maruzen Asia (Pte) Ltd (Republic of Singapore) 309
Maruzen Co Ltd (Japan) 232
Maruzen Co Ltd (Japan) 228
Marva (Switzerland) 349
Marxistische Blätter, Verlag, GmbH (Federal Republic of Germany) 150
Marymar Ediciones SA (Argentina) 6
Marzocco, Editrice Giunti, (Italy) 217
Marzorati Editore SRL (Italy) 217
Masa Baru (Indonesia) 200
Mascareignes, Librairie des, (Mauritius) 249
Mascereel, Frans, Fonds VZW (Belgium) 40
'Mashinostroenie', Izdatelstvo, (Union of Soviet Socialist Republics) 366
Mashreq, Dar-el, (Lebanon) 241
Mason, Kenneth, Publications Ltd (United Kingdom) 396
Masout (Israel) 208
Maspero, François, Editeur (France) 102
Mass, Rubin, (Israel) 208
Mass Culture Publishing House (Democratic People's Republic of Korea) 237
Massada Press Ltd (Israel) 208
Massada Press Ltd (Israel) 210
Massada Publishing Ltd (Israel) 208
Massimo, Editrice, (Italy) 217
Massin, Editions Charles, et Cie (France) 102
Masson do Brasil (Brazil) 53
Masson Editeur (France) 102
Masson Editores (Mexico) 252
Master Storytellers (United Kingdom) 415
Mathews Miller Dunbar (United Kingdom) 396
Matica Slovenská (Czechoslovakia) 72
Matica slovenská (Czechoslovakia) 70
Matice Moravská (Czechoslovakia) 73
Matopo Book Centre (Zimbabwe) 435
Matthaes, Hugo, Druckerei und Verlag GmbH & Co KG (Federal Republic of Germany) 150
Matthes und Seitz Verlag GmbH (Federal Republic of Germany) 150
Matthias-Estienne (France) 110
Matthias-Grünewald-Verlag (Federal Republic of Germany) 150
Matthiesen Verlag Ingwert Paulsen Jr (Federal Republic of Germany) 150
Matze, Editions la, (Switzerland) 349

Mauclert, Librairie, (Niger) 276
Maudrich, Verlag Wilhelm, (Austria) 26
Maudrich, Wilhelm, (Austria) 30
Maugham, Somerset, Award (United Kingdom) 420
Maulana Azad Library (India) 197
Maupetit, Librairie, (France) 110
Mauritanie, Librairie-Papeterie, Nouvelle (Mauritania) 249
Mauritius Archives (Mauritius) 249
Mauritius Institute Public Library (Mauritius) 249
Mauritius Library Association (Mauritius) 249
Maximilian-Verlag (Federal Republic of Germany) 150
May, Karl-, -Verlag, Joachim Schmid & Co (Federal Republic of Germany) 150
May, Verlag A & G de, (Switzerland) 349
Mayela, Librería Editorial Gerardo, (Mexico) 254
Mayer, Edition Hansjörg, (Federal Republic of Germany) 150
Mayer, Ludwig, Ltd (Israel) 210
Mayer'sche, J A, Buchhandlung (Federal Republic of Germany) 150
Mayer'sche Buchhandlung, J A, (Federal Republic of Germany) 170
Mayfair Paperbacks (India) 192
Mayflower Books Ltd (United Kingdom) 396
Mayhew, Kevin, Ltd (United Kingdom) 396
Mayhew-McCrimmon Ltd (United Kingdom) 396
Mazarde, Fernand, Prize (France) 115
Mazarine, Editions, (France) 102
Mazenod, Editions d'Art Lucien, (France) 102
Mazenod Book Centre (Lesotho) 242
Mazenod Institute (Lesotho) 242
Mazzotta, Gabriele, Editore SpA (Italy) 217
McColvin Medal (United Kingdom) 420
McGraw-Hill, Editôra, do Brasil Ltda (Brazil) 53
McGraw-Hill, Editorial, Latino-Americana SA (Panama) 287
McGraw-Hill, Editorial, Latinoamerica SA (Puerto Rico) 302
McGraw-Hill, Editorial, Latinoamericana SA (Colombia) 66
McGraw-Hill, Libros, de Mexico SA de CV (Mexico) 252
McGraw-Hill Book Co (Switzerland) 348
McGraw-Hill Book Co, New Zealand Ltd (New Zealand) 273
McGraw-Hill Book Co (South Africa) (Pty) Ltd (Republic of South Africa) 312
McGraw-Hill Book Co (UK) Ltd (United Kingdom) 395
McGraw-Hill Book Co Australia Pty Ltd (Australia) 16
McGraw-Hill Book Co GmbH (Federal Republic of Germany) 150
McGraw-Hill Inc (France) 102
McGraw-Hill International Book Co (Republic of Singapore) 309
McIndoe, John, Ltd (New Zealand) 273
McKee & Mouche (France) 110
McMillan Memorial Library (Kenya) 236
McPhee Gribble Publishers (Australia) 16
Meadowfield Press Ltd (United Kingdom) 396
Mebso Bookshop (Iran) 202
Meca, Editora, Ltda (Brazil) 53
Meddens, Les Ateliers d'Art graphique, SA (Belgium) 40
Médecine & Hygiène (Switzerland) 349
Médica, Editorial, Panamericana SA (Argentina) 6
Medica, Librería, Paris (Venezuela) 425
Médica, Librería y Editorial La, (Argentina) 6
Medical Friend Co Ltd (Japan) 228
Medical Librarians' Group (Australia) 20
Medical Science Publishing House (Democratic People's Republic of Korea) 237
Medical World Book Co Pte Ltd (Republic of Singapore) 309
Medicala, Editura, (Medical Publishing House) (Romania) 304
Medici, The, Society Ltd (United Kingdom) 396
Medicina Könyvkiadó (Hungary) 182
Medicinsk Forlag ApS (Denmark) 76
Medicinska Knjiga (Yugoslavia) 428
Medicinska Naklada (Yugoslavia) 428
Medicis Foreign Prize (International Literary Prizes) 451
Médicis Prize (France) 115
Medico Farmaceutica, Organizzazione Editoriale, SRL (Italy) 217
Medina, Editorial, SRL (Uruguay) 422
Mediterranea, Librería, (Spain) 327
Mediterranee, Edizioni, SRL (Italy) 217
'Meditsina', Izdatelstvo, (Union of Soviet Socialist Republics) 366
Meditsina i Fizkultura (Bulgaria) 58
Medium, Bokförlaget, AB (Sweden) 335
Medizin, Buchhandlung für, (German Democratic Republic) 120
Medizin, Verlag für, Dr Ewald Fischer GmbH (Federal Republic of Germany) 150
Medizinisch-Literarische Verlagsgesellschaft mbH (Federal Republic of Germany) 150
Meenakshi Prakashan (India) 192

Meerut Publishers' Association (India) 186
Meerwein, Rose M, (Federal Republic of Germany) 169
megapress-Verlag Franz-Joachim Gaber KG (Federal Republic of Germany) 150
Megiddo Publishing Co (Israel) 208
Mehran Library Association (Pakistan) 287
Mei Ya PublicationSs Inc (Sueling, Inc) (China (Taiwan)) 64
Meijer Pers BV (Netherlands) 264
Meili, Buchhandlung, & Co (Switzerland) 356
Meili, Peter, & Co (Switzerland) 349
Meilleure Bibliothèque (France) 110
Meinema/Waltman (Netherlands) 264
Meiner, Felix, Verlag (Federal Republic of Germany) 151
Meisenheim, Verlag Anton, GmbH (Federal Republic of Germany) 151
Meissner, Otto, Verlag (Federal Republic of Germany) 151
Meixner, Friedrich, (Austria) 30
Mejía, Librería-Editorial Juan, Baca (Peru) 289
Mejía, Librería Juan, Baca (Peru) 290
Mekise Nirdamin Society (Israel) 211
Melanchton Verlag (Federal Republic of Germany) 151
Melantrich (Czechoslovakia) 70
Melawai, Toko Buku, (Indonesia) 200
Melayu, Pustaka, Baru (Malaysia) 246
Melbourne House (Publishers) Ltd (United Kingdom) 396
Melbourne University Press (Australia) 16
Melhoramentos, Companhia, de São Paulo (Brazil) 53
Melins, Gustav, AB (Sweden) 335
Melissa Publishing House (Greece) 177
Mella (Dominican Republic) 81
Mellinger, J CH, Verlag GmbH; Wolfgang Militz und Co KG (Federal Republic of Germany) 151
Melrose Press Ltd (United Kingdom) 396
Melzer, Verlag Abi, GmbH (Federal Republic of Germany) 151
Melzer Verlag KG (Federal Republic of Germany) 151
Mendes, Odorico, Prize (Brazil) 57
Menéndez, Librería, (Panama) 288
Menéndez, Ramón, Pidal Prize (International Literary Prizes) 451
Menéndez Pelayo, Biblioteca de, (Spain) 328
Mengès, Editions, (France) 102
Menningarsjóds, Bókaútgáfa, og Thjód vinafélagsins (Iceland) 185
Menno Bookstore (Ethiopia) 84
Mensajero, Ediciones, (Spain) 323
Mensch und Arbeit, Verlag, (Federal Republic of Germany) 151
Mensing en Visser BV (Netherlands) 269
Mentor (United Kingdom) 396
Mentor-Verlag Dr Ramdohr KG (Federal Republic of Germany) 151
Menzies, John, (Holdings) Ltd (United Kingdom) 415
Merbabu, Toko Buku, (Indonesia) 200
Mercantile Guardian Press and Publishers (Pakistan) 285
Mercantile Publishing House (Pvt) Ltd (Zimbabwe) 435
Mercatorfonds-Arcade (Belgium) 40
Mercatorfonds SA (Belgium) 40
Mercier, The, Bookshop Ltd (Republic of Ireland) 205
Mercier, The, Press Ltd (Republic of Ireland) 204
Merck, Johann Heinrich, Prize (Federal Republic of Germany) 173
Merckx, Editeur Paul F, (Belgium) 40
Mercure de France SA (France) 102
Mercurius PVBA (Belgium) 40
Mergus Verlag Hans A Baensch (Federal Republic of Germany) 151
Merian, Christoph, Verlag (Switzerland) 349
Meribérica — Editorial e Comercialização de Direitos Lda (Portugal) 300
Meridiane, Editura, (Romania) 304
Merkaz Le-Chinuch Torani (Israel) 208
Merlin, The, Press Ltd (United Kingdom) 396
Merlin Book Club (United Kingdom) 415
Merlin Library Ltd (Malta) 248
Merlin Verlag Andreas Meyer Verlags GmbH und Co KG (Federal Republic of Germany) 151
Merrill, Charles E, Publishing Co (United Kingdom) 396
Merrion, The, Press (United Kingdom) 396
Merrow Publishing Co Ltd (United Kingdom) 396
Merve Verlag (Federal Republic of Germany) 151
Messageries Centrales du Livre (France) 102
Messeiller, Henri, (Switzerland) 349
Mestre Jou SA (Brazil) 53
Mestre Jou SA (Brazil) 56
Městská knihovna v Praze (Czechoslovakia) 72
Metal Bulletin Books Ltd (United Kingdom) 397
'Metallurgiya', Izdatelstvo, (Union of Soviet Socialist Republics) 366
Methodik-Verlag Manfred Helfrecht (Federal Republic of Germany) 151
Methodist, The, Publishing House and Book Depot (Republic of South Africa) 313
Methodist Book Depot Ltd (Ghana) 175
Methodist Publishing House (United Kingdom) 397

Methuen & Co Ltd (United Kingdom) 397
Methuen Children's Books Ltd (United Kingdom) 397
Methuen New Zealand (New Zealand) 273
Methuen of Australia Pty Ltd (Australia) 16
Metropolitan Book Suppliers Ltd (Trinidad and Tobago) 361
Metz, Max S, Verlag AG (Switzerland) 349
Metzlersche Verlagsbuchhandlung, J B, (Federal Republic of Germany) 151
Metzner, Alfred, Verlag GmbH (Federal Republic of Germany) 151
Meulenhoff, Educatieve Uitgeverij, Educatief BV (Netherlands) 264
Meulenhoff Bruna BV (Netherlands) 269
Meulenhoff Informatief BV (Netherlands) 264
Meulenhoff International BV (Netherlands) 264
Meulenhoff Nederland BV (Netherlands) 264
Mexicana, Editorial, (Mexico) 252
Mexicanos, Editores, Unidos (Mexico) 254
Mexicanos Unidos, Editores, (Edimex) (Mexico) 252
Meyer, Editions d'Art Lucien de, ASBL (Belgium) 40
Meyers-Trefois, D, (Belgium) 40
Meysmans (Belgium) 40
Meyster Verlag (Federal Republic of Germany) 151
Mezhdunarodnaya Kniga (Union of Soviet Socialist Republics) 367
'Mezhdunarodnye Otnosheniya', Izdatelstvo, (Union of Soviet Socialist Republics) 366
Mezőgazdasági Könyvkiadó (Vállalat) (Hungary) 182
Michael, Maurice, (United Kingdom) 397
Michaelmark Books (Israel) 208
Michael's Bookshop (Republic of Singapore) 310
Michaels og Lidt (Denmark) 78
Michaut, Narcisse, Prize (France) 115
Michelin (Département Cartes & Guides) SA (Belgium) 40
Michelin et Cie (Services de Tourisme) (France) 102
Michelin Tyre Co Ltd (United Kingdom) 397
Micolini's, Progress-Verlag Dr, Wtw (Austria) 26
Microfilm Association of Great Britain (United Kingdom) 417
Midas Books (United Kingdom) 397
Middelhauve, Gertraud, Verlag (Federal Republic of Germany) 151
Middle East Book Centre (Egypt) 82
Middle East Librarians Association (International Organizations) 439
Middle East Publishing Co (Lebanon) 241
Middle East Technical University Library (Turkey) 363
Midwest Library Board (Nigeria) 280
Mierlo-Proost, Van, & Co NV (Belgium) 40
Miessner Libreros (Spain) 327
Mifalei Tarbut Vehinuch (Israel) 208
Mihalopoulos, John, & Son (Greece) 178
Miland Publishers (Netherlands) 265
Milano Libri Edizioni (Italy) 217
Militara, Editura, (Romania) 304
Militärverlag, VEB, der DDR (German Democratic Republic) 119
Military Book Society (United Kingdom) 415
Military Guild (United Kingdom) 415
Militz, Wolfgang, und Co KG (Federal Republic of Germany) 151
Millas-Martin, José, (France) 102
Miller, Harvey, Publishers (United Kingdom) 397
Miller, J Garnet, Ltd (United Kingdom) 397
Miller, Louis P, Prize (France) 115
Miller, Maskew, Ltd (Republic of South Africa) 315
Miller, Maskew, Ltd (Republic of South Africa) 312
Millet Library (Turkey) 363
Millî Kütüphane (National Library) (Turkey) 363
Millier, Marcelle, Prize (France) 115
Millington Books (United Kingdom) 397
Milliyet Yaynlari AS (Turkey) 363
Mills & Boon Ltd (United Kingdom) 397
Millwood Press Ltd (New Zealand) 273
Mimbar, Toko Buku Pustaka, (Indonesia) 200
Min Eum Sa (Republic of Korea) 238
Minard, Lettres Modernes, (France) 102
Minard, Librairie, (France) 102
Mindolo Ecumenical Foundation, Hammarskjold Memorial Library (Zambia) 434
Mineral Research and Exploration Institute, Library of the, (Turkey) 363
'Minerva' (Yugoslavia) 428
Minerva, Editor, (Hungary) 183
Minerva, Editora, Central (Mozambique) 256
Minerva, Editorial, (Portugal) 300
Minerva, Editura, (Romania) 304
Minerva, Libreria Editrice, (Italy) 222
Minerva, The, Press Ltd (United Kingdom) 397
Minerva Associates (Publications) Pvt Ltd (India) 192
Minerva Bookshop Ltd (New Zealand) 273
Minerva Central (Mozambique) 256
Minerva Forlag A/S (Norway) 282
Minerva Italica SpA (Italy) 217

Minerva Publishing, The, House (India) 192
Minerva Shobo Co Ltd (Japan) 228
Minerva's Express (Australia) 16
Ministère de l'Education, Bibliothèque centrale du, nationale (Belgium) 44
Ministère de l'Education nationale (Kampuchea) 235
Ministère de l'Information, Bibliothèque du, (Kampuchea) 235
Ministério das Relações Exteriores, Biblioteca do, (Brazil) 56
Ministerio de Cultura (Costa Rica) 68
Ministerio de Educación (El Salvador) 83
Ministerio de Educacion, Editorial del, 'Jose de Pineda Ibarra' (Guatemala) 178
Ministerio de Información y Turismo, Biblioteca del, (Library of the Ministry of Information and Tourism) (Spain) 328
Ministerrat der Deutschen Demokratischen Republik, Ministerium für Kultur, Hauptverwaltung Verlage und Buchhandel (German Democratic Republic) 117
Ministerstvo kultury CSR, Odbor knižní kultury (Czechoslovakia) 69
Ministerstwa Obrony Narodowej, Wydawnictwo, (Publishing House of the Ministry of National Defence) (Poland) 294
Ministry of Agriculture Library (Malaysia) 247
Ministry of Culture, Department of Ancient Literature and Culture., (Burma) 60
Ministry of Culture and Information, Book Publishing Department (Afghanistan) 1
Ministry of Defence Publishing House (Israel) 208
Ministry of Education, Department of Educational Publications (Afghanistan) 1
Ministry of Education Library (Afghanistan) 1
Ministry of Education Library (Cyprus) 69
Ministry of Information (Kuwait) 240
Ministry of Information & Broadcasting (India) 192
Ministry of Justice Library (Egypt) 83
Minjungseogwan (Republic of Korea) 238
Minkoff, Editions, Reprint (Switzerland) 349
Minoas (Greece) 178
Minoas (Greece) 177
'Mintis', Leidykla, (Union of Soviet Socialist Republics) 366
Minuit, Les Editions de, SA (France) 102
Mir, Izdatelstvo, (Union of Soviet Socialist Republics) 366
Mir, S M, (Pakistan) 286
Miracle, Editorial Luis, SA (Spain) 323
Mirananda Publishers BV (Netherlands) 265
Miranda, G, & Sons (Philippines) 292
Mirror Books Ltd (United Kingdom) 397
Mirza Book Agency (Pakistan) 286
Misla (Yugoslavia) 428
Misr, Maktabet, (Misr Bookshop) (Egypt) 82
Misr Bookshop (Egypt) 83
Misr Import & Export Co (Egypt) 83
Misrachi, Galeria de Arte, SA (Mexico) 252
Missionstruppe Frohe Botschaft (Federal Republic of Germany) 151
Mistral, Editora Nacional Gabriela, Ltda (Chile) 62
Misuzu Shobo Publishing Co Ltd (Japan) 229
Miswat Library (People's Democratic Republic of Yemen) 426
Mitchell, The, Library (Glasgow District Libraries) (United Kingdom) 416
Mitchell Beazley Marketing Ltd (United Kingdom) 397
Mitre, Editorial Librería, SRL (Argentina) 6
Mitteldeutscher Verlag (German Democratic Republic) 119
Mittler, E S, und Sohn GmbH (Federal Republic of Germany) 151
Mizrachi, M, Publishers (Israel) 208
Mladá fronta (Czechoslovakia) 70
Mladé letá (Czechoslovakia) 70
Mladé letá Prize (Czechoslovakia) 73
Mladinska Knjiga (Yugoslavia) 431
Mladinska Knjiga (Yugoslavia) 428
Mladost (Yugoslavia) 428
Mladost (Yugoslavia) 428
Mladost (Yugoslavia) 431
Mladost's Book Fans Club (Yugoslavia) 430
Mlodziezowa Agencja Wydawnicza — Polish Youth Publishing Agency (Poland) 296
Mlodziezowa Agencja Wydawnicza (Youth Publishing Agency and Publishing Co-operative) (Poland) 294
Moa Publications (New Zealand) 273
Moadim (Israel) 210
Mockel, Albert, Grand Prize for Poetry (Belgium) 46
Model & Allied Publications (United Kingdom) 397
Modern Book Co Inc (Philippines) 292
Modern Book Company Inc (Philippines) 291
Modern Book Depot (India) 197
Modern Book Store (Republic of Singapore) 310
Modern Cairo Bookshop (Egypt) 83
Modern Educational Research Society Ltd (Hong Kong) 181

Modern Teaching Aids Pty Ltd (Australia) 16
Modern Transport (United Kingdom) 397
Moderne Industrie, Verlag, Wolfgang Dummer und Co (Federal Republic of Germany) 151
Moderne Industrie AG (Switzerland) 349
Moderne Instructie Methoden (MIM) PVBA (Belgium) 40
Moderne Verlags GmbH (MVG) (Federal Republic of Germany) 151
Modernix (New Caledonia) 271
Modtryk, Forlaget, AMBA (Denmark) 76
Modulverlag GmbH (Austria) 26
Mofolo-Plomer Prize (Republic of South Africa) 317
Mohammadi Library (Bangladesh) 32
Mohler, Alfred, Verlag (Switzerland) 349
Mohn, Gütersloher Verlag Gerd, (Federal Republic of Germany) 151
Mohn, Vereinigte Verlagsauslieferung R, oHG (Federal Republic of Germany) 170
Mohr, J C B, (Paul Siebeck) (Federal Republic of Germany) 151
Mohr, Robert, (Austria) 30
Mohrbooks Literary Agency (Switzerland) 356
Moizzi (Italy) 217
Molcho, Solomon, (Greece) 178
Molden, Verlag Fritz, (Federal Republic of Germany) 152
Molden, Verlag Fritz, (Austria) 26
Molendinar, The, Press (United Kingdom) 397
Molino, Editorial, (Spain) 323
Moll, Editorial, (Spain) 323
Mollat, Librairie, (France) 103
Molodaya Gvardiya, Izdatelstvo, (Union of Soviet Socialist Republics) 366
Mombasa Polytechnic Library (Kenya) 236
Momenta Publishing (United Kingdom) 397
Mon Village, Club, SA (Switzerland) 356
Mon Village, Editions, SA (Switzerland) 349
Monas Hieroglyphica Inc Cooperativa Editrice (Italy) 217
Monastery of St-Saviour, Library of the, (Basilian Missionary Order of St-Saviour) (Lebanon) 241
Monceau Prize (International Literary Prizes) 451
Mönch-Verlag GmbH & Co (Federal Republic of Germany) 152
Mondadori, Arnoldo, Editore (Italy) 217
Mondadori, Edizioni Scolastiche Bruno, (Italy) 218
Mondadori Ragazzi (Italy) 218
Mondo, Edizioni del, (Federal Republic of Germany) 152
Mondo SA (Switzerland) 349
Mondoperaio edizioni Avanti SpA (Italy) 218
Mondrup, Svend, International Literary Agency (Denmark) 78
Monfort, Gérard, (France) 103
Mongolgosknigotorg (Mongolian People's Republic) 255
Moniteur, Editions du, (France) 103
Monradske, Den, Medal (Norway) 284
Monselet, Charles, Prize (France) 115
Mont, Du, Buchverlag GmbH und Co KG (Federal Republic of Germany) 152
Mont-Blanc, Les Editions du, SA (Switzerland) 349
Mont Noir, Editions du, (Zaire) 433
Montaigne (New Caledonia) 271
Montaner y Simon SA (Spain) 323
Montchrestien, Editions, Sàrl (France) 103
Monte Avila Editores CA (Venezuela) 424
Montel, Publications Photo-Cinema Paul, (France) 103
Monterrey, Editôra, Ltda (Brazil) 53
Montesó, José, — Editor (Spain) 323
Monteverde, A, y Cia SA (Uruguay) 422
Monthly Review Press (United Kingdom) 397
Montparnasse, Librairie, Edition (France) 110
Montparnasse-Diffusion (France) 103
Montserrat Public Library (Montserrat) 255
Montsouris, Editions de, SA (France) 103
Montyon Prize (France) 115
Moonraker Press (United Kingdom) 397
Moonye Publishing Co (Republic of Korea) 238
Moore, G W, Ltd (New Zealand) 273
Moore, S J, Ltd (Kenya) 236
Moorland Publishing Company Ltd (United Kingdom) 397
Moos, Heinz, Verlag Munich (Federal Republic of Germany) 152
Mor-Carmi, M C, Ltd (Israel) 208
Mora, Marie, OHG (Austria) 30
Móra Ferenc Ifjúsági Könyvkiadó (Hungary) 183
Moraes Editores (Portugal) 300
Morancé, Editions Albert, (France) 103
Morata, Ediciones, SA (Spain) 323
Morawa & Co (Austria) 30
Morcelliana, Editrice, SpA (Italy) 218
Moreau, Editions Alain, (France) 103
Morel Editeurs (France) 103
Morena, Librería, (Argentina) 8
Moreno, Fernando, Poetry Prize (Argentina) 9
Moresheth (Israel) 209

Moreton, Ediciones, SA (Spain) 323
Moretus Plantin, Bibliothèque Universitaire, (Belgium) 44
Morgan-Grampian Book Publishing Co Ltd (United Kingdom) 398
Morgarten-Verlag (Switzerland) 349
Morgen, Buchverlag Der, (German Democratic Republic) 119
Morija Sesuto Book Depot (Lesotho) 242
Morija Sesuto Book Depot (Lesotho) 242
Morikita Shuppan Co Ltd (Japan) 229
Morison Arnold Ltd (Nigeria) 280
Morra, Verlag, (Italy) 218
Morris, William, Organization SpA (Italy) 221
Morsak Verlag (Federal Republic of Germany) 152
Morskie, Wydawnictwo, (Poland) 295
Mortensens, Ernst G, Forlag (Norway) 282
Mortiz, Editorial Joaquín, SA (Mexico) 252
Morus-Verlag (Federal Republic of Germany) 152
Mosaik Verlag (Federal Republic of Germany) 152
Mosca Azul Editores, SRL (Peru) 289
Mosca Hnos (Uruguay) 423
Mosca Hnos SA (Uruguay) 422
'Moskovskii Rabochiy', Izdatelstvo, (Union of Soviet Socialist Republics) 366
Moskovskogo Universiteta, Izdatelstvo, (Union of Soviet Socialist Republics) 366
Mossad Harav Kook (Israel) 209
Mosul Museum, Library of the, (Iraq) 202
Mosul Public Library (Iraq) 202
Motilal Banarsidass (India) 192
Motilal Banarsidass (India) 197
Motive (United Kingdom) 398
Motor Racing Publications Ltd (United Kingdom) 398
Motorbuch-Verlag (Federal Republic of Germany) 152
Motta, Federico, Editore (Italy) 218
Mouj Prakashan Griha (India) 192
Mount Kenya Bookshop (Kenya) 236
Moussault's Uitgeverij BV (Netherlands) 265
Mouton Publishers (Netherlands) 265
Mowbray, A R, & Co Ltd (United Kingdom) 398
Moxon Paperbacks Ltd (Ghana) 175
Moya, José, und Ute Körner de Moya (Spain) 327
Mphala Creative Society (Zambia) 434
Mqhayi, Samuel Edward, Prize (Republic of South Africa) 317
Mr H's Prize (Japan) 234
Mühlemann, Verlag Rudolf, (Switzerland) 349
Muhlethaler, Jacques, (Switzerland) 349
Muiderkring, De, BV (Netherlands) 265
Mukherjee, A, & Co Pvt Ltd (India) 192
Mukherji Book House (India) 192
Mulder en Co (Netherlands) 265
Mulder Holland BV (Netherlands) 265
Mullaya Publications (Australia) 16
Müller, Albert, Verlag AG (Switzerland) 349
Muller, Frederick, Ltd (United Kingdom) 398
Müller, Otto, Verlag KG (Austria) 27
Müller, Rudolf, International Booksellers BV (Netherlands) 269
Müller, Verlag C F, (Federal Republic of Germany) 152
Müller, Verlag Josef, (Federal Republic of Germany) 152
Müller, Verlagsgesellschaft Rudolf, (Federal Republic of Germany) 152
Muller-Groff, Librairie, (Luxembourg) 244
Müller Jüristischer, C F, Verlag GmbH (Federal Republic of Germany) 152
Müller und Kiepenheuer, Verlag, (Federal Republic of Germany) 152
Müller und Schindler, Verlag, (Federal Republic of Germany) 152
Müller und Steinicke, Rudolf, Verlag (Federal Republic of Germany) 152
Mullick Bros (Bangladesh) 32
Mullick Brothers (Bangladesh) 32
Multiling Verlag AG (Switzerland) 349
Multimedia Zambia (Zambia) 433
Mun Woon Dang (Republic of Korea) 238
Munch Bunch (United Kingdom) 398
Münchner Arbeitsgemeinschaft der Verlagshersteller (Munich Association of Publishers' Production Managers) (Federal Republic of Germany) 122
Münchner Verlagsbüro, Horst Hodemacher-Axel Poldner (Federal Republic of Germany) 169
Mundi, Editorial, SAIC y F (Argentina) 6
Mundi-Prensa, Librería, (Spain) 327
Mundi-Prensa Libros SA (Spain) 323
Mundial, Librería, (Venezuela) 425
Mundo, Editorial, Técnico SRL (Argentina) 6
Mundo Nuevo, Editorial, (Chile) 62
Mundus, Österreichische Verlagsgesellschaft GmbH (Austria) 27
Municipal Library (Cyprus) 69
Municipal Library (Cyprus) 69
Municipal Library (Bulgaria) 58
Municipal Library (Socialist Republic of Viet Nam) 426

Municipal Library (Israel) 211
Municipal Prize for Prose and Poetry (Venezuela) 425
Munin Verlag GmbH (Federal Republic of Germany) 152
Munksgaard, International Boghandel (Denmark) 78
Munksgaard, International Booksellers & Publishers Ltd (Denmark) 76
Munshiram Manoharlal Publishers Pvt Ltd (India) 192
Münster Verlag (Federal Republic of Germany) 152
Muralla, Editorial La, (Spain) 323
Murby, Thomas, & Co (United Kingdom) 398
Murr, Georges, (Lebanon) 241
Murray, Donald, (Ramboro Books) (United Kingdom) 398
Murray, Donald, (Ramboro Books) (United Kingdom) 413
Murray, John, (Publishers) Ltd (United Kingdom) 398
Murrays Childrens Books (United Kingdom) 398
Murrays Remainder Books (United Kingdom) 413
Murrays Remainder Books Ltd (United Kingdom) 398
Mursia, Ugo, Editore SpA (Italy) 218
Muscat, Giov, & Co Ltd (Malta) 248
Musée de l'Affiche, Publications du, et du Tract (France) 103
Musée de l'Homme, Bibliothèque du, (France) 111
Musée royal de Mariemont, Bibliothèque du, (Belgium) 44
Musées Nationaux, Editions de la Réunion des, (France) 103
Museo, Biblioteca del, Histórico Nacional (Library of the National Historical Museum) (Uruguay) 423
Museo de Zoologia, Biblioteca del, (Library of the Zoological Museum) (Cuba) 69
Museo y Biblioteca Municipal (Ecuador) 81
Museum, Perpustakaan, Nasional, Departemen Pendidikan dan Kebudayaan (Library of the National Museum, Ministry of Education and Culture) (Indonesia) 201
Muséum Calvet, Bibliothèque (France) 111
Muséum national, Bibliothèque centrale du, d'Histoire naturelle (France) 111
Muséum national, Editions du, d'Histoire naturelle (France) 103
Museum Plantin-Moretus (Belgium) 44
Music Sales Ltd (United Kingdom) 398
Musica, Editio, (Hungary) 183
Musica, Editorial, Moderna (Spain) 323
Musikverleger Union Österreich (Austria) 24
Musin, Louis, Editeur (Belgium) 40
Müskaki Könyvklub (Hungary) 183
Muskett, Netta, Award (United Kingdom) 420
Muslim Welfare House (United Kingdom) 398
Musterschmidt-Verlag (Federal Republic of Germany) 152
Müszaki Könyvkiadó Vállalat (Hungary) 183
Mutiara (Indonesia) 200
Mutual Books Inc (Philippines) 291
Mutualidad Laboral de Escritores de Libros (Book Writers' Friendly Society) (Spain) 328
Muusses, J, BV (Netherlands) 265
Müvelt nép könyvterjesztő vállalat (Hungarian Educated People Book-Distributing Enterprise) (Hungary) 183
'Muzica', Darzhavno Izdatelstvo, (Bulgaria) 58
Muzicala, Editura, (Romania) 304
Muzička Naklada (Yugoslavia) 428
Muzyczne, Polskie Wydawnictwo, (Polish Music Publishers) (Poland) 295
'Muzyka', Izdatelstvo, (Union of Soviet Socialist Republics) 366
Myna Press (India) 192
Mysl, Izdatelstvo, (Union of Soviet Socialist Republics) 366
Mysore State Publishers' and Booksellers' Association (India) 186
Mystery Guild (United Kingdom) 415

N A G Press (United Kingdom) 398
N C C Publications (United Kingdom) 398
N D V (Neue Darmstädter Verlagsanstalt) (Federal Republic of Germany) 152
N E L (United Kingdom) 398
N F E R Publishing Co Ltd (United Kingdom) 398
N F F (Nouvelles Feuilles Familiales) (Belgium) 40
N G Kerk-Uitgewers en Boekhandel (Republic of South Africa) 313
N G Kerkboekhandel Transvaal (Republic of South Africa) 315
N G Kerkboekhandel Transvaal (DRC Publishers) (Republic of South Africa) 313
N I B, Uitgeverij, (Netherlands) 265
N I S H Shtypshkronjave 'Mihal Duri' (Albania) 1
N K I-forlaget (Norway) 282
N S T (Nová sovietska tvorba) (Czechoslovakia) 72
N Z E I (New Zealand) 273
N Z N — Buchverlag (Switzerland) 349
Nå Forlag A/S (formerly Elingaard Forlag) (Norway) 282

Nabco Pendidekan Sdn Bhd (Malaysia) 247
Nachiketa Publications Ltd (India) 192
Nachrichten-Verlags-GmbH (Federal Republic of Germany) 152
Nación, Premio de 'La, ' Prize (Argentina) 9
Nacional, El, Annual Story Award (Venezuela) 425
Nacional de Chile de la Dirección, Biblioteca, de Bibliotecas, Archivos y Museos (Chile) 63
Nacionalna i Sveučilišna Biblioteka (Yugoslavia) 431
Nadal, Eugenio, Prize (Spain) 329
Nadjuri (Australia) 16
Nafees Academy (Pakistan) 285
Nagai Shoten Co Ltd (Japan) 229
Nagel, Les Editions, SA (Switzerland) 349
Nagin, S, & Co (India) 192
Nagoya University Library (Japan) 232
Nah Shperndarjes Të Librit (NST) (Albania) 1
Nahda, Dar al-, al Arabia (Egypt) 82
Naim Frasheri (Albania) 1
Nairoshni (Pakistan) 285
Nakamori Prize (Japan) 234
Nakladni Zavod Matice Hrvatske (Yugoslavia) 428
Nalanda Co Ltd (Mauritius) 249
Nan-ching t'u shu kuan (Nanking Library) (People's Republic of China) 64
Nankodo Co Ltd (Japan) 229
Nanyang University Library (Republic of Singapore) 310
Nanzando Co Ltd (Japan) 229
Naoki Prize (Japan) 234
Napoletana, Società Editrice, SRL (Italy) 218
Naprijed (Yugoslavia) 428
Naranco, Ediciones, SA (Spain) 323
Narcea SA de Ediciones (Spain) 323
Nardini Editore — Centro Internazionale del Libro SpA (Italy) 218
narodna biblioteka, Centralna, SR Crne Gore (Yugoslavia) 431
Narodna biblioteka NR Bosne i Hercegovine (Yugoslavia) 431
Narodna biblioteka SR Srbije (Yugoslavia) 431
Narodna Biblioteka Srbije (Yugoslavia) 428
Narodna in univerzitetna knjižnica (Ljubljana) (Yugoslavia) 431
Narodna in univerzitetna knjižnica (Zagreb) (Yugoslavia) 431
Narodna Knjiga (Yugoslavia) 428
Narodna Kultura (Bulgaria) 58
Narodna Mladezh (Bulgaria) 58
'Narodna Prosveta', Darzhavno Izdatelstvo, (Bulgaria) 58
Narodne Novine (Yugoslavia) 428
Narongsarn (Thailand) 359
Narosa Publishing House (India) 192
Narr, Gunter, Verlag (Federal Republic of Germany) 152
Naša Djeca (Yugoslavia) 429
Naša Kniga (Yugoslavia) 429
Nascimento, Editorial, SA (Chile) 62
Naše Vojsko, Nakladatelství a distribuce knih, (Czechoslovakia) 70
Naše vojsko Prizes (Czechoslovakia) 73
Nasional, Pustaka, (Republic of Singapore) 310
Nasional, Pustaka, Pte Ltd (Republic of Singapore) 309
Nasionale Boekhandel (SWA) (Pty) Ltd (Namibia) 257
Nasionale Boekhandel Ltd (Republic of South Africa) 313
Nasionale Boekwinkels Bpk (Republic of South Africa) 315
Nasou Ltd (Republic of South Africa) 313
Nassau, Editions, (Mauritius) 249
Nassau Public Library (Bahamas) 32
'Nasza Ksiegarnia', Instytut Wydawniczy, (Poland) 295
Nateev-Printing and Publishing Enterprises Ltd (Israel) 209
Nathan, Fernand, Editeur (France) 103
Nation, Verlag der, (German Democratic Republic) 119
National Academy of Arts (Republic of Korea) 240
National Academy of Letters (Sahitya Akademi) Rabindra Bhavan (India) 198
National Archives (Egypt) 83
National Archives (Libya) 242
National Archives (New Zealand) 275
National Archives (Sri Lanka) 330
National Archives (Trinidad and Tobago) 361
National Archives and Records Centre (Republic of Singapore) 310
National Archives Division (Thailand) 360
National Archives of Fiji (Fiji) 85
National Archives of India (India) 197
National Archives of Malawi (Malawi) 245
National Archives of Malaysia (Malaysia) 247
National Archives of Nigeria Library (Nigeria) 280
National Archives of Pakistan (Pakistan) 286
National Archives of Rhodesia (Zimbabwe) 435
National Archives of Tanzania (Tanzania) 358
National Archives of Zambia (Zambia) 434
National Assembly Library (Republic of Korea) 239
National Assembly Library (Egypt) 83
National Award for Book Design (Romania) 305

National Award for Poetry and the Novel (Portugal) 302
National Bank, Library of the, (Afghanistan) 1
National Bank of Pakistan Prize for Literature (Pakistan) 287
National Book, The, Co (China (Taiwan)) 64
National Book, The, League (United Kingdom) 418
National Book Council (Australia) 10
National Book Council Awards (Australia) 22
National Book Council of Pakistan (Pakistan) 284
National Book Development Council of Singapore (Republic of Singapore) 308
National Book Development Council of Singapore Book Awards (Republic of Singapore) 310
National Book Institute Prizes (Brazil) 57
National Book Store (Republic of Singapore) 310
National Book Store (Philippines) 291
National Book Store (Philippines) 292
National Book Trust (India) 192
National Bookshop and Branches (Bahrain) 32
National Central Library (China (Taiwan)) 64
National Centre on Archives (Iraq) 202
National Christian Education Council (United Kingdom) 398
National Computing Centre (United Kingdom) 398
National Council of Applied Economic Research, Publications Division (India) 192
National Council of Educational Research & Training, Publication Department (India) 192
National Council of Ethnographic Arts and Literature of China (China (Taiwan)) 65
National Council of Social Services (United Kingdom) 398
National Cultural Awards (Brazil) 57
National Diet Library (Japan) 232
National Educational Company of Zambia Ltd (Zambia) 434
National Essay Award (Portugal) 302
National Federation of Retail Newsagents (United Kingdom) 369
National Federation of Retail Newsagents (Republic of Ireland) 203
National Foundation for Educational Research in England & Wales (United Kingdom) 398
National Free Library Service (Zimbabwe) 435
National Grand Prize of Letters (France) 115
National House for Distributing and Advertising (Iraq) 202
National Information and Documentation Centre (Egypt) 83
National Information and Documentation Centre (Egypt) 83
National Institute, Division of Documentation,, of Science and Technology (Philippines) 292
National Institute for Compilation and Translation (China (Taiwan)) 65
National Institute of Administration Library (Socialist Republic of Viet Nam) 426
National Institute of Education Library (Uganda) 364
National Library (Thailand) 360
National Library (Republic of Singapore) 310
National Library (Saudi Arabia) 306
National Library (Burma) 60
National Library (Philippines) 292
National Library (Pakistan) 286
National Library (Libya) 242
National Library (Nepal) 257
National Library (Iraq) 202
National Library (Iran) 202
National Library (Guyana) 179
National Library, Central, (Republic of Korea) 239
National Library, The, Government of India (India) 197
National Library and Archives of Ethiopia (Ethiopia) 84
National Library 'Ivan Vazov' (Bulgaria) 58
National Library of Australia (Australia) 16
National Library of Australia (Australia) 20
National Library of Greece (Greece) 178
National Library of Higher Education and Culture (Somalia) 310
National Library of Ireland (Republic of Ireland) 205
National Library of Ireland Society (Republic of Ireland) 205
National Library of Jamaica, Institute of Jamaica (Jamaica) 225
National Library of Latakia (Syria) 357
National Library of Malaysia (Malaysia) 247
National Library of Malta (Malta) 248
National Library of New Zealand (New Zealand) 275
National Library of Nigeria (Nigeria) 280
National Library of Scotland (United Kingdom) 416
National Library Service (Belize) 46
National Literary Awards (Burma) 60
National Literary Awards (Malaysia) 248
National Magazine Co Ltd (United Kingdom) 398
National Minorities Publishing House (People's Republic of China) 63
National Museum Library (Sri Lanka) 330
National Museums, Department of, (Sri Lanka) 329

498 INDEX

National Press, The, (Republic of Ireland) 204
National Press Library (Jordan) 234
National Prize for Literature (Mexico) 255
National Prize for Literature (Venezuela) 425
National Prize of Bibliophily (Romania) 305
National Prize on Literature on Physical Education (India) 198
National Publishing House (India) 192
National Story Prize (Colombia) 67
National Technological University, Library of the, of Athens (Greece) 178
National Tourism Prize (International Literary Prizes) 451
National Trust Children's Series (United Kingdom) 398
National University of Lesotho Library (Lesotho) 242
National War College Library (China (Taiwan)) 64
Nationale, Librairie, (Ministère Education National) (Benin) 47
Nationale Forschungs- und Gedenkstätten der klassischen deutschen Literatur — Zentralbibliothek der deutschen Klassik (German Democratic Republic) 120
Native Language Bureau (Namibia) 257
Native Language Bureau (Namibia) 257
Natoli and Stefan Literary Agency (Italy) 221
Natsionalniya Savet, Izdatelstvo na, na Otetchestveniya Front (Bulgaria) 58
Natur och Kultur, Bokförlaget, (Sweden) 335
Natura, Editorial, SRL (Venezuela) 424
Natura-Verlag (Switzerland) 349
Natural History Museum (United Kingdom) 398
Natural Resources Development College Library (Zambia) 434
Naučna biblioteka (Yugoslavia) 431
Naučna Knjiga (Yugoslavia) 429
Naučno Delo (Yugoslavia) 429
Nauka, Darzhavno Izdatelstvo, i Izkustvo (Bulgaria) 58
'Nauka', Izdatelstvo, (Union of Soviet Socialist Republics) 366
Naukowe, Państwowe Wydawnictwo, (Poland) 295
Naukowo-Techniczne, Wydawnictwa, (Poland) 295
Naumann, Ulrich, (Republic of South Africa) 315
Nauta, Ediciones, SA (Spain) 323
Nautic, AB, (Sweden) 335
Nautical Publishing Co Ltd (United Kingdom) 398
Nautiska Förlaget Sjökortshallen AB (Sweden) 335
Nauwelaerts, NV Uitgeverij, Edition SA (Belgium) 40
Navajivan Trust (India) 192
Navers, Rasmus, Forlag (Denmark) 76
Naville & Cie SA (Switzerland) 349
Navoi, Gosudarstvennaya biblioteka UzSSR im Alishera, (Union of Soviet Socialist Republics) 367
Navyug Publishers (India) 192
Naya Prokash (India) 192
Ndanda Mission Press (Tanzania) 358
Ndebele Readers' Book Club (Zimbabwe) 435
Ndërmarrja e Botimeve Ushtarake (Albania) 1
Ndërmarrja e Librit (Albania) 1
Ndola Public Library (Zambia) 434
Near East School, Library of the, of Theology (Lebanon) 241
Nebelspalter Verlag (Switzerland) 349
Nederlands Bibliotheek en Lektuurcentrum (NBLC = Netherlands Centre for Public Libraries and Literature) (Netherlands) 270
Nederland's Boekhuis BV (Netherlands) 265
Nederlandsche Boekhandel, De, NV (Belgium) 40
Nederlandsche Vereeniging voor Druk- en Boekkunst (Netherlands Society for the Art of Printing and Book Production) (Netherlands) 258
Nederlandsche Vereniging van Antiquaren (Netherlands Association of Antiquarian Booksellers) (Netherlands) 258
Nederlandsche Zondagsschool Vereeniging (Netherlands) 265
Nederlandse Boekenclub (Netherlands Book Club) (Netherlands) 269
Nederlandse Boekverkopersbond (Dutch Booksellers' Association) (Netherlands) 258
Nederlandse Lezerskring Boek en Plaat BV (Netherlands) 265
Nederlandse Vereniging van Bedrijfsarchivarissen (Netherlands Association of Business Archivists) (Netherlands) 270
Nederlandse Vereniging van Bibliothecarissen, Documentalisten en literatuuronderzoekers (NVB) (Netherlands Librarians' Society) (Netherlands) 270
'Nedra', Izdatelstvo, (Union of Soviet Socialist Republics) 366
Née, Alfred, Prize (France) 115
Neff, Paul, Verlag KG (Federal Republic of Germany) 152
Neff, Paul, Verlag KG (Austria) 27
Negara, Perpustakaan, (State Library) (Indonesia) 201
Nègre, Librairie SA Gaston, (Benin) 47
Neguri Editorial SA (Editorial Cartográfica) (Spain) 323
Neilson, John Shaw, Poetry Award (Australia) 23

Nejat Yalki Kitabevi (Turkey) 363
Nelissen, Uitgeverij H, BV (Netherlands) 265
Nelson, Thomas, & Sons Ltd (United Kingdom) 398
Nelson, Thomas, (Australia) Pty Ltd (Australia) 16
Nelson, Thomas, (Nigeria) Ltd (Nigeria) 278
Nelson Memorial Public Library (Western Samoa) 426
Nem Chand & Brothers (India) 192
Nena, Librería La, (Argentina) 8
Nepal Academy (Nepal) 257
Nepal-Bharat Sanskritik Kendra Pustakalay (Nepal) 257
Nepal Booksellers (Nepal) 257
Nepal Library Association (Nepal) 257
Neptun-Verlag (Switzerland) 349
Neruda, Librería e Importadora, (El Salvador) 83
Nerva-Verlag (Federal Republic of Germany) 152
Neske, Verlag Günther, (Federal Republic of Germany) 152
Netzach (Israel) 209
Neue Berlin, Verlag das, (German Democratic Republic) 119
Neue Darmstädter Verlagsanstalt (Federal Republic of Germany) 152
Neue Diana Press AG (Switzerland) 349
Neue Gesellschaft, Verlag, GmbH (Federal Republic of Germany) 152
Neue Kritik, Verlag, KG (Federal Republic of Germany) 152
Neue Mitte, Edition, (Austria) 27
Neue Presse Agentur (NPA) (Switzerland) 356
Neue Schulmann, Verlag Der, (Federal Republic of Germany) 153
Neue Schweizer Bibliothek (Switzerland) 356
Neue Stadt, Verlag, (Switzerland) 349
Neue Stadt, Verlag, GmbH (Federal Republic of Germany) 153
Neue Wirtschafts-Briefe, Verlag, GmbH (Federal Republic of Germany) 153
Neue Zürcher Zeitung (Switzerland) 349
Neuer Jugendschriften-Verlag (Federal Republic of Germany) 153
Neuer Weg, Verlag, (Federal Republic of Germany) 153
Neues Leben, Verlag, (German Democratic Republic) 119
Neufeld Verlag und Galerie (Switzerland) 350
Neufeld-Verlag und Galerie (Austria) 27
Neugebauer, Verlag Claus, (Federal Republic of Germany) 153
Neugebauer, Werner, OHG (Austria) 30
Neugebauer, Wolfgang, (Austria) 27
Neugebauer, Wolfgang, (Austria) 27
Neugebauer Press Verlag für bibliophile Drucke (Austria) 27
Neukirchener Verlag des Erziehungsvereins GmbH (Federal Republic of Germany) 153
Neumann-Neudamm, Verlag J, KG (Federal Republic of Germany) 153
Neureuter Baumann mbH (Federal Republic of Germany) 153
Neustadt International Prize for Literature (International Literary Prizes) 451
New Africa Booksellers (Somalia) 310
New Aqua, P T, Press/Aries Lima (Indonesia) 200
New Australian Library Pty Ltd (Australia) 16
New Book Publishing House (Lebanon) 241
New Cavendish Books (United Kingdom) 399
New Caxton Library Service Ltd (United Kingdom) 399
New City, London (United Kingdom) 399
New Countryside Book Club (Poland) 296
New Educational Books (United Kingdom) 399
New English Library, The, Ltd (United Kingdom) 399
New Fiction, The, Society (United Kingdom) 415
New Guinea Book Depot (Papua New Guinea) 288
New Horn Press (Nigeria) 278
New Interlitho SpA (Italy) 218
New Leaf Books Ltd (United Kingdom) 399
New Left Books (United Kingdom) 399
New Light Publishers (IBI) (India) 192
New Order Book Co (India) 192
New Portway (United Kingdom) 399
New South Wales Booksellers' Association (Australia) 10
New University Education (United Kingdom) 399
New World Publications (Pty) Ltd (Republic of South Africa) 313
New Writers', The, Group (Zambia) 434
New Writers' Press (Republic of Ireland) 204
New Writers Stipendium for Literature (Austria) 31
New Zealand Anzac Fellowships (Australia) 23
New Zealand Book Awards (New Zealand) 276
New Zealand Book Council (New Zealand) 272
New Zealand Book Trade Organization (New Zealand) 272
New Zealand Council for Educational Research (New Zealand) 273
New Zealand Educational Institute (NZEI) (New Zealand) 273

New Zealand Government Printing Office (New Zealand) 273
New Zealand Library Association (New Zealand) 275
New Zealand Literary Fund (New Zealand) 276
New Zealand Women Writers' Society (New Zealand) 275
Newdigate, Sir Roger, Prize for English Verse (United Kingdom) 420
Newman, M, (Israel) 209
Newman Art (Republic of South Africa) 313
Newnes Books (United Kingdom) 399
Newnes-Butterworths (United Kingdom) 399
Newnes-Technical (United Kingdom) 399
Newrick Associates Ltd (New Zealand) 273
Newservice Ltd (Seychelles) 307
Newspread International (Kenya) 236
Newton Compton Editori SRL (Italy) 218
Nexus Books (New Zealand) 273
Ney's Libros and Revistas (Honduras) 180
Nha Xuat Ban Van Hoc (Literature Publishing House) (Socialist Republic of Viet Nam) 426
Nibondh (Thailand) 359
Nibondh (Gaysorn) (Thailand) 360
Nicholson, Robert, Publications Ltd (United Kingdom) 399
Nici (Belgium) 40
Nicolai, M, (Laos) 240
Nicolaische Verlagsbuchhandlung GmbH und Co KG (Federal Republic of Germany) 153
Niederösterreichisches Pressehaus, Verlag, mbH (Austria) 27
Niedersächsische Staats- und Universitätsbibliothek (Federal Republic of Germany) 171
Niedieck Linder AG (Switzerland) 356
Niemeyer, Max, Verlag (Federal Republic of Germany) 153
Niemeyer, VEB Max, Verlag (German Democratic Republic) 119
Niemeyer, Verlag C W, (Federal Republic of Germany) 153
Nigar, Librería y Editorial, SRL (Argentina) 6
Niger (Acada) Bookshop Ltd (Nigeria) 280
Nigeria Educational Research, The, Council (Nigeria) 281
Nigerian Baptist Book Stores (Nigeria) 280
Nigerian Book Suppliers Ltd (Nigeria) 280
Nigerian Booksellers' Association (Nigeria) 277
Nigerian Broadcasting Corporation (Nigeria) 281
Nigerian Library Association (Nigeria) 280
Nigerian Publishers' Association (Nigeria) 277
Nigerian Trade Review (Nigeria) 278
Niggli, Verlag Arthur, AG (Switzerland) 350
Nihon Bunka Kagakusha Co Ltd (Japan) 229
Nihon Eibungakkai (English Literary Society of Japan) (Japan) 233
Nihon Shoten Kumiai Rengokai (Japan) 225
Nihon Vogue (Publishing) Co Ltd (Japan) 229
Nijgh en Van Ditmar, BV Uitgeverij, (Netherlands) 265
Nijhoff, Martinus, BV (Netherlands) 269
Nijhoff, Martinus, Prize (International Literary Prizes) 451
Nijhoff, Martinus, Publishers (Netherlands) 265
Nikas (Greece) 177
Nile & Mackenzie Ltd (United Kingdom) 399
Niloe, Bokforlaget, AB (Sweden) 335
Nine, The, Prize (Sweden) 339
Niove (Dominican Republic) 81
Nippon Bungaku Kyokai (Japan) 233
Nippon Dokubungakkai (Japan) 233
Nippon Dokumentesyon Kyokai (Japan Documentation Society) (Japan) 232
Nippon Furansu-go Furansu-bungaku Kai (Japan) 233
Nippon Hikaku Bungakukai (Japan) 233
Nippon Igaku Toshokan Kyokai (The Japan Medical Library Association) (Japan) 233
Nippon Nogaku Toshokan Kyogikai (Japan Association of Agricultural Librarians and Documentalists) (JAALD) (Japan) 233
Nippon Romazikai (Japan) 233
Nippon Rosiya Bungakkai (Japan) 233
Nippon Shuppan Hanbai KK (Japan) 232
Nippon Toshokan Gakkai (Japan Society of Library Science) (Japan) 233
Nippon Toshokan Kyokai (Japan Library Association) (Japan) 233
Nippon Yakugaku Toshokan Kyogikai (Japan Pharmaceutical Library Association) (Japan) 233
Nisbet, James, & Co Ltd (United Kingdom) 399
Nitzaninn (Israel) 209
Niven, Frederick, Literary Award (United Kingdom) 420
Niyom Vidhya (Thailand) 359
Nizet, Librairie A-G, (France) 103
Nizza, Agencia de Librerías, (Paraguay) 289
Nizza, Ediciones, (Paraguay) 289
Njala University College Bookshop (Sierra Leone) 308
Njala University College Library (University of Sierra Leone) (Sierra Leone) 308
Njala University Publishing Centre (Sierra Leone) 308
Njogu Gitene Publications (Kenya) 236

Nkrumah Teachers' College Library (Zambia) 434
Nnamdi Azikiwe Library (Nigeria) 280
Nobel, Livraría, (Brazil) 56
Nobel, Livraría, SA Editôra (Brazil) 53
Nobel Prize, The, Library (United Kingdom) 415
Nobel Prize for Literature (International Literary Prizes) 451
Nobele, F De, (France) 103
Noblet Editora e Distribuidora Ltda (Brazil) 53
Noguer, Editorial, SA (Spain) 324
Nolit (Yugoslavia) 431
Nolit Publishing House (Yugoslavia) 429
Nolte, Verlag Friedrich, (Federal Republic of Germany) 153
Noma Prize for Juvenile Novel (Japan) 234
Noma Prize for Literature (Japan) 234
Nomath (Belgium) 40
Nomos Verlagsgesellschaft mbH und Co KG (Federal Republic of Germany) 153
Nonesuch, The, Library (United Kingdom) 399
Noord-Hollandsche Uitgeversmaatschappij BV (North Holland Publishing Company) (Netherlands) 265
Noordhoff International Publishing (Netherlands) 265
Noordnederlands Boekbedrijf, Het, NV (Belgium) 40
Noorduijn BV (Netherlands) 265
Nord, Editrice, Sdf (Italy) 218
Nord-Süd Verlag (Switzerland) 350
Nordbok, AB, (Sweden) 335
Norddeutscher Verleger- und Buchhändler-Verband eV (North German Publishers' and Booksellers' Federation) (Federal Republic of Germany) 122
Norden, Förlagshuset, AB (Sweden) 335
Nordic Council Literary Prize (International Literary Prizes) 451
Nórdica, Editorial, Ltda (Brazil) 53
Nordisk Boghandel (Denmark) 78
Nordisk Kolportage Forlag A/S (Denmark) 76
Nordisk Musikforleggerunion (Nordic Music Publishers Union) (International Organizations) 439
Nordisk Romanforlag A/S (Denmark) 77
Nordiska Bokhandeln, AB, (Sweden) 338
Nordiska Bokhandeln, AB, (Sweden) 335
Nordiska Musikförlaget, AB, (Edition Wilhelm Hansen Stockholm) (Sweden) 335
Nordiska Teaterforlaget Edition Wilhelm Hansen (Denmark) 337
Nordiska Teaterförlaget/Edition Wilhelm Hansen (Sweden) 337
Nordiska Vetenskapliga Bibliotekarieförbundet (Scandinavian Association of Research Librarians) (International Organizations) 439
Nordjyske Landsbibliotek, Det, (Denmark) 78
Nordstedt, AB P A, och Söners Förlag (Sweden) 335
Norfolk Press (United Kingdom) 399
Norges Boklag (Norway) 282
Norges Landbrukshøgskoles Bibliotek (Library of the Agricultural University of Norway) (Norway) 283
Norges Tekniske Høgskole, Biblioteket (Library of the Norwegian Institute of Technology, affiliated to the University of Trondheim) (Norway) 283
Noria, Editions La, (France) 103
Norildis, N R L —, (Spain) 327
Norlis, Olaf, Bokhandel A/S (Norway) 283
Norlis, Olaf, Forlag A/S (Norway) 282
Norma, Editorial, y Cia SCA (Colombia) 66
Norma PVBA (Belgium) 40
Normalizacyjne, Wydawnictwa, (Standardization Publishers) (Poland) 295
Norman, Jill, Ltd (United Kingdom) 399
Normanns, M, Forlag A/S (Denmark) 77
Normans Förlag AB (Sweden) 335
Norn (Thailand) 359
Norsk Antikvarbokhandlerforening (Norwegian Antiquarian Booksellers' Association) (Norway) 281
Norsk Bibliotekarlag (Norwegian Librarians' Association) (Norway) 284
Norsk Bibliotekforening (Norwegian Library Association) (Norway) 284
Norsk Bokhandler Medhjelper Forening (Norwegian Book Trade Employees' Association) (Norway) 281
Norsk Bokhandlersamband (Norwegian Christians Booksellers' Union) (Norway) 281
Norsk Bokimport A/S (Norway) 281
Norsk Bokkeucci A/S (Norway) 283
Norsk Dokumentasjonsgruppe (Norwegian Documentation Society) (Norway) 284
Norsk Forleggersamband (Norwegian Christians Publishers' Union) (Norway) 281
Norsk Kunstforlag A/S (Norway) 282
Norsk Musikkforleggerforening (Norwegian Music Publishers' Association) (Norway) 281
Norske Akademi for Sprog og Litteratur (Norwegian Academy for Language and Literature) (Norway) 284
Norske Bokhandlerforening (Norwegian Booksellers' Association) (Norway) 281
Norske Bokklubben, Den, A/S (Norway) 283

Norske Deitidsbibliotekarers Yrkeslag (Norwegian Association for Part-Time Librarians) (Norway) 284
Norske Forfatterforening (Norwegian Authors' Association) (Norway) 284
Norske Forleggerforening, Den, (Norwegian Publishers' Association) (Norway) 281
Norske Forskningsbibliotekarers Forening (Norwegian Research Librarians' Association) (Norway) 284
Norske Samlaget, Det, (Norway) 282
Norske Videnskaps-Akademi, Det, (The Norwegian Academy of Science and Letters) (Norway) 284
Norte, Editorial, SAIC (Argentina) 6
Norte, Librería, (Argentina) 8
North West Arts Publication Awards (United Kingdom) 420
Northern Nigerian Publishing Co Ltd (Nigeria) 278
Northern Technical College Library (Zambia) 434
Northwood Books (United Kingdom) 399
Norwegian Association of Children's and Young Peoples' Authors (Norway) 284
Norwegian Association of Translators (Norway) 284
Nostrand, Van, Reinhold Australia Pty Ltd (Australia) 16
Nostrand Reinhold, Van, Co Ltd (United Kingdom) 399
Nostromo Editores SA (Spain) 324
Nota, Mip, (Yugoslavia) 429
Notre Dame, Librairie, (Benin) 47
Notre Dame, Librairie, (Chad) 62
Nottbeck, Verlag Wissenschaft und Politik, Berend von, (Federal Republic of Germany) 153
Nouveau Cercle parisien du Livre (France) 110
Nouveautés de l'Enseignement-éditions andré casteilla (France) 103
Nouvel Office d'Edition et de Diffusion (Les Productions de Paris — NOE) (France) 103
Nouvelle, Librairie, (Gabon) 116
Nouvelle Agence, La, (France) 110
Nouvelle Cité (France) 103
Nouvelle Diffusion — Complexe (Belgium) 40
Nouvelles Editions, Les, Africaines (Senegal) 307
Nouvelles Editions, Les, Africaines (Ivory Coast) 224
Nouvelles Editions Françaises (France) 103
Nouvelles Editions Latines (France) 103
Nouvelles Editions Marabout, Les, SA (Belgium) 40
Nouvelles Editions Rationalistes SA (France) 103
Nouvelles Editions Vokaer SA (Belgium) 40
Nouvelles feuilles familiales (Belgium) 40
Nova, Editorial, SACI (Argentina) 6
Nova Aguilar, Editora, SA (Brazil) 53
Nova Epoca Editorial Ltda (Brazil) 53
Nova Fronteira, Editora, (Brazil) 53
Nova Hrvatska Ltd (United Kingdom) 399
Nova Knjiga (Yugoslavia) 429
Nova-Press International Publishers Ltd (Switzerland) 350
Nova Rico SpA (Italy) 218
Nova Terra, Editorial, (Spain) 324
Novalis Verlag AG (Switzerland) 350
NovaPart Verlag GmbH (Federal Republic of Germany) 153
Novaro, Organización Editorial, SA (Mexico) 252
Novel Prize (France) 115
Novel Prize (Republic of Ireland) 205
Novello & Co Ltd (United Kingdom) 399
Novelty Trading Co (Jamaica) 224
Novissima, Edizioni di, (Italy) 218
Novos, Editions, SA (Switzerland) 350
'Novosti', Agentstvo Pechati, (Apn) (Union of Soviet Socialist Republics) 366
Novus Forlag A/S (Norway) 282
Nüchtern, Verlag Monika, (Federal Republic of Germany) 153
Nuestra Tierra, Editorial, (Uruguay) 422
Nueva Editorial Interamericana SA de CV (Mexico) 252
Nueva Imagen, Editorial, SA (Mexico) 252
Nueva Visión (Argentina) 8
Nueva Visión, Ediciones, SAIC (Argentina) 6
Nuevo, Editorial, Continente (Honduras) 180
Nuevos Horizontes, Editorial, (Nicaragua) 276
Numismatischer Verlag P N Schulten (Federal Republic of Germany) 153
Nunes, Livraria, (Portugal) 301
Nuova Foglio, La, SpA (Italy) 218
Nuova Italia, La, Editrice (Italy) 218
Nuova Vallecchi Editore SpA (Italy) 218
Nurnberg, Andrew, Associates Ltd (United Kingdom) 413
Nusa Indah (Indonesia) 200
Nusser Verlag (Federal Republic of Germany) 153
Nwamife Publishers Ltd (Nigeria) 278
Nyatsime College Library (Zimbabwe) 435
Nybloms Förlag (Sweden) 335
Nye Bøker (New Book Club) (Norway) 283
Nymphenburger Verlagshandlung GmbH (Federal Republic of Germany) 153

O N K Copyright Agency (Turkey) 363
O R S T O M (France) 103
O S (Organizzazioni Speciali SRL) (Italy) 218
Oasis, Ediciones, SA (Mexico) 252
Oasis Books (United Kingdom) 399
Obelisk, Nakladatelství, (Czechoslovakia) 70
Obelisk-Verlag (Austria) 27
Oberbaumverlag (Federal Republic of Germany) 154
Oberösterreichischer Landesverlag (Austria) 27
Obod (Yugoslavia) 429
Obra, La, (Argentina) 6
O'Brien, The, Press (Republic of Ireland) 204
O'Brien Educational (Republic of Ireland) 204
Obunsha Co Ltd (Japan) 229
Obzor (Yugoslavia) 429
Obzor, vydavatel'stvo knih a casopisov národní podnik (Czechoslovakia) 70
Ocean Interpol Publishing Ltd (United Kingdom) 399
Oceania Printers (Fiji) 85
Octagon, The, Press Ltd (United Kingdom) 399
Octopus Books Ltd (United Kingdom) 399
Octopus Verlag (Austria) 27
Odense Centralbibliotek (Denmark) 78
Odense Universitetsbibliotek (Denmark) 78
Odeon (United Kingdom) 400
Odeon, nakladatelství krásné literatury a umění (Czechoslovakia) 70
Odeon Book Club (Czechoslovakia) 72
Odeon Store LP (Thailand) 359
Odhams Books (United Kingdom) 400
O'Donovan, Anne, Pty Ltd (Australia) 16
Odörfer-Verlags GmbH (Federal Republic of Germany) 154
Odusote Bookstores Ltd (Nigeria) 280
Oeil, L', Ouvert (France) 110
Oekumenischer Verlag Dr R–F Edel (Federal Republic of Germany) 154
Oesch, Emil, Verlag AG (Switzerland) 350
Oetinger, Verlag Friedrich, (Federal Republic of Germany) 154
Oetker, August, (Federal Republic of Germany) 154
Oeuvre Gravée, L', (Switzerland) 350
Ofer Publishing House (Israel) 209
Offene Worte, Verlag, (Federal Republic of Germany) 154
Office Arabe de Presse et de Documentation (Syria) 357
Office Central de Librairie Sàrl (France) 103
Office Central de Lisieux SA (France) 103
Office de Documentation Bibliographique et de Diffusion (France) 103
Office de la Recherche Scientifique et Technique Outre-Mer (Office of Scientific and Technical Research Overseas) (French Guiana) 116
Office de la Recherche Scientifique et Technique Outre Mer (ORSTOM) (France) 103
Office de Promotion de L'Edition Française (France) 88
Office du Livre Malagasy (Democratic Republic of Madagascar) 244
Office du Livre SA (Buchhaus AG) (Switzerland) 350
Office international de Librairie (Belgium) 44
Office national de Planification et de Developpement des Bibliotheques (National Office of Planning and Development of Libraries) (Kampuchea) 235
Office national des Librairies (Popular Republic of Congo) 67
Oficiul de Informare Documentara in Stiintele Sociale si Politice (Office of Information and Documentation in Social and Political Sciences) (Romania) 305
Ofiria, Edizioni, (Italy) 218
Ogbalu, F C, (Nigeria) 279
Ogunsanya Press, Publishers and Bookstores Ltd (Nigeria) 278
Ohlssons, AB Håkan, Förlag (Sweden) 335
Ohm, Karl, Verlag (Federal Republic of Germany) 154
Ohm-, The, Sha Ltd (Japan) 229
Ohridski, Narodna i univerzitetska biblioteka 'Kliment,' (Yugoslavia) 431
Oikos-Tau SA Ediciones (Spain) 324
Oireachtas Library (Republic of Ireland) 205
Oiseau-Lyre, Editions de l', (Monaco) 255
Okapi Centre de Diffusion (Zaire) 433
'Oktobar', Literary Club, (Yugoslavia) 432
Oktoberförlaget AB (Sweden) 335
Olamenu (Israel) 209
Oldenbourg, R, Verlag GmbH (Federal Republic of Germany) 154
Oldenbourg, Verlag, (Austria) 27
Oleander, The, Press (United Kingdom) 400
Oliphants (United Kingdom) 400
Olive Books of Israel (Israel) 209
Oliver & Boyd (United Kingdom) 400
Oliver & Boyd (Australia) 16
Olle und Wolter, Verlag, (Federal Republic of Germany) 154
Olms, Edition, AG (Switzerland) 350
Olms, Georg, Verlag (Federal Republic of Germany) 154
Olschki, Leo S, (Italy) 218

Ölschläger, Verlag, GmbH (Federal Republic of Germany) 154
Ölschläger, Verlag für Wirtschaftsskripten, Dipl Kfm C, GmbH (Federal Republic of Germany) 154
Olympia, Nakladatelství CSTV, (Czechoslovakia) 71
Olympia Press Italia (Italy) 218
Olympio, Livraria José, Editora SA (Brazil) 53
Olzog, Günter, Verlag GmbH (Federal Republic of Germany) 154
O'Mahony & Co Ltd (Republic of Ireland) 205
Omega (United Kingdom) 400
Omega, Ediciones, SA (Spain) 324
Omega Boek BV (Netherlands) 265
Omega NV (Belgium) 40
Omnia, Edizioni, Medica (Italy) 218
Omniboek, Uitgeverij, (Netherlands) 265
Omnibus Book Service (United Kingdom) 400
Omun Kak (Republic of Korea) 239
Oncken Verlag KG (Federal Republic of Germany) 154
Ondori Sha Publishers Co Ltd (Japan) 229
O'Neil, Lloyd, Pty Ltd (Australia) 16
Ongaku No Tomo Sha Corporation (Japan) 229
Onibonoje Book Club (Nigeria) 279
Onibonoje Press & Book Industries (Nigeria) Ltd (Nigeria) 279
Ontwikkeling, Uitgeverij S V, (Belgium) 40
Oosthoek (Netherlands) 265
Opal, Bokförlaget, AB (Sweden) 335
Opdebeek, L, Uitgeversfirma NV (Belgium) 40
Open Books Publishing Ltd (United Kingdom) 400
Open University, The, Press (Open University Educational Enterprises Ltd) (United Kingdom) 400
Openbare Bibliotheek (Public Library) (Netherlands) 269
Openbare Leeszaal en Bibliotheek (Public Reading Room and Library) (Netherlands Antilles) 271
Openbare Leeszaal en Boekerij (Public Reading Room and Library) (Netherlands Antilles) 271
Opera Mundi SA (France) 103
Operaie, Nuove Edizioni, SRL (Italy) 218
Ophrys, Editions, (France) 103
Oppersdorff, Inigo von, Verlag (Switzerland) 350
Opta Editions (France) 110
Opus Records and Publishing House (Czechoslovakia) 71
Orac, Wirtschaftsverlag Dr Anton, (Austria) 27
Orangerie Galerie und Verlag, Gerhard F Reinz (Federal Republic of Germany) 154
Orante, Editions de l', (France) 104
Orban, Editions Oliver, (France) 104
Orbe, Editorial, (Cuba) 68
Orbe, Editorial y Distribuidora, (Chile) 62
Orbis, Nakladatelství, (Czechoslovakia) 71
Orbis Boekhandel NV (Belgium) 40
Orbis Publishing Ltd (United Kingdom) 400
Orbit (United Kingdom) 400
Orbit NV (Netherlands) 265
Ordfront tryckeri & förlag AB (Sweden) 336
Ordina Editions (Belgium) 41
Ordnance Survey (United Kingdom) 400
Orell Füssli (Switzerland) 356
Orell Füssli Verlag (Switzerland) 350
Orellana, Librería, (Chile) 63
Oresko Books (United Kingdom) 400
Organisation, Les Editions d', (France) 104
Organisation for Economic Cooperation and Development (OECD) (International Organizations) 443
Organisator, Verlag, AG (Switzerland) 350
Organización Bienestar Estudiantes (OBE) (Venezuela) 425
Organization for African Unity Library (Ethiopia) 84
Organizzazioni Speciali SRL (Italy) 218
Orhan Özsisman (Turkey) 363
Oriel Press Ltd (United Kingdom) 400
Orient Book Club (India) 197
Orient Longman Ltd (India) 192
Orient Paperbacks (Division of Vision Books) (India) 193
Oriental & Religious, The, Publishing Corp Ltd (Pakistan) 285
Oriental Book Service (Bangladesh) 32
Oriental Books Reprint Corporation (India) 193
Oriental Economist Ltd (K K Toyo Keizai Shimposha) (Japan) 229
Oriental Press BV (APA) (Netherlands) 265
Orientalia Christiana, Edizioni, (Italy) 218
Orientalia Publishers (Pakistan) 285
Orientaliste, Uitgeverij, PVBA (Belgium) 41
Oriente, Editorial, (Cuba) 68
Origo-Verlag (Switzerland) 350
Orion, Ediciones, (Argentina) 7
Orion, Editorial, (Mexico) 252
Orion, Uitgeverij, (Belgium) 41
Orion-Heimreiter Verlag GmbH (Federal Republic of Germany) 154
Orion Press (Japan) 232
Orisun Editions (Nigeria) 279
Ormeraie, Michel de l', (France) 104
Örn og Örlygur HF (Iceland) 185
Orpan Export (Poland) 296

Országos Műszaki Könyvtár és Dokumentációs Központ (Hungarian Central Technical Library and Documentation Centre) (Hungary) 184
Országos Széchényi Könyvtár (Hungary) 183
Orte-Verlag (Switzerland) 350
Ortells, Alfredo, Ferriz (Spain) 324
Orvieto, Laura, Prize (Italy) 223
Orwell, George, Memorial Prize (United Kingdom) 420
Osaka Gakuin University Library (Japan) 232
Osaka Prefectural Nakanoshima Library (Japan) 232
Oslobodenje, NIP, (Yugoslavia) 429
Osprey Publishing Ltd (United Kingdom) 400
Ossolińskich, Zaklad Narodowy im, Wydawnictwo Polskiej Akademii Nauk (Poland) 295
Ossolińskich Biblioteka, Zaklad Narodowy im, Polska Akademia Nauk (Library of the Ossoliński National Institute of the Polish Academy of Science) (Poland) 297
Österreichische Exlibris-Gesellschaft (Austria) 31
Österreichische Gesellschaft für Dokumentation und Information (Austria) 30
Österreichische Gesellschaft für Literatur (Austria) 31
Österreichische Nationalbibliothek (Austria) 30
Österreichische Verlagsanstalt GmbH (Austria) 27
Österreichischen Akademie der Wissenschaften, Bibliothek der, (Austria) 30
österreichischen Akademie der Wissenschaften, Verlag der, (Austria) 27
österreichischen Gewerkschaftsbundes, Verlag des, GmbH (Austria) 27
Österreichischen Patentamtes, Bucherei des, (Austria) 30
Österreichischer Agrarverlag, Druck- und Verlags- GmbH (Austria) 27
Österreichischer Buchklub der Jugend (Austria) 30
Österreichischer Bundesverlag GmbH (Austria) 27
Österreichischer Schriftstellerverband (Austria) 31
Österreichischer Verlegerverband (Austria) 24
Österreichisches Institut für Bibliographie (Austria) 31
Österreichisches Institut für Bibliotheksforschung, Dokumentations- und Informationswesen (Austria) 30
Österreichisches Katholisches Bibelwerk (Austria) 27
Österreichisches Staatsarchiv (Austria) 30
Osterrieth, Verlag, (Federal Republic of Germany) 154
Ostrowiak, Rebecca, School of Reading (Republic of South Africa) 313
Osveta (Czechoslovakia) 71
Oswald, Editions Pierre Jean, (France) 104
Otago University Library (New Zealand) 275
Otava Kustannusosakeyhtiö (Finland) 86
Other, The, Award (United Kingdom) 420
Otokar Kersovani-Rijeka (Yugoslavia) 429
Otpaz (Israel) 209
Ott Verlag AG Thun (Switzerland) 350
Ottaviano, Edizioni, (Italy) 218
Otzar Hamoreh (Israel) 209
Oude, De, Linden NV (Belgium) 41
Oudiovista Productions (Pty) Ltd (Republic of South Africa) 313
Ouest-Publicité (Annuaire de Versailles) (France) 104
Oulun Yliopiston Kirjasto (Finland) 87
Outback Press Pty Ltd (Australia) 17
Outrigger Publishers Ltd (New Zealand) 273
Ouvrières, Les Editions, SA (France) 104
Overseas Publications Interchange Ltd (United Kingdom) 400
Overseas Publishers' Representatives Association of Southern Africa (Republic of South Africa) 311
Owen, Peter, Ltd (United Kingdom) 400
Owlet (United Kingdom) 400
Oxford & I B H Publishing Co (India) 193
Oxford Bibliographical Society (United Kingdom) 417
Oxford Book and Stationery Co (India) 197
Oxford Illustrated Press Ltd (United Kingdom) 400
Oxford Microform Publications Ltd (United Kingdom) 400
Oxford Railway, The, Publishing Co (United Kingdom) 400
Oxford University (United Kingdom) 416
Oxford University Press (United Kingdom) 400
Oxford University Press (Republic of Singapore) 309
Oxford University Press (Tanzania) 358
Oxford University Press (India) 193
Oxford University Press (Hong Kong) 181
Oxford University Press (New Zealand) 273
Oxford University Press (Pakistan) 285
Oxford University Press (Pakistan) 286
Oxford University Press (Kenya) 236
Oxford University Press (Malaysia) 246
Oxford University Press (Australia) 17
Oxford University Press Southern Africa (Republic of South Africa) 313
Oxford University Press Southern Africa (Zimbabwe) 435
Oxonian Press (P) Ltd (India) 193
Oya Soichi Nonfiction Prize (Japan) 234
Oyez Publishing Ltd (United Kingdom) 401
Oyez SA (Belgium) 41

P A C, Editions, (Presse-Auto-Conseil) (France) 104
P E N, Centro del, Internacional (International PEN Centre) (Peru) 290
P E N, Dacca Centre for International, Madhura (Bangladesh) 33
P E N, Hong Kong Chinese, Centre (Hong Kong) 181
P E N, Hong Kong English, Centre (Hong Kong) 181
P E N, International, (Melbourne Centre) (Australia) 21
P E N, International, (Sydney Centre) (Australia) 21
P E N, International, Centre (Iceland) 186
P E N, International, Centre (Philippines) 293
P E N, International, Centre (Venezuela) 425
P E N, International (A World Association of Writers) (International Organizations) 439
P E N, Irish, (Republic of Ireland) 205
P E N, Israeli, Centre (Israel) 211
P E N, Japan, Club (Japan) 233
P E N, Korean, Centre (Republic of Korea) 240
P E N, Lebanese, Club (Lebanon) 241
P E N, Magyar, Club (Hungarian PEN Club) (Hungary) 184
P E N, Mexican, Club (Mexico) 254
P E N, Netherlands Centre of the International, (Netherlands) 270
P E N, Polish, Club (Poland) 297
P E N, Portuguese, Centre (Portugal) 302
P E N, Senegal, Centre (Senegal) 307
P E N, South African, Centre (Cape) (Republic of South Africa) 316
P E N, Spanish, Club (Spain) 328
P E N, Spanish, Club (Cataluña) (Spain) 328
P E N, Svenska Pennklubben (Swedish Centre of International,) (Sweden) 339
P E N All—India Centre (India) 198
P E N Centre (Greece) 178
P E N Centre (Liechtenstein) 243
P E N Centre of Zimbabwe-Rhodesia (Zimbabwe) 436
P E N Club (Monaco) 255
P E N Club (Jamaica) 225
P E N Club (Romania) 305
P E N Club, Flemish Centre, International, (Belgium) 45
P E N Club, International, Belgian French Centre (Belgium) 45
P E N-Club, Österreichischer, (Austria) 31
P E N Club, Yugoslav, (Yugoslavia) 432
P E N Club Award, Yugoslav, (International Literary Prizes) 451
P E N Club de Bolivia (Centro Internacional de Escritores) (International PEN Centre) (Bolivia) 48
P E N Club de la Argentina (Argentina) 9
P E N Club de Puerto Rico (Puerto Rico) 303
P E N Club de Suisse romande (Switzerland) 357
P E N Club di Italian Romansch (Switzerland) 357
P E N Club Français (France) 112
P E N Club International Centre de Côte d'Ivoire (Ivory Coast) 224
P E N Club Medal, Hungarian, (International Literary Prizes) 451
P E N Club of Iran (Iran) 202
P E N Club Prizes, Polish, (International Literary Prizes) 451
P E N Clube do Brasil (Associação Universal de Escritores) (International PEN Centre) (Brazil) 57
P E N English Centre (United Kingdom) 418
P E N Internacional de Escritores de Colombia (Colombia) 67
P E N International Centre (Italy) 223
P E N International New Zealand Centre (New Zealand) 275
P E N International-Thailand Centre (Thailand) 360
P E N-Klubb, Den Norske, (Norwegian Centre of International PEN) (Norway) 284
P E N Scottish Centre (United Kingdom) 418
P E N Yazarlar Dernegi (Turkey) 364
P E N Zentrum, Deutsche Demokratische Republik (German Democratic Republic) 121
P E N Zentrum Bundesrepublik Deutschland (Federal Republic of Germany) 173
P F B (Malaysia) 246
P G Medical Books (Republic of Singapore) 309
P I A G (Federal Republic of Germany) 154
P I C S (Publishers' Information Card Services) (United Kingdom) 369
P O F (France) 104
P P C, Librerías, (Propaganda Popular Católica) (Spain) 327
P P C (Propaganda Popular Católica) (Spain) 324
P P C Ltd (Barbados) 33
P R O N I (Public Record Office of Northern Ireland) (United Kingdom) 416
P R Verlag Wiesbaden, H G Schwieger (Federal Republic of Germany) 154
P U F (France) 104
P U L (France) 104
P W N (Panstwowe Wydawnictwo Naukowe) (Poland) 295
P Y C Edition (France) 104

Pacific Book Centre (Republic of Singapore) 310
Pacific Publications (Australia) Pty Ltd (Australia) 17
Pacifica Ltd (Japan) 229
Pacifico, Editorial del, SA (Chile) 62
Pacifique, Les Editions du, (France) 104
Pacifique, Les Editions du, (French Polynesia) 116
Packard Publishing Ltd (United Kingdom) 401
Päd extra buchverlag in der pädex Verlags GmbH (Federal Republic of Germany) 154
Pädagogischer Verlag Schwann GmbH (Federal Republic of Germany) 154
Paddington Press Ltd (United Kingdom) 401
Padilla, Editorial, (Dominican Republic) 81
Padilla, Editorial, (Dominican Republic) 80
Paedagogiki Academia, Library of the, (Institute of Education Library) (Cyprus) 69
Paes Barreto, Rômulo, (Brazil) 55
Pagan Publishing House (Burma) 59
Pahl-Rugenstein Verlag (Federal Republic of Germany) 154
Pahlavi Library (Iran) 202
Pahlavi University Libraries (Iran) 202
Paico Ltd (Nigeria) 279
Paico Publishing House (India) 193
Paideia Editrice (Italy) 218
Paidós, Editorial, (Argentina) 7
Paintaway (United Kingdom) 401
Pak American Commercial Inc (Pakistan) 286
Pak Book Corporation (Pakistan) 286
Pak Kitab Ghar (Bangladesh) 32
Pak Publishers (Pakistan) 285
Pakistan Board for Advancement of Literature (Pakistan) 287
Pakistan Board for Advancement of Literature Awards (Pakistan) 287
Pakistan Forest Institute, Central Forest Library (Pakistan) 286
Pakistan Institute of Nuclear Science & Technology Library (Pakistan) 286
Pakistan Law Times Publications (Pakistan) 285
Pakistan Library Association (Pakistan) 287
Pakistan Publications (Pakistan) 285
Pakistan Publishers' and Booksellers' Association (Pakistan) 284
Pakistan Publishing Co Ltd (Pakistan) 286
Pakistan Publishing House (Pakistan) 286
Pakistan Scientific and Technological Information Centre (PASTIC) (Pakistan) 286
Pakistan Writers' Guild (Pakistan) 287
Pakpassak Kanphin (Laos) 240
Pala SA (Spain) 324
Palacio, Biblioteca del, Real (Library of the Royal Palace) (Spain) 328
Palácio, Biblioteca do, Nacional de Mafra (Portugal) 301
Palacio, El, del Libro (Venezuela) 425
Palacio del Libro (Uruguay) 423
Paladin Books (United Kingdom) 401
Palanca, Carlos, Memorial Awards for Literature (Philippines) 293
Palatina, Biblioteca, (Italy) 222
Pallas SA (Brazil) 54
Pallas, Vydavatel'stvo SFVU, (Czechoslovakia) 71
'Pallottinum' Wydawnictwo Stowarzyszenia Apolstolstwa Katolickiego (Publishers of the Catholic Apostolate Association) (Poland) 295
Palmerston North Public Library (New Zealand) 275
Paludans, Erik, Boghandel (Denmark) 78
Paludans, Jörgen, Forlag A/S (Denmark) 77
Palumbo, G B, e C Editore SpA (Italy) 218
Památník národního písemnictví, Strahovská knihovna (Czechoslovakia) 72
Pamplona and its Culture Prize (Colombia) 67
Pan Books Ltd (United Kingdom) 401
Pan Library ('Circle of the Friends of Progress') (Greece) 178
Pan Malayan Publishing Co Sdn Bhd (Malaysia) 246
Pan Pacific Book Distributors (S) Pte Ltd (Republic of Singapore) 309
Pancaldi, Libreria Commissionaria Internazionale di Raffaele, (Italy) 222
Panda Press SRL (Italy) 218
Panero, Leopoldo, Prize (International Literary Prizes) 451
Panini, Edizioni, SpA (Italy) 219
Panjab University Publication Bureau (India) 193
Panmun Book Co Ltd (Republic of Korea) 239
Panmun Book Co Ltd (Republic of Korea) 239
Pannedille, Ediciones, (Argentina) 7
Panorama, Editions du, (Switzerland) 350
Panorama, Nakladatelství a vydavatelství, (Czechoslovakia) 71
Pansegrau, Wilhelm, Verlag (Federal Republic of Germany) 154
Pantarei, Edizioni, (Switzerland) 350
Pantelides (Greece) 178
Panther, Penerbitan Buku, (Panther Books Malaysia) (Malaysia) 246

Panther Books Ltd (United Kingdom) 401
Panton (Czechoslovakia) 71
Paoline, Edizioni, (Italy) 219
Papachrysanthou Chryss SA (Greece) 177
Papacito, Ediciones, (Uruguay) 422
Papacito, Librerías, (Uruguay) 423
Papaioannou (Greece) 177
Papazissis Publishers SA (Greece) 177
Paper Tiger (United Kingdom) 401
Paperback Centre (Republic of Ireland) 205
Paperfronts (United Kingdom) 401
Papeterie Centrale (Central African Republic) 61
Papua New Guinea Library Association (Papua New Guinea) 288
Papyros Press (Greece) 177
'Papyrus' (Central African Republic) 61
Parabel Verlag GmbH und Co KG (Federal Republic of Germany) 154
Paracelsus Verlag GmbH (Federal Republic of Germany) 155
Paradise Book Stall (Pakistan) 286
Paramount Book Corporation (Bangladesh) 32
Paramount Book Stall (Pakistan) 286
Paraninfo, Editorial, SA (Spain) 324
Pardo, Casa, SAC (Argentina) 7
Pardo, Librería General de Tomas, (Argentina) 8
Parera, Librería, (Chile) 63
Parey, Verlag Paul, (Federal Republic of Germany) 155
Parimal Prakashan (India) 193
Paris Grand Prize for Literature (France) 115
Paris Prize (France) 115
Parissianos, Grigorios, 'Epistemonikai Ekdoseis' (Greece) 177
Park & Roche Establishment (Liechtenstein) 243
Park and Roche Establishment (Switzerland) 350
Parker & Son Ltd (United Kingdom) 415
Parkland Verlag GmbH und Co Verlags- & Vertriebs-KG (Federal Republic of Germany) 155
Parlement, Bibliothèque du, (Belgium) 44
Parliament Library (Greece) 178
Parliament Library (Iran) 202
Parma, Editora, Ltda (Brazil) 54
Parnfah Pittaya (Thailand) 359
Parramon, Instituto, (Spain) 324
Parrish, Walter, Ltd (United Kingdom) 401
Parry's Book Center (Malaysia) 247
Parsons, Roy, (New Zealand) 274
Partenon, Ediciones, (Spain) 324
Parthenón, Livraria, (Brazil) 56
Passavia, Verlag, (Federal Republic of Germany) 155
Passim, Libreria, (Spain) 327
Paternoster, The, Press Ltd (United Kingdom) 401
Paterson, Banjo, Awards (Australia) 23
Paterson, Mark, & Associates (United Kingdom) 413
Patio, Galerie, Verlag (Federal Republic of Germany) 155
Patmos, Uitgeverij, (Belgium) 41
Patmos Verlag GmbH (Federal Republic of Germany) 155
Patria, Editorial, SA (Mexico) 252
Patria, Librería, (Mexico) 254
Patria, Libreria, SA (Mexico) 252
Pàtron, Casa Editrice, SAS (Italy) 219
Pàtron, Libreria Internazionale, (Italy) 222
Pattloch, Paul, Verlag (Federal Republic of Germany) 155
Patwa (Embakasi) Ltd (Kenya) 236
Paul, Stanley, & Co Ltd (United Kingdom) 401
Pauli SA (Belgium) 41
Paulinas, Ediciones, (Chile) 62
Paulinas, Ediciones, (Argentina) 7
Paulinas, Ediciones, (Spain) 324
Paulinas, Ediciones, SA (Mexico) 252
Paulinas, Edições, (Brazil) 54
Paulinus Verlag (Federal Republic of Germany) 155
Pauls University Bookshop Ltd (New Zealand) 274
Paulusverlag (Switzerland) 350
Pause, Firmin, (Réunion) 303
Pauvert, Jean-Jacques, Editeur (France) 104
Pavillon, Le, Roger Maria Editeur (France) 104
Pawel Pan Presse (Federal Republic of Germany) 155
Pawlak, Manfred, Grossantiquariat und Verlagsgesellschaft mbH (Federal Republic of Germany) 155
Pax, Editorial, México (Mexico) 252
Pax, Instytut Wydawniczy, (Poland) 295
Pax, Livraria Editora, Lda (Portugal) 300
Pax-Chile, Librería, (Chile) 63
Pax Forlag A/S (Norway) 282
Payot, Editions, (France) 104
Payot, Librairie, SA (Switzerland) 350
Payot, Librairie, SA (Switzerland) 350
Paz, Editorial, Montalvo (Spain) 324
Paz e Terra, Editôra, (Brazil) 54
Peace and Socialism International Publishers (Czechoslovakia) 71
Pédagogie Moderne (France) 104
Pedagogika (Union of Soviet Socialist Republics) 366
Pedagogisk Forlag A/S (Norway) 282

Pedagoško-književni zbor, pedagoško društvo SR Hrvatske (Pedagogical and Literary Union of Croatia) (Yugoslavia) 432
Pediátrica, Editorial, (Spain) 324
Pédone, Editions, (France) 104
Pedrazzini, Carlo, (Switzerland) 351
Pedrick, Don, Memorial Literary Award (Sri Lanka) 330
Pe'er Hatora (Israel) 209
Peeters SPRL (Belgium) 41
Pegaso, Ediciones, (Mexico) 253
Pegaso, Ediciones, (Spain) 324
Pegasus Books (Australia) 17
Pegasus Press Ltd (New Zealand) 273
Pei-ching ta hsueh t'u shu kuan (Peking University Library) (People's Republic of China) 64
Pei-ching t'u shu kuan (National Library of Peking) (People's Republic of China) 64
Peiffer, Librairie Armand, (Luxembourg) 244
Peisa, Ediciones, (Peru) 289
Pelajar (Indonesia) 200
Pelham Books Ltd (United Kingdom) 401
Peli, Alexander, Ltd (Israel) 209
Pelican (United Kingdom) 401
Pelita Masa (Indonesia) 200
Pelmas (Israel) 209
Pembangunan (Indonesia) 200
Pemberton Publishing Co Ltd (United Kingdom) 401
Pembimbing, P T, Masa (Indonesia) 200
Pembimbing Masa (Indonesia) 200
Pembinaan, Pusat, Perpustakaan, Departemen P dan K Bidang. Bibliografi and Deposit (Indonesia) 201
Peña, A, Lillo SA (Argentina) 7
Pendidekan, Pustaka, Sdn Bhd (Malaysia) 246
Pendo-Verlag (Switzerland) 351
Penguin Books (NZ) Ltd (New Zealand) 274
Penguin Books Australia Ltd (Australia) 17
Penguin Books Ltd (United Kingdom) 401
Penguin Publishing Co Ltd (United Kingdom) 401
Peninsula, Ediciones, (Spain) 324
Penman, The, Club (International Organizations) 439
Pensamento, Editôra, SA (Brazil) 54
Pensée Moderne Jacques Grancher (France) 104
'Pensiero Scientifico' SRL (Italy) 219
Pentacle (Australia) 17
Pentecost (New Caledonia) 271
Pentos Ltd (United Kingdom) 401
People's Literature Publishing House (People's Republic of China) 63
People's Physical Culture Publishing House (People's Republic of China) 63
People's Publishing Co Ltd (Nigeria) 279
People's Publishing House (Pakistan) 286
People's Publishing House (P) Ltd (India) 193
Pequeña, Una, Librería (Ecuador) 81
Pereira, Parceria A M, Lda (Portugal) 300
Peretz, Y L, Publishing Co (Israel) 209
Perfecting Press (Hong Kong) 181
Pergamon Press (Australia) Pty Ltd (Australia) 17
Pergamon Press Ltd (United Kingdom) 401
Periféria, Ediciones, SRL (Argentina) 7
Périodiques, Les, Parisiens (France) 104
Permanent Press (United Kingdom) 401
Perpessicius Prize (Romania) 305
Perpétuo, Editorial, Socorro (Portugal) 300
Perrin, Editions G M, SA (France) 104
Perrin, Librairie Académique, (France) 104
Perrin, Olivier, Editeur (France) 104
Persatuan Perpustakaan Malaysia (Library Association of Malaysia) (Malaysia) 247
Perskor Books (Pty) Ltd (Republic of South Africa) 313
Perskor Bookshop (Republic of South Africa) 315
Perskor Prize for Literature (Republic of South Africa) 317
Perskor Prize for Youth Literature (Republic of South Africa) 317
Perspectiva, Editôra, (Brazil) 54
Peryer, N M, Ltd (New Zealand) 274
Pestalozzi-Verlag graphische Gesellschaft mbH (Federal Republic of Germany) 155
'Petar Kočić' (Yugoslavia) 429
Peter, Verlag J P, Gebr Holstein (Federal Republic of Germany) 155
Peterborough Literary Agency (United Kingdom) 414
Peters, A D, & Co Ltd (United Kingdom) 414
Peters, C F, Musikverlag GmbH und Co KG (Federal Republic of Germany) 155
Peters, Dr Hans, Verlag (Federal Republic of Germany) 155
Petersen, Hans Heinrich, Buchimport GmbH (Federal Republic of Germany) 170
Petitdidier Prize (France) 115
Petiwala and Co (Pakistan) 286
Pevsner Public Library (Israel) 211
Pfaffenweiler Presse (Federal Republic of Germany) 155

Pfanneberg, Fachbuchverlag Dr. & Co (Federal Republic of Germany) 155
Pfeiffer, Verlag J. (Federal Republic of Germany) 155
Pfister, E, GmbH (Federal Republic of Germany) 155
Pflaum, Richard, Verlag KG (Federal Republic of Germany) 155
Pfriem, Engelbert, Verlag (Federal Republic of Germany) 155
Pfriemer, Udo, Verlag GmbH (Federal Republic of Germany) 155
Phaethon, The, Press (United Kingdom) 401
Phaidon Press Ltd (United Kingdom) 401
Phaneromeni, Library of, (Cyprus) 69
Pharos-Verlag (Switzerland) 351
Phébus, Editions, (France) 104
Philip, David-, Publisher (Pty) Ltd (Republic of South Africa) 313
Philip & Son, George, Ltd (United Kingdom) 402
Philip & Tacey Ltd (United Kingdom) 402
Philip Alexander, George, Ltd (United Kingdom) 402
Philippine Arts and Architecture (Philippines) 291
Philippine Book Co (Philippines) 292
Philippine Book Co (Philippines) 291
Philippine Book Dealers' Association (Philippines) 291
Philippine Education Co Inc (Philippines) 292
Philippine Education Co Inc (Philippines) 292
Philippine Educational Publishers' Association (Philippines) 291
Philippine International Publishing Co (Philippines) 292
Philippine Library Association (Philippines) 292
Philips GmbH, Fachbuch-Verlag (Federal Republic of Germany) 155
Phillimore & Co Ltd (United Kingdom) 402
Philo Press-van Heusden-Hissink & Co CV (APA) (Netherlands) 265
Philograph Publications Ltd (United Kingdom) 402
Philosophisch-Anthroposophischer Verlag (Switzerland) 351
Philpott & Collins (1978) (Pvt) Ltd (Zimbabwe) 435
Pho Thong (Popularization) Publishing House (Socialist Republic of Viet Nam) 426
Phoebus Publishing Co (United Kingdom) 402
Phoebus-Verlag GmbH (Switzerland) 351
Phoenix Book Society (United Kingdom) 415
Phoenix Verlag AG (Switzerland) 351
Physica-Verlag Rudolf Liebing GmbH und Co (Federal Republic of Germany) 155
Physik Verlag GmbH (Federal Republic of Germany) 156
Piatkus Books (United Kingdom) 402
Picador (United Kingdom) 402
Picard, Editions A & J, Sàrl (France) 104
Piccin Editore sas (Italy) 219
Piccoli, Editrice, SpA (Italy) 219
Piccolo (United Kingdom) 402
Pickering & Inglis Ltd (United Kingdom) 402
Pied Piper (United Kingdom) 402
Piedra Santa (Guatemala) 179
Piedra Santa (Guatemala) 178
Pierce, Lorne, Medal (International Literary Prizes) 451
Pierron, Editions Marcel, (France) 104
Pierrot, Editions, SA (Switzerland) 351
Pierrot Publishing Ltd (United Kingdom) 402
Pietra, La, (Italy) 219
Pietsch, Buch- & Verlagshaus Paul, GmbH & Co KG (Federal Republic of Germany) 156
Pigmalión (Argentina) 8
Pike, James, Ltd (EJP Publications) (United Kingdom) 402
Pikkhanet (Thailand) 359
Pilgrim Award (International Literary Prizes) 451
Pilgrim Books Ltd (Nigeria) 279
Pilgrim Publishers (India) 193
Pilgrims Booksellers (Pty) (Republic of South Africa) 315
Pimodan, De, Prize (France) 115
Pinchgut Press (Australia) 17
Pineda Libros (Chile) 62
Pinguin-Verlag, Pawlowski KG (Austria) 27
Pink and Blue Editora Ltda (Brazil) 54
Pink Editions & Productions (Belgium) 41
Pinter, Frances, Ltd (United Kingdom) 402
Pioneer Design Studio Pty Ltd (Australia) 17
Piper, R, & Co Verlag GmbH (Switzerland) 351
Piper, R, und Co Verlag (Federal Republic of Germany) 156
Pirámide, Ediciones, SA (Spain) 324
'Pishchevaya Promyshlennost', Izdatelstvo, (Union of Soviet Socialist Republics) 366
Pitambar Book Depot (India) 193
Pitkin Pictorials Ltd (United Kingdom) 402
Pitman Medical Publishing Co Ltd (United Kingdom) 402
Pitman Publishing Co SA (Pty) Ltd (Republic of South Africa) 313
Pitman Publishing Ltd (United Kingdom) 402
Pitman Publishing NZ Ltd (New Zealand) 274
Pitman Publishing Pty Ltd (Australia) 17
Pitou, Charles, Prize (France) 115

Pittayakarn (Thailand) 359
Pizzi, Amilcare, SpA (Italy) 219
Place, Editions Jean-Michel, (France) 104
Plambeck & Co, Druck und Verlag GmbH (Federal Republic of Germany) 156
Planeta, Editorial, SA (Spain) 324
Planeta Prize (International Literary Prizes) 451
Planeta Publishers (Union of Soviet Socialist Republics) 366
Planning Commission Library (Pakistan) 286
Plantyn, Editions, SA (France) 105
Plantyn, Uitgeverij, SA NV (Belgium) 41
Plata, Editorial, SA (Peru) 289
Plata, Editorial, SA (Venezuela) 424
Platano Editora SARL (Portugal) 300
Playfair (United Kingdom) 402
Playor (Spain) 324
Plaza & Janés, Editorial Argentina, SA (Argentina) 7
Plaza y Janés SA (Spain) 324
Pleamar, Editorial, (Argentina) 7
Plessl, Gerd, Agency (Federal Republic of Germany) 169
Plexus Publishing Ltd (United Kingdom) 402
Ploegsma, Uitgeverij, (Netherlands) 265
Ploetz, Ernst, (Austria) 27
Ploetz GmbH und Co KG (Federal Republic of Germany) 156
Plon, Librairie, SA (France) 105
Plough Publishing House (United Kingdom) 402
Pluim Book Club (Republic of South Africa) 315
Pluma, Editorial, Ltda (Colombia) 66
Plume (United Kingdom) 402
Plus, Bokförlaget, (Sweden) 336
Plus Ultra, Editorial, SAI & C (Argentina) 7
Pluto Press (United Kingdom) 402
Pobjeda (Yugoslavia) 429
Pochinjae (Republic of Korea) 239
Pock, Max, Universitätsbuchhandlung (Austria) 30
Pocket, Presses, (France) 105
Poder, Biblioteca del, Legislativo (Library of the Legislative Power) (Uruguay) 423
Podzun-Pallas Verlag GmbH (Federal Republic of Germany) 156
Poe, Edgar, Prize (International Literary Prizes) 451
Poeschel, C E, Verlag (Federal Republic of Germany) 156
Poètes Présents (France) 110
Poetry Book Society (United Kingdom) 415
Poetry in Irish Award (International Literary Prizes) 451
Poetry Society (United Kingdom) 418
Poetry Society of Australia (Australia) 21
Pohjalainen Kirjakauppa Oy (Finland) 87
Pohl Druckerei und Verlagsanstalt Otto Pohl (Federal Republic of Germany) 156
Poincaré, Raymond, Prize (France) 115
Point d'Interrogation, Librairie du, (Senegal) 307
'Pojezierze', Wydawnictwo Stowarzyszenia Społeczno-Kulturalnego, (Poland) 295
Polak, Emil, Prize (Belgium) 46
Polak en Van Gennep Uitg Mij BV (Netherlands) 265
Polana AG (Switzerland) 351
Polding, The, Press (Australia) 17
Poldner, Axel, (Federal Republic of Germany) 169
Policy Studies Institute (United Kingdom) 402
Poligrafa, Ediciones, SA (Spain) 324
Poligraficheskata Promishlenost i Kulturnite Instituti, Sekciya na Bibliotechnite Rabotnitsi pri Centralniya Komitet na Profesionalniya Sŭyuz na Rabotnitsite ot, (Bulgaria) 59
Polish Academy of Sciences (Poland) 297
Polish Authors' Prizes (International Literary Prizes) 451
Polish Bibliography, Editorial Office for, (formerly Karol Estreicher Research Centre of Polish 19th Century Bibliography) (Poland) 293
Polish Ministry of National Defence Prize (Poland) 297
Polish Prime Minister Award for Literature for Children and Youth (Poland) 297
Polish Union of Socialist Youth Prose Award (Poland) 297
Politécnica Moulines, Librería, (Venezuela) 425
Politica, Editura, (Romania) 304
Political and Social History, Library of, (Indonesia) 201
Politik und Wirtschaft, Verlag für, (Federal Republic of Germany) 156
Politikens Forlag A/S (Denmark) 77
Politizdat (Union of Soviet Socialist Republics) 366
Polke, Bernd, GmbH (Federal Republic of Germany) 156
Pollinger, Laurence, Ltd (United Kingdom) 414
Polskie Towarzystwo Wydawców Ksiazek (Polish Publishers' Association) (Poland) 293
Polybooks Ltd (United Kingdom) 402
Polyglott-Verlag Dr Bolte KG (Federal Republic of Germany) 156
Polyglotte Buch- und Schallplatten-Verlag und Vertrieb (Federal Republic of Germany) 156
Polygraph Verlag GmbH (Federal Republic of Germany) 156
Polytantric Press (United Kingdom) 402
Polytechnic Institute Library (Ethiopia) 84

Polyteknisk Boghandel og Forlag (Denmark) 78
Pomaire, Editorial, SA (Colombia) 66
Pomaire, Editorial, SA (Chile) 62
Pomaire, Editorial, SA (Spain) 324
Pomaire, Editorial, SA (Mexico) 253
Pomaire, Editorial, SA (Uruguay) 422
Pomaire SA (Argentina) 7
Pomaire Venezuela (Venezuela) 424
Pompidou, Centre Georges, Edition (France) 105
Pomso Publishers (Republic of Korea) 239
Pomurski Tisk (Yugoslavia) 429
Pond Press (United Kingdom) 402
Pontificia Universidad Nacional, Biblioteca Central de la, Católica del Perú (Peru) 290
Poolbeg Press Ltd (Republic of Ireland) 204
Poona Booksellers' Association (India) 186
Poplar Publishing Co Ltd (Japan) 229
Popp, Edition Georg, (Federal Republic of Germany) 156
Populaires (Switzerland) 351
Popular Army Publishing House (Socialist Republic of Viet Nam) 426
Popular Book Depot (India) 197
Popular Bookstore (Philippines) 292
Popular Dogs Publishing Co Ltd (United Kingdom) 402
Popular Prakashan Pvt Ltd (India) 193
Popular Publications (Malawi) 245
Pordes, H, (United Kingdom) 402
Pordes, H, (United Kingdom) 413
Porrúa, Ediciones José, Turanzas SA (Spain) 324
Porrúa, Editorial, SA (Mexico) 253
Porrúa, Librería de, Hnos y Cía (Mexico) 254
Porrúa, Librería de Manuel, (Mexico) 253
Porrúa, Librería José, Turanzas SA (Spain) 327
Porte, Editions La, (Morocco) 256
Porter, Libros, (Spain) 328
Pórtic, Editorial, (Spain) 324
Portico, Editorial, (Portugal) 300
Porto Editora Lda (Portugal) 300
Portugal, Livraria, Dias & Andrade Lda (Portugal) 301
Portugalia Editôra Lda (Portugal) 300
Possev-Verlag V Gorachek KG (Federal Republic of Germany) 156
Pourfina Prize (Greece) 178
Powszechna Ksiegarnia Wysylkowa (General Delivery Bookshop) (mail order) (Poland) 296
Poyser, T & A D, Ltd (United Kingdom) 403
Poznan Poetical November Prize (Poland) 297
Poznańskie, Wydawnictwo, (Poznań Publishers) (Poland) 295
Pozza, Neri, (Italy) 219
Pra Cha Chang & Co Ltd (Thailand) 359
'Práca', Vydavateľstvo ROH, (Czechoslovakia) 71
Práce (Czechoslovakia) 71
Prachner, Georg, (Austria) 27
Prachner, Georg, KG (Austria) 30
Pradnya Paramita (Indonesia) 200
Pradnya Paramita (Indonesia) 200
Prae Pittaya Ltd (Thailand) 359
Praepittaya Ltd (Thailand) 360
Praesentverlag Heinz Peter (Federal Republic of Germany) 156
Pragati Prakashan (India) 193
Pragopress (Czechoslovakia) 71
Prague Literary Prize (Czechoslovakia) 73
Prakash Prakashan (India) 193
Pramual Sarn Book Centre Ltd (Thailand) 360
Pramuansarn Publishing House (Thailand) 359
Praphansarn Book Centre (Thailand) 359
Prasarnmitr (Thailand) 359
Präsenz-Verlag der Jesus Bruderschaft (Federal Republic of Germany) 156
Pravda, Nakladatelstvo, (Czechoslovakia) 71
Pravda Publishing House (Union of Soviet Socialist Republics) 366
Prawnicze, Wydawnictwo, (Law Publishers) (Poland) 295
Praxis Libros (Spain) 328
Pre-School Publishing Co (United Kingdom) 403
Preduzeće Matice Srpske, Izdavačko, (Yugoslavia) 429
Preduzeće Sloboda, Izdavačko, (Yugoslavia) 429
Prélat, Julien, Sàrl (France) 105
Prelo Editora Sarl (Portugal) 300
Premier, Librerías, (Argentina) 8
Premio de Remuneraciones Literarias (Uruguay) 423
Premio Nacional de Literatura (Uruguay) 423
Prensa, Biblioteca Pública Gratuita de 'La, ' (Argentina) 8
Prensa, Editorial, Española (Spain) 325
Prensa Editora, La, de Periodicos SCL (Mexico) 253
Prensa Médica, La, Mexicana (Mexico) 253
Prentice-Hall International (United Kingdom) 403
Prentice-Hall of Australia Pty Limited (Australia) 17
Prentice-Hall of India Pvt Ltd (India) 193
Prentice-Hall of Japan Inc (Japan) 229
Prentice-Hall of Southeast Asia Pte Ltd (Republic of Singapore) 309

INDEX 503

Presbyterian Book Depot and Printing Press Ltd (PRESBOOK) (United Republic of Cameroun) 61
Presbyterian Book Depot Ltd (Ghana) 175
Presbyterian Book Depot Ltd (Ghana) 175
Presença, Editorial, (Portugal) 300
Présence Africaine, Société Nouvelle, (France) 105
President Publishers (Republic of South Africa) 313
President's Award for Pride of Performance (Pakistan) 287
Press Agency (Kuwait) 240
Press Department, Library of the, (Afghanistan) 1
Presse, La, Internationale (Belgium) 41
Presse, Verlag, Informations Agentur GmbH (PIAG) (Federal Republic of Germany) 156
Presse-Auto-Conseil (France) 105
Presses, Les, Africaines (Upper Volta) 422
Presses, Librairie des, universitaires (Zaire) 433
Presses Africaines, Les, (Zaire) 433
Presses agronomiques de Gembloux ASBL (Belgium) 41
Presses Centrales Lausanne SA (Switzerland) 351
Presses de la Cité, Les, (France) 105
Presses de la Connaissance, Les, (Switzerland) 351
Presses de la Fondation Nationale des Sciences Politiques (France) 105
Presses de la Renaissance (France) 105
Presses d'Ile-de-France, Les, Sàrl (France) 105
Presses d'Or (France) 110
Presses Monastiques, Les, (France) 105
Presses universitaires de Bruxelles ASBL (Belgium) 41
Presses universitaires de France (France) 111
Presses universitaires de France (PUF) (France) 105
Presses universitaires de Grenoble (France) 105
Presses universitaires de Liège ASBL (Belgium) 41
Presses Universitaires de Lille (PUL) (France) 109
Presses Universitaires de Lyon (France) 105
Presses universitaires de Namur (Belgium) 41
Presses universitaires du Zaïre et l'Office du Livre (PUZ) (Zaire) 433
Pressler, Guido, Verlag (Federal Republic of Germany) 156
Prestel Verlag (Federal Republic of Germany) 156
Prestige Booksellers (Kenya) 236
Preston Corporation Ltd (Malaysia) 246
Preston-Times Printing & Publishing (Malaysia) 247
Pretoria Boekhandel Ltd (Republic of South Africa) 313
Preussler, Helmut, Verlag (Federal Republic of Germany) 156
Price Milburn & Co Ltd (New Zealand) 274
Pride (Republic of South Africa) 313
Primary Education (Publishing) Pty Ltd (Australia) 17
Primor, Editôra, Ltda (Brazil) 54
Primor, Gráfica Editora, SA (Brazil) 54
Primorski Tisk (Yugoslavia) 429
Prince Pierre de Monaco Prize for Literature (International Literary Prizes) 451
Princeton University Press (United Kingdom) 403
Prins en Prins (Netherlands) 269
Prinsen, Reina, -Geerlings Prize for South Africa (Republic of South Africa) 317
Prinsen-Geerlings, Reina, Prize (Netherlands) 271
Printing and Publishing Industry Training Board (United Kingdom) 369
Printox (India) 193
Prior, George, Associated Publishers Ltd (United Kingdom) 403
Priory Press Ltd (United Kingdom) 403
Príroda, vydavateľ stvo kníh a časopisov (Czechoslovakia) 71
Prism Books (Poetry Society of Australia) (Australia) 17
Prism Press (United Kingdom) 403
Prisma, Bokförlaget, AB (Sweden) 336
Prisma, Het, NV (Belgium) 41
Prisma Verlag GmbH (Federal Republic of Germany) 156
Prisma-Verlag Zenner und Gürchott (German Democratic Republic) 119
Priuli e Verlucca, Editori (Italy) 219
Privat, Editions Edouard, SA (France) 105
Private Libraries Association (PLA) (International Organizations) 439
Privredni Pregled (Yugoslavia) 429
Prix Internationale des Editeurs (International Literary Prizes) 451
Prizes for Manuscripts for Juveniles (Pakistan) 287
Pro Civitate (Belgium) 41
Pro Juventute Verlag (Switzerland) 351
Pro Media Literaturvertrieb GmbH (Federal Republic of Germany) 170
Pro Rege Press Ltd (Republic of South Africa) 313
Pro Schola, Editions, (Switzerland) 351
Pro Schule Verlag GmbH (Federal Republic of Germany) 156
Problem-Verlag (Switzerland) 351
Procure, La, (Belgium) 41
Procure scolaire (Zaire) 433
Prodim SPRL (Belgium) 41
Production et Diffusion medico-techniques SPRL (Belgium) 41

Professional Publications (New Zealand) 274
Profil, Nakladatelství, (Czechoslovakia) 71
Profile Books Ltd (United Kingdom) 403
Profizdat (Union of Soviet Socialist Republics) 366
Profizdat, Izdatelstvo, (Bulgaria) 58
Progrès, Editions le, (Egypt) 82
Progreso, Editorial, SA (Mexico) 253
Progress (Thailand) 359
Progress Press (Malta) 248
Progress Publishers (Union of Soviet Socialist Republics) 366
Progressive Corporation Pvt Ltd (India) 193
Prolam SRL (Ediciones Economia y Empresa) (Argentina) 7
Prometeo, Ediciones, (Spain) 325
Prometheus Publishing Co (Zambia) 434
Promoción, Ediciones de, Cultural SA (Spain) 325
Promoculture, Librairie, (Luxembourg) 244
Promotion Littéraire (France) 110
Proost, Henri, & Co (Belgium) 41
Pröpster, Albert, (Federal Republic of Germany) 156
Propyläen Verlag (Federal Republic of Germany) 157
Prospice (United Kingdom) 403
'Prosveshchenie', Izdatelstvo, (Union of Soviet Socialist Republics) 366
Prosveta (Yugoslavia) 431
Prosveta (Yugoslavia) 429
Prosvetno Delo (Yugoslavia) 429
Prosvjeta (Yugoslavia) 429
Prosvjeta (Novinsko-izdavačko i Štamparsko) (Yugoslavia) 429
Protestante, Librairie, (Benin) 47
Protestantse Stichting tot Bevordering van het Bibliotheekwezen en de Lectuurvoorlichting in Nederland (Protestant Foundation for the Promotion of Librarianship and Reading Information in the Netherlands) (Netherlands) 270
Proteus (Publishing) Ltd (United Kingdom) 403
proTHESE, edition, (Switzerland) 351
Provence, Librairie de, (France) 111
Provincial Book Depot (Bangladesh) 33
Provincial Booksellers Fairs Association Annual Book Awards (United Kingdom) 420
Provincial Library (Bangladesh) 33
Provincial Literature Bureau (Senegal) 307
Proyección, Editorial, SRL (Argentina) 7
Prugg Verlag (Austria) 28
Prva Književna Komuna (Yugoslavia) 429
P S A (Republic of South Africa) 313
Psyche, Bookclub, (Japan) 232
Psychic Press Ltd (United Kingdom) 403
Psychologie, Verlag fur, Dr C J Hogrefe (Switzerland) 351
Psychologie, Verlag für, Dr C J Hogrefe (Federal Republic of Germany) 157
Psychosophische Gesellschaft (Switzerland) 351
Psykologiförlaget AB (Sweden) 336
Publi-Union (France) 105
Public Lending Right Committee (Australia) 20
Public Libraries Board (Uganda) 364
Public Library (Afghanistan) 1
Public Library (Barbados) 33
Public Library (Jordan) 234
Public Library (Jordan) 234
Public Library (Libya) 242
Public Library, Central, Dacca (Bangladesh) 33
Public Organization, The, for Books and Scientific Appliances (Egypt) 82
Public Organization, The, for Books and Scientific Appliances, Cairo University (Egypt) 82
Public Record Office (United Kingdom) 416
Public Record Office of Ireland (Republic of Ireland) 205
Publicaciones Cultural SA (Mexico) 253
Publicaciones Españolas SA (Venezuela) 425
Publicações Científicas, Editôra de, Ltda (Brazil) 54
Publication Board (India) 193
Publications Appeal Board (Republic of South Africa) 311
Publications Central Africa (Zimbabwe) 435
Publications Filmées d'Art et d'Histoire (France) 105
Publications India (India) 197
Publications International (Nigeria) Ltd (Nigeria) 279
Publications Orientalistes de France (POF) (France) 105
Publishers' & Booksellers' Association of Andhra Pradesh (India) 186
Publishers' and Booksellers' Association of Bengal (India) 186
Publishers' and Booksellers' Association of Thailand (Thailand) 359
Publishers' and Booksellers' Guild (India) 186
Publishers Association (United Kingdom) 369
Publishers' Association for Cultural Exchange (Japan) 225
Publishers' Association of India (India) 186
Publishers' Association of South India (India) 186
Publisher's Bookshop (Poland) 296
Publisher's Club (Poland) 296

Publishers International (Pakistan) 286
Publishers' Overseas Circle (United Kingdom) 369
Publishers Publicity Circle (United Kingdom) 369
Publishers United Ltd (Pakistan) 286
Publishers/Booksellers Delivery Service (PBDS) (United Kingdom) 369
Publishing Council of the Academy of Sciences of the USSR (Union of Soviet Socialist Republics) 365
Publishing Department (People's Republic of China) 63
Pucci, Christa, (Italy) 221
Pudoc, Centre for Agricultural Publishing and Documentation (Netherlands) 266
Pueblo, Editorial, y Educación (Cuba) 68
Pueyo, Librería Pedro, (Spain) 328
Puffin, The, Club (United Kingdom) 415
Punjab Advisory Board for Books Prizes (Pakistan) 287
Punjab Public Library (Pakistan) 286
Punjab Text Board (Pakistan) 287
Punjab University Library (Pakistan) 286
Punjabi Publishers' Association (India) 186
Punjabi Pustak Bhandar (India) 193
Punktum (Switzerland) 356
Punnoose, Kunnuparampil P, (India) 193
Punnoose, Kunnuparampil P, (India) 197
Purnell & Sons (SA) (Pty) Ltd (Republic of South Africa) 313
Purnell Books (United Kingdom) 403
Pushtu Toulana, Afghan Academy (Afghanistan) 1
Pustet, Anton, München (Federal Republic of Germany) 157
Pustet, Universitätsverlag Anton, (Austria) 28
Pustet, Verlag Friedrich, (Federal Republic of Germany) 157
Puthigar Limited (Bangladesh) 33
Putnam & Co Ltd (United Kingdom) 403
Putnam Awards (International Literary Prizes) 451
Putsj Publications Antwerpen (Netherlands) 266
Pygmalion, Editions, — Gérard Watelet (France) 105
Pyungwha Press (Republic of Korea) 239

Q E D Publishing Ltd (United Kingdom) 403
Q Press Ltd (United Kingdom) 403
Qatari Public Library (National Library) (Qatar) 303
Qaumi Kutab Khana (Pakistan) 286
Quadragono Libri (Italy) 219
Quality Book Club (United Kingdom) 415
Quartet Books Ltd (United Kingdom) 403
Quartier-Latin (Monaco) 255
Quartier-Latin, Librairie, (French Polynesia) 116
Quarto Press (Liechtenstein) 243
Quarto Publishing Ltd (United Kingdom) 403
Queen Anne Press Ltd (United Kingdom) 403
Queen Victoria Memorial Library (Zimbabwe) 435
Queen's, The, Gold Medal for Poetry (United Kingdom) 420
Queensland Book Depot (Head Office) (Australia) 19
Queensland Booksellers' Association (Australia) 10
Queensway Bookshop and Stores (Ghana) 175
Quell-Verlag (Federal Republic of Germany) 157
Quelle Press (Federal Republic of Germany) 169
Quelle und Meyer Verlag (Federal Republic of Germany) 157
Quentin Press Ltd (United Kingdom) 403
Querido's, Em, Uitgeverij BV (Netherlands) 266
Queriniana, Editrice, (Italy) 219
Queromón Editores SA (Mexico) 253
Quet, Mme Janine, (France) 110
Quillet, Librairie Aristide, SA (France) 105
Quintero, Alvarez, Prize (Spain) 329
Quisqueyana, Editora Colegial, SA (Dominican Republic) 80
Quisqueyana, Editora Colegial, SA (Dominican Republic) 81
Quoi de Nouveau (France) 106
Qurinna Library (Libya) 243
Qvist, Erik, Bokhandel A/S (Norway) 283

'R', Editions, (France) 106
R A I, Edizioni, Radiotelevisione Italiana (ERI) SpA (Italy) 219
R C P (Private) Ltd (Zimbabwe) 435
R E C T A Foldex (France) 106
R E M I (France) 106
R Editore (Italy) 219
R I B A Publications Ltd (United Kingdom) 403
R N A Major Award (United Kingdom) 420
R S T, Editions, (France) 106
R S W (Robotnicza Spółdzielnia Wydawnicza) (Poland) 293
R V (Federal Republic of Germany) 157
R A Verlag (Switzerland) 351

Rabaul Newsagency (Papua New Guinea) 288
rabe verlag zürich (Switzerland) 356
Rabe Verlag Zurich (Switzerland) 351
Rabén och Sjögren, AB, Bokförlag (Sweden) 336
Rache, André de, (Belgium) 41
Racine Prize (France) 115
Rad, Izdavačka Organizacija, (Yugoslavia) 429
Radha Krishna Prakashan (India) 194
Radia i Telewizji, Wydawnictwo, (Radio and Television Publishers) (Poland) 295
Radiant Publishers (India) 194
Radical Book Club (India) 197
Radical Reprints (United Kingdom) 404
Radio, Société des Editions, (France) 106
Radio Plays Prize (Republic of South Africa) 317
Radius-Verlag GmbH (Federal Republic of Germany) 157
Radnička Štampa (Yugoslavia) 429
Raeber AG Luzern (Switzerland) 351
Ragman Productions (Australia) 17
Ragot, A. (New Caledonia) 271
Rahman Brothers (Bangladesh) 32
Railway, The, Book Club (United Kingdom) 415
Rainbird, The, Publishing Group (United Kingdom) 404
Rainbow Photo & Book Store (Brunei) 57
Rainer Verlag (Federal Republic of Germany) 157
Raio, Editôra, X Ltda (Brazil) 54
Raith Verlag (Federal Republic of Germany) 157
Rajasthan Pustak Vyavasayee Sangh (India) 186
Rajesh Publications (India) 194
Rajhans Prakashan Mandir (India) 194
Rajkamal Prakashan Pvt Ltd (India) 194
Rajneesh Foundation Ltd (India) 194
Rajpal & Sons (India) 194
Ram Prasad & Sons (India) 194
Ramakrishna, Sri, Math (India) 194
Ramboro Enterprises Ltd (United Kingdom) 404
Ramboro Enterprises Ltd (United Kingdom) 413
Ramdor Publishing Co Ltd (Israel) 209
Ramesh Sondhi (India) 194
Ramos, Edições António, (Portugal) 300
Ramsay, Editions, (France) 106
Ramsay, The, Head Press (United Kingdom) 404
Ramsden, Barbara, Award (Australia) 23
Ranchi District Publishers' and Booksellers' Association (India) 186
Randi, Libreria all' Accademia SNC di, Pietro (Italy) 222
Randow, Dokument und Analyse Verlag Bogislaw von, (Federal Republic of Germany) 157
Ranelagh Editions (United Kingdom) 404
"Rango", Distribuidora, de Publicaciones (Venezuela) 425
Ranner, Verlag Dr Herta, (Austria) 28
Rapp & Whiting Ltd (United Kingdom) 404
'Rast Gufter' Press (Pakistan) 286
Rastogi Publications (India) 194
Rathgeber Verlag (Federal Republic of Germany) 157
Rational Bookshops (Nigeria) (Nigeria) 280
Rationalisierungs-Kuratorium der Deutschen Wirtschaft eV (RKW) (Federal Republic of Germany) 157
Rationalist Press Association (United Kingdom) 404
Ratna Pustak Bhandar (Nepal) 257
Ratna Pustak Bhandar (Nepal) 257
Ratnabharati (India) 194
Ratnakara Press Ltd (Sri Lanka) 329
Rau, Walter, Verlag (Federal Republic of Germany) 157
Rauch, Felizian, Verlagsbuchhandlung (Austria) 28
Rauch, Karl, Verlag KG (Federal Republic of Germany) 157
Rauhen Hauses, Agentur des, GmbH (Federal Republic of Germany) 157
Rautenberg, Druckerei und Verlag Gerhard, (Federal Republic of Germany) 157
Rav Kook Institute (Israel) 209
Ravan Press (Pty) Ltd (Republic of South Africa) 313
Raven Books (United Kingdom) 404
Ravensburger Graphische Betriebe Otto Maier GmbH (Federal Republic of Germany) 157
Ravensburger Verlag GmbH (Federal Republic of Germany) 157
Ravenstein Verlag GmbH (Federal Republic of Germany) 157
Rayas (Greece) 177
Razon, Editora La, (Dominican Republic) 80
Read It Again (Australia) 17
Readers' Book Shop (Jamaica) 224
Readers Choice (United Kingdom) 415
Reader's Choice (Australiana Book Club) (Australia) 19
Reader's Digest, Det Bedste fra, A/S (Denmark) 78
Reader's Digest, Selecciones del, (Iberia) SA (Spain) 325
Reader's Digest, Sélection du, Sàrl (France) 110
Reader's Digest, The, Association Ltd (United Kingdom) 404
Reader's Digest, The, of Japan Limited (Japan) 229
Reader's Digest, Verlag Das Beste GmbH, (Federal Republic of Germany) 170
Readers' Digest AB (Sweden) 338

Reader's Digest Condensed Book Services Pty Ltd (Australia) 19
Reader's Digest NV, Uitgeversmaatschappij,, (Netherlands) 269
Reader's Digest SA (Belgium) 41
Reader's Digest Services Pty Ltd (Australia) 17
Reader's Digest:, Selezione dal, Grandi Opere di Selezione (Italy) 221
Readers Union Ltd (United Kingdom) 415
Real Academia de Ciencias, Bellas Letras y Nobles Artes (Royal Academy of Science, Literature and Fine Arts) (Spain) 328
Real Academia Sevillana de Buenas Letras (Seville Royal Academy of Belles Lettres) (Spain) 328
Real Biblioteca de San Lorenzo de El Escorial (Escorial Library) (Spain) 328
Réalisations pour l'Enseignement Multilingue International (France) 106
Realizações Artis Lda (Portugal) 300
Recalde, Libreria, (Nicaragua) 276
Recht und Gesellschaft, Verlag für, AG (Switzerland) 351
Recht und Wirtschaft, Verlagsgesellschaft, mbH (Federal Republic of Germany) 157
Reclam, Philipp, Jun (Federal Republic of Germany) 157
Reclam, Verlag Philipp, jun (German Democratic Republic) 119
'Recognition Prize' (Austria) 31
Record, Distribuidora, de Serviços de Imprensa SA (Brazil) 54
Redhouse Kitabevi (Turkey) 363
Redhouse Press (Turkey) 363
Rediviva, Bokförlaget, Facsimileförlaget (Sweden) 336
Reed, A H & A W, Ltd Publishers (New Zealand) 274
Reed, A H & A W, Pty Ltd (Australia) 17
Reemst, van, (Netherlands) 266
Reference International Publishers Ltd (United Kingdom) 404
Reforma, Editorial y Librería La, (Puerto Rico) 302
Regain, Editions, (Monaco) 255
Regal Publishing Co (Philippines) 292
Regenbogen-Verlag (Switzerland) 351
Regimprensa (Portugal) 301
Regina Medal (International Literary Prizes) 451
Regional Literature Awards (Pakistan) 287
Regra, A, do Jogo (Portugal) 300
Reich, Kinderbuchverlag, Luzern AG (Switzerland) 351
Reich Verlag AG (Switzerland) 351
Reichert, Dr Ludwig, Verlag (Federal Republic of Germany) 157
Reichl, Otto, Verlag (Federal Republic of Germany) 158
Reichman, Livraría Científica Ernésto, (Brazil) 56
Reid, Professor J C, Award for Excellence in Arts Criticism (New Zealand) 276
Reidel, D, Publishing Co (Netherlands) 266
Reim, Verlag Knut, (Federal Republic of Germany) 158
Reinaert Uitgaven (Belgium) 41
Reinhardt, Ernst, GmbH & Co Verlag (Federal Republic of Germany) 158
Reinhardt, Ernst, Verlag AG (Switzerland) 351
Reinhardt, Max, Ltd (United Kingdom) 404
Reinhardt, Verlag Friedrich, AG (Switzerland) 351
Reinheimer, Verlag Wilhelm G, (Federal Republic of Germany) 158
Reise- und Verkehrsverlag (RV) (Federal Republic of Germany) 158
Reiter, Elisabeth, (Austria) 30
Reitzels, C A, Forlag (Denmark) 77
Reitzels, Hans, Forlag A/S (Denmark) 77
Reka-Or Production and Publishing Ltd (Israel) 209
Relief-Verlag-Eilers (Federal Republic of Germany) 158
Religious Education Press (United Kingdom) 404
Religious Revival Organization (Thailand) 359
Remaja Karya (Indonesia) 200
Rembrandt Verlag GmbH (Federal Republic of Germany) 158
Remembrance Award (International Literary Prizes) 451
Remzi Kitabevi (Turkey) 363
Renacimiento, Editorial, SA (Mexico) 253
Renacimiento, Librería, SA de CV (El Salvador) 83
Renaissance, La, du Livre SA (Belgium) 41
Renaitour, J-M, Prize (France) 115
Renard, Fondation André, (Belgium) 41
Renaudot, Théophraste, Prize (France) 115
Rencontre, Editions, (Belgium) 44
Rencontre, Editions, SA (Switzerland) 351
Renmin-Jiyou-Chuban-She (People's Education Publishing Co) (People's Republic of China) 63
Renner, Verlag Klaus G, (Federal Republic of Germany) 158
Rentsch, Eugen, Verlag AG (Switzerland) 351
Representaciones y Servicios de Ingeniería SA (Mexico) 253
Representative Church Body Library (Republic of Ireland) 205
Reprographia (United Kingdom) 404
Republički Zavod za Unapredivanje Školstva (Yugoslavia) 429

Research Library on African Affairs (Ghana) 175
Research Publishing Co (United Kingdom) 404
Resenha, Editôra, Tributaria Ltda (Brazil) 54
Residenz Verlag (Austria) 28
Restrepo, Felix, Prize (International Literary Prizes) 452
Retail Book, Stationery and Allied Trades Employers' Association (United Kingdom) 369
Retail Bookselling and Stationery Wages Council (Great Britain) (United Kingdom) 369
Retz (France) 106
Réunies, Imprimeries, SA (Switzerland) 351
Reus, Editorial, SA (Spain) 325
Reuter-Verlag (Federal Republic of Germany) 158
Revelation Awards (Poetry and Prose) (Portugal) 302
Reverté, Editora, Colombiana SA (Colombia) 66
Reverté, Editora, Ltda (Brazil) 54
Reverté, Editorial, Mexicana SA (Mexico) 253
Reverté, Editorial, SA (Spain) 325
Reverté, Editorial, Venezolana SA (Venezuela) 424
Review Publications Pty Ltd (Australia) 17
Revisematic (France) 106
Revista, Editôra, dos Tribunais Ltda (Brazil) 54
Revista de Occidente SA (Spain) 325
Revista Mexicana de Seguros (Mexico) 253
Revolución, Ediciones, (Cuba) 68
Revue, La, nouvelle ASBL (Belgium) 41
Rex (United Kingdom) 404
Rex Book Store (Malaysia) 247
Rex Bookstore (Brunei) 57
Rex-Verlag (Switzerland) 352
Reyes, Librería Universitaria Jose T, (Honduras) 180
Rezzonico, Edizioni Raimondo, (Switzerland) 352
Rheingauer Verlagsgesellschaft mbH (Federal Republic of Germany) 158
Rheinland-Palatinate Prize (Federal Republic of Germany) 173
Rheinland-Verlag GmbH (Federal Republic of Germany) 158
Rhodesia Library Association (Zimbabwe) 435
Rhodesian Christian Press (Zimbabwe) 435
Rhodesian Publications (Zimbabwe) 435
Rhodos, International Science and Art Publishers (Denmark) 77
Rhombus-Verlag, Edition Dumreicher (Austria) 28
Rhys, John Llewelyn, Memorial Prize (International Literary Prizes) 452
Rialp, Ediciones, SA (Spain) 325
Riband Books (United Kingdom) 404
Riber, Editions Scientifiques, Sàrl (France) 106
Riccardiana, Biblioteca, (Italy) 222
Ricci, Franco Maria, (France) 106
Ricci, Franco Maria, Editore (Italy) 219
Ricciardi, Riccardo, Editore SpA (Italy) 219
Richards Publishing (New Zealand) 274
Richards Publishing Consultants (New Zealand) 274
Richelieu, Editions, SA (France) 106
Richmond, The, Publishing Co Ltd (United Kingdom) 404
Richmond Hill Press (Australia) 17
Rico SpA (Italy) 219
Ricordi, Arti Grafiche, SpA (Italy) 219
Ricordi, G e C, SpA (Italy) 219
Ricordi Americana SAEC (Argentina) 7
Ridder, Peter de, Press BV (Netherlands) 266
Rider & Co (United Kingdom) 404
Riederer, Dr, Verlag GmbH (Federal Republic of Germany) 158
Riemaecker, De, Uitgeverij (Belgium) 41
Rigby Ltd (Australia) 17
Rigby Ltd (Australia) 19
Right Way Books (United Kingdom) 404
Rigmarole of the Hours (Australia) 18
Rigsarkivet (Denmark) 79
Rihani Printing & Publishing House (Lebanon) 241
Rijksmuseum Meermanno-Westreenianum/Museum van het Boek (Book Museum) (Netherlands) 269
Rijksuniversiteit, Bibliotheek der, (Netherlands) 269
Rijksuniversiteit te Gent, Bibliotheek van de, (Belgium) 44
Rijksuniversiteit te Groningen, Bibliotheek der, (Netherlands) 269
Rijksuniversiteit te Leiden, Bibliotheek der, (Netherlands) 269
Rikisútgáfa Námsbóka (Iceland) 185
Riksarkivet (National Archives of Norway) (Norway) 283
Riksarkivet (National Record Office) (Sweden) 338
Riksbibliotektjenesten (National Office for Research and Special Libraries) (Norway) 284
Rilindja (Yugoslavia) 429
Rinder, Karl und Ina, (Austria) 28
Ringier & Co AG (Switzerland) 352
Rio Grafica e Editora SA (Brazil) 54
Riomar Editores y Distribuidores S de CV (Mexico) 253
Riotor, Léon, Prize (France) 115
Riquier, Jacques, Editions (France) 106
Risosha Ltd (Japan) 229
Ristin Voitto ry (Finland) 86

Ristin Voitto ry (Finland) 86
Rithöfundasamband Íslands (Iceland) 186
Ritter Verlag GmbH (Federal Republic of Germany) 158
Ritzau KG Verlag Zeit und Eisenbahn (Federal Republic of Germany) 158
Riunti, Editori, (Italy) 219
Rivadeneyra Prizes (Spain) 329
River Niger Commission, Documentation and Analysis Centre (Niger) 276
Rivers Press (United Kingdom) 404
Rivière, Librairie Marcel, et Cie (France) 106
Rivingtons (Publishers) Ltd (United Kingdom) 404
Riyadh Modern Bookshop (Saudi Arabia) 306
Rizzoli, Libreria, (Italy) 222
Rizzoli Editore SpA (Italy) 221
Rizzoli Editore SpA (Italy) 219
Roberge Prizes (France) 115
Robert, Dictionnaire Le, (France) 106
Robert, Editions E. (France) 106
Roberts Stationery Ltd (Barbados) 33
Robin Books (Australia) 18
Robinson, J. & Co (Israel) 210
Robinson & Watkins Books Ltd (United Kingdom) 404
Robson Books Ltd (United Kingdom) 404
'Roche', Editiones, (Switzerland) 352
Rocher, Les Editions du, (Monaco) 255
Rocom (Switzerland) 352
Rodana Verlag (Switzerland) 352
Rodas, Ediciones, SA (Spain) 325
Röderberg-Verlag GmbH (Federal Republic of Germany) 158
Rodopi, Editions, NV (Netherlands) 266
Rodríguez, Librería, (Argentina) 8
Roebuck Books (Australia) 18
Roeland Kamer Fonds VZW (Belgium) 41
Roerdomp, De, (Belgium) 41
Rogan, Barbara, Literary Agency (Israel) 210
Rogers, Deborah, Ltd (United Kingdom) 414
Rogers Prize (United Kingdom) 420
Rogner und Bernhard GmbH & Co Verlags KG (Federal Republic of Germany) 158
Rohr, Buchhandlung Hans, (Switzerland) 356
Rohr, Hans, (Switzerland) 352
Rojas, Pablo, Paz Prize (Argentina) 9
Rojas, Ricardo, Prize (Argentina) 9
Rökkur, bókaútgáfan (Iceland) 185
Rolfs, Rudolf, (Federal Republic of Germany) 158
Rolnicze i Leśne, Państwowe Wydawnictwo, (State Agricultural and Forestry Publishers) (Poland) 295
Romance Book Club (United Kingdom) 415
Romanian Literature Museum Award (Romania) 305
Romanian Society of Bibliophiles (Romania) 305
Romantic Novelists' Association (United Kingdom) 418
Rombach und Co GmbH, Verlag & Buchdruckerei (Federal Republic of Germany) 158
Rombaldi, Ediclub, (France) 110
Rombaldi, Éditions, SA (France) 106
Romen (Netherlands) 266
Romero, Litografia A, SA (Italy) 219
Ronald, George, (United Kingdom) 404
Roorkee Press (India) 194
Rosa, Editôra Ana, (Brazil) 54
Rosda (Indonesia) 200
Rose, Barry, (Publishers) Ltd (United Kingdom) 404
Rose of French Poets Prize (International Literary Prizes) 452
Rose-Verlag und Edition Rose-Verlag (Federal Republic of Germany) 158
Rosenberg e Sellier srl (Italy) 219
Rosenberg e Sellier Srl (Italy) 222
Rosenheimer Verlagshaus Alfred Förg GmbH & Co KG (Federal Republic of Germany) 158
Rosenkilde og Bagger (Denmark) 77
Rosenwald, E S F. (France) 106
Rosepierre SA (Switzerland) 352
Rösler und Zimmer Verlag (Federal Republic of Germany) 158
Rosmini, Libreria, di R Maly (Italy) 222
Ross, Libreria, (Argentina) 8
Rossel, Victor, Prize (Belgium) 46
Rossel Edition (France) 106
Rossel Edition SA (Belgium) 41
Rostock, Wilhelm-Pieck-Universität, Universitätsbibliothek (German Democratic Republic) 120
Rotapfel-Verlag AG (Switzerland) 352
Rotbuch Verlag GmbH (Federal Republic of Germany) 158
Rotep, Edições, (Portugal) 300
Roter Morgen, Verlag, (Federal Republic of Germany) 158
Roter Stern, Verlag, (Federal Republic of Germany) 158
Röth, Erich, -Verlag, Kassel (Federal Republic of Germany) 158
Roth et Sauter SA (Switzerland) 352
Rother, Bergverlag Rudolf, (Federal Republic of Germany) 158
Rotten-Verlags AG (Switzerland) 352

Rotterdam University Press (Netherlands) 266
Rötzer, E, Verlag (Austria) 28
Roucoules Foundation Grand Prize for Poetry (France) 115
Roudil, Editions, (France) 106
Rouff, Editions, SA (France) 106
Rouge et Or, G P, (France) 106
Roularta NV (Belgium) 41
Roulet, Editions, & Cie (Switzerland) 352
Roundwood, The, Press (1978) Ltd (United Kingdom) 404
Rousseau, Librairie, (Switzerland) 352
Routledge & Kegan Paul Ltd (United Kingdom) 404
Röver, Verlag Friedrich, (Federal Republic of Germany) 158
Rowohlt Taschenbuch Verlag GmbH (Federal Republic of Germany) 159
Rowohlt Verlag GmbH (Federal Republic of Germany) 159
Roxby Press Ltd (United Kingdom) 404
Roy, K K, (Pvt) Ltd (India) 194
Roy, Publications, (France) 106
Roya Boudewijn (Belgium) 41
Royal Afghanistan Press Department (Afghanistan) 1
Royal Book Co (Pakistan) 286
Royal Book Co (Pakistan) 286
Royal College of Surgeons in Ireland Library (Republic of Ireland) 205
Royal Dublin Society Library (Republic of Ireland) 205
Royal Gazette Ltd (Bermuda) 47
Royal Literary Fund (United Kingdom) 418
Royal Palace, Library of the, (Afghanistan) 1
Royal Prize (Sweden) 339
Royal Society of Literature of the United Kingdom (United Kingdom) 418
Royal Society of South Africa Library (Republic of South Africa) 316
Ruamsarn (1977) Co Ltd (Thailand) 360
Ruamsarn(1977) Co Ltd (Thailand) 359
Rubber Research Institute of Malaysia Library (Malaysia) 247
Rubens (Belgium) 41
Rubinstein, E, (Israel) 209
Rubsamen, Verlag Wilhelm, (Federal Republic of Germany) 170
Ruedo Ibérico (France) 106
Ruhland Verlag (Federal Republic of Germany) 159
Ruiz, Editorial, Romero (Portugal) 300
Runa Press (Republic of Ireland) 204
Rune Forlag (Norway) 282
Rungvit Sawarn-Apichon (Thailand) 359
Ruota, Edizioni La, (Italy) 219
Rupa & Co (India) 194
Rusbet, Ediciones, (Mexico) 253
Rusconi Editore (Italy) 219
Russell, George, (AE) Memorial Award (Republic of Ireland) 205
Russky Yazyk (Union of Soviet Socialist Republics) 366
Rustem, K, & Bro (Cyprus) 69
Rütten, Elsbeth, Verlag (Federal Republic of Germany) 159
Rütten und Loening, Verlag, Berlin (German Democratic Republic) 119
Rütten und Loening Verlag GmbH (Switzerland) 352
Ruy Diaz SAEIC (Argentina) 7
ruže, Nakladatelství, (Czechoslovakia) 71
Rwandaises, Editions, (Rwanda) 306
Ryborsch, VWK, GmbH (Federal Republic of Germany) 159
Rylands, John, University Library of Manchester (United Kingdom) 416
Ryosho-Fukyu-Kai Co Ltd (Japan) 229

S A Cultural Holdings (Pty) Ltd (Republic of South Africa) 314
S A D E, Medalla de Oro de la, (Sociedad Argentina de Escritores) (Argentina) 9
S A D E (Sociedad Argentina de Escritores) (Argentina) 9
S A G E P (Italy) 220
S A G E Publications Ltd (United Kingdom) 404
S A I E Editrice (Italy) 220
S A Kultuurbeleggings (Republic of South Africa) 314
S A M — förlaget (Sweden) 336
S A S S-Verlagsgesellschaft mbH und Co KG (Federal Republic of Germany) 159
S B I (Switzerland) 340
S C E M I (Société Continentale d'Editions Modernes Illustrées) Sàrl (France) 106
S C M Press Ltd (United Kingdom) 405
S C O D E (Italy) 220
S E A P (Société d'Edition d'Annuaires Professionnels) (France) 106

S E C A (Société d'Exploitation et de Diffusion des Codes Rousseau Sàrl) (France) 106
S E D E (Société d'Edition de Dictionnaires et d'Encyclopédies) (France) 106
S E D E S (France) 106
S E I (Società Editrice Internationale) (Italy) 220
S E M I C Förlags AB (Sweden) 336
S E P, Ediciones, Setentas (Secretaria de Educacion Publica (Mexico) 253
S E R T (Société d'Edition, de Publicité, de Radio et Télévision) SA (France) 106
S I M Bookshop (Ethiopia) 84
S I M E P SA (France) 106
S I S A R Edizioni (Società italiana stampati affini reclame) SpA (Italy) 220
S K E A B Förlag AB (Sweden) 336
S M D, Uitgeverij, BV (Spruyt, Van Mantgem en De Does) (Netherlands) 266
S N E D, Librairie, (Societe nationale d'Edition et de Diffusion) (Algeria) 2
S N L (France) 106
S N T L Nakladatelstvi technické literatury (Czechoslovakia) 71
S N-Verlag, Salzburger Nachrichten Verlags GmbH & Co KG (Austria) 28
S O S, Editions, (Editions du Secours Catholique) (France) 106
S P C K (The Society for Promoting Christian Knowledge) (United Kingdom) 405
S P E L D (France) 107
S P K K (Spoločnosť priateľov' krásnych kníh) (Czechoslovakia) 72
S R A (Société de Recherche appliquée à l'Education) (France) 107
S T E M-Mucchi (Società Tipografica Editrice Modenese) (Italy) 220
S T L Books (United Kingdom) 405
S T M (International Organizations) 439
S T P Distributors Sdn Bhd (Republic of Singapore) 310
s t v (Federal Republic of Germany) 159
S U D E L (Société Universitaire d'Editions et de Librairie) (France) 107
S U N socialistische Uitgeverij (Netherlands) 266
Sa Tu-Thu Dich-Thuat Va An-Loat (Socialist Republic of Viet Nam) 426
Saar SRL (Italy) 220
Sabah State Library (Malaysia) 247
Sabe U (Burma) 59
Sabzerou, Shahrokh, (Iran) 202
Sachs, Nelly, Prize (Federal Republic of Germany) 173
Sächsische Landesbibliothek (German Democratic Republic) 120
Sadan Publishing House Ltd (Israel) 209
Sadoveanu, Biblioteca Municipala 'Mihail, (Romania) 305
Saeed, H M, Co (Pakistan) 286
Saeftinge (Belgium) 41
Safari Verlag (Reinhard Jaspert) (Federal Republic of Germany) 159
Safran, Sheri, Associates Ltd (United Kingdom) 414
Saga Publishing Co (Iceland) 185
Sageret, Editions, (France) 107
Saggiatore, Il, SpA (Italy) 220
Sagi, Victor, Servicios Editoriales (Spain) 325
Sagitario SA (Spain) 325
Sagittaire, Les Editions du, — Union des Techniques d'Editions (France) 107
Sagittaire, Librairie du, (French Polynesia) 116
Sagner, Verlag Otto, (Federal Republic of Germany) 159
Sahayogi Prakashan (Nepal) 257
Sahitya Akademi Award (India) 198
Sahitya Bhawan (India) 194
Saiful (Indonesia) 200
Saint-Albert, Librairie, le Grand (Switzerland) 352
Saint-André, Publications de, (Belgium) 41
Saint Andrew Press (United Kingdom) 405
Saint-Augustin, Société de l'Oeuvre, (Switzerland) 352
Saint-Genois Prize (Belgium) 46
Saint-Germain-des-Prés, Editions, SA (France) 107
Saint James Press (United Kingdom) 405
Saint-Joseph (Gabon) 116
Saint Louis, Publications des Facultés universitaires, (Belgium) 41
Saint Louis de Gonzague, Bibliothèque, (Haiti) 180
Saint Michael's Mission (Lesotho) 242
Saint-Paul (Switzerland) 352
Saint-Paul, Departement Les Classiques Africains, Editions, (France) 107
Saint Paul, Editions, (Zaire) 433
Saint-Paul, Editions, SA (France) 107
Saint-Paul, Imprimerie, SA (Luxembourg) 244
Saint Paul, Librairie, (Zaire) 433
Saint Paul, Librairie, (United Republic of Cameroun) 61
Saint Paul, Librairie, (Burundi) 60
Saint Paul, Librairie/Imprimerie, (United Republic of Cameroun) 61
Saint Paul Book Centre (Uganda) 364

Sainte-Devote (Monaco) 255
Sainte-Geneviève, Bibliothèque, (France) 111
Saintour Prize (France) 115
Sajha Prakashan, Co-operative Publishing Organization (Nepal) 257
Sal Terrae, Editorial, (Spain) 325
Saladdine Publications & Distributors (Egypt) 83
Salama Publications Ltd (Kenya) 236
Salamander Books Ltd (United Kingdom) 405
Salamandra, La, (Italy) 220
Salamon e Agustoni Editori (Italy) 220
Salani, Adriano, SpA (Italy) 220
Salesian Publications & Don Bosco Film Strips (United Kingdom) 405
Salesianas, Edições, (Portugal) 300
Salisbury Polytechnic Library (Zimbabwe) 435
Salle, Otto, Verlag (Federal Republic of Germany) 159
Salterain, Biblioteca Municipal 'Dr Joaquín de, ' (Uruguay) 423
Saltire, The, Society (United Kingdom) 405
Saltykova-Schedrina, Gosudarstvennaya publichnaya biblioteka im M E, (Union of Soviet Socialist Republics) 367
Salutiste, Librairie, (Zaire) 433
Salvadoreña, Distribuidora, (El Salvador) 83
Salvat Editores SA (Spain) 325
Salvat SA de Ediciones (Spain) 325
Salvatella, Editorial Miguel A, (Spain) 325
Salvationist Publishing & Supplies Ltd (United Kingdom) 405
Salvator, Editions, Sàrl (France) 107
Salvator Verlag GmbH (Federal Republic of Germany) 159
Salvioni & Co (Switzerland) 352
Salzburger Druckerei, Verlag der, (Austria) 28
Salzer, Eugen, Verlag (Federal Republic of Germany) 159
Sam Carlos, Livraria, (Portugal) 301
Sam Joong Dang Publishing Co (Republic of Korea) 239
Sam-sung Publishing Co (Republic of Korea) 239
Saman Publishers Ltd (Sri Lanka) 329
Samfund til Udgivelse af Gammel Nordisk Litteratur (Denmark) 79
Samfundet de Nio (Sweden) 339
Samil Cultural Award (Republic of Korea) 240
Samlerens Bogklub (Denmark) 78
Samlerens Forlag A/S (Denmark) 77
Sammenslutningen af Danmarks Forskningsbiblioteker (Denmark) 79
Sammler, Verlag für, (Austria) 28
'Samopomoc Chlopska', Zaklad Wydawnictw CRS, (Publishing Institute of the 'Samopomoc Chlopska' — Peasant Cooperative) (Poland) 295
Samouhos, A, Bookstore (Greece) 178
Sampson Low (United Kingdom) 405
Samsom (CED) (Belgium) 42
Samsom Uitgeverij BV (Netherlands) 266
Samwha Publishing Co (Republic of Korea) 239
San José, Editorial, (Nicaragua) 276
San Martin, Editorial, (Spain) 325
San Min Book Co (China (Taiwan)) 64
San Pablo, Librería, (Colombia) 66
San Pablo, Librería, (Chile) 63
Sanchi Prakashan (India) 194
Sanctus, Förlaget, (Sweden) 336
Sandbergs, AB, Bokhandel (Sweden) 338
Sander Kitabevi (Turkey) 363
Sander Yayınları (Turkey) 363
Sanderus PVBA (Belgium) 42
Sandesa Ltd (Sri Lanka) 329
Sändig, Dr Martin, GmbH (Federal Republic of Germany) 159
Sandkühler, Martin, (Federal Republic of Germany) 170
Sandy Beach Book Store (Barbados) 33
Sane, Lennart, Agency (Sweden) 337
Sang-e-Meel Publications (Pakistan) 286
Sangam Books (India) 194
Sangam Sarada Printing Press (Fiji) 85
Sangeet Natak Akademi Prize (India) 198
Sangna Vuddhichai Sarananda (Thailand) 359
Sangster's Book Stores Ltd (Jamaica) 225
Sanguily, Biblioteca 'Manuel, ' (Cuba) 69
Sangyo Tosho Publishing Co Ltd (Japan) 229
Sankei, The, Shimbun Shuppankyoku Co (Japan) 229
Sankei Juvenile Literature Prize (Japan) 234
Sanket Library Yojna (India) 197
Sankore, Librairie, (Senegal) 307
Sankt-Benno Verlag GmbH (German Democratic Republic) 119
Sankt Gabriel, Verlag, (Austria) 28
Sankt-Johannis-Druckerei, Verlag der, C Schweickhardt (Federal Republic of Germany) 159
Sankt Otto Verlag GmbH (Federal Republic of Germany) 159
Sankt Peter, Verlag, (Austria) 28
'Sanlian Shudian' Publishing House (People's Republic of China) 63

Sanseido Co Ltd (Japan) 229
Sanskriti (India) 194
Sansoni, Casa Editrice G C, SpA (Italy) 220
Sanssouci Verlag (Switzerland) 352
Sansyusya Publishing Co Ltd (Japan) 229
Santa Fe, Librería, (Argentina) 8
Santiago, Editorial, Rueda SRL (Argentina) 7
Santillana SA de Ediciones (Spain) 325
Säntis Verlag (Switzerland) 352
Santo Domingo, Biblioteca Municipal de, (Dominican Republic) 81
Sanyo Shuppan Boeki Co Inc (Japan) 230
Sapienza's Library (Malta) 248
Sapphire Books Pty Ltd (Australia) 18
Sappl, Paul, Schulbuch- und Lehrmittelverlag (Austria) 28
Saraiva SA, Livreiros Editores (Brazil) 54
Saraswat Library (India) 194
Sarawak State Library (Malaysia) 247
Sari Agung, Toko Buku, (Indonesia) 200
Sarita Prakashan (India) 194
Sarkar, M C, & Sons (P) Ltd (India) 194
Sarma, Librairie, (Zaire) 433
Sarmiento, Librería, (Argentina) 8
Sarmiento Prize (Argentina) 9
Sarpay Beikman Best Manuscripts Awards (Burma) 60
Sarpay Beikman Board (Burma) 59
Sarpay Beikman Book Club (Burma) 59
Sarpay Beikman Bookshop (Burma) 59
Sarpay Lawka (Burma) 59
Sarvier — Editôra de Livros Medicos Ltda (Brazil) 54
Sassafras Verlag (Federal Republic of Germany) 159
Sasta Sahitya Mandal (India) 194
Sastra Hudaya (Indonesia) 200
Satellite Books Publishers (United Kingdom) 405
Satire Verlag GmbH (Federal Republic of Germany) 159
Saudi Library (Saudi Arabia) 306
Saudi Publishing and Distributing House (Saudi Arabia) 306
Sauer, I H, Verlag GmbH (Federal Republic of Germany) 159
Sauerländer, H R, und Co (Federal Republic of Germany) 159
Sauerländer AG (Switzerland) 352
Sauerländer's, J D, Verlag (Federal Republic of Germany) 159
Saunders, W B, Co Ltd (United Kingdom) 405
Saur, K G, Éditeur Sàrl (France) 107
Saur, K G, Verlag KG (Federal Republic of Germany) 159
Saurambes, Librairie, (France) 111
Sauret, Editions du Livre André, (Monaco) 255
Sautoy, De, College Library (United Republic of Cameroon) 62
Savez bibliotečkih radnika Srbije (Yugoslavia) 431
Savez društava bibliotekara Jugoslavije (Serbo-Croatian) (Yugoslavia) 431
Savez Inženjera i Tehničara Jugoslavije (Yugoslavia) 429
Savolan Kirjakauppa Oy (Finland) 87
Savremena Administracija (Yugoslavia) 429
Saxon House (United Kingdom) 405
Sayam Paritat (Thailand) 359
Scala Istituto Fotografico Editoriale (Italy) 220
Scene Book Club (United Kingdom) 415
Schäfer, Karl A, Buch-und Offsetdruckerei-Goldstadtverlag (Federal Republic of Germany) 159
Schaffstein, Hermann, Verlag (Federal Republic of Germany) 159
Schaik, J L van, (Pty) Ltd (Republic of South Africa) 314
Schaik's, Van, Bookstore (Pty) Ltd (Republic of South Africa) 314
Schapire Editor SRL (Argentina) 7
Schattauer, F K, Verlag GmbH (Federal Republic of Germany) 159
Schaubroeck PVBA (Belgium) 42
Schauenburg, Moritz, Verlag GmbH und Co KG (Federal Republic of Germany) 160
Scheepers Prize (Republic of South Africa) 317
Scheffler, Verlag Heinrich, (Federal Republic of Germany) 160
Scheidegger, Dr A, (Switzerland) 356
Scheltema, Boekhandel, Holkema Vermeulen BV (Netherlands) 269
Scheltema Holkema Vermeulen, Boekhandel, BV (Netherlands) 266
Schendl, Dr A, GmbH & Co KG (Austria) 28
Scherpe Verlag (Federal Republic of Germany) 160
Scherz, Buchhandlung, AG (Switzerland) 356
Scherz Verlag AG (Switzerland) 352
Scherz Verlag GmbH (Federal Republic of Germany) 160
Scheuerer, Gertrud E, Verlag (Federal Republic of Germany) 160
Schibsteds, Chr, Forlag (Norway) 282
Schiele und Schön, Fachverlag, GmbH (Federal Republic of Germany) 160
Schifferli, Verlag der Arche Peter, (Switzerland) 352

Schildts, Holger, Förlagsaktiebolag (Finland) 86
Schiller Prize (Federal Republic of Germany) 174
Schilling, Kurt, (Federal Republic of Germany) 160
Schindele, G, Verlag GmbH (Federal Republic of Germany) 160
Schipper (Netherlands) 266
Schirmer/Mosel Verlag GmbH (Federal Republic of Germany) 160
Schlaefli, Otto, Verlag (Switzerland) 352
Schläpfer & Co AG (Switzerland) 352
Schlegel-Tieck Prize (United Kingdom) 420
Schlender, Verlag Bert, (Federal Republic of Germany) 160
Schlueck, Thomas, (Federal Republic of Germany) 169
Schmid, Joachim, und Co (Karl-May Verlag) (Federal Republic of Germany) 160
Schmidt, Erich, Verlag (Federal Republic of Germany) 160
Schmidt, Richard Carl, und Co (Federal Republic of Germany) 160
Schmidt, Verlag Dr Otto, KG (Federal Republic of Germany) 160
Schmidt-Römhild, Max, Verlag (Federal Republic of Germany) 160
Schmidt-Römhild, Verlag für polizeiliches Fachschrifttum Georg, (Federal Republic of Germany) 160
Schmiere, Die, — Rudolf Rolfs (Federal Republic of Germany) 160
Schmitz, Wilhelm, Verlag (Federal Republic of Germany) 160
Schmücking, Galerie, Verlag (Federal Republic of Germany) 160
Schneekluth, Franz, Verlag (Federal Republic of Germany) 160
Schneider, Franz, Verlag (Austria) 28
Schneider, Franz, Verlag GmbH und Co KG (Federal Republic of Germany) 160
Schneider, Lambert, Verlag GmbH (Federal Republic of Germany) 160
Schnell und Steiner (Switzerland) 352
Schnell und Steiner, Verlag, GmbH und Co (Federal Republic of Germany) 160
Schocken Publishing House Ltd (Israel) 209
Schoelcher, Bibliothèque Victor, (Martinique) 249
Schoenbergske Forlag, Det, A/S (Nyt Nordisk Forlag Arnold Busck A/S) (Denmark) 77
Schofield & Sims Ltd (United Kingdom) 405
Scholar Publications International (Nigeria) Ltd (Nigeria) 279
Scholarship, The, in Letters (New Zealand) 276
Scholastic Publications (United Kingdom) 405
Schöldström, Birger, Prize (Sweden) 339
Scholtens en Zoon BV (Netherlands) 269
Schönbrunn-Verlag GmbH (Austria) 28
Schöne Wissenschaften, Verlag fur, (Belles Lettres Publishing Co — Albert Steffen Foundation) (Switzerland) 352
Schönen Bücher, Verlag Die, Dr Wolf Strache KG (Federal Republic of Germany) 161
Schöningh, Ferdinand, Verlag (Federal Republic of Germany) 161
School Bookshop Association (United Kingdom) 369
School Library Association (United Kingdom) 417
School Library Association of Papua New Guinea (Papua New Guinea) 288
School of Oriental & African Studies (United Kingdom) 405
School of Oriental and African Studies Library (United Kingdom) 416
School Projects Ltd (Australia) 18
School Supplies Ltd (New Zealand) 274
Schoolmaster Publishing Co Ltd (United Kingdom) 405
Schoolpers (Netherlands) 266
Schott Frères Sàrl (France) 107
Schott Frères SPRL (Éditeurs de Musique) (Belgium) 42
Schottentor (Austria) 30
Schott's, B, Söhne, Musikverlag (Federal Republic of Germany) 161
Schreiber, Verlag J F, (Federal Republic of Germany) 161
Schreiner, Olive, Prize for English Literature (Republic of South Africa) 317
Schriftenmission, Verlag und, der Ev Ges für Deutschland GmbH (Federal Republic of Germany) 161
Schriftenmissions-Verlag (Federal Republic of Germany) 161
Schroedel, Hermann, Verlag AG (Switzerland) 352
Schroedel, Hermann, Verlag KG (Federal Republic of Germany) 161
Schroeder, Kurt, Verlag (Federal Republic of Germany) 161
Schroeder, Marion von, Verlag GmbH (Federal Republic of Germany) 161
Schroll, Anton, & Co (Austria) 28
Schroll, Anton, und Co GmbH (Federal Republic of Germany) 161
Schubiger Verlag AG (Switzerland) 352

Schück, Henrik, Prize (Sweden) 339
Schule und Elternhaus, Verlag, (Federal Republic of Germany) 161
Schuler, F. (Switzerland) 352
Schuler Verlagsgesellschaft mbH (Federal Republic of Germany) 161
Schulte, Hermann, (Federal Republic of Germany) 161
Schultheis, Ludwig, Verlag Haus und Heim (Federal Republic of Germany) 161
Schulthess Polygraphischer Verlag AG (Switzerland) 352
Schultz, A/S J H, Forlag (Denmark) 77
Schulz, Verlag R S, (Federal Republic of Germany) 161
Schünemann, Carl Ed, KG (Federal Republic of Germany) 161
Schutter, De, SA (Belgium) 42
Schütz, Verlag K W, KG (Federal Republic of Germany) 161
Schuyt en Co CV (Netherlands) 266
Schwabe & Co Ltd (Switzerland) 353
Schwabe und Co GmbH Verlag (Federal Republic of Germany) 161
Schwabenverlag AG (Federal Republic of Germany) 161
Schwalbach, Verlag Haus, (Federal Republic of Germany) 161
Schwaneberger Verlag GmbH (Federal Republic of Germany) 161
Schwann, Edition, (Federal Republic of Germany) 161
Schwann, Pädagogischer Verlag, GmbH (Federal Republic of Germany) 161
Schwartz, Uitgeverij Gary, (Netherlands) 266
Schwartz, Verlag Otto, und Co (Federal Republic of Germany) 161
Schwarz, Verlag Elke, (Federal Republic of Germany) 162
Schwarze, Dr Wolfgang, Verlag (Federal Republic of Germany) 162
Schwarzer, Verlagsbüro Karl, (Austria) 28
Schweickhardt, Verlag der Sankt-Johannis-Druckerei G, (Federal Republic of Germany) 162
Schweitzer, Dr Albert, Prize (France) 115
Schweitzer, J, Verlag (Federal Republic of Germany) 162
Schweiz Verlag Arbeitsgemeinschaft für die Bergbevölkerung (SAB) (Switzerland) 353
Schweizer Buchwerbung und -Information (S B I) (Switzerland) 340
Schweizer Buchzentrum (Switzerland) 340
Schweizer Jugend, Aare-Verlag/, -Verlag (Switzerland) 353
Schweizer Spiegel Verlag AG & Rodana Verlag (Switzerland) 353
Schweizer Verband der Musikalienhändler und Verleger (Switzerland) 340
Schweizer Verlagshaus AG (Switzerland) 353
Schweizer Volksbuchgemeinde AG (Switzerland) 356
Schweizerbart'sche Verlagsbuchhandlung, E, (Federal Republic of Germany) 162
Schweizerische Bibliophilen-Gesellschaft (Switzerland) 357
Schweizerische Landesbibliothek (Bibliothèque nationale suisse) (Swiss National Library) (Switzerland) 356
Schweizerische Stiftung für Alpine Forschungen (Swiss Foundation for Alpine Research) (Switzerland) 353
Schweizerische Zentralstelle für Stahlbau (Switzerland) 353
Schweizerischen Schallplattenmission, Verlag der, (Switzerland) 353
Schweizerischer Adressbuchverleger-Verband (Switzerland) 340
Schweizerischer Buchhändler- und Verleger-Verband (SBVV) (Switzerland) 340
Schweizerischer Bühnenverleger-Verband (Association of Swiss Publishers for the Stage) (Switzerland) 340
Schweizerischer Schriftsteller-Verband (Switzerland) 357
Schweizerisches Jugendschriftenwerk (Switzerland) 353
Schweizerisches katholisches Bibelwerk, Verlag, (Switzerland) 353
Schweizerisches Ost-Institut (Switzerland) 353
Schweizerisches Wirtschaftsarchiv (Archives économiques suisses) (Swiss Economic Archives) (Switzerland) 356
Schwengler-Verlag (Switzerland) 353
Schwieger, H G, (Federal Republic of Germany) 162
Schwinghammer, Verlag Junge Gemeinde E, KG (Federal Republic of Germany) 162
Schwitter Edition GmbH (Switzerland) 353
Schwitter Holding, F P, Inc (Switzerland) 353
Scialtiel, Bureau littéraire international Marguerite, (France) 110
Sciascia, Salvatore, (Italy) 220
Science Fiction Book Club (United Kingdom) 415
Science Publications Centre (Republic of Korea) 239
Science Research Associates Ltd (United Kingdom) 405
Science Research Associates Pty Ltd (Australia) 18
Sciences et Lettres, Editions, SA (Belgium) 42
Scientechnica (Publishers) Ltd (United Kingdom) 405
Scientia Verlag und Antiquariat Kurt Schilling (Federal Republic of Germany) 162
Scientific Book Agency (India) 194
Scientific Book Club (United Kingdom) 415

Scientific Documentation Centre (Iraq) 202
Scientific Library and Documentation Division (Philippines) 292
Scientific Publishing House (Socialist Republic of Viet Nam) 426
Scientific Translations International Ltd (Israel) 211
Scientifica Editrice, Libreria, (Italy) 220
Scientifiche Italiane, Edizioni, (Italy) 220
Scientology Publications Organization (AOSH DK Publ Dept ApS) (Denmark) 77
Scipione Autores Editores Ltda (Brazil) 54
Scolar Press (United Kingdom) 405
Scolastiche, Edizioni, APE SpA (Italy) 220
Scolavox (France) 107
Scorpion Publications Ltd (United Kingdom) 405
Scott, John, Educational Books Supply (Australia) 19
Scott-Moncrieff Prize (United Kingdom) 421
Scottish Academic Press Ltd (United Kingdom) 406
Scottish Arts Council Book Awards (United Kingdom) 421
Scottish General Publishers' Association (United Kingdom) 369
Scottish Library Association (United Kingdom) 417
Scottish Record Office (United Kingdom) 416
Scrépel (Switzerland) 353
Scriptar, Editions, SA (Switzerland) 353
Scriptor Verlag (Federal Republic of Germany) 162
Scripts Publications (Australia) 18
Scripture Union (United Kingdom) 406
'Scrisul Românesc', Editura, ('Romanian Writing' Publishing House) (Romania) 304
Scuola, Editrice La, SpA (Italy) 220
Se Kwang Musical Publication Co (Republic of Korea) 239
Seafarer Books (United Kingdom) 406
Seale, Patrick, Books Ltd (United Kingdom) 414
Sealy, J C, (Trinidad and Tobago) 361
Seara, Empresa de Publicidade, Nova SARL (Portugal) 301
Search Press Ltd and Burns & Oates Ltd (United Kingdom) 406
Secker & Warburg, Martin, Ltd (United Kingdom) 406
Second Back Row Press Pty Ltd (Australia) 18
Secours, Editions du, Catholique (France) 107
Secretaría de Estado de Relaciones Exteriores, Biblioteca de la, (Dominican Republic) 81
Século, Editorial o, (Portugal) 301
Sécuritas, La Société, SA (France) 107
Seditas (Société d'Editions et de Diffusion Tambourinaire-Sofradel) (France) 107
Sedmay Ediciones SA (Spain) 325
See-saw Book Club (United Kingdom) 415
Seeber, Libreria, (Italy) 222
Seefeld, Edition, (Switzerland) 353
Seeley, Service & Co Ltd (United Kingdom) 406
Seelig, AB, och Co (Sweden) 338
Seemann, E A, Verlag (Federal Republic of Germany) 162
Seemann, VEB E A, Buch- und Kunstverlag (German Democratic Republic) 119
Seewald Verlag (Federal Republic of Germany) 162
Seghers, Editions, SA (France) 107
Seibundo Shinkosha Publishing Co Ltd (Japan) 230
Seiwa Shoten Co Ltd (Japan) 230
Seix, Editorial, Barral SA (Spain) 325
Seizando-Shoten Publication Co Ltd (Japan) 230
Seizoenen, De, PVBA (Belgium) 42
Sejong Daewang Kinyom Saophoe (Republic of Korea) 239
Sekai Bunka Publishing Inc (Japan) 230
Selangor Public Library (Malaysia) 247
Selcon SAEC & I (Selección Contable) (Argentina) 7
Selecciones, Biblioteca de, (Spain) 327
Selecciones, Librería, (Bolivia) 47
Selecciones, Librería, (Ecuador) 81
Selecciones Editoriales SA (Spain) 325
Selecciones SA Comercial (Paraguay) 289
Seleções Editora Ltda (Brazil) 54
Selecta, Librería, (Venezuela) 425
Sélection, Editions, J Jacobs SA (France) 107
Selimiye Library (Turkey) 363
Selina Publishers (India) 194
Sella, Shalom, (Israel) 210
Sellerio Editore (Italy) 220
Sellevolds Bokhandel A/S (Norway) 283
Sellier Verlag GmbH (Federal Republic of Germany) 162
Sembrador, Editorial El, (Chile) 62
Sembrador, Librería El, (Chile) 63
Semences, Editions, Africaines (United Republic of Cameroun) 61
Semic Press (Netherlands) 266
Seminar on the Acquisition of Latin American Library Materials (SALALM) (International Organizations) 439
Seminario, Librería del, (Colombia) 66
Seminario de Integración Social Guatemalteca (Guatemala) 178

Semper, Uitgeverij, Agendo BV (Netherlands) 266
Senate Library (Ketabkhaneh Majles Sena) (Iran) 202
Sendler, Verlag Jürgen, (Federal Republic of Germany) 162
Sénevé, Les Editions du, (France) 107
Senmon Toshokan Kyogikai (SENTOKYO) (Japan Special Libraries Association) (Japan) 233
Senouhy Publishers (Egypt) 82
Sentis, Santiago, Melendo (Argentina) 7
Sentral Bokhandel A/S (Norway) 281
Sentral Bokhandel a/s (Norway) 283
Seomun Dang (Republic of Korea) 239
Seonjin Publishing Co (Republic of Korea) 239
Seoul National University Library (Republic of Korea) 239
Sept Couleurs, Les, (France) 107
Septuaginta BV Uitgeverij (Netherlands) 266
Serg, Editions, SRP (France) 107
Sermwit Barnakarn (Thailand) 359
Service des Bibliothèques, Ministère des Universités (France) 111
Service SC (Belgium) 42
Service Technique pour l'Education (Fonds Social Juif Unifié) (France) 107
Services, Direction générale des, de Bibliothèques, Archives et Documentation (Popular Republic of Congo) 67
Services interbancaires SA (Belgium) 42
Servicio Continental de Publicaciones (Panama) 288
Servicio de Bibliotecas de la Diputación Provincial de Barcelona (Spain) 328
Servicio de Documentación y Biblioteca (Dominican Republic) 81
Servicio de Lewis (Panama) 288
Servire BV Uitgevers (Netherlands) 269
Servire BV Uitgevers (Netherlands) 266
Setberg (Iceland) 185
Settern, Bokförlaget, (Sweden) 336
Seuil, Editions du, (France) 107
Seungmun-gak (Republic of Korea) 239
Seven Seas Publishers (German Democratic Republic) 119
Sevenseas Publishing Pty Ltd (New Zealand) 274
Severin Presse (Austria) 28
Severn House Publishers Ltd (United Kingdom) 406
Severoceské nakladatelství (Czechoslovakia) 71
Sha'b, Al-, Bookshop (Saudi Arabia) 306
Shadeed's Educational & General Supplies (Jamaica) 225
Shakai Shiso-Sha (Japan) 230
Shaker, Ahmed, Al Ansary (Egypt) 83
Shakespeare Head Press (United Kingdom) 406
Shakespeare Head Press (Australia) 18
Shakespearean Authorship Society (United Kingdom) 418
Shang-hai t'u shu kuan (Shanghai Library) (People's Republic of China) 64
Shanghai Book Co Ltd (Hong Kong) 181
Shanghai Book Co Pte Ltd (Republic of Singapore) 310
Sharbain's Bookshop (Israel) 210
Shaw, Pat, Associates (formerly EMBLA) (Norway) 283
Shaw Centre, Bernard, (United Kingdom) 418
Shaw Society, Bernard, (United Kingdom) 418
Shazar Prize (Israel) 211
Shearwater Press Limited (United Kingdom) 406
Sheed & Ward Ltd (United Kingdom) 406
Sheil, Anthony, Associates Ltd (United Kingdom) 414
Sheldon Press (United Kingdom) 406
Shell Book of the Year Award (Australia) 23
Shepheard-Walwyn (Publishers) Ltd (United Kingdom) 406
Sheppard Press Ltd (United Kingdom) 406
Sherratt & Hughes (Bowes & Bowes) (United Kingdom) 415
Sheth, R R, & Co (India) 197
Sheth, R R, and Co (India) 194
Shikmona Publishing Co Ltd (Israel) 209
Shiko-Sha Co Ltd (Japan) 230
Shiksha Bharati (India) 195
Shimoni, Joseph, (Israel) 209
Shincho Prizes (Japan) 234
Shinchosha Co (Japan) 230
Shindan to Chiryo Co Ltd (Japan) 230
Shinkenchiku-Sha Co Ltd (Japan) 230
Shire Publications Ltd (United Kingdom) 406
Shkencore e Universitetit Shtetëror, Biblioteka, të Tiranës (Scientific Library of the State University of Tirana) (Albania) 1
Shkodër Public Library (Albania) 1
Shmulik (Israel) 209
Shogakukan Literary Prize (Japan) 234
Shogakukan Publishing Co Ltd (Japan) 230
Shokabo Publishing Co Ltd (Japan) 230
Shokoku-Sha Publishing Co Ltd (Japan) 230
Shona Readers' Book Club (Zimbabwe) 435
Shona/Ndebele Writers' Association (Zimbabwe) 436
Shortland Educational Publications (New Zealand) 274
Shri Ram Centre for Industrial Relations and Human Resources (India) 195

Shriram Awards (India) 198
Shueisha Publishing Co Ltd (Japan) 230
Shufu-to-Seikatsu Sha Ltd (Japan) 230
Shufunotomo Co Ltd (Japan) 230
Shumawa Book House (Burma) 59
Shumawa Publishing House (Burma) 59
Shuter & Shooter (Pty) Ltd (Republic of South Africa) 314
Shuter and Shooter (Pty) (Republic of South Africa) 315
Shwepyidan Printing & Publishing House (Burma) 59
Si-Sa-Yong-O-Sa (Republic of Korea) 239
Siam, The, Society (Thailand) 360
Siam Book House (Thailand) 360
Siam Directory (Thailand) 359
Siamandas (Greece) 177
Sibelius-Akatemian Kirjasto (Finland) 87
Sideris, J. OE Ekdoseis (Greece) 177
Sidgwick & Jackson Ltd (United Kingdom) 406
Siebdruck Süd GmbH, Druck und Verlagshaus (Federal Republic of Germany) 162
Sieber, Wilfried Th. (Federal Republic of Germany) 169
Siebert und Engelbert Dessart Verlag GmbH (Federal Republic of Germany) 162
Siebert Verlag GmbH (Federal Republic of Germany) 162
Sierra Leone, The, Diocesan Bookshop (Sierra Leone) 308
Sierra Leone Library Association (Sierra Leone) 308
Sierra Leone Library Board (Sierra Leone) 308
Sierra Leone University Press (Sierra Leone) 308
Sifrait Haminhal (Israel) 209
Sifriat Poalim Ltd (Israel) 209
Sifriat Poalim Ltd (Israel) 210
Siglo, Club del Libro Nicaragüense, Librería y Editorial, XX (Nicaragua) 276
Siglo XX, Ediciones, SAC & I (Argentina) 7
Siglo XXI Editores de Colombia Ltda (Colombia) 66
Siglo XXI Editores de España SA (Spain) 325
Siglo XXI Editores SA (Mexico) 253
Siglos, Editorial V, SA (Mexico) 253
Sigmar, Editorial, SACI (Argentina) 7
Signal-Verlag Hans Frevert (Federal Republic of Germany) 162
Sigueme, Ediciones, (Spain) 326
Sijthoff & Noordhoff International Publishers (Netherlands) 266
Sijthoff's Uitg. A W, Mij BV (Netherlands) 266
Sikkel, Uitgeverij De, NV (Belgium) 42
Silex (Spain) 326
Silliman University Library (Philippines) 292
Sillon, Editions Le, d'Or (Belgium) 42
Siloë, Editions, Sàrl (France) 107
Silogos Ecdoton Bibliopolon (Greek Publishers' Association) (Greece) 176
Silva, K V G De, & Sons (Kandy) (Sri Lanka) 330
Silvaire, Editions André, (France) 107
Silvana Editoriale Srl (Italy) 220
Silver Dagger Award (United Kingdom) 421
Silvio Romero Prize (Brazil) 57
Sima, Ediciones, (Spain) 326
Siman Krai (Israel) 209
Símbolo, Edições, (Brazil) 54
Simmat, S. (Federal Republic of Germany) 162
Simon, Verlag Ludwig, (Federal Republic of Germany) 162
Simon Stevin NV (Belgium) 42
Simondium Publishers (Pty) Ltd (Republic of South Africa) 314
Simson, Samuel, Ltd (United Kingdom) 407
Simul, The, Press Inc (Japan) 230
Sinag-Tala Publishers Inc (Philippines) 292
Sinai Publishing Co (Israel) 209
Sind University Central Library (Pakistan) 286
Sindacàto Italiano Editori (Italy) 212
Sindbad (France) 107
Sindhi Adabi Board (Pakistan) 287
Sindicato Nacional dos Editores de Livros (Brazil) 48
Singapore Book Store (Republic of Singapore) 310
Singapore Booksellers' Association (Republic of Singapore) 308
Singapore Chinese Booksellers' Association (Republic of Singapore) 308
Singapore University Press Pte Ltd (Republic of Singapore) 309
Singer, BP, Features Inc (Federal Republic of Germany) 169
Singhbhum District Booksellers' Association (India) 186
Singu Munwha Sa (Republic of Korea) 239
Sinite Parvulos (Belgium) 42
Sino-Malay Publishing Co (Malaysia) 247
Sinodalno Izdatelstvo (Bulgaria) 58
Sinpattana (Thailand) 359
Sint-Ignatius, Bibliotheek der Universitaire Faculteiten, (Belgium) 44
Sintal (Belgium) 42
Sintes, Editorial, SA (Spain) 326
Sinwel-Buchhandlung Verlag (Switzerland) 353

Sir Robert Ho Tung, Biblioteca, (Sir Robert Ho Tung's Chinese Library) (Macao) 244
Sirey, Editions, (France) 107
Siriraj Medical Library (Thailand) 360
Sistem, Pustaka, Pelajaran (Malaysia) 247
Sistema Bibliotecario (Librarians' System) (Honduras) 180
Sitti, A B, Syamsiyah (Indonesia) 200
Skalholt (Iceland) 185
Skandinavia Verlag (Federal Republic of Germany) 170
Skarabee, Uitgeverij, BV (Netherlands) 267
Skaraveos (Greece) 177
Skarv- Nature Publications ApS (Denmark) 77
Skattekartoteket, A/S, (Denmark) 77
Sketch Publishing Co (Nigeria) 279
Skilton, Charles, Ltd (United Kingdom) 406
Skilton & Shaw (United Kingdom) 406
Skinner, Thomas, Directories (United Kingdom) 407
Skira, Editions D'Art Albert, SA (Switzerland) 353
Skjaldborg, Bókaútgáfan, sf (Iceland) 185
'Skladnica Ksiegarska', Państwowe, Przedsiebiorstwo, (Poland) 296
Skolförlaget Gävle AB (Sweden) 336
'Školska knjiga' (Yugoslavia) 430
Sktachnica Ksiegarska (Poland) 296
Skuggsja bókaforlag (Iceland) 185
Skylark ChildreN's Book Club (United Kingdom) 415
Skypress International (Federal Republic of Germany) 162
'Slask', Wydawnictwo, (Poland) 295
Slaska kjiegarnia Techniczna (Poland) 295
Slatkine Reprints (Switzerland) 353
Slezak, Josef Otto, (Austria) 28
Sloboda (Yugoslavia) 430
Slovart Ltd (Czechoslovakia) 72
Slovenská kartografia NP (Czechoslovakia) 71
Slovenská knižničná (Czechoslovakia) 73
Slovenská technická knižnica (Czechoslovakia) 72
Slovenské pedagogické nakladatelstvo (Czechoslovakia) 71
Slovenské ústredie knižnej kultúry (Czechoslovakia) 70
Slovenské vydavatel'stvo podohospodarskej literatúry (Czechoslovakia) 71
Slovenskej Akademie Vied, Vydavatel'stvo, (Czechoslovakia) 71
Slovenský spisovatel' (Czechoslovakia) 71
Slovo Ljubve (Yugoslavia) 430
Službeni List (Yugoslavia) 430
Smålänningens Forlag AB (Sweden) 336
Smart & Mookerdum (Burma) 59
Smeets Illustrated Projects (Netherlands) 267
Smena (Czechoslovakia) 71
Smith, John, & Son (Glasgow) Ltd (United Kingdom) 415
Smith, Lawrence, (Argentina) 8
Smith, Pauline, Prize for Prose (Republic of South Africa) 317
Smith, W H, & Son Ltd (United Kingdom) 415
Smith & Son Children's Literary Competition, W H, (United Kingdom) 421
Smith & Son Literary Award, W H, (United Kingdom) 421
Smythe, Colin, Ltd (United Kingdom) 407
Snaefell, Bókaútgáfan, (Iceland) 185
Snoeck-Ducaju & Zoon NV (Belgium) 42
Snøfugl Forlag (Norway) 283
Sobrier-Arnould Prize (France) 115
Social Science Association Press (Thailand) 359
Social Sciences Library (Socialist Republic of Viet Nam) 426
Socialistisk Bogklub ApS (Denmark) 78
Sociedad de Bibliófilos Chilenos (Chile) 63
Sociedad de Bibliotecarios de Puerto Rico (Society of Librarians of Puerto Rico) (Puerto Rico) 303
Sociedad de Ciencias, Letras y Artes (Scientific, Literary and Art Society) (Spain) 328
Sociedad de Libreros del Ecuador (Ecuador) 81
Sociedad General de Autores de España (Spain) 328
Sociedad General de Autores de la Argentina ('Argentores') (Argentina) 9
Sociedad Mexicana de Bibliografía (Mexican Bibliographical Society) (Mexico) 254
Sociedad Puertorriqueña de Escritores (Puerto Rican Society of Writers) (Puerto Rico) 303
Sociedade Brasileira, Biblioteca da, de Cultura Inglesa (Brazil) 56
Società Dante Alighieri (Italy) 223
Società Dantesca Italiana (Italy) 223
Società Editori della Svizzera Italiana (SESI) (Switzerland) 340
Società Letteraria (Italy) 223
Societäts-Verlag (Federal Republic of Germany) 162
Société africaine de Librairie-Papeterie (African Society of the Stationery and Book Trade) (International Organizations) 439
Société Africaine d'Edition (Senegal) 307

Société belge des Auteurs, Compositeurs et Editeurs (SABAM) (Belgium) 45
Société Biblique belge asbl (Belgium) 42
Société Continentale d'Editions Modernes Illustrées (France) 107
Société de Distribution et de Culture (Martinique) 249
Société de Langue et de Littérature wallones ASBL (Belgium) 45
Société de Presse et d'Edition de Madagascar (Democratic Republic of Madagascar) 245
Société de Recherche appliquée à l'Education (France) 107
Société d'Edition, de Publicité, de Radio et Télévision (France) 107
Société d'Edition d'Afrique Nouvelle (Senegal) 307
Société d'Edition d'Annuaires Professionnels (France) 107
Société d'Edition de Dictionnaires et d'Encyclopédies (France) 107
Société d'Edition d'Enseignement Supérieur (France) 107
Société d'Editions Scientifiques, Dimedia (France) 107
Société des anciens Textes Français (Society of Ancient French Texts) (France) 112
Société des Bibliophiles (France) 110
Société des Gens de Lettres (Society of Men and Women of Letters) (France) 112
Société des Libraries et Editeurs de la Suisse romande (SLESR) (Switzerland) 340
Société des Poètes français (Society of French Poets) (France) 112
Société d'Etudes dantesques (France) 112
Société d'Etudes morales, sociales & juridiques (Belgium) 42
Société d'Exploitation et de Diffusion des Codes Rousseau (France) 107
Société d'Histoire littéraire de la France (France) 112
Société d'Information médicale et d'enseignement post-universitaire (France) 107
Société du Nouveau Littré (SNL) Dictionnaire 'Le Robert' (France) 108
Société du Vieux Montmartre (France) 112
Société Editions Internationales Sàrl (France) 110
Société Encyclopédique Française (SEF) (France) 108
Société française des Traducteurs (French Union of Translators) (France) 116
Société internationale de Bibliographie classique (International Organizations) 439
Société internationale des Bibliothèques-Musées des Arts du Spectacle (SIBMAS) (International Society of Libraries and Museums for the Performing Arts) (International Organizations) 439
Société Kenkoson d'Etudes Africaines (United Republic of Cameroun) 61
Société Librairie nouvelle (Tunisia) 362
Société Malgache d'Edition (Democratic Republic of Madagascar) 245
Société Malgache d'Edition (Democratic Republic of Madagascar) 244
Société nationale d'Edition et de Diffusion (Tunisia) 362
Société nationale d'Edition et de Diffusion (Tunisia) 362
Société nationale d'Edition et de Diffusion (SNED) (Algeria) 2
Société Nouvelle de l'Imprimerie Centrale (Democratic Republic of Madagascar) 244
Société royale des Bibliophiles et Iconophiles de Belgique (Belgium) 45
Société Universitaire d'Editions et de Librairie (France) 108
Society, The, for Promoting Christian Knowledge (United Kingdom) 407
Society for the Promotion and Improvement of Libraries (Pakistan) 287
Society for the Promotion of Japanese Literature (Japan) 233
Society for the Study of Medieval Languages and Literature (United Kingdom) 418
Society of Aesthetes, Art and Literary Critics (Bulgaria) 59
Society of Archivists (United Kingdom) 417
Society of Arts, Literature and Welfare (Bangladesh) 33
Society of Australian Writers (Australia) 21
Society of Authors (United Kingdom) 369
Society of County Librarians (United Kingdom) 417
Society of Editors (Australia) 10
Society of Indexers, The, (United Kingdom) 369
Society of Metropolitan & County Chief Librarians (United Kingdom) 417
Society of Women Writers (Australia) 21
Society of Young Publishers (United Kingdom) 369
Sodel (Editeur) SA (France) 108
Söderström ja Co Förlagsaktiebolag (Finland) 86
Sodexport-Grem (France) 111
Sodimca, Libraires, (Zaire) 433
Soeroengan (Indonesia) 200
Soethoudt, Walter, (Belgium) 42
Sofia City and District State Archives (Bulgaria) 58
Sofia Press Agency (Bulgaria) 58

INDEX 509

Sofiac (Sociéte Française des Imprimeries Administratives Centrales) (France) 108
Sofiiski Universitet 'Kliment Ohridsky' Biblioteka (University of Sofia Library) (Bulgaria) 58
Sofradel-Seditas (France) 108
Sofradif Editions Philippe Auzou (France) 108
Sogalivre, Librairie, (Gabon) 116
Sogensha Publishing Co Ltd (Japan) 230
Sohlmans Förlag AB (Sweden) 336
S O I, Verlag, (Schweizerisches Ost-Institut) (Switzerland) 352
Sojuz na društvata na bibliotekarite na Jugoslavija (Macedonian) (Yugoslavia) 431
Sojuz na društvata za makedonski jazik i literatura (Yugoslavia) 432
Sol, Ediciones del, SA (Argentina) 7
Solar (France) 108
Soledi (Imprimeur-Editeur) SA (Belgium) 42
Soleil Noir, Editions, (France) 108
Solidaridad Publishing House (Philippines) 292
Solum Forlag A/S (Norway) 283
Somaiya Publications Pvt Ltd (India) 195
Somalia d'Oggi (Somalia) 310
Somec-Rwanda (Rwanda) 306
Sommai Press (Thailand) 359
Sommer & Sörensen Forlag ApS (Denmark) 77
Somogy, Editions d'Art Aimery, (France) 108
Soncino Press Ltd (United Kingdom) 407
Sondagskool Boekhandel (Republic of South Africa) 314
Sonnenweg-Verlag Schäfer und Brandt (Federal Republic of Germany) 162
Sonneville Press (Uitgeversmij) PVBA (Belgium) 42
Sonrisa Vertical Prize, La (International Literary Prizes) 452
Sonzé, Editions, (France) 108
Sonzogno SpA (Italy) 220
Sopena, Editorial, Colombiana SA (Mexico) 253
Sopena, Editorial Ramon, av Rio de la Plata SAI y C (Argentina) 7
Sopena, Ramón, SA (Spain) 326
Sopena Colombiana SA (Colombia) 66
Sopena Venezolana, Editorial Ramón, SA (Venezuela) 424
Soprep (Editions de Bussac) (France) 108
Soprode (France) 108
Sorbonne, Bibliothèque de la, (France) 111
Sorgente, La, Srl (Italy) 220
Sorrett Publishing Pty Ltd (Australia) 18
Sotano, Librería del, (Mexico) 254
Sotheby Parke Bernet Publications (United Kingdom) 407
Soulanges, Editions Louis, 'Le Livre Ouvert' (France) 108
Source, Les Editions de la, SA (France) 108
Sousa, Luisa Claudio de, Prize (Brazil) 57
Sousa e Almeida, Livraria, (Portugal) 301
South African Academy of Science and Arts Prizes (Republic of South Africa) 317
South African Indian Library Association (Republic of South Africa) 316
South African Library (Republic of South Africa) 316
South African Library Association (Republic of South Africa) 316
South African Natural History Publications Co (Republic of South Africa) 314
South African Publishers' Association (Republic of South Africa) 311
South Australia Biennial Literature Prize (Australia) 23
South Australia Booksellers' Association (Australia) 10
South Australian Government Literature Prize (Australia) 23
South East Asian Regional Branch of the International Council on Archives (SARBICA) (International Organizations) 439
South Head Press (Australia) 18
South Pacific Commission Library (New Caledonia) 271
Southeast Asian Ministers of Education Organization (SEAMEO) (Republic of Singapore) 309
Southeast Book Co (China (Taiwan)) 64
Southside (United Kingdom) 407
Souvenir Press Ltd (United Kingdom) 407
'Sovetskaya Entsiklopediya', Izdatelstvo, (Union of Soviet Soleiil Republics) 366
'Sovetskaya Rossiya', Izdatelstvo, (Union of Soviet Socialist Republics) 366
'Sovetskii Khudozhnik', Izdatelstvo, (Union of Soviet Socialist Republics) 366
'Sovetskii Kompozitor', Izdatelstvo, (Union of Soviet Socialist Republics) 366
'Sovetskoe Radio', Izdatelstvo, Glavnyi Pochtamt p/ya693 (Union of Soviet Socialist Republics) 366
Soviet Land Nehru Awards (India) 198
Sovietskii Pisatel, Izdatelstvo, (Union of Soviet Socialist Republics) 366
Sovremennik Publishers (Union of Soviet Socialist Republics) 366
Spangenberg (Federal Republic of Germany) 162
Spanish Book Center (Spain) 317
Spanish Book Club (United Kingdom) 415

Spanos, Costas, (Greece) 177
Sparevirke, A/S, (Denmark) 77
Sparfrämjandet, Förlagsaktiebolag (Sweden) 336
Spearman, Neville, (United Kingdom) 407
Spectrum, Het, NV (Belgium) 42
Spectrum, Scherz Taschenbuch Verlag, (Switzerland) 353
Spectrum, Uitgeverij Het, BV (Netherlands) 267
Spectrum Amsterdam (Netherlands) 267
Spectrum Publications (India) 195
Spectrum Publications Pty Ltd (Australia) 18
Spectrum Verlag Stuttgart GmbH (Federal Republic of Germany) 162
Spee — Buchverlag GmbH (Federal Republic of Germany) 162
Speer-Verlag (Switzerland) 353
Spektra, Bokförlaget, AB (Sweden) 336
Spemann, W, Verlag (Federal Republic of Germany) 162
Sperling & Kupfer, Libreria, (Italy) 222
Sperling e Kupfer Editori SpA (Italy) 220
Spes SA (Switzerland) 353
Sphere Books Ltd (United Kingdom) 407
Sphinx, Le, SA (Belgium) 42
Sphinx, The, (Egypt) 82
Sphinx Verlag (Switzerland) 353
Spiegelserie (Netherlands) 269
Spiess, Verlag Volker, (Federal Republic of Germany) 162
Splichal, Anciens Etablissements, SA (Belgium) 42
Společnost přátel knihy pro mládež (Czechoslovakia) 73
Společnost pro Československou literaturu, Index-, v zahraničí (Czechoslovakia) 73
Společnost pro krásné písmo a typografii (Czechoslovakia) 70
Spolek Českých bibliofilu (Czechoslovakia) 73
Spon, E & F N, Ltd (United Kingdom) 407
Sponholtz, Adolf, Verlag (Federal Republic of Germany) 162
Sport (Czechoslovakia) 71
Sport i Turystyka, Wydawnictwo, (Sport and Tourism Publishers) (Poland) 295
Sport Verlags AG (Switzerland) 353
Sporting Handbooks Ltd (United Kingdom) 407
Sportska Knjiga (Yugoslavia) 430
Sportsman's Book Club (United Kingdom) 415
Sportverlag (German Democratic Republic) 119
Spotlight Publications (Israel) 209
Sprachmethodik, Verlag für, (Federal Republic of Germany) 162
Språkförlaget Skriptor AB (Sweden) 336
Språktjänst (Translation Agencies and Associations) (Sweden) 339
Spring Books (United Kingdom) 407
Springer-Verlag Berlin-Heidelberg-New York (Federal Republic of Germany) 163
Springer-Verlag KG (Austria) 28
Springwood Books Ltd (United Kingdom) 407
Spruyt, van Mantgem en de Does BV (Netherlands) 267
Spur (Federal Republic of Germany) 163
Spurbooks Ltd (United Kingdom) 407
Sreberk, J, (Israel) 209
Sreberk, S, (Israel) 209
Sree Rama Publishers (India) 195
Sri Jaya, Pustaka, Sdn Bhd (Malaysia) 247
Sri Lanka, Booksellers' Association of, (Sri Lanka) 329
Sri Lanka Library Association, University of Sri Lanka (Sri Lanka) 330
Sri Lanka National Library Services Board (Sri Lanka) 330
Sri Lanka Publishers' Association (Sri Lanka) 329
Sri Lanka Publishing Co (Sri Lanka) 330
Sri Nakharinwirot University Library (Thailand) 360
Srpska Knjižvena Zadruga (Yugoslavia) 430
Srpske, Biblioteka, Akademije Nauka i Umetnosti (Yugoslavia) 431
Staackmann, L, Verlag KG (Federal Republic of Germany) 163
Staatlich Genehmigte Gesellschaft der Autoren, Komponisten und Musikverleger (AKM) reg Gen mbH (Austria) 24
Staatlich genehmigte Literarische Verwertungsgesellschaft (LVG) reg Gen mbH (Austria) 24
Staats- und Universitätsbibliothek (Federal Republic of Germany) 171
Staatsarchiv, Zentrales, (German Democratic Republic) 120
Staatsbibliothek Bamberg (Federal Republic of Germany) 171
Staatsbibliothek Preussischer Kulturbesitz (Federal Republic of Germany) 171
Staatsdrukkerij en Uitgeverijbedrijf (Netherlands) 267
Staatsverlag der Deutschen Demokratischen Republik (German Democratic Republic) 119
Stabenfeldt Forlag (Norway) 283
Stacey International (United Kingdom) 407
Stadion, Editura, (Sports and Tourism Publishing House) (Romania) 304
Stadsbibliotheek (Belgium) 44

Stadt- und Bezirksbibliothek Leipzig (German Democratic Republic) 120
Stadt- und Universitätsbibliothek (Federal Republic of Germany) 171
Stadt- und Universitätsbibliothek (Switzerland) 356
Städte-Verlag, E v Wagner und J Mitterhuber (Federal Republic of Germany) 162
Stafleu's Wetenschappelijke Uitgeversmaatschappij BV (Netherlands) 267
Stage 1 (United Kingdom) 407
Stäheli, Buchhandlung Kurt, & Co (Switzerland) 356
Stähle und Friedel Verlagsgesellschaft mbH und Co (Federal Republic of Germany) 163
Stahleisen, Verlag, mbH (Federal Republic of Germany) 163
Stainer & Bell Ltd (United Kingdom) 407
Stalling Verlag GmbH, Druck und Verlagshaus (Federal Republic of Germany) 163
Stam Press Ltd (United Kingdom) 407
Stam Technische Boeken (Netherlands) 267
Stam Tijdschriften BV (Netherlands) 267
Stam/Robijns (Netherlands) 267
Stamford College Publishers (Republic of Singapore) 309
Stümpfli, Verlag, & Cie AG (Switzerland) 353
Standaard Hoofdstadboekhandel (Belgium) 44
Standaard Uitgeverij (NV Scriptoria) (Belgium) 42
Standaard Uitgeverij en Distributie BV (Netherlands) 267
Standard, The, Book Depot (India) 195
Standard, The, Bookshop (Tanzania) 358
Standard Book Numbering Agency Ltd (United Kingdom) 369
Standard Books Ltd (Zambia) 434
Standartov, Znak Pochyota Order Izdatelstvo, (Union of Soviet Socialist Republics) 366
Standing Conference of African Library Schools (SCALS) (International Organizations) 439
Standing Conference of African University Libraries (SCAUL) (International Organizations) 440
Standing Conference of National and University Libraries (SCONUL) (United Kingdom) 417
Standing Conference on Library Materials on Africa (SCOLMA) (International Organizations) 440
Stanford Maritime Ltd (United Kingdom) 407
Stanké, Les Editions Internationales Alain, (France) 108
Stanton, Ernest, Publishers (Pty) Ltd (Republic of South Africa) 314
Stapp Verlag Wolfgang Stapp (Federal Republic of Germany) 163
Stappaerts, NV Uitgeverij, (Belgium) 42
Star, Pustaka, (Indonesia) 200
Star, The, Press (Brunei) 57
Star Book Bank (India) 197
Star Books (United Kingdom) 407
Star Publications (P) Ltd (India) 197
Star Publications (P) Ltd (India) 195
Starczewski, Hanns-Joachim, Verlag/Künstlerhof-Galerie (Federal Republic of Germany) 163
Starke, Harold, Ltd (United Kingdom) 407
State Archives (Mongolian People's Republic) 255
State Book Trading Office (Mongolian People's Republic) 255
State Central Library (Democratic People's Republic of Korea) 171
State Central Library (India) 197
State Librarians' Council (Australia) 20
State Library (Burma) 60
State Library (Republic of South Africa) 316
State Library of New South Wales, The, (Australia) 20
State Library of Queensland (Australia) 20
State Library of South Australia (Australia) 20
State Library of Tasmania (Australia) 20
State Library of Victoria (Australia) 20
State of Victoria Short Story Awards (Australia) 23
State Press (Mongolian People's Republic) 255
State Prize for Children's and Youth Literature (Netherlands) 271
State Prize for Literature (also known as Pieter Cornelisz Hooft Prize) (Netherlands) 271
State Prizes for Literature (Finland) 88
State Stipendium for Literature (Austria) 31
Stationery & Educational Book Centre (Jamaica) 225
Stationery Office (Oifig an tSolathair) (Republic of Ireland) 204
Statistical Publications and Printing Board of the Central Statistical Office (Poland) 295
Statisticke a evidencní vydavatelství tiskopisu (Czechoslovakia) 71
Statistics Library (Finland) 87
Statistika (Union of Soviet Socialist Republics) 366
Statistisk Sentralbyras Bibliotek (Library of the Central Bureau of Statistics) (Norway) 284
Statistiska Centralbyråns Bibliotek (Sweden) 338
Statisztikai Kiadó Vállalat (Hungary) 183
Státní pedagogické nakladatelství (Czechoslovakia) 71
Štátní technická knihovna (Czechoslovakia) 73
Štátní technická knihovna v Brně (Czechoslovakia) 73
Státní vědecká knihovna (Czechoslovakia) 73

Státní vědecká knihovna (Czechoslovakia) 73
Statní zemědělské nakladatelství (Czechoslovakia) 72
Statsbiblioteket (Denmark) 79
Stauda, Johannes, Verlag (Federal Republic of Germany) 163
Stavanger Bibliotek (Stavanger Municipal Library) (Norway) 284
Steamships Trading Co (Papua New Guinea) 288
Stechert-Macmillan Inc (France) 111
Steensballes, P F, Boghandels Eftg (Norway) 283
Stegeland, Leif, Förlag AB (Sweden) 336
Steimatzky's Agency Ltd (Israel) 209
Steimatzky's Agency Ltd (Israel) 210
Steindecker, Editions Robert, (Editions RST) (France) 108
Steiner, Franz, Verlag GmbH (Federal Republic of Germany) 163
Steiner, Rudolf, Press (United Kingdom) 407
Steiner, Rudolf, Verlag (Switzerland) 353
Steinhauser, Dr Karl, (Austria) 28
Steinkopf, J F, Verlag GmbH (Federal Republic of Germany) 163
Steinkopff, Dr Dietrich, Verlag (Federal Republic of Germany) 163
Steintor Verlag, Rudolf Jüdes (Federal Republic of Germany) 163
Stella, Editorial, (Argentina) 7
Stella, Editorial, (Dominican Republic) 80
Stelle, Le, SRL (Italy) 220
Stenersen, Rolf, Prize (Norway) 284
Stenvalls, Frank, Förlag (Sweden) 336
Stenvert, Uitgeverij M, en Zoon BV (Netherlands) 267
Stephanus Edition Verlags GmbH (Federal Republic of Germany) 163
Stephens, Patrick, Ltd (United Kingdom) 407
Stephens Book Department (Trinidad and Tobago) 361
Stephenson, Carl, Verlag (Federal Republic of Germany) 163
Steppe (Belgium) 42
Ster, De, PVBA (Belgium) 42
Sterling Publishers Pvt Ltd (India) 195
Sterling Publishers Pvt Ltd (India) 197
Stern-Verlag Janssen und Co (Federal Republic of Germany) 163
Stern-Verlag Janssen und Co (Federal Republic of Germany) 170
Sternberg-Verlag (Federal Republic of Germany) 164
Stevens & Sons Ltd (United Kingdom) 408
Stewart, Bertrand, Prize (United Kingdom) 421
Steyler Verlag (Federal Republic of Germany) 164
Stichting Bibliotheek en Documentatieacademies (Foundation for Library and Documentation Academies) (Netherlands) 258
Stichting Speurwerk betreffende het Boek (Book Research Foundation) (Netherlands) 258
Stichting Wetenschappelijke Bibliotheek (Scientific Library Foundation) (Netherlands Antilles) 271
Stiehm, Lothar, Verlag GmbH (Federal Republic of Germany) 164
Stiftelsen Svenska Barnboksinstitutet (Sweden) 338
Stiftsbibliothek (Switzerland) 356
Stiintifica si Enciclopedica, Editura, (Romania) 304
Stillitron (United Kingdom) 408
Stobart & Son Ltd (United Kingdom) 408
Stock, Editions, (France) 108
Stocker, Josef, AG (Switzerland) 353
Stocker, Leopold, Verlag (Austria) 28
Stocker-Schmid, Verlag, AG (Switzerland) 353
Stockholm International Peace Research Institute (SIPRI) (International Organizations) 443
Stockholm Universitets Bibliotek (Stockholm University Library) (Sweden) 338
Stockholms Stadsbibliotek (Sweden) 338
Stockton House (New Zealand) 274
Stockum, Uitgeverij W P Van, en Zoon NV (Netherlands) 267
Stok, Ad M C, -Zuid-Hollandsche Uitgeversmaatschappij BV (Netherlands) 267
Stollfuss Verlag GmbH & Co KG (Federal Republic of Germany) 164
Story, E, -Scientia PVBA (Belgium) 44
Story, E, -Scientia PVBA (Belgium) 42
Stowarzyszenie Autorow Zaiks (Poland) 297
Stowarzyszenie Bibliotekarzy Polskich (Poland) 297
Stowarzyszenie Ksiegarzy Polskich (Association of Polish Booksellers) (Poland) 293
Strakosch, Carl, & Olaf Nordgreen (Denmark) 78
Strandbergs Forlag (Denmark) 77
Strassova, Mme Hélèna, (France) 110
Středočeské nakladatelství knihkupectví (Czechoslovakia) 72
Strega Prize (Italy) 223
Strengholt's, A J G, Boeken Anno 1928 BV (Netherlands) 267
Strom-Verlag (Switzerland) 354
Stroyizdat Publishing House (Union of Soviet Socialist Republics) 366

Strubes Forlag og Boghandel A/S (Denmark) 77
Stručna Štampa (Yugoslavia) 430
Struik, C, Booksellers (Republic of South Africa) 315
Struik (Pty) Ltd (Republic of South Africa) 314
Student Christian Movement Press (United Kingdom) 408
Studentlitteratur AB (Sweden) 336
Students', The, Book Co (India) 195
Studia, Editions, SA (France) 108
Studia Croatica (Argentina) 7
Studio, Librería, (Chile) 63
Studio, Librería, (Mexico) 254
Studio Book Club (Chile) 62
Studio Editoriale (Italy) 221
Studio Publications (Ipswich) Ltd (United Kingdom) 408
Studio Vista (United Kingdom) 408
Studium, Edizioni, (Vita Nova SpA) (Italy) 221
Studium, Librería, (Peru) 290
Studium, Librería, SA (Peru) 289
Studium, Verlag für das, der Arbeiterbewegung (Federal Republic of Germany) 164
Studium Ediciones (Spain) 326
Stürtz Verlag (Federal Republic of Germany) 164
Stuttgarter Verlagskontor GmbH (Federal Republic of Germany) 164
Stvarnost (Yugoslavia) 430
Styria (Austria) 30
Styria, Verlag, (Austria) 28
Su Hoc (Historical) Publishing House (Socialist Republic of Viet Nam) 426
Su Librería (Ecuador) 81
Su That (Truth) Publishing House (Socialist Republic of Viet Nam) 426
Succes BV (Netherlands) 267
Success Publications (Kenya) 236
Sud Editions (Tunisia) 362
Sudan, The, Bookshop (Sudan) 330
Sudan Library Association (Sudan) 331
Südbuch Vertriebsgesellschaft mbH (Federal Republic of Germany) 164
Süddeutsche Verlagsgesellschaft Ulm (Federal Republic of Germany) 164
Süddeutscher Verlag Buchverlag (Federal Republic of Germany) 164
Sudha Publications Pvt Ltd (India) 195
'Sudostroenie', Izdatelstvo, (Union of Soviet Socialist Republics) 366
Sudri, Bókaútgáfan, (Iceland) 185
Südwest Verlag GmbH und Co KG (Federal Republic of Germany) 164
Suenson, Finn, Forlag (Denmark) 77
Sufi Publishing Co Ltd (United Kingdom) 408
Sugar and Snails Books (Australia) 18
Sugarco Edizioni SRL (Italy) 221
Suhrkamp Verlag KG (Federal Republic of Germany) 164
Suksapan Panich (Business Organization of Teachers' Institute) (Thailand) 359
Suksit Siam Co Ltd (Thailand) 359
Suksit Siam Co Ltd (Thailand) 360
Süleymaniye Kütüphanesi Müdürlügü (Library of the Süleymaniye) (Turkey) 363
Sulina, Livraria, (Brazil) 56
Sulina, Livraría, Editôra (Brazil) 54
Sultan Chand and Sons (India) 195
Sultan's Library (Cyprus) 69
Suma, Librería, (Venezuela) 425
Suman Prakashan (P) Ltd (India) 195
Sumatera (Indonesia) 200
Summit Books (Australia) 18
Sumur Bandung (Indonesia) 200
Sumus Verlag Jutta Gütermann (Switzerland) 354
Sun Books Pty Ltd (Australia) 18
'Sun News-Pictorial' Holiday Short Story Festival Awards (Australia) 23
Sun Yat-Sen Library (Hong Kong) 181
Sundems, H, Bokhandel A/S (Norway) 283
Sundial (United Kingdom) 408
Suomalainen Kirjakauppa (Finland) 87
Suomalainen Tiedeakatemia (Finland) 88
Suomalaisen Kirjallisuuden Seura (Finland) 88
Suomalaisen Kirjallisuuden Seura (Finland) 87
Suomalaisen Kirjallisuuden Seura (Finnish Literature Society) (Finland) 86
Suomen Antikvariaattiyhdistys-Finska Antikvariatiyhdistys (Finland) 85
Suomen Arvostelijain Liitto (Finland) 88
Suomen Kääntäjäin Yhdists (Finnish Translators' Association) (Finland) 88
Suomen Kirjailijaliitto (Finland) 88
Suomen Kirjallisuuspalvelun Seura (Finland) 87
Suomen Kirjastonhoitajat — Finlands Bibliotekarier ry (Finland) 87
Suomen Kirjastoseura (Finland) 87
Suomen Kustannusyhdistys (Finland) 85
Suomen Nortenkirjaneuvosto (Finland) 85
Suomen Nuortenkirjaneuvosto ry (Finland) 88
Suomen Tieteellinen Kirjastoseura (Finland) 87
Supraphon (Czechoslovakia) 72

Sur, Editorial, SA (Argentina) 7
Sur Prize (India) 199
Surinam Publishers' Association (Suriname) 331
Suriwongs Book Centre (Thailand) 360
Suriyaban Publishers (Thailand) 359
Surjeet Book Depot (India) 195
Surrey University Press (United Kingdom) 408
Susaeta, Ediciones, SA (Spain) 326
Sussex University Press (United Kingdom) 408
Sutpaisarn (Thailand) 359
Suuri Suomalainen Kirjakerho Oy (Finland) 87
Suva Book Shop (Fiji) 85
Suva City Library (Fiji) 85
Suyuz Knigoizdatelite i Knizharite (Bulgaria) 58
Svalan, Bokklubben (Sweden) 338
Svaz českých spisovatelu (Czechoslovakia) 73
Svensk Kartjänst AB (Sweden) 336
Svenska Antikvariatföreningen (Sweden) 331
Svenska Arkivsamfundet (Swedish Association of Archivists) (Sweden) 338
Svenska Bibliotekariesamfundet (Sweden) 338
Svenska Bokförläggareföreningen (Sweden) 331
Svenska Bokhandels-Medhjälpare-Föreningen (Sweden) 331
Svenska Bokhandlareföreningen (Sweden) 331
Svenska Folkbibliotekarieförbundet (Sweden) 338
Svenska Litteratursällskapet i Finland (Finland) 88
Svenska Musikförläggareföreningen (Swedish Music Publishers' Association) (Sweden) 331
Svenska Österbottens Litteraturförening (Sweden) 339
Svenska Österbottens Litteraturförening (Finland) 88
Svenska Utbildningsförlaget Liber AB (Sweden) 336
Svepomoc (Czechoslovakia) 72
Sveriges Allmänna Biblioteksförening (Swedish Library Association) (Sweden) 338
Sveriges B-Bokhandlareförbund (Swedish Association of Smaller Booksellers) (Sweden) 331
Sveriges Exportrads Förlag (Sweden) 336
Sveriges Författarförbund (Sweden) 339
Sveriges Lantbruksuniversitets Bibliotek (Libraries of the Swedish University of Agricultural Sciences) (Sweden) 338
Sveriges Radios Förlag (Sweden) 336
Sveriges Vetenskapliga Specialbiblioteks Förening (Association of Special Research Libraries) (Sweden) 338
Svet Knjige (Yugoslavia) 430
Svjetlost (Yugoslavia) 431
Svjetlost (Yugoslavia) 430
Svoboda (Czechoslovakia) 72
Svoboda Book Club (Czechoslovakia) 72
'Svyaz', Izdatelstvo, (Union of Soviet Socialist Republics) 367
Św Wojciecha, Ksiegarnia, (St Adalbert's Bookshop) (Poland) 295
Swan (India) 195
Swan Book Store (Brunei) 57
Swan Productions AG (Switzerland) 354
Swanin, Anni, Prize (Finland) 88
Swaziland National Library Service (Swaziland) 331
Swaziland News Agency (Swaziland) 331
Swedenborg Institut (Switzerland) 354
Swedish Academy Prizes (Sweden) 339
Swedish into Foreign Language Translation Prize (Sweden) 339
Swedish Linguistics Prize (Sweden) 339
Sweet & Maxwell Ltd (United Kingdom) 408
Sweet and Maxwell (NZ) Ltd (New Zealand) 274
Swets en Zeitlinger BV (Netherlands) 267
Swindon Book Co (Hong Kong) 181
Syarikat Cultural Supplies Sdn Bhd (Malaysia) 247
Syarikat Dian Sdn Bhd (Malaysia) 247
Syarikat United Book Sdn Bhd (Malaysia) 247
Sydney University Press (Australia) 18
Symposion-Verlag GmbH (Federal Republic of Germany) 164
Syndicat belge de la Librairie ancienne et moderne (Belgium) 42
Syndicat de la Librairie ancienne et du Commerce de l'Estampe en Suisse (Vereinigung der Buchantiquare und Kupferstichhändler in der Schweiz) (Switzerland) 340
Syndicat des Critiques littéraires (Association of Literary Critics) (France) 112
Syndicat des Editeurs du Maroc (Federation of Moroccan Publishers) (Morocco) 256
Syndicat des Libraires (Socialist Republic of Viet Nam) 425
Syndicat des Librairies d'Algérie (Algeria) 2
Syndicat des Librairies de Tunisie (Tunisian Booksellers' Association) (Tunisia) 361
Syndicat des Librairies du Moroc (Morocco) 256
Syndicat des Réprésentants littéraires français (Association of French Literary Agents) (France) 112
Syndicat National de la Librairie ancienne et moderne (France) 88

Syndicat national de l'Edition (French Publishers' Association) (France) 89
Syndicat national des Annuaires et Supports divers de Publicité (France) 89
Syndicat national des Importateurs et Exportateurs de Livres (France) 89
Syndikat Autoren- und Verlagsgesellschaft (Federal Republic of Germany) 164
Syokabo Publishing Co Ltd (Japan) 230
Syrian Documentation Papers (Syria) 357
Syrian Patriarchal Seminary, Library of the, (Lebanon) 241
Syropoulos Adelfoi OE Ekdotikos Oikos (Greece) 177
Systems Publications Ltd (United Kingdom) 408
Szabó, Fővárosi, Ervin Könyvtár (Ervin Szabó Municipal Library) (Hungary) 183
Szent benedekrend (Library of the Benedictine Abbey) (Hungary) 183
Szépirodalmi Kiadó (Publishing House of Belles Lettres) (Hungary) 183
Szkolne i Pedagogiczne, Wydawnictwa, (The Publishing House for School and Pedagogical Books) (Poland) 296
Szot Literary Prizes (Hungary) 184

T B L (Tübinger Beiträge zur Linguistik) Verlag (Federal Republic of Germany) 164
T E A (Tipográfica Editora Argentina) (Argentina) 7
T E B R O C (Tehran Book Processing Centre) (Iran) 202
T M P Book Department (Tanzania) 358
T M P Book Department (Tanzania) 358
T R-Verlagsunion GmbH (Federal Republic of Germany) 164
Tabajara, Edições, (Brazil) 55
Tabard Press Ltd (United Kingdom) 408
Table Ronde (Les Editions de la) (France) 108
Tabor Publications (United Kingdom) 408
Taeguk Publishing Co (Republic of Korea) 239
Tafelberg Publishers Ltd (Republic of South Africa) 314
Tages-Nachrichten (Switzerland) 354
Tah Chung Book Co (China (Taiwan)) 64
Tai Kuen Book Co (Hong Kong) 181
Taipei Municipal Library (China (Taiwan)) 64
Taipei Publications Trading Co (China (Taiwan)) 64
Taishukan Publishing Co Ltd (Taishukan Shoten) (Japan) 230
Tait, Gordon, Bookseller Ltd (New Zealand) 275
Taiwan Branch Library, National Central Library (China (Taiwan)) 64
Taizé, Les Presses de, (France) 108
Taj Co Ltd (Pakistan) 286
Tájékoztatási tudományos társaság (Information Science Society) (Hungary) 184
Takahashi Shoten Co Ltd (Japan) 230
Takariva, Imprimerie, (Democratic Republic of Madagascar) 244
Talbot Press Ltd (Republic of Ireland) 204
Tallandier, Librairie Jules, (France) 108
Tallboy Publications (Australia) 18
Taller Ediciones JB (Spain) 326
Talleres Graficos Mundial SRL (Argentina) 7
Tallis Press Ltd (United Kingdom) 408
Talmudic Encyclopaedia Publications (Israel) 209
Talmy, Franklin Ltd (United Kingdom) 408
Tamaraw Publishing Co (Philippines) 292
Tamayo, Franz, Prize (Bolivia) 48
Tamburini Editore SpA (Italy) 221
Tamgu Dang Book Centre (Republic of Korea) 239
Tammi Kustannusosakeyhtiö (Finland) 86
Tampere Prize (Finland) 88
Tampereen Kirjakauppa Oy (Finland) 87
Tampereen Yliopiston Kirjasto (Finland) 87
Táncsics Szakszervezeti Kiadó (Publishing House of the Trade Union Movement) (Hungary) 183
Tandem Publishing Limited (United Kingdom) 408
Tanizaki Junichiro Prize (Japan) 234
Tanko-Sha Publishing Co Ltd (Japan) 231
Tankönyvkiadó Vállalat (Hungary) 183
Tantivy Press (United Kingdom) 408
Tanum-Norli (Johan Grundt Tanum Forlag og Olaf Norlis Forlag A/S) (Norway) 283
Tanum/Cammermeyer (Norway) 283
Tanzania Elimu Supplies (Tanzania) 358
Tanzania Library Association (Tanzania) 358
Tanzania Library Service (Tanzania) 358
Tanzania Library Service (Tanzania) 358
Tanzania Library Service (Tanzania) 358
Tanzania Mission Press (Tanzania) 358
Tanzania Mission Press (Tanzania) 358
Tanzania Publishing House (Tanzania) 358
Tapir (Norway) 283
Tara Press (Fiji) 85
Taraporevala Publishing Industries Pvt Ltd (India) 195
Taraporevala Sons & Co Pvt Ltd (India) 195

Tarate (Indonesia) 200
Tarbut Vehinuch (Israel) 209
Tardy, Editions, SA (France) 108
Target (United Kingdom) 408
Target Publishers (Edms) Bpk (Republic of South Africa) 314
Taride, Editions, Sàrl (France) 108
Tarshish Books (Israel) 209
Tartu Riikliku Ulikooli Teaduslik Raamatükogu (Union of Soviet Socialist Republics) 367
Tasmanian Booksellers' Association (Australia) 10
Tassier, Suzanne, Prize (Belgium) 46
Tata McGraw-Hill Publishing Co Ltd (India) 195
Tate Gallery Publications (United Kingdom) 408
Tatran (Czechoslovakia) 72
Tattoo (United Kingdom) 408
Tavistock Publications Ltd (United Kingdom) 408
Tawjih, al-, Press (Syria) 357
Taxation (Pakistan) 286
Taylor, Alister, Publishers (New Zealand) 274
Taylor, Peter, & Co Ltd (Guyana) 179
Taylor, Reginald, Prize (United Kingdom) 421
Taylor & Francis Ltd (United Kingdom) 408
Taylor-Whitehead, W J, (France) 110
Taylorix Fachverlag Stiegler und Co (Federal Republic of Germany) 164
Tcherikover Publishers Ltd (Israel) 209
Tchernichowsky Prize (Israel) 211
Tchou, Claude, Editeur (France) 108
Teach Yourself Books (United Kingdom) 408
Teachers' Book Centre Ltd (Jamaica) 225
Teacher's Bookshelf (Australia) 19
Teachers' Club Library (People's Democratic Republic of Yemen) 426
Teachers' Union (Israel) 210
Teakfield Ltd (United Kingdom) 408
Technica (Bulgaria) 58
Technical Chamber, Library of the, of Greece (Greece) 178
Technical Chamber of Greece (Greece) 177
Technical High School Library (Namibia) 257
Technical Institutes, Central Library of the Higher, (Bulgaria) 59
Technical Library, Central, (Bulgaria) 59
Technical Press, The, Ltd (United Kingdom) 408
Technical University Library (Turkey) 363
Techniek, De, (Belgium) 42
Technik, VEB Verlag, (German Democratic Republic) 119
Technik Tabellen Verlag Fikentscher und Co (Federal Republic of Germany) 164
Technip, Société des Éditions, (France) 108
Technique et Documentation (Librairie Lavoisier) (France) 108
Technique et Vulgarisation SA (France) 108
Techniques de l'Ingénieur Sàrl (France) 108
Techniques Professionels, Editions, (France) 108
Technitrain (Pty) Ltd (Republic of South Africa) 314
Tecni Ciencia Libros (Venezuela) 425
Tecnicos e Cientificos, Livros, Editora SA (Brazil) 55
Tecnoprint SA (Brazil) 55
Tecnos, Editorial, SA (Spain) 326
Teduca Tecnicas Educativas (Venezuela) 424
Teenage (Australia) 19
Tegopoulos (Greece) 177
Tehnica, Editura, (Romania) 304
Tehnička Knjiga (Yugoslavia) 430
Tehnička Knjiga (Yugoslavia) 431
Tehnička Knjiga (Yugoslavia) 430
Tehnika (Yugoslavia) 430
Tehran, Central Library and Documentation Centre of, University (Iran) 202
Tehran Book Processing Centre (TEBROC) (Iran) 201
Tehran Economist (Iran) 202
Tehran University Press (Iran) 202
Teide, Editorial, SA (Spain) 326
Teikoku-Shoin Co Ltd (Japan) 231
Teirlinck, Auguste, Prize (Belgium) 46
Teissonnière, Paul, Prize (France) 115
Teixeira, A M, e Cia (Filhos) Lda (Livraria Classica Editora) (Portugal) 301
Tejerina, Alfonso, Ltda (Bolivia) 47
Tek Translation & International Print Ltd (United Kingdom) 421
Teknisk Forlag A/S (Denmark) 77
Tekniska Litteratursällskapet (Swedish Society for Technical Documentation) (Sweden) 338
Teknografiska Institutet AB (Sweden) 337
Teknologisk Forlag (Norway) 283
Teknologisk Instituts Forlag (Denmark) 77
Tel Aviv University, Publications Sales Division (Israel) 210
Tel Aviv University Library (Israel) 211
Télédition, La, (France) 108
Téléscope, Le, (France) 110
Telex-Verlag Jaeger Waldmann (Federal Republic of Germany) 164

Telford, Thomas, Ltd (United Kingdom) 408
Tella, Instituto Torcuato di, (Argentina) 7
Teloeken, Alf, Verlag KG (Federal Republic of Germany) 164
Telos series of Paperbacks (Federal Republic of Germany) 164
Telstar, Ediciones, (Spain) 326
Tema — Editions (France) 109
Temco Publishing Ltd (Zambia) 434
Temis, Editorial, Ltda (Colombia) 66
Temis, Librería, Ltda (Colombia) 66
Tempel, Uitgeverij De, (Belgium) 42
Temple Press (United Kingdom) 408
Temple Smith, Maurice, Ltd (United Kingdom) 408
Tengler, A & G, (Austria) 30
Ténicos Asociados, Editores, SA (Spain) 326
Tenri Central Library (Japan) 232
Tequi, Librairie Pierre, et Editions Tequi (France) 109
Tercer, Ediciones, Mundo Ltda (Colombia) 66
Tercer Mundo, Librería, (Colombia) 66
Teredo Books Ltd (United Kingdom) 409
Terra Sancta Arts (Israel) 210
Tertulia, Librería La, (Puerto Rico) 302
Tessloff, Ernst, Verlag (Federal Republic of Germany) 164
Tests, Editions, (France) 109
Teti, Nicola, e C Editore SRL (Italy) 221
Tetrad Press (United Kingdom) 409
Teubner, B G, GmbH (Federal Republic of Germany) 164
Teubner, BSB B G, Verlagsgesellschaft (German Democratic Republic) 119
Text Book Centre Ltd (Kenya) 236
Text Books Malaysia Sdn Bhd (Malaysia) 247
Text und Kritik, Edition, GmbH (Federal Republic of Germany) 164
Textbook, The, Centre Ltd (Kenya) 236
Textbook Publishers' Association of Japan (Kyokasho Kyokai) (Japan) 225
Thacker & Co Ltd (India) 196
Thai Commercial Printing Press (Thailand) 359
Thai Inc (Thailand) 359
Thai Library Association (Thailand) 360
Thai National Documentation Centre (TNDC) (Thailand) 360
Thai Watana Panich (Thailand) 359
Thames & Hudson Ltd (United Kingdom) 409
Thames Translations (United Kingdom) 421
Thammasat University Library (Thailand) 360
Than Myit Baho Publishing House (Burma) 59
Thaning og Appels Forlag (Denmark) 77
Theatrum Orbis Terrarum (Netherlands) 267
Theiss, Konrad, Verlag GmbH (Federal Republic of Germany) 164
Thekes, Librería, (Puerto Rico) 302
Theodor (Haiti) 179
Theologischer Verlag (wholesaler) (Switzerland) 356
Theologischer Verlag AG (Switzerland) 354
Theologischer Verlag R Brockhaus (Federal Republic of Germany) 164
Theoria, Ediciones, SRL (Argentina) 7
Theosophical Publishing, The, House (India) 196
Thesen Verlag Vowinckel und Co (Federal Republic of Germany) 164
Theseus Verlag AG (Switzerland) 354
Thiele und Schwarz, Druck- und Verlagshaus, (Federal Republic of Germany) 165
Thielen, Verlag-Buchhandlung Joseph, (Luxembourg) 244
Thieme, BV Uitgeverij en Boekhandel W J, & Cie (Netherlands) 267
Thieme, Georg, Verlag KG (Federal Republic of Germany) 165
Thieme, VEB Georg, (German Democratic Republic) 119
Thiemig, Verlag Karl, AG (Federal Republic of Germany) 165
Thienemanns, K, Verlag (Federal Republic of Germany) 165
Thin, James, Bookseller (United Kingdom) 415
Third World First Publications (Nigeria) 279
Þjóðsaga, Bókaútgáfan, (Iceland) 185
Þjóðskjalasafn (National Archives) (Iceland) 186
Thomas, A, (United Kingdom) 409
Thomas-Verlag (Switzerland) 354
Thompson, Henry, Ltd (United Kingdom) 409
Thomson Book Ltd (United Kingdom) 409
Thomson Press (India) Ltd (India) 196
Thomson Publications South Africa (Pty) Ltd (Republic of South Africa) 314
Thone, Imprimerie-Editions Georges, Sciences et Lettres (Belgium) 42
Thorbecke, Jan, Verlag KG (Federal Republic of Germany) 165
Thornes, Stanley, (Publishers) Ltd (United Kingdom) 409
Thornhill Press Ltd (United Kingdom) 409
Thornton Cox Ltd (United Kingdom) 409
Thorpe, D W, Pty Ltd (Australia) 18
Thorpe, F A, (Publishing) Ltd (United Kingdom) 409

Thorsons Publishers Ltd (United Kingdom) 409
Three Hierarchs, Library of the, (Greece) 178
Thriller Book Club (United Kingdom) 415
Thu Viên Quóc Gia Viet Nam (Socialist Republic of Viet Nam) 426
Thudhammawaddy Press (Burma) 59
Thule, The, Press (United Kingdom) 409
Thun, Verlags und Versandbuchhandlung, AG (Switzerland) 354
Thwe Thauk (Burma) 59
Tiden, Bokförlags AB, (Sweden) 337
Tiden Norsk Forlag (Norway) 283
Tidnings AB Dagen (Sweden) 337
Tiempo, Editorial, Nuevo SA (Venezuela) 424
Tiempo Contemporaneo, Editorial, (Argentina) 7
Tiempo de Hoy, Ediciones, (Argentina) 7
Tiers Monde, Librairie du, (Algeria) 2
Tieteellisen Informoinnin Neuvosto (Finland) 87
Tieteellisten Kirjastojen Virkailijat — Vetenskapliga Bibliotekens Tjänstemannaförening ry (Finland) 87
Tieteellisten Seurain Kirjasto (Finland) 87
Tietoteos Publishing Co (Finland) 86
Tiger (United Kingdom) 409
Tijdstroom, NV Uitgeversmaatschappij de, (Netherlands) 267
Tilburg University Press (Netherlands) 267
Time — Life International de México, SA (Mexico) 253
Time-Life Books (Netherlands) 267
Times Book Centre (Hong Kong) 181
Times Book Club (Nigeria) 279
Times Books Ltd (United Kingdom) 409
Times Bookshop Ltd (Malawi) 245
Times Distributors Sdn Bhd (Malaysia) 247
Times Educational Co Ltd (Malaysia) 247
Times Educational Co Ltd (Hong Kong) 181
'Times Educational Supplement', The, Information Book Awards (International Literary Prizes) 452
Times Stores Ltd (Jamaica) 225
Timmins, Howard B, (Pty) Ltd (Republic of South Africa) 314
Timun, Editorial, Mas SA (Spain) 326
Tin Fung Book Co (Hong Kong) 181
Tintamas Indonesia PT (Indonesia) 200
Tipografia Nacional (Netherlands Antilles) 271
Tipografia Poliglotta Vaticana (Vatican City State) 423
Tipografia Stazionne SA (Switzerland) 354
"Tips für Trips", Verlag, (Federal Republic of Germany) 165
Tiranti, Alec, Ltd (United Kingdom) 409
Tirona, Ramona S, Memorial Library (Philippines) 292
Tiskarna Ljudske Pravice (Yugoslavia) 430
Tisserand, Lucien, Prize (France) 115
Tiszánínneni Református Egyházkerület Nagykönyvtára (Library of the Cistibiscan Reformed Church District) (Hungary) 183
Titania-Verlag (Federal Republic of Germany) 165
Titiwangsa, Penerbit, Sdn Bhd (Malaysia) 247
Tjeenk, H D, Willink BV (Netherlands) 268
Tjeenk Willink, W E J, BV (Netherlands) 268
Tjeenk Willink-Noorduijkn BV (Netherlands) 268
Tman Batjaan dan Perpustakaan Umum (Public Library Jakarta) (Indonesia) 201
Tobin Music Books (United Kingdom) 409
Today and Tomorrow's Book Agency (India) 196
Toeche-Mittler, S, Verlag (Federal Republic of Germany) 165
Togolaise, Nouvelle Librairie, (Togo) 360
Tohoku University Library (Japan) 232
Toison, Libris, d'Or SA (Belgium) 44
Tokai University Press (Japan) 231
Toko Messir (Indonesia) 200
Tokuma-Shoten (Japan) 231
Tokyo Kagaku Dozin Co Ltd (Japan) 231
Tokyo Metropolitan Central Library (Japan) 232
Tokyo News Service Ltd (Japan) 231
Tokyo Shuppan Hanbai Co Ltd (Distributors) (Japan) 232
Tokyo Sogensha Co Ltd (Japan) 231
Tokyo Tosho Co Ltd (Japan) 231
Tolkien, The, Society (United Kingdom) 418
Tolly Publishing Co (United Kingdom) 409
Tom-Gallon Trust Award (United Kingdom) 421
Tomas Förlag AB (Sweden) 337
Tomneub (Kampuchea) 235
Tomus Verlag GmbH (Federal Republic of Germany) 165
Tong-In Sunsawat (Thailand) 360
Tonger, P J, Musikverlag (Federal Republic of Germany) 165
Toonder, Marten, Award (Republic of Ireland) 205
Toorts, Uitgeverij De, (Netherlands) 268
Top Stone Books (United Kingdom) 409
Topaz Publishing Ltd (United Kingdom) 409
Topelius Prize (Finland) 88
Topi, Edizioni Giulio, (Switzerland) 354
Topos Verlag AG (Liechtenstein) 243
Toppan Co (Singapore) Private Ltd (Republic of Singapore) 309

Toppan Co Ltd (Japan) 231
Toppan Co Ltd (Japan) 232
Toray, Ediciones, SA (Spain) 326
Toray-Masson SA (Spain) 326
Toro, G del, Editor (Spain) 326
Torpis Publishing Co (Republic of South Africa) 314
Torres, João Romano, & Cia Lda (Portugal) 301
Torroja, Instituto Eduardo, (Spain) 326
Totius, Editio, Mundi E E Maenner (Austria) 28
Toulon (Belgium) 42
Touret, Editions, SA (France) 109
Touropa-Urlaubsberater (Federal Republic of Germany) 165
'Tout pour l'Ecole', Librairie, (Democratic Republic of Madagascar) 245
Towarzystwo Literackie im Mickiewicza (The Mickiewicz Literary Society) (Poland) 297
Towarzystwo Przyjaciól Ksiazki (Society of Friends of Books) (Poland) 297
Towarzystwo Przyjaciól Ksiazki (TPK) (Society of Friends of Books) (Poland) 296
Towarzystwo Przyjaciól Nauk w Przemyślu (Poland) 297
Towfigh (Iran) 202
Town & Gown Press (Nigeria) 279
Townsend & Co (Pvt) Ltd (Zimbabwe) 435
Townson, Editions, (Switzerland) 354
Townsville Foundation for Australian Literary Studies Award (Australia) 23
Toyo, The, Bunko (Japan) 231
Toyo Keizai Shinposha Ltd (Japan) 231
Traber Verlag (Switzerland) 354
Trachsel Verlag (Switzerland) 354
Tradexim SA (Switzerland) 354
Tradis Verlag und Vertrieb GmbH (Federal Republic of Germany) 165
Trano Printy Loterana (Democratic Republic of Madagascar) 245
Trano Printy Loterana-Trano Printy Fiangonana Loterana Malagasy (TPFLM)-(Imprimerie Luthérienne) (Democratic Republic of Madagascar) 244
Trans-Pacific Publishers (Fiji) 85
Trans Tech Publications SA (Switzerland) 354
Transafrica (Italy) 221
Transafrica (Italy) 223
Transafrica Book Distributors (Kenya) 236
Transatlantik Verlags- und Vertriebsgesellschaft mbH (Federal Republic of Germany) 165
Translation into Swedish Prize (Sweden) 339
Translation Prize (Republic of South Africa) 317
Translation Prize (Norway) 284
Translation Prize (International Literary Prizes) 452
Translatørforeningen (Denmark) 80
Translators Association (United Kingdom) 421
Translators' Guild (United Kingdom) 421
Translegal AG (Switzerland) 354
'Transport', Izdatelstvo, (Union of Soviet Socialist Republics) 367
Transport Library (Republic of Korea) 239
Transportation Publishing House (Democratic People's Republic of Korea) 237
Transpress, VEB Verlag für Verkehrswesen (German Democratic Republic) 119
Transworld Publishers (Australia) Pty Ltd (Australia) 18
Transworld Publishers Ltd (United Kingdom) 409
Trauner, Rudolf, Verlag (Austria) 28
Trautvetter und Fischer Nachf (Federal Republic of Germany) 165
Travel Aid Services Ltd (United Kingdom) 409
Travel Book Club (United Kingdom) 415
Tre Böcker, Bokklubben, (Sweden) 87
Trec Edizioni Pregiate (Italy) 221
Treffer-Boekklub (Republic of South Africa) 315
Treffer Uitgewers (Edms) Ltd (Republic of South Africa) 314
Trèfle, Librairie du, (Mauritius) 249
Trejos, Libreria, (Costa Rica) 69
Trelingue, Edizioni, Luigi Rusconi (Switzerland) 354
Tres Americas, Distribuidora, SAC (Argentina) 7
Tres Américas Libros (Argentina) 8
Tres Tiempos, Ediciones, SRL (Argentina) 8
trèves, éditions, (Federal Republic of Germany) 165
Trevi, Bokförlaget, AB (Sweden) 337
Trévise, Editions de, (France) 109
Triangulo, Livraria, Ltda (Brazil) 56
Trianon Press (France) 109
Tribhuvan University Library (Nepal) 257
Tribune Editions (Switzerland) 354
Tricorne, Editions du, (Switzerland) 354
Triennial Prize for Bibliography (International Literary Prizes) 452
Trikont Verlag GmbH (Federal Republic of Germany) 165
Trillas, Editorial, SA (Mexico) 253
Trimurti Publications Pvt Ltd (India) 196
Trinidad and Tobago, Central Library of, (County Library Department of the Government) (Trinidad and Tobago) 361

Trinidad and Tobago, Library Association of, (Trinidad and Tobago) 361
Trinidad Public Library (Trinidad and Tobago) 361
Trinidad Publishing Co (Trinidad and Tobago) 361
Trinity College Library (Republic of Ireland) 205
Trinity College Library (United Kingdom) 416
Tripathi, N M, Pvt Ltd (India) 196
Tripathi, N M, Pvt Ltd (India) 197
Triple Crown Club (Malaysia) 247
Tripode, Edizioni Il, SRL (Italy) 221
Trois Arches (Belgium) 42
Trois Collines, Editions des, (Switzerland) 354
Trois Continents, Editions des, (Switzerland) 354
Trois Fleuves, Editions des, (Senegal) 307
Tropen, CV Toko Buku, (Indonesia) 200
Trophy (United Kingdom) 409
Troquel, Editorial, SA (Argentina) 8
Troubador (United Kingdom) 409
Trubert, Maurice, Prize (France) 115
Trung-Tam San Xuat Hoc-Lieu (Socialist Republic of Viet Nam) 426
Tryma Book Shop (Bahamas) 32
Tsakalos Prize (Greece) 178
Tsuru-Shobo Co Ltd (Japan) 231
Tübinger Vereinigung für Volkskunde eV (Federal Republic of Germany) 165
Tucar Ediciones SA (Spain) 326
tuduv Verlagsgesellschaft mbH (Federal Republic of Germany) 165
Tun Razak Library (Malaysia) 247
Tuncho, Libreria, Granados G (Guatemala) 179
Turismo Editorial (Argentina) 8
Turistička Štampa (Yugoslavia) 430
Türk Editörler Birligi (Turkey) 362
Türk Kütuphaneciler Dernegi (Turkey) 364
Turkish Public Library (Cyprus) 69
Turm-Verlag (Federal Republic of Germany) 165
Turmberg-Verlag (Federal Republic of Germany) 165
Turnbull, Alexander, Library (New Zealand) 275
Turner Ediciones SRL (Argentina) 8
Turner Memorial Library (Zimbabwe) 435
Turnstone Books (United Kingdom) 409
Turton and Armstrong (Australia) 18
Turun Kansallinen (Finland) 87
Turun Yliopiston Kirjasto (Finland) 87
Tusch, Edition, (Austria) 28
Tusquets Editores (Spain) 326
Tuttle, Charles E, Co Inc (Japan) 231
Tuttle, Charles E, Co Inc (Japan) 232
Tuttle-Mori Agency Inc (Japan) 232
Twentieth Century Classics (Australia) 19
Two Tone Poetry Awards (Zimbabwe) 436
Txertoa, Editorial, (Spain) 326
Tyndale Press (United Kingdom) 409
Typos (Greece) 177
Tyrolia (Austria) 30
Tyrolia, Verlagsanstalt, (Austria) 28

U B S Publishers Dist Pvt Ltd (India) 196
U B S Publisher's Distributors Ltd (India) 197
U Bar Verlag (Switzerland) 354
U C A Editores (El Salvador) 83
U D E F (France) 89
U G A, Editions, (Uitgeverij voor Gemeente-Administratie) (Belgium) 43
U G E (France) 109
U h l, Verlag Dr Alfons, (Federal Republic of Germany) 165
U K B (Samenwerkingsverband van de Universiteits- en Hogeschoolbibliotheken en de Koninklijke Bibliotheek) (Netherlands) 270
U N A C Tokyo (Japan) 231
U N E S C O (International Organizations) 440
U N E S C O Institute for Education (UIE) (International Organizations) 440
U N Economic Commission for Africa Library (Ethiopia) 84
U O P C (Belgium) 43
U O P C (Belgium) 44
U P Indonesia (Indonesia) 200
U P N-Volksverlag (Federal Republic of Germany) 165
U R G S, Edições, (Universidade Federal do Rio Grande do Sul) (Brazil) 55
U S I S Library (Sierra Leone) 308
U S S R Library Council (Union of Soviet Socialist Republics) 367
U S S R Union of Writers (Union of Soviet Socialist Republics) 368
U T B (Federal Republic of Germany) 165
U T E T (Unione Tipografico-Editrice Torinese) (Italy) 221
Überreuter, Verlag Carl, (Austria) 29
Uganda Bookshop (Uganda) 364

Uganda Library Association (Uganda) 364
Uganda Publishing House (Uganda) 364
Uganda Schools Library Association (Uganda) 364
Uganda Special Library Association (Uganda) 364
Uganda Technical College Library (Uganda) 364
Ullstein, Verlag, GmbH (Federal Republic of Germany) 165
Ulmer, Verlag Eugen, GmbH & Co (Federal Republic of Germany) 165
Ultima Hora (Dominican Republic) 80
Ultramar Editores SA (Spain) 326
Ulverscroft Large Print Books Ltd (United Kingdom) 409
Umschau Verlag Breidenstein GmbH (Federal Republic of Germany) 166
Ungarischer Kultureller und Sozialer Fonds eV in der B R D (Federal Republic of Germany) 166
Ungdommens Forlag & Aamodts Forlag A/S (Denmark) 77
Unges, De, Forlag, Unitas Forlag (Denmark) 77
Uni Books (United Kingdom) 409
Uni-Taschenbücher (UTB) GmbH (Federal Republic of Germany) 166
Uni-Text Book Co (Malaysia) 247
União Gráfica Sarl (Portugal) 301
Unicart Kartografisk Produktion AB (Sweden) 337
Unieboek NV (Netherlands) 268
Unifacmanu Trading Co Ltd (China (Taiwan)) 64
Unión, Editorial, (Nicaragua) 276
Union, The, Press (Sri Lanka) 330
Union Book Club (Denmark) 78
Union Classics Library (Denmark) 78
Union Continentale d'Editions SA (Monaco) 255
Union Crime Club (Denmark) 78
Union dals Grischs (Switzerland) 354
Unión de Escritores y Artistas de Cuba (Union of Writers and Artists of Cuba) (Cuba) 69
Union d'Editeurs Français (France) 89
Union des Ecrivains algériens (Algeria) 2
Union des Ecrivains algériens (Union of Algerian Writers) (Algeria) 2
Union des Ecrivains et Artistes latins (Union of Latin Writers and Artists) (France) 112
Union des Editeurs de Langue française (Union of French-language Publishers) (International Organizations) 440
Union des Industries graphiques et du Livre (UNIGRA) (Belgium) 33
Union et Orientation de Presse et de Culture (UOPC) SA (Belgium) 43
Union Harlekin Library (Denmark) 78
Union Helvetia Fachbuchverlag (Switzerland) 354
Union Latine d'Editions SA (France) 109
Union Novel Library (Denmark) 78
Union of Bulgarian Writers (Bulgaria) 59
Union of International Associations (International Organizations) 443
Union of Welsh Publishers and Booksellers (United Kingdom) 369
Union of Writers and Artists of Albania (Albania) 1
Union of Writers of the African Peoples (Union des Ecrivains Negro-Africains) (International Organizations) 440
Union Press Ltd (Hong Kong) 181
Unión Tipográfica Editorial Hispanoamericana (UTEHA) (Mexico) 253
Union tunisienne des Ecrivains (Tunisian Writers' Union) (Tunisia) 362
Union Verlag Berlin VOB (German Democratic Republic) 119
Union Verlag Stuttgart (Federal Republic of Germany) 166
Union Verlagsvereinigung (Switzerland) 354
Unione Editori di Musica Italiani (UNEMI) (Italy) 212
Unipax (Norway) 283
Unipress (France) 89
United Africa Press Ltd (Kenya) 236
United Bank Prize for Literature (Pakistan) 287
United Book Distributors (Pty) Ltd (Republic of South Africa) 315
United Book Shop & Stationers (Bahamas) 32
United Christian Council Literature Bureau (Sierra Leone) 308
United Nations (International Organizations) 441
United Nations, Economic and Social Commission for Asia and the Pacific Library (Thailand) 360
United Nations Depository Library (Republic of Korea) 239
United Nations Educational, Scientific and Cultural Organization (UNESCO) (International Organizations) 441
United Nations Institute for Training and Research (UNITAR) (International Organizations) 441
United Nations Library (Switzerland) 356
United Protestant Publishers (Pty) Ltd (Republic of South Africa) 314
United Publishers (India) 197
United Publishers Services (M) Sdn Bhd (Malaysia) 247

United Publishers Services Ltd (Japan) 232
United Publishers Services Ltd (Japan) 232
United Publishing House and Stationers Sdn Bhd (Malaysia) 247
United States Book Association (Australia) 10
Unites SRL, Annuario Politecnico Italiano (Italy) 221
Unity Books Ltd (New Zealand) 275
Uniunea Scriitorilor din Republica Socialista România (Romania) 305
Univers, Editura, (Romania) 304
Universa PVBA (Belgium) 43
Universal (United Kingdom) 410
Universal Books (Australia) 18
Universal Bookstore, Librería, (Bolivia) 47
Universal Edition AG (Austria) 29
Universal Library (Israel) 210
Universal Paper Products and Distributors Ltd (Ghana) 175
Universal Postal Union (UPU) (International Organizations) 441
Universal Publications Agency Ltd (Republic of Korea) 239
Universal Publications Agency Ltd (Republic of Korea) 239
Universal Publications Sdn Bhd (Malaysia) 247
Universidad, Biblioteca de la, de Panama (Panama) 288
Universidad', Nicholas Ojeda Fierro e Hijos, Librería 'La, SCR Ltda (Peru) 290
Universidad Autónoma, Biblioteca General,, de Barcelona (Spain) 328
Universidad Autónoma de Santo Domingo, Biblioteca de la, (Dominican Republic) 81
Universidad Autónoma de Santo Domingo, Ciudad Universitaria (Dominican Republic) 80
Universidad Católica, Departamento de Publicaciones de la, Madre y Maestra (Dominican Republic) 80
Universidad Católica, Fondo Editorial de la, (Peru) 290
Universidad Católica, Pontificia, de Ecuador (Ecuador) 81
Universidad Católica de Chile, Biblioteca Central de la, (Chile) 63
Universidad Católica de Valparaiso, Biblioteca de la, (Chile) 63
Universidad Central, Biblioteca Central de la, de Venezuela (Venezuela) 425
Universidad Central, Biblioteca General de la, de las Villas (Cuba) 69
Universidad Central de Ecuador, Biblioteca de la, (Ecuador) 81
Universidad Central de la Villas, Carretera de Camajuani (Cuba) 68
Universidad Central del Ecuador (Ecuador) 81
Universidad Centroamericana José Simeón Cañas, Biblioteca de la, (El Salvador) 84
Universidad Complutense, Biblioteca Central,, de Madrid (Spain) 328
Universidad Complutense de Madrid, Biblioteca de la, (Spain) 328
Universidad de Buenos Aires, Instituto Bibliotecológico,, (Argentina) 8
Universidad de Chile, Biblioteca Central de la, (Chile) 63
Universidad de Concepción, Biblioteca Central de la, (Chile) 63
Universidad de Costa Rica (Costa Rica) 68
Universidad de Costa Rica, Biblioteca de la, (Costa Rica) 68
Universidad de El Salvador, Biblioteca Central de la, (El Salvador) 84
Universidad de Granada (Spain) 326
Universidad de Guayaquil (Ecuador) 81
Universidad de Guayaquil, Biblioteca General,, (Ecuador) 81
Universidad de la Habana (Cuba) 68
Universidad de la Habana, Biblioteca Central 'Rubén Martínez Villena' de la, (Cuba) 69
Universidad de los Andes (Colombia) 66
Universidad de Malaga (Spain) 326
Universidad de Navarra, Ediciones, SA (Spain) 326
Universidad de Oriente, Biblioteca Central de la, (Cuba) 69
Universidad de Panama, Escuela de Bibliotecologia (University of Panama, School of Library Science) (Panama) 288
Universidad de San Carlos (Guatemala) 178
Universidad de San Carlos, Biblioteca Central de la, (Guatemala) 179
Universidad de Zulia, Biblioteca Central de la, (Venezuela) 425
Universidad del Salvador, Biblioteca de la, (Argentina) 8
Universidad Iberoamericana, Biblioteca de la, (Mexico) 254
Universidad Mayor de San Andrés, Biblioteca Central de la, (Bolivia) 48
Universidad Mayor de San Francisco Xavier, Biblioteca Central de la, (Bolivia) 48
Universidad Mayor de San Simón, Biblioteca Central de la, (Bolivia) 48

Universidad Nacional, Biblioteca Central del, de Nicaragua (Nicaragua) 276
Universidad Nacional, Librería y Editorial,, de Nicaragua (Nicaragua) 276
Universidad Nacional Autónoma de México (UNAM) (Mexico) 253
Universidad Nacional de Colombia, Biblioteca Central (Colombia) 66
Universidad Nacional de Córdoba, Biblioteca Mayor de la, (Principal Library of the National University of Córdoba) (Argentina) 8
Universidad Nacional de Cuzeco, Biblioteca Central de la, (Peru) 290
Universidad Nacional de La Plata, Biblioteca Pública de la, (Argentina) 8
Universidad Nacional de San Agustín, Biblioteca Central de la, (Peru) 290
Universidad Nacional Mayor, Librería de la, de San Marcos (Peru) 290
Universidad Nacional Mayor de San Marcos (Peru) 290
Universidad Nacional Mayor de San Marcos, Biblioteca Central de la, (Peru) 290
Universidad Pontificia, Biblioteca Universitaria,, de Salamanca (Spain) 328
Universidad SRL (Argentina) 8
Universidade, Biblioteca Geral da, de Coimbra (Portugal) 301
Universidade de Brasília, Biblioteca Central (Brazil) 56
Universidade de Brasília, Editora, (Brazil) 55
Universidade de Luanda Biblioteca (Angola) 2
Universidade de São Paulo, Divisão de Biblioteca e Documentação da, (Brazil) 56
Universidade de São Paulo, Editôra da, (Brazil) 55
Universidade Eduardo Mondlane (Mozambique) 256
Universidade Federal do Rio de Janeiro, Biblioteca da Faculdade Nacional de Medicina da, Centro de Ciencias Medicas (Brazil) 56
Universidade Federal do Rio Grande do Sul, Biblioteca Central (Brazil) 56
Università degli Studi di Firenze, Biblioteca della Facolta di Lettere e Filosofia (Italy) 222
Universidad Mayor de San Andres (Bolivia) 47
Universitaire Boekhandel Nederland (Netherlands) 269
Universitaire Boekhandel NV (Belgium) 43
Universitaria, Editrice, (Italy) 221
Universitaria, Librería, de la Universidad de El Salvador (El Salvador) 83
Universitaria, Librería, UCA (El Salvador) 83
Universitaria de Barcelona, Biblioteca, (Spain) 328
Universitária de Direito, Livraria e Editora, Ltda (Brazil) 55
Universitarias de Valparaiso, Ediciones, (Chile) 62
Universitaire Pers Leiden (Netherlands) 268
Universitas Books (Pty) Ltd (Republic of South Africa) 315
Universitas Verlag Dr Klaus Schweitzer KG (Federal Republic of Germany) 166
Universität Basel, Öffentliche Bibliothek der, (Switzerland) 356
Universitäts- und Landesbibliothek Sachsen-Anhalt (German Democratic Republic) 120
Universitäts- und Stadtbibliothek (Federal Republic of Germany) 171
Universitätsbibliothek (Federal Republic of Germany) 171
Universitätsbibliothek (German Democratic Republic) 120
Universitätsbibliothek der Eberhard-Karls-Universität (Federal Republic of Germany) 171
Universitätsbibliothek der Technischen Universität (German Democratic Republic) 120
Universitätsbibliothek Erlangen-Nürnberg (Federal Republic of Germany) 171
Universitätsbibliothek Graz (Austria) 30
Universitätsbibliothek Heidelberg (Federal Republic of Germany) 171
Universitätsbibliothek Innsbruck (Austria) 30
Universitätsbibliothek Wien (Austria) 30
Universitätsbuchhandlung (German Democratic Republic) 120
Universitätsbuchhandlung (German Democratic Republic) 120
Universitätsbuchhandlung (German Democratic Republic) 120
Universitätsverlag (Switzerland) 354
Université, Bibliothèque de l', nationale du Gabon (Gabon) 116
Université, Bibliothèque de l', Nationale du Rwanda (Rwanda) 306
Université, Editions de l', de Bruxelles (Belgium) 43
Université, Librairie de l', (France) 111
Université Al Quarawiyin, Bibliothèque de l', (Morocco) 256
Université Catholique de Leuven, Bibliothèque centrale de l', (Belgium) 44
Université de Constantine, Bibliothèque de l', (Algeria) 2
Université de Dakar, Bibliothèque (Senegal) 307
Université de Liège, Bibliothèque générale de l', (Belgium) 44

Université de Niamey, Bibliothèque de l', (Niger) 276
Université de Tunis, Bibliothèque de l', (Tunisia) 362
Université de Yaoundé, Bibliothèque de l' (United Republic of Cameroun) 61
Université d'Oran, Bibliothèque (Algeria) 2
Université du Benin, Bibliothèque de l', (Benin) 47
Université du Burundi, Bibliothèque de l', (Burundi) 60
Université du Tchad, Bibliothèque de l', (Chad) 62
Université Jean-Bédel Bokassa, Bibliothèque de l', (National Library) (Central African Republic) 61
Université libre de Bruxelles, Bibliothèques de l', (Belgium) 44
Université Mohammed V, Bibliothèque de l', (Morocco) 256
Université nationale, Campus de Kinshasa, Bibliothèque centrale de l', (Zaire) 433
Université nationale, Campus de Kisangani, Bibliothèque centrale de l', (Zaire) 433
Université nationale, Campus de Lubumbashi, Bibliothèque centrale de l', (Zaire) 433
Université Nationale de Côte d'Ivoire (Ivory Coast) 224
Universiteitsbibliotheek van Amsterdam (Netherlands) 269
Universités de Paris, Bibliothèques des, (Paris University Libraries) (France) 111
Universitetsbibliotheket, 1 afd: Humanities (Denmark) 79
Universitetsbibliotheket, 2 afd: Science and Medicine (Denmark) 79
Universitetsbiblioteket i Bergen (The University Library of Bergen) (Norway) 284
Universitetsbiblioteket i Oslo (The Royal University Library) (National Library) (Norway) 284
Universitetsbiblioteket i Trondheim, Avd B(Kongelige Norske Videnskabers Selskab Biblioteket) (Norway) 284
Universitetsbogladen (Panumbogladen/Naturfagsbogladen/Latinerbogladen) (Denmark) 78
Universitetsbokhandeln (Norway) 283
Universitetsforlaget (Norway) 283
Universities Administration Office (Burma) 59
Universities' Central Library (Burma) 60
Univerzitná knižnica (Czechoslovakia) 73
University Book Agency (Pakistan) 286
University Book Shop (Papua New Guinea) 288
University Book Shop (Auckland) Ltd (New Zealand) 275
University Book Shop (Canterbury) Ltd (New Zealand) 275
University Book Shop (Otago) Ltd (New Zealand) 275
University Book Store (Hong Kong) 181
University Bookshop (Ghana) 175
University Bookshop (Ghana) 175
University Bookshop (Zambia) 434
University Bookshop (Nigeria) Ltd (Nigeria) 280
University Bookstore (Liberia) 242
University Bookstore (Republic of Singapore) 310
University Co-op Bookshop Ltd (Australia) 20
University College Cork Library (Republic of Ireland) 205
University College Dublin Library (Republic of Ireland) 205
University College Galway Library (Republic of Ireland) 205
University College of Swaziland Library (Swaziland) 331
University Education Press (Republic of Singapore) 310
University Karlovy, Knihovny fakult a ústavu, (Czechoslovakia) 73
University Libraries (Saudi Arabia) 306
University Library (Afghanistan) 1
University Microfilms International (United Kingdom) 410
University of Alexandria Library (Egypt) 83
University of Asmara Library (Ethiopia) 84
University of Auckland Library (New Zealand) 275
University of Baghdad, Central Library of the, (Iraq) 202
University of Baluchistan Library (Pakistan) 286
University of Botswana and Swaziland Library (Botswana) 48
University of Cairo (Sudan) 330
University of Cairo Library (Egypt) 83
University of Canterbury Publications (New Zealand) 274
University of Cape Coast Library (Ghana) 175
University of Cape Town Libraries (Republic of South Africa) 316
University of Chicago Press Ltd (United Kingdom) 410
University of Dar es Salaam Library (Tanzania) 358
University of Engineering and Technology (Pakistan) 286
University of Ferdowsi Library (Iran) 202
University of Garyounis Library (Libya) 243
University of Ghana Library (Ghana) 175
University of Haifa Library (Israel) 211
University of Hong Kong Main Library (Hong Kong) 181
University of Ife Bookshop Ltd (Nigeria) 280
University of Ife Library (Nigeria) 280
University of Ife Press (Nigeria) 279
University of Isfahan Library (Iran) 202
University of Jordan Library (Jordan) 234

University of Kabul Bookstores (Afghanistan) 1
University of Khartoum Bookshop (Sudan) 330
University of Khartoum Library (Sudan) 331
University of Lagos Bookshop (Nigeria) 280
University of Lagos Library (Nigeria) 280
University of Lagos Press (Nigeria) 279
University of Liberia Libraries (Liberia) 242
University of Libya (Libya) 243
University of London Library (United Kingdom) 416
University of London Press (Nigeria) 279
University of London Press Ltd (United Kingdom) 410
University of Malawi Library (Malawi) 245
University of Malaya Co-operative Bookshop Ltd (Malaysia) 247
University of Malaya Library (Malaysia) 247
University of Malaya Press Ltd (Malaysia) 247
University of Malta Library (Malta) 248
University of Manila Central Library (Philippines) 292
University of Mauritius Library (Mauritius) 249
University of Melbourne Library (Australia) 20
University of Nairobi Bookshop (Kenya) 236
University of Nairobi Library (Kenya) 236
University of Natal Library (Republic of South Africa) 316
University of Natal Press (Republic of South Africa) 314
University of New South Wales Library (Australia) 20
University of New South Wales Press Ltd (Australia) 18
University of Nigeria Bookshop (Nigeria) 280
University of Otago Press (New Zealand) 274
University of Papua New Guinea Library (Papua New Guinea) 288
University of Peradeniya Library (Sri Lanka) 330
University of Peshawar Library (Pakistan) 286
University of Pretoria, Merensky Library (Republic of South Africa) 316
University of Puerto Rico, General Library (Puerto Rico) 303
University of Puerto Rico, General Library, Mayaguez Campus (Puerto Rico) 303
University of Puerto Rico, Medical Sciences Campus Library (Puerto Rico) 303
University of Puerto Rico Press (UPRED) (Puerto Rico) 302
University of Queensland Library (Australia) 20
University of Queensland Press (Australia) 18
University of Rajshahi Library (Bangladesh) 33
University of Rhodesia (Zimbabwe) 435
University of Rhodesia Library (Zimbabwe) 435
University of Salonika, Library of the, (Greece) 178
University of San Carlos Library (Philippines) 292
University of Santo Tomas Library (Philippines) 292
University of Science and Technology Library (Ghana) 175
University of Singapore Library (Republic of Singapore) 310
University of South Africa (Republic of South Africa) 314
University of South Africa Library (Republic of South Africa) 316
University of Sydney Library (Australia) 20
University of Tabriz, Central Library,. (Iran) 202
University of the East Library (Philippines) 292
University of the Philippines (Philippines) 292
University of the Philippines Library (Philippines) 292
University of the Philippines Press (Philippines) 292
University of the West Indies (Barbados) 33
University of the West Indies Library (Trinidad and Tobago) 361
University of the Witwatersrand Library (Republic of South Africa) 316
University of Tokyo Library (Japan) 232
University of Tokyo Press (Japan) 231
University of Tripoli (Libya) 243
University of Wales Press (United Kingdom) 410
University of Western Australia Library (Australia) 20
University of Western Australia Press (Australia) 18
University of Zambia Library (Zambia) 434
University Press Amsterdam BV (APA) (Netherlands) 268
University Press Ltd (Nigeria) 279
University Press of Africa Ltd (Kenya) 236
University Presses of Columbia and Princeton (United Kingdom) 410
University Publishers (India) 196
University Publishers & Booksellers (Pty) Ltd (Republic of South Africa) 314
University Publishing Co (Nigeria) 279
University Publishing Co (Philippines) 292
University Publishing Co (Israel) 210
University Tutorial Press Ltd (United Kingdom) 410
Universo, Editorial, SA (Peru) 290
Universo, Premio, (Peru) 290
Universo, Società Editrice, (Italy) 221
Uniwersytecka w Toruniu, Biblioteka, (Poland) 297
Uniwersytecka w Warszawie, Biblioteka, (Poland) 297
Uniwersytecka w Wrocławiu, Biblioteka, (Library of the University of Wrocław) (Poland) 297
Upper India, The, Publishing House Pvt Ltd (India) 196

Uppsala Universitetsbibliotek (Sweden) 338
Urachhaus, Verlag, Johannes M Mayer GmbH und Co KG (Federal Republic of Germany) 166
Urania-Verlag (German Democratic Republic) 120
Uranium Verlag (Switzerland) 354
Urban Council Libraries (Hong Kong) 181
Urban und Schwarzenberg (Austria) 30
Urban und Schwarzenberg (Austria) 29
Urban und Schwarzenberg, Verlag, (Medical Publishers) (Federal Republic of Germany) 166
Urdang, Laurence, Associates Ltd (United Kingdom) 410
Urdu Academy Sind (Pakistan) 286
Urdu Akademy Awards (India) 199
Ure Smith (Australia) 18
Urmo SA de Ediciones (Spain) 327
Urs Graf-Verlag GmbH (Switzerland) 354
Usborne Publishing Ltd (United Kingdom) 410
Ústřední knihovnická rada ČSSR (Czechoslovakia) 73
Utbildningsbolaget M M AB (Sweden) 337
Utusan Publications and Distributions Sdn Bhd (Malaysia) 247
Uusi Kirjakerho Oy (Finland) 87
Uusi Tie, Kustannus Oy, (Finland) 86
Uzima Press Ltd (Kenya) 236

V A A P (Union of Soviet Socialist Republics) 367
V A M, Stichting, (Netherlands) 268
V A P Verlag (Federal Republic of Germany) 166
V C L (Netherlands) 269
V C T A Publishing Pty Ltd (Australia) 19
V D E-Verlag GmbH (Federal Republic of Germany) 166
V D I-Verlag GmbH (Verlag des Vereins Deutscher Ingenieure) (Federal Republic of Germany) 166
V-Dia-Verlag GmbH (Federal Republic of Germany) 166
V E D A, vydavateľstvo Slovenskej akadémie vied (Czechoslovakia) 72
V F P (Verlag Frauenpolitik) GmbH (Federal Republic of Germany) 166
V M B (Federal Republic of Germany) 166
V N U (Verenigde Nederlandse Uitgeversbedrijven) NV (Netherlands) 268
V N U Business Press Group (Netherlands) 268
V P A (Vjesnikova Press Agencija) (Yugoslavia) 430
V S A (Verlag für das Studium der Arbeiterbewegung GmbH (Federal Republic of Germany) 166
V V A (Vereinigte Verlagsauslieferung) Reinhard Mohn (Federal Republic of Germany) 170
V W K (Verlag für Wirtschafts-und-Kartographie Publikationen) Ryborsch GmbH (Federal Republic of Germany) 166
Vaad Hayeshivot Be'eretz Israel (Israel) 210
Vaar, De, bv Dordrecht (Netherlands) 268
Vaco NV (Suriname) 331
Vaco NV (Suriname) 331
Vademecum de Pharmacie (Belgium) 43
Vadhana Panich (Thailand) 360
Vahlen, Franz, GmbH (Federal Republic of Germany) 166
Vaillant, Editions de, — IGO (France) 109
Vaillant Carmanne, Imprimerie H, SA (Belgium) 43
Vajarindra (Thailand) 360
Vakils Feffer & Simons Ltd (India) 196
Valabrègue, Antony, Prize (France) 115
Valafell, Bókaútgáfan, (Iceland) 185
Vale, The Helen, Foundation (Australia) 19
Valiant Publishers (Pty) Ltd (Republic of South Africa) 314
Vallardi, Antonio, Editore (Italy) 221
Vallardi Industrie Grafiche (Italy) 221
Vallentine, Mitchell & Co Ltd (United Kingdom) 410
Vallerini, Augusto, Editore di Alberto Vallerini (Italy) 221
Valtionarkisto (National Archives) (Finland) 87
Vandenhoeck und Ruprecht (Federal Republic of Germany) 166
Vander-Oyez SA (France) 109
Vander Publishing (Belgium) 43
Vanderlinden, Librairie, (Belgium) 44
Vanderlinden, Librairie, SA (Belgium) 43
Vanmelle, L, (Drukkerij) NV (Belgium) 43
Vannini, Società Editrice, (Italy) 221
Vår Bok AB (Sweden) 338
Vår Skola Förlag AB (Sweden) 337
Vargas, Fundação Getúlio, (Brazil) 55
Varia Books (Republic of South Africa) 314
Variorum Reprints (United Kingdom) 410
Varsity Book Club (Nigeria) 279
Varsity Industrial Press (Nigeria) 279
Vasco, Editorial, Americana SA (EVA) (Spain) 327

INDEX 515

Vasiliou, J, Bibliopoleion (Greece) 177
Vassallo, A, and Sons Ltd (Malta) 248
Västra, Förlagsaktiebolaget, Sverige (Sweden) 337
Vaticana, Libreria Editrice, (Vatican City State) 423
Vavrín (Czechoslovakia) 72
Vecchi, Editions de, (France) 109
Vecchi, Editôra, SA (Brazil) 55
Vecchi, Editorial De, (Spain) 327
Vecchi, Giovanni de, Editore SpA (Italy) 221
Veen, Uitgeverij L J, BV (Netherlands) 268
Vega, Ediciones, SRL (Venezuela) 424
Vega, Librería Técnica, (Venezuela) 425
Velber Verlag GmbH (Federal Republic of Germany) 167
Velde, Editions Francis Van de, (France) 109
Velde, Editions Van de, (France) 109
Velhagen und Klasing (Federal Republic of Germany) 167
Venceremos, Edition, (Federal Republic of Germany) 167
Ventura Publishing Ltd (United Kingdom) 410
Vera-Reyes Inc (Philippines) 292
Verband bayerischer Buch- und Zeitschriftenhändler eV (Bavarian Booksellers' and Newsagents' Federation) (Federal Republic of Germany) 122
Verband bayerischer Verlage und Buchhandlungen eV (Bavarian Publishers' and Booksellers' Federation) (Federal Republic of Germany) 122
Verband der Antiquare Österreichs (Austria) 24
Verband der Bibliotheken des Landes Nordrhein-Westfalen (Federal Republic of Germany) 172
Verband der Bühnenverleger Österreichs (Austria) 24
Verband der Schulbuchverlage eV (Association of Publishers of Schoolbooks) (Federal Republic of Germany) 122
Verband der Verlage und Buchhandlungen in Baden-Württemberg eV (Federation of Publishers and Booksellers in Baden-Württemberg) (Federal Republic of Germany) 122
Verband der Verlage und Buchhandlungen in Nordrhein-Westfalen eV (Federal Republic of Germany) 122
Verband der wissenschaftlichen Gesellschaften Österreichs (Austria) 29
Verband des werbenden Buch- und Zeitschriftenhandels Gross-Berlin eV (Greater Berlin Federation of the Promotional Book and Periodical Trade) (Federal Republic of Germany) 122
Verband deutscher Adressbuchverleger eV (Association of German Directory Publishers) (Federal Republic of Germany) 122
Verband deutscher Antiquare eV (German Antiquarian Booksellers' Association) (Federal Republic of Germany) 122
Verband deutscher Bahnhofsbuchhändler (Federal Republic of Germany) 122
Verband deutscher Buch-Zeitungs- und Zeitschriften-Grossisten eV (Federation of German Wholesalers of Books, Newspapers and Periodicals) (Federal Republic of Germany) 122
Verband deutscher Bühnenverleger eV (Federation of German Theatrical Publishers) (Federal Republic of Germany) 122
Verband deutscher Schulbuchhändler eV (Federal Republic of Germany) 122
Verband deutscher Werkbibliotheken eV (Federal Republic of Germany) 122
Verband deutschsprachiger Übersetzer literarischer und wissenschaftlicher Werke eV (VDÜ) (Federal Republic of Germany) 174
Verband evangelischer Buchhandlungen und Verlage der Schweiz (Switzerland) 340
Verband katholischer Verleger und Buchhändler eV (Federal Republic of Germany) 122
Verband norddeutscher Buch- und Zeitschriftenhändler eV (Federation of North German Booksellers and Newsagents) (Federal Republic of Germany) 122
Verband österreichischer Archivare (Austria) 31
Verband österreichischer Kommissionäre. Grossobuchhändler und Auslieferer (Austria) 24
Verband österreichischer Volksbüchereien und Volksbibliothekare (Austria) 31
Verband schweizerischer Antiquare und Kunsthändler (Association of Swiss Secondhand Booksellers and Art Dealers) (Switzerland) 340
Verband schweizerischer Schreinermeister und Möbelfabrikanten Verlag und Fachbüchervertrieb (Switzerland) 354
Verband schweizerischer Zeitungsagenturen und Büchergrossisten (Union d'Agences suisses de Journaux et Livres en Gros) (Association of Swiss Newspaper Distributors and Book Wholesalers) (Switzerland) 340
Verband westdeutscher Buch- und Zeitschriftenhändler eV (West German Booksellers' and Newsagents' Federation) (Federal Republic of Germany) 122
Verbandsdruckerei. Buchverlag der, /Editions Imprimerie Fédérative SA Berne (Switzerland) 354
Verbeke-Loys, Uitgaven, (Belgium) 43
Verbo, Editôra, Ltda (Brazil) 55

Verbo, Editorial, Divino (Spain) 327
Verbo Sarl (Portugal) 301
Verbruikersunie, Uitgaven van de, VZW (Editions de Association des Consommateurs ASBL) (Belgium) 43
Verbum (Sweden) 337
Verdade e Vida, Livraria, Editora (Portugal) 301
Vereeniging der Antwerpsche Bibliophielen (Belgium) 45
Vereeniging ter bevordering van de belangen des Boekhandels (Association for the Promotion of the Interests of Booksellers and Publishers) (Netherlands) 258
Verein Angehörige des mittleren und nichtdiplomierten Bibliotheksdienstes eV (Association of Nonprofessional Librarians) (Federal Republic of Germany) 172
Verein der Bibliothekare an öffentlichen Büchereien eV (Federal Republic of Germany) 172
Verein der Diplom-Bibliothekare an Wissenschaftlichen Bibliotheken eV (Federal Republic of Germany) 172
Verein Deutscher Archivare (VdA) (Federal Republic of Germany) 172
Verein deutscher Bibliothekare eV (Federal Republic of Germany) 172
Verein deutscher Dokumentare eV (Federal Republic of Germany) 172
Verein für Verkehrsordnung im Buchhandel (Federal Republic of Germany) 122
Vereinigung der Schweizerischen Buchgemeinschaften (Association of Swiss Book Clubs) (Switzerland) 340
Vereinigung evangelischer Buchhändler eV (Association of Protestant Booksellers) (Federal Republic of Germany) 122
Vereinigung katholischer Buchhändler und Verleger der Schweiz (Switzerland) 340
Vereinigung österreichischer Bibliothekare (Austria) 31
Vereinigung Schweizerischer Archivare (Association of Swiss Archivists) (Switzerland) 357
Vereinigung selbständiger Verlagsvertreter (Federal Republic of Germany) 122
Verenigde Protestantse Uitgewers (Edms) Bpk (Republic of South Africa) 314
Vereniging ter Bevordering van het Vlaamse Boekwezen (Belgium) 33
Vereniging van Archivarissen in Nederland (Association of Archivists in the Netherlands) (Netherlands) 270
Vereniging van de belgische medische Wetenschappelijke Genootschappen VZW (Belgium) 43
Vereniging van Religieus-Wetenschappelijke Bibliothecarissen (Belgium) 44
Vereniging van Uitgevers van Nederlandstalige Boeken (Belgium) 34
Vereniging van Uitgeversvertegenwoordigers (Association of Publishers' Representatives) (Netherlands) 258
Vereniging voor het Theologisch Bibliothecariaat (Association for Theological Librarianship) (Netherlands) 270
Vergadis, M, (Greece) 177
Vergara, Javier, Editor SRL (Argentina) 8
Vergara, José Ma, y Vergara Prize (Colombia) 67
Verissimo, José, Prize (Brazil) 57
Veritas Publications (Republic of Ireland) 204
Veritas-Verlag (Austria) 29
Verkehrshaus der Schweiz (Switzerland) 355
Verkenner, Uitgeverij De, NV (Netherlands) 268
Verlag für polizeiliches Fachschrifttum (Federal Republic of Germany) 156
Verlagsgenossenschaft (Switzerland) 355
Verlain, Valentine Abraham, Prize (France) 115
Verlaine, Paul, Prize (France) 115
Verlegervereinigung Rechtsinformatik eV (Association of Publishers of Legal Documentation) (Federal Republic of Germany) 122
Verne, Jules, Circle (United Kingdom) 418
Veron Editor (Spain) 327
Verrycken, Editions, (Belgium) 43
Verseau, Editions du, (Switzerland) 355
Versluys', W, Uitg Mij BV (Netherlands) 268
Verso Editions (United Kingdom) 410
Vertente Editora Ltda (Brazil) 55
Verve, Editions de la Revue, Sàrl (France) 109
Vervuert, Klaus Dieter, Buchhandel und Verlag (Federal Republic of Germany) 167
Verzekeringswereld, De, PVBA (Belgium) 43
Vesaas, Tarjei, Debutant Prize (Norway) 284
Veselin Masleša (Yugoslavia) 430
Veselin Masleša (Yugoslavia) 431
Vesti (Yugoslavia) 430
Vetch & Lee Ltd (Hong Kong) 181
Vetenskapliga Bibliotekens Tjänstemannaförening VBT (Sweden) 338
Vetter, Verlag Alfred F, (Switzerland) 355
Veyrier (France) 109
Via Afrika Book Store (Republic of South Africa) 315
Via Afrika Botswana Ltd (Botswana) 48
Via Afrika Ltd (Republic of South Africa) 314
Vial, Editions André, (France) 109
Vialetay, Editions, Sàrl (France) 109
Viareggio Prizes (Italy) 223

Vicaire, Gabriel, Prize (France) 115
Vicens-Vives, Editorial, (Spain) 327
Victor, Leo, (Suriname) 331
Victoria Booksellers' Association (Australia) 10
Victory Press (United Kingdom) 410
Vidyarthi Book Depot (India) 197
Vidyarthi Mithram Press (India) 196
Vie, Les Editions, ouvrière ASBL (Belgium) 43
Vieng Krung (Laos) 240
Vienna Art Foundation (Wiener Kunstfonds) (Austria) 31
Vienna Prize for children's and young people's literature (Austria) 31
Vienna Übersetzungsbüro und Sprachinstitut (Austria) 31
Vietnamese Publishing House (Socialist Republic of Viet Nam) 426
Vieweg, Friedr, und Sohn Verlagsgesellschaft mbH (Federal Republic of Germany) 167
Vigília, Editôra, Ltda (Brazil) 55
Vigot, Editions, Frères (France) 109
Vijverberg Prize (Netherlands) 271
Vikas Publishing Co Ltd (United Kingdom) 410
Vikas Publishing House Pvt Ltd (India) 196
Viking Sevensea Ltd (New Zealand) 274
Viktoria Verlag (Switzerland) 355
Villa Benia Prize (Italy) 223
Villaurrutia Prize (Mexico) 255
Ville de Paris, Service des Travaux Historiques de la, et Bibliothèque historique de la Ville de Paris (France) 111
Villepastour, Librarie, (Ivory Coast) 224
Vilnius, The Scientific Library of the, Vincas Kapsukas State University (Union of Soviet Socialist Republics) 367
Vilo, Editions, SA (France) 109
Vincent, Dominique, et Cie (France) 109
Vincentz, Curt R, Verlag (Federal Republic of Germany) 167
Vine Books Ltd (United Kingdom) 410
Vingtième Siècle (France) 109
Vinten's Forlag (Denmark) 77
Vipopremo Agencies (Kenya) 236
Virago Ltd (United Kingdom) 410
Viratham (Thailand) 360
Virdi, Major Tek Singh, Literary Prizes (India) 199
Virenque, Claire, Prize (France) 115
Virtue & Co Ltd (United Kingdom) 410
Visa (Australia) 19
Visão, Editora, Ltda (Brazil) 55
Visentini, Olga, Prize (Italy) 223
Vishal Publications (India) 196
Vision Books Pvt Ltd (India) 196
Vision Press Ltd (United Kingdom) 410
Vision Publishing Corporation (Philippines) 292
Visscher, Albert de, Editeur (Belgium) 43
Visuals of the Australian Environment (Australia) 19
Vitte, Emmanuel, Editeur SA (France) 109
Vives, Editorial Luis, (Edelvives) (Spain) 327
Vivliofilia (Greece) 177
Vivliografiki Etaireia tis Ellados (Bibliographical Society of Greece) (Greece) 178
Vlaamse Bijbelstichting (Belgium) 43
Vlaamse Toeristenbond VZW (Belgium) 43
Vlaamse Vereniging van Bibliotheek-, Archief en Documentatie-Personeel (Belgium) 44
Vlasis, Frères, (Greece) 177
Vlijt, De, NV (Belgium) 43
'Vneshtorgizdat', Vsesoyuznoe Obyedineniye, (Union of Soviet Socialist Republics) 367
Voenno Izdatelstvo (Bulgaria) 58
Vogel, Buchhandlung W, (Switzerland) 356
Vogel-Verlag KG (Federal Republic of Germany) 167
Vogt-Schild AG Druck & Verlag (Switzerland) 355
Voix, Editions La, de l'Ain (France) 109
Vojnoizdavački Zavod (Yugoslavia) 430
Vokaer, Nouvelles Editions, SA (Belgium) 43
Volcans, Librairie Les, (Zaire) 433
Volcans, Librairie Les, (Zaire) 433
Volk, Boekhandel het, (Belgium) 44
Volk, Het, NV (Belgium) 43
Volk und Gesundheit, VEB Verlag, (German Democratic Republic) 120
Volk und Welt, Verlag, (German Democratic Republic) 120
Volk und Wissen Volkseigener Verlag Berlin (German Democratic Republic) 120
Volksbuchverlag GmbH (Austria) 30
Volksdrukkerij NV (Netherlands Antilles) 271
Volksverband der Bücherfreunde Verlag GmbH (Federal Republic of Germany) 170
Vollmer, Emil, Verlag (Federal Republic of Germany) 167
Vollmer/Löwit Verlagsgruppe (Federal Republic of Germany) 167
Volney Prize (France) 115
Voltaire Foundation (United Kingdom) 410
Volturna Press (United Kingdom) 410
Voluntad Editores Ltda y Cía SCA (Colombia) 66
Voorhoeve, J N, (Netherlands) 268

Voortrekker-Boekklub (Republic of South Africa) 315
Vora & Co Publishers Pvt Ltd (India) 196
Vorarlberger Verlagsanstalt GmbH (Austria) 29
Voss, Hartfrid, Verlag (Federal Republic of Germany) 167
Voss, Johann Heinrich, Translation Prize (Federal Republic of Germany) 174
Vowinckel, Kurt, Verlag (Federal Republic of Germany) 167
Voyenizdat (Union of Soviet Socialist Republics) 367
Vozes Editôra Ltda (Brazil) 55
Vries, C De, Brouwers PVBA (Belgium) 43
Vrin, Librairie Philosophique J, (France) 109
Vroente, De, (Belgium) 43
Vsesoyuznaya Knichnaya Palata (Union of Soviet Socialist Republics) 365
Vsesoyuznoe agenstvo po avtorskim pravam (VAAP) (Union of Soviet Socialist Republics) 367
Vuibert, Librairie, SA (France) 109
Vuk Karadžic (Yugoslavia) 430
Vuk Karadžic (Yugoslavia) 431
Východoslovenské vydavatel'stvo np (Czechoslovakia) 72
Vyncke, PVBA Imprimerie-Editions, (Belgium) 43
Vyšehrad (Czechoslovakia) 72
'Vysshaya Shkola', Izdatelstvo, (Union of Soviet Socialist Republics) 367

W R S — Verlag (Federal Republic of Germany) 167
Waage, Verlag Die, Zurich und Hamburg (Switzerland) 355
Wachholtz, Karl, Verlag (Federal Republic of Germany) 167
Wadih M Captan Bookstores (Liberia) 242
Wagenbach, Verlag Klaus, (Federal Republic of Germany) 167
Wagner, Gebrüder, & Co Verlag (Switzerland) 355
Wagner, Universitätsverlag, GmbH (Austria) 29
Wagner'sche Universitätsbuchhandlung (Austria) 30
Wahab, Dakr Abdul, (Syria) 357
Wahbah, Ali, Bookshop (Saudi Arabia) 306
Wahle, Eugène, (Belgium) 43
Wahlström och Widstrand, AB, (Sweden) 337
Wahlströms, B, Bokförlag AB (Sweden) 337
Waiwen Shudian (People's Republic of China) 63
Walburg, De, Pers (Netherlands) 268
Waldia, AB, Förlag (Sweden) 337
Wales Tourist Board (United Kingdom) 410
Walmap Prize (International Literary Prizes) 452
Walraven, Uitgeverij Van, BV (Netherlands) 268
Walsingham (United Kingdom) 410
Walt, J P van der, & Seun (Pty) Ltd (Republic of South Africa) 315
Walt Disney, Clube, (Portugal) 301
Walt Disney Wonderful World of Reading (Denmark) 78
Walter, Henry E, Ltd (United Kingdom) 410
Walter Verlag AG (Switzerland) 355
Walter-Verlag (Federal Republic of Germany) 167
Wangels Forlag A/S (Denmark) 77
Wanyee Bookshop Ltd (Kenya) 236
Wapler, Dominique, (France) 109
Warana Writers' Awards (Australia) 23
Warburg, The, Institute (United Kingdom) 410
Ward Lock Educational Ltd (United Kingdom) 410
Ward Lock Ltd (United Kingdom) 410
Warga (Indonesia) 200
Warne, Frederick, & Co Ltd (United Kingdom) 411
Warsaw City Prize (Poland) 297
Warsaw City Prize for Young Poets (Poland) 297
Was Is Press (Australia) 19
Waseda University Library (Japan) 232
Wasmuth, Ernst, Verlagsbuchhandlung KG (Federal Republic of Germany) 167
Wastiau-Jeukens (Belgium) 43
Watelet, Gerard, (France) 109
Waterlow (London) Ltd (United Kingdom) 411
Waterville Publishing House (Ghana) 175
Watkins Publishing (United Kingdom) 411
'Watra', Wydawnictwa Kultura Zycia Codziennego, (Poland) 296
Watson, W, & Co (United Kingdom) 411
Watt, A P, Ltd (United Kingdom) 414
Wattana Panich (Thailand) 360
Wattie, James, Award for the New Zealand Book of the Year (New Zealand) 276
Watts, Franklin, Ltd (United Kingdom) 411
Wayfarer Book Store Ltd (Barbados) 33
Wayland Publishers (United Kingdom) 411
Wayzgoose, The, Press (United Kingdom) 411
Weatherhill, John, Inc (Japan) 231
Webb & Bower (Publishers) Ltd (United Kingdom) 411
Weber (France) 109
Weber, Anna, (Austria) 30
Weber SA d'Editions (Switzerland) 355

Weber-Stumfohl, Herta, (Federal Republic of Germany) 170
Weekes, A, (United Kingdom) 411
Wehr und Wissen Verlagsgesellschaft mbH (Federal Republic of Germany) 167
Wehrenalp, v, & Co (Switzerland) 355
Weichert, A, Verlag (Federal Republic of Germany) 167
Weickhardt, Con, Award (Australia) 23
Weickhardt, Patricia, Award (Australia) 23
Weidenfeld & Nicolson, George, Ltd (United Kingdom) 411
Weidlich, Wolfgang, Verlag (Federal Republic of Germany) 167
Weilburg-Verlag (Austria) 29
Weilin, Amer-yhtymä Oy, (Finland) 86
Weill, Galerie Lucie, (France) 109
Weill Publishers Ltd (Israel) 210
Weinert, Erich-, -Buchhandlung (German Democratic Republic) 120
Weinmann, Verlag, (Federal Republic of Germany) 167
Weis, Rupertusbuchhandlung Augustin, und Söhne KG (Austria) 30
Weismann Verlag-Frauenbuchverlag GmbH (Federal Republic of Germany) 167
Weiss, Gebrüder, Verlag (Federal Republic of Germany) 167
Weiss, J J, Prize (France) 115
Weitbrecht GmbH (Federal Republic of Germany) 167
Weizmann, The, Science Press of Israel (Israel) 210
Weizmann Institute of Science Libraries (Israel) 211
Wellcome Institute for the History of Medicine Library (United Kingdom) 416
Wellington Public Library (New Zealand) 275
Wells, H G, Society (United Kingdom) 418
Wellsiana—The World of Wells (United Kingdom) 418
Welsermühl, Verlag, (Federal Republic of Germany) 168
Welsh Arts Council Awards to Writers (United Kingdom) 421
Welsh Books Council (Cyngor Llyfrau Cymraeg) (United Kingdom) 369
Welsh Library Association (United Kingdom) 417
Welt im Heim Morawa & Co (Austria) 30
Weltkreis-Verlags-GmbH (Federal Republic of Germany) 168
Weltrundschau Verlag AG (Switzerland) 355
Welz, Verlag Galerie, Salzburg (Austria) 29
'Wema', Wydawnictwa Przemyslu Maszynowego, (Poland) 296
Wendelin, Buchhandlung, Niedlich KG (Federal Republic of Germany) 170
Wentworth Books Pty Ltd (Australia) 19
Wepf, Verlag, & Co (Switzerland) 355
Wepf & Co Buchhandlung und Antiquariat (Switzerland) 356
Wereldbibliotheek BV (Netherlands) 268
Wereldbibliotheek NV (Belgium) 43
Wereldvenster, Het, BV Internationale Uitg Mij (Netherlands) 268
Werner & Bischoff AG (Switzerland) 355
Werner Söderström Osakeyhtiö (WSOY) (Finland) 86
Werner Söderström Osakeyhtiö (WSOY) (Finland) 86
Werner Verlag GmbH (Federal Republic of Germany) 168
Wesmael-Charlier, Maison d'Editions Ad, SA (Belgium) 43
West, John, Publications Ltd (Nigeria) 279
West African Book Publishers Ltd (Nigeria) 279
West African Library Association (WALA) (International Organizations) 440
'West-Friesland', Uit-Mij, (Netherlands) 268
West Pakistan Publishing Co Ltd (Pakistan) 286
Westbooks Pty Ltd (Australia) 19
Westdeutscher Verlag GmbH (Federal Republic of Germany) 168
Westerbergs, Ernst, Förlags AB (Sweden) 337
Westermann, Georg, Verlag, Druckerei & Kartographische Anstalt GmbH & Co (Federal Republic of Germany) 168
Western Australian Booksellers' Association (Australia) 10
Western Book Club (United Kingdom) 415
Westers, Uitgeverij, (Netherlands) 268
Westminster City Libraries (United Kingdom) 416
Wetenschappelijke Uitgeverij (Netherlands) 268
Wettergrens Bokhandel AB (Sweden) 338
Wetzikon, Buchverlag der Druckerei, AG (Switzerland) 355
Wever, Uitgeverij, BV (Netherlands) 268
Wewel, Erich, Verlag (Federal Republic of Germany) 168
Wezäta Förlag (Sweden) 337
Wheatley Medal (United Kingdom) 421
Wheaton, A, & Co Ltd (United Kingdom) 411
Wheeler-Pitman Publishing Co Pvt Ltd (India) 196
Whitaker, J, & Sons Ltd (United Kingdom) 411
Whitbread Literary Awards (United Kingdom) 421
Whitcombe & Tombs Pty Ltd (Australia) 20
Whitcombe & Tombs Pty Ltd (Australia) 19

Whitcoulls Ltd (New Zealand) 275
Whitcoulls Ltd (New Zealand) 274
White, Patrick, Award (Australia) 23
White, Sir Thomas, Memorial Prize (Australia) 23
White Eagle Publishing Trust (United Kingdom) 411
White Horse Books (United Kingdom) 411
White Lion Publishers Ltd (United Kingdom) 411
Whitman (New Zealand) 274
Whizzard, G, Publications Ltd (United Kingdom) 411
Wholesale Book Distributors (New Zealand) 275
Wholesale Booksellers Association of Australia (Australia) 10
Who's Who — Book & Publishing Company (Federal Republic of Germany) 168
Who's Who of Southern Africa (Republic of South Africa) 315
Wiart, Carton de, Prize (Belgium) 46
Wichmann, Herbert, Verlag (Federal Republic of Germany) 168
Widescope International Publishers Pty Ltd (Australia) 19
Widjaja (Indonesia) 200
'Wiedza Powszechna' Państwowe Wydawnictwo (Poland) 296
Wieland, Richard Rudolf, (Switzerland) 355
Wiener Bibliophilen-Gesellschaft (Austria) 31
Wiener Dom-Verlag (Austria) 29
Wiener Goethe-Verein (Austria) 31
Wiener Stadt- und Landesarchiv (Austria) 30
Wiener Stadt und Landesbibliothek (Austria) 30
Wiener Urtext Edition-Musikverlag GmbH & Co KG (Austria) 29
Wilco Publishing House (India) 196
Wild, Alexander, (Switzerland) 355
Wild & Woolley Pty Ltd (Australia) 19
Wild Geese (Republic of Ireland) 204
Wildgans, Anton, Prize of Austrian Industry (Austria) 31
Wildwood House Ltd (United Kingdom) 411
Wiley, John, & Sons Australasia Pty Ltd (Australia) 19
Wiley, John, & Sons Ltd (United Kingdom) 411
Wiley Eastern Ltd (India) 196
Wilfion Books Publishers (United Kingdom) 411
Wilke Literary Award (Australia) 23
Wilkenschildts Forlag (Denmark) 77
Williams, Joseph, (United Kingdom) 411
Williams & Norgate (United Kingdom) 411
Williams Book Illustration Award, Francis, (United Kingdom) 421
Williams Memorial Prize, Griffith John, (Gwobr Goffa Griffith John Williams) (United Kingdom) 421
Willing Verlag GmbH (Federal Republic of Germany) 168
Willis Bookshops (Republic of Ireland) 205
Willshaw, W H, Ltd (United Kingdom) 415
Wilson, John Rowan, Award (International Literary Prizes) 452
Wilson, Philip, Publishers (United Kingdom) 412
Wilson & Horton Ltd (New Zealand) 274
Wilton Publications (United Kingdom) 412
Wilwers, Librairie Jos, (Luxembourg) 244
Wimmer, J, Druckerei und Zeitungshaus GmbH & Co (Austria) 29
Windhoek Public Library (Namibia) 257
Wine, The, Book Club (United Kingdom) 415
Wine & Spirit Publications Ltd (United Kingdom) 412
Wingate, Allan, (Publishers) Ltd (United Kingdom) 412
Wingate Series (United Kingdom) 412
Winkel, Rosa, Verlags-und-Versand GmbH (Federal Republic of Germany) 168
Winkelhaak PVBA (Belgium) 43
Winkler-Verlag (Federal Republic of Germany) 168
Winter, Alfred, Verlag (Austria) 29
Winter, Carl, Universitätsverlag GmbH (Federal Republic of Germany) 168
Winter, Herta, (Austria) 30
Winthers Forlag ApS (Denmark) 77
Wirtschaft, Recht, Steuern (Federal Republic of Germany) 168
Wirtschaft, Verlag Die, (German Democratic Republic) 120
Wirtschaft und Recht, Fachbuchhandlung für, (Austria) 30
Wirtschafts- und Kartographie, Verlag für, -Publikationen, Ryborsch (Federal Republic of Germany) 168
Wirtschaftsskripten, Verlag für, (Federal Republic of Germany) 168
Wirtschaftsverlag (Federal Republic of Germany) 168
Wison Verlag GmbH (Federal Republic of Germany) 168
Wissen Verlag GmbH (Federal Republic of Germany) 168
Wissenschaft, Verlag für, Technik und Industrie AG (Switzerland) 355
Wissenschaft, Wirtschaft und Technik, Verlag für, GmbH und Co KG (Federal Republic of Germany) 168
Wissenschaft und Politik, Verlag, (Federal Republic of Germany) 168
Wissenschaftliche Buchgesellschaft (Federal Republic of Germany) 170

INDEX 517

Wissenschaftliche Buchgesellschaft (Federal Republic of Germany) 168
Wissenschaftliche Verlagsgesellschaft mbH (Federal Republic of Germany) 168
Witherby, H F & G, Ltd and Witherby & Co Ltd (United Kingdom) 412
Wittig, Friedrich, Verlag (Federal Republic of Germany) 168
Wittwer, Buchhandlung Konrad, KG (Federal Republic of Germany) 171
Wittwer, Verlag Konrad, KG (Federal Republic of Germany) 169
Witwatersrand University Press (Republic of South Africa) 315
Witzstrock, Gerhard, GmbH (Federal Republic of Germany) 169
Wkallat Matbouat (Kuwait) 240
Wobbledagger (Australia) 19
Woburn, The, Press (United Kingdom) 412
Wöldikes Forlag (Denmark) 78
Wolfe Medical Publications Ltd (United Kingdom) 412
Wolfe Publishing Ltd (United Kingdom) 412
Wolff, Oswald, (Publishers) Ltd (United Kingdom) 412
Wolfhound Press (Republic of Ireland) 204
Wolfrum, Kunstverlag, (Austria) 30
Wolfrum, Kunstverlag, (Austria) 29
Wolfsbergdrucke, Verlag der, (Switzerland) 355
Wolfson History Awards (United Kingdom) 421
Wolmar, Valentine de, Prize (France) 116
Wolters Leuven, J B, NV (Belgium) 43
Wolters-Noordhoff BV (Netherlands) 268
Wolters Noordhoff Longman BV (Netherlands) 268
Women Writers' Association (Japan) 233
Women's, The, Press Ltd (United Kingdom) 412
Women's Literary Society (Greece) 178
Women's Literary Society Prizes (Greece) 178
Women's Movement Children's Literature Co-op Ltd (Australia) 19
Womm-Press (Federal Republic of Germany) 169
Woodhead-Faulkner (Publishers) Ltd (United Kingdom) 412
Word and Vision Ltd (Greece) 177
Word Books (Word (UK) Ltd) (United Kingdom) 412
Workers' Press (People's Republic of China) 63
Workshop Press Ltd (United Kingdom) 412
World, The, Book Company (Macao) 244
World, The, Press Pvt Ltd (India) 196
World Academy of Art and Science (International Organizations) 443
World Book-Childcraft International Inc (United Kingdom) 412
World Book Co (Hong Kong) 181
World Book Co (China (Taiwan)) 64
World Book Co Ltd (Republic of Singapore) 310
World Books (United Kingdom) 415
World Council of Churches (WCC) (International Organizations) 444
World Distributors (Manchester) Ltd (United Kingdom) 412
World Federation for Mental Health (Fédération mondiale pour la Santé mentale) (International Organizations) 444
World Festival of Negro Arts Literary Prizes (International Literary Prizes) 452
World Health Organization (WHO) (International Organizations) 441
World Intellectual Property Organization (WIPO) (Organisation Mondiale de la Propriété Intellectuelle) (International Organizations) 444
World Medical Association (Association médicale mondiale) (International Organizations) 444
World Meteorological Organization (WMO) (International Organizations) 441
World Microfilms Publications Ltd (United Kingdom) 412
World of Islam Festival Trust (United Kingdom) 412
World of Nature (United Kingdom) 415
World Psychiatric Association (Association mondiale de Psychiatrie) (International Organizations) 444
World Reporting Ltd (United Kingdom) 412
World University Library (United Kingdom) 412
World Veterinary Association (Association mondiale Vétérinaire) (International Organizations) 444
World's Work Ltd (United Kingdom) 412
Wort und Welt Verlag (Austria) 29
Woursell, Abraham, Prize (University of Vienna) (International Literary Prizes) 452
Wren Publishing Pty Ltd (Australia) 19
Wright, Gordon, Publishing (United Kingdom) 412
Wright, John, & Sons Ltd (United Kingdom) 412
Wright, Mme Ellen, (France) 110
Writers', The, Group (Malawi) 245
Writers and Readers Publishing Co-operative (United Kingdom) 413
Writers' Guild of Great Britain (United Kingdom) 418
Writers' Guild Publishing House (Pakistan) 286
Writers' Publishing House (People's Republic of China) 63

Writers' Union Prize (Romania) 305
Writers Workshop (India) 196
'Wspólna Sprawa', Wydawniczo Oświatowa Spółdzielnia Inwalidów, (Educational Publishing Cooperative of the Disabled) (Poland) 296
Wunderlich, Rainer, Verlag Hermann Leins (Federal Republic of Germany) 169
Wüpper, Edgar, (Federal Republic of Germany) 169
Württembergische Bibliotheksgesellschaft (Federal Republic of Germany) 172
Württembergische Landesbibliothek (Federal Republic of Germany) 171
Wykeham Publications (London) Ltd (United Kingdom) 413
Wyndham Publications Ltd (United Kingdom) 413
Wyss, K J, Erben AG (Switzerland) 355

Xarait Editorial (Spain) 327
Xarait Libros (Spain) 328
Xenos Verlagsgesellschaft mbH & Co (Federal Republic of Germany) 169
Xerox Publishing Group Ltd (United Kingdom) 413
Xunhasoba (Socialist Republic of Viet Nam) 426

Y Hoc Publishing House (Socialist Republic of Viet Nam) 426
Y M C A-Press (France) 110
Yachdav, United Publishers Co Ltd (Israel) 210
Yad Eliahu Chitov (Israel) 210
Yad Vashem — Martyrs' and Heroes' Remembrance Authority (Israel) 210
Yaffa Syndicate Pty Ltd (Australia) 19
Yale University Press (United Kingdom) 413
Yama-Kei (Publishers) Co Ltd (Japan) 231
Yamada Shoin (Yamada Publishing Co) (Japan) 231
Yañez, J F, Agencia Literaria (Universitas) (Spain) 327
Yarmouk University Library (Jordan) 234
Yasaguna, C V, (Indonesia) 200
Yavneh Ltd (Israel) 210
Yayasan Buku (Malaysia) 247
Yedioth Ahronoth Enterprises (Book Dept) (Israel) 210
Yee Wen Publishing Co Ltd (China (Taiwan)) 64
Yeshurun (Israel) 210
Yesod (Israel) 210
Yiannakis, Iakovou, (Cyprus) 69
Yliopistokirjakauppa Oy (Finland) 87
Yohan Publications Inc (Japan) 232
Yokendo Ltd (Japan) 231
Yomiuri Literature Prize (Japan) 234
Yonsei University Library (Republic of Korea) 239
Yonsei University Press (Republic of Korea) 239
Yorkshire Arts Association Literary Awards (United Kingdom) 421
'Yorkshire Post' Book of the Year Award (International Literary Prizes) 452
Yoruba (Barbados) 33
Yoseloff, Thomas, Ltd (United Kingdom) 413
Yoshikawa Prize for Popular Novel (Japan) 234
Young People's Book Prize (International Literary Prizes) 452
Young Publishers' Association, Munshiram Monoharial Publishers Pvt Ltd (India) 186
Young Writers' Incentive Awards (New Zealand) 276
Youth Publishing House (People's Republic of China) 63
Youth's Library Mohamad Ahmed Sharareh (Jordan) 234
Yritystieto Oy — Foretagsdata AB (Finland) 86
Yuhikaku Publishing Co Ltd (Japan) 231
Yulwha Dang (Republic of Korea) 239
Yundum College Library (The Gambia) 117
Yunnan Provincial Library (People's Republic of China) 64
'Yuridicheskaya Literatura', Izdatelstvo, (Union of Soviet Socialist Republics) 367
Yushodo Booksellers Ltd (Japan) 231
Yuval (Israel) 210
Yvert et Tellier, Editions Philateliques, (France) 110

Z A Reprints (German Democratic Republic) 120
Z I R A L (Zajednica Izdanja Ranjeni Labud) (Italy) 221
Z O E (Greece) 177
Z-Verlag, Genossenschaft, (Switzerland) 355
Zahar Editores (Brazil) 55
Zahiriah, Al, (National Library) (Syria) 357
Zaïre, Librairie du, (Zaire) 433
Zak, S, & Co (Israel) 210
Založba Obzorja (Yugoslavia) 430
Zambia Catholic Bookshop (Zambia) 434
Zambia Educational Distributors Ltd (Zambia) 434
Zambia Institute of Technology Library (Zambia) 434
Zambia Library Association (Zambia) 434
Zambia Library Service (Zambia) 434

Zambon, Dr, (Federal Republic of Germany) 169
Zanichelli, Nicola, SpA (Italy) 221
Zanzibar Government Archives (Tanzania) 358
Západočeské nakladatelství (Czechoslovakia) 72
Zaruski, Mariusz, Literary Prize (Poland) 298
Zattera, Casa Editrice La, (Italy) 221
Zauho, The, Press (Japan) 231
Zavalía, Victor P de, Editor (Argentina) 8
Zavod za Izdavanje Udžbenika (Yugoslavia) 430
Zavod za obrazovanje kadrova za administrativne poslove SR Srbije (Yugoslavia) 430
Zavod za udžbenike i nastavna sredstva (Yugoslavia) 430
Zavod za Udžbenike i Nastavna Sredstva Sap Kosovo (Yugoslavia) 430
Zbinden Druck und Verlag AG (Switzerland) 355
Zebra Books for Children (India) 196
Zechner und Hüthig Verlag GmbH (Federal Republic of Germany) 169
Zed Press (United Kingdom) 413
Zeit, Verlag, im Bild (German Democratic Republic) 120
Zelkowitz (Israel) 210
Zell, Hans, (Publishers) Ltd (United Kingdom) 413
Zemizdat, Darzhavno Izdatelstvo, (Bulgaria) 58
Zeneműkiadó, Editio Musica Budapest, (Hungary) 183
Zeno Booksellers & Publishers (United Kingdom) 413
Zentralantiquariat der DDR — Reprintabteilung (ZA Reprints) (German Democratic Republic) 120
Zentralbibliothek der deutschen Klassik (German Democratic Republic) 120
Zentralbibliothek Zürich (Switzerland) 356
Zentralgesellschaft für buchgewerbliche und graphische Betriebe (Austria) 30
Zentralinstitut für Bibliothekswesen (German Democratic Republic) 121
Zentralinstitut für Information und Dokumentation (German Democratic Republic) 121
Zentralstelle für maschinelle Dokumentation (Federal Republic of Germany) 172
Zero SA (Spain) 327
Zero-Zyx, Editorial, SA (Spain) 327
Zettner, Verlag Andreas, KG (Federal Republic of Germany) 169
Zibet Prize (Sweden) 339
Zig-Zag, Empressa Editora, SA (Chile) 62
Zimmer, Verlag Wolfgang, (Federal Republic of Germany) 169
Zindermans Förlag (Sweden) 337
Zip Editora Ltda (Brazil) 55
Zjednoczenie Ksiegarstwa (Poland) 296
Zjednoczenie Przedsiebiorstw Wydawniczych Naczelny Zarzad Wydawnictw (United Publishers — Central Publishing Board) (Poland) 293
Zluhan, Verlagsgemeinschaft Friedrich, (Federal Republic of Germany) 169
Zmora, Bitan, Modan Publishers (Israel) 210
'Znak', Spoleczny Instytut Wydawniczy, (Social Publishing Institute) (Poland) 296
Znanie (Union of Soviet Socialist Republics) 367
'Znanje', Nakladni Zavod, (Yugoslavia) 430
Zodiaque (France) 110
Zodiaque, La Pierre-qui-Vire (Switzerland) 355
Zolindakis, Har, (Greece) 177
Zollikofer Fachverlag AG (Switzerland) 355
Zomer en Keuning Boeken BV (Netherlands) 268
Zora (Yugoslavia) 430
Zorn Prize (Sweden) 339
Zoshindo Juken-Kenkyusha (Japan) 232
Zrinyi Katonai Kiadó (Publishing House of the Hungarian Army) (Hungary) 183
Zsolnay, Paul, Verlag GmbH (Federal Republic of Germany) 169
Zsolnay, Paul, Verlag GmbH (Austria) 29
Zuckmayer, Carl, Medal (Federal Republic of Germany) 174
Zuidgroep BV (formerly Hippobook/Studio de Zuid) (Netherlands) 269
Zuidnederlandse Uitgeverij NV (Belgium) 43
Zumstein & Cie (Switzerland) 355
Zur & Zur (Israel) 210
Zuri Book Shop (Afghanistan) 1
Zväz slovenských knihovníkov a informatikov (Czechoslovakia) 73
Zväz slovenských spisovateľov (Czechoslovakia) 73
Zveza društev bibliotekarjev Jugoslavije (Slovene) (Yugoslavia) 431
Zwei-Bären Verlag der VDB (Switzerland) 355
Zweipunkt Verlag KG (Federal Republic of Germany) 169
Zweitausendeins Versand (Federal Republic of Germany) 169
Zwemmer, A, Ltd (United Kingdom) 413
Zwiazek Literatów Poliskich (Union of Polish Writers) (Poland) 297
Zwijsen, Uitgeverij, BV (Netherlands) 269
'Zycie Literackie' Prize (Poland) 298
Zytglogge Verlag (Switzerland) 355

Z
291.5
I 5
1980

JUL 8 1980

Z
291.5
I 5
1980

ND H. FOGLER LIBRARY